HIGH PRAISE FOR

ROGET'S 21ST CENTURY THESAURUS
in Dictionary Form

"Exceptional . . . unique words and groupings . . .
this source is a gem!"
—Booklist

"OUTSTANDING!"
—American Bookseller

"INNOVATIVE . . . CLEAN, THOROUGH . . . a word that
can be almost tasted is accessed in nanoseconds.
It's close to instant gratification, and
a perfect adjunct to the dictionary . . .
This thesaurus fits the meaning of the word.
IT'S A TREASURE."
—San Diego Writers' Monthly

"A SOLID FRAME OF REFERENCE."
—USA Today

TOMORROW'S CLASSIC FOR TODAY'S USER

ROGET'S 21ST CENTURY THESAURUS

IN DICTIONARY FORM

Third Edition

The Essential Reference for
Home, School, or Office

EDITED BY THE PRINCETON LANGUAGE INSTITUTE
Barbara Ann Kipfer, Ph.D., Head Lexicographer

Produced by The Philip Lief Group, Inc.

A Dell Book

ROGET'S 21ST CENTURY THESAURUS, 3RD EDITION
A Dell Book

Published by arrangement with The Philip Lief Group, Inc.

PUBLISHING HISTORY
Dell mass market edition published May 2005
Dell mass market reissue / June 2006

Published by Bantam Dell
A Division of Random House, Inc.
New York, New York

Library of Congress Catalog Card Number: 2005041339

ISBN-13: 978-0-440-24269-7
ISBN-10: 0-440-24269-X

Printed in the United States of America
Published simultaneously in Canada

www.bantamdell.com

OPM   11   10   9   8   7   6   5   4   3   2

CONTENTS

PREFACE

More than ever before, our language and our ideas about language are changing as rapidly as the world around us. Our Information Age has been made possible, of course, by the ever-expanding technology of computers and the extraordinary explosion of information from the Internet and World Wide Web. We are receiving more information than we had ever imagined possible.

But how do we process this information—and articulate it in speech and writing? With expanded research and development of artificial intelligence systems, we have been able to examine more closely the complex cognitive relationships human beings form between their ideas and the words they choose. We now know more about how this process works, and how it can be re-created. Learning from this, current lexicographical research must go beyond traditional methods and techniques to develop effective and contemporary reference materials for students, linguists, and writers.

Most people learn a new word by guessing, based on context, what that word means. Recent studies on students' ability to develop reference skills bear this out. Combining this proven pattern with the advanced theories of language gained through electronic media, we have arrived at an "onomasiological" approach to understanding American English. That is, we are capable of traveling successfully from a meaning to a word instead of the straightforward dictionary approach of going from word to meaning. Onomasiologically, readers move from the concepts of "yellow" and "flower" to a selection of words that describe the combination, or from the notion of a "positive state of mind" to its qualities, actions, and conditions.

We have searched for a method of presenting this lexical theory in a format that provides diversified access to words within one resource. In *Roget's 21st Century Thesaurus, Third Edition,* the text is designed to do just that: allowing users to search both from word to meaning and from meaning to word. The dictionary format is familiar to use, and the Concept Index provides helpful links between words as it illustrates the language's semantic structure. The A-to-Z listings further amplify the resonances between words with their parts of speech and different sense divisions.

This third edition of *Roget's 21st Century Thesaurus* has been greatly expanded with the addition of antonyms and several hundred new headwords reflecting the dynamic changes in our language and the fabric of our lives. It is the most complete and comprehensive selection of synonyms and antonyms published today.

—Barbara Ann Kipfer, Ph.D.

INTRODUCTION

The history of *Roget's Thesaurus* is a long and fascinating one. It began
in 1805, when P. M. Roget, a British surgeon and inventor, took up a
peculiar hobby: the classification of words according to ideas. He hoped to
create a kind of verbal catalogue that would assist writers and linguists in
their search for the right expression. His work was perhaps inspired by two
earlier texts: the ancient Sanskrit *Amarakosha,* arguably the first arrangement of words by subject, and the French *Pasigraphie* (published in 1797),
which was an attempt to order words so they could be understood universally, without translation. Roget called his own work a "thesaurus"—a Latin
word meaning "treasury" or "storehouse of knowledge."

Gradually, Roget's casual pastime became his lifelong passion.
In 1852, some forty-seven years of work culminated in the publication of
Roget's *Thesaurus of English Words and Phrases, Classified and Arranged
so as to Facilitate the Expression of Ideas and Assist in Literary Composition.* This new reference book (published when Roget was seventy-three)
became enormously popular, and a second edition was published only a
year after the first. By the time of his death in 1869, there had been twenty-
eight editions and printings. Today, his name is literally "synonymous"
with the thesaurus.

RENOVATING THE ORIGINAL THESAURUS

Although Roget's original idea was brilliant, his thesaurus assumed that
all users shared the compiler's ideas about language. Its classifications
and indexes presented a labyrinth of possibilities in which each route
could end in a disappointing or inappropriate selection of synonyms.
The classification of terms made the text almost impenetrable and forced
the reader to rely on the index, which did not even include every synonym.
All too often, the right word remained elusive, or the thesaurus remained
on the shelf. And today, Roget's nineteenth-century thesaurus is difficult
for many twenty-first-century readers to use or even understand.

For over a century, thesaurus editors have strived to redefine the
nature and function of the thesaurus. Essentially, their goal has been
to present accurate information in a highly usable format. Attempts to
improve Roget's thesaurus began with Roget's own son, John Lewis,
who expanded the selection of synonyms. Later, Thomas Y. Crowell
acquired publishing rights to the thesaurus. His 1886 edition of *Roget's*
provided a clearer page design and format that enhanced the book's read-
ability. Subsequent generations of Crowells have added Americanisms,
foreign expressions, slang and nonstandard speech, prefixes, suffixes, and

quotations. Although these changes were indeed improvements, *Roget's* original structure of categories, cross-references, and indexes actually became *more* complicated by the addition of an elaborately conceived type design, boldface entries, numbered paragraphs, and a decimal system that required an explanatory diagram.

One of the most important breakthroughs in the evolution of the thesaurus came in the early twentieth century when C. O. Sylvester Mawson attempted to simplify and reorganize *Roget's Thesaurus* into a dictionary-like format. Roget's original work and the early revisions had not been arranged alphabetically. In 1911, Mawson radically changed the book's organization by issuing his alphabetical presentation of the famous Roget system. Twentieth-century editors quickly followed his lead, eager to find an easier method for frustrated thesaurus users.

Even with this improvement, the thesaurus still lacked something, for it did not suggest any relationships between words beyond the simple group of synonyms listed with a main entry. Although it did offer a more straightforward presentation than the index-reliant *Roget's,* it neither helped users organize thoughts nor provided broad conceptual links between ideas as expressed through language in words.

A THESAURUS FOR TODAY'S WORLD

Roget's 21st Century Thesaurus achieved what no other thesaurus has been able to do: combine the simplicity of the dictionary format with the utility of arranging words according to ideas. This revolutionary design has become the new standard for thesaurus users. It is, simultaneously, a fast and efficient handbook for writers and a medium to facilitate the expression of ideas—both of Roget's original objectives brought forward and reinterpreted for the twenty-first-century user.

This third edition of *Roget's 21st Century Thesaurus* has been electronically compiled using state-of-the-art techniques. It lists over 20,000 main entries, or headwords, in alphabetical order. These generate over 500,000 synonyms—more than any other thesaurus in dictionary form.

Reflecting the most recent changes in language, *Roget's 21st Century Thesaurus, Third Edition* is the most contemporary and useful thesaurus in history. The final selection of main entry words and synonyms was derived with today's practices of speaking and writing in mind. Reflecting contemporary usage, obsolete terms have been replaced by timely words and phrases. You will find terms from all areas of our experience, particularly the high-tech world of computers (such as "artificial intelligence," "computerese," "hacker," and "on-line"), the Internet and World Wide Web ("bootleg," "chat room," "cyberpunk"), video and multimedia ("digital library," "telecast," "TV"), medicine ("additive," "AIDS," "attention deficit disorder," "facelift"), political and civil spheres ("affirmative action," "out of the closet," "politically correct," "right-wing"), the environment ("ecosystem," "recycle"), and money and business ("desk jockey," "mutual fund," "shopping center," "white-collar"). A nonsexist, nonracist approach to language replaces outmoded epithets. Foreign words and phrases that reflect our global consciousness have been included ("au pair," "éclat," "kibosh," "schlemiel"), as well as hundreds of Americanisms ("foodie," "pot belly," "psyched," "puke," "rubberneck"). Synonyms that represent colloquial or slang terms are marked with an asterisk.

Roget's 21st Century Thesaurus, Third Edition is not just ultra-contemporary but also eminently usable. Drawing upon computer technology and recent innovations in typesetting and design, the pages are printed in a highly readable and contemporary format so the reader can make quick and effective choices. The synonym lists are not littered with cross-references, usage labels, or abbreviations, all of which can come between the user and the words themselves. Like main entries, the synonym lists are arranged in alphabetical order, completely objective, and not prescriptive, leaving the user to choose from the wealth of synonym choices available.

USING ROGET'S 21ST CENTURY THESAURUS, THIRD EDITION

The book's sensible format ensures swift access to the right alternatives. For quick identification, each headword in the A-to-Z listing is printed in boldface; its part of speech follows in bracketed italics. Some headwords have more than one listing; separate entries are included for each different part of speech—adjectives, nouns, and verbs, as well as adverbs, conjunctions, and prepositions. "Pass," for example, has thirteen entries—four noun forms and nine verb forms. Each sense of the word "pass" is treated individually to help writers pinpoint the precise sense of the word desired.

Concise definitions accompany the headwords, supplying users with a basic reference point and helping them to evaluate synonym choices. Semicolons sometimes appear within definitions to denote fine points of sense for a word's particular usage when the differences are too subtle to warrant a separate entry. .

Remember that no two words mean exactly the same thing. No two words are directly interchangeable. It is the subtle nuance and flavor of particular words that give the English language its rich and varied texture. We turn to a thesaurus to find different, more expressive ways of speaking and writing, but we must turn to a dictionary, a sophisticated semantic tool, to determine meaning. Always consider synonyms in their desired context and consult a dictionary if you have any doubt about the application of a word or phrase.

USING THE CONCEPT INDEX

The entries in *Roget's 21st Century Thesaurus, Third Edition* are enriched by directing users to related concepts in the Concept Index. This unique index offers users an up-to-the-minute language hierarchy that bridges the gap between thought and expression. The Concept Index actually helps writers organize their thoughts by generating possibilities for millions of word choices—far beyond the capabilities of a traditional thesaurus.

Each of the book's approximately 20,000 headwords is referenced to at least one of the 837 individually numbered concepts in the index. The words "CONCEPT(S)" appear in small caps at the end of a main entry, followed by the numbers for all relevant concepts for that word. When an initial search does not yield the desired results, the Concept Index automatically provides users with alternative places to look.

For example, if none of the synonyms listed with the word "scintillating" seems appropriate, the Concept Index directs the writer to concepts #401, "attributes of behavior"; #529, "cognitive qualities"; and #617, "visual brightness." Each concept gathers together scores of headwords that share the same characteristics. Persistent writers or linguists can turn back to the A-to-Z listing to find the synonyms for any of these headwords, allowing them to locate even more word choices.

The Concept Index follows the alphabetical listing of headwords and begins with a reference key. The concepts appear in the index in numerical order and are divided into ten overarching categories of interest: Actions, Causes, Fields of Human Activity, Life Forms, Objects, The Planet, Qualities, Senses, States, and Weights and Measures. All headwords grouped under a specific concept are ordered alphabetically and by different parts of speech, if applicable.

The most advanced theories of communication and learning available have been used to determine concept names and classifications. The word hierarchies in *Roget's 21st Century Thesaurus, Third Edition* have been streamlined into categories that reflect contemporary ways of thinking. It is clear what concepts mean and how they are organized. Whether performing a speedy search through the concepts or entering the index with just a vague notion in mind, users will find the Concept Index to be a fast and reliable research tool.

A CLASSIC FOR TODAY AND TOMORROW

In the minds of writers and linguists, Roget has always been the trademark of a dependable thesaurus. As we are in an era unimagined by P. M. Roget two hundred years ago, *Roget's 21st Century Thesaurus, Third Edition* upholds that reputation. Adapting Roget's thesaurus to reflect today's concerns, this new text represents a fresh and vital reference of American English.

ROGET'S
21ST CENTURY THESAURUS

Third Edition

A

aback |adv| *taken unawares* confused, surprised, thrown off, thrown off guard*; CONCEPT 403

abaft |adj| *to the rear* astern, back, behind, rearward; CONCEPTS 586,820

abandon |n| *careless disregard for consequences* disregard, freedom, impulse, licentiousness, recklessness, spontaneity, thoughtlessness, uninhibitedness, unrestraint, wantonness, wildness; CONCEPTS 633,645 —*Ant.* restraint, self-restraint

abandon |v1| *leave behind, relinquish* abdicate, back out, bail out*, bow out*, chicken out*, cop out*, cut loose*, desert, discard, discontinue, ditch*, drop, drop out, duck*, dump*, dust*, flake out*, fly the coop*, give up the ship*, kiss goodbye*, leave, leg it*, let go, opt out, pull out, quit, run out on, screw*, ship out, stop, storm out*, surrender, take a powder*, take a walk*, throw over*, vacate, walk out on, wash hands of*, withdraw, yield; CONCEPT 195 —*Ant.* cherish, defend, keep, pursue, retain, support

abandon |v2| *leave in troubled state* back out, desert, disown, forsake, jilt, leave, leave behind, quit, reject, renounce, throw over*, walk out on; CONCEPTS 7,19,195 —*Ant.* assert, assert, favor, uphold

abandoned |adj1| *left alone, deserted* alone, cast aside, cast away, deserted, discarded, dissipated, dropped, dumped, eighty-sixed*, eliminated, empty, forgotten, forsaken, given up, godforsaken*, jilted, left, left in the cold*, left in the lurch*, neglected, on the rocks*, outcast, passed up*, pigeon-holed*, rejected, relinquished, shunned, sidelined*, side-tracked*, unoccupied, vacant, vacated; CONCEPT 577 —*Ant.* adopted, cherished, defended, maintained, supported

abandoned |adj2| *free from moral restraint; uninhibited* corrupt, depraved, dissolute, immoral, incontinent, incorrigible, licentious, profligate, shameless, sinful, uncontrolled, unprincipled, unrestrained, wanton, wicked, wild; CONCEPT 545 —*Ant.* chaste, innocent, moral, pure, restrained, virtuous

abase |v| *deprive of self-esteem, confidence* belittle, debase, degrade, demean, diminish, disgrace, dishonor, humble, humiliate, lower, mortify, reduce, shame; CONCEPTS 7,19 —*Ant.* cherish, dignify, exalt, extol, honor, respect

abasement |n| *disgrace* degradation, dishonor, downgrade, humiliation, shame; CONCEPT 388

abashed |adj| *exhibiting mental discomfort, ill at ease* ashamed, bewildered, bugged*, chagrined, confounded, confused, crushed, discombobulated*, disconcerted, embarrassed, fazed*, fuddled, humbled, humiliated, in a tizzy*, mortified, rattled, shamed, taken aback; CONCEPT 403 —*Ant.* at ease, composed, emboldened, proud, reassured

abate |v| *lessen, grow or cause to grow less* allay, chill out*, coast*, cool, cool it*, decline, decrease, diminish, dull, dwindle, ebb, go with the flow*, hang easy*, hang loose*, lay back*, let go, let it all hang out*, let up, mellow out*, moderate, quell, recede, reduce, slacken, slow, subdue, subside, take it easy*, taper, taper

off, unlax*, wane; CONCEPTS 240,698 —*Ant.* amplify, enhance, enlarge, extend, increase, intensify, magnify, prolong, revive, rise

abbey |n| *building that houses monks, nuns, or priests; church* cloister, convent, friary, ministry, monastery, nunnery, priory, temple; CONCEPTS 368,439

abbreviate |v1| *shorten* abridge, abstract, boil down*, clip, compress, condense, contract, cut, cut back, cut down, cut off, cut out, digest, encapsulate, get to the meat*, pare, prune, put in a nutshell*, reduce, summarize, take out, trim; CONCEPTS 236,247 —*Ant.* amplify, enlarge, expand, extend, increase, lengthen

abbreviate |v2| *cut short an activity* abort, curtail, restrict, stop short, truncate; CONCEPT 234 —*Ant.* expand, extend, increase, lengthen

abbreviation |n| *something shortened* abridgement, abstract, abstraction, clipping, compendium, compression, condensation, contraction, digest, outline, precis, reduction, sketch, summary, syllabus, synopsis; CONCEPTS 283,652 —*Ant.* augmentation, enlargement, expansion, extension, increase

abdicate |v| *give up a right, position, or power* abandon, abjure, abnegate, bag it*, bail out*, cede, demit, drop, forgo, give up, leave, leave high and dry*, leave holding the bag*, leave in the lurch*, opt out*, quit, quitclaim, relinquish, renounce, resign, retire, sell out*, step down, surrender, vacate, waive, withdraw, yield; CONCEPTS 133,298 —*Ant.* assert, assume, challenge, claim, defend, defy, hold, maintain, remain, retain, treasure, usurp

abdomen |n| *the stomach and area directly below in an animate being* bay window*, belly, bowels, breadbasket*, corporation, gut*, guts, intestines, middle, midriff, midsection, paunch, pot*, potbelly*, spare tire*, tummy, venter, viscera; CONCEPT 393

abdominal |adj| *concerning the stomach and the area below it* belly, duodenal, gastric, intestinal, stomachic, ventral, visceral; CONCEPT 393

abduct |v| *take by force and without permission* carry off, dognap*, grab, kidnap, make off with, put the snatch on*, remove, seize, shanghai*, snatch, sneeze*, spirit away*; CONCEPT 139 —*Ant.* give up, let go, release

abducted |adj| *taken away by force* appropriated, kidnapped, seized, snatched, stolen; CONCEPTS 90,139

abduction |n| *taking away by force* appropriation, kidnapping, rape, seizure, theft; CONCEPTS 90,139

abend |n| *abnormal end of task* abort, crash, loss; CONCEPTS 658,674

aberrant |adj| *not normal; varying from the usual* abnormal, atypical, bizarre, deviant, different, flaky*, mental*, nonstandard, odd, off-base, off-color, out of line*, peculiar, psycho*, strange, unusual, weird; CONCEPT 547 —*Ant.* normal, same, true

aberration |n1| *state of abnormality* delusion, eccentricity, oddity, peculiarity, quirk, strangeness, weirdness; CONCEPT 647 —*Ant.* conformity, normality, regularity, soundness

aberration |n2| *different from that expected* departure, deviation, difference, distortion, divergence, diversion, irregularity, lapse,

straying, wandering; CONCEPT 665 —*Ant.*
conformity, sameness

abet [v] *assist, help in wrongdoing* advocate,
back, condone, egg on*, encourage, endorse,
goad, incite, instigate, prod, promote, provoke,
sanction, spur, support, urge; CONCEPTS 14,110
—*Ant.* counter, deter, discourage, frustrate,
hinder, hurt, impede, obstruct, resist

abettor [n] *assistant* accessory, accomplice,
co-conspirator, confederate, cooperator, helper,
partner in crime*, second, supporter; CONCEPT
348

abeyance [n] *being inactive or suspended
temporarily* deferral, discontinuation, dormancy,
inactivity, intermission, latency, postponement,
quiescence, recess, remission, suspension, waiting; CONCEPTS 681,705 —*Ant.* action, activity,
continuance, continuation, operation, renewal,
revival

abhor [v] *regard with contempt or disgust*
abominate, be allergic to*, be down on*,
be grossed out by*, despise, detest, hate,
have no use for*, loathe, scorn; CONCEPT 29
—*Ant.* admire, adore, approve, cherish, desire,
enjoy, like, love, relish

abhorrence [n] *disgust* detestation, enmity,
hate, hatred, horror, loathing, malice, odium,
repugnance, revulsion; CONCEPTS 410,720

abhorrent [adj] *disgusting* despicable,
detestable, execrable, loathsome, offensive,
repulsive, revolting; CONCEPTS 485,548

abide [v1] *submit to, put up with* accept,
acknowledge, bear, bear with*, be big about*,
concede, consent, defer, endure, hang in*,
hang in there*, hang tough*, live with*, put
up with*, receive, sit tight*, stand, stand for,
stomach, suffer, swallow, take, tolerate, withstand; CONCEPTS 23,35 —*Ant.* despise, dispute,
pass, quit, reject, resist, shun

abide [v2] *live in a certain place* bide, bunk*,
bunk out*, crash*, dwell, hang out*, inhabit,
lodge, nest, perch, reside, room, roost, settle,
squat, stay; CONCEPT 226 —*Ant.* depart, go,
leave, migrate, move, reject, resist

abide [v3] *remain or continue in a state* continue, endure, keep on, last, persevere, persist,
remain, survive; CONCEPTS 23,239 —*Ant.*
leave, quit, refuse, stop

abide [v4] *stop temporarily and wait for* anticipate, bide, expect, linger, pause, remain, rest,
sojourn, stay, stick around*, stop, tarry, wait;
CONCEPT 119,681 —*Ant.* carry on, continue,
go, move

abiding [adj] *continuing or existing for an
indefinite time* constant, continuing, enduring,
eternal, everlasting, fast, indissoluble, lasting,
permanent, perpetual, persistent, persisting,
steadfast, steady; CONCEPT 551 —*Ant.*
ephemeral, fleeting, transient

ability [n1] *power to act, perform* aptitude,
capability, capacity, competence, competency,
comprehension, dexterity, endowment, facility,
faculty, intelligence, might, potentiality, qualification, resourcefulness, skill, strength, talent,
understanding; CONCEPT 630 —*Ant.* impotence,
inability, limitation, paralysis

ability [n2] *natural or acquired power in a
particular activity* adeptness, adroitness, bent,
capability, cleverness, command, craft, deftness,

expertise, expertness, finesse, flair, genius,
gift, handiness, ingenuity, knack, know-how,
mastery, mind for, proficiency, savvy, skill,
skillfulness, strength, talent, the goods*, the
right stuff*, what it takes*; CONCEPT 706 —*Ant.*
clumsiness, ignorance, inability, inadequacy,
inanity, incompetence, stupidity, weakness

abject [adj] *hopeless and downtrodden* base,
contemptible, degraded, dejected, deplorable,
dishonorable, fawning, forlorn, groveling, hangdog, humiliated, low, miserable, outcast, pitiable,
servile, submissive, worthless, wretched;
CONCEPT 571 —*Ant.* commendable, exalted,
excellent, magnificent, noble, proud, worthy

abjure [v] *give up* abstain from, forswear,
recant, renege, renounce, retract, take back,
withdraw; CONCEPTS 30,54,195

ablate [v] *wear away* erode, evaporate, melt,
vaporize; CONCEPTS 252,469

ablaze [adj1] *on fire* afire, aflame, alight,
blazing, burning, conflagrant, fiery, flaming,
flaring, ignited, lighted; CONCEPTS 485,605

ablaze [adj2] *very excited* afire, angry, aroused,
enthusiastic, fervent, frenzied, fuming, furious,
heated, impassioned, incensed, intense, on
fire, passionate, raging, stimulated, vehement;
CONCEPT 550 —*Ant.* dull, unexcited

ablaze [adj3] *brightly illuminated* aflame,
aglow, brilliant, flashing, gleaming, glowing,
incandescent, luminous, radiant, refulgent,
sparkling; CONCEPT 617 —*Ant.* dark, dim

able [adj1] *capable of performing; having an
innate capacity* adept, adequate, adroit, agile,
alert, apt, bright, capable, competent, cunning,
deft, dexterous, easy, effortless, endowed,
equipped, facile, fitted, good, intelligent,
knowing, powerful, ready, smart, strong,
worthy; CONCEPTS 402,527 —*Ant.* ineffective,
inept, infirm, powerless, unable, useless

able [adj2] *able to perform well; having a
proven capacity* accomplished, adroit, agile,
artful, au fait, brilliant, capable, clever, deft,
dexterous, effective, effectual, efficient, equal
to, experienced, expert, facile, gifted,
ingenious, intelligent, keen, know backwards
and forwards*, know one's onions*, know the
ropes*, learned, masterful, masterly, powerful,
practiced, prepared, proficient, qualified, responsible, savvy, sharp, skilled, skillful, smart,
talented, there*, trained, up to it*, up to snuff*,
up to speed*, with it*; CONCEPTS 402,528
—*Ant.* delicate, feeble, inept, stupid, weak

able-bodied [adj] *physically strong and
capable* firm, fit, hale, hardy, healthy, hearty,
lusty, powerful, robust, staunch, stout, strapping*, sturdy, vigorous; CONCEPTS 314,489
—*Ant.* delicate, infirm, weak

ablution [n] *washing* bath, cleansing, deconta-
mination, lavation, purification, shower,
showering; CONCEPTS 161,165

ably [adv] *capably* adroitly, capably,
competently; CONCEPT 527

abnegate [v] *renounce* abstain, decline,
forbear, forgo, give up, refrain, reject;
CONCEPTS 30,54,195

abnegation [n] *denial, renouncement of something* abandonment, abstinence, eschewal, forbearance, giving up, nixing, refusal, rejection,
relinquishment, renunciation, sacrifice, self-

denial, stonewall*, surrender, temperance; CONCEPTS *18,25* —*Ant.* acquiescence, admittance, surrender, yielding

abnormal [*adj*] *different from standard or norm* aberrant, anomalistic, anomalous, atypical, bizarre, curious, deviant, deviate, deviating, divergent, eccentric, exceptional, extraordinary, fantastic, funny, gawky*, gross, heteroclite, heterodox, heteromorphic, irregular, odd, off-base, off-color, out of line, peculiar, preternatural, queer, screwy*, spastic*, strange, uncommon, unexpected, unnatural, unorthodox, unusual, weird; CONCEPT *547* —*Ant.* customary, normal, standard, straight, usual

abnormality [*n*] *being different from standard or norm* aberrancy, aberration, anomalism, anomaly, atypicalness, bizarreness, deformity, deviance, deviancy, deviation, eccentricity, exception, extraordinariness, flaw, irregularity, oddity, peculiarity, preternaturalness, singularity, strangeness, uncommonness, unnaturalness, unusualness, weirdness; CONCEPT *647* —*Ant.* normality, normalness, sameness, standard

aboard [*adj*] *on or in a transportation object* boarded, consigned, embarked, en route, in transit, loaded, on, on board, traveling; CONCEPT *583* —*Ant.* not on, off

abode [*n*] *building or place where one resides* address, apartment, base, casa, condo, co-op, crash pad*, crib*, den, digs*, domicile, dwelling, flat, flop*, habitat, haunt, headquarters, hearth, hole*, home, homestead, house, joint*, lodging, pad, quarters, residence, roost*, sanctuary, seat; CONCEPT *515*

abolish [*v*] *do away with or put an end to* abate, abrogate, annihilate, annul, call off, cancel, destroy, disestablish, dissolve, end, eradicate, erase, expunge, extinguish, extirpate, finish, inhibit, invalidate, kill, negate, nix, nullify, obliterate, overthrow, overturn, prohibit, put an end to, put kibosh on*, put the kibosh on*, quash, repeal, repudiate, rescind, revoke, scrub*, set aside, squelch, stamp out, subvert, supersede, suppress, terminate, undo, vacate, vitiate, void, wipe out, zap*; CONCEPTS *121,252,298* —*Ant.* confirm, continue, enact, establish, institute, legalize, promote, ratify, support, uphold

abolition [*n*] *formal act of putting an end to, annulling* abolishment, abrogation, annihilation, annulment, cancellation, destruction, dissolution, elimination, end, ending, eradication, extirpation, invalidation, negation, nullification, obliteration, overthrow, overturning, quashing, repeal, repudiation, rescinding, rescindment, rescission, revocation, subversion, suppression, termination, voiding, wiping out, withdrawal; CONCEPTS *121,252,298* —*Ant.* confirmation, establishment, establishment, institution, legalization, promotion

abolitionist [*n*] *person wanting something ended* activist, advocate, opponent, revolutionary; CONCEPT *366*

A-bomb [*n*] *atomic bomb* nuclear bomb, nuclear weapon, physics package*, thermonuclear bomb; CONCEPT *500*

abominable [*adj*] *awful, detestable* abhorrent, atrocious, awful, bad, base, beastly, contemptible, cursed, despicable, disgusting, foul, grim, grody*, gross*, hairy*, hateful, heinous,

hellish, horrible, horrid, loathsome, lousy, nauseating, obnoxious, odious, offensive, repellent, reprehensible, repugnant, repulsive, revolting, rotten, sleazy*, stinking, terrible, vile, wretched; CONCEPTS *29,544,571* —*Ant.* alluring, appealing, delightful, desirable, enjoyable, likeable, lovable, pleasant, sweet, wonderful

abominate [*v*] *detest* abhor, despise, dislike, hate, loathe; CONCEPT *29*

abomination [*n1*] *object of extreme dislike, hate* anathema, aversion, bother, curse, detestation, evil, horror, nuisance, plague, shame, torment; CONCEPTS *29,666* —*Ant.* beauty, blessing, delight, enjoyment, esteem, joy, love, treat

abomination [*n2*] *wrongdoing* crime, offense, wrong; CONCEPT *691* —*Ant.* benefit, right

aboriginal [*adj*] *belonging to one, existing in a place since prehistory* ancient, earliest, endemic, first, indigenous, native, original, primary, primeval, primitive, primordial; CONCEPT *549* —*Ant.* foreign

aborigine [*n*] *first inhabitant* aboriginal, autochthon, bushman*, indigene, native, primitive; CONCEPT *413*

abort [*v1*] *stop or cancel something* arrest, break off, call it quits*, call off, check, cut off, drop, end, fail, halt, interrupt, knock it off*, lay off*, nullify, scrap, scratch, scrub*, terminate; CONCEPT *121* —*Ant.* continue, keep

abort [*v2*] *terminate or fail to complete pregnancy* miscarry; CONCEPTS *121,304,308* —*Ant.* carry to term, keep

abortion [*n1*] *expulsion of fetus* aborticide, feticide, misbirth, miscarriage, termination; CONCEPTS *230,699*

abortion [*n2*] *failure* disappointment, disaster, fiasco, misadventure, premature delivery; CONCEPTS *304,308,674* —*Ant.* continuation, success

abortive [*adj*] *failing to achieve a goal* failed, failing, fruitless, futile, ineffective, ineffectual, miscarried, unavailing, unproductive, unsuccessful, useless, vain, worthless; CONCEPT *528* —*Ant.* complete, consummated, effectual, efficient, fruitful, productive, successful

abound [*v*] *exist in abundance* be alive with, be all over the place*, be knee deep in*, be no end to*, be plentiful, be thick with*, be up to one's ears in*, crawl with*, crowd, flourish, flow, have a full plate*, infest, overflow, proliferate, swarm, swell, teem, thrive; CONCEPT *141* —*Ant.* deficient, fail, lack, need, short, want

abounding [*adj*] *plentiful* abundant, bountiful, copious, filled, flush, plenteous, prodigal, profuse, prolific, replete, teeming; CONCEPTS *762,781*

about [*adv1*] *in an opposite direction* around, back, backward, in reverse, round; CONCEPT *581*

about [*adv2*] *lying anywhere without order, arrangement* anyhow, any which way*, around, here and there; CONCEPT *583*

about [*prep1*] *near an amount, quantity* almost, approximately, in general, in the ball park*, in the neighborhood*, nearly, practically, pretty nearly, roughly; CONCEPT *771*

about [*prep2*] *concerning, relating to* apropos, as concerns, as respects, dealing with, in connection with, in relation to, in respect to, referring to, regarding, relative to, touching, touching on; CONCEPT 532

about [prep3] *near or close to in position* adjacent, beside, nearby; CONCEPTS 586,778 —Ant. afar, away, distant, far, remote

about [prep4] *on every side, in every direction* around, encircling, round, surrounding, through, throughout; CONCEPT 586

about-face [n] *change in direction* changeabout, double, doubleback, reversal, reverse, turn, turnabout, volte-face; CONCEPT 697

above [prep1] *higher in position* aloft, atop, beyond, high, on high, on top of, over, overhead, raised, superior, upon; CONCEPT 752 —Ant. below, under

above [prep2] *more, higher in amount, degree* beyond, exceeding, greater than, larger than, over; CONCEPT 793 —Ant. below, deficient, fewer, less

above [prep3] *superior to* before, beyond, exceeding, prior to, superior to, surpassing; CONCEPT 567 —Ant. inferior, under

aboveboard [adj] *candid* forthright, frank, honest, open, overt, right on*, square, straight, straightforward, straight from shoulder*, true, trustworthy, truthful, up front*, veracious; CONCEPT 404 —Ant. deceitful, devious, lying, shady, underhanded

aboveboard [adv] *candidly* frankly, honestly, on the up and up*, openly, overtly, truly, truthfully, veraciously; CONCEPT 404 —Ant. deceitful, devious, lying, shady, underhanded

above suspicion [adj] *innocent* above reproach, blameless, guiltless, having clean hands*, inculpable, irreproachable, scrupulous, sinless; CONCEPT 545

abracadabra [n] *magic word* hocus-pocus, incantation, invocation, mumbo jumbo, open sesame, spell; CONCEPTS 370,673,689

abrade [v] *scrape* chafe, erode, grate, rub, rub off, scuff, triturate, wear, wear down; CONCEPTS 165,186,215

abrasion [n1] *scraped area* chafe, injury, scrape, scratch, scuff; CONCEPT 309

abrasion [n2] *scraping or wearing down by friction* abrading, chafing, erosion, grating, rubbing, scratching, scuffing; CONCEPT 186

abrasive [adj1] *irritating in manner* annoying, biting, caustic, cutting, galling, hard to take*, hateful, hurtful, nasty, rough, rubbing the wrong way*, sharp, spiky*, unpleasant; CONCEPT 404 —Ant. likeable, pleasant, pleasing

abrasive [adj2] *scraping or wearing* cutting, erosive, grinding, polishing, rough, scratching, scratchy, scuffing, sharpening, smoothing; CONCEPT 606 —Ant. smooth, soft

abreast [adv1] *next to, alongside* beside, equal, in alignment, in line, level, opposite, shoulder to shoulder, side by side; CONCEPT 586

abreast [adv2] *up-to-date* acquainted, au courant, au fait, contemporary, familiar, informed, in touch, knowledgeable, up*, versed; CONCEPT 402 —Ant. lost, out of touch, unaware

abridge [v] *shorten* abbreviate, abstract, blue pencil*, chop, clip, compress, concentrate, condense, contract, curtail, cut, decrease, digest, diminish, downsize, lessen, limit, narrow, put in

nutshell*, reduce, restrict, slash, snip*, summarize, trim, truncate; CONCEPTS 236,247 —Ant. add, enlarge, expand, extend, increase, lengthen

abridgement [n] *shortening, summary* abbreviation, abstract, brief, compendium, condensation, conspectus, contraction, curtailment, cutting, decrease, digest, diminishment, diminution, lessening, outline, precis, reducing, reduction, synopsis; CONCEPTS 283,652 —Ant. addition, enlargement, expansion, extension, increase, lengthening, padding

abroad [adj] *in a foreign country* away, elsewhere, in foreign lands, in foreign parts, out of the country, overseas, touring, traveling; CONCEPT 583 —Ant. at home

abrogate [v] *formally put an end to* abate, abolish, annul, cancel, dissolve, do in*, end, finish off*, invalidate, knock out*, negate, nix, nullify, quash, reject, renege, repeal, retract, revoke, scrub*, torpedo*, undo, vacate, vitiate, void; CONCEPT 121 —Ant. approve, establish, fix, institute, legalize, ratify, sanction, support

abrogation [n] *cancellation* annulment, discontinuation, ending, invalidation, quashing, repudiation, rescission, retraction, reversal, voiding, withdrawal; CONCEPT 119

abrupt [adj1] *rude or brief in manner* brash, brusque, crude, crusty, curt, direct, discourteous, gruff, impetuous, impolite, matter-of-fact, rough, short, snappy, snippy, uncivil, ungracious; CONCEPT 542 —Ant. calm, kind, nice

abrupt [adj2] *happening suddenly and unexpectedly* hasty, hurried, jerky, precipitate, precipitous, quick, rushing, sudden, surprising, unanticipated, unceremonious, unexpected, unforeseen; CONCEPT 820 —Ant. at ease, deliberate, expansive, gradual, leisurely

abscess [n] *swelling* boil, carbuncle, pustule, ulcer; CONCEPTS 306,309

abscond [v] *run away, depart secretly* beat it*, bolt*, break, clear out*, cut and run*, decamp, disappear, dog it*, duck out, escape, fade*, flee, fly the coop*, get, go AWOL*, go south*, hightail*, jump*, leave, make a break*, make off, make scarce*, pull out, quit, run off, scram*, skedaddle*, skip out*, slip, sneak away, split*, steal away, take off*, vamoose*, vanish; CONCEPTS 102,195 —Ant. abide, continue, endure, give up, remain, stay, stop, yield

absconder [n] *person who escapes* absentee, bolter, escapee, quitter, truant; CONCEPTS 403,583

absence [n1] *state of not being present* absenteeism, AWOL, cut*, French leave*, hooky*, nonappearance, nonattendance, no show*, truancy, vacancy; CONCEPT 746 —Ant. existence, presence

absence [n2] *state of lacking something needed or usual* dearth, deficiency, drought, inadequacy, insufficiency, lack, need, omission, privation, unavailability, void, want; CONCEPT 646 —Ant. abundance, enough, plenty

absent [adj1] *not present* astray, away, AWOL*, elsewhere, ghost, gone, hooky*, missing, nobody home*, no-show*, removed, vanished; CONCEPT 583 —Ant. attending, existing, present

absent [adj2] *deficient in something needed or usual* bare, blank, devoid, empty, hollow, lacking, minus, missing, nonexistent, omitted, unavailable, vacant, vacuous, wanting; CONCEPT 546 —*Ant.* sufficient

absentee [*adj*] *not being present* absent, distant, oblivious, remote; CONCEPTS 403,583

absenteeism [*n*] *state of not being present* absence, defection, desertion, skipping, truancy; CONCEPT 746 —*Ant.* attendance, presence

absent-minded [*adj*] *unaware of events, surroundings* absent, absorbed, abstracted, airheaded*, bemused, daydreaming, distracted, distrait, dreaming, dreamy, engrossed, faraway, forgetful, goofing off*, heedless, inattentive, inconscient, lost, mooning*, moony*, oblivious, out to lunch*, pipe dreaming*, preoccupied, remote, removed, space cadet*, spacey*, unconscious, unheeding, unmindful, unobservant, unthinking, withdrawn, woolgathering*; CONCEPT 403 —*Ant.* alert, attentive, aware, aware

absent-mindedness [*n*] *preoccupation* absorption, abstraction, distraction, dreaminess, forgetfulness, heedlessness, inattention; CONCEPTS 293,410,532,690

absolute [*adj1*] *without limit* complete, consummate, downright, entire, flat out*, free, full, infinite, no catch*, no fine print*, no holds barred*, no ifs ands or buts*, no joke*, no strings attached*, outright, plenary, pure, sheer, simple, straight out, supreme, thorough, total, unabridged, unadulterated, unconditional, unlimited, unqualified, unrestricted, utter; CONCEPT 554 —*Ant.* accountable, circumscribed, limited, restricted, tractable

absolute [*adj2*] *in control or complete authority* absolutist, arbitrary, authoritarian, autocratic, autonomous, despotic, dictatorial, full, monocratic, preeminent, sovereign, supreme, totalitarian, tyrannical, tyrannous; CONCEPT 536 —*Ant.* accountable, complaisant, compliant, restricted, submissive, yielding

absolute [*adj3*] *certain* actual, categorical, conclusive, consummate, decided, decisive, definite, exact, factual, fixed, genuine, infallible, positive, precise, sure, unambiguous, undeniable, unequivocal, unmitigated, unquestionable; CONCEPT 535 —*Ant.* conditional, dependent, limited, partial

absolute [*adj4*] *excellent, perfect* categorical, complete, faultless, flawless, ideal, impeccable, thorough, ultimate, unblemished, unflawed, untarnished; CONCEPT 574 —*Ant.* flawed, imperfect

absolutely [*adv1*] *certainly, without question* actually, categorically, come hell or high water*, conclusively, decidedly, decisively, definitely, doubtless, easily, exactly, for sure*, no ifs ands or buts*, no strings attached*, on the button*, on the money*, on the nose*, positively, precisely, really, right on*, straight out*, sure as can be*, sure as hell*, sure enough*, surely, sure thing*, the very thing*, truly, unambiguously, unconditionally, unquestionably; CONCEPT 535 —*Ant.* doubtful, indefinite, not certain, not sure, questionable

absolutely [*adv2*] *in a complete manner, degree* completely, consummately, entirely, fully, thoroughly, utterly, wholly; CONCEPT 531 —*Ant.* incomplete, partially

absolution [*n*] *forgiveness* acquittal, amnesty, compurgation, exculpation, forgiveness, mercy, pardon, release; CONCEPTS 685,689

absolve [*v*] *free from responsibility, duty* acquit, bleach, blink at, clear, discharge, exculpate, excuse, exempt, exonerate, forgive, free, go easy on, launder*, let off*, let off easy*, let off the hook*, let up on*, liberate, lifeboat*, loose, pardon, release, relieve, sanitize*, set free, spare, spring*, vindicate, whitewash, wink at*, wipe it off*, wipe the slate clean*, write off*; CONCEPTS 83,317 —*Ant.* bind, blame, charge, condemn, convict, hold, impeach, incriminate, obligate, punish, sentence

absorb [*v1*] *physically take in a liquid* blot, consume, devour, drink in, imbibe, ingest, ingurgitate, osmose, soak up, sop up*, sponge up*, suck in*, swallow, take in; CONCEPT 256 —*Ant.* disperse, dissipate, eject, emit, exude, spew, vomit

absorb [*v2*] *mentally take in information* assimilate, comprehend, digest, follow, get, get into*, grasp, incorporate, latch onto, learn, sense, soak up, take in, understand; CONCEPT 31 —*Ant.* misunderstand, not get

absorb [*v3*] *occupy complete attention* captivate, concern, consume, employ, engage, engross, fascinate, fill, hold, immerse, involve, monopolize, obsess, preoccupy, rivet; CONCEPT 17 —*Ant.* distract

absorbed [*adj*] *being completely occupied mentally* captivated, consumed, deep in thought, engaged, engrossed, fascinated, fixed, gone*, head over heels*, held, immersed, intent, involved, lost, preoccupied, rapt, really into*, up to here*, wrapped up*; CONCEPT 403 —*Ant.* bored, disinterested, distracted, indifferent, uninterested

absorbent [*adj*] *capable of physically taking in a liquid* absorptive, bibulous, dry, imbibing, penetrable, permeable, porous, pregnable, retentive, spongy, thirsty; CONCEPT 603 —*Ant.* impermeable

absorbing [*adj*] *holding one's attention* arresting, captivating, consuming, engrossing, enthralling, exciting, fascinating, gripping, interesting, intriguing, monopolizing, preoccupying, riveting, spellbinding; CONCEPT 403 —*Ant.* boring, irksome

absorption [*n1*] *assimilation, incorporation* consumption, digestion, drinking in, exhaustion, fusion, imbibing, impregnation, ingestion, inhalation, intake, osmosis, penetration, reception, retention, saturation, soaking up, suction, taking in; CONCEPTS 169,256

absorption [*n2*] *total attention toward something* captivation, concentration, engagement, engrossment, enthrallment, fascination, hang-up*, holding, immersion, intentness, involvement, occupation, preoccupation, raptness; CONCEPT 410 —*Ant.* boredom, distraction

abstain [*v*] *hold back from doing* abjure, abnegate, avoid, cease, constrain, curb, decline, deny oneself, do without, eschew, evade, fast, fence-sit*, forbear, forgo, give the go by*, give up, go on the wagon*, keep from, pass, pass up, quit, refrain, refuse, renounce, shun, sit on one's hands*, sit on the fence*, sit out, spurn, starve, stop, take the cure*, take the pledge*, withhold; CONCEPTS 25,121 —*Ant.* indulge, use

abstemious [adj] restraining behavior or appetite abstinent, ascetic, austere, continent, frugal, moderate, moderating, restrained, self-denying, self-restrained, sober, sparing, temperate; CONCEPT 401 —Ant. gluttonous, greedy, hungry

abstention [n] refraining abstaining, abstinence, avoidance, non-indulgence, self-control, self-denial, self-restraint, sobriety; CONCEPT 633

abstinence [n] restraint from desires, especially physical desires abnegation, abstaining, abstemiousness, asceticism, avoidance, chastity, continence, fasting, forbearance, frugality, moderation, refraining, renunciation, self-control, self-denial, self-restraint, soberness, sobriety, teetotalism, temperance; CONCEPT 633 —Ant. drunkenness, excess, indulgence, intemperance, intoxication, revelry, self-indulgence

abstract [adj] conceptual, theoretical abstruse, complex, deep, hypothetical, ideal, indefinite, intellectual, nonconcrete, philosophical, recondite, transcendent, transcendental, unreal; CONCEPT 582 —Ant. actual, concrete, factual, material, objective, physical, real

abstract [n] short document prepared from a longer one abridgment, brief, compendium, condensation, conspectus, digest, outline, précis, résumé, summary, synopsis; CONCEPT 283 —Ant. document, manuscript

abstract [v1] take away from detach, disconnect, disengage, dissociate, extract, isolate, part, remove, separate, steal, take out, uncouple, withdraw; CONCEPTS 135,211 —Ant. add, combine, fill, insert, introduce, unite

abstract [v2] prepare short document from longer one abbreviate, abridge, condense, digest, outline, review, shorten, summarize; CONCEPTS 79,236,247 —Ant. complete, expand, insert, lengthen, strengthen

abstracted [adj] preoccupied absent-minded, daydreaming, inattentive, lost in thought, out in space*, out to lunch*, remote, withdrawn; CONCEPT 403

abstraction [n] state of being lost in thought absorption, aloofness, brooding, cogitation, consideration, contemplation, daydreaming, detachment, engrossment, entrancement, musing, pensiveness, pondering, preoccupation, reflecting, reflection, remoteness, reverie, ruminating, thinking, trance; CONCEPT 410

abstruse [adj] difficult to understand abstract, clear as dishwater*, complex, complicated, deep, enigmatic, esoteric, Greek to me*, heavy*, hidden, incomprehensible, intricate, involved, muddy, obscure, perplexing, profound, puzzling, recondite, subtle, unfathomable, vague; CONCEPTS 402,562 —Ant. clear, concrete, easy, lucid, obvious, plain, simple

absurd [adj] ridiculous, senseless batty, campy, crazy, daffy, dippy*, flaky*, fooling around, foolish, for grins*, freaky, gagged up*, goofy*, idiotic, illogical, inane, incongruous, irrational, jokey, joshing, laughable, loony, ludicrous, nonsensical, nutty, off the wall*, preposterous, sappy*, screwy*, silly, stupid, tomfool, unreasonable, wacky; CONCEPTS 544,552,558 —Ant. certain, logical, rational, reasonable, sensible, wise

absurdity [n] ridiculous situation or behavior

applesauce*, BS*, bull*, crap*, craziness, farce, flapdoodle*, folly, foolishness, hot air*, idiocy, illogicality, illogicalness, improbability, inanity, incongruity, insanity, irrationality, jazz*, jive*, ludicrousness, ridiculousness, senselessness, silliness, stupidity, unreasonableness; CONCEPTS 650,656 —Ant. logic, reason, reasonableness, sense

abundance [n] great amount or supply affluence, ampleness, bounty, copiousness, fortune, myriad, opulence, plenitude, plenty, plethora, profusion, prosperity, prosperousness, riches, thriving, wealth; CONCEPTS 710,767 —Ant. dearth, deficiency, inadequacy, lack

abundant [adj] plentiful, large in number abounding, ample, bounteous, bountiful, copious, crawling with*, cup runs over with*, eco-rich, exuberant, filled, full, generous, heavy, lavish, liberal, lousy with*, luxuriant, mucho*, no end of*, overflowing, plate is full of*, plenteous, plenty, profuse, rich, rolling in*, stinking with*, sufficient, teeming; CONCEPT 781 —Ant. lacking, rare, scarce, sparse

abuse [n1] wrong use corruption, crime, debasement, delinquency, desecration, exploitation, fault, injustice, misapplication, misconduct, misdeed, mishandling, mismanage, misuse, offense, perversion, prostitution, sin, wrong, wrongdoing; CONCEPT 156

abuse [n2] physical hurting, injuring crime, damage, defilement, harm, hurt, impairment, injury, malevolence, maltreatment, manhandling, misdeed, offense, pollution, violation, wrongdoing; CONCEPT 246 —Ant. aid, help, preservation, respect

abuse [n3] verbal attack bad-mouthing*, blame, castigation, censure, curse, curses*, defamation, derision, hosing*, insults, invective, kicking around*, knifing*, libel, obloquy, opprobrium, pushing around*, put-down, quinine*, reproach, revilement, scolding, signifying, slander, swearing, tirade, upbraiding, vilification, vituperation; CONCEPT 54 —Ant. acclamation, adulation, approval, commendation, plaudit, praise

abuse [v1] physically hurt or injure bang up*, beat up, bung up*, corrupt, cut up*, damage, defile, deprave, desecrate, harm, hose*, ill-treat, impair, maltreat, mar, mess up*, mishandle, mistreat, misuse, molest, oppress, persecute, pollute*, roughhouse, rough up, ruin, shake up*, spoil, taint, total*, victimize, violate, wax*; CONCEPT 246 —Ant. cherish, defend, help, preserve, protect, respect

abuse [v2] use wrongly dissipate, exhaust, misemploy, mishandle, misuse, overburden, overtax, overwork, prostitute, spoil, squander, taint, waste; CONCEPT 156 —Ant. benefit, care for, esteem, prize, respect, revere

abuse [v3] attack with words backbite, bad-mouth, bash, belittle, berate, blow off*, calumniate, cap*, castigate, cuss out*, cut down*, cut to the quick*, decry, defame, derogate, discount, do a number on*, dump on*, give a black eye*, hurl brickbat*, insult, knock*, minimize, nag, offend, oppress, persecute, pick on, put down*, rag on*, reproach, revile, ride*, rip up*, run down*, scold, signify, slam*, slap*, sling mud*, smear*, sound*, swear at*, tear apart*, trash*, upbraid, vilify, vituperate, zing*; CONCEPTS *52,54* —*Ant.* acclaim, adulate, approve, commend, compliment, praise

abuse [v4] *take advantage of* do an injustice to, exploit, impose on, use, wrong; CONCEPTS *156,384* —*Ant.* cherish, esteem, honor, respect, revere, treasure

abusive [adj] *exhibiting unkind behavior or words* calumniating, castigating, censorious, contumelious, defamatory, derisive, disparaging, insolent, insulting, invective, libelous, maligning, obloquious, offensive, opprobrious, reproachful, reviling, rude, sarcastic, scathing, scolding, scurrilous, sharp-tongued, slanderous, traducing, upbraiding, vilifying, vituperative; CONCEPT *267* —*Ant.* complimentary, kind, respectful

abut [v] *touch or be next to something* adjoin, be adjacent to, border on, butt against, join, neighbor; CONCEPT *749*

abutment [n] *masonry mass* arch end, bridge end, end piece, jutting piece, support, vault end; CONCEPTS *745,827,833*

abysmal [adj1] *great extent; immeasurable* bottomless, boundless, complete, deep, endless, extreme, illimitable, incalculable, infinite, profound, thorough, unending, unfathomable, vast; CONCEPTS *772,793* —*Ant.* infinite

abysmal [adj2] *extending deeply* bottomless, fathomless, plumbless, plummetless; CONCEPT *777* —*Ant.* low

abyss [n] *something very deep, usually a feature of land* abysm, chasm, crevasse, depth, fissure, gorge, gulf, hole, pit, void; CONCEPTS *509,514*

academia [n] *scholarly world* academe, academic community, academicians, college, savants, school; CONCEPTS *287,288,289*

academic [adj1] *relating to schooling, learning* bookish, book-learned, college, collegiate, erudite, intellectual, learned, pedantic, scholarly, scholastic, studious, university; CONCEPT *536* —*Ant.* ignorant, untaught

academic [adj2] *relating to theories, philosophy* abstract, closet, conjectural, formalistic, hypothetical, notional, speculative, theoretical; CONCEPTS *402,529* —*Ant.* ordinary, plain, practical, simple

academic [n] *scholar or university/college teacher* academician, lecturer, professor, pupil, scholar, scholastic, student, tutor; CONCEPT *350* —*Ant.* ignoramus

academy [n1] *school, especially for higher education* boarding school, brainery*, finishing school, halls of ivy*, institute, military school, preparatory school, prep school, secondary school, seminary; CONCEPT *289*

academy [n2] *society or institution interested in learning* alliance, association, circle, council, federation, foundation, fraternity, institute, league; CONCEPT *288*

accede [v] *agree or consent* accept, acquiesce, admit, allow, assent, be game for*, cave in*, comply, concede, concur, cooperate, cry uncle*, endorse, enter into, fold, give the go-ahead*, give the green light*, go along with, grant, let, okay, permit, play ball*, roll over and play dead*, subscribe, throw in the towel*, yield; CONCEPTS *8,50,82,88* —*Ant.* condemn, demur, denounce, denounce, deny, protest, refuse

accelerate [v] *increase speed, timing* advance,

drive, dust*, expedite, fire up*, forward, further, gun*, hammer on*, hasten, hurry, impel, lay a patch*, lean rubber*, make tracks*, nail it*, open up*, peel rubber*, precipitate, put on afterburners*, put pedal to metal*, quicken, railroad*, rev, rev up, roll*, speed up, spur, step on gas*, step up, stimulate, tool*; CONCEPTS *234,242* —*Ant.* decelerate, defer, hinder, impede, postpone, retard, slow down

acceleration [n] *increasing speed, timing* dispatch, expedition, hastening, hurrying, quickening, speeding up, spurring, stepping up, stimulation; CONCEPT *234* —*Ant.* deceleration, deferral, hindrance, retardation, slowing down

accent [n1] *importance, emphasis* significance, stress, weight; CONCEPT *668* —*Ant.* unimportance

accent [n2] *stress or pitch in pronunciation* accentuation, articulation, beat, cadence, emphasis, enunciation, force, inflection, intonation, meter, modulation, pronunciation, rhythm, stroke, timbre, tonality, tone; CONCEPT *77*

accent [v] *place emphasis, importance* accentuate, draw attention to, emphasize, highlight, intensify, stress, underline, underscore; CONCEPTS *69,243* —*Ant.* disacknowledge, minimize

accentuate [v] *focus attention on* accent, bring attention to, call attention to, draw attention to, emphasize, feature, give prominence to, highlight, point up, spotlight, stress, underline, underscore; CONCEPT *77* —*Ant.* divert attention from, mask

accept [v1] *receive something given physically* acquire, gain, get, obtain, secure, take, welcome; CONCEPT *124* —*Ant.* deny, discard, refuse, reject

accept [v2] *allow into group* admit, receive, welcome; CONCEPT *384* —*Ant.* blackball, decline, deny, reject

accept [v3] *believe the goodness, realness of something* acknowledge, affirm, approbate, approve, buy*, countenance, fancy, favor, go for*, hold, hold with, like, recognize, relish, swallow*, take as gospel truth*, take stock in*, trust; CONCEPT *12* —*Ant.* disagree, dispute, reject, renounce, repudiate

accept [v4] *put up with* acknowledge, acquiesce, agree, assent, bear, bear with, bow, capitulate, defer to, don't make waves*, don't rock the boat*, endure, fit in, go along with, live with, play the game*, recognize, respect, sit still for*, stand, stand for, stomach, submit to, suffer, swallow, take, tolerate, yield to; CONCEPT *23* —*Ant.* demur, disallow, reject

accept [v5] *receive by agreeing, consenting* accede, acknowledge, acquiesce, admit, adopt, affirm, agree to, approve, assent, assume, avow, bear, buy, check out*, comply, concur with, cooperate with, give stamp of approval*, give the go-ahead*, give the green light*, give the nod*, go for*, lap up*, okay, recognize, rubberstamp*, set store by*, sign, sign off on*, take on*, take one up on*, thumbs up*, undertake; CONCEPTS *8,82* —*Ant.* decline, disapprove, refuse

acceptable [adj] *satisfactory, agreeable* adequate, admissible, all right, A-OK*, average, big*, common, cooking with gas*, cool*, copacetic, decent, delightful, fair, hep*, hip*, hunky-dory*, in the swim*, kosher*, large, okay, on the ball*, on the beam*, passable, peachy keen*, pleasant, pleasing, respectable, right on*, standard, sufficient, swell*, tolerable, trendy, unexceptional, unobjectionable, up to code*, up to snuff*; welcome; CONCEPTS 533,558 —*Ant.* disagreeable, disturbing, unacceptable, unsatisfactory, unwelcome

acceptance [n1] *agreement, taking* accepting, acknowledgment, acquiring, admission, approval, assent, compliance, consent, cooperation, gaining, getting, go-ahead*, green light*, nod*, obtaining, okay, permission, receipt, receiving, reception, recognition, securing, taking on, undertaking, yes; CONCEPTS 8,124 —*Ant.* disagreement, dissent, refusal

acceptance [n2] *belief in goodness of something* accedence, accession, acknowledgment, acquiescence, admission, adoption, affirmation, agreement, approbation, approval, assent, concession, concurrence, favor, recognition, seal of approval; CONCEPTS 12,32 —*Ant.* disbelief

accepted [adj] *generally agreed upon* accustomed, acknowledged, allowed, approved, arrived at, authorized, card-carrying*, chosen, confirmed, conventional, credited, current, customary, endorsed, established, fashionable, in vogue, kosher*, legit*, normal, okayed, orthodox, passed, popular, preferred, received, recognized, regular, sanctioned, standard, straight*, time-honored, touted, universal, unopposed, usual, welcomed; CONCEPTS 547,558 —*Ant.* irregular, questionable, unconventional, unorthodox

access [n] *admission, means of entry, approach* admittance, approach, avenue, connection, contact, course, door, entrance, entree, entry, in, ingress, introduction, key, open arms*, open door*, passage, path, road, route, way; CONCEPTS 501,631 —*Ant.* egress, outlet

accessible [adj] *approachable; ready for use* attainable, available, door's always open*, employable, exposed, getatable, handy, near, obtainable, open, operative, possible, practicable, public, reachable, susceptible, unrestricted, usable; CONCEPT 576 —*Ant.* inaccessible, limited, restricted

accession [n1] *something that augments, adds to* accretion, addition, augmentation, enlargement, extension, increase, increment, raise, rise; CONCEPTS 700,775

accession [n2] *coming to power* assumption, attainment, inauguration, induction, investment, succession, taking on, taking over; CONCEPTS 133,298 —*Ant.* decline, fall

accession [n3] *agreement* accedence, acceptance, acquiescence, assent, concurrence, consent; CONCEPTS 8,410 —*Ant.* disagreement, dispute, repudiation

accessorize [v] *add ornament* accent, add on, adorn, equip, supplement; CONCEPTS 162,177

accessory [n1] *ornament; accompanying item; supplementary part* accent, addition, adjunct, adornment, appendage, appendix, appliance, appurtenance, attachment, component, decoration, extension, extra, frill, help, supplement, trim, trimming; CONCEPT 834 —*Ant.* principal

accessory [n2] *person peripherally involved in illegal activity* abettor, accomplice, aid, aide, assistant, associate, co-conspirator, colleague,

confederate, conspirator, helper, insider, partner, plant*, ringer*, shill*, stall*, subordinate; CONCEPT 412

accident [n1] *unexpected, undesirable event; often physically injurious* blow, calamity, casualty, collision, crack-up*, disaster, fender-bender*, fluke*, hazard, misadventure, misfortune, mishap, pileup*, rear ender*, setback, smash*, smashup*, stack-up*, total*, wrack-up*; CONCEPT 674 —*Ant.* intent, intention, necessity, plan, provision

accident [n2] *chance event* adventure, circumstance, contingency, fate, fluke*, fortuity, fortune, happening, luck, occasion, occurrence, turn; CONCEPT 679 —*Ant.* calculation, decision, decree, plan

accidental [adj] *happening unexpectedly* adventitious, casual, chance, coincidental, contingent, fluky*, fortuitous, inadvertent, incidental, random, uncalculated, unexpected, unforeseen, unintended, unintentional, unplanned; CONCEPTS 530,552 —*Ant.* decided, designed, essential, intended, intentional, planned, premeditated

accidentally [adv] *by chance* by mistake, fortuitously, haphazardly, unintentionally, unwittingly; CONCEPTS 548,552

accident-prone [adj] *clumsy* all thumbs*, bungling, inept, klutzy*, two left feet*; CONCEPTS 401,402,584

acclaim [n] *expression of approval* acclamation, acknowledgment, applause, approbation, celebration, cheering, clapping, commendation, eulogizing, exaltation, honor, kudos, pat on the back*, pat on the head*, plaudits, PR, praise, puff, pumping up*, rave, recognition, strokes*, stroking*; CONCEPT 69 —*Ant.* beratement, criticism, disapproval, jeering, vituperation

acclaim [v] *give approval* applaud, approve, blow horn*, boost, celebrate, cheer, clap, commend, compliment, eulogize, exalt, extol, give a bouquet*, give a posy*, give kudos*, hail, hand it to*, hear it for*, honor, laud, praise, puff up*, push*, rave, recommend, root, salute, stroke*; CONCEPT 69 —*Ant.* berate, censure, damn, denounce, disapprove, dishonor, vituperate

acclaimed [adj] *praised* cheered, extolled, hailed, lauded, renowned; CONCEPTS 568,574

acclamation [n] *enthusiastic expression of approval* acclaim, adulation, applause, approbation, big hand*, cheer, cheering, cheers, hand, honor, jubilation, laudation, ovation, plaudits, salutation, standing O*, tribute; CONCEPTS 69,377 —*Ant.* disapproval

acclimate [v] *make or become adjusted, adapted* acclimatize, accommodate, acculture, accustom, climatize, conform, get used to, habituate, harden, season, toughen; CONCEPTS 202,701

accolade [n] *strong praise, recognition of achievement* approval, award, badge, decoration, distinction, honor, kudos*, laurels; CONCEPT 69

accommodate [v1] *make room, lodging available* board, contain, domicile, entertain, furnish, harbor, hold, house, put up*, quarter, receive, rent, shelter, supply, take in, welcome; CONCEPT 226 —*Ant.* turn away, turn out

accommodate [v2] *make, become suitable for*

something accord, accustom, adapt, adjust, agree, attune, bend over backwards*, comply, compose, conform, coordinate, correspond, don't make waves*, don't rock the boat*, fit, go by the book*, go with the flow*, harmonize, integrate, make consistent, modify, play the game*, proportion, reconcile, settle, shape up, suit, tailor, tailor-make, tune; CONCEPTS *23,126* —*Ant.* disarrange, unsuit

accommodate [v3] *perform service* afford, aid, arrange, assist, avail, benefit, bow, comfort, convenience, defer, favor, furnish, gratify, help, humor, indulge, oblige, pamper, please, provide, serve, settle, submit, suit, supply, support, sustain, yield; CONCEPT *136* —*Ant.* bar, block, frustrate, hinder, impede, limit, obstruct, prevent, stop

accommodating [adj] *willing to help* considerate, cooperative, friendly, generous, handy, helpful, hospitable, kind, neighborly, obliging, on deck*, on tap*, polite, unselfish, user friendly*; CONCEPTS *542,555* —*Ant.* alienating, disobliging, estranged

accommodation [n] *adjustment for different situation, circumstances* adaptation, compliance, composition, compromise, conformity, fifty-fifty deal*, fitting, modification, reconciliation, settlement; CONCEPT *697*

accommodations [n] *place of residence, usually temporary* apartment, board, boardinghouse, crash pad*, crib*, digs*, hotel, house, housing, lodging, motel, pad*, quarters, roof, room and board, rooming house, shelter; CONCEPT *516*

accompaniment [n1] *necessary part or embellishment* accessory, adjunct, appendage, appurtenance, attachment, attendant, attribute, augmentation, complement, concomitant, enhancement, enrichment, supplement; CONCEPTS *834,835*

accompaniment [n2] *music that supports a theme or performer in a composition* back, background, backing, back-up, harmony, instrument, part; CONCEPT *262*

accompany [v1] *go or be with something* associate with, attend, chaperon, come along, conduct, consort, convoy, date, dog*, draft*, drag*, escort, follow, go along, guard, guide, hang around with*, hang out*, keep company, lead, look after, shadow, shlep along*, show about, show around, spook, squire, stick to*, string along*, tag along*, tailgate*, take out, usher; CONCEPTS *113,224* —*Ant.* abandon, desert, leave, withdraw

accompany [v2] *occur with something* add, appear with, append, be connected, belong to, characterize, coexist, coincide with, come with, complete, co-occur, follow, go together, happen with, join with, occur with, supplement, take place with; CONCEPT *643*

accomplice [n] *helper, especially in committing a crime* abettor, accessory, aid, aide, ally, assistant, associate, co-conspirator, collaborator, colleague, confederate, conspirator, insider, partner, plant*, stall*; CONCEPT *412* —*Ant.* adversary, enemy, opponent

accomplish [v] *succeed in doing* achieve, arrive, attain, bring about, bring off, carry out, conclude, consummate, do, do a bang-up job*, do

justice, do one proud*, do the trick*, effect, finish, fulfill, gain, get someplace*, get there*, hit*, make hay*, make it, manage, nail it*, perform, produce, pull off*, put it over*, rack up*, reach, realize, score*, sew up*, take care of, win; CONCEPTS *91,706* —*Ant.* abandon, fail, give up, not finish, nullify, relinquish

accomplished [adj] *skilled in activity* able, adept, brainy, consummate, cool*, cultivated, expert, gifted, hep*, hip*, masterly, polished, practiced, proficient, savvy, sharp, skillful, talented, wised up*, with it*; CONCEPTS *326,528* —*Ant.* inept, skilless, unable

accomplishment [n] *something successfully done, completed* ability, achievement, act, art, attainment, bringing about, capability, carrying out, completion, conclusion, consummation, coup, deed, effecting, effort, execution, exploit, feat, finish, fulfillment, performance, production, proficiency, realization, skill, stroke, talent, triumph; CONCEPT *706* —*Ant.* defeat, failure, frustration, nullification

accord [n] *agreement, mutual understanding (often written)* 10-4*, accordance, concert, concord, concurrence, conformity, congruence, correspondence, deal, good vibes*, good vibrations*, harmony, okay, pact, rapport, reconciliation, sympathy, treaty, unanimity; CONCEPT *684* —*Ant.* antagonism, denial, disagreement, dissension, opposition, refusal

accord [v1] *give approval, grant* accede, acquiesce, admit, allow, award, bestow, concede, confer, endow, give, present, render, tender, vouchsafe; CONCEPTS *50,83,88* —*Ant.* argue, challenge, deny, disallow, disapprove, oppose, question, refuse, withhold

accord [v2] *come to agreement* affirm, agree, assent, be in tune, concur, conform, correspond, fit, harmonize, jibe, match, square, suit, tally; CONCEPTS *8,664* —*Ant.* contest, deny, disagree, withhold

accordant [adj] *in agreement* agreeing, conforming, congruous, harmonious, in concert; CONCEPTS *558,563*

accordingly [adv] *in an appropriate, suitable way* appropriately, as a consequence, as a result, consequently, correspondingly, duly, equally, ergo, fitly, hence, in consequence, in respect to, in that event, properly, proportionately, respectively, resultantly, so, subsequently, suitably, then, therefore, thus, under the circumstances; CONCEPT *558* —*Ant.* inappropriately, unsuitably

accordion [n] *musical instrument* concertina, groanbox*, melodeon, squeezebox*, stomach Steinway*, windbox*; CONCEPTS *463,499*

accost [v] *approach for conversation or solicitation* address, annoy, bother, brace*, buttonhole*, call, challenge, confront, cross, dare, entice, face, flag, greet, hail, proposition, run into, salute, welcome, whistle for*; CONCEPTS *48,51* —*Ant.* avoid, dodge, evade, ignore, scorn, shun

account [n1] *written description of past events* ABCs*, annal, blow by blow*, bulletin, chronicle, detail, explanation, history, lowdown*, make*, narration, narrative, play by play*, recital, report, run-down, score, story, tab, take, tale, the picture*, the whole picture*, version; CONCEPT *282*

account [n2] *record of finances, fees, or charges* bad news*, balance, bill, book, books, charge, check, computation, cuff*, grunt*, inventory, invoice, IOU*, ledger, reckoning, record, register, report, score, statement, tab, tally; CONCEPTS 331,332

account [n3] *basis or consideration for action* cause, ground, grounds, interest, justification, motive, rationale, rationalization, reason, regard, sake; CONCEPT 229

accountability [n] *responsibility* answerability, blameworthiness, liability; CONCEPT 645

accountable [adj] *responsible for having done answerable*, charged with, culpable, liable, obligated, obliged, on the hook*; CONCEPT 527 —Ant. blameless, innocent, irresponsible, unaccountable, unreliable, untrustworthy

accountant [n] *person who maintains financial accounts of a business* actuary, analyst, auditor, bookkeeper, calculator, cashier, clerk, comptroller, CPA, examiner, public accountant, reckoner, teller; CONCEPTS 348,353

account for [v] *offer reason, explanation* answer for, clarify, elucidate, explain, illuminate, justify, rationalize, resolve; CONCEPT 57 —Ant. underestimate

accounting [n] *keeping financial accounts* auditing, balancing the books*, bookkeeping, calculating, computing, reckoning; CONCEPTS 28,764

accredit [v1] *attribute responsibility or achievement* ascribe, assign, charge, credit, refer; CONCEPTS 49,69

accredit [v2] *give authorization or control* appoint, approve, authorize, certify, commission, empower, enable, endorse, entrust, guarantee, license, okay, recognize, sanction, vouch for; CONCEPTS 50,88 —Ant. deny, disapprove, reject

accretion [n] *gradual growth, addition* accession, accumulation, augmentation, build-up, increase, increment, raise, rise; CONCEPT 780 —Ant. decrease, deduction, shrinkage

accrual [n] *growth* accumulation, amassing, amassment, buildup, increase; CONCEPTS 432,780

accrue [v] *increase by addition or growth, often financial* accumulate, amass, build up, collect, enlarge, flow, gather, grow, increase; CONCEPTS 763,780 —Ant. decrease, lose

acculturation [n] *adjustment to culture* acclimatization, assimilation, culture shock, nationalization, naturalization; CONCEPTS 202,701

accumulate [v] *gather or amass something* accrue, acquire, add to, agglomerate, aggregate, amalgamate, assemble, bring together, cache, clean up*, collect, collocate, compile, concentrate, cumulate, draw together, expand, gain, gather, grow, heap, heap together, hoard, incorporate, increase, load up*, lump*, make a bundle*, make a killing*, mass, pile*, pile up*, procure, profit, rack up*, roll up*, round up*, scare up*, stack up, stockpile, store, store up, swell, unite; CONCEPTS 236,245 —Ant. disperse, dissipate, dwindle, lessen, lose, spend, squander, waste

accumulation [n] *gathering or amassing* accession, accretion, addition, agglomeration, aggrandizement, aggregation, amassment, augmentation, build-up, chunk, collecting, collection, conglomeration, enlargement, gob, growth, heap, hoarding, hunk, increase, inflation, intensification, mass, multiplication, pile, quantity, stack, stock, store, trove, up, upping; CONCEPTS 432,780 —Ant. dispersal, dispersion, dissipation, scattering

accuracy [n] *precision or correctness* accurateness, carefulness, certainty, closeness, definiteness, definitiveness, definitude, efficiency, exactitude, exactness, faultlessness, incisiveness, mastery, meticulousness, preciseness, sharpness, skill, skillfulness, strictness, sureness, truthfulness, veracity, verity; CONCEPTS 638,654 —Ant. erroneousness, falsehood, inaccuracy, mistake

accurate [adj1] *precise* authentic, careful, close, concrete, correct, defined, definite, deft, detailed, discriminating, discriminative, distinct, exact, explicit, factual, faithful, genuine, judicious, just, literal, matter-of-fact, methodical, meticulous, on the button*, on the money*, on the nose*, particular, proper, punctilious, punctual, regular, right, rigid, rigorous, scientific, scrupulous, severe, sharp, skillful, solid, specific, strict, systematic, true, ultraprecise, unerring, unmistakable, veracious; CONCEPT 535 —Ant. careless, faulty, inaccurate, lax, vague

accurate [adj2] *correct, without error* absolute, actual, authentic, authoritative, certain, conclusive, definite, definitive, errorless, exact, factual, faultless, final, flawless, genuine, infallible, irrefutable, official, perfect, right, straight, strict, true, truthful, undeniable, undisputed, unimpeachable, unquestionable, unrefuted, valid, veracious; CONCEPT 557 —Ant. doubtful, erroneous, false, inaccurate, misleading, mistaken, questionable, untruthful, wrong

accurately [adv] *correctly* exactly, flawlessly, meticulously, precisely, scrupulously, veraciously; CONCEPTS 535,557

accursed [adj] *cursed* bedeviled, condemned, damned, done for*, doomed, hexed, ill-fated, star-crossed, unfortunate; CONCEPTS 548,571

accusation [n] *charge of wrongdoing, fault* allegation, arraignment, attribution, beef*, blast*, bum rap*, censure, citation, complaint, denunciation, dido, exposé, gripe, impeachment, imputation, incrimination, indictment, insinuation, recrimination, roar*, rumble*, slur, squawk*, stink*; CONCEPT 54 —Ant. exculpation, praise

accuse [v] *place blame for wrongdoing, fault* allege, apprehend, arraign, arrest, attack, attribute, betray, blame, blow the whistle*, brand, bring charges, censure, charge, cite, complain, criminate, denounce, file claim, finger*, frame, hang something on*, hold accountable, impeach, implicate, impute, incriminate, inculpate, indict, lay at door*, let have it*, libel, litigate, lodge complaint, name, pin on*, point finger at*, prosecute, recriminate, serve summons, slander, slur, sue, summon, tax; CONCEPT 44 —Ant. absolve, exculpate, exonerate, praise, vindicate

accuser [n] *person laying blame* indicter, informer, prosecutor, rat*, tattletale*; CONCEPTS 412,423

accustom [v] *get used to* acclimatize, acculturate, acquaint, adapt, familiarize, habituate, season; CONCEPTS 35,202

accustomed [adj1] *be or become prepared,*

ac
ac

used to acclimatized, acquainted, adapted, addicted, confirmed, disciplined, familiar, familiarized, given to, grooved*, habituated, habituated in, in the habit, inured, seasoned, settled in, trained; CONCEPT 403 —**Ant.** unaccustomed

accustomed [*adj2*] *normal, usual* accepted, chronic, common, conventional, customary, established, everyday, expected, general, habitual, ordinary, orthodox, regular, routine, set, traditional, typical; CONCEPT 547 —**Ant.** abnormal, unaccustomed, unusual

AC-DC [*adj*] *bisexual* ambidextrous, androgynous, bi*, double-gaited, epicene, gay, gynandrous, hermaphroditic, hits both ways*, intersexual, monoclinous, swings both ways*, switch-hitting*; CONCEPT 372

ace [*adj*] *exhibiting expertise in some activity* brilliant, champion, distinguished, excellent, expert, first-rate, great, master, outstanding, superb, virtuoso; CONCEPT 528 —**Ant.** inept, unskilled

ace [*n*] *expert in some activity* champion, genius, master, pro, star, virtuoso, winner, wizard; CONCEPT 416 —**Ant.** clod, ignoramus

ace in the hole [*n*] *secret weapon* card up one's sleeve, reserve; CONCEPTS 274,340

acerbate [*v*] *exasperate* aggravate, annoy, disturb, perturb, provoke, rattle one's cage*; CONCEPTS 7,19

acerbic [*adj*] *bitter, sharp, or sour* acidic, acrid, astringent, caustic, harsh, sharp, tart; CONCEPT 613

acerbity [*n1*] *bitterness of taste* acidity, asperity, astringency, mordancy, sourness, tartness; CONCEPTS 462,613 —**Ant.** mellowness, mildness, sweetness

acerbity [*n2*] *harsh speech, behavior* acrimoniousness, causticity, ill temper, irritability, rancor, rudeness, sarcasm, sarcasticness, vitriolicism; CONCEPTS 267,401 —**Ant.** kindness, sweetness

aces [*adj*] *great* excellent, fabulous, peachy, wonderful; CONCEPTS 527,528,574

ache [*n*] *sore feeling; dull pain* anguish, hurt, misery, pang, pounding, smarting, soreness, spasm, suffering, throb, throbbing, throe, twinge; CONCEPTS 316,410,728 —**Ant.** comfort, ease, health, relief

ache [*v*] *feeling soreness or dull pain, often physical* be sore, hurt, pain, pound, smart, suffer, throb, twinge; CONCEPTS 13,17,303,308,313

achievable [*adj*] *doable* attainable, feasible, obtainable; CONCEPTS 528,552,558

achieve [*v*] *bring to successful conclusion; reach a goal* accomplish, acquire, actualize, attain, bring about, bring off*, bring to pass, cap, carry out, carry through, close, complete, conclude, consummate, deliver, discharge, dispatch, do, earn, earn wings*, effect, effectuate, enact, end, execute, finish, follow through, fulfill, gain, get, get done, manage, negotiate, obtain, perfect, perform, procure, produce, rack up*, reach, realize, resolve, score, seal, see through, settle, sign, solve, win, wind up, work out; CONCEPT 706 —**Ant.** fail, lose, miss

achievement [*n*] *something completed successfully; goal reached* accomplishment, acquirement, acquisition, act, actualization, attainment, completion, conquest, consummation, con-

trivance, creation, deed, effectuation, effort, enactment, encompassment, execution, exploit, feat, fulfillment, hit, masterpiece, performance, production, realization, stroke, success, tour de force, triumph, victory; CONCEPT 706 —**Ant.** defeat, failure, forfeit, injury, miscue, misfortune, neglect, negligence

Achilles' heel [*n*] *vulnerability* chink in the armor*, deficiency, frailty, handicap, soft underbelly*, susceptibility, weakness; CONCEPTS 101,230,411,580

acid [*adj1*] *bitter, sour in taste* acerbic, acidulous, biting, piquant, pungent, sharp, tart, vinegarish, vinegary; CONCEPT 613 —**Ant.** bland, sweet

acid [*adj2*] *having acidic, corrosive properties* acerbic, acidulous, acrid, anti-alkaline, biting, bleaching, corroding, disintegrative, dissolvent, eating away, eroding, erosive, oxidizing, rusting; CONCEPT 485 —**Ant.** basic

acid [*adj3*] *bitter in words or behavior* acerbic, biting, caustic, cutting, dry, harsh, hateful, hurtful, mordant, nasty, offensive, sarcastic, sharp, stinging, trenchant, vitriolic; CONCEPTS 267,401 —**Ant.** kind, nice

acid [*n*] *lysergic acid diethylamide, LSD* black tabs*, blotter*, blue acid*, blue dot*, blue Owsley*, California sunshine*, candy*, cubes*, dot*, electric Kool Aid*, green dragon*, hallucinogen, instant Zen*, Lucy in the sky with diamonds*, magic mushrooms, mescalin, microdots*, mushrooms, orange sunshine*, Owsley's acid*, peyote, purple haze*, strawberry fields*, sugar cubes*, yellow sunshine*; CONCEPT 307

acidity [*n*] *bitterness* acerbity, acridness, astringency, causticity, pungency, sourness, tartness; CONCEPT 614

acid test [*n*] *test of value, genuineness* proof, proving ground, substantiation, trial, verification; CONCEPTS 87,290,291

acidulous [*adj1*] *bitter, sour* acerb, acerbic, acetose, dry, piquant, sharp, tart; CONCEPT 613 —**Ant.** sugary, sweet

acidulous [*adj2*] *bitter in speech* biting, cutting, ironical, mocking, sarcastic; CONCEPT 267 —**Ant.** kind, nice, sweet

acknowledge [*v1*] *verbally recognize authority* accede, accept, acquiesce, agree, allow, approve, attest to, certify, defend, defer to, endorse, grant, own, ratify, recognize, subscribe to, support, take an oath, uphold, yield; CONCEPTS 8,50,88 —**Ant.** forswear, ignore, refuse, renounce, repudiate

acknowledge [*v2*] *admit truth or reality of something* accede, accept, acquiesce, allow, avow, come clean*, come out of closet*, concede, confess, cop a plea*, crack*, declare, fess up*, get off chest*, grant, let on*, open up*, own, profess, recognize, yield; CONCEPTS 12,49 —**Ant.** abjure, contradict, disavow, renounce

acknowledge [*v3*] *verbally recognize receipt of something* address, answer, greet, hail, notice, react, remark, reply, respond, return, salute, thank; CONCEPTS 38,45,51,60 —**Ant.** disregard, ignore

acknowledgment [*n1*] *act of recognizing authority or truth of something* acceptance, accession, acquiescence, admission, admitting, affirmation, allowance, allowing, assent, assertion, asseveration, avowal, compliance, conceding, concession, concurrence, confession, confirmation, corroboration, declaration, profession, ratification, realization, recognition, yielding; CONCEPTS 8,50,88

acknowledgment [n2] *physical symbol of recognition* acclamation, addressing, answer, apology, applause, appreciation, bestowal, bow, card, confession, contract, credit, gift, gratitude, greeting, guarantee, hail, hailing, letter, nod, notice, reaction, receipt, reply, response, return, salutation, salute, signature, statement, support, thanks, token; CONCEPTS 595,628

acme [n] *pinnacle of achievement or physical object* apogee, capstone, climax, culmination, height, highest point, high point, meridian, optimum, peak, summit, top, ultimate, vertex, zenith; CONCEPTS 706,836 —*Ant.* nadir

acne [n] *blemishes* blackheads, pimples, pizzaface*, pustules, rosacea, skin inflammation, whiteheads, zits*; CONCEPT 580

acolyte [n] *attendant, usually in a church* aid, assistant, follower, helper; CONCEPT 361

acoustic [adj] *sound* audible, audio, auditory, aural, hearing, phonic; CONCEPTS 591,594

acoustics [n] *sound quality* echo, noise, sound, sound properties, sound transmission; CONCEPT 595

acquaint [v] *inform oneself or another about something new* accustom, advise, apprise, bring out, clue, come out with*, disclose, divulge, enlighten, familiarize, fill in, fix up*, get together*, habituate, inform, intro*, introduce, knock down*, let know, make familiar, notify, post, present, reveal, tell, warn; CONCEPTS 31,60 —*Ant.* conceal, deceive, falsify, hide, hold back, mislead, misrepresent, withhold

acquaintance [n1] *a person known informally* associate, association, colleague, companion, contact, friend, neighbor; CONCEPT 423 —*Ant.* stranger

acquaintance [n2] *knowledge of something through experience* awareness, cognizance, conversance, familiarity, fellowship, grasp, intimacy, ken, relationship, understanding; CONCEPT 409 —*Ant.* ignorance, strangeness, unfamiliarity

acquainted [adj] *aware* abreast, advised, apprised of, clued in*, conversant, enlightened, familiarized, familiar with, informed, in the know*, versed in; CONCEPT 402

acquiesce [v] *agree with some reluctance* accede, accept, accommodate, adapt, adjust, agree, allow, approve, bow to, buy, cave in*, come across, come around, comply, concur, conform, consent, cry uncle*, cut a deal*, ditto*, give in, give out, go along, jibe*, okay, pass, play ball*, reconcile, roll over and play dead*, say uncle*, set, shake on, submit, subscribe, yes, yield; CONCEPTS 8,10,23,82 —*Ant.* disagree, dissent, object, protest

acquiescence [n] *reluctant agreement* acceptance, accession, approval, assent, compliance, concurrence, conformity, consent, giving in, obedience, permission, resignation, submission, submissiveness, yielding; CONCEPTS 8,10 —*Ant.* disagreement, insubordination, rebellion

acquire [v] *obtain or receive* access, achieve, amass, annex, attain, bring in, buy, catch, collect, cop*, corral*, earn, gain, gather, get, get hands on, get hold of, grab, have, hustle, land, latch onto, lock up, pick up, procure, promote, rack up*, scare up*, secure, snag*, take, take possession of*, wangle*, win; CONCEPTS 120,124,142 —*Ant.* fail, forfeit, forgo, lose, relinquish, surrender, yield

acquisition [n1] *obtaining or receiving* accretion, achievement, acquirement, acquiring, addition, attainment, buy, gain, gaining, learning, obtainment, possession, prize, procuration, procurement, procuring, property, purchase, pursuit, recovery, redemption, retrieval, salvage, winning; CONCEPTS 120,124,142 —*Ant.* dearth, lack, loss, need, want

acquisition [n2] *something obtained, received* accomplishment, achievement, allowance, annuity, award, benefit, bonus, commission, dividend, donation, earnings, fortune, gain, gift, grant, income, increment, inheritance, net, premium, prize, proceeds, profit, remuneration, return, reward, riches, salary, security, wages, wealth, winnings; CONCEPTS 120,337,710

acquisitive [adj] *eager to obtain knowledge or things* avaricious, avid, covetous, demanding, desirous, grabbing, grabby, grasping, greedy, predatory, prehensile, rapacious; CONCEPT 542

acquit [v1] *announce removal of blame* absolve, blink at*, clear, deliver, discharge, disculpate, exculpate, excuse, exonerate, free, let go, let off, let off the hook*, liberate, release, relieve, vindicate, whitewash*, wink at*, wipe off*; CONCEPTS 50,83,88,317 —*Ant.* blame, censure, condemn, convict, damn, denounce, doom, sentence

acquit [v2] *behave some way* act, bear, carry, comport, conduct, deport, perform; CONCEPT 633

acquittal [n] *declaration removing blame* absolution, acquitting, amnesty, clearance, deliverance, discharge, discharging, dismissal, dismissing, exculpation, exemption, exoneration, freeing, letting off, liberation, pardon, release, releasing, relief from, reprieve, vindication; CONCEPTS 127,317,318 —*Ant.* blame, censure, conviction, denunciation, doom, sentence

acre [n] *piece of land, unit of area* acreage, bit, estate, grounds, manor, plot, property; CONCEPT 792

acreage [n] *land* back forty*, expanse, holding, parcel, plot, property, real estate; CONCEPT 509

acrid [adj1] *bitter, sour to taste* acid, amaroidal, astringent, biting, burning, caustic, harsh, irritating, pungent, sharp, stinging; CONCEPT 613 —*Ant.* delicious, savory, sweet

acrid [adj2] *nasty in behavior or words* acrimonious, austere, biting, bitter, caustic, cutting, harsh, mordant, sarcastic, sharp, trenchant, vitriolic; CONCEPTS 267,401 —*Ant.* complimentary, kind, nice

acrimonious [adj] *nasty in behavior, speech* acerbic, acid, angry, astringent, belligerent, biting, bitter, caustic, censorious, churlish, crabby, cranky, cross, cutting, indignant, irascible, irate, ireful, mad, mordant, peevish, petulant, rancorous, sarcastic, sharp, spiteful, splenetic, tart, testy, trenchant, wrathful; CONCEPTS 267,401 —*Ant.* kind, kindly, peaceable

acrimony [n] *nasty behavior, speech* acerbity, animosity, antipathy, asperity, astringency, belligerence, bitterness, churlishness, crankiness, harshness, ill will, irascibility, malevolence, malice, mordancy, peevishness, rancor, rudeness, sarcasm, spite, tartness, unkindness, virulence; CONCEPTS 633,657 —*Ant.* civility, courtesy, diplomacy, flattery, kindness, politeness, sweetness

acrobat [n] *performer who does tricks, physical feats* aerialist, artist, athlete, balancer, clown, contortionist, dancer, funambulist, gymnast, performer, stunt person, trapezist, tumbler; CONCEPT 352 —*Ant.* clod

acrobatics [n] *athletic floor exercises* balancing, feats, gymnastics, somersaults, stunts, tumbling; CONCEPT 363

across [prep] *traversing a space, side to side* athwart, beyond, cross, crossed, crosswise, opposite, over, transversely; CONCEPT 581

across-the-board [adj] *all* all-inclusive, blanket, complete, comprehensive, everything, sweeping, total; CONCEPTS 513,772

act [n1] *something done* accomplishment, achievement, action, deed, doing, execution, exploit, feat, move, operation, performance, step, thing, undertaking; CONCEPT 1 —*Ant.* cessation, idleness, inactivity, inertia, quiet, quiet, repose, rest, stoppage, suspension

act [n2] *legislative document* amendment, announcement, bill, clause, code, commitment, decree, edict, enactment, judgment, law, measure, order, ordinance, resolution, statute, subpoena, summons, verdict, warrant, writ; CONCEPTS 271,318

act [n3] *part of a performance* bit*, curtain, epilogue, gag*, introduction, number, piece, prologue, routine, scene, schtick*, show, sketch, spot, turn; CONCEPT 264

act [n4] *pretended behavior* affectation, attitude, bit*, chaser*, dissimulation, fake, false front*, feigning, front, performance, phony, pose, posture, pretense, put-on, sham, show, shuck and jive*, simulation, soft soap*, stall, stance, stunt, sweet talk*; CONCEPT 633

act [v1] *do something* accomplish, achieve, begin, carry on, carry out, consummate, cook, create, develop, do, do a number*, do one's thing*, enforce, execute, function, get in there*, go about, go for broke*, go for it*, go in for*, go that route*, go to town*, intrude, knock off*, labor, make progress, maneuver, move, officiate, operate, percolate*, perk*, perpetrate, persevere, persist, practice, preside, pursue, respond, serve, take effect, take part, take steps, take up, transort, undertake, work out; CONCEPTS 1,4 —*Ant.* abstain, cease, discontinue, give up, halt, hesitate, idle, refrain, stop

act [v2] *behave in a certain way* appear, behave, carry, carry oneself, carry out, comport, conduct, do, enact, execute, exert, perform, give the appearance, go about, impress as, operate, perform, play part, react, represent oneself, seem, serve, strike, take on; CONCEPT 633

act [v3] *entertain by playing a role* be on*, bring down the house*, burlesque, characterize, do a turn*, dramatize, emote, enact, feign, go on, go over, ham*, ham it up*, impersonate, lay an egg*, make debut, mime, mimic, mug, parody, perform, personate, personify, play, play act, play gig, play part, play role, portray, pretend, put it over*, rehearse, represent, say one's piece*, simulate, star, stooge*, strut*, take part, tread the boards*; CONCEPT 292

acting [adj] *substituting in a role* ad interim, adjutant, alternate, assistant, delegated, deputy, interim, pro tem, pro tempore, provisional, surrogate, temporary; CONCEPT 560 —*Ant.* permanent

acting [n] *entertaining, performing* assuming, characterization, depiction, dramatics, dramatizing, enacting, enactment, feigning, hamming*, histrionics, imitating, imitation, impersonation, improvisation, mime, mimicry, pantomime, performance, play acting, playing, portrayal, portraying, posing, posturing, pretending, pretense, putting, rendition, seeming, showing off, simulating, stagecraft, stooging*, theatre, theatricals; CONCEPT 292

action [n1] *something done* activity, agility, alacrity, alertness, animation, bag*, ballgame*, big idea*, bit*, business, bustle, commotion, dash, deal, energy, enterprise, flurry, force, functioning, game, going, happening, haste, hoopla*, hopper*, industry, in the works, life, liveliness, motion, movement, occupation, operation, plan, power, process, proposition, racket*, reaction, response, rush, scene, spirit, stir, stunt, trip, turmoil, vigor, vim, vitality, vivacity; CONCEPT 1 —*Ant.* cessation, idleness, inaction, inactivity, inertia, repose, rest, stoppage

action [n2] *individual deed* accomplishment, achievement, act, blow, commission, dealings, doing, effort, enterprise, execution, exercise, exertion, exploit, feat, handiwork, maneuver, manipulation, move, operation, performance, procedure, step, stroke, thrust, transaction, undertaking; CONCEPTS 91,706

action [n3] *a legal process* case, cause, claim, lawsuit, litigation, proceeding, prosecution, suit; CONCEPT 317

action [n4] *an aggressive military deed* battle, combat, conflict, contest, encounter, engagement, fight, fighting, fray, skirmish, warfare; CONCEPT 320

activate [v] *initiate something; start a function* actify, actuate, arouse, call up, energize, impel, mobilize, motivate, move, prompt, propel, rouse, set in motion, start, stimulate, stir, switch on, take out of mothballs*, trigger, turn on; CONCEPT 234 —*Ant.* arrest, stop

active [adj1] *having movement* alive, astir, at work, bustling, effective, efficacious, exertive, flowing, functioning, going, hasty, impelling, in force, in play, in process, mobile, movable, moving, operating, operative, progressive, pushing, rapid, restless, rolling, running, rushing, rustling, shifting, simmering, speeding, speedy, streaming, swarming, traveling, turning, walking, working; CONCEPT 542 —*Ant.* abeyant, dormant, immobile, inactive, inert, lazy, sluggish

active [adj2] *very involved in activity* aggressive, agile, alert, alive, animated, assiduous, bold, brisk, bustling, busy, chipper, daring, dashing, determined, dexterous, diligent,

dynamic, eager, energetic, engaged, enlivened, enterprising, enthusiastic, eventful, fireball*, forceful, forcible, fresh, frisky, hard-working, high-spirited, hyper*, industrious, intense, inventive, jumping, keen, lively, nimble, on the move, perky, persevering, purposeful, pushing, quick, rapid, ready, resolute, sharp, sprightly, spry, whiz*, zealous; CONCEPTS 401,542
—Ant. disinterested, idle, indifferent, lazy, quiescent, quiet

activism [n] action for change advocacy, boycotting, championing, effecting change, influence peddling, involvement, logrolling, militancy, moving and shaking*, picketing, striking; CONCEPT 689

activity [n1] state of being active action, activeness, animation, bustle, enterprise, exercise, exertion, hustle, labor, life, liveliness, motion, movement; CONCEPT 1,748 —Ant. idleness, immobility, inactivity, indolence, inertia, laziness, sluggishness

activity [n2] special interest or pursuit act, avocation, bag*, ballgame*, bit*, deed, endeavor, enterprise, entertainment, game, hobby, job, labor, occupation, pastime, project, racket, scene*, scheme, stunt, task, trip, undertaking, venture, work, zoo*; CONCEPT 32 —Ant. hate

act of God [n] natural disaster accident, earthquake, freak accident, hurricane, tornado, unforeseen event; CONCEPTS 674,675

actor [n] person who performs, entertains by role-playing amateur, artist, barnstormer, bit player, character, clown, comedian, entertainer, extra, foil, ham*, hambone*, headliner, idol, impersonator, ingénue, lead, mime, mimic, pantomimist, performer, play-actor, player, soubrette, stand-in, star, stooge*, straight person, thesp*, thespian, trouper, understudy, ventriloquist, villain, walk-on; CONCEPT 352
—Ant. audience, fan

actress [n] woman actor diva, ingenue, leading lady, prima donna, starlet; CONCEPT 352

actual [adj1] truly existing, real absolute, authentic, categorical, certain, concrete, confirmed, definite, factual, for real*, genuine, hard, honest injun*, honest to God*, indisputable, indubitable, kosher*, physical, positive, realistic, substantial, substantive, sure enough*, tangible, true, truthful, undeniable, unquestionable, verified; CONCEPT 582
—Ant. counterfeit, false, fictitious, imaginary, legendary, pretended, unreal

actual [adj2] existing at the present time current, exact, existent, extant, live, living, original, prevailing; CONCEPT 799 —Ant. hypothetical, imaginary, nominal, past, reputed, theoretical, unreal

actuality [n] something that truly exists, is real achievement, actualization, attainment, brass tacks*, fact, materiality, materialization, reality, real world*, straight stuff*, substance, substantiality, truth, what it is*; CONCEPT 725

actualize [v] make real accomplish, bring about, engineer, produce, realize; CONCEPT 91

actually [adj] truly real, existent absolutely, as a matter of fact, de facto, genuinely, indeed, in fact, in point of fact, in reality, in truth, literally, really, veritably, very; CONCEPT 582

actuate [v] start a function or action, motivate activate, animate, arouse, cause, drive, egg on*, energize, excite, fire up*, impel, incite, induce, influence, inspire, instigate, key up*, mobilize, motivate, move, prompt, propel, put up to*, quicken, rouse, spur, stimulate, turn on*, work into lather*, work up*; CONCEPTS 221,234
—Ant. impede, stop

act up [v] misbehave act out*, carry on, raise hell*, rebel, sow one's wild oats*; CONCEPTS 106,633

acumen [n] ability to understand and reason acuity, acuteness, astuteness, awareness, brains, brilliance, cleverness, comprehension, cunning, discernment, discrimination, farsightedness, good taste, grasp, guile, ingenuity, insight, intellect, intelligence, intuition, judgment, keenness, perception, percipience, perspicacity, perspicuity, refinement, sagacity, sensitivity, sharpness, shrewdness, smartness, smarts*, understanding, vision, wisdom, wit; CONCEPT 409 —Ant. denseness, ignorance, inability, ineptness, obtuseness, stupidity

acute [adj1] deeply perceptive astute, canny, clever, discerning, discriminating, incisive, ingenious, insightful, intense, intuitive, judicious, keen, observant, penetrating, perspicacious, piercing, quick-witted, sensitive, sharp, smart, subtle; CONCEPT 402 —Ant. dense, imperceptive, insensitive, obtuse, slow, stupid

acute [adj2] very important afflictive, critical, crucial, dangerous, decisive, desperate, dire, essential, grave, serious, severe, sudden, urgent, vital; CONCEPT 568 —Ant. not serious, unimportant

acute [adj3] severe, intense cutting, distressing, excruciating, exquisite, fierce, keen, overpowering, overwhelming, piercing, poignant, powerful, racking, severe, sharp, shooting, stabbing, sudden, violent; CONCEPT 569

acute [adj4] having a sharp end or point acicular, aciculate, acuminate, acuminous, cuspate, cuspidate, knifelike, needle-shaped, peaked, piked, pointed, sharpened, spiked; CONCEPT 485
—Ant. blunt, dull

adage [n] saying or proverb aphorism, apothegm, axiom, byword, dictum, maxim, motto, precept, saw; CONCEPT 276

adamant [adj1] unyielding determined, firm, fixed, hanging tough*, hard-nosed, immovable, inexorable, inflexible, insistent, intransigent, obdurate, pat*, relentless, resolute, rigid, set, set in stone*, standing pat*, stiff, stubborn, unbendable, unbending, uncompromising, unrelenting, unshakable, unswayable; CONCEPT 401 —Ant. flexible, pliant, submissive, yielding

adamant [adj2] hard like rock adamantine, flinty, impenetrable, indestructible, rock-hard, tough, unbreakable; CONCEPT 604 —Ant. flexible, soft, supple

adapt [v] adjust to a different situation or condition acclimate, accommodate, accustom, alter, change, come around, comply, conform, familiarize, fashion, fit, get act together*, get used to, grow used to, habituate, harmonize, make, match, modify, play the game*, prepare, qualify, readjust, reconcile, remodel, revise, roll with punches*, reshape, shape up*, square, suit, tailor; CONCEPTS 232,697 —Ant. disarrange, dislocate, disorder, disturb, unfit

adaptable [adj] *able and usually willing to change* AC-DC*, adjustable, all around, alterable, can-do*, changeable, compliant, conformable, convertible, ductile, easy-going, flexible, hanging loose*, malleable, modifiable, moldable, plastic, pliable, pliant, resilient, supple, switch-hitting, tractable, variable, versatile; CONCEPTS 550,576 —**Ant.** inflexible, intractable, nonconforming, unadaptable

adaptation [n1] *act of adapting* adjustment, adoption, alteration, conversion, modification, refitting, remodeling, reworking, shift, transformation, variation; CONCEPT 697

adaptation [n2] *condition of something resulting from change* acclimatization, accustomedness, agreement, compliance, correspondence, familiarization, habituation, naturalization; CONCEPT 230

adaptive [adj] *adjusting* flexible, modifying, robust; CONCEPTS 314,489,613

add [v1] *simple arithmetical process of increase; accumulation* calculate, cast, compute, count, count up, do addition, enumerate, figure, reckon, reckon up, sum, summate, tally, tot*, total, tote*, tot up*; CONCEPT 764 —**Ant.** subtract

add [v2] *adjoin, increase; make further comment* affix, annex, ante, append, augment, beef up*, boost, build up, charge up, continue, cue in*, figure in, flesh out*, heat up*, hike, hike up*, hitch on*, hook on*, hook up with*, include, jack up*, jazz up*, join together, pad, parlay, piggyback*, plug into*, pour it on*, reply, run up*, say further, slap on*, snowball*, soup up*, speed up, spike, step up, supplement, sweeten*, tack on*, tag; CONCEPTS 51,113,236,245 —**Ant.** decrease, deduct, diminish, lessen, reduce, remove, withdraw

addendum [n] *something conjoined, added* addition, adjunct, appendage, appendix, attachment, augmentation, codicil, extension, extra, postscript, rider, supplement; CONCEPTS 270,827

addict [n] *person who has compulsion toward activity, often injurious* aficionado, buff, devotee, enthusiast, fan, fanatic, fiend, follower, freak*, habitué, hound*, junkie*, nut, practitioner, zealot; CONCEPTS 412,423

addicted [adj] *dependent on something, compulsive* absorbed, accustomed, attached, dependent, devoted, disposed, fanatic, fond, given over to, given to, habituated, hooked, hyped*, imbued, inclined, obsessed, predisposed, prone to, spaced out*, strung out*, under the influence, used to, wedded to; CONCEPT 542 —**Ant.** disinclined, independent, opposed, unaccustomed

addiction [n] *a habit of activity, often injurious* bag*, bent, craving, dependence, enslavement, fixation, hang-up*, hook, inclination, jones*, kick*, monkey*, monkey on back*, obsession, shot*, sweet tooth*, thing*; CONCEPTS 20,316, 709

addictive [adj] *habit-forming* enslaving, hooking, obsessive; CONCEPTS 530,547

addition [n1] *process of conjoining, adding* accession, adding, adjoining, affixing, annexation, attachment, augmentation, enlargement, extension, inclusion, increasing; CONCEPTS 236,245 —**Ant.** decrease, deduction, lessening, loss, reduction, shrinkage, subtraction, withdrawal

addition [n2] *something conjoined to or enlargement of something* accession, accessory, accretion, accrual, addendum, additive, adjunct, aggrandizement, annex, appendage, appendix, attachment, augmentation, bonus, boost, commission, dividend, enhancement, enlargement, expansion, extension, extra, gain, hike, increase, increment, option, profit, raise, reinforcement, rise, supplement, wing; CONCEPTS 640,835

addition [n3] *arithmetical process of augmentation* accretion, accruing, adding, computing, counting, enlarging, expanding, increasing, reckoning, summation, summing, tabulating, totaling, toting*; CONCEPT 764 —**Ant.** subtraction

additional [adj] *extra, supplementary* added, affixed, appended, further, increased, more, new, on the side, option, other, over-and-above, padding, perk, spare, supplementary; CONCEPT 771 —**Ant.** necessary

additive [n] *added ingredient* accompaniment, addition, add-on, extra, flavor enhancer, preservative, supplement; CONCEPTS 640,835

addled [adj] *confused* balled up*, befuddled, bewildered, fouled up*, gone*, mixed up, out of it, punchy, rattled, shaken, shook, shook up, slap-happy, thrown, unglued*, woozy*; CONCEPT 403 —**Ant.** clear, understanding

address [n1] *place of residence or business where one can be contacted* abode, box number, direction, domicile, dwelling, headquarters, home, house, living quarters, location, lodging, number, place of business, place of residence, street, whereabouts, zip code; CONCEPT 516

address [n2] *speech given to formal gathering* chalk talk*, discourse, dissertation, lecture, oration, pep talk*, pitch, sermon, soapbox*, spiel*, talk; CONCEPT 278

address [v1] *write directions for delivery* consign, dispatch, forward, inscribe, label, mark, postmark, remit, route, send, ship, superscribe, transmit; CONCEPTS 60,79

address [v2] *speak to a formal gathering* approach, bespeak, call, deliver speech, deliver talk, discourse, discuss, get on a soapbox*, give speech, give talk, greet, hail, lecture, memorialize, orate, pitch, pontificate, root for, sermonize, spiel*, spout, stump*, take the floor, talk; CONCEPTS 60,266,285

address [v3] *devote effort to something* apply oneself to, attend to, concentrate on, devote oneself to, dig, direct, engage in, focus on, give, go at*, go for*, hammer away*, have a go at*, have at*, knuckle down to*, peg away*, pitch into*, plug away at*, take care of, take up, throw oneself into, try, turn, turn to, undertake; CONCEPT 100 —**Ant.** avoid, cut, disregard, ignore, overlook, pass, shun, slight

adduce [v] *affirm* cite, illustrate, point out, prove, show; CONCEPTS 49,50,88

adept [adj] *very able* accomplished, ace*, adroit, brainy, capable, clean*, crack*, crackerjack*, deft, dexterous, expert, hot*, hotshot*, know stuff*, masterful, masterly, nobody's fool*, no dummy*, no slouch*, on the ball*, on the beam*, practiced, proficient, quick, savvy, sharp, sharp as a tack*, skilled, skillful, slick, smooth, there*, up to speed*, versed, whiz*, wizard*; CONCEPTS 402,527 —**Ant.** awkward, clumsy, incompetent, inept, unskilled

adequacy [n] *ability, competency in some action* capability, capacity, commensurateness, competence, enough, fairness, plenty, requisiteness, satisfactoriness, sufficiency, suitableness, tolerableness; CONCEPTS 636,656 —*Ant.* inadequacy, inadequateness, insufficiency

adequate [adj] *enough, able* acceptable, all right, capable, comfortable, commensurate, competent, decent, equal, fair, passable, requisite, satisfactory, sufficient, sufficing, suitable, tolerable, unexceptional, unobjectionable; CONCEPTS 533,558 —*Ant.* inadequate, inferior, insufficient, unequal, unfit, unqualified, unsuitable, useless

adequately [adv] *sufficiently* abundantly, acceptably, appropriately, capably, competently, copiously, decently, fairly well, fittingly, modestly, pleasantly enough, presentably, satisfactorily, sufficiently, suitably, to an acceptable degree, tolerably, well enough; CONCEPTS 558,560 —*Ant.* inadequately, insufficiently, unequally, unsatisfactorily, unsuitably

adhere [v1] *conform to or follow rules exactly* abide by, be attached, be constant, be devoted, be devoted to, be faithful, be loyal, be true, cleave to, comply, follow, fulfill, heed, keep, maintain, mind, obey, observe, practice, respect, stand by, support; CONCEPTS 87,636 —*Ant.* disjoin, not conform

adhere [v2] *stick or become stuck to, either physically or mentally* attach, cement, cleave, cling like ivy*, cohere, fasten, fix, freeze to*, glue, hold fast, hold on like bulldog*, paste, stay put, stick like a barnacle*, stick like glue*, unite; CONCEPTS 85,113,160 —*Ant.* loose, loosen, separate, unfasten

adherent [n] *supporter or follower* advocate, aficionado, backer, believer, card-carrying member*, devotee, disciple, enthusiast, fan, hanger-on; CONCEPTS 352,366,423

adhesion [n] *holding fast* adherence, adhesiveness, attachment, bond, cling, grip, stickiness, sticking; CONCEPTS 85,160

adhesive [adj] *sticking* adherent, adhering, agglutinant, attaching, clinging, clingy, gelatinous, glutinous, gooey, gummed, gummy, holding, hugging, mucilaginous, pasty, resinous, sticky, tenacious, viscid, viscous, waxy; CONCEPTS 488,606 —*Ant.* inadhesive, loose, open, separated, unattachable

ad hoc [adj] *for a specific purpose* impromptu, provisional, special, specific, specified; CONCEPTS 535,557,564

adieu [n] *parting remark or action* adios*, congé, farewell, goodbye, leave-taking, parting, so long, valediction; CONCEPT 276 —*Ant.* greeting, hello

ad infinitum [adj] *neverending* ceaselessly, endlessly, forever, perpetually; CONCEPT 798

adjacent [adj] *next to, abutting* adjoining, alongside, beside, bordering, close, close by, contiguous, near, neighboring, next door, touching; CONCEPT 586 —*Ant.* apart, away, detached, disconnected, distant, far, faraway, nonadjacent, remote, separate

adjective [n] *word that modifies a noun* accessory, additional, adjunct, adnoun, attribute, attributive, dependent, descriptive, identifier, modifier, qualifier; CONCEPT 275

adjoin [v1] *be next to* abut, approximate, be adjacent to, border, butt, communicate, connect, join, lie, lie beside, link, neighbor, touch, verge; CONCEPT 747

adjoin [v2] *attach* add, affix, annex, append, combine, connect, couple, interconnect, join, link, unite; CONCEPTS 85,113,160 —*Ant.* detach

adjoining [adj] *being next to* abutting, adjacent, approximal, bordering on, connecting, conterminous, contiguous, coterminous, impinging, interconnecting, joined, joining, juxtaposed, near, neighboring, next door, touching, verging; CONCEPT 586 —*Ant.* detached, divided, separate

adjourn [v] *stop a proceeding* curb, defer, delay, discontinue, hold off, hold over, hold up, postpone, prorogue, put off, recess, restrain, shelve, stay, suspend; CONCEPTS 121,234 —*Ant.* begin, convene, convoke, encourage, further, keep on, open, rally, stimulate, urge

adjournment [n] *discontinuation or delay of a proceeding* break, deferment, deferral, intermission, interruption, pause, postponement, prorogation, putting off, recess, stay, suspension; CONCEPTS 121,703 —*Ant.* beginning, commencement, continuance

adjudicate [v] *formally judge* adjudge, arbitrate, decide, determine, mediate, referee, settle, umpire; CONCEPTS 18,317 —*Ant.* defer, dodge, ignore, not judge

adjudication [n] *judgment* conclusion, decision, determination, finding, pronouncement, ruling, settlement, verdict; CONCEPT 103,689

adjunct [n] *addition; help* accessory, addendum, appendage, appendix, appurtenance, associate, auxiliary, complement, detail, partner, subordinate, supplement; CONCEPTS 484,835 —*Ant.* detriment, lessening, subtraction

adjure [v] *command* beseech, charge, entreat, implore, obligate, order, require, supplicate; CONCEPT 53

adjust [v1] *become or make prepared, adapted* acclimatize, accommodate, accustom, adapt, alter, arrange, compose, conform, dispose, do as Romans do*, doctor*, fiddle with*, fine-tune, fit, fix, fix up, get act together*, get it together*, grin and bear it*, habituate, harmonize, make conform, modify, order, quadrate, reconcile, rectify, redress, regulate, remodel, settle, suit, swim with the tide*, tailor, tailor-make, tune; CONCEPTS 35,232,697 —*Ant.* confuse, derange, disarrange, disorder, disorganize, upset

adjust [v2] *mechanically alter, especially to improve* accommodate, align, balance, bring into line, calibrate, connect, correct, fine-tune, fit, fix, focus, grind, improve, mend, overhaul, polish, put in working order, readjust, rectify, regulate, renovate, repair, service, set, sharpen, square, tighten, troubleshoot, tune up; CONCEPTS 202,212 —*Ant.* derange, disarrange, unsuit

adjust [v3] *bring into agreement or to a standard* accord, allocate, arrange, clarify, conclude, conform, coordinate, doctor*, fiddle with*, fine-tune, fix up, grade, methodize, modify, organize, reconcile, regulate, settle, sort, standardize, straighten, systematize, tally; CONCEPTS 84,117 —*Ant.* confuse, derange, unfit, unsuit

adjustable [adj] *alterable* accommodating, adaptable, changeable, conformable, flexible, malleable, modifiable, pliable, tractable; CONCEPT 534

adjustment [n1] *adaptation* acclimation, acclimatization, alteration, arrangement, balancing, conformance, correcting, fitting, fixing, improvement, mending, modification, ordering, organization, organizing, orientation, readjustment, redress, regulating, regulation, repairing, setting, shaping, standardization; turning; CONCEPT 697

adjustment [n2] *financial retribution, payment of claim* agreement, allotment, apportionment, benefit, compensation, compromise, pay, reconciliation, reimbursement, remuneration, settlement, share, stake, stipulation; CONCEPT 332

adjutant [n] *assistant* aide, auxiliary, helper; CONCEPT 348

ad-lib [adj] *improvised* extemporaneous, extempore, extemporized, impromptu, made-up, off-the-cuff*, spontaneous, unprepared, unrehearsed; CONCEPT 267 —*Ant.* deliberate, planned, prepared, rehearsed, written

ad-lib [adv] *in an improvised manner* extemporaneously, extempore, impromptu, off the cuff*, off the top of one's head*, spontaneously, without preparation, without rehearsal; CONCEPT 267 —*Ant.* deliberately, planned, prepared, rehearsed, written

ad-lib [v] *improvise speech* extemporize, invent, make up, speak extemporaneously, speak impromptu, speak off the cuff*; CONCEPT 266 —*Ant.* plan, prepare, rehearse, write

administer [v1] *manage an organization or effort* administrate, be in the driver's seat*, be in the saddle*, boss*, carry out, conduct, control, crack the whip*, direct, execute, govern, head, head up*, hold the reins*, oversee, pull the strings*, pull the wires*, render, ride herd on*, run, run the show*, sit on top of*, superintend, supervise; CONCEPTS 117,298 —*Ant.* forego, mismanage, neglect

administer [v2] *dispense something needed* apply, apportion, authorize, bring, contribute, deal, deliver, disburse, distribute, dole out, execute, extend, furnish, give, impose, inflict, issue, measure out, mete out, offer, perform, portion, proffer, provide, regulate, serve, supply, tender; CONCEPTS 108,136 —*Ant.* deny, frustrate, refuse, withhold

administration [n1] *management of an organization or effort* administering, agency, application, authority, charge, command, conduct, conducting, control, directing, direction, dispensation, disposition, distribution, enforcement, execution, governing, government, guidance, handling, jurisdiction, legislation, order, organization, overseeing, oversight, performance, policy, power, provision, regulation, rule, running, strategy, superintendence, supervision, surveillance; CONCEPTS 117,298

administration [n2] *human or group who manages effort of an organization* admiral, advisers, board, bureau, cabinet, chair, chairperson, chargé d'affaires, command, commander, committee, consulate, department, directors, embassy, executive, executives, feds*, front office*, general, governing body, headquarters, legislature, management, ministry, officers, officials, powers, presidency, president,

presidium, stewards, superintendents, supervisors, top brass*, upstairs*; CONCEPT 299

administration [n3] *period during which a particular human group is in power* dynasty, incumbency, presidency, regime, reign, stay, tenure, term; CONCEPTS 298,816

administrative [adj] *involved in managing or using power* authoritative, bureaucratic, central, commanding, controlling, deciding, decisive, departmental, directing, directive, directorial, executive, governing, governmental, in charge, in control, jurisdictional, legislative, managerial, official, organizational, policy-making, presiding, regulative, regulatory, ruling, superintending, supervising, supervisory; CONCEPTS 319,536

administrator [n] *person who manages organization* ambassador, authority, boss, bureaucrat, captain, CEO, chair, chairperson, chief, commander, consul, controller, custodian, dean, director, exec*, executive, front office*, governor, head, head honcho*, head person*, inspector, judge, leader, manager, mayor, minister, officer, official, organizer, overseer, person upstairs*, premier, president, prez*, producer, superintendent, supervisor; CONCEPTS 347,354 —*Ant.* employee, worker

admirable [adj] *held in great respect* A-1*, ace*, A-OK*, attractive, best ever, cat's pajamas*, choice, commendable, cool*, copacetic*, crackerjack*, deserving, dream*, estimable, excellent, exquisite, fine, good, great, greatest, hunky dory*, keen*, laudable, meritable, meritorious, neat*, out of sight*, out of this world*, peachy*, praiseworthy, rare, solid, super, superduper*, superior, unreal*, valuable, wicked*, wonderful, worthy, zero cool*; CONCEPTS 572,574 —*Ant.* contemptible, despicable, detestable, hateful, loathsome, repugnant, repulsive, shameful, unworthy

admiration [n] *great respect* account, adoration, affection, applause, appreciation, approbation, approval, deference, delight, esteem, estimation, favor, fondness, glorification, homage, honor, idolatry, idolization, liking, love, marveling, obeisance, pleasure, praise, prizing, recognition, regard, reverence, valuing, veneration, wonder, wonderment, worship; CONCEPT 32 —*Ant.* aversion, contempt, disapproval, disgust, dislike, disregard, hate, hatred, loathing

admire [v] *hold in high regard* adore, applaud, appreciate, approve, be crazy about*, be crazy for*, be mad about*, be nuts about*, be stuck on*, be sweet on*, be wild about*, cherish, commend, credit, delight in, esteem, eulogize, extol, fall for*, get high on*, glorify, go for*, groove on*, hail, hold in respect, honor, idolize, laud, look up to, marvel at, moon over*, pay homage to, praise, prize, rate highly, respect, revere, take pleasure in, think highly of, treasure, value, venerate, wonder at, worship; CONCEPT 32 —*Ant.* abhor, condemn, despise, detest, dislike, execrate, hate, scorn

admirer [n] *person who holds someone in high regard* adherent, beau, believer, booster, boyfriend, buff, bug*, cat*, devotee, disciple, enthusiast, fan, fancier, fiend*, follower, freak*, girlfriend, groupie*, hound*, junkie*, lover, nut*, partisan, patron, rooter*, suitor, supporter, swain, sweetheart, wooer, worshiper; CONCEPT 423 —*Ant.* critic, enemy, opponent

admissible [*adj*] *able or deserving of consideration; allowable* acceptable, allowed, applicable, appropriate, concedable, fair, fitting, just, justifiable, lawful, legal, legitimate, licit, likely, logical, not impossible, not unlikely, okay, passable, permissible, permitted, pertinent, possible, probable, proper, rational, reasonable, relevant, right, suitable, tolerable, tolerated, warranted, worthy; CONCEPT 533 —*Ant.* illegitimate, inadmissible, inapplicable, irrelevant, unfair, unjust, unsuitable, wrong

admission [*n1*] *entering or allowing entry* acceptance, access, admittance, certification, confirmation, designation, door, entrance, entree, ingress, initiation, introduction, permission, reception, recognition, way, welcome; CONCEPT 83 —*Ant.* denial, exclusion, expulsion, refusal

admission [*n2*] *confession or acknowledgment* accession, admittance, affidavit, affirmation, allowance, assent, assertion, attestation, averment, avowal, concession, confirmation, declaration, deposition, disclosure, divulgence, profession, revelation, statement, testimonial, testimony; CONCEPT 57 —*Ant.* denial, disallowance, refusal, repudiation

admit [*v1*] *allow entry or use* accept, be big on*, bless, buy, concede, enter, entertain, give access, give the nod*, give thumbs up*, grant, harbor, house, initiate, introduce, let, let in, lodge, okay, permit, receive, shelter, sign*, sign off on*, suffer, take, take in; CONCEPT 83 —*Ant.* debar, deny, dismiss, eject, exclude, expel, oust, refuse, reject, repel, shut

admit [*v2*] *confess, acknowledge* accept, accord, acquiesce, adopt, affirm, agree, allow, approve, avow, bare, bring to light*, communicate, concede, concur, confide, confirm, consent, cop a plea*, credit, declare, disclose, divulge, enumerate, expose, go into details*, grant, indicate, let, let on, make known, narrate, number, open up, own, own up*, permit, proclaim, profess, recite, recognize, relate, reveal, spill*, subscribe to, talk, tell, tolerate, uncover, unveil, yield; CONCEPT 57 —*Ant.* confute, deny, dispute, dissent, gainsay, refuse

admittance [*n*] *permission to enter* access, entrance, entrée, entry, ingress, pass, passage, reception; CONCEPTS 388,685

admixture [*n*] *blending* amalgamation, blend, combination, commixture, compound, fusion, mélange, mingling, mixture; CONCEPT 432

admonish [*v*] *warn, strongly criticize* advise, berate, call down, call on the carpet*, censure, check, chide, come down hard on*, counsel, ding*, draw the line*, enjoin, exhort, forewarn, give a going over*, give a piece of one's mind*, glue*, growl*, hoist*, jack up*, notice, rap*, rap on knuckles*, rebuke, reprimand, reprove, scold, sit on, slap on wrist*, speak to, talk to, tell a thing or two*, tell off*, upbraid, warn; CONCEPTS 52,78 —*Ant.* applaud, approve, commend, compliment, extol, flatter, laud, praise

admonition [*n1*] *caution* advice, appraisal, counsel, forewarning, warning; CONCEPTS 78,274

admonition [*n2*] *scolding* berating, dressing down*, rebuke, reprimand, reproach, reproval, talking to*, upbraiding; CONCEPTS 44,52

ad nauseam [*adv*] *to the point of illness* more than one can stomach, to a sickening degree, too much; CONCEPTS 529,571

ado [*n*] *fuss* bother, confusion, excitement, flurry, hubbub, to-do*, travail, trouble, turmoil; CONCEPTS 46,106,388,633

adolescence [*n*] *state of puberty, preadulthood* boyhood, girlhood, greenness, juvenility, minority, pubescence, spring, teens, youth, youthfulness; CONCEPT 817 —*Ant.* adulthood, infancy

adolescent [*adj*] *preadult or immature* boyish, girlish, growing, juvenile, pubescent, puerile, teen, teenage, young, youthful; CONCEPTS 401,578,797 —*Ant.* adult, infant

adolescent [*n*] *person in puberty, preadulthood* juvenile, minor, stripling, sweet sixteen*, teen, teenager, teenybopper*, youngster, youth; CONCEPT 424 —*Ant.* adult, infant

adopt [*v1*] *choose or take something as one's own* accept, adapt, affiliate, affirm, appropriate, approve, assent, assume, borrow, embrace, endorse, espouse, follow, go down the line*, go in for*, imitate, maintain, mimic, opt, ratify, seize, select, support, take on, take over, take up, tap, use, utilize; CONCEPT 18 —*Ant.* disown, leave alone, reject, repudiate, repulse

adopt [*v2*] *legally care for another's child* choose, foster, naturalize, pick, raise, select, take in; CONCEPT 317

adoption [*n1*] *choosing or taking something as one's own* acceptance, approbation, appropriation, approval, assumption, choice, confirmation, embracement, embracing, enactment, endorsement, espousal, following, maintenance, ratification, selection, support, taking on, taking over, taking up; CONCEPT 18 —*Ant.* pass, rejection, repudiation

adoption [*n2*] *legal taking of another's child* adopting, fosterage, fostering, naturalizing, raising, taking in; CONCEPT 317

adorable [*adj*] *cute, lovable* ambrosial, appealing, attractive, captivating, charming, cute, darling, dear, delectable, delicious, delightful, dishy*, dreamy*, fetching, heavenly, hot*, luscious, pleasing, precious, sexy, suave; CONCEPTS 579,589 —*Ant.* cursed, despicable, detestable, hateable, hateful

adoration [*n*] *intense love* admiration, amore, ardor, attachment, crush, devotion, esteem, estimation, exaltation, glorification, hankering, honor, idolatry, idolization, infatuation, pash*, passion, puppy love*, reverence, shine*, veneration, weakness*, worship, worshipping, yen*; CONCEPT 32 —*Ant.* abhorrence, detestation, disrespect, hate

adore [*v*] *love intensely* admire, be crazy about*, be gone on*, be mad for*, be nuts about*, be serious about*, be smitten with*, be stuck on*, be sweet on*, be wild about*, cherish, delight in, dig*, dote on, esteem, exalt, fall for, flip over*, glorify, go for*, honor, idolize, prize, revere, reverence, treasure, venerate, worship; CONCEPT 32 —*Ant.* abhor, condemn, despise, detest, hate

adorn [*v*] *decorate* array, beautify, bedeck, deck, doll up*, dress up, embellish, enhance, enrich, fix up, furbish, garnish, grace, gussy up*, ornament, spruce up, trim; CONCEPTS 162,

177 —*Ant.* damage, deform, hurt, leave plain, mar

adornment [*n1*] *decorating, enhancing* beautification, decoration, embellishment, gilding, ornamentation, trimming; CONCEPTS 162,177 —*Ant.* plainness

adornment [*n2*] *a decoration* accessory, dingbat, doodad, embellishment, fandangle*, floss*, frill, frippery, furbelow*, gewgaw*, jazz*, ornament, thing, trimming; CONCEPTS 446,484

adrift [*adv1*] *floating out of control* afloat, drifting, loose, unanchored, unmoored; CONCEPT 488 —*Ant.* anchored, stable, tied down

adrift [*adv2*] *without purpose* aimless, directionless, goalless, purposeless; CONCEPT 542 —*Ant.* determined, purposeful

adrift [*adv3*] *off course* amiss, astray, erring, wrong; CONCEPT 581 —*Ant.* on course, on target

adroit [*adj*] *very able or skilled* adept, apt, artful, clean, clever, crack*, crackerjack*, cunning, cute, deft, dexterous, expert, foxy*, good, handy, hot tamale*, ingenious, masterful, neat*, nifty*, nimble, on the ball*, on the beam*, proficient, quick on the trigger*, quick on the uptake*, quick-witted, savvy, sharp, skillful, slick, smart, up*, up to speed*, whiz*, wizard; CONCEPT 527 —*Ant.* awkward, clumsy, dense, inept, stupid, unskilled

adulate [*v*] *flatter* apple polish*, brown-nose*, fall all over*, fawn, gush, kiss feet*, praise, worship; CONCEPTS 59,69

adulation [*n*] *overenthusiastic praise* applause, audation, blandishment, bootlicking*, commendation, fawning, flattery, sycophancy, worship; CONCEPTS 32,69 —*Ant.* abuse, criticism

adult [*adj*] *being mature, fully grown* developed, grown, grown-up, of age, ripe, ripened; CONCEPT 406 —*Ant.* adolescent, infant

adult [*n*] *a mature, fully grown person* gentleperson, grownup, man, person, woman; CONCEPTS 394,424 —*Ant.* adolescent, infant

adulterate [*v*] *alter or debase, often for profit* alloy, amalgamate, attenuate, blend, cheapen, commingle, contaminate, cook, corrupt, cut*, defile, degrade, denature, depreciate, deteriorate, devalue, dilute, dissolve, doctor*, doctor up*, falsify, impair, infiltrate, intermix, irrigate, lace*, make impure, mingle, mix, phony up*, plant*, pollute, shave*, spike*, taint, thin, transfuse, vitiate, water down*, weaken; CONCEPTS 240,254 —*Ant.* clarify, clean, cleanse, distill, filter, free, purify, refine

adulterated [*adj*] *debased or dirty* attenuated, blended, contaminated, corrupt, defiled, degraded, depreciated, deteriorated, devalued, diluted, dissolved, impaired, mixed, polluted, tainted, thinned, vitiated, watered down, weakened; CONCEPT 485 —*Ant.* clean, moral, virtuous

adulterous [*adj*] *unfaithful* cheating, double-crossing*, extracurricular*, fast and loose*, illicit, immoral, moonlighting*, speedy*, two-faced*, two-timing*, unchaste; CONCEPT 372 —*Ant.* chaste, clean, pure, virginal

adultery [*n*] *extramarital affair* affair, carrying on*, cheating, extracurricular activity*, fling, fornication, hanky-panky*, immorality, infidelity, matinee*, playing around*, relationship,

thing*, two-timing*; CONCEPT 633 —*Ant.* faithfulness

advance [*adj*] *ahead in position or time* beforehand, earlier, early, first, foremost, forward, in front, in the forefront, in the lead, leading, previously, prior; CONCEPTS 583,585,799 —*Ant.* after, behind

advance [*n1*] *forward movement* advancement, headway, impetus, motion, progress, progression; CONCEPTS 152,208 —*Ant.* halt, hesitation, recession, stop, withdrawal

advance [*n2*] *improvement, progress in development* advancement, amelioration, betterment, boost, break*, breakthrough, buildup, development, enrichment, furtherance, gain, go-ahead*, growth, headway, increase, progress, promotion, rise, step, up, upgrade, upping; CONCEPTS 700,704 —*Ant.* block, failure, impediment, recession, stagnation

advance [*n3*] *money given beforehand* accommodation, allowance, bite*, credit, deposit, down payment, floater*, front money*, hike, increase, loan, prepayment, retainer, rise*, score, stake, take*, touch*; CONCEPTS 340,344

advance [*v1*] *move something forward, often quickly* accelerate, achieve, bring forward, come forward, conquer, continue ahead, continue on, dispatch, drive, elevate, forge ahead, gain ground, get ahead, get green light*, get there*, get with it*, go ahead, go forth, go forward, go great guns*, go places*, go to town*, hasten, launch, make headway, make the scene*, march, move on, move onward, move up, press on, proceed, progress, promote, propel, push ahead, push on, quicken, send forward, skyrocket*, speed, step forward, storm; CONCEPTS 152,208,704 —*Ant.* back down, halt, hesitate, recede, retreat, retrogress, stop, turn, withdraw, yield

advance [*v2*] *promote or propose an idea* adduce, allege, ballyhoo, beat the drum for, benefit, boost, cite, encourage, foster, further, get ink for*, hype*, introduce, lay forward, make a pitch for*, offer, plug*, present, proffer, puff*, push, put forward, put on the map*, serve, set forth, splash, spot, submit, suggest, throw spotlight on*, urge; CONCEPTS 49,60,68 —*Ant.* hesitate, stop, withdraw

advance [*v3*] *give money beforehand* furnish, lend, loan, pay, provide; CONCEPT 341

advance [*v4*] *increase in amount, number, or position* boost, break the bank*, develop, elevate, enlarge, get fat*, get rich*, grade, grow, hit pay dirt*, hit the jackpot*, improve, magnify, make a killing*, make out*, multiply, pan out*, prefer, prosper, raise, strike gold*, strike it rich*, thrive, up, upgrade, uplift; CONCEPTS 236,244,245 —*Ant.* decrease, take back, withdraw

advanced [*adj*] *ahead in position, time, manner* avant-garde, breakthrough, cutting-edge*, excellent, exceptional, extreme, first, foremost, forward, higher, late, leading, leading-edge*, liberal, precocious, progressive, radical, state-of-the-art*, unconventional; CONCEPTS 574,578,585,797 —*Ant.* after, behind

advancement [*n1*] *promotion, progress* advance, amelioration, betterment, elevation, gain, growth, headway, improvement, preference, preferment, prelation, rise, upgrading; CONCEPTS *700,704* —*Ant.* cessation, decline, descent, downfall, regression, retreat, retrogression, stoppage

advancement [n2] *forward movement* advance, anabasis, gain, headway, march, progress, progression; CONCEPTS *152,208* —*Ant.* cessation, decline, descent, halt, retreat, retrogression, return, reversion, stop, stoppage

advance(s) [n4] *desirous pursuit of someone* approach, move, overture, proposal, proposition, suggestion; CONCEPTS *20,384* —*Ant.* disinterest, ignorance

advantage [n] *benefit, favored position or circumstance* aid, ascendancy, asset, assistance, authority, avail, blessing, boon, break, choice, comfort, convenience, dominance, edge, eminence, expediency, favor, gain, good, gratification, help, hold, improvement, influence, interest, lead, leeway, leg-up*, leverage, luck, mastery, odds, position, power, precedence, pre-eminence, preference, prestige, prevalence, profit, protection, recognition, resources, return, sanction, starting, superiority, support, supremacy, upper hand*, utility, wealth; CONCEPT *574* —*Ant.* disadvantage, drawback, handicap, hindrance, loss, obstacle, restriction

advantageous [adj] *favorable* auspicious, beneficial, expedient, for the best, fortunate, helpful, opportune, profitable, propitious, worthwhile; CONCEPTS *537,558,572*

advent [n] *beginning or arrival of something anticipated* appearance, approach, arrival, coming, entrance, occurrence, onset, visitation; CONCEPTS *119,159* —*Ant.* departure, end

adventure [n] *risky or unexpected undertaking* chance, contingency, emprise, endangerment, enterprise, experience, exploit, feat, happening, hazard, incident, jeopardy, occurrence, peril, scene, speculation, trip, undertaking, venture; CONCEPTS *384,386* —*Ant.* avoidance, inaction, inactivity, inertia, latency, passiveness, stillness

adventurer [n] *person who takes risks* charlatan, daredevil, entrepreneur, explorer, fortune-hunter, gambler, globetrotter, hero, heroine, madcap, mercenary, opportunist, pioneer, pirate, romantic, speculator, stunt person, swashbuckler, traveler, venturer, voyager, wanderer; CONCEPT *423*

adventurous [adj] *daring, risk-taking* adventuresome, audacious, bold, brave, courageous, dangerous, daredevil, enterprising, foolhardy, hazardous, headstrong, intrepid, rash, reckless, risky, temerarious, venturesome, venturous; CONCEPTS *404,542* —*Ant.* careful, cautious, prudent, unadventurous

adverb [n] *word modifying a verb* limiter, modifier, qualifier; CONCEPT *275*

adversary [n] *opponent* antagonist, attacker, bad person, bandit, competitor, contestant, enemy, foe, match, opposer, opposite number*, oppugner, rival; CONCEPT *412* —*Ant.* ally, assistant, backer, friend, helper, helpmate, supporter

adverse [adj] *unfavorable, antagonistic* allergic to*, conflicting, contrary, detrimental, disadvantageous, down on*, down side*, have no use for*, inimical, injurious, inopportune, negative, opposed, opposing, opposite, oppugning,

ornery*, reluctant, repugnant, stuffy*, unfortunate, unfriendly, unlucky, unpropitious, unwilling; CONCEPT *570* —*Ant.* advantageous, aiding, auspicious, favorable, fortunate, helpful, lucky, propitious

adversity [n] *bad luck, situation* affliction, bad break*, bummer*, calamity, can of worms*, catastrophe, clutch, contretemps, crunch*, difficulty, disaster, distress, downer*, drag*, evil eye*, hard knocks*, hardship, hard times, hurting, ill fortune, jam, jinx, kiss of death*, misery, misfortune, mishap, on the skids*, pain in the neck*, poison*, reverse, sorrow, suffering, the worst*, tough luck*, trial, trouble; CONCEPT *674* —*Ant.* aid, encouragement, favor, fortune, good luck, help, prosperity

advertise [v] *publicize for the purpose of selling or causing one to want* acquaint, advance, advise, announce, apprise, ballyhoo*, beat the drum for*, bill, blazon, boost*, build up, circularize, communicate, declare, disclose, display, divulge, drum*, endorse, exhibit, expose, flaunt, get on soapbox for*, hard sell, herald, hype*, inform, make a pitch*, make known, notify, pitch, plug, press agent*, proclaim, promote, promulgate, puff*, push, put on the map*, reveal, show, soft sell, splash*, sponsor, spot, tout, uncover, unmask; CONCEPTS *60,324* —*Ant.* hide, keep secret

advertisement [n] *public notice of sale* ad, announcement, bill, blurb, broadcast, circular, classified ad, commercial, communication, declaration, display, endorsement, exhibit, exhibition, flyer, literature, notice, notification, placard, plug, poster, proclamation, promotion, promulgation, propaganda, publication, publicity, squib, throwaway, want ad; CONCEPTS *270,277,278,280*

advertising [n] *public notice of sale; notices to increase consumer desire* announcement, announcing, ballyhoo*, billing, blasting*, broadcasting, buildup, displaying, exhibiting, exhibition, exposition, hard sell, hoopla*, hype*, pitch, plug, posting, PR, proclamation, promo*, promoting, promotion, publicity, puff*, screamer*, spread, squib; CONCEPTS *97, 138,324*

advice [n] *recommendation* admonition, advisement, advocacy, aid, bum steer*, caution, charge, consultation, counsel, directions, dissuasion, encouragement, exhortation, forewarning, guidance, help, information, injunction, input, instruction, judgment, lesson, news, opinion, persuasion, prescription, proposal, proposition, recommendation, steer, suggestion, teaching, telltale, tidings, tip, tip-off*, two cents' worth*, view, warning, word, word to the wise*; CONCEPTS *75,274* —*Ant.* betrayal, deceit, deception, falsehood, lie, misinformation, misrepresentation

advisable [adj] *recommended, wise* appropriate, apt, commendable, desirable, expedient, fit, fitting, judicious, politic, prudent, seemly, sensible, sound, suggested, suitable, tactical; CONCEPT *574* —*Ant.* improper, imprudent, inadvisable, inappropriate, injudicious, uncorrect, unwise

advise [v/] *offer recommendation* admonish, advocate, caution, charge, commend, counsel,

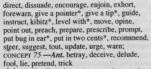

direct, dissuade, encourage, enjoin, exhort, forewarn, give a pointer*, give a tip*, guide, instruct, kibitz*, level with*, move, opine, point out, preach, prepare, prescribe, prompt, put bug in ear*, put in two cents*, recommend, steer, suggest, tout, update, urge, warn; CONCEPT 75 —*Ant.* betray, deceive, delude, fool, lie, pretend, trick

advise [v2] *offer information* acquaint, apprise, clue*, clue in*, fill in, give the word*, inform, keep posted*, lay it out*, let in on*, make known, notify, post*, put next to*, put on the line*, put on to*, report, show, tell, tip off*, update, warn; CONCEPT 60 —*Ant.* keep mum, keep quiet, keep secret

advisedly [adv] *with due consideration* carefully, cautiously, consciously, deliberately, discreetly, intentionally, prudently, thoughtfully; CONCEPT 544

adviser/advisor [n] *person who recommends, teaches, or otherwise helps* aide, attorney, authority, backseat driver*, buttinski*, clubhouse lawyer*, coach, confidant, consultant, counsel, counselor, director, doctor, Dutch uncle*, expert, friend, guide, helper, instructor, judge, kibitzer*, lawyer, mentor, monitor, partner, priest, quarterback*, referee, righthand person, second-guesser, teacher, tutor; CONCEPTS 348,350

advisory [adj] *able, authorized to recommend* advising, consultative, consultive, counseling, helping, recommending; CONCEPT 537

advocacy [n] *support for an idea or cause* advancement, aid, assistance, backing, campaigning for, championing, defense, encouragement, justification, pleading for, promotion, promulgation, propagation, proposal, recommendation, upholding, urging; CONCEPT 689 —*Ant.* attack, opposition, protest

advocate [n] *person supporting an idea or cause publicly* apostle, attorney, backer, campaigner, champion, counsel, defender, exponent, expounder, lawyer, pleader, promoter, proponent, proposer, speaker, spokesperson, supporter, upholder; CONCEPTS 359,423 —*Ant.* antagonist, assailant, enemy, opposition, protestor

advocate [v] *support idea or cause publicly* advance, advise, argue for, back, be in corner*, bless, bolster, boost*, brace up*, build up, campaign for, champion, countenance, defend, encourage, favor, further, get on bandwagon*, give a leg up*, give a lift*, go for, go to bat for*, go with, hold with, justify, plead for, plug*, plump for*, press for, promote, propose, push, recommend, ride shotgun for*, root for*, run interference for*, say so*, side, speak for, spread around*, stump for*, support, tout, uphold, urge, vindicate; CONCEPTS 10,49,75 —*Ant.* assail, attack, criticize, impugn, oppose, protest

aegis [n] *protection* auspices, backing, patronage, shelter, sponsorship, wing*; CONCEPTS 94,376

aerial [adj] *occurring in the air* aeriform, aeronautical, airy, atmospheric, birdlike, ethereal, flying, lofty, pneumatic, up above, vaporous; CONCEPT 583 —*Ant.* ground

aerobics/aerobic [n/adj] *exercise regime designed to increase heart and lung activity while*

toning muscles aquarobics, dance workout, drill, exercise, high impact, low impact, slimnastics, step, warm-up, workout; CONCEPT 363

aesthetic/esthetic [adj] *beautiful or artful* artistic, creative, gorgeous, inventive; CONCEPTS 485,579 —*Ant.* displeasing, ugly

afar [adv] *a great distance away* distant, far away, far off, remote; CONCEPT 778 —*Ant.* close, near

affable [adj] *friendly* amiable, amicable, approachable, benevolent, benign, breezy, civil, clubby*, congenial, cordial, courteous, genial, gentle, good-humored, good-natured, gracious, kindly, mild, nice, obliging, pleasant, polite, sociable, urbane, warm; CONCEPT 401 —*Ant.* complaining, disdainful, grouchy, grumbling, impolite, miserable, reserved, surly, unfriendly

affair [n1] *matter or business to be taken care of; happening* activity assignment, avocation, calling, case, circumstance, concern, duty, employment, episode, event, hap, happening, incident, interest, job, mission, obligation, occupation, occurrence, office function, proceeding, profession, project, province, pursuit, question, realm, responsibility, subject, task, thing*, topic, transaction, undertaking; CONCEPTS 2,349,362

affair [n2] *illicit sexual relationship* affaire, amour, carrying on*, extracurricular activity*, fling, goings-on*, hanky-panky*, intimacy, intrigue, liaison, love, playing around*, relationship, rendezvous, romance, thing together*, two-timing*; CONCEPTS 32,375

affair [n3] *party or celebration* do, entertainment, function, gathering, reception, shindig, soiree; CONCEPTS 377,383

affect [v1] *influence, affect emotionally* act on, alter, change, disturb, impinge, impress, induce, influence, inspire, interest, involve, modify, move, overcome, perturb, prevail, regard, relate, stir, sway, touch, transform, upset; CONCEPTS 7,19,22,228

affect [v2] *pretend, imitate* act, adopt, aspire to, assume, bluff, contrive, counterfeit, do a bit*, fake, feign, lay it on thick, make out like*, playact, put on, put up a front*, sham*, simulate, take on; CONCEPT 59

affectation [n] *pretended behavior to make an impression* air, airs, appearance, artificiality, facade, false front*, front, going Hollywood*, imitation, insincerity, mannerism, pose, pretense, pretension, pretentiousness, put-on, putting on airs*, sham*, show, showing off, simulation; CONCEPT 633 —*Ant.* naturalness, simplicity

affected [adj1] *deeply moved or hurt emotionally* afflicted, altered, changed, compassionate, concerned, damaged, distressed, excited, grieved, impaired, impressed, influenced, injured, overwhelmed, overwrought, sorry, stimulated, stirred, sympathetic, tender, touched, troubled, upset; CONCEPT 403 —*Ant.* calm, unmoved, unperturbed, unswayed, untroubled

affected [adj2] *changed in a bad or artificial way* apish, artificial, assumed, awkward, campy*, chichi*, conceited, contrived, counterfeit, counterfeited, faked, false, feigned, fraud*, gone Hollywood*, ham*, hammy*, high falutin'*, hollow, imitated, insincere, melodramatic, ostentatious, overdone, pedantic, phony, playacting, pompous, precious, pretended, pretentious, put-on*, schmaltzy*, self-conscious, shallow, sham*, simulated, spurious, stiff, stilted, studied, superficial, theatrical, unnatural; CONCEPTS *401,570* —*Ant.* ok, unchanged, unhurt, unimpaired, uninjured

affection [n] *strong fondness* amore, ardor, attachment, care, case*, closeness, concern, crush, desire, devotion, emotion, endearment, feeling, friendliness, friendship, good will, hankering*, heart, inclination, itch*, kindness, liking, love, passion, predilection, propensity, puppy love*, regard, sentiment, shine*, soft spot*, solicitude, tenderness, warmth, weakness*, yen*; CONCEPT *32* —*Ant.* animosity, antipathy, dislike, enmity, hate, hatred, ill will

affectionate [adj] *having or showing fondness* all over*, attached, caring, crazy over*, dear, devoted, doting, fond, friendly, huggy*, kind, lovey-dovey*, loving, mushy*, nutty about*, partial, soft on*, sympathetic, tender, warm, warmhearted; CONCEPTS *401,403* —*Ant.* antagonistic, cold, cool, disliking, undemonstrative

affective [adj] *concerning feelings and intuition* emotional, emotive, feeling, intuitive, noncognitive, perceptual, visceral; CONCEPT *529*

affidavit [n] *written legal declaration* affirmation, oath, sworn statement, testimony; CONCEPTS *271,318*

affiliate [n] *organization that is associated with another* affil*, associate, branch, offshoot, partner, sibling; CONCEPT *381*

affiliate [v] *associate or be associated with a larger organization* ally, amalgamate, annex, associate, band together, combine, come aboard, confederate, connect, form connection, go partners*, hook up*, incorporate, join, line up*, plug into*, relate*, team up, throw in with*, tie up, unite; CONCEPTS *113,114* —*Ant.* disjoin, separate, stay away

affiliation [n] *association with an organization* alliance, amalgamation, banding together, bunch, cahoots*, clan, coalition, combination, confederation, conjunction, connection, crew, crowd, gang, hookup*, incorporation, joining, league, merging, mob, outfit, partnership, relationship, ring, syndicate, tie-in, union; CONCEPT *381*

affinity [n1] *liking or inclination toward something* affection, attraction, closeness, compatibility, cotton*, cup of tea*, druthers*, fondness, good vibrations*, leaning, partiality, rapport, same wavelength, simpatico, sympathy, thing*, weakness*; CONCEPTS *20,32,709* —*Ant.* dislike, hatred

affinity [n2] *similarity* alikeness, alliance, analogy, association, closeness, connection, correspondence, kinship, likeness, relation, relationship, resemblance, semblance, similitude; CONCEPT *670* —*Ant.* dissimilarity

affirm [v] *declare the truth of something* assert, asseverate, attest, aver, avouch, avow, certify, cinch, clinch, confirm, cross heart, declare, guarantee, have a lock on*, ice*, insist, lock up*, maintain, nail down*, okay, predicate, profess, pronounce, put on ice*, ratify, repeat, rubber-stamp*, say so, set, state, swear, swear on bible*, swear up and down*, testify, vouch,

witness; CONCEPTS *49,50,88* —*Ant.* deny, negate, nullify, veto

affirmation [n] *declaration of the truth of something* affidavit, assertion, asseveration, attestation, averment, avouchment, avowal, certification, confirmation, declaration, green light*, oath, okay, pronouncement, ratification, stamp of approval*, statement, sworn statement, testimonial, testimony; CONCEPT *49* —*Ant.* denial, negation, nullification, veto

affirmative [adj] *being agreeable or assenting* acknowledging, acquiescent, affirmatory, affirming, approving, complying, concurring, confirmative, confirmatory, confirming, consenting, corroborative, endorsing, favorable, positive, ratifying, supporting; CONCEPTS *542,572* —*Ant.* dissenting, negative

affirmative action [n] *equal rights policy* anti-discrimination, equal opportunity, fair hiring, fair treatment, quota system, reverse discrimination; CONCEPTS *388,645,667*

affix [v] *attach or stick* add, annex, append, bind, fasten, glue, hitch on*, join, paste, put on, rivet, slap on*, subjoin, tack, tack on*, tag, tag on*; CONCEPTS *85,113,160* —*Ant.* detach, let go, loosen

afflict [v] *cause or become hurt* agonize, annoy, beset, bother, burden, crucify, distress, grieve, harass, harrow, harry, irk, lacerate, martyr, oppress, pain, pester, plague, press, rack, smite, strike, torment, torture, trouble, try, vex, worry, wound; CONCEPTS *7,19,246,313* —*Ant.* aid, comfort, help, solace, stay away from, take care of

affliction [n] *hurt condition; something that causes hurt* adversity, anguish, calamity, cross, crux, depression, difficulty, disease, disorder, distress, grief, hardship, illness, infirmity, misery, misfortune, ordeal, pain, plague, plight, scourge, sickness, sorrow, suffering, torment, trial, tribulation, trouble, woe; CONCEPTS *306,309,674,728* —*Ant.* aid, comfort, consolation, health, help, relief

affluence [n] *wealth* abundance, fortune, luxury, opulence, plenty, prosperity, riches, wealthiness; CONCEPTS *340,710*

affluent [adj] *wealthy* flush*, loaded*, moneyed*, opulent, prosperous, rich, stinking rich*, upper class, upscale, well-off, well-to-do; CONCEPT *334* —*Ant.* destitute, impoverished, needy, penniless, poor

affluent [adj2] *plentiful* abundant, bountiful, copious, full, plenteous; CONCEPT *771* —*Ant.* insufficient, lacking, needy, suffering, wanting

afford [v1] *able to have or do; within financial means* allow, be able to, bear, be disposed to, have enough for, have the means for, incur, manage, spare, stand, support, sustain; CONCEPTS *335,713*

afford [v2] *give, produce* bestow, furnish, grant, impart, offer, provide, render, supply, yield; CONCEPTS *108,143* —*Ant.* take away

affront [n] *an insult* abuse, backhanded compliment*, brickbat*, dirty deed*, indignity, injury, left-handed compliment*, offense, outrage, provocation, put-down*, slap*, slap in the face*, slight, slur, vexation, wrong; CONCEPTS *7,19,44,54* —*Ant.* appeasement, compliment, pleasantry

affront [v] *insult or involve in entanglement* abuse, anger, annoy, confront, criticize, displease, dispraise, dump on*, encounter, face, give a zinger*, give the cold shoulder*, hit where one lives*, meet, offend, outrage, pique, provoke, put down*, slander, slight, taunt, vex; CONCEPTS 7,19,44,54 —*Ant.* appease, assuage, compliment, gratify, mollify, placate, please, satisfy, soothe

aficionado [n] *fan* connoisseur, devotee, enthusiast, fanatic; CONCEPTS 352,366,423

afraid [adj1] *fearful* abashed, aghast, alarmed, anxious, apprehensive, aroused, blanched, cowardly, cowed, daunted, discouraged, disheartened, dismayed, distressed, disturbed, faint-hearted, frightened, frozen, have cold feet*, horrified, in awe, intimidated, nervous, panic-stricken, perplexed, perturbed, petrified, rattled, run scared*, scared, scared stiff*, scared to death*, shocked, spooked, startled, stunned, suspicious, terrified, terror-stricken, timid, timorous, trembling, upset, worried; CONCEPTS 403,690 —*Ant.* bold, brave, composed, confident, cool, courageous, fearless, heroic, intrepid, unafraid, undaunted, valiant

afraid [adj2] *reluctant, regretful* averse, backward, disinclined, hesitant, indisposed, loath, reluctant, sorry, uneager, unhappy, unwilling; CONCEPT 529 —*Ant.* confident, eager, happy, undismayed, venturesome

afresh [adj] *new or repeated* again, anew, de novo, lately, newly, of late, once again, once more, over, over again, recently; CONCEPTS 578,797

Afro [n] *frizzy hairstyle* curly hair, fro; CONCEPT 718

after [adj] *following in position or time* afterwards, back, back of, behind, below, ensuing, hind, hindmost, in the rear, later, next, posterior, postliminary, rear, subsequential, subsequently, succeeding, thereafter; CONCEPTS 586,820 —*Ant.* before

after-effect [n] *repercussion* aftermath, aftershock, consequence, followup, hangover*, offshoot, trail, wake; CONCEPT 230

afterlife [n] *life after death* eternity, heaven, hereafter, immortality, the great beyond*; CONCEPTS 370,410,435

aftermath [n] *situation following an event, occurrence* after-effects, causatum, chain reaction*, consequences, end, eventuality, flak*, impact, issue, outcome, payoff*, remainder, residual, residuum, results, upshot, waves*; CONCEPT 230

afternoon [n] *period after 12 noon and before sunset* cocktail hour, P.M., post meridian, siesta, teatime; CONCEPTS 801,806,810

afterthought [n] *idea that occurs after it is timely* reconsideration, review, second thought; CONCEPT 529 —*Ant.* forethought

afterward/afterwards [adv] *following a time, event* after, another time, at a later time, a while later, behind, by and by, ensuingly, eventually, in a while, intra, late, later, latterly, next, on the next day, soon, subsequently, then, thereafter, thereon, ultimately; CONCEPT 799 —*Ant.* beforehand

again [adv1] *another time; repeated* afresh, anew, anon, bis, come again, encore, freshly, newly, once more, one more time, over, over and over, recurrently, reiteratively, repeatedly; CONCEPTS 553,799

again [adv2] *in addition* additionally, also, besides, further, furthermore, moreover, on the contrary, on the other hand, then; CONCEPT 577

against [prep] *opposite to* across, adjacent, contra, contrary to, counter to, facing, in contrast to, in opposition to, opposed to, opposing, versus; CONCEPT 564

age [n1] *period of animate existence* adolescence, adulthood, boyhood, childhood, dotage, elderliness, girlhood, infancy, life, lifetime, majority, maturity, middle age, milestone, old age, senility, seniority, wear and tear*, youth; CONCEPTS 816,817

age [n2] *a period of time* aeon, blue moon*, century, date, day, duration, epoch, era, generation, interim, interval, life, lifetime, millennium, span; CONCEPT 807

age [v] *become older* decline, deteriorate, develop, get along, grow, grow feeble, grow old, grow up, mature, mellow, push, put mileage on*, ripen, wane; CONCEPT 105

aged [adj] *old* age-old, ancient, antediluvian, antiquated, antique, been around*, creaky*, elderly, getting on*, gray, moth-eaten*, oldie*, over the hill*, passé*, rusty*, senescent, senior citizen, shot*, timeworn, venerable, worn, worse for wear*; CONCEPTS 578,797 —*Ant.* new, unripe, young, youthful

ageism [n] *age-based discrimination* age bias, generation gap; CONCEPT 689

agency [n1] *organization, often business-related* bureau, company, department, firm, office; CONCEPTS 325,381,441

agency [n2] *power, instrumentality* action, activity, auspices, channel, efficiency, force, influence, instrument, instrumentality, intercession, intervention, means, mechanism, mediation, medium, operation, organ, vehicle, work; CONCEPTS 376,658

agenda [n] *list of things to do* calendar, card, diary, docket, lineup, plan, program, schedule, timetable; CONCEPT 283

agent [n1] *person representing an organization or person in business* abettor, actor, advocate, ambassador, assignee, assistant, attorney, broker, commissioner, delegate, deputy, doer, emissary, envoy, executor, factor, factotum, functionary, go-between, handler, intermediary, lawyer, mediary, middleperson, minister, mover, negotiator, officer, operative, operator, principal, proctor, promoter, proxy, representative, salesperson, servant, steward, substitute, surrogate, ten percenter*, worker; CONCEPT 348

agent [n2] *power, instrument for achievement* cause, channel, factor, force, means, medium, organ, power, vehicle; CONCEPTS 376,658

agent provocateur [n] *instigator* agitator, goad, incendiary, rabble-rouser, troublemaker; CONCEPT 412

agglomeration [n] *collection* cluster, heap, jumble, load, mass, pile; CONCEPTS 432,786

aggrandize [v] *cause something to seem or be greater, bigger* acclaim, applaud, augment, beef up*, boost, commend, dignify, distinguish, enlarge, ennoble, expand, extend, glorify, heighten, hike, hike up*, honor, hype, increase, intensify, jack up*, jump, magnify, multiply, parlay, praise; CONCEPTS 50,69,88,236,245 —*Ant.* belittle, debase, degrade, depress, disgrace, humble, lower

aggravate [v1] *annoy* be at*, be' on the back of*, bother, bug, bum*, dog, drive up the wall*, exasperate, gall, get, get on one's nerves, get to, give a hard time, grate, hack, irk, irritate, nag, needle, nettle, peeve, pester, pick on, pique, provoke, tease, vex, wig*; CONCEPTS 7,19 —*Ant.* appease, gladden, make happy, mollify, soften

aggravate [v2] *cause to become worse* complicate, deepen, enhance, exacerbate, exaggerate, heighten, increase, inflame, intensify, magnify, mount, rise, rouse, worsen; CONCEPT 240 —*Ant.* alleviate, help, improve, relieve, soothe

aggravation [n1] *annoyance* affliction, aggro*, bother, botheration*, difficulty, distress, exasperation, hang-up*, headache*, irksomeness, irritation, pain, pain in the neck*, pet peeve*, provocation, teasing, vexation, worry; CONCEPT 410

aggravation [n2] *worsening of a situation, condition* deepening, exacerbation, exaggeration, heightening, increase, inflaming, inflammation, intensification, magnification, sharpening, strengthening, worsening; CONCEPT 240

aggregate [adj] *forming a collection from separate parts* accumulated, added, amassed, assembled, collected, collective, combined, composite, corporate, cumulative, heaped, mixed, piled, total; CONCEPT 781 —*Ant.* individual, part, particular

aggregate [n] *collection* accumulation, agglomerate, agglomeration, all, amount, assemblage, body, bulk, combination, conglomeration, gross, heap, lump, mass, mixture, pile, quantity, sum, the works*, total, totality, whole, whole ball of wax*, whole enchilada*, whole schmear*, whole shooting match*; CONCEPT 432 —*Ant.* individual, one, part

aggregate [v] *combine into a collection* accumulate, add up, amass, amount, assemble, collect, combine, come, heap, mix, number, pile, sum, total; CONCEPT 109 —*Ant.* break up, disperse, divide

aggression [n1] *attack, often military* assailment, assault, blitz, blitzkrieg, encroachment, injury, invasion, offense, offensive, onset, onslaught, push, raid; CONCEPTS 86,320

aggression [n2] *hostile or forceful behavior, attitude* aggressiveness, antagonism, belligerence, blitz, combativeness, destructiveness, fight, hostility, pugnacity, push; CONCEPTS 29,411

aggressive [adj1] *belligerent, hostile* advancing, antipathetic, assailing, attacking, barbaric, bellicose, combative, contentious, destructive, disruptive, disturbing, encroaching, hawkish, intruding, intrusive, invading, martial, militant, offensive, pugnacious, quarrelsome, rapacious, threatening, warlike; CONCEPT 550 —*Ant.* calm, easy-going, laid-back

aggressive [adj2] *assertive* assertory, bold, brassy*, cheeky*, cocky*, come on*, domineering, dynamic, energetic, enterprising, flip*, forceful, fresh*, get up and go*, go after, hard sell, imperious, masterful, militant, nervy*, pushing, pushy, sassy, shooting from the hip*, smart*, smart alecky*, strenuous, tough, vigorous, zealous; CONCEPTS 404,542 —*Ant.* complaisant, laid-back

aggressor [n] *attacker* assailant, initiator, instigator, intruder, invader, provoker, raider, trespasser; CONCEPT 412

aggrieved [adj] *very distressed* afflicted, depressed, disturbed, grieving, harmed, hurt, injured, oppressed, pained, peeved, persecuted, saddened, unhappy, woeful, wronged; CONCEPT 403 —*Ant.* happy, pleased

aghast [adj] *horrified; very surprised* afraid, agape, agog, alarmed, amazed, anxious, appalled, astonished, astounded, awestruck, confounded, dismayed, dumbfounded, frightened, horror-struck, overwhelmed, shocked, startled, stunned, terrified, thunderstruck; CONCEPTS 403,690 —*Ant.* unsurprised

agile [adj] *physically or mentally nimble, deft* active, acute, alert, athletic, brisk, buoyant, bustling, clever, dexterous, easy-moving, energetic, fleet, frisky, limber, lithe, lively, mercurial, prompt, quick, quick on the draw*, quick on the trigger*, quick-witted, rapid, ready, sharp, spirited, sportive, spright, sprightly, spry, stirring, supple, swift, twinkle toes*, vigorous, vivacious, winged, zippy; CONCEPTS 485,527, 588 —*Ant.* brittle, clumsy, stiff

agility [n] *physical or mental nimbleness, deftness* activity, acuteness, adroitness, alacrity, alertness, briskness, celerity, cleverness, dexterity, dispatch, expedition, fleetness, friskiness, litheness, liveliness, promptitude, promptness, quickness, quickwittedness, sharpness, sprightliness, spryness, suppleness, swiftness; CONCEPTS 410,630,748 —*Ant.* clumsiness, stiffness

aging [n] *becoming older* crumbling, declining, developing, fading, fermenting, getting along*, getting on*, maturing, mellowing, senescent, slumping, stale, waning, wearing out*; CONCEPT 701

agitate [v1] *shake physically* beat, churn, concuss, convulse, disturb, rock, rouse, stir, toss; CONCEPT 152 —*Ant.* calm, lull, quiet, soothe, tranquilize

agitate [v2] *disturb, trouble someone* alarm, argue, arouse, bug*, bug up*, burn up*, confuse, craze*, debate, discompose, disconcert, discuss, dispute, disquiet, distract, disturb, egg on*, examine, excite, ferment, flurry, fluster, get to*, incite, inflame, make flip*, move, perturb, psych*, push buttons*, rouse, ruffle, spook, stimulate, stir, trouble, turn on*, unhinge*, upset, ventilate*, work up*; worry; CONCEPTS 7,19,46 —*Ant.* calm, not bother, quiet, soothe

agitation [n] *shaking, mixing* churning, commotion, discomposure, disturbance, rocking, stirring, tizzy, tossing, turbulence, turmoil, unrest, upheaval; CONCEPTS 158,170

agitator [n] *person who disturbs, causes trouble* adjy, advocate, agent, anarchist, champion, demagogue, disrupter, dissident, dogmatist, fighter, firebrand*, fomenter, heretic, incendiary, inciter, instigator, leftist, malcontent, mover, partisan, propagandist, provocateur, pusher, rabble-rouser, radical, reactionary, rebel, reformer, revisionist, revolutionary, ringleader, sparkplug*, troublemaker, wave maker*, zealot; CONCEPT 412

agnostic [n] *person unsure that God exists* doubter, freethinker, materialist, skeptic, unbeliever; CONCEPT *361* —*Ant.* believer

ago [adv] *in the past* ages ago, back, back when, before, from way back, from year one*, gone, since, since God knows when*, time was; CONCEPT *820*

agog [adj] *enthralled* anxious, avid, breathless, eager, enthusiastic, excited, expectant, impatient, in suspense, on tenterhooks; CONCEPTS *401,542*

agonize [v] *suffer or cause another to suffer* afflict, bleed, carry on, crucify, distress, disturb, eat heart out*, excruciate, harrow, hurt, labor, lament, martyr, pain, rack, sing the blues*, squirm, stew over, strain, strive, struggle, take it badly*, torment, torture, try, wince, worry, writhe; CONCEPTS *7,19,410* —*Ant.* not worry

agonizing [adj] *difficult and painful, suffering* disturbing, excruciating, extreme, fierce, harrowing, intense, racking, struggling, tearing, tormenting, tortuous, torturing, vehement, violent; CONCEPTS *403,565*

agony [n] *suffering, pain* affliction, anguish, distress, dolor, misery, pangs, passion, throes, torment, torture, woe; CONCEPTS *410,728* —*Ant.* comfort, happiness, health, peace, success

agrarian [adj] *concerning land, farming* agricultural, natural, peasant, rural, rustic, uncultivated, undomesticated; CONCEPT *536*

agree [v1] *be in unison, assent with another* accede, acknowledge, acquiesce, admit, allow, be of the same mind*, bury the hatchet*, buy into*, check, clinch the deal*, come to terms, comply, concede, concur, consent, cut a deal*, engage, give blessing*, give carte blanche*, give green light*, give the go-ahead*, go along with, grant, make a deal*, okay, pass on, permit, play ball*, recognize, see eye to eye*, set, settle, shake on*, side with, sign*, subscribe, take one up on*, yes*; CONCEPTS *8,10,45,235* —*Ant.* contend, contradict, decline, disagree, dispute, dissent, oppose, protest, refuse

agree [v2] *be similar or consistent* accord, answer, attune, be in harmony, blend, click, cohere, coincide, concert, concord, concur, conform, consort, correspond, equal, fall in with*, fit, get along with, go hand in hand*, go together, go well with, harmonize, jibe, match, parallel, square, suit, synchronize, tally; CONCEPTS *118,656,670* —*Ant.* differ

agreeable [adj1] *pleasing* acceptable, dandy, delicious, delightful, enjoyable, fair, fine, gratifying, hunky-dory*, mild, nice, peach*, peachy*, pleasant, pleasurable, pleasureful, pussycat*, ready, satisfying, spiffy*, swell*, to one's liking, to one's taste, welcome; CONCEPT *572* —*Ant.* disagreeable, discordant, distasteful, harsh, hateful, mean, nasty, offensive, unpleasant

agreeable [adj2] *appropriate, in keeping* befitting, compatible, congruous, consistent, consonant, fitting, proper; CONCEPT *558* —*Ant.* disagreeable, discordant, incompatible, incongruous, unsuitable

agreeable [adj3] *willing to be in unison, assent* acquiescent, amenable, approving, complying, concurring, congenial, consenting, favorable, grateful, in accord, responsive, sympathetic, well-disposed, willing; CONCEPTS *401,542* —*Ant.* disagreeable, incongruous, repugnant, unwilling

agreeably [adv] *willingly, assenting; pleasantly; in keeping* affably, affirmatively, amiably, amicably, appropriately, benevolently, charmingly, cheerfully, convivially, favorably, genially, good-humoredly, good-naturedly, graciously, happily, kindly, mutually, obligingly, peacefully, pleasingly, politely, satisfactorily, sympathetically, well, wonderfully; CONCEPTS *401,572* —*Ant.* dissenting, unpleasantly, unwillingly

agreement [n1] *concurrence* acceding, accession, accommodation, accord, accordance, acknowledging, adjustment, affiliation, affinity, alliance, amity, approving, arbitration, arrangement, assenting, authorizing, bargaining, compatibility, compliance, complying, compromise, concert, concession, concord, concordance, concurring, conformity, congruity, consistency, correspondence, endorsing, granting, harmony, mediation, ratifying, reconciliation, similarity, suitableness, sympathy, understanding, union, unison, verification, verifying; CONCEPT *684* —*Ant.* disagreement

agreement [n2] *document of concurrence, contract* acknowledgment, adjudication, affidavit, approval, arrangement, assent, avowal, bargain, bond, cartel, charter, codicil, compact, compromise, confirmation, covenant, deal, indenture, lease, negotiation, note, oath, okay, pact, piece of paper*, protocol, recognition, settlement, stipulation, the nod*, transaction, treaty, understanding, writ; CONCEPTS *271,331*

agricultural [adj] *concerning farming, land* aggie*, agronomical, arboricultural, floricultural, gardening, horticultural, ranch, rural, rustic; CONCEPTS *536,583*

agriculture [n] *farming, crop production* agronomics, agronomy, cultivation, culture, horticulture, husbandry, tillage; CONCEPTS *205,257*

aground [adv] *on the bottom of* ashore, beached, disabled, foundered, grounded, high and dry*, marooned, reefed, shipwrecked, stranded, stuck, swamped, wrecked; CONCEPT *583* —*Ant.* afloat

ahead [adv] *in front or advance of* advanced, advancing, ahead, along, ante, antecedently, at an advantage, at the head, before, beforehand, earlier, first, fore, foremost, forward, forwards, in the foreground, in the lead, leading, on, onward, onwards, precedent, precedently, preceding, previous, progressing, to the fore; CONCEPTS *586,632,820* —*Ant.* behind

aid [n1] *help, support* advancement, advice, advocacy, alleviation, allowance, assist, assistance, attention, backing, backup, benefaction, benefit, benevolence, bounty, care, charity, comfort, compensation, cooperation, deliverance, encouragement, endowment, favor, furtherance, gift, giving, guidance, hand, handout, leg up*, lift, ministration, ministry, patronage, promotion, reinforcement, relief, rescue, reward, salvation, service, shot in the arm*, subsidy, sustenance, treatment; CONCEPT *110* —*Ant.* blockage, hindrance, impediment, injury, obstruction

aid [v] *help, support* abet, alleviate, assist, bail

out, befriend, benefact, encourage, favor, go to bat for*, go with*, lend a hand*, lighten, mitigate, open doors for*, promote, relieve, serve, stick up for*, straighten out*, subsidize, sustain; CONCEPT *110* —*Ant.* block, hinder, hurt, impede, injure, obstruct

aid/aide [n2] *person who helps* abettor, adjutant, aide-de-camp, assistant, attendant, coadjutant, coadjutor, crew, deputy, helper, lieutenant, second, supporter; CONCEPT *348*

AIDS [n] *immunological disorder* acquired immune deficiency syndrome, HIV, HIV-positive, sexually transmitted disease, STD, virus; CONCEPT *306*

ail [v] *hurt* afflict, annoy, bother, distress, pain, sicken, trouble, upset; CONCEPTS *14,246*

ailing [adj] *not feeling well* below par, debilitated, diseased, down, down with, enfeebled, feeble, feeling awful, ill, indisposed, rocky*, run down*, sick, sick as a dog*, sickly, under the weather*, unwell, wasting, weak; CONCEPT *314* —*Ant.* healthy

ailment [n] *mild sickness* ache, bug, complaint, condition, disease, disorder, dose*, flu, illness, indisposition, infirmity, malady, syndrome; CONCEPTS *306,316* —*Ant.* health

aim [n] *goal* ambition, aspiration, course, desideratum, design, desire, direction, end, intent, intention, mark, object, objective, plan, purpose, scheme, target, where one is heading*, wish; CONCEPT *659* —*Ant.* aimlessness, avoidance, neglect, purposelessness, thoughtlessness

aim [v] *point or direct at a goal* address, angle, aspire, attempt, cast, concentrate, contemplate, covet, design, direct, endeavor, essay, fix, focus, intend, level, mean, plan, propose, purpose, set one's sights on*, sight, slant, steer, strive, target, train, try, want, wish, zero in on, zoom in; CONCEPTS *20,41,201*

aimless [adj] *having no goal* accidental, any which way*, bits-and-pieces*, blind, capricious, careless, casual, chance, desultory, directionless, drifting, erratic, fanciful, fickle, fits and starts*, flighty, fortuitous, frivolous, goalless, haphazard, heedless, hit-or-miss*, indecisive, indiscriminate, irresolute, objectless, pointless, purposeless, random, shiftless, stray, thoughtless, unavailing, undirected, unguided, unplanned, unpredictable, vagrant, wandering, wanton, wayward; CONCEPTS *401,535,544* —*Ant.* determined, directed, goal-oriented, motivated, pointed, purposeful, resolute

air [n1] *gases forming the atmosphere* blast, breath, breeze, draft, heavens, ozone, puff, sky, stratosphere, troposphere, ventilation, waft, whiff, wind, zephyr; CONCEPT *437*

air [n2] *distinctive quality or character; style* address, affectation, ambience, appearance, atmosphere, aura, bearing, comportment, demeanor, deportment, effect, feel, feeling, flavor, impression, look, manner, mannerism, mien, mood, pose, presence, property, quality, semblance, tone; CONCEPTS *644,673*

air [n3] *musical tune* aria, descant, lay, melody, song, strain, theme; CONCEPTS *77,595*

air [v1] *put into the atmosphere; freshen* aerate, aerify, air-condition, circulate, cool, eject, expel, expose, fan, open, oxygenate, purify, refresh, ventilate; CONCEPT *255* —*Ant.* close up, hide

air [v2] *express opinion publicly* broadcast, circulate, communicate, declare, disclose, display, disseminate, divulge, exhibit, expose, make known, make public, proclaim, publicize, publish, put, reveal, speak, state, tell, utter, ventilate, voice; CONCEPTS *51,52* —*Ant.* be quiet, suppress

aircraft [n] *airplane* airliner, airship, balloon, blimp, chopper*, dirigible, flying machine, flying saucer, helicopter, jet, UFO, zeppelin; CONCEPT *504*

airplane [n] *vehicle that transports cargo or passengers through the air* aeroplane, airbus, aircraft, airliner, airship, cab*, crate*, jet, kite*, plane, ramjet*, ship*; CONCEPT *504*

airport [n] *center for transportation by air* aerodome, airdrome, airfield, airstrip, hangar, helipad, heliport, home plate*, installation, landing strip, runway, strip; CONCEPTS *325,439*

airs [n] *affectation; pretended behavior* affectedness, arrogance, false front, front, haughtiness, hauteur, mannerism, ostentation, pomposity, pose, pretense, pretension, pretentiousness, put-on*, show, superciliousness; CONCEPT *633* —*Ant.* personality, realness, truthfulness

airtight [adj1] *sealed* closed, impenetrable, impermeable, shut; CONCEPTS *483,490* —*Ant.* loose, open, penetrable, permeable, unclosed, unsealed

airtight [adj2] *certain* incontestable, indisputable, invulnerable, irrefutable, unassailable; CONCEPT *535* —*Ant.* possible, questionable, uncertain

airy [adj1] *open to the atmosphere* aerial, atmospheric, blowy, breezy, drafty, exposed, fluttering, fresh, gaseous, gusty, light, lofty, out-of-doors, uncluttered, vaporous, ventilated, well-ventilated, windy; CONCEPT *583* —*Ant.* close, closed, oppressive, stuffy

airy [adj2] *delicate or ethereal* dainty, diaphanous, flimsy, fragile, frail, frivolous, illusory, imaginary, immaterial, intangible, light, rare, rarefied, tenuous, thin, vaporous, visionary, volatile, weightless, wispy; CONCEPTS *490,582* —*Ant.* heavy

airy [adj3] *buoyant, light, or lively in nature* animated, blithe, bouncy, cheerful, cheery, effervescent, elastic, fanciful, flippant, frolicsome, gay, graceful, happy, high-spirited, jaunty, light, light-hearted, merry, nonchalant, resilient, sprightly, volatile, whimsical; CONCEPTS *404,550* —*Ant.* burdensome, heavy

aisle [n] *passageway dividing something* alley, artery, avenue, clearing, corridor, course, egress, gangway, hallway, ingress, lane, opening, passage, path, walk, way; CONCEPTS *440,513,830*

ajar [adj/adv] *slightly open* open, unclosed, unlatched, unshut; CONCEPT *586* —*Ant.* closed

akin [adj] *related or connected* affiliated, agnate, alike, allied, analogous, cognated, comparable, connate, consonant, corresponding, incident, kindred, like, parallel, similar; CONCEPTS *487,563,573* —*Ant.* alien, disconnected, unconnected, unrelated

alacrity [n] *liveliness; promptness* alertness, avidity, briskness, cheerfulness, dispatch, eagerness, enthusiasm, expedition, fervor, gaiety, hilarity, joyousness, promptitude, quickness, readiness, speed, sprightliness, willingness, zeal; CONCEPTS 633,657 —Ant. apathy, aversion, disinclination, dullness, indifference, reluctance, slowness, unwillingness

alarm [n1] *feeling of sudden fear* anxiety, apprehension, cold feet*, consternation, dismay, distress, dread, fright, horror, nervousness, panic, scare, strain, stress, tension, terror, trepidation, unease, uneasiness; CONCEPTS 410,690 —Ant. assurance, calmness, composure, confidence, peace, quietness, repose, security

alarm [n2] *warning, signaling device* alert, bell, blast, buzzer, call, caution, clock, cry, drum, flap*, flash*, forewarning, gong, high sign*, horn, Mayday*, nod*, scramble*, scream, shout, sign, signal, siren, SOS, squeal, tip, tip off*, tocsin, trumpet, warning, whistle, wink*, yell; CONCEPTS 269,463

alarm [v] *upset* amaze, astonish, chill, daunt, dismay, distress, frighten, give a turn*, make jump*, panic, scare, scare silly*, scare stiff*, scare to death*, spook, startle, surprise, terrify, unnerve; CONCEPTS 7,14,19,42 —Ant. assure, calm, gladden, reassure, repose, soothe

alarmist [n] *person who spreads alarm* Cassandra, Chicken Little*, pessimist, scaremonger, voice of doom*; CONCEPTS 412,423

albatross [n] *burden* cross to bear, disgrace, load, millstone, misery, woe; CONCEPTS 532,690

album [n] *blank book for collecting; holder* anthology, collection, depository, index, memento, memory book, miscellany, notebook, portfolio, register, registry, scrapbook; CONCEPTS 271,446

alchemy [n] *medieval science* black arts, black magic, hermetics, magic, pseudo science, sorcery, thaumaturgy, witchcraft, wizardry; CONCEPTS 367,370,689

alcohol [n] *intoxicating, flammable liquid* alky*, booze*, canned heat*, cocktail, drink, ethanol, firewater*, hard stuff*, hootch*, intoxicant, liquor, methanol, moonshine*, palliative*, red-eye*, rotgut*, sauce*, smoke*, spirits, tipple*, toddy*; CONCEPTS 454,467

alcoholic [adj] *intoxicating* brewed, distilled, fermented, hard, inebriant, inebriating, sprituous, vinous; CONCEPT 462 —Ant. non-alcoholic

alcoholic [n] *drunk* bar fly*, boozer*, dipsomaniac, hard drinker, inebriate, lush*, problem drinker, sot, souse, substance abuser, tippler, wino; CONCEPT 423

alcoholism [n] *alcohol abuse* addiction, alcohol addiction, alcohol dependence, crapulence, dipsomania, drunkenness, methomania, problem drinking, substance abuse, vinosity; CONCEPTS 20,316,709

alcove [n] *nook, secluded spot* anteroom, bay, bower, compartment, corner, cubbyhole, cubicle, niche, recess, study; CONCEPTS 440,448,513

ale [n] *intoxicating, fermented beverage* beer, brew, hops, malt, suds*; CONCEPT 454

alert [adj] *attentive, lively* active, all ears*, bright, cagey*, careful, circumspect, clever, fast on the draw*, good hands*, heads up*, heedful, hip, intelligent, jazzed*, observant, on guard*, on one's toes*, on the ball*, on the job*, on the lookout*, on the qui vive*, perceptive, psyched up*, quick, ready, sharp, spirited, switched on*, vigilant, wary, watchful, wide-awake, wired*,

wise, with it*; CONCEPTS 402,403 —Ant. asleep, drowsy, inattentive, lethargic, sluggish, unobservant, weary

alert [n] *warning* admonition, alarm, flap*, high sign*, Mayday*, sign, signal, siren, SOS, tip off, wink*; CONCEPTS 78,278,595,628

alert [v] *warn* alarm, flag, forewarn, give the high sign*, inform, notify, put on guard, signal, tip, tip off, wave flag*; CONCEPT 78

algae [n] *rootless, leafless plants living in water* dulse, kelp, scum, seaweed; CONCEPT 429

alias [adv] *otherwise known as* also called, also known as, otherwise; CONCEPT 582

alias [n] *false name* AKA, anonym, assumed name, handle*, moniker, nickname, nom de guerre, nom de plume, pen name, pseudonym, stage name, summer name*; CONCEPT 683 —Ant. name

alibi [n] *defense against charges of wrongdoing; evidence of absence* account, affirmation, airtight case*, allegation, answer, assertion, assurance, avowal, case, cop-out*, cover, declaration, excuse, explanation, fish story*, justification, plea, pretext, profession, proof, reason, reply, retort, song and dance*, stall, statement, vindication; CONCEPT 661

alien [adj] *foreign* conflicting, contrary, estranged, exotic, extraneous, extrinsic, inappropriate, incompatible, incongruous, opposed, remote, separate, unusual; CONCEPT 564 —Ant. akin, appropriate, native, proper

alien [n] *foreign being* blow in*, floater*, foreigner, greenhorn*, guest, immigrant, incomer*, interloper, intruder, invader, migrant, newcomer, noncitizen, outsider, refugee, settler, squatter, stranger, visitor, weed*; CONCEPT 423 —Ant. citizen, countryman, national, native, settler

alienate [v] *cause unfriendliness, hostility* break off, come between, disaffect, disunite, divide, divorce, estrange, make indifferent, part, separate, set against, turn away, turn off, wean, withdraw the affections of; CONCEPTS 7,19,231 —Ant. be friendly, disarm

alienation [n] *unfriendliness* breach, breaking off, coolness, disaffection, diverting, division, divorce, estrangement, indifference, remoteness, rupture, separation, setting against, turning away, variance, withdrawal; CONCEPT 410 —Ant. charm, endearment, friendliness

alight [v] *land* come down, debark, descend, disembark, dismount, get off, light, perch, settle, touch down; CONCEPTS 159,181

align [v1] *line up, arrange next to* adjust, allineate, coordinate, even, even up, fix, make parallel, order, range, regulate, straighten; CONCEPT 158 —Ant. divide, mess up, separate

align [v2] *join; bring to agreement* affiliate, agree, ally, associate, cooperate, enlist, follow, join sides, sympathize; CONCEPTS 8,114 —Ant. disjoin

alignment [n] *lining up* adjustment, arrangement, calibration, order, positioning, sequence, sighting; CONCEPTS 721,727

alike [adj] *similar* akin, allied, analogous, approximate, associated, carbon copy*, cognate, comparable, concurrent, corresponding, corresponding, dead ringer*, ditto*, double, duplicate, equal, equivalent, even, facsimile, identical, indistinguishable, kindred, like, look-alike, matched, matching, mated, parallel, proportionate, related, resembling, same, same difference*, similar, spitting image*, undifferentiated, uniform, Xerox*; CONCEPTS 487,566, 573 —*Ant.* different, dissimilar, distinct, diverse, opposite, unlike

alike [adv] *similarly* analogously, comparably, comparatively, consonantly, correspondingly, equally, equivalently, evenly, identically, in accordance with, in common, in the same degree, in the same manner, likewise, similarly, the same way, uniformly; CONCEPTS 487,566, 573 —*Ant.* differently, dissimilarly, unequally, unevenly

alimentary [adj] *digestive* comestible, dietary, digestible, nourishing, nutrient, nutritional, nutritious, nutritive, peptic, salutary, sustaining, sustentative; CONCEPTS 406,485

alimony [n] *money paid in support of a former spouse* keep, livelihood, living, maintenance, provision, remittance, subsistence, sustenance, upkeep; CONCEPT 344

alive [adj1] *being animately existent* animate, around, awake, breathing, cognizant, conscious, dynamic, existing, extant, functioning, growing, knowing, live, living, mortal, operative, running, subsisting, viable, vital, working, zoetic; CONCEPT 539 —*Ant.* dead, deceased, inanimate, lifeless

alive [adj2] *being active, full of life* abounding, alert, animated, awake, brisk, bustling, cheerful, dynamic, eager, energetic, lively, overflowing, quick, ready, replete, rife, sharp, spirited, sprightly, spry, stirring, swarming, teeming, vigorous, vital, vivacious, zestful; CONCEPTS 401,542 —*Ant.* dispirited, dull, lifeless, morose, sluggish, spiritless

alkali [n] *soluble base; opposite of an acid* antacid, caustic soda, salt; CONCEPT 472

alkaline [adj] *being basic, not acid (chemically)* acrid, alkalescent, alkali, antacid, bitter, caustic, neutralizing, salty, soluble; CONCEPT 472

all [adj1] *whole quantity* complete, entire, full, greatest, gross, outright, perfect, total, utter; CONCEPT 771 —*Ant.* none, zero

all [adj2] *each; every one of a class* any, bar none*, barring no one, complete, each and every, entire, every, every bit of, every single, sum, total, totality, whole; CONCEPT 772

all [adj3] *exclusively* alone, nothing but, only, solely; CONCEPT 554 —*Ant.* incompletely

all [adv] *completely, without exception* all in all, altogether, entirely, exactly, fully, just, purely, quite, totally, utterly, wholly; CONCEPTS 771, 772 —*Ant.* incompletely

all [n] *whole; totality* accumulation, across the board, aggregate, aggregation, collection, ensemble, entirety, everyone, everything, gross, group, integer, jackpot*, lock stock and barrel*, mass, quantity, sum, sum total, total, unit, utmost, wall to wall*, whole ball of wax*, whole enchilada*, whole nine yards*, whole schmear*, whole shooting match*, whole show*, works; CONCEPTS 787,837 —*Ant.* none, zero, zilch, zip

all-around [adj] *multifaceted* comprehensive, diverse, inclusive, versatile; CONCEPTS 527,542

allay [v] *reduce something, usually a pain or a problem* abate, alleviate, assuage, calm, compose, cool out*, decrease, ease, lessen, lighten, make nice*, mitigate, moderate, mollify, pacify, play up to*, pour oil on*, quiet, square, take the bite out*, take the sting out*; CONCEPTS 7,22,244 —*Ant.* intensify, provoke, stir, worsen

allegation [n] *assertion placing blame* accusation, affirmation, asseveration, avowal, charge, claim, declaration, deposition, overment, plea, profession, statement; CONCEPT 49

allege [v] *assert; claim* adduce, advance, affirm, asseverate, aver, avouch, avow, charge, cite, declare, depose, lay, maintain, offer, plead, present, profess, put forward, recite, recount, state, testify; CONCEPT 49 —*Ant.* contradict, deny, disagree, dissent, object, protest, repudiate

alleged [adj] *asserted, often doubtful* averred, declared, described, dubious, ostensible, pretended, professed, purported, questionable, so-called, stated, supposed, suspect, suspicious; CONCEPT 552 —*Ant.* certain, definite, sure

allegiance [n] *loyalty* adherence, ardor, consecration, constancy, dedication, deference, devotion, duty, faithfulness, fealty, fidelity, homage, honor, obedience, obligation, piety; CONCEPT 689 —*Ant.* disloyalty, enmity, sedition, treachery, treason

allegorical [adj] *symbolic* emblematic, figurative, illustrative, metaphorical, parabolic, symbolizing, typifying; CONCEPT 582 —*Ant.* not representative, untypical

allegory [n] *indirect representation, storytelling* apologue, emblem, fable, figuration, moral, myth, parable, story, symbol, symbolism, symbolization, tale, typification; CONCEPT 282

allergen [n] *irritant* antigen, dander, dust mite, foreign substance, immune trigger, irritant, pollen, ragweed; CONCEPT 478

allergic [adj] *having a reaction to food, material, etc.* affected, averse to, dyspathetic, hypersensitive, immune sensitive, sensitive, sensitized, susceptible; CONCEPTS 403,542

allergy [n] *reaction to certain food, material, etc.* allergic reaction, aversion, hay fever, hypersensitivity, sensitivity, susceptibility, vulnerability; CONCEPTS 405,410

alleviate [v] *relieve; lessen* allay, assuage, ease, lighten, mitigate, mollify, pacify, pour oil on*, soft-pedal*, take the bite out*, take the edge off*, take the sting out*; CONCEPTS 7,22,110,236,247 —*Ant.* aggravate, heighten, increase, intensify, magnify

alley [n] *narrow passage* alleyway, back street, lane, passageway, path, pathway, walk; CONCEPT 501

alliance [n] *friendly association, agreement* accord, affiliation, affinity, betrothal, bond, coalition, coherence, collaboration, collusion, combination, communion, compact, concord, concurrence, confederacy, confederation, congruity, conjunction, connection, consanguinity, cooperation, engagement, entente, federation, fraternization, friendship, interrelation, kinship, league, marriage, matrimony, membership, mutuality, pact, participation, partnership, relation, support, tie, treaty, union; CONCEPTS 301,423,684 —*Ant.* antagonism, discord, disunion, divorce, estrangement, hostility, rebellion, separation, war

allied [adj] *friendly; united* affiliated, agnate, akin, amalgamated, associated, bound, cognate, combined, confederate, connate, connected, incident, in league, joined, joint, kindred, linked, married, related, unified, wed; CONCEPTS 555,563 —Ant. disunited, estranged, unfriendly

allocate [v] *assign; divide among* admeasure, allot, apportion, appropriate, budget, cut, designate, dish out*, divvy*, earmark, give, mete, set aside, share, slice; CONCEPTS 41,98,108,129 —Ant. keep, keep together

allocation [n] *distribution* allotment, apportionment, appropriation, portion, quota, ration, share; CONCEPT 835

allot [v] *assign; give portion* admeasure, allocate, appoint, apportion, appropriate, assign, budget, cut, cut the pie*, designate, distribute, divvy*, dole, earmark, mete, set aside, share, shell out*, slice, split up; CONCEPTS 41,108 —Ant. disallow, keep, retain, withhold

allotment [n] *portion assigned or given* allocation, allowance, apportionment, appropriation, bite, chunk, cut, cut of pie*, end, grant, lot, measure, part, piece, piece of the action*, quota,rake off*, ration, share, slice, split, stint*; CONCEPT 835

all-out [adj] *complete* absolute, determined, entire, exhaustive, full, full-blown, full-fledged, full-scale, maximum, optimum, resolute, supreme, thorough, total, undivided, unlimited, utmost, utter; CONCEPTS 531,772 —Ant. half-hearted, halfway

allow [v1] *admit; acknowledge* acquiesce, avow, concede, confess, grant, let on, own; CONCEPTS 60,82 —Ant. deny, refuse, reject

allow [v2] *permit an action* accord, accredit, admit, approve, authorize, bear, be big*, be game for*, brook, certify, commission, consent, empower, endorse, endure, favor, free up*, give a blank check*, give carte blanche, give leave, give permission, give the go-ahead, give the green light*, go along with, grant permission, hear of, hold with, indulge, let, license, live with*, oblige, okay, pass, pass on, put up with, recognize, release, sanction, sit still for*, stand, suffer, support, take kindly to, tolerate, warrant; CONCEPTS 83,99 —Ant. deny, disallow, disapprove, forbid, prohibit, protest, refuse, reject, resist, withstand

allow [v3] *set aside* admeasure, allocate, allot, apportion, assign, deduct, give, grant, lot, mete, provide, remit, spare; CONCEPTS 41,108 —Ant. hold, keep

allowance [n1] *amount of money or other supply* aid, alimony, allocation, allotment, annuity, apportionment, bequest, bite*, bounty, commission, contribution, cut, endowment, fee, fellowship, gift, grant, honorarium, inheritance, interest, legacy, lot, measure, part, pay, pension, piece, portion, prize, quantity, quota, ration, recompense, remittance, salary, scholarship, share, slice, stint, stipend, subsidy, taste, wage; CONCEPTS 337,340

allowance [n2] *discount; concession* accommodation, adaptation, adjustment, admission, advantage, cut, deduction, rebate, reduction, sanction, sufferance, toleration; CONCEPT 274

alloy [n] *mixture, usually of two metals* admixture, adulterant, adulteration, amalgam, amalga-

al
al

mation, blend, combination, composite, compound, debasement, denaturant, fusion, hybrid, intermixture, reduction;CONCEPTS 260,476

alloy [v1] *mix metals* admix, amalgamate, blend, combine, compound, fuse, intermix, mix; CONCEPTS 109,113 —Ant. clear, not mix, purify

alloy [v2] *adulterate* debase, denature, devalue, diminish, impair, reduce; CONCEPT 240 —Ant. clean, clear, purify

all right [adj1] *satisfactory* acceptable, adequate, appropriate, average, decent, fair, fit, fitting, good, hunky-dory*, okay, okey-dokey*, passable, proper, satisfying, standard, swell*, tolerable, unexceptional, unobjectionable; CONCEPTS 547,558 —Ant. unsatisfactory

all right [adj2] *in good condition or health* hale, healthy, safe, sound, unharmed, unhurt, unimpaired, well, whole; CONCEPT 572 —Ant. sick, unhealthy

all right [adj3] *correct; excellent* accurate, exact, good, great, precise, right; CONCEPTS 557,574 —Ant. wrong

all right [adv1] *satisfactorily* acceptably, adequately, okay, passably, tolerably, unobjectionably, well enough; CONCEPTS 547,558

all right [adv2] *yes* agreed, certainly, definitely, of course, okay, positively, surely, very well, without a doubt; CONCEPT 572 —Ant. no

all-time [adj] *unsurpassed and permanent* best, champion, enduring, everlasting, perpetual; CONCEPTS 574,798

allude [v] *hint at* advert, bring up, imply, insinuate, intimate, point, refer, suggest; CONCEPTS 60,66

allure [n] *appeal* attraction, bedroom eyes*, charisma, charm, come-hither look*, come-on*, enchantment, enticement, glamor, inveiglement, lure, magnetism, seductiveness, temptation, the jazz*; CONCEPTS 673,720

allure [v] *entice* attract, bait, beguile, bewitch, cajole, captivate, charm, coax, come on*, decoy, draw, enchant, entrap, fascinate, hook*, inveigle, lead on, lure, magnetize, persuade, pull, seduce, suck in*, sweep off feet*, tempt, turn on*, wile, win over; CONCEPTS 7,22 —Ant. deter, discourage, dissuade, prevent, repel, threaten, turn off, warn

alluring [adj] *attractive* beguiling, bewitching, captivating, charming, enticing, magnetic, seductive, tempting, winning; CONCEPTS 529,579

allusion [n] *indirect reference; hint* casual remark, charge, citation, connotation, denotation, figure of speech, implication, imputation, incidental mention, indication, inference, innuendo, insinuation, intimation, mention, play on words, quotation, remark, statement, suggestion; CONCEPTS 60,274 —Ant. reality

ally [n] *something united with another, especially by treaty* accessory, accomplice, associate, coadjutor, collaborator, colleague, confederate, co-worker, friend, helper, partner; CONCEPTS 299,322,354,359 —Ant. antagonist, enemy

alma mater [n] *school from which one has graduated* academy, college, institution, old school, place of graduation, place of matriculation, university; CONCEPTS 288,289

almanac [n] *document containing information for a year* annual, calendar, chronicle,

almighty [adj1] having complete power, control absolute, all-powerful, invincible, mighty, omnipotent, puissant, supreme, unlimited; CONCEPT 540 —Ant. insignificant, powerless, weak

almighty [adj2] godlike all-knowing, all-seeing, boundless, celestial, deathless, deific, divine, enduring, eternal, everlasting, godly, heavenly, illimitable, immortal, infinite, omnipotent, omnipresent, omniscient, pervading; CONCEPT 539 —Ant. lay, lowly

almighty [adj3] severe awful, desperate, enormous, excessive, extreme, great, intense, loud, terrible; CONCEPT 569 —Ant. weak

almost [adv] nearly, very nearly about, about to, all but, approximately, around, as good as, bordering on, close to, close upon, essentially, for all practical purposes, for the greatest part, in effect, in the neighborhood of, in the vicinity of, just about, most, much, near to, nigh, not far from, not quite, on the brink of, on the edge of, on the point of, on the verge of, practically, pretty near, relatively, roughly, substantially, virtually, well-nigh, within sight of; CONCEPTS 531,586,799

alms [n] handout aid, assistance, benefaction, charity, contribution, dole, donation, offering; CONCEPTS 337,657

alone [adj1] separate; apart abandoned, batching it*, by itself/oneself, companionless, deserted, desolate, detached, forlorn, forsaken, friendless, hermit, individual, in solitary*, isolated, lone, lonely, lonesome, me and my shadow*, me myself and I*, onliest*, only, on one's own, shag*, single, sole, solitary, solo, stag, traveling light*, unaccompanied, unaided, unassisted, unattached, unattended, unescorted, unmarried, widowed; CONCEPTS 577,583 —Ant. together

alone [adj2] to the exclusion of; unique incomparable, matchless, peerless, singly, singular, solely, unequalled, unique, unmatched, unparalleled, unrivaled, unsurpassed; CONCEPT 556

along [adv1] ahead forth, forward, on, onward; CONCEPT 581

along [adv2] together with accompanying, additionally, also, as companion, as well, at same time, besides, coupled with, furthermore, in addition to, likewise, moreover, side by side, simultaneously, too, with; CONCEPT 577 —Ant. apart, separate

along [adv3] near adjacent, at, by; CONCEPT 586 —Ant. far

alongside [prep] close, near side of along the side of, apace with, at the side of, beside, by, by the side of, close at hand, close by, equal with, in company with, next to, parallel to, side by side; CONCEPT 586 —Ant. away

aloof [adj] remote above, apart, casual, chilly, cold, cold fish*, cool, detached, distant, forbidding, hard-boiled*, hard-hearted, haughty, incurious, indifferent, laid back*, loner*, lone wolf*, offish*, on ice*, putting on airs*, reserved, secluded, solitary, standoffish*, stuck up*, supercilious, thick-skinned*, unapproachable, unconcerned, unfriendly, uninterested, unresponsive, unsociable, unsympathetic, uppity*,

withdrawn; CONCEPTS 401,542 —Ant. concerned, friendly, sociable

aloud [adv] in a spoken voice, usually not softly audibly, clearly, distinctly, intelligibly, loudly, lustily, noisily, out loud, plainly, vociferously; CONCEPT 594 —Ant. inaudibly, silently

alphabet [n] letters of a writing system ABCs, characters, elements, fundamentals, graphic representation, hieroglyphs, ideograph, morphemes, phonemes, pictograph, rune, signs, syllabary, symbols; CONCEPT 276

alphabetical [adj] in ascending order of a writing system A to Z, consecutive, graded, indexed, logical, ordered, progressive; CONCEPT 585 —Ant. unalphabetical

alphabetize [v] place in order of a writing system index, order, systematize; CONCEPT 84

alpine [adj] mountaintop; high altitude aerial, elevated, high, high-reaching, in the clouds, lofty, montane, mountainous, rangy, snow-capped, soaring, towering; CONCEPTS 779,836

already [adv] before expected time as of now, at present, before, before now, but now, by now, by that time, by then, by the time mentioned, by this time, earlier, even now, formerly, heretofore, in the past, just now, now, once, previously, then, up to now; CONCEPT 799

also [adv] in addition to additionally, again, along, along with, and, as well, as well as, besides, conjointly, further, furthermore, including, in conjunction with, in like manner, likewise, more, moreover, more than that, on top of, over and above, plus, still, to boot*, together with, too, withal; CONCEPT 577

altar [n] church table, pedestal chantry, font, reredos, retable, shrine, tabernacle; CONCEPT 443

alter [v1] change adapt, adjust, amend, change, convert, cook, correct mid-course*, develop, dial back*, diversify, doctor, fine tune*, make different, metamorphose, modify, mutate, phony up*, recalibrate, recast, reconstruct, refashion, reform, remodel, renovate, reshape, revamp, revise, shift, transform, transmute, turn, vary; CONCEPT 232 —Ant. continue, fix, keep, let stand, maintain, preserve, remain, retain, sustain

alter [v2] sterilize animal caponize, castrate, change, desexualize, emasculate, fix, geld, mutilate, neuter, spay, unsex; CONCEPTS 310,375

alteration [n] change about-face, accommodation, adaptation, adjustment, amendment, conversion, correction, difference, diversification, exchange, fixing, flip-flop*, metamorphosis, mid-course correction*, modification, mutation, reformation, remodeling, reshaping, revision, shift, switch, switch-over*, transformation, transmutation, turn, variance, variation; CONCEPT 701

altercation [n] fight, often verbal argument, beef*, bickering, blowup*, bone of contention*, brawl*, brush*, combat, contest, controversy, dispute, embroilment, flap*, fracas*, fuss, go*, hassle, quarrel, row, rumble*, run-in*, set-to*, squabbling, tiff*, words*, wrangle; CONCEPTS 46,106 —Ant. agreement, concord, harmony, peace, union, unity

altered [adj] changed adapted, adjusted, amended, converted, cooked, corrected, diversified, doctored, fitted, fixed, modified, qualified, redone, refitted, reformed, remade, remodeled, renovated, reshaped, retailored, revised, spiked, transformed, turned, updated; CONCEPT 564 —Ant. continued, fixed, held, kept, maintained, preserved, retained, sustained

alter ego [n1] *other side to personality* doppelganger, evil twin*, second self; CONCEPTS 410,423

alter ego [n2] *companion* buddy, chum, confidante, counterpart, doppelganger*, pal, soul mate; CONCEPT 423

alternate [adj1] *every other* alternating, every second, intermittent, periodic, recurrent, recurring, rotating; CONCEPT 553

alternate [adj2] *substitute* alternative, another, backup, different, interchanging, makeshift, second, surrogate, temporary; CONCEPT 566 —Ant. necessary

alternate [n] *substitute* backup, double, equivalent, fill-in, proxy, replacement, stand-in, sub*, surrogate; CONCEPT 667 —Ant. necessity

alternate [v] *take turns, change back and forth* act reciprocally, alter, blow hot and cold*, change, come and go, exchange, fill in for, fluctuate, follow, follow in turn, interchange, intersperse, oscillate, relieve, rotate, seesaw, shift, shilly-shally*, substitute, sway, vacillate, vary, waver, yo-yo*; CONCEPTS 13,104,232, 701 —Ant. continue

alternative [adj] *other, alternate* another, back-up, different, flipside, other side, second, substitute, surrogate; CONCEPT 564

alternative [n] *possible choice* back-up, druthers*, opportunity, option, other, other fish in sea*, other fish to fry*, pick, preference, recourse, redundancy, selection, sub*, substitute, take it or leave it*; CONCEPT 529 —Ant. compulsion, constraint, necessity, obligation, restraint

although [conj] *even though* admitting, albeit, despite, despite the fact, even if, even supposing, granting, granting all this, in spite of, much as, notwithstanding, still, supposing, though, when, whereas, while; CONCEPT 544

altitude [n] *height in the sky* apex, distance, elevation, eminence, loftiness, peak, summit; CONCEPTS 739,752,791 —Ant. depth

altogether [adv1] *as a whole* all, all in all, all things considered, all told, bodily, by and large, collectively, conjointly, en masse, everything considered, everything included, for the most part, generally, in all, in sum, in toto, on the whole, taken together; CONCEPT 771 —Ant. partly

altogether [adv2] *completely* absolutely, fully, perfectly, quite, thoroughly, totally, utterly, well, wholly; CONCEPT 531 —Ant. incompletely

altruism [n] *unselfish concern* benevolence, charity, humanitarianism, kindness, magnanimity, philanthropy, public spirit, selflessness, social conscience; CONCEPT 633

altruistic [adj] *unselfish* all heart*, benevolent, big*, big-hearted*, bleeding heart*, charitable, considerate, generous, good, good scout, human, humane, humanitarian, kind, magnanimous, openhanded, philanthropic, Robin Hood*, self-sacrificing; CONCEPT 404 —Ant. selfish, unsacrificing

alumnus/alumna [n] *graduate* alum, old grad*, postgraduate; CONCEPT 350

always [adv] *forever; continually* consistently, constantly, eternally, ever, everlastingly, evermore, forevermore, for keeps, in perpetuum, invariably, perpetually, regularly, repeatedly, till blue in the face*, till cows come home*, till hell freezes over*, unceasingly, without exception; CONCEPTS 551,798 —Ant. at no time, never

amalgam [n] *mixture* admixture, alloy, amalgamation, blend, combination, combo*, composite, compound, fusion, mishmash*, soup; CONCEPT 432 —Ant. division, separation

amalgamate [v] *blend* admix, alloy, ally, coalesce, combine, come together, compound, consolidate, fuse, hook up with*, incorporate, integrate, interface, intermix, join together, meld, merge, mingle, network, pool, team up*, tie in, tie up*, unite; CONCEPT 113 —Ant. divide, separate

amass [v] *gather, accumulate* aggregate, assemble, clean up*, collect, compile, corral*, garner, heap*, hoard, lay up*, make a killing*, make a pile*, pile, round up*, scare up*, stockpile, store; CONCEPTS 109,120 —Ant. disburse, disperse, dissipate, divide, dole, scatter, spend

amateur [n] *casual participant* abecedarian, apprentice, aspirant, beginner, bush leaguer*, dabbler, dilettante, greenhorn, ham*, hopeful, layperson, learner, neophyte, nonprofessional, novice, probationer, putterer, recruit, Sunday driver*, tenderfoot*, tyro; CONCEPT 366 —Ant. professional

amateurish [adj] *unprofessional* bush-league*, incompetent, inept, inexperienced, inexpert, insipid, unskilled, untrained; CONCEPTS 527,538

amatory [adj] *affectionate, desirous* admiring, amorous, aphrodisiac, ardent, attracted, devoted, doting, erotic, fervent, fond, languishing, lovesick, loving, passionate, rapturous, romantic, sentimental, tender, wooing, yearning; CONCEPTS 372,403 —Ant. hateful, unfriendly

amaze [v] *surprise* affect, alarm, astonish, astound, bewilder, blow away*, blow one's mind*, bowl over*, daze, dumbfound, electrify, flabbergast*, impress, move, perplex, put one away*, shock, stagger, startle, strike, stun, stupefy, touch*; CONCEPT 42

amazement [n] *state of surprise* admiration, astonishment, awe, bewilderment, confoundment, confusion, marvel, one for the books*, perplexity, shock, something else*, stopper*, stunner*, stupefaction, wonder, wonderment; CONCEPTS 230,410 —Ant. calmness, composure, cool, coolness, indifference, preparation

amazing [adj] *astonishing* awesome, fascinating, incredible, marvelous, prodigious, shocking, stunning, surprising, unbelievable, wonderful; CONCEPTS 547,572

ambassador [n] *representative to a foreign country* agent, consul, deputy, diplomat, emissary, envoy, minister, plenipotentiary; CONCEPT 354

amber [n/adj] *gold-colored* brown, golden, tan, yellowish; CONCEPT 618

ambience [n] *environment* ambient, atmosphere, climate, medium, surroundings; CONCEPT 673

ambiguity [n] *uncertainty of meaning* doubleentendre, double meaning, doubt, doubtfulness, dubiety, dubiousness, enigma, equivocacy,

equivocality, equivocation, incertitude, inconclusiveness, indefiniteness, indeterminateness, obscurity, puzzle, tergiversation, uncertainty, unclearness, vagueness; CONCEPTS 638,682
—Ant. certainty, clarity, clearness, definiteness, explicitness, lucidity

ambiguous [adj] having more than one meaning clear as dishwater*, cryptic, doubtful, dubious, enigmatic, enigmatical, equivocal, inconclusive, indefinite, indeterminate, inexplicit, muddy, obscure, opaque, puzzling, questionable, tenebrous, uncertain, unclear, unintelligible, vague; CONCEPTS 267,535
—Ant. clear, definite, explicit, lucid

ambition [n1] strong desire for success appetite, ardor, aspiration, avidity, craving, desire, drive, eagerness, earnestness, emulation, energy, enterprise, enthusiasm, fire in belly*, get up and go*, hankering*, hope, hunger, initiative, itch*, keenness, longing, love, lust, moxie*, passion, pretension, push, right stuff*, spirit, striving, thirst, vigor, yearning, zeal; CONCEPT 20 —Ant. apathy, contentment, diffidence, humility, indifference, laziness, satisfaction

ambition [n2] something desired aim, aspiration, desire, dream, end, enterprise, goal, hope, intent, mark, objective, purpose, target, wish; CONCEPT 659

ambitious [adj1] desiring success aggressive, anxious, ardent, aspiring, avid, ball of fire*, bent upon, climbing, come on, come on strong, designing, desirous, determined, driving, eager, eager beaver*, earnest, energetic, enterprising, enthusiastic, fireball*, get up and go*, goal-oriented, go-getter*, hard ball*, high-reaching, hopeful, hungry, industrious, inspired, intent, longing, power-loving, purposeful, pushing, pushy*, resourceful, self-starting, sharp, soaring, striving, thirsty, vaulting, zealous; CONCEPTS 326,542 —Ant. content, fulfilled, satisfied, unassuming

ambitious [adj2] requiring great effort, ability arduous, bold, challenging, demanding, difficult, elaborate, energetic, exacting, formidable, grandiose, hard, impressive, industrious, lofty, pretentious, severe, strenuous, visionary; CONCEPT 538 —Ant. easy, facile

ambivalence [n] equivocation confusion dilemma, doubt, fluctuation, haze, hesitancy, hesitation, iffiness*, inconclusiveness, indecision, irresoluteness, muddle, quandary, tentativeness, uncertainty, unsureness; CONCEPT 564 —Ant. certainty, decisiveness

ambivalent [adj] conflicting clashing, contradictory, debatable, doubtful, equivocal, fluctuating, hesitant, inconclusive, irresolute, mixed, opposed, uncertain, undecided, unresolved, unsure, vacillating, warring, wavering; CONCEPTS 534,564 —Ant. certain, definite, resolved, settled, sure, unequivocal

amble [v] walk casually ankle*, boogie*, dawdle, drift, gander*, hoof it*, loiter, meander, mosey*, percolate*, ramble, sashay*, saunter, stroll, toddle*, wander; CONCEPT 151 —Ant. run

ambulance [n] emergency vehicle EMS, hospital wagon, rescue, transport; CONCEPT 505

ambulatory [adj] changing position; able to move under own power ambulant, itinerant,

nomadic, perambulant, perambulatory, peripatetic, roving, vagabond, vagrant; CONCEPT 584 —Ant. steady, stiff, unchanging

ambush [n] lying in wait; concealed position ambuscade, ambushment, camouflage, concealment, deception, hiding, hiding place, lurking, pitfall, shelter, trap, trick*, waiting, waylaying; CONCEPTS 86,188

ambush [v] lie in wait; attack ambuscade, assail, assault, box in*, bushwhack*, decoy, dry gulch*, ensnare, entrap, hem in*, hide, hook*, jap*, jump, lay for, lurk, net, set trap, surprise, surround, trap, wait, waylay; CONCEPTS 86,188

ameliorate [v] make, become better alleviate, amend, help, improve, lighten, meliorate, mitigate, relieve, step up, upgrade; CONCEPT 244 —Ant. worsen

amenable [adj1] willing, cooperative acquiescent, agreeable, biddable, docile, influenceable, manageable, obedient, open, persuadable, pliable, responsive, susceptible, tractable; CONCEPT 404 —Ant. intractable, nonconforming, uncooperative, unwilling

amenable [adj2] able to be judged; responsible accountable, answerable, chargeable, liable, subject; CONCEPT 402 —Ant. irresponsible, not responsible, unaccountable, unanswerable, unchargeable

amend [v] improve, correct alter, ameliorate, better, change, elevate, enhance, fix, help, lift, make up for, mend, modify, pay one's dues*, raise, rectify, reform, remedy, repair, revise, right, square*; CONCEPTS 126,244 —Ant. blemish, corrupt, debase, depress, harm, impair, injure, mar, reduce, subtract, worsen

amendment [n1] correction, improvement alteration, amelioration, betterment, change, correction, enhancement, improvement, mending, modification, rectification, reform, reformation, remedy, repair, revision; CONCEPT 700 —Ant. worsening

amendment [n2] addition to a document act, addendum, adjunct, alteration, attachment, bill, clarification, clause, codicil, measure, modification, motion, revision, rider, suggestion, supplement; CONCEPT 270

amends [n] compensation apology, atonement, expiation, indemnification, indemnity, quittance, recompense, redress, reparation, reprisal, requital, restitution, restoration, satisfaction; CONCEPTS 67,104,384

amenity [n1] pleasant thing advantage, betterment, comfort, convenience, enhancement, enrichment, excellence, extravagance, facility, frill, improvement, luxury, merit, quality, service, superfluity, virtue; CONCEPT 712 —Ant. abomination, inconvenience

amenity [n2] pleasing, agreeable behavior affability, agreeableness, amiability, attention, attractiveness, charity, charm, complaisance, cordiality, courtesy, delightfulness, enjoyableness, etiquette, gallantry, geniality, gentility, gratefulness, kindness, mildness, pleasantness, politeness, refinement, suavity, sweetness; CONCEPT 633 —Ant. disruption, misbehavior

amiable [adj] friendly, agreeable affable, amicable, attractive, benign, breezy, buddy-buddy*, charming, cheerful, clubby*, complaisant, cool*, copacetic*, cordial, cozy, delightful, downright neighborly*, easy, engaging, friendly, genial, good-humored, good-natured, gracious, home cooking*, kind, kindly, lenient, lovable, mellow, mild, obliging, palsy-walsy*, pleasant, pleasing, princely*, pussycat*, responsive, right, righteous, sociable, sweet-tempered, swell*, tight*, warm, warmhearted, winning; CONCEPT 401 —*Ant.* crabby, disagreeable, gloomy, hateful, irritable, mean, quarrelsome, rude, surly, testy, unfriendly

amicable [adj] *friendly, especially regarding an agreement* accordant, agreeable, amiable, civil, clubby*, concordant, cordial, courteous, cozy, empathic, good-humored, harmonious, kind, kindly, like-minded, mellow, neighborly, pacific, peaceable, peaceful, polite, regular, right nice*, sociable, square shooting*, sympathetic, understanding; CONCEPTS 529,542 —*Ant.* hostile, unfriendly

amid/amidst [prep] *in middle of; among* amongst, between, during, in the midst of, in the thick of, mid, over, surrounded by, throughout; CONCEPTS 586,820 —*Ant.* away from, outside, separate

amiss [adj] *wrong; defective* awry, bad, confused, crooked, erring, erroneous, fallacious, false, faulty, flawed, foul, glitched up*, haywire, imperfect, improper, inaccurate, inappropriate, incorrect, mistaken, out of order, sick, unfair, unlawful, unsuitable, untoward; CONCEPT 570 —*Ant.* good, right

amiss [adv] *wrongly; defectively* afield, afoul, badly, erringly, erroneously, faultily, improperly, inappropriately, incorrectly, mistakenly, out of turn, unfavorably, unsuitably; CONCEPT 570 —*Ant.* good, right, well

amity [n] *friendship* amicableness, benevolence, comity, concord, cordiality, friendliness, good vibrations*, goodwill, harmony, hitting it off*, kindliness, neighborliness, same wavelength*, simpatico*, togetherness*; CONCEPT 388 —*Ant.* discord, dislike, hatred, hostility

ammonia [n] *pungent gas, liquid* alkali, salts, spirits, vapor; CONCEPT 472

ammunition [n] *projectiles for weaponry* ammo*, armament, ball, bomb, buckshot, bullet, cannonball, cartridge, charge, chemical, confetti*, explosive, fuse, grenade, gunpowder, iron rations*, materiel, missile, munition, napalm, powder, rocket, round, shell, shot, shrapnel, torpedo; CONCEPTS 498,500

amnesty [n] *pardon, often by government* absolution, condonation, dispensation, forgiveness, immunity, reprieve; CONCEPTS 298,300

among [prep1] *in the middle of; between* amid, amidst, betwixt, encompassed by, in dispersion through, in the midst of, in the thick of, mid, surrounded by, with; CONCEPT 586 —*Ant.* away from, outside, separate

among [prep2] *in a group* by all of, by the whole of, in association with, in connection with, in the class of, in the company of, mutually, out of, together with, with, with one another; CONCEPT 785 —*Ant.* separate

amorous [adj] *loving, affectionate* amative, amatory, aphrodisiac, ardent, attached, boy crazy*, doting, enamored, erotic, fond, girl crazy*, have a crush on*, horny*, hot, hot and heavy*, impassioned, infatuated, in love, lovesick,

lovey dovey*, lustful, passionate, romantic, sexy, sweet for*, sweet on*, tender, turned on*; CONCEPTS 372,403,555 —*Ant.* cold, cool, frigid, hateful, indifferent, unfriendly

amorphous [adj] *without definite shape, character* baggy, blobby, characterless, formless, inchoate, indeterminate, irregular, nebulous, nondescript, shapeless, unformed, unshaped, unstructured, vague; CONCEPTS 404,490 —*Ant.* definite, distinct, distinctive, shaped, shapely

amount [n1] *quantity* aplenty, bags*, bulk, bundle, chunk, expanse, extent, flock, gob*, heap, hunk, jillion*, load, lot, magnitude, mass, measure, mess*, mint*, mucho*, number, oodles*, pack, passel, peck, pile, scads*, score, slat*, slew*, supply, ton*, volume, whopper*; CONCEPTS 787,837

amount [n2] *total* addition, aggregate, all, bad news*, body, budget, cost, damage*, entirety, expense, extent, list, lot, net, outlay, output, price tag*, product, quantum, score, set-back*, sum, tab*, tidy sum*, whole; CONCEPTS 329,784,787

amount [n3] *whole effect* body, burden, core, full value, import, matter, purport, result, sense, significance, substance, thrust, upshot, value; CONCEPT 676

amount [v] *equal, add up to* aggregate, approach, approximate, become, be equivalent to, be tantamount to, check with, come to, correspond, develop into, effect, extend, grow, match, mean, number, purport, reach, rival, sum, tally, total, touch; CONCEPT 667

amour [n] *romance* affair, entanglement, liaison, love, love affair, passion, relationship; CONCEPT 32 —*Ant.* dislike, hate, hatred

amphetamine [n] *hard drug* analeptic, benny*, crank*, crystal, dexy*, pep pill*, speed*, stimulant, STP*, tab*, upper*; CONCEPT 307

ample [adj] *more than necessary, sufficient* abounding, abundant, big, bounteous, bountiful, broad, capacious, commodious, copious, enough, expansive, extensive, full, galore, generous, great, heavy, large, lavish, liberal, no end, plenteous, plentiful, plenty, profuse, rich, roomy, spacious, spare, substantial, unrestricted, voluminous, wide; CONCEPTS 558, 781 —*Ant.* insufficient, meager, not enough

amplification [n] *increase in size or effect* addition, augmentation, boost, boosting, buildup, deepening, development, elaboration, enlargement, exaggeration, expansion, expatiation, extension, fleshing out, heightening, intensification, lengthening, magnification, padding, raising, strengthening, stretching, supplementing, upping, widening; CONCEPTS 236,245,780 —*Ant.* abridgement, compression, condensation, contraction, decrease, lessening, shortening

amplify [v] *increase in size or effect* add, augment, beef up*, boost, build up, deepen, develop, elaborate, enlarge, exaggerate, expand, expatiate, extend, flesh out*, heighten, hike up*, inflate, intensify, jack up*, lengthen, magnify, pad, pyramid, raise, soup up*, strengthen, stretch, supplement, swell, up, widen; CONCEPTS 236,245 —*Ant.* abridge, compress, condense, contract, curtail, decrease, lessen, reduce, shorten, summarize

amply [adv] *fully, sufficiently* abundantly,

acceptably, adequately, appropriately, bountifully, capaciously, completely, copiously, enough, extensively, fittingly, generously, greatly, lavishly, liberally, plenteously, plentifully, profusely, properly, richly, rightly, satisfactorily, substantially, suitably, thoroughly, well; CONCEPTS 558,771 —*Ant.* illiberal, inadequately, insufficiently

amputate [v] *remove a limb* cut away, cut off, dismember, eliminate, excise, lop, separate, sever, truncate; CONCEPTS 176,211

amuck [adv] *crazily* berserk, destructively, ferociously, frenziedly, in a frenzy, insanely, madly, maniacally, murderously, savagely, uncontrollably, violently, wildly; CONCEPT 401

amulet [n] *charm* fetish, lucky piece, ornament, talisman; CONCEPTS 260,446

amuse [v] *entertain; make laugh* break one up*, charm, cheer, crack up*, delight, divert, fracture*, gladden, grab*, gratify, interest, kill*, knock dead*, make roll in the aisles*, occupy, panic*, please, put away*, regale, slay*, tickle, wow*; CONCEPTS 9,292,384 —*Ant.* anger, annoy, bore, dull, tire, upset

amusement [n1] *entertaining, making someone laugh* action, ball*, beguilement, cheer, delight, diversion, enjoyment, entertainment, field day*, fun, fun and games*, gladdening, gratification, grins*, high time*, hilarity, hoopla*, laughs*, laughter, merriment, merry go round*, mirth, picnic*, play, pleasing, pleasure, regalement, whoopee*; CONCEPT 292 —*Ant.* boredom

amusement [n2] *game, pastime* distraction, diversion, entertainment, hobby, interest, joke, lark, play, prank, recreation, sport; CONCEPT 364 —*Ant.* work

amusing [adj] *entertaining, funny* agreeable, boffo*, campy, charming, cheerful, cheering, comical, cut up*, delightful, diverting, droll, enchanting, engaging, enjoyable, entertaining, for grins*, fun, gladdening, gratifying, gut-busting*, humorous, interesting, jocular, jokey*, joshing*, laughable, lively, merry, pleasant, pleasing, priceless, screaming*, sidesplitting*, too funny for words*, witty; CONCEPTS 267,548 —*Ant.* annoying, boring, tiring, unfunny

anachronism [n] *error in time placement* chronological error, metachronism, misdate, misplacement, postdate, prolepsis, solecism; CONCEPT 818

analgesic [n] *pain remover* anesthetic, anodyne, painkiller, soother; CONCEPT 307

analogous [adj] *agreeing, similar* akin, alike, comparable, consonant, convertible, correspondent, corresponding, equivalent, homologous, interchangeable, kindred, like, parallel, related, resembling, undifferentiated, uniform; CONCEPTS 487,573 —*Ant.* disagreeing, disparate, dissimilar, unalike, unlike, unrelated

analogy [n] *agreement, similarity* affinity, alikeness, comparison, correlation, correspondence, equivalence, homology, likeness, metaphor, parallel, relation, relationship, resemblance, semblance, simile, similitude; CONCEPTS 278,670 —*Ant.* disagreement, dissimilarity, unlikeness

analysis [n1] *examination and determination* assay, breakdown, dissection, dissolution, division, inquiry, investigation, partition, reasoning, resolution, scrutiny, search, separation, study, subdivision, test; CONCEPTS 24,103

analysis [n2] *statement of results from examination* estimation, evaluation, finding, interpretation, judgment, opinion, outline, reasoning, report, study, summary; CONCEPTS 271,274

analyst [n] *person who examines and determines; psychoanalyst* accountant, couch doctor*, examiner, guru*, head shrinker*, inquisitor, investigator, number cruncher*, psychiatrist, psychotherapist, questioner, shrink*, therapist; CONCEPTS 348,357

analytic/analytical [adj] *examining and determining* cogent, conclusive, detailed, diagnostic, discrete, dissecting, explanatory, expository, inquiring, inquisitive, interpretive, investigative, judicious, logical, organized, penetrating, perceptive, perspicuous, precise, problemsolving, questioning, ratiocinative, rational, reasonable, scientific, searching, solid, sound, studious, subtle, systematic, thorough, valid, well-grounded; CONCEPT 402

analyze [v1] *examine and determine* assay, beat a dead horse*, chew over*, confab*, consider, estimate, evaluate, figure, figure out, get down to brass tacks*, hash*, inspect, interpret, investigate, judge, kick around*, rehash, resolve, scrutinize, sort out, spell out, study, talk game*, test, think through; CONCEPTS 24,37,103

analyze [v2] *break down to components* anatomize, break up, cut up, decompose, decompound, determine, disintegrate, dissect, dissolve, divide, electrolyze, hydrolyze, lay bare, parse, part, resolve, separate, x-ray; CONCEPTS 135,310 —*Ant.* assemble, combine, synthesize

anarchist [n] *person who opposes the idea of government and laws* agitator, insurgent, insurrectionist, malcontent, mutineer, nihilist, rebel, revolter, revolutionary, terrorist; CONCEPTS 359,412

anarchy [n] *lawlessness; absence of government* chaos, confusion, disorder, disorganization, disregard, hostility, misrule, mob rule, nihilism, nongovernment, rebellion, reign of terror, revolution, riot, turmoil, unrest; CONCEPTS 29,674 —*Ant.* lawfulness, order, rule

anathema [n1] *something hated* abomination, bane, bugbear, detestation, enemy, hate, pariah; CONCEPT 529 —*Ant.* love

anathema [n2] *denouncement* ban, censure, commination, condemnation, curse, damnation, denunciation, excommunication, execration, imprecation, malediction, proscription, reprehension, reprobation, reproof, taboo; CONCEPT 278

anatomy [n1] *study of animal, plant structure* analysis, biology, cytology, diagnosis, dissection, division, embryology, etiology, examination, genetics, histology, inquiry, investigation, medicine, morphology, physiology, zoology; CONCEPT 349

anatomy [n2] *physical structure of animals, plants* build, composition, figure, form, frame, framework, makeup, physique, shape; CONCEPT 733

ancestor [n] *predecessor in family* antecedent, antecessor, ascendant, forebear, forefather, foregoer, foremother, forerunner, founder, precursor, primogenitor, progenitor; CONCEPT 414 —*Ant.* descendant

ancestral [*adj*] *related to previous family or family trait* affiliated, born with, congenital, consanguine, consanguineous, familial, genealogical, inborn, inbred, inherited, innate, in the family, lineal, maternal, old, past, paternal, running in the family, totemic, tribal; CONCEPT 549

ancestry [*n*] *family predecessors; family history* ancestor, antecedent, antecessor, blood, breed, breeding, derivation, descent, extraction, forebear, forefather, foregoer, foremother, forerunner, genealogy, heritage, house, kindred, line, lineage, origin, parentage, pedigree, precursor, primogenitor, progenitor, race, source, stock; CONCEPTS 414,648

anchor [*n*] *something used to hold another thing securely* ballast, bower, comfort, defense, fastener, foothold, grapnel, grappling iron, grip, hold, hook, kedge, mainstay, mooring, mud hook, pillar, protection, safeguard, security, staff, stay, support; CONCEPTS 464,502,731

anchor [*v*] *hold, be held securely* attach, berth, catch, dock, drop, fasten, fix, imbed, make port, moor, plant, secure, stay, tie, tie up; CONCEPTS 85,160,190 —*Ant.* detach, let go, loosen, unfasten

ancient [*adj*] *old, often very old* aged, age-old, antediluvian, antiquated, antique, archaic, back number*, been around*, bygone, creaky*, early, elderly, few miles on*, fossil*, hoary, lot of mileage*, moth-eaten*, obsolete, older, old-fashioned, old goat*, oldie*, outmoded, out-of-date, primal, primeval, primordial, relic, remote, rusty, superannuated, timeworn, venerable, worse for wear*; CONCEPTS 578,797 —*Ant.* modern, new, young

ancillary [*adj*] *extra; supplementary* accessory, accompanying, additional, adjuvant, appurtenant, attendant, attending, coincident, collateral, concomitant, contributory, incident, satellite, secondary, subordinate, subservient, subsidiary; CONCEPT 835 —*Ant.* necessary, needed

and [*conj*] *in addition to; plus* along with, also, as a consequence, as well as, furthermore, including, moreover, together with; CONCEPT 577

androgynous [*adj*] *having male and female traits* bisexual, cross-sexual, epicene, hermaphrodite, trans-sexual, unisexual; CONCEPT 372

anecdotal [*adj*] *informal* based on hearsay, unreliable, unscientific; CONCEPT 589 —*Ant.* scientific

anecdote [*n*] *interesting or amusing story* chestnut*, episode, fairy tale*, fish story*, gag*, incident, long and short of it*, narration, narrative, old chestnut*, recital, relation, reminiscence, short story, sketch, tale, tall story*, tall tale*, yarn; CONCEPT 282

anemic [*adj*] *weak and pale* bloodless, feeble, frail, infirm, pallid, sickly, wan, watery; CONCEPTS 314,483,618 —*Ant.* flushed, strong

anesthesia/anaesthesia [*n*] *induced sleep; induced absence of feeling* analgesia, insentience, numbness, stupor, unconsciousness; CONCEPTS 313,315,728

anesthetic/anaesthetic [*n*] *sleep-inducing or numbing drug* analgesic, anodyne, dope*, gas,

hypnotic, inhalant, narcotic, opiate, pain-killer, shot, soporific, spinal; CONCEPT 307

anew [*adj/adv*] *fresh; again* afresh, another time, come again, de novo, from scratch, from the beginning, in a different way, in a new way, lately, new, newly, once again, once more, one more time, over, over again, recently; CONCEPT 820

angel [*n1*] *attendant of God* archangel, celestial being, cherub, divine messenger, God's messenger, guardian, heavenly being, holy being, seraph, spirit, spiritual being, sprite, supernatural being; CONCEPTS 361,370 —*Ant.* devil

angel [*n2*] *sweet, kind person* beauty, darling, dear, dream, gem, ideal, jewel, paragon, saint, treasure; CONCEPT 416 —*Ant.* demon, savage, fiend

angel dust [*n*] *phencyclidine, PCP* angel hair*, angel mist*, aurora borealis*, black whack, crystal*, cyclones*, devil dust*, dummy dust*, embalming fluid*, hallucinogen, horse tranquilizer*, jet fuel*, magic dust*, rocket fuel*, star dust*; CONCEPT 307

angelic [*adj*] *sweet, kind, and usually beautiful* adorable, archangelic, beatific, beneficent, celestial, cherubic, devout, divine, entrancing, ethereal, godly, good, heavenly, holy, humble, innocent, lovely, otherworldly, pure, radiant, rapturous, righteous, saintly, self-sacrificing, seraphic, virtuous; CONCEPT 572 —*Ant.* demonic, devilish, fiendish, unkind

anger [*n*] *state of being mad, annoyed* acrimony, animosity, annoyance, antagonism, blow up*, cat fit*, chagrin, choler, conniption, dander*, disapprobation, displeasure, distemper, enmity, exasperation, fury, gall, hatred, hissy fit*, huff, ill humor, ill temper, impatience, indignation, infuriation, irascibility, ire, irritability, irritation, mad, miff, outrage, passion, peevishness, petulance, pique, rage, rankling, resentment, slow burn*, soreness, stew, storm, tantrum, temper, tiff, umbrage, vexation, violence; CONCEPTS 29,410 —*Ant.* agreeability, calmness, contentment, enjoyment, good nature, happiness, joy, peace, pleasantness

anger [*v*] *make someone mad; become mad* acerbate, affront, aggravate, agitate, annoy, antagonize, arouse, bait, blow up*, boil*, boil over*, bristle, burn, burn up, chafe, craze*, cross, displease, egg on*, embitter, enrage, exacerbate, exasperate, excite, fret, gall, get mad, get on one's nerves*, goad, incense, inflame, infuriate, irritate, lose one's temper, madden, make sore*, miff, nettle, offend, outrage, pique, provoke, raise hell*, rankle, rant, rave, rile, ruffle, seethe, steam up*, stew, stir up*, tempt, umbrage, vex; CONCEPTS 7,19 —*Ant.* calm, forbear, make happy, quiet, soothe

angle [*n1*] *shape formed by two lines meeting at a point* bend, corner, crook, crotch, cusp, decline, divergence, dogleg, edge, elbow, flare, flection, flexure, fork, incline, intersection, knee, nook, notch, obliquity, point, slant, turn, turning, twist, V, Y; CONCEPT 436

angle [*n2*] *personal approach, purpose* aim, approach, aspect, direction, hand, intention, outlook, perspective, plan, point of view, position, side, slant, standpoint, viewpoint; CONCEPT 660

angle [*v*] *fish* cast, dangle a line*, drop a line*; CONCEPT 363

angle for [v] *attempt to get* aim for, be after, cast about for, connive, conspire, contrive, fish for, hint, hunt, invite, look for, maneuver, plan, plot, scheme, seek, solicit, strive, try for; CONCEPTS 20,87

angry [adj] *being mad, often extremely mad* affronted, annoyed, antagonized, bitter, chafed, choleric, convulsed, cross, displeased, enraged, exacerbated, exasperated, ferocious, fierce, fiery, fuming, furious, galled, hateful, heated, hot, huffy, ill-tempered, impassioned, incensed, indignant, inflamed, infuriated, irascible, irate, ireful, irritable, irritated, maddened, nettled, offended, outraged, piqued, provoked, raging, resentful, riled, sore, splenetic, storming, sulky, sullen, tumultous/tumultuous, turbulent, uptight, vexed, wrathful; CONCEPT 403 —Ant. calm, collected, content, happy, joyful, joyous

angst [n] *feeling of anxiety* agony, apprehension, blues, depression, dread, mid-life crisis*, misgiving, nervousness, uneasiness, Weltschmerz; CONCEPTS 410,532,690

anguish [n] *severe upset or pain* affliction, agony, distress, dole, dolor, grief, heartache, heartbreak, hurting, misery, pang, rue, sorrow, suffering, throe, torment, torture, woe, wretchedness; CONCEPT 410 —Ant. comfort, contentment, happiness, joy, joyfulness, solace

angular [adj1] *bent* akimbo, bifurcate, cornered, crooked, crossing, crotched, divaricate, forked, intersecting, jagged, oblique, sharp-cornered, skewed, slanted, staggered, V-shaped, Y-shaped, zigzag; CONCEPT 486 —Ant. straight

angular [adj2] *thin, especially referring to people* awkward, bony, gangling, gaunt, lank, lanky, lean, rangy, rawboned, scrawny, sharp, skinny, spare; CONCEPT 773 —Ant. fat, heavy, thick, weighted

animal [adj] *beastlike; carnal* beastly, bestial, bodily, brute, brutish, corporeal, earthly, earthy, feral, fleshy, mammalian, muscular, natural, physical, sensual, untamed, wild, zoological; CONCEPT 406

animal [n] *animate being; mammal* beast, being, brute, bum*, creature, critter, invertebrate, living thing, mutt*, pet, stray, varmint*, vertebrate, wild thing; CONCEPT 394 —Ant. mineral, plant

animate [adj1] *alive* breathing, live, living, mortal, moving, viable, vital, zoetic; CONCEPT 539 —Ant. dead

animate [adj2] *lively* activated, active, alert, animated, dynamic, energized, gay, happy, spirited, vivacious; CONCEPT 401 —Ant. discouraged, dull, quiet, shy, spiritless

animate [v] *bring to life* activate, arouse, cheer, embolden, encourage, energize, enliven, exalt, excite, fire, gladden, hearten, impel, incite, inform, inspire, inspirit, instigate, invigorate, kindle, liven, make alive, move, quicken, revive, revivify, rouse, spark, spur, stimulate, stir, urge, vitalize, vivify; CONCEPTS 231,241 —Ant. deaden, discourage, kill

animated [adj] *lively* activated, active, alert, animate, ardent, brisk, buoyant, dynamic, ebullient, elated, energetic, energized, enthusiastic, excited, fervent, gay, happy, passionate, peppy, quick, snappy, spirited, sprightly, vibrant, vigorous, vital, vitalized, vivacious, vivid, zealous, zestful, zingy, zippy; CONCEPT 401

animation [n] *liveliness; activity* action, ardor, bounce, brio, briskness, buoyancy, dash, dynamism, ebullience, élan, elation, energy, enthusiasm, esprit, excitement, exhilaration, fervor, gaiety, high spirits, life, oomph*, passion, pep*, sparkle, spirit, sprightliness, verve, vibrancy, vigor, vim, vitality, vivacity, zap*, zeal, zest, zing*, zip*; CONCEPT 657 —Ant. discouragement, dullness, inactivity

animosity [n] *extreme dislike, hatred* acrimony, animus, antagonism, antipathy, bad blood, bitterness, displeasure, enmity, hate, hostility, ill will, malevolence, malice, malignity, rancor, resentment, virulence; CONCEPT 29 —Ant. good will, love

ankle [n] *joint between leg and foot* anklebone, astragalus, bone, talus, tarsus; CONCEPTS 392,418

annal(s) [n] *history, records* account, archive, chronicle, journal, memorial, record, register; CONCEPTS 271,281

annex [n] *something added; extension* addendum, addition, adjunct, affix, appendix, arm, attachment, ell, subsidiary, supplement, wing; CONCEPTS 440,441,484

annex [v] *join or add* adjoin, affix, append, appropriate, associate, attach, connect, fasten, hitch on*, hitch up*, hook on*, hook up*, link, slap on*, subjoin, tack on*, tag, tag on*, take on, take over, unite; CONCEPTS 85,113, 160 —Ant. detach, leave off, leave out

annexation [n] *adding, joining* addition, annexing, appropriation, attachment, grab, incorporation, increase, increment, merger, takeover; CONCEPTS 113,324 —Ant. detachment, subtraction

Annie Oakley [n] *complimentary ticket* Chinese ducket*, free admission, freebie*, free pass, free seats, free ticket; CONCEPTS 271,685

annihilate [v] *destroy completely* abate, abolish, abrogate, annul, blot out*, crush*, decimate, demolish, do in*, eradicate, erase, expunge, exterminate, extinguish, extirpate, finish off, invalidate, liquidate, massacre, murder, negate, nullify, obliterate, quash, quell, raze, root out*, rub out*, ruin, slaughter, take out*, undo, vitiate, wipe out*, wrack*, wreck; CONCEPT 252 —Ant. help, preserve, revive, save

anniversary [n] *yearly observance, celebration* ceremony, commemoration, feast day, festival, holiday, jubilee, recurrence, red-letter day; CONCEPTS 800,801,815,823

annotate [v] *write explanatory notes* comment, commentate, construe, define, elucidate, explain, expound, footnote, gloss, illustrate, interpret, note, remark; CONCEPTS 51,57,79

annotation [n] *explanatory note* comment, commentary, definition, elucidation, exegesis, explanation, explication, footnote, gloss, glossary, illustration, interpretation, note, observation; CONCEPTS 274,283 —Ant. blank

announce [v1] *make a proclamation* advertise, annunciate, blast, blazon, broadcast, call, communicate, declare, disclose, disseminate, divulge, drum*, give out, impart, intimate, issue, make known, make public, pass the word*, proclaim, promulgate, propound, publicize, publish, release, report, reveal, run off at mouth*, sound off*, spread around*, state, tell, trumpet; CONCEPT 49 —*Ant.* bottle up, conceal, keep secret, refrain, repress, suppress, withhold

announce [v2] *declare arrival* augur, forebode, forecast, forerun, foreshow, foretell, harbinger, herald, indicate, portend, predict, presage, signal, signify; CONCEPTS 60,70 —*Ant.* be quiet, hide, withhold

announcement [n] *proclamation, declaration* advertisement, advice, briefing, broadcast, broadcasting, bulletin, communication, communiqué, disclosure, dissemination, divulgence, edict, exposing, exposition, expression, intimation, message, narration, news, notice, notification, prediction, promulgation, publication, publishing, recitation, release, report, reporting, revelation, statement; CONCEPTS 49,274

announcer [n] *media commentator* anchorperson, broadcaster, communicator, deejay, disc jockey, DJ, leader of ceremonies, newscaster, reporter, rip and reader*, spieler*, talker, telecaster, veejay*, VJ; CONCEPT 348

annoy [v] *irritate, upset* abrade, agitate, ask for it*, badger, be at*, bedevil, beleaguer, be on the back of*, bore, bother, break, bug, burn up, chafe, displease, distress, disturb, egg on*, exasperate, fire up*, gall, get, gnaw, harass, harry, heat up*, henpeck, hit where one lives*, irk, madden, make waves*, miff, nag, needle, nettle, nudge, peeve, perturb, pester, plague, provoke, push button*, ride, rile, ruffle, tease, tick off*, T-off*, trouble, turn off*, vex, work on*, worry; CONCEPTS 7,19 —*Ant.* aid, gratify, make happy, please, soothe

annual [adj1] *occurring, done yearly* anniversary, each year, every year, once a year, year end; CONCEPTS 541,823

annual [adj2] *lasting for a year* a year's worth, yearlong; CONCEPT 798

annual [n] *book produced once a year* annuary, report, summary, yearbook; CONCEPT 271

annually [adv] *occurring, done yearly* by the year, each year, every year, once a year, per annum, per year, year after year; CONCEPT 541

annul [v] *void an agreement* abate, abolish, abrogate, annihilate, blot out, call off, cancel, countermand, declare, delete, discharge, dissolve, efface, erase, expunge, get off the hook*, invalidate, kill, negate, neutralize, nix, nullify, obliterate, quash, recall, render null and void, repeal, rescind, retract, reverse, revoke, scrub*, undo, vacate, vitiate, wipe out*; CONCEPTS 252,297,317 —*Ant.* keep, restore, retain, revalidate, validate

annulment [n] *voiding an agreement* abatement, abolition, abrogation, annihilation, breakup, cancellation, countermanding, dedomiciling, deletion, discharge, dissolution, erasing, going phfft*, invalidation, negation, neutralization, nullification, obliteration, recall, repeal, rescinding, rescindment, rescission, retraction, reversal, revocation, split*, split up*, undoing*, vitiation, voiding; CONCEPTS 297,317,691 —*Ant.* enactment, restoration, retention, validation

anoint [v] *bless, usually with oil or water* bless, consecrate, daub, embrocate, grease, hallow, rub, sanctify, smear; CONCEPT 367

anomalous [adj] *deviating from normal, usual* aberrant, abnormal, atypical, bizarre, divergent, eccentric, exceptional, foreign, heteroclite, incongruous, inconsistent, irregular, odd, peculiar, preternatural, prodigious, rare, strange, unnatural, unorthodox, unrepresentative, untypical, unusual; CONCEPT 547 —*Ant.* conforming, normal, regular, standard, usual

anomaly [n] *deviation from normal, usual* aberration, abnormality, departure, deviation, eccentricity, exception, incongruity, inconsistency, irregularity, oddity, peculiarity, rarity, unconformity, unorthodoxy; CONCEPT 647 —*Ant.* conformity, normality, regularity, standard, usual, usualness

anonymous [adj] *unknown, usually by choice* bearding*, incognito, innominate, Jane/John Doe*, nameless, pseudo, pseudonymous, secret, so and so*, such and such*, unacknowledged, unattested, unavowed, unclaimed, uncredited, undesignated, undisclosed, unidentified, unnamed, unsigned, unspecified, whatchamacallit*, what's his/her name*, whatsis*, X*, you know who*; CONCEPT 683 —*Ant.* identified, known, named

anorexic [adj] *starving* bulimic, emaciated, malnourished, sickly looking, thin, without appetite; CONCEPTS 490,491

another [n] *other person* addition, a different person, one more, someone else, something else; CONCEPT 423

another [prep/det] *additional, different* added, a distinct, a further, a separate, else, farther, fresh, further, more, new, one more, other, some other, that; CONCEPT 564

answer [n] *reply; reaction* acknowledgment, antiphon, backcap*, back talk, band-aid*, close, comeback, comment, cooler*, counterclaim, crack, defense, disclosure, echo, elucidation, explanation, feedback, guff*, interpretation, justification, key, lip*, observation, parting shot*, pay dirt*, plea, quick fix*, rebuttal, refutation, rejoinder, remark, repartee, report, resolution, response, result, retort, return, riposte, sign, solution, statement, thank-you note*, the ticket*, topper*, vindication, wisecrack; CONCEPTS 274,278 —*Ant.* question

answer [v1] *reply, react* acknowledge, answer back, argue, bark at you*, back talk, be in touch*, claim, comeback, contest, counterclaim, defend, deny, disprove, dispute, echo, explain, feedback, field the question*, get back at*, get back to*, give a snappy comeback*, parry, plead, rebut, refute, rejoin, remark, resolve, respond, retaliate, retort, return, sass*, say, settle, shoot back*, solve, squelch, talk back, top*; CONCEPTS 45,266 —*Ant.* ask, question

answer [v2] *solve; fulfill* clarify, conform, correlate, correspond, crack*, deal with*, do*, dope, dope out*, elucidate, fill, fit*, lick*, measure up, meet, pass, qualify, satisfy, serve, suffice, suit, unzip*, work, work through; CONCEPTS 87,664

answerable [adj] *responsible* accountable, amenable, bound, chargeable, compelled, constrained, liable, obligated, obliged, subject, to blame; CONCEPT 545 —*Ant.* irrefutable, unaccountable, unprovable

antagonism [n] *causing problem; opposition* animosity, animus, antipathy, antithesis, clashing, competition, conflict, contention, contradistinction, contrariety, difference, disagreement, discord, dissension, enmity, friction, hatred, hostility, incongruity, oppugnancy, rancor, resistance, rivalry; CONCEPT 29 —*Ant.* accord, agreement, harmony, rapport, sympathy, understanding

antagonist [n] *person causing problem* adversary, angries*, bad person*, bandit*, competitor, contender, crip*, enemy, foe, match, opponent, opposer, opposite number*, oppugnant, rival; CONCEPT 412 —*Ant.* ally, protagonist, supporter

antagonize [v] *cause problem; oppose* alienate, anger, annoy, counteract, estrange, insult, irritate, neutralize, offend, repel, struggle, work against; CONCEPTS 7,19,231 —*Ant.* agree, aid, help

antecedent [adj] *prior* anterior, earlier, foregoing, former, past, precedent, preceding, precursory, preliminary, previous; CONCEPT 820 —*Ant.* after, following

antecedent(s) [n] *predecessor(s) in family* ancestor, ancestry, antecessor, blood, descent, extraction, forebears, forefather/mother, genealogy, line, primogenitor, progenitor, stock; CONCEPT 414 —*Ant.* descendant

antedate [v] *occur or cause to occur earlier* accelerate, anachronize, antecede, backdate, date back, forerun, misdate, pace, precede, predate; CONCEPT 84 —*Ant.* predate

antediluvian [adj] *out-of-date; prehistoric* age-old, ancient, antiquated, antique, archaic, hoary, obsolete, old, old-fashioned, passé, primeval, primitive, primordial, timeworn, venerable; CONCEPTS 578,797,799 —*Ant.* modern, new, up-to-date, young

antenna [n] *appendages for sensing, usually on insects or electronics* aerial, bird snapper*, bullwhip*, ears*, feelers*, rabbit ears, receiver, sky wire*, whip*, wire; CONCEPT 464

anterior [adj] *beginning, prior* antecedent, foregoing, former, past, precedent, preceding, previous; CONCEPT 799 —*Ant.* ending, posterior, subsequent

anthem [n] *song* canticle, chant, chorus, hymn, melody, paean; CONCEPTS 263,595

anthology [n] *literary collection* album, analect, compendium, compilation, digest, garland, omnibus, selection, treasury; CONCEPTS 280,432

anthropology [n] *study of humans and their culture* folklore, sociology; CONCEPT 349

antibiotic [n] *medicine* amoxicillin, ampicillin, erythromycin, penicillin, streptomycin, sulfa drug, sulfonamide, tetracycline, wonder drug*; CONCEPT 307

antic [n] *funny act* caper, dido, frolic, joke, lark, romp, shenanigan, tomfoolery, trick; CONCEPT 292

anticipate [v1] *expect; predict* assume, await, bargain for*, be afraid*, conjecture, count chickens*, count on, cross the bridge*, divine, entertain*, figure, forecast, foresee, foretaste, foretell, have a hunch*, hope for, jump the gun*, look for, look forward to, plan on, prepare for, prevision, prognosticate, promise oneself,

prophesy, see, see coming*, see in the cards*, suppose, visualize, wait, wait for; CONCEPTS 26,70 —*Ant.* be amazed, be surprised, doubt

anticipate [v2] *act in advance of* apprehend, beat someone to it*, be early, be one step ahead of*, block, delay, forestall, hinder, hold back, intercept, precede, preclude, prepare for, prevent, provide against; CONCEPTS 100,121 —*Ant.* be unready

anticipation [n1] *expectation* apprehension, awaiting, contemplation, expectancy, foresight, foretaste, high hopes, hope, impatience, joy, looking forward, outlook, preconception, premonition, preoccupation, prescience, presentiment, promise, prospect, trust; CONCEPTS 26,689 —*Ant.* amazement, astonishment, doubt, fear, sensation, surprise, wonder

anticipation [n2] *readiness; forethought* apprehension, awareness, foreboding, forecast, foreseeing, foresight, foretaste, forethought, inkling, intuition, preconception, premonition, prescience, presentiment, prevision, prior knowledge, realization; CONCEPTS 409,410 —*Ant.* doubt, unreadiness

anticlimax [n] *ineffective conclusion* bathos, comedown, decline, descent, disappointment, drop, letdown, slump; CONCEPTS 230,674 —*Ant.* climax

antidote [n] *counteracting agent* antitoxin, antivenin, corrective, counteractant, counteragent, countermeasure, counterstep, cure, medicine, negator, neutralizer, nullifier, preventive, remedy; CONCEPT 307

antipathy [n] *strong dislike, disgust* abhorrence, allergy, animosity, animus, antagonism, aversion, avoidance, bad blood*, contrariety, distaste, dyspathy, enmity, escape, eschewal, evasion, hate, hatred, hostility, ill will, incompatibility, loathing, opposition, rancor, repellency, repugnance, repulsion; CONCEPT 29 —*Ant.* admiration, appreciation, approval, esteem, honor, like, liking, love, rapport, regard, respect, sympathy

antiquarian [adj] *old, ancient* aged, antique, archaic, hoary, obsolete, primitive, timeworn, venerable; CONCEPTS 578,797 —*Ant.* modern, new, young

antiquated [adj] *obsolete* aged, ancient, antediluvian, antique, archaic, dated, elderly, fusty*, hoary, moldy, obsolescent, old, old-fangled, old-fashioned, old hat*, outmoded, out-of-date, outworn, superannuated; CONCEPTS 530,578,797 —*Ant.* forward-looking, modern, new, recent

antique [adj1] *old* aged, ancient, elderly, obsolescent, obsolete, outdated, out-of-date, prehistoric, superannuated; CONCEPTS 578,797 —*Ant.* modern, new, recent, up-to-date

antique [adj2] *old-fashioned* antiquarian, archaic, classic, obsolete, olden, outdated, vintage; CONCEPTS 530,578,797 —*Ant.* current, fresh, modern

antique [n] *old object, often of great value* antiquity, artifact, bygone, heirloom, monument, objet d'art, rarity, relic, ruin, vestige; CONCEPTS 259,443

antiquity [n1] *old object* antique, relic, ruin; CONCEPT 259

antiquity [n2] *oldness* age, ancientness,

antiqueness, archaicism, archaism, elderliness, hoariness, old age, venerableness; CONCEPT 715 —*Ant.* convention, modernity, newness

antiquity [*n3*] *distant past* ancient time(s), classical times, days of old, days of yore, former age, old days, olden days, remote time, time immemorial; CONCEPT 807 —*Ant.* now

antiseptic [*adj*] *completely clean, uncontaminated; decontaminating* antibacterial, antibiotic, aseptic, bactericidal, clean, disinfectant, germ-destroying, germ-free, germicidal, hygienic, medicated, prophylactic, pure, purifying, sanitary, sterile, sterilized, sterilizing, unpolluted; CONCEPT 485 —*Ant.* contaminated, polluted, unclean, unsanitary, unsterile

antiseptic [*n*] *decontaminating agent* bactericide, detergent, disinfectant, germicide, preservative, preventative, preventive, prophylactic, purifier, sterilizer; CONCEPTS 307,472,492

antisocial [*adj*] *nonparticipating; avoiding company* alienated, ascetic, asocial, austere, cold, cynical, eremetic, hermitlike, introverted, misanthropic, reclusive, remote, reserved, retiring, solitary, standoffish, uncommunicative, unfriendly, unsociable, withdrawn; CONCEPT 555 —*Ant.* friendly, fun-loving, participating, sociable

antithesis [*n1*] *exact opposite* antipode, antipole, contra, contradictory, contrary, contrast, converse, counter, flip side*, inverse, other side, reverse; CONCEPT 665 —*Ant.* same

antithesis [*n2*] *contrast, opposition* antagonism, contradiction, contradistinction, contraposition, contrariety, inversion, opposure, reversal; CONCEPTS 633,665 —*Ant.* same

antithetical [*adj*] *reverse* contradictory, contrary, contrasted, converse, counter, inverse, opposed, opposite, polarized, poles apart*; CONCEPT 542

antitoxin [*n*] *agent for negating the effect of an infection or poison* antibiotic, antibody, antipoison, antiseptic, antiserum, antivenin, counteractant, counteragent, medicine, neutralizer, preventive, serum, vaccine; CONCEPT 307

antonym [*n*] *word with opposite meaning to another word* opposite, reverse; CONCEPT 275 —*Ant.* synonym

antsy [*adj*] *fidgety* anxious, edgy, impatient, on pins and needles*, restless; CONCEPT 401

anxiety [*n*] *worry, tension* all-overs*, angst, ants in pants*, apprehension, botheration*, butterflies*, care, cold sweat*, concern, creeps*, disquiet, disquietude, distress, doubt, downer*, drag*, dread, fidgets*, flap*, foreboding, fretfulness, fuss, goose bumps*, heebie-jeebies*, jitters, jumps*, misery, misgiving, mistrust, nail-biting*, needles*, nervousness, panic, pins and needles*, restlessness, shakes*, shivers*, solicitude, suffering, suspense, sweat*, trouble, uncertainty, unease, uneasiness, watchfulness, willies*; worriment; CONCEPTS 410,532,690 —*Ant.* assurance, calmness, composure, contentment, ease, happiness, nonchalance, peace, tranquility

anxious [*adj1*] *worried, tense* afraid, aghast, antsy*, apprehensive, basket case*, bugged*, butterflies, careful, choked*, clutched*, concerned, disquieted, distressed, disturbed, dreading, fearful, fidgety, fretful, hacked*, hyper*, in

a state*, in a tizzy*, in suspense*, jittery, jumpy, nervous, nervy, overwrought, restless, scared, shaking, shaky, shivery, shook up*, shot to pieces*, solicitous, spooked*, strung out*, sweating bullets*, taut, troubled, uneasy, unglued*, unquiet, uptight*, watchful, wired*, worried sick*, wreck*; CONCEPTS 403,690 —*Ant.* assured, calm, content, cool, happy, indifferent, peaceful, tranqil, unconcerned, unworried

anxious [*adj2*] *eager* agog, ardent, avid, breathless, desirous, enthusiastic, expectant, fervent, impatient, intent, itching*, keen, thirsty, yearning, zealous; CONCEPTS 401,542 —*Ant.* dreading, unwilling

any [*det*] *one, some; unspecified, indiscriminate* a bit, a little, all, each, each and every, either, in general, part of, several, whatever; CONCEPT 762

anybody [*n*] *one, some unspecified person or people* all, any of, anyone, anyone at all, any person, a person, each and every one, everybody, everyone, masses, one, public, whole world; CONCEPT 417

anyhow [*adv*] *by any means* about, anyway, any which way, around, at any rate, at random, haphazard, haphazardly, helter-skelter, however, in any case, in any respect, in any way, in either way, in one way or another, in whatever way, nevertheless, random, randomly, regardless, under any circumstances, whatever happens, willy-nilly; CONCEPT 544

anyone [*n*] *one, some unspecified person* all, anybody, anybody at all, any of, any person, a person, each and every one, everybody, everyone, masses, one, public, whole world; CONCEPT 417

anyplace [*n*] *unspecified area* all over, anywhere, everywhere, in any place, in whatever place, wherever; CONCEPT 198

anything [*n*] *unspecified object or event* all, any one thing, anything at all, everything, whatever; CONCEPTS 2,433

anytime [*n*] *unspecified moment, period* at all, at any moment, at one's convenience, everytime, no matter when, whenever, when one will; CONCEPTS 807,819

anyway [*adv*] *by any means* anyhow, at all, at any rate, ever, however, in any case, in any event, in any manner, nevertheless, once; CONCEPT 544

anywhere [*n*] *unspecified area* all over, anyplace, everywhere, in any place, in whatever place, wherever; CONCEPT 198

apart [*adv*] *separate* afar, alone, aloof, aside, away, by itself, cut off*, disassociated, disconnected, distant, distinct, divorced, excluded, exclusively, freely, independent, independently, individually, isolated, lone wolf*, separated, separately, singly, special, to itself, to one side; CONCEPTS 586,785 —*Ant.* together

apartheid [*n*] *racial segregation* discrimination, racism, separation; CONCEPT 689

apartment [*n*] *set of rooms for rent* accommodation, cave*, chambers, cold-water*, condo, coop, cooperative, crash pad*, den*, digs*, dump*, flat, living quarters, lodging, pad*, penthouse, rental, residence, suite, walk-up; CONCEPTS 448,516

apathetic [*adj*] *uncaring, disinterested* blah*,

callous, cold, cool, could care less*, couldn't care less*, don't give a damn*, draggy*, emotionless, flat, impassive, indifferent, insensible, laid-back*, languid, moony*, passive, stoic, stolid, unconcerned, unemotional, unfeeling, uninterested, unmoved, unresponsive, untouched, what the hell*, wimpy*; CONCEPT 401 —*Ant.* caring, concerned, interested, responsive

apathy [n] *uncaring attitude, lack of interest* aloofness, coldness, coolness, detachment, disinterest, dispassion, disregard, dullness, emotionlessness, halfheartedness, heedlessness, indifference, insensibility, insensitivity, insouciance, lassitude, lethargy, listlessness, passiveness, passivity, stoicism, unconcern, unresponsiveness; CONCEPTS 410,633 —*Ant.* care, concern, feeling, interest, passion, sensitivity, sympathy, warmth

ape [v] *mimic* affect, caricature, copy, counterfeit, ditto*, do*, do like*, echo, emulate, go like*, imitate, impersonate, make like*, mirror, mock, parody, parrot, take off*, travesty; CONCEPTS 111,171

aperture [n] *hole* breach, break, chasm, chink, cleft, crack, cut, eye, fissure, gap, gash, interstice, opening, orifice, outlet, passage, perforation, pinhole, puncture, rift, rupture, slash, slit, slot, space, vent; CONCEPT 757

apex [n] *top, high point* acme, apogee, climax, crest, crown, culmination, cusp, greatest, height, max*, maximum, meridian, most*, ne plus ultra, peak, pinnacle, point, roof, spire, sublimity, summit, tip, tops, up there*, vertex, zenith; CONCEPTS 706,836 —*Ant.* nadir

aphorism [n] *saying expressing a belief, often true* adage, apothegm, axiom, dictum, maxim, moral, precept, proverb, rule, saw, saying, truism; CONCEPTS 275,278,689

aphrodisiac [n/adj] *seductive; inducing sex* amative, amatory, amorous, erotic, love drug, popper*, Spanish fly*, turn-on*, wampole*; CONCEPTS 372,537

apiece [adv] *each* all, a pop*, aside, for each, from each, individually, one by one, per, respectively, severally, singly, successively, to each; CONCEPT 762

apocalypse [n] *mass destruction* annihilation, Armageddon, cataclysm, catastrophe, decimation, devastation, end of the world, holocaust; CONCEPT 674

apocryphal [adj] *questionable; fake* counterfeit, doubtful, dubious, equivocal, false, fictitious, inaccurate, mythical, spurious, unauthenticated, ungenuine, unsubstantiated, untrue, unverified, wrong; CONCEPTS 570,582 —*Ant.* authentic, doubtless, real, true

apologetic [adj] *expressing remorse, regret* atoning, attritional, compunctious, conciliatory, contrite, expiatory, explanatory, on one's knees*, penitent, penitential, propitiatory, regretful, remorseful, repentant, rueful, self-effacing, self-incriminating, sorry, supplicating; CONCEPT 267 —*Ant.* defiant, defying

apologize [v] *express remorse, regret* admit guilt, ask forgiveness, ask pardon, atone, beg pardon, bow to*, clear oneself, confess, cop a plea*, cop out*, crawl*, excuse oneself, get down on knees*, give satisfaction*, make amends, make reparations, make up for, make

up with, offer compensation, offer excuse, purge, retract, say one is sorry, square*, withdraw; CONCEPTS 48,67 —*Ant.* defy

apology [n] *offering of remorse, regret* acknowledgment, admission, amends, atonement, concession, confession, defense, excuse, explanation, extenuation, justification, mea culpa, mitigation, plea, redress, reparation, vindication; CONCEPTS 48,67 —*Ant.* accusation, censure, charge, complaint, condemnation, criticism, defiance, indictment

apoplexy [n] *loss of consciousness from blockage in vein or artery* occlusion, seizure, stroke, thrombosis; CONCEPTS 316,720 —*Ant.* consciousness

apostate [n] *traitor* backslider, defector, deserter, dissenter, heretic, nonconformist, rat*, recreant, renegade, turncoat; CONCEPTS 359,412 —*Ant.* adherent, faithful, loyalist

apostle [n] *preacher; supporter* advocate, champion, companion, converter, evangelist, follower, herald, messenger, missionary, pioneer, propagandist, proponent, proselytizer, witness; CONCEPTS 359,361

apotheosis [n] *glorification* deification, elevation, idolization, immortalization; CONCEPTS 69,367

appall/appal [v] *horrify* alarm, amaze, astound, awe, consternate, daunt, disconcert, dishearten, dismay, faze, frighten, get to*, gross out*, insult, intimidate, outrage, petrify, scare, shake, shock, terrify, throw, unnerve; CONCEPTS 7,19,42 —*Ant.* comfort, encourage, reassure, satisfy

appalling [adj] *horrifying* alarming, astounding, awful, bad, daunting, dire, disheartening, dismaying, dreadful, fearful, formidable, frightening, frightful, ghastly, grim, grody*, gross*, harrowing, heavy*, hideous, horrible, horrid, horrific, intimidating, mean, petrifying, scaring, shocking, terrible, terrifying, the end*, unnerving; CONCEPT 529 —*Ant.* comforting, encouraging, reassuring, satisfying

apparatus [n1] *equipment with a purpose* accoutrement, appliance, black box*, contraption, device, dingbat, doodad*, doohickey*, furnishings, gaff*, gear, gimcrack*, gimmick, gizmo*, grabber*, habiliments, idiot box*, implement, jigger*, job*, machine, machinery, means, mechanism, outfit, paraphernalia, provisions, setup, stuff, supplies, tackle, thingamajig*, tools, utensils, whatchamacallit*, whatsis*, whosis*, widget*; CONCEPTS 260,463,499

apparatus [n2] *organization or system* bureaucracy, chain of command, hierarchy, network, setup, structure; CONCEPTS 381,770

apparel [n] *clothing; covering* accoutrement, array, attire, clothes, costume, drapery, dress, duds*, equipment, garb, garment, gear*, getup*, habiliment, habit, outfit, raiment, rig*, robe, suit, threads*, trapping, vestment; CONCEPTS 451,473

apparent [adj1] *seeming, not proven real* credible, illusive, illusory, likely, ostensible, outward, plausible, possible, probable, semblant, specious, superficial, supposed, suppositious; CONCEPTS 552,582 —*Ant.* doubtful, dubious, equivocal, hidden, improbable, obscure, questionable, real, uncertain, unclear, unlikely

apparent [adj2] *obvious* barefaced, big as life*, clear, clear cut, conspicuous, crystal clear, discernible, distinct, evident, glaring, indubitable, make no bones*, manifest, marked, noticeable, observable, open, open and shut*, out in the open*, overt, palpable, patent, perceivable, plain, self-evident, transparent, unambiguous, under one's nose*, understandable, unequivocal, unmistakable, visible; CONCEPTS 535,582

apparently [adv1] *seemingly* allegedly, as if, as though, at a glance, at first sight, in all likelihood, intuitively, it appears that, it seems that, most likely, on the face of it, ostensibly, outwardly, plausibly, possibly, probably, professedly, reasonably, reputably, speciously, superficially, supposedly, tangibly, to all appearances; CONCEPTS 552,582 —*Ant.* dubiously, equivocally, improbably, questionably, uncertain, unlikely

apparently [adv2] *obviously* clearly, conspicuously, evidently, expressly, indubitably, in plain sight, manifestly, officially, openly, overtly, palpably, patently, perceptibly, plainly, transparently, unmistakably; CONCEPT 535

apparition [n] *ghost* bogeyman, bump in the night*, chimera, delusion, hallucination, haunt, illusion, phantasm, phantom, revenant, specter, spirit, spook, visitant; CONCEPTS 370,689 —*Ant.* animate, being

appeal [n1] *request for help* address, adjuration, application, bid, call, claim, demand, entreaty, imploration, importunity, invocation, overture, petition, plea, prayer, proposal, proposition, question, recourse, requisition, solicitation, submission, suit, supplication; CONCEPT 48 —*Ant.* denial, disavowal, disclaimer, refusal, retraction, revocation

appeal [n2] *power to attract, interest* allure, attraction, attractiveness, beauty, charm, charmingness, engagingness, fascination, glamor, interestingness, pleasingness, seductiveness; CONCEPTS 655,673 —*Ant.* ugliness

appeal [v1] *request* address, adjure, advance, apply, ask, beg, beseech, bid, call, call upon, claim, contest, crave, demand, entreat, hit on, implore, importune, petition, plead, pray, propose, proposition, question, refer, require, resort to, solicit, strike, submit, sue, supplicate, urge; CONCEPT 48 —*Ant.* deny, disclaim, recall, refuse, renounce, retract, revoke

appeal [v2] *attract, interest* allure, beguile, captivate, catch the eye, charm, enchant, engage, entice, fascinate, intrigue, invite, please, tantalize, tempt; CONCEPTS 7,19,22, 384 —*Ant.* disgust, turn away, turn off

appear [v1] *come into sight* arise, arrive, attend, be present, be within view, blow in*, bob up*, break through, breeze in*, check in*, clock in*, come, come forth, come into view, come out, come to light*, crop up*, develop, drop in*, emerge, expose, issue, loom, make the scene*, materialize, occur, pop in*, pop up*, prance, punch in*, punch the clock*, recur, ring in*, rise, roll in*, show, show up, spring, surface, time in*, turn out, turn up; CONCEPTS 159,261 —*Ant.* disappear, hide

appear [v2] *seem* have the appearance, look as if, look like, occur, resemble, sound, strike one as; CONCEPTS 543,716 —*Ant.* be real

appear [v3] *be obvious, clear* be apparent, be evident, be manifest, be patent, be plain; CONCEPT 725

appear [v4] *be published; perform* become available, be created, be developed, be invented, come into being, come into existence, come on, come on stage*, come out, enter, make an appearance, oblige, perform, play, play a part, present oneself, take part; CONCEPTS 292,324

appearance [n1] *coming into sight* actualization, advent, appearing, arrival, coming, debut, display, emergence, entrance, exhibition, introduction, manifestation, materialization, presence, presentation, representation, rise, showing up, turning up, unveiling; CONCEPT 159 —*Ant.* absence, departure, disappearance, leaving

appearance [n2] *outward aspect, characteristic* air, attitude, bearing, blind, carriage, cast, character, condition, countenance, demeanor, dress, expression, face, fashion, feature, figure, form, front, guise, image, look, looks, manner, mannerism, mien, mode, outline, pose, presence, presentation, screen, semblance, shape, stamp; CONCEPTS 543,716

appearance [n3] *outward show; pretense* aura, beard*, blind, countenance, dream, facade, front, guise, idea, illusion, image, impression, mirage, phenomenon, reflection, screen, seeming, semblance, sound, specter, vision; CONCEPT 673 —*Ant.* reality

appease [v] *satisfy, pacify* allay, alleviate, assuage, be enough, blunt, calm, compose, conciliate, content, diminish, do*, ease, gratify, lessen, lull, make matters up, meet halfway, mitigate, mollify, patch things up, placate, propitiate, quell, quench, quiet, serve, soften, soothe, subdue, sweeten, tranquilize; CONCEPTS 7,22,126 —*Ant.* aggravate, annoy, incite, irritate, provoke, tease

appeasement [n] *satisfaction; pacification* abatement, acceding, accommodation, adjustment, amends, appeasing, assuagement, blunting, compromise, concession, conciliation, easing, grant, lessening, lulling, mitigation, moderation, mollification, peace offering, placation, propitiation, quelling, quenching, quieting, reconciliation, reparation, restoration, settlement, softening, solace, soothing, tranquilization; CONCEPTS 7,22,126 —*Ant.* aggravation, annoyance, irritation, provocation, resistance

appellation [n] *name* designation, epithet, handle*, label, moniker*, nickname, sobriquet, title; CONCEPTS 268,683

append [v] *add, join* adjoin, affix, annex, attach, conjoin, fasten, fix, hang, subjoin, supplement, tack on*, tag on*; CONCEPTS 85,113,160 —*Ant.* disjoin, subtract, take away

appendage [n] *limb; accessory* addendum, addition, adjunct, ancillary, annex, appendix, appurtenance, attachment, auxiliary, extremity, member, projection, protuberance, supplement; CONCEPT 835 —*Ant.* body, trunk

appendix [n] *added material at end of document* addendum, addition, adjunct, appendage, appurtenance, attachment, codicil, excursus, index, notes, postscript, rider, sample, supplement, table, verification; CONCEPT 270

appertain [v] *belong, be connected* apply, bear, be characteristic of, be part of, be pertinent, be

ap
ap

proper, be relevant, have to do with, pertain, refer, relate, touch upon, vest; CONCEPT 532

appetite [n] *desire for food, worldly goods* appetence, appetency, appetition, big eyes*, craving, demand, fondness, gluttony, greed, hankering, hunger, inclination, itch*, liking, longing, lust, passion, penchant, proclivity, propensity, ravenousness, relish, soft spot*, stomach, sweet tooth*, taste, thirst, urge, voracity, weakness, willingness, yearning, yen, zeal, zest; CONCEPTS 20,32 —*Ant.* antipathy, aversion, disgust, dislike, distaste, hatred, indifference, loathing, repulsion, revulsion

appetizer [n] *snack before meal* antipasto, aperitif, canapé, cocktail, dip, finger food, hors d'oeuvre, munchies*, relish, sample, spread, taste, tidbit; CONCEPTS 457,828 —*Ant.* meal

appetizing [adj] *tasting very good* aperitive, appealing, delectable, delicious, delish*, divine*, flavorsome, heavenly, inviting, luscious, mouthwatering, palatable, saporous, savory, scrumptious, succulent, sugar-coated*, sweetened, tantalizing, tasty, tempting, toothsome, yummy*; CONCEPT 613 —*Ant.* disgusting, distasteful, unappetizing, unsavory

applaud [v] *clap for; express approval* acclaim, approve, boost, cheer, commend, compliment, encourage, eulogize, extol, give a hand*, give ovation, glorify, hail, hear it for*, kudize*, laud, magnify, plug, praise, rave, recommend, root*; CONCEPTS 10,69,189 —*Ant.* keep silent

applause [n] *clapping; expression of approval* acclaim, acclamation, accolade, approbation, big hand, bring down the house*, cheering, cheers, commendation, eulogizing, hand, handclapping, hurrahs, kudos, laudation, ovation, plaudits, praise, rooting, round, standing ovation; CONCEPTS 69,189 —*Ant.* silence

appliance [n] *machine, usually with domestic purpose* apparatus, device, gadget, implement, instrument, mechanism, tool; CONCEPT 463

applicable [adj] *appropriate* applicative, applicatory, apposite, apropos, apt, associable, befitting, felicitous, fit, fitting, germane, kosher, legit*, material, on target*, on the button*, on the nose*, pertinent, relevant, right on*, suitable, suited, that's the idea*, that's the ticket*, to the point, to the purpose, useful; CONCEPTS 558,563 —*Ant.* inapplicable, inappropriate, unsuitable

applicant [n] *person trying for position* appellant, aspirant, candidate, claimant, hopeful, inquirer, petitioner, postulant, seeker, suitor, suppliant; CONCEPTS 348,359 —*Ant.* boss, manager

application [n1] *use* appliance, appositeness, employment, exercise, exercising, function, germaneness, operation, pertinence, play, practice, purpose, relevance, usance, utilization, value; CONCEPTS 680,694

application [n2] *request* appeal, blank, claim, demand, draft, entreaty, form, inquiry, letter, paper, petition, requisition, solicitation, suit; CONCEPT 48

application [n3] *hard work* assiduity, attention, attentiveness, busyness, commitment, concentration, consideration, dedication, deliberation, diligence, effort, industry, perseverance, study, zeal; CONCEPTS 91,410

application [n4] *putting substance on another* administering, administration, applying, creaming, dosing, oiling, rubbing, treatment; CONCEPT 200

applied [adj] *used* activated, adapted, adjusted, brought to bear, correlated, devoted, enforced, exercised, practiced, related, tested, utilized; CONCEPTS 538,546

apply [v1] *put into use* administer, assign, bring into play, bring to bear, employ, engage, execute, exercise, exploit, handle, implement, practice, utilize; CONCEPT 225

apply [v2] *be appropriate, relevant* affect, allude, appertain, be applicable, bear upon, be pertinent, concern, connect, fit, involve, pertain, refer, regard, relate, suit, touch; CONCEPT 532

apply [v3] *put substance on another* administer, affix, anoint, bestow, cover, fasten, join, lay on, massage, paint, place, put on, rub, smear, spread, touch; CONCEPT 200

apply [v4] *ask, request* appeal, claim, demand, inquire, petition, put in, put in for, requisition, solicit, sue; CONCEPT 48

apply [v5] *work hard* address, bear down, be diligent, be industrious, bend, buckle down*, commit, concentrate, dedicate, devote, dig, direct, give, give all one's got*, give best shot*, give old college try*, grind, hammer away*, hit the ball*, hustle*, knuckle down*, make effort, peg away*, persevere, plug*, pour it on*, pull out all stops*, scratch, study, sweat*, throw, try, turn; CONCEPTS 87,100

appoint [v1] *assign responsibility; decide* accredit, allot, assign, choose, command, commission, decree, delegate, designate, determine, direct, elect, enjoin, establish, finger, fix, install, name, nominate, ordain, select, set, settle, tap; CONCEPTS 41,50,88 —*Ant.* dismiss, fire, refuse, reject

appoint [v2] *furnish* arm, equip, fit, fit out, gear, outfit, provide, rig, supply, turn out; CONCEPT 140 —*Ant.* not give, unfurnish

appointment [n1] *arrangement for meeting; prearranged meeting* assignation, assignment, blind date*, consultation, date, engagement, errand, gig, interview, invitation, meet, rendezvous, session, tryst, zero hour*; CONCEPTS 324,384

appointment [n2] *assignment of responsibility* allotment, approval, assigning, authorization, certification, choice, choosing, commissioning, delegation, deputation, designation, election, empowering, installation, naming, nomination, ordination, promotion, selection; CONCEPT 41

appointment [n3] *job, position of responsibility* appointee, assignment, berth, candidate, delegate, employment, nominee, office, officeholder, place, post, representative, situation, station, work; CONCEPT 349

appointment [n4] *furnishing(s)* accoutrement, appurtenance, equipage, fitting, fixture, gear, outfit, paraphernalia, trappings; CONCEPT 475

apportion [v] *divide into shares* accord, admeasure, administer, allocate, allot, assign, bestow, cut, cut up, deal, dispense, distribute, divvy, divvy up, dole out, give, lot, measure, mete, parcel, part, partition, piece up, prorate, ration, slice, split, split up; CONCEPTS 98,108 —*Ant.* hold, keep, monopolize, withhold

ap
ap

appraisal [n] *judgment, estimation* appraisement, assessment, estimate, evaluation, opinion, pricing, rating, reckoning, stock, survey, valuation; CONCEPTS 18,328,766

appraise [v] *judge, estimate* adjudge, assay, assess, audit, calculate, check, check out*, deem, evaluate, examine, eye*, figure, figure in, figure out, gauge, guesstimate*, have one's number*, inspect, look over, peg, price, rate, read, review, set at, size, survey, take account of, valuate, value; CONCEPTS 18,764

appreciable [adj] *easily noticed; considerable* apparent, ascertainable, clear-cut, definite, detectable, discernible, distinguishable, estimable, evident, goodly, good-sized, healthy, large, manifest, marked, material, measurable, noticeable, observable, obvious, perceivable, perceptible, plain, pronounced, recognizable, sensible, significant, sizable, substantial, tangible, visible; CONCEPTS 619,781 —Ant. imperceptible, inconsiderable, negligible, unappreciable, unnoticed

appreciate [v1] *be grateful, thankful* acknowledge, be appreciative, be indebted, be obliged, enjoy, flip over*, freak out on*, get high on*, give thanks, groove on*, welcome; CONCEPTS 12,32,76 —Ant. be critical, criticize, disparage, disregard, neglect, overlook

appreciate [v2] *increase in worth* enhance, gain, grow, improve, inflate, raise the value of, rise; CONCEPT 763 —Ant. decrease, depreciate, lose value

appreciate [v3] *recognize worth* acknowledge, apprehend, be aware of, be cognizant of, be conscious of, catch the drift, comprehend, dig, fathom, grasp, know, perceive, read, realize, recognize, savvy, see daylight*, sympathize with, take account of, understand; CONCEPT 15

appreciate [v4] *value highly* admire, adore, applaud, apprise, cherish, enjoy, esteem, extol, honor, like, look up to, love, praise, prize, rate highly, regard, relish, respect, savor, treasure; CONCEPTS 10,32

appreciation [n1] *thankfulness* acknowledgment, gratefulness, gratitude, indebtedness, obligation, recognition, testimonial, thanks, tribute; CONCEPTS 12,32 —Ant. criticism, disparagement, disregard, neglect

appreciation [n2] *increase in worth* enhancement, gain, growth, improvement, inflation, rise; CONCEPTS 346,763 —Ant. decrease, depreciation, loss

appreciation [n3] *recognition of worth* admiration, aesthetic sense, affection, appraisal, assessment, attraction, awareness, cognizance, commendation, comprehension, enjoyment, esteem, estimation, grasp, high regard, knowledge, liking, love, perception, realization, recognition, regard, relish, respect, responsivenesss, sensibility, sensitiveness, sensitivity, sympathy, understanding; CONCEPTS 15,409

appreciative [adj1] *thankful* beholden, grateful, indebted, obliged, responsive; CONCEPT 403 —Ant. unappreciative, ungrateful

appreciative [adj2] *understanding, recognizing worth* admiring, affectionate, alive, aware, cognizant, conscious, considerate, cooperative, cordial, enlightened, enthusiastic, favorable, friendly, generous, keen, kindly, knowledgeable, magnanimous, mindful, perceptive, pleased, receptive, regardful, respectful, responsive, satisfied, sensitive, supportive, sympathetic, understanding; CONCEPT 402 —Ant. ignorant, neglectful

apprehend [v1] *catch and arrest* bag*, bust*, capture, collar, cop*, grab, nab, nail*, place under arrest, run in, seize, take in, take into custody, take prisoner; CONCEPTS 90,191,317 —Ant. lose, not catch

apprehend [v2] *understand* absorb, accept, appreciate, believe, catch, comprehend, conceive, digest, fathom, get, get the picture*, grasp, have, imagine, know, perceive, read, realize, recognize, sense, think; CONCEPT 15 —Ant. misunderstand

apprehension [n1] *anxiety, fear* alarm, apprehensiveness, concern, disquiet, doubt, dread, foreboding, misgiving, mistrust, premonition, presage, presentiment, suspicion, trepidation, uneasiness, worry; CONCEPTS 27,690 —Ant. calmness, ease

apprehension [n2] *catching and arresting* booking, capture, collaring, detention, seizure, taking; CONCEPTS 90,317

apprehension [n3] *understanding* awareness, comprehension, grasp, idea, intellect, intelligence, judgment, ken, knowledge, notion, perception, perspicacity, thought; CONCEPT 409 —Ant. imperception, misunderstanding

apprehensive [adj] *anxious, fearful* afraid, alarmed, biting nails*, butterflies*, concerned, disquieted, doubtful, feel in bones*, foreboding, frozen*, get vibes*, have a hunch*, have cold feet*, have funny feeling*, have stage fright*, hung up*, in a cold sweat*, in a dither*, in a sweat*, jellyfish*, jittery, jumpy, lily-livered*, mistrustful, running scared*, scaredy-cat*, shaky*, stiff, suspicious, troubled, uncertain, uneasy, uptight, weak, worried, worried sick*; CONCEPT 403 —Ant. at ease, calm, quiet, unafraid, undoubting, unfearful, unsuspicious, unworried

apprentice [n] *novice/learner of a trade* amateur, beginner, flunky*, greenhorn*, heel*, neophyte, newcomer, new kid on block*, novitiate, probationer, pupil, rook*, rookie*, starter, student, tenderfoot*, tyro; CONCEPTS 348,423 —Ant. mentor, teacher

apprise [v] *tell* advise, brief, enlighten, fill in, inform, notify, tip off; CONCEPTS 57,60,75

approach [n1] *way, means of arriving* access, accession, advance, advent, avenue, coming, drawing near, entrance, gate, landing, nearing, passage, path, reaching, road, way; CONCEPTS 159,501 —Ant. departure, distancing, leaving

approach [n2] *request, suggestion* advance, appeal, application, offer, overture, proposal, proposition; CONCEPT 278

approach [n3] *plan of attack, resolution* attitude, concept, course, crack, fling, go*, idea, lick, manner, means, method, mode, modus operandi, new wrinkle*, offer, procedure, program, shot, stab, style, technique, way, whack*, wrinkle*; CONCEPTS 655,660

approach [v1] *come nearer* advance, approximate, bear, be comparable to, be like, belly up to*, border, buzz*, catch up, close in, come, come at, come close, compare with, contact, converge, correspond to, creep up, draw near, equal, gain on, go toward, impend, loom up, match, meet, move in on, move toward, near, progress, reach, resemble, surround, take after, threaten, verge upon; CONCEPTS *159,198,701* —*Ant.* depart, distance, go away, leave

approach [v2] *make request, suggestion* accost, address, advise, appeal to, apply to, beseech, confer, consult, entreat, feel, feel one out*, give a play*, give a tumble*, greet, implore, make advance, make overture, make up to, plead, propose, sound out, speak to, supplicate, take aside, talk to, thumb, tumble; CONCEPTS *48,75*

approach [v3] *begin* commence, embark, set about, start, undertake; CONCEPT *234*

approachable [adj1] *accessible* attainable, come-at-able*, convenient, door's always open*, getable*, obtainable, reachable; CONCEPT *576* —*Ant.* formal, inaccessible, unapproachable, unreachable

approachable [adj2] *friendly* affable, agreeable, congenial, cordial, open, receptive, sociable; CONCEPT *404* —*Ant.* uncongenial, unfriendly, unsociable

approbation [n] *praise* admiration, approval, bells*, consent, endorsement, esteem, favor, go-ahead*, high regard, okay, permission, recognition, sanction, support, the nod*; CONCEPTS *10, 69* —*Ant.* criticism, disapprobation

appropriate [adj] *suitable* adapted, applicable, appurtenant, apropos, apt, becoming, befitting, belonging, congruous, convenient, correct, deserved, desired, due, felicitous, fit, fitting, germane, good, just, on the button*, on the nose*, opportune, pertinent, proper, relevant, right, rightful, seemly, tailor-made, true, useful, well-suited, well-timed; CONCEPT *558* —*Ant.* improper, unbecoming, unfitting, unseemly, unsuitable, unsuited

appropriate [v1] *set aside; allocate* allot, allow, appoint, apportion, assign, budget, devote, disburse, earmark, reserve, set apart; CONCEPT *135* —*Ant.* keep, refuse, reject

appropriate [v2] *steal* annex, borrow, clap*, confiscate, cop, embezzle, filch, get fingers on*, get hands on*, glom on to*, grab, grab hold of*, hijack, liberate, lift, misappropriate, moonlight requisition*, pilfer, pocket, secure, snatch, swipe*, take over, usurp; CONCEPT *139* —*Ant.* bequeath, bestow, give, return

appropriation [n1] *allocation, setting aside* allotment, allowance, apportionment, assignment, budgeting, concession, donation, earmarking, endowing, funding, giving, grant, provision, setting apart, sponsoring, stipend, stipulation, subsidy; CONCEPTS *135,340* —*Ant.* keeping, refusal, rejection

appropriation [n2] *stealing* confiscation, embezzlement, expropriation, grab, misappropriation, pilfering, seizure, takeover, taking, usurpation; CONCEPT *139* —*Ant.* bestowal, giving, return

approval [n1] *authorization* acquiescence, assent, bells*, blessing, compliance, concurrence, confirmation, consent, countenance, endorsement, go-ahead*, green light*, leave, license, mandate, okay, permission, ratification, recommendation, sanction, support, the nod*, validation; CONCEPTS *10,685* —*Ant.* disapproval, opposition, refusal, rejection

approval [n2] *good opinion* acclaim, admiration, applause, appreciation, approbation, commendation, esteem, favor, liking, pat on the back*, pat on the head*, PR*, praise, puff, pumping up, regard, respect, strokes, stroking, wow*; CONCEPT *32* —*Ant.* disapproval, disfavor, dislike, hatred

approve [v1] *agree something is good* accept, acclaim, admire, applaud, appreciate, approbate, be big on*, commend, countenance, esteem, face it, favor, go along with, grin and bear it*, handle, like, live with*, praise, put up with, regard highly, respect, roll with punches*, string along with*, take up on*, think highly of; CONCEPT *10* —*Ant.* disagree, disapprove

approve [v2] *allow, authorize* accede, accept, accredit, acquiesce, advocate, affirm, agree, assent, authorize, back*, bless*, boost, buy, buy into*, certify, charter, concur, confirm, consent, dig*, empower, encourage, endorse, establish, get behind, give go-ahead*, go along with, groove*, hats off to*, lap up*, license, maintain, make law, make valid, mandate, okay, permit, pronounce, push for, ratify, recommend, sanction, seal, second, sign, sign off on, stump for, subscribe to, support, thumbs up*, uphold, validate; CONCEPTS *50,83,88* —*Ant.* disallow, disapprove, invalidate, oppose, refuse, reject

approximate [adj1] *almost accurate, exact* almost, close, comparative, near, proximate, relative, rough; CONCEPT *557* —*Ant.* accurate, clear, definite, exact, precise

approximate [adj2] *inexact* estimated, guessed, imperfect, imprecise, loose, rough, surmised, uncertain, unprecise, unscientific; CONCEPT *557*

approximate [adj3] *similar* alike, analogous, close, comparable, like, matching, near, relative, resembling, verging on; CONCEPTS *487,573* —*Ant.* dissimilar, exact, same

approximate [adj4] *near* adjacent, bordering, close together, contiguous, nearby, neighboring; CONCEPT *586* —*Ant.* away, far

approximate [v] *come close* approach, border on, come near, estimate, near, reach, resemble, touch, verge on; CONCEPT *664*

approximately [adv] *nearly* about, almost, around, ballpark figure*, bordering on, circa, closely, close to, comparatively, generally, in the ballpark*, in the neighborhood of, in the region of, in the vicinity of, just about, loosely, more or less, most, much, not far from, not quite, proximately, relatively, roughly, upwards of*, very close; CONCEPT *566* —*Ant.* accurately, clearly, definitely, exactly, precisely

apropos [adj] *relevant, suitable* applicable, apposite, appropriate, apt, befitting, belonging, correct, fit, fitting, germane, kosher*, legit*, material, on the button*, on the nose*, opportune, pertinent, proper, related, right, right on*, seemly; CONCEPT *558* —*Ant.* inappropriate, irrelevant, unsuitable

apropos [adv] *relevantly, suitably* appropriately, aptly, opportunely, pertinently, suitably, timely; CONCEPT *558* —*Ant.* inappropriately, irrelevantly, unsuitably

apropos [prep] *in respect of* about, against, as for, as regards, as to, concerning, on the subject of, regarding, respecting, touching, toward, with reference to, with respect to; CONCEPT 532

apt |adj1| *suitable* applicable, apposite, appropriate, apropos, befitting, correct, felicitous, fit, fitting, germane, happy, just, pertinent, proper, relevant, seemly, suitable, timely; CONCEPT 558 —Ant. incorrect, unsuitable

apt |adj2| *tending, inclined* disposed, given, liable, likely, of a mind, prone, ready; CONCEPT 542 —Ant. disinclined, inapt

apt |adj3| *quick to learn* able, adept, astute, bright, clever, expert, gifted, ingenious, intelligent, nobody's fool*, no dummy*, not born yesterday*, prompt, quick on the trigger*, quick on the uptake*, ready, savvy, sharp, skilled, skillful, smart, talented, teachable; CONCEPT 402 —Ant. incapable, stupid, unskilled

aptitude |n1| *inclination* bent, disposition, drift, leaning, predilection, proclivity, proneness, propensity, tendency; CONCEPT 657 —Ant. disinclination, inaptitude, skillessness

aptitude |n2| *quickness at learning* ability, capability, capacity, cleverness, competence, faculty, flair, gift, giftedness, intelligence, knack, proficiency, savvy, smarts, stuff*, talent, what it takes*; CONCEPT 409 —Ant. incapacity, stupidity

aquarium |n| *fish tank* aquatic museum, fishbowl, marine exhibit; CONCEPTS 396,438,514

aquatic |adj| *occurring in water* amphibian, amphibious, floating, marine, maritime, natatory, oceanic, of the sea, sea, swimming, watery; CONCEPTS 396,536

aqueduct |n| *canal* channel, conduit, course, duct, pipeline, water passage, waterworks; CONCEPT 514

arbiter |n| *person who settles dispute* adjudicator, arbitrator, fixer, go-between, holdout, judge, maven, mediator, middleperson, moderator, referee, umpire; CONCEPT 354

arbitrary |adj1| *whimsical, chance* approximate, capricious, discretionary, erratic, fanciful, frivolous, inconsistent, injudicious, irrational, irresponsible, offhand, optional, random, subjective, supercilious, superficial, unaccountable, unreasonable, unscientific, wayward, willful; CONCEPTS 534,542 —Ant. circumspect, rational, reasonable, reasoned, supported

arbitrary |adj2| *dictatorial* absolute, autocratic, bossy, despotic, dogmatic, domineering, downright, flat out*, high-handed, imperious, magisterial, monocratic, no ifs ands or buts*, no joke*, overbearing, peremptory, straight out*, summary, tyrannical, tyrannous; CONCEPT 401 —Ant. democratic

arbitrate |v| *achieve settlement* adjudge, adjudicate, adjust, bring to terms, come to school, come to terms, conciliate, decide, determine, hammer out a deal*, intervene, intervene, judge, make a deal, mediate, meet halfway, negotiate, parley, pass judgment, placate, play ball*, reconcile, referee, settle, smooth, soothe, step in, straighten out, strike happy medium*, trade off, umpire, work out a deal; CONCEPTS 126,300 —Ant. let ride

arbitration |n| *settlement of dispute* adjudication, adjustment, agreement, compromise, decision, determination, judgment, mediation; CONCEPTS 126,300

arbitrator |n| *settler of a dispute* adjudicator, arbiter, fixer, go-between, holdout, judge, maven, mediator, middleperson, referee, umpire; CONCEPTS 348,359

arc |n| *curve* arch, bend, bow, crescent, curvation, curvature, half-moon, round; CONCEPT 436

arcade |n| *covered way* cloister, colonnade, gallery, loggia, mall, passageway, piazza, portico, stoa, walkway; CONCEPT 501

arcane |adj| *hidden, secret* cabalistic, esoteric, impenetrable, mysterious, mystic, occult, recondite, unaccountable, unknowable; CONCEPT 576 —Ant. common, commonplace, known, normal, outward

arch |adj1| *principal, superior* accomplished, champion, chief, consummate, expert, finished, first, foremost, greatest, head, highest, leading, main, major, master, preeminent, premier, primary, top; CONCEPT 574 —Ant. inferior

arch |adj2| *knowing, coy* artful, frolicsome, mischievous, pert, playful, roguish, saucy, sly, waggish, wily; CONCEPT 401

arch |n| *curve, curved structure* arc, archway, bend, bow, curvature, dome, semicircle, span, vault; CONCEPT 436

arch |v| *curve* arc, bend, bow, bridge, camber, extend, form, hook, hump, hunch, round, shape, span, stretch; CONCEPT 184

archaeologist |n| *student of the physical remains of ancient cultures or eras* archaeologian, classicist, excavator, paleologist, paleontologist, prehistorian; CONCEPT 348

archaeology |n| *study of the physical remains of ancient cultures or eras* antiquarianism, excavation, paleohistory, paleology, paleontology, prehistory; CONCEPT 349

archaic |adj| *very old* ancient, antiquated, antique, bygone, obsolete, olden, old-fashioned, outmoded, out of date, passé, primitive, superannuated; CONCEPTS 578,797 —Ant. current, modern, new, present, young

arched |adj| *vaulted* bowed, curved, domed, embowed, rounded; CONCEPT 486

archetypal |adj| *most typical* average, classic, clichéd, conventional, exemplary, hackneyed, model, most characteristic, paradigmatic, prime, quintessential, representative, standard, stereotypical, stock, textbook, trite; CONCEPT 530 —Ant. atypical, unique

archetype |n| *typical example* classic exemplar, form, ideal, model, original, paradigm, pattern, perfect specimen, prime example, prototype, standard; CONCEPTS 636,686 —Ant. atypical

architect |n| *person who designs buildings* artist, builder, creator, designer, draftsperson, engineer, inventor, maker, master builder, originator, planner, prime mover; CONCEPT 348

architecture |n1| *design of buildings* architectonics, building, construction, engineering, planning; CONCEPTS 349,439

architecture |n2| *design, structure of something* composition, constitution, construction, formation, framework, make-up, style; CONCEPTS 660,733

archive |n| *collection, usually of records* annals, chronicles, clippings, documents, excerpts, extracts, files, papers, registers, roll, scrolls, writings; CONCEPTS 271,281,432

archives [n] *place where records are stored* athenaeum, library, museum, office, registry, repository, storage, treasury, vault; CONCEPT 439

archway [n] *curved opening* entrance, passage; CONCEPT 440

arctic [adj] *very cold* chill, chilly, cool, freezing, frigid, frosty, frozen, gelid, glacial, icy, nippy, polar; CONCEPT 605 —*Ant.* tropic

ardent [adj1] *very enthusiastic* agog, avid, blazing, burning, desirous, eager, fervent, fervid, fierce, fiery, horny*, hot*, hungry, impassioned, intense, keen, lovey-dovey*, lusty, passionate, spirited, thirsty, vehement, warm, zealous; CONCEPTS 401,404 —*Ant.* cold, cold-blooded, cool, dispassionate, frigid, indifferent, lukewarm, unenthusiastic

ardent [adj2] *loyal* allegiant, constant, devoted, faithful, resolute, steadfast, true; CONCEPT 404 —*Ant.* disloyal

ardor [n] *enthusiasm* avidity, devotion, eagerness, earnestness, feeling, fervor, fierceness, fire, gusto, heat, intensity, jazz*, keenness, oomph*, passion, pep talk*, spirit, turn on*, vehemence, verve, warmth, weakness*, zeal, zest, zing; CONCEPT 411 —*Ant.* coldness, coolness, frigidity, indifference

arduous [adj] *difficult, hard to endure* backbreaking, burdensome, exhausting, fatiguing, formidable, grueling, harsh, heavy, labored, laborious, murder, no picnic*, onerous, painful, punishing, rigorous, rough, severe, strenuous, taxing, tiring, toilsome, tough, troublesome, trying, uphill; CONCEPT 565 —*Ant.* easy, facile, motivating

area [n1] *extent, scope of a surface* breadth, compass, distance, expanse, field, operation, range, size, space, sphere, stretch, width; CONCEPTS 651,792

area [n2] *region, district* belt, block, city, county, division, domain, dominion, enclosure, field, kingdom, locality, neck of the woods*, neighborhood, parcel, patch, plot, precinct, principality, quarter, section, sector, sphere, square, state, stretch, territory, township, tract, turf, vicinity, ward, zone; CONCEPT 508

arena [n1] *building or enclosure for entertainment or sports* amphitheatre, boards*, bowl*, circus, coliseum, course, diamond, field, gridiron, ground, gym, gymnasium, hippodrome, ice, park, pit, platform, ring, rink, square, stadium, stage; CONCEPT 438

arena [n2] *area of activity* battlefield, battleground, domain, field, province, realm, scene, sector, sphere, territory, theatre; CONCEPT 198

argot [n] *jargon* cant, dialect, idiom, lingo, parlance, patois, slang, terminology, vernacular, vocabulary; CONCEPT 276

arguable [adj1] *tenable* able to hold water*, assertable, believable, conceivable, credible, defendable, defensible, feasible, imaginable, maintainable, rational, reasonable, supportable, sustainable, viable, workable; CONCEPT 552 —*Ant.* untenable

arguable [adj2] *debatable* contentious, controversial, disputable, doubtful, dubious, moot, open to question, questionable, uncertain, unsure; CONCEPT 267 —*Ant.* certain

argue [v1] *verbally fight* altercate, bandy, battle, bicker, break with, buck, bump heads, contend, cross, cross swords, disagree, dispute, face down, face off, feud, gang up on, get in one's face*, go one on one, hammer, hammer away, hash, hash over, hassle, have at each other, have at it, jump, jump on, knock around, lock horns*, mix it up*, pettifog, pick an argument, put up a fight, put up a struggle, quarrel, quibble, rehash, row, sass, set to, sock it to*, squabble, stick it to, talk back, wrangle; CONCEPT 46 —*Ant.* agree, harmonize, ignore, overlook

argue [v2] *try to convince; present support* appeal, assert, attest, claim, contend, controvert, defend, demonstrate, denote, display, elucidate, establish, evince, exhibit, explain, hold, imply, indicate, justify, maintain, manifest, persuade, plead, present, prevail upon, reason, show, suggest, talk into, testify, vindicate, warrant, witness; CONCEPT 68 —*Ant.* agree, comply

argue [v3] *discuss* agitate, canvass, clarify, debate, dispute, expostulate, hold, maintain, question, reason, remonstrate, talk about; CONCEPTS 46,56 —*Ant.* abstain, keep quiet, keep silent

argument [n1] *verbal fight* altercation, beef, bickering, blowup, bone, bone of contention, bone to pick*, brannigan*, brawl, brush, clash, controversy, crusher*, debate, difference of opinion, disagreement, dispute, donnybrook, dustup*, exchange, face-off, falling, feud, finisher*, flap, fuss, gin*, go*, hassle, knockdown*, knock down and drag out*, out, quarrel, rhubarb*, romp, row, ruckus, ruction, rumpus, run-in, scene, scrap, set-to, shindy*, spat, squabble, static*, stew*, talking heads*, tiff, words, wrangle; CONCEPT 46

argument [n2] *effort to convince; presentation of support* argumentation, assertion, case, claim, contention, debate, defense, discussion, exchange, expostulation, grounds, line of reasoning, logic, plea, pleading, polemic, proof, questioning, reason, reasoning, remonstrance, remonstration; CONCEPT 68

argumentative [adj] *wanting to quarrel* belligerent, combative, contentious, contrary, controversial, disputatious, factious, fire-eating, having a chip on one's shoulder*, litigious, opinionated, pugnacious, quarrelsome, salty, scrappy, spiky, touchy; CONCEPT 401 —*Ant.* agreeable, complaisant, friendly

aria [n] *operatic solo* descant, hymn, song; CONCEPTS 263,595

arid [adj1] *dry* barren, bone-dry, desert, dry as a bone, dry as dust, dusty, moistureless, parched, thirsty, waterless; CONCEPT 603 —*Ant.* damp, humid, moist, wet

arid [adj2] *uninterested, spiritless* boring, colorless, drab, dreary, dry, dull, flat, insipid, lackluster, lifeless, tedious, unanimated, uninspired, vapid, wearisome; CONCEPT 542 —*Ant.* interested, lively, spirited

arise [v1] *come into being; proceed* appear, begin, come to light, commence, crop up, derive, emanate, emerge, ensue, flow, follow, happen, head, issue, occur, originate, result, rise, set in, spring, start, stem; CONCEPT 105

arise [v2] *get, stand, or go up* ascend, climb, jump, mount, move upward, pile out*, rise, rise and shine*, roll out*, soar, stand, tower, turn out, wake up; CONCEPTS 154,166 —*Ant.* lay, lie, sit

ar
ar

aristocracy [n] *privileged class, government* elite, gentility, gentry, haut monde, high society, nobility, noblesse, patricians, patriciate, peerage, society, upper class, upper crust*; CONCEPTS 296,423 —*Ant.* commoners, plebites, proletariat

aristocrat [n] *privileged person* blueblood, gentleperson, lace curtain*, noble, patrician, peer, silk stocking, swell*, upper cruster*; CONCEPT 423 —*Ant.* commoner, plebian, proletariat

aristocratic [adj] *privileged, elegant* aloof, blue-blooded, courtly, dignified, elegant, elite, fine, haughty, noble, patrician, polished, refined, snobbish, stylish, upper-class, well-born, well-bred; CONCEPT 555 —*Ant.* low-born, low-life, poor, unprivileged, vulgar, wanting

arithmetic [n] *mathematics* addition, calculation, computation, division, estimation, figuring, multiplication, reckoning, subtraction; CONCEPTS 349,764

arm [n1] *limb, appendage* bender, bough, bow, branch, fin, flapper, flipper, handle, hook, member, offshoot, projection, prong, rod, stump, wing; CONCEPTS 392,471

arm [n2] *subdivision, annex* affiliate, authority, block, branch, command, department, detachment, division, ell, extension, force, offshoot, power, projection, section, sector, wing; CONCEPTS 824,835 —*Ant.* body, division, main

arm [n3] *narrow body of water* branch, brook, channel, creek, estuary, firth, fjord, inlet, rivulet, sound, strait, stream, subdivision, tributary; CONCEPT 514

arm [v] *equip with weapon or power* accouter, appoint, array, deck, equalize, fortify, furnish, gear, gird, guard, heel*, heel up*, issue, load, load up, lug iron*, make ready, mobilize, outfit, pack, pack a rod*, prepare, prime, protect, provide, rig, rod up*, strengthen, supply, tote; CONCEPTS 50,88,182 —*Ant.* disarm

armada [n] *group of ships or aircraft* fleet, flotilla, force, navy, squadron; CONCEPTS 432,504,506

armament(s) [n] *weapon(s)* ammunition, arms, defense, gun, hardware, heat*, material, materiel, munitions, ordnance, protection, security, weaponry; CONCEPT 500

armed [adj] *with weapon* accoutered, equipped, fitted out, girded, loaded, outfitted, packing*, steeled, supplied; CONCEPT 182

armistice [n] *peace-establishing agreement* ceasefire, suspension, treaty, truce; CONCEPTS 230,684 —*Ant.* dispute, fight, war

armor [n] *protective covering, often made of metal* bulletproof vest, defense, guard, mail, plate, protection, security, sheath, shield; CONCEPTS 451,476

armory [n] *military building, usually for storing weapons* arsenal, center, depot, dump, factory, headquarters, magazine, plant, range; CONCEPTS 321,439

arms [n1] *weaponry* accoutrements, armaments, artillery, equipment, firearms, guns, munitions, ordnance, panoply, weapons; CONCEPT 500

arms [n2] *family crest* blazonry, coat, emblazonry, emblem, ensign, escutcheon, heraldry, insignia, shield, signet; CONCEPTS 284,625

army [n1] *military force, usually for land* armed force, artillery, battalion, battery, brigade, cavalry, column, command, company, corps, detail, division, flight, formation, infantry, legion, outfit, patrol unit, platoon, regiment, soldiers, soldiery, squad, troops, wing; CONCEPT 322

army [n2] *group resembling military force* array, cloud, company, crowd, division, flock, horde, host, legion, mob, multitude, outfit, pack, regiment, scores, swarm, throng, unit; CONCEPT 417

aroma [n] *distinctive smell* balm, bouquet, fragrance, incense, odor, perfume, redolence, scent, spice; CONCEPT 599

aromatic [adj] *distinctive smelling* ambrosial, balmy, fragrant, odoriferous, perfumed, pungent, redolent, savory, scented, spicy, sweet, sweet-smelling; CONCEPT 598 —*Ant.* acrid, bland, unsavory

around [adv1] *situated on sides, circumference, or in general area* about, all over, any which way, encompassing, everywhere, in the vicinity, in this area, neighboring, over, throughout; CONCEPT 581

around [adv2] *close to a place* about, almost, approximately, close at hand, near, nearby; CONCEPT 586

arouse [v] *excite, entice* agitate, alert, animate, awaken, call, challenge, electrify, enliven, fire up, foment, foster, goad, heat up, incite, inflame, instigate, kindle, move, provoke, rally, rouse, send, spark, spur, stimulate, stir, thrill, turn on, waken, wake up, warm, whet, whip up, work up; CONCEPTS 7,19,22 —*Ant.* bore, calm, lull, quiet

arraign [v] *accuse* blame, charge, criminate, hang on, incriminate, inculpate, indict, lay at one's door*, pin it on*, point the finger at*, summon; CONCEPTS 44,317 —*Ant.* discharge, exonerate, free, let go

arraignment [n] *accusation* bill of indictment, charge, citation, denunciation, impeachment, indictment, prosecution, summons, trial; CONCEPT 54 —*Ant.* acquittal

arrange [v1] *put in an order* align, array, class, classify, clear the decks, dispose, file, fix up, form, group, line up, methodize, organize, police, police up, position, put in good shape*, put in order*, put to rights*, range, rank, regulate, sort, spruce, spruce up, systematize, tidy, whip into shape*; CONCEPTS 84,158 —*Ant.* confuse, derange, disarrange, disorder, disorganize, disperse, disturb, mix up, scatter

arrange [v2] *make plans, come involving agreement* adapt, adjust, agree to, blueprint, chart, come to terms, compromise, concert, construct, contrive, decide, design, determine, devise, direct, draft, establish, frame*, get act together*, get ready, hammer out a deal*, harmonize, iron out*, lay out, line up, make a connection, make ready, manage, map out, negotiate, organize, prepare, project, promote, provide, pull a wire, pull things together, quarterback*, resolve, schedule, scheme, set stage, settle, shape up, tailor, work out, work out a deal; CONCEPTS 36,84 —*Ant.* disorganize, not plan

arrange [v3] *prepare musical composition differently* adapt, instrument, orchestrate, score; CONCEPT 292

arrangement [n1] *an understanding* adjustment, agreement, compact, compromise, deal, frame-up*, game plan*, layout*, organization, package*, package deal*, plan, preparation, provision, schedule, settlement, setup, terms; CONCEPT 684

arrangement [n2] *something that has been ordered* alignment, array, classification, combination, composition, design, display, disposition, distribution, form, grouping, lineup, method, ordering, organization, pattern, pecking order*, ranging, rank, sequence, setup, structure, system; CONCEPTS 84,727

arrangement [n3] *musical adaptation* chart, composition, instrumentation, interpretation, lead sheet, orchestration, score, version; CONCEPTS 262,595

arrant [adj] *flagrant* absolute, blatant, glaring, notorious, out-and-out, unmitigated, unregenerate; CONCEPTS 401,545,576

array [n1] *collection, considerable group* arrangement, batch, body, bunch, bundle, clump, cluster, design, display, disposition, exhibition, formation, host, lineup, lot, multitude, order, parade, pattern, set, show, supply, throng; CONCEPTS 432,769,787

array [n2] *fine clothes* apparel, attire, drapes*, dress, duds*, finery, full dress, garb, garments, getup*, rig*, threads*; CONCEPT 451

array [v1] *arrange in collection or order* align, display, exhibit, form, group, line up, methodize, organize, parade, range, set, show, systematize; CONCEPT 84

array [v2] *dress in fine clothes* attire, bedeck, clothe, deck, deck out, decorate, dog out*, drape, dud, dude up*, fit, fit out, garb, outfit, suit up, tog, try on, turn out, wrap; CONCEPT 167

arrears [n] *debt* back payment, balance due, claim, debit, deficiency, deficit, liability, obligation, unpaid bill; CONCEPTS 332,335

arrest [n1] *taking into custody* accommodation, apprehension, appropriation, bag*, booby trap*, bust, captivity, capture, collar, commitment, confinement, constraint, crimp*, detention, drop*, fall*, gaff*, glom*, grab*, heat*, hook*, imprisonment, incarceration, jailing, mitt*, nab*, nail*, nick*, nip*, pickle*, pick up*, pinch*, preventive custody, protective custody, pull*, pull in*, restraining, run in*, sequestering, snare, sweep*; CONCEPTS 90,317

arrest [n2] *slowing or stopping* blockage, cessation, check, checking, delay, end, halt, hindrance, inhibition, interruption, obstruction, prevention, restraining, restraint, stalling, stay, staying, stoppage, suppression, suspension; CONCEPTS 121,234 —Ant. activation, encouragement, letting go, release

arrest [v1] *take into authorized custody* apprehend, bag*, book, brace*, bust, capture, catch, collar, detain, drop*, gaff*, get*, glom*, grab*, hook*, imprison, incarcerate, jail, kick*, nab*, nail*, net*, nick*, pick up*, pinch*, pull*, pull in*, put the arm on*, put the cuffs on*, round up*, roust*, run in*, secure*, seize*, sidetrack*, snag*, tab*, tag*, take in, take prisoner, toss in jail*; CONCEPTS 90,317

arrest [v2] *stop or slow* block, can, check, delay, drop, end, freeze, halt, hinder, hold, inhibit, interrupt, knock off, obstruct, prevent, restrain, restrict, retard, scrub*, shut down, stall, stay, suppress; CONCEPTS 121,234 —Ant. activate, encourage, let go, release

arrest [v3] *get someone's attention* absorb,

catch, engage, engross, fascinate, grip; CONCEPTS 7,19,22

arrival [n1] *coming to a destination* accession, advent, alighting, appearance, approach, arriving, debarkation, disembarkation, dismounting, entrance, happening, homecoming, influx, ingress, landing, meeting, occurrence, return; CONCEPT 159 —Ant. departure, disappearance, leave

arrival [n2] *something that makes it to a destination* addition, arriver, caller, cargo, comer, conferee, delegate, delivery, entrant, envoy, freight, guest, mail, newcomer, package, parcel, passenger, representative, shipment, tourist, traveler, visitant, visitor; CONCEPTS 337,423,712

arrive [v1] *come to a destination* access, alight, appear, attain, barge in, blow in, bob up*, breeze in*, bust in*, buzz*, check in*, clock in*, disembark, dismount, drop anchor, drop in, enter, fall by, fall in, get to, hit*, hit town*, land*, make it*, make the scene*, pop in*, pop up*, pull in*, punch the clock*, reach, report, roll in*, show, show up, sign in, sky in*, take place, turn up, visit, wind up at; CONCEPT 159 —Ant. depart, disappear, go, leave

arrive [v2] *achieve recognition* accomplish, become famous, flourish, make good, make it, make the grade, prosper, reach the top, score, succeed, thrive; CONCEPT 706

arrogance [n] *exaggerated self-opinion* airs, aloofness, audacity, bluster, braggadocio, brass*, cheek*, chutzpah*, conceit, conceitedness, contemptuousness, crust*, disdain, disdainfulness, ego, egotism, gall, haughtiness, hauteur, high-handedness, hubris, imperiousness, insolence, loftiness, nerve, ostentation, overbearance, pomposity, pompousness, presumption, pretension, pretentiousness, pride, priggishness, scornfulness, self-importance, self-love, smugness, superciliousness, swagger, vanity; CONCEPTS 411,633 —Ant. humility, meekness, servility

arrogant [adj] *having exaggerated self-opinion* aloof, assuming, audacious, autocratic, biggety*, bossy, bragging, cavalier, cheeky, cocky, cold-shoulder*, conceited, contemptuous, cool*, disdainful, domineering, egotistic, haughty, high and mighty*, high-handed, imperious, insolent, know-it-all*, lordly, on an ego trip*, overbearing, peremptory, pompous, presumptuous, pretentious, proud, puffed up*, scornful, self-important, smarty, smug, sniffy*, snippy*, snooty*, snotty*, stuck up*, supercilious, superior, swaggering, uppity*, vain, wise guy*; CONCEPTS 401,404 —Ant. humble, meek, servile, unconceited

arrogate [v] *claim without justification* accroach, appropriate, assume, commandeer, confiscate, demand, expropriate, preempt, presume, seize, take, usurp; CONCEPTS 142, 266 —Ant. appropriate, give, hand over

arrow [n] *pointed weapon or symbol* bolt, cursor, dart, indicator, missile, pointer, projectile, shaft; CONCEPT 500

arsenal [n] *storage of weapons* armory, depository, depot, dump, factory, magazine, ordnance, plant, repository, stock, stockpile, store, storehouse, supply, warehouse; CONCEPTS 432,439

arson [n] *intentional burning* firing, incendiarism, pyromania, setting fire, torching, touching off; CONCEPT 249

art [n1] *skill, creativity* adroitness, aptitude, artistry, craft, craftsmanship, dexterity, expertise, facility, imagination, ingenuity, inventiveness, knack, know-how, knowledge, mastery, method, profession, trade, virtuosity; CONCEPT 706 —*Ant.* lack, unskill

art [n2] *cunning* artfulness, artifice, astuteness, canniness, craftiness, deceit, duplicity, guile, slyness, trickery, wiliness; CONCEPT 411

art [n3] *creation meant to communicate or appeal to senses or mind* abstraction, carving, description, design, illustration, imitation, modeling, molding, painting, pictorialization, portrayal, representation, sculpting, shaping, simulation, sketching, symbolization; CONCEPT 349 —*Ant.* science

artery [n] *channel* avenue, boulevard, canal, conduit, corridor, course, duct, highway, line, passage, pathway, road, route, sewer, thoroughfare, track, tube, way; CONCEPT 501

artful [adj] *skillful; cunning* adept, adroit, clever, crafty, designing, dexterous, foxy*, ingenious, masterly, politic, proficient, resourceful, scheming, sharp, shrewd, slick*, sly, smart, smooth*, tricky, wily; CONCEPTS 404,528 —*Ant.* artless, ingenuous, naive, unskillful

article [n1] *item, object* commodity, dojigger*, gizmo*, piece, substance, thing, thingamabob*, thingamajig*, unit; CONCEPT 433

article [n2] *piece of writing* beat*, blurb*, column, commentary, composition, discourse, editorial, essay, exposition, feature, item, paper, piece, scoop*, spread, story, theme, think piece*, treatise, write-up; CONCEPTS 270,271, 280

article [n3] *section of document* branch, chapter, clause, detail, division, element, head, heading, item, matter, paragraph, part, passage, piece, point, portion, provision; CONCEPTS 270,318

articulate [adj] *clearly, coherently spoken* clear, coherent, comprehensible, definite, distinct, eloquent, expressive, fluent, intelligible, lucid, meaningful, understandable, well-spoken; CONCEPT 267 —*Ant.* misrepresented, unclear, unintelligible

articulate [v1] *say clearly, coherently* enunciate, express, mouth, pronounce, say, sound off*, speak, state, talk, utter, verbalize, vocalize, voice; CONCEPTS 47,55 —*Ant.* bumble, misrepresent, misspeak

articulate [v2] *connect* concatenate, couple, fit together, hinge, integrate, join, link; CONCEPT 113 —*Ant.* disconnect

articulation [n1] *clear, coherent speech* delivery, diction, enunciation, expression, pronunciation, saying, speaking, statement, talking, utterance, verbalization, vocalization, voicing; CONCEPT 55 —*Ant.* mispronunciation

articulation [n2] *connection* coupling, hinge, joining, joint, junction, juncture, unification, union; CONCEPT 113 —*Ant.* disconnection

artifice [n1] *hoax; clever act* con, contrivance, device, dodge, expedient, gambit, gimmick*, machination, maneuver, play, ploy, racket*, ruse, savvy, scam*, stratagem, subterfuge, tactic, wile; CONCEPT 59 —*Ant.* candor, frankness,

honesty, honor, ingenuousness, innocence, openness, reality, sincerity, truthfulness

artifice [n2] *cunning; deception* artfulness, chicanery, craftiness, dishonesty, duplicity, guile, scheming, slyness, trickery, wiliness; CONCEPT 411 —*Ant.* candor, frankness, honesty, honor, ingenuousness, innocence, openness, reality, sincerity, truthfulness

artifice [n3] *skill, cleverness* ability, adroitness, deftness, facility, finesse, ingenuity, invention, inventiveness, know-how*, skill; CONCEPT 630 —*Ant.* artlessness, inability, incapacity, simplicity, uncleverness

artificial [adj1] *fake; imitation* bogus, counterfeit, ersatz, fabricated, factitious, faked, false, falsie*, hyped up*, manufactured, mock, phony*, plastic, sham, simulated, specious, spurious, substitute, synthetic, unnatural, unreal; CONCEPT 582 —*Ant.* genuine, natural, real

artificial [adj2] *pretended; affected* assumed, contrived, false, feigned, forced, hollow, insincere, labored, mannered, meretricious, phony*, put-on, spurious, theatrical, unnatural; CONCEPT 401 —*Ant.* genuine, natural, unaffected, unpretentious

artificial intelligence [n] *development of "thinking" computer systems* AI, expert system, natural language processing, neural network, robotics; CONCEPTS 269,463

artillery [n] *weaponry or military unit* arms, battery, bazooka, big guns*, cannon, cannonry, force, gunnery, heavy stuff*, munitions, ordnance, rainmakers*, stovepipe, weapons; CONCEPTS 322,500

artist [n] *person skilled in creative activity* artisan, artiste, authority, composer, craftsperson, creator, expert, handicrafter, inventor, painter, virtuoso, whiz*; CONCEPT 352 —*Ant.* scientist

artistic [adj1] *beautiful, satisfying to senses* aesthetic, creative, cultivated, cultured, decorative, dramatic, elegant, exquisite, fine, graceful, grand, harmonious, ideal, imaginative, musical, ornamental, pictorial, picturesque, pleasing, poetic, refined, rhythmical, sensitive, stimulating, stylish, sublime, tasteful; CONCEPT 579 —*Ant.* distasteful, horrible, inelegant, ugly

artistic [adj2] *being skilled in creative activity* accomplished, artful, artsy-craftsy*, arty, crafty, discriminating, gifted, imaginative, inventive, skillful, talented; CONCEPT 527 —*Ant.* scientific

artistry [n] *great skill in creative endeavors* ability, accomplishment, artfulness, brilliance, craftship, creativity, finesse, flair, genius, mastery, proficiency, style, talent, taste, touch, virtuosity, workmanship; CONCEPTS 630,655 —*Ant.* inability, incapacity, ineptitude

artless [adj] *simple* direct, genuine, guileless, honest, ingenuous, innocent, naive, natural, open, plain, pure, sincere, straight, straightforward, talking turkey*, true, unadorned, unaffected, uncontrived, unpretentious, unsophisticated, up front*; CONCEPTS 267,562 —*Ant.* artful, complicated, contrived, pretentious, sophisticated

arty [adj] *pretended expertise in art; affected interest* affected, deceptive, ephemeral, false, flaunting, illusory, imitative, overblown, popular, popularized, pretentious, pseudo, tasteless; CONCEPT 582

as [conj1] *while, when* at the time that, during the time that, in the act of, in the process of, just as, on the point of; CONCEPT 544

as [conj2] *in the way that; to a degree* acting as, being, by its nature, comparatively, equally, essentially, for instance, functioning as, in the manner that, in the same manner with, just as, just for, like, serving as, similarly, such as; CONCEPT 544

as [conj3] *because* as long as, being, cause, considering, for, for the reason that, inasmuch as, now, seeing that, since, whereas; CONCEPT 544

as [prep] *in the role of* being, in the character of, under the name of; CONCEPT 544

ascend [v] *go up* arise, climb, escalate, float, fly, lift off, mount, move up, rise, scale, soar, sprout, take off, tower; CONCEPTS 149,166 —Ant. decline, descend, go down, lower

ascendancy/ascendency [n] *domination* advantage, authority, command, control, dominance, dominion, edge, influence, jump*, leg up*, mastery, on top, power, predominance, preeminence, prepotence, prevalence, reign, rule, sovereignty, superiority, supremacy, sway, upper hand*, whip hand*; CONCEPTS 376,671 —Ant. decline, inferiority, powerlessness, subordination

ascension [n] *going up* ascent, climbing, escalating, flying, mounting, rise, rising, scaling, soaring, towering; CONCEPTS 149,166 —Ant. declension, decline, descendancy

ascent [n1] *upward movement* ascendance, ascending, ascension, clambering, climb, climbing, lift, mounting, rise, rising, scaling, spring, take off; CONCEPT 166 —Ant. decline, descent, lowering

ascent [n2] *upward slope* acclivity, grade, gradient, incline, ramp, rise; CONCEPTS 738, 757 —Ant. decline, descent

ascertain [v] *make sure* catch on, check, check out*, check up on*, confirm, determine, dig*, discover, divine, double-check*, establish, eye*, eyeball*, find out, fix, get down cold*, get down pat*, get hold of*, get it down*, get the hang of*, identify, learn, learn the ropes*, look-see*, make certain, make sure, peg*, pick up*, pick up on*, read, see, settle, size, size up*, tell, verify; CONCEPTS 31,34,38

ascetic [adj] *self-denying* abstaining, abstemious, abstinent, austere, disciplined, puritanical, Spartan, strict; CONCEPT 401

ascribe [v] *assign to source* accredit, attribute, charge, credit, hang on, impute, lay, pin on*, refer, reference, set down; CONCEPTS 39,49

ashamed [adj] *regretting, remorseful* abashed, apologetic, bashful, blushing, chagrined, compunctious, conscience-stricken, contrite, crestfallen, debased, demeaned, discomfited, disconcerted, distraught, distressed, embarrassed, flustered, guilty, hesitant, humble, humbled, humiliated, meek, mortified, muddled, penitent, regretful, reluctant, repentant, shamed, shamefaced, sheepish, shy, sorry, stammering, stuttering, submissive; CONCEPT 550 —Ant. bold, defiant, immodest, not sorry, shameless, unregretful, unremorseful, unself-conscious

ashen [adj] *gray* anemic, blanched, cadaverous, colorless, ghastly, gray, leaden, pale, pallid, pasty, sallow, wan, white; CONCEPT 618

ash(es) [n] *remains of burning* charcoal, cinders, dust, embers, powder, relics, remains, ruins, slag, soot; CONCEPT 260

ashore [adv] *toward, onto land from water* aground, beached, on dry land, on land, on shore, shorewards; CONCEPT 583 —Ant. asea

aside [adv] *away from; to the side* abreast, afar, alone, alongside, apart, away, beside, by oneself, down, in isolation, in reserve, near, nearby, neck and neck, out, out of the way, privately, separately, sidewise; CONCEPT 586 —Ant. middle

aside [n] *confidential statement* departure, digression, discursion, interpolation, interposition, parenthesis, tangent, throwaway*; CONCEPT 51

asinine [adj] *senseless* absurd, cretinous, daft, foolish, half-witted, idiotic, inane, moronic, silly, sophomoric, stupid; CONCEPTS 402,548

ask [v1] *question* buzz*, canvass, catechize, challenge, cross-examine, demand, direct, enjoin, examine, give the third degree*, go over, grill*, hit*, hunt for*, inquire, institute, interrogate, investigate, needle*, pick one's brains*, pop the question*, pry into, pump, put the screws to*, put through the wringer*, query, quiz, request, roast*, sweat*; CONCEPT 48 —Ant. answer, claim, command, insist, reply, repudiate, tell

ask [v2] *request* angle, appeal, apply, beg, beseech, bite*, bum*, call for, charge, claim, command, contend for, crave, demand, entreat, file for, hit*, hustle*, implore, impose, knock*, levy, mooch*, order, petition, plead, pray, promote*, request, requisition, seek, solicit, sue, supplicate, touch*, urge; CONCEPT 53 —Ant. answer, claim, command, insist, tell

ask [v3] *invite* bid, call upon, propose, suggest, summon, urge; CONCEPT 75 —Ant. disinvite, ignore

askance [adv] *sideways* askew, disapprovingly, disdainfully, dubiously, obliquely, sidelong, sideways, skeptically, suspiciously; CONCEPTS 581,583

askew [adj] *crooked* askance, askant, aslant, awry, bent, buckled, catawampus*, cockeyed*, crookedly, curved, knotted, lopsided, oblique, obliquely, off-center, slanted, slanting, to one side, topsy-turvey*, turned, twisted, yaw ways*, zigzag*; CONCEPT 586

asleep [adj] *unconscious* catching some zzz's*, comatose, conked*, crashed*, dormant, dozing, dreaming, flaked out*, getting shut-eye*, hibernating, inactive, in dreamland*, inert, in repose, napping, on the kip*, out*, out cold*, out like a light*, out of it*, reposing, resting, sacked out*, sleeping, slumbering, snoozing, snoring, somnolent, taking forty winks*; CONCEPTS 210,315,681 —Ant. attentive, awake, conscious

aspect [n1] *visible feature* air, appearance, attitude, bearing, condition, countenance, demeanor, expression, face, facet, form, look, manner, mien; CONCEPTS 434,628,673

aspect [n2] *element to consider* angle, bearing, direction, facet, feature, gimmick, hand, outlook, perspective, phase, point of view, position, prospect, regard, scene, side, situation, slant, switch, twist, view, vista; CONCEPT 668 —Ant. whole

asperity [n] *harshness; bad temper* acerbity, acrimony, bitterness, churlishness, crabbiness, crossness, difficulty, disagreeableness, irascibility, irritability, meanness, moroseness, peevishness, roughness, sharpness, sourness, sullenness, tartness; CONCEPT 633 —*Ant.* calmness, happiness, kindness, mildness

aspersion [n] *verbal exhibition of bad temper* abuse, animadversion, backbiting, backhanded compliment, black eye*, calumny, defamation, detraction, dirty dig*, hit*, invective, knock*, libel, obloquy, put-down*, rap*, slam*, slander, smear*, vituperation; CONCEPTS 52,54,58 —*Ant.* calmness, happiness, kindness, mildness

asphyxiate [v] *cut off air* choke, drown, smother, stifle, strangle, strangulate, suffocate; CONCEPTS 121,246 —*Ant.* breathe, loosen

aspirant [n] *person with wish, dream* applicant, candidate, competitor, contestant, hopeful, postulant, striver, wannabe; CONCEPTS 366,423

aspiration [n] *goal, hope* aim, ambition, ambitiousness, craving, desire, direction, dream, eagerness, endeavor, fire in the belly*, hankering, inclination, longing, object, objective, passion, pursuit, push, right stuff*, urge, vocation, wish, work, yearning; CONCEPTS 20,659

aspire [v] *aim, hope* be ambitious, be eager, crave, desire, dream, hanker, long, pursue, seek, strive, struggle, try, want, wish, yearn; CONCEPT 20

aspiring [adj] *hopeful* ambitious, aspirant, eager, eager beaver*, endeavoring, enthusiastic, impassioned, longing, on the make*, striving, wishful, would-be, zealous; CONCEPT 403

ass [n] *stupid person* blockhead*, dolt, donkey*, dope, dunce, fool, idiot, imbecile, jackass*, jerk*, nitwit*, numbskull*, simpleton*, twit*; CONCEPT 412

assail [v] *attack, usually with words* abuse, assault, bash, berate, beset, blast, blister, bust, charge, come at, criticize, encounter, have at*, impugn, invade, lambaste, lay into*, malign, maltreat, molest, revile, set upon*, trash*, vilify, work over; CONCEPTS 52,86

assailant [n] *attacker* aggressor, antagonist, assaulter, bushwhacker*, enemy, foe, goon*, hit person, invader, mugger, opposite number*, trigger person; CONCEPT 412

assassin [n] *murderer of prominent or important person* butcher*, clipper*, dropper*, eliminator, enforcer, executioner, guerrilla*, gun*, gun person, hatchet person, hit person, killer, liquidator, piece person*, plugger*, slayer, soldier, torpedo*, trigger person; CONCEPT 412 —*Ant.* victim

assassinate [v] *murder prominent or important person* bump off*, do in*, eliminate, execute, gun down, hit, kill, knock off*, liquidate, slaughter, slay; CONCEPT 252

assault [n] *attack* advance, aggression, charge, incursion, invasion, offensive, onset, onslaught, rape, storm, storming, strike, violation; CONCEPT 86

assault [v] *attack* abuse, advance, assail, bash, beset, blast, blitz, bushwhack, charge, come down on*, go for, haul off on*, invade, jump, jump down one's throat*, jump on one's case*, lay into, let have it*, light into*, rape, ruin, set

upon, shoot down, slam, slap around, storm, strike, trash, violate, work over, zap*; CONCEPTS 52,86

assay [n] *analysis* appraisal, assessment, estimation, evaluation, examination, inspection, investigation, measurement, rating, survey, test, trial, valuation; CONCEPTS 24,103,290

assay [v] *analyze* appraise, apprise, assess, check, check out, estimate, evaluate, examine, eyeball*, inspect, investigate, measure, peg*, prove, rate, read, see, size, size up*, survey, test, try, valuate, value, weigh; CONCEPTS 24,103

assemblage [v] *gathering of people* aggregation, assembly, association, collection, company, congregation, convergence, crowd, group, throng; CONCEPT 417 —*Ant.* dispersal, scattering

assemble [v1] *congregate* accumulate, agglomerate, amass, bring together, bunch, bunch up, call, call together, capture*, collect, come together, convene, convoke, corral*, flock, gang up*, gather, group, hang around*, hang out*, huddle, lump, make the scene*, meet, meet up, mobilize, muster, rally, reunite, round up, scare up*, summon, unite; CONCEPT 114 —*Ant.* disperse, scatter

assemble [v2] *put together* compile, connect, construct, contrive, erect, fabricate, fashion, fit, form, join, make, manufacture, model, mold, piece together, produce, set up, shape, unite, weld; CONCEPT 113 —*Ant.* divide, separate, take apart

assembly [n1] *congregation* accumulation, aggregation, assemblage, association, band, body, bunch, clambake*, cluster, coffee klatch*, collection, company, conclave, confab*, conference, convocation, council, crew, crowd, faction, flock, gathering, get-together*, group, huddle, mass, meet*, meeting, multitude, rally, sit-in*, throng, turnout*; CONCEPTS 381,432

assembly [n2] *putting together* adjustment, attachment, building, collection, connecting, construction, erection, fabrication, fitting together, joining, manufacture, manufacturing, modeling, molding, piecing together, setting up, shaping, welding; CONCEPT 113

assent [n] *agreement* acceptance, accession, accord, acknowledgment, acquiescence, admission, affirmation, approval, authorization, compliance, concurrence, consent, nod, permission, sanction; CONCEPTS 8,684 —*Ant.* disagreement, dissent, rejection

assent [v] *agree* accede, accept, accord, acquiesce, adopt, allow, approve, buy, cave in*, comply, concur, conform, consent, cut a deal*, defer, ditto*, embrace, espouse, give five*, give in, go along with, grant, knuckle under*, okay*, pass on*, permit, recognize, sanction, say uncle*, shake on*, subscribe; CONCEPT 8 —*Ant.* disagree, disallow, disapprove, dissent, reject

assert [v] *insist, declare, maintain* advance, affirm, allege, argue, asseverate, attest, aver, avouch, avow, butt in*, cite, claim, contend, defend, horn in, justify, mouth off*, pop off*, predicate, press, proclaim, profess, pronounce, protest, put forward, say, shoot off one's mouth*, shoot one's wad*, stand up for, state, stress, swear, uphold, vindicate, warrant; CONCEPT 49 —*Ant.* deny, reject

assertion [n] *declaration, positive statement* affirmation, allegation, asservation, attestation, avowal, contention, defense, insistence, maintenance, mouthful, okay, predication, profession, pronouncement, report, say so*, stamp of approval, stressing, two cents' worth*, vindication; CONCEPTS 49,278 —*Ant.* denial, rejection

assertive [adj] *aggressive* absolute, assured, certain, confident, decided, decisive, demanding, dogmatic, domineering, emphatic, firm, forceful, forward, insistent, militant, overbearing, positive, pushy, self-assured, self-confident, strong-willed, sure; CONCEPT 404 —*Ant.* diffident, quiet, shy, unconfident

assess [v1] *evaluate, determine* appraise, apprise, assay, check*, check out*, compute, determine, dig it*, estimate, figure*, fix, gauge, guess, judge, nick*, peg*, rate, reckon, set, size*, size up, survey, take measure*, valuate, value, weigh; CONCEPT 24

assess [v2] *assign fee* amount charge, demand, evaluate, exact, fix, impose, levy, rate, tax, value; CONCEPT 330

assessment [n1] *evaluation* appraisal, computation, determination, estimate, estimation, judgment, rating, reckoning, valuation, value judgment; CONCEPT 24

assessment [n2] *assignment of fee, amount* appraisal, charge, demand, duty, estimate, fee, levy, rate, rating, tariff, tax, taxation, toll, valuation; CONCEPT 332

asset [n1] *advantage* aid, benefit, blessing, boon, credit, distinction, help, resource, service, treasure; CONCEPT 661 —*Ant.* disadvantage, liability

asset(s) [n2] *property or money possessed* ace in the hole*, ace up sleeve*, backing, bankroll, budget, capital, credit, equity, estate, funds, goods, holdings, kitty*, mattress*, means, nest egg*, nut*, possessions, rainy day*, reserve(s), resources, riches, sock*, something put aside, something put away, stake, stash*, stuff, valuables, wealth; CONCEPTS 332,340,710 —*Ant.* liability

assiduous [adj] *hard-working* active, attentive, busy, constant, diligent, eager beaver*, exacting, grinding, indefatigable, industrious, laborious, persevering, plugging, scrupulous, sedulous, steady, studious, unflagging, untiring, whiz, zealous; CONCEPTS 538,542 —*Ant.* lazy, neglectful, negligent

assign [v1] *select and give a responsibility* accredit, allow, appoint, ascribe, attach, attribute, authorize, cast, charge, choice, commission, commit, credit, delegate, deputize, designate, downlink, download, draft, elect, empower, enroll, entrust, hang on*, hire, hold responsible, impute, name, nominate, ordain, pin on*, refer, reference, select, slot, tab, tag; CONCEPTS 41,50,88

assign [v2] *set apart for a reason* allocate, allot, appoint, apportion, appropriate, consign, designate, detail, determine, dish out*, distribute, divide, earmark, fix, fork out*, give, grant, hand out*, hand over, indicate, mete, prescribe, relegate, shell out*, specify, stipulate; CONCEPTS 129,135 —*Ant.* keep

assignation [n] *clandestine meeting* affair, appointment, date, engagement, heavy date*,

illicit meeting, love nest*, one-night stand*, quickie*, rendezvous, secret meeting, tryst; CONCEPTS 375,386

assignment [n1] *responsibility, task* appointment, beat, charge, chore, commission, drill, duty, homework, job, mission, position, post, practice, stint; CONCEPT 362

assignment [n2] *selecting or setting apart* allocation, allotment, appointment, apportionment, appropriation, ascription, assignation, attribution, authorization, choice, consignment, delegation, designation, determination, distribution, giving, grant, nomination, selection, specification, stipulation; CONCEPTS 41,129 —*Ant.* keeping

assimilate [v1] *absorb mentally* comprehend, digest, grasp, incorporate, ingest, learn, osmose, sense, soak up, take in, take up, understand; CONCEPT 15 —*Ant.* misunderstand, reject, unlearn

assimilate [v2] *become adjusted; adjust* acclimatize, accommodate, acculturate, accustom, adapt, become like, become similar, blend in, conform, fit, go native*, homogenize, homologize, intermix, match, mingle, parallel, standardize; CONCEPTS 232,701 —*Ant.* not adapt

assist [n] *help* abetment, aid, assistance, backing, benefit, boost, collaboration, comfort, compensation, cooperation, facilitation, furtherance, hand, helping hand, lift, reinforcement, relief, service, support; CONCEPT 110 —*Ant.* hindrance, hurt, stop, stoppage, thwarting

assist [v] *help* abet, aid, back, bail out, benefit, boost, collaborate, cooperate, do for*, expedite, facilitate, further, give a boost*, give a leg up*, give a lift*, go down the line for*, go for, go to bat for*, go with, grease the wheels*, hype*, lend a hand*, make a pitch for*, open doors*, plug*, puff*, push*, put on the map*, reinforce, relieve, ride shotgun*, root for*, run interference for*, serve, stand up for*, stump*, support, sustain, take care of, thump*, work for, work with; CONCEPT 110 —*Ant.* hinder, hurt, stop, thwart

assistance [n] *help* abetment, aid, assist, backing, benefit, boost, collaboration, comfort, compensation, cooperation, facilitation, furtherance, hand, help, helping hand, lift, reinforcement, relief, service, support, sustenance; CONCEPT 110 —*Ant.* hindrance, hurt, injury, stop, stoppage

assistant [n] *helper* abettor, accessory, accomplice, adherent, adjunct, aide, ally, appointee, apprentice, associate, attendant, auxiliary, backer, backup*, coadjutant, coadjutor, collaborator, colleague, companion, confederate, cooperator, deputy, fellow worker, flunky*, follower, friend, gofer*, help, helpmate, mate, partner, patron, peon*, representative, right-hand person, secretary, subordinate, supporter, temp*, temporary worker; CONCEPTS 348,423

associate [n] *colleague* accessory, accomplice, affiliate, aid, ally, assistant, auxiliary, branch, buddy, chum, clubber*, comrade*, collaborator, companion, compatriot, comrade, confederate, consort, cooperator, co-worker, crony, fellow, friend, helper, joiner, kissing cousin, mate, offshoot, one of the folks*, pal, pard*, partner, peer, playmate, sidekick; CONCEPTS 348,423 —*Ant.* antagonist, competitor, enemy, foe, opponent, rival, stranger

associate [v1] *connect in the mind* affiliate, blend, bracket, combine, concord, conjoin, correlate, couple, group, identify, join, league, link, lump together, mix, pair, relate, think of together, unite, yoke; CONCEPT 39 —*Ant.* disconnect, disjoin, dissociate, disunite, divide, part, separate, sever

associate [v2] *befriend* accompany, amalgamate, be friends, be in cahoots*, buddy up, bunch up, come together, confederate, consort, fraternize, gang up, get in on, get into, get in with, get together, go along with, go partners*, hang around, hang out, hang out with*, hobnob, join, join up with, line up with, mingle, mix, pal up, play footsie with*, pool, run around with, run with, string along with, swing with, take up with, team up, throw in together, tie in, tie up, truck with, work with; CONCEPTS 114,384 —*Ant.* avoid, disassociate, disjoin, disunite, divorce

association [n1] *group with common interest or pursuit* affiliation, alliance, band, bunch, circle, clan, clique, club, coalition, combination, combo, company, confederacy, confederation, congress, cooperative, corporation, crew, crowd, family, federation, fellowship, fraternity, gang, guild, hookup*, league, mob, order, organization, outfit, partnership, pool, rat pack*, ring, society, sodality, sorority, syndicate, tie-in, tie-up, tribe, troops, troupe, union, zoo*; CONCEPTS 323,325,387

association [n2] *friendship* acquaintance, acquaintanceship, affiliation, agreement, assistance, camaraderie, companionship, comradeship, conjunction, cooperation, familiarity, fellowship, fraternization, frequenting, friendliness, hookup*, intimacy, membership, participation, partnership, relation, relationship; CONCEPTS 387,388 —*Ant.* aloneness, antagonism, disunion, isolation, opposition, rivalry, seclusion, separation, solitude

association [n3] *mental connection* bond, combination, concomitance, concordance, connotation, correlation, identification, impression, joining, juxtaposition, linkage, linking, lumping together, mixing, mixture, pairing, recollection, relation, remembrance, tie, train of thought, union; CONCEPT 39 —*Ant.* disassociation, division, separation

assorted [adj] *various* different, diverse, diversified, heterogeneous, hybrid, indiscriminate, miscellaneous, mixed, motley, sundry, varied, variegated; CONCEPT 564 —*Ant.* same

assortment [n] *variety* array, choice, collection, combination, combo, diversity, garbage, group, hodgepodge, jumble, kind, medley, mélange, miscellany, mishmash, mixed bag, mixture, potpourri, selection, sort; CONCEPTS 432,665

assuage [v] *soothe, relieve* allay, alleviate, appease, calm, compose, conciliate, cool*, ease, fill, lessen, lighten, lull, make nice*, mitigate, moderate, mollify, pacify, palliate, placate, pour oil on*, propitiate, quench, quiet, sate, satisfy, soften, still, surfeit, sweeten, take the edge off*, take the sting out*, temper, tranquilize; CONCEPTS 7,22,244 —*Ant.* exacerbate, upset

assume [v1] *believe, take for granted* accept, ascertain, be afraid, be inclined to think, conclude, conjecture, consider, count upon, deduce,

deem, divine, estimate, expect, fall for, fancy, find, gather, get the idea*, guess, have a hunch*, have sneaking suspicion, hypothesize, imagine, infer, judge, posit, postulate, predicate, presume, presuppose, speculate, suppose, surmise, suspect, theorize, think, understand; CONCEPTS 12,26 —*Ant.* doubt, not believe

assume [v2] *take, undertake* accept, acquire, appropriate, arrogate, attend to, begin, confiscate, don, embark upon, embrace, enter upon, seize, set about, take on, take over, take up; CONCEPTS 87,142 —*Ant.* not do

assume [v3] *pretend* act, adopt, affect, bluff, counterfeit, fake, feign, imitate, impersonate, mimic, pretend, put on, simulate; CONCEPT 59

assume [v4] *adopt, acquire* annex, appropriate, arrogate, borrow, clap hands on*, commandeer, confiscate, expropriate, get fingers on*, get hands on*, glom onto*, grab, grab hold of*, hijack, kipe*, liberate, moonlight requisition*, preempt, seize, snatch, swipe, take over, usurp; CONCEPTS 139,142 —*Ant.* leave, let alone, not take

assumed [adj1] *pretended* affected, artificial, bogus, counterfeit, fake, false, feigned, fictitious, imitation, made-up, make-believe, phony, pretended, put-on, sham, simulated, spurious; CONCEPT 582 —*Ant.* genuine, natural, real

assumed [adj2] *expected* accepted, conjectured, connoted, counted on, given, granted, hypothesized, hypothetical, inferred, postulated, presumed, presupposed, supposed, suppositional, surmised, tacit, taken as known, taken for granted, understood; CONCEPTS 403,689 —*Ant.* unassumed, unexpected

assuming [adj] *presumptuous, arrogant* bold, conceited, disdainful, domineering, egotistic, forward, haughty, imperious, overbearing, pushy, rude; CONCEPT 404 —*Ant.* doubting, unassuming

assumption [n1] *taking something for granted; something expected* acceptance, accepting, assuming, belief, conjecture, expectation, fancy, guess, hunch, hypothesis, inference, posit, postulate, postulation, premise, presumption, presupposition, shot*, shot in the dark*, sneaking suspicion, stab, supposal, supposition, surmise, suspicion, theorization, theory; CONCEPT 689 —*Ant.* doubt, unexpected

assumption [n2] *assuming possession, power* acceptance, accepting, acquisition, adoption, appropriation, arrogation, assuming, embracing, grab, seizure, shouldering, takeover, taking, taking on, taking up, undertaking, usurpation; CONCEPTS 129,142

assumption [n3] *arrogance* brass*, chutzpah*, cockiness, conceit, imperiousness, insolence, nerve, presumption, pride, sass*, self-importance; CONCEPT 411 —*Ant.* genuineness, naturalness, reality, realness

assurance [n1] *statement to relieve doubt* affirmation, assertion, declaration, guarantee, insurance, lock*, lock on*, oath, pledge, profession, promise, rain or shine*, security, shoo-in*, support, sure thing*, vow, warrant, warranty, word, word of honor; CONCEPTS 71,278 —*Ant.* distrust, doubt

assurance [n2] *confidence* aggressiveness, aplomb, arrogance, assuredness, audacity, boldness, bravery, certainty, certitude, conviction, coolness, courage, effrontery, faith, firmness, impudence, nerve, poise, positiveness, presumption, security, self-confidence, self-reliance, sureness, surety, temerity, trust; CONCEPT 410 —*Ant.* confusion, distrust, doubt, fear, hesitancy, misgiving, shyness, uncertainty

assure [v1] *convince, relieve doubt* bag*, bet on*, comfort, encourage, hearten, inspire, persuade, reassure, satisfy, sell*, sell on*, soothe; CONCEPT 68

assure [v2] *promise* affirm, attest, aver, brace up, buck up, certify, confirm, give one's word, guarantee, pledge, swear, vouch for, vow; CONCEPT 71

assure [v3] *make certain* cinch, clinch, complete, confirm, ensure, guarantee, have a lock on*, ice*, insure, lock, lock on, lock up, make sure, nail down*, put on ice*, seal, secure, set; CONCEPTS 36,91

assured [adj1] *absolutely certain* beyond doubt, cinched, clear-cut, clinched, confirmed, decided, definite, dependable, ensured, fixed, guaranteed, indubitable, insured, in the bag*, irrefutable, made certain, nailed down*, on ice*, pronounced, racked*, sealed, secure, set, settled, sewed up*, sure, surefire, undoubted, unquestionable; CONCEPT 535 —*Ant.* doubted, doubtful, feared, uncertain

assured [adj2] *confident* assertive, audacious, bold, brazen, cocksure*, collected, complacent, composed, confident, cool, gung ho*, gutsy*, high*, imperturbable, nonconfident, poised, positive, puffed up*, pumped up*, pushy, rosy*, sanguine, secure, self-assured, self-confident, self-possessed, sure, unflappable, unhesitating, upbeat*; CONCEPTS 401,404 —*Ant.* confused, dismayed, distrustful, doubtful, doubting, fearful, hesitant, nervous

astern [adv] *backward* abaft, aft, rear, rearward; CONCEPT 581 —*Ant.* forward

astonish [v] *surprise* amaze, astound, bewilder, blow away*, blow one's mind*, boggle, bowl over*, confound, daze, dumbfound, flabbergast, floor*, knock over*, overwhelm, put one away*, shock, spring on, stagger, startle, stun, stupefy, take aback, throw a curve*; CONCEPT 42 —*Ant.* bore, calm, expect

astonishing [adj] *surprising* amazing, astounding, bewildering, breathtaking, extraordinary, impressive, marvelous, miraculous, spectacular, staggering, startling, striking, stunning, stupefying, stupendous, wonderful, wondrous; CONCEPTS 547,572 —*Ant.* boring, dull, expected

astonishment [n] *state of surprise* amazement, astoundment, awe, bewilderment, confusion, consternation, dumbfoundment, one for the books*, shock, something else*, stunner, stupefaction, wonder, wonderment; CONCEPTS 230,410 —*Ant.* dullness, expectation, unexcitement

astound [v] *amaze* astonish, bewilder, blow away, bowl over*, confound, confuse, daze, dumbfound, flabbergast, knock over with feather*, overwhelm, shock, stagger, startle, stun, stupefy, surprise, take aback; CONCEPT 42 —*Ant.* bore, dull

astounding [adj] *amazing* astonishing, breathtaking, confounding, eye-popping*, mind-blowing*, mind-boggling*, overwhelming, shocking, startling, stupefying, surprising, wondrous; CONCEPTS 548,571

astray [adj] *off the path or right direction* adrift, afield, amiss, awry, gone, lost, off, off course, off the mark, roaming, straying, vanished, wandering, wrong; CONCEPTS 545,581 —*Ant.* on course, right, straight

astride [adj] *with a leg on either side* astraddle, athwart, on the back of, piggyback, sitting on, straddling; CONCEPT 583

astringent [adj] *harsh* acetic, acrid, biting, bitter, cutting, sharp, tonic; CONCEPTS 598,613 —*Ant.* bland, mild

astrology [n] *prophesy of the future by observation of stars and planets* astrometry, horoscope; CONCEPT 70

astronaut [n] *space explorer* cosmonaut, moonwalker, pilot, rocketeer, rocket scientist, space person, star person; CONCEPT 348

astronomical [adj] *huge* astronomic*, colossal, considerable, enormous, epic, gigantic, ginormous*, humongous*, jumbo, mammoth, massive, mega*, monster*, monumental, prodigious, sizeable, tremendous, vast, very big, very large, whopping*; CONCEPT 771 —*Ant.* insignificant, small

astronomy [n] *study of the stars and planets other than Earth* astrochemistry, astrography, astrolithology, astrometry, astrophysics, selenology, sky-watching, stargazing, uranology; CONCEPT 349

astute [adj] *perceptive* adroit, brainy, bright, calculating, canny, clever, crafty, discerning, foxy, insightful, intelligent, keen, knowing, not born yesterday*, on the ball*, perspicacious, quick on the uptake*, sagacious, savvy, sharp, sharp as a tack*, shrewd, sly; CONCEPT 402 —*Ant.* asinine, idiotic, ignorant, imbecile, obtuse, shallow, stupid, thick, unintelligent

asunder [adv] *apart; into pieces* disconnected, disjoined, divided, in half, loose, separated, split, torn, to shreds; CONCEPT 785 —*Ant.* together

asylum [n1] *refuge* cover, den, harbor, haven, hideaway, hideout, hole, ivory tower*, port, preserve, refuge, retreat, safe house, safety, sanctuary, security, shelter; CONCEPTS 435,515

asylum [n2] *psychiatric hospital* institution, loony bin*, madhouse*, mental hospital, mental institution, sanatorium; CONCEPTS 312,439,516

asymmetrical [adj] *uneven* awry, crooked, disproportional, gibbous, lacking correspondence, not proportionate, not uniform, unbalanced, unequal, unsymmetrical; CONCEPTS 480,566,606

at [prep] *about; in the direction of* appearing in, by, found in, in the vicinity of, near to, on, placed at, situated at, through, toward; CONCEPTS 581,583,799

atheism [n] *belief that no God exists* disbelief, doubt, freethinking, godlessness, heresy, iconoclasm, impiety, infidelity, irreligion, irreverence, nihilism, nonbelief, paganism, skepticism, unbelief; CONCEPT 689 —*Ant.* belief, godliness, piety, religion

atheist [n] *nonbeliever* agnostic, free thinker, heathen, infidel, irreligionist, pagan, skeptic; CONCEPTS 361,423

athlete [n] *person involved in sports* amateur, animal, challenger, competitor, contender, contestant, games player, gorilla*, iron person*, jock, jockey, muscle person*, player, professional, shoulders, sport, sportsperson, super-jock*; CONCEPT 366

athletic [adj1] *agile; prepared to participate in sports* able-bodied, active, brawny, energetic, fit, lusty, muscular, powerful, robust, strapping, strong, sturdy, vigorous; CONCEPTS 406,489 —*Ant.* unathletic

athletic [adj2] *relating to sports* competitive, contesting, exercise-related, recreational, sporting, team; CONCEPT 536

athletics [n] *sports* contest, drill, events, exercises, games, practice, races, recreation, workout; CONCEPT 363

atmosphere [n1] *gases around the earth* air, envelope, heavens, pressure, sky, substratosphere, troposphere; CONCEPT 437

atmosphere [n2] *general feeling or mood* air, ambience, aura, background, character, climate, color, environment, feel, feeling, flavor, impression, local color, medium, mood, place, property, quality, scene, semblance, sense, space, spirit, surroundings, taste, tone; CONCEPT 673

atom [n] *smallest part of something* bit, crumb, dot, fragment, grain, iota, jot, minimum, mite, modicum, molecule, morsel, mote, ounce, particle, scintilla, scrap, shred, smidgen, speck, spot, tittle, trace, whit; CONCEPT 831

atom bomb [n] *nuclear weapon* A-bomb, backpack nuke*, doomsday machine*, fission bomb, H-bomb, hydrogen bomb, neutron bomb, nuclear bomb, nuke*, thermonuclear weapon; CONCEPT 500

atomic [adj1] *tiny* diminutive, fragmentary, granular, microscopic, minute; CONCEPT 773

atomic [adj2] *nuclear* atom-powered, fissionable, thermonuclear; CONCEPT 485

atone [v] *compensate; make amends for former misdoing* absolve, answer, apologize, appease, balance, correct, counterbalance, do penance, expiate, make amends, make redress, make reparation, make up for, offset, outweigh, pay, pay one's dues*, propitiate, recompense, reconcile, redeem, redress, repair, set off, square, take one's medicine*; CONCEPTS 108,126

atonement [n] *compensation* amends, expiation, indemnification, payment, penance, propitiation, recompense, redemption, redress, reparation, restitution, satisfaction; CONCEPTS 126,337

atrocious [adj1] *outrageous; widely condemned* awful, bad, barbaric, beastly, desperate, diabolical, fiendish, flagrant, godawful*, grody*, gross*, hairy*, heinous, lousy, monstrous, nefarious, rotten, scandalous, shocking, villainous, wicked; CONCEPTS 545,571

atrocious [adj2] *offensive* appalling, awful, bad, beastly, detestable, disgusting, dreadful, execrable, foul, godawful*, grody*, gross*, horrible, horrid, horrifying, icky*, loathsome, noisome, obscene, repulsive, rotten, sickening, terrible; CONCEPTS 548,571 —*Ant.* inoffensive

atrocity [n1] *outrageous behavior* atrociousness, barbarity, barbarousness, enormity, fiendishness, heinousness, horror, monstrousness, nefariousness, shockingness, villainous-

ness, wickedness; CONCEPTS 411,657 —*Ant.* good behavior, pleasantry

atrocity [n2] *cruelness, offensiveness; widely condemned action* abomination, barbarity, brutality, crime, enormity, evil, horror, infamy, inhumanity, iniquity, monstrosity, offense, outrage, ruthlessness, savagery, viciousness, wrong; CONCEPTS 29,645 —*Ant.* kindness, pleasantness

atrophy [n] *wasting away, disintegration* decline, degeneracy, degeneration, deterioration, diminution, downfall, downgrade; CONCEPTS 674,698

attach [v1] *join, fasten* add, adhere, affix, annex, append, bind, connect, couple, fix, hitch on, hitch up, hook on, hook up, latch onto, link, make fast, prefix, rivet, secure, slap on*, stick, tag on*, tie, unite; CONCEPTS 85,113,160 —*Ant.* detach, disconnect, disjoin, remove, separate, sever, unfasten

attach [v2] *socially join* accompany, affiliate, associate, become associated with, combine, enlist, join forces with, latch onto*, sign on with, sign up with, unite with; CONCEPT 114 —*Ant.* disjoin, disunite, divorce

attach [v3] *attribute, ascribe* allocate, allot, appoint, assign, associate, connect, consign, designate, detail, earmark, impute, invest with, lay, name, place, put, second, send; CONCEPTS 62,73 —*Ant.* disunite, take away

attachment [n1] *fastening* adapter, bond, clamp, connection, connector, coupling, fastener, joint, junction, link, tie; CONCEPT 471

attachment [n2] *something joined, fastened to another* accessory, accoutrement, adapter, addition, adjunct, annex, appendage, appurtenance, auxiliary, extension, extra, fitting, fixture, part, supplement; CONCEPT 824

attachment [n3] *affection, high regard* affinity, amore, attraction, bond, case, crush, devotion, fidelity, fondness, friendship, hankering*, liking, love, loyalty, partiality, possessiveness, regard, shine*, tenderness, weakness, yen*; CONCEPT 32 —*Ant.* alienation, animosity, aversion, dislike, divorce, enmity, estrangement, hate, hatred, opposition

attack [n1] *physical assault* advance, aggression, assailing, assailment, barrage, blitz, blitzkrieg, charge, defilement, dirty deed*, drive, encounter, encroachment, foray, incursion, initiative, inroad, intervention, intrusion, invasion, irruption, mugging, offense, offensive, onrush, onset, onslaught, outbreak, push, raid, rape, rush, skirmish, storming, strike, thrust, violation, volley; CONCEPT 86 —*Ant.* aid, defense, flight, protection, resistance, retreat, shelter, shield, support, surrender, sustenance

attack [n2] *verbal assault* abuse, aggression, belligerence, blame, calumny, censure, combativeness, criticism, denigration, denunciation, impugnment, libel, pugnacity, slander, vilification; CONCEPTS 52,54 —*Ant.* defense, reprisal, resistance, retreat, submission, surrender

attack [n3] *sudden dysfunction or disorder* access, ailment, bout, breakdown, convulsion, disease, failure, fit, illness, paroxysm, relapse, seizure, spasm, spell, stroke, throe; CONCEPT 308 —*Ant.* health

attack [v1] *assault physically* advance, aggress,

as at

ambush, assail, assault, bash, bat, bean*, beat, beset, besiege, biff*, blast, blister, boff*, bombard, boot*, bop*, brain*, bust, charge, chop down, clip, clock*, club, combat, cook*, harm, hit, hurt, infiltrate, invade, jump, kick, knock block off*, knock cold*, knock for a loop*, larrup*, lay siege to, light into*, molest, mug, overwhelm, pounce upon, punch, raid, rush, set upon, slog, soak, stab, storm, strike, take the offensive, turn on, wallop*, whop*; CONCEPT 86 —Ant. aid, defend, protect, resist, retreat, shelter, shield, submit, support, surrender, sustain

attack [v2] *assault verbally* abuse, berate, blame, blitz, censure, criticize, impugn, jump down one's throat*, jump on one's case*, lay into, malign, refute, reprove, revile, shoot down*, stretch, vilify; CONCEPTS 52,54 —Ant. defend, resist, submit, withstand

attack [v3] *set to work* buckle down*, deal with, dive into, plunge into, set to, start in on, tackle, take up, tear into*; CONCEPT 112 —Ant. be lazy, slough off

attacker [n] *aggressor* assailant, assaulter, mugger, raider, traducer; CONCEPT 412

attain [v] *achieve, accomplish* accede to, acquire, arrive, arrive at, bring off, come through, complete, cop*, earn, effect, fulfill, gain, get*, get fat*, get hands on, get there, glom onto*, grasp, hit, latch onto, make it, obtain, procure, promote, pull off*, rack up, reach, realize, reap, score, secure, snag, succeed, unzip*, win; CONCEPTS 120,706 —Ant. abandon, desert, fail, forfeit, give in, give up, lose, miss, surrender

attainable [adj] *within reach; achievable* accessible, accomplishable, at hand, available, cherry pie*, duck soup*, easy, feasible, gettable, likely, no problem*, no sweat*, obtainable, piece of cake*, possible, potential, practicable, probable, procurable, reachable, realizable, securable; CONCEPTS 528,552 —Ant. unachievable, unattainable, unreachable

attainment [n] *achievement, accomplishment* acquirement, acquisition, arrival, completion, feat, finish, fulfillment, gaining, getting, obtaining, procurement, reaching, realization, reaping, securing, succeeding, winning; CONCEPT 706 —Ant. failure, forfeit, loss, miss, surrender

attempt [n] *try, effort* all one's got*, attack, bid*, crack*, dry run*, endeavor, exertion, experiment, fling, go, header*, lick*, one's all, one's darnedest*, one's level best*, pursuit, shot, stab, striving, struggle, trial, try, tryout, undertaking, venture, whack*, workout; CONCEPT 87 —Ant. certainty, laziness, success

attempt [v] *try, make effort* aim, attack, do level best*, endeavor, essay, exert oneself, experiment, give a fling*, give a whirl*, give best shot*, give it a go*, give it a try*, give old college try*, go the limit*, have a crack*, have a go at*, make a run at*, pursue, push, seek, shoot the works*, solicit, strive, tackle, take a stab at*, take best shot*, take on, try one's hand at*, undertake, venture; CONCEPT 87 —Ant. be lazy

attend [v1] *be present at* appear, be a guest, be at, be present, be there, bob up*, catch, check in, clock in*, come to light*, drop in, frequent, go to, haunt, make an appearance, make it*, make the scene*, pop up*, punch in*, punch the

clock*, ring in*, show, show up, sit in on, time in, turn up, visit; CONCEPT 114 —Ant. be absent

attend [v2] *care for* be in the service of, doctor, do for, look after, mind, minister to, nurse, serve, take care of, tend, wait upon, watch, work for; CONCEPT 110 —Ant. ignore, neglect

attend [v3] *pay attention; apply oneself* catch, concentrate on, devote oneself, follow, get a load of*, hear, hearken, heed, keep one's eye on*, lend an ear*, listen, listen up*, look after, look on, mark, mind, note, notice, observe, occupy oneself with, pay heed, pick up, regard, see to, watch; CONCEPTS 34,596,623 —Ant. be lazy, disregard, ignore, neglect

attend [v4] *accompany* bear, be associated with, be connected with, catch, follow, issue from, make the scene, occur with, result from; CONCEPT 714

attend [v5] *escort* accompany, chaperon, companion, consort, convoy, escort, guard, squire, usher; CONCEPTS 114,714

attendance [n1] *being present* appearance, attending, being in evidence, being there, participation, presence; CONCEPT 388 —Ant. absence

attendance [n2] *people present at event* assemblage, assembly, audience, box office, company, congregation, crowd, draw, gate, gathering, gross, house, observers, onlookers, patrons, public, spectators, turnout, witnesses; CONCEPT 417

attendant [adj] *being present or related* accessory, accompanying, ancillary, associated, attending, coincident, concomitant, consequent, incident; CONCEPT 577 —Ant. absent, detached

attendant [n] *person who serves others* aide, alarm clock*, assistant, auxiliary, baby sitter, bird dog, chaperon, companion, custodian, domestic, escort, follower, guide, helper, lackey, nurse, orderly, secretary, servant, understudy, usher, waitperson; CONCEPT 348 —Ant. boss, manager

attention [n1] *concentration* absorption, application, assiduity, consideration, contemplation, debate, deliberation, diligence, engrossment, heed, heedfulness, immersion, industry, intentness, mind, scrutiny, study, thinking, thought, thoughtfulness; CONCEPT 409 —Ant. disregard, ignorance, neglect, negligence

attention [n2] *consideration, care* awareness, big rush*, brace, concern, consciousness, looking after, ministration, notice, observation, recognition, regard, spotlight, tender loving care, TLC*, treatment; CONCEPTS 32,410 —Ant. disregard, neglect, negligence

attention deficit disorder [n] *learning disability* ADD, ADHD, hyperactiveness, hyperactivity, short attention span; CONCEPT 403

attention(s) [n3] *courtesy* amenity, assiduities, care, civility, compliment, consideration, deference, gallantry, mindfulness, politeness, regard, respect, service; CONCEPT 644 —Ant. disregard

attentive [adj] *concentrating* alert, all ears*, awake, aware, conscientious, enrapt, enthralled, fascinated, glued, hanging on every word*, heedful, hooked, immersed, intent, interested, listening, mindful, observant, on one's toes*, on the ball*, on the job*, on the lookout*, on the qui vive*, preoccupied, regardful, studious, vigilant, watchful; CONCEPT 403

—*Ant.* disregarding, heedless, ignorant, inattentive, inconsiderate, neglectful, neglecting

attentive [adj2] *considerate* accommodating, civil, courteous, devoted, gallant, gracious, kind, obliging, polite, respectful, solicitous, thoughtful; CONCEPTS 401 —*Ant.* heedless, ignorant, inconsiderate, neglectful, unattentive

attenuate [v] *weaken* abate, constrict, contract, cripple, debilitate, deflate, disable, dissipate, enfeeble, extenuate, lessen, mitigate, sap, shrink, thin, undermine, vitiate; CONCEPT 240 —*Ant.* expand, increase, intensify, strengthen

attest [v] *affirm, vouch for* adjure, announce, argue, assert, asservate, authenticate, aver, bear out, bear witness, certify, confirm, corroborate, countersign, declare, demonstrate, display, exhibit, give evidence, indicate, prove, ratify, seal, show, substantiate, support, sustain, swear, testify, uphold, verify, warrant, witness; CONCEPT 49 —*Ant.* deny

attic [n] *space under the roof of a house* garret, loft, sky parlor*, top floor; CONCEPTS 440,448

attire [n] *clothing* accoutrements, apparel, array, bib and tucker*, clothes, costume, drapes, dress, duds*, garb, garments, gear, getup, habiliments, habit, outfit, raiment, things, threads*, togs, uniform, vestment, wear; CONCEPT 451

attire [v] *clothe* accoutre, array, clad, costume, deck, deck out*, doll up*, drape, dress, dud*, dude up*, equip, fit out, outfit, suit up, tog, turn out; CONCEPT 167 —*Ant.* disrobe

attitude [n1] *mental outlook* air, angle, approach, belief, bent, bias, character, demeanor, disposition, frame of mind, headset*, inclination, leaning, like it is*, mental state, mindset*, mindtrip*, mood, notion, opinion, perspective, philosophy, point of view, position, posture, predilection, prejudice, proclivity, reaction, routine, say so*, sensibility, sentiment, set, slant, stance, stand, standing, standpoint, temper, temperament, twist, view, where one is at*; CONCEPTS 410,689

attitude [n2] *stance* aspect, bearing, carriage, manner, mien, pose, position, posture, stand; CONCEPT 757

attorney [n] *lawyer* advocate, ambulance chaser*, barrister, counsel, counselor, DA, fixer, front, legal beagle*, legal eagle*, lip*, mouthpiece*, pleader*, proxy, spieler*; CONCEPT 355

attract [v] *draw attention* allure, appeal to, bait, beckon, beguile, bewitch, bring, captivate, charm, come on*, court, drag, draw, enchant, endear, engage, enthrall, entice, entrance, exert influence, fascinate, freak out*, give the come-on*, go over big, grab, hook, induce, interest, intrigue, inveigle, invite, kill, knock dead*, knock out*, lure, magnetize, make a hit with*, mousetrap*, pull, rope in*, score, seduce, send*, slay*, solicit, spellbind, steer, suck in*, sweep off one's feet*, tempt, turn on, vamp, wile, wow*; CONCEPTS 7,11,22 —*Ant.* repel, repulse

attraction [n] *ability to draw attention; something that draws attention* allure, allurement, appeal, attractiveness, bait, captivation, charm, chemistry, come-on*, courting, draw, drawing power, enchantment, endearment, enthrallment, enticement, fascination, gravitation, inclination, inducement, interest, invitation, it*, lure, magnetism, pull, seduction, solicitation, temptation, tendency; CONCEPTS 14,676 —*Ant.* repulsion, revulsion

attractive [adj] *appealing, drawing attention* adorable, agreeable, alluring, beautiful, beckoning, bewitching, captivating, charming, comely, enchanting, engaging, enthralling, enticing, fair, fascinating, fetching, glamorous, good-looking, gorgeous, handsome, hunky*, interesting, inviting, looker*, lovely, luring, magnetic, mesmeric, pleasant, pleasing, prepossessing, pretty, provocative, seductive, stunning, taking, tantalizing, teasing, tempting, winning, winsome; CONCEPTS 529,579 —*Ant.* repellent, repulsive, ugly, unappealing, unattractive

attribute [n] *feature* aspect, character, characteristic, facet, idiosyncrasy, indication, mark, note, particularity, peculiarity, point, property, quality, quirk, sign, speciality, symbol, trait, virtue; CONCEPTS 411,673,834

attribute [v] *ascribe, assign to source* account for, accredit, apply, associate, blame, charge, connect, credit, fix upon, hang on, hold responsible, impute, lay, pin on, refer, reference, trace; CONCEPT 73

attrition [n1] *wearing down or away* abrasion, attenuation, debilitation, depreciation, disintegration, erosion, grinding, rubbing, thinning, weakening, wear; CONCEPTS 469,776 —*Ant.* building, strengthening

attrition [n2] *regret* contriteness, penance, penitence, remorse, remorsefulness, repentance; CONCEPTS 410,689 —*Ant.* happiness

attune [v] *adjust* acclimatize, accommodate, accord, accustom, adapt, balance, compensate, conform, coordinate, counterbalance, familiarize, harmonize, integrate, make agree, proportion, reconcile, regulate, tune; CONCEPT 232

atypical [adj] *nonconforming* aberrant, abnormal, anomalous, deviant, different, divergent, exceptional, heteroclite, irregular, odd, peculiar, preternatural, strange, unnatural, unrepresentative; CONCEPTS 547,564 —*Ant.* conforming, normal, ordinary, standard, typical, usual

auburn [n] *reddish-brown color* chestnut, copper, hazel, henna, nut, russet, rust, tawny, titian; CONCEPT 622

au courant [adj] *up-to-date* aware, current, enlightened, hip*, informed, up to speed*, well-informed; CONCEPTS 530,820

auction [n] *competitive sale; sale by bid* bargain, jam*, sell-off; CONCEPTS 324,345

audacious [adj1] *reckless, daring* adventurous, aweless, bold, brassy, brave, cheeky*, courageous, daredevil, dauntless, enterprising, fearless, foolhardy, gutty*, intrepid, nervy, rash, resolute, risky, smart ass*, unafraid, uncurbed, undaunted, ungoverned, valiant, venturesome; CONCEPT 401 —*Ant.* cautious, gentle, humble, meek, mild, modest, reserved, timid, yielding

audacious [adj2] *arrogant, presumptuous* assuming, bantam, bold, brash, brassy, brazen, cheeky*, defiant, disrespectful, forward, impertinent, impudent, insolent, nervy, rude, saucy, shameless; CONCEPTS 401,404 —*Ant.* humble, modest, reserved, shy, timid

audacity [n1] *recklessness, daring* adventurousness, audaciousness, boldness, bravery, courage, dauntlessness, enterprise, fearlessness, guts, intrepidity, nerve, rashness, valor, venturesomeness; CONCEPT 633 —*Ant.* care, carefulness, caution, reserve, timidity

audacity [*n2*] *arrogance, presumptuousness* assurance, audaciousness, brass, cheek*, chutzpah*, cockiness*, crust, defiance, disrespectfulness, effrontery, forwardness, gall, guts*, gutsiness, hardiness, impertinence, impudence, insolence, moxie, nerve, rudeness, shamelessness, spunk, stuff*, temerity; CONCEPTS 411,633 —*Ant.* gentility, humility, meekness, modesty, timidity, yielding

audible [*adj*] *able to be heard* aural, auricular, clear, deafening, detectable, discernible, distinct, hearable, loud, loud enough, perceptible, plain, resounding, roaring, sounding, within earshot; CONCEPTS 591,594 —*Ant.* inaudible

audience [*n1*] *group observing an entertainment or sporting event* admirers, assemblage, assembly, congregation, crowd, devotees, fans, following, gallery, gathering, hearers, house, listeners, market, moviegoers, onlookers, patrons, playgoers, public, showgoers, spectators, theatergoers, turnout, viewers, witnesses; CONCEPT 417

audience [*n2*] *hearing* audition, conference, consideration, consultation, conversation, discussion, interview, meeting, reception; CONCEPT 266

audit [*n*] *inspection of financial records* analysis, balancing, check, checking, examination, investigation, report, review, scrutiny, survey, verification, view; CONCEPT 330

audit [*v*] *inspect financial records* analyze, balance, check, examine, go over, go through, investigate, report, review, scrutinize, sit in, survey, verify; CONCEPTS 103,330

audition [*n*] *test of ability* audience, demo, hearing, reading, trial, try on, tryout; CONCEPT 290

auditor [*n*] *person who inspects financial records* accountant, actuary, bookkeeper, cashier; CONCEPT 348

auditorium [*n*] *room, building for entertainment events* amphitheater, assembly hall, barn*, concert hall, hall, movie house, music hall, opera house, playhouse, reception hall, theater; CONCEPTS 293,439,448

augment [*v*] *make greater; improve* add to, aggrandize, amplify, beef up*, boost, build, build up, compound, develop, enhance, enlarge, expand, extend, grow, heighten, increase, inflate, intensify, magnify, mount, multiply, pad, piggyback*, progress, raise, reinforce, strengthen, sweeten, swell, tag on; CONCEPTS 236,244,245 —*Ant.* decrease, degrade

augmentation [*n*] *making greater; improving* accession, accretion, addition, amplification, beefing up*, boost, buildup, development, enhancement, enlargement, enrichment, expansion, extension, fleshing out, growth, heightening, hike, increase, increment, inflation, intensification, magnification, multiplication, raise, reinforcement, rise, strengthening, swelling, up, upping; CONCEPTS 244,245 —*Ant.* decrease, degradation

augur [*n*] *predictor* diviner, forecaster, harbinger, herald, oracle, prognosticator, prophet, seer, soothsayer; CONCEPT 423

augur [*v*] *predict; be an omen of* adumbrate, bespeak, bode, call it*, call the shots*, crystal-ball, figure out, forecast, foreshadow, foretell, harbinger, have a hunch, herald, portend, presage, prognosticate, promise, prophesy, psych out*, read, signify, soothsay; CONCEPT 70

augury [*n1*] *omen* auspice, boding, forerunner, foretoken, forewarning, harbinger, herald, portent, precursor, presage, prognostication, promise, prophecy, sign, token, warning; CONCEPT 284

augury [*n2*] *prediction* divination, prediction, prophecy, soothsaying; CONCEPT 70

august [*adj*] *dignified, noble* baronial, brilliant, eminent, exalted, glorious, grand, grandiose, highfalutin'*, high-minded, high-ranking, honorable, imposing, impressive, lofty, lordly, magnificent, majestic, monumental, pompous, regal, resplendent, stately, superb, venerable; CONCEPTS 404,567 —*Ant.* undignified

au pair [*n*] *live-in nanny* babysitter, caregiver, day care provider, domestic servant, governess, housekeeper, live-in; CONCEPT 295

aura [*n*] *air, character* ambience, appearance, aspect, atmosphere, background, emanation, feel, feeling, mood, quality, scent, semblance, suggestion, tone; CONCEPT 673

auspices [*n*] *protection; support* advocacy, aegis, authority, backing, care, charge, control, countenance, guidance, influence, patronage, sponsorship, supervision; CONCEPTS 94,376

auspicious [*adj*] *encouraging; favorable* advantageous, bright, favorable, felicitous, fortunate, golden, halcyon, happy, hopeful, lucky, opportune, promising, propitious, prosperous, rosy, timely, well-timed; CONCEPT 572 —*Ant.* inauspicious, inopportune, ominous, unfortunate, unhappy, unlucky

austere [*adj1*] *severe in manner* ascetic, astringent, cold, earnest, exacting, forbidding, formal, grave, grim, hard, harsh, inexorable, inflexible, obdurate, rigid, rigorous, serious, sober, solemn, somber, stern, stiff, strict, stringent, unfeeling, unrelenting; CONCEPT 550 —*Ant.* bland, calm, gentle, meek, mild

austere [*adj2*] *refraining; abstinent* abstemious, ascetic, chaste, continent, economical, puritanical, self-denying, self-disciplined, sober, straightlaced, strict, subdued, unrelenting; CONCEPT 401 —*Ant.* elaborate, encouraging, extravagant, indulgent, spending

austere [*adj3*] *grim, barren* bald, bare, bare-bones, bleak, clean, dour, plain, primitive, rustic, severe, simple, spare, spartan, stark, subdued, unadorned, unembellished, vanilla*; CONCEPT 485 —*Ant.* extravagant, luxurious

austerity [*n1*] *severity* acerbity, asperity, astringence, coldness, exactingness, exactness, formality, formalness, gravity, grimness, hardness, harshness, inclemency, inflexibility, obduracy, rigidity, rigor, seriousness, solemnity, sternness, stiffness, strictness, stringency; CONCEPT 644 —*Ant.* blandness, calmness, gentility, meekness, mildness

austerity [*n2*] *refraining; abstinence* abstemiousness, asceticism, chasteness, chastity, continence, determination, economy, prudence, puritanism, self-denial, self-discipline, sobriety, stoicism, strictness, temperance; CONCEPT 633

—*Ant.* elaborateness, extravagance, indulgence, spending

austerity [n3] *grimness, barrenness* baldness, bareness, dourness, economy, plainness, primitiveness, rusticity, severity, simplicity, spareness, spartanism, starkness, unadornment; CONCEPT 723 —*Ant.* elaborateness, luxuriousness

authentic [adj] *real, genuine* accurate, actual, authoritative, bona fide, certain, convincing, credible, creditable, dependable, factual, faithful, for real*, legit*, legitimate, official, original, pure, reliable, sure, true, trustworthy, trusty, twenty-four carat*, valid, veritable; CONCEPT 582 —*Ant.* counterfeit, fake, false, falsified, unauthorized, ungenuine, unreal

authenticate [v] *establish as real, genuine* accredit, attest, authorize, bear out, certify, confirm, corroborate, endorse, guarantee, justify, prove, substantiate, validate, verify, vouch, warrant; CONCEPTS 12,103

author [n] *composer of written work* biographer, columnist, composer, creator, essayist, ghost, journalist, ink slinger*, journalist, originator, playwright, poet, producer, prose writer, reporter, scribbler*, scribe, scripter, word slinger*, wordsmith, work-for-hire*, writer; CONCEPT 348

authoritarian [adj] *domineering* absolute, authoritative, autocratic, despotic, dictatorial, disciplinarian, doctrinaire, dogmatic, harsh, imperious, magisterial, rigid, severe, strict, totalitarian, tyrannical, unyielding; CONCEPTS 319,401 —*Ant.* democratic, liberal

authoritarian [n] *domineering person* absolutist, autocrat, despot, dictator, disciplinarian, tyrant; CONCEPTS 354,412

authoritative [adj1] *recognized as true, valid* accurate, attested, authentic, authenticated, circumstantiated, confirmed, definitive, dependable, documented, factual, faithful, learned, legit*, proven, reliable, righteous, scholarly, sound, straight from horse's mouth*, supported, trustworthy, truthful, validated, verified, veritable; CONCEPT 582 —*Ant.* democratic

authoritative [adj2] *domineering* assertive, authoritarian, autocratic, commanding, confident, decisive, dictatorial, doctrinaire, dogmatic, dominating, imperative, imperious, imposing, masterly, officious, peremptory, self-assured; CONCEPT 550 —*Ant.* democratic

authoritative [adj3] *official, authorized* administrative, approved, bureaucratic, canonical, departmental, ex cathedra, executive, ex officio, imperial, lawful, legal, legitimate, magisterial, mandatory, ruling, sanctioned, sovereign, supreme; CONCEPTS 319,536 —*Ant.* democratic

authority [n1] *power, control* ascendancy, authorization, beef*, charge, clout*, command, credit, domination, dominion, edge, esteem, force, goods*, government, guts*, influence, juice*, jump, jurisdiction, leg up*, license, mastery, might, might and main*, permission, permit, pizzazz*, pow*, powerhouse, prerogative, prestige, punch, right, ropes*, rule, say, say-so*, steam, strength, strong arm*, stuff*, supremacy, sway, upper hand*, warrant, weight, what it takes*, whip hand*, word, zap*; CONCEPTS 376,685,688

authority [n2] *expert, animate or inanimate* arbiter, aristocrat, bible, big cheese*, big shot*, big wig*, boss, brains*, brass*, buff*, CEO, city hall*, connoisseur, czar, egghead*, establishment*, exec*, executive, expert, feds*, front office*, governor, guru, ivory dome*, judge, kingfish*, kingpin*, law*, power elite, pro, professional, professor, pundit, scholar, specialist, textbook*, top brass*, top dog*, top hand*, upstairs*, veteran, virtuoso, whiz, wizard; CONCEPTS 280,348,354

authorize [v1] *give power or control* accredit, bless, commission, empower, enable, entitle, give authority, give the go-ahead*, give the green light*, give the word*, invest, license, okay, rubber-stamp*, say the word*, vest; CONCEPTS 50,88 —*Ant.* deny, reject

authorize [v2] *permit, allow* affirm, approve, confirm, countenance, endorse, give leave, let, license, qualify, ratify, sanction, suffer, tolerate, warrant; CONCEPTS 10,83 —*Ant.* deny, disallow, reject

authorized [adj] *approved* accredited, certified, commissioned, lawful, legal, legitimate, licensed, licit, official, recognized, sanctioned, warranted; CONCEPT 535 —*Ant.* unofficial

autobiography [n] *written account of one's own life* adventures, bio, biography, confession, diary, experience, journal, letter, letters, life, life story, memoir, personal history, reminiscences, self-portrayal; CONCEPT 280

autocracy [n] *government by one* absolutism, czarism, despotism, dictatorship, monarchy, monocracy, oppression, totalitarian government, tyranny; CONCEPTS 354,691 —*Ant.* democracy

autocrat [n] *dictator* authoritarian, Caesar*, despot, Fascist, Hitler*, overlord, totalitarian, tyrant; CONCEPT 354

autocratic [adj] *holding power exclusively* absolute, all-powerful, arbitrary, bossy, czarlike, despotic, dictatorial, domineering, driving, imperious, monocratic, pushing, tyrannical, tyrannous; CONCEPTS 319,536 —*Ant.* democratic

autograph [n] *handwritten signature* endorsement, handwriting, inscription, John Hancock*, seal, token, undersignature, writing; CONCEPT 284

autograph [v] *write signature* endorse, engross, handwrite, ink, inscribe, pen, sign, signature, subscribe, write by hand; CONCEPT 79

automated [adj] *made or done by a machine* automatic, computerized, electrical, electronic, mechanical, mechanized, motorized, programmed, robotic; CONCEPTS 538,549 —*Ant.* by hand, manual

automatic [adj1] *done or made by machine* automated, electric, electronic, mechanical, mechanized, motorized, robotic, self-moving, self-regulating, self-starting; CONCEPTS 538,549 —*Ant.* by hand, manual

automatic [adj2] *done by habit* autogenetic, habitual, impulsive, instinctive, instinctual, intuitive, involuntary, knee-jerk, mechanical, natural, perfunctory, reflex, routine, spontaneous, unconscious, unforced, unintentional, unmeditated, unthinking, unwilled; CONCEPTS 403,538 —*Ant.* thought-out

automatic [adj3] *occurring as natural consequence* assured, certain, inescapable, inevitable, necessary, routine, unavoidable; CONCEPTS 530,535 —*Ant.* stilted, unnatural

automation [*n*] *machine control* computerization, industrialization, mechanization; CONCEPT 770

automobile [*n*] *land vehicle; car* auto, bucket of bolts*, bug*, buggy*, bus, clunker*, compact, convertible, crate*, four-wheeler*, gas guzzler*, go-cart*, hardtop, hatchback, heap*, jalopy*, junker*, lemon*, limousine, motor car, oil burner*, passenger car, pickup truck, ride*, sedan, sports car, station wagon, subcompact, taxi, transportation, truck, tub*, van, wheels*, wreck*; CONCEPT 505

autonomous [*adj*] *independent* free, self-determining, self-governing, self-ruling, sovereign, uncontrolled; CONCEPT 554 —*Ant.* dependent, subject

autonomy [*n*] *independence* freedom, liberty, self-determination, self-government, self-rule, sovereignty; CONCEPT 652 —*Ant.* dependence

autopsy [*n*] *examination of dead body* dissection, necropsy, pathological examination, post-mortem; CONCEPTS 103,310

autumn [*n*] *season between summer and winter* autumnal equinox, fall, harvest; CONCEPT 814 —*Ant.* spring

auxiliary [*adj*] *supplementary* abetting, accessory, adjuvant, ancillary, appurtenant, backup, complementary, contributory, extra, reserve, secondary, spare, subordinate, subservient, subsidiary, supporting; CONCEPTS 546,824 —*Ant.* body, main

auxiliary [*n*] *helper* accessory, accomplice, adjutant, ally, assistant, associate, companion, confederate, crutch*, partner, reserve, subordinate, supporter; CONCEPT 423

avail [*n*] *use* account, advantage, applicability, appropriateness, fitness, service, usefulness; CONCEPT 680

avail [*v*] *be of use; use* account, advantage, answer, be adequate, benefit, fill, fulfill, meet, profit, satisfy, serve, suffice, work; CONCEPT 91

available [*adj*] *ready for use* accessible, achievable, applicable, at hand, at one's disposal*, attainable, come-at-able*, convenient, derivable from, feasible, free, getatable*, handy, obtainable, on deck*, on hand*, on tap*, open to, possible, prepared, procurable, purchasable, reachable, ready willing and able*, realizable, securable, serviceable, up for grabs*, usable, vacant; CONCEPT 576 —*Ant.* unavailable, unhandy, unobtainable

avalanche [*n*] *falling large mass; sudden rush of large quantity* barrage, deluge, flood, inundation, landslide, landslip, snowslide, torrent; CONCEPTS 509,524,787

avant-garde [*adj*] *unconventional, forward-looking* beat*, experimental, head*, hip*, innovative, lead, leading-edge*, liberal, new, new wave, pioneering, progressive, radical, state-of-the-art, vanguard; CONCEPTS 564,585 —*Ant.* conservative, conventional

avarice [*n*] *extreme greed* avidity, close-fistedness*, covetousness, cupidity, frugality, grabbiness, greediness, miserliness, niggardliness, parsimony, penny-pinching*, penuriousness, rapacity, stinginess, thrift; CONCEPTS 335,410 —*Ant.* generosity, philanthropy

avaricious [*adj*] *greedy* covetous, gluttonous, hoarding, money-grubbing*, pleonectic, predatory, rapacious, selfish, tight*; CONCEPTS 404,542

avenge [*v*] *retaliate* chasten, chastise, come back at, even the score, get back at, get even, payback, punish, redress, repay, requite, retribute, revenge, stick it to, take satisfaction, take vengeance, venge, vindicate; CONCEPTS 122,126

avenue [*n*] *street; path* access, alley, approach, boulevard, channel, course, drive, entrance, entry, exit, outlet, parkway, passage, pathway, promenade, road, route, thoroughfare, way; CONCEPT 501

average [*adj1*] *normal, typical* boilerplate*, common, commonplace, customary, dime a dozen*, everyday, fair, fair to middling*, familiar, garden*, garden-variety*, general, humdrum*, intermediate, mainstream, mediocre, medium, middle of the road*, middling, moderate, nowhere*, ordinary, passable, plastic*, regular, run of the mill*, so-so*, standard, tolerable, undistinguished, unexceptional, usual; CONCEPT 547 —*Ant.* abnormal, atypical, exceptional, extraordinary, extreme, outstanding, unusual

average [*adj2*] *numerical mean* intermediate, median, mean, middle; CONCEPT 762

average [*n*] *normal, typical amount* mean, median, medium, middle, midpoint, norm, par, rule, standard, usual; CONCEPTS 647,787 —*Ant.* abnormality, exception, extreme, unusual

average [*v*] *obtain numerical mean* balance, equate, even out; CONCEPT 764

averse [*adj*] *opposing* afraid, allergic, antagonistic, antipathetic, contrary, disinclined, disliking, having no use for*, hesitant, hostile, ill-disposed, indisposed, inimical, loath, nasty, perverse, reluctant, uneager, unfavorable, unfriendly, unwilling; CONCEPTS 403,564 —*Ant.* caring, liking, loving, sympathetic

aversion [*n*] *dislike; opposition* abhorrence, abomination, allergy, animosity, antagonism, antipathy, detestation, disfavor, disgust, disinclination, disliking, displeasure, dissatisfaction, distaste, dread, hate, hatred, having no use for*, horror, hostility, indisposition, loathing, odium, reluctance, repugnance, repulsion, revulsion, unwillingness; CONCEPT 29 —*Ant.* affection, attachment, care, fondness, kindness, like, liking, love, sympathy

avert [*v*] *thwart; avoid by turning away* avoid, deflect, deter, divert, fend off, foil, forestall, frustrate, halt, look away, preclude, prevent, rule out, shove aside, shunt, stave off, turn, turn aside, turn away, ward off; CONCEPTS 121,623 —*Ant.* aid, help

aviation [*n*] *flying an aircraft; study of flying aircraft* aerodynamics, aeronautics, flight, navigation, piloting; CONCEPTS 148,187,324

aviator [*n*] *person who flies aircraft* ace, aeronaut, airperson, barnstormer, bird legs*, eagle*, flier, hotshot*, jockey*, navigator, pilot; CONCEPTS 348,366

avid [*adj*] *enthusiastic* ardent, athirst, avaricious, breathless, covetous, desirous, devoted, dying to*, eager, fanatical, fervent, gotta have*, grasping, greedy, hungry, impatient, insatiable, intense, keen, passionate, rapacious, ravenous, thirsty, voracious, zealous; CONCEPTS 20,401,403 —*Ant.* dispassionate, indifferent, unenthusiastic

avocation [n] *hobby* amusement, diversion, kick*, occupation, pastime, recreation, schtick*, shot*, side interest, sideline, thing*; CONCEPT 364 —*Ant.* profession, vocation, work

avoid [v] *refrain or stay away from; prevent* abstain, avert, bypass, circumlocute, circumvent, deflect, desist, ditch, divert, dodge, duck, elude, escape, eschew, evade, fake out*, fend off, flee, give the slip*, hide, hold off, jump, keep clear, lay low*, obviate, recoil, run for cover*, shake, shake and bake*, shake off, shirk, shrink from, shuffle off, shun, shy, sidestep, skip*, skip out on*, skip town*, skirt*, stay away, stay out, steer clear of*, step aside, turn aside, ward off, weave, withdraw; CONCEPTS 102,121 —*Ant.* face, meet, seek, want

avoidable [adj] *preventable* avertible, escapable, needless, stoppable, unnecessary; CONCEPT 121 —*Ant.* inescapable, inevitable

avoidance [n] *eluding; preventing* absention, circumvention, delay, departure, dodge, dodging, elusion, escape, escapism, eschewal, evasion, flight, forbearance, nonparticipation, parry, passive resistance, prevention, recession, recoil, restraint, retreat, run-around, self-restraint, shirking, shunning, steering clear of*; CONCEPTS 102,121 —*Ant.* meeting

avow [v] *state; profess* acknowledge, admit, affirm, allow, assert, aver, avouch, concede, confess, cross one's heart*, declare, grant, maintain, own up, proclaim, swear, swear on bible*, swear up and down*; CONCEPTS 49,60,71 —*Ant.* censure, condemn, deny, disclaim, disown, dispute, renounce, repudiate

avowal [n] *acknowledgment* admission, affirmation, announcement, assertion, confession, declaration, oath, proclamation, testimony; CONCEPTS 8,50,88

await [v] *wait with expectation* anticipate, attend, be prepared for, be ready for, cool one's heels*, count on, hang around*, hang in*, hang out*, hope, look for, look forward to, stay, sweat*, sweat it out*; CONCEPT 26

awake [adj] *conscious; alert* alive, aroused, attentive, awakened, aware, cognizant, excited, heedful, knowing, observant, on guard, roused, vigilant, wakeful, waking, watchful; CONCEPTS 402,406 —*Ant.* asleep, unconscious

awake [v1] *become alert or cause to rise from sleep* arise, awaken, call, gain consciousness, get up, roll out*, rouse, stir, wake, wake up; CONCEPTS 250,315 —*Ant.* go to sleep, sleep

awake [v2] *become or make aware* activate, alert, animate, arouse, awaken, call forth, enliven, excite, incite, kindle, provoke, revive, stimulate, stir up, vivify; CONCEPT 231 —*Ant.* deaden, lull

awaken [v] *make conscious or alert* activate, animate, arouse, awake, call, enliven, excite, fan, incite, kindle, pile out*, provoke, rally, revive, rise and shine*, roll out*, rouse, show a leg*, stimulate, stir up, turn out*, vivify, wake; CONCEPTS 7,19,22,105,231 —*Ant.* deaden, go to sleep, hypnotize

awakening [n] *making conscious or alert* activation, animating, arousal, awaking, birth, enlivening, incitement, kindling, provocation, rebirth, renewal, revival, rousing, stimulation, stirring up, vivication, waking, waking up; CONCEPTS 13,105,231 —*Ant.* sleep, sleeping

award [n] *prize or reward* accolade, adjudication, allotment, bestowal, citation, conferment, conferral, decision, decoration, decree, distinction, donation, endowment, feather in cap*, gift, gold, gold star*, grant, honor, order, presentation, scholarship, trophy, verdict; CONCEPT 337

award [v] *give prize or reward* accord, adjudge, allocate, allot, apportion, assign, bestow, concede, confer, decree, dish out*, distribute, donate, endow, fork out*, gift, grant, hand out, present, render, reward, shell out*, sweeten the kitty*; CONCEPT 132

aware [adj] *knowledgeable* acquainted, alert, alive, appraised, appreciative, apprehensive, apprised, attentive, au courant, awake, cognizant, conscious, cool*, enlightened, familiar, go-go*, groovy*, grounded*, heedful, hip*, informed, in the know*, in the picture*, into*, know-how, knowing, know the score*, know what's what*, latched on*, mindful, on the beam*, on to*, perceptive, plugged in*, receptive, savvy, sensible, sentient, sharp, tuned in, up on, wise, wised up*, wise to*, with it*; CONCEPT 402 —*Ant.* ignorant, insensitive, unaware, unconscious

awareness [n] *knowledge* acquaintance, acquaintanceship, alertness, aliveness, appreciation, apprehension, attention, attentiveness, cognizance, comprehension, consciousness, discernment, enlightenment, experience, familiarity, information, keenness, mindfulness, perception, realization, recognition, sensibility, sentience, understanding; CONCEPT 409 —*Ant.* ignorance, insensitivity, unconsciousness

away [adv1] *in another direction; at a distance* abroad, absent, afar, apart, aside, beyond, distant, elsewhere, far afield, far away, far off, far remote, from here, from here, hence, not present, off, out of, out of the way, over, to one side; CONCEPTS 581,778

away [adv2] *continuously* endlessly, forever, incessantly, interminably, on and on, relentlessly, repeatedly, tirelessly, unremittingly, without break, without end, without rest, without stopping; CONCEPT 553

awe [n] *amazement* admiration, apprehension, astonishment, consternation, dread, esteem, fear, fright, horror, regard, respect, reverence, shock, stupefaction, terror, veneration, wonder, wonderment, worship; CONCEPTS 230,410 —*Ant.* calmness, coolness, expectation, familiarity, intimacy, steadiness

awe [v] *amaze* alarm, appall, astonish, blow away*, cow*, daunt, dazzle, flabbergast, frighten, grandstand, horrify, hotdog*, impress, intimidate, knock socks off*, overawe, scare, showboat*, startle, strike, stun, stupefy, terrify; CONCEPTS 7,19,22,42 —*Ant.* expect

awesome [adj] *amazing* alarming, astonishing, awe-inspiring, awful, beautiful, breathtaking, daunting, dreadful, exalted, fearful, fearsome, formidable, frantic, frightening, grand, hairy*, horrible, horrifying, imposing, impressive, intimidating, magnificent, majestic, mean,

mind-blowing*, moving, nervous, overwhelming, real gone*, shocking, something else*,
striking, stunning, stupefying, terrible,
terrifying, wonderful, wondrous, zero cool*;
CONCEPTS 537,572 —*Ant.* unamazing

awful [*adj*] *very bad; terrible* abominable,
alarming, appalling, atrocious, deplorable,
depressing, dire, disgusting, distressing, dreadful, fearful, frightful, ghastly, grody*, gross*,
gruesome, grungy*, harrowing, hideous, horrendous, horrible, horrific, horrifying, nasty,
offensive, raunchy, repulsive, shocking, stinking, synthetic, tough, ugly, unpleasant, unsightly; CONCEPTS 570,571 —*Ant.* beautiful,
good, ok, pleasing

awfully [*adv1*] *badly* clumsily, disgracefully,
disreputably, dreadfully, inadequately, incompletely, poorly, reprehensibly, shoddily, unfor-
givably, unpleasantly, wickedly, wretchedly;
CONCEPTS 570,571

awfully [*adv2*] *very badly* dreadfully, excessively, extremely, greatly, hugely, immensely,
indeed, much, quite, terribly, truly, very much;
CONCEPT 569

awhile [*adv*] *for a short period* briefly, for a bit,
for a little while, for a moment, for a spell, for
a while, for the moment, momentarily, not for
long, temporarily, transiently; CONCEPT 798

awkward [*adj1*] *clumsy, inelegant* all thumbs*,
amateurish, artless, blundering, bulky, bumbling, bungling, butterfingers*, coarse, floundering, gawky, graceless, green*, having two
left feet*, having two left hands*, incompetent,
inept, inexpert, klutzy*, lumbering, maladroit,
oafish, rude, stiff, stumbling, uncoordinated,
uncouth, unfit, ungainly, ungraceful, unhandy,
unpolished, unrefined, unskilled, unskillful;
CONCEPTS 406,480,527 —*Ant.* adroit, artful,
dexterous, elegant, graceful, handy, skillful

awkward [*adj2*] *difficult to handle* annoying,
bulky, chancy, cramped, cumbersome, dangerous, disagreeable, discommodious, hard to
use, hazardous, incommodious, inconvenient,
perilous, risky, troublesome, uncomfortable,
unhandy, unmanageable, unwieldy; CONCEPT
558 —*Ant.* convenient, easy, straightforward

awkward [*adj3*] *embarrassing* compromising,
delicate, difficult, embarrassed, ill at ease, inconvenient, inopportune, painful, perplexing,
sticky*, thorny*, ticklish*, troublesome, trying,
uncomfortable, unpleasant, untimely; CONCEPT
555 —*Ant.* clever

awkwardness [*n1*] *clumsiness; inelegance*
amateurishness, artlessness, boorishness, clod-
dishness, coarseness, crudeness, gawkiness,
gracelessness, greenness*, ignorance, inability,
incompetence, ineptitude, ineptness, inexpertness, maladroitness, oafishness, rudeness,
tactlessness, uncoordination, uncouthness,
ungainliness, unskillfulness; CONCEPTS
405,630,717 —*Ant.* artfulness, dexterity,
elegance, grace, handiness, skill

awkwardness [*n2*] *difficulty* bulkiness, chanci-
ness, cumbersomeness, danger, hazardousness,
inconvenience, peril, perilousness, risk, troublesomeness, uncomfortableness, unhandiness,
unmanageability, unwieldiness; CONCEPTS
656,666 —*Ant.* convenience, ease, easiness,
straightforwardness

awkwardness [*n3*] *embarrassment* delicacy,
difficulty, discomfort, inconvenience, inoppor-
tuneness, painfulness, stickiness*, thorniness*,
ticklishness*, trouble, uncomfortableness,
unpleasantness, untimeliness; CONCEPT 388
—*Ant.* cleverness

awning [*n*] *canopy* covering, door cover,
marquee, protection, shade, shelter, sunshade,
tent; CONCEPTS 440,473

awry [*adj*] *off course; amiss* afield, askance,
askew, aslant, astray, badly, bent, cockeyed,
crooked, curved, slanting, turned, wrong,
zigzag; CONCEPTS 537,581 —*Ant.* ok, on
course

ax/axe [*n*] *large cutting tool* adz, chopper,
hatchet, tomahawk; CONCEPT 499

ax/axe [*v1*] *cut with large blade* chop, cut,
cut down, fell, hew; CONCEPT 176

ax/axe [*v2*] *dismiss from service* boot*,
bounce*, can*, cancel, cut back, discharge,
dispense with, eliminate, fire, get rid of, give
a pink slip*, give the boot*, kick out, lay off,
remove, sack*, terminate, throw out; CONCEPT
351 —*Ant.* hire

axiom [*n*] *principle* adage, aphorism, apothegm,
device, dictum, fundamental, law, maxim,
moral, postulate, precept, proposition, proverb,
saying, theorem, truism, truth; CONCEPTS 278,
688,689 —*Ant.* absurdity, ambiguity, foolishness, nonsense, paradox

axiomatic [*adj*] *understood; aphoristic*
absolute, accepted, aphoristic, apothegmatic,
assumed, certain, fundamental, given, indubitable, manifest, obvious, presupposed,prover-
bial, self-evident, unquestioned; CONCEPT 529
—*Ant.* misunderstood, questionable, uncertain

axis [*n*] *point around which something revolves*
arbor, axle, hinge, pivot, pole, shaft, spindle,
stalk, stem, support, turning point; CONCEPT 830

axle [*n*] *shaft around which wheels rotate* arbor,
axis, gudgeon, mandrel, pin, pivot, pole, rod,
shaft, spindle, stalk, stem, support; CONCEPTS
464,830

ax to grind [*n*] *hidden motive* agenda, driving
force, hidden agenda, incentive, motivation,
motive, reason, score to settle*; CONCEPTS 20,
661,689

B

babble [*n*] *trivial talk, often incessant* blubbering, burble, chatter, clamor, drivel, gab, gabble,
gibberish, gossip, gushing, idle talk, jabber,
jabbering, jargon, murmur, muttering, prattle,
ranting, tattling; CONCEPTS 266,278 —*Ant.*
quiet, sense, wisdom

babble [*v*] *talk trivially, often incessantly* blab,
blubber, blurt, burble, cackle, chat, chatter,
gibber, go on, gossip, gush, jabber, mumble,
murmur, mutter, patter, prate, prattle, rant, rave,
run off at the mouth*, run on, spill the beans*,
squeal*, talk foolishly, talk incoherently, talk
nonsensically, tattle, trivialize, yak*, yakkety
yak*; CONCEPTS 51,266 —*Ant.* be quiet

babe [*n*] *baby* bairn, child, infant, little one,
newborn, suckling; CONCEPTS 414,424 —*Ant.*
adolescent, adult

baby [*adj*] *miniature* babyish, diminutive,

dwarf, little, midget, mini*, minute, petite, small, tiny, wee, youthful; CONCEPT 773 —*Ant.* big, giant, large

baby [n] *infant* angelface*, babe, bairn, bambino, bundle, buttercup*, button, cherub, chick, child, crawler*, deduction*, dividend*, dumpling*, kid, little angel*, little darling*, little doll*, little one*, newborn, nipper*, nursling, papoose, preemie*, suckling, tad*, toddler, tot, write-off*, youngster; CONCEPTS 414,424 —*Ant.* adolescent, adult

baby [v] *treat like a child* cater to, cherish, coddle, cosset, cuddle, dandle, dote on, foster, humor, indulge, nurse, overindulge, pamper, pet, please, satisfy, serve, spoil; CONCEPTS 110,295

babyhood [n] *period of infancy* childhood, diaper days*, infanthood; CONCEPT 817 —*Ant.* adolescence, adulthood

babyish [adj] *acting like an infant* baby, childish, foolish, immature, infantile, juvenile, kid stuff, puerile, silly, sissy, spoiled; CONCEPTS 401,550 —*Ant.* grown-up, mature

baby-sit [v] *care for a child* guard, sit, take care, tend, watch; CONCEPT 295

bachelor [n] *unmarried man or woman* available*, celibate, single*, single person, stag*, unattached; CONCEPTS 415,419,423 —*Ant.* groom, husband, spouse

back [adj 1] *end* aback, abaft, aft, after, astern, back of, backward, behind, final, following, hind, hindmost, in the wake of, posterior, rear, rearmost, rearward, tail; CONCEPTS 827,833 —*Ant.* front

back [adj2] *from earlier time* delayed, elapsed, former, overdue, past, previous; CONCEPT 820 —*Ant.* future

back [n] *end part* back, back end, backside, extremity, far end, hindpart, hindquarters, posterior, rear, reverse, stern, tail, tail end, tailpiece; CONCEPTS 392,471,827,833 —*Ant.* front

back [v1] *support* abet, abide by, advocate, ally, angel*, assist, bankroll, boost, champion, countenance, encourage, endorse, favor, finance, give a boost, give a leg up*, give a lift*, go to bat for*, grubstake, sanction, second, side with, sponsor, stake, stand behind, stick by, stick up for, subsidize, sustain, underwrite, uphold; CONCEPTS 8,50,88 —*Ant.* discourage, dissuade

back [v2] *put in reverse direction* backtrack, drive back, fall back, recede, regress, repel, repulse, retire, retract, retreat, reverse, turn tail, withdraw; CONCEPTS 195,208 —*Ant.* advance, go forward

backbiting [n] *hateful talk* abuse, aspersion, backstabbing*, belittlement, calumniation, calumny, cattiness, defamation, denigration, depreciation, detraction, disparagement, gossip, invective, lie, malice, obloquy, scandal, slander, spite, spitefulness, tale, traducement, vilification, vituperation; CONCEPTS 54,58,63 —*Ant.* encouragement, praise

backbone [n1] *strength of character* courage, determination, firmness, fortitude, grit, guts, hardihood, heart, intestinal fortitude*, mettle, moral fiber, nerve, pluck, resolution, resolve, spunk, stamina, steadfastness, tenacity, toughness, will, willpower; CONCEPT 411 —*Ant.* ineptness, powerlessness, spinelessness, weakness

backbone [n2] *spinal column of vertebrate* base, basis, foundation, spine, support, vertebrae, vertebral column; CONCEPTS 420,442

backbreaking [adj] *strenuous* arduous, exhausting, grueling, hard, laborious, punishing, taxing, toilsome, wearisome; CONCEPT 538

back door [n] *secretive or illicit method* back entrance, back way, indirect access, means of entry, trap door; CONCEPTS 274,631

back down [v] *withdraw from agreement or statement* abandon, accede, admit, back off, back out, back pedal*, backtrack, balk, beg off*, cancel, chicken out*, concede, cop out*, demur, give in, give up, go back on, hold back, recant, recoil, renege, resign, retreat, surrender, take back, withdraw, yield; CONCEPTS 266,697 —*Ant.* go forward

backer [n] *supporter* advocate, ally, angel*, benefactor, champion, endorser, follower, grubstaker, meal ticket*, money, patron, promoter, protagonist, sponsor, staker, underwriter, well-wisher; CONCEPT 359 —*Ant.* antagonist, opponent, opposer

backfire [v] *have an opposite effect* backlash, boomerang, bounce back, disappoint, fail, flop, miscarry, rebound, recoil, ricochet, spring back; CONCEPTS 42,701

background [n] *experience or circumstances* accomplishments, acquirement, actions, atmosphere, attainment, aura, backdrop, breeding, capacity, credentials, cultivation, culture, deeds, education, environment, framework, grounding, history, practice, preparation, qualification, rearing, seasoning, tradition, training, upbringing; CONCEPTS 673,678,706 —*Ant.* foreground

backhanded [adj] *underhanded* ambiguous, double-edged, equivocal, sarcastic, sardonic, two-edged; CONCEPTS 401,544

backing [n] *support* abetment, accompaniment, adherence, advocacy, aegis, aid, assistance, auspices, championing, championship, encouragement, endorsement, funds, grant, help, patronage, reinforcement, sanction, secondment, sponsorship, subsidy; CONCEPTS 110, 332 —*Ant.* disfavor, opposition

backlash [n] *adverse reaction* backfire, boomerang, counteraction, kickback, reaction, recoil, repercussion, resentment, resistance, response, retaliation, retroaction, tangle; CONCEPT 230

backlog [n] *uncompleted work; accumulation* excess, hoard, inventory, quantity, reserve(s), reservoir, resources, stock, stockpile, store, supply; CONCEPTS 432,787

back out [v] *withdraw* avoid, back down, back pedal*, beg off*, blow it off*, cancel, chicken out*, cop out*, get cold feet*, give up, go back on, recant, renege, resign, scratch, shy from, surrender, throw in the towel*, weasel out*, welsh, wiggle out, worm out*; CONCEPTS 50, 88,121,266,697

backpack [n] *sack carried on the back* haversack, knapsack, pack, rucksack; CONCEPT 446

back-pedal [v] *change mind* back out of, change opinion, default on, do an about-face, do a U-turn, fail to honor, go back on, go into reverse, have second thoughts, reconsider, renege, shift one's ground, sing a different song*, take back; CONCEPT 13

backside [n] *rear end* behind, bottom, butt*,

aw
ba

buttocks, derrière, fanny*, posterior, rear, rump*, seat*, tail*, tush*; CONCEPT 392 —Ant. front

backslide [v] *go astray* apostatize, deviate, fall from grace, lapse, leave the straight and narrow*, relapse, revert, sin, slip; CONCEPTS 195, 665,697

backstab [v] *attack indirectly* backbite, betray, double-cross*, play Judas*, sell down the river*, slander, smear; CONCEPTS 54,192

back talk [n] *nasty reply* cheek, guff, lip, mouth, sass; CONCEPTS 46,278

backup [n] *auxiliary* alternate, extra, substitute; CONCEPTS 546,824

backward [adj1] *toward the rear* astern, behind, inverted, rearward, regressive, retrograde; CONCEPT 581 —Ant. ahead, forward, to the front

backward [adj2] *bashful* afraid, averse, demure, diffident, disinclined, hesitant, hesitating, humble, indisposed, late, loath, modest, reluctant, reserved, retiring, shy, sluggish, tardy, timid, uneager, unwilling, wavering; CONCEPT 401 —Ant. aggressive, forward, precocious, unshy

backward [adj3] *slow in growth* arrested, behind, checked, delayed, dense, dull, feeble-minded, imbecile, late, moronic, stupid, subnormal, underdeveloped, underprivileged, undeveloped; CONCEPTS 402,562 —Ant. developing, fast, intelligent, smart

backward [adv] *toward the rear* aback, abaft, about, astern, back, behind, in reverse, inverted, rearward, turned around; CONCEPT 581 —Ant. forward

backwash [n] *repercussion* aftermath, result, wake; CONCEPTS 230,674

backwoods [n/adj] *forests; land distant from settled area* backcountry, boondocks*, frontier, hinterland, interior, isolation, outback, rural area, sticks*, timberland, woodland; CONCEPT 509

backyard [n] *expanse behind house* courtyard, garden, grass, lawn, patio, play area, terrace, yard; CONCEPT 513 —Ant. front yard

bacteria [n] *microorganisms* bacilli, germs, microbes, organisms, pathogens; CONCEPTS 306,393

bad [adj1] *poor quality* abominable, amiss, atrocious, awful, bad news*, beastly, blah*, bottom out, bummer*, careless, cheap, cheesy*, crappy*, cruddy*, crummy*, defective, deficient, diddly*, dissatisfactory, downer*, dreadful, erroneous, fallacious, faulty, garbage, godawful*, grody*, gross*, grungy*, icky*, imperfect, inadequate, incorrect, inferior, junky*, lousy*, not good, off, poor, raunchy*, rough, sad, slipshod, stinking, substandard, synthetic, the pits*, unacceptable, unsatisfactory; CONCEPT 571 —Ant. good, honest, reputable, right, upright, virtuous, worthy

bad [adj2] *harmful* damaging, dangerous, deleterious, detrimental, hurtful, injurious, ruinous, unhealthy; CONCEPTS 537,570 —Ant. advantageous, beneficial, benevolent, good, honest, profitable, virtuous

bad [adj3] *immoral* base, corrupt, criminal, delinquent, evil, iniquitous, mean, reprobate, sinful, vicious, vile, villainous, wicked, wrong; CONCEPT 545 —Ant. good, honest, just, reputable, right, true, virtuous

bad [adj4] *mischievous* disobedient, ill-behaved, misbehaving, naughty, unruly, wrong; CONCEPT 401

bad [adj5] *decayed* moldy, off, putrid, rancid, rotten, sour, spoiled; CONCEPTS 485,613 —Ant. good, ok, undecayed

bad [adj6] *severe* disastrous, distressing, grave, harsh, intense, painful, serious, terrible; CONCEPT 569

bad [adj7] *sick* ailing, diseased, ill, in pain, unwell; CONCEPT 314

bad [adj8] *sorry* apologetic, conscience-stricken, contrite, crestfallen, dejected, depressed, disconsolate, down, downcast, downhearted, guilty, low, regretful, remorseful, sad, upset, woebegone; CONCEPT 403

bad [adj9] *distressing* adverse, disagreeable, discouraged, discouraging, displeasing, distressed, gloomy, grim, melancholy, troubled, troubling, unfavorable, unfortunate, unhappy, unpleasant; CONCEPTS 403,529

bad blood [n] *ill will* acrimony, anger, animosity, antagonism, bad feeling, bitterness, dislike, distrust, enmity, hard feelings, hatred, hostility, malevolence, malice, nastiness, odium, rancor, resentment, unfriendliness, venom; CONCEPT 29

bad form [n] *bad style* barbarism, impropriety, indecorum, inelegance, infelicity, solecism; CONCEPTS 275,633

badge [n] *emblem worn* brand, cordon, device, identification, insignia, mark, marker, medallion, motto, pin, ribbon, scepter, shield, sign, stamp, symbol, token; CONCEPTS 260,284,476

badger [v] *nag, bother* annoy, bait, bug, bully, eat*, give the business*, goad, harass, harry, hassle, heckle, hound, importune, insist on, needle, nudge, pester, plague, ride, tease, torment, work on; CONCEPTS 14,51

bad luck [n] *adversity* blow, hard luck, hard time, mischance, misfortune, reverse, setback; CONCEPTS 388,674,679

badly [adv1] *inadequately* abominably, awkwardly, blunderingly, carelessly, clumsily, crudely, defectively, erroneously, faultily, feebly, haphazardly, imperfectly, incompetently, ineffectively, ineptly, maladroitly, negligently, poorly, shoddily, stupidly, unfavorably, unfortunately, unsatisfactorily, unskillfully, unsuccessfully, weakly, wrong, wrongly; CONCEPT 571 —Ant. adequately

badly [adv2] *immorally* criminally, evilly, improperly, naughtily, shamefully, unethically, wickedly; CONCEPT 545 —Ant. morally

badly [adv3] *very much; desperately* acutely, deeply, exceedingly, extremely, gravely, greatly, hard, intensely, painfully, roughly, seriously, severely; CONCEPT 569 —Ant. calmly, little, mildly

bad manners [n] *improper behavior* boorishness, discourtesy, disrespect, impoliteness, inconsideration, unmannerliness; CONCEPTS 29,633

bad-mouth [v] *to denigrate* belittle, criticize, cut down to size*, dis*, disparage, dump on*, find fault, knock*, malign, mudsling*, pan, pooh pooh*, put down*, rap, rip, roast*, run down*, slam, slander, take a dig at*, take down a peg*, tear down*, tear to pieces*; CONCEPTS 52,54

bad news [*n*] *trouble* bind, bother, concern, danger, deep trouble, difficulty, dilemma, dire straits, disappointment, distress, grief, headache*, hindrance, hot water*, inconvenience, mess, misfortune, nuisance, pain, predicament, problem, struggle, torment, woe; CONCEPTS 532,674,675, 690,728

bad scene [*n*] *misfortunate event* bad trip*, bummer*, bum trip*, depressing experience, disaster, downer*, drag*, raw deal, rotten hand, unhappy situation, unpleasant experience, unpleasant situation; CONCEPTS 674,675

bad time [*n*] *agony* going-over, grief, grilling, hard time, third degree, torture; CONCEPTS 410,728

bad trip [*n*] *unpleasant experience* bad scene, bummer*, bum trip*, disaster, downer*, drag*, freak-out*, unhappy situation, unpleasant drug experience, unpleasant situation; CONCEPTS 674,675

baffle [*v1*] *perplex* addle, amaze, astound, befuddle, bewilder, buffalo*, confound, confuse, daze, disconcert, dumbfound, elude, embarrass, faze, floor*, get, mix up, muddle, mystify, nonplus, puzzle, rattle, stick*, stump*, stun, throw; CONCEPTS 7,19,42 —*Ant.* clear up, enlighten, explain

baffle [*v2*] *hinder* beat, block, check, circumvent, dash, defeat, disappoint, foil, frustrate, impede, obstruct, prevent, ruin, thwart, upset; CONCEPT 121 —*Ant.* abet, aid, assist, encourage, help, relieve, support

baffling [*adj*] *puzzling* abstruse, bewildering, beyond one, confusing, difficult to understand, enigmatic, hard to understand, incomprehensible, mystifying, over one's head, perplexing, unclear, unfathomable; CONCEPT 403 —*Ant.* clear, comprehensible

bag [*n1*] *container for one's possesions* attaché, backpack, briefcase, carryall, carry-on, case, duffel, gear, handbag, haversack, holdall, kit, knapsack, pack, packet, pocket, pocketbook, poke, pouch, purse, rucksack, sac, sack, saddlebag, satchel, suitcase, tote; CONCEPTS 339,450

bag [*n2*] *special interest* expertise, favorite activity, hobby, preference, speciality, thing*; CONCEPTS 32,529

bag [*v1*] *catch* acquire, apprehend, capture, collar, gain, get, hook, kill, land, nab, nail, net, seize, shoot, take, trap; CONCEPT 90 —*Ant.* lose

bag [*v2*] *droop* balloon, billow, bulge, flap, flop, hang, lop, sag, swell; CONCEPTS 754,757

baggage [*n*] *gear* accoutrements, bags, belongings, carry-on, effects, equipment, fortnighter, gear, impedimenta, luggage, overnighter*, paraphernalia, parcels, slough, suitcases, things, tote, tote bag, trappings, two-suiter; CONCEPT 494

baggy [*adj*] *drooping* billowing, bulging, droopy, flabby, floppy, ill-fitting, loose, oversize, roomy, sagging, slack, unshapely; CONCEPTS 486,490 —*Ant.* firm, fitting, tight

bail [*n*] *money for assurance* bond, collateral, guarantee, pawn, pledge, recognizance, security, surety, warrant, warranty; CONCEPTS 318,332

bail out [*v1*] *help* aid, deliver, release, relieve, rescue, spring; CONCEPT 110 —*Ant.* ignore, refuse

bail out [*v2*] *escape* flee, quit, retreat, withdraw; CONCEPT 102 —*Ant.* stay

bait [*n*] *something for luring* allurement, attraction, bribe, come-on*, drag, enticement, inducement, lure, seducement, shill, snare, temptation, trap; CONCEPT 709

bait [*v1*] *lure* allure, attract, bedevil, beguile, draw, entice, fascinate, lead on, seduce, tempt; CONCEPTS 9,14

bait [*v2*] *needle* anger, annoy, badger, bother, gall, harass, heckle, hound, irk, irritate, nag, persecute, provoke, tease, torment; CONCEPTS 7,19

bake [*v*] *cook in oven* heat, melt, scorch, simmer, stew, warm; CONCEPT 170

baked [*adj*] *cooked in oven* dried, heated, melted, scorched, simmered, stewed, warmed; CONCEPT 462

baker [*n*] *person who cooks baked goods* chef, cook, dough puncher*, pastry maker; CONCEPT 348

bakery [*n*] *cooking business where baked goods are produced* bake shop, confectionery, pastry shop, pâtisserie; CONCEPTS 325,439,449

balance [*n1*] *equilibrium* antithesis, correspondence, counterbalance, equity, equivalence, evenness, even-steven*, hang, harmony, parity, proportion, stasis, symmetry, tension; CONCEPTS 664,667 —*Ant.* disproportion, imbalance, instability

balance [*n2*] *composure* equanimity, poise, self-control, self-possession, stability, steadfastness; CONCEPT 633 —*Ant.* imbalance, noncomposure

balance [*n3*] *money remaining in account* difference, dividend, excess, profit, remainder, residue, rest, surplus; CONCEPT 332

balance [*v1*] *make equal; cause to have equilibrium* accord, adjust, attune, cancel, collate, come out, come out even, compensate, correspond, counteract, counterbalance, equalize, equate, even, harmonize, level, make up for, match, neutralize, nullify, offset, oppose, pair off, parallel, poise, readjust, redeem, set, square, stabilize, steady, tie, weigh; CONCEPTS 197,697 —*Ant.* disproportion, overbalance, unbalance

balance [*v2*] *compare* assess, consider, deliberate, estimate, evaluate, weigh; CONCEPT 17 —*Ant.* unbalance

balance [*v3*] *make equal numerically* adjust, audit, calculate, compute, count, enumerate, equate, estimate, figure, settle, square, sum up, tally, total; CONCEPT 764 —*Ant.* unbalance

balanced [*adj1*] *equalized* counterbalanced, equitable, equivalent, evened, fair, just, offset, proportional, stabilized, symmetrical, uniform; CONCEPT 566 —*Ant.* disproportioned, imbalanced, unequal, unsymmetrical

balanced [*adj2*] *settled financially* certified, confirmed, validated; CONCEPT 334 —*Ant.* unbalanced

balance sheet [*n*] *financial statement including gains and losses for a period* account, annual report, assets and liabilities, budget, ledger, report; CONCEPTS 271,332

balcony [*n*] *porch or structure above the ground* balustrade, box*, catwalk, gallery, mezzanine, piazza, platform, porch, portico, stoop, terrace, veranda; CONCEPT 440

bald [*adj1*] *having no covering* baldheaded, bare, barren, depilated, exposed, glabrous, hairless, head*, naked, shaven, skin head*, smooth, stark, uncovered; CONCEPT 485 —*Ant.* hairy, hirsute

bald [*adj2*] *simple, unadorned* austere, bare, blunt, direct, downright, forthright, outright, plain, severe, straight, straightforward, unembellished; CONCEPTS 485,589 —*Ant.* adorned, decorated

bale [*n*] *bunch* bundle, package, parcel; CONCEPT 432

baleful [*adj*] *menacing* calamitous, deadly, dire, evil, foreboding, harmful, hurtful, injurious, malevolent, malignant, noxious, ominous, pernicious, ruinous, sinister, threatening, venomous, vindictive, woeful; CONCEPTS 537,570 —*Ant.* advantageous, auspicious, favorable, good, helping, promising

balk [*v1*] *stop short* cramp, crimp, demur, desist, dodge, evade, flinch, hesitate, recoil, refuse, resist, shirk, shrink from, shy, turn down, upset apple cart*; CONCEPTS 119,121,188

balk [*v2*] *thwart* baffle, bar, beat, check, circumvent, counteract, cramp, cramp one's style*, dash, defeat, disappoint, disconcert, foil, forestall, frustrate, hinder, obstruct, prevent, ruin, stall, stop, throw a curve*, throw monkey wrench in*, upset the apple cart*; CONCEPT 121 —*Ant.* aid, help, make easier

balky [*adj*] *uncooperative* averse, contrary, hesitant, immovable, indisposed, inflexible, intractable, loath, negative, negativistic, obstinate, ornery, perverse, reluctant, stubborn, unbending, unmanageable, unpredictable, unruly; CONCEPT 401 —*Ant.* cooperative

ball [*n1*] *dance party* hoedown, hoodang, hop, jump, mingle, prom, promenade, reception, shindig; CONCEPT 386

ball [*n2*] *globe, sphere* apple, balloon, drop, globule, orb, pellet, pill, round, spheroid; CONCEPT 436

ballad [*n*] *narrative song* carol, chant, ditty, serenade; CONCEPT 595

ballast [*n*] *something giving balance* balance, brace, bracket, counterbalance, counterweight, equilibrium, sandbag, stability, stabilizer, support, weight; CONCEPT 712

ballet [*n*] *graceful, expressive dancing* choreography, dance, toe dancing; CONCEPT 263

ballet dancer [*n*] *person who performs graceful dancing* company, coryphee, dancer, danseur, danseuse, figurant, figurante, hoofer*, prima ballerina; CONCEPT 352

balloon [*n*] *inflated material or vehicle* airship, bladder, blimp, dirigible, zeppelin; CONCEPTS 293,504

balloon [*v*] *billow out; bloat* belly, blow up, bulge, dilate, distend, enlarge, expand, inflate, puff out, swell; CONCEPTS 208,756

ballot [*n1*] *voting; recording of vote* election, franchise, plebiscite, poll, polling, referendum, slate, tally, ticket; CONCEPTS 300,301

ballot [*n2*] *candidates from political party* choice, lineup, slate, ticket; CONCEPT 301

balm [*n1*] *oily substance* analgesic, application, balsam, cerate, compound, cream, demulcent, dressing, embrocation, emollient, formula, lotion, medicine, ointment, potion, poultice, preparation, prescription, salve, soother, soothing agent, unction, unguent; CONCEPTS 307,466

balm [*n2*] *something soothing* alleviation, anodyne, assuagement, comfort, consolation, curative, cure, easement, mitigation, palliative, refreshment, relief, remedy, restorative, solace, soother; CONCEPTS 337,529

balmy [*adj1*] *comfortable with respect to weather* mild, moderate, moist, pleasant, refreshing, summerlike, summery, temperate, tropical; CONCEPTS 603,605 —*Ant.* cool, inclement, wintery

balmy [*adj2*] *insane* absurd, bugged out*, cracked*, crazed, crazy, daft, deranged, dotty*, foolish, harebrained*, idiotic, loony, mentally incompetent, moronic, nuts*, nutty*, odd, potty*, preposterous, silly, stupid, wacky; CONCEPT 403 —*Ant.* balanced, rational, sane, sensible

bamboozle [*v*] *fool; cheat* baffle, befuddle, bilk, con, confound, confuse, deceive, defraud, delude, dupe, flimflam*, hoax, hoodwink*, hornswoggle*, mystify, perplex, puzzle, stump, swindle, trick; CONCEPT 59 —*Ant.* be honest

ban [*n*] *official forbiddance* a thou-shalt-not*, boycott, censorship, don't*, embargo, injunction, interdiction, limitation, no-no*, off limits*, out of bounds*, prohibition, proscription, refusal, restriction, stoppage, suppression, taboo; CONCEPTS 50,88,121,688 —*Ant.* allowance, permission

ban [*v*] *officially forbid* banish, bar, blackball*, close down, close up, curse, declare illegal, disallow, enjoin, exclude, halt, ice out*, illegalize, inhibit, interdict, outlaw, pass by, pass up, prevent, prohibit, proscribe, restrict, shut out; suppress; CONCEPTS 50,88,121 —*Ant.* allow, permit

banal [*adj*] *commonplace* blah*, bland, bromidic, clichéd, common, conventional, cornball*, cornfed*, corny, dull as dishwater*, dumb, everyday, flat, hackneyed, ho hum*, hokey*, humdrum*, insipid, mundane, noplace, nothing, nowhere, old hat*, ordinary, pabulum*, pedestrian, platitudinous, square, stale, stereotyped, stock, stupid, tired, tripe, trite, unimaginative, unoriginal, vapid, watery, wishy-washy*, zero*; CONCEPT 530 —*Ant.* fresh, new, original

banality [*n*] *common saying* adage, boiler*, buzzword, chestnut*, cliché, corn*, dullsville*, familiar tune*, high camp*, hokum*, old chestnut*, old saw*, plate*, platitude, prosaicism, prosaism, saw*, trite phrase, trivia, triviality, truism; CONCEPT 275 —*Ant.* coinage, nuance, original saying

band [*n1*] *something which encircles* bandage, bandeau, belt, binding, bond, braid, cable, chain, circle, circuit, copula, cord, fillet, harness, hoop, ligature, line, link, manacle, ribbon, ring, rope, sash, scarf, shackle, snood, stay, strap, string, strip, tape, tie, truss; CONCEPTS 470,751

band [*n2*] *group of people with same interest* assembly, association, bevy, body, bunch, clique, club, cluster, collection, company, corps, coterie, covey, crew, gang, gathering, horde, menagerie, outfit, party, society, troop, troupe; CONCEPTS 387,391,417

band [*n3*] *musical group* combo, ensemble,

orchestra, philharmonic, symphony, troupe; CONCEPT *294*

band [v] *group or join group* affiliate, ally, amalgamate, belt, coadjute, combine, conjoin, consolidate, federate, gather, league, merge, team, unite; CONCEPTS *113,114*

bandage [n] *covering for wound* cast, compress, dressing, gauze, plaster; CONCEPT *311*

bandage [v] *cover a wound* bind, dress, swathe, truss, wrap; CONCEPT *310*

bandanna [n] *colorful scarf* handkerchief, kerchief, neckerchief, silk; CONCEPT *450*

bandit [n] *thief* brigand, criminal, crook, desperado, forager, gangster, gunperson, highwayperson, hijacker, holdup person, hooligan, marauder, mobster, outlaw, pillager, pirate, plunderer, racketeer, raider, ravager, robber, villain; CONCEPT *412* —*Ant.* law, police

bandwidth [n] *frequency range* high frequency, low frequency, radio band, radio band-width, transmission capacity; CONCEPT *279*

bane [n] *cause of misery* affliction, bête noire, blight, burden, calamity, curse, despair, destruction, disaster, downfall, fatal attraction, misery, nuisance, pest, plague, poison, ruin, ruination, scourge, torment, trial, trouble, undoing, venom, woe; CONCEPTS *529,674* —*Ant.* advantage, blessing, fortune, good luck

baneful [adj] *ruinous, injurious* baleful, calamitous, deadly, deleterious, destructive, disastrous, evil, fatal, harmful, hurtful, malefic, noxious, pernicious, pestilent, pestilential, poisonous, venomous, wicked; CONCEPTS *537,570* —*Ant.* advantageous, beneficial, beneficent, fortunate, helpful, lucky

bang [adv] *suddenly, with force* abruptly, hard, headlong, head on, noisily, precisely, smack, straight, suddenly; CONCEPT *540* —*Ant.* slowly

bang [n1] *explosive noise* blast, boom, burst, clang, clap, clash, crack, detonation, discharge, howl, peal, pop, report, roar, roll, rumble, salvo, shot, slam, smash, sound, thud, thump, thunder, wham; CONCEPT *595* —*Ant.* whimper

bang [n2] *loud hit or knock* bash, bat, belt, blow, box, bump, collide, crack, cuff, punch, slam, smack, smash, sock, stroke, wallop, whack, whop; CONCEPT *189* —*Ant.* tap

bang [n3] *thrilling situation* enjoyment, excitement, kick*, pleasant feeling, smash, wallop, wow*; CONCEPT *230*

bang [v1] *hit or knock loudly* boom, burst, clang, clatter, crash, detonate, drum, echo, explode, make noise, peal, rattle, resound, sound, thump, thunder; CONCEPTS *65,189* —*Ant.* tap

bang [v2] *moving by hitting hard* bash, beat, bump, clatter, collide, crash, hammer, hit, knock, pound, pummel, rap, slam, smash, strike, thump, whack; CONCEPT *189*

banish [v] *expel from place or situation* ban, cast out, deport, discard, discharge, dislodge, dismiss, dispel, drive away, eject, eliminate, eradicate, evict, exclude, excommunicate, exile, expatriate, expulse, extradict, get rid of, isolate, ostracize, oust, outlaw, proscribe, release, remove, rusticate, sequester, shake off, shut out, transport; CONCEPTS *121,217* —*Ant.* allow, keep, welcome

banister [n] *railing of stairs* baluster, balustrade, handrail, rail, support; CONCEPT *443*

bank [n1] *financial institution* coffer, counting-house, credit union, depository, exchequer, fund, hoard, investment firm, repository, reserve, reservoir, safe, savings, stock, stockpile, store, storehouse, thrift, treasury, trust company, vault; CONCEPTS *333,339,439*

bank [n2] *ground bounding waters* beach, cay, cliff, coast, edge, embankment, lakefront, lakeshore, lakeside, ledge, levee, oceanfront, reef, riverfront, riverside, seabank, seaboard, seafront, shore, strand, streamside, waterfront; CONCEPT *509*

bank [n3] *row or tier of objects* array, dashboard, group, line, rank, row, sequence, series, succession; CONCEPT *464*

bank [v1] *collect money or advantage* amass, deposit, heap, hill, hoard, invest, lay aside, lay away, mass, mound, pile, put by, salt away, save, sock away, speculate, squirrel, stash; CONCEPTS *109,330* —*Ant.* disburse, spend

bank [v2] *lean or tilt* bend, camber, cant, incline, pitch, slant, slope; CONCEPTS *148,213* —*Ant.* straighten

banker [n] *professional in financial institution* broker, capitalist, croupier, dealer, financier, house, investor, manager, money-lender, officer, teller, treasurer, usurer; CONCEPTS *347,348,353*

bank on [v] *depend upon* assume, believe in, be sure about, bet on, build on, count on, gamble on, lean on, look to, reckon on, rely on, stake, trust, venture, wager; CONCEPT *12*

bankrupt [adj] *unable to pay debts* broke, depleted, destitute, exhausted, failed, impoverished, in Chapter 11*, insolvent, lacking, lost, out of business, ruined, spent, tapped out; CONCEPT *334* —*Ant.* rich, solvent, wealthy

bankruptcy [n] *inability to pay debts* Chapter 11*, defalcation, default, destituteness, destitution, disaster, exhaustion, failure, indebtedness, indigence, insolvency, lack, liquidation, loss, nonpayment, overdraft, pauperism, privation, repudiation, ruin, ruination; CONCEPT *335* —*Ant.* richness, solvency, wealth

banner [adj] *successful* exceptional, foremost, leading, outstanding, red-letter; CONCEPT *528*

banner [n1] *flag, usually with message* banderole, burgee, colors, emblem, ensign, gonfalon, heading, headline, pennant, pennon, standard, streamer; CONCEPTS *270,277,278*

banner [n2] *ad on Web/Internet page* advertisement, burst page, headline, streamer; CONCEPTS *270,277,278,280*

banquet [n] *formal dinner, usually ceremonial* feast, festivity, fete, meal, reception, regale, repast, spread, treat; CONCEPTS *377,459*

bantam [adj] *small* diminutive, little, petite, tiny; CONCEPTS *491,773* —*Ant.* big, huge, large

banter [n] *teasing* badinage, chaff, chaffing, chitchat, derision, dissing*, exchange, fun, gossip, jeering, jesting, joking, joshing, kidding, mockery, persiflage, play, raillery, repartee, ribbing, ridicule, small talk; CONCEPTS *59,278*

banter [v] *tease* chaff, deride, fool, fun, jeer, jest, jive*, joke, josh, kid, make fun of, mock, rag*, razz*, rib, ridicule, satirize, taunt; CONCEPTS *59,273*

baptism [n] *church rite; initiation* ablution, baptismal, christening, debut, dedication, dunking, immersion, introduction, launching, lustration, purgation, purge, purification, rite of passage, ritual, sanctification, sprinkling; CONCEPTS 367,377

baptize [v] *initiate in church rite* admit, asperse, besprinkle, call, christen, cleanse, denominate, dip, dub, entitle, immerse, name, purify, regenerate, sprinkle, term, title; CONCEPT 367

bar [n1] *rod; straight length of material* batten, billet, boom, crossbar, crosspiece, ingot, lever, paling, pig, pole, rail, rib, rule, shaft, slab, spar, spoke, stake, stick, streak, strip, stripe, stroke; CONCEPTS 470,471

bar [n2] *barrier; blockage* barricade, blank wall, block, clog, deterrent, encumbrance, fence, hindrance, hurdle, impediment, obstacle, obstruction, pale, rail, railing, restraint, road block, snag, stop, stumbling block, traverse, wall; CONCEPTS 470,652,680 —*Ant.* advantage, aid, help

bar [n3] *establishment serving alcohol* alehouse, barroom, beer garden, bistro, canteen, cocktail lounge, drinkery, inn, lounge, pub, public house, rathskeller, saloon, tap, taproom, tavern, watering hole*; CONCEPTS 325,439

bar [n4] *legal system* attorneys, barristers, bench, counsel, counselors, court, courtroom, dock, judgment, judiciary, jurists, law, law court, law practice, lawyers, legal profession, solicitors, tribunal; CONCEPTS 318,381

bar [v1] *secure, usually with a length of material* barricade, block, blockade, bolt, caulk, clog, close, dam, deadbolt, dike, fasten, fence, jam, latch, lock, plug, seal, secure, trammel, wall; CONCEPTS 121,130 —*Ant.* loosen, open, unfasten

bar [v2] *prohibit* ban, boycott, circumvent, condemn, debar, deny, disallow, discountenance, discourage, eliminate, enjoin, except, exclude, exile, forbid, freeze out, frustrate, hinder, interdict, interfere, keep out, limit, obstruct, ostracize, outlaw, override, preclude, prevent, refuse, reject, restrain, rule out, segregate, shut out, stop, suspend; CONCEPTS 50,61,88 —*Ant.* advocate, allow, open, permit

barb [n1] *point* arrow, bristle, dart, prickle, prong, quill, shaft, spike, spur, thistle, thorn; CONCEPTS 434,836

barb [n2] *pointed comment* affront, criticism, cut, dig, gibe, insult, rebuff, sarcasm, scoff, sneer; CONCEPTS 52,54 —*Ant.* kindness, praise

barbarian [adj] *crude, savage* barbaric, barbarous, boorish, brutal, coarse, cruel, inhuman, lowbrow, merciless, philistine, primitive, rough, rude, uncivil, uncivilized, uncouth, uncultivated, uncultured, unsophisticated, untamed, vicious, vulgar, wild; CONCEPT 401 —*Ant.* civilized, cultured, educated, humane, kind, nice, polite, refined, sophisticated

barbarian [n] *crude, savage person* beast, bigot, boor, brute, cannibal, clod, hooligan, hun, ignoramus, lout, monster, philistine, rascal, ruffian, troglodyte, vandal; CONCEPT 412 —*Ant.* sophisticated

barbaric [adj] *crude, savage* barbarian, barbarous, boorish, brutal, coarse, cruel, fierce, graceless, inhuman, lowbrow, primitive, rough, rude, tasteless, uncivilized, uncouth, vulgar, wild; CONCEPT 401

barbarism [n] *crudity, savagery, especially in speech* atrocity, barbarity, brutality, catachresis, coarseness, corruption, cruelty, impropriety,

inhumanity, localism, malapropism, misusage, misuse, primitive culture, provincialism, solecism, uncivilizedness, vernacularism, vernacularity, vulgarism; CONCEPTS 275,633 —*Ant.* kindness, praise

barbarity [n] *crudity, savagery* boorishness, brutality, crudeness, cruelty, inhumanity, ruthlessness, savageness, viciousness, vulgarity; CONCEPT 633 —*Ant.* kindness

barbarous [adj] *crude, savage* atrocious, barbarian, barbaric, brutal, brutish, coarse, cruel, ferocious, heartless, ignorant, inhuman, inhumane, monstrous, primitive, rough, rude, ruthless, sadistic, truculent, uncivil, uncivilized, uncouth, uncultured, unsophisticated, vicious, vulgar, wicked, wild, wolfish; CONCEPT 401 —*Ant.* civilized, cultured, educated, kind, nice, polite, refined, sophisticated

barbecue [n1] *meal cooked on grill* bake, clam bake, cookout, party, picnic, wienie roast; CONCEPT 459

barbecue [n2] *grill for cookout* broiler, charcoal grill, fireplace, gas grill, griddle, pit of coals, roaster, spit; CONCEPT 493

barbecue [v] *cook outside, usually on a grill* broil, charcoal, fry, grill, rotisserie, sear; CONCEPT 170

barber [n] *hair cutter* beautician, coiffeur, coiffeuse, cosmetologist, hairdresser, hair stylist, shaver, tonsorial artist; CONCEPT 348

bare [adj1] *without clothing* bald, bareskinned, denuded, disrobed, divested, exposed, in one's birthday suit*, naked, nude, peeled, shorn, stripped, unclad, unclothed, uncovered, undressed, unrobed; CONCEPT 485 —*Ant.* clothed, robed

bare [adj2] *without covering or content* arid, barren, blank, bleak, clear, desert, desolate, empty, lacking, mean, open, poor, scanty, scarce, stark, unfurnished, vacant, vacuous, void, wanting; CONCEPT 490 —*Ant.* covered, full

bare [adj3] *simple, unadorned* austere, bald, basic, blunt, chaste, cold, essential, hard, literal, meager, mere, modest, scant, severe, sheer, simple, spare, stark, unembellished, unornamented; CONCEPT 562 —*Ant.* adorned, decorated

bare [v] *reveal* disclose, divulge, exhibit, expose, publish, show, uncover, unroll, unveil; CONCEPTS 60,138 —*Ant.* cloak, hide, secret

barefaced [adj] *shameless; open* apparent, arrant, audacious, blatant, blunt, bold, brash, brassy, brazen, candid, clear, flagrant, frank, glaring, immodest, impudent, insolent, manifest, naked, obvious, palpable, temerarious, transparent, unabashed, unconcealed; CONCEPT 401 —*Ant.* careful, quiet, shamed

barefoot [adj] *wearing no shoes* barefooted, discalceate, discalced, shoeless, unshod; CONCEPT 406 —*Ant.* shod

barely [adj] *not quite* almost, hardly, just, only just, scantily, scarcely; CONCEPT 772

bareness [n] *state of being unclothed* dishabille, nakedness, nudity, starkness, unadornment, undress; CONCEPT 453 —*Ant.* clothed

bargain [n1] *agreement* arrangement, bond, business, compact, contract, convention, covenant, deal, engagement, negotiation, pact, pledge, promise, stipulation, transaction, treaty, understanding; CONCEPT 684

bargain [n2] *something bought at cheap price* budget price, buy, closeout, deal, discount, giveaway, good buy, good deal, good value, low price, markdown, nominal price, reduction, steal, value; CONCEPTS *332,338* —*Ant.* rip-off

bargain [v] *negotiate terms of sale or agreement* agree, arrange, barter, buy, compromise, confer, contract, covenant, deal, dicker, do business, haggle, make terms, palter, promise, sell, stipulate, trade, traffic, transact; CONCEPTS *56,330*

bargain for [v] *expect* aim for, anticipate, contemplate, count on, foresee, imagine, look for, plan on, reckon on; CONCEPT *26*

barge [n] *large work boat* ark, canal boat, dory, flatboat, freight ship, lighter, raft, scow; CONCEPT *506*

barge in/barge into [v] *charge* break in, burst in, collide, infringe, interrupt, intrude, muscle in, push, shove, stumble; CONCEPTS *150,208* —*Ant.* wait

bark [n1] *plant covering* case, casing, coat, cortex, crust, husk, peeling, rind, shell, skin; CONCEPT *428*

bark [n2] *animal yelp* bay, growl, grunt, howl, roar, snarl, woof, yap, yip; CONCEPT *64*

bark [v1] *yelp* arf, bay, cry, gnarl, growl, howl, snap, snarl, woof, yap, yip; CONCEPT *64*

bark [v2] *shout* bawl, bellow, clamor, cry, growl, grumble, mutter, roar, snap, snarl, yell; CONCEPT *77*

barn [n] *animal shelter* farm building, outbuilding, shed; CONCEPTS *439,517*

baroque [adj] *decorative, especially architecture* bizarre, convoluted, elaborate, embellished, extravagant, flamboyant, florid, gilt, grotesque, ornamented, ornate, overdecorated, rich, rococo; CONCEPTS *562,589* —*Ant.* plain, unadorned, undecorated

barracks [n] *shelter for military* billet, bivouac, camp, cantonment, dormitory, encampment, enclosure, garrison, headquarters, hut, prefab, quarters, Quonset hut, tent; CONCEPTS *321,516*

barrage [n1] *weapon fire* battery, blast, bombardment, broadside, cannonade, crossfire, curtain of fire, discharge, enfilade, fire, fusillade, gunfire, hail, salvo, shelling, shower, storm, volley; CONCEPT *320*

barrage [n2] *profusion of something* assault, attack, blast, bombardment, burst, deluge, hail, mass, onslaught, plethora, rain, shower, storm, stream, surge, torrent; CONCEPT *787*

barrel [n] *cylindrical container* butt, cask, cylinder, drum, firkin, hogshead, keg, pipe, receptacle, tub, tun, vat, vessel; CONCEPT *494*

barren [adj1] *unable to support growth* arid, depleted, desert, desolate, dry, effete, empty, fallow, fruitless, impotent, impoverished, infecund, infertile, parched, sterile, unbearing, uncultivable, unfertile, unfruitful, unproductive, waste; CONCEPTS *485,527* —*Ant.* developing, fecund, fertile, filled, full, growing, productive, useful

barren [adj2] *unprofitable* dull, flat, fruitless, futile, lackluster, profitless, stale, uninspiring, unproductive, unrewarding, useless, vain, vapid; CONCEPT *560* —*Ant.* developing, growing, productive, profitable

barricade [n] *blocking object* bar, barrier, blank wall, block, blockade, bulwark, fence, obstruction, palisade, rampart, roadblock, stockade, stop, wall; CONCEPT *470* —*Ant.* opening

barricade [v] *block, usually to protect* bar, blockade, defend, fortify, obstruct, shut in; CONCEPTS *130,201* —*Ant.* allow, open

barrier [n1] *obstruction* bar, barricade, blank wall, blockade, bound, boundary, confines, curtain, ditch, enclosure, fence, fortification, gully, hurdle, impediment, limit, moat, obstacle, pale, palisade, railing, rampart, roadblock, stop, trench, wall; CONCEPTS *435,470,513* —*Ant.* opening

barrier [n2] *obstruction to goal* bar, check, difficulty, drawback, encumbrance, handicap, hindrance, hurdle, impediment, limitation, obstacle, pale, preventive, restraint, restriction, stumbling block; CONCEPT *532* —*Ant.* opening

barring [adj] *except for* apart from, aside from, bar, but for, discounting, excepting, excluding, other than, outside of, save for, short of, with the exception of; CONCEPT *25*

barter [v] *trade goods or services* bargain, exchange, haggle, swap, trade, traffic, truck; CONCEPT *104*

base [adj] *vulgar, low* abject, abominable, cheap, coarse, common, contemptible, corrupt, depraved, despicable, disgraceful, dishonorable, disreputable, foul, grovelling, humble, ignoble, immoral, indelicate, loathsome, lowly, mean, menial, offensive, paltry, pitiful, plebeian, poor, scandalous, servile, shameful, shoddy, sleazy, sordid, sorry, squalid, trashy, ugly, unworthy, vile, worthless, wretched; CONCEPTS *542,570* —*Ant.* good, honest, moral, noble

base [n1] *foundation* basement, basis, bed, bedrock, bottom, foot, footing, ground, groundwork, infrastructure, pedestal, rest, root, seat, seating, stand, substratum, substructure, support, underpinning; CONCEPT *442* —*Ant.* top

base [n2] *fundamental part* authority, backbone, basis, chief constituent, core, essence, essential, evidence, foundation, fundamental, groundwork, heart, important part, infrastructure, key, origin, primary element, principal, principle, root, source, underpinning; CONCEPT *826*

base [n3] *headquarters* camp, center, depot, dock, field, garrison, hangar, harbor, home, port, post, settlement, site, starting point, station, strip, terminal; CONCEPTS *435,449* —*Ant.* annex, branch

base [v] *build plan or opinion on* construct, depend, derive, establish, found, ground, hinge, locate, plant, predicate, prop, rest, set up, station, stay; CONCEPT *36*

baseless [adj] *without substantiation* bottomless, flimsy, foundationless, gratuitous, groundless, reasonless, unconfirmed, uncorroborated, unfounded, ungrounded, unjustifiable, unjustified, unsubstantiated, unsupported, untenable, unwarranted; CONCEPT *582* —*Ant.* based

basement [n] *room on lower floor of building* bottom, cellar, crypt, excavation, furnace room, storage, substructure, subterranean room, underbuilding, understructure, vault; CONCEPT *440* —*Ant.* attic

bash [n] *party* celebration, spree, wing-ding*; CONCEPT *383*

bash [v] *hit* clobber*, pop*, punch, slam, slug, smash, strike, whack; CONCEPTS *189,200*

bashful [adj] shy abashed, backward, blushful, blushing, chary, confused, constrained, coy, demure, diffident, embarrassed, humble, modest, nervous, overmodest, recoiling, reserved, reticent, retiring, self-conscious, self-effacing, shamefaced, sheepish, shrinking, silent, timid, timorous, unassertive; CONCEPT 404 —*Ant.* confident, unabashed, unshy

bashing [n] abuse against a group or individual based on identity or ideological beliefs assault, attack, beating, beating up, bias crime, censure, charge, condemnation, criticism, denigration, harassment, hate crime, hounding, jumping, offensive, persecution, strike, torment; CONCEPT 86

basic [adj] elementary, fundamental basal, capital, central, chief, elemental, essential, indispensable, inherent, intrinsic, key, main, necessary, primary, primitive, principal, radical, substratal, underlying, vital; CONCEPT 568 —*Ant.* additional, extra, inessential, nonessential, outside, peripheral, secondary

basically [adv] fundamentally at heart, at the bottom, essentially, firstly, in essence, inherently, in substance, intrinsically, mostly, primarily, radically; CONCEPT 568 —*Ant.* additionally, extra, inessentially

basin [n] container or area where water is held bay, bowl, concavity, depression, dip, ewer, gulf, hole, hollow, lagoon, pan, pool, pot, sag, sink, sinkage, sinkhole, tub, valley, vessel, watershed; CONCEPTS 494,509,514

basis [n1] physical foundation base, bed, bottom, foot, footing, ground, groundwork, rest, resting place, seat, substructure, support; CONCEPT 442

basis [n2] foundation for belief, action antecedent, assumption, authority, axiom, backbone, background, backing, base, bedrock, cause, center, chief ingredient, core, crux, data, dictum, essence, essential, evidence, explanation, footing, fundamental, hard fact, heart, infrastructure, justification, keynote, keystone, law, nexus, nucleus, postulate, premise, presumption, presupposition, principal element, principle, proof, reason, root, rudiment, sanction, security, source, substratum, support, theorem, theory, underpinning, warrant; CONCEPTS 661,688,689

bask [v1] lie in sunlight laze, loll, lounge, relax, sun, sunbathe, swim in, toast oneself*, warm oneself; CONCEPTS 162,210 —*Ant.* cover, hide

bask [v2] lie in glory delight in, derive pleasure, enjoy, indulge, luxuriate, relish, revel, rollick, savor, take comfort, take pleasure, wallow, welter; CONCEPT 32

basket [n] woven container bassinet, bin, box, bushel, cradle, crate, creel, hamper, nacelle, pannier; CONCEPT 494

basketball [n] team sport ball, B-ball*, brownball*, hoops*; CONCEPT 363

bastard [adj] illegitimate adulterated, baseborn, counterfeit, fake, false, imperfect, impure, inferior, irregular, misbegotten, misborn, mixed, mongrel, natural, phony, sham, spurious, suppositious, ungenuine; CONCEPT 549 —*Ant.* legitimate

bastardize [v] debase adulterate, bestialize, brutalize, corrupt, debauch, declare illegitimate, degrade, demoralize, deprave, pervert, vitiate, warp; CONCEPT 44 —*Ant.* appreciate, praise, value

baste [v1] moisten during cooking brush with liquid, drip, grease, lard, season; CONCEPT 170

baste [v2] sew temporarily catch, fasten, stitch, tack; CONCEPT 218

baste [v3] pummel, thrash batter, beat, berate, blister, clobber, club, drub, lambaste, lash, maul, pelt, revile, scold, trounce, wallop, whip, whomp; CONCEPTS 52,189

bastion [n] support; fortified place breastwork, bulwark, citadel, defense, fortification, fortress, mainstay, parapet, prop, protection, rock, stronghold, support, tower of strength; CONCEPT 712 —*Ant.* weakness, weak spot

bat [n/v] a hit with a solid object bang, belt, blow, bop, crack, knock, rap, slam, smack, sock, strike, swat, thump, thwack, wallop, whack, whop; CONCEPT 189

batch [n] group of same objects accumulation, aggregation, amount, array, assemblage, assortment, bunch, bundle, clump, cluster, clutch, collection, crowd, group, lot, pack, parcel, quantity, set, shipment, volume; CONCEPTS 432,787 —*Ant.* individual

bath [n1] washing with water and, usually, soap ablution, cleansing, dip, douche, dousing, gargle, laving, scrubbing, shower, soak, soaking, soaping, sponging, tub, wash; CONCEPTS 161,165

bath [n2] room for bathing bathroom, lavatory, powder room, restroom, sauna, shower, shower room, spa, steam room, toilet, washroom; CONCEPT 448

bathe [v] wash with water and, usually, soap bath, clean, cleanse, dip, douse, dunk, flood, hose, imbathe, imbue, immerse, moisten, rinse, scour, scrub, shower, soak, soap, sponge, steep, submerge, suffuse, tub, water, wet; CONCEPTS 161,165 —*Ant.* dirty

bathing suit [n] clothing for swimming, sunning bathing costume, beach costume, bikini, maillot, one-piece, swimsuit, trunks, two-piece; CONCEPT 451

bathos [n] sentimentality anticlimax, comedown, letdown, melodrama, mush, schmaltz*; CONCEPTS 32,410,689

bathroom [n] room for bathing, toilet use bath, lavatory, powder room, restroom, sauna, shower, shower room, spa, steam room, toilet, washroom, water closet; CONCEPT 448

baton [n] stick used for conducting or for protection billy, billy club, blackjack, club, cudgel, mace, nightstick, rod, staff, truncheon, wand; CONCEPTS 262,470,500

battalion [n] military division army, brigade, company, contingent, corps, force, horde, host, legion, multitude, regiment, squadron, throng, unit; CONCEPT 322

batten [v1] fasten securely board up, clamp down, cover up, fix, nail down, secure, tie, tighten; CONCEPTS 85,160 —*Ant.* loosen, unfasten, unfix

batten [v2] grow fat burgeon, feed on, grow, prosper, thrive, wax; CONCEPT 704

batter [n] mixture before baking concoction, dough, mix, mush*, paste, preparation, recipe; CONCEPTS 457,466

batter [*v*] *strike and damage* assault, bash, beat, break, bruise, buffet, clobber, contuse, cripple, crush, dash, deface, demolish, destroy, disable, disfigure, drub, hurt, injure, lacerate, lambaste, lame, lash, mangle, mar, maul, mutilate, pelt, pommel, pound, pummel, punish, ruin, shatter, smash, thrash, wallop, wreck; CONCEPTS 189,246,252

battery [*n1*] *series of similar things* array, batch, body, bunch, bundle, chain, clot, clump, cluster, group, lot, ring, sequence, set, suite; CONCEPT 432 —*Ant.* individual

battery [*n2*] *physical abuse* assault, attack, beating, mayhem, mugging, onslaught, thumping, violence; CONCEPTS 189,246

battery [*n3*] *group of weapons* artillery, cannon, cannonry, gunnery unit, guns; CONCEPTS 321,500

battle [*n1*] *military fight* action, assault, attack, barrage, blitzkreig, bloodshed, bombing, brush, campaign, carnage, clash, combat, conflict, contention, crusade, encounter, engagement, fighting, fray, havoc, hostility, onset, onslaught, press, ravage, scrimmage, significant contact, skirmish, sortie, strife, struggle, war, warfare; CONCEPT 106 —*Ant.* truce

battle [*n2*] *struggle* agitation, campaign, clash, conflict, contest, controversy, crusade, debate, disagreement, dispute, strife; CONCEPTS 46,106

battle [*v*] *fight, struggle* argue, clamor, combat, contend, contest, dispute, feud, oppugn, skirmish, strive, tug, war, wrestle; CONCEPTS 46,106 —*Ant.* make peace

battlefield [*n*] *location of military fights* arena, Armageddon, battleground, combat zone, field, front, front line, salient, theater of operations, theater of war; CONCEPTS 198,321

bawdy [*adj*] *vulgar, dirty* blue, cheap, coarse, erotic, gross, indecent, indecorous, indelicate, lascivious, lecherous, lewd, libidinous, licentious, lustful, obscene, off-color, prurient, ribald, risqué, rude, salacious, suggestive; CONCEPT 545 —*Ant.* chaste, clean, decent, proper, virginal

bawl [*v1*] *yell* bark, bellow, bluster, call, cheer, clamor, holler, howl, roar, rout, scream, screech, shout, shriek, vociferate; CONCEPT 77

bawl [*v2*] *cry* blubber*, boohoo*, howl, shed tears, sob, squall, wail, weep, yowl; CONCEPTS 77,185

bay [*n1*] *shoreline indentation* anchorage, arm, basin, bayou, bight, cove, estuary, fiord, firth, gulf, harbor, inlet, lagoon, loch, mouth, narrows, sound, strait; CONCEPTS 509,514

bay [*n2*] *alcove in wall* bow window, compartment, niche, nook, opening, oriel, recess; CONCEPT 440

bay [*n3*] *howl* bark, bellow, clamor, cry, growl, howl, ululation, wail, yelp; CONCEPT 64

bazaar [*n*] *fair; sale place* exchange, exposition, fete, market, marketplace, mart; CONCEPTS 345,438,449

bboard [*n*] *electronic messaging system* BBS, board, bulletin board, bulletin board system; CONCEPTS 349,770

be [*v1*] *exist* abide, act, be alive, breathe, continue, do, endure, go on, have being, have place, hold, inhabit, last, live, move, obtain, persist, prevail, remain, rest, stand, stay, subsist, survive; CONCEPT 407

be [*v2*] *happen* befall, come about, come to pass, occur, take place, transpire; CONCEPT 2

beach [*n*] *sandy area by body of water* bank, coast, lakeshore, lakeside, littoral, margin, oceanfront, seaboard, seafront, seashore, seaside, shingle, shore, strand, waterfront; CONCEPTS 509,514

beached [*adj*] *grounded* abandoned, aground, ashore, deserted, high and dry, marooned, stranded, wrecked; CONCEPT 583 —*Ant.* at sea

beacon [*n*] *light used as signal, guide* alarm, alert, balefire, beam, bonfire, flare, guidepost, heliograph, lamp, lantern, lighthouse, lodestar, pharos, radar, rocket, sign, signal fire, smoke signal, warning signal, watchtower; CONCEPT 628

bead [*n*] *droplet, blob* bean, bubble, dab, dot, driblet, drop, globule, grain, particle, pea, pellet, pill, shot, speck, spherule, stone; CONCEPT 436

beads [*n*] *string of small, often round, objects* chaplet, choker, necklace, necklet, pearls, pendant, rosary, wampum; CONCEPTS 368,446

beak [*n*] *nose of animal* bill, mandible, muzzle, neb, nib, nozzle, pecker, proboscis, projection, prow, snout; CONCEPT 392

beam [*n1*] *length of material used as support* axle, bail, balk, bolster, boom, brace, cantilever, column, crossbar, crosspiece, girder, jamb, joist, lath, lintel, pile, piling, pillar, plank, pole, post, prop, rafter, reach, scaffolding, scantling, shaft, sill, spar, stanchion, stay, stringer, strip, strut, stud, timber, transverse, trestle, two-by-four; CONCEPTS 471,479

beam [*n2*] *ray of light* bar, beacon, chink, column, dartle, emission, finger, flicker, glare, gleam, glimmer, glint, glitter, glow, laser, radiation, ray, shaft, shimmer, shoot, sparkle, streak, stream, twinkle; CONCEPTS 624,628

beam [*v1*] *broadcast on air waves* emit, give off, give out, glare, glimmer, glow, radiate, send, shed, shine, throw off, transmit; CONCEPTS 519,624

beam [*v2*] *smile broadly* gleam, glow, grin, laugh, radiate, shine, smirk; CONCEPT 185 —*Ant.* frown, scowl

beam [*v3*] *shine, as a light* burn, emit, glare, gleam, glitter, glow, radiate, yield; CONCEPT 624 —*Ant.* be dark

beam [*v4*] *make electronic transfer* emit, radiate, send out, transfer file, transmit, transmit signal; CONCEPT 266

beaming [*adj1*] *radiant; beautiful* bright, brilliant, effulgent, flashing, fulgent, gleaming, glistening, glittering, glowing, incandescent, lambent, lucent, luminous, refulgent, scintillating, sparkling; CONCEPT 617 —*Ant.* ugly

beaming [*adj2*] *very happy* animated, cheerful, genial, grinning, joyful, radiant, shining, smiling, sparkling, sunny; CONCEPT 401 —*Ant.* frowning, sad, sullen, unhappy

bean counter [*n*] *number cruncher* accountant, actuary, analyst, auditor, bookkeeper, certified public accountant, comptroller, CPA, financial executive, statistician, treasurer; CONCEPTS 348,353

beanpole [*n*] *a tall, thin person* beanstalk*, broomstick*, hatrack*, stick*, string bean*; CONCEPT 417

bear [*v1*] *bring* buck, carry, convey, deliver, ferry, fetch, lug, move, pack, take, tote, transfer, transport; CONCEPTS *108,143* —*Ant.* refuse, take, throw away

bear [v2] *support mentally* cherish, entertain, exhibit, harbor, have, hold, hold up, maintain, possess, shoulder, sustain, uphold, weigh upon; CONCEPTS *8,12*

bear [v3] *endure* abide, admit, allow, brook, encounter, experience, permit, put up with, stomach, suffer, tolerate, undergo; CONCEPTS *23,239* —*Ant.* avoid, dodge, evade, shun

bear [v4] *give birth* be delivered of, beget, breed, bring forth, create, develop, engender, form, fructify, generate, invent, make, parturitate, produce, propagate, provide, reproduce, yield; CONCEPTS *173,251,302,373* —*Ant.* be unproductive

bearable [adj] *endurable* acceptable, admissible, allowable, livable, manageable, passable, satisfactory, sufferable, supportable, sustainable, tolerable; CONCEPT *529* —*Ant.* intolerable, unbearable, unendurable, unmanageable

beard [n1] *facial hair on human* bristles, brush, five-o-clock shadow*, fuzz, goatee, imperial, muttonchops, Santa Claus*, stubble, Vandyke*; CONCEPT *418*

beard [n2] *decoy* false face, front, mask; CONCEPT *716*

beard [v] *confront* brave, face, oppose, stand up to; CONCEPTS *46,96*

bearded [adj] *having facial hair* barbate, beardy, bewhiskered, bristly, bushy, goateed, hairy, hirsute, shaggy, stubbled, stubbly, unshaven, whiskered; CONCEPTS *406,485* —*Ant.* unbearded, unhirsute

bear down [v] *close in on* advance on, approach, converge on, near, press, weigh down; CONCEPTS *152,208,704*

bearer [n1] *person who carries messages or deliveries* agent, beast of burden*, carrier, conveyor, courier, drogher, emissary, envoy, internuncio, messenger, porter, runner, servant, shipper, transporter; CONCEPT *348*

bearer [n2] *person who requests payment of bill* beneficiary, casher, collector, consignee, payee; CONCEPT *353*

bearing [n1] *person's conduct, posture* address, air, aspect, attitude, behavior, carriage, comportment, demeanor, deportment, display, front, look, manner, mien, poise, port, pose, presence, set, stand; CONCEPTS *411,633*

bearing [n2] *significance* application, connection, import, meaning, pertinence, reference, relation, relevance, weight; CONCEPT *668*

bearing/bearings [n3] *position, usually of water vehicle* aim, course, direction, location, orientation, point of compass, position, situation, track, way, whereabouts; CONCEPTS *739,746*

bear in mind [v] *be aware of* be cognizant of, be mindful of, beware, consider, heed, mind, note, remember; CONCEPTS *17,623*

bear on/bear upon [v] *concern* affect, appertain to, apply, belong to, involve, pertain to, refer to, relate to, touch upon; CONCEPT *532*

bear out [v] *substantiate* authenticate, confirm, corroborate, endorse, justify, prove, substantiate, support, uphold, validate, verify, vindicate; CONCEPTS *50,88,97*

bear up [v] *endure* carry on, persevere, soldier on, suffer, withstand; CONCEPT *23*

bear with [v] *tolerate* be patient, endure, forbear, make allowance, put up with, suffer, wait; CONCEPT *23* —*Ant.* not bear, not tolerate

bear witness [v] *vouch for* attest, confirm, corroborate, demonstrate, depose, evidence, evince, prove, show, testify, testify to; CONCEPTS *49,71,317*

beast [n] *large wild animal; brute* barbarian, beastie*, creature, critter*, fiend, gargoyle, glutton, lower animal, monster, monstrosity, pig, quadruped, swine, varmint*; CONCEPT *394*

beastly [adv1] *savage; vulgar* abominable, animal, barbarous, base, bestial, boorish, brutal, brute, brutish, carnal, coarse, cruel, degraded, depraved, disgusting, feral, ferine, foul, gluttonous, gross, inhuman, irrational, loathsome, low, monstrous, obscene, piggish, prurient, repulsive, sadistic, swinish, unclean, vile; CONCEPT *401* —*Ant.* good, kind, nice, superior

beastly [adv2] *offensive* awful, disagreeable, disgusting, foul, gross, mean, nasty, revolting, rotten, terrible, unpleasant, vile; CONCEPTS *537,542* —*Ant.* good, inoffensive, kind, nice

beat [adj] *very tired* dog tired*, exhausted, fatigued, kaput*, wearied, weary, worn out; CONCEPTS *316,720* —*Ant.* rested

beat [n1] *throbbing* cadence, cadency, flow, flutter, measure, meter, oscillation, palpitation, pound, pressure, pulsation, pulse, quake, quiver, rhyme, rhythm, ripple, shake, surge, swell, swing, throb, thump, tick, undulation, vibration; CONCEPTS *150,185*

beat [n2] *blow, stroke* hit, lash, punch, shake, slap, strike, swing, thump; CONCEPT *189*

beat [n3] *area of responsibility* circuit, course, march, path, patrol, precinct, rounds, route, walk, way; CONCEPTS *513,532*

beat [v1] *injure by striking* bang, bash, bat, batter, belt, box, break, bruise, buffet, cane, castigate, clout, club, collide, crush, cudgel, drub, flagellate, flail, flog, hammer, hit, knock, lambaste*, lash, lick*, maltreat, mash, maul, pelt, pound, pummel, punch, punish, ram, rap, slap, slug, smack, spank, strike, swat, thrash, thresh, thump, thwack, trounce, wallop, whale*, whip; CONCEPTS *189,246* —*Ant.* aid, assist, guard, help, protect

beat [v2] *defeat, surpass* best, better, be victorious, conquer, exceed, excel, outdo, outplay, outrival, outrun, outshine, outstrip, overcome, overtake, overwhelm, shoot ahead of, subdue, top, transcend, triumph, vanquish, whip; CONCEPTS *95,141* —*Ant.* cede, lose, relinquish, retreat, surrender

beat [v3] *forge* fashion, form, hammer, malleate, model, pound, shape, work; CONCEPTS *137,175*

beat [v4] *throb* agitate, alternate, bob, bounce, buffet, flap, flicker, fluctuate, flutter, heave, jerk, jounce, oscillate, palpitate, pitch, pound, pulsate, pulse, quake, quaver, quiver, ripple, shake, shiver, swing, thrill, throb, thump, tremble, twitch, undulate, vibrate, writhe; CONCEPTS *150,185*

beat [v5] *mix* stir, whip; CONCEPT *170*

beaten [adj1] *defeated* baffled, bested, circumvented, conquered, cowed, crushed, disappointed, discomfited, disheartened, frustrated, humbled, licked, mastered, overcome, overpowered, overthrown, overwhelmed, routed, ruined, subjugated, surmounted, thwarted, trounced, undone, vanquished, worsted; CONCEPTS 403,674

beaten [adj2] *forged* formed, hammered, milled, pounded, rolled, shaped, stamped, tamped, tramped, tramped down, trodden, worked; CONCEPTS 486,490

beaten [adj3] *mixed* aerated, blended, bubbly, churned, creamy, foamy, frothy, meringued, stirred, whipped, whisked; CONCEPTS 491,606

beat it [v] *go away* leave, scram, shoo, skedaddle, vamoose; CONCEPT 195

beatitude [n] *blessedness* bliss, ecstasy, felicity, happiness, peace, serenity; CONCEPT 410

beatnik [n] *uncoventional, free-sprited person* beat, Bohemian, demonstrator, dropout, flower child*, hippie, iconoclast, maverick, nonconformist, peacenik*, protester, radical; CONCEPT 423

beat up [v] *assault* attack, batter, do over, hammer, knock around, pulverize, thrash; CONCEPTS 52,86

beau [n] *boyfriend* admirer, beloved, cavalier, escort, fiancé, flame, gentleman caller, gentleman friend, honey, inamorato, love, lover, paramour, squire, steady, suitor, swain, sweetheart, true love; CONCEPT 423 —*Ant.* girlfriend, mistress

beautiful [adj] *physically attractive* admirable, alluring, angelic, appealing, beauteous, bewitching, charming, classy, comely, cute, dazzling, delicate, delightful, divine, elegant, enticing, excellent, exquisite, fair, fascinating, fine, foxy*, good-looking, gorgeous, graceful, grand, handsome, ideal, lovely, magnificent, marvelous, nice, pleasing, pretty, pulchritudinous, radiant, ravishing, refined, resplendent, shapely, sightly, splendid, statuesque, stunning, sublime, superb, symmetrical, taking, well-formed; CONCEPTS 485,579,589 —*Ant.* disgusting, grotesque, hideous, homely, offensive, plain, repulsive, ugly, unattractive

beautifully [adv] *in an attractive or pleasing manner* alluringly, appealingly, attractively, bewitchingly, celestially, charmingly, cutely, delightfully, divinely, elegantly, entrancingly, excellently, exquisitely, gorgeously, gracefully, handsomely, ideally, magnificently, prettily, seductively, splendidly, sublimely, superbly, tastefully, wonderfully; CONCEPT 544

beautify [v] *make more physically attractive* adorn, array, bedeck, deck, decorate, dress up, embellish, enhance, garnish, gild, glamorize, grace, improve, make up, ornament, prettify, set off, trim; CONCEPT 162 —*Ant.* disfigure, harm, injure, mar, spoil

beauty [n1] *physical attractiveness* adorableness, allure, allurement, artistry, attraction, bloom, charm, class, comeliness, delicacy, elegance, exquisiteness, fairness, fascination, glamor, good looks, grace, handsomeness, loveliness, polish, pulchritude, refinement, shapeliness, style, symmetry, winsomeness; CONCEPT 718 —*Ant.* homeliness, offensiveness, ugliness

beauty [n2] *good-looking person* Adonis*, Apollo*, beaut*, charmer, dream, dreamboat*, enchanter, eyeful*, good-looker*, head turner*, looker*, ornament*, stunner*, Venus*, vision; CONCEPT 424 —*Ant.* dog

beauty [n3] *advantage* asset, attraction, benefit, blessing, boon, excellent, feature, good thing, importance, merit, value, worth; CONCEPT 668 —*Ant.* disadvantage

because [conj/prep] *on account of* as, as a result of, as long as, as things go, being, by cause of, by reason of, by virtue of, considering, due to, for, for the reason that, for the sake of, in as much as, in behalf of, in that, in the interest of, in view of, now that, on the grounds that, over, owing to, seeing, since, thanks to, through, whereas; CONCEPT 676

beckon [v] *call, signal, or lure* allure, ask, attract, bid, coax, command, demand, draw, entice, gesticulate, gesture, invite, motion, nod, pull, sign, summon, tempt, wave; CONCEPTS 7,22,53,74

become [v1] *evolve into* alter to, assume form of, be converted to, be reduced to, be reformed, be remodeled, be transformed into, change into, come, come to be, convert, develop into, emerge as, eventually be, grow into, incline, mature, metamorphose, pass into, ripen into, shift, turn into, turn out, wax; CONCEPT 701

become [v2] *enhance* accord, adorn, agree, augment, be appropriate, belong to, display, embellish, enrich, fit, flatter, garnish, go together, go with, grace, harmonize, heighten, make handsome, match, ornament, set off, suit; CONCEPT 244

becoming [adj1] *flattering* acceptable, agreeable, attractive, beautiful, comely, cute, effective, enhancing, excellent, fair, graceful, handsome, neat, nice, presentable, pretty, seemly, tasteful, welcome, well-chosen; CONCEPTS 579,589 —*Ant.* indecorous, tasteless, ugly, unattractive, unbecoming, unfitting, unsuitable

becoming [adj2] *suitable; appropriate* befitting, comme il faut, compatible, conforming, congruous, correct, decent, decorous, fit, fitting, in keeping, nice, proper, right, seemly, worthy; CONCEPT 558 —*Ant.* improper, inappropriate, unbecoming, unfitting, unseemly, unsuitable

bed [n1] *furniture for sleeping* bassinet, bedstead, berth, bunk, chaise, cot, couch, cradle, crib, davenport, divan, mattress, pallet, platform, sack, trundle; CONCEPT 443

bed [n2] *patch of ground for planting* area, border, frame, garden, piece, plot, row, strip; CONCEPTS 509,513

bed [n3] *base, foundation* basis, bedrock, bottom, ground, groundwork, rest, seat, substratum, understructure; CONCEPT 442

bed [v] *plant* base, embed, establish, fix, found, implant, insert, settle, set up; CONCEPTS 234,257

bedazzle [v] *captivate* astound, bewilder, blind, confuse, daze, dazzle, dumbfound, enchant, overwhelm, stagger, stun; CONCEPTS 7,22,42

bedding [n] *covering for sleeping furniture* bedclothes, bed linen, bedspread, blanket, comforter, cover, coverlet, eiderdown, electric blanket, linen, pillow, pillowcase, quilt, sheet, spread, thermal blanket; CONCEPTS 444,473

bedlam [n] *chaotic situation* chaos, clamor, commotion, confusion, din, disquiet, disquietude, furor, hubbub, madhouse, maelstrom, noise, pandemonium, racket, shambles, tumult, turmoil, uproar; CONCEPTS 230,674 —*Ant.* calm, peace, quiet

bedraggled [*adj*] *unkempt* decrepit, dilapidated, dirty, disheveled, disordered, dowdy, drenched, dripping, faded, messy, muddied, muddy, run-down, seedy, shabby, sloppy, slovenly, sodden, soiled, stained, sullied, tacky, tattered, threadbare, untidy, wet; CONCEPT 589 —*Ant.* clean, neat, tidy

bedridden [*adj*] *sick in bed* ailing, disabled, flat on one's back*, ill, incapacitated, infirm, invalid, laid up*, prostrate; CONCEPTS 314,485,489

bedroom [*n*] *place for sleeping* bedchamber, bunk room, chamber, cubicle, guest room; CONCEPT 448

bedspread [*n*] *thick, often quilted, covering for bed* bedcover, blanket, counterpane, cover, coverlet, spread; CONCEPT 444

bee [*n1*] *honey-making, stinging insect* bumblebee, drone, honey bee, killer bee, queen bee; CONCEPT 398

bee [*n2*] *collective task* communal gathering, harvest, party, social, work party; CONCEPT 362

beef [*n1*] *strong physical makeup* arm, brawn, flesh, force, heftiness, meat, might, muscle, physique, power, robustness, sinew, steam, strength, thew, vigor; CONCEPT 757

beef [*n2*] *complaint* bickering, criticism, dispute, grievance, gripe, grouse, grumble, objection, protestation, quarrel, rhubarb*, squabble; CONCEPT 52 —*Ant.* compliment, praise

beep [*n*] *sound from electronic device* bell sound, bleep, breedle, computer sound, ding, eep, feep, signal, tone, warning; CONCEPTS 74,284,529,685

beep [*v*] *call for electronically* call, page, summon, track down, warn; CONCEPT 74

beer [*n*] *alcoholic beverage made from malted grain* ale, amber brew*, barley pop*, brew, brewski*, brown bottle*, chill*, cold coffee*, cold one*, hops, lager, malt, malt liquor, oil*, stout*, suds*; CONCEPT 455

befall [*v*] *happen to; take place* action, bechance, betide, break, chance, come down, come off, come to pass, cook*, cook up a storm*, cook with gas*, develop, ensue, fall, fall out, follow, gel, go, go down, hap*, happen, jell*, materialize, occur, shake*, smoke*, supervene, transpire; CONCEPT 4

befitting [*adj*] *appropriate according to Hoyle**, apt, becoming, behooving, beseeming, comme il faut, conforming, correct, decent, decorous, felicitous, fit, fitting, happy, just, kosher*, nice, on the button*, on the nose*, proper, right, right on*, seemly, suitable, what the doctor ordered*; CONCEPTS 533,558 —*Ant.* improper, inappropriate, incorrect, unbecoming, unfitting, unsuitable

before [*adv*] *earlier* afore, aforetime, ahead, ante, antecedently, anteriorly, back, before present, ere, fore, former, formerly, forward, gone, gone by, heretofore, in advance, in days of yore, in front, in old days, in the past, past, precendently, previous, previously, since, sooner, up to now; CONCEPT 820 —*Ant.* after, afterward, behind, later

before [*prep*] *earlier than* ahead of, ante, antecedent to, anterior to, ere, in advance of,

in front of, preceding, previous to, prior to, since; CONCEPT 820 —*Ant.* after, afterward, behind, later

beforehand [*adj/adv*] *early* advanced, ahead, ahead of time, already, ante, antecedently, before, before now, earlier, fore, in advance, in anticipation, precedently, precocious, previous, previously, sooner; CONCEPT 820 —*Ant.* after, afterward, behind, later

befriend [*v*] *make social acquaintance; support* advise, aid, assist, back, benefit, buddy up*, case out*, come on to*, cotton to*, encourage, favor, get chummy with, get in with*, help, hit it off*, patronize, side with, stand by, sustain, take under one's wing*, take up with, uphold, welcome; CONCEPTS 110, 384 —*Ant.* ignore, neglect

befuddle [*v*] *confuse* addle, baffle, ball up*, bewilder, bother, daze, disorient, distract, dumbfound, fluster, inebriate, intoxicate, make punchy*, mix up, muddle, puzzle, shake, stupefy, throw off*; CONCEPTS 7,19,42 —*Ant.* clear up, explain

beg [*v1*] *request* abjure, advocate, apply to, ask, beseech, besiege, call to, canvass, conjure, crave, desire, entreat, impetrate, implore, importune, invoke, nag, obsecrate, obtest, petition, plead, pray, press, requisition, solicit, sue, supplicate, urge, woo, worry; CONCEPT 48 —*Ant.* answer

beg [*v2*] *seek charity* ask alms, benefit, bite*, brace, bum*, burn*, buzz*, cadge*, call on, call upon, chisel*, clamor for, dime up*, ding*, freeload*, hit up*, hustle, knock, live hand to mouth*, mendicate, mooch*, nick*, nickel up*, panhandle, pass the hat*, put the bite on*, put the touch on*, score*, scrounge, solicit charity, sponge*, sponge on*, tap, touch, want; CONCEPT 53 —*Ant.* give

beget [*v*] *create, bear* afford, breed, bring, bring about, cause, effect, engender, father, generate, get, give rise to, multiply, occasion, procreate, produce, progenerate, propagate, reproduce, result in, sire; CONCEPTS 173,251, 374

beggar [*n1*] *person asking for charity* asker, borrower, bum, deadbeat, hobo, mendicant, panhandler, rustler, scrounger, supplicant, supplicator, tramp, vagabond; CONCEPTS 412,423

beggar [*n2*] *person in financial trouble* alms person, bankrupt, dependent, down-and-out*, guttersnipe*, indigent, mendicant, pauper, poor person, poverty-stricken person, street person*, suppliant, vagrant, ward of state; CONCEPT 423

begin [*v1*] *start* activate, actualize, break ground, break the ice*, bring about, bring to pass, cause, commence, create, do, drive, effect, embark on, enter on, enter upon, establish, eventuate, found, generate, get going, give birth to, give impulse, go ahead, go into, impel, inaugurate, induce, initiate, instigate, institute, introduce, launch, lay foundation for, lead, make, make active, motivate, mount, occasion, open, originate, plunge into, prepare, produce, set about, set in motion, set up, trigger, undertake; CONCEPTS 234,241 —*Ant.* complete, conclude, consummate, end, finish

begin [*v2*] *come into being; become functional* appear, arise, be born, bud, come forth, come

be
be

into existence, come out, commence, crop up, dawn, derive from, emanate, emerge, enter, germinate, get going, get show on road*, get under way, grow out of, happen, issue forth, kick off, make tick*, occur, originate, proceed from, result from, rise, sail, send off, set, spring, sprout, start, stem from, take off; CONCEPTS 105, 680 —*Ant.* die, end

beginner [n] *person unskilled in something* abecedarian, amateur, apprentice, buckwheater*, catechumen, colt, fish*, fledgling, greenhorn, greenie*, initiate, learner, neophyte, newcomer, new kid on the block*, new person, novice, novitiate, probationer, recruit, starter, student, tenderfoot*, trainee, tyro; CONCEPTS 423,424 —*Ant.* expert, old hand, professional, veteran

beginning [n1] *start of an event or action* alpha, basis, birth, blastoff*, commencement, creation, dawn, dawning, day one*, genesis, inauguration, inception, induction, infancy, initiation, installation, introduction, kickoff, onset, opener, opening, origin, origination, outset, point of departure, preface, prelude, presentation, rise, root, rudiment, source, spring, square one*, starting point, takeoff, threshold, top; CONCEPTS 815,833 —*Ant.* completion, conclusion, consummation, end, ending, finish, goal, termination

beginning [n2] *origin, cause* antecedent, birth, conception, egg, embryo, font, fount, fountain, fountainhead, generation, genesis, germ, heart, principle, resource, root, seed, stem, well; CONCEPT 229 —*Ant.* conclusion, outcome, result

begrudge [v] *wish that someone did not have* be jealous, be reluctant, be stingy, covet, eat one's heart out, envy, grudge, pinch, resent, stint; CONCEPTS 17,21

beguile [v1] *fool* betray, bluff, burn*, cheat, chisel, con, deceive, delude, double-cross, dupe, entice, exploit, finesse, flimflam*, gyp*, have, hoodwink*, impose on, jockey, juggle, lure, manipulate, mislead, play, play for a sucker*, rook*, rope in*, scam, seduce, shave*, snow*, stick*, string along, suck in*, take, take in, trick; CONCEPT 59

beguile [v2] *charm* amuse, attract, cheer, delight, distract, divert, engross, entertain, entice, knock dead, knock out, lure, occupy, seduce, send, slay, solace, sweep off one's feet, tickle, tickle pink*, tickle to death*, turn on, vamp, wow*; CONCEPTS 7,19,22

behalf [n] *personal interest* account, advantage, aid, assistance, benefit, cause, concern, countenance, defense, encouragement, favor, furtherance, good, help, part, place, profit, recommendation, representation, sake, service, side, stead, support, welfare; CONCEPTS 410,532

behave [v1] *function* act, operate, perform, react, run, take, work; CONCEPTS 1,4

behave [v2] *act reasonably, properly* act correctly, act one's age, act with decorum, be civil, be good, be nice, be on best behavior*, be orderly, comport oneself, conduct oneself properly, control, demean oneself, deport oneself, direct, discipline oneself, keep one's nose clean*, keep the peace, live up to, manage, manage oneself, mind one's manners*, mind one's p's and q's*, observe golden rule*, observe the law, play fair, shape up, toe the

mark*, watch one's step*; CONCEPT 633 —*Ant.* act up, misbehave

behavior [n] *manner of conducting oneself* act, action, address, air, attitude, bag*, bearing, carriage, code, comportment, conduct, convention, course, dealings, decency, decorum, deed, delivery, demeanor, deportment, ethics, etiquette, expression, form, front, guise, habits, management, mien, mode, morals, nature, observance, performance, practice, presence, propriety, ritual, role, routine, savoir-faire, seemliness, social graces, speech, style, tact, talk, taste, tenue, tone, way, way of life, ways, what's done*; CONCEPTS 633,655

behead [v] *decapitate* bring to the block, decollate, execute, guillotine, head, kill, neck; CONCEPT 176

behest [n] *order; personal decree* bidding, charge, command, commandment, demand, dictate, direction, expressed desire, injunction, instruction, mandate, order, precept, prompting, request, solicitation, wish, word; CONCEPTS 20,53

behind [adv1/prep1] *position farther back; following back*, after, afterwards, at the heels of*, at the rear of, back of, bringing up the rear*, eating the dust*, in the background, in the wake, later than, next, off the pace, subsequently, trailing; CONCEPTS 586,820 —*Ant.* front

behind [adv2] *in debt; late* backward, behindhand, behind schedule, behind time, belated, delayed, dilatory, have to play catch up*, in arrears, laggard, overdue, slow, sluggish, tardy; CONCEPTS 334,799 —*Ant.* paid

behind [n] *buttocks* backside, bottom, breech, can*, derrière, fanny*, fundament, posterior, rear, rump, seat, tail, tush*; CONCEPT 392 —*Ant.* front

behind [prep2] *being the reason for* at the bottom of, causing, concerning the circumstances, initiating, instigating, responsible for; CONCEPT 532

behind [prep3] *in support* backing, for, in agreement, on the side of, supporting; CONCEPT 388

behind one's back [adv] *deceitfully* covertly, secretly, sneakily, sub rosa, surreptitiously; CONCEPTS 267,548

behind the times [adj] *old-fashioned* antiquated, dated, obsolete, old hat*, outdated, outmoded, out of date, passe, square; CONCEPTS 578,589,797,799

behold [v] *regard; look at* catch, consider, contemplate, descry, discern, distinguish, earmark, eye, eyeball*, feast one's eyes*, flash*, lay eyes on*, note, notice, observe, perceive, regard, scan, see, spot, spy, survey, view, watch, witness; CONCEPTS 34,626

beholden [adj] *indebted* bound, grateful, in hock, into, obligated, obliged, on a string*, on the arm*, on the cuff*, on the tab*, owe one, owing, responsible, under obligation; CONCEPT 403 —*Ant.* ingrateful

behoove [v] *be necessary, proper* be expected, befit, be fitting, be incumbent upon, be needful, be one's obligation, be required, be requisite, be right, beseem, owe it to, suit; CONCEPT 646

beige [n/adj] *light brown color* biscuit, buff,

café au lait, camel, cream, ecru, fawn, khaki, mushroom, neutral, oatmeal, off-white, sand, tan, taupe; CONCEPTS 618,622

being [n1] *existence* actuality, animation, journey, life, living, presence, reality, subsistence, vitality, world; CONCEPT 407 —*Ant.* deadness

being [n2] *essential nature* character, entity, essence, essentia, essentiality, individuality, marrow, personality, quintessence, self, soul, spirit, substance, texture; CONCEPTS 411,673

being [n3] *animate object* animal, beast, body, conscious thing, creature, entity, human, human being, individual, living thing, mortal, organism, person, personage, soul, thing; CONCEPT 389 —*Ant.* abstract, inanimate

belabor [v] *dwell on* beat a dead horse*, go on about, hammer home, overwork, pound, rehash, repeat; CONCEPT 56

belated [adj] *late, slow* behindhand, behind time, delayed, long-delayed, overdue, remiss, tardy, unpunctual; CONCEPT 820 —*Ant.* early, on time, punctual, timely

belch [v] *burp; spew* discharge, disgorge, emit, eruct, eructate, erupt, give off, gush, hiccup, irrupt, repeat, ventilate, vomit; CONCEPT 185

beleaguer [v] *harass, besiege* annoy, badger, bedevil, beset, blockade, bother, gnaw, harry, nag, persecute, pester, plague, put upon, set upon, siege, storm, tease, vex, worry; CONCEPTS 7,19

belfry [n] *tower; part of tower* bell tower, campanile, carillon, clocher, cupola, dome, head, minaret, spire, steeple, turret; CONCEPT 440

belie [v1] *disprove* confute, contradict, contravene, controvert, deny, disaffirm, disagree, explode, gainsay, negate, negative, oppose, repudiate; CONCEPTS 54,58 —*Ant.* attest, prove

belie [v2] *deceive* color, conceal, disguise, distort, falsify, garble, give the lie to, gloss over, hide, miscolor, mislead, misrepresent, misstate, pervert, trump up, twist, warp; CONCEPT 63 —*Ant.* be honest

belief [n1] *putting regard in as true* acceptance, admission, assent, assumption, assurance, avowal, axiom, certainty, conclusion, confidence, conjecture, conviction, credence, credit, deduction, divination, expectation, faith, fancy, feeling, guess, hope, hypothesis, idea, impression, intuition, judgment, knowledge, mind, mindset, notion, opinion, persuasion, position, postulation, presumption, presupposition, profession, reliance, supposition, surmise, suspicion, theorem, theory, thesis, thinking, trust, understanding, view; CONCEPTS 410,529 —*Ant.* disbelief

belief [n2] *something regarded as true* assumption, concept, credence, credo, creed, doctrine, dogma, faith, fundamental, gospel, gospel truth*, hypothesis, idea, ideology, law, opinion, postulate, precept, principle, say-so*, tenet, theorem, theory; CONCEPT 689 —*Ant.* disbelief, nonbelief

believable [adj] *trustworthy* aboveboard, acceptable, authentic, colorable, conceivable, convincing, credential, credible, creditable, fiduciary, honest-to-God*, imaginable, impressive, likely, persuasive, plausible, possible, presumable, presumptive, probable, rational, reasonable, reliable, satisfying, straight, supposable,

tenable, tried, trusty, unquestionable, up front*; CONCEPTS 403,582 —*Ant.* inconceivable, incredible, unbelieveable, unconvincing, unreliable, unthinkable

believe [v1] *trust, rely on* accept, accredit, admit, affirm, attach weight to, be certain of, be convinced of, be credulous, be of the opinion, buy*, conceive, conclude, consider, count on, credit, deem, fall for*, give credence to, have, have faith in, have no doubt, hold, keep the faith, lap up*, place confidence in, posit, postulate, presume true, presuppose, reckon on, regard, rest assured, suppose, swallow*, swear by, take as gospel*, take at one's word, take for granted, take it, think, trust, understand; CONCEPT 12 —*Ant.* disbelieve, distrust

believe [v2] *assume or suppose* conjecture, consider, credit, deem, expect, feel, gather, guess, hold, imagine, judge, maintain, postulate, presume, reckon, sense, speculate, suppose, suspect, take, think, understand; CONCEPT 28

believer [n] *person who has faith in something* acceptor, adherent, apostle, canonist, convert, devotee, disciple, doctrinaire, dogmatist, follower, freak, orthodox, prophet, proselyte, religionist, religious person, supporter, upholder, zealot; CONCEPTS 361,423 —*Ant.* agnostic, atheist, disbeliever, non-believer

belittle [v] *detract* bad-mouth, blister, criticize, cut down to size*, cut to the quick*, decry, deprecate, depreciate, deride, derogate, diminish, discount, discredit, disparage, dispraise, downgrade, downplay, dump on*, knock*, lower, minimize, pan, pooh pooh*, poor mouth*, put down, rip*, roast*, run down, scoff at, scorch*, scorn, shoot down*, shoot full of holes*, slam*, smear, sneer at, sour grapes*, squash*, squelch, take a swipe at*, take down, take down a peg*, tear down*, underestimate, underrate, undervalue, write off; CONCEPTS 52,54 —*Ant.* build up, exaggerate, praise, value

bell [n] *signaling object or sound* alarm, buzz, buzzer, carillon, chime, clapper, curfew, dingdong*, dinger*, gong, peal, ringer, siren, tintinnabulum, tocsin, toll, vesper; CONCEPT 595

belligerent [adj] *nasty, argumentative* aggressive, antagonistic, ardent, at loggerheads*, battling, bellicose, cantankerous, combative, contentious, fierce, fighting, flip, have a bone to pick*, have chip on shoulder*, have it in for*, hostile, hot, hot-tempered, mean, militant, on the outs*, ornery, pugnacious, quarrelsome, scrappy, truculent, warlike; CONCEPTS 401,404 —*Ant.* cooperative, helping, kind, nice

bellow [v] *holler* bark, bawl, bay, beller, blare, bluster, bray, call, clamor, cry, howl, low, roar, rout, scream, shout, shriek, wail, whoop, yawp, yell, yelp; CONCEPT 77

bells and whistles [n] *added-value features* accessories, added features, attractive features, chrome, dressing, extras, gongs, trappings; CONCEPTS 386,829

belly [n] *stomach* abdomen, bay window*, beer belly*, breadbasket*, corporation*, front porch*, gut, insides, intestines, paunch, pelvis, pot*, pot belly*, solar plexus, spare tire*, tank, tummy, venter; CONCEPT 393

belong [v1] *be part of, be in proper place* accord, agree, appertain, apply, associate, attach to, be a component, be a constituent, be akin, be an adjunct of, be a part, bear, bear upon, become, be connected with, befit, be fitting, be linked with, be related, be relevant, chime, concern, correlate, correspond, exist, fit, go, go with, harmonize, have relationship to, have respect to, have to do with, inhere, match, permeate, pertain, refer, regard, reside, set, suit, touch, vest; CONCEPTS 532,543

belong [v2] *be affiliated with* be allied to, be a member, be a member of, be associated with, be classified among, be contained in, be included in, be one of, be one of the family, be part of, fit in, have a place, in, in with, owe allegiance, owe support, run with*, swing with*, take one's place with; CONCEPTS 114,388

belonging [n] *sense of security in friendship* acceptance, affinity, association, attachment, inclusion, kinship, loyalty, rapport, relationship; CONCEPTS 388,410 —*Ant.* antipathy, insecurity

belongings [n] *personal possessions* accouterments, appurtenances, assets, chattels, effects, gear, goods, paraphernalia, personal property, property, stuff, things; CONCEPTS 446,710

belonging to [adj] *owned by* affiliated with, associated with, essential to, held by, inherent in, intrinsic in, native to; CONCEPTS 404,549

beloved [adj] *adored* admired, cared for, cherished, darling, dear, dearest, doted on, endeared, esteemed, fair-haired, favorite, hallowed, highly regarded, highly valued, idolized, loved, near to one's heart*, pet*, pleasing, popular, precious, prized, respected, revered, sweet, treasured, venerated, well-liked, worshiped; CONCEPTS 568,572 —*Ant.* despised, disliked, hated

beloved [n] *someone adored* baby*, beau, boyfriend, darling, dear, dearest, fiancé, flame, girlfriend, heartbeat*, heartthrob, honey, idol, inamorato, love, love of my life*, lover, number one*, numero uno*, object of affection, one and only, pet*, prize, rave*, significant other, steady, sugar*, sweetheart, tootsie*, treasure, true love; CONCEPT 423 —*Ant.* hate

below [adv/prep] *lower* beneath, down, down from, under, underneath; CONCEPTS 581,586,735 —*Ant.* above, over

below [prep2] *less than; beneath* inferior, lesser, lower, subject, subordinate, unworthy; CONCEPTS 567,771 —*Ant.* above, more, over

below par [adj] *second-rate in quality* below average, imperfect, inferior, lacking, not oneself, off, off-form, poor, substandard, under the weather*, wanting; CONCEPT 574

below the belt [adj/adv] *nastily and unfairly* cowardly, dirty, dishonest, foul, unjust, unscrupulous, unsportsmanlike; CONCEPTS 411,674,732

belt [n1] *supporting band* cincture, cummerbund, girdle, ribbon, ring, sash, strap, string, waistband; CONCEPT 450

belt [n2] *strip of land with characteristic feature* area, district, layer, region, stretch, territory, tract, zone; CONCEPTS 513,517.

belt [v] *hit hard* bash, bat, biff, blast, blow, bop, clobber, slam, slug, smack, smash, sock, strap, switch, wallop, whip, whop; CONCEPT 189 —*Ant.* pat, tap

bemoan [v] *express sorrow* beat one's breast*, bewail, complain, cry over spilled milk*, de-

plore, grieve for, lament, moan over, mourn, regret, rue, sing the blues*, weep for; CONCEPTS 49,51 —*Ant.* be happy, gloat

bemuse [v] *confuse* addle, amaze, bewilder, daydream, daze, gather wool*, moon, muddle, overwhelm, paralyze, perplex, pipe dream*, puzzle, stun, stupefy; CONCEPTS 7,19,22 —*Ant.* clear up, enlighten, explain, illuminate, tell

bench [n1] *furniture for sitting* bank, chair, form, lawn seat, pew, seat, settee, settle, stall; CONCEPT 443

bench [n2] *large table* board, counter, desk, easel, ledge, shelf, trestle, workbench, work table; CONCEPT 443

bench [n3] *group of judges* court, courtroom, judiciary, magistrate, the bar, tribunal, your honors; CONCEPTS 318,355

benchmark [n] *reference point* criterion, gauge, measure, standard, touchstone, yardstick; CONCEPT 688

bend [n] *curve* angle, arc, bending, bow, corner, crook, curvation, curvature, deflection, deviation, flection, flexure, hook, lean, loop, round, sag, shift, tack, tilt, turn, twist, yaw, zigzag; CONCEPT 436 —*Ant.* line

bend [v1] *form or cause a curve* angle away, angle off, arch, bow, buckle, camber, careen, circle, contort, crimp, crinkle, crook, crouch, curl, deflect, deform, detour, double, droop, flex, genuflect, hook, incline, incurvate, lean, loop, pervert, round, spiral, stoop, swerve, tilt, turn, twist, veer, verge, warp, waver, wilt, wind, yaw, zigzag; CONCEPTS 149,184 —*Ant.* straighten

bend [v2] *persuade; influence* change mind, compel, direct, mold, shape, subdue, submit, sway, yield; CONCEPT 68

beneath [adv] *in a lower place* below, underneath; CONCEPT 586 —*Ant.* above, higher, over

beneath [prep] *inferior* below, lesser, less than, lower than, subject, subordinate, unbefitting, under, underneath, unworthy of; CONCEPT 567 —*Ant.* above, higher, over, superior

benediction [n] *closing prayer* amen, approbation, approval, beatitude, benedictus, benison, blessing, consecration, favor, grace, gratitude, invocation, laying on of hands, okay, orison, praise, sanctification, thanks, thanksgiving; CONCEPT 69 —*Ant.* anathema, execration

benefactor [n] *donor* aid, altruist, angel, assistant, backer, contributor, fairy godparent*, fan, good Samaritan, grubstaker, helper, humanitarian, mark*, patron, philanthropist, promoter, protector, Santa Claus*, sponsor, subscriber, subsidizer, supporter, well-wisher; CONCEPTS 416,423 —*Ant.* antagonist, opponent, opposer

beneficial [adj] *advantageous* benign, constructive, favorable, favoring, gainful, good, good for what ails you*, healthful, helpful, profitable, propitious, salubrious, salutary, serviceable, toward, useful, valuable, what the doctor ordered*, wholesome, worthy; CONCEPTS 567,572 —*Ant.* disadvantageous, harmful, hurting, unfortunate, unhelpful, unrewarding

beneficiary [n] *person who gains, benefits* almsperson, assignee, devisee, donee, grantee, heir, heiress, inheritor, legatee, payee, possessor, receiver, recipient, stipendiary, successor; CONCEPTS 355,423 —*Ant.* giver, payer

be
be

benefit [n1] *advantage, profit* account, aid, asset, assistance, avail, benediction, betterment, blessing, boon, cream*, egg in one's beer*, extras, favor, gain, godsend*, good, gravy*, help, interest, perk*, profit, prosperity, use, welfare, worth; CONCEPTS 337,346,661 —*Ant.* disadvantage, handicap, harm, hindrance, hurt, loss, misfortune

benefit [n2] *event to raise money* ball, bazaar, charitable affair, charity performance, concert, dance, dinner, exhibit, exhibition, fair, pancake breakfast, raffle; CONCEPT 386

benefit [v] *help, enhance* advance, advantage, aid, ameliorate, assist, avail, be good for, better, build, contribute to, do for one, do the trick, favor, fill the bill*, further, improve, make a killing*, make it*, pay, pay off*, profit, promote, relieve, serve, succor, work for; CONCEPTS 110,244 —*Ant.* handicap, harm, hinder, hurt, injure

benevolence [n] *charity* altruism, amity, comity, compassion, feeling, friendliness, friendship, generosity, gift, goodness, good will, humanity, kindheartedness, kindness, sympathy; CONCEPT 633 —*Ant.* animosity, greediness, ill will, malevolence, meanness, selfishness, spite, unkindness

benevolent [adj] *charitable, kind* all heart, altruistic, beneficent, benign, big, big-hearted, bounteous, bountiful, caring, chivalrous, compassionate, considerate, generous, helpful, humane, humanitarian, kindhearted, liberal, magnanimous, philanthropic, tenderhearted, warmhearted, well-disposed; CONCEPT 401 —*Ant.* greedy, malevolent, mean, selfish, spiteful, unkind

benign [adj1] *kindly* amiable, beneficent, benevolent, benignant, complaisant, congenial, favorable, friendly, generous, genial, gentle, good, goodhearted, gracious, kind, liberal, merciful, mild, obliging, sympathetic; CONCEPT 542 —*Ant.* hateful, hostile, hurtful, injurious, malignant, unkind

benign [adj2] *mild, especially describing weather* auspicious, balmy, bright, favorable, fortunate, gentle, healthful, propitious, refreshing, temperate, warm; CONCEPT 605 —*Ant.* bad, severe

benign [adj3] *advantageous* auspicious, beneficent, benevolent, bright, charitable, dexter, encouraging, favorable, fortunate, good, lucky, merciful, propitious, salutary, smiling; CONCEPTS 537,572 —*Ant.* disadvantageous, harmful, hurtful

benign [adj4] *not cancerous* curable, early stage, harmless, limited, remediable, slight, superficial; CONCEPT 314 —*Ant.* cancerous, malignant

bent [adj1] *curved* angled, arced, arched, arciform, bowed, contorted, crooked, curvilinear, doubled over, drooping, droopy, hooked, humped, hunched, inclined, limp, looped, round, rounded, sinuous, slouchy, slumped, stooped, twined, twisted, warped, wilted; CONCEPT 486 —*Ant.* straight

bent [adj2] *determined* bound, decided, decisive, dedicated, disposed, firm, fixed, inclined, insistent, intent, leaning, predisposed, resolute, resolved, set, settled, tending; CONCEPT 403 —*Ant.* uncaring, undecided

bent [n] *inclination; talent* ability, aim, aptitude, bag*, disposition, druthers*, facility, faculty, flair, forte, genius, gift, head-set*, inclining, knack, leaning, mind-set*, nose, penchant, predilection, predisposition, preference, proclivity, propensity, set, tack, tendency, thing for*, tilt, turn, weakness for; CONCEPTS 409,630

bequeath [v] *give in a will* bestow, commit, devise, endow, entrust, grant, hand down, hand on, impart, leave, leave to, legate, pass on, transmit, will; CONCEPTS 108,317 —*Ant.* take

bequest [n] *something given in will* bequeathal, bequeathment, bestowal, devisal, devise, dower, endowment, estate, gift, heritage, inheritance, legacy, settlement, trust; CONCEPTS 318,337

berate [v] *criticize hatefully* bawl out*, blister, call down, castigate, censure, chew*, chew out*, chide, cuss out*, eat out*, give one hell*, give what for*, jaw*, jump all over*, rail at*, rake over the coals*, rate, rebuke, reprimand, reproach, reprove, revile, scold, scorch, tell off, tongue-lash, upbraid, vituperate; CONCEPT 52 —*Ant.* compliment, hail, praise

bereavement [n] *death; loss* affliction, deprivation, distress, misfortune, sorrow, tribulation; CONCEPTS 230,674

bereft [adj] *lacking; missing* beggared, bereaved, cut off, deprived, destitute, devoid, dispossessed, divested, fleeced, impoverished, left without, minus, naked, parted from, robbed, shorn, stripped, wanting, without; CONCEPTS 546,576 —*Ant.* full, happy

berry [n] *small fruit* bean, drupe, drupelet, grain, haw, hip, kernel, pome, seed; CONCEPT 426

berserk [adj] *crazed* crazy, demented, deranged, insane, mad, maniacal, manic, violent; CONCEPT 403

berth [n1] *harbor; bunk* anchorage, bed, bedroom, billet, compartment, cot, dock, hammock, haven, jetty, levee, pier, port, quay, slip, wharf; CONCEPTS 513,516

berth [n2] *position of responsibility* appointment, billet, capacity, connection, employment, job, living, office, place, post, profession, situation, spot; CONCEPTS 362,668

beseech [v] *beg* adjure, appeal, ask, call upon, crave, entreat, implore, importune, invoke, petition, plead, pray, solicit, sue, supplicate; CONCEPT 48 —*Ant.* give, offer

beset [v] *plague; hem in* aggress, assail, attack, badger, bedevil, beleaguer, besiege, bug*, circle*, compass, dog*, drive up the wall*, embarrass, encircle, enclose, encompass, entangle, environ, fall on, fall upon, girdle, give a bad time*, give a hard time*, give one the business*, give the needle*, harass, harry, hassle, infest, invade, jump on one's case*, nag, nudge, overrun, perplex, pester, pick on, put the squeeze on*, ride, ring, start in on, storm, strike, surround; CONCEPTS 7,19

beside [adv/prep] *next to* abreast of, adjacent to, adjoining, alongside, aside, a step from, at one's elbow, at the edge of, at the side of, bordering on, by, cheek by jowl*, close at hand, close to, close upon, connected with, contiguous to, fornent, in juxtaposition, near, nearby, neck and neck*, neighboring, next door to, nigh, opposite, overlooking, round, side by side, verging on, with; CONCEPT 586

beside oneself [adj] *very upset* berserk, crazed, delirious, demented, distraught, frantic, frenetic, insane, mad, unbalanced, unhinged; CONCEPTS 403,485,570

besides [adv] *in addition; as well* added to, additionally, along with, also, and all, apart from, aside from, as well as, beyond, conjointly, else, exceeding, exclusive of, extra, further, furthermore, in conjunction with, in distinction to, in excess of, in other respects, likewise, more, moreover, more than, not counting, on the side*, on top of everything, other than, otherwise, over and above, plus, secondly, supplementary to, to boot*, together with, too, what's more*, with the exception of, yet; CONCEPT 772

besides [prep1] *apart from* aside from, bar, barring, beside, but, except, excepting, excluding, exclusive of, in addition to, other than, outside of, over and above, save, without; CONCEPT 772

besides [prep2] *in addition to* added to, along with, as well as, beside, beyond, in excess of, more than, on top of, other than, over and above, plus, supplementary, together with; CONCEPT 772

beside the point [adj] *not important* extraneous, immaterial, inapplicable, incidental, inconsequential, irrelevant, pointless, unimportant, unrelated; CONCEPT 575

besiege [v1] *surround; assault* assail, attack, beleaguer, beset, blockade, come at from all sides, confine, congregate, encircle, encompass, environ, hem in, invest, lay siege to, shut in, trap, work on, work over; CONCEPTS 86,90 —Ant. leave alone

besiege [v2] *bother* badger, beleaguer, bug*, buttonhole*, harass, harry, hound*, importune, nag, pester, plague, trouble; CONCEPTS 7,19 —Ant. leave alone

best [adj1] *most excellent* 10*, A-1*, ace, bad*, beyond compare, boss*, capital, champion, chief, choicest, cool*, culminating, finest, first, first-class, first-rate, foremost, greatest, highest, incomparable, inimitable, leading, matchless, nonpareil, number 1*, optimum, out-of-sight*, outstanding, paramount, peerless, perfect, preeminent, premium, prime, primo*, principal, sans pareil, second to none, super, superlative, supreme, terrific, tops, tough, transcendent, unequaled, unparalleled, unrivaled, unsurpassed; CONCEPTS 568,572 —Ant. worst

best [adj2] *correct, right* advantageous, apt, desirable, golden, most desirable, most fitting, preferred, presentable; CONCEPT 558 —Ant. incorrect, not right

best [adj3] *most* biggest, bulkiest, greatest, largest; CONCEPT 771 —Ant. fewest, least

best [adv] *most excellently* advantageously, attractively, creditably, extremely, gloriously, greatly, honorably, illustriously, magnanimously, most deeply, most fortunately, most fully, most highly, sincerely; CONCEPTS 568, 572 —Ant. worst

best [n1] *most outstanding thing in class* choice, cream, cream of the crop*, elite, fat, favorite, finest, first, flower, gem, model, nonpareil, paragon, pick, prime, prize, select, top; CONCEPT 668 —Ant. worst

best [n2] *highest personal effort* all one's got, best shot, hardest, highest endeavor, level best*, Sunday best*, utmost; CONCEPT 411

best [v] *defeat; gain advantage* beat, beat up*, better, blank*, blast*, bulldoze*, clobber*, conquer, cream*, deck*, drub*, exceed, excel, flax*, floor*, get the better of, knock off*, KO*, lambaste, let have it*, lick*, master, outclass, outdo, outshine, outstrip, overcome, prevail, put away, shoot down*, shut down*, surpass, take care of, take down*, tan*, thrash*, top, total, transcend, trash*, triumph, triumph over, trounce, wallop, waste*, wax*, whip*, whomp*, whop*, wipe*, wipe out, wipe the floor with*, zap*; CONCEPT 95 —Ant. give up, lose, relent, surrender

bestow [v] *give, allot* accord, apportion, award, bequeath, come through, commit, confer, devote, donate, entrust, favor, gift, give away, grant, hand out, honor with, impart, kick in, lavish, offer, present, put out, render to; CONCEPTS 98,108 —Ant. deprive, refuse, take

best-seller [n] *top-selling item* a top ten, chart-buster, favorite, hit*, hot item*, hot seller, mover*, number one, record-breaker, success, winner; CONCEPTS 423,446 —Ant. failure, flop

best-selling [adj] *top-selling* chart-topping, hit, number one, smash, very popular, very successful; CONCEPT 528 —Ant. failing

best shot [n] *all-out try* all one's got, best effort, best one can do, maximum effort, one's all, one's damndest, optimum effort; CONCEPTS 87,362,677,724

bet [n] *game of chance; money gambled* action, ante, betting, chance, down on, hazard, long shot, lot, lottery, odds, odds on, parlay, play, pledge, plunge, pot, raffle, random shot, risk, shot, shot in the dark*, speculation, stake, sweepstakes, uncertainty, venture, wager; CONCEPTS 28,293,329

bet [v] *gamble* ante, buy in on, chance, dice, game, hazard, lay down, lay odds, play against, play for, play the ponies*, pledge, pony up*, put, put money on, risk, set, speculate, tempt fortune*, toss up, trust, venture, wager; CONCEPTS 292,330

beta [adj] *being tested* dubious, experimental, flaky, mostly working, new, pre-release, suspect, testing, unready; CONCEPTS 529,582

bête noire [n] *trouble* adversary, anathema, antagonist, bad news*, bane, curse, devil, enemy, pet hate, plague; CONCEPTS 532,674, 675,690,728

betray [v1] *be disloyal* abandon, be unfaithful, bite the hand that feeds you*, blow the whistle*, bluff, break faith, break promise, break trust, break with, commit treason, cross, deceive, deliver up*, delude, desert, double-cross, finger*, forsake, go back on, inform against, inform on, jilt, knife*, let down, mislead, play false*, play Judas*, seduce, sell down the river*, sell out, stab in the back*, take in*, trick, turn in, turn informer, turn state's evidence, walk out on; CONCEPT 384 —Ant. be faithful, be loyal, defend, protect, support

betray [v2] *divulge, expose information* blurt out, dime*, disclose, evince, fink on*, give away, inform, lay bare, let slip, make known, manifest, rat on*, reveal, show, sing*, snitch*,

80

spill, squeal*, stool*, tattle, tell, tell on, turn in, uncover, unmask; CONCEPTS 44,60 —*Ant.* be quiet, hide, keep secret

betrayal [n1] *exhibition of disloyalty* deception, dishonesty, double-crossing, double-dealing, duplicity, falseness, giveaway, Judas kiss*, let-down, perfidy, sellout, treachery, treason, trickery, unfaithfulness; CONCEPT 633 —*Ant.* faithfulness, loyalty, protection, support

betrayal [n2] *divulgence of information* blurting out, diming*, disclosure, giving away, ratting*, revelation, snitching*, spilling*, squealing*, tattling, telling; CONCEPTS 44,60 —*Ant.* quiet, secret

betroth [v] *marry* affiance, become engaged, bind, commit, contract, engage, espouse, give one's hand, make compact, plight faith, plight troth, promise, tie oneself to, vow; CONCEPT 297 —*Ant.* divorce, leave, separate

betrothal [n] *marriage* affiancing, betrothing, engagement, espousal, plight, promise, troth, vow; CONCEPT 297 —*Ant.* divorce, separation

better [adj1] *excelling, more excellent* bigger, choice, exceeding, exceptional, finer, fitter, greater, higher quality, improved, larger, more appropriate, more desirable, more fitting, more select, more suitable, more useful, more valuable, preferable, preferred, prominent, sharpened, sophisticated, souped up*, superior, surpassing, worthier; CONCEPTS 568,572 —*Ant.* worse

better [adj2] *improved in health* convalescent, cured, fitter, fully recovered, healthier, improving, less ill, mending, more healthy, on the comeback trail*, on the mend, on the road to recovery*, out of the woods*, over the hump*, progressing, recovering, stronger, well; CONCEPT 314 —*Ant.* more ill, sicker, unhealthy, worse

better [adj3] *larger* bigger, greater, longer, more, preponderant, weightier; CONCEPTS 771,773 —*Ant.* littler, smaller, tinier

better [adv] *in a more excellent manner* finer, greater, in a superior way, more, more advantageously, more attractively, more competently, more completely, more effectively, more thoroughly, preferably, to a greater degree; CONCEPTS 568,572 —*Ant.* worse

better [v] *improve performance; outdo* advance, ameliorate, amend, beat, best, cap, correct, enhance, exceed, excel, forward, further, help, meliorate, mend, outshine, outstrip, promote, raise, rectify, refine, reform, revamp, surpass, top, transcend; CONCEPTS 141,244 —*Ant.* deteriorate, get worse, worsen

betterment [n] *improvement* advancement, amelioration, mastery, melioration, progress, prosperity, upgrading; CONCEPT 244 —*Ant.* deterioration, impairment, unhealthiness, worsening

between [adv/prep] *middle from two points* amid, amidst, among, at intervals, betwixt, bounded by, centrally located, enclosed by, halfway, in, inserted, interpolated, intervening, in the middle, in the midst of, in the seam, in the thick of, medially, mid, midway, separating, surrounded by, 'tween, within; CONCEPTS 586,820 —*Ant.* around, away, away from, outside, separate

beverage [n] *liquid refreshment* cooler, draft, drink, drinkable, libation, liquor, potable, potation; CONCEPT 454 —*Ant.* food, victuals

bevy [n] *swarm* assembly, band, bunch, cluster, collection, company, covey, crew, crowd, flight, flock, gathering, group, pack, party, troupe; CONCEPT 432 —*Ant.* individual, one

bewail [v] *cry over, lament* bemoan, deplore, eat heart out*, express sorrow, grieve for, moan, mourn, regret, repent, rue, sing the blues*, take on, wail, weep over; CONCEPT 266 —*Ant.* be happy, be joyous, exalt, gloat, praise, vaunt

beware [v] *be careful* attend, avoid, be cautious, be wary, guard against, heed, keep eyes open*, keep one's distance, keep on one's toes*, look out, mind, mind p's and q's*, notice, refrain from, shun, steer clear of*, take care, take heed, walk on eggs*, watch one's step, watch out; CONCEPT 34 —*Ant.* court, invite, risk, take on

bewilder [v] *confuse* addle, baffle, ball up*, befuddle, bemuse, confound, daze, disconcert, distract, floor*, fluster, mess with one's head*, mix up, muddle, mystify, perplex, puzzle, rattle, snow*, stump, stupefy, throw, upset; CONCEPTS 14,42 —*Ant.* clear up, explain, orient

bewildered [adj] *confused* addled, agape, aghast, agog, appalled, astonished, astounded, awed, awe-struck, baffled, befuddled, bowled over*, dazed, dazzled, disconcerted, dizzy, dumbfounded, dumbstruck, flabbergasted, flipped out*, floored*, flustered, giddy, in a dither*, lost, misled, muddled, mystified, perplexed, punchy*, puzzled, rattled, reeling, shocked, shook up, speechless, staggered, startled, stumped, stunned, stupefied, surprised, taken aback, thrown, thunderstruck*, uncertain, unglued*; CONCEPTS 402,403 —*Ant.* clear, oriented, understanding

bewilderment [n] *puzzlement* bafflement, confusion, daze, discombobulation*, disorientation, perplexity, surprise; CONCEPT 14

bewitch [v] *charm* allure, attract, bedevil, beguile, captivate, capture, control, dazzle, draw, enchant, enrapture, enthrall, entrance, fascinate, hex, hypnotize, knock dead*, knock out, put horns on*, put the whammy on*, put under magic spell*, send*, slay*, spell*, spellbind, sweep off one's feet*, take, tickle*, tickle pink*, tickle to death*, trick, turn on*, vamp, voodoo, wile, wow*; CONCEPTS 7,22 —*Ant.* disenchant, disgust, turn off

bewitched [adj] *charmed* captivated, enamored, enchanted, enraptured, ensorcelled, entranced, fallen for, fascinated, gaga about*, have a bug in one's ear*, have a thing about*, head over heels*, hooked*, hung up*, mad about, mesmerized, possessed, spellbound, transformed, turned on*, under a spell; CONCEPT 32 —*Ant.* disenchanted, disgusted, turned off

beyond [adv/prep] *further; outside limits* above, after, ahead, apart from, as well as, at a distance, away from, before, behind, besides, beyond the bounds, clear of, farther, free of, good way off, hyper, in addition to, in advance of, long way off, moreover, more remote, on the far side, on the other side, out of range, out of reach, outside, over, over and above, over there, past, remote, superior to, without, yonder; CONCEPTS 554,772,778 —Ant. close, inside

bias [n1] *belief in one way; partiality* bent, bigotry, chauvinism, disposition, favoritism, flash, head-set*, illiberality, inclination, intolerance, leaning, mind-set*, mind trip*, narrowmindedness, one-sidedness, penchant, preconception, predilection, predisposition, preference, prejudice, prepossession, proclivity, proneness, propensity, spin, standpoint, tendency, tilt, turn, unfairness, viewpoint; CONCEPT 689 —Ant. fairness, impartiality, justness

bias [n2] *diagonal weave of fabric* angle, cant, cross, incline, oblique, slant; CONCEPT 606

bias [v] *cause to favor* distort, incline, influence, make partial, prejudice, prepossess, slant, sway, twist, warp, weight; CONCEPTS 7,19 —Ant. be fair, be impartial, be just

bible [n] *holy book; authoritative book* authority, creed, doctrine, guide, guidebook, handbook, manual, sacred writ, sacred writings, scripture, testament, text, the good news; CONCEPTS 280,368

bicker [v] *nastily argue* altercate, brawl, caterwaul, cause a scene*, cavil, dig, disagree, dispute, fall out, fight, hassle, pick at, quarrel, quibble, row, scrap, scrape, spar, spat, squabble, tiff, trade zingers*, wrangle; CONCEPT 46 —Ant. agree, concede, discuss

bicycle [n] *pedal-driven recreational vehicle* bike, cycle, tandem, two-wheeler, velocipede, wheels; CONCEPTS 364,505

bid [n1] *offering of money or services* advance, amount, declaration, feeler, hit, invitation, offer, pass, price, proffer, proposal, proposition, request, submission, suggestion, sum, summons, tender; CONCEPTS 67,330

bid [n2] *endeavor* attempt, crack, effort, essay, try, venture; CONCEPT 87

bid [v1] *offer money or services* present, proffer, propose, render, submit, tender, venture; CONCEPTS 67,330

bid [v2] *say* call, greet, tell, wish; CONCEPT 266

bid [v3] *ask for; command* call, charge, demand, desire, direct, enjoin, instruct, invite, make a pass at*, make a pitch*, make a play for*, order, proposition, request, require, solicit, summon, tell, warn; CONCEPT 53

bidding [n1] *command* behest, call, charge, demand, dictate, direction, injunction, instruction, invitation, mandate, order, request, summons, word; CONCEPT 53 —Ant. answer

bidding [n2] *offering of money, services* advance, auction, invitation, offer, proffering, proposal, proposition, request, submission, suggestion, tender; CONCEPTS 67,330

bide [v] *wait* abide, attend, await, continue, dwell, hang around, hang in*, hang out*, hold the phone*, lie in wait*, linger, live, remain, reside, sit tight*, stay, stick around, sweat it*, tarry, watch for; CONCEPT 681 —Ant. go, hurry, move

big [adj1] *large, great* ample, awash, a whale of a*, brimming, bulky, bull*, burly, capacious, chock-full*, colossal, commodious, considerable, copious, crowded, enormous, extensive, fat, full, gigantic, heavy-duty*, heavyweight, hefty, huge, hulking, humongous*, husky, immense, jumbo, mammoth, massive, mondo*,

monster*, oversize, packed, ponderous, prodigious, roomy, sizable, spacious, strapping, stuffed, substantial, super colossal*, thundering, tremendous, vast, voluminous, walloping, whopper, whopping; CONCEPTS 771,773 —Ant. itsy, little, small, tiny

big [adj2] *important* big league*, big-time*, consequential, considerable, eminent, heavy-duty*, heavyweight, influential, leading, main, major league*, material, meaningful, momentous, paramount, popular, powerful, prime, principal, prominent, serious, significant, substantial, super, super colossal*, valuable, weighty; CONCEPT 568 —Ant. blah, bland, dull, unimportant

big [adj3] *grown* adult, elder, full-grown, grown-up, mature, tall; CONCEPTS 578,797 —Ant. adolescent, baby, babyish, infant, infantile, juvenile

big [adj4] *generous* altruistic, benevolent, big-hearted, chivalrous, considerate, free, gracious, greathearted, heroic, liberal, lofty, magnanimous, noble, princely, unselfish; CONCEPT 404 —Ant. selfish, ungenerous, ungiving

big [adj5] *arrogant* arty, boastful, bragging, conceited, flamboyant, haughty, high-sounding, imperious, imposing, inflated, overblown, pompous, presumptuous, pretentious, proud; CONCEPT 401 —Ant. humble, shy, unconfident

big deal [n] *something or someone important* big cheese*, big enchilada*, big fish*, biggie*, big gun*, big shot*, big wheel*, bigwig*, boss, boss man*, head honcho*, hotshot*, important person, top dog*, tycoon, very important person, VIP; CONCEPT 347

big-hearted [adj] *very kind* altruistic, benevolent, compassionate, generous, giving, gracious, noble; CONCEPTS 404,542

big league [adj] *important* big-time, chief, critical, crucial, exceptional, four-star, front-page*, grave, great, heavy, high-power, major-league, playing hard ball*, professional, serious, strictly business; CONCEPTS 567,568

bigmouth [n] *a loudmouth* bag of wind*, big talker*, blowhard*, blusterer, boaster, brag, braggart, bragger, bull artist*, bull-thrower*, gasbag*, gossiper, grandstander, know-it-all, show-off, swelled head*, trumpeter*, windbag*; CONCEPTS 412,423

bigot [n] *intolerant, prejudiced person* chauvinist, diehard, doctrinaire, dogmatist, enthusiast, extremist, fanatic, fiend, maniac, monomaniac, opinionated person, partisan, persecutor, puritan, racist, sectarian, segregationist, sexist, stickler, superpatriot, zealot; CONCEPTS 359,423 —Ant. humanitarian, liberal, tolerator

bigoted [adj] *intolerant, prejudiced* biased, chauvinistic, dogmatic, narrow, narrow-minded, obstinate, opinionated, partial, partisan, sectarian, slanted, small-minded, twisted, unfair, warped; CONCEPTS 403,555 —Ant. broad-minded, fair, humanitarian, just, open-minded, tolerant, unprejudiced

bigotry [n] *intolerance, prejudice* bias, discrimination, dogmatism, fanaticism, injustice, Jim Crowism*, narrow-mindedness, partiality, provincialism, racialism, racism, sectarianism, sexism, unfairness; CONCEPTS 388,410 —Ant. broad-mindedness, fairness, open-mindedness, tolerance

be
bi

big shot [n] *important person* big cheese*, big gun*, big wheel*, bigwig*, celebrity, dignitary, heavy-hitter*, heavyweight*, mogul, personage, somebody, VIP; CONCEPT 423

big win [n1] *overwhelming success or victory* coup, coup d'etat, obliteration; CONCEPT 706

big win [n2] *desirable chance discovery* accidental discovery, chance discovery, good fortune, luck, serendipity; CONCEPT 693

bilateral [adj] *having two sides* mutual, reciprocal, respective, two-sided; CONCEPT 562 —Ant. multilateral, unilateral

bilk [v] *cheat* bamboozle*, beat, circumvent, con, deceive, defraud, disappoint, do*, fleece*, flimflam*, foil, frustrate, gyp*, overreach, rook*, ruin, snow*, swindle, thwart, trick; CONCEPTS 59,139 —Ant. give, give away

bill [n1] *account of charges; money owed* bad news*, check, chit, damage*, debt, invoice, IOU, itemized account, knock*, note, reckoning, request for payment, score, statement, statement of indebtedness, tab; CONCEPTS 329,332

bill [n2] *list; circular* advertisement, affiche, agenda, bulletin, card, catalogue, flyer, handbill, handout, inventory, leaflet, listing, notice, placard, playbill, poster, program, roster, schedule, syllabus; CONCEPTS 280,283

bill [n3] *piece of legislation* act, draft, measure, projected law, proposal, proposed act; CONCEPTS 271,318

bill [n4] *piece of paper money* bank note, buck, certificate, currency, dollar, greenback*, long green*, skin*; CONCEPT 340 —Ant. coin

bill [n5] *beak of animal* mandible, neb, nib, pecker, projection; CONCEPT 399

bill [v1] *charge money for goods, services* bone, chase, debit, draw upon, dun, figure, invoice, put the arm on*, put the bite on*, put the squeeze on*, reckon, record, render, solicit; CONCEPTS 330,342

bill [v2] *advertise* announce, book, give advance notice, post; CONCEPTS 60,292

billow [n] *surging mass* beachcomber, breaker, crest, roller, surge, swell, tide, wave; CONCEPTS 437,514

billow [v] *surge* balloon, belly, bloat, bounce, bulge, ebb and flow, heave, pitch, puff up, ripple, rise and fall, rise up, rock, roll, swell, toss, undulate, wave; CONCEPTS 159,208

billowy [adj] *surging* bouncing, bouncy, bulgy, distended, ebbing and flowing, heaving, puffy, rippled, rippling, rising, rising and falling, rolling, swelling, swirling, swollen, undulating, waving, wavy; CONCEPTS 486,584

bind [n] *predicament* between a rock and a hard place*, crunch*, difficulty, dilemma, hot water*, no-win situation*, nuisance, pickle*, predicament, quandary, sticky situation*, tight situation, tight spot*; CONCEPTS 230,674

bind [v1] *fasten, secure* adhere, attach, bandage, border, chain, cinch, clamp, connect, constrict, cover, dress, edge, encase, enchain, enfetter, fetter, finish, fix, fold, furl, glue, hamper, handcuff, hem, hitch, hitch on, hobble, hook on, hook up, lace, lap, lash, leash, manacle, moor, muzzle, peg down, pin, pin down, pinion, put together, restrain, restrict, rope, shackle, stick, strap, swathe, tack on, tether, tie, tie up, trammel, trim, truss, unite, wrap,

yoke; CONCEPTS 85,160 —Ant. free, loose, loosen, release, set free, unbind, unfasten, untie

bind [v2] *obligate; restrict* compel, confine, constrain, detain, engage, enslave, force, hamper, hinder, hogtie*, indenture, lock up, necessitate, oblige, prescribe, put half nelson on*, put lock on*, require, restrain, restrict, yoke; CONCEPTS 14,130 —Ant. allow, free, let, permit, set free

binding [adj1] *necessary* bounden*, compulsory, conclusive, counted upon, essential, imperative, incumbent on, indissoluble, irrevocable, mandatory, obligatory, required, requisite, unalterable; CONCEPT 546

binding [adj2] *confining* attached, enslaved, fastened, indentured, limiting, restraining, tied, tying; CONCEPT 554 —Ant. alterable, breakable, revocable, unbinding, unconfining, unnecessary

binding [n] *cover; something which fastens* adhesive, belt, fastener, jacket, tie, wrapper; CONCEPT 475

binge [n] *spree* affair, bender, blind*, bout*, carousal, compotation, drunk*, fling, jag*, orgy*, toot*; CONCEPT 386 —Ant. saving

biography [n] *account of person's life* adventures, autobiography, bio, biog, close-up, confessions, diary, experiences, journal, letters, life, life history, life story, memoir, personal account, personal anecdote, personal narrative, personal record, picture, profile, résumé, saga, sketch, vita; CONCEPTS 280,282

bird [n] *flying animal* feathered creature, fowl, game; CONCEPT 395

birds of a feather [n] *two of a kind* Bobbsey twins, close friends, compadres, comrades, friends, two minds thinking as one; CONCEPT 423

birth [n1] *becoming alive* bearing, beginning, birthing, blessed event*, childbearing, childbirth, creation, act of God, delivery, labor, nascency, natality, nativity, parturition, producing, travail, visit from stork*; CONCEPTS 302, 373 —Ant. death

birth [n2] *beginning* commencement, dawn, dawning, emergence, fountainhead, genesis, onset, opening, origin, outset, rise, source, start; CONCEPT 119 —Ant. conclusion, death, end, ending, finish

birth [n3] *heritage* ancestry, background, blood, breeding, derivation, descent, extraction, forebears, genealogy, heritance, legacy, line, lineage, parentage, pedigree, position, race, rank, station, status, stock, strain; CONCEPTS 296,648

birth control [n] *method of preventing pregnancy* abstinence, condom, contraception, contraceptive, diaphragm, IUD, pill, planned parenthood, rhythm method, rubber, safety*, tied tubes, vasectomy; CONCEPTS 121,375

birth defect [n1] *congenital defect* abnormality, congenital malformation, deformity; CONCEPT 580

birthmark [n] *blemish one is born with* angioma, beauty mark, hemangioma, mole, mother's mark, nevus, port wine stain; CONCEPT 580

bisect [v] *divide in two* bifurcate, branch off, cleave, cross, cut across, cut in half, cut in two, dichotomize, dimidiate, divaricate, divide in two, fork, furcate, halve, hemisect, intersect, separate, split, split down the middle; CONCEPTS 98,137,176 —*Ant.* combine, join

bisexual [*adj*] *having relations with either gender* AC-DC*, androgynous, bi*, epicene, gynandrous, hermaphroditic, intersexual, monoclinous, swings both ways*; CONCEPT 372 —*Ant.* heterosexual, homosexual

bistro [*n*] *drinkery with food* bar, lounge, restaurant, tavern; CONCEPTS 439,448,449

bit [*n1*] *tiny piece* atom, butt, chicken feed*, chip, chunk, crumb, dab, dash, division, dollop, dose, dot, driblet, droplet, end, excerpt, flake, fraction, fragment, grain, iota, item, jot, lick*, lump, mite, modicum, moiety, molecule, morsel, niggle, parcel, part, particle, peanuts*, pinch, portion, sample, scale, scintilla, scrap, section, segment, shard, share, shaving, shred, slice, sliver, smidgen, snatch, snip, snippet, specimen, speck, splinter, sprinkling, stub, stump, taste, tittle, trace, trickle; CONCEPT 831 —*Ant.* whole

bit [*n2*] *short period of time* instant, jiffy, little while, minute, moment, second, space, spell, stretch, tick, while; CONCEPT 807

bit [*n3*] *computer information* 0, 1, binary digit, binary unit, data; CONCEPT 274

bite [*n1*] *injury from gripping, tearing* chaw*, chomp*, gob*, itch*, laceration, nip, pain, pinch, prick, smarting, sting, tooth marks*, wound; CONCEPT 309

bite [*n2*] *mouthful of food* brunch, drop, light meal, morsel, nibble, nosh*, piece, refreshment, sample, snack, sop*, taste; CONCEPTS 457,459

bite [*n3*] *pungency; stinging sensation* burn, edge, guts*, kick, piquancy, punch, spice, sting, zap*, zip*; CONCEPT 614

bite [*n4*] *allotment* allowance, cut, lot, part, piece, portion, quota, share, slice; CONCEPT 835

bite [*v1*] *grip or tear with teeth* champ, chaw, chaw on, chew, chomp, clamp, crunch, crush, cut, eat, gnaw, hold, lacerate, masticate, munch, nibble, nip, pierce, pinch, rend, ruminate, seize, sever, snap, take a chunk out of*, taste, tooth, wound; CONCEPTS 185,616

bite [*v2*] *corrode, eat away* burn, consume, decay, decompose, deteriorate, dissolve, eat into, engrave, erode, etch, oxidize, rot, rust, scour, sear, slash, smart, sting, tingle, wear away; CONCEPTS 215,250

bite [*v3*] *take a chance* be victim, get hooked*, nibble, risk, volunteer; CONCEPT 384 —*Ant.* be careful

bite the bullet [*v*] *take it* be forced, bow to fate, face the music*, have no choice, know no alternative, pay the piper*, stand up and take it, swallow the pill*, take one's medicine*, take the rap; CONCEPTS 23,96

biting [*adj1*] *piercing, sharp* bitter, bleak, blighting, cold, crisp, cutting, freezing, harsh, nipping, penetrating, raw; CONCEPTS 569,605 —*Ant.* bland, calm, mild

biting [*adj2*] *sarcastic* acerbic, acrimonious, bitter, caustic, cutting, incisive, mordant, scathing, severe, sharp, stinging, trenchant, withering; CONCEPT 267 —*Ant.* kind, nice, sweet

bitter [*adj1*] *pungent, sharp* absinthal, absinthian, acerb, acerbic, acid, acrid, amaroidal, astringent, harsh, sour, tart, unsweetened, vinegary; CONCEPT 613 —*Ant.* bland, mild, pleasant, sweet

bitter [*adj2*] *hostile, nasty* acrimonious, alienated, antagonistic, begrudging, biting, caustic, crabby, divided, embittered, estranged, fierce, freezing, hateful, intense, irreconcilable, morose, rancorous, resentful, sardonic, severe, sore, sour, stinging, sullen, virulent, vitriolic, with chip on shoulder*; CONCEPT 267 —*Ant.* agreeable, content, genial, kind, nice, pleasant, sweet

bitter [*adj3*] *painful, distressing* afflictive, annoying, bad, brutal, calamitous, cruel, dire, disagreeable, displeasing, distasteful, disturbing, galling, grievous, hard, harsh, heartbreaking, hurtful, inclement, intemperate, intense, merciless, offensive, poignant, provoking, rigorous, rugged, ruthless, savage, severe, sharp, stinging, unpalatable, unpleasant, vexatious, woeful; CONCEPT 537 —*Ant.* good, helping, wonderful

bitterness [*n1*] *sourness* acerbity, acidity, acridity, astringency, brackishness, brininess, piquancy, pungency, sharpness, tartness, vinegariness; CONCEPT 614 —*Ant.* sweetness

bitterness [*n2*] *agony* acrimoniousness, anguish, asperity, distress, grievousness, harshness, hostility, mordancy, pain, painfulness, sarcasm, venom, virulence; CONCEPTS 410,633 —*Ant.* contentment, geniality, happiness, sweetness

bizarre [*adj*] *strange, wild* bugged out*, camp*, comical, curious, eccentric, extraordinary, fantastic, far-out*, freakish, grody*, grotesque, kooky, ludicrous, odd, oddball, offbeat, off the wall*, outlandish, outré, peculiar, queer, ridiculous, singular, unusual, way-out*, weird; CONCEPTS 547,564 —*Ant.* normal, reasonable, usual

blab [*v*] *gossip* babble, betray, blather, blurt out, chatter, disclose, divulge, gab, gabble, give away, go on, jabber, let out, let slip, mouth, peach*, prattle, reveal, run off at the mouth*, run on, shoot the breeze*, spill*, spill the beans*, squeal*, talk through one's hat*, tattle, tell, tell on, yak*, yakkety-yak*; CONCEPTS 55,60 —*Ant.* be quiet, shut up

blabbermouth [*n*] *someone who talks too much* babblemouth, babbler, bag of wind*, bigmouth, blabber, blabberer, blowhard*, chatterbox, chatterer, gabber, gasbag*, gossiper, gossipmonger, jabberer, loudmouth, motor-mouth, squealer*, tattletale, windbag*, yapper; CONCEPTS 412,423

black [*adj1*] *dark, inky* atramentous, brunet, charcoal, clouded, coal, dingy, dusky, ebon, ebony, inklike, jet, livid, melanoid, murky, obsidian, onyx, piceous, pitch, pitch-dark, raven, sable, shadowy, slate, sloe, somber, sombre, sooty, starless, stygian, swart, swarthy; CONCEPT 618 —*Ant.* white

black [*adj2*] *hopeless* atrocious, bleak, depressing, depressive, dismal, dispiriting, distressing, doleful, dreary, foreboding, funereal, gloomy, horrible, lugubrious, mournful, ominous, oppressive, sad, sinister, sombre, threatening; CONCEPTS 529,570 —*Ant.* hopeful, optimistic

black [*adj3*] *dirty* dingy, filthy, foul, grimy, grubby, impure, nasty, soiled, sooty, spotted, squalid, stained, unclean, uncleanly; CONCEPT 589 —*Ant.* clean

black [*adj4*] *angry* enraged, fierce, furious, hostile, menacing, resentful, sour, sullen, threatening; CONCEPT 403 —*Ant.* happy

bi
bl

black [adj5] evil bad, diabolical, iniquitous, mean, nefarious, villainous, wicked; CONCEPT 545 —Ant. good

black [n] African-American African, Afro-American, Negro; CONCEPT 380 —Ant. Caucasian, white

blackball [v] expel from group ban, blacklist, debar, exclude, ostracize, oust, reject, repudiate, snub, veto; CONCEPTS 25,384

blacken [v1] darken befoul, begrime, blot, cloud, deepen, ebonize, grow dark, grow dim, ink, make dark, shade, smudge, soil; CONCEPT 250 —Ant. bleach, lighten, whiten

blacken [v2] malign; smear asperse, attack, bad-mouth*, blot, blotch, calumniate, decry, defame, defile, denigrate, dishonor, do a number on*, give a black eye*, knock*, libel, malign, rip*, rip up and down*, slander, slur, smudge, stain, sully, taint, tarnish, traduce, vilify; CONCEPT 54 —Ant. compliment, enhance, praise

black hole [n] abyss great void, supernova, theoretical mass, void; CONCEPTS 509,514

blacklist [v] ban blackball, boycott, debar, exclude, expel, hit list*, ostracize, preclude, proscribe, put on hit list*, reject, repudiate, snub, thumbs down*, vote against; CONCEPT 25 —Ant. accept, allow, ask in, permit, welcome

black magic [n] sorcery diabolism, magic, necromancy, voodoo, witchcraft, wizardry; CONCEPTS 370,689

blackmail [n] intimidation for money; money to quiet informer bribe, bribery, exaction, extortion, hush money*, milking*, payoff, protection, ransom, slush fund*, tribute; CONCEPTS 123,192

blackmail [v] intimidating for money badger, bleed, coerce, compel, demand, exact, extort, force, hold to ransom, milk*, put the shake on*, ransom, shake*, shake down*, squeeze*, threaten; CONCEPTS 192,342

black market [n] illegal sales bootleg market, underground, underground market, underworld market; CONCEPT 323

black out [v1] delete; cover batten, conceal, cover up, cross out, cut off, darken, eclipse, eradicate, erase, hold back, make dark, obfuscate, rub out, shade, squash, squelch; CONCEPT 250 —Ant. add, pencil in, uncover

black out [v2] faint collapse, crap out*, draw a blank*, go out like a light*, lose consciousness, pass out*, slip into coma, swoon*, zonk out*; CONCEPT 303 —Ant. resuscitate, revive

black sheep [n] disgraceful person ne'er-do-well, outcast, pariah, prodigal, reject, reprobate; CONCEPT 423

blade [n] cutting tool brand, cutlass, edge, épée, knife, shank, sword; CONCEPTS 495,499

blah [adj] dull, lifeless banausic, bland, boring, dim, dreary, humdrum, monotone, monotonous, pedestrian, plodding, yawn producing*; CONCEPT 544 —Ant. exciting, full of life, spirited

blame [n1] condemnation accusation, animadversion, arraignment, attack, attribution, castigation, censure, charge, chiding, complaint, criticism, denunciation, depreciation, diatribe, disapprobation, disapproval, disfavor, disparagement, expostulation, exprobation, impeachment, implication, imputation, incrimination, inculpation, indictment, invective, objurgation, obloquy, opposition, rebuke, recrimination, remonstrance, reprehension, reprimand, reproach, reprobation, reproof, repudiation, slur, tirade; CONCEPT 54 —Ant. applause, commendation, exaltation, exculpation, exoneration, praise, thanks

blame [n2] responsibility accountability, answerability, burden, culpability, fault, guilt, incrimination, liability, onus, rap*; CONCEPTS 639,661

blame [v] accuse; place responsibility admonish, ascribe, attribute, blast, blow the whistle on*, censure, charge, chide, climb all over*, condemn, criticize, denounce, denunciate, disapprove, express disapprobation, find fault with, finger*, frame, hold responsible, impute, indict, jump all over*, jump down one's throat*, knock*, lay a bad trip on*, lay at one's door*, lay to*, let one have it*, lower the boom*, pass the buck*, point the finger*, rap, rebuke, reprehend, reproach, reprove, roast*, saddle, skin*, stick it to*, tax, upbraid; CONCEPT 44 —Ant. applaud, commend, exalt, exculpate, exonerate, praise, thank

blameless [adj] not responsible above suspicion, clean, clean-handed, clear, crimeless, exemplary, faultless, good, guilt-free, guiltless, immaculate, impeccable, inculpable, innocent, in the clear*, irreprehensible, irreproachable, not guilty, perfect, pure, righteous, stainless, unblemished, unimpeachable, unoffending, unspotted, unsullied, untarnished, upright, virtuous; CONCEPT 555 —Ant. culpable, guilty, impeachable, reproachable, responsible

blanch [v] become afraid flinch, pale, recoil, shrink, start, wince; CONCEPT 27 —Ant. be brave

bland [adj1] tasteless; undistinctive banal, blah*, boring, dull, dull as dishwater*, flat, flavorless, ho hum*, humdrum, insipid, milk-and-water*, monotonous, nerdy*, nothing, pabulum*, sapless*, tame, tedious, unexciting, uninspiring, uninteresting, unstimulating, vanilla*, vapid, waterish, watery, weak, wimpy*, wishy-washy*, zero*; CONCEPTS 589,613 —Ant. delicious, distinctive, sharp, tasty, yummy

bland [adj2] friendly, gracious affable, amiable, civilized, congenial, courteous, gentle, good-natured, ingratiating, oily, pleasant, smooth, suave, unctuous, unemotional, urbane; CONCEPT 401 —Ant. blase, dull, unfriendly, ungracious

bland [adj3] mild, temperate balmy, calm, calmative, clear, lenient, mollifying, nonirritant, nonirritating, smooth, soft, soothing; CONCEPTS 485,605 —Ant. bitter, caustic, severe, sharp, zingy

blank [adj1] clear bare, barren, clean, empty, fresh, new, pale, plain, spotless, uncompleted, unfilled, unmarked, untouched, unused, vacant, vacuous, virgin, virginal, void, white; CONCEPTS 485,562 —Ant. filled, full, habited, occupied

blank [adj2] expressionless deadpan, dull, empty, fruitless, hollow, immobile, impassive, inane, inexpressive, inscrutable, lifeless, masklike, meaningless, noncommittal, poker-faced, stiff, stupid, uncommunicative, unexpressive, vacant, vacuous, vague; CONCEPT 406 —Ant. animated

blank [*adj*3] *dumbfounded* at a loss, awestruck, bewildered, confounded, confused, dazed, disconcerted, muddled, nonplussed, stupefied, uncomprehending, wonderstruck; CONCEPT 402 —*Ant.* aware, excited, understanding

blank [*adj*4] *absolute, utter* complete, downright, out-and-out, outright, perfect, regular, sheer, straight-out, thorough, total, unconditional, unqualified; CONCEPT 531

blank [*n*] *empty space* abyss, cavity, chasm, emptiness, gap, gulf, hiatus, hole, hollow, hollowness, interstice, interval, lacuna, nihility, nothingness, nullity, omission, opening, preterition, pretermission, skip, tabula rasa, vacancy, vacuity, vacuum, void, womb; CONCEPT 513

blank check [*n*] *carte blanche* free hand, free rein, license, permission, permit, say-so, the run of, total freedom, unconditional authority, unconditional right; CONCEPT 376

blanket [*adj*] *comprehensive* absolute, across-the-board, all-inclusive, overall, powerful, sweeping, unconditional, wide-ranging; CONCEPT 772 —*Ant.* incomplete, uncomprehensive

blanket [*n*] *cover, covering* afghan, carpet, cloak, coat, coating, comforter, covering, coverlet, envelope, film, fleece, layer, mat, puff, quilt, rug, sheath, sheet, throw, wrapper; CONCEPTS 473,475

blanket [*v*] *cover* bury, cloak, cloud, coat, conceal, crown, eclipse, envelop, hide, mask, obscure, overcast, overlay, overspread, suppress, surround; CONCEPT 172 —*Ant.* lay bare, uncover

blare [*v*] *make loud noise* bark, bellow, blast, boom, bray, clamor, clang, honk, hoot, peal, resound, roar, scream, shout, shriek, sound out, toot, trumpet; CONCEPTS 65,77 —*Ant.* toot

blarney [*n*] *flattery* adulation, a line*, baloney*, blandishment, cajolery, coaxing, compliments, exaggeration, eyewash*, fawning*, honey*, incense, ingratiation, inveiglement, oil*, overpraise, soft soap*, soft words, sweet talk*, wheedling; CONCEPT 69

blasé [*adj*] *nonchalant* apathetic, been around twice*, bored, cloyed, cool*, disenchanted, disentranced, done it all*, fed up*, glutted, indifferent, jaded, knowing, laid-back*, lukewarm*, mellow*, mundane, offhand, satiated, sick of, sophisticate, sophisticated, surfeited, unconcerned, unexcited, uninterested, unmoved, weary, worldly, world-weary; CONCEPT 404 —*Ant.* enthusiastic, excited

blasphemous [*adj*] *irreverent* cursing, disrespectful, godless, impious, insulting, irreligious, profanatory, profane, sacrilegious, swearing, ungodly; CONCEPT 545 —*Ant.* godly, pious, religious, respectful, reverent

blasphemy [*n*] *irreverence* abuse, cursing, cussing, desecration, execration, heresy, impiety, impiousness, imprecation, indignity, lewdness, profanation, profaneness, profanity, reviling, sacrilege, scoffing, scurrility, swearing, vituperation; CONCEPT 645 —*Ant.* godliness, piety, religion, religiousness, reverence

blast [*n*1/*v*1] *loud sound; make loud sound* bang, blare, blow, burst, clang, clap, crack, din, honk, peal, roar, scream, slam, smash, toot, trumpet, wail, wham; CONCEPTS 65,521,595

blast [*n*2] *explosion* bang, blow-up, burst, crash, detonation, discharge, dynamite, eruption, outbreak, outburst, salvo, volley; CONCEPTS 179,521

blast [*n*3] *gust of wind* blow, draft, gale, squall, storm, strong breeze, tempest; CONCEPTS 437,524 —*Ant.* breeze, quiet, stillness

blast [*n*4] *fun time* amusement, bash*, blow out*, excitement, good time, great time, party, riot*; CONCEPT 386

blast [*v*2] *explode* annihilate, blight, blow up, bomb, break up, burst, damage, dash, demolish, destroy, detonate, dynamite, injure, kill, ruin, shatter, shrivel, spoil, stunt, torpedo, wither, wreck; CONCEPTS 86,179

blast [*v*3] *lambaste; defeat mentally* attack, beat, castigate, clobber*, criticize, drub*, flay, lash out at, lick*, rail at, shellac*, whip*; CONCEPT 52 —*Ant.* boost, compliment, praise, uphold

blatant [*adj*1] *obvious; brazen* arrant, bald, barefaced, brassy, clear, conspicuous, crying, flagrant, flashy, flaunting, garish, gaudy, glaring, glitzy, impudent, loud, meretricious, naked, obtrusive, ostentatious, outright, overbold, overt, plain, prominent, pronounced, protrusive, screaming, shameless, sheer, showy, snazzy, unabashed, unblushing, unmitigated; CONCEPTS 540,569 —*Ant.* inconspicuous, quiet, subtle, unpronounced

blatant [*adj*2] *deafening* boisterous, clamorous, crying, ear-splitting, harsh, loud, loudmouthed, noisy, obstreperous, obtrusive, piercing, screaming, scurrilous, strident, vociferant, vociferous, vulgar; CONCEPTS 592,594 —*Ant.* quiet, silent

blaze [*n*1] *fire* bonfire, burning, combustion, conflagration, flame, flames, holocaust, wildfire; CONCEPTS 478,521

blaze [*n*2] *flash of light* beam, brilliance, burst, flare, glare, gleam, glitter, glow, radiance; CONCEPT 628

blaze [*n*3] *torrent* blast, burst, eruption, flare-up, flash, fury, outbreak, outburst, rush, storm; CONCEPT 673

blaze [*v*] *burn brightly* beam, burst out, coruscate, explode, fire, flame, flare, flash, flicker, fulgurate, glare, gleam, glow, illuminate, illumine, incandesce, jet, light, radiate, scintillate, shimmer, shine, sparkle; CONCEPT 249

bleach [*v*] *whiten* achromatize, blanch, blench, decolor, decolorize, etiolate, fade, grow pale, lighten, make pale, peroxide, wash out; CONCEPT 250 —*Ant.* blacken, darken, yellow

bleachers [*n*] *seating for watching event* benches, boxes, grandstand, Ruthville*, seats, stands; CONCEPTS 440,443

bleak [*adj*1] *barren* austere, bare, blank, blighted, bombed, bulldozed, burned, chilly, cleared, cold, deforested, desert, deserted, desolate, dreary, exposed, flat, gaunt, grim, open, raw, scorched, stripped, unpopulated, unsheltered, weather-beaten, wild, windswept; CONCEPT 490 —*Ant.* appealing, bright, comfortable, nice, pleasant, sunny

bleak [*adj*2] *depressing* black, cheerless, comfortless, dark, discouraging, disheartening, dismal, drear, dreary, funereal, gloomy, grim, hard, harsh, hopeless, joyless, lonely, melancholy, mournful, oppressive, sad, somber, unpromising; CONCEPTS 403,537 —*Ant.*

cheerful, comforting, congenial, encouraging, nice, pleasant

bleed [v1] *cause blood to flow* drain, exude, gush, hemorrhage, leech, ooze, open vein, phlebotomize, run, seep, shed, spurt, trickle, weep; CONCEPT 185

bleed [v2] *extort* blackmail, confiscate, deplete, drain, exhaust, extract, fleece, impoverish, leech*, milk*, mulct, overcharge, pauperize, put the screws to*, rook*, sap*, skin*, squeeze*, steal, stick*, strong-arm; CONCEPTS 192,342

bleed [v3] *grieve* ache, agonize, be in pain, feel for, pity, suffer, sympathize; CONCEPTS 12,17

blemish [n] *flaw* beauty spot, birthmark, blackhead, blister, bloom*, blot, blotch, blot on the landscape*, blur, brand, bruise, bug*, catch, chip, cicatrix, defacement, defect, deformity, dent, discoloration, disfigurement, disgrace, dishonor, eyesore, fault, freckle, hickey*, imperfection, impurity, lentigo, lump, macula, maculation, mark, mole, nevus, nodule, patch, pimple, pock, pockmark, scar, second, sight, smudge, snag, speck, speckle, spot, stain, stigma, taint, tarnish, vice, wart, whitehead, zit*; CONCEPT 580 —Ant. adornment, decoration, embellishment, ornament

blemish [v] *flaw, disfigure* blot, blotch, blur, damage, deface, distort, harm, hurt, impair, injure, maim, mangle, mar, mark, mutilate, pervert, prejudice, scar, smudge, spoil, spot, stain, sully, taint, tarnish, twist, vitiate, wrench; CONCEPTS 54,246 —Ant. adorn, beautify, decorate, embellish, ornament

blend [n] *composite, mix* alloy, amalgam, amalgamation, brew, combination, commixture, composite, compound, concoction, fusion, interfusion, intermixture, mixture, synthesis, union; CONCEPT 432 —Ant. natural element, separation

blend [v1] *mix* amalgamate, cement, coalesce, combine, commingle, commix, compound, fuse, integrate, interblend, intermix, meld, merge, mingle, synthesize, unite, weld; CONCEPT 109 —Ant. disperse, divide, separate, unmix

blend [v2] *harmonize* arrange, complement, fit, go well, go with, integrate, orchestrate, suit, symphonize, synthesize, unify; CONCEPT 656 —Ant. disharmonize, unmix

bless [v1] *sanctify* absolve, anoint, baptize, beatify, canonize, commend, confirm, consecrate, cross, dedicate, enshrine, eulogize, exalt, extol, give thanks to, glorify, hallow, honor, invoke benefits, invoke happiness, laud, magnify, make holy, offer, offer benediction, ordain, panegyrize, praise, pray for, pronounce holy, sacrifice, sign, sprinkle, thank; CONCEPTS 69,367 —Ant. condemn, curse, damn

bless [v2] *grant, bestow* celebrate, endow, favor, give, glorify, grace, laud, magnify, praise, provide; CONCEPTS 50,88 —Ant. deny, disallow, disapprove, refuse, veto

blessed [adj1] *sanctified* adored, among the angels, beatified, consecrated, divine, enthroned, exalted, glorified, hallowed, holy, inviolable, redeemed, resurrected, revered, rewarded, sacred, sacrosanct, saved, spiritual, unprofane; CONCEPTS 536,568 —Ant. condemned, cursed, damned, disapproved

blessed [adj2] *happy* blissful, content, contented, endowed, favored, fortunate, glad, granted, joyful, joyous, lucky; CONCEPT 404 —Ant. condemned, cursed, damned, unblessed, unfavored, unhappy, unlucky

blessing [n1] *sanctification* absolution, benedicite, benediction, benison, commendation, consecration, dedication, divine sanction, grace, invocation, laying on of hands, thanks, thanksgiving; CONCEPT 367 —Ant. blight, condemnation, curse, damnification, disapproval

blessing [n2] *good wishes, approval* approbation, backing, concurrence, consent, favor, Godspeed, leave, okay*, permission, regard, sanction, support, valediction; CONCEPTS 10,50,88 —Ant. condemnation, curse, damnation, disapproval, ill will

blessing [n3] *advantage* asset, benediction, benefit, boon, bounty, break, favor, gain, gift, godsend, good, good fortune, good luck, help, kindness, lucky break, manna from heaven*, miracle, profit, service, stroke of luck*, windfall; CONCEPTS 230,679 —Ant. bad fortune, bad luck, curse, disadvantage

blight [n] *disease; plague* affliction, bane, blot on the landscape*, canker, contamination, corruption, curse, decay, dump, evil, eyesore, fungus, infestation, mildew, pest, pestilence, pollution, rot, scourge, sight, withering, woe; CONCEPTS 306,674 —Ant. blessing, boon, health, prosperity

blight [v] *ruin, destroy* annihilate, blast, crush, damage, dash, decay, disappoint, foul up*, frustrate, glitch up*, injure, mar, mess up*, nip in the bud*, nullify, shrivel, spoil, taint, trash*, wither, wreck; CONCEPT 252 —Ant. aid, bless, guard, help, prosper, protect

blimp [n] *airship* aircraft, dirigible, zeppelin; CONCEPT 504

blind [adj1] *sightless* amaurotic, blind as a bat*, dark, destitute of vision, eyeless, groping, in darkness, purblind, typhlotic, undiscerning, unseeing, unsighted, visionless; CONCEPT 619 —Ant. seeing, sighted

blind [adj2] *indifferent* careless, heedless, ignorant, imperceptive, inattentive, inconsiderate, indiscriminate, injudicious, insensitive, myopic, nearsighted, neglectful, oblivious, thoughtless, unaware, unconscious, undiscerning, unmindful, unobservant, unperceiving, unreasoning, unseeing; CONCEPT 402 —Ant. aware, cunning, quick, sharp, understanding

blind [adj3] *uncontrolled* hasty, heedless, impetuous, inconsiderate, irrational, mindless, rash, reckless, senseless, shortsighted, thoughtless, unseeing, unthinking, violent, wild; CONCEPT 544 —Ant. controlled

blind [adj4] *hidden or covered* blocked, closed, closed at one end, concealed, dark, dead-end, dim, disguised, impassable, leading nowhere, obscured, obstructed, secluded, unmarked, without egress, without exit; CONCEPTS 490,576 —Ant. open, revealed, uncovered

blind [n] *screen, covering* blinder, blindfold, blinker, camouflage, cloak, cover, curtain, facade, front, mask, trap, veil; CONCEPT 716

blindly [adv1] *without direction, purpose* aimlessly, at random, confusedly, frantically, in all directions, indiscriminately, instinctively,

madly, pell-mell, purposelessly, wildly;
CONCEPT 542 —*Ant.* carefully, cautiously,
purposely, reasonably, sensibly

blindly [*adv2*] *carelessly* foolishly, heedlessly,
impulsively, inconsiderately, obtusely, passionately, purblindly, recklessly, regardlessly,
senselessly, thoughtlessly, tumultuously,
unreasonably, unreasoningly, willfully, without
rhyme or reason*; CONCEPT 401 —*Ant.* carefully, cautiously, considerately, sensibly

blindness [*n*] *sightlessness* amaurosis, anopsia,
astigmatism, cataracts, darkness, defect, myopia,
presbyopia, purblindness, typhlosis; CONCEPT
629 —*Ant.* sight, sightedness

blind-side [*v*] *attack by surprise* bushwhack,
catch unaware, hit unexpectedly, sucker-punch*;
CONCEPTS 86,189,200

blink [*v1*] *wink of eye; twinkle* bat, flash, flicker,
flutter, glimmer, glitter, nictate, nictitate,
scintillate, shimmer, sparkle, squint; CONCEPTS
185,624

blink [*v2*] *ignore* bypass, condone, connive,
cushion, discount, disregard, fail, forget, neglect, omit, overlook, overpass, pass by, slight,
turn a blind eye*; CONCEPT 30 —*Ant.* attend,
be aware, pay attention

bliss [*n*] *ecstasy* beatitude, blessedness, cool*,
euphoria, felicity, gladness, gone*, happiness,
heaven*, joy, paradise, rapture; CONCEPTS
32,230 —*Ant.* grief, misery, sorrow, unhappiness, upset

blissful [*adj*] *happy* beatific, cool*, crazy,
delighted, dreamy, ecstatic, elated, enchanted,
enraptured, euphoric, floating*, flying*, gone*,
heavenly, in ecstasy, in seventh heaven*, in the
twilight zone*, joyful, joyous, mad*, on cloud
nine*, rapturous, sent*, spaced-out*, turned-
on*; CONCEPT 403 —*Ant.* grieving, miserable,
sorrowful, unhappy, upset, wretched

blister [*n*] *swelling* abscess, blain, bleb, boil,
bubble, bulla, burn, canker, carbuncle, cyst,
furuncle, pimple, pustule, sac, sore, ulcer,
vesication, vesicle, wale, weal, welt, wheal;
CONCEPT 309

blithe [*adj*] *happy* animated, buoyant, carefree,
cheerful, cheery, chirpy, gay, gladsome, gleeful, jaunty, jocund, jolly, jovial, joyful, lighthearted, merry, mirthful, sprightly, sunny,
vivacious; CONCEPT 404 —*Ant.* heavyhearted,
morose, sad, sorrowful, unhappy

blitz [*n*] *heavy attack* assault, blitzkrieg, bombardment, bombing, lightning attack, offensive,
onslaught, raid, shelling, strike; CONCEPTS
86,320 —*Ant.* let-up

blizzard [*n*] *snow storm* blast, gale, precipitation, snowfall, squall, tempest, whiteout;
CONCEPT 526

bloat [*v*] *blow up like a balloon* balloon, belly,
bilge, billow, dilate, distend, enlarge, expand,
inflate, puff up, swell; CONCEPTS 184,208
—*Ant.* deflate, shrink, shrivel, tighten

blob [*n*] *drop, spot* ball, bead, blot, blotch,
bubble, dab, daub, dot, droplet, glob*, globule,
splash, splotch*; CONCEPT 432

block [*n1*] *mass of material* bar, brick, cake,
chunk, cube, hunk, ingot, loaf, lump, oblong,
piece, section, segment, slab, slice, solid,
square; CONCEPTS 470,471

block [*n2*] *obstruction* bar, barrier, blank wall,

blockage, chunk, clog, hindrance, impediment,
jam, mass, obstacle, obstruction, roadblock,
snag, stop, stoppage, wall; CONCEPTS 470,652
—*Ant.* opening

block [*v*] *obstruct* arrest, bar, barricade, blockade, block out, brake, catch, charge, check,
choke, clog, close, close off, close out, congest,
cut off, dam, deter, fill, halt, hang up*, hinder,
hold up, impede, intercept, interfere with,
occlude, plug, prevent, shut off*, shut out,
stall, stonewall, stop, stopper, stop up*, stymie,
tackle, take out of play*, thwart; CONCEPTS
121,130 —*Ant.* let go, let up, open, unblock

blockade [*n*] *barrier* bar, barricade, blank
wall, clog, closure, embolus, encirclement,
hindrance, impediment, infarct, infarction,
obstacle, obstruction, restriction, roadblock,
siege, snag, stop, stoppage, wall; CONCEPTS
470,652 —*Ant.* opening

block out [*v1*] *plan course* arrange, chart,
map out, outline, prepare, sketch; CONCEPT 36

block out [*v2*] *try to forget* close, conceal,
cover, hide, obscure, obstruct, screen, shroud,
shut off, shut out; CONCEPT 40 —*Ant.* recall,
remember

blond/blonde [*adj*] *having light-colored hair*
albino, auricomous, bleached, champagne, fair,
fair-haired, flaxen, golden-haired, light, pale,
pearly, platinum, sallow, sandy-haired, snowy,
straw, strawberry, towheaded*, washed-out,
yellow-haired; CONCEPT 618 —*Ant.* brunet,
brunette

blood [*n1*] *red body fluid* claret, clot, cruor,
gore, hemoglobin, juice, plasma, sanguine
fluid, vital fluid; CONCEPTS 393,420

blood [*n2*] *ancestry* birth, consanguinity,
descendants, descent, extraction, family,
kindred, kinship, line, lineage, origin, pedigree,
relations, stock; CONCEPT 296

bloodless [*adj1*] *unfeeling* anesthetic, cold,
coldhearted, dull, impassive, indolent, insensible, insensitive, languid, lazy, lifeless, listless,
passionless, slow, sluggish, spiritless, torpid,
unemotional, unkind; CONCEPT 404 —*Ant.*
caring, feeling, sensitive

bloodless [*adj2*] *pale* anemic, ashen, cadaverous, chalky, colorless, ghostly, lifeless, pallid,
pasty, sallow, sickly, wan, watery; CONCEPT 618
—*Ant.* blushing, flushed, rosy, ruddy, sanguine

bloodthirsty [*adj*] *murderous* barbaric, cruel,
homicidal, inhuman, ruthless, sanguinary,
savage, slaughterous; CONCEPT 401

bloody [*adj1*] *bleeding* blood-soaked, blood-
spattered, bloodstained, crimson, ensanguined,
gaping, gory, grisly, hematic, hemic, imbrued,
open, raw, sanguinary, sanguine, unstaunched,
unstopped, wounded; CONCEPT 485

bloody [*adj2*] *hard-fought* bloodthirsty, cruel,
cutthroat, decimating, ferocious, fierce, gory,
grim, heavy, homicidal, murderous, sanguinary,
sanguine, savage, slaughterous; CONCEPTS
540,569

bloom [*n*] *flower* blossom, blossoming, bud,
efflorescence, floret, flourishing, flower,
floweret, opening; CONCEPT 425

bloom [*v*] *flower; flourish* bear fruit, be in
flower, blossom, blow, bud, burgeon, burst,
develop, effloresce, fare well, fructify, germinate, grow, open, prosper, sprout, succeed,

tassel out, thrive, wax; CONCEPTS *427,706*
—*Ant.* shrink, shrivel, wither

blooper [*n*] *blunder* boner*, boo-boo*, bungle, error, faux pas, fluff*, gaffe, impropriety, indecorum, lapse, mistake, slip, solecism, trip*; CONCEPTS *384,674*

blossom [*n*] *flower* bloom, bud, efflorescence, floret, floweret, inflorescence, posy, spike; CONCEPT *425*

blossom [*v1*] *flower* bloom, blow, burgeon, burst, effloresce, leaf, open, outbloom, shoot, unfold; CONCEPT *427* —*Ant.* fade, shrink, shrivel, wither

blossom [*v2*] *flourish* batten, bloom, develop, grow, mature, progress, prosper, succeed, thrive; CONCEPT *706* —*Ant.* deteriorate, die, fade, shrink

blot [*n*] *mark; flaw* black eye*, blemish, blotch, blur, brand, defect, discoloration, disgrace, fault, odium, onus, patch, slur, smear, smudge, speck, spot, stain, stigma, taint; CONCEPTS *230,580* —*Ant.* blank, clarity

blot [*v1*] *disgrace, disfigure* bespatter, blemish, dirty, discolor, mark, smudge, smut, soil, spoil, spot, stain, sully, tarnish; CONCEPT *240* —*Ant.* beautify, grace, prettify

blot [*v2*] *soak up* absorb, dry, take up; CONCEPT *211* —*Ant.* dampen, moisten, soak, wet

blotch [*n*] *smudge* acne, blemish, blot, breakout, eruption, mark, mottling, patch, splash, spot, stain, stigma; CONCEPT *580* —*Ant.* blank, clarity, cleanness

blouse [*n*] *shirt for woman* bodice, bodysuit, middy, pullover, shell, slipover, T-shirt, turtleneck, V-neck; CONCEPT *451*

blow [*n1*] *blast, rush of air, wind* draft, flurry, gale, gust, hurricane, puff, squall, strong breeze, tempest, typhoon; CONCEPT *526*

blow [*n2*] *hard hit* bang, bash, bat, belt, biff, blindside, bop*, buffet, bump, clip, clout, clump, collision, concussion, crack, cut, ding*, impact, jab, jar, jolt, kick, knock, knockout, knuckle sandwich*, KO*, lick, percussion, poke, pound, punch, rap, shock, slam, slap, slug, smack, smash, sock, strike, stroke, swat, swing, swipe, thrust, thump, thwack*, uppercut, wallop, whack, whomp*, zap*; CONCEPT *189*

blow [*n3*] *catastrophe* affliction, balk, bolt from the blue*, bombshell*, calamity, casualty, chagrin, comedown, debacle, disappointment, disaster, disgruntlement, frustration, jolt, letdown, misadventure, misfortune, mishap, reverse, setback, shock, tragedy, upset; CONCEPT *674* —*Ant.* good fortune, luck

blow [*v1*] *blast, rush of air, wind* breathe, buffet, drive, exhale, fan, flap, flow, flutter, gasp, heave, huff, inflate, pant, puff, pump, ruffle, rush, stream, swell, swirl, waft, wave, whiff, whirl, whisk, whisper, whistle; CONCEPTS *185,526*

blow [*v2*] *make sound, usually with instrument* blare, blast, honk, mouth, pipe, play, sound, toot, trumpet, vibrate; CONCEPT *65*

blow [*v3*] *leave suddenly* depart, go, hit the road*, split*, take a hike*, take a powder*; CONCEPT *195* —*Ant.* arrive, come, come in

blow [*v4*] *ruin chance* fail, flounder, goof*, miscarry, miss; CONCEPT *699* —*Ant.* do well, succeed

blow [*v5*] *use up money* dissipate, lay out, pay out, spend, squander, waste; CONCEPT *341* —*Ant.* save

blowout [*n1*] *explosion; something exploded* blast, break, burst, detonation, eruption, escape, flat tire, leak, puncture, rupture, tear; CONCEPT *179*

blowout [*n2*] *wild party* bash, binge, feast, riot*, shindig, spree; CONCEPT *383*

blow over [*v*] *disappear slowly* cease, die down, dissipate, end, finish, fizzle out, pass, peter out*, subside, vanish; CONCEPT *699*

blow up [*v1*] *inflate* billow, bloat, distend, enlarge, expand, fill, inflate, puff up, pump up, swell; CONCEPTS *208,236,245* —*Ant.* deflate, let out, shrink, shrivel

blow up [*v2*] *explode* blast, bomb, burst, detonate, dynamite, erupt, go off, mushroom, rupture, shatter; CONCEPTS *179,320* —*Ant.* deflate

blow up [*v3*] *magnify importance* enlarge, exaggerate, heighten, overstate; CONCEPTS *49,59* —*Ant.* ignore, let go

blow up [*v4*] *burst with anger* become angry, become enraged, erupt, go off the deep end*, hit the roof*, lose control, lose temper, rage, rave; CONCEPTS *29,44* —*Ant.* be calm

blue [*adj1*] *sky, sea color* azure, beryl, cerulean, cobalt, indigo, navy, royal, sapphire, teal, turquoise, ultramarine; CONCEPT *618*

blue [*adj2*] *sad* dejected, depressed, despondent, disconsolate, dismal, dispirited, downcast, downhearted, down in the dumps*, fed up*, gloomy, glum, low, melancholy, moody, unhappy, woebegone; CONCEPT *403* —*Ant.* gay, happy, joyful, joyous, lighthearted, upbeat

blue [*adj3*] *vulgar* bawdy, dirty, indecent, lewd, naughty, obscene, off-color, racy, risqué, salty, shady, smutty, spicy, suggestive, wicked; CONCEPT *545* —*Ant.* clean, decent, unvulgar

blueprint [*n*] *plan* archetype, architectural plan, design, draft, game plan, layout, master plan, model, prototype, rendering, scheme, sketch; CONCEPTS *268,271,625*

blues [*n*] *depression* dejection, despondency, doldrums, dumps*, gloom, gloominess, glumness, heavy heart*, low spirits, melancholy, moodiness, mournfulness, sadness, the dismals*, the mopes*, unhappiness; CONCEPT *410* —*Ant.* euphoria, gaiety, gladness, happiness

bluff [*adj*] *abrupt* barefaced, bearish, blunt, blustering, breviloquent, brief, brusque, candid, crusty, curt, direct, downright, forthright, frank, gruff, hearty, honest, laconic, no-nonsense, open, outspoken, plain-spoken, rough, rude, short, short-spoken, sincere, snippety, snippy, straightforward, tactless, tart, terse, unceremonious; CONCEPT *267*

bluff [*n1*] *boast; deceit* bluster, braggadocio, bragging, bravado, deception, delusion, facade, fake, false colors, false front, feint, fraud, front, humbug*, jiving*, lie, pretense, pretext, ruse, sham, show, snow*, stall, subterfuge, trick; CONCEPTS *58,59*

bluff [*n2*] *precipice* bank, cliff, crag, escarpment, headland, hill, mountain, peak, promontory, ridge, rock; CONCEPT *509*

bluff [*v*] *deceive* affect, beguile, betray, bunco*, con, counterfeit, defraud, delude, double-cross, fake*, fake out*, feign, fool, humbug*, illude, jive*, juggle, lie, mislead, pretend, psych out*, put on*, sham*, shuck*, simulate, snow*, take in*, trick; CONCEPTS 58,59 —Ant. come clean, reveal, tell truth

blunder [n] *mistake* blooper*, boner*, boo-boo*, bungle, dumb move*, dumb thing to do*, error, fault, faux pas, flub*, flub-up*, fluff*, gaffe, goof*, howler*, impropriety, inaccuracy, indiscretion, lapse, muff*, oversight, slip, slip-up, solecism, trip*; CONCEPTS 101,230 —Ant. accuracy, correction, fix, restitution

blunder [v] *make mistake* ball up*, blow, bobble, botch, bumble, bungle, confuse, drop the ball*, err, flounder, flub*, foul up, fumble, gum up*, louse up, mess up, misjudge, screw up*, slip up, stumble; CONCEPT 101 —Ant. correct, fix, restore

blunt [adj1] *not sharp* dull, dulled, edgeless, insensitive, obtuse, pointless, round, rounded, unsharpened; CONCEPTS 485,486 —Ant. needled, pointed, sharp

blunt [adj2] *straightforward* abrupt, bluff, brief, brusque, candid, crusty, curt, discourteous, explicit, forthright, frank, gruff, impolite, matter-of-fact, outspoken, plain-spoken, rude, short, snappy, snippy, tactless, trenchant, unceremonious, uncivil, unpolished; CONCEPT 267 —Ant. polite, subtle, tactful

blunt [v] *make dull* attenuate, benumb, cripple, dampen, deaden, debilitate, desensitize, disable, enfeeble, numb, obtund, sap, soften, take the edge off, undermine, water down, weaken; CONCEPT 240 —Ant. needle, point, sharpen

blur [v1] *cloud, fog* becloud, bedim, befog, blear, blind, darken, daze, dazzle, dim, glare, make hazy, make indistinct, make vague, mask, muddy, obscure, shade, soften; CONCEPT 627 —Ant. clear, uncloud, unsmudge

blur [v2] *make dirty* besmear, blemish, blot, discolor, smear, smudge, spot, stain, taint, tarnish; CONCEPT 254 —Ant. clarify, clean, cleanse, purify

blurt [v] *utter suddenly* babble, betray, blab, burst out with, call out, come out with, cry out, disclose, divulge, exclaim, give away, jabber, leak, let on, let out, let slip, let the cat ouf of the bag*, reveal, run off at the mouth*, spill the beans*, spout; CONCEPT 47 —Ant. keep quiet

blush [n] *pink coloring* bloom, blossom, burning, color, flush, flushing, glow, glowing, mantling, pink tinge, reddening, redness, rosiness, rosy tint, ruddiness, scarlet; CONCEPT 622 —Ant. paleness, pallidity, whiteness

blush [v] *become colored, pinken* color, crimson, flush, glow, have rosy cheeks, mantle, redden, rouge, turn red, turn scarlet; CONCEPT 250 —Ant. blanch, pale

bluster [n] *bullying, intimidation* bluff, boasting, boisterousness, bombast, braggadocio, bragging, bravado, crowing, rabidity, rampancy, swagger, swaggering; CONCEPT 633

bluster [v] *bully, intimidate* badger, boast, brag, brazen, browbeat, bulldoze*, cow*, crow*, domineer, gloat, hector, rant, rave, ride the high horse*, roar, roister, shoot off one's mouth*, show off, storm, strut, swagger, swell, talk big*, vapor*, vaunt, yap*; CONCEPTS 49,78

blustery [adj] *stormy* gusting, gusty, howling, inclement, raging, roaring, rough, tempestuous,

turbulent, violent, wild, windy; CONCEPT 525 —Ant. calm, still

board [n1] *piece of wood* lath, panel, plank, slat, strip, timber; CONCEPT 479

board [n2] *meal* daily bread*, eats*, fare, food, keep*, mess, provisions, victuals; CONCEPT 459

board [n3] *group of advisers* advisers, advisory group, brass, cabinet, committee, conclave, council, directorate, directors, execs*, executives, executive suite, front office*, jury, panel, trustees, upstairs*; CONCEPTS 323,333,417 —Ant. individual, one

board [v1] *embark on vehicle* catch, climb on, embus, emplane, enter, entrain, get on, hop on, mount; CONCEPTS 159,195 —Ant. disembark, get off, leave

board [v2] *provide food and sleeping quarters* accommodate, bed, canton, care for, feed, harbor, house, let crash*, lodge, put up, quarter, room; CONCEPT 136 —Ant. turn out

boast [n] *brag; source of pride* avowal, bluster, bombast, braggadocio, bravado, exaggeration, gasconade, grandiloquence, heroics, joy, pretension, pride, pride and joy, self-satisfaction, swank, treasure, vaunt; CONCEPTS 410,710 —Ant. deprecation, modesty

boast [v1] *brag* advertise, aggrandize, attract attention, blow, blow one's own horn*, blow smoke*, bluster, bully, cock-a-doodle-doo*, con, congratulate oneself, crow, exaggerate, exult, fake, flatter oneself, flaunt, flourish, gasconade, give a good account of oneself, gloat, glory, grandstand*, hug oneself*, jive*, lay on thick*, prate, preen, psych*, puff*, shoot*, shovel*, showboat*, show off, shuck*, sling*, sound off, strut, swagger, talk big*, triumph, vapor*; CONCEPT 49 —Ant. be modest, deprecate

boast [v2] *to have advantage* be proud of, claim, exhibit, have in keeping, own, possess, pride oneself on, show off; CONCEPT 261

boastful [adj] *bragging* arrogant, big, big-headed, bombastic, cocky, conceited, crowing, egotistic, egotistical, exultant, full of hot air*, hifalutin*, hot stuff*, know-it-all, loudmouth, on ego trip*, pompous, pretentious, puffed-up, self-aggrandizing, self-applauding, smart-alecky*, snooty, strutting, stuck-up, swaggering, swanky, swollen-headed, too big for one's britches*, vainglorious, vaunting, windbag*; CONCEPTS 267,404 —Ant. deprecating, modest

boat [n] *vehicle for water travel* ark, barge, bark, bateau, bottom, bucket, canoe, catamaran, craft, dinghy, dory, hulk, ketch, launch, lifeboat, pinnace, raft, sailboat, schooner, scow, ship, skiff, sloop, steamboat, tub, yacht; CONCEPT 506

boating [n] *travel, recreation in water* canoeing, cruising, drifting, paddling, rowing, sailing, sculling, trawling, yachting; CONCEPT 363

bob [v] *bounce up and down* bow, duck, genuflect, hop, jerk, jounce, leap, nod, oscillate, quaver, quiver, ricochet, seesaw, skip, waggle, weave, wobble; CONCEPT 147

bodily [adj] *concerning animate structure* actual, animal, carnal, corporal, corporeal, fleshly, gross, human, material, natural, normal, organic, physical, sensual, somatic, substantial, tangible, unspiritual; CONCEPT 406 —Ant. mental, soulful, spiritual

bl
bc

bodily [adv] *totally* absolutely, altogether, as a body, as a group, collectively, completely, en masse, entirely, fully, wholly; CONCEPTS 531,772

body [n1] *physique* anatomy, bag of bones*, beefcake*, bod*, boody*, build, carcass, chassis, constitution, embodiment, figure, form, frame, makeup, mortal part, protoplasm, shaft, shape, tenement, torso, trunk; CONCEPT 405 —*Ant.* mind, soul, spirit

body [n2] *corpse* ashes, bones, cadaver, carcass, carrion, clay, corpus delicti, dead body, deceased, dust, relic, remains, stiff*; CONCEPT 390

body [n3] *human being* being, creature, human, individual, mortal, party, person, personage, soul; CONCEPT 389 —*Ant.* abstract, concept, fantasy, immateriality, inanimate, thought

body [n4] *bulk; central portion* assembly, basis, bed, box, chassis, core, corpus, crux, essence, frame, fuselage, gist, gravamen, groundwork, hull, main part, majority, mass, material, matter, pith, skeleton, staple, substance, substructure, sum, tenor, total, trunk, whole; CONCEPT 829 —*Ant.* nothing, nothingness

body [n5] *crowd* array, batch, bunch, bundle, clump, cluster, group, horde, lot, majority, mass, mob, multitude, parcel, party, set, society, throng; CONCEPT 417 —*Ant.* individual, one

body [n6] *main part of written work* argument, burden, core, discourse, dissertation, evidence, exposition, gist, heart, material, meat, pith, sense, substance, text, thesis, treatise, upshot; CONCEPT 270

bodyguard [n] *protector* bouncer, escort, guardian, minder, muscle*, praetorian, security guard; CONCEPT 348

bog [n] *swamp* fen, lowland, marsh, marshland, mire, morass, moss, peat, quag, quagmire, slough, sump, wetlands; CONCEPT 509

bog down [v] *stick; become stuck* decelerate, delay, detain, halt, hang up, impede, retard, set back, sink, slacken, slow down, slow up, stall; CONCEPT 121

boggle [v] *astonish* amaze, astound, bowl over*, fill with wonder, flabbergast*, overwhelm, shock, startle; CONCEPT 42

bogus [adj] *counterfeit* artificial, dummy, ersatz, fake, false, fictitious, forged, fraudulent, imitation, not what it is cracked up to be*, phony, pretended, pseudo, sham, simulated, spurious; CONCEPT 582 —*Ant.* authentic, genuine, real

bohemian [n] *nonconformist* artist, beatnik*, dilettante, flower child*, free spirit, gypsy, hippie*, iconoclast, writer; CONCEPT 423

boil [n] *blister* abscess, blain, blister, carbuncle, excrescence, furuncle, pimple, pustule, sore, tumor, ulcer; CONCEPT 309

boil [v1] *heat to bubbling* agitate, bubble, churn, coddle, cook, decoct, effervesce, evaporate, fizz, foam, froth, parboil, poach, seethe, simmer, smolder, steam, steep, stew; CONCEPTS 170,255 —*Ant.* freeze

boil [v2] *be angry* be indignant, blow up, bristle, burn, flare, foam at the mouth*, fulminate, fume, rage, rave, sputter, storm; CONCEPT 29 —*Ant.* be happy

boiling [adj1] *very hot* baking, blistering, broiling, burning, fiery, hot, red-hot, roasting, scalding, scorching, sizzling, torrid, tropical, warm; CONCEPT 605 —*Ant.* freezing

boiling [adj2] *angered* angry, enraged, fuming, furious, incensed, indignant, infuriated, mad, raging; CONCEPT 403 —*Ant.* happy

boisterous [adj] *noisy and mischievous* bouncy, brawling, clamorous, disorderly, effervescent, impetuous, loud, obstreperous, rambunctious, raucous, riotous, rollicking, rowdy, strident, tumultous/tumultuous, unrestrained, unruly, uproarious, vociferant, vociferous, wild; CONCEPT 401 —*Ant.* calm, quiet, restrained, silent

bold [adj1] *brave* adventurous, assuming, audacious, aweless, bantam, courageous, daring, dauntless, enterprising, fearless, forward, gallant, heroic, intrepid, resolute, unafraid, undaunted, valiant, valorous; CONCEPT 401 —*Ant.* afraid, cowardly, fearful, meek, shy, timid, weak

bold [adj2] *brazen, insolent* assuming, audacious, barefaced, brash, brassy, cheeky, coming on strong*, confident, forward, fresh, gritty, gutsy, immodest, impudent, insolent, nervy, pert, presumptuous, rude, sassy, saucy, shameless, smart, smart-alecky*, spunky; CONCEPTS 401,404 —*Ant.* meek, quiet, reticent, retiring, shy, timid, timorous

bold [adj3] *bright, striking* clear, colorful, conspicuous, definite, evident, eye-catching, flashy, forceful, lively, loud, manifest, plain, prominent, pronounced, showy, spirited, strong, vivid; CONCEPTS 589,617,618 —*Ant.* faint, fair, light

bolster [v] *help* aid, assist, bear up, boost, brace, buck up, bulwark, buoy, buttress, carry, cushion, help, hold up, maintain, pick up, pillow, prop, reinforce, shore up, stay, strengthen, support, sustain, uphold; CONCEPT 110 —*Ant.* hinder, not support, obstruct, prevent, undermine

bolt [n1] *lock; part of lock* bar, brad, catch, coupling, dowel, fastener, lag, latch, lock, nut, padlock, peg, pin, pipe, rivet, rod, screw, skewer, sliding bar, spike, stake, staple, stud; CONCEPTS 470,471,680 —*Ant.* key

bolt [n2] *flash; projectile* arrow, dart, fulmination, missile, shaft, thunderbolt, thunderstroke; CONCEPTS 624,687

bolt [n3] *large roll of material* coil, curl, cylinder, package, spindle, spiral, twist; CONCEPT 432

bolt [v1] *run quickly away* abscond, bail out*, bound, cop out*, cut loose*, cut out*, dart, dash, ditch*, drop out*, dump*, escape, flee, flight, fly, hightail*, hotfoot*, hurtle, jump, kiss goodbye*, leap, leave flat*, leave high and dry*, leave holding the bag*, leave in the lurch*, make a break for it*, make off*, make tracks*, opt out*, run like scared rabbit*, run out on, rush, scamper, scoot, skedaddle*, skip, split*, spring, sprint, start, startle, step on it*, take flight, take off*, walk out on; CONCEPTS 150,195 —*Ant.* stay, wait

bolt [v2] *fasten securely* bar, deadbolt, latch, lock, secure; CONCEPT 225 —*Ant.* loosen, open, unbolt, unfasten, unlock

bolt [v3] *eat very fast* consume, cram, devour, englut, gobble, gorge, gulp, guzzle, ingurgitate, inhale, scarf*, slop, slosh, stuff, swallow whole, wolf*; CONCEPT 169 —*Ant.* dawdle

bomb [n] *exploding weapon* atom bomb, bombshell, charge, device, explosive, grenade, hydrogen bomb, mine, missile, Molotov cocktail, nuclear bomb, projectile, rocket, shell, ticker*, torpedo; CONCEPT 500

bomb [v1] *detonate weapon* attack, blast, blitz, blow up, bombard, cannonade, destroy, napalm, prang, raid, rain destruction*, rake, shell, strafe, torpedo, wipe out*, zero in*; CONCEPTS 86,252

bomb [v2] *fail miserably* blow it*, flop, flummox, go out of business, lose, wash out*, wipe out*; CONCEPT 699 —*Ant.* do well, succeed, win

bombard [v] *assault, attack* assail, barrage, batter, beset, besiege, blast, blitz, bomb, cannonade, catapult, fire upon, harass, hound, launch, open fire, pester, pound, shell, strafe, strike; CONCEPTS 7,19,86

bombastic [adj] *pompous, grandiloquent* aureate, balderdash, big-talking*, declamatory, euphuistic, flowery, full of hot air*, fustian, grandiose, highfalutin*, high-flown, histrionic, inflated, loudmouthed, magniloquent, orotund, ostentatious, overblown, ranting, rhapsodic, rhetorical, sonorous, stuffed shirt*, swollen, tumid, turgid, verbose, windbag*, windy, wordy; CONCEPT 267 —*Ant.* humble, quiet, reserved, restrained

bona fide [n] *genuine* actual, authentic, honest, kosher, legitimate, real, true, valid; CONCEPT 582

bonanza [n] *windfall* cash cow*, gold mine, treasure trove; CONCEPTS 332,337,446,710

bond [n1] *binder or fastener* band, binding, chain, connection, cord, fastening, fetter, gunk, handcuff, hookup, irons, ligature, link, linkage, manacle, network, nexus, rope, shackle, stickum*, tie, tie-in, wire; CONCEPT 497

bond [n2] *association, relation* affiliation, affinity, attachment, connection, connective, friendship, hookup, interrelationship, liaison, link, marriage, network, obligation, relationship, restraint, tie, tie-in, union; CONCEPT 388

bond [n3] *guarantee; contract* agreement, bargain, certificate, collateral, compact, convention, covenant, debenture, guaranty, obligation, pact, pledge, promise, security, transaction, warrant, warranty, word; CONCEPTS 318,684

bond [v] *fasten; stick* bind, connect, fix, fuse, glue, gum, paste, stickum*; CONCEPTS 85,160 —*Ant.* let go, loosen, open, unfasten, unstick

bondage [n] *slavery* chains, enslavement, helotry, peonage, serfage, serfdom, servility, servitude, subjection, subjugation, thrall, thralldom, villenage, yoke; CONCEPTS 136,652 —*Ant.* freedom, independence

bone [n] *piece of animate skeleton* bony process, cartilage, ossein, osseous matter; CONCEPTS 393,420

boner [n] *a mistake* blooper*, blunder, bonehead play, boo-boo*, bungle, error, false move, faux pas*, flub, flummox, foulup, gaffe, goof-up, miscalculation, miscue, misstep, muddle, muff, oversight, screw-up, slipup*, snafu*, whoops; CONCEPTS 101,230,410

boneyard [n] *burial ground* boot hill*, catacomb, cemetery, charnel, charnel house, churchyard, city of the dead*, crypt, eternal home*, funerary grounds, garden, God's acre*, Golgotha, grave, graveyard, marble town*, memorial park, mortuary, necropolis, ossuary, polyandrium, potter's field, resting place, sepulcher, tomb, vault; CONCEPTS 305,368

bonfire [n] *large prepared fire* beacon, conflagration, feu de joie, pyre; CONCEPTS 478,521

bonus [n] *unexpected extra* additional compensation, benefit, bounty, commission, dividend, fringe benefit, frosting*, gift, golden parachute*, goody*, gratuity, gravy*, hand-out*, honorarium, ice*, perk*, plus*, premium, prize, reward, special compensation, tip; CONCEPT 337

boo boo [n1] *small hurt* black and blue mark, bruise, cut, injury, laceration, scratch, sore; CONCEPTS 309,728

boo boo [n2] *small mistake* blunder, error, gaffe, goof*, misstep, oversight, screw-up*, slip; CONCEPTS 101,230,410

book [n1] *published document* album, atlas, bestseller, bible, booklet, brochure, codex, compendium, copy, dictionary, dissertation, edition, encyclopedia, essay, fiction, folio, handbook, hardcover, leaflet, lexicon, magazine, manual, monograph, nonfiction, novel, octavo, offprint, omnibus, opus, opuscule, pamphlet, paperback, periodical, portfolio, preprint, primer, publication, quarto, reader, reprint, roll, scroll, softcover, speller, text, textbook, thesaurus, tome, tract, treatise, vade mecum, volume, work, writing; CONCEPT 280

book [n2] *account; diary* agenda, album, list, notebook, pad, record, register, roster; CONCEPTS 271,331

book [v1] *register, arrange for* bespeak, bill, charter, engage, enroll, enter, hire, line up*, make reservation, order, organize, pencil in*, preengage, procure, program, reserve, schedule, set up, sew up*; CONCEPT 36 —*Ant.* bow out, cancel

book [v2] *arrest* accuse, charge, prefer charges, take into custody; CONCEPT 317 —*Ant.* exonerate, free, let go

booking [n] *engagement* gig, performance date, play date, tour date; CONCEPT 384

booklet [n] *pamphlet* brochure, circular, flyer, handbill, handout, leaflet, mailer, notice, tract; CONCEPT 280

boom [n1] *loud sound; crash* bang, barrage, blare, blast, burst, cannonade, clap, crack, drumfire, explosion, reverberation, roar, rumble, slam, smash, thunder, wham; CONCEPTS 521,595

boom [n2] *prosperity* advance, boost, development, expansion, gain, growth, improvement, increase, inflation, jump, prosperousness, push, rush, spurt, upsurge, upswing, upturn; CONCEPTS 230,335,700 —*Ant.* collapse, failure, loss

boom [v1] *crash; make loud sound* bang, blast, burst, clap, crack, drum, explode, resound, reverberate, roar, roll, rumble, slam, smash, sound, thunder, wham; CONCEPT 65

boom [v2] *prosper* appreciate, bloom, develop, enhance, expand, flourish, flower, gain, grow, increase, intensify, rise in value, spurt, strengthen, succeed, swell, thrive; CONCEPTS 700,704 —*Ant.* collapse, fail, fade, lose

boom box [n] *portable music machine* audio system, CD player, ghetto blaster*, ghetto box*, radio, stereo, tape player; CONCEPT 463

boomerang [v] *backfire* backlash, bounce back, come back, come home to roost*, kick back, react, rebound, recoil, return, reverse, ricochet; CONCEPTS 242,695 —*Ant.* work

boon [n] *advantage* benefaction, benefit, benevolence, blessing, break, compliment, donation, favor, gift, godsend, good, good fortune, grant, gratuity, help, largess, present, windfall; CONCEPTS 337,661 —Ant. disadvantage

boor [n] *clod* barbarian, bear, boob*, brute, buffoon, cad, churl, dork*, goon*, lout, oaf, peasant, philistine, rube*, vulgarian; CONCEPT 423 —Ant. charmer, enthusiast, exciter

boorish [adj] *crude, awkward* bad-mannered, barbaric, bearish, cantankerous, churlish, cloddish, clodhopping*, clownish, clumsy, coarse, countrified, gross*, gruff, ill-bred, ill-mannered, impolite, inurbane, loud, loutish, lowbred, oafish, ornery, out-of-line, out-of-order, provincial, rough, rude, rustic, swinish, tasteless, ugly, uncivilized, uncouth, uncultured, uneducated, ungracious, unpoised, unpolished, unrefined, vulgar; CONCEPT 404 —Ant. charming, cultured, exciting, polite, refined, sophisticated

boost [n1] *increase* addition, advance, breakthrough, expansion, hike, improvement, increment, jump, lift, raise, rise, step-up, up, upgrade, wax; CONCEPTS 700,780 —Ant. blow, decrease, hindrance, setback

boost [n2] *encouragement* aid, assistance, backup, buildup, goose*, hand*, handout, help, helping hand, improvement, leg*, leg up*, lift, praise, promotion, shot in the arm*, support; CONCEPT 110 —Ant. discouragement, hindrance

boost [n3] *push, usually up* advance, goose*, heave, hoist, lift, raise, shove, thrust; CONCEPTS 196,208

boost [v1] *further, improve* advance, advertise, assist, encourage, foster, inspire, plug, praise, promote, push, support, sustain; CONCEPT 244 —Ant. discourage, halt, hinder, hurt, prevent, undermine

boost [v2] *push, usually up* advance, elevate, heave, heighten, hoist, lift, raise, shove, thrust, upraise, uprear; CONCEPTS 196,208

boost [v3] *increase* add to, aggrandize, amplify, augment, beef up*, develop, enlarge, expand, extend, heighten, hike, jack up*, jump, magnify, multiply, put up, raise, up; CONCEPTS 236,245 —Ant. blow, decrease, hinder, set back

boot [n] *heavy, often tall, shoe* brogan, footwear, galoshes, mukluk, oxford, snow shoes, waders, waters*; CONCEPT 450

boot [v1] *kick; oust* ax, bounce, can*, chase, chuck*, cut, discharge, dismiss, drive, dropkick*, eighty-six*, eject, evict, expel, extrude, fire, heave, kick out, knock, punt*, sack*, shove, terminate, throw out; CONCEPTS 180,189

boot [v2] *start operating system* bootstrap, cold boot, load, reboot, reset, restart, start, start computer, warm boot; CONCEPT 221

booth [n] *small enclosure or building* berth, box, carrel, compartment, coop, corner, cote, counter, cubbyhole, cubicle, dispensary, hut, hutch, nook, pen, pew, repository, shed, stall, stand; CONCEPTS 439,440,443

bootleg [adj] *illegal* black-market, bootlegged, contraband, illicit, pirated, smuggled, unauthorized, under-the-counter, unlawful, unofficial, unsanctioned; CONCEPT 319 —Ant. legal

booty [n] *loot* boodle, gain, goods, haul*, pickings*, plunder, spoils, swag, takings*; CONCEPTS 337,710

border [n1] *outermost edge, margin* bound, boundary, bounds, brim, brink, circumference, confine, end, extremity, fringe, hem, limit, line, lip, outskirt, perimeter, periphery, rim, selvage, skirt, trim, trimming, verge; CONCEPTS 484,827 —Ant. center, inside, interior, middle

border [n2] *boundary; frontier* beginning, borderline, door, edge, entrance, line, march, marchland, outpost, pale, perimeter, sideline, threshold; CONCEPTS 484,513 —Ant. mainland, region, territory

border [v] *bound on; be on the edge* abut, adjoin, be adjacent to, bind, circumscribe, communicate, contour, decorate, define, delineate, edge, encircle, enclose, flank, frame, fringe, hem, join, line, march, margin, mark off, neighbor, outline, rim, set off, side, skirt, surround, touch, trim, verge; CONCEPT 747 —Ant. be inside, center

borderline [adj] *inexact* ambiguous, ambivalent, doubtful, dubitable, equivocal, indecisive, indefinite, indeterminate, marginal, open, problematic, uncertain, unclassifiable, unclear, undecided, unsettled; CONCEPT 534 —Ant. certain, definite, exact, sure

border on [v] *come close to; approximate* abut, adjoin, approach, be like, be similar to, come near, compare, connect, contact, echo, impinge, join, lie near, lie next to, march, match, near, neighbor, parallel, resemble, touch, verge on; CONCEPTS 667,749 —Ant. not touch

bore [n] *nuisance* bother, bromide, bummer*, creep*, deadhead*, downer*, drag*, drip*, dull person, flat tire*, headache, nag, nudge, pain, pain in the neck*, pest, pill*, soporific, stuffed shirt*, tedious person, tiresome person, wet blanket*, wimp*, yawn*; CONCEPT 423 —Ant. charmer, exciter, pleasure

bore [v1] *drill hole* burrow, gouge out, mine, penetrate, perforate, pierce, pit, prick, punch, puncture, ream, riddle, sink, tunnel; CONCEPT 178

bore [v2] *cause weariness, disinterest* afflict, annoy, bend one's ear*, be tedious, bother, burn out, cloy, discomfort, drag, exhaust, fatigue, irk, irritate, jade, pall, pester, put to sleep*, send to sleep*, talk one's ear off*, tire, trouble, turn one off*, vex, wear, wear out, weary, worry; CONCEPTS 7,19 —Ant. amuse, charm, excite, interest, please

boredom [n] *disinterest; weariness* apathy, detachment, disgust, distaste, doldrums, dullness, ennui, fatigue, flatness, incuriosity, indifference, irksomeness, jadedness, lack of interest, lassitude, lethargy, listlessness, monotony, pococurantism, sameness, taedium vitae, tediousness, tedium, tiresomeness, unconcern, world-weariness, yawn; CONCEPT 410 —Ant. excitement, interest, pleasure

boring [adj] *uninteresting* arid, bomb*, bromidic, bummer*, characterless, cloying, colorless, commonplace, dead*, drab, drag*, drudging, dull, flat*, ho hum*, humdrum, insipid, interminable, irksome, lifeless, monotonous, moth-eaten*, mundane, nothing, nowhere, platitudinous, plebeian, prosaic, repetitious, routine, spiritless, stale, stereotyped, stodgy, stuffy, stupid, tame, tedious, threadbare, tiresome, tiring, trite, unexciting, uninteresting, unvaried, vapid, wearisome, well-worn, zero*; CONCEPT 529 —Ant. exciting, fascinating, interesting

born [adj] *innate* built-in, congenital, constitutional, deep-seated, essential, inborn, inbred, ingenerate, inherent, intrinsic, natural; CONCEPTS 549,550

borrow [v1] *take for temporary use* accept loan of, acquire, beg, bite, bum, cadge*, chisel*, give a note for*, hire, hit up*, lift, mooch*, negotiate, obtain, pawn, pledge, raise money, rent, run into debt, scrounge, see one's uncle*, soak, sponge, take on loan, tap, touch, use temporarily; CONCEPT 225 —Ant. give, lend, pay, return

borrow [v2] *adopt from another source; appropriate* acquire, adopt, assume, copy, filch, imitate, make one's own, obtain, pilfer, pirate, plagiarize, simulate, steal, take, use, usurp; CONCEPT 225 —Ant. give, return

bosom [n1] *breast* bust, chest, rib cage, teats; CONCEPT 418

bosom [n2] *heart; core* affections, center, circle, conscience, emotions, feelings, inside, interior, sentiments, soul, spirit, sympathies; CONCEPTS 410,826 —Ant. exteriority, outside

boss [adj] *great* awesome*, bang-up*, capital, champion, excellent, fine, first-rate, fly*, top, whiz-bang*, wonderful; CONCEPT 572

boss [n] *manager over other employees* administrator, big cheese*, big gun*, big person*, chief, chieftain, controller, director, dominator, employer, exec*, executive, foreperson, head, head honcho*, helmer, honcho*, leader, overseer, owner, person in charge, superintendent, supervisor, taskperson, top dog*, wheel*; CONCEPT 347 —Ant. employee, worker

boss [v] *control; command* administer, administrate, chaperon, direct, employ, manage, overlook, oversee, quarterback*, run, superintend, supervise, survey, take charge; CONCEPT 117 —Ant. behave, follow

boss around [v] *bully* browbeat, bulldoze, dominate, domineer, dragoon, oppress, order around, push around, tyrannize; CONCEPT 14

bossy [adj] *domineering* authoritarian, commanding, controlling, despotic, dictatorial, high-handed, imperious, iron-handed, oppressive, overbearing, overpowering, pushy, strict, tyrannical; CONCEPTS 401,404

botany [n] *study of plants* anatomy, cytology, dendrology, ecology, floristics, genetics, horticulture, morphology, natural history, paleobotany, pathology, physiology, phytogeography, phytology, pomology, study of flora, study of vegetation, taxonomy; CONCEPT 349

botch [v] *blunder* blow*, bobble*, boggle*, bollix*, boot, bumble, bungle, butcher*, distort, err, fall down*, flounder, flub*, fumble, goof up*, gum up*, louse up*, mar, mend, mess, mess up*, misapply, miscalculate, miscompute, misconjecture, misconstrue, mishandle, misjudge, mismanage, muck up*, muddle, muff, mutilate, patch, pull a boner*, ruin, screw up*, spoil, stumble, wreck; CONCEPT 101 —Ant. accomplish, achieve, do well, succeed

both [det] *two together* one and the other, the couple, the pair, the two, twain; CONCEPT 714

bother [n] *trouble, inconvenience* ado, aggravation, annoyance, anxiety, bellyache*, botheration, bustle, care, concern, difficulty, distress, drag*, exasperation, flurry, fuss, headache*, irritant, irritation, molestation, nudge, nuisance, pain, pain in the neck*, perplexity, pest, plague, pother*, pressure, problem, strain, to-do*, trial, trouble, vexation, worriment, worry; CONCEPT 532 —Ant. aid, convenience, help

bother [v1] *harass, annoy; give trouble* afflict, aggravate, agitate, alarm, badger, bedevil, bore, browbeat, carp at, concern, cross, discommode, disconcert, disgust, dismay, displease, disquiet, distress, disturb, eat, embarrass, exacerbate, exasperate, goad, grate on, grieve, harry, hinder, hurt, impede, inconvenience, insult, intrude upon, irk, irritate, molest, nag, needle, nudge, pain, perplex, perturb, pester, pick on, plague, provoke, pursue, put out, ride, scare, spite, tantalize, taunt, tease, torment, trouble, upset, vex, worry; CONCEPTS 7,19 —Ant. aid, help, please

bother [v2] *take the trouble* be concerned about, concern oneself, exert oneself, fuss over, go out of one's way*, make a fuss about*, make an effort, put oneself out*, take pains, try, worry about; CONCEPT 87 —Ant. ignore, neglect

bothersome [adj] *troubling* aggravating, annoying, distressing, disturbing, exasperating, incommodious, inconvenient, irritating, rebarbative, remote, tiresome, troublesome, vexatious, vexing; CONCEPT 529 —Ant. convenient, helpful, untroubling

bottle [n] *container, usually for liquids* canteen, carafe, cruet, dead soldier*, decanter, ewer, flagon, flask, glass, jar, jug, phial, soldier, urn, vacuum bottle, vial; CONCEPT 494

bottleneck [n] *obstacle* barrier, block, blockage, clog, congestion, hindrance, hold-up, impediment, jam, obstruction, snag, traffic jam; CONCEPTS 470,532,666,674

bottle up [v] *keep feeling inside oneself* box up, check, collar, contain, coop up, corner, cramp, curb, keep back, restrain, restrict, shut in, suppress, trap; CONCEPT 35 —Ant. confide, reveal, tell

bottom [adj] *lowest; fundamental* basal, base, basement, basic, foundational, ground, last, lowermost, lowest, meat-and-potatoes*, nethermost, primary, radical, rock-bottom, underlying, undermost; CONCEPTS 585,586,735,799 —Ant. highest, top, unnecessary

bottom [n1] *foundation* base, basement, basis, bed, bedrock, belly, deepest part, depths, floor, foot, footing, ground, groundwork, lowest part, nadir, nether portion, pedestal, pediment, rest, seat, sole, substratum, substructure, support, terra firma, underbelly, underneath, underside; CONCEPT 442 —Ant. top

bottom [n2] *base, core* basis, bottom line, cause, essence, essentiality, ground, heart, mainspring, marrow, origin, pith, principle, quintessence, root, soul, source, stuff, substance, virtuality; CONCEPTS 648,826 —Ant. exteriority, outside

bottom [n3] *rear end* backside, behind, breech, bum*, butt*, buttocks, derriere, fanny*, fundament, posterior, rear, rump, seat, tail, tush*; CONCEPT 418

bottom feeder [n] *lowlife* base person, bottom fish, hungry puppy, lowest common denominator, riffraff, scum*, slopsucker; CONCEPT 412

bottomless pit [n] *extremely hopeless situation* abysm, abyss, chasm, crevasse, fire and brimstone*, gulf, Hades, Hell, infernal regions; CONCEPTS 370,435,674

bottom line [n] *conclusion* determination, final decision, income, last word, loss, main point, net, profit; CONCEPT 230

bough [n] *branch* arm, fork, limb, offshoot, shoot, sprig, sucker; CONCEPT 428

boulevard [n] *street, often lined with trees* artery, avenue, drag, highway, passage, path, road, thoroughfare, track, way; CONCEPT 501

bounce [n] *spring* animation, bound, dynamism, elasticity, energy, give, go, life, liveliness, pep, rebound, recoil, resilience, springiness, vigor, vitality, vivacity, zip; CONCEPTS 150,411

bounce [v1] *spring up; rebound* backlash, bob, boomerang, bound, buck, bump, carom, fly back, glance off, hop, hurdle, jerk up and down*, jounce, jump, kick back, leap, rebound, recoil, resile, ricochet, saltate, snap back, spring back, thump, vault; CONCEPTS 150,194

bounce [v2] *evict ax*, boot out*, can*, discharge, dismiss, eighty-six*, eject, fire, give one notice, give the heave ho*, heave*, kick out*, oust, sack*, terminate, throw; CONCEPTS 211,351,384 —Ant. allow, let in, permit

bound [adj] *obligated; destined* apprenticed, articled, bent, bounden, certain, coerced, compelled, constrained, contracted, doomed, driven, duty-bound, enslaved, fated, firm, forced, having no alternative, impelled, indentured, intent, made, necessitated, obligated, obliged, pledged, pressed, required, restrained, sure, under compulsion, under necessity, urged; CONCEPT 554 —Ant. allowed, free, permitted, unbounded, unobliged, unrestricted

bound [v1] *jump, bounce* bob, caper, frisk, gambol, hop, hurdle, leap, pounce, prance, recoil, ricochet, saltate, skip, spring, vault; CONCEPT 194

bound [v2] *restrict* circumscribe, confine, define, delimit, delimitate, demarcate, determine, encircle, enclose, hem in, limit, mark, mark out, measure, restrain, restrict, surround, terminate; CONCEPT 130 —Ant. allow, let go, permit, unbind, unrestrict

boundary [n] *outer limit* abuttals, ambit, barrier, beginning, border, borderland, borderline, bounds, brink, circumference, circumscription, compass, confines, edge, end, environs, extent, extremity, frame, fringe, frontier, hem, horizon, limits, line, line of demarcation, march, margin, mark, mere, mete, outline, outpost, pale, perimeter, periphery, precinct, purlieus, radius, rim, side, skirt, terminal, termination, terminus, verge; CONCEPTS 5,484,745 —Ant. inside, interior, minimum

bound/bounds [n] *farthest limit* boundary, compass, confine, edge, end, environs, extremity, fringe, limit, limitation, line, march, margin, pale, periphery, precinct, purlieus, rim, term, termination, verge; CONCEPTS 484,788 —Ant. inside, interior, minimum

bounded [adj] *limited, confined* belted, bordered, boundaried, circumscribed, compassed, contiguous, defined, definite, delimited, determinate, edged, encircled, enclosed, encompassed, enveloped, fenced, finite, flanked, fringed, girdled, hedged, hog-tied*, limitary, restricted, rimmed, ringed, surrounded, walled; CONCEPTS 554,772 —Ant. free, loose, unbounded, unconfined, unlimited

boundless [adj] *endless, without limit* great, illimitable, immeasurable, immense, incalculable, indefinite, inexhaustible, infinite, limitless, measureless, no catch*, no end of, no end to, no holds barred*, no strings*, no strings attached*, tremendous, unbounded, unconfined, unending, unlimited, untold, vast, wide open; CONCEPTS 554,772 —Ant. limited, restricted

bountiful [adj] *abundant* ample, aplenty, bounteous, copious, crawling with*, dime a dozen*, exuberant, free, galore*, generous, handsome, lavish, liberal, luxuriant, magnanimous, munificent, no end of*, plenteous, plentiful, plenty, prolific, stink with*, unsparing; CONCEPT 771 —Ant. insufficient, lacking, meagre, sparse, wanting

bounty [n] *bonus; compensation* donation, gift, grant, gratuity, largess, pay, premium, present, prize, recompense, reward; CONCEPTS 337,344

bouquet [n1] *flower arrangement* boutonniere, buttonhole, corsage, festoon, garland, lei, nosegay, posy, pot, spray, vase, wreath; CONCEPTS 425,429

bouquet [n2] *aroma* aura, balm, fragrance, incense, odor, perfume, redolence, savor, scent, smell, spice; CONCEPT 599

bourgeois [adj] *commonplace* common, conservative, conventional, hidebound, illiberal, materialistic, middle-class, old-line, Philistine, traditional, Victorian; CONCEPTS 530,589 —Ant. adventurous, imaginative, inspired, nonconforming, original, untraditional

bout [n1] *period of time in which something occurs* course, fit*, go*, round, run, session, shift, spell, stint, stretch, tear, term, tour, trick*, turn; CONCEPT 807

bout [n2] *competitive fight* bat, battle, boxing match, competition, contest, encounter, engagement, go, match, round, set-to, struggle; CONCEPTS 92,106

boutique [n] *shop* booth, concession, exclusive shop, franchise, gift store, specialty shop, store; CONCEPTS 441,448,449

bow [n1] *bend from waist* angle, arc, arch, bend, bending, bob, curtsy, curvation, curvature, curve, flection, flexure, genuflection, inclination, kowtow*, nod, obeisance, round, salaam, turn, turning; CONCEPTS 154,201 —Ant. straighten

bow [n2] *front of boat* beak, bowsprit, fore, forepart, head, nose, prow, stem; CONCEPT 502

bow [v1] *bend over* arch, bob, cower, crook, curtsy, curve, debase, dip, do obeisance, droop, duck, genuflect, hunch, incline, nod, round, stoop; CONCEPT 213

bow [v2] *submit, concede* accept, acquiesce, bend, be servile, capitulate, cave, comply, defer, give in, knuckle*, knuckle under*, kowtow*, relent, succumb, surrender, yield; CONCEPT 23 —Ant. defend, fight, overpower

bowels [n] *insides* belly, core, deep, depths, entrails, guts, hold, innards, interior, intestines, penetralia, recesses, viscera, vitals; CONCEPT 393

bowl [n] *hollow, concave container* basin, boat, casserole, crock, deep dish, dish, porringer, pot, saucer, tureen, urn, vessel; CONCEPTS 493,494

bowl [v] *roll a ball down a lane* fling, hurl, pitch, play duckpins, play tenpins, revolve, rotate, spin, throw, trundle, whirl; CONCEPT 363

bowl over [v] *amaze* astonish, astound, dumbfound, flabbergast, floor, stagger, startle, stun, surprise; CONCEPT 42

box [n] *container, often square or rectangular* bin, carton, case, casket, chest, coffer, crate, pack, package, portmanteau, receptacle, trunk; CONCEPT 494

box [v1] *place in square or rectangular container* case, confine, crate, encase, pack, package, wrap; CONCEPT 209 —*Ant.* unbox

box [v2] *punch competitively* buffet, clout, cuff, duke*, exchange blows, hit, mix, scrap, slap, slug, sock, spar, strike, wallop, whack*; CONCEPTS 106,189

boxing [n] *punching competition* battle, glove game*, mill*, prelim*, prizefighting, pugilism, slugfest*, sparring, the ring*; CONCEPTS 92,363

boy [n] *young man* buck, cadet, chap, child, dude*, fellow, gamin, guy, half-pint*, junior, lad, little guy*, little shaver*, master, punk*, puppy*, runt*, schoolboy, shaver*, small fry*, sonny*, sprout*, squirt*, stripling, tadpole*, whippersnapper*, youngster, youth; CONCEPTS 419,424 —*Ant.* girl

boycott [v] *ban; refrain from using* avoid, bar, blackball*, blacklist, brush off, cut off, embargo, exclude, hold aloof from, ice out*, ostracize, outlaw, pass by*, pass up*, prohibit, proscribe, refuse, reject, shut out*, snub, spurn, strike, withhold patronage; CONCEPTS 25,130 —*Ant.* buy, encourage, support, use

boyfriend [n] *male acquaintance or romantic companion* admirer, beau, companion, confidant, date, escort, fiancé, flame*, follower, friend, intimate, partner, soul mate, steady, suitor, swain, sweetheart, young man; CONCEPTS 419,423 —*Ant.* girlfriend

brace [n] *support* arm, band, bar, bearing, block, bolster, boom, bracer, bracket, buttress, cantilever, clamp, girder, grip, guy, lever, mainstay, peg, prop, rafter, reinforcement, rib, shore, skid, splice, splint, staff, stanchion, stave, stay, stirrup, strengthener, strut, sustainer, truss, underpinning, vice; CONCEPTS 470,475,499

brace [v] *support* bandage, bind, bolster, buttress, fasten, fortify, gird, hold up, prepare, prop, ready, reinforce, shove, steady, steel, strap, strengthen, support, tie, tighten, uphold; CONCEPT 191 —*Ant.* let go, loosen, unfasten

bracelet [n] *wrist jewelry* arm band, armlet, bangle, circlet, manacle, ornament, trinket, wristlet; CONCEPT 446

bracing [adj] *brisk; exhilarating* animating, chilly, cool, crisp, energizing, exhilarative, fortifying, fresh, invigorating, lively, quickening, refreshing, restorative, reviving, rousing, stimulating, stimulative, tonic, vigorous*; CONCEPTS 537,605 —*Ant.* debilitating, exhausting, tiring

brag [v] *talk boastingly* blow one's own horn*, bluster, boast, crow*, exult, gasconade, gloat, grandstand*, hotdog*, jive*, mouth*, pat oneself on the back*, prate, puff*, rodomontade, showboat*, shuck*, swagger, vaunt; CONCEPTS 49,51 —*Ant.* be modest, be quiet, deprecate

braggart [n] *person who talks boastingly* bag of wind*, bigmouth, big talker*, big-timer*, blowhard*, blusterer, boaster, brag, braggadocio, bragger, egotist, exhibitionist, gasbag*,

gascon*, grandstander*, hotshot*, know-it-all, peacock*, ranter, raver, show-off, strutter, swaggerer, swashbuckler*, swelled head*, trumpeter*, windbag*; CONCEPTS 412,423

braid [n] *interwoven hair style* pigtail, plait, ponytail, queue; CONCEPTS 418,716

braid [v] *interweave* complect, cue, entwine, interknit, interlace, intertwine, lace, mesh, pigtail, plait, ravel, twine, twist, weave; CONCEPTS 184,202 —*Ant.* unbraid

brain [n1] *very smart person* academician, doctor, egghead*, Einstein*, genius, highbrow, intellect, intellectual, mastermind, prodigy, pundit, sage, scholar; CONCEPT 350 —*Ant.* dumbo, dumdum, simpleton

brain [n2] *mind, intelligence* cerebellum, cerebrum, encephalon, gray matter*, head, intellect, medulla oblongata, mentality, upper story*, wit; CONCEPTS 393,409,420 —*Ant.* body, physicality

brain drain [n] *loss of important personnel* departure, mass exodus, turnover; CONCEPT 195

brainstorm [v] *problem-solve* analyze, conceive, conceptualize, conjure up, create, deliberate, dream up, invent, plan, ponder, put heads together*, rack brains*, share ideas, think; CONCEPTS 35,173,251

brainwash [v] *force to believe or do things* alter, catechize, condition, convert, convince, educate, indoctrinate, influence, instill, persuade, proselytize, teach; CONCEPT 14

brainy [adj] *intelligent* bright, brilliant, clever, intellectual, sapient, smart; CONCEPT 402

brake [n] *stopping device; check* anchor, binders, cinchers, constraint, control, curb, damper, deterrent, discouragement, hamper, hindrance, hurdle, obstacle, rein, restraint, retarding device; CONCEPTS 130,463 —*Ant.* accelerator

brake [v] *check; stop* bar, block, dam, decelerate, halt, hinder, impede, moderate, obstruct, reduce speed, slacken, slow, slow down, stop; CONCEPT 121 —*Ant.* accelerate

bramble [n] *thorny bush* brier, burr, catch weed, cleaver, furze, goose grass, gorse, hedge, nettle, prick, prickly shrub, shrub, spray, thistle, thistle sage, thorn; CONCEPT 429

branch [n1] *department* annex, arm, bureau, category, chapter, classification, connection, dependency, derivative, division, extension, local, member, office, outpost, part, portion, section, subdivision, subsection, subsidiary, tributary, wing; CONCEPTS 325,378 —*Ant.* company

branch [n2] *arm, limb* bough, branchlet, bug, detour, divergence, extension, fork, growth, offshoot, prong, scion, shoot, spray, sprig, wing; CONCEPTS 392,428,471,835

branch off/branch out [v] *extend beyond main part* add to, develop, diverge, diversify, divide, enlarge, expand, extend, fork, grow, increase, multiply, part, proliferate, ramify, separate, spread out; CONCEPT 756 —*Ant.* lessen, shrink

brand [n1] *type, kind* cast, character, class, description, grade, make, quality, sort, species, variety; CONCEPT 378

brand [n2] *distinctive label, mark* brand name, emblem, hallmark, heraldry, imprint, logo, logotype, marker, sign, stamp, symbol, trademark, welt; CONCEPT 284

brand [n3] *stigma* bar sinister, black eye, blot, blur, disgrace, infamy, mark, mark of Cain, odium, onus, reproach, slur, smirch, spot, stain, stigma, taint; CONCEPT 388

brand [v] *label negatively* disgrace, mark, stigmatize, taint; CONCEPTS 62,79

brandish [v] *flaunt, swing around* come on strong*, display, disport, exhibit, expose, flash, gesture, parade, raise, shake, show, show off, sport, swing, threaten, throw weight around*, trot out*, warn, wield; CONCEPT 261 —Ant. not show

brash [adj] *impulsive, brazen* audacious, bold, brazenfaced, cheeky*, cocksure, cocky*, effervescent, flip, foolhardy, forward, hasty, headlong, heedless, hotheaded, ill-advised, impertinent, impetuous, impolitic, impudent, incautious, inconsiderate, indiscreet, insolent, madcap, maladroit, nervy, precipitate, presuming, presumptuous, pushing, rash, reckless, rude, self-asserting, self-assertive, tactless, thoughtless, undiplomatic, untactful, uppity, vivacious; CONCEPTS 401,404 —Ant. afraid, careful, cautious, discreet, fearful, reserved

brass [n] *impulsiveness; nerve* assumption, audacity, brashness, cheek*, chutzpah*, confidence, effrontery, gall, impertinence, impudence, insolence, presumption, rudeness; CONCEPT 633 —Ant. carefulness, caution, circumspection, prudence

brassy [adj] *vulgar, loud to the senses* arrant, barefaced, blaring, blatant, bold, brash, brazen, flashy, flirtatious, forward, garish, gaudy, grating, hard, harsh, impudent, insolent, jarring, jazzy, loudmouthed, noisy, obtrusive, overbold, pert, piercing, rude, saucy, shameless, showy, shrill, strident, unabashed, unblushing; CONCEPTS 401,589,592,594 —Ant. careful, cautious, circumspect, humble, prudent

brat [n] *spoiled child* devil*, enfant terrible*, holy terror*, impudent child, kid, punk*, rascal, unruly child, urchin, whippersnapper*, wild one*, youngster; CONCEPT 424 —Ant. angel

bravado [n] *boastfulness* blowing, bluff, bluster, boasting, bombast, braggadocio, bragging, bullying, crowing*, fancy talk*, fuming*, gasconade, grandiosity, guts*, hot air*, pomposity, pretension, raging, railing, rant, selfglorification, storming, swaggering, swelling, talk, tall talk*; CONCEPTS 49,51 —Ant. cowardice, fear, fearfulness, modesty, restraint

brave [adj] *bold* adventurous, audacious, chinup*, chivalrous, confident, courageous, daring, dashing, dauntless, defiant, doughty, fearless, firm, foolhardy, forward, gallant, game, gritty, gutsy, hardy, heroic, herolike, imprudent, indomitable, intrepid, lionhearted, militant, nervy, plucky, reckless, resolute, spirited, spunky, stalwart, stout, stouthearted, strong, unabashed, unafraid, unblinching, undauntable, undaunted, undismayed, unfearful, valiant, valorous, venturesome; CONCEPT 401 —Ant. afraid, cautious, fearful, frightened, humble, meek, reticent, retiring, shy, timid

brave [v] *endure bad situation* bear, beard, challenge, confront, court, dare, defy, face, face off, fly in the face of*, go through, outdare, risk, stand up to, suffer, support, take on, venture, withstand; CONCEPT 23 —Ant. break

down, capitulate, complain, dodge, fear, give up, hide, run away, skip

bravery [n] *boldness* courage, daring, dauntlessness, fearlessness, fortitude, gallantry, grit, guts, hardiness, heroism, indomitability, intrepidity, mettle, pluck, pluckiness, spirit, spunk, valor; CONCEPTS 411,633 —Ant. cowardice, diffidence, humility, timidity

brawl [n] *nasty fight* affray, altercation, argument, battle, battle royal*, bickering, broil, clash, disorder, dispute, donnybrook, duke out*, feud, fight, fracas, fray, free-for-all*, fuss, hassle, melee, quarrel, rhubarb*, riot, row, ruckus*, rumble*, rumpus, scrap, scuffle, squabble, tumult, uproar, wrangle; CONCEPTS 46,106 —Ant. peace, truce

brawl [v] *fight nastily* altercate, argue, battle, bicker, buck*, caterwaul, dispute, kick up a row*, quarrel, raise Cain*, roughhouse*, row, rumble*, scrap, scuffle, spat, squabble, tussle, wrangle, wrestle; CONCEPTS 46,106 —Ant. make peace

brawn [n] *muscular strength and breadth* beef, beefiness, clout, energy, flesh, kick, meat, might, moxie*, muscle, muscularity, power, punch, robustness, sinews, sock, steam, thew, vigor; CONCEPTS 723,732 —Ant. frailness, skinniness, slightness, thinness

brawny [adj] *muscular, strong* able-bodied, athletic, beefy, bulky, burly, fleshy, hardy, hefty, husky, powerful, robust, sinewy, stalwart, strapping, sturdy, thewy, tough, vigorous, vital; CONCEPTS 485,489 —Ant. frail, skinny, slight, thin, weak

brazen [adj] *brash, unashamed* audacious, barefaced, blatant, bold, brassy, cheeky, cocky, contumelious, defiant, flashy, flip, forward, gritty, gutsy, hotshot*, immodest, impertinent, impudent, indecent, insolent, loud, meretricious, nervy, overbold, pert, saucy, shameless, smart-alecky*, smart-ass*, spunky, tawdry, unabashed, unblushing; CONCEPTS 267,401 —Ant. humble, meek, shamed, shamefaced, shy, timid

breach [n1] *gap* aperture, break, chasm, chip, cleft, crack, discontinuity, fissure, hole, opening, rent, rift, rupture, slit, split; CONCEPT 513 —Ant. bridge, connection

breach [n2] *violation of a law* contravention, delinquency, dereliction, disobedience, disregard, infraction, infringement, neglect, noncompliance, nonobservance, offense, transgression, trespass, violation; CONCEPT 192 —Ant. upholding

breach [n3] *change from friendly to unfriendly relationship* alienation, break, difference, disaffection, disagreement, discord, disharmony, dissension, disunity, division, estrangement, falling-out, fissure, fracture, parting of the ways*, quarrel, rent, rift, rupture, schism, secession, separation, severance, split, strife, variance, withdrawal; CONCEPT 388

bread [n1] *daily food* aliment, bed and board, comestibles, diet, fare, feed, grub*, necessities, nourishment, nurture, nutriment, provender, provisions, shingle*, staff of life*, subsistence, sustenance, viands, victuals; CONCEPT 457

bread [n2] *money* cabbage*, cash, coin, dollars, dough*, finance, funds, greenbacks*, mazuma*, scratch*; CONCEPT 340

breadth [n1] *width* broadness, diameter, distance across, latitude, span, spread, wideness; CONCEPT 760

breadth [n2] *extent* amplitude, area, compass, comprehensiveness, dimension, expanse, extensiveness, fullness, gamut, greatness, inclusiveness, largeness, magnitude, measure, orbit, range, reach, scale, scope, size, space, spread, stretch, sweep, vastness; CONCEPTS 651,756,788

break [n1] *fissure, opening* breach, cleft, crack, discontinuity, disjunction, division, fracture, gap, gash, hole, rent, rift, rupture, schism, split, tear; CONCEPTS 230,757 —Ant. association, attachment, binding, combination, fastening, juncture

break [n2] *interruption of activity* blow, breather, breathing space, caesura, coffee break, cutoff, downtime*, halt, hiatus, interlude, intermission, interval, lacuna, layoff*, letup*, lull, pause, recess, respite, rest, suspension, ten*, time off, time out; CONCEPT 807 —Ant. continuation, continuity

break [n3] *change from friendly to unfriendly relationship* alienation, altercation, breach, clash, difference of opinion, disaffection, dispute, divergence, estrangement, fight, misunderstanding, rift, rupture, schism, separation, split, trouble; CONCEPT 388

break [n4] *lucky happening* accident, advantage, chance, favorable circumstances, fortune, good luck, luck, occasion, opening, opportunity, shot, show, stroke of luck, time; CONCEPT 679 —Ant. bad luck, misfortune

break [v1] *destroy; make whole into pieces* annihilate, batter, burst, bust, bust up, crack, crash, crush, damage, demolish, disintegrate, divide, eradicate, finish off, fracture, fragment, make hash of*, make mincemeat of*, part, pull to pieces, rend, separate, sever, shatter, shiver, smash, snap, splinter, split, tear, torpedo, total, trash*; CONCEPT 252 —Ant. attach, fasten, fix, join, mend, put together, secure

break [v2] *violate law* breach, contravene, disobey, disregard, infract, infringe, offend, renege on, transgress, violate; CONCEPT 192 —Ant. agree, obey

break [v3] *weaken, cause instability* bankrupt, bust, confound, confute, controvert, cow, cripple, declass, degrade, demerit, demoralize, demote, disconfirm, dispirit, disprove, downgrade, enervate, enfeeble, humiliate, impair, impoverish, incapacitate, pauperize, reduce, refute, ruin, subdue, tame, undermine; CONCEPT 240 —Ant. stabilize, strengthen

break [v4] *stop an action* abandon, cut, discontinue, give up, interrupt, pause, rest, suspend; CONCEPT 121 —Ant. allow, cause

break [v5] *tell news* announce, come out, communicate, convey, disclose, divulge, impart, inform, let out, make public, pass on, proclaim, reveal, tell, transmit; CONCEPT 60 —Ant. hide, keep quiet, secret

break [v6] *better a performance* beat, cap, exceed, excel, go beyond, outdo, outstrip, surpass, top; CONCEPT 141

break [v7] *emerge, happen* appear, befall, betide, burst out, chance, come forth, come off, come to pass, develop, erupt, go, occur, transpire; CONCEPT 4

break [v8] *run away* abscond, bust out*, clear out*, cut and run*, dash, decamp, escape, flee, fly, get away, get out; CONCEPTS 102,195 —Ant. stay, wait

break [v9] *cushion something's effect* diminish, lessen, lighten, moderate, reduce, soften, weaken; CONCEPT 110

breakable [adj] *easily hurt or destroyed* brittle, crisp, crispy, crumbly, delicate, flimsy, fracturable, fragile, frail, frangible, friable, shatterable, shattery, splintery, vitreous, weak; CONCEPTS 489,606 —Ant. durable, sturdy, unbreakable

break away [v] *depart* escape, flee, fly, leave, part company*, quit, run away, split*; CONCEPT 195

breakdown [n1] *nervous collapse* basket case*, crackup*, disintegration, disruption, failure, mishap, nervous prostration, neurasthenia, neurosis, psychasthenia; CONCEPT 410 —Ant. mental health

breakdown [n2] *account of finances or other business* analysis, categorization, classification, detailed list, diagnosis, dissection, itemization, resolution; CONCEPT 283

break even [v] *be or become equal* balance books, equalize, experience no loss, recover cost, recover expense; CONCEPTS 126,232

break in [v1] *intrude* barge in, breach, break and enter, burglarize, burgle, burst in*, butt in*, interfere, interject, interrupt, intervene, invade, meddle, raid, rob, steal, trespass; CONCEPTS 139,192

break in [v2] *train in new skill* accustom, condition, educate, gentle, get used to, habituate, initiate, instruct, prepare, tame; CONCEPT 285

breakneck [adj] *extremely fast* at full tilt, dangerously fast, excessive, flat out, headlong, high-speed, lightning, precipitate, rapid, reckless, speedy, whirlwind; CONCEPT 588 —Ant. extremely slow

break off [v1] *snap off something* detach, disassemble, divide, part, pull off, separate, sever, splinter, take apart; CONCEPT 211 —Ant. combine, join, mend

break off [v2] *end activity* cease, desist, discontinue, end, finish, halt, pause, stop, suspend, terminate; CONCEPT 234 —Ant. begin, start

break out [v1] *happen, emerge* appear, arise, begin, burst forth, commence, erupt, explode, occur, set in, spring up, start; CONCEPT 701

break out [v2] *escape* abscond, bolt, break loose, burst out, bust out*, depart, flee, get free, leave; CONCEPTS 102,195

break the ice [v] *be friendly and talkative* lead the way, oil the works*, set at ease, socialize, start the ball rolling; CONCEPT 384

breakthrough [n] *advance, progress* boost, development, discovery, find, finding, gain, hike, improvement, increase, invention, leap, progress, quantum leap*, rise, step forward; CONCEPT 704 —Ant. step back, step backward

breakup [n] *end of relationship* breakdown, breaking, crackup*, disintegration, dispersal, dissolution, divorce, ending, parting, rift, separation, split, splitsville*, splitting, termination, wind-up; CONCEPT 385 —Ant. reconciliation

break up [v] *end relationship, activity* adjourn, disassemble, disband, dismantle, disperse, disrupt, dissolve, divide, divorce, end, halt, part, put an end to, scatter, separate, sever, split, stop, sunder, suspend, take apart, terminate; CONCEPT 234 —*Ant.* reconcile

break with [v] *part ways* ditch, drop, jilt, reject, renounce, separate; CONCEPTS 21,30,180

breast [n1] *front of upper body* bosom, bust, chest, front, mammary glands, mammilla, nipple, teat, udder; CONCEPT 418

breast [n2] *feelings, conscience* being, bosom, character, core, emotions, essential nature, heart, mind, psyche, seat of affections, sentiments, soul, spirit, thoughts; CONCEPTS 410,529

breath [n1] *respiration* animation, breathing, eupnea, exhalation, expiration, gasp, gulp, inhalation, inspiration, insufflation, pant, wheeze; CONCEPT 163

breath [n2] *wind or something in the air* aroma, faint breeze, flatus, flutter, gust, odor, puff, sigh, smell, vapor, waft, whiff, zephyr; CONCEPTS 437,599

breath [n3] *respite, break* blow*, breather, breathing space*, instant, moment, pause, rest, second, ten*; CONCEPT 807

breath [n4] *hint, suggestion* dash, murmur, shade, soupçon, streak, suspicion, touch, trace, undertone, whiff, whisper; CONCEPTS 278,831

breathe [v1] *take air in and let out* draw in, exhale, expire, fan, gasp, gulp, inhale, insufflate, open the floodgates*, pant, puff, respire, scent, sigh, sniff, snore, snort, use lungs, wheeze; CONCEPTS 163,601

breathe [v2] *inspire action* imbue, impart, infuse, inject, instill, transfuse; CONCEPT 242

breathe [v3] *tell information* articulate, confide, express, murmur, say, sigh, utter, voice, whisper; CONCEPT 60 —*Ant.* hide, secret

breathless [adj1] *unable to respire normally* asthmatic, blown, choking, emphysematous, exhausted, gasping, gulping, out of breath, panting, short of breath, short-winded, spent, stertorous, wheezing, winded; CONCEPT 406 —*Ant.* breathy, calm

breathless [adj2] *astounded* agog, anxious, avid, eager, excited, flabbergasted, open-mouthed, thunderstruck, with bated breath; CONCEPT 403

breathtaking [adj] *beautiful, awesome* amazing, astonishing, awe-inspiring, exciting, hair-raising, heart-stirring, heart-stopping, impressive, magnificent, moving, overwhelming, spine-tingling, stunning, thrilling; CONCEPT 529 —*Ant.* disgusting, ugly

breed [n] *kind, class* brand, character, extraction, family, feather, genus, ilk, likes, line, lineage, lot, nature, number, pedigree, progeny, race, sort, species, stamp, stock, strain, stripe, type, variety; CONCEPT 378

breed [v1] *generate, bring into being* bear, beget, bring about, bring forth, cause, create, deliver, engender, give birth to, give rise to, hatch, impregnate, induce, make, multiply, originate, procreate, produce, progenerate, propagate, reproduce; CONCEPTS 173,251,302,373 —*Ant.* not produce

breed [v2] *raise, nurture* bring up, cultivate, develop, discipline, educate, foster, instruct, nourish, rear; CONCEPTS 285,295

breeding [n] *cultivation of person* ancestry, civility, conduct, courtesy, culture, development,

gentility, grace, lineage, manners, nurture, polish, raising, rearing, refinement, schooling, training, upbringing, urbanity; CONCEPT 388

breeze [n] *light wind* air, airflow, breath, current, draft, flurry, gust, puff, waft, whiff, zephyr; CONCEPTS 437,524

breeze [v] *work quickly through task* cruise, flit, glide, hurry, move, pass, sail, sally, skim, slide, slip, sweep, trip, waltz, zip; CONCEPT 704

breezy [adj1] *windy* airy, blowing, blowy, blusterous, blustery, drafty, fresh, gusty, squally, stormy; CONCEPT 525 —*Ant.* calm, peaceful, quiet, still

breezy [adj2] *easy, lighthearted* airy, animated, blithe, buoyant, carefree, casual, cheerful, debonair, easy-going, effervescent, free and easy*, gay, informal, jaunty, light, lively, low-pressure, peppy, racy, relaxed, sparkling, spicy, spirited, sprightly, sunny, unconstrained, vivacious; CONCEPT 544 —*Ant.* difficult

brevity [n] *shortness, briefness* conciseness, concision, condensation, crispness, curtness, economy, ephemerality, impermanence, pithiness, pointedness, succinctness, terseness, transience, transitoriness; CONCEPTS 730,804 —*Ant.* lengthiness, longevity, permanence

brew [n] *concoction* beverage, blend, broth, compound, distillation, drink, fermentation, hash, hodgepodge*, infusion, instillation, liquor, melange, miscellany, mishmash*, mixture, potpourri, preparation; CONCEPTS 260,454,457

brew [v1] *prepare by boiling* boil, concoct, cook, ferment, infuse, mull, seethe, soak, steep, stew; CONCEPT 170

brew [v2] *plan, devise* breed, compound, concoct, contrive, develop, excite, foment, form, gather, hatch, impend, loom, mull, plot, project, scheme, start, stir up, weave; CONCEPT 36

bribe [n] *payoff to influence illegal or wrong activity* allurement, bait, blackmail, blandishment, compensation, contract, corrupting gift, corrupt money, enticement, envelope*, feedbag*, fringe benefit, gift, goody*, graft, gratuity, gravy*, grease*, hush money*, ice*, incentive, inducement, influence peddling, kickback, lagniappe, lure, payola*, perk*, perquisite, present, price, protection*, remuneration, reward, sop*, sweetener*, sweetening*, take; CONCEPTS 192,329

bribe [v] *request silence, action, or inaction for money* approach, buy, buy back, buy off, coax, corrupt, do business*, entice, fix*, get at, get to, grease palm*, influence, instigate, lubricate, lure, make a deal, oil palm*, pay off, pervert, reward, seduce, soap*, square, suborn, sugar, sweeten the pot*, take care of, tamper, tempt, tip; CONCEPTS 53,192

bridal [adj] *concerning marriage* conjugal, connubial, epithalamic, espousal, hymeneal, marital, matrimonial, nubile, nuptial, pre-wedding, prothalamic, spousal; CONCEPT 536 —*Ant.* divorce

bride [n] *female marriage partner* helpmate, mate, newly married woman, newlywed, old woman*, spouse, wife; CONCEPTS 296,415 —*Ant.* bridegroom, groom

bridegroom [n] *male marriage partner* benedict, groom, helpmate, husband, mate, newlywed, old man*, spouse; CONCEPTS 296,419 —*Ant.* bride

bridge [n] *structure or something that makes connection* arch, bond, branch, catwalk, connection, extension, gangplank, link, overpass, platform, pontoon, scaffold, span, tie, transit, trestle, viaduct, wing; CONCEPTS 501,721

bridge [v] *connect, extend* arch over, attach, bind, branch, couple, cross, cross over, go over, join, link, reach, span, subtend, traverse, unite; CONCEPTS 113,756 —Ant. detach, disconnect, disjoin, disunite, unlink

bridle [n] *restraining device* check, control, curb, deterrent, hackamore, halter, headstall, leash, rein, restraint, trammels; CONCEPT 497

bridle [v] *check, hold back* constrain, control, curb, govern, inhibit, keep in check, master, moderate, repress, restrain, rule, subdue, suppress, withhold; CONCEPT 121 —Ant. let go, release, set free

brief [adj1] *short, compressed* abrupt, bluff, blunt, boiled down*, breviloquent, brusque, compendiary, compendious, concise, crisp, curt, hasty, laconic, limited, little, pithy, sharp, short and sweet*, skimpy, small, snippy, succinct, surly, terse, to the point; CONCEPTS 267,773 —Ant. lengthy, long

brief [adj2] *short in time* concise, curtailed, ephemeral, fast, fleeting, hasty, instantaneous, little, meteoric, momentary, passing, quick, short-lived, short-term, swift, temporary, transient, transitory; CONCEPT 798 —Ant. enduring, lasting, lengthy, long, long-lived

brief [n] *abridgment* abstract, argument, boildown*, case, condensation, conspectus, contention, data, defense, digest, epitome, outline, précis, sketch, summary, synopsis; CONCEPTS 283,318

brief [v] *inform of facts* abridge, advise, apprise, edify, enlighten, epitomize, explain, fill in, give rundown*, give the lowdown*, inform, initiate, instruct, let in on*, orient, prepare, prime, recapitulate, show the lay of the land*, show the ropes*, summarize, tip off*, update; CONCEPT 60 —Ant. hide, secret

briefcase [n] *carrier for work papers* attaché, bag, baggage, case, dispatch, folder, portfolio, valise; CONCEPTS 446,494

briefing [n] *preparation by informing of facts* background meeting, conference, directions, discussion, guidance, information, initiation, instruction, meeting, preamble, priming, rundown, update; CONCEPT 60

brigade [n] *fleet of trained people* army, band, body, company, contingent, corps, crew, detachment, force, group, organization, outfit, party, posse, squad, team, troop, unit; CONCEPTS 322,381 —Ant. individual, one

bright [adj1] *shining, glowing in appearance* ablaze, aglow, alight, argent, auroral, beaming, blazing, brilliant, burning, burnished, coruscating, dazzling, effulgent, flashing, fulgent, fulgid, glaring, gleaming, glistening, glittering, glossy, golden, illuminated, illumined, incandescent, intense, irradiated, lambent, light, lighted, limpid, luminous, lustrous, mirrorlike, moonlit, phosphorescent, polished, radiant, relucent, resplendent, scintillating, shimmering, shiny, silvery, sparkling, sunlit, sunny, twinkling, vivid; CONCEPT 617 —Ant. dark, dreary, dull, obscure, somber

bright [adj2] *sunny, clear (weather)* clement, cloudless, fair, favorable, limpid, lucid, mild, pellucid, pleasant, translucent, transparent, unclouded; CONCEPT 525 —Ant. black, cloudy, dark, dreary, dusky, gloomy, murky

bright [adj3] *intelligent* acute, advanced, alert, astute, aware, brainy, brilliant, clear-headed, clever, discerning, eggheaded*, Einstein*, having smarts*, ingenious, inventive, keen, knowing, precocious, quick, quick-witted, sharp, smart, whiz kid*, wide-awake; CONCEPT 402 —Ant. dull, stupid, unaware, unintelligent

bright [adj4] *hopeful, promising* airy, auspicious, benign, breezy, cheering, encouraging, excellent, favorable, golden, good, optimistic, palmy, propitious, prosperous, rosy; CONCEPT 537 —Ant. depressing, horrible, threatening, unpromising

bright [adj5] *cheerful* alert, animated, gay, genial, glad, happy, jolly, joyful, joyous, keen, lighthearted, lively, merry, optimistic, sanguine, spirited, sprightly, vivacious; CONCEPT 404 —Ant. depressed, depressing, doleful, dreary, gloomy, unhappy

bright [adj6] *famous, outstanding* distinguished, eminent, glorious, illustrious, magnificent, prominent, remarkable, splendid; CONCEPT 568 —Ant. normal, typical

bright [adj7] *vivid in color* brave, brilliant, clear, colored, colorful, deep, flashy, fresh, gay, glitzy*, hued, intense, psychedelic, razzle-dazzle, rich, ruddy, sharp, showy, tinged, tinted; CONCEPT 618 —Ant. light, pale, pastel

brighten [v1] *make shine or glow* buff up, burnish, clear up, enliven, gleam, grow sunny, illuminate, illumine, intensify, kindle, lighten, light up, polish, punch up*, spiff up*; CONCEPTS 244,250 —Ant. darken, deepen, dull, fade

brighten [v2] *make happy, feel better* become cheerful, buck up, buoy up, cheer, cheer up, clear up, encourage, enliven, gladden, hearten, improve, look up, perk up; CONCEPTS 7,22 —Ant. depress, upset

brilliant [adj1] *shining, glowing in appearance* ablaze, bright, coruscating, dazzling, effulgent, flashy, fulgent, gleaming, glittering, glossy, incandescent, intense, lambent, lucent, luminous, lustrous, radiant, refulgent, resplendent, scintillating, showy, sparkling, vivid; CONCEPT 617 —Ant. dark, dull, dulled

brilliant [adj2] *famous, outstanding* celebrated, distinguished, eminent, excellent, exceptional, glorious, illustrious, magnificent, prominent, splendid, superb; CONCEPT 568 —Ant. normal, typical

brilliant [adj3] *very intelligent* accomplished, acute, astute, brainy, bright, clever, discerning, eggheaded*, Einstein*, expert, genius, gifted, ingenious, intellectual, inventive, knowing, knowledgeable, masterly, penetrating, profound, quick, quick-witted, sharp, smart, talented, whip, whiz kid*; CONCEPT 402 —Ant. stupid, unaware, unintelligent

brim [n] *edge of object, usually the top* border, brink, circumference, fringe, hem, lip, margin, perimeter, periphery, rim, skirt, verge; CONCEPT 836 —Ant. center, interior, middle

brim [v] *flow over the top* fill, fill up, hold no more, overflow, run over, spill, swell, teem, well over; CONCEPT 740

brimming/brimful [adj] *overflowing; up to the top* awash, chock-full, crammed, crowded, filled, flush, full, full to the top, jammed, level with, loaded, overfull, packed, running over, stuffed, topfull; CONCEPTS 481,771,774 —*Ant.* empty, unfilled

brine [n] *salt solution* alkali, blue, brackish water, deep, drink, marinade, ocean, pickling solution, preservative, saline, salt water, sea water, sodium chloride solution, vinegar; CONCEPT 514

bring [v1] *transport or accompany* attend, back, bear, buck*, carry, chaperon, companion, conduct, consort, convey, deliver, escort, fetch, gather, guide, gun*, heel*, import, lead, lug, pack, pick up, piggyback*, ride, schlepp*, shoulder, take, take along, tote, transfer, transport, truck, usher; CONCEPT 143 —*Ant.* drop, leave, quit, refuse, shun, take

bring [v2] *cause; influence* begin, compel, contribute to, convert, convince, create, dispose, effect, engender, force, induce, inflict, lead, make, move, occasion, persuade, prevail on, prevail upon, produce, prompt, result in, sway, wreak; CONCEPT 242 —*Ant.* avoid, back out, desist, give up, hold back, pass up

bring [v3] *command a price* afford, bring in, draw, earn, fetch, gross, net, produce, return, sell for, take, yield; CONCEPTS 330,335

bring [v4] *file charges in court* appeal, arraign, cite, declare, indict, initiate legal action, institute, prefer, serve, sue, summon, take to court; CONCEPT 317

bring about [v] *cause success* accomplish, achieve, beget, bring to pass, compass, create, do, draw on, effect, effectuate, engender, generate, give rise to, make happen, manage, occasion, produce, realize, secure, succeed; CONCEPTS 244,706 —*Ant.* halt, kill, stop

bring around [v] *convince, induce* argue, convert, draw, get, indoctrinate, persuade, prevail upon, prompt, prove, talk into, win over; CONCEPT 68

bring down [v] *reduce or hurt* abase, cut down, damage, drop, fell, floor, injure, knock down, KO*, lay low, level, lower, mow down, murder*, overthrow, overturn, prostrate, pull down, shoot down, slay*, throw down, tumble, undermine, upset, wound; CONCEPTS 7,19,252 —*Ant.* aid, encourage, help, raise

bring in [v] *make a profit* accrue, acquire, bear, be worth, bring, cost, earn, fetch, gain, get, gross, make, pay, produce, realize, return, sell, yield; CONCEPTS 124,330 —*Ant.* decrease, lose

bring off [v] *accomplish* achieve, bring home the bacon*, bring to pass, carry off, carry out, discharge, effect, effectuate, execute, perform, pull off, realize, succeed; CONCEPTS 704,706 —*Ant.* fail, lose

bring on [v] *provoke* accelerate, advance, cause, expedite, generate, give rise to, induce, inspire, lead to, occasion, precipitate, prompt; CONCEPTS 7,19

bring out [v] *draw out* bring to light, emphasize, expose, highlight, introduce, publish, utter; CONCEPTS 49,57

bring up [v1] *raise youngster* breed, cultivate,

develop, discipline, educate, feed, form, foster, nourish, nurture, provide for, rear, school, support, teach, train; CONCEPT 295

bring up [v2] *initiate, mention in conversation* advance, advert, allude to, broach, discuss, introduce, moot, move, offer, point out, propose, put forward, raise, raise a subject, refer, submit, tender, touch on, ventilate*; CONCEPT 51

brink [n] *edge of an object or area* border, boundary, brim, fringe, frontier, limit, lip, margin, perimeter, periphery, point, rim, skirt, threshold, verge; CONCEPTS 484,513 —*Ant.* center, interior, middle

brisk [adj1] *fast-moving; active* adroit, agile, alert, animated, bustling, busy, energetic, lively, nimble, quick, speedy, sprightly, spry, vigorous, vivacious, zippy; CONCEPTS 542,584 —*Ant.* inactive, slow, sluggish, unenergetic

brisk [adj2] *chilly, refreshing (weather)* biting, bracing, crisp, exhilarating, fresh, invigorating, keen, nippy, sharp, snappy, stimulating; CONCEPT 605 —*Ant.* temperate, warm

bristle [n] *short, prickly hair* barb, feeler, fiber, point, prickle, quill, spine, stubble, thorn, vibrissa, whisker; CONCEPT 418

bristle [v] *become upset, excited* be angry, be infuriated, be maddened, blow up*, boil, boil over, bridle, flare, flare up, fume, get one's dander up*, rage, rise, ruffle, see red*, seethe, spit*, stand on end*, swell; CONCEPT 410

brittle [adj1] *fragile* breakable, crisp, crumbling, crumbly, delicate, frail, frangible, friable, inelastic, shatterable, shivery, vitreous, weak; CONCEPTS 488,606 —*Ant.* durable, flexible, moveable, resilient, supple

brittle [adj2] *tense* curt, edgy, irritable, nervous, prim, short, stiff, stilted; CONCEPT 401 —*Ant.* relaxed, resilient

broach [v1] *bring up a topic* advance, approach, bring up, hint at, interject, interpose, introduce, mention, moot, move, offer, open up, propose, raise subject, speak of, submit, suggest, talk of, touch on, ventilate*; CONCEPT 51 —*Ant.* not mention

broach [v2] *open, pierce* begin, crack, decant, draw off, puncture, start, tap, uncork; CONCEPTS 142,225 —*Ant.* close, close up

broad [adj1] *wide* ample, capacious, deep, expansive, extended, extensive, full, generous, immense, large, latitudinous, outspread, outstretched, roomy, spacious, splay, squat, thick, vast, voluminous, widespread; CONCEPTS 773,796 —*Ant.* narrow, small

broad [adj2] *extensive* all-embracing, all-inclusive, comprehensive, copious, encyclopedic, expansive, extended, far-flung, far-reaching, general, inclusive, nonspecific, scopic, sweeping, ubiquitous, undetailed, universal, unlimited, wide, wide-ranging, widespread; CONCEPT 772 —*Ant.* narrow, small

broad [adj3] *full, obvious* apparent, clear, explicit, open, plain, straightforward, undisguised, unequivocal; CONCEPT 576 —*Ant.* empty, restricted

broad [adj4] *liberal-minded* advanced, cultivated, experienced, open, open-minded, permissive, progressive, radical, tolerant, unbiased, wide; CONCEPT 403 —*Ant.* close-minded, small-minded

broad [*adj5*] *vulgar* blue, coarse, dirty, gross, improper, indecent, indelicate, low-minded, off-color, purple, racy, risqué, salty, saucy, smutty, spicy, suggestive, unrefined, unrestrained, wicked; CONCEPT 545

broad [*n*] *a woman* babe*, bimbo*, chick*, dame, dish, doll*, doxy, female, floozy, gal, girl, honey*, lady, lassie, miss, moll, skirt*, sweet thing*, tootsie*; CONCEPTS 414,415

broadcast [*n*] *information on electronic media* advertisement, air time, announcement, newscast, performance, program, publication, radiocast, show, simulcast, telecast, transmission; CONCEPTS 274,293

broadcast [*v1*] *put forth on electronic media* air, announce, beam, be on the air, cable, circulate, colorcast, communicate, get out*, go on the air, go on the airwaves, put on the air, radio, radiograph, relay, send, show, simulcast, telecast, telegraph, telephone, televise, transmit; CONCEPTS 60,292

broadcast [*v2*] *make public* advertise, announce, annunciate, blare, blazon, circulate, communicate, declare, disseminate, distribute, proclaim, promulgate, publish, report, sow, spread, strew, troll; CONCEPT 60 —*Ant.* hide, keep quiet, secret

broadcasting [*n*] *informing via electronic media* airing, air time, announcing, auditioning, newscasting, performing, posting online, putting on program, radio, reporting, telecasting, television, transmission, transmitting; CONCEPTS 263,293

broaden [*v*] *extend, supplement* augment, breadthen, develop, enlarge, expand, fatten, grow, increase, open up, ream, spread, stretch, swell, widen; CONCEPT 239 —*Ant.* decrease, narrow, restrict

broad-minded [*adj*] *liberal* advanced, catholic, cosmopolitan, dispassionate, flexible, free-thinking, indulgent, liberal, open, open-minded, permissive, progressive, radical, receptive, responsive, tolerant, unbiased, unbigoted, undogmatic, unprejudiced, wide; CONCEPT 403 —*Ant.* close-minded, small-minded

brochure [*n*] *short, printed document* advertisement, booklet, circular, flyer, folder, handbill, handout, leaflet, pamphlet; CONCEPT 280

broil [*v*] *cook under direct heat* burn, melt, roast, scorch, sear, swelter; CONCEPT 170 —*Ant.* freeze

broiling [*adj*] *very hot* baking, burning, fiery, on fire, red-hot, roasting, scalding, scorching, sizzling, sweltering, torrid; CONCEPT 605 —*Ant.* freezing

broke [*adj*] *without money* bankrupt, beggared, bust*, cleaned out*, destitute, dirt poor*, flat broke*, impoverished, in Chapter 11*, in debt, indebted, indigent, insolvent, needy, penniless, penurious, poor, ruined, stone broke*, strapped*, tapped out; CONCEPT 334 —*Ant.* affluent, rich, solvent, wealthy

broken [*adj1*] *destroyed; made into pieces from a whole* burst, busted, collapsed, cracked, crippled, crumbled, crushed, damaged, defective, demolished, disintegrated, dismembered, fractured, fragmentary, fragmented, hurt, injured, in pieces, mangled, mutilated, pulverized, rent, riven, ruptured, separated, severed, shattered, shivered, shredded, slivered, smashed, split; CONCEPT 485 —*Ant.* complete, connected, fixed, ok, unbroken, whole

broken [*adj2*] *discontinuous* disconnected, disturbed, erratic, fragmentary, incomplete, intermittent, interrupted, irregular, spasmodic, spastic; CONCEPT 482 —*Ant.* complete, connected, continuous, unbroken

broken [*adj3*] *mentally defeated* beaten, browbeaten, crippled, crushed, defeated, demoralized, depressed, discouraged, disheartened, heartsick, humbled, oppressed, overpowered, subdued, tamed, vanquished; CONCEPT 403 —*Ant.* happy, satisfied, uplifted

broken [*adj4*] *not working* busted, coming unglued, coming unstuck, defective, disabled, down, exhausted, fallen apart, faulty, feeble, gone, gone to pieces*, gone to pot*, haywire, imperfect, in disrepair, in need of repair, inoperable, in the shop*, kaput*, not functioning, on the blink*, on the fritz*, on the shelf*, out, out of commission*, out of kilter*, out of order, out of whack*, ruined, run-down, screwed up*, shot, spent, unsatisfactory, weak, wracked*, wrecked; CONCEPTS 485,560 —*Ant.* fixed, unbroken, working

broken [*adj5*] *forgotten, ignored (promise)* abandoned, dishonored, disobeyed, disregarded, ignored, infringed, isolated, retracted, traduced, transgressed, violated; CONCEPT 544 —*Ant.* kept

broken [*adj6*] *stuttering in speech* disjointed, halting, hesitant, hesitating, imperfect, incoherent, mumbled, muttered, stammering, unintelligible, weak; CONCEPT 267 —*Ant.* continuous, flowing

brokenhearted [*adj*] *devastated* crestfallen, crushed, desolate, despairing, despondent, disappointed, disconsolate, grief-stricken, grieved, heartbroken, heartsick, heartsore, inconsolable, miserable, mournful, prostrated, sorrowful, wretched; CONCEPT 403 —*Ant.* happy, lighthearted, pleased

broker [*n*] *financial expert* agent, business person, dealer, entrepreneur, factor, financier, go-between, interagent, interceder, intercessor, intermediary, intermediate, mediator, merchant, middleperson, negotiator, stockbroker; CONCEPTS 348,353

bronze [*adj*] *coppery-brown color* brownish, burnished, chestnut, copper, copper-colored, metallic brown, reddish-brown, reddish-tan, russet, rust, tan; CONCEPT 618

brooch [*n*] *ornamental pin* bar pin, breastpin, clip, cluster, jewelry; CONCEPT 446

brood [*n*] *cluster of children* begats, breed, chicks, clutch, descendants, family, flock, hatch, infants, issue, litter, offspring, posterity, progeniture, progeny, scions, seed, young; CONCEPT 296 —*Ant.* child

brood [*v*] *agonize over* be in brown study*, bleed, chafe inwardly*, consider, daydream, deliberate, despond, dream, dwell upon, eat one's heart out*, fret, gloom, grieve, lament, languish, meditate, mope, mull over, muse, ponder, reflect, repine, ruminate, sigh, speculate, stew over*, sulk, sweat out*, sweat over*, think about, think upon, worry; CONCEPT 17 —*Ant.* not worry

brook [n] *stream of water* beck, branch, burn, creek, rill, rindle, river, rivulet, run, runnel, streamlet, watercourse; CONCEPT *514*

brook [v] *endure, accept* abide, allow, bear, be big*, countenance, go, hang in, hang in there*, hear of, live with, put up with, sit tight*, stand, stomach, suffer, support, swallow, take, tolerate, withstand; CONCEPT *23*

broom [n] *device for cleaning floors* besom, carpet sweeper, feather duster, floor brush, mop, swab, sweeper, whisk; CONCEPT *499*

broth [n] *soup, usually clear* borscht, bouillon, bowl, brew, chowder, concoction, consommé, decoction, dishwater*, distillation, elixir, fluid, gumbo, hodge-podge*, olio, porridge, potage, potpourri, pottage, puree, splash, stock, vichyssoise; CONCEPTS *457,467*

brothel [n] *house of prostitution* bagnio, bawdy house*, bordello, call house*, cathouse*, den of iniquity*, house of assignation, house of ill-repute, house with red doors*, massage parlor, red-light district, whorehouse; CONCEPT *449*

brother [n1] *male sibling* blood brother, kin, kinsperson, relation, relative, twin; CONCEPTS *414,419* —*Ant.* sister

brotherhood [n] *association* affiliation, alliance, clan, clique, community, comradeship, confederacy, coterie, fellowship, fraternity, guild, kinship, league, society, union; CONCEPTS *387,388* —*Ant.* sisterhood

brow [n] *forehead* countenance, eyebrow, face, frons, front, mien, temple, top; CONCEPT *418*

browbeat [v] *castigate, nag* badger, bludgeon, bluster, bulldoze*, bully, coerce, cow, despotize, domineer, dragoon, frighten, harass, hector, intimidate, lean on*, lord it over*, oppress, overawe, overbear, put heat on*, put the chill on*, put through the wringer*, threaten, tyrannize; CONCEPTS *14,52* —*Ant.* boost, coax, compliment, praise

brown [adj] *dark, burnished color* amber, auburn, bay, beige, bister, brick, bronze, buff, burnt sienna, chestnut, chocolate, cinnamon, cocoa, coffee, copper, drab, dust, ecru, fawn, ginger, hazel, henna, khaki, mahogany, nut, ochre, puce, russet, rust, sepia, snuff-colored, sorrel, tan, tawny, terra-cotta, toast, umber; CONCEPT *618*

brownnose [v] *suck up to* apple-polish, backscratch, bootlick, curry favor, fawn on, flatter, get on the right side of, kiss ass, scratch one's back, suck up to, toady; CONCEPTS *59,69*

brownnoser [n] *sycophant, toady* apple-polisher, ass-kisser, backscratcher*, backslapper*, bootlicker*, brownnose*, doter, fawner, flatterer, flunky*, kiss-ass, kowtower, lackey, minion, teacher's pet, yes-man, yes-person; CONCEPT *423*

browse [v] *look around; look through* check over, dip into*, examine cursorily, feed, flip through, get the cream*, give the once over*, glance at, graze, hit the high spots*, inspect loosely, leaf through, nibble*, once over lightly*, pass an eye over*, peruse, read, read here and there, riffle through, riff through, run through, scan, skim, skip through, survey, thumb through wander; CONCEPT *623*

browser [n] *Internet /Web viewing software* display program, gateway, Internet service

provider, portal, search engine, web crawler, web directory, web spider; CONCEPTS *349,770*

bruise [n] *black and blue mark under skin* black eye, black mark, blemish, boo-boo*, contusion, discoloration, injury, mark, mouse*, swelling, wale, wound; CONCEPT *309*

bruise [v] *break blood vessel; discolor* bang up, batter, beat, black, blacken, blemish, bung up*, contuse, crush, damage, deface, do a number on*, injure, mar, mark, pound, pulverize, wound, zing*; CONCEPTS *137,246,250*

brunette/brunet [adj] *dark hair and/or skin* bistered, brown, dusky, pigmented, swart, swarthy, tanned, tawny; CONCEPTS *406,618* —*Ant.* blond/blonde

brunt [n] *bad end of a situation* burden, force, full force, impact, pressure, shock, strain, stress, tension, thrust, violence; CONCEPT *674*

brush [n1] *tool with bristles for cleaning* besom, broom, hairbrush, mop, polisher, sweeper, toothbrush, waxer, whisk; CONCEPT *499*

brush [n2] *fight* clash, conflict, confrontation, encounter, engagement, fracas, rub, run-in, scrap, set-to, skirmish, tap, touch, tussle; CONCEPT *106*

brush [n3] *scrappy bushes* boscage, bracken, brushwood, chaparral, coppice, copse, cover, dingle, fern, gorse, grove, hedge, scrub, sedge, shrubbery, spinney, thicket, undergrowth, underwood; CONCEPT *429*

brush [v1] *touch lightly* caress, contact, flick, glance, graze, kiss, scrape, shave, skim, smooth, stroke, sweep, tickle; CONCEPT *612*

brush [v2] *clean, prepare by whisking* buff, clean, paint, polish, sweep, wash, whisk, wipe; CONCEPTS *165,202*

brush aside/brush off [v] *ignore; refuse* boycott, cold-shoulder*, contradict, cut, deny, disclaim, dismiss, disown, disregard, get rid of, have no time for*, ostracize, override, rebuff, reject, repudiate, scorn, send away, slight, snub, spurn, sweep aside; CONCEPT *30* —*Ant.* attend, pay attention, see

brush up [v] *improve condition* clean up, cram, go over, look over, polish up, read up, refresh one's memory, refurbish, relearn, renovate, reread, retouch, review, revise, study, touch up; CONCEPTS *202,244* —*Ant.* forget

brusque [adj] *curt, surly* abrupt, bluff, blunt, brief, crusty, discourteous, gruff, hasty, impolite, sharp, short, snappy, snippy, tart, terse, unmannerly; CONCEPTS *267,401* —*Ant.* courteous, kind, polite, tactful

brutal [adj1] *cruel, remorseless* barbarous, bloodthirsty, callous, ferocious, gruff, hard, harsh, heartless, impolite, inhuman, insensitive, merciless, pitiless, remorseless, rough, rude, ruthless, savage, severe, uncivil, uncivilized, unfeeling, unmannerly, unmerciful, vicious; CONCEPT *401* —*Ant.* generous, humane, kind, nice

brutal [adj2] *crude, rough* animal, bearish, beastly, bestial, brute, brutish, carnal, coarse, feral, ferine, inhuman, inhumane, rude, savage, swinish, unfeeling; CONCEPT *544* —*Ant.* gentle, kind, nice

brutality [n] *cruel treatment* atrocity, barbarism, barbarity, bloodthirstiness, brutishness, choke hold*, cruelty, ferocity, fierceness, grossness, inhumanity, ruthlessness, sadism, savageness, savagery, third degree*, unfeelingness, viciousness; CONCEPTS *14,86* —*Ant.* gentleness, humaneness, kindness, niceness

brutally [*adv*] *cruelly, without remorse* atrociously, barbarically, barbarously, brutishly, callously, demoniacally, diabolically, ferally, ferociously, fiercely, hardheartedly, heartlessly, in cold blood, inexorably, inhumanely, inhumanly, meanly, mercilessly, murderously, pitilessly, relentlessly, remorselessly, ruthlessly, savagely, something fierce, something terrible, unkindly, unrelentingly, viciously; CONCEPT *544* —*Ant.* gently, humanely, kindly, nicely

brute [*adj*] *very strong; animal-like* animal, beastly, bestial, bodily, carnal, feral, ferine, fleshly, instinctive, mindless, physical, senseless, swinish, unthinking; CONCEPTS *489,540* —*Ant.* gentle, mild, weak

brute [*n*] *barbarian* animal, beast, cannibal, creature, critter*, degenerate, devil, fiend, lout, monster, ogre, ruffian, sadist, savage, swine, wild animal; CONCEPTS *394,423* —*Ant.* gentleman, humanitarian

bubble [*n*] *globule of air* air ball*, balloon, barm, bead, blister, blob, drop, droplet, effervescence, foam, froth, lather, sac, spume, vesicle; CONCEPT *437*

bubble [*v*] *foam, froth up, especially with sound* boil, burble, churn, eddy, effervesce, erupt, fester, fizz, gurgle, gush, issue, moil, murmur, percolate, ripple, seep, seethe, simmer, smolder, sparkle, spume, stir, swash, trickle, well; CONCEPTS *179,469*

bubbly [*adj1*] *sparkling* aerated, bubbling, carbonated, effervescent, fizzy, gassy, spumante; CONCEPT *462* —*Ant.* flat, still

bubbly [*adj2*] *vivacious* animated, bubbling, dynamic, effervescent, energetic, enthusiastic, full of beans*, full of life, high-spirited, lively, peppy*, perky, sparkling, spirited, vibrant, zesty; CONCEPT *401* —*Ant.* dull, listless

buck [*n*] *male animal* bull, stag; CONCEPTS *394,419*

buck [*v*] *resist, kick off* bound, combat, contest, dislodge, dispute, duel, fight, jerk, jump, leap, oppose, prance, repel, start, throw, traverse, trip, unseat, vault, withstand; CONCEPTS *180,222*

bucket [*n*] *container, often for liquids, with handle* brazier, can, canister, cask, hod, kettle, pail, pot, scuttle, vat; CONCEPT *494*

buckle [*n*] *fastener with long pin* catch, clamp, clasp, clip, fastening, fibula, harness, hasp; CONCEPT *450*

buckle [*v*] *contort, warp* bend, bulge, cave in, collapse, crumple, distort, fold, twist, yield; CONCEPT *702* —*Ant.* flatten, smooth

buckle down [*v*] *concentrate on* address, apply oneself, attend to, bend, dedicate oneself to, devote oneself to, exert oneself, give, give oneself over to, keep close to, keep one's mind on, launch into, occupy oneself with, pitch in, set to, throw, turn; CONCEPTS *17,87* —*Ant.* be lazy, ignore, relax

bucolic [*adj*] *rural or rustic* agrarian, agricultural, Arcadian, countrified, country, pastoral; CONCEPTS *536,583*

bud [*n*] *new sprout on plant* bloom, blossom, embryo, floret, germ, incipient flower, nucleus, shoot, spark; CONCEPT *428*

bud [*v*] *sprout* burgeon, burst forth, develop, grow, pullulate, shoot; CONCEPT *427* —*Ant.* die, shrink, waste, wither

budding [*adj*] *developing, flowering* beginning, blossoming, burgeoning, bursting forth, embryonic, fledgling, fresh, germinal, germinating, growing, incipient, maturing, nascent, opening, potential, promising, pubescent, pullulating, shooting up, sprouting, vegetating, young; CONCEPT *490* —*Ant.* dying, shrinking, withering

buddy [*n*] *friend* associate, chum, co-mate, companion, comrade, confidant, co-worker, crony, intimate, mate, pal, peer, sidekick; CONCEPT *423* —*Ant.* enemy

budge [*v*] *dislodge from staid position* bend, change, change position, convince, give way, inch, influence, locomote, move, persuade, propel, push, remove, roll, shift, slide, stir, sway, yield; CONCEPTS *68,147*

budget [*n*] *financial plan* account, aggregate, allocation, allowance, bulk, cost, estimated expenses, finances, fiscal estimate, funds, means, planned disbursement, quantity, quantum, resources, spending plan, statement, total; CONCEPT *332*

budget [*v*] *plan money or action* allocate, apportion, calculate, compute, cost, estimate, predict, ration; CONCEPTS *36,330*

buff [*adj*] *sandy color* bare, blonde, canary, ecru, lemon, light brown, nude, ochre, straw, tan, tawny, yellow-brown, yellowish; CONCEPT *618*

buff [*n*] *enthusiast* addict, admirer, aficionado, connoisseur, devotee, expert, fan, fiend*, freak*, habitué, hound, lover, votary; CONCEPTS *352,423* —*Ant.* detractor, opponent

buff [*v*] *polish to a shine* brush, burnish, furbish, glaze, gloss, pumice, rub, sandpaper, scour, shine, smooth; CONCEPTS *202,215*

buffer [*n*] *safeguard* bulwark, bumper, cushion, defense, fender, intermediary, screen, shield, shock absorber; CONCEPTS *484,729*

buffet [*n*] *meal set out on table for choosing* café, cafeteria, cold table, counter, cupboard, lunch wagon, salad bar, shelf, sideboard, smorgasbord, snack bar; CONCEPTS *443,459*

buffet [*v*] *hit repeatedly* bang, batter, beat, blow, box, bump, clobber, cuff, flail, jolt, knock, pound, pummel, push, rap, shove, slap, smack, spank, strike, thrash, thump, wallop; CONCEPT *189*

buffoon [*n*] *clownlike person* antic, bozo*, clown, comedian, comic, droll, fool, harlequin, jester, joker, merry-andrew, wag, zany; CONCEPT *423*

bug [*n1*] *bacterium, microorganism* bacillus, disease, germ, infection, microbe, virus; CONCEPT *306*

bug [*n2*] *insect* ant, beetle, cootie, flea, gnat, louse, pest, vermin; CONCEPT *398*

bug [*n3*] *obsession* craze, enthusiasm, fad, mania, rage, zeal; CONCEPT *532*

bug [*n4*] *computer glitch* breakdown, computer malfunction, defect, error, failure, fault, flaw, hitch, problem, something wrong, trouble; CONCEPTS *580,674*

bug [*v1*] *bother, disturb* abrade, annoy, badger, chafe, gall, get on someone's*, harass, irk, irritate, needle, nettle, pester, plague, provoke, vex; CONCEPTS *7,19* —*Ant.* not bother

br
bu

bug [v2] *listen to without permission* eavesdrop, listen in, overhear, spy, tap, wiretap; CONCEPTS 192,596

bugle [n] *musical horn* clarion, cornet, misery pipe*, trumpet; CONCEPT 262

build [n] *physical structure, form* body, conformation, constitution, figure, frame, habit, habitus, physique, shape; CONCEPT 757 —*Ant.* mind

build [v1] *construct structure* assemble, bring about, carpenter, cast, compile, compose, contrive, engineer, erect, evolve, fabricate, fashion, fit together, forge, form, frame, jerry-build, knock together*, make, manufacture, model, prefabricate, produce, put together, put up, raise, rear, reconstruct, sculpture, set up, superstruct, synthesize, throw together*, throw up*; CONCEPT 168 —*Ant.* demolish, destroy, dismantle, knock down, raze, ruin, take down

build [v2] *initiate, found* base, begin, constitute, establish, formulate, inaugurate, institute, originate, set up, start; CONCEPT 234 —*Ant.* destroy, overthrow, overturn, ruin

build [v3] *increase, accelerate* aggrandize, amplify, augment, boost, compound, develop, enlarge, escalate, expand, extend, heighten, improve, intensify, magnify, mount, multiply, strengthen, swell, wax; CONCEPTS 236,245 —*Ant.* decelerate, decrease, destroy, ruin

builder [n] *construction worker* architect, artisan, constructor, contractor, craftsperson, erector, fabricator, framer, inventor, maker, manufacturer, mason, originator, producer; CONCEPT 348 —*Ant.* wrecker

building [n] *constructed dwelling* architecture, construction, domicile, edifice, erection, fabric, framework, home, house, hut, pile, superstructure; CONCEPTS 439,441

buildup [n] *development; accumulation* accretion, advertising, enlargement, escalation, expansion, gain, growth, heap, hype, increase, load, mass, plug, promotion, publicity, puff*, stack, stockpile, store; CONCEPTS 230,704,787 —*Ant.* decrease, destruction, reduction

build up [v] *amplify, advertise* add to, boost, develop, enhance, expand, extend, fortify, heighten, hype, improve, increase, intensify, plug*, promote, publicize, puff*, reinforce, spotlight, strengthen; CONCEPTS 236,245,266 —*Ant.* lessen, let down, play down, weaken

built-in [adj] *included* congenital, constitutional, deep-seated, essential, implicit, inborn, inbred, in-built, incorporated, indwelling, ingrained, inherent, innate, inseparable, integral, part and parcel*; CONCEPT 549 —*Ant.* added, extra, not included

bulb [n] *globular object* ball, bunch, corm, corn, globe, head, knob, nodule, nub, protuberance, swelling, tuber, tumor; CONCEPT 436

bulge [n] *swollen object* appendage, bagginess, blob, bump, bunch, bunching, convexity, dilation, distention, excess, excrescence, gibbosity, growth, hump, intumescence, jut, lump, nodulation, nodule, outgrowth, outthrust, projection, prominence, promontory, protrusion, protuberance, sac, sagging, salience, salient, superfluity, swelling, tuberosity, tumefaction, tumor, wart; CONCEPTS 436,470 —*Ant.* depression

bulge [v] *project outward* bag, balloon, beetle, belly, bilge, billow, bloat, blob, bug out, dilate,

distend, enlarge, expand, extrude, jut, overhang, poke, pop out, pouch, protrude, protuberate, puff out, sag, stand out, stick out, swell; CONCEPTS 208,780 —*Ant.* cave in, depress

bulk [n1] *size, largeness* aggregate, amount, amplitude, bigness, dimensions, extent, immensity, magnitude, mass, massiveness, quantity, quantum, substance, total, totality, volume, weight; CONCEPT 730

bulk [n2] *main part, most* best part, better part, biggest share, body, generality, greater number, greater part, gross, lion's share*, majority, major part, mass, nearly all, plurality, predominant part, preponderance, principal part; CONCEPTS 635,829

bulky [adj] *huge* awkward, beefy, big, colossal, cumbersome, cumbrous, enormous, gross, heavy, hefty, high, hulking, immense, large, long, mammoth, massive, ponderous, substantial, unhandy, unmanageable, unwieldy, voluminous, weighty; CONCEPT 781 —*Ant.* insubstantial, miniature, small, thin, tiny

bulldoze [v1] *demolish* drive, elbow, flatten, force, jostle, level, press, propel, push, raze, shove, thrust; CONCEPTS 208,252 —*Ant.* build, construct

bulldoze [v2] *bully, intimidate* bludgeon, bluster, browbeat, coerce, cow, dragoon, harass, hector; CONCEPT 14 —*Ant.* leave alone

bullet [n] *small missile* ammo*, ammunition, ball, bolt, cap, cartridge, dose*, lead, love letter*, pellet, projectile, rocket, round, shot, slug, trajectile; CONCEPT 500

bulletin [n] *message, notification* account, announcement, break, calendar, communication, communiqué, dispatch, flash*, handout, hot wire*, item, list, news, news flash*, notice, program, publication, release, report, scoop*, skinny*, statement, the dope*, what's going down*, what's happening*; CONCEPTS 271,274

bulletin board [n] *electronic messaging system* bboard, BBS, board, bulletin board system; CONCEPTS 349,770

bully [n] *domineering person* annoyer, antagonizer, browbeater, bulldozer, coercer, harrier, hector, insolent, intimidator, oppressor, persecutor, pest, rascal, rowdy, ruffian, tease, tormenter, tough; CONCEPT 423

bully [v] *intimidate, push around* bludgeon, bluster, browbeat, buffalo, bulldoze, coerce, cow, despotize, domineer, dragoon, enforce, harass, hector, lean on, menace, oppress, overbear, persecute, ride roughshod*, showboat*, swagger, terrorize, threaten, torment, torture, turn on the heat*, tyrannize, walk heavy*; CONCEPT 14 —*Ant.* allow, leave alone

bulwark [n] *fortification, support* barrier, bastion, buffet, buttress, citadel, defense, embankment, fort, fortress, guard, mainstay, outwork, parapet, partition, protection, rampart, redoubt, safeguard, security, stronghold, vallation; CONCEPTS 96,729 —*Ant.* weak point

bum [n] *beggar* bindle*, black sheep*, derelict, drifter, floater, gutterpup*, guttersnipe*, hobo, stiff*, tramp, transient, vagabond, vagrant; CONCEPTS 412,423

bummer [n] *bad experience* disappointment, disaster, downer*, drag*, misfortune; CONCEPTS 674,679

bump [v1] *collide, hit, usually with sound* bang, bounce, box, buck, bunt, butt, carom, clap, clatter, crack, crash, impinge, jar, jerk, jolt, jostle, jounce, knock, pat, plop, plunk, pound, punch, rap, rattle, shake, slam, slap, smack, smash into, strike, thud, thump, thunder, thwack, whack; CONCEPT 189

bump [v2] *move over, dislodge* budge, displace, remove, shift; CONCEPT 213

bump [v3] *increment* increase, raise, step up; CONCEPTS 236,245,780

bump into [v] *happen upon* chance upon, come across, encounter, hit, light, light upon, luck, meet, meet up with, run across, run into, stumble, tumble; CONCEPT 114

bumpy [adj] *rough* choppy, corrugated, jarring, jerky, knobby, lumpy, potholed*, rugged, rutted, uneven; CONCEPTS 485,606

bum rap [n] *rotten deal* bad break*, bad deal, bad rap*, bum deal*, bummer*, drag*, frame-up, lousy deal, misfortune, raw deal, stroke of bad luck*, the shaft*; CONCEPTS 674,679

bun [n] *baked roll* bread, cruller, Danish, doughnut, eclair, muffin, pastry, scone, sweet roll; CONCEPT 457

bunch [n] *collection of something* agglomeration, assemblage, assortment, band, batch, bevy, blob, bouquet, bundle, caboodle*, chunk, clump, cluster, covey, crew, crowd, fascicle, flock, galaxy, gang, gathering, group, heap, host, hunk, knot, lot, mass, mess, mob, multitude, number, oodles*, pack, parcel, party, passel*, pile, quantity, sheaf, shebang*, shock, shooting match*, spray, stack, swarm, team, thicket, troop, tuft; CONCEPT 432 —Ant. individual, one

bunch [v] *gather in group* assemble, bundle, cluster, collect, congregate, cram, crowd, flock, group, herd, huddle, mass, pack; CONCEPT 109 —Ant. disperse, divide, scatter, separate, spread

bundle [n] *accumulation, package of something* array, assortment, bag, bale, batch, box, bunch, carton, clump, cluster, collection, group, heap, lot, mass, pack, package, packet, pallet, parcel, pile, quantity, roll, set, stack, wad; CONCEPTS 432,787

bundle [v] *accumulate, package* bale, bind, clothe, fasten, pack, palletize, tie, truss, wrap; CONCEPTS 158,202 —Ant. disperse, divide, let go, scatter, separate, spread

bungle [v] *blunder, mess up* ball up*, boggle, botch, butcher*, drop the ball*, err, flub, foul up*, fudge*, fumble, goof up*, gum up*, louse up*, make a mess of, mar, mess up, miscalculate, mishandle, mismanage, muff*, ruin, screw up*, spoil; CONCEPT 101 —Ant. do well, fix, manage, succeed

bungler [n] *person who blunders* addlebrain*, blockhead*, blunderer, bonehead*, botcher*, bumbler, butcher*, butterfingers*, clod, clumsy oaf*, dolt, donkey*, duffer*, dunce, featherbrain*, fool, foul-up*, fumbler*, goofball*, goof off*, harebrain*, idiot, ignoramus, incompetent, klutz*, mismanager, muddler, muffer*, numskull*, screw up*, spoiler; CONCEPTS 412,423 —Ant. success

bunk [n1] *nonsense* applesauce*, balderdash, baloney*, bilge*, claptrap, eyewash*, flimflam*, garbage*, hogwash*, hooey*, horsefeathers*, jazz*, piffle*, poppycock*, rot*,

rubbish, tomfoolery*, tommyrot*, trash*, twaddle*; CONCEPTS 63,278 —Ant. sense

bunk [n2] *twin bed, usually stacked; place to sleep* berth, cot, doss, hay, kip, pallet, sack; CONCEPT 443

bunt [v] *hit half-heartedly* butt, lay it down*, meet, sacrifice, throw, toss; CONCEPTS 189,363

buoy [n] *floating device* beacon, drift, float, guide, marker, signal; CONCEPT 628

buoyancy/buoyance [n1] *lightness in weight* airiness, ethereality, floatability, levity, weightlessness; CONCEPT 734 —Ant. heaviness

buoyancy/buoyance [n2] *lightness in spirit* animation, bounce, cheerfulness, cheeriness, ebullience, effervescence, exuberance, gaiety, good feeling, good humor, happiness, high spirits, jollity, liveliness, pep, spiritedness, sunniness, vim and vigor*, zing*, zip; CONCEPTS 410,411 —Ant. blues, depression, heaviness

buoyant [adj1] *light in weight* afloat, airy, bouncy, floatable, floating, resilient, supernatant, unsinkable, weightless; CONCEPT 491 —Ant. heavy, weighted

buoyant [adj2] *light in spirit* animated, blithe, bouncy, breezy, bright, carefree, cheerful, debonair, effervescent, elastic, expansive, full of zip, gay, happy, invigorated, jaunty, jovial, joyful, laid back*, lighthearted, lively, peppy, resilient, sunny, supple, vivacious; CONCEPTS 403,404 —Ant. depressed, down, heavy, heavy-hearted

buoy (up) [v] *make light, encourage* bolster, boost, buck up, cheer, cheer up, encourage, hearten, keep afloat, lift, prop, raise, support, sustain, uphold; CONCEPTS 7,22 —Ant. bring down, depress

burden [n] *mental weight; stress* accountability, affliction, albatross*, anxiety, ball and chain*, blame, care, charge, clog, concern, deadweight, difficulty, duty, encumbrance, excess baggage*, grievance, hardship, Herculean task, hindrance, load, millstone, misfortune, mishap, obstruction, onus, punishment, responsibility, sorrow, strain, task, tax, thorn in one's side*, trial, trouble, weary load, work, worry; CONCEPTS 532,690 —Ant. aid, help, relief

burden [v] *encumber, strain* afflict, bear down on, bother, crush, cumber, depress, dish it out*, dish out*, dump on*, encumber, give it to, hamper, handicap, hinder, impede, lade, load, make heavy, obligate, oppress, overcharge, overload, overwhelm, pile, press, saddle with, snow*, snow under*, stick it to, strain, tax, trouble, try, vex, weigh down, worry; CONCEPTS 7,14,19 —Ant. aid, help, relieve

burdensome [adj] *troublesome* carking, crushing, demanding, difficult, disturbing, exacting, exigent, heavy*, irksome, onerous, oppressive, superincumbent, taxing, tough, trying, wearing, wearying, weighty; CONCEPT 529 —Ant. aiding, helpful, helping, relieving, unburdensome

bureau [n1] *branch of an organization* agency, authority, board, commission, committee, department, division, front office*, office, salt mines*, service, setup, shop, store; CONCEPTS 325,441,449

bureau [n2] *chest of drawers* chiffonier, commode, desk, dresser, highboy, sideboard, writing desk; CONCEPT 443

bureaucracy [n] *system which controls organization* administration, authority, beadledom*, city hall*, civil service, directorate, government, management, ministry, officialdom, officials, powers that be*, red tape*, regulatory commission, the Establishment*, the system*; CONCEPTS 325,770

bureaucrat [n] *government official* administrator, civil servant, desk-jockey*, functionary, office-holder, pencil-pusher*, politician, public servant; CONCEPTS 347,354

burglar [n] *person who steals* cat burglar, crook, filcher*, housebreaker, midnighter*, owl*, picklock*, pilferer*, porch-climber*, prowler, robber, safecracker, sneakthief*, thief; CONCEPT 412

burglary [n] *stealing from residence, business* break-in, breaking and entering, caper, crime, filching, heist, housebreaking, larceny, owl job*, pilferage, prowl, robbery, safecracking, second-story work*, sting, theft, thieving; CONCEPT 139

burial [n] *laying in of dead body* burying, deep six*, deposition, entombment, exequies, funeral, inhumation, interment, last rites, obsequies, sepulture; CONCEPT 367

burlesque [adj] *farcical* caricatural, comic, ironical, ludicrous, mock, mocking, parodic, satirical, travestying; CONCEPT 555

burlesque [n] *bawdy show; vaudeville* burly*, caricature, farce, lampoon, lampoonery, mock, mockery, parody, pastiche, peep show, revue, satire, send-up, spoof, strip, takeoff, travesty, vaudeville; CONCEPT 263

burly [adj] *husky able-bodied, athletic, beefcake*, beefy*, big, brawny, bruising, bulky, gorillalike, hefty, hulking, hulky, hunk, muscular, portly, powerful, stocky, stout, strapping, strong, sturdy, thickset, well-built; CONCEPT 773 —**Ant.** light, slim, small, thin

burn [v1] *be on fire; set on fire* bake, be ablaze, blaze, brand, broil, calcine, cauterize, char, combust, conflagrate, cook, cremate, enkindle, flame, flare, flash, flicker, glow, heat, ignite, incinerate, kindle, light, melt, parch, reduce to ashes, rekindle, roast, scald, scorch, sear, set a match to, singe, smoke, smolder, toast, torch, wither; CONCEPT 249 —**Ant.** cool, extinguish, put out, quench, smother, wet

burn [v2] *feel stinging pain* bite, hurt, pain, smart, sting, tingle; CONCEPT 590

burn [v3] *be excited about; yearn for* be angry, be aroused, be inflamed, be passionate, be stirred up, blaze, boil, breathe fire*, bristle, desire, eat up*, fume, lust, rage, seethe, simmer, smoulder, tingle, yearn; CONCEPTS 20,29,34 —**Ant.** stifle, subdue

burn [v4] *cheat* beat, bilk, chisel, cozen, deceive, defraud, gyp, overreach, ream, swindle, take, trick, use; CONCEPTS 59,142 —**Ant.** aid, help

burning [adj1] *blazing, flashing* afire, aflame, alight, blistering, broiling, conflagrant, enkindled, fiery, flaming, flaring, gleaming, glowing, heated, hot, ignited, illuminated, incandescent, in flames, kindled, on fire, oxidizing, red-hot*, scorching, searing, sizzling, smoking, smouldering, torrid, white-hot*; CONCEPTS 485,605 —**Ant.** cold, cool

burning [adj2] *fervent, excited* all-consuming,

ardent, blazing, eager, earnest, fervid, feverish, frantic, frenzied, heated, hectic, impassioned, intense, passionate, red-hot*, vehement, white-hot*, zealous; CONCEPT 403 —**Ant.** apathetic, cold, cool, unexcited, unimportant

burning [adj3] *stinging, painful* acrid, biting, caustic, irritating, painful, piercing, prickling, pungent, reeking, sharp, smarting, tingling; CONCEPTS 314,537

burning [adj4] *important* acute, clamant, clamorous, compelling, critical, crucial, crying, dire, essential, exigent, imperative, importunate, instant, pressing, significant, urgent, vital; CONCEPT 568 —**Ant.** unimportant

burnish [v] *polish, brighten* buff, furbish, glance, glaze, gloss, luster, patina, put on a finish, rub, sheen, shine, smooth, wax; CONCEPTS 202,215 —**Ant.** dull, tarnish

burrow [n] *hole dug by animal* couch, den, hovel, lair, retreat, shelter, tunnel; CONCEPT 517

burrow [v] *dig a hole* delve, excavate, hollow out, scoop out, tunnel, undermine; CONCEPT 178 —**Ant.** cover, fill

burst [n] *blow-up, blast* access, bang, barrage, blowout, bombardment, breach, break, cannonade, crack, discharge, eruption, explosion, fit, flare, fusillade, gush, gust, outbreak, outpouring, round, rupture, rush, sally, salvo, shower, spate, split, spurt, storm, surge, torrent, volley; CONCEPTS 86,179,208

burst [v] *blow up, break out* barge, blow, break, crack, detonate, discharge, disintegrate, erupt, explode, fly open, fracture, fragment, gush forth, perforate, pierce, pop, prick, puncture, rend asunder, run, rupture, rush, shatter, shiver, splinter, split, spout, tear apart; CONCEPTS 179

bury [v1] *lay to rest after death* consign to grave, cover up, deposit, embalm, ensepulcher, enshrine, entomb, hold last rites for*, hold services for, inearth, inhume, inter, inurn, lay out, mummify, plant*, put away*, put six feet under*, sepulcher, sepulture, tomb; CONCEPT 367 —**Ant.** dig out, disinter, uncover

bury [v2] *conceal, cover* cache, cover up, ensconce, enshroud, hide, occult, plant, screen, secrete, shroud, stash, stow away; CONCEPTS 172,188 —**Ant.** dig out, reveal, uncover

bury [v3] *plant in ground* drive in, embed, engulf, implant, sink, submerge; CONCEPTS 172,257 —**Ant.** dig out

bury [v4] *engross oneself* absorb, concentrate, engage, immerse, interest, occupy, rivet, throw oneself into; CONCEPT 24

bush [n] *shrubs; woodland* backcountry, backwoods, boscage, bramble, briar, brush, chaparral, creeper, forest, hedge, hinterland, jungle, outback, plant, scrub, scrubland, shrubbery, the wild, thicket, vine, wilderness; CONCEPT 429

bush-league [adj] *second-rate* minor league*, small potatoes*; CONCEPTS 334,567,574

bushy [adj] *shaggy, unkempt* bristling, bristly, disordered, feathery, fluffy, fringed, full, furry, fuzzy, hairy, heavy, hirsute, leafy, luxuriant, nappy, prickly, rough, rumpled, spreading, stiff, thick, tufted, unruly, wiry, woolly; CONCEPTS 406,606 —**Ant.** bald, neat, well-kept

busily [adv] *actively; intently* agilely, animatedly, ardently, arduously, assiduously, briskly, carefully, diligently, eagerly, earnestly, energetically, enthusiastically, expeditiously, fervently, hastily, hurriedly, indefatigably, industriously, laboriously, like all get out*, like the devil*, like the dickens*, nimbly, painstakingly, perseveringly, persistently, purposefully, restlessly, seriously, speedily, spiritedly, strenuously, studiously, unremittingly, unweariedly, vigilantly, vigorously, vivaciously, zealously; CONCEPT 544 —*Ant.* idly, inactively, quietly

business [n1] *job, profession* bag*, biz*, calling, career, craft, dodge*, employment, field, function, game, line, livelihood, métier, occupation, pursuit, racket*, specialty, trade, vocation, what one is into*, work; CONCEPT 360 —*Ant.* avocation, recreation, unemployment

business [n2] *company, enterprise* cartel, concern, corporation, establishment, factory, firm, fly-by-night operation*, house, institution, market, megacorp*, mill, Mom and Pop*, monopoly, organization, outfit, partnership, setup, shoestring operation*, shop, store, syndicate, trust, venture; CONCEPTS 325,449

business [n3] *commerce, trade* affairs, bargaining, barter, buying and selling, capital and labor, commercialism, contracts, deal, dealings, exchange, free enterprise, game, industrialism, industry, manufacturing, market, merchandising, production and distribution, racket*, sales, selling, trading, traffic, transaction, undertaking; CONCEPTS 325,770

business [n4] *personal concern* affair, assignment, beeswax*, carrying on, duty, function, goings-on*, hanky-panky*, happening, interest, issue, lookout, matter, palaver, point, problem, question, responsibility, subject, task, topic; CONCEPT 532

businesslike [adj] *efficient, professional* accomplished, careful, concentrated, correct, diligent, direct, disciplined, earnest, effective, enterprising, expeditious, hardworking, industrious, intent, matter-of-fact, methodical, orderly, organized, painstaking, practical, practiced, purposeful, regular, routine, sedulous, serious, skillful, systematic, thorough, well-ordered, workaday; CONCEPTS 326,544 —*Ant.* amateur, disorganized, inefficient, unbusinesslike, unprofessional

businessperson [n] *professional working person* baron, big-time operator*, big wheel*, capitalist, dealer, employer, entrepreneur, executive, financier, franchiser, gray flannel suit*, industrialist, manager, merchandiser, merchant, operator, organization person, small potatoes*, storekeeper, suit*, the bacon*, tradesperson, trafficker, tycoon, wheeler-dealer*; CONCEPTS 347,348

bust [n1] *chest of human* bosom, breast, chest, front; CONCEPT 392

bust [n2] *arrest for illegal action* apprehension, arrest, capture, cop, detention, nab, pickup, pinch, raid, search, seizure; CONCEPTS 298,317 —*Ant.* exoneration

bust [v1] *ruin, impoverish* become insolvent, break, crash, fail, fold up, go bankrupt, go into Chapter 11*, pauperize; CONCEPT 330 —*Ant.* aid, help

bust [v2] *arrest for illegal action* apprehend, catch, collar, cop*, detain, nab, pick up, pinch,

pull in, raid, run in, search; CONCEPTS 298,317 —*Ant.* exonerate, let go

bust [v3] *physically break* burst, fold, fracture, rupture; CONCEPT 252 —*Ant.* fix, mend

bustle [n] *quick and busy activity* ado, agitation, clamor, commotion, do*, excitement, flurry, furor, fuss, haste, hubbub, hurly-burly*, hurry, pother, rumpus, stir, to-do*, tumult, turmoil, uproar, whirl, whirlpool, whirlwind; CONCEPT 386 —*Ant.* laziness, relaxation

bustle [v] *move around quickly, busily* bestir, dash, dust, flit, flutter, fuss, hasten, hum, hurry, hustle, run, rush, scamper, scramble, scurry, scuttle, stir, tear, whirl, whisk; CONCEPT 150

busy [adj1] *engaged, at work* active, already taken*, assiduous, at it*, buried, diligent, employed, engaged, engrossed, having a full plate*, having enough on one's plate*, having fish to fry*, having many irons in the fire*, hustling, in a meeting, in conference, industrious, in someone else's possession*, in the field, in the laboratory, occupied, on assignment, on duty, on the go, overloaded, persevering, slaving, snowed*, swamped*, tied up, unavailable, up to one's ears*, with a customer, working; CONCEPTS 326,544,555 —*Ant.* idle, quiet, unbusy, unemployed, unengaged

busy [adj2] *active, on the go* bustling, busy as a beaver*, energetic, full, fussy, hectic, humming*, hustling, lively, popping*, restless, strenuous, tireless, tiring; CONCEPT 542 —*Ant.* idle, inactive, lazy

busy [adj3] *nosy, impertinent* butting in, curious, forward, inquisitive, interfering, intrusive, meddlesome, meddling, nebby, obtrusive, officious, prying, pushy, snoopy, stirring, troublesome; CONCEPT 404

busybody [n] *nosy, impertinent person* backseat driver*, butt-in*, buttinsky*, eavesdropper, fink*, fussbudget, gossip, intermeddler, intruder, meddler, newsmonger*, nosey parker*, rubberneck*, scandalmonger*, sidewalk superintendent*, snoop, snooper, tattletale, troublemaker, yenta*; CONCEPT 423

butcher [n] *meat killer, seller* boner*, meatmarket person, meat person, processor, skinner*, slaughterer, slayer*; CONCEPT 348

butcher [v1] *slay and prepare animal for meat* beef up, carve, clean, cure, cut, cut down, dress, joint, liquidate, salt, slaughter, smoke, stick; CONCEPTS 170,252

butcher [v2] *ruin* bollix up*, botch, destroy, goof up*, louse up*, make a mess of*, mutilate, screw up*, spoil, wreck; CONCEPT 101

butt [n1] *end, shaft* base, bottom, edge, extremity, fag end, foot, fundament, haft, handle, hilt, shank, stock, stub, stump, tail, tip; CONCEPT 827

butt/buttocks [n2] *animate rear end* back end, backside, behind, bottom, bum*, derrière, fanny*, fundament, gluteus maximus, haunches, hindquarters, posterior, rear, rump, seat, tush*; CONCEPT 392

butt [n3] *object of joking* chump*, clay pigeon*, derision, dupe*, easy mark*, fall guy*, fool, goat, jestee*, joke, laughingstock, mark, patsy, pigeon*, sap, setup*, sitting duck*, softie*, subject, sucker, target, turkey, victim; CONCEPT 423

butt [n4] *cigarette* cancer stick*, cig*, coffin nail*, fag*, smoke*, tobacco; CONCEPT 293

butt [v1] *bang up against with head* batter, buck, buffet, bump, bunt, collide, gore, hook, horn, jab, knock, poke, prod, punch, push, ram, run into, shove, smack, strike, thrust, toss; CONCEPT 189

butt [v2] *touch, adjoin* abut, border, bound, communicate, join, jut, meet, neighbor, project, protrude, verge; CONCEPTS 113,747

butterfingers [n] *a clumsy person* bull in a china shop*, bungler, clod, clumsy oaf*, clunker, dolt, duffer*, foozle, fumbler, klutz, lummox, muffer*, schlep; CONCEPTS 412,423

butt in [v] *meddle* barge in, bother, burst in, charge in, chisel in*, cut in, disturb, get into the act*, interject, interrupt, intrude, muscle in, pester, poke one's face in*, pry, put one's two cents in*; CONCEPTS 14,159,208,266,384

button [n1] *fastener* catch, clasp, fastening, frog, knob, stud; CONCEPTS 445,471

button [n2] *pushbutton* adjuster, dial, knob, on/off, power switch, switch, toggle, tuner; CONCEPT 201

buttress [n] *brace, support* abutment, column, mainstay, pier, prop, reinforcement, shore, stanchion, stay, strut, underpinning; CONCEPT 440

buttress [v] *support, bolster* back up, beef up*, brace, build up, bulwark, carry, jack up, jazz up*, prop, reinforce, shore, step up, strengthen, sustain, uphold; CONCEPT 250 —*Ant.* let down, weaken

buxom [adj] *bosomy* ample, built, busty, chubby, comely, curvaceous, curvy, full-bosomed, full-figured, healthy, hearty, lusty, plump, robust, shapely, stacked*, voluptuous, well-made, well-proportioned, well-rounded, zaftig*; CONCEPT 406 —*Ant.* flat, petite, small

buy [n] *something purchased* acquisition, bargain, closeout, deal, good deal, investment, purchase, steal, value; CONCEPT 710

buy [v1] *purchase* acquire, bargain for, barter for, contract for, get, get in exchange, go shopping, invest in, market, obtain, pay for, procure, purchase, redeem, score, secure, shop for, sign for, take; CONCEPT 327 —*Ant.* market, sell

buy [v2] *bribe* corrupt, fix, grease palm*, have, land, lubricate, oil palm*, ransom, reach, redeem, sop*, square, suborn, tamper; CONCEPTS 192,341

buyer [n] *someone who purchases* client, consumer, customer, easy make*, emptor, end user, patron, prospect, purchaser, representative, shopper, sucker*, user, vendee; CONCEPT 348 —*Ant.* marketer, seller

buzz [n1] *droning sound* drone, fizz, fizzle, hiss, hum, murmur, purr, ring, ringing, sibilation, whir, whisper; CONCEPT 595

buzz [n2] *gossip* comment, cry, grapevine*, hearsay, news, report, rumble*, rumor, scandal, scuttlebutt, talk, whisper; CONCEPT 274

buzz [v1] *make droning sound* bombinate, bumble, drone, fizz, fizzle, hum, murmur, reverberate, ring, sibilate, whir, whisper, whiz; CONCEPT 65

buzz [v2] *gossip* call, chatter, inform, natter, rumor, tattle; CONCEPT 60

buzzword [n] *popular word or phrase* argot, cant, doublespeak, fuzzword, jargon, lingo,

mediaspeak, phraseology, policyspeak, slang; CONCEPT 275

by [adv] *near* aside, at hand, away, beyond, close, handy, in reach, over, past, through, to one side; CONCEPT 586

by [prep1] *next to* along, alongside, beside, by way of, close to, near, nearby, nigh, over, past, round CONCEPT 586

by [prep2] *by means of* at the hand of, in the name of, on, over, supported by, through, through the agency of, through the medium of, under the aegis of, via, with, with the assistance of; CONCEPT 544

bygone [adj] *in the past* ancient, antiquated, archaic, belated, dated, dead, defunct, departed, down memory lane*, erstwhile, extinct, forgotten, former, gone, gone by, in oblivion, late, lost, of old, of yore, olden, oldfangled, old-fashioned, old-time, one-time, out-of-date, previous, quondam, sometime, vanished, water over the dam*, water under the bridge*; CONCEPT 820 —*Ant.* modern, new, recent

by hand [v] *manually* arduously, laboriously, strenuously, the hard way, tooth and nail; CONCEPT 544

bypass [v] *avoid* blink at, burke, circumnavigate, circumvent, depart from, detour, deviate from, finesse, get around, go around, go around the barn*, ignore, let go, neglect, omit, outflank, pass around, sidestep, skirt, take back road*, wink at; CONCEPTS 30,102

by-product [n] *side product* after-effect, consequence, fall-out, offshoot, outgrowth, repercussion, result, side effect, spinoff; CONCEPTS 230,260

bystander [n] *person who watches* eyewitness, gaper*, kibitzer*, looker-on, observer, onlooker, passerby, spectator, viewer, watcher, witness; CONCEPT 423 —*Ant.* participant

byte [n] *unit of computer memory* data, eight bits, unit; CONCEPT 274

byword [n] *saying* adage, aphorism, apophthegm, axiom, catchphrase, catchword, dictum, epithet, gnome, gnomic saying, handle, maxim, motto, nickname, precept, proverb, saw, shibboleth, slogan, standing joke; CONCEPT 275

C

cab [n] *car for hire* carriage, hack, hackney, jitney, taxi, taxicab, tourist car; CONCEPT 505

cabaret [n] *nightclub with musical performances* after-hours joint*, bar, café, disco, discothèque, dive, hideaway, hot spot*, nightery, night spot, speakeasy, supper club, tavern, watering hole*; CONCEPTS 447,449

cabin [n] *tiny house; lodging* berth, box, caboose, camp, chalet, compartment, cot, cottage, crib, deckhouse, home, hovel, hut, lodge, log house, quarters, room, shack, shanty, shed, shelter; CONCEPT 516

cabinet [n1] *cupboard for storage* case, chiffonier, closet, commode, container, depository, dresser, escritoire, locker, repository, wardrobe; CONCEPTS 443,494

cabinet [n2] *executives serving a leader* administration, administrators, advisers, assembly, assistants, authority, brain trust*, bureau, bureaucracy, committee, council, counselors, department heads, governing body, government, kitchen cabinet*, ministry, official family; CONCEPT 299

cabin fever [n] *claustrophobia* climbing the walls*, distress, neurosis, restlessness, SAD, seasonal affective disorder, temporary insanity, winter blues; CONCEPTS 410,657,748

cache [n] *hidden supply* accumulation, assets, drop, drop joint, drop-off, fund, hideout, hiding place, hoard, kitty*, nest egg*, plant, repository, reserve, shade, stake, stash, stockpile, store, storehouse, supplies, treasure, treasury, wealth; CONCEPTS 446,710

cache [v] *hide a supply of something* accumulate, bury, conceal, cover, ditch, duck, ensconce, lay away, maintain, park, plant, put away, put in the hole*, save, screen, secrete, squirrel*, squirrel away*, stash, stash away, store; CONCEPT 188

cackle [n] *a loud laugh* chortle, chuckle, cluck, crow, gibber, giggle, gobble, guffaw, quack, snicker, snigger, titter; CONCEPT 77

cackle [v] *laugh irritatingly* babble, blather, burble, chortle, chuckle, cluck, crow, gibber, giggle, gobble, jabber, quack, snicker, snigger, titter; CONCEPT 77

cacophonous [adj] *harsh sounding* clinking, discordant, disharmonic, dissonant, grating, ill-sounding, immusical, inharmonious, jangly, jarring, noisy, raucous, sour, strident, unmusical; CONCEPTS 592,594 —Ant. quiet

cad [n] *sly, dastardly person* boor, bounder*, clown, creep, cur*, dog*, heel, louse, lout, rake, rascal, rat*, rotter*, rounder*, scoundrel, stinker, worm; CONCEPT 412 —Ant. gentleman, helper

cadaver [n] *dead body* body, cage, carcass, corpse, deceased, mort*, remains, skeleton, stiff*; CONCEPT 390 —Ant. being

cadaverous [adj] *pale, corpselike* ashen, bag of bones, blanched, bloodless, consumptive, dead, deathlike, deathly, emaciated, exsanguinous, gaunt, ghastly, ghostly, haggard, pallid, peaked, peaky, sallow, shadowy, sick, skeletal, skeletonlike, skin and bones*, spectral, thin, wan, wasted; CONCEPTS 406,491,618 —Ant. flushed, lifelike, lively

cadence [n] *rhythm* accent, beat, count, inflection, intonation, lilt, measure, meter, modulation, pulse, rhythmus, swing, tempo, throb; CONCEPT 65

cadre [n] *nucleus of effort* core, force, framework, infrastructure, key group, officers, organization, personnel, staff; CONCEPTS 417,432

café [n] *small, informal restaurant* bistro, burger joint, cafeteria, cake shop, chophouse, coffee bar, coffee shop, diner, eating house, grease joint*, greasy spoon*, hash house*, luncheonette, lunchroom, noshery*, pit stop*, quick-lunch, snack bar, soup house, tearoom; CONCEPT 449

cafeteria [n] *restaurant* café, commissary, lunch counter, lunchroom, snack bar, tea room; CONCEPT 449

cage [n] *enclosure with bars* coop, corral, crate, enclosure, fold, jail, mew, pen, pinfold, pound; CONCEPT 494

cage [v] *hold in enclosure* close in, confine, coop up, enclose, envelop, fence in, hem,

immure, impound, imprison, incarcerate, jail, lock up, mew, pen, restrain, shut in, shut up; CONCEPT 191 —Ant. free, let go, let out, release

cagey [adj] *tricky* cagey, careful, circumspect, crafty, cunning, leery, secretive, shrewd, sly, wary, wily; CONCEPTS 401,545

cahoots [n] *conspiracy* alliance, collusion, league, partnership; CONCEPTS 14,660

cajole [v] *attempt to coax; flatter* apple polish*, argue into, banter, beguile, blandish, bootlick*, brownnose*, build up, butter up*, con, crowd, deceive, decoy, delude, dupe, entice, entrap, get around, get next to*, hand a line*, induce, influence, inveigle, jolly, lay it on thick*, lure, make up to, maneuver, massage, mislead, oil*, play up to, push, rub the right way*, seduce, snow*, soap*, soften, soft-soap*, spread it on*, stroke, suck up to*, sweeten up*, sweet-talk*, tantalize, tempt, urge, wheedle, work on, work over*; CONCEPTS 59,68,75 —Ant. bully, force, repel

cake [n] *bar of something* block, brick, loaf, lump, mass, slab; CONCEPT 470

calamitous [adj] *disastrous; tragic* adverse, afflictive, blighting, cataclysmic, catastrophic, deadly, deplorable, devastating, dire, fatal, grievous, harmful, heartbreaking, lamentable, messy, pernicious, regrettable, ruinous, unfavorable, unfortunate, woeful; CONCEPT 537 —Ant. blessed, comforting, favorable, fortunate, happy, joyous, wonderful

calamity [n] *disaster; tragedy* adversity, affliction, blue ruin*, cataclysm, catastrophe, collapse, cross, curtains, distress, downfall, hardship, holy mess*, misadventure, mischance, misfortune, mishap, reverse, ruin, scourge, the worst*, trial, tribulation, unholy mess*, visitation, waterloo*, woe, wreck, wretchedness; CONCEPTS 674,675 —Ant. advantage, blessing, boon, comfort, fortune, good fortune, good luck, happiness, joy, profit

calculable [adj] *able to be computed or estimated* accountable, ascertainable, computable, countable, discoverable, estimable, foreseeable, measurable, predictable, reckonable; CONCEPTS 402,762 —Ant. incalculable, inestimable, uncomputable

calculate [v1] *compute or estimate amount* account, add, adjust, appraise, assay, cast, cipher, consider, count, determine, divide, dope out*, enumerate, figure, forecast, foretell, gauge, guess, judge, keep tabs*, measure, multiply, number, rate, reckon, size up, subtract, sum, take account of, tally, tot, tote up*, value, weigh, work out; CONCEPT 764

calculate [v2] *plan on* aim, anticipate, assume, bank on, build, count on, depend on, design, intend, judge, plan, reckon, rely on, suppose, think likely, trust; CONCEPTS 26,36

calculating [adj] *scheming to manipulate* artful, canny, careful, cautious, chary, circumspect, considerate, contriving, crafty, cunning, designing, devious, discreet, gingerly, guarded, guileful, intelligent, Machiavellian, manipulative, politic, premeditating, safe, scheming, sharp, shrewd, sly, wary, wily; CONCEPTS 401,403 —Ant. artless, naive, unassuming, uncalculating

calculation [n1] *computing, estimating amount* adding, arithmetic, ciphering, computation, counting, dividing, estimate, estimation, figuring, forecast, judgment, multiplying, prediction, reckoning, subtracting, summation, totaling; CONCEPTS 28,764

calculation [n2] *computed or estimated amount* answer, computation, divination, estimate, estimation, figuring, forecast, judgment, prediction, prognosis, prognostication, reckoning, reply; CONCEPT 787

calculation [n3] *forethought* canniness, caution, circumspection, contrivance, deliberation, discretion, foresight, planning, precaution, prudence, thought; CONCEPT 660

calculator [n] *adding machine* computer, number cruncher*, PDA, personal digital assistant; CONCEPTS 269,463

calendar [n] *schedule of events* agenda, almanac, annal, bulletin, card, chronology, daybook, diary, docket, journal, lineup, list, log, logbook, menology, pipeline, program, record, register, sked, system of reckoning, tab, table, time, timetable; CONCEPTS 274,281,809

calf [n1] *leg between knee and ankle* foreleg, shin; CONCEPT 392

calf [n2] *baby cow* dogie, freemartin, heifer, maverick, veal, yearling, young bull, young cow; CONCEPT 394

caliber [n1] *capacity; character* ability, appetency, capability, competence, constitution, dignity, distinction, endowment, essence, faculty, force, gifts, habilitation, merit, nature, parts, power, quality, scope, stature, strength, talent, value, virtue, worth, worthiness; CONCEPT 411

caliber [n2] *size of ammunition* bore, class, diameter, gauge, grade, length, measure, measurement, quality, striking power, weight; CONCEPT 730

call [n1] *yelled statement* alarm, calling, command, cry, hail, holler*, scream, shout, signal, whoop, yawp, yell; CONCEPT 278

call [n2] *demand, announcement* appeal, bidding, command, invitation, notice, order, plea, proposal, request, solicitation, subpoena, summons, supplication, visit; CONCEPT 53

call [n3] *need, cause for action* claim, excuse, grounds, justification, necessity, obligation, occasion, reason, right, urge; CONCEPT 709

call [n4] *normal sound of animal* cheep, chirp, cry, note, peep, roar, shriek, song, tweet, twitter, warble; CONCEPT 64

call [v1] *yell declaration* announce, arouse, awaken, bawl, bellow, cry, cry out, exclaim, hail, holler*, hoot, howl, proclaim, roar, rouse, scream, screech, shout, shriek, vociferate, waken, whoop, yawp*, yoo hoo*, yowl; CONCEPT 47 —*Ant.* conceal, listen, refrain

call [v2] *arrange meeting* ask, assemble, bid, collect, contact, convene, convoke, gather, invite, muster, phone*, rally, request, ring up, subpoena, summon, telephone; CONCEPT 114 —*Ant.* cancel, stop

call [v3] *entitle* address, baptize, christen, denominate, describe as, designate, dub, label, name, style, term, title; CONCEPT 62

call [v4] *demand or announce action* appeal to, appoint, ask, challenge, charge, claim, command, declare, decree, elect, entreat, exact, ordain, order, postulate, pray to, proclaim, require, requisition, set apart, solicit, summon; CONCEPT 53 —*Ant.* stop

call [v5] *estimate, consider* adumbrate, approximate, augur, forecast, foretell, guess, judge, make rough guess, place, portend, predict, presage, prognosticate, prophesy, put, reckon, regard, think, vaticinate; CONCEPTS 28,70 —*Ant.* ignore

call [v6] *attempt to communicate by telephone* beep, blast*, bleep, buzz, contact, get back to*, phone, ring, telephone; CONCEPTS 74,266 —*Ant.* receive

call [v7] *visit at residence or business* come by, come over, crash, drop by, drop in, fall by, fall down, hit, look in on, look up, play, pop in*, run in, see, stop by, stop in, swing by; CONCEPT 227

call for [v] *demand; entail* ask for, inquire, involve, lack, necessitate, need, occasion, request, require, suggest, want; CONCEPT 646

calling [n] *chosen profession* art, business, career, craft, day gig*, do*, dodge*, employment, gig*, go*, handicraft, hang*, life's work, lifework, line, métier, mission, nine-to-five*, occupation, play, province, pursuit, racket*, rat race*, slot*, swindle*, trade, vocation, walk of life, work; CONCEPT 360 —*Ant.* amusement, avocation, entertainment, hobby, recreation

call off [v] *discontinue* abandon, abort, break off, cancel, desist, drop, kill*, postpone, scrub*, withdraw; CONCEPTS 18,211,234

callous [adj] *cruel, insensitive* apathetic, blind to, careless, case-hardened, cold, cold-blooded, deaf to, hard, hard-bitten, hard-boiled, hardened, hardhearted, heartless, impassive, impenitent, indifferent, indurated, inflexible, insensate, insensible, insensitive, insentient, inured, obdurate, soulless, spiritless, stiff, stony, stubborn, thick-skinned, torpid, tough, toughened, unaffected, unbending, uncaring, uncompassionate, unconcerned, unfeeling, unimpressionable, unresponsive, unsusceptible, unsympathetic; CONCEPT 404 —*Ant.* compassionate, feeling, kind, nice, sensitive, sympathetic, tender

callow [adj] *immature* crude, green, guileless, inexperienced, infant, jejune, jellybean*, juvenile, kid, low tech*, naive, not dry behind ears*, puerile, raw, sophomore, tenderfoot, unbaked, unfledged, unripe, unsophisticated, untrained, untried, young; CONCEPTS 578,678, 797 —*Ant.* experienced, initiated, mature, sophisticated

calm [adj1] *peaceful, quiet (inanimate)* at a standstill, at peace, bland, bucolic, cool, halcyon, harmonious, hushed, inactive, in order, low-key, mild, motionless, pacific, pastoral, placid, quiescent, reposeful, reposing, restful, rural, serene, slow, smooth, soothing, still, stormless, tranquil, undisturbed, unruffled, waveless, windless; CONCEPTS 544,705 —*Ant.* excited, fierce, frenzied, rough, stormy, turbulent, violent, wild

calm [adj2] *composed, cool (animate)* aloof, amiable, amicable, civil, collected, cool as cucumber*, cool-headed, detached, disinterested, dispassionate, equable, gentle, impassive, imperturbable, inscrutable, kind, laid-back*, levelheaded, listless, moderate, neutral, patient, placid, pleased, relaxed, restful, satisfied, sedate, self-possessed, serene, still, temperate, unconcerned, undisturbed, unemotional, unexcitable, unexcited, unflappable, unimpressed, unmoved, unruffled, untroubled; CONCEPTS 401,404 —*Ant.* agitated, angry, excitable, excited, furious, mad, passionate, roused, ruffled, wild, worried

calm [n] *quietness, composure* calmness, dispassion, doldrums, hush, impassivity, imperturbation, lull, patience, peace, peacefulness, peace of mind, placidity, quiet, repose, rest, restraint, serenity, silence, stillness, stoicism, tranquility; CONCEPTS 388,411,720 —*Ant.* agitation, anger, madness, restlessness, storminess, terror, turbulence, violence

calm [v] *make composed, quiet* allay, alleviate, appease, assuage, balm, becalm, compose, cool, cool it*, cool out*, hush, lay back*, lull, mitigate, mollify, pacify, placate, quiet, quieten, relax, relieve, sedate, settle, simmer down, softpedal*, soothe, steady, still, stroke, take it easy*, take the edge off*, tranquilize; CONCEPT 231 —*Ant.* agitate, anger, disquiet, distract, excite, inflame, irritate, outrage, rouse, ruffle, worry

camaraderie [n] *friendship* cheer, companionability, companionship, comradeship, conviviality, esprit de corps, fellowship, gregariousness, intimacy, jollity, sociability, togetherness; CONCEPT 388 —*Ant.* bad blood, dislike, hate

camera [n] *photographic equipment* 35mm, camcorder, Kodak*, Polaroid*, video camera; CONCEPTS 446,463

camouflage [n] *disguise* beard*, blind, cloak, concealment, cover, coverup, deceit, deceptive marking, dissimulation, faking, false appearance, front, guise, mask, masking, masquerade, mimicry, paint, plain brown wrapper*, protective coloring, red herring*, screen, shade, shroud, smokescreen, veil; CONCEPT 260

camouflage [v] *disguise, cover* beard*, becloud, befog, cloak, conceal, cover up, deceive, dim, dissemble, dissimulate, dress up, hide, mask, obfuscate, obscure, screen, throw on makeup, veil; CONCEPTS 172,188 —*Ant.* reveal, show, uncover

camp [adj] *consciously affecting the unfashionable, weird, or bizarre* affected, arch, artificial, avant-garde, Daliesque*, far out*, in*, mannered, mod, ostentatious, pop, posturing, wild; CONCEPT 544

camp [n] *site for outdoor living* bivouac, campfire, campground, camping ground, caravansary, chalet, cottage, encampment, hut, lean-to, lodge, log cabin, shack, shanty, shed, summer home, tent, tent city, tepee, tilt, wigwam; CONCEPTS 198,516

campaign [n] *attempt to win; attack* crusade, drive, expedition, fight, movement, offensive, operation, push, warfare; CONCEPTS 87,320

campaign [v] *attempt to win political election* agitate, barnstorm, canvass, contend for, contest, crusade, electioneer, go to grass roots*, hit the trail*, lobby, mend fences*, muckrake, mudsling*, politick, press the flesh*, ring doorbells*, run, run for, shake hands and kiss babies*, solicit votes, stand for, stump*, tour, whistle-stop*; CONCEPT 300

camper [n] *mobile home* recreational vehicle, RV, tin can*, Winnebago*; CONCEPT 503

campus [n] *school grounds* dorm, grounds, quad, quadrangle, square, yard; CONCEPT 509

can [n1] *container, usually metallic* aluminum, bottle, bucket, canister, cannikin, gunboat*, gutbucket*, jar, package, pop top*, receptacle, tin, vessel; CONCEPTS 476,494

can [n2] *toilet* head*, john*, johnny*, latrine, lavatory, litter box*, outhouse, pot*, potty*, privy, restroom, sandbox*, throne*, washroom, water closet; CONCEPT 443

can [n3] *buttocks* backside, behind, butt*, derrière, fanny*, fundament, gluteus maximus, hind end, posterior, rump, seat, tush*; CONCEPT 418

can [v1] *preserve fruit, vegetable* bottle, keep, put up; CONCEPT 170

can [v2] *be able* be capable of, be equal to, be up to, be within one's area, be within one's control, can do*, commit, could, cut the mustard*, have it made*, lie in one's power, make it*, make out, make the grade*, manage, may, take care of; CONCEPT 630 —*Ant.* cannot

can [v3] *fire from job* ax*, boot*, bounce*, cashier, discharge, dismiss, expel, give the heave ho*, kick out*, let go, sack*, terminate; CONCEPT 351 —*Ant.* employ, hire

canal [n] *waterway* aqueduct, bottleneck, channel, choke point, conduit, course, cove, ditch, duct, estuary, firth, trench, water, watercourse; CONCEPT 514

cancel [v1] *call off; erase* abolish, abort, abrogate, annul, ax, black out, blot out, break, break off, countermand, cross out, cut, deface, delete, destroy, do away with, do in, efface, eliminate, eradicate, expunge, finish off*, go back on one's word*, kill, obliterate, off*, omit, quash, remove, render invalid, repeal, repudiate, rescind, revoke, rub out, scratch out, scrub*, sink*, smash, squash, stamp across, strike out, torpedo*, total*, trash*, trim*, undo, wash out*, wipe out*, wipe slate clean*, X-out*, zap*; CONCEPTS 18,211,234 —*Ant.* allow, approve, arrange, establish, permit, uphold

cancel [v2] *equal out* abort, abrogate, annul, balance out, call off, compensate for, counteract, counterbalance, countercheck, countermand, counterpoise, declare invalid, discard, discharge, frustrate, ignore, invalidate, make up for, negate, neutralize, nullify, offset, overthrow, put an end to, recall, recant, redeem, redress, refute, render inert, render null and void, repeal, repudiate, rescind, retract, revoke, rule out, set aside, suppress, vacate, void; CONCEPTS 232,667 —*Ant.* imbalance, tip

cancellation [n] *calling off; erasure* abandoning, abandonment, abolishing, abolition, abrogation, annulment, canceling, deletion, dissolution, dissolving, elimination, invalidating, invalidation, nullification, overruling, quashing, recall, recalling, repeal, repudiation, retirement, retracting, retraction, reversal, reversing, revocation, revoking, undoing, withdrawing; CONCEPT 119 —*Ant.* allowance, approval, arrangement, establishment, permission

cancer [n] *malignant growth* big C*, C*, canker, carcinoma, corruption, disease, long illness, malignancy, sickness, tumor; CONCEPT 306 —*Ant.* benignity

candid [adj] *honest* aboveboard, bluff, blunt, equal, equitable, fair, forthright, frank, free, frontal, genuine, guileless, impartial, ingenuous, just, objective, open, outspoken, plain, right up front*, scrupulous, sincere, straightforward, talking turkey*, telling it like it is*, truthful, unbiased, uncolored, unequivocal, unprejudiced, unpretended, up front*, upright; CONCEPT 267 —*Ant.* artful, deceitful, devious, lying, tricky

candidate [n] *person desiring political office, job* applicant, aspirant, bidder, claimant, competitor, contender, contestant, dark horse*, entrant, favorite son*, handshaker*, hopeful*, job-hunter, nominee, office-seeker, petitioner, possibility, possible choice, pothunter*, runner, seeker, solicitant, stumper*, successor, suitor, whistle-stopper*, write-in*; CONCEPT 359

candlestick [n] *holder for candles* candelabra, candelabrum, menorah, pricket, sconce, taper holder; CONCEPT 444

candor [n] *complete honesty* artlessness, directness, fairness, forthrightness, frankness, glasnost, guilelessness, honesty, impartiality, ingenuousness, naiveté, openness, outspokenness, probity, simplicity, sincerity, straightforwardness, truthfulness, unequivocalness, uprightness, veracity; CONCEPT 411 —*Ant.* artifice, deception, falsehood, guile, lying

candy [n] *confection* bonbon, confectionery, confit, hokum*, jawbreaker*, sweet, sweetmeat; CONCEPT 457

cane [n] *stick to aid walking of disabled* pikestaff, pole, rod, staff, vade mecum, walking stick; CONCEPT 479

canker [n] *blistered infection* bane, blight, blister, boil, cancer, corrosion, corruption, lesion, rot, scourge, smutch, sore, ulcer; CONCEPT 306

canker [v] *blight, corrupt* animalize, bestialize, consume, corrode, debase, debauch, demoralize, deprave, embitter, envenom, inflict, pervert, poison, pollute, rot, ruin, scourge, sore, stain, ulcer, vitiate; CONCEPT 240

cannibal [n] *beast, beastlike human* aborigine, anthropophaginian, anthropophagite, anthropophagus, brute, bush dweller, cruel person, head-hunter, ogre, ogress, primitive, ruffian, savage; CONCEPT 412

cannon [n] *large gun* Big Bertha*, heavy artillery, howitzer, Long Tom*, mortar, ordnance; CONCEPT 500

canny [adj] *clever, artful* able, acute, adroit, astute, cagey, careful, cautious, circumspect, cunning, dexterous, discreet, foxy*, frugal, having fancy footwork*, hep*, ingenious, intelligent, judicious, knowing, nimble-witted, perspicacious, prudent, quick, quick-witted, sagacious, shrewd, skillful, slick, slippery*, sly, smart, smooth*, street smart*, streetwise*, subtle, wary, watchful, wise, with it*, worldly-wise; CONCEPT 402 —*Ant.* foolish, inept, silly

canoe [n] *light, paddled boat* coracle, dugout, kayak, outrigger, piragua, pirogue; CONCEPT 506

can of worms [n] *troublesome problem* complication, difficulty, entanglement, Gordian knot, hot water*, Pandora's box, predicament, quagmire, quandary, trouble; CONCEPTS 532,674,690

canon [n1] *rule, edict* assize, catalogue, command, commandment, criterion, declaration, decree, decretum, dictate, doctrine, dogma, formula, law, list, maxim, order, ordinance, precept, principle, regulation, roll, screed, standard, statute, table, tenet, touchstone, yardstick; CONCEPTS 318,688

canon [n2] *a body of the most important, influential or superior works in music, literature, or art* ana, analects, anthology, chrestomathy, classics, collected works, delectus, library, miscellanea, oeuvre, works; CONCEPTS 280,432

canonical [adj] *accepted, recognized* approved, authoritative, authorized, lawful, legal, official, orthodox, received, sanctioned, sound, statutory; CONCEPTS 319,535 —*Ant.* unacceptable, unauthorized, uncanonical, unorthodox, unrecognized, unsanctioned

canonize [v] *sanctify; idolize* apotheosize, beatify, besaint, bless, consecrate, dedicate, deify, glorify, idolatrize, love, put on a pedestal*, saint, worship; CONCEPTS 32,367

canopy [n] *overhanging covering* awning, baldachin, cover, marquee, shade, sunshade, umbrella; CONCEPTS 440,444

cant [n1] *hypocritical statement* affected piety, deceit, dishonesty, humbug, hypocrisy, hypocriticalness, insincerity, lip service*, pecksniffery, pharisaicalness, pious platitudes, pomposity, pretense, pretentiousness, sanctimoniousness, sanctimony, sham holiness, show; CONCEPT 63

cant [n2] *jargon* argot, dialect, diction, idiom, language, lingo, patois, patter, phraseology, slang, vernacular, vocabulary; CONCEPTS 275,278 —*Ant.* standard

cant [v] *lean, slant* angle, bevel, careen, grade, heel, incline, list, recline, rise, slope, tilt, tip; CONCEPTS 154,201

cantankerous [adj] *difficult, crabby* bad-tempered, bearish, captious, choleric, contrary, cranky, critical, cross, crotchety*, crusty*, disagreeable, dour, grouchy*, grumpy*, huffy*, ill-humored, ill-natured, irascible, irritable, morose, obstinate, ornery*, peevish, perverse, petulant, prickly, quarrelsome, snappish, sour, stuffy*, testy, vinegarish, vinegary; CONCEPT 401 —*Ant.* easy, good-natured, happy, nice, pleasant

canteen [n1] *portable kitchen* chuck wagon, mobile kitchen, snack bar, snack shop; CONCEPT 449

canteen [n2] *container for liquids, used in travels* bota, bottle, flacon, flask, flasket, jug, thermos, water bottle; CONCEPT 494

canvas [n1] *coarse material* awning cloth, duck, fly, sailcloth, shade, tarp, tarpaulin, tenting; CONCEPT 473

canvas [n2] *painting on coarse material* art, artwork, oil, picture, piece, portrait, still life, watercolor; CONCEPT 259

canvass [v] *poll; discuss issues* agitate, analyze, apply, argue, campaign, check, check over, consult, debate, dispute, electioneer, examine, inspect, investigate, review, run, scan, scrutinize, sift, solicit, study, survey, ventilate; CONCEPTS 24,48,56,300

canyon [n] *gulf in mountain area* coulee, glen, gorge, gulch, gully, ravine, valley; CONCEPTS 509,513 —*Ant.* mountain

cap [n] *small hat* beanie*, beret, bonnet, dink*, fez, pillbox, skullcap, tam, tam o'shanter; CONCEPT 450

cap [v] *outdo a performance* beat, best, better, button down*, button up*, can*, clinch*, cob*, complete, cover, crest, crown, do to a T*, eclipse, exceed, excel, finish, outshine, outstrip, pass, put the lid on*, surmount, surpass, top, top it off*, transcend, trump, wrap up*; CONCEPT 141

capability [n] *ability to perform* adequacy, aptitude, art, capacity, competence, craft, cunning, effectiveness, efficacy, efficiency, facility, faculty, means, might, potency, potential, potentiality, power, proficiency, qualification, qualifiedness, skill, wherewithal; CONCEPT 630 —*Ant.* impotence, inability, incompetence, ineptness

capable [adj] *able to perform* able, accomplished, adapted, adept, adequate, apt, au fait, clever, competent, dynamite, efficient, experienced, fireball*, fitted, gifted, good, green thumb*, has what it takes*, having know-how*, having the goods*, having the right stuff*, intelligent, knowing the ropes*, knowing the score*, like a one-man band*, like a pistol*, masterly, old hand*, old-timer*, on the ball*, proficient, proper, qualified, skillful, suited, talented, there*, up*, up to it*, up to snuff*, up to speed*, veteran; CONCEPT 527 —*Ant.* impotent, incapable, incompetent, inept, unable, unskilled, unskillful

capacious [adj] *ample, extensive* abundant, broad, comfortable, commodious, comprehensive, dilatable, distensible, expandable, expansive, extended, generous, liberal, plentiful, roomy, sizable, spacious, substantial, vast, voluminous, wide; CONCEPTS 481,772,773,774 —*Ant.* cramped, small, squeezed, tiny

capacity [n1] *volume; limit of volume held* accommodation, amplitude, bulk, burden, compass, contents, dimensions, expanse, extent, full, holding ability, holding power, latitude, magnitude, mass, measure, proportions, quantity, range, reach, retention, room, scope, size, space, spread, standing room only*, sufficiency, sweep; CONCEPTS 481,736,774,794

capacity [n2] *ability; competency* adequacy, aptitude, aptness, bent, brains, caliber, capability, cleverness, compass, competence, efficiency, facility, faculty, forte, genius, gift, inclination, intelligence, knack, might, power, qualification, readiness, skill, stature, strength, talent, the goods*, up to it*, what it takes*; CONCEPTS 409,630 —*Ant.* impotence, inability, incompetence

cape [n1] *promontory into water* arm, beak, bill, chersonese, finger, foreland, head, headland, jetty, jutty, mole, naze, neck, ness, peninsula, point, tongue; CONCEPTS 509,514

cape [n2] *sleeveless coat* bertha, capote, cardinal, cloak, cope, dolman, fichu, gabardine, manteau, mantelletta, mantilla, mantle, overdress, paletot, pelerine, pelisse, poncho, shawl, tabard, talma, tippet, Vandyke, victorine, wrap, wrapper; CONCEPT 451

caper [n] *antic, lark* escapade, gag*, gambol, high jinks*, hop, hot foot*, jest, joke, jump, leap, mischief, monkeyshines*, practical joke, prank, put on*, revel, rib*, rollick, shenanigan*, sport, stunt, tomfoolery*, trick; CONCEPT 386

caper [v] *frolic, cavort* blow the lid off*, bounce, bound, cut capers*, cut loose*, dance, frisk, gambol, go on a tear*, hop, horse

around*, jump, kick up one's heels*, leap, let loose*, play, raise hell*, rollick, romp, skip, spring, whoop it up*; CONCEPT 384

capital [adj1] *main, essential* basic, cardinal, central, chief, controlling, dominant, first, foremost, fundamental, important, leading, major, number one*, outstanding, overruling, paramount, predominant, preeminent, primary, prime, principal, prominent, underlying, vital; CONCEPTS 546,568,829 —*Ant.* extra, minor, nonessential, secondary, unimportant

capital [adj2] *superior* best, champion, choice, crack, dandy, delightful, deluxe, excellent, famous, fine, first, first-class*, first-rate*, five-star*, fly, great, prime, splendid, superb, top, top-notch*, world-class*; CONCEPT 574 —*Ant.* inferior, low-class, minor, poor, unimportant

capital [n1] *financial assets* business, cash, CD, estate, finances, financing, fortune, funds, gold, interests, investment, IRA, kitty*, means, money, nest egg*, principal, property, resources, savings, stake, stock, substance, treasure, ways and means*, wealth, wherewithal; CONCEPTS 332,710

capital [n2] *city of governmental seat* control, county seat, metropolis, municipality, political front, principal city, the Hill*; CONCEPTS 507,512

capital [n3] *upper case written symbol* cap, initial, majuscule; small cap, uncial; CONCEPT 284 —*Ant.* small

capitalism [n] *economic system of private ownership* commercialism, competition, democracy, free enterprise, free market, industrialism, laissez faire economics, mercantilism, private enterprise; CONCEPTS 299,689,770 —*Ant.* communism

capitalist [n] *person engaged in private ownership of business* backer, banker, bourgeois, businessperson, entrepreneur, financier, investor, landowner, moneybags*, one who signs the checks*, plutocrat, the boss*, the money*; CONCEPT 347 —*Ant.* communist

capitalize [v] *benefit from situation* avail oneself of, exploit, gain, make capital of, obtain, profit, realize, subsidize, take advantage of; CONCEPT 120

capitol [n] *building or buildings housing chief governmental offices* Capitol Hill, center, dome, legislative hall, political scene*, seat of government, statehouse; CONCEPTS 299,449

capitulate [v] *give in* bow, buckle under, cave in, cede, come across, come to terms, concede, defer, fold, give away the store*, give out, give up, knuckle under, put out, relent, submit, succumb, surrender, yield; CONCEPTS 35,83 —*Ant.* defend, fight

capitulation [n] *giving in* accedence, bowing, buckling, conceding, giving up, knuckling under, relenting, resignation, submission, succumbing, surrender, yielding; CONCEPTS 83,410 —*Ant.* defending, fighting

caprice [n] *sudden change of behavior* bee*, caper*, changeableness, contrariety, crotchet, fad, fancy, fickleness, fitfulness, fool notion*, freak, gag*, humor, impulse, inconsistency, inconstancy, jerk, kink, mood, notion, peculiarity, perversity, put on*, quirk, rib*, temper, thought, vagary, vein, whim, whimsy;

CONCEPTS 13,410 —*Ant.* constancy, constant, dependability, steadfastness

capricious [*adj*] *given to sudden behavior change* any way the wind blows*, arbitrary, blowing hot and cold*, careless, changeful, contrary, crotchety, effervescent, erratic, every which way*, fanciful, fickle, fitful, flaky*, flighty, freakish, gaga*, helter-skelter*, humorsome, impulsive, inconstant, kinky*, lubricious, mercurial, moody, mutable, notional, odd, picky*, punchy*, queer, quirky, temperamental, ticklish, unpredictable, unreasonable, unstable, up and down*, vagarious, variable, volatile, wayward, whimsical, yo-yo*; CONCEPT 401 —*Ant.* constant, dependable, sensible, staid, steadfast, steady

capsize [*v*] *overturn* invert, keel over, roll, tip over, turn over, turn turtle*, upset; CONCEPTS 150,152

capsule [*adj*] *shortened form* abridged, canned, condensed, epitomized, pocket, potted, tabloid; CONCEPTS 531,773

capsule [*n*] *tablet, usually medicine* bolus, cap, dose, lozenge, pellet, pill, troche; CONCEPTS 260,307

captain [*n*] *chief of vehicle, effort* authority, boss, cap, CEO, CFO, chieftain, commander, director, exec*, executive, four-striper*, guide, head, head honcho*, higher up*, leader, master, mistress, number one*, officer, operator, owner, pilot, royalty, skip*, skipper*, top*, top dog*; CONCEPT 347

caption [*n*] *heading; short description* explanation, head, inscription, legend, rubric, subtitle, title, underline; CONCEPT 283

captious [*adj*] *very critical* acrimonious, cantankerous, carping, caviling, cavillous, censorious, contrary, crabby, cross, demanding, deprecating, disparaging, exacting, exceptive, fault-finding, finicky, hypercritical, irritable, nagging, nitpicking, overcritical, peevish, perverse, petulant, sarcastic, severe, testy, touchy; CONCEPTS 267,404 —*Ant.* commendatory, complimentary, encouraging, flattering, laudatory, praising

captivate [*v*] *attract, enchant* allure, beguile, bewitch, charm, dazzle, delight, draw, enamour, enrapture, enslave, ensnare, entertain, enthrall, entrance, fascinate, gratify, grip, hold, hook, hypnotize, infatuate, intrigue, lure, magnetize, make a hit with*, mesmerize, please, rope in*, seduce, spellbind, sweep off one's feet*, take, turn one on, vamp, wile, win; CONCEPTS 7,22 —*Ant.* disgust, disillusion, offend, repel, repulse

captive [*adj1*] *physically held by force* bound, caged, confined, enslaved, ensnared, imprisoned, incarcerated, incommunicado, in custody, jailed, locked up, penned, restricted, subjugated, under lock and key*; CONCEPTS 536,554 —*Ant.* free, independent, loose

captive [*adj2*] *mentally enchanted, held* beguiled, bewitched, charmed, delighted, enraptured, enthralled, fascinated, hypnotized, infatuated; CONCEPT 403 —*Ant.* disillusioned, uninterested

captive [*n*] *person held physically* bondman, bondservant, bondwoman, con, convict, detainee, hostage, internee, prisoner, prisoner of war, slave; CONCEPTS 412,423 —*Ant.* free man, independent

captivity [*n*] *physical detention by force* bondage, committal, confinement, constraint, custody, durance, duress, enslavement, enthrallment, entombment, impoundment, imprisonment, incarceration, internment, jail, limbo, restraint, serfdom, servitude, slavery, subjection, thralldom, vassalage; CONCEPTS 191,652 —*Ant.* freedom, independence, liberty, license

capture [*n*] *catching, forceful holding* abduction, acquirement, acquisition, apprehension, appropriating, appropriation, arrest, bag*, bust*, catch, collar, commandeering, confiscation, drop*, ensnaring, fall, gaining, grab*, grasping, hit the jackpot*, hook*, imprisonment, knock off*, laying hold of*, nab*, nail*, obtaining, occupation, pick up*, pinch*, pull*, run in*, securing, seizing, seizure, snatching*, sweep*, taking, taking captive, taking into custody, trapping, trip, winning; CONCEPT 90 —*Ant.* freeing, letting go, liberalization, release

capture [*v*] *catch and forcefully hold* apprehend, arrest, bag*, bust*, catch, collar, conquer, cop, gain control, get, grab*, hook*, land, nab*, nail*, net, occupy, overwhelm, pick up*, pinch*, prehend, pull in, put the cuffs on*, round up*, run in*, secure, seize, snare, snatch, take, take captive, take into custody, take prisoner, trap, tumble; CONCEPT 90 —*Ant.* free, let go, liberate, lose, release

car [*n*] *vehicle driven on streets* auto, automobile, bucket*, buggy*, bus, clunker*, compact, convertible, conveyance, coupe, gas guzzler*, hardtop, hatchback, heap*, jalopy*, jeep, junker*, limousine, machine, motor, motorcar, pickup, ride*, roadster, sedan, station wagon, subcompact, touring car, truck, van, wagon, wheels*, wreck*; CONCEPT 505

caravan [*n*] *group traveling together* band, camel train, campers, cavalcade, convoy, expedition, procession, safari, train, troop; CONCEPTS 432,503 —*Ant.* individual

carbohydrate [*n*] *organic compound composed of carbon, hydrogen, and oxygen* cellulose, dextrin, dextrose, disaccharide, fructose, galactose, glucose, glycogen, lactose, maltose, monosaccharide, polysaccharide, starch, sucrose, sugar; CONCEPT 478

carcass/carcase [*n*] *dead body; framework, base structure* body, cadaver, corpse, framework, hulk, mort*, remains, shell, skeleton, stiff*; CONCEPTS 390,434

carcinogen [*n*] *cancer-causing agent* deadly chemical, health hazard, killer*, mutagen, poison, toxin; CONCEPT 675

card [*n*] *piece of paper, often with purposeful writing* agenda, badge, billet, calendar, cardboard, check, docket, fiberboard, identification, label, pass, poster, program, schedule, sheet, square, tally, ticket, timetable, voucher; CONCEPTS 260,271

cardiac arrest [*n*] *heart stoppage* coronary thrombosis, heart attack, heart failure, myocardial infarction; CONCEPT 308

cardinal [*adj*] *important, key* basal, basic, central, chief, constitutive, essential, first, foremost, fundamental, greatest, highest, indispensable, leading, main, overriding, overruling, paramount, pivotal, preeminent, primary, prime, principal, ruling, vital;

CONCEPTS 568,574 —*Ant.* inessential, insignificant, minor, negligible, secondary, unimportant

care [n1] *personal interest, concern* affliction, aggravation, alarm, anguish, annoyance, anxiety, apprehension, bother, burden, chagrin, charge, consternation, discomposure, dismay, disquiet, distress, disturbance, encumbrance, exasperation, fear, foreboding, fretfulness, handicap, hardship, hindrance, impediment, incubus, load, misgiving, nuisance, onus, oppression, perplexity, pressure, responsibility, solicitude, sorrow, stew, strain, stress, sweat, tribulation, trouble, uneasiness, unhappiness, vexation, woe, worry; CONCEPTS 410,532 —*Ant.* carelessness, disregard, ignorance, inattention, neglect, negligence, oversight

care [n2] *carefulness, attention to detail* alertness, caution, circumspection, concentration, concern, conscientiousness, consideration, diligence, direction, discrimination, effort, enthusiasm, exactness, exertion, fastidiousness, forethought, heed, interest, management, meticulousness, nicety, pains, particularity, precaution, prudence, regard, scrupulousness, solicitude, thought, trouble, vigilance, wariness, watchfulness; CONCEPT 657 —*Ant.* carelessness, neglect, negligence, omission, oversight

care [n3] *custody of person, usually child* administration, aegis, auspices, charge, control, direction, guardianship, keeping, management, ministration, protection, safekeeping, superintendence, supervision, trust, tutelage, ward, wardship; CONCEPTS 285,295,388

care [v1] *tend to* attend, baby sit, consider, foster, keep an eye on*, keep tabs on*, look after, mind, mind the store*, minister, mother, nurse, nurture, pay attention to, protect, provide for, ride herd on*, sit, take pains, tend, treasure, wait on, watch, watch over; CONCEPTS 110,295 —*Ant.* disregard, ignore, neglect

care [v2] *regard highly* be crazy about*, be fond of*, cherish, desire, enjoy, find congenial, hold dear, like, love, prize, respect, take to, want; CONCEPTS 20,32 —*Ant.* dislike, hate, not care

careen [v] *tilt; move wildly down path* bend, lean, lurch, pitch, sway, tilt; CONCEPT 147

career [n1] *occupation* bag*, calling, course, dodge*, employment, field, game*, job, lifework, livelihood, number*, pilgrimage, profession, pursuit, racket*, specialty, thing*, vocation, work; CONCEPTS 349,360 —*Ant.* amusement, avocation, entertainment, recreation

career [n2] *course, path* course, orbit, passage, pilgrimage, procedure, progress, race, walk; CONCEPTS 501,678,692

carefree [adj] *lighthearted, untroubled* airy, at ease, blithe, breezy, buoyant, calm, careless, cheerful, cheery, cool, easy, easy-going, feelgood*, happy, happy-go-lucky, insouciant, jaunty, jovial, laid back*, radiant, secure, sunny, unanxious, unbothered; CONCEPT 404 —*Ant.* anxious, heavyhearted, troubled, worried

careful [adj] *cautious; painstaking* accurate, alert, apprehensive, assiduous, attentive, chary, choosy, circumspect, concerned, conscientious, conservative, cool, deliberate, discreet, exacting, fastidious, finicky, fussy, going to great lengths*, guarded, heedful, judicious, leery, meticulous, mindful, observant, particular,

playing safe*, precise, prim, protective, provident, prudent, punctilious, regardful, religious, rigorous, scrupulous, selfdisciplined, shy, sober, solicitous, solid, thorough, thoughtful, vigilant, wary; CONCEPTS 326,542 —*Ant.* careless, inattentive, incautious, thoughtless, uncareful, unconcerned, unscrupulous

carefully [adv] *cautiously; painstakingly* anxiously, attentively, circumspectly, concernedly, conscientiously, correctly, deliberately, delicately, dependably, discreetly, exactly, faithfully, fastidiously, fully, gingerly, guardedly, heedfully, honorably, in detail, laboriously, meticulously, particularly, precisely, providently, prudently, punctiliously, regardfully, reliably, rigorously, scrupulously, solicitously, thoroughly, thoughtfully, trustily, uprightly, vigilantly, warily, watchfully, with forethought, with reservations; CONCEPT 542 —*Ant.* carelessly, incautiously, thoughtlessly, uncarefully

caregiver [n] *person caring for child* au pair, babysitter, caretaker, custodian, father, governess, mother, nanny, nurse, parent; CONCEPT 348

careless [adj1] *without sufficient attention* absent-minded, abstracted, casual, cursory, disregardful, forgetful, hasty, heedless, improvident, imprudent, inaccurate, inadvertent, incautious, inconsiderate, indifferent, indiscreet, indolent, injudicious, irresponsible, lackadaisical, lax, loose, mindless, napping, negligent, nonchalant, oblivious, offhand, perfunctory, pococurante, reckless, regardless, remiss, slipshod, sloppy, thoughtless, uncircumspect, unconcerned, unguarded, unheeding, unmindful, unobservant, unreflective, unthinking, wasteful; CONCEPT 542 —*Ant.* accurate, attentive, careful, cautious, concerned, mindful, painstaking, prudent, ready, thoughtful

careless [adj2] *artless* casual, modest, naive, natural, nonchalant, simple, unstudied; CONCEPT 557 —*Ant.* cautious, guarded, kind, mindful, scrupulous

caress [n] *loving touch* cuddle, embrace, endearment, feel, fondling, hug, kiss, pat, pet, petting, snuggle, squeeze, stroke; CONCEPTS 375,590

caress [v] *touch lovingly* bear hug*, brush, buss, clinch, clutch, coddle, cosset, cuddle, dandle, embrace, feel, fondle, graze, handle, hug, kiss, make love, massage, mug, neck, nestle, nuzzle, pat, pet, play around*, rub, squeeze, stroke, toy; CONCEPTS 375,612

caretaker [n] *person who maintains something* baby sitter, concierge, curator, custodian, house-sitter, janitor, keeper, porter, sitter, super*, superintendent, supervisor, warden, watchperson; CONCEPT 348

cargo [n] *baggage; something to be delivered* burden, consignment, contents, freight, goods, haul, lading, load, merchandise, payload, shipload, shipment, tonnage, ware; CONCEPTS 338,446

caricature [n] *exaggerated description in writing, drawing* burlesque, cartoon, distortion, farce, imitation, lampoon, libel, mimicry, mockery, parody, pasquinade, pastiche, put-on*, ridicule, satire, send-up*, sham, takeoff*, travesty; CONCEPTS 271,386,625

carillon [n] *set of bells* angelus, chimes,

glockenspiel, gong, lyra, peal, tintinnabulation, tocsin; CONCEPT 595

carnage [n] *massacre* annihilation, blitz, blood, blood and guts*, blood bath*, bloodshed, butchering, butchery, crime, extermination, gore, havoc, hecatomb, holocaust, homicide, killing, liquidation, manslaughter, mass murder, murder, offing*, rapine, search and destroy*, shambles, slaughter, slaying, taking out*, warfare, wasting; CONCEPT 252

carnal [adj] *erotic, sensual* animal, bodily, corporal, corporeal, earthly, fleshly, genital, impure, lascivious, lecherous, lewd, libidinous, licentious, lustful, physical, prurient, salacious, sensuous, temporal, unchaste, venereal, voluptuous, vulgar, wanton, worldly; CONCEPTS 372,403 —Ant. chaste, clean, intellectual, pure, spiritual

carnival [n] *outdoor celebration* amusement park, bacchanal, carny*, carousal, circus, conviviality, exposition, fair, feasting, festival, fete, fiesta, frolic, gala, grind show*, heyday, jamboree, jollification, jubilee, Mardi Gras, masquerade, merrymaking, orgy, ragbag*, revelry, rout, saturnalia, side show, spree, street fair; CONCEPTS 377,386

carnivorous [adj] *eating animal flesh* cannibal, flesh-eating, hungry, omnivorous, predatory, rapacious; CONCEPT 401 —Ant. vegetarian

carol [n] *joyful hymn* ballad, canticle, canzonet, chorus, Christmas song, ditty*, lay, madrigal, noel, song, strain; CONCEPTS 263,595

carouse [v] *make merry, often with liquor* booze, drink, frolic, go on a spree*, have fun, imbibe, paint the town*, paint the town red*, play, quaff, raise Cain*, revel, riot, roister, wassail, whoop it up*; CONCEPT 384 —Ant. be sad, grieve

carp [v] *nag* bother, cavil, censure, complain, criticize, find fault, fuss, grumble, hypercriticize, knock, nitpick*, objurgate, pan, peck*, pick at, quibble, reproach; CONCEPT 52 —Ant. ignore, let go

carpal tunnel syndrome [n] *wrist irritation* repetitive motion disorder, repetitive motion injury, sensorimotor disorder; CONCEPT 306

carpenter [n] *person who works with wood* artisan, builder, cabinetmaker, carps*, chips*, craftsperson, joiner, laborer, mason, woodworker, worker; CONCEPT 348

carpet [n] *nappy floor covering* carpeting, matting, rug, runner, tapestry, throw rug, wall-to-wall*; CONCEPT 473

carping [adj] *complaining* bellyaching*, caviling, censorious, critical, criticizing, deprecatory, disparaging, fault-finding, griping, grouchy, grousing, grumbling, hypercritical, kvetching*, moaning, nagging, niggling, nit-picking*, overcritical, quibbling, scathing, whining; CONCEPT 52 —Ant. complimentary, forgiving

carriage [n1] *delivery of freight* carrying, conveyance, conveying, delivering, freight, transit, transport, transportation; CONCEPTS 148,217

carriage [n2] *posture, physical and mental* air, aspect, attitude, bearing, behavior, cast, comportment, conduct, demeanor, deportment, gait, look, manner, mien, pace, positure, presence, stance, step; CONCEPTS 633,720

carry [v1] *transport physical object* backpack*, bear, bring, cart, channel, conduct, convey, convoy, displace, ferry, fetch, freight, funnel, give, haul, heft, hoist, import, lift, lug*, move, pack, pipe, portage, relay, relocate, remove, schlepp*, shift, shoulder*, sustain, take, tote, traject, transfer, transmit, transplant, truck, waft; CONCEPTS 148,217

carry [v2] *win; accomplish* affect, be victorious, capture, drive, effect, gain, get, impel, impress, influence, inspire, move, prevail, secure, spur, strike, sway, touch, urge; CONCEPTS 68,706 —Ant. fail, lose

carry [v3] *broadcast electronically* air, bear, communicate, conduct, convey, display, disseminate, give, offer, pass on, publish, relay, release, send, transfer, transport; CONCEPTS 217,266

carry on [v1] *continue activity* achieve, endure, hang on, keep going, last, maintain, perpetuate, persevere, persist, proceed; CONCEPT 239 —Ant. discontinue, stop

carry on [v2] *manage operations* administer, conduct, direct, engage in, keep, operate, ordain, run; CONCEPT 117 —Ant. mismanage

carry on [v3] *lose control emotionally* act up, be indecorous, blunder, cut up, lose it*, make a fuss*, misbehave, rage, raise Cain*; CONCEPT 633 —Ant. be calm

carry out [v] *complete activity* accomplish, achieve, carry through, consummate, discharge, effect, effectuate, execute, finalize, fulfill, implement, meet, perform, realize; CONCEPT 706 —Ant. leave, not finish, stop

cart [n] *small attachment for transporting* barrow, buggy, curricle, dolly, dray, gig, gurney, handcart, palanquin, pushcart, rickshaw, tilbury, truck, tumbrel, two-wheeler, wagon, wheelbarrow; CONCEPTS 499,505

cart [v] *carry* bear, bring, convey, ferry, haul, move, schlepp*, take, tote; CONCEPTS 148,217

carte blanche [n] *full power, authority* blank check, freedom, free hand, free rein, license, permission, power of attorney, prerogative, sanction, say, say-so, unconditional right; CONCEPT 376

cartel [n] *group which shares business interest* bunch*, chain, combine, conglomerate, consortium, corporation, crew*, crowd*, gang*, holding company, megacorp*, mob*, monopoly, multinational*, outfit*, plunderbund*, pool, ring*, syndicate, trust; CONCEPTS 323,325

carton [n] *box for holding items* bin, case, casket, chest, coffer, container, corrugated box, crate, pack, package, packet; CONCEPT 494

cartoon [n] *funny drawing, often with dialogue or caption* animation, caricature, comic strip, drawing, lampoon, parody, representation, satire, sketch, takeoff; CONCEPTS 280,625

cartoonist [n] *person who draws cartoons* artist, caricaturist, comic artist, gag person*, gagster*, illustrator, social critic; CONCEPT 348

carve [v] *cut carefully with sharp instrument* block out, chip, chisel, cleave, dissect, dissever, divide, engrave, etch, fashion, form, grave, hack, hew, incise, indent, insculpt, model, mold, mould, pattern, rough-hew, sculpt, shape, slash, slice, stipple, sunder, tool, trim, whittle; CONCEPTS 137,176,184

carved in stone [adj] *fixed* established, etched

in stone*, firm, immutable, permanent, set in concrete*, set in stone*, unchangeable; CONCEPTS 488,551,583,649,798

cascade [n] *something falling, especially water* avalanche, cataract, chute, deluge, downrush, falls, flood, force, fountain, outpouring, precipitation, rapids, shower, spout, torrent, watercourse, waterfall; CONCEPTS 514,787

cascade [v] *fall in a rush* descend, disgorge, flood, gush, heave, overflow, pitch, plunge, pour, spew, spill, spit up, surge, throw up, tumble, vomit; CONCEPT 179

case [n1] *container; items in container* bag, baggage, basket, bin, box, cabinet, caddy, caisson, canister, capsule, carton, cartridge, casing, casket, chamber, chassis, chest, coffer, compact, cover, covering, crate, crating, crib, drawer, envelope, folder, grip, holder, integument, jacket, receptacle, safe, scabbard, sheath, shell, suitcase, tray, trunk, wallet, wrapper, wrapping; CONCEPT 494

case [n2] *circumstance, conditions* context, contingency, crisis, dilemma, event, eventuality, fact, incident, occurrence, plight, position, predicament, problem, quandary, situation, state, status; CONCEPT 696

case [n3] *example* case history, exemplification, illustration, instance, occasion, occurrence, representative, sample, sampling, specimen; CONCEPT 686

case [n4] *matter brought before a court* action, argument, cause, claim, dispute, evidence, lawsuit, litigation, petition, proceedings, process, proof, suit, trial; CONCEPT 318

case [v] *check something in detail* canvass, check out, check over, check up, examine, inspect, scrutinize, study, view; CONCEPT 103

cash [n] *money; assets* banknote, bread*, buck*, bullion, cabbage*, chicken feed*, coin, coinage, currency, dinero*, dough*, funds, green stuff*, investment, legal tender, lot, mazumah*, note, payment, pledge, principal, ready assets, refund, remuneration, reserve, resources, riches, savings, scratch*, security, skins*, stock, supply, treasure, wampum*, wherewithal; CONCEPTS 340,710

cash [v] *exchange for real money* acknowledge, break a bill*, change, discharge, draw, honor, liquidate, make change, pay, realize, redeem; CONCEPT 330

cashier [n] *bank worker* accountant, banker, bursar, clerk, collector, paymaster, purser, receiver, teller, treasurer; CONCEPT 348

cashier [v] *discard, expel* ax*, boot*, bounce, break, can*, cast off, discharge, dismiss, displace, drum out*, fire, give a pink slip*, give the heave ho*, heave*, remove, sack*, terminate; CONCEPTS 211,324

casing [n] *covering* hull, jacket, sheath, skin, wrapper; CONCEPTS 484,750

casino [n] *gambling establishment* bank, betting house, big store*, club, clubhouse, dance hall, dice joint*, dive, gambling den, hall, honky-tonk, house, joint, Monte Carlo, pool hall, roadhouse, rotunda, saloon, track; CONCEPT 447

cask [n] *rounded container for liquids* barrel, barrelet, butt, firkin, hogshead, keg, pipe, tun, vat; CONCEPT 494

casket [n] *burial box* bin, carton, case, chest,

coffer, crate, funerary box, pine box, pinto, sarcophagus, wood overcoat*; CONCEPTS 368,494

casserole [n] *dish consisting of a combination of cooked food* covered dish, goulash, hash, meat pie, pot pie, pottage, stew, stroganoff; CONCEPT 457

cast [n1] *a throw to the side* casting, ejection, expulsion, fling, flinging, heave, heaving, hurl, hurling, launching, lob, lobbing, pitch, pitching, projection, propulsion, shooting, sling, slinging, thrust, thrusting, toss, tossing; CONCEPT 222 —*Ant.* catch, keeping, retention

cast [n2] *appearance; shade of color* air, complexion, countenance, demeanor, embodiment, expression, face, hue, look, manner, mien, semblance, stamp, style, tinge, tint, tone, turn, visage; CONCEPTS 622,716

cast [n3] *actors in performance* actors, actresses, artists, characters, company, dramatis personae, list, parts, players, roles, troupe; CONCEPT 294

cast [n4] *molded structure* conformation, copy, duplicate, embodiment, facsimile, figure, form, mold, plaster, replica, sculpture, shape; CONCEPTS 470,475

cast [v1] *throw aside* boot, bung*, chuck*, drive, drop, fire*, fling, heave, hurl, impel, launch, lob, peg, pitch, project, shed, shy, sling, thrust, toss; CONCEPT 222 —*Ant.* catch, gather

cast [v2] *emit, give* aim, bestow, deposit, diffuse, direct, distribute, point, radiate, scatter, shed, spatter, spray, spread, sprinkle, strew, train; CONCEPTS 108,62 —*Ant.* receive, take

cast [v3] *calculate* add, compute, count, figure, foot, forecast, number, reckon, sum, summate, tot, total; CONCEPT 764

cast [v4] *select for activity* allot, appoint, arrange, assign, blueprint, chart, choose, decide upon, delegate, design, designate, detail, determine, devise, give parts, name, pick, plan, project; CONCEPT 41

caste [n] *social class* cultural level, degree, estate, grade, lineage, order, position, race, rank, social order, species, sphere, standing, station, status, stratum; CONCEPTS 378,388

castigate [v] *criticize severely* baste, bawl out*, beat, berate, blister, cane, censure, chasten, chastise, chew out*, come down on*, correct, criticize, discipline, drag over the coals*, dress down*, drub, excoriate, flay, flog, jump down one's throat*, lambaste, lash, lay out*, lean on*, penalize, pummel, punish, rail, rate, read the riot act*, ream, rebuke, reprimand, scarify, scathe, scold, scorch, scourge, thrash, tongue-lash*, upbraid, whip; CONCEPT 52 —*Ant.* compliment, laud, praise

castle [n] *magnificent home, often for royalty* acropolis, alcazar, château, citadel, donjon, estate house, fasthold, fastness, fort, fortification, fortress, hold, keep, manor, mansion, palace, peel, safehold, seat, stronghold, tower, villa; CONCEPT 516

castrate [v] *remove sexual organs* alter, asexualize, caponize, change, cut, deprive of virility, desexualize, emasculate, eunuchize, fix, geld, mutilate, neuter, spay, sterilize, unsex; CONCEPT 310

casual [adj1] *chance, random* accidental, adventitious, by chance, contingent, erratic, extemporaneous, extempore, fluky, fortuitous, impromptu, improvised, impulsive, incidental, infrequent, irregular, occasional, odd, offhand, serendipitous, spontaneous, uncertain, unexpected, unforeseen, unintentional, unplanned, unpremeditated; CONCEPTS *541,544 —Ant.* deliberate, painstaking, planned, premeditated

casual [*adj2*] *nonchalant, relaxed in manner* aloof, apathetic, blasé, breezy, cool*, cursory, detached, down home*, easygoing, folksy*, homey*, incurious, indifferent, informal, insouciant, lackadaisical, laid-back*, loose*, low-pressure, mellow, offhand, perfunctory, pococurante, purposeless, remote, unconcerned, unfussy, uninterested, withdrawn; CONCEPTS *401,542,589 —Ant.* formal, serious

casualty [*n1*] *accident* blow, calamity, catastrophe, chance, contingency, debacle, disaster, misadventure, misfortune, mishap; CONCEPT *674*

casualty [*n2*] *victim* dead, death toll, fatality, injured, killed, loss, missing, prey, sufferer, wounded; CONCEPTS *407,423*

casuistry [*n*] *overgeneral reasoning* chicanery, deception, deceptiveness, delusion, equivocation, evasion, fallacy, lie, oversubtleness, sophism, sophistry, speciousness, spuriousness, trick; CONCEPTS *54,63*

cat [*n*] *feline animal, sometimes a pet* bobcat, cheetah, cougar, grimalkin, jaguar, kitten, kitty, leopard, lion, lynx, malkin, mouser, ocelot, panther, puma, puss, pussy, tabby, tiger, tom, tomcat; CONCEPTS *394,400*

cataclysm [*n*] *disaster* calamity, cataract, catastrophe, collapse, convulsion, crunch*, curtains*, debacle, deluge, disturbance, double trouble*, flood, flooding, holy mess*, inundation, misadventure, ruin, torrent, tragedy, unholy mess*, upheaval, waterloo*, woe; CONCEPTS *674,675 —Ant.* boon, good fortune, happiness, miracle, wonder

catalog/catalogue [*n*] *written or printed matter featuring a selection of objects* archive, brief, bulletin, calendar, cartulary, charts, classification, compendium, directory, docket, draft, enumeration, gazette, gazetteer, hit list*, index, inventory, list, prospectus, record, register, roll, roster, schedule, slate, specification, syllabus, synopsis, table; CONCEPTS *271,280*

catalyst [*n*] *something which incites activity* adjuvant, agitator, enzyme, goad, impetus, impulse, incendiary, incentive, incitation, incitement, motivation, radical stimulus, reactant, reactionary, spark plug*, spur, stimulant, synergist, wave maker*; CONCEPT *712 —Ant.* block, blockage, preventer, prevention

catapult [*n*] *implement for shooting weapon* arbalest, ballista, heaver, hurler, pitcher, propeller, shooter, sling, slingshot, tosser, trebuchet; CONCEPTS *463,500*

catastrophe [*n*] *calamity; unhappy conclusion* accident, adversity, affliction, alluvion, bad luck, bad news*, blow, calamity, casualty, cataclysm, contretemps, crash, culmination, curtains*, debacle, denouement, desolation, devastation, disaster, emergency, end, failure, fatality, fiasco, finale, grief, hardship, havoc, ill, infliction, meltdown*, misadventure, mischance, misery, misfortune, mishap, reverse, scourge, stroke, termination, the worst*, tragedy, trial, trouble, upshot, waterloo*,

wreck; CONCEPT *674 —Ant.* benefit, blessing, favor, good fortune, good luck, happiness, miracle, success, wonder

catatonic [*adj*] *unaware* comatose, confused, hung, suspended, unconscious, wedged; CONCEPT *402*

catcall [*n*] *heckle* boo, Bronx cheer*, derision, gibe, hiss, hoot, jeer, raspberry*, shout, whistle; CONCEPTS *44,47*

catch-22 [*n*] *no-win situation* contradiction, dilemma, lose-lose, paradox, quagmire; CONCEPT *532*

catch [*n1*] *fastener* bolt, buckle, clamp, clasp, clip, hasp, hook, hook and eye, latch, snap; CONCEPT *497*

catch [*n2*] *trick, hidden disadvantage* Catch-22, conundrum, deception, decoy, drawback, fly in the ointment*, hitch, joke, puzzle, puzzler, snag, stumbling block, trap; CONCEPTS *674,679*

catch [*v1*] *ensnare, apprehend* arrest, bag, bust*, capture, clasp, claw, clench, clutch, collar, cop, corral, entangle, entrap, get one's fingers on*, glom, glove, grab, grasp, grip, hook, lasso, lay hold of, nab, nail, net, pick, pluck, pounce on, prehend, secure, seize, snag, snare, snatch, take, take hold of, trap; CONCEPT *90 —Ant.* free, let go, let off, lose, misplace, miss, release

catch [*v2*] *find out, discover* descry, detect, encounter, expose, hit upon, meet with, spot, surprise, take unawares, turn up, unmask; CONCEPT *31 —Ant.* miss, misunderstand

catch [*v3*] *contract an illness* become infected with, break out with, come down with, develop, fall ill with, fall victim to, get, incur, receive, sicken, succumb to, suffer from, take; CONCEPTS *93,308 —Ant.* be immune

catch [*v4*] *come from behind and grab* board, climb on, come upon, cotch, get, go after, grab, hop on, jump, make, overhaul, overtake, pass, ram, reach, run down, take; CONCEPT *164 —Ant.* let go, push

catch [*v5*] *hear and understand* accept, apprehend, comprehend, discern, feel, follow, get, grasp, perceive, recognize, see, sense, take in, understand; CONCEPT *15*

catching [*adj*] *contagious (disease)* communicable, dangerous, endemic, epidemic, epizootic, infectious, infective, miasmatic, pandemic, pestiferous, pestilential, taking, transferable, transmittable; CONCEPT *314 —Ant.* uncontagious

catchword [*n*] *motto* byword, catchphrase, household word, maxim, password, refrain, shibboleth, slogan, watchword; CONCEPTS *275,278*

catchy [*adj*] *captivating, addictive* fetching, haunting, having a good hook*, memorable, popular; CONCEPT *544 —Ant.* boring, dull, ignorable

catechize [*v*] *instruct and question* ask, cross-examine, drill, educate, examine, grill, inquire, interrogate, query, quiz, teach, train; CONCEPTS *48,285 —Ant.* answer, listen

categorical [*adj*] *explicit, unconditional* absolute, all out*, certain, clear-cut, definite, definitive, direct, downright, emphatic, express, flat out*, forthright, no holds barred*, no strings attached*, positive, specific, straight out, sure, ultimate, unambiguous, unequivocal, unmitigated, unqualified, unreserved; CONCEPT *535*

—Ant. ambiguous, conditional, equivocal, implied, qualified, questionable, tentative, uncategorical, vague

categorize [v] *sort by type, classification* assort, button down*, class, classify, group, identify, peg*, pigeonhole*, put down as, rank, tab, typecast; CONCEPT 39

category [n] *classification, type* class, department, division, grade, group, grouping, head, heading, kind, league, level, list, order, pigeonhole*, rank, section, sort, tier; CONCEPT 378

cater [v] *provide, help* baby, coddle, cotton, furnish, gratify, humor, indulge, minister to, outfit, pamper, pander to, procure, provision, purvey, spoil, supply, victual; CONCEPT 136

caterwaul [v] *make screeching, crying noise* bawl, bicker, howl, quarrel, scream, screech, shriek, squall, wail, yell, yowl; CONCEPT 77

catharsis [n] *purging, purification* ablution, abreaction, cleansing, expurgation, lustration, purgation, purification, release; CONCEPTS 13,165,230 **—Ant.** dirtying

cathedral [n] *large church* basilica, bishop's seat, chancel, holy place, house of God, house of prayer, house of worship, minster, place of worship, sanctuary, temple; CONCEPTS 368,439

catholic [adj] *all-embracing, general* all-inclusive, broad-minded, charitable, comprehensive, cosmic, cosmopolitan, diffuse, eclectic, ecumenical, extensive, generic, global, inclusive, indeterminate, large-scale, liberal, open-minded, planetary, receptive, tolerant, unbigoted, universal, unprejudiced, unsectarian, whole, wide, world-wide; CONCEPTS 557,772 **—Ant.** narrow, narrow-minded, specific

cattle [n] *bovine animals* beasts, bovid mammals, bulls, calves, cows, dogies*, herd, livestock, longhorn*, moo cows*, oxen, shorthorns, stock, strays; CONCEPT 394

catty [adj] *nasty, malicious* backbiting, evil, hateful, ill-natured, malevolent, mean, rancorous, spiteful, venomous, vicious, wicked*; CONCEPT 404 **—Ant.** kind, nice, pleasant

caucus [n] *group gathered to make decision* assembly, conclave, convention, council, gathering, get-together, meeting, parley, session; CONCEPTS 301,417

cause [n1] *agent, originator* account, agency, aim, antecedent, author, basis, beginning, causation, consideration, creator, determinant, doer, element, end, explanation, foundation, genesis, ground, grounds, incitement, inducement, instigation, leaven, mainspring, maker, matter, motivation, motive, object, occasion, origin, prime mover, principle, producer, purpose, root, source, spring, stimulation; CONCEPTS 229,661 **—Ant.** consequence, development, effect, end, fruit, issue, outcome, outgrowth, product, result

cause [n2] *belief; undertaking for belief* attempt, conviction, creed, enterprise, faith, goal, ideal, intention, movement, object, objective, plan, principles, purpose; CONCEPT 689

cause [v] *bring into being; bring about* be at the bottom of*, begin, brainstorm*, break in*, break the ice*, breed, bring to pass, come out with*, compel, cook up*, create, dream up*, effect, elicit, engender, evoke, fire up*, generate, get things rolling*, give rise to, hatch,

incite, induce, introduce, kickoff*, kindle, lead to, let, make, make up, motivate, muster, occasion, open, originate, precipitate, produce, provoke, result in, revert, secure, sow the seeds, start the ball rolling*, think up, work up; CONCEPTS 228,231,241

cause célèbre [n] *controversial issue* bone of contention, celebrated case, controversy, debate, grist for the gossip mill*, hot potato*, moot point, political football*, scandal, war of words; CONCEPTS 46,278,665

caustic [adj1] *burning, corrosive* abrasive, acerbic, acid, acrid, alkaline, astringent, biting, corroding, erosive, keen, mordant, pungent, tart; CONCEPT 485 **—Ant.** calm, mild, soothing

caustic [adj2] *sarcastic* acerb, acerbic, acrimonious, bitter, cutting, harsh, incisive, pithy, pungent, rough, salty, satiric, scathing, severe, sharp, stinging, trenchant, virulent; CONCEPT 267 **—Ant.** kind, unsarcastic

caution [n1] *alertness, carefulness* attention, canniness, care, circumspection, deliberation, discreetness, discretion, Fabian policy, foresight, forethought, heed, heedfulness, providence, prudence, vigilance, watchfulness; CONCEPT 410 **—Ant.** heedlessness, imprudence, indiscretion, neglect, negligence, thoughtlessness

caution [n2] *warning* admonition, advice, bug in one's ear*, caveat, commonition, counsel, forewarning, hint, injunction, monition, notice, omen, premonition, sign, tip*; tip-off*; CONCEPTS 78,274

caution [v] *warn, advise* admonish, alert, exhort, flag, forewarn, give the high sign*, give the lowdown on*, pull one's coat*, put one wise*, tip*, tip off*, urge, wave a red flag*, wise one up*; CONCEPT 78

cautionary tale [n] *event illustrating a hazard* admonition, advisory, caveat, message, omen, portent, red flag*, sign of things to come*, wake-up call*, warning, word to the wise*; CONCEPTS 78,274

cautious [adj] *careful, guarded* alert, all ears*, cagey, calculating, chary, circumspect, considerate, discreet, forethoughtful, gingerly, hedging one's bets*, heedful, judicious, keeping on one's toes*, leery, on the lookout*, playing it cool*, playing safe*, politic, provident, prudent, pussyfoot*, safe, shrewd, taking it easy, taking it slow*, tentative, thinking twice*, vigilant, walking on eggs*, wary, watchful, watching one's step*, watching out, with one's eyes peeled*; CONCEPTS 401,403 **—Ant.** careless, hasty, heedless, imprudent, incautious, rash, thoughtless, uncareful, unguarded, unobservant

cavalcade [n] *parade* array, drill, march-past, procession, promenade, review, spectacle, train; CONCEPT 432

cavalier [adj] *arrogant* condescending, curt, disdainful, haughty, high-and-mighty*, insolent, lofty, lordly, offhand, overbearing, proud, scornful, snooty*, snotty*, supercilious, superior; CONCEPT 401 **—Ant.** humble, reticent, shy

cavalry [n] *troops riding horses* army, bowlegs*, chasseurs, cuirassiers, dragoons, horse, horse soldiers, hussars, lancers, mounted troops, Mounties, rangers, squadron, uhlans; CONCEPT 322

cave [n] *hole in land formation* cavern, cavity, den, grotto, hollow, pothole, rock shelter, subterrane, subterranean area; CONCEPT *509*

caveat [n] *warning* admonition, alarm, caution, commonition, forewarning, monition, sign; CONCEPTS *78,274*

cavern [n] *hollow in land formation* cave, grotto, hole, pothole, subterrane, subterranean area; CONCEPT *509*

cavernous [adj] *hollow and large* alveolate, broad, chambered, chasmal, commodious, concave, curved inward, deep, deep-set, echoing, gaping, huge, resonant, reverberant, roomy, sepulchral, socketed, spacious, sunken, vast, wide, yawning; CONCEPTS *490,773,796* —*Ant.* filled

cavity [n] *sunken or decayed area* atrium, basin, bursa, caries, chamber, crater, decay, dent, depression, gap, hole, hollow, pit, pocket, sinus, socket, vacuity, void; CONCEPT *513*

cavort [v] *frolic, prance* caper, caracole, carry on*, cut loose*, cut up*, dance, fool around*, frisk, gambol, go places and do things*, horse around*, horseplay, monkey around*, play, revel, rollick, romp, roughhouse*, sport; CONCEPTS *114,384*

cease [v] *stop, conclude* back off, break off, bring to an end, call it a day*, call it quits*, close, close out, come to an end, culminate, cut it out*, desist, die, discontinue, drop, end, fail, finish, give over, halt, intermit, knock off*, leave off, pack in*, quit, quit cold turkey*, refrain, shut down, stay, surcease, terminate, wind up*; CONCEPT *234* —*Ant.* begin, commence, continue, go, initiate, keep on, start

cease-fire [n] *stop in fighting* armistice, suspension of hostilities, truce; CONCEPTS *230,298,684*

ceaseless [adj] *never-ending* amaranthine, constant, continual, continuous, day and night*, endless, eternal, everlasting, incessant, indefatigable, interminable, nonstop, on a treadmill*, perennial, perpetual, round the clock*, unceasing, unending, uninterrupted, unremitting, untiring, world-without-end*; CONCEPT *798* —*Ant.* ceasing, completed, concluded, ending, finished, infrequent, irregular, occasional

cede [v] *abandon, surrender* abalienate, abdicate, accord, alien, alienate, allow, capitulate, come across with*, communicate, concede, convey, deed, drop, fold*, fork over*, give in*, give up, grant, hand over*, leave, make over, part with, relinquish, remise, renounce, resign, sign over, throw in the sponge*, throw in the towel*, transfer, vouchsafe, waive, yield; CONCEPTS *108,127* —*Ant.* defend, fight, gain, guard, take over, win

ceiling [n1] *top of a room* baldachin, beam, canopy, covert, dome, fan vaulting, groin, highest point, housetop, plafond, planchement, plaster, roof, roofing, timber, topside covering; CONCEPT *440* —*Ant.* floor

ceiling [n2] *maximum* legal price, record, superiority, top; CONCEPT *836* —*Ant.* minimum

celebrate [v] *commemorate occasion, achievement* beat the drum*, bless, blow off steam*, carouse, ceremonialize, commend, consecrate, dedicate, drink to, eulogize, exalt, extol, feast, fete, glorify, hallow, have a ball*, honor, jubilate, keep, kick up one's heels*, laud, let loose*, lionize, live it up*, make merry, make whoopee*, mark with a red letter*, memorialize, observe, paint the town red*, party*, perform, praise, proclaim, publicize, raise hell*, rejoice, revel, revere, ritualize, signalize, solemnize; CONCEPT *377* —*Ant.* disregard, forget, ignore, neglect, overlook

celebrated [adj] *distinguished, famous* acclaimed, big*, eminent, famed, glorious, great, high-powered, illustrious, immortal, important, large, laureate, lionized, notable, number one*, numero uno*, outstanding, popular, preeminent, prominent, renowned, revered, storied, up there*, well-known, w. k.*; CONCEPT *568* —*Ant.* inexalted, inglorious, obscure, plain, unknown

celebration [n] *commemoration of occasion, achievement* anniversary, bash*, birthday, blast*, blowout*, carousal, ceremony, conviviality, festival, festivity, fete, frolic, gaiety, gala, glorification, hilarity, honoring, hoopla, hullabaloo*, jollification, joviality, jubilation, jubilee, keeping, magnification, memorialization, merriment, merrymaking, observance, party, performance, recognition, remembrance, revelry, saturnalia, solemnization, spree, triumph, wingding*; CONCEPT *377*

celebrity [n1] *dignitary* ace, big cheese*, big deal*, big gun*, big name*, big shot*, big stuff*, bigwig*, celeb*, cynosure, famous person, figure, heavyweight, hero, hotshot*, immortal, lion*, luminary, magnate, mahatma, major leaguer*, name, notable, personage, personality, somebody, someone, star, superstar, the cheese*, VIP, worthy; CONCEPT *423* —*Ant.* nobody

celebrity [n2] *fame, notoriety* distinction, éclat, eminence, glory, honor, notability, popularity, preeminence, prestige, prominence, renown, reputation, repute, stardom; CONCEPTS *388,668* —*Ant.* obscurity

celerity [n] *swiftness* alacrity, briskness, dispatch, expedition, expeditiousness, fleetness, gait, haste, hurry, hustle, legerity, promptness, quickness, rapidity, speed, speediness, swiftness, velocity, vivacity; CONCEPT *755* —*Ant.* slowness, sluggishness

celestial [adj] *heavenly* angelic, astral, beatific, blessed, divine, elysian, empyral, empyrean, eternal, ethereal, godlike, hallowed, holy, immortal, Olympian, otherworldly, seraphic, spiritual, sublime, supernal, supernatural, transcendental, transmundane; CONCEPTS *536, 673* —*Ant.* earthly, hellish, infernal, mortal

celibacy [n] *abstinence from sexual activity* abstention, chastity, continence, frigidity, impotence, maidenhood, purity, singleness, virginity, virtue; CONCEPT *388* —*Ant.* promiscuousness

celibate [adj] *abstaining from sexual activity* chaste, continent, pure, virgin, virginal, virtuous; CONCEPT *372* —*Ant.* active, promiscuous

cell [n1] *smallest living organism* bacterium, cellule, corpuscle, egg, embryo, follicle, germ, haematid, microorganism, spore, unit, utricle, vacuole; CONCEPTS *389,478*

cell [n2] *small room, container* alcove, antechamber, apartment, bastille, booth, burrow, cage, cavity, chamber, cloister, closet, compartment, coop, crib, crypt, cubicle, den, dungeon, hold, hole, keep, lockup, nook, pen, receptacle, recess, retreat, stall, tower, vault; CONCEPTS 448,494,513

cellar [n] *underground story of building* apartment, basement, subbasement, subterrane, underground room, vault; CONCEPTS 440,448 —*Ant.* attic

cement [n] *gluing, binding material* adhesive, binder, birdlime, bond, concrete, epoxy, glue, grout, gum, gunk*, lime, lute, mortar, mucilage, mud*, paste, plaster, putty, rubber cement, sand, sealant, size, solder, stickum*, tar; CONCEPT 475

cement [v] *attach securely, often with sticky material* bind, blend, bond, cohere, combine, connect, fasten, fuse, glue, gum, join, merge, mortar, paste, plaster, seal, solder, stick together, unite, weld; CONCEPTS 85,160 —*Ant.* divide, separate, unfix

cemetery [n] *burial ground* boot hill*, catacomb, charnel, charnel house, churchyard, city of the dead*, crypt, eternal home*, funerary grounds, garden, God's acre*, Golgotha, grave, graveyard, marble town*, memorial park, mortuary, necropolis, ossuary, polyandrium, potter's field, resting place, sepulcher, tomb, vault; CONCEPTS 305,368

censor [v] *forbid; ban; selectively remove* abridge, blacklist, black out*, bleach, bleep*, blue-pencil*, bowdlerize, clean up, conceal, control, cork*, criticize, cut, decontaminate, delete, drop the iron curtain*, edit, examine, excise, expurgate, exscind, inspect, launder*, narrow, oversee, prevent publication, purge, purify, put the lid on*, refuse transmission, repress, restrain, restrict, review, revile, sanitize, scissor out*, squelch, sterilize, strike out, supervise communications, suppress, withhold; CONCEPTS 121,266 —*Ant.* allow, approve, endorse, permit, sanction

censorious [adj] *very critical* accusatory, captious, carping, caviling, cavillous, chiding, complaining, condemnatory, condemning, critical, culpatory, denouncing, disapproving, disparaging, fault-finding, hypercritical, overcritical, reprehending, reproaching, severe; CONCEPT 267 —*Ant.* complimentary, encouraging, flattering, laudatory, praising

censorship [n] *forbiddance; ban* blackout*, blue pencil*, bowdlerization, control, forbidding, hush up*, infringing on rights, iron curtain*, restriction, suppression, thought control*; CONCEPTS 376,388 —*Ant.* approval, compliment, encouragement, endorsement, praise, recommendation, sanction

censure [n] *severe criticism* admonishment, admonition, blame, castigation, condemnation, disapproval, dressing down, objection, obloquy, rebuke, remonstrance, reprehension, reprimand, reproach, reproof, stricture; CONCEPTS 52,410 —*Ant.* approval, compliment, encouragement, endorsement, praise, ratification, recommendation, sanction

censure [v] *condemn; criticize severely* abuse, admonish, animadvert, asperse, attack, backbite, berate, blame, carp at, castigate, cavil, chastise, chide, contemn, cut up*, denigrate, denounce, deprecate, disapprove, discipline, disparage, exprobate, find fault with, get after, impugn, incriminate, judge, knock, lecture, look

askance, ostracize, pick apart, pull apart, read out*, rebuff, rebuke, remonstrate, reprehend, reprimand, reproach, reprove, scold, take to task*, tear apart*, tell off, upbraid; CONCEPT 52 —*Ant.* allow, approve, compliment, endorse, laud, permit, sanction

census [n] *head count* demographics, demography, enumeration, poll, population tally, statistics, stats; CONCEPTS 283,786

center [adj] *middle* at halfway point, centermost, deepest, equidistant, inmost, inner, innermost, inside, interior, intermediary, intermediate, internal, mean, medial, mid, middlemost, midpoint, midway; CONCEPTS 583,585,830 —*Ant.* bordering, edging, exterior, marginal, outside, peripheral

center [n1] *middle point* axis, bull's-eye, centrality, centriole, centrum, core, cynosure, equidistance, essence, focal point, focus, gist, heart, hotbed, hub, inside, interior, intermediacy, kernel, mainstream*, marrow, middle of the road*, midpoint, midst, nave, navel, nucleus, omphalos, pith, pivot, place, polestar, quick, radial point, root, seat; CONCEPT 830 —*Ant.* border, boundary, edge, exterior, exteriority, margin, outside, outskirts, periphery, rim, surroundings

center [n2] *point of attraction for visitors, shoppers, travelers* capital, city, club, concourse, crossroads, focal point, focus, heart, hub, mall, market, marketplace, mart, meeting place, metropolis, nerve center, plaza, polestar, shopping center, social center, station, town, trading center; CONCEPTS 435,438,507

center [v] *concentrate, draw together* attract, bring to a focus, bring together, centralize, close on, collect, concenter, consolidate, converge upon, focalize, focus, gather, intensify, join, medialize, meet, unify; CONCEPTS 35,84 —*Ant.* disperse, dissipate

centerpiece [n] *highlight* best part, center of attention, climax, focal point, heart, high point, high spot, hub, keynote, main event, main feature, nucleus; CONCEPT 832

central [adj] *main, principal; in the middle* axial, basic, cardinal, center, centric, centroidal, chief, dominant, equidistant, essential, focal, foremost, fundamental, important, inmost, inner, interior, intermediate, key, leading, master, mean, median, mid, middle, middlemost, midmost, midway, nuclear, outstanding, overriding, paramount, pivotal, predominant, primary, prime, radical, ruling, salient, significant, umbilical; CONCEPTS 567,583,830 —*Ant.* exterior, minor, outside, peripheral, secondary

centralize [v] *concentrate, draw toward a point* accumulate, amalgamate, assemble, compact, concenter, condense, consolidate, converge, focus, gather, incorporate, integrate, organize, rationalize, streamline, systematize, unify; CONCEPTS 35,84 —*Ant.* decentralize, disperse, scatter

centrifugal [adj] *radiating from a central point* deviating, diffusive, divergent, diverging, eccentric, efferent, outward, radial, spiral, spreading; CONCEPTS 581,584 —*Ant.* centripetal

ceramics [n] *pottery* china, pots, slipware, terracotta, wares; CONCEPT 174

cereal [n] *edible grain* bran, breakfast food,

ca
ce

corn, grain, oats, rice, rye, wheat; CONCEPTS
428,831
cerebral [*a*] *using one's brain* analytical,
brainy, deep, erudite, intellectual, intelligent,
recondite, scholarly, smart; CONCEPT *402*
ceremonial [*adj*] *ritual, formal* august, conventional, imposing, liturgical, lofty, mannered,
ritualistic, solemn, stately, studied, stylized;
CONCEPT *548* —*Ant.* informal, unceremonial
ceremonious [*adj*] *ritual, formal* civil, courteous, courtly, decorous, deferential, dignified,
exact, grandiose, impressive, majestic, moving,
precise, proper, punctilious, seemly, solemn,
starchy, stately, stiff, striking; CONCEPT *548*
—*Ant.* informal, relaxed, unceremonious,
unobserved
ceremony [*n1*] *ritual; celebratory observation*
ceremonial, commemoration, custom, formality, function, liturgy, observance, ordinance,
parade, rite, sacrament, service, show, solemnity, tradition; CONCEPT *386*
ceremony [*n2*] *etiquette* ceremonial, conformity, decorum, form, formal courtesy, formalism, formality, nicety, politeness, pomp,
preciseness, prescription, propriety, protocol,
strictness, usage; CONCEPT *388*
certain [*adj1*] *confident* assertive, assured,
believing, calm, cocksure, convinced, positive,
questionless, sanguine, satisfied, secure, self-
confident, sure, unconcerned, undisturbed, undoubtful, undoubting, unperturbed, untroubled;
CONCEPT *403* —*Ant.* doubtful, doubting, hesitant, uncertain, unconfident, unsure
certain [*adj2*] *undoubtable, valid* absolute,
ascertained, authoritative, clear, conclusive,
confirmable, definite, demonstrable, destined,
determined, establishable, evident, firm, fixed,
genuine, guaranteed, having down pat*, incontrovertible, indubitable, infallible, in the bag*,
irrefutable, known, on ice*, plain, positive, predestined, provable, real, reliable, safe, salted
away*, set, sound, supreme, sure, sure-thing*,
true, trustworthy, unambiguous, undeniable, undoubted, unequivocal, unerring, unmistakable,
verifiable; CONCEPTS *535,582* —*Ant.* doubtful,
dubious, faltering, questionable, uncertain,
unreliable, unsure
certain [*adj3*] *fixed* assured, bound, certified,
concluded, decided, definite, determined,
ensured, established, guaranteed, insured, set,
settled, stated, stipulated, sure, warranted;
CONCEPT *535* —*Ant.* uncertain, undecided,
unfixed, unpredictable
certain [*adj4*] *referring to a specifically known
amount* a couple, a few, defined, divers, express, individual, many, marked, numerous,
one, particular, precise, regular, several, singular, some, special, specific, specified, sundry,
upwards of, various; CONCEPT *557*
certainly [*adv*] *without doubt* absolutely, assuredly, cert*, exactly, for a fact, of course,
positively, posolutely*, right on*, surely, unquestionably, without fail; CONCEPT *535* —*Ant.*
doubtfully, dubiously, equivocally, questioningly
certainty [*n1*] *positive assurance* all sewn
up*, authoritativeness, belief, certitude, cinch,
confidence, conviction, credence, definiteness,
dogmatism, faith, firmness, indubitableness, inevitability, lock*, lockup*, open and shut case*,

positiveness, positivism, rain or shine*, setup,
shoo-in*, staunchness, steadiness, stock, store,
sure bet*, surefire*, sureness, sure thing*,
surety, trust, validity, wrap-up; CONCEPTS
638,725 —*Ant.* ambiguity, doubt, hesitation,
questionableness, uncertainty
certainty [*n2*] *fact, resulting truth* consequence,
foregone conclusion, inevitable result, reality,
sure thing*, surety; CONCEPT *230* —*Ant.*
concept, idea, theory
certificate [*n*] *authorizing document* affidavit,
affirmation, attestation, authentication, authorization, certification, coupon, credential, deed,
diploma, docket, documentation, endorsement,
guarantee, license, paper, pass, permit, receipt,
record, sheepskin*, shingle, testament, testifica-
tion, testimonial, testimony, ticket, voucher,
warrant, warranty; CONCEPTS *271,685*
certify [*v*] *declare as true* accredit, approve,
ascertain, assure, attest, authenticate, authorize,
aver, avow, commission, confirm, corroborate,
endorse, guarantee, license, notify, okay, profess, reassure, rubber-stamp*, sanction, show,
state, swear, testify, validate, verify, vouch,
witness; CONCEPTS *50,88* —*Ant.* contradict,
counteract, deny, disavow, discredit, invalidate,
reject, repudiate
cessation [*n*] *ending* abeyance, arrest, break,
break-off*, breather*, cease, ceasing, close,
conclusion, cutoff*, desistance, discontinuance,
downtime*, end, finish, freeze*, grinding halt,
halt, halting, hiatus, intermission, interruption,
interval, layoff*, let-up*, pause, recess, remission, respite, rest, screaming halt*, standstill,
stay, stop, stoppage, suspension, termination,
time off, time-out*; CONCEPT *119* —*Ant.*
beginning, commencement, start
chafe [*v1*] *rub, grind against* abrade, bark,
corrode, damage, erode, excoriate, gall, grate,
graze, hurt, impair, inflame, irritate, peel, ruffle,
scrape, scratch, skin, wear; CONCEPT *215*
chafe [*v2*] *annoy* abrade, anger, annoy, bother,
exasperate, exercise, fret, fume, gall, grate, harass, incense, inflame, irk, irritate, itch, offend,
provoke, rage, rasp, rub, ruffle, scrape, scratch,
vex, worry; CONCEPTS *7,19* —*Ant.* make happy
chaff [*n*] *waste* crust, debris, dregs, husks, pod,
refuse, remains, rubbish, shard, shell, trash;
CONCEPT *679*
chaff [*v*] *joke, ridicule* banter, deride, fun, jeer,
jolly, josh, kid, mock, rag*, rally, razz*, rib*,
scoff, taunt, tease; CONCEPT *273*
chagrin [*n*] *displeasure* annoyance, balk, blow,
crushing, discomfiture, discomposure, disgruntlement, dismay, disquiet, dissatisfaction,
embarrassment, fretfulness, frustration, humiliation, ill-humor, irritation, letdown, mortification, peevishness, shame, spleen, upset,
vexation; CONCEPTS *410,674* —*Ant.* delight,
gladness, happiness, joy, pleasure, triumph
chagrin [*v*] *cause displeasure* abash, annoy,
confuse, crush, discomfit, discompose, disconcert, disgrace, dismay, displease, disquiet,
dissatisfy, embarrass, humiliate, irk, irritate,
mortify, peeve, perturb, shame, upset, vex;
CONCEPTS *7,19* —*Ant.* delight, make happy,
please
chain [*n1*] *succession, series* alternation, catena,
concatenation, conglomerate, consecution,

continuity, group, order, progression, row, sequence, set, string, syndicate, train, trust; CONCEPTS 432,727,769

chain [n2] *connected metal links; jewelry made of such links* bond, bracelet, cable, clinker*, connection, coupling, fetter, iron, lavaliere, link, locket, manacle, pendant, shackle, trammel; CONCEPTS 446,476,499

chain [v] *manacle in metal* attach, bind, confine, connect, enslave, fetter, handcuff, hold, moor, restrain, shackle, tether, tie up, trammel; CONCEPTS 85,160

chair [n1] *single-seat furniture* armchair, bench, cathedra, recliner, rocker, sling*; CONCEPT 443

chair [n2] *person in or position of authority* captain, chairperson, director, fellowship, helm, instructorship, leader, monitor, position of control, principal, professorate, professorship, throne, tutor, tutorship; CONCEPTS 348,376

chairperson [n] *person in charge of proceedings* administrator, captain, chair, director, introducer, leader, moderator, monitor, president, presider, principal, prolocutor, speaker, spokesperson, symposiarch; CONCEPTS 348,376

challenge [n] *dispute, question* claiming, confrontation, dare, defiance, demanding, demur, interrogation, objection, protest, provocation, remonstrance, summons to contest, test, threat, trial, ultimatum; CONCEPTS 53,532 —*Ant.* agree, answer, decide, win

challenge [v] *dispute, question* accost, arouse, ask for, assert, beard, brave, call for, call out, claim, confront, cross, dare, defy, demand, denounce, exact, face down, face off, face the music*, fly in the face of*, hang in*, impeach, impose, impugn, inquire, insist upon, investigate, invite competition, make a point of, make a stand, object to, provoke, query, reclaim, require, search out, stand up to, stick it out, stimulate, summon, tax, test, throw down the gauntlet*, try, vindicate; CONCEPT 53 —*Ant.* agreement, answer, decision, victory

chamber [n1] *small compartment, room* alcove, antechamber, apartment, bedchamber, bedroom, box, case, cavity, cell, chest, container, cubicle, enclosure, flat, hall, hollow, lodging, pocket, room, socket; CONCEPTS 448,494

chamber [n2] *legislative body* assembly, council, legislature, organization, representatives; CONCEPT 299

champion [adj] *best, excellent* blue-ribbon, boss*, capital, chief, choice, cool, dandy, distinguished, first, greatest, head, illustrious, out of sight*, out of this world*, outstanding, premier, prime, principal, prize-winning, splendid, super, superior, tip top*, top drawer*, topflight*, top-notch*, tops*, unbeaten, undefeated, world class*; CONCEPT 574 —*Ant.* poorest, worst

champion [n] *defeater in competition; preeminent supporter* advocate, ally, backer, challenger, champ, conqueror, defender, endorser, exponent, expounder, guardian, hero, heroine, medalist, nonpareil, number one*, numero uno*, paladin, partisan, patron, proponent, protector, supporter, sympathizer, the greatest*, titleholder, top dog*, upholder, vanquisher, victor, vindicator, warrior, winner; CONCEPT 366 —*Ant.* loser

champion [v] *advocate, support* back, battle, contend, defend, espouse, fight for, go to bat

for*, patronize, plead for, promote, put in a good word for*, ride shotgun for*, side with, stand behind, stand up for, support, thump for, uphold; CONCEPTS 10,69 —*Ant.* be against, oppose

championship [n] *contest for ultimate victor* crown, crowning achievement, elimination, playoffs, showdown, title match, tournament, winner takes all*; CONCEPT 363

chance [adj] *accidental, unforeseeable* adventitious, at random, casual, contingent, fluky, fortuitous, fortunate, happy, inadvertent, incidental, lucky, odd, offhand, unforeseen, unintentional, unlooked for, unplanned; CONCEPT 552 —*Ant.* designed, foreseeable, planned, understood

chance [n1] *possibility, probability* break, contingency, fair shake*, fighting chance*, indications, liability, likelihood, long shot*, look-in, occasion, odds, opening, opportunity, outlook, prospect, scope, shot*, show, squeak, time, wager; CONCEPT 650 —*Ant.* assurance, certainty, design, law, plan, scheme

chance [n2] *fate, luck* accident, advantage, adventure, bad luck, break, cast, casualty, coincidence, contingency, destination, destiny, doom, even chance, fluke, fortuity, fortune, future, gamble, good luck, hap*, haphazard, happening, hazard, heads or tails*, hit*, in the cards*, kismet, lot, lottery, luck out*, lucky break, misfortune, occurrence, odds, outcome, peradventure, peril, providence, risk, stroke of luck*, throw of the dice*, toss-up*, turn of the cards*, way the cookie crumbles*, wheel of fortune*; CONCEPT 679 —*Ant.* aim, design, plan, scheme

chance [n3] *gamble, risk* bet, craps game*, fall of the cards*, hazard, jeopardy, lottery, raffle, speculation, stake, throw of the dice*, try, venture, wager; CONCEPT 363

chance [v1] *risk, endanger* attempt, cast lots, draw lots, gamble, go out on a limb, have a fling at, hazard, jeopardize, play with fire*, plunge, put eggs in one basket*, put it on the line*, roll the dice*, run the risk, skate on thin ice*, speculate, stake, stick one's neck out*, take shot in the dark*, tempt fate*, tempt fortune*, toss up*, try, venture, wager, wildcat; CONCEPT 87 —*Ant.* aim, design, plan, scheme, understand

chance [v2] *happen* arrive, befall, be one's fate, betide, blunder on, break, bump, come, come about, come off, come to pass, fall out, fall to one's lot, go, hap*, hit upon, light, light upon, luck, meet, occur, stumble, stumble on, transpire, tumble, turn up; CONCEPT 4

chancy [adj] *dangerous, risky* capricious, contingent, dicey, erratic, fluctuant, fluky, hazardous, iffy*, incalculable, precarious, problematic, problematical, rocky, speculative, ticklish, touchy, tricky, uncertain, unpredictable, unsound, whimsical; CONCEPTS 552,587 —*Ant.* certain, not dangerous, safe, secure, sure, tried

chandelier [n] *light hanging from ceiling* candelabrum, candleholder, corona, crown, electrolier, gasolier, light fixture, luster; CONCEPT 444

change [n1] *something made different; alteration* about-face*, addition, adjustment, advance, break, compression, contraction, conversion, correction, development, difference, distortion, diversification, diversity, innovation, metamorphosis, modification, modulation, mutation, novelty, permutation, reconstruction, refinement, remodeling, reversal, revision, revolution, shift, surrogate, switch, tempering, transformation, transition, transmutation, turn, turnover, variance, variation, variety, vicissitude; CONCEPTS 230,260,701

change [n2] *substitution; replacement* conversion, exchange, flip-flop*, interchange, swap, switch, trade, turnaround; CONCEPT 128

change [n3] *smaller currency in exchange for larger* chicken feed*, coins, copper, dimes, nickels, pennies, pin money*, pocket money, quarters, silver, spending money; CONCEPT 340 —*Ant.* bill, dollar

change [v1] *make or become different* accommodate, adapt, adjust, alter, alternate, commute, convert, diminish, diverge, diversify, evolve, fluctuate, make innovations, make over, merge, metamorphose, moderate, modify, modulate, mutate, naturalize, recondition, redo, reduce, reform, regenerate, remake, remodel, renovate, reorganize, replace, resolve, restyle, revolutionize, shape, shift, substitute, tamper with, temper, transfigure, transform, translate, transmute, transpose, turn, vacillate, vary, veer, warp; CONCEPTS 228,232,235,701 —*Ant.* continue, hold, keep, persist, remain, stay

change [v2] *substitute, replace* alternate, barter, convert, displace, exchange, interchange, invert, remove, reverse, shift, supplant, swap, switch around, trade, transmit, transpose; CONCEPT 128

changeable [adj] *erratic* agitated, capricious, changeful, commutative, convertible, fickle, fitful, flighty, fluctuating, fluid, impulsive, inconstant, indecisive, irregular, irresolute, irresponsible, kaleidoscopic, mercurial, mobile, movable, mutable, permutable, protean, restless, reversible, revocable, shifting, skittish, spasmodic, transformable, transitional, uncertain, unpredictable, unreliable, unsettled, unstable, unsteady, vacillating, vagrant, variable, variant, varying, versatile, volatile, wavering, whimsical; CONCEPT 534 —*Ant.* certain, changeless, constant, fixed, lasting, reliable, stable, steady, sure, unchangeable, undeviating

channel [n1] *pathway, usually containing water* approach, aqueduct, arroyo, artery, avenue, canal, canyon, carrier, chamber, chase, conduit, course, dig, ditch, duct, fluting, furrow, gouge, groove, gully, gutter, main, means, medium, pass, passage, pipe, raceway, route, runway, sewer, slit, sound, strait, tideway, trough, tube, tunnel, vein, watercourse, way; CONCEPTS 501, 514

channel [n2] *means* agency, agent, approach, avenue, course, instrument, instrumentality, instrumentation, medium, ministry, organ, route, vehicle, way; CONCEPTS 6,660,770

channel [v] *direct, guide* carry, conduct, convey, funnel, pipe, route, send, siphon, traject, transmit, transport; CONCEPTS 187,217

chant [n] *chorus of song* carol, croon, hymn, incantation, intonation, lilt, melody, psalm, shout, singing, song, trill, tune, warble; CONCEPTS 263

chant [v] *sing simple song or song part* cantillate, carol, chorus, croon, descant, doxologize, drone, intone, recite, shout, tune, vocalize, warble; CONCEPTS 65,77

chaos [n] *utter confusion* anarchy, ataxia, bedlam, clutter, disarray, discord, disorder, disorganization, entropy, free-for-all*, holy mess*, lawlessness, misrule, mix-up, mobocracy, muddle, pandemonium, rat's nest*, snarl, topsy-turviness*, tumult, turmoil, unruliness; CONCEPTS 230,674 —*Ant.* calm, harmony, normality, order, organization, quiet, system

chaotic [adj] *utterly confused* anarchic, deranged, disordered, disorganized, every which way*, harum-scarum*, helter-skelter*, lawless, purposeless, rampageous, riotous, topsy-turvy*, tumultuous, turbid, turbulent, uncontrolled; CONCEPT 548 —*Ant.* calm, harmonized, normal, ordered, organized, quiet, systematic

chaperon [n] *person who accompanies for supervision* alarm clock*, babysitter*, bird dog*, companion, escort; CONCEPT 423

chaperon [v] *accompany for supervision* attend, carry, conduct, consort with, convoy, escort, guide, oversee, protect, safeguard, shepherd, supervise, watch over; CONCEPTS 114,714

chaplain [n] *minister in church* cleric, member of clergy, pastor, preacher, priest, rabbi, turnaround collar*; CONCEPT 361

chapter [n] *section of book or group of items* affiliate, branch, clause, division, episode, member, offshoot, part, period, phase, stage, topic, unit, wing; CONCEPTS 270,382,832

char [v] *scorch, sear* burn, carbonize, cauterize, singe; CONCEPT 249

character [n1] *individuality* appearance, aspect, attribute, badge, bent, caliber, cast, complex, complexion, constitution, crasis, disposition, emotions, estimation, ethos, frame, frame of mind, genius, grain, habit, humor, kind, makeup, mettle, mood, morale, mystique, nature, personality, quality, record, reputation, repute, sense, set, shape, singularity, sort, specialty, spirit, standing, streak, style, temper, temperament, tone, trait, turn, type, vein; CONCEPT 411

character [n2] *integrity* courage, fame, honor, intelligence, mind, name, place, position, rank, rectitude, rep, report, reputation, repute, standing, station, status, uprightness; CONCEPT 668

character [n3] *odd person* card*, case*, clown, crank*, customer*, duck*, eccentric, figure, freak, nut, oddball, oddity, original*, personage, personality, queer, spook*, wack*, weirdo, zombie*; CONCEPTS 412,423

character [n4] *written symbol* cipher, device, emblem, figure, hieroglyph, letter, logo, mark, monogram, number, numeral, rune, sign, type; CONCEPT 284

character [n5] *portrayal of another* impersonation, part, personification, role; CONCEPT 263

characteristic [adj] *typical; distinguishing* appropriate, diagnostic, differentiating, discriminating, discriminative, distinctive, distinguishing, emblematic, especial, essential, exclusive, fixed, idiosyncratic, inborn, inbred, indicative, individual, individualistic, individualizing, ingrained, inherent, innate, local, marked, native, normal, original, particular, peculiar, personal, private, proper, regular, representative, singular, special, specific, symbolic, symptomatic, unique; CONCEPTS 542,547,550 —*Ant.* abnormal, uncharacteristic, untypical

characteristic [n] *typical feature, trait* affection, aspect, attribute, badge, bag, bearing, bent, caliber, cast, complexion, component, differentia, disposition, distinction, earmark, endowment, essence, essential, faculty, flavor, frame, idiosyncrasy, inclination, individuality, lineament, mannerism, mark, mood, nature, originality, particularity, peculiarity, personality, point, property, quality, singularity, specialty, streak, stripe, style, symptom, temperament, tendency, thing, thumbprint, tinge, tone, trademark, turn, virtue; CONCEPT *411* —*Ant.* abnormality

characterize [v] *typify, distinguish* belong to, brand, button down*, constitute, define, delineate, describe, designate, differentiate, discriminate, feature, identify, indicate, individualize, individuate, inform, make up, mark, outline, peculiarize, peg, personalize, pigeonhole*, portray, represent, signalize, singularize, stamp, style, symbolize, tab, typecast; CONCEPT *644*

charade [n] *pretense* deception, disguise, fake, farce, make-believe, mimicry, pageant, pantomime, parody, pretension, pretentiousness, put-on, travesty, trick; CONCEPT *59*

charge [n1] *accusation* allegation, beef*, complaint, gripe, imputation, indictment, plaint, stink*; CONCEPTS *44,317* —*Ant.* exculpation, exoneration, freeing

charge [n2] *attack* assault, blitz, blitzkrieg, invasion, mugging, onset, onslaught, outbreak, push, rush, sortie; CONCEPT *86* —*Ant.* retreat

charge [n3] *burden* care, commitment, committal, concern, custody, deadweight, duty, millstone, must, need, obligation, office, onus, ought, responsibility, right, safekeeping, task, tax, trust, ward, weight; CONCEPTS *532,709*

charge [n4] *price asked for something* amount, bad news*, bite, cost, damage, expenditure, expense, nick, outlay, payment, price, price tag, rate, squeeze, tab, tariff, tick; CONCEPT *329*

charge [n5] *command* behest, bidding, dictate, direction, exhortation, injunction, instruction, mandate, order, precept, word; CONCEPTS *53,274*

charge [n6] *supervisory responsibility* care, conduct, custody, handling, intendance, management, oversight, running, superintendence, superintendency, supervision, ward; CONCEPT *117*

charge [v1] *accuse* arraign, blame, blow the whistle on*, censure, criminate, drag into court*, finger*, hang something on*, impeach, impugn, impute, incriminate, inculpate, indict, involve, peg, point the finger at*, reprehend, reproach, tax, turn on, whistle-blow*; CONCEPTS *44,317* —*Ant.* exculpate, exonerate, free

charge [v2] *attack* assail, assault, blindside, bolt, buck, bushwhack*, chase, dash, invade, jump on, lunge, mug, rush, smash, stampede, storm, tear; CONCEPT *86* —*Ant.* retreat

charge [v3] *load, tax* afflict, burden, choke, clog, commit, cram, crowd, cumber, encumber, entrust, fill, heap, impregnate, instill, lade, pack, penetrate, permeate, pervade, pile, ram, saddle, saturate, suffuse, transfuse, weigh; CONCEPTS *107,156,740*

charge [v4] *order something done* adjure, ask, bid, command, direct, enjoin, entrust, exhort,

instruct, request, require, solicit, tell, warn; CONCEPTS *53,78*

charge [v5] *ask a price* demand, fix price at, impose, levy, price, require, sell for; CONCEPTS *330,345* —*Ant.* pay

charge [v6] *pay with credit card* book, buy on credit, chalk up, cuff, debit, encumber, go into hock*, incur debt, nick*, paste*, put on account, put on one's card, put on the cuff, put on the tab, receive credit, run up; CONCEPTS *327,330* —*Ant.* pay by check, pay cash

charisma [n] *great personal charm* allure, animal magnetism*, appeal, dazzle, drawing power, fascination, flash, glamour, it*, magnetism, pizzazz*, something*, star quality, witchcraft, witchery; CONCEPT *411*

charismatic [adj] *charming* alluring, appealing, hypnotic, larger than life*, magnetic, mesmerizing, poised; CONCEPTS *529,537*

charitable [adj1] *giving, generous* accommodating, all heart, altruistic, beneficent, benevolent, benign, big*, bighearted*, bountiful, eleemosynary, good, helpful, humane, humanitarian, kind, kindly, lavish, liberal, obliging, philanthropic, sympathetic; CONCEPTS *334,542* —*Ant.* inhumane, malevolent, mean, uncharitable, unkind, unsympathetic

charitable [adj2] *kind, lenient* all heart*, benevolent, big*, bighearted*, broad-minded, clement, considerate, easy, favorable, forbearing, forgiving, gracious, humane, indulgent, kindly, lenient, magnanimous, merciful, sympathetic, thoughtful, tolerant, understanding; CONCEPT *404* —*Ant.* hard, harsh, inhumane, mean, rough, severe, tough

charity [n1] *generosity, gift* alms, alms-giving, assistance, benefaction, beneficence, contribution, dole, donation, endowment, fund, gifting, hand*, hand-out, helping hand*, largesse, oblation, offering, philanthropy, relief, write-off; CONCEPTS *337,657* —*Ant.* stealing, taking

charity [n2] *kindness, compassion* affection, agape, altruism, amity, attachment, benevolence, benignity, bountifulness, bounty, caritas, clemency, fellow feeling, generosity, goodness, goodwill, grace, humaneness, humanity, indulgence, kindliness, lenity, love, magnanimity, mercy, tenderheartedness; CONCEPTS *32,411* —*Ant.* malevolence, uncharitableness, unkindness

charlatan [n] *swindler* cheat, con, con artist, fake, fraud, imposter, mountebank, phony, pretender, quack, rip-off artist*, sham; CONCEPTS *260,412*

charm [n1] *enchantment, allure* agreeableness, allurement, appeal, attraction, attractiveness, beauty, bewitchery, charisma, chemistry, conjuration, delightfulness, desirability, fascination, glamour, grace, it*, lure, magic, magnetism, pizzazz*, something*, sorcery, spell, star quality, witchery; CONCEPTS *411,673* —*Ant.* repulsion

charm [n2] *talisman* amulet, fetish, good-luck piece, juju, lucky piece, madstone, mascot, phylactery, rabbit's foot, trinket, zemi; CONCEPTS *284,446*

charm [v] *enchant* allure, attract, beguile, bewitch, cajole, captivate, delight, draw, enamor, enrapture, ensorcell, enthrall, entrance, fascinate, grab, hex, hypnotize, inveigle, kill*, knock

ch
ch

dead*, knock out*, magnetize, mesmerize, please, possess, put under a spell*, send*, slay*, spell*, sweep off feet*, take*, tickle, tickle pink*, transport, turn on*, vamp, voodoo, wile, win, win over, wow*; CONCEPTS 7,22 —*Ant.* displease, irritate, offend, repel, repulse, turn off

charming [adj] *captivating* absorbing, alluring, amiable, appealing, attractive, bewitching, charismatic, choice, cute, dainty, delectable, delicate, delightful, desirable, electrifying, elegant, enamoring, engaging, engrossing, enthralling, entrancing, eye-catching, fascinating, fetching, glamorous, graceful, infatuating, inviting, irresistible, likable, lovable, lovely, magnetizing, nice, pleasant, pleasing, provocative, rapturous, ravishing, seducing, seductive, sweet, tantalizing, tempting, titillating, winning, winsome; CONCEPT 404 —*Ant.* frightening, irritating, offensive, repellent, repulsing, repulsive, terrifying

chart [n] *map, plan* blueprint, diagram, graph, outline, plat, plot, rough draft, scheme, sketch, table, tabulation; CONCEPTS 625,660

chart [v] *plan, map out* arrange, block out, blueprint, cast, delineate, design, devise, draft, graph, lay out, outline, plot, project, shape, sketch; CONCEPTS 36,174

charter [n] *treaty, agreement* allotment, bond, code, concession, constitution, contract, conveyance, deed, document, endowment, franchise, grant, indenture, license, pact, patent, permit, prerogative, privilege, right, settlement; CONCEPTS 684,685

charter [v] *reserve, commission* allow, authorize, borrow, contract, employ, engage, hire, lease, let, license, permit, rent, sanction; CONCEPTS 48,50,88,89 —*Ant.* cancel

chary [adj] *careful, cautious* cagey, calculating, canny, circumspect, considerate, constrained, discreet, economical, fastidious, frugal, gingerly, guarded, heedful, hesitant, inhibited, leery, loath, miserly, particular, prudent, reluctant, restrained, safe, scrupulous, sparing, stingy, suspicious, thrifty, uneasy, wary, watchful; CONCEPTS 401,587 —*Ant.* careless, hasty, heedless, incautious, rash, uncareful, willing

chase [n] *pursuit* hunt, hunting, quest, race, venery; CONCEPT 207 —*Ant.* escape, retreat

chase [v] *run after, pursue* bird-dog*, charge, chivy, course, drive, drive away, expel, follow, go after, hound, hunt, run down, rush, seek, shag*, speed, take off after*, tear, track, track down, trail; CONCEPT 207 —*Ant.* escape, retreat, run away

chasm [n] *gap, abyss* abysm, alienation, arroyo, blank, breach, cavity, cleavage, cleft, clough, clove, crater, crevasse, fissure, flume, gorge, gulch, gulf, hiatus, hole, hollow, omission, opening, oversight, penetration, ravine, rent, rift, schism, skip, split, void, yawn; CONCEPT 513 —*Ant.* closure, junction, juncture

chaste [adj] *pure, incorrupt* austere, celibate, clean, continent, controlled, decent, decorous, elegant, immaculate, impotent, inexperienced, innocent, intemerate, modest, monogamous, moral, neat, platonic, proper, prudish, quiet, refined, restrained, simple, spotless, stainless, subdued, unaffected, unblemished, uncontaminated, undefiled, unstained, unsullied, unwed,

vestal, virginal, virtuous, wholesome; CONCEPTS 372,404 —*Ant.* corrupt, defiled, dirty, lewd, unchaste, wanton

chasten [v] *correct, humiliate* abase, admonish, afflict, berate, call down, castigate, chastise, chide, cow, curb, discipline, exprobate, fulminate against, have on the carpet*, humble, objurgate, penalize, punish, rake over the coals*, rebuke, reprehend, repress, reprimand, reproach, reprove, restrain, scold, scourge, soften, subdue, take to task, tame, tonguelash*, try, upbraid; CONCEPTS 52,122 —*Ant.* aid, animate, assist, boost, cheer, comfort, embolden, encourage, help, honor, uplift

chastise [v] *scold, discipline* baste, beat, berate, castigate, censure, chasten, chew out*, climb all over*, correct, ferule*, flog*, lash*, lay into*, lean on*, pummel, punish, ream, scourge, skelp, slap down*, spank, thrash, upbraid, whip; CONCEPTS 52,122 —*Ant.* cheer, comfort, compliment, encourage, forgive, inspirit, promote

chastity [n] *celibacy, purity* abstemiousness, abstinence, chasteness, cleanness, continence, decency, demureness, devotion, honor, immaculacy, innocence, integrity, modesty, monogamy, morality, naiveté, restraint, singleness, sinlessness, spotlessness, temperance, uprightness, virginity, virtue; CONCEPT 633 —*Ant.* dirtiness, fornication

chat [n] *talk, often short* babble, bull session, chatter, conversation, converse, gab*, gas*, gossip, heart-to-heart*, hot air*, jabber*, palaver, prattle*, rap*, rap session*, tête-à-tête, visit, yak*; CONCEPT 278 —*Ant.* quiet, silence

chat [v] *talk, gossip* babble, blab*, burble, cackle, chatter, chew the fat*, chew the rag*, converse, gab*, go on*, jaw*, prate, prattle*, run on*, shoot the breeze*, yap*; CONCEPT 266 —*Ant.* be quiet

chat room [n] *interaction via computer* data communication channel, live discussion, net event, room; CONCEPTS 349,770

chatter [n] *constant or rapid talk* babble, blather, chat, chitchat, gas*, gossip, jabber*, palaver, prattle*, twaddle, yakking*; CONCEPTS 266,278 —*Ant.* drawl

chatter [v] *speak fast and non-stop* babble, blab*, blather, cackle, chat, chitchat, clack, gab*, gabble, gas*, gibber, go on and on, gossip, jabber, jaw*, natter, palaver, prate, prattle*, tattle, twaddle, twiddle, yak*; CONCEPT 266 —*Ant.* drawl

chatty [adj] *talkative* colloquial, communicative, conversational, familiar, friendly, gabby, garrulous, gossipy, informal, intimate, looselipped, loquacious, multieloquent, spontaneous, talky; CONCEPT 267 —*Ant.* quiet, silent, untalkative

chauvinism [n] *extreme devotion to a belief or nation* bellicism, ethnocentricity, fanatical patriotism, fanaticism, jingoism, narrowness, nationalism, zealotry; CONCEPT 689 —*Ant.* unbias

cheap [adj] *inexpensive* at a bargain, bargain, bargain-basement*, bargain-counter, bought for a song*, budget, buy, cheapo*, competitive, cost next to nothing*, cut-price, cut-rate, depreciated, dime a dozen*, easy on the pocketbook*, economical, half-priced, irregular, low-cost, lowered, low-priced, low tariff, marked down, moderate, nominal, on sale, popularly priced, real buy*, reasonable, reduced, sale, slashed, standard, steal, uncostly, undear, utility, worth the money*; CONCEPT 334 —*Ant.* costly, dear, expensive

cheap [adj2] *inferior, low in quality* bad, base, bogus, catchpenny, cheesy, common, commonplace, crappy*, cruddy, dud, flashy, garbage, garish, glitzy*, junky*, lousy, mangy, mean, mediocre, meretricious, no bargain*, no good, ordinary, paltry, poor, ratty, raunchy, rinkydink*, rotten, rubbishy, scroungy, second-rate, shoddy, sleazy, small-time*, tatty, tawdry, terrible, trashy, trumpery, two-bit, valueless, white elephant*, worthless; CONCEPT 589 —*Ant.* excellent, noble, precious, priceless, superior, valuable, worthy

cheap [adj3] *low, vulgar* abject, base, beggarly, contemptible, despicable, dirty, dishonest, mean, pitiable, scurvy, shabby, sordid, sorry, tawdry, vile; CONCEPT 542 —*Ant.* sophisticated, superior, upper

cheap [adj4] *concerned with saving money* mean, mingy, miserly, penny-pinching, stingy, thrifty, tight*, tight-wad*; CONCEPT 332

cheapen [v] *diminish worth* abase, beat down, belittle, corrupt, damage, debase, decline, decry, degrade, demean, denigrate, depreciate, derogate, devalue, discredit, disparage, downgrade, drop, fall, lose value, lower, mar, mark down, minimize, reduce, render worthless, ruin, spoil, undervalue, write off; CONCEPT 240 —*Ant.* appreciate, enhance, increase, raise, upgrade

cheat [n1] *person who fools others* bluff, charlatan, chiseler, con artist, confidence operator, conniver, cozener, crook, deceiver, decoy, defrauder, dodger, double-crosser*, double-dealer*, enticer, fake, hypocrite, impostor, inveigler, jockey, masquerader, pretender, quack, rascal, scammer*, shark, sharper, shyster, swindler, trickster; CONCEPT 412

cheat [n2] *trick* artifice, baloney, bamboozlement*, bill of goods*, bunco, chicanery, con, con game, cover up, cozening, deceit, deception, dirty pool*, dirty trick*, dodge, double-dealing*, fake, fast one, fast shuffle*, fix, flimflam, frame, fraud, gyp, hanky-panky*, hoax, hoaxing, humbug, hustle, imposture, jazz, jive, plant, put-on, racket, rip-off, run around, scam, sell, shady deal, sham, shell game, snow job*, spoof, sting, stunt, swindle, trickery, whitewash, wrong; CONCEPT 59

cheat [v1] *defraud, fool* bamboozle*, beat, beguile, bilk, bleed, bunco, burn, caboodle, chisel, con, cozen, crib, cross, deceive, defraud, delude, diddle*, do*, do a number on*, double-cross, double-deal, dupe, fast talk, finagle, fleece, flimflam, fudge*, give bum steer*, gouge, gyp*, hoodwink, hose, jerk around, milk, mislead, pull one's leg*, ream*, rip off*, rook*, rope in*, sandbag, scam, screw, shaft, short, shuck, skin, snow, stiff, sucker, swindle, take, take for a ride*, take in, take out, trick, trim, two-time, victimize; CONCEPTS 59,139,192

cheat [v2] *frustrate, thwart* baffle, check, defeat, deprive, foil, prevent; CONCEPT 121

check [n1] *inspection, examination* analysis, audit, checkup, control, inquiry, investigation,

poll, rein, research, review, scrutiny, test; CONCEPT 103

check [n2] *restraint, hindrance* blow, constraint, control, curb, damper, disappointment, frustration, grunt, harness, holdup, impediment, inhibition, limitation, obstruction, rebuff, rejection, restrainer, reversal, reverse, setback, stoppage, trouble; CONCEPTS 121,130,230 —*Ant.* aid, allowance, assistance, help, indulgence, liberation, permission

check [n3] *symbol for ticking off* cross, dot, line, mark, score, sign, stroke, tick, X*; CONCEPT 284

check [n4] *pattern of squares* checkerboard, patchwork, plaid, quilt, tartan; CONCEPT 436

check [v1] *inspect, examine* analyze, ascertain, audit, balance account, candle, case, compare, confirm, correct, count, enquire about, eyeball*, find out, frisk, go through, investigate, keep account, look at, look over, look see*, make sure, monitor, note, overlook, probe, prove, quiz, review, scout out, scrutinize, study, take stock, tell, test, try, verify; CONCEPTS 24,103

check [v2] *hinder, restrain* arrest, baffle, bar, bit, bottleneck*, bridle, checkmate, choke, circumvent, constrain, control, counteract, curb, cut short, delay, discourage, foil, frustrate, halt, harness, hold, hold back, hold down, hold in, impede, inhibit, interrupt, keep back, limit, moderate, neutralize, nip in the bud*, obstruct, obviate, pause, play for time, preclude, prevent, rebuff, reduce, rein in, repress, repulse, retard, slacken pace, slow down, snub, squelch, stay, stop, suppress, tame, terminate, thwart, withhold; CONCEPTS 121,130 —*Ant.* allow, assist, expedite, help, indulge, liberate, permit

checkered [adj] *patterned* checky, diversified, motley, mutable, patchwork, plaid, quilted, spotted, variegated; CONCEPT 486

cheek [n1] *side of human face* chop*, choppers*, gill, jowl; CONCEPT 418

cheek [n2] *audacity, boldness* brashness, brass*, brazenness, chutzpah*, confidence, disrespect, effrontery, gall, impertinence, impudence, insolence, lip*, nerve*, presumption, rudeness, sauce*, temerity; CONCEPT 633 —*Ant.* humbleness, meekness, timidity

cheeky [adj] *impudent* audacious, ballsy*, bold, brash, brazen, disrespectful, forward, impertinent, insolent, insulting, nervy, saucy; CONCEPTS 401,404

cheep [v] *vocalize as a bird* chip, chipper, chirp, chirrup, peep, tweedle, tweet, twitter; CONCEPT 64

cheer [n1] *happiness* animation, buoyancy, cheerfulness, cheeriness, comfort, delight, encouragement, exuberance, gaiety, geniality, gladness, glee, good cheer, hilarity, hopefulness, jauntiness, jocundity, joy, joyousness, lightheartedness, liveliness, merriment, merrymaking, mirth, optimism, solace; CONCEPT 410 —*Ant.* depression, gloom, gravity, melancholy, sadness, seriousness, unhappiness

cheer [n2] *applause, supportive yell* acclamation, approbation, approval, cry, encouragement, hurrah, hurray, huzzah, ovation, plaudits, roar, shout; CONCEPTS 69,77 —*Ant.* boo

cheer [v1] *make someone feel happier* animate, brace up, brighten, buck up*, buoy, comfort, console, elate, elevate, embolden, encourage, enliven, exhilarate, give a lift*, gladden, hearten, help, incite, inspirit, let the sun shine in*, perk up, pick up, put on cloud nine*, put on top of the world*, snap out of it*, solace, steel, strengthen, uplift, upraise, warm; CONCEPTS 7,22 —*Ant.* bring down, depress, dishearten, make unhappy

cheer [*v2*] *encourage in activity* acclaim, applaud, clap, hail, hurrah, plug*, rise to, root, salute, sound off for, support, yell; CONCEPT 69 —*Ant.* discourage, dishearten, dissuade

cheerful [*adj*] *happy* airy, animated, blithe, bouncy, bright, bucked, buoyant, cheery, chipper, chirpy, contented, effervescent, enlivening, enthusiastic, full of pep, gay, glad, gladsome, good-humored, good-natured, hearty, high, hilarious, hopeful, in good spirits, in high spirits, jaunty, jocund, jolly, joyful, lighthearted, lively, merry, optimistic, peppy, perky, pleasant, roseate, rosy, sanguine, snappy, sparkling, sprightly, sunny, sunny side up*, up*, upbeat, vivacious, winsome, zappy, zingy, zippy; CONCEPTS 403,404 —*Ant.* cheerless, depressed, gloomy, grave, heavy, melancholy, sad, serious, unhappy

cheering [*adj*] *encouraging* auspicious, bright, comforting, heartening, hopeful, promising, propitious; CONCEPT 529 —*Ant.* dejecting, depressing, discouraging, disheartening

cheerless [*adj*] *depressing, unhappy* austere, black, bleak, blue, comfortless, dark, dejected, dejecting, depressed, desolate, despondent, disconsolate, dismal, dispiriting, dolorous, drab, draggy, drearisome, dreary, dull, forlorn, funereal, gloomy, grim, in the dumps*, jarring, joyless, melancholy, miserable, mopey, mournful, oppressive, sad, somber, sorrowful, sullen, tenebrific, uncomfortable, wintry, woebegone, woeful; CONCEPT 403 —*Ant.* bright, cheerful, happy, uplifting

chef [*n*] *cook* chief cook and bottle washer*, cuisinier, culinary artist, gourmet chef, hash slinger*, sous chef; CONCEPT 348

chemical [*adj*] *concerned with atom and molecule change* actinic, alchemical, enzymatic, synthesized, synthetic, synthetical; CONCEPT 536

cherish [*v*] *care about deeply* admire, adore, appreciate, apprize, care for, clasp, cleave to, cling to, coddle, comfort, cosset, cultivate, defend, dote on, embrace, encourage, enshrine, entertain, fancy, fondle, foster, guard, harbor, hold dear, hold in high esteem, honor, hug, idolize, like, love, nourish, nurse, nurture, pet, preserve, prize, revere, reverence, safeguard, shelter, shield, support, sustain, treasure, value, venerate, worship; CONCEPT 32 —*Ant.* abandon, denounce, forsake, not care, renounce

cherry [*adj*] *bright red color* blooming, blushing, bright red, cerise, claret, crimson, dark red, erubescent, incarnadine, reddish, rosy, rubescent, rubicund, ruddy; CONCEPT 618

cherry-picker [*n*] *truck with raisable boom* boom, cable truck, telephone truck, utility truck; CONCEPT 505

chest [*n1*] *box for storage* bin, bureau, cabinet, carton, case, casket, chiffonier, coffer, commode, crate, exchequer, pyxis, receptacle, reliquary, strongbox, treasury, trunk; CONCEPT 494

chest [*n2*] *upper front of body* bosom, breast,

bust, heart, mammary glands, peritoneum, pulmonary cavity, rib cage, ribs, thorax, upper trunk; CONCEPT 392 —*Ant.* back

chew [*v1*] *grind with teeth* bite, champ, chaw, chomp, crunch, dispatch, feast upon, gnaw, gulp, gum, manducate, masticate, munch, nibble, rend, ruminate, scrunch; CONCEPTS 169,185

chew [*v2*] *think about deeply* consider, deliberate, meditate, mull, mull over, muse on, ponder, reflect upon, ruminate, weigh; CONCEPT 24 —*Ant.* ignore

chew out [*v*] *scold* bawl out, carpet*, criticize, dress down, jaw, revile, tell off, tongue-lash*, vituperate, wig, yell at; CONCEPT 52 —*Ant.* compliment, laud, praise

chic [*adj*] *fashionable* chichi*, clean*, current, dap*, dapper, dashing, elegant, exclusive, faddish, last word*, latest thing*, mod*, modern, modish, natty, sharp, smart, stylish, swank, trendy, voguish, with-it*; CONCEPT 589 —*Ant.* dull, old-fashioned, out-moded, unfashionable

chicanery [*n*] *deception, trickery* artifice, cheating, chicane, deviousness, dishonesty, dodge, double-crossing, double-dealing*, duplicity, feint, fourberie, fraud, furtiveness, gambit, hanky-panky*, intrigue, machination, maneuver, plot, ploy, ruse, sharp practice, skullduggery, sophistry, stratagem, subterfuge, surreptitiousness, underhandedness, wiles; CONCEPTS 59,660 —*Ant.* forthrightness, honesty, truthfulness

chicken [*n1*] *person afraid to try something* coward, craven, dastard, funk, poltroon, quitter, recreant, scaredy cat*, yellow belly*; CONCEPT 423

chicken [*n2*] *farm fowl* banty, barnyard fowl, biddy, capon, chick, cock, cock-a-doodle-do*, cockalorum, cockerel, gump*, heeler, hen, poultry, pullet, rooster; CONCEPTS 394,395

chicken feed [*n*] *small amount of money* coins, nickles and dimes*, paltry sum, peanuts*, pin money*, pocket money, small change, small potatoes*, spending money; CONCEPT 340

chicken out [*v*] *back out* avoid, back down, back pedal*, beg off*, blow it off*, cancel, chicken out*, cop out*, get cold feet*, give up, go back on, recant, renege, scrap, scratch, shy from, surrender, throw in the towel*, turn yellow*, weasel out, welsh, wiggle out, withdraw, worm out*; CONCEPTS 50,88,121,266,697

chide [*v*] *criticize, lecture* admonish, berate, blame, call down*, call on the carpet*, castigate, censure, check, condemn, exprobate, find fault, flay, give a hard time*, lesson, monish, rate, rebuke, reprehend, reprimand, reproach, reprove, scold, slap on the wrist*, speak to, take down*, take down a peg*, talk to, tell off, tick off*, upbraid; CONCEPT 52 —*Ant.* compliment, laud, praise

chief [*adj*] *most important, essential* arch, capital, cardinal, central, champion, consequential, controlling, crucial, effective, especial, first, foremost, grand, head, highest, key, leading, main, major, momentous, number one*, outstanding, paramount, potent, predominant, preeminent, premier, primal, primary, prime, principal, ruling, significant, star, stellar, superior, supreme, telling, uppermost, vital, weighty; CONCEPTS 568,574,829 —*Ant.* inessential, minor, secondary, subordinate, unimportant, unnecessary

chief [n] *person in charge* big cheese*, big gun*, big wheel*, bigwig*, boss, captain, chieftain, commander, dictator, director, foreperson, general, governor, head, head honcho*, head person*, honcho*, key player*, leader, manager, monarch, overlord, overseer, president, principal, proprietor, ringleader, ruler, sovereign, superintendent, supervisor, suzerain, top brass*, top cat*; CONCEPTS 347,376 —*Ant.* apprentice, employee, servant, subordinate, underling, worker

chiefly [adv] *most importantly* above all, especially, essentially, in general, in the first place, in the main, largely, mainly, mostly, on the whole, overall, predominantly, primarily, principally, usually; CONCEPTS 567,772 —*Ant.* unimportantly

child [n] *very young person* adolescent, anklebiter*, babe, baby, bairn, bambino, brat, cherub, chick, cub, descendant, dickens*, imp, infant, innocent, issue, juvenile, kid, kiddie*, lamb*, little angel*, little darling*, little doll*, little one, minor, mite, moppet, neonate, nestling, newborn, nipper, nursling, offspring, preteen, progeny, pubescent, shaver, small fry*, sprout, squirt, stripling, suckling, tadpole, teen, teenager, teenybopper*, toddler, tot, tyke, urchin*, whippersnapper*, young one, youngster, youth; CONCEPTS 414,424 —*Ant.* adult

childbirth [n] *giving birth* accouchement, bearing children, blessed event*, childbed, confinement, delivering, delivery, labor, lying-in, nativity, parturience, parturition, procreation, producing, propagation, reproduction, travail, visit from the stork*; CONCEPTS 302,373

childhood [n] *period of being young* adolescence, babyhood, cradle, immaturity, infancy, juniority, juvenility, minority, nonage, nursery, puberty, pupilage, schooldays, teens, tender age, youth; CONCEPTS 816,817 —*Ant.* adulthood

childish [adj] *immature, silly* adolescent, baby, babyish, callow, childlike, foolish, frivolous, green, infantile, infantine, innocent, jejune, juvenile, kid stuff*, naive, puerile, unsophisticated, young, youthful; CONCEPTS 401,402,424, 578,797 —*Ant.* adult, mature, sensible, serious, wise

childlike [adj] *innocent, naive* artless, childish, credulous, guileless, immature, ingenuous, natural, simple, spontaneous, trustful, trusting, unaffected, unfeigned; CONCEPT 404 —*Ant.* complicated, untrusting

chill [adj1] *cold, raw* arctic, biting, bleak, brisk, chilly, cool, freezing, frigid, frosty, gelid, glacial, icy, nippy, sharp, wintry; CONCEPT 605 —*Ant.* hot, warm

chill [adj2] *unfriendly, aloof* cool, depressing, discouraging, dismal, dispiriting, distant, emotionless, formal, frigid, glacial, hateful, hostile, icy, indifferent, reserved, solitary, standoffish, stony, uncompanionable, unemotional, ungenial, unhappy, unresponsive, unwelcoming, wintry, withdrawn; CONCEPTS 401,404 —*Ant.* friendly, responsive, sympathetic, warm

chill [n] *cold conditions* bite, coldness, coolness, crispness, frigidity, gelidity, iciness, nip, rawness, rigor, sharpness; CONCEPT 524 —*Ant.* heat, warmth

chill [v1] *make cold* air-condition, congeal, cool,

freeze, frost, ice, refrigerate; CONCEPTS 255,521 —*Ant.* heat, warm

chill [v2] *discourage* cloud, dampen, dash, deject, demoralize, depress, dishearten, dismay, disparage, dispirit; CONCEPTS 7,19 —*Ant.* encourage, hearten, incite, inspirit

chilly [adj1] *cold* arctic, biting, blowy, breezy, brisk, cool, crisp, drafty, freezing, fresh, frosty, glacial, hawkish, icebox, icy, nippy, penetrating, sharp, snappy, wintry; CONCEPT 605 —*Ant.* hot, tropical, warm

chilly [adj2] *unfriendly, aloof* cold, frigid, hostile, unfriendly, unresponsive, unsympathetic, unwelcoming; CONCEPT 404 —*Ant.* friendly, responsive, sympathetic, warm, welcoming

chime [v] *ring, peal* bell, bong, boom, clang, dong, jingle, knell, sound, strike, tinkle, tintinnabulate, toll; CONCEPT 65

chimera [n] *dream, fantasy* bogy, bubble, delusion, fabrication, fancy, fata morgana, figment, fool's paradise*, hallucination, ignis fatuus, illusion, mirage, monster, monstrosity, pipe dream*, rainbow*, snare, specter, virtual reality; CONCEPT 529 —*Ant.* reality, truth

chimney [n] *smokestack for building* chase, chimney pot, chimney stack, fireplace, flue, funnel, furnace, hearth, pipe, smokeshaft, stack, vent, ventilator; CONCEPT 440

chin [n] *area under mouth* button, jaw, jawbone, mandible, mentum, point; CONCEPT 399

china [n] *dishes, often valuable* ceramics, crockery, porcelain, pottery, service, stoneware, tableware, ware; CONCEPT 493

chink [n] *opening* aperture, cleft, crack, crevice, cut, fissure, gap, hole, rift, slit, slot, space; CONCEPT 513

chintzy [adj] *cheap-looking* cheap, frowzy, schlocky*, shabby, sleazy, tacky; CONCEPT 485

chip [n] *shard, flaw* dent, flake, fragment, gobbet, nick, notch, paring, part, scrap, scratch, shaving, slice, sliver, wafer, wedge; CONCEPTS 580,831

chip [v] *knock a piece out of* break, chisel, chop, clip, crack, crack off, crumble, cut away, cut off, damage, flake, fragment, gash, hack, hackle, hew, incise, nick, notch, shape, shear, slash, slice, sliver, snick, snip, splinter, split, whack, whittle; CONCEPTS 137,189,246,250

chip in [v] *contribute* ante up*, break in*, chime in*, come through*, conate, go Dutch*, interpose, interrupt, pay, pitch in, subscribe; CONCEPT 110 —*Ant.* pilfer, take, take away

chipper [adj] *happy* alert, animate, animated, bright, brisk, gay, in good spirits, keen, lively, spirited, sprightly, vivacious; CONCEPT 403 —*Ant.* unhappy

chips [n] *substitute for money; money* coin, currency, markers, play money, scratch; CONCEPT 340

chirp [v] *peep, cheep* call, chip, chipper, chirrup, lilt, pipe, purl, quaver, roll, sing, sound, trill, tweedle, tweet, twitter, warble; CONCEPT 64

chisel [n] *shaping tool* adze, blade, edge, gouge, knife; CONCEPTS 495,499

chisel [v] *cut, wear away* carve, hew, incise, roughcast, roughhew, sculpt, sculpture, shape; CONCEPTS 137,176,184

chivalrous [adj] *valiant* benevolent, big, bold, brave, considerate, courageous, courteous, courtly, gallant, gentlemanlike, great-hearted, heroic, high-minded, honorable, intrepid, lofty, magnanimous, manly, noble-minded, polite, quixotic, spirited, sublime, true, valorous; CONCEPT 401 —*Ant.* afraid, cowardly, fearful, frightened, humble, unchivalrous

chivalry [*n*] *valor, gallantry* courage, courtesy, courtliness, fairness, politeness, valiance; CONCEPT 633 —*Ant.* cowardice, fear, humbleness, humility

choice [*adj*] *best, superior* 10*, 24-karat*, A-1*, elect, elite, excellent, exceptional, exclusive, exquisite, fine, first-class, hand-picked, nice, popular, precious, preferential, preferred, prime, prize, rare, select, solid gold*, special, top-drawer*, uncommon, unusual, valuable, winner; CONCEPT 574 —*Ant.* inferior, poor, sad, worst

choice [*n*] *power to select; selection* alternative, appraisal, choosing, cull, cup of tea*, decision, determination, discretion, discrimination, distinction, druthers*, election, evaluation, extract, favorite, finding, free will, judgment, opportunity, option, pick, preference, rating, say, substitute, variety, verdict, volition, vote, weakness; CONCEPTS 41,376

choke [*v*] *smother, block* asphyxiate, bar, check, clog, close, congest, constrict, dam, die, drown, fill, gag, garrote, gasp, gibbet, kill, noose, obstruct, occlude, overpower, retard, squeeze, stifle, stop, stopper, strangle, strangulate, stuff, stunt, suffocate, suppress, throttle, wring; CONCEPTS 121,219 —*Ant.* release, unblock, unconstrict

choose [*v*] *pick, select* accept, adopt, appoint, call for, cast, commit oneself, co-opt, crave, cull, decide on, designate, desire, determine, discriminate between, draw lots, elect, embrace, espouse, excerpt, extract, fancy, favor, feel disposed to, finger, fix on, glean, judge, love, make choice, make decision, make up one's mind, name, opt for, predestine, prefer, see fit, separate, set aside, settle upon, sift out, single out, slot, sort, tab, tag, take, take up, tap, want, weigh, will, winnow, wish, wish for; CONCEPT 41

choosy [*adj*] *fussy, discriminating* dainty, eclectic, exacting, fastidious, finical, finicky, nice, overparticular, particular, persnickety*, picky, prissy, select, selective; CONCEPT 404 —*Ant.* undemanding, unfastidious, unfussy

chop [*v*] *cut up with tool* axe, cleave, clip, cube, dice, divide, fell, fragment, hack, hackle, hash, hew, lop, mangle, mince, sever, shear, slash, truncate, whack; CONCEPT 176

choppy [*adj*] *wavy* inclement, ripply, rough, uneven, violent, wild; CONCEPT 488 —*Ant.* calm, smooth

chore [*n*] *task* assignment, burden, devoir, duty, effort, errand, grind, housework, job, KP*, routine, scutwork, stint, trial, tribulation, workout; CONCEPT 362

chortle [*v*] *laugh gleefully* cackle, chuckle, crow, giggle, guffaw, hee-haw*, snicker, sniggle, snort, teehee*, titter; CONCEPT 77

chorus [*n1*] *group of singers* carolers, choir, chorale, choristers, ensemble, glee club, singing group, vocalists, voices; CONCEPT 294

chorus [*n2*] *refrain* bob, burden, chorale, main section, melody, motif, music, recurrent verse,

response, ritornelle, song, strain, theme, tune, undersong; CONCEPT 264

chorus [*n3*] *agreement* accord, concert, concord, consonance, harmony, tune, unison; CONCEPTS 673,684

chosen [*adj*] *preferred* called, conscript, elect, exclusive, got the nod*, named, pegged, pick, picked, popular, preferential, select, selected, tabbed; CONCEPTS 546,567,574 —*Ant.* ignored, inferior

christen [*v*] *named in religious rite* asperse, baptize, bless, call, dedicate, denominate, designate, dub, entitle, godparent, immerse, sprinkle, style, term, title; CONCEPTS 62,367

chronic [*adj*] *incessant, never-ending* abiding, ceaseless, confirmed, constant, continual, continuing, continuous, deep-rooted, deep-seated, enduring, ever-present, fixed, habitual, inborn, inbred, incurable, ineradicable, ingrained, inveterate, lasting, lifelong, lingering, long-lived, long-standing, obstinate, perennial, persistent, persisting, prolonged, protracted, recurrent, recurring, rooted, routine, settled, stubborn, sustained, tenacious, unabating, unmitigated, unyielding, usual; CONCEPTS 534,551,798 —*Ant.* curable, eradicable, intermittent, occasional, temporary

chronicle [*n*] *account, narrative* annals, archives, diary, history, journal, narration, prehistory, recital, record, recountal, register, report, story, version; CONCEPTS 271,282

chronicle [*v*] *report, recount* enter, narrate, record, register, relate, set down, tell; CONCEPTS 60,79 —*Ant.* hide, secret

chronological [*adj*] *in consecutive time order* archival, chronographic, chronologic, chronometric, chronometrical, chronoscopic, classified, dated, historical, horological, horometrical, in due course, in due time, in order, in sequence, junctural, ordered, progressive, sequent, sequential, tabulated, temporal; CONCEPTS 548,585

chubby [*adj*] *slightly fat* ample, bearish, big, butterball*, buxom, chunky, fatty, flabby, fleshy, full-figured, hefty, husky, pleasingly plump*, plump, plumpish, podgy, portly, pudgy, roly-poly*, rotund, round, stout, tubby, zaftig*; CONCEPTS 491,773 —*Ant.* skinny, slim, thin

chuck [*v*] *throw aside, throw away, throw out* abandon, can, cast, desert, discard, ditch, eighty-six*, eject, fire, fling, flip, forsake, give the heave ho*, heave, hurl, jettison, junk, launch, pitch, quit, reject, relinquish, renounce, scrap, shed, shy, sling, slough, toss; CONCEPTS 180,222 —*Ant.* keep

chuckle [*v*] *giggle* cackle, chortle, crow, exult, guffaw, hee-haw*, laugh, smile, snicker, snigger, sniggle, teehee*, titter; CONCEPT 77

chug [*v*] *drink quickly* chug-a-lug, down, drink in one draft; CONCEPT 169

chum [*n*] *friend* associate, bro*, buddy, co-mate, companion, comrade, crony, mate, pal, playmate, sis*; CONCEPT 423 —*Ant.* enemy

chummy [*adj*] *friendly* affectionate, buddy-buddy*, close, confidential, constant, cozy, familiar, intimate, pally*, palsy-walsy*, thick*; CONCEPTS 401,555 —*Ant.* unfriendly, unsociable

chunk [*n*] *mass, slab of something* block, clod,

ch
ci

dollop, glob, gob, hunk, lump, nugget, part, piece, portion, wad; CONCEPT 471

chunky [adj] *fat, plump* beefy, chubby, dumpy, heavyset, husky, rotund, scrub, squat, stocky, stout, stubby, thick-bodied, thickset; CONCEPTS 491,773 —*Ant.* skinny, slim, thin

church [n1] *religious institution, building* abbey, basilica, bethel, cathedral, chancel, chantry, chapel, fold, house of God, house of prayer, house of worship, Lord's house, minster, mission, mosque, oratory, parish, sacellum, sanctuary, shrine, synagogue, tabernacle, temple; CONCEPTS 368,449

church [n2] *religious belief, group* affiliation, body, chapter, communion, congregation, connection, creed, cult, denomination, doctrine, faction, faith, gathering, ism, order, persuasion, religion, schism, sect, society; CONCEPTS 369,689

churl [n] *rude and ill-bred, a boor; person overly concerned with saving money* beast, chuff, clodhopper*, miser, mucker*, niggard*, oaf, peasant, provincial, rustic, tightwad, yokel; CONCEPT 423

churlish [adj] *crude, boorish* base, blunt, brusque, cantankerous*, cloddish, clodhopping*, crabbed, crude, crusty, curt, cussed*, discourteous, dour, grouchy, gruff, grumpy, harsh, ill-tempered, impolite, loutish, lowbred, mean, miserly, morose, oafish, ornery*, rude, rustic, snippy*, sullen, surly, touchy*, ugly, uncivil, uncivilized, uncultured, unmannerly, unneighborly, unpolished, unsociable, vulgar; CONCEPT 404 —*Ant.* gentle, nice, pleasant, polite

churn [v] *mix up, beat* agitate, boil, bubble, convulse, ferment, foam, froth, jolt, moil, seethe, simmer, stir up, swirl, toss; CONCEPTS 147,170

chute [n] *ramp, slope* channel, course, fall, gutter, incline, rapid, runway, slide, trough; CONCEPTS 440,471

chutzpah [n] *fearlessness* arrogance, audacity, backbone*, balls*, boldness, brass, gall, nerve, spine*; CONCEPT 633

cinch [n] *easy accomplishment* breeze, cakewalk, child's play*, duck soup*, no sweat*, piece of cake*, snap; CONCEPT 693

cinder [n] *hot ash* clinker, ember, hot coal, soot; CONCEPT 260

cinema [n] *movie industry; movie arena* big screen*, bijou, cine, drive-in, film, flicks*, motion pictures, movie house, movie theater, moving pictures, nabes*, photoplay, pictures, picture show, playhouse, show, silver screen*; CONCEPTS 293,349

cipher [n] *zero; nothingness* blank, diddly squat*, goose egg*, insignificancy, nada*, naught, nil, nobody, nonentity, nothing, nought, nullity, squat, zilch, zip, zippo*, zot*; CONCEPTS 668,787

cipher [v] *figure out code* break, calculate, clear up, compute, count, decipher, estimate, figure, reckon, resolve, solve, unravel; CONCEPT 37 —*Ant.* code

circa [prep] *approximately* about, around, close on, in the region of, near, nearby, nigh, roughly; CONCEPT 820

circle [n1] *orb, loop, round figure* amphitheater, aureole, band, belt, bowl, bracelet, circlet, circuit, circumference, circus, cirque, coil, colure,

compass, cordon, corona, crown, cycle, disc, disk, ecliptic, enclosure, equator, full turn, globe, halo, hoop, horizon, lap, meridian, orbit, parallel of latitude, perimeter, periphery, record, revolution, ring, ringlet, round, sphere, stadium, tire, turn, vortex, wheel, wreath, zodiac; CONCEPT 436

circle [n2] *group of close friends, associates* assembly, bunch, cabal, camarilla, camp, clan, class, clique, club, companions, company, comrades, coterie, crew, cronies, crowd, crush, fraternity, gang, in-group, insiders, intimates, lot, Mafia, mob, outfit, party, posse, ring, school, set, society, sorority; CONCEPTS 387,417

circle [v] *go around, circumnavigate* begird, belt, cincture, circuit, circulate, circumduct, circumscribe, coil, compass, curve, embrace, encircle, enclose, encompass, ensphere, envelop, gird, girdle, gyrate, gyre, hem in, loop, mill around, pivot, revolve, ring, roll, rotate, round, spiral, surround, tour, wheel, whirl, wind about; CONCEPT 758

circuit [n] *revolution, track, boundary* ambit, area, bounds, circle, circling, circulation, circumference, circumnavigation, circumscription, circumvolution, compass, course, cycle, district, gyration, gyre, journey, lap, limit, line, orbit, perambulation, perimeter, periphery, range, region, round, route, tour, tract, turn, turning, twirl, way, wheel, whirl, wind, winding, zone; CONCEPTS 484,501,770

circuitous [adj] *going around, indirect* back road*, by way of, circular, collateral, complicated, devious, labyrinthine, long way*, long way around*, meandering, oblique, rambling, roundabout, tortuous, winding around; CONCEPTS 544,581 —*Ant.* direct, in line, straight

circular [adj] *going around* annular, circling, disklike, indirect, oblique, orbicular, round, rounded, spheroid; CONCEPT 486

circular [n] *handbill* advertisement, booklet, broadside, brochure, flyer, handout, insert, leaflet, literature, notice, pamphlet, poster, publication, throwaway*; CONCEPT 271

circulate [v1] *make known* bring out, broadcast, diffuse, disperse, disseminate, distribute, exchange, interview, issue, promulgate, propagate, publicize, publish, radiate, report, spread, strew, troll; CONCEPTS 60,138

circulate [v2] *flow* actuate, circle, fly about, get about, get around, go about, gyrate, mill around, mobilize, move around, radiate, revolve, rotate, set off, travel, wander; CONCEPT 147 —*Ant.* block

circulation [n1] *distribution* apportionment, currency, dissemination, spread, transmission; CONCEPTS 631,651

circulation [n2] *moving circularly* circling, circuit, circumvolution, current, flow, flowing, gyration, gyre, motion, revolution, rotation, round, turn, twirl, wheel, whirl; CONCEPTS 147,738 —*Ant.* blockage

circumference [n] *edge, perimeter* ambit, border, boundary, bounds, circuit, compass, confines, extremity, fringe, girth, limits, lip, margin, outline, periphery, rim, verge; CONCEPT 484 —*Ant.* inside, interior, middle

circumlocution [n] *indirect speech* beating around the bush*, circumambages, diffuseness, discursiveness, euphemism, gassiness, indirectness, periphrase, periphrasis, pleonasm, prolixity, roundabout, tautology, verbal evasion, verbality, verbiage, wordiness; CONCEPTS 51,266 —*Ant.* conciseness, directness, straightforwardness, terseness

circumscribe [*v*] *mark off, delimit* bar, bound, confine, define, delineate, demarcate, encircle, enclose, encompass, environ, girdle, hamper, hem in*, limit, nail down*, outline, prelimit, restrain, restrict, surround, trammel; CONCEPTS 18,130 —*Ant.* free, loose, open

circumspect [*adj*] *cautious, discreet* attentive, cagey, calculating, canny, careful, chary, considerate, deliberate, discriminating, gingerly, guarded, heedful, judicious, meticulous, observant, politic, prudent, punctilious, safe, sagacious, sage, scrupulous, vigilant, wary, watchful; CONCEPTS 403,544 —*Ant.* audacious, bold, careless, incautious, indiscreet, rash, uncareful, uncircumspect, unheedful

circumstance [*n*] *situation, condition* accident, action, adjunct, affair, article, case, cause, coincidence, concern, contingency, crisis, destiny, detail, doom, element, episode, event, exigency, fact, factor, fate, feature, fortuity, go, happening, happenstance, incident, intervention, item, juncture, kismet, lot, matter, Moira, occasion, occurrence, particular, phase, place, point, portion, proviso, respect, scene, status, stipulation, supervention, thing, time, where it's at*; CONCEPT 696

circumstances [*n*] *state of affairs in one's life* assets, capital, chances, class, command, degree, dowry, financial status, footing, income, lifestyle, lot, means, net worth, outlook, position, precedence, prestige, property, prospects, prosperity, rank, rating, resources, situation, sphere, standing, state, station, status, substance, times, way of life, worldly goods; CONCEPTS 335,388

circumstantial [*adj*] *incidental* amplified, coincidental, concomitant, concurrent, conjectural, contingent, detailed, environmental, fortuitous, inconclusive, indirect, inferential, presumptive, provisional, uncertain; CONCEPTS 556,582,653 —*Ant.* direct

circumvent [*v*] *fool, mislead* avoid, beat, beguile, bilk, bypass, circumnavigate, cramp, crimp, deceive, detour, disappoint, dodge, dupe, elude, ensnare, entrap, escape, evade, foil, frustrate, get around, hoodwink, outflank, outwit, overreach, prevent, queer, ruin, shun, sidestep, skirt, stave off, steer clear of*, stump, stymie, thwart, trick, ward off; CONCEPTS 59,102,121 —*Ant.* aid, allow, assist, help, permit

circus [*n*] *fair with entertainment* bazaar, big top, festival, gilly*, hippodrome, kermis, show, spectacle, three-ring*; CONCEPT 293

citadel [*n*] *top, tower* bastion, blockhouse, castle, fastness, fort, fortification, keep, manor, redoubt, stronghold; CONCEPTS 321,836

citation [*n1*] *excerpt* example, illustration, mention, passage, quotation, quote, quoting, reference, saying, source; CONCEPT 283

citation [*n2*] *award* bidding, charge, commendation, encomium, mention, panegyric, reward, salutation, summons, tribute; CONCEPTS 69,337 —*Ant.* demerit

cite [*v1*] *note, quote* adduce, advance, allege, allude to, appeal to, enumerate, evidence, excerpt, exemplify, extract, get down to brass tacks*, give as example, illustrate with, indicate, instance, lay, mention, name, number, offer, point out, present, recite, recount, reference, refer to, rehearse, remember, reminisce, repeat, specify, spell out, tell; CONCEPT 57

cite [*v2*] *subpoena* arraign, call, command, name, order, summon; CONCEPT 317

citizen [*n*] *person native of country* aborigine, burgess, burgher, civilian, commoner, cosmopolite, denizen, dweller, freeman/woman, householder, inhabitant, John/Jane Q. Public*, member of body politic, member of community, national, native, naturalized person, occupant, resident, settler, subject, taxpayer, townsperson, urbanite, villager, voter; CONCEPT 413 —*Ant.* alien, foreigner, immigrant

city [*adj*] *metropolitan* burghal, citified, civic, civil, interurban, intraurban, megalopolitan, municipal, urban; CONCEPT 536 —*Ant.* rural

city [*n*] *large town* apple*, boom town, borough, burg, capital, center, conurbation, downtown, megalopolis, metropolis, metropolitan area, municipality, place, polis, port, urban place, urbs*; CONCEPT 507

civic [*adj*] *community* borough, civil, communal, local, metropolitan, municipal, national, public, urban; CONCEPTS 536,583

civil [*adj1*] *civic, community* civilian, domestic, governmental, home, interior, local, municipal, national, political, public; CONCEPTS 536,583

civil [*adj2*] *obliging, kind* accommodating, affable, civilized, complaisant, cordial, courteous, courtly, cultivated, diplomatic, formal, genteel, gracious, mannerly, polished, polite, politic, refined, suave, urbane, wellbred, wellmannered; CONCEPT 401 —*Ant.* ill-mannered, impolite, rude, unkind

civilian [*adj*] *nonmilitary* noncombatant, noncombative, nonmilitant, not in armed forces, pacificist, private, unhostile; CONCEPT 555 —*Ant.* military

civilian [*n*] *nonmilitary person* citizen, civ*, civvie*, commoner, noncombatant, private citizen, subject; CONCEPT 423

civilization [*n1*] *culture, sophistication* acculturation, advancement, breeding, civility, cultivation, development, edification, education, elevation, enlightenment, illumination, polish, progress, refinement, social well-being; CONCEPT 388 —*Ant.* barbarism, primitiveness

civilization [*n2*] *society* civilized life, community, customs, literate society, modern humanity, mores, nation, people, polity, way of life; CONCEPTS 388,417

civilize [*v*] *make cultured; develop* acculturate, acquaint, advance, better, cultivate, edify, educate, elevate, enlighten, ennoble, enrich, ethicize, foster, help forward, humanize, idealize, improve, indoctrinate, inform, instruct, polish, promote, reclaim, refine, sophisticate, spiritualize, tame, uplift; CONCEPTS 244,385

civilized [*adj*] *refined* advanced, civil, cultured, educated, enlightened, humane, refined, sophisticated, urbane; CONCEPT 562

civil rights [*n*] *freedoms of citizens* civil liberties, constitutional rights, freedom of religion, freedom of speech, freedoms, God-given rights, rights; CONCEPT 376

claim [n] *property, right demanded or reserved* affirmation, allegation, application, assertion, birthright, call, case, counterclaim, declaration, demand, dibs, due, entreaty, interest, lien, part, petition, plea, postulation, prerogative, pretense, pretension, privilege, profession, protestation, reclamation, request, requirement, requisition, suit, title, ultimatum; CONCEPTS 278,318, 376,709

claim [v] *demand, maintain property or right* adduce, advance, allege, ask, assert, believe, call for, challenge, collect, declare, defend, exact, have dibs on something*, hit, hit it up*, hold, hold out for*, insist, justify, knock, lay claim to, need, pick up, pop the question*, postulate, pretend, profess, pronounce, require, requisition, solicit, stake out, take, uphold, vindicate; CONCEPTS 53,129 —Ant. deny, disclaim, question

clairvoyance [n] *intuition* acumen, discernment, ESP*, feeling, foreknowledge, insight, omen, penetration, perception, precognition, premonition, psyche, sixth sense*, telepathy; CONCEPTS 409,410

clairvoyant [adj] *intuitive, psychic* clear-sighted, discerning, extrasensory, farseeing, far-sighted, fey, judicious, long-sighted, new age*, oracular, penetrating, perceptive, prescient, prophetic, second-sighted, sibylline, spiritualistic, telepathic, vatic, visionary; CONCEPTS 402,403

clairvoyant [n] *person who is psychic* augur, channeller, diviner, fortune-teller, haruspex, horoscopist, medium, oracle, palm reader, prophet, seer, sibyl, soothsayer, telepath, telepathist, visionary, voodoo doctor*; CONCEPT 423

clam [n] *bivalve living in ocean* cherrystone, littleneck, mollusk, quahog; CONCEPT 394

clammy [adj] *damp* close, dank, drizzly, moist, mucid, mucous, muculent, pasty, slimy, soggy, sticky, sweating, sweaty, wet; CONCEPT 603 —Ant. dry

clamor [n] *loud cry; commotion* agitation, babel, blare, brouhaha*, bustle, buzz, clinker, complaint, convulsion, din, discord, exclamation, ferment, hassle, hoo-ha*, hubba-hubba*, hubbub, hullabaloo*, hurly-burly*, lament, noise, outcry, pandemonium, protesting, racket, remonstrance, row, ruckus, shout, shouting, to-do, tumult, turmoil, upheaval, uproar, vociferation; CONCEPTS 386,595,674 —Ant. quiet, silence

clamor [v] *cry out, make commotion* agitate, bark, bawl, bellow, bluster, claim, debate, demand, dispute, holler, put up a howl*, raise Cain*, raise the roof*, roar, rout, shout; CONCEPTS 77,106 —Ant. be quiet, be silent

clamp [n] *fastener* brace, catch, clasp, grip, hold, lock, nipper, press, snap, vice; CONCEPT 499

clamp [v] *fasten* brace, clench, clinch, fix, impose, make fast, secure; CONCEPTS 85,160 —Ant. loosen, open, unbuckle, unclamp, unfasten, unlock

clan [n] *family, clique* association, band, bunch, club, coterie, crew, crowd, crush, faction, folks, gang, group, house, insiders, kinfolks, mob, moiety, organization, outfit, race, ring, sect, set,

society, sodality, stock, tribe; CONCEPTS 296,387

clandestine [adj] *secret, sly* artful, cloak-and-dagger, closet, concealed, covert, foxy, fraudulent, furtive, hidden, hush-hush*, illegitimate, illicit, in holes and corners*, on the Q. T.*, on the quiet, private, sneaky, stealthy, surreptitious, undercover, underground, underhand, under-the-counter*, under wraps*; CONCEPTS 555,576 —Ant. aboveboard, forthright, open, truthful

clank [n] *metallic noise* bang, bong, clash, clink, jangle, ring; CONCEPT 595

clank [v] *clang, clatter* bong, clash, clink, jangle, make noise, resound, reverberate, ring, toll; CONCEPT 65

clannish [adj] *exclusive, select* akin, alike, associative, cliquish, close, insular, like, narrow, related, reserved, restricting, restrictive, sectarian, unfriendly, unreceptive; CONCEPT 555 —Ant. friendly, open, welcoming

clap [n] *loud hitting noise* applause, bang, blast, boom, burst, crack, crash, handclap, pat, slam, slap, smash, strike, thrust, thunder, thunderclap, thwack, wallop, whack, wham; CONCEPTS 189,595

clap [v] *applaud; slap with approbation* acclaim, approve, bang, cheer, give a big hand*, give a hand*, hear it for*, pat, praise, slap, strike gently, thwack, whack; CONCEPTS 185,189

clarification [n] *explanation* description, elucidation, exposition, illumination, interpretation, resolution, simplification, solution, unravelment, vivification; CONCEPTS 57,274 —Ant. complication, misunderstanding, muddle

clarify [v1] *explain, make clear* analyze, break down, clear up, define, delineate, draw a picture, elucidate, formulate, illuminate, illustrate, interpret, make perfectly clear, make plain, resolve, settle, shed light on*, simplify, spell out*, straighten out, throw light on; CONCEPT 57 —Ant. confuse, muddle

clarify [v2] *purify* clean, cleanse, depurate, distill, filter, rarefy, refine; CONCEPT 165 —Ant. dirty, muddle, muddy

clarion [adj] *clear, stirring sound* blaring, definite, inspiring, loud, ringing, sharp, shrill, strident; CONCEPTS 562,592,594

clarity [n] *clearness* accuracy, articulateness, brightness, certainty, cognizability, comprehensibility, conspicuousness, decipherability, definition, directness, distinctness, evidence, exactitude, exactness, explicability, explicitness, intelligibility, legibility, limpidity, limpidness, lucidity, manifestness, obviousness, openness, overtness, palpability, penetrability, perceptibility, perspicuity, plainness, precision, prominence, purity, salience, simplicity, tangibility, transparency, unambiguity, unmistakability; CONCEPTS 409,638 —Ant. dirtiness, obscurity, unintelligiblity

clash [n1] *disagreement or fight, often brief* affray, argument, battle, brawl, break, broil, brush, bump, collision, concussion, conflict, confrontation, crash, difference of opinion, discord, discordance, disharmony, dispute, donnybrook*, embroilment, encounter, engagement, fracas, fray, have a go at each other*, impact, jam, jar, jolt, jump, melee, misunderstanding, mix up, opposition, rift, riot, row, rumpus,

ci
cl

run-in, rupture, scrap, scrimmage, set-to, shock, showdown, skirmish, smash, wallop; CONCEPTS 46,106

clash [v1] *hit with a loud noise* bang, bump, clang, clank, clatter, collide, crash, grate, grind, jangle, jar, jolt, prang, rattle, scrap, scrimmage, shock, smash, wallop; CONCEPTS 65,189

clash [v2] *fight about, often verbally* argue, bang heads*, battle, brawl, buck, combat, conflict, contend, cross swords, differ, disagree, encounter, feud, fret, gall, grapple, grate, mix it up*, quarrel, raise Cain*, row, try, war, wrangle; CONCEPTS 46,106 —*Ant.* agree

clash [v3] *do not match* be dissimilar, conflict, contrast, differ, disaccord, discord, disharmonize, mismatch, not go with; CONCEPTS 655,664 —*Ant.* match

clasp [n] *fastener; hold on something* brooch, buckle, catch, clamp, clench, clinch, clip, clutch, embrace, fastening, fibula, grapple, grasp, grip, hasp, hold, hook, hug, pin, safety pin, snap; CONCEPTS 497,641

clasp [v] *grab tightly* attack, bear hug*, buckle, clamp, clinch, clip, clutch, coil, concatenate, connect, embrace, enfold, fasten, glom onto*, grapple, grasp, grip, hold, hug, pin, press, seize, snatch, squeeze, take; CONCEPTS 85,160,191,219 —*Ant.* let go, loose

class [adj] *stylish; with panache* chic, classy, dashing, fashionable, fine, fly*, foxy*, sharp; CONCEPT 589 —*Ant.* plain, unstylish

class [n1] *kind, sort, category* branch, brand, breed, cast, caste, character, classification, collection, color, degree, denomination, department, description, designation, distinction, division, genus, grade, grain, grouping, hierarchy, humor, ilk, kidney, league, make, mold, name, nature, order, origin, property, province, quality, range, rank, rate, school, sect, section, selection, set, source, species, sphere, standing, status, stripe, style, suit, temperament, value, variety; CONCEPT 378

class [n2] *societal group, background* ancestry, birth, bourgeoisie, breed, caliber, caste, circle, clan, clique, club, company, condition, connection, coterie, cultural level, degree, derivation, descent, estate, extraction, family, genealogy, grade, hierarchy, influence, intelligentsia, league, lineage, moiety, nobility, origin, pecking order*, pedigree, pigeonhole*, place, position, prestige, quality, sect, social rank, source, sphere, standing, state, station, status, stock, strain, stratum, the right stuff*, tier, title; CONCEPTS 296,387,388,417

class [n3] *group in school* academy, colloquium, course, course of study, division, form, grade, homeroom, lecture group, line, quiz group, recitation, room, round table, section, seminar, seminary, session, study, study group, subdivision, subject; CONCEPTS 286,287,288,289

class [v] *categorize* account, allot, appraise, assess, assign, assort, brand, classify, codify, consider, designate, divide, evaluate, gauge, grade, group, hold, identify, judge, mark, part, pigeonhole*, rank, rate, reckon, regard, score, separate; CONCEPTS 39,135

classic [adj2] *characteristic, regular* prototypal, prototypical, representative, simple, standard,

time-honored, typical, usual, vintage; CONCEPTS 533,547 —*Ant.* abnormal, irregular, uncharacteristic

classic [n] *model* chef d'oeuvre, exemplar, magnum opus, paradigm, prototype, standard, tour de force; CONCEPTS 259,655,686

classical [adj1] *concerning ancient culture* academic, Attic, Augustan, belletristic, bookish, canonic, canonical, classic, classicistic, Doric, Grecian, Greek, Hellenic, Homeric, humanistic, Ionic, Latin, Roman, scholastic, Virgilian; CONCEPTS 536,549

classical [adj2] *simple, chaste* classic, elegant, harmonious, pure, refined, restrained, symmetrical, understated, well-proportioned; CONCEPT 589 —*Ant.* complicated, modern, unclassical

classic/classical [adj1] *best, model* archetypal, capital, champion, consummate, definitive, distinguished, esthetic, excellent, exemplary, famous, fine, finest, first-rate, flawless, ideal, master, masterly, paradigmatic, paramount, perfect, prime, quintessential, ranking, standard, superior, top, top-notch, vintage, well-known; CONCEPT 574 —*Ant.* inferior, worst

classicism [n] *simple style; regularity, restraint* aesthetic principle, Atticism, balance, Ciceronianism, clarity, class, classicalism, conventional formality, dignity, elegance, excellence, finish, formality, formal style, grandeur, grand style, Hellenism, high art, lucidity, majesty, neoclassicism, nobility, objectivity, polish, proportion, propriety, pure taste, purity, rationalism, refinement, rhythm, severity, simplicity, sobriety, sublimity, symmetry; CONCEPT 655

classification [n] *categorization* allocation, alloting, allotment, analysis, apportionment, arrangement, assignment, assortment, cataloguing, categorizing, codification, collocation, consignment, coordination, denomination, department, designation, disposal, disposition, distributing, distribution, division, echelon, gradation, grade, grading, graduation, group, grouping, kind, order, ordering, ordination, organization, pigeonholing*, regulation, sizing, sorting, systematization, tabulating, taxonomy, typecasting; CONCEPTS 18,39,135,378

classified [adj] *top-secret* confidential, private, restricted, secret; CONCEPTS 267,576

classify [v] *categorize* allocate, allot, alphabetize, analyze, arrange, assort, brand, break down, button down*, catalogue, class, codify, collocate, coordinate, correlate, dispose, distinguish, distribute, divide, docket, embody, file, grade, group, incorporate, index, label, match, name, number, order, organize, peg*, pigeonhole*, put away, put down as, put down for, range, rank, rank out, rate, regiment, segregate, size, size up, sort, systematize, tab, tabulate, tag, take one's measure, ticket, type, typecast; CONCEPTS 18,39

classy [adj] *stylish, having panache* chic, dashing, elegant, exclusive, fashionable, high-class, in, in vogue, mod, modish, posh, select, sharp, superior, swank, swanky, tony, uptown; CONCEPT 589 —*Ant.* inelegant, inferior, plain, unstylish

clatter [n] *loud noise* ballyhoo*, bluster, clack, clangor, hullabaloo*, pandemonium, racket, rattle, rumpus, shattering, smashing; CONCEPTS 181,189,595

clatter [v] *crash; make racket* bang, bluster, bump, clang, clank, clash, hurtle, noise, rattle, roar, shatter, smash; CONCEPTS 65,181,189

clause [n] *provision in document* article, catch*, chapter, codicil, condition, fine print*, heading, item, joker*, kicker*, limitation, paragraph, part, passage, point, provision, proviso, requirement, rider, section, small print*, specification, stipulation, string attached to something*, ultimatum; CONCEPTS 270,275

claw [n] *nail of animal; tool shaped like nail of an animal* barb, cant hook, clapperclaw, crook, fang, fingernail, grapnel, grappler, hook, manus, nail claw, nipper, paw, pincer, retractile, spur, talon, tentacle, unguis, ungula; CONCEPT 392

claw [v] *using sharp nail* break, dig, graze, hurt, itch, lacerate, mangle, maul, open, rip, scrabble, scrap, scrape, scratch, tear; CONCEPTS 178,214,220

clay [n] *workable earth material* adobe, argil, argillaceous earth, bole, brick, china material, clunch, earth, kaolin, loam, loess, marl, mud, porcelain material, pottery, slip, terra cotta, till, wacke; CONCEPT 509

clean [adj1] *not dirty; uncluttered* apple-pie order*, blank, bright, cleansed, clear, delicate, dirtless, elegant, faultless, flawless, fresh, graceful, hygienic, immaculate, laundered, neat, neat as a button*, neat as a pin*, orderly, pure, sanitary, shining, simple, snowy, sparkling, speckless, spic and span*, spotless, squeaky, stainless, taintless, tidy, trim, unblemished, unpolluted, unsmudged, unsoiled, unspotted, unstained, unsullied, untarnished, vanilla*, washed, well-kept, white; CONCEPT 485 —Ant. cluttered, dirty, filthy, foul, polluted, stained, tarnished

clean [adj2] *sterile* antiseptic, aseptic, clarified, decontaminated, disinfected, hygienic, pure, purified, sanitary, sterilized, unadulterated, uncontaminated, uninfected, unpolluted, unsullied, wholesome; CONCEPTS 314,485 —Ant. adulterated, dirty, impure, unsterile

clean [adj3] *chaste, virtuous* blameless, crimeless, decent, exemplary, faultless, good, guiltless, honorable, inculpable, innocent, modest, moral, respectable, sinless, undefiled, unguilty, unsullied, upright, wholesome; CONCEPT 404 —Ant. besmirched, defiled, impure, unchaste, unvirtuous

clean [adj4] *precise, sharp* clear, clear-cut, correct, definite, distinct, legible, neat, plain, readable, simple, trim, uncluttered; CONCEPT 535 —Ant. imprecise, indefinite, muddled

clean [adj5] *complete, thorough* absolute, conclusive, decisive, entire, final, perfect, total, unimpaired, whole; CONCEPT 531 —Ant. incomplete

clean [v] *make undirty, uncluttered* absterge, bath, bathe, blot, brush, cauterize, clarify, cleanse, clear the decks*, clear up, deodorize, depurate, deterge, disinfect, do up*, dredge, dust, edulcorate, elutriate, erase, expunge, expurgate, flush, hackle, launder, lave, mop, neaten, pick, pick up, polish, purge, purify, rake, rasp, refine, rinse, rout out, sanitize, scald, scour, scrape, scrub, shake out, shampoo, soak, soap, sponge, spruce up*, sterilize, straighten up, swab, sweep, tidy up, vacuum, wash, whisk, winnow, wipe; CONCEPTS 161,

165 —Ant. adulterate, defile, dirty, foul, soil, stain

clean-cut [adj] *neat, clearly outlined* categorical, chiseled, clear, definite, definitive, etched, explicit, express, sharp, specific, unambiguous, well-defined; CONCEPTS 490,535 —Ant. ruffled

cleanse [v] *make undirty; wash* absolve, clarify, clean, clear, depurgate, disinfect, expurgate, launder, lustrate, purge, purify, refine, restore, rinse, sanitize, scour, scrub, sterilize; CONCEPT 165 —Ant. dirty, soil, spot

cleanser [n] *strong disinfectant, solvent* abrasive, abstergent, antiseptic, cathartic, deodorant, detergent, fumigant, lather, polish, purgative, purifier, scourer, soap, soap powder, suds; CONCEPT 492

clear [adj1] *cloudless, bright* clarion, crystal, fair, fine, halcyon, light, luminous, pleasant, rainless, shining, shiny, sunny, sunshiny, unclouded, undarkened, undimmed; CONCEPTS 525,617,627 —Ant. cloudy, dark, dim, dull, fuzzy, gloomy, shadowy, unclear

clear [adj2] *understandable, apparent* apprehensible, audible, clear-cut, coherent, comprehensible, conspicuous, crystal, definite, distinct, evident, explicit, express, graspable, incontrovertible, intelligible, knowable, legible, loud enough, lucent, lucid, manifest, obvious, open and shut*, palpable, patent, perceptible, perspicuous, plain, precise, pronounced, readable, recognizable, sharp, simple, spelled out*, straightforward, transparent, transpicuous, unambiguous, unblurred, uncomplicated, unequivocal, unmistakable, unquestionable; CONCEPTS 402,562 —Ant. ambiguous, indistinct, mysterious, obscure, unintelligible, vague

clear [adj3] *open, unhindered* bare, empty, free, smooth, stark, unhampered, unimpeded, unlimited, unobstructed, vacant, vacuous, void; CONCEPT 490 —Ant. blocked, clogged, closed, congested, hindered

clear [adj4] *transparent* apparent, cloudless, crystal, crystal clear, crystalline, glassy, limpid, pellucid, pure, see-through, thin, tralucent, translucent, translucid; CONCEPT 618 —Ant. clouded, cloudy, foggy, obscured, smudged

clear [adj5] *not guilty* absolved, blameless, clean, cleared, discharged, dismissed, exculpated, exonerated, guiltless, immaculate, innocent, pure, sinless, stainless, unblemished, uncensurable, undefiled, untarnished, untroubled; CONCEPTS 319,404 —Ant. culpable, guilty, responsible

clear [adj6] *certain in one's mind* absolute, confirmed, convinced, decided, definite, positive, resolved, satisfied, sure; CONCEPT 403 —Ant. uncertain, unclear, unintelligible

clear [v1] *clean, clear away* ameliorate, break up, brighten, burn off, clarify, cleanse, disencumber, disengage, disentangle, eliminate, empty, erase, extricate, free, lighten, loosen, lose, meliorate, open, purify, refine, rid, rule out, shake off, sweep, throw off, tidy, unblock, unburden, unclog, unload, unloose, unpack, untie, vacate, void, wipe; CONCEPTS 165,211 —Ant. clutter, pile up

clear [v2] *liberate; free from uncertainty* absolve, acquit, clarify, defog*, discharge, disculpate, emancipate, exculpate, exonerate, explain, find innocent, let go, let off, let off the hook*, release, relieve, set free, vindicate; CONCEPTS 7,22,127 —Ant. condemn, find guilty, sentence

clear [v3] *pass over, often by jumping* hurdle, leap, miss, negotiate, overleap, surmount, vault; CONCEPT 194 —Ant. hit, run into

clear [v4] *profit* accumulate, acquire, clean up*, earn, gain, gather, get, glean, make, net, obtain, pick up, realize, reap, receive, secure, win; CONCEPTS 129,342

clearance [n1] *permission for activity* approval, authorization, consent, endorsement, go-ahead*, green light*, leave, okay, sanction, say-so*; CONCEPT 376 —Ant. denial, grounding, refusal, veto

clearance [n2] *gap above something* allowance, assart, defoliated area, empty space, expanse, gap, headroom, margin, opening, open space; CONCEPT 513

clear-cut [adj] *definite* assured, categorical, crystalline, decided, definitive, distinct, evident, explicit, express, indubitable, lucent, lucid, obvious, plain, precise, pronounced, sharp-cut, specific, straightforward, unambiguous, undisputed, undoubted, unequivocal, unquestioned, well-defined; CONCEPT 535 —Ant. ambiguous, fuzzy, indefinite, vague

clearing [n] *gap in area* allowance, assart, clearance, defoliated area, dell, empty space, expanse, gap, glade, headroom, margin, opening, open space; CONCEPT 513

clearly [adv] *without any doubt* acutely, apparently, audibly, beyond doubt, certainly, conspicuously, decidedly, definitely, discernibly, distinctly, evidently, incontestably, incontrovertibly, indubitably, lucidly, manifestly, markedly, noticeably, obviously, openly, overtly, patently, penetratingly, perceptibly, plainly, positively, precisely, prominently, purely, recognizably, seemingly, sharply, sonorously, surely, translucently, transparently, undeniably, undoubtedly, unmistakably; CONCEPTS 535,552 —Ant. indefinitely, indistinctly, mysteriously, vaguely

clear out [v1] *empty something* clean out, dispose of, eliminate, exhaust, get rid of, remove, sort, tidy up; CONCEPT 211 —Ant. fill, fill up, put

clear out [v2] *leave, often quickly* beat it*, begone, decamp, depart, go, hightail*, kite*, make oneself scarce*, remove oneself, retire, scram, skedaddle*, split*, take a hike*, take off, vamoose*, withdraw; CONCEPT 195 —Ant. arrive, rush in

clear up [v1] *explain; resolve* answer, cipher, clarify, decipher, dissolve, elucidate, figure out, illuminate, illustrate, make plausible, make reasonable, puzzle out, resolve, solve, straighten out, tidy, unfold, unravel; CONCEPTS 37,57 —Ant. complicate, question

clear up [v2] *become improved* become fair, become sunny, blow over, brighten, die away, die down, improve, lapse, lift, pick up, run its course*; CONCEPT 700 —Ant. worsen

cleavage [n] *gap* break, chasm, cleft, discontinuity, divide, division, fracture, hole, rift, schism, separation, severance, split, valley; CONCEPT 513

cleave [v1] *divide, split* carve, chop, crack, cut, dissect, dissever, disunite, divorce, hack, hew, open, part, pierce, rend, rip, rive, separate, sever, slice, stab, sunder, tear asunder, whack; CONCEPTS 98,137,176 —Ant. join, meld, unite

cleave [v2] *stand by, stick together* abide by, adhere, agree, associate, attach, be devoted to, be tight with*, be true*, cling, cohere, combine, freeze to*, hold, join, link, remain, stay put, unite; CONCEPTS 8,113

cleft [adj] *separated, split* broken, cloven, cracked, crannied, crenelated, parted, perforated, pierced, rent, riven, ruptured, separated, sundered, torn; CONCEPT 490 —Ant. joined, joint, united

cleft [n] *break, gap* aperture, arroyo, breach, canyon, chasm, chink, cleavage, clough, clove, crack, cranny, crevasse, crevice, fissure, fracture, gorge, gulch, opening, ravine, rent, rift, rima, rimation, rime, schism, slit; CONCEPT 513 —Ant. closing, closure, solid

clemency [n] *forgiveness* caritas, charity, compassion, endurance, equitableness, fairness, forbearance, gentleness, grace, humanity, indulgence, justness, kindness, lenience, leniency, lenity, lifesaver, mercifulness, mercy, mildness, moderation, soft-heartedness, sufferance, tenderness, tolerance, toleration; CONCEPTS 410,644 —Ant. no mercy

clement [adj1] *calm, mild (weather)* balmy, clear, fair, fine, moderate, peaceful, temperate, warm; CONCEPT 525 —Ant. harsh, severe, violent

clement [adj2] *forgiving* benevolent, benign, benignant, charitable, compassionate, easy, forbearing, gentle, humane, humanitarian, indulgent, kind, kind-hearted, kindly, lenient, merciful, mild, soft-hearted, sympathetic, tender, tolerant; CONCEPTS 404,550 —Ant. hard-hearted, harsh, mean, unforgiving

clench [v] *grasp* clamp, clasp, clinch, clutch, constrict, contract, double up, draw together, grapple, grip, hold; CONCEPT 191 —Ant. let go, loose, loosen, release

clergy [n] *ministry of church* canonicate, canonry, cardinalate, churchpersons, clerics, conclave, deaconry, diaconate, ecclesiastics, first estate, holy order, pastorate, prelacy, priesthood, rabbinate, the cloth, the desk, the pulpit; CONCEPT 369

clergyperson [n] *minister of church* abbey, archbishop, bishop, blackcoat*, cardinal, cassock, chaplain, churchperson, cleric, clerk, curate, dean, divine, ecclesiast, ecclesiastic, evangelist, father, missionary, monsignor, padre, parson, pastor, person of God, person of the cloth, pontiff, preacher, predicant, priest, primate, pulpitarian, pulpiteer, rabbi, rector, reverend, sermonizer, shepherd, vicar; CONCEPT 361

clerical [adj1] *secretarial* accounting, bookkeeping, clerkish, clerkly, office, pink collar*, scribal, stenographic, subordinate, typing, white collar*, written; CONCEPT 536

clerical [adj2] *concerning clergy* apostolic, canonical, churchly, cleric, ecclesiastic, ecclesiastical, episcopal, holy, ministerial, monastic, monkish, papal, parsonical, parsonish, pastoral, pontifical, prelatic, priestly, rabbinical, sacerdotal, sacred, theocratical; CONCEPT 536

clerk [n] *assistant* agent, amanuensis, auditor, bookkeeper, cashier, copyist, counter jumper*, counterperson, employee, notary, office helper, operator, paper pusher*, paper shuffler*, pencil pusher*, pen pusher*, receptionist, recorder, registrar, salesperson, secretary, seller, shopperson, stenographer, teller, transcriber, white collar*, worker; CONCEPT 348

clever [adj] *bright, ingenious* able, adept, adroit, alert, apt, astute, brainy, brilliant, cagey, canny, capable, competent, crackerjack*, cunning, deep, dexterous/dextrous, discerning, egghead*, expert, foxy*, gifted, good, handy, intelligent, inventive, keen, knowing, knowledgeable, many-sided, nimble, nobody's fool*, pretty, pro, qualified, quick, quick on trigger*, quick-witted, rational, resourceful, sagacious, savvy, sensible, sharp, shrewd, skilled, skillful, slick, sly, smart, sprightly, talented, versatile, wise, witty; CONCEPT 402 —Ant. awkward, foolish, idiotic, ignorant, naive, senseless, stupid, unclever

cleverness [n] *brightness, ingenuity* ability, adroitness, astuteness, brains, calculation, canniness, dexterity, discernment, flair, gift, gumption, intelligence, quickness, quick wit, resourcefulness, sagacity, sense, sharpness, shrewdness, skill, smartness, talent, wisdom, wit; CONCEPT 409 —Ant. foolishness, ignorance, naievety, senselessness, stupidity

cliché [n] *overused, hackneyed phrase* adage, banality, boiler plate*, bromide, buzzword, chestnut*, commonplace, corn*, counterword, familiar tune, motto, old story*, platitude, potboiler, prosaism, proverb, rubber stamp*, saying, shibboleth, slogan, stale saying, stereotype, threadbare phrase, triteness, trite remark, triviality, truism, vapid expression; CONCEPTS 275,278 —Ant. coinage, nuance

click [n/v] *metallic sound* bang, beat, clack, snap, tick; CONCEPTS 65,595

click [v2] *fall into place* become clear, be compatible, be on same wavelength*, come off*, feel a rapport*, get on*, go, go off well*, go over, hit it off*, make a hit*, make sense, match, meet with approval, pan out*, prove out, succeed, take to each other*; CONCEPT 704

client [n] *customer* applicant, believer, buyer, chump, consumer, dependent, disciple, follower, front, habitué, head, mark, patient, patron, protégé, protégée, purchaser, shopper, walk-in, ward; CONCEPT 348 —Ant. manager, owner

clientele [n] *customers of business* audience, business, clientage, clientry, clients, constituency, cortege, dependents, following, market, patronage, patrons, public, regulars, trade; CONCEPTS 325,417 —Ant. management, ownership

cliff [n] *overhang on hill or mountain* bluff, crag, escarpment, face, precipice, rock face, rocky height, scar, scarp, steep rock, wall; CONCEPT 509

cliffhanger [n] *something suspenseful* close call, close shave*, narrow escape, shocker, spine-chiller, squeaker*, thriller, white knuckle*; CONCEPTS 410,679

climactic/climacteric [adj] *decisive* acute, climactical, critical, crucial, desperate, dire,

paramount, peak; CONCEPT 567 —Ant. anticlimacteric, anticlimactic, bathetic, indecisive, trivial, undecided

climate [n1] *weather of region* altitude, aridity, atmospheric conditions, characteristic weather, clime, conditions, humidity, latitude, meteorological character, meteorologic conditions, temperature; CONCEPT 524

climate [n2] *mood of situation* ambience, ambient, atmosphere, disposition, environment, feeling, medium, milieu, mise-en-scène, mood, surroundings, temper, tendency, trend; CONCEPT 673

climax [n] *peak, culmination* acme, apex, apogee, ascendancy, capsheaf, capstone, climacteric, crest, crowning point, extremity, head, height, highlight, high spot, intensification, limit, maximum, meridian, ne plus ultra, orgasm, payoff*, pinnacle, pitch, summit, tiptop, top, turning point, utmost, zenith; CONCEPTS 706,836 —Ant. anticlimax, cliffhanger

climax [v] *come to top; culminate* accomplish, achieve, break the record*, cap, come, come to a head*, conclude, content, crown, end, finish, fulfill, hit high spot, orgasm, peak, please, reach a peak, reach the zenith, rise to crescendo*, satisfy, succeed, terminate, top, tower; CONCEPTS 375,704,706 —Ant. delve, dip, drop, fall off

climb [v] *crawl, move up* ape up*, ascend, clamber, escalade, escalate, go up, mount, rise, scale, soar, top; CONCEPT 166 —Ant. descend, dismount, go down, retreat

clinch [v1] *secure a goal* assure, cap, conclude, confirm, decide, determine, seal, seize, set, settle, sew up, verify; CONCEPT 706

clinch [v2] *hold securely; grab* bolt, clamp, clasp, clench, clutch, cuddle, embrace, enfold, fasten, fix, grab hold of, grapple, grasp, grip, hug, lay hands on, make fast, nail, press, rivet, secure, seize, snatch, squeeze; CONCEPTS 191,219 —Ant. let go

clincher [n] *settling event* capper, closer, coup de grâce, crowning blow*, culmination, deathblow*, deciding moment, finisher, finishing touch; CONCEPTS 230,635,676

cling [v] *attach to* adhere, be true to, cherish, clasp, cleave to, clutch, cohere, continue, embrace, endure, fasten, freeze to, grasp, grip, hang in, hang onto, hold fast, hug, last, linger, squeeze, stay put, stick, stick like glue*; CONCEPTS 85,160,190 —Ant. detach, let go, unfasten

clinic [n] *medical center* dispensary, hospital, infirmary, sick bay, surgery center; CONCEPTS 312,439,449

clinical [adj] *dispassionate* analytic, antiseptic, cold, detached, disinterested, emotionless, impersonal, objective, scientific, unemotional; CONCEPT 404 —Ant. feeling, passionate, subjective

clink [n/v] *bang against, ring* chink, clang, jangle, jingle, sound, tingle, tinkle; CONCEPTS 65,595

clip [v1] *cut short* bob, crop, curtail, cut, cut back, decrease, dock, lower, mow, pare, prune, reduce, shave, shear, shorten, skive, slash, snip, trim, truncate; CONCEPT 137 —Ant. lengthen

clip [v2/n] *punch* blow, box, clout, cuff, knock, punch, smack, sock, thump, wallop, whack; CONCEPT 189

clique [n] *group of friends* bunch, cabal, camar-illa, camp, circle, clan, club, coterie, crew, crowd, crush, faction, gang, in-group, insiders, lobby, Mafia, mob, organization, outfit, pack, posse, ring, set, society; CONCEPTS 387,417

cloak [n] *cover; coat* beard, blind, camouflage, cape, capote, disguise, facade, face, front, guise, manteau, mantle, mask, pretext, semblance, shawl, shield, show, veneer, wrap; CONCEPTS 451,475,680

cloak [v] *disguise* blanket, camouflage, coat, conceal, cover, curtain, dissemble, dissimulate, dress up, hide, mask, obscure, pretext, screen, shroud, veil; CONCEPT 188 —Ant. reveal, un-cloak, uncover

clobber [v] *hit, beat* belt, blast, drub, lambaste*, lick, shellac*, slam, slug, smash, smear, smother, thrash, trim, wallop, whip; CONCEPTS 189,252

clock [n] *timekeeping device* alarm, Big Ben*, chroniker*, chronograph, chronometer, digital watch, hourglass, pendulum, stopwatch, sun-dial, tattler, ticker*, tick-tock*, timekeeper, timemarker, timepiece, timer, turnip*, watch; CONCEPTS 463,819

clockwork [n] *being on time; precision* accu-racy, consistency, perfect timing, regularity, smoothness; CONCEPT 818

clod [n] *stupid person* blockhead*, boor, chump, clown, dimwit*, dolt, dope*, dumbbell, dummy, dunce, fool, imbecile, lame-brain*, lout, oaf, simpleton; CONCEPTS 412,423

clog [n] *blockage* bar, block, blockade, burden, cumbrance, dead weight, drag, encumbrance, hindrance, impedance, impediment, obstruc-tion, snag; CONCEPTS 121,674 —Ant. clearance, opening

clog [v] *block, hinder* burden, choke, close, congest, curb, dam up, encumber, entrammel, fetter, fill, glut, hamper, impede, jam, leash, obstruct, occlude, plug, seal, shackle, stopper, stop up, stuff, tie, trammel; CONCEPTS 121,130, 190 —Ant. clear, free, open, unblock, unclog, unencumber, unstop

cloister [n] *secluded religious place* abbey, cell, chapter house, convent, friary, hermitage, house, lamasery, monastery, nunnery, order, priorate, priory, religious community, retreat, sanctuary; CONCEPTS 368,516

cloistered [adj] *secluded* cloistral, confined, hermitic, hidden, insulated, recluse, reclusive, restricted, secluse, seclusive, sequestered, shel-tered, shielded, shut off, withdrawn; CONCEPTS 554,583 —Ant. free, open, unsecluded

clone [n] *exact duplicate* act-alike, copy, double, duplicate, look-alike computer, reproduction, twin; CONCEPTS 664,667,716

clone [v] *copy exactly* copy, duplicate, repeat, replicate, reproduce; CONCEPTS 91,171

close [adj1] *near, nearby* abutting, across the street, adjacent, adjoining, approaching, around the corner, at hand, contiguous, convenient, give or take a little*, handy, hard by, immedi-ate, imminent, impending, in spitting dis-tance*, in the ball park*, near-at-hand, nearest, nearly, neighboring, next, nigh, proximate, under one's nose*, warm; CONCEPT 586 —Ant. away, beyond, detached, far, faraway

close [adj2] *dense, cramped* circumscribed,

close-grained, compact, confined, confining, congested, consolidated, cropped, crowded, firm, impenetrable, impermeable, jam-packed, narrow, packed, restricted, short, solid, substan-tial, thick, tight; CONCEPTS 481,483,774 —Ant. loose, open, uncramped

close [adj3] *accurate, precise* conscientious, exact, faithful, lifelike, literal, resembling, similar, strict; CONCEPTS 535,563 —Ant. far, imprecise, inaccurate

close [adj4] *intimate* attached, buddy-buddy*, chummy, confidential, cozy with, dear, devoted, familiar, inseparable, kissing cousins*, loving, making it with*, on top of each other*, palsy-walsy*, private, related, thick*, thick as thieves*, thick with*; CONCEPTS 372,555 —Ant. unfriendly

close [adj5] *oppressive, humid* airless, breath-less, choky, confined, fusty, heavy, moldy, motionless, muggy, musty, stagnant, stale, stale-smelling, sticky, stifling, stuffy, suffocat-ing, sultry, sweltering, sweltry, thick, tight, uncomfortable, unventilated; CONCEPTS 525, 605 —Ant. cool, dry

close [adj6] *secret, reserved* buttoning one's lip*, buttoning up*, clamming up*, close-lipped, closemouthed, hidden, hush-hush*, mum's the word*, on the Q. T.*, private, reticent, retired, secluded, secretive, silent, taciturn, tight chops*, tight-lipped*, uncommunicative, unforthcom-ing, zipping one's lips*; CONCEPTS 267,576 —Ant. open, unreserved

close [adj7] *stingy* chintzy*, closefisted, illiberal, mean, mingy, miserly, narrow, niggardly, parsi-monious, penny-pinching, penurious, skimpy, skinflint*, tight, tight-fisted, ungenerous; CONCEPTS 334,404 —Ant. generous, giving

close [n] *ending* adjournment, cease, cessation, completion, conclusion, culmination, denoue-ment, desistance, end, finale, finish, period, stop, termination, windup; CONCEPTS 119,832 —Ant. beginning, commencement, opening, start

close [v1] *obstruct, seal* bang, bar, block, bolt, button, caulk, choke, clap, clench, clog, con-fine, congest, cork, dam, exclude, fasten, fill, lock, occlude, plug, prevent passage, put to, retard flow, screen, secure, shut, shut off, shutter, slam, stopper, stop up, stuff, turn off; CONCEPTS 113,121,201 —Ant. open, release, unclose, unplug, unseal, unstop

close [v2] *complete, finish, stop* button down*, button up*, call it a day*, call off, cap, cease, clear, clinch, conclude, consummate, culminate, cut loose, determine, discontinue, do, drop the curtain*, end, fold, fold up, halt, pack it in*, put a lid on*, put to bed*, sew up*, shut down, shutter, terminate, ultimate, wind down*, wind up*, wrap up*; CONCEPT 234 —Ant. begin, continue, not finish, open, start

close [v3] *join, unite* agree, bind, chain, coalesce, come together, connect, couple, encounter, fuse, grapple, inclose, meet, put together, tie, tie up; CONCEPT 113 —Ant. disjoin, disunite, open

close call [n] *narrow escape* cliffhanger, close shave*, heart stopper*, near miss, photofinish, squeaker*, white-knuckler*; CONCEPT 102

closed [adj1] *shut, out of service* bankrupt, dark, fastened, folded, gone fishing*, locked, not open, out of business*, out of order*, padlocked, sealed, shut down; CONCEPT 576 —*Ant.* in business, open, running, working

closed [*adj2*] *finished, terminated* concluded, decided, ended, final, over, resolved, settled; CONCEPT 548 —*Ant.* beginning, continuing, open, started, starting, unsettled

closed [*adj3*] *exclusive, independent* restricted, self-centered, self-contained, self-sufficient, self-sufficing, self-supported, self-supporting, self-sustained, self-sustaining; CONCEPT 550 —*Ant.* open, welcoming

closely [*adv*] *approximately, carefully* by the skin of one's teeth*, exactly, firmly, hard, heedfully, in conjunction with, intently, intimately, jointly, meticulously, mindfully, minutely, nearly, punctiliously, scrupulously, searchingly, sharply, similarly, strictly, thoughtfully; CONCEPTS 487,557,573

closemouthed [*adj*] *silent, reserved* buttoned up*, clammed up*, close, close-lipped, dummied up, have tight chops*, hush-hush, on the Q. T.*, quiet, reticent, sedate, taciturn, tight-lipped, uncommunicative, zipped one's lips*; CONCEPT 267 —*Ant.* chatty, open, talkative

closet [*n*] *storage cupboard, usually tall* ambry, bin, buffet, cabinet, chest of drawers, clothes room, cold storage, container, depository, locker, receptacle, recess, repository, room, safe, sideboard, vault, walk-in, wardrobe; CONCEPT 440

closure [*n1*] *conclusion* cease, cessation, close, closing, desistance, end, ending, finish, stop, stoppage, termination; CONCEPT 119 —*Ant.* beginning, introduction, opening, start

closure [*n2*] *plug, seal* blockade, bolt, bung, cap, cork, fastener, latch, lid, obstruction, occludent, occlusion, padlock, stop, stopper, stopple, tampon, tap; CONCEPTS 471,680 —*Ant.* opening

clot [*n*] *blockage, mass of coagulation* array, batch, battery, body, bulk, bunch, bundle, clotting, clump, cluster, coagulum, coalescence, conglutination, consolidation, curd, curdling, embolism, embolus, glob, gob, group, grume, lump, occlusion, precipitate, set, thickness, thrombus; CONCEPTS 432,466, 470 —*Ant.* opening

clot [*v*] *coagulate* clabber, coalesce, congeal, curdle, gel, gelate, gelatinize, glop up*, jell, jellify, jelly, lopper*, lump, set, solidify, thicken; CONCEPT 469 —*Ant.* loose, thin

cloth [*n*] *fabric* bolt, calico, cotton, dry goods, goods, material, stuff, synthetics, textiles, tissue, twill, weave, yard goods; CONCEPT 473

clothe [*v*] *cover with apparel* accouter, apparel, array, attire, bedizen, bedrape, breech, bundle up, caparison, cloak, coat, costume, dandify, deck, disguise, dizen, do up*, drape, dress, dress up, dud*, endow, endue, enwrap, equip, fit, fit out, garb, gown, guise, habilitate, habit, invest, jacket, livery, mantle, outfit, primp, raiment, rig, robe, spruce, suit up, swaddle, swathe, tog, turn out, vest; CONCEPT 167 —*Ant.* reveal, take off, unclothe, uncover

clothes/clothing [*n*] *personal attire* accouterment, apparel, array, caparison, civvies*, costume, covering, drag*, drapery, dress, duds*, ensemble, equipment, finery, frippery, frock, full feather*, garb, garments, gear,

get-up*, habiliment, habit, hand-me-downs, livery, mufti, outfit, overclothes, panoply, rags*, raiment, regalia, rigging*, sack*, sportswear, Sunday best*, tailleur, tatters*, things*, threads*, toggery*, togs, tout ensemble, trappings, trousseau, underclothes, vestment, vesture, vines*, wardrobe, wear, weeds*, zoot suit*; CONCEPT 451

cloud [*n1*] *mass of water particles in air* billow, brume, darkness, dimness, film, fog, fogginess, frost, gloom, haze, haziness, mare's tail*, mist, murk, nebula, nebulosity, obscurity, ol' buttermilk sky*, overcast, pea soup*, pother, puff, rack, scud, sheep, smog, smoke, smother, steam, thunderhead, vapor, veil, woolpack; CONCEPTS 437,524

cloud [*n2*] *crowd* army, dense mass, flock, horde, host, legion, multitude, rout, scores, shower, swarm, throng; CONCEPTS 417,432

cloud [*v1*] *become foggy or obscured* adumbrate, becloud, befog, blur, darken, dim, eclipse, envelop, fog, gloom, mist, obfuscate, overcast, overshadow, shade, shadow, veil; CONCEPTS 469,526 —*Ant.* clear, unfog, unveil

cloud [*v2*] *confuse* addle, becloud, befuddle, disorient, distort, distract, impair, muddle, muddy, obscure, perplex, puzzle; CONCEPTS 7,19 —*Ant.* clear up, explain, explicate

cloudy [*adj*] *hazy; darkened* blurred, confused, dark, dense, dim, dismal, dull, dusky, emulsified, foggy, gloomy, heavy, indefinite, indistinct, leaden, lowering, misty, mucky, muddy, murky, mushy, nebulous, nontranslucent, nontransparent, not clear, nubilous, obscure, opaque, overcast, somber, sullen, sunless, vaporous; CONCEPT 525 —*Ant.* clear, cloudless

clout [*n*] *power* authority, influence, prestige, pull*, standing, sway, weight; CONCEPT 686

clout [*v*] *hit* blow, box, clip, clobber, cuff, rap, slap, smack, sock, strike, thump, wallop, whack; CONCEPTS 189,200

clown [*n1*] *joking person* antic, buffoon, comedian, comic, cut-up*, dolt, droll, farceur, fool, funnyperson, funster, gagman*, gagster*, harlequin, humorist, jester, joker, jokesmith, jokester, life of the party*, madcap, merryandrew, merrymaker, mime, mountebank, mummer, picador, pierrot, prankster, punch, punchinello*, quipster, ribald, wag, wisecracker, wit*, zany*; CONCEPT 423

clown [*n2*] *stupid, ignorant person* blockhead*, boor, bucolic, buffoon, bumpkin*, chuff, churl, clodhopper*, gawk, hayseed*, hick*, hind, jake, lout, mucker*, oaf, peasant, rube, rustic, swain, yahoo*, yokel; CONCEPTS 412,423

clown [*v*] *joke* act crazy, act the fool*, bug out*, cut up*, fool around, have fun, jest, kid around; CONCEPT 386

cloy [*v*] *overfill* disgust, fill, glut, gorge, jade, nauseate, pall, sate, satiate, satisfy, sicken, stall, stodge, suffice, surfeit, weary; CONCEPT 740

cloying [*adj*] *sickly sweet* cheesy*, cornball*, corny*, cutesy*, drippy*, gooey*, honeyed, mushy*, over-sentimental, oversweet, saccharine, sappy, sentimental, sugary, syrupy; CONCEPT 401

club [*n1*] *bat, stick* baton, billy*, blackjack, bludgeon, business*, conk buster*, convincer*, cosh, cudgel, hammer, hickory, mace, mallet, nightstick, persuader*, quarterstaff, rosewood, sap, shill, shillelagh, staff, swatter, truncheon, works*; CONCEPTS 470,499

club [n2] *social organization* affiliation, alliance, association, bunch, circle, clique, company, crew, faction, gang, guild, hangout*, league, lodge, meeting, mob, order, outfit, ring, set, society, sodality, stamping ground*, union; CONCEPTS 387,439

club [n3] *golfing tool* brassie, cleek, driver, iron, mashie, midiron, niblick, putter, spoon, stick, wedge, wood; CONCEPT 364

club [v] *hit hard with object* bash, baste, batter, beat, blackjack, bludgeon, clobber, clout, cosh, cudgel, fustigate, hammer, pommel, pound, pummel, strike, whack; CONCEPT 189

clue [n] *hint, evidence* cue, dead giveaway*, hot lead*, indication, inkling, intimation, key, lead, mark, notion, pointer, print, proof, sign, solution, suggestion, suspicion, telltale, tip, tip-off*, trace, track, wind; CONCEPT 274

clue [v] *give information* acquaint, advise, apprise, fill in, give the lowdown*, give the skinny on*, hint, indicate, inform, intimate, lead to, leave evidence, leave trace, leave tracks, notify, point to, post, suggest, tell, warn, wise up; CONCEPT 60 —*Ant.* hide, keep secret

clump [n1] *mass of something* array, batch, blob, body, bunch, bundle, chunk, cluster, clutter, gob, group, hodgepodge, hunk, jumble, knot, lot, lump, nugget, parcel, set, shock, wad; CONCEPTS 432,470

clump [n2] *thumping noise* clatter, clomp, galumph, scuff, stomp, stumble, thud; CONCEPT 595

clump [v] *make thumping noise* barge, bumble, clatter, clomp, galumph, hobble, limp, lumber, plod, scuff, stamp, stomp, stumble, stump, thud, thump, tramp; CONCEPTS 65,595

clumsy [adj] *not agile; awkward* all thumbs*, blundering, blunderous, bulky, bumbling, bungling, butterfingered*, clownish, crude, elephantine, gauche, gawkish, gawky, graceless, ham-handed*, heavy, heavy-handed, helpless, hulking, ill-shaped, incompetent, inelegant, inept, inexperienced, inexpert, lubberly, lumbering, lumpish, maladroit, oafish, ponderous, splay, stumbling, unable, unadept, uncoordinated, uncouth, undexterous, uneasy, ungainly, unhandy, unskillful, untactful, untalented, untoward, unwieldy, weedy; CONCEPTS 401,402, 584 —*Ant.* adroit, agile, athletic, clever, coordinated, couth, dexterous, expert, graceful

cluster [n] *group of something* array, assemblage, band, batch, bevy, blob, body, bunch, bundle, chunk, clump, clutch, collection, covey, crew, gathering, hunk, knot, lot, pack, party, set; CONCEPT 432 —*Ant.* individual, one

cluster [v] *assemble, group* accumulate, aggregate, associate, bunch, bunch up, bundle, collect, crowd around, cumulate, flock, gang around, gather, package, parcel, round up; CONCEPT 109 —*Ant.* disperse, dissemble, let go, scatter

clutch [n] *strong hold* clamp, clasp, clench, clinch, connection, coupling, grapple, grasp, grip, gripe, link; CONCEPT 190

clutch [v] *grab, snatch* catch, cherish, clasp, clench, clinch, cling to, collar, embrace, fasten,

glom*, grapple, grasp, grip, harbor, hold, hook, keep, nab, nail*, put the snare on*, seize, snag, snatch, take; CONCEPTS 190,191 —*Ant.* let go, unfasten

clutches [n] *personal power* claws, control, custody, grasp, grip, hands, keeping, possession, sway; CONCEPTS 388,641,710

clutter [n] *disarray, mess* ataxia, chaos, confusion, derangement, disorder, hodgepodge, huddle, jumble, litter, medley, melange, muddle, rummage, scramble, shuffle, tumble, untidiness; CONCEPTS 432,674 —*Ant.* neatness, order, tidiness

clutter [v] *cause mess, disarray* dirty, jumble, litter, muddle, scatter, snarl, strew; CONCEPT 254 —*Ant.* array, clean up, neaten, order, tidy

coach [n1] *instructor, usually in recreation* drill instructor, educator, mentor, physical education instructor, skipper, teacher, trainer, tutor; CONCEPTS 350,366 —*Ant.* player, pupil, student

coach [n2] *carriage* bus, car, chaise, charabanc, fourwheeler, gocart, perambulator, stage, tallyho*, train, vehicle, victoria; CONCEPT 505

coach [v] *instruct, usually in recreation* break in*, cram, drill, educate, hone, lay it out for*, lick into shape*, prepare, pull one's coat*, put through the grind*, put through the mill*, ready, school, teach, train, tutor; CONCEPTS 285,363 —*Ant.* accept, learn, listen

coagulate [v] *clot* clabber, coalesce, compact, concentrate, concrete, condense, congeal, consolidate, curdle, dry, gel, gelate, gelatinize, glop up*, harden, inspissate, jell, jellify, jelly, lopper*, set, solidify, thicken; CONCEPT 469 —*Ant.* dilute, dissolve, melt, open, thin, unclot

coagulation [n] *clotting* agglomeration, caseation, concentration, concretion, condensation, congelation, consolidation, curdling, embolism, gelatination, incrassation, inspissation, jellification, thickening; CONCEPT 469 —*Ant.* dissolution, melting, opening, thinning

coalesce [v] *blend, come together* adhere, amalgamate, associate, bracket, cleave, cling, cohere, combine, commingle, commix, conjoin, connect, consolidate, fuse, hook up with*, incorporate, integrate, join, join up with, link, merge, mingle, mix, relate, stick, tie in with*, unite, wed; CONCEPTS 112,113 —*Ant.* divide, separate

coalition [n] *allied group, association* affiliation, alliance, amalgam, amalgamation, anschluss, bloc, coadunation, combination, combine, compact, confederacy, confederation, conjunction, consolidation, conspiracy, faction, federation, fusion, integration, league, melding, mergence, merger, merging, party, ring, unification, union; CONCEPT 381 —*Ant.* disassociation

coarse [adj1] *not fine, crude* base, bawdy, blue*, boorish, brutish, cheap, common, crass, crude, dirty, earthy, filthy, foul, foul-mouthed, gross, gruff, immodest, impolite, improper, impure, incult, indelicate, inelegant, loutish, low, lowbred, lowdown and dirty*, mean, nasty, obscene, off-color, offensive, raffish, raunchy, raw, ribald, rough, roughneck*, rude, scatological, smutty*, tacky, uncivil, uncouth, uncultivated, uncultured, unrefined, vulgar, vulgarian; CONCEPTS 401,545 —*Ant.* gentle, nice, polite, refined, sophisticated

cl
co

coarse [adj2] *rough, unrefined* chapped, coarse-grained, crude, grainy, granular, harsh, home-spun, impure, inferior, loose, lumpy, mediocre, particulate, poor quality, rough-hewn, rugged, unfinished, unpolished, unprocessed, unpurified; CONCEPTS 574,606 —*Ant.* delicate, refined, smooth, soft

coarseness [n] *rudeness, vulgarity* bawdiness, boorishness, callousness, crassness, crudity, earthiness, harshness, indelicacy, offensiveness, poor taste, rawness, ribaldry, roughness, smut*, smuttiness*, uncouthness, unevenness, unrefinement; CONCEPTS 633,645 —*Ant.* delicacy, manners, politeness, refinement, sophistication

coast [n] *border by water* bank, beach, coast-line, littoral, margin, seaboard, seacoast, seashore, seaside, shore, shoreline, strand; CONCEPTS 509,514

coast [v] *glide along without much effort* cruise, drift, float, freewheel, get by*, ride on current, sail, skate, slide, smooth along*; taxi; CONCEPTS 150,704

coastal [adj] *bordering the water* along a coast, littoral, marginal, marshy, riverine, seaside, skirting; CONCEPT 583

coat [n1] *animal hair* crust, ectoderm, epidermis, felt, fleece, fur, hide, husk, integument, leather, membrane, pelage, pellicle, pelt, peltry, protective covering, rind, scale, scarfskin, shell, skin, wool; CONCEPT 399

coat [n2] *covering* bark, coating, crust, finish, glaze, gloss, lacquer, lamination, layer, overlay, painting, plaster, priming, roughcast, set, tinge, varnish, wash, whitewashing; CONCEPT 259

coat [n3] *personal outerwear* cape, cloak, cut-away, flogger, frock, greatcoat, jacket, mackinaw, mink, overcoat, pea, raincoat, slicker, suit, tails, threads, topcoat, trench, tux, tuxedo, ulster, windbreaker, wrap; CONCEPT 451

coat [v] *cover with layer of material* apply, cover, crust, enamel, foil, glaze, incrust, laminate, paint, plaster, plate, smear, spread, stain, surface, varnish; CONCEPTS 172,202 —*Ant.* reveal, uncover

coating [n] *covering* blanket, bloom, coat, crust, dusting, encrustation, film, finish, glaze, lamination, layer, membrane, patina, sheet, skin, varnish, veneer; CONCEPT 475

coax [v] *persuade* allure, argue into, arm-twist*, barter, beguile, blandish, blarney, butter up*, cajole, come on, con, decoy, entice, flatter, get, hook, importune, induce, influence, inveigle, jawbone*, lure, pester, plague, press, prevail upon, rope in*, soft-soap*, soothe, sweet-talk, talk into, tease, tempt, urge, wangle, wheedle, work on, worm; CONCEPT 68 —*Ant.* allow, not care

cobweb [n] *entanglement; filament* fiber, gossamer, labyrinth, mesh, net, network, snare, tissue, toil, web, webbing; CONCEPTS 517,674

cocaine [n] *illegal drug* blow*, coke*, controlled substance, crack*, crystal*, freebase*, happy dust*, ice*, joy powder*, mojo*, narcotic, nose candy*, poison*, snort*, snow*, speedball*, stardust*, stuff*, sugar*, white horse*, white lady*, wings*; CONCEPT 307

cock [n] *rooster* capon, chanticleer, chicken, cock-a-doodle-doo*, cockalorum, cockerel; CONCEPT 394

cock [v] *aim up toward* erect, hump, perk up, pile, prick, raise, stack, stand erect, stand up, stick up; CONCEPT 201

cockeyed [adj] *crooked, askew* absurd, askance, askant, asymmetrical, awry, cam, canted, crazy, crooked, cross-eyed, lopsided, ludicrous, nonsensical, preposterous, squint, strabismic; CONCEPT 586 —*Ant.* level, straight

cocky/cocksure [adj] *self-assured, full of oneself* arrogant, brash, bumptious, certain, conceited, confident, egotistical, hotdogging*, hotshot*, hubristic, know-it-all*, lordly, nervy, overconfident, overweening, positive, presumptuous, self-confident, smart aleck*, smart guy*, smarty*, smarty pants*, sure, swaggering, swollen-headed, vain, wise guy*; CONCEPTS 401,404 —*Ant.* humble, modest, uncertain, unself-confident, unsure

cocoon [v] *protect with covering* cushion, encase, envelop, insulate, pad, swaddle, swathe, truss, wrap; CONCEPTS 130,134

coddle [v1] *indulge, pamper* baby, caress, cater to, cosset, cotton, favor, humor, make much of, mollycoddle, nurse, pet, play up to, spoil; CONCEPTS 110,295 —*Ant.* ignore, turn away

coddle [v2] *boil lightly, usually eggs* brew, cook, poach, simmer, steam; CONCEPT 170

code [n1] *secret language system* cipher, cryptograph; CONCEPTS 276,284

code [n2] *law, rule* canon, charter, codex, constitution, convention, custom, digest, discipline, ethics, etiquette, manners, maxim, method, regulation, system; CONCEPTS 318,688

co-dependent [adj] *unhealthy psychological reliance of one person on another* addicted, attached, hooked, interconnected, interdependent, mutually dependent, slavish trust, unhealthy confidence; CONCEPTS 404,542

codicil [n] *added part to document* addendum, addition, appendix, postscript, rider, supplement; CONCEPT 270

codify [v] *systematize* arrange, catalogue, classify, code, collect, condense, digest, order, organize, summarize, tabulate; CONCEPTS 39,84 —*Ant.* disorganize, unsystematize

coerce [v] *compel, press* beset, browbeat, bulldoze*, bully, concuss, constrain, cow, dragoon, drive, force, high pressure*, hinder, impel, intimidate, lean on, make, make an offer they can't refuse*, menace, oblige, pressurize, push, put the squeeze on*, repress, restrict, shotgun*, strong-arm, suppress, terrorize, threaten, twist one's arm*, urge; CONCEPTS 14,68 —*Ant.* leave alone

coercion [n] *compulsion, pressure* browbeating, bullying, constraint, duress, force, intimidation, menace, menacing, persuasion, restraint, strong-arm tactic*, threat, threatening, violence; CONCEPTS 14,68

coexistence [n] *happening or being at same time, place* accord, coetaneousness, coevality, coincidence, concurrence, conformity, conjunction, contemporaneousness, harmony, order, peace, simultaneousness, synchronicity; CONCEPT 407

coffee [n] *hot beverage made from beans of a tree* battery acid*, brew, café, café au lait, café noir, cappuccino, decaf, decoction, demitasse, espresso, forty weight*, hot stuff*, ink*, jamocha*, java*, joe*, mocha*, mud*, perk*, varnish remover*; CONCEPT 454

coffer [n] *large box* case, casket, chest, exchequer, repository, strongbox, treasure chest, treasury, war chest*; CONCEPT 494

coffin [n] *box for dead person* casket, catafalque, crate, funerary box, pall, pine box, pine drape*, sarcophagus; CONCEPTS 368,479, 494

cog [n] *main part of device* cogwheel, differential, fang, gear, pinion, prong, rack, ratchet, tine, tooth, transmission, tusk, wheel; CONCEPT 464

cogency [n] *effectiveness* bearing, concern, connection, conviction, convincingness, force, forcefulness, pertinence, point, potency, power, punch, relevance, strength, validity, validness; CONCEPTS 376,676 —Ant. impotence, ineffectiveness, invalidity, weakness

cogent [adj] *effective* apposite, apt, compelling, conclusive, consequential, convictive, convincing, fitting, forceful, forcible, inducing, influential, irresistible, justified, meaningful, momentous, persuasive, pertinent, potent, powerful, puissant, relevant, satisfactory, satisfying, significant, solid, sound, strong, suasive, telling, urgent, valid, weighty, well-grounded; CONCEPT 537 —Ant. impotent, ineffective, invalid, weak

cogitate [v] *think deeply about* brainstorm*, cerebrate, chew the cud*, conceive, consider, contemplate, deliberate, envisage, envision, figure, flash on*, imagine, kick around*, meditate, mull over, muse, noodle around*, ponder, reason, reflect, ruminate, speculate, stew over*; CONCEPTS 17,24 —Ant. ignore

cogitation [n] *deep thought* brainwork, cerebration, consideration, contemplation, deliberation, meditation, reflection, rumination, speculation; CONCEPT 410 —Ant. ignorance

cognate [adj] *alike, associated* affiliated, agnate, akin, allied, analogous, comparable, connate, connatural, connected, consanguine, general, generic, incident, kindred, like, related, same, similar, universal; CONCEPTS 487,573 —Ant. disassociated, dissimilar, unalike, unallied, unconnected, unlike

cognizance/cognition [n] *understanding* acknowledgment, apprehension, attention, awareness, comprehension, discernment, insight, intelligence, knowledge, mind, need, note, notice, observance, observation, perception, percipience, reasoning, recognition, regard; CONCEPT 409 —Ant. ignorance, misunderstanding

cognizant [adj] *aware* acquainted, alive, apprehensive, au courant, awake, conscious, conversant, down with, familiar, grounded, hep to*, hip to*, informed, in on, in the know, in the picture*, judicious, knowing, knowledgeable, observant, on the beam*, on to*, perceptive, plugged in, savvy, sensible, sentient, tuned in*, up on*, versed, wise to*, with it*, witting; CONCEPT 402 —Ant. ignorant, unaware, unfamiliar, uninformed, unknowledgeable, unwitting

cohabit [v] *live together* be roommates with, conjugate, couple, have relations, live illegally, live with, mingle, play house*, room together, shack up*, share address, take up housekeeping*; CONCEPTS 226,375,384

cohere [v1] *stick to, cling* adhere, associate, bind, blend, cleave, coalesce, combine, connect, consolidate, fuse, glue, hold, join, merge, unite; CONCEPTS 85,113,160 —Ant. divide, fall off, separate

cohere [v2] *agree, conform* accord, be connected, be consistent, check, check out, comport, conform, correspond, dovetail, fit in, go, hang together, harmonize, hold, hold water, make sense, relate, square; CONCEPTS 8,636, 667 —Ant. disagree, dispute, not conform

coherence [n] *agreement* adherence, attachment, bond, cementation, cling, clinging, comprehensibility, concordance, conformity, congruity, connection, consistency, consonance, construction, continuity, correspondence, inseparability, inseparableness, integrity, intelligibility, rationality, relations, solidarity, stickage, tenacity, union, unity; CONCEPTS 388,684 —Ant. disagreement, incoherence, incongruity, nonsense, unintelligibility

coherent [adj] *understandable* articulate, comprehensible, consistent, identified, intelligible, logical, lucid, meaningful, orderly, organized, rational, reasoned, sound, systematic; CONCEPT 402 —Ant. disorganized, incomprehensible, irrational, not understandable, unintelligible, unrational, unsystematic

cohort [n] *partner in activity* accomplice, adherent, aide, ally, assistant, associate, companion, company, comrade, confrere, consociate, contingent, disciple, follower, friend, hand, legion, mate, myrmidon, pal, partisan, regiment, satellite, sidekick, stall, supporter; CONCEPT 423 —Ant. enemy, opponent

coiffure [n] *hairstyle* afro, beehive, blow dry*, braids, corn rows, crew cut, DA*, dreadlocks, dreads, flip, fuzz cut*, hair, hair-comb, haircut, hairdo, permanent, pigtails, plait, ponytail, razor cut*, tail, tease, trim, wave; CONCEPTS 418,718

coil [n] *thread that curls* bight, braid, circle, convolution, corkscrew, curlicue, gyration, helix, involution, lap, loop, ring, roll, scroll, spiral, tendril, turn, twine, twirl, twist, whorl, wind; CONCEPT 436

coil [v] *curl around, entwine* convolute, convolve, corkscrew, fold, intertwine, intervolve, lap, loop, make serpentine, rotate, scroll, sinuate, snake, spiral, spire, turn, twine, twist, wind, wrap around, wreathe, writhe; CONCEPTS 201,758

coin [n] *metallic money* bread*, cash, change, chicken feed*, chips*, coinage, copper, currency, dough, gold, jack*, legal tender, meter money*, mintage, money, piece, scratch*, silver, small change*, specie; CONCEPT 340 —Ant. bill, dollar

coin [v] *create, invent* brainstorm*, compose, conceive, contrive, counterfeit, dream up, fabricate, forge, formulate, frame, head trip*, make up, make up off the top of one's head*, manufacture, mint, mold, originate, spark, spitball*, stamp, strike, think up, trump up*; CONCEPTS 36,173

coincide [v] *go along with; coexist* accompany, accord, acquiesce, agree, be concurrent, befall, be the same, come about, concert, concur, correspond, equal, eventuate, harmonize, identify, jibe, match, occur simultaneously, quadrate, square, sync, synchronize, tally; CONCEPTS 667,714; —*Ant.* clash, deviate, differ, disagree, diverge, mismatch

coincidence [n1] *agreement; coexistence* accompaniment, accord, accordance, collaboration, concomitance, concurrence, conformity, conjunction, consonance, correlation, correspondence, parallelism, synchronism, union; CONCEPTS 667,684,714 —*Ant.* clash, deviation, difference, disagreement, divergence, mismatch

coincidence [n2] *accidental happening* accident, chance, eventuality, fate, fluke, fortuity, happening, happy accident, incident, luck, stroke of luck; CONCEPTS 4,230 —*Ant.* design, plan, scheme

coincident [adj] *concurring, happening together* ancillary, attendant, attending, coinciding, collateral, concomitant, consonant, contemporaneous, contemporary, coordinate, correspondent, incident, satellite, simultaneous, synchronous; CONCEPTS 548,820

coincidental [adj] *accidental* casual, chance, circumstantial, fluky, fortuitous, incidental, unintentional, unplanned; CONCEPT 548 —*Ant.* decided, deliberate, designed, planned

cold [adj1] *chilly, freezing* algid, arctic, below freezing, below zero, benumbed, biting, bitter, blasting, bleak, boreal, brisk, brumal, chill, chilled, cool, crisp, cutting, frigid, frore, frosty, frozen, gelid, glacial, have goose bumps*, hawkish, hiemal, hyperborean, icebox, iced, icy, inclement, intense, keen, nipping, nippy, numbed, numbing, one-dog night*, penetrating, piercing, polar, raw, rimy, severe, sharp, shivery, Siberian, sleety, snappy, snowy, stinging, two-dog night*, wintry; CONCEPT 605 —*Ant.* hot, warm

cold [adj2] *aloof, unresponsive* apathetic, cold-blooded, cool, dead, distant, emotionless, frigid, frosty, glacial, icy, impersonal, imperturbable, indifferent, inhibited, inhospitable, joyless, lukewarm, matter-of-fact, passionless, phlegmatic, reserved, reticent, spiritless, standoffish, stony, unconcerned, undemonstrative, unenthusiastic, unfeeling, unimpassioned, unmoved, unresponsive, unsympathetic; CONCEPT 404 —*Ant.* animated, ardent, eager, enthusiastic, excited, fervid, friendly, interested, sympathetic, warm, zealous

cold [n] *frigid conditions* ague, algidity, algor, chill, chilliness, coldness, congelation, draft, freeze, frigidity, frost, frostbite, frostiness, frozenness, gelidity, gelidness, glaciation, goose flesh, iciness, inclemency, rawness, refrigeration, shivering, shivers, snow, wintertime, wintriness; CONCEPTS 524,610 —*Ant.* heat, warmth

cold-blooded [adj] *cruel, heartless* barbarous, brutal, callous, cold, dispassionate, hard-boiled, hardened, hard-hearted, imperturbable, inhuman, matter-of-fact, merciless, obdurate, pitiless, relentless, ruthless, savage, steely, stony-hearted, uncompassionate, unemotional, unfeeling, unmoved; CONCEPT 542 —*Ant.* compassionate, demonstrative, feeling, friendly, merciful, nice, sympathetic, warm-blooded

cold feet [n] *fear of carrying out an activity* anxiety, fear, reservations, second thoughts, timidity; CONCEPT 27

cold fish [n] *unemotional person* aloof person, iceberg*, unfeeling person; CONCEPT 412

cold-hearted [adj] *unfeeling* cold, detached, hard, hard-hearted, harsh, heartless, indifferent, insensitive, stony-hearted, uncaring, unemotional, unfriendly, unkind, unloving, unsympathetic; CONCEPT 403 —*Ant.* warm-hearted

cold shoulder [n] *snub* aloofness, brush-off, coldness, dismissal, disregard, iciness; CONCEPTS 30,633

coliseum [n] *arena for events* amphitheater, bowl, hippodrome, open-air theater, stade, stadium, theater; CONCEPT 438

collaborate [v] *work together* be in cahoots*, coact, cofunction, collude, come together, concert, concur, conspire, cooperate, coproduce, do business with, get together, glue oneself to*, go partners*, hook on, hook up*, interface, join forces, join together, join up with, participate, team up, throw in together*, throw in with*, tie in, work with; CONCEPTS 100,351,384 —*Ant.* disagree, divorce, part

collaboration [n] *cooperation* alliance, association, collusion, combination, concert, fraternization, joint effort, participation, partnership, teamwork, working together; CONCEPT 110 —*Ant.* noncooperation

collaborator [n] *person who works with another* assistant, associate, colleague, confederate, co-worker, fellow traveller, helper, partner, quisling, running dog, teammate, team player*; CONCEPTS 348,423

collage [n] *mixture of pictures* abstract composition, found art, photomontage; CONCEPT 259

collapse [n] *downfall, breakdown* bankruptcy, basket case*, cataclysm, catastrophe, cave-in, conk out*, crackup*, crash, debacle, destruction, disintegration, disorganization, disruption, exhaustion, failure, faint, flop, prostration, ruination, ruining, smash, smashup, subsidence, undoing, wreck; CONCEPTS 230,316,410,674 —*Ant.* build-up, increase, rise, success

collapse [v] *fall apart, break down* belly up*, bend, break, cave in, conk out*, crack up*, crumple, deflate, disintegrate, droop, drop, exhaust, fail, faint, fall down, flag, flake out, fold, founder, give, give in, give out, give way, go*, go to pieces*, keel over, languish, shatter, subside, succumb, tire, topple, weaken, weary, wilt, yield; CONCEPTS 252,469,702 —*Ant.* build, increase, rise

collar [n] *neck attire* bertha, choker, dicky, Eton, fichu, fraise, frill, jabot, neckband, ruff, torque, Vandyke; CONCEPTS 450,452

collar [v] *apprehend* abduct, appropriate, arrest, bag, capture, catch, cop*, corner, get, grab, hook, lay hands on, nab, nail*, prehend, secure, seize, take, tree; CONCEPTS 90,317 —*Ant.* let go, lose, release

collate [v] *sort collection* adduce, analogize, assemble, bracket, collect, compare, compose, contrast, examine, gather, group, match, order, relate, verify; CONCEPTS 84,158

collateral [adj] *indirect, secondary* accessory, accompanying, added, adjunctive, adjuvant, ancillary, appurtenant, attendant, auxiliary, circuitous, coincident, complementary, concomitant, concurrent, confirmatory, coordinate, corresponding, corroborative, dependent, incident, lateral, not lineal, parallel, related, roundabout, satellite, side, sub, subordinate, subservient, subsidiary, supporting, tributary, under; CONCEPTS 546,567,831 —Ant. chief, direct, main, primary, principal

collateral [n] *monetary deposit* assurance, bond, endorsement, guarantee, pledge, promise, security, surety, warrant, wealth; CONCEPT 344

colleague [n] *associate, fellow worker* aide, ally, assistant, auxiliary, buddy, chum, coadjutor, cohort, collaborator, companion, compatriot, compeer, comrade, confederate, confrere, coworker, crony, friend, helper, pal, partner, teammate, workmate; CONCEPTS 348,423 —Ant. antagonist, detractor, enemy, opponent, opposer

collect [v1] *accumulate, come together* aggregate, amass, array, assemble, cluster, compile, congregate, congress, convene, converge, convoke, corral, flock, flock together, gather, get hold of, group, heap, hoard, muster, rally, rendezvous, round up, save, scare up, stockpile; CONCEPTS 109,114 —Ant. dispense, disperse, disseminate, distribute, divide, scatter, share

collect [v2] *obtain (money)* acquire, dig up, muster, pass the hat*, raise, requisition, secure, solicit; CONCEPT 342 —Ant. compensate, give, meed

collected [adj] *composed, calm* confident, cool, easy, easygoing, levelheaded, nonchalant, peaceful, placid, poised, possessed, quiet, sanguine, self-possessed, serene, still, sure, temperate, together, tranquil, unflappable, unperturbable, unperturbed, unruffled; CONCEPT 401 —Ant. agitated, disorganized, excited, mixed up, upset, worried

collection [n] *group, accumulation* accumulating, acquiring, acquisition, agglomeration, amassing, amassment, anthology, assemblage, assembling, assembly, assortment, batch, bringing together, caboodle, clump, cluster, collation, combination, company, compilation, congeries, congregation, convocation, crowd, cumulation, digest, gathering, heap, hoard, kit, levy, lot, mass, medley, mess, miscellany, mobilization, muster, number, obtaining, omnibus, pile, quantity, securing, selection, set, stack, stock, stockpile, store; CONCEPTS 109,432

collective [adj] *composite* aggregate, assembled, collated, combined, common, compiled, concentrated, concerted, conjoint, consolidated, cooperative, corporate, cumulative, gathered, grouped, heaped, hoarded, joint, massed, mutual, piled, shared, unified, united; CONCEPT 585 —Ant. divided, separate

college [n] *institution of higher education* alma mater, association, brainery*, halls of ivy*, halls of knowledge*, institute, lyceum, organization, seminary, university; CONCEPTS 287,288,289

college student [n] *person studying at institution of higher education* first year student, grad student*, graduate student, junior, senior, sophomore, undergrad*, undergraduate student; CONCEPT 350

collide [v] *slam into* bang, beat, break up, bump, clash, conflict, crash, crunch*, disagree, fenderbend*, fragment, hit, jolt, meet head-on*, pile up*, plow into*, pulverize*, scrap*, shatter, sideswipe, smash, splinter, strike, wrack up*; CONCEPTS 189,248

collision [n] *accident* blow, bump, butt, concussion, contact, crash, demolishment, destruction, dilapidation, encounter, fender bender*, head-on*, hit, impact, jar, jolt, knock, percussion, pileup*, rap, ruin, shock, sideswipe, slam, smash, strike, thud, thump, wreck; CONCEPTS 189,230,674

collocate [v] *compile* accumulate, assemble, collect, collimate, gather, parallel; CONCEPT 84

colloquial [adj] *particular, familiar to an area, informal* chatty, common, conversational, demotic, dialectal, everyday, idiomatic, jive*, popular, street*, vernacular; CONCEPT 267 —Ant. correct, formal, standard, stilted

colloquy [n] *conversation, debate* buzz session, chat, chinfest*, chitchat, clambake*, colloquium, confab*, confabulation, conference, converse, dialogue, discourse, discussion, flap*, gab fest*, gam*, groupthink*, huddle*, palaver, parley, powwow*, rap*, rap session*, seminar, talk, talkfest*; CONCEPT 266

collusion [n] *secret understanding, often with intent to defraud* bait and switch*, bill of goods*, bunco*, cahoots*, complicity, con game*, connivance, conspiracy, craft, deceit, diddling*, dodge, double-cross, fast shuffle, flam*, flimflam*, fradulent artifice, graft, guilt, guiltiness, gyp, intrigue, plot, racket, scam, scheme, shell game*, skunk*, sting*, trick, whitewash; CONCEPTS 114,660

cologne [n] *fragrance product* fragrance, perfume, scent, toilet water; CONCEPTS 599,600

colonial [adj] *pioneering, relating to a nonindependent or new territory* crude, dependent, dominion, early American, emigrant, frontier, immigrant, new, outland, pilgrim, pioneer, prerevolutionary, primitive, provincial, puritan, territorial, transplanted, uncultured, unsettled, unsophisticated, wild; CONCEPTS 549,799 —Ant. modern, new

colonization [n] *settlement of area* clearing, establishment, expanding, expansion, founding, immigration, migration, opening up, peopling, pioneering, populating, settlement, settling, squatting, transplanting; CONCEPTS 198,298

colony [n] *community* antecedents, clearing, dependency, dominion, mandate, new land, offshoot, outpost, possession, protectorate, province, satellite, settlement, subject state, swarm, territory; CONCEPTS 379,512

color [n1] *pigment, shade* blush, cast, chroma, chromaticity, chromatism, chromism, colorant, coloration, coloring, complexion, dye, glow, hue, intensity, iridescence, luminosity, paint, pigmentation, polychromasia, saturation, stain, tinct, tincture, tinge, tint, undertone, value, wash; CONCEPT 622

color [n2] *deceptive appearance* deception, disguise, excuse, facade, face, false show, front, guise, mask, plea, pretense, pretext, put-on, semblance, show; CONCEPTS 59,716

color [v1] *make pigmented; shade* adorn, blacken, bloom, blush, burn, chalk, crayon, crimson, darken, daub, dye, embellish, emblazon, enamel, enliven, flush, fresco, gild, glaze, gloss, illuminate, imbue, infuse, lacquer, paint, pigment, pinken, redden, rouge, stain, stipple, suffuse, tinge, tint, tone, variegate, wash; CONCEPTS 250,469 —Ant. discolor, pale, whiten

color [v2] *distort, exaggerate* angle*, belie, cook up*, disguise, doctor*, embroider*, fake, falsify, fudge*, garble, gloss over, magnify, misrepresent, misstate, overstate, pad*, pervert, prejudice, slant*, taint, twist*, warp*; CONCEPTS 49,63 —*Ant.* be truthful, represent

colored [adj1] *not white* dyed, flushed, glowing, hued, shaded, stained, tinged, tinted, washed; CONCEPT 618 —*Ant.* white

colored [adj2] *distorted* angled, biased, false, falsified, misrepresented, one-sided, partial, partisan, perverted, prejudiced, prepossessed, tampered with, tendentious, warped*; CONCEPT 582 —*Ant.* genuine, honest, real, truthful

colorful [adj1] *brilliant, intensely hued* bright, chromatic, flashy, florid, gaudy, gay, hued, intense, jazzy, kaleidoscopic, loud, motley, multicolored, picturesque, prismatic, psychedelic, rich, showy, splashy, variegated, vibrant, vivid; CONCEPTS 617,618 —*Ant.* colorless, drab, dreary, faded, plain, uncolored, uncolorful

colorful [adj2] *full of life, interesting* brave, characterful, distinctive, flaky*, gay, glamorous, graphic, jazzy, lively, picturesque, rich, stimulating, unusual, vivid; CONCEPT 404 —*Ant.* boring, dull, lifeless, plain, uninteresting

colorless [adj1] *without hue* achromatic, achromic, anemic, ashen, ashy, blanched, bleached, cadaverous, doughy, drab, dull, faded, flat, ghastly, livid, lurid, neutral, pale, sickly, uncolored, wan, washed out, waxen, white; CONCEPT 618 —*Ant.* brilliant, colored, colorful, motley, rich, stimulating, vibrant, vivid

colorless [adj2] *unlively, uninteresting* characterless, dreary, dull, insipid, lackluster, lifeless, prosaic, run-of-the-mill*, tame, unmemorable, unpassioned, vacuous, vapid; CONCEPT 404 —*Ant.* brilliant, distinctive, intense, interesting, lively, stimulating, vibrant

colossal [adj] *very large* barn door*, behemothic, blimp*, cyclopean, elephantine, enormous, gargantuan, giant, gigantic, huge, humongous*, immense, jumbo, mammoth, mondo*, monstrous, mountainous, super, titanic, vast; CONCEPT 781 —*Ant.* small, teeny, tiny

colossus [n] *giant thing* behemoth, Cyclops, Gargantua, giant, Godzilla, Goliath, Hercules, leviathan, mammoth, Samson, titan; CONCEPT 424

colt [n] *young horse* filly, fledgling, foal, rookie, sapling, yearling, youngling, youngster; CONCEPT 394

column [n1] *line, procession* cavalcade, company, file, list, platoon, queue, rank, row, string, train; CONCEPTS 432,727

column [n2] *pillar* brace, buttress, caryatid, colonnade, cylinder, mast, minaret, monolith, monument, obelisk, pedestal, peristyle, pier, pilaster, post, prop, pylon, shaft, standard, stay, stele, support, totem, tower, underpinning, upright; CONCEPT 440

coma [n] *deep unconsciousness* blackout, dullness, faint, hebetude, insensibility, lethargy, oblivion, sleep, slumber, somnolence, stupor, swoon, syncope, torpidity, torpor, trance; CONCEPT 315 —*Ant.* alertness, consciousness, wakefulness

comatose [adj] *unconscious* cold, dead, dead to the world*, dopey, drowsy, drugged, hebetudinous, inconscious, insensible, lethargic, out, out cold*, out to lunch*, senseless, sleepy, sluggish, slumberous, somnolent, soporose, stupefied, stupid, stuporous, torpid, vegged out*; CONCEPT 539 —*Ant.* alert, awake, conscious

comb [v1] *arrange hair* adjust, card, cleanse, curry, disentangle, dress, groom, hackle, hatchel, lay smooth, rasp, scrape, separate, smooth, sort, straighten, tease, untangle; CONCEPT 162

comb [v2] *search by ransacking* beat, beat the bushes*, examine, finecomb*, forage, go through with fine-tooth comb*, grub, hunt, inspect, investigate, leave no stone unturned*, look high and low*, probe, rake, ransack, rummage, scour, screen, scrutinize, search high heaven*, sift, sweep, turn inside out*, turn upside down*; CONCEPT 216

combat [n] *battle* action, affray, battle royal*, brush, brush-off, conflict, contest, encounter, engagement, fight, flap, fray, jackpot*, mix-up*, run-in*, service, shoot-out*, skirmish, struggle, war, warfare; CONCEPTS 86,106 —*Ant.* accord, compromise, peace, retreat, surrender, truce

combat [v] *fight* battle, buck, clash, contend, contest, cope, cross swords with*, defy, dispute, do battle with, duel, engage, fight, go up against, oppose, put up a fight*, repel, resist, shoot it out*, strive, struggle, traverse, war, withstand; CONCEPTS 86,106 —*Ant.* agree, compromise, retreat, surrender

combatant [n] *fighter* adversary, antagonist, assailant, attacker, battler, belligerent, contender, enemy, foe, serviceman, soldier, warrior; CONCEPT 358

combative [adj] *aggressive* antagonistic, bellicose, belligerent, cantankerous, contentious, cussed, energetic, fire-eating*, gladiatorial, hawkish, militant, ornery*, pugnacious, quarrelsome, ructious, scrappy, strenuous, trigger-happy*, truculent, warlike, warring; CONCEPTS 401,404 —*Ant.* agreeable, compromising, peaceful, peaceloving

combination [n1] *mixture, blend* aggregate, amalgam, amalgamation, blending, brew, coalescence, combo, composite, compound, connection, consolidation, everything but kitchen sink*, fusion, junction, medley, merger, miscellany, mishmash*, mix, olio, order, sequence, solution, soup, stew, succession, synthesis, unification, union; CONCEPT 432 —*Ant.* detachment, division, parting, separation

combination [n2] *alliance, association* affiliation, bloc, cabal, cahoots, camarilla, cartel, circle, clique, club, coadunation, coalition, combine, compound, confederacy, confederation, conjunction, connection, consolidation, consortium, conspiracy, coterie, faction, federation, gang, guild, hookup*, mafia, melding, mergence, merger, merging, partnership, party, pool, ring, set, syndicate, tie-up*, trust, unification, union; CONCEPT 381 —*Ant.* dissolution, disunion, separation, severance

combine [v] *connect, integrate* amalgamate, associate, band, bind, blend, bond, bracket, bunch up, coadjute, coalesce, commingle, compound, conjoin, cooperate, couple, dub, fuse, get together, glue oneself to, hitch on*, hook on*, incorporate, interface, join, league, link, marry, merge, mingle, mix, network, plug into, pool, put together, relate, slap on*, stand in with, synthesize, tack on*, tag on*, team up with*, throw in together*, tie up with*, unify, unite, wed; CONCEPT 113 —Ant. detach, disconnect, dissolve, divide, part, separate

combustible [adj] *able to be exploded* burnable, comburent, combustive, explosive, fiery, firing, flammable, ignitable, incendiary, inflammable, kindling, volatile; CONCEPTS 485,537 —Ant. noncombustible, nonexplosive

combustion [n] *explosion; on fire* agitation, candescence, disturbance, thermogenesis, flaming, ignition, kindling, oxidization, thermogenesis, tumult, turmoil; CONCEPTS 521,676,724

come [v1] *advance, approach* appear, arrive, attain, be accessible, be at disposal, become, be convenient, be handy, be obtainable, be ready, blow in*, bob up, breeze in*, burst, buzz*, check in*, clock in*, close in, draw near, drop in, enter, fall by, fall in, flare*, get, get in, happen, hit, hit town*, make it, make the scene*, materialize, move, move toward, near, occur, originate, pop in*, pop up*, punch in*, punch the clock*, reach, ring in*, roll in*, show, show up, sign in, sky in*, spring in, turn out, turn up, wind up at; CONCEPT 159 —Ant. depart, go, leave, recede, retreat

come [v2] *happen* befall, betide, break, chance, come to pass, develop, fall, hap*, occur, take place, transpire, turn out; CONCEPT 4

come [v3] *extend, reach* add up, aggregate, amount, become, come over, develop, expand, get, go, grow, join, mature, number, run, run into, spread, stretch, sum to, total, turn, wax; CONCEPTS 239,701

come about [v] *happen* arise, befall, come to pass, occur, result, take place, transpire; CONCEPT 701

come across [v] *encounter, find* bump into, chance upon, discover, happen upon, hit upon, light upon, meet, notice, stumble upon, uncover, unearth; CONCEPTS 38,183

come along [v] *progress, develop* do well, get on, improve, mend, perk up, pick up, rally, recover, recuperate, show improvement; CONCEPT 700

come at [v1] *reach, attain* accomplish, achieve, discover, feel for, find, grasp, succeed, touch, win; CONCEPTS 34,706

come at [v2] *attack* assail, assault, charge, fall upon, fly at, go for, invade, light into*, rush; CONCEPT 86

comeback [n1] *recovery, triumph* improvement, rally, rebound, resurgence, return, revival, victory, winning; CONCEPT 706 —Ant. failure

comeback [n2] *snappy retort* answer back, quip, rejoinder, repartee, reply, response, retaliation, riposte; CONCEPT 278

come back [v] *return* come again, do better, reappear, recover, recur, re-enter, remigrate, resume, triumph; CONCEPT 239 —Ant. depart, go, leave

come between [v] *alienate* divide, estrange, interfere, interpose, interrupt, intervene, meddle, part, put at odds, separate; CONCEPTS 14,386 —Ant. bring together, join, unite

come by [v1] *acquire* get, lay hold of, obtain, procure, secure, take possession of, win; CONCEPTS 124,129 —Ant. give, lose, miss

come by [v2] *visit someone* call, come over, drop by, drop in, look in, look up, meet, pay a call, pop in, run in, see, step in, stop by, visit; CONCEPT 227

come clean [v] *acknowledge information* admit, confess, explain, make clean breast*, own up, reveal; CONCEPTS 49,57 —Ant. hide, hold, secret

comedian [n] *funny person, often professional* actor, banana*, card*, clown, comic, cutup, droll, entertainer, farceur, humorist, jester, joker, jokester, laugh, merry-andrew, million laughs*, quipster, stand-up comic, stooge*, top banana*, wag, wisecracker, wit*, zany*; CONCEPTS 352,423

comedown [n] *letdown, blow* anticlimax, blow, collapse, comeuppance, crash, cropper*, decline, defeat, deflation, demotion, descent, disappointment, discomfiture, dive, down, downfall, failure, fall, flop*, humiliation, pratfall*, reverse, ruin, setback, undoing, wreck; CONCEPTS 674,699 —Ant. ascent, boon, boost, fortune, promotion

come down [v] *worsen* decline, decrease, degenerate, descend, deteriorate, fail, fall, go downhill, reduce, suffer; CONCEPT 698 —Ant. boost, improve

come down on [v] *criticize strongly* attack, dress down, jump on, land on, rebuke, reprimand, scold; CONCEPT 52 —Ant. compliment, laud, praise

come down with [v] *contract illness* be stricken with, catch, contract, fall ill, fall victim to, sicken, take, take sick; CONCEPTS 93,303 —Ant. be immune

comedy [n] *funny entertainment* ball*, burlesque, camp, chaffing, comicality, comicalness, comic drama, drollery, drollness, facetiousness, farce, field day*, fun, fun and games*, funnies*, funniness, gag show, grins, high camp*, high time, hilarity, hoopla, humor, humorousness, interlude, jesting, joking, laughs, light entertainment, merry-go-round*, picnic, play on, satire, schtick*, send-up, sitcom*, slapstick, takeoff, travesty, vaudeville, wisecracking, witticism, wittiness; CONCEPTS 263,293 —Ant. tragedy

come forward [v] *volunteer services* appear, make proposal, offer services, present oneself, proffer oneself; CONCEPT 67

come from [v] *arise, emanate* accrue, derive from, ejaculate, emerge, end up, flow, hail from, issue, originate, proceed, result, rise, spring, stem, turn out; CONCEPTS 105,179

come in [v] *enter place* alight, appear, arrive, cross threshold, disembark, finish, immigrate, intrude, land, pass in, reach, set foot in, show up; CONCEPT 159 —Ant. depart, exit, go, leave

come in for [v] *be eligible for something* acquire, bear brunt, endure, get, receive, suffer; CONCEPTS 23,124

comely [adj] *beautiful* a ten*, attractive, beauteous, becoming, blooming, buxom, fair, fine, good-looking, gorgeous, graceful, handsome,

CO
CO

nice, pleasing, pretty, pulchritudinous, stunning, wholesome, winsome; CONCEPT 579 —*Ant.* bad-looking, despicable, disagreeable, offensive, repellent, repulsive, revolting, ugly, unattractive

come off [v] *transpire* befall, betide, break, chance, click, come about, develop, go, go off, go over, hap*, happen, occur, pan out, prove out, succeed, take place; CONCEPT 4 —*Ant.* not happen

come on [v1] *advance, progress* develop, gain, improve, increase, make headway, proceed; CONCEPT 704 —*Ant.* decline, deteriorate, fall, reduce, retreat, worsen

come on [v2] *appear, enter* begin, come across, come into, come upon, encounter, meet, pass in, set foot in*, take place; CONCEPT 119 —*Ant.* depart, exit, go, leave

come out [v1] *make public* appear, be announced, be brought out, be disclosed, be divulged, be exposed, be issued, be made known, be promulgated, be published, be released, be reported, be revealed, break*, debut, get out, leak*, out, transpire; CONCEPT 60 —*Ant.* hide

come out [v2] *conclude* end, result, terminate, transpire; CONCEPT 119

come out with [v] *disclose information* acknowledge, bring out, chime in*, come clean, declare, deliver, divulge, lay open, own, own up, say, state, tell, throw out, utter; CONCEPT 60 —*Ant.* hide, secret

come through [v1] *accomplish goal* achieve, be successful, be victorious, carry out, chip in, contribute, kick in, pitch in, prevail, score, succeed, triumph, win; CONCEPT 706 —*Ant.* fail

come through [v2] *survive bad situation* endure, live through, persist, pull through, ride, ride out, survive, weather storm*, withstand; CONCEPT 23 —*Ant.* fail

come unglued [v] *go to pieces* break down, come apart at the seams*, come unstuck, come unwrapped, disintegrate, fall apart, fall to bits*, fall to pieces*, malfunction; CONCEPTS 252,469

come up [v] *happen suddenly* arise, crop up, occur, rise, spring up, turn up; CONCEPT 119

come upon [v] *happen upon* bump into*, chance, come across, encounter, meet; CONCEPTS 38,384

comeuppance [n] *deserved fate* due, due reward, just deserts, just punishment, recompense, requital, retribution; CONCEPT 679

come up to [v] *meet expectations* admit of comparison with, approach, arrive, bear comparison with, come near, compare with, equal, extend, get near, match, measure up to, rank with, reach, resemble, rival, stand comparison with; CONCEPT 667

come up with [v] *suggest, create* advance, bring forth, compose, detect, discover, find, furnish, invent, offer, originate, present, produce, propose, provide, recommend, stumble upon, submit, uncover; CONCEPTS 75,173

comfort [n1] *good feeling; ease* abundance, alleviation, amenity, assuagement, bed of roses*, cheer, cheerfulness, complacency, contentment, convenience, coziness, creature comforts*, enjoyment, exhilaration, facility, gratification, happiness, luxury, opulence, peacefulness, pleasure, plenty, poise, quiet,

relaxation, relief, repose, rest, restfulness, satisfaction, snugness, succor, sufficiency, warmth, well-being; CONCEPTS 230,410,720 —*Ant.* aggravation, annoyance, bother, botheration, distress, exasperation, irritation, torment, torture

comfort [n2] *aid, help* alleviation, assist, compassion, compensation, consolation, encouragement, hand, lift, pity, relief, secours, solace, succor, support, sympathy; CONCEPTS 337,712 —*Ant.* hindrance, hurt, injury, torment, torture

comfort [v] *make to feel better* abate, aid, allay, alleviate, ameliorate, assist, assuage, bolster, buck up*, calm, cheer, commiserate with, compose, condole, confirm, console, delight, divert, ease, encourage, enliven, free, gladden, grant respite, hearten, help, inspirit, invigorate, lighten burden, make well, mitigate, nourish, put at ease, quiet fears, reanimate, reassure, refresh, relieve, remedy, revitalize, revive, salve, soften, solace, soothe, strengthen, stroke, succor, support, sustain, sympathize, uphold, upraise; CONCEPTS 7,22,572 —*Ant.* aggravate, annoy, bother, distress, exasperate, hurt, irritate, provoke, torment, torture, trouble, vex

comfortable [adj1] *good feeling* adequate, agreeable, appropriate, at rest, cared for, cheerful, complacent, contented, convenient, cozy, delightful, easy, enjoyable, enjoying, gratified, hale, happy, healthy, hearty, loose, loose-fitting, made well, pleasant, pleased, protected, relaxed, relaxing, relieved, rested, restful, restored, satisfactory, satisfying, serene, sheltered, snug, snug as a bug in a rug*, soft, soothed, strengthened, untroubled, useful, warm, well-off; CONCEPT 572 —*Ant.* discontented, hopeless, miserable, neglected, uncomfortable, unhappy, upset

comfortable [adj2] *affluent, wealthy* ample, easy, enough, prosperous, substantial, sufficient, suitable, well-heeled*, well-off, well-to-do; CONCEPT 334 —*Ant.* destitute, hopeless, needy, pitiable, poor, uncomfortable, wretched

comfortable [adj3] *more than adequate* ample, commodious, cushy, luxurious, palatial, rich, roomy, spacious; CONCEPT 485

comfort food [n] *satisfying food* home cooking, meat and potatoes, Mom's food, plain food, prepackaged food; CONCEPTS 457,460,461

comforting [adj] *cheering* abating, allaying, alleviating, analeptic, assuaging, consolatory, consoling, curing, encouraging, freeing, healthgiving, heart-warming, inspiriting, invigorating, lightening, mitigating, reassuring, refreshing, relieving, remedying, restoring, revitalizing, reviving, softening, solacing, soothing, succoring, sustaining, tranquilizing, upholding, warming; CONCEPT 529 —*Ant.* aggravating, depressing, dispiriting, distressing, disturbing, irritating, upsetting, worrying

comic [n] *funny person, often professional* banana*, buffoon*, card*, clown, comedian, droll, humorist, jester, joker, jokester, life of the party*, million laughs*, quipster, stand-up comic, stooge*, top banana*, wag*, wit*; CONCEPTS 352,423 —*Ant.* tragedian

comic/comical [adj] *amusing* absurd, batty, boffo*, camp*, comical, crazy, dippy, diverting, dizzy, droll, entertaining, facetious, farcical, flaky*, fool, foolheaded, for grins*, freaky, funny, gelastic, goofus*, goofy, gump*, horse's tail*, humorous, ironic, jerky, jocular, joking, joshing, laughable, light, loony, ludicrous, Mickey Mouse*, nutty, off the wall*, priceless, ridiculous, risible, schtick*, screwy, side-splitting, silly, wacky, waggish, whimsical, witty; CONCEPTS 401,529 —*Ant.* sad, serious, sober, solemn, tragic, unfunny

coming [adj] *approaching, promising* about to happen, advancing, almost on one, anticipated, aspiring, at hand, certain, close, converging, deserving, docking, drawing near, due, en route, eventual, expected, fated, foreseen, forthcoming, future, gaining upon, getting near, immediate, imminent, impending, in prospect, instant, in store, in the offing, in the wind*, in view, marked, near, nearing, next, nigh, oncoming, ordained, predestined, preparing, progressing, prospective, pursuing, running after, subsequent, to be, up-and-coming; CONCEPTS 537,799

coming [n] *arrival* accession, advent, approach, landing, reception; CONCEPTS 119,159 —*Ant.* departing, departure, exit, going, leaving

command [n1] *directive, instruction* act, adjuration, ban, behest, bidding, call, canon, caveat, charge, citation, commandment, decree, demand, devoir, dictate, dictation, dictum, direction, duty, edict, enactment, exaction, fiat, imperative, imposition, injunction, interdiction, law, mandate, notification, obligation, order, ordinance, precept, prescript, proclamation, prohibition, proscription, regulation, request, requirement, requisition, responsibility, rule, subpoena, summons, ultimatum, warrant, will, word, writ; CONCEPTS 274,662 —*Ant.* contradiction, countermand, opposition, recall, reversal, revocation

command [n2] *rule, power* ability, absolutism, aplomb, authority, authorization, charge, coercion, compulsion, constraint, control, despotism, domination, dominion, expertise, expertism, expertness, government, grasp, grip, hold, jurisdiction, know-how*, leadership, management, might, prerogative, primacy, restraint, right, royalty, skill, sovereignty, strings*, supervision, supremacy, sway, tyranny, upper hand*; CONCEPT 376 —*Ant.* subordination

command [v1] *demand* adjure, appoint, authorize, ban, bar, beckon, bid, call, call for, call on, call the signals*, call upon, charge, check, cite, compel, debar, dictate, direct, enact, enjoin, exact, forbid, force upon, give directions, give orders, grant, impose, inflict, inhibit, instruct, interdict, lay down the law, mark out, oblige, ordain, order, ordinate, proclaim, prohibit, put foot down*, require, requisition, restrain, rule out, send for, set, subpoena, summon, take charge, take lead, task, tell, warn; CONCEPT 53 —*Ant.* contradict, countermand, oppose, recall, reverse, revoke

command [v2] *rule, have power* administer, boss, charge, check, coach, coerce, compel, conduct, conquer, constrain, control, curb, determine, dictate, direct, dominate, domineer, exact, exercise power, force, govern, guide, have authority, head, hinder, hold office, influence, lead, manage, officiate, oppress, overbear, override, overcome, predominate, preside over,

prevail, push, regulate, reign, reign over, repress, restrain, run, stop, subdue, superintend, supervise, sway, take over, tyrannize, wield; CONCEPTS 133,298 —*Ant.* follow

commandeer [v] *seize, take over* accroach, activate, annex, appropriate, arrogate, assume, confiscate, conscript, draft, enslave, expropriate, grab, hijack, liberate, moonlight requisition*, preempt, requisition, sequester, sequestrate, snatch, take, usurp; CONCEPTS 90,142

commander [n] *leader of military or other organization* administrator, big cheese*, boss, captain, chief, CO*, commandant, czar, director, don, exec, guru, head, head honcho*, head person, higher up, high priest/priestess*, kingfish*, kingpin*, lead-off person*, mastermind, officer, point person*, ruler, skipper, top banana*, top brass*, top dog*; CONCEPTS 347,358 —*Ant.* follower

commanding [adj] *superior, authoritative* advantageous, arresting, assertive, autocratic, bossy, compelling, controlling, decisive, dictatorial, dominant, dominating, forceful, imperious, imposing, impressive, in charge, lofty, peremptory, striking; CONCEPTS 536,574 —*Ant.* indecisive, inferior, unassertive, uncontrolling

commemorate [v] *honor, observe occasion* admire, celebrate, immortalize, keep, memorialize, monument, monumentalize, observe, pay tribute to, perpetuate, remember, salute, solemnize; CONCEPTS 69,377,384 —*Ant.* dishonor, forget, neglect

commemoration [n] *honoring, observance* celebration, ceremony, custom, memorial service, monumentalization, recognition, remembrance, tribute; CONCEPT 377 —*Ant.* forgetting, neglect, negligence, unobservance

commemorative [adj] *in honor of something* celebratory, commemoratory, dedicatory, in memory of, in remembrance, memorial, observing; CONCEPT 555 —*Ant.* dishonoring, forgetful, neglectful, neglecting

commence [v] *start action* arise, begin, come into being, come into existence, embark on, enter upon, get cracking*, get going, get one's feet wet*, get show on road*, hit the ground running*, inaugurate, initiate, jump into, kick off*, launch, lead off, open, originate, start the ball rolling*, take up, tear into; CONCEPTS 119, 234 —*Ant.* cease, complete, end, finish, stop

commencement [n] *ceremony marking the beginning of stage* admission, alpha, birth, bow, celebration, convocation, countdown, curtain-raiser*, dawn, dawning, genesis, graduation, initiation, kickoff*, onset, opener, opening, outset, proem, services, start, starting point, tee off*; CONCEPT 377 —*Ant.* cessation, completion, end, ending, finish, stop

commend [v1] *recommend, praise* acclaim, accredit, advocate, applaud, approve, boost, build, build up, compliment, countenance, endorse, eulogize, extol, give a posy*, gold star*, hail, hand it to*, hats off to*, hear it for*, kudize, laud, pat on the back*, puff up, sanction, speak highly of, stroke, support; CONCEPTS 69,75 —*Ant.* censure, criticize, disapprove, rebuke, reprimand

commend [v2] *hand over with confidence* assign, commit, confer, confide, consign, deliver, entrust, proffer, relegate, resign, tender, trust, turn over, yield; CONCEPTS *108,132* —*Ant.* deny, keep, refuse

commendable [*adj*] *praiseworthy* admirable, creditable, deserving, estimable, excellent, exemplary, laudable, meritable, meritorious, praisable, thankworthy, worthy; CONCEPTS *527,572* —*Ant.* blameworthy, poor, unworthy

commendation [*n*] *giving of praise; acclaim* acclamation, approbation, approval, award, bouquet, Brownie points*, credit, encomium, encouragement, good opinion, honor, panegyric, pat on the back*, pat on the head*, pay, plum, points*, posy, PR*, puff, pumping up*, rave, recommendation, shot in the arm*, stroke, stroking, tribute; CONCEPTS *69,337* —*Ant.* blame, censure, criticism, disapproval, reprimand

commensurate [*adj*] *adequate, corresponding* appropriate, coextensive, comparable, compatible, consistent, due, equal, equivalent, fit, fitting, in accord, proportionate, sufficient, symmetrical; CONCEPTS *563,566* —*Ant.* inadequate, inappropriate, incommensurate, unacceptable, unfitting

comment [*n*] *statement of opinion; explanation* animadversion, annotation, backtalk*, buzz*, comeback*, commentary, crack*, criticism, dictum, discussion, editorial, elucidation, exposition, footnote, gloss, hearsay, illustration, input, judgment, mention, mouthful, note, obiter, observation, opinion, remark, report, review, two cents' worth*, wisecrack*; CONCEPTS *51,278* —*Ant.* quiet, silence

comment [*v*] *make statement of opinion, explanation* affirm, animadvert, annotate, assert, bring out, clarify, commentate, conclude, construe, criticize, disclose, elucidate, explain, explicate, expound, express, gloss, illustrate, interject, interpose, interpret, mention, note, notice, observe, opine, pass on, point out, pronounce, reflect, remark, say, state, touch upon; CONCEPTS *51,57* —*Ant.* keep quiet, remain

commentary [*n*] *analysis* annotation, appreciation, comment, consideration, criticism, critique, description, discourse, exegesis, explanation, exposition, gloss, narration, notes, obiter dictum, observation, remark, review, treatise, voice-over; CONCEPTS *51,278*

commentator [*n*] *reporter* analyst, annotator, announcer, correspondent, critic, expositor, interpreter, observer, pundit, reviewer, sportscaster, writer; CONCEPT *356*

commerce [*n*] *buying and selling* business, dealing, dealings, economics, exchange, industry, marketing, merchandising, merchantry, retailing, trade, traffic, truck, wholesaling; CONCEPTS *325,770*

commercial [*adj1*] *concerning business, marketing* across the counter*, bartering, commissary, economic, exchange, financial, fiscal, for sale, in demand, in the market, market, marketable, mercantile, merchandising, monetary, pecuniary, popular, profitable, profit-making, retail, retailing, saleable, sales, supplying, trade, trading, wholesale, wholesaling; CONCEPT *536* —*Ant.* noncommercial

commercial [*adj2*] *intended for financial gain* exploited, for profit, investment, materialistic, mercenary, monetary, money-making,

pecuniary, profitmaking, venal, Wall Street*; CONCEPT *334* —*Ant.* noncommercial, not-for-profit

commercialize [*v*] *prepare for saleability* advertise, cheapen, degrade, depreciate, develop as business, lessen, lower, make bring returns, make marketable, make pay, make profitable, make saleable, market, sell; CONCEPT *324*

commingle [*v*] *blend* amalgamate, combine, commix, compound, inmix, integrate, intermingle, intermix, join, merge, mingle, unite; CONCEPT *109* —*Ant.* divide, separate

commiserate [*v*] *listen to woes of another* ache, compassionate, condole, console, feel, feel for, have mercy, pity, share sorrow, sympathize; CONCEPTS *110,596* —*Ant.* be indifferent, turn away

commission [*n1*] *task, duty* agency, appointment, authority, brevet, certificate, charge, consignment, delegation, deputation, diploma, embassy, employment, errand, function, instruction, legation, mandate, mission, obligation, office, permit, power of attorney, proxy, trust, warrant, work; CONCEPT *362*

commission [*n2*] *share of a profit* allowance, ante, bite*, bonus, brokerage, chunk, compensation, cut, cut-in*, discount, end*, factorage, fee, indemnity, juice, pay, payment, percentage, piece, piece of the action*, rake-off*, remuneration, royalty, salary, slice*, stipend, taste, vigorish; CONCEPTS *329,344*

commission [*n3*] *group working together toward goal* board, commissioners, committee, delegation, deputation, representative; CONCEPT *381*

commission [*v*] *authorize or delegate task* accredit, appoint, assign, bespeak, bid, charge, command, commit, confide to, consign, constitute, contract, crown, depute, deputize, dispatch, employ, empower, enable, engage, enlist, enroll, entrust, hire, inaugurate, induct, instruct, invest, license, name, nominate, ordain, order, select, send; CONCEPTS *50,88,324,351* —*Ant.* retract, unauthorize

commit [*v1*] *perform an action* accomplish, achieve, act, carry out, complete, contravene, do, effectuate, enact, execute, go for broke*, go in for*, go out for*, offend, perpetrate, pull, pull off*, scandalize, sin, transgress, trespass, violate, wreak; CONCEPTS *6,87* —*Ant.* cease, desist, end, idle, loaf, rest, stop, wait

commit [*v2*] *deliver, entrust* allocate, allot, apportion, authorize, charge, commend, commission, confer trust, confide, consign, convey, delegate, deliver, depend upon, deposit, depute, deputize, destine, dispatch, employ, empower, engage, give, give to do, grant authority, hand over, hold, ice, imprison, institutionalize, intrust, invest, leave to, make responsible for, move, offer, ordain, promise, put away, put in the hands of, relegate, rely upon, remove, send, shift, submit, transfer, turn over to, vest; CONCEPTS *108,143,217* —*Ant.* keep, keep from

commitment [*n*] *assurance; obligation* charge, committal, devoir, duty, engagement, guarantee, liability, must, need, ought, pledge, promise, responsibility, undertaking, vow, word; CONCEPTS *71,271,274* —*Ant.* broken promise, denial, refusal

committee [n] *group working on project*
board, bureau, cabinet, chamber, commission,
consultants, convocation, council, investigators,
jury, panel, representatives, task force, trustees;
CONCEPT 381

commodious [adj] *ample, spacious* big,
capacious, comfortable, convenient, expansive,
extensive, large, loose, roomy, wide; CONCEPTS
773,781 —*Ant.* confined, cramped, inconvenient, small, squeezed, uncomfortable

commodity [n] *merchandise, possession*
article, asset, belonging, chattel, goods, line,
material, object, produce, product, property,
specialty, stock, thing, vendible; ware;
CONCEPTS 338,710

common [adj1] *average, ordinary* accepted,
banal, bourgeois, casual, characteristic, colloquial, comfortable, commonplace, conventional, current, customary, daily, everyday,
familiar, frequent, general, habitual, hackneyed,
homely, humdrum, informal, mediocre, monotonous, natural, obscure, passable, plain, prevailing, prevalent, probable, prosaic, regular,
routine, run-of-the-mill*, simple, stale, standard,
stereotyped, stock, trite, trivial, typical, undistinguished, universal, unvaried, usual, wearisome,
workaday, worn-out; CONCEPT 547 —*Ant.* abnormal, extraordinary, infrequent, noteworthy,
rare, scarce, uncommon, unusual, valuable

common [adj2] *generally known; held in common* accepted, coincident, collective, communal,
communistic, community, commutual, congruous, conjoint, conjunct, constant, corporate,
correspondent, customary, general, generic,
in common, intermutual, joint, like, mutual,
popular, prevailing, prevalent, public, reciprocal, shared, social, socialistic, united, universal,
usual, well-known, widespread; CONCEPT 530

common [adj3] *low, coarse* baseborn, characterless, cheap, colorless, crass, declassé, hack,
hackneyed, impure, inferior, low-grade, mean,
middling, nondescript, passable, pedestrian,
Philistine, plebeian, poor, prosy, raffish, second-
class, second-rate, shoddy, sleazy, stale, trite,
undistinguished, vulgar; CONCEPTS 401,545
—*Ant.* aristocratic, cultured, excellent, high,
noble, refined, sophisticated, superior

commonly [adv] *usually* as a rule, by ordinary,
frequently, generally, more often than not,
ordinarily, regularly; CONCEPTS 530,541
—*Ant.* uncommonly, unusually

commonplace [adj] *usual, everyday* boiler
plate*, characterless, clichéd, colorless, conventional, corny*, customary, dime-a-dozen*,
familiar, familiar tune, garden variety*, hackneyed, humdrum, lowly, mainstream, matter-
of-course, mediocre, middle-of-the-road*, middling, mundane, natural, normal, obvious, ordinary, pedestrian, plebeian, prevalent, prosaic,
run-of-the-mill*, stale, starch, stereotyped,
threadbare, trite, typical, uneventful, unexceptional, uninteresting, unnoteworthy, vanilla*,
widespread, workaday, worn-out; CONCEPT 530
—*Ant.* exceptional, infrequent, peculiar, rare,
uncommon, unusual

commonplace [n] *clichéd saying or idea*
banality, bromide*, chestnut*, cliché, corn*,
inanity, motto, platitude, prosaicism, prosaism,
prose, rubber stamp*, shallowness, shibboleth,
stereotype, tag, triteness, triviality truism;
CONCEPTS 278,689

common-sense [adj] *reasonable* astute, commonsensical, cool, down-to-earth, hard-headed,
judicious, levelheaded, matter-of-fact, practical,
rational, realistic, sane, sensible, shrewd, sound;
CONCEPT 402 —*Ant.* foolish, impractical,
insane, unreasonable, unsensible, unsound

common sense [n] *good reasoning* acumen,
cool, good sense, gumption, horse sense*, intelligence, levelheadedness, practicality, prudence,
reasonableness, sense, sound judgment, soundness, wisdom, wit; CONCEPT 409 —*Ant.* foolishness, impracticality, insanity, unreasonableness

commonwealth [n] *political or geographic
area* body politic, citizenry, citizens, commonality, democracy, federation, nation, people,
polity, republic, society; CONCEPTS 301,512

commotion [n] *clamor, uproar* ado, agitation,
annoyance, backwash, ballyhoo*, bedlam, big
scene*, big stink*, brouhaha, bustle, clatter,
combustion, confusion, convulsion, discomposure, disquiet, dither, excitement, ferment,
fermentation, flap, flurry, furor, fuss, hell broke
loose*, hubbub, hurly-burly, insurgence, insurrection, lather*, mutiny, outcry, pandemonium,
perturbation, pother, racket, rebellion, revolt,
riot, rumpus, stew, stir, to-do, tumult, turbulence, upheaval, uprising, upset, upturn,
vexation, welter, whirl; CONCEPTS 388,674
—*Ant.* calm, calmness, peace, quiet, quietude,
repose, silence, stillness, tranquility

communal [adj] *collective; shared* common,
communistic, community, conjoint, conjunct,
cooperative, general, intermutual, joint, mutual,
neighborhood, public; CONCEPTS 536,708
—*Ant.* individual, personal, private, unshared

commune [n] *group living together* collective,
commonage, commonality, community, cooperative, family, kibbutz, municipality, neighborhood, rank and file, village; CONCEPT 379

commune [v] *communicate, experience with
another* confer, confide in, contemplate,
converse, discourse, discuss, mediate, muse,
parley, ponder, reflect; CONCEPTS 17,266

communicable [adj] *able to be contracted*
catching, communicative, contagious, expansive, infectious, pandemic, taking, transferable,
transmittable; CONCEPT 314 —*Ant.* incon-
tractable, noncommunicable, noncontagious

communicate [v1] *give or exchange information, ideas* acquaint, advertise, advise, announce, be in touch, betray, break, broadcast,
carry, connect, contact, convey, correspond,
declare, disclose, discover, disseminate,
divulge, enlighten, get across, get through,
hint, impart, imply, inform, interact, interface,
keep in touch, let on, let out, make known,
network*, pass on, phone, proclaim, publicize,
publish, raise, reach out, relate, report, reveal,
ring up, signify, spread, state, suggest, tell,
touch base*, transfer, transmit, unfold, write;
CONCEPT 266 —*Ant.* bottle up, conceal, cover,
keep, keep quiet, suppress, withhold

communicate [v2] *mutually exchange information* answer, associate with, be close to, be in
touch, be near, buzz, cable, chat, commune with,
confabulate, confer, converse, correspond, discourse, drop a line*, drop a note*, establish

contact, get on the horn*, give a call, give a ring*, have confidence of, hear from, reach, reply, talk, telephone, wire, write; CONCEPT 56

communication [n1] *giving, exchanging information, ideas* advice, advisement, announcing, articulation, assertion, communion, connection, contact, conversation, converse, correspondence, corresponding, declaration, delivery, disclosing, dissemination, elucidation, expression, intelligence, interchange, intercommunication, intercourse, link, making known, mention, notifying, publication, reading, reception, revelation, talk, talking, telling, transfer, translating, transmission, utterance, writing; CONCEPT 266 —*Ant.* concealment, cover, quiet, suppression, withholding

communication [n2] *information transmitted* account, advice, announcement, briefing, bulletin, communiqué, conversation, converse, declaration, directive, disclosure, dispatch, excerpt, goods*, hot story*, ideas, info*, information, inside story*, intelligence, language, lowdown, message, missive, news, note, pipeline, poop*, précis, prophecy, publicity, report, revelation, scoop*, skinny*, speech, statement, summary, tidings, translation, utterance, warning, word, work; CONCEPT 274

communications [n] *systems of information exchange* information technology, means, media, publicity, public relations, route, telecommunications, transport, travel; CONCEPTS 349,770

communicative [adj] *informative* candid, chatty, communicable, conversable, conversational, demonstrative, effusive, enlightening, expansive, forthcoming, frank, garrulous, gushing, loquacious, open, outgoing, talkative, unreserved, voluble; CONCEPT 267 —*Ant.* close-mouthed, reserved, reticent, unfriendly, uninformative, unsociable

communion [n1] *affinity, agreement* accord, association, closeness, close relationship, communing, concord, contact, converse, fellowship, harmony, intercommunication, intercourse, intimacy, participation, rapport, sympathy, togetherness, unity; CONCEPT 684 —*Ant.* antagonism, contention, disagreement, discord, disunity, division, hostility, variance

communion [n2] *sacrament in church; body of believers sharing a sacrament* breaking of bread, church, creed, denomination, Eucharist, faith, Lord's Supper, Mass, persuasion, religion, sacrament; CONCEPT 367

communism [n] *socialist government* Bolshevism, collectivism, Leninism, Marxism, rule of the proletariat, socialism, state ownership, totalitarianism; CONCEPT 301 —*Ant.* capitalism, democracy

community [n1] *society, area of people* association, body politic, center, colony, commonality, commonwealth, company, district, general public, hamlet, locality, nation, neck of the woods*, neighborhood, people, populace, public, residents, society, state, stomping ground*, territory, turf; CONCEPTS 379,512

community [n2] *agreement, similarity* affinity, identity, kinship, likeness, sameness, semblance; CONCEPTS 664,670 —*Ant.* disagreement, dissimilarity

commute [v1] *travel to work* drive, go back and

forth, take the bus/subway/train; CONCEPT 224

commute [v2] *reduce punishment* alleviate, curtail, decrease, mitigate, modify, remit, shorten, soften; CONCEPTS 236,247,317 —*Ant.* increase, lengthen

commute [v3] *exchange, trade* barter, change, convert, interchange, metamorphose, substitute, switch, transfer, transfigure, transform, translate, transmogrify, transmute, transpose; CONCEPTS 104,232 —*Ant.* keep

commuter [n] *daily traveler, usually for work* city worker, driver, straphanger*, suburbanite, traveler; CONCEPT 348

compact [adj1] *condensed* appressed, bunched, close, compressed, crowded, dense, firm, hard, impenetrable, impermeable, packed, pressed, solid, thick, tight; CONCEPTS 481,483,774 —*Ant.* loose, slack, uncondensed

compact [adj2] *short, brief* boiled down, compendious, concise, epigrammatic, in a nutshell*, laconic, make a long story short*, marrowy, meaty, pithy, pointed, short and sweet*, succinct, terse, to the point; CONCEPTS 773,798 —*Ant.* big, large, lengthy, long, unabridged

compact [n] *agreement* alliance, arrangement, bargain, bond, concordat, contract, convention, covenant, deal, engagement, entente, indenture, pact, settlement, stipulation, transaction, treaty, understanding; CONCEPTS 271,684 —*Ant.* disagreement

compact [v] *make condensed* combine, compress, concentrate, condense, consolidate, contract, cram, integrate, pack, set, solidify, stuff, unify, unite; CONCEPTS 137,208 —*Ant.* enlarge, loosen, slacken, thin, uncondense

compact disc [n] *recording of music or speech* album, CD, cut*, cylinder, demo, digital recording, disk, laser disk, record, release, track; CONCEPT 262

companion [n] *helper, friend* accompaniment, accomplice, aide, ally, assistant, associate, attendant, buddy, chaperon, colleague, comate, complement, comrade, concomitant, confederate, consort, convoy, counterpart, cousin, co-worker, crony, cuz*, double, escort, guide, match, mate, nurse, pal, pard*, partner, playmate, protector, roomie*, safeguard, sidekick; CONCEPT 423 —*Ant.* enemy, foe, foreigner, opponent, stranger

companionable [adj] *friendly* affable, amicable, buddy buddy*, clubby*, complacent, congenial, conversable, convivial, cordial, cozy, cozy with, familiar, genial, good-natured, gregarious, intimate, mellow, neighborly, outgoing, pally, palsy*, sociable, social, tight, tight with*; CONCEPT 555 —*Ant.* antagonistic, foreign, opposing, unfriendly

companionship [n] *friendship, accompaniment* affiliation, alliance, amity, camaraderie, company, comradeship, conviviality, esprit de corps, rapport, society, togetherness, union; CONCEPT 388 —*Ant.* antagonism, strangeness

company [n1] *crowd of people* aggregation, assemblage, assembly, association, band, body, circle, clan, clique, club, collection, community, concourse, congregation, convention, corps, cortege, coterie, crew, ensemble, gang*, gathering, group, horde, jungle*, league, mob*, muster, order, outfit, pack, party, retinue, ring, ruck, set, team, throng, troop, troupe, turnout, zoo*; CONCEPT *417*

company [*n2*] *business concern* association, business, concern, corporation, enterprise, establishment, firm, house, megacorp*, multinational, outfit, partnership, syndicate; CONCEPT *325*

company [*n3*] *social friend, guest* boarder, caller, companionship, cortege, party, presence, retinue, society, visitor; CONCEPTS *417,423*

comparable [*adj1*] *worthy of comparison* a match for, as good as, commensurable, commensurate, equal, equipollent, equipotential, equivalent, in a class with, on a par, proportionate, tantamount; CONCEPT *566* —*Ant.* incomparable, unequal, unworthy

comparable [*adj2*] *corresponding, similar* agnate, akin, alike, analogous, cognate, consonant, corresponding, like, parallel, related, relative, undifferenced, uniform; CONCEPTS *487,573* —*Ant.* dissimilar, unalike, unlike

comparative [*adj*] *approximate, close to* allusive, analogous, approaching, by comparison, comparable, conditional, connected, contingent, contrastive, correlative, corresponding, equivalent, in proportion, like, matching, metaphorical, near, not absolute, not positive, parallel, provisional, qualified, related, relative, restricted, rivaling, similar, vying, with reservation; CONCEPT *487* —*Ant.* unequal, unlike

compare [*v1*] *examine in contrast* analyze, approach, balance, bracket, collate, confront, consider, contemplate, contrast, correlate, divide, equal, examine, hang, hold a candle to*, inspect, juxtapose, match, match up, measure, observe, oppose, parallel, place in juxtaposition, ponder, rival, scan, scrutinize, segregate, separate, set against, set side by side, size up, stack up against*, study, touch, weigh, weigh against another; CONCEPTS *24,103*

compare [*v2*] *liken, equate* allegorize, approach, approximate to, assimilate, balance, bear comparison, be in the same class as*, be on a par with*, bring near, come up to, compete with, connect, correlate, distinguish between, draw parallel, equal, equate, hold a candle to*, identify with, link, make like, match, notice similarities, parallel, put alongside, relate, resemble, show correspondence, stack up with*, standardize, tie up, vie; CONCEPT *39*

comparison [*n*] *contrasting; corresponding* allegory, analogizing, analogy, analyzing, association, balancing, bringing together, collating, collation, comparability, connection, contrast, correlation, discrimination, distinguishing, dividing, estimation, example, exemplification, identification, illustration, juxtaposition, likeness, likening, measuring, metaphor, observation, opposition, paralleling, ratio, relating, relation, resemblance, segregation, separation, similarity, testing, weighing; CONCEPTS *24,39,529*

compartment [*n*] *section, subdivision* alcove, area, bay, berth, booth, carrel, carriage, category, cell, chamber, corner, cubbyhole, cubicle, department, division, hole, locker, niche, nook, part, piece, pigeonhole, place, portion, slot, stall; CONCEPT *434*

compass [*n*] *boundary, periphery* ambit, area, bound, circle, circuit, circumference, circum-

scription, confines, domain, enclosure, environs, expanse, extent, field, limit, limitation, orbit, perimeter, precinct, purlieus, purview, radius, range, reach, realm, restriction, round, scope, sphere, stretch, sweep, zone; CONCEPTS *484,651,788*

compass [*v1*] *enclose* beset, besiege, blockade, circle, circumscribe, encircle, encompass, environ, gird, girdle, hem in, ring, round, surround; CONCEPT *758*

compass [*v2*] *achieve, get* accomplish, annex, attain, bring about, effect, execute, fulfill, gain, have, land, obtain, perform, procure, realize, secure, win; CONCEPTS *142,706* —*Ant.* fail, lose

compassion [*n*] *tender feeling* benevolence, charity, clemency, commiseration, compunction, condolence, consideration, empathy, fellow feeling, grace, heart, humaneness, humanity, kindness, lenity, mercy, softheartedness, softness, sorrow, sympathy, tenderheartedness, tenderness, yearning; CONCEPTS *410,633* —*Ant.* cruelty, harshness, hatred, indifference, meanness, mercilessness, tyranny

compassionate [*adj*] *having tender feelings* all heart, being big*, benevolent, bleeding heart*, charitable, commiserative, forbearing, going easy on*, humane, humanitarian, indulgent, kindhearted, kindly, lenient, living with, merciful, old softie*, piteous, pitying, responsive, softhearted, soft shell*, sparing, sympathetic, tender, tenderhearted, understanding, warm, warmhearted; CONCEPTS *401,403* —*Ant.* cruel, hard, harsh, hateful, indifferent, mean, merciless, tyrannous

compatibility [*n*] *harmony in relationship* affinity, agreeableness, agreement, amity, congeniality, congruity, consonance, empathy, fit, like-mindedness, rapport, single-mindedness, sympathy, unity; CONCEPT *388* —*Ant.* disharmony, incompatibility

compatible [*adj*] *agreeable, in harmony* accordant, adaptable, appropriate, congenial, congruent, congruous, consistent, consonant, cooperative, cotton to*, fit, fitting, getting along with, harmonious, having good vibes*, hitting it off*, in keeping, in sync with*, in the groove*, like-minded, meet, on the same wavelength*, proper, reconcilable, simpatico, suitable, sympathetic, together; CONCEPT *555* —*Ant.* antagonistic, antipathetic, disagreeable, incompatible, inharmonious, unsuitable, unsuited

compel [*v*] *force to act* bulldoze*, coerce, concuss, constrain, crack down, dragoon, drive, enforce, exact, hustle, impel, make, make necessary, necessitate, oblige, put the arm on*, put the chill on*, restrain, shotgun*, squeeze, throw weight around*, turn on the heat*, urge; CONCEPTS *14,384* —*Ant.* block, check, delay, deter, hinder, impede, obstruct, stop

compendious [*adj*] *abridged* abbreviated, breviloquent, brief, close, compact, compendiary, comprehensive, concise, condensed, contracted, curt, inclusive, laconic, short, short and sweet*, succinct, summarized, summary, synoptic; CONCEPTS *773,789* —*Ant.* enlarged, lengthened, unabridged

compendium [*n*] *abridgment* abstract, aperçu, brief, conspectus, digest, epitome, essence, guide, handbook, manual, overview, pandect, précis, sketch, summary, survey, syllabus, sylloge; CONCEPT 283

compensate [v1] *make restitution* atone, come down with*, commit, guerdon, indemnify, make good*, pay, pay up, plank out*, pony up*, recompense, recoup, refund, reimburse, remunerate, repay, requite, reward, satisfy, shell out*, take care of, tickle the palm*; CONCEPTS 108,126,341 —*Ant.* deprive, fine, forfeit, lose

compensate [v2] *offset, make up for* abrogate, annul, atone for, balance, better, cancel out, counteract, counterbalance, counterpoise, countervail, fix, improve, invalidate, make amends, negate, negative, neutralize, nullify, outweigh, redress, repair, set off; CONCEPTS 126,212 —*Ant.* damage, deprive, penalize

compensation [n] *repayment; rectification* advantage, allowance, amends, atonement, benefit, bonus, bread*, consideration, counterclaim, coverage, damages, defrayal, deserts*, earnings, fee*, gain, honorarium, indemnification, indemnity, meet, pay, payment, payoff, premium, profit, quittance, reciprocity, reckoning, recompense, recoupment, redress, reimbursement, remittal, remittance, remuneration, reparation, reprisal, requital, restitution, reward, salary, salt, satisfaction, scale, settlement, shake, stipend, take*, take-home*, wage; CONCEPTS 337,344 —*Ant.* damage, deprivation, fine, forfeiture, loss, penalty

compete [v] *go up against in contest* attempt, bandy, battle, be in the running*, bid, challenge, clash, collide, contend, contest, cope with, emulate, encounter, essay, face, fence, fight, go after, go for*, go for broke*, go for the gold*, grapple, in the hunt*, jockey for position*, joust, lock horns*, match strength, match wits*, oppose, participate in, pit oneself against*, play, rival, run for, scramble for*, seek prize, spar, strive, struggle, take on, take part, tilt, try, tussle, vie, wrestle; CONCEPT 92

competence [n] *ability* adequacy, appropriateness, capability, capacity, competency, cutting it*, cutting the mustard*, expertise, fitness, hacking it*, know-how, makings, making the grade*, might, moxie, proficiency, qualification, qualifiedness, savvy, skill, suitability, the goods*, the right stuff*, what it takes*; CONCEPT 630 —*Ant.* inability, inadequacy, incapability, incompetence, inefficiency, ineptness

competent [adj] *able* adapted, adequate, all around, appropriate, au fait, being a pistol*, capable, clever, complete, crisp, decent, dynamite, efficient, endowed, enough, equal, fireball*, fit, fool, good, know ins and outs*, know one's business*, know one's stuff*, know the answers*, know the ropes*, know the score*, no slouch*, on the ball*, paid one's dues*, pertinent, polished, proficient, qualified, satisfactory, savvy, skilled, sufficient, suitable, there*, up to it, up to snuff*, up to speed*, wicked*; CONCEPT 527 —*Ant.* inadequate, incapable, incompetent, inefficient, inept, unable

competition [n] *contest* antagonism, athletic event, bout, candidacy, championship, clash, concours, contention, controversy, counteraction, dog eat dog*, do or die*, emulation, encounter, engagement, event, fight, game, go for it, go for the gold*, horse race*, jungle*, match, matchup, meeting, one on one*, one-upping, opposition, pairing off, puzzle, quiz, race, racing, rat race*, rivalry, run, sport, strife, striving, struggle, tilt, tournament, trial, tug-of-war, warfare; CONCEPTS 92,363

competitive [adj] *willing to oppose* aggressive, ambitious, antagonistic, at odds, combative, competing, cutthroat, dog-eat-dog*, emulous, killer*, killer instinct*, opposing, rival, streetwise, vying; CONCEPT 542 —*Ant.* noncompetitive, unambitious

competitor [n] *person willing to enter contest* adversary, antagonist, challenger, competition, contestant, corival, dark horse*, emulator, favorite, opponent, opposition, rival; CONCEPTS 366,423

compilation [n] *assemblage* accumulating, accumulation, aggregating, anthology, assembling, assortment, collecting, collection, collocating, combining, compiling, consolidating, garner, garnering, gathering, incorporating, joining, treasury, unifying; CONCEPTS 109,432

compile [v] *assemble, accumulate* abridge, amass, anthologize, arrange, assemble, bring together, collate, collect, colligate, collocate, compose, concentrate, congregate, consolidate, cull, draw together, edit, garner, gather, get together, glean, group, heap up, marshal, muster, organize, put together, recapitulate, unite; CONCEPTS 79,84,109 —*Ant.* disassemble, disperse, scatter, separate

complacent [adj] *contented* conceited, confident, easy-going, egoistic, egotistic, gratified, happy, obsequious, pleased, satisfied, self-assured, self-contented, self-pleased, self-possessed, self-righteous, self-satisfied, serene, smug, unconcerned; CONCEPTS 401,403 —*Ant.* concerned, discontented, discontented, dissatisfied

complain [v] *grumble about* accuse, ascribe, attack, beef*, bellyache*, bemoan, bewail, bitch, carp, cavil, charge, contravene, criticize, defy, demur, denounce, deplore, deprecate, differ, disagree, disapprove, dissent, expostulate, find fault, fret, fuss, gainsay, grieve, gripe, groan, grouse, growl, grumble, impute, indict, kick up a fuss*, lament, lay, look askance, make a fuss, moan, nag, object, oppose, protest, refute, remonstrate, repine, reproach, snivel, sound off, take exception to, wail, whimper, whine, yammer; CONCEPT 52 —*Ant.* applaud, approve, be content, be happy, commend, praise, recommend, sanction

complaint [n1] *statement of disagreement, discontent* accusation, annoyance, beef*, cavil, CC*, charge, clamor, criticism, dissatisfaction, expostulation, fault-finding, grievance, gripe, grouse, grumble, guff*, jeremiad, kick, lament, moan, objection, plaint, protest, protestation, rap, remonstrance, remonstration, representation, reproach, rumble*, squawk, stink, trouble, wail, whine; CONCEPTS 52,689 —*Ant.* applause, approval, commendation, contentedness, happiness, praise, recommendation, sanction

complaint [n2] *illness, affliction* affection, ailment, condition, disease, disorder, ill, indisposition, infirmity, malady, sickness, syndrome, upset; CONCEPTS 306,316 —*Ant.* health

complaisance [n] *agreeableness* accommodativeness, acquiescence, compliance, courtesy, deference, friendliness, kindness, obligingness, politeness, respect; CONCEPT 633 —Ant. antagonism, disagreeableness, discontent, dissatisfaction, obstinacy

complaisant [adj] agreeable accommodating, amiable, compliant, conciliatory, deferential, easy, easy-going, friendly, generous, good-humored, good-natured, good-tempered, indulgent, lenient, mild, obliging, polite, solicitous, submissive; CONCEPT 401 —Ant. antagonistic, disagreeable, discontented, dissatisfied, obstinate

complement [n] companion, counterpart accompaniment, addition, aggregate, augmentation, balance, capacity, completion, consummation, correlate, correlative, counterpart, enhancement, enrichment, entirety, filler, finishing touch, makeweight, pendant, quota, remainder, rest, rounding-off*, supplement, total, totality; CONCEPTS 635,824

complement [v] complete accomplish, achieve, cap, clinch, conclude, consummate, crown, finish, fulfill, integrate, perfect, round off, top off; CONCEPTS 91,119,234 —Ant. take away

complementary [adj] filling, completing commutual, complemental, completing, completory, conclusive, correlative, correspondent, corresponding, crowning, equivalent, fellow, integral, integrative, interconnected, interdependent, interrelated, interrelating, matched, mated, paired, parallel, reciprocal; CONCEPTS 577,824 —Ant. independent, unrelated

complete [adj1] total, not lacking all, entire, exhaustive, faultless, full, full-dress, gross, hook line and sinker*, imperforate, intact, integral, integrated, lock stock and barrel*, organic, outright, plenary, replete, the works*, thorough, thoroughgoing, unabbreviated, unabridged, unbroken, uncondensed, uncut, undiminished, undivided, undocked, unexpurgated, unimpaired, unitary, unreduced, whole, whole enchilada*, whole-hog*, whole-length, whole nine yards*; CONCEPT 531 —Ant. defective, deficient, imperfect, incomplete, lacking, missing, needy, short, wanting

complete [adj2] finished accomplished, achieved, all-embracing, all-inclusive, all over, all over but the shouting*, attained, compassed, concluded, consummate, done, done with, down, effected, ended, entire, executed, fini*, finished off, full, full-fledged, home free*, perfect, plenary, realized, sweeping, terminated, that's it*, through; CONCEPT 528 —Ant. imperfect, incomplete, unfinished

complete [adj3] utter, absolute blank, blanket, categorical, consummate, downright, dyed-in-the-wool*, flawless, impeccable, out-and-out, outright, perfect, positive, sheer, thorough, thoroughgoing, total, unblemished, unconditional, unmitigated, unqualified, whole; CONCEPTS 531,535

complete [v] carry out action accomplish, achieve, actualize, bring to fruition, bring to maturity, call it a day*, cap, carry off, close, conclude, consummate, crown, determine, develop, discharge, do, do thoroughly, effect, effectuate, elaborate, end, equip, execute, fill, finalize, finish, fulfill, furnish, get through, go the limit*, go through with, go whole hog*, halt, make good*, make up, perfect, perform,

put to bed*, realize, refine, round off, round out, settle, sew up*, supplement, terminate, ultimate, wind up*, wrap up*; CONCEPT 91 —Ant. forget, give up, halt, ignore, neglect, stop

completely [adv] entirely absolutely, all the way*, altogether, competently, comprehensively, conclusively, effectively, en masse, exclusively, exhaustively, extensively, finally, from A to Z*, from beginning to end*, fully, heart and soul*, hook line and sinker*, in all, in entirety, in full, in toto*, on all counts*, painstakingly, perfectly, quite, solidly, thoroughly, totally, to the end, to the limit, to the max*, to the nth degree*, ultimately, unabridged, unanimously, unconditionally, undividedly, utterly, wholly, without omission; CONCEPT 531

completion [n] accomplishment, finishing achievement, attainment, close, conclusion, consummation, culmination, curtains*, dispatch, end, expiration, finalization, finis, finish, fruition, fulfillment, hips*, integration, perfection, realization, swan song*, windup*, wrap-up; CONCEPTS 119,706 —Ant. anticlimax, imperfection

complex [adj1] involved, intricate circuitous, complicated, composite, compound, compounded, confused, conglomerate, convoluted, elaborate, entangled, heterogeneous, knotty, labyrinthine, manifold, mingled, miscellaneous, mixed, mixed-up, mosaic, motley, multifarious, multiform, multiple, multiplex, tangled, tortuous, variegated; CONCEPT 562 —Ant. clear, easy, evident, homogeneous, obvious, plain, simple, uniform

complex [adj2] difficult to understand abstruse, bewildering, Byzantine, circuitous, complicated, confused, convoluted, crabbed, cryptic, Daedalean, discursive, disordered, disturbing, enigmatic, entangled, excursive, Gordian, hidden, impenetrable, inscrutable, interwoven, intricate, involved, jumbled, knotted, knotty, labyrinthine, mazy, meandering, mingled, mixed, muddled, obscure, paradoxical, perplexing, puzzling, rambling, recondite, round-about, sinuous, snarled, sophisticated, tangled, tortuous, undecipherable, unfathomable, winding; CONCEPTS 402,529 —Ant. apparent, clear, direct, discernible, easy, evident, obvious, plain

complex [n1] composite, aggregate association, compound, conglomerate, ecosystem, entanglement, group, network, organization, scheme, structure, syndrome, synthesis, system, totality; CONCEPTS 432,770

complex [n2] psychological problem anxiety, a thing about something*, exaggerated reaction, fear, fixation, fixed idea, hang-up*, idée fixe, insanity, mania, neurosis, obsession, phobia, preoccupation, repression; CONCEPT 410

complexion [n1] skin coloring, appearance cast, color, coloration, coloring, flush, front, glow, hue, looks, mug*, phiz*, pigmentation, skin, skin tone, texture, tinge, tint, tone; CONCEPTS 405,622

complexion [n2] someone's character appearance, aspect, cast, countenance, disposition, guise, humor, ilk, individualism, individuality, kind, light, look, make-up, nature, personality, seeming, semblance, sort, stamp, style, temper, temperament, type; CONCEPT 411

complexity [n] *complicatedness* complication, convolution, elaboration, entanglement, intricacy, involvement, multiplicity, ramification; CONCEPT 663 —**Ant.** clarity, directness, ease, obvious, simplicity

compliance [n] *agreement* acquiescence, amenability, assent, complaisance, concession, concurrence, conformity, consent, deference, docility, obedience, observance, passivity, resignation, submission, submissiveness, tractability, yielding; CONCEPTS 411,684 —**Ant.** defiance, denial, disagreement, disobedience, dissension, dissent, fight, nonconformity, refusal, veto

complicate [v] *confuse, make difficult* add fuel to fire*, bedevil, clog, combine, confound, convolute, derange, disarrange, disorder, elaborate, embroil, entangle, fold, foul up*, handicap, impede, infold, interfuse, interrelate, interweave, involve, jumble, make intricate, make waves*, mix up, muck up*, muddle, multiply, obscure, open can of worms*, perplex, ravel, render unintelligible, screw up*, snafu*, snag, snarl up*, tangle, twist, upset; CONCEPTS 7,19 —**Ant.** disentangle, ease, explain, facilitate, make simple, untangle

complicated [adj] *difficult, complex* abstruse, arduous, Byzantine, can of worms*, convoluted, Daedalean, difficult, elaborate, entangled, fancy, gasser*, Gordian, hard, hi-tech*, interlaced, intricate, involved, knotty, labyrinthine, mega factor*, mixed, perplexing, problematic, puzzling, recondite, sophisticated, troublesome, various, wheels within wheels*; CONCEPTS 562,565 —**Ant.** easy, facile, simple

complication [n] *difficult situation* aggravation, complexity, confusion, development, difficulty, dilemma, drawback, embarrassment, entanglement, factor, intricacy, obstacle, problem, snag, web; CONCEPTS 230,674 —**Ant.** ease, peace, simplicity

complicity [n] *conspiracy* abetment, agreement, collaboration, collusion, complot, concurrence, confederacy, connivance, engineering, guilt, guiltiness, implication, intrigue, involvement, machination, manipulation, partnership; CONCEPTS 388,660 —**Ant.** ignorance, innocence, noninvolvement, refusal

compliment [n] *praise, flattery* acclaim, acclamation, admiration, adulation, applause, appreciation, approval, blessing, bouquet*, buttering up*, cajolery, commendation, comp, confirmation, congratulations, courtesy, encomium, endorsement, eulogy, favor, felicitation, good word, homage, honor, kudo, laud, laudation, laurels, notice, orchid*, ovation, panegyric, pat on the back*, posy*, regard, respects, sanction, sentiment, tribute, veneration, warm fuzzy*; CONCEPTS 69,278 —**Ant.** blame, censure, complaint, criticism, denunciation, insult, libel, slander

compliment [v] *praise, flatter* acclaim, adulate, applaud, butter up*, cajole, celebrate, charm, cheer, commemorate, commend, congratulate, endorse, eulogize, exalt, extol, fawn upon, felicitate, give bouquet*, glorify, hail, hand it to*, honor, ingratiate oneself with, kudize*, laud, magnify, make much of, panegyrize, pat on the

back*, pay respects, pay tribute to, please, puff up*, recommend, roose, salute, sanction, satisfy, sing praises of, soothe, speak highly of, take off hat to*, toast, trade last*, wish joy to, worship; CONCEPT 69 —**Ant.** blame, censure, complain, criticize, denounce, insult, libel, slander

complimentary [adj] *flattering* adulatory, appreciative, approbative, approbatory, approving, celebrating, commendatory, congratulatory, courtly, encomiastic, encomiastical, eulogistic, fair-spoken, fawning, highly favorable, honeyed, honoring, laudatory, panegyrical, plauditory, polite, praiseful, respectful, sycophantic, unctuous, well-wishing, with highest recommendation, with high praise; CONCEPT 267 —**Ant.** blaming, censuring, critical, denouncing, disparaging, insulting, reproachful, unflattering

complimentary [adj2] *free as a perk*, chargeless, comp, costless, courtesy, donated, free lunch*, free of charge, gratis, gratuitous, honorary, on the house*; CONCEPT 334 —**Ant.** for sale

comply [v] *abide by, follow agreement or instructions* accede, accord, acquiesce, adhere to, agree to, cave in, come around, conform to, consent to, cry uncle*, defer, discharge, ditto*, don't make waves*, don't rock the boat*, fit in, fold, fulfill, give in, give out, give up, go along with, go with the flow*, keep, knuckle to*, knuckle under*, mind, obey, observe, perform, play ball*, play the game*, put out, quit, respect, roll over and play dead*, satisfy, shape up, stay in line*, straighten up, submit, throw in towel*, toss it in*, yes one*; yield; CONCEPTS 8,35,91 —**Ant.** decline, deny, disobey, oppose, rebuff, refuse, reject, resist

component [adj] *constituent* basic, composing, elemental, fundamental, inherent, integral, intrinsic, part and parcel of*, part of; CONCEPTS 546,567

component [n] *part, element* constituent, factor, fixings, ingredient, item, making, makings, peripheral, piece, plug-in, segment, unit; CONCEPTS 831,834 —**Ant.** whole

compose [v1] *be part of construction* be an adjunct, be an element of, belong to, be made of, build, compound, comprise, consist of, constitute, construct, enter in, fashion, form, go into, make, make up, merge in; CONCEPTS 168,642 —**Ant.** destroy, disarrange, disperse, ruin, scatter

compose [v2] *create writing, artwork, or music* author, bang out*, cast, clef*, coin a phrase, comp, conceive, contrive, cook up*, design, devise, discover, draw up, dream up, fabricate, forge, form, formulate, frame*, fudge together*, ghost*, ghostwrite, imagine, indite, invent, knock off*, knock out*, make up, note down, orchestrate, originate, pen, poetize, produce, push pencil*, put down, put pen to paper*, score, scribble, script, set type, set up, time, turn out, whip up*, write; CONCEPTS 79,173,174

compose [v3] *calm, bring under control* adjust, allay, appease, arrange, assuage, balm, becalm, check, collect, comfort, console, contain, control, cool, ease, ease up, hold in, lessen, let up, lull, mitigate, moderate, modulate, pacify, placate, quell, quiet, re-collect, reconcile, regulate, rein, relax, repress, resolve, restrain, settle, simmer down, slacken, smother, soften, solace, soothe, still, suppress, temper, tranquilize, tune down; CONCEPTS 7,22,117 —Ant. agitate, anger, arouse, distress, excite, upset

composed [adj] *calm, collected* at ease, calmed, clearheaded, commonsensical, confident, cool, cool as cucumber*, disimpassioned, dispassionate, easy, easygoing, have one's act together*, imperturbable, keeping a stiff upper lip*, keeping one's shirt on*, levelheaded, nonchalant, not turn a hair*, placid, poised, possessed, quieted, relaxed, repressed, sedate, self-assured, self-possessed, sensible, serene, serious, soothed, staid, suppressed, sure of oneself, temperate, together, tranquil, unflappable, unruffled, untroubled; CONCEPT 401 —Ant. agitated, angered, annoyed, aroused, distressed, excited, perturbed, upset, worried

composer [n] *songwriter* melodist, serialist, singer-songwriter, songsmith, songster, tunesmith, writer; CONCEPT 352

composite [adj] *combined, mixed* blended, complex, compound, conglomerate, melded, synthesized; CONCEPT 490 —Ant. homogeneous, simple, unblended, uncombined, uniform, unmixed

composite [n] *combination, mixture* amalgam, amalgamation, blend, combo, commixture, complex, compost, compound, conglomerate, fusion, immixture, intermixture, medley, mix, olio, pasteup*, stew*, synthesis, union; CONCEPTS 260,432

composition [n1] *structure, arrangement* agreement, architecture, balance, beauty, combination, concord, configuration, consonance, constitution, content, design, distribution, form, formation, harmony, layout, make-up, placing, proportion, relation, rhythm, spacing, style, symmetry, weave; CONCEPTS 733,757

composition [n2] *written or musical creation* arrangement, article, chart, concerto, dissertation, drama, essay, exercise, exposition, fiction, getup*, literary work, manuscript, melody, music, novel, number, opus, paper, piece, play, poetry, rhapsody, romance, score, setup*, short story, song, stanza, study, symphony, theme, thesis, tune, verse, work, writing; CONCEPTS 259,260,263,271

compost [n] *organic material* admixture, blend, commixture, composition, compound, fertilizer, fusion, humus, manure, mix, mixture, mulch, ordure, pile; CONCEPT 509

composure [n] *calmness, collectedness* accord, aplomb, assurance, balance, calm, contentment, control, cool*, cool head*, coolheadedness, coolness, dignity, dispassion, ease, equanimity, equilibrium, evenness, even temper, fortitude, harmony, imperturbability, inexcitability, levelheadedness, moderation, nonchalance, peace of mind, placidity, poise, polish, presence of mind, quiet, quietude, repose, sang-froid, sedateness, self-assurance, self-control, self-possession, serenity, sobriety, stability, tranquility; CONCEPT 410 —Ant. agitation, arousal, discomposure, excitement, perturbedness, upset

compound [n] *combination, mixture* admixture, aggregate, alloy, amalgam, amalgamation, blend, combo, commixture, composite, composition, compost, conglomerate, fusion, goulash,

medley, mishmash*, soup, stew, synthesis, union; CONCEPTS 260,432

compound [v1] *mix, combine* admix, amalgamate, associate, blend, bracket, coagment, coalesce, commingle, commix, concoct, connect, couple, fuse, immix, intermingle, join, link, make up, meld, mingle, synthesize, unite; CONCEPT 109 —Ant. divide, separate, unmix

compound [v2] *make difficult; complicate* add to, aggravate, augment, confound, confuse, exacerbate, extend, heighten, intensify, magnify, make complex, make intricate, multiply, worsen; CONCEPTS 231,240 —Ant. better, make easy, uncomplicate

comprehend [v1] *understand* appreciate, apprehend, assimilate, capiche*, catch, click, cognize, conceive, dig*, discern, envisage, envision, fathom, get*, get the picture*, gotcha*, grasp, have, know, make out*, perceive, read, savvy*, see, take in, tumble*; CONCEPT 15 —Ant. misinterpret, mistake, misunderstand

comprehend [v2] *include* comprise, contain, embody, embrace, enclose, encompass, have, involve, subsume, take in; CONCEPT 118 —Ant. exclude, not include

comprehensible [adj] *understandable* apprehensible, clear, coherent, comprehendible, conceivable, explicit, fathomable, graspable, intelligible, knowable, lucid, luminous, plain; CONCEPTS 402,529 —Ant. exclusive, incomplete, nonunderstandable, unintelligible

comprehension [n] *understanding* aha*, apperception, apprehension, awareness, capacity, cognizance, conception, discernment, double take*, grasp, intelligence, judgment, ken, knowledge, perception, prehension, realization, sense, slow take*, take*; CONCEPT 409 —Ant. incomprehension, misinterpretation, mistake, misunderstanding

comprehensive [adj] *inclusive* absolute, across the board*, all-embracing, all-inclusive, blanket, broad, catholic, compendious, complete, comprising, containing, discursive, encircling, encyclopedic, exhaustive, expansive, extensive, far-reaching, full, general, global, in depth, infinite, lock stock and barrel*, of great scope, overall, sweeping, synoptic, the big picture*, the whole shebang*, the works*, thorough, umbrella, wall-to-wall*, whole, wide, widespread; CONCEPTS 531,772 —Ant. exclusive, incomprehensive, particular, selective, specific

compress [v] *compact, condense* abbreviate, abridge, abstract, bind, boil down, coagulate, concentrate, consolidate, constrict, contract, cram, cramp, crowd, crush, decrease, dehydrate, densen, densify, epitomize, force into space, make brief, narrow, pack, press, press together, ram, reduce, restrict, shorten, shrink, shrivel, squash, squeeze, stuff, summarize, syncopate, telescope, tighten, wedge, wrap; CONCEPTS 208,236,247 —Ant. blow up, expand, extend, fill, increase, loosen, stretch, uncompress, uncondense

comprise [v] *make up, consist of* add up to, amount to, be composed of, be contained in, compass, compose, comprehend, constitute, contain, cover, embody, embrace, encircle, enclose, encompass, engross, form, hold, include, incorporate, involve, span, subsume, sum up, take in; CONCEPT 643 —*Ant.* except, exclude, fail, fall short, lack, need, want

compromise [n] *agreement, give-and-take* accommodation, accord, adjustment, arrangement, bargain, compact, composition, concession, contract, copout*, covenant, deal, fifty-fifty*, half and half, half measure, happy medium*, mean, middle course, middle ground, pact, sellout, settlement, trade-off, understanding, win-win situation*; CONCEPTS 230,684 —*Ant.* contest, controversy, difference, disagreement, dispute, dissension, dissent, quarrel

compromise [v1] *give and take* adjust, agree, arbitrate, compose, compound, concede, conciliate, find happy medium*, find middle ground*, go fifty-fifty*, make a deal, make concession, meet halfway, negotiate, play ball with*, settle, split the difference*, strike balance, trade off; CONCEPT 8 —*Ant.* contest, differ, disagree, dispute, dissent, quarrel

compromise [v2] *put in jeopardy* blight, cop out*, discredit, dishonor, embarrass, endanger, explode, expose, give in, hazard, imperil, implicate, jeopardize, mar, menace, peril, prejudice, put under suspicion, risk, ruin, sell out, spoil, weaken; CONCEPTS 101,240 —*Ant.* guard, protect, save

compulsion [n] *drive, obligation* coercion, constraint, demand, drive, driving, duress, duty, engrossment, exigency, force, hang-up, have on the brain*, monkey*, necessity, need, obsession, preoccupation, prepossession, pressure, tiger by the tail*, urge, urgency; CONCEPTS 410,532 —*Ant.* freedom, free will, independence, liberty, license

compulsive [adj] *driving, obsessive* besetting, compelling, enthusiastic, irresistible, overwhelming, passionate, uncontrollable, urgent; CONCEPT 401 —*Ant.* controlled, easy-going, free, independent

compulsory [adj] *binding* compulsory, de rigueur, forced, imperative, imperious, mandatory, necessary, obligatory, required, requisite; CONCEPT 546 —*Ant.* free, liberalized, liberated, optional, unstipulated, voluntary

compunction [n] *regret, sorrow* attrition, conscience, contrition, misgiving, penitence, penitency, pity, punctiliousness, qualm, reluctance, remorse, repentance, rue, ruth, second thoughts, shame, stab of conscience, sympathy; CONCEPT 410 —*Ant.* defiance, meanness, no remorse

computation [n] *performing arithmetic* calculation, ciphering, computing, counting, data processing, estimating, estimation, figuring, gauge, guess, reckoning, summing, totalling; CONCEPT 764 —*Ant.* conjecture, guesstimation

compute [v] *calculate, estimate* add up, cast up, cipher, count, count heads, count noses, cut ice*, dope out*, enumerate, figure, figure out, gauge, keep tabs*, measure, rate, reckon, run down, size up, sum, take account of, take one's measure, tally, tot*, total, tote*, tote up*; CONCEPT 764 —*Ant.* conjecture, guess, guesstimate, surmise

computer [n] *calculating, data processing machine* abacus, adding machine, analog, artificial intelligence, brain*, calculator, clone, CPU, data processor, digital, electronic brain*, laptop*, MAC, mainframe, micro*, microcomputer, mini*, minicomputer, number cruncher*, PC, personal computer, thinking machine*; CONCEPTS 269,463

computerese [n] *computer technical language* computer jargon, computer terminology, computer terms, hacker talk, tech talk; CONCEPT 275

computer geek [n] *computer expert* computer specialist, engineer, guru, hacker, programmer, techie; CONCEPT 348

comrade [n] *ally* associate, bosom buddy, buddy, chum, colleague, comate, companion, compatriot, compeer, confederate, confidant, confidante, co-worker, crony, friend, intimate, mate, pal, partner, sidekick; CONCEPT 423 —*Ant.* enemy, foe, opponent

con [n] *trick* bluff, cheat, crime, deception, double-cross, dupe, fraud, gold brick*, graft, mockery, swindle, take in; CONCEPT 59 —*Ant.* honesty, truthfulness

con [v] *deceive, defraud* bamboozle*, bilk, cajole, cheat, chicane, coax, double-cross, dupe, flimflam*, fool, hoax, hoodwink, hornswoggle*, humbug, inveigle, mislead, rip off*, rook, sweet-talk*, swindle, trick, wheedle; CONCEPT 59 —*Ant.* be forthright, be honest

concatenation [n] *connection, sequence* chain, connecting, continuity, integration, interlocking, link, linking, nexus, series, succession, uniting; CONCEPTS 721,727 —*Ant.* interruption

concave [adj] *curved, depressed* biconcave, cupped, dented, dimpled, dipped, excavated, hollow, hollowed, incurvate, incurvated, incurved, indented, round, rounded, sagging, scooped, sinking, sunken; CONCEPT 486 —*Ant.* convex, distended

conceal [v] *hide, disguise* beard, burrow, bury, cache, camouflage, cloak, couch, cover, cover up, dissemble, ditch, duck, ensconce, enshroud, harbor, hole up*, keep dark, keep secret, lie low*, lurk, mask, masquerade, obscure, plant*, put in a hole*, screen, secrete, shelter, skulk, slink, sneak, stash, stay out of sight, stow, tuck away, veil, wrap; CONCEPT 188 —*Ant.* disclose, divulge, expose, lay bare, let out, open, reveal, show, tell, uncover

concealed [adj] *hidden, secret* buried, cached, camouflaged, covered, covered up, covert, enshrouded, guarded, holed up, hushed up, hush-hush*, incog*, incognito, inconspicuous, masked, obscure, obscured, on the Q. T.*, perdu, planted, privy, put in the hole*, recondite, screened, secreted, shrouded, stashed, tucked away, ulterior, under wraps*, unseen, veiled; CONCEPTS 576,619 —*Ant.* bare, clear, disclosed, exposed, obvious, open, plain, revealed, shown, told, uncovered

concealment [n] *hiding, secrecy* beard, blind, camouflage, cover, covering, cover-up, curtain, disguise, dissimulation, fig leaf*, front, hideaway, hide-out, laundromat, mask, obliteration, obscuration, occultation, privacy, red herring*, secretion, smoke screen*, veil, wraps*; CONCEPTS 188,631 —*Ant.* disclosure, divulgence, exposition, revelation, showing, telling

concede [v] *acknowledge, give in* accept, accord, admit, allow, avow, award, bury the hatchet*, capitulate, cave in, cede, confess, cry uncle*, ditto*, fess up*, fold, give up, go along with, go with the flow*, grant, hand over, knuckle under, let on, own, own up, play ball with*, quit, relinquish, say uncle*, surrender, throw in the towel*, waive, yes one*, yield; CONCEPTS 35,57,82,235 —*Ant.* contradict, disacknowledge, disagree, dispute, dissent, fight, refuse, reject, repudiate

conceit [n] *egotism* amour-propre, arrogance, complacence, complacency, consequence, immodesty, narcissism, outrecuidance, pomposity, pride, self-admiration, self-exaltation, self-importance, self-love, self-regard, smugness, snottiness, stuffiness, swagger, swelled head*, vainglory, vainness, vanity; CONCEPT 411 —*Ant.* humility, meekness, modesty, self-consciousness, shyness, timidity, unself-confidence

conceited [adj] *egotistical* arrogant, big-headed*, big talking, cocky, conceity, full of hot air*, gall, ham*, hot stuff*, immodest, know-it-all, loudmouth, narcissistic, overweening, phony, puffed up*, self-important, smart-alecky*, snotty*, stuck up*, swollen-headed*, vain, vainglorious, windbag*; CONCEPT 404 —*Ant.* diffident, humble, meek, modest, self-conscious, shy, timid, unself-confident

conceivable [adj] *reasonable, easy to understand* believable, convincing, credible, earthly, imaginable, likely, mortal, possible, probable, supposable, thinkable; CONCEPTS 529,552 —*Ant.* difficult, inconceivable, unbelievable, unimaginable, unreasonable, unthinkable

conceive [v1] *understand* accept, appreciate, apprehend, assume, believe, catch, compass, comprehend, deem, dig, envisage, expect, fancy, feel, follow, gather, get, grasp, imagine, judge, perceive, realize, reckon, suppose, suspect, take, twig; CONCEPT 15 —*Ant.* misunderstand, not believe

conceive [v2] *create* become pregnant, brainstorm, cogitate, consider, contrive, cook up*, depicture, design, develop, devise, dream up, envisage, envision, fancy, feature, form, formulate, head trip*, image, imagine, make up, meditate, originate, ponder, produce, project, purpose, realize, ruminate, spark, speculate, spitball, think up, trump up*, visualize; CONCEPTS 35,173,251 —*Ant.* abort, destroy

concentrate [v1] *think about closely* apply, attend, be engrossed in, bring to bear, brood over, center, consider closely, contemplate, crack one's brains*, direct attention, establish, examine, fixate, fix attention, focus, focus attention, get on the beam*, give attention, hammer*, hammer away at*, head trip*, intensify, knuckle down, meditate, muse, need, occupy thoughts, peruse, ponder, pour it on*, put, put mind to, rack one's brains*, rivet, ruminate, scrutinize, set, settle, study, sweat, think hard, weigh; CONCEPT 17

concentrate [v2] *gather, collect* accumulate, agglomerate, aggregate, amass, assemble, bunch, center, centralize, cluster, coalesce, collect, combine, compact, compress, congest, conglomerate, congregate, consolidate, constrict, contract, converge, cramp, crowd, draw together, eliminate, embody, focalize, focus, forgather, garner, get to the meat*, heap, heap up, hoard, huddle, integrate, intensify, localize, mass, muster, narrow, pile, reduce, salt away,

store, strengthen, swarm, unify, zero in*; CONCEPTS 84,109 —*Ant.* disperse, scatter

concentrated [adj1] *condensed, reduced* boiled down, complete, crashed*, entire, evaporated, fixed, full-bodied, lusty, potent, rich, robust, straight, strong, stuffed*, telescoped*, thick, thickened, total, unadulterated, undiffused, undiluted, undivided, unmingled, unmixed, whole; CONCEPTS 483,554 —*Ant.* diffuse, loose, thin

concentrated [adj2] *intense* all-out, deep, desperate, exquisite, fierce, furious, hard, intensive, terrible, vehement, vicious; CONCEPTS 326,569 —*Ant.* diffuse, diluted, free, loose

concentration [n1] *consolidation of effort* absorption, amassing, application, assembly, bringing to bear, centering, centralization, close attention, clustering, coalescing, combination, compacting, compression, concern, congregation, consolidation, convergence, converging, debate, deliberation, fixing, flocking, focusing, heed, huddling, intensification, massing, narrowing, need, single-mindedness, study, unity; CONCEPT 677

concentration [n2] *aggregation* accumulation, army, array, audience, band, cluster, collection, company, concourse, convergence, flock, group, herd, horde, mass, miscellany, mob, party; CONCEPT 432 —*Ant.* dispersal, scattering, separation

concept [n] *idea* abstraction, apprehension, approach, big idea*, brainchild*, brain wave*, conceit, conception, conceptualization, consideration, fool notion*, hypothesis, image, impression, intellection, notion, perception, slant, supposition, theory, thought, twist, view, wrinkle; CONCEPTS 532,689 —*Ant.* being, concrete

conception [n1] *understanding; idea* apperception, appreciation, apprehension, clue, cogitating, cognition, communing, comprehension, conceit, concentrating, concept, consideration, considering, deliberating, design, dreaming, envisaging, explanation, exposition, fancy, fancying, image, imagining, impression, inkling, intellection, interpretation, meditating, meditation, mental grasp, musing, notion, perception, philosophizing, picture, plan, realization, representation, speculating, speculation, thought, version; CONCEPTS 409,410,689 —*Ant.* being, concrete

conception [n2] *beginning, birth* fertilization, formation, germination, impregnation, inception, initiation, insemination, invention, launching, origin, outset, start; CONCEPTS 119,302,373,375 —*Ant.* abortion, death

concern [n1] *business, responsibility* affair, burden, care, charge, company, corporation, deportment, entanglement, enterprise, establishment, field, firm, house, interest, involvement, job, jungle*, matter, megacorp*, mission, multinational, occupation, organization, outfit, shooting match*, task, thing, transaction, worry, zoo*; CONCEPTS 325,362,532

concern [n2] *interest; anxiety* apprehension, attention, bearing, care, carefulness, concernment, consideration, disquiet, disquietude, distress, heed, heedfulness, important matter, matter, reference, regard, relation, relevance, solicitude, tender loving care, unease, worry; CONCEPTS 410,690 —*Ant.* disinterest, unconcern

concern [v1] *affect personally* apply to, bear on, become involved, be relevant to, bother, disquiet, distress, disturb, interest, involve, make anxious, make uneasy, pertain to, perturb, regard, take pains, touch, trouble, worry; CONCEPTS 7,19,22

concern [v2] *relate to, have reference to* answer to, appertain to, apply to, be about, be applicable to, bear on, bear upon, be connected with, be dependent upon, be interdependent with, belong to, be pertinent to, be well taken, deal with, depend upon, have a bearing on, have connections with, have implications for, have relation to, have significance for, have to do with, involve, pertain to, refer to, regard; CONCEPT 532 —Ant. unconcern

concerned [adj1] *worried* anxious, biting one's nails*, bothered, butterflies in stomach*, distressed, disturbed, exercised, in a stew*, on pins and needles*, perturbed, tied up in knots*, troubled, uneasy, upset, uptight, worried sick*; CONCEPT 403 —Ant. happy, undisturbed, unperturbed, untroubled, unworried

concerned [adj2] *involved with* active, affected, attentive, caring, down with, implicated, in on, interested, mixed up, privy to, solicitous; CONCEPTS 401,403 —Ant. disinterested, inattentive, uncaring, unconcerned, uninvolved

concerning [prep] *having to do with* about, anent, apropos of, as regards, germane to, in regard to, in the matter of, pertaining to, re, regarding, relating to, relevant to, respecting, touching, with reference to, with regard to; CONCEPT 563

concert [n1] *musical performance* gig, jam session, musical, musicale, recital, rockfest, selections, show; CONCEPT 263

concert [n2] *agreement, harmony* accord, chorus, collaboration, concord, concordance, consonance, joint, league, togetherness, tune, unanimity, union, unison; CONCEPTS 388,684 —Ant. disagreement, disharmony, disunity

concerted [adj] *coordinated* agreed upon, collaborative, combined, joint, mutual, planned, prearranged, united; CONCEPT 538 —Ant. disarranged, disordered, disorganized, separate, uncoordinated

concession [n] *yielding, adjustment* acknowledgment, admission, allowance, assent, authorization, boon, buyback, compromise, confession, copout*, deal, giveback, giving in, grant, indulgence, permission, permit, privilege, rollback, sellout, surrender, trade-off, warrant; CONCEPTS 13,50,67,88 —Ant. denial, difference, disagreement, disputation, fighting, protest, refusal, repudiation

conciliatory [adj] *placid, yielding* appeasing, assuaging, calm, civil, disarming, irenic, mollifying, pacific, peaceable, placating, placatory, propitiative, quiet, willing; CONCEPT 401 —Ant. antagonistic, fighting, refusing, stubborn

concise [adj] *short, to the point* abridged, boiled down*, breviloquent, brief, compact, compendiary, compendious, compressed, condensed, curt, epigrammatic, in a nutshell*, laconic, lean, marrowy, meaty, pithy, short and sweet*, succinct, summary, synoptic, terse; CONCEPTS 773,798 —Ant. expansive, lengthy, long, long-winded, redundant, repetitive, wordy

conclave [n] *secret meeting* assembly, buzz session*, cabinet*, confab*, conference, council, encounter, gathering, get-together, huddle, meet, parley, powwow*, private meeting, session; CONCEPTS 324,384

conclude [v1] *finish, come to an end* achieve, bring down curtain*, call it a day*, cease, cinch, clinch, close, close out, complete, consummate, crown, desist, draw to close, end, halt, knock off, put the lid on*, put to bed*, round off, stop, terminate, top off, ultimate, wind up, wrap up; CONCEPTS 119,234 —Ant. begin, commence, introduce, preface, start

conclude [v2] *decide, deduce* add up to, adjudge, analyze, assume, be afraid, boil down to*, collect, derive, draw, figure, gather, have a hunch*, infer, intuit, judge, make, make out, presume, ratiocinate, reason, reckon, sum up, suppose, surmise, the way one sees it*; CONCEPTS 18,37

conclude [v3] *settle, resolve* accomplish, achieve, bring about, carry out, clinch, confirm, decide, determine, effect, establish, fix, pull off, rule, work out; CONCEPT 18 —Ant. unsettle

conclusion [n1] *end* cease, cessation, close, closure, completion, consequence, culmination, denouement, desistance, development, ending, end of the line*, eventuality, finale, finish, issue, outcome, payoff, period, result, stop, termination, upshot, windup, wrap; CONCEPTS 119,832 —Ant. beginning, commencement, introduction, preface, prelude, start

conclusion [n2] *judgment, decision* agreement, conviction, corollary, deduction, determination, illation, inference, opinion, ratiocination, resolution, resolve, sequitur, settlement, verdict; CONCEPT 689 —Ant. concept, theory

conclusive [adj] *definite, final* absolute, all out*, clear, clinching, cogent, compelling, convincing, deciding, decisive, demonstrative, determinant, determinative, flat out*, incontrovertible, indisputable, irrefragable, irrefrangible, irrefutable, irrevocable, litmus test*, precise, resolving, revealing, settling, straight out, telling, ultimate, unambiguous, unanswerable, unarguable, unconditional, undeniable, unmistakable, unquestionable, what you see is what you get*; CONCEPT 535 —Ant. inconclusive, indefinite

concoct [v] *formulate, think up* ad lib, batch*, brew*, compound, contrive, cook up, create, design, devise, discover, dream up, envisage, envision, fabricate, frame*, hatch, invent, make up, mature, originate, plan, plot, prefab*, prepare, project, scheme, slap together*, throw together*, vamp; CONCEPTS 36,173,251

concoction [n] *creation, blend* brew, combination, compound, contrivance, intention, medley, mixture, plan, preparation, project, solution; CONCEPTS 260,432,660

concomitant [adj] *contributing, accompanying* accessory, adjuvant, agreeing, ancillary, associated with, associative, attendant, attending, belonging, coefficient, coetaneous, coeval, coexistent, coincident, coincidental, collateral, complementary, concordant, concurrent, conjoined, conjoined with, connected, contemporaneous, contemporary, coordinate, corollary, coterminous, coupled with, fellow, incident, in tempo, in time, isochronal, isochronous, joint, satellite, synchronal, synchronous, synergetic, synergistic; CONCEPT 577 —Ant. accidental, chance, unrelated

concord [n1] *unity, harmony* accord, agreement, amity, calmness, chime, comity, concert, concordance, consensus, consonance, friendship, goodwill, peace, placidity, rapport, serenity, tranquility, tune, unanimity, understanding, unison; CONCEPT 388 —Ant. discord, disunity

concord [n2] *agreement, treaty* compact, concordat, contract, convention, entente, pact, protocol; CONCEPTS 271,684 —Ant. disagreement, discord

concourse [n1] *passageway* avenue, boulevard, entrance, foyer, hall, highway, lobby, lounge, meeting place, path, rallying point*, road, street; CONCEPTS 440,501

concourse [n2] *crowd, group* assemblage, assembly, collection, concursion, confluence, convergence, crush, gang, gathering, joining, junction, linkage, meeting, mob, multitude, rout, throng; CONCEPT 432

concrete [adj1] *actual, factual* accurate, corporeal, definite, detailed, explicit, material, objective, particular, precise, real, sensible, solid, specific, substantial, tangible; CONCEPT 535 —Ant. abstract, ideal, immaterial, intangible

concrete [adj2] *hardened* caked, calcified, cemented, compact, compressed, congealed, conglomerated, consolidated, dried, firm, indurate, monolithic, petrified, poured, precast, set, set in stone*, solid, solidified, steeled, strong, unyielding; CONCEPT 604 —Ant. bending, flexible, pliable

concur [v] *agree, approve* accede, accord, acquiesce, assent, band, be consonant with, be in harmony, coadjute, coincide, collaborate, combine, come together, consent, cooperate, cut a deal*, equal, harmonize, jibe*, join, league*, meet, okay*, pass on*, shake on*, unite; CONCEPTS 8,10,82 —Ant. argue, differ, disagree, disapprove, dispute, object, oppose, reject

concurrent [adj1] *simultaneous* circumstantial, coeval, coexisting, coincident, concerted, concomitant, contemporaneous, incidental, in sync, parallel, synchronal, synchronous; CONCEPT 799

concurrent [adj2] *agreeing, converging* allied, at one, centrolineal, coinciding, compatible, concerted, confluent, consentient, consistent, convergent, cooperating, coterminous, harmonious, in agreement, in rapport, joined, likeminded, meeting, mutual, of the same mind, unified, uniting; CONCEPT 563 —Ant. disagreeing, divergent, nonconcurrent

concussion [n] *collision, shaking* blast, blow, buffeting, bump, clash, clout, crack, crash, hit, impact, injury, jar, jarring, jolt, jolting, jounce, pounding, punch, shock, trauma; CONCEPT 189

condemn [v] *blame, convict* adjudge, belittle, blow whistle on*, call down*, castigate, censure, chide, come down on*, criticize, damn, decry, denounce, denunciate, deprecate, depreciate, disapprove, disparage, doom, find fault with, find guilty, frame, hang something on*, judge, knock, lay at one's door*, let have it*, name, pass sentence on*, pin it on*, point finger at*, pronounce, proscribe, punish, put away, put down, reprehend, reproach, reprobate, reprove, send up, send up the river*, sentence, skin, thumbs down on*, upbraid; CONCEPTS 44,52,317

—Ant. absolve, acquit, approve, clear, discharge, exonerate, free, pardon, release, set free

condemnation [n] *blaming, conviction* accusation, blame, censure, damnation, denouncement, denunciation, disapproval, doom, judgment, proscription, reproach, reprobation, reproof, sentence, stricture; CONCEPTS 44,52,317 —Ant. absolution, acquittal, clearance, discharge, exoneration, freeing, pardon, release

condensation [n1] *abridgment* abstract, boildown*, breviary, brief, compendium, compression, concentration, consolidation, conspectus, contraction, curtailment, digest, epitome, essence, précis, reduction, summary, synopsis; CONCEPTS 283,730 —Ant. unabridgment

condensation [n2] *water buildup* condensate, crystallization, deliquescence, dew, distillation, liquefaction, precipitate, precipitation, rainfall; CONCEPT 514 —Ant. dryness

condense [v] *abridge* abbreviate, blue pencil*, boil down, chop, coagulate, compact, compress, concentrate, constrict, contract, curtail, cut, cut down, decoct, densen, digest, edit, encapsulate, epitomize, inventory, precipitate, précis, press together, put in a nutshell*, reduce, shorten, shrink, snip, solidify, sum, summarize, summate, synopsize, telescope, thicken, trim; CONCEPTS 236,247 —Ant. enlarge, expand, lengthen

condescend [v] *stoop, humble oneself* accommodate, accord, acquiesce, agree, be courteous, bend, come down off high horse*, comply, concede, degrade oneself, deign, demean oneself, descend, favor, grant, high hat*, lower oneself, oblige, see fit, submit, talk down to, toss a few crumbs*, unbend, vouchsafe, yield; CONCEPT 633 —Ant. rise above

condescending [adj] *snobby, lordly* arrogant, complaisant, disdainful, egotistic, la-dee-da*, lofty, patronizing, snobbish, snooty*, snotty*, supercilious, superior, uppish, uppity; CONCEPT 401 —Ant. approachable, friendly, humble

condescension [n] *disdain, superiority* airs, civility, deference, haughtiness, loftiness, lordliness, patronage, patronizing attitude, superciliousness, toleration; CONCEPT 633 —Ant. friendliness, humility, inferiority

condiment [n] *flavoring* catsup, dressing, gravy, horseradish, ketchup, mustard, pepper, relish, salsa, salt, sauce, seasoning, spice, zest; CONCEPTS 457,461

condition [n1] *circumstances* action, ballgame*, case, estate, happening, how it goes*, how things are*, how things stack up*, lay of the land*, like it is*, mode, order, plight, position, posture, predicament, quality, rank, repair, reputation, riff, scene, shape, situation, size of it*, sphere, spot, standing, state, state of affairs, status, status quo, trim, way things are*, way things shape up*, where it's at*; CONCEPTS 639,696

condition [n2] *requirement, limitation* arrangement, article, catch, codicil, contingency, demand, essential, exception, exemption, fine print*, kicker*, modification, must, necessity, postulate, precondition, prerequisite, provision, proviso, qualification, requisite, reservation, rule, sine qua non, small print*, stipulation, strings*, terms; CONCEPTS 270,688

condition [n3] *physical shape, fitness* appearance, aspect, build, constitution, fettle, form, health, kilter, mint, order, phase, repair, state, status, tone, trim; CONCEPTS 316,757

condition [n4] *illness* affection, ailment, complaint, disease, ill, infirmity, malady, predicament, problem, syndrome, temper, weakness; CONCEPT 306

condition [v] *adapt, prepare* accustom, brainwash, build up, educate, equip, habituate, inure, loosen up, make ready, modify, practice, program, ready, shape up, sharpen, tone up, toughen up, train, warm up, whip into shape*, work out, work over; CONCEPTS 35,202

conditional [adj] *dependent* codicillary, contingent, depending on, fortuitous, granted on certain terms, guarded, iffy*, incidental, inconclusive, limited, modified, not absolute, obscure, provisional, provisory, qualified, relative, reliant, relying on, restricted, restrictive, subject to, tentative, uncertain, with grain of salt*, with reservations, with strings attached*; CONCEPT 554 —*Ant.* independent, unconditional, unlimited, unqualified, unrestricted

condolence [n] *sympathy* comfort, commiseration, compassion, condolement, consolation, fellow feeling, solace; CONCEPT 633

condom [n] *birth control* contraceptive, French letter*, johnny*, prophylactic, protection, raincoat*, rubber*, safe, sheath; CONCEPT 307

condominium [n] *tenant-owned apartment house* apartment, condo, co-op, timeshare, townhouse; CONCEPT 516

condone [v] *make allowance for* buy*, disregard, excuse, forget, forgive, give green light*, go along with, ignore, lap up*, let it come*, let it go by*, let pass*, look the other way*, nod at*, okay, overlook, pardon, pass over, remit, wink at*; CONCEPTS 10,23 —*Ant.* censure, condemn, forbid, not allow, prevent

conducive [adj] *favorable for* accessory, calculated to produce, contributive, contributory, helpful, leading, productive of, promotive, tending, useful; CONCEPT 542 —*Ant.* adverse, discouraging, hindering, unconducive, unfavorable, unhelpful

conduct [n1] *administration* care, carrying on*, channels, charge, control, direction, execution, guidance, handling, intendance, leadership, management, manipulation, organization, oversight, plan, policy, posture, red tape*, regimen, regulation, rule, running, strategy, superintendence, supervision, tactics, transaction, treatment, wielding; CONCEPT 117

conduct [n2] *behavior* address, attitude, bearing, carriage, comportment, demeanor, deportment, manner, manners, mien, posture, stance, tenue, ways; CONCEPT 633

conduct [v1] *administer* accompany, attend, call the tune*, carry on*, chair, chaperon, control, convey, direct, engineer, escort, govern, guide, handle, head, keep, lead, manage, operate, ordain, order, organize, oversee, pilot, preside over, regulate, ride herd on*, rule, run, run things, shepherd, steer, supervise, trailblaze*, usher, wield baton*; CONCEPT 117

conduct [v2] *comport oneself* acquit, act, bear, behave, carry, demean, deport, go on, quit; CONCEPT 384

conduct [v3] *transport* accompany, attend, bring, carry, chaperon, companion, convoy, escort, guide, lead, move, pass on, pilot, route, send, shepherd, show, steer, transfer; CONCEPT 187 —*Ant.* leave

conductor [n] *leader* director, guide, maestro, manager, marshal, master, supervisor; CONCEPTS 347,350,354

conduit [n] *passage* aqueduct, cable, canal, channel, conductor, course, culvert, duct, flow, flume, gully, gutter, lead-in, lead-out, main, pipe, pipeline, race, sewer, spout, trough, tube, watercourse; CONCEPTS 499,501

cone [n] *circular-shaped object with pointed end* conoid, pyramid, raceme, strobile, strobiloid; CONCEPT 436

confection [n] *sweet food* cake, candy, dainty, jam, pastry, sweet; CONCEPT 457

confederacy [n] *coalition* alliance, anschluss, bond, compact, confederation, conspiracy, covenant, federation, government, league, organization, union; CONCEPTS 299,301

confederate [adj] *allied* amalgamated, associated, combined, corporate, federal, federated, in alliance, incorporated, leagued, organized, syndicated, unionized; CONCEPT 536

confederate [n] *abettor* accessory, accomplice, ally, associate, coconspirator, collaborator, colleague, conspirator, fellow, fellow traveler, partner; CONCEPT 412

confer [v1] *discuss, deliberate* advise, argue, bargain, blitz*, brainstorm*, breeze*, collogue, confab*, confabulate, consult, converse, deal, debate, discourse, flap*, gab*, get heads together*, give meeting*, groupthink*, huddle, jaw, kick ideas around*, negotiate, parley, pick one's brain*, powwow*, speak, talk, toss ideas around*, treat; CONCEPT 56

confer [v2] *giving honor, award* accord, allot, award, bestow, donate, gift with, give, grant, lay on, present, provide, sweeten the kitty*, vouchsafe; CONCEPT 132 —*Ant.* dishonor, taking

conference [n1] *convention, colloquium* appointment, argument, chat, colloquy, confabulation, conferring, congress, consultation, conversation, convocation, deliberation, discussion, forum, gabfest*, groupthink*, huddle, interchange, interview, meeting, palaver, parley, powwow*, round robin, round table, seminar, symposium, talk, think-in*, ventilation; CONCEPTS 56,324,386

conference [n2] *league of athletic teams* association, athletic union, circuit, league, loop, organization, ring; CONCEPT 365

confess [v] *admit, confirm* acknowledge, affirm, allow, assert, attest, aver, avow, blow, blurt out, chirp, clue in, come clean*, come out, concede, confide, declare, disclose, divulge, dump on*, evince, finger*, fink*, grant, humble oneself, leak*, let on*, level with, make clean breast of*, manifest, narrate, open one's heart*, own, own up, post, profess, prove, rat on*, recognize, relate, reveal, sing*, snitch*, sound off*, spill the beans*, spit out*, squeal*, tip hand*, unload*, vent, weasel*; CONCEPT 60 —*Ant.* conceal, deny, disavow, disown, hide, mask, repudiate, secrete

confession [n] *admittance of information* acknowledgment, admission, affirmation, allowance, assenting, assertion, avowal, concession, declaration, disclosing, disclosure, divulgence, enumeration, exposé, exposure, making public, narration, owning up, proclamation, profession, publication, recitation, relation, revealing, revelation, song*, squawk*, squeal*, statement, story, telling, unbosoming, utterance; CONCEPTS 60,274 —**Ant.** concealment, cover, denial, disavowal, secret

confidant [n] *close friend* acquaintance, adherent, adviser, alter ego, bosom buddy, companion, crony, familiar, intimate, mate, pal; CONCEPT 423 —**Ant.** enemy, foe

confide [v1] *divulge information* admit, bend an ear*, breathe, buzz*, confess, crack to, disclose, hint, impart, insinuate, intimate, lay it on*, lay the gaff*, let in on*, reveal, spill to*, suggest, tell, unload on*, whisper; CONCEPT 57 —**Ant.** conceal, hide, secrete, suppress

confide [v2] *entrust* bestow, charge, commend, commit, consign, delegate, hand over, present, relegate, trust; CONCEPT 108 —**Ant.** keep

confidence [n1] *belief in oneself* aplomb, assurance, backbone, boldness, brashness, certainty, cool, courage, daring, dash, determination, elan, faith in oneself, fearlessness, firmness, fortitude, grit, hardihood, heart, impudence, intrepidity, mettle, morale, nerve, pluck, poise, presumption, reliance, resoluteness, resolution, self-possession, self-reliance, spirit, spunk, sureness, tenacity; CONCEPT 411 —**Ant.** uncertainty, unconfidence

confidence [n2] *belief in something* assurance, credence, dependence, faith, hope, reliance, stock, store, sure bet*, trust; CONCEPT 689 —**Ant.** apprehension, distrust, doubt, fear, uncertainty, unconfidence

confident [adj] *certain, assured* bet on*, bold, brave, cocksure, convinced, counting on, courageous, dauntless, depending on, expectant, expecting, fearless, having faith in, high*, hopeful, intrepid, positive, presuming, presumptuous, puffed up*, pushy, racked, sanguine, satisfied, secure, self-assured, self-reliant, self-sufficient, sure, trusting, unafraid, undaunted, upbeat, uppity*, valiant; CONCEPTS 403,404 —**Ant.** uncertain, unsure

confidential [adj] *secret* arcane, backdoor, classified, closet, hushed, hush-hush*, inside, intimate, off the record*, private, privy; CONCEPTS 267,576 —**Ant.** common, familiar, known, public, well-known

confidentially [adv] *in secret* behind closed doors*, between ourselves, between us, between you and me*, covertly, don't breathe a word*, hushedly, in confidence, in on the ground floor*, off the cuff*, off the record*, personally, privately, sub rosa; CONCEPTS 267,576 —**Ant.** commonly, familiarly, openly, publicly

configuration [n] *arrangement* composition, contour, disposition, figure, form, Gestalt, outline, shape, structure; CONCEPTS 84,727

confine [v] *enclose, limit* bar, bind, bound, cage, circumscribe, constrain, cool, cool down, cramp, delimit, detain, enslave, fix, hem in, hinder, hog-tie*, hold back, ice*, immure, imprison, incarcerate, intern, jail, keep, put a lid on*, put away, put on ice*, repress, restrain, restrict, send up, shorten, shut up; CONCEPTS 121,130 —**Ant.** free, let go, liberate, release

confined [adj] *limited, enclosed* bedfast, bedridden, bottled up, bound, chilled, circumscribed, compassed, cooped up, cramp, cramped, detained, flattened out, grounded, hampered, held, hog-tied*, iced*, immured, imprisoned, incarcerated, in chains, incommodious, indisposed, in jail, invalided, jailed, laid up, locked up, on ice*, pent, restrained, restricted, sealed up, shut in, sick; CONCEPT 554 —**Ant.** free, liberated, unlimited

confinement [n] *imprisonment; restriction* bonds, bounding, bounds, check, circumscription, coercion, constrainment, constraint, control, cramp, curb, custody, delimitation, detention, immuration, incarceration, internment, jail, keeping, limitation, repression, safekeeping, trammels; CONCEPTS 90,191 —**Ant.** freedom, liberation

confines [n] *boundaries* borders, bounds, circumference, compass, country, dimension, edge, end, environs, extent, limits, orbit, periphery, precinct, proportions, purlieus, purview, radius, range, reach, region, scope, sweep, term, terrain, territory; CONCEPTS 484,745,788 —**Ant.** open

confirm [v1] *validate, prove* affirm, approve, attest, authenticate, back, bear out, bless, buy, certify, check, check out, circumstantiate, corroborate, debunk, double-check, endorse, establish, explain, give green light*, give high sign*, give stamp of approval*, give the go-ahead*, give the nod*, justify, lap up, make good*, make sure, okay, rubber-stamp*, sanction, settle, sign, sign off on*, size up, subscribe, substantiate, support, thumbs up*, underpin, uphold, verify, vouch, warrant, witness; CONCEPTS 57,103 —**Ant.** annul, cancel, contradict, destroy, disprove, invalidate, oppose, veto, void

confirm [v2] *reinforce* assure, buttress, clinch, establish, fix, fortify, invigorate, make firm, settle, strengthen; CONCEPTS 244,250 —**Ant.** contradict, deny, destroy, oppose, repudiate, void

confirmation [n] *ratification, validation, proof* acceptance, accepting, accord, admission, affirmation, affirming, agreement, approval, assent, attestation, authenticating, authentication, authorization, authorizing, avowal, consent, corroborating, corroboration, endorsement, evidence, go ahead*, green light*, nod, okay, passage, passing, proving, recognition, sanction, sanctioning, stamp of approval*, substantiation, support, supporting, testament, testimonial, testimony, validating, verification, verifying, visa, witness; CONCEPTS 661,685 —**Ant.** annulment, cancellation, contradiction, denial, destruction, opposition, veto, void

confirmed [adj] *habitual; rooted* accepted, accustomed, chronic, deep-rooted, deep-seated, dyed-in-the-wool*, entrenched, firmly established, fixed, habituated, hardened, hard-shell*, ingrained, inured, inveterate, long-established, proved, seasoned, settled, staid, valid, worn; CONCEPTS 542,798 —**Ant.** indefinite, infrequent, sporadic, uncommitted, unconfirmed, undecided

confiscate [v] *steal; seize* accroach, annex, appropriate, arrogate, assume, commandeer, confisticate, expropriate, glom on to*, grab, hijack, impound, liberate, moonlight requisition*, possess oneself of, preempt, sequester, sequestrate, swipe, take, take over, usurp; CONCEPTS 139,142 —*Ant.* give, offer

conflagration [*n*] *large fire* blaze, bonfire, burning, flaming, holocaust, inferno, rapid oxidation, up in smoke*, wildfire; CONCEPTS 249,478

conflict [*n1*] *fight, warfare* battle, clash, collision, combat, competition, contention, contest, emulation, encounter, engagement, fracas, fray, rivalry, set-to, strife, striving, struggle, tug-of-war, war; CONCEPTS 106,388,674 —*Ant.* accord, agreement, concord, harmony, peace

conflict [*n2*] *disagreement, discord* affray, animosity, antagonism, bad blood*, brush, competition, concours, contention, contest, dance, difference, disaccord, dispute, dissension, dissent, dissidence, disunity, divided loyalties, faction, factionalism, flap, fray, friction, fuss, hassle, hostility, interference, meeting, opposition, row, ruckus, run-in, set-to, strife, variance; CONCEPTS 106,388,674 —*Ant.* accord, agreement, concord, harmony, peace

conflict [*v*] *be at odds* brawl, bump heads with*, clash, collide, combat, contend, contest, contrast, cross swords with, differ, disaccord, disagree, discord, disharmonize, disturb, fight, interfere, jar, lock horns with*, mismatch, oppose, romp, run against tide*, scrap, slug, square off with, strive, struggle, tangle, vary; CONCEPTS 46,106 —*Ant.* agree, be calm, harmonize

conflicting [*adj*] *contradictory* adverse, antagonistic, antipathetic, at odds with, clashing, contrariant, contrary, disconsonant, discordant, discrepant, dissonant, incompatible, incongruent, incongruous, inconsistent, inconsonant, opposed, opposing, paradoxical, unfavorable, unmixable; CONCEPTS 542,570 —*Ant.* agreeable, harmonious, nonconflicting, peaceful

confluence [*n*] *coming together* assemblage, assembly, concourse, concurrence, concursion, conflux, convergence, crowd, gathering, host, junction, meeting, mob, multitude, union; CONCEPTS 109,114

conform [*v1*] *adjust, adapt* accommodate, attune, be guided by, clean up act*, comply, coordinate, don't make waves*, don't rock the boat*, fall in with, fit, follow, follow beaten path*, follow the crowd, go by the book*, go with the flow*, harmonize, integrate, keep, make room, meet halfway, mind, move over, obey, observe, play the game*, proportion, quadrate, reconcile, reconciliate, roll with punches*, run with the pack*, shape up, square, straighten up, suit, tailor, tailor-make*, toe the line*, tune, yield; CONCEPT 13 —*Ant.* differ, fight, refuse

conform [*v2*] *correspond, match* accord, agree, assimilate, be regular, dovetail, fit in, fit the pattern, go, harmonize, jibe, square, suit, tally; CONCEPT 664 —*Ant.* mismatch, not correspond

conformable [*adj*] *appropriate; matching* adapted, agreeable, alike, amenable, applicable, assorted, comparable, compliant, consistent, docile, fitted, fitting, harmonious, in agreement, like, matched, obedient, orderly, proper, regular, resembling, similar, submissive, suitable, suited, tractable, unified, useable, well-regu-

lated; CONCEPTS 487,558,563,573 —*Ant.* inappropriate, mismatched, nonconforming

conformation [*n*] *shape* anatomy, arrangement, build, cast, configuration, figure, form, formation, frame, framework, outline, structure, symmetry, type; CONCEPTS 754,757

conformist [*n*] *person in agreement* Babbit, bourgeois, brick in a wall*, conventionalist, emulator, follower, one of the herd*, rubber stamp*, sheep*, traditionalist, yes man*; CONCEPTS 361,423

conformity [*n1*] *compliance* acquiescence, allegiance, assent, consent, conventionality, docility, obedience, observance, orthodoxy, resignation, submission, willingness; CONCEPTS 13,689 —*Ant.* difference, fight, noncomformity, refusal

conformity [*n2*] *correspondence, harmony* accord, affinity, agreement, coherence, conformance, congruity, consistency, consonance, likeness, resemblance, similarity; CONCEPT 664 —*Ant.* disagreement, discord, nonconformity

confound [*v*] *confuse* abash, amaze, astonish, astound, baffle, befog, bewilder, blend, bug*, commingle, confute, discombobulate*, discomfit, discountenance, dumbfound, embarrass, faze, fiddle, flabbergast, jumble, metagrobolize, misidentify, mix, mix up*, mystify, nonplus, perplex, pose, puzzle, rattle, screw up*, startle, surprise, throw*; CONCEPTS 16,42 —*Ant.* clarify, clear up, enlighten, explain, make clear, relate

confront [*v*] *challenge* accost, affront, beard, brave, call one's bluff*, come up against*, dare, defy, encounter, face down*, face up to*, face with*, flout, front, go one-on-one*, go up against*, make my day*, meet, meet eyeball-to-eyeball*, oppose, repel, resist, scorn, stand up to, tell off, withstand; CONCEPTS 46,52,54 —*Ant.* back down

confrontation [*n*] *conflict* affray, battle, contest, crisis, dispute, encounter, fight, meeting, set-to, showdown, strife; CONCEPTS 46,106 —*Ant.* calm, peace

confuse [*v1*] *bewilder someone* abash, addle, amaze, astonish, baffle, becloud, bedevil, befuddle, bemuse, cloud, clutter, complicate, confound, darken, daze, demoralize, discomfit, discompose, disconcert, discountenance, disorient, distract, embarrass, faze, fluster, fog, frustrate, fuddle, involve, lead astray, mess up*, misinform, mislead, mortify, muddle, mystify, nonplus, obscure, perplex, perturb, puzzle, rattle, render uncertain, shame, stir up, stump, throw off, throw off balance*, trouble, unhinge, unsettle, upset, worry; CONCEPT 16 —*Ant.* clarify, clear up, enlighten, explain

confuse [*v2*] *mix up; involve* bedlamize, blend, clutter, confound, disarrange, disarray, discombobulate*, discreate, disorder, disorganize, embroil, encumber, entangle, intermingle, involve, jumble, litter, mess up*, mingle, mistake, muddle, muss up, rumple, snarl up, tangle, tousle, tumble; CONCEPT 112 —*Ant.* order, organize, separate

confused [*adj1*] *disoriented mentally* abashed, addled, at a loss*, at sea*, at sixes and sevens*, baffled, befuddled, bewildered, come apart*, dazed, discombobulated*, disconcerted, disorganized, distracted, flummoxed, flustered, fouled up*, glassy-eyed*, gone*, misled, mixed up, muddled, nonplussed, not with it*, out to lunch*, perplexed, perturbed, punch-drunk*, punchy*, puzzled, screwy*, shook up*, shot to pieces*, slaphappy, spaced out*, stumped, taken aback, thrown, thrown off balance*, unglued*, unscrewed*, unzipped*; CONCEPT 403 —Ant. clear, organized, oriented, understanding

confused [adj2] mixed up, disordered anarchic, blurred, chaotic, disarranged, disorderly, disorganized, haywire, in a muddle, in disarray, involved, jumbled, messy, miscalculated, miscellaneous, mistaken, misunderstood, obscured, out of order, snafu*, snarled, topsyturvy, unsettled, untidy; CONCEPT 585 —Ant. methodical, ordered, organized, separated, systematic

confusion [n1] disorientation abashing, abashment, addling, agitation, befuddlement, befuddling, bemusement, bewilderment, blurring, chagrin, cluttering, commotion, confounding, demoralization, disarranging, discomfiting, discomfiture, disorientation, distraction, disturbing, dither, dumbfounding, embarrassing, embarrassment, embroiling, flap, fluster, lather, mixup mystification, obscuring, perplexing, perplexity, perturbation, pother, puzzlement, stew, stirring up, tangling, tumult, turbulence, turmoil, unsettling, upsetting; CONCEPT 14 —Ant. clarity, order, organization, orientation, sense

confusion [n2] disoriented state abashment, ado, anarchy, astonishment, bustle, chaos, clutter, commotion, complexity, complication, consternation, daze, difficulty, disarray, discomposure, dislocation, disorganization, distraction, emotional upset, ferment, fog, fracas, haze, hodge-podge, imbroglio, intricacy, jumble, labyrinth, mess, mistake, muddle, mystification, pandemonium, perturbation, racket, riot, row, shambles, stir, stupefaction, surprise, tangle, trouble, tumult, turmoil, untidiness, upheaval, uproar, wilderness; CONCEPTS 410,727 —Ant. calm, clarity, composure, method, order, organization, orientation, system

confute [v] disprove, refute blow sky high*, break, bring to naught, confound, contradict, controvert, defeat, demolish, dismay, disprove, expose, invalidate, knocks props out from under*, negate, oppugn, overcome, overthrow, overturn, overwhelm, parry, prove false, prove wrong, put down, rebut, set aside, shut up, silence, subvert, tap, upset, vanquish; CONCEPTS 46,95 —Ant. affirm, attest, confirm, endorse, prove, verify

congeal [v] coagulate cake, clabber, clot, concrete, condense, curdle, dry, freeze, gel, gelate, gelatinate, gelatinize, glob up*, harden, indurate, jell, jellify, jelly, refrigerate, set, solidify, stiffen, thicken; CONCEPTS 250,469 —Ant. dissolve, liquify, melt, separate, thin

congenial [adj] friendly, compatible adapted, affable, agreeable, amical, clubby, companionable, compatible, complaisant, congruous, consistent, consonant, conversable, convivial, cooperative, cordial, delightful, favorable, fit, genial, good-humored, gracious, happy, harmonious, jovial, kindly, kindred, like-minded, mellow, pleasant, pleasing, regular fellow,

right neighborly, sociable, social, suitable, sympathetic, well-suited; CONCEPT 555 —Ant. disagreeable, ill-suited, incompatible, uncongenial, unfriendly, unsympathetic

congenital [adj] inborn complete, connate, connatural, constitutional, inbred, indigenous, indwelling, ingrained, inherent, inherited, innate, intrinsic, inveterate, latent, native, natural, thorough, unacquired, utter; CONCEPTS 314,549 —Ant. contracted

congested [adj] blocked, clogged chock-full, choked, closed, crammed, crowded, filled, glutted, gorged, gridlocked, jam-full, jammed, jam-packed, massed, mobbed, obstructed, occluded, overcrowded, overfilled, overflowing, packed, packed like sardines*, plugged, stopped, stoppered, stuffed, stuffed-up, teeming, up to the rafters*; CONCEPTS 481,483,774 —Ant. clear, free, open, unblocked, unclogged, uncongested, uncrowded

congestion [n] blockage bottleneck*, clogging, crowdedness, crowding, excess, jam, mass, overcrowding, overdevelopment, overpopulation, press, profusion, rubber-necking*, snarl-up*, surfeit, surplus, traffic jam; CONCEPTS 230,432 —Ant. opening

conglomerate [adj] composite amassed, assorted, blended, clustered, heterogeneous, indiscriminate, massed, melded, miscellaneous, mixed, motley, multifarious, promiscuous, varied, variegated; CONCEPTS 490,589 —Ant. individual, separate, single

conglomerate [n] composite organization agglomerate, agglomeration, aggregate, aggregation, cartel, chain, combine, conglomeration, group, multinational, pool, syndicate, trust; CONCEPTS 323,325

conglomeration [n] accumulation, potpourri agglomeration, aggregate, aggregation, amassment, assortment, collection, combination, combo*, composite, cumulation, everything but the kitchen sink*, hoard, hodge-podge, mass, medley, miscellany, mishmash*, mixed bag*, trove; CONCEPT 432

congratulate [v] compliment on achievement, luck applaud, bless, boost, felicitate, give a big cigar*, give bouquet*, give regards, gold star*, hand it to*, hear it for*, laud, pat on back, praise, rejoice with, salute, stroke*, toast, wish happy returns*, wish joy to, wish one well; CONCEPTS 51,69 —Ant. commiserate, criticize, harp

congratulations [n] complimentation on achievement, luck best wishes, compliments, felicitations, give a " hear-hear"*, good going*, good wishes, good work, greetings, hail; CONCEPTS 69,278 —Ant. commiseration, condolences, criticism

congregate [v] assemble, come together besiege, bunch up*, collect, concentrate, congress, convene, converge, convoke, corral, flock*, forgather, gang around, gang up, gather, hang out*, make the scene*, mass, meet, meet up, muster, pack, raise, rally, rendezvous, round up, swarm, teem, throng; CONCEPTS 109,114 —Ant. divide, scatter, separate

congregation [n] assembled group, especially concerned with church-going aggregation, assemblage, assembly, audience, churchgoers, collection, company, confab*, crowd, disciples, flock, following, gathering, get-together, group, host, laity, meet, meeting, multitude, muster, parish, parishioners, public, sit-in, throng, turnout; CONCEPTS 369,387,417

congress [n] *delegation of representatives* assembly, association, caucus, chamber, club, committee, conclave, conference, convention, convocation, council, delegates, government, guild, league, legislative body, legislature, meeting, order, parliament, senate, society, the Hill, the house, union; CONCEPTS 299,387

congruent [adj] *agreeable, harmonious* coinciding, compatible, concurring, conforming, consistent, corresponding, identical, in agreement; CONCEPT 563 —**Ant.** disagreeable, incongruent, unharmonious

congruous [adj] *corresponding, suitable* accordant, appropriate, apt, becoming, coincidental, compatible, concordant, congruent, consistent, consonant, correspondent, fit, fitting, harmonious, meet, proper, seemly, sympathetic; CONCEPTS 558,563 —**Ant.** disagreeing, incongruous, unfitting, unharmonious, unsuitable

conical/conic [adj] *shaped cylindrically and with a point* coned, cone-shaped, conoid, conoidal, funnel-shaped, pointed, pyramidal, sharp, strobilate, strobiloid, tapered, tapering; CONCEPT 486

conjectural [adj] *speculative* academic, assumed, doubtful, figured, guessing, guesstimated*, hypothetical, on a hunch*, on a long shot*, putative, reputed, supposed, suppositional, suppositious, suppositive, surmised, surmising, suspect, tentative, theoretical, uncertain, unresolved; CONCEPT 582 —**Ant.** certain, factual, proven, real, truthful

conjecture [n] *speculation, assumption* conclusion, fancy, guess, guesstimate*, guesswork, hunch, hypothesis, inference, notion, opinion, perhaps, presumption, shot in the dark*, sneaking suspicion, stab in the dark*, supposition, surmise, theorizing, theory; CONCEPTS 28,274, 689 —**Ant.** fact, proof, reality, truth

conjecture [v] *speculate* assume, believe, conceive, conclude, deem, estimate, expect, fancy, feel*, figure, gather, glean, guess, guesstimate*, hazard a guess*, hypothesize, imagine, infer, judge, presume, pretend, suppose, surmise, suspect, take a shot*, take a stab*, take for granted, theorize, think; CONCEPTS 28,51 —**Ant.** prove

conjugal [adj] *marital* bridal, connubial, hymeneal, married, matrimonial, nuptial, spousal, wedded; CONCEPT 555

conjunction [n] *combination* affiliation, agreement, alliance, association, cahoots, coincidence, concomitance, concurrence, congruency, conjointment, hookup*, juxtaposition, parallelism, partnership, tie-up*, union; CONCEPTS 388,714 —**Ant.** detachment, disconnection, division, separation

conjure [v1] *appeal to, implore* adjure, ask, beg, beseech, brace, crave, entreat, importune, pray, supplicate, urge; CONCEPT 48 —**Ant.** disgust, turn off

conjure [v2] *cast spell* bewitch, call upon, charm, enchant, ensorcel, entrance, exorcise, fascinate, invoke, levitate, play tricks, raise, rouse, summon, voodoo; CONCEPT 14

conjure up [v] *bring to mind* call, contrive,

create, evoke, materialize, produce as by magic, recall, recollect, remember, review, summon, urge; CONCEPT 38 —**Ant.** forget, ignore, neglect

connect [v] *combine, link* affix, ally, associate, attach, bridge, cohere, come aboard, conjoin, consociate, correlate, couple, equate, fasten, get into, hitch on, hook on, hook up, interface, join, join up with, marry, meld with, network with, plug into, relate, slap on, span, tack on, tag, tag on, tie in, tie in with, unite, wed, yoke; CONCEPTS 85,113,160 —**Ant.** disconnect

connected [adj] *related, affiliated* akin, allied, applicable, associated, banded together, bracketed, coherent, combined, consecutive, coupled, in on with*, joined, linked, pertinent, undivided, united; CONCEPTS 482,577 —**Ant.** disconnected, disjoined, unaffiliated, uncombined, unconnected, unrelated

connection [n1] *person who aids another in achieving goal* acquaintance, agent, ally, associate, association, contact, friend, go-between, intermediary, kin, kindred, kinship, mentor, messenger, network, reciprocity, relation, relative, sponsor; CONCEPTS 348,423 —**Ant.** disconnection, gap, opening

connection [n2] *something that connects, links* affiliation, alliance, association, attachment, bond, combination, conjointment, conjunction, coupling, fastening, hookup, joining, joint, junction, juncture, link, linkage, network, partnerhip, seam, tie, tie-in, tie-up, union; CONCEPTS 499,720 —**Ant.** disconnection

connection [n3] *something that communicates, relates* affinity, application, association, bearing, bond, commerce, communication, correlation, correspondence, intercourse, interrelation, kinship, link, marriage, nexus, partnership, reciprocity, relation, relationship, relevance, tie-in, togetherness; CONCEPTS 388,664

connive [v] *plot, scheme* angle, be in cahoots with*, cabal, cogitate, collude, conspire, contrive, cook up, devise, diddle*, finagle, frame, frame up, intrigue, machinate, operate, promote, wangle, wire, work hand in glove*; CONCEPT 36

connoisseur [n] *authority* adept, aesthete, aficionado, appreciator, arbiter, bon vivant, buff*, cognoscente, critic, devotee, dilettante, epicure, expert, fan, freak*, gourmet, judge, maven*, nut*, one into*, savant, specialist; CONCEPTS 352,376 —**Ant.** ignoramus

connotation [n] *implication* association, coloring, essence, hint, meaning, nuance, overtone, significance, suggestion, undertone; CONCEPTS 682,689 —**Ant.** denotation

connote [v] *imply* add up to, betoken, denote, designate, evidence, express, hint at, import, indicate, insinuate, intend, intimate, involve, mean, signify, spell, suggest; CONCEPTS 75,118 —**Ant.** denote

connubial [adj] *marital* conjugal, hymeneal, married, matrimonial, nuptial, spousal, wedded; CONCEPT 555

conquer [v1] *defeat, overcome* beat, bring to knees*, checkmate, circumvent, clobber, control, cream*, crush, discomfit, drub, foil, frustrate, get the better of*, humble, lick, master, outwit, overmaster, overpower, override, overthrow, prevail, quell, reduce, rout, shut down, subdue, subjugate, succeed, surmount, throw, thwart, total*, trample underfoot, trash, triumph, vanquish, whip, wipe off map*, worst, zap*; CONCEPT 95 —Ant. capitulate, fail, give up, lose, retreat, succumb, surrender, yield

conquer [v2] *win; obtain* achieve, acquire, annex, best, master, occupy, overcome, overrun, prevail, seize, succeed, triumph; CONCEPTS 90,141,706 —Ant. forfeit, lose, surrender

conqueror [n] *champion* conquistador, defeater, hero, subduer, subjugator, vanquisher, victor, winner; CONCEPTS 354,358 —Ant. loser

conquest [n1] *defeat, victory* acquisition, annexation, appropriation, big win*, clean sweep*, conquering, coup, defeating, discomfiture, grand slam*, invasion, killing*, occupation, overthrow, rout, routing, score, splash*, subdual, subjection, subjugation, success, takeover, triumph, vanquishment, win; CONCEPTS 95,706 —Ant. failure, forfeit, loss, surrender, yielding

conquest [n2] *enchantment; person enchanted* acquisition, adherent, admirer, captivation, catch, enthrallment, enticement, fan, feather in cap*, follower, prize, seduction, supporter, worshiper; CONCEPTS 410,423

consanguinity [n] *family relationship* affiliation, affinity, agnate, blood-relationship, brotherhood, cognate, connection, family tie, filiation, kin, kindred, kindredship, kinship, lineage, race, sisterhood, strain; CONCEPTS 296,388

conscience [n] *moral sense* censor, compunction, demur, duty, inner voice, morals, principles, qualms, right and wrong, scruples, shame, small voice*, squeam, still small voice*, superego; CONCEPTS 645,689 —Ant. immorality

conscientious [adj1] *thorough, careful* complete, diligent, exact, exacting, faithful, fastidious, fussy, hanging in*, hanging tough*, heart and soul into*, heedful, meticulous, minding p's and q's*, painstaking, particular, playing safe, punctilious, punctual, reliable, tough, walking on eggs*; CONCEPTS 531,538 —Ant. careless, inexact, irresponsible, uncareful, unconscientious, unscrupulous

conscientious [adj2] *moral, upright* conscionable, high-minded, high-principled, honest, honorable, incorruptible, just, pious, principled, responsible, right, scrupulous, straightforward, strict, true; CONCEPT 545 —Ant. corrupt, dishonest, immoral, unjust, vulgar

conscious [adj1] *alert, awake* able to recognize, acquainted, aesthetic, alive to, apperceptive, apprised, assured, attentive, au courant, aware, certain, cognizant, conversant, discerning, felt, hep to*, informed, in on*, in right mind, keen, knowing, known, mindful, noticing, noting, observing, on to*, perceiving, percipient, recognizing, remarking, responsive, seeing, sensible, sensitive to, sentient, supraliminal, sure, understanding, vigilant, watchful, wise to*, with it*, witting; CONCEPTS 402,539 —Ant. ignorant, impassive, indifferent, senseless, unaware, unconscious, unmindful, unresponsive

conscious [adj2] *intentional* affected, calculated, deliberate, knowing, mannered, premeditated, rational, reasoning, reflective, responsible, self-conscious, studied, willful; CONCEPTS

403,535 —Ant. indifferent, not deliberate, unconscious, unfeeling, unintentional, unstudied

consciousness [n] *knowledge* alertness, apprehension, awareness, care, carefulness, cognizance, concern, heed, heedfulness, mindfulness, realization, recognition, regard, sensibility; CONCEPT 409 —Ant. senselessness, stupidity, unconsciousness

consecrate [v] *hold in high religious regard* anoint, beatify, bless, dedicate, devote, exalt, hallow, honor, ordain, sanctify, set apart, venerate; CONCEPTS 69,367 —Ant. deprecate

consecutive [adj] *in sequence* after, chronological, connected, constant, continuing, continuous, ensuing, following, going on, increasing, in order, in turn, later, logical, numerical, one after another, progressive, running, sequent, sequential, serial, serialized, seriate, seriatim, succedent, succeeding, successional, successive, understandable, uninterrupted; CONCEPTS 585,799 —Ant. broken, discontinuous, infrequent, intermittent, innumerical, unconsecutive

consensus [n] *general agreement* accord, concord, concurrence, consent, harmony, unanimity, unison, unity; CONCEPTS 684,689 —Ant. disagreement

consent [n] *agreement; concession* accord, acquiescence, allowance, approval, assent, authorization, blank check*, blessing, carte blanche*, compliance, concurrence, go-ahead*, green light*, leave, okay*, permission, permit, right on*, sanction, say so*, stamp of approval*, sufferance, understanding, yes; CONCEPTS 684,685 —Ant. difference, disagreement, disapproval, dissension, objection, opposition, protest, refusal

consent [v] *agree* accede, accept, acquiesce, allow, approve, assent, bless, comply, concede, concur, fold, give in, give the nod*, give up, knuckle under, let, make a deal, okay*, permit, roll over, sanction, say uncle*, say yes, sign off on*, subscribe, throw in the towel*, yes*, yield; CONCEPTS 8,50,88 —Ant. differ, disagree, disapprove, dissent, object, oppose, protest, refuse

consequence [n1] *result, outcome of action* aftereffect, aftermath, bottom line*, can of worms*, chain reaction*, effect, end, event, fallout, follow through, follow-up, issue, outgrowth, payback, reaction, repercussion, sequel, sequence, spin-off, upshot, waves*; CONCEPT 230 —Ant. beginning, cause, commencement, inception, origin, rise, source, start

consequence [n2] *importance, significance* account, concern, exigency, fame, honor, import, interest, magnitude, moment, momentousness, need, note, pith, portent, renown, reputation, repute, signification, value, weight, weightiness; CONCEPT 668 —Ant. insignificance, unimportance, worthlessness

consequence [n3] *person's status* cachet, dignity, distinction, eminence, notability, position, prestige, rank, repute, standing, state, stature, status; CONCEPT 388

consequent [adj] *resultant* consistent, ensuing, following, indirect, inferable, intelligent, logical, rational, reasonable, resulting, sensible, sequential, sound, subsequent, successive, understandable; CONCEPTS 537,548 —Ant.

beginning, causal, commencing, originating, preparatory, starting

consequential [adj] *significant* big, considerable, eventful, far-reaching, grave, important, material, meaningful, momentous, serious, substantial, weighty; CONCEPT 568 —*Ant.* inconsequential, insignificant, uneventful, unimportant

conservation [n] *preservation* attention, care, cherishing, conservancy, conserving, control, custody, directing, economy, governing, guardianship, guarding, keeping, maintenance, management, managing, preserval, preserving, protecting, protection, safeguarding, safekeeping, salvation, saving, stewardship, storage, supervising, supervision, sustentation, upkeep; CONCEPTS 134,257 —*Ant.* destruction, neglect, spending, squandering, waste

conservationist [n] *environmental activist* environmentalist, green*, guardian, preservationist, tree hugger*; CONCEPTS 414,423

conservative [adj] *cautious, moderate, tending to preserve the status quo* bourgeois, constant, controlled, conventional, die-hard, fearful, firm, fogyish*, fuddy-duddy*, guarded, hard hat*, hidebound, holding to, illiberal, in a rut*, inflexible, middle-of-the-road*, not extreme, obstinate, old guard*, old line*, orthodox, quiet, reactionary, redneck*, right, right of center*, right-wing, sober, stable, steady, timid, Tory*, traditional, traditionalistic, unchangeable, unchanging, uncreative, undaring, unimaginative, unprogressive, white bread*; CONCEPT 542 —*Ant.* exaggerated, incautious, left-wing, liberal, progressive, radical

conservative [n] *person who is cautious, moderate; an opponent of change* bitter-ender*, classicist, conserver, conventionalist, diehard, hard hat*, middle-of-the-roader*, moderate, moderatist, obstructionist, old guard*, old liner*, preserver, reactionary, redneck*, right, rightist, right-winger, silk-stocking*, standpat, stick-in-the-mud*, Tory*, traditionalist, unprogressive; CONCEPT 359 —*Ant.* left-winger, liberal, progressive, radical

conservator [n] *caretaker of collection* curator, custodian, guardian, keeper, protector, restorer; CONCEPT 348

conservatory [n] *greenhouse* cold frame, glasshouse, hot house, nursery; CONCEPT 439

conserve [v] *save, protect* cut back, cut down on, go easy on*, hoard, keep, maintain, nurse, preserve, safeguard, scrimp, skimp, sock away*, squirrel*, squirrel away*, stash, steward, store up, support, sustain, take care of, use sparingly; CONCEPT 134 —*Ant.* destroy, neglect, spend, squander, use, waste

consider [v1] *turn over in one's mind* acknowledge, allow for, assent to, chew over*, cogitate, concede, consult, contemplate, deal with, deliberate, dream of, envisage, examine, excogitate, favor, flirt with*, grant, inspect, keep in mind, look at, meditate, mull over, muse, perpend, ponder, provide for, reason, reckon with, recognize, reflect, regard, revolve, ruminate, scan, scrutinize, see, see about, speculate, study, subscribe to, take into account, take under advisement, take up, think out, think over, toss around*; CONCEPTS 17,24 —*Ant.* discard, dismiss, forget, ignore, neglect, reject

consider [v2] *regard a certain way* analyze, appraise, bear in mind, believe, care for, count, credit, deem, estimate, feel, hold, hold an opinion, judge, keep in view, look upon, make allowance for, reckon with, reflect, remember, respect, sense, set down, suppose, take for, take into account, think, think of, view; CONCEPT 12 —*Ant.* abandon, dismiss, disregard, ignore, leave, reject

considerable [adj1] *abundant, large* ample, appreciable, astronomical, big, bountiful, comfortable, commodious, extensive, goodly, great, hefty, huge, large-scale, lavish, major, marked, much, noticeable, plentiful, pretty, reasonable, respectable, sizable, substantial, tidy, tolerable; CONCEPT 781 —*Ant.* inconsiderable, insignificant, little, slight, small, undistinguished, unnoticeable

considerable [adj2] *important* big, consequential, distinguished, doozie*, dynamite, essential, fab*, fat, influential, material, meaningful, momentous, mondo*, noteworthy, renowned, significant, solid gold*, something, something else*, substantial, super, super-duper*, to the max*, unreal*, venerable, weighty; CONCEPT 568 —*Ant.* insignificant, unimportant, unnoteworthy, unnoticeable

considerably [adv] *significantly* appreciably, far, greatly, markedly, noticeably, quite, rather, remarkably, somewhat, substantially, very much, well; CONCEPT 569 —*Ant.* insignificantly, little, slightly, unappreciably, unremarkably

considerate [adj] *respectful of others* accommodating, amiable, attentive, benevolent, big, charitable, chivalrous, circumspect, compassionate, complaisant, concerned, cool, discreet, forbearing, generous, kind, kindly, like a sport*, magnanimous, mellow, mindful, obliging, patient, polite, solicitous, sympathetic, tactful, tender, thoughtful, unselfish, warmhearted; CONCEPT 401 —*Ant.* disrespectful, impatient, inattentive, inconsiderate, mean, scornful, selfish, thoughtless, unfeeling, unmindful

consideration [n1] *mental analysis* application, attention, cogitation, concentration, contemplation, debate, deliberation, discussion, examination, forethought, heed, reflection, regard, review, scrutiny, study, thinking, thought; CONCEPT 24 —*Ant.* disregard, disrespect, failure, heedlessness, ignorance, neglect, negligence, omission, thoughtlessness

consideration [n2] *concern; something mentally examined* development, difficulty, emergency, estate, evidence, exigency, extent, factor, fancy, idea, incident, issue, items, judgment, magnitude, minutiae, notion, occasion, occurrence, particulars, perplexity, plan, point, problem, proposal, puzzle, scope, situation, state, thought, trouble; CONCEPT 532 —*Ant.* omission

consideration [n3] *high regard* attentiveness, awareness, concern, considerateness, esteem, estimation, favor, forbearance, friendliness, heed, heedfulness, kindliness, kindness, mercy, mindfulness, respect, solicitude, tact, thoughtfulness, tolerance; CONCEPTS 32,410 —*Ant.* disdain, disregard

consideration [n4] *payment* baksheesh, commish*, commission, fee*, payback, percentage, perk, perquisite, recompense, remuneration, reward, salary, something to sweeten pot*, tip, wage; CONCEPT 344 —*Ant.* debt

considered [*adj*] *deliberate, thought-out* advised, aforethought, contemplated, designed, designful, examined, express, given due consideration, gone into, intentional, investigated, mediated, premeditated, prepense, studied, studious, thought-about, thought-through, treated, voluntary, weighed, well advised, well chosen, willful; CONCEPTS 402,529 —*Ant.* disregarded, forgotten, neglected, unplanned, unstudied

considering [*adj*] *taking everything in mind* all in all, all things considered, as, as long as, because, everything being equal, for, forasmuch as, inasmuch as, in consideration of, in light of, insomuch as, in view of, now, pending, seeing, since, taking into account; CONCEPT 529

consign [*v*] *entrust, hand over for care* address, appoint, assign, authorize, commend to, commission, commit, confide, convey, delegate, deliver, deposit with, dispatch, forward, give, issue, put in charge of, relegate, remit, route, send, ship, transfer, transmit, turn over; CONCEPTS 108,143,217 —*Ant.* hold, keep, receive, retain

consignment [*n1*] *entrusting, handing over* assignment, committal, dispatch, distribution, relegation, sending shipment, transmittal; CONCEPTS 108,143,217 —*Ant.* holding, keeping, retention

consignment [*n2*] *something entrusted to another's care* batch, delivery, goods, shipment; CONCEPT 338

consist [*v*] *exist, reside* abide, be, be contained in, be expressed by, be found in, dwell, inhere, lie, repose, rest, subsist; CONCEPT 539

consistency [*n1*] *thickness* bendability, bendableness, compactness, density, elasticity, fabric, firmness, flexibility, frangibility, hardness, limberness, moldability, organization, plasticity, pliability, softness, solidity, suppleness, texture, viscidity, viscosity, viscousness; CONCEPTS 611,722

consistency [*n2*] *constancy, regularity* accord, agreement, apposition, appropriateness, aptness, coherence, cohesion, compatibility, concord, concurrence, conformability, congruity, consonance, correspondence, evenness, fitness, harmony, homogeneity, invariability, likeness, proportion, similarity, stability, steadfastness, steadiness, suitability, symmetry, uniformity, union, unity; CONCEPTS 637,656,670 —*Ant.* erraticism, incongruity, inconsistency, inconstancy, irregularity, variation

consistent [*adj1*] *constant, regular* dependable, even, expected, homogeneous, invariable, logical, of a piece, persistent, rational, same, steady, true, true to type, unchanging, undeviating, unfailing, uniform, unvarying; CONCEPT 534 —*Ant.* disagreeing, erratic, incongruous, inconsistent, inconstant, irregular, varying

consistent [*adj2*] *agreeing, compatible* accordant, according to, agreeable, all of a piece, coherent, conforming with, congenial, congruous, consonant, equable, harmonious, like, logical, matching, sympathetic; CONCEPT 563 —*Ant.* disagreeing, incompatible, inconsistent, unfitting, unsuitable

consist of [*v*] *made up of* amount to, be composed of, comprise, contain, embody, include, incorporate, involve; CONCEPT 643

consolation [*n*] *relief, comfort* alleviation, assuagement, cheer, comfort, compassion, ease, easement, encouragement, fellow feeling, help, lenity, pity, solace, succor, support, sympathy; CONCEPTS 32,410 —*Ant.* agitation, annoyance, antagonism, discouragement, disturbance, trouble, upset

console [*v*] *relieve, comfort* animate, assuage, buck up*, calm, cheer, condole with, encourage, express sympathy, gladden, inspirit, lift, solace, soothe, tranquilize, untrouble, upraise; CONCEPTS 7,22 —*Ant.* agitate, annoy, antagonize, depress, discourage, dispirit, disturb, hurt, sadden, trouble, upset

consolidate [*v*] *combine; make firm* add to, amalgamate, amass, band, bind, blend, build up, bunch up, cement, centralize, compact, compound, concatenate, concentrate, condense, conjoin, connect, densen, develop, federate, fortify, fuse, harden, hitch, hitch on, hook up with, incorporate, join, league, mass, meld, mix, plug into, pool, reinforce, render solid, secure, set, slap on, solidify, stabilize, strengthen, tack on, tag on, team up with*, thicken, throw in together*, tie in, tie up with, unify; CONCEPTS 109,250 —*Ant.* disjoin, disperse, divide, part, separate

consolidation [*n*] *combination, fortification* alliance, amalgamation, association, coadunation, coalition, compression, concentration, condensation, federation, fusion, incorporation, melding, mergence, merger, merging, reinforcement, solidification, strengthening, unification; CONCEPTS 109,469 —*Ant.* dispersal, division, parting, severance, weakening

consonance [*n*] *agreement, consistency* accord, chime, chorus, concert, concord, conformity, congruence, congruity, correspondence, harmony, suitableness, tune; CONCEPT 664 —*Ant.* disagreement, discord, dissonance, incompatibility, incongruence, incongruity, nonconformity

consonant [*adj*] *agreeing, consistent* accordant, according, agnate, akin, alike, analogous, blending, coincident, comparable, compatible, concordant, conformable, congenial, congruous, correspondent, corresponding, harmonious, in agreement, in rapport, like, parallel, similar, suitable, sympathetic, uniform; CONCEPT 563 —*Ant.* disagreeing, dissonant, incompatible, incongruent, incongruous, inconsistent, inconsonant

consort [*n*] *associate, partner* accompaniment, companion, concomitant, friend, husband, mate, spouse, wife; CONCEPT 423 —*Ant.* antagonist, enemy, foe

consort [*v1*] *be friendly with; fraternize* accompany, associate, attend, bear, befriend, bring, carry, chaperon, chum together*, chum with*, clique with, company, conduct, convoy, gang up with*, go around with*, hang around with*, hang out with*, hang with*, join, keep company, mingle, mix, pal, pal around with, pal with, run around with*, run with, take up with, tie up with; CONCEPTS 114,384

consort [*v2*] *agree* accord, coincide, comport,

concur, conform, correspond, dovetail, harmonize, march, square, tally; CONCEPT 664 —*Ant.* disagree

conspectus [*n*] *summary* abstract, digest, outline, overview, précis, resume, review, rundown*, summation, synopsis; CONCEPT 283

conspicuous [*adj1*] *obvious, easily seen* apparent, clear, discernible, distinct, evident, manifest, noticeable, open-and-shut*, patent, perceptible, plain, visible; CONCEPT 619 —*Ant.* concealed, hidden, imperceptible, inconspicuous, obscure, secret, unnoticeable, unremarkable, unseen

conspicuous [*adj2*] *important, prominent* arresting, arrestive, blatant, celebrated, commanding, distinguished, eminent, famed, famous, flagrant, flashy, garish, glaring, glitzy*, illustrious, influential, jazzy, loud, marked, notable, noted, notorious, outstanding, pointed, rank, remarkable, renowned, salient, screaming, showy, signal, splashy, stick out like sore thumb*, striking, tony*, well-known; CONCEPTS 542,567 —*Ant.* inconspicuous, obscure, unimportant, unknown, unremarkable

conspiracy [*n*] *collusion in plan* cabal, complot, confederacy, connivance, countermine, counterplot, covin, disloyalty, fix, frame*, game*, hookup*, intrigue, league, little game*, machination, perfidy, plot, practice, put-up job*, scheme, sedition, treacherousness, treachery, treason, trick, trickery; CONCEPT 660

conspirator [*n*] *schemer* accomplice, backstabber*, betrayer, caballer, collaborator, colluder, highbinder, plotter, subversive, traitor; CONCEPT 412

conspire [*v1*] *plot, scheme with someone* be in cahoots*, cabal, cogitate, collogue, collude, confederate, connive, contrive, cook up*, cooperate, devise, get in bed with*, hatch, intrigue, machinate, maneuver, operate, promote, put out a contract*, wangle, wire, work something out*; CONCEPTS 36,192

conspire [*v2*] *agree, concur* cabal, colleague, combine, complot, conduce, consort, contribute, cooperate, join, tend, unite, work together; CONCEPT 8 —*Ant.* disagree

constancy [*n*] *fixedness* abidingness, adherence, allegiance, ardor, attachment, certainty, decision, dependability, determination, devotedness, devotion, doggedness, eagerness, earnestness, endurance, faith, fealty, fidelity, firmness, honesty, honor, integrity, love, loyalty, permanence, perseverance, principle, regularity, resolution, stability, staunchness, steadfastness, steadiness, surety, tenacity, trustiness, trustworthiness, truthfulness, unchangeableness, unfailingness, uniformity, zeal; CONCEPTS 32,410,637 —*Ant.* change, changeableness, fluctuation, inconstancy, instability, irregularity, unsteadiness

constant [*adj1*] *fixed* connected, consistent, continual, equable, even, firm, habitual, homogeneous, immutable, invariable, like the Rock of Gibralter*, monochrome, monophonic, monotonous, nonstop, of a piece, permanent, perpetual, regular, regularized, solid as rock*, stable, stable, standardized, steadfast, steady, together, unalterable, unbroken, unchanging, unflappable, unfluctuating, uniform, uninterrupted,

unvarying; CONCEPT 534 —*Ant.* changeable, fickle, fluctuating, inconstant, irregular, unstable, unsteady, varying, wavering

constant [*adj2*] *neverending* abiding, ceaseless, chronic, continual, continuous, endless, enduring, eternal, everlasting, incessant, interminable, lasting, nonstop, perpetual, persistent, persisting, relentless, sustained, unending, uninterrupted, unrelenting, unremitting; CONCEPTS 649,798 —*Ant.* concluding, ending, interrupted, stopping, terminable, terminating

constant [*adj3*] *loyal, determined* allegiant, attached, dependable, devoted, dogged, faithful, fast, persevering, resolute, staunch, tried-and-true, true, trustworthy, trusty, unfailing, unflagging, unshaken, unwavering; CONCEPT 542 —*Ant.* disloyal, fickle, flagging, inconstant, undecided, undetermined, untrue, untrustworthy

consternation [*n*] *dismay, distress* alarm, amazement, anxiety, awe, bewilderment, confusion, distraction, dread, fear, fright, horror, muddle, muddlement, panic, perplexity, shock, stupefaction, terror, trepidation, trepidity, wonder; CONCEPT 230 —*Ant.* calm, composure, happiness, peacefulness, tranquility

constituency [*n*] *voting public* balloters, body of voters, body politic, citizenry, city, county, district, electorate, electors, faction, nation, people, precinct, state, system, voters, voting area, ward; CONCEPT 379

constituent [*adj1*] *component, part* basic, combining, composing, constituting, division, elemental, essential, factor, forming, fraction, fundamental, ingredient, integral, portion; CONCEPTS 826,834,835 —*Ant.* whole

constituent [*adj2*] *voting* balloter, citizen, electing, electoral, official, overruling; CONCEPT 536

constituent [*n*] *element* board, component, division, essential, factor, fixins*, fraction, ingredient, makings, part, part and parcel*, plug-in*, portion, principle, unit; CONCEPTS 826,834 —*Ant.* whole

constitute [*v1*] *comprise, form* aggregate, complement, complete, compose, compound, construct, cook up*, create, develop, dream up*, embody, enact, establish, fill out, fix, flesh out*, found, frame, fudge together*, incorporate, integrate, make, make up, set up; CONCEPTS 173,184,251

constitute [*v2*] *authorize* appoint, commission, decree, delegate, depute, deputize, designate, draft, empower, enact, establish, legislate, make, name, nominate, ordain, order; CONCEPTS 50,88 —*Ant.* deny, refuse

constitution [*n1*] *physical make-up and health* architecture, build, character, composition, construction, content, contents, design, disposition, essence, form, formation, frame, habit, habitus, nature, physique, structure, temper, temperament, type, vitality; CONCEPT 757

constitution [*n2*] *establishment* charter, code, composition, custom, formation, lawmaking, legislation, organization, written law; CONCEPTS 271,318

constitutional [*adj1*] *inherent* built-in, congenital, deep-seated, essential, inborn, inbred, ingrained, innate, intrinsic, natural, organic, vital; CONCEPT 549 —*Ant.* contracted, learned

constitutional [adj2] *provided for by law* approved, chartered, democratic, ensured, lawful, legal, representative, statutory, vested; CONCEPT 319

constitutional [n] *walk* airing, ambulation, footwork, legwork, perambulation, ramble, saunter, stroll, turn, walk; CONCEPT 149

constrain [v] *force; restrain* ban, bar, bind, bottle up, bridle, chain, check, coerce, compel, concuss, confine, constrict, cool off*, cork, curb, deny, deprive, disallow, drive, hem in*, hog-tie*, hold back, hold down, hold in, immure, impel, imprison, incarcerate, inhibit, intern, jail, keep lid on*, make, necessitate, oblige, pressure, pressurize, put half nelson on*, shotgun*, stifle, urge, withhold; CONCEPTS 14,121,130 —*Ant.* free, let go, release

constraint [n1] *force* a must*, coercion, compulsion, driving, duress, goad, hang-up*, impelling, impulsion, monkey*, motive, necessity, no-no*, pressure, repression, restraint, spring, spur, suppression, violence; CONCEPTS 14,121

constraint [n2] *shyness* bashfulness, diffidence, embarrassment, hang-up*, humility, inhibition, modesty, repression, reservation, reserve, restraint, timidity; CONCEPT 411 —*Ant.* aggression

constraint [n3] *restriction* arrest, captivity, check, circumscription, confinement, constrainment, cramp, curb, damper, detention, deterrent, hindrance, limitation, restraint; CONCEPTS 130,652 —*Ant.* allowance, permission

constrict [v] *inhibit* astringe, choke, circumscribe, clench, compress, concentrate, condense, confine, constringe, contract, cramp, curb, draw together, limit, narrow, pinch, restrain, restrict, shrink, squeeze, strangle, strangulate, tauten, tense, tighten, tuck; CONCEPTS 130,191,219 —*Ant.* expand, free, let go, loosen, open, release

constriction [n] *blockage* binding, choking, compression, constraint, contraction, cramp, impediment, limitation, narrowing, pressure, reduction, restriction, squeezing, stenosis, stricture, tightness; CONCEPTS 130,191,219 —*Ant.* opening

construct [v] *assemble, build* build up, cobble up*, compose, compound, constitute, cook up*, create, design, dream up*, elevate, engineer, envision, erect, establish, fabricate, fashion, forge, form, formulate, found, frame, fudge together*, hammer out*, hoke up*, imagine, invent, make, manufacture, organize, prefab*, produce, put out, put together, put up, raise, rear, set up, shape, throw together, throw up*, trump up*, uprear, whip up*; CONCEPTS 168,173,251 —*Ant.* annihilate, break, demolish, destroy, dismantle, raze, ruin

construction [n1] *creation, building* architecture, arrangement, assembly, build, cast, composition, conception, constitution, contour, cut, development, disposition, edifice, elevation, erecting, erection, fabric, fabricating, fabrication, figuration, figure, form, format, formation, foundation, improvisation, invention, makeup, making, manufacture, mold, origination, outline, plan, planning, prefab, prefabrication, putting up, raising, rearing, roadwork, shape, structure, system, systematization, turn, type;

CONCEPTS 168,439,757 —*Ant.* destruction, disfigurement, disorganization, ruin, ruins

construction [n2] *explanation* apprehension, construal, definition, exegesis, explication, exposé, exposition, inference, interpretation, reading, rendering, rendition, translation, version; CONCEPT 274

constructive [adj] *helpful* effective, positive, practical, productive, useful, valuable; CONCEPT 401 —*Ant.* destructive, hurting, injurious, negative, unhelpful

construe [v] *deduce; explain* analyze, decipher, define, explicate, expound, figure it to be*, infer, interpret, one's best guess*, parse, read, render, spell out, take, translate, understand; CONCEPTS 37,57

consul [n] *representative* delegate, emissary, envoy, lawyer, legate; CONCEPTS 354,355

consulate [n] *embassy* consular office, government office, ministry; CONCEPTS 439,449

consult [v] *ask, confer* argue, ask advice of, be closeted with, brainstorm*, call in, cogitate, collogue, commune, compare notes, confab, confabulate, consider, debate, deliberate, discuss, examine, flap*, groupthink*, huddle, interrogate, interview, kick ideas around*, negotiate, parlay, pick one's brains*, powwow*, put heads together*, question, refer to, regard, respect, review, seek advice, seek opinion of, take account of, take a meeting*, take counsel, talk over, toss ideas around*, treat, turn to; CONCEPTS 17,48,56

consultant [n] *professional advisor* advisor, authority, counsel, expert, freelancer, guide, master, maven, mentor, pro*, specialist, veteran; CONCEPTS 348,350

consultation [n] *asking, conference* appointment, argument, buzz session*, clambake*, confab*, conference, council, deliberation, dialogue, discussion, examination, groupthink*, hearing, huddle, interview, meeting, powwow*, second opinion*, session; CONCEPTS 48,114,324

consume [v1] *use up* absorb, apply, avail oneself of, deplete, devour, dissipate, dominate, drain, drivel, eat up, employ, engross, exhaust, expend, finish, finish up, fritter away, frivol away, go, go through, have recourse to, lavish, lessen, monopolize, obsess, preoccupy, profit by, put away, put to use, run out of, run through, spend, squander, throw away, trifle, utilize, vanish, wash up, waste, wear out; CONCEPT 225 —*Ant.* accumulate, collect, gather, neglect, not use, store

consume [v2] *eat, drink* absorb, bolt, chow down*, devour, down, eat up, feed, gobble*, gorge, gulp, guzzle, hoover*, ingest, ingurgitate, inhale, meal, mow*, nibble, partake, polish off*, punish, put away*, put down*, scarf*, snack, stuff one's face*, swallow, swill, take, toss down*, wolf*; CONCEPT 169 —*Ant.* fast, starve

consume [v3] *destroy* annihilate, crush, decay, demolish, devastate, eat up, exhaust, expend, extinguish, lay waste, overwhelm, ravage, raze, ruin, suppress, waste, wreck; CONCEPT 252 —*Ant.* build, construct

consumer [n] *person who buys merchandise, services* buyer, customer, end user, enjoyer, purchaser, shopper, user; CONCEPT 348 —*Ant.* marketer, merchandiser

consummate [adj] ultimate, best able, absolute, accomplished, complete, conspicuous, downright, faultless, finished, flawless, gifted, ideal, impeccable, inimitable, matchless, out-and-out*, peerless, perfect, perfected, polished, positive, practiced, ripe, skilled, superb, superlative, supreme, talented, thoroughgoing, total, trained, transcendent, unmitigated, unqualified, unsurpassable, utter, virtuosic, whole; CONCEPTS 528,572 —Ant. incomplete, unfinished, worst

consummate [v] achieve, finish accomplish, button down*, call a day*, can*, carry out, clean up, clinch, close, come, come through, compass, complete, conclude, crown, drop curtain*/, effectuate, end, fold up, get it together*, go the distance*, halt, knock off, mop up, perfect, perform, polish off*, put away*, put finishing touch on*, put lid on*, put to bed*, sew up, sign, take care of, terminate, top it off, ultimate, wind up, wrap, wrap up; CONCEPTS 234,704,706 —Ant. neglect

consummation [n] achievement, fulfillment cleanup, completion, culmination, doing it to a T*, end, mop-up, payoff, perfection, realization, to a finish, wind-up*, wrap, wrap-up*; CONCEPT 706 —Ant. failure, unfulfillment

consumption [n] devouring; use burning, consuming, damage, decay, decrease, depletion, desolation, destruction, devastation, diminution, dispersion, dissipation, drinking, eating, exhaustion, expenditure, loss, misuse, ruin, swallowing, using up, utilization, waste, wear and tear; CONCEPTS 156,169,225,252 —Ant. fasting, starvation

contact [n1] form of communication acquaintance, association, channel, commerce, communion, companionship, connection, influence, intercourse, junction, meeting, network, touch, union, unity; CONCEPTS 278,388,687

contact [n2] touching approximation, closeness, collision, connection, contiguity, contingence, hit, impingement, junction, juxtaposition, nearness, propinquity, proximity, relation, strike, taction, touch, union; CONCEPT 747 —Ant. avoidance

contact [v] communicate with approach, be in touch with, buzz*, call, check with, connect, get, get ahold of, get in touch with, interact, interface, network*, phone, reach, reach out, relate, speak to, talk, telephone, touch base*, visit, write to; CONCEPT 266 —Ant. avoid

contagion [n] infection bane, contamination, corruption, illness, miasma, pestilence, plague, poison, pollution, taint, transmission, venom, virus; CONCEPT 306

contagious [adj] communicable catching, deadly, endemic, epidemic, epizootic, impartible, infectious, inoculable, pestiferous, pestilential, poisonous, spreading, taking, transmissible, transmittable; CONCEPT 314 —Ant. noncommunicable

contain [v1] include, hold accommodate, be composed of, comprehend, comprise, consist of, embody, embrace, enclose, encompass, have, have capacity for, hold, incorporate, involve, seat, subsume, take in; CONCEPTS 112,736,742 —Ant. exclude

contain [v2] hold back, control bottle up*, check, collect, compose, cool*, cork*, curb,

harness, hog-tie*, hold in, keep back, keep lid on*, put half nelson on*, rein, repress, restrain, restrict, simmer down, smother, stifle, stop; CONCEPTS 94,191

container [n] holder for physical object alembic, bag, beaker, bin, bottle, bowl, box, bucket, bunker, caisson, can, canister, canteen, capsule, carafe, carton, cask, casket, cauldron, chamber, chest, churn, cistern, cradle, crate, crock, dish, ewer, firkin, flask, hamper, hod, hopper, humidor, hutch, jar, jeroboam, jug, kettle, magnum, package, packet, pail, pit, pod, poke, pot, pottery, pouch, purse, receptacle, reliquary, repository, sac, sack, scuttle, stein, storage, tank, tub, utensil, vase, vat, vessel, vial; CONCEPT 494

contaminate [v] adulterate alloy, befoul, corrupt, debase, debauch, defile, deprave, desecrate, dirty, harm, infect, injure, muck up, pervert, poison, pollute, profane, radioactivate, soil, spoil, stain, sully, taint, tarnish, vitiate; CONCEPTS 252,254 —Ant. clean, cure, heal, purify, sterilize

contamination [n] adulteration contagion, corruption, decay, defilement, dirtying, disease, epidemic, filth, foulness, impurity, infection, pestilence, plague, poisoning, pollution, radioactivation, rottenness, spoliation, taint; CONCEPTS 230,306,674 —Ant. cleaning, cure, healing, purification, sterilization

contemplate [v1] think about seriously; plan aim, aspire to, brood over, chew over, consider, cool out*, deliberate, design, envisage, excogitate, expect, foresee, intend, kick around*, mean, meditate on, mind, mull over, muse over, observe, percolate, perpend, ponder, propose, purpose, reflect upon, ruminate, size up, speculate, study, take in, think of, weigh; CONCEPTS 17,36 —Ant. discard, disregard, forget, neglect, scorn, slight

contemplate [v2] gaze at audit, behold, consider, examine, eye, inspect, notice, observe, peer, penetrate, peruse, pierce, pore over, probe, pry, regard, scan, scrutinize, see, stare at, study, survey, view, witness; CONCEPT 623 —Ant. disregard, look away, scorn

contemplation [n1] deep thought; planning ambition, cogitation, consideration, deliberation, design, intention, meditation, musing, plan, pondering, purpose, reflection, reverie, rumination, study; CONCEPT 410 —Ant. disdain, disregard, neglect, rejection, slight

contemplation [n2] gazing at examination, inspection, looking at, observation, scrutiny, survey, viewing; CONCEPT 623 —Ant. avoidance, disregard

contemplative [adj] deep in thought attentive, cogitative, in brown study*, intent, introspective, lost, meditative, musing, pensive, pondering, rapt, reflecting, reflective, ruminative, speculative, thinking, thoughtful; CONCEPTS 402,403 —Ant. disdainful, disregarding, negligent, rejecting, scornful, shallow, unreflective

contemporary [adj] modern abreast, à la mode*, au courant, contempo*, current, existent, extant, hot off press*, in fashion, instant, in vogue, just out*, latest, leading-edge*, mod*, new, newfangled, now, present, present-day, recent, red-hot*, state-of-the-art*, today's, topical, ultramodern, up*, up-to-date, up-to-the-minute, voguish, with it*; CONCEPTS 578,589,797 —*Ant.* old, old-fashioned, past, preceding

contemporary [*adj2*] *existing, occurring at same time* accompanying, associated, attendant, coetaneous, coeval, coexistent, coexisting, coincident, concomitant, concurrent, connected, contemporaneous, current, linked, present, related, simultaneous, synchronal, synchronic, synchronous; CONCEPT 820 —*Ant.* future, past, preceding, succeeding

contempt [*n1*] *disdain, disrespect* antipathy, audacity, aversion, condescension, contumely, defiance, derision, despisal, despisement, despite, disesteem, disregard, distaste, hatred, indignity, malice, mockery, neglect, recalcitrance, repugnance, ridicule, scorn, slight, snobbery, stubbornness; CONCEPT 29 —*Ant.* admiration, affection, approbation, approval, endorsement, love, regard, respect, sanction

contempt [*n2*] *state of disgrace* discredit, disesteem, disfavor, dishonor, disrepute, humiliation, ignominy, infamy, insignificancy, opprobrium, shame, stigma; CONCEPTS 388,674 —*Ant.* endorsement, regard, respect

contemptible [*adj*] *despicable, shameful* abhorrent, abject, abominable, bad, base, beggarly, cheap, crass, currish, degenerate, despisable, detestable, dirty, disgusting, hateful, heel, ignoble, ignominious, inferior, low, low-down*, lowest, mean, odious, outcast, paltry, pitiable, pitiful, poor, sad, scummy*, scurvy*, shabby, sordid, sorry*, swinish, unworthy, vile, worthless, wretched; CONCEPT 550 —*Ant.* admirable, admired, good, honorable, loved, respectable, worthy

contemptuous [*adj*] *arrogant, insolent* audacious, bold, cavalier, cheeky, cold-shoulder, condescending, contumelious, cool, derisive, derisory, disdainful, disrespectful, dog it*, hard, hard-nosed, haughty, high and mighty*, high hat*, insulting, on high horse*, opprobrious, sardonic, scornful, sneering, snippy, snobbish, snooty*, snotty*, supercilious, temperamental, uppity, upstage; CONCEPT 401 —*Ant.* humble, polite, respected, shy

contend [*v1*] *compete, fight* argue, battle, clash, confront, contest, controvert, cope, dispute, emulate, encounter, face, give all one's got*, give one's all*, go after, go for, go for broke*, go for it*, go for jugular*, grapple, have at*, jockey for position*, jostle, knock oneself out*, litigate, lock horns*, make play for*, meet, mix it up with*, oppose, oppugn, push, push for, resist, rival, scramble for, shoot at, shoot for, skirmish, stand, strive, struggle, tangle with, tug, vie, withstand; CONCEPTS 92,106 —*Ant.* abandon, desert, give up, leave, retreat

contend [*v2*] *argue* affirm, allege, assert, aver, avow, blast, charge, claim, come at, cross, debate, defend, dictate, dispute, enjoin, fly in face of*, gang up on, go at, have at*, have bone to pick*, hold, insist, jump on, justify, lace into*, lay into*, let have it*, light into*, lock horns with*, maintain, mix, mix it up*, prescribe, put up argument, report, rip*, say, set to, sock it to one*, stick it to*, take on, tell, urge, vindicate, warrant, zap*; CONCEPT 46 —*Ant.* cede, give in, give up, surrender

content [*adj*] *happy, agreeable* appeased, at ease, can't complain*, comfortable, complacent, contented, fat dumb and happy*, fulfilled, gratified, pleased as punch*, satisfied, smug, tickled pink*, willing; CONCEPT 403 —*Ant.* depressed, disagreeable, discontent, dissatisfied, disturbed, needy, unhappy, upset, wanting

content [*n1*] *comfort, happiness* contentment, ease, gratification, peace, peace of mind, pleasure, satisfaction; CONCEPT 410 —*Ant.* discontent, displeasure, uncomfortableness, unhappiness

content [*n2*] *essence, meaning* burden, composition, constitution, gist, idea, matter, significance, subject, subject matter, substance, text, thought; CONCEPT 682

content [*n3*] *capacity, volume* filling, load, measure, packing, size; CONCEPTS 719,740

content [*v*] *please* appease, bewitch, captivate, charm, delight, enrapture, gladden, gratify, humor, indulge, make happy, mollify, placate, reconcile, satisfy, suffice, thrill, tickle; CONCEPTS 7,22 —*Ant.* anger, displease, disturb, upset

contented [*adj*] *at ease; happy* at peace, cheerful, comfortable, complacent, content, glad, gratified, pleased, satisfied, serene, thankful; CONCEPT 403 —*Ant.* depress, discontent, discontented, dissatisfied, disturbed, unhappy, unsatisfied, upset

contention [*n1*] *competition* altercation, argument, battle, beef*, belligerency, bone of contention*, bone to pick*, combat, conflict, contest, controversy, difference, disaccord, discord, dispute, dissension, dissent, dissidence, disunity, enmity, feuding, fight, flak*, hassle, hostility, quarrel, rivalry, run-in, scene, scrap, set-to*, squabble, static, strife, struggle, variance, war, wrangle, wrangling; CONCEPTS 92,106 —*Ant.* affection, consideration, friendliness, friendship, good will, kindness, sympathy

contention [*n2*] *argument for idea* advancement, affirmation, allegation, assertion, asseveration, avowal, belief, charge, claim, contestation, declaration, demurrer, deposition, discussion, explanation, ground, hurrah, hypothesis, idea, maintaining, opinion, plea, position, predication, profession, rumpus, stand, thesis, view; CONCEPTS 46,278,689

contentious [*adj*] *quarrelsome* antagonistic, argumentative, belligerent, combative, disagreeable, factious, perverse, petulant, querulous, testy; CONCEPTS 401,542

contentment [*n*] *comfort, happiness* complacency, content, contentedness, ease, equanimity, fulfillment, gladness, gratification, peace, pleasure, repletion, satisfaction, serenity; CONCEPT 410 —*Ant.* discomfort, discontent, displeasure, dissatisfaction, misery, sadness, unhappiness

contents [*n*] *elements of larger object* capacity, cargo, chapters, connotation, constituents, details, divisions, essence, filling, freight, furnishing, gist, guts, implication, ingredients, innards, inside, lading, load, meaning, nub, packing, shipment, significance, size, space, stuffing, subject matter, subjects, substance, sum, text, themes, topics, volume; CONCEPT 835

contest [*n1*] *competition* challenge, concours, discussion, game, match, meet, meeting, proving, rencounter, sport, testing, tournament, trial, trying; CONCEPTS *92,363*

contest [n2] *fight, struggle* action, affray, altercation, battle, battle royal*, beef*, brawl, brush, combat, conflict, controversy, debate, discord, dispute, emulation, encounter, engagement, fray, go*, hassle, rivalry, row, rumble*, run-in, scrap, set-to*, shock, skirmish, static, strife, striving, tug-of-war, warfare, wrangle; CONCEPTS *106,320* —*Ant.* agreement, calm, peace, quiet, stillness, tranquility

contest [v1] *argue, challenge* blast, call in question, debate, dispute, doubt, give it one's all*, go for it*, go for jugular*, jockey for position*, jump on, litigate, mix it up with*, object to, oppose, push, question, scramble for, shoot for*, stand up for, tangle; CONCEPT *46* —*Ant.* agree, allow, give up, resign

contest [v2] *fight* altercate, attack, battle, brawl, break with, buck, compete, conflict, contend, cross, defend, duel, feud, fight over, gang up on, hassle, knuckle with, lay a finger on*, lay out, put on gloves*, put up dukes*, quarrel, repel, rival, row, rumpus, scrap, scuffle, set to, sock*, square off, strike, struggle, take on, tilt, traverse, vie, withstand, wrangle; CONCEPT *106* —*Ant.* agree

contestant [n] *competitor* adversary, antagonist, aspirant, battler, candidate, challenger, combatant, contender, contester, dark horse*, disputant, entrant, favorite, hopeful, member, participant, player, rival, scrapper*, team member, warrior; CONCEPT *366*

context [n] *framework, circumstances* ambience, background, conditions, connection, frame of reference, lexicon, relation, situation, substance, text, vocabulary; CONCEPTS *682,696*

contiguous [adj] *adjacent, in contact* abutting, adjoining, approximal, beside, bordering, close, contactual, conterminous, juxtaposed, juxtapositional, meeting, near, near-at-hand, nearby, neighboring, next, next door to, next to, touching; CONCEPT *586* —*Ant.* divided, separated

continence [n] *self-restraint* abstemiousness, abstinence, asceticism, celibacy, chastity, forbearance, moderation, refraining, self-control, sobriety, temperance, virtue; CONCEPT *633*

continent [adj] *chaste, pure* abstemious, abstentious, abstinent, ascetic, austere, bridled, celibate, curbed, inhibited, modest, restrained, self-restrained, sober, temperate; CONCEPT *550* —*Ant.* impure, incontinent, unchaste

contingency [n] *chance happening; possibility* accident, break, chance, crisis, crossroads, emergency, event, eventuality, exigency, fortuity, happening, if it's cool*, incident, juncture, likelihood, occasion, odds, opportunity, pass, pinch, predicament, probability, strait, turning point, uncertainty, zero hour*; CONCEPTS *650,679,693* —*Ant.* certainty, definiteness, reality, surety, truth

contingent [adj] *conditional; possible* accidental, casual, chance, controlled by, dependent, fluky, fortuitous, haphazard, incidental, likely, odd, probable, probably, random, subject to, unanticipated, uncertain, unexpected, unforeseeable, unforeseen, unpredictable; CONCEPT *552* —*Ant.* certain, definite, real, sure, truthful, unconditional

contingent [n] *group of followers* batch, body, bunch, deputation, detachment, disciples, mission, quota, sect, section, set; CONCEPT *417*

continual [adj] *constant, incessant* aeonian, around-the-clock, ceaseless, connected, consecutive, continuous, dateless, endless, enduring, eternal, everlasting, frequent, interminable, oft-repeated, permanent, perpetual, persistent, persisting, recurrent, regular, relentless, repeated, repetitive, running, staying, steady, timeless, unbroken, unceasing, unchanging, unending, unfailing, unflagging, uninterrupted, unremitting, unvarying, unwaning; CONCEPTS *534,798* —*Ant.* broken, ceasing, checked, halting, inconstant, infrequent, intermittent, interrupted, occasional, temporary

continuance [n] *duration* constancy, continuation, endurance, extension, guts*, longevity, period, permanence, perpetuation, protraction, run, survival, term, vitality; CONCEPTS *637,804,807* —*Ant.* arrest, end, ending, finish, hindrance, obstruction, stop, stoppage

continuation [n] *addition; maintenance* assiduity, augmenting, continuance, continuing, continuity, duration, endurance, enduring, extension, furtherance, going on, increase, increasing, line, maintaining, perpetuating, perpetuation, persisting, postscript, preservation, preserving, producing, production, prolongation, prolonging, propagation, protracting, protraction, sequel, succession, supplement, sustaining, sustenance, tenacity; CONCEPTS *640,651,804* —*Ant.* cessation, end, finish, halt, stop, termination

continue [v1] *persist, carry on* abide, advance, carry forward, draw out, endure, extend, forge ahead, get on with it*, go on, hang in*, keep at, keep on, keep on truckin'*, keep the ball rolling*, keep up, last, lengthen, linger, live on, loiter, maintain, make headway, move ahead, never cease, outlast, outlive, perdure, persevere, persist in, press on, progress, project, prolong, promote, pursue, push on, reach, remain, rest, ride, run on, stand, stay, stay on, stick at, stick to, survive, sustain, uphold; CONCEPT *239* —*Ant.* cease, complete, desist, discontinue, end, finish, halt, stop

continue [v2] *begin again; resume* begin over, begin where one left off, carry on, carry over, go on with, pick up, proceed, recapitulate, recommence, reestablish, reinstate, reinstitute, renew, reopen, restart, restore, return to, take up; CONCEPT *234* —*Ant.* complete, desist, discontinue, end, finish

continuity [n] *progression* chain, cohesion, connection, constancy, continuance, continuousness, continuum, dovetailing, durability, duration, endurance, extension, flow, interrelationship, linking, perpetuity, persistence, prolongation, protraction, sequence, stability, stamina, succession, survival, train, uniting, unity, vitality, whole; CONCEPT *721* —*Ant.* break, discontinuity, intermittence, interruption, stoppage

continuous [adj] *constant, unending* connected, consecutive, continued*day and night*, endless, everlasting, extended, for ever and ever, interminable, looped, no end of*, no end to, on a treadmill*, perpetual, prolonged, regular, repeated, stable, steady, timeless, unbroken, unceasing, undivided, unfaltering, uninterrupted; CONCEPTS 482,798 —*Ant.* ceasing, completed, discontinuous, ending, finished, halting, intermittent, interrupted, sporadic, stopping

contort [v] *disfigure, distort* bend, convolute, curve, deform, gnarl, knot, misshape, torture, twist, warp, wind, wrench, writhe; CONCEPTS 147,184 —*Ant.* beautify, smooth

contortion [n] *distortion, mutilation* anamorphosis, crookedness, deformation, deformity, dislocation, grimace, malformation, misproportion, misshapement, pout, twist, ugliness, unsightliness, wryness; CONCEPTS 436,580 —*Ant.* beauty, smoothness

contour [n] *outline, profile* curve, delineation, figuration, figure, form, lineament, lines, relief, shape, silhouette; CONCEPT 436

contraband [adj] *black-market; unlawful* banned, bootleg, bootlegged, disapproved, excluded, forbidden, hot*, illegal, illicit, interdicted, prohibited, proscribed, shut out, smuggled, taboo, unauthorized, verboten; CONCEPTS 319,545 —*Ant.* allowed, lawful, legal, permitted

contraband [n] *black-market production* bootlegging, counterfeiting, crime, dealing, goods*, moonshine*, piracy, plunder, poaching, rum-running*, smuggling, stuff, swag, theft, trafficking, violation, wetbacking*; CONCEPTS 192,338 —*Ant.* legal goods

contraceptive [n] *birth control method* armor, barrier method, coil, condom, diaphragm, foam, hormone, intrauterine device, IUD, jelly, loop, pill, planned parenthood, preventative, preventive medicine, prophylactic, rhythm method, ring, rubber, safety, shield, spermicidal cream, sponge, vaginal suppository; CONCEPTS 307,446

contract [n] *agreement, deal* arrangement, bargain, bond, commission, commitment, compact, concordat, convention, covenant, deposition, dicker*, engagement, evidence, guarantee, handshake*, indenture, liability, mise, obligation, pact, paper, pledge, promise, proof, record, settlement, stipulation, treaty, understanding; CONCEPTS 271,684 —*Ant.* disagreement, misunderstanding

contract [v1] *condense* abate, abbreviate, abridge, become smaller, clench, compress, confine, constrict, consume, curtail, decline, decrease, deflate, draw in, dwindle, ebb, edit, epitomize, evaporate, fall away, fall off, grow less, lessen, lose, narrow, omit, purse, recede, reduce, shrink, shrivel, subside, syncopate, take in, tighten, wane, waste, weaken, wither, wrinkle; CONCEPTS 169,236,247 —*Ant.* amplify, dilate, enlarge, expand, extend, increase, lengthen, spread, stretch

contract [v2] *come to terms* accept offer, adjust, agree, arrange, assent, bargain, become indebted, bound, buy, circumscribe, clinch, close, come around, commit, consent, covenant, dicker*, engage, enter into, firm a deal*, give one's word, go along with*, hammer out deal*, initial*, ink*, it's a deal*, limit, make terms, negotiate, obligate, owe, pact, pledge, promise, put in writing, set, settle, shake hands on it*, sign for, sign papers, sign up, stipulate, swear

to, undertake, work out details*; CONCEPTS 8,50,88 —*Ant.* break off, disagree

contract [v3] *catch disease* acquire, afflict, be afflicted with, become infected with, be ill with, bring on, cause, come down with, decline, derange, develop, disorder, fall, fall victim to, get, go down with, incur, indispose, induce, obtain, sicken, sink, succumb to, take, take one's death, upset, weaken; CONCEPTS 93,308 —*Ant.* give

contraction [n] *drawing in; shortening* abbreviating, abbreviation, abridging, abridgment, compression, condensation, condensing, confinement, confining, constriction, curtailing, curtailment, cutting down, decrease, decreasing, deflating, deflation, diminishing, diminution, drawing together, dwindling, elision, evaporating, evaporation, lessening, lopping, narrowing, omission, omitting, receding, recession, reducing, reduction, shrinkage, shrinking, shrivelling, tensing, tightening, withdrawal, withdrawing; CONCEPTS 469,776 —*Ant.* amplification, dilation, enlargement, expansion, extension, increase, lengthening, spread, stretch

contradict [v] *be at variance with* belie, buck, call in question*, challenge, confront, contravene, controvert, counter, counteract, cross, dare, deny, differ, disaffirm, disclaim, disprove, dispute, fly in the face of*, gainsay, have bone to pick*, impugn, negate, negative, oppose, refuse to accept, repudiate, take on, thumbs down*, traverse; CONCEPTS 46,54,665 —*Ant.* accept, agree, approve, concede, confirm, corroborate, OK, reconcile, sign, verify, vouch

contradiction [n] *variance to something* bucking, conflict, confutation, contravention, defiance, denial, difference, disagreement, discrepancy, dispute, dissension, gainsaying, incongruity, inconsistency, negation, opposite, opposition; CONCEPTS 46,278,665 —*Ant.* acceptance, agreement, approval, concession, confirmation, corroboration, OK, reconcilement, verification

contradictory [adj] *antagonistic* adverse, against, agin, anti, antipodal, antipodean, antithetic, antithetical, con, conflicting, contrary, converse, counter, counteractive, diametric, discrepant, incompatible, incongruous, inconsistent, irreconcilable, negating, no go*, nullifying, opposing, opposite, ornery*, paradoxical, polar, repugnant, reverse; CONCEPT 542 —*Ant.* agreeing, confirming, consistent, reconcilable, reconciled, vouching

contraption [n] *device* apparatus, appliance, contrivance, doohickey*, gadget, gizmo*, machine, mechanism, rig, Rube Goldberg device*, thingamajig*, widget; CONCEPTS 463,499

contrary [adj] *antagonistic; opposite* adverse, anti, antipathetic, antipodal, antipodean, antithetical, askew, clashing, conflicting, contradictory, contrariant, contumacious, converse, counter, diametric, discordant, dissentient, dissident, froward, headstrong, hostile, inconsistent, inimical, insubordinate, intractable, negative, nonconforming, nonconformist, obstinate, opposed, ornery*, paradoxical, perverse, rebellious, recalcitrant, recusant, refractory, restive, reverse, stubborn, unruly, wayward, wrongheaded; CONCEPT 401 —*Ant.* accommodating, agreeing, alike, concordant, correspondent, harmonious, homogeneous, like, obliging, similar

contrast [n] *difference* adverse, antithesis, comparison, contradiction, contradistinction, contraposition, contrariety, converse, differentiation, disagreement, disparity, dissimilarity, dissimilitude, distinction, divergence, diversity, foil, heterogeneity, incompatibility, incongruousness, inconsistency, inequality, inverse, oppositeness, opposition, reverse, unlikeness, variance, variation; CONCEPTS 561,665 —*Ant.* agreement, conformity, copy, equality, facsimile, homogeneousness, likeness, similarity, uniformity, unity

contrast [v] *compare, differ* balance, be a foil to*, be contrary to, be dissimilar, be diverse, be unlike, be variable, bracket, collate, conflict, contradict, depart, deviate, differentiate, disagree, distinguish, diverge, hang, hold a candle to*, match up, mismatch, oppose, separate, set in opposition, set off, stack up against*, stand out, vary, weigh; CONCEPTS 39,561,665 —*Ant.* accord, agree, be alike, be equal, be similar, coincide, concur, conform

contravene [v] *go against, contradict* abjure, breach, break, combat, conflict with, counteract, cross, defy, disaffirm, disobey, encroach, exclude, fight, gainsay, hinder, impugn, infract, infringe, interfere, interpose, intrude, negate, offend, oppose, overstep, refute, reject, repudiate, resist, spurn, thwart, transgress, traverse, trespass, violate; CONCEPTS 46,106,121,192 —*Ant.* agree, aid, allow, approve, assent, assist, concur, consent, endorse, help, permit, uphold

contribute [v1] *donate, provide* accord, add, afford, ante up, assign, bequeath, bequest, bestow, chip in, come through, commit, confer, devote, dispense, dole out*, dower, endow, enrich, furnish, give, give away, go Dutch*, grant, hand out, kick in*, pitch in*, pony up*, present, proffer, sacrifice, share, subscribe, subsidize, supply, sweeten the kitty*, tender, will; CONCEPTS 108,140 —*Ant.* harm, hurt, neglect, oppose, shun, subtract, take, take away, withdraw, withhold

contribute [v2] *be partly responsible for* add to, advance, aid, assist, augment, be conducive, be instrumental, conduce, do one's bit*, finger in the pie*, fortify, get in the act*, have a hand in*, help, lead, put in two cents*, redound, reinforce, sit in on, strengthen, supplement, support, tend, uphold; CONCEPTS 83,110,244 —*Ant.* counteract, disapprove, neglect, shun, withhold

contribution [n] *gift, offering* addition, a hand, alms, augmentation, benefaction, beneficence, bestowal, charity, donation, do one's part*, gifting, grant, handout, helping hand, improvement, increase, input, present, significant addition, subscription, supplement, write-off*; CONCEPTS 337,340

contrite [adj] *regretful* apologetic, attritional, chastened, compunctious, conscience-stricken, humble, penitent, penitential, remorseful, repentant, sorrowful, sorry; CONCEPT 403 —*Ant.* hurtful, indifferent, mean, unrepentant

contrition [n] *regret* attrition, compunction, contriteness, humiliation, penance, penitence, penitency, remorse, repentance, rue, ruth,

self-reproach, sorrow; CONCEPT 410 —*Ant.* hurtfulness, indifference, meanness

contrivance [n1] *plan, fabrication* angle, artifice, brainchild, coinage, design, dodge, expedient, formation, gimmick, intrigue, invention, inventiveness, machination, measure, plot, project, ruse, scheme, slant, stratagem, switch, trick, twist; CONCEPT 660 —*Ant.* disorganization

contrivance [n2] *gadget* apparatus, appliance, brainchild, coinage, contraption, convenience, creation, device, discovery, engine, equipment, gear, gimcrack*, harness, implement, instrument, invention, machine, material, mechanism, tackle, thingamabob*, thingamajig*, tool, utensil, whatsis*, widget*; CONCEPTS 260,463,499

contrive [v1] *invent, design* come up with, concoct, construct, cook up, create, devise, dream up*, engineer, fabricate, fashion, forge, form, formulate, frame*, handle, hatch, improvise, make, make up*, manipulate, manufacture, move, plan, plot, project, rig*, scheme, throw together*, trump up*, vamp, wangle, whip up*; CONCEPTS 36,173 —*Ant.* disorganize

contrive [v2] *bring about, succeed with difficulty* achieve, angle, arrange, carry out, cogitate, collude, compass, concoct, connive, develop, devise, effect, elaborate, engineer, execute, finagle*, hatch, hit upon, intrigue, jockey*, machinate, manage, maneuver, manipulate, mastermind, negotiate, pass, plan, play games*, plot, project, scheme, shift, swing, work out, wrangle; CONCEPTS 36,91,94 —*Ant.* demolish, destroy, ruin, stop, waste, wreck

contrived [adj] *overly planned* affected, artificial, elaborate, fake, false, forced, labored, manipulated, overdone, phony, recherché, strained, unnatural, unspontaneous; CONCEPTS 564,582

control [n] *command, mastery* ascendancy, authority, bridle, charge, check, clout, containment, curb, determination, direction, discipline, domination, dominion, driver's seat*, force, government, guidance, inside track, juice, jurisdiction, limitation, management, manipulation, might, oversight, predomination, qualification, regimentation, regulation, restraint, restriction, ropes, rule, strings*, subjection, subordination, superintendence, supervision, supremacy, sway, upper hand*, weight, wire pulling*; CONCEPT 376 —*Ant.* helplessness, powerlessness, relinquishment, renouncement, weakness

control [v1] *have charge of* administer, administrate, advise, be in saddle*, boss, bully, call, call the signals*, command, conduct, deal with, direct, discipline, dominate, domineer, govern, guide, handle, head, head up*, hold purse strings*, hold sway over*, hold the reins*, instruct, lead, manage, manipulate, overlook, oversee, pilot, predominate, push buttons*, quarterback*, regiment, regulate, reign over, rule, run*, run the show*, run things*, steer, subject, subjugate, superintend, supervise; CONCEPT 117 —*Ant.* abandon, forsake, give up, let go, relinquish, renounce, resign

control [v2] *curb, hold back* adjust, awe, bridle, check, collect, compose, constrain, contain, cool, corner, cow, limit, monopolize, quell, regulate, rein in, repress, restrain, simmer down*, smother, subdue; CONCEPT 130 —*Ant.* chance, jump in, let go, risk, rush

controversial [adj] *at issue* arguable, argumentative, contended, contentious, controvertible, debateable, disputable, disputatious, disputed, doubtable, doubtful, dubious, dubitable, in dispute, litigious, moot, open to discussion*, open to question*, polemical, questionable, suspect, uncertain, under discussion; CONCEPTS 535,546 —*Ant.* agreeable, incontrovertible, peaceful, uncontroversial, undisputed, undoubted, unquestionable

controversy [n] *debate, dispute* altercation, argument, beef*, bickering, brush, contention, difference, discussion, disputation, dissention, embroilment, falling-out*, flak, fuss, hurrah, miff, polemic, quarrel, row, rumpus, scene, scrap, squabble, strife, tiff*, words, wrangle, wrangling; CONCEPTS 46,278,665 —*Ant.* accord, agreement, forbearance, harmony, peace, quiet

controvert [v] *oppose, argue* break, challenge, confound, confute, contest, contradict, counter, debate, deny, disconfirm, discuss, disprove, dispute, oppugn, question, rebut, refute, wrangle; CONCEPTS 21,46 —*Ant.* agree, forbear, harmonize, make peace, restrain

contumacious [adj] *headstrong, obstinate* alienated, contrary, disaffected, estranged, factious, froward, haughty, inflexible, insubordinate, insurgent, intractable, intransigent, irreconcilable, mutinous, obdurate, perverse, pig-headed, rebellious, recalcitrant, refractory, seditious, stubborn, unyielding; CONCEPT 401 —*Ant.* following, obedient, subordinate, tractable, willing

contusion [n] *bruise, injury* bang, bump, cut, discoloration, knock, mouse, swelling, wale, wound; CONCEPT 309

conundrum [n] *puzzle* brain-teaser, closed book*, enigma, mystery, mystification, poser*, problem, puzzlement, riddle, why*; CONCEPTS 532,666,690

convalescent [adj] *improving, recuperating* ambulatory, discharged, dismissed, gaining strength, getting better, getting over something*, getting well, healing, mending, on the mend*, past crisis, perked up*, rallying, recovering, rejuvenated, rejuvenating, released, restored, strengthening; CONCEPT 314 —*Ant.* failing, faltering, regressing, sickly, weak, worsening

convene [v] *bring together; meet* assemble, call, call in, collect, come together, congregate, convoke, corral, gather, get together, hold meeting, muster, open, rally, round up, scare up*, sit, summon, unite; CONCEPTS 60,114,324 —*Ant.* adjourn, call off, cancel, disperse, dissemble

convenience [n1] *availability, usefulness; useful thing* accessibility, accessory, accommodation, advancement, advantage, agreeableness, aid, amenity, appliance, appropriateness, assistance, avail, benefit, comfort, comforts, contribution, cooperation, decency, ease, enjoyment, facility, fitness, furtherance, handiness, help, life, luxury, means, ministration, ministry, openness, opportuneness, promotion, receptiveness, relief, satisfaction, service, serviceability, succor, suitability, suitableness, support, time saver, use, utility; CONCEPTS 658,712 —*Ant.* inconvenience, inexpedience, inutility, unsuitability, uselessness, waste

convenience [n2] *spare time* chance, freedom, hour, leisure, liberty, occasion, one's own sweet time*, opportunity, place, preference, spare moment*, suitable time, whenever; CONCEPT 807

convenient [adj1] *appropriate, useful* acceptable, accommodating, adaptable, adapted, advantageous, agreeable, aiding, assisting, available, beneficial, comfortable, commodious, conducive, contributive, decent, favorable, fit, fitted, good, handy, helpful, in public interest, opportune, proper, ready, roomy, seasonable, serviceable, suitable, suited, timely, time-saving, user-friendly*, well-planned; CONCEPT 560 —*Ant.* awkward, inappropriate, inconvenient, ineffectual, inopportune, unadaptable, unhandy, unsuited, unuseful

convenient [adj2] *nearby* accessible, adjacent, adjoining, all around, at elbows*, at fingertips*, at hand, available, central, close, close at hand, close-by, contiguous, easy to reach, handy, immediate, in neighborhood, next, next door, nigh, on deck*, on tap*, under one's nose*, within reach; CONCEPT 586 —*Ant.* distant, far, inconvenient, out-of-the-way, unavailable

convent [n] *nunnery* abbey, cloister, monastery, religious community, retreat, school; CONCEPTS 368,516

convention [n1] *conference* assemblage, assembly, clambake, confab*, congress, convocation, council, delegates, delegation, get together, meet*, meeting, members, powwow*, rally, representatives, show; CONCEPTS 114,324,417

convention [n2] *practice, tradition* canon, code, covenance, custom, etiquette, fashion, form, formality, habit, law, percept, precept, propriety, rule, understanding, usage; CONCEPT 688 —*Ant.* strangeness

convention [n3] *agreement* bargain, bond, compact, concord, concordat, contract, covenant, pact, protocol, stipulation, transaction, treaty; CONCEPTS 271,684 —*Ant.* disagreement, discord

conventional [adj1] *common, normal* accepted, accustomed, button-down, commonplace, correct, current, customary, decorous, everyday, expected, fashionable, formal, general, habitual, in established usage, ordinary, orthodox, plain, popular, predominant, prevailing, prevalent, proper, regular, ritual, routine, square, standard, stereotyped, straight, traditional, tralatitious, typical, usual, well-known, wonted; CONCEPTS 530,547 —*Ant.* abnormal, exotic, foreign, irregular, strange, uncommon, unconventional, uncustomary, unusual

conventional [adj2] *unoriginal* bigoted, bourgeois, commonplace, conforming, conservative, demure, doctrinal, dogmatic, drippy, hackneyed, hidebound, humdrum, illiberal, inflexible, in rut, insular, isolationist, lame, literal, moderate, moral, narrow, narrow-minded, not heretical, obstinate, parochial, pedestrian, prosaic, puritanical, rigid, routine, rube*, run-of-the-mill, sober, solemn, square, stereotyped, straight, straight-laced, strict, stuffy, uptight; CONCEPT 550 —*Ant.* different, exotic, foreign, new, original, strange, unique

converge [v] *gather* assemble, coincide, combine, come together, concenter, concentrate, concur, encounter, enter in, focalize, focus, join, meet, merge, mingle, rally, unite;

CONCEPTS *113,114* —*Ant.* disperse, diverge, divide, scatter, separate, spread

conversant [*adj*] *experienced, familiar with* abreast, acquainted, alive, apprehensive, au courant, au fait, aware, cognizant, comprehending, conscious, cool*, down with*, hep*, hip*, informed, into, kept posted, knowing, knowledgeable, learned, on the beam*, perceptive, percipient, plugged in*, practiced, proficient, sensible, sentient, skilled, up*, up-to-date, versant, versed, well-informed, witting; CONCEPT *402* —*Ant.* ignorant, inexperienced, quiet, silent

conversation [*n*] *dialogue, discourse* chat, colloquy, comment, communication, communion, confab*, confabulation, conference, consultation, converse, debate, discussion, exchange, expression, gab*, gossip, hearing, intercourse, jive*, observation, palaver, parley, pillow talk*, powwow*, questioning, remark, repartee, speech, talk, talkfest*, tête-à-tête*, ventilation*, visit, yak*; CONCEPT *266* —*Ant.* quiet, quietude, silence

converse [*adj*] *opposite* antipodal, antipodean, antithetical, contradictory, contrary, counter, counterpole, different, reverse, reversed, transposed; CONCEPT *564* —*Ant.* complementary, equal, same, similar

converse [*n*] *opposite* antipode, antipole, antithesis, contra, contrary, counter, counterpole, inverse, obverse, other side, reverse; CONCEPT *665* —*Ant.* equal, same, similarity

converse [*v*] *talk* chat, chew the fat*, chitchat*, commune, confer, discourse, exchange, gab*, parley, rap*, schmooze*, speak, use, yak*; CONCEPT *266* —*Ant.* be quiet, be silent

conversion [*n*] *change, adaptation* about-face*, alteration, born again*, change of heart*, changeover, exchange, flip-flop*, flux, growth, innovation, metamorphosis, metanoia, metasis, modification, novelty, passage, passing, permutation, progress, proselytization, qualification, reclamation, reconstruction, reformation, regeneration, remodelling, reorganization, resolution, resolving, reversal, see the light*, switch, transfiguration, transformation, translation, transmogrification, transmutation, turning, turning around; CONCEPTS *232,701* —*Ant.* idleness, sameness

convert [*n*] *new believer* catechumen, disciple, follower, neophyte, novice, novitiate, proselyte; CONCEPT *361*

convert [*v1*] *change; adapt* alter, apply, appropriate, commute, downlink, download, interchange, make, metamorphose, modify, remodel, reorganize, restyle, revise, switch, switch over, transfigure, transform, translate, transmogrify, transmute, transpose, turn; CONCEPTS *232,701* —*Ant.* endure, hold, idle, keep, persist, remain, stay, wait

convert [*v2*] *change belief, especially regarding religion* actuate, alter conviction, assimilate to, baptize, be born again*, bend, bias, brainwash, bring, bring around, budge, cause to adopt, change into, change of heart*, convince, create anew, impel, incline, lead, lead to believe, make over, move, persuade, proselyte, proselytize, redeem, reform, regenerate, save, see the light*, sway, turn; CONCEPTS *12,14,35* —*Ant.* hold, remain

convertible [*adj*] *changeable* able to be changed, adaptable, adjustable, exchangeable, modifiable, swappable, switchable; CONCEPT *534*

convex [*adj*] *rounded, curving outward* arched, bent, biconvex, bulged, bulging, bulgy, gibbous, outcurved, protuberant, raised; CONCEPT *486* —*Ant.* concave, depressed, sinking

convey [*v1*] *transport* back, bear, bring, carry, channel, conduct, dispatch, ferry, fetch, forward, funnel, grant, guide, hump, lead, lug, move, pack, pipe, ride, schlepp*, send, shoulder, siphon, support, tote, traject, transfer, transmit, truck; CONCEPTS *187,217* —*Ant.* hold, keep, maintain, retain

convey [*v2*] *express message* break, carry, communicate, conduct, disclose, impart, make known, pass on, project, put across, relate, reveal, send, tell, transmit; CONCEPT *60* —*Ant.* keep secret, refrain, withhold

conveyance [*n*] *transport* car, carriage, carrying, communication, machine, movement, transfer, transference, transmission, transportation, vehicle; CONCEPTS *143,501,503* —*Ant.* hold, possession

convict [*n*] *criminal* captive, con, culprit, felon, jailbird*, long-termer*, loser*, malefactor, prisoner, repeater*; CONCEPT *412* —*Ant.* victim

convict [*v*] *find guilty* adjudge, attaint, bring to justice, condemn, declare guilty, doom, frame, imprison, pass sentence on, pronounce guilty, put away, put the screws to*, rap*, send up*, send up the river*, sentence, throw the book at*; CONCEPTS *18,317* —*Ant.* exonerate, free, liberate, release

conviction [*n1*] *belief, opinion* confidence, creed, doctrine, dogma, eye, faith, feeling, judgment call, mind, persuasion, principle, reliance, say so*, sentiment, slant, tenet, view; CONCEPT *689*

conviction [*n2*] *guilty sentence; assurance* assuredness, certainty, certitude, condemnation, condemning, confidence, determining guilt, earnestness, fall, fervor, firmness, rap, reliance, sureness, surety, unfavorable verdict; CONCEPTS *317,410* —*Ant.* overturning

convince [*v*] *gain the confidence of* argue into, assure, brainwash, bring around, bring home to*, bring to reason*, change, demonstrate, draw, effect, establish, get, hook*, induce, make a believer*, overcome, persuade, prevail upon, prompt, prove, put across, refute, satisfy, sell*, sell one on*, sway, talk into, turn, twist one's arm*, win over; CONCEPT *68*

convincing [*adj*] *persuasive* acceptable, authentic, believeable, cogent, conclusive, credible, dependable, faithful, hopeful, impressive, incontrovertible, likely, moving, plausible, possible, powerful, presumable, probable, rational, reasonable, reliable, satisfactory, satisfying, solid, sound, swaying, telling, trustworthy, trusty, valid; CONCEPTS *267,537,552* —*Ant.* doubtful, dubious, implausible, improbable, incredible, unconvincing, unlikely, unpersuasive

convivial [*adj*] *fun-loving* back-slapping*, cheerful, clubby*, companionable, conversible, entertaining, festal, festive, friendly, gay, genial, glad-handering*, happy, hearty, hilarious, holiday, jocund, jolly, jovial, lively, merry, mirthful,

pleasant, sociable, vivacious;CONCEPTS *401,404*
—**Ant.** blah, dull, serious, solemn, staid

convocation [*n*] *assembly* assemblage, conclave, concourse, confab*, conference, congregation, congress, convention, council, diet, get-together, meet, meeting, powwow*, synod, turnout; CONCEPT *114*

convoluted [*adj*] *complicated* baffling, complex, confused, elaborate, impenetrable, intricate, involved, labyrinthine, perplexing, puzzling, serpentine, tangled, tortuous; CONCEPT *562* —**Ant.** simple, straightforward

convolution [*n*] *loop, spiral* coil, coiling, complexity, contortion, curlicue, flexing, gyration, helix, intricacy, involution, serpentine, sinuosity, sinuousness, snaking, swirl, tortuousness, twist, undulation, winding; CONCEPT *436* —**Ant.** line, straightness

convoy [*n*] *guard, escort* attendance, attendant, companion, protection; CONCEPT *423*

convoy [*v*] *protect, escort* accompany, attend, bear, bring, chaperon, companion, company, conduct, consort, defend, guard, pilot, safeguard, shepherd, shield, usher, watch; CONCEPTS *96,110*—**Ant.** ignore, neglect

convulsion [*n1*] *muscle spasm* algospasm, attack, contortion, contraction, cramp, epilepsy, fit, paroxysm, seizure, throe, tremor; CONCEPT *308*

convulsion [*n2*] *disturbance* agitation, cataclysm, clamor, commotion, disaster, ferment, furor, outcry, quaking, rocking, seism, shaking, shock, tottering, trembling, tumult, turbulence, upheaval, upturn; CONCEPTS *152,748* —**Ant.** harmony, peace

cook [*n*] *person who prepares food* baker, chef, hash slinger*, mess sergeant, servant, sous chef; CONCEPT *348*

cook [*v*] *prepare food, usually using heat* bake, barbecue, blanch, boil, braise, brew, broil, brown, burn, coddle, curry, decoct, deep fry, devil, doctor*, escallop, fix, French fry, fricassee, fry, griddle, grill, heat, imbue, melt, microwave, mull, nuke*, panfry, parboil, parch, percolate, poach, pressure-cook, reduce, roast, ruin*, sauté, scald, scorch, sear, seethe, simmer, sizzle, spoil*, steam, steep, stew, toast, warm up; CONCEPT *170*

cook up [*v*] *devise* arrange, concoct, contrive, dream up, fabricate, falsify, formulate, frame, hatch, improvise, invent, make up, plan, plot, prepare, scheme, vamp; CONCEPTS *17,36*

cool [*adj1*] *cold, nippy* air-conditioned, algid, arctic, biting, chill, chilled, chilling, chilly, coldish, frigid, frore, frosty, gelid, hawkish, nipping, refreshing, refrigerated, shivery, snappy, wintry; CONCEPT *605* —**Ant.** hot, temperate, warm

cool [*adj2*] *calm, collected* assured, composed, coolheaded, deliberate, detached, dispassionate, impassive, imperturbable, levelheaded, nonchalant, philosophical, phlegmatic, placid, quiet, relaxed, self-controlled, self-possessed, serene, stolid, together, tranquil, unagitated, unemotional, unexcited, unflappable, unruffled; CONCEPT *401* —**Ant.** agitated, annoyed, excited, upset

cool [*adj3*] *aloof, disapproving* annoyed, apathetic, distant, frigid, impertinent, impudent,

incurious, indifferent, insolent, lukewarm, offended, offhand, offish, procacious, reserved, solitary, standoffish, unapproachable, uncommunicative, unenthusiastic, unfriendly, uninterested, unresponsive, unsociable, unwelcoming, withdrawn; CONCEPT *404* —**Ant.** approving, friendly, kind, responsive, warm

cool [*adj4*] *excellent* boss*, dandy, divine, glorious, hunky-dory*, keen, marvelous, neat, nifty, sensational, swell; CONCEPT *572* —**Ant.** poor, square, uncool, unpopular

cool [*v1*] *chill* abate, air-condition, air-cool, ally, calm, freeze, frost, infrigidate, lessen, lose heat, mitigate, moderate, reduce, refrigerate, temper; CONCEPT *255*—**Ant.** heat, warm

cool [*v2*] *take a break; abate* allay, assuage, calm, calm down, chill, compose, control, dampen, lessen, mitigate, moderate, quiet, reduce, rein, repress, restrain, simmer down, suppress, temper; CONCEPTS *240,384*—**Ant.** continue, go on, increase, step up

coop [*n*] *pen* birdcage, cage, corral, enclosure, hutch, lock-up, mew, pound; CONCEPT *494*

coop [*v*] *confine* cage, close in, corral, detain, enclose, fence in, hem in, hold captive, hold prisoner, impound, imprison, incarcerate, intern, keep, lock up, pen, put under lock and key*, shut in, shut up, trap; CONCEPT *191* —**Ant.** set free

cooperate [*v*] *aid, assist* abet, advance, agree, back up, band, befriend, be in cahoots*, chip in, coadjute, coincide, collaborate, combine, comply with, concert, concur, conduce, conspire, contribute, coordinate, espouse, forward, further, go along with, help, join forces, join in, league*, lend a hand*, participate, partner, pitch in*, play ball*, pool resources, pull together, second, share in, show willingness, side with, stick together, succor, take part, unite, uphold, work side by side, work together; CONCEPTS *110,112*—**Ant.** block, delay, disturb, encumber, handicap, hinder, impede, obstruct, prevent, stop

cooperation [*n*] *mutual effort* aid, alliance, assistance, cahoots*, coaction, coadjuvancy, coalition, collaboration, combination, combined effort, communion, company, concert, concurrence, confederacy, confederation, confunction, conspiracy, doing business with, esprit de corps, federation, fusion, give-and-take, harmony, help, helpfulness, logrolling*, participation, partisanship, partnership, playing ball*, reciprocity, responsiveness, service, society, symbiosis, synergism, synergy, teaming, teamwork, unanimity, union, unity; CONCEPTS *110,112, 388,677*—**Ant.** blockage, delay, encumbrance, handicap, hindrance, obstruction, prevention, stoppage

cooperative [*adj1*] *joint, unified* agreeing, coacting, coactive, coadjuvant, coefficient, collaborating, collaborative, collective, collegial, collusive, combined, combining, common, concerted, concurring, coordinated, hand in glove*, harmonious, in league, interdependent, joining, participating, reciprocal, shared, symbiotic, synergetic, synergic, team, united, uniting; CONCEPT *538* —**Ant.** disjoint, disobliging, disunited, divided, separate, uncooperative, uncoordinated

cooperative [*adj2*] *helpful* accommodating, companionable, obliging, responsive, sociable,

CO
CO

supportive, useful; CONCEPTS 538,555
—Ant. disobliging, encumbering, hindering,
hurting, preventing, uncooperative, unhelpful,
unsupportive

co-opt [v] *to assimilate in order to take over or
appropriate* absorb, accept, admit, adopt, bring
in, bring into line, bring into the fold, connatu-
ralize, convert, draw in, elect, embrace, encompass, enfold, homogenize, homologize, include,
incorporate, make one's own, take in, take over;
CONCEPTS 232,701

coordinate [adj] *equivalent* alike, coequal,
correlative, correspondent, counterpart, equal,
equalized, like, parallel, same, tantamount;
CONCEPT 566 —Ant. different, dissimilar,
unequal, unparallel

coordinate [v] *match, relate* accommodate,
adjust, agree, attune, combine, conduce, conform, correlate, get it together*, get one's act
together*, harmonize, integrate, mesh, organize,
pool, proportion, pull together, quarterback*,
reconcile, reconciliate, regulate, shape up,
synchronize, systematize, team up; CONCEPTS
36,84,158 —Ant. disintegrate, mismatch,
uncoordinate, unrelate

cop [n] *policeperson* deputy, flatfoot*, fuzz*,
lawman, officer of the law, patrolman, patrol-
woman, peace officer, policeman, police officer, policewoman, sheriff, the man*; CONCEPTS
299,354

cope [v] *manage, contend* battle with, buffet,
carry on, confront, deal, dispatch, encounter,
endure, face, get a handle on*, get by, grapple,
hack*, hack it*, handle, hold one's own*, live
with, make go of it*, make it*, make out*, make
the grade*, pit oneself against*, rise to occasion,
struggle, struggle through, survive, weather,
tangle, tussle, weather, wrestle; CONCEPTS 23,35

copious [adj] *abundant* alive with, a mess of*,
ample, aplenty, bounteous, bountiful, coming
out of ears*, crawling with*, extensive, exuberant, full, galore, generous, heavy, lavish,
liberal, lush, luxuriant, no end*, overflowing,
plenteous, plentiful, plenty, profuse, prolix,
replete, rich, superabundant, thick with, verbose,
wordy; CONCEPT 771 —Ant. lacking, meager,
needing, needy, poor, rare, scarce, wanting

copiousness [n] *abundance* affluence, amplitude, bountifulness, bounty, cornucopia, exuberance, fullness, horn of plenty*, lavishness,
luxuriance, plentifulness, plenty, richness,
superabundance; CONCEPT 767 —Ant. lack,
need, poorness, rareness, scarcity, want

cop out [v] *abandon, quit* back down, back
off, back out, backpedal, desert, dodge, excuse,
give the slip*, have alibi, rationalize, renege,
renounce, revoke, skip, use pretext, welsh,
withdraw; CONCEPTS 121,156 —Ant. be ready,
face, ready, take on

copulate [v] *have sexual relations* be carnal,
bed, breed, cohabit, conjugate, couple, do it*,
fool around*, fornicate, go all the way*, go to
bed*, have coition, have relations, have sex,
lay*, lie with, make it*, make love, make out*,
mate, sleep together, sleep with, unite; CONCEPT
375 —Ant. abstain, refrain

copy [n] *duplicate, imitation* archetype, carbon,
carbon copy*, cast, clone, counterfeit, counterpart, ditto*, ectype, effigy, ersatz, facsimile,

forgery, hard copy, image, impersonation,
impression, imprint, likeness, microfiche,
mimeograph, miniature, mirror, model, offprint,
parallel, pattern, photocopy, photograph, photostat, portrait, print, reflection, replica, replication, representation, reprint, reproduction,
rubbings, similarity, simulacrum, simulation,
study, tracing, transcript, transcription, type,
Xerox*; CONCEPTS 269,667,716 —Ant. original,
origination, source

copy [v1] *duplicate* carbon, cartoon, clone,
counterfeit, delineate, depict, ditto, draw, dupe,
engrave, engross, fake, forge, imitate, knock
off*, limn, manifold, mimeo, mirror, mold,
paint, paraphrase, photocopy, photostat, picture,
plagiarize, portray, reduplicate, reflect, repeat,
replicate, represent, reproduce, rewrite, sculpture, simulate, sketch, stat, trace, transcribe,
Xerox*; CONCEPT 171

copy [v2] *imitate* act like, ape, burlesque, do, do
a take-off*, do like*, echo, embody, emulate,
epitomize, fake, follow, follow example, follow
suit, go like*, illustrate, incarnate, knock off*,
make like*, mimic, mirror, mock, model, parody, parrot, personify, phony, pirate, play a
role, prefigure, repeat, sham, simulate, steal,
take leaf out of book*, take off*, travesty, typify; CONCEPTS 59,139,242 —Ant. be original

coquet [v] *tease* dally, flirt, fool, gold-dig*,
lead on, make eyes at*, operate, philander,
string along, titillate, toy, trifle, vamp, wanton,
wink at*; CONCEPTS 375,384 —Ant. be shy

cord [n] *rope* bond, connection, cordage, fiber,
line, link, string, tendon, tie, twine; CONCEPTS
470,680

cordial [adj] *friendly, sociable* affable, affectionate, agreeable, amicable, buddy-buddy*,
cheerful, clubby, companionable, congenial,
convivial, cozy, earnest, genial, glowing, gracious, happy, heartfelt, heart-to-heart, hearty,
invigorating, jovial, mellow, neighborly, palsy-
walsy*, polite, red-carpet*, responsive, sincere,
social, sympathetic, tender, warm, warmhearted, welcoming, wholehearted; CONCEPT
401 —Ant. aloof, cool, disagreeable, hostile,
indifferent, inhospitable, uncordial, unfriendly,
unpleasant, unsociable

cordiality [n] *friendliness, sociability* affability, agreeability, agreeableness, amenity,
amiability, approbation, approval, earnestness,
enjoyableness, favor, geniality, gratefulness,
heartiness, mutuality, pleasantness, reciprocity,
responsiveness, sincerity, sweetness and light*,
sympathy, understanding, warmth, wholeheartedness; CONCEPT 633 —Ant. aloofness,
coolness, hostility, ill will, indifference,
unfriendliness, unsociability

core [n] *center, gist* amount, base, basis, body,
bottom line, bulk, burden, consequence, corpus,
crux, essence, focus, foundation, heart, import,
importance, kernel, main idea, mass, meat*,
meat and potatoes*, middle, midpoint, midst,
nitty gritty*, nub, nucleus, origin, pith, pivot,
purport, quick, root, significance, staple, substance, thrust, upshot; CONCEPTS 442,668,826
—Ant. covering, exterior, exteriority, outside,
perimeter, surface

corner [n1] *angle* bend, branch, cloverleaf,
crook, crossing, edge, fork, intersection, joint,

180

junction, projection, ridge, rim, shift, V*, veer, Y*; CONCEPTS *436,484,513*

corner [n2] *niche* angle, cavity, compartment, cranny, hideaway, hide-out, hole, indentation, nook, recess, retreat; CONCEPTS *440,471,513*

corner [n3] *predicament* box, difficulty, dilemma, distress, fix, hole, impasse, impediment, jam, knot, pickle, plight, scrape, tight spot; CONCEPTS *674,675*

corner [v] *trap* bottle, bring to bay, capture, catch, collar*, fool, get on ropes*, have up a tree*, mousetrap*, nab, put out, seize, tree, trick, trouble; CONCEPTS *59,90* —*Ant.* allow, let go, release

cornerstone [n] *vital element* anchor, base, essential, foundation, key element, keystone, linchpin, main ingredient, mainspring, mainstay, pillar; CONCEPTS *442,826*

corny [adj] *trite, clichéd* banal, commonplace, dull, feeble, hackneyed, mawkish, melodramatic, old-fashioned, old hat*, sentimental, shopworn, stale, stereotyped, stupid, tired, warmed-over; CONCEPT *550* —*Ant.* new, original, unique

corollary [n] *conclusion, deduction* aftereffect, analogy, consequence, culmination, effect, end, end product, induction, inference, issue, precipitate, result, sequel, sequence, upshot; CONCEPTS *230,410,529*

corporal [adj] *bodily, physical* anatomical, carnal, corporeal, fleshly, fleshy, gross, human, material, objective, phenomenal, sensible, somatic, substantial, tangible; CONCEPT *542* —*Ant.* cerebral, immaterial, intangible, mental, spiritual

corporate [adj] *allied* amalgamated, associated, collaborative, collective, combined, common, communal, concerted, incorporated, joint, pooled, shared, united; CONCEPTS *563,577*

corporation [n] *business organization, usually large* association, bunch, business, clan, company, corporate body, crew, crowd, enterprise, gang, hookup*, jungle*, legal entity, megacorp*, mob, multinational, octopus*, outfit, partnership, ring, shell, society, syndicate, zoo*; CONCEPT *325*

corporeal [adj] *bodily, physical* anatomical, carnal, corporal, fleshly, fleshy, human, material, mortal, objective, phenomenal, sensible, somatic, substantial, tangible; CONCEPT *542* —*Ant.* cerebral, immaterial, intangible, mental, spiritual

corps [n] *group trained for action* band, body, brigade, company, contingent, crew, detachment, division, outfit, party, posse, regiment, squad, squadron, team, troop, troupe, unit; CONCEPTS *294,322,417*

corpse [n] *dead body* body, bones*, cadaver, carcass, carrion, deceased, departed, mort*, remains, stiff*; CONCEPTS *390,417*

corpulent [adj] *fat, chubby* baby elephant*, beefy*, blimp*, bulky, burly, embonpoint, fat, fleshy, gross, having a bay window*, having a spare tire*, heavy, hefty, husky, large, lusty, obese, overblown, overweight, plump, portly, roly-poly*, rotund, stout, tubby, weighty, well-padded*; CONCEPTS *406,491,773* —*Ant.* skinny, slender, slight, thin

corpus [n] *body of text* bulk, collection, compi-

lation, complete works, core, entirety, extant works, mass, oeuvre, opera omnia, staple, substance, whole; CONCEPT *271*

corral [n] *enclosure* compound, paddock, pen, pound, stockade; CONCEPT *494*

corral [v] *enclose* cage, confine, coop up, fence in, lock up, pen, shut in, shut up; CONCEPT *191* —*Ant.* set free

correct [adj] *accurate, exact* according to Hoyle*, actual, amen*, appropriate, cooking with gas*, dead on*, equitable, factual, faithful, faultless, flawless, for sure, free of error, impeccable, just, legitimate, nice, okay, on target*, on the ball*, on the beam*, on the button*, on the money*, on the nose*, on track*, perfect, precise, proper, regular, right, right as rain*, righteous, right on*, right stuff*, rigorous, stone, strict, true, undistorted, unmistaken, veracious, veridical; CONCEPTS *542,557,574* —*Ant.* flawed, imprecise, inaccurate, incorrect, inexact, wrong

correct [adj2] *proper, appropriate* acceptable, becoming, careful, comme il faut, conforming, conventional, decent, decorous, diplomatic, done, fitting, meticulous, nice, okay, punctilious, right, right stuff*, scrupulous, seemly, standard, suitable; CONCEPTS *401,558* —*Ant.* improper, inappropriate, incorrect, unfitting, unsuitable

correct [v1] *fix, adjust* alter, ameliorate, amend, better, change, clean up, clean up act*, cure, debug*, doctor*, do over, edit, emend, fiddle with, fix up, get with it*, go over, help, improve, launder, make over, make right, make up for, mend, pay dues*, pick up, polish, put in order, reclaim, reconstruct, rectify, redress, reform, regulate, remedy, remodel, reorganize, repair, retouch, review, revise, right, scrub*, set right, set straight, shape up, straighten out, touch up, turn around, upgrade; CONCEPT *126* —*Ant.* blow, blunder, mistake

correct [v2] *discipline, chastise* administer, admonish, castigate, chasten, chide, penalize, punish, reprimand, reprove; CONCEPTS *52,122* —*Ant.* be permissive, coddle, indulge, pamper, pet, spoil

correction [n1] *adjustment; fixing* alteration, amelioration, amending, amendment, changing, editing, emendation, improvement, indemnification, mending, modification, rectification, redress, reexamination, remodeling, repair, reparation, rereading, revisal, revising, righting; CONCEPT *126* —*Ant.* blunder, goof, mistake

correction [n2] *discipline* admonition, castigation, chastisement, punishment, punition, reformation, reproof, rod; CONCEPT *122* —*Ant.* allowance, coddling, indulgence, permissiveness, petting, spoiling

corrective [adj] *healing, curing* antidotal, counteracting, curative, disciplinary, palliative, penal, punitive, reformatory, rehabilitative, remedial, restorative, therapeutic; CONCEPT *537* —*Ant.* harmful, hurtful, hurting, injurious, paining

correctly [adv] *right* accurately, befittingly, decently, decorously, fitly, fittingly, justly, nicely, perfectly, precisely, properly, rightly, to a T*, well; CONCEPT *558* —*Ant.* flawed, inaccurately, incorrectly, mistakenly, wrongly

correctness [n1] *accuracy* definiteness, definitiveness, definitude, exactitude, exactness, faultlessness, fidelity, preciseness, precision, regularity, truth; CONCEPTS 638,654 —*Ant.* fault, flaw, imperfection, impreciseness, inaccuracy, incorrectness, inexactness, wrong

correctness [n2] *propriety* bon ton, civility, correctitude, decency, decorousness, decorum, fitness, good breeding, order, orderliness, properness, rightness, seemliness; CONCEPTS 633,656 —*Ant.* impropriety, incorrectness, infidelity, unacceptableness, unseemliness, unsuitableness

correlate [v] *equate, compare* associate, be on same wavelength*, connect, coordinate, correspond, have good vibes*, interact, parallel, relate mutually, tie in*, tune in on*; CONCEPT 39 —*Ant.* differ, dissassociate, disconnect, imbalance

correlation [n] *equating, equivalence* alternation, analogue, complement, correspondence, correspondent, counterpart, interaction, interchange, interconnection, interdependence, interrelation, interrelationship, match, parallel, pendant, reciprocity, relationship; CONCEPTS 388,667 —*Ant.* difference, disassociation, disconnection, imbalance

correspond [v1] *agree, complement* accord, amount, approach, assimilate, be consistent, be identical to, be similar to, coincide, compare, conform, correlate, dovetail, equal, fit, harmonize, lip sync, match, partake of, reciprocate, resemble, rival, square, tally, touch; CONCEPT 664 —*Ant.* differ, disagree

correspond [v2] *communicate in writing* answer, drop a kite*, drop a line*, drop a note*, epistolize, exchange letters, have pen pal, hear from, keep in touch, pen, put pen to paper*, reply, scribble, send letter, send word, write; CONCEPTS 79,266

correspondence [n1] *agreement* accord, analogy, coherence, coincidence, comparability, comparison, concurrence, conformity, congruity, consistency, correlation, equivalence, fitness, harmony, likeness, match, regularity, relation, resemblance, similarity, symmetry; CONCEPT 664 —*Ant.* difference, disagreement

correspondence [n2] *communication by writing* exchange of letters, letters, mail, messages, post, reports, writing; CONCEPTS 79,277,278

correspondent [n] *person communicating in writing* contributor, epistler, epistolarian, freelancer, gazetteer, journalist, letter writer, pen pal, reporter, stringer*, writer; CONCEPTS 348,423

corresponding [adj] *equivalent, matching* agnate, akin, alike, analogous, answering, comparable, complementary, consonant, correlative, correspondent, coterminous, identical, interrelated, kin, kindred, like, parallel, reciprocal, similar, synonymous, undifferentiated; CONCEPT 566 —*Ant.* differing, disparaging, dissimilar, mismatched, unlike

corridor [n] *hallway* aisle, couloir, entrance hall, entranceway, foyer, hall, ingress, lobby, passage, passageway; CONCEPT 440

corroborate [v] *back up information, story* approve, authenticate, bear out, certify, check on, check out, check up, confirm, declare true, document, double check, endorse, establish, give nod*, justify, okay, prove, ratify, rubber-stamp*,

strengthen, substantiate, support, sustain, validate, verify; CONCEPTS 49,57 —*Ant.* contradict, deny, disallow, disclaim, refute, reject

corrode [v] *wear away; eat away* bite, canker, consume, corrupt, destroy, deteriorate, erode, gnaw, impair, oxidize, rot, rust, scour, waste; CONCEPTS 156,169,186,250 —*Ant.* aid, build, fortify, help

corrosion [n] *disintegration* decay, decomposition, degeneration, deterioration, erosion, oxidation, rust, wear; CONCEPTS 309,720

corrosive [adj] *consuming, wearing; bitter* acerb, acerbic, acrid, biting, caustic, corroding, cutting, destructive, erosive, incisive, sarcastic, strongly acid, trenchant, venomous, virulent, wasting; CONCEPT 537 —*Ant.* contributing, fortifying, supporting

corrugated [adj] *ridged, grooved* channelled, creased, crinkled, crumpled, flexed, fluted, folded, furrowed, puckered, roughened, rumpled, wrinkled; CONCEPTS 485,606 —*Ant.* flat, smooth

corrupt [adj1] *dishonest* base, bent, bribable, crooked, debauched, double-dealing, exploiting, extortionate, faithless, fast and loose*, fixed, foul, fraudulent, gone to the dogs*, inconstant, iniquitous, knavish, mercenary, nefarious, on the take*, open, padded*, perfidious, praetorian, profiteering, racket up*, reprobate, rotten, shady, snide, suborned, tainted, treacherous, two-faced, underhanded, unethical, unfaithful, unprincipled, unscrupulous, untrustworthy, venal, wide open*; CONCEPT 545 —*Ant.* decent, honest, honorable, principled, pure, trustworthy, truthful, uncorrupt, upright

corrupt [adj2] *debased, vicious* abandoned, abased, baneful, boorish, degenerate, degraded, deleterious, depraved, dishonored, dissolute, evil, flagitious, infamous, loose, low, miscreant, monstrous, nefarious, perverse, profligate, rotten, villainous; CONCEPTS 401,545 —*Ant.* clean, decent, helpful, high, kind, noble, sound, wholesome

corrupt [adj3] *adulterated, rotten* altered, contaminated, decayed, defiled, distorted, doctored, falsified, foul, infected, noxious, polluted, putrescent, putrid, tainted; CONCEPTS 485,613 —*Ant.* clean, pure, purified, sound, wholesome

corrupt [v] *pervert; pollute* abase, abuse, adulterate, animalize, bastardize, blemish, blight, bribe, contaminate, damage, debase, debauch, decay, decompose, deface, defile, deform, degrade, demean, demoralize, deprave, depreciate, despoil, disfigure, disgrace, dishonor, fix, grease palm*, harm, hurt, ill-treat, impair, infect, injure, lower, lure, maltreat, mar, mistreat, misuse, outrage, pull down, putrefy, ravage, reduce, rot, ruin, spoil, square, stain, suborn, subvert, taint, undermine, violate, vitiate, warp, waste; CONCEPTS 14,240 —*Ant.* better, chasten, cleanse, dignify, improve, purify

corruption [n1] *dishonesty* breach of trust, bribery, bribing, crime, crookedness, demoralization, exploitation, extortion, fiddling, fraud, fraudulency, graft, jobbery, malfeasance, misrepresentation, nepotism, on the take*, payoff, payola*, profiteering, racket*, shadiness*, shady deal*, shuffle, skimming, squeeze*,

unscrupulousness, venality; CONCEPT 645
—*Ant.* decency, honesty, honor, truthfulness,
wholesomeness

corruption [n2] *baseness* atrocity, decadence,
degeneration, degradation, depravity, evil, immorality, impurity, infamy, iniquity, looseness,
lubricity, perversion, profligacy, sinfulness,
turpitude, vice, viciousness, vulgarity, wickedness; CONCEPTS 633,645 —*Ant.* decency, goodness, honor, kindness, wholesomeness

corruption [n3] *adulteration* debasement,
decay, defilement, distortion, doctoring, falsification, foulness, infection, noxiousness, pollution, putrefaction, putrescence, rot, rottenness;
CONCEPT 723 —*Ant.* cleanliness, cleanness,
pureness, purification, purity, sterility

cosmetic [adj] *beautifying; relating to appearance* corrective, gooky*, improving, makeup,
nonessential, painted, remedial, restorative,
superficial, surface, touching-up; CONCEPT 579
—*Ant.* disfiguring

cosmic [adj] *limitless; universal* catholic,
cosmogonal, cosmogonic, cosmopolitan,
ecumenical, empyrean, global, grandiose,
huge, immense, infinite, measureless, planetary, vast, worldwide; CONCEPT 772 —*Ant.*
bounded, limited

cosmopolitan [adj] *worldly-wise* catholic,
cultivated, cultured, ecumenical, global, gregarious, metropolitan, planetary, polished, public,
smooth, sophisticated, universal, urbane, well-
travelled, worldly, worldwide; CONCEPT 589
—*Ant.* country, rural, rustic

cosmos [n1] *universe* creation, galaxy, macrocosm, macrocosmos, megacosm, nature, solar
system, star system, world; CONCEPTS 511,770

cosmos [n2] *ordered system* harmony, order,
organization, scheme, structure; CONCEPTS
727,770

cost [n1] *expense; price paid* amount, arm and a
leg*, bad news*, bite*, bottom dollar*, bottom
line*, charge, damage*, disbursement, dues,
expenditure, figure, line, nick*, nut*, outlay,
payment, price, price tag, rate, score*, setback*,
squeeze*, tab, tariff, ticket, toll, top dollar*,
value, worth; CONCEPTS 328,336

cost [n2] *penalty, sacrifice* damage, deprivation, detriment, expense, forfeit, forfeiture, harm,
hurt, injury, loss, suffering; CONCEPTS 676,679
—*Ant.* repayment, retribution

cost [v1] *command a price of* amount to be
asked, be demanded, be given, be marked at,
be needed, be paid, be priced at, be received, be
valued at, be worth, bring in, come to, mount
up, move back, nick*, rap*, require, sell at,
sell for, set back, take, to the tune of*, yield;
CONCEPTS 328,336

cost [v2] *harm; exact a penalty* do disservice
to, expect, hurt, infuriate, lose, necessitate,
obligate, require; CONCEPT 246

cost-effective [adj] *economical* practical,
profitable, worthwhile; CONCEPT 542

costly [adj1] *expensive* an arm and leg*, cher*,
dear, excessive, executive, exorbitant, extortionate, extravagant, fancy, high, highly priced,
high-priced, inordinate, precious, premium,
pricey, steep, stiff*, top, valuable; CONCEPT 334
—*Ant.* cheap, inexpensive, reasonable

costly [adj2] *priceless* gorgeous, inestimable,

invaluable, lavish, luxurious, opulent, precious,
rich, splendid, sumptuous, valuable; CONCEPT
567 —*Ant.* cheap, not valuable, poor

costly [adj3] *harmful, damaging* catastrophic,
deleterious, disastrous, loss-making, ruinous,
sacrificial; CONCEPT 537 —*Ant.* aiding, helpful

costume [n] *set of clothes* apparel, attire, clothing, dress, duds*, ensemble, fashion, garb,
getup*, guise, livery, mode, outfit, rig*, robes*,
style, suit, uniform, wardrobe; CONCEPT 451

cot [n] *temporary bed* army bed, berth, bunk,
camp bed, folding bed, gurney, small bed,
trundle; CONCEPT 443

cottage [n] *tiny house; lodging* box, bungalow,
cabana, cabin, caboose, camp, carriage house,
chalet, cot, home, hut, lean-to, lodge, ranch,
shack, shanty, small house; CONCEPT 516

couch [n] *sofa; long, upholstered furniture* bed,
chair, chaise longue, chesterfield, davenport,
daybed, divan, lounge, love seat, ottoman,
resting place, settee; CONCEPT 443

couch [v] *express in particular way* formulate,
frame, phrase, put, set forth, utter, word;
CONCEPT 51

couch potato [n] *inactive person* bystander,
goof-off*, idler, laggard, lazy person, loafer,
lotuseater*, lounger, observer, slouch, sluggard,
spectator, televiewer*, TV viewer, viewer;
CONCEPT 423

cough [n] *expelled air with sound* ahem, bark,
cold, croup, frog in throat*, hack, hem, tickle
in throat*, whoop; CONCEPTS 65,316

cough [v] *expelling air with sound* bark, choke,
clear throat, convulse, expectorate, hack, hawk,
hem, spit up, vomit, whoop; CONCEPTS 65,308*

council [n] *people assembled for purpose*
assembly, board, body, brain trust*, cabinet,
chamber, clan, committee, conclave, confab*,
conference, congregation, congress, convention, convocation, diet, directorate, gang, gathering, governing body, groupthink*, huddle*,
kitchen cabinet*, meet, ministry, mob, official
family, outfit, panel, parliament, powwow*,
ring, senate, synod; CONCEPTS 299,325,381

counsel [n1] *guidance* admonition, advice, advisement, caution, consideration, consultation,
deliberation, direction, forethought, information,
instruction, kibitz*, recommendation, steer,
suggestion, tip, tip-off*, two cents' worth*,
warning, word to the wise*; CONCEPTS 75,274

counsel [n2] *legal representative* adviser,
advocate, attorney, barrister, bomber*, counselor, legal adviser, legal beagle*, legal eagle*,
lip*, mouthpiece*, patch*, shyster*, solicitor;
CONCEPT 355

counsel [v] *give advice* admonish, advise, advocate, caution, charge, confab*, direct, enjoin,
exhort, give pointer, give two cents*, guide,
huddle*, inform, instruct, keep posted, kibitz*,
order, prescribe, prompt, put bug in ear*, put
heads together*, put on to, recommend, reprehend, show the ropes*, steer, suggest, teach,
tip, tip off*, tout, urge, warn, wise one up*;
CONCEPTS 75,317

counselor [n] *legal representative; adviser*
advocate, ambulance chaser*, attorney, counsel,
front*, guide, instructor, legal beagle*, legal
eagle*, lip*, mentor, mouthpiece*, pleader,
solicitor, squeal*, teacher*; CONCEPT 355

CO
CO

count [n] *tally; number* calculation, computation, enumeration, numbering, outcome, poll, reckoning, result, sum, toll, total, whole; CONCEPT 766 —*Ant.* estimate, guess

count [v1] *add, check in order* add up, calculate, cast, cast up, cipher, compute, enumerate, estimate, figure, foot, keep tab, number, numerate, reckon, run down, score, sum, take account of, tally, tell, tick off, total, tot up; CONCEPT 764 —*Ant.* estimate, guess

count [v2] *consider, deem* await, esteem, expect, hope, impute, judge, look, look upon, rate, regard, think; CONCEPTS 18,43 —*Ant.* disregard, ignore

count [v3] *have importance* carry weight, cut ice*, enter into consideration, import, matter, mean, militate, rate, signify, tell, weigh; CONCEPT 668

count [v4] *include* await, expect, hope, look, number among, take into account, take into consideration; CONCEPTS 26,112 —*Ant.* exclude

countenance [n1] *appearance, usually of the face* aspect, biscuit*, cast, demeanor, expression, face, features, gills*, kisser*, look, looks, map*, mask, mien, mug*, phizog*, physiognomy, poker face*, potato*, puss*, visage; CONCEPTS 716,718

countenance [n2] *self-control* calmness, composure, presence of mind, self-composure; CONCEPT 633

countenance [v] *approve, support* abet, accept, advocate, aid, applaud, approbate, back, bear with, champion, commend, condone, confirm, cope, encourage, endorse, favor, get behind, give green light*, give stamp of approval*, give the nod*, go along with, go for, grin and bear it*, handle, help, hold with, invite, live with*, nod at, okay*, put John Hancock on*, put up with, sanction, sign off on*, sit still for*, smile on*, stand for, stomach something*, swallow*, thumbs up*, uphold; CONCEPTS 10,50,88 —*Ant.* deny, disagree, disapprove, discourage, fight, oppose, refuse

counter [adj] *opposite, opposing* adverse, against, antagonistic, anti, antipodal, antipodean, antithetical, conflicting, contradictory, contrary, contrasting, converse, diametric, hindering, impeding, obstructive, obverse, opposed, polar, reverse; CONCEPTS 544,581 —*Ant.* agreeing, concurring, corresponding, corroborating, equal, same, similar

counter [adv] *contrary, reverse* against, at variance with, contrarily, contrariwise, conversely, in defiance of, opposite, versus; CONCEPTS 544, 581 —*Ant.* equally, same, similarly

counter [v] *answer, respond in retaliation* backtalk, beat, bilk, buck, circumvent, contravene, counteract, counterwork, cross, dash, disappoint, fly in the face of*, foil, frustrate, have bone to pick*, hinder, hit back, match, meet, offset, oppose, parry, pit, play off, resist, respond, retaliate, return, ruin, take on, thumbs down*, vie, ward off; CONCEPTS 45,121

counteract [v] *do opposing action* annul, buck, cancel, cancel out, check, contravene, correct, counterbalance, countercheck, counterwork, cross, defeat, fix, foil, frustrate, go against, halt, hinder, invalidate, negate, negative, neutralize, offset, oppose, prevent,

rectify, redress, resist, right, thwart; CONCEPTS 87,96,126 —*Ant.* aid, approve, assist, help, support

counterbalance [v] *offset an action* amend, atone for, balance, cancel, compensate, correct, counteract, counterpoise, countervail, equalize, make up for, outweigh, rectify, redeem, set off; CONCEPTS 87,96,126

counterfeit [adj] *fake, simulated* affected, assumed, bent, bogus*, brummagem, copied, crock, deceptive, delusive, delusory, ersatz, faked, false, feigned, fictitious, fishy*, forged, framed, fraudulent, Hollywood*, imitation, misleading, mock, not genuine, not kosher*, phony*, pirate, plant*, pretended, pretentious, pseudo, put-on*, queer, sham, snide, soft shell*, spurious, supposititious, two-faced*, won't fly*, wrong; CONCEPTS 549,582 —*Ant.* genuine, real, true

counterfeit [n] *fake, forgery* actor, bogus*, bum, copy, deceit, deception, dummy, facsimile, fraud, gyp, hoax, humbug, imitation, imposture, junque*, phony, pseudo, put-on*, reproduction, sell*, sham, simulacrum; CONCEPTS 648,725 —*Ant.* reality, real thing

counterfeit [v] *make deceitful imitation* act like, affect, ape, assume, bluff, carbon, cheat, circulate bad money, clone, coin, copy, defraud, delude, ditto, do like*, dupe, fabricate, fake, feign, forge, go like*, imitate, impersonate, knock off*, make like*, make money, mimeo, mimic, mint, phony*, phony up*, pretend, put on*, sham, simulate, stat, Xerox*; CONCEPTS 59,171 —*Ant.* be honest

countermand [v] *annul, cancel a command* override, recall, repeal, rescind, retract, retreat, reverse, revoke; CONCEPTS 50,53,88 —*Ant.* allow, approve, permit, sanction

counterpart [n] *match; identical part or thing* analogue, carbon copy*, complement, copy, correlate, correlative, correspondent, dead ringer*, ditto*, doppelganger, duplicate, equal, equivalent, fellow, like, look alike, mate, obverse, opposite, opposite number, peas in a pod*, pendant, ringer*, spit and image*, spitting image*, supplement, tally, twin, two of a kind; CONCEPTS 667,834 —*Ant.* opposite

countless [adj] *innumerable* bags of*, endless, gobs*, heap*, immeasurable, incalculable, infinite, innumerous, jillion*, legion, limitless, loads*, lots of, many, measureless, mess*, mint*, mucho*, multitudinous, myriad, numberless, oodles*, passel of*, peck, pile, raft*, scads*, slew*, stack*, tidy sum, umpteen*, uncountable, uncounted, untold, wad*, whole slew*, zillion*; CONCEPTS 762,781 —*Ant.* calculable, countable, counted, limited, measurable, numbered, numerable

count on/count upon [v] *depend on; rely* aim for, bank on, bargain for, believe, believe in, bet bottom dollar*, bet on, expect from, heed, lean on, pin faith on, place confidence in, plan on, reckon on, rest on, score, stake on, swear by, tab, take as gospel truth*, take for granted, take on trust, trust; CONCEPTS 12,26 —*Ant.* disbelieve, distrust, not expect

count out [v] *disregard, exclude* bar, bate, debar, eliminate, except, get rid of, leave out, leave out of account, mark off, pass over, rule out, suspend; CONCEPT 25 —Ant. consider, figure on, include, regard

country [adj] *rural, pastoral* agrarian, agrestic, Arcadian, bucolic, campestral, countrified, georgic, homey, out-country, outland, provincial, rustic, uncultured, unpolished, unrefined, unsophisticated; CONCEPTS 401,536,589 —Ant. city, metropolitan, urban

country [n1] *political territory; nation* citizenry, citizens, commonwealth, community, constituents, electors, grass roots, homeland, inhabitants, kingdom, land, native land, patria, people, polity, populace, public, realm, region, society, soil, sovereign state, state, terrain, voters; CONCEPTS 379,508,510

country [n2] *rural area; area away from city* back country, backwoods, boondocks*, boonies*, bush, countryside, cow country*, farmland, farms, forests, green belt*, hinterland, middle of nowhere*, outback, outdoors, province, sticks*, up country*, wide open space*, wilderness, wilds, woodlands, woods; CONCEPTS 508,513 —Ant. city, metropolis, urbanity

country mile [n] *long distance* far piece, good way, great distance; CONCEPTS 651,739,790

countryside [n] *non-city environment* back roads*, boonies*, country, environment, land, landscape, non-urban area, scenery, setting, sticks*, surroundings, terrain; CONCEPT 508

county [n] *province or district of area* canton, constituency, division, shire; CONCEPTS 508,513

coup [n] *achievement, often by maneuver* accomplishment, action, coup de maître, coup d'état, deed, exploit, feat, overthrow, plot, revolution, stratagem, stroke, stroke of genius*, stunt, successful stroke, tour de force, upset; CONCEPT 706

coup de grâce [n] *finishing blow* blow, clincher*, comeuppance, deathblow, defeat, final blow, final stroke, kill, knockout, mercy stroke, mortal blow, quietus; CONCEPTS 95,252

coup d'état [n] *violent seizure* coup, overthrow, palace revolution, power play*, putsch*, rebellion, revolt, revolution, takeover; CONCEPTS 86,90,320

couple [n] *pair of things* brace, couplet, deuce*, doublet, duo, dyad, husband and wife, item, newlyweds, set, span, team, twain, twosome, yoke; CONCEPTS 432,766

couple [v] *join two things* bracket, bring together, buckle, clasp, coalesce, cohabit, come together, conjoin, conjugate, connect, copulate, harness, hitch, hook up, link, marry, match, pair, unite, wed, yoke; CONCEPTS 113,114,297,375 —Ant. disconnect, disjoin, divide, separate, unbuckle, uncouple

coupon [n] *discount ticket* advertisement, box top*, card, certificate, credit slip, detachable portion, order blank, premium certificate, ration slip, redeemable part, redemption slip, slip, token, voucher; CONCEPT 331

courage [n] *boldness, braveness* adventuresomeness, adventurousness, audacity, backbone, bravery, bravura, daring, dash, dauntlessness, determination, élan, endurance, enterprise, fearlessness, firmness, fortitude, gallantry, gameness, grit, guts, hardihood, heroism, intrepidity, lion-heartedness, mettle, nerve, pluck, power, prowess, pugnacity, rashness, recklessness, resolution, spirit, spunk, stoutheartedness, temerity, tenacity, valor, venturesomeness; CONCEPTS 411,633 —Ant. cowardice, faintheartedness, fear, meekness, timidity, weakness

courageous [adj] *brave, bold* adventuresome, adventurous, assured, audacious, cool, daredevil, daring, dauntless, doughty, fearless, fiery, fire-eating*, gallant, game, gritty*, gutsy*, hardy, heroic, high-spirited, impavid, indomitable, intrepid, lionhearted, martial, nervy, plucky*, red-blooded*, resolute, Spartan, stalwart, stand tall*, stouthearted, strong, tenacious, tough, Trojan*, unafraid, undaunted, valiant, valorous, venturesome, venturous; CONCEPTS 401,404 —Ant. cowardly, fainthearted, fearful, fearing, meek, shy, timid, weak

courier [n] *messenger* bearer, carrier, dispatcher, emissary, envoy, express, go-between, gofer*, gopher*, herald, intelligencer, internuncio, runner; CONCEPT 348 —Ant. receiver, sender

course [n1] *progress, advance* advancement, chain, channels, consecution, continuity, development, flow, furtherance, line, manner, march, movement, order, plan, policy, polity, procedure, program, progression, red tape*, row, scheme, sequel, sequence, series, string, succession, system, unfolding, way; CONCEPTS 704,727

course [n2] *path, channel* aisle, aqueduct, boards, byway, canal, circuit, conduit, direction, duct, flow, groove, itinerary, lap, line, movement, orbit, passage, range, road, route, run, rut, scope, stream, tack, track, trail, trajectory, watercourse, way; CONCEPTS 501,514

course [n3] *length of action* duration, elapsing, lapse, passage, passing, progress, sweep, term, time; CONCEPT 804

course [n4] *plan of study* class, conference, curriculum, discussion group, interest, laboratory, lecture, matriculation, meeting, method, period, preparation, procedure, program, regimen, schedule, seminar, session, speciality, subject; CONCEPT 287

course [v] *flow; run* career, chase, dart, dash, follow, gallop, gush, hasten, hunt, hurry, hustle, pursue, race, rush, scamper, scoot, scurry, speed, spring, stream, surge, tumble; CONCEPTS 150,152

court [n1] *yard, garden of building* cloister, close, compass, courtyard, curtilage, enclosure, forum, patio, piazza, plaza, quad, quadrangle, square, street; CONCEPTS 509,513

court [n2] *ruler's attendants* castle, cortege, entourage, hall, lords and ladies, palace, retinue, royal household, staff, suite, train; CONCEPTS 296,348

court [n3] *judicial system* bar, bench, court of justice, forum, judge, justice, kangaroo court*, law court, magistrate, seat of judgment, session, tribunal; CONCEPTS 299,318

court [n4] *building for legal proceedings* bar, bench, city hall, county courthouse, courthouse, courtroom, federal building, hall of justice, justice building, law court, municipal building, tribunal; CONCEPTS 318,439

court [n5] *wooing* address, attention, homage, love, respects, suit; CONCEPT 32

court [v] *fawn over, pay attention to* allure, ask in marriage, attract, beseech, bid, bootlick, captivate, charm, chase, cultivate, curry favor, date, entice, entreat, flatter, follow, gallant, go out with, go steady, go together, go with, grovel, importune, invite, keep company with, make love to, make overture, make time with*, pander to, pay addresses to, pay court to, please, pop the question*, praise, propose, pursue, run after*, seek, seek the hand of, serenade, set one's cap*, solicit, spark, spoon*, sue, sweetheart, take out, woo; CONCEPTS *32, 384* —*Ant.* disregard, ignore

courteous [*adj*] *gentle, mannerly* affable, attentive, ceremonious, civil, civilized, complaisant, considerate, courtly, cultivated, debonair, elegant, gallant, genteel, gracious, polished, polite, refined, respectful, soft-spoken, suave, thoughtful, urbane, well-behaved, well-bred, well-mannered, well-spoken; CONCEPTS *267,401* —*Ant.* bad-mannered, discourteous, impolite, rude, uncivil, uncourteous, unmannerly, unrefined

courtesy [*n1*] *good manners* address, affability, amenities, amiability, attentiveness, ceremony, chivalry, civility, comity, complaisance, consideration, cordiality, courteousness, courtliness, cultivation, culture, deference, elegance, familiarity, favor, friendliness, gallantness, gallantry, generosity, geniality, gentleness, good behavior, good breeding, graciousness, indulgence, kindness, polish, politeness, refinement, respect, reverence, solicitude, suavity, sympathy, tact, thoughtfulness, urbanity; CONCEPTS *633,644* —*Ant.* bad manners, discourtesy, impoliteness, pompousness, rudeness, unmannerliness

courtesy [*n2*] *favor, indulgence* accommodation, benevolence, bounty, charity, chivalry, compassion, consent, consideration, dispensation, generosity, kindness, liberality, service, unselfishness; CONCEPTS *337,388,633* —*Ant.* discourtesy, disfavor, disregard

courtly [*adj*] *refined manner* adulatory, affable, aristocratic, august, ceremonious, chivalrous, civil, civilized, complimentary, conventional, cultured, decorous, dignified, elegant, flattering, formal, gallant, gracious, high-bred, imposing, lofty, obliging, polished, polite, preux, prim, refined, stately, studied, urbane; CONCEPT *401* —*Ant.* impolite, indecorous, inelegant, low-bred, provincial, rough, uncivil, unpolished, unrefined

courtship [*n*] *dating, romance* courting, engagement, keeping company*, love, lovemaking, pursuit, suit, wooing; CONCEPT *388*

cove [*n*] *inlet, small niche* anchorage, arm, bay, bayou, bight, cave, cavern, creek, estuary, firth, frith, gulf, harbor, hole, lagoon, nook, retreat, slough, sound, wash; CONCEPT *509*

covenant [*n*] *pact, promise* agreement, arrangement, bargain, bond, commitment, compact, concordat, contract, convention, deal, deed, dicker*, handshake*, papers, stipulation, transaction, treaty, trust; CONCEPT *684* —*Ant.* disagreement

covenant [*v*] *agree* bargain, concur, contract, engage, pledge, plight, promise, stipulate, swear, undertake, vow; CONCEPTS *8,71,317* —*Ant.* break, disagree

cover [*n1*] *wrapping, cover-up* awning, bark, binding, camouflage, canopy, canvas, cap, caparison, case, ceiling, cloak, clothing, coating,

covering, coverlet, disguise, dome, dress, drop, envelope, facade, false front*, fig leaf, front, guise, hood, integument, jacket, lid, marquee, mask, masquerade, overlay, paint, parasol, polish, pretense, put-on*, roof, screen, seal, semblance, sheath, sheet, shroud, smoke screen*, spread, stopper, tarp, tarpaulin, tegument, tent, top, umbrella, varnish, veil, veneer, window-dressing, wrapper, wraps; CONCEPTS *484,750*

cover [*n2*] *hiding place* asylum, camouflage, concealment, covert, defense, drop, front, guard, harbor, harborage, haven, port, protection, refuge, retreat, safety, sanctuary, screen, security, shelter; CONCEPT *198*

cover [*v1*] *wrap, hide* blanket, board up, bury, bush up, cache, camouflage, canopy, cap, carpet, cloak, clothe, coat, conceal, cover up, crown, curtain, daub, disguise, do on the sly*, dress, eclipse, encase, enclose, enfold, ensconce, enshroud, envelop, hood, house, invest, layer, mantle, mask, obscure, overcast, overlay, overspread, protect, put on, screen, secrete, set on, shade, shield, shroud, stash*, superimpose, superpose, surface, veil; CONCEPT *172* —*Ant.* lay bare, lay out, reveal, uncover, unwrap

cover [*v2*] *protect, guard* bulwark, defend, fend, house, reinforce, safeguard, screen, secure, shelter, shield, watch over; CONCEPT *96* —*Ant.* abandon, disregard, forget, ignore, leave alone

cover [*v3*] *include, contain* be enough, comprehend, comprise, consider, deal with, embody, embrace, encompass, examine, incorporate, involve, meet, provide for, reach, refer to, suffice, survey, take account of; CONCEPT *643* —*Ant.* exclude

cover [*v4*] *describe in published writing* broadcast, detail, investigate, narrate, recount, relate, report, tell of, write up; CONCEPTS *60,79* —*Ant.* disregard, forget, ignore

cover [*v5*] *fill in for, compensate* balance, counterbalance, double for, insure, make good, make up for, offset, relieve, stand in for*, substitute, take over, take the rap for*; CONCEPTS *110,126*

cover [*v6*] *travel across area* cross, do, journey over, pass over, pass through, range, track, traverse, trek; CONCEPT *224*

covert [*adj*] *clandestine, underhanded* buried, camouflaged, cloaked, concealed, disguised, dissembled, furtive, hidden, hush-hush*, incog*, incognito, masked, obscured, private, privy, QT*, secret, shrouded, stealthy, sub rosa, surreptitious, ulterior, undercover, underhand, under-the-table*, under wraps*, unsuspected, veiled; CONCEPTS *544,548* —*Ant.* aboveboard, candid, frank, honest, open, overt, public, unconcealed

covertly [*adv*] *clandestine, underhandedly* by stealth, clandestinely, furtively, hush-hush*, in camera, in holes and corners*, on the QT*, on the quiet, on the sly, privately, secretly, slyly, stealthily, sub rosa, surreptitiously, undercover, under wraps*, wildcat*; CONCEPTS *544,548* —*Ant.* candidly, frankly, honestly, openly, overtly, publicly

cover-up [*n*] *concealment* burial*, camouflage, closeting, complicity, conspiracy, disguising, dissimulation, evasion, front, masking, pretense, smoke-screen, whitewash; CONCEPT *188*

covet [*v*] *desire strongly* aspire to, begrudge, choose, crave, desiderate, envy, fancy, hanker for*, have eye on*, have hots for*, itch for*, long for, lust after, spoil for, thirst for, want, wish for, yearn for, yen for*; CONCEPT 20 —Ant. abjure, be generous, give, not want

covetous [adj] *greedy; very desirous* acquisitive, avaricious, avid, close-fisted, eager, ensurient, envious, gluttonous, grabby, grasping, green-eyed*, grudging, hogging, itchy*, jealous, keen, mercenary, piggish*, prehensile, rapacious, ravenous, selfish, swinish*, voracious, yearning; CONCEPT 401 —Ant. benevolent, generous, giving

cow [v] *browbeat, intimidate* abash, appall, awe, bludgeon, bluster, buffalo, bulldoze, bully, daunt, discomfit, disconcert, dishearten, dismay, dragoon, embarrass, enforce, faze, frighten, hector, lean on*, overawe, push around*, rattle, scare, showboat*, strong-arm*, subdue, terrorize, turn on the heat*, unnerve, walk heavy*; CONCEPTS 7,19,52 —Ant. encourage, hearten, inspirit

coward [n] *person who is scared, easily intimidated* alarmist, baby*, caitiff, chicken*, chicken heart*, chicken liver*, craven, cur, dastard, deserter, faintheart, faint-of-heart, fraidy-cat*, funk, gutless*, invertebrate*, jellyfish*, lily liver, malingerer, mouse*, pessimist, poltroon, quitter, rabbit*, recreant, scaredy cat*, shirk, shirker, skulker, sneak, weakling, white liver*, wimp*, yellow*, yellow belly*; CONCEPT 423 —Ant. aggressor, hero

cowardice [n] *timidity* cold feet*, faintheartedness, fear, fearfulness, funk, gutlessness, mousiness, pusillanimity, wimpiness; CONCEPT 27

cowardly [adj] *fearful* afraid, anxious, apprehensive, backward, base, caitiff, chickenhearted, cowering, cowhearted, craven, dastardly, diffident, dismayed, fainthearted, frightened, gutless, having the willies*, jittery, lacking courage, lily-livered*, nervous, no guts, panicky, paper tiger*, pigeonhearted*, pusillanimous, recreant, retiring, running scared, scared, shrinking, shy, soft*, spineless*, timid, timorous, weak, weak-kneed*, worthless, yellow*, yellow-bellied*; CONCEPT 401 —Ant. bold, brave, courageous, daring, dauntless, unafraid, undaunted, unfearful

cowboy [n] *mounted cattle hand* bronco, bronco-buster, buckaroo, cattle herder, cattleman, cowhand, cowpoke, cowpuncher, drover, gaucho, herdsman, rancher, stockman, vaquero, wrangler; CONCEPT 258

cower [v] *hide, hover in fear* apple-polish*, blench, bootlick*, brownnose*, cringe, crouch, draw back, fawn, flinch, grovel, honey*, kowtow*, quail*, recoil, shrink, skulk, sneak, toady*, tremble, truckle, wince; CONCEPTS 188,384 —Ant. come out

coy [adj] *very modest* backward, bashful, blushing, coquettish, demure, diffident, evasive, flirtatious, humble, kittenish, overmodest, prudish, rabbity, reserved, retiring, self-effacing, shrinking, shy, skittish, timid, unassertive; CONCEPTS 401,404 —Ant. aggressive, forward, immodest, impudent, unshy

cozy [adj] *comforting, soft, warm* comfortable, comfy, cuddled up, cushy, easeful, in clover, intimate, in velvet*, on bed of roses*, restful, safe, secure, sheltered, snug, snug as bug in

rug*, snuggled down, tucked up; CONCEPTS 485,605,606 —Ant. uncomfortable

crabby/crabbed [adj] *in a bad mood* acid, acrid, acrimonious, awkward, bad-tempered, blunt, brusque, captious, choleric, churlish, cranky*, cross, crotchety, crusty*, cynical, difficult, dour, fretful, gloomy, glum, grouchy*, harsh, huffy, ill-humored, ill-tempered, irascible, irritable, misanthropic, morose, nasty-tempered, peevish, perverse, petulant, prickly, saturnine, snappish, snappy, sour, splenetic, sulky, sullen, surly, tart, testy, tough, trying, unsociable; CONCEPTS 401,403 —Ant. happy

crack [adj] *super, first-rate* able, ace, adept, best, capital, choice, crackerjack*, deluxe, elite, excellent, expert, first-class, handpicked, pro*, proficient, skilled, skillful, superior, talented; CONCEPTS 528,542,574 —Ant. bad, inferior, poor

crack [n1] *break, crevice* breach, chink, chip, cleft, cranny, crevasse, cut, discontinuity, division, fissure, fracture, gap, hole, interstice, interval, rent, rift, rima, rimation, rime, split; CONCEPTS 469,513

crack [n2] *loud sound, usually from hitting* bang, bash, belt, blast, blow, boom, buffet, burst, clap, clip, clout, crash, cuff, explosion, go, noise, pop, report, shot, slam, slap, smack, smash, snap, splintering, splitting, stab, stroke, thump, thwack, wallop, whack, wham; CONCEPTS 189,595

crack [n3] *attempt to do something* fling, go, opportunity, pop, shot, stab, try, whack, whirl; CONCEPT 87

crack [n4] *joke* dig, funny remark, gag, insult, jest, jibe, quip, remark, return, smart remark, wisecrack, witticism; CONCEPT 273

crack [v1] *break, usually into parts* burst, chip, chop, cleave, crackle, crash, damage, detonate, explode, fracture, hurt, impair, injure, pop, ring, rive, sever, shiver, snap, splinter, split; CONCEPT 248 —Ant. fix, mend

crack [v2] *lose self-control* become deranged, become insane, blow one's mind*, blow up, break down, bug out*, collapse, flip*, give way*, go bonkers*, go crazy, go to pieces*, lose it*, succumb, yield; CONCEPT 13 —Ant. be calm, compose

crack [v3] *hit very hard* bash, buffet, clip, clout, cuff, slap, thump, thunder, wallop, whack; CONCEPT 189

crack [v4] *discover meaning, answer* break, cryptanalyze, decipher, decode, decrypt, fathom, figure out, get answer, solve, work out; CONCEPTS 37,38 —Ant. misunderstand

crackdown [n] *restraint* clampdown, crush, end, repression, stop, strike, suppression; CONCEPTS 240,832

cracker [n] *hard, often salted, baked wafer* biscuit, bun, cookie, hardtack, pretzel, rusk, saltine; CONCEPT 457

crack up [v] *break down mentally* become demented, become psychotic, blow a fuse*, collapse, come apart at seams*, decline, derange, deteriorate, fail, flip out*, freak out*, go bonkers*, go crazy, go nuts, go off deep end*, go off rocker*, go out of mind*, go to pieces*, have breakdown, schizz out*, sicken; CONCEPT 13 —Ant. be calm

cradle [n1] *small bed for baby* baby bed, bassinet, cot, crib, hamper, Moses basket, pannier, trundle bed; CONCEPT 443

cradle [n2] *early childhood; origins* babyhood, beginning, birthplace, fount, fountain, fountainhead, infancy, nativity, nursery, origin, source, spring, ultimate cause, wellspring; CONCEPTS 648,817

cradle [v] *hold in arms; nurture* lull, nestle, nourish, nurse, rock, support, tend, watch over; CONCEPTS 190,295

craft [n1] *expertise, skill* ability, adeptness, adroitness, aptitude, art, artistry, cleverness, competence, cunning, dexterity, expertness, ingenuity, knack, know-how*, proficiency, technique; CONCEPTS 409,706

craft [n2] *deceit, scheme* art, artfulness, artifice, cageyness, canniness, contrivance, craftiness, cunning, disingenuity, duplicity, foxiness, guile, ruse, shrewdness, slyness, stratagem, strategy, subterfuge, subtlety, trickery, wiles, wiliness; CONCEPTS 645,660 —*Ant.* honesty, openness

craft [n3] *business, discipline* art, calling, career, employment, handicraft, line, métier, occupation, profession, pursuit, trade, vocation, work; CONCEPT 360 —*Ant.* avocation, entertainment, recreation

craft [n4] *water or air vehicle* aircraft, airplane, air ship, barge, blimp, boat, bottom, plane, ship, shipping, spacecraft, vessel, watercraft, zeppelin; CONCEPTS 504,506

craftsperson [n] *person skilled in art* artificer, artisan, journeyperson, machinist, maker, manufacturer, mechanic, skilled worker, smith, specialist, technician, wright; CONCEPT 348 —*Ant.* bumbler, unskilled

crafty [adj] *clever, scheming* adroit, artful, astute, cagey, calculating, canny, crazy like fox*, cunning, deceitful, deep, designing, devious, disingenuous, duplicitous, foxy*, fraudulent, guileful, insidious, intelligent, keen, knowing, sharp, shrewd, slick, slippery*, sly, smart, smooth, street smart*, streetwise*, subtle, tricky, vulpine, wily; CONCEPT 401 —*Ant.* honest, naive, unclever

craggy [adj] *jagged* asperous, broken, cragged, harsh, precipitous, rock-bound, rocky, rough, rugged, scabrous, scraggy, stony, uneven, unlevel, unsmooth; CONCEPTS 490,606 —*Ant.* flat, smooth

cram [v1] *fill to overflowing; compress* charge, chock, choke, compact, crowd, crush, devour, drive, force, gobble, gorge, guzzle, heap, ingurgitate, jam, jam-pack*, load, overcrowd, overeat, overfill, pack, pack 'em in*, pack in, pack it in*, pack like sardines*, press, ram, sardine*, satiate, shove, slop, slosh, squash, squeeze, stive, stuff, tamp*, thrust, wedge, wolf*; CONCEPTS 208,740 —*Ant.* let out, open, release

cram [v2] *study intensely* burn midnight oil*, heavy booking*, hit the books*, megabook*, mug up*, read, review, revise; CONCEPT 17

cramp [n] *muscle spasm* ache, charley horse*, circumscription, confinement, constipation, contraction, convulsion, crick, hindrance, impediment, kink, obstruction, pain, pang, restriction, shooting pain, stiffness, stitch, stricture, twinge; CONCEPTS 308,728

cramp [v] *hinder, restrain* bottle up*, box up*, check, circumscribe, clamp, clasp, clog, confine, constrain, coop up*, encumber, fasten, grip, hamper, hamstring, handicap, impede, inhibit, limit, object, obstruct, restrict, shackle, stymie, thwart; CONCEPTS 130,191 —*Ant.* allow, let go, release

cramped [adj] *congested, overcrowded* awkward, circumscribed, close, closed in, confined, crabbed, crowded, hemmed in*, illegible, incommodious, indecipherable, irregular, jammed in, little, minute, narrow, packed, pent, restricted, small, squeezed, tight, tiny, tucked up, two-by-four*, uncomfortable; CONCEPTS 483,773 —*Ant.* free, open, uncongested, uncramped, uninhibited, unobstructed

cranky [adj] *in bad mood* bad-humored, bearish, cantankerous, choleric, crabby, cross, crotchety, cussed, disagreeable, got up on wrong side of bed*, grouchy, grumpy, hot-tempered, ill-humored, irascible, irritable, like a bear*, mean, ornery*, out of sorts, perverse, quick-tempered, ratty, snappish, tetchy, ugly, vinegary; CONCEPTS 401,403 —*Ant.* amiable, cheerful, happy

cranny [n] *nook, opening* breach, byplace, chink, cleft, crack, crevice, fissure, gap, hole, interstice, niche; CONCEPTS 440,513

crappy [adj] *poor* cheap, inferior, junky, lousy, shoddy, sub-par, trashy, useless, worthless; CONCEPT 571

crapshoot [n] *big chance* iffy proposition, risk, risky business, shot in the dark*, spin of the roulette wheel*; CONCEPTS 675,693

crash [n1/v1] *bang; banging sound* blast, boom, burst, clang, clap, clash, clatter, clattering, crack, din, peal, racket, slam, smash, smashing, sound, thunder, thunderclap, wham; CONCEPTS 65,521,595

crash [n2] *collision, accidental hitting* accident, bump, collapse, concussion, crack-up*, crunch, debacle, ditch, fender bender*, fender tag*, impact, jar, jolt, percussion, pileup, ram, rear-ender*, shock, sideswipe, smash, smashup*, splashdown*, stack-up*, thud*, thump*, total*, washout*, wreck; CONCEPT 189

crash [n3] *computer system failure* abend, head crash, program crash, program error, program failure, system crash, system error; CONCEPTS 699,706

crash [v2] *break into pieces* bang into, crack up, crunch, dash, disintegrate, fracture, fragment, pile up, shatter, shiver, sideswipe, smash, smash up, splinter, total*, wrack up*;CONCEPT 248

crash [v3] *fall down; bite the dust** bump, collapse, collide, crash-land, ditch, dive into, drop, fall flat*, fall headlong, fall prostrate, give way, go in*, hurtle, lurch, meet, overbalance, overturn, pancake*, pitch, plough into*, plunge, prang, slip, smash, splash down, sprawl, topple, tumble, upset, washout*; CONCEPT 181

crass [adj] *coarse, insensitive* asinine, blundering, boorish, bovine, churlish, dense, doltish, gross, indelicate, inelegant, loutish, lowbrow, lumpish, oafish, obtuse, Philistine, raw, rough, rude, stupid, uncouth, unrefined, vulgar, witless; CONCEPT 401 —*Ant.* careful, delicate, kind, nice, refined, sensitive, tactful

crate [n] *wooden container* box, cage, carton, case, chest, package; CONCEPT 494

co
cr

crave [v1] *desire intensely* ache for, covet, cry out for, die for*, dream, eat one's heart out*, fancy, give eyeteeth for*, hunger for*, itch for*, long for, lust after, need, pine for*, require, sigh for, spoil for, suspire, thirst for*, want, yearn for, yen for*; CONCEPT 20 —*Ant.* abjure, dislike, hate, not want, spurn

crave [v2] *beg* ask, beseech, call for, demand, entreat, implore, necessitate, petition, plead for, pray for, require, seek, solicit, supplicate, take; CONCEPTS 48,53 —*Ant.* not want

craven [adj] *weak, timid* chicken*, cowardly, dastardly, fearful, gutless, lily-livered*, mean-spirited, poltroonish, pusillanimous, scared, timorous, weak-kneed*, wimpish*, wimpy*, wussy*, yellow*, yellow-bellied*; CONCEPTS 401,550 —*Ant.* bold, brave, courageous, heroic, strong

craven [n] *timid person* caitiff, chicken*, coward, dastard, fraidy cat*, nebbish, poltroon, quitter, recreant, scaredy cat*, weakling, wheyface, wimp*, wuss*, yellow belly*; CONCEPT 423

craving [n] *strong desire* appetite, appetition, hankering, hunger, hurting, itch*, longing, lust, munchies*, need, passion, thirst, urge, yearning, yen*; CONCEPTS 20,709 —*Ant.* dislike, distaste, hate, indifference

crawl [v1] *move very slowly* clamber, creep, drag, drag oneself along, go on all fours, go on belly, grovel, hang back, inch, lag, loiter along, lollygag*, move at snail's pace*, move on hands and knees, plod, poke, pull oneself along, scrabble, slide, slither, squirm, worm, wriggle, writhe; CONCEPT 151

crawl [v2] *humble oneself* abase oneself, apple-polish*, brownnose*, cringe, fawn, grovel, toady, truckle; CONCEPTS 35,48

craze [n] *fad, strong interest* chic, cry, enthusiasm, fashion, fever, furor, infatuation, in thing*, kick*, mania, mode, monomania, newest wrinkle*, novelty, passion, preoccupation, rage, the last word*, the latest thing*, trend, vogue, wrinkle; CONCEPTS 532,690

craze [v] *make insane* bewilder, confuse, dement, derange, distemper, distract, drive mad, enrage, frenzy, infatuate, inflame, madden, unbalance, unhinge; CONCEPTS 7,19 —*Ant.* balance, clear up, steady

crazed [adj] *insane* berserk, certifiable, crazy, demented, deranged, frenzied, hysterical, lunatic, mad, maniac, manic, mental*, out of one's mind, psychopathic, raving; CONCEPT 403 —*Ant.* sane

crazy [adj1] *mentally strange* ape, barmy, batty, berserk, bonkers*, cracked, crazed, cuckoo, daft, delirious, demented, deranged, dingy*, dippy*, erratic, flaky, flipped*, flipped out*, freaked out*, fruity*, idiotic, insane, kooky, lunatic, mad, maniacal, mental*, moonstruck*, nuts, nutty, nutty as fruitcake*, of unsound mind, out of one's mind, out of one's tree*, out to lunch*, potty*, psycho*, round the bend*, schizo*, screwball*, screw loose*, screwy*, silly, touched*, unbalanced, unglued*, unhinged*, unzipped*, wacky; CONCEPT 403 —*Ant.* balanced, realistic, reasonable, responsible, sane, sensible, smart

crazy [adj2] *unrealistic, fantastic* absurd, balmy, beyond all reason, bizarre, cockeyed, derisory, eccentric, fatuous, foolhardy, foolish, goofy*, half-baked*, harebrained*, idiotic, ill-conceived, impracticable, imprudent, inane, inappropriate, insane, irresponsible, loony, ludicrous, nonsensical, odd, out of all reason, outrageous, peculiar, preposterous, puerile, quixotic, ridiculous, senseless, short-sighted, silly, strange, unworkable, weird, wild; CONCEPT 529 —*Ant.* believable, realistic, reasonable, sensible

crazy [adj3] *infatuated, in love* ardent, beside oneself*, devoted, eager, enamored, fanatical, hysterical, keen, mad, passionate, smitten, wild, zealous; CONCEPT 403 —*Ant.* dislike, hate

creak [v] *grind, grate with high noise* chirr, crepitate, groan, rasp, scrape, scratch, screech, sound, squeak, squeal; CONCEPTS 65,186,215

cream [n1] *lotion, oil* cerate, chrism, cosmetic, demulcent, emulsion, essence, jelly, liniment, moisturizer, ointment, paste, salve, unction, unguent; CONCEPTS 466,467,468

cream [n2] *the best* choice, crème de la crème*, elite, fat, favorite, finest, flower, pick, pride, prime*, prize, skim*, top; CONCEPT 668 —*Ant.* worst

creamy [adj] *smooth, buttery* creamed, feathery, fluffy, gloppy*, gooey, gooky*, goopy*, greasy, gunky, luscious, lush, milky, oily, rich, soft, velvety; CONCEPT 606

crease [n] *fold, wrinkle* bend, bulge, cockle, corrugation, furrow, groove, line, overlap, pleat, plica, pucker, ridge, rimple, rivel, ruck, rugosity, tuck; CONCEPTS 452,757

crease [v] *fold, rumple* bend, cockle, corrugate, crimp, crinkle, crumple, dog-ear*, double up, plait, pleat, pucker, purse, ridge, ruck up, screw up*, wrinkle; CONCEPTS 158,219

create [v] *develop in mind or physically* actualize, author, beget, bring into being, bring into existence, bring to pass, build, cause to be, coin, compose, conceive, concoct, constitute, construct, contrive, design, devise, discover, dream up, effect, erect, establish, fabricate, fashion, father, forge, form, formulate, found, generate, give birth to, give life to, hatch, imagine, initiate, institute, invent, invest, make, occasion, organize, originate, parent, perform, plan, procreate, produce, rear, set up, shape, sire, spawn, start; CONCEPTS 173,239,251 —*Ant.* destroy, ruin

creation [n1] *development of entity* conception, constitution, establishment, formation, formulation, foundation, generation, genesis, imagination, inception, institution, laying down, making, nascency, nativity, origination, procreation, production, setting up, siring; CONCEPT 173 —*Ant.* destruction, ruin

creation [n2] *all living things* cosmos, life, living world, macrocosm, macrocosmos, megacosm, nature, totality, universe, world; CONCEPTS 389,429 —*Ant.* death

creation [n3] *invention, concoction* achievement, brainchild, chef-d'oeuvre, concept, handiwork, magnum opus, opus, piece, pièce de résistance, production, work, work of genius; CONCEPTS 259,260

creative [adj] *artistic, imaginative* clever, cool*, demiurgic, deviceful, fertile, formative, gifted, hip*, ingenious, innovational, innovative, innovatory, inspired, inventive, leading-edge*, original, originative, productive, prolific, stimulating, visionary, way out*; CONCEPT 402 —*Ant.* uncreative, ungifted, unimaginative, uninspired, unproductive, untalented

creativity [n] *artistry* cleverness, genius, imagination, imaginativeness, ingenuity, inspiration, inventiveness, originality, resourcefulness, talent, vision; CONCEPTS 409,410

creator [n] *inventor; God* architect, author, begetter, brain, deity, designer, founder, framer, generator, initiator, maker, originator, prime mover, producer, sire; CONCEPTS 348,352,361 —*Ant.* destroyer, destructor

creature [n] *being, beast* animal, body, brute, creation, critter*, fellow, individual, living being, living thing, lower animal, man, mortal, party, person, personage, quadruped, soul, varmint*, woman; CONCEPT 389 —*Ant.* abstract, inanimate

credence [n] *trust, acceptance* accepting, admission, admitting, assurance, belief, certainty, confidence, credit, dependence, faith, reliance, stock, store; CONCEPT 689 —*Ant.* distrust, faithlessness

credentials [n] *references, attestation* accreditation, authorization, card, certificate, character, deed, diploma, docket, document, documentation, endorsement, letter of credence, letter of introduction, license, missive, papers, passport, proof, recommendation, sanction, testament, testimonial, title, token, voucher, warrant; CONCEPTS 271,685

credibility [n] *believeableness* believability, chance, integrity, likelihood, plausibility, possibility, probability, prospect, reliability, satisfactoriness, solidity, solidness, soundness, tenability, trustworthiness, validity; CONCEPTS 650,725 —*Ant.* implausibility, improbability, unreasonableness

credible [adj] *believable* aboveboard, colorable, conceivable, conclusive, creditable, dependable, determinative, honest, honest to God*, imaginable, likely, plausible, possible, probable, probably, rational, reasonable, reliable, satisfactory, satisfying, seeming, sincere, solid, sound, straight, supposable, tenable, thinkable, trustworthy, trusty, up front*, valid; CONCEPTS 552,582 —*Ant.* implausible, impossible, improbable, inconceivable, incredible, unbelievable, unimaginable, unlikely, untenable

credit [n1] *recognition; trust* acclaim, acknowledgment, approval, attention, belief, Brownie points*, commendation, confidence, credence, distinction, faith, fame, glory, honor, kudos*, merit, notice, pat on the back*, points*, praise, reliance, strokes*, thanks, tribute; CONCEPTS 69,410 —*Ant.* disacknowledgement, disapproval, disbelief, disclaimer, discredit, dishonor, disregard, disrespect

credit [n2] *reputation, status* authority, character, clout, esteem, estimation, fame, good name, influence, position, prestige, regard, renown, repute, standing, weight; CONCEPT 388 —*Ant.* discredit, disrespect, ill repute

credit [n3] *deferred payment arrangement; assets* balance, bond, capital outlay, continuance, debenture, extension, installment buying, installment plan, lien, loan, mortgage, on

account, on the arm*, on the cuff*, plastic*, respite, securities, stock, surplus cash, tab, trust, wealth; CONCEPT 335 —*Ant.* cash

credit [v1] *believe, depend on* accept, bank on, buy, consider, deem, fall for*, feel, hand it to one, have faith in, hold, pat on back, rely on, sense, swallow*, take as gospel truth*, take stock in*, think, trust; CONCEPT 12 —*Ant.* disbelieve, mistrust, not buy, not subscribe

credit [v2] *accredit, assign to* ascribe to, attribute to, chalk up to, charge to, defer, impute, lay, refer; CONCEPT 18 —*Ant.* discredit, renege

creditable [adj] *praiseworthy* admirable, batting a thousand*, believeable, commendable, decent, deserving, estimable, excellent, exemplary, honest, honorable, laudable, meritorious, nasty*, not too shabby*, organic, palmary, reputable, reputed, respectable, salt of the earth*, satisfactory, suitable, well-thought-of*, worthy; CONCEPT 542 —*Ant.* disrespected, unworthy

credulous [adj] *gullible, naive* accepting, believing, born yesterday*, dupable, easy mark*, falling for*, green, overtrusting, simple, swallow whole, taken in, trustful, trusting, uncritical, unquestioning, unsophisticated, unsuspecting, unsuspicious, unwary; CONCEPT 404 —*Ant.* skeptical, suspecting, suspicious, untrusting

creed [n] *belief, principles* articles of faith, canon, catechism, church, confession, conviction, cult, doctrine, dogma, faith, ideology, persuasion, profession, religion, tenet, weltanschauung; CONCEPTS 688,689

creek [n] *stream of water* brook, brooklet, burn, crick, ditch, race, rill, rindle, river, rivulet, run, runnel, spring, streamlet, tributary, watercourse; CONCEPT 514

creep [v] *crawl along, usually on ground* approach unnoticed, crawl on all fours, edge, glide, grovel, gumshoe*, inch, insinuate, lurk, pussyfoot, scrabble, scramble, skulk, slink, slither, snake*, sneak, squirm, steal, tiptoe, worm, wriggle, writhe; CONCEPT 151

creepy [adj] *nasty, scary* awful, direful, disgusting, disturbing, dreadful, eerie, frightening, ghoulish, gruesome, hair-raising, horrible, itching, itchy, macabre, menacing, nightmarish, ominous, shuddersome, sinister, terrifying, threatening, unpleasant, weird; CONCEPT 570 —*Ant.* good, nice, normal, pleasant, pleasing, unscary

crescendo [n] *increase to climax* apex, ascension, building, climb, crest, critical mass, culmination, elevation, escalation, intensification, peak, pinnacle, rise, summit, surge, upsurge, zenith; CONCEPT 836

crescent [adj] *sickle-shaped* bowed, bow-shaped, concave, convex, crescentic, crescentiform, curved, falcate, semicircular; CONCEPT 486

crescent [n] *sickle-shaped object* bow, concave figure, convex figure, crescentoid, curve, demilune, half-moon, horned moon, lune, meniscus, new moon, old moon, sickle; CONCEPT 436

crest [n1] *highest point* acme, apex, apogee, climax, crescendo, crown, culmination, fastigium, head, height, noon, peak, pinnacle, ridge, roof, summit, top, vertex; CONCEPT 836 —*Ant.* bottom, nadir

Cr
Cr

crest [n2] *emblem, symbol* badge, bearings, charge, device, insignia; CONCEPT 284

crest [n3] *topknot on head of animal* aigrette, caruncle, chine, cockscomb, comb, crown, feather, hogback, mane, panache, plume, ridge, tassel, tuft; CONCEPT 399

crestfallen [adj] *disappointed* ass in a sling*, blue, cast down, chapfallen, dejected, depressed, despondent, disconsolate, discouraged, disheartened, dispirited, down, downcast, downhearted, down in the dumps*, in a funk*, inconsolable, low, sad, singing the blues*, taken down*; CONCEPT 403 —*Ant.* cheered, elated, encouraged, excited, happy, hearted, inspirited

cretin [n] *obnoxious stupid person* creep, fool, idiot, imbecile, loser, moron; CONCEPTS 350,423

crevice/crevasse [n] *crack, gap* abyss, chasm, chink, cleft, crack, cranny, cut, division, fissure, fracture, hole, interstice, opening, precipice, rent, rift, slit, split; CONCEPTS 509,513

crew [n] *group working together* aggregation, assemblage, band, bevy, bunch, cluster, collection, company, complement, congregation, corps, covey, crowd, faction, gang, hands, herd, horde, lot, mob, organization, pack, party, posse, retinue, sailors, sect, set, squad, swarm, team, troop, troupe, workers, working party; CONCEPTS 381,417

crib [n] *baby bed* bassinet, bin*, box*, bunk, cot, cradle, manger, Moses basket*, rack*, stall*, trundle bed; CONCEPT 443

crick [n] *muscle spasm* ache, charley horse*, convulsion, cramp, jarring, kink, pain, stitch, twinge, wrench; CONCEPTS 308,728

crime [n] *offense against the law* abomination, antisocial behavior, atrocity, breach, break, caper, case, corruption, criminality, delict, delictum, delinquency, depravity, dereliction, enormity, evil, evil behavior, fast one*, fault, felony, hit, illegality, immorality, infraction, infringement, iniquity, job, lawlessness, malefaction, malfeasance, misconduct, misdeed, misdemeanor, mortal sin, outrage, racket, scandal, sneak, tort, transgression, trespass, unlawful act, vice, villainy, violation, wickedness, wrong, wrongdoing; CONCEPT 192 —*Ant.* good deed, kindness

criminal [adj] *lawless, felonious* bent, caught, corrupt, crooked, culpable, deplorable, dirty, heavy, hung up*, illegal, illegitimate, illicit, immoral, indictable, iniquitous, nefarious, off base*, out of line*, peccant, racket, scandalous, senseless, shady*, smoking gun*, unlawful, unrighteous, vicious, villainous, wicked, wildcat*, wrong; CONCEPT 545 —*Ant.* correct, lawful, legal, moral, right, righteous

criminal [n] *person who breaks the law* bad actor*, blackmailer, black marketeer, con, convict, crook, culprit, delinquent, desperado, deuce, evildoer, ex-con, felon, fugitive, gangster, guerilla, heavy*, hood*, hoodlum, hooligan*, hustler, inside person*, jailbird, lawbreaker, malefactor, mobster, mug, muscle*, offender, outlaw, racketeer, repeater, scofflaw, sinner, slippery eel*, thug*, transgressor, trespasser, wrongdoer, yardbird*; CONCEPT 412 —*Ant.* law, police

crimp [v] *fold or curl* coil, crease, crimple, crinkle, crisp, crumple, flow, frizz, pleat,

rimple, ruck, screw, scrunch, set, swirl, undulate, wave, wrinkle; CONCEPTS 137,213,250 —*Ant.* straighten

cringe [v] *flinch, recoil from danger* blench, cower, crawl, crouch, dodge, draw back, duck, eat dirt, grovel, kneel, quail, quiver, shrink, shy, start, stoop, tremble, wince; CONCEPTS 188,195 —*Ant.* come forward

crinkle [v] *crumple, ruffle* cockle, coil, crackle, crease, crimp, crimple, curl, fold, hiss, pucker, ruck, rumple, rustle, scallop, screw, scrunch, seam, swish, twist, whisper, wind, wreathe, wrinkle; CONCEPTS 65,137,213,250 —*Ant.* straighten

cripple [v1] *disable; make lame* attenuate, blunt, debilitate, disarm, dislimb, dismember, enfeeble, hamstring*, hurt, immobilize, incapacitate, injure, lame, maim, mangle, mutilate, palsy, paralyze, prostrate, sap, sideline*, stifle, undermine, unstrengthen, weaken; CONCEPT 246 —*Ant.* aid, assist, enable, help, strengthen, support

cripple [v2] *hinder action, progress* bring to standstill, cramp, damage, destroy, halt, hamstring*, impair, put out of action*, ruin, spoil, stifle, vitiate; CONCEPT 121 —*Ant.* aid, allow, assist, capacitate, encourage, help

crippled [adj] *disabled* bedridden, broken, damaged, defective, deformed, enfeebled, game, gimp*, halt, hamstrung*, handicapped, harmed, hog-tied*, housebound, impaired, incapacitated, laid up*, lame, maimed, mangled, marred, mutilated, out of commission*, paralyzed, sidelined*; CONCEPTS 314,485 —*Ant.* healthy, walking

crisis [n] *critical situation* big trouble*, catastrophe, change, climacteric, climax, confrontation, contingency, corner, crossroad, crunch*, crux, culmination, deadlock, dilemma, dire straits*, disaster, embarrassment, emergency, entanglement, exigency, extremity, height, hot potato*, hour of decision*, imbroglio, impasse, juncture, mess, moment of truth*, necessity, pass, perplexity, pickle*, pinch*, plight, point of no return*, predicament, pressure, puzzle, quandary, situation, stew, strait, trauma, trial, trouble, turning point, urgency; CONCEPT 674 —*Ant.* calm, peace

crisp [adj1] *brittle, dry* crispy, crumbly, crunchy, crusty, firm, fresh, friable, green, plump, ripe, short, unwilted; CONCEPT 606 —*Ant.* flexible, limp, soft

crisp [adj2] *fresh, chilly* bracing, brisk, clear, cloudless, invigorating, refreshing, stimulating; CONCEPTS 525,605 —*Ant.* temperate, warm

crisp [adj3] *short, curt in presentation* abrupt, biting, brief, brusque, clear, clear-cut, cutting, incisive, penetrating, piquing, pithy, provoking, stimulating, succinct, tart, terse; CONCEPT 267 —*Ant.* lengthy, long

crisp [adj4] *smart, snappy in appearance* clean-cut, neat, orderly, spruce, tidy, well-groomed, well-pressed; CONCEPT 579 —*Ant.* ruffled, rumpled

criterion [n] *test, gauge for judgment* archetype, basis, benchmark, canon, example, exemplar, fact, foundation, law, measure, model, norm, opinion, original, paradigm, pattern, point of comparison, precedent, principle, proof, prototype, rule, scale, standard, touchstone, yardstick; CONCEPTS *290,688* —*Ant.* change, conjecture, fancy, guess, possibility, probability

critic [*n1*] *analyst, interpreter* analyzer, annotator, arbiter, authority, caricaturist, cartoonist, commentator, connoisseur, diagnostic, evaluator, expert, expositor, judge, pundit, reviewer, sharpshooter; CONCEPT *348*

critic [*n2*] *faultfinder, detractor* aristarch, attacker, backseat driver*, belittler, blamer, carper, caviler, censor, censurer, complainant, complainer, defamer, disapprover, disparager, disputer, doubter, fretter, hypercritic, maligner, muckraker, mud-slinger*, nagger*, nit-picker*, panner*, quibbler, reviler, scolder, sidewalk superintendent*, slanderer, vilifier, worrier, zapper*; CONCEPT *412* —*Ant.* complimenter, praiser

critical [*adj1*] *fault-finding, detracting* analytical, belittling, biting, calumniatory, captious, carping, caviling, cavillous, censorious, censuring, choleric, condemning, critic, cutting, cynical, demanding, demeaning, derogatory, diagnostic, disapproving, discerning, discriminating, disparaging, exacting, exceptive, finicky, fussy, hairsplitting, humbling, hypercritical, lowering, nagging, niggling, nit-picking*, overcritical, particular, penetrating, reproachful, sarcastic, satirical, scolding, severe, sharp, trenchant, withering; CONCEPT *267* —*Ant.* complimentary, laudatory, praising

critical [*adj2*] *urgently important* acute, all-important, climacteric, conclusive, consequential, crucial, dangerous, deciding, decisive, desperate, determinative, dire, exceptive, grave, hairy*, hazardous, high-priority, integral, momentous, perilous, pivotal, precarious, pressing, risky, serious, significant, strategic, urgent, vital, weighty; CONCEPT *568* —*Ant.* trivial, uncritical, unimportant

critical mass [*n*] *crisis point* critical point, critical stage, crossroads*, crunch time, do or die time*, high noon*, irreversible momentum, moment of truth, point of no return, sink or swim time*, the Rubicon, turning point; CONCEPT *674*

criticism [*n1*] *interpretation, analysis* appraisal, appreciation, assessment, comment, commentary, critique, elucidation, essay, estimate, evaluation, examination, exposition, judgment, notice, observation, opinion, pan*, rating, rave*, review, reviewal, scorcher, sideswipe*, sleighride*, study, write-up; CONCEPTS *271,277, 278* —*Ant.* estimation, guess, supposition

criticism [*n2*] *verbal disapproval* animadversion, aspersion, bad press*, blast, brickbats, Bronx cheer*, call down*, carping, cavil, caviling, censure, critical remarks, cut*, denunciation, disparagement, faultfinding, flak*, hit*, knock*, nit-picking, objection, opprobrium, pan*, panning, put down, quibble, rap on knuckles*, reproof, roast*, slam*, slap*, slap on wrist*, static, stricture, swipe*, vitriol, zapper*; CONCEPT *52* —*Ant.* approval, compliment, praise

criticize [*v1*] *disapprove, judge as bad* animadvert on, bash, blame, blast, blister, carp, castigate, censure, chastise, chide, clobber, come down on, condemn, cut down*, cut to bits*, cut up*, denounce, denunciate, disparage, do a number on*, dress down*, excoriate, find fault, fluff*, fulminate against, fustigate, give bad press*, hit, jump on*, knock*, lambaste*, nag at, nit-pick, pan, pick at, rap*, reprehend, reprimand, reprobate, reprove, rip*, roast*, scathe, scorch*, skin*, skin alive*, slam*, slog*, slug*, take down*, trash*, trim*, zap*; CONCEPT *52* —*Ant.* approve, compliment, laud, praise

criticize [*v2*] *analyze, interpret* appraise, assess, comment upon, evaluate, examine, give opinion, judge, pass judgment on, probe, review, scrutinize, study; CONCEPTS *37,103* —*Ant.* estimate, guess, suppose

critique [*n*] *analysis, essay* appraisal, assessment, comment, commentary, criticism, editorial, examination, exposition, flak*, judgment, notice, pan*, putdown*, rap*, rave*, review, reviewal, slam*, slap*, study, take-down*, write-up, zapper*; CONCEPTS *51,52, 271* —*Ant.* compliment, praise

croak [*v*] *make husky, squawking noise* caw, crow, gasp, grunt, quack, squawk, utter huskily, utter throatily, wheeze; CONCEPT *77*

crony [*n*] *ally, companion* accomplice, acquaintance, associate, bosom buddy*, buddy, chum, colleague, comate, comrade, confidant, friend, good buddy*, intimate, mate, pal, partner, sidekick*; CONCEPT *423* —*Ant.* enemy, foe

crook [*n*] *criminal, thief* cheat, filcher, knave, pilferer, purloiner, racketeer, robber, rogue, scoundrel, shark*, shyster*, swindler, villain; CONCEPT *412* —*Ant.* law, police

crook [*v*] *bend, angle* bow, curve, flex, fork, hook, meander, notch, round, slither, snake, wind, zigzag; CONCEPTS *213,738* —*Ant.* straighten

crooked [*adj1*] *bent, angled* agee, anfractuous, angular, asymmetric, awry, bowed, catawampus*, circuitous, cockeyed*, contorted, crippled, curved, curving, deformed, deviating, devious, disfigured, distorted, errant, gnarled, hooked, incurving, indirect, irregular, kinky, knurly, lopsided, meandering, misshapen, not straight, oblique, out of shape, rambling, roundabout, screwy*, serpentine, sinuous, skewed, slanted, snaky, spiral, tilted, topsy-turvy*, tortile, tortuous, twisted, twisting, uneven, warped, winding, zigzag; CONCEPTS *486,490, 581* —*Ant.* straight

crooked [*adj2*] *evil, corrupt* crafty, criminal, deceitful, devious, dishonest, dishonorable, double-dealing, dubious, fraudulent, illegal, indirect, iniquitous, lying, nefarious, questionable, ruthless, shady, shifty, suborned, treacherous, underhand, unlawful, unprincipled, unscrupulous, untruthful; CONCEPT *545* —*Ant.* good, honest, law-abiding, lawful, moral

crop [*n*] *harvest of fruit, vegetable* annual production, byproduct, crops, fruitage, fruits, gathering, gleaning, output, produce, product, reaping, season's growth, vintage, yield; CONCEPT *429*

crop [*v*] *cut, trim off* chop, clip, curtail, detach, detruncate, disengage, hew, lop, mow, pare, pollard, prune, reduce, shave, shear, shorten, skive, slash, snip, top, truncate; CONCEPT *176*

cross [*adj*] *very angry; in a bad mood* annoyed, cantankerous, captious, caviling, choleric, churlish, crabby*, cranky, crotchety*, crusty, disagreeable, faultfinding, fractious, fretful, grouchy, grumpy, ill-humored, ill-tempered,

impatient, irascible, irritable, jumpy, out of
humor, peeved, peevish, pettish, petulant, put
out*, querulous, quick-tempered, ratty, short,
snappy, splenetic, sullen, surly, testy, tetchy,
touchy, vexed, waspish; CONCEPTS 401,403
—*Ant.* animated, cheerful, happy, pleasant

cross [v1] *traverse an area* bridge, cruise, cut
across, extend over, ford, go across, meet, move
across, navigate, overpass, pass over, ply, sail,
span, transverse, voyage, zigzag; CONCEPTS
159, 224 —*Ant.* remain, stay

cross [v2] *intersect, lie across* bisect, crisscross,
crosscut, decussate, divide, intercross, intertwine, lace, lie athwart of, rest across; CONCEPTS
738,747 —*Ant.* divide, part, separate

cross [v3] *hybridize, mix* blend, crossbreed,
cross-fertilize, cross-mate, cross-pollinate,
interbreed, intercross, mingle, mongrelize;
CONCEPTS 250,257 —*Ant.* unmix

cross [v4] *betray, hinder* backtalk, block, bollix,
buck, crab, cramp, crimp, deny, double-cross,
flummox, foil, foul up*, frustrate, have bone
to pick*, impede, interfere, knock props out*,
louse up*, obstruct, oppose, resist, sell*, sell
out*, snafu*, stab in the back*, stonewall*,
stump, stymie, take on, take wind out of sails*,
thwart; CONCEPTS 7,19,59,121 —*Ant.* abet, aid,
assist, help

cross-examine [v] *ask pointed questions*
catechize, check, cross-question, debrief,
examine, grill, interrogate, investigate, pump,
put the screws to*, question, quiz, sweat,
third-degree*; CONCEPTS 48,53,317

crossing [n] *pathway to traverse larger path*
bridge, cloverleaf, crossroad, crosswalk, crossway, decussation, exchange, grade crossing,
grating, gridiron, interchange, intersection,
junction, loop, network, overpass, passage,
screen, traversal, traverse, underpass; CONCEPTS
501,513

crosswise/crossways [adj] *across, at an angle*
angular, aslant, athwart, at right angles, awry,
contrariwise, crisscross, cross, crossing, diagonally, from side to side, horizontally, longways,
on the bias, over, perpendicular, sideways,
thwart, transversal, transverse, transversely,
traverse, vertically; CONCEPT 581

crotchety [adj] *irritable, often due to old age*
awkward, bad-tempered, bearish, cantankerous,
contrary, crabby*, cranky, cross, cross-grained,
crusty, curmudgeonly, difficult, disagreeable,
eccentric, fractious, grouchy, grumpy, irritable,
obstinate, obstreperous, odd, ornery*, peevish,
queer, surly, testy, unusual, vinegary*, waspish;
CONCEPTS 401,403 —*Ant.* cheerful,
happy, pleasant

crouch [v] *stoop low; cringe* bend, bend down,
bow, cower, dip, duck, grovel, huddle, hunch,
hunker down, kneel, quail, squat, scrooch down,
squat, stoop, wince; CONCEPT 213 —*Ant.* stretch

crow [v] *brag, exult* babble, blow, bluster,
boast, cackle, caw, cock-a-doodle-doo*, cry,
flourish, gas, gloat, glory in, gurgle, jubilate,
mouth, prate, puff, rodomontade, squawk, strut,
swagger, triumph, vaunt, whoop; CONCEPT 49

crowd [n1] *large assembly* army, array,
blowout, bunch, cattle, circle, clique, cloud,
cluster, company, concourse, confluence,
conflux, congeries, congregation, coterie, crew,

crush, deluge, drove, faction, flock, flood, gaggle, great unwashed*, group, herd, horde, host,
jam, legion, lot, mass, masses, meet, mob,
multitude, muster, organization, pack, party,
people, posse, press, rabble, rank and file*,
scores, sellout, set, stream, surge, swarm,
throng, troupe, tumult; CONCEPTS 381,417

crowd [n2] *special group of friends* bunch,
circle, clique, coterie, faction, group, in-crowd,
lot, posse, push, set; CONCEPTS 387,417

crowd [v] *cram, press into area* bear, bunch,
bundle, chock, cluster, congest, congregate,
crush, deluge, elbow, flock, gather, huddle, jam,
jam-pack*, justle, mass, muster, overcrowd,
pack, pack 'em in*, pack like sardines*, pile,
push, ram, sardine*, shove, squash, squeeze,
squish*, stream, surge, swamp, swarm, throng,
top off, troop; CONCEPTS 208,740 —*Ant.* abandon, leave, retreat

crowded [adj] *busy, congested* awash, brimful,
brimming, chock-full, clean, close, compact,
crammed, cramped, crushed, dense, elbow-to-
elbow*, filled to the rafters*, fit to bust*, full,
full house*, full up*, huddled, jammed, jam-
packed*, loaded, lousy with*, massed, mobbed,
mob scene*, overflowing, packed, populous,
sardined*, sold out, SRO*, standing room
only*, stiff with*, stuffed, swarming, teeming,
thick, thickset, thronged, tight, topped off, up to
here*, up to the hilt*, wall-to-wall*; CONCEPTS
481,483,774 —*Ant.* empty, uncongested, uncrowded, unfilled

crown [n1] *top; best* acme, apex, climax, crest,
culmination, fastigium, head, meridian, peak,
perfection, pinnacle, roof, summit, tip, top,
ultimate, vertex, zenith; CONCEPTS 706,836
—*Ant.* bottom, worst

crown [n2] *tiara for royalty* chaplet, circlet,
coronal, coronet, diadem, garland, headband,
headdress, wreath; CONCEPT 452

crown [n3] *royalty* crowned head, monarch,
monarchy, potentate, ruler, sovereign, sovereignty, supreme ruler, the throne; CONCEPT 422

crown [v1] *reward, dignify* adorn, arm, authorize, commission, coronate, delegate, determine, dower, enable, endow, endue, ennoble,
enthrone, erect, establish, exalt, festoon, fix,
heighten, honor, inaugurate, induct, install,
invest, raise, sanction, settle, set up, stabilize,
strengthen; CONCEPTS 50,69,88 —*Ant.* dishonor,
disregard, fine, punish

crown [v2] *be the culmination of* cap, climax,
complete, consummate, crest, finish, fulfill, perfect, put finishing touch on, round off, surmount,
terminate, top, top off; CONCEPTS 234,706

crown [v3] *hit, usually on head* biff, box, cuff,
knock, punch, smite, strike; CONCEPT 189

crowning [adj] *climactic* consummate, culminating, excellent, final, paramount, principal,
sovereign, supreme, ultimate; CONCEPTS 531,548

crucial [adj] *critical, important* acute, central,
clamorous, climacteric, climatic, compelling,
deciding, decisive, desperate, dire, essential,
hanging by thread*, high-priority, imperative,
insistent, momentous, necessary, on thin ice*,
pivotal, pressing, searching, showdown*,
touch and go*, touchy, urgent, vital; CONCEPT
568 —*Ant.* inessential, trivial, uncritical,
unimportant

crucify [v1] *execute; torture near to death* excruciate, hang, harrow, kill, martyr, martyrize, nail to cross, persecute, rack, torment, torture; CONCEPT 252 —Ant. exalt

crucify [v2] *browbeat, destroy with words* afflict, agonize, bedevil, bother, harrow, ill-treat, lampoon, pan, ridicule, smite, tear to pieces*, torment, torture, try, wipe the floor with*; CONCEPTS 7,19,52 —Ant. compliment, exalt, laud, praise

crude [adj1] *vulgar, unpolished in manner* awkward, backward, barnyard*, boorish, cheap, cloddish, clumsy, coarse, crass, dirty, earthy, filthy, foul, grody*, gross*, ignorant, ill-bred, indecent, indelicate, inelegant, insensible, lewd, loud, loud-mouthed, loutish, lowbred, oafish, obscene, raunchy*, raw, rough, rude, savage, smutty*, tacky*, tactless, uncouth, unenlightened, ungainly, unskillful; CONCEPTS 267,401 —Ant. gentle, nice, polished, refined, tasteful

crude [adj2] *unrefined, natural* amateurish, callow, coarse, green, harsh, homemade, homespun, immature, impure, inexpert, in the rough*, makeshift, outline, prentice, primitive, raw, rough, rough-hewn, rude, rudimentary, rustic, simple, sketchy, thick, undeveloped, unfinished, unformed, ungraded, unmatured, unmilled, unpolished, unprepared, unprocessed, unproficient, unsorted, untaught, untrained, unworked, unwrought; CONCEPTS 562,578, 589,797 —Ant. formal, planned, refined, sophisticated, stilted

cruel [adj] *vicious, pitiless; causing pain* atrocious, barbarous, bestial, bitter, bloodthirsty, brutal, brutish, callous, cold-blooded, degenerate, demoniac, depraved, evil, excruciating, ferocious, fierce, flinty, hard, hard-hearted, harsh, hateful, heartless, hellish, implacable, inexorable, inhuman, inhumane, malevolent, merciless, monstrous, painful, pernicious, poignant, rancorous, relentless, revengeful, ruthless, sadistic, sinful, spiteful, tyrannical, unfeeling, unkind, unnatural, unrelenting, vengeful, vicious, virulent, wicked; CONCEPTS 401,570 —Ant. charitable, compassionate, considerate, feeling, gentle, kind, merciful, sympathetic, thoughtful, uncruel

cruelty [n] *brutality, harshness* animality, barbarism, barbarity, bestiality, bloodthirstiness, brutishness, callousness, coarseness, coldness, depravity, despotism, ferocity, fiendishness, fierceness, hard-heartedness, heartlessness, inhumanity, insensibility, insensitiveness, malice, malignity, masochism, mercilessness, murderousness, persecution, rancor, ruthlessness, sadism, savageness, savagery, severity, spite, spitefulness, torture, truculence, unfeelingness, unkindness, venom, viciousness, wickedness; CONCEPT 633 —Ant. charity, compassion, consideration, feeling, gentility, kindness, mercy, niceness, thoughtfulness

cruise [n] *sailing expedition* boat trip, crossing, jaunt, journey, sail, sailing, sea trip, voyage; CONCEPTS 224,292,363

cruise [v] *sail* boat, coast, drift, fare, gad, gallivant, go, hie, jaunt, journey, keep steady pace, meander, navigate, pass, proceed, push on, repair, travel, voyage, wander about, wend; CONCEPTS 147,151,159,224

crumb [n] *tiny bit, morsel* atom, dab, dash, dram, drop, grain, iota, jot, mite, ounce, particle, pinch, scrap, seed, shred, sliver, smidgen, snippet, soupçon, speck; CONCEPT 831

crumble [v] *break or fall into pieces* break up, collapse, crumb, crush, decay, decompose, degenerate, deteriorate, disintegrate, dissolve, fragment, go to pieces, granulate, grind, molder, perish, powder, pulverize, putrefy, triturate, tumble; CONCEPTS 181,248,469 —Ant. build, put together

crumbly [adj] *brittle* breakable, corroded, crisp, crunchy, decayed, degenerated, deteriorated, deteriorating, disintegrated, eroded, fragile, frail, frangible, friable, oxidized, perishing, powdery, pulverizable, rotted, rotten, rusted, shivery, short, soft, worn; CONCEPTS 485,606 —Ant. flexible, pliable, soft

crummy [adj] *lousy* cheap, contemptible, crappy*, grotty, inferior, miserable, pathetic, poor, rotten, second-rate, shabby, sub-par, third-rate, useless, worthless; CONCEPT 571

crumple [v] *make or become wrinkled* break down, buckle, cave in, collapse, crease, crimp, crimple, crinkle, crush, fall, fold, give way, go to pieces, pucker, rimple, ruck, rumple, screw, scrunch, shrivel, wad, wrinkle; CONCEPTS 184,208,252 —Ant. straighten

crunch [n] *crucial point* crisis, critical point, crux, difficulty, emergency, hour of decision*, moment of truth*, problem, test, trouble, trying time*; CONCEPTS 388,674,675 —Ant. trivia

crunch [v] *grind, chew* beat, bite, champ, chaw, chomp, crush, gnaw, masticate, munch, ruminate, scrunch; CONCEPTS 169,186

crunchy [adj] *brittle* chewy, crackling, crisp, crispy, crumbly, crusty; CONCEPT 606

crusade [n] *campaign for cause* cause, demonstration, drive, evangelism, expedition, holy war, jihad, march, movement, push; CONCEPT 300

crush [n1] *crowd of animate beings* drove, gathering, horde, huddle, jam, multitude, party, press, push, throng, tumult; CONCEPTS 417,432

crush [n2] *infatuation* beguin, desire, flame, love affair, passion, puppy love*, torch; CONCEPT 20 —Ant. dislike, hate, hatred

crush [v1] *compress, smash* beat, bray, break, bruise, buck, comminute, contriturate, contuse, crease, crowd, crumble, crunch, embrace, enfold, express, hug, jam, kablooey*, mash, pound, powder, press, pulverize, push, romp, rumple, squash, squeeze, squish, total*, trample, tread, triturate, wrinkle; CONCEPTS 208,219,246,252 —Ant. let go, release, uncompress, unwrinkle

crush [v2] *defeating soundly* annihilate, bear down, beat, blot out*, blow away*, conquer, defeat, demolish, extinguish, force down, ice*, kill, obliterate, overcome, overpower, overwhelm, quelch, quell, reduce, ruin, squelch, stamp out*, strangle, subdue, subjugate, suppress, vanquish, wreck; CONCEPTS 95,252 —Ant. lose, surrender, yield

crush [v3] *humiliate* abash, browbeat, chagrin, dispose of, dump, hurt, mortify, overwhelm, put away*, put down*, quash, quell, shame, suppress; CONCEPTS 7,19 —Ant. build up, compliment, encourage, inspirit, praise

crust [n] *stiff outer layer; coating* band, bloom, border, caking, coat, concretion, covering, edge, encrustation, film, hull, incrustation, integument, layer, outside, rind, scab, shell, skin, surface, verge; CONCEPT 484

crusty [adj1] *irritable, often due to old age* abrupt, bluff, blunt, brief, brusque, cantankerous, captious, choleric, crabbed, crabby*, cranky, cross, curt, dour, gruff, harsh, illhumored, irascible, peevish, prickly, sarcastic, saturnine, scornful, short, short-tempered, snappish, snarling, snippety, snippy, splenetic, surly, testy, touchy, vinegary*; CONCEPT 401 —*Ant.* cheerful, happy, nice, pleasant

crusty [adj2] *brittle on outside* crisp, crispy, crunchy, friable, hard, short, well-baked,. well-done; CONCEPTS 462,606 —*Ant.* flexible, pliable, pliant, soft, soggy

crux [n] *most important part* body, bottom line*, core, decisive point, essence, gist, heart, kernel, matter, meat*, meat and potatoes*, nitty-gritty, nub, pith, purport, substance, thrust; CONCEPTS 668,826 —*Ant.* trivia

cry [n1] *weeping and making sad sounds* bawl, bawling, bewailing, blubber, blubbering, howl, howling, keening, lament, lamentation, mourning, shedding tears, snivel, snivelling, sob, sobbing, sorrowing, tears, the blues*, wailing, weep, whimpering, yowl; CONCEPTS 77,469

cry [n2] *calling out; yelling* acclamation, bark, bawl, bay, bellow, cackle, call, caw, chatter, cheer, clack, clamor, cluck, coo, crow, ejaculation, exclamation, expletive, fuss, gobble, groan, grunt, hiss, holler, hoot, howl, hullabaloo, hurrah, meow, mewling, moo, motto, nicker, note, outcry, pipe, quack, report, roar, ruckus, scream, screech, shout, shriek, song, squall, squawk, squeak, trill, uproar, vociferation, wail, whine, whinny, whistle, whoop, yammer, yawp*, yell, yelp, yoo-hoo; CONCEPTS 47,77,278

cry [v1] *weep and make sad sounds* bawl, bemoan, bewail, blub, blubber, boohoo*, break down, burst into tears*, caterwaul, choke up, complain, crack up*, deplore, dissolve in tears*, fret, grieve, groan, howl, keen, lament, let go, let it all out*, mewl, moan, mourn, put on the weeps*, regret, ring the blues*, shed bitter tears*, shed tears, sigh, sniff, snivel, sob, sorrow, squall, turn on waterworks*, wail, weep, whimper, whine, yammer, yowl; CONCEPTS 77,469

cry [v2] *call out, yell* bark, bawl, bay, bellow, bleat, cackle, call, caw, chatter, cheer, clack, clamor, cluck, coo, croak, crow, ejaculate, exclaim, gabble, growl, grunt, hail, hiss, holler, holler out, hoot, howl, low, meow, moo, nicker, pipe, quack, roar, scream, screech, shout, shriek, sing out, snarl, squawk, trill, tweet, twitter, vociferate, whinny, whistle, whoop, yawp*, yelp; CONCEPTS 47,77

cry [v3] *advertise* announce, bark*, broadcast, build up, hawk, hype*, press-agent*, proclaim, promulgate, publicize, publish, puff*, trumpet*; CONCEPT 324

crybaby [n] *malcontent* bellyacher, complainer, critic, faultfinder, griper, grumbler, moaner, sissy, softy*, whiner, wimp*, wuss*; CONCEPT 412

crypt [n] *burial place* catacomb, cave, cavern, cell, chamber, compartment, grave, grotto, mausoleum, room, sepulcher, tomb, undercroft, vault; CONCEPT 305

cryptic [adj] *secret; obscure in meaning* abstruse, ambiguous, apocryphal, arcane, cabalistic, dark, Delphian, Delphic, enigmatic, equivocal, esoteric, evasive, hidden, incomprehensible, inexplicable, murky, mysterious, mystic, mystical, mystifying, occult, opaque, oracular, perplexing, puzzling, recondite, secretive, strange, tenebrous, unclear, unfathomable, uninformative, vague, veiled; CONCEPTS 267, 576,682 —*Ant.* clear, obvious, plain, seen, straightforward

crystal [adj] *clear, transparent* clear-cut, limpid, lucent, lucid, luminous, pellucid, translucent, transpicuous, unblurred; CONCEPTS 617,618 —*Ant.* clouded, foggy

cubicle [n] *office compartment* booth, cell, chamber, cubbyhole, desk, nook, office, pigeonhole, room, stall, work area; CONCEPT 434

cuddle [v] *hold fondly, closely* bundle, burrow, caress, clasp, cosset, curl up, dandle, embrace, enfold, feel up*, fondle, huddle, hug, kiss, love, nestle, nuzzle, pet, snug, snuggle, touch; CONCEPTS 190,375 —*Ant.* push away

cuddly [adj] *huggable, embraceable* caressible, cuddlesome, kissable, lovable, plump, snuggly, soft, warm; CONCEPT 485 —*Ant.* despicable, disgusting

cudgel [n] *baton for hitting* bastinado, bat, billy*, billyclub, birch, blackjack, bludgeon, cane, club, cosh*, ferule, mace, nightstick, paddle, rod, sap, shill, shillelagh, spontoon, stick, switch, truncheon; CONCEPT 500

cue [n] *signal to act* catchword, clue, hint, hot lead*, idea, indication, inkling, innuendo, in the wind*, intimation, job, key, lead, mnemonic, nod, notion, prod, prompt, prompting, reminder, sign, suggestion, telltale*, tip-off, warning; CONCEPTS 278,284,628

cuff [n] *beating with hands* belt, biff, box, buffet, chop, clip, clout, hit, knock, poke, punch, rap, slap, smack, sock, thump, wallop, whack; CONCEPT 189

cuff [v] *beat with hands* bat, belt, biff, box, buffet, clap, clobber*, clout, hit, knock, pummel, punch, slap, smack, spank, thump, whack; CONCEPT 189

cuisine [n] *food* cooking, dishes, eats*, fare, grub*, meal, menu; CONCEPT 459

cull [v1] *pick out for reason* choose, discriminate, elect, extract, glean, mark, optate, opt for, pluck, prefer, select, sift, single out, take, thin, thin out, winnow; CONCEPTS 41,142

cull [v2] *gather* accumulate, amass, collect, extract, garner, glean, pick up, round up; CONCEPT 109

culminate [v] *come to a climax* cap, climax, close, come to a head*, conclude, crown, end, end up, finish, go over the mountain*, go the route*, rise to crescendo, round off, shoot one's wad*, terminate, top off*, wind up*; CONCEPT 119 —*Ant.* begin, commence, open, start

culmination [n] *conclusion; climactic stage* acme, all the way*, apex, apogee, blow off*, capper*, climax, completion, consummation, critical mass, crown, crowning touch, finale, finish, height, limit, maximum, meridian, ne plus ultra, noon, payoff, peak, perfection, pinnacle, punch line*, summit, top, zenith; CONCEPTS 230,635,676 —Ant. beginning, commencement, opening, start

culpable [adj] responsible for action amiss, answerable, at fault, blamable, blameful, blameworthy, caught, caught in the act*, caught red-handed*, censurable, demeritorious, dirty, found wanting, guilty, hung up, impeachable, indictable, in the wrong, liable, off base, out of line*, punishable, reprehensible, responsible, sinful, smoking gun*, to blame, unholy, wrong; CONCEPTS 404,545 —Ant. blameless, inculpable, innocent, not guilty, right

culprit [n] person responsible for wrongdoing con, convict, criminal, delinquent, evildoer, ex-con, felon, fugitive, guilty party, jailbird*, malefactor, miscreant, offender, rascal, sinner, transgressor, wrongdoer, yardbird*; CONCEPT 412

cult [n1] group sharing belief band, body, church, clan, clique, creed, denomination, faction, faith, following, party, persuasion, religion, school, sect; CONCEPTS 369,382

cult [n2] worship; form of ceremony admiration, ceremony, craze, creed, cultus, devotion, faddism, faith, idolization, liturgy, persuasion, religion, reverence, rite, ritual, veneration; CONCEPTS 410,689

cultivate [v1] develop land for growing breed, crop, dress, farm, fertilize, garden, harvest, labor, manage, mature, plant, plow, prepare, propagate, raise, ripen, seed, tend, till, work; CONCEPTS 253, 257 —Ant. destroy, ignore, neglect

cultivate [v2] enrich situation; give special attention advance, ameliorate, better, bolster, bring on, brownnose*, butter up*, cherish, civilize, court, develop, discipline, elevate, encourage, enrich, foster, further, get in with*, get next to*, get on good side of*, improve, nourish, nurse, nurture, play up to*, polish, promote, refine, run after, seek friendship, shine up to*, suck up to*, take pains with, train; CONCEPTS 244,384 —Ant. ignore, neglect

cultivate [v3] nurture, take care of aid, ameliorate, better, cherish, devote oneself to, educate, encourage, forward, foster, further, help, improve, instruct, nurse, patronize, promote, pursue, raise, rear, refine, support, teach, train; CONCEPTS 110,295 —Ant. ignore, neglect

cultivation [n1] development of land for growing agrology, agronomics, agronomy, farming, gardening, horticulture, planting, plowing, tillage, tilling, working; CONCEPT 257

cultivation [n2] culture, sophistication, education advancement, aestheticism, breeding, civility, civilization, delicacy, discernment, discrimination, enlightenment, gentility, good taste, grounding, improvement, learning, letters, manners, polish, progress, refined taste, refinement, schooling, taste; CONCEPTS 411,655,673 —Ant. ignorance, unsophistication

cultivation [n3] nurture, help advancement, advocacy, development, encouragement, enhancement, fostering, furtherance, patronage, promotion, support; CONCEPTS 110,657 —Ant. destruction, harm, hurt, neglect

cultural [adj] educational, enlightening adorning, advancing, artistic, beautifying, beneficial, broadening, civilizing, constructive, corrective, developmental, dignifying, disciplining, edifying, educative, elevating, ennobling, enriching, expanding, glorifying, helpful, humane, humanizing, influential, inspirational, instructive, learned, liberal, liberalizing, nurturing, ornamenting, polishing, promoting, raising, refined, refining, regenerative, socializing, stimulating, uplifting, widening; CONCEPTS 537,555,589

culture [n1] breeding, education, sophistication ability, accomplishment, address, aestheticism, art, capacity, civilization, class, courtesy, cultivation, delicacy, dignity, discrimination, dress, elegance, elevation, enlightenment, erudition, experience, fashion, finish, gentility, good taste, grace, improvement, kindness, learning, manners, nobility, perception, polish, politeness, practice, proficiency, refinement, savoir-faire, science, skill, tact, training, urbanity; CONCEPTS 388,633,678

culture [n2] ideas, values of a people arts and sciences, civilization, convention, customs, development, ethnology, folklore, folkways, grounding, habit, humanism, knowledge, lifestyle, mores, society, the arts, way of life; CONCEPTS 388,689

culture [n3] development of land agriculture, agrology, agronomics, agronomy, cultivation, farming, gardening, raising, tending; CONCEPT 257

cultured [adj] well-bred, experienced able, accomplished, advanced, aesthetic, appreciative, au courant, blue-stocking*, chivalrous, civilized, courteous, cultivated, distingue, educated, elegant, enlightened, erudite, gallant, genteel, highbrow*, high-class, informed, intellectual, intelligent, knowledgeable, lettered, liberal, literary, literate, mannerly, polished, polite, refined, savant, scholarly, sensitive, sophisticated, tasteful, tolerant, traveled, understanding, up-to-date, urbane, versed, well-informed; CONCEPT 550 —Ant. ignorant, inexperienced, stupid, unsophisticated

culvert [n] ditch for flow of water canal, channel, conduit, drain, duct, gutter, pipe, watercourse; CONCEPT 509

cumbersome [adj] clumsy, awkward bulky, burdensome, clunker, clunking, clunky, cumbrous, embarrassing, galumphing, heavy, hefty, incommodious, inconvenient, leaden, massive, oppressive, ponderous, tiresome, unhandy, unmanageable, unwieldy, wearisome, weighty; CONCEPTS 544,773 —Ant. graceful

cumulative [adj] accruing; growing in size or effect accumulative, additive, additory, advancing, aggregate, amassed, augmenting, chain, collective, heaped, heightening, increasing, increscent, intensifying, magnifying, multiplying, snowballing*, summative; CONCEPTS 540,548,786 —Ant. decreasing, subtracting

cunning [adj1] clever acute, artful, astute, cagey, canny, crafty, crazy like fox*, deep, fancy footwork*, foxy, guileful, insidious, keen, knowing, Machiavellian, sharp, shifty, shrewd, slick, slippery, sly, sly boots*, smart, smarts, smooth, street-smart*, streetwise*, subtle, tricky, wary, wily; CONCEPTS 401,545 —Ant. gullible, kind, naive, shy

cr
cu

cunning [adj2] *imaginative* able, adroit, canny, clever, crackerjack*, deft, dexterous, ingenious, intelligent, masterful, skillful, slighty, sly, smart, smooth, subtle, well-laid, well-planned; CONCEPT 402 —Ant. unclever, unimaginative

cup [n] *container for drinking* beaker, bowl, cannikin, chalice, cupful, demitasse, draught, drink, goblet, grail, mug, potion, stein, taster, teacup, tumbler, vessel; CONCEPT 494

cupboard [n] *storage cabinet* buffet, closet, depository, facility, locker, press, repository, sideboard, storeroom, wardrobe; CONCEPT 443

cupidity [n] *greed, strong desire* acquisitiveness, avarice, avariciousness, avidity, covetousness, craving, eagerness, graspingness, greediness, hunger, infatuation, itching*, longing, lust, passion, possessiveness, rapaciousness, rapacity, voracity, yearning; CONCEPTS 20,709 —Ant. dislike, distaste

cur [n1] *rotten, lowly animate being* blackguard, black sheep*, bum, cad, coward, dog*, good-for-nothing*, heel*, hound*, ne'er-do-well*, rat*, riffraff*, scoundrel, scum*, skunk*, snake*, stinker*, toad*, villain, worm*, wretch, yellow dog*; CONCEPTS 389,412

cur [n2] *animal of mixed breed* crossbreed, hybrid, mongrel, mutt; CONCEPT 394

curable [adj] *able to be improved, fixed* amenable, capable, correctable, corrigible, healable, improvable, mendable, not hopeless, not too bad, reparative, restorable, subject to cure; CONCEPTS 314,485 —Ant. incurable, unhelpable

curative [adj] *healing, health-giving* alleviative, beneficial, corrective, curing, healthful, helpful, invigorating, medicable, medicative, medicinal, pick-me-up*, remedial, remedying, restorative, salutary, sanative, shot in the arm*, therapeutic, tonic, vulnerary, what the doctor ordered*, wholesome; CONCEPTS 314,537 —Ant. harmful, hurting, injurious, painful

curator [n] *caretaker of collection* administrator, conservator, custodian, director, guardian, keeper, manager, steward; CONCEPT 348

curb [n] *restraining device; check* barrier, border, brake, bridle, chain, control, deterrent, edge, harness, hindrance, ledge, limitation, lip, rein, restrainer, restraint, restriction, rim; CONCEPTS 376,497,652,745 —Ant. encouragement, opening

curb [v] *repress, restrict* abstain, bit, bottle up*, box in, bridle, bring to screeching halt*, check, clog, constrain, contain, control, cook*, cool down, cool off, deny, entrammel, fetter, hamper, hinder, hobble, hog-tie*, hold back, hold down, hold in, ice*, impede, inhibit, keep lid on*, keep tight rein on*, leash, manacle, moderate, muzzle, refrain, rein in, restrain, retard, scrub*, send up, shackle, subdue, suppress, tame, tie, tie up, withhold; CONCEPTS 121,130 —Ant. aid, assist, encourage, foster, help

curdle [v] *sour; change into coagulated substance* acerbate, acidify, acidulate, clabber, clot, coagulate, condense, congeal, curd, ferment, go off, spoil, thicken, turn, turn sour; CONCEPT 456

cure [n] *solution to problem, often health* aid, alleviation, antidote, assistance, catholicon, corrective, counteractant, counteragent, countermeasure, drug, elixir, elixir vitae, fix, healing,

healing agent, help, medicament, medicant, medication, medicine, nostrum, panacea, pharmacon, physic, placebo, proprietary, quick fix*, recovery, redress, remedy, reparation, restora-tive, therapeutic, treatment; CONCEPTS 110,307,311 —Ant. disease, problem

cure [v1] *heal, ease bad situation* alleviate, ameliorate, attend, better, cold turkey*, correct, doctor, dose, dress, dry out*, help, improve, kick, kick the habit*, make better, make healthy, make whole, medicate, mend, minister to, nurse, palliate, quit cold*, rectify, redress, rehabilitate, relieve, remedy, repair, restore, restore to health, right, shake, sweat it out*, treat; CONCEPTS 126,244,310 —Ant. depress, hurt, injure

cure [v2] *cook, age food* dry, fire, harden, keep, kipper, pickle, preserve, salt, smoke, steel, temper; CONCEPT 170

curio [n] *knickknack* antique, bauble, bibelot, bygone, collectible, collector's item, objet d'art, toy, trifle, trinket, whatnot; CONCEPT 446

curiosity [n1] *intense desire to know, understand* concern, eagerness, inquiring mind, inquiringness, inquisitiveness, interest, interestingness, intrusiveness, investigation, meddlesomeness, meddling, mental acquisitiveness, nosiness, officiousness, prying, questioning, regard, searching, snoopiness, snooping, thirst for knowledge; CONCEPTS 20,410 —Ant. disinterest, indifference

curiosity [n2] *odd item* anomaly, bibelot, bygone, conversation piece, curio, exoticism, freak, knickknack, marvel, monstrosity, nonesuch, objet d'art, oddity, peculiar object, prodigy, rarity, singular object, trinket, unusual object, wonder; CONCEPT 260 —Ant. normality

curious [adj1] *desiring knowledge, understanding* analytical, disquisitive, examining, impertinent, inquiring, inquisitive, inspecting, interested, interfering, intrusive, investigative, meddlesome, meddling, nosy, peeping, peering, prurient, prying, puzzled, questioning, scrutinizing, searching, snoopy*, tampering; CONCEPTS 403,542 —Ant. disinterested, incurious, indifferent, uninterested

curious [adj2] *very odd* bizarre, exotic, extraordinary, marvelous, mysterious, novel, oddball, peculiar, puzzling, quaint, queer, rare, remarkable, singular, strange, unconventional, unexpected, unique, unorthodox, unusual, weird, wonderful; CONCEPTS 547,564 —Ant. average, normal, ordinary, usual

curl [n] *loop, ringlet, curve* coil, crimp, crispation, curlicue, flourish, frizz, kink, quirk, spiral, swirl, twist, wave, whorl; CONCEPTS 418,436 —Ant. line

curl [v] *bend, loop* buckle, coil, contort, convolute, corkscrew, crimp, crinkle, crisp, crook, curve, entwine, fold, form into ringlets, frizz, indent, kink, lap, meander, ringlet, ripple, roll, scallop, snake, spiral, swirl, turn, twine, twirl, twist, undulate, wave, wind, wreathe, writhe, zigzag; CONCEPTS 147,184,213 —Ant. straighten

curly [adj] *looping, forming ringlets* coiled, convoluted, corkscrew, crimped, crimpy, crinkling, crinkly, crisp, curled, curling, frizzed, frizzy, fuzzy, kinky, looped, permed, spiralled, waved, waving, wavy, winding, wound; CONCEPTS 406,486 —*Ant.* straight

currency [*n*] *paper and coin money of a country* almighty dollar*, bills, bread*, cabbage*, cash, chicken feed*, coinage, coins, cold cash*, dinero*, dough*, folding money, green stuff*, legal tender, medium of exchange, moolah*, notes, piece of change*, roll*, specie, wad*; CONCEPT 340

current [*adj*] *contemporary; common* accepted, accustomed, afoot, circulating, common knowledge, customary, cutting-edge*, doing, existent, extant, fad, fashionable, general, going around, hot*, in, in circulation, in progress, instant, in the mainstream, in the news, in use, in vogue, leading-edge*, mod*, modern, now*, on front burner*, ongoing, popular, present, present-day, prevailing, prevalent, rampant, regnant, rife, ruling, state-of-the-art, swinging, topical, trendy, up-to-date, widespread; CONCEPTS 530,820 —*Ant.* antiquated, old, old-fashioned, past, uncommon, uncontemporary

current [*n*] *flow of something, usually water* course, draught, drift, ebb and flow, flood, flux, jet, juice, progression, river, run, rush, spate, stream, tidal motion, tide; CONCEPTS 514,519,738

curriculum [*n*] *course of study* educational program, modules, program of studies, schedule, studies, subjects, syllabus; CONCEPT 287

curse [*n1*] *hateful, swearing remark* anathema, ban, bane, blaspheming, blasphemy, commination, cursing, cussing*, cuss word*, damning, denunciation, dirty name*, dirty word*, double whammy*, execration, expletive, four-letter word*, fulmination, imprecation, malediction, malison, naughty words*, no-no*, oath, objuration, obloquy, obscenity, profanation, profanity, sacrilege, swearing, swear word, vilification, whammy*; CONCEPTS 54,278 —*Ant.* compliment, praise

curse [*n2*] *misfortune wished upon someone* affliction, bane, burden, calamity, cancer, cross, disaster, evil, evil eye*, hydra, jinx, ordeal, pestilence, plague, scourge, torment, tribulation, trouble, vexation, voodoo; CONCEPTS 674,675

cursed [*adj1*] *damned, doomed for bad ending* accursed, bedeviled, blankety-blank*, blasted, blessed, blighted, cast out, confounded, doggone*, excommunicate, execrable, fey, foredoomed, hell fire*, ill-fated, infernal, snakebit*, star-crossed, unholy, unsanctified, villainous, voodooed*; CONCEPTS 548,571 —*Ant.* blessed

cursed [*adj2*] *detestable, hateful* abominable, accursed, atrocious, damnable, devilish, disgusting, execrable, fiendish, heinous, infamous, infernal, loathsome, odious, pernicious, pestilential, vile; CONCEPTS 404,571 —*Ant.* great, kind, nice, sweet

cursory [*adj*] *casual, hasty* brief, careless, depthless, desultory, fast, half-assed*, half-baked*, haphazard, hit or miss*, hurried, offhand, passing, perfunctory, quick, random, rapid, shallow, short, sketchy, slapdash, slight, sloppy, speedy, summary, superficial, swift, uncritical; CONCEPTS 562,588,589 —*Ant.* complete, meticulous, painstaking, perfect, thorough, unhurried

curt [*adj*] *abrupt, rude* blunt, breviloquent, brief, brusque, churlish, compendiary, compendious, concise, crusty, gruff, imperious, laconic, offhand, peremptory, pithy, sharp, short, short and sweet, snappish, snippety, snippy, succinct, summary, tart, terse, unceremonious, uncivil, ungracious; CONCEPT 267 —*Ant.* ceremonious, civil, gracious, lengthy, polite

curtail [*v*] *cut short; abridge* abbreviate, boil down, chop, clip, contract, cramp, cut, cut back, decrease, diminish, dock, downsize, get to meat*, halt, lessen, lop, minify, pare down, put in nutshell*, reduce, retrench, roll back, shorten, slash, trim, truncate; CONCEPTS 130,236,247 —*Ant.* extend, increase, lengthen, prolong

curtain [*n*] *window covering* blind, decoration, drape, drapery, film, hanging, jalousie, oleo, portiere, rag, roller, screen, shade, shield, shroud, shutter, valance, veil, Venetian blind; CONCEPT 444

curtains [*n*] *the end* bitter end, death, end of life, end of the line*, exit, extinction, lights out*, taps*; CONCEPTS 195,304

curvaceous [*adj*] *voluptuous, full-figured* bosomy, buxom, curvesome, curvilinear, curvy, rounded, shapely, statuesque, well-developed, well-proportioned, well-rounded, zaftig*; CONCEPTS 406,490 —*Ant.* flat

curvature [*n*] *rounded part of thing, usually body part* arc, arch, arching, bend, bow, curve, curving, curvity, deflection, flexure, incurvation, round, shape; CONCEPTS 754,757

curve [*n*] *arched, rounded line or object* ambit, arc, arch, bend, bight, bow, camber, catenary, chord, circle, circuit, circumference, compass, concavity, contour, crook, curlicue, curvation, curvature, ellipse, festoon, flexure, hairpin, half-moon, helix, horseshoe, hyperbola, incurvation, incurvature, loop, meniscus, ogee, parabola, quirk, rondure, round, sinuosity, sweep, swerve, trajectory, turn, vault, whorl; CONCEPT 436 —*Ant.* line

curve [*v*] *bending in a shape or course* arc, arch, bend, bow, buckle, bulge, coil, concave, convex, crook, crumple, curl, deviate, divert, gyrate, hook, incurve, inflect, loop, round, skew, snake, spiral, stoop, swerve, turn, twist, veer, wind, wreathe; CONCEPTS 147,184,213,738 —*Ant.* straighten

curved [*adj*] *bowed, bent* arced, arched, arciform, arrondi, biflected, circular, compass, crooked, curly, curvaceous, curvilinear, declinate, elliptical, embowed, humped, incurvate, incurved, looped, loopy, round, rounded, serpentine, sigmoid, sinuous, skewed, snaky, S-shaped, sweeping, swirly, turned, twisted, twisting, twisty, wreathed; CONCEPTS 486,490 —*Ant.* straight

cushion [*n*] *pillow, pad* beanbag, bolster, buffer, bumper, fender, hassock, headrest, mat, rest, seat, sham, squab, woolsack; CONCEPTS 444,464,484

cushion [*v*] *pad, protect from blow* bolster, buttress, cradle, dampen, deaden, insulate, muffle, pillow, seclude, soften, stifle, support, suppress; CONCEPT 680

cushy [*adj*] *lush, comfortable* agreeable, comfy*, easy, pleasant, plum, soft*, undemanding; CONCEPT 334

custodian [n] *caretaker, maintenance person* baby sitter, bodyguard, Cerberus, claviger, cleaner, cleaning person, concierge, curator, escort, guardian, housesitter, keeper, maintenance person, manager, overseer, protector, sitter, steward, super*, superintendent, supervisor, swamper*, warden, watchdog, watchperson; CONCEPT 348

custody [n1] *supervision, charge of something* aegis, auspices, care, conservation, custodianship, guardianship, keeping, management, observation, preservation, protection, safekeeping, salvation, superintendence, trusteeship, tute-lage, ward, wardship, watch; CONCEPT 117

custody [n2] *confinement, jailing* arrest, detention, duress, imprisonment, incarceration, jail, keeping; CONCEPTS 90,691 —Ant. freedom, liberation, liberty

custom [n1] *habitual action* addiction, beaten path*, characteristic, consuetude, daily grind*, fashion, form, grind*, groove, habit, habitude, hang-up*, into*, manner, matter of course, mode, observance, practice, praxis, precedent, procedure, proprieties, routine, rule, second nature*, shot, swim, thing, trick, usage, use, way, wont; CONCEPT 633 —Ant. departure, deviation, difference, divergence, irregularity

custom [n2] *ritual, traditional action* attitude, canon, ceremony, character, convention, conventionalism, design, dictates, established way, etiquette, fashion, folkways, form, formality, inheritance, manner, matter of course, method, mode, mold, mores, observance, observation, pattern, performance, policy, practice, praxis, precedent, precept, rite, routine, rule, second nature*, style, system, taste, type, unwritten law, unwritten rule, usage, use, vogue, way; CONCEPTS 644,688 —Ant. departure, deviation

customarily [adv] *ordinarily; as a rule* as a matter of course, as usual, commonly, consistently, conventionally, frequently, generally, habitually, naturally, normally, regularly, routinely, traditionally, usually, wontedly; CONCEPTS 530,547 —Ant. differently, divergently, occasionally, rarely, sometimes

customary [adj] *usual, established* accepted, according to Hoyle*, accustomed, acknowledged, by the numbers*, chronic, common, confirmed, conventional, established, everyday, familiar, fashionable, frequent, general, habitual, household, in a rut*, in the groove*, normal, ordinary, orthodox, playing it safe*, popular, prescriptive, recognized, regular, regulation, routine, same old*, SOP*, standard, standard operating procedure*, stipulated, traditional, understood, universal, wonted; CONCEPTS 530,547 —Ant. abnormal, different, irregular, occasional, rare, sometime, unusual

customer [n] *buyer of goods, services* client, clientele, consumer, habitué, patron, prospect, purchaser, regular shopper; CONCEPT 348 —Ant. owner

cut [n1] *incision* carving, chip, chop, cleavage, cleft, dissection, fissure, furrow, gash, graze, groove, intersection, kerf, laceration, mark, nick, nip, notch, opening, passage, penetration, pierce, prick, rabbet, rent, rip, scarification, sculpture, section, shave, slash, slit, slot, snip, stab, stroke, trench, trim, wound; CONCEPT 309

cut [n2] *reduction, diminution* cutback, decrease, decrement, downsize, economy, fall, lessening, lowering, reduction, saving; CONCEPTS 698,776 —Ant. increase

cut [n3] *portion of profit* allotment, allowance, bite, chop*, division, kickback*, lot, member, moiety, part, partage, percentage, piece, quota, section, segment, share, slice; CONCEPT 344

cut [n4] *style, shape of clothing* configuration, construction, fashion, figure, form, look, mode; CONCEPTS 655,754

cut [n5] *insult* abuse, hateful remark, indignity, offense; CONCEPT 52 —Ant. compliment, nicety, praise

cut [n6] *type, kind* cast, description, feather, ilk, lot, mold, sort, stamp; CONCEPT 378

cut [v1] *sever, chop with sharp instrument; incise* amputate, behead, bisect, bite, carve, chine, chip, chisel, cleave, clip, crop, curtail, decussate, dice, dispatch, dissect, dissever, divide, facet, fell, flitch, gash, guillotine, hack, hash, hew, intersect, lacerate, lay open, level, lop, massacre, mince, mow, mow down, nick, notch, part, penetrate, perforate, pierce, prune, puncture, quarter, rabbet, raze, reap, rend, rip, rive, saber, saw, scarify, scissor, score, scythe, separate, shave, shear, sickle, skive, slash, slaughter, slay, slice, slit, sliver, snip; CONCEPT 252

cut a deal [v] *make a deal* bargain, barter, bicker, dicker*, do business, hammer out a deal*, negotiate, trade, work out a deal*; CONCEPT 324

cutback [n] *decrease* abatement, belt-tightening, curtailment, decline, decrement, economy, lessening, lowering, reduction, reversal; CONCEPT 698 —Ant. increase, raise

cute [adj] *perky, attractive* adorable, beautiful, charming, dainty, delightful, pleasant, pretty; CONCEPTS 404,579 —Ant. homely, ugly

cut in [v] *interrupt* break in, butt in*, chisel in*, horn in*, interfere, interpose, intervene, intrude, move in, obtrude; CONCEPT 234 —Ant. allow

cut off [v1] *prevent; interrupt* block, break in, bring to end, catch, close off, disconnect, discontinue, halt, insulate, intercept, intersect, intervene, intrude, isolate, obstruct, renounce, segregate, separate, sequester, suspend; CONCEPT 234 —Ant. allow, encourage, permit

cut off [v2] *disinherit in will* cut out of will, disown, renounce; CONCEPT 317 —Ant. give

cut out [v] *excise, remove* carve, cease, delete, displace, eliminate, exclude, exsect, extirpate, extract, give up, oust, pull out, refrain from, sever, stop, supersede, supplant, usurp; CONCEPT 211 —Ant. add, include

cut out for [adj] *adapted* adequate, competent, designed, equipped, fit, fitted, good for, qualified, suitable, suited; CONCEPT 558 —Ant. inadequate, incompetent, unfitted, unqualified, unsuitable, unsuited, wrong

cut short [v] *bring to an end; leave unfinished* abbreviate, abort, abridge, break off, check, diminish, end, finish, halt, hinder, intercept, interrupt, postpone, quit, shorten, stop, terminate; CONCEPTS 121,234 —Ant. continue, lengthen, prolong

cutthroat [adj] *ruthless* barbarous, blood-thirsty, cruel, dog-eat-dog*, ferocious, hard as nails*, merciless, pitiless, relentless, savage, unprincipled, vicious; CONCEPTS 401, 404

cutting [adj] *nasty, hateful* acerbic, acid, acrimonious, barbed, biting, bitter, caustic, clear-cut, crisp, hurtful, incisive, ingoing, malicious, penetrating, piercing, pointed, probing, raw, sarcastic, sardonic, scathing, severe, sharp, stinging, trenchant, wounding; CONCEPT 267 —*Ant.* kind, nice, pleasant

cutting edge [n] *newest technology* advancement, avant-garde, fore, forefront, front line, innovation, invention, leading edge, new wave, point, vanguard; CONCEPT 668

cut up [v1] *make fun of; criticize* censure, condemn, crucify, denounce, give a rough time*, knock, pan*, rap, reprehend, reprobate, ridicule, skin, vilify; CONCEPT 52

cut up [v2] *be rowdy* act up, caper, carry on*, cavort, clown, fool around, joke, misbehave, play, play jokes, romp, roughhouse, show off, whoop it up*; CONCEPT 384 —*Ant.* be serious

cut up [v3] *chop, mince* carve, dice, divide, slice; CONCEPT 176

cybernetics [n] *science studying brain function to design analogous mechanical systems* artificial intelligence, automatic technology, automation, autonetics, electronic communication, radiodynamics, robotization, telemechanics; CONCEPTS 274,349

cyberpunk [n] *computer hacker* computer nerd, engineer, geek, hacker, programmer; CONCEPT 348

cyberspace [n] *computer world* communications, computer network, data bank, data network, electronic highway, electronic mail, email, global village, infobahn*, information space, information superhighway*, information technology, Internet, online community, virtual community, virtual library, virtual reality, Web, World Wide Web, WWW; CONCEPTS 349,770

cycle [n] *era, phase* aeon, age, alternation, chain, circle, circuit, course, eon, isochronism, loop, orbit, period, periodicity, revolution, rhythm, ring, rotation, round, run, sequel, sequence, series, succession, wheel; CONCEPTS 816,817

cyclical [adj] *happening at regular intervals* circular, patterned, periodic, recurrent, recurring, regular, repeated, repetitive, seasonal; CONCEPTS 816, 817

cynic [n] *nonbeliever* carper, caviler, detractor, disbeliever, doubter, doubting Thomas*, egoist, egotist, flouter, misanthrope, misanthropist, misogamist, misogynist, mocker, pessimist, questioner, satirist, scoffer, skeptic, sneerer, unbeliever; CONCEPTS 361,423 —*Ant.* believer, optimist

cynical [adj] *nonbelieving; doubtful* contemptuous, derisive, ironic, misanthropic, misanthropical, mocking, pessimistic, sarcastic, sardonic, scoffing, scornful, skeptical, sneering, suspicious, unbelieving, wry; CONCEPTS 267,403 —*Ant.* believing, hopeful, optimistic, trusting, undoubting

cyst [n] *unusual growth* bag, bleb, blister, injury, pouch, sac, sore, vesicle, wen; CONCEPT 306

D

dab [n] *small quantity* bit, blob, dollop, drop, fleck, flick, pat, peck, smidgen, smudge, speck, spot, stroke, tap, touch; CONCEPT 835 —*Ant.* glob, mass

dab [v] *blot up; touch lightly* bedaub, besmear, daub, pat, peck, plaster, smear, smudge, stipple, swab, tap, wipe; CONCEPT 612

dabble [v] *play at; tinker* amuse oneself with, be amateur, dally, dilly-dally*, fiddle with*, flirt with*, horse around*, idle, kid around*, mess around*, monkey*, monkey around*, muck around*, not be serious*, play, play around*, play games with, toy with, trifle, trifle with, work superficially; CONCEPT 87 —*Ant.* take seriously

dabbler [n] *amateur* abecedarian, beginner, dilettante, loafer, nonprofessional, novice, potterer, pretender, smatterer, tinkerer, trifler, tyro, uninitiate; CONCEPTS 348,366 —*Ant.* professional

dad [n] *father* daddy*, old man*, pa*, papa*, pappy*, parent, pop; CONCEPTS 394,400,414, 419,423

daffy [adj] *silly, crazy* clownish, crackers*, daft, demented, deranged, dotty, foolish, goofy* loony*, nuts, nutty*; CONCEPT 403

daft [adj] *stupid; crazy* absurd, asinine, bedlamite, bonkers, cracked*, crackers*, daffy*, demented, deranged, dopey*, flaky*, foolish, fried*, giddy, half-baked*, idiotic, inane, insane, in the ozone*, lunatic, mad, mental*, nuts, nutty*, off the wall*, out of one's gourd*, ridiculous, screwy*, silly, simple, touched, unbalanced, unhinged*, unsound, wacky, whacko*, witless*; CONCEPT 403 —*Ant.* brainy, bright, intelligent, smart, understanding

dagger [n] *knife* anlace, bayonet, blade, bodkin, cutlass, dirk, poniard, sidearm, skean, stiletto, stylet, switchblade, sword; CONCEPTS 495,499

daily [adj] *occurring every day; during the day* circadian, common, commonplace, constantly, cyclic, day after day, day by day, day-to-day, diurnal, everyday, from day to day, often, once a day, once daily, ordinary, per diem, periodic, quotidian, regular, regularly, routine; CONCEPTS 541,801 —*Ant.* at night, nightly, nocturnal

dainty [adj1] *delicate, fragile, fine* airy, attractive, beautiful, bonny, charming, choice, comely, cute, darling, delectable, delicious, delightful, diaphanous, elegant, ethereal, exquisite, fair, feeble, frail, graceful, lacy, light, lovely, neat, nice, palatable, petite, pleasing, precious, pretty, rare, recherché, refined, savory, select, soft, subtle, superior, sweet, tasteful, tasty, tender, thin, toothsome, trim, well-made; CONCEPTS 490,491,606 —*Ant.* clumsy, coarse, harsh, heavy, rough

dainty [adj2] *finicky, particular* acute, choosy, delicate, fastidious, finical, finicking, fussy, mincing, nice, perceptive, persnickety*, refined, scrupulous, tasteful; CONCEPT 404 —*Ant.* accepting, easy

dairy [n] *producer of milk products* buttery, cow barn, creamery, dairy farm, factory, farm, pasteurizing plant; CONCEPTS 449,517

dalliance [n1] *dawdling* dabbling, delay,

delaying, dilly-dallying*, frittering, frivoling, idling, loafing, loitering, playing, poking*, procrastinating, procrastination, puttering, toying, trifling; CONCEPTS 151,210,681 —*Ant.* hastening, hurrying, push, rush

dalliance [n2] *love affair* affair, a little on the side*, amorous play, carrying on*, fling, fooling around*, frolicking, hanky-panky*, messing around*, relationship, seduction, toying*, working late at office*; CONCEPTS 114,375,388

dally [vi] *dawdle, delay* boondoggle*, drag, fool around, fool with, fritter away, hang about*, horse around*, idle, jerk off*, lag, linger, loiter, lollygag*, play around*, play games with*, procrastinate, put off, putter, tarry, trail, trifle with, waste time, while away; CONCEPTS 151,210,681 —*Ant.* hasten, hurry, push, rush

dally/dally with [v2] *have love affair* be insincere with, carry on, cosset, fool around*, frivol, frolic, gambol, have a fling, lead on, play around*, rollick, romp, tamper, wanton; CONCEPTS 114,375

dam [n] *embankment, wall* bank, barrage, barrier, dike, ditch, gate, grade, hindrance, levee, milldam, millpond, obstruction, weir; CONCEPT 470

dam [v] *hold back; block* bar, barricade, brake, check, choke, clog, close, confine, hinder, hold in, impede, obstruct, repress, restrain, restrict, retard, slow, stop up, suppress; CONCEPTS 130,191 —*Ant.* free, let go, liberate, release, unblock, unclog, unloose

damage [n1] *injury, loss* accident, adulteration, adversity, affliction, bane, blemish, blow, breakage, bruise, casualty, catastrophe, cave-in, contamination, corruption, debasement, depreciation, deprivation, destruction, deterioration, detriment, devastation, disservice, disturbance, evil, hardship, harm, hurt, illness, impairment, infliction, knockout, marring, mischief, mishap, mutilation, outrage, pollution, ravage, reverse, ruin, ruining, spoilage, stroke, suffering, waste, wound, wreckage, wrecking, wrong; CONCEPTS 309,674 —*Ant.* advantage, benefit, blessing, boon, favor, improvement, profit

damage [v] *cause injury, loss* abuse, bang up*, batter, bleach, blight, break, burn, contaminate, corrode, corrupt, crack, cripple, deface, defile, dirty, discolor, disfigure, disintegrate, dismantle, fade, gnaw, harm, hurt, impair, incapacitate, infect, injure, lacerate, maim, maltreat, mangle, mar, mutilate, pollute, ravage, rot, ruin, rust, scathe, scorch, scratch, smash, split, spoil, stab, stain, tamper with, tarnish, tear, undermine, vitiate, weaken, wear away, wound, wreak havoc on*, wreck, wrong; CONCEPTS 246,252 —*Ant.* benefit, bless, enhance, favor, fix, improve, mend, perfect, repair

damaged [adj] *broken, not working* beat-up, bent, blemished, busted, dinged, down, flawed, flubbed*, fouled up, glitched*, gone, hurt, impaired, imperfect, injured, in need of repair, in poor condition, in smithereens*, kaput*, loused up*, marred, messed up*, mucked up*, no go*, on the blink*, on the fritz*, out of action*, out of kilter*, out of whack*, run-down, screwed up*, shot, snafued*, spoiled, sunk*, totaled*, unsound; CONCEPTS 485,560

—*Ant.* fixed, mended, ok, perfect, repaired, unbroken, undamaged, working

damage(s) [n2] *cost for problem* amends, bill, charge, compensation, expense, fine, forfeit, indemnity, reimbursement, reparation, satisfaction, total; CONCEPTS 123,329 —*Ant.* award, compensation, profit, recompense, reward

damaging [adj] *hurtful to reputation* bad, deleterious, detrimental, disadvantageous, evil, harmful, injurious, mischievous, nocent, nocuous, prejudicial, ruinous; CONCEPT 537 —*Ant.* beneficial, favorable, helpful

damn [v] *condemn, denounce* abuse, anathematize, attack, ban, banish, blaspheme, blast, castigate, cast out, censure, complain of, confound, convict, criticize, cry down, curse, cuss*, darn, denunciate, doom, drat, excommunicate, excoriate, execrate, expel, flame, fulminate against, imprecate, inveigle against, jinx, object to, objurgate, pan*, penalize, proscribe, punish, revile, sentence, slam, swear, thunder against*; CONCEPTS 52,54 —*Ant.* bless, cherish, commend, elevate, exalt, favor, glorify, laud, praise, promote

damnable [adj] *atrocious, horrible* abhorrent, abominable, accursed, blamed, blessed, culpable, cursed, dang*, darn, depraved, despicable, detestable, dratted, execrable, hateful, odious, offensive, outrageous, wicked; CONCEPTS 545,570 —*Ant.* admirable, blessed, cherished, exalted, favorable, favored, good, laudatory, loveable, praiseworthy

damnation [n] *everlasting punishment* condemnation, doom, hell, perdition, suffering, torment; CONCEPT 679

damned [adj] *hateful, unwelcome* accursed, all-fired*, anathematized, bad, blankety-blank*, blasted, blessed*, bloody*, blooming*, condemned, confounded, cursed, cussed*, damnable, dang*, darn*, darned*, despicable, detestable, doggone*, done for*, doomed, dratted*, execrable, gone to blazes*, infamous, infernal*, loathsome, lost, lousy, reprobate, revolting, unhappy, voodooed*; CONCEPTS 545,570 —*Ant.* blessed, cherished, favored, likeable, loveable, nice, praiseworthy, welcome

damp [adj] *wet, humid* clammy, cloudy, dank, dewy, drenched, dripping, drippy, drizzly, irriguous, misty, moist, muggy, oozy, saturated, soaked, soaking, sodden, soggy, sopping, steam bath*, steamy, sticky, vaporous, waterlogged, wettish; CONCEPT 603 —*Ant.* arid, dessicated, dried, dry, parched

dampen [v1] *make wet* bedew, besprinkle, dabble, humidify, moisten, rinse, spray, sprinkle, water, wet; CONCEPT 256 —*Ant.* dry

dampen [v2] *spoil spirits* allay, check, chill, cloud, cool, curb, dash, deaden, deject, depress, diminish, discourage, dismay, dispirit, dull, humble, inhibit, moderate, muffle, mute, restrain, stifle; CONCEPTS 7,19 —*Ant.* brighten, encourage, hearten, inspirit, uplift

damsel [n] *maiden* colleen, lady, lass, lassie, miss, virgin, woman, young girl, young woman; CONCEPTS 414,415

dance [n1/v] *moving feet and body to music* bob*, boogie, boogie down*, bunny hop, caper, careen, cavort, Charleston, conga, cut a rug*, disco, flit*, foot it*, foxtrot, frolic, gambol, get down*, hoof it*, hop, hustle, jig, jitter*, jitterbug, jive*, jump, leap, one-step, prance, promenade, rhumba, rock, rock 'n' roll, samba, shimmy, skip, spin, step, strut, sway, swing, tango, tap, tread, trip, trip the light fantastic*, twist, two-step, waltz, whirl; CONCEPTS 292,363

dance [n2] *party for moving to music* ball, brawl, disco, formal, hoedown, hop, jump, masquerade, mingle, prom, promenade, shindig, social, sock hop; CONCEPT 383

dancer [n] *ballerina* ballet dancer, belly-dancer, chorus girl, coryphee, danseur, danseuse, go-go dancer, hoofer*, line-dancer, prima ballerina, show girl, tap-dancer; CONCEPT 352

dandle [v] *caress, cuddle* amuse, cosset, cradle, dance, fondle, love, nuzzle, pet, play, ride on knee, rock, sport, toss, toy*, toy with*; CONCEPTS 147,190

dandruff [n] *scurf* flakes, seborrhea; CONCEPT 831

dandy [adj] *fine, excellent* capital, cool*, exemplary, famous, first-class, first-rate, five-star*, fly*, glorious, grand, great, groovy*, hunky-dory*, keen, marvelous, model, neat, nifty, paragon, peachy*, prime, splendid, superior, swell, terrific; CONCEPT 574 —Ant. bad, inferior, not good, second-rate, unacceptable

danger [n] *hazard, troublesome situation* clouds, crisis, double trouble*, dynamite, emergency, endangerment, exigency, exposure, hot potato*, insecurity, instability, jeopardy, menace, peril, pitfall, possibility, precariousness, precipice, probability, risk, risky business*, slipperiness, storm, thin ice*, threat, uncertainty, venture, vulnerability; CONCEPT 675 —Ant. care, carefulness, guard, preservation, safety, security

dangerous [adj] *hazardous, troubling* alarming, bad, breakneck*, chancy, critical, dangersome, deadly, delicate, dynamite, exposed, fatal, formidable, hairy*, heavy*, hot*, impending, impregnable, insecure, jeopardous, loaded, malignant, menacing, mortal, nasty, on collision course*, parlous, perilous, portentous, precarious, pressing, queasy, risky, serious, serpentine, shaky, speculative, terrible, thorny*, threatening, ticklish*, touch-and-go*, touchy, treacherous, ugly*, unhealthy, unsafe, unstable, urgent, viperous, vulnerable, wicked; CONCEPT 548 —Ant. careful, guarded, safe, secure, unhazardous, untroubled

dangerously [adv] *precariously* alarmingly, carelessly, critically, daringly, desperately, gravely, harmfully, hazardously, perilously, precariously, recklessly, riskily, seriously, severely, unsafely, unsecurely; CONCEPT 548 —Ant. carefully, on guard, safely, securely

dangle [v] *suspend* brandish, depend, droop, entice, flap, flaunt, flourish, hang, hang down, lure, sling, sway, swing, tantalize, tempt, trail, wave; CONCEPTS 153,190

dangling [adj] *supported from above* drooping, droopy, hanging, pendent, pendulous, suspended; CONCEPT 485

dank [adj] *clammy* chilly, close, damp, dewy, dripping, humid, moist, muggy, slimy, soggy, steamy, sticky, wet, wettish; CONCEPT 603 —Ant. dry, parched

dapper [adj] *well-groomed, neat* bandbox,

brisk, chic, chichi, classy, clean, dainty, dashing, doggy*, dressed to kill*, dressed to nines*, jaunty, natty, nice, nifty, nimble, nobby, posh, prim, rakish, ritzy, sassy, sharp, showy, smart, snazzy*, snug, spiff, spiffy, spruce, spry, stylish, swank, swanky, swell, trim, turned out, well turned out; CONCEPT 579 —Ant. dirty, dishevelled, ruffled, rumpled, scruffy, shabby, sloppy, tousled, ungroomed, wrinkled

dappled [adj] *mottled, freckled* brindle, brindled, checkered, discolored, flecked, motley, multicolor, multicolored, multihued, parti-colored, piebald, pied, speckled, spotted, stippled, varicolored, variegated, versicolor, versicolored; CONCEPT 618 —Ant. uncolored, unflecked, unspotted

dare [n] *challenge, defiance* cartel, defy, provocation, stump, taunt; CONCEPTS 53,87

dare [v1] *challenge, defy someone* beard, brave, bully, call one's bluff, confront, cope, denounce, disregard, face, face off, front, goad, insult, knock chip off shoulder*, laugh at, make my day*, meet, mock, muster courage, oppose, outdare, provoke, resist, run the gauntlet, scorn, spurn, square off, step over the line, take one on, taunt, threaten, throw down gauntlet; CONCEPTS 14,53

dare [v2] *take a risk; be courageous* adventure, attempt, be bold, brave, endanger, endeavor, gamble, go ahead, hazard, make bold, pluck up, presume, risk, run the risk, speculate, stake, take a chance, take heart, try, try one's hand*, undertake, venture; CONCEPTS 35,87 —Ant. be careful, hold back, refrain

daredevil [n] *thrill-seeker* adventurer, hotdog*, madcap, risk-taker, show-off, stuntman, stuntperson, stuntwoman; CONCEPT 423

daring [adj] *adventurous* adventuresome, audacious, bold, brassy*, brave, cheeky, cocky, courageous, crusty, fearless, fire eating*, foolhardy, forward, game, go for broke*, gritty, gutsy*, gutty*, hot shot*, impudent, impulsive, intrepid, nervy, obtrusive, out on a limb*, plucky, rash, reckless, salty*, smart, smart-alecky*, spunky*, temerarious, valiant, venturesome; CONCEPT 401 —Ant. afraid, bashful, chicken, cowardly, fearful, meek, shy, timid, unadventurous, unwilling

dark [adj1] *lack of light* aphotic, atramentous, black, blackish, caliginous, Cimmerian, clouded, cloudy, crepuscular, darkened, dim, dingy, drab, dull, dun, dusk, dusky, faint, foggy, gloomy, grimy, ill-lighted, indistinct, inky, lightless, lurid, misty, murky, nebulous, obfuscous, obscure, opaque, overcast, pitch-black, pitch-dark, pitchy, rayless, shaded, shadowy, shady, somber, sooty, stygian, sunless, tenebrous, unlighted, unlit, vague; CONCEPT 617 —Ant. bright, brilliant, illuminated, light, lucid, luminous, radiant, shining, visible, vivid

dark [adj2] *shaded complexion, hair* adumbral, bistered, black, brunet, brunette, dark-complexioned, dark-skinned, dusky, ebon, ebony, sable, swart, swarthy, tan; CONCEPTS 406,618 —Ant. light

dark [adj3] *hidden, secret* abstruse, anagogic, arcane, cabalistic, complicated, concealed, cryptic, deep, Delphian, enigmatic, esoteric, intricate, knotty, mysterious, mystic, mystical,

da
da

mystifying, not known, obscure, occult, puzzling, recondite; CONCEPTS 402,576,582 —Ant. apparent, distinct, evident, manifest, plain, visible

dark [adj4] *grim, hopeless* bleak, cheerless, dismal, doleful, drab, foreboding, gloomy, joyless, morbid, morose, mournful, ominous, sinister, somber, unpropitious; CONCEPT 548 —Ant. bright, brilliant, encouraging, hopeful, shining

dark [adj5] *evil, satanic* atrocious, bad, corrupt, damnable, foul, hellish, horrible, immoral, infamous, infernal, nefarious, sinful, sinister, vile, wicked; CONCEPT 545 —Ant. good, moral

dark [adj6] *ignorant* benighted, uncultivated, unenlightened, unlettered, unread; CONCEPT 402

dark [adj7] *angry, upset* dour, forbidding, frowning, glowering, glum, ominous, scowling, sulky, sullen, threatening; CONCEPT 401 —Ant. cheerful, happy, pleased

dark [n1] *place, time without light* caliginosity, darkness, dead of night, dimness, dusk, duskiness, evening, gloom, midnight, murk, murkiness, night, nightfall, nighttime, obscurity, opacity, semidarkness, shade, shadows, twilight, witching hour; CONCEPTS 620,810 —Ant. brightness, day, daylight, daytime, illumination, light, lightness, morning

dark [n2] *ignorance; mystery* concealment, denseness, inscrutability, seclusion, secrecy, thickness; CONCEPTS 409,410 —Ant. cognizance, enlightening, intelligence, sense, sensibility, understanding

darken [v] *become shaded, unlit* becloud, bedim, blacken, cloud over, cloud up, deepen, dim, eclipse, fog, gray, haze, make dim, murk, obfuscate, obscure, overcast, overshadow, shade, shadow, tone down*; CONCEPT 469 —Ant. brighten, illuminate, lighten, whiten

dark horse [n] *long shot* hundred-to-one shot, improbability, outside chance, sleeper, small chance, underdog, unexpected winner, unknown, unlikelihood, unlikely winner; CONCEPTS 366,423

darkness [n1] *place, time that is unlit* black, blackness, blackout, brownout, caliginosity, Cimmerian shade, cloudiness, crepuscule, dark, dimness, dusk, duskiness, eclipse, gloom, lightlessness, murk, murkiness, nightfall, obscurity, pitch darkness, shade, shadiness, shadows, smokiness, tenebrosity, twilight; CONCEPT 620 —Ant. brightness, day, daylight, daytime, illumination, light, lightness, morning

darkness [n2] *ignorance; mystery* blindness, concealment, denseness, inscrutability, isolation, privacy, seclusion, secrecy, unawareness; CONCEPT 409 —Ant. cognizance, enlightening, intelligence, sense, sensibility, understanding

darling [n] *sweetheart, favorite person* angel*, apple of one's eye*, baby*, beloved, boyfriend, dear, dearest, dearie*, dear one, fair-haired boy*, flame, friend, girlfriend, heart's desire*, honeybunch, lamb*, light of my life*, love, lover, one and only*, pet*, precious, sugar*, sweetie, treasure*, truelove; CONCEPT 423 —Ant. enemy, foe

darn [interj] *damn* confound it, cripes, damn it, dang*, darnation, doggone, drat*, gosh-darn; CONCEPTS 52,54

dart [v] *race away; propel* bound, career, cast, course, dash, flash, fling, flit, float, fly, gallop, hasten, heave, hurry, hurtle, launch, move quickly, pitch, plunge, run, rush, sail, scamper, scoot, scud, scurry, shoot, skim, speed, spring, sprint, spurt, start, tear, throw, thrust, whiz; CONCEPTS 150,195,222

dash [n1] *fast race for short distance* birr, bolt, dart, haste, onset, run, rush, sortie, sprint, spurt, zip; CONCEPT 150

dash [n2] *flair, style* animation, birr, brio, éclat, élan, energy, esprit, flourish, force, impressiveness, intensity, life, might, oomph*, panache, power, spirit, strength, vehemence, verve, vigor, vim, vivacity, zing, zip; CONCEPTS 411,655,673 —Ant. drab, dullness, frumpiness

dash [n3] *small amount; suggestion* bit, drop, few drops, flavor, grain, hint, lick, little, part, pinch, scattering, seasoning, smack, smidgen, soupçon, sprinkle, sprinkling, squirt, streak, suspicion, taste, tincture, tinge, touch, trace, trifle, zest; CONCEPT 831 —Ant. glob, lump

dash [v1] *run very fast for short distance* boil, bolt, bound, career, charge, chase, course, dart, fly, gallop, get on it*, haste, hasten, hurry, lash, make a run for it*, make it snappy*, race, rush, rush at, scamper, scoot, scurry, shoot, speed, spring, sprint, tear; CONCEPT 150

dash [v2] *break by hitting or throwing violently* beat, bludgeon, cast, charge, crash, cudgel, destroy, fling, hit, hurl, hurtle, lunge, plunge, shatter, shiver, slam, sling, smash, splash, splatter, splinter, throw; CONCEPTS 189,222,248 —Ant. aid, assist, encourage, help, inspirit

dash [v3] *discourage, frustrate* abash, baffle, balk, beat, blast, blight, chagrin, chill, circumvent, cloud, confound, dampen, disappoint, discomfort, dismay, dispirit, foil, nip, ruin, spoil, thwart; CONCEPTS 7,19,121

dashboard [n] *instrument panel* control panel, indicator panel, instrument board; CONCEPTS 463,499

dashing [adj] *bold, flamboyant* adventurous, alert, animated, chic, dapper, daring, dazzling, debonair, elegant, exclusive, exuberant, fashionable, fearless, gallant, gay, jaunty, keen, lively, modish, plucky, rousing, showy, smart, spirited, sporty, stylish, swank, swashbuckling, swish, vivacious; CONCEPTS 404,589 —Ant. boring, calm, drab, dull, plain, unimpressive, unstylish

dastardly [adj] *rotten* base, contemptible, cowardly, craven, despicable, low, mean, pusillanimous, underhanded, vile; CONCEPTS 404,545,570,571,574

data [n] *information in visible form* abstracts, brass tacks*, chapter and verse*, circumstances, compilations, conclusions, details, documents, dope, dossier, evidence, experiments, facts, figures, goods, info, input, knowledge, materials, measurements, memorandums, notes, picture, proof, reports, results, scoop, score, statistics, testimony, whole story*; CONCEPT 274

data bank [n] *database* computerized information, data processing, storage; CONCEPT 274

data processor [n] *computer* calculator, CPU, laptop, MAC, Macintosh, mainframe, microcomputer, number-cruncher, PC, personal computer, word processor; CONCEPTS 269,463

date [n1] *point in time; particular day or time* age, century, course, day, duration, epoch, era, generation, hour, juncture, moment, period, quarter, reign, span, spell, stage, term, time, while, year; CONCEPTS 800,801,802,815

date [n2] *social engagement* appointment, assignation, call, interview, meeting, rendezvous, tryst, visit; CONCEPTS 114,386

date [n3] *person accompanying another socially* blind date, boyfriend, companion, escort, friend, girlfriend, lover, partner, steady, sweetheart; CONCEPT 423

date [v1] *assign a time* affix a date to, belong to, carbon-date, chronicle, come from, determine, exist from, fix, fix the date of, isolate, mark, measure, originate in, put in its place, record, register; CONCEPTS 18,37

date [v2] *see person socially* associate with, attend, consort with, court, deuce it*, escort, fix up, go around together*, go around with*, go out with, go steady, go together, keep company, make a date, see, step around, take out, woo; CONCEPT 114

date [v3] *become obsolete* antiquate, archaize, obsolesce, obsolete, outdate, show one's age; CONCEPT 105

dated [adj] *out-of-date* antiquated, archaic, behind the times, obsolescent, obsolete, old-fashioned, old hat, outdated, outmoded, out of style, passé, unfashionable; CONCEPTS 530,578,797

daub [v] *coat; make dirty* begrime, besmear, bespray, blur, cover, dab, deface, dirty, fleck, grime, paint, plaster, slap on, smear, smirch, smudge, spatter, speckle, s̲p̲latter, spot, spread, stain, sully, variegate, varnish; CONCEPTS 172,250

daughter [n] *female child* offspring, girl, offspring, woman; CONCEPTS 415,424

daunt [v] *frighten, alarm* appall, baffle, browbeat, bully, consternate, cow, deter, discourage, dishearten, dismay, dispirit, foil, horrify, intimidate, overawe, put off*, scare, shake, subdue, terrify, thwart; CONCEPTS 7,19 —Ant. aid, assist, embolden, encourage, hearten, help, incite, inspirit, stimulate, undaunt, urge

dauntless [adj] *bold, courageous* aweless, brave, daring, doughty, fearless, gallant, game, heroic, indomitable, intrepid, invincible, lionhearted, resolute, stouthearted, unafraid, unconquerable, undaunted, unfearing, unflinching, valiant, valorous; CONCEPT 401 —Ant. afraid, daunted, discouraged, disheartened, fearful, frightened, intimidated, scared, terrified

davenport [n] *sofa; small desk* chesterfield, convertible sofa, couch, daybed, futon, secretary, sofa bed, writing desk; CONCEPT 443

dawdle [v] *delay; waste time* amble, bum around*, dally, diddle-daddle*, dilly-dally*, drag, fool around*, fritter away*, get no place fast*, goof off*, hang around*, hang out*, idle, lag, laze, lazy, loaf, loiter, loll, lounge, mosey*, poke*, procrastinate, put off, saunter, scrounge around, shlep along*, sit around*, sit on one's butt*, stay, stroll, tarry, toddle, trifle, wait, warm a chair*; CONCEPTS 210,681 —Ant. forward, hasten, hurry, push, rush, speed

dawn [n1] *beginning of day* aurora, break of day, bright, cockcrow, crack of dawn, dawning, daybreak, daylight, day peep, early bright, first blush, first light, light, morn, morning, sunrise, sunup, wee hours*; CONCEPTS 810,815 —Ant. dusk, end, evening, eventide, setting, sundown, sunset

dawn [n2] *a beginning* advent, alpha, birth, commencement, dawning, emergence, foundation, genesis, head, inception, onset, opening, origin, outset, outstart, rise, source, start, unfolding; CONCEPT 832 —Ant. conclusion, end, ending, finish

dawn [v] *start* appear, begin, develop, emerge, glimmer, initiate, lighten, loom, open, originate, rise, show itself, unfold; CONCEPT 119 —Ant. end, finish, set

day [n1] *light part of every 24 hours* astronomical day, bright, dawn-to-dark, daylight, daytime, diurnal course, early bright, light, light of day, mean solar day, nautical day, sidereal day, sunlight, sunrise-to-sunset, sunshine, working day; CONCEPTS 801,803,810,821 —Ant. evening, night

day [n2] *era* age, ascendancy, cycle, epoch, generation, height, heyday, period, prime, term, time, years, zenith; CONCEPTS 802,816

daybook [n] *journal* album, datebook, diary, FilofaxTM, ledger, log, logbook, memo pad, notebook, record, scrapbook; CONCEPTS 280,283

daybreak [n] *beginning of light hours* aurora, break of day, bright, cockcrow, crack of dawn, dawn, dawning, daylight, day peep, dayspring, early bright, first light, morn, morning, sunrise, sunup; CONCEPTS 810,815 —Ant. darkness, eventide, sundown, sunset

daycare [n] *child care center* babysitter, kindergarten, nursery school, playgroup, pre-K, pre-school; CONCEPT 295

daydream [n] *fantasy* thought of when awake castle in the air*, conceiving, dream, fancy, fancying, figment of imagination, fond hope, fool's paradise*, head trip*, imagination, imagining, in a zone*, mind trip*, musing, phantasm, phantasy, pie in the sky*, pipe dream, reverie, stargazing, trip*, vision, wish, woolgathering; CONCEPT 529 —Ant. reality

daydream [v] *make up fantasy* build castles in air*, conceive, dream, envision, fancy, fantasize, hallucinate, imagine, moon, muse, pipe dream*, stargaze, trip out*, woolgather; CONCEPTS 17,36

daylight [n] *light part of 24 hours* aurora, dawn, day, daybreak, daytime, during the day, light, light of day, sunlight, sunrise, sunshine; CONCEPT 810 —Ant. darkness, evening, night, sunset

daze [n] *confusion* befuddlement, bewilderment, distraction, gauze, glaze, haze, lala-land*, maze, muddledness, nadaville*, narcosis, shock, stupefaction, stupor, trance; CONCEPT 410 —Ant. expectation, understanding

daze [v] *confuse, shock* addle, amaze, astonish, astound, befog, befuddle, benumb, bewilder, blind, blur, confound, dazzle, disorder, distract, dizzy, dumbfound, flabbergast, fuddle, mix up, muddle, mystify, numb, overpower, overwhelm, paralyze, perplex, petrify, puzzle, rock, stagger, startle, stun, stupefy, surprise; CONCEPTS 16,42 —Ant. expect

da
da

dazzle [v] *confuse, amaze* astonish, awe, bedazzle, blind, blur, bowl over*, daze, excite, fascinate, glitz*, hypnotize, impress, overawe, overpower, overwhelm, razzle-dazzle, strike dumb*, stupefy, surprise; CONCEPTS *16,42* —*Ant.* bore

dazzling [adj] *radiant* beaming, bright, brilliant, flashy, glaring, glittering, ravishing, resplendent, sensational, shining, sparkling, splendid, stunning; CONCEPT *617*

deacon [n] *clergyperson* church officer, cleric, elder, priest; CONCEPT *361*

deactivate [v] *decommission* demilitarize, disband, make inactive, shut down, shut off; CONCEPTS *25,121,188*

dead [adj1] *no longer alive* asleep, bereft of life, bloodless, bought the farm*, breathless, buried, cadaverous, checked out*, cold, cut off, deceased, defunct, departed, done for*, erased, expired, extinct, gone, gone to meet maker*, gone to reward*, inanimate, inert, late, lifeless, liquidated, mortified, no more, not existing, offed*, out of one's misery*, passed away, perished, pushing up daisies*, reposing, resting in peace, spiritless, stiff, unanimated, wasted; CONCEPT *539* —*Ant.* alive, animated, being, existent, existing, live, living, subsisting

dead [adj2] *indifferent, cold* anesthetized, apathetic, asleep, boring, callous, deadened, dull, flat, frigid, glazed, inert, insensitive, insipid, lukewarm, numb, numbed, paralyzed, senseless, spiritless, stagnant, stale, still, tasteless, torpid, unfeeling, uninteresting, unresponsive, vapid, wooden; CONCEPT *550* —*Ant.* active, animated, interested, live, living, responsive, spirited, warm

dead [adj3] *not working* barren, bygone, defunct, departed, exhausted, extinct, gone, inactive, inoperable, inoperative, lost, obsolete, spent, stagnant, sterile, still, tired, unemployed, unprofitable, useless, vanished, wearied, worn, worn out; CONCEPT *560* —*Ant.* active, alive, animate, animated, live, operative, working

dead [adj4] *complete, total* absolute, bloody, downright, entire, final, out-and-out*, outright, perfect, sure, thorough, unconditional, unmitigated, unqualified, utter, whole; CONCEPT *531* —*Ant.* continuing, enduring, incomplete, unfinished

dead [adv] *completely, totally* absolutely, direct, directly, due, entirely, exactly, right, straight, straightly, undeviatingly, wholly; CONCEPTS *531,772* —*Ant.* incompletely

deadbeat [n] *freeloader* bum, debtor, leech, loafer, moocher, parasite, sponge; CONCEPTS *412,423*

deaden [v] *diminish, muffle, quiet* abate, alleviate, anesthetize, benumb, blunt, check, chloroform, consume, cushion, damp, dampen, depress, deprive, desensitize, destroy, devitalize, dim, dope, drown, dull, etherize, exhaust, freeze, frustrate, gas, hush, impair, incapacitate, injure, knock out, KO*, lay out, lessen, mute, numb, paralyze, put out of order*, put to sleep, quieten, reduce, repress, retard, slow, smother, soften, stifle, stun, stupefy, suppress, tire, tone down, unnerve, weaken; CONCEPTS *130,240* —*Ant.* animate, build, enliven, increase, strengthen

dead end [n] *cul-de-sac; deadlock* blank wall, blind alley, Catch-22, corner, draw, impasse, nowhere to turn, obstacle, road block, stalemate, standoff, stumbling block; CONCEPT *674*

deadline [n] *due date* bound, cutoff, limit, period, target date, time frame, time limit, zero hour; CONCEPTS *513,745,815,832*

deadlock [n] *stalemate, impasse* box*, Catch-22*, cessation, checkmate, corner, dead end, dead heat, dilemma, draw, full stop, gridlock, halt, hole, pause, pickle, plight, posture, predicament, quandary, standoff, standstill, tie, wall*; CONCEPT *674* —*Ant.* agreement, breakthrough

deadly [adj1] *causing end of life* baleful, baneful, bloodthirsty, bloody, cannibalistic, carcinogenic, cruel, dangerous, death-dealing, deathly, deleterious, destroying, destructive, fatal, grim, harmful, homicidal, injurious, internecine, killing, lethal, malignant, mortal, mortiferous, murderous, noxious, pernicious, pestiferous, pestilent, pestilential, poisonous, ruthless, savage, slaying, suicidal, toxic, unrelenting, venomous, violent, virulent; CONCEPT *537* —*Ant.* animating, energizing, harmless, healthful, healthy, invigorating, wholesome

deadly [adj2] *ghostly* ashen, corpselike, dead-center, deadened, deathlike, deathly, ghastly, pallid, wan, white; CONCEPT *539* —*Ant.* lively

dead-on [adj] *accurate* by the book, dead-center, definite, direct, exact, on the button*, on the mark*, on the money*, on the nose*, precise, to the point; CONCEPT *535*

deadpan [adj] *expressionless* blank, impassive, nobody home*, poker-faced, serious, stony, straight-faced, unreadable, vacant, wooden; CONCEPT *406*

deaf [adj1] *without hearing* deafened, earless, hard of hearing, stone deaf*, unable to hear; CONCEPT *591* —*Ant.* hearing

deaf [adj2] *unwilling* bullheaded*, headstrong, indifferent, intractable, mulish*, oblivious, obstinate, pertinacious, perverse, pigheaded*, self-willed, strong-willed, stubborn, to listen blind, unaware, unconcerned, unhearing, unmoved; CONCEPT *401* —*Ant.* attentive, aware, conscious, listening, willing

deafening [adj] *very loud* at full volume, blaring, booming, ear-piercing*, ear-popping*, ear-splitting*, noisy, ringing, roaring, rowdy, screaming, thunderous, turned up, vociferous; CONCEPTS *592,594*

deal [n1] *agreement, bargain* accord, arrangement, buy, compromise, conception, contract, pact, pledge, prearrangement, transaction, understanding; CONCEPT *684* —*Ant.* disagreement, misunderstanding

deal [n2] *amount, share* abundance, degree, distribution, extent, plenty, plethora, portion, quantity, shake, superabundance, transaction; CONCEPTS *344,787,835*

deal [n3] *distribution of playing cards* appointment, chance, cut and shuffle*, fresh start, game, hand, opportunity, round; CONCEPT *363*

deal [v2] *do business* bargain, barter, bicker, buy and sell, dicker*, hammer out deal*, handle, horse trade*, knock down price*, negotiate, sell, stock, swap, trade, traffic, treat, work out deal; CONCEPT *324* —*Ant.* deny, refuse

deal [v3] *distribute* administer, allot, apportion, assign, bestow, come across with*, deliver, disburse, dish out*, dispense, disperse, disseminate, divide, divvy*, dole out*, drop, fork out*, fork over*, give, hand out, impart, inflict, measure, mete out, partake, participate, partition, render, reward, share, strike; CONCEPTS 108,140 —*Ant.* hold, keep

deal/deal with [v1] *handle, manage* act, approach, attend to, behave, behave toward, clear, concern, conduct oneself, consider, control, cope with, direct, discuss, get a handle on something*, hack it*, handle, have to do with, live with*, make a go of it*, make it*, oversee, play, review, rid, see to, serve, take, take care of, treat, unburden, use; CONCEPTS 94,117 —*Ant.* mismanage

dealer [n] *business owner* banker, bursar, businessperson, chandler, changer, dispenser, marketer, merchandiser, merchant, retailer, trader, tradesperson, trafficker, vendor, wholesaler; CONCEPT 347 —*Ant.* customer

dealings [n] *business relations* affairs, balls in air*, business, commerce, concerns, doings, intercourse, irons in fire*, matters, proceedings, ropes*, sale, strings*, things, trade, traffic, transactions, truck, wire pulling*, wires*; CONCEPT 324

dean [n] *leader of institution* administrator, authority, dignitary, doyen, ecclesiastic, guide, lead, legislator, pilot, president, principal, professor, senior, tack; CONCEPT 350 —*Ant.* pupil, student

dear [adj1] *beloved, favorite* cherished, close, darling, doll face, endeared, esteemed, familiar, intimate, loved, pet, precious, prized, respected, treasured; CONCEPTS 555,567 —*Ant.* common, despised, hateful, unimportant, valueless, worthless

dear [adj2] *very expensive* an arm and a leg*, at a premium, cher*, costly, fancy, high, high-priced, out of sight*, overpriced, pretty penny*, pricey*, prized, steep, stiff*, valuable; CONCEPT 334 —*Ant.* cheap, inexpensive, low-priced, valueless, worthless

dear [n] *beloved person* darling, favorite, heartthrob, honey, love, loved one, lover, pet, precious, sweetheart, treasure; CONCEPT 423 —*Ant.* despised, hate

dearly [adv1] *extremely* greatly, profoundly, to a great extent, very, very much; CONCEPT 772

dearly [adv2] *lovingly* affectionately, devotedly, fondly, tenderly, yearningly; CONCEPT 403 —*Ant.* hatefully

dearth [n] *insufficiency, scarcity* absence, default, defect, deficiency, exiguousness, famine, inadequacy, infrequency, lack, meagerness, miss, need, paucity, poverty, privation, rareness, scantiness, scantness, shortage, slim pickings*, sparsity, uncommonness, want; CONCEPTS 646,674,709 —*Ant.* abundance, excess, plentifulness, plenty, sufficiency

death [n] *end of life* afterlife, annihilation, bereavement, casualty, cessation, curtains*, darkness, decease, demise, departure, destruction, dissolution, downfall, dying, end, ending, eradication, eternal rest, euthanasia, exit, expiration, extermination, extinction, fatality, finis*, finish, grave, grim reaper*, heaven, loss,

mortality, necrosis, obliteration, oblivion, paradise, parting, passing, passing over, quietus, release, repose, ruin, ruination, silence, sleep, termination, tomb; CONCEPT 304 —*Ant.* being, birth, entity, existence, life, living

deathly [adj1] *suggesting end of life* appalling, cadaverous, corpselike, deathlike, defunctive, dreadful, gaunt, ghastly, grim, gruesome, haggard, horrible, macabre, pale, pallid, wan, wasted; CONCEPTS 579,618 —*Ant.* animated, beginning, blooming, blossoming, lively

deathly [adj2] *fatal* deadly, extreme, intense, lethal, mortal, mortiferous, noxious, pestilent, pestilential, terrible; CONCEPT 537 —*Ant.* benign, harmless, healthful, healthy, life-giving, strengthening

debacle [n] *catastrophe* beating, blue ruin*, breakdown, collapse, crack-up*, crash, defeasance, defeat, devastation, disaster, dissolution, downfall, drubbing, failure, fiasco, havoc, licking, overthrow, reversal, rout, ruin, ruination, shellacking*, smash, smashup, trouncing, vanquishment, washout, wreck; CONCEPT 674 —*Ant.* boon, miracle, wonder

debase [v1] *degrade, shame* abase, bemean, cast down, cheapen, corrupt, cripple, debauch, debilitate, demean, demoralize, deprave, devaluate, devalue, disable, disgrace, dishonor, drag down*, dump on*, enfeeble, fluff off*, humble, humiliate, lower, put away, put down, reduce, sap, shoot down, sink, take down*, take down a peg*, undermine, weaken; CONCEPTS 7,19,52,54 —*Ant.* elevate, honor, laud, praise, upgrade, value

debase [v2] *adulterate* abase, animalize, bastardize, bestialize, contaminate, corrupt, damage, defile, depreciate, doctor, dope up*, impair, load, pervert, pollute, sophisticate, spoil, taint, vitiate, weight, worsen; CONCEPTS 240,250 —*Ant.* clean, clear, enhance, improve, purify

debatable [adj] *controversial* arguable, between rock and hard place*, between sixes and sevens*, betwixt and between*, bone of contention*, borderline, chancy*, contestable, disputable, doubtful, dubious, iffy*, in dispute, moot, mootable*, open to question, problematic, problematical, questionable, the jury's out*, touch and go*, uncertain, undecided, unsettled, up for discussion; CONCEPTS 267,535 —*Ant.* certain, inarguable, incontrovertible, indubious, questionable, sure, uncontestable, undoubted

debate [n] *discussion of issues; consideration* agitation, altercation, argument, argumentation, blah-blah*, cogitation, contention, contest, controversy, controverting, deliberation, dialectic, disputation, dispute, forensic, hassle, match, meditation, mooting, polemic, rebutting, reflection, refuting, tiff, words, wrangle; CONCEPTS 56,532 —*Ant.* agreement

debate [v] *argue, discuss* agitate, altercate, answer, bandy, bicker, bump heads*, canvass, chew the fat*, cogitate, confab*, confute, consider, contend, contest, controvert, cross swords*, deliberate, demonstrate, differ, discept, disprove, dispute, hammer away at*, hash over*, hassle, have at it*, kick around*, knock around*, lock horns*, moot, oppose, pettifog, pick a bone*, prove, put up argument, question, reason, rebut, refute, rehash, set to, talk back*,

da
de

talk game*, thrash out*, toss around*, wrangle; CONCEPTS 24,56 —Ant. agree, go along

debauch [v] *deprave, corrupt* abuse, bastardize, bestialize, betray, brutalize, debase, defile, deflower, demoralize, fornicate, fraternize, go bad*, go to hell*, intrigue, inveigle, lead astray*, live in the gutter*, lure, pervert, pollute, ravish, ruin, seduce, subvert, tempt, violate, vitiate, warp; CONCEPTS 14,240,375 —Ant. clean, cleanse, improve, purify, upgrade

debauched [adj] *violated, corrupted* abandoned, corrupt, debased, defiled, degenerate, degraded, depraved, deteriorated, dissipated, dissolute, fast, gone bad*, gone to the dogs*, immoral, in the gutter*, licentious, perverted, profligate, reprobate, vitiate, vitiated, wanton, wicked; CONCEPT 545 —Ant. clean, cleansed, improved, pure, purified, uncorrupt, unpolluted, virtuous

debauchery [n] *immoral self-indulgence* bender*, binge, blowout*, burning candle at both ends*, bust, carousal, depravity, dissipation, dissoluteness, drunk*, excess, fast living*, fornication, gluttony, incontinence, indulgence, intemperance, intimacy, la dolce vita*, lasciviousness, lechery, lewdness, license, licentiousness, life in fast lane*, lust, orgy, overindulgence, revel, revelry, seduction, sensuality, sybaritism, tear*; CONCEPTS 633, 645 —Ant. benevolence, giving, mercifulness, unselfishness

debenture [n] *certificate of debt* bond, I.O.U., promise to pay, voucher; CONCEPTS 318,684

debilitate [v] *incapacitate* attenuate, blunt, cripple, devitalize, disable, enervate, enfeeble, eviscerate, exhaust, extenuate, harm, hurt, injure, mar, prostrate, relax, sap, spoil, unbrace, undermine, unstrengthen, weaken, wear out; CONCEPTS 240,246 —Ant. aid, assist, cure, energize, help, invigorate, mend, strengthen

debility [n] *incapacity, weakness* decrepitude, disease, enervation, enfeeblement, exhaustion, faintness, feebleness, frailty, infirmity, languor, malaise, sickliness, unhealthiness; CONCEPT 316 —Ant. ability, capability, health, strength, vigor

debonair [adj] *charming, elegant* affable, buoyant, casual, cheerful, courteous, dashing, detached, happy, jaunty, lighthearted, nonchalant, pleasant, refined, smooth, sprightly, suave, urbane, well-bred; CONCEPT 401 —Ant. awkward, clumsy, inelegant, uncharming, undebonair

debrief [v1] *question* ask questions, cross-examine, examine, gather intelligence, give the third degree*, grill, interrogate, interview, investigate, probe, put through the wringer*, quiz, work over; CONCEPTS 48,53

debrief [v2] *silence* censor, dummy up*, gag, hold one's tongue*, hush up, mute, muzzle, put the lid on, quash, say nothing, shut up, sit on*, soft-pedal*, squelch, stifle, suppress; CONCEPT 266

debris [n] *litter, waste* bits, crap*, detritus, dregs, dross, fragments, garbage, junk, offal, pieces, refuse, remains, riffraff, rubbish, rubble, ruins, trash, wreck, wreckage; CONCEPT 260 —Ant. cleanliness, neatness, purity

debt [n] *money owed to others* albatross*, arrearage, arrears, bad news*, baggage*, below the line*, bill, bite*, capital, check, chit*, claim,

commitment, credit, cuff*, damage*, dead horse*, debenture, debit, deficit, due, dues, duty, encumbrance, indebtedness, in hock*, in the hole*, in the red*, invoice, IOU, liability, manifest, mortgage, note, obligation, outstandings*, price tag*, promissory note, receipt, reckoning, red ink*, responsibility, score, tab, tally, voucher; CONCEPTS 329,344 —Ant. asset, cash, credit, excess, profit

debug [v] *troubleshoot* adjust, correct, fix, iron out, remedy, remove errors, repair, sort out, straighten out, unravel, unscramble, untangle, work the bugs out of; CONCEPTS 126,212

debunk [v] *disprove, ridicule* cut down to size*, deflate, demystify, discover, disparage, expose, lampoon, mock, puncture, show up*, uncloak, unmask, unshroud; CONCEPTS 49,60 —Ant. prove, uphold

debut [n] *first public appearance* admission, appearance, beginning, bow, coming out*, coming out party*, entrance, entree, first step*, graduating, graduation, inauguration, incoming, initiation, introduction, launching, opener, presentation; CONCEPT 386 —Ant. closing, finale

debutante [n] *young woman* deb, teenage girl, young girl, young lady; CONCEPTS 415,424

decadence [n] *perversion; deterioration of morality* corruption, debasement, decay, declension, decline, degeneracy, degeneration, degradation, devolution, dissipation, dissolution, downfall, downgrade, evil, excess, fall, gluttony, incontinence, intemperance, lasciviousness, lechery, lewdness, licentiousness, regression, sensuality, sybaritism; CONCEPT 645 —Ant. humility, morality

decadent [adj] *corrupt, self-indulgent* debased, debauched, decaying, declining, degenerate, degraded, depraved, dissolute, effete, evil, gone bad, gone to the dogs*, immoral, lost, moribund, overripe, perverted, wanton, wicked; CONCEPT 545 —Ant. benevolent, good, humble, kind, moral

decal [n] *sticker* advertisement, decalcomania, decorative picture, emblem, symbol, token; CONCEPTS 259,284,625

decamp [v] *depart suddenly* beat it, bolt, break camp, clear out, depart, disappear, escape, evacuate, flee, head for the hills*, hightail*, hit the road*, make a break for it, make oneself scarce*, make tracks*, run away, scram, skedaddle*, slip away, vamoose; CONCEPTS 102,150,195

decanter [n] *vessel* bottle, canteen, carafe, container, cruet, flask, jug, magnum, pitcher, wine bottle; CONCEPT 494

decapitate [v] *behead* ax, bring to the block*, chop off one's head, decollate, execute, guillotine; CONCEPT 176

decay [n] *breaking down, collapse* adulteration, atrophy, blight, caries, consumption, corrosion, crumbling, decadence, decline, decomposition, decrease, decrepitude, degeneracy, degeneration, depreciation, deterioration, dilapidation, disintegration, disrepair, dissolution, downfall, dying, extinction, fading, failing, gangrene, impairment, mortification, perishing, putrefaction, putrescence, putridity, putridness, rot, rotting, ruin, ruination, rust, senescence, spoilage, spoilation, wasting, wasting away, withering;

CONCEPTS 230,674,716 —Ant. development, flourish, germination, growth, improvement, ripening, strength, strengthening

decay [v] *deteriorate, crumble* atrophy, become contaminated, be impaired, blight, break up, collapse, corrode, curdle, decline, decompose, defile, degenerate, depreciate, discolor, disintegrate, dissolve, dry-rot, dwindle, fade, fail, get worse, go bad, go to seed*, go to the dogs*, hit rock bottom*, hit the skids*, lessen, mildew, mold, molder, mortify, pejorate, perish, pollute, putrefy, putresce, reach depths, rot, sap, shrivel, sicken, sink, slump, spoil, suppurate, turn, wane, waste away, weaken, wear away, wither; CONCEPTS 240,246,469 —Ant. develop, flourish, germinate, grow, improve, ripen, strengthen

decayed [adj] *rotten, falling apart* addled, bad, carious, carrion, corroded, decomposed, effete, gangrenous, moldered, overripe, perished, putrefied, putrescent, putrid, rank, riddled, rotted, ruined, spoiled, wasted, withered; CONCEPT 485 —Ant. developing, flourishing, germinating, growing, improving, ripening

decease [n] *death* buying the farm*, curtains*, defunction, demise, departure, dissolution, dying, grim reaper*, passing, passing away, passing over, quietus, release, silence, sleep, taps*, the end; CONCEPT 304 —Ant. birth

decease [v] *pass away; expire* buy a one-way ticket*, call off all bets*, cease, check out*, cool off*, croak*, deep six*, depart, die, drop, go, pass, pass away, pass on, pass over, perish, succumb; CONCEPT 304 —Ant. bear, be born

deceased [adj] *dead* asleep, bit the dust*, cold*, defunct, departed, exanimate, expired, extinct, finished, former, gave up the ghost*, gone, inanimate, kicked the bucket*, late, lifeless, lost, passed on, pushing up daisies*; CONCEPT 539 —Ant. alive, born, lively, living

deceit [n1] *practice of misleading* ambidexterity, ambidextrousness, artifice, cheating, chicane, chicanery, cozening, craft, craftiness, cunning, deceitfulness, deception, defrauding, dirty dealing*, dirty pool*, dishonesty, dissemblance, dissimulation, double-dealing, duplicity, entrapping, fraud, fraudulence, guile, hypocrisy, imposition, overreaching, pretense, slyness, smoke and mirrors*, trapping, treachery, trickery, two-facedness*, two-timing*, underhandedness; CONCEPTS 59,633 —Ant. frankness, honesty, openness, truth, truthfulness, uprightness

deceit [n2] *particular type of trick, misleading* artifice, blind, cheat, chicanery, crocodile tears*, deception, dirty trick*, dirty work*, duplicity, fake, feint, flimflam*, fraud, fraudulence, hoax, humbug, imposture, misrepresentation, pretense, ruse, sell, sellout, sham, shift, smoke and mirrors*, snow job*, soft soap*, spoof, stratagem, subterfuge, sweet talk*, swindle, trick, whitewash*, wile; CONCEPTS 59,660

deceitful [adj] *dishonest, insincere* artful, astucious, astute, beguiling, clandestine, counterfeit, crafty, cunning, deceiving, deceptive, delusive, delusory, designing, disingenuous, double-dealing, duplicitous, fallacious, false, feline, foxy, fraudulent, furtive, guileful, hypocritical, illusory, impostrous, indirect, insidious, knavish, lying, mendacious, misleading, rascal, roguish, shifty, slick, sly, sneaky, stealthy, subtle, treacherous, tricky, two-faced*, underhand, underhanded, untrustworthy, untruthful, wily; CONCEPT 401 —Ant. faithful, frank, honest, loyal, open, sincere, trustworthy, truthful, upright

deceive [v] *mislead; be dishonest* bamboozle*, beat, beat out of*, beguile, betray, bilk, buffalo*, burn, cheat, circumvent, clip, con, cozen, cross up, defraud, delude, disappoint, double-cross, dupe, ensnare, entrap, fake, falsify, fleece, fool, gouge, gull, hoax, hoodwink, hook*, humbug, impose upon, lead on, outwit, play joke on, pull fast one*, put on, rob, scam, screw, sell, skin, suck in*, swindle, take advantage of, take for, take for ride*, take in, take to cleaners*, trick, victimize; CONCEPTS 7,19,59 —Ant. be honest

decency [n] *respectable behavior* appropriateness, ceremoniousness, civility, conventionality, correctness, courtesy, decorum, dignity, etiquette, fitness, fittingness, formality, good form, good manners, honesty, modesty, propriety, respectability, righteousness, seemliness, virtue; CONCEPT 633 —Ant. immodesty, immorality, impropriety, indecency, obsceneness, obscenity

decent [adj1] *respectable, appropriate* approved, becoming, befitting, chaste, clean, comely, comme il faut, conforming, continent, correct, decorous, delicate, ethical, fit, fitting, good, honest, honorable, immaculate, mannerly, modest, moral, nice, noble, on the up and up*, polite, presentable, proper, prudent, pure, reserved, right, seemly, spotless, stainless, standard, straight, straight arrow*, straight shooting*, suitable, trustworthy, unblemished, undefiled, untarnished, upright, virtuous, worthy; CONCEPTS 401,558 —Ant. inappropriate, indecent, poor, unrespectable, unsuitable, unsuited

decent [adj2] *kind, generous* accommodating, courteous, friendly, gracious, helpful, obliging, thoughtful, virtuous; CONCEPTS 404,542 —Ant. disobliging, indecent, unaccommodating, ungenerous, unkind

decent [adj3] *sufficient, tolerable* acceptable, adequate, all right, ample, average, comfortable, common, competent, enough, fair, fair to middling*, good, mediocre, middling, moderately good, passable, presentable, reasonable, respectable, right, satisfactory, sufficing, unexceptional, unimpeachable, unobjectionable; CONCEPTS 533,558,572 —Ant. indecent, insufficient, intolerable, unsuitable

deception [n1] *misleading; being dishonest* beguilement, betrayal, blarney*, boondoggle*, cheat, circumvention, cozenage, craftiness, cunning, deceit, deceitfulness, deceptiveness, defraudation, dirt, disinformation, dissimulation, double-dealing, dupery, duplicity, equivocation, falsehood, fast one*, flimflam*, fraud, fraudulence, guile, hokum*, hypocrisy, imposition, insincerity, juggling, legerdemain, lying, mendacity, pretense, prevarication, snow job*, sophism, treachery, treason, trickery, trickiness, trumpery, untruth; CONCEPTS 7,19,59 —Ant. frankness, honesty, honor, openness, trustworthiness, truth, truthfulness, uprightness

deception [n2] *trick* artifice, bilk, bluff, catch, cheat, chicane, con, confidence game, con game*, cover-up, crock, decoy, device, dodge, fallacy, fast one*, fast shuffle*, feint, fib, fraud, gimmick, hoax, hogwash*, hustle, illusion, imposture, jive*, lie, malarkey*, mare's-nest*, pretext, ride*, ruse, scam, sham, shift, shuck, snare, snow job*, stall, sting, story, stratagem, subterfuge, swindle, trap, trick, whitewash*, wile, wrinkle*; CONCEPTS 59,230

deceptive [adj] *dishonest* ambiguous, astucious, beguiling, bum*, catchy, crafty, cunning, deceitful, deceiving, deluding, delusive, delusory, designing, disingenuous, fake, fallacious, false, fishy, foxy, fraudulent, illusory, imposturous, indirect, insidious, lying, misleading, mock, oblique, off*, phony, plausible, rascal, roguish, scheming, seeming, serpentine, shifty, slick, slippery, sly, sneaky, snide, specious, spurious, subtle, treacherous, tricky, two-faced*, underhand, underhanded, unreliable, wily; CONCEPTS 401,582 —*Ant.* forthright, frank, honest, open, truthful, upright

decide [v] *make a determination; settle an issue* adjudge, adjudicate, agree, arrive at conclusion, award, call shots*, cast the die*, choose, cinch, clinch, come to agreement, come to conclusion, come to decision, commit oneself, conclude, conjecture, decree, determine, draw a conclusion, elect, end, establish, figure, fix upon, form opinion, gather, go down line*, guess, have final word*, judge, make a decision, make up mind, mediate, opt, poll, purpose, reach decision, resolve, rule, select, set, surmise, take a stand, tap, vote, will; CONCEPT 18 —*Ant.* defer, delay, hesitate, postpone, procrastinate, put off, wait

decided [adj] *certain, definite* absolute, assured, categorical, cinched, clear, clear-cut, clinched, destined, determined, distinct, emphatic, explicit, express, fated, for sure*, indisputable, in the bag*, nailed*, on ice*, positive, prearranged, predetermined, pronounced, resolved, runaway*, settled, sure, unalterable, unambiguous, undeniable, undisputed, unequivocal, unmistakable, unquestionable; CONCEPT 535 —*Ant.* indefinite, uncertain, undecided

decided [adj2] *determined, strong-willed* assertive, bent, certain, cocksure, decisive, deliberate, earnest, emphatic, established, firm, fixed, inflexible, intent, iron-jawed*, mulish, positive, purposeful, resolute, resolved, serious, set, settled, strong-minded, sure, unbending, unfaltering, unhesitating, unwavering, unyielding; CONCEPTS 401,403 —*Ant.* deferential, delaying, hesitant, postponing, procrastinating, undecided

decidedly [adv] *certainly* absolutely, bloody*, by all means, clearly, decisively, determinedly, distinctly, downright, emphatically, flat out*, for a fact*, in spades*, no catch*, no holds barred*, no ifs ands or buts*, no mistake*, no strings attached*, of course, positively, powerful, real, really, right, straight out, strongly, sure, surely, terribly, terrifically, unequivocally, unmistakably; CONCEPT 535

deciding [adj] *determining* chief, conclusive, critical, crucial, decisive, important, influential, key, necessary, prime, principal, significant; CONCEPTS 546,568 —*Ant.* inconclusive, insignificant, secondary, trivial, uncritical, unimportant

decimate [v] *destroy* annihilate, butcher*, commit genocide, execute, exterminate, kill off, massacre, obliterate, slaughter, stamp out, wipe out; CONCEPT 252

decipher [v] *figure out, understand* analyze, break, break down, bring out, cipher, construe, crack, decode, deduce, disentangle, dope out, elucidate, encipher, explain, expound, find the key, interpret, make clear, make out, puzzle out, read, render, reveal, solve, spell, translate, unfold, unravel, unriddle; CONCEPTS 15,31,37 —*Ant.* code, encode, scramble

decision [n1] *conclusion; resolution reached* accommodation, accord, adjudication, adjudicature, adjustment, agreement, arbitration, arrangement, choice, compromise, declaration, determination, end, finding, judgment, opinion, outcome, prearrangement, preference, reconciliation, resolution, result, ruling, selection, sentence, settlement, showdown, the call, the nod, understanding, verdict; CONCEPTS 278,689 —*Ant.* deferment, deferral, delay, indecision, postponement

decision [n2] *strength of mind or will* backbone, decidedness, decisiveness, determination, doggedness, earnestness, firmness, fortitude, grit, iron will, obstinacy, obstinance, perseverance, persistence, pluck*, purpose, purposefulness, resoluteness, resolution, resolve, seriousness, spine, stubbornness, volition, will, will power; CONCEPTS 410,411 —*Ant.* indecision, indefiniteness, indetermination, procrastination, wavering

decisive [adj] *definite* absolute, all out*, assured, bent, certain, conclusive, crisp, critical, crucial, decided, definitive, determined, fateful, final, firm, flat out*, forceful, imperative, imperious, incisive, influential, litmus test*, momentous, peremptory, positive, resolute, resolved, set, settled, significant, straight out*, strong-minded, trenchant; CONCEPT 535 —*Ant.* indecisive, indefinite, procrastinating, unpositive

deck [v] *put on clothing, usually new* accouter, adorn, appoint, array, attire, beautify, bedeck, clothe, decorate, dress, dress up, embellish, festoon, garland, garnish, grace, gussy up*, ornament, prettify, primp, slick, trim; CONCEPT 167 —*Ant.* disrobe, unclothe

declaim [v] *proclaim; get on a soapbox* attack, bloviate, blow hot air*, declare, decry, denounce, harangue, hold forth, inveigh, lecture, mouth, orate, perorate, pile it on*, proclaim, rail, rant, recite, soapbox*, speak, spiel*, spout*, talk big*; CONCEPTS 49,51

declaration [n1] *assertion of belief or knowledge* acknowledgment, admission, advertisement, affirmation, allegation, announcement, answer, attestation, averment, avowal, bomb*, broadcast, communication, deposition, disclosure, enunciation, explanation, exposition, expression, hot air*, information, notice, notification, oath, pitch, presentation, profession, promulgation, protestation, publication, remark, report, revelation, saying, say so*, spiel*, statement, story, testimony, two cents' worth*, utterance; CONCEPTS 49,274,278 —*Ant.* denial, disavowal, retraction

declaration [n2] *official proclamation* acclamation, affidavit, allegation, announcement, article, attestation, bulletin, canon, charge, confirmation, constitution, credo, creed, denunciation, deposition, document, edict, gospel, indictment, manifesto, notice, notification, plea, proclamation, profession, promulgation, pronouncement, pronunciamento, resolution, testament, testimony, ultimatum; CONCEPTS *271,274,278* —*Ant.* denial, retraction

declare [v1] *make known clearly or officially* acknowledge, advance, advocate, affirm, allegate, allege, announce, argue, assert, asservate, attest, aver, avow, be positive, blaze, bring forward, certify, cite, claim, confess, confirm, contend, convey, demonstrate, disclose, enunciate, give out, inform, insist, maintain, manifest, notify, pass, proclaim, profess, promulgate, pronounce, propound, publish, put forward, reaffirm, reassert, render, repeat, reveal, set forth, show, sound, state, stress, swear, tell, testify, validate, vouch; CONCEPTS *49,60* —*Ant.* deny, disavow, retract

declare [v2] *claim as possession* acknowledge, admit, avouch, avow, confess, convey, disclose, divulge, impart, indicate, manifest, notify, own, profess, represent, reveal, state, swear; CONCEPTS *57,60* —*Ant.* deny, disclaim

declassify [v] *open to the public* display, exhibit, make available, make public, publicize, show; CONCEPT *261*

decline [n1] *lessening* abatement, backsliding, comedown, cropper*, decay, decrepitude, degeneracy, degeneration, descent, deterioration, devolution, diminution, dissolution, dive, downfall, downgrade, downturn, drop, dwindling, ebb, ebbing, enfeeblement, failing, failure, fall, falling off, flop, lapse, on the skids*, pratfall, recession, relapse, senility, skids*, slump, wane, waning, weakening, worsening; CONCEPTS *674,698,699* —*Ant.* betterment, improvement, increase, rise

decline [n2] *downward change in value, position* declivity, decrease, depression, descent, dip, downslide, downswing, downtrend, downturn, drop, drop-off, fall-off, hill, incline, lapse, loss, lowering, pitch, sag, slide, slip, slope, slump; CONCEPTS *336,346,738* —*Ant.* ascent, increase, rise

decline [v1] *say no* abjure, abstain, avoid, balk, beg to be excused, bypass, demur, deny, desist, disapprove, dismiss, don't buy*, forbear, forgo, gainsay, nix*, not accept, not hear of, not think of, pass on*, refrain, refuse, reject, renounce, reprobate, repudiate, send regrets, shy, spurn, turn down, turn thumbs down*; CONCEPTS *45, 51* —*Ant.* accept, say yes

decline [v2] *lessen, become less* abate, backslide, cheapen, decay, decrease, degenerate, depreciate, deteriorate, diminish, disimprove, disintegrate, droop, drop, dwindle, ebb, fade, fail, fall, fall off, flag, go downhill*, go to pot*, go to the dogs*, hit the skids*, languish, lapse, lose value, lower, pine, recede, relapse, retrograde, return, revert, rot, sag, settle, shrink, sink, slide, subside, wane, weaken, worsen; CONCEPTS *240,698* —*Ant.* improve, increase, rise

decline [v3] *descend* dip, droop, drop, fall, go down, lower, sag, set, settle, sink, slant, slope; CONCEPTS *151,181* —*Ant.* ascend, go up, rise

decode [v] *decipher* break, clear up, crack, crack the code, decrypt, figure out, find the solution, interpret, make clear, read, solve, translate, unravel, unriddle, unscramble, untangle, work out; CONCEPTS *15,31,37*

decommission [v] *withdraw from active service* deactivate, demilitarize, make inactive, retire, shut down, shut off; CONCEPTS *25,121*

decompose [v1] *rot, break up* break down, crumble, decay, disintegrate, dissolve, fall apart, fester, molder, putrefy, putresce, spoil, taint, turn; CONCEPT *469* —*Ant.* combine, develop, grow, improve

decompose [v2] *analyze by taking apart* anatomize, atomize, break down, break up, decompound, disintegrate, dissect, dissolve, distill, resolve, separate; CONCEPTS *24,103* —*Ant.* combine, join, put together, unite

decomposition [n] *rot, breakdown* atomization, corruption, decay, disintegration, dissipation, dissolution, division, putrefaction, putrescence, putridity; CONCEPTS *230,674* —*Ant.* combination, development, growth, improvement

deconstructionist [n/adj] *exposing a text's multiple meanings* critical, debunking, demystifying, demythifying, hermeneutical, reinterpreting, revisionist; CONCEPT *268*

decontaminate [v] *clean* antisepticize, cleanse, disinfect, fumigate, make sterile, purify, sanitize, sterilize, wash; CONCEPTS *161,165*

decor [n] *colors, furnishings of a place* adornment, color scheme, decoration, interior design, ornamentation; CONCEPTS *622,723*

decorate [v1] *beautify, embellish* add finishing touches, adorn, bedeck, bedizen, brighten, burnish, color, deck, do up*, dress out*, dress up*, enhance, enrich, festoon, finish, fix up, frill, furbish, garnish, gild, grace, gussy up*, idealize, illuminate, jazz up*, ornament, paint, perfect, prank, renovate, spruce up*, trim; CONCEPTS *162,177*

decorate [v2] *honor and give medal* cite, laureate, pin medal on, plume; CONCEPT *132*

decoration [n1] *beautification, embellishment* adornment, beautifying, bedecking, bedizenment, designing, elaboration, enhancement, enrichment, festooning, flounce, flourish, frill, furbelow, garnish, garnishing, illumination, improvement, ornament, ornamentation, redecorating, spangle, trimming; CONCEPTS *162,177* —*Ant.* eyesore

decoration [n2] *particular type of embellishment* appliqué, arabesque, bauble, braid, color, curlicue, design, dingbat*, doodad*, extravagance, fandangle*, festoon, filigree, finery, flounce, flourish, fretwork, frill, frippery, furbelow, fuss, garbage*, garnish, garniture, gewgaws, gilt, gimcracks*, gingerbread, inlay, jazz*, lace, ornament, parquetry, plaque, ribbon, scroll, sequin, spangle, thing*, tinsel, tooling, trimming, trinket, wreath; CONCEPTS *259,260*

decoration [n3] *medal of honor* accolade, award, badge, bays, citation, colors, cross, distinction, emblem, garter, kudos, laurels, medal, mention, order, Purple Heart, ribbon, star; CONCEPT *337*

decorative [adj] *beautifying* adorning, cosmetic, embellishing, enhancing, fancy, florid, nonfunctional, ornamental, prettifying, pretty; CONCEPT 579 —*Ant.* ugly

decorous [*adj*] *appropriate, suitable* au fait, becoming, befitting, ceremonial, ceremonious, civilized, comely, comme il faut, conforming, conventional, correct, decent, demure, de rigueur, dignified, done, elegant, fit, fitting, formal, good, mannerly, meet, moral, nice, polite, prim, proper, punctilious, refined, respectable, right, seasonable, sedate, seemly, staid, well-behaved; CONCEPTS 401,558 —*Ant.* impolite, inappropriate, indecent, indecorous, unbecoming, unfit, unrefined, unseemly, unsuitable

decorum [*n*] *appropriate behavior, good manners* breeding, civility, conduct, convenance, convention, correctitude, correctness, courtliness, decency, demeanor, deportment, dignity, etiquette, form, formality, gentility, good grace, gravity, habits, order, orderliness, politeness, politesse, properness, propriety, protocol, punctilio, respectability, seemliness, tact, usage; CONCEPT 633 —*Ant.* bad behavior, bad manners, impoliteness, indecency, rudeness

decoy [*n*] *bait, trap* allurement, attraction, beard*, blind, blow off*, booster, camouflage, catch, chicane, chicanery, come-on, deception, drawing card, ensnarement, enticement, facade, fake, front, imitation, inducement, inveiglement, lure, nark, plant, pretense, seducement, shill, sitting duck*, snare, stick, stoolie*, stool pigeon*, temptation, trick, trickery; CONCEPTS 59,230,680

decoy [*v*] *bait, entrap* allure, come on, con, deceive, delude, egg one on*, ensnare, ensorcell, entice, inveigle, lead on*, lead up garden path*, lure, mislead, mousetrap*, rope in*, seduce, shill, steer, suck in*, tempt, toll, tout, trap, wile; CONCEPTS 16,59

decrease [*n*] *diminishing, lessening* abatement, compression, condensation, constriction, contraction, cutback, decline, declining, decrescence, depression, diminution, discount, downturn, dwindling, ebb, falling off, loss, reduction, shrinkage, striction, subsidence, waning; CONCEPT 698 —*Ant.* addition, development, enlargement, expansion, growth, increase, raise

decrease [*v*] *grow less or make less* abate, calm down, check, contract, crumble, curb, curtail, cut down, decay, decline, degenerate, depreciate, deteriorate, devaluate, die down, diminish, droop, drop, drop off, dry up, dwindle, ease, ebb, evaporate, fade, fall off, lessen, let up, lighten, lose edge, lower, modify, narrow down, peter out, quell, quiet, reduce, restrain, run low, settle, shrink, shrivel, sink, slacken, slack off, slash, slow down, slump, soften, subside, tail off, wane, waste, weaken, wear away, wear down, wither; CONCEPTS 240,698 —*Ant.* add, develop, enlarge, expand, grow, increase, raise

decree [*n*] *mandate, legal order* act, announcement, behest, bidding, charge, charging, command, commandment, declaration, decretum, dictum, direction, directive, edict, enactment, injunction, instruction, judgment, law, order, ordinance, precept, prescript, proclamation, promulgation, pronouncement, rap*, regulation, rule, ruling, say, statute, the riot act*, the word*; CONCEPTS 318,685

decree [*v*] *order rule or action* announce, command, compel, constrain, decide, declare, demand, determine, dictate, enact, force, impose, lay down the law*, oblige, ordain, prescribe, proclaim, pronounce, put one's foot down*, read the riot act*, require, rule, set; CONCEPTS 50,53,81,88,317

decrepit [*adj*] *deteriorated, debilitated, especially as a result of age* aged, anile, antiquated, battered, bedraggled, broken-down, creaky, crippled, dilapidated, doddering, effete, feeble, flimsy, fragile, frail, haggard, incapacitated, infirm, insubstantial, old, quavering, ramshackle, rickety, run-down, seedy, senile, shabby, shaking, superannuated, tacky, threadbare, tired, tottering, tumble-down, unsound, used, wasted, weak, weakly, weather-beaten, worn, worn-out; CONCEPTS 406,485 —*Ant.* fit, healthy, young

decriminalize [*v*] *legalize* allow, declare lawful, legitimize, make legal, permit, regulate, sanction; CONCEPTS 298,317

decry [*v*] *criticize, blame* abuse, asperse, badmouth*, belittle, calumniate, censure, condemn, cry down, defame, denounce, depreciate, derogate, detract, devalue, diminish, discount, discredit, disgrace, disparage, do a number on*, downgrade, dump on*, hit*, knock*, lower, malign, mark down, minimize, opprobriate, pan*, poor-mouth*, put down, rail against, rap, reprehend, reprobate, run down, slam*, take away, take swipe at*, throw stones at*, traduce, underestimate, underrate, undervalue, vilify, write off; CONCEPTS 44,52 —*Ant.* applaud, compliment, exalt, laud, praise

dedicate [*v1*] *donate, set aside for special use* address, allot, apply, apportion, appropriate, assign, commit, consign, devote, give, give over to, inscribe, offer, pledge, restrict, surrender; CONCEPTS 18,50,88,135 —*Ant.* misapply, misuse, steal, take

dedicate [*v2*] *sanctify* anoint, bless, consecrate, hallow, set apart; CONCEPTS 69,367 —*Ant.* alienate, desecrate, misuse

dedicated [*adj*] *loyal, hard-working* committed, devoted, enthusiastic, faithful, given over to, old faithful*, purposeful, single-hearted, single-minded, sworn, true blue*, true to the end*, wholehearted, zealous; CONCEPTS 404, 542 —*Ant.* apathetic, lazy

dedication [*n1*] *faithfulness, loyalty* adherence, allegiance, commitment, devotedness, devotion, single-mindedness, wholeheartedness; CONCEPTS 411,657 —*Ant.* disloyalty, unfaithfulness

dedication [*n2*] *speech of praise; sanctification* address, celebration, consecration, devotion, envoy, glorification, hallowing, inscription, message; CONCEPTS 69,367 —*Ant.* apathy

deduce [*v*] *figure out, understand* add up, analyze, assume, be afraid, boil down, cogitate, collect, conceive, conclude, consider, deduct, deem, derive, draw, fancy, figure, gather, glean, have a hunch*, imagine, infer, judge, make, make out, presume, presuppose, ratiocinate, read into, reason, regard, surmise, take to mean; CONCEPTS 15,24

deducible [*adj*] *understandable* a priori, consequent, deductive, derivable, dogmatic, following, inferable, inferential, provable, reasoned, traceable; CONCEPTS 402,529

deduct [v] *take away or out; reduce* abstract, allow, bate, cut back, decrease by, diminish, discount, dock, draw back, knock off, lessen, rebate, reduce, remove, roll back, subtract, take, take from, take off, withdraw, write off; CONCEPTS 236,247 —*Ant.* add, increase, raise

deduction [n1] *conclusion, understanding* answer, assumption, cogitation, concluding, consequence, consideration, contemplation, corollary, deliberation, derivation, finding, illation, inference, inferring, judgment, meditation, mulling, musing, opinion, pondering, ratiocination, reasoning, reflection, result, rumination, sequitur, speculation, thinking, thought; CONCEPTS 15,24,689 —*Ant.* confusion

deduction [n2] *something subtracted* abatement, abstraction, allowance, credit, cut, decrease, decrement, depreciation, diminution, discount, dockage, excision, rebate, reduction, removal, subtraction, withdrawal, write-off; CONCEPTS 763,776 —*Ant.* addition, increase, rise

deed [n1] *achievement* accomplishment, act, action, adventure, ballgame, big idea*, bit,- byplay, cause, commission, crusade, do, enterprise, exploit, fact, feat, follow through, game, happenin'*, performance, plan, quest, reality, securing, stunt, thing*, tour de force, truth, winning; CONCEPTS 4,706

deed [n2] *legal paper assigning property; contract* agreement, bargain, certificate, charter, compact, conveyance, covenant, document, indenture, instrument, lease, papers, proof, record, release, security, title, transaction, voucher, warranty; CONCEPTS 271,318

deem [v] *regard, consider* account, allow, appraise, assume, be afraid, believe, calculate, conceive, conjecture, credit, daresay, divine, esteem, estimate, expect, feel, guess, hold, imagine, judge, know, presume, reckon, sense, set store by, suppose, surmise, suspect, think, understand, view; CONCEPTS 12,28

deep [adj1] *extending very far, usually down* abysmal, abyssal, below, beneath, bottomless, broad, buried, deep-seated, distant, downreaching, far, fathomless, immersed, inmost, low, profound, rooted, subaqueous, submarine, submerged, subterranean, sunk, underground, unfathomable, wide, yawning; CONCEPTS 737,777 —*Ant.* shallow

deep [adj2] *abstract, complicated in meaning* abstruse, acute, arcane, complex, concealed, Delphic, difficult, discerning, esoteric, hard to understand, heavy*, hermetic, hidden, incisive, intricate, learned, mysterious, obscure, occult, Orphic, penetrating, profound, recondite, sagacious, secret, serious, Sibylline, wise; CONCEPTS 402,529 —*Ant.* frivolous, ignorant, shallow, superficial, trivial, unintelligent

deep [adj3] *scheming, devious* acute, artful, astute, canny, contriving, crafty, cunning, designing, foxy, guileful, insidious, intriguing, keen, knowing, plotting, sharp, shrewd, sly, tricky, wily; CONCEPT 404 —*Ant.* aboveboard, artless, open

deep [adj4] *absorbed, engrossed in activity* abstracted, centered, concentrated, enfolded, engaged, fixed, focused, immersed, intent, into, lost, musing, preoccupied, rapt, set, wrapped, wrapped up; CONCEPT 542 —*Ant.* flighty, superficial

deep [adj5] *intense in effect on senses* bass, booming, dark, extreme, full-toned, grave, great, hard, low, low-pitched, low-toned, profound, resonant, rich, sonorous, strong, vivid; CONCEPTS 537,594,618 —*Ant.* light, pale, quiet, soft

deep [n] *the sea* blue*, brine, briny*, Davy Jones's locker*, drink*, main, middle, ocean, Poseidon's realm*, the high seas; CONCEPT 514

deepen [v1] *make depth greater* dig, dig out, dredge, excavate, expand, extend, hollow, scoop out, scrape out; CONCEPT 250 —*Ant.* fill

deepen [v2] *make more intense* aggravate, develop, enhance, expand, extend, grow, heighten, increase, intensate, intensify, magnify, mount, redouble, reinforce, rise, rouse, strengthen; CONCEPTS 236,245,697 —*Ant.* lighten, pale, quieten, soften

deeply [adv] *completely, intensely* acutely, affectingly, distressingly, feelingly, genuinely, gravely, intensely, mournfully, movingly, passionately, profoundly, sadly, seriously, severely, surely, thoroughly, to the quick; CONCEPTS 531,772 —*Ant.* incompletely, little, slightly

deep-seated [adj] *ingrained* built-in, chronic, confirmed, deep down, deeply felt, deep-rooted, dyed-in-the-wool, established, fixed, habitual, inborn, inbred, inherent, lodged in one's brain*, longstanding, longtime, subconscious; CONCEPTS 535,549

deep space [n] *region beyond Earth's solar system* intergalactic space, interplanetary space, interstellar space, outer space; CONCEPTS 370,511

deface [v] *mar, mutilate* blemish, contort, damage, deform, demolish, destroy, dilapidate, disfigure, distort, harm, impair, injure, mangle, misshape, obliterate, ruin, scratch, spoil, sully, tarnish, trash*, vandalize, wreck; CONCEPTS 246,252 —*Ant.* adorn, beautify, decorate, embellish, fix, mend, ornament, repair

de facto [adv] *in reality* actual, actually, existing, genuinely, in effect, in fact, real, really, tangible, truly, veritably; CONCEPT 582

defamation [n] *libel, slander* aspersion, backbiting, backstabbing, belittlement, black eye*, calumny, character assassination, cheap shot*, denigration, depreciation, detraction, dirt, dirty laundry*, disparagement, dump*, dynamite, hit, knock, lie, low-down dirty*, mud, obloquy, opprobrium, scorcher, slam*, slap in face*, slime, slur, smear, tale, traducement, vilification; CONCEPT 54 —*Ant.* approval, commendation, compliment, exaltation, praise

defamatory [adj] *libelous, slanderous* abusive, calumnious, contumelious, denigrating, derogatory, detracting, detractive, disparaging, injurious, insulting, maligning, opprobrious, traducing, vilifying, vituperative; CONCEPTS 267,537 —*Ant.* approving, commending, complimentary, exalting, praising

defame [v] *inflict libel or slander* asperse, bad-mouth*, belie, besmirch, blacken, blister, calumniate, cast aspersions on, cast slur on, denigrate, detract, discredit, disgrace, dishonor, disparage, do a number on*, knock, malign, pan*, put zingers on*, roast, scandalize, scorch, slam, smear, speak evil of*, stigmatize, throw mud at*, traduce, vilify, villainize, vituperate; CONCEPTS 7,19,54 —*Ant.* approve, commend, compliment, exalt, praise

default [n] *failure; want* absence, blemish, blunder, dearth, defect, deficiency, delinquency, dereliction, disregard, error, fault, imperfection, inadequacy, insufficiency, lack, lapse, miss, neglect, nonpayment, offense, omission, overlooking, oversight, privation, shortcoming, slight, transgression, vice, weakness, wrongdoing; CONCEPTS 335,699,709 —*Ant.* advantage, payment, perfection, satisfaction, success

default [v] *dodge payment* bilk, defraud, dishonor, evade, fail, leave town*, meet under arch*, neglect, put on the cuff*, rat*, repudiate, run out on*, see in the alley, shirk, skate*, skip, skip out on*, stiff*, swindle, welch, welsh; CONCEPTS 59,63,330 —*Ant.* pay

defeat [n1] *overthrow, beating* ambush, annihilation, beating, blow, break, breakdown, check, collapse, conquest, count, debacle, defeasance, destruction, discomfiture, downthrow, drubbing*, embarrassment, extermination, failure, fall, insuccess, killing*, KO*, lacing, licking, loss, massacre, mastery, nonsuccess, paddling, rebuff, repulse, reverse, rout, ruin, scalping, setback, shellacking*, slaughter, subjugation, thrashing, trap, trashing, trimming, triumph, trouncing, vanquishment, waxing, whaling, whipping, whitewashing*; CONCEPT 95 —*Ant.* conquest, success, triumph, victory, win

defeat [n2] *frustration* disappointment, discomfiture, downfall, failure, foil, loss, rebuff, repulse, reversal, reverse, setback, thwarting; CONCEPT 410 —*Ant.* attainment, mastery, success, triumph

defeat [v1] *conquer in military manner* ambush, annihilate, bar, bear down, beat, best, block, butcher, crush, decimate, demolish, discomfit, drown, entrap, finish off, halt, hinder, impede, lick, mow down, obliterate, obstruct, outflank, outmaneuver, overpower, overrun, overthrow, overwhelm, parry, prevail over, quell, reduce, repel, repress, repulse, roll back, rout, route, sack, scatter, shipwreck, sink, slaughter, smash, subdue, subjugate, suppress, surmount, swamp, torpedo*, trample, trash, upset, vanquish, whip, wipe out; CONCEPTS 95,320 —*Ant.* give up, lose, surrender

defeat [v2] *conquer in athletic contest* beat, bust*, clobber*, cream*, deck*, drop*, drub*, edge, flax*, flog*, floor*, knock out*, KO*, lambaste*, lick, outhit, outjump, outplay, outrun, overpower, plow under*, pommel*, pound*, powder*, pulverize*, run roughshod over*, skin*, steamroll*, take, take it all*, take to cleaners*, tan*, thrash, total, trounce, wallop*, whack*, whomp*, win, work over*, zap*; CONCEPTS 95,363 —*Ant.* give up, lose, surrender

defeat [v3] *frustrate* baffle, balk, beat down*, beat the system*, blank, block, bury, cast down, cause setback, checkmate, circumvent, confound, contravene, cook*, counterplot, cross, disappoint, discomfit, disconcert, disprove, edge out*, foil, invalidate, neutralize, nonplus, nose out*, nullify, outwit, overturn, put end to*, puzzle, quell, reduce, refute, ruin, scuttle,

shave*, shellac*, skunk*, spoil, squash, stump, subdue, subjugate, surmount, take wind out of sails*, throw for loop*, thwart, undo, victimize; CONCEPTS 14,121 —*Ant.* abet, aid, encourage, help, inspirit

defect [n] *blemish, imperfection* birthmark, blot, blotch, break, bug, catch, check, crack, deficiency, deformity, discoloration, drawback, error, failing, fault, flaw, foible, frailty, gap, glitch, gremlin, hole, infirmity, injury, irregularity, kink, knot, lack, mark, marring, mistake, patch, rift, rough spot, scar, scarcity, scratch, seam, second, shortage, shortcoming, sin, speck, spot, stain, taint, unsoundness, vice, want, weakness, weak point; CONCEPTS 309,580,646 —*Ant.* advantage, improvement, perfection, strength

defect [v] *break from belief, faith* abandon, abscond, apostatize, back out, break faith*, change sides, depart, desert, fall away from*, forsake, go, go back on, go over, go over the fence*, lapse, leave, pull out, quit, rat*, rebel, reject, renege, renounce, revolt, run out, schism, sell out*, spurn, take a walk*, tergiversate, tergiverse, turn, turn coat*, walk out on, withdraw; CONCEPTS 198,362 —*Ant.* come in, join

defection [n] *abandonment* alienation, apostasy, backsliding, deficiency, dereliction, desertion, disaffection, disloyalty, disownment, divorce, estrangement, failing, failure, faithlessness, forsaking, lack, parting, rebellion, recreancy, rejection, repudiation, retreat, revolt, separation, severance, sundering, tergiversation, withdrawal; CONCEPTS 195,198 —*Ant.* joining

defective [adj] *broken, not working* abnormal, amiss, blemished, damaged, deficient, faulty, flawed, impaired, imperfect, inadequate, incomplete, injured, insufficient, lacking, on the bum*, out of order, poor, seconds, sick, subnormal, unfinished, unhealthy, unsound, wanting; CONCEPTS 560,565 —*Ant.* excellent, faultless, flawless, perfect, unbroken

defend [v1] *protect* avert, battle, beat off, bulwark, care for, cherish, conserve, contend, cover, entrench, espouse, fend off, fight, fight for, fortify, foster, garrison, guard, guard against, hedge, hold, hold at bay, house, insure, keep safe, look after, maintain, mine, nourish, oppose, panoply, preserve, prevent, provide sanctuary, repel danger, resist, retain, safeguard, save, screen, secure, shelter, shield, stave off, sustain, take in, uphold, war, ward off, watch, watch over, withstand; CONCEPTS 96,110 —*Ant.* abandon, attack, desert, leave, quit, relinquish, resign, surrender

defend [v2] *show support for* advocate, aid, apologize for, argue, assert, back, back up, bear one out*, befriend, champion, come to defense of, cover for, endorse, espouse, exculpate, exonerate, explain, go to bat for*, guarantee, justify, maintain, plead, prove a case, put in a good word*, rationalize, recommend, ride shotgun for*, say in defense, second, speak up for, stand by, stand up for, stick up for, stonewall*, support, sustain, thump for, uphold, vindicate, warrant; CONCEPTS 10,49 —*Ant.* deny, forsake, renounce

defendant [n] *accused* appellant, litigant, offender, prisoner, suspect; CONCEPT 412

defense [n1] *armament; protection system* aegis, armor, arms, barricade, bastille, bastion, bulwark, buttress, citadel, cover, deterrence, dike, embankment, fastness, fence, fort, fortification, fortress, garrison, guard, immunity, munitions, palisade, parapet, position, protection, rampart, redoubt, resistance, safeguard, security, shelter, shield, stockade, stronghold, trench, wall, ward, warfare, weaponry, weapons; CONCEPTS 321,322,500 —*Ant.* desertion, flight, surrender

defense [n2] *explanation, justification* answer, apologetics, apologia, apologizing, apology, argument, cleanup, copout*, exculpation, excuse, excusing, exoneration, explaining, extenuation, fish story*, jive, off-time*, plea, rationalization, rejoinder, reply, response, retort, return, song and dance*, story, vindication, whitewash*; CONCEPTS 57,278 —*Ant.* betrayal, capitulation, yielding

defenseless [adj] *powerless, vulnerable* caught, endangered, exposed, hands tied*, helpless, indefensible, in line of fire*, like a clay pigeon*, like a sitting duck*, naked*, on the line*, on the spot*, open, out on limb*, pigeon*, poor, unarmed, unguarded, unprotected, up the creek*, weak, wide open*; CONCEPTS 555,576 —*Ant.* powerful, strong

defensible [adj] *justifiable* condonable, defendable, excusable, fit, logical, pardonable, permissible, plausible, proper, tenable, valid, vindicable, warrantable; CONCEPT 528 —*Ant.* indefensible, invalid, unjustifiable, unvindicable

defensive [adj] *protective, watchful* arresting, averting, balking, checking, conservative, coping with, defending, foiling, forestalling, frustrating, guarding, in opposition, interrupting, opposing, preservative, preventive, protecting, resistive, safeguarding, thwarting, uptight*, warding off, withstanding; CONCEPTS 401,550 —*Ant.* undefensive, unprotective, unwary, unwatchful

defer [v1] *hold off, put off* adjourn, block, delay, detain, extend, give rain check*, hang fire*, hinder, hold up, impede, intermit, lay over, lengthen, obstruct, postpone, procrastinate, prolong, prorogue, protract, put on back burner*, put on hold*, put on ice*, remit, retard, set aside, shelve, slow, stall, stay, suspend, table, waive; CONCEPTS 121,130 —*Ant.* advance, expedite, forge, forward, hasten, hurry

defer [v2] *yield* accede, accommodate, acquiesce, adapt, adjust, admit, agree, assent, bow, buckle, capitulate, cave, comply, concede, cringe, fawn, give in to, knuckle*, knuckle under*, kowtow*, obey, submit, succumb, truckle; CONCEPT 83 —*Ant.* advance, force, forge

deference [n1] *obedience, compliance* acquiescence, capitulation, complaisance, condescension, docility, obeisance, submission, yielding; CONCEPT 633 —*Ant.* disobedience, impoliteness, noncompliance

deference [n2] *attention, homage* acclaim, civility, consideration, courtesy, esteem, honor, obeisance, politeness, regard, respect, reverence, thoughtfulness, veneration; CONCEPTS 10,410 —*Ant.* dishonor, disregard, ignorance

deferential [adj] *respectful, considerate* civil, complaisant, courteous, disarming, duteous, dutiful, ingratiating, ingratiatory, insinuating, insinuative, obedient, obeisant, obsequious, polite, regardful, reverential, saccharine, silken, silky, submissive; CONCEPT 401 —*Ant.* arrogant, disobedient, disrespectful, immodest, impolite, inconsiderate, noncompliant

deferment/deferral [n] *postponement* adjournment, delay, holdover*, moratorium, pause, putting off*, stay, suspension; CONCEPTS 121,130 —*Ant.* advance, expedition, forging

deferred [adj] *put off till a later time* adjourned, assessed, charged, delayed, funded, held up, indebted, in waiting, negotiated, on hold*, on the shelf*, pigeonholed*, postponed, prolonged, protracted, remanded, renegotiated, retarded, scrubbed*, stalled, staved off, temporized; CONCEPT 820 —*Ant.* advanced, forwarded, furthered, hastened, hurried

defiance [n] *disobedience, disregard* affront, audacity, back talk*, big talk*, boldness, bravado, brazenness, call, cartel, challenge, command, confrontation, contempt, contrariness, contumacy, dare, defy, effrontery, enjoinder, factiousness, gas*, guts*, hot air*, impudence, impugnment, insolence, insubordination, insurgence, insurgency, intractableness, lip*, muster*, opposition, order, perversity, provocation, rebellion, rebelliousness, recalcitrance, revolt, sass*, spite, stump, summons, temerity, throwing of the gauntlet*, unruliness; CONCEPTS 633,657 —*Ant.* acquiescence, obedience, regard, respect, submission, subordination

defiant [adj] *disobedient, disregardful* aggressive, audacious, bold, challenging, contumacious, daring, gutsy*, insolent, insubmissive, insubordinate, mutinous, obstinate, provocative, rebellious, recalcitrant, reckless, refractory, resistant, resistive, sassy*, truculent; CONCEPT 401 —*Ant.* acquiescent, obedient, respectful, submissive, submitting, subordinating

deficiency [n] *imperfection, inadequacy* absence, bug*, dearth, defalcation, default, defect, deficit, demerit, dereliction, failing, failure, fault, flaw, frailty, glitch*, inability to hack it*, insufficience, insufficiency, lack, loss, need, neglect, paucity, privation, scantiness, scarcity, shortage, shortcoming, sin, want, weakness; CONCEPTS 635,666,674 —*Ant.* adequacy, enough, faultlessness, perfection, plenty, satisfaction, sufficiency, superfluity

deficient [adj] *imperfect, inadequate* amiss, bad, damaged, defective, exiguous, faulty, flawed, found wanting, impaired, incomplete, inferior, infrequent, injured, insufficient, lacking, marred, meager, not cut out for*, not enough, not make it*, not up to scratch*, outta gas*, rare, scant, scanty*, scarce, second fiddle*, second string, short, shy, sketchy, skimpy, third string*, unassembled, unequal, unfinished, unsatisfactory, wanting, weak; CONCEPTS 531,565 —*Ant.* adequate, ample, enough, excessive, faultless, flawless, perfect, satisfactory, sufficient, superfluous

deficit [n] *shortage of something needed, required* arrears, dead horse*, defalcation, default, deficiency, due bill, dues, inadequacy, in hock*, insufficience, insufficiency, in the hole*, in the red, lack, loss, paucity, red ink*, scantiness, shortcoming, shortfall, underage; CONCEPTS 335,646 —*Ant.* enough, excess, plenty, superfluousness

deficit spending [n] *paying out in excess of income* debt, debt explosion, deficit financing, in the red, megadebt, negative cash flow, no assets, overspending; CONCEPTS 324,330,344

defile [v] *corrupt, violate* abuse, adulterate, befoul, besmirch, contaminate, debase, deflower, degrade, desecrate, dirty, discolor, disgrace, dishonor, hurt, maculate, make foul, mess up*, molest, muck up*, pollute, profane, rape, ravish, scuzz up*, seduce, shame, smear, soil, stain, sully, taint, tar, tarnish, trash, vitiate; CONCEPTS 54,156,246 —*Ant.* clean, cleanse, hallow, honor, purify, sanctify

defiled [adj] *corrupted, violated* besmirched, common, cooked, desecrated, dirty, dishonored, exposed, impure, mucked up*, polluted, profaned, ravished, spoilt, tainted, trashed*, unclean, vitiated; CONCEPT 570 —*Ant.* clean, cleansed, hallowed, honorable, pure, purified, sanctified

define [v1] *give description* ascertain, assign, call a spade a spade*, characterize, construe, decide, delineate, denominate, denote, describe, designate, detail, determine, dub, elucidate, entitle, etch, exemplify, explain, expound, formalize, illustrate, interpret, label, lay it out*, nail it down*, name, prescribe, represent, specify, spell out, tag, translate; CONCEPTS 55,57,62 —*Ant.* confuse, distort, tangle, twist

define [v2] *delimit, outline* belt, border, bound, circumscribe, compass, confine, curb, delineate, demarcate, distinguish, edge, encircle, enclose, encompass, envelop, establish, fence in, fix, flank, gird, girdle, limit, mark, mark out, rim, set, set bounds to, settle, stake out, surround, verge, wall in; CONCEPTS 18,60,758

definite [adj1] *exact, clear* audible, bold, categorical, clean-cut, clear-cut, clearly defined, complete, crisp, definitive, determined, distinct, distinguishable, downright, explicit, express, fixed, forthright, full, graphic, incisive, marked, minute, not vague, obvious, palpable, particular, plain, positive, precise, pronounced, ringing, severe, sharp, silhouetted, specific, straightforward, tangible, unambiguous, undubitable, unequivocal, unmistakable, visible, vivid, well-defined, well-grounded, well-marked; CONCEPT 557 —*Ant.* imprecise, indefinite, indistinct, inexact, not clear, obscure, uncertain, unclear, undefined, vague

definite [adj2] *fixed, certain, positive* assigned, assured, beyond doubt, circumscribed, convinced, decided, defined, determinate, determined, established, guaranteed, limited, narrow, precise, prescribed, restricted, set, settled, sure; CONCEPT 535 —*Ant.* indeterminate, inexact, uncertain, unfixed, unlimited, vague

definitely [adv] *certainly* absolutely, beyond any doubt, categorically, clearly, decidedly, doubtless, doubtlessly, easily, explicitly, expressly, far and away*, finally, indubitably, no ifs ands or buts about it*, obviously, plainly, positively, specifically, surely, undeniably, unequivocally, unmistakably, unquestionably, without doubt, without fail, without question; CONCEPTS 535,552 —*Ant.* doubtfully, dubiously, indefinitely, questionably

definition [n] *description* analogue, annotation, answer, characterization, clarification, clue, comment, commentary, cue, delimitation, delineation, demarcation, denotation, determination, diagnosis, drift, elucidation, exemplification, explanation, explication, exposition, expounding, fixing, formalization, gloss, individuation, interpretation, key, outlining, rationale, rendering, rendition, representation, settling, signification, solution, statement of meaning, terminology, translation; CONCEPTS 274,278,689 —*Ant.* ambiguity, nonsense, vagueness

definitive [adj] *authoritative* absolute, actual, categorical, clear-cut, closing, complete, completing, concluding, conclusive, decisive, definite, determining, downright*, ending, exhaustive, express, final, finishing, flat out*, last, limiting, nailed down, perfect, plain, precise, real, reliable, settling, specific, straight out, terminal, terminating, ultimate, unambiguous; CONCEPTS 531,535,574 —*Ant.* incomplete, inconclusive, inexact, interim, temporary, unreliable

deflate [v1] *reduce or cause to contract* collapse, decrease, depreciate, depress, devalue, diminish, empty, exhaust, flatten, puncture, shrink, squash, void; CONCEPTS 236,247,776 —*Ant.* blow up, expand, inflate

deflate [v2] *humiliate* chasten, cut down to size*, dash, debunk, discount, dispirit, humble, kick in the teeth*, knock down*, let down easy*, let wind out of sails*, mortify, puncture balloon*, put down*, shoot down*, take down*; CONCEPTS 7,19 —*Ant.* boost, build up, inflate

deflect [v] *bounce off; turn aside* avert, bend, cover up, curve, deviate, disperse, diverge, divert, fend, glance off, hold off, hook, keep off, parry, pivot, ricochet, sheer, shy, sidetrack, slew, slip, swerve, twist, veer, volte-face, wheel, whip, whirl, wind; CONCEPTS 147,189,194

deflower [v] *ravish; take away beauty* assault, defile, deflorate, depredate, desecrate, despoil, devour, force, harm, have, mar, molest, outrage, possess, ravage, ravish, ruin, seduce, spoil, violate; CONCEPT 375

deforestation [n] *clear-cutting* denuding, desertification, erosion, logging; CONCEPTS 252,257,698

deform [v] *distort, disfigure* batter, blemish, buckle, contort, cripple, damage, deface, flaw, gnarl, grimace, impair, injure, knot, maim, malform, mangle, mar, misshape, mutilate, ruin, skew, spoil, twist, warp, wince; CONCEPTS 246,250 —*Ant.* beautify, improve

deformed [adj] *disfigured, distorted* askew, awry, bent, blemished, bowed, buckled, contorted, cramped, crippled, crooked, curved, damaged, disjointed, gnarled, grotesque, humpbacked, hunchbacked, ill-made, irregular, knotted, maimed, malformed, mangled, marred, misproportioned, misshapen, out of shape, scarred, twisted, ugly, warped; CONCEPTS 485,486 —*Ant.* beautified, beautiful, graceful, improved, shapely, symmetrical

deformity [n] *disfigurement, distortion* aberration, abnormality, asymmetry, buckle, contortion, corruption, crookedness, damage, defacement, defect, depravity, evil, grossness, hideousness, impairment, injury, irregularity, knot, malconformation, malformation, misproportion, misshape, misshapenness, repulsiveness, ugliness, unattractiveness, unnaturalness, unsightliness, warp; CONCEPT 580 —Ant. beauty, grace, shapeliness

defraud [v] *cheat, bilk* bamboozle, beguile, burn, chouse, circumvent, clip, con, cozen, deceive, delude, do, do number on*, do out of*, dupe, embezzle, fleece, flimflam, foil, hoax, jive*, milk*, outwit, pull fast one*, rip off*, rob, shaft*, shuck*, stick*, sucker into*, swindle, take*, take in*, take to the cleaner's*, trick, victimize; CONCEPT 59 —Ant. contribute, help, repay, support

defray [v] *pay* bear the cost*, chip in*, cover cost, finance, foot the bill*, fund, pay for, pick up the bill*, pick up the check*, pick up the tab*, settle; CONCEPTS 108,115,327,341,351

deft [adj] *agile, clever* able, adept, adroit, apt, crack, cute, dexterous, expert, fleet, handy, having good hands, having know-how, ingenious, neat, nimble, proficient, prompt, quick, ready, skilled, skillful; CONCEPT 527 —Ant. awkward, clumsy, inept, unhandy, unskillful

defunct [adj] *extinct, not functioning* asleep, bygone, cold, dead, deceased, departed, done for*, down the drain*, exanimate, expired, gone, had it*, inanimate, inoperative, invalid, kaput*, late, lifeless, lost, nonexistent, obsolete, out of commission*, vanished; CONCEPTS 539, 560 —Ant. alive, existent, existing, functioning, live, operating, operative, valid, working

defuse [v] *disarm; smooth over* alleviate, cripple, deactivate, demilitarize, diminish, disable, lessen, moderate, mollify, pacify, pad, restrain, soften, soothe, subdue, weaken; CONCEPTS 7,22,142,211,320

defy [v] *challenge, frustrate* baffle, beard, brave, confront, contemn, dare, defeat, deride, despise, disregard, elude, face, flout, fly in face of*, foil, front, gibe*, hang tough*, hurl defiance at, ignore, insult, make my day*, mock, oppose, outdare, provoke, repel, repulse, resist, ridicule, scorn, slight, spurn, stick*, stick fast*, take one on*, thwart, venture, violate, withstand; CONCEPTS 78,87 —Ant. give in, obey, surrender, yield

degeneracy [n1] *corruption* abasement, decadence, degradation, depravity, dissoluteness, downfall, immorality, inferiority, meanness, poorness; CONCEPT 645 —Ant. morality

degeneracy [n2] *decay, deterioration* atrophy, debasement, declination, decline, decrease, depravation, devolution, downfall, downgrade; CONCEPTS 230,469 —Ant. development, improvement

degenerate [adj] *corrupt, deteriorated* base, debased, debauched, decadent, decayed, degenerated, degraded, demeaned, depraved, dissolute, effete, failing, fallen, flatitious, immoral, infamous, low, mean, miscreant, nefarious, overripe, perverted, retrograde, retrogressive, rotten, sinking, unhealthy, vicious, villainous, vitiated, wicked, worsen; CONCEPTS 545,570 —Ant. moral, upright, virtuous

degenerate [v] *decay, deteriorate* backslide, come apart at seams*, corrode, corrupt, decline, decrease, deprave, descend, die on vine*, disimprove, disintegrate, fall off, go downhill*,

go to pieces*, go to the dogs*, lapse, lessen, regress, retrogress, return, revert, rot, sink, slip, vitiate, worsen; CONCEPTS 469,698,702 —Ant. develop, improve

degradation [n] *depravity, shame* abasement, debasement, decadence, decline, degeneracy, degeneration, demotion, derogation, deterioration, discredit, disgrace, dishonor, downgrading, evil, humiliation, ignominy, mortification, perversion, reduction; CONCEPTS 230,410 —Ant. admiration, approval, elevation, honor, promotion, upgrade

degrade [v] *shame, humiliate* abase, belittle, bemean, bench, break, bump, bust, canker, cast down, cheapen, corrupt, cut down to size*, debase, debauch, declass, decry, degenerate, demean, demote, depose, deprave, derogate, deteriorate, detract, diminish, disbar, discredit, disgrace, dishonor, disparage, downgrade, humble, impair, injure, lessen, lower, mudsling*, pan*, pervert, put down, reduce, rule out, run down*, shoot down*, sink, slam, take down*, take down a peg*, tear down*, vitiate, weaken; CONCEPTS 7,19,240 —Ant. admire, approve, elevate, honor, promote, upgrade

degrading [adj] *debasing* cheapening, demeaning, derogatory, disgraceful, downgrading, humiliating, lowering; CONCEPTS 267,555,570

degree [n1] *unit of measurement* amount, amplitude, caliber, dimension, division, expanse, extent, gauge, gradation, grade, height, intensity, interval, length, limit, line, link, mark, notch, period, plane, point, proportion, quality, quantity, range, rate, ratio, reach, rung, scale, scope, severity, shade, size, space, stage, stair, standard, step, stint, strength, tenor, term, tier; CONCEPTS 651,783,792

degree [n2] *recognition of achievement; rank or grade of position* approbation, approval, baccalaureate, caliber, class, compass, credentials, credit, dignification, dignity, distinction, eminence, grade, height, honor, level, magnitude, order, pitch, point, position, potency, qualification, quality, quantity, range, rank, reach, scope, sheepskin, shingle, sort, stage, standard, standing, station, status, strength, testimonial, testimony; CONCEPTS 388,706

dehydrate [v] *take moisture out of* cottonmouth, desiccate, drain, dry, dry out, dry up, evaporate, exsiccate, parch, sear; CONCEPTS 250,469 —Ant. hydrate, moisten, wet

deify [v] *elevate, glorify* adore, apotheosize, consecrate, ennoble, enthrone, exalt, extol, idealize, idolize, immortalize, venerate, worship; CONCEPTS 69,367 —Ant. degrade, dishonor, lower

deign [v] *lower oneself* condescend, consent, deem worthy, patronize, see fit*, stoop, think fit*, vouchsafe; CONCEPT 35 —Ant. be proud, hold head high

deity [n] *god, worshiped being* celestial, celestial being, creator, divine being, divinity, goddess, godhead, idol, immortal, supreme being; CONCEPTS 368,370

déjà vu [n] *already seen or experienced* familiarity, past-life experience, recall, recognition, remembrance; CONCEPTS 40,529

dejected [adj] *depressed, blue* abject, all torn up*, atrabilious, black, bleak, broody, bummed out*, cast down, cheerless, clouded, crestfallen, dampened, dashed, despondent, disconsolate, discouraged, disheartened, dismal, dispirited, doleful, down, downcast, downhearted, down in the dumps*, down in the mouth*, dragged, drooping, droopy, gloomy, glum, heavyhearted, hurting*, in the pits*, low, low-spirited, melancholy, miserable, moody, mopey*, mopish*, morose, sad, sagging, shot down*, spiritless, woebegone, wretched; CONCEPT 403 —*Ant.* cheerful, encouraged, happy, joyous

delay [n] *deferment, interruption* adjournment, bind, check, cooling-off period*, cunctation, dawdling, demurral, detention, discontinuation, downtime*, filibuster, hangup*, hindrance, holding, holding pattern*, hold-up*, impediment, interval, jam, lag, lingering, logjam*, loitering, moratorium, obstruction, postponement, problem, procrastination, prorogation, putting off*, remission, reprieve, retardation, retardment, setback, showstopper*, stall, stay, stop, stoppage, surcease, suspension, tarrying, tie-up, wait; CONCEPTS 121,130,666 —*Ant.* advance, dispatch, expedition, furtherance, hastening, hurry, rush, speed

delay [v] *cause stop in action* adjourn, arrest, bar, bide time, block, check, choke, clog, confine, curb, dawdle, defer, detain, deter, dilly-dally*, discourage, drag, encumber, filibuster, gain time, hamper, hold, hold over, impede, inhibit, interfere, intermit, keep, keep back, lag, lay over, linger, loiter, obstruct, postpone, prevent, procrastinate, prolong, prorogue, protract, put off, remand, repress, restrict, retard, shelve, slacken, stall, stave off, stay, suspend, table, tarry, temporize, withhold; CONCEPTS 121,130,237 —*Ant.* advance, dispatch, expedite, further, hasten, hurry, rush, speed

delectable [adj] *delicious, enjoyable* adorable, agreeable, ambrosial, appetizing, charming, choice, dainty, darling, delicate, delightful, delish, divine, enticing, exquisite, gratifying, heavenly, inviting, luscious, lush, palatable, pleasant, pleasurable, rare, sapid, satisfying, savory, scrumptious, tasty, toothsome, yummy; CONCEPTS 574,579,613 —*Ant.* bad, disagreeable, horrible, nauseating, offensive, repulsive, sickening, unpleasant, unsatisfying

delegate [n] *representative, often governmental* agent, alternate, ambassador, appointee, catchpole*, commissioner, consul, deputy, emissary, envoy, factor, front*, legate, member, member of congress, minister, mouthpiece, nominee, people's choice, pinch hitter*, plenipotentiary, proxy, regent, rep*, replacement, senator, spokesperson, stand-in, substitute, surrogate, vicar, viceroy; CONCEPT 354

delegate [v1] *give authority; empower* accredit, appoint, assign, authorize, cast, charge, choose, commission, constitute, depute, deputize, designate, elect, give nod, invest, license, mandate, name, nominate, ordain, place trust in, select, swear in, warrant; CONCEPTS 50,88 —*Ant.* keep

delegate [v2] *assign responsibility* authorize, consign, devolve, entrust, give, hand over, hold responsible for, parcel out*, pass on*, relegate, send on errand, send on mission, shunt, transfer; CONCEPTS 50,88,143 —*Ant.* keep

delegation [n1] *assignment of responsibility* appointment, apportioning, authorization, charge, commissioning, committal, consigning, consignment, conveyance, conveying, deputation, deputization, deputizing, devolution, entrustment, giving over, installation, investiture, mandate, nomination, ordination, reference, referring, relegation, sending away, submittal, submitting, transferal, transference, transferring, trust; CONCEPTS 50,88,143,685 —*Ant.* keeping

delegation [n2] *group of representatives* commission, contingent, deputation, embassy, envoys, gathering, legation, mission, organization; CONCEPTS 299,301

delete [v] *erase, remove* annul, black out, bleep, blot out, blue-pencil*, cancel, clean, clean up, cross out, cut, cut out, decontaminate, destroy, drop, edit, efface, eliminate, exclude, expunge, obliterate, omit, pass up, rub, rub out, rule out, sanitize, snip, squash, squelch, sterilize, strike out, trim, wipe out, X-out*; CONCEPT 211 —*Ant.* add, put in

deleterious [adj] *harmful, damaging* bad, destroying, destructive, detrimental, hurtful, injurious, mischievous, nocent, nocuous, pernicious, prejudicial, prejudicious, ruining, ruinous; CONCEPTS 537,570 —*Ant.* aiding, assisting, helpful

deliberate [adj] *intentional* advised, aforethought, calculated, careful, cautious, cold-blooded, conscious, considered, cut-and-dried*, designed, designful, done on purpose, express, fixed, intended, judged, meticulous, planned, pondered, prearranged, predesigned, predeterminate, predetermined, premeditated, prepense, projected, provident, prudent, purposed, purposeful, purposive, reasoned, resolved, schemed, scrupulous, studied, studious, thoughtful, thought out, voluntary, wary, weighed, willful, with forethought, witting; CONCEPTS 401,542 —*Ant.* chance, indeterminate, unintentional, unmethodical, unsystematic, unwitting

deliberate [v] *think about seriously; discuss* argue, bat it around*, cerebrate, chew over*, cogitate, consider, consult, contemplate, debate, excogitate, hammer away at*, judge, kick around, knock around, meditate, mull over, muse, ponder, pour it on*, put on thinking cap*, rack brains*, reason, reflect, revolve, roll, ruminate, run up a flagpole*, speculate, stew over*, study, sweat over*, talk over, turn over, weigh; CONCEPTS 17,24,56

deliberately [adv] *intentionally* advisedly, after consideration, apurpose, by design, calculatingly, consciously, designed, determinedly, emphatically, freely, in cold blood, independently, knowingly, meaningfully, on purpose, pointedly, premeditatively, prepensely, purposely, purposively, resolutely, studiously, to that end, voluntarily, willfully, with a view to, with eyes wide open*, with malice aforethought*, without qualms, wittingly; CONCEPTS 401,542 —*Ant.* indeterminedly, unintentionally, unwittingly

deliberation [n] *serious thought, discussion* application, attention, brainwork, calculation, care, carefulness, caution, cerebration, circumspection, cogitation, confabulation, conference, consideration, consultation, debate, forethought, heed, meditation, prudence, purpose, rap, ratiocination, reflection, speculation, study, ventilation, wariness; CONCEPTS 17,24,56

delicacy [n1] *daintiness, fineness of structure* airiness, debility, diaphaneity, elegance, etherealness, exquisiteness, fragility, frailness, frailty, gossameriness, infirmity, lightness, slenderness, smoothness, softness, subtlety, tenderness, tenuity, translucency, transparency, weakness; CONCEPTS 611,733 —*Ant.* coarseness, heaviness, indelicacy, inelegance, robustness, roughness

delicacy [n2] *delicious, gourmet food* ambrosia, banquet, bonne bouche, dainty, delight, dessert, feast, goody, indulgence, luxury, morsel, nectar, pleasure, rarity, regale, relish, savory, special, sweet, tidbit, treat; CONCEPT 457

delicate [adj1] *dainty, weak* aerial, balmy, breakable, choice, delectable, delicious, delightful, elegant, ethereal, exquisite, faint, filmy, fine, fine-grained, finespun, flimsy, fracturable, fragile, frail, frangible, gauzy, gentle, gossamery, graceful, hairline, mild, muted, nice, pale, pastel, rare, recherché, select, shatterable, shattery, slight, soft, subdued, subtle, superior, tender; CONCEPTS 490,574,606 —*Ant.* coarse, harsh, heavy, indelicate, inelegant, robust, rough, strong

delicate [adj2] *sickly* ailing, debilitated, decrepit, feeble, flimsy, fragile, frail, infirm, shatterable, shattery, slender, slight, susceptible, tender, unhealthy, weak; CONCEPT 314 —*Ant.* healthful, healthy, strong

delicate [adj3] *fussy, discriminating* alert, careful, critical, dainty, fastidious, finical, finicking, finicky, gentle, nice, particular, persnickety, prudish, pure, refined, scrupulous, sensitive, squeamish, thin-skinned; CONCEPT 404 —*Ant.* imprecise, indelicate, indiscriminating, uncritical

delicate [adj4] *difficult, sticky (situation)* critical, hair-trigger*, precarious, sensitive, ticklish, touchy, tricky, uncertain, unpredictable, volatile; CONCEPT 565

delicate [adj5] *careful, tactful* accurate, adept, cautious, considerate, deft, detailed, diplomatic, discreet, expert, foresighted, heedful, masterly, minute, politic, precise, proficient, prudent, sensitive, skilled, tactical, wary; CONCEPTS 401,542 —*Ant.* indelicate, inelegant, insensitive, uncareful, unscrupulous

delicately [adv] *carefully* beautifully, cautiously, daintily, deftly, elegantly, exquisitely, fastidiously, finely, gracefully, lightly, precisely, sensitively, skillfully, softly, subtly, tactfully; CONCEPTS 542,544 —*Ant.* indelicately, strongly, uncarefully

delicatessen [n] *eatery* café, cafeteria, charcuterie, deli, restaurant, sandwich shop, subway shop; CONCEPT 449

delicious [adj] *pleasing, especially to the taste* adorable, ambrosial, appetizing, choice, dainty, darling, delectable, delightful, delish*, distinctive, divine, enjoyable, enticing, exquisite, fit for king*, good, gratifying, heavenly, luscious, lush, mellow, mouthwatering, nectarous, nice, palatable, piquant, pleasant, rare, rich, sapid, savory, scrumptious, spicy, sweet, tasteful, tasty, tempting, titillating, toothsome, well-prepared, well-seasoned, yummy*; CONCEPTS

572,613 —*Ant.* disagreeable, distasteful, horrible, unpleasant, unsavory

delight [n] *enjoyment, happiness* contentment, delectation, ecstasy, enchantment, felicity, fruition, gladness, glee, gratification, hilarity, jollity, joy, joyance, mirth, pleasure, rapture, relish, satisfaction, transport; CONCEPT 410 —*Ant.* depression, disappointment, dismay, melancholy, misery, pain, sorrow, trouble, unhappiness

delight [v] *make happy; experience happiness* allure, amuse, arride, attract, be the ticket*, charm, cheer, content, delectate, divert, enchant, enrapture, entertain, exult, fascinate, freak out*, gladden, glory, go over big*, gratify, groove*, hit the spot*, jubilate, knock dead*, knock out*, please, pleasure, ravish, rejoice, satisfy, score, send, slay, thrill, tickle pink*, tickle to death*, turn on, wow; CONCEPTS 7,22 —*Ant.* depress, disappoint, dismay, distress, pain, trouble

delighted [adj] *very happy* captivated, charmed, ecstatic, elated, enchanted, entranced, excited, fulfilled, gladdened, gratified, joyous, jubilant, overjoyed, pleasantly surprised, pleased, thrilled; CONCEPT 403 —*Ant.* depressed, disappointed, dismayed, melancholy, miserable, pained, sorrowful, troubled, unhappy

delightful [adj] *pleasant, charming* adorable, agreeable, alluring, ambrosial, amusing, attractive, beautiful, captivating, cheery, clever, congenial, darling, delectable, delicious, enchanting, engaging, enjoyable, entertaining, fair, fascinating, gratifying, heavenly, ineffable, lovely, luscious, lush, pleasing, pleasurable, rapturous, ravishing, refreshing, satisfying, scrumptious, thrilling, yummy*; CONCEPTS 401,404 —*Ant.* bad, disappointing, horrible, unamusing, unenjoyable, unhappy, unpleasant

delight in [v] *take pleasure from* admire, adore, amuse oneself, appreciate, be content, be pleased, cherish, dig*, eat up*, enjoy, feast on, get a kick out of*, get high on*, get off on*, glory in, groove on*, indulge in, like, live a little*, live it up*, love, luxuriate in, relish, revel in, savor; CONCEPTS 32,410 —*Ant.* dislike, hate

delineate [v] *describe; outline* characterize, chart, define, depict, detail, draft, draw, figure, lay out, limn, mark, plot, portray, represent, sketch out, trace; CONCEPTS 36,55,174

delinquency [n] *misconduct* crime, default, dereliction, failure, fault, lapse, misbehavior, misdeed, misdemeanor, neglect, nonobservance, offense, oversight, weakness, wrongdoing; CONCEPTS 192,645 —*Ant.* good behavior

delinquent [adj] *irresponsible, defaulting* behind, blamable, blameworthy, careless, censurable, criminal, culpable, defaultant, derelict, disregardful, faulty, guilty, lax, neglectful, negligent, offending, overdue, procrastinating, red-handed*, remiss, reprehensible, shabby, slack, tardy, unpaid; CONCEPTS 401,570 —*Ant.* behaving, careful, responsible

delinquent [n] *criminal, often young* behind, blackguard, black sheep*, culprit, dawdler, deadbeat*, deadhead*, debtor, defaulter, derelict, desperado, evader, fallen angel*, felon, hoodlum*, jailbird*, JD*, juvenile delinquent, juvie*, lawbreaker, loafer, lounger, malefactor,

miscreant, neglecter, no show*, offender, outlaw, punk*, recreant, reprobate, sinner, wrongdoer, young offender; CONCEPT 412

delirious [adj1] *mentally imbalanced* aberrant,
bewildered, confused, crazed, crazy, demented,
deranged, deviant, disarranged, disordered, distracted, disturbed, flipped*, flipped
out*, hallucinatory, incoherent, insane, irrational, lightheaded, lunatic, mad, maniac, maniacal, manic, off one's head*, out of one's head*,
out of one's skull*, rambling, raving, unhinged,
unreasonable, unsettled, wandering; CONCEPT
402 —*Ant.* balanced, collected, normal, sane

delirious [adj2] *excited; very happy* beside
oneself*, carried away*, corybantic, crazy,
delighted, drunk*, ecstatic, enthused, frantic,
frenetic, frenzied, furious, hysterical, intoxicated, mad, overwrought, rabid*, rapturous,
thrilled, transported, wild; CONCEPTS 401,403
—*Ant.* unexcited, unhappy

delirium [n] *madness* aberration, ardor,
dementia, derangement, ecstasy, enthusiasm,
fervor, fever, frenzy, furor, fury, hallucination,
hysteria, insanity, lunacy, mania, passion,
rage, raving, transport, zeal; CONCEPT 410
—*Ant.* balance, calmness, saneness

deliver [v1] *transfer, carry* bear, bring, cart,
come across with*, convey, dish out*, distribute, drop, fork over*, gimme*, give, hand,
hand-carry, hand over, pass, put on, put out,
remit, transport, truck; CONCEPTS 108,217
—*Ant.* hold, keep, retain

deliver [v2] *relinquish possession* abandon,
cede, commit, give up, grant, hand over,
let go, resign, surrender, transfer, turn over,
yield; CONCEPTS 116,131 —*Ant.* capture,
limit, restrain, restrict

deliver [v3] *free, liberate* acquit, discharge,
emancipate, loose, ransom, redeem, release,
rescue, save, unshackle; CONCEPT 127 —*Ant.*
confine, detain, imprison, restrain, restrict

deliver [v4] *announce, proclaim* address, bring
out, broach, chime in, come out with, communicate, declare, express, give, give forth, impart,
present, pronounce, publish, read, say, state,
tell, throw out, utter, vent, voice; CONCEPTS
51,60 —*Ant.* be quiet, keep, withhold

deliver [v5] *administer; throw* aim, deal,
direct, dispatch, fling, give, hurl, inflict, launch,
pitch, send, strike, transmit; CONCEPTS 217,222

deliver [v6] *discharge, give forth* accouch,
bear, birth, born, dispense, feed, find, hand,
hand over, produce, provide, release, supply,
turn over; CONCEPTS 179,374

deliverance [n] *liberation* acquittal, delivery,
emancipation, extrication, freeing, redemption,
release, rescue, salvation, saving; CONCEPT 134

delivery [n1] *transfer, transmittal* carting,
commitment, consignment, conveyance,
dispatch, distribution, drop, freighting, giving
over, handing over, impartment, intrusting,
mailing, parcel post, portage, post, rendition,
shipment, surrender, transmission; CONCEPTS
108,217 —*Ant.* hold, keeping, retention

delivery [n2] *articulation of message* accent,
diction, elocution, emphasis, enunciation, inflection, intonation, modulation, pronunciation,
speech, utterance; CONCEPTS 47,595 —*Ant.*
quiet, secrecy

delivery [n3] *childbirth* accouchement,
bearing, birth, birthing, bringing forth,
Caesarian section, childbearing, confinement,
geniture, labor, lying-in, parturition, travail;
CONCEPTS 302,373,374

delivery [n4] *giving of freedom* deliverance,
emancipation, escape, freeing, liberation,
pardon, release, rescue, salvage, salvation;
CONCEPT 127 —*Ant.* capture, confinement,
imprisonment, restraint

delivery room [n] *birthing room* birthing
center, hospital room; CONCEPTS 312,439,449

delude [v] *deceive, fool* beguile, betray, bluff,
caboodle*, cheat, con, cozen, disinform, do a
number on*, double-cross, dupe*, gull*, hoax*,
hoodwink*, illude, impose on, jive*, juggle*,
lead up garden path*, misguide, mislead,
mousetrap*, outfox, play trick on, snow*,
string along, sucker*, take in, trick; CONCEPT
59 —*Ant.* be truthful

deluge [n] *downpour, flood of something*
avalanche, barrage, cataclysm, cataract,
drencher, flux, inundation, niagara, overflowing, overrunning, pour, rush, spate, torrent;
CONCEPTS 432,524,787

deluge [v1] *inundate with water* douse, drench,
drown, engulf, flood, flush, gush, overflow,
overrun, overwhelm, pour, sluice, soak, sop,
souse, steam, submerge, swamp, wet, whelm;
CONCEPT 256

deluge [v2] *overwhelm* abound, crowd, engulf,
flood, glut, inundate, overcome, overcrowd,
overload, overrun, oversupply, snow*, snow
under*, swamp, teem; CONCEPTS 42,140

delusion [n] *misconception, misbelief* apparition, blunder, casuistry, chicanery, daydream,
deception, deceptiveness, dream, eidolon, error,
fallacy, false impression, fancy, fantasy, figment*, fool's paradise*, ghost, hallucination,
head trip*, ignis fatuus, illusion, lapse, mirage,
misapprehension, mistake, optical illusion,
oversight, phantasm, phantom, pipe dream*,
self-deception, shade, speciousness, spuriousness, trickery, trip, vision; CONCEPT 689 —*Ant.*
actuality, certainty, fact, reality, surety, truth

delusive [adj] *deceptive* apparent, beguiling,
chimerical, deceiving, deluding, fallacious,
false, fanciful, fantastic, illusive, illusory,
imaginary, misleading, ostensible, quixotic,
seeming, specious, spurious, visionary;
CONCEPT 582 —*Ant.* actual, certain, factual,
honest, real, truthful

deluxe [adj] *superior, plush* choice, costly,
dainty, delicate, elegant, exclusive, expensive,
exquisite, first-class, grand, luscious, lush,
luxuriant, luxurious, opulent, palatial, posh,
rare, recherché, rich, ritzy, select, special,
splendid, sumptuous, super, swank, swanky;
CONCEPT 574 —*Ant.* inferior, poor

delve [v] *dig into task, action* burrow, dig,
dredge, examine, excavate, explore, ferret out*,
go into, gouge out, inquire, investigate, jump
into, leave no stone unturned*, look into, probe,
prospect, ransack, really get into*, research,
rummage, scoop out, search, seek, shovel,
sift, spade, trowel, turn inside out*, unearth;
CONCEPTS 87,103,216

demagogue [n] *agitating person* agitator,
fanatic, firebrand*, fomenter, haranguer,

hothead*, incendiary, inciter, inflamer, instigator, politician, rabble-rouser*, radical, rebel, revolutionary, soapbox orator*, troublemaker; CONCEPTS 359,412

demand [n] *question, request* appeal, application, arrogation, bid, bidding, call, call for, charge, claim, clamor, command, counterclaim, entreatment, entreaty, exaction, impetration, imploration, importunity, imposition, inquiry, insistence, interest, interrogation, lien, necessity, need, occasion, order, petition, plea, prayer, pursuit, requirement, requisition, rush, sale, search, solicitation, stipulation, suit, supplication, trade, ultimatum, use, vogue, want; CONCEPT 662 —*Ant.* grant, offer, reply

demand [v] *ask strongly for something* abuse, appeal, apply, arrogate, badger, beg, beseech, besiege, bid, challenge, charge, cite, claim, clamor for, coerce, command, compel, constrain, counterclaim, direct, dun, enjoin, entreat, exact, expect, force, hit, hit up, impetrate, implore, importune, inquire, insist on, interrogate, knock, nag, necessitate, oblige, order, pester, petition, postulate, pray, press, question, request, require, requisition, solicit, stipulate, sue for, summon, supplicate, tax, urge, whistle for; CONCEPT 53 —*Ant.* give, grant, offer, reply

demand [v2] *require* ask, call for, command, crave, cry out for, fail, involve, lack, necessitate, need, oblige, take, want; CONCEPTS 26,646 —*Ant.* give, present, supply

demanding [adj] *challenging, urgent* ambitious, backbreaker*, bothersome, clamorous, critical, dictatorial, difficult, exacting, exhausting, exigent, fussy, grievous, hard, imperious, importunate, insistent, nagging, onerous, oppressive, pressing, querulous, strict, stringent, taxing, tough, troublesome, trying, wearing, weighty; CONCEPTS 542,565 —*Ant.* easy, facile, trivial, unchallenging, undemanding

demarcation [n] *boundary, division* bound, confine, delimitation, differentiation, distinction, enclosure, limit, margin, separation, split, terminus; CONCEPT 745

demean [v] *humble, humiliate* abase, badmouth*, belittle, bemean, cast down, contemn, cut down to size*, cut rate, debase, decry, degrade, derogate, descend, despise, detract, dis*, disparage, dump on*, knock down*, lower, pan*, poor-mouth*, scorn, sink, stoop*; CONCEPTS 7,19,54 —*Ant.* boost, enhance, improve, upgrade

demeanor [n] *behavior, manner* address, air, attitude, bearing, carriage, comportment, conduct, deportment, disposition, mien, poise, port, presence, set; CONCEPTS 411,633

demented [adj] *crazy, insane* bananas*, bemused, crackbrained*, daft, delirious, deranged, distracted, distraught, flipped out*, foolish, frenzied, fruity*, hysterical, idiotic, in the ozone*, lunatic, mad, maniac, maniacal, manic, non compos mentis, nutty as a fruitcake*, out of one's gourd*, out of one's tree*, psycho, psychopathic, psychotic, schitzy*, schizoid*, unbalanced, unglued*, unhinged*, unsound, whacko*; CONCEPT 403 —*Ant.* balanced, rational, reasonable, sane, sensible

dementia [n] *senility* Alzheimer's disease, derangement, insanity, madness, mental decay, mental deterioration, mental disorder, personality change, softening of the brain*, unbalance; CONCEPTS 316,410

demise [n] *fate, usually death* annihilation, collapse, curtains, decease, departure, dissolution, downfall, dying, end, ending, expiration, extinction, failure, fall, final thrill*, last out*, last roundup*, lights out*, number's up*, passing, quietus, ruin, silence, sleep, termination; CONCEPTS 105,304,679 —*Ant.* birth

democracy [n] *government in which people participate* commonwealth, egalitarianism, emancipation, equalitarianism, equality, freedom, justice, liberal government, representative government, republic, suffrage; CONCEPTS 299, 688,629

democratic [adj] *representative, self-governing* autonomous, common, communal, constitutional, egalitarian, equal, free, friendly, individualistic, informal, just, libertarian, orderly, popular, populist, self-ruling, socialist; CONCEPTS 319,536

demography [n] *study of human population* anthropology, census-taking, population analysis, population density, population growth, population size, population studies, population vital statistics; CONCEPT 349

demolish [v] *destroy; consume* annihilate, break, bulldoze, burst, crack, crush, decimate, defeat, devastate, devour, dilapidate, dismantle, eat, flatten, gobble up, knock down, level, obliterate, overthrow, overturn, pulverize, put away, put in toilet*, raze, ruin, sink, smash, take apart, take out, tear down, torpedo*, total*, trash*, undo, wax*, wipe off map*, wrack, wreck; CONCEPTS 169,252 —*Ant.* build, construct, fix, produce, rebuild, repair, restore

demolition [n] *destruction* annihilation, bulldozing, explosion, extermination, knocking down, leveling, razing, wrecking; CONCEPT 252 —*Ant.* building, construction, fixing, production, repair

demon [n] *evil, devilish being or influence* archfiend, beast, brute, fiend, goblin, hellion, imp, incubus, little devil*, malignant spirit, monster, rascal, rogue, Satan, succubus, vampire, villain; CONCEPTS 370,412 —*Ant.* angel, god

demonic [adj] *evil* aroused, bad, crazed, demoniac, demoniacal, devilish, diabolic, diabolical, fiendish, fired, frantic, frenetic, frenzied, hellish, impious, infernal, insane, inspired, mad, maniacal, manic, possessed, satanic, serpentine, unhallowed, violent, wicked; CONCEPTS 404,545 —*Ant.* angelic, godlike, good, moral

demonstrable [adj] *provable, evident* ascertainable, attestable, axiomatic, certain, conclusive, deducible, evincible, incontrovertible, indubitable, inferable, irrefutable, obvious, palpable, positive, self-evident, undeniable, unmistakable, verifiable; CONCEPTS 529,535 —*Ant.* distorted, doubtful, obscure, undemonstrable, unverifiable, vague

demonstrate [v1] *display, show* authenticate, determine, establish, evidence, evince, exhibit, expose, flaunt, indicate, make evident, make out, manifest, prove, roll out*, show and tell*, test, testify to, trot out*, try, validate; CONCEPT 97 —*Ant.* conceal, hide

demonstrate [v2] *explain, illustrate* confirm, debunk, describe, express, give for instance, make clear, ostend, proclaim, set forth, show how, teach, testify to, walk one through*; CONCEPT 57 —*Ant.* confuse, distort, falsify, misrepresent

demonstrate [v3] *display or take public action for a cause* exhibit, fast, lie in, manifest, march, march on, parade, picket, protest, rally, sit in, stage walkout, strike, walkout; CONCEPTS 261,300

demonstration [n1] *display of proof* affirmation, confirmation, description, evidence, exhibition, explanation, exposition, expression, illustration, induction, manifestation, presentation, proof, show, spectacle, substantiation, test, testimony, trial, validation; CONCEPT 261 —*Ant.* concealment, hiding

demonstration [n2] *display of belief in cause by taking public action* fast, lie-in*, love-in*, march, mass lobby, parade, peace march, picket, picket line, protest, rally, sit-in*, strike, teach-in*, walkout; CONCEPTS 261,300

demonstrative [adj1] *expressive, communicative* affectionate, candid, effusive, emotional, evincive, expansive, explanatory, expository, frank, gushing, histrionic, illustrative, indicative, loving, open, outgoing, outpouring, outspoken, plain, profuse, symptomatic, tender, unconstrained, unreserved, unrestrained, warmhearted; CONCEPTS 267,401 —*Ant.* cold, cool, inexpressive, reserved, restrained, uncommunicative, undemonstrative, unemotional

demonstrative [adj2] *conclusive* authenticating, certain, convincing, decisive, definite, final, proving, showing, specific, validating; CONCEPTS 531,537 —*Ant.* anticlimactic, confusing, inconclusive, mysterious

demonstrator [n] *protester* agitator, boycotter, disrupter, dissenter, marcher, objector, picketer, radical, revolter, revolutionary, rioter, striker, troublemaker; CONCEPT 412

demoralize [v1] *depress, unnerve* abash, blow out, blow up, chill, cripple, damp, dampen, daunt, debilitate, deject, disarrange, disconcert, discountenance, discourage, dishearten, disorder, disorganize, disparage, dispirit, disturb, embarrass, enfeeble, get to*, jumble, muddle, nonplus, psych out*, rattle, sap, send up*, shake, snarl, take apart*, take steam out*, undermine, unglue*, unman, unsettle, unzip*, upset, weaken; CONCEPTS 7,19 —*Ant.* boost, comfort, encourage, uplift

demoralize [v2] *corrupt, pervert* bastardize, bestialize, brutalize, debase, debauch, deprave, lower, vitiate, warp; CONCEPT 14 —*Ant.* make good, moralize, purify

demote [v] *downgrade, lower in rank* bench*, break, bump, bust, declass, degrade, demean, demerit, dismiss, disrate, hold back, kick downstairs*, lower, reduce, relegate, set back; CONCEPTS 233,351 —*Ant.* improve, promote, rate, upgrade

demur [v] *disagree* balk, cavil, challenge, combat, complain, deprecate, disapprove, dispute, doubt, fight, hem and haw*, hesitate, object, oppose, pause, protest, pussyfoot*, refuse, remonstrate, resist, scruple, shy, stick, stickle, strain, take exception*, vacillate, wait and see*, waver; CONCEPTS 46,54 —*Ant.* accept, agree, consent, go along

demure [adj] *reserved, affected* backward, bashful, blushing, close, coy, decorous, diffident, earnest, humble, modest, nice, prim, prissy, proper, prudish, reticent, retiring, sedate, serious, shy, silent, skittish, sober, solemn, staid, strait-laced, timid, unassertive, unassuming, unassured; CONCEPTS 401,404 —*Ant.* aggressive, bold, extroverted, outgoing, shameless, strong

den [n1] *cavern, hideaway* atelier, burrow, cave, cloister, couch, cubbyhole, haunt, hideout, hole, hotbed, lair, lodge, nest, retreat, sanctuary, sanctum, shelter, snuggery, study; CONCEPTS 448,513

den [n2] *room for relaxation or informal entertaining* family room, library, media room, playroom, recreation room, rec room*, rumpus room, studio, TV room; CONCEPTS 440,448

denial [n] *dismissal, refusal of belief in statement* abnegation, abstaining, abjuration, brush-off, cold shoulder*, contradiction, controversion, declination, disallowance, disapproval, disavowal, disclaimer, dismissing, disproof, dissent, forswearing, gainsaying, nay, negation, negative, nix*, nonacceptance, noncommittal, no way*, prohibition, protestation, rebuff, rebuttal, refraining, refusing, refutal, refutation, rejecting, rejection, renegement, renouncement, renunciation, repudiating, repudiation, repulse, retraction, turndown, veto; CONCEPTS 45,54 —*Ant.* affirmation, agreement, approval, avowal, claim, corroboration, vouching

denigrate [v] *belittle, malign* asperse, bad mouth*, besmirch, blacken, blister, calumniate, decry, defame, dis*, disparage, give black eye*, impugn, knock*, libel, mudsling*, put down*, revile, rip up*, roast*, run down*, scandalize, slander, tear down*, traduce, vilify; CONCEPTS 52,54 —*Ant.* boost, cherish, compliment, praise

denizen [n] *resident* citizen, dweller, habitant, indweller, inhabitant, inhabiter, liver, national, native, occupant, resider, subject; CONCEPT 413 —*Ant.* alien, foreigner, immigrant

denomination [n1] *religious belief* church, communion, connection, creed, cult, faith, group, persuasion, religion, school, sect; CONCEPTS 368,689

denomination [n2] *classification* body, category, class, grade, group, size, type, unit, value; CONCEPT 378

denomination [n3] *name* appellation, appellative, brand, cognomen, compellation, designation, flag, handle, identification, label, moniker, nomen, slot, style, surname, tab, tag, term, title; CONCEPT 683

denotation [n] *meaning, description* designation, explanation, implication, indication, signification, specification; CONCEPTS 268,682

denote [v] *designate, mean* add up, announce, argue, bespeak, betoken, connote, evidence, express, finger, flash, hang sign on*, imply, import, indicate, insinuate, intend, make, mark, peg, prove, put down for, put finger on*, show, signify, spell, stand for, symbol, symbolize, tab, tag, typify; CONCEPTS 55,682

denouement [n] *the end result* climax, close, completion, conclusion, culmination, end, final curtain*, finale, last act*, resolution, windup*; CONCEPT 832

denounce [v] *condemn, attack* accuse, adjudicate, arraign, blacklist, blame, boycott, brand, castigate, censure, charge, charge with, criticize, damn, declaim, decry, denunciate, derogate, dress down, excoriate, expose, finger*, hang something on*, impeach, implicate, impugn, incriminate, indict, inveigh against, knock, ostracize, proscribe, prosecute, rap, rat*, rebuke, reprehend, reprimand, reproach, reprobate, reprove, revile, scold, show up, skin*, smear, stigmatize, take to task, threaten, upbraid, vilify, vituperate; CONCEPTS 44,52 —*Ant.* approve, commend, compliment, praise

dense [adj1] *compressed, thick* close, close-knit, compact, condensed, crammed, crowded, heaped, heavy, impenetrable, jammed, jam-packed*, massed, opaque, packed, packed like sardines*, piled, solid, substantial, thickset; CONCEPT 483 —*Ant.* open, scattered, sparse, thin, uncompressed

dense [adj2] *slow, stupid* blockheaded*, boorish, doltish, dull, dumb, fatheaded*, ignorant, imbecilic, impassive, lethargic, numskulled*, oafish, obtuse, phlegmatic, simple, slow-witted, sluggish, stolid, thick, torpid; CONCEPT 402 —*Ant.* brainy, clever, intelligent, smart

density [n] *bulk, mass* body, closeness, compactness, concretion, consistency, crowdedness, denseness, frequency, heaviness, impenetrability, massiveness, quantity, solidity, substantiality, thickness, tightness; CONCEPT 722 —*Ant.* openness, sparsity, thinness

dent [n] *depression, scrape, chip* cavity, concavity, crater, crenel, cut, dimple, dint, dip, embrasure, furrow, hollow, impression, incision, indentation, nick, notch, pit, scallop, score, scratch, sink, trough; CONCEPT 580 —*Ant.* bulge

dent [v] *chip, scrape, depress* dig, dimple, dint, furrow, gouge, hollow, imprint, indent, make concave, mark, nick, notch, perforate, pit, press in, push in, ridge, scratch; CONCEPTS 176,189, 208,246 —*Ant.* bulge

dentures [n] *false teeth* artificial teeth, bridge, choppers*, dental plate, implants, partial, set of teeth; CONCEPT 393

denude [v] *strip* bare, disrobe, expose, fleece, lay bare*, peel, uncover, undress; CONCEPT 211

denunciation [n] *condemnation, criticism* accusation, arraignment, blame, castigation, censure, charge, cursing, damning, denouncement, derogation, dressing down*, fulmination, incrimination, indictment, invective, knock*, obloquy, rap*, reprehension, reprimand, reprobation, smearing, stigmatization, upbraidment, vilification; CONCEPT 52 —*Ant.* appreciation, approval, commendation, compliment, praise

deny [v] *disagree, renounce, decline* abjure, abnegate, ban, begrudge, call on, contradict, contravene, controvert, curb, disacknowledge, disallow, disavow, disbelieve, discard, disclaim, discredit, disown, disprove, doubt, enjoin from, eschew, exclude, forbid, forgo, forsake, gainsay, hold back, keep back, negate, negative, not buy, nullify, oppose, rebuff, rebut, recant, refuse, refute, reject, repudiate, restrain, revoke, sacrifice, say no to, spurn, taboo, take exception to, turn down, turn thumbs down*, veto, withhold;

CONCEPTS 46,49,52 —*Ant.* accede, acknowledge, admit, affirm, agree, allow, concede, confess, corroborate, go along, grant

deodorant [n] *something that freshens* air freshener, antiperspirant, cleanser, cosmetic, deodorizer, disinfectant, fumigant, fumigator, smoke screen*; CONCEPT 492

deodorize [v] *freshen* aerate, air, depollute, disinfect, fumigate, neutralize, purify, sanitize, sterilize, sweeten, ventilate; CONCEPTS 161,244

depart [v1] *leave, retreat* abandon, abdicate, absent, beat it*, blast off*, cut and run*, cut out*, decamp, desert, disappear, emigrate, escape, evacuate, exit, get away, git*, go, go away, go forth, hit the bricks*, hit the road*, hit the trail*, make a break*, march out, migrate, move on, move out, part, perish, pull out, quit, remove, retire, sally forth*, say goodbye*, scram*, secede, set forth, shove off*, slip away*, split*, start, start out, take leave, tergiversate, troop*, vacate, vanish, withdraw; CONCEPT 195 —*Ant.* arrive, come, enter

depart [v2] *diverge from normal, expected* abandon, cast, desert, deviate, differ, digress, disagree, discard, dissent, excuse, forsake, ramble, reject, repudiate, stray, swerve, turn aside, vary, veer, wander; CONCEPTS 665,697 —*Ant.* continue, keep to, linger, stay, wait

departed [adj] *dead* bought the farm*, buried, deceased, expired, gone, in the grave*, laid to rest*, late, passed away, pushing up daisies*, six feet under*, stiff; CONCEPT 539

department [n1] *section of organization, area* administration, agency, area, arena, beat, board, branch, bureau, canton, circuit, commission, commune, constituency, division, force, office, parish, precinct, quarter, range, staff, station, subdivision, territory, tract, unit, ward; CONCEPTS 381,440,508

department [n2] *area of interest, expertise* activity, administration, assignment, avocation, bailiwick, berth, bureau, business, capacity, class, classification, domain, dominion, duty, field, function, incumbency, jurisdiction, line, niche, occupation, office, province, realm, responsibility, slot, specialty, sphere, spot, station, vocation, walk of life, wing; CONCEPT 349

department store [n] *retail store* anchor store, chain store, dime store, discount store, five-and-dime store, outlet store, shop, store; CONCEPTS 325,439,448,449

departure [n1] *leaving* abandonment, adieu, bow out*, congé, decampment, desertion, egress, egression, embarkation, emigration, escape, evacuation, exit, exodus, expatriation, farewell, flight, getaway*, going, going away, goodbye*, hegira, migration, parting, passage, powder*, quitting, recession, removal, retirement, retreat, sailing, separation, setting forth, setting out, stampede, start, takeoff, taking leave, taking off, vacation, vanishing act*, walkout, withdrawal, withdrawing; CONCEPT 195 —*Ant.* arrival, coming, entrance

departure [n2] *deviation from normal, expected* aberration, branching off, branching out, change, declination, deflection, difference, digression, divergence, diversion, innovation, in thing*, last word*, latest thing*, new wrinkle*, novelty, rambling, shift, straying, turning, variance, variation, veering, wandering; CONCEPTS 665,697 —*Ant.* abidance, continuation, keeping, stay

depend [v1] *count on, rely upon* bank on*, bet bottom dollar on*, bet on*, build upon, calculate on, confide in, gamble on*, lay money on*, lean on*, reckon on, trust in, turn to;CONCEPT 26

depend [v2] *be contingent on* be at mercy of, be based on, be conditioned, be connected with, be determined by, be in control of, be in the power of, be subject to, be subordinate to, bottom, found, ground, hang, hang in suspense, hang on, hinge on, pend, rest, rest on, rest with, revolve around, revolve on, stand on, stay, trust to, turn on; CONCEPT 711

dependable [adj] *reliable, responsible* always there, carrying the load*, certain, constant, faithful, good as one's word*, loyal, rocklike*, secure, stable, staunch, steadfast, steady, sturdy, sure, to be counted on, tried, tried-and-true, true, trustworthy, trusty, unfailing; CONCEPTS 542,560 —*Ant.* dishonest, irresponsible, uncertain, undependable, unreliable, unsteady, unsure

dependence/dependency [n1] *confidence, reliance* assurance, belief, credence, expectation, faith, hope, interdependence, responsibility, responsibleness, stability, steadiness, stock, trust, trustiness, trustworthiness; CONCEPTS 410, 689 —*Ant.* freedom, independence, strength

dependence/dependency [n2] *addiction, need* attachment, contingency, habit, helplessness, hook, inability, security blanket, servility, subjection, subordination, subservience, vulnerability, weakness, yoke; CONCEPTS 20,709 —*Ant.* independence, subtraction, want

dependent [adj1] *weak, helpless* abased, clinging, counting on, debased, defenseless, humbled, immature, indigent, inferior, lesser, minor, poor, reliant, relying on, secondary, subordinate, tied to apron strings*, under, under thumb*, unsustaining, vulnerable; CONCEPTS 404,574 —*Ant.* independent, mature, strong, unreliant

dependent [adj2] *contingent, determined by* accessory to, ancillary, appurtenant, conditional, controlled by, counting, depending, incidental to, liable to, provisory, reckoning, regulated by, relative, reliant, relying, subject to, subordinate, subservient, susceptible, sustained by, trusting, under control of; CONCEPT 546 —*Ant.* free, independent

depict [v] *describe, render in drawing or writing* characterize, delineate, design, detail, illustrate, image, interpret, limn, narrate, outline, paint, picture, portray, relate, report, represent, reproduce, sculpt, sketch, state; CONCEPTS 79,174 —*Ant.* confuse, distort, mix up

depiction [n] *description, rendering* delineation, drawing, illustration, image, likeness, outline, picture, portraiture, portrayal, presentment, representation, sketch; CONCEPTS 259,268

deplete [v] *consume, exhaust supply* bankrupt, bleed*, decrease, dig into, diminish, drain, draw, dry up, empty, evacuate, expend, finish, impoverish, lessen, milk*, reduce, sap, spend, squander, suck dry*, undermine, use up, wash up, waste, weaken; CONCEPTS 142,169,225 —*Ant.* add, augment, expand, fill, give, increase

depleted [adj] *consumed, exhausted* all in*, bare, bleary*, collapsed, decreased, depreciated,

destitute, devoid of, drained, effete, emptied, far-gone*, in want, kaput*, lessened, out of, pooped out*, reduced, sapped, short of, sold, sold out, spent, sucked out*, used, used up, vacant, washed out, wasted, weakened, without resources, worn, worn out;CONCEPTS 576,771 —*Ant.* augmented, enlarged, increased, unconsumed, unused

deplorable [adj] *unfortunate, shameful* afflictive, awful, blameworthy, bummer*, calamitous, dire, dirty, disastrous, disgraceful, dishonorable, disreputable, distressing, dolorous, downer*, dreadful, execrable, faulty, godawful*, grievous, grim, heartbreaking, heartrending, horrifying, intolerable, lamentable, lousy, melancholy, miserable, mournful, opprobrious, overwhelming, pitiable, poor, regrettable, reprehensible, rotten, sad, scandalous, sickening, stinking, terrible, tragic, unbearable, unsatisfactory, woeful, wretched; CONCEPTS 529,570,574 —*Ant.* cheerful, delightful, excellent, good, happy, shameless

deplore [v] *regret; condemn* abhor, be against, bemoan, bewail, carry on, censure, complain, cry, denounce, deprecate, disapprove of, eat one's heart out*, grieve for, hate, hurt, lament, moan, mourn, object to, repent, rue, sing the blues*, sorrow over, take on, weep; CONCEPTS 21,29 —*Ant.* approve, be happy, delight, praise, rejoice, revel

deploy [v] *redistribute, station troops or weapons* arrange, display, dispose, expand, extend, fan out, form front, open, position, put out patrol, set out, set up, spread out, take battle stations, unfold, use, utilize; CONCEPTS 158,213,320 —*Ant.* not use, withhold

deport [v] *banish* cast out, dismiss, displace, exile, expatriate, expel, expulse, extradite, oust, relegate, ship out, transport; CONCEPTS 198,211,217 —*Ant.* allow, permit, stay

deportation [n] *banishment* displacement, eviction, exile, expatriation, expulsion, extradition, ostracism, relegation, removal, transportation; CONCEPTS 198,211,217 —*Ant.* approval, permission

deportment [n] *carriage, manner of person* actions, address, air, appearance, aspect, bearing, behavior, cast, comportment, conduct, demeanor, mien, port, posture, set, stance; CONCEPT 633

depose [v] *oust from position* boot out, bounce, break, can*, cashier, chuck, degrade, demote, dethrone, disown, dismiss, displace, downgrade, drum out, eject, freeze out*, give heave-ho*, impeach, kick out*, overthrow, remove from office, ride out on rail*, run out of town*, send packing*, subvert, throw out, throw out on ear*, uncrown, unfrock, unmake, unseat, upset; CONCEPTS 133,298,320

deposit [n1] *down payment; money saved* drop, installment, money in the bank, partial payment, pledge, retainer, security, stake, warranty; CONCEPTS 340,344 —*Ant.* debit, withdrawal

deposit [n2] *accumulation of solid* alluvium, delta, deposition, dregs, drift, grounds, lees, precipitate, precipitation, sediment, settlings, silt; CONCEPTS 432,470,471

deposit [v] *locate, put in place for safekeeping* accumulate, amass, bank, collect, commit, deliver, ditch, drop, entrust, garner, give in trust, hoard, install, invest, keep, lay, lay away, park, place, plant*, plop*, plunk*, plunk down*, precipitate, put aside, put by, repose, rest, salt away*, save, settle, sit down, sock away*, squirrel away*, stash, stock up, store, stow, transfer, treasure; CONCEPTS *134,201,330* —*Ant.* take away, take out

deposition [n1] *dethroning, ousting* degradation, discharge, dismissal, displacement, ejection, impeachment, overthrow, removal, unfrocking; CONCEPTS *133,298,320*

deposition [n2] *attestation of truth, especially in legal matters* affidavit, affirmation, allegation, announcement, declaration, evidence, sworn statement, testimony; CONCEPTS *271,318*

depository [n] *storage place* archive, arsenal, bank, bunker, cache, collection, depot, gallery, magazine, museum, repertory, repository, safe, safe-deposit box, store, storehouse, tomb, vault, warehouse; CONCEPT *435*

depot [n] *storage place; station* annex, armory, base, depository, destination, garage, halting-place, haven, junction, loft, lot, magazine, office, repository, stopping-place, store, storehouse, storeroom, terminal, terminus, waiting room, warehouse, yard; CONCEPTS *435,449*

deprave [v] *corrupt, lead astray* bastardize, bestialize, brutalize, debase, debauch, degrade, demoralize, pervert, seduce, subvert, vitiate, warp; CONCEPT *14* —*Ant.* ennoble, improve, moralize

depraved [adj] *corrupt, immoral* abandoned, bad, base, debased, debauched, degenerate, degraded, dirty*, dirty-minded, dissolute, evil, fast*, filthy*, flagitious, gone to the dogs*, kinky*, lascivious, lewd, licentious, low, mean, miscreant, nefarious, perverted, profligate, putrid, rotten, shameless, sinful, twisted, unhealthy, unnatural, vicious, vile, villainous, vitiate, vitiated, wanton, warped, wicked; CONCEPT *545* —*Ant.* good, honorable, just, moral, noble, pure, uncorrupt, upright, virtuous

depravity [n] *corruption, immorality* abandonment, baseness, contamination, criminality, debasement, debauchery, degeneracy, degradation, depravation, evil, iniquity, lewdness, licentiousness, perversion, profligacy, sensuality, sinfulness, vice, viciousness, vitiation, wickedness; CONCEPT *645* —*Ant.* good, honor, justice, morality, nobility, purity, uprightness, virtue

deprecate [v] *belittle, condemn* cut down to size*, depreciate, derogate, detract, disapprove of, discommend, discountenance, disesteem, disfavor, disparage, expostulate, frown, mud-sling*, not go for*, object, pooh-pooh*, poor mouth*, protest against, put down*, rip*, run down*, take dim view of, take down, take exception to; CONCEPTS *7,19,52* —*Ant.* approve, build up, commend, compliment, endorse, laud, praise

depreciate [v1] *devalue, lose value* abate, cheapen, decay, decrease, decry, deflate, depress, deteriorate, devalorize, diminish, downgrade, drop, dwindle, erode, fall, lessen, lower, mark down, reduce, soften, underrate, undervalue, worsen, write down, write off; CONCEPTS *698,776* —*Ant.* gain value, increase, overrate, raise, rate

depreciate [v2] *belittle, ridicule* abuse, asperse, attack, calumniate, censure, clamor against, condemn, contemn, decry, defame, denigrate, denounce, deprecate, deride, derogate, detract, discount, discountenance, discredit, disgrace, disparage, dispraise, fault, find fault with, humble, knock, look down on*, lower, malign, minimize, put down, rap, revile, roast*, run down*, scoff at, scorn, slam, slander, slight, slur, smear, sneer at, spurn, take down a peg*, traduce, underestimate, underrate, undervalue, vilify; CONCEPTS *7,19,52* —*Ant.* approve, commend, compliment, exalt, laud, praise, recommend

depreciation [n] *devaluation* accounting allowance, deflation, fall, loss of value, reduction, slump; CONCEPTS *137,236,240,247*

depredation [n] *devastation, destruction* burglary, crime, desecration, desolation, despoiling, laying waste, marauding, pillage, plunder, ransacking, rapine, ravaging, robbery, sacking, spoliation, stealing, theft, wasting; CONCEPTS *192,252* —*Ant.* boon, construction, goodness, miracle, wonder

depress [v1] *deject, make despondent; exhaust* abase, afflict, ail, bear down, beat, beat down*, bother, bug*, bum out*, cast down, chill*, cow*, damp, dampen, darken, daunt, debase, debilitate, degrade, desolate, devitalize, discourage, dishearten, dismay, dispirit, distress, disturb, drag*, drain, dull, enervate, faze, keep under, lower, mock, mortify, oppress, perturb, press, put down*, reduce, reduce to tears*, run down*, sadden, sap*, scorn, slow, throw cold water on*, torment, trouble, try, turn one off*, upset, weaken, weary, weigh down*; CONCEPTS *7,19,240* —*Ant.* cheer, comfort, encourage, excite, lift, make happy, stimulate

depress [v2] *devalue* cheapen, debase, depreciate, diminish, downgrade, impair, lessen, lower, reduce; CONCEPTS *240,330* —*Ant.* increase, raise

depress [v3] *push down* couch, demit, dip, droop, flatten, let down, level, lower, press down, settle, sink, smoosh, squash; CONCEPT *208* —*Ant.* push up, raise, uplift

depressant [n] *sedative* calmant, downer, intoxicant, relaxant, tranquilizer; CONCEPT *7*

depressed [adj1] *discouraged* bad, bleeding*, blue*, bummed out*, cast-down, crestfallen, crummy*, dejected, despondent, destroyed, disconsolate, dispirited, down, down and out*, downcast, downhearted, down in the dumps*, down in the mouth*, dragged*, fed up*, glum, grim, hurting, in a blue funk*, in pain*, in the dumps*, in the pits*, in the toilet*, let down, low, low-down, low-spirited, lugubrious, melancholy, moody, morose, on a downer*, pessimistic, ripped, sad, sob story*, spiritless, taken down*, torn up*, unhappy, weeping, woebegone; CONCEPT *403* —*Ant.* cheerful, comforted, encouraged, happy, satisfied, unburdened

depressed [adj2] *concave, pushed down* hollow, indented, recessed, set back, sunken; CONCEPT *490* —*Ant.* bulging, convex, pushed up, raised

depressed [adj3] *disadvantaged* cheapened, depreciated, deprived, destitute, devalued, distressed, ghetto, ghost, impaired, needy, poor, poverty-stricken, run-down, shanty, skid row*, underprivileged, weakened; CONCEPTS 334,555 —Ant. blessed, flourishing, prosperous, rich

depressing [adj] discouraging, upsetting
black, bleak, daunting, dejecting, disheartening, dismal, dispiriting, distressing, dreary, funereal, gloomy, heartbreaking, hopeless, joyless, melancholic, melancholy, mournful, oppressive, sad, saddening, somber; CONCEPT 529 —Ant. cheering, encouraging, happy

depression [n1] low spirits; despair abasement, abjection, abjectness, blahs*, bleakness, blue funk*, bummer, cheerlessness, dejection, desolation, desperation, despondency, disconsolation, discouragement, dispiritedness, distress, dole, dolefulness, dolor, downheartedness, dreariness, dullness, dumps, ennui, gloom, gloominess, heaviness of heart, heavyheartedness, hopelessness, lowness, lugubriosity, melancholia, melancholy, misery, mortification, qualm, sadness, sorrow, the blues*, trouble, unhappiness, vapors*, woefulness, worry; CONCEPT 410 —Ant. cheerfulness, encouragement, happiness, hope, hopefulness

depression [n2] economic decline bad times*, bankruptcy, bear market*, big trouble*, bottom out*, bust, crash, crisis, deflation, dislocation, downturn, drop, failure, hard times*, inactivity, inflation, overproduction, panic, paralysis, rainy days*, recession, retrenchment, sag, slide, slowness, slump, stagflation, stagnation, unemployment; CONCEPTS 324,330,335 —Ant. recovery, surge

depression [n3] concavity, cavity basin, bowl, crater, dent, dimple, dip, excavation, hole, hollow, impression, indentation, pit, pocket, sag, scoop, sink, sinkage, sinkhole, vacuity, vacuum, valley, void; CONCEPT 513 —Ant. bulge, convexity, protuberance

deprivation [n] taking, keeping away; need denial, deprival, destitution, detriment, disadvantage, dispossession, distress, divestiture, divestment, expropriation, hardship, loss, privation, removal, seizure, want, withdrawal, withholding; CONCEPTS 121,142,709 —Ant. bestowal, endowment, giving, indulgence, offer, offering, presentation, supply

deprive [v] keep or take away something wanted, needed bankrupt, bare, bereave, denude, despoil, disinherit, dismantle, dispossess, disrobe, divest, dock, expropriate, hold back, lose, oust, rob, seize, skim, stiff, strip, wrest; CONCEPTS 121,142 —Ant. appropriate, bestow, confer, endow, give, indulge, offer, present, supply

depth [n1] distance down or across base, bottom, declination, deepness, draft, drop, expanse, extent, fathomage, intensity, lower register, lowness, measure, measurement, pit, pitch, profoundness, profundity, remoteness, sounding; CONCEPTS 737,790 —Ant. height

depth [n2] insight, wisdom acuity, acumen, astuteness, brain, discernment, intellect, intelligence, keenness, penetration, profoundness, profundity, sagacity, sense, sharpness, weightiness; CONCEPT 409

deputize [v] appoint as a deputy assign, authorize, commission, consign, delegate, depute, entrust, mandate; CONCEPT 50

deputy [n] assistant, agent aide, ambassador, appointee, assembly member, backup, commissioner, councilor, delegate, dogcatcher*, factor, legate, lieutenant, minister, proxy, regent, replacement, representant, representative, second-in-command, sub, subordinate, substitute, surrogate; CONCEPT 348 —Ant. chief, manager

derange [v] make crazy; confuse confound, craze*, dement, disarrange, disarray, discommode, discompose, disconcert, disorder, disorganize, displace, distract, disturb, drive mad, frenzy, madden, make insane, mess up*, misplace, muss*, perplex, ruffle, rummage, unbalance, unhinge*, unsettle, upset; CONCEPTS 16,84 —Ant. calm, comfort

deranged [adj] crazy, insane ape*, baked*, bananas*, berserk, cracked*, crazed, delirious, demented, disarranged, disconcerted, disordered, displaced, distracted, dotty*, flipped*, flipped out*, frantic, frenzied, fried*, irrational, loco*, lunatic, mad, maddened, maniac, maniacal, nuts*, perplexed, schizzo*, unbalanced, unglued*, unhinged*, unscrewed*, unsettled, unsound, unzipped*, whacko*; CONCEPT 403 —Ant. balanced, calm, ok, sane

deregulate [v] remove imposed controls on a system decontrol, denationalize, leave be, let alone, not interfere, not meddle, not tamper; CONCEPTS 94,117

deregulation [n] the removal of imposed controls on a system disinvolvement, free competition, free enterprise, free trade, isolationism, laissez-faire, liberalism, noninterference, nonintervention, self-regulating market; CONCEPT 299

derelict [adj1] careless, negligent behindhand, delinquent, disregardful, irresponsible, lax, regardless, remiss, slack, undependable, unreliable, untrustworthy; CONCEPT 542 —Ant. careful, caring

derelict [adj2] deserted, forsaken abandoned, castoff, desolate, dilapidated, dingy, discarded, faded, lorn, neglected, ownerless, relinquished, ruined, run-down, seedy, shabby, solitary, threadbare, uncouth; CONCEPT 560 —Ant. improved, populated

derelict [n] destitute or down-and-out person beggar, bum, castaway, dawdler, drifter, floater, grifter, hobo, ne'er-do-well*, outcast, renegade, skidrow bum, stiff, stumblebum*, tramp, vagabond, vagrant; CONCEPTS 412,423

deride [v] make fun of; insult banter, chaff, contemn, detract, dis*, disdain, disparage, do a number on*, dump on*, flout, gibe, jeer, jolly, kid, knock, laugh at, lout, mock, pan, pooh-pooh*, put down*, quiz, rag*, rally, razz*, rib*, ridicule, roast*, scoff, scorn, slam, sneer, taunt, twit; CONCEPTS 52,54 —Ant. commend, compliment, flatter, praise, revere

de rigueur [adj] proper, right au fait, becoming, comme il faut, conventional, correct, decent, decorous, done, fitting, necessary, required; CONCEPT 558 —Ant. improper, wrong

derision [n] insult, disrespect backhanded compliment*, brickbat*, Bronx cheer*, butt*, comeback, contempt, contumely, crack, dig*, disdain, disparagement, dump*, jab, jest, joke, laughingstock, laughter, mockery, object of ridicule, parting shot, pilgarlic, put-down, raillery, ridicule, satire, scoffing, scorn, slam*, slap, sneering; CONCEPTS 52,278 —Ant. adulation, commendation, compliment, flattery, praise

derisive [adj] ridiculing cheeky*, cocky, contemptuous, crusty, disdainful, flip*, fresh, gally, insulting, jeering, mocking, nervy, out-of-line, rude, sarcastic, sassy, scoffing, scornful, smart*, smart-alecky*, taunting; CONCEPT 267 —Ant. complimentary, flattering, praising, respectful

derivable [adj] deducible a priori, attributable, available, determinable, dogmatic, extractable, inferable, likely, obtainable, reasoned, resultant, traceable; CONCEPT 529 —Ant. inconcludable, underivable

derivation [n] root, source ancestry, basis, beginning, descent, etymology, foundation, genealogy, inception, origin, provenance, provenience, spin-off, well, wellspring, whence it came; CONCEPT 648 —Ant. conclusion, consequence, effect, end, outgrowth, result

derivative [adj] borrowed, transmitted from source acquired, ancestral, caused, cognate, coming from, connate, copied, evolved, hereditary, imitative, inferential, inferred, not original, obtained, plagiaristic, plagiarized, procured, rehashed, secondary, secondhand, subordinate, uninventive, unoriginal; CONCEPT 549 —Ant. inventive, original, unborrowed, unique

derivative [n] product, descendant by-product, offshoot, outgrowth, spin-off, wave; CONCEPT 260 —Ant. invention, original, root, source

derive [v] deduce a conclusion acquire, arrive, assume, collect, determine, develop, draw, educe, elaborate, elicit, evolve, excogitate, extract, follow, formulate, gain, gather, get, glean, infer, judge, make, make out, obtain, procure, put together, reach, receive, trace, work out; CONCEPTS 15,18 —Ant. create, invent

derive from [v] come from; arise descend, emanate, flow, head, issue, originate, proceed, rise, spring from, stem from; CONCEPT 648

dernier cri [n] the latest thing fad, look, the last word*, the newest fashion, vogue; CONCEPT 655

derogatory [adj] offensive, uncomplimentary aspersing, belittling, calumnious, censorious, contumelious, critical, damaging, decrying, defamatory, degrading, demeaning, deprecatory, depreciative, despiteful, detracting, disdainful, dishonoring, disparaging, fault-finding, humiliating, injurious, malevolent, malicious, maligning, minimizing, opprobrious, reproachful, sarcastic, scornful, slanderous, slighting, spiteful, unfavorable, unflattering, vilifying; CONCEPTS 267,570 —Ant. appreciative, complimentary, favorable, flattering, praising

derriere [n] backside ass, bottom, buns, buttocks, can, cheeks, fanny, heinie, keister, posterior, rear, rear end, seat; CONCEPT 392

descend [v1] move down, lower a cascade, cataract, cave in*, coast, collapse, crash, crouch, decline, deplane, detrain, dip, disembark, dismount, dive, dribble*, drop, fall, fall prostrate, get down, get off, go down, gravitate, ground, incline, light, lose balance, penetrate, pitch, plop, plummet, plunge, prolapse, set, settle, sink, slant, slide, slip, slope, slough off, slump, stoop, stumble, submerge, subside, swoop, toboggan, topple, trickle, trip, tumble, weep; CONCEPTS 147,181,213 —Ant. ascend, go up, increase, rise

descend [v2] condescend abase oneself, concede, degenerate, deteriorate, humble oneself, lower oneself, patronize, stoop; CONCEPTS 23,35

descend [v3] trace ancestry from; be passed or handed down arise, derive, issue, originate, proceed, spring; CONCEPT 108

descendant [n] person in line of ancestry brood, child, children, chip off old block*, get*, heir, issue, kin, offshoot, offspring, posterity, product, progeniture, progeny, scion, seed, spin-off*; CONCEPTS 296,414 —Ant. ascendant, predecessor

descent [n1] moving down; lowering cave-in, coast, coming down, crash, declension, declination, decline, declivity, dip, downgrade, droop, drop, drop-off, fall, falling, grade, gradient, header, hill, inclination, incline, landslide, plummeting, plunge, plunging, precipitation, prolapse, sag, settlement, sinkage, sinking, slant, slide, slip, slope, swoop, tailspin, topple, tumble; CONCEPTS 147,181,213,738 —Ant. ascension, ascent, elevation, increase, rise, upgrade

descent [n2] line of ancestry blood, extraction, family, family tree, genealogy, heredity, lineage, origin, parentage, pedigree, relationship; CONCEPT 296

descent [n3] deterioration abasement, anticlimax, cadence, comedown, debasement, decadence, decline, degradation, discomfiture, down, downcome, downfall, lapse, pathos, slump; CONCEPTS 230,674 —Ant. improvement, upgrade

descent [n4] assault, attack advance, foray, incursion, invasion, pounce, raid, swoop; CONCEPTS 86,320

describe [v] explain in speech, writing call, characterize, chronicle, communicate, construe, convey image, define, delineate, depict, detail, distinguish, draw, elucidate, epitomize, exemplify, explicate, expound, express, illuminate, illustrate, image, impart, interpret, label, limn, make apparent, make clear, make sense of, make vivid, mark out, name, narrate, outline, paint, particularize, picture, portray, recite, recount, rehearse, relate, report, represent, sketch, specify, state, tell, term, trace, transmit, write up; CONCEPT 55 —Ant. confuse, misrepresent, mix up

description [n1] account in speech, writing ABCs*, blow by blow, brief, characterization, chronicle, confession, declaration, definition, delineation, depiction, detail, explanation, explication, fingerprint, information, make, monograph, narration, narrative, picture, portraiture, portrayal, presentment, recital, recitation, record, recountal, rehearsal, report, representation, rundown, sketch, specification, statement, story, summarization, summary, tale, version, vignette, writeup, yarn; CONCEPT 268 —Ant. misrepresentation

description [n2] class, kind brand, breed, category, character, classification, feather, genre, genus, ilk, kidney, nature, order, sort, species, stripe, type, variety; CONCEPT 378

descriptive [adj] explanatory anecdotic, characteristic, characterizing, circumstantial, classificatory, clear, definitive, delineative, depictive, describing, designating, detailed, eloquent, explicative, expository, expressive, extended, graphic, identifying, illuminating, illuminative, illustrative, indicative, interpretive, lifelike, narrative, particularized, pictorial, picturesque, revealing, specific, true to life, vivid; CONCEPTS 267,557 —*Ant.* confusing, cursory, undescriptive

desecrate [v] *abuse, violate* befoul, blaspheme, commit sacrilege, contaminate, defile, depredate, desolate, despoil, devastate, devour, dishonor, make lose face*, mess up*, pervert, pillage, pollute, profane, prostitute, ravage, sack*, spoil, spoliate, waste; CONCEPTS 246,252 —*Ant.* honor, praise, sanctify

desecration [n] *violation, abuse* blasphemy, debasement, defilement, impiety, irreverence, profanation, sacrilege; CONCEPTS 246,252 —*Ant.* honor, praise, sanctification

desegregate [v] *eliminate segregation* abolish segregation, commingle, give equal access, integrate, open, unify; CONCEPTS 113,114

desensitize [v] *dull* anesthetize, benumb, deaden, make inactive, make less sensitive, numb, render insensible; CONCEPTS 130,240

desert [adj] *barren, uncultivated* arid, bare, desolate, infertile, lonely, solitary, sterile, uninhabited, unproductive, untilled, waste, wild; CONCEPT 560 —*Ant.* cultivated, fertile, productive

desert [n] *wasteland; dry area* arid region, badland, barren, barren land, flats, lava bed, Sahara, sand dunes, solitude, wild, wilderness, wilds; CONCEPTS 508,517 —*Ant.* wetland

desert [v] *abandon, defect* abscond, apostatize, bail out*, beach, betray, bolt, check out*, chuck, cop out*, crawl out, decamp, depart, duck*, escape, flee, fly, forsake, give up, go, go AWOL*, go back on, go over the hill*, go west*, jilt, leave, leave high and dry*, leave in the lurch*, light, maroon, opt out, play truant, pull out, quit, relinquish, renounce, resign, run out on*, sneak off*, split*, strand, take a hike*, take off, transversate, throw over, vacate, violate oath, walk; CONCEPTS 195,297 —*Ant.* aid, assist, come back, help, stay, support

deserted [adj] *abandoned, unoccupied* bare, barren, bereft, cast off, derelict, desolate, empty, forlorn, forsaken, godforsaken*, isolated, left, left in the lurch*, left stranded, lonely, lorn, neglected, relinquished, solitary, uncouth, uninhabited, vacant; CONCEPTS 485,577 —*Ant.* busy, crowded, populated, populous

deserter [n] *fugitive from responsibility* absconder, apostate, AWOL*, backslider, betrayer, criminal, defector, delinquent, derelict, escapee, escaper, hookey player*, lawbreaker, maroon, no-show*, recreant, refugee, renegade, runaway, shirker, slacker, traitor, truant; CONCEPTS 358,412,423

desertion [n] *abandonment* abrogation, absconding, apostasy, avoidance, backsliding, betrayal, castoff, defecting, departing, departure, derelict, dereliction, disaffection, disavowal, disavowing, divorce, elusion, escape, evasion, falling away, falseness, flight, forsaking, going back on*, leaving, marooning, perfidy, recreancy, rejection, relinquishment, renunciation, repudiation, resignation, retirement, retreat, running out on*, secession, tergiversation,

treachery, truancy, withdrawal; CONCEPTS 195,297 —*Ant.* aid, assistance, help, staying

deserts [n] *what is due one* chastening, chastisement, comeuppance, compensation, deserving, discipline, disciplining, due, get hers*, get his*, guerdon, lumps*, meed, merit, payment, penalty, punishment, recompense, requital, retribution, return, revenge, reward, right, talion, what is coming to one*, what one is asking for*; CONCEPTS 129,710

deserve [v] *be entitled to* be given one's due*, be in line for*, be worthy of, demand, earn, gain, get, get comeuppance*, get what is coming to one*, have it coming*, have the right to, justify, lay claim to, merit, procure, rate, warrant, win; CONCEPT 129

deserving [adj] *worthy, meritorious* admirable, commendable, due, estimable, fitting, laudable, needy, praisable, praiseworthy, righteous, rightful, thankworthy; CONCEPT 404 —*Ant.* undeserving, unworthy

desiccate [v] *take moisture out of* anhydrate, dehydrate, deplete, devitalize, divest, drain, dry, dry up, evaporate, exsiccate, parch, sear, shrivel, wither, wizen; CONCEPTS 137,250 —*Ant.* moisten, moisturize, wet

design [n1] *sketch, draft* architecture, arrangement, blueprint, chart, comp, composition, conception, constitution, construction, delineation, depiction, diagram, doodle, drawing, dummy, form, formation, idea, layout, makeup, map, method, model, outline, paste-up, pattern, perspective, picture, plan, scheme, study, tracery, tracing, treatment; CONCEPTS 268,625,660

design [n2] *artful conception* arrangement, configuration, construction, depiction, device, doodle, drawing, figure, form, illustration, motif, motive, organization, painting, pattern, picture, portrait, shape, sketch, style; CONCEPT 259

design [n3] *intention* action, aim, angle, animus, big picture*, brainchild*, child*, conation, conspiracy, deliberation, end, enterprise, game plan*, gimmick, goal, intendment, intrigue, lay of the land*, machination, meaning, notion, object, objective, picture, pitch, plan, play, plot, point, project, proposition, purport, purpose, recipe, reflection, scenario, scene, schema, scheme, setup, story, target, thinking, thought, trick, undertaking, view, volition, what's cooking*, will; CONCEPTS 410,660

design [v1] *plan, outline* accomplish, achieve, arrange, block out, blueprint, cast, chart, construct, contrive, create, delineate, describe, devise, diagram, dope out, draft, draw, effect, execute, fashion, form, frame, fulfill, invent, lay out, perform, produce, project, set out, sketch, sketch out, trace, work out; CONCEPT 36 —*Ant.* disorder, disorganize

design [v2] *create, conceive* compose, contrive, cook up*, devise, dream up*, fabricate, fashion, form, frame, invent, make up, originate, produce, think up; CONCEPTS 43,173

design [v3] *intend, mean to do* aim, contemplate, contrive, destine, devise, make, mind, plan, prepare, project, propose, purpose, scheme, tailor; CONCEPTS 35,36

designate [v1] *name, entitle* baptize, call, christen, cognominate, denominate, dub, label, nickname, nominate, style, term, title; CONCEPT 62

designate [v2] *specify as selection* allocate, allot, appoint, apportion, appropriate, assign, authorize, button down*, characterize, charge, choose, commission, connote, constitute, define, delegate, denote, depute, deputize, describe, dictate, earmark*, elect, evidence, favor, finger*, indicate, individualize, make, mark, mete, name, nominate, opt, peg*, pick, pin down, pinpoint, prefer, put down for*, reseve, set apart, set aside, show, single, slot, stipulate, tab*, tag*, tap*; CONCEPTS 41,129

designation [n1] *name, label, mark* appellation, appellative, class, classification, cognomen, compellation, denomination, description, epithet, identification, key word, moniker, nickname, nomen, style, title; CONCEPT 683

designation [n2] *delegation, selection* appointment, classification, identification, indication, pigeonhole*, recognition, specification; CONCEPT 41

designedly [adv] *intentionally* apurpose, by design, calculatedly, deliberately, knowingly, on purpose, prepensely, purposedly, purposely, purposively, studiously, willfully, wittingly; CONCEPTS 402,535 —Ant. innocently, unconsciously, unintentionally, unknowingly, unwittingly

designer [n] *creator* architect, author, costumier, couturier, deviser, engineer, fabricator, fashion designer, fashioner, inventor, maker, originator, planner, producer; CONCEPT 352

designing [adj] *plotting, crafty* artful, astute, conniving, beautiful*, conspiring, crooked, cunning, deceitful, devious, heedful, intriguing, Machiavellian, observant, scheming, sharp, shrewd, sly, treacherous, tricky, unscrupulous, wily; -CONCEPT 542 —Ant. aboveboard, artless, honest, not clever, unplanned

desirable [adj1] *attractive, seductive* adorable, alluring, beautiful*, charming, covetable, enticing, fascinating, fetching, sexy; CONCEPTS 372,579 —Ant. bad, disagreeable, disgusting, unattractive, undesirable

desirable [adj2] *advantageous, good* acceptable, advisable, agreeable, beneficial, covetable, eligible, enviable, expedient, grateful, gratifying, helpful, pleasing, preferable, profitable, useful, welcome, worthwhile; CONCEPTS 560,572 —Ant. bad, detrimental, disadvantageous, evil, harmful, hurtful, injurious, unprofitable

desire [n1] *want, longing* admiration, ambition, appetite, ardor, aspiration, attraction, avidity, concupiscence, covetousness, craving, craze, cupidity, devotion, doting, eagerness, fancy, fascination, fervor, fondness, frenzy, greed, hankering*, hunger, inclination, infatuation, itch*, lasciviousness, lechery, libido, liking, love, lust, mania, motive, need, passion, predilection, proclivity, propensity, rapaciousness, rapture, ravenousness, relish, salacity, solicitude, thirst, urge, voracity, will, wish, yearning; CONCEPTS 20,709 —Ant. aversion, disgust, dislike, distaste, hate, hatred, repulsion

desire [n2] *request* appeal, entreaty, hope, importunity, petition, solicitation, supplication, want, wish; CONCEPT 662 —Ant. answer, antagonism, reply

desire [v1] *want, long for* aim, aspire to, be smitten, be turned on by*, choose, cotton to, covet, crave, desiderate, die over*, enjoy, fall for*, fancy, give eyeteeth for*, go for*, hanker after*, have eyes for*, have the hots for*, hunger for, like, lust after, make advances to, partial to, pine, set heart on*, spoil for, sweet on*, take a liking to*, take a shine to*, take to*, thirst, wish for, yearn for; CONCEPT 20 —Ant. not want

desire [v2] *ask, request* beg, bespeak, entreat, importune, petition, seek, solicit; CONCEPT 48 —Ant. answer

desirous [adj] *aspiring, hopeful* acquisitive, ambitious, amorous, anxious, avid, covetous, craving, desiring, eager, enthusiastic, grasping, greedy, hot*, itchy*, keen, longing, lustful, passionate, prehensile, ready, stimulated, turned on*, willing, wishful, wishing, yearning; CONCEPT 529 —Ant. reluctant, unambitious, unenthusiastic, unhopeful

desist [v] *stop, refrain from* abandon, abstain, avoid, break off, cease, discontinue, end, forbear, give over, give up, halt, have done with*, knock off*, leave off, not do, pause, quit, relinquish, resign, surcease, suspend, yield; CONCEPT 119 —Ant. carry on, continue, endure, go on, keep on, persevere, restart, resume

desk [n] *table* counter, davenport, escritoire, lectern, reading stand, rolltop, school desk, secretary, workspace, writing desk; CONCEPT 443

desk jockey [n] *an office worker* clerical worker, desk worker, pencil driver, pencil pusher, pen pusher, white-collar worker; CONCEPT 348

desktop publishing [n] *producing publications with computer software* desktop*, electronic publishing, formatting, outputting, typesetting; CONCEPT 277

desolate [adj1] *unused, barren* abandoned, bare, bleak, derelict, desert, destroyed, dreary, empty, forsaken, godforsaken*, isolated, lonely, lonesome, lorn, ruined, solitary, unfrequented, uninhabited, unoccupied, vacant, waste, wild; CONCEPTS 485,560 —Ant. cultivated, populated, used

desolate [adj2] *depressed, despondent* abandoned, acheronian, bereft, black, bleak, blue, cheerless, comfortless, companionless, dejected, disconsolate, dismal, dolorous, down, downcast, forlorn, forsaken, funereal, gloomy, hurting, in a blue funk*, inconsolable, joyless, lonely, lonesome, lorn, melancholy, miserable, somber, tragic, wretched; CONCEPT 403 —Ant. cheerful, happy, pleased

desolate [v] *ravage, destroy* depopulate, depredate, desecrate, despoil, devastate, devour, lay low, lay waste, pillage, plunder, ruin, sack, spoliate, waste; CONCEPT 252 —Ant. build, construct, improve

desolation [n1] *uninhabited area; barrenness* bareness, bleakness, desert, devastation, dissolution, extinction, forlornness, isolation, loneliness, ruin, solitariness, solitude, waste, wildness, wreck; CONCEPTS 517,710 —Ant. civilization

desolation [n2] *distress, unhappiness* anguish, dejection, despair, gloom, gloominess, loneliness, melancholy, misery, mourning, sadness, sorrow, woe, wretchedness; CONCEPT 410 —Ant. cheer, comfort, happiness, joy

despair [n] *depression, hopelessness* anguish, dashed hopes, dejection, desperation, despondency, discouragement, disheartenment, forlornness, gloom, melancholy, misery, ordeal, pain, sorrow, trial, tribulation, wretchedness; CONCEPT 410 —Ant. cheer, cheerfulness, confidence, faith, happiness, hopefulness, joy, joyfulness, trust

despair [v] *give up hope* abandon, be hopeless, despond, destroy, drop, flatten, give way, have heavy heart*, let air out*, lose faith, lose heart, relinquish, renounce, resign, surrender, take down, yield; CONCEPT 21 —Ant. anticipate, expect, have faith, hope, wish for

despairing [adj] *upset, despondent* anxious, at end of one's rope*, blue, brokenhearted, can't win*, cynical, dejected, depressed, desperate, disconsolate, downcast, forlorn, frantic, grief-stricken, hopeless, inconsolable, in pain*, in the dumps*, in the pits*, in the soup*, melancholy, miserable, not a prayer*, no-win*, oppressed, pessimistic, sad, shot down*, strabilious, suicidal, sunk*, weighed down*, wretched; CONCEPT 403 —Ant. confident, encouraged, expectant, hopeful

desperado [n] *criminal* bandit, convict, cutthroat, gangster, hoodlum, lawbreaker, mugger, outlaw, ruffian, thug; CONCEPT 412

desperate [adj1] *reckless, outrageous* atrocious, audacious, bold, careless, dangerous, daring, death-defying, determined, devil-may-care, foolhardy, frantic, frenzied, furious, hasty, hazardous, headlong, headstrong, heinous, impetuous, incautious, madcap, monstrous, precipitate, rash, risky, scandalous, shocking, venturesome, violent, wild; CONCEPT 401 —Ant. confident, content, satisfied, secure, unworried

desperate [adj2] *extreme, intense* acute, climacteric, concentrated, critical, crucial, dire, drastic, exquisite, fierce, furious, great, terrible, urgent, vehement, very grave, vicious, violent; CONCEPTS 537,540,569 —Ant. calm, content, contented, satisfactory, satisfied

desperate [adj3] *hopeless* at end of one's rope*, back to the wall*, can't win*, dead duck*, despairing, despondent, desponding, downcast, forlorn, futile, gone*, goner*, hard up*, inconsolable, in the soup*, in the toilet*, irrecoverable, irremediable, irretrievable, no-chance*, no-way*, no-win*, running out of time*, sad, sunk*, up against it*, up the creek*, useless, vain, wretched; CONCEPT 548 —Ant. hopeful

desperately [adv1] *severely* badly, carelessly, dangerously, dramatically, fiercely, gravely, greatly, harmfully, hysterically, like crazy*, like mad*, perilously, seriously; CONCEPT 569 —Ant. calmly, easily, trivially

desperately [adv2] *frightfully* appallingly, fearfully, hopelessly, shockingly; CONCEPT 403

desperation [n1] *hopelessness* agony, anguish, anxiety, concern, dejection, depression, desolation, despair, despondency, discomfort, disconsolateness, distraction, distress, fear, gloom, grief, heartache, melancholy, misery, pain, pang, sorrow, torture, trouble, unhappiness, worry; CONCEPT 410 —Ant. confidence, contentment, security

desperation [n2] *rashness* carelessness, defiance, foolhardiness, frenzy, heedlessness, impetuosity, madness, recklessness; CONCEPT 633 —Ant. calm, cautiousness, collectedness, peace, peacefulness

despicable [adj] *hateful; beyond contempt* abject, awful, base, beastly, cheap, contemptible, degrading, detestable, dirty, disgraceful, disreputable, down, ignominious, infamous, insignificant, loathsome, low, low-life*, mean,no-good*, pitiful, reprehensible, shameful, slimy*, sordid, vile, worthless, wretched; CONCEPTS 404,570 —Ant. desirous, honorable, likeable, loveable, respectable, virtuous, worthy

despise [v] *look down on* abhor, abominate, allergic to*, contemn, deride, detest, disdain, disregard, eschew, execrate, feel contempt for, flout, hate, have no use for*, loathe, look down nose at*, misprize, neglect, put down*, reject, renounce, repudiate, revile, scorn, shun, slight, snub, spurn, undervalue, wipe out*; CONCEPT 29 —Ant. admire, appreciate, cherish, like, love

despite [prep] *in spite of, regardless of* against, although, even though, even with, in contempt of, in defiance of, in the face of, notwithstanding, undeterred by; CONCEPT 544

despoil [v] *ravage, destroy* denude, depopulate, depredate, deprive, desecrate, desolate, devastate, devour, dispossess, divest, loot, maraud, pillage, plunder, raid, rifle, rob, sack, spoil, spoliate, strip, vandalize, waste, wreak havoc, wreck; CONCEPT 252 —Ant. build, construct, improve

despondent [adj] *depressed* all torn up*, blue*, bummed-out*, cast-down, dejected, despairing, disconsolate, discouraged, disheartened, dispirited, doleful, down, downcast, downhearted, forlorn, gloomy, glum, grief-stricken, grieving, hopeless, in a blue funk*, in despair, in the pits*, low, low-spirited, melancholy, miserable, morose, mourning, sad, shot down*, sorrowful, woebegone, wretched; CONCEPT 403 —Ant. cheerful, elated, happy, hopeful, spirited, up

despot [n] *dictator* autocrat, Hitler*, monocrat, oppressor, slavedriver, tyrant; CONCEPTS 354,412

despotism [n] *absolute power* authoritarianism, autocracy, dictatorship, tyranny; CONCEPT 133

dessert [n] *sweet treat* cake, candy, confection, cookie, frozen dessert, frozen treat, fruit, ice cream, last course, pastry, pie, pudding, sweet, sweet course, tart; CONCEPT 457

destination [n] *goal; place one wants to go* aim, ambition, design, end, harbor, haven, intention, journey's end, landing-place, object, objective, purpose, resting-place, station, stop, target, terminal, terminus; CONCEPTS 198,659 —Ant. beginning, source, start

destine [v] *predetermine, ordain* allot, appoint, assign, consecrate, decide, decree, dedicate, design, determine, devote, doom, doom to, earmark*, fate, foreordain, intend, mark out, predestine, preform, preordain, purpose, reserve; CONCEPT 18

destined [adj1] *bound for, fated in near future* at hand, brewing*, certain, closed, coming, compelled, compulsory, condemned, designed, directed, doomed, foreordained, forthcoming, hanging over*, impending, ineluctable, inescapable, inevitable, inexorable, in prospect, instant, in store, intended, in the cards*, in the wind*, looming, meant, menacing, near, ordained, overhanging, predesigned, predestined, predetermined, que sera sera*, sealed, settled, stated, that is to be, that will be, threatening, to come, unavoidable, way the ball bounces*; CONCEPT 537 —Ant. avoidable, unscheduled

destined [adj2] en route, on the road to appointed, appropriated, assigned, bent upon, booked, bound for, chosen, consigned, delegated, designated, determined, directed, entrained, heading, ordered to, prepared, routed, scheduled, specified; CONCEPT 584

destiny [n] fate afterlife, break*, breaks*, certainty, circumstance, conclusion, condition, constellation, course of events, cup, design, divine decree, doom, expectation, finality, foreordination, fortune, future, happenstance, hereafter, horoscope, inevitability, intent, intention, karma, kismet*, lot, luck, Moirai, objective, ordinance, portion, predestination, predetermination, prospect, serendipity, the stars*, way the ball bounces*, way the cookie crumbles*, what is written*, wheel of fortune*, world to come*; CONCEPT 679 —Ant. choice, free will, volition

destitute [adj] down and out; wanting bankrupt, beggared, bereft, busted, dead broke*, deficient, depleted, deprived of, devoid of, dirt poor*, divested, drained, empty, exhausted, flat*, flat broke*, impecunious, impoverished, indigent, in need of, insolvent, lacking, moneyless, necessitous, needy, on the breadline*, on the rocks*, penniless, penurious, pinched, played out*, poor, poverty-stricken, stony, strapped, stripped, totaled, wiped out*, without; CONCEPT 334 —Ant. lucky, prosperous, rich, secure, wealthy

destroy [v] demolish, devastate abort, annihilate, annul, axe*, blot out, break down, butcher*, consume, cream*, crush, damage, deface, desolate, despoil, dismantle, dispatch, end, eradicate, erase, exterminate, extinguish, extirpate, gut*, impair, kill, lay waste, level, liquidate, maim, mar, maraud, mutilate, nuke*, nullify, overturn, quash, quell, ravage, ravish, raze, ruin, sabotage, shatter, slay, smash, snuff out*, spoliate, stamp out, suppress, swallow up*, tear down, torpedo*, total, trash*, vaporize, waste, wax*, wipe out, wreck, zap*; CONCEPT 252 —Ant. build, construct, create, improve, repair, restore

destruction [n] demolition, devastation abolishing, abolition, annihilation, assassinating, bane, carnage, crashing, crushing, disintegrating, disrupting, dissolving, downfall, elimination, end, eradication, extermination, extinction, extinguishing, extirpation, havoc, invalidating, invalidation, liquidation, loss, massacre, murder, overthrow, ravaging, ruin, ruination, sacking, shattering, slaughter, slaying, subjugation, subversion, subverting, undoing, wreckage, wrecking; CONCEPTS 230, 252 —Ant. building, construction, creation, improvement, reparation, restoration

destructive [adj1] injurious, devastating annihilative, baleful, baneful, calamitous, cancerous, cataclysmic, catastrophic, consumptive, cutthroat, damaging, deadly, deleterious, detrimental, dire, disastrous, eradicative, evil, extirpative, fatal, fell, harmful, hurtful, internecine, lethal, lethiferous, mortal, noisome, noxious, pernicious, pestiferous, pestilential, ruinous, slaughterous, suicidal, toxic, venomous, wrackful, wreckful; CONCEPT 537 —Ant. aiding, assisting, building, creative, helpful, productive

destructive [adj2] hurtful, disparaging abrasive, adverse, antagonistic, cankerous, caustic, contrary, corrosive, deleterious, derogatory, detrimental, discouraging, discrediting, erosive, hostile, injurious, invalidating, negative, offensive, opposed, troublesome, undermining, vicious; CONCEPTS 267,537 —Ant. encouraging, hopeful, positive

desultory [adj] random aimless, chance, chaotic, deviating, erratic, haphazard, orderless, rambling, unmethodical, unstable, unsystematic, without purpose; CONCEPTS 535,548,557

detach [v] disconnect, cut off abstract, disaffiliate, disassemble, disassociate, disengage, disentangle, disjoin, dismount, dissociate, disunite, divide, divorce, free, isolate, loose, loosen, part, remove, segregate, separate, sever, sunder, take apart, tear off, uncouple, unfasten, unfix, unhitch, withdraw; CONCEPT 135 —Ant. attach, combine, connect, couple, link, merge, unite

detached [adj1] disconnected alone, apart, discrete, disjoined, divided, emancipated, free, isolate, isolated, loose, loosened, removed, separate, severed, unaccompanied, unconnected; CONCEPT 490 —Ant. attached, combined, connected, coupled, linked, merged, united

detached [adj2] aloof, disinterested; neutral abstract, apathetic, casual, cool*, dispassionate, distant, impartial, impersonal, incurious, indifferent, laid-back*, objective, out of it*, poker-faced*, remote, removed, reserved, spaced-out, spacey*, staid, stolid, unbiased, uncommitted, unconcerned, uncurious, uninvolved, unpassioned, unprejudiced, withdrawn; CONCEPTS 401,404 —Ant. biased, compassionate, engaged, interested, sympathetic

detachment [n1] disconnection disengagement, disjoining, dissolution, disunion, division, divorce, divorcement, partition, rupture, separation, severing, split-up; CONCEPTS 388,747 —Ant. attachment, combination, connection, linkage, merger

detachment [n2] aloofness brown study*, coldness, coolness, disinterestedness, dreaminess, impartiality, incuriosity, indifference, neutrality, nonpartisanship, objectivity, preoccupation, remoteness, reverie, unconcern, woolgathering*; CONCEPT 633 —Ant. bias, compassion, interest, kindness, sympathy

detachment [n3] military troop army, body, detail, division, force, organization, party, patrol, special force, squad, task force, troupe, unit; CONCEPT 322

detail [n1] feature, specific aspect ABCs*, accessory, article, brass tacks*, chapter and verse*, circumstantiality, component, count, cue, design, dope*, element, fact, factor, fine point, fraction, item, meat and potatoes*, minor point, minutia, nicety, nitty-gritty*, nuts and bolts*, part, particular, peculiarity, plan, point, portion, respect, schedule, singularity, specialty, specification, structure, technicality, thing, trait, trivia, triviality; CONCEPT 831 —*Ant.* whole

detail [*n2*] *military troop* army, assignment, body, detachment, duty, fatigue, force, kitchen police, KP*, organization, party, special force, squad, unit; CONCEPT 322

detail [*v1*] *specify, make clear* analyze, catalog, circumstantiate, communicate, delineate, depict, describe, designate, elaborate, embellish, enumerate, epitomize, exhibit, fly speck*, get down to brass tacks*, individualize, itemize, lay out, narrate, particularize, portray, produce, quote chapter and verse*, recapitulate, recite, recount, rehearse, relate, report, reveal, set forth, show, specialize, spell out, spread, stipulate, summarize, sweat details*, tell, uncover; CONCEPTS 55,57,60 —*Ant.* hide, misrepresent, suppress, withhold

detail [*v2*] *assign specific task* allocate, appoint, charge, commission, delegate, detach, send; CONCEPTS 50,88

detailed [*adj*] *itemized, particularized* abundant, accurate, all-inclusive, amplified, at length, blow-by-blow*, circumstantial, circumstantiated, clocklike, complete, complicated, comprehensive, copious, definite, described, developed, disclosed, elaborate, elaborated, enumerated, exact, exhausting, exhaustive, finicky*, full, fussy*, individual, individualized, intricate, meticulous, minute, narrow, nice, point-by-point, precise, seriatim, specific, specified, thorough, unfolded; CONCEPT 557 —*Ant.* brief, cursory, inexhaustive, nonspecific, sparing, uncomplicated, undetailed

detain [*v*] *hold, keep back; arrest* apprehend, bog down*, bust*, buttonhole*, check, confine, constrain, decelerate, delay, hang up*, hinder, hold up*, ice*, impede, inhibit, intern, jail, mire, nab*, pick up, pinch*, pull in*, put away*, reserve, restrain, retard, run in, send up, set back, slow down, slow up, withhold; CONCEPTS 191,317 —*Ant.* free, let go, liberate, release

detect [*v*] *discover* ascertain, catch, descry, dig up*, disclose, distinguish, encounter, espy, expose, find, hit on*, hit upon*, identify, meet, meet with, nose out*, note, notice, observe, recognize, reveal, scent, see, smell out*, smoke out*, spot, stumble on, track down, tumble into, turn up, uncover, unmask, wise up to*; CONCEPTS 38,183 —*Ant.* miss, not see, overlook, pass by

detection [*n*] *discovery* apprehension, disclosure, espial, exposé, exposure, ferreting out, find, revelation, strike, tracking down, uncovering, unearthing, unmasking; CONCEPTS 38, 183 —*Ant.* failure, miss, mistake

detective [*n*] *investigator of crime* agent, analyst, bird dog*, bloodhound*, bull*, constable, cop, dick*, eavesdropper, eye*, fed*, fink*, flatfoot*, gumshoe*, informer, nark*, peeper*, P. I.*, plainclothes officer, police officer, private eye, private investigator, prosecutor, reporter, roper, scout, sergeant, shadow*, shamus*, Sherlock Holmes*, shoofly*, sleuth, slewfoot*, snoop*, spy, tail*; CONCEPT 348

détente [*n*] *peace* amity, cooling off, equal power, harmony, relaxation, relief, tranquility, truce; CONCEPTS 388,691

detention [*n*] *confinement, imprisonment* apprehension, arrest, arrestation, bust*, custody, delay, detainment, hindrance, holding back, holding pen*, immurement, impediment, incarceration, internment, keeping in, nab, pen*, pickup, pinch*, quarantine, restraint, retention, time up the river*, withholding; CONCEPTS 191,317 —*Ant.* freedom, liberation, release

deter [*v*] *check, inhibit from action* act like a wet blanket*, avert, block, caution, chill, cool, damp, dampen, daunt, debar, disadvise, discourage, dissuade, divert, forestall, forfend, frighten, hinder, impede, intimidate, obstruct, obviate, preclude, prevent, prohibit, put a damper on, put off, restrain, rule out, scare, shut out, stave off, stop, talk out of, throw cold water on*, turn off, warn; CONCEPT 121 —*Ant.* encourage, instigate, persuade, promote, put on to, stimulate, support, turn on, urge

detergent [*n*] *soap* cleaner, solvent; CONCEPT 492

deteriorate [*v*] *decay, degenerate* adulterate, alloy, become worse, be worse for wear*, break, corrode, corrupt, crumble, debase, debilitate, decline, decompose, degrade, deprave, depreciate, descend, disimprove, disintegrate, ebb, fade, fail, fall apart, flag, go downhill*, go to pieces*, go to pot*, go to the dogs*, hit the skids*, impair, injure, languish, lapse, lessen, lose it, lose quality, lower, mar, pervert, regress, retrograde, retrogress, rot, sink, skid, slide, spoil, undermine, vitiate, weaken, wear away, worsen; CONCEPT 698 —*Ant.* build, construct, develop, get better, improve

deterioration [*n*] *decay, degeneration* abasement, adulteration, atrophy, corrosion, crumbling, debasement, decadence, decaying, declension, declination, decline, decomposition, degradation, degringolade, depreciation, descent, devaluation, dilapidation, disintegration, dislocation, disrepair, downfall, downgrade, downturn, drop, fall, lapse, lessening, perversion, retrogression, rotting, ruin, slump, spoiling, vitiation, worsening; CONCEPTS 230,698 —*Ant.* betterment, building, construction, development, improvement

determination [*n1*] *perseverance* assurance, backbone*, boldness, bravery, certainty, certitude, constancy, conviction, courage, dauntlessness, decision, dedication, doggedness, dogmatism, drive, energy, fearlessness, firm-ness, fortitude, grit, guts*, hardihood, heart*, independence, indomitability, intrepidity, nerve*, obstinacy, persistence, pluck*, purpose, purposefulness, resoluteness, resolution, resolve, self-confidence, single-mindedness, spine*, spunk*, steadfastness, stiff upper lip*, stubbornness, tenacity, valor, willpower; CONCEPTS 411,657 —*Ant.* disinterest, doubt, hesitation, irresolution, spinelessness, vacillation

determination [*n2*] *conclusion* decision, judgment, measurement, opinion, perception, purpose, resolution, resolve, result, settlement, solution, verdict, visualization; CONCEPTS 685,689 —*Ant.* beginning, start

determine [*v1*] *conclude, decide* actuate, arbitrate, call the shots*, cinch, clinch, complete, dispose, drive, end, figure, finish, fix upon, halt, impel, incline, induce, move, nail down*, opt, ordain, persuade, pin down*, predispose, regulate, resolve, rule, settle, take a decision, tap, terminate, ultimate, wind up*, wrap up*; CONCEPTS *18,35,234* —*Ant.* begin, start

determine [v2] *discover, find out* add up to*, ascertain, boil down to*, catch on, certify, check, demonstrate, detect, divine, establish, figure, figure out, have a hunch*, hear, learn, make out, see, size up, tell, tumble, unearth, verify, work out; CONCEPTS *15,31* —*Ant.* miss, overlook

determine [v3] *choose, decide* destine, doom, elect, establish, fate, finger*, fix, foreordain, make up mind, predestine, predetermine, preform, preordain, purpose, resolve, settle; CONCEPT *18* —*Ant.* doubt, hesitate, waver

determine [v4] *dictate, govern, regulate* affect, bound, circumscribe, command, condition, control, decide, delimit, devise, direct, impel, impose, incline, induce, influence, invent, lead, limit, manage, mark off, measure, modify, plot, rule, shape; CONCEPT *94*

determined [adj] *driven, persistent* bent, bent on, buckled down*, constant, decided, decisive, dogged, earnest, firm, fixed, hard-as-nails*, hardboiled*, intent, mean business*, obstinate, on ice*, pat, persevering, purposeful, resolute, resolved, serious, set, set on, settled, single-minded, solid, steadfast, strong-minded, strong-willed, stubborn, tenacious, unfaltering, unflinching, unhesitating, unwavering; CONCEPTS *404,542* —*Ant.* flexible, hesitating, irresolute, vacillating, wavering, weak

deterrent [n] *impediment, restraint* bridle, check, curb, defense, determent, discouragement, disincentive, hindrance, leash, obstacle, preventative, preventive, rein, shackle; CONCEPT *680* —*Ant.* catalyst, encouragement, incentive

detest [v] *hate; feel disgust toward* abhor, abominate, be allergic to, despise, dislike intensely, down on, execrate, feel aversion toward, feel hostility toward, feel repugnance toward, have no use for*, loathe, recoil from, reject, repudiate; CONCEPT *29* —*Ant.* adore, cherish, like, love, prize, respect

detestable [adj] *loathsome, abominable* abhorred, abhorrent, accursed, atrocious, awful, despicable, disgusting, execrable, godawful*, grody*, gross*, hateable, hateful, heinous, horrid, lousy, low-down, maggot, monstrous, obnoxious, odious, offensive, outrageous, repugnant, repulsive, revolting, rotten, shocking, sorry, vile; CONCEPTS *529,542* —*Ant.* admirable, adorable, adored, cherished, likeable, loveable, prized, respectable, respected

dethrone [v] *oust* degrade, depose, discrown, dismiss, displace, uncrown, unmake; CONCEPTS *298,320* —*Ant.* crown, enthrone, put in power

detonate [v] *set off bomb* bang, blast, blow up, burst, discharge, explode, fulminate, kablooey*, let go, mushroom*, push the button*, shoot off, touch off, va-voom*; CONCEPT *179* —*Ant.* dismantle

detonation [n] *explosion* bang, blast, blowout, blow-up, boom, discharge, ignition; CONCEPTS *179,320,521*

detour [n] *indirect course* alternate route, back road, branch, bypass, bypath, byway,

circuit, circuitous route, circumbendibus*, circumnavigation, circumvention, crotch, deviation, divergence, diversion, fork, roundabout way, runaround, secondary highway, service road, substitute, temporary route; CONCEPT *501*

detract [v] *take away a part; lessen* backbite*, belittle, blister, cheapen, cut rate, decrease, decry, depreciate, derogate, devaluate, diminish, discount, discredit, disesteem, draw away, knock*, laugh at, lower, minimize, misprize, reduce, subtract from, underrate, undervalue, vilipend, withdraw, write off; CONCEPTS *52,54,236,247* —*Ant.* add to, increase, optimize

detraction [n] *misrepresentation; slander* abuse, aspersion, backbiting*, backstabbing*, belittlement, calumny, damage, defamation, denigration, deprecation, derogation, disesteem, disparagement, harm, hit, hurt, injury, injustice, innuendo, insinuation, knock*, libel, libeling, lie, maligning, minimization, muckraking*, obloquy, pejorative, revilement, ridicule, running down*, scandal, scandalmongering, scurrility, slam, smear campaign*, tale, traducement, traducing, vilification, vituperation, wrong; CONCEPTS *52,54,63* —*Ant.* admiration, adulation, flattery, praise

detriment [n] *disadvantage* damage, disability, disservice, drawback, handicap, harm, hurt, impairment, injury, liability, loss, marring, mischief, prejudice, spoiling; CONCEPTS *309,674* —*Ant.* advantage, assistance, benefit, gain, help, profit

detrimental [adj] *damaging, disadvantageous* adverse, bad, baleful, deleterious, destructive, disturbing, evil, harmful, hurtful, ill, inimical, injurious, mischievous, negative, nocuous, pernicious, prejudicial, unfavorable; CONCEPTS *537,570* —*Ant.* advantageous, assisting, beneficial, helpful, profitable

detritus [n] *debris* deposit, fragments, grains, leavings, rubble, scree, sediment, shavings; CONCEPT *260*

devalue [v] *depreciate* cheapen, cut rate, debase, decrease, decry, devalorize, devaluate, knock off, lower, mark down, nose dive, revalue, take down, underrate, undervalue, write down, write off; CONCEPTS *330,335* —*Ant.* increase, overvalue, raise

devastate [v] *demolish, destroy* depredate, desecrate, desolate, despoil, devour, do one in*, lay waste, level, pillage, plunder, raid, ravage, raze, ruin, sack, smash, spoil, spoliate, stamp out*, take apart, total*, trash*, waste, wipe off map*, wreck; CONCEPTS *246,252* —*Ant.* build, construct, enrich, help, improve

devastation [n] *destruction* confusion, defoliation, demolition, depredation, desolation, havoc, loss, pillage, plunder, ravages, ruin, ruination, spoliation, waste; CONCEPT *674* —*Ant.* building, construction, creation

develop [v1] *cultivate, prosper* advance, age, enroot, establish, evolve, expand, flourish, foster, grow, grow up, maturate, mature, mellow, progress, promote, ripen, thrive; CONCEPTS *253,427,704* —*Ant.* halt, repress

develop [v2] *expand, work out* actualize, advance, amplify, augment, beautify, broaden, build up, cultivate, deepen, dilate, elaborate, enlarge, enrich, evolve, exploit, extend, finish, heighten, improve, intensify, lengthen, magnify, materialize, perfect, polish, promote, realize, refine, spread, strengthen, stretch, unfold, widen; CONCEPTS 700,775 —*Ant.* circumscribe, compress, confine, decrease, lessen, narrow

develop [v3] *begin; occur* acquire, arise, befall, betide, break, break out, breed, chance, come about, come off, commence, contract, ensue, establish, follow, form, generate, go, happen, invest, originate, pick up, result, start, transpire; CONCEPT *119* —*Ant.* cease, discontinue, end, halt, stop

develop [v4] *unfold; be made known* account for, acquire, actualize, disclose, disentangle, elaborate, evolve, exhibit, explain, explicate, foretell, form, materialize, produce, reach, realize, recount, state, uncoil, uncover, unfurl, unravel, unroll, untwist, unwind; CONCEPTS *60,261*

developer [n] *real estate developer* builder, planner, real estate investor; CONCEPT *348*

development [n1] *growth* adding to, addition, adulthood, advance, advancement, advancing, augmentation, augmenting, boost, buildup, developing, elaborating, enlargement, evolution, evolvement, evolving, expansion, fl owering, hike, improvement, increase, increasing, making progress, maturation, maturing, maturity, ongoing, perfecting, progress, progression, reinforcement, reinforcing, ripening, spread, spreading, unfolding, unraveling, upgrowth, upping; CONCEPTS *700,704,775* —*Ant.* decline, decrease, stoppage

development [n2] *happening, incident* change, circumstance, conclusion, denouement, event, eventuality, eventuation, issue, materialization, occurrence, outcome, phenomenon, result, situation, transpiration, turn of events, upshot; CONCEPT *3*

deviant [adj] *abnormal, different* aberrant, anomalous, atypical, bent, devious, divergent, freaky, heretical, heteroclite, irregular, kinky, off-key, perverse, perverted, preternatural, queer, twisted, unorthodox, unrepresentative, untypical, variant, varying, wandering, wayward, weird; CONCEPT *564* —*Ant.* normal, regular, standard, usual

deviate [v] *stray from normal path* aberrate, angle off, avert, bear off, bend, bend the rules*, break pattern, circumlocate, contrast, deflect, depart, depart from, differ, digress, divagate, diverge, drift, edge off*, err, get around, go amiss, go haywire*, go off on tangent*, go out of control*, go out of way, leave beaten path*, not conform, part, shy, swerve, swim against stream*, take a turn, turn, turn aside, vary, veer, wander; CONCEPTS *195,665,697* —*Ant.* go straight, keep, stay

deviation [n] *change, departure* aberration, alteration, anomaly, breach, crotch, deflection, detour, difference, digression, discrepancy, disparity, divergence, diversion, fluctuation, fork, hereticism, inconsistency, irregularity, modification, shift, transgression, turning, variance, variation; CONCEPTS *665,697,738* —*Ant.* conformity, sameness, straightforwardness, uniformity

device [n1] *instrument, tool* accessory, agent, apparatus, appliance, arrangement, article, construction, contraption, contrivance, creation,

doohickey*, equipment, expedient, gadget, gear, gimmick, implement, invention, machine, makeshift, material, means, mechanism, medium, outfit, resort, resource, rigging*, Rube Goldberg invention*, shift, tackle, thingamabob*, utensil, whatchamacallit*, whatnot*, whatsit*; CONCEPTS *463,499*

device [n2] *ploy, scheme, maneuver* artifice, cabal, chicanery, clever move, craft, craftiness, cunningness, design, dodge, evasion, expedient, fake, feint, finesse, gambit, game, gimmick, improvisation, loophole*, machination, method, pattern, plan, plot, project, proposition, purpose, racket, ruse, shift, stratagem, strategy, stunt, subterfuge, trap, trick, wile; CONCEPT *660*

device [n3] *symbol, emblem* badge, colophon, crest, design, ensign, figure, insignia, logo, motif, motto, pattern, scroll, sign, slogan, token; CONCEPT *284*

devil [n] *demon* adversary, archfiend, beast, Beelzebub, bête noire, brute, common enemy, dastard, diablo, djinn, dybbuk, enfant terrible*, evil one, fiend, genie, hellion, imp, knave, Lucifer, Mephistopheles, monster, ogre, Prince of Darkness, rogue, Satan, scamp, scoundrel, the dickens*, the Erinyes, the Furies, villain; CONCEPTS *370,412* —*Ant.* angel, god

devilish [adj] *wicked* accursed, atrocious, bad, brutish, cloven-footed, cursed, damnable, demoniac, demonic, detestable, diabolic, diabolical, evil, execrable, fiendish, hellborn, hellish, infernal, inhuman, iniquitous, Mephistophelian, nefarious, satanic, serpentine, unhallowed, villainous; CONCEPT *545* —*Ant.* angelic, godlike, good, moral

devil's advocate [n] *mediator* apologist, pleader, polemicist, sophist; CONCEPTS *348,423*

devious [adj1] *dishonest, crafty* artful, calculating, crooked, deceitful, double-dealing, duplicitous, errant, erring, evasive, faking one out*, fishy*, foxy*, fraudulent, guileful, indirect, insidious, insincere, not straightforward, oblique, obliquitous, playing games, playing politics*, put on, roundabout, scheming, shady, shifty, shrewd, sly, sneaking, sneaky, surreptitious, treacherous, tricky, underhanded, wily; CONCEPTS *401,404* —*Ant.* artless, frank, honest, open, straightforward, trustworthy, truthful

devious [adj2] *crooked; indirect* ambiguous, bending, circuitous, confounding, confusing, curving, detouring, deviating, digressing, digressory, diverting, errant, erratic, excursive, flexuous, misleading, obscure, out-of-the-way, rambling, remote, removed, roundabout, serpentine, straying, tortuous, twisting, wandering; CONCEPT *581* —*Ant.* direct, straight

devise [v] *conceive, dream up* ad-lib, arrange, blueprint*, brainstorm*, cast, chart, cogitate, come up with, concoct, construct, contrive, cook up*, craft, create, design, discover, dope out*, fake it, forge, form, formulate, frame*, get off*, hatch, head trip*, imagine, improvise, intrigue, invent, machinate, make up, mastermind*, plan, play it by ear*, plot, prepare, project, scheme, shape, spark, think up, throw together, trump up*, vamp, whip up*, work out; CONCEPTS *36,43* —*Ant.* borrow

devoid [adj] *empty, wanting* bare, barren, bereft, deficient, denuded, destitute, free from,

innocent, lacking, needed, sans*, unprovided
with, vacant, void, without; CONCEPTS 483,485
—Ant. complete, filled, full

devote [v] *commit one's energies, thoughts*
allot, apply, apportion, appropriate, assign,
bestow, bless, concern oneself, confide,
consecrate, consign, dedicate, donate, enshrine,
entrust, give, give away, hallow, hand out,
occupy oneself, pledge, present, reserve,
sanctify, set apart, vow; CONCEPTS 17,108,112
—Ant. misappropriate, misuse, waste

devoted [adj] *committed, loyal* adherent, affectionate, ardent, behind one, caring, concerned,
consecrated, constant, crazy about*, dear, dedicated, devout, doting, dutiful, faithful, fervid,
fond, gone on*, lovesome, loving, staunch,
steadfast, stuck on*, thoughtful, true, true-blue*,
wild about*, zealous; CONCEPT 542 —Ant.
apathetic, disloyal, inconstant, neglectful, negligent, uncommitted, unfaithful, untrustworthy

devotee [n] *ardent supporter; fan* addict,
adherent, admirer, aficionado, amateur,
believer, booster, buff, disciple, enthusiast,
fanatic, fancier, fiend, follower, groupie,
habitué, junkie, lover, rooter, supporter,
votarient, votary; CONCEPT 423 —Ant.
adversary, antagonist, enemy

devotion [n] *commitment; loyalty* adherence,
adoration, affection, allegiance, ardor, attachment, consecration, constancy, dedication,
deference, devotedness, devotement, devoutness, earnestness, enthusiasm, faithfulness,
fealty, fervor, fidelity, fondness, intensity, love,
observance, passion, piety, reverence, sanctity,
service, sincerity, spirituality, worship, zeal;
CONCEPTS 32,657 —Ant. apathy, carelessness,
indifference, neglect, negligence

devour [v] *swallow, consume* absorb, annihilate, appreciate, be engrossed in, be preoccupied, bolt, bolt down*, chow down*, cram*,
delight in, destroy, dispatch, do compulsively,
do voraciously, drink in, eat, enjoy, exhaust,
feast on, feed on, gloat over, gobble, gorge*,
go through, gulp, guzzle, hoover*, imbibe,
ingest, inhale, partake of, pig out*, polish off*,
ravage, rejoice in, relish, revel in, scarf down*,
spend, stuff, take, take in, use up, waste, wipe
out, wolf*, wolf down*; CONCEPTS 169,225
—Ant. abstain, pick

devout [adj] *sincerely believing; devoted* adherent, adoring, ardent, deep, earnest, faithful,
fervent, fervid, genuine, godly, goody-goody*,
goody two-shoes*, heart-and-soul, heartfelt,
holy, intense, orthodox, passionate, pietistic,
pious, prayerful, profound, religious, reverent,
revering, serious, sincere, venerating, worship-
ing, zealous; CONCEPT 542 —Ant. insincere,
irreligious, unbelieving

dew [n] *moisture* condensation, water droplets;
CONCEPTS 467,524

dewy-eyed [adj] *innocent* dovelike, green, inexperienced, naive, pure, sinless, uncorrupted,
undefiled, unworldly, wide-eyed; CONCEPT 404

dexterity [n] *aptitude, ability* address, adroitness, aptness, art, artistry, cleverness, craft,
cunning, deftness, effortlessness, expertise, expertness, facility, finesse, handiness, ingenuity,
knack, know-how, mastery, neatness, nimbleness, proficiency, readiness, skill, skillfulness,

smoothness, tact, touch; CONCEPTS 409,630
—Ant. awkwardness, clumsiness, inability,
ineptness

dexterous [adj] *ingenious, proficient* able,
active, acute, adept, adroit, agile, apt, artful,
canny, clever, crack*, crackerjack*, deft,
effortless, expert, facile, handy, having the
know-how*, masterly, neat, nimble, nimble-
fingered, prompt, quick, savvy, skilled,
skillful, slick, sly, smooth; CONCEPTS 402,
527 —Ant. awkward, clumsy, inept, inexpert,
unable, unhandy, unskilled

diabolic [adj] *evil, fiendish* atrocious, cruel,
damnable, demoniac, demonic, devilish, hellish,
impious, infernal, Mephistophelian, monstrous,
nasty, nefarious, satanic, serpentine, shocking,
unhallowed, unpleasant, vicious, vile, villainous,
wicked; CONCEPT 545 —Ant. gentle, kind,
moral, nice

diagnose [v] *identify problem, disease* analyze,
determinate, determine, diagnosticate, distinguish, interpret, investigate, pinpoint, place,
pronounce, recognize, spot; CONCEPTS 38,310
—Ant. misdiagnose

diagnosis [n] *identification of problem, disease*
analysis, conclusion, examination, interpretation, investigation, opinion, pronouncement,
scrutiny, summary; CONCEPTS 283,689

diagonal [adj] *angled* askew, bevel, beveled,
bias, biased, cater-cornered, catty-cornered,
cornerways, cross, crossways, crosswise, inclining, kitty-cornered*, oblique, skewing, slanted,
slanting, transversal, transverse; CONCEPT 581

diagonally [adv] *at an angle* askew, aslant,
cater-corner, catty-corner, cornerwise, crosswise, kitty-corner*, obliquely, on a slant, on
the bias, slantingways, slantways, slantwise,
slaunchways; CONCEPT 581

diagram [n] *drawing, sketch of form or plan*
big picture*, blueprint, chart, description,
design, draft, figure, floor plan, game, game
plan, ground plan, layout, outline, perspective,
representation, rough draft; CONCEPTS 625,660

dial [v] *tune to desired position* punch, ring,
rotate, turn, twist, wheel, zero in on*;
CONCEPT 201

dialect [n] *local speech* accent, argot, cant,
idiom, jargon, language, lingo, localism,
patois, patter, pronunciation, provincialism,
regionalism, slang, terminology, tongue,
vernacular, vocabulary; CONCEPT 276

dialectic [adj] *logical, rational* analytic,
argumentative, controversial, dialectical,
persuasive, polemical, rationalistic; CONCEPT
529 —Ant. illogical, irrational

dialectic [n] *logic, reasoning* argumentation,
contention, debate, deduction, discussion, disputation, forensic, logical argument, mooting,
persuasion, polemics, question-and-answer
method, ratiocination; CONCEPT 37

dialogue/dialog [n] *talk, exchange of ideas*
chat, colloquy, communication, confab*, confabulation, conference, conversation, converse,
discourse, discussion, duologue, interlocution,
lines*, parlance, parley, powwow, remarks,
repartee, script, sides, small talk*; CONCEPT 56

diameter [n] *measurement across object* bore,
breadth, broadness, caliber, module, width;
CONCEPT 760

diametric/diametrical [adj] opposed, conflicting adverse, antipodal, antipodean, antithetical, contradictory, contrary, contrasting, converse, counter, facing, opposite, polar, reverse; CONCEPT 564 —Ant. approving, coinciding, like, same, similar

diaphanous [adj] fine, see-through chiffon, clear, cobweblike, delicate, filmy, flimsy, gauzy, gossamer, light, pellucid, pure, sheer, thin, translucent, transparent; CONCEPTS 490,606 —Ant. opaque, thick

diarrhea [n] loose bowels dysentery, flux, Montezuma's revenge*, the runs*, the trots*; CONCEPT 306

diary [n] recounting of activities in writing account, agenda, appointment book, chronicle, daily record, daybook, engagement book, journal, log, minutes, notebook, record; CONCEPT 283

diaspora [n] the spreading out of a group of people disbandment, dispersal, dispersion, dissolution, escape, exodus, mass exodus, refugee flow; CONCEPT 195

diatribe [n] harangue, criticism abuse, castigation, denunciation, disputation, invective, jeremiad, objection, onslaught, philippic, reviling, screed, stricture, tirade, vituperation; CONCEPT 52 —Ant. praise, recommendation

dibs [n] claim dueness, entitlement, preemptive declaration, privilege, request, rights; CONCEPTS 278,318,376,709

dicey [adj] risky capricious, chancy, dangerous, difficult, erratic, fluctuant, iffy*, incalculable, ticklish, tricky, uncertain, unpredictable, whimsical; CONCEPTS 535,552 —Ant. certain, safe, sure

dichotomy [n] division difference, difference of opinion, disagreement, disunion, separation, split; CONCEPTS 98,135

dicker [v] bargain; argue about barter, buy and sell, chaffer, cut a deal*, haggle*, hammer out a deal*, huckster*, negotiate, palter, trade, work out a deal*; CONCEPTS 46,330 —Ant. agree

dictate [n] command; rule behest, bidding, code, decree, dictum, direction, edict, fiat, injunction, law, mandate, order, ordinance, precept, principle, requirement, statute, ultimatum, word; CONCEPTS 274,318,688 —Ant. request

dictate [v1] command; give instructions bid, bulldoze*, call the play*, call the shots*, call the tune*, charge, control, decree, direct, enjoin, govern, guide, impose, instruct, lay down, lay down the law, lead, manage, ordain, order, prescribe, pronounce, put foot down*, read the riot act*, regiment, rule, set, take the reins*, walk heavy*; CONCEPTS 53,60 —Ant. ask, implore, request

dictate [v2] read out for the record compose, deliver, draft correspondence, emit, formulate, give account, give forth, interview, orate, prepare draft, say, speak, talk, transmit, utter, verbalize; CONCEPTS 60,324

dictator [n] absolute ruler absolutist, adviser, authoritarian, autocrat, boss, chief, commander, despot, disciplinarian, fascist, Hitler*, leader, magnate, mogul, oligarch, oppressor, ringleader, slavedriver, totalitarian, tycoon, tyrant, usurper; CONCEPT 354

dictatorial [adj] tyrannical, authoritarian absolute, arbitrary, arrogant, autocratic, bossy,

clamorous, crack-the-whip*, despotic, dictative, doctrinaire, dogmatic, domineering, egotistic, firm, haughty, imperative, imperious, iron-handed, oppressive, overbearing, peremptory, pompous, proud, stern, throwing weight around, totalitarian, unlimited, unrestricted; CONCEPT 542 —Ant. democratic, docile, passive

dictatorship [n] absolute rule authoritarianism, autocracy, coercion, despotism, fascism, garrison state, Nazism, reign of terror*, totalitarianism, tyranny, unlimited rule; CONCEPTS 133, 299,641 —Ant. democracy

diction [n] style of speech; articulation command of language, delivery, elocution, eloquence, enunciation, expression, fluency, gift of gab*, inflection, intonation, language, line, lingo, locution, oratory, parlance, phrase, phraseology, phrasing, pronunciation, rhetoric, usage, verbalism, verbiage, vocabulary, wordage, wording; CONCEPTS 47,276

dictionary [n] book of word meanings concordance, cyclopedia, encyclopedia, glossary, language, lexicon, palaver, promptory, reference, terminology, vocabulary; CONCEPT 280

dictum [n1] saying; proverb adage, aphorism, apothegm, axiom, brocard, gnome, maxim, moral, motto, precept, rule, saw, truism; CONCEPTS 278,689

dictum [n2] decree, pronouncement affirmation, assertion, command, declaration, dictate, edict, fiat, order; CONCEPT 278

didactic [adj] educational academic, advisory, donnish, edifying, enlightening, exhortative, expository, homiletic, hortative, instructive, moral, moralizing, pedagogic, pedantic, preachy, preceptive, schoolmasterist, sermonic, sermonizing, teacherish, teacherly, teachy; CONCEPT 548

die [v1] pass away; stop living be no more*, be taken, breathe one's last*, cease to exist, conk*, croak*, decease, demise, depart, drop, drop off, drown, expire, finish, give up the ghost*, go way of all flesh*, kick the bucket*, perish, relinquish life, rest in peace, succumb, suffocate; CONCEPT 304 —Ant. be born, begin, live

die [v2] wither, dwindle abate, fade, break down, crumble, decay, decline, degenerate, deteriorate, dilapidate, diminish, disappear, droop, ease off, ebb, end, expire, fade, fade away, fade out, fail, fall, fizzle out*, go bad*, go downhill*, halt, lapse, let up, lose power, melt away, moderate, molder, pass, peter out*, rankle, recede, retrograde, rot, run down, run low, run out, sink, slacken, stop, subside, vanish, wane, weaken, wear away, wilt; CONCEPTS 469,698 —Ant. develop, flourish, grow, improve

die-hard [adj] uncompromising conservative, convinced, dyed-in-the-wool*, extremist, firm, fogyish, immovable, inflexible, intransigent, old-line*, orthodox, Philistine, reactionary, right, standpat, Tory*, traditionalistic, ultraconservative, unreconstructed; CONCEPTS 404,542 —Ant. compromising, conceding, flexible

diehard [n] overenthusiastic person bitter ender*, Bourbon*, dyed-in-the-wool*, extremist, fanatic, fogy, fundamentalist, intransigent, mossback*, old liner*, praetorian, pullback*, reactionary, right, rightist, right-winger, standpat, standpatter, stick-in-the-mud*, Tory*, true blue*, ultraconservative, zealot; CONCEPTS 359,423

diet [n1] *abstinence from food* dietary, fast, nutritional therapy, regime, regimen, restriction, starvation, weight-reduction plan; CONCEPT 660 —*Ant.* indulgence

diet [n2] *daily intake of food* aliment, bite, comestibles, commons, daily bread, edibles, fare, goodies, grubbery, menu, nourishment, nutriment, nutrition, provisions, rations, snack, subsistence, sustenance, viands, victuals; CONCEPTS 457,459

diet [v] *abstain from food* count calories*, eat sparingly, fall off, fast, go without, lose weight, reduce, skinny down*, slim, slim down, starve, tighten belt*, watch weight*; CONCEPT 169 —*Ant.* gorge, indulge

differ [v1] *be dissimilar, distinct* alter, bear no resemblance, be distinguished from, be off the beaten path*, be unlike, clash with, conflict with, contradict, contrast, depart from, deviate from, digress, disagree, divaricate from, diverge, diversify, jar with, lack resemblance, modify, not conform, not look like, qualify, reverse, run counter to, show contrast, sing a different tune*, stand apart, take exception, turn, vary; CONCEPT 665 —*Ant.* agree, be same, conform

differ [v2] *clash; hold opposing views* bicker*, bump heads*, contend, debate, demur, disaccord, disagree, discept, discord, dispute, dissent, divide, fight, go after each other, go at it*, hit a clinker*, hit a sour note*, jar*, lock horns*, object, oppose, protest against, quarrel, squabble, take issue, vary, war; CONCEPT 46 —*Ant.* agree, consent, harmonize

difference [n1] *dissimilarity, distinctness* aberration, alteration, anomaly, antithesis, asymmetry, change, characteristic, contrariety, contrariness, contrast, departure, deviation, digression, discongruity, discrepancy, disparity, dissemblance, distinction, divergence, diversity, exception, heterogeneity, idiosyncrasy, inequality, irregularity, nonconformity, opposition, particularity, peculiarity, separateness, separation, singularity, unconformity, unlikeness, unorthodoxness, variance, variation, variety; CONCEPT 665 —*Ant.* accord, agreement, alikeness, concurrence, conformity, likeness, sameness, similarity, uniformity

difference [n2] *opposing views* argument, beef*, blowup*, bone to pick*, brannigan, brawl, brush*, brush-off*, catamaran, clash, conflict, contention, contrariety, contretemps, controversy, debate, disaccord, disagreement, discord, discordance, dispute, dissension, dissent, dissidence, disunity, dustup*, estrangement, hassle, quarrel, row*, run-in*, scrap*, set-to*, spat*, strife, tiff*, variance, words*, wrangle; CONCEPTS 46,388 —*Ant.* agreement, assent, concurrence, consent

different [adj1] *dissimilar, unlike* a far cry from*, altered, antithetic, at odds, at variance, changed, clashing, colorful, contradictinct, contradistinctive, contrary, contrasting, contrastive, deviating, differential, discrepant, disparate, distant, distinct, distinctive, divergent, divers, diverse, incommensurable, incomparable, inconsistent, individual, like night and day*, mismatched, mismated, offbeat, opposed,

other, otherwise, particular, peculiar, poles apart*, single, unalike, unequal, unrelated, unsimilar, variant, various; CONCEPTS 487,564, 573 —*Ant.* alike, correspondent, homogeneous, like, resembling, same, similar

different [adj2] *separate, distinct* another, another story, atypical, bizarre, discrete, diverse, especial, express, extraordinary, individual, novel, original, other, out of the ordinary, particular, peculiar, rare, several, singular, something else, special, specialized, specific, startling, strange, uncommon, unconventional, unique, unusual, various; CONCEPT 564 —*Ant.* conventional, correspondent, harmonious, normal, same, standard, unified, united

different [adj3] *miscellaneous, various* anthologized, assorted, asymmetrical, collected, disparate, dissonant, divergent, divers, diverse, diversified, diversiform, heterogeneous, incongruous, inconsistent, indiscriminate, jarring, manifold, many, multifarious, multiform, numerous, omnifarious, omniform, several, some, sundry, varicolored, varied, variegated, varietal, variform; CONCEPT 772 —*Ant.* normal, same, similar, standard, uniform

differentiate [v1] *make a distinction* antithesize, characterize, comprehend, contrast, demarcate, discern, discrepate, discriminate, extricate, individualize, individuate, know, know what's what*, mark, mark off, redline*, separate, set apart, set off, sever, severalize, split hairs*, tell apart, understand; CONCEPTS 15,38 —*Ant.* associate, confuse, connect, group, link, mix up

differentiate [v2] *change; make different* adapt, alter, assort, convert, diversify, mismatch, mismate, modify, transform, variegate, vary; CONCEPT 232 —*Ant.* allow, leave

differently [adv] *in another way; otherwise* abnormally, adversely, antagonistically, antithetically, asymmetrically, conflictingly, contradictorily, contrarily, contrastingly, contrastively, discordantly, disparately, dissimilarly, distinctively, divergently, diversely, hostilely, in a different manner, incompatibly, incongruously, individually, negatively, nonconformably, on the contrary, on the other hand, oppositely, poles apart, separately, uniquely, unorthodoxly, unusually, variously, vice versa; CONCEPT 564

difficult [adj1] *hard on someone; hard to do* ambitious, arduous, backbreaker*, bothersome, burdensome, challenging, crucial, demanding, difficile, easier said than done*, effortful, exacting, formidable, galling, Gargantuan*, hard-won, heavy, Herculean*, immense, intricate, irritating, labored, laborious, no picnic*, not easy, onerous, operose, painful, problem, problematic, prohibitive, rigid, severe, stiff, strenuous, titanic, toilsome, tough, troublesome, trying, unyielding, uphill, upstream, wearisome; CONCEPT 538 —*Ant.* calm, easy, free, manageable, plain, simple, uncomplicated

difficult [adj2] *complicated; hard to comprehend* abstract, abstruse, baffling, bewildering, complex, confounding, confusing, dark, deep, delicate, enigmatic, enigmatical, entangled, esoteric, formidable, hard to explain, hard to solve, hidden, inexplicable, intricate, involved, knotty, labyrinthine, loose, meandering, mysterious, mystical, mystifying, nice, obscure, obstinate, paradoxical, perplexing, problematical, profound, puzzling, rambling, subtle, tangled, thorny, ticklish, troublesome, unclear, unfathomable, unintelligible, vexing; CONCEPT 529 —Ant. easy, simple, straightforward, uncomplicated

difficult [adj3] *unmanageable socially* argumentative, bearish, boorish, dark, demanding, fastidious, finicky, fractious, fussy, grim, hard to please, impolite, intractable, irritable, oafish, obstreperous, perverse, picky, refractory, rigid, rude, tiresome, tough, troublesome, trying, unaccommodating, unamenable; CONCEPTS 404,542,555 —Ant. calm, friendly, sociable

difficulty [n1] *problem; situation requiring great effort* adversity, arduousness, awkwardness, barricade, check, complication, crisis, crux, dead end, deadlock, deep water*, dilemma, distress, emergency, exigency, fix*, frustration, hardship, hazard, hindrance, hitch*, hot water*, impasse, knot*, labor, laboriousness, mess, misfortune, muddle, obstacle, obstruction, pain, painfulness, paradox, perplexity, pickle*, predicament, quagmire, quandary, scrape*, snag*, stew*, strain, strait, strenuousness, struggle, stumbling block*, tribulation, trouble; CONCEPTS 674,677 —Ant. calm, ease, felicity, peace, tranquility

difficulty [n2] *mental burden* ado, aggravation, annoyance, anxiety, bafflement, bother, care, charge, complication, crisis, depression, discouragement, distress, embarrassment, emergency, exigency, frustration, grievance, hangup, harassment, imbroglio, inconvenience, irritation, jam, maze, mess, millstone*, misery, oppression, perplexity, pickle*, pinch, predicament, pressure, puzzle, quandary, ramification, responsibility, scrape*, setback, strain, strait, stress, strife, struggle, to-do*, trouble, vicissitude, weight, worry; CONCEPTS 410,532,690 —Ant. calmness, contentment, peace, pleasure, satisfaction

difficulty [n3] *argument* altercation, beef*, bickering, controversy, dispute, falling-out*, fight, hassle, misunderstanding, quarrel, squabble, strife, trouble; CONCEPT 46 —Ant. harmony, peace

diffidence [n] *hesitancy; lack of confidence* backwardness, bashfulness, constraint, doubt, fear, hesitation, humility, insecurity, meekness, modesty, mousiness, reluctance, reserve, self-consciousness, sheepishness, shyness, timidity, timidness, timorousness, unassertiveness; CONCEPT 633 —Ant. boldness, confidence

diffident [adj] *hesitant; unconfident* backward, bashful, blenching, chary, constrained, coy, demure, distrustful, doubtful, dubious, flinching, humble, insecure, meek, modest, mousy, rabbity, reluctant, reserved, retiring, self-conscious, self-effacing, sheepish, shrinking, shy, suspicious, timid, timorous, unassertive, unassuming, unassured, unobtrusive, unpoised, unsure, withdrawn; CONCEPT 401 —Ant. bold, confident

diffuse [adj1] *spread out* broadcast, catholic, circulated, diluted, dispersed, disseminated, distributed, expanded, extended, general, prevalent, propagated, radiated, scattered, separated, strewn, thin, unconcentrated, universal, widespread; CONCEPTS 530,583,772 —Ant. compact, compressed, concentrated, confined, limited, restricted

diffuse [adj2] *wordy* circumlocutory, copious, diffusive, digressive, discursive, dull, exuberant, lavish, lengthy, long, long-winded, loose, meandering, palaverous, profuse, prolix, rambling, random, redundant, vague, verbose, waffling, windy; CONCEPT 267 —Ant. abbreviated, abridged, brief, short, succinct

diffusion [n] *spread; wide distribution* circulation, dispersal, dispersion, dissemination, dissipation, expansion, propaganda, propagation, scattering; CONCEPTS 634,651 —Ant. collection, concentration

dig [n] *insult* crack, cut, cutting remark, gibe, innuendo, jeer, quip, slur, sneer, taunt, wisecrack; CONCEPT 54 —Ant. compliment, flattery, praise

dig [v1] *delve into; hollow out* bore, break up, bulldoze, burrow, cat, channel, clean, concave, deepen, depress, dig down, discover, dredge, drill, drive, enter, excavate, exhume, fork out, go into, gouge, grub, harvest, hoe, investigate, mine, penetrate, pierce, pit, probe, produce, quarry, root, root out, rout, sap, scoop, scoop out, search, shovel, sift, spade, till, tunnel, turn over, uncover, undermine, unearth; CONCEPT 178 —Ant. fill

dig [v2] *thrust object into* drive, gouge, jab, jog, nudge, plunge, poke, prod, punch, ram, sink, stab, stick; CONCEPT 208

dig [v3] *investigate; discover* bring to light*, come across, come up with, delve, dig down, expose, extricate, find, go into, inquire, look into, probe, prospect, research, retrieve, root, search, search high and low*, shake down*, sift*, turn inside out*, turn upside down*, uncover, unearth; CONCEPTS 31,103,216

dig [v4] *enjoy, like* appreciate, follow, go for*, groove*, love, mind, relish, understand; CONCEPT 32 —Ant. dislike

dig [v5] *understand* accept, apprehend, catch, comprehend, follow, grasp, recognize, see, take, take in; CONCEPT 15 —Ant. misunderstand, not get

digest [n] *abridgement of something written* abstract, aperçu, brief, compendium, condensation, epitome, pandect, précis, résumé, short form, sketch, summary, survey, syllabus, sylloge, synopsis; CONCEPT 271 —Ant. unabridgement

digest [v1] *assimilate food* absorb, chymify, consume, dissolve, eat, incorporate, macerate, swallow, take; CONCEPT 169

digest [v2] *make shorter; abridge* abbreviate, abstract, boil down, classify, codify, compress, condense, cut, cut down, cut to bone*, decrease, epitomize, get to the meat*, inventory, methodize, nutshell*, put in a nutshell*, reduce, shorten, sum, summarize, summate, sum up, survey, synopsize, systematize, tabulate, trim; CONCEPTS 236,247 —Ant. detail, enlarge, expand, lengthen

digest [v3] *come to understand* absorb, analyze, assimilate, consider, contemplate, deliberate, grasp, master, meditate, ponder, study, take in, think about, think over; CONCEPT 15 —Ant. misunderstand

digest [v4] *tolerate, endure* abide, bear, brook, go, stand, stomach, swallow, take; CONCEPT 23

dig in [v] *begin with enthusiasm* bite, burrow, chew, commence, consume, delve, eat, rise, set about, spring, start eating; CONCEPTS 100,169 —*Ant.* avoid, delay, postpone, procrastinate

digit [n1] *number* Arabic, chiffer, cipher, figure, integer, notation, numeral, symbol, whole number; CONCEPTS 765,784

digit [n2] *small appendage of animate being* claw, extremity, fang, feeler, finger, fork, hook, index finger, phalange, pinkie, pointer, ring finger, thumb, toe; CONCEPT 392

digital library [n] *multimedia library* digital object library, electronic library, information superhighway, national information infrastructure, virtual library; CONCEPT 274

dignified [adj] *honorable* aristocratic, august, courtly, decorous, distingué, distinguished, eminent, formal, grand, grave, great, highbrow*, highfalutin'*, imperial, imperious, lofty, magisterial, magnificent, nifty*, noble, proud, refined, regal, reserved, respected, solemn, somber, stately, superior, upright; CONCEPTS 404,555,574 —*Ant.* dishonorable, indecorous, undignified

dignify [v] *make honorable; glorify* adorn, advance, aggrandize, distinguish, elevate, ennoble, erect, exalt, grace, honor, magnify, prefer, promote, raise, sublime, uprear; CONCEPTS 244,700 —*Ant.* belittle, condemn, degrade, demote, detract, disgrace, humiliate, insult, shame

dignitary [n] *high ranking person* big gun*, big kahuna*, bigshot*, bigwig*, celebrity, luminary, official, person of influence, star, top cat*, VIP*; CONCEPTS 388,668

dignity [n] *excellence, nobility* address, cachet, character, consequence, courtliness, culture, decency, decorum, distinction, elevation, eminence, ethics, etiquette, glory, grace, grandeur, gravity, greatness, hauteur, honor, importance, loftiness, majesty, merit, morality, nobleness, perfection, poise, prestige, propriety, quality, rank, regard, renown, respectability, seemliness, self-respect, significance, solemnity, splendor, standing, state, stateliness, station, stature, status, sublimity, virtue, worth, worthiness; CONCEPTS 388,411,668 —*Ant.* lowliness

digress [v] *stray, deviate* aberrate, beat about the bush*, be diffuse, circumlocute, depart, divagate, drift, excurse, get off the point, get off the subject, get sidetracked, go by way of*, go off on a tangent*, long way*, meander, ramble, roam, swerve, turn aside, veer, wander, wander away; CONCEPTS 195,266,697 —*Ant.* be direct, stay

digression [n] *deviation; straying* apostrophe, aside, deflection, departure, detour, difference, discussion, divagation, divergence, diversion, drifting, episode, excursion, excursus, footnote, incident, note, obiter dictum, parenthesis, rambling, variation, wandering; CONCEPTS 278,665,697 —*Ant.* directness, straightness

dilapidated [adj] *falling apart; in ruins* battered, beat-up, broken-down, crumbling, crumbly, crummy*, damaged, decayed, decaying, decrepit, derelict, dingy, dog-eared*, faded, fallen-in, impaired, in a bad way*, injured, marred, neglected, old, ramshackle, ratty*, raunchy, rickety, rinky-dink*, run-down, seedy, shabby, shaky, slummy, tacky,

threadbare, tumble-down, uncared for, unimproved, unkempt,used-up, worn-out; CONCEPTS 485,560 —*Ant.* in good repair, rebuilt

dilate [v] *stretch, widen* amplify, augment, be profuse, be prolix, broaden, develop, distend, enlarge, expand, expatiate, expound, extend, increase, inflate, lengthen, prolong, protract, puff out, spin off, swell; CONCEPT 57 —*Ant.* compress, constrict, contract, lessen, reduce

dilatory [adj] *procrastinating* backward, behindhand, dallying, delaying, deliberate, laggard, late, lax, lazy, leisurely, lingering, loitering, moratory, neglectful, negligent, putting off, remiss, slack, slow, sluggish, snail-like*, tardy, tarrying, time-wasting, unhasty, unhurried; CONCEPTS 542,799 —*Ant.* diligent, eager, enthusiastic, hard-working, ready, zealous

dilemma [n] *crisis* bind*, box*, Catch-22*, corner, difficulty, double bind*, embarrassment, fix, hole, hooker*, impasse, jam, mess, mire, perplexity, pickle*, plight, predicament, problem, puzzle, quandary, scrape, spot, strait, tight corner*; CONCEPTS 674,675 —*Ant.* miracle, solution, wonder

dilettante [adj] *amateurish* artsy fartsy*, dabbling, green*, half-baked*, half-cocked*, rookie, tenderfoot*, unaccomplished, ungifted, unskilled; CONCEPT 527 —*Ant.* professional

dilettante [n] *amateur* abecedarian, aesthete, connoisseur, dabbler, dallier, greenhorn*, nonprofessional, rookie, smatterer, tenderfoot*, trifler, tyro, uninitiate; CONCEPT 423 —*Ant.* professional

diligence [n] *perseverance in carrying out action* activity, alertness, application, assiduity, assiduousness, attention, attentiveness, briskness, care, carefulness, constancy, earnestness, exertion, heed, heedfulness, industry, intensity, intent, intentness, keenness, laboriousness, pertinacity, quickness, sedulousness, vigor; CONCEPTS 657,677 —*Ant.* inactivity, indifference, laziness, lethargy, neglect

diligent [adj] *persevering, hard-working* active, assiduous, attentive, busy, careful, conscientious, constant, eager, eager beaver*, earnest, grind*, indefatigable, industrious, laborious, occupied, operose, painstaking, persistent, persisting, pertinacious, plugging*, sedulous, steadfast, studious, tireless, unflagging, unrelenting, untiring; CONCEPTS 326,538,542 —*Ant.* inactive, indifferent, languid, lazy, lethargic, negligent

dilly-dally [v] *waste time* dawdle, delay, hem and haw*, hesitate, linger, loiter, meander, mosey, move slowly, procrastinate, vacillate; CONCEPTS 151,210,681

dilute [v] *make thinner; weaken* adulterate, alter, attenuate, cook, cut, decrease, deliquesce, diffuse, diminish, doctor*, doctor up*, irrigate, lace, lessen, liquefy, mitigate, mix, moderate, modify, needle*, phony up*, plant, qualify, reduce, shave*, spike, temper, water, water down; CONCEPT 250 —*Ant.* concentrate, strengthen, thicken

diluted/dilute [adj] *thinned, weakened* adulterated, attenuated, cut, impaired, impoverished, laced, light, moderated, reduced, shaved*, spiked, tempered, washy, watered down, waterish, watery, wishy-washy*; CONCEPTS 485,606 —*Ant.* concentrated, strengthened, thickened

dim [adj1] *darkish* blah, bleary, blurred, caliginous, cloudy, dark, dingy, dreary, dull, dusk, dusky, faded, faint, flat, fuzzy, gloomy, gray, ill-defined, indistinct, lackluster, lightless, mat, monotone, monotonous, murky, muted, obscured, opaque, overcast, pale, poorly lit, shadowy, sullied, tarnished, tenebrous, unclear, unilluminated, vague, weak; CONCEPT 617 —*Ant.* bright, brilliant, clear, distinct, light

dim [adj2] *unfavorable with regard to opinion* depressing, disapproving, discouraging, gloomy, skeptical, somber, suspicious, unpromising; CONCEPT 542 —*Ant.* favorable, good

dim [adj3] *not very intelligent* boorish, dense, dim-witted, doltish, dull, dumb, oafish, obtuse, slow, slow on uptake*, stupid, thick*, weak-minded; CONCEPT 402 —*Ant.* bright, intelligent, smart

dim [v] *darken; obscure* becloud, bedim, befog, blear, blur, cloud, dull, eclipse, fade, fog, haze, lower, muddy, obfuscate, pale, tarnish, turn down; CONCEPTS 250,627 —*Ant.* brighten, lighten

dimensions/dimension [n] *proportions; range* admeasurement, ambit, amplitude, bigness, bulk, capacity, compass, depth, dimensionality, extension, extensity, extent, greatness, height, importance, largeness, length, magnitude, measure, measurement, reach, scale, scope, size, volume, width; CONCEPTS 730,792

diminish [v1] *become or cause to be less* abate, abbreviate, attenuate, become smaller, close, contract, curtail, cut, decline, decrease, depreciate, die out, drain, dwindle, ebb, extenuate, fade away, lessen, lower, minify, moderate, peter out, recede, reduce, retrench, shrink, shrivel, slacken, subside, taper, temper, wane, weaken; CONCEPTS 698,776 —*Ant.* develop, enlarge, expand, extend, grow, increase, lengthen, prolong

diminish [v2] *belittle* abuse, bad-mouth*, cheapen, cut down to size*, decry, demean, depreciate, derogate, detract from, devalue, dispraise, dump on*, give comeuppance*, knock off high horse*, minimize, pan*, poormouth*, put away*, put down*, run down*, tear down*; CONCEPT 54 —*Ant.* compliment, flatter, praise

diminution [n] *lessening, reduction* abatement, alleviation, contraction, curtailment, cut, cutback, decay, decline, decrease, deduction, retrenchment, weakening; CONCEPTS 698,776 —*Ant.* development, enlargement, expansion, growth, increase

diminutive [adj] *tiny, petite* bantam, bitsy*, bitty*, button*, Lilliputian, little, midget, mini, miniature, minute, peewee*, pint-sized, pocket, pocket-sized, small, teensy*, teensy-weensy*, teeny*, teeny-weeny*, undersize, wee*, weeny*; CONCEPT 789 —*Ant.* big, huge, large, tall

dimple [n] *indentation* cleft, concavity, dent, depression, divot, hollow, pit; CONCEPT 490

dimwit [n] *a stupid person* blockhead, bonehead, dolt, dullard, dunce, fool, idiot, ignoramus, imbecile, moron, numskull, simpleton, twit; CONCEPT 412

din [n] *loud, continuous noise* babel, bedlam, boisterousness, brouhaha, buzz, clamor, clangor, clash, clatter, commotion, confusion, crash, disquiet, hoo-ha*, hubbub, hullabaloo*, hurly-burly*, jangle, music, outcry, pandemonium, percussion, racket, row, shout, sound, stridency, tintamarre*, tintinnabulation, tumult, uproar; CONCEPT 595

dine [v] *eat, often formally* banquet, breakfast, consume, do lunch*, eat out*, fall to*, feast, feed on, lunch, sup, supper; CONCEPT 169 —*Ant.* abstain

diner [n] *casual restaurant with varied menu* Automat*, bistro, booth, café, canteen, chuck wagon*, coffee shop, concession, dump*, eatery*, eating house, facility, fast-food outlet, greasy spoon*, grill, hash house*, ice-cream parlor, lunch counter, lunchroom, lunch wagon, mess hall, quick-lunch, saloon, sandwich shop, snack bar, tearoom; CONCEPT 449

dingy [adj] *soiled, tacky* bedimmed, broken-down, colorless, dark, darkish, dilapidated, dim, dirty, discolored, drab, dreary, dull, dusky, faded, gloomy, grimy, muddy, murky, obscure, run-down, seedy, shabby, smirched, somber, sullied, tarnished, threadbare, tired; CONCEPTS 485,617 —*Ant.* bright, clean, immaculate, neat, pure, spotless

dinky [adj] *tiny, small* bush-league*, dainty, insignificant, lesser, Lilliputian, mini, miniature, minor, minor-league*, neat, petite, secondary, second rate*, small-fry*, small-time*, trim; CONCEPT 789 —*Ant.* big, huge, large

dinner [n] *evening meal* banquet, blowout*, chow*, collation, din-din*, eats*, feast, feedbag*, fete, main meal, major munch*, potluck, principal meal, refection, regale, repast, ribs*, spread*, supper, table d'hôte; CONCEPT 459

dip [n1] *submersion in liquid* bath, dive, douche, drenching, ducking, immersion, plunge, soak, soaking, swim; CONCEPT 256

dip [n2] *something for dunking* concoction, dilution, infusion, mixture, preparation, solution, suffusion, suspension; CONCEPTS 260,466

dip [n3] *depression; decline* basin, concavity, declivity, descent, downslide, downswing, downtrend, drop, fall, fall-off, hole, hollow, inclination, incline, lowering, pitch, sag, sink, sinkage, sinkhole, slip, slope, slump; CONCEPTS 513,697,738 —*Ant.* ascent, increase, rise

dip [v1] *put into liquid* baptize, bathe, douse, drench, duck, dunk, immerse, irrigate, lave, lower, moisten, pitch, plunge, rinse, slop, slosh, soak, souse, splash, steep, submerge, submerse, wash, water, wet; CONCEPTS 201,256

dip [v2] *lower, descend* bend, decline, disappear, droop, drop down, fade, fall, go down, incline, nose-dive, plummet, plunge, reach, recede, sag, set, settle, sheer, sink, skew, slant, slip, slope, slue, slump, spiral, subside, swoop, tilt, tumble, veer, verge; CONCEPT 181 —*Ant.* ascend, raise

dip [v3] *scoop, ladle* bail, bale, bucket, decant, dish, draft off, draw, draw out, dredge, handle, lade, lift, offer, reach into, shovel, spoon, strain; CONCEPTS 196,225

dip into [v] *try, sample* appropriate, browse, dabble, flip through, get, glance at, glance over, leaf through, peruse, play at, rifle through*, run over, run through, scan, seize, skim, take, taste, thumb through*; CONCEPTS 87,623

diploma [n] *certificate for achievement* authority, award, charter, commission, confirmation, credentials, degree, honor, recognition, sheep-skin, shingle, voucher, warrant; CONCEPTS 271,337

diplomacy [n] *tact* address, artfulness, craft, delicacy, delicatesse, discretion, expedience, finesse, negotiation, poise, politics, savoir-faire, skill, statecraft, subtlety; CONCEPTS 388,633 —*Ant.* bad manners, impoliteness, rudeness

diplomat [n] *politician, consul* agent, ambassador, attaché, cabinet member, chargé d' affaires, conciliator, emissary, envoy, expert, go-between, legate, mediator, minister, moderator, negotiator, plenipotentiary; public relations person, representative, tactician; CONCEPTS 354,359

diplomatic [adj] *politic, tactful* adept, arch, artful, astute, bland, brainy, cagey, calculating, capable, clever, conciliatory, conniving, contriving, courteous, crafty, cunning, deft, delicate, dexterous, discreet, gracious, guileful, intriguing, opportunistic, polite, prudent, savvy, scheming, sensitive, sharp, shrewd, sly, smooth, strategic, suave, subtle, wily; CONCEPTS 401,542 —*Ant.* artless, impolite, rude, tactless

dire [adj1] *urgent; crucial* acute, burning, clamant, clamorous, climacteric, critical, crying, desperate, drastic, exigent, extreme, immoderate, imperative, importunate, instant, pressing; CONCEPTS 546,568,799 —*Ant.* trivial, unimportant

dire [adj2] *terrible, ominous* afflictive, alarming, appalling, awful, black, calamitous, cataclysmic, catastrophic, cruel, deplorable, depressing, disastrous, dismal, distressing, dreadful, fearful, fierce, frightful, gloomy, grievous, grim, heart-breaking, horrible, horrid, lamentable, oppressing, portentous, redoubtable, regrettable, ruinous, scowling, shocking, terrific, ugly, unfortunate, woeful; CONCEPTS 537,548,570 —*Ant.* fortunate, good, lucky, nice

direct [adj1] *honest* absolute, bald, blunt, candid, categorical, downright, explicit, express, forthright, frank, matter-of-fact, open, outspoken, person-to-person, plain, plainspoken, point-blank, sincere, straight, straightforward, straight from the shoulder*, talk turkey*, unambiguous, unconcealed, undisguised, unequivocal, unreserved; CONCEPT 267 —*Ant.* devious, dishonest, indirect, wily

direct [adj2] *undeviating; uninterrupted* beeline*, continuous, even, horizontal, in bee line*, in straight line, linear, nonstop, not crooked, point-blank, right, shortest, straight, straight ahead, straightaway, through, true, unbroken, unswerving; CONCEPTS 482,581 —*Ant.* changing, deviating, indirect, intermittent, interrupted, varying

direct [adj3] *face-to-face; next to* contiguous, firsthand, head-on, immediate, lineal, next, personal, primary, prompt, proximate, resultant, succeeding; CONCEPTS 585,586 —*Ant.* indirect

direct [v1] *manage, oversee* administer, advise, be in the driver's seat*, boss, call the shots*, carry on, conduct, control, control the affairs of, dispose, dominate, govern, guide, handle, have the say, head up*, influence, keep, lead, operate, ordain, preside over, quarterback*, regulate, rule, run, run the show*, run things*, shepherd, superintend, supervise, take the reins*; CONCEPTS 94,117 —*Ant.* misguide, mismanage, neglect

direct [v2] *give instructions; teach* address, advise, bid, charge, command, deliver, dictate, enjoin, give directions, give orders, inform, instruct, lecture, order, read, tell, warn; CONCEPTS 53,61 —*Ant.* misguide, mislead

direct [v3] *point in a direction; guide* address, aim, beam, cast, conduct, escort, fix, focus, head, incline, indicate, intend, lay, lead, level, mean, move in, pilot, point, point the way, present, route, see, set, shepherd, show, sight, sight on, slant, steer, target, train, turn, zero in; CONCEPTS 187,201 —*Ant.* diverge, misdirect

direct [v4] *send, usually by mail system* address, designate, inscribe, label, mail, mark, route, superscribe; CONCEPT 217

direct [v5] *put all of efforts toward* address, aim, apply, bend, buckle down, devote, endeavor, fix, give, set, settle, strive, throw, try, turn; CONCEPT 87,677

direction [n1] *management* administration, charge, command, control, government, guidance, leadership, order, oversight, superintendence, supervision; CONCEPTS 299,325

direction [n2] *course, route* aim, angle, area, aspect, bearing, beeline*, bent, bias, current, drift, end, inclination, line, objective, orientation, outlook, path, point of compass, proclivity, range, region, road, set, side, slant, spot, standpoint, stream, tack, tendency, that-a-way*, tide, track, trajectory, trend, viewpoint, way; CONCEPTS 657,738 —*Ant.* deviation, misdirection, wrong way

direction(s) [n3] *instructions, guidance* advice, advisement, assignment, briefing, directive, guidelines, indication, lowdown*, notification, plan, prescription, recommendation, regulation, sealed order, specification, specs*, steer*, summons, tip, word*; CONCEPTS 271,274 —*Ant.* misdirection, misinstruction

directive [n] *command, instruction* charge, communication, decree, dictate, edict, injunction, mandate, memo, memorandum, message, notice, order, ordinance, regulation, ruling, ukase, word; CONCEPTS 271,274,662 —*Ant.* answer

directly [adv1] *the shortest route* as a crow flies*, beeline*, dead, direct, due, exactly, plump, precisely, right, slam bang*, slap, smack, smack dab*, straight, straightly, undeviatingly, unswervingly, without deviation; CONCEPTS 581,778 —*Ant.* indirectly

directly [adv2] *as soon as possible* anon, at once, contiguously, dead*, due, first off, forthwith, immediately, in a second, instantaneously, instanter, instantly, presently, promptly, pronto*, quickly, right away, shortly, speedily, straightaway, straight off; CONCEPT 820

directly [adv3] *straightforwardly* candidly, face-to-face, honestly, in person, literally, openly, personally, plainly, point-blank, truthfully, unequivocally, verbatim, without prevarication, word for word; CONCEPT 267 —*Ant.* indirectly

director [n] *manager* administrator, big person*, boss, chair, chief, controller, exec, executive, executive officer, governor, head, head honcho*, helmer, key player*, kingpin*, leader, organizer, overseer, person upstairs*, player, principal, producer, skipper*, supervisor, top dog*, top person*; CONCEPTS 347,352

directory [n] *reference book; guide* agenda, almanac, atlas, blue book, book, catalogue, charts, gazeteer, hit list*, index, laundry list*, lineup, list, little black book*, record, register, roster, scorecard, short list*, social register, syllabus, white pages*, who's who*, yellow pages*; CONCEPTS 280,283

direful [adj] *fearful; horrible* apocalyptic, appalling, awful, baleful, baneful, calamitous, dreadful, fateful, ghastly, gloomy, horrid, ill-boding, inauspicious, ominous, shocking, terrible, terrific, unlucky, unpropitious; CONCEPTS 537,570 —Ant. good, nice

dirge [n] *sad song* chant, coronach, cry, death march, death song, elegy, funeral song, hymn, jeremiad, keen, lament, march, monody, requiem, threnody; CONCEPT 595

dirigible [n] *airship* blimp, hot-air balloon, zeppelin; CONCEPT 504

dirt [n1] *grime, impurity* crud*, dreck, dregs, excrement, feculence, filth, filthiness, gook*, ground, gunk*, mire, muck, mud, rottenness, scuz*, sleaze, slime, smudge, smut, soil, stain, tarnish; CONCEPT 509 —Ant. cleanliness, pureness, purity, sterility

dirt [n2] *obscenity; immorality* chicanery, double-dealing, filth, fourberie, fraud, indecency, lubricity, pornography, smut; CONCEPT 645 —Ant. morality

dirt [n3] *soil* clay, dust, earth, loam, real estate, terra firma; CONCEPT 509

dirt [n4] *gossip* buzz, intimate intelligence, juicy morsel, news, rumor, talk, the lowdown*; CONCEPTS 274,278

dirty [adj1] *soiled, unclean* bedraggled, begrimed, black, contaminated, cruddy*, crummy, defiled, disarrayed, dishabille, disheveled, dreggy, dungy, dusty, filthy, foul, fouled, greasy, grimy, grubby, grungy*, icky*, lousy, messy, mucky*, muddy, mung*, murky, nasty, pigpen*, polluted, raunchy, scummy*, scuzzy*, slatternly, slimy, sloppy, slovenly, smudged, smutty, sooty, spattered, spotted, squalid, stained, straggly, sullied, undusted, unhygienic, unkempt, unlaundered, unsanitary, unsightly, unswept, untidy, unwashed, yucky*; CONCEPT 485 —Ant. clean, pure, spotless, sterile

dirty [adj2] *obscene, pornographic* base, blue, coarse, contemptible, despicable, filthy, immoral, impure, indecent, lewd, low, mean, nasty, off-color, ribald, risqué, salacious, scatological, scurvy, smutty, sordid, squalid, unchaste, unclean, uncleanly, vile, vulgar; CONCEPTS 542,545 —Ant. clean, moral, upright

dirty [adj3] *dishonest* below the belt*, cheating, corrupt, crooked, deceitful, double-dealing, foul, shabby, shady, shifty, sleazy, sneaky, sordid, underhanded, unethical, unscrupulous, untruthful; CONCEPT 267 —Ant. clean, nice

dirty [v] *cause to be soiled* begrime, besoil, blacken, blotch, blur, botch, coat, contaminate, corrupt, debase, decay, defile, discolor, draggle, encrust, foul, grime, make dusty, make impure, mess up, mold, muddy, pollute, rot, smear, smirch, smoke, smudge, smutch, spatter, spoil, spot, stain, sully, sweat, taint, tar,

tarnish; CONCEPT 254 —Ant. clean, cleanse, purify, sterilize

dirty old man [n] *pervert* degenerate, lecher, sex maniac, sleazebag; CONCEPT 412

dirty tricks [n] *dishonest practices* dirty pool*, funny business*, malicious tactics, monkey business*, shady business, skullduggery, unethical behavior; CONCEPTS 59,633,657

disability [n] *disadvantage, restriction* affliction, ailment, defect, detriment, disqualification, drawback, impairment, inability, incapacity, incompetency, inexperience, infirmity, injury, invalidity, lack, unfitness, weakness; CONCEPTS 309,316,410 —Ant. advantage, fitness, strength

disable [v] *render inoperative; cripple* attenuate, batter, blunt, damage, debilitate, disarm, disenable, disqualify, enervate, enfeeble, exhaust, hamstring*, handicap, harm, hock*, hogtie*, hurt, immobilize, impair, incapacitate, invalidate, kibosh*, knock out*, maim, mangle, mar, mutilate, muzzle, paralyze, pinion, prostrate, put out of action*, render incapable, ruin, sabotage, sap, shatter, shoot down*, spoil, take out*, throw monkey wrench in*, total*, unbrace, undermine, unfit, unstrengthen, weaken, wreck; CONCEPTS 130,246 —Ant. aid, assist, enable, help, improve

disabled [adj] *incapacitated* broken-down, confined, decrepit, disarmed, hamstrung*, handicapped, helpless, hurt, incapable, infirm, laid-up, lame, maimed, out-of-action*, out-of-commission*, paralyzed, powerless, run-down, sidelined, stalled, weakened, worn-out, wounded, wrecked; CONCEPTS 314,527 —Ant. able, healthy

disadvantage [n2] *hurt, loss* damage, deprivation, detriment, disservice, harm, injury, prejudice; CONCEPTS 230,309,679 —Ant. advantage, benefit, blessing, gain, profit

disadvantaged [adj] *underprivileged* deprived, discriminated against, handicapped, hindered, impaired, impoverished, poor; CONCEPT 334 —Ant. privileged, prosperous, rich, wealthy

disadvantageous [adj] *detrimental, inconvenient* adverse, contrary, damaging, debit-side, deleterious, depreciative, depreciatory, derogatory, detracting, disparaging, downside, dyslogistic, harmful, hurtful, ill-timed, inexpedient, injurious, inopportune, objectionable, on the debit side, pejorative, prejudicial, slighting, uncomplimentary, unfavorable, unprofitable; CONCEPTS 334,537,555 —Ant. advantageous, convenient, helpful, well-timed

disadvantage(s) [n1] *difficulty, trouble* adverse circumstance, bar, blocking, burden, defect, deficiency, deprivation, detriment, disability, discommodity, drawback, failing, fault, flaw, fly in the ointment*, hamper, handicap, hardship, hindrance, impediment, imperfection, imposition, inadequacy, inconvenience, inutility, lack, liability, limitation, minus, nuisance, opposition, obstacle, privation, problem, restraint, snag, stumbling block*, weakness, weak point; CONCEPTS 666,674 —Ant. advantage, good fortune

disaffect [v] *lose affection for, estrange* agitate, alienate, antagonize, discompose, disquiet, disturb, disunify, disunite, divide, repel, upset, wean; CONCEPTS *7,19,135,384* —*Ant.* content, make happy, please

disaffected [*adj*] *alienated, estranged* antagonistic, discontented, disloyal, dissatisfied, hostile, indifferent, mutinous, rebellious, seditious, uncompliant, unfriendly, unsubmissive; CONCEPT *403* —*Ant.* contented, happy, pleased

disaffection [*n*] *alienation, estrangement* animosity, antagonism, antipathy, aversion, breach, disagreement, discontent, dislike, disloyalty, dissatisfaction, hatred, hostility, ill will, repugnance, resentment, unfriendliness; CONCEPTS *388,410* —*Ant.* attraction, happiness, harmony, pleasure

disagree [*v1*] *be different* be discordant, be dissimilar, clash, conflict, contradict, counter, depart, deviate, differ, discord, disharmonize, dissent, diverge, run counter to, vary, war; CONCEPT *665* —*Ant.* agree, coincide, harmonize

disagree [*v2*] *argue; hold differing opinion* altercate, battle, bicker, brawl, break with, bring action, clash, contend, contest, controversialize, controvert, debate, differ, disaccord, discept, discord, dispute, dissent, divide, fall out*, feud, fight, go for the jugular*, haggle, have words*, jump on*, lay into*, let have it, mischannel, object, oppose, palter, quarrel, quibble, rip, row, scrap, set to, skirmish, spar, spat, sue, take issue, take on, war, wrangle, zap*; CONCEPTS *12,46* —*Ant.* accept, acquiesce, agree, concur, consent

disagree [*v3*] *be injurious* be distasteful, be disturbing, be sickening, be unsuitable, bother, discomfort, distress, go against the grain*, hurt, injure, make ill, nauseate, sicken, trouble, upset; CONCEPT *246* —*Ant.* aid, help

disagreeable [*adj1*] *bad-tempered, irritable* bellicose, brusque, cantankerous, churlish, contentious, contrary, cross, difficult, disobliging, disputatious, eristic, grouchy, ill-natured, nasty, obnoxious, offensive, out of sorts, peevish, pettish, petulant, querulous, rude, snappy, surly, ugly, unfriendly, ungracious, unlikable, unpleasant, uptight, waspish, whiny; CONCEPT *401* —*Ant.* agreeable, friendly, happy, nice, pleasant

disagreeable [*adj2*] *disgusting, offensive* annoying, awful, bad, bothersome, displeasing, distasteful, distressing, drag, nasty, objectionable, obnoxious, pain, repellent, repugnant, repulsive, rotten, sour, unhappy, uninviting, unpalatable, unpleasant, unsavory, upsetting, woeful; CONCEPTS *537,548* —*Ant.* agreeable, inoffensive, nice, pleasant, pleasing

disagreement [*n1*] *dispute, quarrel* altercation, animosity, antagonism, argument, atmospherics, bickering, breach, break, clash, clashing, conflict, contention, contest, controversy, cross-purposes, debate, difference, discord, dissent, dissidence, disunion, disunity, division, divisiveness, falling out, feud, fight, friction, hassle, hostility, ill feeling, ill will, jarring, misunderstanding, opposition, rupture, spat, split, squabble, strife, tension, variance, vendetta, words, wrangle; CONCEPTS *46,388* —*Ant.* acquiescence, agreement, harmony, peace

disagreement [*n2*] *difference, unlikeness* clash, disaccord, discordance, discrepancy, disharmonism, disharmony, disparity, dissimilarity, dissimilitude, divergence, divergency, diversity, incompatibility, incongruity, incongruousness,

inconsistency, variance; CONCEPT *665* —*Ant.* agreement, likeness, sameness, similarity

disallow [*v*] *reject, prohibit* abjure, cancel, censor, debar, deny, disacknowledge, disavow, disclaim, dismiss, disown, embargo, exclude, forbid, keep back, kill, nix*, pass on, proscribe, put down, rebuff, refuse, repudiate, shut out, taboo*, veto, withhold, zing*; CONCEPTS *21,25, 30* —*Ant.* allow, permit

disappear [*v*] *vanish; cease* abandon, abscond, be done for, be gone, be lost, be no more*, be swallowed up, cease to exist, clear, come to naught, decamp, dematerialize, depart, die, die out, disperse, dissipate, dissolve, drop out of sight*, ebb, end, end gradually, escape, evanesce, evanish, evaporate, exit, expire, fade, fade away, flee, fly, go, go south*, leave, leave no trace, melt, melt away, pass, pass away, perish, recede, retire, retreat, sink, take flight, vacate, vamoose*, wane, withdraw; CONCEPTS *102,105,195* —*Ant.* appear, arrive, come in

disappearance [*n*] *vanishing* ceasing to exist, decline and fall, dematerialization, departure, desertion, disappearing act, disintegration, dispersal, dissipation, dissolution, ebbing, eclipse, escape, evanescence, evaporation, exit, exodus, fading, flight, going, loss, melting, passing, receding, recession, removal, retirement, wane, wearing away, withdrawal; CONCEPTS *102,105, 195* —*Ant.* appearance, arrival, coming, entrance

disappoint [*v*] *sadden, dismay; frustrate* abort, baffle, balk, bring to naught, bungle, cast down, chagrin, circumvent, come to nothing, dash, dash hopes*, deceive, delude, disconcert, disenchant, disgruntle, dishearten, disillusion, dissatisfy, dumbfound, embitter, fail, fall down on, fall flat, fall short of, foil, founder, hamper, hinder, leave in the lurch*, let down, miscarry, mislead, not show, put out, ruin prospects, stand up, tease, thwart, torment, vex; CONCEPTS *7,19,699* —*Ant.* delight, excite, make happy, please, satisfy

disappointed [*adj*] *let down, saddened* aghast, balked, beaten, chapfallen, complaining, crestfallen, defeated, depressed, despondent, disconcerted, discontented, discouraged, disenchanted, disgruntled, disillusioned, dissatisfied, distressed, down, downcast, downhearted, down in the dumps*, foiled, frustrated, hopeless, objecting, shot down, taken down, thwarted, unhappy, unsatisfied, upset, vanquished, worsted; CONCEPT *403* —*Ant.* delighted, excited, happy, pleased, satisfied

disappointment [*n1*] *saddening situation; letdown* bitter pill*, blind alley*, blow, blunder, bringdown, bummer, bust*, calamity, defeat, disaster, discouragement, downer*, downfall, drag, dud, error, failure, false alarm*, faux pas*, fiasco, fizzle, flash in the pan*, impasse, inefficacy, lemon*, miscalculation, mischance, misfortune, mishap, mistake, obstacle, old one-two*, setback, slip, washout; CONCEPTS *230,674* —*Ant.* boost, comfort, happiness, help, miracle, pleasure, relief, success, wonder

disappointment [*n2*] *mental upset; displeasure* adverse fate, adversity, bafflement, blow, chagrin, defeat, despondency, discontent, discouragement, disenchantment, disgruntlement, disillusion, disillusionment, dissatisfaction, distress, failure, frustration, lack of success, letdown, mortification, nonsuccess, regret, setback, the knocks*, unfulfillment; CONCEPT 410 —*Ant.* delight, encouragement, euphoria, happiness, pleasure, satisfaction

disapproval [n] *condemnation* blackball*, black list*, blame, boo*, boycott, brickbat,call down, castigation, catcall*, censure, criticism, denunciation, deprecation, disapprobation, discontent, disfavor, dislike, disparagement, displeasure, dissatisfaction, hiss*, nix*, objection, opprobrium, ostracism, reproach, reproof, slap on wrist*, stricture, thumbs down*, vitriol, zing*; CONCEPTS 278,689 —*Ant.* agreement, approval, endorsement, sanction

disapprove [v] *condemn* blame, censure, chastise, criticize, damn, decry, denounce, deplore, deprecate, detract, disallow, discommend, discountenance, disesteem, disfavor, dislike, dismiss, dispraise, expostulate, find fault with, find unacceptable, frown on, look askance at, look down on, nix*, object to, oppose, pan*, pass on, refuse, reject, remonstrate, reprehend, reprobate, reprove, set aside, slam, spurn, take dim view of, take exception to, turn down, veto, zing*; CONCEPTS 18,21,52 —*Ant.* agree, approve, endorse, like, love, sanction

disarm [v1] *render defenseless* conciliate, cripple, deactivate, debilitate, deescalate, demilitarize, demobilize, disable, disband, disqualify, incapacitate, invalidate, neutralize, occupy, pacify, paralyze, prostrate, skin, strip, subdue, subjugate, unarm, weaken; CONCEPTS 142,211,320 —*Ant.* arm

disarm [v2] *persuade* allure, attract, bewitch, captivate, charm, coax, convince, enchant, fascinate, seduce, set at ease, unarm, urge, win over; CONCEPTS 7,19,22,68

disarmament [n] *reduction of weapons* arms limitation, arms reduction, conquest, crippling, de-escalation, demilitarization, demobilization, disablement, disqualification, freeze, neutralizing, occupation, pacification, paralyzing, rendering powerless, subjugation; CONCEPTS 142,211,320 —*Ant.* arming, buildup

disarming [adj] *charming* bewitching, convincing, deferential, ingratiating, ingratiatory, insinuating, insinuative, inveigling, irresistible, likable, persuasive, saccharine, seductive, silken, silky, winning; CONCEPT 401 —*Ant.* despicable, disgusting

disarrange [v] *disorder* derange, discompose, disturb, get out of order, jumble, mess, mix up, ruffle, scramble, shuffle, unsettle, untidy; CONCEPTS 240,250

disarray [n] *disorder, confusion, mess* anarchy, ataxia, chaos, clutter, disarrangement, discomposure, disharmony, dishevelment, disorganization, holy mess*, indiscipline, jumble, muddle, shambles*, snarl, tangle, topsy-turviness*, unholy mess*, unruliness, untidiness, upset; CONCEPTS 230,727 —*Ant.* arrangement, harmony, order, orderliness, organization

disaster [n] *accident, trouble* act of God*, adversity, affliction, bad luck, bad news*, bale, bane, blight, blow, bust, calamity, casualty, cataclysm, catastrophe, collapse, collision, crash, debacle, defeat, depression, emergency,

exigency, failure, fall, fell stroke*, fiasco, flood, flop, grief, hard luck, harm, hazard, holocaust, hot water*, ill luck, misadventure, mischance, misfortune, mishap, reverse, rock, rough, ruin, ruination, setback, slip, stroke, the worst*, tragedy, undoing, upset, washout*, woe; CONCEPTS 674,675 —*Ant.* blessing, good fortune, good luck, miracle, prosperity, success, triumph, win, wonder

disaster area [n] *scene of destruction* area of devastation, chaos, confusion, crisis zone, earthquake zone, emergency area, flood zone, havoc, hot spot, war zone; CONCEPTS 230,674

disastrous [adj] *detrimental, devastating* adverse, calamitous, cataclysmal, cataclysmic, catastrophic, destructive, dire, dreadful, fatal, fateful, hapless, harmful, ill-fated, ill-starred, luckless, ruinous, terrible, tragic, unfavorable, unfortunate, unlucky, unpropitious, untoward; CONCEPTS 537,548 —*Ant.* blessed, fortunate, lucky, miraculous, prosperous, successful, triumphant, winning, wondrous

disavow [v] *reject* abjure, contradict, deny, disacknowledge, disallow, disclaim, disown, drop out, forswear, gainsay, go back on word*, impugn, negate, negative, refuse, renege, renig, repudiate, wash hands of*, weasel out of*, welsh, worm out of*; CONCEPTS 18,25 —*Ant.* agree, approve, sanction, vouch for, vow

disband [v] *break up* demobilize, destroy, disperse, dissolve, fold, scatter, separate, thin out; CONCEPT 234

disbelief [n] *doubt, skepticism* atheism, distrust, dubiety, incredulity, mistrust, nihilism, rejection, repudiation, spurning, unbelief, unbelievingness, unfaith; CONCEPTS 21,689 —*Ant.* belief, trust

disbelieve [v] *doubt* discount, discredit, distrust, eschew, give no credence to, mistrust, not accept, not buy, not credit, not swallow*, question, reject, repudiate, scoff at, scorn, scout, suspect, unbelieve; CONCEPT 21 —*Ant.* believe, trust

disbelieving [adj] *suspicious, doubting* aporetic, cagey, cynical, incredulous, leery, mistrustful, questioning, quizzical, show-me*, skeptical, unbelieving; CONCEPT 403 —*Ant.* believing, trusting, unquestioning, unsuspicious

disburse [v] *spend money* acquit, ante up*, come across, come through, come up with, contribute, cough up*, deal, defray, dispense, disperse, distribute, divide, divvy*, dole out*, expend, foot the bill*, give, lay out*, measure out, outlay, partition, pay out, pony up*, put out, shell out*; CONCEPTS 108,341 —*Ant.* deposit, hoard, hold, retain, save, set aside

disbursement [n] *payment* cost, disposal, expenditure, expense, outgoing, outlay, spending; CONCEPT 344 —*Ant.* deposit, hoard, savings

discard [v] *get rid of* abandon, abdicate, abjure, adios*, banish, can*, cancel, cashier, cast aside, chuck, deep-six*, desert, dispatch, dispense with, dispose of, dispossess, ditch, divorce, do away with, drop, dump, eject, eliminate, expel, forsake, free of, give up, have done with, jettison, junk*, oust, part with, protest, put by, reject, relinquish, remove, renounce, repeal, repudiate, scrap, shake off, shed, sweep away, throw away, throw out, throw overboard*, toss aside, write off; CONCEPT 180 —*Ant.* embrace, keep, retain

discern [*v*] *catch sight of; recognize and understand* anticipate, apprehend, ascertain, behold, descry, detect, determine, difference, differentiate, discover, discrepate, discriminate, distinguish, divine, espy, extricate, figure out, find out, focus, foresee, get a load of*, get the picture*, get wise to, judge, know, make distinction, make out, note, notice, observe, perceive, pick out, read, remark, rubberneck*, secern, see the light*, see through, separate, severalize, spot, take in, view; CONCEPTS 15,38 —*Ant.* disregard, neglect, overlook

discernible [*adj*] *recognizable; distinct* apparent, appreciable, audible, clear, detectable, discoverable, distinguishable, noticeable, observable, obvious, palpable, perceivable, perceptible, plain, sensible, tangible, visible; CONCEPTS 535,576,619 —*Ant.* indistinct, invisible, obscured, unnoticeable, unrecognizable

discerning [*adj*] *discriminating* acute, astute, bright, brilliant, clear-sighted, clever, critical, gnostic, ingenious, insighted, insightful, intelligent, judicious, knowing, knowledgeable, penetrating, perceptive, percipient, perspicacious, piercing, sagacious, sage, sensitive, sharp, shrewd, subtle, wise; CONCEPT 402 —*Ant.* disregardful, neglectful, negligent, overlooking, undiscerning, undiscriminating

discharge [*n1*] *setting free* acquittal, clearance, disimprisonment, exoneration, liberation, pardon, parole, probation, release, remittance; CONCEPT 127 —*Ant.* hold, imprisonment, incarceration, keep, retention

discharge [*n2*] *dismissal from responsibility* ax, bounce, bum's rush*, congé, demobilization, ejection, gate, old heave ho*, pink slip*, the boot*, the door*, walking papers*; CONCEPTS 324,351 —*Ant.* assignment, delegation, employment, engagement, hiring

discharge [*n3*] *detonation* barrage, blast, burst, explosion, firing, fusillade, report, salvo, shot, shower, volley; CONCEPT 521 —*Ant.* loading

discharge [*n4*] *pouring forth* elimination, emission, emptying, excretion, exudation, flow, ooze, pus, secretion, seepage, shower, suppuration, vent, voiding; CONCEPTS 179,748 —*Ant.* damming

discharge [*n5*] *unloading* disburdening, emptying, unburdening, unlading; CONCEPT 211 —*Ant.* loading

discharge [*n6*] *carrying out of responsibility* accomplishment, achievement, execution, fulfillment, observance, performance; CONCEPT 706

discharge [*n7*] *payment of debt* acquittal, disbursement, liquidation, satisfaction, settlement; CONCEPTS 341,344 —*Ant.* indebtedness, owing

discharge [*v1*] *set free* absolve, acquit, allow to go*, clear, disimprison, dismiss, emancipate, exonerate, expel, liberate, loose, loosen, manumit, oust, pardon, release, unbind, unchain, unshackle; CONCEPT 127 —*Ant.* detain, hold, imprison, keep

discharge [*v2*] *dismiss from responsibility* absolve, ax, boot out*, bounce, bump, bust, can*, cashier, disburden, discard, disencumber, dispense, displace, eject, excuse, exempt, expel, fire, freeze out*, give one notice, kick out, lay off, let go, let off, let one go, let out, lock out*, nix*, oust, privilege from, relieve, remove, replace, ride out on rail*, run out of town*, show the door*, spare, supersede, supplant, terminate, unload; CONCEPTS 324,351 —*Ant.* assign, delegate, employ, engage, hire

discharge [*v3*] *detonate weapon* blast, explode, fire, let off, set off, shoot, shoot off; CONCEPT 179 —*Ant.* load

discharge [*v4*] *pour forth* break out, disembogue, dispense, ejaculate, emit, empty, erupt, excrete, exude, give off, gush, leak, ooze, release, send forth, spew, void, vomit; CONCEPTS 152,179 —*Ant.* dam

discharge [*v5*] *unload* carry away, disburden, empty, off-load, remove, remove cargo, send, take away, take off, unburden, unlade, unpack, unship, unstow; CONCEPT 211 —*Ant.* load

discharge [*v6*] *carry out responsibility* accomplish, achieve, do, execute, fulfill, meet, observe, perform; CONCEPT 91

discharge [*v7*] *pay, settle debt* clear, honor, liquidate, meet, pay up, quit, relieve, satisfy, square up; CONCEPT 341 —*Ant.* owe

discharge [*v8*] *invalidate agreement* abrogate, annul, cancel, dissolve, quash, render void, vacate, void; CONCEPT 121

disciple [*n*] *believer, follower* adherent, apostle, attendant, booster, buff, bug*, catechumen, cohort, convert, devotee, enthusiast, fan, fanatic, fiend, freak, groupie, hound*, junkie*, learner, nut*, partisan, proselyte, pupil, rooter*, satellite, sectary, sectator, student, supporter, votary, witness, zealot; CONCEPTS 361,423 —*Ant.* god

disciplinarian [*n*] *person who makes others work hard* authoritarian, bully, despot, drill sergeant, enforcer, formalist, master, sergeant, stickler, strict teacher, sundowner, teacher, trainer, tyrant; CONCEPTS 350,354,423

discipline [*n1*] *regimen, training* conduct, control, cultivation, curb, development, domestication, drill, drilling, education, exercise, inculcation, indoctrination, limitation, method, orderliness, practice, preparation, regulation, restraint, self-command, self-control, self-government, self-mastery, self-restraint, strictness, subordination, will, willpower; CONCEPTS 94,326,410 —*Ant.* chaos, confusion, disorder, disorganization, neglect, negligence, permissiveness

discipline [*n2*] *punishment* castigation, chastisement, comeuppance, correction, getting yours*, hell to pay*, punition, rod; CONCEPTS 122,123 —*Ant.* award, reward

discipline [*n3*] *field of study; subject of interest* area, branch of knowledge, course, curriculum, specialty; CONCEPT 349

disc jockey [*n*] *radio personality* announcer, broadcaster, deejay*, dj*, pancake turner*, radio performer, shock jock*, video jockey, vj*; CONCEPT 348

disclaim [*v*] *deny* abandon, abjure, abnegate, belittle, contradict, contravene, criticize, decline, deprecate, disacknowledge, disaffirm, disallow, disavow, discard, disown, disparage, divorce oneself from, forswear, gainsay, minimize, negate, recant, refuse, reject, renounce, repudiate, retract, revoke, spurn, traverse, turn back on, wash hands of*; CONCEPT 54

—Ant. accept, acknowledge, admit, allow, claim, own

disclaimer [n] *repudiation* abjuration, abnegation, clause, denial, disavowal, dissociation, renunciation, retraction, waiver; CONCEPT 45

disclose [v] *reveal, make public* acknowledge, admit, avow, bare, betray, blab, bring to light*, broadcast, come out of the closet*, communicate, confess, discover, display, divulge, exhibit, expose, give away, impart, lay bare, leak, let slip, make known, mouth*, open, own, publish, relate, reveal, show, snitch*, spill, spill the beans*, squeal*, tell, uncover, unfurl, unveil, utter; CONCEPT 60 —Ant. conceal, hide, secrete, withhold

disclosure [n] *announcement, revelation* acknowledgment, admission, advertisement, betrayal, blow-by-blow*, broadcast, confession, declaration, discovery, divulgation, divulgence, enlightenment, exposal, exposé, exposure, handout, impartance, impartation, leak, make, picture, publication, revealing, revealment, rundown, snitch*, squeal*, tip*, tip-off*, uncovering, unveilment, ventilation; CONCEPT 274 —Ant. secret

disco [n] *discotheque* club, dance hall, nightclub, nightspot; CONCEPTS 293,439,449

discolor [v] *fading, dirtying of hue* besmear, besmirch, blot, defile, mar, mark, rust, smear, soil, stain, streak, sully, tar, tarnish, tinge; CONCEPTS 250,469 —Ant. brighten, color

discomfit [v] *defeat, frustrate; confuse* abash, annoy, baffle, balk, beat, bother, checkmate, confound, demoralize, discompose, disconcert, discountenance, disturb, embarrass, faze, fluster, foil, irk, outwit, overcome, perplex, perturb, prevent, rattle, ruffle, take aback, thwart, trump, unsettle, upset, vex, worry, worst; CONCEPTS 7,19,95 —Ant. surrender, yield

discomfiture [n] *embarrassment, frustration* abashment, agitation, beating, chagrin, comedown, confusion, conquest, defeasance, defeat, demoralization, descent, disappointment, discomposure, disconcertion, disconcertment, disquiet, failure, humiliation, overthrow, perturbation, rout, ruin, shame, undoing, unease, uneasiness, upset, vanquishment, vexation; CONCEPTS 410,674 —Ant. surrender, yielding

discomfort [n] *irritation, pain* ache, annoyance, discomfiture, discomposure, displeasure, disquiet, distress, embarrassment, hardship, hurt, inquietude, malaise, nuisance, soreness, trouble, uneasiness, unpleasantness, upset, vexation; CONCEPTS 410,728 —Ant. comfort, ease, easiness, pleasure, relief

discomfort [v] *irritate; cause pain* discomfit, discompose, disquiet, distress, disturb, embarrass, make uncomfortable, nettle, perturb, upset, vex; CONCEPTS 7,19,246,313 —Ant. aid, alleviate, comfort, ease, help, relieve

discommode [v] *annoy* bother, burden, disoblige, disquiet, disturb, fluster, harass, incommode, inconvenience, irk, molest, perturb, put out, trouble, upset, vex; CONCEPTS 7,19 —Ant. make happy, please

discompose [v] *provoke, agitate* annoy, bewilder, bother, confuse, discombobulate, discomfit, disconcert, dismay, disorganize, displease, disquiet, disturb, embarrass, faze, flurry, fluster,

harass, harry, irk, irritate, nettle, perplex, perturb, pester, plague, rattle, ruffle, unhinge, unsettle, upset, vex, worry; CONCEPTS 7,19 —Ant. calm, compose, soothe

disconcert [v] *shake up; confuse* abash, agitate, baffle, balk, bewilder, bug, confound, demoralize, disarrange, discombobulate, discomfit, discompose, discountenance, disturb, embarrass, faze, fluster, foul up, frustrate, get to, hinder, nonplus, perplex, perturb, psych out*, put off, puzzle, rattle, ruffle, take aback, throw off balance, trouble, unbalance, undo, unsettle, upset, upset apple cart*, worry; CONCEPTS 7,16, 19 —Ant. calm, comfort, soothe

disconcerted [adj] *confused; shaken* annoyed, bewildered, caught off balance, come apart, distracted, disturbed, embarrassed, fazed, flustered, in botheration, messed-up, mixed-up, nonplussed, out of countenance, perturbed, psyched-out*, rattled, ruffled, shook-up*, spaced-out*, taken aback, thrown, troubled, unglued, unsettled, unzipped*, upset; CONCEPT 403 —Ant. calm, composed, concerted, soothed, unworried

disconnect [v] *take apart; uncouple* abstract, break it off, break it up, cut off, detach, disassociate, disengage, disjoin, dissever, dissociate, disunite, divide, drop it, part, separate, sever, sideline, unfix; CONCEPTS 98,135 —Ant. attach, connect, couple, hitch, hook, join, link, plug

disconnected [adj] *confused; discontinuous* broken, detached, disjointed, disordered, garbled, illogical, inchoate, incoherent, incohesive, interrupted, irrational, irregular, jumbled, loose, mixed-up, muddled, rambling, separated, uncontinuous, uncoordinated, unintelligible, wandering; CONCEPTS 267,482 —Ant. attached, coherent, connected, continuous, intelligible, joined, understandable

disconsolate [adj] *depressed, unhappy* bad, black, blue, cheerless, cold, comfortless, crestfallen, crushed, dark, dejected, desolate, despairing, destroyed, dispirited, distressed, doleful, down, downcast, downhearted, dreary, forlorn, gloomy, grief-stricken, heartbroken, hopeless, hurting, inconsolable, in pain*, in the pits*, low, melancholy, miserable, ripped*, sad, somber, sorrowful, torn-up*, woebegone, woeful, wretched; CONCEPT 403 —Ant. cheerful, consoled, happy, solaced, soothed

discontent [n] *dissatisfaction* depression, discontentment, displeasure, envy, fretfulness, regret, restlessness, uneasiness, unhappiness, vexation; CONCEPT 410 —Ant. contentedness, easiness, happiness, patience, pleasure, satisfaction

discontented/discontent [adj] *unhappy, dissatisfied* blue, complaining, crabby, disaffected, disgruntled, displeased, disquieted, disturbed, exasperated, fed up, fretful, griping, kvetching*, malcontent, malcontented, discontented, perturbed, picky, restless, ungratified, upset, vexed; CONCEPT 403 —Ant. content, contented, happy, patient, pleased, satisfied, uncomplaining

discontinuance [n] *stop, suspension of activity* adjournment, alternation, cease, cessation, close, closing, desistance, desuetude, discontinuation, disjunction, disruption, ending, finish, intermission, interruption, separation, stopping, termination; CONCEPT *119* —*Ant.* continuation, restarting, retry

discontinue [*v*] *prevent activity from going on* abandon, bag it*, blow off*, break off*, call it quits, cease, close, desist, disconnect, disjoin, dissever, disunite, drop, end, finish, give over, give up, halt, interpose, interrupt, intervene, kill, knock off*, leave off, part, pause, put an end to, quit, refrain from, scrub, separate, stop, surcease, suspend, terminate; CONCEPTS *121,234* —*Ant.* carry on, continue, restart, retry

discontinuous [*adj*] *broken; intermittent* alternate, desultory, disconnected, disjointed, disordered, fitful, gaping, inchoate, incoherent, incohesive, interrupted, irregular, muddled, spasmodic, unconnected, unorganized; CONCEPT *482* —*Ant.* connected, contiguous, continuous, regular, unbroken

discord [*n1*] *conflict, disagreement* animosity, antagonism, antipathy, clash, clashing, collision, contention, difference, disaccord, discordance, discrepancy, disharmony, dispute, dissension, dissent, dissidence, dissonance, disunion, disunity, division, enmity, friction, fuss, hassle, hostility, incompatibility, incongruity, inharmony, lack of concord, mischief, opposition, polarization, rancor, row, ruckus, rupture, scene, spat, split, static, strife, variance, wrangling; CONCEPT *388* —*Ant.* accord, agreement, cooperation, harmony, peace

discord [*n2*] *noise* cacophony, clamor, clinker, din, disharmony, dissonance, harshness, jangle, jarring, racket, sour note, tumult; CONCEPT *595* —*Ant.* harmoniousness, harmony

discordant [*adj*] *not in harmony; conflicting* antagonistic, antipathetic, at odds, cacophonous, clashing, contradictory, contrarient, contrary, different, disagreeing, discrepant, dissonant, divergent, grating, harsh, incompatible, incongruous, inconsistent, inconsonant, inharmonious, jangling, jarring, on a sour note*, opposite, quarreling, strident, uncongenial, unharmonious, unmelodious, unmixable; CONCEPTS *558,564,592,594* —*Ant.* agreeable, agreeing, concordant, cooperating, harmonious

discount [*n*] *reduction in cost* abatement, allowance, commission, concession, cut, cut rate, decrease, deduction, depreciation, diminution, drawback, exemption, knock-off*, markdown, modification, percentage, premium, qualification, rebate, remission, rollback, salvage, something off, subtraction, tare; CONCEPTS *335,763* —*Ant.* increase, mark-up, premium, rise

discount [*v1*] *lower, reduce cost* abate, allow, deduct, depreciate, diminish, hold a sale, knock off*, make allowance for, mark down, modify, rebate, redeem, remove, sell at discount, strike off, subtract, take away, take off, undersell; CONCEPT *236* —*Ant.* increase, mark up, raise

discount [*v2*] *ignore; treat as insignificant* belittle, blink at*, brush off*, depreciate, derogate, detract from, disbelieve, discredit, dispraise, disregard, doubt, fail, forget, minimize, mistrust, neglect, omit, overlook, overpass, pass over, question, reject, scoff at, scout, slight; CONCEPTS *21,30* —*Ant.* attend, pay attention, recognize

discountenance [*v1*] *reject, oppose* condemn, count me out*, deprecate, disapprove, discommend, discourage, disesteem, disfavor, dispute,

frown on*, hold no brief for*, not go for*, not stand for*, object to, put down, resist, take a dim view of*, take exception to*; CONCEPT *21* —*Ant.* approve, back, countenance, sanction, support

discountenance [*v2*] *embarrass, disconcert* abash, chagrin, confuse, discomfit, discompose, faze, humiliate, rattle, shame; CONCEPTS *7,19,54*

discourage [*v1*] *dishearten, dispirit* abash, afflict, alarm, appall, awe, beat down, bother, break one's heart*, bully, cast down, chill, confuse, cow, dampen, dash, daunt, deject, demoralize, deprecate, depress, dismay, disparage, distress, droop, frighten, intimidate, irk, overawe, prostrate, repress, scare, throw cold water on*, trouble, try, unnerve, vex, weigh; CONCEPT *14* —*Ant.* encourage, hearten, inspire, inspirit

discourage [*v2*] *deter, dissuade; restrain* check, chill, control, curb, deprecate, disadvise, discountenance, disfavor, disincline, divert, frighten, hinder, hold back, hold off, impede, indispose, inhibit, interfere, keep back, obstruct, prevent, put off, quiet, repress, scare, shake, talk out of, throw cold water on*, turn aside, turn off, warn, withhold; CONCEPTS *68,121* —*Ant.* encourage, inspire, spur on

discouraged [*adj*] *disheartened* beat, beat-down, blue, caved-in, come-apart, crestfallen, dashed, daunted, depressed, deterred, dismayed, dispirited, down, downbeat, downcast, down-in-mouth*, glum*, gone to pieces*, in a funk*, in blue funk*, in the dumps*, lost momentum, pessimistic, sad; CONCEPT *403* —*Ant.* encouraged, heartened, inspired

discouragement [*n1*] *despondency* cold feet*, dejection, depression, despair, disappointment, discomfiture, dismay, downheartedness, hopelessness, loss of confidence, low spirits, melancholy, pessimism, sadness, the blues*; CONCEPT *410* —*Ant.* cheerfulness, happiness, hopefulness

discouragement [*n2*] *restraint* bar, constraint, curb, damper, deterrent, disincentive, hindrance, impediment, obstacle, opposition, rebuff, setback; CONCEPT *674* —*Ant.* catalyst, encouragement, incentive

discouraging [*adj*] *upsetting* black, bleak, dampening, daunting, depressing, depressive, deterring, disadvantageous, disappointing, disheartening, dismal, dismaying, dispiriting, dissuading, dreary, gloomy, hindering, inopportune, off-putting, oppressive, repressing, unfavorable, unpropitious; CONCEPTS *403,529* —*Ant.* auspicious, encouraging, favorable, heartening, inspiring, inspiriting

discourse [*n*] *dialogue; dissertation* address, article, chat, communication, conversation, converse, descant, discussion, disquisition, essay, gabfest*, homily, huddle, lecture, memoir, monograph, monologue, oration, paper, rhetoric, sermon, speaking, speech, talk, thesis, tractate, treatise, utterance, verbalization; CONCEPT *266* —*Ant.* quiet, silence

discourse [*v*] *discuss, speak about* argue, chew*, comment, commentate, confab*, confer, converse, debate, declaim, descant, develop, dilate upon, dispute, dissert, dissertate, elaborate, enlarge, expand, expatiate, explain, expound, give a meeting, harangue, hold forth, lecture, modulate, orate, perorate,

di
di

remark, sermonize, talk, treat, voice; CONCEPTS 51,56 —*Ant.* be quiet

discourteous [*adj*] *rude, impolite* abrupt, bad-mannered, boorish, brusque, cavalier, cheeky*, churlish, contumelious, crude, crusty*, curt, disrespectful, flip, fresh, ill-bred, ill-mannered, impertinent, inaffable, indelicate, insolent, inurbane, oafish, offhand, rustic, sassy, smart-alecky*, uncivil, uncouth, ungenteel, ungracious, unmannerly, unrefined; CONCEPT 401 —*Ant.* civil, courteous, gracious, mannered, polite, refined, respectful, well-bred

discover [*v*] *find, uncover* ascertain, bring to light, catch, come across, come upon, conceive, contrive, debunk, design, detect, determine, devise, dig up, discern, disclose, distinguish, elicit, espy, explore, ferret out*, get wind of*, get wise to*, glimpse, hear, identify, invent, learn, light upon, locate, look up, nose out*, notice, observe, originate, perceive, pick up on*, pioneer, realize, recognize, reveal, see, sense, smoke out*, spot, think of, turn up, unearth; CONCEPTS 31,183 —*Ant.* lose, miss, pass by

discovery [*n1*] *finding, uncovering* analysis, ascertainment, authentication, calculation, certification, detection, determination, diagnosis, discernment, disclosure, distinguishing, empiricism, encounter, espial, experimentation, exploration, exposition, exposure, feeling, hearing, identification, introduction, invention, learning, locating, location, origination, perception, revelation, sensing, sighting, strike, unearthing, verification; CONCEPTS 31,183 —*Ant.* loss, miss

discovery [*n2*] *treasure; invention* algorithm, bonanza*, breakthrough, conclusion, contrivance, coup, data, design, device, find, finding, formula, godsend*, innovation, law, luck, luck out*, machine, method, principle, process, result, secret, theorem, way; CONCEPTS 260,532 —*Ant.* loss

discredit [*v1*] *blame, detract from* blow up*, bring into disrepute, bring to naught, censure, defame, degrade, destroy, disesteem, disfavor, disgrace, dishonor, disparage, disprove, explode, expose, frown upon*, knock bottom out of*, mudsling*, poke full of holes*, pooh-pooh*, puncture, put down, reflect on, reproach, ruin, run down, shoot, show up, slander, slur, smear, take rug out from under*, tear down*, vilify; CONCEPTS 44,54 —*Ant.* commend, credit, honor, praise

discredit [*v2*] *doubt, question* challenge, deny, disbelieve, discount, dispute, distrust, put under suspicion, reject, scoff at; CONCEPT 21 —*Ant.* believe, credit, trust

discreet [*adj*] *cautious, sensible* alert, attentive, awake, cagey, calculating, careful, chary, circumspect, civil, conservative, considerate, controlled, diplomatic, discerning, discriminating, gingerly, guarded, having foresight, heedful, intelligent, judicious, like a clam*, moderate, noncommittal, not rash, observant, on lookout*, politic, precautious, prudent, reasonable, reserved, restrained, safe, sagacious, strategic, tactful, temperate, thoughtful, vigilant, wary, watchful, wise, worldly-wise; CONCEPT 401 —*Ant.* careless, foolish, incautious, indiscreet, rash, reckless, thoughtless, uncareful, undiscerning

discrepancy [*n*] *conflict, disagreement* alterity, contrariety, difference, discordance, disparity, dissemblance, dissimilarity, dissimilitude, dissonance, distinction, divergence, divergency, error, far cry*, incongruity, inconsistency, miscalculation, otherness, split, unlikeness, variance, variation; CONCEPT 665 —*Ant.* agreement, concordance, concurrence, consistency, harmony, parity

discrepant [*adj*] *disagreeing* at variance, conflicting, contradictory, contrary, different, differing, disconsonant, discordant, disparate, dissonant, divergent, diverse, incompatible, incongruent, incongruous, inconsistent, inconsonant, unmixable, varying; CONCEPT 564 —*Ant.* agreeing, concurring, consistent, harmonious

discrete [*adj*] *individual* detached, different, disconnected, discontinuous, distinct, diverse, separate, several, unattached, various; CONCEPT 564 —*Ant.* attached, combined, joined

discretion [*n*] *caution, judgment* acumen, attention, calculation, canniness, care, carefulness, chariness, circumspection, concern, considerateness, consideration, deliberation, diplomacy, discernment, discrimination, foresight, forethought, good sense, gumption, heed, heedfulness, judiciousness, maturity, observation, perspicacity, precaution, presence of mind, providence, prudence, responsibility, sagacity, sense, shrewdness, solicitude, tact, thoughtfulness, vigilance, wariness, warning, watchfulness, wisdom; CONCEPT 657 —*Ant.* carelessness, indiscretion, thoughtlessness

discretionary [*adj*] *open to choice* at the call*, elective, facultative, judge and jury, leftover, nonmandatory, nonobligatory, open, optional, unrestricted; CONCEPT 546 —*Ant.* nondiscretionary

discriminate [*v1*] *show prejudice* be bigot, be partial, contradistinguish, disfavor, favor, hate, incline, judge, segregate, separate, set apart, show bias, single out, treat as inferior, treat differently, victimize; CONCEPTS 32,384

discriminate [*v2*] *differentiate, distinguish* assess, collate, compare, contradistinguish, contrast, difference, discern, discrepate, evaluate, extricate, judge, know, know what's what*, make out*, note, perceive, remark, segregate, separate, sever, severalize, sift, specify, split hairs*, tell apart, tell the difference; CONCEPTS 15,38 —*Ant.* confuse, mix up

discriminating [*adj*] *critical* acute, astute, careful, choicy, choosy, cultivated, discerning, distinctive, eclectic, fastidious, finical, finicky, fussy, individualizing, judicious, keen, opinionated, particular, persnickety*, picky, prudent, refined, select, selective, sensitive, tasteful, wise; CONCEPTS 404,542 —*Ant.* uncritical, undiscriminating

discrimination [*n1*] *bias* bigotry, favoritism, hatred, inequity, injustice, intolerance, partiality, prejudice, unfairness, wrong; CONCEPTS 29,689 —*Ant.* fairness, tolerance

discrimination [*n2*] *particularity in taste* acumen, acuteness, astucity, astuteness, bias, clearness, decision, difference, differentiation, discernment, distinction, judgment, keenness, penetration, perception, percipience, perspicacity, preference, refinement, sagacity, sense, separation, shrewdness, subtlety, taste, understanding; CONCEPTS *32,410,655* —*Ant.* indifference

discursive [*adj*] *rambling* deviating, digressive, erratic, excursive, long-winded, meandering, prolix, roaming, roving, spreading, wandering; CONCEPT *267*

discuss [*v*] *talk over with another* altercate, argue, bounce off*, canvass, compare notes, confabulate, confer, consider, consult with, contend, contest, converse, debate, deliberate, descant, discept, discourse about, dispute, dissert, dissertate, examine, exchange views on*, explain, figure, get together, go into, groupthink*, hash over*, hold forth, jaw*, kick about*, knock around*, moot, put heads together*, reason about, review, sift, take up, thrash out*, toss around*, ventilate, weigh; CONCEPT *56* —*Ant.* be quiet

discussion [*n*] *talk with another* altercation, analysis, argument, argumentation, canvass, colloquy, confabulation, conference, consideration, consultation, contention, controversy, conversation, debate, deliberation, dialogue, discourse, disputation, dispute, dissertation, examination, exchange, excursus, groupthink*, huddle, interview, meet, meeting, powwow*, quarrel, review, scrutiny, symposium, ventilation, wrangling; CONCEPT *56* —*Ant.* quiet, silence

disdain [*n*] *hate; indifference* antipathy, arrogance, aversion, contempt, contumely, derision, despisal, despisement, despite, dislike, disparagement, hatred, haughtiness, hauteur, insolence, loftiness, pride, ridicule, scorn, sneering, snobbishness, superbity, superciliousness; CONCEPT *29* —*Ant.* admiration, esteem, favor, like, love, praise, respect

disdain [*v*] *scorn* abhor, be allergic to*, belittle, chill, contemn, deride, despise, disregard, hate, ignore, look down nose at*, look down on, misprize, pooh-pooh*, put down*, refuse, reject, scout, slight, sneer at, spurn, undervalue; CONCEPTS *29,30* —*Ant.* admire, approve, esteem, favor, praise, respect

disdainful [*adj*] *scornful* aloof, antipathetic, arrogant, averse, cavalier, contemning, contemptuous, cool, derisive, despising, egotistic, haughty, high-and-mighty*, hoity-toity*, indifferent, insolent, lordly, overbearing, proud, rejecting, repudiating, scouting, sneering, snooty*, supercilious, superior, toplofty, unsympathetic, uppity*; CONCEPT *401* —*Ant.* esteemable, favoring, loving, praising, respectful

disease [*n*] *ailment, affliction* ache, affection, attack, blight, breakdown, bug*, cancer, canker, collapse, complaint, condition, contagion, contamination, convulsions, debility, decrepitude, defect, disorder, distemper, endemic, epidemic, feebleness, fever, fit, flu, hemorrhage, ill health, illness, indisposition, infection, infirmity, inflammation, malady, misery, pathosis, plague, seizure, sickliness, sickness, spell, stroke, syndrome, temperature, unhealthiness, unsoundness, upset, virus, visitation; CONCEPT *306* —*Ant.* health

diseased [*adj*] *unhealthy* afflicted, ailing, indisposed, infected, infectious, infirm, rotten, sick, sickly, tainted, unsound, unwell, unwholesome; CONCEPT *314* —*Ant.* fit, healthy

disembark [*v*] *get off transportation* alight, anchor, arrive, come ashore, debark, deplane, detrain, dismount, go ashore, land, put in, step out of; CONCEPT *159* —*Ant.* embark, get on, leave

disembowel [*v*] *gut* clean, disbowel, draw, empty, eviscerate, exenterate, extract; CONCEPTS *206,211*

disenchanted [*adj*] *let down* blasé, cynical, disappointed, disenthralled, disentranced, disillusioned, embittered, indifferent, jaundiced, knowing, mondaine, out of love, sick of, sophisticate, sophisticated, soured, undeceived, worldly, worldly-wise; CONCEPT *403* —*Ant.* enchanted, encouraged

disengage [*v*] *free from connection* abstract, back off, back out, cut loose, cut out, detach, disassociate, disconnect, disentangle, disjoin, dissociate, disunite, divide, drop out, ease, extricate, liberate, loose, loosen, opt out, pull the plug, release, separate, set free, unbind, uncouple, undo, unfasten, unfix, unloose, untie, weasel out*, withdraw; CONCEPT *135* —*Ant.* attach, bind, connect, engage, fasten, join, unite

disentangle [*v*] *unwind, disconnect; solve* bail one out*, clear up, detach, discumber, disembroil, disencumber, disengage, disinvolve, emancipate, expand, extricate, free, let go, let off, loose, open, part, resolve, separate, sever, simplify, sort out, sunder, unbraid, undo, unfold, unravel, unscramble, unsnarl, untangle, untie, untwine, untwist, work out; CONCEPTS *127,135* —*Ant.* entangle, entwine, twist, wind

disfavor [*n*] *dislike; disgrace* aversion, disapprobation, disapproval, discredit, disesteem, dishonor, disinclination, displeasure, disregard, disrepute, disrespect, dissatisfaction, distaste, distrust, doghouse*, indisposition, mistrust, shame, thumbs down*, unpopularity; CONCEPT *29* —*Ant.* approval, endorsement, favor, like

disfigure [*v*] *make ugly* blemish, damage, deface, defile, deform, disfashion, disfeature, distort, hurt, injure, maim, mangle, mar, mutilate, scar; CONCEPTS *137,246,250* —*Ant.* adorn, beautify, decorate, ornament

disgorge [*v*] *vomit* be sick*, discharge, lose one's lunch*, regurgitate, retch, spew, throw up, upchuck*; CONCEPTS *179,185,308*

disgrace [*n*] *state of shame; bad reputation* abasement, abuse, baseness, black eye*, blemish, blur, brand, comedown, contempt, contumely, corruption, culpability, debasement, debasing, defamation, degradation, derision, disbarment, discredit, disesteem, disfavor, dishonor, disrepute, disrespect, humbling, humiliation, ignominy, ill repute, infamy, ingloriousness, meanness, obloquy, odium, opprobrium, pollution, prostitution, put-down, reproach, scandal, scorn, slander, slight, slur, spot, stain, stigma, taint, tarnish, turpitude, venality; CONCEPT *388* —*Ant.* esteem, exaltation, honor, respect

disgrace [*v*] *bring shame upon* abase, attaint, besmirch, blot, debase, defame, defile, degrade, depress, deride, derogate, desecrate, discredit, disfavor, dishonor, disparage, disregard, disrespect, expel, give a black eye*, humble, humiliate, libel, lose face*, lower, mock, put down, reduce, reproach, ridicule, slander, slur, snub, stain, stigmatize, sully, taint, take down a peg*, tar and feather*, tarnish; CONCEPTS *14,54,384* —*Ant.* esteem, exalt, honor, respect

disgraceful [*adj*] *shameful, low* blameworthy, contemptible, degrading, detestable, discreditable, dishonorable, disreputable, ignoble, ignominious, infamous, inglorious, mean, offensive, opprobrious, scandalous, shabby, shady, shocking, shoddy, unrespectable, unworthy; CONCEPT *555* —*Ant.* exalted, honorable, respectable

disgruntled [*adj*] *unhappy; critical* annoyed, bad tempered, bellyaching*, crabbing*, crabby, cranky, disappointed, discontent, discontented, displeased, dissatisfied, griping, grouchy, grousing, grumpy, irritable, irritated, kicking, kvetching*, malcontent, malcontented, peeved, peevish, petulant, put out, sulky, sullen, testy, uncontent, ungratified, vexed; CONCEPTS *401,403* —*Ant.* contented, happy, pleased, satisfied, uncritical

disguise [*n*] *covering, makeup for deception* beard, blind, camouflage, charade, cloak, color, coloring, concealment, costume, counterfeit, cover-up, dissimulation, dress, facade, face, faking, false front*, fig leaf*, front*, get-up, guise, illusion, make-believe, mask, masquerade, pageant, pen name, pretense, pretension, pretentiousness, pseudonym, put-on, red herring*, screen, semblance, smoke screen*, trickery, veil, veneer; CONCEPTS *446,451,680*

disguise [*v*] *mask; misrepresent* affect, age, alter, antique, assume, beard, belie, camouflage, change, cloak, color, conceal, counterfeit, cover, cover up, deceive, dissemble, dissimulate, doctor up*, dress up, fake, falsify, feign, front, fudge*, garble, gloss over, hide, make like, make up, masquerade, muffle, obfuscate, obscure, pretend, put on a false front*, put on a front*, put on an act*, put up a front*, redo*, screen, secrete, sham, shroud, simulate, touch up, varnish, veil, wear cheaters*, whitewash*; CONCEPTS *59,137,172,188,202* —*Ant.* expose, open, represent, reveal, uncover, unmask

disguised [*adj*] *unrecognizable* camouflaged, changed, cloaked, covered, covert, fake, false, feigned, hidden, incog, masked, pretend, undercover; CONCEPTS *547,619* —*Ant.* bare, open, recognizable, revealed, uncovered, unmasked

disgust [*n*] *aversion; repulsion* abhorrence, abomination, antipathy, detestation, dislike, distaste, hatefulness, hatred, loathing, nausea, nauseation, nauseousness, objection, repugnance, revolt, revulsion, satiation, satiety, sickness, surfeit; CONCEPTS *410,720* —*Ant.* admiration, appeal, desire, esteem, fondness, like, liking, loving, respect, reverence

disgust [*v*] *cause aversion; repel* abominate, be repulsive, bother, cloy on, disenchant, displease, disturb, fill with loathing, gross out*, insult, irk, make one sick*, nauseate, offend, offend morals of, outrage, pall, pique, put off, reluct, repulse, revolt, scandalize, shock, sicken, surfeit, turn off, turn one's stomach*, upset; CONCEPTS *7,19* —*Ant.* admire, appeal, desire, esteem, like, love, respect, revere

disgusted [*adj*] *sickened; offended* abhorred, appalled, displeased, fastidious, fed up*, full up*, grossed out*, had bellyful*, had enough*, had it*, nauseated, nauseous, outraged, overwrought, queasy, repelled, repulsed, revolted,

satiated, scandalized, sick, sick and tired of*, sick of*, squeamish, teed off*, tired, turned off*, unhappy, up to here*, weary; CONCEPT *403* —*Ant.* attracted, delighted, desirous, happy, pleased

disgusting [*adj*] *sickening; repulsive* abominable, awful, beastly, cloying, creepy, detestable, distasteful, foul, frightful, ghastly, grody*, gross*, gruesome, hateful, hideous, horrid, horrific, icky*, loathsome, lousy, macabre, monstrous, nasty, nauseating, nerdy*, noisome, objectionable, obnoxious, odious, offensive, outrageous, repellent, repugnant, revolting, rotten, satiating, scandalous, scuzzy*, shameless, shocking, sleazeball*, sleazy*, stinking, surfeiting, vile, vulgar, yecchy*, yucky*; CONCEPTS *485,548* —*Ant.* attractive, desirous, pleasant, pleasing

dish [*n1*] *eating receptacle* bowl, casserole, ceramic, china, container, cup, mug, pitcher, plate, platter, porringer, pot, pottery, salver, saucer, tray, vessel; CONCEPT *494*

dish [*n2*] *main part of meal* course, eats*, entrée, fare, food, helping, recipe, serving; CONCEPTS *457,460,461*

dish [*n3*] *attractive woman* angel, babe*, bathing beauty, beauty queen, broad*, bunny*, centerfold, chick*, cover girl, cupcake*, cutie, cutie-pie*, doll*, dollface, dreamboat*, dream girl, fox*, glamor girl, good-looking woman, honey*, hot dish*, hot number*, peach*, pin-up, raving beauty, sex bunny*, sex kitten*, sex pot*, tomato*; CONCEPTS *415,424*

disharmony [*n*] *conflict, discord* clash, contention, difference, disaccord, dissension, dissonance, dissonancy, friction, inharmoniousness, strife, variance; CONCEPTS *388, 665* —*Ant.* accord, agreement, compatibility, concord, harmony

dishearten [*v*] *depress, ruin one's hopes* cast down, chill*, crush, damp, dampen, dash, daunt, deject, demoralize, deter, discourage, disincline, dismay, disparage, dispirit, get down*, humble, humiliate, indispose, put a damper on*, put down, shake, throw a pall over*; CONCEPTS *7,19* —*Ant.* encourage, hearten, inspirit

disheveled [*adj*] *wrinkled, unkempt in appearance* bagged out*, beat up*, bedraggled, blowzy*, dirty, disarranged, disarrayed, disordered, frowzy*, grubby*, messed up, messy, mussed up*, mussy, ruffled, rumpled, scuzzy, slipshod, sloppy, slovenly, tousled, unbuttoned, uncombed, unfastidious, untidy, unzipped*; CONCEPTS *485,579* —*Ant.* neat, ordered, orderly, tidy, unwrinkled

dishonest [*adj*] *lying, untruthful* backbiting*, bent, bluffing, cheating, corrupt, crafty, crooked, cunning, deceitful, deceiving, deceptive, designing, disreputable, double-crossing, double-dealing, elusive, false, fraudulent, guileful, hoodwinking*, mendacious, misleading, perfidious, recreant, shady, shifty, sinister, slippery*, sneaking, sneaky, swindling, traitorous, treacherous, tricky, two-faced*, two-timing*, unctuous, underhanded, unfair, unprincipled, unscrupulous, untrustworthy, villainous, wily; CONCEPT *267* —*Ant.* aboveboard, ethical, fair, frank, honest, moral, open, principled, scrupulous, trustworthy, truthful

dishonesty [n] *lying; unwillingness to tell the truth* artifice, bunk, cheating, chicane, chicanery, corruption, craft, criminality, crookedness, cunning, deceit, double-dealing, duplicity, faithlessness, falsehood, falsity, flimflam*, fourberie, fraud, fraudulence, graft, guile, hanky-panky*, hocus-pocus*, improbity, infamy, infidelity, insidiousness, mendacity, perfidiousness, perfidy, racket, rascality, sharp practice*, slyness, stealing, swindle, treachery, trickery, trickiness, unscrupulousness, wiliness; CONCEPTS 59,633,657 —*Ant.* fairness, frankness, honesty, openness, scrupulousness, sincerity, truthfulness

dishonor [n] *state of shame* abasement, abuse, affront, blame, degradation, discourtesy, discredit, disesteem, disfavor, disgrace, disrepute, ignominy, indignity, infamy, insult, obloquy, odium, offense, opprobrium, outrage, reproach, scandal, slight; CONCEPT 388 —*Ant.* credit, esteem, honor

dishonor [v] *shame, degrade* abase, attaint, blot, corrupt, debase, debauch, defame, defile, disconsider, discredit, disgrace, disoblige, give a black eye*, libel, make lose face*, reflect on, slander, sully; CONCEPT 54 —*Ant.* credit, esteem, honor, upgrade

dishonorable [adj] *shameful, corrupt* base, blackguardly, contemptible, crooked, deceitful, despicable, devious, discreditable, disgraceful, disreputable, fraudulent, ignoble, ignominious, infamous, inglorious, low, miscreant, offensive, opprobrious, putrid, scandalous, shabby, shady, treacherous, unprincipled, unrespectable, unscrupulous, untrustworthy; CONCEPT 555 —*Ant.* blameless, ethical, honorable, principled, respectable, trustworthy, uncorrupt, worthy

dish out [v] *distribute* allocate, deliver, dispense, dole out*, fork over*, furnish, give out, hand, hand out, hand over, inflict, ladle, mete out, present, produce, scoop, serve, serve up, spoon, supply, transfer, turn over; CONCEPT 140 —*Ant.* take

disillusioned [adj] *disappointed* blasé, broken, brought down to earth*, debunked, disabused, disenchanted, disenthralled, disentranced, embittered, enlightened, freed, indifferent, knowing, let-down, mondaine, out of love*, punctured, sadder and wiser*, shattered, sophisticated, undeceived, worldly, worldly-wise*; CONCEPT 403 —*Ant.* enchanted, encouraged, enthusiastic

disinclination [n] *unwillingness to do or believe something* alienation, antipathy, aversion, demur, disfavor, dislike, disliking, displeasure, disrelish, dissatisfaction, distaste, hatred, hesitance, indisposition, lack of desire, lack of enthusiasm, loathness, objection, opposition, reluctance, repugnance, resistance; CONCEPTS 29,410,657 —*Ant.* bent, desire, enthusiasm, incentive, inclination, willingness

disinclined [adj] *unwilling* afraid, antipathetic, averse, backward, balking, doubtful, dubious, hesitating, indisposed, loath, not in the mood*, objecting, opposed, protesting, reluctant, resistant, shy, shying, slow, sticking, uneager, unsympathetic; CONCEPTS 403,542 —*Ant.* bent, desirous, disposed, enthusiastic, inclined, leaning, willing

disinfect [v] *make clean, pure* antisepticize, cleanse, decontaminate, deodorize, fumigate, purify, sanitize, sterilize; CONCEPT 165 —*Ant.* dirty, pollute

disingenuous [adj] *insincere* artful, crooked, cunning, deceitful, designing, dishonest, duplicitous, false, feigned, foxy, guileful, indirect, insidious, mendacious, oblique, shifty*, sly, tricky, two-faced*, uncandid, underhanded, unfair, unfrank; wily; CONCEPTS 401,542 —*Ant.* frank, honest, ingenuous, naive, sincere

disinherit [v] *cut off in will of bequeathal* bereave, cut off without a cent*, deprive, disaffiliate, disown, dispossess, divest, evict, exclude, exheridate, neglect, oust, repudiate, rob; CONCEPTS 25,317 —*Ant.* bequeath, give

disintegrate [v] *fall apart; reduce to pieces* atomize, break apart, break down, break up, come apart, crumble, decay, decline, decompose, degenerate, deliquesce, descend, detach, dilapidate, disband, disconnect, disimprove, dismantle, disorganize, disperse, disunite, divide, fade away, fall to pieces*, molder, pulverize, putrefy, rot, separate, sever, shatter, sink, splinter, spoil, taint, take apart, turn, turn to dust*, wash away, wash out, wither, worsen; CONCEPTS 252,469 —*Ant.* combine, meld, unite

disinterested [adj] *detached, uninvolved* aloof, candid, casual, dispassionate, equitable, even-handed, impartial, impersonal, incurious, indifferent, just watching the clock*, lackadaisical, negative, neutral, nonpartisan, not giving a damn*, outside, perfunctory, remote, unbiased, unconcerned, uncurious, unprejudiced, unselfish, withdrawn; CONCEPTS 401,403 —*Ant.* biased, concerned, interested, involved, passionate, prejudiced

disjointed [adj] *loose, disconnected* aimless, confused, cool, discontinuous, disordered, displaced, disunited, divided, far-out, fitful, fuzzy, inchoate, incoherent, incohesive, irrational, jumbled, muddled, out-of-it*, out-to-lunch*, rambling, separated, spaced-out*, spacey*, spasmodic, split, unattached, unconnected, unorganized; CONCEPTS 267,482,585 —*Ant.* coherent, connected, contiguous, jointed, ordered, united

disk [n] *round object* circle, disc, discoid, discoidal, discus, dish, flan, plate, platter, quoit, sabot, saucer, shell; CONCEPT 436

dislike [n] *antagonism, hatred toward something* animosity, animus, antipathy, aversion, deprecation, detestation, disapprobation, disapproval, disesteem, disfavor, disgust, disinclination, displeasure, dissatisfaction, distaste, enmity, hostility, indisposition, loathing, objection, offense, opposition, prejudice, repugnance; CONCEPT 29 —*Ant.* approval, like, liking, love

dislike [v] *be antagonistic toward something; hate* abhor, abominate, antipathize, avoid, be allergic to*, bear malice toward, be averse to, be turned off to*, condemn, contemn, deplore, despise, detest, disapprove, disesteem, disfavor, disrelish, eschew, execrate, grossed out on*, have hard feelings*, have no stomach for*, have no taste for, loathe, look down on, lose interest in, make faces at*, mind, not appreciate, not care for, not endure, not feel like, not take kindly to, object to, regret, resent, scorn, shudder at, shun; CONCEPT 29 —*Ant.* approve, like, love

dislocate [v] *displace* break, disarticulate, disconnect, disengage, disjoint, disorder, disrupt, disturb, disunite, divide, jumble, misplace, mix up, move, put out of joint, remove, rummage, separate, shift, transfer, unhinge, upset; CONCEPTS 135,147 —*Ant.* keep together, order

dislocation [n] *displacement* break, confusion, disarray, disarticulation, disconnection, discontinuity, disengagement, disorder, disorganization, disruption, disturbance, division, luxation, misplacement, unhinging; CONCEPTS 316,720,727 —*Ant.* order, ordering

dislodge [v] *knock loose* dig out, disentangle, dislocate, displace, disturb, eject, evict, extricate, force out, oust, uproot; CONCEPTS 147,213

disloyal [adj] *unfaithful* alienated, apostate, cheating, disaffected, double-crossing, estranged, faithless, false, perfidious, recreant, seditious, snaky*, subversive, traitorous, treacherous, treasonable, two-faced*, two-timing*, unloyal, unpatriotic, untrue, untrustworthy, wormlike*; CONCEPT 401 —*Ant.* faithful, loyal, true, trustworthy

disloyalty [n] *unfaithfulness* apostasy, bad faith, betrayal of trust, breach of trust, breaking of faith, deceitfulness, disaffection, double-dealing, faithlessness, falseness, falsity, inconstancy, infidelity, perfidiousness, perfidy, recreancy, sedition, seditiousness, subversive activity, treachery, treason, untrueness, violation; CONCEPT 633 —*Ant.* faithfulness, loyalty, trueness, trustworthiness

dismal [adj] *bleak, dreary, gloomy* afflictive, black, boring, cheerless, cloudy, dark, depressed, depressing, desolate, despondent, dim, dingy, disagreeable, discouraging, disheartening, dispiriting, doleful, dolorous, dull, forlorn, frowning, funereal, ghastly, gruesome, hopeless, horrible, horrid, inauspicious, in the pits*, joyless, lonesome, lowering, lugubrious, melancholy, miserable, monotonous, morbid, murky, oppressive, overcast, sad, shadowy, somber, sorrowful, tedious, tenebrous, troublesome, unfortunate, unhappy; CONCEPTS 525,536,548 —*Ant.* bright, cheerful, glad, happy, hopeful, light, pleasant

dismantle [v] *take apart* annihilate, bankrupt, bare, break down, break up, decimate, demolish, denudate, denude, deprive, destroy, disassemble, dismember, dismount, disrobe, divest, fell, knock down, level, part out, pull down, raze, ruin, strike, strip, subvert, take down, take to pieces, tear down, undo, unrig, wrack, wreck; CONCEPTS 135,168,252 —*Ant.* assemble, build, combine, construct, put together, raise

dismay [n] *disappointed feeling; distress* agitation, alarm, anxiety, apprehension, blue funk*, blues*, bummer*, chagrin, cold feet*, consternation, discouragement, disheartenment, disillusionment, downer*, dread, dumps*, fear, fright, funk*, hassle, horror, letdown, panic, terror, the blahs*, trepidation, upset; CONCEPTS 27,410,690 —*Ant.* assurance, confidence, encouragement, happiness

dismay [v] *disappoint, fill with consternation* abash, affright, agitate, alarm, appall, bewilder,

bother, chill, confound, daunt, discomfit, discompose, disconcert, discourage, dishearten, disillusion, dispirit, disquiet, distress, disturb, dumbfound, embarrass, faze, flummox*, fluster, foul up*, frighten, get to, horrify, louse up*, mess up*, muck up*, mystify, nonplus, paralyze, perplex, put off, puzzle, rattle, scare, screw up*, shake, snafu*, take aback, terrify, terrorize, throw, throw into a tizzy*, unhinge*, unnerve, upset; CONCEPTS 7,19 —*Ant.* assure, encourage, make happy

dismember [v] *cut into pieces* amputate, anatomize, cripple, disassemble, disjoint, dislimb, dislocate, dismantle, dismount, dissect, divide, maim, mutilate, part, rend, sever, sunder, take down; CONCEPTS 98,135,176 —*Ant.* join

dismiss [v1] *send away, remove; free* abolish, banish, boot*, brush off*, bundle, cast off*, cast out*, chase, chuck, clear, decline, deport, detach, disband, discard, dispatch, dispense with, disperse, dispose of, dissolve, divorce, do without, drive out, eject, expel, force out, have done with*, kick out*, let go, let out, lock out*, outlaw, push aside, push back, reject, release, relegate, relinquish, repel, repudiate, rid, send off, send packing*, shed, show out*, slough off, supersede, sweep away*, turn out; CONCEPTS 127,217 —*Ant.* accept, hold, keep, maintain, preserve, welcome

dismiss [v2] *remove from job, responsibility* ax*, boot*, boot out*, bounce*, bump*, can*, cashier*, defrock, depone, depose, deselect, discharge, disemploy, disfrock, displace, disqualify, drop, fire, furlough, give notice to, give the ax*, give the gate*, give the heave-ho*, give walking papers*, give warning, impeach, kick out*, lay off, let go*, let out*, oust, pension, pink-slip*, put away*, recall, retire, sack*, send packing*, shelve*, shut out*, suspend, terminate, turn away, unfrock, unseat, wash out*; CONCEPTS 324,351 —*Ant.* appoint, employ, engage, hire, keep, secure

dismiss [v3] *put out of one's mind* banish, contemn, deride, despise, discard, disdain, dispel, disregard, drop, flout, gibe, gird, jeer, kiss off*, laugh away*, lay aside, mock, pooh-pooh*, rally, reject, relegate, repudiate, repulse, ridicule, scoff, scorn, scout, set aside, shelve*, spurn, taunt, twit; CONCEPT 35 —*Ant.* accept, welcome

dismissal [n] *release* adjournment, banishment, bounce, brush-off, cold shoulder*, congé, deportation, deposal, deposition, discharge, dislodgment, displacement, dispossession, dissolution, door*, end, eviction, exile, exorcism, expatriation, expulsion, freedom, freeing, housecleaning*, kiss-off*, layoff, liberation, marching orders*, notice, old heave-ho*, ostracism, ouster, permission, pink slip*, relegation, removal, suspension; CONCEPTS 127,217,351 —*Ant.* acceptance, appointment, employment, hiring, maintainance, retention, welcome

dismount [v] *get off something higher* alight, debark, deplane, descend, detrain, disembark, get down, light; CONCEPT 195 —*Ant.* get up, mount

disobedience [n] *misbehavior; noncompliance with rules* defiance, dereliction, disregard, indiscipline, infraction, infringement, insubmission, insubordination, insurgence, intractableness, mutiny, neglect, nonobservance, perversity, rebellion, recalcitrance, refractoriness, revolt, revolution, riot, sabotage, sedition, strike, stubbornness, transgression, unruliness, violation, waywardness; CONCEPT 633 —*Ant.* behavior, obedience, observance, submission

disobedient [*adj*] *defiant, mischievous* contrary, contumacious, disorderly, fractious, froward, headstrong, insubordinate, intractable, naughty, noncompliant, nonobservant, obstreperous, perverse, recalcitrant, refractory, resistive, uncompliant, undisciplined, unruly, wayward, willful; CONCEPT 401 —*Ant.* accepting, behaving, nice, obedient, observant, submitting

disobey [*v*] *disregard rules; refuse to conform* balk, be remiss, break rules, contravene, counteract, dare, decline, defy, desert, differ, disagree, evade, flout, fly in face of*, go counter to, ignore, infringe, insurrect, misbehave, mutiny, neglect, not heed, not listen, not mind, object, overstep, pay no attention to, rebel, recalcitrate, resist, revolt, revolution, revolutionize, riot, rise in arms*, run riot*, set aside, shirk, strike, take law into own hands*, transgress, violate, withstand; CONCEPTS 30,192,384 —*Ant.* conform, go along, obey, oblige, regard, submit

disoblige [*v*] *displease, annoy* affront, bother, discommode, disturb, incommode, inconvenience, insult, offend, put about, put out, slight, trouble, upset, vex; CONCEPTS 7,19 —*Ant.* agree, oblige, please

disobliging [*adj*] *rude, annoying* awkward, disagreeable, discourteous, ill-disposed, ill-natured, unaccommodating, unamiable, uncivil, uncongenial, uncooperative, unhelpful, unpleasant; CONCEPT 401 —*Ant.* accommodating, agreeable, civil, cooperative, courteous, mannered, mannerly, polite

disorder [*n1*] *chaos, clutter* anarchy, ataxia, confusion, derangement, disarrangement, disarray, discombobulation, disorderliness, disorganization, huddle, irregularity, jumble, mess, muddle, rat's nest*, shambles, snarl, topsy-turviness*, untidiness; CONCEPT 230 —*Ant.* arrangement, conformity, method, order, orderliness, organization, system

disorder [*n2*] *social commotion; mental confusion* agitation, anarchism, anarchy, brawl, bustle, chaos, clamor, complication, convulsion, discombobulation*, discord, disorganization, distemper, disturbance, dither, entanglement, fight, flap, fracas, fuss, hubbub, hullabaloo*, imbroglio, insurrection, lawlessness, mayhem, misrule, mob rule*, quarrel, rebellion, reign of terror*, revolution, riot, rioting, ruckus, rumpus, static, strike, terrorism, tizzy*, trouble, tumult, turbulence, turmoil, unrest, unruliness, uproar; CONCEPTS 388,410 —*Ant.* health

disorder [*n3*] *illness* affliction, ailment, cachexia, complaint, disease, diseasedness, indisposition, infirmity, malady, sickness, unhealth, upset; CONCEPT 306 —*Ant.* health

disorder [*v*] *mix up, disarrange* clutter, confound, confuse, derange, discompose, discreate, dishevel, disjoint, dislocate, disorganize, disrupt, distemper, disturb, embroil, jumble, mess up, muddle, muss up*, rummage, rumple,

scatter, shuffle, tumble, unsettle, upset; CONCEPTS 240,250 —*Ant.* arrange, conform, neaten, order, regulate, systematize

disordered [*adj*] *in a mess* all over the place*, confused, deranged, disarranged, discombobulated, disconnected, discontinuous, disjointed, dislocated, disorganized, displaced, incoherent, in confusion, jumbled, mislaid, misplaced, molested, moved, muddled, out-of-place, removed, roiled, ruffled, rumpled, shifted, shuffled, stirred up, tampered-with, tangled, tossed, tousled, tumbled, unsettled, untidy; CONCEPTS 485,535 —*Ant.* arranged, methodical, neat, ordered, orderly, organized, systematic, systematized, trim

disorderly [*adj1*] *messy, untidy* all over the place*, chaotic, cluttered, confused, dislocated, disorganized, heterogeneous, indiscriminate, irregular, jumbled, mixed up, out-of-control*, out-of-line*, out-of-step*, out-of-whack*, scattered, scrambled, slovenly, topsy-turvy*, tumult, uncombed, undisciplined, unkempt, unmethodical, unrestrained, unsystematic, untrained; CONCEPTS 485,535 —*Ant.* arranged, neat, ordered, orderly, organized, systematized, trim

disorderly [*adj2*] *causing trouble; unlawful* boisterous, disobedient, disruptive, drunk, fractious, indisciplined, intemperate, noisy, obstreperous, off-base*, on-a-tear*, out-of-line*, out-of-order*, raucous, rebellious, refractory, riotous, rowdy, stormy, termagant, tumultous/tumultuous, turbulent, uncompliant, uncontrollable, ungovernable, unmanageable, unruly, wayward; CONCEPTS 401,545 —*Ant.* behaved, conforming, disciplined, manageable, orderly, well-behaved

disorganization [*n*] *unordered situation or thing* anarchy, chaos, confusion, derangement, disarray, disjointedness, disorder, disruption, dissolution, disunion, foul-up*, incoherence, mix-up, rat's nest*, screw-up*, unconnectedness, unholy mess*; CONCEPTS 674,727 —*Ant.* coherence, method, neatness, order, organization, plan, system, tidiness

disorganize [*v*] *disrupt arrangement; make shambles of* break down, break up, clutter, complicate, confound, confuse, demobilize, derange, destroy, disarrange, disarray, disband, discompose, discreate, dishevel, dislocate, disorder, disperse, disturb, embroil, jumble, litter, mess up, mislay, misplace, muddle, perturb, put out of order, scatter, scramble, shuffle, toss, turn topsy-turvy, unsettle, upset; CONCEPTS 250,252,384 —*Ant.* compose, neaten, order, organize, plan, systematize, tidy

disorganized [*adj*] *unmethodical; messed up* chaotic, confused, disordered, disorderly, haphazard, jumbled, mixed up, muddled, screwed up*, shuffled, unsystematic; CONCEPTS 485,585 —*Ant.* methodical, neat, ordered, organized, planned, regulated, systematic, systematized, tidy

disoriented [*adj*] *confused, unstable* adrift, all at sea*, astray, bewildered, discombobulated, lost, mixed-up, not adjusted, off-beam*, off-course, out-of-joint*, perplexed, unbalanced, unhinged, unsettled; CONCEPT 403 —*Ant.* balanced, oriented, settled, understanding, unpuzzled

disown [v] *refuse to acknowledge* abandon, abjure, abnegate, cast off, deny, disacknowledge, disallow, disavow, discard, disclaim, divorce oneself from, refuse to recognize, reject, renounce, repudiate, retract; CONCEPTS 50,54,88 —Ant. accept, acknowledge, allow, avow, claim

disparage [v] *criticize; detract from* abuse, belittle, chill*, cry down, decry, defame, degrade, deject, demoralize, denigrate, deprecate, depreciate, deride, derogate, dis*, discourage, discredit, disdain, dishearten, dismiss, dispirit, dispraise, downcry, dump on*, lower, malign, minimize, pan*, put down, put hooks in*, rap*, ridicule, roast*, run down*, scorch, scorn, slam*, slander, smear*, sour grapes*, tear down, traduce, underestimate, underrate, undervalue, vilify, write off; CONCEPTS 7,19,52,54 —Ant. approve, commend, compliment, flatter, laud, praise, sanction

disparagement [n] *strong criticism; detraction* aspersion, backbiting*, backstabbing*, belittlement, blame, calumny, censure, condemnation, contempt, contumely, debasement, degradation, denunciation, depreciation, derision, derogation, discredit, disdain, impairment, lessening, lie, prejudice, reproach, ridicule, scandal, scorn, slander, tale, underestimation; CONCEPTS 52,54 —Ant. approval, commendation, compliment, flattery, praise, sanction

disparate [adj] *at odds, different* at variance, contrary, contrasting, discordant, discrepant, dissimilar, distant, distinct, divergent, diverse, far cry, incommensurate, incompatible, inconsistent, inconsonant, like night and day*, poles apart, separate, unalike, unequal, unequivalent, uneven, unlike, unsimilar, various; CONCEPT 564 —Ant. alike, equal, like, same, similar

disparity [n] *difference* alterity, discrepancy, disproportion, dissemblance, dissimilarity, dissimilitude, distinction, divergence, divergency, diverseness, gap, imbalance, imparity, incongruity, inequality, otherness, unevenness, unlikeness, variation; CONCEPT 665 —Ant. alikeness, equality, likeness, sameness, similarity

dispassionate [adj] *unfeeling, impartial* abstract, aloof, calm, candid, cold-blooded, cold-fish*, collected, composed, cool, cool cat*, couldn't care less*, detached, disinterested, fair, iceberg*, impersonal, imperturbable, indifferent, judicial, just, laid back, moderate, neutral, nondiscriminatory, nonpartisan, objective, poker-faced*, quiet, serene, sober, temperate, tough, unbiased, unemotional, unexcitable, unexcited, unflappable, uninvolved, unmoved, unprejudiced, unruffled; CONCEPTS 401,404 —Ant. biased, emotional, excited, feeling, involved, moved, partial, passionate, prejudiced, subjective

dispatch [n1] *speed in carrying out action* alacrity, celerity, expedition, expeditiousness, haste, hurry, hustle, precipitateness, promptitude, promptness, quickness, rapidity, rustle, speediness, swiftness; CONCEPTS 755,818 —Ant. retention, slowing

dispatch [n2] *communication* account, bulletin, communiqué, document, instruction, item, letter, message, missive, news, piece, report, story; CONCEPTS 271,277,278

dispatch [v1] *hurry, send fast* accelerate, address, consign, dismiss, express, forward, hand-carry, hasten, issue, quicken, railroad*, remit, route, run with, run with ball*, ship, speed, transmit, walk through; CONCEPTS 152,217 —Ant. hold, hold back, keep, prohibit, retain

dispatch [v2] *finish; consume* conclude, devour, discharge, dispose of, eat up, expedite, lay low, perform, polish off*, scarf down*, settle; CONCEPTS 169,234

dispatch [v3] *kill* assassinate, bump off*, butcher*, destroy, eliminate, execute, finish, finish off*, murder, put away*, put end to, slaughter, slay, take out*; CONCEPTS 238,252

dispel [v] *drive away thought, belief* allay, banish, beat off*, break it up*, break up*, bust up*, cancel, chase away, crumble, deploy, disband, disintegrate, dismiss, disperse, dissipate, distribute, eject, eliminate, expel, oust, repel, resolve, rout, scatter, scramble, split up*; CONCEPTS 14,35 —Ant. accumulate, collect, garner, gather, recall

dispensable [adj] *not necessary; able to be thrown away* disposable, excessive, expendable, minor, needless, nonessential, removable, superfluous, trivial, unimportant, unnecessary, unrequired, useless; CONCEPT 546 —Ant. indispensable, irreplaceable, necessary, needed, useful

dispensation [n1] *allocation of supply* allotment, appointment, apportionment, award, bestowal, conferment, consignment, courtesy, dealing out, disbursement, distribution, dole, endowment, favor, indulgence, kindness, part, portion, quota, service, share; CONCEPTS 140,337

dispensation [n2] *management* administration, direction, economy, plan, regulation, scheme, stewardship, system; CONCEPTS 325,660,770

dispensation [n3] *permission* exception, exemption, immunity, indulgence, license, privilege, relaxation, relief, remission, reprieve; CONCEPT 685 —Ant. denial, veto

dispense [v1] *dole out supply* allocate, allot, apportion, assign, come across with, deal, deal out, disburse, dish out*, distribute, divide, divvy*, fork out*, furnish, give, give away, give with, hand out, hand over, lot, measure, mete out, partition, portion, prepare, prorate, share, shell out*; CONCEPT 140 —Ant. receive, take

dispense [v2] *operate, administer* apply, carry out, command, direct, discharge, enforce, execute, handle, implement, manage, maneuver, manipulate, swing, undertake, wield; CONCEPT 117

dispense [v3] *exempt from responsibility* absolve, discharge, except, excuse, exonerate, let off, privilege from, release, relieve, reprieve, spare; CONCEPT 110

dispense with [v] *omit; do away with* abolish, abstain from, brush aside, cancel, dispose of, disregard, do without, forgo, get rid of, give up, ignore, pass over, relinquish, render needless, shake off, waive; CONCEPT 30 —Ant. accept, keep, regard, retain, take, use

disperse [v] *distribute; scatter* banish, besprinkle, break up, broadcast, cast forth, circulate, deal, diffuse, disappear, disband, disburse, discharge, dislodge, dismiss, dispel, disseminate, dissipate, dissolve, divvy*, dole out, eject, intersperse, measure out, partition, propagate, radiate, rout, scatter, scramble, send off, separate, shed, sow, split up, spray, spread, strew, take off in all directions*, vanish; CONCEPTS 135,217 —Ant. arrange, assemble, collect, garner, gather

dispirited [adj] dejected, sad blue*, bummed-out*, crestfallen, depressed, despondent, disconsolate, discouraged, disheartened, down*, downbeat, downcast, downhearted, dragged*, funky*, gloomy, glum, in the doldrums, low, melancholy, morose, shot-down*, spiritless, woebegone; CONCEPT 403 —Ant. encouraged, enthused, happy, heartened, inspirited

displace [v1] move, remove from normal place change, crowd out, derange, disarrange, disestablish, dislocate, dislodge, displant, dispossess, disturb, eject, evict, expel, expulse, force out, lose, mislay, misplace, relegate, shift, transpose, unsettle, uproot; CONCEPTS 147,213 —Ant. leave

displace [v2] remove from position of responsibility banish, can*, cashier*, cut out*, deport, depose, dethrone, discard, discharge, disthrone, disenthrone, dismiss, disthrone, exile, expatriate, fire, oust, relegate, remove, replace, sack*, step into shoes of*, succeed, supersede, supplant, take over, take the place of, transport, uncrown, unmake, usurp; CONCEPTS 133,298, 300 —Ant. leave

display [n] public showing; spectacle act, affectation, arrangement, array, arrayal, blaze, bravura, dash, demonstration, example, exhibit, exhibition, expo*, exposition, exposure, fanfare, flourish, for show, frame-up*, frippery, front, grandstand play*, layout, manifestation, ostentation, ostentatiousness, pageant, panorama, parade, pedantry, pomp, presentation, pretension, pretentiousness, revelation, sample, scheme, shine, showboat*, splash, splendor, splurge, spread, unfolding, vanity; CONCEPTS 261,386 —Ant. hiding

display [v] show for public viewing, effect advertise, arrange, bare, betray, boast, brandish, bring to view, demonstrate, disclose, emblazon, evidence, evince, exhibit, expand, expose, extend, feature, flash, flaunt, flourish, glaze, grandstand*, illustrate, impart, lay bare*, lay out, make clear, make known, manifest, model, open, open out, parade, perform, present, promote, promulgate, publish, represent, reveal, set out, showcase, show off, sport, spread out, stretch out, trot out*, uncover, unfold, unfurl, unmask, unroll, unveil, vamp; CONCEPT 261 —Ant. conceal, cover, hide, secrete, withhold

displease [v] make unhappy aggravate, anger, annoy, antagonize, bother, cap, chagrin, cool, curdle*, cut to the quick*, disappoint, discontent, disgruntle, disgust, disoblige, dissatisfy, enrage, exasperate, fret, frustrate, gall, hurt, incense, irk, irritate, nettle, offend, perplex, pique, play dirty, provoke, put out, repel, revolt, rile, roil, sound, turn off*, upset, vex, wing*, worry, zing*; CONCEPTS 7,19 —Ant. appease, calm, compose, delight, humor, make happy, please, satisfy

displeasure [n] unhappiness, anger annoyance, aversion, disapprobation, disapproval, discontentment, disfavor, disgruntlement, disinclination, dislike, disliking, disrelish, dissatisfaction, distaste, incensement, indignation, indisposition, irritation, offense, pique, resentment, umbrage, vexation, wrath; CONCEPT 410 —Ant. calm, composure, delight, happiness, pleasure, satisfaction

disposal [n1] parting with or throwing something away auctioning, bartering, chucking, clearance, conveyance, demolishing, demolition, destroying, destruction, discarding, dispatching, dispensation, disposition, dumping, ejection, jettison, jettisoning, junking, relegation, relinquishment, removal, riddance, sacrifice, sale, scrapping, selling, trading, transfer, transference, vending; CONCEPT 180 —Ant. hold, keeping, retention

disposal [n2] conclusion, settlement of situation action, allocation, arrangement, array, assignment, assortment, bequest, bestowal, consignment, control, conveyance, determination, dispensation, disposition, distribution, division, effectuation, end, gift, grouping, order, ordering, placing, position, provision, sequence, transfer, winding up; CONCEPTS 119,230 —Ant. beginning, start

dispose [v] place, order; deal with actuate, adapt, adjust, arrange, array, bend, bias, call the tune*, condition, determine, distribute, fix, govern, group, incline, induce, influence, lay down the law*, lead, locate, make willing, marshal, methodize, motivate, move, organize, predispose, prepare, promote, prompt, put, put one's foot down*, put to rights, range, rank, read the riot act*, regulate, ride herd on*, set, set in order, settle, shepherd, stand, sway, systematize, tailor, tempt; CONCEPTS 84,117,158,180 —Ant. disarrange, disorder, displace, disturb, mismanage

disposed [adj] inclined to a type of behavior apt, at drop of hat*, biased, fain, game*, game for, given, liable, likely, minded, of a mind to*, partial, predisposed, prone, ready, subject, tending toward, willing; CONCEPTS 542,552 —Ant. indisposed, unlikely, unready, unwilling

dispose of [v1] throw away adiós*, bestow, chuck*, deep six*, destroy, discard, dump, eighty-six*, eliminate, file in circular file*, get rid of, give, jettison, junk*, kiss*, kiss off*, make over, part with, relinquish, scrap, sell, transfer, unload; CONCEPT 180 —Ant. hold, keep, retain

dispose of [v2] settle a matter chop, cut, cut off, deal with, decide, determine, do the trick*, end, finish, knock off*, polish off*, put away, take care of; CONCEPTS 18,234 —Ant. begin, continue, start

disposition [n1] personal temperament bag*, being, bent, bias, cast, character, complexion, constitution, cup of tea*, druthers*, emotions, flash, frame of mind, groove*, habit, humor, identity, inclination, individualism, individuality, leaning, make-up, mind-set*, mood, nature, penchant, personality, predilection, predisposition, proclivity, proneness, propensity, readiness, spirit, stamp, temper, tendency, tenor, thing*, tone, type, vein; CONCEPT 411

disposition [n2] arrangement, management of a situation adjustment, classification, control, decision, direction, disposal, distribution, grouping, method, order, ordering, organization, placement, plan, regulation, sequence; CONCEPTS 6,660 —*Ant.* disarrangement, mismanagement

dispossess [v] *deprive* appropriate, eject, evict, expel, expropriate, oust, put out, throw into the street*; CONCEPTS 121,142

disproportion [n] *imbalance* asymmetry, difference, discrepancy, disparity, imparity, inadequacy, inequality, insufficiency, irregularity, lopsidedness, unevenness, unsuitableness; CONCEPTS 665,667 —*Ant.* balance, equality, evenness, parity, proportion

disproportionate [adj] *out of balance* asymmetric, excessive, incommensurate, inordinate, irregular, lopsided, nonsymmetrical, out of proportion, overbalanced, superfluous, too much, unequal, uneven, unreasonable, unsymmetrical; CONCEPTS 564,566,771 —*Ant.* balanced, equal, even, proportionate

disprove [v] *prove false* belie, blow sky high*, blow up*, break, confound, confute, contradict, contravene, controvert, deny, disconfirm, discredit, explode, expose, find unfounded, impugn, invalidate, knock bottom out of*, knock props out*, negate, negative, overthrow, overturn, poke holes in*, puncture, rebut, refute, set aside, shoot, shoot holes in*, tear down*, throw out, traverse, weaken; CONCEPT 58 —*Ant.* credit, prove, validate

disputable [adj] *debatable; open to discussion* arguable, controversial, doubtful, dubious, moot, mootable, problematic, questionable, uncertain; CONCEPTS 529,535 —*Ant.* inarguable, indisputable, unquestionable

disputation [n] *controversy* argumentation, debate, dialectic, dispute, dissension, forensic, mooting, polemics; CONCEPTS 278,532 —*Ant.* harmony

disputatious [adj] *argumentative* cantankerous, captious, caviling, contentious, controversial, dissentious, litigious, polemical, pugnacious, quarrelsome; CONCEPTS 401,542 —*Ant.* agreeable,*calm, peaceful

dispute [n] *argument* altercation, beef*, bickering, bone of contention*, brawl, broil, brouhaha, commotion, conflict, contention, controversy, debate, difference of opinion, disagreement, discord, discussion, dissension, disturbance, embroilment, falling-out, feud, fireworks*, flare-up, fracas, friction, fuss, hubbub, miff*, misunderstanding, polemic, quarrel, row, rumpus*, squabble, squall, strife, tiff, uproar, variance, words, wrangle; CONCEPTS 46,106,278 —*Ant.* agreement

dispute [v] *argue* agitate, altercate, bicker, brawl, bump heads*, canvass, challenge, clash, confute, contend, contest, contradict, controvert, debate, deny, disaffirm, discept, discuss, disprove, doubt, gainsay, hassle, have at*, impugn, jump on one's case*, kick around*, lock horns*, moot, negate, pick a bone*, quarrel, question, quibble, rebut, refute, squabble, take on, thrash out, toss around*, wrangle; CONCEPT 46 —*Ant.* agree, give in, go along

disqualification [n] *disability; rejection for participation* awkwardness, clumsiness, debarment, disenablement, disentitlement,

elimination, exclusion, incapacitation, incapacity, incompetence, incompetency, ineligibility, ineptitude, lack, unfitness, unproficiency; CONCEPT 630 —*Ant.* ability, aptitude, capability

disqualify [v] *be unfit for; be ineligible* bar, bate, debar, disable, disenable, disentitle, disfranchise, eighty-six*, except, exclude, impair, incapacitate, invalidate, nix*, not make the cut*, paralyze, preclude, prohibit, rule out, suspend, unfit, weaken; CONCEPTS 121,699 —*Ant.* allow, be eligible, capacitate, fit, permit, qualify

disquiet [n] *worry; mental upset* ailment, alarm, angst, anxiety, care, concern, concernment, disquietude, distress, disturbance, fear, ferment, foreboding, fretfulness, inquietude, nervousness, restiveness, restlessness, solicitude, storm, trouble, turmoil, uneasiness, unrest; CONCEPTS 410,532,690 —*Ant.* calm, collectedness, ease, peace

disquiet [v] *worry; make uneasy* agitate, annoy, bother, concern, discompose, distress, disturb, fluster, fret, harass, incommode, perplex, perturb, pester, plague, trouble, unhinge, unsettle, upset, vex; CONCEPTS 7,19 —*Ant.* calm, ease, please, settle, soothe

disquieting [adj] *upsetting* annoying, bothersome, disconcerting, distressing, disturbing, irritating, perplexing, perturbing, troublesome, troubling, unnerving, unsettling, vexing, worrying; CONCEPT 529 —*Ant.* calming, pleasing, settling, soothing

disregard [n] *ignoring* apathy, brush-off*, contempt, disdain, disesteem, disfavor, disinterest, disrespect, forgetting, heedlessness, inadvertence, inattention, indifference, insouciance, lassitude, lethargy, listlessness, neglect, neglecting, negligence, oblivion, omission, omitting, overlooking, oversight, scorn, slight, slighting, the cold shoulder*, unconcern, unmindfulness; CONCEPTS 30,633 —*Ant.* attention, esteem, honor, note, regard, respect

disregard [v] *ignore; make light of* blink at*, brush aside, brush away, brush off, coldshoulder*, contemn, despise, discount, disdain, disobey, disparage, fail, forget, have no use for*, laugh off*, leave out of account, let go, let off easy*, let pass*, live with*, look the other way*, miss, neglect, omit, overlook, overpass, pass over, pay no attention to, pay no heed to, pay no mind*, pooh-pooh*, scorn, shut eyes to*, slight, snub, take no notice of, tune out*, turn a blind eye*, turn a deaf ear*, vilipend, wink at*; CONCEPT 30 —*Ant.* attend, esteem, note, pay attention, regard, respect

disrepair [adj] *broken; deteriorated* busted*, damaged, dead, decayed, decrepit, down, kaput*, not functioning, on the blink*, on the fritz*, out of commission*, out of order, worn out, wracked*; CONCEPT 485 —*Ant.* good, unbroken

disrepair [n] *state of deterioration* collapse, decay, decrepitude, dilapidation, ruination; CONCEPT 230 —*Ant.* good condition, repair

disreputable [adj] *dishonorable, lowly* abject, bad, base, beggarly, cheap, contemptible, derogatory, despicable, discreditable, disgraceful, disorderly, dissolute, ignominious, in bad, infamous, inglorious, in low esteem, in the doghouse*, lewd, libidinous, licentious, mean, no good*, notorious, opprobrious, pitiable, scandalous, scurvy, shabby, shady, shameful, shocking, shoddy, sordid, sorry, unprincipled, vicious, vile; CONCEPT 404 —Ant. decent, ethical, honorable, principled, reputable, respected

disrepute [n] dishonor, shame blemish, blot, brand, cloud, discredit, disesteem, disfavor, disgrace, ignominy, ill fame, ill favor, ill repute, infamy, ingloriousness, notoriety, obloquy, odium, opprobrium, reproach, scandal, scar, slur, smear, spot, stain, stigma, taint, unpopularity; CONCEPT 411 —Ant. esteem, good reputation, honor

disrespect [n] disregard, rudeness toward someone boldness, coarseness, contempt, discourtesy, dishonor, flippancy, hardihood, impertinence, impiety, impoliteness, impudence, incivility, insolence, insolency, insolentness, irreverence, lack of respect, sacrilege, unmannerliness; CONCEPTS 29,633 —Ant. civility, esteem, honor, regard, respect, reverence

disrespectful [adj] insulting, rude aweless, bad-mannered, blasphemous, bold, cheeky*, contemptuous, discourteous, disgracious, flip*, flippant, fresh, ill-bred, ill-mannered, impertinent, impious, impolite, impudent, insolent, irreverent, misbehaved, nervy*, out-of-line*, profanatory, profane, sacrilegious, sassy*, saucy*, smart-alecky*, snippy*, uncivil, unfilial, ungracious; CONCEPTS 267,401 —Ant. civil, courteous, mannered, mannerly, nice, respectful

disrobe [v] take off one's clothes bare, denudate, denude, deprive, dismantle, divest, doff, husk*, peel*, remove, shed, shuck*, slip out of, strip, take it off, unbutton*, unclothe, uncover, undress; CONCEPT 167 —Ant. clothe, put on

disrupt [v1] upset, disorganize agitate, bollix, confuse, disarray, discombobulate, discompose, disorder, disturb, mess up, mix up, muck up*, muddle, muddy the waters*, psych out*, put off, rattle, rattle one's cage*, rummage, screw up*, shake, spoil, throw, unsettle, upset the apple cart*; CONCEPTS 16,84,234 —Ant. arrange, organize, ready

disrupt [v2] break, interrupt breach, break into, break up, fracture, hole, interfere with, intrude, obstruct, open, rupture, unsettle, upset; CONCEPTS 98,135

disruptive [adj] causing trouble, confusion disorderly, distracting, disturbing, obstreperous, off-base*, out-of-line*, out-of-order*, rowdy, troublemaking, troublesome, unruly, unsettling, upsetting; CONCEPTS 401,537 —Ant. calming, disciplined, settling, soothing, well-behaved

dissatisfaction [n] discontent, unhappiness annoyance, anxiety, aversion, boredom, chagrin, complaint, desolation, disapproval, discomfort, discouragement, disfavor, disgruntlement, disinclination, dislike, disliking, dismay, displeasure, disquiet, disrelish, distaste, distress, ennui, envy, exasperation, fretfulness, frustration, heartburn, hopelessness, indisposition, irritation, jealousy, lamentation, malcontent, malcontentment, oppression, querulousness, regret, resentment, trouble, uneasiness, weariness, worry; CONCEPTS 29,410 —Ant. contentment, happiness, pleasure, satisfaction

dissatisfactory [adj] unsatisfactory bad, damaged, deficient, disappointing, displeasing, distressing, inadequate, insufficient, junky*, lame,

mediocre, no good, not satisfying, not up to par*, offensive, poor, rotten, unacceptable, unsatisfying, unsuitable, unworthy, useless; CONCEPTS 529,558,570

dissatisfied [adj] discontented, unhappy annoyed, begrudging, bothered, complaining, crabby*, critical, disaffected, disappointed, disgruntled, displeased, ennuied, envious, faultfinding, fed-up*, fretful, fretting, frustrated, griping, grudging, grumbling, grumpy*, insatiable, irked, jaundiced, jealous, kvetching*, malcontent, malcontented, not satisfied, offended, picky, plaintive, put-out*, querulous, sniveling, sulky, sullen, unappeased, unassuaged, unfulfilled, ungratified, unsated, unsatisfied, vexed; CONCEPT 403 —Ant. contented, fulfilled, gratified, happy, pleased, satisfied

dissect [v1] cut up; take apart anatomize, break up, cut, dichotomize, disjoin, disjoint, dislimb, dismember, dissever, divide, exscind, exsect, lay open, operate, part, prosect, quarter, section, sever, slice, sunder; CONCEPTS 98,176 —Ant. connect, join, mend, sew

dissect [v2] analyze anatomize, break down, decompose, decompound, examine, explore, inquire about, inspect, investigate, resolve, scrutinize, study; CONCEPT 24

dissection [n1] cutting up, particularly of a dead body anatomization, anatomy, autopsy, dismemberment, examination, necropsy, operation, postmortem, vivisection; CONCEPTS 176,310 —Ant. connection, joining, mending, sewing

dissection [n2] thorough analysis breakdown, breakup, criticism, critique, examination, inquest, inspection, investigation, resolution, review, scrutiny, study; CONCEPTS 24,290

dissemble [v] disguise, pretend affect, camouflage, cloak, conceal, counterfeit, cover, cover up, dissimulate, doublespeak*, double-talk*, dress up, fake, falsify, feign, four-flush*, hide, let on*, make like*, mask, pass, play possum*, pussyfoot*, put on a false front*, put on a front*, put on an act*, put up a front*, put up a smoke screen*, sham*, shroud, shuck and jive*, signify, simulate, stonewall*, whitewash*; CONCEPTS 59,188,716 —Ant. admit, allow

disseminate [v] distribute, scatter advertise, announce, annunciate, blaze, blazon, broadcast, circulate, declare, diffuse, disject, disperse, dissipate, proclaim, promulgate, propagate, publicize, publish, radiate, sow, spread, strew; CONCEPTS 108,140,201,222 —Ant. collect, gather

dissemination [n] distribution airing, broadcasting, circulation, diffusion, dissipation, promulgation, propagation, publication, publishing, spread; CONCEPTS 651,746 —Ant. collection, gathering

dissension [n] conflict of opinion altercation, argument, bad vibes*, bickering, clinker*, contention, controversy, difference, disaccord, disagreement, discord, discordance, dispute, dissent, dissidence, disunity, faction, factionalism, flak*, friction, fuss, quarrel, scene, sour note*, static, strife, trouble, variance, wrangle; CONCEPTS 46,278,665 —Ant. agreement, approval, authorization, concurrence, confirmation, peace, ratification

dissent [n] *disagreement, disapproval* bone*, bone of contention*, bone to pick*, clinker*, conflict, contention, denial, difference, disaccord, discord, dissension, dissidence, disunity, far cry*, flak*, hassle, heresy, heterodoxy, misbelief, nonagreement, nonconcurrence, nonconformism, nonconformity, nope*, objection, opposition, poles apart*, protest, refusal, resistance, schism, sour note*, spat, split, strife, unorthodoxy, variance; CONCEPTS 29,665,689 —*Ant.* agreement, approval, authorization, concurrence, endorsement, ratification, sanction

dissent [v] *disagree* argue, balk, break with, buck, contradict, decline, demur, differ, disaccord, discord, divide, fly in the face of*, object, oppose, pettifog, protest, put up a fight*, put up an argument, refuse, say not a chance*, say nothing doing*, say no way*, shy, stickle, vary, wrangle; CONCEPTS 21,46 —*Ant.* agree, approve, assent, authorize, concur, consent, endorse, ratify, sanction

dissertation [n] *scholarly thesis* argumentation, commentary, critique, discourse, disputation, disquisition, essay, exposition, memoir, monograph, tractate, treatise; CONCEPTS 271,287

disservice [n] *unkindness* bad turn, detriment, disfavor, harm, hurt, injury, injustice, insult, outrage, prejudice, wrong; CONCEPTS 309,645, 674 —*Ant.* benevolence, favor, giving, good turn, kindness, service

dissidence [n] *difference of opinion* bad vibes*, contention, disaccord, disagreement, discordance, disharmony, dispeace, dispute, dissension, dissent, feud, heresy, heterodoxy, misbelief, nonconformism, nonconformity, rupture, schism, sour note*, strife, unorthodoxy; CONCEPTS 278,633,689 —*Ant.* agreement, harmony, peace

dissident [adj] *disagreeing, differing* discordant, dissentient, dissenting, heretical, heterodox, nonconformist, schismatic, sectarian, unorthodox; CONCEPT 403 —*Ant.* agreeing, conforming

dissident [n] *person who holds different belief* agitator, dissenter, heretic, misbeliever, nonconformist, protester, rebel, recusant, schismatic, schismatist, sectary, separatist; CONCEPTS 359,423 —*Ant.* yes-man

dissimilar [adj] *not alike; not capable of comparison* antithetical, antonymous, contradictory, contrary, disparate, distant, divergent, diverse, far cry*, heterogeneous, individual, like night and day*, march to a different drummer*, mismatched, mismated, not similar, offbeat, opposite, poles apart*, unequal, unique, unlike, unrelated, unsimilar, various, weird*; CONCEPT 564 —*Ant.* alike, compatible, equal, matched, related, same, similar

dissimilarity [n] *unlikeness* alterity, contrast, difference, discord, discordance, discrepancy, disparity, dissemblance, dissimilitude, distance, distinction, divarication, divergence, divergency, diversity, heterogeneity, incomparability, incongruity, inconsistency, inconsonance, nonuniformity, offset, otherness, separation, severance, unrelatedness, variance, variation; CONCEPT 665 —*Ant.* compatibility, equality, likeness, relatedness, sameness, similarity

dissimulate [v] *conceal, disguise* beard*,

camouflage, cloak, deceive, dissemble, dress up, fake, feign, hide, make-believe, mask, present a false face*, present a false front*, pretend; CONCEPTS 59,172,188 —*Ant.* be honest

dissipate [v1] *expend, spend* be wasteful with, blow*, burn up*, consume, deplete, dump*, fritter away, indulge oneself, kiss goodbye*, lavish, misspend, misuse, run through, squander, throw away, trifle away, use up, waste; CONCEPTS 156,169 —*Ant.* accumulate, collect, gather, hoard, save

dissipate [v2] *disappear* dispel, disperse, dissolve, drive away, evanesce, evaporate, melt away, run dry, scatter, spread, vanish; CONCEPTS 105,469 —*Ant.* appear

dissipated [adj1] *used up* blown, burnt out*, consumed, destroyed, exhausted, kaput*, played out*, scattered, spent, squandered, wasted; CONCEPTS 560,576 —*Ant.* accumulated, gathered, hoarded, saved, stored

dissipated [adj2] *self-indulgent* abandoned, corrupt, debauched, dissolute, gone bad*, gone to seed*, gone to the dogs*, hellbent*, intemperate, profligate, rakish, wicked; CONCEPTS 401,545 —*Ant.* conservative, unselfish, virtuous

dissipation [n1] *amusement, entertainment, occasionally to excess* bender*, binge, blowout, bust*, celebration, circus, distraction, diversion, divertissement, gratification, party, recreation, self-indulgence, tear*, toot*, wingding*; CONCEPTS 363,386

dissipation [n2] *wantonness* abandonment, debauchery, dissoluteness, dissolution, drunkenness, evil, excess, extravagance, free-living, high-living*, indulgence, intemperance, lavishness, life in the fast lane*, prodigality, profligacy, self-gratification, squandering, to hell in handbasket*, waste; CONCEPT 633 —*Ant.* unselfishness, virtue

dissipation [n3] *disappearance* diffusion, disintegration, dispersal, dispersion, dissemination, dissolution, distribution, emission, extravagance, improvidence, radiation, scattering, spread, vanishing, wastage, waste; CONCEPTS 230,651,720 —*Ant.* appearance

dissociate [v] *part company with; separate* abstract, alienate, break off, detach, disassociate, disband, disconnect, disengage, disjoin, disperse, disrupt, distance, disunite, divide, divorce, estrange, isolate, quit, scatter, segregate, set apart, uncouple, unfix; CONCEPTS 135,384 —*Ant.* associate, attach, join

dissociation [n] *detachment, separation* break, disconnection, disengagement, disjunction, distancing, disunion, division, divorce, isolation, segregation, severance; CONCEPT 388 —*Ant.* association, attachment, connection, union

dissolute [adj] *lacking restraint, indulgent* abandoned, corrupt, debauched, degenerate, depraved, dissipated, evil, fast*, fast and loose*, gone bad*, high living*, intemperate, in the fast lane*, lascivious, lax, lecherous, lewd, libertine, licentious, light, loose*, nighthawk*, night owl*, on the take*, open, player*, profligate, raffish, rakish, reprobate, slack, swift, sybaritic, unconstrained, unprincipled, unrestrained, vicious, wanton, wayward, wicked, wild; CONCEPTS 401,545 —*Ant.* chaste, good, moral, pure, resolute, respectful, virtuous

dissolution [n1] *separation, rupture* breaking up, detachment, disintegration, disunion, division, divorce, divorcement, parting, partition, resolution, split-up; CONCEPTS 230,388 —*Ant.* combination, connection, solution, unification

dissolution [n2] *death; destruction* adjournment, conclusion, curtains, decay, decease, decomposition, defunction, demise, disappearance, disbandment, discontinuation, dismissal, dispersal, end, ending, evaporation, extinction, finish, liquefaction, melting, overthrow, passing, quietus, release, resolution, ruin, silence, sleep, solution, suspension, termination; CONCEPTS 105,304,469,703 —*Ant.* beginning, commencement, construction, start

dissolve [v1] *melt from solid to liquid; mix* in defront, deliquesce, diffuse, fluidify, flux, fuse, liquefy, liquesce, render, run, soften, thaw, waste away; CONCEPTS 469,702 —*Ant.* coagulate, concentrate, solidify, unmix

dissolve [v2] *disappear, disintegrate* break down, break into pieces, break up, crumble, decline, decompose, diffuse, dilapidate, disband, disperse, dissipate, dwindle, evanesce, evaporate, fade, melt away, perish, separate, unmake, vanish, waste away; CONCEPTS 105,469 —*Ant.* appear, assemble, integrate, put together, unite

dissolve [v3] *annul, discontinue* abrogate, adjourn, annihilate, break up, cancel, collapse, decimate, demolish, destroy, destruct, discharge, dismiss, disorganize, disunite, divorce, do away with, end, eradicate, invalidate, loose, overthrow, postpone, put an end to, quash, render void, repeal, resolve into, ruin, separate, sever, shatter, shoot, suspend, terminate, unmake, vacate, void, wind up, wrack, wreck; CONCEPTS 121,234,252 —*Ant.* continue, marry, resolve

dissonance [n1] *disagreement* antagonism, conflict, contention, controversy, difference, disaccord, discord, discrepancy, disharmony, disparity, dissension, dissidence, incongruity, inconsistency, strife, variance; CONCEPTS 278,665,689 —*Ant.* agreement, concord, harmony

dissonance [n2] *noise, discord* cacophony, harshness, jangle, jarring, unmelodiousness; CONCEPT 595 —*Ant.* accord, consonance, harmony, peacefulness, resonance

dissonant [adj1] *different, conflicting* anomalous, at variance, differing, disagreeing, disconsonant, discordant, discrepant, dissentient, incompatible, incongruent, incongruous, inconsistent, inconsonant, irreconcilable, irregular, sour note*, unmixable; CONCEPT 564 —*Ant.* coinciding, compatible, complementary, consonant, similar

dissonant [adj2] *unharmonious* cacophonic, cacophonous, discordant, disharmonic, disharmonious, grating, harsh, inharmonic, inharmonious, jangling, jarring, out of tune, raucous, strident, tuneless, unmelodious, unmusical; CONCEPTS 592,594 —*Ant.* concordant, harmonious

dissuade [v] *talk out of* advise against, caution against, chicken out*, counsel, cry out against, deprecate, derail, deter, disadvise, discourage, disincline, divert, exhort, expostulate, faze, hinder, lean on*, persuade not to, prevent, prick, put off, remonstrate, throw a wet blanket on*, throw cold water on*, throw off, thwart,

turn off*, urge not to, warn; CONCEPTS 68,78 —*Ant.* incite, persuade, talk into

distance [n1] *interval, range* absence, ambit, amplitude, area, bit, breadth, compass, country mile*, expanse, extension, extent, farness, far piece*, gap, good ways*, heavens, hinterland, horizon, lapse, length, objective, orbit, outpost, outskirts, provinces, purlieu, purview, radius, reach, remoteness, remove, scope, separation, size, sky, space, span, spread, stretch, sweep, way, width; CONCEPTS 651,739,790

distance [n2] *aloofness* coldness, coolness, frigidity, reserve, restraint, stiffness; CONCEPT 633 —*Ant.* affection, friendliness, sympathy, warmth

distance [v] *dissociate oneself; leave behind* break away from the pack, outdo, outpace, outrun, outstrip, pass, put in proportion, separate oneself; CONCEPT 195 —*Ant.* associate, be friendly, go to

distant [adj1] *faraway* abroad, abstracted, apart, a piece, arm's length*, asunder, away, backwoods, beyond range, far, far back, far-flung, far-off, farther, further, inaccessible, indirect, in the background, in the boonies*, in the distance, in the sticks*, isolated, middle of nowhere*, not home*, obscure, outlying, out of earshot*, out of range, out of reach, out-of-the-way, remote, removed, retired, secluded, secret, separate, sequestered, telescopic, unapproachable, ways*, wide of*, yonder*; CONCEPTS 576,778 —*Ant.* adjacent, close, near, nearby, open

distant [adj2] *aloof* arrogant, ceremonious, cold, cool, formal, haughty, insociable, laid back, modest, offish, on ice*, proud, put on airs*, remote, reserved, restrained, reticent, retiring, shy, solitary, standoff, standoffish, stiff, stuck-up*, unapproachable, uncompanionable, unconcerned, unfriendly, unsociable, uppity*, withdrawn; CONCEPTS 401,404 —*Ant.* friendly, kind, sympathetic, warm

distaste [n] *dislike, hate* abhorrence, antipathy, aversion, detestation, disfavor, disgust, disinclination, displeasure, disrelish, dissatisfaction, hatred, horror, hostility, indisposition, loathing, repugnance, repulsion, revolt, revulsion; CONCEPT 29 —*Ant.* desire, like, love, loving

distasteful [adj] *repulsive, unpleasant* abhorrent, abominable, afflicting, bitter, detestable, disagreeable, dislikable, displeasing, flat, flavorless, galling, grievous, grody*, gross*, hateful, icky*, insipid, loathsome, nauseous, objectionable, obnoxious, odious, offensive, painful, repellent, repugnant, savorless, tasteless, unappetizing, undesirable, uninviting, unlikable, unpalatable, unsavory, yicky*, yucky*; CONCEPTS 529,589,613 —*Ant.* agreeable, delectable, delicious, palatable, pleasant, pleasing

distend [v] *bulge, swell* amplify, augment, balloon, bloat, dilate, distort, enlarge, expand, increase, inflate, lengthen, puff, stretch, widen; CONCEPTS 157,469,780 —*Ant.* cave in, contract, deflate, fall, shrink

distended [adj] *swollen* bloated, bulging, enlarged, expanded, inflated, puffed out, puffy, stretched, tumescent, tumid, turgid; CONCEPT 485

distill [v] *make pure; draw out something* boil

down, brew, clarify, concentrate, condense, cook, cut, cut down, cut to the bone*, dribble, drip, drop, evaporate, express, extract, ferment, get to the meat*, infuse, precipitate, press, press out, purify, rarefy, rectify, refine, squeeze out, steam, sublimate, trickle, trim, vaporize, volatilize; CONCEPTS 165,170,211,219 —*Ant.* dirty, pollute

distillation [n] *distillate* cleansing, purification, refining; CONCEPTS 165,367

distinct [adj1] *apparent, obvious* audible, categorical, clean-cut, clear, clear-cut, decided, definite, enunciated, evident, explicit, express, incisive, lucid, manifest, marked, noticeable, palatable, patent, perspicuous, plain, prescribed, recognizable, sharp, sharp-cut, specific, transparent, trenchant, unambiguous, unequivocal, unmistakable, well-defined; CONCEPTS 535, 591,619 —*Ant.* ambiguous, fuzzy, hazy, indistinct, obscure, undefined, vague

distinct [adj2] *different; unconnected* detached, discrete, disparate, dissimilar, distinctive, disunited, divergent, diverse, especial, individual, offbeat, particular, peculiar, poles apart*, separate, separated, several, single, sole, special, specific, unassociated, unattached, unique, various; CONCEPT 564 —*Ant.* connected, like, resembling, similar

distinction [n1] *differentiation; feature* acumen, acuteness, alterity, analysis, characteristic, clearness, contrast, diagnosis, difference, differential, discernment, discrepancy, discreteness, discretion, discrimination, dissemblance, dissimilarity, dissimilitude, divergence, divergency, division, earmark, estimation, individuality, judgment, mark, marking, nicety, otherness, particularity, peculiarity, penetration, perception, qualification, quality, refinement, sensitivity, separation, sharpness, tact, unlikeness; CONCEPTS 411,665

distinction [n2] *prominence; achievement* accolade, account, award, badge, bays, celebrity, consequence, credit, decoration, eminence, excellence, fame, flair, greatness, illustriousness, importance, kudos, laurels, manner, merit, name, note, perfection, preeminence, prestige, quality, rank, renown, reputation, repute, style, superiority, worth; CONCEPTS 388,671,706 —*Ant.* insignificance, lowliness, mediocrity, unimportance

distinctive [adj] *different, unique* characteristic, cool, diacritic, diagnostic, discrete, distinguishing, excellent, extraordinary, far cry, gnarly*, idiosyncratic, individual, like night and day*, offbeat, original, outstanding, peculiar, perfect, poles apart*, proper, separate, single, singular, special, superior, typical, uncommon, unreal, weird, wicked; CONCEPTS 564,574 —*Ant.* common, normal, resembling, same, similar, standard

distinguish [v1] *tell the difference* analyze, ascertain, categorize, characterize, classify, collate, decide, demarcate, determinate, determine, diagnose, diagnosticate, differentiate, discriminate, divide, estimate, extricate, figure out, finger*, identify, individualize, individuate, judge, know, label, make out, mark, mark off, name, part, pinpoint, place, qualify, recognize, select, separate, set apart, set off, sift, signalize, single out, singularize, sort out, specify, spot,

tag, tell apart, tell between, tell from; CONCEPTS 15,18,38

distinguish [v2] *discern, identify* beam*, catch, descry, detect, dig, discover, discriminate, eye, eyeball*, flash*, focus, get a load of*, get an eyeful*, know, make out, mark, note, notice, observe, perceive, pick out, pick up on*, read, recognize, remark, see, spot, spy, take in, tell, view; CONCEPTS 38,626

distinguish [v3] *make famous* acknowledge, admire, celebrate, dignify, honor, immortalize, pay tribute to, praise, signalize; CONCEPT 69

distinguished [adj] *famous, outstanding* acclaimed, aristocratic, arresting, big name*, brilliant, celebrated, conspicuous, dignified, distingué, eminent, especial, esteemed, extraordinary, famed, foremost, glorious, great, highly regarded, honored, illustrious, imposing, marked, memorable, name, noble, nonpareil, notable, noted, noteworthy, peerless, prominent, remarkable, renowned, reputable, royal, salient, shining, signal, singular, special, stately, striking, superior, talked of, unforgettable, venerable, well-known; CONCEPT 574 —*Ant.* common, insignificant, ordinary, standard, unextraordinary, unknown

distort [v] *deform; falsify* alter, angle, belie, bend, bias, buckle, change, collapse, color, con, contort, crush, curve, deceive, decline, deteriorate, deviate, disfigure, doctor*, fake, fudge*, garble, gnarl, knot, lie, make out like, mangle, melt, misconstrue, misinterpret, misrepresent, misshape, pervert, phony up*, put one on, sag, scam*, slant, slump, snow*, torture, trump up*, twist, warp, whitewash*, wind, wrench, writhe; CONCEPTS 63,137,232, 250 —*Ant.* beautify, shape nicely, straight

distortion [n] *deformity; falsification* baloney*, bend, bias, BS*, buckle, coloring, contortion, crock, crookedness, exaggeration, intorsion, jazz*, jive*, lie, line, malconformation, malformation, misinterpretation, misrepresentation, misshape, misstatement, misuse, mutilation, perversion, slant, smoke*, story*, tall story*, torture, twist, twistedness, warp; CONCEPTS 63,580 —*Ant.* beauty, clarity, perfection

distract [v] *divert attention; confuse* abstract, addle, agitate, amuse, befuddle, beguile, bewilder, call away, catch flies*, confound, derange, detract, discompose, disconcert, disturb, divert, draw away, engross, entertain, fluster, frenzy, harass, lead astray*, lead away, madden, mislead, mix up, occupy, perplex, puzzle, sidetrack, stall, throw off*, torment, trouble, turn aside, unbalance, unhinge*; CONCEPTS 14,16 —*Ant.* clarify, explain

distraction [n] *having one's attention drawn away* aberration, abstraction, agitation, amusement, beguilement, bewilderment, commotion, complication, confusion, disorder, dissipation, disturbance, diversion, divertissement, engrossment, entertainment, frenzy, game, interference, interruption, pastime, perplexity, preoccupation, recreation; CONCEPTS 293,410,532,690

distraught [adj] *very upset, worked-up* addled, agitated, anxious, beside oneself, bothered, concerned, confused, crazed*, crazy, discomposed, distracted, distrait, distressed, flustered, frantic, harassed, hysterical, in a panic, like a chicken with its head cut off*, mad, muddled, non-plussed, nuts*, out of one's mind*, over-wrought, perturbed, rattled, raving, shook up, thrown*, tormented, troubled, unglued*, un-screwed*, unzipped*, wild, worried; CONCEPTS 401,403,690 —**Ant.** calm, gladdened, happy, pleased, untroubled

distress [n1] *pain, agony* ache, affliction, anguish, anxiety, bad news*, blues*, care, concern, cross, dejection, desolation, disap-pointment, discomfort, disquietude, dolor, embarrassment, grief, headache, heartache, heartbreak, irritation, malaise, misery, mortifica-tion, ordeal, pang, perplexity, sadness, shame, sorrow, stew, suffering, throe, torment, torture, trial, tribulation, trouble, twinge, unconsolabil-ity, unhappiness, vexation, visitation, woe, worriment, worry, wretchedness; CONCEPTS 410, 532 —**Ant.** comfort, happiness, health, pleasure

distress [n2] *hardship, adversity* bad luck, bummer*, calamity, can of worms*, catastro-phe, crunch*, destitution, difficulty, disaster, downer*, drag*, exigency, hard knocks*, hard time*, holy mess*, hot water*, indigence, jam*, misfortune, need, pickle*, pinch*, poverty, privation, rigor, rotten luck*, scrape*, straits, throe, ticklish spot*, tough break*, tough luck*, trial, trouble, unholy mess*, vicissitude, want; CONCEPT 674 —**Ant.** advantage, benefit, miracle

distress [v] *worry, upset* afflict, aggrieve, ago-nize, ail, be on one's case*, bother, break, bug, burn up, depress, desolate, discombobulate*, disquiet, disturb, do a number on*, dog*, eat*, get*, get to*, give a hard time*, grieve, harass, harry, hound, hurt, injure, irk, irritate, make it tough for*, miff, nag, needle, nit-pick, oppress, pain, peeve, perplex, pester, pick on, plague, push, push buttons*, rack, sadden, strain, strap, stress, tick off*, torment, torture, trouble, try, vex, weigh, wound; CONCEPTS 7,19,313 —**Ant.** assist, calm, comfort, help, soothe

distressed [adj] *upset* afflicted, agitated, all torn up*, antsy, anxious, basket case*, both-ered, bugged, bummed out*, bundle of nerves*, concerned, cut up*, discombobulated*, discon-solate, distracted, distrait, distraught, dragged, exercised, fidgety, harassed, hyper*, in a stew*, in a tizzy*, inconsolable, jittery, jumpy, miffed, peeved, perturbed, ripped*, saddened, shaky, shook*, shook up*, shot down*, spooked*, strung out*, tormented, troubled, unconsolable, unglued*, up the wall*, uptight*, wired, wor-ried, wrecked*, wretched; CONCEPT 403 —**Ant.** calm, collected, comforted, glad, happy, joyful

distress signal [n] *alarm* burglar alarm, call for help*, danger signal, fire alarm, mayday, SOS, warning signal; CONCEPTS 269,463

distribute [v1] *allocate, deliver, spread* admin-ister, allot, apportion, appropriate, assign, bestow, circulate, consign, convey, cut up, deal, deal out, diffuse, disburse, dish out*, dispense, disperse, dispose, disseminate, divide, divvy up*, dole out*, donate, endow, fork out*, give, give away, hand out, issue, lot out, measure out, mete, parcel, partition, pass out, pay out, present, prorate, radiate, ration, scatter, share, shell out*, slice up, sow, strew; CONCEPTS 98,140,217 —**Ant.** collect, gather, hoard, hold, keep, maintain, preserve, store

distribute [v2] *classify* arrange, assort, catego-rize, class, file, group, order; CONCEPT 84

distribution [n1] *allocation, dispersion* admin-istration, alloting, allotment, apportioning, apportionment, assessment, assigning, circulat-ing, circulation, dealing, delivery, diffusion, dispensation, dispersal, disposal, disposing, dissemination, dissipating, division, dole, hand-ing out, handling, mailing, marketing, partition, partitioning, propagation, prorating, rationing, scattering, sharing, spreading, trading, trans-port, transportation; CONCEPTS 98,140,217 —**Ant.** collection, gathering, hoard, hoarding, maintenance, store

distribution [n2] *classification* arrangement, assortment, disposal, disposition, grouping, location, order, ordering, organization, placement, sequence; CONCEPTS 109,727

distributor [n] *wholesaler* dealer, jobber, merchandiser, middleperson, salesperson, trader; CONCEPT 347

district [n] *geographical area* commune, com-munity, department, locale, locality, neck of the woods*, neighborhood, parcel, parish, precinct, quarter, region, section, sector, stomping ground*, territory, turf*, vicinage, vicinity, ward; CONCEPT 508

distrust [n] *lack of faith in something* disbelief, doubt, misdoubt, misgiving, mistrust, qualm, question, skepticism, suspicion, wariness; CONCEPTS 21,689 —**Ant.** assurance, belief, certainty, confidence, credit, faith, surety, trust

distrust [v] *be suspicious, skeptical of* be wary of, disbelieve, discredit, doubt, misbelieve, mistrust, question, smell a rat*, suspect, wonder about; CONCEPT 21 —**Ant.** be confident, believe, credit, trust

distrustful [adj] *disbelieving* been hit before*, cagey, cautious, chary, cynical, doubtful, doubt-ing, dubious, fearful, jealous, leery, mistrustful, skeptical, suspicious, uneasy, uptight, wary; CONCEPTS 403,542 —**Ant.** assured, believing, certain, faithful, trustful, trusting, unsuspecting

disturb [v1] *bother, upset* afflict, agitate, ail, alarm, amaze, annoy, arouse, astound, badger, burn up*, complicate, confound, confuse, de-press, discompose, dishearten, disrupt, distract, distress, excite, fluster, frighten, gall, grieve, harass, interfere, interrupt, intrude, irk, irritate, make uneasy, molest, muddle, outrage, pain, perplex, perturb, pester, pique, plague, provoke, puzzle, rattle, rouse, ruffle, shake, shake up*, startle, tire, trouble, unhinge*, unnerve, unset-tle, vex, worry; CONCEPTS 7,19 —**Ant.** appease, calm, comfort, pacify, quiet, reassure, soothe

disturb [v2] *disorder; dislocate* confuse, derange, disarrange, disarray, discompose, disorganize, displace, distort, foul up*, inter-fere, jumble, louse up*, mess up, mix up, move, muddle, remove, replace, shift, tamper, unsettle, upset; CONCEPTS 84,137,250 —**Ant.** arrange, locate, order, organize, sort

disturbance [n] *commotion; upset* agitation, annoyance, big scene*, big stink*, bother, brawl, brouhaha, clamor, confusion, convul-sion, derangement, disarrangement, disorder, disruption, distraction, eruption, explosion, ferment, fisticuffs, flap, fracas, fray, fuss, hindrance, hubbub, hullabaloo*, insurrection, interruption, intrusion, molestation, perturbation, quake, quarrel, racket, rampage, restlessness, riot, ruckus, rumble, shock, spasm, stink*, stir*, storm, to-do*, tremor, tumult, turmoil, upheaval, uprising, uproar, violence; CONCEPTS 388,410,674,720 —Ant. calm, order, peace, quiet, tranquility

ditch [n] *gulley* canal, channel, chase, cut, dike, drain, excavation, furrow, gutter, mine, moat, trench, watercourse; CONCEPTS 509,513

ditch [v] *get rid of* abandon, desert, discard, dispose of, drop, dump*, eighty-six*, forsake, jettison, junk*, leave, reject, scrap*, throw away, throw out, throw overboard*; CONCEPT 180 —Ant. pick up

ditsy [adj] *silly* airbrained, airheaded, daffy*, dippy*, dipsy*, dizzy*, dopey, eccentric, empty, giddy, goofy*, inane, kooky*, rattlebrained, scatterbrained; CONCEPTS 314,401

ditto [n] *the same; duplicate* clone, copy, double, duplication, facsimile, likewise, reproduction, the above, the very words*; CONCEPTS 664,667,716

ditty [n] *song* ballad, composition, jingle, tune; CONCEPT 595

ditz [n] *scatterbrain* airbrain, airhead, birdbrain*, dingbat*, fluffhead*, ninny, rattlebrain, silly person, space case; CONCEPTS 412,423

diva [n] *prima donna* famous singer, lead singer, opera singer; CONCEPT 352

dive [n1] *descent, usually underwater* belly flop*, dash, dip, duck, ducking, fall, header* headlong* jump, leap, lunge, nosedive, pitch, plunge, spring, submergence, submersion, swoop; CONCEPTS 147,181 —Ant. ascent, jump

dive [n2] *dirty, sleazy establishment* bar, barroom, beer garden* cabaret, dump, flea trap*, flophouse*, hangout, hole, honky-tonk*, joint, lounge, night club, pool hall, pub, saloon, taproom, tavern; CONCEPT 449

dive [v] *descend, usually going underwater* belly flop*, dip, disappear, drop, duck, fall, go headfirst, gutter, header*, jump, leap, lunge, nose-dive, pitch, plumb, plummet, plunge, spring, submerge, swoop, vanish, vault; CONCEPTS 147,181,194 —Ant. ascend, go up, jump

diverge [v1] *go in different directions* bend, bifurcate, branch, branch off, depart, deviate, digress, divagate, divaricate, divide, excurse, fork, part, radiate, ramble, separate, split, spread, stray, swerve, veer, wander; CONCEPTS 195,738 —Ant. agree, converge, join, parallel

diverge [v2] *be different from; be at odds* argue, conflict, contrast, depart, deviate, differ, digress, disagree, disapprove, dissent, oppose, stray, swerve, turn aside, vary, wander; CONCEPTS 46,665 —Ant. agree, concur

divergence [n] *branching out; difference* aberration, alteration, alterity, crotch, deflection, departure, detour, deviation, digression, disagreeing, discrepancy, disparity, dissemblance, dissimilarity, dissimilitude, distinction, divagation, divergency, diversity, division, fork, mutation, otherness, parting, radiation, ramification, separation, turning, unlikeness, variety, varying; CONCEPTS 665,738 —Ant. accord, agreement, concord, convergence, harmony, sameness

divergent [adj] *differing* aberrant, abnormal, anomalous, antithetical, atypical, conflicting, contradictory, contrary, deviating, different, disagreeing, disparate, dissimilar, dissonant, distant, diverging, diverse, factional, factious, irregular, off-key, opposite, poles apart*, separate, unalike, unequal, unlike, unnatural, unsimilar, untypical, variant, various; CONCEPT 564 —Ant. agreeing, convergent, similar

diverse [adj] *different; various* assorted, contradictory, contrary, contrasted, contrasting, contrastive, differing, discrete, disparate, dissimilar, distant, distinct, divergent, diversified, diversiform, incommensurable, like night and day*, manifold, miscellaneous, mixed bag*, multifarious, opposite, separate, several, sundry, unalike, unequal, unlike, varied, varying; CONCEPTS 564,772 —Ant. alike, conforming, identical, like, parallel, similar, uniform

diversify [v] *spread out; branch out* alter, assort, change, expand, mix, modify, transform, variegate, vary; CONCEPTS 232,697 —Ant. conform, stay same, unvary

diversion [n1] *change in a course, path* aberration, alteration, deflection, departure, detour, deviation, digression, divergence, fake out*, red herring*, turning, variation; CONCEPTS 501, 738 —Ant. conforming, staying

diversion [n2] *entertainment, recreation* amusement, ball, beguilement, delectation, delight, disport, dissipation, distraction, divertissement, enjoyment, field day*, frivolity, fun, fun and games*, game, gratification, grins*, high time*, hoopla*, laughs*, levity, merry-go-round*, pastime, picnic*, play, pleasure, relaxation, relish, sport, whoopee*; CONCEPTS 292,363,386 —Ant. chore, task, vocation, work

diversity [n] *variety, difference* assortment, dissimilarity, distinction, distinctiveness, divergence, diverseness, diversification, heterogeneity, medley, mixed bag*, multeity, multifariousness, multiformity, multiplicity, range, unlikeness, variance, variegation, variousness; CONCEPTS 651,665 —Ant. identicalness, sameness, similarity, uniformity

divert [v1] *turn a different direction* alter, avert, change, deflect, modify, pivot, redirect, sheer, swerve, switch, turn aside, veer, volte-face, wheel, whip, whirl; CONCEPTS 187,213 —Ant. be direct, keep to, maintain, stay

divert [v2] *amuse, entertain* beguile, break one up*, delight, fracture one*, get one's jollies*, gladden, gratify, knock 'em dead*, make happy, panic, please, put 'em away*, recreate, regale, relax, slay, tickle, wow; CONCEPT 9 —Ant. anger, irritate, make mad, upset

divert [v3] *take attention away* abstract, attract attention, bend the rules*, catch flies*, circumlocute, detach, deter, detract, disadvise, discourage, disengage, dissuade, distract, disturb, draw away, get around, lead astray, lead away, send on a wild-goose chase*, sidetrack, stall; CONCEPTS 7,19,22

divest [v] *dispossess; take off* bankrupt, bare, bereave, bleed, denudate, denude, deprive, despoil, disinherit, dismantle, disrobe, ditch*, doff, dump*, eighty-six*, lose, milk*, oust, plunder, remove, rob, seize, spoil, strip, take from, unclothe, uncover, undress, unload; CONCEPTS

139,142,211 —*Ant.* clothe, cover, invest, possess, take

divide [*v1*] *separate, disconnect* abscind, bisect, branch, break, break down, carve, chop, cleave, cross, cut, cut up, demarcate, detach, dichotomize, disengage, disentangle, disjoin, dislocate, dismember, dissect, dissever, dissociate, dissolve, disunite, divorce, halve, intersect, isolate, loose, part, partition, pull away, quarter, rend, rupture, section, segment, segregate, sever, shear, split, subdivide, sunder, tear, unbind, undo; CONCEPTS *98,135,137* —*Ant.* append, attach, collect, combine, connect, couple, gather, join, link, unite

divide [*v2*] *distribute* allocate, allot, apportion, articulate, cut, cut in*, cut one in*, cut up, deal, deal out, disburse, dish out*, dispense, disperse, divvy up*, dole out*, factor, fork out*, go fifty-fifty*, hand out, hand over, lot out, measure out, parcel, partition, piece up, portion, prorate, quota, ration, share, shell out*, shift, slice, slice up, split up; CONCEPTS *98,140* —*Ant.* hold, keep, maintain, retain

divide [*v3*] *put in order; classify* arrange, categorize, grade, group, separate, sort; CONCEPT *84* —*Ant.* disarrange, disorganize

divide [*v4*] *disagree, alienate* break up, cause to disagree, come between, differ, disaccord, dissent, disunite, estrange, part, pit against, separate, set against, set at odds*, sow dissension*, split, vary; CONCEPTS *46,266* —*Ant.* agree, convince, persuade

dividend [*n*] *one's share, profit* allotment, allowance, appropriation, bonus, carrot*, check, coupon, cut*, dispensation, divvy*, extra, gain, gravy*, guerdon, interest, lagniappe*, meed, pay, portion, premium, prize, proceeds, remittance, returns, reward, surplus, taste*; CONCEPTS *337,344* —*Ant.* loss

divination [*n*] *fortune-telling* augury, clairvoyancy, horoscope, occultism, palmistry, prediction, premonition, prognostication, prophecy, soothsaying; CONCEPTS *70,278,689*

divine [*adj*] *godlike, perfect* all-powerful, almighty, ambrosial, angelic, beatific, beautiful, blissful, celestial, consecrated, deific, deistic, eternal, exalted, excellent, glorious, godly, hallowed, heavenly, holy, immaculate, magnificent, marvelous, mystical, omnipotent, omnipresent, omniscient, rapturous, religious, sacramental, sacred, sacrosanct, sanctified, spiritual, splendid, superhuman, superlative, supernatural, supreme, theistic, transcendent, transcendental, transmundane, unearthly, wonderful; CONCEPTS *568,574*

divine [*v*] *prophesy* anticipate, apprehend, conjecture, deduce, discern, forebode, forefeel, foreknow, foresee, foretell, go out on a limb*, guess, infer, intuit, perceive, predict, previse, prognosticate, see, see in the cards*, suppose, surmise, suspect, take a shot*, take a stab*, understand, visualize; CONCEPT *28*

divinity [*n*] *absolute being; divine nature* celestial, deity, genius, god, goddess, godhead, godhood, godliness, godship, guardian spirit, higher power, holiness, lord, prime mover, sanctity, spirit; CONCEPTS *368,370* —*Ant.* devil, evil

division [*n1*] *separation, disconnection* analysis, apportionment, autopsy, bisection, break-

ing, breaking down, breaking up, carving, contrasting, cutting up, demarcation, departmentalizing, detaching, detachment, diagnosis, disjuncture, dismemberment, disparting, disseverance, dissolution, distinguishing, distribution, disunion, disuniting, dividing, divorce, parceling, parting, partition, reduction, rending, rupture, segmentation, selection, separating, severance, splitting up, subdivision, vivisection; CONCEPTS *98,135* —*Ant.* accord, agreement, connection, unification, unison, unity

division [*n2*] *something produced from separating* affiliate, associate, border, boundary, branch, category, chunk, class, compartment, cut, degree, demarcation, department, divide, dividend, divider, dividing line, divvy*, end, fraction, fragment, grouping, head, kind, lobe, lump, member, moiety, offshoot, parcel, partition, piece, piece of action*, portion, rake-off*, ramification, section, sector, segment, share, slice, sort, split, subdivision, wedge; CONCEPTS *378,382,710,835* —*Ant.* system, whole

division [*n3*] *breach, estrangement* conflict, difference of opinion, difficulty, disaccord, disagreement, discord, disharmony, dispute, dissension, dissent, dissidence, dissonance, disunion, feud, rupture, split, trouble, variance, words; CONCEPT *388* —*Ant.* agreement, juncture, unification

divisive [*ad*] *dissenting* alienating, at odds, discordant, disruptive; CONCEPTS *401,537*

divorce [*n*] *split-up of marriage* annulment, breach, break, breakup, decree nisi, dedomiciling, detachment, disparateness, dissociation, dissolution, disunion, division, divorcement, on the rocks*, parting of the ways*, partition, rupture, separate maintenance, separation, severance, split, splitsville*; CONCEPT *297* —*Ant.* marriage

divorce [*v*] *split up a marriage* annul, break up, cancel, disconnect, disjoin, dissever, dissociate, dissolve, disunite, divide, nullify, part, put away, separate, sever, split, sunder, unmarry; CONCEPT *297* —*Ant.* marry

divulge [*v*] *make known; confess* admit, betray, blab, blow the whistle*, broadcast, communicate, cough up*, declare, disclose, discover, exhibit, expose, fess up*, give away, go public*, gossip, impart, leak, let hair down*, let slip*, mouth, open up*, own up*, proclaim, promulgate, publish, reveal, spill, spill the beans*, spring, tattle, tell, tip off*, uncover; CONCEPT *60* —*Ant.* conceal, hide, keep, secrete

divvy up [*v*] *divide* allocate, apportion, cut, cut up the pie*, dole out, go halves*, measure out, mete out, share, split; CONCEPTS *98,140*

dizzy [*adj1*] *light-headed, confused* addled, befuddled, bemused, bewildered, blind, blinded, dazed, dazzled, distracted, disturbed, dumb, dumbfounded, faint, gaga*, giddy, groggy*, hazy, light, muddled, off balance*, out of control*, punch-drunk*, punchy*, puzzled, reeling, shaky, slap-happy*, staggered, staggering, swimming*, tipsy, unsteady, upset, vertiginous, weak in the knees*, weak-kneed*, whirling, wobbly, woozy; CONCEPTS *314,480* —*Ant.* clear, clear-headed, unconfused

dizzy [*adj2*] *flighty, scatterbrained* capricious, changeable, crazy, empty-headed, fatuous, feather-brained, fickle, foolish, frivolous, giddy, harebrained, heady, inane, light-headed, silly, skittish, unstable; CONCEPT 402 —Ant. clear-thinking, sensible, smart

DNA [n] *deoxyribonucleic acid* chromosome, gene, genetic code, heredity, nucleic acid, RNA; CONCEPT 648

do [v1] *carry out* accomplish, achieve, act, arrange, be responsible for, bring about, cause, close, complete, conclude, cook*, create, determine, discharge, do one's thing*, effect, end, engage in, execute, finish, fix, fulfill, get ready, get with it*, go for it*, look after, make, make ready, move, operate, organize, perform, prepare, produce, pull off*, see to, succeed, take care of business*, take on, transact, undertake, wind up*, work, wrap up*; CONCEPT 91 —Ant. defer, destroy, fail, idle, lose, miss, neglect, pass, put off, undo

do [v2] *be sufficient* answer, avail, be adequate, be enough, be good enough for, be of use, be useful, give satisfaction*, pass muster*, satisfy, serve, suffice, suit; CONCEPTS 646,656

do [v3] *figure out, solve* adapt, decipher, decode, interpret, puzzle out, render, resolve, translate, transliterate, transpose, work out; CONCEPT 15

do [v4] *act, behave* acquit oneself, appear, bear, carry, come on like*, comport, conduct, demean, deport, discourse, enact, fare, get along, get by, give, go on, impersonate, make out*, manage, muddle through*, operate, perform, personate, play, playact, portray, present, produce, put on*, quit, render the role, seem, stagger along*; CONCEPT 633

do [v5] *travel, visit* cover, explore, journey, look at, pass through, stop in, tour, track, traverse; CONCEPT 224

do [v6] *cheat* beat, bilk, chouse, con, cozen, deceive, defraud, dupe, fleece*, flimflam*, gyp*, hoax, overreach, swindle, take for a ride*, trick; CONCEPT 59

do away with [v] *get rid of; destroy* abolish, bump off*, cancel, discard, discontinue, do in*, eliminate, exterminate, finish, kill, liquidate, murder, put an end to, put to death, remove, slaughter, slay, take away, wipe out*; CONCEPTS 180,252 —Ant. build, construct, get, keep

docile [adj] *compliant, submissive* accommodating, acquiescent, adaptable, agreeable, amenable, biddable, childlike, complacent, cool, docious, ductile, easily influenced, easy, easygoing, gentle, governable, humble, laid-back, manageable, meek, mellow, mild, obedient, obliging, orderly, pliable, pliant, quiet, resigned, soft, tame, teachable, tractable, usable, weak-kneed*, well-behaved, willing, yielding; CONCEPTS 401,404 —Ant. determined, headstrong, inflexible, intractable, obstinate, opinionated, stubborn, uncooperative, unyielding

dock [n] *waterfront* berth, embarkment, harbor, jetty, landing, landing pier, levee, lock, marina, pier, quay, slip, wharf; CONCEPT 439

dock [v] *land on the waterfront* anchor, berth, drop anchor, hook up, join, link up, moor, put in, rendezvous, tie up, unite; CONCEPT 159 —Ant. set sail, ship out

docket [n] *program, agenda* calendar, card, schedule, tab, tally, ticket, timetable; CONCEPT 271

doctor [n] *medical practitioner* bones*, doc*, expert, general practitioner, healer, intern, MD, medic, medical person, medico, physician, professor*, quack*, scientist, specialist, surgeon; CONCEPT 357 —Ant. patient

doctor [v1] *fix up, treat* administer, apply medication, attend, do up, fix, give treatment, medicate, mend, overhaul, patch up*, rebuild, recondition, reconstruct, repair, revamp, supply; CONCEPTS 110,310 —Ant. harm, hurt, injure

doctor [v2] *adulterate, pervert* add to, alter, change, cut, deacon, debase, dilute, disguise, dope up*, falsify, fudge*, gloss, load, misrepresent, mix with, sophisticate, spike*, tamper with, water down, weight; CONCEPT 240 —Ant. clean, purify

doctrinaire [adj] *dogmatic, opinionated* authoritarian, authoritative, biased, bigoted, bullheaded*, dictative, dictatorial, dogged, fanatical, impractical, inflexible, insistent, magisterial, mulish, obstinate, one-sided, pertinacious, pigheaded*, rigid, speculative, stiff-necked*, stubborn, unrealistic; CONCEPTS 267,401 —Ant. amenable, flexible, manageable, obedient, submissive

doctrine [n] *opinion; principle* article, article of faith, attitude, axiom, basic, belief, canon, concept, convention, conviction, credenda, creed, declaration, dogma, fundamental, gospel, implantation, inculcation, indoctrination, instruction, position, precept, pronouncement, propaganda, proposition, regulation, rule, statement, teaching, tenet, tradition, universal law, unwritten rule; CONCEPTS 688,689 —Ant. disbelief, heterodoxy, skepticism, unbelief

document [n] *written communication* archive, certificate, credentials, deed, diary, evidence, form, instrument, language, pages, paper, record, report, script, testimony, token; CONCEPT 271 —Ant. speech

documentary [n] *investigative report* account, broadcast, docudrama, feature, film, information, narrative; CONCEPTS 271,282

dodder [v] *shake* quiver, shiver, shudder, stagger, sway, teeter, totter, tremble, wobble; CONCEPTS 150,152

doddering [adj] *aged, feeble* anile, decrepit, dotard, faltering, floundering, infirm, senile, shaky, tottering, trembling, unsteady, weak; CONCEPTS 314,488,578,797 —Ant. agile, young, youthful

dodge [n] *trick, feint* contrivance, device, machination, method, plan, plot, ploy, ruse, scheme, stratagem, strategy, subterfuge, wile; CONCEPT 660

dodge [v] *avoid* circumlocute, dark, deceive, ditch, duck, elude, equivocate, escape, evade, fence, fend off, fudge*, get around, get out of, give the slip*, hedge, juke, lurch, malinger, move to the side*, parry, pussyfoot*, put the move on*, shake, shake off*, shift, shirk, short-circuit, shuffle, sidestep, skip out on*, skirt, slide, slip, swerve, tergiversate, tergiverse, trick, turn aside, weasel*; CONCEPTS 59,102 —Ant. confront, encounter, face, meet, stand up to

doer [n] *go-getter* achiever, busy person, dynamo*, energetic person, man of action, motivator, mover and shaker*, risk-taker, woman of action; CONCEPT 706

doff [v] *remove* cast off, discard, disrobe, peel, put aside, shed, shuck, slip off, strip, take off, undress; CONCEPTS 211,453

do for [v1] *destroy* defeat, deprive, finish, kill, ruin, shatter, slaughter, slay; CONCEPTS 238,252 —*Ant.* bear, create

do for [v2] *help* abet, aid, assist, benefact, care for, help out, lend a hand*, look after, provide for, steady, support; CONCEPT 110 —*Ant.* deny, refuse

dog [n] *canine mammal* bitch, bowwow*, cur, doggy, fido*, flea bag*, hound, man's best friend*, mongrel, mutt, pooch*, pup, puppy, stray, tail-wagger*, tyke; CONCEPT 400

dog [v] *chase after; bother* bedog, haunt, hound, plague, pursue, shadow, tag, tail, track, trail, trouble; CONCEPT 207 —*Ant.* leave alone, let go

dog-eat-dog [adj] *competitive* aggressive, brutal, cutthroat, every person for themselves*, fierce, ruthless, vicious; CONCEPT 542

dogged [adj] *determined, persistent* adamant, bullheaded*, firm, hanging tough*, hardheaded*, hard-nosed*, indefatigable, inexorable, inflexible, insistent, mulish, obdurate, obstinate, perseverant, persevering, persevering, pertinacious, pigheaded*, relentless, resolute, rigid, single-minded, staunch, steadfast, steady, stubborn, tenacious, tough nut*, unbending, unflagging, unshakable, unyielding; CONCEPTS 401,542 —*Ant.* indifferent, irresolute, undetermined, yielding

dogleg [n] *bend* curve, hairpin curve, sharp turn; CONCEPT 436

dogma [n] *belief, principle* article, article of faith, canon, conviction, credenda, credo, creed, doctrine, gospel, opinion, persuasion, precept, rule, teachings, tenet, view; CONCEPTS 688,689 —*Ant.* ambiguity, doubt, indecision, unbelief, uncertainty

dogmatic [adj1] *dictatorial, opinionated* arbitrary, arrogant, assertive, bigoted, bullheaded*, categorical, cocksure*, confident, definite, despotic, determined, dictative, doctrinaire, domineering, downright, egotistical, emphatic, fanatical, fascistic, formal, high and mighty*, imperious, intolerant, magisterial, narrowminded, obdurate, obstinate, one-sided, overbearing, peremptory, pigheaded*, prejudiced, stiff-necked, stubborn, tenacious, tyrannical, unequivocal, wrong-headed; CONCEPTS 267, 542 —*Ant.* amenable, doubting, flexible, indecisive, manageable, obedient, questioning, skeptical, submissive

dogmatic [adj2] *based on absolute truth* a priori, as a matter of course, assertive, authoritarian, authoritative, axiomatic, by fiat, by natural law, by nature, canonical, categorical, deducible, deductive, derivable, doctrinaire, doctrinal, eternal, excathedra, formal, imperative, inevitable, on faith, oracular, orthodox, peremptory, positive, pragmatic, prophetic, reasoned, systematic, theoretical, unchangeable, unerring, unqualified; CONCEPTS 530,567, 582 —*Ant.* ambiguous, doubtful, dubious, equivocal, fluctuating, indecisive, not positive, uncertain, vacillating

do-gooder [n] *idealist* altruist, bleeding heart, good Samaritan, humanitarian, philanthropist, volunteer; CONCEPTS 416,423

do in [v] *destroy; exhaust* assassinate, bankrupt, bump off*, butcher*, cool*, dilapidate, dispatch, do away with*, eliminate, execute, fatigue, finish, frazzle*, kill, knock out*, liquidate, murder, put away*, ruin, shatter, slaughter, slay, tire, wear out, weary, wreck; CONCEPTS 137,250,252 —*Ant.* bear, create, invent

doing [n] *achievement* accomplishing, accomplishment, achieving, act, action, carrying out, deed, execution, exploit, handiwork, implementation, performance, performing, thing; CONCEPT 706

doings [n] *actions* acts, affairs, deal, deed, events, goings-on, happenings, matters, proceeding; CONCEPT 1

doldrums [n] *depression* apathy, black mood*, blahs*, blue funk*, blues*, boredom, bummer*, dejection, disinterest, dismals, downer, dullness, dumps*, ennui, funk*, gloom, inactivity, indifference, inertia, lassitude, letdown, listlessness, malaise, mopes*, slump, stagnation, stupor, tedium, torpor, yawn*; CONCEPT 410 —*Ant.* elation, gladness, glee, happiness, joy

dole [n] *allowance, allocation* allotment, alms, apportionment, benefit, charity, dispensation, distribution, division, donation, gift, grant, gratuity, handout, living wage, mite, modicum, parcel, pittance, portion, quota, relief, share, subsistence, trifle; CONCEPTS 337,344

doleful [adj] *depressing* afflicted, cast down, cheerless, crestfallen, dejected, depressed, dirgeful, dismal, dispirited, distressing, dolent, dolorous, down, downcast, downhearted, down in the mouth*, dreary, forlorn, funereal, gloomy, grieving, lamentable, lugubrious, melancholy, mournful, painful, piteous, pitiful, plaintive, rueful, sad, somber, sorrowful, woebegone, woeful, wretched; CONCEPTS 403,529 —*Ant.* cheerful, elated, glad, gleeful, happy, joyful

dole out [v] *allocate, distribute* administer, allot, apportion, assign, deal, deal out, dispense, disperse, divide, divvy*, give, hand out, lot, measure, mete, mete out, parcel, partition, share, share out; CONCEPTS 108,140 —*Ant.* collect, gather, hoard, hold

doll [n1] *toy person* baby, dolly, effigy, figure, figurine, manikin, marionette, model, moppet*, puppet; CONCEPT 446

doll [n2] *generous person* darling, decent person, helpful person, honey*, prince*, sweetheart, sweetie; CONCEPTS 296,423

doll [n3] *attractive woman* angel, babe*, bathing beauty, brood*, bunny*, centerfold, chick*, cover girl, cupcake*, cutie, cutiepie*, dish*, dollface, dreamboat*, dream girl, fox*, glamour girl, good-looking woman, honey*, hot dish*, hot number*, peach*, pin-up, raving beauty, sex bunny*, sex kitten*, sexpot*, tomato*; CONCEPTS 415,424

dollar [n] *paper money* ace*, bank note, bill, buck*, certificate, clam*, cucumber*, currency, folding money, greenback*, legal tender, note, one-spot*, single; CONCEPT 340 —*Ant.* change, coin

dollop [n] *lump* bit, blob, glob, gob, mass, piece, portion; CONCEPTS 432,786,835

doll up [v] *beautify oneself; dress up* deck out*, fix up, gussy up*, preen, primp, put on best

clothes, smarten up*, spiff*, spruce up*;
CONCEPTS 162,167,202 —Ant. dress down

dolly [n] handtruck carrier, cart, pushcart;
CONCEPTS 499,505

dolor [n] misery, anguish agony, distress, grief,
heartache, heartbreak, passion, ruth, sadness,
sorrow, suffering; CONCEPT 410 —Ant. cheer,
happiness, hopefulness

dolorous [adj] miserable, anguished afflicted,
afflictive, calamitous, deplorable, dire, distressing, doleful, dolent, dolesome, grievous, harrowing, heart-rending, lamentable, lugubrious,
melancholy, mournful, painful, plaintive,
regrettable, rueful, ruthful, sad, sorrowful,
woebegone, woeful, wretched; CONCEPTS
401,403 —Ant. cheery, happy, hopeful

dolt [n] stupid person airhead*, blockhead*,
boob*, chump*, dimwit*, dodo*, dope, dork*,
dumbbell*, dumdum*, dunce, fool, goon*,
idiot, ignoramus, lamebrain*, lunkhead*,
meathead*, nitwit*, sap*, simpleton, stupid,
yo-yo*; CONCEPTS 412,423 —Ant. brain, genius

domain [n] area of expertise, rule authority,
bailiwick, concern, demesne, department, discipline, district, dominion, empire, estate, field,
home park*, jurisdiction, land, neck of the
woods*, occupation, orbit*, power, province,
quarter, realm, region, scope, slot, specialty,
sphere, stomping grounds*, terrain, territory,
turf, walk, wing; CONCEPTS 349,518,710

dome [n] arched part of ceiling arcade, arch,
bubble, bulge, covering, cupola, mosque, roof,
span, top, vault; CONCEPT 440

domestic [adj1] household calm, devoted,
domiciliary, family, home, homelike, home-
loving, homely, indoor, pet, private, sedentary,
settled, stay-at-home, subdued, submissive,
tame, trained, tranquil; CONCEPT 542 —Ant.
business, industrial, office

domestic [adj2] not foreign handcrafted, homegrown, homemade, indigenous, inland, internal,
intestine, intramural, municipal, national, native; CONCEPTS 536,549 —Ant. alien, foreign

domesticate [v] tame; habituate acclimatize,
accustom, break, break in, breed, bring up, bust,
corral, domiciliate, familiarize, gentle, herd,
hitch, housetrain, naturalize, raise, reclaim,
round up, subdue, teach, train, yoke; CONCEPTS
202,285

domesticity [n] home life domestication,
family life, staying at home; CONCEPT 516

domestic partner [n] live-in significant other
beneficiary, cohabitant, companion, housemate,
longtime companion, lover, partner, spouse;
CONCEPT 414

domicile [n] human habitat abode, accommodation, apartment, castle, commorancy, condo*,
condominium, co-op, crash pad*, dump,
dwelling, habitation, home, house, joint, legal
residence, mansion, pad*, rack*, residence,
residency, roof over head*, roost*, settlement;
CONCEPTS 439,516

dominance [n] supremacy ascendancy, authority, command, control, domination, dominion,
government, influence, paramountcy, power,
preeminence, preponderance, prepotence, prepotency, rule, sovereignty, sway, upper hand,
whip hand; CONCEPTS 376,668 —Ant. modesty,
subordination, weakness

dominant [adj1] superior, controlling ascendant, assertive, authoritative, bossy, chief, commanding, demonstrative, despotic, domineering,
effective, first, foremost, governing, imperative,
imperious, leading, main, obtaining, outweigh-
ing, overbalancing, overbearing, overweighing,
paramount, powerful, predominant, predominate, preeminent, preponderant, presiding, prevailing, prevalent, principal, regnant, reigning,
ruling, sovereign, supreme, surpassing, transcendent; CONCEPT 574 —Ant. humble, inferior,
modest, reserved, retiring, unaggressive, unassuming, uncontrolling

dominant [adj2] main, primary capital, chief,
influential, major, number one*, outstanding,
paramount, predominant, preeminent, prevailing, prevalent, principal, prominent, stellar;
CONCEPT 568 —Ant. inferior, secondary,
subordinate

dominate [v1] govern, rule boss, call the
shots*, command, control, detract from,
dictate, direct, domineer, eclipse, handle,
have one's way*, have upper hand*, head,
hold sway over*, influence, keep under
thumb*, lay down the law*, lead, lead by the
nose*, manage, monopolize, outshine, overbear, overrule, overshadow, play first fiddle*,
predominate, preponderate, prevail, prevail
over, reign, rule the roost*, run, run the show*,
sit on top of*, subject, subjugate, superabound,
sway, tyrannize; CONCEPTS 94,117,298 —Ant.
follow, go along, submit, surrender, yield

dominate [v2] tower above bestride, look
down upon, loom over, overlie, overlook,
overtop, stand over, survey; CONCEPTS 741,
752 —Ant. be below

domination [n] control; subjection ascendancy, authority, command, despotism,
dictatorship, dominance, dominion, influence,
jurisdiction, might, oppression, power, preponderancy, prepotence, prepotency, repression,
rule, sovereignty, strings*, subordination,
superiority, suppression, supremacy, sway,
tyranny; CONCEPT 376 —Ant. following,
submission, surrender, yielding

domineer [v] oppress; assume authority be in
the saddle*, bend, bluster, boss around*, browbeat, bulldoze*, bully*, call the shots*, dominate, hector, henpeck*, in the driver's seat*,
intimidate, keep under thumb*, kick around*,
lead by the nose*, menace, overbear, predominate, preponderate, prevail, push the buttons*,
reign, rule, rule the roost*, run the show*,
run things*, swagger, threaten, throw weight
around*, tyrannize; CONCEPTS 14,94 —Ant.
follow, submit, surrender, yield

domineering [adj] oppressive, authoritarian
arrogant, autocratic, bossy, coercive, crack the
whip*, despotic, dictatorial, egotistic, high-
handed, imperative, imperial, imperious, in
driver's seat*, insolent, iron-handed*, on high
horse*, overbearing, peremptory, tyrannical;
CONCEPT 401 —Ant. submissive, surrendering,
yielding

dominion [n] area of rule; authority ascendancy, authorization, bailiwick, command,
commission, control, country, demesne,
district, domain, dominance, domination, empire, enclave, field, government, jurisdiction,

management, power, preeminence, prepotence, prepotency, prerogative, privilege, property, province, realm, regency, regiment, regimentation, region, reign, rule, seniority, sovereignty, sphere, state, stomping grounds*, supremacy, sway, terrain, territory, turf, walk; CONCEPTS 198,376,710 —Ant. outside

donate [v] *make a gift of* accord, ante up*, award, bequeath, bestow, chip in*, confer, contribute, devote, dole out*, do one's part*, feed the kitty*, get in the act*, get it up*, give, give away, grant, hand out, lay on, pass the hat*, present, provide, subscribe, sweeten the pot*; CONCEPT 108 —Ant. keep, renege

donation [n] *gift* a hand*, aid, allowance, alms, appropriation, assistance, benefaction, beneficence, bequest, boon, charity, contribution, dole, do one's part*, endowment, gifting, grant, gratuity, handout, help, helping hand* largess, lump, offering, philanthropy, pittance, present, presentation, ration, relief, subscription, subsidy, subvention, write-off*; CONCEPTS 337,340

done [adj1] *accomplished, finished* all in*, all over*, a wrap*, brought about, brought to pass, buttoned up*, compassed, complete, completed, concluded, consummated, depleted, down, drained, effected, effete, ended, executed, exhausted, fixed, fulfilled, over, perfected, performed, realized, rendered, set, spent, succeeded, terminated, through, used up, wired, wrought; CONCEPTS 528,531 —Ant. incomplete, undone, unfinished, unperfected

done [adj2] *thoroughly cooked* baked, boiled, brewed, broiled, browned, crisped, fried, ready, stewed; CONCEPTS 462,613 —Ant. rare, raw, undone

done [adj3] *approved, agreed upon* compacted, determined, okay, settled, you're on*; CONCEPT 558 —Ant. denied, vetoed

done for [adj] *beaten, defeated* broken, conquered, dashed, destroyed, doomed, finished, foiled, lost, ruined, through, undone, vanquished, washed-up*, wrecked; CONCEPTS 537,570 —Ant. accomplished, successful

done in [adj] *exhausted* all in*, bushed*, dead, depleted, done, effete, fagged, far-gone*, on last leg*, ready to drop*, spent, tired, used up, washed-out*, weary, worn-out; CONCEPTS 314,485 —Ant. rested

Don Juan [n] *ladies' man* Casanova*, charmer, lady-killer*, libertine, lover, philanderer, playboy, Romeo*, seducer, skirt chaser, smooth operator, stud, woman chaser; CONCEPT 423

donkey [n] *small domestic horselike mammal* ass, burro, horse, jackass, jennet, jenny, maud, moke, mule, neddy, pony, Rocky Mountain canary*; CONCEPT 400

donnybrook [n] *brawl* battle royal, fight, fracas, fray, free-for-all, hoedown*, melee, rhubarb*, riot, row, rumble, shindig, slugfest*, turmoil, uproar; CONCEPTS 46,106

donor [n] *giver of gift* almsgiver, altruist, angel*, backer, benefactor, benefactress, bestower, conferrer, contributor, donator, grantor, heavy hitter*, patron, philanthropist, presenter, Santa Claus*, savior, subscriber; CONCEPT 359

do-nothing [n] *bum* couch potato*, goof-off*, idler, lazybones, lazy person, loafer, moocher, slacker; CONCEPTS 412,423

doodad [n] *gadget* contraption, contrivance, doohickey*, gismo, object, thing, thingamabob*, thingamajig*, whatchamacallit*, widget; CONCEPTS 463,499

doohickey [n] *gadget* contraption, contrivance, doodad*, gismo, object, thing, thingamabob*, thingamajig*, whatchamacallit*, widget; CONCEPTS 463,499

doom [n] *fate or decision, usually unpleasant* annihilation, calamity, cataclysm, catastrophe, circumstance, conclusion, condemnation, death, decree, destination, destiny, destruction, disaster, downfall, end, fixed future, foreordination, fortune, handwriting on wall*, judgment, Judgment Day, karma, kismet, lap of the gods*, lot, Moira, opinion, portion, predestination, predetermination, ruin, sentence, tragedy, verdict, way the ball bounces*, way the cookie crumbles*; CONCEPT 679

doomed [adj] *condemned, hopeless* bedeviled, bewitched, convicted, cursed, cut down, damned, dead duck*, destroyed, done, done for*, fated, foreordained, ill-fated, ill-omened, in the cards*, kiss of death*, lost, luckless, menaced, overthrown, overwhelmed, predestined, que sera sera*, reprobate, ruined, sentenced, star-crossed, sunk, suppressed, threatened, thrown down, undone, unfortunate, unredeemed, wrecked; CONCEPT 537 —Ant. hopeful, lucky

doomsayer [n] *alarmist* Chicken Little, doom merchant, pessimist, scaremonger; CONCEPTS 412,423

door [n] *entrance to room, building or more;* egress, entry, entryway, exit, gate, gateway, hatch, hatchway, ingress, opening, portal, postern, slammer; CONCEPT 440

doorbell [n] *chime* buzzer, door knocker, ringer; CONCEPTS 74,284,529,685

do out of [v] *cheat* balk, beat out of*, bilk, con, deceive, deprive, steal, swindle, trick; CONCEPTS 59,139

doozy [n] *winner* beauty, humdinger*, killer*, lulu*, smash hit, something; CONCEPTS 366,416

dope [n1] *stupid person* ass, blockhead*, dimwit*, dolt, donkey*, dunce, fool, idiot, lame-brain*, simpleton; CONCEPTS 412,423 —Ant. brain, genius

dope [n2] *drug* narcotic, opiate, stimulant; CONCEPT 307

dope [n3] *inside news* account, details, developments, facts, info*, information, knowledge, lowdown*, tip*; CONCEPT 274

dope [v] *drug someone* adulterate, anesthetize, deaden, debase, inject, knock out*, load, narcotize, put to sleep, sedate, soak, sophisticate, stupefy; CONCEPTS 156,310

dopey [adj] *stupid* comatose, dense, dumb, foolish, heavy, hebetudinous, idiotic, lethargic, senseless, silly, simple, slow, sluggish, slumberish, thick, torpid; CONCEPT 402 —Ant. brainy, intelligent, sensible, smart

dormant [adj] *inactive; sleeping* abeyant, asleep, closed down, comatose, down, fallow, hibernating, inert, inoperative, latent, lethargic, lurking, on the shelf*, out of action*, passive, potential, prepatent, quiescent, sidelined, slack, sluggish, slumbering, smoldering, suspended, torpid; CONCEPT 539 —Ant. active, lively

dormitory [n] *living quarters* bedroom, dorm, dorm room, sleeping quarters; CONCEPT *448*

dose [n] *portion of drug or other consumable* application, dosage, dram, draught, fill, fix*, hit*, lot, measure, measurement, nip*, potion, prescription, quantity, share, shot*, slug*, spoonful; CONCEPTS *307,835*

dossier [n] *file* archives, information, personal account, portfolio, profile, record, recorded information, report, summary; CONCEPTS *271,281*

dot [n] *tiny mark, drop* atom, circle, dab, droplet, fleck, flyspeck, grain, iota, jot, mite, mote, particle, period, pinpoint, point, speck, spot, tittle; CONCEPTS *284,831*

dot [v] *make spot(s)* bespeckle, dab, dabble, fleck, freckle, pepper, pimple, sprinkle, stipple, stud; CONCEPTS *79,174*

dotage [n] *feebleness, old age* advanced age, decrepitude, elderliness, fatuity, imbecility, infirmity, second childhood*, senectitude, senility, weakness; CONCEPTS *405,715* —*Ant.* childhood, strength, youngness, youth, youthfulness

dote on/dote upon [v] *lavish affection on* admire, adore, be fond of, be infatuated with, be sweet on*, cherish, enjoy, fancy, hold dear, idolize, like, love, pet, prize, treasure, worship; CONCEPT *32* —*Ant.* ignore, neglect

doting [adj] *indulgent; serving* adoring, affectionate, devoted, fascinated, fatuous, fond, foolish, lovesick, lovesome, loving, silly, simple, struck; CONCEPT *401* —*Ant.* ignorance, neglect, negligence

dotty [adj] *crazy* absurd, daft, demented, disturbed, eccentric, foolish, goofy*, loony*, mentally unbalanced, nuts*, nutty, odd, peculiar, queer, ridiculous, strange, twisted, unconventional, weird; CONCEPT *403*

double [adj] *in a pair* as much again, bifold, binary, binate, coupled, dual, dualistic, duple, duplex, duplicate, duplicated, geminate, paired, repeated, second, twice, twin, twofold, two times; CONCEPT *771* —*Ant.* single

double [n] *something which exactly resembles another* angel, clone, companion, coordinate, copy, counterpart, dead ringer*, duplicate, image, impersonator, lookalike*, match, mate, picture, portrait, reciprocal, replica, ringer*, simulacrum, spitting image*, stand-in*, twin; CONCEPTS *664,716*

double [v] *make two of; make twice as large* amplify, augment, dualize, dupe, duplicate, duplify, enlarge, fold, grow, increase, infold, loop, magnify, multiply, plait, pleat, plicate, redouble, repeat, replicate, supplement; CONCEPTS *236,245* —*Ant.* disect, divide, halve

double back [v] *reverse path* backtrack, circle, dodge, loop, retrace one's steps, return, turn; CONCEPTS *224,232* —*Ant.* forge, forward, go forward

double-cross [v] *betray* beguile, bluff, cheat, con, cross, deceive, defraud, four-flush*, hoodwink*, humbug*, illude, juggle, mislead, sell, sell out*, split, swindle, take in, trick, two-time*; CONCEPTS *7,19,59* —*Ant.* be open, tell truth

double-dealing [adj] *cheating, deceitful* ambidextrous, crooked, dishonest, double, duplicitous, fraudulent, hypocritical, insincere, left-handed*, lying, perfidious, sneaky, swindling,

treacherous, tricky, two-faced*, two-timing*, underhanded, untrustworthy, wily; CONCEPT *401* —*Ant.* forthright, honest, truthful

double-dealing [n] *betrayal, cheating* bad faith, chicane, chicanery, deceit, deception, dishonesty, duplicity, foul play*, fourberie, fraud, hanky-panky*, hypocrisy, mendacity, perfidy, sharp practice*, treachery, trickery, two-timing*; CONCEPT *59* —*Ant.* forthrightness, honesty, truthfulness

double entendre [n] *play on words* ambiguity, amphibiology, double meaning, equivocality, equivocation, equivoque, innuendo, joke, pun, tergiversation; CONCEPTS *278,682*

double standard [n] *contrasting principles* contradictory standard, two sets of rules; CONCEPTS *46,278,665*

double-talk [n] *nonsense communicated* amphibiology, balderdash, baloney*, bull*, drivel, equivocation, flimflam*, gibberish, jazz*, mumbo jumbo*, rigmarole; CONCEPT *278* —*Ant.* sense, straight talk

doubt [n] *lack of faith, conviction; questioning* agnosticism, ambiguity, apprehension, confusion, demurral, difficulty, diffidence, dilemma, disbelief, discredit, disquiet, distrust, dubiety, dubiousness, faithlessness, faltering, fear, hesitancy, hesitation, incertitude, incredulity, indecision, irresolution, lack of confidence, misgiving, mistrust, perplexity, problem, qualm, quandary, rejection, reluctance, scruple, skepticism, suspense, suspicion, uncertainty, vacillation, wavering; CONCEPTS *21,410,689, 690* —*Ant.* belief, certainty, confidence, dependence, faith, reliance, trust

doubt [v] *lack confidence in; question* be apprehensive of, be curious, be dubious, be in a quandary, be puzzled, be uncertain, be undetermined, call in question, challenge, demur, disbelieve, discredit, dispute, distrust, fear, fluctuate, give no credence, harbor suspicion, have qualms, hesitate, imagine, impugn, insinuate, misdoubt, misgive, mistrust, not buy*, query, read differently, scruple, shilly-shally*, skepticize, smell a rat*, surmise, suspect, take dim view of, vacillate, waver, wonder at; CONCEPT *21* —*Ant.* be certain, believe, not question, rely, trust

doubter [n] *person who does not believe* agnostic, cynic, disbeliever, headshaker*, questioner, skeptic, unbeliever, zetetic; CONCEPTS *361,423* —*Ant.* believer, truster

doubtful [adj1] *questionable, unclear* ambiguous, borderline, chancy, clouded, contingent, debatable, dicey, disreputable, doubtable, dubious, dubitable, equivocal, far-fetched, fat chance, fishy*, hazardous, hazy, iffy*, impugnable, inconclusive, indecisive, indefinite, indeterminate, indistinct, insecure, long shot*, obscure, on thin ice*, open, pending, precarious, problematic, shady, sneaky*, speculative, suspect, suspicious, touch-and-go*, touchy, uncertain, unconfirmed, undecided, uneasy, unsettled, unstable, unsure, up for grabs*; CONCEPTS *529,535* —*Ant.* certain, clear, confirmed, decided, definite, exact, resolved, settled, unquestionable

doubtful [adj2] *not believing* agnostic, baffled, confused, discomposed, disconcerted, distracted, distrustful, disturbed, doubting, dubious, equivocal, faithless, faltering, flustered, hesitant, hesitating, in a quandary, in clouds*, indecisive, in dilemma, irresolute, like doubting Thomas*, lost, not following, of two minds*, perplexed, puzzled, questioning, skeptical, suspicious, tentative, theoretical, troubled, uncertain, unconvinced, undecided, unresolved, unsettled, unsure, vacillating, wavering, without belief; CONCEPTS 403,542 —Ant. believing, certain, confident, convinced, sure, trusting

doubting Thomas [n] *skeptic* disbeliever, doubter, questioner, unbeliever; CONCEPTS 361, 423

doubtless [adv] *certainly; most likely* absolutely, apparently, assuredly, clearly, easily, for sure, indisputably, no ifs ands or buts*, of course, ostensibly, positively, precisely, presumably, probably, seemingly, supposedly, surely, truly, undoubtedly, unequivocally, unquestionably, without doubt; CONCEPTS 535, 552 —Ant. doubted, doubtedly, dubious, improbably, questionable, uncertain, unlikely

dough [n] *money* beans*, boodle*, bread*, bucks*, cabbage*, cash, change, chips, clams*, coin, coinage, cold cash, currency, dinero, funds, greenback*, hard cash*, legal tender, lettuce*, loot, moola, pesos*; CONCEPT 340

doughnut [n] *sweet ring-shaped fried cake* bun, cruller, danish, dunker*, pastry, sinker*, sweet roll; CONCEPTS 457,461

do up [v] *physically prepare; fix* clean, doctor, enclose, finish, gift-wrap, launder, mend, overhaul, package, patch, rebuild, recondition, reconstruct, repair, revamp, wash, wrap; CONCEPTS 126,165,182 —Ant. hurt, injure, ruin

dour [adj] *gloomy, grim* bleak, crabbed, dismal, dreary, forbidding, glum, hard, harsh, morose, saturnine, severe, sour, stringent, sulky, sullen, surly, ugly, unfriendly; CONCEPTS 401,542 —Ant. bright, cheerful, cheery, happy

douse [v] *drench, extinguish with liquid* blow out, deluge, drown, duck, dunk, immerse, plunge, put out, quench, saturate, slop, slosh, smother, snuff, snuff out, soak, sop, souse, spatter, splash, splatter, squench, steep, submerge, submerse, wet; CONCEPTS 250,256 —Ant. dry

dovetail [v] *link, fit together* accord, agree, check out, coincide, conform, correspond, go, harmonize, interlock, jibe, join, match, mortise, square, sync*, sync up*, tally, tenon, unite; CONCEPTS 113,664 —Ant. disconnect, disunite, unlink

dowdy [adj] *poorly dressed; old-fashioned* antiquated, archaic, baggy, bedraggled, blowsy*, bygone, dated, dingy, drab, dull, frowzy*, frumpy*, homely, moldy, old hat*, outdated, outmoded, out-of-date, passé, plain, run-down, scrubby*, shabby, slatternly, sloppy, slovenly, stodgy, tacky, tasteless, unfashionable, unkempt, unseemly, unstylish, untidy, vintage, wrinkled; CONCEPT 589 —Ant. chic, classy, fashionable, modern

do without [v] *get along without* abstain from, dispense, endure, forgo, give up; CONCEPTS 23, 646

down [adj1/adv] *below; physically lower* bottomward, cascading, declining, depressed,

descending, downgrade, downhill, downward, dropping, earthward, falling, gravitating, groundward, inferior, nether, precipitating, sagging, sinking, sliding, slipping, slumping, subjacent, to the bottom, under, underneath; CONCEPTS 583,586,735 —Ant. above, higher

down [adj2] *unhappy* bad, blue*, cast down, chapfallen, crestfallen, dejected, depressed, disheartened, dispirited, downcast, downhearted, low, miserable, off, sad, slack, sluggish; CONCEPT 403 —Ant. cheerful, cheery, happy, heartened

down-and-out [adj] *poverty-stricken* beaten, beggared, defeated, derelict, destitute, finished, impoverished, needy, outcast, penniless, ruined, vagabond, vagrant; CONCEPT 334 —Ant. rich, wealthy, well-to-do

downbeat [adj] *pessimistic* cheerless, defeatist, dejected, dispirited, gloomy, hopeless, negative, unhappy, unhopeful; CONCEPTS 403,548

downcast [adj] *depressed, unhappy* bad, blue, brooding, bummed out*, cast down, chapfallen, cheerless, crestfallen, daunted, dejected, despondent, disappointed, disconsolate, discouraged, disheartened, dismayed, dispirited, distressed, doleful, down, downhearted, down in the dumps*, down-in-the-mouth*, dragged*, droopy, dull, forlorn, gloomy, glum, heartsick, in pain, listless, low, low-spirited, miserable, moody, mopey*, morose, oppressed, sad, shot down*, singing the blues*, sunk*, troubled, weighed down*, woebegone; CONCEPT 403 —Ant. cheerful, elated, glad, happy, heartened, satisfied

downer [n] *depressing experience* bad deal*, bad scene*, bad trip*, bummer*, drag*, misfortune, raw deal, rotten hand; CONCEPTS 674,679

downfall [n] *disgrace, ruin* atrophy, bane, breakdown, cloudburst, collapse, comedown, comeuppance, debacle, decadence, declension, degeneracy, degeneration, deluge, descent, destruction, deterioration, devolution, discomfiture, down, drop, failure, fall, flood, on the rocks*, overthrow, rack and ruin*, road to ruin*, ruination, storm, the skids*, undoing; CONCEPTS 674,679,699 —Ant. accomplishment, ascent, rise, success

downgrade [n] *slope* decline, declivity, descent, dip, hill, inclination, pitch; CONCEPTS 509,738 —Ant. upgrade

downgrade [v] *lower in opinion or rank* abase, bench*, break*, bump*, bust*, declass, decrease, decry, degrade, demerit, demote, denigrate, depreciate, detract from, devalorize, devalue, disparage, disrate, humble, mark down, minimize, reduce, run down, set back, take down a peg*, undervalue, write off*; CONCEPTS 7,19,54,240 —Ant. improve, promote, raise, upgrade

downhearted [adj] *depressed, unhappy* blue*, chapfallen, crestfallen, dejected, despondent, disconsolate, discouraged, disheartened, dismayed, dispirited, down, downcast, low, low-spirited, sad, sorrowful, spiritless, woebegone; CONCEPT 403 —Ant. cheered, happy, heartened, uplifted

downhill [adj] *descending* declining, dipping, dropping, falling, sloping downward; CONCEPTS 583,586,735

do
do

downlink [n] *transmission path for data* circuit, communications pathway, network, pathway, signal route; CONCEPT 269

download [v] *transfer data from one computer system to another* boot up, compute, computerize, crunch numbers*, digitize, initialize, input, keyboard, key in, load, log in, log out, program, run; CONCEPTS 211,217,223

downplay [v] *minimize* attach little importance to, deemphasize, devalue, give little weight to, lessen, make light of, play down, soften, think nothing of, whitewash; CONCEPTS 54,240,247

downpour [n] *tremendous pouring of rain* cloudburst, deluge, drencher, flood, inundation, monsoon, rainstorm, storm, torrential rain; CONCEPT 526 —*Ant.* sprinkle

downright [adj] *thorough, absolute* blatant, blunt, categorical, certain, clear, complete, damned, explicit, flat, gross, honest, indubitable, open, out-and-out, outright, plain, positive, simple, sincere, straight, straightforward, sure, thoroughgoing, total, undisguised, unequivocal, unmitigated, unqualified, unquestionable, utter, whole; CONCEPT 531

downside [n] *a negative aspect of a situation* defect, disadvantage, drawback, fault, flaw, inconvenience, minus, problem, trouble; CONCEPTS 666,674

downsize [v] *to decrease in size, especially of a workforce* curtail, cut, cut back, cut down, decrease, deduct, diminish, phase down, phase out, reduce, retrench, roll back, roll down, scale back, scale down, shrink, step down, trim, trim away, tune down; CONCEPTS 236,240,247

downtime [n] *time during which an activity is stopped* break, breathing spell, freedom, free time, halt, interim, interlude, intermission, letup, lull, pause, recess, repose, respite, rest, spare time, spell, stay, suspension, time on one's hands, time out, time to burn, time to kill; CONCEPT 807

down-to-earth [adj] *reasonable, practical* common, commonsense, easy, hard, hard-boiled, hardheaded, matter-of-fact, mundane, no-nonsense, plainspoken, pragmatic, rational, realistic, sane, sensible, sober, unfantastic, unidealistic, unsentimental; CONCEPTS 402,558 —*Ant.* excitable, excited, impractical, unreasonable, unsensible

downtrodden [adj] *afflicted, abused* abject, a slave to*, at one's beck and call*, at one's feet*, at one's mercy*, destitute, distressed, exploited, have-not, helpless, in one's clutches*, in one's pocket*, in one's power*, led by the nose*, maltreated, mistreated, needy, oppressed, overcome, persecuted, subjugated, subservient, suppressed, tyrannized, underdog*, underfoot*, under one's thumb*; CONCEPT 542 —*Ant.* happy, respected, satisfied

downturn [n] *drop* decline, descent, deterioration, dip, downtick, fall, plunge, retreat, sinking, slide, slump; CONCEPTS 336,346,738

downy [adj] *fluffy* featherlike, feathery, fleecy, fuzzy, light, plumate, plumose, pubescent, silky, soft, velutinous, velvety, woolly; CONCEPTS 604,606

doze [n] *light sleep* catnap, drowse, forty winks*, nap, shut-eye*, siesta, slumber, snooze*; CONCEPTS 315,681

doze [v] *take a nap* catch a wink*, catnap, cop some z's*, drift off*, drop off*, drowse, nod off*, sleep, sleep lightly, slumber, snooze; CONCEPTS 315,681

drab [adj] *dull, colorless* arid, blah*, bleak, boring, brown, characterless, cheerless, desolate, dingy, dismal, dreary, dry, dull as dishwater*, faded, flat, gloomy, gray, grungy, lackluster, lusterless, muddy, murky, run-down, same, shabby, somber, subfuse, unchanging, uninspired, vapid, zero*; CONCEPTS 536,617,618 —*Ant.* bright, colorful, inspired

draconian [adj] *harsh* brutal, cruel, drastic, exorbitant, extreme, heavy-handed, oppressive, rough, severe, strict, very severe; CONCEPT 401

draft [n1] *something formulated; plan* abstract, blueprint, delineation, outline, preliminary form, rough sketch, version; CONCEPTS 271,660

draft [n2] *check for paying money* bank draft, bill, bond, cheque, coupon, debenture, IOU, letter of credit, money order, order, promissory note, receipt, warrant; CONCEPTS 332,344

draft [n3] *gust of air* breeze, current, eddy, puff, wind; CONCEPT 437

draft [n4] *military conscription* allotment, assignment, call of duty, call-up*, greetings*, impressment, induction, letter from Uncle Sam*, levy, lottery, recruiting, registration, roll call*, selection, selective service; CONCEPT 321

draft [n5] *drink of beverage* drag*, drain, drench, glass, peg*, quaff, swallow, swig*, swill*; CONCEPTS 169,454

draft [v1] *formulate* adumbrate, block out, characterize, compose, concoct, contrive, delineate, design, devise, draw, draw up, fabricate, fashion, forge, form, frame, invent, make, manufacture, outline, plan, prepare, project, rough, shape, skeleton, sketch; CONCEPTS 36,79,173

draft [v2] *select for military force* call up, choose, conscribe, conscript, dragoon, enlist, enroll, impress, indite, induct, muster, press, recruit, sign on, sign up; CONCEPTS 8,320

drag [n1] *bad situation* annoyance, bore, bother, burden, encumbrance, hang-up, hindrance, impediment, nuisance, pain, pest, pill, sway, trouble; CONCEPT 674

drag [n2] *a puff while smoking* breathing, draw, inhalation, pull, smoke; CONCEPT 185

drag [v1] *haul something to a new place* draw, hale, lug, magnetize, move, pull, schlepp*, tow, trail, transport, truck, tug, yank; CONCEPTS 206,213

drag [v2] *move very slowly* be delayed, be quiescent, crawl, creep, dally*, dawdle*, delay, encounter difficulty*, hang*, inch*, lag, lag behind, limp along, linger, loiter, mark time*, poke*, procrastinate, put off*, sag, shamble, shuffle, slow down, stagnate, straggle, tarry, trail behind*, traipse; CONCEPTS 151,681 —*Ant.* rush

dragging [adj] *tiresome, monotonous* boring, drawn-out, dull, going slowly, humdrum, lengthy, long, overlong, prolonged, protracted, tedious, wearisome; CONCEPTS 482,798 —*Ant.* energizing, lively

dragnet [n] *manhunt* all points bulletin, chase, pursuit, search; CONCEPT 207

drag on/drag out [v] *extend time of action* continue, draw out, endure, extend, go on slowly, keep going, lengthen, persist, prolong, protract, spin out, stretch out; CONCEPT 239 —*Ant.* complete

drag queen [*n*] *cross-dresser* female impersonator, transvestite; CONCEPT 412

drain [*n*] *channel through which liquid runs off* cesspool, cloaca, conduit, culvert, ditch, duct, outlet, pipe, sewer, sink, trench, watercourse; CONCEPT 501

drain [*v1*] *remove liquid; remove supply* abate, bankrupt, bleed, bleed dry*, catheterize, consume, debilitate, decrease, deplete, devitalize, diminish, dissipate, divert, draft, draw off, drink up, dry, empty, evacuate, exhaust, expend, fatigue, filter off, finish, free from, get last drop*, get rid of, gulp down, impoverish, lessen, milk*, pump, pump out, quaff, reduce, sap, siphon, spend, strain, suck, suck dry*, swallow, tap, tax, tire out, use up, waste, wear down, weary, withdraw; CONCEPTS 142,211, 225 —*Ant.* fill, pour

drain [*v2*] *seep, discharge liquid* abate, decline, decrease, diminish, dwindle, effuse, exude, filter off, flow, flow out, leak, leave dry, ooze, osmose, percolate, reduce, run off, taper off, trickle, well; CONCEPTS 179,698 —*Ant.* fill

drained [*adj*] *used up; exhausted* all in*, beat*, bleary, burned out*, dead, dead tired*, depleted, dragging, effete, far-gone, hacked*, pooped*, spent, washed-out, weary, wiped-out*, worn-out; CONCEPTS 485,560 —*Ant.* energized, full, lively

drama [*n1*] *theatrical piece; acting* boards*, Broadway*, climax, comedy, dramatic art, dramatization, dramaturgy, farce, footlights, histrionic art, melodrama, play, production, scene, show, show business, showmanship, stagecraft, stage show, tear-jerker*, theater, theatricals, thespian art, tragedy, vehicle*; CONCEPTS 263,271,293 —*Ant.* comedy

drama [*n2*] *turmoil in real life* climax, comedy, crisis, dramatics, emotion, excitement, farce, histrionics, melodrama, scene, spectacle, tension, theatrics, tragedy; CONCEPT 674

dramatic [*adj*] *exciting, moving* affecting, breathtaking, climactic, comic, effective, electrifying, emotional, expressive, farcical, histrionic, impressive, melodramatic, powerful, sensational, startling, striking, sudden, suspenseful, tense, theatrical, thespian, thrilling, tragic, vivid; CONCEPTS 537,548 —*Ant.* comedic, normal, ordinary, undramatic, unexciting, unmoving, usual

dramatization [*n*] *drama* dramatics, entertainment, melodrama; CONCEPTS 263,271,293

dramatize [*v*] *make a performance of* act, amplify, burlesque, enact, exaggerate, execute, farcialize, give color to, ham it up*, lay it on*, make a production of, melodramatize, overdo, overstate, perform, playact, play on heartstrings*, play to gallery, play up, present, produce, show, splash, stage, tragedize; CONCEPTS 49,59,292

drape [*v*] *hang over, adorn* array, cloak, clothe, cover, dangle, display, don, dress, droop, drop, enclose, enswathe, envelop, enwrap, fold, hang, lean over, let fall, line, model, roll, sprawl, spread, spread-eagle, suspend, swathe, wrap; CONCEPT 172 —*Ant.* undrape

drastic [*adj*] *severe, extreme* desperate, dire, exorbitant, extravagant, forceful, harsh, immoderate, radical, strong; CONCEPTS 537,569 —*Ant.* calm, collected, easy, mild

draw [*n*] *tie in competition* dead end*, dead heat*, deadlock, even steven*, photo finish*, stalemate, standoff, tie; CONCEPT 706

draw [*v1*] *move something by pulling* attract, bring, carry, convey, cull, draft, drag, drain, educe, elicit, evoke, extract, fetch, gather, haul, hook, jerk, lug, magnetize, pick, pluck, pump, rake, siphon, tap, tow, trail, trawl, tug, wind in, wrench, yank; CONCEPT 206 —*Ant.* exhale, propel, push, repel, repulse

draw [*v2*] *create a likeness in a picture* caricature, chart, compose, crayon, delineate, depict, describe, design, draft, engrave, etch, express, form, formulate, frame, graph, limn, map out, mark, model, outline, paint, pencil, portray, prepare, profile, sketch, trace, write; CONCEPTS 79,174

draw [*v3*] *deduce* collect, conclude, derive, gather, get, infer, judge, make, make out, take; CONCEPT 15

draw [*v4*] *allure, influence* argue into, attract, bewitch, bring around, bring forth, call forth, captivate, charm, convince, elicit, enchant, engage, entice, evoke, fascinate, get, induce, invite, lure, magnetize, persuade, prompt, take, wile, win over; CONCEPTS 7,19,22,68 —*Ant.* alienate, estrange, push away, rebuff, reject, repel, repulse, turn off

draw [*v5*] *take out, extend* attenuate, choose, drain, elongate, extort, extract, lengthen, pick, pull out, respire, select, single out, stretch, suck, take; CONCEPT 142 —*Ant.* put in, shorten

drawback [*n*] *disadvantage* check, defect, deficiency, detriment, difficulty, disability, evil, failing, fault, flaw, fly in the ointment*, handicap, hindrance, hitch, ill, impediment, imperfection, inconvenience, lack, nuisance, obstacle, shortcoming, snag, stumbling block*, trouble, weakness; CONCEPTS 666,674 —*Ant.* advantage, benefit, boon, extra, perfection

draw back [*v*] *retract from position* deduct, discount, pull back, recede, recoil, reel in, retreat, sheathe, shrink, start back, subtract, take away, withdraw; CONCEPTS 195,213 —*Ant.* forge, go forward, start

drawing [*n*] *illustration* cartoon, commercial art, comp, delineation, depiction, design, doodle, etching, graphics, layout, likeness, outline, painting, picture, portrayal, representation, sketch, storyboard, study, tracing, work of art; CONCEPT 625

drawl [*v*] *lengthen, draw out* chant, drag out, drone, extend, intone, nasalize, prolong, pronounce slowly, protract, utter; CONCEPTS 77,239 —*Ant.* clip, shorten

drawn [*adj*] *tense, fatigued* fraught, haggard, harassed, harrowed, peaked, pinched, sapped, starved, strained, stressed, taut, thin, tired, worn; CONCEPT 485 —*Ant.* relaxed, unstressed

draw on [*v*] *use to advantage* effect, employ, exploit, extract, fall back on, have recourse to, make use of, rely on, require, take from; CONCEPT 225

draw out [*v*] *prolong* attract, continue, drag, drag out, elongate, extend, lead on, lengthen,

do
dr

make longer, prolongate, protract, pull, spin, spin out*, stretch, string out*, tug; CONCEPTS 236,239,245 —Ant. clip, shorten

draw up [v] *draft document* compose, formulate, frame, indite, make, prepare, write, write out; CONCEPT 79

dread [adj] *horrible, terrifying* alarming, awe-inspiring, awful, creepy*, dire, frightening, frightful, shuddersome, terrible;CONCEPT 537 —Ant. pleasant, pleasing, welcomed, wonderful

dread [n] *fear* affright, alarm, apprehension, aversion, awe, cold feet*, consternation, creeps*, dismay, fright, funk*, goose bumps*, horror, jitters, panic, phobia, stage fright, terror, trepidation, trepidity, worriment; CONCEPT 27 —Ant. bravery, confidence, courage, encouragement, want, welcoming

dread [v] *anticipate with horror* apprehend, be afraid, cringe, fear, have cold feet*, misdoubt, quake, shrink from, shudder, tremble; CONCEPT 27 —Ant. encourage, want, welcome

dreadful [adj] *horrible, frightening* abominable, alarming, appalling, atrocious, awful, bad, beastly, creepy*, dire, distressing, fearful, formidable, frightful, frozen, ghastly, godawful*, grievous, grim, grody*, gross*, hideous, horrendous, horrific, icky*, lousy, mean, monstrous, rotten, shameful, shocking, shuddersome, spooky, terrible, terrific, tragic, tremendous, wicked; CONCEPTS 537,550 —Ant. pleasant, pleasing, welcomed, wonderful

dream [n1] *illusion, vision* bubble*, castle in the air*, chimera, daydream, delusion, fancy, fantasy, hallucination, head trip*, idea, image, imagination, impression, incubus, mental picture, nightmare, pie in the sky*, pipe dream*, rainbow, reverie, specter, speculation, thought, trance, vagary, wraith; CONCEPT 529 —Ant. actuality, certainty, existence, fact, reality, substance, truth

dream [n2] *goal* ambition, aspiration, design, desire, flight of fancy*, hope, notion, pipe dream*, wish; CONCEPT 659

dream [v] *conjure up scenario* be delirious, be moonstruck, be up in clouds*, brainstorm, build castles in air*, conceive, concoct, cook up*, crave, create, daydream, devise, envisage, fancy, fantasize, formulate, hallucinate, hanker*, hatch*, have a flash*, have a nightmare*, have a notion*, have a vision, hunger, idealize, imagine, invent, long, lust, make up, picture, pine, search for pot of gold*, sigh, stargaze*, sublimate, think, think up, thirst, visualize; CONCEPTS 17,529

dreamer [n] *visionary* daydreamer, escapist, fantasizer, idealist, romantic, star-gazer, theorizer, Walter Mitty*; CONCEPTS 361,416

dreamland [n] *sleep, fantasy world* cloud cuckoo land, ideal place, land of Nod, never-never land, seventh heaven, Shangri-La, slumber, Utopia; CONCEPT 315 —Ant. real world, wakefulness

dream up [v] *concoct plan* contrive, cook up*, create, devise, frame, hatch*, imagine, invent, make up, spin*, think up; CONCEPTS 17,36

dreamy [adj] *illusory, romantic* abstracted, astral, calming, chimerical, daydreaming, excellent, fanciful, fantastic, gentle, idealistic, imaginary, immaterial, impractical, intangible, introspective, introvertive, lulling, marvelous, misty, musing, mythical, nightmarish, otherworldly, out of this world*, pensive, phantasmagoric, phantasmagorical, preoccupied, quixotic, relaxing, shadowy, soothing, speculative, unreal, unsubstantial, utopian, vague, visionary, whimsical; CONCEPT 582 —Ant. horrible, terrible, unromantic

dreary [adj] *gloomy, lifeless* black, blah, bleak, boring, cheerless, colorless, comfortless, damp, depressing, depressive, dingy, dismal, dispiriting, doleful, downcast, drab, dull, forlorn, funereal, glum, humdrum, joyless, lonely, lonesome, melancholy, monotonous, mournful, oppressive, pedestrian, raw, routine, sad, somber, sorrowful, tedious, uneventful, uninteresting, wearisome, windy, wintry, wretched; CONCEPTS 525,544 —Ant. bright, clear, happy, light, pleasant

dredge [v] *deepen* bring up, clean, dig up, raise, unearth, widen; CONCEPT 178

dregs [n1] *sediment* deposits, dirt, draff, lees, residue, settlings, slag, waste; CONCEPT 260

dregs [n2] *bad person* loser, outcast, rabble, riffraff, scum, trash; CONCEPT 412

drench [v] *wet thoroughly* deluge, dip, douse, drown, duck, dunk, flood, imbrue, immerse, impregnate, inundate, pour, saturate, seethe, soak, sodden, sop, souse, steep, submerge, teem; CONCEPT 256 —Ant. dry, parch

dress [n] *clothing; woman's garment* accouterment, apparel, attire, attirement, civvies*, costume, covering, drape, dry goods, duds*, ensemble, evening clothes, frock, garb, gear, gown, guise, habiliment, habit, muumuu, outfit, raiment, robe, shift, skirt, smock, suit, Sunday best*, things*, threads*, tog, toga, toggery, trappings, uniform, vestment, wardrobe; CONCEPT 451

dress [v1] *put on clothing* adorn, apparel, array, attire, bedeck, bundle up, change, clad, clothe, costume, cover, deck, decorate, don, drape, embellish, fit out, furbish, garb, ornament, outfit, primp, put on, raiment, rig, robe, slip into, slip on, spruce up, suit up, trim, turn out, wear; CONCEPT 167 —Ant. bare, disrobe, lay bare, unclothe, undress

dress [v2] *physically prepare; groom* adjust, align, arrange, comb, decorate, dispose, do up, fit, make ready, ornament, set, straighten, trim; CONCEPT 202 —Ant. disarray, mess up, rumple, wrinkle

dress [v3] *cover a wound* attend, bandage, bind, cauterize, cleanse, give first aid, heal, plaster, sew up, sterilize, treat; CONCEPTS 172, 310 —Ant. open, uncover, undress

dress down [v] *scold* bawl out, berate, carpet, castigate, censure, chew out*, lash, rail, rake over coals*, ream, rebuke, reprimand, reprove, tear into*, tell off*, tongue-lash*, upbraid; CONCEPT 52 —Ant. compliment, flatter, praise

dresser [n] *chest of drawers* bureau, cabinet, chiffonier, closet, highboy, wardrobe; CONCEPT 443

dressing-down [n] *severe scolding* bawling-out, castigation, chiding, lambasting, reprimand, reproach, tongue-lashing, upbraiding; CONCEPTS 123,278

dress up [v] *put on one's best clothes* array, attire, beautify, clothe, deck out*, embellish, fit out*, fix up, gussy up*, improve, overdress, preen, prettify, primp, prink, slick, smarten, spiff up*, spruce up*, titivate; CONCEPT 167 —Ant. dress casually, dress down

dressy [*adj*] *formal, fashionable* chic, classy, dressed to kill*, dressed to the nines*, dressed up*, elaborate, elegant, fancy, in high feather*, looking sharp, ornate, ritzy, smart, stylish; CONCEPTS 579,589 —Ant. casual, dowdy, inelegant, informal, unstylish

dribble [*v*] *trickle* distill, drip, drivel, drizzle, drool, drop, fall in drops, leak, ooze, run, salivate, seep, slaver, slobber, spout, squirt, trill, weep; CONCEPTS 179,185 —Ant. pour

drift [*n1*] *accumulation* alluvion, bank, batch, bunch, bundle, clump, cluster, deposit, heap, hill, lot, mass, mound, mountain, parcel, pile, set, shock, stack; CONCEPTS 432,524

drift [*n2*] *meaning, significance of communication* aim, design, direction, end, gist, implication, import, intention, object, progress, progression, purport, scope, significance, tendency, tenor; CONCEPT 682

drift [*v*] *move aimlessly* accumulate, aim, amass, amble, be carried along, coast, dance, draw near, flicker, flit, flitter, float, flow, flutter, gad*, gallivant*, gather, go-that-a-way*, go with the tide*, gravitate, hover, kick around*, linger, malinger, meander, mosey*, muck*, ride, sail, saunter, scud, skim, slide, stray, stroll, tend, waft, wander, wash*; CONCEPT 147 —Ant. decide, direct, guide, set

drifter [*n*] *wanderer* derelict, hobo, itinerant, nomad, rolling stone, tramp, transient, vagabond, vagrant; CONCEPTS 412,423

drill [*n1*] *practice, exercise* assignment, call, conditioning, constitutional, daily dozen*, discipline, dress, drilling, dry run*, gym, homework, instruction, learning by doing, maneuvers, marching, preparation, repetition, run-through*, shakedown*, training, tryout, warm-up, workout; CONCEPTS 87,290

drill [*n2*] *tool for boring* auger, awl, bit, borer, corkscrew, countersink, dibble, gimlet, implement, jackhammer, punch, riveter, rotary tool, trepan, trephine, wimble; CONCEPT 499

drill [*v1*] *train, discipline* accustom, break, break in, exercise, get into shape, habituate, hone, instruct, lick into shape, practice, rehearse, teach, tune up, walk through, work out; CONCEPTS 117,285

drill [*v2*] *bore hole* dig, penetrate, perforate, pierce, prick, punch, puncture, sink in; CONCEPT 220

drink [*n*] *beverage; alcoholic beverage* alcohol, booze*, brew, cup, draft, glass, gulp, libation, liquid, liquor, potable, potation, potion, refreshment, shot, sip, slug*, spirits, spot*, swallow, swig, taste, thirst quencher*, toast; CONCEPT 454 —Ant. food

drink [*v*] *take in liquid* absorb, belt*, booze*, consume, dissipate, down, drain, gargle, gulp, guzzle*, hit the bottle*, imbibe, indulge, inhale, irrigate, lap*, liquor up*, nip*, partake of, put away, quaff, sip, slosh, slurp, soak up, sop, sponge, suck, sup, swallow, swig, swill, tank up*, thirst, tipple*, toast, toss off*, wash down*, wet whistle*; CONCEPT 169

drip [*v*] *drop, trickle* dribble, drizzle, exude,

filter, plop, rain, splash, sprinkle, trill, weep; CONCEPT 181 —Ant. pour

drive [*n1*] *journey by vehicle* airing, commute, excursion, expedition, hitch, jaunt, joyride, lift, outing, pickup, ramble, ride, run, spin, Sunday drive*, tour, trip, turn, whirl; CONCEPT 224

drive [*n2*] *campaign for cause* action, advance, appeal, crusade, effort, enterprise, get-up-and-go*, initiative, push, surge; CONCEPTS 87,300

drive [*n3*] *person's will to achieve* ambition, clout, effort, energy, enterprise, fire in belly*, get-up-and-go, goods*, gumption*, guts*, impellent, impetus, impulse, initiative, momentum, motivation, motive, moxie*, pep, pressure, punch*, push*, right stuff*, spunk*, steam*, stuff*, vigor, vitality, what it takes*, zip*; CONCEPTS 411,706

drive [*v1*] *move or urge on* actuate, act upon, animate, arouse, bulldoze*, chase, coerce, compel, constrain, dog*, egg on*, encourage, force, goad, goose*, harass, hasten, herd, hound*, hurl, hurry, hustle, impel, induce, inspire, instigate, kick, lean on*, make, motivate, nag, oblige, overburden, overwork, pound, press, pressure, prod, prompt, propel, provoke, push, put up to*, railroad*, ride herd on*, rouse, rush, send, shepherd, shove, spirit up, spur, steamroll*, stimulate, work on, worry; CONCEPTS 68,147,208 —Ant. check, curb, discourage, dissuade, halt, repress, retard, stop

drive [*v2*] *moving, controlling a vehicle* actuate, advance, bear down, bicycle, bike, burn rubber*, burn up the road*, coast, cruise, cycle, dash, direct, drag, fire up*, floor it*, fly, guide, handle, impel, lean on it*, make sparks fly*, manage, mobilize, motor, operate, pour it on*, propel, push, ride, roll, run, send, speed, spin, start, steer, step on it*, step on the gas*, tailgate, tool*, transport, travel, turn, vehiculate*, wheel; CONCEPTS 148,187 —Ant. halt, stop

drive [*v3*] *hit with heavy blow* batter, beat, butt, dash, dig, hammer, jackhammer, knock, maul, plunge, pop, punch, ram, run, shoot, sink, smite, sock, stab, stick, strike, throw, thrust, thump, twack*, whack*, wham*; CONCEPT 189

drive at [*v*] *mean, suggest as meaning* aim, allude to, contemplate, design, get at, have in mind, hint at, imply, indicate, intend, intimate, propose, refer to, signify; CONCEPTS 73,682

drivel [*n*] *foolish talk* babble, balderdash*, blather, bunk*, double-talk, gibberish, gobbledygook*, Greek*, hogwash*, hooey*, jabber*, nonsense, poppycock*, prating, rot*, rubbish*, tripe*, twaddle*; CONCEPT 278 —Ant. sense

drivel [*v1*] *talk foolishly* babble, blabber, blather*, blethe, gab, gabble, prate, prattle, ramble, twaddle*, waffle*; CONCEPT 266

drivel [*v2*] *drool* dribble, salivate, slaver, slobber; CONCEPTS 185,256

driver [*n*] *person who engineers vehicle* autoist, automobilist, cabbie, chauffeur, coach person, hack*, handler, jockey, leadfoot*, motorist, operator, road hog*, trainer, whip*; CONCEPT 423 —Ant. passenger

driving [*adj*] *forceful* active, compelling, dynamic, energetic, enterprising, galvanic, impellent, lively, propulsive, sweeping, urging,

drizzle [v] *fine rain* dribble, drip, drop, mist, mizzle, shower, spit, spray, sprinkle; CONCEPT 526 —*Ant.* downpour

droid [n] *robot* android, clone, cyborg, drone; CONCEPT 463

droll [adj] *amusing, farcical* absurd, camp, campy, clownish, comic, comical, crack-up, diverting, eccentric, entertaining, for grins*, funny, gagged up*, gelastic, humorous, jocular, joshing, laffer, laughable, ludicrous, odd, preposterous, quaint, queer, quizzical, ridiculous, riot, risible, waggish, whimsical; CONCEPTS 267,548 —*Ant.* dramatic, serious, traumatic, unfunny

drone [n1] *person who is lazy* idler, leech, loafer, lounger, parasite, slug, sluggard, sponger*; CONCEPT 412 —*Ant.* overachiever, workaholic

drone [n2] *continuous noise* buzz, hum, murmur, purr, sound, vibration, whirr; CONCEPT 595 —*Ant.* quiet, silence

drone [v] *making noise continuously* bombinate, buzz, chant, drawl, hum, intone, nasalize, purr, sound, strum, thrum, vibrate, whirr; CONCEPTS 65,77 —*Ant.* be quiet, silence

drool [n] *saliva* drivel, expectoration, salivation, slaver, slobber, spit, spittle; CONCEPT 467

drool [v1] *drivel* dribble, lick one's chops*, salivate, slaver, slobber, water at the mouth; CONCEPT 467

drool [v2] *salivate* dribble, drivel, froth, ooze, run, slabber, slaver, slobber, spit, water, water at the mouth; CONCEPTS 185,256

drool [v3] *desire, lust after* dote on, enthuse, fondle, gush, lick chops*, make much of, pet, rave, rhapsodize, rhapsody, slobber over*, spoil, want; CONCEPT 20

droop [v] *hang down; languish* bend, dangle, decline, depress, diminish, drop, fade, fail, faint, fall down, flag, lean, let down, loll, lop, sag, settle, sink, sling, slouch, slump, subside, suspend, weaken, wilt, wither; CONCEPTS 181,699 —*Ant.* inflate, rise

droopy [adj] *limp* bent, drooping, flabby, floppy, languid, languorous, lassitudinous, pendulous, sagging, saggy, slouchy, stooped, wilting; CONCEPT 485 —*Ant.* full, inflated, raised

drop [n1] *globule* bead, bit, bubble, crumb, dab, dash, dewdrop, driblet, drip, droplet, iota, molecule, morsel, nip, ounce, particle, pearl, pinch, sip, smidgen, speck, splash, spot, taste, tear, teardrop, trace, trickle; CONCEPTS 467, 468

drop [n2] *steep decline; hole* abyss, chasm, declivity, deepness, depth, descent, dip, fall, plunge, precipice, slope, tumble; CONCEPTS 181,509 —*Ant.* incline, mound, mountain, rise

drop [n3] *decrease* cut, decline, descent, deterioration, dip, downfall, downslide, downswing, downtrend, downturn, fall, fall-off, landslide, lapse, lowering, precipitation, reduction, sag, slide, slip, slump, tumble, upset; CONCEPTS 698,776 —*Ant.* increase, rise

drop [v1] *fall in globules* bead, bleed, descend, distill, drain, dribble, drip, emanate, hail, leak, ooze, percolate, precipitate, seep, snow, splash, trickle, trill; CONCEPT 179 —*Ant.* downpour, pour

drop [v2] *let go of; fall* abandon, bring down, cave in, collapse, decline, depress, descend, dive, duck, dump, fell, floor, flop, give up, go down, ground, keel over*, knock, loosen, lower, nose-dive*, pitch, plummet, plunge, plunge, release, relinquish, shed, shoot, sink, slide, slip, slump, topple, tumble, unload; CONCEPTS 181,200 —*Ant.* ascend, mount, rise, take up

drop [v3] *abandon; ignore* adios, bag, be alienated from, break with, call off, cancel, cast off, cease, desert, discontinue, dismiss, disown, ditch*, divorce, dust off*, eighty-six*, end, forfeit, forget about, forsake, give up, have done with*, interrupt, jilt, kick*, leave, lose, part from, part with, quit, reject, relinquish, remit, renounce, repudiate, resign, sacrifice, scratch*, scrub*, separate, shake, stop, terminate, throw over, wash out*, waste one*, wipe out*, write off*; CONCEPTS 30, 121,195 —*Ant.* continue, do, mount, pursue, take up

drop in [v] *visit* blow in*, call, call upon, come by, come over, go and see*, look in on, look up, pop in*, run in*, stop, stop by, stop in, turn up; CONCEPT 227

drop in the bucket [n] *small amount* bit, drop in the ocean*, not enough, pittance, small change*, small potatoes*, small quantity, speck, trivial amount; CONCEPT 831

drop off [v1] *decrease* decline, diminish, dwindle, fall away, fall off, lessen, sag, slacken, slide, slip, slump; CONCEPTS 698,776 —*Ant.* go up, increase, rise

drop off [v2] *deliver* deposit, give, hand over, leave, let off, present, set down, unload; CONCEPT 108 —*Ant.* receive, take away

drop off [v3] *fall asleep* catnap, doze, doze off*, drowse, have forty winks*, nod, nod off*, snooze; CONCEPTS 210,315 —*Ant.* awake, wake

drop out [v] *stop doing an activity* abandon, back out, cease, forsake, give notice, give up, leave, quit, renege, retreat, withdraw; CONCEPT 121 —*Ant.* begin, carry out, engage, join

droppings [n] *excrement* cow pies*, cowplop*, crap, dung, feces, fertilizer, guano, manure, meadow muffin*, night soil*, ordure, poop*; CONCEPT 260

drought [n] *dryness; shortage of supply* aridity, dearth, deficiency, dehydration, desiccation, dry spell, insufficiency, lack, need, parchedness, rainlessness, scarcity, want; CONCEPTS 607,646 —*Ant.* monsoon, wetness

drove [n] *large gathering* collection, company, crowd, crush, drive, flock, herd, horde, mob, multitude, pack, press, rout, run, swarm, throng; CONCEPTS 397,432

drown [v] *submerge in liquid; submerge and die* asphyxiate, deluge, dip, douse, drench, engulf, flood, go down, go under, immerse, inundate, knock over, obliterate, overcome, overflow, overpower, overwhelm, plunge, prostrate, sink, soak, sop, souse, stifle, suffocate, swamp, whelm, wipe out; CONCEPTS 252,256 —*Ant.* float, rescue, save

drowsy [adj] *sleepy* comatose, dazed, dopy, dozing, dozy, dreamy, drugged, half asleep, heavy, indolent, lackadaisical, languid, lazy, lethargic, lulling, napping, nodding, out of it*,

restful, sluggish, slumberous, snoozy, somnolent, soothing, soporific, tired, torpid; CONCEPTS 406,539 —*Ant.* alert, awake, energized, lively

drub [v] *thrash* beat, cane, clobber, defeat, flog, hit, lash, pound, spank, strike, tan, trounce, wallop, whip; CONCEPT 95

drudge [n] *slave, very hard worker* factotum, grind*, laborer, menial, nose to grindstone*, peon*, plodder*, servant, toiler, workaholic, worker; workhorse; CONCEPT 348 —*Ant.* idler, laze

drudge [v] *work very hard* back to the salt mines*, dig, grind*, hammer*, keep nose to grindstone*, labor, muck*, perform, plod, plow, plug away*, pound*, schlepp*, slave, slog, sweat, toil, travail; CONCEPTS 87,100,324 —*Ant.* avoid, be lazy, dodge, hesitate, idle

drudgery [n] *hard, tedious work* backbreaker*, chore, daily grind*, elbow grease*, grind*, gruntwork*, labor, menial labor, rat race, slavery, struggle, sweat, toil, travail, workout; CONCEPT 362 —*Ant.* snap

drug [n] *medication* biologic, cure, depressant, dope, essence, medicament, medicinal, medicine, narcotic, opiate, pharmaceutical, physic, pill, poison, potion, prescription, remedy, sedative, stimulant, tonic; CONCEPT 307

drug [v] *put under influence of medication* analgize, anesthetize, benumb, blunt, deaden, desensitize, dope*, dope up, dose, dose up*, fix, hit, knock out*, medicate, narcotize, numb, poison, relax, sedate, stupefy, treat; CONCEPT 310

drugged [adj] *under the influence of medication* benumbed, blown away*, coked*, comatose, dazed, doped, dopey*, floating*, flying*, high*, junked-up*, loaded*, narcotized, on a trip*, out of it*, ripped*, smashed*, spaced-out*, stoned*, strung out*, stupefied, unconscious; CONCEPT 314 —*Ant.* clean, undrugged

druggist [n] *pharmacist* apothecary, pharmacologist, posologist; CONCEPT 357

drum [v] *beat, tap a beat* boom*, pulsate, rap, reverberate, roar, strum, tattoo, throb, thrum, thunder*; CONCEPTS 65,189

drum into [v] *make a point strongly* din into, drive home*, hammer away*, harp on*, instill, reiterate; CONCEPTS 49,75

drum up [v] *gather support for something* attract, bid for, canvass, discover, obtain, petition, round up, solicit, succeed in finding; CONCEPTS 68,300 —*Ant.* dissuade, repulse, turn off

drunk [adj] *intoxicated by alcohol* bashed, befuddled, boozed up*, buzzed*, crocked*, feeling no pain*, flushed*, flying*, fuddled, glazed*, groggy, high*, inebriated, juiced*, laced*, liquored up*, lit*, lush, muddled, plastered*, potted*, seeing double*, sloshed*, stewed*, stoned*, tanked*, three sheets to the wind*, tight*, tipsy, totaled*, under the influence, under the table*, wasted*; CONCEPTS 314,545 —*Ant.* sober, straight

drunk/drunkard [n] *person who is inebriated* alcoholic, boozer*, carouser*, dipsomaniac, drinker, guzzler*, inebriate, lush*, sot*, sponge*, wino*; CONCEPT 423

dry [adj1] *moistureless* anhydrous, arid, athirst, baked, bald, bare, barren, dehydrated, depleted,

desert, desiccant, desiccated, drained, dried-up, droughty, dusty, evaporated, exhausted, hard, impoverished, juiceless, not irrigated, parched, rainless, sapless, sapped, sear, shriveled, stale, thirsty, torrid, unmoistened, waterless; CONCEPT 603 —*Ant.* damp, dripping, humid, juicy, moist, soaked, soggy, watery, wet

dry [adj2] *dull, uninteresting* apathetic, blah, boring, bromidic, draggy, dreary, dull as dishwater*, dusty, ho hum*, impassive, inelaborate, insipid, matter-of-fact, modest, monotonous, naked, phlegmatic, plain, simple, tedious, tiresome, trite, wearful, wearisome; CONCEPT 529 —*Ant.* exciting, interesting, juicy, lively, untiring

dry [adj3] *sarcastic, sharp-tongued* acerbic, arcane, biting, caustic, cutting, cynical, deadpan, droll, harsh, humorous, ironical, keen, low-key, restrained, salty, sardonic, satirical, sharp, sly, sour, subtle, tart; CONCEPT 267

dry [v] *take moisture out of* anhydrate, bake, blot, concentrate, condense, dehumidify, dehydrate, deplete, desiccate, drain, empty, evaporate, exhaust, exsiccate, freeze-dry, harden, kiln, mummify, parch, scorch, sear, shrivel, soak up, sponge, stale, swab, torrefy, towel, wilt, wipe, wither, wizen; CONCEPTS 250,469 —*Ant.* dampen, soak, water, wet

dual [adj] *two-fold* bifold, binal, binary, coupled, double, doubleheader, duplex, duplicate, matched, paired, twin; CONCEPT 762

dub [v] *name, label something* baptize, bestow, call, christen, confer, denominate, designate, entitle, knight, nickname, style, tag, term, title; CONCEPT 62

dubious [adj1] *doubtful* arguable, chancy, debatable, diffident, disputable, dubitable, equivocal, far-fetched, fishy*, fly-by-night*, hesitant, iffy*, improbable, indecisive, moot, mootable, open, perplexed, problematic, questionable, reluctant, shady, skeptical, suspect, suspicious, touch and go*, trustless, unassured, uncertain, unclear, unconvinced, undecided, undependable, unlikely, unreliable, unsure, untrustworthy, untrusty, wavering; CONCEPT 552 —*Ant.* certain, definite, doubtless, positive, reliable, sure, trustworthy, trusty, undoubtful

dubious [adj2] *vague, unclear* ambiguous, debatable, disinclined, doubtful, equivocal, indefinite, indeterminate, mistrustful, obscure, open, problematic, problematical, undecided, unsettled; CONCEPTS 535,576 —*Ant.* certain, clear, definite, unambiguous, unobscure

duck [v] *drop down; avoid* bend, bob, bow, crouch, dip, dive, dodge, double, elude, escape, evade, fence, lower, lurch, move to side, parry, plunge, shirk, shun, shy, sidestep, stoop, submerge; CONCEPTS 102,154,181 —*Ant.* face, jump, meet

duck soup [n] *easily accomplished task* a breeze, a snap, cakewalk, child's play, easy thing, easy to do, piece of cake; CONCEPT 693

duct [n] *channel, pipe* aqueduct, canal, conduit, course, funnel, passage, tube, vessel, watercourse; CONCEPT 501

ductile [adj] *pliant, flexible* adaptable, amenable, biddable, docile, extensile, malleable, manageable, moldable, plastic, pliable, responsive, submitting, supple, tractable, yielding;

CONCEPTS 488,490 —*Ant.* hard, inflexible, intractable, stiff, unyielding

dud [*n*] *failure* bomb, bummer, bust, debacle, flop, lemon, loser, washout; CONCEPT 674 —*Ant.* success

dude [*n1*] *friend* buddy, chap, fellow, guy; CONCEPT 423

dude [*n2*] *dapper man* Beau Brummel*, coxcomb, dandy, fancy Dan*, fashion plate, fine gentleman, fop, slicker*, stud; CONCEPT 423

duds [*n*] *clothes* accoutrement, apparel, array, civvies*, costume, covering, dress, finery, frippery, frock, garb, garments, habiliment, outfit, rags*, raiment, sportswear, Sunday best*, tatters*, threads*, wardrobe; CONCEPT 451

due [*adj1*] *unpaid; owing money* chargeable, collectible, expected, in arrears, IOU, mature, not met, outstanding, overdue, owed, payable, receivable, scheduled, to be paid, unliquidated, unsatisfied, unsettled; CONCEPT 334 —*Ant.* paid

due [*adj2*] *appropriate, proper* becoming, coming, condign, deserved, earned, equitable, fair, fit, fitting, good, just, justified, merited, obligatory, requisite, rhadamanthine, right, rightful, suitable; CONCEPT 558 —*Ant.* improper, inappropriate, insufficient, unjustified, unmerited, unrightful, unsuitable

due [*adv*] *directly* dead, direct, exactly, right, straight, straightly, undeviatingly; CONCEPTS 581,799 —*Ant.* indirectly

due [*n*] *expected reward* be in line for*, claim, comeuppance, compensation, deserts*, entitlement, guerdon, interest, merits, need, payment, perquisite, prerogative, privilege, rate, recompense, repayment, reprisal, retaliation, retribution, revenge, right, rights, satisfaction, title, vengeance, what is coming to one*; CONCEPTS 337,710

duel [*n*] *fight* affair of honor, bout, challenge, engagement, fencing, joust, shootout, single combat, sword fight; CONCEPTS 53,532

dues [*n*] *payment for membership* ante, arrearage, assessment, charge, charges, collection, contribution, custom, debit, debt, duty, fee, kickback, levy, liability, obligation, pay, protection, rates, tax, toll; CONCEPTS 344,679

duff [*n*] *rear end* ass, backside, behind, buns*, butt*, buttocks, cheeks*, derriere, fanny*, gluteus maximus, heinie*, keister, posterior, seat*; CONCEPT 392

dulcet [*adj*] *melodious* agreeable, musical, pleasing to the ear, pleasurable, sweet, sweet-sounding; CONCEPT 594

dull [*adj1*] *unintelligent* addled, backward, besotted, boring, brainless, daffy, daft, dense, dim, dim-witted, doltish, dumb, feeble-minded, half-baked, ignorant, imbecile, indolent, insensate, low, moronic, not bright, numskulled, obtuse, scatterbrained, shallow, simple, simple-minded, slow, sluggish, stolid, stupid, tedious, thick, unintellectual, vacuous, wearisome, witless; CONCEPT 402 —*Ant.* intelligent, keen, sharp, smart, witty

dull [*adj2*] *insensitive* accustomed, apathetic, blank, boring, callous, colorless, dead, depressed, empty, even, flat, heavy, impassible, inactive, indifferent, inert, insensible, jejune, languid, lifeless, listless, lumpy, monotonous, passionless, placid, prosaic, quiet, regular, routine, slack, slow, sluggish, spiritless, stagnant, still, stolid, torpid, unexciting, unresponsive, unsympathetic, usual, vacuous; CONCEPT 542 —*Ant.* lively, quick, sensitive, vivacious

dull [*adj3*] *boring, uninteresting* abused, archaic, arid, big yawn*, blah, colorless, common, commonplace, dead, dismal, dreary, driveling, dry, familiar, flat, hackneyed, heavy, hoary, ho hum*, humdrum*, insipid, jejune, longwinded, monotonous, oft-repeated*, ordinary, out-of-date, plain, pointless, prolix, prosaic, prosy, repetitious, repetitive, routine, run-of-the-mill*, soporific, stale, stock, stupid, tame, tedious, tired, tiresome, trite, unimaginative, uninspiring, usual, usual thing, vapid, worn-out; CONCEPTS 529,530 —*Ant.* active, exciting, interesting, lively

dull [*adj4*] *not sharp* blunt, blunted, edentate, edgeless, flat, not keen, obtuse, pointless, round, square, toothless, turned, unpointed, unsharpened; CONCEPT 486 —*Ant.* knifelike, pointed, serrated, sharp

dull [*adj5*] *uneventful* accustomed, apathetic, blah, boring, dead, depressed, draggy*, even, falling off, flat, inactive, inert, languid, lifeless, listless, monotonous, placid, quiet, regular, routine, sitting tight*, slack, slothful, slow,* sluggish, stagnant, still, stolid, tight, torpid, unexciting, unresponsive, usual, without incident, yawn; CONCEPT 548 —*Ant.* active, eventful, exciting, interesting, lively

dull [*adj6*] *drab, lackluster in effect on senses* ashen, black, blind, cloudy, cold, colorless, dark, dead, dim, dingy, dismal, dun, dusky, faded, feeble, flat, grimy, hazy, indistinct, leaden, lifeless, low, matte, mousy, muddy, muffled, murky, muted, obscure, opaque, overcast, plain, shadowy, sober, soft, softened, somber, sooty, subdued, subfusc, toned-down, unlit; CONCEPTS 594,617 —*Ant.* bright, clear, light, luminous, lustrous

dullard [*n*] *dolt* airhead*, blockhead*, boob*, dimwit, dope*, dork*, dumbbell*, dunce, fool, idiot, imbecile, lamebrain*, lunkhead*, meathead*, nitwit, simpleton, stupid person; CONCEPTS 412,423

dullsville [*adj*] *boring* blah*, dead*, deadsville, dragsville, hicksville, tedious; CONCEPTS 529,548

duly [*adv*] *accordingly, properly* appropriately, at the proper time, befittingly, correctly, decorously, deservedly, on time, punctually, rightfully, suitably; CONCEPTS 558,799 —*Ant.* improperly, unduly, unsuitably

dumb [*adj1*] *unable to speak* at a loss for words*, inarticulate, incoherent, mousy*, mum, mute, quiet, silent, soundless, speechless, tongue-tied, uncommunicative, voiceless, wordless; CONCEPT 593 —*Ant.* speaking

dumb [*adj2*] *stupid, unintelligent* dense, dim-witted, doltish, dull, feebleminded, foolish, moronic, simple-minded, thick*; CONCEPT 402 —*Ant.* bright, intelligent, sharp, smart

dumbbell [*n*] *stupid person* dodo*, dolt, dullard, dumbo*, dumdum*, dummy, dunce, idiot, ignoramus, moron, simpleton; CONCEPTS 412,423 —*Ant.* brain, genius

dumbfound [*v*] *astound, confuse* amaze, astonish, bewilder, blow away*, blow one's mind*, boggle, bowl over*, confound, flabbergast, knock over with feather*, nonplus, overwhelm, puzzle, stagger, startle, stun, surprise, take aback, throw, throw into a tizzy*; CONCEPTS 16,42 —Ant. clear up, explain, explicate, lay out

dumbfounded [adj] *astounded, confused* agape, aghast, amazed, astonished, bamboozled*, beat, bewildered, blown away*, bowled over*, breathless, buffaloed*, confounded, dismayed, dumb, flabbergasted, floored, knocked, licked, nonplused, overcome, overwhelmed, puzzled, shocked, speechless, staggered, startled, stuck, stumped, stunned, surprised, taken aback, thrown, thunderstruck*; CONCEPT 403 —Ant. aware, expectant, unsurprised

dumbstruck [adj] *shocked* amazed, astonished, astounded, blown away, dumbfounded, flabbergasted, jolted, rendered speechless, startled, stunned, stupefied; CONCEPT 42

dummy [n1] *mannequin* copy, counterfeit, duplicate, figure, form, imitation, manikin, model, ringer*, sham*, stand-in, sub, substitute; CONCEPTS 436,716 —Ant. being, entity

dummy [n2] *stupid person* blockhead*, dimwit*, dolt*, dullard*, dunce, fool, idiot, ignoramus, moron, numskull, oaf, simpleton; CONCEPTS 412,423 —Ant. brain, genius

dump [n1] *junkyard* ash heap*, cesspool, depot, dumping ground, garbage lot, junk pile*, magazine, refuse heap, rubbish pile, swamp; CONCEPTS 438,449,680

dump [n2] *slummy establishment* hole, hovel, joint*, mess*, pigpen*, pigsty*, shack, shanty, slum, sty; CONCEPTS 449,673

dump [v] *drop, throw away* cast, chuck, clear out, deep-six*, deposit, discard, discharge, dispose of, ditch, drain, eject, empty, evacuate, expel, exude, fling, fling down, get rid of, jettison, junk, leave, let fall, scrap, throw down, throw out, throw overboard*, tip, unload, unpack; CONCEPTS 180,181 —Ant. hold, keep, maintain, save

dumps [n] *depression* blahs*, blues*, bummer, cheerlessness, doldrums, dreariness, gloom, gloominess, low spirits, melancholy, sulks, the blues*, trouble, unhappiness, woefulness; CONCEPT 410

dumpy [adj] *short and stout* chubby, chunky, fat, homely, plump, podgy, pudgy, roly-poly, squat, stocky, stumpy, tubby; CONCEPT 491

dunce [n] *stupid person* ass, birdbrain*, blockhead*, bonehead*, buffoon, dimwit*, dolt, donkey*, dope, dork*, drip*, dullard, dunderhead*, fool, goof, goof ball*, half-wit, idiot, ignoramus, imbecile, jerk, knucklehead*, lame-brain*, lightweight*, moron, nerd*, nincompoop*, ninny*, nitwit, numskull, oaf, pinhead*, scatter-brain*, schnook*, simpleton, twit*; CONCEPTS 412,423 —Ant. brain, genius

dune [n] *hill* hillock, hummock, knoll, ridge, sand drift, sand dune, sand pile; CONCEPT 509

dung [n] *excrement* cow pies*, cowplop*, crap, droppings, feces, fertilizer, guano, manure, meadow muffin*, night soil*, ordure, poop*; CONCEPT 260

dungarees [n] *blue jeans* denims, jeans, pants, trousers; CONCEPT 451

dungeon [n] *prison* cell, oubliette, torture chamber, vault; CONCEPTS 439,449,516

dunk [v] *dip in liquid* douse, duck, immerse, saturate, soak, sop, souse, submerge, submerse; CONCEPT 256

duo [n] *twosome* brace, couple, doublet, dyad, pair; CONCEPT 787

dupe [n] *person who is fooled* butt*, chump*, easy mark*, fish*, fool, mark*, patsy*, pigeon*, pushover*, sap*, sitting duck*, sucker, victim; CONCEPT 423 —Ant. cognizant

dupe [v] *fool someone* baffle, bamboozle*, beguile, betray, catch, cheat, chicane, circumvent, con, cozen, deceive, defraud, delude, double-cross, dust*, flimflam*, gull, hoax, hoodwink*, hornswoggle, jerk around*, kid, mislead, outwit, overreach, pull one's leg*, pull something*, rip off*, rook*, rope in*, shaft, spoof, swindle, trick, victimize; CONCEPT 59

duplex [adj] *twofold* double, paired, twin; CONCEPT 771

duplicate [adj] *matching* alike, corresponding, dualistic, duple, duplex, equal, equivalent, identic, identical, indistinguishable, same, self-same, tantamount, twin, twofold, very; CONCEPTS 563,566 —Ant. different, unmatching

duplicate [n] *copy, reproduction* analogue, carbon, carbon copy*, chip off the old block*, clone, companion, coordinate, copycat*, correlate, counterfeit, counterpart, counter-script, dead ringer*, ditto*, double, dupe*, duplication, facsimile, fake, fellow, germination, imitation, knockoff*, likeness, lookalike, match, mate, obverse, parallel, phony, photocopy, photostat, pirate, reciprocal, recurrence, repetition, replica, replication, repro*, ringer*, second, similarity, spitting image*, stat, twin, Xerox*; CONCEPTS 664,667,716 —Ant. archetype, model, original, prototype

duplicate [v] *make a copy; repeat* act like, clone, copy, counterfeit, ditto*, do again, do a takeoff*, do like*, double, dualize, dupe, echo, fake, go like*, imitate, knock off*, make like*, make replica, make twofold, manifold, mimeo, mirror, multiply, phony, photocopy, photostat, pirate*, redo, redouble, reduplicate, remake, replicate, repro, reproduce, rework, stat, take off as*, trace, Xerox*; CONCEPTS 91,171

duplicitous [adj] *deceptive* cheating, deceitful, dishonest, double-dealing, shady, two-faced, two-timing; CONCEPTS 401,582

duplicity [n] *deception* artifice, chicanery, cunning, deceit, dirty dealing*, dirty pool*, dirty trick, dirty work*, dishonesty, dissemblance, dissimulation, double-dealing, dualism, duality, faithlessness, falsehood, fraud, guile, hypocrisy, Judas kiss*, one-upmanship, perfidiousness, perfidy, skullduggery, stab in back*, treacherousness, treachery, two-facedness*, twoness; CONCEPTS 59,63 —Ant. forthrightness, honesty, trustworthiness

durability [n] *sturdiness over time* backbone, constancy, durableness, endurance, grit, guts*, gutsiness, hard as nails*, heart*, imperishability, intestinal fortitude, lastingness, moxie*, permanence, persistence, stamina, starch*, staying power*, stick-to-itiveness*; CONCEPTS 721,731,732 —Ant. impermanency, poorness, unreliability, weakness

durable [adj] *sturdy, long-lasting* abiding, constant, dependable, diuturnal, enduring, fast, firm, fixed, impervious, lasting, long-continued, perdurable, perduring, permanent, persistent, reliable, resistant, sound, stable, stout, strong, substantial, tenacious, tough;CONCEPTS 482, 488,489 —Ant. fragile, impermanent, poorly made, temporary, undependable, unsturdy, weak

duration [n] *length of action, event* continuance, continuation, continuity, endurance, extent, period, perpetuation, persistence, prolongation, run, span, spell, stretch, term, tide, time; CONCEPT 804

duress [n] *threat, hardship* bondage, captivity, coercion, compulsion, confinement, constraint, control, detention, discipline, force, imprisonment, incarceration, pressure, restraint, violence; CONCEPTS 14,674

during [prep] *concurrently with an activity, event* all along, all the while, amid, as, at the same time as, at the time, for the time being, in the course of, in the interim, in the meanwhile, in the middle of, in the time of, meanwhile, mid, midst, over, pending, the time between, the whole time, throughout, until, when, while; CONCEPT 820

dusk [n] *early evening* dark, dimday, dimmet, eventide, gloaming, gloom, night, nightfall, sundown, sunset, twilight; CONCEPT 810 —Ant. dawn

dusky [adj] *dark-hued; murky* adusk, bistered, bleak, brunette, caliginous, cheerless, cloudy, crepuscular, dark, dark-complexioned, darkish, desolate, dim, dismal, dull, funereal, gloomy, joyless, lightless, obscure, overcast, sable, shadowy, shady, swart, swarthy, tenebrous, twilight, twilit, unilluminated, veiled; CONCEPTS 617,618 —Ant. bright, clear, light

dust [n] *tiny particles in the air* ashes, cinders, dirt, dust bunnies*, earth, filth, flakes, fragments, gilings, granules, grime, grit, ground, lint, loess, powder, refuse, sand, smut, soil, soot; CONCEPT 437

dust [v] *sprinkle tiny particles* besprinkle, cover, dredge, powder, scatter, sift, spray, spread; CONCEPTS 172,222

dusty [adj] *filled with or covered with powdery particles* arenaceous, arenose, chalky, crumbly, dirty, friable, granular, grubby, sandy, sooty, unclean, undusted, unswept, untouched; CONCEPT 485 —Ant. clean, clear

dutiful [adj] *obedient* binding, compliant, conscientious, deferential, devoted, docile, duteous, faithful, incumbent on, obligatory, punctilious, regardful, respectful, reverential, submissive; CONCEPT 542 —Ant. betraying, disobedient, faithless, irresponsible, undutiful, unfaithful, unrespectful

duty [n1] *responsibility, assignment* burden, business, calling, charge, chore, commission, commitment, committal, contract, devoir, dues, engagement, function, hook*, job, load, millstone*, minding the store*, mission, must, need, obligation, occupation, office, onus, ought*, pains, part, province, role, service, station, string*, taking care of business*, task, trouble, trust, undertaking, weight, work;CONCEPTS 362,376,679 —Ant. disregard, irresponsibility

duty [n2] *tax on foreign goods* assessment, custom, customs, due, excise, impost, levy, rate, revenue, tariff, toll; CONCEPT 329

duty [n3] *moral obligation* accountability, accountableness, allegiance, amenability, answerability, burden, call of duty, charge, conscience, deference, devoir, faithfulness, good faith, honesty, integrity, liability, loyalty, obedience, pledge, respect, reverence; CONCEPT 388 —Ant. faithlessness, inconstancy, treachery

dwarf [adj] *miniature, tiny* baby, diminutive, low, petite, pocket, small, undersized; CONCEPT 773 —Ant. big, giant, huge, large

dwarf [n] *very small person* bantam, dwarfling, homunculus, Lilliputian*, midget, Tom Thumb*; CONCEPT 424 —Ant. giant

dwarf [v] *minimize* belittle, check, detract from, dim, diminish, dominate, hinder, look down upon, lower, make small, micrify, minify, overshadow, predominate, retard, rise above, stunt, suppress, tower above, tower over; CONCEPTS 7,19,698,741 —Ant. maximize, oversize

dwell [v] *live in* abide, bide, bunk*, continue, crash*, establish oneself, exist, flop*, hang one's hat*, hang out*, hole up*, inhabit, keep house, locate, lodge, make one's home, nest, occupy, park*, perch*, pitch tent*, quarter, remain, rent, reside, rest, room, roost*, settle, sojourn, squat*, stay, stop, tarry, tenant, tent; CONCEPT 226

dwelling [n] *home* abode, castle, commoracy, den, digs*, domicile, dump*, establishment, habitat, habitation, haunt, hole in the wall*, house, lodging, pad, quarters, residence, residency; CONCEPT 516

dwell on/dwell upon [v] *linger over; be engrossed in* consider, continue, elaborate, emphasize, expatiate, harp on*, involve oneself, tarry over; CONCEPTS 17,239 —Ant. forget, ignore, miss, pass

dwindle [v] *waste away; taper off* abate, bate, become smaller, close, contract, decay, decline, decrease, die away, die down, die out, diminish, drain, drop, ebb, fade, fall, grow less, lessen, peter out*, pine, shrink, shrivel, sink, slack off*, subside, taper, wane, weaken, wither; CONCEPTS 698,776 —Ant. develop, enlarge, expand, extend, grow, increase, save, swell

dye [n] *coloring agent* color, colorant, dyestuff, pigment, stain, tincture, tinge, tint; CONCEPT 259 —Ant. bleach, whitener

dye [v] *change color with mixture* impregnate, pigment, stain, tincture, tinge, tint; CONCEPT 250 —Ant. bleach, fade, whiten

dyed-in-the-wool [adj] *through and through* absolute, complete, deep-down, deeply ingrained, deep-rooted, die-hard, entrenched, fixed, genuine, hardened, long-standing, to the core*, unchangeable, uncompromising; CONCEPT 554

dying [adj] *failing, expiring* at death's door*, at end of rope*, decaying, declining, disintegrating, done for*, doomed, ebbing, fading, fated, final, giving up the ghost*, going, in extremis, moribund, mortal, one foot in grave*, on last leg*, passing, perishing, sinking, vanishing, withering; CONCEPT 539 —Ant. creating, developing, growing, living, reviving

dynamic [adj] *active, vital* activating, aggressive, changing, charismatic, coming on strong*, compelling, driving, effective, electric, energetic, energizing, enterprising, forceful, forcible, go-ahead*, go-getter*, go-getting*, highpowered, hyped-up, influential, intense, lively, lusty, magnetic, peppy*, play for keeps*, play hard ball*, potent, powerful, productive, progressive, red-blooded*, strenuous, vehement, vigorous, vitalizing, zippy*; CONCEPTS 404,540,542 —*Ant.* apathetic, boring, dull, inactive, passive, unexciting

dynamite [n] *explosive* gelignite, nitroglycerin, TNT, trinitrotoluene; CONCEPT 500

dynamo [n] *go-getter* achiever, ball of fire*, bundle of energy*, busy person, doer, eager beaver*, energetic person, fireball*, generator, hard worker, hot shot, live wire*, mover and shaker*, pistol*, risk-taker, spark plug*, whiz kid*; CONCEPT 706

dynasty [n] *area of rule* absolutism, ascendancy, dominion, empire, government, house, regime, sovereignty, sway; CONCEPTS 435,508

dysfunctional [adj] *socially impaired* broken, debilitated, decayed, defective, deteriorated, flawed, inhibited, maladjusted, malfunctional, sick, undermined, unfit, wounded; CONCEPT 314

E

each [adj] *every* all, any, exclusive, individual, one by one*, particular, personal, piece by piece*, respective, separate, several, single, specific, various, without exception; CONCEPT 577 —*Ant.* none

each [adv] *apiece; for one* all, a pop*, a shot*, aside, a throw*, by the, every, individually, per, per capita, per head, per person, per unit, proportionately, respectively, separately, singly, without exception; CONCEPT 577

each [pron] *each one* each and every one*, each other, every last one, every one, one, one and all*, one another; CONCEPT 577 —*Ant.* none

eager [adj] *anxious, enthusiastic* acquisitive, agog, ambitious, antsy, appetent, ardent, athirst, avid, breathless, champing at the bit*, covetous, craving, desiring, desirous, dying to, earnest, fervent, fervid, greedy, gung ho*, hankering, heated, hot*, hot to trot*, hungry*, impatient, intent, keen, longing, pining, rarin' to go*, ready and willing*, restive, restless, self-starting, solicitous, thirsty, vehement, voracious, warmblooded*, wild, wishful, yearning, zealous; CONCEPTS 326,401,542 —*Ant.* apathetic, disinterested, dispassionate, unconcerned, uneager, unenthusiastic

eager beaver [n] *active person* ambitious person, ball of fire*, busy bee*, busy person, doer, dynamo, fireball*, go-getter, hot shot, live wire*, pistol*, self-starter, spark plug*, workhorse; CONCEPT 706

eagerness [n] *enthusiasm, anxiousness* alacrity, ambition, anticipation, ardor, avidity, earnestness, excitement, fervor, greediness, gusto, heartiness, hunger, impatience, impetuosity, intentness, keenness, longing, promptness, quickness, solicitude, thirst, vehemence, voracity, yearning, zeal, zest, zing*; CONCEPTS 20,633,657 —*Ant.* apathy, disinterest

eagle-eyed [adj] *keen-eyed* clear-sighted, hawk-eyed, observant, perceptive, perspicacious, sharp-eyed, X-ray eye;CONCEPTS 402,542

ear [n] *attention* appreciation, consideration, discrimination, hearing, heed, mark, mind, note, notice, observance, observation, perception, regard, remark, sensitivity, taste; CONCEPT 532

early [adj1] *in the beginning* a bit previous, aboriginal, ancient, antecedent, antediluvian, antiquated, brand-new, budding, early bird*, fresh, initial, new, original, preceding, premier, prevenient, previous, primal, prime, primeval, primitive, primordial, prior, pristine, proleptical, raw, recent, undeveloped, young; CONCEPTS 799,828 —*Ant.* late

early [adj2] *sooner than expected* advanced, ahead of time, anticipative, anticipatory, before appointed time, beforehand, direct, immature, immediate, matinal, on short notice*, on the dot*, overearly, oversoon, preceding, precipitant, precocious, preexistent, premature, previous, prompt, pronto, punctual, quick, seasonable, soon, speedy, unanticipated, unexpected, untimely; CONCEPT 820 —*Ant.* later

early [adv1] *sooner than expected* a bit previous, ahead of time, anon, beforehand, before long, betimes, briefly, bright and early*, directly, early bird*, ere long, far ahead, immediately, in advance, in good time*, in the bud*, in time, on short notice*, on the dot*, oversoon, prematurely, presently, previous, promptly, pronto, proximately, quick, shortly, soon, too soon, unexpectedly, with time to spare*; CONCEPT 820 —*Ant.* later

early [adv2] *immediately* at once, betimes, directly, first, freshly, in a jiffy*, in an instant*, in no time*, instantaneously, instantly, newly, presto, primitively, promptly, recently, right away, seasonably, soon, straightaway, summarily, thereon, thereupon, timely, without delay; CONCEPTS 799,828 —*Ant.* late

earmark [n] *signature characteristic* attribute, differential, distinction, feature, hallmark, label, marking, peculiarity, quality, stamp, tag, token, trademark, trait; CONCEPT 644

earmark [v] *reserve* allocate, designate, keep back, label, maintain, mark out, name, set aside, slot, tab, tag; CONCEPT 129 —*Ant.* throw away, use, waste

earn [v1] *make money* acquire, attain, be gainfully employed, be in line for*, bring home*, bring home the bacon*, bring home the groceries*, bring in, clean up*, clear*, collect, consummate, cop*, derive, draw, effect, gain, gather, get, gross, hustle, make, make fast buck*, make it big*, net, obtain, pay one's dues*, perform, pick up, procure, profit, pull*, pull down*, rate, realize, reap, receive, scare up*, score*, scrape together*, secure, snag*, sock*, turn, win, wrangle; CONCEPTS 330,351 —*Ant.* cost, lose, spend, throw away

earn [v2] *deserve a reward* acquire, attain, bag, be entitled to, be worthy of, come by, gain, harvest, merit, net, rate, reap, score, warrant, win; CONCEPTS 120,129

earnest [adj1] *very enthusiastic* ardent, busy, devoted, diligent, eager, fervent, fervid, heartfelt, impassioned, industrious, keen, passionate, perseverant, purposeful, sedulous, sincere, urgent, vehement, warm, wholehearted, zealous; CONCEPTS 326,401,542 —*Ant.* flippant, unconcerned, unenthusiastic, unpassionate, unpurposeful, unthoughtful

earnest [adj2] *serious; very important* close, constant, determined, firm, fixed, for real, grave, intent, mean business, meaningful, no-fooling, no-nonsense, playing hard ball*, resolute, resolved, sedate, sincere, sober, solemn, somber, stable, staid, steady, thoughtful, weighty; CONCEPT 568 —*Ant.* flippant, insincere, thoughtless, trivial, unimportant, unserious

earnestness [n] *determination; seriousness* absorption, ardor, attentiveness, concentration, decision, deliberation, devotion, doggedness, eagerness, engrossment, enthusiasm, fervor, firmness, gravity, intensity, intentness, keenness, passion, perseverance, persistence, purposefulness, resolution, resolve, seriousmindedness, sincerity, sobriety, solemnity, stress, tenacity, urgency, vehemence, warmth, zeal; CONCEPTS 633,657 —*Ant.* flippancy, insincerity, unimportance

earnings [n] *money for work performed* balance, bottom line*, emolument, gain, gate, groceries*, income, in the black*, lucre, net, pay, payoff, piece of the pie*, proceeds, profit, receipts, remuneration, return, revenue, reward, salary, salt*, stipend, take-home*, takings, wages; CONCEPT 344 —*Ant.* bills, debt, losses, payout

earsplitting [adj] *loud* blaring, deafening, noisy, penetrating, piercing, ringing, shrill, strident, thunderous; CONCEPTS 592,594

Earth [n1] *the world* apple*, big blue marble*, cosmos, creation, dust*, globe, macrocosm, orb, planet, sphere, star, sublunary world, terra, terra firma, terrene, terrestrial sphere, universe, vale; CONCEPT 511

earth [n2] *ground, soil* alluvium, clay, clod, coast, compost, deposit, dirt, dry land, dust, fill, glebe, gravel, humus, land, loam, marl, mold, muck, mud, peat moss, sand, shore, sod, subsoil, surface, terra firma, terrain, terrane, topsoil, turf; CONCEPT 509

earthling [n] *human being* earth dweller, humankind, man, person, tellurian, woman; CONCEPT 417

earthly [adj1] *physically concerning land or its inhabitants* alluvial, carnal, corporeal, geotic, global, human, in all creation, material, mortal, mundane, nonspiritual, physical, profane, secular, subastral, sublunary, tellurian, telluric, temporal, terraqueous, terrene, terrestrial, uncelestial, under the sun*, unspiritual, worldly; CONCEPT 536 —*Ant.* heavenly, immaterial, spiritual, unearthly

earthly [adj2] *conceivable* feasible, imaginable, likely, mortal, possible, potential, practical, probable; CONCEPT 552 —*Ant.* inconceivable

earthmover [n] *bulldozer* backhoe, excavator, grader, heavy machinery, tracked vehicle; CONCEPT 505

earthquake [n] *tremor from inside the earth* convulsion, fault, macroseism, microseism, movement, quake, quaker*, seimicity, seism, seismism, shake, shock, slip, temblor, trembler*, undulation, upheaval; CONCEPTS 144,526

earthy [adj] *unsophisticated* bawdy, coarse, crude, down, down home*, down-to-earth*,

dull, easygoing, folksy, funky*, hard-boiled*, home folk*, homely, homey, indelicate, lowbred, lusty, mundane, natural, pragmatic, ribald, robust, rough, simple, unidealistic, uninhibited, unrefined; CONCEPT 542 —*Ant.* cultured, elegant, refined, sophisticated

ease [n1] *peace, quiet; lack of difficulty* affluence, ataraxia, bed of roses*, calm, calmness, comfort, content, contentment, easiness, enjoyment, gratification, happiness, idleness, inactivity, inertia, inertness, leisure, luxury, passivity, peace of mind*, prosperity, quietness, quietude, relaxation, repose, requiescence, rest, restfulness, satisfaction, security, serenity, supinity, tranquility; CONCEPTS 388,410,673 —*Ant.* difficulty, disquiet, excitableness, furor, strife, turmoil, uneasiness, unrest

ease [n2] *facility, freedom* adroitness, affability, aplomb, breeze, child's play*, cinch, cleverness, composure, dexterity, dispatch, duck soup*, easygoingness, efficiency, effortlessness, expertise, expertness, familiarity, flexibility, fluency, informality, insouciance, knack, liberty, naturalness, nonchalance, poise, pushover, quickness, readiness, relaxedness, setup, simplicity, skillfulness, smoothness, smooth sailing*, snap, unaffectedness, unconstraint, unreservedness; CONCEPTS 376,388,630 —*Ant.* difficulty, effort, inhibition, perplexity, restriction

ease [v1] *alleviate, help* abate, aid, allay, ameliorate, anesthetize, appease, assist, assuage, attend to, calm, cheer, clear the way*, comfort, cure, disburden, disengage, doctor, expedite, facilitate, forward, free, further, improve, lessen, let up on, lift, lighten, make easier, meliorate, mitigate, moderate, mollify, nurse, open the door*, pacify, palliate, promote, quiet, relax, release, relent, relieve, run interference for*, simplify, slacken, smooth, soften, soothe, speed, speed up, still, tranquilize, untighten; CONCEPTS 110,310 —*Ant.* annoy, increase, irritate, perplex, vex, worsen

ease [v2] *guide, move carefully* disentangle, edge, extricate, facilitate, handle, inch, induce, insert, join, loose, loosen, maneuver, relax, remove, right, set right, slack, slacken, slide, slip, squeeze, steer, untighten; CONCEPT 187 —*Ant.* make difficult, vex

easel [n] *stand* frame, mount, tripod; CONCEPTS 442,733,757

easement [n] *right of way* access, legal right, means of access, passage; CONCEPTS 318,685

easily [adv1] *without difficulty* calmly, comfortably, competently, conveniently, coolly, dexterously, efficiently, effortlessly, evenly, facilely, fluently, freely, handily, hand over fist*, hands down*, just like that*, lightly, like nothing*, no sweat*, nothing to it*, piece of cake*, plainly, quickly, readily, regularly, simply, smoothly, steadily, surely, swimmingly, uncomplicatedly, well, with ease, with no effort, without a hitch*, without trouble; CONCEPT 565 —*Ant.* difficulty

easily [adv2] *without a doubt* absolutely, actually, almost certainly, assuredly, beyond question, by far, certainly, clearly, decidedly, definitely, doubtless, doubtlessly, far and away, indeed, indisputably, indubitably, no doubt, plainly, positively, probably, really, surely, truly, undeniably, undoubtedly, unequivocally,

unquestionably; CONCEPTS 535,552
—*Ant.* doubtedly, dubitably, questionably

easy [*adj1*] *not difficult* accessible, apparent, basic, child's play*, cinch, clear, easily done, effortless, elementary, evident, facile, inconsiderable, light, little, manageable, manifest, mere, no bother*, no problem*, no sweat*, not burdensome, nothing to it*, no trouble*, obvious, painless, paltry, picnic*, piece of cake*, plain, plain sailing*, pushover*, royal, simple, simple as ABC*, slight, smooth, snap, straightforward, uncomplicated, undemanding, uninvolved, untroublesome, wieldy, yielding; CONCEPT 565 —*Ant.* arduous, complex, complicated, demanding, difficult, hard, intricate, involved, laborious, uneasy

easy [*adj2*] *leisurely, relaxed* at ease, calm, carefree, comfortable, comfy, commodious, composed, content, contented, cozy, cursive, cushy, easeful, effortless, flowing, fluent, forthright, gentle, in clover*, languid, light, mild, moderate, peaceful, pleasant, prosperous, quiet, running, satisfied, secure, serene, slow, smooth, snug, soft, spontaneous, substantial, successful, temperate, thriving, tranquil, undemanding, undisturbed, unexacting, unhurried, untroubled, unworried, well-to-do; CONCEPTS 542,544 —*Ant.* difficult, exhausting, hard, oppressive, trying, uneasy, unleisurely, unrelaxed

easy [*adj3*] *tolerant, permissive* accommodating, amenable, benign, biddable, charitable, clement, compassionate, compliant, condoning, deceivable, deludable, dupable, easygoing, excusing, exploitable, fleeceable, flexible, forbearing, forgiving, gentle, gullible, humoring, indulgent, kindly, lax, lenient, liberal, light, merciful, mild, moderate, mollycoddling*, naive, pampering, pardoning, soft, spoiling, submissive, susceptible, sympathetic, temperate, tractable, trusting, unburdensome, unoppressive, unsuspicious; CONCEPT 401 —*Ant.* difficult, impossible, intolerant, onery, strict, unpermissive

easy [*adj4*] *good-humored* affable, amiable, at ease, carefree, casual, complaisant, diplomatic, familiar, friendly, gentle, good-natured, good-tempered, graceful, gracious, gregarious, informal, mild, natural, obliging, open, pleasant, polite, relaxed, secure, smooth, sociable, suave, tolerant, unaffected, unanxious, undemanding, unforced, unpretentious, urbane; CONCEPT 404 —*Ant.* difficult, unhappy

easy as pie [*adj*] *very easy* duck soup, easily done, easily managed, easy as can be, like falling off a log*, like shooting fish in a barrel*, like stealing candy from a baby*, no sweat*, simple, simple as ABC; CONCEPTS 527,565

easygoing [*adj*] *complacent, permissive* amenable, breezy, calm, carefree, casual, collected, complaisant, composed, devil-may-care*, even-tempered*, flexible, free and easy*, hang-loose*, happy-go-lucky*, indolent, indulgent, informal, insouciant, laid-back*, lazy, lenient, liberal, low-pressure, mild, moderate, nonchalant, offhand, outgiving, patient, placid, poised, relaxed, self-possessed, serene, tolerant, tranquil, unconcerned, uncritical, undemanding, unhurried, uninhibited; CONCEPT 404 —*Ant.* agitated, critical,

demanding, hurried, hyped, intolerant, nervous, strict, upset, worried

eat [*v1*] *consume food* absorb, attack, banquet, bite, bolt*, break bread*, breakfast, chew, chow down*, cram*, devour, dine, dispatch, dispose of, fall to, feast upon, feed, gobble up*, gorge, gormandize, graze*, have a bite*, have a meal, have for, ingest, inhale*, lunch, make pig of oneself*, masticate, munch, nibble, nosh*, partake of, peck at*, pick, pig out*, polish off*, pork out*, put away*, ruminate, scarf*, scoff, snack, sup, swallow, take food, take in, take nourishment, wolf; CONCEPT 169

eat [*v2*] *erode, wear away; use up* bite, condense, corrode, crumble, decay, decompose, disappear, disintegrate, dissipate, dissolve, drain, exhaust, gnaw, liquefy, melt, nibble, rot, run through, rust, spill, squander, vanish, waste away; CONCEPTS 225,469 —*Ant.* build, maintain, preserve

eatable [*adj*] *able to be consumed* appetizing, comestible, culinary, delicious, delish*, dietary, digestible, edible, esculent, fit, good, harmless, kosher*, nutritious, nutritive, palatable, piquant, safe, satisfying, savory, scrumptious, succulent, tasty, tempting, wholesome, yummy*; CONCEPTS 462,613 —*Ant.* inedible, undelicious, uneatable, unpalatable, unwholesome

eat high on the hog [*v*] *live well* be in fat city*, be in hog heaven*, be sitting pretty, have it good, have it made, sit pretty; CONCEPT 5

eating disorder [*n*] *unhealthy disturbance in eating behavior* anorexia nervosa, bingeing, bulimarexia, bulimia, compulsive eating, hypheragia, pica, psychological disorder, purging; CONCEPT 316

eats [*n*] *food* chow, comestibles, eatables, fare, grub*, meals, nosh*, nourishment, nutriment, provisions, rations, snacks, sustenance, tidbits, victuals, vittles; CONCEPT 457

eat up [*v*] *to accept* buy, stand still for, swallow; CONCEPT 12

eavesdrop [*v*] *listen without permission* be all ears*, bend an ear*, bug, ears into*, listen in, monitor, overhear, pry, snoop, spy, tap, tune in on*, wire, wiretap; CONCEPTS 188,596 —*Ant.* ignore

ebb [*n*] *regression; decline* abatement, backflow, decay, decrease, degeneration, depreciation, deterioration, diminution, drop, dwindling, fading away, flagging, going out, lessening, low tide, low water, outward flow, petering out*, recession, refluence, reflux, retreat, retrocession, retroflux, shrinkage, sinking, slackening, subsidence, sweep, wane, waning, weakening, withdrawal; CONCEPTS 195,698 —*Ant.* flow, incline, increase, rise

ebb [*v*] *subside; decline* abate, decay, decrease, degenerate, deteriorate, die down, die out, diminish, drop, dwindle, ease off, fade away, fall, fall away, fall back, flag, flow back, go out, languish, lessen, let up, melt, moderate, peter out, recede, relent, retire, retreat, retrocede, shrink, sink, slacken, wane, weaken, withdraw; CONCEPTS 195,698 —*Ant.* flow, increase, rise

ebullience [*n*] *enthusiasm* agitation, animation, buoyancy, effervescence, effusiveness, elation, excitement, exhilaration, exuberance, exuberancy, ferment, gaiety, high-spiritedness, high spirits, liveliness, vitality, vivaciousness, vivacity, zest; CONCEPT 633 —*Ant.* apathy, disinterest

ebullient [adj] *enthusiastic* agitated, bouncy, brash, buoyant, chipper*, chirpy*, effervescent, effusive, elated, excited, exhilarated, exuberant, frothy*, gushing, high-spirited, in high spirits*, irrepressible, vivacious, zestful, zippy*; CONCEPT 401 —*Ant.* apathetic, disinterested, unenthusiastic

eccentric [adj] *bizarre, unusual* aberrant, abnormal, anomalous, beat*, bent*, bizarre, capricious, characteristic, cockeyed, crazy, curious, droll, erratic, far out*, flaky, freak, freakish, funky*, funny, idiosyncratic, irregular, kooky, nutty, odd, oddball, offbeat, off-center, off the wall*, out in left field*, outlandish, peculiar, quaint, queer, quirky, quizzical, singular, strange, uncommon, unconventional, unnatural, way out*, weird, whimsical, wild; CONCEPTS 547,564 —*Ant.* boring, common, dull, normal, ordinary, plain, regular, standard, unexciting, usual

eccentric [n] *person who is bizarre, unusual* beatnik, character, freak, hippie, kook, loner, maverick, nonconformist, nut*, oddball, oddity, odd person, original, queer duck*, rare bird*, three-dollar bill*, weirdo; CONCEPT 423 —*Ant.* normal, standard

eccentricity [n] *bizarreness, unusualness* aberration, abnormality, anomaly, caprice, capriciousness, foible, freakishness, hereticism, idiocrasy, idiosyncrasy, irregularity, kink, nonconformity, oddity, oddness, outlandishness, peculiarity, queerness, quirk, singularity, strangeness, unconventionality, unorthodoxness, waywardness, weirdness, whimsicality, whimsicalness; CONCEPTS 647,665 —*Ant.* commonality, dullness, normality, regularness, standard, uniformity, usual, usualness

ecclesiastical [adj] *churchly* clerical, diaconal, episcopal, holy, ministerial, orthodox, parochial, pastoral, religious, sectarian, spiritual; CONCEPTS 536,582

echelon [n] *class, level* degree, file, grade, line, office, place, position, queue, rank, row, string, tier; CONCEPTS 378,388

echo [n] *repeat, copy* answer, imitation, mirror, mirror image, onomatopoeia, parallel, parroting, rebound, reflection, reiteration, repercussion, repetition, reply, reproduction, reverberation, ringing, rubber stamp*; CONCEPTS 595,695,716

echo [v] *repeat, copy* ape, ditto*, do like*, go like*, imitate, impersonate, make like*, mimic, mirror, parallel, parrot, react, recall, redouble, reflect, reiterate, reproduce, resemble, resound, respond, reverberate, ring, rubber-stamp*, second, vibrate; CONCEPTS 91,171

éclat [n] *style* brio, dash, dynamism, élan, flair, flourish, gusto, oomph*, panache, pizzazz*, stylishness, verve, vigor, vitality, vivaciousness, vivacity, zest, zing*; CONCEPT 655

eclectic [adj] *comprehensive, general* all-embracing, assorted, broad, catholic, dilettantish, diverse, diversified, heterogeneous, inclusive, liberal, many-sided, mingled, mixed, multifarious, multiform, selective, universal, varied, wide-ranging; CONCEPTS 537,772 —*Ant.* incomprehensive, narrow, particular, specific, unvaried

eclipse [n] *shadowing of the sun* concealment, darkening, decline, diminution, dimming, extinction, extinguishment, obliteration, obscuration, occultation, penumbra, shading, shroud, veil; CONCEPTS 522,624

eclipse [v1] *obscure, veil* adumbrate, becloud, bedim, blot out, cloud, darken, dim, extinguish, murk, overshadow, shadow, shroud; CONCEPT 250 —*Ant.* clear, explain, lay out

eclipse [v2] *surpass achievement* exceed, excel, outdo, outshine, overrun, surmount, tower above, transcend; CONCEPT 141 —*Ant.* fall behind

ecology [n] *environmental science* bionomics, conservation, preservation; CONCEPTS 134,257

economic [adj] *business-related; financial* bread-and-butter*, budgetary, commercial, fiscal, industrial, material, mercantile, monetary, money-making, pecuniary, productive, profitable, profit-making, remunerative, solvent, viable; CONCEPTS 334,536

economical [adj1] *conservative with resources; careful* avaricious, canny, chary, circumspect, close, closefisted, cost-effective, curmudgeonly, efficient, frugal, meager, mean, methodical, miserly, money-saving, niggardly*, on the rims*, parsimonious, penny-pinching*, pennywise*, penurious, practical, provident, prudent, prudential, saving, scrimping, skimping, spare, sparing, stingy, thrifty, tight, time-saving, unwasteful, watchful, work-saving; CONCEPT 542 —*Ant.* careless, expensive, uncareful, uneconomical, wasteful

economical [adj2] *inexpensive* bought for a song*, cheap, cost next to nothing*, cost nothing, cut rate, dime a dozen*, dirt cheap*, dog cheap*, fair, low, low-priced, low tariff, marked down, moderate, modest, on sale, quite a buy*, reasonable, reduced, sound, steal*; CONCEPT 334 —*Ant.* expensive, uneconomical, unreasonable

economize [v] *save money* be frugal, be prudent, be sparing, conserve, cut back, cut corners*, cut down, keep within means, make ends meet*, manage, meet a budget, pay one's way*, pinch pennies*, retrench, run tight ship*, scrimp, shepherd, skimp, stint, stretch a dollar*, tighten one's belt*; CONCEPT 330 —*Ant.* spend, squander, throw away

economy [n] *saving, frugality* abridgement, austerity, care, carefulness, caution, curtailment, cutback, decrease, deduction, direction, discretion, husbandry, layoff, meanness, miserliness, moratorium, niggardliness, parcity, parsimony, providence, prudence, recession, reduction, regulation, restraint, retrenchment, rollback, scrimping, shrinkage, skimping, sparingness, stinginess, supervision, thrift, thriftiness; CONCEPTS 117,330,335 —*Ant.* spending, squandering

eco-rich [adj] *possessing an abundance of natural resources* bountiful, clean, flowing, full, green, natural, plentiful, pure, rich; CONCEPT 518

ecosystem [n] *environment* ecological community, environs; CONCEPTS 515,673,696

ecstasy [n] *bliss* beatitude, blessedness, cool*, delectation, delight, delirium, ebullience, elation, enchantment, enthusiasm, euphoria, exaltation, felicity, fervor, frenzy, gladness, happiness, heaven, inspiration, intoxication, joy, joyfulness, paradise, rapture, ravishment, rhapsody, seventh heaven*, trance, transport, twilight zone*; CONCEPT 410 —Ant. despair, sorrow, torment, trouble, unhappiness

ecstatic [adj] very happy, blissful athrill, beatific, crazy, delirious, dreamy, elated, enraptured, enthusiastic, entranced, euphoric, fervent, floating, flying high*, frenzied, gone*, high*, in exaltation, in seventh heaven*, joyful, joyous, mad, on cloud nine*, out, overjoyed, pleased as punch*, rapturous, ravished, rhapsodic, sent*, sunny, thrilled, tickled pink*, tickled to death*, transported*, turned on*, upbeat, wild; CONCEPT 403 —Ant. despaired, sorrowful, tormented, troubled, unhappy

ecumenical [adj] general all-comprehensive, all-inclusive, all-pervading, catholic, comprehensive, cosmic, cosmopolitan, global, inclusive, planetary, unifying, universal, worldwide; CONCEPTS 537,772

eddy [n] current swirl, tide, vortex, whirlpool; CONCEPT 514

Eden [n] Paradise Arcadia, garden, Garden of Eden, heaven, heaven on earth, promised land, Shangri-La, Utopia; CONCEPTS 370,410,515

edge [n1] border, outline bend, berm, bound, boundary, brim, brink, butt, circumference, contour, corner, crook, crust, curb, end, extremity, frame, fringe, frontier, hem, hook, ledge, limb, limit, line, lip, margin, molding, mouth, outskirt, peak, perimeter, periphery, point, portal, rim, ring, shore, side, skirt, split, strand, term, threshold, tip, trimming, turn, verge; CONCEPTS 484,513 —Ant. center, inside, interior, middle, surface

edge [n2] advantage allowance, ascendancy, bulge, dominance, draw, handicap, head start, lead, odds, start, superiority, upper hand*, vantage; CONCEPT 712 —Ant. block, disadvantage

edge [v1] border, trim bind, bound, decorate, fringe, hem, margin, outline, rim, shape, skirt, surround, verge; CONCEPTS 751,758 —Ant. center

edge [v2] defeat narrowly creep, ease, inch, infiltrate, nose out*, sidle, slip by, slip past, squeeze by*, squeeze past*, steal, worm*; CONCEPT 95 —Ant. lose, wallop

edge [v3] sharpen file, grind, hone, polish, sharpen, strop, whet; CONCEPTS 137,250 —Ant. blunt, dull, thicken

edgy [adj] nervous anxious, critical, excitable, excited, high-strung, ill at ease, impatient, irascible, irritable, on edge*, overstrung, restive, restless, skittish, tense, touchy, uneasy, uptight; CONCEPT 401 —Ant. calm, composed, easy-going, laid-back

edible [adj] able to be eaten comestible, digestible, eatable, esculent, fit, good, harmless, nourishing, nutritious, nutritive, palatable, savory, succulent, tasty, toothsome, wholesome; CONCEPTS 462,613 —Ant. harmful, inedible, poisonous, unpalatable

edict [n] pronouncement, order act, canon, command, commandment, decree, decretum, dictate, dictum, directive, enactment, fiat, injunction, instrument, judgment, law, mandate, manifesto, ordinance, precept, prescript, procla-

mation, pronunciamento, regulation, rule, ruling, statute, ukase, writ; CONCEPTS 278,662,688

edification [n] improvement, education betterment, elevation, elucidation, enhancement, enlightenment, guidance, illumination, information, instruction, irradiation, knowledge, learning, nurture, schooling, teaching, tuition, uplifting; CONCEPTS 31,287,700 —Ant. destruction, worsening

edifice [n] structure building, construction, erection, habitation, house, monument, pile, rockpile*, skyscraper, towers; CONCEPT 439

edit [v] rewrite, refine adapt, alter, amplify, analyze, annotate, arrange, assemble, assign, blue-pencil*, boil down*, butcher, censor, check, choose, compile, compose, condense, correct, cut, delete, discard, doctor, draft, emend, excise, feature, fine-tune, finish, fly speck*, go over, make up, massage*, polish, prepare, prescribe, proofread, publish, put together, rearrange, recalibrate, rectify, redact, regulate, rehash, rephrase, report, revise, scrub*, select, set up, strike out, style, tighten, trim, write over; CONCEPTS 79,126,203

edition [n] issue of publication copy, impression, imprint, number, printing, program, publication, reissue, release, reprint, reprinting, version, volume; CONCEPT 280

editorial [n] commentary article, critique, opinion, report, review; CONCEPTS 51,278

educate [v] teach information, experience brainwash*, brief, civilize, coach, cultivate, develop, discipline, drill, drum into, edify, enlighten, exercise, explain, foster, improve, indoctrinate, inform, instruct, let in on, mature, nurture, put hip*, put through the grind*, rear, school, show the ropes*, train, tutor; CONCEPTS 61,285 —Ant. learn

educated [adj] learned, experienced accomplished, acquainted with, brainy, civilized, coached, corrected, cultivated, cultured, developed, enlightened, enriched, erudite, expert, finished, fitted, formed, informed, initiated, instructed, intelligent, knowledgeable, lettered, literary, literate, nurtured, polished, prepared, professional, refined, scholarly, schooled, scientific, shaped, skilled, tasteful, taught, trained, tutored, versed in, well-informed, well-read, well-taught, well-versed; CONCEPT 402 —Ant. ignorant, illiterate, inexperienced, stupid, uncultured, uneducated, unsophisticated

education [n] instruction, development of knowledge apprenticeship, background, book learning*, brainwashing*, breeding, catechism, civilization, coaching, cultivation, culture, direction, discipline, drilling, edification, enlightenment, erudition, finish, guidance, improvement, inculcation, indoctrination, information, learnedness, learning, literacy, nurture, pedagogy, preparation, propagandism, proselytism, reading, rearing, refinement, scholarship, schooling, science, study, teaching, training, tuition, tutelage, tutoring; CONCEPTS 285,287,409 —Ant. ignorance

educational [adj] instructional academic, cultural, didactic, informational, informative, instructive, scholarly, scholastic, tutorial; CONCEPT 536

educator [n] *teacher* coach, dean, department head, educationist, instructor, lecturer, mentor, monitor, professor, schoolteacher, trainer, tutor; CONCEPT 350

educe [v] *bring out, elicit* come out, conclude, deduce, derive, develop, distill, drag, draw, draw out, evince, evoke, evolve, excogitate, extort, extract, gain, get, infer, milk*, obtain, procure, pull, reason, secure, think out, wrest, wring; CONCEPTS 37,142

eerie [adj] *spooky* awesome, bizarre, crawly, creepy, fantastic, fearful, frightening, ghostly, mysterious, scary, spectral, strange, supernatural, superstitious, uncanny, unearthly, weird; CONCEPT 537 —*Ant.* funny, normal, ordinary, silly

efface [v] *erase* blot out, blue-pencil, cancel, cross out, delete, destroy, edit, eliminate, expunge, fade, obliterate, rub out, scratch out, white out, wipe out; CONCEPTS 211,215

effect [n1] *result* aftereffect, aftermath, backlash, backwash, can of worms*, causatum,chain reaction*, conclusion, consequence, corollary, denouement, development, end, end product, event, eventuality, fallout, flak*, follow through, follow-up, fruit, issue, outcome, outgrowth, precipitate, pursuance, ramification, reaction, reflex, repercussion, response, sequel, sequence, side effect, spin-off, upshot*, waves*; CONCEPT 230 —*Ant.* beginning, cause, commencement, foundation, origin, source, start

effect [n2] *impact, impression* action, clout, drift, effectiveness, efficacy, efficiency, enforcement, essence, execution, fact, force, implementation, import, imprint, influence, mark, meaning, power, purport, purpose, reality, sense, significance, strength, tenor, use, validity, vigor, weight; CONCEPT 687

effect [v] *carry out, accomplish* achieve, actualize, actuate, begin, bring about, bring off, bring on, buy, carry through, cause, complete, conceive, conclude, consummate, create, do a number*, do one's thing*, do the job*, do the trick*, do to a T*, draw on, effectuate, enact, enforce, execute, fulfill, generate, get across, get to, give rise to, implement, induce, initiate, invoke, make, make it*, make waves*, perform, procure, produce, pull it off*, put across, realize, render, secure, sell, turn out, turn the trick*, unzip*, yield; CONCEPTS 91,706 —*Ant.* fail, forget, ignore, neglect, overlook

effective [adj1] *productive, persuasive* able, active, adequate, capable, cogent, compelling, competent, convincing, direct, effectual, efficacious, efficient, emphatic, energetic, forceful, forcible, having lead in pencil*, impressive, live, moving, on the ball*, operative, playing hardball*, potent, powerful, powerhouse*, practical, producing, resultant, serviceable, serving, sound, striking, sufficient, telling, trenchant, useful, valid, virtuous, wicked*, yielding; CONCEPT 537 —*Ant.* fruitless, impotent, incapable, ineffective, unproductive, useless, weak

effective [adj2] *in use at the time* active, actual, current, direct, dynamic, in effect, in execution, in force, in operation, operative, real; CONCEPTS 560,582,799 —*Ant.* inoperative, useless

effectiveness [n] *influence* capability, clout, cogency, effect, efficacy, efficiency, force,

forcefulness, performance, point, potency, power, punch, strength, success, use, validity, validness, verve, vigor, weight; CONCEPTS 676, 687 —*Ant.* ineffectiveness, unproductivity, uselessness

effects [n] *belongings* accouterments, chattels, goods, holdings, paraphernalia, possessions, property, stuff, things, trappings; CONCEPTS 446,710

effectual [adj] *influential; authoritative* accomplishing, achieving, adequate, binding, capable, conclusive, decisive, determinative, effecting, effective, efficacious, efficient, forcible, fulfilling, in force, lawful, legal, licit, potent, powerful, practicable, productive, qualified, serviceable, sound, strong, successful, telling, useful, valid, virtuous, workable; CONCEPTS 319,528,537 —*Ant.* impotent, incapable, ineffectual, unproductive, unsuccessful, useless, weak

effeminate [adj] *having female qualities* epicene, feminine, womanish, womanlike, womanly; CONCEPTS 401,404 —*Ant.* manly, masculine

effervescence [n1] *fizz, foam* bubbles, bubbling, ebullition, ferment, fermentation, froth, frothing, sparkle; CONCEPTS 437,522

effervescence [n2] *enthusiasm, vivacity* animation, buoyancy, ebullience, excitedness, excitement, exhilaration, exuberance, exuberancy, gaiety, happiness, high spirits, joy, liveliness, vim, virility, volatility, zing*; CONCEPTS 633, 657 —*Ant.* dullness, flatness

effervescent [adj1] *fizzing, foaming* airy, boiling, bouncy, bubbling, bubbly, carbonated, elastic, expansive, fermenting, frothing, frothy, resilient, sparkling, volatile; CONCEPTS 462,485 —*Ant.* flat, stale

effervescent [adj2] *enthusiastic, vivacious* animated, bouncy, brash, bubbly, buoyant, ebullient, excited, exhilarated, exuberant, gleeful, happy, high-spirited, hilarious, in high spirits*, irrepressible, jolly, joyous, lively, merry, mirthful, sprightly, vital, zingy; CONCEPT 401 —*Ant.* dull, inactive, serious, sober, unenthusiastic

effete [adj1] *spoiled, exhausted* burnt out*, corrupt, debased, decadent, decayed, declining, decrepit, degenerate, dissipated, dissolute, drained, enervated, enfeebled, far-gone*, feeble, immoral, obsolete, overrefined, overripe, played out*, soft, spent, vitiated, washed-out*, wasted, weak, worn out; CONCEPT 560 —*Ant.* capable, tireless

effete [adj2] *unproductive* barren, fruitless, impotent, infecund, infertile, sterile, unfruitful, unprolific; CONCEPT 527 —*Ant.* productive, useful, working

efficacious [adj] *efficient, productive* active, adequate, capable, competent, effective, effectual, energetic, influential, operative, potent, powerful, puissant, serviceable, strong, successful, useful, virtuous; CONCEPTS 528,537 —*Ant.* incapable, inefficacious, inefficient, unproductive, unsuccessful, useless

efficacy [n] *efficiency; productiveness* ability, adequacy, capability, capableness, capacity, competence, effect, effectiveness, efficaciousness, energy, force, influence, performance, potency, power, strength, success, sufficiency, use, vigor, virtue, weight; CONCEPTS *641,676, 706* —*Ant.* failure, inefficacy, inefficiency, unproductiveness, uselessness, weakness

efficiency [n] *adeptness, effectiveness* ability, abundance, adaptability, address, adequacy, capability, capableness, competence, competency, completeness, economy, effectuality, efficacy, energy, expertise, facility, faculty, know-how, performance, potency, power, powerfulness, productiveness, productivity, proficiency, prowess, quantity, readiness, resourcefulness, response, skill, skillfulness, suitability, suitableness, talent, thoroughness; CONCEPTS *409,630,658* —*Ant.* helplessness, impotence, inability, incompetence, ineffectiveness, inefficiency, weakness

efficient [adj] *adept, effective* able, accomplished, active, adapted, adequate, apt, businesslike, capable, clever, competent, conducive, decisive, deft, dynamic, economic, economical, effectual, efficacious, energetic, equal to, experienced, expert, familiar with, fitted, good at, good for, handy, masterly, organized, potent, powerful, practiced, productive, proficient, profitable, qualified, ready, saving, shrewd, skilled, skillful, systematic, talented, tough, useful, valuable, virtuous, well-organized; CONCEPTS *402,527,560* —*Ant.* helpless, impotent, incompetent, ineffective, inefficient, powerless, unable, weak

effigy [n] *dummy* figure, icon, idol, image, likeness, model, picture, portrait, puppet, representation, statue; CONCEPT *436* —*Ant.* being, entity

effort [n] *work, exertion* accomplishment, achievement, act, aim, application, aspiration, attempt, battle, crack*, creation, deed, discipline, drill, elbow grease*, endeavor, energy, enterprise, essay, exercise, feat, fling*, force, go*, industry, intention, job, labor, old college try*, pains, power, product, production, pull, purpose, push, resolution, shot*, spurt, stab*, strain, stress, stretch, strife, striving, struggle, sweat, tension, toil, training, travail, trial, trouble, try, tug*, undertaking, venture, whack*; CONCEPTS *87,362,677,724* —*Ant.* hesitation, idleness, inactivity, laziness, passivity

effortless [adj] *easy* child's play*, cursive, duck soup*, facile, flowing, fluent, light, no problem*, no sweat*, offhand, painless, picnic*, piece of cake*, royal, running, simple, smooth, snap*, uncomplicated, undemanding, untroublesome; CONCEPT *565* —*Ant.* complicated, demanding, difficult, effortful, hard, labored

effrontery [n] *nerve, boldness* arrogance, assurance, audacity, backtalk, brashness, brass*, brazenness, cheek*, cheekiness, chutzpah*, crust*, disrespect, face, gall, guff, hardihood, impertinence, impudence, incivility, insolence, lip*, presumption, rudeness, sass, sauce*, self-assurance, self-confidence, shamelessness, smart talk, temerity; CONCEPTS *411, 633* —*Ant.* manners, modesty, shame, shyness

effulgent [adj] *glowing, luminous* beaming, blazing, bright, brilliant, dazzling, flaming, fluorescent, incandescent, lambent, lucent, lustrous, radiant, resplendent, shining, splendid, vivid; CONCEPT *617*

effusion [n] *outpouring* address, diffusion, discharge, effluence, effluvium, efflux, emanation, emission, exudate, gush, gushing, ooze, outflow, pouring, shedding, stream, verbosity, wordiness; CONCEPTS *179,266*

effusive [adj] *gushing, profuse* all jaw*, big mouthed*, demonstrative, ebullient, enthusiastic, expansive, extravagant, exuberant, free-flowing, fulsome, gabby*, gushy*, lavish, outpouring, overflowing, prolix, talkative, unconstrained, unreserved, unrestrained, verbose, windbag*, windy*, wordy; CONCEPTS *267,542*

egalitarian [adj] *equal* democratic, equitable, even-handed, impartial, just, unbiased; CONCEPTS *319,536*

egg [n] *seed, cell; embryo of an animal* bud, cackle*, cackleberry*, germ, nucleus, oospore, ovum, roe, rudiment, spawn, yellow eye*; CONCEPTS *389,392*

egghead [n] *intellectual* bluestocking, bookworm*, brain*, geek*, genius, highbrow, know-it-all*, longhair*, rocket scientist*, scholar, thinker; CONCEPTS *350,416*

egg on [v] *push to do something* agitate, arouse, drive, encourage, excite, exhort, goad, incite, instigate, pique, prick, prod, prompt, propel, rally, sic, spur, stimulate, stir up, urge, whip up; CONCEPT *68* —*Ant.* discourage, dissuade, hold back, talk out of

ego [n] *personality* character, psyche, self, self-admiration, selfdom, self-pride; CONCEPT *411*

egocentric [adj] *thinking very highly of oneself* conceited, egoistic, egoistical, egomaniacal, egotistic, egotistical, individualist, individualistic, megalomaniac, narcissistic, pompous, self-absorbed, self-centered, self-concerned, self-indulgent, self-interested, selfish, self-loving, self-serving, stuck-up, vainglorious, wrapped up in oneself; CONCEPT *404* —*Ant.* altruistic, humble, modest, reserved, selfless, shy, submissive, timid, unassuming

egoism/egotism [n] *self-centeredness* arrogance, assurance, boastfulness, boasting, bragging, conceit, conceitedness, egocentricity, egomania, gasconade, haughtiness, insolence, megalomania, narcissism, ostentation, overconfidence, preoccupation with self, presumption, pride, self-absorption, self-admiration, self-confidence, self-importance, self-interest, selfishness, self-love, self-possession, self-regard, self-worship, superiority, swellheadedness, vainglory, vanity, vaunting; CONCEPT *411* —*Ant.* altruism, humility, selflessness

egotistic/egoistic [adj] *thinking very highly of oneself* affected, aloof, autocratic, boastful, boasting, bragging, conceited, egocentric, egomaniacal, haughty, individualistic, inflated, inner-directed, intimate, intrinsic, introverted, isolated, narcissistic, obsessive, opinionated, personal, pompous, prideful, proud, puffed up*, self-absorbed, self-admiring, self-centered, self-important, snobbish, stuck on oneself*, stuck-up*, subjective, superior, swollen, vain, vainglorious; CONCEPT *404* —*Ant.* altruistic, humble, modest, reserved, selfless, shy, submissive, timid, unassuming

egregious [adj] *outstandingly bad; outrageous* arrant, atrocious, capital, deplorable, extreme, flagrant, glaring, grievous, gross*, heinous, infamous, insufferable, intolerable, monstrous, nefarious, notorious, outright, preposterous,

rank, scandalous, shocking, stark; CONCEPTS
545,548 —Ant. little, minor, secondary, slight

egress [n] *passage out* departure, doorway, emanation, emergence, escape, exit, exiting, exodus,
issue, opening, outlet, setting-out, vent, way out,
withdrawal; CONCEPTS 195,440 —Ant. entrance

ejaculate [v] *eject semen* climax, come*,
discharge, have an orgasm, spurt; CONCEPTS
152,179

eject [v] *throw or be thrown out* banish,
bounce*, bump, cast out, debar, disbar, discharge, disgorge, dislodge, dismiss, displace,
dispossess, ditch, do away with*, drive off,
dump*, eighty-six*, ejaculate, eliminate, emit,
eradicate, eruct, erupt, evict, exclude, expel,
expulse, extrude, fire, force out, get rid of, give
the boot*, heave out*, irrupt, kick out*, kiss
goodbye*, oust, reject, rout, sack, send packing*, show the gate to*, spew, spit out, spout,
squeeze out, throw overboard*, turn out, unloose, vomit; CONCEPTS 179,222 —Ant. take in

ejection [n] *expulsion* banishment, disbarment,
discharge, dismissal, elimination, eviction, exile,
ouster, removal, the boot*, the heave-ho*, the
sack*, throwing out; CONCEPTS 179,748

eke out [v] *make something last* barely exist,
be economical with, be frugal with, be sparing
with, economize on, get by*, stretch out;
CONCEPT 239 —Ant. use up, waste

elaborate [adj] *intricate; involved* busy,
careful, complex, complicated, decorated,
detailed, elegant, embellished, exact, extensive,
extravagant, fancy, fussy, garnished, highly
wrought, high tech*, imposing, knotty, labored,
labyrinthine, luxurious, many-faceted, minute,
ornamented, ornate, ostentatious, overdone,
overworked, painstaking, perfected, plush,
posh, precise, prodigious, refined, showy, skillful, sophisticated, studied, thorough, with all the
extras*, with all the options*, with bells
and whistles*; CONCEPT 562 —Ant. general,
normal, plain, regular, simple, uncomplicated,
unelaborate, uninvolved, usual

elaborate [v] *make detailed; expand* amplify,
bedeck, clarify, comment, complicate, deck,
decorate, develop, devise, discuss, embellish,
enhance, enlarge, evolve, expatiate, explain,
expound, flesh out, garnish, improve, interpret,
ornament, particularize, polish, produce, refine,
specify, unfold, work out; CONCEPT 57 —Ant.
make simple, simplify

élan [n] *vivacity* animation, ardor, brio,
dash, esprit, flair, impetuosity, impetus, life,
oomph*, panache, spirit, style, verve, vigor,
vim, zest, zing*; CONCEPT 411 —Ant. dullness,
lifelessness

elapse [v] *go by; slip away* expire, flow, glide
by, lapse, pass, pass away, pass by, roll by,
roll on, run out, transpire, vanish; CONCEPT 6

elastic [adj1] *pliant, rubbery* adaptable, bouncy,
buoyant, ductile, extendible, extensible, flexible, irrepressible, limber, lithe, malleable,
moldable, plastic, pliable, resilient, rubberlike,
springy, stretchable, stretchy, supple, tempered,
yielding; CONCEPTS 490,606 —Ant. inelastic,
rigid, stiff, tense, unflexible, unyielding

elastic [adj2] *adaptable, tolerant* accommodating, adjustable, airy, animated, bouncy, buoyant,
complaisant, compliant, ebullient, effervescent,

expansive, flexible, gay, high-spirited, lively,
recuperative, resilient, soaring, spirited,
sprightly, supple, variable, vivacious, volatile,
yielding; CONCEPT 404 —Ant. difficult,
inflexible, intolerant, unadaptable, ungiving

elasticity [n] *stretchiness* adaptability, adjustability, flexibility, fluidity, give*, malleability,
plasticity, pliancy, resilience, rubberiness,
springiness, suppleness; CONCEPT 731
—Ant. rigidity

elated [adj] *very happy* animated, aroused,
blissful, cheered, delighted, ecstatic, elevated,
enchanted, enraptured, euphoric, exalted,
excited, exhilarated, exultant, fired up*, flying*,
flying high*, gleeful, high, hopped up*, in
heaven*, in high spirits*, in seventh heaven*,
intoxicated, joyful, joyous, jubilant, looking
good*, on cloud nine*, overjoyed, proud,
puffed up*, roused, set up, transported, turned-
on*; CONCEPTS 22,403 —Ant. depressed, down,
sad, sorrowful, unhappy

elation [n] *extreme happiness* bliss, buoyancy,
buzz, charge, cloud nine*, delight, ecstasy,
enthusiasm, euphoria, exaltation, excitement,
exhilaration, exultation, glee, high, high spirits,
intoxication, jollies*, joy, joyfulness, joyousness, jubilation, kick*, kicks*, rapture, stars in
one's eyes*, transport, triumph, up*, upper*;
CONCEPT 410 —Ant. depression, sadness,
sorrow, unhappiness

elbow [n] *angular part of arm; angularly
shaped item* arc on, angle, bend, bow, corner,
crazy bone*, crook, crutch, curve, fork, funny
bone*, half turn, hinge, joint, turn; CONCEPTS
418,436

elbow [v] *push aside* bend, bulldoze, bump,
crowd, hook, hustle, jostle, knock, nudge,
press, rough and tumble*, shoulder, shove;
CONCEPT 208

elbow grease [n] *physical effort* effort, exertion, labor, muscle, oomph*, strain, strength,
sweat, toil; CONCEPTS 87,100,351,360,362

elbow room [n] *room to maneuver* breathing
space, clearance, freedom, latitude, leeway, license, margin, play, room, space; CONCEPT 739

elder [adj] *born earlier* ancient, earlier, first-
born, more mature, older, senior; CONCEPTS
578,797 —Ant. last-born, younger, youngest

elder [n] *older person* ancestor, ancient,
forebearer, golden ager*, matriarch, oldest,
old fogey*, oldster*, patriarch, senior, senior
citizen, superior, veteran; CONCEPT 424
—Ant. junior, minor, youngster, youth

elderly [adj] *in old age* aged, aging, ancient,
been around*, declining, gray*, hoary, long
in tooth*, lot of mileage*, no spring chicken*,
old, olden, on last leg*, over the hill*, retired,
tired, venerable; CONCEPTS 578,797 —Ant.
young, youth

elect [v] *select as representative; choose* accept,
admit, appoint, ballot, conclude, cull, decide
upon, designate, determine, go down the line,
judge, mark, name, nominate, optate, opt for,
pick, pick out, prefer, receive, resolve, settle,
settle on, single out, take, tap, vote, vote for;
CONCEPTS 41,300 —Ant. ignore, vote down,
vote out

election [n] *choosing; voting* alternative,
appointment, ballot, balloting, choice, decision,

determination, franchise, judgment, option, poll, polls, preference, primary, referendum, selection, ticket, vote-casting; CONCEPTS *41,300*

electioneering [*n*] *campaigning* barnstorming*, canvassing, polling, voting; CONCEPT *87*

elective [*adj*] *able to be chosen* constituent, discretionary, electoral, facultative, nonobligatory, not compulsory, optional, selective, voluntary, voting; CONCEPT *535* —**Ant.** required

electric/electrical [*adj*] *charged; energetic* AC, DC, dynamic, electrifying, exciting, juiced*, magnetic, motor-driven, power-driven, rousing, stimulating, stirring, tense, thrilling, voltaic; CONCEPT *540* —**Ant.** boring, uncharged, unenergetic, unexciting

electricity [*n*] *energized matter, power* AC, current, DC, electromagneticism, electron, galvanism, heat, hot stuff*, ignition, juice*, light, magnetic ism, service, spark, tension, utilities, voltage; CONCEPT *520*

electrify [*v*] *thrill, stimulate* amaze, animate, astonish, astound, charge, commove, disturb, dynamize, energize, enthuse, excite, fire, frenzy, galvanize, invigorate, jar, jolt, magnetize, power, provoke, rouse, send, shock, stagger, startle, stir, strike, stun, take one's breath away*, wire*; CONCEPTS *7,22,42* —**Ant.** bore, dull

electronics [*n*] *electronic devices* camcorders, CD players, computer chips, computers, electronic components, integrated circuitry, radios, stereos, televisions, transistors, VCRs, video cameras; CONCEPTS *463,499*

elegance [*n*] *cultivated beauty, taste* breeding, charm, class, courtliness, cultivation, culture, delicacy, dignity, discernment, distinction, exquisiteness, felicity, gentility, good taste, grace, gracefulness, grandeur, hauteur, lushness, luxury, magnificence, nicety, nobility, noblesse, ornateness, polish, politeness, poshness, propriety, purity, refinement, restraint, rhythm, sophistication, splendor, style, sumptuousness, symmetry, tastefulness; CONCEPTS *655,671,718* —**Ant.** crudeness, inelegance, poor taste, roughness, ugliness

elegant [*adj*] *beautiful, tasteful* affected, appropriate, apt, aristocratic, artistic, august, chic, choice, classic, clever, comely, courtly, cultivated, cultured, dainty, delicate, dignified, effective, exquisite, fancy, fashionable, fine, genteel, graceful, grand, handsome, ingenious, luxurious, majestic, modish, neat, nice, noble, opulent, ornamented, ornate, ostentatious, overdone, polished, rare, recherché, refined, rich, select, simple, stately, stuffy, stylish, stylized, sumptuous, superior, turgid, wellbred; CONCEPTS *574,579,589* —**Ant.** crude, inelegant, rough, ugly, unfashionable, unrefined, unsophisticated, untasteful

elegiac [*adj*] *lamenting* doleful, funereal, melancholy, mournful, sad, sorrowful, threnodial; CONCEPT *403*

elegy [*n*] *dirge* death song, funeral song, knell, lament, plaint, requiem, threnody; CONCEPTS *262,293,595*

element [*n1*] *essential feature* aspect, basic, basis, bit, component, constituent, detail, drop, facet, factor, fundamental, hint, ingredient, item, material, matter, member, part, particle, particular, piece, portion, principle, root,

section, stem, subdivision, trace, unit, view; CONCEPTS *668,826,829*

element [*n2*] *place where one feels comfortable* domain, environment, field, habitation, medium, milieu, sphere; CONCEPTS *198,516* —**Ant.** foreign land

elementary [*adj*] *simple, basic* ABCs, abecedarian, basal, beginning, child's play*, clear, duck soup*, easy, elemental, essential, facile, foundational, fundamental, initial, introductory, meat and potatoes*, original, plain, prefatory, preliminary, primary, primitive, primo*, rudimentary, simplest, simplex, simplified, straightforward, substratal, uncomplex, uncomplicated, underlying; CONCEPTS *546, 562* —**Ant.** abstruse, advanced, complex, complicated, compound, difficult, hard, intricate, involved, secondary

elephantine [*adj*] *huge* behemothic, big, colossal, enormous, extensive, gargantuan, giant, gigantic, grand, great, humongous, immense, jumbo*, large, mammoth, massive, monstrous, monumental, mountainous, titanic, towering; CONCEPTS *771,773*

elevate [*v1*] *lift up* erect, fetch up*, heighten, hike up*, hoist, jack up*, levitate, poise, pump, put up, pyramid*, raise, ramp, rear, shoot up*, stilt, take up, tilt, uphold, uplift, upraise; CONCEPT *196* —**Ant.** decrease, depress, drop, lessen, lower, push down

elevate [*v2*] *promote; augment* advance, aggrandize, appoint, boost, build up, dignify, enhance, ennoble, exalt, further, glorify, heighten, honor, increase, intensify, magnify, prefer, put up, swell, upgrade; CONCEPTS *69,351,700* —**Ant.** condemn, demote, denounce, deprecate, disdain, lessen, lower, spurn

elevate [*v3*] *raise spirits* animate, boost, brighten, bring up, buoy up*, cheer, elate, excite, exhilarate, glorify, hearten, inspire, lift up*, perk up*, refine, rouse, sublimate, uplift; CONCEPTS *7,22* —**Ant.** depress, disgrace, distress, lower, shame, trouble, upset

elevated [*adj1*] *highly moral or dignified* animated, big-time*, bright, elated, eloquent, eminent, ethical, exalted, exhilarated, formal, grand, grandiloquent, heavy, high, high-flown*, high-minded, honorable, inflated, lofty, noble, righteous, stately, sublime, superb, upright, upstanding, virtuous; CONCEPTS *402,545,567* —**Ant.** base, immoral, lowly, undignified

elevated [*adj2*] *raised up* aerial, high, high-rise, lifted, raised, stately, tall, towering, upheaved, uplifted, upraised, uprisen; CONCEPT *779* —**Ant.** base, decreased, dropped, lessened, lowered, lowly

elevation [*n1*] *height; high ground* acclivity, altitude, ascent, boost, eminence, heave, hill, hillock, hoist, levitation, mountain, platform, ridge, rise, roof, top, uplift, upthrow; CONCEPTS *509,741* —**Ant.** depression, lowness

elevation [*n2*] *advancement, promotion* aggrandizement, apotheosis, boost, deification, eminence, ennoblement, exaltation, exaltedness, glorification, grandeur, immortalization, lionization, loftiness, magnification, nobility, nobleness, preference, preferment, prelation, raise, sublimity, upgrading; CONCEPTS *69,351, 668* —**Ant.** demotion, disdain, spurning

eg
el

elevator [n] *lift* conveyor, dumbwaiter, escalator, hoist; CONCEPT 196

elf [n] *small, fairytale character* brownie, elfin, fairy, fay, leprechaun, nisse, pixie; CONCEPT 370 —*Ant.* giant

elfin [adj] *mischievous; small* delicate, devilish, disobedient, elfish, frolicsome, impish, little, minute, misbehaving, naughty, petite, playful, prankish, puckish, puny, rascally, slight, sprightly, tiny; CONCEPTS 401,545

elicit [v] *draw out* arm-twist*, badger, bite*, bring, bring forth, bring out, bring to light*, call forth, cause, derive, educe, evince, evoke, evolve, exact, extort, extract, fetch, give rise to, milk*, obtain, put muscle on*, put the arm on*, rattle, shake, shake down*, squeeze, wrest, wring; CONCEPTS 68,142 —*Ant.* cover, hide, keep, repress, supress

eligible [adj] *fit, worthy* acceptable, appropriate, becoming, capable of, desirable, discretionary, elective, employable, equal to, fitted, in line for*, in the running*, licensed, likely, preferable, privileged, proper, qualified, satisfactory, seemly, suitable, suited, trained, up to*, usable; CONCEPTS 527,558 —*Ant.* improper, inappropriate, ineligible, unfit, unsuitable, unsuited, unworthy

eliminate [v] *remove, throw out* annihilate, blot out*, bump off*, cancel, cast out, count out, cut out, defeat, discard, discharge, dismiss, dispense with, dispose of, disqualify, disregard, do away with, drive out, drop, eject, eradicate, erase, evict, exclude, expel, exterminate, get rid of, ignore, invalidate, kill, knock out*, leave out, liquidate, murder, omit, oust, phase out, put out, reject, rub out*, rule out, set aside, shut the door on*, slay, stamp out*, take out, terminate, waive, waste, wipe out*; CONCEPTS 30,211 —*Ant.* accept, choose, include, keep, ratify, sanction, welcome

elimination [n] *removal* cut, destruction, discard, displacement, dropping, ejection, eradication, exclusion, expulsion, extermination, omission, rejection, riddance, taking away, weeding out, withdrawal; CONCEPT 180

elite [adj] *best, first-class* aristocratic, choice, cool*, crack*, elect, exclusive, gilt-edged, greatest, noble, out of sight*, out of this world*, pick, selected, super, tip-top*, top, top drawer*, topflight, top-notch, upper-class, world-class; CONCEPTS 555,574 —*Ant.* common, low-class, lower, lower-class, ordinary, poor, worst

elite [n] *high-class persons* aristocracy, beautiful people*, best, blue blood*, carriage trade*, celebrity, choice, country club set*, cream, crème de la crème*, crowd, elect, establishment, fast lane*, fat*, flower, gentility, gentry, glitterati, high society*, in-crowd*, jet-set*, main line*, nobility, old money*, optimacy, pride, prime, prize, quality, select, society, top, upper class, upper crust*; CONCEPTS 387,388, 417 —*Ant.* commonality, lower class, low-life, ordinary

elitist [n] *snob* highbrow, name-dropper, pompous ass, pompous person, social climber, stiff, stuffed shirt; CONCEPT 423

elixir [n] *remedy* cure-all, elixir of life, extract, medicine, mixture, panacea, philosopher's stone, potion, principle, solution; CONCEPTS 307,311,693,712

elliptical [adj] *oval-shaped* egg-shaped, ellipsoidal, oblong, ovoid; CONCEPT 486

elocution [n] *articulation* declamation, delivery, diction, dramatic, eloquence, enunciation, expression, locution, oratory, pronunciation, public speaking, reading, rhetoric, speech, speechcraft, speechmaking, utterance, voice culture, voice production; CONCEPT 47 —*Ant.* inarticulation, mispronouncement

elongate [v] *make longer* drag one's feet*, drag out, draw, draw out, extend, fill, lengthen, let out, pad*, prolong, prolongate, protract, put rubber in*, spin out, stretch; CONCEPTS 137,239,250 —*Ant.* constrict, contract, shorten

elongated [adj] *lengthened* dragged out, drawn out, expanded, extended, increased, made longer, outstretched, prolonged, protracted, stretched, strung out; CONCEPTS 482,779,798

elope [v] *run away to be married* abscond, bolt, decamp, disappear, escape, flee, fly, go secretly, go to Gretna Green*, leave, run off, skip*, slip away, slip out, steal away; CONCEPT 297

eloquence [n] *skillful way with words* ability, appeal, articulation, command of language, delivery, diction, dramatic, expression, expressiveness, expressivity, facility, fervor, flow, fluency, force, forcefulness, gift of gab*, grandiloquence, loquacity, meaningfulness, mellifluousness, oration, oratory, passion, persuasiveness, poise, power, rhetoric, spirit, style, vigor, vivacity, volubility, wit, wittiness; CONCEPTS 68,278,630 —*Ant.* dullness, inarticulateness

eloquent [adj] *having a skillful way with words* affecting, ardent, articulate, expressive, facund, fervent, fervid, fluent, forceful, glib, grandiloquent, graphic, impassioned, impressive, indicative, magniloquent, meaningful, moving, outspoken, passionate, persuasive, poignant, potent, powerful, revealing, rhetorical, sententious, significant, silver-tongued*, smooth-spoken*, stirring, suggestive, telling, touching, vivid, vocal, voluble, well-expressed; CONCEPT 267 —*Ant.* dull, inarticulate

elsewhere [adv] *in another place* abroad, absent, away, formerly, gone, hence, not here, not present, not under consideration, otherwhere, outside, remote, removed, somewhere, somewhere else, subsequently; CONCEPT 586

elucidate [v] *explain in detail* annotate, clarify, clear, clear up, decode, demonstrate, draw a picture*, enlighten, exemplify, explicate, expound, get across*, gloss, illuminate, illustrate, interpret, make perfectly clear, make plain, make see daylight*, prove, shed light on*, spell out*, throw light on*, unfold; CONCEPT 57 —*Ant.* be vague, confuse, distract, make ambiguous, mix up, mystify, obscure

elude [v] *avoid; escape* baffle, beat around the bush*, be beyond someone*, bilk, circumvent, confound, cop out*, ditch, dodge, double, duck, eschew, evade, flee, fly, foil, frustrate, get around, get away from, give the runaround*, give the slip*, give wide berth to*, hem and haw*, not touch, outrun, outwit, pass the buck*, pass up, puzzle, run around, shirk, shuck, shun, shy, stall, stay shy of*, steer clear of*, stonewall*, stump, thwart; CONCEPTS 30,38, 59,102 —*Ant.* attract, confront, encounter, entice, face, invite, meet, take on

elusive [*adj*] *evasive, mysterious* ambiguous, baffling, cagey, deceitful, deceptive, difficult to catch, elusory, equivocal, evanescent, fallacious, fleeting, fraudulent, fugacious, fugitive, greasy, illusory, imponderable, ˈincomprehensible, indefinable, insubstantial, intangible, misleading, occult, phantom, puzzling, shifty, shy, slippery, stonewalling*, subtle, transient, transitory, tricky, unspecific, volatile; CONCEPTS 529,542 —*Ant.* attracting, confronting, encountering, enticing, facing, inviting

emaciated [*adj*] *undernourished; thin* anorexic, atrophied, attenuate, attenuated, bony, cadaverous, consumptive, famished, gaunt, haggard, lank, lean, like a bag of bones*, meager, peaked, pinched, scrawny, skeletal, skeletonlike, skin-and-bones*, skinny, starved, thin as rail*, underfed, wasted, wizened; CONCEPTS 490,491 —*Ant.* fat, heavy, overnourished, overweight, plump

e-mail [*n*] *electronic mail* chat message, online correspondence, online mail, voice mail; CONCEPT 266

emanate [*v*] *come forth; give off* arise, birth, derive, discharge, egress, emerge, emit, exhale, exit, exude, flow, initiate, issue, originate, proceed, radiate, rise, send forth, spring, stem; CONCEPTS 179,221,648 —*Ant.* take, withdraw

emanation [*n*] *emergence, discharge* arising, beginning, derivation, drainage, effluence, effluent, efflux, effusion, ejaculation, emerging, emission, escape, exhalation, exudation, flow, flowing, gush, issuance, issuing, leakage, oozing, origin, origination, outflow, outpour, proceeding, radiation, springing, welling; CONCEPTS 179,221 —*Ant.* taking, withdrawal

emancipate [*v*] *set free* affranchise, deliver, discharge, disencumber, disenthral, enfranchise, liberate, loose, loosen, manumit, release, unbind, unchain, unfetter, unshackle; CONCEPT 127 —*Ant.* hold, imprison, incarcerate

emancipation [*n*] *freedom* deliverance, delivery, enfranchisement, independence, liberation, liberty, release, setting free; CONCEPT 691

emasculate [*v*] *weaken, deprive of force* alter, debilitate, devitalize, enervate, fix*, impoverish, vitiate; CONCEPTS 240,250 —*Ant.* aid, assist, help

embalm [*v*] *preserve, immortalize* anoint, cherish, consecrate, conserve, enshrine, freeze, lay out, mummify, prepare, process, store, treasure, wrap; CONCEPT 202

embargo [*n*] *prohibition, restriction* ban, bar, barrier, blockage, check, hindrance, impediment, interdict, interdiction, proscription, restraint, stoppage; CONCEPTS 119,130

embark [*v*] *get on transportation object* board, commence, emplane, enter, entrain, go aboard ship, launch, leave port, plunge into, put on board, set about, set out, set sail, take on board, take ship; CONCEPTS 159,195,224 —*Ant.* disembark, stay

embark on [*v*] *begin undertaking, journey* broach, commence, engage, enter, get off, initiate, jump off, launch, open, plunge into,

set about, set out, set to, start, take up, tee off*; CONCEPTS 100,221

embarrass [*v*] *cause mental discomfort* abash, agitate, annoy, bewilder, bother, bug, catch one short*, chagrin, confuse, discombobulate*, discomfit, discompose, disconcert, discountenance, distract, distress, disturb, dumbfound, faze, fluster, give a bad time*, give a hard time*, hang up*, irk, let down*, make a monkey of*, mortify, nonplus, perplex, perturb, plague, put in a hole*, put in a spot*, put on the spot*, put out of countenance*, puzzle, rattle, shame, show up*, stun, tease, throw, throw into a tizzy*, upset; CONCEPTS 7,19,54 —*Ant.* comfort, gladden, help, please

embarrassing [*adj*] *humiliating, shaming* awkward, bewildering, compromising, confusing, delicate, difficult, disagreeable, discomfiting, discommoding, discommodious, disconcerting, distracting, distressing, disturbing, equivocal, exasperating, impossible, incommodious, inconvenient, inopportune, mortifying, perplexing, puzzling, rattling, sensitive, shameful, sticky, ticklish, touchy, tricky, troublesome, troubling, uncomfortable, uneasy, unpropitious, unseemly, upsetting, worrisome; CONCEPTS 537,548 —*Ant.* comfortable, unshameful

embarrassment [*n*] *humiliation, shame* awkwardness, awkward situation, bashfulness, bind, boo boo*, chagrin, clumsiness, complexity, confusion, destitution, difficulty, dilemma, discomfiture, discomposure, disconcertion, distress, egg on face*, faux pas, fix, hitch, hot seat*, hot water*, impecuniosity, indebtedness, indiscretion, inhibition, mess, mistake, mortification, pickle*, pinch, plight, poverty, predicament, puzzle, quandary, scrape, self-consciousness, shyness, snag, stew, strait, tangle, timidity, unease, uneasiness; CONCEPTS 410,674 —*Ant.* comfort, confidence

embassy [*n*] *residence, offices of overseas representatives* commission, committee, consular office, consulate, delegation, diplomatic office, legation, ministry, mission; CONCEPTS 439,449, 516

embattle [*v*] *prepare for battle* arm, array, equip, fortify, furnish, make ready, militarize, mobilize, prepare for combat, strengthen, supply; CONCEPT 202

embed [*v*] *sink, implant* bury, deposit, dig in, drive in, enclose, fasten, fix, hammer in, impact, infix, ingrain, inlay, insert, install, lodge, pierce, plant, plunge, press, put into, ram in, root, set, stick in, stuff in, thrust in, tuck in; CONCEPTS 178,188 —*Ant.* dig up

embellish [*v*] *make beautiful; decorate* add bells and whistles*, adorn, amplify, array, beautify, bedeck, color, deck, dress up*, elaborate, emblaze, embroider, enhance, enrich, exaggerate, festoon, fix up*, fudge*, garnish, gild, give details, grace, gussy up*, magnify, ornament, overstate, spiff up*, spruce up*, trim; CONCEPTS 49,162,177,700 —*Ant.* deface, disfigure, mar, simplify, spoil, uglify

embellishment [*n*] *beautification; decorating* adornment, coloring, decoration, doodad*, elaboration, embroidering, embroidery, enhancement, enrichment, exaggeration, fandangle*, floridity, flowery speech, frill, froufrou*, fuss*, garnish, gilding, ginger-bread*, hyperbole, icing on the cake*, jazz*, ornament, ornamentation, ostentation, over-statement; CONCEPTS 177,278,700,718 —*Ant.* disfigurement, injury, simplification, spoliation

embers [n] *hot ashes from fire* ash, brand, cinders, clinkers, coals, firebrand, live coals, slag, smoking remnants, smoldering remains; CONCEPTS 260,478

embezzle [v] *steal money, often from employer* abstract, appropriate, defalcate, filch, forge, loot, misapply, misappropriate, misuse, pecu-late, pilfer, purloin, put hand in cookie jar*, put hand in till*, skim, thieve; CONCEPT 139 —*Ant.* compensate, give, pay, reimburse, return

embezzlement [n] *stealing money, often from employer* abstraction, appropriation, defalca-tion, filching, fraud, larceny, misapplication, misappropriation, misuse, peculation, pilfer-age, pilfering, purloining, skimming, theft, thieving; CONCEPT 139 —*Ant.* compensation, pay, reimbursement, return

embitter [v] *upset, alienate* acerbate, acidulate, aggravate, anger, annoy, bitter, bother, disaf-fect, disillusion, envenom, exacerbate, exasper-ate, irritate, make bitter, make resentful, poison, sour, venom, worsen; CONCEPTS 7,14,19 —*Ant.* calm, comfort, make happy, pacify

embittered [adj] *resentful* bitter, disaffected, full of hate, irritated, rancorous, sore, spiteful; CONCEPTS 267,404

emblazon [v] *adorn* add finishing touches, beautify, brighten, color, deck, decorate, do up*, embellish, fix up, gussy up*, jazz up*, ornament, paint, spruce up; CONCEPTS 162,177

emblem [n] *crest* adumbration, arms, attribute, badge, banner, brand, character, coat of arms, colophon, colors, design, device, figure, flag, hallmark, identification, image, impress, in-signia, logo, mark, marker, medal, memento, miniature, monogram, motto, pennant, regalia, reminder, representation, scepter, seal, sign, standard, symbol, token, trademark, type; CONCEPTS 259,284,625

embodiment [n] *representation, manifestation* apotheosis, archetype, cast, collection, compre-hension, conformation, embracement, encom-passment, epitome, example, exemplar, exemplification, expression, form, formation, incarnation, inclusion, incorporation, integra-tion, matter, organization, personification, prosopopoeia, quintessence, realization, reification, structure, symbol, systematization, type; CONCEPTS 118,686 —*Ant.* exclusion

embody [v1] *represent; materialize* actualize, complete, concretize, demonstrate, emblematize, epitomize, evince, exemplify, exhibit, express, exteriorize, externalize, hypostatize, illustrate, incarnate, incorporate, manifest, mirror, objec-tify, personalize, personify, realize, reify, show, stand for, substantiate, symbolize, typify; CONCEPT 118 —*Ant.* disembody, exclude

embody [v2] *include, integrate* absorb, amalga-mate, assimilate, blend, bring together, codify, collect, combine, comprehend, comprise, con-centrate, consolidate, contain, embrace, encom-pass, establish, fuse, have, incorporate, involve, merge, organize, subsume, systematize, take in,

unify; CONCEPTS 112,113 —*Ant.* disembody, disintegrate, exclude

embolden [v] *encourage* boost, buoy, cheer, energize, enhearten, exhilarate, give courage, give pep talk*, goad, inspire, inspirit, invigo-rate, psyche up, push, rally, reassure, refresh, revitalize, spur, stir, sway; CONCEPTS 7,22

emboss [v] *imprint* adorn, carve, decorate, etch, impress, punch, sculpt, stamp; CONCEPT 79

embrace [v1] *hold tightly in one's arms* bear hug*, clasp, clinch, cling, clutch, cradle, cud-dle, encircle, enfold, entwine, envelop, fold, fondle, grab, grasp, grip, hug, lock, nuzzle, press, seize, snuggle, squeeze, take in arms*, wrap; CONCEPTS 190,191 —*Ant.* let go, release

embrace [v2] *include in one's beliefs; take into account* accept, accommodate, admit, adopt, avail oneself of, comprehend, comprise, contain, cover, deal with*, embody, enclose, encompass, espouse, get into*, go in for*, grab, have, incorporate, involve, make use of, provide for, receive, seize, subsume, take advantage of, take in, take on, take up, welcome; CONCEPTS 12,15,112 —*Ant.* disbelieve, distrust, exclude, reject, shun

embroider [v1] *add fancy stitching, adornment* beautify, bedeck, braid, color, cross-stitch, deck, decorate, embellish, fix up, garnish, gild, gussy up*, knit, ornament, pattern, quilt, spruce up*, stitch, weave pattern, work; CONCEPTS 177,218

embroider [v2] *exaggerate information* aggrandize, amplify, blow-up*, build up, color, distend, dramatize, elaborate, embellish, enhance, enlarge, expand, falsify, fudge*, heighten, hyperbolize, lie, magnify, make federal case*, make mountain out of molehill*, overdo, overelaborate, overembellish, overem-phasize, overestimate, overstate, pad*, play up*, puff*, romanticize, spread on thick*, stretch, stretch the truth*, yeast*; CONCEPT 58

embroidery [n] *fancy stitching* adornment, appliqué, arabesque, bargello, brocade, crewel, crochet, cross-stitch, decoration, lace, lacery, needlepoint, needlework, quilting, sampler, tapestry, tatting, tracery; CONCEPTS 218,259

embroil [v] *involve in dispute; complicate* cause trouble, compromise, confound, confuse, derange, disorder, disturb, disunite, encumber, enmesh, ensnare, entangle, implicate, incrimi-nate, involve, mire, mix up, muddle, perplex, snarl, tangle, trouble; CONCEPTS 7,19,86 —*Ant.* exclude, uncomplicate

embryonic [adj] *rudimentary* beginning, developing, early, elementary, evolving, germinal, immature, incipient, undeveloped; CONCEPTS 485,578,797

emend [v] *correct* alter, amend, better, edit, emendate, improve, polish, rectify, redact, retouch, revise, right, touch up; CONCEPT 126 —*Ant.* make mistake, worsen

emerge [v] *come out, arise* appear, arrive, become apparent, become known, become visible, come forth, come into view, come on the scene, come to light, come up, crop up, dawn, derive, develop, egress, emanate, flow, gush, issue, loom, make appearance, material-ize, originate, proceed, rise, show, spring, spring up, spurt, steam, stem, surface, transpire, turn up; CONCEPTS *105,118* —*Ant.* disappear, fade, go away, leave

emergency [n] *crisis, danger* accident, climax, clutch*, compulsion, crossroad, crunch*, depression, difficulty, distress, exigency, extremity, fix, hole, impasse, juncture, meltdown*, misadventure, necessity, pass, pinch*, plight, predicament, pressure, push, quandary, scrape, squeeze, strait, tension, turning point, urgency, vicissitude, zero hour*; CONCEPTS *674,675* —*Ant.* calm, peace

emergency room [n] *trauma center* critical care facility, emergency clinic, ER, ICU, intensive care unit, triage room; CONCEPT *312*

emergent [adj] *resulting* appearing, budding, coming, developing, efflorescent, emanant, emanating, issuing forth, outgoing, rising; CONCEPT *537* —*Ant.* declining, dependent

emigrant [n] *person who leaves his or her native country* alien, colonist, departer, displaced person, émigré, evacuee, exile, expatriate, fugitive, migrant, migrator, outcast, pilgrim, refugee, traveler, wanderer, wayfarer; CONCEPTS *413,423* —*Ant.* nationalist, native

emigrate [v] *move to new country* depart, migrate, move abroad, quit, remove, transmigrate; CONCEPT *198* —*Ant.* remain, stay

émigré [n] *emigrant* displaced person, DP, exile, expatriate, foreigner, migrant, refugee; CONCEPT *413*

eminence [n1] *importance, fame* authority, celebrity, credit, dignity, distinction, esteem, famousness, glory, greatness, honor, illustriousness, influence, kudos, loftiness, notability, note, power, preeminence, prepotency, prestige, prominence, prominency, rank, renown, reputation, repute, significance, standing, superiority, weight; CONCEPTS *388,668,671* —*Ant.* inferiority, unimportance

eminence [n2] *high ground* altitude, elevation, height, highland, highness, hill, hillock, knoll, loftiness, peak, project, prominence, promontory, raise, ridge, rise, summit, upland; CONCEPTS *509,741* —*Ant.* flat, low ground

eminent [adj] *very important; famous* august, big-gun*, big-league*, big-name*, big-time*, celeb*, celebrated, celebrious, conspicuous, distinguished, dominant, elevated, esteemed, exalted, famed, grand, great, high, high-ranking, illustrious, lionlike, lofty, name, noble, notable, noted, noteworthy, of note, outstanding, page-oner*, paramount, preeminent, prestigious, prominent, redoubted, renowned, star, superior, superstar, VIP*, well-known; CONCEPTS *555,568* —*Ant.* disrespected, inferior, undistinguished, unimportant, unnotable

eminently [adv] *exceptionally; well* conspicuously, exceedingly, extremely, greatly, highly, notably, outstandingly, prominently, remarkably, strikingly, suitably, surpassingly, very; CONCEPT *574* —*Ant.* unimportantly, unremarkably

emir [n] *prince* amir, chieftain, governor, leader, shah, sheik; CONCEPTS *347,354*

emissary [n] *deputy* agent, ambassador, bearer, carrier, consul, courier, delegate, envoy, front, go-between, herald, hired gun*, intermediary, internuncio, legate, messenger, rep*, representative, scout, spy; CONCEPTS *348,423*

emission [n] *issuance, diffusion* discharge, ejaculation, ejection, emanation, exhalation, exudation, issue, radiation, shedding, transmission, utterance, venting; CONCEPT *179* —*Ant.* concealment, containment, refrain, repression, suppression, withholding

emit [v] *diffuse, discharge* afford, beam, belch, breathe, cast out, disembogue, drip, eject, emanate, erupt, evacuate, excrete, exhale, expectorate, expel, expend, expire, extrude, exude, give off, give out, give vent to, gush, issue, jet, let off, loose, ooze, pass, perspire, pour, pronounce, purge, radiate, reek, secrete, send forth, send out, shed, shoot, speak, spew, spill, spit, squirt, throw out, transmit, utter, vent, voice, void, vomit, yield; CONCEPTS *108,179, 266* —*Ant.* conceal, contain, refrain, repress, suppress, withhold

emollient [adj] *soothing* balsamic, demulcent, healing, lenitive, palliative, relieving, remedial, softening; CONCEPTS *7,22,110,384*

emollient [n] *lotion* balm, cream, lenitive, liniment, moisturizer, oil, ointment, salve, soothing agent, unguent; CONCEPTS *311,446, 466*

emote [v] *express emotion* act, dramatize, exaggerate, ham it up*, overact, overdramatize, overplay; CONCEPT *292*

emoticon [n] *keyboard symbol code, :-)* emotag, smiley, winkey; CONCEPT *284*

emotion [n] *mental state* affect, affection, affectivity, agitation, anger, ardor, commotion, concern, desire, despair, despondency, disturbance, drive, ecstasy, elation, empathy, excitability, excitement, feeling, fervor, grief, gut reaction, happiness, inspiration, joy, love, melancholy, passion, perturbation, pride, rage, remorse, responsiveness, sadness, satisfaction, sensation, sensibility, sensitiveness, sentiment, shame, sorrow, sympathy, thrill, tremor, vehemence, vibes, warmth, zeal; CONCEPT *410* —*Ant.* physicality

emotional [adj] *demonstrative about feelings* affecting, ardent, disturbed, ecstatic, emotive, enthusiastic, excitable, exciting, falling apart*, fanatical, feeling, fervent, fervid, fickle, fiery, heartwarming, heated, histrionic, hot-blooded*, hysterical, impassioned, impetuous, impulsive, irrational, moving, nervous, overwrought, passionate, pathetic, poignant, responsive, roused, sensitive, sentient, sentimental, spontaneous, stirred, stirring, susceptible, tear-jerking*, temperamental, tender, thrilling, touching, warm, zealous; CONCEPTS *403,542* —*Ant.* physical

emotionless [adj] *unfeeling, undemonstrative* blank, chill, cold, cold-blooded*; cold fish*, cool, cool cat*, deadpan, detached, dispassionate, distant, flat, frigid, glacial*, heartless, icy, immovable, impassive, impersonal, in cold blood*, indifferent, laid back*, matter-of-fact, nonemotional, nowhere*, poker face*, remote, reserved, stony-eyed*, thick-skinned*, toneless, unemotional, unimpassioned, with straight face; CONCEPTS *401,403,542* —*Ant.* demonstrative, emotional, feeling, passionate, sympathetic

empathize [v] *identify with* comprehend, feel for, imagine, put oneself in another's place, relate to, share, stand in one's shoes*, suffer with, sympathize, understand; CONCEPTS *34,110*

empathy [n] *understanding* affinity, appreciation, being on same wavelength*, being there for someone*, communion, community of interests, compassion, comprehension, concord, cottoning to*, good vibrations*, hitting it off*, insight, picking up on*, pity, rapport, recognition, responsiveness, soul, sympathy, warmth; CONCEPTS 32,409,411 —Ant. apathy, misunderstanding, unfeelingness

emperor [n] *ruler* czar, dictator, empress, king, monarch, prince, sovereign, sultan; CONCEPTS 347,354

emphasis [n] *importance, prominence* accent, accentuation, attention, decidedness, force, headline, highlight, impressiveness, insistence, intensity, moment, positiveness, power, preeminence, priority, significance, strength, stress, underlining, underscoring, weight; CONCEPTS 668,682 —Ant. insignificance, unimportance

emphasize [v] *stress, give priority to* accent, accentuate, affirm, articulate, assert, bear down, charge, dramatize, dwell on, enlarge, enunciate, headline, highlight, hit*, impress, indicate, insist on, italicize, labor the point*, limelight*, maintain, make a point, make clear, make emphatic, make much of*, mark, pinpoint, play up*, point out*, point up*, press, pronounce, punctuate, put accent on*, reiterate, repeat, rub in*, spotlight*, underline, underscore, weight; CONCEPTS 49,57 —Ant. depreciate, forget, ignore, play down, understate

emphatic [adj] *insistent, unequivocal* absolute, accented, assertive, assured, categorical, certain, cogent, confident, decided, definite, definitive, determined, direct, distinct, dogmatic, dynamic, earnest, energetic, explicit, express, flat, for a face*, forceful, forcible, important, impressive, marked, momentous, no mistake*, pointed, positive, potent, powerful, pronounced, resounding, significant, sober, solemn, stressed, striking, strong, sure, telling, trenchant, unmistakable, vigorous; CONCEPTS 267,535 —Ant. equivocal, indefinite, indistinct, insignificant, reserved, understated, unpronounced

empire [n] *place ruled by sovereign; rule* authority, command, commonwealth, control, domain, dominion, federation, government, people, power, realm, sovereignty, supremacy, sway, union; CONCEPTS 198,299,376

empirical/empiric [adj] *practical; based on experience* experient, experiential, experimental, factual, observational, observed, pragmatic, provisional, CONCEPTS 548,582 —Ant. hypothetical, impractical, speculative, theoretical, unobserved

employ [v1] *make use of* apply, bestow, bring to bear*, engage, exercise, exert, exploit, fill, handle, keep busy*, manipulate, occupy, operate, put to use*, spend, take up*, use, use up*, utilize; CONCEPT 225 —Ant. ignore, misuse, shun, unemploy

employ [v2] *give money in exchange for work performed* bring on board*, come on board*, commission, contract, contract for, engage, enlist, hire, ink*, obtain, place, procure, put on*, retain, secure, sign on*, sign up*, take on, truck with*; CONCEPT 351 —Ant. fire, lay off, let go

employed [adj] *working* active, at it*, at work, busy, engaged, hired, in a job, in collar*, in

harness*, inked*, in place, laboring, occupied, on board*, on duty*, on the job*, on the payroll*, operating, plugging away*, selected, signed*; CONCEPTS 538,560 —Ant. idle, inactive, unemployed, unengaged, unoccupied

employee [n] *person being paid for working for another or a corporation* agent, apprentice, assistant, attendant, blue collar*, breadwinner*, clerk, cog*, company person, craftsperson, desk jockey*, domestic, hand, help, hired gun*, hired hand*, hireling, jobholder, laborer, member, operator, pink collar*, plug*, representative, sales help, salesperson, servant, slave, staff member, wage-earner, white collar*, worker, working stiff*; CONCEPT 348

employer [n] *person, business who hires workers* big cheese*, big shot*, boss, businessperson, capitalist, CEO*, chief, CO*, company, corporation, director, entrepreneur, establishment, executive, firm, front office, head, head honcho*, juice*, kingpin*, management, manager, manufacturer, meal ticket*, organization, outfit, overseer, owner, patron, president, proprietor, slavedriver*, superintendent, supervisor; CONCEPT 347

employment [n1] *working for a living; engagement in activity* application, assignment, avocation, awarding, business, calling, carrying, commissioning, contracting, craft, employ, engaging, enlistment, enrollment, exercise, exercising, exertion, field, function, game*, hire, hiring, job, line, métier, mission, number, occupation, occupying, office, position, post, profession, pursuit, racket*, recruitment, retaining, service, servicing, setup, signing on*, situation, taking on, thing*, trade, using, vocation, what one is into*, work; CONCEPTS 349, 351;360 —Ant. idleness, inactivity, unemployment

employment [n2] *using something* adoption, appliance, application, disposition, exercise, exercising, exertion, exploitation, handling, operation, play, purpose, usage, usance, use, utilization; CONCEPTS 225,658,694 —Ant. misuse

emporium [n] *market* bazaar, boutique, chain, co-op, cut-rate store*, discount store, five-and-dime*, flea market, galleria, mall, mart, outlet, outlet store, shop, shopping center, shopping plaza, stand, store, supermarket, thrift shop; CONCEPT 449

empower [v] *authorize, enable* accredit, allow, capacitate, charge, commission, delegate, entitle, entrust, grant, invest, legitimize, license, okay, permit, privilege, qualify, sanction, vest, warrant; CONCEPTS 50,88 —Ant. disenfranchise, refuse, reject, revoke

empress [n] *female ruler* princess, queen, sovereign; CONCEPTS 347,354

emptiness [n1] *void, bareness* blank, blankness, chasm, depletedness, desertedness, desolation, destitution, exhaustion, gap, hollowness, inanition, vacancy, vacuity, vacuum, waste; CONCEPTS 720,733 —Ant. capacity, fill, fullness

empty [adj1] *containing nothing* abandoned, bare, barren, blank, clear, dead, deflated, depleted, desert, deserted, desolate, despoiled, destitute, devoid, dry, evacuated, exhausted, forsaken, godforsaken*, hollow, lacking, stark, unfilled, unfurnished, uninhabited, unoccupied, vacant, vacated, vacuous, void, wanting, waste; CONCEPTS 481,774,786 —*Ant.* complete, entire, filled, full, replete, sated, satisfied

empty [*adj2*] *fruitless, ineffective* aimless, banal, barren, cheap, dead, deadpan, devoid, dishonest, dumb, expressionless, fatuous, flat, frivolous, futile, hollow, idle, ignorant, inane, ineffectual, inexpressive, insincere, insipid, jejune, meaningless, nugatory, otiose, paltry, petty, purposeless, senseless, silly, trivial, unintelligent, unreal, unsatisfactory, unsubstantial, vacuous, vain, valueless, vapid, worthless; CONCEPTS 402,570,575 —*Ant.* abundant, copious, effective, fruitful, productive, sufficient

empty [*adj3*] *hungry* famished, ravenous, starving, unfed, unfilled; CONCEPT 406 —*Ant.* filled, full, sated, satisfied

empty [*v*] *remove contents* clear, consume, decant, deplete, discharge, disgorge, drain, drink, dump, ebb, eject, escape, evacuate, exhaust, expel, flow out, gut, leak, leave, make void, pour out, purge, release, run out, rush out, tap, unburden, unload, use up, vacate, void; CONCEPT 211 —*Ant.* fill

empty-headed [*adj*] *flighty, scatterbrained* brainless, dizzy, featherbrained, frivolous, giddy, harebrained, ignorant, illiterate, inane, know-nothing, silly, skittish, stupid, uneducated, unschooled, untaught, vacant, vacuous; CONCEPT 402 —*Ant.* cognizant, intelligent, sensible, slick, smart

emulate [*v*] *copy the actions of* challenge, compete, compete with, contend, contend with, ditto*, do*, do like*, follow, follow in footsteps*, follow suit*, follow the example of*, go like*, imitate, make like*, mimic, mirror, outvie, pattern after*, rival, rivalize, take after*, vie with; CONCEPTS 87,171

enable [*v*] *allow, authorize* accredit, approve, capacitate, commission, condition, empower, endow, facilitate, fit, give power, implement, invest, let, license, make possible, permit, prepare, provide the means*, qualify, ready, sanction, set up, warrant; CONCEPTS 50,83,88, 99 —*Ant.* block, disallow, halt, hinder, inhibit, oppose, prevent, stop

enact [*v1*] *act out; accomplish* achieve, appear as, depict, discourse, do, execute, go on*, perform, personate, play, playact, play the part of, portray, represent; CONCEPTS 91,292 —*Ant.* fail, hinder, repeal, stop

enact [*v2*] *authorize, legislate* accomplish, appoint, bring about, carry through, command, constitute, decree, determine, dictate, effect, effectuate, establish, execute, fix, formulate, get the floor*, institute, jam through*, make, make into law, make laws, ordain, order, pass, proclaim, put in force, put through, railroad*, railroad through*, ratify, sanction, set, steamroll*,transact, vote favorably*, vote in*; CONCEPTS 50,88,298,317 —*Ant.* hinder, prevent, refuse, veto

enactment [*n1*] *playacting* achievement, acting, depiction, execution, impersonation, performance, personation, personification, playing, portrayal, representation; CONCEPTS 263,292

enactment [*n2*] *law; authorization* command, commandment, decree, dictate, edict, execution,

legislation, order, ordinance, proclamation, ratification, regulation, statute; CONCEPTS 318, 685 —*Ant.* block, disallowance, hindrance, stop, veto

enamel [*n*] *paint, often shiny* cloisonné, coating, finish, glaze, gloss, japan, lacquer, polish, stain, topcoat, varnish, veneer; CONCEPTS 259,260,467

enamor [*v*] *fascinate, captivate* attract, bewitch, charm, enchant, endear, enrapture, enthrall, entice, entrance, fall in love with*, grab, infatuate, make hit with*, please, slay*, sweep off feet*, turn on*; CONCEPTS 7,22, 375 —*Ant.* dislike, hate

enamored [*adj*] *in love* amorous, attracted, besotted, bewitched, captivated, charmed, crazy about*, devoted, dotty, enchanted, enraptured, entranced, fascinated, fond, gone*, has a thing about*, hooked*, infatuated, loving, nuts about*, silly about*, smitten, stuck on*, swept off one's feet*, taken*, wild about*; CONCEPTS 32,403 —*Ant.* disliked, hated

encampment [*n*] *camp* bivouac, campground, campsite, rest area, site; CONCEPTS 198,516

encapsulate [*v1*] *encase* box, cover, enclose, envelop, sheathe, wrap; CONCEPTS 112,209,758

encapsulate [*v2*] *epitomize* abbreviate, abridge, capsulize, condense, cut, digest, précis, shorten, summarize, sum up, synopsize; CONCEPTS 236, 247

enchant [*v*] *delight, mesmerize* allure, beguile, bewitch, captivate, carry away*, cast a spell on*, charm, delectate, draw, enamor, enrapture, ensorcell, enthrall, entice, entrance, fascinate, grab, gratify, hex, hypnotize, kill*, knock dead*, magnetize, make a hit with*, make happy*, please, send*, slay*, spell, spellbind, sweep off feet*, take, thrill, turn on*, voodoo*, wile, wow*; CONCEPTS 7,22 —*Ant.* bother, disenchant, disgust, repel, repulse

enchanting [*adj*] *fascinating, delightful* alluring, appealing, attractive, beguiling, bewitching, captivating, charming, delectable, endearing, enthralling, entrancing, exciting, glamorous, intriguing, lovely, pleasant, pleasing, ravishing, seductive, siren, sirenic, winsome; CONCEPTS 404,529 —*Ant.* bothering, disenchanting, disgust, repellent, repulsive

enchantress [*n*] *sorceress* charmer, diviner, femme fatale, seductress, siren, vamp, witch; CONCEPTS 361,412,415

encircle [*v*] *circumscribe* band, begird, cincture, circle, circuit, compass, cover, enclose, encompass, enfold, enring, envelop, environ, gird in, girdle, halo, hem in*, inclose, invest, ring, surround, wreathe; CONCEPT 758 —*Ant.* let go, unloose

enclose [*v*] *put inside, surround* blockade, block off, bound, box up, cage, circle, circumscribe, close in, confine, coop, corral, cover, encase, encircle, encompass, enfold, enshroud, environ, fence, fence off*, hedge, hem in*, imbue, immure, implant, impound, imprison, include, induct, insert, intern, jail, limit, lock in*, lock up*, mew, mure, pen, restrict, set apart, shut in, veil, wall in, wrap;CONCEPTS 112,209,758 —*Ant.* free, let go, release, unloose

enclosure [*n1*] *area bounded by something* asylum, aviary, bowl, building, cage, camp, cell, close, coliseum, coop, corral, court, courtyard, den, dungeon, garden, ghetto, hutch, jail, pale, park, patch, pen, place, plot, pound, precinct, prison, quad, quadrangle, region, room, stadium, stockade, sty, vault, walk, yard, zone; CONCEPTS *439,448,513* —*Ant.* open

enclosure [*n2*] *something included with a letter* check, circular, copy, document, form, information, money, printed matter, question- naire; CONCEPT *271*

encode [*v*] *encrypt* cipher, conceal, cryptograph, make secret, put into code; CONCEPT *188*

encompass [*v1*] *surround, circumscribe* beset, circle, compass, encircle, enclose, envelop, environ, gird, girdle, hem in, ring; CONCEPT *758*

encompass [*v2*] *include, contain* admit, com- prehend, comprise, cover, embody, embrace, have, hold, incorporate, involve, subsume, take in; CONCEPT *112* —*Ant.* exclude

encore [*n*] *another round of applause; repeat* acclamation, cheers, number, plaudits, praise, reappearance, repeat performance, repetition, response, return; CONCEPT *264*

encounter [*n1*] *chance meeting* appointment, brush, concurrence, confrontation, interview, rendezvous; CONCEPT *384* —*Ant.* avoidance, evasion, retreat

encounter [*n2*] *fight, argument* action, battle, bout, brush, clash, collision, combat, conflict, contention, contest, dispute, engagement, flap*, fray, hassle, quarrel, rumpus*, run-in*, scrap, set-to*, skirmish, velitation, violence; CONCEPTS *46,86,106* —*Ant.* surrender, yielding

encounter [*v1*] *happen upon* alight upon, bear, bump into, chance upon, close, come across, come upon, confront, cross the path*, descry, detect, espy, experience, face, fall in with*, find, front, hit upon, meet, meet up with, rub eyeballs*, run across, run into, run smack into*, suffer, sustain, turn up, undergo; CONCEPTS *38,384* —*Ant.* avoid, evade, retreat, run away

encounter [*v2*] *fight, attack* affront, battle, clash with, collide, combat, conflict, confront, contend, cross swords*, do battle*, engage, face, grapple, meet, strive, struggle; CONCEPTS *86,106* —*Ant.* let go, surrender, yield

encourage [*v1*] *stimulate spiritually* animate, applaud, boost, brighten, buck up*, buoy, cheer, cheer up, comfort, console, embolden, energize, enhearten, enliven, excite, exhilarate, fortify, galvanize, give shot in arm*, gladden, goad, hearten, incite, inspire, inspirit, instigate, praise, prick, prop up*, psych up*, push, rally, reas- sure, refresh, restore, revitalize, revivify, rouse, spur, steel, stir, strengthen, sway; CONCEPTS *7,22* —*Ant.* dampen, deject, depress, deter, discourage, dispirit, dissuade, uninspire

encourage [*v2*] *give support; help* abet, ad- vance, advocate, aid, approve, assist, back, back up, befriend, bolster, boost, brace, com- fort, console, countenance, develop, ease, egg on*, endorse, favor, fortify, forward, foster, further, get behind, give a leg up*, go for*, improve, instigate, invite, pat on the back, prevail, promote, pull for*, push, reassure, reinforce, relieve, root for*, sanction, second, serve, side with*, smile upon*, solace, spur, strengthen, subscribe to, subsidize, succor,

support, sustain, uphold; CONCEPTS *8,110* —*Ant.* block, confuse, deter, discourage

encouragement [*n*] *help, support* advance, advocacy, aid, animation, assistance, backing, boost, cheer, comfort, confidence, consolation, consoling, easement, enlivening, faith, favor, firmness, fortitude, helpfulness, hope, incentive, incitement, inspiration, inspiritment, invigora- tion, optimism, promotion, reassurance, reas- suring, refreshment, relief, relieving, reward, shot in the arm*, softening, solacing, stimula- tion, stimulus, succor, supporting, trust, urging; CONCEPTS *7,22,110,410* —*Ant.* denunciation, derision, deterrent, discouragement

encroach [*v*] *invade another's property, busi- ness* appropriate, arrogate, barge in*, butt in*, crash, elbow in*, entrench, horn in*, impinge, infringe, interfere, interpose, intervene, intrude, make inroads*, meddle, muscle in*, overstep, put two cents in*, squeeze in*, stick nose into*, trench, trespass, usurp, work in, worm in*; CONCEPTS *7,19,86,159* —*Ant.* keep off

encumber [*v*] *bother, burden* block, charge, clog, cramp, discommode, embarrass, hamper, handicap, hang up, hinder, hog-tie*, hold up, impede, incommode, inconvenience, lade, load, make difficult, obstruct, oppress, overburden, overload, retard, saddle, saddle with*, slow down, tax, trammel, weigh down, weight; CONCEPTS *121,130* —*Ant.* aid, assist, help

encumbrance [*n*] *burden* albatross, ball and chain*, cross, debt, duty, guilt, handicap, hindrance, impediment, load, millstone, monkey on one's back*, obstruction, responsi- bility, saddle, thorn in one's side*, weight, worry; CONCEPTS *532,690*

encyclopedic [*adj*] *comprehensive* all-embrac- ing, all-encompassing, all-inclusive, broad, catholic, complete, discursive, exhaustive, extensive, general, thorough, thorough-going, universal, vast, wide-ranging, widespread; CONCEPTS *267,772* —*Ant.* brief, incomplete, summary, uncomprehensive

end [*n1*] *extreme, limit* borderline, bound, boundary, butt end, confine, cusp, deadline, edge, extent, extremity, foot, head, heel, limitation, neb, nib, point, prong, stub, stub, stump, tail, tail end, term, terminal, termina- tion, terminus, tip, top, ultimate; CONCEPT *745* —*Ant.* beginning, cause, foundation, origin

end [*n2*] *completion, stop* accomplishment, achievement, adjournment, attainment, bottom line*, cease, cessation, close, closing, closure, conclusion, consequence, consummation, culmination, curtain, denouement, desistance, desuetude, determination, discontinuance, execution, expiration, expiry, finale, finis, finish, fulfillment, issue, last word*, omega, outcome, payoff, perfection, realization, resolution, result, retirement, sign-off*, target, termination, terminus, upshot*, windup, wrap-up*; CONCEPTS *119,230,832* —*Ant.* beginning, commencement, opening, start

end [*n3*] *intention, aim* aspiration, design, drift, goal, intent, mark, object, objective, point, purpose, reason, where one's heading*; CONCEPT *659* —*Ant.* means

end [*n4*] *leftover part* bit, butt end, dregs, fragment, leaving, lees, particle, piece, portion, remainder, remnant, residue, scrap, share, side, stub, tag end; CONCEPT 835

end [n5] *death, destruction* annihilation, demise, dissolution, doom, expiration, extermination, extinction, finish, passing, ruin, ruination; CONCEPT 304 —*Ant.* birth, construction, creation

end [v1] *bring to an end* abolish, abort, accomplish, achieve, break off, break up, call it a day*, call off*, cease, close, close out, complete, conclude, consummate, crown, culminate, cut short, delay, determine, discontinue, dispose of, dissolve, drop, expire, finish, get done, give up, halt, interrupt, pack it in*, perorate, postpone, pull the plug*, put the lid on*, quit, relinquish, resolve, settle, sew up*, shut down*, stop, switch off*, terminate, top off*, ultimate, wind up*, wrap, wrap up*; CONCEPT 234 —*Ant.* begin, commence, create, start

end [v2] *die or kill* abolish, annihilate, cease, depart, desist, destroy, die, expire, exterminate, extinguish, lapse, put to death, ruin, run out, wane; CONCEPTS 252,304 —*Ant.* bear, create, give birth

endanger [v] *put in jeopardy* be careless, chance, chance it*, expose, hazard, imperil, lay on the line*, lay open*, leave defenseless, leave in the middle*, make liable, menace, peril, play into one's hands*, put at risk, put in danger, put on the spot*, risk, stick one's neck out*, subject to loss, threaten, venture; CONCEPTS 246,252,384 —*Ant.* aid, assist, comfort, help, save, take care

endangered [adj] *imperiled* at risk, facing extinction, in danger, threatened; CONCEPTS 231,407

endear [v] *attract attention* attach, bind, captivate, charm, cherish, engage, prize, treasure, value, win; CONCEPTS 7,22,32 —*Ant.* disenchant, repulse

endearing [adj] *lovable* adorable, captivating, charming, dear, irresistible, sweet, winning; CONCEPT 404

endeavor [n] *attempt to achieve something* aim, all*, best shot*, crash project*, dry run*, effort, enterprise, essay, exertion, fling, full blast*, full court press*, full steam*, go, header*, labor, lick*, old college try*, one's all*, one's level best*, push, shot*, stab*, striving, struggle, toil, travail, trial, try, try-on*, undertaking, venture, whack*, whirl*, work; CONCEPT 87 —*Ant.* idleness, laziness

endeavor [v] *attempt to achieve something* address, aim, apply, aspire, assay, bid for, buck, determine, dig, do one's best*, drive at, essay, go for*, go for broke*, grind, hammer away*, hassle, have a crack*, have a shot at*, have a swing at*, hump*, hustle, intend, labor, make an effort, make a run at*, offer, peg away*, plug, pour it on*, purpose, push, risk, scratch, seek, strain, strive, struggle, sweat, take on, take pains*, try, undertake, venture; CONCEPT 87 —*Ant.* be idle, ignore, laze, procrastinate, put off

endemic [adj] *native* local, regional; CONCEPT 536

ending [n] *conclusion* catastrophe, cessation, close, closing, closure, completion, consummation, coup de grace, culmination, denouement,

desistance, dissolution, epilogue, expiration, finale, finish, lapse, omega, outcome, period, resolution, stop, summation, swan song*, termination, terminus, upshot, wane, windup; CONCEPTS 119,230,832 —*Ant.* beginning, commencement, introduction, opening, start

endless [adj] *not stopping, not finishing* amaranthine, boundless, ceaseless, constant, continual, continuous, countless, deathless, enduring, eternal, everlasting, illimitable, immeasurable, immortal, incalculable, incessant, indeterminate, infinite, interminable, limitless, measureless, monotonous, multitudinous, never-ending, no end of, no end to, numberless, overlong, perpetual, self-perpetuating, unbounded, unbroken, undivided, undying, unending, unfathomable, uninterrupted, unlimited, unsurpassable, untold, without end; CONCEPTS 482,551,798 —*Ant.* bounded, completing, ending, finishing, limited, passing, stopping, terminable

endorse [v1] *support, authorize* accredit, advocate, affirm, approve, attest, authenticate, back, back up*, bless, boost, certify, champion, commend, confirm, countenance, defend, favor, give a boost to, give green light*, give one's word*, give the go-ahead*, give the nod*, go along with*, go to bat for*, go with, guarantee, lend one's name to, okay, praise, push, ratify, recommend, rubber-stamp*, sanction, second, stand behind, stand up for*, stump for*, subscribe to, sustain, underwrite, uphold, vouch for, warrant, witness; CONCEPTS 10,50,69, 88,300 —*Ant.* censure, disapprove, oppose, protest, reject, repel, unauthorize

endorse [v2] *countersign a check* add one's name to, authenticate, autograph, cosign, notarize, put John Hancock on*, put signature on, rubber-stamp*, say amen to*, sign, sign off on, sign on dotted line*, subscribe, superscribe, undersign, underwrite; CONCEPTS 50,79,88,330

endorsement [n] *support, authorization* advocacy, affirmation, approbation, approval, backing, championing, commercial, confirmation, countersignature, favor, fiat, go-ahead*, green light*, hubba-hubba*, okay, pat on back*, permission, qualification, ratification, recommendation, sanction, seal of approval, signature, stroke, subscription to, superscription, the nod*, warrant; CONCEPT 685 —*Ant.* censure, disapproval, opposition, rejection

endow [v] *give large gift* accord, award, back, bequeath, bestow, come through with, confer, contribute, donate, empower, enable, endue, enhance, enrich, establish, favor, finance, found, fund, furnish, grant, heighten, invest, lay on*, leave, make over*, organize, promote, provide, settle on, sponsor, subscribe, subsidize, supply, support, vest in, will; CONCEPTS 108, 341 —*Ant.* receive, take

endowment [n1] *large gift* award, benefaction, benefit, bequest, bestowal, boon, bounty, dispensation, donation, fund, funding, gifting, grant, gratuity, income, inheritance, largess, legacy, nest egg, pension, presentation, property, provision, revenue, stake, stipend, subsidy, trust; CONCEPTS 337,340 —*Ant.* loss

endowment [n2] *personal talent, ability* aptitude, attribute, capability, capacity, faculty, flair, genius, gift, habilitation, power, qualification, quality, turn; CONCEPTS *411,630* —*Ant.* drawback, inability, weakness

end up [*v*] *become eventually; come to a close* arrive finally, cease, come to a halt, finish, finish as, finish up, stop, turn out to be, wind up; CONCEPT *119*

endurable [*adj*] *tolerable* bearable, livable, sufferable, supportable, sustainable; CONCEPT *548* —*Ant.* changeable, intolerable, tiring, unendurable

endurance [*n1*] *bearing hardship; staying power* ability, allowance, backbone, bearing, capacity, continuing, cool, coolness, courage, enduring, forebearance, fortitude, grit, guts, gutsiness, heart*, holding up*, intestinal fortitude, mettle, moxie*, patience, perseverance, persistence, pertinacity, pluck, resignation, resistance, resolution, restraint, spunk, stamina, standing, starch*, strength, submission, sufferance, suffering, tenacity, tolerance, toleration, undergoing, vitality, will, withstanding; CONCEPTS *411,633*

endurance [*n2*] *continuity, lastingness* continuance, continuation, durability, duration, immutability, longevity, permanence, persistence, stability; CONCEPT *804* —*Ant.* end, fleetingness

endure [*v1*] *bear hardship* abide, accustom, allow, bear the brunt*, be patient with, brave, brook, cope with, countenance, eat, encounter, experience, face, feel, go through, grin and bear it*, hang in*, keep up, know, live out, live through, meet with, never say die*, permit, put up with, repress feelings, resign oneself, ride out*, sit through, stand, stick, stick it out*, stomach*, subject to, submit to, suffer, support, sustain, swallow*, take, take it*, take patiently, tolerate, undergo, weather, withstand; CONCEPT *23*

endure [*v2*] *continue; be durable* abide, be, be left, be long lived, be timeless, bide, carry on, carry through, cling, exist, go on, hang on*, have no end, hold, hold on, hold out, keep on, last, linger, live, live on, never say die*, outlast, outlive, perdure, persist, prevail, remain, ride out*, run on, stand, stay, stay on, stick to*, superannuate, survive, sustain, wear, wear on, wear well*; CONCEPTS *239,407,804* —*Ant.* discontinue

enemy [*n*] *someone hated or competed against* adversary, agent, antagonist, archenemy, asperser, assailant, assassin, attacker, backbiter, bad person*, bandit, betrayer, calumniator, competitor, contender, criminal, defamer, defiler, detractor, disputant, emulator, falsifier, fifth column*, foe, guerrilla, informer, inquisitor, invader, murderer, opponent, opposition, other side*, prosecutor, rebel, revolutionary, rival, saboteur, seditionist, slanderer, spy, terrorist, traducer, traitor, vilifier, villain; CONCEPTS *322,412* —*Ant.* aide, ally, assistant, confidante, friend, helper

energetic [*adj*] *full of life; forceful* active, aggressive, animated, ball of fire*, breezy, brisk, demoniac, driving, dynamic, enterprising, forcible, fresh, hardy, high-powered, indefatigable, industrious, kinetic, lively, lusty, peppy, potent, powerful, red-blooded*, rugged, snappy, spirited, sprightly, spry, stalwart, strenuous, strong, sturdy, tireless, tough, unflagging,

untiring, vigorous, vital, vivacious, zippy*; CONCEPTS *404,542* —*Ant.* idle, inactive, lazy, lethargic, lifeless, slow, sluggish, tired

energize [*v*] *activate; give more life* actify, activize, animate, arm, build up, electrify, empower, enable, enliven, excite, fortify, goose*, innervate, inspirit, invigorate, jazz up*, juice up*, liven up, motivate, pep up, prime, pump up*, put zip into*, quicken, reinforce, start up, stimulate, strengthen, sustain, switch on, trigger, turn on, vitalize, work up, zap*; CONCEPTS *7,22,231,700* —*Ant.* deactivate, debilitate, sap, tire, weaken, weary

energy [*n1*] *person's spirit and vigor* activity, animation, application, ardor, birr, dash, drive, effectiveness, efficacy, efficiency, élan, endurance, enterprise, exertion, fire, force, forcefulness, fortitude, get-up-and-go*, go, hardihood, initiative, intensity, juice, life, liveliness, might, moxie*, muscle, operativeness, pep, pizzazz, pluck, potency, power, puissance, punch, spirit, spontaneity, stamina, steam, strength, toughness, tuck, vehemence, verve, vim, virility, vitality, vivacity, zeal, zest, zing, zip*; CONCEPT *411* —*Ant.* idleness, inactivity, laziness, lethargy, tiredness

energy [*n2*] *generated power* application, burn, conductivity, current, dynamism, electricity, force, friction, gravity, heat, horsepower, juice, kilowatts, magnetism, potential, pressure, radioactivity, rays, reaction, response, service, steam, strength, voltage, wattage; CONCEPT *520*

enervate [*v*] *tire, wear out* debilitate, devitalize, disable, enfeeble, exhaust, fatigue, incapacitate, jade, paralyze, sap, unnerve, vitiate, weaken, weary; CONCEPTS *156,225,250* —*Ant.* activate, animate, empower, energize, invigorate, liven, strengthen

enervated [*adj*] *exhausted, worn out* debilitated, deteriorated, devitalized, done in, enfeebled, fatigued, feeble, gone to seed*, incapacitated, lackadaisical, languid, languishing, languorous, limp, listless, on the ropes*, out of condition*, out of gas*, out of shape*, paralyzed, prostrate, prostrated, run-down, rusty, sapped, soft, spent, spiritless, tired, undermined, unnerved, vitiated, washed out, weak, weakened; CONCEPTS *485,560* —*Ant.* activated, active, animated, energized, enthusiastic, invigorated, lively, strengthened

enfeeble [*v*] *make very weak* attenuate, blunt, cripple, debilitate, deplete, devitalize, diminish, disable, exhaust, fatigue, incapacitate, sap, undermine, unhinge, unnerve, weaken, wear out; CONCEPTS *240,252* —*Ant.* strengthen

enfold [*v*] *embrace, hug* bear hug, cinch, clasp, clinch, clutch, cover, drape, encase, enclose, encompass, enshroud, envelop, envelope, enwrap, fold, girdle, grab, hold, invest, press, shroud, squeeze, surround, swathe, veil, wrap, wrap up; CONCEPTS *191,219* —*Ant.* let go

enforce [*v*] *put a rule, plan in force* accomplish, administer, administrate, apply, carry out, coerce, commandeer, compel, constrain, crack down, demand, dictate, discharge, dragoon, drive, effect, egg on*, emphasize, exact, execute, exert, expect, extort, force upon, fortify, fulfill, goad, hound, impel, implement, impose, incite, insist on, invoke, lash, lean on, make, necessitate, oblige, perform, press, prosecute, put into effect, put screws to*, reinforce, require, sanction, spur, strain, stress, strong-arm, urge, whip, wrest; CONCEPTS 50,88,133,298,317 —*Ant.* abandon, disregard, drop, forego, forget, give up, neglect, overlook

enforcement [n] *requirement to obey; implementation of rule(s)* administration, application, carrying out, coercion, compulsion, compulsory law, constraint, duress, enforcing, exaction, execution, fulfilling, imposition, impulsion, insistence, lash, martial law, necessitation, obligation, prescription, pressure, prosecution, reinforcement, spur, whip; CONCEPTS 133,298, 317,685 —*Ant.* abandon, disregard, forgetfulness, neglect, renunciation, slight

enfranchise [v] *set free* citizenize, emancipate, empower, free, give rights to, grant citizenship to, liberate, manumit, naturalize, release; CONCEPT 110 —*Ant.* enslave

engage [v1] *hire for job, use* appoint, bespeak, book, bring on board*, charter, come on board*, commission, contract, employ, enlist, enroll, ink*, lease, place, prearrange, put on, rent, reserve, retain, secure, sign on, sign up, take on, truck with*; CONCEPTS 129,351 —*Ant.* banish, discharge, dismiss, eject, expel, fire, let go, oust, release

engage [v2] *occupy oneself; engross* absorb, allure, arrest, bewitch, busy, captivate, catch, charm, draw, embark on, employ, enamor, enchant, enter into, enthrall, fascinate, give a try*, give a whirl*, go for broke*, go in for*, go out for*, grip*, have a fling at*, have a go at*, have a shot at*, imbue, immerse, interest, involve, join, keep busy, monopolize, partake, participate, pitch in, practice, preengage, preoccupy, set about, soak, tackle*, take part, tie up, try on for size*, undertake; CONCEPTS 87,363 —*Ant.* decline, refuse, reject, shun

engage [v3] *promise to marry* affiance, agree, betroth, bind, catch, commit, contract, covenant, give one's word*, guarantee, hook, obligate, oblige, pass, pledge, tie, troth, turn on*, undertake, vouch, vow; CONCEPT 297 —*Ant.* break off, break up

engage [v4] *start a fight; attack* assail, assault, combat, do battle with, encounter, face, fall on, give battle to, join battle with, launch, meet, strike, take on; CONCEPTS 86,106,320 —*Ant.* give up, surrender, yield

engage [v5] *interconnect; bring into operation* activate, apply, attach, dovetail, energize, fasten, get going, interact, interlace, interlock, intermesh, interplay, join, lock, mesh, switch on; CONCEPTS 85,113,160,221 —*Ant.* cancel, defuse, disconnect

engaged [adj1] *promised to be married* affianced, asked for, betrothed, bound, committed, contracted, future, given one's word*, going steady*, hooked*, intended, matched, pinned, pledged, plighted, ringed, spoken for, steady*; CONCEPT 555 —*Ant.* available, uninvolved

engaged [adj2] *operating; busy* absorbed, at work, committed, connected with, dealing in, deep, doing, employed, engrossed, immersed, in place, intent, interested, in use, involved, occupied, performing, practicing, preoccupied, pursuing, rapt, signed, tied up, unavailable,

working, wrapped up*; CONCEPTS 542,555,576 —*Ant.* disengaged, inoperable, not working

engagement [n1] *pledge to marry* assurance, betrothal, betrothing, betrothment, bond, commitment, compact, contract, espousal, match, oath, obligation, pact, plight, promise, troth, undertaking, vow, word; CONCEPT 297 —*Ant.* break-up, disengagement

engagement [n2] *meeting; date* appointment, arrangement, assignation, blind date*, commission, commitment, date, errand, get-together, gig, going out*, interview, invitation, meet, seeing about*, stint, tryst, visit; CONCEPT 384

engagement [n3] *battle* action, combat, conflict, confrontation, contest, encounter, fight, fray, skirmish; CONCEPTS 106,320 —*Ant.* surrender

engaging [adj] *charming* agreeable, alluring, appealing, attractive, bewitching, captivating, enchanting, enticing, entrancing, fascinating, fetching, glamorous, interesting, intriguing, inviting, likable, lovable, magnetic, mesmeric, pleasant, pleasing, prepossessing, siren, sweet, winning, winsome; CONCEPT 404 —*Ant.* boring, repulsive, tiresome, undesirable, unlikeable

engender [v] *cause to happen; cause an action* arouse, beget, breed, bring about, bring forth, create, develop, excite, foment, generate, give birth to, give rise to, hatch, incite, induce, instigate, lead to, make, muster, occasion, precipitate, procreate, produce, propagate, provoke, quicken, rouse, spawn, stimulate, stir, work up; CONCEPTS 221,242 —*Ant.* destroy, finish, halt, kill, stop

engine [n] *device that drives a machine* agent, apparatus, appliance, barrel, contrivance, cylinder, diesel, dynamo, fan, generator, horses*, implement, instrument, means, mechanism, motor, piston, pot*, powerhouse, power plant, power train, putt-putt*, rubber band*, tool, transformer, turbine, weapon, what's under the hood*; CONCEPTS 463,464

engineer [n] *person who puts together things* architect, builder, contriver, designer, deviser, director, inventor, manager, manipulator, originator, planner, schemer, sights*, surveyor, techie*, technie*; CONCEPT 348

engineer [v] *devise; bring about* angle, arrange, cause, come up with, con, conceive, concoct, contrive, control, cook*, create, direct, doctor, effect, encompass, finagle*, jockey*, machinate, manage, maneuver, manipulate, negotiate, operate, organize, originate, plan, plant, play games*, plot, pull strings*, pull wires*, put one on*, put one over*, put over*, put through, rig*, scam, scheme, set up, superintend, supervise, swing, upstage, wangle, work; CONCEPTS 36,173,251

engrave [v] *carve letters or designs into* bite, burn, chase, chisel, crosshatch, cut, diaper, embed, enchase, etch, fix, grave, hatch, impress, imprint, infix, ingrain, initial, inscribe, instill, intaglio, lithograph, lodge, mezzotint, ornament, print, scratch, stipple; CONCEPTS 79,174,176

engraving [n] *carving of letters or design into something* blocking, chasing, chiselling, cutting, dry point, enchasing, etching, illustration, impression, inscribing, inscription, intaglio, lithograph, mezzotint, photoengraving, photogravure, print, rotogravure, scratch, woodcut; CONCEPTS 79,174,176,625

engross [v] hold one's attention absorb, apply, arrest, assimilate, attract, become lost, be hung*, bewitch, busy, captivate, consume, corner, engage, engulf, enrapture, enthrall, fascinate, fill, grip, hog*, immerse, involve, monopolize, occupy, preoccupy, sew up*, soak, take up, up on*; CONCEPTS 14,17 —Ant. forget, ignore, reject, repulse, turn off

engrossed [adj] preoccupied; attentive to absorbed, all wound up*, assiduous, bugged*, busy, captivated, caught up, caught up in, consumed, deep, diligent, engaged, enthralled, fascinated, fiend for*, gone*, gripped, head over heels*, heavily into*, hooked, hung up, immersed, industrious, intent, into*, intrigued, lost, monopolized, occupied, rapt, really into*, riveted, sedulous, submerged, taken up with, tied up, turned on*, up to here in*, wrapped up*; CONCEPTS 403,542 —Ant. bored, disenthralled, disinterested, ignoring, inattentive, oblivious, uncaring, uninterested, unoccupied

engrossing [adj] very interesting absorbing, all-consuming, captivating, compelling, consuming, controlling, enthralling, exciting, fascinating, gripping, intriguing, monopolizing, obsessing, preoccupying, provoking, riveting, stimulating; CONCEPT 529 —Ant. boring, repellent, repulsive, uninteresting

engulf [v] absorb, overwhelm bury, consume, deluge, drown, encompass, engross, envelop, flood, imbibe, immerse, inundate, overflow, overrun, overwhelm, plunge, submerge, swallow up, swamp, whelm; CONCEPTS 169,172,256

enhance [v] improve, embellish add to, adorn, aggrandize, amplify, appreciate, augment, beautify, boom, boost, build up, complement, elevate, embroider, enlarge, exaggerate, exalt, flesh out*, heighten, increase, intensify, lift, magnify, pad*, pyramid*, raise, reinforce, strengthen, swell, upgrade; CONCEPTS 162, 177, 244 —Ant. decrease, fix, lower, minimize, reduce, worsen

enigma [n] mystery bewilderment, cliffhanger, conundrum, crux, cryptogram, Gordian knot*, grabber*, knot*, mind-boggler*, mind-twister*, mystification, parable, perplexity, problem, puzzle, puzzlement, puzzler, question, question mark, riddle, secret, sixty-four dollar question*, sphinx*, sticker, stickler, stumper, teaser, tough nut to crack*, twister, why*; CONCEPT 532

enigmatic/enigmatical [adj] mysterious ambiguous, cryptic, dark, Delphian*, doubtful, equivocal, incomprehensible, indecipherable, inexplicable, inscrutable, obscure, occult, oracular, perplexing, puzzling, recondite, secret, Sibylline*, sphinxlike, stickling, stumping, teasing, uncertain, unfathomable, unintelligible; CONCEPTS 529,576,582 —Ant. clear, obvious, unmysterious

enjoin [v1] order, command adjure, admonish, advise, appoint, bid, call upon, caution, charge, counsel, decree, demand, dictate, direct, forewarn, impose, instruct, ordain, prescribe, require, rule, tell, urge, warn; CONCEPTS 53,78

enjoin [v2] forbid ban, bar, deny, disallow, inhibit, interdict, outlaw, place injunction on,

preclude, prohibit, proscribe, restrain, taboo; CONCEPTS 50,53,88,130 —Ant. allow, permit

enjoy [v1] take pleasure in, from something adore, appreciate, be entertained, be fond of, be pleased, cotton to*, delight in, dig*, dote on*, drink in*, eat up*, fancy, flip over*, freak out on*, get a charge out of*, get a kick out of*, get high on*, go, have a ball*, have a good time, have fun, like, live a little*, live it up*, love, luxuriate in, mind, paint the town*, rejoice in, relish, revel in, savor, take joy in, thrill to; CONCEPTS 32,384 —Ant. detest, dislike, hate

enjoy [v2] have the benefit or use of be blessed, be favored, boast, command, experience, have, hold, maintain, occupy, own, possess, process, reap the benefits*, retain, use; CONCEPT 710 —Ant. lack, need, want

enjoyable [adj] pleasing; to one's liking agreeable, amusing, clear sailing*, delectable, delicious, delightful, entertaining, fun, genial, gratifying, groovy*, just for grins*, just for kicks*, just for laughs*, just for the heck of it*, likable, lots of laughs*, pleasant, pleasurable, preferable, relishable, satisfying, welcome; CONCEPTS 529,548 —Ant. disagreeable, displeasing, unenjoyable, unhappy, unpleasant, unsatisfying

enjoyment [n1] delight in something amusement, delectation, diversion, enjoying, entertainment, fruition, fun, gladness, gratification, gusto, happiness, hedonism, indulgence, joy, loving, luxury, pleasure, recreation, rejoicing, relaxation, relish, satisfaction, savor, self-indulgence, sensuality, thrill, triumph, zest; CONCEPTS 32,410 —Ant. displeasure, dissatisfaction, misery, sorrow, unhappiness, woe

enjoyment [n2] possession; use of advantage, benefit, exercise, having, indulgence, ownership, spending, using; CONCEPT 710 —Ant. lack, need, want

enlarge [v] make or grow bigger; increase add to, aggrandize, amplify, augment, beef up*, blow up*, boost, broaden, build, bulk, develop, diffuse, dilate, distend, elaborate, elongate, embroider, exaggerate, expand, expatiate, extend, give details, grow, grow larger, heighten, inflate, jack up*, jazz up*, lengthen, magnify, make larger, mount, multiply, pad*, pyramid*, rise, slap on*, snowball*, spread, stretch, swell, upsurge, wax, widen; CONCEPTS 137,236,245,780 —Ant. abridge, compress, condense, curtail, decrease, diminish, lessen, lower, reduce, shrink

enlargement [n] increase, expansion aggrandizement, amplification, augmentation, blow up, elongation, extension, growth, spread; CONCEPT 780 —Ant. abridgment, compression, decrease, lessening, lowering, reduction, shrinkage

enlighten [v] explain thoroughly; make aware acquaint, advise, apprise, brief, catechize, cause to understand, civilize, convert, counsel, direct, disclose, divulge, edify, educate, elucidate, give faith*, give the lowdown*, give the word*, guide, illume, illuminate, illumine, imitate, improve, inculcate, indoctrinate, inform, inspirit, instruct, let in on, open up, persuade, preach, put on to*, reveal, save, school, teach, tell, train, update, uplift; CONCEPTS 57,60,75

—*Ant.* be vague, bewilder, confound, confuse, delude, mislead, obscure, puzzle

enlightened [*adj*] *informed, educated* aware, broad-minded, civilized, cultivated, hip to*, instructed, in the picture*, knowing what's what*, knowledgeable, learned, liberal, literate, open-minded, plugged in*, reasonable, refined, savvy, sharp, sophisticated, tuned in*, wised up*; CONCEPT 402 —*Ant.* confounded, confused, in the dark, misled, perplexed, uneducated, unenlightened, uninformed

enlightenment [*n*] *awareness, understanding* broad-mindedness, civilization, comprehension, cultivation, culture, edification, education, information, insight, instruction, knowledge, learning, literacy, open-mindedness, refinement, sophistication, teaching, wisdom; CONCEPT 409 —*Ant.* bewilderment, confusion, ignorance, puzzlement

enlist [*v*] *sign up for responsibility* admit, appoint, assign, attract, call to arms, call up, conscribe, conscript, draft, embody, employ, engage, enroll, enter, enter into, gather, get, hire, hitch, incorporate, induct, initiate, inscribe, interest, join, join up, levy, list, mobilize, muster, oblige, obtain, place, press into service, procure, record, recruit, register, reserve, secure, serve, sign on, take on, volunteer; CONCEPTS 8, 320 —*Ant.* avoid, dodge, shun

enliven [*v*] *inspire, vitalize* animate, brace up, brighten, buck up, buoy, cheer, cheer up, divert, entertain, excite, exhilarate, fire, fire up, galvanize, give a lift, give life to, gladden, hearten, inspirit, invigorate, jazz up*, juice up*, let sunshine in*, pep up*, perk up*, pick up, put pep into, quicken, recreate, refresh, rejuvenate, renew, restore, rouse, snap out of it*, spark, spice, spice up*, stimulate, vivificate, vivify, wake up, work up*, zap*; CONCEPTS 7, 22 —*Ant.* bore, dull, enervate, exhaust, fatigue, subdue, tire

en masse [*adj*] *all at once* all in all, all together, altogether, as a body, as a group, as a whole, as one, bodily, by and large*, ensemble, generally, in a body, in a group, in a mass, jointly, on the whole, together; CONCEPT 577 —*Ant.* one at a time, singly

enmesh [*v*] *involve in a situation* box in, catch, drag into*, draw in, embroil, ensnare, entangle, entrap, hook, implicate, incriminate, lay a trap for*, lay for*, make party to*, net, snare, snarl, tangle, trammel, trap; CONCEPTS 59,112 —*Ant.* exclude, leave out

enmity [*n*] *hatred, animosity* acrimony, alienation, animus, antagonism, antipathy, aversion, bad blood*, bitterness, daggers*, detestation, dislike, hate, hostility, ill will, loathing, malevolence, malice, malignancy, malignity, rancor, spite, spleen, uncordiality, unfriendliness, venom; CONCEPT 29 —*Ant.* affinity, fellowship, friendship, good will, kindness, love

ennui [*n*] *boredom* apathy, blahs, blues, dejection, depression, dissatisfaction, doldrums, dumps*, fatigue, ho hums*, lack of interest, languidness, languor, lassitude, listlessness, melancholy, sadness, satiety, spiritlessness, surfeit, tedium, weariness, yawn*; CONCEPT 410 —*Ant.* energy, enthusiasm, excitement, liveliness, vigor

enormity [*n1*] *horribleness* abomination, atrociousness, atrocity, crime, depravity, disgrace, evil, evilness, flagrancy, grossness, heinousness, horror, monstrosity, monstrousness, nefariousness, outrage, outrageousness, rankness, turpitude, vice, viciousness, vileness, villainy, wickedness; CONCEPTS 645,666 —*Ant.* goodness

enormity [*n2*] *extreme largeness* bigness, bulk, enormousness, greatness, hugeness, immensity, magnitude, massiveness, size, tremendousness, vastness; CONCEPT 730 —*Ant.* smallness, tininess, triviality

enormous [*adj*] *very large* astronomic, barn door*, blimp*, colossal, excessive, gargantuan, gigantic, gross, huge, humongous, immense, jumbo*, mammoth, massive, monstrous, mountainous, prodigious, stupendous, supercolossal*, titanic*, tremendous, vast, whopping; CONCEPT 773 —*Ant.* insignificant, little, minute, small, tiny

enough [*adj*] *plenty* abundant, acceptable, adequate, all right already*, ample, bellyful*, bounteous, bountiful, comfortable, competent, complete, copious, decent, enough already*, fed up*, full, had it*, last straw*, lavish, plenteous, plentiful, replete, satisfactory, satisfying, sick and tired of*, sufficient, sufficing, suitable, unlimited, up to here*; CONCEPTS 546,771 —*Ant.* inadequate, insufficient

enough [*adv*] *adequately* abundantly, acceptably, admissibly, amply, averagely, barely, commensurately, decently, fairly, moderately, passably, proportionately, rather, reasonably, satisfactorily, so-so*, sufficiently, tolerably; CONCEPTS 546,558,771 —*Ant.* inadequately

enough [*n*] *plenty* abundance, adequacy, ampleness, ample supply, competence, plenitude, right amount, sufficiency, sufficient; CONCEPTS 646,767 —*Ant.* inadequacy, insufficiency

enquire [*v*] *ask about* analyze, check, examine, explore, go over, inquire, inspect, investigate, look into, probe, pry, query, question, scrutinize, search, seek, seek an answer, want to know; CONCEPTS 24,48

enquiry [*n*] *inquest* analysis, examination, exploration, inquiry, inquisition, inspection, interrogation, investigation, probe, query, questioning, research, study; CONCEPTS 24,48,290

enrage [*v*] *make very upset* aggravate, anger, ask for it*, exasperate, get under skin*, hack*, incense, incite, inflame, infuriate, ire, irritate, madden, make blood boil*, make see red*, needle, provoke, rile, steam up*, T-off*, umbrage, whip up*; CONCEPTS 7,14,19 —*Ant.* appease, calm, compose, pacify, placate, please, soothe

enraged [*adj*] *furious* aggravated, angered, angry, boiling*, exasperated, fuming, incensed, inflamed, infuriated, irate, livid, mad, pushed too far*, riled, upset; CONCEPT 403

enrapture [*v*] *captivate* allure, attract, beguile, bewitch, charm, delight, elate, enamor, enchant, enthrall, entrance, fascinate, gladden, gratify, please, ravish, rejoice, score, send, spellbind, transport; CONCEPTS 7,22 —*Ant.* disgust, displease, offend, repel

enrich [*v*] *improve, embellish* adorn, aggrandize, ameliorate, augment, beef up*, better, build, build up, cultivate, decorate, develop, endow, enhance, figure in, flesh out*, grace, hike up*, hop up*, jack up*, jazz up*, make rich, ornament, pad, parlay, pour it on*, pyramid*, refine, run up*, soup up*, spike*, step up, supplement, sweeten*, up*, upgrade; CONCEPTS 177,244 —Ant. decrease, deplete, impoverish, reduce, take

enroll [v1] *sign up for membership* accept, admit, become student, call up, employ, engage, enlist, enter, join, join up, matriculate, muster, obtain, recruit, register, serve, sign on, subscribe, take course, take on;CONCEPTS 114,129 —Ant. avoid, dodge, ignore, pass, reject

enroll [v2] *list, record* affix, bill, book, catalog, chronicle, engross, enlist, enter, file, fill out, index, inscribe, insert, inventorize, mark, matriculate, note, poll, register, schedule, slate; CONCEPTS 79,125 —Ant. cancel, dismiss, neglect

enrollment [n] *registration for membership* acceptance, accession, admission, conscription, engagement, enlistment, entrance, entry, induction, influx, listing, matriculation, rally, reception, record, recruitment, response, student body, students, subscription; CONCEPTS 288,388,417

en route [adj] *on the way to destination* advancing, along the way, bound, driving, entrained, en voyage*, flying, heading toward, in passage, in transit, making headway*, midway, on the road*, pressing on, progressing, traveling; CONCEPTS 577,586 —Ant. derailed, detained, off the path, sidetracked

ensconce [v] *hide; tuck away* bury, cache, conceal, cover, curl up, ditch, establish, fix, install, locate, nestle, place, plant, protect, screen, seat, secrete, set, settle, shelter, shield, situate, snuggle up, stash, station; CONCEPTS 188,201 —Ant. reveal, take out, uncover, unveil

ensemble [adv] *at the same time* all at once, altogether, as a body, as a group, as a whole, as one, at once, en masse, in concert; CONCEPT 577

ensemble [n1] *collection* aggregate, assemblage, band, cast, choir, chorus, company, composite, entirety, gathering, glee club, group, octet, orchestra, organization, outfit, quartet, quintet, set, sextet, sum, total, totality, trio, troupe, whole; CONCEPTS 294,432

ensemble [n2] *clothing outfit* coordinates, costume, garb*, get-up*, suit, togs*; CONCEPT 451

enshrine [v] *hold as sacred* apotheosize, bless, cherish, consecrate, dedicate, embalm, exalt, hallow, idolize, preserve, revere, sanctify, treasure; CONCEPTS 69,367 —Ant. defile, desecrate, disrespect

enshroud [v] *cover* cloak, conceal, hide, mask, pall, shroud; CONCEPTS 172,188

ensign [n] *flag* banderole, banner, colors, emblem, gonfalon, insignia, pennant, standard, streamer, symbol; CONCEPTS 284,473

enslave [v] *make someone a servant* bind, capture, chain, check, circumscribe, coerce, compel, confine, deprive, disenfranchise, disfranchise, dominate, enchain, enclose, enthrall, fetter, get hooks into*, hobble, hold, immune, imprison, incarcerate, indenture, jail, keep under thumb*, oppress, put in irons*, reduce, restrain, restrict, secure, shackle, shut

in, subdue, subject, subjugate, suppress, tether, tie, yoke; CONCEPTS 14,90,130,191 —Ant. allow, emancipate, free, let go, liberate

ensnare [v] *trap* bag*, bat eyes at*, capture, catch, cheat, come on, deceive, decoy, embroil, enmesh, entangle, entice, entrap, hook, inveigle, lure, mislead, net, rope in, snag, snare, snarl, suck in*, tangle, trick; CONCEPTS 59,90 —Ant. free, let go, liberate, release

ensue [v] *start to happen; come to pass* appear, arise, attend, be consequent on, befall, be subsequent to, come after, come next, come up, derive, develop, emanate, eventualize, eventuate, flow, follow, issue, occur, proceed, result, stem, succeed, supervene, turn out, turn up; CONCEPTS 119,242 —Ant. antecede, precede

ensuing [adj] *resultant* after, coming, coming up, consequent, consequential, following, later, next, next off, posterior, postliminary, subsequent, subsequential; CONCEPTS 548,820 —Ant. antecedent, preceding

ensure [v] *guarantee; make secure* arrange, assure, certify, cinch, clinch, confirm, effect, establish, guard, insure, lock on*, lock up*, make certain, make safe, make sure, nail down*, okay, protect, provide, put on ice*, safeguard, secure, set out, warrant; CONCEPT 71

entail [v] *require; result in* bring about, call for, cause, demand, encompass, entangle, evoke, give rise to, impose, involve, lead to, necessitate, occasion, require, tangle; CONCEPTS 242,646

entangle [v] *involve, mix up* bewilder, burden, catch, clog, come on, complicate, compromise, confuse, corner, dishevel, duke in, embarrass, embrangle, embroil, enchain, enmesh, ensnare, entrap, fetter, hamper, hook, impede, implicate, intertangle, intertwine, interweave, jumble, knot, lead on, mat, muddle, perplex, puzzle, ravel, rope in, set up, snag, snare, snarl, swindle, tangle, trammel, trap, twist, unsettle; CONCEPTS 59,90,112 —Ant. disentangle, exclude, explain, untangle, untwist

entanglement [n] *complication, predicament* affair, association, cobweb, complexity, confusion, difficulty, embarrassment, embroilment, enmeshment, ensnarement, entrapment, imbroglio, intricacy, intrigue, involvement, jumble, knot, liaison, mesh, mess, mix-up, muddle, snare, tangle, tie-up, toil, trap, web; CONCEPTS 666,674 —Ant. disentanglement, simplicity

entente [n] *agreement* accord, arrangement, deal, pact, settlement, treaty, understanding; CONCEPTS 271,331

enter [v1] *come, put into a place* access, arrive, barge in*, blow in*, break in, breeze in*, burst in, bust in*, butt in*, come in, crack, crawl, creep, crowd in*, drive in, drop in, fall into, gain entrée, get in, go in, horn in*, immigrate, infiltrate, ingress, insert, insinuate, introduce, intrude, invade, jump in, make an entrance, make way, move in, pass into, penetrate, pierce, pile in, pop in*, probe, rush in, set foot in, slip, sneak, work in, worm in*, wriggle; CONCEPT 159 —Ant. depart, exit, go, leave, withdraw

enter [v2] *embark on; take part in* become member, begin, commence, commit oneself, enlist, enroll, get oneself into*, inaugurate, join, join up, lead off, muster*, open, participate in, set about, set out on, set to, sign on, sign up, start, subscribe, take up, tee off*; CONCEPTS 114,234 —Ant. abstain, forget, refrain, stop

enter [v3] *record, list* admit, docket, inject, inscribe, insert, intercalate, interpolate, introduce, log, note, post, put in, register, set down, take down; CONCEPT 125 —Ant. delete, erase

enterprise [n1] *adventure, undertaking* action, activity, affair, attempt, baby*, bag*, ballgame*, biggie*, big idea*, bit*, business, campaign, cause, company, concern, crusade, deal, deed, do*, effort, endeavor, engagement, essay, establishment, firm, flier*, follow through*, game*, happening, hazard, house, move, operation, outfit, performance, pet project*, plan, plunge*, program, project, proposition, purpose, pursuit, risk, scheme, speculation, stake, striving, stunt, task, thing*, trade, try, venture, work; CONCEPTS 87,324,325,362 —Ant. idleness, inactivity, unemployment

enterprise [n2] *resourcefulness, energy* activity, adventurousness, alertness, ambition, audacity, boldness, courage, daring, dash, drive, eagerness, enthusiasm, force, foresight, get-up-and-go*, gumption, hustle, industry, initiative, inventiveness, pluck, push, readiness, resource, self-reliance, spirit, venturesomeness, vigor, zeal; CONCEPTS 411,657 —Ant. apathy, idleness, indolence, passiveness, passivity

enterprising [adj] *resourceful, energetic* active, advancing, adventurous, aggressive, alert,ambitious, aspiring, audacious, bold, busy, coming on strong*, craving, daring, dashing, diligent, driving, eager, enthusiastic, go-ahead*, go-go*, gumptious, hard ball*, hardworking, hungry, hustling, industrious, intrepid, itching, keen, lively, lusting, peppy, progressive, pushing, ready, self-starting, snappy, spanking, spark plug*, spirited, stirring, take-over, up-and-coming*, venturesome, vigorous, yearning, zealous, zippy*; CONCEPTS 326,404,542 —Ant. inactive, passive, unadventurous, unambitious, unenthused, unimaginative, unresourceful

entertain [v1] *amuse* absorb, beguile, captivate, charm, cheer, comfort, crack up*, delight, distract, divert, ecstasize, elate, engross, enliven, enthrall, gladden, grab, gratify, humor, indulge, inspire, inspirit, interest, knock dead*, make merry, occupy, pique, please, recreate, regale, relax, satisfy, slay, solace, stimulate, tickle; CONCEPTS 9,292 —Ant. bore, tire

entertain [v2] *accommodate visitors* admit, be host, board, chaperone, dine, do the honors*, feed, foster, give a party, harbor, have a do*, have a get-together*, have company, have guests, have visitors, house, invite, lodge, nourish, pick up the check*, pop for*, put up*, quarter, receive, recreate, regale, room, show hospitality, spring for*, throw a party*, treat, welcome, wine and dine*; CONCEPTS 377,384 —Ant. refuse, reject, turn away

entertain [v3] *think about seriously* cherish, cogitate on, conceive, consider, contemplate, deliberate, foster, harbor, heed, hold, imagine, keep in mind, maintain, muse over, ponder, recognize, support, think over; CONCEPT 17 —Ant. disregard, forget, reject

entertaining [adj] *amusing, pleasing* absorbing, affecting, be a ball*, captivating, charming,

cheerful, cheering, clever, compelling, delightful, diverting, droll, enchanting, engaging, engrossing, enjoyable, enthralling, enticing, entrancing, exciting, fascinating, fun, funny, gas*, gay, humorous, impressive, inspiring, interesting, lively, moving, piquant, pleasant, pleasurable, poignant, priceless, provocative, recreative, relaxing, restorative, riot, rousing, scream, side-splitting, stimulating, stirring, striking, thrilling, witty; CONCEPTS 529,537 —Ant. boring, dull, laborious, sad, tiring, unamusing, unfunny, unpleasant

entertainment [n] *amusement, pleasure* ball*, bash*, big time*, blast*, blow out*, celebration, cheer, clambake*, delight, dissipation, distraction, diversion, divertissement, enjoyment, feast, frolic, fun, fun and games*, gaiety, game, good time*, grins*, high time*, laughs*, leisure activity, lots of laughs*, merriment, merrymaking, party, pastime, picnic, play, recreation, regalement, relaxation, relief, revelry, satisfaction, shindig*, sport, spree, surprise, treat, wingding*; CONCEPTS 383,384,386,388 —Ant. chore, drudgery, labor, task, work

enthrall [v] *captivate* absorb, bewitch, charm, enchant, engage, enrapture, enslave, entrance, fascinate, grab, grip, hold spellbound, hook, hypnotize, intrigue, mesmerize, preoccupy, rivet, spellbind, subdue, subject, subjugate; CONCEPTS 7,19,22 —Ant. bore, dull, tire, turn off, weary

enthusiasm [n] *keen interest, excitement* activity, ardency, ardor, avidity, conviction, craze, dash, devotion, eagerness, earnestness, ecstasy, élan, emotion, energy, exhilaration, fad, fanaticism, feeling, fervor, fever, fieriness, fire, flame, flare, frenzy, fury, gaiety, glow, go*, heat, hilarity, hobby, impetuosity, intensity, interest, joy, joyfulness, keenness, life, mania, mirth, nerve, oomph*, orgasm, passion, pep, rapture, red heat*, relish, snap, spirit, transport, vehemence, verve, vim, vivacity, warmth, zeal, zealousness, zest; CONCEPTS 633,657 —Ant. aloofness, apathy, coldness, coolness, doubt, indifference, lethargy, pessimism, weariness

enthusiast [n] *person active in interest* addict, admirer, aficionado, believer, buff, bug*, bum*, devotee, eccentric, fan, fanatic, follower, freak, habitué, lover, maniac, monomaniac, nut*, optimist, participant, partisan, rooter, supporter, votary, worshiper, zealot; CONCEPT 423 —Ant. critic, detractor, pessimist

enthusiastic [adj] *interested, excited* agog, animated, anxious, ardent, athirst, attracted, avid, bugged*, concerned, crazy about*, devoted, dying to*, eager, earnest, ebullient, exhilarated, exuberant, fanatical, fascinated, fervent, fervid, forceful, gaga*, gone on*, gung ho*, hearty, intent, keen, keyed up*, lively, nutty*, obsessed, passionate, pleased, rabid, red-hot*, rhapsodic, spirited, tantalized, thrilled, titillated, unqualified, vehement, vigorous, wacky*, warm, wholehearted, willing, zealous; CONCEPTS 401,542 —Ant. apathetic, disinterested, doubting, indifferent, lethargic, pessimistic, unenthusiastic, unexcited, weary

entice [v] *allure; persuade* attract, bait, bat eyes at*, beguile, cajole, coax, decoy, draw, entrap, inveigle, lead on, lure, prevail on, seduce, tempt,

toll, turn on*, wheedle; CONCEPTS *7,19,22,68*
—*Ant.* disgust, dissuade, repel,
repulse, turn away, turn off

enticement [n] *allurement; persuasion* attraction, bait, blandishment, cajolery, coaxing, come hither*, come-on*, decoy, fascination, inducement, inveiglement, lure, mousetrap*, promise, seduction, snare, sweetener*, sweetening, temptation, trap; CONCEPTS *7,19,22,68*
—*Ant.* disgust, dissuasion, repulsion

entire [adj] *complete, whole* absolute, all, choate, consolidated, continuous, full, gross, intact, integral, integrated, outright, perfect, plenary, sound, thorough, total, unbroken, undamaged, undiminished, undivided, unified, unimpaired, uninjured, unmarked, unmarred, unmitigated, unreserved, unrestricted, untouched; CONCEPTS *482,531* —*Ant.* abridged, incomplete, limited, part

entirely [adv] *completely* absolutely, alone, altogether, exclusively, fully, in every respect, only, perfectly, plumb, quite, reservedly, solely, thoroughly, totally, undividedly, uniquely, utterly, well, wholly, without exception, without reservation; CONCEPTS *531,535* —*Ant.* incompletely, partially

entirety [n] *wholeness, whole* absoluteness, aggregate, all, allness, collectiveness, collectivity, completeness, complex, comprehensiveness, ensemble, entireness, entirety, everything, fullness, gross, intactness, integrality, integrity, omneity, omnitude, oneness, perfection, plenitude, sum, sum total, the works*, total, totality, undividedness, unity, universality, whole ball of wax*, whole bit*, whole enchilada*, whole nine yards*; CONCEPTS *635,837* —*Ant.* fraction, incompleteness, part, partiality, section

entitle [v1] *name, label* baptize, call, characterize, christen, denominate, designate, dub, nickname, style, subtitle, term, title; CONCEPT *62*

entitle [v2] *hold right to* accredit, allow, authorize, be in line for*, confer a right, empower, enable, enfranchise, fit for, have coming*, let, license, make eligible, permit, qualify for, rate, warrant; CONCEPTS *50,83,88,129*

entity [n1] *object that exists* article, being, body, creature, existence, individual, item, material, matter, organism, presence, quantity, single, singleton, something, stuff, subsistence, substance, thing; CONCEPT *433* —*Ant.* abstract, concept, idea

entity [n2] *nature of a being* actuality, essence, existence, integral, integrate, quiddity, quintessence, reality, subsistence, substance, sum, system, totality; CONCEPTS *411,644* —*Ant.* abstract

entomb [v] *bury* embalm, ensepulcher, enshrine, hold last rites for*, hold services for*, inhume, inter, inurn, lay to rest*, put six feet under*, sepulcher, sepulture, tomb; CONCEPT *367*

entourage [n] *followers* associates, attendants, companions, company, cortege, court, courtiers, escort, following, groupies*, hangers-on*, retainers, retinue, staff, suite, sycophants, toadies*, train; CONCEPTS *387,417* —*Ant.* leader

entrails [n] *internal organs* bowels, guts, innards, insides, internal parts, viscera, vitals; CONCEPT *393*

entrance [n1] *a way into a place* access, approach, archway, avenue, corridor, door,

doorway, entry, entryway, gate, gateway, hall, hallway, ingress, inlet, lobby, opening, passage, passageway, path, porch, port, portal, portico, staircase, threshold, vestibule, way; CONCEPT *440* —*Ant.* exit

entrance [n2] *coming into a place; introduction* access, accession, adit, admission, admittance, appearance, approach, arrival, baptism, beginning, commencement, debut, enlistment, enrollment, entrée, entry, immigration, import, importation, inception, incoming, ingoing, ingress, ingression, initiation, invasion, outset, passage, penetration, progress, start, trespass; CONCEPTS *119,159* —*Ant.* conclusion, departure, exit, leave

entrance [v] *captivate, hypnotize* anesthetize, attract, bewitch, charm, delight, enchant, enrapture, enthrall, fascinate, gladden, mesmerize, please, put in a trance, ravish, rejoice, spellbind, transport; CONCEPTS *7,14,22* —*Ant.* disgust, repel, repulse, turn off

entrant [n] *person entering competition, starting new activity* aspirant, beginner, candidate, competitor, contestant, convert, entry, incomer, initiate, neophyte, newcomer, new member, novice, participant, petitioner, player, probationer, rival, solicitor, tenderfoot*; CONCEPTS *366,423* —*Ant.* fan, spectator

entrap [v] *capture, involve* allure, bag*, beguile, benet, box in*, catch, decoy, embroil, enmesh, ensnare, entangle, entice, hook, implicate, inveigle, lay for*, lead on, lure, net, reel in*, rope in*, seduce, set up, snare, suck in*, tempt, trap, trick; CONCEPTS *59,90,112* —*Ant.* clear, disentangle, exclude, free, liberate, release

entreat [v] *plead with* appeal to, ask, beg, beseech, blandish, coax, conjure, crave, enjoin, exhort, implore, importune, invoke, pester, petition, plague, pray, press, request, supplicate, urge, wheedle; CONCEPTS *48,53* —*Ant.* answer, command, demand

entreaty [n] *plea* appeal, application, imploration, imprecation, petition, prayer, request, suit, supplication; CONCEPTS *318,662* —*Ant.* answer, command, demand

entrée [n] *admittance* access, adit, admission, connection, contact, debut, door, entrance, entry, importation, in, incoming, induction, ingress, introduction, open arms*, open door*, way; CONCEPTS *388,685* —*Ant.* blackballing, rejection

entrench [v1] *establish, make inroads* anchor, confirm, define, dig in, embed, ensconce, fence, fix, fortify, found, ground, hole up, implant, infix, ingrain, install, lodge, plant, protect, root, seat, set, settle, strengthen; CONCEPTS *518,710*

entrench [v2] *trespass* break in on, encroach, impinge, infringe, interfere, interlope, intervene, intrude, invade, make inroads*, stick nose into*; CONCEPT *192* —*Ant.* stay off

entrepreneur [n] *person who starts a business alone* administrator, backer, businessperson, contractor, executive, founder, impressario, industrialist, manager, organizer, producer, promoter, undertaker; CONCEPT *347*

entropy [n] *deterioration* breakup, collapse, decay, decline, degeneration, destruction, falling apart, worsening; CONCEPTS *230,698*

entrust |v| *give custody, authority to* allocate, allot, assign, authorize, bank, bend an ear*, charge, commend, commit, confer, confide, consign, count, delegate, deliver, depend, deposit with, hand over, impose, invest, leave with, reckon, relegate, rely, trust, turn over; CONCEPTS 50,88,108

entry |n1| *way in to a place* access, adit, approach, avenue, door, doorway, entrance, foyer, gate, hall, ingress, ingression, inlet, lobby, opening, passage, passageway, portal, threshold, vestibule; CONCEPT 440 —*Ant.* egress, exit

entry |n2| *introduction; permission to enter* access, adit, admission, admittance, appearance, coming in, entering, entrance, entrée, free passage*, ingress, initiation, introgression, way; CONCEPTS 388,685 —*Ant.* blackballing, conclusion, refusal, rejection

entry |n3| *person participating in competition; effort* attempt, candidate, competitor, contestant, entrant, participant, player, submission; CONCEPT 366 —*Ant.* fan, spectator

entry |n4| *listing in a record* account, item, jotting, memo, memorandum, minute, note, registration; CONCEPT 270

entwine |v| *twist around* braid, coil, corkscrew, curl, embrace, encircle, enmesh, entangle, interlace, interplait, intertwine, interweave, knit, lace, plait, spiral, surround, twine, weave, wind, wreathe; CONCEPTS 147,201,754 —*Ant.* unravel, untwist, unwind

enumerate |v| *list, count* add up, calculate, cite, compute, count noses*, detail, figure, identify, inventory, itemize, keep tabs*, mention, name, number, particularize, quote, recapitulate, recite, reckon, recount, rehearse, relate, run down, run off*, specialize, specify, spell out, sum, take account of, tally, tell, tick off*, total; CONCEPTS 57,125,764 —*Ant.* not count

enunciate |v| *speak clearly* affirm, announce, articulate, declare, deliver, develop, enounce, express, intone, lay down, modulate, outline, phonate, postulate, proclaim, promulgate, pronounce, propound, publish, say, show, sound, state, submit, utter, vocalize, voice; CONCEPTS 47,51 —*Ant.* mispronounce, muffle, mumble

envelop |v| *encase, hide* blanket, cage, cloak, conceal, contain, coop, corral, cover, drape, embrace, encircle, enclose, encompass, enfold, engulf, enshroud, enwrap, fence, gird, girdle, guard, hem, immure, invest, obscure, overlay, overspread, pen, protect, roll, sheathe, shield, shroud, shut in, superimpose, surround, swaddle, swathe, veil, wrap, wrap up; CONCEPTS 172,188 —*Ant.* free, let go, let loose, open, release, uncover, unwrap

envelope |n| *wrapper* bag, box, case, casing, cloak, coat, coating, container, cover, covering, enclosure, hide, jacket, pocket, pouch, receptacle, sheath, shell, skin, vesicle, wrapping; CONCEPT 494

enviable |adj| *desired, blessed* advantageous, covetable, desirable, excellent, favored, fortunate, good, lucky, privileged, superior, welcome; CONCEPT 574 —*Ant.* disadvantaged, undesirable, undesired, unenviable, unfavored, unlucky

envious |adj| *jealous, resentful* appetent, aspiring, begrudging, coveting, covetous, craving,

desiring, desirous, distrustful, fain, grasping, greedy, green-eyed*, green with envy*, grudging, hankering, invidious, jaundiced, longing for, malicious, spiteful, suspicious, umbrageous, watchful, wishful, yearning; CONCEPTS 401,403 —*Ant.* comfortable, confident, content, kind, pleased, unenvious

environment |n| *surroundings, atmosphere* ambiance, aura, backdrop, background, circumstances, climate, conditions, context, domain, element, encompassment, entourage, habitat, hood*, jungle*, locale, medium, milieu, neck of the woods*, neighborhood, purlieus, scene, scenery, setting, situation, status, stomping ground*, surroundings, terrain, territory, turf, zoo*; CONCEPTS 515,673,696

environment |n| *Earth's system of natural resources* atmosphere, biosphere, ecosphere, ecosystem, environs, Gaia; CONCEPTS 511,515

environmentalist |n| *conservationist* eagle freak*, ecologist, greenie*, naturalist, preservationist, tree-hugger*; CONCEPTS 515,673,696

environs |n| *neighborhood* bound, boundary, compass, confine, district, fringes*, limits, locality, outskirts, precinct, purlieus, suburb, surroundings, territory, turf, vicinity; CONCEPT 516

envisage/envision |v| *picture in one's mind* anticipate, behold, conceive, conceptualize, contemplate, externalize, fancy, feature, foresee, form mental picture of*, grasp, have a picture of*, image, imagine, look upon, materialize, objectify, predict, realize, regard, see, survey, think up, view, view in mind's eye*, vision, visualize; CONCEPTS 17,43

envoy |n| *deputy* agent, ambassador, attaché, bearer, carrier, chargé d'affaires, consul, courier, delegate, diplomat, emissary, intermediary, internuncio, legate, medium, messenger, minister, nuncio, plenipotentiary, representative, vicar; CONCEPTS 348,354

envy |n| *jealousy* backbiting, coveting, covetousness, enviousness, evil eye*, green-eyed monster*, grudge, grudging, grudgingness, hatred, heartburn, ill will, invidiousness, jaundiced eye*, lusting, malevolence, malice, maliciousness, malignity, opposition, prejudice, resentfulness, resentment, rivalry, spite; CONCEPT 410 —*Ant.* comfort, confidence, contentedness, good will, kindness, pleasure

envy |v| *be jealous of another* be envious, begrudge, covet, crave, desire, die over*, eat one's heart out*, grudge, hanker, have hard feelings*, hunger, long, lust, object to, resent, thirst, turn green*, want, yearn; CONCEPTS 10,20 —*Ant.* be confident, be content

eon |n| *an age* aeon, ages, time period, years; CONCEPT 807

ephemeral |adj| *momentary, passing* brief, episodic, evanescent, fleeting, flitting, fugacious, fugitive, impermanent, short, short-lived, temporary, transient, transitory, unenduring, volatile; CONCEPTS 798,801 —*Ant.* enduring, eternal, everlasting, interminable, lasting, long, permanent, perpetual

epic |n| *long story* heroic poem, legend, narrative, saga, tale; CONCEPT 282 —*Ant.* short story

epicure |n| *gourmet* bon vivant, connoisseur, Epicurean, gastronome, gastronomer, gastronomist, gourmand; CONCEPTS 348,423

epicurean |adj| *loving food and finer things* gluttonous, gourmandizing, gourmet, hedonistic, libertine, lush, luxurious, pleasure-seeking, self-indulgent, sensual, sensuous, sybaritic, voluptuous; CONCEPT 401

epicurean |n| *gourmet* bon vivant, connoisseur, critic, epicure, gastronome, gastronomer, glutton, gourmand, hedonist, pleasure seeker, sensualist, specialist, sybarite; CONCEPT 423

epidemic |adj| *widespread* catching, communicable, contagious, endemic, general, infectious, pandemic, prevailing, prevalent, rampant, rife, sweeping, wide-ranging; CONCEPTS 314,537 —*Ant.* limited

epidemic |n| *widespread disease* contagion, endemic, growth, outbreak, pest, pestilence, plague, rash, scourge, spread, upsurge, wave, what's going around*; CONCEPTS 306,316

epigram |n| *witticism* aphorism, bon mot, joke, motto, pithy saying, quip, quirk; CONCEPT 278

epilogue |n| *afterword* coda, concluding speech, conclusion, ending, finale, follow-up, peroration, postlude, postscript, sequel, summation, swan song*; CONCEPTS 264,270,278 —*Ant.* foreword, introduction, preface

episode |n| *adventure; scene* affair, business, chapter, circumstance, doings, event, experience, goings-on*, happening, incident, installment, interlude, matter, occasion, occurrence, part, passage, section, thing*, what's going down*; CONCEPTS 3,4

episodic |adj| *intermittent; composed of several tales* anecdotal, digressive, disconnected, discursive, disjointed, incidental, irregular, occasional, picaresque, rambling, roundabout, segmented, soap opera*, sporadic, wandering; CONCEPT 482 —*Ant.* connected, lasting, permanent, regular, unbroken

epistle |n| *letter* billet doux*, cannonball*, card, communication, dispatch, FYI*, get-well, invite, kite*, line*, love letter, memo, message, missive, note, poison pen*, postcard, scratch*, tab*, thank-you; CONCEPT 271

epitaph |n| *inscription on a gravestone* commemoration, elegy, epigraph, eulogy, hic jacet, legend, memorial, monument, remembrance, requiescat in pace, sentiment; CONCEPT 278

epithet |n| *nickname* appellation, description, designation, name, sobriquet, tag, title; CONCEPT 683

epitome |n1| *perfect example* apotheosis, archetype, embodiment, essence, exemplar, exemplification, illustration, last word*, personification, quintessence, representation, type, typification, ultimate; CONCEPT 686

epitome |n2| *abbreviation* abridgment, abstract, brief, compendium, condensation, conspectus, contraction, digest, précis, recapitulation, résumé, summary, summation, syllabus, synopsis; CONCEPT 283 —*Ant.* addition, enlargement, expansion, extension, increase, unabridgement

epitomize |v1| *typify* characterize, embody, exemplify, illustrate, mean, model, personify, represent, stand for, symbolize; CONCEPT 644

epitomize |v2| *encapsulate* abbreviate, abridge, capsulize, compress, condense, contract, cut, digest, reduce, shorten, summarize, sum up, synopsize; CONCEPTS 236,247

epoch |n| *period* age, date, era, span, time; CONCEPTS 807,822

equable |adj| *steady, calm* agreeable, composed, consistent, constant, easy-going, even, even-tempered, imperturbable, level-headed, methodical, orderly, placid, regular, serene, smooth, stabile, stable, systematic, temperate, tranquil, unchanging, unexcitable, unflappable, unfluctuating, uniform, unruffled, unvarying; CONCEPTS 401,542,544 —*Ant.* changeable, excitable, fluctuating, irregular, spasmodic, vacillating, variable, varying, wavering

equal |adj1| *alike* according, balanced, break even, commensurate, comparable, coordinate, correspondent, corresponding, double, duplicate, egalitarian, equivalent, evenly matched, fifty-fifty*, homologous, identic, identical, indistinguishable, invariable, level, look-alike, matched, matching, one and the same, parallel, proportionate, same, same difference*, spit and image*, stack up with*, tantamount, to the same degree, two peas in pod*, uniform, unvarying; CONCEPTS 487,566,573 —*Ant.* different, not alike, unequal, unlike, unmatched, variable, varying

equal |adj2| *fair, unbiased* dispassionate, egalitarian, equable, even-handed, impartial, just, nondiscriminatory, nonpartisan, objective, uncolored, unprejudiced, without distinction; CONCEPTS 401,542 —*Ant.* biased, disproportionate, unequal, unequitable, unfair, unjust

equal |n| *peer* alter ego, coequal, companion, compeer, competitor, complement, copy, counterpart, double, duplicate, equivalent, like, likeness, match, mate, parallel, rival, twin; CONCEPT 423 —*Ant.* inferior

equal |v| *make even, be even with* agree, amount to, approach, balance, be commensurate, be identical, be level, be tantamount, break even, come up to, compare, comprise, consist of, coordinate, correspond, emulate, equalize, equate, equipoise, equiponderate, keep pace with*, level, live up to*, match, measure up, meet, parallel, partake of, rank with, reach, rise to, rival, run abreast, square with, tally, tie, touch; CONCEPT 667 —*Ant.* disproportion, imbalance, unmatch, vary

equality |n| *similarity, balance; egalitarianism* adequation, civil rights, commensurateness, coordination, correspondence, equal opportunity, equatability, equilibrium, equipoise, equivalence, evenness, fairness, fair play*, fair practice, fair shake*, homology, identity, impartiality, isonomy, likeness, par, parallelism, parity, sameness, tolerance, uniformity; CONCEPTS 388,645,667 —*Ant.* difference, disproportion, dissimilarity, imbalance, inequality, unfairness

equalize |v| *make the same; balance* adjust, commeasure, communize, compare, coordinate, democratize, emulate, equal, equate, establish, even, even up, handicap, level, match, parallel, regularize, rival, smooth, socialize, square, standardize, trim; CONCEPTS 126,232 —*Ant.* disproportion, imbalance, unmatch, vary

equanimity |n| *levelheadedness* aplomb, assurance, ataraxia, ataraxy, calm, calmness, composure, confidence, cool, coolness, detachment, equability, imperturbability, patience, peace, phlegm, placidity, poise, presence of mind*, sangfroid, self-possession, serenity, steadiness, tranquillity; CONCEPTS 410,633 —*Ant.* agitation, alarm, anxiety, discompose, excitableness, upset, worry

equate [v] *balance; think of together* agree, assimilate, associate, average, be commensurate, compare, consider, correspond to, correspond with, equalize, even, hold, level, liken, make equal, match, offset, pair, paragon, parallel, regard, relate, represent, similize, square, tally, treat; CONCEPTS 37,39,667 —*Ant.* disagree, imbalance, unliken

equilibrium [n] *balance; evenness* calm, calmness, composure, cool, coolness, counterbalance, counterpoise, equanimity, equipoise, poise, polish, rest, serenity, stability, stasis, steadiness, steadying, symmetry; CONCEPTS 633,731 —*Ant.* imbalance, unevenness

equip [v] *make ready with supplies* accouter, adorn, appoint, arm, array, attire, deck, deck out*, decorate, dress, endow, feather nest*, fit out, fix up, furnish, gear, gear up*, heel*, implement, line nest*, man, outfit, prep*, prepare, provide, qualify, ready, rig, set up, stake, stock, supply, turn out; CONCEPTS 140,182

equipment [n] *supplies, gear for activity* accessories, accompaniments, accouterments, apparatus, appliances, appurtenances, articles, attachments, baggage, belongings, contraptions, contrivances, devices, equipage, facilities, fittings, fixtures, furnishings, furniture, gadgets, habiliments, impedimenta, kit and kaboodle*, machinery, material, materiel, miscellaneous, outfit, paraphernalia, provisioning, provisions, rig*, setup, shebang*, stock, store, stuff, tackle, things, tools, trappings, traps, utensils; CONCEPTS 364,446,496

equitable [adj] *impartial* candid, cricket, decent, disinterested, dispassionate, due, ethical, even-handed, even-steven*, fair, fair and square*, fair shake*, fair-to-middling*, honest, impersonal, just, level, moral, nondiscriminatory, nonpartisan, objective, proper, proportionate, reasonable, right, rightful, square, square deal*, stable, unbiased, uncolored, unprejudiced; CONCEPTS 542,545 —*Ant.* biased, disproportionate, partial, prejudiced, unequitable, unfair, unjust, unreasonable

equity [n1] *impartiality* disinterestedness, equitableness, even-handedness, fair-mindedness, fairness, fair play, honesty, integrity, justice, justness, nonpartisanship, piece, reasonableness, rectitude, righteousness, square deal*, uprightness; CONCEPTS 645,657 —*Ant.* bias, inequity, partiality, unfairness, unjustness

equity [n2] *money invested in possession* capital, investment, outlay; CONCEPTS 332,344

equivalence [n] *sameness, similarity* adequation, agreement, alikeness, compatibility, conformity, correlation, correspondence, equality, evenness, exchangeability, identity, interchangeability, interchangeableness, likeness, match, par, parallel, parity, synonym, synonymy; CONCEPTS 667,670 —*Ant.* difference, dissimilarity, inequality, unlikeness

equivalent [adj] *same, similar* agnate, akin, alike, analogous, carbon*, commensurate, comparable, convertible, copy, correlative,

correspondent, corresponding, ditto*, duplicate, equal, even, homologous, identical, indistinguishable, interchangeable, like, of a kind, parallel, proportionate, reciprocal, same difference*, substitute, synonymous, tantamount; CONCEPTS 487,566,573 —*Ant.* changeable, different, dissimilar, mismatched, unequal, unlike

equivalent [n] *equal, counterpart* carbon copy*, correspondent, dead ringer*, ditto, like, match, obverse, opposite, parallel, peer, reciprocal, same difference*, spitting image*, substitute, twin; CONCEPTS 667,670 —*Ant.* difference

equivocal [adj] *doubtful, uncertain* ambiguous, ambivalent, amphibological, borderline, clear as mud*, clouded*, disreputable, dubious, evasive, fishy*, fuzzy*, hazy*, indefinite, indeterminate, indistinct, misleading, muddled, muzzy*, oblique, obscure, open, problematic, puzzling, questionable, suspect, suspicious, tenebrous, unclear, undecided, unexplicit, unintelligible, vague, with mixed feelings*; CONCEPTS 529,535 —*Ant.* certain, clear, definite, determined, obvious, plain, sure, unequivocal, unquestionable

equivocate [v] *avoid an issue* beat around the bush*, beg the question*, blow hot and cold*, cavil, cloud the issue*, con, cop a plea*, cop out*, cover up*, dodge, double-talk, elude, escape, eschew, evade, falsify, fence, fib, flip-flop*, fudge*, give run around*, hedge, hem and haw*, jive*, lie, mince words, palter, parry, pass the buck*, prevaricate, pussyfoot, quibble, run around, shuck, shuffle, sidestep, sit on the fence*, stonewall*, tell white lie*, tergiversate, tergiverse, waffle*, weasel*; CONCEPTS 63,102 —*Ant.* face, meet, speak on

equivocation [n] *avoidance of an issue* ambiguity, amphibology, casuistry, coloring, con, cop out, cover, cover-up, deceit, deception, deceptiveness, delusion, dissimulation, distortion, double entendre, double meaning, double talk, doubtfulness, duplicity, equivocality, evasion, fallacy, fib, fibbing, hedging, lie, line*, lying, misrepresentation, prevarication, quibbling routine, run-around, shuffling, song*, song and dance*, sophistry, speciousness, spuriousness, stall, stonewall*, tergiversation, waffle*; CONCEPTS 63,278 —*Ant.* directness, facing, meeting

era [n] *time period in history* aeon, age, cycle, date, day, days, eon, epoch, generation, stage, term, time; CONCEPTS 807,816

eradicate [v] *destroy; remove* abate, abolish, annihilate, blot out*, demolish, deracinate, do away with, efface, eliminate, erase, expunge, exterminate, extinguish, extirpate, liquidate, mow down*, obliterate, off*, purge, raze, root out*, rub out*, scratch*, scrub, shoot down, squash, stamp out*, take out*, torpedo*, total, trash, unroot, uproot, wash out, waste, weed out*, wipe out*; CONCEPTS 211,252 —*Ant.* aid, assist, bear, create, establish, fix, help, institute, plant

erase [v] *remove; rub out* abolish, annul, black out, blank, blot, blue pencil*, cancel, cross out, cut, cut out, delete, disannul, dispatch, efface, eliminate, excise, expunge, extirpate, gut, kill, launder*, negate, nullify, obliterate, scratch out*, stamp out*, strike, strike out, take out, trim, wipe out*, withdraw, X-out*; CONCEPTS 211,215 —*Ant.* add, insert, put in

erect [*adj*] *straight up* arrect, cocked, elevated, erectile, firm, perpendicular, raised, rigid, standing, stiff, upright, upstanding, vertical; CONCEPTS 485,581,604 —*Ant.* prone, prostrate

erect [*v*] *build; establish* assemble, bring about, cobble up*, cock, compose, construct, create, effect, elevate, fabricate, fashion, fit together, forge, form, found, frame, fudge together*, heighten, hoist, initiate, institute, join, knock together*, lift, make, make up, manufacture, mount, organize, pitch, plant, prefabricate*, produce, put together, put up, raise, rear, run up, set up, shape, stand, stand up, throw together*, throw up, upraise, uprear; CONCEPTS 168,221 —*Ant.* raze, topple

ergo [*adv*] *for that reason* accordingly, consequently, hence, in consequence, so, then, therefore, thereupon, thus, thusly; CONCEPT 544

ergonomics [*n*] *human engineering* comfort design, functional design, human factors, user-friendly systems, workplace efficiency; CONCEPT 349

erode [*v*] *deteriorate; wear away* abrade, bite, consume, corrode, crumble, destroy, disintegrate, eat, gnaw, grind down, scour, spoil, waste, wear down; CONCEPTS 252,469 —*Ant.* build, construct, fix, rebuild

erosion [*n*] *deterioration; wearing away* abrasion, attrition, consumption, corrosion, decrease, desedimentation, despoliation, destruction, disintegration, eating away, grinding down, spoiling, washing away, wear, wearing down; CONCEPTS 252,257,698 —*Ant.* building, construction, rebuilding, strengthening

erotic [*adj*] *sexy* amative, amatory, amorous, aphrodisiac, bawdy, blue*, carnal, concupiscent, earthy, erogenous, fervid, filthy, fleshly, hot*, impassioned, kinky*, lascivious, lecherous, lewd, obscene, off-color*, prurient, purple*, raunchy, raw, romantic, rousing, salacious, seductive, sensual, sexual, spicy, steamy, stimulating, suggestive, titillating, venereal, voluptuous; CONCEPTS 372,545 —*Ant.* bland, cold, dull, frigid, unerotic

erotica [*n*] *pornography* adult literature, adult materials, dirt*, obscene art, obscene literature, porn, sexually explicit art, sexually explicit literature, smut, soft porn, X-rated materials; CONCEPT 280

eroticism [*n*] *sexual excitement* arousal, libido, lust, stimulation, titillation; CONCEPTS 20,709

err [*v*] *make a mistake; do wrong* be inaccurate, be incorrect, be in error, be mistaken, blow*, blunder, bollix*, boo-boo*, deviate, drop the ball*, fall, flub*, foul up*, go astray, goof*, go wrong, lapse, louse up*, make a mess of*, mess up*, misapprehend, misbehave, miscalculate, misjudge, muff*, offend, screw up*, sin, slip up*, snafu*, snarl up, stray, stumble, transgress, trespass, wander; CONCEPT 101 —*Ant.* correct

errand [*n*] *task* assignment, charge, commission, duty, job, message, mission; CONCEPT 362

errant [*adj*] *wrong; deviant* aberrant, deviating, devious, drifting, errable, erratic, erring, fallible, heretic, meandering, misbehaving, mischievous, miscreant, naughty, offending, off straight and narrow*, rambling, ranging, roaming, roving, shifting, sinning, stray, straying, unorthodox, unreliable, wandering, wayward; CONCEPTS 542, 545,581 —*Ant.* correct, righteous

erratic [*adj*] *unpredictable; wandering* aberrant, abnormal, anomalous, arbitrary, bizarre, capricious, changeable, desultory, devious, dicey, directionless, dubious, eccentric, fitful, flaky*, fluctuant, idiosyncratic, iffy*, incalculable, inconsistent, inconstant, irregular, meandering, mercurial, nomadic, oddball*, peculiar, planetary, rambling, roving, shifting, spasmodic, strange, stray, uncertain, undirected, unnatural, unreliable, unstable, unusual, vagarious, variable, volatile, wayward, weird, whimsical; CONCEPTS 535,542,581 —*Ant.* certain, consistent, definite, dependable, predictable, regular, reliable, steady, sure, unchanging

erroneous [*adj*] *wrong, incorrect* all off*, all wet*, amiss, askew, awry, defective, fallacious, false, faulty, flawed, inaccurate, inexact, invalid, misguided, mistaken, off, specious, spurious, unfounded, unsound, untrue, way off, wrong number*; CONCEPTS 267,570,582 —*Ant.* correct, right, true, valid

error [*n*] *mistake; wrong* absurdity, bad job*, blunder, boner*, boo-boo*, delinquency, delusion, deviation, erratum, failure, fall, fallacy, falsehood, falsity, fault, faux pas, flaw, glitch, goof*, howler*, inaccuracy, lapse, misapprehension, misbelief, miscalculation, misconception, miscue, misdeed, misjudgment, mismanagement, miss, misstep, misunderstanding, offense, omission, oversight, screamer*, screw-up*, sin, slight, slip, slipup, solecism, stumble, transgression, trespass, untruth, wrongdoing, X*; CONCEPTS 101,230,674,699 —*Ant.* accuracy, certainty, correction, right, truth, validity

ersatz [*adj*] *artificial* bogus, copied, counterfeit, fake, false, imitation, manufactured, phony, pretended, sham, simulated, spurious, substitute, synthetic; CONCEPT 582 —*Ant.* genuine, real

erstwhile [*adj*] *former* bygone, ex, late, old, once, one-time, past, preceding, previous, quondam, sometime; CONCEPT 820

erudite [*adj*] *well-educated, cultured* brainy, cultivated, educated, highbrow, in the know, into*, knowledgeable, learned, lettered, literate, savvy, scholarly, scholastic, studious, well-read, wise up*; CONCEPT 402 —*Ant.* common, ignorant, uncultured, uneducated

erudition [*n*] *higher education* bookishness, brains, cultivation, culture, enlightenment, intellectuality, knowledge, learnedness, learning, letters, literacy, lore, pedantry, refinement, savvy, scholarliness, scholarship, science, studiousness; CONCEPTS 287,409 —*Ant.* ignorance

erupt [*v*] *give forth, eject with force* appear, belch, blow up, boil, break out, burst, cast out, detonate, discharge, emit, eruct, explode, extravasate, flare up*, go off*, gush, hurl, jet, pour forth, rupture, spew, spit, spout, spurt, throw off*, touch off*, vent, vomit; CONCEPTS 179,222

eruption [*n*] *ejection* access, blast, blow-up, breakout, burst, discharge, explosion, flare-up, flow, gust, outbreak, outburst, sally, venting, vomiting; CONCEPTS 179,467

escalate [*v*] *increase, be increased* amplify, ascend, broaden, climb, enlarge, expand, extend, grow, heighten, intensify, magnify, make worse, mount, raise, rise, scale, step up, widen; CONCEPTS 236,245 —*Ant.* decrease, diminish, lessen, lower, weaken

escapade [n] *adventure, usually lighthearted* antic, caper, fling, folly, frolic, gag, high jinks, lark, mischief, monkeyshines*, prank, rib*, roguery, rollick, romp, scrape, shenanigans*, spree, stunt, trick, vagary; CONCEPTS 384,386

escape [n] *breaking away; getaway* abdication, avoidance, AWOL*, beat, bolt, break, breakout, bypassing, circumvention, decampment, deliverance, departure, desertion, disappearance, dodging, ducking, elopement, elusion, elusiveness, eschewal, evasion, evasiveness, extrication, fadeout, flight, freedom, hegira, lam, leave, liberation, out, outbreak, powder, release, rescue, retreat, runaround, shunning, sidestepping, slip, spring, withdrawal; CONCEPT 102 —*Ant.* capture, maintenance, stay

escape [v] *break away from* abscond, avoid, bail out*, bolt, burst out, circumvent, cut and run*, cut loose*, decamp, depart, desert, disappear, dodge, double, duck, duck out*, elope, elude, emerge, evade, flee, fly, fly the coop*, get away with*, get off*, go scot-free*, leave, make getaway*, make off*, make oneself scarce*, pass, play hooky*, run, run away, run off*, run out on*, shun, skip, slip, slip away, steal away, take a powder*, take flight, take on the lam*, vanish, work out of, wriggle out*; CONCEPT 102 —*Ant.* capture, remain, stay

escapee [n] *fugitive* defector, deserter, dodger, escaped prisoner, hunted person, jail-breaker, refugee, runaway; CONCEPT 412

eschew [v] *have nothing to do with* abandon, abjure, abstain, avoid, double, duck, elude, evade, forgo, forswear, give up, have no truck with*, let well enough alone*, not touch, refrain, renounce, sacrifice, shun, shy, shy away from, steer clear of*, swear off*; CONCEPTS 30,102 —*Ant.* embrace, like, love

escort [n] *protection; accompaniment* alarm clock*, attendant, beau, bird dog*, bodyguard, cavalier, chaperon, companion, company, consort, convoy, conveyor, cortege, date, entourage, fellow, friend, gallant, guard, guide, partner, protector, retinue, safeguard, squire, train, warden*; CONCEPTS 419,423

escort [v] *act as a companion, guard* accompany, attend, bear, bring, carry, chaperon, company, conduct, consort with, convoy, date, direct, drag, go with, guide, lead, partner, pilot, protect, route, see, shepherd, show, squire, steer, take out, usher; CONCEPTS 114,384,714 —*Ant.* abandon, desert, drop, leave, lose, maroon, neglect

escrow [n] *collateral* bond, deed, guarantee, insurance, pledge, security; CONCEPTS 71,271,685

esoteric [adj] *mysterious, obscure* abstruse, acroamatic, arcane, cabalistic, cryptic, deep, Delphic, heavy, hermetic, hidden, inner, inscrutable, mystic, mystical, occult, Orphic, private, profound, recondite, secret, Sibylline; CONCEPTS 529,576,582 —*Ant.* common, familiar, known, obvious, public, unmysterious

especial [adj] *exceptional, particular* chief, distinguished, dominant, exclusive, express, extraordinary, individual, marked, notable, noteworthy, outstanding, paramount, peculiar, personal, predominant, preeminent, preponderant, principal, private, set, signal, singular, special, specific, supreme, surpassing, uncommon, unique, unusual; CONCEPTS 535,564,574 —*Ant.* common, general, normal, ordinary, unexceptional, unspecific, usual

especially [adv] *exceptionally, particularly* abnormally, above all, before all els... chiefly, conspicuously, curiously, eminently, exclusively, expressly, extraordinarily, ... particular in specie, mainly, markedly, notably, ... outstandingly, peculiarly, preeminently, primarily, principally, remarkably, ... singularly, specially, specifically, ... strikingly, supremely, unaccountably, uncommonly, uncustomarily, uniquely, ... wonderfully; CONCEPTS 535,564, ... —*Ant.* commonly, generally, normally, ... unexceptionally, usually

espionage [n] *spying* intelligence, ... nonsance, secret service, shadowing, ... undercover operations, undercover ... underground activities; CONCEPTS ... 412

esplanade [n] *promenade* avenue, ... dwalk, path, walk, walkway; CONCEPTS 6, ...

espouse [v1] *stand up for; support* ...pt, adopt, advocate, approve, back, ch... ...ion, defend, embrace, get into*, go in fo... ...main-tain, stand behind*, take on, take up, ... CONCEPT 10 —*Ant.* forsake, reject

espouse [v2] *marry* betroth, catch, take as spouse, unite, wed; CONCEPT 297 —*Ant.* divorce

esprit de corps [n] *group spirit* camaraderie, common bond, cooperation, group loyalty, morale, solidarity, team spirit; CONCEPT 410

essay [n1] *written discourse* article, composition, discussion, disquisition, dissertation, explication, exposition, manuscript, paper, piece, study, theme, thesis, tract, treatise; CONCEPT 271

essay [n2] *try, attempt* aim, bid, dry run*, effort, endeavor, exertion, experiment, hassle, labor, one's all*, one's level best*, shot*, striving, struggle, test, toil, travail, trial, try on*, tryout, undertaking, venture, whack*, work; CONCEPT 87 —*Ant.* idleness, pass

essay [v] *try, attempt* aim, assay, endeavor, have a crack*, have a go*, have a shot*, have at it*, labor, make a run at*, offer, put to the test*, seek, strive, struggle, take a stab at*, take a whack at*, take on, test, toil, travail, try out, undertake, venture, work; CONCEPT 87 —*Ant.* be idle, forget, neglect, pass

essence [n1] *heart, significance* aspect, attribute, backbone, base, basis, be-all and end-all*, being, bottom, bottom line*, burden, caliber, character, chief constituent, constitution, core, crux, element, entity, essentia, essentiality, fiber, form, fundamentals, germ, grain, kernel, life, lifeblood, main idea, marrow, meaning, meat*, name of game*, nature, nitty-gritty*, nub, nucleus, pith, point, principle, property, quality, quiddity, quintessence, reality, root, soul, spirit, structure, stuff, substance, timber, vein, virtuality; CONCEPTS 411,661,668,688

essence [n2] *distillate, concentrate* balm, cologne, drug, effusion, elixir, extract, fragrance, juice, liquor, perfume, potion, scent, spirits, tincture; CONCEPTS 260,467

essential [adj1] *important, vital* capital, cardinal, chief, constitutive, crucial, foremost, fundamental, imperative, indispensable, leading, main, necessary, necessitous, needed, needful, prerequisite, principal, required, requisite, right-hand, wanted; CONCEPT 567 —*Ant.* accessory, auxiliary, inessential, minor, nonessential, secondary, subsidiary, unimportant

essential [adj2] *basic, fundamental* absolute, basal, cardinal, cold, complete, congenital, connate, constitutional, deep-seated, elemental, elementary, ideal, inborn, inbred, inherent, innate, intrinsic, key, main, material, meat and potatoes*, name of the game*, nitty-gritty*, nub, perfect, primary, prime, primitive, principal, quintessential, substratal, underlying; CONCEPTS 546,549 —*Ant.* atypical, minor, secondary

essential [n] *necessity, basic* ABCs*, bottom line*, brass tacks*, condition, element, essence, fire and ice*, fundamental, groceries*, guts*, heart, meat and potatoes*, must, name of the game*, nitty-gritty*, nuts and bolts*, part and parcel*, precondition, prerequisite, principle, quintessence, requirement, requisite, rudiment, sine qua non, stuff, substance, vital part, where one's at*; CONCEPTS 646,661,826 —*Ant.* accessory, auxiliary, nonessential, subsidiary, throwaway, trivia

establish [v1] *set up, organize* authorize, base, build, constitute, create, decree, domiciliate, enact, endow, ensconce, entrench, erect, fix, form, found, ground, implant, inaugurate, inculcate, install, institute, land, lay foundation, live, lodge, moor, originate, place, plant, practice, provide, put, ring in, rivet, root, secure, set down, settle, stabilize, start, start ball rolling*, station, stick; CONCEPTS 168,173,221 —*Ant.* destroy, disestablish, invalidate, ruin, unsettle

establish [v2] *authenticate; demonstrate* ascertain, authorize, base, certify, circumstantiate, confirm, constitute, corroborate, decree, determine, discover, enact, find out, formulate, learn, legislate, make, make out, predicate, prescribe, prove, ratify, rest, show, stay, substantiate, validate, verify; CONCEPTS 49,50,88,97 —*Ant.* confuse, disprove, invalidate

establishment [n1] *organization; creation* enactment, endowment, formation, formulation, foundation, founding, inauguration, installation, institution, setting up; CONCEPTS 173,221

establishment [n2] *business, institution* abode, building, company, concern, corporation, enterprise, factory, firm, foundation, house, institute, office, organization, outfit, plant, quarters, residence, setup, structure, system, workplace; CONCEPTS 323,325,449

establishment [n3] *ruling class; bureaucracy* authority, city hall*, conservatives, diehards*, established order, Old Guard*, powers that be*, them, the system*; CONCEPTS 347,354 —*Ant.* proletariat

estate [n1] *extensive manor and its property* acreage, area, country home, country place, demesne, domain, dominion, farm, finca, freehold, grounds, holdings, lands, parcel, plantation, quinta, ranch, residence, rural seat, territory, villa; CONCEPT 516

estate [n2] *person's possessions, property, wealth* assets, belongings, bequest, capital, chattels, devise, earthly possessions, effects, endowment, fortune, goods, heritage, inheritance, legacy, patrimony, substance; CONCEPTS 340,710

estate [n3] *class, rank* bracket, caste, category, classification, condition, echelon, footing, form, grade, level, lot, order, period, place, position, quality, repair, shape, situation, sphere, standing, state, station, status, stratum; CONCEPTS 378,388

esteem [v1] *think highly of* admire, appreciate, apprise, be fond of, cherish, consider, hold dear, honor, idolize, like, look up to*, love, prize, regard, regard highly, respect, revere, reverence, think the world of*, treasure, value, venerate, worship; CONCEPT 32 —*Ant.* abuse, dislike, disregard, disrespect, hate, insult, mock, ridicule

esteem [v2] *consider, believe* account, calculate, deem, estimate, hold, judge, rate, reckon, regard, think, view; CONCEPT 12 —*Ant.* deride, disbelieve, disregard, disrespect

estimable [adj] *honorable, worthy* admirable, admired, appreciable, august, big name*, big time*, commendable, decent, deserving, esteemed, excellent, good, high-powered, honored, in limelight*, laudable, major league*, meritorious, meritable, name, noble, palmary, praisable, praiseworthy, reputable, reputed, respectable, respected, sterling, valuable, valued, venerable, well-thought-of*; CONCEPTS 567,572 —*Ant.* bad, dishonorable, inestimable, insignificant, poor, unworthy

estimate [n] *approximate calculation; educated guess* appraisal, appraisement, assay, assessment, ballpark figure*, belief, conclusion, conjecture, estimation, evaluation, gauging, guess, guesstimate*, impression, judgment, measure, measurement, mensuration, opinion, point of view, projection, rating, reckoning, sizing up*, stock, surmise, survey, thought, valuation; CONCEPTS 28,37,689,784

estimate [v] *guess, try to value* account, appraise, assay, assess, believe, budget, calculate roughly, cast, cipher, class, classify, compute, conjecture, consider, count, decide, deduce, determine, enumerate, evaluate, examine, expect, figure, form opinion, gauge, guess, guesstimate*, judge, look into, look upon, number, outline, plan, predict, prophesy, rank, rate, reason, reckon, regard, run over*, scheme, set a figure*, size up*, sum, suppose, surmise, suspect, tax, think, think through*; CONCEPTS 28,37,764

estimation [n] *belief, guess* admiration, appraisal, appreciation, arithmetic, assessment, calculating, ciphering, computation, consideration, considered opinion, credit, esteem, estimate, estimating, evaluation, favor, figuring, impression, judgment, opinion, predicting, reckoning, regard, respect, stock, valuation, veneration, view; CONCEPTS 28,689 —*Ant.* disbelief

estrange [v] *destroy the affections of* alien, alienate, antagonize, break up, disaffect, disunify, disunite, divert, divide, divorce, drive apart, leave, make hostile, part, put on the outs*, separate, set at odds*, sever, split, sunder, turn off*, wean, withdraw, withhold; CONCEPTS 7,19,297,384 —*Ant.* engage, marry, unite

estrangement [n] *destruction of affections* alienation, antagonization, breach, break-up, disaffection, disassociation, disunity, division, divorce, hostility, leave, leaving, parting, removal, schism, separation, split, withdrawal, withholding; CONCEPTS 297,388 —*Ant.* connection, marriage, union

estuary [n] *mouth* arm, creek, firth, fjord, inlet, tidewater, waterway; CONCEPTS 509,514

et cetera [adj] *and so forth* along with others, and all, and on and on, and others, and so on, and the like, and the rest, blah blah blah*, et al., whatever, whatnot; CONCEPTS 267,577

etch [v] *carve* compose, corrode, cut, define, delineate, depict, describe, eat into, engrave, erode, execute, furrow, grave, impress, imprint, incise, ingrain, inscribe, outline, picture, portray, reduce, represent, set forth, stamp; CONCEPTS 174,176

etching [n] *art created by carving* engraving, impression, imprint, inscription, mezzotint, photoengraving, photogravure, print, reproduction, rotogravure, transferring; CONCEPT 259

eternal [adj] *without pause; endless* abiding, ageless, always, amaranthine, boundless, ceaseless, constant, continual, continued, continuous, dateless, deathless, enduring, everlasting, forever, illimitable, immemorial, immortal, immutable, imperishable, incessant, indefinite, indestructible, infinite, interminable, lasting, never-ending, perdurable, perennial, permanent, perpetual, persistent, relentless, termless, timeless, unbroken, unceasing, undying, unending, unfading, uninterrupted, unremitting, without end; CONCEPTS 482,798 —*Ant.* brief, changeable, changing, ending, ephemeral, stopping, temporary, terminable, transient

eternally [adv] *endlessly* always, continually, ever, evermore, forever, forevermore, for ever so long*, for keeps, in perpetuum, perpetually, regularly, till cows come home*; CONCEPT 798 —*Ant.* briefly, changeably, temporarily, transiently

eternity [n] *forever* aeon, afterlife, age, ages, blue moon*, dog's age*, endlessness, endless time, everlastingness, forever and a day*, future, immortality, imperishability, infiniteness, infinitude, infinity, kingdom come*; other world*, perpetuity, timelessness, time without end, wild blue yonder*, world without end*; CONCEPTS 370,804,818

ethereal [adj] *delicate, heavenly* aerial, airy, celestial, dainty, divine, empyreal, empyrean, exquisite, fairy, filmy, fine, gaseous, ghostly, gossamer, impalpable, insubstantial, intangible, light, rarefied, refined, spiritual, sublime, subtle, supernal, tenuous, unearthly, unsubstantial, unworldly, vaporous, vapory; CONCEPTS 491, 549,582,606 —*Ant.* earthly, indelicate, worldly

ethical [adj] *moral, right* Christian, clean, conscientious, correct, decent, elevated, equitable, fair, fitting, good, high-principled, honest, honorable, humane, just, kosher*, moralistic, noble, principled, proper, respectable, right, right-minded, square, straight, true blue*, upright, upstanding, virtuous; CONCEPT 545 —*Ant.* corrupt, dishonest, immoral, improper, unethical, unjust, unrighteous

ethics/ethic [n] *moral philosophy, values* belief, conduct, conscience, convention, conventionalities, criteria, decency, ethos, goodness, honesty, honor, ideal, imperative, integrity, moral code, morality, mores, natural law, nature, practice, principles, right and wrong, rules of conduct, standard, standards, the Golden Rule*; CONCEPTS 645,688,689 —*Ant.* corruption, immorality

ethnic [adj] *racial, cultural* indigenous, national, native, traditional, tribal; CONCEPT 549

etiquette [n] *manners, politeness* amenities, civility, code, convention, courtesy, customs, decency, decorum, deportment, dignity, form, formalities, good behavior*, mores, politesse, proper behavior, propriety, protocol, p's and q's*, rules, seemliness, social graces, suavities, usage; CONCEPT 633 —*Ant.* bad manners

etymology [n] *word history* derivation, development, etymon, origin, phrase history, phrase origin, root, source; CONCEPT 275

eulogize [v] *praise, glorify* acclaim, applaud, bless, celebrate, commend, compliment, cry up, exalt, extol, flatter, give a bouquet*, give a posy*, hymn, idolize, laud, magnify, panegyrize, pay tribute to, sing praises; CONCEPT 69 —*Ant.* calumniate, condemn, criticize

eulogy [n] *praise, acclamation* acclaim, accolade, adulation, applause, citation, commendation, compliment, encomium, exaltation, glorification, laudation, paean, panegyric, plaudit, salutation, tribute; CONCEPTS 69,278 —*Ant.* calumny, condemnation, criticism

euphemism [n] *nice way of saying something* circumlocution, delicacy, floridness, grandiloquence, inflation, pomposity, pretense, purism; CONCEPTS 275,278

euphonious [adj] *pleasing to the ear* agreeable, clear, dulcet, harmonious, mellifluous, melodious, musical, rhythmic, smooth, sweet-sounding, tuneful, well-pitched; CONCEPT 563

euphoria [n] *extreme happiness* bliss, dreamland, ecstasy, elation, exaltation, exhilaration, exultation, frenzy, glee, health, high spirits, intoxication, joy, joyousness, jubilation, madness, rapture, relaxation, transport; CONCEPT 410 —*Ant.* depression, despair, misery, sorrow, unhappiness, woe

euthanasia [n] *mercy killing* assisted suicide, putting out of misery*; CONCEPT 252

evacuate [v] *clear an area; empty* abandon, bail out*, cut out, decamp, depart, desert, discharge, displace, eject, expel, forsake, hightail, leave, move out, pack up, pull out, quit, relinquish, remove, run for the hills*, skidaddle*, vacate, withdraw; CONCEPTS 179, 195 —*Ant.* come in, enter, fill, load, occupy

evade [v] *get away from* avoid, baffle, balk, beat around bush*, beg the question*, bypass, cavil, circumvent, conceal, confuse, cop out, deceive, decline, dodge, double, duck, elude, equivocate, escape, eschew, fence, fend off*, flee, fly, fudge*, get around, give the runaround*, hedge, hide, keep distance*, lay low*, lead on a merry chase*, lie, parry, pass up, pretend, prevaricate, pussyfoot, put off, shift, shirk, shuck, shuffle, shun, shy, sidestep, slip out, sneak away*, steer clear of*,

es
ev

tergiversate, trick, waffle*, weasel*; CONCEPTS
30,102 —Ant. face, meet, take on

evaluate [v] *judge* appraise, assay, assess,
calculate, check, check out, class, classify,
criticize, decide, estimate, figure out, future,
gauge, grade, guesstimate*, look over, peg*,
price out, rank, rate, read, reckon, set at, size,
size up*, survey, take account of, take measure,
valuate, value, weigh; CONCEPTS 18,24,103

evaluation [n] *judgment* appraisal, appraisement, assessment, calculation, decision,
estimate, estimation, guesstimation*, interpretation, opinion, rating, stock, take, valuation;
CONCEPTS 24,103,689

evanescent [adj] *transient* brief, disappearing,
fading, fleeting, momentary, passing, short-
lived, temporary, tenuous, vanishing; CONCEPTS
551,798

evangelism [n] *preaching* ministration, sermonizing, spreading the word, teaching; CONCEPT
361

evangelist [n] *preacher* circuit rider, minister,
missionary, pastor, religious teacher, revivalist,
televangelist, television evangelist, television
preacher, TV evangelist; CONCEPT 361

evaporate [v] *dry up, dissolve* clear, concentrate, dehumidify, dehydrate, dematerialize,
desiccate, disappear, dispel, disperse, dissipate,
evanesce, evanish, fade, fade away, melt, parch,
pass, vanish, vaporize, weaken; CONCEPTS 469,
698 —Ant. dampen, soak, wet

evaporation [n] *drying up; dissolution* dehydration, dematerialization, desiccation, disappearance, dispelling, dispersal, dissipation,
escape, evanescence, fading, melting, vanishing, vaporescence, vaporization; CONCEPTS
469,607,698 —Ant. dampening, soaking,
wetting

evasion [n] *escape, avoidance* artifice, circumvention, cop-out*, cunning, ditch*, dodge*,
dodging, elusion, equivocating, equivocation,
eschewal, evading, evasiveness, excuse, fancy
footwork*, fudging*, jive, lie, obliqueness, pretext, prevarication, quibble, routine, run-around,
ruse, shift, shirking, shuffling, shunning, slip*,
sophism, sophistry, stall, stonewall*, subterfuge,
trick, trickery; CONCEPTS 59,63,102 —Ant.
directness, facing, meeting

evasive [adj] *deceitful, tricky* ambiguous,
cagey, casuistic, casuistical, cunning, deceptive,
devious, dissembling, elusive, elusory, equivocating, false, fugitive, greasy, indirect, intangible, lying, misleading, oblique, prevaricating,
shifty, shuffling, slippery, sly, sophistical,
stonewalling*, unclear, vague; CONCEPTS
267,401,542 —Ant. direct, forthright, honest,
ready, straight, straightforward

even [adj1] *flat, uniform* alike, balanced, consistent, constant, continual, continuous, direct,
equal, flush, homogenous, horizontal, level,
matching, metrical, parallel, planate, plane,
plumb, proportional, regular, right, same,
smooth, square, stabile, stable, steady, straight,
surfaced, true, unbroken, unchanging, undeviating, unfluctuating, uninterrupted, unvaried,
unvarying, unwavering, unwrinkled; CONCEPTS
480,490 —Ant. broken, different, disparate,
irregular, rough, uneven

even [adj2] *calm, undisturbed* composed,

cool, equable, equanimous, even-tempered,
imperturbable, peaceful, placid, serene,
stable, steady, tranquil, unexcitable, unruffled,
well-balanced; CONCEPT 401 —Ant. agitated,
irregular, troubled

even [adj3] *commensurate; having no advantage* balanced, coequal, comparable, coterminous, drawn, equal, equalized, equivalent,
even-steven*, exact, fifty-fifty*, horse to
horse*, identical, level, matching, neck and
neck*, on a par*, parallel, proportional,
proportionate, same, similar, smack in the
middle*, square, tied, uniform; CONCEPT 566
—Ant. irregular, unequal, uneven

even [adj4] *fair, impartial* balanced, disinterested, dispassionate, equal, equitable, fair and
square*, honest, just, matching, nonpartisan,
square, straightforward, unbiased, unprejudiced;
CONCEPTS 267,542 —Ant. biased, partial, unfair

even [adv] *still, yet* all the more, despite,
disregarding, indeed, in spite of, much,
notwithstanding, so much as; CONCEPT 544

even [v] *balance, make smooth* align, equal,
equalize, flatten, flush, grade, lay, level, match,
pancake*, plane, regularize, roll, square, stabilize, steady, symmetrize, uniform; CONCEPTS
231,757 —Ant. break, furrow, lump, roughen

even-handed [adj] *fair* aboveboard, balanced,
disinterested, equitable, honest, honorable,
impartial, just, neutral, nonpartisan, objective,
on the level*, on the up-and-up*, reasonable,
square, straight, unbiased, unprejudiced, upright, virtuous; CONCEPT 542

evening [n] *latter part of a day* black, close,
dark, decline, dim, dusk, duskiness, early
black*, eve, even, eventide, late afternoon,
nightfall, sundown, sunset, twilight; CONCEPTS
801,806,810 —Ant. morning

event [n1] *occurrence, happening* accident, act,
action, advent, adventure, affair, appearance,
business, calamity, case, catastrophe, celebration, ceremony, chance, circumstance, coincidence, conjuncture, crisis, deed, development,
emergency, episode, experience, exploit, fact,
function, holiday, incident, juncture, marvel,
matter, milestone, miracle, misfortune, mishap,
mistake, occasion, occurrence, pass, phase,
phenomenon, predicament, proceeding, shift,
situation, story, thing*, tide, transaction,
triumph, turn, wonder; CONCEPT 2

event [n2] *effect, result* aftereffect, aftermath,
case, causatum, chance, conclusion, consequence, end, end result, eventuality, fortuity,
hap, happenstance, issue, offshoot, outcome,
outgrowth, product, resultant, sequel, sequent,
termination, upshot; CONCEPT 230 —Ant.
cause, source

event [n3] *performance, competition* bout,
contest, game, match, meet, tournament;
CONCEPTS 263,363

even-tempered [adj] *easygoing* calm,
collected, complacent, composed, cool,
level-headed, patient, relaxed, stable, steady,
unexcitable, unruffled; CONCEPTS 401,404

eventful [adj] *significant, busy* active, consequential, critical, crucial, decisive, exciting,
fateful, full, historic, important, lively, memorable, momentous, notable, noteworthy, outstanding, remarkable, signal; CONCEPT 548

—*Ant.* dull, insignificant, normal, ordinary, trivial, uneventful, unnoteworthy, usual

eventual [*adj*] *future, concluding* closing, conditional, consequent, contingent, dependent, down the pike*, down the road*, ending, endmost, ensuing, final, hindmost, indirect, inevitable, in the cards*, last, later, latter, overall, possible, prospective, resulting, secondary, succeeding, terminal, ulterior, ultimate, vicarious; CONCEPTS 552,820 —*Ant.* past

eventuality [*n*] *something that probably will happen* aftereffect, aftermath, any case, case, chance, consequence, contingency, effect, event, go-down*, goings-on*, happening, issue, likelihood, outcome, possibility, probability, result, sequel, toss-up, upshot*; CONCEPTS 230,650 —*Ant.* improbability, unlikelihood

eventually [*adv*] *in the course of time* after all, at last, at the end of the day*, finally, hereafter, in future, in the end, in the long run*, one day, someday, sometime, sooner or later*, ultimately, when all is said and done*, yet; CONCEPTS 552,820

eventuate [*v*] *be a consequence* be consequent, befall, come about, come to pass, end, ensue, eventualize, follow, happen, issue, occur, result, stop, take place, terminate; CONCEPTS 2,242 —*Ant.* cause

ever [*adv*] *always, at any time* anytime, at all, at all times, at any point, by any chance*, consistently, constantly, continually, endlessly, eternally, everlastingly, evermore, forever, for keeps, in any case*, incessantly, in perpetuum, invariably, on any occasion*, perpetually, regularly, relentlessly, till cows come home*, to the end of time*, unceasingly, unendingly, usually; CONCEPTS 798,799

everlasting [*adj*] *infinite, never-ending* abiding, amaranthine, boundless, ceaseless, constant, continual, continuous, deathless, endless, eternal, immortal, imperishable, incessant, indestructible, interminable, lasting, limitless, perdurable, permanent, perpetual, termless, timeless, unceasing, undying, unending, uninterrupted, unremitting; CONCEPT 798 —*Ant.* ceasing, concluding, ending, temporary, terminating, transient

every [*adj*] *each, all* each one, whole, without exception; CONCEPT 531 —*Ant.* none

everybody/everyone [*n*] *all involved, all human beings; the whole world* all, all and sundry*, anybody, each one, each person, every person, generality, masses, people, populace, the public, the whole, young and old*; CONCEPT 417 —*Ant.* nobody/noone

everyday [*adj*] *common* accustomed, average, commonplace, conventional, customary, daily, dime a dozen*, dull, familiar, frequent, garden variety*, habitual, informal, lowly, mainstream, middle-of-the-road*, mundane, normal, ordinary, per diem, plain, prosaic, quotidian, routine, run-of-the-mill*, stock, unexceptional, unimaginative, unremarkable, usual, vanilla*, whitebread*, wonted, workaday; CONCEPTS 530,547 —*Ant.* abnormal, different, exceptional, special, uncommon, unexpected, unfamiliar, unusual

everything [*n*] *entirety* aggregate, all, all in all, all that, all things, business, complex, each

thing, every little thing*, fixins'*, lock stock and barrel*, lot, many things, sum, the works*, total, universe, whole, whole ball of wax*, whole caboodle*, whole enchilada*, whole lot*, whole shebang*; CONCEPTS 432,837 —*Ant.* nothing

everywhere [*adv*] *in all places* all around, all over, all over creation*, all over the map*, far and wide*, here and there*, here till Sunday*, high and low*, in all quarters, in each place, in every direction, in every place, inside and out, near and far*, omnipresent, overall, pole to pole*, the world over*, throughout, ubiquitous, ubiquitously, universally, wherever; CONCEPT 583 —*Ant.* nowhere

evict [*v*] *throw out from residence* boot out*, bounce*, chase, dislodge, dismiss, dispossess, eject, expel, extrude, force out, heave-ho*, kick out*, oust, out, put out, remove, send packing*, show out, show the door*, shut out, toss out on ear*, turn out; CONCEPTS 122,198,211 —*Ant.* admit, board, include, lease, receive, rent, take in, welcome

eviction [*n*] *throwing out of a residence* boot*, bounce*, bum's rush*, clearance, dislodgement, dispossession, ejection, expulsion, kicking out*, ouster, removal, rush, the gate*, walking papers*; CONCEPTS 123,198,211 —*Ant.* admittance, boarding, including, leasing, receiving, renting, welcome, welcoming

evidence [*n*] *proof* affirmation, attestation, averment, cincher*, clincher*, clue, confirmation, corroboration, cue, data, declaration, demonstration, deposition, documentation, dope*, goods*, gospel, grabber*, grounds, index, indication, indicia, info*, information, manifestation, mark, sign, significant, smoking gun*, substantiation, symptom, testament, testimonial, testimony, token, witness; CONCEPTS 274,318 —*Ant.* contradiction, disproof, heresay, refutation

evidence [*v*] *prove* attest, bespeak, betoken, confirm, connote, demonstrate, denote, designate, display, evince, exhibit, expose, illustrate, indicate, manifest, mark, ostend, proclaim, reveal, show, signify, testify to, witness; CONCEPTS 57,97,317 —*Ant.* contradict, disprove, refute

evident [*adj*] *apparent, clear* axiomatic, barefaced*, clear-cut, conspicuous, crystal clear*, distinct, fact, incontestable, incontrovertible, indisputable, logical, manifest, noticeable, obvious, open-and-shut*, palpable, patent, perceptible, plain, plain as day*, reasonable, straightforward, tangible, unambiguous, unmistakable, visible; CONCEPTS 529,535 —*Ant.* disputable, hidden, indefinite, mistakable, obscure, secret, uncertain, unclear, unknown, unsure, vague

evidently [*adv*] *apparently, clearly* doubtless, doubtlessly, incontestably, incontrovertibly, indisputably, it seems, it would seem, manifestly, obviously, officially, ostensibly, outwardly, patently, plainly, professedly, seemingly, to all appearances*, undoubtedly, unmistakably, without question; CONCEPT 535 —*Ant.* doubtfully, mistakably, obscurely, questionably, vaguely

evil [*adj*] *sinful, immoral* angry, atrocious, bad, baneful, base, beastly, calamitous, corrupt, damnable, depraved, destructive, disastrous, execrable, flagitious, foul, harmful, hateful, heinous, hideous, iniquitous, injurious, loathsome, low, maleficent, malevolent, malicious, malignant, nefarious, no good, obscene, offensive, pernicious, poison, rancorous, reprobate, repugnant, repulsive, revolting, spiteful, stinking, ugly, unpleasant, unpropitious, vicious, vile, villainous, wicked, wrathful, wrong; CONCEPTS 545,570 —Ant. auspicious, decent, good, honest, moral, sinless, upright, virtuous

evil [n] *badness, immorality; disaster* affliction, baseness, blow, calamity, catastrophe, corruption, crime, criminality, curse, debauchery, depravity, devilry, diabolism, harm, hatred, heinousness, hurt, ill, impiety, indecency, infamy, iniquity, injury, knavery, lewdness, licentiousness, looseness, malevolence, malignity, meanness, mischief, misery, misfortune, obscenity, outrage, pain, perversity, ruin, sin, sinfulness, sorrow, suffering, turpitude, vice, viciousness, vileness, villainy, wickedness, woe, wrong, wrongdoing; CONCEPT 645 —Ant. good, goodness, morality, virtue

evildoer [n] *wrongdoer* bad person, criminal, devil, evil person, felon, gangster, lawbreaker, murderer, psychopath, sinner, sociopath, troublemaker, villain; CONCEPT 412

evince [v] *manifest* attest, declare, demonstrate, disclose, display, furnish, indicate, prove, reveal, show; CONCEPTS 118,261

evocative [adj] *suggestive* calling up, expressive, graphic, redolent, reminiful of, reminiscent, resonant with; CONCEPT 266

evoke [v] *induce, stimulate* arouse, awaken, call, call forth, conjure, educe, elicit, evince, evolve, excite, extort, extract, give rise to, invoke, milk*, provoke, raise, rally, recall, rouse, stir up, summon, waken; CONCEPTS 228,242 —Ant. halt, quell, repress, silence, stifle, stop, suppress

evolution [n] *development, progress* change, enlargement, evolvement, expansion, flowering, growth, increase, maturation, natural process, progression, transformation, unfolding, working out; CONCEPT 704 —Ant. blockage, decrease, halt, stoppage

evolve [v] *develop, progress* advance, derive, disclose, educe, elaborate, emerge, enlarge, excogitate, expand, get, grow, increase, mature, obtain, open, result, ripen, unfold, work out; CONCEPTS 236,245,704 —Ant. block, decrease, halt, stop

exacerbate [v] *infuriate; make worse* add insult to injury*, aggravate, annoy, egg on*, embitter, enrage, envenom, exasperate, excite, fan the flames*, feed the fire*, go from bad to worse*, heat up*, heighten, hit on*, increase, inflame, intensify, irritate, madden, provoke, push one's button*, rattle one's cage*, rub salt in a wound*, vex, worsen; CONCEPTS 7,19 —Ant. aid, calm, comfort, help, soothe

exact [adj1] *accurate, precise* bull's-eye*, careful, clear, clear-cut, correct, dead on*, definite, distinct, downright, explicit, express, faithful, faultless, identical, literal, methodical, nailed down*, nice, on target*, on the button*, on the money*, on the numbers*, orderly, particular, perfect, right, right on*, rigorous,

sharp, specific, true, unequivocal, unerring, veracious, verbal, verbatim; CONCEPTS 535,557 —Ant. approximate, imprecise, inaccurate, incorrect, indefinite, inexact

exact [adj2] *careful, painstaking* conscientious, conscionable, demanding, exacting, finicky, fussy, heedful, meticulous, punctilious, punctual, rigorous, scrupulous, severe, strict; CONCEPT 542 —Ant. approximate, careless, uncareful, unreliable

exact [v] *demand, call for* assess, bleed, call, challenge, claim, coerce, command, compel, constrain, extort, extract, force, gouge, impose, insist upon, lean on, levy, oblige, pinch, postulate, put on, require, requisition, shake down*, solicit, squeeze, wrench, wrest, wring; CONCEPTS 53,142 —Ant. give

exacting [adj] *demanding* burdensome, by the book*, careful, critical, difficult, exigent, finicky, fussy, grievous, hard, harsh, hypercritical, imperious, nit-picking, onerous, oppressive, painstaking, particular, persnickety, picky, precise, rigid, rigorous, severe, stern, strict, stringent, taxing, tough, trying, unsparing, weighty; CONCEPTS 401,404 —Ant. giving, lending

exactly [adv] *accurately, particularly* absolutely, altogether, bang*, carefully, completely, correctly, definitely, explicitly, expressly, faithfully, faultlessly, for a fact, for certain, for sure*, indeed, in every respect, just, literally, methodically, no mistake, on the dot*, on the money*, on the nail*, on the nose*, positively, precisely, quite, right, rigorously, scrupulously, severely, sharp, specifically, square, strictly, the ticket*, totally, truly, truthfully, unequivocally, unerringly, utterly, veraciously, wholly; CONCEPTS 535,557 —Ant. inaccurately, inexactly

exactness [n] *accuracy, precision* carefulness, correctness, definiteness, definitiveness, definitude, exactitude, faithfulness, faultlessness, nicety, orderliness, painstakingness, preciseness, promptitude, regularity, rigor, rigorousness, scrupulousness, strictness, truth, unequivocalness, veracity; CONCEPTS 638,654 —Ant. carelessness, imprecision, inaccuracy, inexactness, irregularity

exaggerate [v] *overstate, embellish* amplify, blow out of proportion*, boast, boost, brag, build up, caricature, color, cook up*, corrupt, distort, embroider, emphasize, enlarge, exalt, expand, fabricate, falsify, fudge*, go to extremes*, heighten, hike, hyperbolize, inflate, intensify, lay it on thick*, lie, loud talk*, magnify, make too much of*, misquote, misreport, misrepresent, overdo, overdraw, overemphasize, overestimate, pad*, pretty up*, puff, put on, pyramid*, romance, romanticize, scam, stretch, up*; CONCEPT 63 —Ant. depreciate, minimize, play down, reduce, understate

exaggerated [adj] *overstated, embellished* a bit thick*, abstract, amplified, artificial, bouncing, caricatural, distorted, embroidered, exalted, excessive, extravagant, fabricated, fabulous, false, fantastic, farfetched, hammy, highly colored, histrionic, hyperbolic, impossible, inflated, magnified, melodramatic, out of proportion, overblown, overdone, overestimated, overkill, overwrought, preposterous, pretentious, schmaltzy, sensational, spectacular, steep, strained, stylized, tall, too much*, too-too*, unrealistic; CONCEPTS 267,542,562 —*Ant.* depreciated, minimized, played down, reduced, understated, unembellished, unexaggerated

exaggeration [*n*] *overstatement, embellishment* aggrandizement, amplification, baloney*, boasting, caricature, coloring, crock*, elaboration, embroidery, emphasis, enlargement, exaltation, excess, extravagance, fabrication, falsehood, fancy, fantasy, figure of speech, fish story*, flight of fancy*, hogwash*, hyperbole, inflation, jazz*, line*, magnification, misjudgment, misrepresentation, overemphasis, overestimation, pretension, pretentiousness, rant, romance, stretch, tall story*, untruth, whopper*, yarn*; CONCEPTS 63,278,663 —*Ant.* minimization, reduction, understatement, unembellishment

exalt [*v*] *promote, praise* acclaim, advance, aggrandize, apotheosize, applaud, bless, boost, build up*, commend, dignify, distinguish, ennoble, erect, eulogize, extol, glorify, halo, honor, idolize, intensify, laud, magnify, pay homage to, pay tribute to, raise, revere, set on pedestal*, sublime, transfigure, upgrade, uprear, worship; CONCEPTS 10,69 —*Ant.* castigate, condemn, criticize, debase, denounce, humiliate

exaltation [*n1*] *promotion, praise* acclaim, acclamation, advancement, aggrandizement, apotheosis, applause, blessing, dignity, elevation, eminence, ennoblement, extolment, glorification, glory, grandeur, high rank, homage, honor, idolization, laudation, lionization, loftiness, magnification, panegyric, plaudits, prestige, reverence, rise, tribute, upgrading, uplifting, worship; CONCEPTS 69,278 —*Ant.* castigation, condemnation, criticism, debasement, denunciation, humiliation

exaltation [*n2*] *great joy* animation, bliss, delectation, delight, ecstasy, elation, elevation, euphoria, excitement, exhilaration, exultation, inspiration, intoxication, joyousness, jubilation, rapture, stimulation, transport, uplift; CONCEPTS 32,410 —*Ant.* depression, misery, sorrow, unhappiness, woe

exalted [*adj*] *praised; held in high esteem* astral, august, dignified, elevated, eminent, exaggerated, excessive, first, grand, high, highest, highest-ranking, high-minded, high-ranking, honorable, honored, ideal, illustrious, immodest, imposing, inflated, intellectual, leading, lofty, magnificent, noble, number one, outstanding, overblown, pompous, prestigious, pretentious, proud, self-important, sublime, superb, superior, top-drawer*, top-ranking, uplifting; CONCEPTS 404,529 —*Ant.* condemned, criticized, debased, denounced, humiliated

examination [*n1*] *test, analysis* assay, audit, battery, blue book*, breakdown, canvass, catechism, checking, checkup, cross-examination, diagnosis, dissection, exam, experiment, exploration, final, grilling, inquest, inquiry, inquisition, inspection, interrogation, investigation, legwork*, make-up, observation, once-over*, oral, perlustration, perusal, probe, quest, questioning, questionnaire, quiz, raid, reconnaissance, research, review, scan, scrutiny, search, study, survey, the eye*, third degree*, trial, tryout, view, written; CONCEPT 290

examination [*n2*] *medical checkup* autopsy, biopsy, exam, inquiry, observation, physical, postoperative, probe, test; CONCEPTS 103,310

examine [*v1*] *analyze, test* appraise, assay, audit, canvass, case, check, check out, chew over*, consider, criticize, delve into, dig into, explore, eye*, finger*, frisk, go into, go over, go through, gun*, inquire, inspect, investigate, look over, look see*, parse, pat down, peruse, pick at, ponder, pore over, probe, prospect, prove, read, reconnoiter, research, review, scan, scope, screen, scrutinate, scrutinize, search into, sift, size up*, study, survey, sweep, take stock of*, try, turn over*, vet, view, weigh, winnow*; CONCEPTS 24,103

examine [*v2*] *ask questions pointedly* catechize, check, cross-examine, experiment, give the third*, give the third degree*, grill, inquire, interrogate, judge, measure, pump, put through the wringer*, query, quiz, try, try out, weigh; CONCEPT 48

example [*n*] *instance, model* archetype, case, case history, case in point, citation, copy, excuse, exemplar, exemplification, for instance, ideal, illustration, kind of thing, lesson, object, original, paradigm, paragon, part, pattern, precedent, prototype, quotation, representation, sample, sampling, specimen, standard, stereotype, symbol; CONCEPT 686

exasperate [*v*] *upset, provoke* aggravate, agitate, anger, annoy, bug*, disturb, drive up the wall*, embitter, enrage, exacerbate, excite, gall, get*, get under one's skin*, incense, inflame, infuriate, irk, irritate, madden, make waves*, needle*, nettle, peeve, pique, rankle, rile, roil, rouse, T-off*, try the patience of, vex, work up; CONCEPTS 7,19 —*Ant.* calm, comfort, ease, placate, please, soothe

exasperation [*n*] *upset, provocation* aggravation, anger, annoyance, besetment, bother, botheration, displeasure, exacerbation, fury, ire, irritant, irritation, nuisance, passion, pest, pique, plague, rage, resentment, vexation, wrath; CONCEPTS 29,410 —*Ant.* calming, calmness, comfort, ease, placation, pleasing, soothing

excavate [*v*] *dig up* burrow, cut, delve, empty, gouge, grub, hollow, mine, quarry, scoop, scrape, shovel, spade, trench, tunnel, uncover, unearth; CONCEPT 178 —*Ant.* fill

excavation [*n*] *site of digging; digging* blasting, burrow, cavity, cut, cutting, dig, disinterring, ditch, dugout, exhuming, hole, hollow, mine, mining, pit, quarry, removal, scooping, shaft, shoveling, trench, trough, unearthing; CONCEPTS 178,509,513 —*Ant.* filling

excavator [*n*] *earthmover* backhoe, bulldozer, digger, heavy machinery; CONCEPT 505

exceed [*v*] *be superior to; surpass* beat, best, better, break record*, cap, distance, eclipse, excel, get upper hand*, go beyond, go by, have advantage, have a jump on*, have it all over*, out-distance, outdo, outpace, outreach, outrun, outshine, outstrip, overstep, overtake, overtax, pass, rise above*, run circles around*, surmount, top, transcend; CONCEPT 141 —*Ant.* be inferior, fail, fall behind

exceedingly [*adv*] *very; exceptionally* awfully, enormously, especially, excessively, extraordinarily, extremely, greatly, highly, hugely, immoderately, in a marked degree, inordinately, powerful, really, remarkably, strikingly, superlatively, surpassingly, terribly, too much, unusually, vastly, vitally; CONCEPT 569

excel [v] *be superior; surpass* beat, be good, be master of, be proficient, be skillful, best, be talented, better, cap, come through, eclipse, exceed, go beyond, go to town*, improve upon, make it, outdo, outrival, outshine, outstrip, pass, predominate, shine, show talent, surmount, take precedence, top, transcend, wax*; CONCEPTS 141,671,706 —Ant. be inferior, fail

excellence [n] *superiority* arete, class, distinction, éclat, eminence, excellency, fineness, goodness, greatness, high quality, merit, perfection, preeminence, purity, quality, superbness, supremacy, transcendence, virtue, worth; CONCEPT 671 —Ant. failure, imperfection, inferiority

excellent [adj] *superior, wonderful* A-1*, accomplished, admirable, attractive, capital, certified, champion, choice, choicest, desirable, distinctive, distinguished, estimable, exceptional, exemplary, exquisite, fine, finest, first, first-class, first-rate, good, great, high, incomparable, invaluable, magnificent, meritorious, notable, noted, outstanding, peerless, piked*, premium, priceless, prime, select, skillful, sterling, striking, superb, superlative, supreme, tiptop*, top-notch, transcendent, world-class; CONCEPT 574 —Ant. bad, failing, imperfect, indistinguished, inferior, poor, second-class, second-rate, unnoteworthy, unworthy

except [prep] *other than* apart from, aside from, bar, barring, besides, but, excepting, excluding, exclusive of, exempting, if not, lacking, leaving out, minus, not for, omitting, outside of, rejecting, save, saving, short of, without, with the exception of; CONCEPT 577

except [v] *leave out* ban, bar, bate, count out, debar, disallow, eliminate, exclude, exempt, expostulate, inveigh, object, omit, pass over, protest, reject, remonstrate, rule out, suspend, taboo; CONCEPTS 25,30,211 —Ant. admit, allow, include

exception [n1] *leaving out* barring, debarment, disallowment, excepting, exclusion, excusing, expulsion, noninclusion, omission, passing over, rejection, repudiation, reservation; CONCEPTS 25,30,211 —Ant. admittal, admittance, allowance, inclusion

exception [n2] *special case; irregularity* allowance, anomalism, anomaly, departure, deviation, difference, dispensation, eccentricity, exemption, freak, inconsistency, nonconformity, oddity, peculiarity, perquisitor, privilege, privileged person, quirk; CONCEPTS 423,665 —Ant. normality, regularity, usualness

exceptional [adj1] *irregular* aberrant, abnormal, anomalous, atypical, deviant, distinct, extraordinary, inconsistent, infrequent, notable, noteworthy, odd, peculiar, phenomenal, rare, remarkable, scarce, singular, special, strange, uncommon, uncustomary, unheard-of, unimaginable, unique, unordinary, unprecedented, unthinkable, unusual; CONCEPT 564 —Ant. common, conventional, expected, general, normal, ordinary, regular, unexceptional, usual

exceptional [adj2] *excellent, wonderful* brainy, extraordinary, fine, first-class, first-rate, good,

high, marvelous, outstanding, phenomenal, premium, prodigious, remarkable, singular, special, superior, world-class; CONCEPTS 572,574 —Ant. inferior, mediocre, ok, unexceptional, unnoteworthy, unprodigious

excerpt [n] *citation; something taken from a whole* extract, fragment, notation, note, part, passage, pericope, piece, portion, quotation, quote, saying, section, selection; CONCEPTS 270,274,835 —Ant. insert, whole

excerpt [v] *take a part from a whole* choose, cite, cull, extract, glean, note, pick, pick out, quote, select, single out; CONCEPTS 41,142, 211 —Ant. insert

excess [n1] *overabundance of something* balance, by-product, enough, exorbitance, exuberance, fat, fulsomeness, glut, inundation, lavishness, leavings, leftover, luxuriance, nimiety, overdose, overflow, overkill, overload, overmuch, overrun, oversupply, overweight, plenty, plethora, profusion, recrement, redundance, redundancy, refuse, remainder, residue, rest, spare, superabundance, supererogation, superfluity, surfeit, surplus, the limit, too much*, too much of a good thing*, waste, wastefulness; CONCEPTS 787,824,835 —Ant. dearth, deficiency, insufficiency, lack, need, poverty, shortcoming, want

excess [n2] *overindulgence in personal desires* debauchery, dissipation, dissoluteness, exorbitance, extravagance, extreme, extremity, immoderacy, immoderation, indulgence, inordinateness, intemperance, overdoing, prodigality, saturnalia, self-indulgence, unrestraint; CONCEPTS 633,645 —Ant. deprivation, economy, frugality, moderation, privation

excessive [adj] *too much; overdone* boundless, disproportionate, dissipated, dizzying, enormous, exaggerated, exorbitant, extra, extravagant, extreme, immoderate, indulgent, inordinate, intemperate, limitless, more, needless, over, overboard, overkill, overmuch, plethoric, prodigal, profligate, recrementitious, redundant, self-indulgent, sky-high*, steep, stiff, stratospheric*, super, superabundant, superfluous, supernatural, too many, towering, unbounded, unconscionable, undue, unmeasurable, unreasonable, way out*; CONCEPTS 560, 771,781 —Ant. insufficient, moderate, reasonable, underdone

exchange [n1] *trade; deal* barter, buying and selling, castling, change, commerce, commutation, conversion, correspondence, dealing, interchange, interdependence, interrelation, network, quid pro quo, rearrangement, reciprocation, reciprocity, replacement, revision, shift, shuffle, shuffling, substitution, supplanting, supplantment, swap, switch, tit for tat*, traffic, transaction, transfer, transposing, transposition, truck*; CONCEPTS 104,324

exchange [n2] *place where goods are bought, sold* curb, market, net, network, over the counter, stock exchange, store, the Big Board*, the Street*, Wall Street*; CONCEPTS 325,449

exchange [v] *trade* alternate, bandy, bargain, barter, buy and sell, cash in, castle, change, change hands*, commute, contact with, convert into, correspond, deal in, displace, flip-flop*, give and take*, go over to*, hook up, horse trade, interchange, invert, link up, market, network, pass to, pay back, rearrange, reciprocate, replace, return the compliment*, reverse, revise, seesaw, shift, shuffle, shuttle, substitute, swap, swap horses*, switch, traffic, transact, transfer, transpose, truck*, turn the tables*; CONCEPT *104* —*Ant.* hold, keep

excise [*n*] *tax on goods* customs, duty, import tax, levy, surcharge, tariff, toll; CONCEPT *329*

excise [*v*] *remove, delete* amputate, black out, blot out*, blue pencil*, cross out, cut, cut off, cut out, cut up, destroy, edit, elide, eradicate, erase, expunge, exscind, exsect, exterminate, extirpate, extract, gut, knock off*, launder*, lop off*, resect, scissor out, scratch out, slash, stamp out*, strike, trim, wipe out, X out*; CONCEPT *211* —*Ant.* add, put in

excitable [*adj*] *easily upset or inspired* agitable, alarmable, demonstrative, edgy, emotional, enthusiastic, fidgety, fierce, fiery, galvanic, hasty, high-strung, hot-headed, hot-tempered, hysterical, impatient, impetuous, impulsive, inflammable, intolerant, irascible, mercurial, moody, nervous, neurotic, overzealous, passionate, peevish, quick, quick-tempered, rash, reckless, restless, sensitive, short fused, skittish, susceptible, temperamental, testy, touchy, uncontrolled, uneasy, vehement, violent, volatile, volcanic; CONCEPTS *401,404* —*Ant.* calm, easy, easy-going, insensitive, laid-back, passive, unexcitable, uninspired

excite [*v*] *inspire; upset* accelerate, agitate, amaze, anger, animate, annoy, arouse, astound, awaken, bother, chafe, delight, discompose, disturb, electrify, elicit, energize, evoke, feed the fire*, fire, fluster, foment, galvanize, goad, incite, induce, inflame, infuriate, instigate, intensify, irritate, jar, jolt, kindle, madden, mock, move, offend, precipitate, provoke, quicken, rouse, start, stimulate, stir up, taunt, tease, thrill, titillate, touch off, vex, waken, wake up, warm, whet, work up, worry; CONCEPTS *7,14,19,22* —*Ant.* bore, calm, compose, deaden, lull, moderate, pacify, quiet, repress, tranquilize

excited [*adj*] *inspired; upset* aflame, agitated, animated, annoyed, aroused, awakened, beside oneself*, charged, delighted, discomposed, disconcerted, disturbed, eager, enthusiastic, feverish, fired up*, frantic, high*, hot*, hot and bothered*, hyperactive, hysterical, in a tizzy*, inflamed, juiced up*, jumpy*, keyed up*, moved, nervous, on edge*, on fire*, overwrought, passionate, piqued, provoked, roused, ruffled, steamed up*, stimulated, stirred, thrilled, tumultous/tumultuous, wild, wired*, worked up, zipped up*; CONCEPTS *401,403* —*Ant.* bored, calm, composed, easy-going, laid-back, unenthused, unenthusiastic, unexcited, uninspired

excitement [*n*] *enthusiasm; incitement* action, activity, ado, adventure, agitation, animation, bother, buzz*, commotion, confusion, discomposure, disturbance, dither*, drama, elation, emotion, excitation, feeling, ferment, fever, flurry, frenzy, furor, fuss, heat*, hubbub*, hullabaloo*, hurry, hysteria, impulse, instigation, intoxication, kicks*, melodrama, motivation, motive, movement, passion, perturbation, provocation, rage, stimulation, stimulus, stir,

thrill, titillation, to-do*, trepidation, tumult, turmoil, urge, warmth, wildness; CONCEPTS *388,410,633* —*Ant.* apathy, boredom, calm, calmness, dullness, lull, peace

exciting [*adj*] *inspiring, exhilarating* agitative, animating, appealing, arousing, arresting, astonishing, bracing, breathtaking, commoving, dangerous, dramatic, electrifying, exhilarant, eye-popping*, far-out*, fine, flashy, groovy*, hair-raising*, heady*, hectic, impelling, impressive, interesting, intoxicating, intriguing, lively, melodramatic, mind-blowing, moving, neat, overpowering, overwhelming, provocative, racy, rip-roaring*, rousing, sensational, showy, spine-tingling*, stimulating, stirring, thrilling, titillating, wild, zestful; CONCEPTS *529,542,548* —*Ant.* boring, moderate, unenthused, unenthusiastic, unexciting, uninspiring, unpromising, unstimulating

exclaim [*v*] *shout out* assert, bellow, blurt, burst out, call, call aloud, call out, cry, cry out, declare, ejaculate, emit, figure, holler, proclaim, rend the air*, roar, say loudly, shout, state, utter, vociferate, yawp*, yell; CONCEPTS *47,49* —*Ant.* be quiet

exclamation [*n*] *shout; assertion* bellow, call, clamor, cry, ejaculation, expletive, holler, interjection, outcry, roar, utterance, vociferation, yawp*, yell; CONCEPTS *49,77* —*Ant.* quiet, silence

exclude [*v*] *expel, forbid* ban, bar, bate, blackball*, blacklist, block, bounce, boycott, close out, count out, debar, disallow, drive out, eject, eliminate, embargo, estop, evict, except, force out, get rid of, ignore, interdict, keep out, leave out, lock out, obviate, occlude, omit, ostracize, oust, pass over, preclude, prevent, prohibit, proscribe, put out, refuse, refuse admittance, reject, remove, repudiate, rule out, set aside, shut out, shut the door on*, sideline, suspend, throw out, veto, ward off; CONCEPTS *25,30, 121* —*Ant.* accept, add, admit, allow, include, incorporate, take on, welcome

exclusion [*n*] *expulsion; forbiddance* ban, bar, blackball*, blockade, boycott, coventry, cut, debarment, debarring, discharge, dismissal, ejection, elimination, embargo, eviction, exception, excommunication, interdict, interdicting, interdiction, keeping out, lockout, nonadmission, occlusion, omission, ostracism, ousting, preclusion, prevention, prohibition, proscription, refusal, rejection, relegation, removal, repudiation, segregation, separation, suspension, veto; CONCEPTS *25,30,121* —*Ant.* acceptance, addition, admittance, allowance, inclusion, incorporation, welcome

exclusive [*adj*] *unshared, restricted* absolute, aloof, aristocratic, chic, choice, chosen, circumscribed, clannish, classy, cliquish, closed, complete, confined, country club, discriminative, elegant, entire, exclusionary, exclusory, fashionable, full, independent, licensed, limited, narrow, only, particular, peculiar, posh, preferential, private, privileged, prohibitive, restrictive, ritzy, segregated, select, selfish, single, snobbish, socially correct, sole, swank, total, undivided, unique, upper crust*, whole; CONCEPTS *554,567* —*Ant.* divided, part, partial, shared, unlimited, unrestricted

exclusively [adv] *particularly* alone, but, completely, entirely, one and only, onliest, only, singularly, solely, wholly; CONCEPT 554 —Ant. unlimited, unrestricted

exclusive of [prep] *except for* aside from, bar, barring, bating, besides, but, debarring, excepting, excluding, leaving aside, not counting, omitting, outside of, restricting, ruling out, save; CONCEPT 554 —Ant. inclusive of

excogitate [v] *think about seriously* conceive, consider, contemplate, contrive, deliberate, derive, develop, devise, educe, evolve, frame, invent, mind, mull over, perpend, ponder, ruminate, study, think out, think up, weigh, work out; CONCEPTS 17,24 —Ant. disregard, ignore

excommunicate [v] *banish* anathematize, ban, cast out, curse, denounce, dismiss, eject, exclude, expel, oust, proscribe, remove, repudiate, unchurch; CONCEPTS 317,367 —Ant. allow, include, permit, welcome

excoriate [v1] *scrape layers off* abrade, chafe, flay, fret, gall, peel, rub, scarify, scratch, skin, strip; CONCEPTS 211,215

excoriate [v2] *denounce, criticize* attack, berate, blister, castigate, censure, chastise, condemn, flay, lambaste, lash, rebuke, reproach, reprove, revile, scathe, scold, scorch, slash, slash into, upbraid, vilify; CONCEPT 52 —Ant. compliment, laud, praise

excrement [n] *feces* crap, droppings, dung, guano, manure, poop, sewage, stool, waste, waste matter; CONCEPT 260

excrete [v] *discharge, usually liquified substance* defecate, egest, ejaculate, eject, eliminate, emanate, evacuate, exhale, expel, exudate, exude, give off, leak, pass, perspire, produce, remove, secrete, sweat, throw off, urinate, void; CONCEPTS 179,185

excruciating [adj] *torturous, painful* acute, agonizing, burning, chastening, consuming, exquisite, extreme, grueling, harrowing, insufferable, intense, piercing, punishing, racking, rending, searing, severe, sharp, shooting, stabbing, tearing, tormenting, torturesome, torturing, unbearable, unendurable, violent; CONCEPTS 314,548,609 —Ant. bearable, endurable, helpful, pleasant, pleasing, soothing

exculpate [v] *forgive* absolve, acquit, amnesty, clear, condone, discharge, disculpate, dismiss, excuse, exonerate, explain, free, justify, let off*, pardon, rationalize, release, remit, vindicate, wipe slate clean*; CONCEPTS 10,127,317 —Ant. blame, condemn, sentence

excursion [n] *journey* circuit, cruise, day trip, digression, expedition, jaunt, junket, outing, picnic, pleasure trip, ramble, round trip, safari, tour, trek, trip, walk, wandering; CONCEPTS 224,384

excusable [adj] *allowable* all right, condonable, defensible, exculpatory, explainable, fair, forgivable, justifiable, minor, moderate, not too bad*, okay, pardonable, passable, permissible, plausible, reasonable, remittable, reprievable, slight, specious, temperate, tenable, trivial, understandable, venial, vindicable, vindicatory, warrantable, within limits; CONCEPT 558 —Ant. blameable, inexcusable, unallowable, unforgivable, unjustifiable

excuse [n] *reason, explanation* alibi, apology, cleanup*, cop-out*, cover*, cover story*, coverup, defense, disguise, evasion, expedient, extenuation, fish story*, grounds, jive*, justification, makeshift, mitigation, plea, pretext, rationalization, regrets, routine, semblance, shift, song*, song and dance*, stall, stopgap*, story, substitute, subterfuge, trick*, vindication, whitewash*, why and wherefore*; CONCEPTS 59,661

excuse [v] *forgive, absolve; justify* acquit, alibi, apologize for, appease, bear with, clear, condone, cover, defend, discharge, dispense from, exculpate, exempt, exempt from, exonerate, explain, extenuate, forgive, free, give absolution, grant amnesty, indulge, let go*, let off*, liberate, make allowances for, mitigate, overlook, pardon, pass over*, plead ignorance, pretext, purge, rationalize, release, relieve, remit, reprieve, shrive, shrug off*, spare, take rap for*, tolerate, vindicate, whitewash*, wink at*; CONCEPTS 10,57,83

execrable [adj] *horrible, sickening* abhorrent, abominable, accursed, atrocious, confounded, cursed, damnable, defective, deplorable, despicable, detestable, disgusting, foul, hateful, heinous, horrific, loathsome, low, monstrous, nauseous, obnoxious, odious, offensive, repulsive, revolting, vile, wretched; CONCEPT 542 —Ant. nice, pleasant

execrate [v] *hate* abhor, abominate, accurse, anathematize, censure, condemn, curse, damn, denounce, deplore, despise, detest, excoriate, imprecate, loathe, objurgate, reprehend, reprobate, reprove, revile, vilify; CONCEPT 29 —Ant. like, love

execration [n] *hating* abhorrence, abomination, anathema, blasphemy, condemnation, contempt, curse, cursing, cussing, damnation, denunciation, detestation, detesting, excoriation, hatred, imprecation, loathing, malediction, odium, profanity, swearing, vilification; CONCEPT 29 —Ant. liking, loving

execute [v1] *kill* assassinate, behead, bump off*, do in*, electrocute, eliminate, finish, gas, guillotine, hang, knock off*, liquidate, murder, purge, put away*, put to death, shoot; CONCEPT 252 —Ant. bear, create

execute [v2] *carry out a task* accomplish, achieve, act, administer, administrate, bring off, bring to fruition, cause, come through, complete, consummate, deal with, discharge, do, do the job*, do the trick*, do to a T*, earn wings*, effect, enact, enforce, finish, fulfill, get there*, govern, hack it*, hit*, implement, make it*, meet, percolate*, perform, play, polish off*, prosecute, pull off*, put into effect, put over*, put through, realize, render, sail through*, score*, take care of, take care of business*, transact; CONCEPTS 91,706 —Ant. abandon, disregard, fail, forget, ignore, leave, miss, neglect, shirk

execution [n1] *killing* beheading, capital punishment, contract killing*, crucifixion, decapitation, electrocution, gassing, guillotining, hanging, hit, impalement, lethal injection, necktie party*, punishment, rub out*, shooting, strangling, strangulation; CONCEPT 252

execution [n2] *carrying out of a task* accomplishment, achievement, administration, completion, consummation, delivery, discharge, doing, effect, enactment, enforcement, fulfilling, implementation, nuts and bolts*, operation, performance, prosecution, realization, rendering, style; CONCEPTS *91,706* —Ant. abandoning, disregard, failure, forgetting, ignorance, leaving, neglect

executive [adj] *administrative* controlling, decision-making, directing, governing, managerial, managing, ruling; CONCEPT *527*

executive [n] *person who manages an organization* administration, administrator, big wheel*, boss, brass, businessperson, CEO*, chief, CO*, commander, director, directorate, entrepreneur, exec*, government, governor, head, head honcho*, head person*, heavyweight*, hierarchy, higher-up*, industrialist, key player*, leader, leadership, management, manager, officer, official, skipper*, supervisor, top brass*, tycoon, VIP*; CONCEPTS *347,354*

exemplar [n] *ideal* archetype, copy, criterion, epitome, example, exemplification, illustration, instance, mirror, model, paradigm, paragon, pattern, prototype, specimen, standard, type; CONCEPT *686*

exemplary [adj] *ideal* admirable, batting a thousand*, blameless, bueno*, characteristic, classic, classical, commendable, correct, estimable, excellent, good, guiltless, honorable, illustrative, inculpable, innocent, irreprehensible, laudable, meritorious, model, neato*, not bad*, not too shabby*, paradigmatic, praiseworthy, prototypical, punctilious, pure, quintessential, representative, righteous, sterling, typical, virtuous, worthy; CONCEPTS *404,572, 574* —Ant. erring, incorrect, unideal, wrong

exemplify [v] *serve as an example* body, cite, clarify, clear up, demonstrate, depict, display, elucidate, emblematize, embody, enlighten, epitomize, evidence, exhibit, illuminate, illustrate, instance, manifest, mirror, personify, quote, represent, show, spell out, symbolize, typify; CONCEPTS *97,118*

exempt [adj] *freed from responsibility* absolved, beat the rap*, clear, cleared, discharged, excepted, excluded, excused, favored, free, immune, let go*, let off*, liberated, not liable, not responsible, not subject, off the hook*, outside, privileged, released, set apart, spared, special, unbound, unchecked, unrestrained, unrestricted, unshackled, void of, walked*; CONCEPTS *319, 554* —Ant. accountable, answerable, liable, nonexempt, responsible

exempt [v] *relieve, absolve* clear, discharge, dispense, except, excuse, exonerate, free, go easy on*, grant immunity, let off*, let off the hook*, liberate, pass by, privilege from, release, spare, wipe the slate*, write off; CONCEPTS *50, 83,88,127* —Ant. blame

exemption [n] *freedom from a responsibility* absolution, discharge, dispensation, exception, exoneration, immunity, impunity, privilege, release; CONCEPTS *652,685,691* —Ant. accountability, answerability, liability, responsibility

exercise [n1] *work, effort* act, action, activity, calisthenics, constitutional*, daily dozen*, discharge, discipline, drill, drilling, examination, exercising, exertion, gym, labor, lesson, movement, occupation, performance, problem, pursuit, recitation, schoolwork, study, task, test, theme, toil, training, warm-up, workout; CONCEPTS *87,290,362,363*

exercise [n2] *accomplishment, use* application, discharge, employment, enjoyment, exertion, fulfillment, implementation, operation, performance, practice, pursuit, utilization; CONCEPTS *225,706* —Ant. disuse, misuse

exercise [v1] *put to use* apply, bestow, bring to bear, devote, drill, employ, enjoy, execute, exert, exploit, handle, operate, practice, put into practice, rehearse, sharpen, use, utilize, wield; CONCEPT *225* —Ant. ignore, not use

exercise [v2] *do repeatedly, especially to improve* break, break in, condition, cultivate, develop, discipline, drill, dry run*, exert, fix, foster, groom, habituate, hone, improve, inure, labor, lick into shape*, limber up, loosen up, maneuver, ply, practice, prepare, pump iron*, put out, put through grind*, put through mill*, rehearse, run through, set, strain, teach, train, tune up, walk through, warm up, work, work out; CONCEPTS *87,363*

exercise [v3] *upset, worry* abrade, afflict, agitate, annoy, bother, burden, chafe, distress, disturb, gall, irk, occupy, pain, perturb, preoccupy, provoke, trouble, try, vex; CONCEPTS *7,19*

exert [v] *make use of* apply, apply oneself, bring into play*, bring to bear*, dig*, employ, endeavor, exercise, expend, give all one's got*, give best shot*, labor, make effort, peg away*, plug*, ply, pour it on*, push, put forth, put out, strain, strive, struggle, sweat it*, throw, toil, try hard, use, utilize, wield, work; CONCEPTS *87,225*

exertion [n] *hard work* action, activity, application, attempt, effort, elbow grease*, employment, endeavor, exercise, hard pull*, industry, labor, long pull*, operation, pains, strain, stretch, striving, struggle, toil, travail, trial, trouble, use, utilization; CONCEPTS *87,362,677* —Ant. idleness, laziness

exfoliate [v] *peel* desquamate, doff, flake off, scale off, shed; CONCEPTS *142,176,211*

exhale [v] *breathe out* breathe, discharge, eject, emanate, emit, evaporate, expel, give off, issue, let out, respire, steam, vaporize; CONCEPT *163* —Ant. breathe in, inhale

exhaust [v1] *tire or wear out* bankrupt, burn out, conk out*, cripple, debilitate, disable, do in*, drain, draw, enervate, enfeeble, fag, fatigue, frazzle, impoverish, overdo, overexert, overextend, overfatigue, overtire, overwork, peter out*, poop*, poop out*, prostrate, run ragged*, sap*, suck dry*, tucker*, use up, weaken, wear down, weary; CONCEPTS *250, 469* —Ant. animate, invigorate, refresh

exhaust [v2] *consume, use up* bankrupt, bleed dry*, deplete, devour, dispel, disperse, dissipate, drain, draw, dry, eat, eat up*, empty, expend, finish, impoverish, run out, run through, spend, squander, strain, suck dry*, take last of, void, wash up, waste; CONCEPTS *169,225* —Ant. refresh, replenish

exhausted [adj1] *extremely tired* all in*, beat*, bleary, bone-weary, bushed, crippled, dead*, dead tired*, debilitated, disabled, dog-tired*, done for*, done in*, drained, effete, enervated, frazzled, had it*, kaput*, limp, out on one's feet*, outta gas*, prostrated, ready to drop*,

ex
ex

run-down, sapped*, shot*, spent, tired out, wasted*, weak, weakened, wearied, worn, worn out; CONCEPTS 406,485 —Ant. animated, energetic, fresh, invigorated, lively, vigorous

exhausted [adj2] *used up* all gone, at an end, bare, consumed, depleted, dissipated, done, drained, dry, empty, expended, finished, gone, spent, squandered, void, washed-out, wasted; CONCEPTS 560,771 —Ant. plenty, refreshed, restored, saved, stored, unused

exhaustion [n] *tiredness* burnout*, collapse, consumption, debilitation, debility, enervation, expenditure, fatigue, feebleness, lassitude, prostration, weariness; CONCEPTS 410,720 —Ant. energy, liveliness, readiness, vigor

exhaustive [adj] *all-inclusive, complete* all-embracing, all-encompassing, all-out, catholic, comprehensive, embracive, encyclopedic, extensive, far-reaching, from A to Z*, full, full-blown, full-dress*, full-scale, in-depth, intensive, no stone unturned*, out-and-out*, profound, radical, sweeping, the word, thorough, thoroughgoing, total, whole-hog*; CONCEPTS 531,772 —Ant. excluding, incomplete, unfinished

exhibit [n] *viewing; presentation* display, exhibition, exposition, fair, illustration, model, performance, show; CONCEPTS 259,261 —Ant. concealment, cover, hiding

exhibit [v] *put on view; present* advertise, air, brandish, demonstrate, disclose, display, disport, evidence, evince, expose, express, feature, flash, flaunt, illustrate, indicate, let it all hang out*, make clear, make plain, manifest, mark, offer, ostend, parade, parade wares*, proclaim, reveal, roll out, show, show and tell*, showcase, show off, strut stuff*, trot out*, wave around*; CONCEPT 261 —Ant. conceal, cover, hide

exhibition [n] *showing, demonstration* advertisement, airing, an act*, a scene*, carnival, display, exhibit, expo, exposition, fair, fireworks, flash*, front*, manifestation, offering, pageant, performance, presentation, representation, show, sight, spectacle; CONCEPTS 261,386

exhibitionism [n] *attention-seeking behavior* exposing oneself, flashing*, immodesty, indecent exposure, self-display, showing off; CONCEPTS 261,386

exhilarate [v] *make very happy* animate, boost, buoy, cheer, commove, delight, elate, enliven, exalt, excite, gladden, inspire, inspirit, invigorate, juice*, lift, pep up*, perk up*, pick up, put zip into*, quicken, rejoice, send, snap up*, stimulate, thrill, turn on*, uplift, vitalize; CONCEPTS 7,22 —Ant. agitate, depress, discourage, sadden, upset, worry

exhilarating [adj] *stimulating, cheering* animating, animative, bracing, breathtaking, electric, elevating, enlivening, exalting, exciting, exhilarant, exhilarative, exhilaratory, eye-popping*, gladdening, inspiring, inspiriting, intoxicating, invigorating, quickening, rousing, stimulative, stirring, thrilling, tonic, uplifting, vitalizing; CONCEPTS 529,548 —Ant. agitating, boring, depressing, discouraging, upsetting, worrying

exhilaration [n] *great happiness, excitement* animation, a rush*, cheerfulness, delight, elation, electrification, elevation, enlivenment, euphoria, exaltation, excitation, firing, gaiety, galvanization, gladness, gleefulness, head rush*, high spirits*, hilarity, inspiration, invigoration, joy, joyfulness, liveliness, mirth, quickening, sprightliness, stimulation, uplift, vitalization, vivacity, vivification; CONCEPT 410 —Ant. agitation, depression, discouragement, unhappiness, upset, worry

exhort [v] *urge, warn* admonish, advise, beseech, bid, call upon, caution, counsel, egg on*, encourage, enjoin, entreat, goad, incite, insist, persuade, plead, preach, press, pressure, prick, prod, prompt, propel, spur, stimulate; CONCEPTS 75,78

exhortation [n] *warning, urging* admonition, advice, beseeching, bidding, caution, counsel, encouragement, enjoinder, entreaty, goading, incitement, instigation, lecture, persuasion, preaching, sermon; CONCEPTS 75,78,274

exhume [v] *dig up, especially the dead* disclose, disembalm, disentomb, disinhume, disinter, resurrect, reveal, unbury, uncharnel, unearth; CONCEPT 178 —Ant. bury

exigency/exigence [n] *difficulty; demand* acuteness, constraint, contingency, crisis, criticalness, crossroad, demandingness, dilemma, distress, duress, emergency, extremity, fix, hardship, imperativeness, jam, juncture, necessity, need, needfulness, pass, pickle*, pinch, plight, predicament, pressingness, pressure, quandary, requirement, scrape*, stress, turning point*, urgency, vicissitude, want, wont, zero hour*; CONCEPTS 646,674, 709 —Ant. ease, easiness, ordinariness

exigent [adj1] *urgent, pressing* acute, burning, clamant, clamorous, constraining, critical, crucial, crying, imperative, importunate, insistent, instant, menacing, necessary, needful, threatening; CONCEPTS 548,568 —Ant. ordinary, unpressured, usual

exigent [adj2] *difficult, taxing* arduous, burdensome, demanding, exacting, grievous, hard, harsh, onerous, oppressive, rigorous, severe, stiff, strict, stringent, superincumbent, tough, weighty; CONCEPTS 537,542 —Ant. easy, facile, unpressured

exiguous [adj] *scanty* bare, confined, diminutive, inadequate, limited, little, meager, narrow, negligible, paltry, petty, poor, restricted, skimpy, slender, slight, small, spare, sparse, tenuous, thin, tiny; CONCEPTS 771,789 —Ant. plenty

exile [n1] *deportation from a place* banishment, diaspora, dispersion, displacement, exclusion, expatriation, expulsion, extradition, migration, ostracism, proscription, relegation, scattering, separation; CONCEPT 298

exile [n2] *person deported from a place* deportee, displaced person, DP*, émigré, expatriate, expellee, fugitive, nonperson*, outcast, outlaw, person without country*, refugee; CONCEPTS 354,412,423

exile [v] *deport from place* banish, cast out, displace, dispossess, drive out, eject, evacuate, expatriate, expel, expulse, extradite, ostracize, oust, outlaw, proscribe, relegate, transport, turn out; CONCEPTS 122,198,298 —Ant. import, take in, welcome

exist [v1] *be living* abide, be, be extant, be latent, be present, breathe, continue, endure, happen, last, lie, live, move, obtain, occur, prevail, remain, stand, stay, subsist, survive; CONCEPT 407 —Ant. die

exist [v2] *get along in life* consist, dwell, eke out a living*, endure, get by*, go on, inhere, kick*, lie, live, make it*, reside, stay alive*, subsist, survive; CONCEPTS 100,226

existence [n] *life* actuality, animation, being, breath, continuance, continuation, duration, endurance, entity, essence, hand one is dealt*, individuality, journey, lifing, permanence, perseverance, presence, rat race*, reality, real world*, something, subsistence, survival, the big game*, world; CONCEPTS 407,639 —Ant. death, inanimateness

exit [n1] *way out of a place* avenue, door, egress, fire escape, gate, hole, opening, outlet, passage out, vent; CONCEPT 440 —Ant. entrance

exit [n2] *leaving* adieu, death, demise, departure, egress, egression, evacuation, exodus, expiration, expiry, farewell, going, goodbye, leave-taking, offgoing, retirement, retreat, stampede, withdrawal; CONCEPT 195 —Ant. arrival, arriving, coming, entering, entrance

exit [v] *leave a place* bid farewell, blow*, depart, do vanishing act*, flake off*, get*, get away, get off, git*, go, go away, go out, issue, move, move out, quit, retire, retreat, say goodbye, split*, take a hike*, take one's leave*, withdraw; CONCEPT 195 —Ant. arrive, come in, enter, go in

exodus [n] *leaving* departure, egress, egression, emigration, evacuation, exit, exiting, flight, going out, journey, migration, offgoing, retirement, retreat, withdrawal; CONCEPT 195 —Ant. arrival, entrance

exonerate [v] *excuse, clear of responsibility or blame* absolve, acquit, disburden, discharge, dismiss, except, exculpate, exempt, free, justify, let off*, let off hook*, liberate, pardon, release, relieve, sanitize, vindicate, whitewash*, wipe slate clean*; CONCEPTS 10,127,317 —Ant. accuse, blame, charge, condemn, incarcerate, incriminate, sentence

exorbitant [adj] *extravagant, excessive* absonant, dear, enormous, exacting, expensive, extortionate, extreme, high, highway robbery*, immoderate, inordinate, out of sight*, outrageous, overboard, overmuch, over one's head*, preposterous, pricey, steep*, stiff*, towering, unconscionable, undue, unreasonable, unwarranted, up to here*, wasteful; CONCEPTS 334,547,558 —Ant. cheap, inexpensive, low, moderate, reasonable, sensible

exorcise [v] *free from evil spirits* cast out, dismiss, drive out, expel, purge, purify, remove; CONCEPT 179

exorcism [n] *expelling evil spirits* casting out, ceremony, ejection, expulsion, purification, ritual; CONCEPTS 165,367

exotic [adj] *not native or usual; mysterious* alien, alluring, avant garde, bizarre, colorful, curious, different, enticing, external, extraneous, extraordinary, extrinsic, far out*, fascinating, foreign, glamorous, imported, introduced, kinky*, outlandish, outside, peculiar, peregrine, romantic, strange, striking, unfamiliar, unusual, way out*, weird*; CONCEPTS 542,549 —Ant. familiar, normal, ordinary, usual

expand [v1] *extend, augment* aggrandize, amplify, beef up*, bloat, blow up*, bolster, broaden, bulk up*, burgeon, detail, develop, diffuse, dilate, distend, elaborate, embellish, enlarge, explicate, fan out*, fatten, fill out, grow, heighten, hike, increase, inflate, lengthen, magnify, mount, multiply, mushroom, open, open out, outspread, pad, piggyback*, prolong, protract, puff up*, pyramid*, slap on*, soup up*, spread, spread out, stretch, stretch out, swell, tack on*, thicken, unfold, unfurl, unravel, unroll, upsurge, wax*, widen; CONCEPTS 236,245 —Ant. abbreviate, contract, lessen, lower, shorten, shrink

expand [v2] *go into detail* amplify, beef up*, build up, develop, dilate, discourse, drag out*, elaborate, embellish, enlarge, expatiate, expound, extend, flesh out*, spell out, sweeten; CONCEPT 57 —Ant. abbreviate, abridge, shorten

expanse [n] *large space, usually open* amplitude, area, belt, breadth, compass, distance, domain, extension, extent, field, immensity, latitude, length, margin, orbit, plain, radius, range, reach, region, remoteness, room, scope, span, sphere, spread, stretch, sweep, territory, tract, uninterrupted space, width, wilderness; CONCEPTS 509,513,651,788

expansion [n] *growth* amplification, augmentation, breadth, development, diffusion, dilation, distance, distension, enlargement, evolution, expanse, extension, increase, inflation, magnification, maturation, multiplication, opening out, space, spread, stretch, swelling, unfolding, unfurling; CONCEPTS 700,704,780 —Ant. lessening, shrinkage, stagnation

expansionism [n] *growth* development, economic expansion, imperialism, progress; CONCEPTS 427,469,703,704,775

expansive [adj1] *broad, comprehensive* all-embracing, ample, big, dilatant, elastic, expanding, expansile, extensive, far-reaching, great, inclusive, large, scopic, scopious, stretching, thorough, unrepressed, unsuppressed, voluminous, wide, wide-ranging, widespread; CONCEPT 772 —Ant. limited, narrow

expansive [adj2] *talkative* affable, communicative, demonstrative, easy, effervescent, effusive, extroverted, free, friendly, garrulous, generous, genial, gregarious, gushy, lavish, liberal, loquacious, open, outgoing, sociable, unconstrained, uninhibited, unreserved, unrestrained, warm; CONCEPT 267 —Ant. quiet, reserved, silent

expatriate [n] *person thrown out of a country* departer, deportee, displaced person, emigrant, émigré, evacuee, exile, expellee, migrant, outcast, refugee; CONCEPTS 354,412,423

expatriate [v] *throw out of a country* banish, deport, displace, exile, expel, expulse, ostracize, oust, proscribe, relegate, transport; CONCEPTS 130,198,211 —Ant. allow, welcome

expect [v] *believe strongly; anticipate* apprehend, assume, await, bargain for, bargain on, be afraid, calculate, conjecture, contemplate, count on, divine, envisage, feel, figure, forecast, foreknow, foresee, gather, hope, hope for, imagine, in the cards*, look, look ahead to, look for, look forward to*, predict, presume, presuppose, reckon, see coming*, sense, suppose, surmise, suspect, take, think, trust, understand, wait for, watch for; CONCEPTS 12,26

expect [v2] *want, wish* call for, count on, demand, exact, insist on, look for, rely upon, require; CONCEPT 20

expectancy [n] *anticipation* assumption, assurance, belief, calculation, confidence, conjecture, expectation, hope, likelihood, looking forward, outlook, prediction, presentation, presentiment, presumption, probability, prospect, reliance, supposition, surmise, suspense, trust, view, waiting; CONCEPTS 410,689

expectant [adj1] *anticipating* alert, anticipative, anxious, apprehensive, awaiting, breathless, eager, expecting, hopeful, hoping, in suspense, looking for, on edge*, on tenterhooks*, prepared, raring*, ready, vigilant, waiting, waiting on, watchful, with bated breath*; CONCEPTS 403,406

expectant [adj2] *preparing to give birth* enceinte, expecting, gravid, parturient, pregnant, with child*; CONCEPT 485

expectation [n] *belief, anticipation* apprehension, assumption, assurance, calculation, chance, confidence, conjecture, design, expectancy, fear, forecast, hope, intention, likelihood, looking forward, motive, notion, outlook, possibility, prediction, presumption, probability, promise, prospect, reliance, supposition, surmise, suspense, trust, view; CONCEPTS 410,689

expecting [adj] *pregnant* carrying, expectant, in a family way*, with child*; CONCEPTS 406,485

expediency/expedience [n1] *appropriateness; worth* advantage, advantageousness, advisability, appositeness, aptness, benefit, convenience, desirability, effectiveness, efficiency, fitness, helpfulness, judiciousness, meetness, opportunism, opportunity, order, policy, practicality, pragmatism, profitability, profitableness, properness, propitiousness, propriety, prudence, rightness, suitability, usefulness, utilitarianism, utility; CONCEPTS 656,658 —*Ant.* disadvantage, inappropriateness

expediency/expedience [n2] *resource* band-aid*, contrivance, design, device, dodge, easy way out*, gimmick*, makeshift*, maneuver, means, measure, method, recourse, resort, scheme, shift, step, stopgap*, stratagem, strategy, substitute, surrogate, tactic, trick; CONCEPTS 660,712

expedient [adj] *worthwhile, appropriate* ad hoc, advantageous, advisable, beneficial, convenient, desirable, discreet, effective, feasible, fit, fitting, helpful, judicious, meet, opportune, politic, possible, practicable, practical, pragmatic, profitable, proper, prudent, seasonable, suitable, tactical, timely, useful, utilitarian, wise; CONCEPTS 558,560 —*Ant.* inappropriate, inexpedient, unbeneficial, unprofitable, unworthwhile

expedient [n] *resource* contrivance, device, gency, instrument, instrumentality, makeshift, maneuver, means, measure, medium, method, recourse, refuge, resort, scheme, shift, stopgap, stratagem, substitute; CONCEPTS 660,712

expedite [v] *make happen faster* accelerate, advance, assist, cut the red tape*, dispatch, facilitate, fast track*, forward, grease wheels*, hand-carry, handle personally, hand-walk*,

hasten, hurry, precipitate, press, promote, quicken, railroad*, run interference*, run with the ball*, rush, shoot through*, speed, speed up, urge, walk it through*; CONCEPT 242 —*Ant.* block, cease, check, delay, halt, hinder, slow, stop

expedition [n1] *journey; people on a journey* campaign, caravan, cavalcade, company, crew, crowd, cruise, crusade, enterprise, entrada, excursion, exploration, explorers, fleet, jaunt, junket, mission, outing, party, patrol, peregrination, picnic, posse, quest, safari, squadron, swing, team, tour, travel, travellers, trek, trip, undertaking, voyage, voyagers, wayfarers; CONCEPTS 224,417

expedition [n2] *speed; speeding up* alacrity, celerity, dispatch, expeditiousness, goodwill, haste, hurry, hustle, promptitude, promptness, punctuality, quickness, rapidity, readiness, swiftness; CONCEPTS 242,755 —*Ant.* blockage, delay, halt, hindrance, slowing, stoppage

expeditious [adj] *immediate, speedy* active, alert, breakneck, brisk, diligent, effective, effectual, efficient, fast, fleet, hasty, instant, nimble, prompt, punctual, quick, rapid, ready, swift; CONCEPTS 542,588 —*Ant.* pokey, retarded, slow

expel [v1] *discharge* belch, blow out, cast out, disgorge, dislodge, drive out, ejaculate, eruct, erupt, evacuate, exhaust, exudate, exude, get rid of, irrupt, pass, remove, spew, throw out, vomit; CONCEPT 179 —*Ant.* absorb, admit, take in

expel [v2] *throw out, banish* ban, bar, black-ball*, bust, cast out, chase, deport, discharge, dismiss, displace, dispossess, drum out, eject, eliminate, evict, exclude, exile, expatriate, expulse, fire, give the boot*, give the hook*, give walking papers*, kick out, oust, proscribe, send packing*, show the door*, suspend, throw out on ear*, turn out; CONCEPTS 122,130,198 —*Ant.* admit, allow, permit, take in, welcome

expend [v] *exhaust; spend* ante up*, blow*, consume, disburse, dish out*, dispense, dissipate, distribute, employ, finish, foot the bill*, fork over*, give, go through*, lay out, outlay, pay, pay out, put out*, shell out*, splurge, spring for*, throw money at*, use up, wash up*; CONCEPTS 225,341 —*Ant.* hold, keep, save

expendable [adj] *not important* dispensable, disposable, excess, inessential, nonessential, replaceable, superfluous, unimportant; CONCEPTS 546,575 —*Ant.* important, indispensable, necessary, useful

expenditure [n] *payment* amount, application, bottom line*, cash on barrelhead*, charge, come to*, consumption, cost, disbursement, dissipation, expense, figure, investment, kick-back*, outgo, outlay, output, payoff, price, rate, setback*, spending, splurge, squander, throw*, tune*, use, valuation, value, waste; CONCEPT 344 —*Ant.* savings

expense [n] *cost, payment* amount, assessment, bite*, bottom line*, budget, charge, consumption, debit, debt, decrement, deprivation, disbursement, duty, expenditure, forfeit, forfeiture, insurance, investment, liability, loan, loss, mortgage, obligation, outdo*, outlay, out of pocket*, output, overhead, payroll, price, price tag, rate, responsibility, risk, sacrifice, spending, sum, surcharge, tariff, toll, upkeep, use, value, worth; CONCEPTS 328,329,336,344

expensive [adj] *high-priced* an arm and a leg*, at a premium, big-ticket*, costly, dear, excessive, exorbitant, extravagant, fancy, high, highway robbery*, holdup*, immoderate, inordinate, invaluable, lavish, out of sight*, overpriced, plush, posh, pretty penny*, pricey*, rich, ritzy*, sky-high*, steep*, stiff*, swank*, too high, uneconomical, unreasonable, up-scale*, valuable; CONCEPT 334 —*Ant.* cheap, inexpensive, low-priced, moderate, reasonable

experience [n1] *knowledge* acquaintance, action, actuality, background, caution, combat, contact, doing, empiricism, evidence, existence, exposure, familiarity, forebearance, intimacy, involvement, inwardness, judgment, know-how*, maturity, observation, participation, patience, perspicacity, practicality, practice, proof, reality, savoir-faire, seasoning, sense, skill, sophistication, strife, struggle, training, trial, understanding, wisdom, worldliness; CONCEPT 409 —*Ant.* ignorance, immaturity, inexperience

experience [n2] *happening, occurrence* adventure, affair, encounter, episode, event, incident, ordeal, test, trial, trip; CONCEPTS 2,696

experienced [adj] *knowledgeable, knowing* accomplished, accustomed, adept, been around*, been there*, broken in*, capable, competent, cultivated, dynamite, expert, familiar, having something on the ball*, instructed, in the know*, knowing one's stuff*, knowing the score*, mature, matured, old, old hand*, practical, practiced, pro, professional, qualified, rounded, seasoned, skillful, sophisticated, sport, tested, the right stuff*, trained, tried, versed, vet, veteran, well-versed, wise, worldly, worldly-wise*; CONCEPTS 402,527 —*Ant.* green, ignorant, immature, inexperienced, unfamiliar, unknowledgeable, unseasoned, unsophisticated

experiment [n] *investigation, test* agreement, analysis, assay, attempt, check, dissection, dry run*, enterprise, essay, examination, exercise, experimentation, fling*, measure, observation, operation, practice, probe, procedure, proof, quiz, R and D*, rehearsal, research, research and development, scrutiny, search, speculation, study, trial, trial and error*, trial run*, try, try-on, tryout, undertaking, venture, verification; CONCEPTS 103,290

experiment [v] *investigate, test* analyze, assay, diagnose, examine, explore, fool with*, futz around*, mess around*, play around with*, practice with, probe, prove, put to the test*, research, sample, scrutinize, search, shake down*, speculate, study, try, try on, try on for size*, try out, venture, verify, weigh; CONCEPTS 24,87,103

experimental [adj] *exploratory* beginning, developmental, empirical, experiential, first stage, laboratory, momentary, on approval, pilot, preliminary, preparatory, primary, probationary, provisional, speculative, temporary, tentative, test, trial, trial-and-error, unconcluded, under probation, unproved; CONCEPT 535 —*Ant.* proven, tested, tried

expert [adj] *knowledgeable, proficient* able, adept, adroit, apt, big league*, clever, crack, crackerjack*, deft, dexterous, experienced, facile, handy, practiced, professional, qualified, savvy, schooled, sharp, skilled, skillful, slick, trained, virtuoso; CONCEPTS 402,527 —*Ant.* amateur, inexpert, unknowledgeable, unskilled, untrained

expert [n] *master, specialist* ace*, adept, artist, artiste, authority, buff, connoisseur, doyen, graduate, guru*, hot shot*, old hand*, old pro*, phenomenon, pro, professional, proficient, shark*, virtuoso, whiz*, wizard; CONCEPTS 348,350,416 —*Ant.* amateur, apprentice, ignoramus, novice

expertise/expertness [n] *knowledge, proficiency* ability, ableness, adroitness, aptness, art, cleverness, command, competence, craft, cunning, deftness, dexterity, dodge*, facility, finesse, goods*, ingeniousness, judgment, knack*, know-how*, line*, makings*, oil*, one's thing*, prowess, readiness, savvy, sharpness, skill, skillfulness, stuff*; CONCEPTS 409,630 —*Ant.* ignorance, inexpertness, lack

expiate [v] *make amends for* absolve, amend, appease, atone, atone for, compensate, correct, do penance, excuse, forgive, pay one's dues*, rectify, redeem, redress, remedy, square things*; CONCEPTS 67,126

expiration [n] *finish, demise* cessation, close, closing, conclusion, death, decease, departure, dying, elapsing, end, expiry, going, passing, termination, terminus; CONCEPT 119,304 —*Ant.* beginning, birth, commencement, inception, start

expire [v1] *come to an end* bite the dust*, buy it*, cash in chips*, cease, close, conclude, croak*, decease, depart, die, elapse, end, finish, go, kick the bucket*, lapse, pass, pass away, pass on, pass over, perish, quit, run out, stop, strike out*, terminate, up and die*; CONCEPTS 119,304 —*Ant.* bear, begin, commence, start

expire [v2] *breathe out* emit, exhale, expel; CONCEPTS 163,185 —*Ant.* breathe in, inhale

explain [v] *make clear; give a reason for* account for, analyze, annotate, break down, bring out, clarify, clear up, construe, decipher, define, demonstrate, describe, diagram, disclose, elucidate, excuse, explicate, expound, get across*, go into detail, illustrate, interpret, justify, make plain*, manifest, paraphrase, point out, put across, put in plain English*, rationalize, read, refine, render, resolve, reveal, set right, solve, spell out*, teach, tell, throw light upon*, translate, unfold, unravel, untangle; CONCEPT 57 —*Ant.* be vague, complicate, confuse, mystify, obscure, perplex

explanation [n] *clarification; reason* account, annotation, answer, breakdown, brief, cause, comment, commentary, confession, definition, demonstration, description, details, display, elucidation, evidence, example, excuse, explication, exposition, expression, gloss, history, illustration, information, interpretation, justification, meaning, mitigation, motive, narration, note, recital, rendition, report, resolution, sense, showing, significance, specification, statement, story, summary, tale, talking, telling, vindication, writing; CONCEPTS 271,274,661 —*Ant.* complication

explanatory [adj] *descriptive* allegorical, analytical, annotative, critical, declarative, demonstrative, diagrammatic, discursive, elucidatory, enlightening, exegetic, exegetical, explicative, expositional, expository, graphic, guiding, hermeneutic, illuminative, illustrative, informative, informing, instructive, interpretive, justifying, summary, supplementary; CONCEPT 267 —*Ant.* confusing, mysterious, obscure, perplexing, puzzling, vague

expletive [n] *swear word; exclamation* curse, cuss, cuss word, interjection, oath; CONCEPT 275

explicate [v] *clarify, expand* amplify, clear up, construe, demonstrate, develop, dilate, elucidate, enlarge upon, enucleate, expatiate, explain, expound, give the big picture*, illustrate, interpret, make clear, make explicit, make plain*, run down, spell out*, tell why, unfold, untangle, work out; CONCEPT 57 —*Ant.* cloud, complicate, confuse, mystify, obscure, tangle

explicit [adj] *specific, unambiguous* absolute, accurate, categorical, certain, clean-cut, clear, clear-cut, correct, definite, definitive, direct, distinct, exact, express, frank, lucid, obvious, on the nose*, open, outspoken, patent, perspicuous, plain, positive, precise, stated, straightforward, sure, understandable, unequivocal, unqualified, unreserved; CONCEPTS 267,529,535 —*Ant.* ambiguous, confused, equivocal, implicit, indefinite, obscure, unspecific, vague

explode [v1] *blow up* backfire, blast, blaze, blow to kingdom come*, break out, burst, collapse, convulse, detonate, discharge, erupt, flame up, flare up, fracture, jet, kablooey*, let go*, mushroom*, rupture, set off, shatter, shiver, split, thunder; CONCEPTS 179,320 —*Ant.* implode

explode [v2] *discredit* belie, confute, debunk, deflate, discard, disprove, invalidate, puncture, refute, repudiate, shoot down*, shoot full of holes*; CONCEPT 54 —*Ant.* prove

exploit [n] *achievement* accomplishment, adventure, attainment, coup, deed, do, effort, enterprise, escapade, feat, job, maneuver, performance, stroke, stunt, tour de force, venture; CONCEPT 706

exploit [v] *take advantage of; misuse* abuse, apply, avail oneself of, bleed*, capitalize on, cash in on*, employ, exercise, finesse, fleece*, get mileage out of*, handle, impose upon, jockey*, make capital of, maneuver, milk*, mine*, play*, play on, profit by, profit from, put to use, skin*, soak*, stick*, use, utilize, work; CONCEPTS 156,225

exploitation [n] *taking advantage* bleeding*, profiteering, using; CONCEPTS 156,225

exploration [n] *investigation; survey* analysis, examination, expedition, inquiry, inspection, probe, reconnaissance, research, scrutiny, search, study, tour, travel, trip; CONCEPTS 216,224

explore [v] *investigate; survey* analyze, burrow, delve into, dig into, examine, go into*, have a look*, hunt, inquire into, inspect, leave no stone unturned*, look into, probe, prospect, question, reconnoitre, research, scout, scrutinize, search, seek, sift, test, tour, travel, traverse, try, turn inside out*; CONCEPTS 103,216,224

explorer [n] *trailblazer* adventurer, experimenter, inquisitive person, pathfinder, pilgrim, pioneer, searcher, seeker, traveler; CONCEPTS 348,413

explosion [n] *eruption, discharge* access, backfire, bang, blast, blowout, blowup, burst, clap, combustion, concussion, crack, detonation, firing, fit, flare-up, fulmination, gust, ignition, outbreak, outburst, paroxysm, percussion, pop, report, roar, salvo; CONCEPTS 179,320,521 —*Ant.* implosion

explosive [adj] *volatile, dangerous* at the boiling point*, bursting, charged, consequential, convulsive, detonating, detonative, ebullient, eruptive, fiery, forceful, frenzied, fulminant, fulminating, hazardous, impetuous, meteoric, overwrought, perilous, raging, rampant, stormy, tense, touchy, ugly, uncontrollable, unstable, vehement, violent, wild; CONCEPT 542 —*Ant.* calm, peaceful, safe

explosive [n] *something that blows up* ammunition, bomb, booby trap*, charge, detonator, dynamite, fireworks, grease*, grenade, gunpowder, mine, missile, mulligan, munition, nitroglycerin, pineapple*, powder, propellant, shell, shot, soup*, TNT*; CONCEPT 500

exponent [n1] *person who supports, advocates* backer, booster, champion, defender, demonstrator, expositor, expounder, interpreter, partisan, promoter, propagandist, proponent, protagonist, second, seconder, spokesperson, supporter, upholder; CONCEPT 423

exponent [n2] *example* denotation, exemplar, illustration, index, indication, model, representative, sample, sign, specimen, token, type; CONCEPTS 284,686

export [v] *sell or trade abroad* consign, convey, dump, find market, find outlet, freight, send out, ship, smuggle, transport, transship; CONCEPTS 217,324 —*Ant.* buy, import

exposé [n] *disclosure* betrayal, confession, construction, divulgence, exegesis, explanation, explication, exposal, exposition, exposure, interpretation, revelation, truth, uncovering; CONCEPT 274 —*Ant.* secret, silence

expose [v1] *reveal* advertise, air, bare, betray, brandish, bring to light*, broadcast, crack, debunk, denude, dig up*, disclose, display, disport, divulge, exhibit, feature, flash, flaunt, give away, lay bare*, lay open*, leak, let cat out of bag*, let out*, make known, manifest, open, open to view, parade, present, prove, publish, put on view, report, show, show off, smoke out*, spill, streak, tip off*, trot out*, unclothe, uncover, unearth, unfold, unmask, unshroud, unveil; CONCEPTS 60,261 —*Ant.* conceal, cover, hide

expose [v2] *subject to danger* endanger, hazard, imperil, jeopardize, lay open*, leave open*, make liable, make vulnerable, peril, put in harm's way*, risk; CONCEPT 246 —*Ant.* guard, protect, save, shield

exposed [adj1] *made public* apparent, bare, bared, brought to light*, caught, clear, debunked, defined, denuded, disclosed, discovered, divulged, dug up*, evident, exhibited, for show, found out, laid bare*, made manifest, manifest, naked, on display, on the spot*, on view, open, peeled, resolved, revealed, shown,

ex
ex

solved, stripped, unconcealed, uncovered, unhidden, unmasked, unprotected, unsealed, unsheltered, unveiled, visible; CONCEPT 576 —*Ant.* concealed, guarded, private, protected, secret

exposed [*adj2*] *in danger* accessible, in peril, laid bare*, laid open*, left open*, liable, menaced, open, prone, sensitive, subject, susceptible, threatened, unguarded, unprotected, vulnerable; CONCEPTS 485,548 —*Ant.* guarded, protected, safe, sheltered, shielded

exposition [*n1*] *written description* account, analysis, annotation, article, comment, commentary, composition, construal, construction, critique, delineation, details, discourse, discussion, disquisition, dissertation, editorial, elucidation, enucleation, enunciation, essay, exegesis, explanation, explication, exposé, expounding, history, illustration, interpretation, monograph, paper, piece, position paper, presentation, report, review, statement, story, study, tale, text, theme, thesis, tract, tractate, treatise; CONCEPTS 268,271

exposition [*n2*] *fair* bazaar, circus, county fair, demonstration, display, exhibition, expo, marketplace, mart, pageant, presentation, production, show, showing; CONCEPT 386

expository [*adj*] *descriptive* critical, disquisitional, elucidative, exegetic, explanatory, explicative, exploratory, hermeneutic, illustrative, informative, interpretive; CONCEPT 267

expostulate [*v*] *reason with* argue, dissuade, oppose, protest, remonstrate; CONCEPT 46

exposure [*n*] *uncovering; putting in view or danger* acknowledgment, airing, baring, betrayal, confession, defenselessness, denudation, denunciation, disclosure, display, divulgence, divulging, exhibition, exposé, giveaway, hazard, introduction, jeopardy, laying open, liability, manifestation, nakedness, openness, peril, presentation, publicity, revelation, risk, showing, susceptibility, susceptiveness, susceptivity, unfolding, unmasking, unveiling, vulnerability, vulnerableness; CONCEPTS 60,261 —*Ant.* concealment, covering, hiding

expound [*v*] *talk about in great detail* clarify, comment, construe, delineate, describe, discourse, elucidate, enucleate, exemplify, explain, explicate, express, illustrate, interpret, present, set forth, spell out, state, unfold; CONCEPT 57

express [*adj1*] *certain, precise* accurate, categorical, clean-cut*, clear, clear-cut, considered, definite, definitive, deliberate, designful, direct, distinct, especial, exact, explicit, expressed, individual, intended, intentional, out-and-out*, outright, particular, plain, pointed, premeditated, set, singular, special, specific, unambiguous, unconditional, unmistakable, unqualified, uttered, voiced, voluntary, willing, witting; CONCEPTS 535,556,653 —*Ant.* imprecise, indefinite, obscure, uncertain, vague

express [*adj2*] *direct, speedy* accelerated, fast, high-speed, nonstop, quick, rapid, swift, velocious; CONCEPTS 548,588 —*Ant.* indirect, slow

express [*v1*] *articulate; signify, mean* add up to*, air, assert, asseverate, bespeak, broach, circulate, communicate, connote, convey, couch, declare, denote, depict, designate, disclose, divulge, embody, enunciate, evince, exhibit, formulate, frame*, give, hint, import, indicate, insinuate, intend, intimate, make known, manifest, phrase, pop off*, proclaim, pronounce, put, put across, put into words*, represent, reveal, say, show, speak, spell, stand for, state, suggest, symbolize, tell, testify, utter, vent, ventilate, verbalize, voice, word; CONCEPTS 51,682

express [*v2*] *discharge by squeezing or force* crush, dispatch, distill, expel, extract, force out, forward, press out, ship, squeeze out; CONCEPT 179

expression [*n1*] *verbalization* announcement, argument, articulation, assertion, asseveration, choice of words, commentary, communication, declaration, definition, delivery, diction, elucidation, emphasis, enunciation, execution, explanation, exposition, formulation, idiom, interpretation, intonation, issue, language, locution, mention, narration, phrase, phraseology, phrasing, pronouncement, remark, rendition, set phrase, speaking, speech, statement, style, term, turn of phrase, utterance, vent, voice, voicing, word, writ; CONCEPTS 47, 268,276

expression [*n2*] *facial appearance* air, aspect, cast, character, contortion, countenance, face, grimace, grin, look, mien, mug*, pout*, simper, smile, smirk, sneer, visage; CONCEPT 716

expressionless [*adj*] *having a blank look on face* dead*, deadpan, dull, empty, fish-eyed*, impassive, inexpressive, inscrutable, lackluster, lusterless, nobody home*, poker-faced*, stolid, straight-faced, stupid, unexpressive, vacant, vacuous, wooden; CONCEPT 406 —*Ant.* animated, demonstrative, expressive

expressive [*adj*] *telling, revealing* alive, allusive, articulate, artistic, brilliant, colorful, demonstrative, dramatic, eloquent, emphatic, energetic, forcible, graphic, indicative, ingenious, lively, masterly, meaningful, mobile, moving, passionate, pathetic, pictorial, picturesque, poignant, pointed, pregnant, representative, responsive, revelatory, showy, significant, silver-tongued*, spirited, stimulating, stirring, striking, strong, suggestive, sympathetic, tender, thoughtful, touching, understanding, vivid, warm; CONCEPTS 267, 537 —*Ant.* expressionless, inexpressive, passive, undemonstrative

expressly [*adv1*] *purposely* especially, exactly, in specie, intentionally, on purpose, particularly, precisely, specially, specifically; CONCEPT 556

expressly [*adv2*] *definitely, unambiguously* absolutely, categorically, clearly, decidedly, directly, distinctly, explicitly, in no uncertain terms*, manifestly, outright, plainly, pointedly, positively, specifically, unequivocally, unmistakably; CONCEPT 535 —*Ant.* ambiguously

expressway [*n*] *large, well-travelled road* freeway, interstate, parkway, superhighway, thruway, turnpike; CONCEPT 501

expropriate [*v*] *seize* accroach; annex, appropriate, arrogate, assume, commandeer, confiscate, deprive of property, dispossess, impound, preempt, requisition, sequester, take, take over; CONCEPTS 90,142 —*Ant.* appropriate, distribute, give

expulsion [n] *banishing* banishment, boot*, bounce, debarment, deportment, discharge, dislodgment, dismissal, displacement, dispossession, driving out, ejection, eviction, exclusion, exile, expatriation, extrusion, forcing out, ostracism, ouster, ousting, proscription, purge, relegation, removal, rush, suspension; CONCEPTS *130,211,298* —*Ant.* import, welcoming

expunge [v] *destroy, obliterate* abolish, annihilate, annul, black, black out*, blot out, blue pencil*, call all bets off*, call off, cancel, cut, delete, discard, drop, efface, eradicate, erase, exclude, exterminate, extinguish, extirpate, gut, kayo*, kill, knock off*, KO*, launder*, omit, raze, remove, scrub*, strike out, take out, trim, wipe out, X out*, zap*; CONCEPTS *211,252* —*Ant.* bear, build, construct, create

expurgate [v] *censor, cut* bleep*, bleep out*, blip*, blue pencil*, bowdlerize, cleanse, clean up, decontaminate, lustrate, purge, purify, sanitize, screen, scrub*, squash, sterilize; CONCEPTS *165,232* —*Ant.* allow, permit

exquisite [adj1] *beautiful, excellent, finely detailed* admirable, attractive, charming, choice, comely, consummate, cultivated, dainty, delicate, delicious, discerning, discriminating, elegant, errorless, ethereal, fastidious, fine, flawless, impeccable, incomparable, irreproachable, lovely, matchless, meticulous, outstanding, peerless, perfect, pleasing, polished, precious, precise, rare, recherché, refined, select, selective, splendid, striking, subtle, superb, superior, superlative; CONCEPTS *574, 579,589* —*Ant.* crude, flawed, horrible, horrifying, imperfect, inferior, poor, ugly

exquisite [adj2] *intense* acute, concentrated, consummate, desperate, excruciating, extreme, fierce, furious, keen, piercing, poignant, sharp, terrible, transcending, vehement, vicious, violent; CONCEPT *569* —*Ant.* dull, ordinary

extant [adj] *in existence* actual, alive, around, being, contemporary, current, existent, existing, immediate, in current use, instant, living, not lost, present, present-day, real, remaining, subsisting, surviving, undestroyed; CONCEPTS *539,582* —*Ant.* dead, extinct, gone

extemporaneous/extemporary [adj] *unrehearsed, improvised* ad hoc, ad lib, at first glance, automatic, by ear*, casual, expedient, extempore, free, immediate, impromptu, improv*, improvisatory, improviso, informal, jamming*, made-up, makeshift, offhand, off the cuff*, off the top of head*, on impulse, on-the-spot*, snap, spontaneous, spur-of-the-moment*, taking for ride*, thought out loud*, tossed off*, tossed out*, unplanned, unpremeditated, unprepared, unstudied, winging it*; CONCEPTS *267,799* —*Ant.* planned, prepared, read, rehearsed, written

extemporize [v] *improvise* ad-lib, dash out, devise, do offhand*, improvisate, invent, knock off*, make up, play by ear*, toss off*; CONCEPT *51* —*Ant.* plan, prepare, read, rehearse

extend [v1] *make larger, longer* add to, aggrandize, amplify, augment, beef up*, boost, broaden, carry on, continue, crane, develop, dilate, drag one's feet*, drag out, draw, draw out, elongate, enhance, enlarge, expand, fan out, go on, heighten, increase, last, lengthen,

let out, magnify, mantle, multiply, open, pad, prolong, prolongate, protract, run on, spin out, spread, spread out, stall, stretch, string out, supplement, take, unfold, unfurl, unroll, widen; CONCEPTS *236,239,245* —*Ant.* abridge, condense, contract, curtail, cut, decrease, lessen, lower, shorten, shrink

extend [v2] *offer* accord, advance, allocate, allot, award, bestow, bring forward, confer, donate, give, grant, hold out, impart, place at disposal, pose, present, proffer, put forth, put forward, reach out, stretch out, submit, tender, yield; CONCEPTS *66,67* —*Ant.* hold, keep, maintain, take back

extended [adj1] *lengthened* continued, drawn-out, elongate, elongated, enlarged, lengthy, long, prolonged, protracted, spread, spread out, stretched out, unfolded, unfurled, very long; CONCEPTS *782,798* —*Ant.* abbreviated, abridged, compressed, condensed, contracted, curtailed, cut, lessened, reduced, shortened

extended [adj2] *widespread, comprehensive* broad, enlarged, expanded, expansive, extensive, far-flung, far-reaching, large-scale, outspread, scopic, scopious, spread, sweeping, thorough, wide; CONCEPT *772* —*Ant.* abbreviated, abridged, narrow, reduced

extension [n] *enlargement, continuation* addendum, addition, adjunct, amplification, annex, appendage, appendix, arm, augmentation, branch, broadening, compass, continuing, delay, development, dilatation, distension, drawing out, elongation, expansion, extent, increase, lengthening, orbit, postponement, production, prolongation, protraction, purview, radius, reach, scope, span, spread, spreading out, stretch, stretching, supplement, sweep, widening, wing; CONCEPTS *236,245,824* —*Ant.* abbreviation, abridgment, compression, contraction, curtailment, decrease, reduction, shortening

extensive [adj] *far-reaching, thorough* across the board*, all-encompassing, all-inclusive, big, blanket*, boundless, broad, capacious, commodious, comprehensive, comprising, considerable, expanded, extended, far-flung*, general, great, hefty, huge, inclusive, indiscriminate, large, large-scale, lengthy, long, major, pervasive, prevalent, protracted, roomy, scopic, scopious, sizable, spacious, spaciousness, sweeping, unexclusive, universal, unrestricted, vast, voluminous, wall to wall*, wholesale, wide, wide-ranging, widespread; CONCEPTS *772,773* —*Ant.* limited, narrow, restricted, short, uncomprehensive

extent [n] *range, magnitude* admeasurement, ambit, amount, amplitude, area, bounds, breadth, bulk, capaciousness, compass, degree, dimensions, duration, elbowroom*, expanse, expansion, extension, intensity, leeway, length, limit, mass, matter, measure, neighborhood, orbit, order, period of time, play, proliferation, proportions, purview, quantity, radius, reach, scope, size, space, spaciousness, span, sphere, stretch, sweep, term, territory, time, tract, tune, vicinity, volume, wideness, width; CONCEPTS *651,730,743,745,783,000,000*

extenuate [v] *lessen, mitigate* decrease, diminish, downplay, excuse, justify, make allowances, minimize, moderate, palliate, qualify, reduce, soften; CONCEPTS *247,698,776*

extenuating [adj] *serving as an excuse* condoning, diminishing, justifying, lessening, mitigating, moderating, palliating, qualifying, reducing, sanitizing, softening, varnishing, whitewashing*; CONCEPT 537

exterior [adj] *outside* exoteric, external, extraneous, extraterrestrial, extraterritorial, extrinsic, foreign, marginal, outdoor, outer, outermost, outlying, outmost, outward, over, peripheral, superficial, surface; CONCEPT 583 —*Ant.* central, interior, middle

exterior [n] *visible part* appearance, aspect, coating, cover, covering, exteriority, external, facade, face, finish, outside, polish, rind, shell, skin, superficies, superstratum, surface; CONCEPT 484 —*Ant.* center, core, interior, middle

exterminate [v] *kill* abolish, annihilate, blot out*, decimate, erase, execute, extinguish, extirpate, finish off, massacre, obliterate, put an end to*, rub out*, send to kingdom come*, slaughter, stamp out*, wipe out*; CONCEPT 252 —*Ant.* bear, create

external [adj] *outside, extrinsic* alien, apparent, exterior, extraneous, foreign, independent, out, outer, outermost, outmost, outward, over, peripheral, superficial, surface, visible; CONCEPT 583 —*Ant.* inside, internal, intrinsic

extinct [adj] *dead, obsolete* abolished, archaic, asleep, bygone, cold*, dead and gone*, deceased, defunct, departed, disappeared, done for*, doused, ended, exanimate, exterminated, extinguished, fallen, gone, inactive, late, lifeless, lost, no longer known, out, outmoded, passé, passed on, snuffed out*, superseded, terminated, unknown, vanished, vanquished, void; CONCEPT 539 —*Ant.* alive, existing, extant, living

extinction [n] *dying out* annihilation, death, destruction, elimination, end of life, no life, obsolescence, thing of the past*; CONCEPT 252

extinguish [v1] *put out a fire* blot out, blow out, choke, douse, drown, out, quench, smother, snuff out, stamp out, stifle, suffocate, trample; CONCEPT 256 —*Ant.* light

extinguish [v2] *kill; quash* abate, abolish, annihilate, blot out*, check, crush, destroy, eliminate, end, eradicate, erase, expunge, exterminate, extirpate, obliterate, obscure, put down, put the lid on*, quell, remove, squash, stamp out, suppress, wipe out*; CONCEPTS 95,252 —*Ant.* bear, create

extirpate [v] *destroy; uproot* abate, abolish, annihilate, blot out*, cut out, demolish, deracinate, efface, eliminate, eradicate, erase, excise, expunge, exsect, exterminate, extinguish, kill, raze, remove, root out, wipe out*; CONCEPTS 211,252 —*Ant.* help, leave alone

extol [v] *sing the praises of* acclaim, applaud, bless, boost, brag about, celebrate, commend, cry up*, eulogize, exalt, give a boost to, give a bouquet*, glorify, hand it to*, hats off to*, hear it for*, hymn, laud, magnify, make much of, panegyrize, pay tribute to, praise, puff up*, push, rave, root, stroke*; CONCEPT 69 —*Ant.* blame, criticize

extort [v] *cheat; blackmail* bleed*, bully, clip, coerce, demand, educe, elicit, evince, exact, extract, fleece, force, get, gouge, hold up*, ice*,

make pay through nose*, milk*, obtain, pinch, pull one's leg*, put screws to*, put the arm on*, secure, shake down*, skin*, soak, squeeze, stick, sting, wrench, wrest, wring; CONCEPTS 53

extortion [n] *blackmail; cheating* arm, badger, bite, coercion, compulsion, demand, exaction, force, fraud, oppression, payoff, payola*, pressure, protection, racket, rapacity, shake, shakedown*, squeeze, stealing, swindle, theft; CONCEPTS 53,139,192,342

extra [adj] *accessory; excess* added, additional, ancillary, another, auxiliary, beyond, button*, extraneous, extraordinary, fresh, further, fuss*, gingerbread*, gravy*, ice*, in addition, inessential, in reserve, in store, lagniappe*, leftover, more, needless, new, one more, optional, other, over and above*, perk*, plus, redundant, reserve, spare, special, superfluous, supernumerary, supplemental, supplementary, surplus, tip, unnecessary, unneeded, unused; CONCEPTS 546,771 —*Ant.* basic, elementary, essential, fundamental, integral, necessary

extra [adv] *particularly* considerably, especially, exceptionally, extraordinarily, extremely, markedly, noticeably, rarely, remarkably, uncommon, uncommonly, unusually; CONCEPTS 557,569

extra [n] *accessory* addendum, addition, adjunct, affix, appendage, appurtenance, attachment, bonus, complement, extension, supernumerary, supplement; CONCEPT 824 —*Ant.* basic, essential, fundamental, necessity

extract [n] *something condensed from whole* abstract, citation, clipping, concentrate, cutting, decoction, distillate, distillation, elicitation, essence, excerpt, infusion, juice*, passage, quotation, selection; CONCEPTS 270,835 —*Ant.* insertion

extract [v1] *physically remove, draw out* avulse, bring out, catheterize, cull, derive, distill, eke out, elicit, eradicate, evoke, evulse, exact, express, extirpate, extort, extricate, garner, gather, get, glean, obtain, pick up, pluck, press out, pry, pull, reap, secure, select, separate, siphon, squeeze, take, tear, uproot, weed out*, withdraw, wrest, wring, yank; CONCEPTS 206,211 —*Ant.* add, insert, put in

extract [v2] *select a quotation* abridge, abstract, bring forth, choose, cite, condense, copy, cull, cut out, deduce, derive, educe, elicit, evolve, excerpt, glean, quote, shorten; CONCEPTS 79, 142,211 —*Ant.* edit in, insert

extraction [n1] *removal from whole; distillation* abstraction, derivation, drawing, elicitation, eradication, evocation, evulsion, expression, extirpation, extrication, pulling, separation, taking out, uprooting, withdrawal, wrenching, wresting; CONCEPT 211 —*Ant.* addition, insertion, introduction

extraction [n2] *ancestry, origin* birth, blood, derivation, descent, family, lineage, parentage, pedigree, race, stock; CONCEPTS 296,648

extradite [v] *send to another place by force* abandon, apprehend, arrest, bring to justice, bring to trial, deliver, give up, release, surrender; CONCEPTS 217,317

extraneous [adj] *unneeded; irrelevant* accidental, additional, adventitious, beside the point, extra, foreign, immaterial, impertinent, inadmissible, inapplicable, inapposite, inappropriate, incidental, inessential, needless, nonessential, off the subject, peripheral, pointless, redundant, superfluous, supplementary, unconnected, unessential, unnecessary, unrelated; CONCEPT 546 —*Ant.* appropriate, basic, essential, integral, necessary, needed, pertinent, relevant

extraneous [*adj2*] *foreign* adventitious, alien, exotic, external, extrinsic, out of place, strange; CONCEPT 549 —*Ant.* national, native

extraordinary [*adj*] *strange and wonderful* amazing, bizarre, boss*, curious, exceptional, fab*, fantastic, flash*, gnarly*, heavy*, inconceivable, incredible, marvelous, odd, off beaten path*, out of the ordinary, outstanding, particular, peculiar, phenomenal, rare, remarkable, singular, special, strange, stupendous, surprising, terrific, uncommon, unfamiliar, unheard-of, unimaginable, unique, unprecedented, unthinkable, unusual, unwonted, weird, wicked*; CONCEPTS 564,572 —*Ant.* common, commonplace, customary, familiar, normal, ordinary, unextraordinary, unsurprising, usual

extrapolate [*v*] *infer* anticipate, assume, conclude, deduce, envision, figure, foresee, foretell, guess, hypothesize, make an educated guess*, predict, project, see ahead, theorize; CONCEPTS 12,15,37

extrasensory perception [*n*] *psychic powers* clairvoyance, ESP, intuition, keen intuition, second sight, sixth sense, telepathy, vision; CONCEPTS 409,410

extraterrestrial [*n*] *alien* E.T.*, little green man*, Martian, men from outer space*, space being, space inhabitant; CONCEPT 423

extravagance [*n*] *indulgence; waste* absurdity, amenity, dissipation, exaggeration, excess, exorbitance, expenditure, folly, frill, icing on the cake*, immoderation, improvidence, lavishness, luxury, outrageousness, overdoing, overindulgence, overspending, preposterousness, prodigality, profligacy, profusion, recklessness, squander, squandering, superfluity, unreasonableness, unrestraint, unthrift, wastefulness, wildness; CONCEPTS 335,337,787 —*Ant.* economy, moderation, providence, saving, thrift, thriftiness

extravagant [*adj*] *indulgent, wasteful* absurd, bizarre, costly, crazy, exaggerated, excessive, exorbitant, expensive, extortionate, extreme, fanciful, fancy, fantastic, flamboyant, flashy, foolish, garish, gaudy, grandiose, immoderate, implausible, improvident, imprudent, inordinate, lavish, ludicrous, nonsensical, ornate, ostentatious, outrageous, overpriced, preposterous, pretentious, prodigal, profligate, reckless, ridiculous, showy, silly, spendthrift, steep, unbalanced, unconscionable, unreasonable, unrestrained; CONCEPTS 334,560,771 —*Ant.* close, economical, moderate, provident, reasonable, saving, stingy, thrifty, unpretentious

extravaganza [*n*] *spectacle* caricature, display, divertissement, flight of fancy*, pageant, parody, show, spectacular; CONCEPTS 263,293

extreme [*adj1*] *very great* acute, consummate, high, highest, intense, maximal, maximum, severe, sovereign, supreme, top, ultimate, utmost, uttermost; CONCEPTS 569,771,781 —*Ant.* limited, mild, moderate

extreme [*adj2*] *beyond reason and convention* absolute, desperate, dire, downright, drastic, egregious, exaggerated, exceptional, excessive, extraordinary, extravagant, fabulous, fanatical, flagrant, gross, harsh, immoderate, improper, imprudent, inordinate, intemperate, irrational, nonsensical, out-and-out*, out of proportion, outrageous, overkill, preposterous, rabid, radical, remarkable, rigid, severe, sheer, stern, strict, thorough, unbending, uncommon, uncompromising, unconventional, unreasonable, unseemly, unusual, utter, zealous; CONCEPTS 547,558,569 —*Ant.* mild, moderate

extreme [*adj3*] *faraway* far-off, farthest, final, furthermost, last, most distant, outermost, outmost, remotest, terminal, ultimate, utmost, uttermost; CONCEPT 778 —*Ant.* close, near

extreme [*n*] *ultimate; limit* acme, apex, apogee, bitter end, boundary, ceiling, climax, consummation, crest, crown, culmination, depth, edge, end, excess, extremity, height, inordinancy, maximum, nadir, nth degree*, peak, pinnacle, pole, termination, top, utmost, uttermost, zenith; CONCEPTS 484,706,745,836

extremely [*adv*] *greatly, intensely* acutely, almighty, awfully, drastically, exceedingly, exceptionally, excessively, exorbitantly, extraordinarily, highly, hugely, immensely, immoderately, inordinately, intensely, markedly, mortally, notably, over, overly, overmuch, parlous, plenty, powerful, prohibitively, quite, radically, rarely, remarkably, severely, strikingly, surpassingly, terribly, terrifically, to nth degree*, too, too much*, totally, ultra*, uncommonly, unduly, unusually, utterly, very*, violently, vitally; CONCEPTS 569,771,781 —*Ant.* mildly, moderately

extremist [*n*] *person zealous about a belief* agitator, die-hard, fanatic, radical, revolutionary, revolutionist, ultra, ultraist, zealot; CONCEPTS 359,423 —*Ant.* conservative, moderate

extremity [*n1*] *ultimate; limit* acme, acuteness, adversity, apex, apogee, border, bound, boundary, brim, brink, butt, climax, consummation, crisis, depth, dire straits, disaster, edge, end, excess, extreme, extremes, frontier, height, last, margin, maximum, nadir, outside, pinnacle, plight, pole, remote, rim, setback, terminal, termination, terminus, tip, top, trouble, verge, vertex, zenith; CONCEPTS 484,706,745,836

extremity [*n2*] *animate being's appendage* backside, finger, flipper, foot, hand, leg, limb, paw, posterior, toe; CONCEPT 392

extricate [*v*] *get out of a situation; relieve of responsibility* bail out*, clear, deliver, detach, difference, differentiate, disburden, discumber, disembarrass, disencumber, disengage, disentangle, disinvolve, extract, free, get off the hook*, get out from under*, let go, let off*, liberate, loose, loosen, pull out, release, remove, rescue, resolve, save one's neck*, separate, sever, untie, withdraw, wriggle out of*; CONCEPTS 102,127 —*Ant.* entangle, involve

extrinsic [*adj*] *foreign* acquired, alien, exotic, exterior, external, extraneous, gained, imported, outer, outside, outward, superficial; CONCEPT 549 —*Ant.* essential, integral, interior, intrinsic, necessary

extrovert [*n*] *sociable person* character*,

exhibitionist, gregarious person, life of the party*, showboat*, show-off*; CONCEPT *423* —*Ant.* introvert

extroverted |*adj*| *outgoing* congenial, cordial, demonstrative, friendly, gregarious, personable, sociable, social, unreserved; CONCEPT *404*

extrude |*v*| *force out* boot*, chase, dismiss, eject, evict, expel, kick out, press, project, squeeze*, throw out, thrust; CONCEPTS *208,222*

exuberance |*n1*| *energy, enthusiasm* abandon, animation, ardor, bounce, buoyancy, cheerfulness, eagerness, ebullience, effervescence, excitement, exhilaration, fervor, friskiness, gayness, get up and go*, high spirits, juice*, life, liveliness, pep, pepper*, spirit, sprightliness, vigor, vitality, zap*, zest*, zip*; CONCEPT *633* —*Ant.* discouragement, lifelessness

exuberance |*n2*| *profusion* abundance, affluence, copiousness, effusiveness, exaggeration, excessiveness, fulsomeness, lavishness, lushness, luxuriance, plenitude, plenty, prodigality, richness, superabundance, superfluity, teemingness; CONCEPTS *710,767* —*Ant.* insufficiency, lack, need, want

exuberant |*adj1*| *energetic, enthusiastic* animated, ardent, bouncy, brash, buoyant, cheerful, chipper, eager, ebullient, effervescent, elated, excited, exhilarated, feeling one's oats*, frolicsome, gay, high-spirited, lively, passionate, sparkling, spirited, sprightly, vigorous, vivacious, zappy*, zestful, zingy*, zippy*; CONCEPT *401* —*Ant.* depressed, discouraged, lifeless, unenthusiastic, unexcited

exuberant |*adj2*| *profuse* abundant, affluent, copious, diffuse, effusive, exaggerated, excessive, fecund, fertile, fruitful, fulsome, lavish, lush, luxuriant, opulent, overdone, overflowing, plenteous, plentiful, prodigal, prolific, rampant, rich, riotous, superabundant, superfluous, teeming; CONCEPT *781* —*Ant.* insufficient, lacking, needing, wanting

exude |*v*| *display, emit* bleed, discharge, emanate, evacuate, excrete, exhibit, expel, flow out, give forth, give off, issue, leak, manifest, ooze, pass, percolate, radiate, secrete, seep, show, sweat, throw off, trickle, weep; CONCEPTS *118,179* —*Ant.* conceal, hide

exult |*v1*| *be joyful* be delighted, be elated, be happy, be in high spirits*, be jubilant, be overjoyed, celebrate, cheer, jubilate, jump for joy*, make merry*, rejoice; CONCEPTS *32,266* —*Ant.* be sad, grieve, mourn

exult |*v2*| *boast* bluster, brag, bully, crow, gloat, glory, revel, show off, take delight in*, triumph, vaunt; CONCEPT *49* —*Ant.* conceal, hide

exultant |*adj*| *very happy* blown away*, delighted, ecstatic, elated, exulting, flipping, flushed, flying, gleeful, high, joyful, joyous, jubilant, overjoyed, rejoicing, reveling, transported, triumphant, turned on*, wowed*; CONCEPT *403* —*Ant.* depressed, discouraged, sad, sorrowful, unhappy

exultation |*n*| *celebration, reveling* crowing, delight, elation, glee, gloating, glory, happiness, high spirits, joy, joyousness, jubilance, jubilation, merriment, rejoicing, satisfaction, transport, triumph; CONCEPTS *32,410* —*Ant.* discouragement

eye |*n1*| *judgment, opinion* appreciation, belief, conviction, discernment, discrimination, eagle eye*, feeling, mind, perception, persuasion, point of view, recognition, scrutiny, sentiment, surveillance, tab, taste, view, viewpoint, watch; CONCEPTS *411,689*

eye |*n2*| *optical organ of an animate being* baby blue*, blinder*, eyeball, headlight*, lamp*, ocular, oculus, optic, peeper*, pie*; CONCEPT *392*

eye |*v*| *gaze at, scrutinize* check out, consider, contemplate, eyeball*, gape, give the eye*, glance at, have a look, inspect, keep eagle eye on*, leer, look at, ogle, peruse, regard, rubberneck*, scan, size up*, stare at, study, survey, take a look, take in, view, watch; CONCEPTS *17,623,626* —*Ant.* look away

eye-catching |*adj*| *noticeable* attractive, beautiful, can't miss it*, conspicuous, gorgeous, manifest, obvious, showy, spectacular, striking, stunning; CONCEPTS *529,579*

eyeful |*n*| *spectacular-looking person* beauty, dazzler*, knockout*, looker, lovely, show, spectacle, stunner*, vision; CONCEPT *424* —*Ant.* eyesore

eyeglasses |*n*| *glasses* bifocals, cheaters*, contact lenses, contacts, goggles, lorgnette, monocle, pair of glasses, pince-nez, reading glasses, shades, specs*, spectacles, sunglasses, trifocals; CONCEPT *446*

eyesight |*n*| *vision* optics, perceiving, perception, range of view, seeing, sight, view; CONCEPT *629*

eyesore |*n*| *mess, ugliness* atrocity, blemish, blight, blot, blot on landscape*, deformity, disfigurement, disgrace, distortion, dump, horror, monstrosity, sight, ugly thing; CONCEPTS *674,716* —*Ant.* beauty, eyeful, sight

eyewitness |*n*| *person who sees an event occur* beholder, bystander, looker-on, observer, onlooker, passer-by, spectator, viewer, watcher, witness; CONCEPT *423*

F

fable |*n*| *fantasy, story* allegory, apologue, bestiary, bunk*, crock*, fabrication, fairy story, fairy tale, falsehood, fantasy, fib, fiction, figment, fish story*, hogwash*, invention, legend, lie, myth, old chestnut*, old saw*, one for the birds*, parable, romance, tale, tall story, untruth, white lie*, whopper*, yarn; CONCEPT *282* —*Ant.* truth

fabled |*adj*| *legendary* fabulous, famed, famous, fanciful, fictional, mythical, mythological, storied, unreal; CONCEPT *568* —*Ant.* unheard of, unknown

fabric |*n1*| *cloth, material* bolt, fiber, goods, stuff, textile, texture, web; CONCEPT *473*

fabric |*n2*| *structure* building, consistency, constitution, construction, foundation, frame, framework, infrastructure, make-up, mold, organization, shape, substance, texture; CONCEPTS *733,757*

fabricate |*v1*| *manufacture* assemble, brainstorm, build, cobble up*, compose, concoct, construct, contrive, cook up*, create, devise, dream up, erect, fashion, fit together, form, formulate, frame, head trip*, invent, join, knock together*, make, make up, mix,

organize, piece together, prefab*, produce,
put together, shape, structure, think up, throw
together*, throw up*, turn out, whip up*,
whomp up*; CONCEPTS 36,173,205,251
—*Ant.* break, demolish, destroy, ruin, wreck

fabricate [v2] *falsify, make up a story* coin,
concoct, contrive, counterfeit, devise, fake,
feign, fib, forge, form, fudge*, invent, jive*, lie,
make like*, misrepresent, pretend, prevaricate,
trump up*; CONCEPTS 58,63 —*Ant.* tell truth

fabrication [n1] *lie* artifact, concoction, deceit,
fable, fairy story*, fake*, falsehood, fib, fiction,
figment, forgery, hogwash*, invention, jazz*,
jive*, line*, myth, opus, smoke*, song and
dance*, untruth, work, yarn; CONCEPTS 63,278
—*Ant.* truth

fabrication [n2] *something manufactured*
assemblage, assembly, building, construction,
creation, erection, product, production;
CONCEPTS 205,260,338

fabulous [adj] *amazing, wonderful* 10*, A-1*,
aces*, A-OK*, astonishing, astounding, awesome, best, breathtaking, cool*, doozie*, extravagant, fab*, fantastic, fictitious, first-class,
greatest, groovy*, immense, inconceivable,
incredible, legendary, marvelous, mind-
blowing*, out-of-sight*, out-of-this-world*,
outrageous, peachy*, phenomenal, primo*,
prodigious, rad*, remarkable, spectacular,
striking, stupendous, super, superb, terrific,
top drawer*, tops*, turn-on*, unbelievable,
unreal, wicked*; CONCEPTS 529,572
—*Ant.* common, normal, ordinary, simple

facade [n] *appearance, often deceptive* beard*,
bluff, color, disguise, exterior, face, fake, false
colors*, false front*, front, frontage, guise,
look, mask, phony, pretense, put-on*, semblance, show, veneer, window dressing*;
CONCEPT 716 —*Ant.* character, personality

face [n1] *front of something; expression, exterior*
air, appearance, aspect, cast, clock, countenance,
dial*, disguise, display, facet, features, finish*,
frontage*, frontal, frontispiece, frown, glower,
grimace, guise, kisser*, light*, lineaments,
look, makeup, map*, mask, mug*, obverse,
paint*, physiognomy, pout, presentation, profile,
scowl, seeming, semblance, show, showing,
silhouette, simulacrum, smirk, surface, top,
visage; CONCEPTS 484,716,836 —*Ant.* back,
behind, rear

face [n2] *pretense, nerve* air, audacity, boldness,
brass*, cheek*, chutzpah*, cloak, confidence,
cover, disguise, effrontery, facade, false front*,
front, gall, impertinence, impudence, mask,
presumption, semblance, show, veil; CONCEPTS
633,657 —*Ant.* character, personality

face [n3] *authority, status* dignity, honor, image,
prestige, reputation, self-respect, social position, standing; CONCEPT 388

face [v1] *come up against a situation* abide,
accost, affront, allow, bear, beard, be confronted
by, bit the bullet*, brace, brave, brook, challenge, confront, contend, cope with, countenance, court, cross, dare, deal with, defy,
encounter, endure, experience, eyeball*, fight,
fly in face of*, go up against*, grapple with,
make a stand*, meet, oppose, resist, risk, run
into, square off*, stand, stomach*, submit,
suffer, sustain, swallow*, take, take it, take on,

take the bull by the horns*, tell off*, tolerate,
venture, withstand; CONCEPTS 23,35,117
—*Ant.* hide, retreat, run, withdraw

face [v2] *be opposite; look at* be turned toward,
border, confront, front, front onto, gaze, glare,
meet, overlook, stare, watch; CONCEPTS
623,747 —*Ant.* back

face [v3] *put paint or finish on* clad, coat,
cover, decorate, dress, finish, front, level,
line, overlay, plaster, polish, redecorate,
refinish, remodel, sheathe, shingle, side, skin,
smooth, surface, veneer; CONCEPTS 172,202

face-lift [n] *beautification; cosmetic surgery*
new look, nose job, plastic surgery, renovation,
repair, restoration, revival, rhytidectomy;
CONCEPT 162

facet [n] *surface; aspect* angle, appearance,
character, face, feature, front, hand, level,
obverse, part, phase, plane, side, slant, switch,
twist; CONCEPT 835

face the music [v] *face up to* be punished,
bite the bullet*, grin and bear it*, pay the
piper*, swallow the pill*, take one's lumps*,
take one's medicine*; CONCEPT 23

facetious [adj] *tongue-in-cheek, kidding* amusing, blithe, capering, clever, comic, comical,
droll, dry, fanciful, farcical, flip*, flippant, frivolous, funny, gay, humorous, indecorous, ironic,
irreverent, jesting, jocose, jocular, joking, joshing, laughable, ludicrous, merry, not serious,
playful, pleasant, pulling one's leg*, punning,
putting one on*, ridiculous, salty, sarcastic,
satirical, smart, sportive, sprightly, waggish,
whimsical, wisecracking, witty, wry; CONCEPT
267 —*Ant.* formal, grave, serious, unfunny

facile [adj] *easy; easily mastered* accomplished,
adept, adroit, apparent, articulate, breeze, child's
play*, cursory, deft, dexterous, easy as pie*,
effortless, fast talk*, flip*, fluent, glib, hasty,
light, obvious, picnic*, practiced, proficient,
pushover*, quick, ready, shallow, simple, skillful, slick*, smooth, superficial, uncomplicated,
untroublesome, voluble; CONCEPTS 527,565
—*Ant.* arduous, complicated, confusing, difficult, hard, involved, laborious, profound

facilitate [v] *assist the progress of* aid, ease,
expedite, forward, further, grease the wheels*,
hand-carry*, help, make easy, open doors*,
promote, run interference for*, simplify,
smooth, speed, speed up, walk through*;
CONCEPTS 110,242 —*Ant.* block, check, delay,
detain, hinder, prohibit, stop

facility [n1] *ease; ability* address, adroitness,
aptitude, bent, child's play*, competence, dexterity, efficiency, effortlessness, expertness,
fluency, knack, leaning, lightness, poise, proficiency, propensity, quickness, readiness, skill,
skillfulness, smoothness, smooth sailing*,
spontaneity, tact, turn, wit; CONCEPTS 630,666
—*Ant.* difficulty, hardness

facility [n2] *convenience* accommodation,
advantage, aid, amenity, appliance, comfort,
equipment, fitting, material, means, opportunity, resource, tool; CONCEPTS 693,712
—*Ant.* difficulty, hardness

facsimile [n] *reproduction* carbon, carbon
copy*, chip off old block*, clone, copy, copycat*, dead ringer*, ditto*, double, dupe*, duplicate, knock-off*, likeness, look-alike, mimeo,

miniature, mirror, photocopy, photostat, print, reduplication, replica, replication, repro*, ringer*, spitting image*, stat, transcript, twin, Xerox*; CONCEPTS 271,625,716 —Ant. original

fact [n1] *verifiable truth; reality* actuality, appearance, authenticity, basis, bottom line*, brass tacks*, case, certainty, certitude, concrete happening, dope*, evidence, experience, genuineness, gospel, gospel truth*, how it is*, intelligence, law, like it is*, matter*, naked truth*, palpability, permanence, scene, scripture, solidity, stability, substantiality, verity, what's what*; CONCEPTS 688,725 —Ant. fabrication, lie

fact [n2] *event; detail of action* accomplishment, act, action, actuality, adventure, affair, being, case, circumstance, conception, consideration, construction, creation, data, datum, deed, entity, episode, evidence, experience, factor, fait accompli, feature, happening, incident, information, item, manifestation, occurrence, organism, particular, performance, phenomenon, point, proceeding, specific, statistic, transaction, truism; CONCEPTS 2,274,433 —Ant. lie

faction [n1] *group sharing a belief or cause* band, bloc, bunch, cabal, camp, caucus, cell, circle, clan, clique, club, coalition, combination, combine, combo, concern, conclave, confederacy, conspiracy, contingent, coterie, crew, crowd, design, division, entente, gang, guild, insiders, intrigue, junta, knot, lobby, machine, minority, mob, network, offshoot, outfit, partnership, party, pressure group, ring, schism, sect, section, sector, set, side, splinter group, team, unit, wing; CONCEPTS 301,387 —Ant. entirety, total, whole

faction [n2] *conflict, strife* disagreement, discord, disharmony, dissension, disunity, division, divisiveness, friction, infighting, quarrelsomeness, rebellion, sedition, tumult, turbulence; CONCEPTS 106,684 —Ant. agreement, conformity, peace, unity

factious [adj] *conflicting, warring* alienated, belligerent, contending, contentious, contumacious, disaffected, disputatious, dissident, divisive, estranged, fighting, hostile, insubordinate, insurgent, insurrectionary, litigious, malcontent, mutinous, partisan, quarrelsome, rebellious, refractory, rival, sectarian, seditious, troublemaking, tumultous/tumultuous, turbulent; CONCEPT 542 —Ant. agreeing, cooperating, cooperative, peaceful, united

factor [n] *determinant* agency, agent, aid, antecedent, aspect, board, cause, circumstance, component, consideration, constituent, element, fixin's*, influence, ingredient, instrument, instrumentality, item, makin's*, means, part, part and parcel*, point, portion, thing; CONCEPTS 831,835

factory [n] *manufacturing plant* branch, cooperative, firm, forge, foundry, industry, laboratory, machine shop, manufactory, mill, mint, salt mines*, shop, sweatshop*, warehouse, workroom, works, workshop; CONCEPTS 439,441,449

factotum [n] *handyperson* general employee, jack of all trades, man/girl Friday, Mr/Ms Fixit, odd-job person, personal assistant; CONCEPT 348

facts [n] *inside information* bottom line*, brass tacks*, certainty, clue, cue, data, details, dope*, gospel, info*, inside dope*, like it is*, lowdown*, numbers, poop*, reality, scoop*, score*, story, whole story*; CONCEPT 274 —Ant. lies

factual [adj] *real, correct* absolute, accurate, actual, authentic, card-carrying*, certain, circumstantial, close, credible, descriptive, exact, faithful, genuine, hard, kosher*, legit*, legitimate, literal, objective, on the level*, positive, precise, righteous, specific, straight from horse's mouth*, sure, sure-enough*, true, true-to-life*, unadorned, unbiased, undoubted, unquestionable, valid, veritable; CONCEPTS 535,582 —Ant. biased, false, imprecise, incorrect, unfactual, untruthful

faculty [n1] *ability, skill* adroitness, aptitude, aptness, bent, capability, capacity, cleverness, dexterity, facility, flair, forte, genius, gift, instinct, intelligence, knack, knowing way around*, leaning, nose*, peculiarity, penchant, pistol*, power, predilection, proclivity, propensity, property, quality, readiness, reason, right stuff*, sense, strength, talent, turn, what it takes*, wits; CONCEPT 630 —Ant. inability, incompetence, ineptness, lack, need

faculty [n2] *teachers in educational institution* academics, advisers, body, clinic, college, corps, department, employees, institute, instructors, lecturers, literati, mentors, organization, pedagogues, personnel, professoriate, professors, profs*, researchers, scholars, society, staff, tutors, university, workers; CONCEPTS 288,350 —Ant. students

fad [n] *craze* affectation, amusement, caprice, chic, conceit, cry, custom, dernier cri, eccentricity, fancy, fantasy, fashion, fool notion*, frivolity, furor, hobby, humor, in, innovation, in thing*, kick, kink, latest word*, mania, mode, newest wrinkle*, new look*, passing fancy*, passion, quirk, rage, sport, style, thing, trend, vagary, vogue, whim, whimsy, wrinkle; CONCEPT 655 —Ant. standard, tradition

fade [v1] *lose color* achromatize, become colorless, blanch, bleach, blench, clear, decolorize, dim, disappear, discolor, dissolve, dull, etiolate, evanish, evaporate, grow dim, lose brightness, lose luster, muddy, neutralize, pale, tarnish, tone down, vanish, wash out; CONCEPTS 250,469,622 —Ant. brighten, color, sharpen, strengthen

fade [v2] *dwindle, die out* abate, attenuate, clear, decline, deliquesce, deteriorate, die away, die on vine*, dim, diminish, disappear, disperse, dissolve, droop, ebb, etiolate, evanesce, evanish, evaporate, fag out*, fail, fall, flag, fold, hush, languish, lessen, melt, melt away, moderate, perish, peter out*, poop out*, quiet, rarefy, shrivel, sink, slack off*, taper, thin, tire, tucker out*, vanish, wane, waste away, weaken, wilt, wither; CONCEPTS 105,698 —Ant. enhance, improve, recover, strengthen

faded [adj] *bleached; used* achromatic, ashen, bedraggled, dim, dingy, discolored, dull, etiolated, indistinct, lackluster, lusterless, murky, not shiny, pale, pallid, run-down, seedy, shabby, shopworn, tacky, tattered, threadbare, tired, wan, washed out, wasted, worn; CONCEPTS 560,617,618 —Ant. brightened, colored, strengthened

fail [v1] *be unsuccessful* abort, backslide, back wrong horse*, be defeated, be demoted, be found lacking*, be in vain*, be ruined, blunder, break down, come to naught, come to nothing, decline, deteriorate, fall, fall flat*, fall short*, fall through*, fizzle, flop, flounder, fold, founder, go astray*, go down*, go downhill*, go down swinging*, go up in smoke*, go wrong, hit bottom*, hit the skids*, lose control, lose out, lose status, meet with disaster, miscarry, miss, miss the boat*, play into, run aground*, slip, turn out badly; CONCEPT 699 —*Ant.* accomplish, achieve, earn, gain, merit, obtain, prosper, reach, succeed, win

fail [v2] *abandon, forsake* abort, back out, blink, break one's word, desert, disappoint, discount, disregard, fault, forget, funk, go astray, ignore, let down, miscarry, neglect, omit, overlook, overpass, slight, slip; CONCEPTS 7,19 —*Ant.* capture, complete, deliver, finish, obtain, procure

fail [v3] *lose money* be cleaned out*, become insolvent, be in arrears, be ruined, be taken to the cleaners*, break, close, close down*, close one's doors*, crash, defalcate, default, dishonor, drop, drop a bundle*, end, finish, fold, go bankrupt, go belly up*, go broke*, go bust*, go into chapter 11*, go out of business*, go to the wall*, go under*, go up*, lose big*, lose one's shirt*, overdraw, repudiate, terminate; CONCEPTS 330,335 —*Ant.* earn, gain, obtain, win

failing [adj] *not well, weak* declining, defeated, deficient, faint, feeble, inadequate, insufficient, scant, scanty, scarce, short, shy, unavailing, unprosperous, unsuccessful, insufficient, unthriving, vain, wanting; CONCEPTS 485,489 —*Ant.* healthy, ok, rebounding, strong, thriving, well

failing [n] *lapse, shortcoming* blind spot*, defect, deficiency, drawback, error, failure, fault, flaw, foible, frailty, imperfection, infirmity, miscarriage, misfortune, vice, weakness, weak point*; CONCEPTS 411,674 —*Ant.* advantage, strength, strong point

fail-safe [adj] *guaranteed not to fail* confident, covered, foolproof, protected, reliable, reliant, safeguarded, secure, sound, sure; CONCEPTS 535,542,544

failure [n1] *lack of success* abortion, bankruptcy, bomb, botch*, breakdown, bungle*, bust, checkmate, collapse, decay, decline, defeat, deficiency, deficit, deterioration, downfall, failing, false step*, faux pas, fiasco, flash in the pan*, flop*, frustration, implosion, inadequacy, lead balloon*, lemon*, loser, loss, mess, misadventure, miscarriage, misstep, nonperformance, nonsuccess, overthrow, rout, rupture, sinking ship*, stalemate, stoppage, total loss, turkey*, washout*, wreck; CONCEPTS 699,706 —*Ant.* accomplishment, achievement, attainment, earnings, gain, merit, success, win

failure [n2] *person who does not succeed* also-ran*, bankrupt, beat*, born loser*, bum, castaway, deadbeat, defaulter, derelict, disappointment, dud*, flop, good-for-nothing*, has-been, incompetent, insolvent, loafer, loser, lumpy*, might-have-been*, moocher*, nobody, no-good, nonperformer, prodigal, turkey*, underachiever, washout*; CONCEPTS 412,423 —*Ant.* achiever, success

faint [adj1] *having little effect on senses* aside, bated, bland, bleached, blurred, breathless,

deadened, deep, delicate, dim, distant, dull, dusty, faded, faltering, far-off, feeble, gentle, hazy, hoarse, hushed, ill-defined, imperceptible, inaudible, indistinct, lenient, light, low, low-pitched, mild, moderate, muffled, murmuring, muted, muttering, obscure, out of earshot*, padded, pale, piano, quiet, remote, shadowy, slight, smooth, soft, softened, soothing, stifled, subdued, tenuous, thin, unclear, vague, wan, weak, whispered; CONCEPTS 537,594,617 —*Ant.* clear, distinct, heavy, loud, strong

faint [adj2] *weak* delicate, dizzy, drooping, enervated, exhausted, faltering, fatigued, feeble, fragile, languid, lethargic, lightheaded, slight, tender, unenthusiastic, woozy; CONCEPTS 314,485 —*Ant.* bold, brave, courageous, resolute, strong

faint [n] *unconsciousness* blackout, collapse, dizziness, grayout, insensibility, knockout, stupor, swoon, syncope, vertigo; CONCEPTS 308,316 —*Ant.* consciousness

faint [v] *lose consciousness* become unconscious, be overcome, black out, collapse, drop, fade, fail, fall, flicker, go out like light*, keel over, languish, pass out, succumb, swoon, weaken; CONCEPTS 303,308

fainthearted [adj] *timid* afraid, cowardly, cowed, cowering, fearful, frightened, gutless, having cold feet*, intimidated, lily-livered*, meek, mousy, spineless, unassertive, weak, wimpy*, yellow*; CONCEPT 401

fair [adj1] *impartial, unprejudiced* aboveboard, benevolent, blameless, candid, civil, clean, courteous, decent, disinterested, dispassionate, equal, equitable, even-handed, frank, generous, good, honest, honorable, impartial, just, lawful, legitimate, moderate, nonpartisan, objective, on the level*, on up-and-up*, open, pious, praiseworthy, principled, proper, reasonable, respectable, righteous, scrupulous, sincere, square, straight, straightforward, temperate, trustworthy, unbiased, uncolored, uncorrupted, upright, virtuous; CONCEPT 542 —*Ant.* biased, partial, prejudiced, unfair, unjust, unreasonable

fair [adj2] *light-complexioned, light-haired* argent, blanched, bleached, blond, blonde, chalky, colorless, creamy, faded, fair-haired, fair-skinned, flaxen-haired, light, milky, neutral, pale, pale-faced, pallid, pearly, sallow, silvery, snowy, tow-haired, tow-headed, white, whitish; CONCEPTS 406,618 —*Ant.* dark

fair [adj3] *mediocre, satisfactory* adequate, all right, average, common, commonplace, decent, fairish, indifferent, intermediate, mean, medium, middling, moderate, not bad*, okay, ordinary, passable, pretty good*, reasonable, respectable, satisfactory, so-so*, tolerable, up to standard*, usual; CONCEPT 530

fair [adj4] *beautiful* attractive, beauteous, bonny, charming, chaste, comely, dainty, delicate, enchanting, exquisite, good-looking, handsome, lovely, pretty, pulchritudinous, pure; CONCEPT 579 —*Ant.* repulsive, ugly

fair [adj5] *bright, cloudless (weather)* balmy, calm, clarion, clear, clement, dry, favorable, fine, mild, placid, pleasant, pretty, rainless, smiling, sunny, sunshiny, tranquil, unclouded, undarkened, unthreatening; CONCEPT 525 —*Ant.* cloudy, inclement, rainy, stormy

fair [n] *exposition, carnival* bazaar, celebration, centennial, display, exhibit, exhibition, expo*, festival, fete, gala, market, observance, occasion, pageant, show, spectacle; CONCEPTS 377,386

fairly [adv1] *somewhat* adequately, averagely, enough, kind of, moderately, more or less, passably, pretty well, quite, rather, ratherish, reasonably, some, something, sort of, so-so*, tolerably; CONCEPT 786

fairly [adv2] *justly* deservedly, equitably, honestly, honorably, impartially, objectively, properly, reasonably, without favor, without fear; CONCEPT 542 —*Ant.* unfairly, unjustly

fairness [n] *justice* candor, charitableness, charity, civility, consideration, courtesy, decency, decorum, disinterestedness, due, duty, equitableness, equity, exactitude, fair-mindedness, fair shake*, give and take*, good faith, goodness, honesty, honor, humanity, impartiality, integrity, justness, legitimacy, moderation, open-mindedness, propriety, rationality, reasonableness, right, righteousness, rightfulness, rightness, seemliness, square deal*, suitability, tolerance, truth, uprightness, veracity; CONCEPTS 645,657 —*Ant.* inequity, injustice, partiality, unfairness, wrong

fairy [n] *supernatural being* bogie, brownie, elf, enchanter, fay, genie, gnome, goblin, gremlin, hob, imp, leprechaun, mermaid, nisse, nymph, pixie, puck, siren, spirit, sprite, sylph; CONCEPT 370

fait accompli [n] *done deed* accomplished fact, certainty, fact of life, hard facts, irreversible accomplishment, irreversible act, irreversible truth, matter of fact, reality, undeniable fact; CONCEPTS 689,725

faith [n1] *trust in something* acceptance, allegiance, assent, assurance, belief, certainty, certitude, confidence, constancy, conviction, credence, credit, credulity, dependence, faithfulness, fealty, fidelity, hope, loyalty, reliance, stock, store, sureness, surety, troth, truth, truthfulness; CONCEPT 689 —*Ant.* disbelief, distrust, doubt, misgiving, skepticism, suspicion

faith [n2] *belief in a higher being; community of believers* canon, church, communion, confession, connection, conviction, credo, creed, cult, denomination, doctrine, dogma, doxy, gospel, orthodoxy, persuasion, piety, piousness, principle, profession, religion, revelation, sect, teaching, tenet, theism, theology, worship; CONCEPTS 368,689 —*Ant.* agnosticism, denial, doubt, rejection, skepticism, unbelief

faithful [adj1] *loyal, reliable* affectionate, allegiant, ardent, attached, behind one, circumspect, confiding, conscientious, constant, dependable, devoted, dutiful, dyed-in-the-wool*, enduring, fast, firm, genuine, hard-core*, honest, honorable, incorruptible, loving, obedient, on the level*, patriotic, resolute, scrupulous, sincere, staunch, steadfast, steady, straight, string along with*, sure, tried, tried and true*, true, true-blue*, trustworthy, trusty, truthful, unchanging, unswerving, unwavering, upright, veracious; CONCEPTS 401,545 —*Ant.* dishonest, disloyal, false, inconstant, treacherous, unfaithful, unreliable, untrue

faithful [adj2] *authentic, accurate* close, credible, exact, just, lifelike, precise, right, similar, strict, true, trusty, undistorted, veracious, veridical; CONCEPTS 487,573 —*Ant.* different, false, inaccurate, inexact, uncertain

faithfulness [n] *devotion* adherence, adhesion, allegiance, ardor, attachment, care, constancy, dependability, duty, fealty, fidelity, loyalty, piety, trustworthiness, truth; CONCEPTS 633,645,689 —*Ant.* dishonesty, disloyalty, falseness, inconstancy, treachery

faithless [adj] *disloyal* capricious, changeable, changeful, cheating, deceitful, dishonest, double-crossing*, double-dealing*, doubting, dubious, false, fickle, fluctuating, inconstant, perfidious, recreant, skeptical, traitorous, treacherous, two-faced*, two-timing*, unbelieving, unconverted, unfaithful, unloyal, unreliable, unstable, untrue, untrustworthy, untruthful, wavering; CONCEPTS 401,545 —*Ant.* believing, faithful, constant, loyal, reliable, true

faithlessness [n] *disloyalty* betrayal, disbelief, dishonesty, doubt, falseness, fickleness, fraud, inconstancy, infidelity, perfidiousness, perfidy, skepticism, treacherousness, treachery, treason, unfaithfulness; CONCEPTS 633,645 —*Ant.* belief, faithfulness, constancy, loyalty

fake [adj] *false, imitation* affected, artificial, assumed, bogus, concocted, counterfeit, fabricated, fictitious, forged, fraudulent, invented, make-believe, mock, phony, pretended, pseudo*, reproduction, sham, simulated, spurious; CONCEPTS 401,582 —*Ant.* genuine, original, real, true, truthful

fake [n] *imposter, copy* actor, bluffer, charlatan, cheat, counterfeit, deception, fabrication, faker, flimflam*, forgery, four-flusher*, fraud, gold brick*, hoax, imitation, imposition, imposture, junque, make-believe, mountebank, phony, plant*, pretender, pretense, pseudo*, put-on, reproduction, scam, sham*, sleight, spoof, swindle, trick; CONCEPTS 260,412 —*Ant.* original, reality

fake [v] *pretend* act, affect, assume, bluff, copy, counterfeit, disguise, dissimulate, fabricate, feign, forge, put on, put on an act*, sham, simulate, spoof; CONCEPT 59

falderal [n] *folderol, foolishness* absurdity, baloney, bunk*, craziness, garbage, gibberish, gobbledygook*, horse feathers*, lunacy, nonsense, stupidity, twaddle; CONCEPT 633

fall [n1] *descent; lowering* abatement, belly flop*, cut, decline, declivity, decrease, diminution, dip, dive, downgrade, downward slope, drop, dwindling, ebb, falling off, header*, incline, lapse, lessening, nose dive*, plummet, plunge, pratfall*, recession, reduction, slant, slip, slope, slump, spill, tumble; CONCEPTS 152,181,776 —*Ant.* ascent, climb, rise, scaling

fall [n2] *defeat, overthrow* abasement, breakdown, capitulation, collapse, death, degradation, destruction, diminution, disaster, dive, downfall, drop, failure, humiliation, loss, resignation, ruin, surrender, tumble; CONCEPTS 116,230,674,699

fall [v1] *descend; become lower* abate, backslide, be precipitated, break down, buckle, cascade, cave in, collapse, crash, decline, decrease, depreciate, diminish, dip, dive, drag,

droop, drop down, dwindle, ease, ebb, flag,
flop, fold up, go down, gravitate, hit the dirt*,
keel over, land, lapse, lessen, nose-dive, pitch,
plummet, plunge, recede, regress, relapse,
settle, sink, slip, slope, slump, spin, stumble,
subside, take a header*, tip over, topple, totter,
trail, trip, tumble, wane; CONCEPTS *152,181,776*
—*Ant.* ascend, climb, go up, rise, scale

fall [v2] *be overthrown by an enemy; surrender*
back down, be casualty, be destroyed, be killed,
be lost, bend, be taken, capitulate, defer to, die,
drop, eat dirt*, fall to pieces*, give in, give up,
give way, go down, go under, lie down, obey,
pass into enemy hands*, perish, resign, slump,
submit, succumb, yield; CONCEPTS *116,699*
—*Ant.* advance, attain, overcome, overthrow,
reach, win

fall [v3] *happen* arrive, become, befall, chance,
come about, come to pass, occur, take place;
CONCEPT *119*

fallacious [adj] *false, wrong* beguiling, deceiving, deceptive, deluding, delusive, delusory,
erroneous, fictitious, fishy*, fraudulent, illogical, illusory, incorrect, invalid, irrational, mad,
misleading, mistaken, off*, phony, reasonless,
sophistic, sophistical, spurious, unfounded,
ungrounded, unreal, unreasonable, unreasoned,
unsound, untrue, way off*; CONCEPTS
267,570,582 —*Ant.* correct, real, true, truthful

fallacy [n] *illusion, misconception* aberration,
ambiguity, artifice, bias, casuistry, cavil, deceit,
deception, deceptiveness, delusion, deviation,
elusion, equivocation, erratum, erroneousness,
error, evasion, falsehood, faultiness, flaw,
heresy, illogicality, inconsistency, inexactness,
invalidity, misapprehension, miscalculation,
misconstrue, misinterpretation, mistake, non
sequitur, notion, paradox, perversion, preconception, prejudice, quibbling, quirk, solecism,
sophism, sophistry, speciousness, subterfuge,
untruth; CONCEPTS *410,689,725* —*Ant.* certainty, evidence, fact, honesty, reality, right,
surety, truth

fall back [v] *retreat* back, draw back, give
back, recede, recoil, retire, retrocede, retrograde, surrender, withdraw, yield; CONCEPT *195*
—*Ant.* forge, forward, progress

fallen [adj1] *disgraced, ruined* collapsed,
decayed, dishonored, immoral, loose, ruinous,
shaken, shamed, sinful, unchaste; CONCEPTS
539,555 —*Ant.* honorable, honored, lauded

fallen [adj2] *dead* casualty, killed, lost,
perished, slain, slaughtered; CONCEPT *539*

fall for [v] *become infatuated with* desire, fall
in love with, flip over, go head over heels*,
lose one's head over*, succumb; CONCEPT *32*
—*Ant.* repulse

fall guy [n] *scapegoat* chopping block, dupe,
patsy, pigeon, sacrifice, sap, schmuck, stooge,
sucker, victim, whipping boy; CONCEPT *412*

fallible [adj] *able or prone to err* careless,
deceptive, errable, errant, erring, faulty, frail,
heedless, human, ignorant, imperfect, in question, liable, mortal, questionable, uncertain,
unreliable, untrustworthy, weak; CONCEPT
542 —*Ant.* certain, correct, definite, infallible,
perfect, reliable, strong, sure, unerring

falling-out [n] *disagreement* altercation, argument, clash, dispute, exchange, feud, fight,

friction, misunderstanding, quarrel; CONCEPTS
46,388

fall out [v1] *argue* altercate, bicker, clash,
differ, disagree, fight, quarrel, spar, squabble;
CONCEPT *46* —*Ant.* agree, concur

fall out [v2] *come to pass* befall, chance,
happen, occur, result, take place, turn out;
CONCEPT *4*

fallow [adj] *inactive* dormant, idle, inert,
neglected, quiescent, resting, slack, uncultivated, undeveloped, unplanted, unplowed,
unproductive, unseeded, untilled, unused,
vacant, virgin; CONCEPTS *485,560* —*Ant.*
active, cultivated, developed, used

fall to [v] *set about doing* apply oneself to,
begin, be up to, buckle down*, commence,
jump in, pitch in*, start, undertake, wade
into*; CONCEPTS *100,221* —*Ant.* be idle,
forget, ignore, laze, neglect

false [adj1] *wrong, made up* apocryphal, beguiling, bogus, casuistic, concocted, contrary to
fact, cooked-up*, counterfactual, deceitful,
deceiving, delusive, dishonest, distorted, erroneous, ersatz*, fake, fallacious, fanciful, faulty,
fictitious, fishy, fraudulent, illusive, imaginary,
improper, inaccurate, incorrect, inexact, invalid,
lying, mendacious, misleading, misrepresenta-
tive, mistaken, off the mark*, phony, sham,
sophistical, specious, spurious, trumped up*,
unfounded, unreal, unsound, untrue, untruthful;
CONCEPTS *267,570,582* —*Ant.* accurate, actual,
correct, factual, genuine, known, precise, real,
right, substantiated, true, valid

false [adj2] *dishonest, hypocritical* apostate,
base, beguiling, canting, corrupt, crooked,
deceitful, deceiving, deceptive, deluding,
delusive, devious, dishonorable, disloyal,
double-dealing*, duplicitous, faithless, false-
hearted, forsworn, foul, lying, malevolent,
malicious, mean, misleading, mythomaniac,
perfidious, perjured, rascally, recreant, renegade, scoundrelly, traitorous, treacherous, treasonable, two-faced*, underhanded, unfaithful,
unscrupulous, untrustworthy, venal, villainous,
wicked; CONCEPTS *267,401* —*Ant.* genuine,
honest, just, reliable, right, straight, true, truthful

false [adj3] *fake, counterfeit* adulterated,
alloyed, artificial, assumed, bent, bogus*,
brummagem, bum*, colored, contrived,
copied, crock*, deceptive, disguised, ersatz*,
fabricated, factitious, feigned, fishy*, forged,
framed*, hollow, imitation, made-up, make-
believe, manufactured, meretricious, mock,
ostensible, phony, pretended, pseudo*, seeming, shady, sham*, simulated, snide, so-called*,
spurious, substitute, synthetic, unreal, wrong;
CONCEPT *582* —*Ant.* actual, genuine, real, valid

falsehood [n] *lie* canard, cover-up, deceit, deception, dishonesty, dissimulation, distortion,
equivocation, erroneousness, error, fable, fabrication, fakery, fallaciousness, fallacy, falseness,
falsity, feigning, fib, fibbery, fiction, figment,
fraud, half truth, hogwash*, line, mendacity,
misstatement, perjury, pretense, prevarication,
sham*, story, tale, tall tale*, untruism, untruth,
untruthfulness, whopper*, yarn; CONCEPTS
63,278 —*Ant.* truth

falsely [adv] *deceitfully* basely, behind one's
back*, crookedly, dishonestly, dishonorably,

disloyally, faithlessly, falseheartedly, malevolently, maliciously, perfidiously, roguishly, traitorously, treacherously, underhandedly, unfaithfully, unscrupulously; CONCEPTS 267,401 —Ant. honestly, truthfully

false teeth [n] *dentures* artificial teeth, bridge, choppers*, dental plate, implants, partial, set of teeth; CONCEPT 393

falsies [n] *padded bra* props, Wonderbra™; CONCEPT 451

falsify [v] *alter, misrepresent* adulterate, belie, change, color, con, contort, contradict, contravene, cook, counterfeit, deacon, deceive, deny, distort, doctor, dress up*, embroider, equivocate, exaggerate, fake, fake it, fib, forge, fourflush*, frame up*, garble, gloss, lie, misquote, misstate, palter, pervert, phony up*, prevaricate, promote, put on an act*, salt*, tamper with, traverse, trump up*, twist, warp;CONCEPT 63

falsity [n] *dishonesty, deception* canard, cheating, deceit, deceptiveness, disingenuousness, double-dealing, duplicity, erroneousness, error, faithlessness, fake, fallacy, falsehood, fib, fraud, fraudulence, hypocrisy, inaccuracy, infidelity, insincerity, lie, mendacity, misrepresentation, perfidiousness, perfidy, prevarication, sham, story, tale, treachery, uncandidness, unfaithfulness, unreality, untruth; CONCEPTS 278,645,725 —Ant. honesty, truth, truthfulness

falter [v] *stumble, stutter* be undecided, bobble, break, drop the ball*, flounder, fluctuate, fluff, halt, hem and haw*, hesitate, lurch, quaver, reel, rock, roll, scruple, shake, speak haltingly, stagger, stammer, stub toe*, teeter, topple, totter, tremble, trip up, vacillate, waver, whiffle, wobble; CONCEPTS 18,147,266 —Ant. continue, endure, maintain, persist, remain, stay

fame [n] *celebrity* acclaim, acclamation, account, acknowledgment, character, credit, dignity, distinction, éclat, elevation, eminence, esteem, estimation, exaltation, favor, glory, greatness, heyday, honor, illustriousness, immortality, kudos, laurels, luster, majesty, name, nobility, note, notoriety, place, popularity, position, preeminence, prominence, public esteem, rank, recognition, regard, renown, rep*, report, reputation, repute, splendor, standing, stardom, station, superiority; CONCEPT 388

familiar [adj1] *common, well-known* accustomed, commonplace, conventional, customary, domestic, everyday, frequent, garden variety*, habitual, homespun, household, humble, informal, intimate, known, matter-of-fact, mundane, native, natural, old hat*, ordinary, plain, prosaic, proverbial, recognizable, repeated, routine, simple, stock, unceremonious, unsophisticated, usual, wonted, workaday; CONCEPTS 530,547 —Ant. foreign, new, strange, uncommon, undistinguished, unfamiliar, unknown, unremarkable

familiar [adj2] *knowledgeable* abreast, acquainted, apprised, at home with*, au courant, au fait, aware, cognizant, conscious, conversant, grounded*, informed, in on*, in the know*, introduced, kept posted*, mindful, no stranger to*, plugged in*, savvy, tuned in*, up*, up on*, versant, versed in, well up in*, with it*; CONCEPT 402 —Ant. ignorant, unacquainted, unknowledgeable

familiar [adj3] *friendly, bold* affable, amicable,

buddy-buddy*, chummy*, close, comfortable, confidential, cordial, cozy, dear, easy, forward, free, free-and-easy*, fresh, genial, gracious, impudent, informal, intimate, intrusive, near, neighborly, nervy, obtrusive, officious, open, palsy, palsy-walsy*, presuming, presumptuous, relaxed, sassy*, smart, snug, sociable, thick, tight, unceremonious, unconstrained, unreserved, wise; CONCEPT 555 —Ant. aloof, cold, cool, distant, reserved, unapproachable, unfamiliar, unfriendly

familiarity [n1] *friendliness* acquaintance, acquaintanceship, boldness, closeness, ease, fellowship, forwardness, freedom, freshness, friendship, informality, intimacy, liberty, naturalness, openness, presumption, sociability, unceremoniousness; CONCEPT 388 —Ant. aloofness, cool, distance, frigidity, reserve, unfriendliness

familiarity [n2] *knowledgeableness* acquaintance, awareness, cognition, comprehension, experience, feel, grasp, knowledge, sense, understanding; CONCEPT 409 —Ant. ignorance, unfamiliarity

familiarize [v] *make or become acquainted with, knowledgeable about* accustom, adapt, adjust, awaken to, become adept in, become aware of, break the ice*, bring into use, case*, check out, coach, come to know, condition, enlighten, gain friendship, get in, get lay of land*, get lowdown on*, get together, get to know, get with it*, habituate, inform, instruct, inure, let down hair*, let know, let next to, make conversant, make used to, mix, naturalize, popularize, post, prime, put on to*, school, season, tip off*, train, use, wont; CONCEPTS 15,38

family [n] *kin, offspring; classification* ancestors, ancestry, birth, blood, brood, children, clan, class, descendants, descent, dynasty, extraction, folk, forebears, genealogy, generations, genre, group, heirs and assigns, house, household, inheritance, in-laws, issue, kind, kindred, kith and kin, line, lineage, ménage, network, parentage, pedigree, people, progenitors, progeny, race, relations, relationship, relatives, siblings, strain, subdivision, system, tribe; CONCEPTS 296,378,397

family tree [n] *family history* ancestral tree, ancestry, bloodline, descent, genealogical chart, genealogy, heredity, lineage, pedigree; CONCEPT 296

famine [n] *hunger* dearth, destitution, drought, misery, paucity, poverty, scarcity, starvation, want; CONCEPTS 674,709 —Ant. feast, plenty, stores, supply

famished [adj] *starving* could eat a horse*, dog-hungry*, empty, flying light*, having the munchies*, hollow, hungering, hungry, ravening, ravenous, starved, starved to death*, voracious; CONCEPTS 20,406,546 —Ant. full, sated, satiated, satisfied

famous [adj] *legendary, notable to many* acclaimed, applauded, august, brilliant, celebrated, conspicuous, distinguished, elevated, eminent, exalted, excellent, extraordinary, foremost, glorious, grand, great, honored, illustrious, important, imposing, influential, in limelight*, in spotlight*, leading, lionized, memorable, mighty, much-publicized, noble, noted, noteworthy, notorious, of note, outstanding, peerless, powerful, preeminent, prominent, recognized, remarkable, renowned, reputable, signal, splendid, talked about*, well-known; CONCEPT 568 —*Ant.* inconspicuous, obscure, unknown, unnotable, unremarkable

fan [n1] *blower of air* air conditioner, blade, draft, flabellum, leaf, palm leaf, propeller, thermantidote, vane, ventilator, windmill; CONCEPT 463

fan [n2] *person enthusiastic about an interest* addict, adherent, admirer, aficionado, amateur, buff, devotee, follower, freak*, groupie*, habitué, hound, lover, rooter, supporter, votary, zealot; CONCEPTS 352,366,423

fan [v1] *blow on* aerate, air-condition, air-cool, cool, refresh, ruffle, spread, ventilate, wind, winnow; CONCEPTS 199,208

fan [v2] *provoke* add fuel, agitate, arouse, enkindle, excite, expand, extend, impassion, increase, rouse, stimulate, stir up, whip up, work up; CONCEPT 14

fanatic [n] *person overenthusiastic about an interest* activist, addict, bigot, bug*, crank*, crazy, demon, devotee, enthusiast, extremist, fiend*, fool, freak, maniac, militant, monomaniac, nut*, radical, ultraist, visionary, zealot; CONCEPTS 352,359,366

fanatical [adj] *overenthusiastic* biased, bigoted, bugged*, burning*, contumacious, credulous, devoted, dogmatic, domineering, enthusiastic, erratic, extreme, fervent, feverish, fiery, frenzied, headstrong, high on*, immoderate, impassioned, impulsive, incorrigible, infatuated, mad, monomaniacal, narrow-minded, nuts for*, obsessed, obsessive, obstinate, opinionated, partial, partisan, passionate, possessed, prejudiced, rabid, radical, raving, single-minded, stubborn, turned on*, unruly, violent, visionary, wild, willful, zealous; CONCEPT 401 —*Ant.* disinterested, dispassionate, impartial, unenthusiastic

fanaticism [n] *overenthusiasm* abandonment, arbitrariness, bias, bigotry, contumacy, dedication, devotion, dogma, enthusiasm, extremism, faction, frenzy, hatred, illiberality, immoderation, incorrigibility, infatuation, injustice, intolerance, madness, monomania, obsessiveness, obstinacy, partiality, partisanship, passion, prejudice, rage, single-mindedness, stubbornness, superstition, tenacity, transport, unfairness, unreasonableness, unruliness, violence, willfulness, zeal, zealotry; CONCEPTS 633,689 —*Ant.* disinterest, impartiality, unenthusiasm

fanciful [adj] *imaginary, romantic* absurd, aerial, bizarre, blue sky*, capricious, castles in the air*, chimerical, curious, dreamlike, extravagant, fabulous, fairy-tale, fancied, fantastic, fantastical, fictional, fictitious, fictive, flaky*, floating, ideal, illusory, imaginative, imagined, incredible, kinky*, legendary, mythical, notional, offbeat, on cloud nine*, pie in the sky*, pipe dream*, poetic, preposterous, shadowy, suppositious, unreal, visionary, whimsical, wild; CONCEPTS 529,572 —*Ant.* grave, ordinary, real, serious, sincere, unfanciful, unimaginative, unromantic

fancy [adj] *extravagant, ornamental* adorned, baroque, beautifying, chichi*, complicated, cushy, custom, decorated, decorative, deluxe, elaborate, elegant, embellished, fanciful, florid, frilly, froufrou*, garnished, gaudy, gingerbread*, intricate, lavish, ornate, ostentatious, resplendent, rich, rococo, showy, special, spiffy*, sumptuous, unusual; CONCEPTS 562,579 —*Ant.* plain, unfancy, unornamented

fancy [n1] *impulse, urge* caprice, conceit, conception, contrariness, creation, cup of tea*, desire, druthers*, flash, fool's paradise*, groove*, humor, idea, image, imagination, impression, inclination, irrationality, liking, mind, notion, perverseness, pleasure, thing*, thought, vagary, velleity, visualization, weakness for, whim, will; CONCEPTS 20,532 —*Ant.* dislike, hate

fancy [n2] *liking, dream* big eyes*, chimera, conception, daydream, delusion, envisagement, envisioning, eyes for*, fabrication, fantasy, figment, fondness, hallucination, hankering, idea, illusion, imagination, imaginativeness, inclination, invention, itch*, mirage, nightmare, notion, partiality, penchant, phantasm, picture, pie in the sky*, pipe dream*, predilection, preference, relish, reverie, romancing, sweet tooth*, vision, yearning, yen; CONCEPTS 20,32,409 —*Ant.* certainty, fact, reality, truth

fancy [v1] *imagine, create* be inclined to think, believe, conceive, conjecture, dream up, envisage, envision, fantasize, feature*, guess, head trip*, image, infer, make up, make up off top of one's head*, phantom, picture, realize, reckon, spark, spitball*, suppose, surmise, think, think likely, think up, trump up*, vision, visualize; CONCEPT 43

fancy [v2] *love, desire* approve, be attracted to, be captivated by, be enamored of, be in love with, care for, crave, crazy about*, desire, dream of, endorse, fall for, favor, like, long for, lust after, mad for*, prefer, relish, sanction, set one's heart on*, take a liking to*, take to, wild for*, wish for, yearn for; CONCEPTS 17,20,32 —*Ant.* dislike, hate

fanfare [n] *cheering* alarum, array, ballyhoo*, demonstration, display, flourish, hullabaloo*, panoply, parade, pomp, shine, show, trump, trumpet call*; CONCEPT 377

fanny [n] *buttocks* ass, backside, behind*, bottom*, buns*, butt*, cheeks*, derriere, gluteus maximus, heinie*, hindquarters, posterior, rear end, rump*, seat*, tail; CONCEPT 392

fantasize [v] *dream about desires* build castles in air*, daydream, envision, hallucinate, head trip*, imagine, invent, live in a dream world*, moon, romance, trip out*, woolgather*; CONCEPT 17

fantastic [adj1] *strange, different; imaginary* absurd, artificial, capricious, chimerical, comical, crazy, eccentric, erratic, exotic, extravagant, extreme, fanciful, far-fetched, fictional, foolish, foreign, freakish, grotesque, hallucinatory, illusive, imaginative, implausible, incredible, insane, irrational, ludicrous, mad, misleading, nonsensical, odd, outlandish, out of sight*, peculiar, phantasmagorical, preposterous, quaint, queer, ridiculous, singular, suppositious, unbelievable, unlikely, unreal, wacky*, weird, whimsical; CONCEPTS 564,582 —*Ant.* common, commonplace, conventional, customary, familiar, ordinary, plain, usual

fantastic [adj2] *enormous* cracking, extreme,

great, huge, humongous, massive, monstrous, monumental, overwhelming, prodigious, severe, stupendous, towering, tremendous; CONCEPT 781 —*Ant.* little, small, tiny

fantastic [*adj3*] *wonderful, excellent* A-1*, awesome, best, best ever, cat's meow*, delicious, far out*, first-class, first-rate, great, like wow*, marvelous, out of sight*, out of this world*, primo*, sensational, superb, unreal*; CONCEPTS 572,574 —*Ant.* bad, poor, unpleasant

fantasy [*n*] *imagination, dream* air castle, apparition, appearance, Atlantis*, bubble*, chimera, conceiving, creativity, daydream, delusion, envisioning, externalizing, fabrication, fairyland*, fancy, fancying, fantasia, figment*, flight, flight of imagination, fool's paradise*, hallucination, head trip*, illusion, imaginativeness, imagining, invention, mind trip*, mirage, nightmare, objectifying, originality, rainbow*, reverie, trip, Utopia, vagary, vision; CONCEPTS 20,529,689 —*Ant.* reality, truth

FAQ [*n*] *frequently asked questions* common answers, common questions, listed questions and answers; CONCEPTS 48,53

far [*adj/adv1*] *at a great distance* afar, a good way, a long way, bit, deep, distant, end of rainbow*, faraway, far-flung*, far-off, far piece*, far-removed, good ways*, long, middle of nowhere*, miles, outlying, out-of-the-way*, piece, remote, removed, stone's throw*, ways*; CONCEPTS 586,778 —*Ant.* close, near

far [*adv2*] *considerably* decidedly, extremely, greatly, incomparably, much, notably, quite, significantly, somewhat, very, very much, well; CONCEPTS 772,781

faraway [*adj*] *remote, distant* absent, abstracted, beyond the horizon, distant, dreamy, far, far-flung*, far-off, far-removed, lost, outlying, preoccupied, quite a ways*, removed, well away; CONCEPTS 586,778 —*Ant.* close, near

farce [*n*] *nonsense, satire* absurdity, broad comedy, buffoonery, burlesque, camp, caricature, comedy, high camp*, horseplay*, interlude, joke, low camp*, mock, mockery, parody, play, pratfall comedy, ridiculousness, sham*, skit, slapstick, travesty; CONCEPTS 263,293 —*Ant.* sobriety, tragedy

farcical [*adj*] *absurd* amusing, camp, campy*, comic, comical, derisory, diverting, droll, for grins*, funny, gelastic, joshing, laughable, ludicrous, nonsensical, outrageous, preposterous, ridiculous, risible, slapstick, stupid*; CONCEPTS 267,542 —*Ant.* real, reasonable, sensible, serious, tragic

fare [*n1*] *amount charged for transportation* book, charge, check, expense, passage, price, slug, tariff, ticket, token, toll; CONCEPT 329

fare [*n2*] *food served at meals* commons, diet, eatables, eats*, edibles, meals, menu, provision, rations, slop*, sustenance, swill*, table, victuals; CONCEPTS 457,459

fare [*v*] *get along; turn out* advance, do, get by, get on, go, handle, happen, hie, journey, make headway, make out, manage, muddle through, pass, proceed, progress, prosper, prove, shift, stagger; CONCEPTS 100,117,704

farewell [*n*] *departing saying; departure* adieu, adieus, adieux, adios, bye-bye, cheerio, ciao, goodbye, hasta la vista, have a nice day, leave-taking, parting, salutation, sendoff, so long, ta-ta, valediction; CONCEPTS 195,278 —*Agt.* greeting, hello

far-fetched [*adj*] *hard to believe* bizarre, doubtful, dubious, eccentric, fantastic, fishy*, forced, hard to swallow*, illogical, implausible, improbable, incoherent, inconsequential, incredible, labored, preposterous, queer, recondite, strained, strange, suspicious, unbelievable, unconvincing, unlikely, unnatural, unrealistic; CONCEPTS 529,552,582 —*Ant.* believable, natural, plausible, realistic

far-flung [*adj*] *wide-ranging* comprehensive, distant, extensive, far-reaching, global, remote, spacious, widely distributed, widespread; CONCEPTS 576,778

farm [*n*] *land for agriculture or animal breeding* acreage, acres, arboretum, claim, demense, enclosure, estate, farmstead, field, freehold, garden, grange, grassland, holding, homestead, lawn, meadow, nursery, orchard, pasture, patch, plantation, ranch, soil, vineyard; CONCEPTS 258,449,509,517

farm [*v*] *produce crops, raise animals* bring under cultivation, crop, cultivate, direct, dress, garden, graze, grow, harrow, harvest, homestead, husband, landscape, look after, operate, pasture, plant, plow, ranch, reap, run, seed, sow, subdue, superintend, tend, till, till the soil, work; CONCEPTS 117,253,324

farmer [*n*] *person who produces crops, raises animals* agriculturalist, agriculturist, agronomist, breeder, clodhopper*, cob*, country person, cropper, cultivator, feeder, gardener, gleaner, grazer, grower, harvester, hired hand, homesteader, horticulturist, laborer, peasant, planter, plower, producer, rancher, reaper, sharecropper, sower, tender, tiller, villein; CONCEPTS 347,348

farming [*n*] *producing crops, raising animals* agriculture, agronomics, agronomy, breeding, crop-raising, cultivation, culture, feeding, fertilizing, gardening, geoponics, gleaning, grazing, growing, harvesting, homesteading, hydroponics, landscaping, operating, production, ranching, reaping, seeding, sharecropping, soil culture, threshing, tillage; CONCEPTS 117,253,324

far-out [*adj*] *very unconventional* boss*, cool*, deep*, excellent, fabulous, fantastic, groovy*, hip*, neat, nifty, rad*, sensational, strange, super, swell, trendy, unorthodox, way-out, weird, wild, wonderful; CONCEPT 572

far-reaching [*adj*] *broad, widespread* extensive, far-ranging, important, momentous, pervasive, significant, sweeping, wide; CONCEPT 772 —*Ant.* incomprehensible, insignificant, narrow, trivial, unimportant

far-sighted [*adj*] *looking ahead wisely* acute, canny, cautious, clairvoyant, commonsensical, cool-headed*, discerning, judicious, level-headed, perceptive, politic, prescient, provident, prudent, sagacious, sage, shrewd, well-balanced, wise; CONCEPT 402 —*Ant.* incautious, rash, shortsighted, uncareful, unthinking, unwise

fart [*n*] *flatulence* gas, vapors, wind; CONCEPT 465

fart [*v*] *expel gas* break wind, cut one*, cut the cheese*, pass gas, rip one*, toot; CONCEPT 465

farther [adv] *at a greater distance* beyond, further, longer, more distant, more remote, remoter, yon, yonder; CONCEPTS 586,778 —*Ant.* closer, nearer

farthest [adv] *most distant* extreme, farthermost, furthermost, furthest, last, lattermost, outermost, outmost, remotest, ultimate, utmost, uttermost; CONCEPTS 586,778 —*Ant.* closest, nearest

fascinate [v] *captivate, hold spellbound* absorb, allure, animate, arouse, attach, attract, beguile, bewitch, charm, compel, delight, draw, enamor, enchant, engage, engross, enrapture, enslave, ensnare, enthrall, entice, entrance, excite, fire, gladden, hypnotize, infatuate, interest, intoxicate, intrigue, invite, kindle, lure, mesmerize, overpower, overwhelm, pique, please, provoke, ravish, rivet, seduce, spellbind, stimulate, stir, subdue, tantalize, tempt, thrill, titillate, transfix, transport, win; CONCEPTS 7,11,22 —*Ant.* bore, disenchant, disenthrall, disinterest, repel, tire

fascinated [adj] *captivated, spellbound* absorbed, aroused, attracted, beguiled, bewitched, charmed, dazzled, delighted, enamored, enchanted, engrossed, enraptured, enthralled, enticed, entranced, excited, fond of, hypnotized, infatuated, in love with, intoxicated, mesmerized, overpowered, seduced, sent, smitten, sold on*, stuck on*, tantalized, thrilled, titillated, transfixed, transported, under a spell*; CONCEPTS 32,403 —*Ant.* bored, disenchanted, disenthralled, disinterested, repulsed, tired, uninterested

fascinating [adj] *interesting, spellbinding* alluring, appealing, attractive, bewitching, captivating, charming, compelling, delectable, delightful, enchanting, engaging, engrossing, enticing, glamorous, gripping, intriguing, irresistible, ravishing, riveting, seducing, seductive, siren; CONCEPT 529 —*Ant.* boring, repulsive, uninteresting

fascination [n] *strong interest* allure, appeal, attraction, bug*, charisma, charm, enchantment, enthrallment, glamour, grabber*, hang-up*, lure, magic, magnetism, obsession, piquancy, power, pull*, sorcery, spell, thing*, thing for*, trance, witchcraft, witchery; CONCEPTS 20,32,532,690 —*Ant.* boredom, disinterest

fascism [n] *political system of dictatorship* absolutism, authoritarianism, autocracy, bureaucracy, despotism, Nazism, one-party system, party government, racism, regimentation, totalitarianism; CONCEPTS 299,301,689 —*Ant.* democracy

fascist [n] *dictator* authoritarian, autocrat, Nazi, totalitarian, tyrant; CONCEPT 354

fashion [n1] *latest style, prevailing taste* appearance, bandwagon*, chic, configuration, convention, craze, cry, cultism, cultus, custom, cut, dernier cri, fad, faddism, figure, form, furor, in thing*, last word*, latest*, latest thing*, line*, look, make, mode, model, mold, newest wrinkle*, pattern, rage, shape, thing*, tone, trend, usage, vogue; CONCEPT 655

fashion [n2] *attitude, manner* convention, custom, demeanor, device, etiquette, form, formality, formula, guise, method, mode, modus operandi, mores, observance, order, practice, precedent, prescription, prevalence,

procedure, sort, style, system, technique, tendency, tone, trend, usage, vein, vogue, way; CONCEPTS 644,657

fashion [v] *adjust, design, create* accommodate, adapt, build, carve, construct, contrive, cook up*, cut, devise, dream up*, erect, fabricate, fit, forge, form, frame*, knock together*, make, manufacture, model, mold, plan, plot, produce, sculpture, shape, suit, tailor, throw together*, turn out*, work; CONCEPTS 168,173,232

fashionable [adj] *stylish, up-to-date* a go-go*, á la mode*, all the rage*, chic, chichi*, contemporary, current, customary, dashing, faddy*, favored, fly*, genteel, hot*, in style, in-thing*, in vogue, last word*, latest*, latest thing*, mod*, modern, modish*, natty*, new, newfangled, now, popular, prevailing, rakish, smart, swank, trendsetting, trendy, upscale*, up-to-the-minute*, usual, well-liked, with it*; CONCEPTS 579,589 —*Ant.* old-fashioned, out, unfashionable, unpopular

fast [adj1] *speedy* accelerated, active, agile, blue streak*, breakneck*, brisk, chop-chop*, dashing, double-time*, electric, expeditious, expeditive, flashing, fleet, fleeting, flying, hairtrigger*, hasty, hot, hurried, hypersonic, in a jiffy*, in nothing flat*, lickety split*, like a bat out of hell*, like all get out*, like crazy*, like mad*, nimble, on the double*, PDQ*, posthaste, presto, pronto, quick, racing, rapid, ready, screamin'*, snap*, snappy*, speedball*, supersonic, swift, velocious, winged; CONCEPTS 588,799 —*Ant.* plodding, slow, tardy, unhurried

fast [adj2] *fixed, immovable* adherent, ardent, attached, close, constant, constrained, durable, faithful, fastened, firm, fortified, glued, held, impregnable, indelible, inextricable, lasting, loyal, permanent, resistant, resolute, secure, set, sound, stable, staunch, steadfast, stuck, sure, tenacious, tight, true, true blue*, unwavering, wedged; CONCEPTS 488,542 —*Ant.* flexible, impermanent, insecure, loose, movable, unattached, unfixed

fast [adj3] *immoral, promiscuous* bawdy, careless, debauched, depraved, devil-may-care*, dissipated, dissolute, easy, extravagant, flirtatious, frivolous, gadabout*, giddy, incontinent, indecent, intemperate, lascivious, lecherous, lewd, libertine, libidinous, licentious, light, loose, lustful, profligate, rakish, reckless, salacious, self-gratifying, self-indulgent, sportive, sporty, unchaste, wanton, wild; CONCEPT 545 —*Ant.* good, moral, upright

fast [adv1] *speedily* apace, chop-chop*, expeditiously, flat-out*, fleetly, full tilt*, hastily, hurriedly, in a flash*, in haste, in nothing flat*, in short order*, like a flash*, like a shot*, like greased lightning*, like wildfire*, posthaste, presto, promptly, pronto, quick, quickly, rapidly, soon, swift, swiftly; CONCEPTS 588,799 —*Ant.* slow, slowly

fast [adv2] *fixedly* deeply, firm, firmly, hard, securely, solidly, soundly, steadfastly, tight, tightly; CONCEPT 488 —*Ant.* loosely, unfixedly

fast [n] *abstention from eating* abstinence, diet, fasting, xerophagy; CONCEPT 169 —*Ant.* eating, feast, gluttony, gorging, stuffing

fast [v] *go without food* abstain, deny oneself, diet, famish, forbear, go hungry, not eat, refrain, starve; CONCEPT *169* —*Ant.* eat, glut, gorge, stuff

fasten [v] *make secure; join together* adhere, affix, anchor, attach, band, bar, batten, belt, bind, bolt, bond, brace, button, catch, cement, chain, cleave, close, cohere, connect, couple, embed, establish, fix, freeze to*, girth, glue, grip, hitch, hitch on, hold, hook, hook up, implant, infix, jam, knot, lace, leash, link, lock, lodge, make firm, moor, mortise, nail, rivet, rope, screw, seal, set, settle, solder, stay put, stick, strengthen, string, tack on, tag, tie, tighten, truss, unite, wedge, weld; CONCEPTS *85,113,160* —*Ant.* detach, disconnect, loosen, open, release, unchain, unfasten, unlink, unlock

fastener [n] *holder* bolt, buckle, button, catch, clasp, fastening, latch, lock, rivet, screw, snap; CONCEPT *499*

fastidious [adj] *very careful, meticulous* captious, choosy, critical, dainty, demanding, difficult, discriminating, easily disgusted, exacting, finical, finicky, fussbudgety*, fussy, hard to please*, hypercritical, nice, nit-picky, overdelicate, overnice, particular, persnickety*, picky, punctilious, queasy, squeamish, stickling; CONCEPTS *542,550* —*Ant.* indifferent, indiscriminating, uncareful, uncouth, uncritical, undemanding

fat [adj1] *overweight* beefy*, big, blimp, bovine, brawny, broad, bulging, bulky, bull, burly, butterball*, chunky*, corpulent, distended, dumpy, elephantine, fleshy, gargantuan, gross, heavy, heavyset*, hefty, husky, inflated, jelly-belly*, lard, large, meaty*, obese, oversize, paunchy, plump, plumpish, ponderous, porcine, portly, potbellied, pudgy*, roly-poly*, rotund, solid, stout, swollen, thickset*, weighty, whalelike*; CONCEPT *491* —*Ant.* skinny, slender, slight, slim, thin

fat [adj2] *containing an oily substance* adipose, fatlike, fatty, greasy, oleaginous, suety, unctuous; CONCEPT *485* —*Ant.* lean

fat [adj3] *productive, rich* affluent, cushy, fertile, flourishing, fruitful, good, lucrative, lush, profitable, prosperous, remunerative, thriving; CONCEPT *334* —*Ant.* impoverished, poor, unproductive

fat [n] *overweight, adipose tissue* blubber, bulk, cellulite, corpulence, excess, fatness, flab, flesh, grease, lard, obesity, overabundance, overflow, paunch, plethora, suet, superfluity, surfeit, surplus, tallow; CONCEPTS *723,734*

fatal [adj1] *deadly, lethal* baleful, baneful, calamitous, cataclysmic, catastrophic, deathly, destructive, disastrous, fateful, final, ill-fated, ill-starred, incurable, inevitable, killing, malefic, malignant, mortal, mortiferous, noxious, pernicious, pestilent, pestilential, poisonous, ruinous, terminal, virulent; CONCEPT *537* —*Ant.* healthful, life-giving, nourishing, vital, wholesome

fatal [adj2] *critical, very important* crucial, decisive, destined, determining, doomed, fateful, final, foreordained, inevitable, predestined, unlucky; CONCEPTS *531,568* —*Ant.* trivial, unimportant, unnecessary

fatalism [n] *resignation to a fate* acceptance, destinism, determinism, necessitarianism, passivity, predestinarianism, predestination, stoicism; CONCEPT *689*

fatality [n] *death, loss; ability to cause such* accident, casualty, deadliness, destructiveness, disaster, dying, inevitability, lethality, lethalness, mortality, necrosis, noxiousness, poisonousness, virulence; CONCEPTS *304,675* —*Ant.* birth

fat chance [n] *no chance* impossible, not a prayer, no way, snowball's chance in hell*, unthinkable, very little chance, when hell freezes over*; CONCEPT *552*

fat city [n] *paradise* cloud nine*, hog heaven*, pig heaven*; CONCEPTS *370,410,515*

fate [n] *predetermined course* break, chance, circumstance, consequence, cup*, destination, destiny, divine will*, doom, effect, end, ending, fortune, future, handwriting on the wall*, horoscope, inescapableness, issue, karma, kismet, lot, luck, Moirai, nemesis, outcome, portion, predestination, providence, stars*, termination, upshot, wheel of fortune*; CONCEPT *679*

fated [adj] *governed by fate* decided by fate, destined, doomed, foreordained, imminent, impending, inescapable, inevitable, in the stars*, predestined, predetermined, prejudged, preordained, unavoidable; CONCEPTS *548,820*

fateful [adj1] *significant* acute, apocalyptic, conclusive, critical, crucial, decisive, determinative, direful, doomful, eventful, important, inauspicious, momentous, ominous, portentous, resultful; CONCEPT *568* —*Ant.* insignificant, unimportant

fateful [adj2] *deadly* calamitous, cataclysmic, catastrophic, destructive, disastrous, fatal, lethal, mortal, ominous, ruinous; CONCEPT *537* —*Ant.* healthful, healthy, life-giving

father [n1] *male person who begets children* ancestor, begetter, dad, daddy*, forebearer, origin, pa, padre, papa, parent, pop*, predecessor, procreator, progenitor, sire, source; CONCEPTS *394,400,414,419,423* —*Ant.* mother

father [n2] *priest* abbé, clergyman, confessor, curé, ecclesiastic, minister, padre, parson, pastor, preacher, reverend; CONCEPT *361*

father/mother [n3] *founder, inventor* administrator, architect, author, builder, creator, dean, elder, encourager, generator, initiator, introducer, leader, maker, matriarch, motor*, mover, organizer, originator, patriarch, patron, prime mover*, promoter, promulgator, publisher, sire, sponsor, supporter; CONCEPTS *347,423*

father [v] *sire* beget, conceive, create, dream up, engender, establish, found, generate, invent, originate, procreate, produce, sow the seeds of*, spawn, trigger; CONCEPTS *173,239,251* —*Ant.* mother

fatherland [n] *homeland* home, motherland, native land, the old country; CONCEPTS *510,515,648*

fathom [v] *discern, understand* appreciate, apprehend, catch, cognize, comprehend, dig, divine, estimate, figure out, follow, gauge, get, get to the bottom*, grasp, have, interpret, know, measure, penetrate, perceive, pierce, pinpoint, plumb, probe, recognize, savvy, sound, unravel; CONCEPTS *15,38* —*Ant.* misunderstand, not get

fatigue [n] *tiredness* brain fag*, burnout*, debility, dullness, enervation, ennui, exhaustion,

faintness, fatigation, feebleness, heaviness, languor, lassitude, lethargy, listlessness, overtiredness, weakness, weariness; CONCEPTS 316,405
—*Ant.* energy, freshness, liveliness, spirit, vigor

fatigue [v] *tire, wear out* bedraggle, burn out*, bush*, conk out*, debilitate, deplete, disable, drain, droop, drop, enervate, exhaust, fag, fizzle, flag, jade*, knock out*, languish, overtire, peter out*, poop*, poop out*, prostrate, sag, sink, succumb, take, tucker, weaken, wear down, weary; CONCEPTS 137,225,240,250
—*Ant.* energize, envigorate, refresh

fatigued [adj] *tired* all in*, beat*, bedraggled, blasé, burned out*, bushed*, dead*, dead-beat*, dead-tired*, dog-tired*, dog-weary*, done in*, droopy, dropping, enervated, exhausted, fagged out*, jaded*, languid, languorous, lassitudinous, listless, out of gas*, overtired, played out*, pooped*, prostrate, ready to drop*, spent*, tuckered*, washed out*, wasted*, weary, worn, worn-out, zonked*; CONCEPT 485 —*Ant.* alert, energized, keen, lively, refreshed, vivacious

fatness [n] *overweight* adiposity, breadth, bulkiness, corpulence, distension, flab*, flesh, fleshiness, girth, grossness, heaviness, heftiness, inflation, largeness, obesity, plumpness, portliness, protuberance, pudginess, rotundity, size, stoutness, tumidity, weight; CONCEPT 734
—*Ant.* skinniness, slimness, thinness, underweight

fatten [v] *grow or make bigger; nourish* augment, bloat, broaden, build up, coarsen, cram, distend, expand, feed, fill, gain weight, increase, overfeed, plump, put flesh on*, put on weight, round out, spread, stuff, swell, thicken, thrive, wax; CONCEPTS 236,245,250 —*Ant.* thin, undernourish

fatty [adj] *full of adipose tissue* blubbery, fatlike, greasy, lardaceous, lardy, oily, oleaginous, rich, suety, unctuous; CONCEPT 485 —*Ant.* defatted, lean, low-fat, thin

fatuous [adj] *stupid* absurd, asinine, birdbrained*, boneheaded*, brainless*, dense, dull, foolish, idiotic, imbecile, inane, insensate, jerky*, lamebrained*, ludicrous, lunatic, mad, mindless, moronic, puerile, sappy, silly, simple, vacuous, witless; CONCEPT 402 —*Ant.* aware, bright, intelligent, keen, sensible, smart

faucet [n] *spigot* bibb, bibcock, hydrant, nozzle, spout, stopcock, tap, valve; CONCEPTS 445,464

fault [n1] *blame, sin; mistake* accountability, answerability, blunder, crime, culpability, defect, delinquency, dereliction, error, evil doing, failing, flaw, foible, frailty, guilt, impropriety, inaccuracy, indiscretion, infirmity, lapse, liability, loss of innocence, malfeasance, malpractice, misconduct, miscue, misdeed, misdemeanor, negligence, offense, omission, onus, oversight, peccancy, responsibility, slip, slip-up*, solecism, transgression, trespass, vice, weakness, wrong, wrongdoing; CONCEPTS 101,192,699 —*Ant.* advantage, benefit, blessing, correctness, good, perfection

fault [n2] *physical defect* blemish, debility, deficiency, demerit, imperfection, infirmity, lack, pimple, shortcoming, weakness, weak point, zit*; CONCEPT 580 —*Ant.* perfection, soundness, strength

fault-finding [adj] *critical* captious, carping,

fussy, hairsplitting*, hard to please, hypercritical, nagging, niggling, nit-picking, overcritical, pettifogging, quibbling; CONCEPT 267

faultless [adj] *having nothing wrong with it* above reproach, accurate, blameless, classic, clean, correct, crimeless, errorless, exemplary, exquisite, faithful, flawless, foolproof, guiltless, ideal, immaculate, impeccable, inculpable, innocent, intact, irreproachable, model, on target*, perfect, pure, right on*, sinless, spotless, stainless, supreme, textbook*, unblemished, unguilty, unspotted, unsullied, whole; CONCEPTS 545,572 —*Ant.* blemished, flawed, imperfect, tainted

faulty [adj] *not working; incorrect* adulterated, amiss, awry, bad, below par, blamable, blemished, botched, broken, cracked, damaged, debased, defective, deficient, distorted, erroneous, fallacious, fallible, false, flawed, frail, impaired, imperfect, imprecise, inaccurate, inadequate, incomplete, inexact, injured, insufficient, invalid, lame, leaky, lemon, maimed, malformed, malfunctioning, marred, out of order, rank, sick, tainted, unfit, unreliable, unretentive, unsound, warped, weak, wrong; CONCEPTS 560,570 —*Ant.* accurate, correct, perfect, sound, strong, working

faux pas [n] *blunder in etiquette* blooper*, boo-boo*, breach, break, bungle, error, flop, flub*, gaffe*, goof*, impropriety, indecorum, indiscretion, mess-up, misconduct, misjudgment, misstep, mistake, oversight, solecism; CONCEPTS 13,384

favor [n] *approval, good opinion; help* accommodation, account, admiration, aid, approbation, assistance, backing, benediction, benefit, benevolence, benignity, bias, blessing, boon, championship, compliment, consideration, cooperation, courtesy, dispensation, encouragement, esteem, estimation, friendliness, gift, good turn*, good will*, grace, indulgence, kindness, largess, obligement, okay, partiality, patronage, present, regard, respect, service, support, token; CONCEPTS 10,110,689 —*Ant.* disapproval, disfavor

favor [v1] *pamper, reward; help* abet, accommodate, advance, aid, assist, befriend, be partial to, do a kindness, do right by*, esteem, facilitate, further, gratify, humor, indulge, make exception, oblige, play favorites*, promote, pull strings*, show consideration, side with, smile upon*, spare, spoil, treat well, value; CONCEPT 110 —*Ant.* hinder, hurt, thwart

favor [v2] *prefer, like* accept, advocate, appreciate, approbate, approve, back, be in favor of, be on one's side*, buck for*, champion, choose, commend, cotton to*, countenance, encourage, endorse, esteem, eulogize, fancy, flash on*, for, go for*, hold with, honor, incline, lean toward, look up to, opt for, patronize, pick, praise, prize, regard highly, root for, sanction, single out*, support, take a liking to*, take a shine to*, take to*, think well of, tilt toward*, value; CONCEPT 32 —*Ant.* disfavor, dislike

favor [v3] *look like* be the image of*, be the picture of*, feature, resemble, simulate, take after*; CONCEPT 716

favorable [adj] *approving, friendly* acclamatory, affirmative, agreeable, amicable, approbative, approbatory, assenting, benevolent, benign, benignant, commending, complimentary, encouraging, enthusiastic, inclined, in favor of, kind, kindly, laudatory, okay, positive, praiseful, predisposed, reassuring, recommendatory, supportive, sympathetic, understanding, welcoming, well-disposed, well-intentioned; CONCEPT 401 —Ant. bad, disagreeable, unfavorable, unfriendly, unpromising

favorable [adj2] good, timely, advantageous
appropriate, auspicious, benefic, beneficial, benign, bright, cheering, convenient, encouraging, fair, fit, fortunate, full of promise, gratifying, happy, healthful, helpful, hopeful, kindly, lucky, nice, opportune, pleasant, pleasing, pleasurable, pleasureful, promising, propitious, prosperous, providential, reassuring, seasonable, suitable, toward, useful, welcome, well-timed, wholesome, worthy; CONCEPTS 537,558, 572 —Ant. bad, derogatory, detrimental, harmful, hindering, hurtful, hurting, injurious, unfavorable, unhelpful

favorably [adv1] genially, in a kindly manner
agreeably, amiably, approvingly, cordially, courteously, enthusiastically, fairly, generously, graciously, heartily, helpfully, positively, receptively, usefully, willingly, with approbation, with approval, without prejudice; CONCEPT 401 —Ant. unfavorably, unfriendly

favorably [adv2] opportunely, advantageously
auspiciously, conveniently, fortunately, happily, profitably, prosperously, satisfyingly, successfully, swimmingly, to one's advantage, well; CONCEPTS 537,558,572 —Ant. disadvantageously, unfavorably

favored [adj] popular advantaged, best-liked, blessed, chosen, elite, fair-haired*, lucky, pet*, preferred, privileged, recommended, selected, singled out, sweetheart, well-liked; CONCEPTS 529,568 —Ant. disfavored, unpopular

favorite [adj] preferred admired, adored, beloved, best-loved, cherished, choice, darling, dear, dearest, desired, especial, esteemed, favored, intimate, liked, main, number one*, personal, pet*, pleasant, popular, precious, prized, revered, sweetheart*, treasured, wished-for; CONCEPTS 529,568 —Ant. disliked, hated, loathed

favorite [n] something or someone cherished, prized apple of eye*, beloved, chalk*, choice, darling, dear, fave*, front-runner*, ideal, idol, love, main, minion, number one*, paramour, pet*, pick, preference, shoo-in*, teacher's pet*; CONCEPTS 423,446 —Ant. hate, peeve

favoritism [n] bias, partiality discrimination, inclination, inequity, nepotism, one-sidedness, partisanship, preference, preferential treatment, unfairness; CONCEPTS 41,388,645 —Ant. fairness, impartiality, justice

fawn [n] baby deer baby buck, baby doe, yearling; CONCEPTS 394,400

fawn [v] ingratiate oneself to; serve abase, apple-polish*, be at beck and call*, be obsequious, be servile, blandish, bow, brownnose*, buddy up*, butter up*, cajole, cater to, cave in to*, cotton*, court, cower, crawl, creep, cringe, crouch, curry favor*, debase, defer, fall all over, fall on one's knees*, flatter, grovel, honey up*, invite, jolly, kneel, kowtow*, lay it on*,

lick boots*, make up to, massage*, oil*, pander, pay court*, play up to*, scrape, slaver, snow*, stoop, stroke*, submit, toady*, truckle*, woo*, yield; CONCEPTS 110,384 —Ant. ignore

fawning [adj] deferential, groveling abject, adulatory, bootlicking*, bowing, brownnosing*, compliant, cowering, crawling, cringing, flattering, humble, ingratiating, kowtowing*, mealy-mouthed*, obsequious, parasitic, prostrate, scraping, servile, slavish, sniveling, spineless, submissive, subservient, sycophant, sycophantic; CONCEPT 401 —Ant. aloof, cool, disinterested, proud, unfriendly

fax [n] facsimile copy, duplicate, electronic message, reproduction, transmission; CONCEPTS 269,667,716

fax [v] copy deliver, relay, send, transmit; CONCEPTS 269,667,716

faze [v] embarrass abash, annoy, appall, bother, confound, confuse, daunt, discomfit, disconcert, discountenance, dismay, dumbfound, horrify, irritate, muddle, mystify, nonplus, perplex, puzzle, rattle, vex; CONCEPTS 7,19

fear [n] alarm, apprehension abhorrence, agitation, angst, anxiety, aversion, awe, bête noire, chickenheartedness*, cold feet*, cold sweat*, concern, consternation, cowardice, creeps, despair, discomposure, dismay, disquietude, distress, doubt, dread, faintheartedness, foreboding, fright, funk*, horror, jitters, misgiving, nightmare, panic, phobia, presentiment, qualm, recreancy, reverence, revulsion, scare, suspicion, terror, timidity, trembling, tremor, trepidation, unease, uneasiness, worry; CONCEPT 27 —Ant. bravery, courage, fearlessness, heroism, unconcern

fear [v] feel alarm; be scared of anticipate, apprehend, avoid, be afraid, be anxious, be apprehensive, be disquieted, be frightened, be in awe, blanch, break out in a sweat*, cower, crouch, dare not, dread, expect, falter, feel concern, flinch, foresee, fret, have butterflies*, have qualms, lose courage*, quail, quaver, shrink, shudder, shun, shy, start, suspect, tremble, wilt, worry; CONCEPT 27 —Ant. brave

fearful [adj1] alarmed, apprehensive aflutter, afraid, aghast, agitated, anxious, chicken, chickenhearted*, diffident, discomposed, disquieted, disturbed, fainthearted, frightened, goosebumpy*, have cold feet*, hesitant, in a dither*, intimidated, jittery, jumpy, lily-livered*, mousy, nerveless, nervous, nervy, panicky, perturbed, phobic, pusillanimous, quivery, rabbity*, running scared*, scared, shaky, sheepish*, shrinking, shy, skittish, solicitous, spineless, tense, timid, timorous, tremulous, uneasy, unmanly, weak-kneed*, worried, yellow*; CONCEPT 401 —Ant. bold, brave, courageous, inapprehensive, unafraid, unfearful

fearful [adj2] horrifying appalling, astounding, atrocious, awful, baleful, bloodcurdling, creepy, dire, distressing, dreadful, eerie, formidable, frightful, ghastly, ghoulish, grievous, grim, grisly, gruesome, hair-raising*, hideous, horrendous, horrible, horrific, lurid, macabre, monstrous, morbid, overwhelming, redoubtable, shocking, shuddersome, sinister, strange, sublime, terrible, tremendous, unearthly, unspeakable; CONCEPT 529 —Ant. good, nice, pleasant

fearless [adj] *brave, unafraid* assured, aweless, bodacious, bold, brassy, cheeky, chesty*, cocky, confident, cool hand*, courageous, crack*, daring, dashing, dauntless, doughty, flip*, fresh*, gallant, game, gritty, gutsy, heroic, icy*, indomitable, intrepid, lionhearted, nervy, plucky, salty*, sanguine, sassy*, smart, spunky, sure, temerarious, unabashed, undaunted, unflinching, valiant, valorous, wise; CONCEPT 401 —*Ant.* afraid, apprehensive, fearful, timid

feasible [adj] *possible, doable* achievable, advantageous, appropriate, attainable, beneficial, breeze, cinch, duck soup*, easy as pie*, expedient, fit, fitting, likely, no sweat*, performable, pie*, piece of cake*, practicable, practical, probable, profitable, pushover, realizable, reasonable, simple as ABC*, snap, suitable, viable, workable, worthwhile; CONCEPTS 528,552,558 —*Ant.* impossible, inconceivable, unfeasible, unlikely, unpractical, unreasonable

feast [n] *banquet and celebration* barbecue, big feed*, blow*, blowout*, carnival, carousal, clambake, dinner, entertainment, fest, festival, festivity, fete, fiesta, gala, jollification, merry-making, picnic, refreshment, regale, repast, spread, treat, wassail; CONCEPTS 377,459

feast [v] *eat a great amount or very well* banquet, dine, eat sumptuously, entertain, gorge, gormandize, indulge, overindulge, regale, stuff, stuff one's face*, treat, wine and dine*; CONCEPT 169 —*Ant.* abstain, fast

feat [n] *achievement* accomplishment, act, action, adventure, attainment, conquest, consummation, coup, deed, effort, enterprise, execution, exploit, performance, stunt, tour de force, triumph, venture, victory; CONCEPTS 1,706 —*Ant.* failure, idleness, inaction

feather [n] *tuft of bird; plumage* calamus, crest, down, fin, fluff, fringe, penna, pinion, pinna, plume, plumule, pompon, quill, shaft, spike, wing; CONCEPT 399

feature [n1] *characteristic* affection, angle, article, aspect, attribute, character, component, constituent, detail, differential, earmark*, element, facet, factor, gag*, gimmick, hallmark, idiosyncrasy, individuality, ingredient, integrant, item, mark, notability, particularity, peculiarity, point, property, quality, savor, slant*, speciality, specialty, trait, twist*, unit, virtue; CONCEPTS 831,834,835

feature [n2] *highlight, special attraction* big show*, crowd puller*, draw, drawing card*, headliner*, innovation, main item, peculiarity, prominent part, speciality, specialty; CONCEPTS 386,829

feature [n3] *special article in publication* column, comment, item, piece, report, story; CONCEPT 270

feature [v] *give prominence to* accentuate, advertise, blaze*, call attention to, emphasize, headline*, italicize, make conspicuous, mark, play up*, point up*, present, promote, set off*, spotlight*, star, stress, underline, underscore; CONCEPT 60 —*Ant.* disregard, ignore

featureless [adj] *nondescript* bland, characterless, faceless, forgettable, nameless, plain, stark, unadorned; CONCEPTS 485,589

features [n] *facial characteristics* appearance, countenance, face, lineaments, looks, mien, mug*, physiognomy, puss*, visage; CONCEPT 418

featuring [adj] *giving prominence to* calling attention to, displaying, drawing attention to, giving center stage to*, headlining*, highlighting, making much of*, pointing up*, presenting, promoting, pushing, recommending, showing, showing off*, starring, turning, turning the spotlight on*; CONCEPT 292

febrile [adj] *feverish* delirious, fevered, fiery, flushed, hallucinatory, hot, inflamed, pyretic; CONCEPTS 314,605 —*Ant.* cold, freezing, frigid

feckless [adj] *without purpose* aimless, carefree, careless, feeble, fustian, futile, good-for-nothing*, hopeless, incautious, incompetent, ineffective, ineffectual, irresponsible, meaningless, reckless, shiftless, uncareful, useless, weak, wild, worthless; CONCEPTS 404,542 —*Ant.* competent, effective, effectual, efficient, purposeful, responsible, strong, useful

fecund [adj] *productive* breeding, fertile, fructiferous, fruitful, generating, pregnant, proliferant, prolific, propagating, reproducing, rich, spawning, teeming; CONCEPT 537 —*Ant.* impotent, infertile, sterile, unfruitful, unproductive

federation [n] *partnership, organization* alliance, amalgamation, association, bunch, coalition, combination, confederacy, crew, crowd, entente, family, federacy, gang, league, mob, outfit, pool, ring, syndicate, syndication, tribe, union; CONCEPTS 323,381,417

fed up [adj] *disgusted with* annoyed, blasé, blue*, bored, depressed, discontented, dismal, dissatisfied, down, gloomy, glum, jaded, sated, satiated, sick and tired*, surfeited, tired, up to here*, weary; CONCEPT 403 —*Ant.* happy, overjoyed, pleased

fee [n] *charge for service or privilege* account, ante*, bill, bite*, chunk*, commission, compensation, consideration, cost, cut*, emolument, end*, expense, gravy*, handle, hire, honorarium, house*, juice*, pay, payment, percentage, piece*, piece of the action*, price, rake-off*, recompense, remuneration, reward, salary, share, slice*, stipend, take*, take-in*, toll, wage; CONCEPTS 329,344

feeble [adj] *not strong; ineffective* aged, ailing, chicken*, debilitated, decrepit, delicate, doddering, dopey*, effete, emasculated, enervated, enfeebled, etiolated, exhausted, failing, faint, flabby*, flat, fragile, frail, gentle, helpless, impotent, inadequate, incompetent, indecisive, ineffectual, inefficient, infirm, insubstantial, insufficient, lame, languid, low, out of gas*, paltry, poor, powerless, puny, sapless, sickly, slight, strengthless, tame, thin, unconvincing, vitiated, weak, weakened, weakly, wimpy*, woozy*, zero*; CONCEPTS 267,489,527 —*Ant.* able, effective, hardy, healthy, hearty, powerful, solid, sound, strong

feebleminded [adj] *mentally handicapped* dim-witted, dull-witted, dumb, half-witted, imbecilic, moronic, retarded, simple, slow, soft in the head, stupid, unintelligent, weak-minded; CONCEPTS 402,548

feebleness [n] *lack of strength; ineffectiveness* debility, decrepitude, delicacy, disease, effeteness, enervation, etiolation, exhaustion, flimsiness, frailness, frailty, inability, inadequacy, incapacity, incompetence, ineffectualness, infirmity, infirmness, insignificance, insufficiency, lameness, languor, lassitude, malaise, senility, sickliness, unhealthiness, weakness; CONCEPTS 630,676,732 —*Ant.* ability, effectiveness, health, heartiness, power, soundness, strength

feed [*n*] *food* animal food, barley, corn, fodder, forage, grain, grass, grub, hay, meal, pasturage, provender, provisions, silage, straw, vittles; CONCEPTS 457,460,461

feed [*v*] *give nourishment; augment* banquet, bolster, cater, cram, deliver, dine, dish out*, dispense, encourage, fatten, feast, fill, find, foster, fuel, furnish, give, gorge, hand, hand over, maintain, minister, nourish, nurse, nurture, provide, provision, regale, satisfy, stock, strengthen, stuff, supply, support, sustain, victual, wine and dine"; CONCEPTS 107,140 —*Ant.* starve

feedback [*n*] *response* answer, assessment, comeback, comment, criticism, evaluation, observation, reaction, rebuttal, reply, retaliation, sentiment; CONCEPT 278

feed on [*v*] *consume* devour, eat, exist on, fare, feast, graze, have a bite*, ingest, live on*, meal, munch, nibble, nurture, partake, pasture*, peck*, pig out*, prey on, scarf*, snack, sponge, subsist, take, take nourishment; CONCEPT 169

feel [*n*] *texture; air* ambience, atmosphere, aura, feeling, finish, impression, mood, palpation, quality, semblance, sensation, sense, surface, tactility, taction, touch, vibes; CONCEPTS 611, 673

feel [*v1*] *touch, stroke* apperceive, caress, clasp, clutch, explore, finger, fondle, frisk, fumble, grapple, grasp, grip, grope, handle, manipulate, maul, palm, palpate, paw, perceive, pinch, ply, poke, press, run hands over*, sense, squeeze, test, thumb, tickle, try, twiddle, wield; CONCEPT 612

feel [*v2*] *experience* accept, acknowledge, appear, appreciate, be affected, be aware of, be excited, be impressed, be sensible of, be sensitive, be turned on to*, comprehend, discern, encounter, endure, enjoy, exhibit, get*, get in touch*, get vibes*, go through*, have, have a hunch*, have funny feeling*, have vibes*, know, meet, note, notice, observe, perceive, receive, remark, resemble, savor, see, seem, sense, suffer, suggest, take to heart*, taste, undergo, understand, welcome; CONCEPTS 15,34,38

feel [*v3*] *believe* assume, be convinced, be of the opinion, conclude, conjecture, consider, credit, deduce, deem, esteem, gather, guess, have a hunch*, have the impression*, hold, infer, intuit, judge, know, presume, repute, sense, suppose, surmise, suspect, think; CONCEPT 12 —*Ant.* disbelieve

feeling [*n1*] *sensation, especially of touch* activity, awareness, consciousness, enjoyment, excitability, excitation, excitement, feel, innervation, motility, motor response, pain, perceiving, perception, pleasure, reaction, receptivity, reflex, responsiveness, sense, sensibility, sensitivity, sensuality, tactility, tangibility, titillation;

CONCEPT 608 —*Ant.* insensibility, numbness, unconsciousness

feeling [*n2*] *idea, impression* apprehension, belief, consciousness, conviction, eye*, hunch*, inclination, inkling, instinct, mind, notion, opinion, outlook, persuasion, point of view, presentiment, reaction, sense, sentiment, suspicion, thought, view; CONCEPTS 532,689,690 —*Ant.* concrete, solid, thing

feeling [*n3*] *a state of mind, often strong* action, affection, appreciation, ardor, behavior, capacity, compassion, concern, cultivation, culture, delicacy, discernment, discrimination, emotion, empathy, faculty, fervor, fondness, heat, imagination, impression, intelligence, intensity, intuition, judgment, keenness, palpability, passion, pathos, pity, reaction, refinement, sensibility, sensitivity, sentiment, sentimentality, sharpness, spirit, sympathy, tangibility, taste, tenderness, understanding, warmth; CONCEPTS 409,410

feeling [*n4*] *ambience* air, atmosphere, aura, impression, imprint, mood, quality, semblance; CONCEPT 673

feign [*v*] *pretend* act, affect, assume, bluff*, counterfeit, devise, dissemble, dissimulate, do a bit*, fabricate, fake, forge, four-flush*, give appearance of, imagine, imitate, invent, make show of*, phony up*, play, play possum*, put on, put on act*, put up a front*, sham*, simulate, stonewall*; CONCEPT 59 —*Ant.* be true

feigned [*adj*] *pretended* affected, artificial, assumed, counterfeit, fabricated, fake, faked, false, fictitious, imaginary, imagined, imitation, insincere, phony, pretended, pseudo*, put-on*, sham*, simulated, spurious; CONCEPTS 401,582 —*Ant.* genuine, real, sincere

feint [*n*] *pretense* artifice, bait, blind, bluff, cheat, deceit, distraction, dodge, duck, expedient, fake, gambit, hoax, hoodwinking*, imposture, make-believe, maneuver, mock attack, play, ploy, pretension, pretext, ruse, sham*, shift, snare, stall, stratagem, subterfuge, trick, wile; CONCEPTS 633,660,725 —*Ant.* truth

feisty [*adj*] *spirited; touchy* active, alive, bubbly, courageous, difficult, enthusiastic, excitable, fiery, frisky, full of pep, game, gritty, gutsy, gutty, high-strung, hot-blooded, lively, mettlesome, ornery, peppy, quarrelsome, scrappy, sensitive, spunky, thin-skinned, tough, truculent, zestful; CONCEPTS 404,542

felicitate [*v*] *congratulate* commend, compliment, praise, recommend, rejoice with, salute, wish joy to; CONCEPT 69 —*Ant.* condemn, reject

felicitous [*adj*] *appropriate, suitable* applicable, apposite, apropos, apt, convincing, fit, fitting, germane, happy, inspired, just, neat, opportune, pat, pertinent, proper, propitious, relevant, seasonable, telling, timely, well-chosen, well-timed; CONCEPTS 558,799 —*Ant.* improper, inappropriate, infelicitous, inopportune, unfitting, unsuitable, untimely

felicity [*n1*] *happiness* bliss, cheerfulness, contentment, delight, ecstasy, elation, enjoyment, euphoria, exhilaration, exuberance, glee, good spirits, joviality, joy, jubilation, merriment, mirth, pleasure, rapture, well-being; CONCEPT 410

felicity [*n2*] *appropriateness* applicability, aptness, becomingness, suitability; CONCEPT 558

fell [v] *chop down* blow down, bowl over*, bring down, cause to fall, cleave, cut, cut down, dash, demolish, down, drop, flatten, floor*, gash, ground, hack, hew, knock down, knock over, lay low*, level, mangle, mow down*, prostrate, pull down, raze, rive, sever, shoot, shoot down*, slash, split, strike down, sunder, throw down, tumble; CONCEPTS *176,181* —*Ant.* build, construct, erect, raise

fellow [n] *male or female colleague, friend* assistant, associate, cohort, companion, compeer, comrade, concomitant, confrere, consort, coordinate, counterpart*, coworker, double, duplicate, equal, instructor, lecturer, match, mate, member, partner, peer, professor, reciprocal, twin; CONCEPTS *348,423* —*Ant.* enemy

fellowship [n] *sociability, association* acquaintance, affability, alliance, amity, camaraderie, club, communion, companionability, companionship, company, comradeship, conviviality, familiarity, friendliness, guild, intimacy, kindliness, league, order, society, sodality, togetherness; CONCEPTS *387,388*

felon [n] *criminal* con, convict, delinquent, ex-con*, jailbird*, lawbreaker, lifer*, loser*, malefactor, offender, outlaw, yardbird*; CONCEPT *412* —*Ant.* police

felonious [adj] *criminal* base, corrupt, evil, illegal, illicit, lawbreaking, villainous, wrongful; CONCEPT *545*

felony [n] *crime* arson, assault, burglary, criminal offense, foul play, murder, offense, rape, robbery, violation, wrongdoing; CONCEPT *192*

female [adj] *having the qualities or characteristics of a woman* effeminate, fecund, feminine, fertile, maternal, muliebrous, womanish, womanly; CONCEPTS *371,408* —*Ant.* male, masculine

female [n] *woman* daughter, femme, gal, gentlewoman, girl, grandmother, lady, madam, matron, Miss/Mrs./Ms., mother, she, sister; CONCEPT *415* —*Ant.* male, man

femininity/feminine [n/adj] *womanly* effeminate, effete, fertile, gender, gynic, womanhood, womanish, womanliness; CONCEPTS *371,372,408,648* —*Ant.* masculinity

femme fatale [n] *seductress* attractive woman, dangerous woman, enchantress, enticing woman, siren, temptress, vamp; CONCEPTS *361,412,415*

fence [n] *barrier used to enclose a piece of land* backstop, balustrade, bar, barbed wire, barricade, block, boards, chains, Cyclone, defense, dike, guard, hedge, net, paling, palisade, pickets, posts, rail, railing, rampart, roadblock, shield, stakes, stockade, stop, wall; CONCEPTS *260, 476,479*

fence [v1] *enclose or separate an area* bound, cage, circumscribe, confine, coop, corral, defend, encircle, fortify, girdle, guard, hedge, hem, immure, mew, mure, pen, protect, rail, restrict, secure, surround, wall; CONCEPT *758* —*Ant.* release, set free, uncoop

fence [v2] *dodge; beat around the bush* avoid, baffle, cavil, duck, equivocate, evade, feint, foil, hedge, maneuver, outwit, parry, prevaricate, quibble, shift, shirk, sidestep, stonewall*, tergiversate; CONCEPTS *30,59* —*Ant.* face, meet

fend [v] *defend* bulwark, cover, dodge, guard, oppose, parry, protect, repel, resist, safeguard, screen, secure, shield; CONCEPT *96* —*Ant.* surrender, yield

fender [n] *piece protecting part of a vehicle* apron, buffer, bumper, cover, curb, cushion, frame, guard, mask, mudguard*, protector, screen, shield, splashboard, ward; CONCEPT *502*

fend for [v] *take care of* eke out existence*, look after, make do, make provision for, provide for, stay alive*, subsist, support, survive, sustain; CONCEPT *100* —*Ant.* ignore, neglect

fend off [v] *keep at bay* avert, avoid, beat off*, deflect, drive back*, hold at bay*, keep at a distance, keep at arm's length*, keep off, parry, rebuff, rebuke, rebut, refuse, reject, repel, repulse, resist, snub, spurn, stave off, turn aside, ward off; CONCEPT *96* —*Ant.* let in

feral [adj] *untamed* animal, brutal, ferocious, fierce, raging, savage, tameless, uncultivated, undomesticated, wild; CONCEPTS *401,542*

ferment [n1] *substance causing chemicals to split into simpler substances* bacteria, bacterium, barm, ebullition, enzyme, fermentation agent, leaven, leavening, mold, seethe, simmer, yeast; CONCEPT *478*

ferment [n2] *agitation, uprising* ailment, brouhaha, clamor, commotion, convulsion, disquiet, disquietude, disruption, disturbance, excitement, fever, flap, frenzy, furor, fuss, heat, hell broke loose*, hubbub, imbroglio, outcry, restiveness, restlessness, row, rumble, scene, state of unrest, stew*, stink*, stir, storm, to-do*, tumult, turbulence, turmoil, unrest, upheaval, uproar, upturn; CONCEPTS *106,674* —*Ant.* calm, contentedness, happiness, peace, pleasure

ferment [v] *split into simpler substances; be agitated* acidify, be violent, boil, brew, bubble, churn, concoct, dissolve, effervesce, evaporate, excite, fester, fizz, foam, foment, froth, heat, incite, inflame, leaven, moil, overflow, provoke, ripen, rise, rouse, seethe, simmer, sour, sparkle, stir up, work; CONCEPTS *7,19,22,250*

ferocious [adj] *violent, barbaric* barbarous, bloodthirsty, brutal, brutish, cruel, fell, feral, fierce, frightful, grim, implacable, inhuman, inhumane, lupine, merciless, murderous, pitiless, predatory, rapacious, ravening, ravenous, relentless, ruthless, sanguinary, savage, tigerish, truculent, unmerciful, unrestrained, untamed, vehement, vicious, voracious, wild, wolfish; CONCEPTS *401,542* —*Ant.* gentle, innocent, kind, mild, nonviolent, tame, tender

ferocity [adj] *fierceness* barbarity, bloodthirstiness, brutality, cruelty, ferociousness, murderousness, savagery, viciousness, violence, wildness; CONCEPTS *401,542*

ferret out [v] *trace, search out* ascertain, be on to, bring to light*, chase, determine, dig up*, disclose, discover, drive out, elicit, extract, follow, get at*, hunt, learn, nose out*, penetrate, pick up on, pierce, probe, pry, pursue, quest, root out*, seek, smell out*, smoke out*, track down, trail, unearth; CONCEPTS *183,216*

ferry [n] *transportation boat* barge, ferryboat, packet, packet boat, passage boat; CONCEPT *506*

ferry [v] *carry across* bear, buck, carry, chauffeur, convey, lug*, move across, pack, run, schlepp*, send, ship, shuttle, tote*, transport; CONCEPTS *187,217*

fertile [*adj*] *ready to bear, produce* abundant, arable, bearing, black, bountiful, breeding, breedy, bringing forth, childing, fecund, feracious, flowering, flowing with milk and honey*, fruitful, generative, gravid, hebetic, loamy, lush, luxuriant, plenteous, plentiful, pregnant, procreant, producing, productive, proliferant, prolific, puberal, pubescent, rank, rich, spawning, teeming, uberous, vegetative, virile, with child*, yielding; CONCEPTS 372,485 —*Ant.* barren, fruitless, impotent, infertile, sterile, unproductive, useless

fertility [*n*] *readiness to bear, produce* abundance, copiousness, fecundity, feracity, fruitfulness, generative capacity, gravidity, luxuriance, plentifulness, potency, pregnancy, productiveness, productivity, prolificacy, prolificity, puberty, pubescence, richness, uberty, virility; CONCEPTS 372,723 —*Ant.* aridity, childlessness, emptiness, infertility, sterility

fertilize [*v*] *make ready to bear, produce* beget, breed, compost, cover, dress, enrich, fecundate, feed, fructify, generate, germinate, impregnate, inseminate, lime, make fruitful, make pregnant, manure, mulch, pollinate, procreate, propagate, top-dress, treat; CONCEPTS 257,374,375

fertilizer [*n*] *dressing to aid production of crops* buffalo chips*, compost, cow chips*, dung, guano, humus, manure, maul*, mulch, peat moss, plant food, potash, top dressing*; CONCEPTS 260,399,429

fervent/fervid [*adj*] *enthusiastic, excited* animated, ardent, blazing, burning, devout, dying to*, eager, earnest, ecstatic, emotional, enthused, falling all over oneself*, fiery, glowing, go great guns*, heartfelt, hearty, hot*, hot-blooded*, impassioned, intense, passionate, perfervid, pious, religious, responsive, serious, sincere, unfeigned, vehement, warm, warmhearted, wholehearted, zealous; CONCEPTS 401,542 —*Ant.* cool, discouraged, dispirited, impassive, uncaring, unenthusiastic, unexcited

fervor [*n*] *excitement, enthusiasm* animation, ardency, ardor, devoutness, eagerness, earnestness, fervency, fire*, heartiness, heat*, hurrah, intensity, jazz*, love, oomph*, passion, pep talk*, piety, piousness, religiousness, seriousness, sincerity, solemnity, vehemence, warmth, weakness, wholeheartedness, zeal, zealousness; CONCEPTS 633,657 —*Ant.* apathy, coolness, discouragement

fester [*v*] *intensify; become inflamed* aggravate, blister, canker, chafe, decay, gall, gather, irk, maturate, putrefy, rankle, rot, smolder, suppurate, ulcer, ulcerate; CONCEPTS 469,698 —*Ant.* dissipate, get better, heal, lessen

festival [*n*] *celebration* anniversary, carnival, commemoration, competition, entertainment, fair, feast, festivities, fete, field day, fiesta, gala, holiday, jubilee, merrymaking, treat; CONCEPT 377

festive [*adj*] *decorated, celebratory* blithe, bouncy, carnival, cheery, chipper*, chirpy, convivial, festal, gala, gay, gleeful, go-go*, grooving, happy, hearty, holiday, jocund, jolly, jovial, joyful, joyous, jubilant, juiced up*, jumping, lighthearted, merry, mirthful, peppy*, perky, rocking*, snappy*, swinging, upbeat,

zippy*; CONCEPTS 403,548 —*Ant.* depressed, gloomy, somber, undecorated

festivity [*n*] *celebration, revelry* amusement, bash*, blowout*, carousal*, clambake*, conviviality, do*, entertainment, festival, fun, fun and games*, gaiety, happiness, hilarity, hoopla, jamboree, jollity, joviality, joyfulness, levity, merriment, merrymaking, mirth, party, pleasure, revel, reveling, revelment, shindig*, sport, whoopee*, winging*; CONCEPTS 377,383

festoon [*v*] *decorate* adorn, deck, drape, garnish, hang, trim, wreath; CONCEPTS 162,177

fetch [*v*] *go get, bring in* back, bear, be sold for, bring, bring back, bring to, buck, call for, carry, conduct, convey, deliver, draw forth, earn, elicit, escort, get, give rise to, go for, gun, heel, lead, lug*, make, obtain, pack, piggyback*, produce, realize, retrieve, ride, sell, sell for, schlepp*, shoulder*, tote, transport, truck*, yield; CONCEPTS 90,124,131 —*Ant.* free, let go

fetching [*adj*] *alluring, attractive* beautiful, captivating, charming, cute, enchanting, enticing, fascinating, intriguing, luring, pleasing, sweet, taking, tempting, winsome; CONCEPTS 537,579 —*Ant.* repellent, repulsive, ugly, unalluring, unattractive

fete [*n*] *celebration, party* ball, banquet, bazaar, do*, fair, festival, fiesta, gala; CONCEPT 377

fete [*v*] *throw a party for someone* celebrate, entertain, feast, festival, hold reception for, holiday, honor, lionize, make much of*, roll out the red carpet*, treat, wine and dine*; CONCEPT 384

fetid [*adj*] *foul, rancid* corrupt, fusty, grody*, gross*, icky*, loathsome, lousy, malodorous, mephitic, noisome, noxious, offensive, putrid, rank, reeking, repugnant, repulsive, revolting, rotten, smelly, stenchy, stinking, stinky, strong, yecchy*, yucky*; CONCEPT 598 —*Ant.* aromatic, clean, fragrant, pure, sweet

fetish [*n1*] *obsession* bias, craze*, desire, fixation, golden calf*, idée fixe, leaning, luck, mania, partiality, penchant, periapt, predilection, prejudice, preoccupation, prepossession, proclivity, propensity, stimulant, thing*; CONCEPTS 529,689

fetish [*n2*] *object believed to have supernatural powers* amulet, charm, cult object, idol, image, juju*, mascot, phylactery, superstition, talisman, voodoo doll*, zemi; CONCEPTS 446,687

fetter [*v*] *tie up, hold* bind, chain, check, clog, confine, cuff, curb, drag feet, encumber, hamper, hamstring*, handcuff, hang up, hinder, hobble, hog-tie*, hold captive, leash, manacle, put straitjacket on*, repress, restrain, restrict, shackle, throw monkey wrench in*, trammel; CONCEPTS 130,191 —*Ant.* free, let go, loose, loosen, release

fetters [*n*] *bindings; bondage* bilboes, bonds, captivity, chains, check, cuffs, curb, handcuffs, hindrance, irons, manacles, obstruction, restraint, shackles, trammels; CONCEPTS 130,191

fettle [*n*] *spirits* condition, emotional state, mental state, order, shape, sound condition, state of mind; CONCEPTS 407,411

fetus [*n*] *unborn young* blastosphere, blastula, developing infant, embryo, fertilized egg; CONCEPTS 414,424

feud [*n*] *major argument; estrangement* altercation, bad blood*, bickering, broil*, combat, conflict, contention, contest, controversy, disagreement, discord, dispute, dissension, enmity, faction, falling out*, fight, fracas, grudge, hostility, quarrel, rivalry, row, run-in*, squabble, strife, vendetta; CONCEPTS 46,106,388 —*Ant.* agreement, comradeship, friendship

feud [*v*] *fight bitterly; fall out* be at daggers with*, be at odds*, bicker, brawl, clash, contend, dispute, duel, quarrel, row, squabble, war; CONCEPTS 46,106 —*Ant.* agree, make peace, socialize

fever [*n*] *state of high temperature or agitation* burning up*, delirium, ecstasy, excitement, febrile disease, ferment, fervor, fire, flush, frenzy, heat, intensity, passion, pyrexia, restlessness, running a temperature*, the shakes*, turmoil, unrest; CONCEPTS 410,610 —*Ant.* chill, coldness, freeze, frigidity

feverish [*adj1*] *having a high temperature* above normal*, aguey, burning, burning up*, febrile, fevered, fiery, flushed, having the shakes*, hectic, hot, inflamed, on fire, pyretic, running a temperature*; CONCEPT 605 —*Ant.* chilled, chilly, cold, freezing

feverish [*adj2*] *excited, agitated* burning, distracted, fervid, fevered, frantic, frenetic, frenzied, furious, heated, hectic, high-strung*, impatient, keyed up*, nervous, obsessive, overwrought, passionate, restless; CONCEPT 401 —*Ant.* calm, collected, content, cool, easy-going, unexcited

few [*adj*] *hardly any* exiguous, few and far between*, imperceptible, inconsequential, inconsiderable, infrequent, insufficient, lean, less, meager, middling, minor, minority, minute, negligible, not many, not too many*, occasional, paltry, petty, piddling, rare, scant, scanty, scarce, scarcely any, scattered, scattering, seldom, semioccasional, short, skimpy, slender, slight, slim, some, sparse, sporadic, stingy, straggling, thin, trifling, uncommon, unfrequent, widely spaced; CONCEPTS 771,789 —*Ant.* many, much

few [*pron*] *scarcely any* not many, not too many*, scattering, several, slim pickings*, small number, smatter, smattering, some, spattering, sprinkling; CONCEPT 787 —*Ant.* many, much

fiancé/fiancée [*n*] *person engaged to marry* affianced person, betrothed, engaged person, future*, husband-to-be, intended, prospective spouse, steady*, wife-to-be; CONCEPTS 414,423

fiasco [*n*] *catastrophe* abortion, blunder, botched situation, breakdown, debacle, disaster, dumb thing to do*, dumb trick*, embarrassment, error, failure, farce, flap, flop, mess, miscarriage, route, ruin, screwup*, stunt, washout*; CONCEPT 674 —*Ant.* advantage, benefit, blessing, boon, miracle, success, wonder

fiat [*n*] *order, proclamation* authorization, command, decree, dictate, dictum, edict, endorsement, mandate, ordinance, permission, precept, sanction, ukase, warrant; CONCEPT 685 —*Ant.* question, request

fib [*n*] *undetailed lie* canard, crock*, equivocation, evasiveness, fabrication, fairy tale*, falsehood, falsity, fiction, invention, jazz*, line*, mendacity, misrepresentation, prevarication, spinach*, story, tale, untruth, untruthfulness,

white lie*, whopper*, yarn*; CONCEPTS 278,282 —*Ant.* truth

fib [*v*] *tell an undetailed lie* concoct, create fiction, equivocate, fabricate, falsify, invent, jive*, make up, palter, plant, prevaricate, promote, shovel*, speak with forked tongue*, stretch the truth*, tell a little white lie*, trump up*; CONCEPT 63 —*Ant.* be honest, tell truth

fiber [*n1*] *strand of material* cilia, cord, fibril, filament, footlet, grain, grit, hair, shred, staple, string, strip, tendril, thread, tissue, tooth, vein, warp, web, woof; CONCEPTS 392,428,611,831

fiber [*n2*] *texture* essence, fabric, feel, hand, nap, nature, pile, spirit, substance; CONCEPTS 411,682

fibrous [*adj*] *stringy* coarse, fibroid, hairy, muscular, pulpy, ropy, sinewy, stalky, threadlike, tissued, veined, wiry, woody; CONCEPT 606 —*Ant.* nonfibrous

fickle [*adj*] *vacillating, blowing hot and cold* arbitrary, capricious, changeable, cheating, coquettish, double-crossing, faithless, fitful, flighty, frivolous, inconstant, irresolute, lubricious, mercurial, mutable, quicksilver, sneaking, temperamental, ticklish, two-timing, unfaithful, unpredictable, unstable, unsteady, untrue, variable, volatile, whimsical, yo-yo*; CONCEPTS 401,534,545 —*Ant.* aware, cognizant, constant, faithful, reliable, stable, steady

fiction [*n*] *made-up story* anecdote, best seller, book, cliff-hanger*, clothesline*, concoction, crock*, drama, fable, fabrication, falsehood, fancy, fantasy, fib, figment of imagination*, fish story*, hooey*, imagination, improvisation, invention, legend, lie, misrepresentation, myth, narrative, novel, potboiler*, prevarication, romance, smoke*, storytelling, tale, tall story*, terminological inexactitude, untruth, whopper*, work of imagination, yarn*; CONCEPTS 63,271,280,282 —*Ant.* non-fiction, truth

fictitious [*adj*] *untrue, made-up* apocryphal, artificial, assumed, bogus*, chimerical, concocted, cooked-up*, counterfeit, created, deceptive, delusive, delusory, dishonest, ersatz*, fabricated, factitious, fake, faked, false, fanciful, fantastic, fashioned, feigned, fictional, fictive, figmental, hyped up*, illusory, imaginary, imagined, improvised, invented, made, make-believe, misleading, mock, mythical, phony, queer, romantic, sham*, simulated, spurious, suppositious, suppositious, synthetic, trumped-up*, unreal; CONCEPTS 267,582 —*Ant.* actual, certain, confirmed, factual, genuine, proven, real, sincere, sure, true, truthful

fiddle [*v*] *mess with, tinker* dabble, doodle, feel, fidget, finger, fool, handle, interfere, mess, mess around*, monkey*, play, potter, puddle, putter, tamper, touch, toy, trifle, twiddle; CONCEPTS 87,291

fidelity [*n1*] *faithfulness in a relationship* allegiance, ardor, attachment, constancy, dependability, devotedness, devotion, faith, fealty, integrity, loyalty, piety, reliability, staunchness, steadfastness, true-heartedness, trustworthiness; CONCEPTS 32,388 —*Ant.* disloyalty, faithlessness, infidelity, lying, treachery

fidelity [*n2*] *conformity to a standard* accuracy, adherence, adhesion, attachment, closeness, constancy, correspondence, exactitude, exactness, faithfulness, loyalty, naturalism, preciseness, precision, realism, scrupulousness, verism; CONCEPT 636 —*Ant.* inconstancy, nonconformity, unsteadiness, vacillation, wavering

fidget [v] *move restlessly* be antsy*, be hyper*, be nervous, be on pins and needles*, be spooked*, be wired*, bustle, chafe, fiddle, fret, fuss, hitch, jiggle, jitter, joggle, jump, play, squirm, stir, toss, trifle, twiddle, twitch, wiggle, worry; CONCEPT 147 —*Ant.* be still, relax, rest

fidgety [adj] *restlessly moving* antsy*, apprehensive, high-strung*, hyper*, impatient, jerky, jittery, jumpy, nervous, nervous wreck*, nervy, on edge*, on pins and needles*, restive, restless, spooked*, spooky*, twitchy, uneasy, unrestful, up the wall*, wired*; CONCEPT 401 —*Ant.* quiet, relaxed, restful, resting, still, unmoving

field [n1] *open land that can be cultivated* acreage, cropland, enclosure, farmland, garden, glebe, grassland, green, ground, lea, mead, meadow, moorland, pasture, patch, plot, ranchland, range, terrain, territory, tillage, tract, vineyard; CONCEPTS 509,517

field [n2] *persons taking part in competition* applicants, candidates, competition, competitors, contestants, entrants, entries, nominees, participants, possibilities, runners; CONCEPTS 325,365,417

field [n3] *sphere of influence, activity, interest, study* area, avocation, bailiwick, bounds, calling, champaign, circle, compass, confines, cup of tea*, demesne, department, discipline, domain, dominion, environment, job, jurisdiction, limits, line, long suit*, margin, métier, occupation, orbit, precinct, province, purview, racket, range, reach, region, scope, speciality, specialty, sweep, terrain, territory, thing, vocation, walk, weakness, work; CONCEPT 349

field [n4] *arena with special use, as athletics* amphitheater, battlefield, circuit, course, court, diamond, fairground, golf course, green, gridiron, grounds, landing strip, lot, park, playground, playing area, racecourse, race track, range, rink, stadium, terrain, theater, track, turf; CONCEPTS 364,438,449

field [v] *catch a hit or thrown object* cover, deal with, deflect, handle, hold, occupy, patrol, pick up, play, retrieve, return, stop, turn aside; CONCEPT 164

field trip [n] *outing* day trip, excursion, expedition, school outing, school trip; CONCEPTS 224,386

fiend [n1] *dastardly person* barbarian, beast, brute, degenerate, demon, devil, diablo*, evil spirit, hellion, imp, little devil*, Mephistopheles, monster, ogre, Satan, savage, serpent, troll; CONCEPT 412 —*Ant.* angel, friend

fiend [n2] *person overenthusiastic about interest* addict, aficionado, bigot, devotee, enthusiast, fan, fanatic, freak, maniac, monomaniac, nut*, votarist, votary, zealot; CONCEPT 423

fiendish [adj] *diabolical* atrocious, beastly, brutish, cruel, demonic, demonical, devilish, diabolic, evil, hellish, inhuman, malicious, nefarious, sadistic, satanic, savage, vicious, wicked; CONCEPT 545

fierce [adj] *violent, menacing* angry, animal, ape, awful, barbarous, bloodthirsty, blustery, boisterous, bold, brutal, brutish, cruel, cutthroat*, dangerous, enraged, fell, feral, ferocious, fiery, flipped*, frightening, furious, horrible, howling, impetuous, infuriated, intense, malevolent, malign, murderous, passionate, powerful, primitive, raging, raving, relentless, savage, stormy, strong, tempestuous, terrible, threatening, tigerish, truculent, tumultous/tumultuous, uncontrollable, untamed, vehement, venomous, vicious, wild; CONCEPTS 525,537,540 —*Ant.* calm, gentle, kind, meek, nonviolent, peaceful, tame, tender, unthreatening

fiercely [adv] *violently, menacingly* angrily, awfully, boldly, brutally, ferociously, forcefully, forcibly, frantically, frenziedly, frighteningly, furiously, hard, horribly, impetuously, in a frenzy, irresistibly, like cats and dogs*, madly, maleficiently, malevolently, malignly, mightily, monstrous, no holds barred*, passionately, riotously, roughly, savagely, severely, stormily, tempestuously, terribly, threateningly, tigerishly, tooth and nail*, turbulently, uncontrollably, vehemently, venomously, viciously, wildly, with bared teeth*; CONCEPTS 525,537,540 —*Ant.* gently, kindly, mildly, quietly, tamely

fiery [adj] *passionate; on fire* ablaze, afire, aflame, agitable, alight, blazing, burning, choleric, combustible, conflagrant, enthusiastic, excitable, febrile, fervid, fevered, feverish, fierce, flaming, flaring, flickering, flushed, glowing, heated, hot, hot-blooded, hot-headed*, hot-tempered*, igneous, ignited, impassioned, impetuous, impulsive, inflamed, in flames, intense, irascible, irritable, madcap, peppery, perfervid, precipitate, red-hot*, spirited, unrestrained, vehement, violent; CONCEPTS 401,542,605 —*Ant.* cold, cool, dull, flat, impassive, subdued

fiesta [n] *day of rest; religious celebration* carnival, feast, festival, holiday, holy day, saint's day, vacation; CONCEPTS 377,386

fight [n1] *physical encounter* action, affray, altercation, argument, battle, battle royal*, bout, brawl, broil, brush, clash, combat, conflict, confrontation, contention, contest, controversy, difficulty, disagreement, dispute, dissension, dogfight, duel, engagement, exchange, feud, fisticuffs*, fracas, fray, free-for-all*, fuss, hostility, joust, match, melee, quarrel, riot, rivalry, round, row, ruckus, rumble, scrap*, scrimmage, scuffle, set-to*, skirmish, sparring match, strife, struggle, tiff, to-do*, tussle, war, wrangling; CONCEPT 106 —*Ant.* peace

fight [n2] *courage, will to resist* aggression, aggressiveness, attack, backbone, belligerence, boldness, combativeness, gameness, hardihood, mettle, militancy, pluck, pugnacity, resistance, spirit; CONCEPT 411

fight [v1] *engage in physical encounter* altercate, assault, attack, bandy with*, battle, bear arms, bicker, box, brawl, brush with*, buck, carry on war, challenge, clash, contend, cross swords, dispute, do battle, duel, exchange blows, feud, flare up, go to war, grapple, joust, meet, mix it up*, oppugn, ply weapons, protect, quarrel, repel, resist, rowdy, scrap, scuffle, skirmish, spar, strive, struggle, take all comers*, take the field*, take up the gauntlet*, tiff*, tilt*, traverse, tug, tussle, wage war, war, withstand, wrangle, wrestle; CONCEPT 106 —Ant. agree, make peace, surrender, yield

fight [v2] *oppose action, belief* argue, bicker, buck*, buckle down*, carry on, combat, conduct, contest, continue, defy, dispute, effect, endure, engage in, exert oneself, fall out, force, further, hammer away*, hassle, lay into*, light into*, maintain, make a stand against*, oppose, persevere, persist, prosecute, push forward, put up an argument*, repel, resist, row, spare no effort*, squabble, stand up to*, strive, struggle, support, take on, take pains*, tangle with, toil on, travail, traverse, uphold, wage, withstand, wrangle; CONCEPTS 46,100,384 —Ant. agree, believe, support, uphold

fight back/fight off [v] *defend oneself* beat off*, bottle up*, check, contain, control, curb, fend off, hold at bay*, hold back, keep at bay*, oppose, put up fight, repel, reply, repress, repulse, resist, restrain, retaliate, stave off, ward off; CONCEPTS 96,106 —Ant. give in, give up, surrender, yield

fighter [n] *person engaged in hostile encounter* aggressor, antagonist, assailant, battler, belligerent, boxer, brawler, bruiser*, bully, champion, combatant, competitor, contender, contestant, disputant, duelist, GI, gladiator, heavy*, jouster, mercenary, militant, opponent, person-at-arms, pugilist, punching bag*, rival, scrapper, serviceperson, slugger, soldier, tanker*, warrior, wildcat*; CONCEPTS 358,366, 412 —Ant. peacemaker

fighting [adj] *aggressive, warlike* angry, argumentative, battling, bellicose, belligerent, boxing, brawling, combative, contending, contentious, determined, disputatious, disputative, fencing, ferocious, hawkish, hostile, jingoistic, jousting, martial, militant, militaristic, pugnacious, quarrelsome, ready to fight, resolute, scrappy, skirmishing, sparring, tilting, truculent, unbeatable, under arms*, up in arms*, warmongering, wrestling; CONCEPT 401 —Ant. peaceloving

fighting [n] *battle, encounter* argument, battle royal*, beef*, bloodshed, blowup, bout, brannigan, brawling, brush, combat, conflict, contention, dispute, donnybrook*, exchange, flap*, fracas, free-for-all*, go, hassle, hell broke loose*, hostility, joust, match, melee, mix, punch out*, riot, roughhouse*, row, rowdy, rumble, rumpus, run-in*, scramble, scrap*, scrimmage, scuffle, set-to*, spat, strife, struggle, tiff, war, warfare, words, wrangle; CONCEPT 106 —Ant. ceasefire, peace, surrender

figment [n] *creation in one's mind* bubble*, castle in the air*, chimera, daydream, dream, fable, fabrication, falsehood, fancy, fantasy, fiction, illusion, improvisation, invention, lie, nightmare, production; CONCEPT 529 —Ant. reality

figurative [adj] *not literal, but symbolic* allegorical, denotative, descriptive, emblematic, emblematical, fanciful, florid, flowery, illustrative, metaphoric, metaphorical, ornate, pictorial, poetical, representative, signifying, typical; CONCEPTS 267,582 —Ant. literal, real, straightforward

figure [n1] *numeral; numeric value* amount, character, chiffer, cipher, cost, digit, integer, number, price, quotation, rate, sum, symbol, terms, total, worth; CONCEPTS 784,787 —Ant. letter

figure [n2] *form, shape; physical structure* anatomy, appearance, attitude, bod*, body, build, carriage, cast, chassis*, configuration, conformation, constitution, delineation, development, frame, mass, measurements, outline, physique, pose, posture, proportions, shadow, silhouette, substance, torso; CONCEPTS 733,754,757

figure [n3] *object with design; depiction* cast, composition, decoration, device, diagram, drawing, effigy, embellishment, emblem, illustration, image, model, mold, motif, motive, ornamentation, pattern, piece, portrait, representation, sketch, statue; CONCEPTS 259,625

figure [n4] *famous person* celebrity, character, dignitary, force, leader, notability, notable, personage, personality, presence, somebody, worthy; CONCEPTS 354,423 —Ant. commoner

figure [v1] *calculate, compute* add, cast, cipher, count, count heads*, count noses*, cut ice*, dope out*, enumerate, estimate, fix a price, foot*, guess, keep tabs*, number, reckon, run down, sum, summate, take account of, tally, tot*, total, totalize, tote*, tot up*, work out; CONCEPTS 197,764 —Ant. estimate, guess

figure [v2] *understand; decide, infer* catch on to, cipher, clear up, comprehend, conclude, crack, decipher, decode, determine, discover, disentangle, dope out*, fathom, follow, get*, make heads or tails of*, make out*, master, opine, puzzle out, reason, resolve, rule, see, settle, solve, suppose, think, think out, unfold, unravel, unriddle, unscramble, untangle; CONCEPTS 15,18,37

figurehead [n] *person who is leader in name only* cipher, front*, mouthpiece*, nominal head, nonentity, nothing, puppet*, straw boss*, straw person, titular head, token; CONCEPTS 354,423

figure in [v] *contribute to* act, appear, be conspicuous, be featured, be included, be mentioned, have a place in, play a part*; CONCEPT 112

figure of speech [n] *communication that is not meant literally; stylistic device* adumbration, allegory, alliteration, allusion, analogue, anaphora, anticlimax, antistrophe, antithesis, aposiopesis, apostrophe, asyndeton, bathos, comparison, conceit, echoism, ellipsis, euphemism, euphuism, exaggeration, hyperbole, image, imagery, irony, litotes, metaphor, metonymy, onomatopoeia, oxymoron, parable, paradox, parallel, personification, proteron, rhetoric, satire, simile, synecdoche, trope, tropology, turn of phrase, understatement; CONCEPTS 275,278

filch [v] *steal quietly* crib*, embezzle, hustle*, lift*, misappropriate, pilfer*, pinch*, purloin, rip off*, rob, scrounge, sneak, snipe, snitch*, swipe, take, thieve, walk off with*; CONCEPTS 139,142 —Ant. contribute, give

file [n1] *system of order, placement for ease of use* book, cabinet, case, census, charts, circular file*, data, directory, docket, documents, dossier, folder, index, information, list, notebook, pigeonhole*, portfolio, record, register, repository; CONCEPTS 271,770

file [n2] *line, queue* column, echelon, list, parade, rank, row, string, tier, troop; CONCEPT 727

file [v] *put in place, order* alphabetize, arrange, catalog, catalogue, categorize, classify, deposit, docket, document, enter, index, list, pigeonhole*, record, register, slot, tabulate; CONCEPTS 84,158 —*Ant.* disarrange, disorder

file [v] *rub down, grind* abrade, burnish, erode, finish, furbish, grate, level, polish, rasp, raze, refine, scrape, shape, sharpen, smooth; CONCEPTS 137,186,215,250

filibuster [n] *obstruction of progress, especially in verbal argument* delay, hindrance, holding the floor*, interference, opposition, postponement, procrastination, stonewalling*, talkathon*; CONCEPT 298 —*Ant.* catalyst, impetus, incentive, progression

filigree [n] *ornamental art* fretwork, interlace, lacework, lattice, ornamentation, tracery; CONCEPT 473

fill [n] *capacity* all one wants, ample, enough, filler, padding, plenty, satiety, stuffing, sufficiency, sufficient; CONCEPTS 719,736,794 —*Ant.* emptiness

fill [v] *to put in and occupy the whole of* block, blow up, brim over, bulge out, charge, choke, clog, close, congest, cram, crowd, distend, fulfill, furnish, glut, gorge, heap, impregnate, inflate, jam-pack, lade, load, meet, overflow, overspread, pack, pack like sardines*, permeate, pervade, plug, puff up*, pump up, ram, ram in*, replenish, sate, satiate, satisfy, saturate, shoal, stock, stopper*, store, stretch, stuff, supply, swell, take up, top, top off*; CONCEPTS 107,209 —*Ant.* deplete, drain, empty, exhaust, spend, take, use, void

fill [v2] *execute, fulfill* answer, assign, carry out, discharge, dispatch, distribute, elect, engage, fix, hold, meet, name, occupy, officiate, perform, satisfy, take up; CONCEPT 91

fill in [v1] *answer in writing* advise, apprise, clue, complete, fill out, inform, insert, notify, post, sign, tell, warn, write in; CONCEPTS 45,79 —*Ant.* leave blank

fill in [v2] *act as substitute* deputize, insinuate, interject, interpose, replace, represent, stand in, substract, take the place of, understudy; CONCEPT 128

filling/filler [n] *something that takes up capacity* batting, bushing, cartridge, center, content, contents, cylinder, dressing, fill, guts*, impletion, inlay, innards, inside, layer, liner, mixture, pack, packing, pad, padding, refill, replenishment, shim, stuffing, wad, wadding; CONCEPTS 826,830 —*Ant.* emptiness

film [n1] *coating, tissue; mist* blur, brume, cloud, coat, covering, dusting, fabric, foil, fold, gauze, haze, haziness, integument, layer, leaf, membrane, mistiness, nebula, obscuration, opacity, partition, pellicle, scum*, sheet, skin, transparency, veil, web; CONCEPTS 478,524

film [n2] *movie* cinema, dailies*, flick*, footage, motion picture, moving picture, photoplay, picture, picture show, rushes, show, silent*, talkie*; CONCEPT 293

film [v] *take photographs* photograph, put in the can*, record, roll, shoot, take; CONCEPT 173

filmy [adj1] *finespun, fragile* chiffon, cobwebby*, dainty, delicate, diaphanous, fine, fine-grained, flimsy, floaty, gauzy, gossamer, insubstantial, see-through*, sheer, tiffany, transparent, wispy; CONCEPT 606 —*Ant.* nontransparent, opaque, substantial

filmy [adj2] *covered with mist; blurry* bleary, blurred, cloudy, dim, hazy, membranous, milky, misty, opalescent, opaque, pearly; CONCEPTS 525,603 —*Ant.* clean, clear, see-through, translucent, transparent

filter [v] *separate to refine; seep through* clarify, clean, distill, drain, dribble, escape, exude, filtrate, leak, metastasize, ooze, osmose, penetrate, percolate, permeate, purify, refine, screen, sieve, sift, soak through, strain, trickle, winnow; CONCEPTS 135,165 —*Ant.* collect, combine

filth [n] *dirt, pollution* carrion, contamination, corruption, crud*, defilement, dregs, dung, excrement, feces, feculence, filthiness, foul matter, foulness, garbage, grime, impurity, manure, mire, muck, mud, nastiness, ordure, putrefaction, putrescence, putridity, refuse, rottenness, sediment, sewage, silt, sleaze, slime, slop, sludge, slush, smut, trash, uncleanness; CONCEPTS 260,674 —*Ant.* cleanliness, purity, sterility

filthy [adj1] *dirty, polluted* begrimed, black, blackened, cruddy*, crummy*, disheveled, fecal, feculent, foul, grimy*, gross*, grubby*, grungy*, impure, loathsome, miry, mucky*, muddy, nasty, obscene, offensive, putrid, repulsive, revolting, scummy, sleazy, slimy, slipshod, sloppy, slovenly, smoky, soiled, soily, sooty, squalid, unclean, uncleanly, unkempt, unwashed, verminous, vile, yecchy*; CONCEPTS 485,570 —*Ant.* clean, pure, sterile, unpolluted

filthy [adj2] *vulgar, obscene* base, bawdy, blue*, coarse, contemptible, corrupt, depraved, despicable, dirty-minded*, foul, foul-mouthed, impure, indecent, lewd, licentious, low, mean, nasty, offensive, pornographic, raunchy, scatological, scurvy, smutty, suggestive, vicious, vile; CONCEPTS 267,545 —*Ant.* chaste, clean, decent, pure

finagle [v] *maneuver* cheat, contrive, deceive, manipulate, plot, scheme, swindle, trick, wheel and deal*; CONCEPTS 36,59

final [adj1] *last* closing, concluding, crowning, end, eventual, finishing, hindmost, lag, last-minute, latest, latter, supreme, terminal, terminating, ultimate; CONCEPTS 531,820 —*Ant.* beginning, commencing, first, opening, starting

final [adj2] *conclusive, definitive* absolute, decided, decisive, definite, determinate, determinative, finished, incontrovertible, irrefutable, irrevocable, settled, unanswerable, unappealable; CONCEPT 535 —*Ant.* continuing, inconclusive, interim, introductory, persistent, temporary

finale [n] *ending of an event* afterpiece, blow-off*, button*, cessation, chaser*, climax, close, closer*, conclusion, consummation, crowning glory*, culmination, denouement, end, end piece, epilogue, finis, finish, last act, payoff*, peroration, summation, swan song*, termination, windup*; CONCEPT 832 —*Ant.* beginning, debut, first act, opening, start

finality [n] *definiteness, conclusiveness* certitude, completeness, decidedness, decisiveness, entirety, finish, inevitableness, intactness, integrity, irrevocability, perfection, resolution, terminality, totality, unavoidability, wholeness; CONCEPTS 635,638,832 —*Ant.* continuity, inconclusiveness, indefiniteness

finalize [v] *finish, complete action* agree, clinch*, conclude, consummate, decide, settle, sew up*, tie up*, work out, wrap up; CONCEPT 91 —*Ant.* begin, introduce, open, start

finally [adv1] *beyond any doubt* assuredly, beyond recall*, beyond shadow of doubt*, certainly, completely, conclusively, convincingly, decisively, definitely, determinately, done with, enduringly, for all time*, for ever, for good*, in conclusion, inescapably, inexorably, irrevocably, lastly, once and for all*, past regret*, permanently, settled, with conviction; CONCEPT 535 —*Ant.* doubtfully, dubiously, inconclusively

finally [adv2] *in the end; after period of time* after all, after a while, already, as a sequel, at last, at length, at long last*, at the end, at the last moment, belatedly, despite delay*, eventually, in conclusion, in spite of all*, in the eleventh hour*, in the long run*, lastly, someday, sometime, sooner or later*, subsequently, tardily, ultimately, yet; CONCEPT 799

finance [n] *economic affairs* accounts, banking, business, commerce, economics, financial affairs, investment, money, money management; CONCEPTS 360,770

finance [v] *offer loan money; set up in business* back, bank, bankroll, capitalize, endow, float*, fund, go for*, grubstake*, guarantee, juice*, lay on one*, loan shark*, patronize, pay for, pick up the check*, pick up the tab*, prime the pump*, promote, provide funds, provide security, put up money, raise dough*, sponsor, stake, subsidize, support, underwrite; CONCEPTS 108,115,341 —*Ant.* call in, take

finances [n] *person or corporation's money, property* affairs, assets, balance sheet, budget, capital, cash, condition, funds, net, net worth, resources, revenue, wealth, wherewithal, worth; CONCEPTS 340,710

financial [adj] *having to do with money* banking, budgeting, business, commercial, economic, fiscal, monetary, numbers*, numeric, pecuniary, pocket; CONCEPT 334

financier [n] *person who lends money, advises* backer, banker, bankroller, broker, businessperson, capitalist, entrepreneur, fat cat*, grubstaker*, manipulator*, merchant, money, moneybags*, money lender, operator*, person who writes the checks*, rich person, Santa Claus*, speculator, sponsor, staker, stockbroker, tycoon, usurer; CONCEPTS 347,348,353

financing [n] *money for operating expenses* costs, expenditure, funding, loan, matching funds, outgo', outlay, payment; CONCEPTS 340,344

find [n] *discovery* acquisition, asset, bargain, boast, bonanza, catch, gem, good buy, jewel, one in a million*, pride, treasure, treasure trove; CONCEPTS 337,712 —*Ant.* loss

find [v1] *catch sight of, lay hands on* arrive at, bring to light*, bump into*, chance upon, collar*, come across, come upon, come up with*,

corral, descry, detect, dig up*, discern, discover, distinguish, encounter, espy, expose, fall in with*, ferret out, happen upon*, hit upon*, identify, lay fingers on, light upon*, locate, make out, meet, notice, observe, perceive, pinpoint, recognize, recover, run across, run into, scare up*, sight, smoke out*, spot, strike, stumble upon, track down, trip on*, turn up*, uncover, unearth; CONCEPT 183 —*Ant.* fail, lose, miss, pass by

find [v2] *achieve, win* acquire, attain, be one's lot*, earn, fall to the lot*, gain, get, meet, meet with, obtain, procure; CONCEPTS 124,706 —*Ant.* fail, fall short, forfeit, lose

finding [n] *judgment, verdict* award, conclusion, data, decision, decree, discovery, pronouncement, recommendation, sentence; CONCEPT 685

find out [v] *discover, learn* ascertain, catch, catch on, detect, determine, divine, expose, hear, identify, note, observe, perceive, realize, reveal, see, uncover, unearth, unmask; CONCEPTS 31,183 —*Ant.* conceal, cover, hide

fine [adj1] *excellent, masterly* accomplished, aces*, admirable, attractive, beautiful, capital, choice, cool*, crack*, dandy*, elegant, enjoyable, exceptional, expensive, exquisite, fashionable, first-class, first-rate, first-string, five-star*, gilt-edged*, gnarly*, good-looking, great, handsome, lovely, magnificent, mean, neat*, not too shabby*, ornate, outstanding, pleasant, rare, refined, select, showy, skillful, smart, solid, splendid, striking, subtle, superior, supreme, top, top-notch, unreal*, well-made, wicked*; CONCEPTS 528,574,579 —*Ant.* bad, poor

fine [adj2] *cloudless, sunny* balmy, bright, clarion, clear, clement, dry, fair, pleasant, rainless, undarkened; CONCEPT 525 —*Ant.* cloudy, dark, rainy, stormy

fine [adj3] *dainty, delicate; sheer* diaphanous, ethereal, exquisite, filmy, fine-drawn, fine-grained, fine-spun, flimsy, fragile, gauzy, gossamer, gossamery, granular, impalpable, light, lightweight, little, loose, minute, porous, powdered, powdery, pulverized, quality, slender, small, thin, threadlike, transparent; CONCEPTS 491,606 —*Ant.* coarse, rough, thick

fine [adj4] *discriminating, exact* abstruse, acute, clear, critical, cryptic, delicate, distinct, enigmatic, esoteric, fastidious, fine-spun, hairline, hairsplitting, intelligent, keen, minute, nice, obscure, petty, precise, pure, quick, recondite, refined, sensitive, sharp, sterling, strict, subtle, tasteful, tenuous, trifling, unadulterated, unpolluted; CONCEPT 557 —*Ant.* awkward, crude, uncouth, undiscriminating, unrefined

fine [n] *penalty in money* amends, amercement, assessment, damages, forfeit, mulct, punishment, reparation, rip; CONCEPT 123 —*Ant.* amends, award, compensation, reimbursement, reward

fine [v] *penalize in monetary way* alienate, amerce, confiscate, dock*, exact, extort, hit with*, levy, make pay, mulct, pay through the nose*, punish, sconce, seize, sequestrate, slap with*, tax, throw book at*; CONCEPTS 122,342 —*Ant.* award, compensate, reimburse, reward

finery [n] *best clothing* apparel, bib and tucker*, caparison, decoration, fancy dress, formals, frippery*, full dress, gear, regalia, splendor, suit, Sunday best* trappings, trimmings, trinkets; CONCEPT *451* —*Ant.* rags

finesse [*n*] *know-how, maneuver* acumen, adeptness, adroitness, artfulness, artifice, big stick*, bluff, cleverness, competence, con, craft, craftiness, cunning, delicacy, diplomacy, discernment, discretion, feint, gimmick, grift, guile, polish, quickness, racket*, run-around*, ruse, savoir-faire, savvy, skill, sophistication, stratagem, subtlety, tact, trick, wile; CONCEPTS *409,657* —*Ant.* ignorance

finesse [*v*] *maneuver, manipulate* angle, beguile, bluff, exploit, finagle*, jockey*, operate, play, play games*, pull strings*, pull wires*, rig*, wangle; CONCEPTS *36,59* —*Ant.* bobble, mishandle

fine-tune [*v*] *make small adjustments* adjust, calibrate, make improvements, set, tune up, tweak; CONCEPTS *202,212*

finger [*n*] *appendage of hand* antenna*, claw, digit, extremity, feeler*, hook*, pinky*, pointer*, ring finger, tactile member, tentacle*, thumb; CONCEPT *392*

finger [*v1*] *touch lightly* feel, fiddle, grope, handle, manipulate, maul, meddle, palpate, paw, play with, thumb, toy with; CONCEPT *612* —*Ant.* manhandle

finger [*v2*] *choose, designate* appoint, determine, identify, indicate, locate, make, name, nominate, pin down*, point out, specify, tap; CONCEPT *41* —*Ant.* ignore, pass over

finicky [*adj*] *overparticular* choosy, critical, dainty, difficult, fastidious, finical, finicking, fussbudget*, fussy, hard to please, nice, nit-picking, overnice, persnickety*, picky, scrupulous, squeamish, stickling; CONCEPTS *401,404,556* —*Ant.* easy, open, uncritical

finish [*n1*] *conclusion; completion* accomplishment, achievement, acquirement, acquisition, annihilation, attainment, cease, cessation, close, closing, culmination, curtain*, curtains*, death, defeat, denouement, desistance, end, ending, end of the line*, end of the road*, finale, finis, last, last stage, ruin, stop, termination, terminus, winding-up*, wind-up, wrap, wrap-up*; CONCEPTS *119,832* —*Ant.* beginning, commencement, initiation, introduction, start

finish [*n2*] *coating; perfecting* appearance, beauty, burnish, cultivation, culture, elaboration, glaze, grace, grain, lacquer, luster, patina, perfection, polish, refinement, shine, smoothness, surface, texture, veneer; CONCEPTS *611, 655*

finish [*v1*] *bring to a conclusion; get done* accomplish, achieve, bag it*, break up, bring to a close, carry through, cease, clinch, close, complete, conclude, crown*, culminate, deal with, determine, discharge, do, effect, end, execute, finalize, fold, fulfill, get out of the way*, halt, hang it up*, have done with*, make, make short work of*, mop up*, perfect, put finishing touches on*, round off*, round up*, scratch, scrub, settle, sew up*, shut down, shutter*, stop, terminate, top off*, ultimate, wind up*, wrap, wrap up*; CONCEPTS *91,234* —*Ant.* begin, commence, initiate, introduce, start

finish [*v2*] *consume, use up* deplete, devour, dispatch, dispose of, drain, drink, eat, empty,

exhaust, expend, go, run through*, spend, use, wash up*; CONCEPTS *169,225* —*Ant.* keep, maintain, save, store

finish [*v3*] *defeat; kill* annihilate, assassinate, best*, bring down*, carry off*, destroy, dispatch, dispose of, do in*, down, execute, exterminate, get rid of*, liquidate, overcome, overpower, put an end to, put away*, rout, rub out*, ruin, slaughter, slay, take off*, take out*, vaporize, worst*; CONCEPTS *95,252* —*Ant.* bear, create

finish [*v4*] *put a coating on; perfect* coat, develop, elaborate, face, gild, lacquer, polish, refine, smooth, stain, texture, veneer, wax; CONCEPTS *172,202*

finished [*adj1*] *cultivated, refined* accomplished, all-around, classic, consummate, cultured, elegant, expert, exquisite, flawless, impeccable, many-sided, masterly, perfected, polished, professional, proficient, skilled, smooth, suave, urbane, versatile; CONCEPTS *404,528* —*Ant.* crude, uncultivated, unfinished, unrefined, unsophisticated

finished [*adj2*] *complete, done* accomplished, achieved, brought about, ceased, closed, come to an end, compassed, concluded, consummated, decided, discharged, dispatched, disposed of, done for, done, done with, effected, effectuated, elaborated, ended, entire, executed, final, finalized, fulfilled, full, in the past, lapsed, made, over, over and done*, perfected, performed, put into effect*, realized, resolved, satisfied, settled, sewn up*, shut, stopped, terminated, through, tied up*, worked out*, wound up*, wrapped up*; CONCEPTS *528,531* —*Ant.* crude, incomplete, unfinished

finished [*adj3*] *consumed, used up* bankrupt, devastated, done, done for*, done in*, drained, empty, exhausted, gone, liquidated, lost, played out*, ruined, spent, through, undone, washed up*, wiped out*, wrecked*; CONCEPTS *334,560* —*Ant.* held, kept, saved, stored

finite [*adj*] *subject to limitations* bound, bounded, circumscribed, conditioned, confined, definable, definite, delimited, demarcated, determinate, exact, fixed, limited, precise, restricted, specific, terminable; CONCEPTS *535,554* —*Ant.* endless, infinite, interminable, unlimited, unrestricted

fink [*n*] *informer* canary*, narc, nark, rat*, scab, snake*, snitch, squealer, stoolie, stool pigeon, tattletale, tipster, weasel, whistle-blower; CONCEPTS *412,423*

fire [*n1*] *burning* blaze, bonfire, campfire, charring, coals, combustion, conflagration, devouring, element, embers, flame and smoke, flames, flare, glow, hearth, heat, holocaust, hot spot*, incandescence, inferno, luminosity, oxidation, phlogiston, pyre, rapid oxidation, scintillation, scorching, sea of flames*, searing, sparks, tinder, up in smoke*; CONCEPTS *478,521*

fire [*n2*] *barrage of projectiles* attack, bombarding, bombardment, bombing, cannonade, cannonading, crossfire, explosion, fusillade, hail, round, salvo, shelling, sniping, volley; CONCEPTS *86,320*

fire [*n3*] *animation, vigor* ardor, brio, calenture, dash, drive, eagerness, élan, energy, enthusiasm, excitement, exhilaration, fervency, fervor, force, ginger*, gusto, heartiness, heat, impetuosity, intensity, life, light, liveliness, luster, passion, pep*, punch*, radiance, red heat*, scintillation, snap*, sparkle, spirit, splendor, starch, verve, vim, virtuosity, vivacity, white heat*, zeal, zing, zip; CONCEPT 411 —Ant. apathy, dullness, lethargy, spiritlessness

fire [v1] *cause to burn* enkindle, ignite, kindle, light, put a match to*, set ablaze, set aflame, set alight, set fire to, set on fire, start a fire, touch off*; CONCEPT 249

fire [v2] *detonate or throw a weapon* cast, discharge, eject, explode, fling, heave, hurl, launch, let off*, loose, pitch, pull trigger, set off*, shell, shoot, toss, touch off*; CONCEPTS 179,222

fire [v3] *excite, arouse* animate, electrify, enliven, enthuse, exalt, galvanize, heighten, impassion, incite, inflame, inform, inspire, inspirit, intensify, intoxicate, irritate, provoke, quicken, rouse, stir, thrill; CONCEPT 14 —Ant. bore, dull

fire [v4] *dismiss from responsibility* ax*, boot*, can*, discharge, drop, eject, expel, give bum's rush*, give marching orders*, give one notice*, give pink slip*, give the sack*, hand walking papers*, kick out*, lay off, let one go*, oust, pink slip*, sack*, terminate; CONCEPTS 50,88,351 —Ant. hire

fire alarm [n] *smoke detector* danger signal, emergency alarm, fire bell, heat sensor, siren, smoke alarm; CONCEPTS 269,463

firearm [n] *gun* handgun, heat*, musket, pistol, revolver, rifle, shotgun, weapon; CONCEPT 500

firebrand [n] *agitator* demonstrator, guerrilla, instigator, malcontent, protester, rabble-rouser, rebel, revolutionist, troublemaker; CONCEPTS 359,412,432

firecracker [n] *fireworks* bottle rockets, bursts, cherry bomb, fire flowers, illuminations, pyrotechnics, rockets, Roman candles, sparklers; CONCEPT 293

fireplace [n] *hearth for burning wood* bed of coals, blaze, chimney, fireside, furnace, grate, hearthside, hob, ingle, inglenook, ingleside, settle, stove; CONCEPTS 440,443

fireproof [adj] *resistant to burning* asbestos, concrete, fire-resistant, incombustible, noncandescent, noncombustible, nonflammable, noninflammable; CONCEPT 485 —Ant. waterproof

fireworks [n] *pyrotechnic display at celebrations* bottle rockets, bursts, firecrackers, fire flowers, illuminations, rockets, Roman candles, sparklers; CONCEPT 293

firm [adj1] *inflexible* close, close-grained, compact, compressed, concentrated, concrete, condensed, congealed, dense, fine-grained, hard, hardened, heavy, impenetrable, impermeable, impervious, inelastic, jelled, nonporous, refractory, rigid, set, solid, solidified, stiff, sturdy, substantial, thick, tough, unyielding; CONCEPTS 604,606 —Ant. flexible, loose, slack, soft, supple, weak, yielding

firm [adj2] *stable, unmoving* anchored, bolted, braced, cemented, closed, durable, embedded, fast, fastened, fixed, immobile, immovable, motionless, mounted, nailed, petrified, riveted, robust, rooted, screwed, secure, secured, set, settled, soldered, solid, sound, spiked, stationary, steady, strong, sturdy, substantial, taut,

tenacious, tight, tightened, unfluctuating, unshakable, welded; CONCEPT 488 —Ant. moving, unsettled, unstable, wavering

firm [adj3] *unalterable, definite* abiding, adamant, bent, bound, consistent, constant, dead set on*, determined, enduring, established, exact, explicit, fixed, flat, going, hang tough*, inflexible, intent, never-failing, obdurate, persevering, persistent, prevailing, resolute, resolved, set, settled, specific, stable, stand pat*, stated, staunch, steadfast, steady, stipulated, strict, strong, sure, tenacious, true, unbending, unchangeable, undeviating, unflinching, unqualified, unshakable, unshaken, unwavering, unyielding; CONCEPTS 267,403,542 —Ant. alterable, changeable, indefinite, irresolute

firm [n] *business* association, bunch, company, concern, conglomerate, corporation, crew, crowd, enterprise, gang, house, megacorp, mob, multinational, organization, outfit, partnership, ring; CONCEPTS 323,325

firmament [n] *heaven* empyrean, lid*, sky, the blue*, the skies, vault, welkin, wild blue yonder*; CONCEPT 437 —Ant. hell

firmly [adv1] *immovably* durably, enduringly, fast, fixedly, hard, inflexibly, like a rock*, motionlessly, rigidly, securely, solid, solidly, soundly, stably, steadily, stiffly, strongly, substantially, thoroughly, tight, tightly, unflinchingly, unshakeably; CONCEPTS 488,489,604 —Ant. flexibly, movably, weakly

firmly [adv2] *with determination* adamantly, constantly, decisively, doggedly, indefatigably, intently, obdurately, obstinately, perseveringly, persistently, pertinaciously, purposefully, resolutely, staunchly, steadfastly, stolidly, strictly, stubbornly, tenaciously, through thick and thin*, unchangeably, unwaveringly, with heavy hand*; CONCEPTS 534,542 —Ant. changeably, indefinitely, waveringly, weakly

firmness [n1] *stiffness* compactness, density, durability, fixedness, hardness, impenetrability, impermeability, imperviousness, impliability, inelasticity, inflexibility, resistance, rigidity, solidity, temper, tensile strength, toughness; CONCEPTS 722,726 —Ant. flexibility, softness, weakness

firmness [n2] *immovability* durability, solidity, soundness, stability, steadiness, strength, substantiality, tautness, tension, tightness; CONCEPTS 731,732 —Ant. infirmity, instability, movability

firmness [n3] *resolution, resolve* constancy, decidedness, decision, determination, fixedness, fixity, inflexibility, obduracy, obstinacy, purposefulness, purposiveness, staunchness, steadfastness, strength, strictness; CONCEPTS 410,633 —Ant. indefiniteness, uncertainty

first [adj1] *earliest in order* aboriginal, ahead, antecedent, anterior, basic, beginning, cardinal, early, elementary, first off*, front, fundamental, head, headmost, inaugural, inceptive, incipient, initial, in the beginning, introductory, key, leading, lead off*, least, number one*, numero uno*, opening, original, pioneer, premier, primary, prime, primeval, primitive, primogenial, primordial, pristine, right up front*, rudimentary, slightest, smallest; CONCEPTS 585,632,820 —Ant. final, last

first [adj2] *highest in importance* advanced, A-number-1*, arch, champion, chief, dominant, eminent, first-class, first-string*, foremost, greatest, head, head of the line*, leading, main, number one*, outstanding, paramount, predominant, preeminent, premier, primary, prime, primo*, principal, ranking, ruling, sovereign, supreme, top-flight*, top of the list; CONCEPT 568 —*Ant.* last, least

first [adv] *at the beginning* at the outset, before all else, beforehand, initially, in the first place, originally, to begin with, to start with; CONCEPTS 585,820 —*Ant.* finally, last

first-class/first-rate [adj] *superior, excellent* capital, choice, dandy, fine, first-string*, five-star*, in class by itself*, prime*, shipshape, sound, supreme, tiptop*, top, top-notch*, very good; CONCEPT 574 —*Ant.* bad, inferior, lesser, poor, second-class/second-rate

firsthand [adj] *direct* eyewitness, immediate, primary, straight, straight from the horse's mouth*; CONCEPT 267 —*Ant.* hearsay, impersonal, indirect

first name [n] *forename* baptismal name, baptism name, Christian name, given name; CONCEPTS 62,268 —*Ant.* last name, surname

fiscal [adj] *monetary* budgetary, commercial, economic, financial, money, pecuniary, pocket; CONCEPT 334

fish [v] *throwing bait to catch seafood* angle, bait, bait the hook*, bob, cast, cast one's hook*, cast one's net*, chum, extract, extricate, find, go fishing, haul out*, net, produce, pull out, seine, trawl, troll; CONCEPT 363

fisherman [n] *angler* clam digger, fisher, lobsterman, piscator, rodman, trawler, troller; CONCEPT 423

fish for [v] *look for; hint* angle, angle for, elicit, hope for, hunt for, invite, search for, seek, solicit, try to evoke; CONCEPTS 20,75

fishing [n] *angling* fly-fishing, freshwater fishing, piscary, trawling, trolling; CONCEPT 363

fishy [adj] *doubtful, suspicious* ambiguous, doubtable, dubious, dubitable, equivocal, far-fetched, funny, implausible, improbable, odd, problematic, queer, questionable, shady, suspect, uncertain, unlikely; CONCEPT 552 —*Ant.* aboveboard, honest, likely, probable, real, truthful, unquestionable, unsuspicious

fission [n] *splitting* atomic reaction, atom smashing, dividing, division, nuclear fission, parting, severance, splitting the atom, thermonuclear reaction; CONCEPT 500

fit [adj1] *suitable, appropriate* able, adapted, adequate, advantageous, apposite, apt, becoming, befitting, beneficial, capable, comely, comme il faut, competent, conformable, convenient, correct, correspondent, deserving, desirable, due, equipped, equitable, expedient, favorable, feasible, felicitous, fitted, fitting, good enough, happy, just, likely, meet, opportune, practicable, preferable, prepared, proper, qualified, ready, right, rightful, seasonable, seemly, tasteful, timely, trained, well-suited, wise, worthy; CONCEPT 558 —*Ant.* inadequate, incorrect, unfit, unsuitable, unsuited, unworthy

fit [adj2] *healthy, in good physical shape* able-bodied, competent, fit as a fiddle*, hale, in good condition, muscled, robust, slim, sound, strapping*, toned, trim, up to snuff*, well, wholesome, wrapped tight*; CONCEPT 314,485 —*Ant.* inadequate, poor, weak

fit [n] *seizure; sudden emotion* access, attack, blow, bout, burst, caprice, conniption*, convulsion, epileptic attack, frenzy, humor, jumps*, mood, outbreak, outburst, paroxysm, rage, rush, spasm, spate, spell, stroke, tantrum, throe, torrent, turn, twitch, whim, whimsy; CONCEPTS 13,303

fit [v1] *belong, correspond* accord, agree, answer, apply, be apposite, be apt, become, be comfortable, be consonant, befit, be in keeping, click*, concur, conform, consist, dovetail*, go, go together, go with, harmonize, have its place, interlock, join, match, meet, parallel, relate, respond, set, suit, tally; CONCEPT 664

fit [v2] *equip* accommodate, accoutre, arm, fix, furnish, get, implement, kit out*, make, make up, outfit, prepare, provide, ready, rig*; CONCEPT 182

fit [v3] *adapt, change* adjust, alter, arrange, conform, dispose, fashion, modify, place, position, quadrate, reconcile, shape, square, suit, tailor, tailor-make*; CONCEPT 232

fitful [adj] *irregular, sporadic* bits and pieces*, broken, capricious, catchy*, changeable, desultory, disturbed, erratic, flickering, fluctuating, haphazard, herky-jerky*, hit-or-miss*, impulsive, inconstant, intermittent, interrupted, on-again-off-again, periodic, random, recurrent, restive, restless, shifting, spasmodic, spastic*, spotty, unstable, variable; CONCEPTS 482, 534 —*Ant.* constant, continuous, regular, undisturbed, unvarying, even

fitness [n1] *good condition* fettle*, good health, health, kilter*, repair, robustness, shape, strength, trim, vigor; CONCEPTS 316, 723 —*Ant.* poor health

fitness [n2] *appropriateness* accommodation, accordance, adaptation, adequacy, admissibility, agreeableness, applicability, appositeness, aptitude, aptness, assimilation, auspiciousness, compatibility, competence, concurrency, congeniality, congruousness, consistency, consonance, convenience, correspondence, decency, decorum, eligibility, expediency, harmony, keeping, order, patness, pertinence, preparedness, propriety, qualification, readiness, relevancy, rightness, seasonableness, seemliness, suitability, timeliness; CONCEPT 656 —*Ant.* inappropriateness, unsuitability

fitted [adj1] *appropriate, right* adapted, conformable, cut out for, equipped, matched, proper, qualified, suitable, suited, tailor-made; CONCEPT 558 —*Ant.* inappropriate, incorrect, unfit, unprepared, unqualified, wrong

fitted [adj2] *equipped* accoutered, appointed, armed, furnished, implemented, outfitted, provided, rigged out*, set up, supplied; CONCEPTS 560,589 —*Ant.* ill-equipped, lacking, needing, unfitted, unprepared

fitting [adj] *appropriate, suitable* applicable, apt, becoming, comme il faut, correct, decent, decorous, desirable, due, felicitous, happy, just, just what was ordered*, meet, on the button*, on the nose*, proper, right, right on*, seemly, that's the ticket*; CONCEPT 558

—*Ant.* improper, inappropriate, incorrect, unfitting, unseemly, unsuitable

fitting [*n*] *accessory* accoutrement, appointment, attachment, component, connection, convenience, equipment, extra, furnishing, furniture, instrument, paraphernalia, part, piece, trimming, unit; CONCEPT 824

fix [*n*] *difficult or ticklish situation* box*, corner*, dilemma, embarrassment, hole*, hot water*, jam*, mess*, pickle*, plight, predicament, quandary, scrape, spot*; CONCEPT 674
—*Ant.* ease, good, peace

fix [*v1*] *establish, make firm* affix, anchor, attach, bind, catch, cement, congeal, connect, consolidate, couple, embed, entrench, fasten, freeze to*, glue, graft, harden, implant, inculcate, infix, ingrain, install, instill, link, locate, lodge, moor, nail down*, pin, place, plant, position, rigidity, rivet, root, secure, set, settle, solidify, stabilize, stay put, steady, stick, stiffen, thicken, tie; CONCEPTS 85,113,160,201 —*Ant.* change, destroy, disarrange, disorganize, unsettle

fix [*v2*] *determine, decide* agree on, appoint, arrange, arrive at, conclude, define, establish, limit, name, resolve, set, settle, solve, specify, work, work out; CONCEPT 18 —*Ant.* disturb, ignore, neglect

fix [*v3*] *mend, repair* adjust, amend, correct, debug, doctor, do up*, emend, face-lift*, fiddle with, overhaul, patch, put to rights*, rebuild, re-condition, reconstruct, regulate, restore, retread, revamp, revise, see to*, sort, tune up; CONCEPTS 126,212 —*Ant.* break, corrupt, destroy, unfix

fix [*v4*] *prepare, plan ahead* arrange, dispose, frame, prearrange, precontrive, predesign, preorder, preplan, put up, rig*, set up, stack the deck*; CONCEPT 36 —*Ant.* forget, ignore, neglect

fix [*v5*] *focus on* concenter, concentrate, direct, fasten, fixate, level at, put, rivet; CONCEPT 623 —*Ant.* ignore, look away

fix [*v6*] *cook a meal* fit, get, get ready, heat, make, make up, microwave, prepare, ready, warm, whip up*; CONCEPT 170 —*Ant.* eat out

fix [*v7*] *manipulate, influence an event* bribe, buy, buy off, corrupt, fiddle*, have, lubricate, maneuver, pull strings*, reach, square, suborn, tamper with; CONCEPTS 192,232 —*Ant.* play fair

fix [*v8*] *wreak vengeance on* cook someone's goose*, get*, get even, get revenge, hurt, pay back, punish, take retribution; CONCEPT 86 —*Ant.* aid, assist, help

fixate [*v*] *focus* become attached, center on, direct, haunt, infatuate, obsess, rivet one's eyes*, zero in on; CONCEPTS 17,623

fixation [*n*] *obsession* addiction, case, complex, craze, crush, fascination, fetish, hang-up*, idée fixe, infatuation, mania, preoccupation, thing; CONCEPTS 532,690

fixed [*adj1*] *permanent, steady* anchored, attached, established, fast, firm, hitched, hooked, immobile, immotile, immovable, located, locked, made fast, nailed*, quiet, rigid, rooted, secure, set, settled, situated, solid, stable, steadfast, stiff, still, tenacious, tight; CONCEPTS 488,551,583,649 —*Ant.* changeable, impermanent, unfixed, unsteady

fixed [*adj2*] *intent, resolute; established* abiding, agreed, arranged, certain, changeless, circumscribed, confirmed, decided, defined, definite, definitive, determinate, enduring, firm, inalterable, inflexible, in the bag*, inveterate, level, limited, narrow, never-failing, planned, prearranged, precise, resolved, restricted, rigged, rooted, set, settled, set-up, stated, steadfast, steady, still, stipulated, sure, unbending, unblinking, unchangeable, undeviating, unfaltering, unflinching, unmodifiable, unmovable, unqualified, unwavering; CONCEPTS 535,554 —*Ant.* indefinite, irresolute, unestablished, unfixed, variable

fixed [*adj3*] *repaired* back together, going, in order, in working order, mended, put right, rebuilt, refitted, sorted, whole; CONCEPT 560 —*Ant.* broken, in disrepair, unfixed

fixture [*n*] *fitting, appliance* accessory, appendage, appurtenance, attachment, component, device, equipment; CONCEPT 463

fix up [*v*] *prepare, beautify* deck*, dress up, furnish, gussy up*, primp, provide, rehabilitate, repair, smarten, spiff*, spruce up*; CONCEPTS 162,202 —*Ant.* corrupt, deface, defile, uglify

fizz [*v*] *bubble* buzz, effervesce, fizzle, froth, hiss, seethe, sibilate, simmer, sparkle, sputter, whisper, whoosh; CONCEPT 469 —*Ant.* be flat

fizzle [*v*] *collapse, fall through* abort, be a fiasco*, come to nothing*, die, end, end in defeat*, end in disappointment*, fail, fold, miscarry, misfire, miss the mark*, peter out*, wane; CONCEPT 699 —*Ant.* build, develop, progress

fizzy [*adj*] *effervescent* aerated, bubbling, bubbly, carbonated, gassy, sparkling, spumante; CONCEPT 462 —*Ant.* flat, still

flabbergast [*v*] *surprise* abash, amaze, astonish, astound, blow away*, bowl over*, confound, daze, disconcert, dumbfound, make speechless, nonplus, overcome, overwhelm, put away*, shock, stagger, stun, throw, throw for a loop*; CONCEPT 42 —*Ant.* expect

flabby [*adj*] *baggy, fat* drooping, enervated, flaccid, flexuous, floppy*, gone to seed*, hanging, irresilient, lax, limp, loose, out of condition*, out of shape*, pendulous, rusty, sagging, shapeless, slack, sloppy, soft, tender, toneless, unfit, yielding; CONCEPTS 486,490 —*Ant.* firm, lean, slim, taut, thin, tight

flaccid [*adj*] *drooping* debilitated, emasculated, enervated, enfeebled, flabby, flimsy, inelastic, irresilient, lax, limp, loose, nerveless, quaggy, sapped, slack, soft, weak, weakened; CONCEPTS 485,604 —*Ant.* firm, taut, tight

flag [*n*] *pennant, symbol* banderole, banner, bannerol, burgee, colors, emblem, ensign, gonfalon, jack, pennon, standard, streamer; CONCEPTS 284,473

flag [*v1*] *decline, fall off* abate, deteriorate, die, droop, ebb, fade, fail, faint, languish, peter out*, pine, sag, sink, slump, succumb, taper off*, wane, weaken, weary, wilt; CONCEPTS 698,699 —*Ant.* do well, increase, rise, strengthen

flag [*v2*] *signal* gesture, give a sign to, hail, indicate, motion, salute, warn, wave; CONCEPT 74

flagellate [*v*] *whip, lash* beat, beat the living daylights out of*, belt, flay, flog, hit, lash, spank, tan*, tan someone's hide*, thrash; CONCEPT 189

flagrant [*adj*] *flaunting, blatant; without shame*
arrant, atrocious, awful, bare-faced*, bold,
brazen, capital, conspicuous, crying, disgraceful, dreadful, egregious, enormous, flagitious,
flaming, flashy*, glaring, grody*, gross*, hanging out*, heinous, immodest, infamous, noticeable, notorious, obvious, open, ostentatious,
out-and-out*, outrageous, rank, scandalous,
shameful, shameless, shocking, stick out like
sore thumb*, striking, undisguised, wicked;
CONCEPTS 401,545,576 —*Ant.* concealed, disguised, hidden, mild, moral, restrained, secret

flagship [*n*] *leader* bellwether, chief, crown
jewel, flotilla leader, forerunner, front runner,
head, lead ship, mother ship; CONCEPTS 347,354

flail [*v*] *beat, strike* bash, batter, club, flog, hit,
knock, lash, maltreat, pummel, slug, smack,
smash, sock, thrash, thwack, whale; CONCEPTS
189,246

flair [*n*] *talent, style* ability, accomplishment,
aptitude, aptness, bent, chic, dash, elegance,
faculty, feel, genius, gift, glamour, head,
knack, mastery, panache, pizzazz*, presence,
shine*, splash*, taste, turn, zip*; CONCEPTS
630,706 —*Ant.* inability, incapacity, ineptitude, ineptness

flak [*n*] *complaint, criticism* abuse, bad press*,
brickbat*, censure, condemnation, disapprobation, disapproval, disparagement, fault-finding,
hostility, knock*, opposition, pan*, rap*,
swipe*; CONCEPTS 52,278 —*Ant.* compliment,
praise

flake [*n*] *scale, peel* cell, disk, drop, foil,
lamella, lamina, layer, leaf, membrane, pellicle,
plate, scab, section, shaving, sheet, skin, slice,
sliver, wafer; CONCEPT 831

flake [*v*] *peel off* blister, chip, delaminate,
desquamate, drop, exfoliate, pare, scab, scale,
shed, slice, sliver, trim, wear away; CONCEPTS
157,469

flaky [*adj*] *eccentric* birdy*, crazy, goofy*,
half-cracked, haywire, nutty, odd, peculiar,
queer, screwy, unconventional, wacky;
CONCEPTS 547,564

flamboyant [*adj*] *extravagant, theatrical*
baroque, bombastic, brilliant, camp, chichi*,
colorful, dashing, dazzling, elaborate, exciting,
flaky*, flaming, flashy, florid, gassy*, gaudy,
glamorous, jazzy*, luscious, luxuriant, ornate,
ostentatious, peacockish, pretentious, resplendent, rich, rococo, showy, splashy, sporty,
swank*, swashbuckling*; CONCEPTS 401,589
—*Ant.* calm, moderate, modest, restrained,
tasteful, unflashy

flame [*n1*] *fire* blaze, brightness, conflagration,
flare, flash, holocaust, light, rapid oxidation,
wildfire; CONCEPTS 478,521

flame [*n2*] *lover; passion* affection, ardor, baby,
beau, beloved, boyfriend, darling, dear, desire,
enthusiasm, fervor, fire, girlfriend, heartthrob,
honey, inamorata, inamorato, keenness, love,
paramour, spark, steady, swain, sweetheart,
sweetie, truelove; CONCEPTS 32,423 —*Ant.* hate

flame [*n3*] *insulting e-mail message* abusive
e-mail message, abusive newsgroup message,
abusive newsgroup posting, flame-mail, flame
war, insulting newsgroup message, insulting
newsgroup posting; CONCEPTS 52,54,278

flame [*v*] *burn* blaze, coruscate, fire, flare, flare

up, flash, glare, glint, glow, ignite, kindle, light,
oxidize, shine; CONCEPT 249

flaming [*adj1*] *burning* ablaze, afire, aflame,
alight, blazing, brilliant, conflagrant, fiery,
flaring, glowing, ignited, in flames, raging,
red, red-hot*; CONCEPT 485

flaming [*adj2*] *very angry, vehement* ardent,
aroused, blazing, bright, burning, fervent,
frenzied, hot, hot-blooded*, impassioned,
intense, passionate, raging, red-hot*, scintillating, vivid, white-hot*; CONCEPTS 267,403
—*Ant.* gleeful, happy, joyful, pleased

flammable [*adj*] *easily set afire* burnable,
combustible, ignitable, incendiary, inflammable; CONCEPT 485 —*Ant.* fireproof, flameproof,
incombustible, non-flammable

flank [*n*] *haunch of an animate being* ham,
hand, hip, loin, pleuron, quarter, side, thigh,
wing; CONCEPT 392

flap [*n1*] *winged or extended part of an object*
accessory, adjunct, appendage, apron, cover,
drop, fly, fold, hanging, lapel, lobe, lug, overlap, pendant, pendulosity, ply, queue, skirt,
strip, tab, tag, tail, tippet; CONCEPTS 471,824

flap [*n2*] *commotion* agitation, banging,
brouhaha, confusion, dither, fluster, flutter,
fuss, lather*, panic, pother*, state*, stew*,
sweat*, tizzy, to-do, tumult, turbulence,
turmoil, twitter*; CONCEPTS 230,674
—*Ant.* calm, peace, peacefulness

flap [*v*] *flutter* agitate, beat, dangle, flail, flash,
flop, hang, lop, shake, swing, swish, thrash,
thresh, vibrate, wag, wave; CONCEPT 149

flare [*v1*] *erupt, blow* blaze, boil over, break
out, burn, burn up, burst, dart, dazzle, explode,
fire up, flash, flicker, flutter, fume, glare, glow,
go off, lose control, rant, seethe, shimmer,
shoot, waver; CONCEPTS 13,179,249

flare [*v2*] *spread* broaden, grow, splay, widen;
CONCEPT 469

flare-up [*n*] *sudden outbreak* blowup, epidemic,
eruption, explosion, gush, outburst, rise;
CONCEPT 633

flash [*n1*] *shimmer, flicker* beam, bedazzlement,
blaze, burst, coruscation, dazzle, flame, flare,
glance, glare, gleam, glimmer, glint, glisten,
glitter, glow, illumination, imprint, impulse,
incandescence, luster, phosphorescence, quiver,
radiation, ray, reflection, scintillation, shine,
spark, sparkle, streak, stream, twinkle, twinkling, vision; CONCEPTS 521,624

flash [*n2*] *instant, split second* breathing, burst,
jiffy, minute, moment, outburst, shake, show,
trice, twinkling; CONCEPTS 808,821

flash [*n3*] *demonstration* burst, display, manifestation, outburst, show, sign, splash, swank;
CONCEPT 261

flash [*v1*] *shimmer, flicker* beam, bedazzle,
blaze, blink, coruscate, dazzle, flame, flare,
glance, glare, gleam, glimmer, glint, glisten,
glitter, glow, incandesce, light, phosphoresce,
radiate, reflect, scintillate, shine, shoot out,
spangle, spark, sparkle, twinkle; CONCEPT 624

flash [*v2*] *move fast and display* bolt, brandish,
dart, dash, disport, exhibit, expose, flaunt, flit,
flourish, fly, parade, race, shoot, show, show
off, speed, spring, streak, sweep, trot out,
whistle, zoom; CONCEPTS 150,261 —*Ant.*
pause, slow, walk

flashback [n] *remembrance* flash from the past*, hallucination, memory, nostalgia, recall, recollection, reliving, reminiscence, thoughts of the past*, voice from the past*; CONCEPTS 40,529

flash point [n] *crucial moment* breaking point, crisis, critical moment, hour of decision, moment of truth, turning point, zero hour; CONCEPT 674

flashy [adj] *flamboyant, in poor taste* blatant, brazen, catchpenny*, cheap, chintzy, flaunting, florid, garish, gaudy, glaring, glittering, glittery, glitzy, jazzy*, loud, meretricious, ornate, ostentatious, showy, snazzy, sparkling, tacky*, tasteless, tawdry, tinsel, vulgar; CONCEPT 589 —*Ant.* plain, simple, subdued, tasteful, unflamboyant, unflashy, ungaudy, unobtrusive

flask [n] *small container for liquid* alembic, ampulla, bag, beaker, bottle, canteen, carafe, caster, chalice, crock, cruet, crystal, decanter, demijohn, ewer, fiasco, flacon, flagon, flasket, glass, goblet, gourd, horn, jar, jug, noggin, phial, retort, tumbler, urn, vial; CONCEPT 494

flat [adj1] *level, smooth* collapsed, complanate, decumbent, deflated, depressed, empty, even, extended, fallen, flush, horizontal, laid low, low, oblate, outstretched, pancake*, planar, planate, plane, procumbent, prone, prostrate, punctured, reclining, recumbent, splay, spread out, supine, tabular, unbroken; CONCEPTS 486,490 —*Ant.* broken, elevated, raised, rough, rounded, rugged, uneven

flat [adj2] *dull, lackluster to the senses* banal, blah, bland, blind, boring, colorless, dead, dim, drab, draggy, flavorless, ho hum*, inane, innocuous, insipid, jejune, lead balloon*, lifeless, matte, monotonous, muted, pointless, prosaic, prosy, sapless, spiritless, stale, tasteless, tedious, uninteresting, unpalatable, unsavory, unseasoned, vanilla*, vapid, watery, weak, whitebread*; CONCEPTS 529,537 —*Ant.* bubbly, effervescent, sharp

flat [adj3] *absolute, positive* categorical, direct, downright, explicit, final, fixed, indubitable, out-and-out*, peremptory, plain, straight, unconditional, unequivocal, unmistakable, unqualified, unquestionable; CONCEPT 535 —*Ant.* indefinite

flat [n] *apartment* chambers, condo, co-op*, crash pad*, floor-through, go-down, joint*, lodging, pad*, railroad apartment, rental, room, rooms, suite, tenement, walk-up; CONCEPT 516

flat-out [adv] *at top speed* all-out, all the way, at a good clip*, for all one's worth*, full blast, head over heels*, in full gallop*, lickety-split, the whole nine yards*, to the max, unrestrainedly, wide open, without reservation; CONCEPTS 574,762,781

flatten [v] *level out* abrade, beat down, compress, crush, debase, deflate, depress, even out, fell, floor, flush, grade, ground, iron out, knock down, lay, lay low, mow down, plane, plaster*, prostrate, raze, roll, smash, smooth, spread out, squash, straighten, subdue, trample; CONCEPTS 137,250,469,702 —*Ant.* break, elevate, make uneven, raise, round

flatter [v1] *compliment excessively* adulate, beslaver, blandish, bootlick*, brownnose*, build up*, butter up*, cajole, cater to, charm, con, court, fawn*, get next to*, glorify, grovel, humor, inveigle, jolly, lay it on thick*, massage, oil*, overpraise, play up to*, praise, rub the right way*, salve, sell, snow*, soften*, soft-soap*, spread it on*, stroke, suck up to*, sweeten up*, sweet-talk*, toady*, wheedle, work on*, work over*; CONCEPTS 59,69 —*Ant.* belittle, castigate, condemn, criticize, denounce, insult, offend

flatter [v2] *complement, enhance* adorn, beautify, become, decorate, do something for*, embellish, enrich, finish, go with*, grace, ornament, perfect, put in best light*, set off, show to advantage, suit; CONCEPTS 162,664 —*Ant.* mismatch

flatterer [n] *complimenter* apple polisher*, backscratcher, bootlicker*, brownnose*, cajoler, charmer, fawner, flunkey, lackey, puffer*, sweet talker*, sycophant, teacher's pet, toady, yes-person*; CONCEPTS 59,69

flattery [n] *false praise, compliments* adulation, applause, approbation, blandishment, blarney*, bootlicking*, cajolery, commendation, encomium, eulogy, eyewash*, fawning*, flattering, flummery, fulsomeness, gallantry, gratification, hokum*, honeyed words, incense, ingratiation, jive*, laud, mush*, obsequiousness, palaver, plaudits, pretty speech, puffery*, servility, smoke*, snow*, snow job*, soft-soap*, soft words, stroke*, sweet talk*, sycophancy, toadyism, tribute, truckling, unctuousness; CONCEPTS 59,69 —*Ant.* belittlement, castigation, condemnation, criticism, denunciation, insult, offense

flatulent [adj] *pretentious, long-winded* bombastic, inflated, oratorical, overblown, pompous, prolix, shallow, superficial, swollen, tedious, tumescent, tumid, turgid, windy, wordy; CONCEPTS 267,404 —*Ant.* brief, unpretentious

flaunt [v] *make an exhibition, show off* advertise, air, boast, brandish, break out, broadcast, declare, disclose, display, disport, divulge, expose, fan it*, flash, flash about, flourish, gasconade, grandstand*, hotdog*, let it all hang out*, make a scene*, parade, proclaim, put on an act*, reveal, roll out, show and tell, showcase, smack with*, sport, spring on*, streak, throw weight around*, trot out*, vaunt, wave around, whip out*; CONCEPT 261 —*Ant.* conceal, hide, refrain

flavor [n1] *odor and taste* acidity, aroma, astringency, bitterness, essence, extract, gusto, hotness, piquancy, pungency, relish, saltiness, sapidity, sapor, savor, seasoning, smack, sourness, spiciness, sweetness, tang, tartness, twang, vim, wallop, zest, zing; CONCEPT 614

flavor [n2] *aura, essence* aspect, character, feel, feeling, property, quality, soupçon, stamp, style, suggestion, tinge, tone, touch; CONCEPT 673

flavor [v] *add seasoning* add zing, add zip, ginger, hot it up*, imbue, impart, infuse, lace, leaven, pepper, pep up*, salt, season, spice; CONCEPT 170

flavoring [n] *spice, extract added to food* additive, condiment, distillation, essence, herb, quintessence, relish, sauce, seasoning, spirit, tincture, zest; CONCEPT 428.

flaw [n] *imperfection* blemish, bug, catch*,

Catch-22*, defect, disfigurement, failing, fault, foible, glitch*, gremlin*, pitfall, slipup, speck, spot, stain, typo*, vice, wart*, weakness, weak spot; CONCEPTS 580,674 —*Ant.* fine point, perfection, strength

flawless [*adj*] *spotless, intact* absolute, entire, faultless, immaculate, impeccable, irreproach-able, perfect, sound, unblemished, unbroken, undamaged, unimpaired, unmarred, unsullied, whole; CONCEPTS 574,579 —*Ant.* damaged, defective, disfigured, flawed, imperfect

fleck [*n*] *spot, pinpoint mark* bit, dot, mite, mote, patch, pinpoint, speck, speckle, stipple, streak, stripe; CONCEPTS 284,831

fleck [*v*] *mark with spots* bespeckle, besprinkle, dapple, dot, dust, maculate, mottle, speckle, stipple, streak, variegate; CONCEPT 79

fledgling [*n*] *beginner in activity* apprentice, chick, colt, greenhorn*, learner, neophyte, nestling, newcomer, novice, rookie, tender-foot*, trainee, tyro*; CONCEPTS 352,366,424 —*Ant.* expert, professional

flee [*v*] *run away to escape* abscond, avoid, beat a hasty retreat*, blow*, bolt*, break, cut and run*, cut out*, decamp, depart, desert, elude, evade, fly, fly the coop*, get*, get away, get the hell out*, hotfoot*, jump, leave, make a getaway*, make off*, make oneself scarce*, make one's escape*, make quick exit*, make tracks*, retreat, scamper, scoot, scram*, skedaddle*, skip*, split*, step on it*, step on the gas*, take a hike*, take flight, take off, vamoose*, vanish; CONCEPTS 102,150,195 —*Ant.* face, meet, stand, stay, wait

fleece [*v*] *plunder, steal* bleed*, burn*, cheat*, clip*, con, cozen, defraud, despoil, flimflam*, gouge, hustle, jerk around*, milk*, mulct, overcharge, pluck, rifle, rip off*, rob, rook*, rope in*, run a game on*, sell a bill of goods*, shaft*, strip, swindle, take for a ride*, take to the cleaners*; CONCEPTS 59,139,342 —*Ant.* give, offer

fleecy [*adj*] *downy, woolly; like a lamb's coat* floccose, flocculent, fluffy, hairy, hirsute, lanose, pileous, pilose, shaggy, soft, whiskered; CONCEPT 606

fleet [*adj*] *quick in movement* agile, barreling, breakneck*, brisk, expeditious, expeditive, fast, flying, hasty, in nothing flat*, like greased light-ning*, lively, mercurial, meteoric, nimble, nim-ble-footed, on the double*, rapid, screaming, speedball*, speedy, swift, winged; CONCEPTS 584,588 —*Ant.* clumsy, slow

fleet [*n*] *group of ships* argosy, armada, flotilla, formation, line, naval force, navy, sea power, squadron, tonnage, vessels, warships; CONCEPTS 322,432,506

fleeting [*adj*] *brief, transient* cursory, ephemeral, evanescent, fading, flash in the pan*, flitting, flying, fugacious, fugitive, imper-manent, meteoric, momentary, passing, short, short-lived, sudden, temporary, transitory, vanishing, volatile; CONCEPTS 551,798 —*Ant.* constant, continual, endless, enduring, lasting, lengthy, long, long-lived, permanent, perpetual

flesh [*n1*] *body tissue, skin* beef, brawn, cells, corpuscles, fat, fatness, flesh and blood, food, meat, muscle, plasm, plasma, protoplasm, sinews, thews, weight; CONCEPT 392

flesh [*n2*] *humankind* animality, carnality, homo sapiens, humanity, human nature, human race, living creatures, mortality, people, physicality, physical nature, race, sensuality, stock, world; CONCEPTS 407,417

fleshly [*adj1*] *lecherous, desiring sex* animal, animalistic, bodily, carnal, erotic, gross, lascivious, lewd, lustful, profane, sensual, venereal, voluptuous; CONCEPTS 372,529,545 —*Ant.* immaterial, religious, spiritual

fleshly [*adj2*] *bodily* corporal, corporeal, earthly, human, material, mundane, of this world, physical, secular, somatic, terrestrial, worldly; CONCEPT 536 —*Ant.* mentally, spiritual

fleshy [*adj*] *overweight* adipose, ample, beefy*, brawny, chubby*, chunky*, corpulent, fat, gross, heavy, hefty, husky, meaty*, obese, plump, porcine, portly, pudgy*, pulpy, sarcous, stout, tubby*, weighty, well-padded*, zaftig*; CONCEPTS 406,491,773 —*Ant.* skinny, thin, underweight

flex [*v*] *bend* angle, contract, crook, curve, lean, mold, ply, spring, stretch, tighten, tilt, yield; CONCEPTS 147,149 —*Ant.* be stiff, extend, straighten

flexibility [*n*] *elasticity, adaptability* adjustabili-ty, affability, complaisance, compliance, docility, extensibility, flaccidity, flexibleness, give, limberness, litheness, plasticity, pliability, pliancy, resilience, springiness, suppleness, tensility, tractability; CONCEPTS 652,731 —*Ant.* constraint, inelasticity, inflexibility, resistance

flexible [*adj1*] *pliable, bendable* adjustable, bending, ductile, elastic, extensible, extensile, flexile, formable, formative, impressionable, like putty*, limber, lithe, malleable, moldable, plastic, pliant, soft, spongy, springy, stretch, stretchable, stretchy, supple, tensile, tractable, tractile, whippy*, willowy, yielding; CONCEPTS 485,488 —*Ant.* brittle, inflexible, resistant, rigid, stiff, unbendable, unpliable, unyielding

flexible [*adj2*] *adaptable, responsive* acquies-cent, adjustable, amenable, biddable, com-pliant, compliant, discretionary, docile, gentle, going every which way*, hanging loose*, like putty in hands*, manageable, open, rolling with punches*, tractable, variable; CONCEPTS 401,542 —*Ant.* inflexible, obstinate, ornery, stern, stubborn, unaccommodating, unadaptable, unresponsive, unyielding

flick [*v*] *light touch* dab, flicker, flip, hit, pat, snap, tap, tip, touch lightly; CONCEPT 612

flicker [*n*] *spark, glimmer* beam, flare, flash, gleam, oscillation, quivering, ray, scintillation, twinkle, vibration; CONCEPTS 145,624,831

flicker [*v*] *sparkle, flutter* blare, blaze, blink, burn, dance, flare, flash, flit, flitter, fluctuate, glance, gleam, glimmer, glint, glitter, glow, hover, oscillate, quaver, quiver, scintillate, shimmer, swing, tremble, twinkle, vibrate, waver; CONCEPTS 152,624

flier [*n*] *flyer, pilot* ace*, aeronaut, air person, aviator, aviatrix, jet*, navigator; CONCEPT 348

flight [*n1*] *flying; journey* aerial navigation, aeronautics, arrival, aviation, avigation, depar-ture, gliding, hop, jump, mounting, navigation, shuttle, soaring, take-off, transport, trip, volitation, voyage, winging; CONCEPT 224

fl
fl

flight [n2] *fleeing; departure* beat*, break*, breakout, escape, escapement, escaping, exfiltration, exit, exodus, fugue, getaway, getaway car*, lam, out*, powder*, retreat, retreating, running away, slip*, spring*; CONCEPTS 102, 195 —*Ant.* standing, staying, waiting

flightiness [n] *irresponsibility* airheadedness*, capriciousness, changeability, dizziness, fickleness, flippancy, frivolity, giddiness, inconstancy, instability, levity, lightness, mercurialness, variability, volatility, whimsicality, whimsicalness; CONCEPT 633 —*Ant.* responsibility

flighty [adj] *fickle, irresponsible* airheaded*, birdbrained*, bubbleheaded*, capricious, changeable, dingbat*, dingdong*, dizzy*, effervescent, empty-headed, featherbrained*, frivolous, gaga*, giddy, harebrained*, impetuous, impulsive, inconstant, lightheaded, lively, mercurial, scatterbrained, silly, thoughtless, twit, unbalanced, unstable, unsteady, volatile, whimsical, wild; CONCEPT 401 —*Ant.* responsible

flimflam [v] *deceive, swindle* bilk, burn*, cheat, chisel, con, defraud, diddle*, dupe*, fleece, fool, gip*, gull, gyp*, hose*, pull a fast one*, 'rip off*, rook*, sandbag, scam, shaft, steal, take for a ride*, trick; CONCEPTS 59,139,192

flimsy [adj1] *not strong; light, thin* chiffon, cutrate*, decrepit, defective, delicate, diaphanous, feeble, fragile, frail, gauzy, gossamer, house of cards*, inadequate, infirm, insubstantial, meager, papery, rickety, rinkydink*, shaky, shallow, sheer, slapdash*, sleazy, slight, superficial, tacky, transparent, unsound, unsubstantial, weak, wobbly; CONCEPT 606 —*Ant.* firm, heavy, solid, strong, sturdy, substantial, thick, tough

flimsy [adj2] *unconvincing, implausible* assailable, baseless, contemptible, controvertible, fallacious, false, feeble, frivolous, groundless, illogical, improbable, inadequate, inane, inconceivable, incredible, inept, lame, poor, puerile, superficial, thin, transparent, trifling, trivial, unbelievable, ungrounded, unpersuasive, unreasonable, unsatisfactory, unsubstantial, weak, weakly, wishful; CONCEPT 267 —*Ant.* convincing, plausible, reasonable, serious, strong

flinch [v] *shy away, wince* avoid, balk, blanch, blench, blink, cower, cringe, crouch, draw back, duck, elude, escape, eschew, evade, flee, quail, recede, recoil, retire, retreat, shirk, shrink, shun, start, swerve, withdraw; CONCEPTS 102,150 —*Ant.* confront, face, meet

fling [n1] *casual throw* cast, chuck, firing, heave, hurl, launching, lob, peg, pitch, shot, slinging, toss; CONCEPT 222

fling [n2] *unrestrained behavior* affair, attempt, binge, celebration, crack*, essay, fun, gamble, go*, good time, indulgence, orgy, party, rampage, shot*, splurge, spree, stab*, trial, try, venture, whirl; CONCEPT 386

fling [v] *throw with abandon* cast, catapult, chuck*, dump, fire, heave, hurl, jerk, launch, let fly*, lob, peg*, pitch, precipitate, propel, send, shy*, sling, toss; CONCEPT 222

flinty [adj] *stern* cruel, firm, hard, inflexible, rigid, steely, stony, unsympathetic, unyielding; CONCEPT 604

flip [n/v] *throw, jump with abandon* cast, chuck, flick, jerk, pitch, snap, spin, toss, twist; CONCEPTS 194,222

flip-flop [n] *reversal* about-face, change, change of heart, turn-around, U-turn; CONCEPTS 674,679

flip out [v] *lose one's cool* blow a gasket*, blow one's mind*, blow one's stack*, blow one's top*, crack up*, fly off the handle*, freak out*, go ape*, go ballistic*, go berserk*, go crazy*, go haywire*, go nuts*, go off the deep end*, hit the ceiling*, lose control of oneself, lose it*, lose one's composure, lose one's mind, lose one's temper, wig out*; CONCEPT 13

flippancy [n] *irreverence* archness, cheek, cheekiness, cockiness, disrespectfulness, flightiness, freshness, frivolity, impertinence, impishness, impudence, levity, lightness, mischievousness, pertness, playfulness, roguishness, rudeness, sauciness, volatility, waggishness; CONCEPT 633 —*Ant.* courtesy, respect, reverence, seriousness

flippant [adj] *irreverent* brassy, breezy, cheeky*, cocky, disrespectful, flighty, flip*, fresh, frivolous, glib, impertinent, impudent, insolent, lippy*, nervy*, offhand, pert, playful, rude, sassy*, smart*, smart-alecky*, superficial; CONCEPT 401 —*Ant.* courteous, respectful, reverent, serious

flip side [n] *reverse side* back, B-side*, contraposition, opposite side, other side, other side of the fence*; CONCEPT 665

flirt [n] *person who makes advances* coquette, cruiser*, heartbreaker, operator*, philanderer, player, seducer, siren, swinger, tease, trifler, vamp, vixen, wanton, wolf*; CONCEPT 423

flirt [v] *make advances toward someone* banter, bat eyes at*, come hither*, come on*, coquet, dally, disport, eyeball*, fool, gam*, hit on*, lead on, linger with, make a move*, make a pass*, ogle, philander, pick up*, pitch*, proposition, tease, wink at*; CONCEPTS 375, 384 —*Ant.* be faithful

flirtation [n] *amorous advance* amour, coquetry, courting, cruising, dalliance, flirting, intrigue, pickup*, romance, romancing, tease, teasing, toying*, trifling*; CONCEPTS 32,375, 384 —*Ant.* faithfulness

flirtatious [adj] *provocative, teasing* amorous, arch, come-hither*, come-on*, coquettish, coy, dallying, enticing, flirty, libidinous, spoony*, sportive; CONCEPTS 401,404 —*Ant.* cool, modest, shy, unprovocative

flit [v] *flutter, move rapidly* dance, dart, flash, fleet, flicker, float, fly, hover, hurry, pass, run, rush, sail, scud*, skim, speed, sweep, whisk, whiz, wing, zip; CONCEPT 150

float [v] *lie on the surface* be buoyant, bob, drift, glide, hang, hover, move gently, poise, rest on water, ride, sail, skim, slide, slip along, smooth along, stay afloat, swim, waft, wash; CONCEPT 153 —*Ant.* drown, sink

flock [n] *congregation* army, assembly, bevy, brood, cloud, collection, colony, company, convoy, crowd, crush, drift, drove, flight, gaggle, gathering, group, herd, host, legion, litter, mass, multitude, pack, progeny, rout, scores, skein, throng; CONCEPTS 391,432

flock [v] *congregate* collect, converge, crowd, gather, group, herd, huddle, mass, throng, troop; CONCEPTS 109,384 —*Ant.* disperse, separate, spread

flog [v] *whip, lash* beat, belt, cane, castigate, chastise, ferule, flagellate, flax, flay, give the cat o'nine tails*, hide, hit, larrup, lather, leather*, paddle, scourge, spank, strike, stripe, tan one's hide*, thrash, trounce, wax*, whack, whale*, whomp*, whop*; CONCEPT 189

flood [n] *overwhelming flow, quantity* abundance, alluvion, bore, bounty, cataclysm, cataract, current, deluge, downpour, drencher, drift, eager, excess, flow, flux, freshet, glut, inundation, multitude, niagara, outgushing, outpouring, overflow, plenty, pour, profusion, rush, spate, stream, superabundance, superfluity, surge, surplus, tide, torrent, tsunami, wave; CONCEPTS 179,524,787

flood [v] *inundate or submerge* brim over, choke, deluge, drown, engulf, fill, flow, glut, gush, immerse, overflow, oversupply, overwhelm, pour over, rush, saturate, surge, swamp, swarm, sweep, whelm; CONCEPTS 179,209,740

floor [n] *bottom of a room; level of a multistory building* basement, boards, canvas, carpet, cellar, deck, downstairs, flat, flooring, ground, landing, lowest point, mat, mezzanine, nadir, rug, stage, story, tier, upstairs; CONCEPT 440 —*Ant.* ceiling

floor [v] *perplex, confound* baffle, beat, bewilder, bowl over*, bring down*, bring up short*, conquer, defeat, discomfit, disconcert, down, drop, dumbfound, fell, flatten, ground, knock down, lay low*, level, nonplus, overthrow, prostrate, puzzle, stump, throw; CONCEPTS 16,95 —*Ant.* clear up, explain

floor it [v] *drive at full speed* accelerate, barrel, gather momentum, go flat-out, nail it*, open the throttle, put the pedal to the metal*, sprint, step on it*, step on the gas; CONCEPTS 234,242

floozy [n] *sexually promiscuous woman* bimbo, broad, doxy, easy make, hooker, moll, nympho, piece of tail*, prostitute, tramp, whore; CONCEPTS 348,412,415,419

flop [n] *miserable failure* bomb, bust, debacle, disaster, dud*, fiasco, lemon*, loser, miscarriage, nonstarter, washout*; CONCEPTS 674,699 —*Ant.* accomplishment, achievement, success

flop [v1] *fall limply, collapse* dangle, droop, drop, flag, flap, flounder, flutter, hang, jerk, lop, quiver, sag, slump, stagger, teeter, topple, toss, totter, tumble, wave, wiggle; CONCEPTS 144,181

flop [v2] *fail miserably* bomb*, close, come apart*, come to nothing*, fall flat*, fall short*, flummox, fold, founder, miscarry, misfire, wash out*; CONCEPT 699 —*Ant.* accomplish, achieve, succeed

flophouse [n] *cheap hotel* fleabag, fleabox, fleahouse, fleatrap, flop joint, run-down boarding house, run-down hotel; CONCEPTS 439,449,516

floppy [adj] *limp* drooping, droopy, flabby, flaccid, loose, pendulous, relaxed, sagging, saggy, slack; CONCEPT 485 —*Ant.* erect, stiff

floral [adj] *decorated with flowers* blooming, blossoming, blossomy, botanic, decorative, dendritic, efflorescent, flower-patterned, flowery, herbaceous, sylvan, verdant; CONCEPT 589

florid [adj1] *very elaborate* aureate, baroque, busy, decorative, embellished, euphuistic, figurative, flamboyant, flowery, fussy, garnished, grandiloquent, high-flown, luscious, magnilo-

quent, ornamental, ornamented, ornate, overblown, pretentious, rhetorical, rich, sonorous; CONCEPTS 267,589 —*Ant.* inelaborate, natural, plain, undecorated, unornate

florid [adj2] *flushed, ruddy* blowzy, flush, glowing, high-colored, pink, reddened, rubicund, sanguine; CONCEPTS 406,618 —*Ant.* pale, pallid, white

flotilla [n] *small fleet* argosy, armada, group, navy, squadron, unit, vessels; CONCEPTS 322,432,506

flotsam [n] *floating debris* cargo, castoffs, jetsam, junk, odds and ends, sea-drift, wreckage; CONCEPTS 260,674

flounce [v] *bounce; intermittently move* fling, jerk, mince, nancy, prance, sashay, spring, stamp, storm, strut, swish, throw, toss; CONCEPT 149

flounder [v] *struggle; be in the dark* blunder, bobble, cast about, come apart at the seams*, drop the ball*, fall down, flop, flummox, foul up*, fumble, go at backwards*, go to pieces*, grope, labor, lurch, make a mess of, miss one's cue*, muddle, plunge, pratfall*, screw up*, slip up*, snafu*, strive, stub one's toe*, stumble, thrash, toil, toss, travail, trip up*, tumble, wallow, work at; CONCEPTS 101,699 —*Ant.* do well, succeed

flourish [n] *curlicue, decoration* curl, embellishment, furbelow, garnish, ornamentation, plume, quirk, spiral, sweep, twist; CONCEPTS 259,284

flourish [v1] *grow, prosper* amplify, arrive, augment, batten, bear fruit, be on top of heap*, bloom, blossom, boom, burgeon, come along, develop, do well, expand, flower, get ahead, get on*, go, go great guns*, hit it big*, increase, live high on hog*, make out*, multiply, score, succeed, thrive, wax; CONCEPTS 141,704,706 —*Ant.* cease, fail, hinder, languish, stunt

flourish [v2] *wave about* brandish, display, flaunt, flutter, shake, sweep, swing, swish, twirl, vaunt, wag, wield; CONCEPTS 147,152

flourishing [adj] *prospering, going well* blooming, burgeoning, doing well, expanding, exuberant, going strong, growing, in full swing*, in the pink*, in top form*, lush, luxuriant, mushrooming, profuse, prosperous, rampant, rank, rich, roaring, robust, successful, thriving, vigorous; CONCEPT 528 —*Ant.* ceasing, decreasing, failing, languishing, stunted, undeveloping

flout [v] *show contempt for* affront, defy, deride, disregard, gibe, gird, insult, jeer, laugh at, mock, outrage, quip, repudiate, ridicule, scoff, scorn, slight, sneer, spurn, taunt, thumb nose at*; CONCEPT 54 —*Ant.* honor, respect

flow [n] *issue, abundance* breeze, continuance, continuation, continuity, course, current, deluge, discharge, draft, draw, dribble, drift, ebb, effusion, electricity, emanation, flood, flux, gush, juice, leakage, movement, oozing, outflow, outpouring, plenty, plethora, progress, progression, river, run, sequence, series, spate, spout, spurt, stream, succession, tide, train, wind; CONCEPTS 146,179,467,787 —*Ant.* trickle

flow [v] *issue, surge, run out* abound, arise, brim, cascade, circulate, continue, course, deluge, discharge, disembogue, dribble, ebb, emanate, emerge, emit, exudate, exude, flood, glide, gurgle, gush, inundate, jet, leak, move, ooze, overflow, pass, percolate, pour, proceed, progress, pullulate, regurgitate, result, ripple, roll, rush, slide, sluice, smooth along, spew, spill, splash, spring, spurt, sputter, squirt, stream, sweep, swell, swirl, teem, trickle, tumble, void, well forth; CONCEPTS *146,179* —*Ant.* trickle

flowchart [*n*] *sequential diagram* flow diagram, flow sheet; CONCEPTS *625,660*

flower [*n1*] *bloom of a plant* annual, blossom, bud, cluster, efflorescence, floret, floweret, head, herb, inflorescence, perennial, pompon, posy, shoot, spike, spray, vine; CONCEPTS *425,428*

flower [*n2*] *best, choicest part* cream, elite, finest point, freshness, greatest point, height, pick, pride, prime, prize, top; CONCEPTS *668,829* —*Ant.* worst

flower [*v*] *bloom, flourish* batten, blossom, blow, burgeon, effloresce, mature, open, outbloom, prosper, thrive, unfold; CONCEPTS *253,704*—*Ant.* close, die, droop, fade, sag, shrink, shrivel

flowery [*adj*] *ornate, especially referring to speech or writing* aureate, baroque, bombastic, declamatory, diffuse, embellished, euphemistic, euphuistic, fancy, figurative, florid, grandiloquent, high-flown, magniloquent, ornamented, overwrought, prolix, purple, redundant, rhetorical, rococo, sonorous, swollen, verbose, windy, wordy; CONCEPTS *267,589*—*Ant.* inelaborate, plain, unembellished, unflowery, unornate

flowing [*adj*] *gushing, abounding* brimming, continuous, cursive, easy, falling, flooded, fluent, fluid, fluidic, full, issuing, liquefied, liquid, overrun, pouring out, prolific, rich, rippling, rolling, running, rushing, sinuous, smooth, spouting, streaming, sweeping, teeming, tidal, unbroken, uninterrupted; CONCEPTS *482,584* —*Ant.* trickling

fluctuate [*v*] *vacillate, change* alter, alternate, be undecided, blow hot and cold*, ebb and flow, flutter, go up and down*, hem and haw*, hesitate, oscillate, rise and fall*, seesaw*, shift, swing, undulate, vary, veer, vibrate, wave, waver, yo-yo*; CONCEPTS *13,469,697* —*Ant.* hold, persist, remain, stay

flue [*n*] *pipe* channel, chimney, duct, exhaust pipe, passage, smoke duct, tube, vent; CONCEPT *440*

fluent [*adj*] *articulate* chatty, cogent, copious, cursive, declamatory, disputatious, easy, effortless, effusive, eloquent, facile, flowing, garrulous, glib, liquid, loquacious, mellifluent, mellifluous, natural, persuasive, prompt, quick, ready, running, silver-tongued*, smooth, smooth-spoken, talkative, verbose, vocal, voluble, well-versed, wordy; CONCEPTS *267, 584*—*Ant.* effortful, hesitant, inarticulate, unfluent, unprepared

fluff [*n1*] *down* eiderdown, feathers, fleece, floss, fuzz, lint, wool; CONCEPT *606*

fluff [*n2*] *mistake* blooper*, bungling, error, false step, flub*, fumble, miscalculation, miscue, miss, muddle, muff, oversight, slip, slipup*, stumble; CONCEPTS *101,230,410*

fluffy [*adj*] *soft, furry* creamy, downy, featherlike, feathery, fleecy, flocculent, flossy, gossamer, linty, pile, silky, velutinous; CONCEPT *606* —*Ant.* coarse, rough, smooth

fluid [*adj1*] *liquid* aqueous, flowing, fluent, in solution, juicy, liquefied, lymphatic, melted, molten, running, runny, serous, uncongealed, watery; CONCEPTS *603,757*—*Ant.* solid

fluid [*adj2*] *adaptable, changeable* adjustable, changeful, flexible, floating, fluctuating, indefinite, malleable, mercurial, mobile, mutable, protean, shifting, unsettled, unstable, unsteady, variable; CONCEPTS *534,542* —*Ant.* inflexible, stable, unchangeable

fluid [*n*] *liquid* aqua, broth, chaser, cooler, goo*, goop*, juice, liquor, solution, vapor; CONCEPT *467*—*Ant.* solid

fluke [*n*] *chance occurrence* accident, blessing, break, contingency, fortuity, fortunate, fortune, good fortune*, good luck, incident, lucky break*, odd chance, quirk, stroke of luck*, windfall; CONCEPTS *4,679,693* —*Ant.* certainty, design, plan

fluky [*adj*] *chance* accidental, casual, chancy, coincidental, contingent, fortuitous, incalculable, incidental, lucky, odd, uncertain, variable; CONCEPT *552* —*Ant.* certain, designed, planned, sure

flume [*n*] *chute* channel, conduit, run, sluice, spillway; CONCEPTS *501,514*

flummox [*v*] *confuse* baffle, bewilder, buffalo*, confound, discombobulate*, disconcert, mystify, nonplus, perplex, puzzle, stump, throw*, throw off*; CONCEPT *16*

flurry [*n*] *commotion, burst* ado, agitation, brouhaha, bustle, confusion, disturbance, excitement, ferment, flap*, flaw, fluster, flutter, furor, fuss, gust, haste, hurry, outbreak, pother, spell, spurt, squall, stir*, to-do, tumult, turbulence, turmoil, whirl, whirlwind; CONCEPTS *230,524* —*Ant.* calm, calmness, quiet

flurry [*v*] *agitate, confuse* bewilder, bother, bustle, discombobulate*, discompose, disconcert, disquiet, distract, disturb, excite, fluster, flutter, frustrate, fuss, galvanize, hassle, hurry, hustle, perplex, perturb, provoke, quicken, rattle, ruffle, stimulate, unhinge, unsettle, upset; CONCEPTS *7,19*—*Ant.* calm, comfort, quiet

flush [*adj1*] *flat* even, horizontal, level, planate, plane, smooth, square, true; CONCEPTS *486,490* —*Ant.* rough, uneven

flush [*adj2*] *overflowing, abundant* affluent, close, full, generous, lavish, liberal, opulent, prodigal, rich, wealthy, well-off; CONCEPTS *334,771*—*Ant.* lacking

flush [*n*] *blush* bloom, color, freshness, glow, pinkness, redness, rosiness, ruddiness; CONCEPT *622* —*Ant.* pale

flush [*v1*] *become or make pink or red* blush, burn, color, color up, crimson, flame, glow, go red, mantle, pink, pinken, redden, rose, rouge, suffuse; CONCEPTS *250,469*—*Ant.* pale, uncolor

flush [*v2*] *inundate with liquid* cleanse, douche, drench, eject, expel, flood, hose, rinse, swab, wash; CONCEPTS *165,179*

flushed [*adj*] *pink, glowing* ablaze, animated, aroused, blushing, burning, crimson, elated, embarrassed, enthused, exhilarated, feverish, florid, full-blooded, high, hot, inspired, intoxicated, red, rosy, rubicund, ruddy, sanguine, thrilled; CONCEPTS *401,403,618*—*Ant.* pale, pallid

fluster [n] *perturbation, upset* agitation, brouhaha, commotion, disturbance, dither, flap*, flurry, flutter, furor, ruffle, state*, to-do*, turmoil; CONCEPT 410 —*Ant.* calm, calmness, comfort, peace

fluster [v] *upset, perturb* addle, agitate, bewilder, bother, confound, confuse, craze*, discombobulate*, discompose, disquiet, distract, disturb, excite, flip*, flurry, frustrate, fuddle*, get to*, hassle, heat*, hurry, make nervous, make waves*, muddle, mystify, nonplus, perplex, psych*, rattle, ruffle, spook*, stir up*, throw off balance*, unhinge*, work up*; CONCEPTS 7,16,19 —*Ant.* calm, comfort, settle

flutter [v] *wave rapidly, flap* agitate, bat, beat, dance, drift, flicker, flit, flitter, flop, fluctuate, hover, lop, oscillate, palpitate, pulsate, quaver, quiver, ripple, ruffle, shake, shiver, swing, throb, tremble, vibrate, wiggle, wobble; CONCEPTS 150,152

flux [n] *state of constant change* alteration, change, flow, fluctuation, fluidity, instability, modification, motion, mutability, mutation, transition, unrest; CONCEPT 697 —*Ant.* constancy, stability, steadiness

fly [v1] *take to the air, usually employing wings* aviate, barnstorm*, bend the throttle*, buzz*, circle, circumnavigate, climb, control, cross, dart, dash, dive, drift, flat-hat*, fleet, flit, float, flutter, glide, hop, hover, hurry, jet, jet out, jet over, maneuver, mount, operate, pilot, reach, remain aloft, rush, sail, scud*, seagull*, shoot, skim, skirt, sky out*, soar, speed, swoop, take a hop*, take flight, take off, take wing, travel, whisk*, whiz*, whoosh*, wing*, wing in*, zip*, zoom*; CONCEPTS 148,150,224 —*Ant.* land, stay on ground, walk

fly [v2] *run or pass swiftly* barrel, bolt, breeze, career, dart, dash, elapse, flee, flit, glide, go like the wind*, hasten, hurry, hustle, make off*, pass, race, roll, run its course*, rush, scamper, scoot, shoot, slip away*, speed, sprint, tear, whiz*, zoom*; CONCEPTS 150,818

fly [v3] *escape, flee* abscond, avoid, bolt, break, clear, clear out*, cut and run*, decamp, disappear, get away, hasten away, hide, hightail*, light out*, make a getaway*, make a quick exit*, make off, run*, run for it, run from, skedaddle*, skip, steal away, take flight, take off, withdraw; CONCEPTS 102,195 —*Ant.* confront, face, remain, stay

fly-by-night [adj] *undependable* brief, cowboy*, dubious, here-today-gone-tomorrow*, impermanent, questionable, shady, shifty, short-lived, slimy*, slippery*, treacherous, trustless, unreliable, unsure, untrustworthy; CONCEPTS 542,551 —*Ant.* dependable, reliable, reputable, responsible, trustworthy

flyer [n] *person who navigates an aircraft* ace*, air person, aviator, flier, jet*, navigator, pilot; CONCEPT 348

flying [adj] *in the air, winged* aerial, aeronautical, airborne, avian, drifting, express, flapping, fleet, floating, fluttering, gliding, hovering, mercurial, mobile, on the wing, plumed, soaring, speedy, streaming, swooping, volant, volar, volitant, waving, winging, zooming; CONCEPT 584 —*Ant.* ground, grounded

flying saucer [n] *spaceship* extraterrestrial vessel, spacecraft, UFO, unidentified flying object; CONCEPTS 504,506

foam [n] *bubbles formed from a liquid* cream, fluff, froth, head, lather, scum, spray, spume, suds, surf, yeast; CONCEPT 260

foam [v] *become bubbly* aerate, boil, burble, effervesce, ferment, fizz, froth, gurgle, hiss, lather, seethe, simmer, sparkle; CONCEPTS 170,469 —*Ant.* become flat

foamy [adj] *bubbly* barmy, boiling, burbling, carbonated, creamy, ebullient, effervescent, fermented, fizzy, frothy, lathery, scummy*, seething, simmering, spumescent, spumous, spumy, sudsy, yeasty; CONCEPT 485 —*Ant.* flat

focus [n] *center of attraction* bull's eye*, center, core, cynosure, focal point, headquarters*, heart, hub, limelight*, locus, meeting place, nerve center*, point of convergence, polestar, seat, spotlight, target; CONCEPTS 532, 826,829

focus [v] *aim attention at* adjust, attract, bring out, center, centralize, concenter, concentrate, convene, converge, direct, fasten, fix, fixate, get detail, home in*, home in on*, hone in*, join, key on*, knuckle down*, meet, move in, pinpoint, pour it on*, put, rivet, sharpen, spotlight*, sweat*, zero in*, zoom in*; CONCEPTS 17,623 —*Ant.* ignore, neglect

fodder [n] *animal feed* animal food, barley, corn, food, forage, grain, grass, grub, hay, meal, pasturage, provender, provisions, silage, straw, vittles; CONCEPTS 457,460,461

foe [n] *person who is an adversary* antagonist, anti*, enemy, hostile party, rival; CONCEPT 412 —*Ant.* friend

fog [n1] *heavy mist that reduces visibility* brume, cloud, effluvium, film, gloom, grease, ground clouds, haze, London fog, miasma, murk, murkiness, nebula, obscurity, pea soup*, smaze, smog, smoke, smother, soup*, steam, vapor, visibility zero-zero*, wisp; CONCEPTS 524,627 —*Ant.* clearness

fog [n2] *mental unclarity* befuddlement, blindness, confusion, daze, haze, maze, mist, muddledness, muddlement, obscurity, perplexity, stupor, trance, vagueness; CONCEPT 410 —*Ant.* cognizance, understanding

fog [v] *muddle, obscure* addle, becloud, bedim, befuddle, bewilder, blind, blur, cloud, confuse, darken, daze, dim, eclipse, mist, muddy, mystify, obfuscate, perplex, puzzle, steam up, stupefy; CONCEPTS 250,526 —*Ant.* clear up, explain

foggy [adj] *hazy, obscure* blurred, ceiling zero*, closed in, clouded, cloudy, dark, dim, filmy, fogged in, fuzzy, gray, indistinct, misty, murky, mushy, nebulous, pea-soupy*, smazy, smoggy, socked in*, soupy*, unclear, vague, vaporous, vapory, zero-zero*; CONCEPTS 403,525 —*Ant.* clear

foghorn [n] *warning signal* alarm, danger signal, signal, siren; CONCEPTS 269,463

foible [n] *personal imperfection* characteristic, defect, eccentricity, failing, fault, frailty, idiosyncrasy, infirmity, kink, mannerism, oddity, peculiarity, quirk, shortcoming, singularity, vice, weakness, weak point; CONCEPTS 411,644 —*Ant.* strength

fl
fo

foil [n] *contrast* antithesis, background, complement, counterblow, defense, guard, setting; CONCEPT 665

foil [v] *circumvent, nip in the bud* baffle, balk, beat, bilk, bollix*, buffalo*, check, checkmate, counter, crab, cramp, crimp, curb, dash, defeat, disappoint, disconcert, ditch, dodge, duck, elude, faze, foul up*, frustrate, get around*, give the run-around*, give the slip*, hang up*, hinder, juke, nullify, outwit, prevent, rattle, restrain, run circles around*, run rings around*, shake, shake off, shuffle off, skip, stop, stymie, throw monkey wrench in*, thwart, upset the apple cart*; CONCEPTS 121,130 —Ant. abet, aid, assist, help

foist [v] *force upon* compel to accept, fob off, impose, insert fraudulently, palm off, pass off, pull a fast one*, ram down one's throat*, sneak in; CONCEPT 14

fold [n] *double thickness* bend, circumvolution, cockle, convolution, corrugation, crease, crimp, crinkle, dog's ear*, flection, flexure, furrow, gather, gathering, groove, knife-edge*, lap, lapel, layer, loop, overlap, plait, pleat, plica, plication, plicature, ply, pucker, ridge, rimple, rivel, ruche, ruck, ruffle, rumple, shirring, smocking, tuck, turn, wrinkle; CONCEPT 754

fold [v1] *lay in creases* bend, cockle, corrugate, crimp, crisp, crumple, curl, dog-ear*, double, double over, furrow, gather, groove, hem, intertwine, knit, lap, overlap, overlay, plait, pleat, plicate, pucker, purse, replicate, ridge, ruche, ruck, ruffle, telescope, tuck, turn under, wrinkle; CONCEPT 184 —Ant. flatten, leave, unbend

fold [v2] *encase, enclose* do up, enfold, entwine, envelop, involve, wrap, wrap up; CONCEPT 209 —Ant. free, let out, loose, loosen

fold [v3] *fail, close* become insolvent, be ruined, break, bust, collapse, crash, crumple, give, go bankrupt, go bust, go into Chapter 11*, go under*, impoverish, pauper, pauperize, shut down, yield; CONCEPTS 324,699 —Ant. achieve, succeed

folder [n] *paper envelope for holding items* binder, case, file, pocket, portfolio, sheath, wrapper, wrapping; CONCEPT 260

foliage [n] *leaves* frondescence, greenness, growth, herbage, leafage, umbrage, vegetation, verdure; CONCEPT 428

folk [n] *person's relations, acquaintances* body politic, clan, community, confederation, culture group, ethnic group, family, general public, group, house, household, inhabitants, kin, kindred, lineage, masses, ménage, nation, nationality, people, population, proletariat, public, race, settlement, society, state, stock, tribe; CONCEPTS 296,379

folklore [n] *tales from the past* ballad, custom, fable, folk story, legend, myth, mythology, mythos, oral literature, superstition, tradition, wisdom; CONCEPT 282

folks [n] *family* brood, clan, horde, household, kin, parents, people, relatives, tribe; CONCEPTS 296,378,397

folksy [adj] *informal, simple* cozy, down-to-earth*, homely, homey, low-key, modest, natural, plain, rustic, unassuming, unpretentious; CONCEPTS 562,589

follow [v1] *take the place of* be subsequent to, chase, come after, come from, come next, displace, ensue, go after, go next, postdate, proceed from, pursue, replace, result, spring from, succeed, supersede, supervene, supplant; CONCEPTS 128,242,813 —Ant. neglect, pass over, shun, slight

follow [v2] *trail, pursue physically* accompany, attend, bring up the rear*, catenate, chase, come with, concatenate, convoy, dog*, dog the footsteps of*, draggle, escort, freeze, give chase, go after, go with, hound*, hunt, onto*, persecute, put a tail on*, run after, run down, schlepp along*, search, seek, shadow, shag*, spook*, stalk, stick to, string along, tag, tag after*, tag along*, tail, tailgate*, take out after, track; CONCEPT 207 —Ant. go before, lead, precede

follow [v3] *act in accordance with* abide by, accord, adhere to, adopt, attend, be consistent with, be devoted to, be guided by, be in keeping, be interested in, comply, conform, copy, cultivate, do like, emulate, follow suit, give allegiance to, harmonize, heed, hold fast, imitate, keep, keep abreast of, keep an eye on, live up to, match, mimic, mind, mirror, model on, note, obey, observe, pattern oneself upon, reflect, regard, serve, string along*, support, take after, take as an example, watch; CONCEPTS 8,91,171 —Ant. avoid, disregard, scorn

follow [v4] *understand* accept, appreciate, apprehend, catch*, catch on*, comprehend, dig*, fathom, get*, get the picture*, grasp, realize, see, take in*; CONCEPT 15 —Ant. misunderstand, not get

follower [n] *person who believes or has great interest* addict, adherent, admirer, advocate, apostle, attendant, backer, believer, bootlicker*, buff, client, cohort, companion, convert, copycat, devotee, disciple, fan, fancier, freak*, habitué, hanger-on*, helper, imitator, lackey*, member, minion, parasite, participant, partisan, patron, promoter, proselyte, protégé, pupil, representative, satellite, sectary, servant, sidekick, stooge*, supporter, sycophant, toady*, vassal, votary, worshiper, zealot; CONCEPTS 352,366,423 —Ant. leader

following [adj] *happening, being next or after* after a while, afterward, attendant, a while later, back, by and by, coming, coming after, coming next, consecutive, consequent, consequential, directly after, ensuing, henceforth, hinder, in pursuit, in search of, in the wake of, later, later on, latter, next, next off*, on the scent*, posterior, presently, proximate, pursuing, rear, resulting, sequent, sequential, serial, seriate, specified, subsequent, succeeding, successive, supervenient, then, trailing, when; CONCEPTS 585,811, 818,820 —Ant. first, leading, preceding

following [n] *persons of an interest or belief* adherents, audience, circle, clientage, clientele, cortege, coterie, dependents, entourage, fans, group, groupies*, hangers-on*, patronage, patrons, public, retinue, rout, suite, support, supporters, train; CONCEPTS 294,387,417 —Ant. disbelievers

follow through [v] *bring to a conclusion* complete, conclude, consummate, pursue, see through; CONCEPT 91 —Ant. leave, not finish

follow up [v] *make inquiries* check out, find out about, investigate, look into, make sure, pursue; CONCEPT 103 —*Ant.* avoid, dodge, forget

folly [n] *nonsense, ridiculous idea* absurdity, craziness, daftness, dottiness, dumb thing to do*, dumb trick*, fatuity, foolishness, idiocy, imbecility, impracticality, imprudence, inadvisability, inanity, indiscretion, irrationality, lunacy, madness, obliquity, preposterousness, rashness, recklessness, senselessness, silliness, stupidity, triviality, unsoundness, vice, witlessness; CONCEPTS 410,633 —*Ant.* judgment, knowledge, seriousness, understanding, wisdom

foment [v] *instigate, provoke* abet, agitate, arouse, brew, cultivate, encourage, excite, fan the flames*, foster, goad, incite, nurse, nurture, promote, quicken, raise, set, set on, sow the seeds*, spur, start, stimulate, stir up, whip up*; CONCEPTS 14,221 —*Ant.* cease, dampen, discourage, dissuade, stop

fond [adj] *have a liking or taste for* addicted, adoring, affectionate, amorous, attached, caring, devoted, doting, enamored, indulgent, keen on, lovesome, lovey-dovey*, loving, mushy*, partial, predisposed, responsive, romantic, sentimental, silly over, sympathetic, tender, warm; CONCEPTS 32,542 —*Ant.* hating, hostile

fondle [v] *touch lovingly* bear hug*, caress, clutch, cosset, cuddle, dandle, embrace, feel, fool around*, grab, grope, hug, love, make love to, neck, nestle, nuzzle, pat, paw, pet, play footsie*, snuggle, squeeze, stroke; CONCEPTS 190,375

fondness [n] *liking or taste for* affection, attachment, devotion, fancy, kindness, love, partiality, penchant, predilection, preference, soft spot, susceptibility, tenderness, weakness; CONCEPT 32 —*Ant.* dislike, hate, hatred, loathing

font [n1] *source* fount, fountain, genesis, origin, root, seed, wellspring; CONCEPT 648

font [n2] *print type* face, typeface; CONCEPTS 79

food [n] *edible material* aliment, bite*, board, bread, cheer, chow*, comestible, cookery, cooking, cuisine, diet, drink, eatable, eats*, entrée, fare, fast food, feed, fodder*, foodstuff, goodies*, grit*, groceries*, grub*, handout*, home cooking, keep, larder, meal, meat, menu, mess*, moveable feast, nourishment, nutriment, nutrition, pabulum, provision, ration, refreshment, slop*, snack, store, subsistence, support, sustenance, table, take out, tuck, viand, victual, vittles*; CONCEPTS 457,460,461 —*Ant.* beverage, drink

food court [n] *public area where variety of food is sold* cafe, counter, fast food, food festival, restaurant, smorgasbord; CONCEPTS 439,448,449

foodie [n] *lover of food* bon vivant, bon viveur, connoisseur, gastronome, glutton, gourmand, gourmet, hedonist, sensualist; CONCEPT 366

food poisoning [n] *poisoning caused by eating food* botulism, ptomaine poisoning, salmonella; CONCEPT 537

fool [n] *stupid or ridiculous person* ass, birdbrain*, blockhead*, bonehead*, boob*, bore, buffoon, clod*, clown, cretin*, dimwit*, dolt*, dope*, dumb ox*, dunce, dunderhead*, easy mark*, fair game*, fathead*, goose*, halfwit,

idiot, ignoramus, illiterate, imbecile, innocent, jerk*, lamebrain*, lightweight*, loon*, moron, nerd*, nincompoop*, ninny*, nitwit, numskull*, oaf, sap*, schlemiel*, silly, simpleton, stooge*, sucker*, turkey*, twerp*, twit*, victim; CONCEPTS 412,423 —*Ant.* brain

fool [v] *trick, mislead* bamboozle*, bluff, cheat, chicane, con, deceive, delude, diddle, dupe, fake out*, flimflam*, fox*, gull, hoax, hoodwink*, jive*, juke*, kid, lead on, make believe, outfox, play-act*, play a trick on, pretend, put on, put one over on*, scam*, snow*, spoof*, suck in*, take in*, trifle; CONCEPT 59

fool around [v] *waste time* dawdle, hang around*, idle, kill time*, lark, mess around*, play around*; CONCEPT 681 —*Ant.* labor, toil, work

fooled [adj] *tricked* bamboozled*, conned, deceived, deluded, duped, flimflammed*, hornswoggled*, misled, outfoxed*, snowed*, sucked in*; CONCEPT 537 —*Ant.* clear, cognizant, unfooled, untricked

foolhardy [adj] *impetuous, rash* adventuresome, adventurous, audacious, bold, breakneck*, daredevil, daring, devil-may-care*, harebrained*, headstrong, imprudent, incautious, irresponsible, madcap, off deep end*, out on limb*, precipitate, reckless, temerarious, venturesome, venturous, wide open*; CONCEPT 401 —*Ant.* careful, cautious, discreet, thoughtful

fooling [n] *joking, tricks* bluffing, buffoonery, clownishness, farce, frolicking, high jinks*, horseplay, jesting, joshing, kidding, making light*, mockery, nonsense, pretense, roughhouse*, roughhousing*, rowdiness, sham*, skylarking*, spoofing, teasing, trifling; CONCEPT 59 —*Ant.* seriousness

foolish [adj] *nonsensical, idiotic* absurd, asinine, brainless, cockamamy*, crazy, daffy*, daft, dippy*, doltish*, dotty*, fantastic, fatuous, feebleminded*, half-baked*, half-witted*, harebrained*, ill-advised, ill-considered, imbecile, imprudent, incautious, indiscreet, injudicious, insane, irrational, jerky*, kooky*, loony*, ludicrous, lunatic, mad, moronic, nerdy*, nutty*, preposterous, ridiculous, senseless, short-sighted, silly, simple, stupid, unintelligent, unreasonable, unwise, wacky*, weak, witless, zany*; CONCEPTS 401,542,544 —*Ant.* careful, cautious, circumspect, prudent, sensible, serious, thoughtful, unfoolish, wise

foolishly [adv] *idiotic, without due consideration* absurdly, ill-advisedly, imprudently, incautiously, indiscreetly, injudiciously, mistakenly, short-sightedly, stupidly, unwisely; CONCEPTS 401,542,544 —*Ant.* carefully, cautiously, sensibly, thoughtfully, wisely

foolishness [n] *idiocy, nonsense* absurdity, absurdness, bunk*, carrying-on*, claptrap*, craziness, dumb trick*, folly, foolery, fool trick, horse feathers*, impracticality, imprudence, inanity, indiscretion, insanity, insensibility, irrationality, irresponsibility, ludicrousness, lunacy, mistake, poppycock*, preposterousness, rubbish*, senselessness, silliness, stupidity, tommyrot*, twaddle, unreasonableness, unwiseness, weakness, witlessness; CONCEPT 633 —*Ant.* care, carefulness, caution, circumspec-

fo
fo

tion, prudence, sense, seriousness, thoughtfulness, wiseness

foolproof [*adj*] *infallible* certain, dependable, fail-safe, faultless, flawless, goofproof, guaranteed, idiot-proof*, never-failing, perfect, reliable, safe, sure, sure-fire, tested, tried, unassailable, unerring, unfailing; CONCEPTS 535,582

foot [*n1*] *extremity of an animate being* hoof, pad, paw; CONCEPT 392

foot [*n2*] *base of an object* bottom, foundation, lowest point, nadir, pier; CONCEPT 442 —*Ant.* lid, top

foot [*n3*] *twelve inches/30.48 centimeters measured* cubic, square; CONCEPTS 790,791

footing [*n1*] *foundation, basis* basement, bedrock, bottom, establishment, foot, foothold, ground, groundwork, infrastructure, installation, resting place, seat, seating, settlement, substratum, substructure, underpinning, understructure, warrant; CONCEPTS 442,661

footing [*n2*] *social status* capacity, character, condition, grade, place, position, rank, relations, relationship, situation, standing, state, station, terms; CONCEPT 388

footloose [*adj*] *free* easygoing, free and easy, go-as-you-please, loose, unattached, uncommitted, unengaged; CONCEPTS 401,542

footprint [*n*] *footmark* footstep, hoofprint, impression, imprint, spoor, track, trail, tread; CONCEPTS 513,628

fop [*n*] *dandy* beau, Beau Brummel, clotheshorse, coxcomb, dude, fashion plate, macaroni, peacock, popinjay; CONCEPT 423

for [*conj*] *in consequence of the fact that* as, as long as, because, being, considering, inasmuch as, now, since, whereas; CONCEPT 544

for [*prep*] *in consideration of* after, as, beneficial to, concerning, conducive to, during, for the sake of, in contemplation of, in exchange for, in favor of, in furtherance of, in order to, in order to get, in place of, in pursuance of, in spite of, in the direction of, in the interest of, in the name of, notwithstanding, on the part of, on the side of, pro, supposing, to, to counterbalance, to go to, to the amount of, to the extent of, toward, under the authority of, with a view to, with regard to, with respect; CONCEPT 544

forage [*v*] *search madly for* beat, cast about, comb, explore, fine-tooth-comb*, grub, hunt, pilfer, plunder, raid, rake, ransack, ravage, rummage, scour, scrounge, seek; CONCEPT 216

foray [*n*] *incursion, attempt* attack, depredation, descent, inroad, invasion, irruption, raid, reconnaissance, sally, sortie; CONCEPTS 86,90,159 —*Ant.* abstention, idleness, laziness

forbear [*v*] *resist the temptation to* abstain, avoid, bridle, cease, curb, decline, desist, escape, eschew, evade, forgo, go easy*, hold back*, inhibit, keep, keep from, omit, pause, refrain, restrain, sacrifice, shun, stop, withhold; CONCEPTS 35,121,130,681 —*Ant.* continue, indulge, involve, partake, use

forbearance [*n*] *resisting, avoidance* abstinence, endurance, fortitude, going easy on*, living with*, longanimity, moderation, patience, patientness, refraining, resignation, restraint, self-control, temperance, tolerance; CONCEPTS 410,633 —*Ant.* continuation, indulgence, involvement, pursual, use

forbearing [*adj*] *tolerant* being big*, charitable, clement, considerate, easy, forgiving, gentle, going easy on*, going easy with*, humane, humanitarian, indulgent, lenient, living with*, longanimous, long-suffering, merciful, mild, moderate, patient, soft-shell*, thoughtful; CONCEPTS 404,542 —*Ant.* impatient, intolerant, merciless, strict, uncontrolled

forbid [*v*] *outlaw, prohibit an action* ban, block, cancel, censor, check, debar, declare illegal, deny, deprive, disallow, embargo, enjoin, exclude, forestall, forfend, freeze*, halt, hinder, hold up, impede, inhibit, interdict, lock up, nix*, obstruct, obviate, oppose, preclude, prevent, proscribe, put the chill on*, restrain, restrict, rule out, say no*, shut down*, shut out*, spike*, stop, stymie*, taboo*, veto, withhold; CONCEPT 121 —*Ant.* allow, approve, authorize, permit, sanction

forbidden [*adj*] *outlawed, prohibited* banned, closed, closed-down*, closed-up*, contraband, no-no*, off limits, out of bounds, proscribed, refused, taboo*, verboten, vetoed; CONCEPT 548 —*Ant.* allowed, approved, authorized, permitted, sanctioned

forbidden fruit [*n*] *taboo* desired object, golden apple, illicit love, no-no*, prohibition; CONCEPTS 532,687

forbidding [*adj*] *ominous, daunting* abhorrent, disagreeable, dour, foreboding, frightening, glowering, grim, hostile, menacing, odious, offensive, off-putting, repellent, repulsive, sinister, threatening, tough, ugly, unapproachable, unfriendly, unpleasant; CONCEPTS 537,550 —*Ant.* approachable, friendly, undaunting

force [*n1*] *physical energy, power* arm, brunt, clout, coercion, compulsion, conscription, constraint, draft, duress, dynamism, effort, enforcement, exaction, extortion, full head of steam*, fury, horsepower, impact, impetus, impulse, might, momentum, muscle, pains*, potency, potential, pow*, pressure, punch, push, sinew, sock*, speed, steam, stimulus, strain, strength, stress, strong arm*, stuff*, subjection, tension, trouble, velocity, vigor, violence, what it takes*; CONCEPTS 641,724 —*Ant.* powerlessness, weakness

force [*n2*] *mental power, energy* ability, authority, bite*, capability, coercion, cogency, competence, determination, dominance, drive, duress, effect, effectiveness, efficacy, emphasis, fierceness, forcefulness, gumption, guts*, impressiveness, influence, intensity, intestinal fortitude, obligation, persistence, persuasiveness, point, pressure, puissance, punch, push, requirement, sapience, stress, validity, validness, vehemence, vigor, willpower; CONCEPTS 410,677 —*Ant.* incompetence, weakness

force [*n3*] *military organization* armed forces, army, battalion, body, cell, corps, crew, detachment, division, guard, horses, host, legion, patrol, regiment, reserves, shop, soldiers, squad, squadron, troop, unit; CONCEPTS 322,417

force [*v1*] *obligate to do something* apply, bear down, bear hard on, bind, blackmail, bring pressure to bear upon*, burden, cause, charge, choke, coerce, command, compel, concuss, conscript, constrain, contract, demand, draft, drag, dragoon*, drive, enforce, enjoin, exact, extort, fix, impel, impose, impress, inflict, insist, limit, make, move, necessitate, oblige, obtrude, occasion, order, overcome, pin down, press, pressure, pressurize, put screws to*, put squeeze on*, require, restrict, sandbag*, shotgun*, strong-arm*, urge, wrest, wring; CONCEPT 14 —*Ant.* let go

force [v2] *use violence upon* assault, blast, break in, break open, burst, bust open, crack open, defile, extort, jimmy*, propel, pry, push, rape, ravish, spoil, squeeze, thrust, twist, undo, violate, wrench, wrest, wring; CONCEPTS 156, 208 —*Ant.* surrender, yield

forced [adj] *compulsory, strained* affected, artificial, begrudging, binding, bound, coerced, coercive, compelled, conscripted, constrained, contrived, enforced, factitious, false, grudging, inflexible, insincere, involuntary, labored, mandatory, obligatory, peremptory, rigid, slave, stiff, stringent, unnatural, unwilling, wooden*; CONCEPTS 542,548 —*Ant.* noncompulsory, spontaneous, unforced, voluntary

forceful [adj] *effective, powerful* ball of fire*, bullish*, cogent, coming on strong, commanding, compelling, constraining, convincing, dominant, dynamic, electric, elemental, energetic, forcible, gutsy*, mighty, persuasive, pithy, potent, powerhouse, puissant, punchy*, steamroller*, stringent, strong, take-charge, take-over, telling, titanic, vehement, vigorous, violent, virile, weighty; CONCEPTS 267,401,550 —*Ant.* feeble, impotent, ineffective, meek, unforceful, weak

forcible [adj] *powerful, aggressive* active, armed, assertive, coercive, cogent, compelling, compulsory, drastic, effective, efficient, energetic, forceful, impressive, intense, mighty, militant, persuasive, potent, puissant, strong, telling, valid, vehement, vigorous, violent, weighty; CONCEPTS 267,537 —*Ant.* nonaggressive, weak

forcibly [adv] *against one's will* by force, coercively, compulsorily, effectively, energetically, hard, mightily, powerfully, strongly, under protest, vigorously; CONCEPTS 544,548 —*Ant.* noncompulsorily, weakly

fore [adv] *in the front* ahead, ante*, antecedently, before, beforehand, forward, in advance, near, nearest, precedently, previous; CONCEPTS 585,820 —*Ant.* aft, back

forebearer [n] *family predecessor* ancestor, antecedent, ascendant, author, begetter, forerunner, founder, materfamilias, matriarch, originator, parent, paterfamilias, patriarch, precursor, primogenitor, procreator, progenitor, relative, sire; CONCEPT 414

forebode [v] *predict, warn* augur, betoken, bode, divine, forecast, foresee, foreshadow, foretell, foretoken, forewarn, indicate, omen, portend, premonish, presage, prognosticate, promise; CONCEPTS 70,78

foreboding [n] *misgiving, bad omen* anxiety, apprehension, apprehensiveness, augury, bad vibes*, chill, dread, fear, foreshadowing, foretoken, forewarning, funny feeling*, handwriting on the wall*, portent, prediction, premonition, prenotion, presage, presentiment, prognostic, prophecy, sinking feeling*, vibes*, warning, wind change*; CONCEPTS 78,689,690

—*Ant.* fortune, good omen, luck, providence

forecast [n] *prediction, often of weather or business* anticipation, augury, budget, calculation, cast, conjecture, divination, estimate, foreknowledge, foreseeing, foresight, foretelling, forethought, foretoken, guess, outlook, planning, precognition, prescience, prevision, prognosis, prognostication, projection, prophecy; CONCEPTS 28,37,70,78

forecast [v] *predict, guess* adumbrate, anticipate, augur, calculate, call the turn*, conclude, conjecture, demonstrate, determine, divine, dope out*, estimate, figure, figure out*, foresee, foretell, gather, gauge, infer, in the cards*, plan, portend, predetermine, presage, prognosticate, prophesy, reason, see it coming*, soothsay, surmise, telegraph; CONCEPTS 28,37,70,78

forefather [n] *ancestor* antecedent, ascendant, forebearer, patriarch, precursor, predecessor, primogenitor, procreator, progenitor; CONCEPT 414

forefront/foreground [n] *prominence* beginning, center, cutting-edge*, focus, fore, forepart, front, lead, leading-edge*, limelight*, on the line*, spearhead*, state-of-the-art, vanguard; CONCEPT 668 —*Ant.* back, background, rear, unimportance

foregoing [adj] *come before; previous* above, aforementioned, aforesaid, aforestated, antecedent, anterior, former, past, precedent, preceding, prior; CONCEPT 585 —*Ant.* after

foreign [adj1] *from another country, experience* adopted, alien, alienated, antipodal, barbarian, barbaric, borrowed, derived, different, distant, estranged, exiled, exotic, expatriate, external, extralocal, extraneous, extrinsic, far, faraway, far-fetched, far-off, from abroad, immigrant, imported, inaccessible, nonnative, nonresident, not domestic, not native, offshore, outlandish, outside, overseas, remote, strange, transoceanic, unaccustomed, unexplored, unfamiliar, unknown; CONCEPTS 536,549 —*Ant.* local, national, native

foreign [adj2] *irrelevant* accidental, adventitious, extraneous, extrinsic, heterogeneous, immaterial, impertinent, inapposite, incompatible, incongruous, inconsistent, inconsonant, irrelative, repugnant, unassimilable, uncharacteristic, unrelated; CONCEPTS 267,537 —*Ant.* characteristic, familiar, known, regular, relevant

foreigner [n] *person from another country* alien, fresh off the boat*, greenhorn*, immigrant, incomer, newcomer, outlander, outsider, stranger; CONCEPT 413 —*Ant.* citizen, local, national, native

foremost [adj] *first in rank, order* A-1*, A-number-1*, arch, at the cutting edge*, at the leading edge*, champion, chief, front, head, headmost, heavy, heavy stuff*, heavyweight*, highest, hotdog*, hotshot*, hot stuff*, inaugural, initial, leading, most important, number one*, original, paramount, preeminent, premier, primary, prime, primo*, principal, supreme; CONCEPTS 568,585,799 —*Ant.* inferior, last, least, lowest, secondary, unimportant

forensic [adj] *judicial, legal* argumentative, debatable, dialectic, dialectical, disputative, juridical, juristic, moot, polemical, rhetorical; CONCEPTS 267,319

foreordain [v] *doom, fate* destinate, destine, foredoom, foreshadow, foretell, prearrange, predestine, predetermine, preform, preordain, reserve; CONCEPT 70

foreplay [n] *fondling* action*, caress, cuddling, heavy petting, kissing, lovemaking, making out, necking, oral sex, petting, sex, sexual activity; CONCEPTS 375,388

forerunner [n1] *messenger, herald* advertiser, advocate, ancestor, announcer, author, envoy, forebearer, foregoer, harbinger, initiator, originator, pioneer, precursor, progenitor, prognostic, prognostics; CONCEPTS 414,423

forerunner [n2] *example, sign* advertisement, announcement, antecedent, antecessor, augury, exemplar, foregoer, foreshadow, foretoken, forewarning, indication, mark, model, omen, pattern, portent, precursor, predecessor, premonition, presage, prognostic, prototype, sign, token, warning; CONCEPT 529 —*Ant.* result

foresee [v] *anticipate, predict* apprehend, call the turn*, crystal ball it*, discern, divine, dope out*, envisage, espy, expect, forebode, forecast, forefeel, foreknow, foretell, have a hunch*, perceive, preknow, presage, previse, prevision, prognosticate, prophesy, psych out*, see, see it coming*, understand, visualize; CONCEPTS 26,70

foreshadow [v] *indicate* adumbrate, augur, be in the wind*, betoken, bode, forebode, foretell, hint, imply, omen, portend, predict, prefigure, presage, promise, prophesy, shadow, signal, suggest, telegraph; CONCEPTS 70,75,261

foresight [n] *mental preparedness* anticipation, canniness, care, carefulness, caution, circumspection, clairvoyance, discernment, discreetness, discretion, economy, far-sightedness, foreknowledge, forethought, insight, longsightedness, perception, precaution, precognition, preconception, premeditation, premonition, prenotion, prescience, prospect, providence, provision, prudence, sagacity; CONCEPTS 409,410 —*Ant.* hindsight, ignorance, thoughtlessness

forest [n] *area with a large number of trees* backwoods, brake, chase, clump, coppice, copse, cover, covert, grove, growth, jungle, park, shelter, stand, thicket, timber, timberland, weald, wildwood, wood, woodland, woodlot, woods; CONCEPTS 509,517

foretell [v] *predict, warn* adumbrate, announce, anticipate, apprehend, augur, auspicate, betoken, bode, call, call it*, call the shot*, crystal ball it*, declare, disclose, divine, divulge, dope*, dope out*, figure, figure out*, forebode, forecast, foreknow, foreshadow, forewarn, make book*, portend, prefigure, presage, proclaim, prognosticate, prophesy, psych, read, reveal, see something coming*, signify, soothsay, tell; CONCEPTS 70,78

forethought [n] *mental preparedness* anticipation, canniness, caution, deliberation, discreetness, discretion, far-sightedness, foresight, gumption, judgment, planning, precaution, premeditation, providence, provision, prudence, sense; CONCEPT 410 —*Ant.* hindsight, ignorance, thoughtlessness

forever [adv1] *for all time; everlasting* always, durably, endlessly, enduringly, eternally, evermore, everything considered*, for always, forevermore, for good*, for keeps*, for life*, immortally, infinitely, in perpetuity, in perpetuum, interminably, lastingly, now and forever*, on and on*, permanently, perpetually, till blue in the face*, till death do us part*, till Doomsday*, till the cows come home*, till the end of time*, unchangingly, world without end*; CONCEPTS 551,649,798,799 —*Ant.* brief, never, temporary

forever [adv2] *not ceasing, continually* all the time, constantly, endlessly, eternally, everlastingly, incessantly, interminably, perpetually, regularly, unendingly, unremittingly; CONCEPTS 534,798 —*Ant.* ceasing, ending, never

forewarn [v] *caution that something may happen* admonish, advise, alarm, alert, apprise, dissuade, flag, forbode, give fair warning*, give the high sign*, portend, premonish, pull one's coat*, put a bug in one's ear*, put one wise*, put on guard*, telegraph, tip, tip off, wave a red flag*; CONCEPT 78

foreword [n] *introduction to a document* exordium, overture, preamble, preface, preliminary, prelude, prelusion, proem, prolegomenon, prologue; CONCEPT 270 —*Ant.* addendum, epilogue, postscript

forfeit [n] *something given as sacrifice* cost, damages, fine, loss, mulct, penalty, relinquishment; CONCEPT 123 —*Ant.* gain, victory, win

forfeit [v] *give up something in sacrifice* abandon, be deprived of, be stripped of, drop, give over, lose, relinquish, renounce, sacrifice, surrender; CONCEPT 116 —*Ant.* gain, profit, win

forge [v1] *counterfeit* coin, copy, design, duplicate, fabricate, fake, falsify, fashion, feign, frame, imitate, invent, make, phony up*, pirate*, produce, reproduce, scratch, trace, transcribe, trump up*; CONCEPTS 59,171

forge [v2] *make something from scratch* beat, build, construct, contrive, create, devise, fabricate, fashion, form, frame, hammer out*, invent, manufacture, mold, pound, put together, shape, turn out, work; CONCEPTS 168,173,175,205,251

forgery [n] *counterfeiting; counterfeit item* bogus*, carbon*, carbon copy, cheat, coining, copy, fabrication, fake, faking, falsification, fraudulence, imitating, imitation, imposition, imposture, lookalike, phony, pseudo, sham*, twin, workalike*; CONCEPTS 59,171,716

forget [v1] *not be able to remember* blow, clean forget*, consign to oblivion*, dismiss from mind, disremember, draw a blank*, escape one's memory*, fail to remember, let slip from memory*, lose consciousness of, lose sight of*, misrecollect, obliterate, think no more of*; CONCEPT 40 —*Ant.* learn, recall, recollect, remember

forget [v2] *leave behind* blink, discount, disregard, drop, fail, ignore, lose sight of*, neglect, omit, overlook, overpass, pass over, skip, slight, transgress, trespass; CONCEPTS 30, 116 —*Ant.* carry, remember, take

forgetful [adj] *tending to not remember* absent, absent-minded, abstracted, airheaded*, amnemonic, amnesic, asleep on the job*, bemused, careless, distracted, dreamy, heedless, inattentive, lax, like an absent-minded professor*, looking out window*, mooning, moony*, neglectful, negligent, nirvanic, not on the job*, oblivious, out of it*, out to lunch*, pipe dreaming*, preoccupied, remiss, slack, sloppy, unmindful, unwitting, woolgathering*; CONCEPTS 403,530 —Ant. attentive, mindful, recalling, remembering

forgetfulness [n] *consistent inability to remember* absentmindedness, abstraction, amnesia, blackout, blank, blockout, carelessness, dreaminess, fugue, heedlessness, hypomnesia, inattention, lapse of memory, laxness, lethe, limbo, loss of memory, negligence, nirvana, oblivion, obliviousness, paramnesia, repression, short memory, suppression; CONCEPTS 410, 644 —Ant. attentiveness, heed, mindfulness, remembering

forgive [v] *stop blame and grant pardon* absolve, accept apology, acquit, allow for, amnesty, bear no malice*, bear with, bury the hatchet*, clear, commute, condone, dismiss from mind, efface, exculpate, excuse, exempt, exonerate, extenuate, forget, kiss and make up*, laugh off*, let bygones be bygones*, let it go*, let off*, let off easy*, let pass*, let up on*, make allowance, overlook, palliate, pocket, purge, release, relent, remit, reprieve, respite, spring, think no more of*, turn other cheek*, wink at*, wipe slate clean*; CONCEPTS 12,50,88 —Ant. accuse, blame, censure, charge, punish

forgiveness [n] *pardon; end of blame* absolution, acquittal, amnesty, charity, clemency, compassion, condonation, dispensation, exculpation, exoneration, extenuation, grace, immunity, impunity, indemnity, justification, lenience, lenity, mercy, overlooking, palliation, purgation, quarter, quittance, remission, remittal, reprieve, respite, vindication; CONCEPTS 685,689 —Ant. accusation, blame, censure, charge, punishment, sentence

forgo [v] *give up, do without* abandon, abdicate, abjure, abstain, cede, desist, eschew, forbear, forsake, give in, go on the wagon*, leave alone, leave out, pack in*, pass, pass on, pass up, quit, refrain, relinquish, renounce, resign, resist, sacrifice, sit out*, surrender, swear off*, take the cure*, take the oath*, waive, yield; CONCEPTS 121,130,681 —Ant. continue, indulge, keep, use

forgotten [adj] *out of one's mind* abandoned, blanked out*, blotted out*, blown over*, buried, bygone, clean forgot*, consigned to oblivion*, disremembered*, drew a blank*, erased, fell between the cracks*, gone, lapsed, left behind, left out, lost, obliterated, omitted, past, past recollection, repressed, slipped one's mind*, suppressed, unrecalled, unremembered; CONCEPTS 402,403,529 —Ant. recalled, recollected, remembered

fork [v] *go separate ways* angle, bifurcate, branch off, branch out, divaricate, diverge, divide, part, split; CONCEPTS 98,738 —Ant. join

forked [adj] *going separate ways* angled, bifid, bifurcate, bifurcated, branched, branching, dichotomous, dichotonic, divaricate, divided, furcate, furcated, pronged, split, tined, tridented, zigzag; CONCEPTS 485,581 —Ant. joined, unbranched

for keeps [adv] *forever* for good, permanently, till hell freezes over*; CONCEPTS 551,649, 798,799

for kicks [adv] *for fun* for mere pleasure, for no useful reason, for the hell of it; CONCEPTS 537,572

forlorn [adj] *hopeless, inconsolable* abandoned, alone, bereft, blue*, cheerless, comfortless, cynical, defenseless, depressed, deserted, desolate, despairing, desperate, despondent, destitute, destroyed, disconsolate, down and out*, dragging*, forgotten, forsaken, friendless, fruitless, futile, godforsaken*, helpless, homeless, in the dumps*, lonely, lonesome, lost, miserable, oppressed, pathetic, pessimistic, pitiable, pitiful, solitary, tragic, unhappy, vain, weighed down, woebegone, wretched; CONCEPT 403 —Ant. cheerful, comforted, consolable, happy, hopeful, joyful, pleased

form [n1] *shape; arrangement* anatomy, appearance, articulation, cast, configuration, conformation, construction, contour, cut, design, die, embodiment, fashion, figure, formation, framework, mode, model, mold, outline, pattern, plan, profile, scheme, silhouette, skeleton, structure, style, system; CONCEPTS 184,660,754,757 —Ant. shapelessness

form [n2] *animate body and its condition* anatomy, being, build, condition, fettle*, figure, fitness, frame, health, object, outline, person, phenomenon, physique, shape, silhouette, thing, torso, trim*; CONCEPTS 316,389,720

form [n3] *accepted procedure; ceremony* behavior, by the book*, by the numbers*, canon, ceremonial, channels*, conduct, convenance, convention, custom, decorum, done thing*, etiquette, fashion, formality, habit, law, layout, manner, manners, method, mode, practice, precept, proceeding, process, propriety, protocol, regulation, rite, ritual, ropes*, rule, setup, style, usage, way; CONCEPT 688

form [n4] *document that requires answers or information* application, blank, chart, data sheet, letter, paper, questionnaire, sheet; CONCEPT 271

form [n5] *type, kind* arrangement, character, class, description, design, grade, guise, make, manifestation, manner, method, mode, order, practice, rank, semblance, sort, species, stamp, style, system, variety, way; CONCEPTS 6,378

form [n6] *organization, arrangement* format, framework, harmony, order, orderliness, placement, plan, proportion, scheme, structure, symmetry; CONCEPT 727 —Ant. disarrangement, disorganization

form [v1] *bring into existence; make, produce* arrange, assemble, block out, bring about, build, cast, complete, compose, conceive, concoct, constitute, construct, consummate, contrive, cook up*, create, cultivate, cut, design, develop, devise, dream up, erect, establish, fabricate, fashion, finish, fix, forge, found, frame, hammer out*, invent, knock off*, make up, manufacture, model, mold, organize, outline, pattern, perfect, plan, plot, project, put together, scheme, set, set up, shape, structure, throw together, trace, turn out*, work; CONCEPTS 168,173,205,251 —Ant. break, destroy, hurt, ruin

form [v2] *come into being; arise* accumulate, acquire, appear, become a reality, become visible, condense, crystallize, develop, eventuate, fall into place*, grow, harden, materialize, mature, rise, set, settle, shape up, show up, take on character, take shape*; CONCEPTS *105,704* —Ant. destroy, kill, ruin

form [v3] *educate, discipline* breed, bring up, give character, instruct, rear, school, teach, train; CONCEPTS *285,295* —Ant. neglect

form [v4] *comprise, be a part of* act as, compose, constitute, figure in, make, make up, serve as; CONCEPT *643*

formal [adj1] *established, orderly* academic, approved, ceremonial, ceremonialistic, ceremonious, confirmed, conventional, decorous, directed, explicit, express, fixed, formalistic, lawful, legal, methodical, official, precise, prescribed, pro forma, proper, punctilious, regular, rigid, ritual, ritualistic, set, solemn, stately, stereotyped, stereotypical, strict, systematic; CONCEPTS *533,547* —Ant. disorderly, informal, relaxed

formal [adj2] *stiff, affected, correct* aloof, by the numbers*, ceremonious, conventional, decorous, distant, exact, nominal, playing the game*, polite, precise, prim, punctilious, reserved, seemly, sententious, starched*, stilted*, straight arrow*, stuffy*, unbending; CONCEPT *401* —Ant. customary, informal, normal, relaxed, unaffected

formality [n1] *convention, custom* academism, ceremony, convenance, conventionality, form, gesture, liturgy, matter of form*, officialism, procedure, red tape*, rite, ritual, rituality, rubric, rule, service, solemnity, solemnness, stereotype, tradition; CONCEPT *688* —Ant. informality

formality [n2] *etiquette, protocol* ceremoniousness, conventionalism, correctness, decorum, formalism, honors, mummery, politesse, propriety, p's and q's*, punctiliousness; CONCEPT *633* —Ant. informality

format [n] *layout, plan* arrangement, composition, configuration, dimensions, figure, form, formation, formula, look, makeup, pattern, scheme, setup, shape, size; CONCEPTS *625,660*

formation [n] *composition, establishment* accumulation, architecture, arrangement, compilation, configuration, constitution, construction, creation, crystallization, deposit, design, development, dispersal, disposition, embodiment, evolution, fabrication, figure, forming, generation, genesis, grouping, induction, makeup, manufacture, order, organization, pattern, production, rank, structure, synthesis; CONCEPTS *173,260*

formative [adj] *influential, impressionable* determinative, developmental, immature, impressible, malleable, moldable, pliant, sensitive, shaping, susceptible; CONCEPTS *534,537* —Ant. destructive, noninfluential

former [adj] *previous in time or order* above, aforementioned, aforesaid, ancient, antecedent, anterior, bygone, departed, earlier, erstwhile, ex-*, first, foregoing, late, long ago*, long gone, of yore*, old, once, one-time, past, preceding, prior, quondam, sometime, whilom; CONCEPTS *585,820* —Ant. after, current, ensuing, following, future, present, prospective, subsequent, succeeding

formerly [adv] *previously in time or order* aforetime, already, anciently, at one time, away

back, a while back, back, back when*, before, before now, before this, down memory lane*, earlier, eons ago*, erewhile, erstwhile, heretofore, in former times, in the olden days*, in the past, lately, long ago, of old, of yore, olden days*, once, once upon a time*, radically, some time ago, time wars*, used to be*, water under the bridge*; CONCEPTS *585,820* —Ant. currently, future, presently, subsequently

formidable [adj1] *horrible, terrifying* appalling, awful, dangerous, daunting, dire, dismaying, dreadful, fearful, fierce, frightful, horrific, imposing, impregnable, intimidating, menacing, redoubtable, shocking, terrible, terrific, threatening; CONCEPT *537* —Ant. feeble, friendly, harmless, nice, pleasant, powerless, weak

formidable [adj2] *difficult, overwhelming* allpowerful, arduous, awesome, ballbuster, challenging, colossal, dismaying, effortful, great, hard, impressive, indomitable, intimidating, labored, laborious, mammoth, mighty, murder*, onerous, overpowering, powerful, puissant, rough*, rough go*, staggering, strenuous, tall order*, toilsome, tough*, tough proposition*, tremendous, uphill*; CONCEPT *565* —Ant. easy, not hard, pleasant, trivial

formless [adj] *disorganized, vague* amorphous, baggy*, blobby*, chaotic, crude, inchoate, incoherent, indefinite, indeterminate, indistinct, nebulous, obscure, orderless, raw, rough, rude, shapeless, unclear, undefined, unformed, unorganized; CONCEPTS *485,535,589* —Ant. coherent, distinct, formed, organized, shaped, specific

formula [n] *set preparation; rule, recipe* blueprint, canon, code, credo, creed, custom, description, direction, equation, form, formulary, maxim, method, modus operandi, precept, prescription, principle, procedure, rite, ritual, rote, rubric, specifications, theorem, way; CONCEPTS *268,688*

formulate [v] *plan, specify systematically* codify, coin, compose, concoct, contrive, cook up, couch, define, detail, develop, devise, draft, draw up*, dream up*, evolve, express, forge, frame, give form to, hatch, indite, invent, make, make up*, map, originate, particularize, phrase, prepare, put, set down*, systematize, vamp, work, work out; CONCEPTS *36,173,202*

fornicate [v] *have sexual intercourse* be promiscuous, commit adultery, philander, sleep around; CONCEPTS *375,384*

fornication [n] *sexual intercourse* coition, coitus, copulation, intimacy, lovemaking, relations, screwing around, sex, sleeping around; CONCEPTS *375,384*

for openers [adv] *as a beginning* first off, for starters, to begin with; CONCEPTS *815,833*

forsake [v] *abandon, turn one's back on* abdicate, cast off, change one's tune*, desert, disclaim, disown, drift away*, forgo, forswear, give up, have done with, jettison, jilt, kiss goodbye*, leave, leave flat*, leave high and dry*, quit, reject, renounce, repudiate, resign, run out on*, set aside, show the door*, spurn, surrender, take the oath*, throw over*, walk out on*, wash one's hands of*; yield; CONCEPTS *30,195,384* —Ant. go back, rediscover, return, revert

forsaken [adj] abandoned cast off, derelict, deserted, desolate, destitute, disowned, forlorn, friendless, godforsaken*, ignored, isolated, jilted, left at the altar*, left behind, left in the lurch*, lonely, lorn, marooned, outcast, solitary, thrown over*; CONCEPT 555 —Ant. cherished, helped, nurtured, wanted

for sure [adv] definitely certainly, dead sure, for a fact, for certain, for real, no doubt, no question, no two ways about it, really, sure thing, unquestionably; CONCEPTS 535,552

forswear [v] abandon, disavow abjure, deny, disclaim, disown, drop, forgo, forsake, give up, recall, recant, reject, renege, renounce, repudiate, retract, swear off, take back, withdraw; CONCEPTS 44,54 —Ant. go back to, revert

forte [n] person's strong point ability, ableness, aptitude, competence, effectiveness, efficiency, eminency, faculty, gift*, long suit*, medium, métier, oyster*, speciality, strength, strong suit*, talent, thing*; CONCEPTS 409,411 —Ant. weakness

fort/fortress [n] stronghold acropolis, blockhouse, camp, castle, citadel, fastness, fortification, garrison, redoubt, station; CONCEPT 439

forth [adv] outward ahead, alee, along, away, first, forward, into, into the open*, on, onward, out; CONCEPT 581

forthcoming [adj] expected, imminent accessible, anticipated, approaching, at hand, available, awaited, coming, destined, fated, future, impending, inescapable, in evidence, inevitable, in preparation, in prospect, in store*, in the cards*, in the wind*, nearing, obtainable, oncoming, on tap*, open, pending, predestined, prospective, ready, resulting, upcoming; CONCEPTS 548,799 —Ant. bygone, distant, gone, past

forthright [adj] straightforward, honest aboveboard, bald, blunt, call a spade a spade*, candid, categorical, direct, directly, forward, frank, from the hip*, like it is*, no lie*, open, outspoken, plain, plainspoken, real, simple, sincere, straight, undisguised, up front*; CONCEPT 267 —Ant. devious, dishonest, secret, untruthful

forthwith [adv] immediately abruptly, at once, away, directly, instantly, now, quickly, right away*, right now*, straightaway, suddenly, tout de suite, without delay; CONCEPTS 544,820 —Ant. later

fortification [n] reinforced position barricade, barrier, bastion, battlement, block, blockhouse, breastwork, buffer, bulwark, castle, citadel, consolidation, defense, earthwork, embattlement, entrenchment, fastness, fort, fortress, garrison, keep, outpost, parapet, preparation, presidio, protection, reinforcement, stockade, strengthening, stronghold, support, wall; CONCEPTS 439,729

fortify [v1] make strong and secure; add to brace, build up, bulwark, buttress, charge up, consolidate, embattle, entrench, garrison, gird, prepare, prop, protect, punch up*, ready, reinforce, secure, shore up*, soup up*, steel*, step up, strengthen, support; CONCEPT 202 —Ant. decrease, hurt, injure, weaken

fortify [v2] encourage, reassure arouse, brace, buck up*, build up, cheer, confirm, embolden, energize, enliven, hearten, invigorate, pour it on*, punch up*, rally, refresh, reinforce, renew,

restore, rouse, stiffen, stir, strengthen, sustain; CONCEPTS 7,22 —Ant. discourage, dissuade, weaken

fortitude [n] strength of mind; guts backbone*, boldness, braveness, bravery, constancy, courage, courageousness, dauntlessness, determination, endurance, fearlessness, firm☐, grit*, gutsiness, hardihood, heart, intre☐, mettle, moxie, nerve, patience, perseve☐, pith, pluck, resoluteness, resolution, sp☐, spirit, spunk, stamina, starch, staying p☐, stick-to-itiveness*, stomach, southeart☐, tenacity, true grit*, valiancy, valor, valo☐, ness, what it takes*; CONCEPTS 410,411☐ —Ant. cowardice, helplessness, weakne☐

fortuitous [adj] lucky, accidental arbitra☐, casual, chance, contingent, fluke*, fluky☐, fortunate, haphazard, happy, incidental☐, in*, luck out*, lucky-dog*, odd, provide☐☐, random, serendipitous, unforeseen, unpla☐, CONCEPTS 548,552 —Ant. calculated, de☐☐, ate, designed, intentional, planned, unluc☐

fortunate [adj] having good luck advanta☐, geous, affluent, auspicious, blessed, born☐, silver spoon*, bright, charmed, convenien☐, couraging, favorable, favored, felicitous, flo☐, ishing, fortuitous, gaining, get a break*, golden☐, happy, healthy, helpful, hopeful, in luck*, in the gravy*, lucky, on a roll*, opportune, overcoming, profitable, promising, propitious, prosperous, providential, rosy, sitting pretty, successful, sunny side*, thriving, timely, triumphant, victorious, wealthy, well-off, well-todo; CONCEPTS 404,542,572 —Ant. adverse, sad, unfortunate, unhappy, unlucky, untoward, upset

fortunately [adv] luckily auspiciously, by good luck, by happy chance*, favorably, happily, in good time*, in the nick of time*, opportunely, prosperously, providentially, satisfyingly, seasonably, successfully, swimmingly, well; CONCEPTS 537,544,572 —Ant. sadly, unfortunately, unhappily, unluckily

fortune [n1] wealth, possessions affluence, capital, estate, gold mine*, inheritance, opulence, portion, property, prosperity, resources, riches, substance, treasure, worth; CONCEPTS 335,710 —Ant. hardship, misfortune, poverty

fortune [n2] fate, lot in life accident, break*, certainty, chance, circumstances, contingency, destiny, doom, expectation, experience, fiftyfifty*, fighting chance*, fluke*, fortuity, fortunateness, good break, hazard, history, karma*, kismet*, life, luck, lucked into*, lucked out*, luckiness, lucky break*, lucky hit*, Moirai, portion, providence, roll of the dice*, run of luck*, star, streak of luck, success, way the ball bounces*, way the cookie crumbles*, wheel of fortune*; CONCEPT 679

fortune-teller [n] person attempting to tell the future augur, clairvoyant, crystal ball gazer, diviner, medium, mind reader, oracle, palmist, palm reader, predicter, prophet, psychic, seer, soothsayer, spiritualist, tarot reader, tea-leaf reader; CONCEPTS 348,423

forum [n1] meeting assembly, colloquium, conclave, conference, congregation, congress, convention, convocation, council, gathering, get-together*, rally, seminar, symposium; CONCEPT 324

forum [n2] *setting* agency, apparatus, avenue, backdrop, channel, framework, means, mechanism, medium, meeting place, place, scene, stage, vehicle, venue; CONCEPTS 198,263

forward [adj1] *advancing, early* ahead, forth, forward-looking, in advance, leading, onward, precocious, premature, progressing, progressive, propulsive, well-developed; CONCEPT 528 —*Ant.* backward, later, past, reversing

forward [adj2] *in front, first* advance, anterior, facial, fore, foremost, front, head, leading, ventral; CONCEPTS 581,583,585 —*Ant.* back, last

forward [adj3] *brash, impertinent* aggressive, assuming, audacious, bantam, bare-faced, bold, brazen, cheeky*, coming on strong*, confident, familiar, fresh, impudent, nervy*, overassertive, overweening, pert, presuming, presumptuous, pushing, pushy*, rude, sassy*, saucy*, self-assertive, smart, smart-alecky*, uppity*, wise; CONCEPTS 401,404 —*Ant.* meek, reserved, shy, timid

forward [adv] *toward the front in order, time* ahead, alee, along, ante, antecedently, before, beforehand, fore, forth, in advance, into prominence, into view, on, onward, out, precedently, previous, to the fore*, vanward; CONCEPTS 581,585,799 —*Ant.* back, backward, past

forward [v1] *aid, expedite* advance, assist, back, champion, cultivate, encourage, favor, foster, further, hasten, help, hurry, promote, serve, speed, support, uphold; CONCEPTS 68, 110 —*Ant.* cease, halt, hinder, impede, stop

forward [v2] *send, ship* address, consign, deliver, dispatch, express, freight, post, remit, route, transmit, transport; CONCEPT 217 —*Ant.* hold, keep, maintain

fossil [n] *organic remains of a previous time* deposit, eolith, impression, neolith, paleolith, petrifaction, reconstruction, relic, skeleton, specimen, trace; CONCEPTS 429,470,509

foster [v1] *promote, support* advance, back, champion, cherish, cultivate, encourage, feed, foment, forward, further, harbor, nurse, nurture, serve, stimulate, uphold; CONCEPT 110 —*Ant.* condemn, discourage

foster [v2] *give care or accommodation to* assist, bring up, care for, cherish, entertain, favor, harbor, help, house, lodge, minister to, nourish, nurse, oblige, raise, rear, serve, shelter, sustain, take care of; CONCEPTS 110,140,295 —*Ant.* ignore, neglect

foul [adj1] *disgusting, dirty* abhorrent, abominable, base, contaminated, despicable, detestable, disgraceful, dishonorable, egregious, fetid, filthy, gross*, hateful, heinous, horrid, icky*, impure, infamous, iniquitous, loathsome, malodorous, mucky*, nasty, nauseating, nefarious, noisome, notorious, offensive, pigpen*, polluted, putrid, rank*, raunchy*, repellent, repulsive, revolting, rotten, scandalous, shameful, squalid, stinking*, sullied, tainted, unclean, vicious, vile, wicked, yecchy*, yucky*; CONCEPTS 485,529 —*Ant.* clean, fragrant, pleasing, pure, wonderful

foul [adj2] *vulgar, offensive* abusive, blasphemous, blue*, coarse, dirty, filthy, foul-mouthed, gross*, indecent, lewd, low, nasty, obscene, profane, raunchy, scatological, scurrilous, smutty*; CONCEPT 267 —*Ant.* clean, innocent, inoffensive, moral

foul [adj3] *corrupt, dishonest* caitiff, crooked, dirty, fraudulent, inequitable, monstrous, shady, underhand, underhanded, unfair, unjust, unscrupulous, vicious; CONCEPTS 537, 548 —*Ant.* fair, good, honest, incorrupt, just

foul [n] *infraction* breach, encroachment, error, faux pas, infringement, offense, slip*, violation; CONCEPTS 192,691

foul [v] *make or become dirty* befoul, begrime, besmear, besmirch, block, catch, choke, clog, contaminate, defile, desecrate, discolor, ensnare, entangle, fill, jam, pollute, profane, smear, smudge, snarl, soil, spot, stain, sully, taint, tarnish, twist; CONCEPTS 250,469 —*Ant.* clean, purify, sterilize

foul play [n] *treacherous action* bad deed, corruption, crime, cruel act, dirty trick, dirty work, felony, fraud, funny business, lawbreaking, murder, violence, wrong; CONCEPT 645

foul up [v] *make a mess of* botch, bungle, confuse, jumble, mismanage, mix up*, muck up*, muddle, screw up*, snafu*, snarl, tumble; CONCEPTS 16,234 —*Ant.* fix, mend, organize

found [v1] *bring into being* begin, commence, constitute, construct, create, endow, erect, establish, fashion, fix, form, get going, inaugurate, initiate, institute, launch, organize, originate, plant, raise, ring in*, settle, settle up, start, start the ball rolling*, start up; CONCEPT 221 —*Ant.* destroy, end

found [v2] *put on a base* bottom, build, erect, establish, ground, predicate, raise, rear, rest, root, stay, support, sustain; CONCEPTS 168,221

foundation [n1] *basis for something physical or mental* ABCs*, authority, base, basics, bed, bedrock, bottom, bottom line*, brass tacks*, foot, footing, ground, groundwork, guts*, heart*, infrastructure, justification, nitty-gritty*, nub*, nuts and bolts*, prop, reason, root, stay, substratum, substructure, support, underpinning, understructure; CONCEPTS 442,826

foundation [n2] *established institution* association, charity, company, corporation, endowment, establishment, guild, inauguration, institute, organization, plantation, settlement, set-up, society, trusteeship; CONCEPT 381

founder [n] *person who establishes an institution* architect, author, beginner, benefactor, builder, constructor, creator, designer, establisher, forebearer, framer, generator, initiator, institutor, inventor, maker, organizer, originator, patron, planner, prime mover*; CONCEPTS 347,423

founder [v] *go under, fail* abort, be lost, break down, collapse, come to nothing, fall, fall through, go down, go lame, go to bottom, lurch, miscarry, misfire, sink, sprawl, stagger, stumble, submerge, submerse, trip; CONCEPTS 181,699 —*Ant.* accomplish, achieve, succeed

fountain [n] *source, often of liquid* bubbler, cause, font, fount, geyser, gush, inception, inspiration, jet, lode, mainspring, mine, origin, play, provenance, provenience, pump, reservoir, root, spout, spray, spring, stream, well, wellhead, wellspring; CONCEPTS 514,648

fountainhead [n] *principal source; person who originates* administrator, architect, author,

builder, creator, father, fount, fountain, generator, initiator, leader, maker, mother, originator,
spring, wellspring; CONCEPTS 348,350

foxy [adj] *shrewd* artful, astute, canny, crafty,
cunning, deceitful, deep, devious, dishonest,
experienced, guileful, insidious, intelligent,
knowing, retiary, sharp, slick, sly, subtle,
tricky, vulpine, wily; CONCEPTS 401,404
—*Ant.* naive, unclever, unintelligent, unsmart

foyer [n] *receiving area* antechamber, anteroom, entrance hall, lobby, reception, vestibule;
CONCEPTS 440,441,448

fracas [n] *disturbance, fight* affray, altercation,
battle, battle royal*, bickering, brawl, broil*,
brouhaha, dispute, donnybrook*, feud, flap*,
fray, free-for-all*, hassle, knock-down-drag-
out*, melee, mix up*, quarrel, riot, row,
ruction, ruffle, rumpus, run-in*, scrimmage,
scuffle, set-to*, squabble, stew*, trouble,
tumult, uproar, words*; CONCEPTS 46,106
—*Ant.* calm, harmony, peace

fraction [n1] *part* bite, chunk, cut, division,
end, fragment, half, piece, portion, section,
share, slice; CONCEPT 835 —*Ant.* entirety,
total, whole

fraction [n2] *incomplete number* bit, division,
fragment, part, partial, piece, portion, quotient,
ratio, section, segment, slice, subdivision;
CONCEPT 765

fractional [adj] *partial* apportioned, compart-
mental, compartmented, constituent, dismembered, dispersed, divided, fragmentary,
frationary, incomplete, parceled, part, piecemeal, sectional, segmented; CONCEPT 785
—*Ant.* all, entire, total

fractious [adj] *grouchy, cross* awkward, captious, crabby*, disorderly, fretful, froward,
huffy*, indocile, indomitable, intractable,
irritable, mean, ornery*, peevish, perverse,
pettish, petulant, querulous, recalcitrant,
refractory, restive, scrappy, snappish, testy,
thin-skinned, touchy, uncompliant, undisciplined, unmanageable, unruly, wayward,
wild; CONCEPTS 267,401 —*Ant.* agreeable,
complaisant, happy, nice, patient

fracture [n] *break, rupture* breach, cleavage,
cleft, crack, discontinuity, disjunction, displacement, fissure, fragmentation, gap, mutilation,
opening, rent, rift, schism, severance, splinter,
split, wound; CONCEPTS 309,513

fragile [adj] *breakable, dainty* brittle, crisp,
crumbly, decrepit, delicate, feeble, fine, flimsy,
fracturable, frail, frangible, friable, infirm, insubstantial, shatterable, shivery, slight, unsound,
weak, weakly; CONCEPTS 485,489 —*Ant.*
durable, firm, strong, tough, unbreakable

fragment [n] *part, chip* ace, atom, bit, bite,
chunk, crumb, cut, end, fraction, gob*, grain,
hunk, iota, job*, lump*, minim, morsel,
particle, piece, portion, remnant, scrap, share,
shiver, shred, slice, sliver, smithereen*;
CONCEPT 835 —*Ant.* entirety, total, whole

fragment [v] *break into pieces* burst, come
apart, crumble, disintegrate, disunite, divide,
rend, rive, shatter, shiver, smash, splinter,
split, split up; CONCEPTS 98,135,137,246,469
—*Ant.* complete, total

fragmentary [adj] *broken, incomplete* bitty,
disconnected, discrete, disjointed, fractional,

incoherent, part, partial, piecemeal, scattered,
scrappy, sketchy, unsystematic; CONCEPT 785
—*Ant.* all, complete, total, unbroken, whole

fragrance [n] *pleasant odor* aroma, aura, balm,
bouquet, incense, perfume, redolence, scent,
smell, spice; CONCEPT 600 —*Ant.* stench, stink

fragrant [adj] *smelling pleasant* ambrosial,
aromal, aromatic, balmy, delectable, delicious,
delightful, odoriferous, odorous, perfumed,
perfumy, redolent, savory, spicy, sweet,
sweet-scented, sweet-smelling; CONCEPT 598
—*Ant.* noxious, putrid, stale, stinking

frail [adj] *breakable, weak* brittle, dainty,
decrepit, delicate, feeble, fishy, flimsy, fracturable, fragile, frangible, infirm, insubstantial,
puny, sad, shatterable, shattery, sickly, slender,
slight, slim, tender, tenuous, thin, unsound,
unsubstantial, vulnerable, wimpy*, wishy-
washy*, wispy; CONCEPTS 485,489 —*Ant.*
firm, strong, unbreakable

frailty [n] *weakness, flaw* Achilles heel*,
blemish, daintiness, debility, decrepitude,
defect, deficiency, delicacy, error, failing,
fallibility, fault, feebleness, flimsiness, foible,
foil, imperfection, infirmity, peccability,
peccadillo, shortcoming, solecism, suscept-
weak point*; CONCEPTS 101,230,411,580
—*Ant.* firmness, strength

frame [n] *skeleton, casing* anatomy, architecture, body, build, cage, carcass, construction,
enclosure, fabric, flounce, form, framework,
fringe, groundwork, hem, mount, mounting,
outline, physique, scaffold, scaffolding,
scheme, setting, shell, stage, structure,
support, system, trim, trimming, truss, valance;
CONCEPTS 442,733,757

frame [v1] *build* assemble, back, border, constitute, construct, encase, enclose, erect, fabricate,
fashion, forge, form, institute, invent, lath,
make, manufacture, mat, model, mold, mount,
panel, produce, put together, raise, set up,
shingle; CONCEPTS 168,758 —*Ant.* destroy, raze

frame [v2] *compose, plan* block out, conceive,
concoct, contrive, cook up, design, devise,
draft, draw up, dream up*, form, formulate,
hatch, indite, invent, make, make up, map out,
outline, prepare, shape, sketch, vamp, write;
CONCEPTS 36,173

frame of mind [n] *state of mind* attitude,
constitution, disposition, emotions, inner
nature, makeup, mentality, mood, nature,
spirit, state, temperament; CONCEPTS 410,689

framework [n] *foundation, core* bare bones*,
cage, fabric, frame, frame of reference*,
groundwork, plan, schema, scheme, shell,
skeleton, structure; CONCEPTS 439,479,733

franchise [n] *authority, right* authorization,
ballot, charter, exemption, freedom, immunity,
patent, prerogative, privilege, suffrage, vote;
CONCEPT 376

frank [adj] *completely honest* aboveboard, apparent, artless, bare-faced*, blunt, bold, brazen,
call a spade a spade*, candid, direct, downright,
easy, familiar, flat-out*, forthright, free, from
the hip*, guileless, heart-to-heart*, ingenuous,
lay it on the line*, like it is*, matter-of-fact,
naive, natural, open, outright, outspoken, plain,
plain-spoken, real, saying what one thinks*,
scrupulous, sincere, straight, straightforward,

transparent, truthful, unconcealed, undisguised, uninhibited, unreserved, unrestricted, up front*, upright; CONCEPTS 267,582 —*Ant.* devious, dishonest, evasive, insincere, secretive

frankfurter [n] *cylindrical meat sausage* bowwow*, Coney Island*, dog*, footlong*, frank, hot dog, link, weenie*, wiener, wiener-wurst; CONCEPTS 457,460

frankly [adv] *very honestly* bluntly, candidly, dead level*, dead on*, directly, forthrightly, freely, from the hip*, in truth, laid on the line*, level, on the level*, on the line*, openly, plainly, straight, straightforwardly, without reserve; CONCEPT 267 —*Ant.* deviously, dishonestly, insincerely, secretively

frantic [adj] *distressed, distracted* agitated, angry, at wits' end*, berserk, beside oneself*, corybantic, crazy, delirious, deranged, distraught, excited, flipped out*, fraught, freaked out*, frenetic, frenzied, furious, hectic, hot and bothered*, hot under the collar*, hyper*, in a stew*, in a tizzy*, insane, keyed up*, mad, out of control, overwrought, rabid, raging, raving, shook up*, spazzed out*, unglued*, unscrewed*, violent, weird, weirded out*, wigged out*, wild, wired*, worked up*, zonkers*; CONCEPTS 403,542 —*Ant.* calm, collected, composed, docile, peaceful, tranquil

fraternity [n] *brotherhood* affiliation, camaraderie, club, fellowship, frat*, guild, house, kinship, order, sisterhood, society, sorority; CONCEPTS 381,387 —*Ant.* sisterhood, sorority

fraternize [v] *associate with* be friendly, be sociable with, club together, consort with, fall in with, go around with, hang out with, hobnob*, keep company with, make friends, mingle with, mix with, rub elbows with, rub shoulders with, run with, socialize with; CONCEPTS 114,384 —*Ant.* disagree, ignore

fraud [n1] *trickery, deception* artifice, bamboozlement*, blackmail, cheat, chicane, chicanery, con, craft*, deceit, double-dealing*, dupery, duping, duplicity, extortion, fake, fast one*, fast shuffle*, flimflam*, fourberie, fraudulence, graft, guile, hanky-panky*, hoax, hocus-pocus*, hoodwinking*, hustle*, imposture, line, misrepresentation, racket, scam, sell, shakedown*, sham*, sharp practice*, skunk*, smoke*, song*, song and dance*, spuriousness, sting, string, swindle, swindling, treachery; CONCEPTS 59,192,645 —*Ant.* fairness, honesty, justice

fraud [n2] *person who is false, deceitful* bastard, bluffer, charlatan, cheat, counterfeit, crook, deceiver, double-dealer*, fake, forger, four-flusher*, hoaxer, horse trader*, impostor, mechanic*, mountebank, phony, play actor*, pretender, quack*, racketeer, sham*, shark*, swindler; CONCEPT 412

fraudulent [adj] *deceptive, false* bamboozling*, counterfeit, crafty, criminal, crooked, deceitful, devious, dishonest, dishonorable, double-dealing*, duplicitous, fake, forged, mock, phony, pseudo, sham*, spurious, swindling, treacherous, tricky; CONCEPTS 545,582 —*Ant.* authentic, genuine, honest, real, valid

fraught [adj] *full of* abounding, attended, bristling, charged, filled, heavy, laden, replete, stuffed; CONCEPTS 483,771 —*Ant.* empty

fray [n] *fight, battle* affray, battle royal*, brawl, broil*, brouhaha*, clash, combat, conflict, contest, disturbance, donnybrook*, engagement, fracas, melee, quarrel, riot, row, ruckus, rumble, rumpus, scuffle, set-to*; CONCEPTS 86,106 —*Ant.* agreement, harmony, peace

fray [v] *shred, come apart* become ragged, become threadbare, chafe, erode, frazzle, fret, ravel, rip, rub, tatter, tear, unravel, wear, wear away, wear thin; CONCEPT 214

frazzle [n] *exhaustion; something very worn* collapse, enervation, lassitude, prostration, rag, remnant, shred; CONCEPTS 410,720

frazzle [v] *wear out* exhaust, fray, knock out, poop*, prostrate, rip, shred, tear, tire, tucker*, wear; CONCEPTS 156,186 —*Ant.* maintain, preserve

freak [n1] *something, someone very abnormal* aberration, abortion, anomaly, chimera, curiosity, geek*, grotesque, malformation, miscreation, misshape, monster, monstrosity, mutant, mutation, oddity, queer, rarity, sport, weirdo*; CONCEPTS 424,580 —*Ant.* normality, ordinary, regular

freak [n2] *irregularity, whim* caprice, conceit, crochet, fad, fancy, folly, humor, megrim, quirk, turn, twist, vagary, whimsy; CONCEPT 679 —*Ant.* commonality, ordinary, regularity

freak [n3] *person enthused about something* addict, aficionado, buff, bug*, devotee, enthusiast, fan, fanatic, fiend*, maniac, nut*, zealot; CONCEPTS 352,366,423

freak [v] *become extraordinarily upset* flip out*, go beserk, go insane, go mad, lose control, rave, unhinge*, wig out*; CONCEPTS 7,19,80

freakish [adj] *abnormal, unusual* aberrant, arbitrary, bizarre, capricious, crazy, erratic, fantastic, far-out, freaky, grotesque, malformed, monstrous, odd, outlandish, outré, preternatural, queer, strange, unconventional, vagarious, wayward, weird, whimsical, wild; CONCEPT 564 —*Ant.* common, general, natural, normal, ordinary, standard, usual

freak out [v] *lose one's cool* blow a gasket*, blow one's mind*, blow one's stack*, blow one's top*, break down, come unglued, crack up*, flip out*, fly off the handle*, freak out*, go ape*, go ballistic*, go berserk*, go crazy*, go haywire*, go nuts*, go off the deep end*, hit the ceiling*, lose control of oneself, lose it*, lose one's composure, lose one's mind, lose one's temper, wig out*; CONCEPTS 7,19,80

freckle [n] *small discoloration on skin* blemish, blotch, daisy, dot, lentigo, macula, mole, patch, pepper, pigmentation, pit, pock, pockmark, speck, speckle, sprinkle, stipple; CONCEPT 392

free [adj1] *without charge* chargeless, comp*, complimentary, costless, for love*, for nothing*, freebie*, free of cost, free ride*, gratis, gratuitous, handout, on the cuff*, on the house*, paper*, unpaid, unrecompensed; CONCEPT 334 —*Ant.* costly, expensive, high-priced, priced

free [adj2] *unrestrained personally* able, allowed, at large, at liberty, casual, clear, disengaged, easy, escaped, familiar, fancy-free*, footloose*, forward, frank, free-spirited, free-wheeling, independent, informal, lax, liberal, liberated, loose, off the hook*, on one's own*, on the loose*, open, permitted, relaxed, unattached, uncommitted, unconfined, unconstrained, unengaged, unfettered, unhampered, unimpeded, unobstructed, unregulated, unrestricted, untrammeled; CONCEPTS 401,542 —*Ant.* bound, confined, hindered, limited, restrained

free [*adj3*] *unrestrained politically* at liberty, autarchic, autonomic, autonomous, democratic, emancipated, enfranchised, freed, independent, individualistic, liberated, self-directing, self-governing, self-ruling, separate, sovereign, sui juris, unconstrained, unenslaved, unregimented; CONCEPTS 319,536 —*Ant.* barred, bound, enslaved, prevented, suppressed

free [*adj4*] *not busy; unoccupied* at leisure, available, clear, empty, extra, idle, loose, not tied down*, spare, unemployed, unengaged, unhampered, unimpeded, uninhabited, unobstructed, unused, vacant; CONCEPT 485 —*Ant.* busy, occupied, scheduled, tied-up

free [*adj5*] *generous, unsparing* big, big-hearted*, bounteous, bountiful, charitable, eager, handsome, hospitable, lavish, liberal, munificent, open-handed*, prodigal, unstinging, willing; CONCEPT 404 —*Ant.* mean, niggardly, tight-fisted

free [*v1*] *liberate, let go* absolve, acquit, bail, bail out*, clear, cut loose*, deliver, demobilize, discharge, disengage, disenthrall, disimprison, dismiss, emancipate, enfranchise, extricate, let loose*, let off*, let off the hook*, let out, loose, loosen, manumit, pardon, parole, put on the street*, ransom, redeem, release, relieve, reprieve, rescue, save, set free, spring*, turn loose, turn out, unbind, uncage, unchain, undo, unfetter, unfix, unleash, untie; CONCEPT 127 —*Ant.* confine, enslave, hold, incarcerate, restrain

free [*v2*] *take burden from* cast off, clear, cut loose, decontaminate, deliver, discharge, disembarrass, disencumber, disengage, disentangle, empty, excuse, exempt, extricate, put off, ransom, redeem, relieve, rescue, rid, unburden, undo, unlade, unload, unpack, unshackle; CONCEPTS 110,211 —*Ant.* burden, compel, limit, suppress

freebie [*n*] *something for nothing* complimentary ticket, free lunch, free pass, gift, giveaway, handout; CONCEPT 337

freedom [*n1*] *independence, license to do as one wants* abandon, abandonment, ability, bent, carte blanche, compass, discretion, elbowroom*, exemption, facility, flexibility, free rein*, full play*, full swing*, immunity, indulgence, laissez faire, latitude, laxity, leeway, liberty, margin, opportunity, own accord*, play, plenty of rope*, power, prerogative, privilege, profligacy, rampancy, range, rein, right, rope*, scope, sweep, swing, unrestraint; CONCEPT 693 —*Ant.* captivity, confinement, imprisonment, incarceration, limitation, servitude, slavery

freedom [*n2*] *political independence* abolition, abolitionism, autarchy, autonomy, citizenship, deliverance, delivery, democracy, discharge, disengagement, disimprisonment, emancipation, enfranchisement, exemption, extriction, franchise, home rule*, immunity, impunity, liberation, liberty, manumission, parole, prerogative, privilege, probation, redemption, release, relief, representative government,

rescue, salvage, salvation, self-determination, self-government, sovereignty; CONCEPT 691 —*Ant.* communism, government, subjection, subordination, suppression

freedom [*n3*] *easy attitude* abandon, boldness, brazenness, candor, directness, disrespect, ease, facility, familiarity, forthrightness, forwardness, frankness, impertinence, informality, ingenuousness, lack of reserve, lack of restraint, laxity, license, openness, overfamiliarity, presumption, readiness, spontaneity, unconstraint; CONCEPT 633 —*Ant.* difficulty, limitation, reserve, restraint, restriction

free-for-all [*n*] *fight* affray, battle, brawl, broil*, brouhaha*, fracas, fray, knock-down-drag-out*, melee, riot, row, ruction; CONCEPT 106 —*Ant.* calm, harmony, peace

freelance [*adj*] *independent* free agent, non-staff, self-employed, unaffiliated; CONCEPT 554

freely [*adj1*] *without restriction* advisedly, as you please*, at one's discretion, at one's pleasure, at will, candidly, deliberately, designedly, fancy-free*, frankly, intentionally, of one's own accord*, of one's own free will*, openly, plainly, purposely, spontaneously, unchallenged, unreservedly, voluntarily, willingly, without hindrance, without prompting, without reserve, without restraint, without urging; CONCEPT 401 —*Ant.* bound, limited

freely [*adv2*] *easily, smoothly done* abundantly, amply, as one pleases*, bountifully, cleanly, copiously, effortlessly, extravagantly, facilely, lavishly, liberally, lightly, like water*, loosely, open-handedly, readily, unhindered, unobstructedly, unstintingly, well, with a free hand*, without encumbrance*, without hindrance*, without restraint, without stint*; CONCEPT 544 —*Ant.* difficultly

free spirit [*n*] *maverick* bohemian, dissenter, eccentric, nonconformist, radical; CONCEPT 359

freeware [*n*] *free software* public-domain software, shareware; CONCEPTS 274,660

freeway [*n*] *expressway* artery, beltway, highway, interstate, parkway, road, superhighway, thoroughfare, thruway; CONCEPT 501

free will [*n*] *person's full intent and purpose* assent, choice, consent, desire, determination, discretion, free choice, freedom, inclination, intention, mind, option, own say so*, own sweet way*, pleasure, power, say so*, velleity, volition, voluntary decision, willingness, wish; CONCEPTS 20,410 —*Ant.* responsibility

freeze [*v1*] *make cold enough to become solid* benumb, bite, chill, chill to the bone*, congeal, frost, glaciate, harden, ice over, ice up, nip, pierce, refrigerate, solidify, stiffen; CONCEPTS 255,521 —*Ant.* boil, heat

freeze [*v2*] *stop* dampen, depress, discourage, dishearten, fix, hold up, inhibit, peg, suspend; CONCEPTS 14,121 —*Ant.* continue, go

freezer [*n*] *icebox* cold storage, cooler, refrigerator; CONCEPTS 202,255

freezing [*adj*] *very cold* arctic, biting, bitter, chill, chilled, chilly, cutting, frigid, frost-bound, frosty, gelid, glacial, hawkish, icy, nippy, numbing, one-dog night*, penetrating, polar, raw, shivery, Siberian*, snappy*, two-dog night*, wintry; CONCEPT 605 —*Ant.* boiling, heated, hot

freight [n] *goods being shipped* bales, ballast, bulk, burden, carriage, consignment, contents, conveyance, encumbrance, fardel, haul, lading, load, merchandise, pack, packages, payload, shipment, shipping, tonnage, transportation, wares, weight; CONCEPT *338*

frenetic [adj] *maniacal* corybantic, delirious, demented, distraught, excited, fanatical, frantic, frenzied, furibund, furious, hyper*, in a lather*, insane, lost it*, mad, obsessive, overwrought, phrenetic, rabid, unbalanced, unscrewed*, weirded out*, wigged out*, wild, wired*; CONCEPT *403* —**Ant.** balanced, calm

frenzied [adj] *uncontrolled* agitated, berserk, convulsive, corybantic, delirious, distracted, distraught, excited, feverish, frantic, frenetic, furious, hysterical, mad, maniacal, nuts*, rabid, wild; CONCEPTS *542,544* —**Ant.** calm, controlled

frenzy [n] *uncontrolled state or situation* aberration, agitation, blow, blow a fuse*, blow one's cork*, blow one's stack*, blow one's top*, bout, burst, conniption*, convulsion, craze, delirium, derangement, distemper, distraction, dithers*, excitement, ferment, fever, fit, flap*, flip one's lid*, free-for-all*, furor, fury, fuss, hell broke loose*, hysteria, insanity, lather, lunacy, madness, mania, outburst, paroxysm, passion, rage, row, ruckus, ruction, rumble, rumpus, seizure, spasm, stew, stir, to-do*, transport, turmoil, wingding*; CONCEPTS *230,410,674* —**Ant.** calmness, peace, peacefulness

frequency [n] *commonness, repetitiveness* abundance, beat, constancy, density, frequentness, iteration, number, oscillation, periodicity, persistence, prevalence, pulsation, recurrence, regularity, reiteration, repetition, rhythm; CONCEPT *634* —**Ant.** infrequency, irregularity, uncommonness

frequent [adj] *common, repeated* a good many*, commonplace, constant, continual, customary, everyday, expected, familiar, general, habitual, incessant, intermittent, iterated, manifold, many, monotonous, numberless, numerous, periodic, perpetual, persistent, pleonastic, profuse, recurrent, recurring, redundant, reiterated, reiterative, successive, thick, ubiquitous, usual, various; CONCEPT *530* —**Ant.** inconstant, infrequent, irregular, occasional, rare, sporadic, uncommon, unrepeated, unusual

frequent [v] *be a regular customer of* affect, attend, attend regularly, be at home in*, be found at, be often in, drop in, go to, hang about*, hang around*, hang out at*, haunt*, hit*, infest, overrun, patronize, play*, resort, revisit, visit often; CONCEPTS *227,384*

frequently [adv] *commonly, repeatedly* again and again*, as a rule*, at regular intervals, at short intervals, at times, by ordinary, customarily, every now and then*, generally, habitually, in many instances*, in quick succession, intermittently, many a time*, many times, much, not infrequently, not seldom, oft, often, oftentimes, ofttimes, ordinarily, over and over, periodically, recurrently, regularly, spasmodically, successively, thick and fast*, time and again*, usually, very often; CONCEPTS *530,544,799* —**Ant.** infrequently, not much, rarely, seldom, uncommonly

fresh [adj1] *new, just produced* beginning, brand-new*, comer, contemporary, crisp, crude, current, different, gleaming, glistening, green*, hot*, hot off the press*, immature, just out*, late, latest, mint*, modern, modernistic, natural, neoteric, newborn, newfangled*, novel, now, original, radical, raw, recent, sparkling, state-of-the-art, the latest's*, this season's*, unconventional, unprocessed, unseasoned, untouched, unusual, up-to-date, virginal, what's happening*, young, youthful; CONCEPTS *578,797* —**Ant.** old, stale, tired, used

fresh [adj2] *additional* added, another, auxiliary, else, extra, farther, further, increased, more, new, other, renewed, supplementary; CONCEPTS *546,824* —**Ant.** old, used

fresh [adj3] *refreshing to the senses* bracing, bright, brisk, clean, clear, colorful, cool, crisp, definite, fair, invigorating, not stale, pure, quick, sharp, spanking, sparkling, stiff, stimulating, sweet, uncontaminated, unpolluted, vivid; CONCEPT *537* —**Ant.** stale, tired

fresh [adj4] *energetic, healthy* active, alert, blooming, bouncing, bright, bright-eyed, bushy-tailed*, chipper*, clear, dewy, fair, florid, glowing, good, hardy, invigorated, keen, like new, lively, refreshed, rehabilitated, relaxed, relieved, rested, restored, revived, rosy, ruddy, sprightly, spry, stimulated, undimmed, unfaded, unused, unwearied, unwithered, verdant, vigorous, vital, wholesome, young; CONCEPTS *485,542* —**Ant.** exhausted, lifeless, tired, unenergetic, worn

fresh [adj5] *inexperienced* artless, callow, green*, natural, new, raw, tenderfooted*, uncultivated, unpracticed, unskilled, untrained, untried, unversed, young, youthful; CONCEPT *404* —**Ant.** experienced

fresh [adj6] *sassy, brazen* bold, cheeky*, disrespectful, familiar, flip*, flippant, forward, impertinent, impudent, insolent, nervy*, pert, presumptuous, rude, saucy*, smart*, smart-alecky*, snippy*, wise; CONCEPTS *267,401* —**Ant.** gentle, kind, polite

freshen [v] *make like new; revitalize* activate, air, cleanse, enliven, invigorate, purify, refresh, restore, revive, rouse, spruce up, sweeten, titivate, ventilate; CONCEPT *244* —**Ant.** overuse

freshman [n] *first-year student* beginner, frosh*, greenhorn, novice, rookie, underclassman, undergrad*, undergraduate; CONCEPT *348*

freshness [n] *newness* bloom, brightness, callowness, cleanness, clearness, dew, dewiness, glow, greenness, inexperience, innovativeness, inventiveness, novelty, originality, rawness, shine, sparkle, vigor, viridity, youth; CONCEPT *715* —**Ant.** oldness, staleness

fret [v1] *worry, be annoyed* affront, agonize, anguish, bleed, bother, brood, carp, carry a heavy load*, chafe, chagrin, distress oneself, eat one's heart out*, fume, fuss, get into a dither*, grieve, lose sleep over*, mope*, pother*, stew, sweat it out*, take on, torment, upset oneself; CONCEPT *410* —**Ant.** calm, comfort, soothe

fret [v2] *upset someone* abrade, agitate, bother, displease, distress, disturb, gall, get on nerves*, goad, harass, irk, irritate, nag, nettle, peeve, pique, provoke, rile, ruffle, torment, trouble, vex; CONCEPTS *7,19* —**Ant.** appease, pacify, placate, please fret [v3] *rub hard* abrade, chafe, corrode, erode, excoriate, fray, gall, riffle, ripple, wear away, wear threadbare; CONCEPT 215

fretful [adj] *irritable* captious, carping*, caviling, complaining, contrary, crabby*, cranky*, critical, cross, crotchety*, edgy, faultfinding, fractious, huffy*, mean, ornery*, out of sorts*, peevish, perverse, petulant, querulous, short-tempered, snappish*, splenetic, testy, touchy, uneasy, worried, wreck*; CONCEPTS 401,403 —Ant. calm, cheered, easy-going, happy, joyous, laid-back, pleased, relaxed

friction [n1] *rubbing* abrasion, agitation, attrition, chafing, erosion, filing, fretting, grating, grinding, irritation, massage, rasping, resistance, scraping, soreness, traction, trituration, wearing away; CONCEPT 215

friction [n2] *disagreement* animosity, antagonism, bad blood*, bad feeling*, bickering, bone to pick*, conflict, counteraction, discontent, discord, disharmony, dispute, dissension, faction, factionalism, flak*, hassle, hatred, hostility, impedance, incompatibility, interference, opposition, quarrel, resentment, resistance, rivalry, row*, ruckus*, rumpus*, set-to*, sour note*, strife, trouble, wrangling*; CONCEPTS 46,106,674 —Ant. agreement, harmony, peace

friend [n1] *confidant, companion* acquaintance, ally, alter ego, associate, bosom buddy*, buddy, chum*, classmate, cohort, colleague, companion*, compatriot, comrade, consort, cousin, crony, familiar, intimate, mate, pal, partner, playmate, roommate, schoolmate, sidekick, soul mate*, spare*, well-wisher; CONCEPT 423 —Ant. enemy, foe

friend [n2] *benefactor* accomplice, adherent, advocate, ally, associate, backer, partisan, patron, supporter, well-wisher; CONCEPT 348 —Ant. detractor, opponent

friendless [adj] *without companionship or confidant* abandoned, adrift, alienated, all alone*, all by one's self*, alone, cut off*, deserted, estranged, forlorn, forsaken, isolated, lonely, lonesome, marooned*, ostracized, shunned, solitary, unattached, without ties; CONCEPT 555 —Ant. attached, befriended, beloved, liked, loved

friendliness [n] *companionability* affability, amiability, amity, benevolence, camaraderie, comity, comradery, congeniality, conviviality, cordiality, friendship, geniality, goodwill, kindliness, kindness, neighborliness, open arms*, sociability, warmth; CONCEPT 388 —Ant. aloofness, coldness, incompatibility

friendly [adj] *intimate, companionable* affable, affectionate, amiable, amicable, attached, attentive, auspicious, beneficial, benevolent, benign, buddy-buddy*, chummy*, civil, close, clubby, comradely, conciliatory, confiding, convivial, cordial, faithful, familiar, favorable, fond, genial, good, helpful, kind, kindly, loving, loyal, neighborly, on good terms*, outgoing, peaceable, peaceful, propitious, receptive, sociable, solicitous, sympathetic, tender, thick, welcoming, well-disposed*; CONCEPT 555 —Ant. aloof, antagonistic, cold, cool, incompatible, uncompanionable, unfriendly, unreceptive, unsociable

friendship [n] *companionship* accord, acquaintanceship, affection, affinity, agreement, alliance, amiability, amicability, amity, association, attachment, attraction, benevolence, closeness, coalition, comity, company, concord, consideration, consonance, devotion, empathy, esteem, familiarity, favor, favoritism, fondness, friendliness, fusion, good will, harmony, intimacy, league, love, pact, partiality, rapport, regard, sociability, society, sodality, solidarity, understanding; CONCEPTS 388,714 —Ant. enmity, hate, hatred

fright [n1] *extreme apprehension* alarm, cold sweat*, consternation, dismay, dread, fear, horror, panic, quaking, scare, shiver, shock, terror, trepidation, trepidity; CONCEPT 410 —Ant. fearlessness

fright [n2] *horrifying or unpleasant sight* bother, eyesore*, frump*, mess, monstrosity, nuisance, scarecrow, ugliness; CONCEPT 718 —Ant. beauty

frighten [v] *shock, scare* affright, agitate, alarm, appall, astound, awe, browbeat*, bulldoze*, chill, chill to the bone*, cow, curdle the blood*, daunt, demoralize, deter, disburb, discomfort, disconcert, discourage, dishearten, dismay, disquiet, faze, horrify, intimidate, make blood run cold*, make teeth chatter*, panic, perturb, petrify, repel, scare away, scare off, scare to death*, spook, startle, stiff, strike terror into*, terrify, terrorize, unhinge*, unnerve; CONCEPTS 14,42 —Ant. calm, comfort, exhilarate, gladden

frightened [adj] *very scared* abashed, affrighted, afraid, aghast, alarmed, anxious, butterflies*, chicken*, chicken-hearted*, cowed*, dismayed, fearful, frozen, have cold feet*, having kittens*, hung up*, in a cold sweat*, in a panic*, in a sweat*, jellyfish*, jittery, jumpy, lily-livered*, mousy*, numb, panicky, petrified, pushing the panic button*, rabbity*, running scared*, scared stiff*, shaky, shivery, sissy*, spooked, startled, terrified, terrorized, terror-stricken, unnerved, uptight, yellow*; CONCEPTS 403,690 —Ant. calm, comforted, happy

frightful [adj2] *offensive* annoying, awful, bad, calamitous, disagreeable, dreadful, extreme, ghastly, great, hideous, horrible, insufferable, lewd, shocking, terrible, terrific, unpleasant, vile, wicked, wrong; CONCEPTS 529,545 —Ant. delightful, gentle, inoffensive, nice

frightful/frightening [adj1] *scary, shocking* alarming, appalling, atrocious, awesome, awful, chilling, daunting, dire, direful, dismaying, disquieting, dread, dreadful, fearful, fearsome, formidable, ghastly, grabber, grim, grisly, gruesome, hair-raising, hairy, harrowing, hideous, horrendous, horrible, horrid, horrifying, inconceivable, intimidating, lurid, macabre, menacing, morbid, ominous, petrifying, portentous, repellent, spooky, terrible, terrifying, traumatic, unnerving, unspeakable; CONCEPTS 529,537 —Ant. calming, comforting, pleasing

frigid [adj1] *extremely cold* antarctic, arctic, chill, chilly, cool, freezing, frost-bound, frosty, frozen, gelid, glacial, hyperboreal, icebox*, ice-cold, icy, refrigerated, Siberian*, snappy, three-dog night*, wintry; CONCEPT 605 —Ant. hot, warm

frigid [adj2] *unresponsive* aloof, austere, chilly, cold, cold-hearted*, cold-shoulder*, cool,

forbidding, formal, frosty, icy, impotent, indifferent, lifeless, passionless, passive, repellent,
rigid, stiff, unapproachable, unbending, unfeeling, unloving; CONCEPT 404 —*Ant.* amicable,
amorous, lovable, loving, responsive, warm

frill [n] *luxury, nice touch* amenity, decoration,
doodad*, extravagance, fandangle, flounce,
foppery*, frippery*, fuss, garbage*, garnish,
gathering, gimcrack*, gingerbread*, jazz*,
lace, ruffle, superfluity, thing*, tuck; CONCEPTS
646,655,824 —*Ant.* plainness

fringe [n] *border, trimming* binding, borderline,
brim, brink, edge, edging, flounce, hem, limit,
mane, march, margin, outside, outskirts,
perimeter, periphery, rickrack, ruffle, skirt,
tassel, verge; CONCEPTS 484,825 —*Ant.* center,
inside, interior, middle

fringe benefit [n] *additional benefit* extra,
perk, perquisite, plus, privilege; CONCEPT 344

frippery [n] *waste, nonsense* adornment,
bauble, decoration, fanciness, fandangle*,
flashiness, frill, fussiness, gaudiness, knickknack, meretriciousness, ornament, ostentation,
pretentiousness, showiness, tawdriness, toy,
trinket; CONCEPTS 655,824 —*Ant.* plainness

frisk [v] *cavort* bounce, caper, dance, frolic,
gambol, hop, jump, lark, leap, play, prance,
rollick, romp, skip, sport, trip; CONCEPT 384

frisk [v] *search* check, fan, inspect, run over,
shake down; CONCEPT 216

frisky [adj] *full of spirit* active, antic, bouncy,
coltish*, dashing, feeling one's oats*, frolicsome, full of beans*, gamesome, high-spirited,
in high spirits*, jumpy, kittenish*, larkish,
lively, peppy, playful, prankish, rollicking,
romping, spirited, sportive, wicked, zesty,
zippy; CONCEPTS 401,542,555 —*Ant.* depressed,
down, lifeless

fritter [v] *waste away* be wasteful with, blow*,
cast away, consume, dally, diddle away, dissipate, frivol, go through*, idle, lavish, misspend,
run through*, spend like water*, squander,
throw away, trifle; CONCEPTS 156,341 —*Ant.*
hold, save, store

frivolity [n] *silliness, childishness* coquetting,
dallying, flightiness, flippancy, flirting, flummery, folly, fribble, frippery, frivolousness,
fun, gaiety, game, giddiness, jest, levity, lightheartedness, lightness, nonsense, play, puerility,
shallowness, sport, superficiality, toying,
trifling, triviality, volatility, whimsicality,
whimsy; CONCEPTS 388,633 —*Ant.* sensibility,
seriousness, wiseness

frivolous [adj] *trivial, silly* barmy*, childish,
dizzy*, empty-headed*, facetious, featherbrained*, flighty, flip, flippant, foolish, gay,
giddy*, harebrained*, idiotic, idle, ill-considered, impractical, juvenile, light, light-minded,
minor, niggling*, nonserious, not serious,
paltry, peripheral, petty, playful, pointless,
puerile, scatterbrained*, senseless, shallow,
sportive, superficial, tongue-in-cheek*,
unimportant, unprofound, volatile, whimsical;
CONCEPTS 401,402,575 —*Ant.* grave, mature,
sensible, serious, solemn, thoughtful, wise

frock [n] *women's garment* apron, clothing,
dress, gown, habit, muumuu, robe; CONCEPT 451

frog [n] *jumping amphibian* bullfrog, croaker*,
polliwog, toad; CONCEPT 394

frolic [n] *amusement, revel* antic, drollery, escapade, fun, fun and games*, gaiety, gambol,
game, high jinks*, joke, joviality, lark,
merriment, monkeyshines*, play, prank,
romp, shenanigan*, skylarking*, sport, spree,
tomfoolery*, trick; CONCEPTS 59,386

frolic [v] *have fun, make merry* caper, carouse,
cavort, cut capers, cut loose*, fool around*,
frisk, gambol, go on a tear*, kick up one's
heels*, lark, let go*, let loose*, play, prance,
raise hell*, revel, riot, rollick, romp, sport,
spree, whoop it up*; CONCEPTS 384,386

frolicsome [adj] *playful* antic, coltish, frisky,
fun, gamesome, gay, gleeful, happy, impish,
jocular, jovial, kittenish, lively, merry,
mischievous, roguish, rollicking, sportive,
sprightly; CONCEPT 542 —*Ant.* serious,
staid, stiff

from [prep1] *outside of, separating* against,
in distinction to, out of possession of, taken
away; CONCEPT 583

from [prep2] *arising out of* beginning at,
coming out of, deriving out of, originating at,
starting with; CONCEPT 549

from scratch [adv] *from the very beginning*
from square one, from the ground up, from
the top, initially; CONCEPTS 585,799,828

front [adj] *lead, beginning* advanced, ahead,
anterior, facial, first, fore, foremost, forward,
frontal, head, headmost, in the foreground,
leading, obverse, topmost, vanward, ventral;
CONCEPTS 567,583,585,632 —*Ant.* back,
ending, final, finishing, rear

front [n1] *forward, beginning part of something*
anterior, bow, breast, brow, exterior, facade,
face, facing, fore, foreground, forehead,
forepart, frontage, frontal, frontispiece, front
line, head, lead, obverse, proscenium, top,
van, vanguard; CONCEPTS 833,835,836
—*Ant.* back, rear

front [n2] *appearance put on for show* air,
aspect, bearing, blind, carriage, coloring,
countenance, cover, cover-up*, demeanor,
disguise, display, expression, exterior, facade,
face, fake, figure, manner, mask, mien, phony,
port, presence, pretext, put-on*, show, veil,
window dressing*; CONCEPT 716

front [v] *look out on* to border, confront,
cover, encounter, face, look over, meet,
overlay, overlook; CONCEPT 746

frontier [n1] *boundary* borderland, borderline,
bound, confines, edge, limit, march, perimeter,
verge; CONCEPTS 513,745

frontier [n2] *unexplored, unoccupied area of
land* backcountry, backwater, backwoods,
boondocks*, boonies*, bush, hinterland, outback, outskirts, sticks*, unknown*; CONCEPT
509 —*Ant.* metropolis

front runner [n] *leader* best bet*, favorite, first
choice, forerunner, top seed; CONCEPTS 347,354

frost [n] *extreme cold* blight, dip, drop, freeze,
hoarfrost, ice, Jack Frost*, rime; CONCEPTS
524,610 —*Ant.* heat

frosting [n] *icing* covering, glaze, spread, sugar
coating, topping; CONCEPTS 457,460,461

frosty [adj] *very cold* antarctic, arctic, chill,
chilly, cool, frigid, frozen, gelid, glacial, hoar,
ice-capped, icicled, icy, nippy*, rimy, shivery,
wintry; CONCEPT 605 —*Ant.* heated, hot, warm

froth [n] *lather, bubbles* barm, ebullition, effervescence, fizz, foam, head, scud, scum, spindrift, spray, spume, suds, yeast; CONCEPTS 260,467,468

frothy [adj] *bubbly* barmy, bubbling, fermenting, fizzing, fizzy, foaming, foamy, spumescent, spumous, spumy, sudsy, with a head on*, yeasty; CONCEPT 485 —Ant. flat

frown [v1] *scowl* cloud up*, do a slow burn*, give a dirty look*, give the evil eye*, glare, gloom, glower, grimace, knit brows*, look black*, look daggers*, look stern*, lower, pout, sulk; CONCEPT 185 —Ant. grin, smile

frown [v2] *disapprove* deprecate, discommend, discountenance, discourage, disesteem, disfavor, dislike, look askance at*, not take kindly to*, object, show displeasure, take a dim view of*; CONCEPTS 21,29 —Ant. approve, condone, encourage

frozen [adj1] *very cold* antarctic, arctic, chilled, frigid, frosted, icebound, ice-cold, ice-covered, iced, icy, numb, Siberian*; CONCEPT 605 —Ant. boiled, heated, hot

frozen [adj2] *stopped* fixed, pegged, petrified, rooted, stock-still, suspended, turned to stone; CONCEPTS 534,584 —Ant. continual, continued, moving

frugal [adj] *economical* abstemious, canny, careful, chary, conserving, discreet, meager, meticulous, mingy*, niggardly*, parsimonious, penny-pinching*, penny-wise*, preserving, provident, prudent, saving, scrimping, sparing, Spartan*, stingy, thrifty, tight, tightwad*, unwasteful, wary; CONCEPT 334 —Ant. generous, lavish, spendthrifty, uneconomical, wasteful

frugality [n] *economizing* avarice, avariciousness, carefulness, conservation, economy, forehandedness, good management, miserliness, moderation, niggardliness, parsimoniousness, parsimony, penuriousness, providence, prudence, saving, scrimping, stinginess, thrift, thriftiness; CONCEPTS 330,335 —Ant. generosity, lavishness, wastefulness

fruit [n1] *edible part of vegetative growth developed after flowering* berry, crop, drupe, grain, harvest, nut, pome, produce, product, yield; CONCEPTS 426,428

fruit [n2] *result of labor* advantage, benefit, consequence, effect, outcome, pay, profit, result, return, reward; CONCEPTS 230,337

fruitful [adj] *productive* abounding, abundant, advantageous, beneficial, blooming, blossoming, breeding, childing, conducive, copious, effective, fecund, fertile, flourishing, flush, fructiferous, gainful, plenteous, plentiful, profitable, profuse, proliferant, prolific, propagating, reproducing, rewarding, rich, spawning, successful, useful, well-spent, worthwhile; CONCEPTS 528,537,560 —Ant. barren, impotent, sterile, unfruitful, unproductive

fruition [n] *achievement, maturation* accomplishment, actualization, attainment, completion, consummation, enjoyment, fulfillment, gratification, materialization, maturity, perfection, pleasure, realization, ripeness, satisfaction, success; CONCEPTS 704,706 —Ant. failure, unfulfillment

fruitless [adj] *bringing no advantage, product* abortive, barren, empty, futile, gainless, idle, ineffective, ineffectual, infertile, in vain, pointless, profitless, spinning one's wheels*, sterile, to no avail*, to no effect*, unavailable, unavailing, unfruitful, unproductive, unprofitable, unprolific, unsuccessful, useless, vain, wild goose chase*; CONCEPTS 528,537,560 —Ant. copious, fruitful, plentiful, potent, productive, profitable, successful, useful

frumpy [adj] *dowdy* badly dressed, baggy, blowsy*, dingy, drab, dull, frumpish, homely, old-fashioned, outdated, plain, poorly dressed, shabby, sloppy, stodgy, unfashionable, unkempt, unstylish; CONCEPT 589

frustrate [v] *thwart, disappoint* annul, arrest, baffle, balk, bar, beat, block, cancel, check, circumvent, confront, conquer, counter, counteract, cramp, cramp one's style*, crimp, dash, dash one's hope*, defeat, depress, discourage, dishearten, foil, forbid, forestall, foul up*, give the run around*, halt, hang up*, hinder, hold up, impede, inhibit, lick, negate, neutralize, nullify, obstruct, obviate, outwit, overcome, preclude, prevent, prohibit, render null and void*, ruin, stump*, stymie*, upset the applecart*; CONCEPTS 7,19,121 —Ant. aid, assist, cooperate, encourage, facilitate, help, support

frustrated [adj] *disappointed, thwarted* balked*, crabbed*, cramped, crimped, defeated, discontented, discouraged, disheartened, embittered, foiled, fouled up*, hung up on*, irked, resentful, stonewalled*, stymied*, through the mill*, ungratified, unsated, unslaked, up the wall*; CONCEPT 403 —Ant. encourage, fulfilled, inspirited, stimulated, uplifted

frustration [n] *disappointment, thwarting* annoyance, bitter pill*, blocking, blow, bummer, chagrin, circumvention, contravention, curbing, defeat, disgruntlement, dissatisfaction, downer*, drag*, failure, fizzle, foiling, grievance, hindrance, impediment, irritation, letdown, nonfulfillment, nonsuccess, obstruction, old one-two*, resentment, setback, unfulfillment, vexation; CONCEPTS 410,674 —Ant. aid, assistance, cooperation, encouragement, facilitation, help, support

fry [v] *cook in hot oil* brown, french fry, fricassee, frizzle, pan fry, sauté, sear, singe, sizzle; CONCEPT 170

frying pan [n] *skillet* fry pan, gridiron, spider, wok; CONCEPTS 493,494

fuddy-duddy [n] *fussy person* fussbudget, fusspot*, old fogy*, old geezer*, old poop*, square*, stick-in-the-mud*, stuffed shirt*; CONCEPT 423

fudge [v] *fake, misrepresent* avoid, color, cook up*, dodge, embellish, embroider, equivocate, evade, exaggerate, falsify, hedge, magnify, overstate, pad, patch, shuffle, slant, stall; CONCEPTS 59,63 —Ant. tell truth

fuel [n] *something providing energy* ammunition, combustible, electricity, encouragement, food, gas, incitement, juice, material, means, nourishment, propellant, provocation; CONCEPTS 467,520,523,661

fuel [v] *give energy to* charge, fan, feed, fill 'er up*, fill up, fire, gas, gas up*, incite, inflame, nourish, service, stoke up*, supply, sustain, tank up*; CONCEPTS 107,140 —Ant. de-energize, deplete, discourage, unfuel

fugitive [adj] *fleeing, transient* avoiding, brief, criminal, elusive, ephemeral, errant, erratic, escaping, evading, evanescent, fleeting, flitting, flying*, fugacious, hot*, impermanent, lamster, momentary, moving, on the lam*, passing, planetary, running away*, short*, short-lived, temporary, transitory, unstable, volatile, wandering, wanted; CONCEPTS 551,584,798 —*Ant.* confronting, facing, permanent

fugitive [n] *person escaping from law or other pursuer* bolter, derelict, deserter, displaced person, dodger, émigré, escapee, escaper, evacuee, exile, fly-by-night*, hermit, hunted person, outcast, outlaw, recluse, refugee, runagate, runaway, stray, transient, truant, vagabond, waif, walkout; CONCEPT 412

fulfill [v] *bring to completion* accomplish, achieve, answer, be just the ticket*, carry out, comply with, conclude, conform, discharge, do, effect, effectuate, execute, fill, fill the bill*, finish, hit the bull's-eye*, implement, keep, make it*, make the grade*, meet, obey, observe, perfect, perform, please, realize, render, satisfy, score*, suffice, suit; CONCEPTS 7,22,91,706 —*Ant.* fail, miss, neglect

fulfilled [adj] *completed* accomplished, achieved, actualized, attained, brought about, brought to a close, carried out, compassed, concluded, consummated, crowned, delighted, dispatched, effected, effectuated, executed, finished, gratified, made good*, matured, obtained, perfected, performed, pleased, put into effect, reached, realized, satisfied; CONCEPTS 403,531 —*Ant.* disappointed, incomplete, unfinished, unfulfilled, unsatisfied

fulfillment [n] *accomplishment, completion* achievement, attainment, carrying out, carrying through, consummation, contentedness, contentment, crowning, discharge, discharging, effecting, end, gratification, implementation, just the ticket*, kick*, kicks* observance, perfection, realization, you got it*; CONCEPTS 230,706 —*Ant.* disappointment, dissatisfaction, failure, frustration, unfulfillment

full [adj1] *brimming, filled* abounding, abundant, adequate, awash, big, bounteous, brimful, burdened, bursting, chockablock, chock-full, competent, complete, crammed, crowded, entire, extravagant, glutted, gorged, imbued, impregnated, intact, jammed, jammed full*, jam-packed*, laden, lavish, loaded, overflowing, packed, packed like sardines, padded, plenteous, plentiful, plethoric, profuse, replete, running over, sated, satiated, satisfied, saturated, stocked, stuffed, sufficient, suffused, surfeited, teeming, voluminous, weighted; CONCEPTS 481,483,773,774,786 —*Ant.* empty, incomplete, void

full [adj2] *thorough* absolute, abundant, adequate, all-inclusive, ample, blow-by-blow*, broad, choate, circumstantial, clocklike, complete, comprehensive, copious, detailed, entire, exhaustive, extensive, generous, integral, itemized, maximum, minute, particular, particularized, perfect, plenary, plenteous, plentiful, unabridged, unlimited, whole; CONCEPT 531 —*Ant.* incomplete

full [adj3] *deep in sound* clear, distinct, loud, resonant, rich, rounded, throaty; CONCEPT 594

full [adj4] *satiated in hunger* glutted, gorged, jaded, lousy with*, sated, satiate, stuffed, surfeited, up to here*; CONCEPTS 406,481, 774 —*Ant.* empty, hungry, needy, starved, unsatisfied

full-blooded [adj] *purebred; strong* hardy, hearty, powerful, robust, sound, thoroughbred, unmixed, vigorous, virile, vital; CONCEPTS 314,489,613

full-bodied [adj] *robust* concentrated, fruity, full-flavored, heady*, heavy, lusty, mellow, potent, redolent, rich, strong, well-matured; CONCEPTS 489,613 —*Ant.* weak

full-grown/full-fledged [adj] *developed, ripe, ready* adult, full-blown*, grown, grown-up, in one's prime*, marriageable, mature, nubile, of age, perfected, prime, ripened; CONCEPTS 558,578,797 —*Ant.* new, small, underdeveloped, undeveloped, unripe, young

fullness [n] *abundance, breadth* adequateness, ampleness, amplitude, broadness, completeness, completion, comprehensiveness, congestion, copiousness, curvaceousness, dilation, distension, enlargement, entirety, extensiveness, fill, glut, plenitude, plenty, plenum, profusion, repletion, roundness, satiation, satiety, saturation, scope, sufficiency, surfeit, swelling, totality, tumescence, vastness, voluptuousness, wealth, wholeness, wideness; CONCEPTS 635,730 —*Ant.* emptiness, incompleteness, need, void, want

full-scale [adj] *total, all-out* all-encompassing, comprehensive, exhaustive, extensive, full-blown*, full-dress*, full-out*, in-depth, major, proper, sweeping, thorough, thoroughgoing, total, unlimited, wide-ranging; CONCEPTS 531,772 —*Ant.* incomplete, incomprehensive, partial

fully [adv1] *completely, in all respects* absolutely, all out*, all the way*, altogether*, entirely, every inch*, from A to Z*, from soup to nuts*, heart and soul*, intimately, outright, perfectly, positively, quite, royal*, thoroughly, through and through*, totally, utterly, wholly, without exaggeration; CONCEPTS 531,772 —*Ant.* incompletely, partially, partly

fully [adv2] *sufficiently, adequately* abundantly, amply, comprehensively, enough, plentifully, satisfactorily, well; CONCEPT 558 —*Ant.* inadequately, insufficiently, partly

fulminate [v] *criticize harshly* animadvert, berate, blow up, bluster, castigate, censure, condemn, curse, declaim, denounce, denunciate, execrate, explode, fume, intimidate, inveigh against, menace, protest, rage, rail, reprobate, swear at, thunder, upbraid, vilify, vituperate; CONCEPTS 52,54 —*Ant.* compliment, defend, flatter, praise, support

fulmination [n] *tirade, condemnation* blast, curse, denunciation, diatribe, discharge, explosion, intimidation, invective, obloquy, outburst, philippic, reprobation, warning; CONCEPTS 52,54,278 —*Ant.* compliment, defense, flattery, praise, support

fulsome [adj] *sickening or excessive behavior* adulatory, bombastic, buttery*, canting, cloying, coarse, extravagant, fawning, flattering, glib, grandiloquent, hypocritical, immoderate, ingratiating, inordinate, insincere, magniloquent, mealy-mouthed*, nauseating, offensive, oily*, oleaginous, overdone, saccharine, sanctimonious, slick*, slimy*, smarmy*, smooth, suave, sycophantic, unctuous, wheedling*; CONCEPTS 267,401 —Ant. reasonable, sincere

fumble [v] *bumble, mess up* bollix*, botch*, bungle*, err, feel, flounder, flub*, fluff*, goof*, grapple, grope, lose the handle*, louse up*, misfield, mishandle, mismanage, scrabble*, screw up*, spoil, stumble; CONCEPTS 101,181 —Ant. do well

fume [v] *get very upset about* anger, blow up*, boil, bristle, burn, chafe, chomp at the bit*, get hot*, get steamed up*, rage, rant, rave, seethe, smoke*, storm*; CONCEPTS 21,29,410 —Ant. be calm, be happy

fumes [n] *pollution, gas in air* effluvium, exhalation, exhaust, haze, miasma, reek, smog, smoke, stench, vapor; CONCEPTS 437,600

fumigate [v] *disinfect, ventilate* air out, antisepticize, circulate, decontaminate, deodorize, fan, freshen, purify, sanitize, sterilize, vaporize; CONCEPTS 51,60

fun [adj] *good, happy* amusing, boisterous, convivial, diverting, enjoyable, entertaining, lively, merry, pleasant, witty; CONCEPTS 537, 572 —Ant. bad, sad, unfun, unhappy, woeful

fun [n] *amusement, play* absurdity, ball*, big time*, blast*, buffoonery, celebration, cheer, clowning, distraction, diversion, enjoyment, entertainment, escapade, festivity, foolery, frolic, gaiety, gambol, game*, good time*, grins*, high jinks*, holiday, horseplay*, jesting, jocularity, joke, joking, jollity, joy, junketing, laughter, living it up*, merriment, merrymaking, mirth, nonsense, pastime, picnic*, playfulness, pleasure, recreation, rejoicing, relaxation, riot, romp, romping, solace, sport, tomfoolery*, treat, whoopee*; CONCEPTS 386,388 —Ant. sadness, work

function [n1] *capacity, job* action, activity, affair, behavior, business, charge, concern, duty, employment, exercise, faculty, goal, mark, mission, object, objective, occupation, office, operation, part, post, power, province, purpose, raison d'être*, responsibility, role, service, situation, target, task, use, utility, work; CONCEPTS 362,659

function [n2] *social occasion* affair, celebration, do*, gathering, get-together*, meeting, party, reception; CONCEPT 386

function [v] *perform, work* act, act the part*, behave, be in action, be in commission, be in operation, be running, cook, do, do duty*, do one's thing*, get with it*, go, go to town*, move, officialize, officiate, operate, percolate*, react, run, serve, take, take care of business*; CONCEPTS 87,362 —Ant. idle, malfunction

functional [adj] *working* handy, occupational, operative, practicable, practical, serviceable, useful, utile, utilitarian, utility; CONCEPT 560 —Ant. broken, idle, malfunctioning, unfunctional

fund [n] *repository, reserve* armamentarium, capital, endowment, foundation, hoard, inventory, kitty*, mine, pool*, reservoir, source, stock, store, storehouse, supply, treasury, trust, vein; CONCEPTS 332,340,710

fund [v] *provide money for* back, bankroll,

capitalize, endow, finance, float, grubstake*, juice*, patronize, pay for, pick up the check*, pick up the tab*, promote, stake, subsidize, support; CONCEPTS 115,341 —Ant. take

fundamental [adj] *basic, important* axiological, axiomatic, basal, bottom, bottom-line*, cardinal, central, constitutional, constitutive, crucial, elemental, elementary, essential, first, foundational, grass-roots*, indispensable, integral, intrinsic, key, major, meat-and-potatoes*, necessary, organic, original, paramount, primary, prime, primitive, primordial, principal, radical, requisite, rudimentary, significant, structural, substratal, substantive, supporting, sustaining, theoretical, underived, underlying, vital; CONCEPTS 546,567 —Ant. additional, advanced, auxiliary, extra, minor, secondary, subordinate, trivial, unimportant

fundamental [n] *basic, essential part* ABCs*, axiom, basis, bottom line*, brass tacks*, coal and ice*, component, constituent, cornerstone, element, factor, foundation, guts*, heart, law, nitty-gritty*, principium, principle, rock bottom*, rudiment, rule, sine qua non*, theorem; CONCEPTS 668,688,826,829 —Ant. addition, auxiliary, extra, subordinate, trivia

fundraiser [n] *pledge drive* appeal for funds, bazaar, charity event, charity sale, philanthropic enterprise, radiothon, telethon; CONCEPTS 337,657

funds [n] *cash reserve* accounts receivable, affluence, assets, backing, bankroll, belongings, bread*, budget, capital, collateral, currency, dough*, earnings, finance, fluid assets, hard cash*, kitty*, lucre, means, money, money in the bank*, money on hand*, nest egg*, nut*, petty cash, pork barrel*, possessions, proceeds, profits, property, ready money*, resources, revenue, savings, scratch*, securities, specie, stakes*, store*, stuff*, substance, treasure, wealth, wherewithal*, winnings*; CONCEPTS 340,710 —Ant. debt

funeral [n] *ceremony for the dead* burial, cremation, entombment, exequies, funeration, inhumation, interment, last rites, obit, obsequies, planting, requiem, sepulture, services, solemnities; CONCEPTS 172,386 —Ant. baptism, christening

funereal [adj] *depressing* black, bleak, dark, deathlike, dirgelike, disheartening, dismal, doleful, dreary, elegiac, gloomy, grave, grim, lamenting, lugubrious, melancholy, mournful, oppressive, sad, sepulchral, serious, solemn, somber, woeful; CONCEPTS 403,537,542 —Ant. cheerful, happy, joyful, lively, upbeat

funk [n] *fear, depression* alarm, cold sweat*, despondency, fright, gloom, misery, panic, trembling; CONCEPTS 27,410 —Ant. happiness, joy

funnel [v] *direct down a path* carry, channel, conduct, convey, filter, move, pass, pipe, pour, siphon, traject, transmit; CONCEPTS 187,217

funny [adj1] *comical, humorous* absurd, amusing, antic, blithe, capricious, clever, diverting, droll, entertaining, facetious, farcical, for grins*, gas*, gay, gelastic, good-humored, hilarious, humdinger, hysterical, jocose, jocular, joking, jolly, killing*, knee-slapper*, laughable, ludicrous, merry, mirthful, playful, priceless, rich, ridiculous, riot, riotous, risible, screaming,

side-splitting*, silly, slapstick, sportive, waggish, whimsical, witty; CONCEPTS 267,529,537
—*Ant.* dramatic, melancholy, sad, serious, tragic, unamusing, unfunny

funny [*adj2*] *odd, peculiar* bizarre, curious, dubious, fantastic, mysterious, perplexing, puzzling, queer, remarkable, strange, suspicious, unusual, weird; CONCEPTS 552,564
—*Ant.* common, normal, standard, usual

funny money [*n*] *counterfeit money* bad currency, bad money, counterfeit currency, fake currency, fake money, false currency, false money, play money; CONCEPTS 648,725

fur [*n*] *hair on animals* brush, coat, down, fluff, fuzz, hide, jacket, lint, pelage, pelt, pile, skin, wool; CONCEPT 399

furbish [*v*] *polish; renovate* brighten, buff, burnish, clean, deck out*, fix up, glaze, gloss, gussy up*, improve, recondition, refurbish, rehabilitate, renew, restore, rub, shine, smarten up*, spruce up*; CONCEPTS 162,165,700

furious [*adj1*] *extremely angry, very mad* bent*, bent out of shape*, beside oneself*, boiling*, browned off*, bummed out*, corybantic, crazed, demented, desperate, enraged, fierce, fit to be tied*, frantic, frenetic, frenzied, fuming, hacked, hopping mad*, incensed, infuriated, insane, irrational, livid, maddened, maniac, on the warpath*, rabid, raging, smoking*, steamed, unreasonable, up in arms*, vehement, vicious, violent, wrathful; CONCEPT 403 —*Ant.* cheerful, elated, excited, exhilarated, happy, pleased

furious [*adj2*] *stormy, turbulent* agitated, blustering, blustery, boisterous, concentrated, excessive, exquisite, extreme, fierce, flaming, impetuous, intense, intensified, raging, rampageous, rough, savage, tempestuous, terrible, tumultous/tumultuous, ungovernable, unrestrained, vehement, vicious, violent, wild; CONCEPTS 525,537,548 —*Ant.* calm, mild, moderate, peaceful, quiet

furlough [*n*] *leave of absence* layoff, leave, liberty, rest and recreation, rest and recuperation, rest and relaxation, R&R, sabbatical, shore leave, shutdown, vacation; CONCEPTS 802,807

furnace [*n*] *heating mechanism* boiler, calefactor, cinerator, cremator, forge, Franklin stove, heater, heating system, incinerator, kiln, oil burner, smithy, stove; CONCEPT 463 —*Ant.* freezer

furnish [*v1*] *decorate, supply* accoutre, apparel, appoint, arm, array, clothe, endow, equip, feather a nest*, fit, fit out*, fix up*, gear, line a nest*, make habitable, outfit, provide, provision, purvey, rig, stock, store, turn out; CONCEPTS 140,177,182 —*Ant.* leave plain, unfurnish

furnish [*v2*] *give, reveal information* afford, bestow, deliver, dispense, endow, feed, grant, hand, hand over, offer, present, provide, supply, transfer, turn over; CONCEPTS 60,67,108 —*Ant.* conceal, hide, secret

furnishings [*n*] *appliances, furniture* accessories, accoutrements, appointments, décor, equipment, fittings, fixtures, gear, provisions, trappings; CONCEPT 443

furniture [*n*] *household property* appliance, appointment, bed, bookcase, buffet, bureau, cabinet, chair, chattel, chest, commode, couch, counter, cupboard, davenport, desk, dresser,

effect, equipment, fittings, furnishing, goods, highboy, hutch, movables, possession, sideboard, sofa, stool, table, thing, wardrobe; CONCEPT 443

furor [*n*] *disturbance, excitement* ado*, agitation, big scene*, big stink*, bustle, commotion, craze, enthusiasm, fad, ferment, flap*, free-for-all*, frenzy, fury, fuss, hell broke loose*, hullabaloo*, hysteria, lunacy, madness*, mania, outburst, outcry, rage, row, ruckus, stir*, to-do*, tumult, uproar, whirl; CONCEPTS 230,388,410 —*Ant.* calm, peace

furrow [*n*] *ditch* channel, corrugation, crease, crinkle, crow's-foot*, dike, fluting, fold, groove, gutter, hollow, line, plica, rabbet, ridge, rimple, rivel, ruck, rut, seam, trench, wrinkle; CONCEPT 513

further [*adj*] *additional* added, another, else, extra, farther, fresh, in addition, more, new, other, supplementary; CONCEPT 771

further [*adv*] *additionally* again, also, as well as, besides, beyond, distant, farther, in addition, moreover, on top of*, over and above*, then, to boot, what's more*, yet, yonder; CONCEPT 771

further [*v*] *advance, lend support* aid, assist, back up, bail out*, ballyhoo*, champion, contribute, encourage, engender, expedite, facilitate, forward, foster, generate, give a boost to*, go with, hasten, help, lend a hand*, open doors*, patronize, plug, promote, propagate, push, serve, speed, succor, take care of, work for; CONCEPTS 69,87,110 —*Ant.* block, cease, check, curtail, delay, frustrate, halt, hinder, impede, obstruct, prevent, protest, stop

furtherance [*n*] *advancement* advocacy, backing, boosting, carrying-out, championship, progress, progression, promotion, prosecution, pursuit; CONCEPTS 110,704 —*Ant.* blockage, curtailment, delay, hindrance, impediment, stoppage

furthermore [*adv*] *in addition* additionally, along, as well, besides, likewise, moreover, not to mention, to boot, too, what's more*, withal, yet; CONCEPTS 577,824

furthest [*adj*] *most distant* extreme, farthest, most remote, outermost, outmost, remotest, ultimate, uttermost; CONCEPTS 586,778 —*Ant.* closest, nearest

furtive [*adj*] *sneaky, secretive* artful, calculating, cautious, circumspect, clandestine, cloaked, conspiratorial, covert, crafty*, creepy*, cunning, disguised, elusive, evasive, foxy, guileful, hidden, hush-hush*, insidious, masked, scheming, shifty*, skulking, slinking*, sly, stealthy, subrosa*, surreptitious, tricky*, undercover, underhand, underhanded, under-the-table*, under wraps*, wily; CONCEPTS 548,576 —*Ant.* aboveboard, forthright, honest, open, truthful

fury [*n*] *anger, wrath* acerbity, acrimony, asperity, boiling point*, conniption, energy, ferocity, fierceness, fire, flare-up, force, frenzy, furor, impetuosity, indignation, intensity, ire, madness, might, passion, rage, rapidity, rage, rampancy, rise, savagery, severity, slow burn*, sore, stew*, storm*, tempestuousness, turbulence, vehemence, violence; CONCEPTS 29,410 —*Ant.* calm, happiness, peace

fuse [v] *meld, intermix* agglutinate, amalgamate, bind, blend, cement, coalesce, combine, commingle, deliquesce, dissolve, federate, flux, integrate, interblend, interfuse, intermingle, join, liquefy, liquesce, melt, merge, mingle, run, run together, smelt, solder, thaw, unite, weld; CONCEPT 113 —*Ant.* disconnect, divide, separate

fusillade [n] *rapid outburst* barrage, broadside, burst of fire, hail, salvo, volley; CONCEPT 633

fusion [n] *melding; mixture* admixture, alloy, amalgam, amalgamation, blend, blending, coadunation, coalescence, coalition, commingling, commixture, compound, federation, heating, immixture, integration, intermixture, junction, liquefaction, liquification, melting, merger, merging, smelting, soldering, synthesis, unification, union, uniting, welding; CONCEPTS 113,260,432 —*Ant.* disconnection, division, separation

fuss [n] *disturbance, trouble* ado, agitation, altercation, argument, bickering, bother, broil*, bustle, commotion, complaint, confusion, controversy, difficulty, display, dispute, excitement, falling-out*, fight, flap, flurry, flutter, fret, furor, hassle, kick-up*, objection, palaver, perturbation, quarrel, row, ruckus, scene, squabble, stew*, stink*, stir, storm, to-do*, turmoil, unrest, upset, winging*, worry; CONCEPTS 46,106,388,633 —*Ant.* calm, peace

fussy [adj] *meticulous, particular* careful, choosy, conscientious, conscionable, dainty, difficult, discriminating, exact, exacting, fastidious, finical, finicky, fretful, fuddy-duddy*, hard to please*, heedful, nit-picking*, overfastidious, painstaking, persnickety, picky, picky-picky*, punctilious, punctual, querulous, scrupulous, squeamish, stickling; CONCEPTS 401,404 —*Ant.* uncritical, undemanding, unfussy

fustian [adj] *pompous* arrogant, boastful, bombastic, conceited, flaunting, high and mighty*, highfalutin, lofty, ostentatious, pontifical, portentous, pretentious, puffed up*, ranting, self-centered, self-important, vain, vaingloriones; CONCEPTS 267,401,542

futile [adj] *hopeless, pointless* abortive, barren, bootless, delusive, empty, exhausted, forlorn, fruitless, hollow, idle, impracticable, impractical, ineffective, ineffectual, insufficient, in vain, no dice*, nugatory, on a treadmill*, otiose, out the window*, profitless, resultless, save one's breath*, sterile, to no avail*, to no effect*, to no purpose*, trifling, trivial, unavailing, unimportant, unneeded, unproductive, unprofitable, unreal, unsatisfactory, unsubstantial, unsuccessful, useless, vain, valueless, worthless; CONCEPTS 528,548,560 —*Ant.* fruitful, hopeful, productive, profitable

futility [n] *uselessness* emptiness, frivolousness, fruitlessness, hollowness, idleness, ineffectiveness, ineffectuality, meaninglessness, pointlessness, senselessness, unprofitableness, worthlessness; CONCEPT 560

futon [n] *sofa bed* convertible sofa, couch, davenport, daybed, sofa; CONCEPT 443

future [adj] *to come; expected* approaching, booked, budgeted, close at hand*, coming, coming up, destined, down the line*, down the pike, down the road*, eventual, fated, final, forthcoming, from here in, from here on, from here to eternity*, from now on in*, imminent, impending, inevitable, in the cards*, in the course of time, in the offing*, just around the corner*, later, likely, looked toward, near, next, planned, prospective, scheduled, subsequent, to be*, ulterior, ultimate, unborn, unfolding, up; CONCEPT 820 —*Ant.* past

future [n] *time to come* aftertime, afterward, by and by*, destiny, eternity, expectation, fate, futurity, hereafter, infinity, life to come, millennium, morrow, offing, outlook, posterity, prospect, subsequent time, to be*, tomorrow, world to come*; CONCEPTS 679,807,811,818 —*Ant.* past

futuristic [adj] *ahead of one's time* advanced, cutting edge, innovative, modern, pioneering, revolutionary, visionary; CONCEPTS 578,589,797

fuzz [n] *fluff* down, dust ball*, dust bunnies*, fiber, floss, fur, hair, lanugo, lint, nap, pile; CONCEPT 260 —*Ant.* smoothness

fuzzy [adj1] *fluffy* down-covered, downy, flossy, frizzy, furry, hairy, linty, napped, pilate, velutinous, woolly; CONCEPT 606 —*Ant.* smooth

fuzzy [adj2] *out of focus* bleary, blurred, dim, distorted, faint, foggy, hazy, ill-defined, indefinite, indistinct, misty, muffled, murky, obscure, shadowy, unclear, unfocused, vague; CONCEPT 619 —*Ant.* clear

G

gab [n] *conversation* blab*, blather*, chat, chitchat*, gossip, idle talk*, loquacity*, palaver*, prattle, small talk*, talk, tête-à-tête, tongue-wagging*, yak*, yakkety-yak*; CONCEPT 278 —*Ant.* silence

gab [v] *talk a lot* blabber*, blather*, buzz*, chatter, gossip, jabber*, jaw*, prate, prattle, yak*, yakkety-yak*; CONCEPT 266 —*Ant.* be quiet

gabby [adj] *talkative* chattering, chatty, effusive, excitant, garrulous, glib, gossiping, gushing, jabbering, long-winded*, loose-lipped*, loquacious, mouthy*, prattling, prolix, talky, verbose, voluble, windy*, wordy; CONCEPT 267 —*Ant.* close-mouthed, quiet, secretive

gad [v] *roam about* cruise, gallivant, hit the road*, hit the trail*, jaunt, knock about*, knock around*, maunder, mooch*, ramble, range, rove, run around*, stray, traipse, wander; CONCEPTS 149,224

gadfly [n] *goad; nuisance* annoyance, energizer, excitant, irritant, motivator, mover, pest, prod, spur, stimulator; CONCEPTS 412,674

gadget [n] *device, novelty* apparatus, appliance, business, concern, contraption, contrivance, doodad*, doohickey*, gimmick, gizmo*, invention, object, thing*, thingamajig, tool, utensil, whatchamacallit*, widget*; CONCEPTS 463,499

gadgetry [n] *mechanism* appliances, bells and whistles, contraptions, ingenious device, instrumentation, machinery, works; CONCEPTS 463,499

gaffe [n] *mistake, goof* blooper*, blunder, boner*, boo-boo*, faux pas*, howler*, impropriety, indecorum, indiscretion, putting foot in mouth*, slip*, solecism; CONCEPTS 101,230 —*Ant.* correction

gag [*n*] *practical joke* crack, drollery, hoax, jest, quip, ruse, trick, wile, wisecrack, witticism; CONCEPT 59

gag [*v1*] *silence, stop up* balk, bottle up*, choke, constrain, cork*, cork up*, curb, deaden, demur, garrote, keep the lid on*, muffle, muzzle, obstruct, put the lid on*, quiet, repress, restrain, shut down, shy, squash*, squelch, stifle, still, stumble, suppress, tape up*, throttle*, tongue-tie*; CONCEPTS 121,130

gag [*v2*] *vomit, choke* be nauseated, disgorge, gasp, heave, nauseate, pant, puke*, retch, sicken, spew, strain, struggle, throw up; CONCEPTS 179,308

gaiety [*n*] *happiness, celebration* animation, blitheness, brightness, brilliance, cheer, color, colorfulness, conviviality, effervescence, elation, entertainment, exhilaration, festivity, frolic, fun, geniality, gladness, glee, glitter, good humor*, grins*, high spirits*, hilarity, joie de vivre, jollity, joviality, joyousness, lightheartedness, liveliness, merriment, merry-making, mirth, pleasantness, radiance, revel, reveling, revelry, shindig*, showiness, sparkle, sport, sprightliness, vivacity, whoopee*, winging*; CONCEPTS 377,388 —*Ant.* sadness, solemnity, unhappiness

gaily [*adv*] *happily, brightly* blithely, brilliantly, cheerfully, colorfully, flamboyantly, flashily, gleefully, glowingly, joyfully, laughingly, lightheartedly, merrily, showily, sparklingly, spiritedly, splendidly, vivaciously, with élan*, with spirit*; CONCEPTS 542,589 —*Ant.* sadly, solemnly, unhappily

gain [*n*] *acquisition, winnings* accretion, accrual, accumulation, achievement, addition, advance, advancement, advantage, attainment, benefit, boost, buildup, cut, dividend, earnings, emolument, gravy*, growth, headway*, hike*, improvement, income, increase, increment, lucre, payoff, proceeds, produce, profit, progress, receipts, return, rise, share, take, up*, upping*, velvet*, yield; CONCEPTS 337, 344,706, 710 —*Ant.* expenditure, forfeit, forfeiture, loss, waste

gain [*v*] *acquire, win* accomplish, achieve, advance, ameliorate, annex, attain, augment, benefit, boost, bring in, build up, capture, clear, collect, complete, consummate, earn, enlarge, enlist, expand, fulfill, gather, get, glean, grow, harvest, have, improve, increase, land, make, make a killing*, move forward, net, obtain, overtake, parlay, perfect, pick up, procure, produce, profit, progress, promote, rack up*, reach, realize, reap, score*, secure, succeed, win over; CONCEPTS 120,124,129 —*Ant.* exhaust, forfeit, lose, miss, pass, spend, waste

gainful [*adj*] *very productive, profitable* advantageous, beneficial, fat, fruitful, generous, going, going concern*, good, in the black*, lucrative, lush, moneymaking, paid off, paying, remunerative, rewarding, rich, satisfying, substantial, sweet*, useful, well-paying, worthwhile; CONCEPT 334 —*Ant.* disadvantageous, unproductive, unprofitable, useless

gainsay [*v*] *contradict* combat, contravene, controvert, cross, deny, disaffirm, disagree, disclaim, disprove, dispute, fight, impugn, negate, negative, oppose, refute, repudiate, resist, traverse, withstand; CONCEPTS 52,54 —*Ant.* agree, concur, go along

gait [*n*] *way an animal or person moves, walks* amble, bearing, canter, carriage, clip, gallop, get along, lick, march, motion, movement, pace, run, speed, step, stride, tread, trot, walk; CONCEPT 149

gala [*adj*] *celebratory* bright, colorful, convivial, festal, festive, gay, happy, jovial, joyful, merry; CONCEPT 548

gala [*n*] *festival* affair, ball, bash, blast*, blowout*, carnival, celebration, clambake, dance, do, festivity, fete, fiesta, function, get-together*, hop, jamboree, moveable feast, pageant, party, prom, roast, shindig*, stag, to-do*, winging*; CONCEPTS 377,383

galaxy [*n*] *nebula* elliptical galaxy, irregular galaxy, island universe, Milky Way, spiral galaxy, star cluster, star system; CONCEPTS 370,511

gale [*n*] *violent storm* blast, blow, burst, chinook, cyclone, hurricane, mistral, monsoon, outbreak, outburst, squall, tempest, tornado, typhoon, wind, windstorm; CONCEPTS 524,526

gall [*n*] *nerve, brashness* acrimony, animosity, arrogance, bitterness, brass, brazenness, cheek*, chutzpah*, conceit, confidence, crust cynicism, effrontery, guts*, haughtiness, hostility, impertinence, impudence, insolence, malevolence, malice, overbearance, pomposity, presumption, rancor, sauciness, self-importance,spite, venom; CONCEPTS 411,633 —*Ant.* modesty, reservations, shyness

gall [*v1*] *upset, irritate* aggravate, annoy, bedevil, bother, burn, chafe, chide, disturb, exasperate, fret, grate, harass, harry, inflame, irk, nag, peeve, pester, plague, provoke, rile, roil, rub, ruffle, scrape, torment, trouble, vex, worry; CONCEPTS 7,19 —*Ant.* cheer, encourage, enliven, exhilarate, make happy

gall [*v2*] *rub raw* abrade, bark, burn, chafe, corrode, erode, excoriate, file, fray, frazzle, fret, grate, graze, irritate, scrape, scratch, scuff, skin, wear; CONCEPT 215

gallant [*adj*] *brave, splendid* attentive, bold, considerate, courageous, courteous, courtly, daring, dashing, dauntless, dignified, doughty, fearless, fire-eating*, game*, glorious, gracious, grand, gritty*, hairy*, heroic, honorable, intrepid, lionhearted*, lofty, magnanimous, noble, plucky*, polite, quixotic, stately, stouthearted, suave, thoughtful, urbane, valiant, valorous; CONCEPTS 404,542 —*Ant.* afraid, cowardly, fearful, timid, ungentlemanly, unmannerly

gallantry [*n*] *bravery, civility* address, attentiveness, audacity, boldness, courage, courageousness, courteousness, courtesy, daring, dauntlessness, deference, derring-do*, duty, elegance, fearlessness, graciousness, honor, intrepidity, mettle, nerve, nobility, pluck*, poise, politeness, prowess, resolution, reverence, savoir-faire, spirit, tact, urbanity, valiance, valor; CONCEPTS 411,657 —*Ant.* cowardliness, fear

gallery [*n1*] *balcony* arcade, loggia, mezzanine, patio, porch, upstairs, veranda; CONCEPT 440

gallery [*n2*] *showplace for wares* exhibit, exhibition room, hall, museum, salon, showroom, studio, wing; CONCEPTS 448,449

gallery [n3] *audience, usually seated high attendance,* onlookers, peanut gallery*, public, spectators; CONCEPTS 294,417

galling [adj] *very upsetting* acid, afflictive, aggravating, annoying, bitter, bothersome, distasteful, exasperating, grievous, harassing, humiliating, irksome, irritating, nettlesome, painful, plaguing, provoking, rankling, unpalatable, vexatious, vexing; CONCEPTS 7, 19 —*Ant.* cheering, comforting, pleasing, satisfying, soothing, wonderful

gallivant [v] *run around, gad about* cruise, jaunt, meander, mooch, ramble, range, roam, rove, stray, traipse, wander; CONCEPTS 149,224 —*Ant.* behave

gallop [v] *bolt, race with slight jumping motion* amble, canter, career, course, dart, dash, fly, hasten, hurdle, hurry, jump, leap, lope, pace, rack, run, rush, shoot, speed, spring, sprint, stride, tear along, trot, zoom; CONCEPTS 150,194

galvanize [v] *inspire, stimulate* animate, arouse, astonish, awaken, commove, electrify, energize, excite, fire*, frighten, innervate, invigorate, jolt, motivate, move, pique, prime, provoke, quicken, shock, spur, startle, stir, stun, thrill, vitalize, wake, zap*; CONCEPTS 7,14,22 —*Ant.* depress, deter, discourage, disparage, dissuade, retard

gambit [n] *plan, plot* artifice, design, device, gimmick, jig, maneuver, play, ploy, ruse, trick; CONCEPT 660

gamble [n] *chance, speculation* action, bet, fling, leap*, long shot*, lottery, outside chance*, raffle, risk, shot in the dark*, spec*, stab*, throw of the dice*, toss up*, uncertainty, venture, wager; CONCEPTS 28,363 —*Ant.* design, guard, insurance, plan, protection, safeguard

gamble [v] *take a chance on winning* back, bet, brave, buck the odds*, cast lots*, challenge, cut the cards, dare, defy, endanger, face, flip the coin*, game, go for broke*, hazard, imperil, jeopardize, lay money on*, lot, make a bet, play, plunge, put, put faith in, put trust in, risk, set, shoot the moon*, shoot the works*, speculate, stake, stick one's neck out*, take a flyer*, tempt fortune*, trust to luck, try one's luck, venture, wager; CONCEPTS 28,363 —*Ant.* be careful, design, ensure, guard, insure, plan, safeguard

gambol [v] *tumble playfully* bound, caper, carry on, cavort, cut, cut a caper*, cut loose*, fool around*, frisk, frolic, hop, horse around*, jump, kibitz around*, kick up one's heels*, lark, leap, play, prance, revel, roister, rollick, romp, skip, sport, spring, whoop it up*; CONCEPTS 149,194,363

game [adj1] *brave, willing* bold, courageous, dauntless, desirous, disposed, dogged, eager, fearless, gallant, hardy, heroic, inclined, interested, intrepid, nervy*, persevering, persistent, plucky*, prepared, ready, resolute, spirited, spunky, unafraid, unflinching, up for*, valiant, valorous; CONCEPT 404 —*Ant.* afraid, cautious, cowardly, disinclined, fearful, unprepared, unready, unwilling

game [adj2] *debilitated* ailing, bad, crippled, deformed, disabled, incapacitated, injured, lame, maimed, weak; CONCEPTS 314,485 —*Ant.* able, capable, working

game [n1] *entertainment* adventure, amusement, athletics, business, distraction, diversion, enterprise, festivity, frolic, fun, jest, joke, lark, line, merriment, merrymaking, occupation, pastime, plan, play, proceeding, pursuit, recreation, romp, scheme, sport, sports, undertaking; CONCEPTS 292,363

game [n2] *individual sporting event* competition, contest, match, meeting, round, tournament; CONCEPT 364

game [n3] *undomesticated animals chased for food* chase, fish, fowl, kill, meat, prey, quarry, ravin, victim, wild animals; CONCEPTS 394, 457,460

game [n4] *plot, trick* butt, derision, design, device, hoax, joke, object of ridicule, plan, ploy, practical joke, prank, scheme, stratagem, strategy, tactic; CONCEPTS 59,660

gamely [adv] *bravely* boldly, courageously, dauntlessly, eagerly, enthusiastically, fearlessly, stoutly, with one's head held high*; CONCEPT 401

gamut [n] *range* area, catalogue, compass, diapason, extent, field, panorama, scale, scope, series, spectrum, sweep; CONCEPTS 651,788

gamy [adj] *ill-smelling; corrupt* fetid, foul, malodorous, pungent, rancid, rank, reeking, seamy, sordid, strong-flavored, strong-smelling, strong-tasting, tainted; CONCEPT 598

gang [n] *group, mob of people* assemblage, band, bunch, circle, clan, clique, club, cluster, combo*, company, coterie, crew, crowd, herd, horde, knot, lot, organization, outfit, pack, party, posse, ring, set, shift, squad, syndicate, team, tribe, troop, troupe, workers, zoo*; CONCEPT 387

gangling [adj] *rangy* awkward, bony, gawky, lanky, leggy, long-legged, long-limbed, lumbering, skinny, spindly, tall, thin; CONCEPTS 490,491

gangster [n] *person involved in illegal activities* bandit, bruiser*, criminal, crook, dealer, desperado, goon*, hit person, hood, hoodlum, hooligan*, Mafioso*, member of the family, mobster, pusher, racketeer, robber, ruffian, soldier*, thug, tough; CONCEPT 412

gap [n] *break, breach* aperture, arroyo, blank, caesura, canyon, chasm, cleft, clove, crack, cranny, crevice, cut, defile, difference, disagreement, discontinuity, disparity, divergence, divide, division, fracture, gorge, gulch, gully, hiatus, hole, hollow, inconsistency, interlude, intermission, interruption, interspace, interstice, interval, lacuna, lull, notch, opening, orifice, pause, ravine, recess, rent, respite, rest, rift, rupture, separation, slit, slot, space, vacuity, void; CONCEPTS 513,665 —*Ant.* closure

gape [v1] *gawk* beam, bore, eye, eyeball*, focus, get a load of*, get an eyeful*, give the eye*, glare, gloat, goggle*, look, ogle, peer, rubberneck*, size up*, stare, take in*, wonder, yawp*; CONCEPT 623

gape [v2] *be wide open* cleave, crack, dehisce, divide, frondesce, gap, part, split, yaw, yawn; CONCEPT 135 —*Ant.* close

gaping [adj] *wide open* broad, cavernous, chasmal, great, vast, yawning; CONCEPTS 485, 490 —*Ant.* closed, shut

garage [n] *storage building for vehicles, workplace* barn, carport*, car stall*, parking lot, parking space, repair shop, shop, storage; CONCEPTS 439,449

garb [n] *clothing* apparel, appearance, array, attire, clothes, costume, dress, duds*, feathers*, form, garment, gear, guise, habiliment, habit, outfit, rags*, raiment, robes*, semblance, things*, threads*, uniform, vestments, wear; CONCEPT 451

garb [v] *fit with clothes* apparel, array, attire, clad, clothe, cover, deck, deck out*, drape, dress, dud*, fit out*, garment, raiment, rig out*, rig up*, robe, suit up*, tog*, turn out*; CONCEPT 167 —*Ant.* disrobe, unclothe

garbage [n] *refuse, litter* bits and pieces*, debris, detritus, dreck, dregs, dross, filth, junk, muck, odds and ends*, offal, rubbish, rubble, scrap, scrapings, sewage, slop*, sweepings, swill, trash, waste; CONCEPT 260

garble [v] *mix up, misrepresent* belie, color, confuse, corrupt, distort, doctor, falsify, jumble, misinterpret, mislead, misquote, misstate, mutilate, obscure, pervert, slant, tamper with, twist, warp; CONCEPTS 59,63 —*Ant.* decipher, order, pronounce, represent, translate, unscramble

garden [n] *cultivated plants, flowers* back yard, bed, cold frame, conservatory, enclosure, field, greenhouse, hothouse, nursery, oasis, patch, patio, plot, terrace; CONCEPTS 509,517

gargantuan [adj] *very large* big, colossal, elephantine, enormous, giant, gigantic, heavyweight, huge, humongous, immense, jumbo, leviathan, mammoth, massive, monstrous, monumental, mountainous, prodigious, supercolossal*, super-duper*, titanic, towering, tremendous, vast, whopping*; CONCEPTS 491,773 —*Ant.* little, miniscule, small, tiny

gargle [v] *rinse the mouth with liquid* irrigate, swish, trill, use mouthwash; CONCEPTS 169, 308,616

garish [adj] *flashy, tasteless* blatant, brassy, brazen, cheap, chintzy, flaunting, gaudy, glaring, glittering, kitschy*, loud, meretricious, ornate, ostentatious, overdone, overwrought, raffish, screaming*, showy, tawdry, tinsel, vulgar; CONCEPT 589 —*Ant.* discreet, modest, normal, plain, tasteful

garland [n] *strand of material, usually hung* bays, chaplet, coronal, crown, festoon, honors, laurel, palm, wreath; CONCEPTS 260,429

garment [n] *article of clothing* apparel, array, attire, costume, covering, drapes*, dress, duds*, feathers*, garb, gear, get-up*, habiliment, habit, outfit, raiment, robe, things*, threads*, togs*, uniform, vestments, wear, weeds*; CONCEPT 451

garner [v] *collect, accumulate* amass, assemble, cull, cumulate, deposit, extract, gather, glean, harvest, hive, hoard, lay in*, lay up*, pick up, put by*, reap, reserve, roll up*, save, stockpile, store, stow away, treasure; CONCEPTS 109,135 —*Ant.* disperse, dissipate, divide, separate, spread

garnish [v] *embellishment, improvement* adornment, decoration, enhancement, furbelow, gingerbread*, ornament, ornamentation, tinsel, trim, trimming; CONCEPT 824 —*Ant.* decrease, divestment, plainness

garnish [v] *embellish, improve* adorn, beautify, bedeck, deck, decorate, dress up, enhance, fix

up, grace, gussy up*, ornament, set off*, spiff up*, spruce up*, trim; CONCEPT 244 —*Ant.* decrease, divest, harm, hurt, leave plain, strip

garrison [n] *military post, fort* barracks, base, camp, citadel, command post, encampment, fortification, fortress, stronghold; CONCEPTS 321,439

garrulous [adj] *talkative* babbling, blabbermouth*, chattering, chatty, effusive, flap jaw*, gabby, glib, gossiping, gushing, longwinded*, loose-lipped*, loose-tongued*, loquacious, motormouth*, mouthy, prating, prattling, prolix, prosy, running on at the mouth*, verbose, voluble, wind-bag*, windy*, wordy, yakkity*, yakky*; CONCEPTS 267,404 —*Ant.* mum, quiet, reserved, silent, still, untalkative

gas [n] *something not liquid or solid* effluvium, fumes, miasma, smoke, stream, vapor, volatile substance; CONCEPT 465 —*Ant.* liquid, solid

gash [n] *cut made by slicing* cleft, furrow, gouge, incision, laceration, mark, nip, notch, rent, slash, slit, split, tear, wound; CONCEPT 309

gash [v] *cut by slicing* carve, cleave, furrow, gouge, incise, injure, lacerate, lance, mark, nip, notch, pierce, rend, slash, slit, split, tear, wound; CONCEPTS 137,176

gasket [n] *seal* cap, covering, packing, stopper; CONCEPTS 85,160

gasoline [n] *fuel* diesel fuel, gasohol, juice*, oil, petrol, propellant; CONCEPTS 467,520,523,661

gasp [n] *sharply drawn breath* blow, ejaculation, exclamation, gulp, heave, pant, puff, wheeze, whoop; CONCEPTS 163,595

gasp [v] *draw breath in sharply* blow, catch one's breath, choke, convulse, fight for breath, gulp, heave, inhale, inspire, pant, puff, respire, sniffle, snort, wheeze, whoop; CONCEPT 163

gastric [adj] *pertaining to the stomach* abdominal, celiac, duodenal, enteric, gastrocolic, intestinal, stomach, stomachic, stomachical, ventral; CONCEPT 393

gate [n] *movable barrier at entrance* access, bar, conduit, door, doorway, egress, exit, gateway, issue, lock, opening, passage, port, portal, revolving door, slammer*, turnstile, way, weir; CONCEPTS 440,445

gatekeeper [n] *watchperson* doorkeeper, guard, lookout, monitor, protector, security officer, sentinel, sentry; CONCEPT 348

gather [v1] *come or bring together* accumulate, aggregate, amass, assemble, associate, bunch up, capture, choose, close with, cluster, collect, concentrate, congregate, convene, converge, corral, crowd, cull, draw, draw in, flock, forgather, gang up, garner, get together, group, hang around*, hang out*, heap, herd, hoard, huddle, make the scene*, marshal, mass, meet, muster, pick, pile up, pluck, poke*, pour in, punch*, rally, reunite, round up*, scare up*, scrape together*, show up, stack up, stockpile, swarm, throng, unite; CONCEPTS 109,114 —*Ant.* allot, deal, disperse, distribute, divide, scatter, separate, spread

gather [v2] *be led to believe; infer* assume, conclude, deduce, draw, expect, find, hear, imagine, judge, learn, make, presume, reckon, suppose, surmise, suspect, take, think, understand; CONCEPT 15 —*Ant.* misunderstand

gather [v3] *harvest, pick out* crop, cull, draw, extract, garner, glean, heap, ingather, mass, pick up, pile, pluck, reap, select, stack, take in; CONCEPT 257 —*Ant.* grow, plant

gather [v4] *gain, increase* build, deepen, enlarge, expand, grow, heighten, intensify, rise, swell, thicken, wax; CONCEPT 780

gathering [n] *assemblage, accumulation* acquisition, affair, aggregate, aggregation, association, band, body, bunch, caucus, clambake*, collection, company, concentration, conclave, concourse, conference, congregation, congress, convention, convocation, crowd, crush, drove, flock, function, gain, get-together*, group, heap, herd, horde, huddle, junction, knot, levy, mass, meet, meeting, muster, parley, party, pile, powwow*, rally, roundup, social function, society, stock, stockpile, swarm, throng, turnout, union; CONCEPTS 324,386,417

gauche [adj] *tactless, unsophisticated* awkward, bumbling, clumsy, crude, graceless, green, halting, ham-handed*, heavy-handed, ignorant, ill-bred, ill-mannered, inelegant, inept, insensitive, lacking, maladroit, oafish, uncouth, uncultured, unhappy, unpolished, wooden*; CONCEPT 404 —*Ant.* elegant, graceful, mannerly, polished, refined, sophisticated, tactful, tasteful

gaudy [adj] *bright and vulgar* blatant, brazen, brilliant, catchpenny*, chichi*, chintzy, coarse, crude, flashy, flaunting, florid, frou-frou*, garish, gay, glaring, gross, gussied up*, jazzy, kitschy*, loud, meretricious, obtrusive, ostentatious, pizzazz*, pretentious, putting on the ritz*, raffish, ritzy, screaming*, showy, snazzy, splashy, splendiferous, tasteless, tawdry, tinsel; CONCEPTS 589,618 —*Ant.* calm, drab, dull, modest, plain, refined, simple, sophisticated

gauge [n] *measure, standard* barometer, basis, benchmark, bore, capacity, check, criterion, degree, depth, example, exemplar, extent, guide, guideline, height, indicator, magnitude, mark, meter, model, norm, pattern, rule, sample, scale, scope, size, span, test, thickness, touchstone*, type, width, yardstick; CONCEPTS 647, 680,688,792 —*Ant.* estimate, guess

gauge [v] *measure, judge* adjudge, appraise, ascertain, assess, calculate, calibrate, check, check out, compute, count, determine, estimate, evaluate, eye*, figure, figure in, guess, guesstimate, have one's number*, look over, meter, peg*, quantify, quantitate, rate, reckon, scale, size, size up*, take account of, tally, value, weigh; CONCEPTS 37,764 —*Ant.* estimate, guess

gaunt [adj] *skinny* angular, anorexic, attenuated, bare, bleak, bony, cadaverous, desolate, dismal, dreary, emaciated, forbidding, forlorn, grim, haggard, harsh, lank, lean, like a bag of bones*, meager, peaked, peaky, pinched, rawboned, scraggy, scrawny, skeletal, skeleton, skin and bones*, spare, thin, wasted; CONCEPTS 406, 490,491 —*Ant.* plump, thick, well-nourished

gauzy [adj] *see-through, gossamer in texture* delicate, diaphanous, filmy, flimsy, insubstantial, light, lucid, pellucid, sheer, thin, tiffany, translucent, transparent; CONCEPT 606 —*Ant.* cloudy, foggy, heavy, obscured, opaque, thick

gawk [v] *stare at in amazement* bore*, eyeball*, gape, gaze, glare, gloat, goggle*, look, ogle, peer, rubberneck*, yawp*; CONCEPT 623

gawky [adj] *clumsy* awkward, bumbling, clownish, gauche, loutish*, lumbering, lumpish*, lumpy, maladroit, oafish, rude, rustic, splay, uncouth, ungainly; CONCEPTS 550,584 —*Ant.* athletic, graceful, lithe

gay [adj1] *happy* alert, animate, animated, blithe, blithesome, bouncy, brash, carefree, cheerful, cheery, chipper*, chirpy, confident, convivial, devil-may-care*, festive, forward, frivolous, frolicsome, fun-loving, gamesome, glad, gleeful, hilarious, insouciant, jocund, jolly, jovial, joyful, joyous, keen, lighthearted, lively, merry, mirthful, playful, pleasure-seeking, presuming, pushy, rollicking, self-assertive, sparkling, spirited, sportive, sprightly, sunny, vivacious, wild, zippy*; CONCEPTS 403,542 —*Ant.* depressed, discouraged, sad, unhappy, upset, worried

gay [adj2] *colorful, vivid* brave, bright, brilliant, flamboyant, flashy, fresh, garish, gaudy, intense, rich, showy; CONCEPTS 589, 618 —*Ant.* colorless, dull, lifeless, plain, uncolorful

gay [adj3] *homosexual* homoerotic, homophile, lesbian, Sapphic; CONCEPT 372 —*Ant.* heterosexual

gaze [n] *long, fixed stare* fish eye*, glaring, gun*, look, looking, ogling, peek, peep, rubbernecking*, scrutiny, seeing, survey, watching; CONCEPT 623

gaze [v] *stare at* admire, beam*, bore*, contemplate, eye, eyeball*, gape, gawk, get a load of*, get an eyeful*, glare, gloat, inspect, lamp*, look, look fixedly, moon*, observe, ogle, peek, peep, peer, pin*, pipe*, regard, rubber*, rubberneck*, scrutinize, see, size up*, survey, take in*, view, watch, wonder; CONCEPTS 623,626

gazebo [n] *pavilion* arbor, bandstand, belvedere, bower, kiosk, platform, rotunda, summerhouse; CONCEPTS 440,443

gear [n1] *equipment* accessory, accouterment, adjunct, apparatus, appendage, appurtenance, baggage, belongings, contraption, effects, encumbrances, fittings, habiliment, harness, impedimenta, instrument, kit, kit and kaboodle*, luggage, machinery, material, materiel, means, outfit, paraphernalia, possessions, rigging, setup, stuff, supply, tackle, things, tools, trappings; CONCEPT 496

gear [n2] *toothed part of wheel* cog, cogwheel, gearwheel, pinion, ragwheel, sprocket, spurwheel; CONCEPT 464

gear [n3] *clothing* apparel, array, attire, clothes, costume, drapes*, dress, duds*, feathers*, garb, garments, habit, outfit, rags*, threads*, toggery*, togs*, wear; CONCEPT 451

gear [v] *prepare, equip* accouter, adapt, adjust, appoint, arm, blend, fit, fit out*, furnish, harness, match, organize, outfit, ready, regulate, rig*, suit, tailor, turn out; CONCEPTS 182,202

geek [n] *odd person; computer expert* buffoon, computer specialist, curiosity, dolt, dork, freak, goon, guru, nerd, techie, weirdo; CONCEPTS 352,366,423

gelatinous [adj] *coagulated* gluey, glutinous, gummy, jelled, jellied, jelly-like, mucilaginous, pudding*, sticky, thick, viscid, viscous; CONCEPT 606 —*Ant.* liquid

geld [v] *castrate* alter*, emasculate, eunuchize, fix*, neuter, spay, sterilize, unman; CONCEPTS 240,250

gem [n] *precious stone; treasure* bauble*, glass*, hardware*, jewel, jewelry, masterpiece, nonpareil, ornament, paragon, pearl, pick, prize, rock*, sparkler*, stone, trump*; CONCEPTS 337,446,474

gender [n] *grammatical rules applying to nouns that connote sex or animateness* common, feminine, gender-specific, masculine, neuter; CONCEPT 408

genealogy [n] *person's family tree* ancestry, blood line, derivation, descent, extraction, generation, genetics, heredity, history, line, lineage, parentage, pedigree, progeniture, stemma, stirps, stock, strain; CONCEPT 296

general [adj1] *common, accepted* accustomed, broad, commonplace, conventional, customary, everyday, extensive, familiar, generic, habitual, humdrum, inclusive, matter-of-course*, natural, normal, ordinary, popular, prevailing, prevalent, public, regular, routine, run-of-the-mill*, typical, uneventful, universal, usual, wide, widespread, wonted; CONCEPTS 530,547 —*Ant.* abnormal, exceptional, extraordinary, individual, novel, rare, unaccepted, uncommon, unique, unusual

general [adj2] *inexact, approximate* ill-defined, imprecise, inaccurate, indefinite, loose, not partial, not particular, not specific, uncertain, undetailed, unspecific, vague; CONCEPT 557 —*Ant.* circumscribed, definite, exact, individual, limited, particular, singular, specific

general [adj3] *comprehensive* across-the-board*, all-around*, all-embracing*, all-inclusive*, ample, blanket, broad, catholic, collective, comprehending, diffuse, ecumenical, encyclopedic, endless, extensive, far-reaching, generic, global, inclusive, indiscriminate, infinite, limitless, miscellaneous, overall, panoramic, sweeping, taken as a whole, total, ubiquitous, unconfined, universal, unlimited, wide, worldwide; CONCEPTS 537,772 —*Ant.* circumscribed, limited

generality [n] *vague notion* abstraction, abstract principle, generalization, half-truth, law, loose statement, observation, principle, sweeping statement, universality; CONCEPTS 688,689 —*Ant.* detail, specific, specificity

generalize [v] *make a sweeping assumption, statement* be metaphysical, conclude, derive, discern, discover, establish, hypothesize, induce, observe, philosophize, postulate, speculate, stay in the clouds*, theorize, vapor; CONCEPTS 37,49 —*Ant.* except, specifize

generally [adv] *mainly, in most cases* about, all in all, almost always, altogether, approximately, as a rule, broadly, by and large, chiefly, commonly, conventionally, customarily, en masse, extensively, for the most part, habitually, largely, mostly, normally, on average, on the whole, ordinarily, overall, popularly, practically, predominantly, primarily, principally, publicly, regularly, roughly, roundly, thereabouts, typically, universally, usually, widely; CONCEPTS 530,547,772 —*Ant.* exactly, particularly, rarely, seldom, specifically

generate [v] *produce, create* accomplish,

achieve, bear, beget, breed, bring about, bring to pass, cause, develop, effect, engender, form, found, get up, give birth to, give rise to, hatch, inaugurate, induce, initiate, institute, introduce, make, multiply, muster, occasion, originate, parent, perform, procreate, propagate, provoke, reproduce, set up, spawn, whip up*, work up; CONCEPTS 173,205,251,374 —*Ant.* break, destroy

generation [n1] *creation, production* bearing, begetting, breeding, bringing forth, engendering, formation, fructifying, genesis, multiplying, origination, procreation, propagation, reproduction, spawning; CONCEPTS 173,205, 374 —*Ant.* destruction

generation [n2] *era; age group* aeon, breed, contemporaries, crop, day, days, eon, epoch, peers, period, rank, span, step, time, times; CONCEPTS 807,816

generic [adj] *common, general* all-encompassing, blanket, collective, comprehensive, inclusive, nonexclusive, sweeping, universal, wide; CONCEPT 530 —*Ant.* exclusive, individual, particular, specific

generosity [n] *spirit of giving* all heart*, almsgiving, altruism, beneficence, benevolence, bounteousness, bounty, charitableness, charity, free giving, goodness, heart, high-mindedness, hospitality, kindness, largesse, liberality, magnanimity, munificence, nobleness, openhandedness, philanthropy, profusion, readiness, unselfishness; CONCEPTS 411,657 —*Ant.* greed, meanness, selfishness, stinginess

generous [adj1] *giving, big-hearted* acceptable, altruistic, beneficent, benevolent, big, bounteous, bountiful, charitable, considerate, easy, equitable, excellent, fair, free, good, great-hearted, helpful, high-minded, honest, honorable, hospitable, just, kind, kindhearted, kindly, lavish, liberal, lofty, loose, magnanimous, moderate, munificent, noble, open-handed, philanthropic, prodigal, profuse, reasonable, soft-touch*, thoughtful, tolerant, ungrudging, unselfish, unsparing, unstinting, willing; CONCEPTS 404,542 —*Ant.* greedy, mean, miserly, selfish, stingy

generous [adj2] *plentiful* abundant, affluent, ample, aplenty, bounteous, bountiful, copious, dime a dozen*, full, galore, handsome, large, lavish, liberal, luxuriant, no end*, no end in sight*, overflowing, plenteous, rich, stinking with*, unstinting, wealthy; CONCEPTS 334,589, 781 —*Ant.* depleted, wanting

genesis [n] *beginning, creation* alpha, birth, commencement, dawn, dawning, engendering, formation, generation, inception, opening, origin, outset, propagation, provenance, provenience, root, source, start; CONCEPTS 119,832 —*Ant.* conclusion, end, finale, finish

genetic [adj] *coming from heredity* abiogenetic, ancestral, digenetic, eugenic, genesiological, genital, hereditary, historical, matriclinous, patrimonial, phytogenetic, sporogenous, xenogenetic; CONCEPTS 314,549 —*Ant.* acquired

genial [adj] *extremely nice and happy* affable, agreeable, amiable, amicable, blithe, cheerful, cheering, cheery, chipper*, chirpy*, congenial, convivial, cordial, easygoing, enlivening, favorable, friendly, gentle, glad, good-natured, gracious, hearty, high, jocund, jolly, jovial, joyous, kind, kindly, merry, neighborly, perky, pleasant, sociable, sunny*, sunny side up*, up*, upbeat, upper*, warm, warm-hearted; CONCEPTS *401,404* —Ant. aloof, cold, cool, cranky, irritable, moody, unfriendly, unhappy

geniality [n] *extreme niceness* affability, agreeability, agreeableness, amenity, amiability, cheerfulness, cheeriness, congenialness, conviviality, cordiality, enjoyableness, friendliness, gladness, good cheer, good nature, gratefulness, happiness, heartiness, jollity, joviality, joy, joyousness, kindliness, kindness, mirth, pleasance, pleasantness, sunniness*, sweetness and light*, warmheartedness, warmth; CONCEPTS *411,633* —Ant. aloofness, coldness, coolness, irritation, moodiness, unfriendliness, unhappiness

genie [n] *mythical being* demon, djinni, jinnee, jinni, spirit, wizard; CONCEPT *361*

genius [n] *gift of high intellect* ability, accomplishment, acumen, acuteness, adept, aptitude, aptness, astuteness, bent, brain, brilliance, capacity, creativity, discernment, Einstein*, endowment, expert, faculty, flair, grasp, head, imagination, inclination, ingenuity, inspiration, intelligence, inventiveness, knack, mature, originality, percipience, perspicacity, power, precocity, prodigy, propensity, prowess, reach, sagacity, superability, talent, turn, understanding, virtuoso, wisdom; CONCEPTS *350,409, 416* —Ant. idiot, imbecile

genocide [n] *mass extermination* annihilation, carnage, decimation, ethnic cleansing, holocaust, massacre, mass execution, mass murder, race extermination, slaughter; CONCEPT *252*

genre/genus [n] *type, class* brand, category, character, classification, fashion, group, kind, school, sort, species, style; CONCEPTS *378,388, 655*

genteel [adj] *sophisticated, cultured* affected, aristocratic, artificial, chivalrous, civil, confined, courteous, courtly, cultivated, distingué, elegant, fashionable, formal, graceful, hollow, intolerant, la-di-da*, mannerly, noble, ostentatious, polished, polite, pompous, precious, pretentious, priggish, prim, prissy, prudish, refined, respectable, straitlaced, stuffy*, stylish, urbane, well-behaved, well-bred, well-mannered; CONCEPTS *401,404* —Ant. boorish, callous, rough, rude, rugged, uncultured, unrefined, unsophisticated

gentility [n] *sophistication, cultivation* aristocracy, blue blood*, civility, courtesy, courtliness, culture, decorum, elegance, elite, etiquette, flower*, formality, gentle birth*, gentlefolk, gentry, good breeding*, good family*, good manners*, high birth*, mannerliness, nobility, optimacy, polish, politeness, propriety, quality, rank, refinement, respectability, ruling class*, society, upper class, upper crust*, urbanity; CONCEPTS *388,411* —Ant. coarseness, crudeness, roughness, rusticity

gentle [adj] *having a mild or kind nature* affable, agreeable, amiable, benign, biddable, bland, compassionate, considerate, cool*, cultivated, disciplined, docile, domesticated, dovelike*, easy, genial, humane, kindly, laid back*, lenient, manageable, meek, mellow, merciful, moderate, pacific, peaceful, placid, pleasant,

pleasing, pliable, quiet, soft, softhearted, sweet-tempered, sympathetic, tame, taught, temperate, tender, tractable, trained, warm-hearted; CONCEPTS *404,542* —Ant. crude, rough, troubled, unkind, violent, wild

gentle [adj2] *mild, temperate in effect on senses* balmy, bland, calm, clement, delicate, easy, faint, feeble, gradual, halcyon, hushed, imperceptible, lenient, light, low, low-pitched, low-toned, mellow, mild, moderate, muted, peaceful, placid, quiet, sensitive, serene, slight, slow, smooth, soft, soothing, subdued, tender, tranquil, untroubled; CONCEPTS *525,537,594* —Ant. harsh, loud, odorous, putrid, rough, sharp, strong

gentle [adj3] *of noble birth* aristocratic, blue-blooded*, Brahmin*, courteous, cultured, elegant, genteel, highborn, highbred, noble, polished, polite, refined, upper-class, well-born, well-bred; CONCEPT *555* —Ant. crude, low

gentleperson [n] *polite, well-mannered person* aristocrat, brick*, good egg*, good person, nice person, noble, scholar; CONCEPT *423*

genuine [adj1] *authentic, real* 24-carat*, absolute, accurate, actual, authenticated, bona fide, -carat*, certain, certified, demonstrable, exact, existent, factual, for real*, good, hard, honest, honest-to-goodness*, indubitable, in the flesh*, kosher*, legit, legitimate, literal, natural, official, original, palpable, plain, positive, precise, proved, pure, real stuff*, sound, sterling, sure-enough*, tested, true, unadulterated, unalloyed, undoubted, unimpeachable, unquestionable, unvarnished, valid, veritable, very, whole; CONCEPT *582* —Ant. counterfeit, false, illegitimate, sham, unreal

genuine [adj2] *unaffected; honest* actual, artless, candid, earnest, frank, heartfelt, known, natural, open, positive, real, reliable, righteous, sincere, true, trustworthy, undesigning, unfeigned, unimpeachable, unpretended, unquestionable, up front*, valid, well-established; CONCEPTS *267,542* —Ant. affected, deceiving, deceptive, dishonest, insincere, misleading

genus [n] *type* brand, breed, category, class, compartment, department, division, genre, group, kind, make, model, section, sort, style, subdivision, subfamily, variety; CONCEPT *378*

geography [n] *the earth's features; study of land* cartography, chorography, earth science, geology, geopolitical study, geopolitics, physiographics, physiography, topography, topology; CONCEPTS *349,509*

germ [n1] *microscopic organism, often causing illness* antibody, bacterium, bug*, disease, microbe, microorganism, parasite, pathogen, plague, virus, what's going around*; CONCEPTS *306,392*

germ [n2] *beginning* bud, cause, egg, embryo, inception, nucleus, origin, ovule, ovum, root, rudiment, seed, source, spark, spore, sprig, sprout; CONCEPTS *392,648,826,832*

germane [adj] *appropriate* ad rem, akin, allied, applicable, applicative, applicatory, apposite, apropos, apt, cognate, connected, fitting, kindred, kosher*, legit*, material, on target*, on the button*, on the nose*, pertinent, proper, related, relating, relevant, right on*, suitable, that's the ticket*, to the point, to the purpose;

CONCEPT 558 —Ant. improper, inappropriate, irrelevant, unfitting, unrelated, unsuitable

germinate [v] grow bud, develop, generate, live, originate, pullulate, shoot, sprout, swell, vegetate; CONCEPT 427 —Ant. halt, slow, stop, thwart

gestation [n] process of early development evolution, fecundation, gravidity, growth, incubation, maturation, pregnancy, reproduction, ripening; CONCEPTS 316,704,809

gesture [n] motion as communication action, body language, bow, curtsy, expression, genuflection, gesticulation, high sign, indication, intimation, kinesics, mime, nod, pantomime, reminder, salute, shrug, sign, signal, sign language, token, wave, wink; CONCEPTS 74, 185 —Ant. speech

gesture/gesticulate [v] make signs, motions to communicate act out, flag, indicate, mime, pantomime, signal, signalize, use one's hands, use sign language, wave; CONCEPT 74 —Ant. speak

get [v1] come into possession of; achieve access, accomplish, acquire, annex, attain, bag*, bring, bring in, build up, buy into, buy off, buy out, capture, cash in on*, chalk up*, clean up*, clear, come by, compass, cop*, draw, earn, educe, effect, elicit, evoke, extort, extract, fetch, gain, get hands on*, glean, grab, have, hustle*, inherit, land, lock up, make, make a buy, make a killing*, net, obtain, parlay, pick up, procure, pull, rack up*, realize, reap, receive, score, secure, snag*, snap up*, snowball*, succeed to, take, wangle*, win; CONCEPTS 120,706,710 —Ant. fail, lose, miss, pass

get [v2] fall victim to accept, be afflicted with, become infected with, be given, be smitten by, catch, come down with*, contract, get sick, receive, sicken, succumb, take; CONCEPT 93 —Ant. overtake, overthrow

get [v3] seize apprehend, arrest, bag*, beat, capture, catch, collar*, defeat, grab, lay hold of*, lay one's hands on*, nab*, nail*, occupy, overcome, overpower, secure, take, trap; CONCEPT 90 —Ant. give in, surrender, yield

get [v4] come to be achieve, attain, become, come over, develop into, effect, go, grow, realize, run, turn, wax*; CONCEPTS 697,706

get [v5] understand acquire, catch, catch on to, comprehend, fathom, figure out, follow, gain, get into one's head*, hear, know, learn, look at, memorize, notice, perceive, pick up*, receive, see, take in, work out; CONCEPTS 15, 31 —Ant. misconstrue, misunderstand

get [v6] arrive advance, blow in*, come, come to, converge, draw near, land, make it, reach, show, show up, turn up; CONCEPT 159 —Ant. depart, leave

get [v7] contact for communication get in touch, reach; CONCEPT 266 —Ant. lose

get [v8] arrange, manage desired goal adjust, contrive, dispose, dress, fit, fix, make, make up, order, prepare, ready, straighten, succeed, wangle*; CONCEPT 202 —Ant. fail, mismanage

get [v9] convince, induce argue into, beg, bring around, coax, compel, draw, influence, persuade, press, pressure, prevail upon, prompt, provoke, sway, talk into, urge, wheedle, win over; CONCEPT 68 —Ant. discourage, dissuade

get [v10] have an effect on affect, amuse, arouse, bend, bias, carry, dispose, entertain, excite, gratify, impress, influence, inspire, move, predispose, prompt, satisfy, stimulate, stir, stir up, strike, sway, touch; CONCEPTS 7,22

get [v11] produce offspring beget, breed, generate, procreate, produce, propagate, sire; CONCEPT 374

get [v12] irritate, upset aggravate, annoy, bother, bug*, burn, exasperate, gall, get someone's goat*, irk, nettle, peeve, pique, provoke, put out*, rile, rub the wrong way*, try, vex; CONCEPTS 7,19 —Ant. calm, please, soothe

get [v13] confuse baffle, beat, bewilder, buffalo*, confound, discomfit, disconcert, distress, disturb, embarrass, mystify, nonplus, perplex, perturb, puzzle, stick*, stump, upset; CONCEPT 16 —Ant. understand

get across [v] communicate an idea bring home*, convey, get through to, impart, make clear, make understood, pass on, put over, transmit; CONCEPT 60 —Ant. miscommunicate

get ahead [v] excel, succeed advance, be successful, climb, do well, flourish, get on, leave behind, make good, outdo, outmaneuver, overtake, progress, prosper, surpass, thrive; CONCEPTS 141,706 —Ant. fail, fall behind

get a kick out of [v] delight in be pleased, dig*, enjoy, get a bang out of*, get a charge out of*, get pleasure from, gloat over, take pleasure in; CONCEPTS 32,384

get along [v1] make progress cope, develop, do, fare, flourish, get by*, get on*, make out, manage, muddle through*, prosper, shift, succeed, thrive; CONCEPTS 117,704 —Ant. cease, halt, stop

get along [v2] depart advance, be off, go, go away, leave, march, move, move off, move on, proceed, progress, push ahead, take a hike*; CONCEPT 195 —Ant. arrive

get along [v3] be compatible agree, be friendly, get on*, harmonize, hit it off*; CONCEPT 388 —Ant. argue, behave

get at [v1] attain access, achieve, acquire, arrive, ascertain, gain access, get hold of, reach; CONCEPT 120 —Ant. lose, miss, pass

get at [v2] mean, intend aim, hint, imply, lead up to, purpose, suggest; CONCEPT 75

getaway [n] escape break, breakout, decampment, flight, lam, slip; CONCEPT 102

get back [v1] regain reclaim, recoup, recover, repossess, retrieve, salvage; CONCEPT 120 —Ant. lose, miss, pass

get back [v2] return arrive home, come back, come home, reappear, revert, revisit, turn back; CONCEPT 159 —Ant. depart, go away, leave

get back at [v] settle a score be avenged, get even, pay back, retaliate, revenge, take vengeance; CONCEPTS 14,246

get by [v] manage, survive contrive, cope, do, do well enough, exist, fare, flourish, get along, get on, make ends meet*, make out, muddle through*, prosper, shift, subsist, succeed, thrive; CONCEPT 117

get down [v] dismount alight, bring down, climb down, come down, descend, disembark, get off, lower, step down; CONCEPT 154 —Ant. get up, mount

get even [v] *to get revenge* even the score, get back at, get square, settle the score; CONCEPTS 126,384

get in [v] *infiltrate; find a way in* alight, appear, arrive, blow in*, come, embark, enter, gain ingress, get inside, include, insert, interpose, land, mount, penetrate, reach, show, show up, turn up; CONCEPT 159 —*Ant.* get out

get off [v] *depart* alight, blow*, descend, disembark, dismount, escape, exit, go, go away, leave, light, pull out, quit, retire, withdraw; CONCEPTS 154,195 —*Ant.* arrive

get off someone's back [v] *leave alone* back off, get off someone's case, let someone breathe, stop annoying, stop nagging; CONCEPTS 30,83

get on [v1] *mount* ascend, board, climb, embark, enplane, entrain, go up, scale; CONCEPTS 159,166 —*Ant.* dismount, get off

get on [v2] *cope, progress* advance, do, do well enough, fare, get along, get by, make out, manage, muddle through*, prosper, shift, succeed; CONCEPTS 117,704

get on [v3] *be compatible* agree, be friendly, concur, get along, harmonize, hit it off; CONCEPT 388 —*Ant.* disagree

get on [v4] *put clothing on* assume, attire, don, draw on, dress, slip into, throw on, wear; CONCEPT 167 —*Ant.* disrobe, unclothe

get out [v] *escape* alight, avoid, beat it*, begone, be off, break out, bug off*, buzz off*, clear out, decamp, depart, dodge, duck, egress, evacuate, evade, exit, extricate oneself, flee, fly, free oneself, go, hightail*, kite*, leave, make tracks*, run away, scram*, shirk, shun, skedaddle*, split, take a hike*, take, vacate, vamoose*, withdraw; CONCEPTS 102,195 —*Ant.* capture, grab, seize

get over [v] *recover* come round, get better, mend, overcome, pull through, recuperate, shake off, survive; CONCEPT 35

get the lead out [v] *hurry* a move on, get cracking*, get going, get it on, hop to it, hustle, look alive, make it snappy, shake a leg*, snap to it, step on it; CONCEPTS 91,150

get together [v] *gather, accumulate* assemble, collect, congregate, convene, converge, join, meet, muster, rally, unite; CONCEPTS 109,113 —*Ant.* disperse, distribute, divide, scatter, separate

get up [v] *mount; get out of bed* arise, ascend, awake, awaken, climb, increase, move up, pile out*, rise, rise and shine*, roll out, scale, spring out, stand, turn out, uprise, upspring; CONCEPT 154

geyser [n] *fountain* gusher, hot spring, jet, spout, thermal spring; CONCEPTS 514,648

ghastly [adj] *horrifying, dreadful; pale* abhorrent, anemic, appalling, ashen, awful, bloodless, cadaverous, corpselike, deathlike, dim, disgusting, faint, frightening, frightful, funereal, ghostly, ghoulish, grim, grisly, gruesome, haggard, hideous, horrendous, horrible, horrid, livid, loathsome, lurid, macabre, mortuary, nauseating, offensive, pallid, repellent, repulsive, sepulchral, shocking, sickening, spectral, supernatural, terrible, terrifying, uncanny, unearthly, unnatural, unpleasant, wan, weak, wraithlike; CONCEPTS

485,529,537 —*Ant.* delightful, pleasant, pleasing, wonderful

ghetto [n] *slum* public squalor, rundown section of a city; CONCEPTS 334,485,570

ghetto box [n] *large portable stereo* boom box, ghetto blaster, radio; CONCEPT 279

ghost [n] *spirit of the dead* apparition, appearance, banshee, daemon, demon, devil, eidolon, ethereal being, haunt, incorporeal being, kelpie, manes, phantasm, phantom, poltergeist, revenant, shade, shadow, soul, specter, spook, vampire, vision, visitor, wraith, zombie; CONCEPT 370 —*Ant.* being, entity

ghostly [adj] *spooky* apparitional, cadaverous, corpselike, deathlike, divine, eerie, eidolic, ghastly, haunted, holy, illusory, insubstantial, pale, phantasmal, phantom, scary, shadowy, spectral, spiritual, supernatural, uncanny, unearthly, vampiric, wan, weird, wraithlike, wraithy; CONCEPTS 485,537

ghoul [n] *evil demon* bogeyman, devil, evil spirit, fiend, grave robber, monster; CONCEPTS 370,412

ghoulish [adj] *hideous, scary* cruel, demonic, devilish, diabolical, eerie, fiendish, frightening, ghastly, grim, grisly, gruesome, horrible, macabre, monstrous, morbid, revolting, spine-chilling, spooky, terrifying; CONCEPTS 529,548

GI [n] *government issue; soldier* army personnel, doughboy, enlisted person, GI Joe, serviceperson; CONCEPT 358

giant [adj] *very large* big, blimp*, brobdingnagian*, colossal, cyclopean, elephantine*, enormous, gargantuan, gigantic, gross*, Herculean*, huge, hulking, humongous*, immense, jumbo*, mammoth, monstrous*, mountainous, prodigious, super-duper*, titanic, vast, whale of a*, whaling*; CONCEPTS 491, 773,779,781 —*Ant.* dwarf, little, miniature, miniscule, minor, small, teeny, tiny

giant [n] *extremely large person* behemoth, bulk, colossus, cyclops, elephant*, goliath, Hercules*, hulk, jumbo*, leviathan, mammoth, monster*, mountain*, ogre, polypheme, titan, whale*, whopper*; CONCEPT 424 —*Ant.* dwarf, midget, runt

gibberish [n] *nonsense talk* babble, balderdash*, blah-blah*, blather, chatter, claptrap*, double talk*, drivel, gobbledygook*, hocus-pocus*, jabber*, jargon, mumbo jumbo*, palaver*, prattle, scat*, twaddle*, yammer*; CONCEPT 278 —*Ant.* sense

gibe [n] *ridicule* comeback, cutting remark, derision, dig*, dump*, jab, jeer, joke, mockery, parting shot*, put-down*, rank-out*, sarcasm, scoffing, slam*, sneer, swipe, taunt; CONCEPT 278 —*Ant.* commendation, praise

gibe [v] *ridicule* deride, dis*, disrespect, flout, jeer, make fun of*, mock, poke fun at*, scoff, scorn, sneer, taunt; CONCEPTS 52,54 —*Ant.* admire, commend, laud, praise

giddy [adj] *silly, impulsive* bemused, brainless, bubbleheaded*, capricious, careless, changeable, changeful, ditzy*, dizzy, empty-headed*, erratic, fickle, flighty*, flustered, frivolous, gaga*, heedless, inconstant, irresolute, irresponsible, lightheaded*, punchy*, reckless, reeling, scatterbrained*, skittish*, slaphappy*, swimming*, thoughtless, unbalanced, unset-

gift [n1] *something given freely, for no recompense* allowance, alms, award, benefaction, benefit, bequest, bestowal, bonus, boon, bounty, charity, contribution, courtesy, dispensation, donation, endowment, fairing, favor, giveaway, goodie, grant, gratuity, hand, hand-me-down*, handout, honorarium, lagniappe, largesse, legacy, libation, oblation, offering, offertory, philanthropy, pittance, premium, present, presentation, provision, ration, reward, remembrance, remittance, reward, souvenir, subscription, subsidy, tip, token, tribute, write-off*; CONCEPT 337 —*Ant.* forfeit, loss, penalty

gift [n2] *talent, aptitude* ability, accomplishment, acquirement, aptness, attainment, attribute, bent, capability, capacity, endowment, faculty, flair, forte, genius, head*, instinct, knack, leaning, nose*, numen, power, propensity, set, specialty, turn; CONCEPTS 409,630,706

gifted [adj] *talented, intelligent* able, accomplished, adroit, brilliant, capable, class act, clever, expert, got it*, have on the ball*, have smarts*, have the goods*, hot*, hotshot, ingenious, mad, masterly, phenomenal, shining at*, skilled, smart; CONCEPTS 402,527,528 —*Ant.* dull, incapable, inept, unintelligent, untalented

gig [n] *show* appearance, concert, employment, engagement, job, performance, recital; CONCEPT 706

gigantic [adj] *very large* blimp, brobdingnagian*, colossal, cyclopean*, elephantine, enormous, gargantuan, giant, gross*, Herculean*, huge, immense, jumbo*, mammoth, massive, Moby*, monster, monstrous, prodigious, stupendous, super-colossal*, titan, tremendous, vast, whopping*; CONCEPTS 491,773,779,781 —*Ant.* dwarfed, little, miniature, miniscule, small, teeny, tiny

giggle [n/v] *snickering laugh* cackle, chortle, chuckle, guffaw*, hee-haw*, snicker, snigger, teehee*, titter, twitter; CONCEPT 77

gigolo [n] *male escort* Casanova, Don Juan, inamorato, ladies' man, lady-killer, Lothario, lover, male prostitute, seducer; CONCEPT 423

gild [v] *embellish, decorate* adorn, aureate, aurify, beautify, bedeck, begild, brighten, coat, deck, dress up, embroider, engild, enhance, enrich, garnish, glitter, grace, ornament, overlay, paint, plate, tinsel, varnish, wash, whitewash*; CONCEPTS 172,177,202

gimcrack [n] *gewgaw* bagatelle, bauble, curio, doodad*, knickknack, novelty, souvenir, trinket; CONCEPT 446

gimmick [n] *contrived object; scheme* aid, apparatus, artifice, catch, concern, counterfeit, deceit, device, dodge*, fake, feint, fixture, fun, gadget, gambit, game, gizmo*, imposture, instrument, jest, maneuver, means, method, ploy, ruse, secret, shift, sport, stratagem, stunt, trick, widget*, wile; CONCEPTS 59,260,660

gingerly [adj] *careful* calculating, cautious, chary, circumspect, considerate, dainty, delicate, discreet, fastidious, guarded, hesitant, reluctant, safe, squeamish, suspicious, timid,

wary; CONCEPTS 542,550 —*Ant.* careless, rash, rough, uncareful, uncautious

gingerly [adv] *carefully* cautiously, charily, circumspectly, daintily, delicately, discreetly, fastidiously, guardedly, hesitantly, reluctantly, safely, squeamishly, suspiciously, timidly, warily; CONCEPTS 542,550 —*Ant.* carelessly, rashly, roughly, uncarefully, uncautiously

gin mill [n] *barroom* alehouse, beer garden, cocktail lounge, drinkery, pub, public house, saloon, taproom, tavern, watering hole; CONCEPTS 439,448,449

gird [v1] *encircle; strengthen* band, belt, bind, block, blockade, bolster, brace, buttress, cincture, circle, enclose, encompass, enfold, environ, fasten, fortify, girdle, hem in*, make ready, pen, prepare, ready, reinforce, ring, round, secure, steel, support, surround; CONCEPTS 250,758 —*Ant.* let go, weaken

gird [v2] *make fun of* deride, flout, fun at, gibe, jeer, jest, mock, poke, quip, ridicule, scoff, scorn, sneer, taunt; CONCEPTS 52,54 —*Ant.* compliment, flatter, praise

girder [n] *main support beam* I-beam, joist, rafter, tiebeam, truss; CONCEPTS 471,479

girdle [n] *corset* band, belt, sash, undergarment, underwear, waistband; CONCEPT 451

girl [n] *young female person* adolescent, damsel, daughter, lady, lassie, mademoiselle, Ms, schoolgirl, she, teenager, young lady, young woman; CONCEPTS 415,424 —*Ant.* boy, man

girlfriend [n] *female acquaintance or romantic companion* companion, confidante, date, fiancée, flame*, friend, intimate, partner, soul mate, steady, sweetheart; CONCEPTS 415,423

gist [n] *meaning, essence* basis, bearing, bottom line*, burden, core, drift, force, heart, idea, import, kernel*, keynote, marrow, matter, meat*, name of the game*, nature of the beast*, nitty gritty*, nuts and bolts*, pith*, point, punch line, quintessence, score, sense, short, significance, soul, spirit, stuff*, subject, substance, summary, tenor, theme, thrust, topic, upshot; CONCEPT 682

give [v1] *contribute, supply, transfer* accord, administer, allow, ante up, award, bequeath, bestow, cede, come across, commit, confer, consign, convey, deed, deliver, dish out*, dispense, dispose of, dole out, donate, endow, entrust, fork over*, furnish, gift, grant, hand down, hand out, hand over, heap upon, lavish upon, lay upon, lease, let have, make over*, parcel out, part with, pass down, pass out, permit, pony up*, present, provide, relinquish, remit, sell, shell out*, subsidize, throw in, tip, transmit, turn over, vouchsafe, will; CONCEPTS 108,223,243 —*Ant.* hold, keep, take

give [v2] *communicate* air, announce, be a source of, broadcast, carry, deliver, emit, express, furnish, impart, issue, notify, present, pronounce, publish, put, read, render, state, supply, transfer, transmit, utter, vent, ventilate; CONCEPTS 60,266 —*Ant.* conceal, keep, refrain, withhold

give [v3] *demonstrate, proffer* administer, bestow, confer, dispense, display, evidence, extend, furnish, hold out, indicate, issue, manifest, minister, offer, pose, present, produce, provide, put on, render, return, set forth, show, tender, yield; CONCEPTS 97,118 —*Ant.* keep

give [*v4*] *yield, collapse* allow, bend, bow to, break, cave, cede, concede, contract, crumble, crumple, devote, fail, fall, flex, fold, fold up, give way, go, grant, hand over, lend, open, recede, relax, relent, relinquish, retire, retreat, sag, shrink, sink, slacken, surrender, weaken; CONCEPT 13 —*Ant.* fight, hold up, withstand

give [*v5*] *perform action* address, apply, bend, buckle down, cause, devote, direct, do, engender, lead, make, occasion, produce, throw, turn; CONCEPT 100

give-and-take [*n*] *compromise* adaptability, cooperation, exchange, reciprocity, swap, trade-off; CONCEPTS 230,684

give away [*v1*] *reveal* betray, blab*, disclose, discover, divulge, expose, inform, leak, let out, let slip, mouth*, spill, tell, uncover; CONCEPT 60 —*Ant.* conceal, hide, secret

give away [*v2*] *unselfishly transfer* award, bestow, devote, donate, hand out, present; CONCEPT 108 —*Ant.* keep

give in/give up [*v*] *admit defeat* abandon, back down*, bail out*, bow out*, buckle under*, capitulate, cave in*, cease, cede, chicken out*, collapse, comply, concede, cry uncle*, cut out, desist, despair, drop, drop like a hot potato*, fold, forswear, hand over, leave off, pull out, quit, relinquish, resign, stop, submit, surrender, take the oath*, throw in the towel*, waive, walk out on, wash one's hands of*, yield; CONCEPTS 8,45,119,385 —*Ant.* fight, hold out, stand up to, withstand

given to [*adj*] *likely to* accustomed, addicted, apt, disposed, habituated, inclined, in the habit of, inured, liable, obsessed, prone; CONCEPT 542

give off/give out [*v*] *discharge* beam, belch, effuse, emanate, emit, exhale, exude, flow, give forth, issue, pour, produce, radiate, release, send out, smell of, throw out, vent, void; CONCEPT 179

give the cold shoulder [*v*] *snub* act cool*, brush off*, disregard, eject, ignore, make unwelcome, neglect, ostracize, shun, turn up one's nose*, upstage; CONCEPT 30

gizmo [*n*] *gadget* appliance, contraption, contrivance, device, doohickey, instrument, machine, mechanical device, thingamabob, thingamajig, tool, whatchamacallit, widget; CONCEPTS 463,499

glacial [*adj1*] *extremely cold* antarctic, arctic, biting, bitter, chill, chilly, cool, freezing, frigid, frosty, frozen, gelid, icy, nippy, piercing, polar, raw, wintry; CONCEPT 605 —*Ant.* hot, warm

glacial [*adj2*] *unfriendly* aloof, antagonistic, chill, cold, cool, distant, emotionless, frigid, hostile, icy, inaccessible, indifferent, inimical, remote, reserved, seclusive, standoffish, unapproachable, unemotional, withdrawn; CONCEPTS 401,404 —*Ant.* amicable, friendly, warm

glacier [*n*] *mountain of ice, snow* berg, floe, glacial mass, iceberg, icecap, ice field, ice floe, snow slide; CONCEPT 509

glad [*adj*] *happy, delightful* animated, beaming, beautiful, blithesome, bright, can't complain*, cheerful, cheering, cheery, contented, exhilarated, felicitous, floating on air*, gay, genial, gleeful, gratified, gratifying, hilarious, jocund, jovial, joyful, joyous, lighthearted, merry, mirthful, overjoyed, pleasant, pleased, pleased

as punch*, pleasing, radiant, rejoicing, sparkling, tickled, tickled pink*, tickled to death*, up, willing; CONCEPTS 403,529 —*Ant.* sad, unhappy

gladden [*v*] *please* brighten, cheer, delight, elate, hearten, make happy, warm; CONCEPT 22

gladiator [*n*] *combatant* boxer, contender, fighter; CONCEPTS 358,366,412

gladly [*adv*] *happily* acquiescently, ardently, beatifically, blissfully, blithely, cheerfully, cheerily, contentedly, cordially, delightedly, delightfully, ecstatically, enchantedly, enthusiastically, felicitously, freely, gaily, genially, gleefully, gratefully, heartily, jocundly, jovially, joyfully, joyously, lovingly, merrily, paradisiacally, passionately, pleasantly, pleasingly, pleasurably, rapturously, readily, sweetly, warmly, willingly, with good grace, with pleasure, with relish, zealously, zestfully; CONCEPTS 403,538,542 —*Ant.* sadly, unhappily

gladness [*n*] *happiness* animation, blitheness, cheer, cheerfulness, delight, felicity, gaiety, glee, high spirits*, hilarity, jollity, joy, joyousness, mirth, pleasure; CONCEPT 410 —*Ant.* sorrow, unhappiness, woe

glamorous [*adj*] *sophisticated in style* alluring, attractive, bewitching, captivating, charismatic, charming, classy, dazzling, drop-dead gorgeous*, elegant, enchanting, entrancing, exciting, fascinating, flashy, foxy*, glittering, glossy, looking like a million*, lovely, magnetic, nifty, prestigious, righteous, seductive, siren, smart; CONCEPTS 579,589 —*Ant.* dull, lackluster, ugly, unglamorous, unsophisticated

glamour [*n*] *sophisticated style* allure, allurement, animal magnetism, appeal, attraction, beauty, bewitchment, charisma, charm, color, enchantment, fascination, interest, magnetism, prestige, ravishment, razzle-dazzle*, romance, star quality; CONCEPTS 655,718 —*Ant.* drab, dullness, plainness, ugliness

glance [*n1*] *brief look* eye*, eyeball*, flash*, fleeting look, gander, glimpse, lamp*, look, look-see*, peek, peep, quick look, sight, slant*, squint, swivel*, view; CONCEPT 623 —*Ant.* stare

glance [*n2*] *reflection of light* coruscation, flash, gleam, glimmer, glint, glisten, shimmer, sparkle, twinkle; CONCEPTS 624,628

glance [*v1*] *look at briefly* browse, check out, dip into*, flash*, flip through, gaze, get a load of*, glimpse, leaf through, peek, peep, peer, riffle through*, run over, run through, scan, see, skim through*, take a gander*, take in, thumb through*, view; CONCEPT 623 —*Ant.* stare

glance [*v2*] *reflect light* coruscate, flash, gleam, glimmer, glint, glisten, glitter, shimmer, shine, sparkle, twinkle; CONCEPT 624

glance [*v3*] *ricochet, hit off of something* bounce, brush, careen, carom, contact, dart, graze, kiss*, rebound, scrape, shave*, sideswipe, skim, skip, slant, slide, strike, touch; CONCEPT 189

glare [*n1*] *very bright light, shine* blaze, blinding light, brilliance, dazzle, flame, flare, glow; CONCEPT 620 —*Ant.* dullness

glare [*n2*] *dirty look* angry stare, bad eye*, black look*, evil eye*, frown, glower, lower, scowl; CONCEPTS 623,716 —*Ant.* grin, smile

glare [v1] *give a dirty look* bore, do a slow burn*, fix, frown, gape, gawk, gaze, glower, look daggers*, lower, menace, peer, pierce, scowl, stare, stare angrily*, stare icily*, wither; CONCEPT 623 —*Ant.* grin, smile

glare [v2] *shine very brightly* beam, blare, blaze, blind, blur, daze, dazzle, flame, flare, glaze, glow, radiate; CONCEPT 624

glaring [adj1] *obvious, unconcealed* audacious, blatant, brazen, capital, conspicuous, crying, egregious, evident, excessive, extreme, flagrant, gross, inordinate, manifest, noticeable, obtrusive, open, outrageous, outstanding, overt, patent, protrusive, rank, visible; CONCEPTS 576, 619 —*Ant.* concealed, hidden

glaring [adj2] *bright, dazzling; flashy* blatant, blazing, blinding, brazen, chintzy, florid, garish, gaudy, glowing, loud, meretricious, shining, tawdry; CONCEPT 589 —*Ant.* dark, dull, plain

glass [n1] *object that reflects an image* looking glass, mirror, reflector, seeing glass; CONCEPTS 260,470

glass [n2] *object used for drinking liquids* beaker, bottle, chalice, cup, decanter, goblet, highball, jar, jigger, jug, mug, pilsener, pony, snifter, tumbler; CONCEPT 494

glasses [n] *object worn to correct vision* bifocals, blinkers*, cheaters*, contact lenses, eyeglasses, four eyes*, frames, goggles, lorgnette, pince-nez, rims*, shades*, specs*, spectacles, trifocals; CONCEPT 446

glassy [adj1] *polished, smooth* burnished, clear, glazed, glazy, glossy, hyaline, hyaloid, icy, lustrous, shiny, sleek, slick, slippery, transparent, vitreous, vitric; CONCEPT 606 —*Ant.* dull, rough, rugged, uneven

glassy [adj2] *expressionless, especially referring to eyes* blank, cold, dazed, dull, empty, fixed, glazed, lifeless, stupid, vacant; CONCEPTS 406,619 —*Ant.* shining, smiling

glaze [n] *varnish, lacquer coat* enamel, finish, glint, gloss, luster, patina, polish, sheen, shine; CONCEPTS 259,475 —*Ant.* stripper

glaze [v] *varnish, lacquer* buff, burnish, coat, cover, enamel, furbish, glance, glass, gloss, incrust, make lustrous, make vitreous, overlay, polish, rub, shine, vitrify; CONCEPTS 172,202, 215 —*Ant.* strip

gleam [n] *brightness, sparkle* beam, brilliance, coruscation, flash, flicker, glance, glim, glimmer, glint, glitz, gloss, glow, luster, ray, scintillation, sheen, shimmer, splendor, twinkle; CONCEPTS 620,624 —*Ant.* dullness

gleam [v] *sparkle* beam, burn, coruscate, flare, flash, glance, glimmer, glint, glisten, glister, glitter, glow, radiate, scintillate, shimmer, shine, twinkle; CONCEPTS 620,624 —*Ant.* dull

glean [v] *pick out, collect* accumulate, amass, ascertain, conclude, cull, deduce, extract, garner, gather, harvest, learn, pick, reap, select, sift, winnow; CONCEPTS 31,135

glee [n] *extreme happiness* blitheness, cheerfulness, delectation, delight, elation, enjoyment, exhilaration, exuberance, exultation, fun, gaiety, gladness, hilarity, jocularity, jollity, joviality, joy, joyfulness, joyousness, liveliness, merriment, mirth, pleasure, sprightliness, triumph, verve; CONCEPT 410 —*Ant.* discouragement, sadness, unhappiness

gleeful [adj] *very happy* blithe, blithesome, boon, cheerful, delighted, elated, exalted, exuberant, exultant, frolicsome, gay, gratified, hilarious, jocund, jolly, jovial, joyful, joyous, jubilant, lighthearted, merry, mirthful, overjoyed, pleased, triumphant; CONCEPT 403 —*Ant.* discouraged, sad, sorrowful, unhappy, upset, worried

glen [n] *valley* canyon, combe, dale, dell, glade, gorge, vale; CONCEPT 509

glib [adj] *slick, smooth-talking* artful, articulate, easy, eloquent, facile, fast-talking*, flip, fluent, garrulous, hot-air*, insincere, loquacious, plausible, quick, ready, silver-tongued*, slippery*, smooth operator*, smooth-spoken*, smooth-tongued*, suave, talkative, urbane, vocal, vocative, voluble; CONCEPTS 267,404 —*Ant.* inarticulate, quiet, stuttering, tongue-tied, uncommunicative

glide [v] *move smoothly and quickly on a surface* coast, decline, descend, drift, flit, float, flow, fly, glissade, roll, run, sail, scud, shoot, skate, skim, skip, skirr, slide, slink, slip, slither, smooth along, soar, spiral, stream, trip, waft, wing; CONCEPT 150

glimmer [n] *flash, sparkle* blink, coruscation, flicker, glance, gleam, glint, glow, grain, hint, inkling, ray, scintillation, shimmer, suggestion, trace, twinkle; CONCEPTS 624,831 —*Ant.* dullness

glimmer [v] *sparkle* blink, coruscate, fade, flash, flicker, glance, gleam, glint, glisten, glister, glitter; glow, scintillate, shimmer, shine, twinkle; CONCEPT 624

glimpse [n] *brief look* eye, eyeball*, flash*, gander*, glance, glom*, gun*, impression, lamp*, look-see*, peek, peep, quick look, sight, sighting, slant, squint, swivel*; CONCEPT 623 —*Ant.* stare

glimpse [v] *look briefly* catch sight of, check out, descry, espy, eye, flash, get a load of*, get an eyeful*, peek, sight, spot, spy, take a gander*, take in*, view; CONCEPT 623 —*Ant.* stare

glint [n] *sparkle* flash, glance, gleam, glimmer, glitter, look, shine, trace, twinkle; CONCEPTS 411,624,628

glisten [v] *shimmer* coruscate, flash, flicker, glance, glare, gleam, glimmer, glint, glister, glitter, glow, scintillate, shine, sparkle, twinkle; CONCEPT 624

glitch [n] *error* bug*, defect, flaw, hitch, malfunction, misfire, mishap, problem, setback, snafu, snag, something wrong; CONCEPTS 101, 230,674,699

glitter [n] *brilliance, sparkle* beam, brightness, coruscation, display, flash, gaudiness, glamour, glare, gleam, glint, glisten, glister, glitz, luster, pageantry, radiance, scintillation, sheen, shimmer, shine, show, showiness, splendor, tinsel, twinkle, zap*; CONCEPTS 620,655 —*Ant.* dullness

glitter [v] *sparkle* coruscate, flash, glance, glare, gleam, glimmer, glint, glisten, glister, glow, scintillate, shimmer, shine, spangle, twinkle; CONCEPT 624

glitz [n] *showiness* appeal, flashiness, gaudiness, glamour, ostentation, speciousness; CONCEPT 261

gloat [v] *exclaim triumph* celebrate, crow*, exult, glory, rejoice, relish, rub it in*, triumph, vaunt, whoop*; CONCEPT 49 —*Ant.* be sad, commiserate, sympathize

glob [n] *thick lump* batch, blob, chunk, clump, gob, hunk, mass, wad; CONCEPTS 432,470,471

global [adj] *worldwide, all-encompassing* all-around, all-inclusive, all-out, blanket, catholic, comprehensive, cosmic, cosmopolitan, earthly, ecumenical, encyclopedic, exhaustive, general, grand, international, mundane, overall, pandemic, planetary, spherical, sweeping, thorough, total, unbounded, universal, unlimited, world; CONCEPTS 536,772 —*Ant.* individual, limited, local

globe [n] *Earth, sphere* apple*, ball, balloon*, big blue marble*, map, orb, planet, rondure, round, spheroid, terrene, world; CONCEPT 436

gloom [n1] *melancholy, depression* anguish, bitterness, blue devils*, blue funk*, blues*, catatonia, chagrin, cheerlessness, dejection, desolation, despair, despondency, disconsolateness, discouragement, dismals, distress, doldrums, dolor, downheartedness, dullness, dumps*, foreboding, grief, heaviness, heavy-heartedness, horror, low spirits*, malaise, misery, misgiving, mopes, morbidity, mourning, oppression, pensiveness, pessimism, sadness, saturninity, sorrow, unhappiness, vexation, weariness, woe; CONCEPT 410 —*Ant.* animation, cheer, contentedness, encouragement, happiness, joy, sparkle, vivaciousness

gloom [n2] *darkness, blackness* bleakness, cloud, cloudiness, dimness, dullness, dusk, duskiness, gloominess, murk, murkiness, obscurity, shade, shadow, twilight; CONCEPTS 620,622,810 —*Ant.* brightness, light, sunniness

gloomy [adj1] *dark, black* bleak, caliginous, cheerless, clouded, cloudy, crepuscular, desolate, dim, dismal, dreary, dull, dusky, forlorn, funereal, lightless, murky, obscure, overcast, overclouded, sepulchral, shadowy, somber, tenebrous, unilluminated, unlit, wintry; CONCEPTS 525,617 —*Ant.* bright, light, sunny

gloomy [adj2] *feeling down, blue* blue funk*, broody, chapfallen, cheerless, crabbed*, crestfallen, dejected, depressed, desolate, despondent, disconsolate, dismal, dispirited, dour, downcast, downhearted, down in the dumps*, down in the mouth*, dragged, forlorn, glum, in low spirits*, in the dumps*, joyless, low, melancholy, mirthless, miserable, moody, moping, mopish, morose, mournful, oppressed, pessimistic, sad, saturnine, solemn, sulky, sullen, surly, ugly, unhappy, weary, woebegone, woeful; CONCEPT 403 —*Ant.* animated, cheerful, content, encouraged, happy, joyful, sparkling, vivacious

gloomy [adj3] *sad, depressing* acheronian, acherontic, bad, black, bleak, cheerless, cold, comfortless, depressive, desolate, disconsolate, discouraging, disheartening, dismal, dispiriting, drab, dreary, dull, dusky, funereal, joyless, lugubrious, morose, oppressive, saddening, somber, tenebrific; CONCEPTS 537,548 —*Ant.* cheerful, encouraging, exhilarating, happy, uplifting

glorify [v1] *praise* acclaim, bless, boost, build up, celebrate, commend, cry up, eulogize, exalt, extol, hike, honor, hymn, laud, lionize, magnify, panegyrize, put on a pedestal*, put up, sing the praises of*; CONCEPT 69 —*Ant.* castigate, condemn, criticize, debase, degrade

glorify [v2] *adore, idolize* adorn, aggrandize, apotheosize, augment, beatify, bless, canonize, deify, dignify, distinguish, elevate, enhance, ennoble, enshrine, erect, exalt, halo*, honor, illuminate, immortalize, lift up, magnify, pay homage to, raise, revere, sanctify, transfigure, uprear, venerate, worship; CONCEPT 12 —*Ant.* humiliate, lower, mock, shame

glorious [adj] *adored, idolized; divine* august, beautiful, bright, brilliant, celebrated, dazzling, delightful, distinguished, effulgent, elevated, eminent, enjoyable, esteemed, exalted, excellent, famed, famous, fine, gorgeous, grand, gratifying, great, heavenly, heroic, honored, illustrious, immortal, magnificent, majestic, marvelous, memorable, noble, notable, noted, pleasurable, preeminent, radiant, remarkable, renowned, resplendent, shining, splendid, sublime, superb, time-honored, triumphant, venerable, well-known, wonderful; CONCEPTS 568,574,579 —*Ant.* atrocious, awful, bad, contemptible, disgraceful, shameful

glory [n1] *fame, importance* celebrity, dignity, distinction, eminence, exaltation, grandeur, greatness, honor, illustriousness, immortality, kudos, magnificence, majesty, nobility, praise, prestige, renown, reputation, splendor, sublimity, triumph; CONCEPTS 388,668 —*Ant.* unimportance, unknown

glory [n2] *great beauty* brightness, brilliance, effulgence, fineness, gorgeousness, grandeur, luster, magnificence, majesty, pageantry, pomp, preciousness, radiance, resplendence, richness, splendor, sublimity, sumptuousness; CONCEPTS 673,718 —*Ant.* ugliness

glory [v] *boast, exult* crow, gloat, jubilate, pride oneself, relish, revel, take delight, triumph; CONCEPTS 12,49 —*Ant.* condemn, criticize

gloss [n1] *shine, sheen* appearance, brightness, brilliance, burnish, facade, finish, front, glaze, gleam, glint, glossiness, luster, polish, shimmer, silkiness, sleekness, slickness, surface, varnish, veneer; CONCEPTS 611,620 —*Ant.* dullness?

gloss [n2] *definition* annotation, comment, commentary, elucidation, explanation, footnote, interpretation, note, translation; CONCEPT 268 —*Ant.* misinformation

gloss [v1] *make shiny* buff, burnish, finish, furbish, glance, glaze, lacquer, polish, rub, shine, varnish, veneer; CONCEPTS 202,215 —*Ant.* dull

gloss [v2] *conceal truth* belie, camouflage, cover up, deacon, disguise, doctor, explain, extenuate, falsify, hide, justify, mask, misrepresent, palliate, rationalize, smooth over, soft-pedal, sugarcoat*, varnish, veil, veneer, white, whiten, whitewash*; CONCEPTS 49,63 —*Ant.* clear up, explain, reveal

gloss [v3] *define* annotate, comment, construe, elucidate, explain, interpret, justify, translate; CONCEPT 57 —*Ant.* misinform

glossary [n] *word list* dictionary, lexicon, vocabulary, word index; CONCEPT 280

glossy [adj] *shiny* bright, brilliant, burnished, glassy, glazed, gleaming, glistening, lustrous, polished, reflecting, silken, silky, sleek, slick, smooth; CONCEPTS *606,617* —*Ant.* drab, dull, mate, muted

glove [n] *hand covering for warmth, protection* gage, gauntlet, mitt, mitten, muff; CONCEPT *451*

glow [n] *burning, brightness* afterglow, bloom, blossom, blush, brilliance, effulgence, flush, glare, gleam, glimmer, glitter, gusto, heat, incandescence, intensity, lambency, light, luminosity, passion, phosphorescence, radiance, ray, splendor, vividness, warmth; CONCEPTS *610, 620,622,673*

glow [v] *burn, radiate* be suffused, blare, blaze, blush, brighten, color, crimson, fill, flame, flare, flush, gleam, glimmer, glisten, glitter, ignite, kindle, light, mantle, pink, pinken, redden, rose, rouge, shine, smolder, thrill, tingle, twinkle; CONCEPTS *249,469,624*

glower [v] *frown* glare, gloom, look, look daggers*, lower, scowl, stare, sulk, watch; CONCEPT *623* —*Ant.* grin, smile

glowing [adj1] *burning, bright* aglow, beaming, flaming, florid, flush, flushed, gleaming, lambent, luminous, lustrous, phosphorescent, red, rich, rubicund, ruddy, sanguine, suffused, vibrant, vivid, warm; CONCEPTS *617,618*

glowing [adj2] *very happy, enthusiastic* adulatory, ardent, avid, blazing, burning, complimentary, desirous, eager, ecstatic, eulogistic, fervent, fervid, fierce, fiery, flaming, heated, hot-blooded, impassioned, keen, laudatory, panegyrical, passionate, rave, rhapsodic, zealous; CONCEPTS *267,401* —*Ant.* dull, unenthusiastic, unhappy, unsmiling

glue [n] *adhesive* cement, gum, gunk*, mucilage, paste, plaster, spit*, stickum*; CONCEPT *475*

glum [adj] *sullen* blue, bummed out, dejected, depressed, dismal, dispirited, down, gloomy, low, melancholy, morose, sad, sulky; CONCEPT *403*

glut [n] *overabundance* excess, nimiety, oversupply, plenitude, saturation, superfluity, surfeit, surplus, too much*; CONCEPTS *740,787* —*Ant.* insufficiency, lack, need, want

glut [v] *choke; oversupply* burden, clog, cloy, congest, cram, deluge, devour, feast, fill, flood, gorge, hog*, inundate, jade, load, make a pig of*, overfeed, overload, overstock, overwhelm, pack*, pall, raven, sate, satiate, saturate, stuff, surfeit, wolf*; CONCEPTS *140,169,209,740* —*Ant.* abstain, diet, fast, moderate, reduce, repress, suppress

glutton [n] *person who overeats* epicure, gorger*, gormandizer, gourmand, hefty eater, hog*, pig*, sensualist, stuffer*; CONCEPT *412*

gluttonous [adj] *voracious* covetous, devouring, edacious, gorging, gourmandizing, greedy, gross, hoggish*, insatiable, never full, omnivorous, piggish*, piggy*, prodigious, rapacious, ravening, ravenous, sating, starved, starving, unquenchable, wolfish*; CONCEPTS *20,401*

gnarled [adj] *knotted* bent, contorted, crooked, deformed, distorted, gnarly, knurled, leathery, out of shape, rough, rugged, tortured, twisted, weather-beaten, wrinkled; CONCEPTS *485,486* —*Ant.* straight, unbent, uncurled, untwisted

gnarly [adj] *cool, excellent* boss*, finest, great, hairy*, keen, magnificent, marvelous, neat, nifty, sensational, superb, swell, wonderful; CONCEPT *574*

gnash [v] *grind* clamp, crush, grate, grit, rub; CONCEPTS *186,204*

gnaw [v1] *bite, chew* champ, chaw, chomp, consume, corrode, crunch, devour, eat, eat away, erode, gum, masticate, munch, nibble, wear; CONCEPTS *169,185*

gnaw [v2] *be bothered, worried about* annoy, bedevil, beleague, distress, eat at*, fret, harass, harry, haunt, irritate, nag, pester, plague, prey on one's mind*, rankle, tease, trouble, wear down; CONCEPTS *17,34*

gnome [n] *troll* elf, fairy; CONCEPT *424*

go [n1] *spirit, vitality* activity, animation, bang, birr*, drive, energy, force, get-up-and-go*, hardihood, life, moxie*, oomph*, pep, potency, push, snap*, starch*, tuck*, verve, vigor, vivacity, zest; CONCEPT *411*

go [n2] *try, attempt* bid, crack, effort, essay, fling, pop, shot, slap, stab, turn, whack, whirl; CONCEPTS *87,677*

go [v1] *advance, proceed physically* abscond, approach, beat it*, bug out*, cruise, decamp, depart, escape, exit, fare, flee, fly, get away, get going*, get lost, get off*, hie, hightail*, hit the road*, journey, lam, leave, light out*, make a break for it*, make for*, make one's way*, mosey*, move, move out, near, pass, progress, pull out, push off, push on, quit, repair, retire, run along, run away, set off, shove off*, skip out*, split*, take a hike*, take a powder*, take flight, take leave*, take off*, travel, vamoose*, wend, withdraw; CONCEPTS *159,195* —*Ant.* stay, stop

go [v2] *operate, function* act, carry on, click*, continue, flourish, maintain, make out, move, pan out*, perform, persist, prosper, run, score, succeed, thrive, work; CONCEPTS *4,239* —*Ant.* break

go [v3] *span, stretch* connect, cover, extend, fit, give access, lead, make, range, reach, run, spread, vary; CONCEPTS *651,756*

go [v4] *contribute, work towards an end* avail, befall, chance, come, concur, conduce, develop, eventuate, fall out, fare, happen, incline, lead to, occur, persevere, persist, proceed, result, serve, tend, transpire, turn, turn out, wax*, work out; CONCEPTS *87,704*

go [v5] *agree, harmonize* accord, be adapted for, be designed for, belong, blend, chime, complement, conform, correspond, dovetail*, enjoy, fit, jibe*, like, match, mesh, relish, set, square, suit; CONCEPTS *8,664,714* —*Ant.* disagree, mismatch

go [v6] *die, collapse* bend, break, cave, conclude, consume, crumble, decease, decline, demise, depart, deplete, devour, dissipate, drop, exhaust, expend, expire, fail, finish, fold up, fritter, give, pass away*, pass on*, perish, run through*, spend, squander, succumb, terminate, use up, waste, weaken, worsen, yield; CONCEPTS *105,698* —*Ant.* be born, create

go [v7] *elapse* be spent, expire, flow, lapse, pass, pass away, slip away, transpire, waste away; CONCEPT *804*

go [v8] *endure* abide, allow, bear, brook, consent to, let, permit, put up with*, stand, stomach*, suffer, swallow*, take, tolerate; CONCEPT *23* —*Ant.* surrender

go about [v] *undertake* approach, be employed,

begin, devote oneself to, engage in, get busy with, occupy oneself with, set about, tackle, work at; CONCEPT *100*

goad [*n*] *stimulus* catalyst, compulsion, desire, drive, impetus, impulse, impulsion, incentive, incitation, incitement, irritation, lash, lust, motivation, passion, pressure, prod, spur, urge, whip, zeal; CONCEPTS *20,661* —*Ant.* deterrent, discouragement, diversion, restraint

goad [*v*] *egg on, incite* animate, annoy, arouse, bully, coerce, drive, encourage, excite, exhort, fire up*, force, goose*, harass, hound, impel, inspirit, instigate, irritate, key up*, lash, move, needle*, press, prick*, prod, prompt, propel, provoke, push, put up to*, rowel, sic*, sound, spark*, spur, stimulate, sting*, tease, thrust, trigger, turn on*, urge, whip*, work up, worry; CONCEPTS *14,68* —*Ant.* discourage, dissuade

go-ahead [*adj*] *progressive* ambitious, enterprising, entrepreneurial, go-getting*, gumptious*, pioneering, up-and-coming*; CONCEPTS *538,542* —*Ant.* denied, vetoed

go-ahead [*n*] *authorization* assent, consent, green light*, leave, okay, permission; CONCEPT *685* —*Ant.* ban, denial, refusal, veto

go ahead [*v*] *proceed* advance, begin, continue, dash ahead, edge forward, go forward, go on, move on, progress, shoot ahead; CONCEPTS *149,159,704* —*Ant.* cease, discontinue, finish, halt, stop

goal [*n*] *aim, purpose of an action* ambition, design, destination, duty, end, ground zero*, intent, intention, limit, mark, mission, object, objective, target, use, zero*; CONCEPT *659*

go along/go along with [*v*] *agree, cooperate* accompany, acquiesce, act jointly, assent, collaborate, concur, conspire, follow, share in, work together; CONCEPTS *8,18* —*Ant.* disagree, fight

goat [*n1*] *hollow-horned mammal* billy, buck, kid; CONCEPTS *394,400*

go back/go back on [*v*] *break promise; change one's mind* abandon, betray, be unfaithful, desert, forsake, leave in the lurch*, renege, repudiate, retract, return, revert, run out on; CONCEPTS *13,71* —*Ant.* keep, promise

go back to square one [*v*] *start all over* begin again, go back to the drawing board, make a fresh start, make a new beginning, start from scratch, wipe the slate clean; CONCEPTS *221,241*

gobble [*v*] *eat hurriedly* cram*, devour, gorge, gulp*, guzzle, ingurgitate, scarf*, stuff*, suck up*, swallow, wolf*; CONCEPT *169* —*Ant.* nibble

gobbledygook [*n*] *jargon* balderdash*, baloney*, bosh, bull*, bunk*, cant, drivel, gibberish, hooey*, rigmarole, rubbish*; CONCEPTS *275,276*

go-between [*n*] *person acting as an agent* arbitrator, attorney, broker, dealer, delegate, deputy, emissary, entrepreneur, envoy, factor, interagent, interceder, intercessor, intermediary, intermediate, intermediator, liaison, matchmaker, mediator, medium, messenger, negotiator, proxy, referee, representative; CONCEPTS *348,423*

goblin [*n*] *elf* bogeyman, brownie, demon, fiend, gnome, gremlin, imp, kobold, nixie, pixie, spirit, sprite; CONCEPT *370*

go by [*v1*] *elapse* exceed, flow on, make one's way, move onward, pass, proceed; CONCEPT *141*

go by [*v2*] *adopt, conform* abide by, adjust to, agree, be guided by, comply, cooperate, fall in with, follow, heed, judge from, observe, take as guide; CONCEPTS *8,18*

go crazy [*v*] *become insane* blow a gasket*, blow one's mind*, blow one's stack*, blow one's top*, crack up*, flip one's lid*, flip out, fly off the handle*, freak out*, go ballistic*, go bananas*, go batty*, go berserk*, go bonkers*, go buggy*, go cuckoo*, go daffy*, go haywire*, go kooky*, go loco*, go loony*, go mental, go nuts*, go nutty*, go off, go off one's rocker*, go off the deep end*, go off the wall*, go psycho*, go wacko*, go wacky*, lose control of oneself, lose it*, lose one's cool, lose one's mind, wig out*; CONCEPT *13*

god [*n*] *supernatural being worshipped by people* Absolute Being, Allah, All Knowing, All Powerful, Almighty, Creator, daemon, deity, demigod, demon, Divine Being, divinity, Father, God, holiness, Holy Spirit, idol, Infinite Spirit, Jah, Jehovah, King of Kings, Lord, Maker, master, numen, omnipotent, power, prime mover, providence, soul, spirit, totem, tutelary, universal life force, world spirit, Yahweh; CONCEPT *370*

God-fearing [*adj*] *religious* churchgoing, dedicated, devoted, devout, ecclesiastical, faithful, godly, goody-goody*, holy, orthodox, pious, prayerful, reverent, righteous, sacred, spiritual, theological; CONCEPTS *536,545*

godforsaken [*adj*] *desolate* abandoned, backward, deserted, dismal, distant, empty, forgotten, forlorn, gloomy, isolated, lonely, miserable, neglected, out-of-the-way, remote, secluded, wicked; CONCEPTS *485,560*

godless [*adj*] *without a god or divine faith* adiamorphic, agnostic, atheistic, freethinking, iconoclastic, irreligious, nonbelieving, skeptical, undogmatic; CONCEPT *542* —*Ant.* godly, religious

godly [*adj*] *religious* angelic, born-again, celestial, charismatic, deific, devout, divine, godfearing, good, holy, pietistic, pious, prayerful, righteous, saintlike, saintly, virtuous; CONCEPT *542* —*Ant.* godless, hellish, impious, irreligious, sacrilegious, sinful, ungodly, wicked

go down [*v*] *lose, fall* be beaten, be defeated, cave in, collapse, crumple, decline, decrease, descend, droop, drop, fold, founder, go under, keel, lessen, make less, pitch, plunge, reduce, sag, set, sink, slump, submerge, submerse, submit, succumb, suffer defeat, topple, tumble; CONCEPTS *181,698* —*Ant.* gain, go up, increase

godsend [*n*] *gift, benefit* advantage, benediction, blessing, boon, good, manna*, stroke of luck*, windfall; CONCEPTS *337,679* —*Ant.* bad fortune, bad luck, blow, bombshell, setback

go far [*v*] *be successful* achieve, advance, do well, get ahead, get on, make a name*, move up in the world*, progress, rise, succeed; CONCEPTS *704,706* —*Ant.* fail

gofer [*n*] *errand boy or girl* bottom person on the totem pole*, gal Friday, go getter*, grunt, guy Friday, hired help, low person on the totem pole*, office boy, office girl, peon, scrub; CONCEPT *348*

go for [v1] *reach* clutch at, fetch, obtain, outreach, seek, stretch for; CONCEPT *149*

go for [v2] *like, choose* accept, admire, approbate, approve, be attracted to, be fond of, care for, countenance, fancy, favor, hold with, prefer; CONCEPTS *10,32* —*Ant.* dislike, hate

go for [v3] *attack* assail, assault, launch at, run at, rush, rush upon, set upon, spring at; CONCEPT *86* —*Ant.* surrender, yield

go for it [v] *take a risk* bet the farm, bet the ranch, exert oneself, go all out, go for broke, pull out all the stops, put one's heart and soul into it, shoot the works, use every muscle; CONCEPTS *87,100*

go into [v1] *take an interest in; participate* be absorbed in, begin, develop, engage in, enter, get involved with, take on*, take up*, take upon oneself*, undertake; CONCEPT *100* —*Ant.* ignore

go into [v2] *investigate* analyze, consider, delve into, dig*, dig into*, discuss, examine, explore, inquire, look into, probe, prospect, pursue, review, scrutinize, sift, study; CONCEPTS *24,103*

gold/golden [adj1] *dark yellow* aureate, auric, auriferous, aurous, aurulent, blond, blonde, caramel, dusty, flaxen, honeyed, mellow yellow, ochroid, straw, tan, tawny, wheat; CONCEPT *618*

golden [adj2] *beautiful, advantageous* auspicious, best, blissful, bright, brilliant, delightful, excellent, favorable, flourishing, glorious, happy, joyful, joyous, opportune, precious, promising, propitious, prosperous, resplendent, rich, rosy, shining, successful, valuable; CONCEPTS *529,574* —*Ant.* disadvantaged, ugly, unsuccessful

gold mine [n] *very profitable venture* bonanza, cash cow*, golden goose*, goose that laid the golden egg*, gravy train*, license to print money*, mother lode, source of supply, vein; CONCEPTS *334,537,572*

gone [adj] *not present, no longer in existence* absent, astray, away, AWOL*, burned up*, consumed, dead, decamped, deceased, defunct, departed, disappeared, disintegrated, displaced, dissipated, dissolved, done, down the drain*, dried up, elapsed, ended, extinct, finished, flown, lacking, left, lost, missing, moved, no more, nonextant, not a sign of*, not here, out the window*, over, passed, past, quit, removed, retired, run-off, shifted, spent, split, taken a powder*, taken leave*, transferred, traveling, turned to dust*, vanished, withdrawn; CONCEPTS *407,586* —*Ant.* around, current, existing, present, working

gonzo [adj] *bizarre* crazy, far-fetched, insane, odd, strange, unconventional, weird, wild; CONCEPTS *547,564*

goo [n] *sticky substance* crud*, glop, gook*, guck*, gunk*, muck, ooze, sludge, slush, yuck*; CONCEPT *260*

good [adj1] *pleasant, fine* acceptable, ace*, admirable, agreeable, bad, boss*, bully, capital, choice, commendable, congenial, crack*, deluxe, excellent, exceptional, favorable, first-class, first-rate, gnarly*, gratifying, great, honorable, marvelous, neat*, nice, pleasing, positive, precious, prime, rad*, recherché*, reputable, satisfactory, satisfying, select, shipshape*, sound, spanking*, splendid, sterling,

stupendous, super, superb, super-eminent, super-excellent, superior, tip-top*, up to snuff*, valuable, welcome, wonderful, worthy; CONCEPTS *529,572* —*Ant.* bad, detestable, disagreeable, unpleasant

good [adj2] *moral, virtuous* admirable, blameless, charitable, dutiful, estimable, ethical, exemplary, guiltless, honest, honorable, incorrupt, inculpable, innocent, irreprehensible, irreproachable, lily-white*, obedient, praiseworthy, pure, reputable, respectable, right, righteous, sound, tractable, uncorrupted, untainted, upright, well-behaved, worthy; CONCEPT *545* —*Ant.* evil, immoral, noxious, sinful, unvirtuous, vile, wicked

good [adj3] *competent, skilled* able, accomplished, adept, adroit, au fait, capable, clever, dexterous, efficient, expert, first-rate, proficient, proper, qualified, reliable, satisfactory, serviceable, skillful, suitable, suited, talented, thorough, trustworthy, useful; CONCEPT *527* —*Ant.* incompetent, unskilled, unsuitable

good [adj4] *useful, adequate* acceptable, advantageous, all right, ample, appropriate, approving, apt, auspicious, becoming, benefic, beneficial, benignant, brave, commendatory, commending, common, conformable, congruous, convenient, decent, desirable, favorable, favoring, fit, fitting, fruitful, healthful, healthy, helpful, hygienic, meet, needed, opportune, profitable, proper, propitious, respectable, right, salubrious, salutary, satisfying, seemly, serviceable, suitable, tolerable, toward, unobjectionable, wholesome; CONCEPTS *537,558, 560* —*Ant.* inadequate, rotten, unsuitable

good [adj5] *reliable; untainted* dependable, eatable, fit to eat, flawless, fresh, intact, loyal, normal, perfect, safe, solid, sound, stable, trustworthy, unblemished, uncontaminated, uncorrupted, undamaged, undecayed, unhurt, unimpaired, unspoiled, vigorous, whole; CONCEPT *485* —*Ant.* noxious, rotten, tainted, unreliable

good [adj6] *kind, giving* altruistic, approving, beneficent, benevolent, charitable, considerate, friendly, gracious, humane, humanitarian, kindhearted, merciful, obliging, philanthropic, tolerant, well-disposed; CONCEPTS *404,542* —*Ant.* bad, mean, vicious

good [adj7] *authentic, real* bona fide, conforming, dependable, genuine, honest, justified, kosher*, legitimate, loyal, orthodox, proper, regular, reliable, sound, strict, true, trustworthy, valid, well-founded; CONCEPT *582* —*Ant.* fake, forged, unreal

good [adj8] *well-behaved* considerate, decorous, dutiful, kindly, mannerly, obedient, orderly, polite, proper, respectful, seemly, thoughtful, tolerant, tractable, well-mannered; CONCEPT *401* —*Ant.* bad, misbehaving

good [adj9] *considerable* adequate, advantageous, ample, big, complete, entire, extensive, full, great, immeasurable, large, long, lucrative, much, paying, profitable, respectable, sizable, solid, substantial, sufficient, whole, worthwhile; CONCEPTS *334,771,781* —*Ant.* inconsequential, inconsiderable

good [n1] *advantage, benefit* asset, avail, behalf, benediction, blessing, boon*, commonwealth, favor, gain, godsend, good fortune, interest, nugget*, plum*, prize, profit, prosperity, service, treasure, use, usefulness, welfare, well-being, windfall; CONCEPTS 337,658,679 —*Ant.* disadvantage

good [n2] *morality* class, dignity, excellence, ideal, merit, prerogative, probity, quality, rectitude, right, righteousness, straight, uprightness, value, virtue, worth; CONCEPT 645 —*Ant.* evil, immorality, sin, wickedness

goodbye [n] *farewell statement* adieu, adios, bye-bye, cheerio, ciao, godspeed*, leave-taking, parting, so long*, swan song*, toodle-oo*; CONCEPTS 195,278 —*Ant.* hello

good-for-nothing [n] *person who is idle, worthless* bad lot*, black sheep*, bum, loafer, ne'er-do-well*, no-good*, profligate, rapscallion, scalawag, scamp, tramp, vagabond, waster*, wastrel; CONCEPT 412 —*Ant.* hard worker

good-humored [adj] *funny, happy* affable, amiable, buoyant, cheerful, cheery, complaisant, congenial, easy, genial, good-natured, good-tempered, lenient, merry, mild, obliging, pleasant, smiling; CONCEPT 404 —*Ant.* ill-humored, morose, sad, unfunny, unhappy

good-looking [adj] *handsome* attractive, beauteous, beautiful, clean-cut, comely, fair, impressive, lovely, pretty, pulchritudinous, righteous; CONCEPT 579 —*Ant.* dull, homely, ugly

good-natured [adj] *easygoing, easily pleased* acquiescent, agreeable, altruistic, amiable, benevolent, bighearted, breezy, charitable, complaisant, compliant, cordial, easy, even-tempered, friendly, good-hearted, good-humored, gracious, helpful, kind, kindly, lenient, marshmallow*, mild, moderate, nice, obliging, softie*, tolerant, warmhearted, well-disposed, willing to please; CONCEPT 404 —*Ant.* bad, mean

goodness [n] *decency, excellence* advantage, beneficence, benefit, benevolence, ethicality, friendliness, generosity, good will, grace, graciousness, honesty, honor, humaneness, integrity, kindheartedness, kindliness, kindness, mercy, merit, morality, nourishment, obligingness, probity, quality, rectitude, righteousness, rightness, superiority, uprightness, value, virtue, wholesomeness, worth; CONCEPTS 411,645 —*Ant.* evil, indecency, meanness, wickedness

goods [n1] *personal possessions* appurtenances, belongings, chattels, effects, encumbrances, equipment, furnishings, furniture, gear, impedimenta, movables, paraphernalia, property, stuff, things, trappings; CONCEPT 446

goods [n2] *merchandise* bolt, cargo, commodities, fabric, freight, line, load, materials, seconds, stock, stuff, textile, vendibles, wares; CONCEPT 338

good will/goodwill [n] *kindliness* altruism, amity, benevolence, brownie points*, charity, comity, cordiality, favor, friendliness, friendship, generosity, good deed, good side of*, helpfulness, rapport, right side of*, sympathy, tolerance; CONCEPTS 411,645 —*Ant.* meanness

goody-goody [adj] *straight-laced* God-fearing, goody two-shoes*, holier-than-thou*, moral, nice, PC, pious, politically correct,

priggish, prissy, prudish, Puritan, self-righteous, unctuous, Victorian, virtuous; CONCEPT 401

gooey [adj] *sticky, gummy* adhesive, gluey, glutinous, mucilaginous, soft, tacky, viscous; CONCEPT 606 —*Ant.* dry

goof [v] *mistake* blow it, blunder, botch*, bungle, err, flub*, foul up, get wrong, louse up, make a boner*, mess up, miscalculate, mix up, screw up*, slip, snarl; CONCEPTS 101,230,410

go off [v1] *explode* befall, blow, blow up, burst, detonate, discharge, fire, happen, mushroom, occur, pass, take place; CONCEPT 179

go off [v2] *leave* decamp, depart, exit, go away, move out, part, quit; CONCEPT 195 —*Ant.* arrive, come, enter

goof off [v] *avoid work* bum around, coast, diddle, dog it*, doodle, drag one's feet*, featherbed, fiddle around, fluff off, fool around, hang around, hang out, horse around, lollygag, mess around, monkey around, putz around, screw off, shirk, slack, take it easy; CONCEPTS 30,59,681

goofy [adj] *silly* crazy, daffy*, dippy*, ditzy*, dopey, dotty, empty-headed*, flaky*, foolish, idiotic, kooky*, nutty*, screwy, stupid, wacky*, weird; CONCEPTS 401,403,542

goon [n] *ruffian* bozo*, bruiser*, dope, gorilla*, hood*, hooligan*, jerk, lummox, moron, nincompoop, ninny, sap, strong-arm, thug, tough guy*; CONCEPTS 412,423

go on [v] *continue* act, advance, bear, behave, carry on, come about, comport, conduct, deport, endure, execute, go ahead, hang on, happen, hold on, keep on, last, occur, persevere, persist, proceed, ramble, stay, take place; CONCEPTS 100,239 —*Ant.* cease, halt, stop

go out [v1] *become extinguished* become dark, burn out, cease, darken, die, die out, dim, expire, fade out, flicker, stop shining; CONCEPTS 105,469 —*Ant.* inflame

go out [v2] *leave* decamp, depart, exit, go on strike, walk out; CONCEPT 195 —*Ant.* arrive, come back, enter

go over [v1] *review* analyze, examine, inspect, investigate, look at, peruse, practice, read, rehearse, reiterate, repeat, revise, riffle through*, scan, skim, study, thumb through*; CONCEPTS 24,103 —*Ant.* ignore, neglect

go over [v2] *succeed* be impressive, be successful, click*, come off*, go, pan out*, prove*; CONCEPT 706

gore [n] *bloodshed* blood, carnage, slaughter; CONCEPT 252

gore [v] *pierce* gouge, impale, lance, perforate, puncture, spear, stab, stick, wound; CONCEPT 220

gorge [n] *valley* abyss, arroyo, canyon, chasm, cleft, clough, clove, crevasse, fissure, flume, gap, glen, gulch, pass, ravine; CONCEPT 509

gorge [v] *eat voraciously* blimp out*, bolt*, cloy, congest, cram, devour, eat like a horse*, feed, fill, glut, gobble, gormandize, gulp, guzzle, hoover*, jade, jam, make a pig of*, overeat, overindulge, pack, sate, satiate, stuff*, surfeit, swallow, wolf*; CONCEPT 169 —*Ant.* abstain, diet, fast

gorgeous [adj] *beautiful, magnificent* attractive, beaut*, bright, brilliant, centerfold*, colorful, dazzling, delightful, dream, drop-dead*, easy on the eyes*, elegant, enjoyable, exquisite, fine, flamboyant, foxy*, gaudy, glittering, glorious, good-looking, grand, handsome, imposing, impressive, knockout*, lavish, lovely, lulu*, luxuriant, luxurious, opulent, ostentatious, pleasing, plush, pulchritudinous, ravishing, resplendent, showy, splendid, splendiferous, stunning, sublime, sumptuous, superb; CONCEPTS 579,589 —Ant. homely, ugly, undesirable

gormandize [v] gorge binge, devour, eat like a horse*, eat to excess, glut, gluttonize, gobble, gulp, guzzle, hoover*, overeat, overindulge, pig out*, stuff, wolf*; CONCEPTS 169,225

gory [adj] bloody, horrible bleeding, bloodsoaked, bloodstained, imbrued, murderous, offensive, sanguinary, sanguine; CONCEPTS 314,537 —Ant. mild, pleasant, pleasing

gospel [n] fact, doctrine actuality, authority, belief, certainty, credo, creed, dogma, faith, last word, scripture, testament, truism, truth, veracity, verity; CONCEPT 689 —Ant. hypothesis, theory

gossamer [adj] gauzy, thin airy, cobweb, delicate, diaphanous, fibrous, fine, flimsy, light, sheer, silky, tiffany, translucent, transparent; CONCEPT 606 —Ant. coarse, thick

gossip [n1] talk about others; rumor account, babble, back-fence talk*, blather, blether, buzz*, calumny, chatter, chitchat*, chronicle, clothesline*, conversation, cry, defamation, dirty laundry*, dirty linen*, dirty wash*, earful*, grapevine*, hearsay, idle talk, injury, malicious talk, meddling, news, prate, prattle, report, scandal, scuttlebutt*, slander, small talk*, story, tale, talk, whispering campaign*, wire*; CONCEPTS 274,278 —Ant. fact

gossip [n2] person who talks a lot, spreads rumors babbler*, blabbermouth*, busybody, chatterbox, chatterer, circulator, fl ibbertigibbet*, gossipmonger, informer, meddler, newsmonger, parrot*, prattler, rumormonger*, scandalizer*, scandalmonger*, snoop*, talebearer, tattler, telltale; CONCEPT 412

gossip [v] talk about others; spread rumors babble, bad-mouth*, bend one's ear*, blab, blather, blether, chat, chatter, cut to pieces*, cut up*, dish, hint, imply, insinuate, intimate, jaw*, prate, prattle, rattle on*, repeat, report, rumor, schmoose*, spill the beans*, spread*, suggest, talk, talk idly, tattle, tell secrets*, tell tales*, wiggle-waggle*; CONCEPTS 56,60

go straight [v] reform be honorable, go legit, mend one's ways*, turn over a new leaf*, walk the straight and narrow*; CONCEPTS 35,110,126

go through [v1] endure bear, brave, experience, suffer, support, survive, swallow, tolerate, undergo, withstand; CONCEPT 23 —Ant. surrender, yield

go through [v2] use up consume, deplete, exhaust, pay out, spend, squander; CONCEPT 169 —Ant. hoard, save, store

go through [v3] search audit, check, examine, explore, hunt, inspect, investigate, look, pass through; CONCEPT 103

go to bat for [v] show support for back up, cover for, defend, endorse, go to the wall for*, recommend, stand behind, stand by, stand up for, stick up for, support; CONCEPTS 10,49,110

go together/go with [v1] agree, match accompany, accord, become, befit, be suitable,

blend, complement, concur, correspond, fit, go, harmonize, make a pair*, not clash, suit; CONCEPT 664 —Ant. disagree, mismatch

go together/go with [v2] accompany socially attend, be with, court, date, escort, go out with*, go steady with*, keep company with*; CONCEPT 384 —Ant. go solo

gouge [n] groove, hole channel, cut, excavation, furrow, gash, hollow, notch, scoop, score, scratch, trench; CONCEPT 220

gouge [v] cut, scoop burrow, claw, dig, dredge, excavate, gash, groove, scrape, scratch, shovel, tunnel; CONCEPT 220

go under [v] fail, submerge bankrupt, default, die, drown, fall, fold, founder, go down, sink, submerse, submit, succumb, suffocate, surrender; CONCEPTS 181,699 —Ant. accomplish, achieve, succeed

gourmet [n] person who likes, knows about food bon vivant, connoisseur, critic, epicure, epicurean, gastronome, gastronomer, gastronomist, gourmand; CONCEPTS 348,423

govern [v1] take control; rule administer, assume command, be in power, be in the driver's seat*, call the shots*, call the signals*, captain*, carry out, command, conduct, control, dictate, direct, execute, exercise authority, guide, head, head up, hold dominion, hold office, hold sway, lay down the law*, lead, manage, occupy throne, order, overrule, oversee, pilot, pull the strings*, regulate, reign, render, run, serve the people*, steer, superintend, supervise, sway, tyrannize, wear the crown*; CONCEPT 133 —Ant. agree, comply, obey, surrender, yield

govern [v2] influence; hold in check boss, bridle, check, contain, control, curb, decide, determine, direct, directionalize, discipline, dispose, dominate, get the better of*, guide, handle, incline, inhibit, manage, predispose, regulate, restrain, rule, shepherd, steer, subdue, sway, tame, underlie; CONCEPTS 7,19,22,130 —Ant. acquiesce, allow, consent, give way, permit

government [n] management, administration authority, bureaucracy, command, control, direction, domination, dominion, empire, execution, executive, governance, guidance, influence, jurisdiction, law, ministry, patronage, political practice, politics, polity, power, powers-that-be*, predominance, presidency, regency, regime, regimentation, regulation, restraint, rule, sovereignty, state, statecraft, superintendence, superiority, supervision, supremacy, sway, the feds*, Uncle Sam*, union, Washington*; CONCEPT 299 —Ant. anarchy, chaos, coup, insurrection, lawlessness, mutiny, revolt, revolution

governor [n] person administering government administrator, boss, chief, chief of state, commander, comptroller, controller, director, executive, gubernatorial leader, guv*, head, head honcho*, leader, manager, overseer, presiding officer, ruler, superintendent, supervisor; CONCEPT 354

go without [adj] deny or be denied abstain, be deprived of, do without, fall short*, go short*, lack, need, want; CONCEPT 646 —Ant. earn, get, indulge, take, use

gown [n] robe, dress clothes, costume, frock, garb, garment, habit; CONCEPT 451

grab [v] *latch on to* capture, catch, catch hold of, clutch, collar*, corral*, get one's fingers on*, get one's hands on*, glom*, grapple, grasp, grip, hook, land, lay one's hands on*, nab, nail, pluck, seize, snag, snap up, snatch, take, take hold of; CONCEPTS *90,190* —*Ant.* let go, release

grace [n1] *charm, loveliness* address, adroitness, agility, allure, attractiveness, balance, beauty, breeding, comeliness, consideration, cultivation, decency, decorum, dexterity, dignity, ease, elegance, etiquette, finesse, finish, form, gracefulness, lissomeness, lithesomeness, mannerliness, manners, nimbleness, pleasantness, pliancy, poise, polish, propriety, refinement, shapeliness, smoothness, style, suppleness, symmetry, tact, tastefulness; CONCEPTS *633,655,718* —*Ant.* clumsiness, ineptness, tactlessness

grace [n2] *mercy, forgiveness* benefaction, beneficence, benevolence, caritas, charity, clemency, compassion, compassionateness, favor, forbearance, generosity, goodness, good will, indulgence, kindliness, kindness, leniency, lenity, love, pardon, quarter, reprieve, responsiveness, tenderness; CONCEPTS *278,657,685* —*Ant.* mercilessness, unforgiveness

grace [n3] *prayer* benediction, blessing, invocation, petition, thanks, thanksgiving; CONCEPTS *278,368*

grace [v] *beautify, embellish* adorn, bedeck, crown, deck, decorate, dignify, distinguish, elevate, enhance, enrich, favor, garnish, glorify, honor, laureate, ornament, set off; CONCEPTS *202,700* —*Ant.* disgrace, uglify

graceful [adj] *agile, charming, lovely* adroit, aesthetic, artistic, balletic, beautiful, becoming, comely, controlled, curvaceous, dainty, decorative, delicate, dexterous, easy, elastic, elegant, exquisite, fair, fine, flowing, handsome, harmonious, limber, lissome, lithe, natural, neat, nimble, pleasing, pliant, poised, practiced, pretty, refined, rhythmic, seemly, shapely, skilled, slender, smooth, springy, statuesque, supple, symmetrical, tasteful, trim, willowy; CONCEPTS *579,584,589* —*Ant.* awkward, careless, graceless, inept, uncouth, ungraceful, unhandy

graceless [adj] *clumsy, unsophisticated* awkward, barbarian, barbaric, barbarous, boorish, clunky*, coarse, corrupt, crude*, forced, gauche, gawky*, ill-mannered, improper, indecorous, inelegant, inept, infelicitous, klutzy*, loutish, oafish, outlandish, rough, rude, shameless, tasteless, two left feet*, uncouth, uncultured, unfortunate, ungainly, unhappy, unmannered; CONCEPTS *401,584* —*Ant.* beautiful, charming, dexterous, elegant, graceful, sophisticated

gracious [adj] *kind, giving* accommodating, affable, amiable, amicable, approachable, beneficent, benevolent, benign, benignant, big-hearted, bland, bonhomous, charitable, chivalrous, civil, compassionate, complaisant, congenial, considerate, cordial, courteous, courtly, easy, forthcoming, friendly, gallant, genial, good-hearted, good-natured, hospitable, indulgent, lenient, loving, merciful, mild, obliging, pleasing, polite, sociable, stately, suave, tender, unctuous, urbane, well-mannered; CONCEPTS *401,542* —*Ant.* discourteous, hateful, mean, nasty, rude, sarcastic, severe, ungiving, ungracious, unkind, vulgar

gradation [n] *classification, step* arrangement, calibration, change, degree, difference, distinction, divergence, grade, grouping, level, mark, measurement, modification, notch, nuance, ordering, place, point, position, progression, rank, scale, sequence, series, shade, sorting, stage, succession, variation; CONCEPTS *378,665*

grade [n1] *rank, step* brand, caliber, category, class, classification, condition, degree, division, echelon, estate, form, gradation, group, grouping, league, level, mark, notch, order, pigeonhole*, place, position, quality, rung*, size, stage, standard, station, tier; CONCEPTS *286, 378,665,727,744*

grade [n2] *incline, slope* acclivity, ascent, bank, cant, climb, declivity, descent, downgrade, elevation, embankment, gradient, height, hill, inclination, inclined plane, lean, leaning, level, obliquity, pitch, plane, ramp, rise, slant, tangent, tilt, upgrade; CONCEPTS *738,757*

grade [v] *evaluate, rank* arrange, assort, brand, class, classify, group, order, range, rate, sort, value; CONCEPTS *103,291*

gradient [n] *slope* acclivity, angle, bank, cant, declivity, grade, hill, inclination, incline, lean, leaning, pitch, ramp, rise, slant, tilt; CONCEPTS *738,757*

gradual [adj] *happening slowly, evenly* bit-by-bit*, by degrees, continuous, creeping, even, gentle, graduate, moderate, piecemeal, progressive, regular, slow, steady, step-by-step*, successive, unhurried; CONCEPTS *544,588,799* —*Ant.* abrupt, infrequent, intermittent, sudden, uneven

gradually [adv] *happening slowly, evenly* bit by bit*, by degrees, by installments, constantly, continuously, deliberately, gently, imperceptibly, inch by inch*, increasingly, in small doses*, little by little*, moderately, perceptibly, piece by piece*, piecemeal, progressively, regularly, sequentially, serially, steadily, step by step*, successively, unhurriedly; CONCEPTS *544,588,799* —*Ant.* abruptly, fastly, intermittently, suddenly

graduate [n] *person who completes education, pursuit* alum*, alumnus, baccalaureate, bachelor, collegian, diplomate, doctor, former student, grad, holder, licentiate, master, Ph.D., product, recipient; CONCEPT *350* —*Ant.* undergraduate

graduate [v1] *complete education, pursuit* be commissioned, certify, confer degree, earn, finish, get a degree, get out*, give sheepskin*, grant diploma, take a degree, win; CONCEPT *234*

graduate [v2] *classify, grade* arrange, calibrate, class, group, mark off, measure, measure out, order, proportion, range, rank, regulate, sort; CONCEPTS *84,103*

graduation [n] *commencement* commencement exercises, convocation; CONCEPTS *119,706*

graffiti [n] *wall writing* cave painting, defacement, doodles, scribbling; CONCEPTS *79,284*

graft [n1] *transplant* bud*, hybridization, implant, jointure, scion, shoot, slip, splice, sprout, union; CONCEPTS *113,257*

graft [n2] *payoff for fraud* bribe, corruption, gain, hat*, hush money*, juice*, money, money under the table*, pay, payola*, peculation, shake*, share, skimming*, squeeze*, thievery; CONCEPTS *192,344*

go
gr

graft [v] *transplant, splice* affix, implant, ingraft, insert, join, plant, propagate, unite; CONCEPTS *113,257*

grain [n1] *seed, piece* atom, bit, cereal, corn, crumb, drop, fragment, granule, grist, iota, jot, kernel, mite, modicum, molecule, morsel, mote, ounce, particle, pellet, scintilla, scrap, scruple, smidgen, spark, speck, tittle, trace, whit; CONCEPTS *428,831*

grain [n2] *texture of fabric* character, current, direction, fiber, make-up, nap, pattern, staple, striation, surface, tendency, tissue, tooth, warp and woof, weave, weft; CONCEPT *611*

grammar [n] *language rules* ABCs*, accidence, alphabet, elements, fundaments, linguistics, morphology, principles, rudiments, sentence structure, stratification, structure, syntax, tagmemics; CONCEPTS *275,276,770*

grammatical [adj] *pertaining to syntax* acceptable, allowable, correct, linguistic, morphological, phonological, semantic, syntactic, well-formed; CONCEPT *272* —*Ant.* solecistic, ungrammatical

grand [adj1] *impressive, great* admirable, ambitious, august, awe-inspiring, dignified, dynamite, elevated, eminent, exalted, excellent, fab*, fine, first-class, first-rate, glorious, grandiose, haughty, illustrious, imposing, large, lofty, luxurious, magnificent, majestic, marvelous, monumental, noble, opulent, ostentatious, outstanding, palatial, pompous, pretentious, regal, rich, smashing, something else*, splendid, stately, striking, sublime, sumptuous, super, superb, terrific, unreal, very good; CONCEPTS *574,589,773* —*Ant.* bad, common, low, paltry, poor, unimpressive

grand [adj2] *most important* chief, dignified, elevated, exalted, grave, head, highest, leading, lofty, main, majestic, mighty, noble, preeminent, principal, regal, supreme, transcendent; CONCEPT *568* —*Ant.* contemptible, inferior, insignificant, pitiful, poor, unimportant

grandeur [n] *great importance* amplitude, augustness, beauty, breadth, brilliance, celebrity, circumstance, dignity, distinction, elevation, eminence, expansiveness, fame, fineness, glory, grandiosity, gravity, greatness, handsomeness, immensity, impressiveness, inclusiveness, loftiness, luxuriousness, magnificence, majesty, might, nobility, opulence, pomp, preeminence, richness, splendor, state, stateliness, sublimity, sumptuousness, superbity, sway, transcendency, vastness; CONCEPT *668* —*Ant.* insignificance, unimportance

grandiloquent [adj] *pretentious, flowery (communication)* aureate, big-talking*, bombastic, declamatory, euphistic, fustian, high-flown, histrionic, inflated, magniloquent, oratorical, orotund, overblown, pompous, purple*, rhetorical, sonorous, swollen, tall-talking*, verbose, windbag*, windy*; CONCEPT *267* —*Ant.* plain, simple, unadorned, unpretentious

grandiose [adj] *theatrical, extravagant* affected, ambitious, august, bombastic, cosmic, egotistical, flamboyant, fustian, grand, high-falutin'*, high-flown, imposing, impressive, lofty, lordly, magnificent, majestic, monumental, noble, ostentatious, overwhelming, pompous, pretentious, purple*, royal, showy, splashy, stately, unfathomable, vast; CONCEPTS *401,542* —*Ant.* calm, moderate, small, unpretentious

grandstand [v] *show off* be ostentatious, be vain, flaunt it*, hot dog*, parade, play to the crowd, prance, put on airs*, showboat*, strut, swagger; CONCEPT *261*

grange [n] *farm* acreage, farmstead, hacienda, manor, plantation, ranch; CONCEPTS *258,516, 517*

grant [n] *allowance, gift* admission, allocation, allotment, alms, appropriation, assistance, award, benefaction, bequest, boon, bounty, charity, concession, contribution, dole, donation, endowment, fellowship, gratuity, handout, lump, present, privilege, reward, scholarship, stipend, subsidy; CONCEPTS *337,344* —*Ant.* forfeit, loss

grant [v] *authorize, allow* accede, accept, accord, acknowledge, acquiesce, admit, agree to, allocate, allot, assign, assume, avow, award, bestow, bless, cede, come across, come around, come through, concede, confer, consent to, convey, donate, drop, gift with*, give, give in, give out, give the nod*, give thumbs-up*, go along with*, impart, invest, own, own up*, permit, present, profess, relinquish, shake on*, sign off on*, sign on*, stake, suppose, surrender, transfer, transmit, vouchsafe, yield; CONCEPTS *8,50,82,83,88* —*Ant.* condemn, deny, refuse, veto

granted [adv] *allowed, accepted* acknowledged, admitted, assumed, indeed, just so, yes; CONCEPT *558* —*Ant.* unaccepted

granulate [v] *crush into tiny pieces* atomize, comminute, crumble, crystallize, disintegrate, grate, grind, make coarse, make grainy, pound, powder, pulverize, triturate; CONCEPT *186*

graphic [adj1] *clear, explicit* colorful, compelling, comprehensible, concrete, convincing, definite, descriptive, detailed, distinct, eloquent, expressive, figurative, forcible, illustrative, incisive, intelligible, lively, lucid, moving, perspicuous, picturesque, precise, realistic, stirring, striking, strong, telling, unequivocal, vivid; CONCEPTS *267,535,562* —*Ant.* implicit, unclear, vague

graphic [adj2] *pictorial, visible* blocked-out, delineated, depicted, descriptive, diagrammatic, drawn, engraved, etched, iconographic, illustrated, illustrational, illustrative, marked-out, outlined, painted, photographic, pictoric, pictured, portrayed, representational, seen, sketched, traced, visual; CONCEPTS *576,589, 619* —*Ant.* obscure, vague

graphic novel [n] *comic book* cartoon, comic, comic-strip book, manga; CONCEPT *271*

graphics [n] *drawings* artwork, computer graphics, illustrations, pictures, visuals; CONCEPT *625*

grapple [v] *grab, wrestle* attack, battle, catch, clash, clasp, close, clutch, combat, confront, contend, cope, deal with, do battle*, encounter, engage, face, fasten, fight, grasp, grip, hold, hook, hug, nab, nail, scuffle, seize, snatch, struggle, tackle, take, take on*, tussle; CONCEPTS *106,191* —*Ant.* let go, release

grasp [n1] *hold, grip* butt, cinch, clamp, clasp, clench, clinch, clutches, embrace, grapple, lug, possession, purchase, tenure; CONCEPTS *191, 710* —*Ant.* avoidance, release

grasp [n2] *understanding* awareness, comprehension, ken, knowledge, mastery, perception, realization; CONCEPT 409 —*Ant.* ignorance, misconception, misunderstanding

grasp [v1] *grab* bag*, catch, clasp, clinch, clutch, collar*, corral, enclose, glom*, grapple, grip, hold, hook, land, seize, snatch, take, take hold of; CONCEPTS 90,191 —*Ant.* let go, release

grasp [v2] *understand* accept, appreciate, apprehend, catch, catch on*, cognize, compass, comprehend, dig*, envisage, fathom, follow, get, get the drift*, get the picture*, have, know, latch on*, make, perceive, pick up*, realize, see, take, take in*; CONCEPT 15 —*Ant.* misunderstand, not get

grasping [adj] *greedy* acquisitive, avaricious, avid, close-fisted, covetous, desirous, extorting, extortionate, grabby*, itchy*, mean, miserly, niggardly*, penny-pinching*, penurious, prehensile, rapacious, selfish, stingy*, tightfisted*, usurious, venal; CONCEPTS 326,334,542 —*Ant.* generous, unselfish

grass [n] *lawn* barley, grama, hay, meadow, pasture, sod, turf, verdure; CONCEPT 429

grassland [n] *meadow* campo, field, llano, pampas, pasture, plain, prairie, range, savanna, steppe, sward, swarth, veldt; CONCEPT 509

grate [v1] *shred, grind down* abrade, bark, bray, file, fray, gall, mince, pound, pulverize, rasp, raze, rub, scrape, scratch, scuff, skin, triturate; CONCEPTS 186,215

grate [v2] *irritate* aggravate, annoy, burn, chafe, exasperate, fret, gall, get on one's nerves*, irk, nettle, peeve, pique, provoke, rankle, rile, rub the wrong way*, vex; CONCEPTS 7,14,19 —*Ant.* make happy, please

grateful [adj1] *appreciative* beholden, gratified, indebted, obliged, pleased, thankful; CONCEPT 403 —*Ant.* heedless, thankless, unappreciative, ungrateful

grateful [adj2] *pleasing, nice* acceptable, agreeable, comforting, congenial, consoling, delectable, delicious, delightful, desirable, favorable, good, gratifying, pleasant, pleasurable, pleasureful, refreshing, rejuvenating, renewing, restful, restorative, restoring, satisfactory, satisfying, solacing, welcome; CONCEPTS 537,548,572 —*Ant.* abusive, mean, rude, ungrateful

gratification [n] *satisfaction* delight, enjoyment, fruition, fulfillment, glee, hit, indulgence, joy, kicks*, luxury, pleasure, recompense, regalement, relish, reward, sure shock*, thrill; CONCEPT 410 —*Ant.* disappointment, dissatisfaction, upset

gratify [v] *give pleasure; satisfy* appease, arride, baby*, cater to, coddle, content, delectate, delight, do one proud*, do the trick*, enchant, favor, fill the bill*, fulfill*, get one's kicks*, gladden, hit the spot*, humor, indulge, make a hit*, make happy, oblige, pamper, please, recompense, requite, thrill; CONCEPTS 7,22 —*Ant.* annoy, disappoint, disturb, frustrate, offend, pain, upset

grating [adj] *irritating; scraping* annoying, disagreeable, discordant, displeasing, dissonant, dry, grinding, harsh, harsh-sounding, hoarse, irksome, jarring, offensive, rasping, raucous, rough, shrill, squeaky, strident, stridulous,

stridulous, unpleasant, vexatious; CONCEPTS 529,592,594 —*Ant.* pleasing, soothing

gratis [adj] *free* chargeless, complimentary, costless, for love*, for nothing, freebie*, freely given, free of charge, free ride*, gratuitous, on someone*, on the house*, unpaid for, without charge, without recompense; CONCEPT 334 —*Ant.* costly, expensive

gratitude [n] *appreciation* acknowledgment, appreciativeness, grace, gratefulness, honor, indebtedness, obligation, praise, recognition, requital, response, responsiveness, sense of obligation, thankfulness, thanks, thanksgiving; CONCEPTS 32,76,278,410 —*Ant.* ingratitude, thanklessness

gratuitous [adj1] *free* chargeless, complimentary, costless, for nothing, gratis, spontaneous, unasked-for, unpaid, voluntary, willing; CONCEPTS 334,542 —*Ant.* costly, expensive

gratuitous [adj2] *not necessary* assumed, baseless, bottomless, causeless, groundless, indefensible, inessential, needless, reasonless, supererogatory, superfluous, uncalled-for, unessential, unfounded, unjustified, unmerited, unprovoked, unsupportable, unwarranted, wanton; CONCEPT 546 —*Ant.* deserved, needed, reasonable, warranted

gratuity [n] *gift, tip* alms, benefaction, bonus, boon, bounty, contribution, donation, fringe benefit, grease palm*, largesse, little something*, offering, perk*, perquisite, present, recompense, reward, salve*, sweetener*, token; CONCEPTS 337,344

grave [adj1] *serious; gloomy* cold sober*, deadpan*, dignified, dour, dull, earnest, grim, grimfaced, heavy, leaden, long-faced, meaningful, muted, no-nonsense*, ponderous, quiet, sad, sage, saturnine, sedate, sober, solemn, somber, staid, strictly business*, subdued, thoughtful, unsmiling; CONCEPT 401 —*Ant.* cheerful, frivolous, funny, happy, ridiculous, silly

grave [adj2] *crucial, dangerous* acute, afflictive, consequential, critical, deadly, destructive, dire, exigent, fatal, fell, grievous, hazardous, heavy*, important, killing*, life-and-death*, major, momentous, of great consequence, ominous, perilous, pressing, serious, severe, significant, threatening, ugly, urgent, vital, weighty; CONCEPTS 537,548,567 —*Ant.* inconsequential, trivial, unimportant

grave [n] *burial place* catacomb, crypt, final resting place*, last home*, mausoleum, mound, permanent address*, place of interment, resting place, sepulcher, shrine, six feet under*, tomb, vault; CONCEPT 305

graveyard [n] *burial area* boneyard*, burial ground, cemetery, charnel house, God's acre*, memorial park, necropolis; CONCEPT 305

gravitate [v] *be drawn toward; fall to* approach, be attracted, be influenced, be pulled, descend, drift, drop, incline, lean, move, precipitate, settle, sink, tend; CONCEPTS 34,159 —*Ant.* retreat, run away

gravity [n1] *force of attraction* force, heaviness, pressure, weight; CONCEPT 641 —*Ant.* weightedness

gravity [n2] *seriousness, importance* acuteness, concern, consequence, exigency, hazardousness, momentousness, perilousness, severity, significance, solemnity, urgency, weightiness; CONCEPT 668 —*Ant.* frivolity, inconsequentiality, levity, silliness, unimportance

gray/grey [*adj*] *muted silver in color* ash, ashen, battleship*, cinereal, clouded, dingy, dove, drab, dusky, dusty, granite, heather, iron, lead, leaden, livid, mousy, neutral, oyster, pearly, peppery, powder, sere, shaded, silvered, silvery, slate, smoky, somber, stone; CONCEPT 618

graze [*v1*] *touch* abrade, brush, carom, chafe, glance off, kiss*, ricochet, rub, scrape, scratch, shave*, skim, skip; CONCEPT 612 —*Ant.* manhandle

graze [*v2*] *feed on* bite, browse, champ, crop, crunch, eat, forage, gnaw, masticate, munch, nibble, pasture, ruminate, uproot; CONCEPT 169 —*Ant.* abstain

grease [*n*] *fat* animal oil, drippings, lard, lubricant, oil, tallow, vegetable oil; CONCEPTS 723, 734

grease [*v1*] *lubricate* anoint, butter, oil, slick; CONCEPT 202

grease [*v2*] *bribe* buy off, corrupt, do business*, entice, fix*, influence, oil someone's palm*, pay off, take care of, tamper; CONCEPTS 53,192

greasy [*adj*] *slippery, oily* anointed, creamy, daubed, fatty, lubricated, lubricious, oleaginous, pomaded, salved, slick, slimy*, slithery, smeared, swabbed, unctuous; CONCEPT 606 —*Ant.* dry

greasy spoon [*n*] *inexpensive restaurant* beanery, bean wagon, cheap restaurant, dump*, eatery, grease pit*, hashery, hashhouse; CONCEPTS 439,448,449

great [*adj1*] *very large* abundant, ample, big, big league*, bulky, bull, colossal, considerable, decided, enormous, excessive, extended, extensive, extravagant, extreme, fat, gigantic, grievous, high, huge, humongous, husky, immense, inordinate, jumbo*, lengthy, long, major league*, mammoth, mondo*, numerous, oversize, prodigious, prolonged, pronounced, protracted, strong, stupendous, terrible, titanic*, towering, tremendous, vast, voluminous; CONCEPTS 773,781 —*Ant.* few, little, miniature, minute, short, small

great [*adj2*] *important, celebrated* august, capital, chief, commanding, dignified, distinguished, eminent, exalted, excellent, famed, famous, fine, glorious, grand, heroic, highly regarded, high-minded, honorable, idealistic, illustrious, impressive, leading, lofty, magnanimous, main, major, noble, notable, noted, noteworthy, outstanding, paramount, primary, principal, prominent, puissant, regal, remarkable, renowned, royal, stately, sublime, superior, superlative, talented; CONCEPT 568 —*Ant.* infamous, insignificant, powerless, uncelebrated, undignified, unimportant, unknown, weak

great [*adj3*] *excellent, skillful* able, absolute, aces*, adept, admirable, adroit, awesome, bad*, best, brutal, cold*, complete, consummate, crack*, downright, dynamite, egregious, exceptional, expert, fab*, fantastic, fine, first-class*, first-rate*, good, heavy*, hellacious*, marvelous, masterly, number one*, out-and-out*, out of sight*, out of this world*, perfect,

positive, proficient, super-duper*, surpassing, terrific, total, tough, transcendent, tremendous, unmitigated, unqualified, utter, wonderful; CONCEPTS 527,528,574 —*Ant.* ignorant, menial, poor, stupid, unskilled, weak

greatly [*adv*] *considerably* abundantly, by much, conspicuously, eminently, emphatically, enormously, exceedingly, exceptionally, extremely, famously, glaringly, highly, hugely, immeasurably, immensely, incalculably, incomparably, incredibly, indeed, infinitely, in great measure, inimitably, intensely, largely, markedly, mightily, most, much, notably, on a large scale, powerfully, remarkably, strikingly, superlatively, supremely, surpassingly, tremendously, vastly, very much; CONCEPTS 537,569, 772 —*Ant.* inconsiderably, insignificantly, unremarkably

greatness [*n1*] *large size* abundance, amplitude, bigness, bulk, enormity, force, high degree, hugeness, immensity, infinity, intensity, length, magnitude, mass, might, potency, power, prodigiousness, sizableness, strength, vastness; CONCEPTS 730,767 —*Ant.* littleness, smallness, tininess

greatness [*n2*] *nobleness of character; eminence* celebrity, chivalry, dignity, distinction, fame, generosity, glory, grandeur, heroism, high-mindedness, idealism, illustriousness, importance, loftiness, magnanimity, majesty, merit, morality, nobility, note, prominence, renown, stateliness, sublimity, worthiness; CONCEPTS 411,645,668 —*Ant.* insignificance, unimportance

greed [*n*] *overwhelming desire for more* acquisitiveness, avarice, avidity, covetousness, craving, cupidity, eagerness, edacity, esurience, excess, gluttony, gormandizing, graspingness, hunger, indulgence, insatiableness, intemperance, longing, piggishness*, rapacity, ravenousness, selfishness, swinishness*, the gimmies*, voracity; CONCEPT 20 —*Ant.* benevolence, generosity

greedy [*adj*] *desiring excessively* acquisitive, avaricious, avid, carnivorous, close, close-fisted*, covetous, craving, desirous, devouring, eager, edacious, esurient, gluttonous, gobbling, gormandizing, grabby, grasping, grudging, gulping, guzzling, hoggish*, hungry, impatient, insatiable, insatiate, intemperate, itchy*, miserly, niggardly, omnivorous, parsimonious, pennypinching*, penurious, piggish*, prehensile, rapacious, ravening, ravenous, selfish, stingy, swinish, tight*, tight-fisted*, voracious; CONCEPTS 326,403,542 —*Ant.* abstemious, benevolent, charitable, extravagant, generous, liberal, philanthropic

green [*adj1*] *young, new, blooming* bosky, budding, burgeoning, callow, developing, flourishing, foliate, fresh, grassy, growing, half-formed, immature, infant, juvenile, leafy, lush, maturing, pliable, puerile, pullulating, raw, recent, sprouting, supple, tender, undecayed, undried, unfledged, ungrown, unripe, unseasoned, verdant, verduous, youthful; CONCEPTS 485, 578,797 —*Ant.* old, withered

green [*adj2*] *inexperienced* callow, credulous, fresh, gullible, ignorant, immature, inexpert, ingenuous, innocent, naive, new, raw, tenderfoot*, unconversant, unpolished, unpracticed, unseasoned, unskillful, unsophisticated, untrained, unversed, wet behind the ears*, young, youthful; CONCEPT 404 —Ant. experienced, expert, skilled

green [adj3] *emerald in color* apple, aquamarine, beryl, chartreuse, fir, forest, grass, jade, kelly, lime, malachite, moss, olive, pea, peacock, pine, sage, sap, sea, spinach, verdigris, vert, viridian, willow; CONCEPT 618

green [adj4] *referring to practices or policies that do not negatively affect the environment* biodegradable, ecological, environmental, environmentally-safe, environment-friendly; CONCEPT 485

green [n] *square or park in center of town* common, field, grass, grassplot, lawn, plaza, sward, terrace, turf; CONCEPTS 509,513

green around the gills [adj] *sick* blah, crummy, miserable, nauseated, pale, queasy, shaky, sick as a dog*, sick to one's stomach, throwing up, under the weather, vomiting; CONCEPT 314

green card [n] *working card* pass, passport, permit, visa; CONCEPTS 271,376,685

greenhorn [n] *inexperienced person* amateur, apprentice, babe*, beginner, colt*, hayseed*, ingénue, learner, naif, neophyte, newcomer, new hand, novice, recruit, rube*, simpleton, tenderfoot*, tyro*, virgin; CONCEPT 423 —Ant. expert, professional

green light [n] *authorization* agreement, approval, assent, blessing, clearance, consent, dispensation, empowerment, go-ahead*, license, nod*, OK*, permission, rubber stamp, sanction, seal of approval, stamp of approval, thumbs-up*; CONCEPT 685 —Ant. red light, refusal, veto

greet [v] *welcome* accost, acknowledge, address, approach, attend, bow, call to, compliment, curtsy, embrace, exchange greetings, extend one's hand, flag, hail, herald, highball*, high-five*, meet, move to, nod, pay respects, receive, recognize, roll out the red carpet*, salaam*, salute, say hello, say hi*, shake hands, shoulder, speak to, stop, tip one's hat*, usher in*, whistle for; CONCEPT 51 —Ant. say farewell, say goodbye

greeting [n] *welcome; message of kindness* accosting, acknowledgment, address, aloha*, attention, best wishes*, blow*, card*, ciao*, compellation, compliments, good wishes*, hail, hello, heralding, hi, highball*, high five*, how-do-you-do*, howdy*, letter*, nod, note, notice, ovation, reception, regards, respects, rumble, salaam*, salutation, salute, speaking to, testimonial, ushering in, what's happening*; CONCEPT 51 —Ant. farewell, goodbye

gregarious [adj] *friendly* affable, clubby*, companionable, convivial, cordial, fun, outgoing, sociable, social; CONCEPT 404 —Ant. cold, cool, introverted, unfriendly, unhospitable, unsociable

gridlock [n] *traffic jam* barrier, blockage, bottleneck, clog, congestion, impasse, logjam, obstacle, stoppage; CONCEPTS 230,432

grief [n] *mental suffering* affliction, agony, anguish, bemoaning, bereavement, bewailing, care, dejection, deploring, depression, desolation, despair, despondency, discomfort, disquiet, distress, dole, dolor, gloom, grievance,

harassment, heartache, heartbreak, infelicity, lamentation, lamenting, malaise, melancholy, misery, mortification, mournfulness, mourning, pain, purgatory, regret, remorse, repining, rue, sadness, sorrow, torture, trial, tribulation, trouble, unhappiness, vexation, woe, worry, wretchedness; CONCEPTS 410,728 —Ant. delight, ecstasy, exhilaration, happiness

grief-stricken [adj] *sad, sorrowful* anguished, cheerless, dejected, depressed, despairing, devastated, distressed, down, heartbroken, heartsick, heavyhearted, hurting, inconsolable, melancholy, miserable, morose, overcome, troubled, unhappy, woebegone; CONCEPT 403

grievance [n] *complaint, gripe* affliction, ax to grind*, beef*, bellyache*, big stink*, blast, case, cross*, damage, distress, flack*, grief, grouse*, hardship, holler*, hoo-ha*, howl*, injury, injustice, jeremiad*, kick, knock*, objection, outrage, pain, pain in the neck*, rap*, resentment, rigor, roar, rumble, sorrow, squawk*, stink*, trial, tribulation, trouble, unhappiness, violence, wrong, yell; CONCEPTS 52,278,689 —Ant. compliment, flattery, praise

grieve [v1] *mourn, feel deep distress* ache, bear, bemoan, bewail, carry on, complain, cry, cry a river*, deplore, eat one's heart out*, endure, hang crepe*, keen, lament, regret, rue, sing the blues*, sorrow, suffer, take it hard*, wail, weep; CONCEPTS 17,410 —Ant. be glad, be happy

grieve [v2] *upset, distress someone* afflict, aggrieve, agonize, break the heart of*, constrain, crush, hurt, injure, pain, sadden, wound; CONCEPTS 7,19 —Ant. delight, please, satisfy

grievous [adj] *severe, painful; serious* afflicting, agonizing, appalling, atrocious, calamitous, damaging, deplorable, dire, dismal, disquieting, distressing, disturbing, dreadful, egregious, flagrant, glaring, grave, harmful, heart-rending, heavy*, heinous, hurtful, injurious, intolerable, lamentable, monstrous, mournful, offensive, onerous, oppressive, outrageous, pathetic, pitiful, sad, shameful, sharp, shocking, sorrowful, taxing, tough, tragic, troublesome, unbearable, upsetting, villainous, weighty*, wounding; CONCEPTS 537,544,548 —Ant. good, harmless, pleasant

grift [n] *swindle* cheating, confidence game, con game*, deceit, dirty pool*, double-dealing*, extortion, fix, fraud, racket*, rip-off*, scam, shady deal*, shell game*, stealing, sting, trickery; CONCEPTS 59,139,192

grill [v1] *broil food* barbecue, burn, charcoal-broil, cook, cook over an open pit, roast, rotisserie, sear; CONCEPT 170

grill [v2] *ask questions aggressively* catechize, cross-examine, give the third degree*, go over*, inquisition, interrogate, interview, put the pressure on*, put the screws to*, question, roast*, third degree*; CONCEPTS 48, 53 —Ant. answer

grim [adj] *hopeless, horrible in manner, appearance* austere, barbarous, bleak, cantankerous, churlish, crabbed*, cruel, crusty, dogged, ferocious, fierce, forbidding, foreboding, formidable, frightful, funereal, ghastly, gloomy, glowering, glum, grisly, grouchy, gruesome, grumpy*, harsh, hideous, horrid, implacable, inexorable, intractable, merciless, morose, ominous, relentless, resolute, ruthless, scowling, severe, shocking, sinister, somber, sour, splenetic, stern, stubborn, sulky, sullen, surly, terrible, truculent, unrelenting, unyielding; CONCEPTS 534,544,570 —*Ant.* bright, cheerful, happy, hopeful, joyful, sunny

grimace [*n*] *scowling facial expression* face, frown, moue, mouth, mouthing, mug*, scowl, smile, smirk, sneer, wry face; CONCEPT 716 —*Ant.* grin, smile

grimace [*v*] *make a pained expression* contort, deform, distort, frown, make a face, make a wry face, misshape, mouth, mug*, scowl, screw up one's face*, smirk, sneer; CONCEPT 185 —*Ant.* grin, smile

grime [*n*] *dirt* crud*, dust, film, filth, gook*, gunk*, muck*, smudge, smut*, soil, soot, tarnish; CONCEPT 260 —*Ant.* cleanliness, purity

grimy [*adj*] *dirty* begrimed, besmirched, cruddy*, dingy*, filthy, foul, grubby*, grungy*, messy, mucky*, nasty, scuzzy*, sleazy*, smeared, smutty*, soiled, sooty, sordid, squalid, unclean; CONCEPTS 485,621 —*Ant.* clean, pure, sterile

grin [*n/v*] *smile widely* beam, crack, simper, smirk; CONCEPTS 185,716 —*Ant.* frown, growl

grind [*n*] *tedious job* chore, drudgery, groove*, grubwork*, hard work, labor, moil, pace, rote, routine, rut*, sweat*, task, toil, travail, treadmill*; CONCEPT 362

grind [*v1*] *crush, pulverize* abrade, atomize, attenuate, beat, bray, chop up, comminute, crumble, crumple, disintegrate, file, granulate, grate, kibble*, levigate, mill, pestle, pound, powder, pulverize*, rasp, reduce, roll out*, scrape, shiver, triturate; CONCEPTS 186,204

grind [*v2*] *sharpen* abrade, file, give an edge to, gnash, grate, grit, polish, rub, sand, scrape, smooth, whet; CONCEPTS 186,215

grind [*v3*] *oppress* afflict, annoy, harass, hold down, hound, persecute, plague, trouble, tyrannize, vex; CONCEPTS 14,130 —*Ant.* free, liberate

grip [*n1*] *clasp, embrace* anchor, brace, catch, cinch, cincture, clamp, clamping, clench, clinch, clutch, coercion, constraint, crushing, duress, enclosing, enclosure, fastening, fixing, grapnel, grapple, grasp, gripe, handclasp, handgrip, handhold, handshake, hold, hook, ligature, lug, purchase, restraint, snatch, squeeze, strength, tenure, vise, wrench; CONCEPT 191 —*Ant.* release

grip [*n2*] *perception, understanding* clutches*, comprehension, control, domination, grasp, hold, influence, keeping, ken, possession, power, tenure; CONCEPT 409 —*Ant.* misconception, misunderstanding

grip [*v1*] *hold tightly* clap a hand on, clasp, clench, clinch, clutch, get one's hands on*, grasp, latch on to*, lay hands on, nab, seize, snag, snatch, take, take hold of; CONCEPT 191 —*Ant.* let go, release

grip [*v2*] *entrance, enchant* catch up, compel, engross, enthrall, fascinate, hold, hypnotize, involve, mesmerize, rivet, spellbind; CONCEPTS 7,11,22 —*Ant.* disgust, repel

gripe [*n1*] *complaint* ache, aching, affliction, disorder, distress, grievance, groan, grouse, grumble, illness, indisposition, infirmity, moan,

objection, pain, pang; CONCEPTS 52,278,313 —*Ant.* compliment, flattery, praise

gripe [*n2*] *strong hold* clamp, clasp, clench, clinch, clutch, crunch, grab, grapple, grasp, grip, tenure; CONCEPT 191

gripe [*v1*] *complain* bellyache*, blow off*, carp, crab*, fuss, groan, grouch, grouse, grumble, kvetch*, moan, murmur, mutter, nag, squawk, take on*, whine, yammer*, yawp*; CONCEPTS 44,52 —*Ant.* compliment, please

gripe [*v2*] *pain, annoy* bother, compress, cramp, disturb, hurt, irritate, pinch, press, squeeze, vex; CONCEPTS 7,19,219,246 —*Ant.* please, soothe

grisly [*adj*] *horrifying* abominable, appalling, awful, blood-stained, bloody, disgusting, dreadful, eerie, frightful, ghastly, grim, grody*, gross*, gruesome, hideous, horrible, horrid, lurid, macabre, sanguine, shocking, sick, sickening, terrible, terrifying, yucky*; CONCEPTS 537,544,570 —*Ant.* nice, pleasing, pretty

grit [*n1*] *particles of dirt* dust, foreign matter, gravel, lumps, pebbles, powder, sand; CONCEPTS 260,831

grit [*n2*] *courage, determination* backbone, daring, doggedness, fortitude, gameness, guts*, hardihood, intestinal fortitude*, mettle, moxie*, nerve, perseverance, pluck, resolution, spine*, spirit, spunk, steadfastness, tenacity, toughness; CONCEPTS 411,633 —*Ant.* cowardice, timidity, weakness

gritty [*adj1*] *granular* abrasive, branlike, calculous, crumbly, dusty, friable, grainy, gravelly, in particles, loose, lumpy, permeable, porous, powdery, pulverant, rasping, rough, sabulous, sandy, scratchy; CONCEPT 606 —*Ant.* fine, smooth

gritty [*adj2*] *brave* courageous, determined, dogged, game*, hardy, mettlesome, plucky*, resolute, spirited, steadfast, tenacious, tough; CONCEPTS 401,404 —*Ant.* afraid, cowardly, spineless

groan [*n*] *moan, complaint* cry, gripe, grouse, grumble, grunt, objection, sigh, sob, whine; CONCEPTS 278,595

groan [*v*] *moan, complaint* bemoan, cry, gripe, grouse, grumble, keen, lament, mumble, murmur, object, sigh, whine; CONCEPTS 44,52,77

grocery store [*n*] *supermarket* bodega, convenience store, corner store*, food mart, food store, market, mom-and-pop store, retail food store; CONCEPTS 323,333,449

groggy [*adj*] *dizzy, stunned* befuddled, confused, dazed, dopey*, drunken, faint, hazy, out of it*, punch-drunk*, punchy*, reeling, shaky, slaphappy*, staggering, stupefied, swaying, tired, unsteady, weak, whirling, wobbly, woozy*; CONCEPT 314 —*Ant.* clear, clearheaded, cognizant

groom [*n1*] *man being married* benedict, bridegroom, fiancé, husband, spouse, suitor; CONCEPT 419 —*Ant.* bride

groom [*n2*] *stable attendant; servant* equerry, hostler, stable person; CONCEPTS 348,419

groom [*v*] *make ready, prepare physically* brush, clean, coach, comb, curry, dress, drill, educate, lick into shape*, make attractive, make presentable, nurture, preen, prep*, pretty up*, prim, prime, primp, put through grind*, put through mill*, ready, refine, refresh, rub down, shape up, sleek, slick up*, smarten up*, spiff up*, spruce up*, tend, tidy, train, turn out; CONCEPTS 162,202,285 —Ant. forget, ignore

groove [n1] *channel, indentation* canal, corrugation, crease, crimp, cut, cutting, depression, ditch, flute, fluting, furrow, gouge, gutter, hollow, incision, notch, pucker, rabbet, rut, scallop, score, scratch, slit, trench, valley; CONCEPT 513

groove [n2] *daily routine* daily grind*, grind, pace, rote, rut*, same old stuff*, schtick*, slot*; CONCEPTS 362,677

groovy [adj] *cool, wonderful* boss*, chic, deep*, excellent, fabulous, fantastic, far-out*, great, hip, neat*, nifty*, rad*, sensational, splendid, super, swell*, trendy, unorthodox, way-out, wild, with it; CONCEPT 572

grope [v] *feel about for* cast about, examine, explore, feel blindly, finger*, fish*, flounder, fumble, grabble, handle, manipulate, poke, pry, root, scrabble, search, touch; CONCEPTS 34,216,612

gross [adj1] *large, fat* adipose, big, bulky, chubby*, corpulent, dense, fleshy, great, heavy, hulking, husky, lumpish, massive, obese, overweight, porcine, portly, stout, thick, unwieldy, weighty; CONCEPTS 773,781 —Ant. skinny, slender, thin

gross [adj2] *whole* aggregate, all, before deductions, before tax, complete, entire, in sum, outright, total, whole ball of wax*, whole enchilada*, whole nine yards*, whole schmear*, whole shebang*; CONCEPT 785 —Ant. net, part, partial

gross [adj3] *crude, vulgar* barnyard*, boorish, breezy, callous, carnal, cheap, coarse, corporeal, crass, dull, fleshly, foul, ignorant, improper, impure, indecent, indelicate, inelegant, insensitive, in the gutter*, lewd, loudmouthed, low, low-minded, lustful, obscene, offensive, rank, raunchy, raw, ribald, rough, rude, scatological, sensual, sexual, sleazy*, smutty*, swinish*, tasteless, ugly, uncouth, uncultured, undiscriminating, unfeeling, unrefined, unseemly, unsophisticated, voluptuous; CONCEPTS 267,542,545 —Ant. clean, moral, polite

gross [adj4] *obvious, apparent* absolute, arrant, blatant, capital, complete, downright, egregious, excessive, exorbitant, extreme, flagrant, glaring, grievous, heinous, immoderate, inordinate, manifest, out-and-out*, outrageous, outright*, perfect, plain, rank, serious, shameful, sheer, shocking, unmitigated, unqualified, utter; CONCEPTS 535,537 —Ant. hidden, modified, obscured, vague

gross [n] *total, whole* aggregate, all, entirety, sum, sum total, totality; CONCEPTS 344,837 —Ant. net, part

gross [v] *bring in as total* earn, make, take in; CONCEPTS 330,351 —Ant. net

grotesque [adj] *ugly, misshapen* aberrant, abnormal, absurd, antic, bizarre, deformed, distorted, eerie, extravagant, extreme, fanciful, fantastic, flamboyant, freakish, grody*, gross*, incongruous, ludicrous, malformed, monstrous, odd, outlandish, perverted, preposterous, queer, ridiculous, strange, surrealistic, uncanny, unnatural, weird, whimsical; CONCEPTS 486, 537,579 —Ant. beautiful, nice, pretty, shapely

grotto [n] *cave* antre, cavern, cavity, chamber, den, hollow, rock shelter, subterrane, underground chamber; CONCEPT 509

grouch [n] *person who complains a lot* bear*, bellyacher*, bug*, crab*, crank, crosspatch*, curmudgeon, faultfinder, griper, grouser, growler, grumbler, grump*, kicker*, malcontent, moaner, sorehead*, sourpuss*, whiner; CONCEPTS 412,423

grouch [v] *complain a lot* bellyache*, carp, find fault, gripe, grouse, grumble, moan, murmur, mutter, scold, whine; CONCEPT 52 —Ant. compliment, praise

grouchy [adj] *complaining, irritable* cantankerous*, cross, crusty*, discontented, grumbling, grumpy*, ill-tempered, irascible, peevish, petulant, querulous, snappy, sulky, surly, testy; CONCEPTS 267,401 —Ant. complimentary, content, happy, pleased, praising, satisfied

ground [n] *earth, land* arena, dirt, dust, field, landscape, loam, old sod, park, real estate, sand, sod, soil, terra firma, terrain, turf; CONCEPT 509 —Ant. heavens, sky

ground [v1] *base, set; educate* acquaint, bottom, coach, discipline, establish, familiarize, fit, fix, found, indoctrinate, inform, initiate, instruct, introduce, predicate, prepare, prime, qualify, rest, settle, stay, teach, train, tutor; CONCEPTS 18,285

ground [v2] *restrict; drop in place* bar, beach, bring down, dock, down, fell, floor, knock down, land, level, mow down*, prevent, strand; CONCEPTS 130,181 —Ant. free, let go, liberate

groundbreaking [adj] *pioneering* avant-garde, cutting-edge, innovating, innovative, leading-edge, radical, revolutionary, spearheading, trailblazing, trendsetting; CONCEPTS 529,578, 589,797

groundless [adj] *without reason, justification* baseless, bottomless, causeless, chimerical, empty, false, flimsy, foundationless, gratuitous, idle, illogical, illusory, imaginary, unauthorized, uncalled-for, unfounded, unjustified, unprovoked, unsupported, unwarranted; CONCEPTS 267,552 —Ant. called-for, grounded, justified, proven, reasonable, warranted

grounds [n1] *estate, domain* acreage, area, campus, country, district, environs, fields, gardens, habitat, holding, land, lot, premises, property, real estate, realm, sphere, spot, terrace, terrain, territory, tract, zone; CONCEPTS 508,516

grounds [n2] *basis, premise* account, antecedent, argument, base, bedrock*, call, cause, chapter and verse*, demonstration, determinant, dope*, evidence, excuse, factor, footing, foundation, goods*, groundwork, inducement, info*, information*, infrastructure, justification, motive, numbers, occasion, pretext, proof, rationale, reason, root*, seat, straight stuff*, substratum, test, testimony, trial, underpinning, wherefore, why, whyfor; CONCEPTS 274,661

grounds [n3] *sediment* deposit, dregs, grouts, leavings, lees, precipitate, precipitation, residue, settlings; CONCEPT 260

groundwork [n] *basis, fundamentals* ABCs*, background, base, bedrock*, cornerstone*, footing, foundation, ground, infrastructure, origin, preliminaries, preparation, root, substratum, underpinning, understructure; CONCEPTS 274,442,660,661

group [n] *list of individuals collectively* accumulation, aggregation, assemblage, assembly, association, assortment, band, batch, battery, bevy, body, bunch, bundle, cartel, category, chain, circle, class, clique, clot, club, clump, cluster, clutch, collection, combination, combine, company, conglomerate, congregation, coterie, covey, crew, crowd, faction, formation, gang, gathering, grade, league, lot, mess, organization, pack, parcel, party, passel, platoon, pool, posse, set, shooting match, society, sort, suite, syndicate, troop, trust; CONCEPTS 391,432

group [v1] *bring together* arrange, assemble, associate, band together, bracket, bunch, bunch up*, cluster, collect, congregate, consort, corral, crowd, gang around*, gang up*, gather, get together, hang out*, harmonize, huddle, link, make the scene*, meet, organize, poke, punch*, round up*, scare up*, systematize; CONCEPTS 109,114 —Ant. disperse, scatter, spread

group [v2] *classify, sort* arrange, assemble, associate, assort, bracket, categorize, class, dispose, file, gather, marshal, order, organize, pigeonhole*, put together, range, rank; CONCEPTS 18, 84,158 —Ant. jumble, mix up

groupie [n] *devoted fan* admirer, buff, devotee, follower, hanger-on, supporter; CONCEPTS 352,366,423

grove [n] *cluster of trees* brake, coppice, copse, covert, forest, orchard, plantation, spinney, stand, thicket, wood, woodland; CONCEPTS 429,517

grovel [v] *abase, demean oneself* apple-polish*, beg, beg for mercy, beseech, blandish, bootlick*, bow and scrape*, brown-nose*, butter up*, cater to, court, cower, crawl, creep, cringe, crouch, eat crow*, eat dirt*, eat humble pie*, fall all over*, fawn*, flatter, humble oneself, humor, implore, kiss one's feet*, kneel, kowtow*, make much of*, make up to*, pamper, play up to*, prostrate*, revere, snivel, softsoap*, stoop, suck up to*, truckle*, wheedle, yes*; CONCEPTS 384,633 —Ant. boast

grow [v] *become larger, evolve* abound, advance, age, amplify, arise, augment, become, branch out, breed, build, burgeon, burst forth, come, come to be, cultivate, develop, dilate, enlarge, expand, fill out, flourish, gain, germinate, get bigger, get taller, heighten, increase, issue, luxuriate, maturate, mature, mount, multiply, originate, pop up*, produce, propagate, pullulate, raise, ripen, rise, shoot*, spread, spring up, sprout, stem, stretch, swell, thicken, thrive, turn, vegetate, wax*, widen; CONCEPTS 427,469,704,775 —Ant. decline, decrease, diminish, halt, lessen, reduce, stop, stunt

growl [n/v] *animal-like sound* bark, bellow, gnarl, gnarr, grumble, grunt, howl, moan, roar, roll, rumble, snarl, thunder; CONCEPTS 77,595

grown-up [n] *adult* gentleman, grown person, lady, mam, man, Miss, mister, Mr., Mrs., Ms., woman; CONCEPT 424 —Ant. child, youngster

growth [n1] *development, progress* advance, advancement, aggrandizement, augmentation, beefing up*, boost, buildup, crop, cultivation, enlargement, evolution, evolvement, expansion, extension, fleshing out*, flowering, gain, germination, heightening, hike, improvement, increase, maturation, maturing, multiplication, produce, production, proliferation, prosperity, rise, sprouting, stretching, success, surge, swell, thickening, unfolding, up, upping, vegetation, waxing*, widening; CONCEPTS 427,469,703, 704, 775 —Ant. abatement, decrease, diminishment, failure, lessening, reduction, stagnation, underdevelopment

growth [n2] *tumor* cancer, cancroid, excrescence, fibrousness, fibrous tissue, fungus, lump, mole, outgrowth, parasite, polyp, swelling, thickening, wen; CONCEPT 306

grub [n1] *larva* caterpillar, entozoon, maggot, worm; CONCEPT 398

grub [n2] *food* chow*, comestibles, eats*, edibles, feed, nosh*, nurture, provisions, rations, sustenance, viands, victuals, vittles*; CONCEPTS 457,460

grub [v1] *dig, uncover* beat, break, burrow, clean, clear, comb, delve, excavate, ferret, fine-tooth-comb*, forage, hunt, poke, prepare, probe, pull up, rake, ransack, root, rummage, scour, search, shovel, spade, unearth, uproot; CONCEPTS 178,216 —Ant. cover, hide

grub [v2] *work very hard* drudge, grind, labor, moil, plod, slave, slog, sweat, toil; CONCEPT 100 —Ant. idle, laze, tinker

grubby [adj] *dirty, disheveled* besmeared, black, filthy, foul, frowzy*, grimy, grungy*, impure, messy, mucky*, nasty, scruffy, scuzzy*, seedy*, shabby, sloppy, slovenly, smutty*, soiled, sordid, squalid, unclean, uncleanly, unkempt, untidy, unwashed; CONCEPTS 485,621 —Ant. clean, cleanly, dressed-up, neat

grudge [n] *hard feelings* animosity, animus, antipathy, aversion, bad blood*, bitterness, bone to pick*, dislike, enmity, grievance, hate, hatred, ill will, injury, injustice, malevolence, malice, maliciousness, malignancy, peeve, pet peeve*, pique, rancor, resentment, spite, spitefulness, spleen, venom; CONCEPT 29 —Ant. idle, laze, tinker

grudge [v] *feel resentful; give unwillingly* begrudge, be reluctant, be stingy*, complain, covet, deny, envy, hold back, mind, pinch, refuse, resent, stint; CONCEPT 21 —Ant. favor, forgive

grueling [adj] *difficult, taxing* arduous, backbreaking, brutal, chastening, crushing, demanding, excruciating, exhausting, fatiguing, fierce, grinding, hairy*, hard, harsh, heavy*, laborious, punishing, racking, severe, stiff, strenuous, tiring, torturous, trying; CONCEPT 565 —Ant. easy, facile

gruesome [adj] *horrible, awful* abominable, appalling, daunting, fearful, frightful, ghastly, grim, grisly, grody*, gross*, hideous, horrendous, horrid, horrific, horrifying, loathsome, lurid, macabre, monstrous, morbid, offensive, repugnant, repulsive, shocking, sick*, spine-tingling*, terrible, terrifying, ugly, weird*; CONCEPTS 485,548 —Ant. beautiful, pleasant, pretty

gruff [adj1] *bad-tempered, rude* abrupt, bearish, blunt, boisterous, boorish, brusque, churlish, crabbed, crabby*, crude, crusty*, curt, discourteous, dour, fierce, grouchy*, grumpy*, ill-natured, impolite, morose, nasty, offhand, rough, saturnine, short, snappy*, snippy*, sour, sullen, surly, truculent, uncivil, ungracious, unmannerly; CONCEPTS 267,401 —*Ant.* even-tempered, happy, nice, polite

gruff [*adj2*] *rasping in sound* cracked, croaking, croaky, grating, guttural, harsh, hoarse, husky, low, rough, throaty; CONCEPT 594 —*Ant.* pleasant, soft, sweet

grumble [*v1*] *complain* bellyache*, carp, find fault, fuss, gripe, groan, grouch*, grouse, kick, kvetch*, moan, protest, pule, repine, scold, snivel*, squawk*, whine; CONCEPTS 44,52 —*Ant.* compliment, praise

grumble [*v2*] *murmur, rumble* bark, croak, gnarl, gnarr, growl, grunt, gurgle, mumble, mutter, roar, roll, snap, snarl, snuffle, splutter, whine; CONCEPTS 65,77

grump [*n*] *cranky person* bear*, complainer, crab*, curmudgeon, grouch, malcontent, sore-head*, sourpuss*, whiner; CONCEPTS 412,423

grumpy [*adj*] *in a bad mood* bad-tempered, cantankerous*, crabby*, cross, crotchety, disgruntled, dissatisfied, griping, grouchy*, grumbling, irritable, peevish, pettish, petulant, querulous, sulky, sullen, surly, testy, truculent; CONCEPTS 401,403 —*Ant.* happy, nice, pleasant

grungy [*adj*] *dirty and unkempt* cruddy*, dilapi-dated, disgusting, disheveled, filthy, flimsy, foul, greasy, grimy, grubby, messy, nasty, offensive, repellent, revolting, rundown, scummy*, scuzzy*, shoddy, slimy, sloppy, trashy, unclean, unwashed, vile, wretched; CONCEPTS 485,579

guarantee [*n*] *pledge, promise* agreement, assurance, attestation, bail, bargain, bond, certainty, certificate, certification, charter, collateral, contract, covenant, deposit, earnest, gage, guaranty, insurance, lock, oath, pawn, pipe, recognizance, security, sure thing*, surety, testament, token, undertaking, vow, warrant, warranty, word, word of honor; CONCEPTS 71,271,685

guarantee [*v*] *pledge, promise* affirm, angel, answer for, assure, attest, aver, back, bankroll, be surety for, bind oneself, certify, confirm, cosign, endorse, ensure, evidence, evince, get behind*, give bond, grubstake, guaranty, insure, juice*, maintain, make bail*, make certain, make sure, mortgage, pick up the check*, pick up the tab*, protect, prove, reassure, secure, sign for, stake, stand behind*, stand up for*, support, swear, testify, vouch for, wager, war-rant, witness; CONCEPTS 71,110 —*Ant.* break

guaranteed [*adj*] *made certain* affirmed, ap-proved, ascertained, assured, attested, bonded, certified, confirmed, endorsed, for a fact, for sure, have a lock on*, insured, on ice*, pledged, plighted, protected, sealed, secured, sure, sure enough*, sure-fire*, warranted; CONCEPT 535 —*Ant.* indefinite, insecure, uncertain, unsure

guard [*n1*] *protector* bouncer*, chaperon, chap-erone, chaser*, convoyer, custodian, defender, escort, guardian, lookout, picket, sentinel, sentry, shepherd, shield, ward, warden, watch, watchperson; CONCEPT 348

guard [*n2*] *defense* aegis, armament, armor, buffer, bulwark, pad, protection, rampart, safeguard, screen, security, shield, ward; CONCEPT 712

guard [*v*] *protect, watch* attend, baby-sit, bul-wark, chaperon, chaperone, conduct, convoy, cover, cover up, defend, escort, fend, keep, keep an eye on*, keep in view, keep under sur-veillance, look after, lookout, mind, observe, oversee, patrol, police*, preserve, ride shotgun for*, safeguard, save, screen, secure, see after, shelter, shepherd, shield, shotgun, stonewall*, superintend, supervise, tend; CONCEPTS 96,134 —*Ant.* disregard, forget, ignore, neglect

guarded [*adj*] *suspicious* attentive, cagey, calculating, canny, careful, cautious, chary, circumspect, discreet, gingerly, leery, noncom-mittal, on the lookout*, overcautious, prudent, reserved, restrained, reticent, safe, vigilant, wary, watchful, with eyes peeled*; CONCEPT 542 —*Ant.* careless, incautious, unguarded, unsuspicious, unwatchful

guardian [*n*] *keeper, protector* angel*, atten-dant, baby-sitter, bird dog*, cerberus, champion, chaperon, chaperone, conservator, cop*, curator, custodian, defender, escort, guard, keeper, nurse, overseer, paladin, patrol, preserver, safeguard, sentinel, shepherd, sitter, sponsor, superintendent, supervisor, trustee, vigilante, warden, watchdog*; CONCEPTS 414,423

guerrilla [*n*] *bushfighter* commando, freedom fighter, irregular, mercenary, professional soldier, resistance fighter, soldier of fortune, terrorist, underground fighter; CONCEPT 358

guess [*n*] *belief, speculation* assumption, ball-park figure*, conclusion, conjecture, deduction, divination, estimate, fancy, feeling, guessti-mate*, guesswork, hunch*, hypothesis, induc-tion, inference, judgment, notion, opinion, postulate, postulation, prediction, presumption, presupposition, reckoning, shot*, shot in the dark*, sneaking suspicion*, stab*, supposal, supposition, surmisal, surmise, suspicion, theory, thesis, view; CONCEPT 689 —*Ant.* calculation, measurement

guess [*v*] *try to figure out; imagine* believe, calculate, chance, conjecture, dare say, deduce, deem, divine, estimate, fancy*, fathom, go out on a limb*, guesstimate*, happen upon*, hazard*, hypothesize, infer, judge, jump to a conclusion*, lump it*, opine, penetrate, pick, postulate, predicate, predict, presume, pretend, reason, reckon, select, size up*, solve, specu-late, suggest, suppose, surmise, survey, suspect, take a shot at*, take a stab at*, theorize, think, think likely, venture, work out*; CONCEPT 28 —*Ant.* calculate, measure

guest [*n*] *person accommodated, given hospitality* bedfellow, boarder, caller, client, companion, company, customer, frequenter*, habitué, inmate, lodger, mate, out-of-towner*, partaker, patron, recipient, renter, roomer, sharer, sojourner, tenant, transient, vacationer, visitant, visitor; CONCEPT 423

guff [*n*] *nonsense* baloney, bull, bunk, bunkum, crap*, drivel, flapdoodle, foolishness, garbage, hogwash, hooey, poppycock, rubbish; CONCEPTS 230,388,633

guffaw [*n*] *burst of laughter* belly laugh, deep laugh, howl, howling, laughter, loud laugh, roar, shout, shriek, snort; CONCEPTS 77,185

guidance [*n*] *counseling* advice, auspices, conduct, conduction, control, conveyance, direction, government, help, instruction, intelligence, leadership, management, navigation, supervision, teaching; CONCEPTS 75,274,278

guide [n1] *something that or someone who leads* adviser, attendant, captain, chaperon, cicerone, conductor, controller, convoy, counselor, criterion, design, director, docent, escort, example, exemplar, exhibitor, genie, genius, guiding spirit, guru, ideal, inspiration, lead, leader, lodestar, mentor, model, monitor, paradigm, pathfinder, pattern, pilot, pioneer, rudder, scout, standard, superintendent, teacher, usher, vanguard; CONCEPTS 348,423,686

guide [n2] *information, instructions* ABCs*, beacon*, bellwether*, bible, catalog, chapter and verse*, clue, compendium, directory, enchiridion, guidebook, guiding light*, handbook, hot lead*, key, landmark, lodestar, manual, mark, marker, no-no's*, pointer, print, sign, signal, signpost, telltale, the book*, the numbers*, tip-off*, vade mecum; CONCEPT 274

guide [v] *direct, lead* accompany, advise, attend, beacon*, chaperon, command, conduct, contrive, control, convoy, counsel, coxswain, educate, engineer, escort, govern, handle, have a handle on*, influence, instruct, manage, maneuver, marshal, navigate, oversee, pilot, quarterback*, regulate, route, rule, see, shepherd, show, show the way, spearhead*, steer, superintend, supervise, sway, teach, trailblaze*, train, usher; CONCEPTS 75,110,117,187 —*Ant.* abandon, leave, misguide, mislead, neglect

guidebook [n] *handbook* enchiridion, field guide, how-to book, instruction book, manual, map, reference book, road map, travel book, vade mecum; CONCEPT 280

guideline [n] *direction* clue, code, ground rule, guidance, guide, instruction, key, mark, marker, precept, protocol, rule, signal, standard procedure; CONCEPTS 271,274

guild [n] *association, fellowship* club, company, corporation, federation, group, interest group, league, lodge, order, organization, profession, society, sodality, trade, union; CONCEPTS 381,387

guile [n] *slyness, cleverness* artfulness, artifice, chicanery, craft, craftiness, cunning, deceit, deception, dirty dealing*, dirty pool*, dirty trick*, dirty work*, dishonesty, dissemblance, dissimulation, double-cross*, duplicity, foul play*, jive*, run-around*, ruse, sellout*, sharp practice*, stab in the back*, treachery, trickery, trickiness, wiliness; CONCEPTS 645,657 —*Ant.* artlessness, frankness, honesty, naivety, openness, sincerity

guileless [adj] *honest* aboveboard, artless, candid, frank, genuine, ingenuous, innocent, naive, natural, open, simple, simple-minded, sincere, straightforward, truthful, unaffected, undesigning, unsophisticated, unstudied; CONCEPTS 267,542,545 —*Ant.* artful, clever, crafty, cunning, deceitful, dishonest, guileful, tricky

guilt [n] *blame; bad conscience over responsibility* answerability, blameworthiness, contrition, crime, criminality, culpability, delinquency, dereliction, disgrace, dishonor, error, failing, fault, indiscretion, infamy, iniquity, lapse, liability, malefaction, malfeasance, malpractice, misbehavior, misconduct, misstep,

offense, onus, peccability, penitence, regret, remorse, responsibility, self-condemnation, self-reproach, shame, sin, sinfulness, slip, solecism, stigma, transgression, wickedness, wrong; CONCEPTS 101,532,645,690 —*Ant.* innocence

guiltless [adj] *blameless, not responsible* clean, clear, crimeless, exemplary, faultless, free, good, immaculate, impeccable, inculpable, innocent, irreproachable, pure, righteous, sinless, spotless, unimpeachable, unsullied, untainted, untarnished, virtuous; CONCEPT 545 —*Ant.* blameful, corrupt, guilty, immoral, sinful, wrong

guilty [adj] *blameworthy; found at fault* accusable, caught, censurable, censured, chargeable, condemned, conscience-stricken, contrite, convictable, convicted, criminal, culpable, damned, delinquent, depraved, doomed, erring, evil, felonious, hangdog*, impeached, incriminated, in error, iniquitous, in the wrong, judged, liable, licentious, offending, on one's head*, out of line*, proscribed, regretful, remorseful, reprehensible, responsible, rueful, sentenced, sheepish, sinful, sorry, wicked, wrong; CONCEPT 545 —*Ant.* guiltless, innocent, moral, right, sinless, truthful

guinea pig [n] *test subject* examinee, experimental subject, lab animal, laboratory animal, test animal, testee, victim; CONCEPTS 5,290

guise [n] *appearance, pretense* air, aspect, behavior, cloak, color, cover, demeanor, disguise, disguisement, dress, facade, face, false front*, false show*, fashion, form, front, mask, mien, mode, pose, posture, role, seeming, semblance, shape, show, showing, simulacrum; CONCEPTS 645,716 —*Ant.* reality

gulch [n] *small ravine* arroyo, channel, cut, ditch, gap, gorge, gulley, trench, valley; CONCEPTS 509,513

gulf [n1] *sea inlet* basin, bay, bayou, bight, cove, firth, harbor, slough, sound, whirlpool; CONCEPTS 509,514

gulf [n2] *deep, gaping hole* abyss, breach, cave, cavity, chasm, cleft, crevasse, depth, depths, distance, expanse, gap, gulch, hiatus, hollow, opening, pit, ravine, rent, rift, separation, shaft, split, void, well, whirlpool; CONCEPTS 509,513

gullible [adj] *naive, trusting* being a sucker*, believing, biting, credulous, easily taken in*, easy mark*, falling hook line and sinker*, foolish, green*, innocent, kidding oneself*, mark*, silly, simple, sucker, susceptible, swallowing whole*, taken in*, taking the bait*, trustful, tumbling for*, unskeptical, unsophisticated, unsuspecting, wide-eyed*; CONCEPTS 402,542 —*Ant.* astute, discerning, knowledgeable, perceptive, suspicious, unbelieving, untrusting, wise

gully [n] *ravine, ditch* channel, chase, chasm, crevasse, culvert, gutter, notch, trench, watercourse; CONCEPTS 509,513

gulp [n] *swallow* choke, draught, gasp, mouthful, swig, swill; CONCEPT 185 —*Ant.* nibble

gulp [v] *eat, drink fast* belt*, choke down*, chugalug*, consume, devour, dispatch, dispose, drop*, englut, gobble*, guzzle*, imbibe, ingurgitate, inhale*, pour, quaff, scarf down*, slop*, slosh*, stuff, swallow, swig, swill, take in, toss off*, wolf*, wolf down*; CONCEPTS 169,185 —*Ant.* nibble

gum [n] *sticky substance* adhesive, amber, cement, cohesive substance, exudate, glue, mucilage, paste, pitch, plaster, resin, rosin, tar, wax; CONCEPT 466

gumption [n] *nerve, initiative* ability, acumen, astuteness, cleverness, commonsense, discernment, enterprise, get-up-and-go*, good sense, horse sense*, industry, judgment, perspicaciousness, perspicacity, resourcefulness, sagaciousness, sagacity, savvy, sense, shrewdness, spirit, wisdom, wit; CONCEPT 411 —*Ant.* cowardice, naivety

gun [n] *weapon that shoots* 9 mm.*, blaster*, cannon, difference*, equalizer*, flintlock, forty-five*, handgun, hardware*, howitzer, magnum, mortar, musket, ordnance, peashooter*, persuader*, piece*, pistol, revolver, rifle, rod*, Saturday-night special*, shotgun, thirty-eight*, Uzi*; CONCEPT 500

gung ho [adj] *extremely enthusiastic* anxious, ardent, dedicated, eager, enthused, excited, fanatical, fired up*, keyed up*, lively, passionate, spirited, zealous; CONCEPTS 401,542

gurgle [n/v] *burble, murmur* babble, bubble, crow, lap, plash, purl, ripple, slosh, splash, wash; CONCEPTS 65,595

guru [n] *mentor, guide* authority, guiding light*, leader, master, sage, teacher, tutor; CONCEPT 350 —*Ant.* follower, student

guru [n2] *technical expert* computer expert, computer geek, computer specialist, geek, techie; CONCEPTS 348,350,416

gush [n] *outpouring* burst, cascade, flood, flow, flush, issue, jet, run, rush, spate, spout, spring, spurt, stream, surge; CONCEPTS 467,687

gush [v1] *pour out* burst, cascade, emanate, emerge, flood, flow, flush, issue, jet, pour, roll, run, rush, sluice, spew, spout, spring, spurt, stream, surge, well; CONCEPT 179 —*Ant.* trickle

gush [v2] *speak with overwhelming enthusiasm* babble*, blather, carry on about*, chatter, effervesce, effuse, enthuse, fall all over*, go on about*, jabber, make a to-do over*, overstate, prate, prattle, rave; CONCEPT 49 —*Ant.* be quiet

gust [n] *rush, eruption* access, blast, blow, breeze, burst, explosion, fit, flare-up, flurry, gale, outburst, paroxysm, passion, puff, sally, squall, storm, surge; CONCEPTS 524,787 —*Ant.* trickle

gusto [n] *great enthusiasm* appetite, appreciation, ardor, brio, delectation, delight, enjoyment, exhilaration, fervor, heart, liking, palate, passion, pleasure, relish, savor, taste, verve, zeal, zest; CONCEPTS 411,657 —*Ant.* apathy, reluctance, unenthusiasm

gusty [adj] *windy* airy, blowy, blustering, blustery, breezy, hearty, robust, squally, stormy, tempestuous; CONCEPT 525 —*Ant.* calm, quiet

gut [adj] *intuitive* basic, deep-seated, emotional, heartfelt, innate, inner, instinctive, interior, internal, intimate, involuntary, natural, spontaneous, unthinking, visceral, viscerous; CONCEPT 403 —*Ant.* material, physical

gut [n] *stomach and abdomen* belly, bowels, duodenum, entrails, innards, intestines, paunch, tripes, tummy*, venter, viscera; CONCEPT 393

gut [v] *clean out, strip* bowel, decimate, despoil, dilapidate, disembowel, draw, dress, empty, eviscerate, exenterate, loot, pillage, plunder, ransack, ravage, rifle, sack; CONCEPTS 165,211 —*Ant.* fill

gutless [adj] *timid* abject, chicken*, chicken-hearted*, coward, cowardly, craven, faint-hearted*, feeble, irresolute, lily-livered*, pusillanimous, spineless*, submissive, weak, wimpy*, yellow*, yellow-bellied*; CONCEPTS 404,542 —*Ant.* bold, brave, courageous, gutsy, resolute

guts [n] *nerve, boldness* audacity, backbone*, courage, daring, dauntlessness, effrontery, forcefulness, fortitude, grit*, hardihood, heart*, intestinal fortitude*, mettle, moxie*, pluck, resolution, sand*, spine*, spirit, spunk*, willpower; CONCEPTS 411,657 —*Ant.* cowardice, fear, timidity

gutsy [adj] *bold, brave* courageous, determined, gallant, game*, indomitable, intrepid, mettlesome, plucky, resolute, spirited, spunky*, staunch, unfearful, valiant; CONCEPTS 404,542 —*Ant.* cowardly, fearful, timid

gutter [n] *ditch* channel, conduit, culvert, dike, drain, duct, eaves, fosse, funnel, gully, moat, pipe, runnel, sewer, sluice, spout, sulcation, trench, trough, tube, watercourse; CONCEPT 440

guttural [adj] *deep in sound* glottal, grating, gravelly, growling, gruff, harsh, hoarse, husky, inarticulate, low, rasping, rough, sepulchral, thick, throaty; CONCEPT 594 —*Ant.* dulcet

guy [n] *man* bird*, bloke*, boy, brother, bud, buddy, cat*, chap, chum, dude*, feller*, fellow, gentleman, individual, male, person; CONCEPTS 414,419 —*Ant.* girl

guzzle [v] *drink down fast* bolt*, booze*, carouse*, cram, devour, englut, gobble*, gorge, gormandize, imbibe, ingurgitate, knock back*, quaff, slop*, slosh*, soak, swig, swill, tipple; CONCEPT 169 —*Ant.* sip

gymnasium [n] *arena for sports, recreation* alley, amphitheater, athletic club, center, circus, coliseum, course, exercise room, field house, floor, gym, health club, hippodrome, pit, recreation center, ring, rink, spa, stadium, sweatshop*, theater; CONCEPTS 364,438,439 •

gymnastics [n] *acrobatic exercise* aerobatics, balance beam, bars, body-building, calisthenics, floor exercise, free exercise, gym, horse, rings, trampoline, trapeze, tumbling, vaulting, workout; CONCEPT 363

gyp [v] *rip-off* bamboozle, bilk, cheat, deceive, defraud, dupe, fleece, flimflam*, gip, gull, hoodwink, hustle*, pull something*, rook, scam, stick*, swindle, take for a ride*, trick; CONCEPT 59 —*Ant.* be fair, give, offer

gyrate [v] *revolve* circle, circulate, circumduct, gyre, pirouette, purl, roll, rotate, spin, spiral, turn, twirl, whirl, whirligig; CONCEPTS 147,149

H

habit [n1] *tendency, practice* addiction, bent, bias, constitution, consuetude, convention, custom, dependence, disposition, fashion, fixation, fixed attitude, frame of mind*, gravitation, groove, habitude, hangup, impulsion, inclination, make-up*, manner, mannerism, mode, nature, obsession, pattern, penchant, persuasion, praxis, predisposition, proclivity, proneness, propensity, quirk, routine, rule, rut, second nature*, set, style, susceptibility, thing*, turn, usage, use, way, weakness, wont; CONCEPT 644

habit [n2] *dress, clothing, often for a particular purpose* apparel, costume, garb, garment, habiliment, riding clothes, robe, vestment; CONCEPT 451

habitat/habitation [n] *place where someone resides* abode, accommodations, address, apartment, berth, biosphere, cave, commoracy, condo, condominium, co-op, den, digs*, domicile, dwelling, element, environment, fireside, flat, haunt*, haven, hearth, hole*, home, home plate*, homestead, house, housing, locale, locality, lodging, neck of the woods*, nest, nook, occupancy, occupation, pad*, place, quarters, range, residence, residency, roof*, roost*, seat*, settlement, site, stamping ground*, stomping ground*, surroundings, terrain, territory, turf; CONCEPT 515

habitual [adj] *usual, established* accepted, accustomed, addicted, addicting, automatic, chronic, common, confirmed, constant, continual, conventional, customary, cyclic, disciplined, familiar, fixed, frequent, hardened, ingrained, inveterate, iterated, iterative, mechanical, methodical, natural, normal, ordinary, perfunctory, permanent, perpetual, persistent, practiced, recurrent, regular, reiterative, repeated, repetitious, rooted, routine, seasoned, set, standard, steady, systematic, traditional, wonted; CONCEPTS 530,547 —Ant. infrequent, inhabitual, intermittent, occasional, rare, seldom, uncommon, unestablished, unusual

habituate [v] *prepare, accustom* acclimate, acclimatize, addict, adjust, break in, condition, confirm, devote, discipline, endure, familiarize, harden, inure, make used to, school, season, take to, tolerate, train; CONCEPTS 35,202 —Ant. ignore, neglect

hacienda [n] *large estate* cattle ranch, farmhouse, large house, mansion, plantation, ranch; CONCEPTS 439,516

hack [n1] *person who does easy work for money* drudge*, greasy grind*, grind*, hireling, lackey*, old pro*, plodder*, pro*, servant, slave, workhorse*; CONCEPT 348

hack [n2] *taxicab* cab, carriage, coach, hackney, taxi, vehicle; CONCEPT 505

hack [n3/v] *cut without care* chop, clip, fell, gash, hackle, hew, lacerate, mangle, mutilate, notch, slash, whack; CONCEPTS 137,176

hacker [n] *someone proficient at computers, especially a hobbyist* application programmer, computer architect, computer designer, computer jock, key puncher, operator, programmer, systems analyst, systems engineer, systems programmer, systems software specialist, technician; CONCEPTS 360,366

hack it [v] *to succeed* accomplish, avail, be successful, bring home the bacon*, carry off*, come out on top*, come through, cut it, cut the mustard*, deliver the goods*, get to the top*, hit the mark*, make a go of it*, make it*, make the cut*, make the grade*, prevail, pull it off, score, win; CONCEPTS 141,706

hackneyed [adj] *clichéd, tired* antiquated, banal, common, commonplace, conventional, corny*, everyday, familiar tune*, hokey*,

moth-eaten*, obsolete, old, old-chestnut*, old-hat*, old-saw*, outdated, outmoded, out-of-date, overworked, pedestrian*, played-out*, quotidian, run-of-the-mill*, stale, stereotyped, stock, threadbare*, timeworn, tripe, trite, unoriginal, well-worn, worn-out*; CONCEPTS 267,530 —Ant. fresh, new, original, uncommon

haggard [adj] *worn, weakened* ashen, careworn, drawn, emaciated, exhausted, faded, fagged, fatigued, fretted, gaunt, ghastly, lank, lean, pale, pallid, pinched, scraggy, scrawny, shrunken, skinny, spare, starved, thin, tired, wan, wasted, weak, wearied, worn-down, wrinkled; CONCEPTS 314,406,491 —Ant. fresh, healthy, hearty, strong, unworn

haggle [v] *bicker, quarrel* argue, bargain, barter, beat down*, cavil, chaffer, deal, dicker*, dispute, hammer out a deal*, horse-trade*, make a deal*, palter, quibble, squabble, wrangle; CONCEPT 46 —Ant. agree, comply, concur

hail [n] *torrent* barrage, bombardment, broadside, cannonade, hailstorm, pelting, rain, salvo, shower, storm, volley; CONCEPTS 189,524

hail [v1] *call to, yell for* accost, address, flag, flag down*, greet, hello, holler*, salute, shoulder, shout, signal, sing out*, speak to, wave down, welcome, whistle down*, whistle for*, yawp*, yoo-hoo*; CONCEPTS 47,74,77 —Ant. whisper

hail [v2] *honor, salute* acclaim, acknowledge, applaud, cheer, commend, compliment, exalt, glorify, greet, hear it for*, kudize, praise, recognize, recommend, root for*, welcome; CONCEPT 69 —Ant. disdain, dishonor, disparage, slight

hail [v3] *come from; originate* be a native of, be born in, begin, claim as birthplace; CONCEPT 648

hail [v4] *rain down on* barrage, batter, beat down upon, bombard, pelt, shower, storm, volley; CONCEPT 526 —Ant. dribble, drip

hair [n] *threadlike growth on animate being* beard, bristle, cilium, coiffure, cowlick, cut, down, eyebrow, eyelash, feeler, fiber, filament, fluff, fringe, frizzies*, fur, grass, haircut, hairstyle, lock, mane, mop*, moustache, quill, ruff, shock, sideburn, split ends, strand, thatch, tress, tuft, vibrissa, villus, whiskers, wig, wool; CONCEPT 392

hairdresser [n] *hair stylist* barber, beautician, coiffeur, coiffeuse, friseur; CONCEPT 348

hairless [adj] *without growth on body part* bald, baldheaded, beardless, clean-shaven, cue ball*, depilated, egghead*, glabrate, glabrescent, glabrous, shaved, shaven, shorn, skinhead*, smooth, smooth-faced, tonsured, whiskerless; CONCEPT 406 —Ant. furry, hairy, hirsute

hair-raising [adj] *causing excitement* bloodcurdling, breathtaking, chilling, cliff-hanging, electrifying, exciting, frightening, shocking, spine-chilling, spine-tingling, suspenseful, terrifying; CONCEPTS 529,542,548

hairsplitting [n] *nitpicking* bickering, carping, caviling, faultfinding, perfectionism, pettiness, quibbling, sophistry; CONCEPTS 671,706

hairstyle [n] *cut, style of a head of hair* afro*, beehive*, blow dry*, bob*, bouffant, braid, brushcut, bubble*, bun, coiffure, crewcut, cut, do*, dreadlocks, ducktail, fade, feather cut, flattop*, flip, haircut, hairdo, headdress, horse tail, mohawk, natural, pageboy, pigtails, pixie, ponytail, razor cut; CONCEPT 718

hairy [adj1] *having much hair* bearded, be-whiskered, bristly, bushy, downy, fleecy, flocculent, fluffy, furry, fuzzy, hirsute, lanate, pileous, piliferous, pilose, pubescent, rough, shaggy, stubbly, tufted, unshaven, unshorn, villous, whiskered, woolly; CONCEPT 406 —Ant. bald, balding, clean, hairless

hairy [adj2] *dangerous* chancy, difficult, hazardous, jeopardous, perilous, risky, scary, treacherous, uncertain, unhealthy, unsound, wicked; CONCEPT 548 —Ant. calm, safe

halcyon [adj] *calm, peaceful* at peace, balmy, bucolic, gentle, golden, happy, harmonious, palmy, pastoral, quiet, serene, soothing, still, sunny, tranquil, untroubled; CONCEPTS 401,404

hale [adj] *strong and healthy* able-bodied, alive and kicking*, blooming, fit, fit as a fiddle*, flourishing, healthy, hearty, husky, in fine fettle*, in the pink*, right, robust, sane, sound, stout, strapping, strong, trim, vigorous, well, well-conditioned, wholesome; CONCEPTS 314, 489 —Ant. sick, unhealthy, weak

half [adj] *partial* bisected, divided, even-steven*, fifty-fifty*, fractional, halved, incomplete, limited, moderate, partly; CONCEPT 785 —Ant. total, whole

half [n] *one of two equal parts of a whole* bisection, division, fifty percent, fraction, hemisphere, moiety; CONCEPT 835

half-baked [adj] *stupid; not thought through* backward, batty*, birdbrained*, blockheaded*, boneheaded*, brainless, crazy, dumb, feeble-minded, foolish, harebrained*, idiotic, ignorant, ill-conceived, imbecilic, impractical, indiscreet, moronic, poorly planned, retarded, senseless, short-sighted, silly, slow, sophomoric, underdeveloped, witless; CONCEPTS 403,529, 548 —Ant. intelligent, smart, thoughtful, wise

half-breed [n] *mixed creation* amalgam, blend, combination, conglomeration, cross, crossbreed, hodgepodge*, hybrid, medley, mélange, miscegnation, mishmash*, mule, mutt*; CONCEPTS 260,394

halfhearted [adj] *without enthusiasm* apathetic, cool, impassive, indifferent, irresolute, lackluster, listless, lukewarm, neutral, passive, perfunctory, spiritless, tame, tepid, unenthusiastic, uninterested; CONCEPT 401 —Ant. desirous, enthusiastic, interested, warm, whole-hearted

halfway [adj] *not complete; in the middle* betwixt and between*, center, centermost, central, equidistant, imperfect, intermediate, medial, median, mid*, middlemost, midway, moderate, part, partial, part-way, smack dab*, smack in the middle*; CONCEPTS 531,586 —Ant. complete, total, whole

halfway [adv] *not complete; in the middle* comparatively, compromising, conciliatory, half the distance, imperfectly, incompletely, in part, insufficiently, medially, middling, midway, moderately, nearly, partially, partly, pretty*, rather, restrictedly, to a degree, to some extent, to the middle, unsatisfactorily; CONCEPTS 531,586 —Ant. completely, totally, wholly

half-wit [n] *stupid person* blockhead*, cretin, dimwit, dingbat*, dolt, dope*, dork*, dullard, dumbbell*, dummy*, dunce, dunderhead, fool, idiot, ignoramus, imbecile, lamebrain*, moron, nitwit, pea brain*, simpleton; CONCEPTS 350,423

hall [n1] *corridor* anteroom, entrance, entrance-way, entry, foyer, gallery, hallway, lobby, pass, passage, passageway, room, rotunda, vestibule; CONCEPT 440

hall [n2] *room for large affairs* amphitheater, arena, armory, assembly room, auditorium, ballroom, casino, chamber, church, gallery, gym, gymnasium, lounge, lyceum, mart, meeting place, refectory, salon, stateroom, theater; CONCEPTS 438,439,441,448

hallmark [n] *symbol, authentication* badge, certification, device, emblem, endorsement, indication, mark, ratification, seal, sign, signet, stamp, sure sign, telltale sign, trademark; CONCEPTS 284,628

hallowed [adj] *holy, revered* anointed, beatified, blessed, consecrated, dedicated, divine, enshrined, holy, honored, inviolable, sacred, sacrosanct, sanctified, unprofane; CONCEPT 568 —Ant. desecrated, irreligious, profane, unhallowed, unholy, unsanctified

hallucinate [v] *imagine vividly* blow one's mind*, daydream, envision, fantasize, freak out*, have visions, head trip*, hear voices*, trip*, visualize; CONCEPT 34 —Ant. experience

hallucination [n] *dream, delusion* aberration, apparition, fantasy, figment of the imagination*, head trip*, illusion, mirage, phantasm, phantasmagoria, phantom, trip*, vision, wraith; CONCEPTS 529,532,690 —Ant. experience, fact, reality, truth

halo [n] *ring of light* aura, aureola, aureole, aurora, corona, crown of light, glory, halation, nimbus, radiance; CONCEPTS 624,628

halt [n] *end, stoppage* arrest, break, break-off*, close, cutoff, freeze*, grinding halt, impasse, interruption, layoff, letup, pause, screaming halt*, screeching halt*, stand, standstill, stop, termination; CONCEPT 119 —Ant. continuation, endurance, go, perseverance, start

halt [v1] *stop, cause to stop* adjourn, arrest, balk, bar, block, blow the whistle on*, break off*, bring to an end, bring to standstill, call it a day*, cease, cease fire, check, close down, come to an end, cool it*, curb*, cut short, desist, deter, draw up, drop anchor*, end, frustrate, hamper, hold at bay*, hold back, impede, intermit, interrupt, obstruct, pause, pull up*, punctuate, put a cork in*, rest, stall, stand still, stay, stem, stop, suspend, terminate, wait; CONCEPTS 121,234 —Ant. carry on, continue, forge, forward, push

halt [v2] *hesitate, stutter* be defective, dither, falter, hobble, limp, pause, shilly-shally*, stagger, stammer, stumble, vacillate, waver, whiffle*, wiggle-waggle*; CONCEPTS 234,721, 804 —Ant. continue, speak smoothly

halting [adj] *hesitant* awkward, bumbling, clumsy, doubtful, faltering, gauche, imperfect, indecisive, inept, irresolute, labored, limping, lumbering, maladroit, slow, stammering, stumbling, stuttering, tentative, uncertain, unhandy, vacillating, vacillatory, wavering, wooden*; CONCEPTS 534,550 —Ant. flowing, smooth, unhesitating

halve [v] *cut in half* bisect, divide equally, reduce by fifty percent, share equally, split in two; CONCEPT 98 —Ant. combine

ha
ha

hamburger [n] *ground beef sandwich* beef-burger, burger, cheeseburger, chopped beefsteak, ground chuck, ground round, ground sirloin, Salisbury steak; CONCEPTS 457,460

hamlet [n] *small village* community, crossroads, district, small town, suburb; CONCEPT 507

hammer [v] *beat, hit* bang, batter, bear down, clobber, defeat, drive, drub, fashion, forge, form, knock, make, pound, pummel, shape, strike, tap, thrash, trounce, wallop, whack, whomp; CONCEPT 189

hammer away/hammer into [v] *work hard at* continue, drive home*, drub into*, drudge, drum into*, endeavor, grind*, grind into*, impress upon, instruct, keep on, peg away*, persevere, persist, plug away*, pound away*, repeat, stick to*, try hard, try repeatedly, work; CONCEPTS 68,87,239

hammer out [v] *bring to a conclusion* accomplish, bring about, build, complete, construct, erect, establish, excogitate, fight through, finish, form, make, negotiate, produce, settle, set up, sort out, thrash out*, work out; CONCEPTS 91,706

hamper [n] *basket for storage* bassinet, carton, crate, creel, laundry basket, pannier; CONCEPT 494

hamper [v] *impede, restrict* baffle, balk, bar, bind, block, check, clog, cramp, cramp one's style*, cumber, curb, drag one's feet*, embarrass, encumber, entangle, fetter, foil, frustrate, get in the way*, hamstring*, handicap, hang up*, hinder, hobble, hog-tie*, hold up*, inconvenience, inhibit, interfere with, leash, obstruct, prevent, restrain, retard, shackle, slow down, stymie, thwart, tie, tie one's hands*, tie up, trammel; CONCEPT 130 —*Ant.* aid, allow, assist, encourage, expedite, help, permit, promote

hamstring [v] *disable* cripple, debilitate, handicap, hinder, hobble, immobilize, impair, lame, maim, mangle, paralyze, weaken; CONCEPTS 130,246

hand [n1] *appendage at end of human arm, including fingers* duke*, extremity, fin*, fist, grasp, grip, ham*, hold, hook, metacarpus, mitt*, palm, paw*, phalanges, shaker*; CONCEPT 392

hand [n2] *person who does labor* aide, artificer, artisan, craftsperson, employee, help, helper, hired person, laborer, operative, roustabout, worker; CONCEPT 348

hand [n3] *help, aid* ability, agency, assistance, control, direction, guidance, influence, instruction, knack, lift, part, participation, relief, share, skill, succor, support; CONCEPTS 110,630 —*Ant.* check, encumbrance, hindrance, obstruction, prevention

hand [n4] *handwriting* calligraphy, chirography, longhand, script; CONCEPT 79

hand [n5] *round of applause* clap, handclapping, ovation, thunderous reception; CONCEPT 189 —*Ant.* silence

handbag [n] *person's carryall* backpack, bag, clutch, evening bag, grip, hide, knapsack, leather, pocketbook, portmanteau, purse, reticule; CONCEPT 446

handbook [n] *document giving instruction, information* bible, compendium, directory,

enchiridion, encyclopedia, fundamentals, guide, guidebook, instruction book, manual, text, textbook, vade mecum; CONCEPT 280

handful [adj] *a small quantity* few, scattering, small number, smattering, some, spattering, sprinkling; CONCEPT 789 —*Ant.* lot, mass

handicap [n1] *disadvantage* affliction, baggage*, barrier, block, burden, detriment, disability, drawback, encumbrance, hangup*, hindrance, impairment, impediment, injury, limitation, load, millstone, obstacle, psychological baggage*, restriction, shortcoming, stumbling block*; CONCEPTS 666,674 —*Ant.* advantage, benefit, help

handicap [n2] *advantage* bulge, edge*, favor, head start*, odds, penalty, points*, start, upper hand*, vantage; CONCEPT 693 —*Ant.* disadvantage, drawback, impairment, limitation, restriction, shortcoming

handicap [v] *give disadvantage* burden, cripple, encumber, hamper, hamstring*, hinder, hog-tie*, hold back, impede, limit, put out of commission*, restrict, sideline*, take out*; CONCEPTS 130,246 —*Ant.* aid, assist, benefit, further, give advantage, help, promote

handicraft [n] *artwork, skill* achievement, art, artifact, artisanship, calling, craft, craftship, creation, design, handiwork, invention, métier, product, production, profession, result, trade, vocation; CONCEPTS 259,630

handle [n1] *something to grip* arm, bail, crank, ear, grasp, haft, handgrip, helve, hilt, hold, holder, knob, shaft, stem, stock, tiller; CONCEPTS 445,502,831

handle [n2] *nickname* appellation, byname, by-word, cognomen, denomination, designation, moniker, name, nomen, sobriquet, style, title; CONCEPT 683

handle [v1] *touch* check, examine, feel, finger*, fondle, grasp, hold, manipulate, maul, palpate, paw*, pick up, poke, test, thumb*, try; CONCEPT 612

handle [v2] *manage, take care of* administer, advise, apply, behave toward, bestow, call the shots*, command, conduct, control, cope with, cut the mustard*, deal with, direct, discuss, dispense, dominate, employ, exercise, exploit, get a handle on*, govern, guide, hack it*, make out*, make the grade*, maneuver, manipulate, operate, play, ply, run things, serve, steer, supervise, swing, take, treat, use, utilize, wield, work; CONCEPTS 91,117 —*Ant.* disregard, mismanage, misuse, neglect

handle [v3] *carry as merchandise* deal in, market, offer, retail, sell, stock, trade, traffic in; CONCEPT 345 —*Ant.* not carry

handling [n] *management* administration, approach, care, charge, conduct, direction, manipulation, running, styling, superintendence, supervision, treatment; CONCEPT 117 —*Ant.* mismanagement

hand-me-down [adj] *secondhand* not new, passed down, previously owned, used; CONCEPTS 575,585

hand out [v] *give to others* bestow, deal out, deliver, devote, disburse, dish out, dispense, disseminate, distribute, donate, give away, give out, hand over, mete, present, provide; CONCEPTS 108,140 —*Ant.* receive, take

hand over [v] *give back; release* abandon, cede, commend, commit, consign, deliver, dispense, donate, entrust, feed, find, fork out*, fork up*, give up, hand, leave, present, provide, relegate, relinquish, supply, surrender, transfer, turn over, waive, yield; CONCEPTS *108,131* —*Ant.* hold, keep, retain

handsome [adj1] *attractive* admirable, aristocratic, athletic, august, beautiful, becoming, clean-cut, comely, dapper, elegant, fair, fashionable, fine, good-looking, graceful, impressive, lovely, majestic, noble, personable, pulchritudinous, robust, sharp, smart, smooth, spruce, stately, strong, stylish, suave, virile, well-dressed, well-proportioned; CONCEPT *579* —*Ant.* homely, ugly, unattractive

handsome [adj2] *abundant* ample, bounteous, bountiful, considerable, extensive, full, generous, gracious, large, lavish, liberal, magnanimous, munificent, openhanded, plentiful, princely, sizable, unsparing; CONCEPT *781* —*Ant.* insignificant, poor, small, stingy, ungiving

handsomely [adv] *abundantly* amply, bountifully, generously, lavishly, liberally, magnanimously, munificently, nobly, plentifully, richly; CONCEPT *781* —*Ant.* insignificantly, poorly

handwriting [n] *the way a person writes* autography, calligraphy, chicken scratch*, chirography, ductus,'griffonage, hand, hieroglyphics, longhand, manuscript, manuscription, mark, pencraft, penscript, scratching*, scrawl, scribble, script, scription, scrivenery, scrivening, style, writing; CONCEPTS *284,625,628*

handy [adj1] *nearby* accessible, adjacent, at hand, available, close, close-at-hand, close by, convenient, near, near-at-hand, on hand, ready, within reach; CONCEPT *586* —*Ant.* faraway, inconveniently, unhandy

handy [adj2] *easy to use* adaptable, advantageous, available, beneficial, central, convenient, functional, gainful, helpful, manageable, neat, practicable, practical, profitable, ready, serviceable, useful, utile, wieldy; CONCEPT *560* —*Ant.* awkward, hard, inconvenient, unhandy, useless

handy [adj3] *adept physically* able, adroit, clever, deft, dexterous, expert, fit, ingenious, nimble, proficient, ready, skilled, skillful; CONCEPT *527* —*Ant.* awkward, bumbling, bungling, clumsy, inept, unhandy

hang [v1] *suspend or be suspended* adhere, attach, beetle, be fastened, be in' mid-air, be loose, bend, be pendent, be poised, bow, cling, cover, dangle, deck, decorate, depend, drape, drift, droop, drop, fasten, fix, flap, float, flop, furnish, hold, hover, impend, incline, lean, loll, lop, lower, nail, overhang, pin, project, remain, rest, sag, stay up, stick, swing, tack, trail, wave; CONCEPTS *144,201,746*

hang [v2] *kill by suspension from a rope* execute, gibbet, hoist, lynch, noose, scrag, send to the gallows, stretch*, string up*, swing*; CONCEPT *252*

hang [v3] *depend on future action* await, be conditional upon, be contingent on, be dependent on, be determined by, be in limbo, be in suspense, cling, hinge, pend, rest, turn on; CONCEPT *681*

hang about/hang around/hang out [v] *associate with; be residing in* abide, affect, dally, frequent, get along with, haunt, have relations with, linger, live, loiter, reside, resort, roam, spend time, stand around, swell, tarry, waste time; CONCEPTS *114,226* —*Ant.* condemn

hangdog [adj] *shamefaced* ashamed, browbeaten, conscience-stricken, cowering, defeated, downcast, guilty, intimidated, sheepish, wretched; CONCEPT *403*

hanger-on [n] *person who attends the powerful for status or benefit* dependent, flunky*, follower, freeloader*, lackey*, leech*, nuisance, parasite, sponger*, sycophant, truckler*; CONCEPT *423*

hang on [v] *continue, endure* be tough, carry on, cling, clutch, go on, grasp, grip, hold fast, hold on, hold out, persevere, persist, remain; CONCEPTS *23,239* —*Ant.* cease, give up, let go, stop

hangout [n] *place for socializing* bar, den*, dive*, haunt*, home, honky-tonk*, joint*, purlieu, resort, stomping ground*, watering hole*; CONCEPTS *439,447,449*

hangover [n] *result of heavy drinking* aftereffect, big head*, delirium tremens, drunkenness, DTs*, headache, morning after*, shakes*, under the weather*, willies*, withdrawal; CONCEPT *316* —*Ant.* sobriety

hang tough [v] *endure* bear, bear the brunt*, be patient with, brave, cope with, face, go through, grin and bear it*, gut it out*, hang in*, hang in there, keep up, live out, live through, meet with, never say die*, put up with, ride out*, sit through, stand, stick in there, stick it out*, stomach*, suffer, swallow*, take, take it*, tough it out*, weather, withstand; CONCEPT *23*

hang-up [n] *preoccupation* block, difficulty, dilemma, disturbance, impasse, inhibition, obsession, predicament, problem, reserve, restraint, thing; CONCEPTS *532,674,690*

hanker after/hanker for [v] *desire strongly* ache, covet, crave, hunger, itch, long, lust, partial to, pine, sigh, thirst, want, wish, yearn, yen; CONCEPT *20* —*Ant.* dislike, hate

hankering [n] *strong desire* ache, craving, druthers*, fire in belly*, hunger, itch*, longing, munchies*, pining, thirst, urge, want, weakness, wish, yearning, yen; CONCEPTS *20,709* —*Ant.* dislike, hate, hatred

hanky-panky [n] *mischief* chicane, chicanery, deception, devilry, double-dealing, fourberie, fraud, funny business*, knavery, machinations, monkey business*, sharp practice*, shenanigans*, skullduggery*, subterfuge, trickery; CONCEPTS *59,384* —*Ant.* faithfulness, honesty

haphazard [adj] *without plan or organization* accidental, aimless, all over the map*, any old way*, any which way*, arbitrary, careless, casual, chance, designless, desultory, devil-may-care*, disorderly, disorganized, erratic, fluke, helter-skelter*, hit-or-miss*, incidental, indiscriminate, irregular, loose, offhand, purposeless, random, reckless, slapdash, slipshod, spontaneous, sudden, unconcerned, unconscious, uncontrolled, uncoordinated, unexpected, unmethodical, unorganized, unpremeditated, unsystematic, unthinking, willy-nilly*; CONCEPTS *535,581* —*Ant.* careful, designed, intentional, methodical, organized, planned, straight, systematic, thought-out

hapless [adj] *unfortunate* behind the eightball*, cursed, hexed, ill-fated, ill-starred, infelicitous, jinxed, jonah*, loser, luckless, miserable, poor fish*, sad sack*, snakebit*, star-crossed*, unhappy, unlucky, untoward, voodooed*, woeful, wretched; CONCEPT 548 —Ant. fortuitous, fortunate, lucky, well-off

happen [v] *come to pass; occur* appear, arise, arrive, become a fact, become known, become of, befall, be found, betide, bump, chance, come about, come after, come into being, come into existence, come off, crop up*, develop, down, ensue, eventuate, fall, follow, go on, hit, issue, light, luck, materialize, meet, pass, present itself, proceed, recur, result, shake, smoke*, spring, stumble, stumble upon, supervene, take effect, take place, transpire, turn out, turn up, what goes*; CONCEPT 4

happening [n] *occurrence* accident, adventure, affair, case, chance, circumstance, episode, event, experience, go*, incident, milestone, occasion, phenomenon, proceeding, scene, thing*; CONCEPT 4 —Ant. method, plan, system

happily [adv1] *with joy, pleasure* agreeably, blissfully, blithely, brightly, buoyantly, cheerfully, contentedly, delightedly, delightfully, devotedly, elatedly, enthusiastically, exhilaratingly, exultantly, freely, gaily, gladly, gleefully, graciously, heartily, hilariously, jovially, joyfully, joyously, laughingly, lightheartedly, lightly, lovingly, merrily, optimistically, peacefully, playfully, sincerely, smilingly, sportively, vivaciously, willingly, with relish, with zeal, zestfully; CONCEPTS 403,542 —Ant. unhappily

happily [adv2] *successfully* appropriately, aptly, auspiciously, favorably, felicitously, fortunately, gracefully, propitiously, prosperously, providentially, satisfyingly, seasonably, swimmingly, well; CONCEPT 548 —Ant. unhappily, unluckily, unsuccessfully

happiness [n] *high spirits, satisfaction* beatitude, blessedness, bliss, cheer, cheerfulness, cheeriness, content, contentment, delectation, delight, delirium, ecstasy, elation, enchantment, enjoyment, euphoria, exhilaration, exuberance, felicity, gaiety, geniality, gladness, glee, good cheer, good humor, good spirits, hilarity, hopefulness, joviality, joy, jubilation, laughter, lightheartedness, merriment, mirth, optimism, paradise, peace of mind, playfulness, pleasure, prosperity, rejoicing, sanctity, seventh heaven*, vivacity, well-being; CONCEPT 410 —Ant. depression, gloom, misery, pain, sadness, sorrow, unhappiness, woe

happy [adj1] *in high spirits; satisfied* blessed, blest, blissful, blithe, can't complain*, captivated, cheerful, chipper, chirpy, content, contented, convivial, delighted, ecstatic, elated, exultant, flying high*, gay, glad, gleeful, gratified, intoxicated, jolly, joyful, joyous, jubilant, laughing, light, lively, looking good*, merry, mirthful, on cloud nine*, overjoyed, peaceful, peppy, perky, playful, pleasant, pleased, sparkling, sunny, thrilled, tickled, tickled pink*, up, upbeat, walking on air*; CONCEPT 403 —Ant. depressed, discouraged, dissatisfied, miserable, morose, pained, sad, sorrowful, unhappy

happy [adj2] *lucky* accidental, advantageous, appropriate, apt, auspicious, befitting, casual, convenient, correct, effective, efficacious, enviable, favorable, felicitous, fitting, fortunate, incidental, just, meet, nice, opportune, promising, proper, propitious, providential, right, satisfactory, seasonable, successful, suitable, timely, well-timed; CONCEPT 558 —Ant. forsaken, hopeless, troubled, unfortunate, unhappy, unlucky

happy-go-lucky [adj] *carefree and untroubled* blithe, casual, cheerful, cool, devil-may-care*, easy, easygoing, feckless, free-minded, heedless, improvident, insouciant, irresponsible, lackadaisical*, lighthearted, nonchalant, reckless, unconcerned; CONCEPTS 404,542 —Ant. disconsolate, discontented, dissatisfied, distressed, troubled, upset, worried

hara-kiri [n] *ritual suicide* belly cutting, ceremonious suicide, disembowelment, self-immolation, seppuku; CONCEPTS 192,252

harangue [n] *long lecture* address, chewing out*, declamation, diatribe, discourse, exhortation, hassle, jeremiad, oration, philippic, reading out*, screed, sermon, speech, spiel*, spouting, tirade; CONCEPTS 51,278

harangue [v] *give a long lecture* accost, address, apostrophize, buttonhole*, chew out*, declaim, exhort, get on a soapbox*, go on about*, hold forth, orate, perorate, rant, rave, soapbox*, spiel*, spout, stump, talk to, yell at; CONCEPT 51

harass [v] *badger* annoy, attack, bait, bedevil, beleaguer, bother, bug*, burn*, despoil, devil*, distress, disturb, eat*, exasperate, exhaust, fatigue, foray, get to*, give a bad time*, give a hard time*, gnaw*, harry, hassle, heckle, hound*, intimidate, irk, irritate, jerk around*, macerate, maraud, noodge*, pain*, perplex, persecute, pester, plague, raid, rattle one's cage*, ride, strain, stress, tease, tire, torment, trouble, try, vex, weary, work on*, worry; CONCEPTS 7,14,19 —Ant. aid, assist, facilitate, help, support

harassment [n] *badgering* aggravation, annoyance, bedevilment, bother, bothering, disturbance, exasperation, hassle, irking, irritation, molestation, nuisance, persecution, perturbation, pestering, provocation, provoking, torment, trouble, vexation, vexing; CONCEPTS 14, 313 —Ant. aid, assistance, facilitation, furtherance, help, support

harbinger [n] *indication* augury, forerunner, foretoken, herald, messenger, omen, portent, precursor, sign, signal; CONCEPTS 74,284,529

harbor [n1] *place for storing boats in the water* anchorage, arm, bay, bight, breakwater, chuck, cove, dock, embankment, firth, gulf, haven, inlet, jetty, landing, mooring, pier, port, road, roadstead, wharf; CONCEPTS 439,509,514

harbor [n2] *place for seclusion* asylum, cover, covert, harborage, haven, port, refuge, retreat, sanctuary, sanctum, security, shelter; CONCEPT 515

harbor [v1] *hide, protect* accommodate, board, bunk, conceal, defend, domicile, entertain, guard, hold back, house, lodge, nurse, nurture, provide refuge, put up, quarter, relieve, safeguard, screen, secrete, secure, shelter, shield, suppress, withhold; CONCEPTS 134,188 —Ant. eject, let out, uncover

harbor [v2] *hold in imagination* believe, brood

over, cherish, cling to, consider, entertain, foster, hold, imagine, maintain, nurse, nurture, regard, retain; CONCEPT *17* —*Ant.* disregard, ignore

hard [*adj1*] *rocklike* adamantine, callous, compact, compacted, compressed, concentrated, consolidated, dense, firm, hardened, impenetrable, indurate, indurated, inflexible, iron*, packed, rigid, rocky, set, solid, stiff, stony, strong, thick, tough, unyielding; CONCEPT *604* —*Ant.* flexible, malleable, pliable, pliant, soft, yielding

hard [*adj2*] *difficult, exhausting* arduous, backbreaking, bothersome, burdensome, complicated, demanding, difficile, distressing, effortful, exacting, fatiguing, formidable, grinding, hairy*, heavy*, Herculean*, intricate, involved, irksome, knotty*, labored, laborious, mean, merciless, murder, onerous, operose, rigorous, rough, rugged, scabrous, serious, severe, slavish, sticky, strenuous, terrible, tiring, toilful, toilsome, tough, troublesome, unsparing, uphill*, uphill battle*, wearing, wearisome, wearying; CONCEPTS *529,538,565* —*Ant.* easy, facile, mild, simple

hard [*adj3*] *cruel, ruthless* acrimonious, angry, antagonistic, austere, bitter, bleak, brutal, callous, cold, cold-blooded*, cold fish*, dark, disagreeable, distressing, dour, exacting, grievous, grim, hard as nails*, hard-boiled*, harsh, hostile, inclement, intemperate, intolerable, obdurate, painful, perverse, pitiless, rancorous, resentful, rigorous, rugged, severe, stern, strict, stringent, stubborn, thick-skinned*, tough, unfeeling, unjust, unkind, unpleasant, unrelenting, unsparing, unsympathetic, vengeful; CONCEPTS *401,542* —*Ant.* merciful, mild, nice, pleasant, sensitive, sympathetic

hard [*adj4*] *true, indisputable* absolute, actual, bare, cold, definite, down-to-earth, genuine, plain, positive, practical, pragmatic, realistic, sure, undeniable, unvarnished, verified; CONCEPTS *535,582* —*Ant.* disputable, doubtful, inexact, questionable, uncertain, untrue

hard [*adv1*] *with great force* actively, angrily, animatedly, boisterously, briskly, brutally, cruelly, earnestly, energetically, ferociously, fiercely, forcibly, frantically, furiously, heavily, intensely, keenly, like fury, madly, meanly, painfully, powerfully, relentlessly, rigorously, roughly, rowdily, savagely, seriously, severely, sharply, spiritedly, sprightly, stormily, strongly, tumultously/tumultuously, turbulently, uproariously, urgently, viciously, vigorously, violently, vivaciously, wildly, with all one's might; CONCEPT *540* —*Ant.* gently, softly

hard [*adv2*] *with determination* assiduously, closely, diligently, doggedly, earnestly, exhaustively, industriously, intensely, intensively, intently, painstakingly, persistently, searchingly, sharply, steadily, strenuously, thoroughly, unremittingly, untiringly; CONCEPT *538* —*Ant.* unenthusiastically

hard [*adv3*] *with difficulty* agonizingly, arduously, awkwardly, badly, burdensomely, carefully, cumbersomely, cumbrously, distressingly, exhaustingly, gruelingly, hardly, harshly, inconveniently, laboriously, painfully, ponderously, roughly, severely, strenuously, tiredly,

toilsomely, unwieldily, vigorously, with great effort; CONCEPT *565* —*Ant.* easily, moderately

hard [*adv4*] *with resentment* bitterly, hardly, keenly, rancorously, reluctantly, slowly, sorely; CONCEPT *403* —*Ant.* indulgently, tolerantly

hard [*adv5*] *in a fixed manner* close, fast, firm, firmly, solidly, steadfastly, tight, tightly; CONCEPTS *488,586* —*Ant.* unfixedly, yielding

hard-boiled [*adj*] *tough* callous, firm, hard as nails*, hard-line*, hard-nosed*, hard-shelled*, headstrong, inflexible, obdurate, obstinate, rough, stern, strict, unbending, unfeeling; CONCEPTS *403,542*

hard-core [*adj*] *dedicated* determined, devoted, die-hard*, dyed-in-the-wool*, explicit, extreme, faithful, intransigent, obstinate, resolute, rigid, staunch, steadfast, stubborn, uncompromising, unwavering, unyielding; CONCEPTS *535,542* —*Ant.* indulgent, mild, moderate, soft-core, tolerant, undedicated

harden [*v1*] *make or become solid* amalgamate, anneal, bake, brace, buttress, cake, calcify, callous, cement, close, clot, coagulate, compact, congeal, consolidate, contract, crystallize, curdle, densify, dry, firm, fix, fortify, fossilize, freeze, gird, indurate, jell, nerve, ossify, petrify, precipitate, press, reinforce, set, settle, solidify, starch, steel, stiffen, strengthen, temper, thicken, toughen, vitrify; CONCEPTS *250,469* —*Ant.* liquefy, melt, soften

harden [*v2*] *accustom* acclimate, acclimatize, adapt, adjust, blunt, brutalize, callous, callus, case-harden, climatize, coarsen, conform, deaden, develop, discipline, dull, embitter, habituate, indurate, inure, make callous, numb, paralyze, render insensitive, roughen, season, steel, stiffen, strengthen, stun, stupefy, teach, train; CONCEPTS *35,235* —*Ant.* be intolerant, indulge, spoil

hardened [*adj*] *unfeeling* accustomed, benumbed, callous, case-hardened, coldhearted*, contemptuous, cruel, disdainful, habituated, hard-as-nails*, hard-bitten*, hard-boiled*, hardhearted*, heartless, impenetrable, impious, inaccessible, indurated, inured, irreverent, obdurate, obtuse, prepared, resistant, seasoned, steeled, toughened, unashamed, unbending, uncaring, uncompassionate, unemotional, unrepenting, unsubmissive; CONCEPTS *404, 542* —*Ant.* compassionate, feeling, kind, nice, sympathetic

hardhearted [*adj*] *cold, cruel* brutish, callous, cold-blooded*, coldhearted*, hard, hard-boiled*, heartless, indifferent, inhuman, insensitive, intolerant, merciless, obdurate, pitiless, stony, uncaring, uncompassionate, unemotional, unfeeling, unkind, unsympathetic; CONCEPTS *401,404* —*Ant.* compassionate, kind, nice, softhearted, warm

hard-line [*adj*] *firm* adamant, hard-boiled*, hard-core, hard-nosed*, inflexible, militant, stand pat*, staunch, steadfast, stern, stiff, strict, unbending, uncompromising, ungiving, unyielding; CONCEPTS *267,403,542*

hardly [*adv*] *scarcely; with difficulty* almost inconceivably, almost not, barely, by a hair, by no means, comparatively, detectably, faintly, gradually, imperceptibly, infrequently, just, little, no more than, not a bit, not at all, not by much, not likely, not markedly, not measurably, not much, not notably, not noticeably, not often, not quite, no way, once in a blue moon*, only, only just, perceptibly, practically, pretty near, rarely, scantly, seldom, simply, slightly, somewhat, sparsely, sporadically, with trouble; CONCEPTS 541,552,771 —*Ant.* very

hard-nosed/hardheaded [*adj*] stubborn · astute, bullheaded*, hard*, hard-boiled*, headstrong, intractable, levelheaded, locked in*, mulish, obstinate, pertinacious, perverse, pigheaded*, practical, pragmatic, rational, realistic, resolute, sensible, shrewd, sober, stand pat, tough, tough-nut*, unsentimental, unyielding, willful; CONCEPTS 404,542 —*Ant.* easy, easygoing, laid-back, merciful

hardship [*n*] personal burden accident, adversity, affliction, asperity, austerity, calamity, case, catastrophe, curse, danger, destitution, difficulty, disaster, discomfort, distress, drudgery, fatigue, grief, grievance, hard knocks*, hazard, Herculean task*, injury, labor, mischance, misery, misfortune, need, oppression, peril, persecution, privation, rainy day*, rigor, rotten luck*, sorrow, suffering, toil, torment, tough break*, tough luck*, travail, trial, tribulation, trouble, uphill battle*, vicissitude, want, worry; CONCEPT 674 —*Ant.* advantage, assistance, benefit, blessing, ease, favor, gain, good, profit

hardware [*n*] tools; fittings, especially made of metal accoutrements, appliances, fasteners, fixtures, household furnishings, housewares, implements, ironware, kitchenware, metalware, plumbing, utensils; CONCEPTS 338,499

hardy [*adj*] strong, tough able, able-bodied, acclimatized, brawny, burly, capable, enduring, firm, fit, fresh, hale, hardened, healthy, hearty, hefty, indefatigable, in fine fettle*, in good condition, in good shape, inured, lusty, mighty, muscular, physically fit, powerful, resistant, robust, rugged, seasoned, solid, sound, stalwart, staunch, stout, sturdy, substantial, tenacious, unflagging, vigorous, well; CONCEPTS 314,485, 489 —*Ant.* feeble, infirm, invalid, sick, tender, unhealthy, weak

harebrained [*adj*] stupid, unthinking absurd, asinine, barmy, bizarre, careless, changeable, crazy, dizzy*, empty-headed*, featherbrained*, flighty, foolish, frivolous, giddy, half-baked*, heedless, inane, irresponsible, loony*, mindless, preposterous, rash, rattlebrained, reckless, scatterbrained*, unstable, unsteady, wacky*, wild; CONCEPTS 402,529 —*Ant.* brainy, intelligent, reasonable, sensible, smart, thoughtful

harlot [*n*] prostitute call girl, concubine, courtesan, fallen woman*, floozy*, hooker, hussy, lady of the evening, loose woman, nymphomaniac*, painted woman, slut, streetwalker, strumpet, tramp, whore; CONCEPTS 348,412,415,419

harm [*n*] injury, evil abuse, banefulness, damage, deleteriousness, detriment, disservice, foul play*, hurt, ill, immorality, impairment, infliction, iniquity, loss, marring, mischance, mischief, misfortune, misuse, noxiousness, outrage, perniciousness, prejudice, ravage, ruin, ruination, sabotage, sin, sinfulness, vandalism, vice, violence, wear and tear*, wickedness, wrong; CONCEPTS 309,674,728 —*Ant.* advantage, benefit, blessing, good, pleasure

harm [*v*] injure; cause evil abuse, blemish, bruise, cripple, crush, damage, dilapidate, discommode, disserve, do violence to, dump on*, get, hurt, ill-treat, impair, incommode, inconvenience, louse up*, maim, maltreat, mangle, mar, mess up*, misuse, molest, muck up*, mutilate, nick, outrage, prejudice, put down, ruin, sabotage, sap*, scathe, shatter, shock, spoil, stab, tarnish, total, trample, traumatize, tweak*, undermine, vandalize, vitiate, wing*, wound, wreck, wrench, wrong, zing*; CONCEPTS 7,19,246,313 —*Ant.* aid, assist, benefit, care, fix, help, improve, mend

harmful [*adj*] injurious, hurtful adverse, bad, baleful, baneful, calamitous, cataclysmic, catastrophic, consumptive, corroding, corrupting, crippling, damaging, deleterious, destructive, detrimental, dire, disadvantageous, disastrous, evil, harassing, incendiary, inimical, internecine, malefic, malicious, malignant, menacing, mischievous, murderous, nocuous, noxious, painful, pernicious, pestiferous, pestilential, risky, ruinous, sinful, sinister, subversive, toxic, undermining, unhealthy, unsafe, unwholesome, virulent; CONCEPT 537 —*Ant.* aiding, assisting, helpful, nice, unharmful

harmless [*adj*] not injurious or dangerous controllable, disarmed, gentle, guiltless, hurtless, innocent, innocuous, innoxious, inoffensive, inoperative, kind, manageable, naive, nonirritating, nontoxic, painless, paper-tiger*, powerless, pussycat*, reliable, safe, sanitary, simple, soft*, softie*, sound, sure, trustworthy, unobjectionable, unoffensive; CONCEPT 537 —*Ant.* bad, destructive, evil, harmful, hurtful, injurious, sinful, wicked

harmonious [*adj*] agreeable, corresponding; friendly accordant, adapted, amicable, balanced, compatible, concordant, congenial, congruous, consonant, coordinated, cordial, dulcet, euphonious, harmonic, harmonizing, in accord, in chorus, in concert, in harmony, in step, in tune, in unison, like, matching, mellifluous, melodic, melodious, mix, musical, of one mind*, on same wavelength*, peaceful, rhythmical, silvery, similar, simpatico, sonorous, suitable, sweet-sounding, symmetrical, sympathetic, symphonic, symphonious, tuneful; CONCEPT 563 —*Ant.* cacophonous, disagreeable, discordant, dissonant, harsh, inharmonious, opposed, unfriendly, unlike

harmonize [*v*] correspond, match accord, adapt, adjust, agree, arrange, attune, be in unison, be of one mind*, blend, carol, chime with, cohere, combine, compose, cooperate, coordinate, correlate, fit in with*, integrate, orchestrate, proportion, reconcile, reconciliate, relate, set, sing, suit, symphonize, synthesize, tune, unify, unite; CONCEPTS 77,664 —*Ant.* clash, disagree, fight

harmony [*n*] social agreement accord, affinity, amicability, amity, compatibility, concord, conformity, consensus, consistency, cooperation, correspondence, empathy, friendship, good will, kinship, like-mindedness, meeting of minds*, peace, rapport, sympathy, tranquility, unanimity, understanding, unity; CONCEPT 388 —*Ant.* clash, disagreement, discord, fighting

harmony [n2] *correspondence, balance* accord, agreement, articulation, chime, concord, concordance, conformance, conformity, congruity, consistency, consonance, fitness, form, integration, integrity, oneness, order, parallelism, proportion, regularity, suitability, symmetry, togetherness, tune, unity; CONCEPT 664 —*Ant.* disproportion, imbalance

harmony [n3] *musical accordance* arrangement, attunement, blend, blending, chime, chord, chorus, composition, concentus, concert, concinnity, concurrence, consonance, diapason, euphony, harmonics, mellifluousness, melodiousness, melody, organum, overtone, piece, polyphony, richness, symphony, triad, tune, tunefulness, unison, unity; CONCEPTS 65,262, 595 —*Ant.* cacophony, discord, jangling

harness [n] *gear for controlling an animal* belt, equipment, strap, tack, tackle, trappings; CONCEPT 496

harness [v] *rein in; control* accouter, apply, bind, bridle, channel, check, cinch, collar, constrain, couple, curb, domesticate, employ, equip, exploit, fasten, fetter, fit, furnish, gear, govern, hitch, hold, leash, limit, make productive, mobilize, muzzle, outfit, put in harness, render useful, rig, saddle, secure, strap, tackle, tame, tie, utilize, yoke; CONCEPTS 94,130,191 —*Ant.* release, unharness

harried [adj] *pressured* agitated, anxious, at wit's end*, beset, bothered, distressed, harassed, hard-pressed, stressed, troubled, worried; CONCEPTS 403,690

harrowing [adj] *dangerous, frightening* agonizing, alarming, chilling, distressing, disturbing, excruciating, heartbreaking, heart-rending, nerve-racking, painful, racking, soaring, tearing, terrifying, tormenting, torturing, torturous, traumatic; CONCEPTS 529,548 —*Ant.* calming, pleasant, pleasing, unfrightening

harry [v] *pester, annoy* attack, badger, bedevil, beleaguer, chivy, depredate, devastate, disturb, fret, gnaw, harass, hassle, irk, irritate, lay waste, molest, persecute, perturb, pillage, plague, plunder, ravage, sack, tease, torment, trouble, upset, vex, worry; CONCEPTS 7,19 —*Ant.* aid, assist, help, support

harsh [adj1] *rough, crude (to the senses)* acrid, asperous, astringent, bitter, bleak, cacophonous, caterwauling, clashing, coarse, cracked, craggy, creaking, croaking, disagreeing, discordant, dissonant, disturbing, earsplitting, flat, glaring, grating, grim, guttural, hard, hoarse, incompatible, jagged, jangling, jarring, noisy, not smooth, off-key*, out-of-key*, out-of-tune*, rasping, raucous, rigid, rugged, rusty, screeching, severe, sharp, sour, strident, stridulous, tuneless, uneven, unlevel, unmelodious, unmusical, unrelenting; CONCEPTS 537,569 —*Ant.* easy, gentle, mild, peaceful, pleasing, smooth, soft

harsh [adj2] *nasty, abusive* austere, bitter, brutal, comfortless, cruel, cussed, discourteous, dour, grim, gruff, hairy*, hard, hard-boiled, hard-nosed*, hard-shell*, mean, pitiless, punitive, relentless, rude, ruthless, severe, sharp, stern, stringent, tough, uncivil, unfeeling, ungracious, unkind, unpleasant, unrelenting, wicked; CONCEPTS 267,542 —*Ant.* courteous, kind, nice, polite

harum-scarum [adj] *reckless* carefree, careless, daring, disorderly, erratic, flighty, foolhardy, giddy, haphazard, hasty, imprudent, irresponsible, light-minded, negligent, rash, regardless, romping, scatty, thoughtless, wild; CONCEPTS 401,542

harvest [n] *crops; taking in of crops* autumn, by-product, consequence, cropping, effect, fall, fruitage, fruition, garnering, gathering, harvesting, harvest-time, ingathering, intake, output, produce, reaping, repercussion, result, return, season, storing, summer, yield, yielding; CONCEPTS 257,338,429

harvest [v] *gathering of produce* accumulate, acquire, amass, bin, cache, collect, crop, cull, cut, garner, gather, get, glean, harrow, hoard, mow, pick, pile up, plow, pluck, reap, squirrel*, stash, store, stow, strip, take in; CONCEPTS 142, 257 —*Ant.* plant, seed

hash [n] *mess, mix-up* assortment, clutter, confusion, hodgepodge*, hotchpotch*, jumble, litter, medley, mélange, miscellany, mishmash*, muddle*, salmagundi*, shambles*, stew*; CONCEPTS 260,432

hashish [n] *cannabis resin* black hash*, black oil*, cannabis, dope, drug, ganja*, grass*, hash, hemp, marijuana, narcotic, pot*; CONCEPT 307

hassle [n] *problem, fight* altercation, argument, bickering, bother, clamor, commotion, difficulty, disagreement, dispute, inconvenience, quarrel, row, run-in*, squabble, struggle, trial, trouble, try, tumult, turmoil, tussle, uproar, upset, whirl, wrangle; CONCEPTS 46,106,674 —*Ant.* agreement, peace

hassle [v] *bother, harass* annoy, argue, argufy, badger, bedevil, beleaguer, bicker, dispute, dun, harry, hound, pester, plague, quibble, squabble, worry, wrangle; CONCEPTS 14,16,46 —*Ant.* agree, concur, make peace

haste [n] *extreme speed, hurry* alacrity, briskness, bustle, carelessness, celerity, dash, dispatch, drive, expedition, expeditiousness, fleetness, flurry, foolhardiness, hastiness, heedlessness, hurly-burly*, hurriedness, hustle, hustling, impatience, impetuosity, incautiousness, nimbleness, pace, precipitancy, precipitateness, prematureness, press, promptitude, promptness, quickness, rapidity, rapidness, rashness, recklessness, rush, scamper, scramble, scurry, scuttle, swiftness, urgency, velocity; CONCEPTS 755,818 —*Ant.* delay, leisure, lingering, rest, slowness

hasten [v] *speed something; hurry* accelerate, advance, bolt, bound, burn, bustle, clip*, cover ground*, dash, dispatch, expedite, express, flee, fly, gallop, get cracking*, get the lead out*, goad, haste, hie, hustle, leap, make haste, make tracks*, move quickly, not lose a minute*, pace, plunge, precipitate, press, push, quicken, race, run, rush, scamper, scoot, scurry, scuttle, shake a leg*, skip, sprint, spurt, step on it*, step up*, take wing*, tear, trot, urge, waste no time*, whip around*; CONCEPTS 150,152 —*Ant.* go slow, lag, linger, loiter, procrastinate, rest, tarry

hastily [adv] *with great speed* agilely, apace, carelessly, double-quick, expeditiously, fast, flat-out*, heedlessly, hurriedly, impetuously, impulsively, lickety-split*, nimbly, on spur of the moment*, posthaste, precipitately, prematurely, promptly, quickly, rapidly, rashly, recklessly, speedily, straightaway, subito, suddenly, swiftly, thoughtlessly, too quickly, unpremeditatedly; CONCEPTS *544,588* —Ant. delayed, slowly

hasty [adj] *speedy; without much thought* abrupt, agile, brash, breakneck*, brief, brisk, careless, chop-chop*, cursory, eager, expeditious, fast, fiery, fleet, fleeting, foolhardy, harefooted*, headlong, heedless, hurried, ill-advised, impatient, impetuous, impulsive, incautious, inconsiderate, madcap*, on the double*, passing, PDQ*, perfunctory, precipitate, prompt, pronto*, quick, quickened, quickie, rapid, rash, reckless, rushed, short, slambang*, slapdash*, snappy*, sudden, superficial, swift, thoughtless, urgent; CONCEPTS *542,588,799* —Ant. delayed, lazy, lingering, loitering, slow

hat [n] *covering for the head* boater, bonnet, bowler, bucket, chapeau, fedora, headgear, headpiece, helmet, lid*, millinery, Panama, sailor*, skimmer, sombrero, Stetson, stove pipe*, straw*, tam, tam o'shanter*, ten-gallon*, topper*; CONCEPT *451*

hatch [v] *create, plan* bear, brainstorm*, breed, bring forth, brood, cause, come up with, conceive, concoct, contrive, cook up*, design, devise, dream up*, engender, formulate, generate, get up, give birth, incubate, induce, invent, lay eggs, make, make up, occasion, originate, parent, plot, prepare, procreate, produce, project, provoke, scheme, set, sire, spawn, spitball*, think up*, throw together*, trump up*, whip up*, work up*; CONCEPTS *36,173,251*

hate [n] *extreme dislike* abhorrence, abomination, anathema, animosity, animus, antagonism, antipathy, aversion, bête noire*, black beast*, bother, bugbear*, detestation, disgust, enmity, execration, frost*, grievance, gripe, hatred, horror, hostility, ill will, irritant, loathing, malevolence, malignity, mislike, nasty look, no love lost*, nuisance, objection, odium, pain, rancor, rankling, repugnance, repulsion, resentment, revenge, revulsion, scorn, spite, trouble, venom; CONCEPT *29* —Ant. liking, love, loving

hate [v] *dislike very strongly* abhor, abominate, allergic to*, anathematize, bear a grudge against, be disgusted with, be hostile to, be loath, be reluctant, be repelled by, be sick of, be sorry, can't stand*, contemn, curse, deprecate, deride, despise, detest, disapprove, disdain, disfavor, disparage, down on*, execrate, feel malice to, have an aversion to*, have enough of*, have no use for*, loathe, look down on, nauseate*, not care for*, object to, recoil from, scorn, shudder at, shun, spit upon*, spurn; CONCEPT *29* —Ant. like, love

hateful [adj] *nasty, obnoxious* abhorrent, abominable, accursed, awful, bitter, blasted, catty*, confounded, cursed, cussed, damnable, damned, despicable, despiteful, detestable, disgusting, evil, execrable, forbidding, foul, gross, heinous, horrid, infamous, invidious, loathsome, malevolent, malign, mean, odious, offensive, ornery*, pesky, pestiferous, repellent, repugnant, repulsive, resentful, revolting, shuddersome, spiteful, uncool*, undesirable, vicious, vile; CONCEPTS *267,404* —Ant.

friendly, kind, likable, lovable, nice, pleasant, polite

hatred [n] *severe dislike* abhorrence, abomination, acrimony, alienation, allergy to*, animosity, animus, antagonism, antipathy, aversion, bitterness, coldness, contempt, detestation, disapproval, disfavor, disgust, displeasure, distaste, enmity, envy, execration, grudge, hard feelings*, hate, horror, hostility, ignominy, ill will, invidiousness, loathing, malevolence, malice, malignance, militancy, no use for*, odium, pique, prejudice, rancor, repugnance, repulsion, revenge, revulsion, scorn, spite, spleen, venom; CONCEPT *29* —Ant. like, liking, love, loving

haughtiness [n] *air of supremacy* aloofness, arrogance, conceit, contempt, contemptuousness, disdain, disdainfulness, hauteur, insolence, loftiness, pomposity, pride, snobbishness, superbity, superciliousness; CONCEPT *633* —Ant. humility, meekness

haughty [adj] *arrogant* assuming, cavalier*, conceited, contemptuous, detached, disdainful, distant, egotistic, egotistical, high, high and mighty*, hoity-toity*, imperious, indifferent, lofty, on high horse*, overbearing, overweening, proud, reserved, scornful, sniffy*, snobbish, snooty*, snotty*, stuck-up*, supercilious, superior, uppity*; CONCEPT *401* —Ant. humble, meek, shy, timid

haul [n] *something obtained or moved* booty, burden, cargo, catch, find, freight, gain, harvest, lading, load, loot*, payload*, spoils, takings*, yield; CONCEPTS *337,338*

haul [v] *move, pull to another spot* back, boost, bring, buck, carry, cart, convey, drag, draw, elevate, gun, heave, heel, hoist, hump, jag, lift, lug, pack, piggy back*, raise, rake, remove, ride, shift, schlepp*, shoulder, tote, tow, trail, transport, trawl, truck, tug; CONCEPTS *147,148*

haunt [n] *place for socializing* abode, bar, clubhouse, cubbyhole*, den, dwelling, gathering place, habitat, hangout*, headquarters, home, lair, living quarters, locality, meeting place, niche, place, purlieu, range, rendezvous, resort, retreat, site, stomping ground*, trysting place, watering hole*; CONCEPTS *435,516*

haunt [v1] *visit as a spirit* agitate, agonize, annoy, appall, appear, bedevil, be ever present, beset, besiege, come back, disquiet, dwell, float, frighten, harass, harrow, hound*, hover, infest, inhabit, intrude, madden, manifest, materialize, molest, nettle, obsess, overrun, permeate, pervade, pester, plague, possess, prey on, rack*, reappear, recur, return, rise, spook*, stay with, tease, terrify, terrorize, torment, trouble, vex, voodoo*, walk, weigh on, worry; CONCEPT *14*

haunt [v2] *spend a lot of time at affect,* frequent, habituate, hang about*, hang around*, hang out*, infest, repair, resort, tarry at, visit; CONCEPT *384*

haunting [adj] *unforgettable* eerie, memorable, nagging, nostalgic, obsessive, ongoing, persistent, recurrent, repeated, spooky; CONCEPTS *529,537*

hauteur [n] *arrogance* airs, audacity, conceit, conceitedness, condescension, contempt, disdain, disdainfulness, egotism, gall, haughtiness, high-handedness, nerve, pomposity, pompousness, presumption, pride, self-importance, snobbishness, vanity; CONCEPTS 411,633

have [v1] *be in possession* accept, acquire, admit, annex, bear, carry, chalk up, compass, corner, enjoy, gain, get, get hands on*, get hold of*, have in hand, hog*, hold, include, keep, land, latch on to*, lock up*, obtain, occupy, own, pick up, possess, procure, receive, retain, secure, sit on*, take, take in, teem with; CONCEPTS 124,142,710 —*Ant.* lack, need, want

have [v2] *endure, bear* allow, become, be compelled to, be forced to, be one's duty to, be up to, consider, enjoy, entertain*, experience, fall on, feel, know, leave, let, meet with, must, need, ought, permit, put up with*, rest with, see, should, suffer, sustain, think about, tolerate, undergo; CONCEPTS 23,83,646

have [v3] *contain* comprehend, comprise, embody, embrace, encompass, include, involve, subsume, take in; CONCEPTS 642,742 —*Ant.* exclude

have [v4] *cheat, trick* buy off*, deceive, dupe*, fix*, fool, outfox, outmaneuver, outsmart, outwit, overreach, swindle, take in*, tamper with, undo*; CONCEPTS 59,192

have [v5] *bring into the world* bear, beget, bring forth, deliver, give birth; CONCEPT 374 —*Ant.* kill

have a ball [v] *have fun* beat the drum*, cut loose, enjoy, feast, get down*, get it on*, go to town*, jubilate, kick up one's heels*, let loose*, let off steam*, live it up*, make merry, paint the town red*, party, raise hell*, raise the roof*, rejoice, revel, revere; CONCEPT 377

haven [n] *refuge, port* anchorage, asylum, cover, covert, harbor, harborage, retreat, roadstead, sanctuary, sanctum, shelter; CONCEPTS 435,515

have someone's number [v] *know someone's motives* be onto someone, be wise to someone*, have someone pegged*, have someone sized up*, know what makes someone tick*, read someone; CONCEPTS 15,18,37

havoc [n] *chaotic situation* calamity, cataclysm, catastrophe, chaos, confusion, damage, desolation, despoiling, destruction, devastation, dilapidation, disorder, disruption, loss, mayhem, plunder, rack and ruin*, ravages, ruination, shambles*, vandalism, waste, wreck, wreckage; CONCEPT 674 —*Ant.* peace

hawker [n] *peddler* colporteur, costermonger, huckster, pitchperson, salesperson, seller, street seller, street vendor; CONCEPTS 347,348

hayseed [n] *bumpkin, yokel* · backwoodsman/woman, boor*, clodhopper*, country boy/girl, country bumpkin, country cousin*, hick*, hillbilly, rustic; CONCEPT 413

haywire [adj] *broken; crazy* amiss, amok, batty, berserk, bonkers*, chaotic, confused, cracked, crazed, defective, disordered, disorganized, erratic, flipped, in a mess*, in pieces, insane, mad, messy, nuts, orderless, out of order, out of whack*, out to lunch*, psycho*, schizo*, screwball*, screwy*, touched*, unbalanced, unglued*, unhinged, wacky; CONCEPTS 403,485

hazard [n1] *danger* double trouble*, dynamite, endangerment, hot potato*, imperilment, jeopardy, peril, risk, risky business*, thin

ice*, threat; CONCEPT 675 —*Ant.* protection, safeguard, safety

hazard [n2] *luck, chance* accident, adventure, coincidence, dynamite, fling*, fluke*, go*, hundred-to-one*, long shot, lucky break*, lucky hit*, misfortune, mishap, possibility, risk, risky business*, stroke of luck*, toss-up, venture, wager, way the ball bounces*, way the cookie crumbles*; CONCEPT 693 —*Ant.* assurance, certainty, determination, fact, proof, reality, surety

hazard [v] *take a chance; risk* adventure, conjecture, dare, endanger, gamble, go for broke*, go out on limb*, guess, imperil, jeopardize, presume, proffer, skate on thin ice*, speculate, stake, submit, suppose, take a plunge*, throw out, try, venture, volunteer, wager; CONCEPTS 28,87

hazardous [adj] *dangerous, unpredictable* chancy, dicey*, difficult, hairy*, haphazard, hot*, insecure, parlous, perilous, precarious, risky, touchy, uncertain, unhealthy, unsafe, unsound, venturesome, wicked; CONCEPT 548 —*Ant.* certain, guarded, predictable, protected, safe, secure

haze [n] *cloudy air* brume, cloud, dimness, film, fog, fumes, ground clouds, haziness, indistinctness, miasma, mist, murk, obscurity, smog, smokiness, smother, soup*, steam, vapor; CONCEPT 524 —*Ant.* clarity, clearness

hazy [adj1] *cloudy* bleared, bleary, blurred, blurry, clouded, crepuscular, dim, dull, dusky, faint, foggy, frosty, fuliginous, fumy, fuzzy, gauzy, indefinite, indistinct, misty, murky, mushy*, nebulous, obfuscated, obfuscous, obscure, opaque, overcast, rimy, screened, shadowy, smoggy, smoky, soupy*, steaming, thick, unclear, vague, vaporous, veiled; CONCEPT 525 —*Ant.* clear, sunny, uncloudy, unhazy

hazy [adj2] *confused* dazed, dizzy, dreamy, groggy, ill-defined, indefinite, indistinct, muddled, murky, nebulous, obscure, stuporous, tranced, uncertain, unclear, unintelligible, unsound, vague, whirling; CONCEPTS 402,529 —*Ant.* certain, definite, distinct, explained, sure, unconfused

head [adj] *most important; chief* arch, champion, first, foremost, front, highest, leading, main, pioneer, preeminent, premier, prime, principal, stellar, supreme, topmost; CONCEPTS 568,574 —*Ant.* auxiliary, inferior, lower, second, secondary, trivial, unimportant

head [n1] *top part of an animate body* attic*, belfry*, brain, coconut*, cranium, crown, dome*, gray matter, noggin*, noodle*, pate, scalp, skull, thinker*, think tank*, top story*, upper story*, upstairs*; CONCEPT 392 —*Ant.* foot

head [n2] *leader* boss, captain, chief, chieftain, commander, commanding officer, director, dominator, executive, honcho*, lead-off person*, manager, officer, president, principal, superintendent, supervisor, top dog*; CONCEPT 347 —*Ant.* follower

head [n3] *top part* apex, banner, beak, bill, cap, cork, crest, crown, heading, headline, height, peak, pitch, point, promontory, streamer, summit, tip, vertex; CONCEPT 836 —*Ant.* bottom, end, rear

ha
he

head [n4] *front, beginning* commencement, first place, fore, forefront, fountainhead, origin, rise, source, start, van, vanguard; CONCEPTS 648,727 —*Ant.* conclusion, end, ending, finish

head [n5] *ability, intelligence* aptitude, aptness, bent, brains, capacity, faculty, flair, genius, gift, intellect, knack, mentality, mind, talent, thought, turn, understanding; CONCEPTS 409,630 —*Ant.* ignorance, inability, stupidity

head [n6] *turning point* acme, climax, conclusion, crisis, culmination, end; CONCEPT 832

head [v] *manage, oversee* address, be first, be in charge, command, control, direct, dominate, go first, govern, guide, hold sway over*, lead, lead the way*, pioneer, precede, rule, run, supervise; CONCEPT 117 —*Ant.* follow, obey

headache [n1] *difficulty, problem* annoyance, bane, bother, dilemma, frustration, hassle, hindrance, inconvenience, nuisance, pain in the neck*, pest, predicament, quagmire, trouble, vexation, worry; CONCEPTS 674,677

headache [n2] *migraine* cephalalgia, megrim, pounding head, splitting headache, throbbing head; CONCEPTS 316,728

headhunting [n] *recruiting* executive recruiting, executive recruitment, recruitment, talent search; CONCEPT 351

heading [n1] *title* caption, description, descriptor, headline, label, legend, lemma, rubric; CONCEPT 283

heading [n2] *course* aim, angle, bearing, compass reading, direction, line, point, point of compass, route, track, trajectory, way; CONCEPTS 501,514

headlong [adj] *dangerous, reckless* abrupt, brash, breakneck, daredevil, daring, foolhardy, hasty, hurried, impetuous, impulsive, inconsiderate, precipitant, precipitate, rash, rough, rushing, sudden, tempestuous, thoughtless; CONCEPTS 542,588 —*Ant.* careful, cautious, thoughtfully, wary

headquarters [n] *center of operations* base, base of operations, central station, command post, company headquarters, high command, HQ, main office, nerve center; CONCEPTS 312,439,441,448,449

headstrong [adj] *stubborn* bullheaded*, contrary, determined, foolhardy, froward, hard-core*, hard-nosed, hard-shell*, heedless, imprudent, impulsive, intractable, locked-in*, mule, mulish, murder, obstinate, perverse, pigheaded*, rash, reckless, refractory, self-willed, strong-minded, uncontrollable, ungovernable, unruly, unyielding, willful; CONCEPTS 401,403 —*Ant.* calm, docile, moderate, obedient, submissive, tolerant

headway [n] *progress* advance, advancement, anabasis, ground, improvement, increase, march, proficiency, progression, promotion, way; CONCEPTS 230,704 —*Ant.* block, hindrance, stoppage

heady [adj] *thrilling, intoxicating* exciting, exhilarating, inebriating, overwhelming, potent, powerful, provocative, spirituous, stimulating, strong; CONCEPT 529 —*Ant.* dull, unenthused, unexcited

heal [v] *cure, recover* alleviate, ameliorate, attend, bring around, compose, conciliate, convalesce, doctor, dress, fix, free, get well,

harmonize, improve, knit, make healthy, make sound, make well, make whole, medicate, meliorate, mend, minister to, patch up, physic, put on feet again*, reanimate, rebuild, reconcile, regenerate, rehabilitate, rejuvenate, remedy, renew, renovate, repair, restore, resuscitate, revive, revivify, salve, set, settle, soothe, treat; CONCEPTS 308,310 —*Ant.* harm, hurt, injure

healer [n] *faith healer* curer, doctor, medicine man, mender, physician, shaman, therapist; CONCEPT 357

health [n] *physical, mental wellness* bloom*, clean bill*, complexion, constitution, energy, eupepsia, euphoria, fettle, fine feather*, fitness, form, good condition, haleness, hardihood, hardiness, healthfulness, healthiness, lustiness, pink*, prime*, robustness, salubriousness, salubrity, shape, soundness, stamina, state, strength, tone, tonicity, top form, verdure, vigor, well-being, wholeness; CONCEPTS 316,410,720 —*Ant.* disease, illness, infirmity, sickness

healthful/healthy [adj1] *good for one's wellness* advantageous, aiding, aseptic, beneficial, benign, body-building, bracing, cathartic, clean, compensatory, conducive, corrective, desirable, disease-free, energy-giving, fresh, harmless, healing, health-giving, helpful, hygienic, innocuous, invigorating, mitigative, nourishing, nutritious, nutritive, profitable, pure, restorative, salubrious, salutary, sanatory, sanitary, stimulating, sustaining, tonic, unadulterated, unpolluted, untainted, useful, wholesome; CONCEPT 537 —*Ant.* bad, corrupt, diseased, noxious, rotten, sickening, unhealthful, unhealthy

healthy [adj2] *in good condition* able-bodied, active, all right, athletic, blooming, bright-eyed*, bushy-tailed*, chipper*, firm, fit, flourishing, fresh, full of life*, hale, hardy, healthful, hearty, husky, in fine feather*, in fine fettle*, in good shape, in the pink*, lively, lusty, muscular, normal, physically fit, potent, restored, robust, rosy-cheeked*, safe and sound*, sound, stout, strong, sturdy, tough, trim, unimpaired, vigorous, virile, well, whole; CONCEPTS 314, 403 —*Ant.* delicated, diseased, fragile, ill, indisposed, infirm, poor, sick, sickly, unhealthy, worn

heap [n] *pile, accumulation* abundance, agglomeration, aggregation, a lot*, amassment, assemblage, bank, batch, bulk, bunch, bundle, cargo, clump, cluster, collection, concentration, congeries, deposit, fullness, gathering, gobs*, great deal, harvest, haul, hill, hoard, jumble, load, lot, lots, lump, mass, million, mint, mound, mountain, much, ocean, oodles*, plenty, pot, profusion, quantity, scad*, stack, stock, stockpile, store, sum, thousand, ton, total, trillion, volume, whole; CONCEPTS 432, 787 —*Ant.* bit

heap [v] *amass, collect in pile* accumulate, add, arrange, augment, bank, bunch, concentrate, deposit, dump, fill, fill up, gather, group, hoard, increase, load, lump, mass, mound, pack, stack, stockpile, store, swell; CONCEPT 109

hear [v1] *detect by perceiving sound* apprehend, attend, auscultate, be all ears*, become aware, catch, descry, devour, eavesdrop, get*, get an earful*, get wind of*, give an audience to*, give attention, give ears*, hark, hearken, heed, listen, make out*, overhear, pick up*, read, strain, take in*; CONCEPTS 590,596

hear [v2] *become aware of information* apperceive, ascertain, be advised, be informed, be led to believe, be told of, catch, catch on, descry, determine, discover, find out, gather, get the picture*, get wind of*, get wise to*, glean, have on good authority*, learn, pick up*, receive, see, tumble*, understand, unearth; CONCEPTS 15,31 —*Ant.* ignore

hearing [n1] *ability to perceive sound* audition, auditory, auditory range, detecting, distinguishing, ear, earshot, effect, extent, faculty, hearing distance, listening, perception, range, reach, recording, sense; CONCEPT 597

hearing [n2] *opportunity to present views, knowledge, or skill* admittance, attendance, attention, audience, audit, audition, chance, conference, congress, consultation, council, discussion, inquiry, interview, investigation, meeting, negotiation, notice, parley, performance, presentation, reception, review, test, trial, tryout; CONCEPTS 48,103,317,693

hearsay [n] *unsubstantiated information* clothesline*, comment, cry, gossip, grapevine*, leak*, mere talk*, noise*, report, rumble*, rumor, scandal, scuttlebutt*, talk, talk of the town*, word of mouth*; CONCEPTS 51,278 —*Ant.* evidence, proof, reality, testimony, truth

heart [n1] *person's emotions* affection, benevolence, character, compassion, concern, disposition, feeling, gusto, humanity, inclination, love, nature, palate, pity, relish, response, sensitivity, sentiment, soul, sympathy, temperament, tenderness, understanding, zest; CONCEPT 410 —*Ant.* head

heart [n2] *courage* boldness, bravery, dauntlessness, fortitude, gallantry, guts*, mettle, mind, moxie*, nerve, pluck, purpose, resolution, soul, spirit, spunk*, will; CONCEPT 411 —*Ant.* cowardice, fear

heart [n3] *essence, central part* basic, bosom, bottom line*, center, coal and ice*, core, crux, focal point, focus, gist, hub, kernel, marrow, middle, nitty-gritty*, nub, nucleus, pith, polestar*, quick*, quintessence, root, seat, soul; CONCEPT 826 —*Ant.* exterior, exteriority, outside, periphery, surface

heart [n4] *blood-pumping organ in an animate being* cardiac organ, clock*, ticker*, vascular organ; CONCEPTS 393,420

heartache [n] *anguish, sorrow* affliction, agony, bitterness, broken heart, dejection, depression, despair, despondency, distress, dolor, grief, heartbreak, heavy heart, hurting, misery, pang, remorse, sadness, suffering, torment, torture; CONCEPT 410

heart attack [n] *acute myocardial infarction* angina pectoris, cardiac arrest, cardiovascular disease, coronary, coronary thrombosis; CONCEPT 308

heartbreak [n] *mental or emotional misery* affliction, agony, anguish, bale, bitterness, broken heart, care, desolation, despair, distress, grief, heartache, heartsickness, heavy heart*, pain, regret, remorse, rue, sorrow, suffering, torment, torture, woe; CONCEPTS 410,728 —*Ant.* happiness, joy, love

heartbreaking [adj] *disappointing* affecting, afflictive, agonizing, bitter, calamitous, cheerless, deplorable, dire, distressing, grievous, heart-rending, joyless, lamentable, moving, pitiful, poignant, regrettable, sad, touching, tragic, unfortunate; CONCEPTS 529,537 —*Ant.* exhilarating, heartwarming, joyous, wonderful

hearten [v] *raise someone's spirits* animate, arouse, assure, buck up, buoy, cheer, comfort, console, embolden, encourage, energize, enliven, incite, inspire, inspirit, rally, reassure, revivify, rouse, steel, stimulate, stir, strengthen; CONCEPTS 7,22 —*Ant.* bring down, depress, discourage, dishearten

heartfelt [adj] *genuine* ardent, bona fide, cordial, deep, devout, earnest, fervent, heart-to-heart, hearty, honest, profound, sincere, true, unfeigned, warm, wholehearted; CONCEPTS 267,582 —*Ant.* false, insincere, unreal

heartless [adj] *without feeling; cold* brutal, callous, cold-blooded*, cold fish*, cold-hearted*, cruel, hard, hard as nails*, hard-boiled*, hard-hearted*, harsh, inhuman, insensitive, merciless, obdurate, pitiless, ruthless, savage, thick-skinned*, uncaring, uncompassionate, unemotional, unfeeling, unkind, unsympathetic; CONCEPTS 401,542 —*Ant.* caring, compassionate, considerate, feeling, kind, nice, sympathetic, warmhearted

heartrending [adj] *arousing deep sympathy* agonizing, distressing, doleful, excruciating, harrowing, heartbreaking, heartsickening, moving, piteous, pitiful, sad, tear-jerking, touching, tragic; CONCEPTS 529,537

heartsick [adj] *despondent* all torn up*, blue, bummed-out*, dejected, depressed, despairing, disappointed, disconsolate, disheartened, down, forlorn, grieving, heavy-hearted, inconsolable, low, melancholy, mournful, sad, unhappy, woebegone; CONCEPT 403

heartwarming [adj] *pleasant* cheering, encouraging, exhilarating, gladdening, heartening, heartfelt, inspiring, joyous, loving, stirring, sweet; CONCEPTS 542,548,572

hearty [adj1] *energetic, enthusiastic* affable, animated, ardent, avid, back-slapping*, cheerful, cheery, cordial, deep, deepest, deep-felt, devout, eager, earnest, ebullient, effusive, exuberant, frank, friendly, gay, generous, genial, genuine, glad, gushing, heartfelt, honest, impassioned, intense, jolly, jovial, neighborly, passionate, profuse, real, responsive, sincere, true, unfeigned, unreserved, unrestrained, vivacious, warm, warmhearted, wholehearted, zealous; CONCEPTS 401,542 —*Ant.* apathetic, emotionless, lazy, lethargic, unenthusiastic

hearty [adj2] *healthy, full* active, ample, energetic, filling, glowing, good, hale, hardy, nourishing, robust, sizable, solid, sound, square, strong, substantial, vigorous, well; CONCEPTS 314,773 —*Ant.* feeble, small, unhealthy, weak

heat [n1] *high temperature* calefaction, calidity, dog days*, fever, fieriness, heatwave, hotness, hot spell, hot weather, incalescence, incandescence, sultriness, swelter, torridity, torridness, warmness, warmth; CONCEPT 610 —*Ant.* cold, cool

heat [n2] *anger, passion* agitation, ardor, desire, earnestness, excitement, ferocity, fervor, fever, fury, impetuosity, intensity, rage, vehemence, violence, warmth, zeal; CONCEPTS 410,657 —*Ant.* coolness, disinterest, frigidity

heat [*v*] *make or become hot* bake, bask, blaze, boil, broil, calorify, chafe, char, enflame, enkindle, fire, flame, flush, frizzle, fry, glow, grill, grow hot, grow warm, ignite, incandesce, incinerate, inflame, kindle, melt, oxidate, oxidize, perspire, raise the temperature, reheat, roast, scald, scorch, sear, seethe, set on fire, singe, smelt, steam, sun, swelter, tepefy, thaw, toast, warm, warm up; CONCEPTS 255,469 —*Ant.* cool, freeze

heated [*adj1*] *angry* acrimonious, ardent, avid, bitter, excited, fervent, fervid, feverish, fierce, fiery, frenzied, furious, hectic, impassioned, indignant, intense, irate, ireful, mad, passionate, raging, stormy, tempestuous, vehement, violent, wrathful; CONCEPT 267 —*Ant.* calm, peaceful

heated [*adj2*] *warmed* baked, baking, boiling, broiled, broiling, burned, burning, burnt, cooked, fiery, fired, fried, hot, parched, scalding, scorched, scorching, sizzling, toasted; CONCEPT 605 —*Ant.* cooled, frozen

heathen [*adj*] *not believing in Christian god* agnostic, atheistic, barbarian, godless, idolatrous, infidel, irreligious, nonbeliever, pagan, profane, skeptic; CONCEPT 545 —*Ant.* godly, religious

heave [*v1*] *lift, throw with effort* boost, cast, chuck, drag, elevate, fling, haul, heft, hoist, hurl, launch, pitch, pull, raise, send, sling, toss, tug; CONCEPTS 196,222

heave [*v2*] *discharge with force; expel from digestive system by mouth* billow, breathe, cast, dilate, disgorge, exhale, expand, gag, groan, huff, palpitate, pant, puff, puke*, retch, rise, sign, sob, spew, spit up, surge, suspire, swell, throb, throw up, upchuck*, vomit; CONCEPTS 163,179

heaven [*n*] *place where God lives; wonderful feeling* afterworld, Arcadia, atmosphere, azure*, beyond, bliss, Canaan, dreamland, ecstasy, Elysium, empyrean, enchantment, eternal home, eternal rest, eternity, fairyland*, felicity, firmament, glory, great unknown*, happiness, happy hunting ground*, harmony, heights, hereafter, immortality, kingdom, kingdom come, life everlasting, life to come, next world, nirvana, paradise, pearly gates*, promised land*, rapture, Shangri-la*, sky*, the blue*, transport, upstairs*, Utopia, wonderland*, Zion; CONCEPTS 370,410,435 —*Ant.* hell

heavenly [*adj*] *very pleasant* adorable, alluring, ambrosial, angelic, beatific, beautiful, blessed, blissful, celestial, cherubic, darling, delectable, delicious, delightful, divine, empyrean, enjoyable, entrancing, excellent, exquisite, extraterrestrial, glorious, godlike, holy, immortal, lovely, luscious, lush, paradisaical, rapturous, ravishing, scrumptious, seraphic, sublime, superhuman, supernal, supernatural, sweet, wonderful, yummy; CONCEPTS 537,572 —*Ant.* hellish

heavy [*adj1*] *having great weight* abundant, ample, awkward, beefy*, big, built, bulky, burdensome, chunky*, considerable, copious, corpulent, cumbersome, cumbrous, elephantine, enceinte, excessive, expectant, fat, fleshy, gravid, gross*, hefty, huge, laden, large, lead-footed*, loaded, lumbering, massive, obese, oppressed, overweight, parturient, ponderous, porcine, portly, pregnant, stout, substantial, top-heavy, two-ton*, unmanageable, unwieldy, weighted, weighty, zaftig*; CONCEPT 491 —*Ant.* airy, light, lightweight, little, slight, small

heavy [*adj2*] *difficult, severe* abstruse, acroamatic, arduous, boisterous, burdensome, complex, complicated, confused, effortful, esoteric, formidable, grave, grievous, hard, harsh, intolerable, knotty*, labored, laborious, onerous, oppressive, profound, recondite, rough, serious, solemn, stormy, strenuous, tedious, tempestuous, toilsome, tough, troublesome, turbulent, vexatious, violent, wearisome, weighty, wild; CONCEPTS 538,565,569 —*Ant.* easy, inconsequential, insignificant, trivial, unimportant

heavy [*adj3*] *depressed, gloomy* close, cloudy, crestfallen, damp, dark, dejected, despondent, disconsolate, dismal, downcast, dull, grieving, leaden, lowering, melancholy, oppressive, overcast, sad, sodden, soggy, sorrowful, stifling, wet; CONCEPTS 403,525,548 —*Ant.* gay, happy, joyful

heavy [*adj4*] *listless, slow* apathetic, comatose, dull, hebetudinous, indifferent, lethargic, sluggish, slumberous, torpid; CONCEPT 584 —*Ant.* light, moving, smoooth

heckle [*v*] *jeer* badger, bait, bother, bully, chivy, dis*, discomfit, disconcert, disrupt, disturb, embarrass, faze, gibe, hound*, interrupt, pester, plague, rattle, ride*, ridicule, shout at, taunt, tease, torment, worry; CONCEPTS 44,47 —*Ant.* encourage, help, promote, support

hectic [*adj*] *frantic, turbulent* animated, boisterous, burning, chaotic, confused, disordered, excited, exciting, fervid, fevered, feverish, flurrying, flustering, frenetic, frenzied, furious, hassle, heated, hell broke loose*, jungle*, madhouse*, nutsy*, restless, riotous, riproaring, tumultuous, unsettled, wild, woolly*, zoolike*; CONCEPT 548 —*Ant.* calm, easeful, leisurely, unhurried

hedge [*n*] *boundary, obstacle, especially one made of plants* barrier, bush, enclosure, fence, guard, hedgerow, hurdle, protection, quickset, screen, shrubbery, thicket, windbreak; CONCEPTS 429,470

hedge [*v1*] *avoid, dodge* beat around the bush*, be noncommittal, blow hot and cold*, cop a plea*, cop out*, duck, equivocate, evade, flip-flop*, fudge*, give the run around*, hem and haw*, jive*, pass the buck*, prevaricate, pussyfoot*, quibble, run around, shilly-shally*, shuck*, shuffle, sidestep, sit on the fence*, stall, stonewall*, temporize, tergiversate, tergiverse, waffle*; CONCEPTS 18,30 —*Ant.* confront, face, meet

hedge [*v2*] *enclose* block, border, cage, confine, coop, corral, edge, fence, girdle, hem in, hinder, immure, obstruct, pen, restrict, ring, siege, surround; CONCEPT 758 —*Ant.* release

hedonist [*n*] *person who seeks pleasure above other values* bon vivant, debauchee, epicure, epicurean, glutton, gourmand, lecher, libertine, pleasuremonger, pleasureseeker, profligate, sensualist, sybarite, thrill-seeker, voluptuary; CONCEPT 423 —*Ant.* ascetic

heed [n] *care, thought* application, attention, carefulness, caution, cognizance, concentration, concern, consideration, debate, deliberation, ear*, heedfulness, interest, listen up*, mark, mind*, note, notice, observance, observation, regard, remark, respect, spotlight*, study, tender loving care*, TLC*, watchfulness; CONCEPTS 17,532 —*Ant.* carelessness, disregard, heedlessness, inattention, indifference, neglect, negligence, thoughtlessness

heed [v] *give care, thought to* attend, baby-sit, bear in mind, be aware, be guided by, catch, consider, dig*, do one's bidding*, follow, follow orders, get a load of*, give ear*, hark, hear, hearken, keep eye peeled*, keep tabs*, listen, mark, mind, mind the store*, note, obey, observe, pay attention, pick up, regard, ride herd on*, see, sit, spot, stay in line*, take notice of, take to heart*, toe the line*, watch, watch one's step*, watch out, watch over, watch the store*; CONCEPTS 17,623 —*Ant.* disregard, ignore, neglect, overlook

heedless [adj] *careless* asleep at the switch*, daydreaming, disregardful, fast and loose*, feckless, foolhardy, goofing off*, impetuous, imprudent, inadvertent, inattentive, incautious, inconsiderate, irreflective, neglectful, negligent, oblivious, out to lunch*, precipitate, rash, reckless, slapdash*, sloppy, thoughtless, uncaring, unmindful, unobservant, unthinking, unwary; CONCEPT 401 —*Ant.* attentive, careful, caring, cautious, concerned, heedful, observant, thoughtful

hefty [adj] *big, bulky* ample, awkward, beefy*, brawny, burly, colossal, cumbersome, extensive, fat, forceful, heavy, hulking, husky, large, large-scale, major, massive, muscular, ponderous, powerful, robust, sizable, strapping*, strong, sturdy, substantial, thumping*, tremendous, unwieldy, vigorous, weighty; CONCEPTS 491, 773 —*Ant.* slight, small, thin, tiny

height [n1] *altitude, top part* acme, apex, apogee, brow, ceiling, crest, crown, cusp, elevation, extent, highness, hill, loftiness, mountain, peak, pinnacle, pitch, prominence, rise, solstice, stature, summit, tallness, tip, tiptop, vertex, zenith; CONCEPTS 741,743,791,836 —*Ant.* bottom, depth, lowness

height [n2] *climax; importance* acme, crest, crisis, crowning point, culmination, dignity, eminence, end, exaltation, extremity, grandeur, heyday*, high point, limit, loftiness, maximum, ne plus ultra*, prominence, sublimity, top, ultimate, utmost degree, uttermost; CONCEPTS 388,668,832 —*Ant.* bottom, nadir, unimportance

heighten [v] *intensify* add to, amplify, augment, boost, build up, elevate, enhance, enlarge, exalt, extend, improve, increase, lift, magnify, make higher, raise, send up, strengthen; CONCEPT 233

heinous [adj] *horrifying, monstrous* abhorrent, abominable, accursed, atrocious, awful, bad, beastly, crying, cursed, evil, execrable, flagitious, flagrant, frightful, godawful*, grave, gross*, hateful, hideous, horrendous, infamous, iniquitous, nefarious, odious, offensive, outrageous, raunchy, revolting, scandalous, shocking, stinking*, unspeakable, vicious, villainous; CONCEPTS 529,548,570 —*Ant.* glorious, good, lovely, magnificent

heir [n] *person who inherits possessions* beneficiary, crown prince/princess, devisee, grantee, heritor, inheritor, next in line, scion, successor; CONCEPTS 355,414 —*Ant.* heiress

heirloom [n] *something inherited, often antique* antique, bequest, birthright, gift, heritage, inheritance, legacy, patrimony, reversion; CONCEPT 337

heist [n] *burglary, robbery* break-in, breaking and entering, caper, crime, five-finger discount, holdup, larceny, pilferage, rip-off, stickup, sting, theft; CONCEPT 139

helicopter [n] *aircraft* autogiro, chopper, copter, eggbeater*, whirlybird; CONCEPT 504

hell [n] *place of the condemned; bad situation* Abaddon*, abyss, affliction, agony, anguish, blazes*, bottomless pit*, difficulty, everlasting fire*, fire and brimstone*, Gehenna*, grave, Hades, hell-fire, infernal regions, inferno, limbo, lower world, misery, nether world, nightmare, ordeal, pandemonium, perdition, pit, place of torment, purgatory, suffering, torment, trial, underworld, wretchedness; CONCEPTS 370,435,674 —*Ant.* heaven

hell-bent [adj] *determined* bent on and determined, constant, decided, driven, firm, fixed, intent, obsessed, persevering, persistent, resolute, resolved, serious, set on, steadfast, strong-minded, strong-willed, stubborn, tenacious, unhesitating, unwavering; CONCEPTS 404,542

hellion [n] *troublemaker* agent provocateur, agitator, demon, evildoer, firebrand*, heel*, incendiary, inciter, inflamer, instigator, loose cannon*, mischief-maker, punk*, rabble-rouser*, rascal, recreant, rogue, rowdy*, smart aleck*, wise guy*; CONCEPT 412

hellish [adj] *fiendish; unpleasant* abominable, accursed, atrocious, barbarous, cruel, damnable, damned, demonic, devilish, diabolical, horrible, infernal, monstrous, nefarious, satanic, terrible, vicious, wicked; CONCEPTS 529,570

helm [n] *wheel* command, control, controls, driver's seat, leadership, reins, rudder, steering wheel, tiller; CONCEPTS 436,464,502

helmet [n] *headgear* armor, busby, crash helmet, hard hat, hat, head protector, kepi, safety helmet, shako; CONCEPT 451

help [n1] *assistance, relief* advice, aid, assist, avail, balm*, benefit, comfort, cooperation, corrective, cure, guidance, hand, helping hand*, lift*, maintenance, nourishment, remedy, service, succor, support, sustenance, use, utility; CONCEPTS 658,694 —*Ant.* blockage, check, counteraction, harm, hindrance, hurt, injury, obstruction, stop

help [n2] *employee* abettor, adjutant, aide, ally, ancilla, assistant, attendant, auxiliary, collaborator, colleague, deputy, domestic, hand, helper, helpmate, mate, partner, representative, right-hand person*, servant, subsidiary, supporter, worker; CONCEPT 348 —*Ant.* management, ownership

help [v1] *aid, assist* abet, accommodate, advocate, back, ballyhoo*, befriend, benefit, be of use, bolster, boost, buck up*, cheer, cooperate, do a favor, do a service, do one's part*, encourage, endorse, further, go to bat for*, go with, hype*, intercede, lend a hand*, maintain, open doors*, patronize, plug*, promote, prop, puff*, push, relieve, root for*, sanction, save, second, see through, serve, stand by, stick up for*, stimulate, stump for*, succor, support, sustain, take under one's wing*, uphold, work for; CONCEPT *110* —*Ant.* block, check, counteract, harm, hinder, hurt, injure, obstruct, stop

help [*v2*] *improve* alleviate, ameliorate, amend, attend, better, cure, doctor, ease, facilitate, heal, meliorate, mitigate, nourish, palliate, relieve, remedy, restore, revive, treat; CONCEPT *244* —*Ant.* decrease, harm, hinder, hurt, injure, worsen

helper [*n*] *assistant* abettor, accessory, accomplice, adherent, adjunct, aide, ally, appointee, apprentice, attendant, backer, backup*, coadjutant, coadjutor, collaborator, colleague, companion, deputy, fellow worker, follower, friend, gal Friday*, girl Friday*, gofer*, help, helpmate, henchman, man Friday*, paraprofessional, partner, right-hand man/woman, right-hand person, secretary, servant, subordinate, supporter, temp*, temporary worker; CONCEPTS *348,423*

helpful [*adj*] *beneficial, beneficent* accessible, accommodating, advantageous, applicable, benevolent, bettering, caring, conducive, considerate, constructive, contributive, convenient, cooperative, crucial, effectual, efficacious, essential, favorable, fortunate, friendly, good for, important, improving, instrumental, invaluable, kind, neighborly, operative, practical, pragmatic, productive, profitable, serendipitous, serviceable, significant, suitable, supportive, symbiotic, sympathetic, timely, usable, useful, utilitarian, valuable; CONCEPTS *537,560* —*Ant.* disadvantageous, harmful, hurtful, injurious, unconstructive, unhelpful, useless, worthless

helping [*n*] *portion of food* allowance, course, dollop, meal, order, piece, plateful, ration, serving, share; CONCEPT *457*

helpless [*adj*] *incapable, incompetent; vulnerable* abandoned, basket-case*, debilitated, defenseless, dependent, destitute, disabled, exposed, feeble, forlorn, forsaken, friendless, handcuffed, impotent, inefficient, inexpert, infirm, invalid, over a barrel*, paralyzed, pinned*, powerless, prostrate, shiftless, tapped, tapped out*, unable, unfit, unprotected, up creek without paddle*, weak, with hands tied*; CONCEPTS *401,542* —*Ant.* able, capable, competent, enterprising, independent, resourceful, skilled, strong

helter-skelter [*adv*] *carelessly, confused* about, anyhow, any which way*, anywise, around, at random, cluttered, disorderly, haphazard, hastily, headlong, higgledy-piggledy*, hit-or-miss*, hotfoot*, hurriedly, impetuously, incautiously, in confusion, incontinently, irregular, jumbled, muddled, pell-mell*, random, randomly, rashly, recklessly, topsy-turvy*, tumultous/tumultuous, unmindfully, wildly; CONCEPT *544* —*Ant.* carefully, methodical, organized, straight, systematic

hem [*n*] *border, edge* brim, brink, define, edging, fringe, margin, perimeter, periphery, piping, rim, selvage, skirt, skirting, trimming, verge; CONCEPTS *484,513* —*Ant.* body, center, interior

he-man [*adj*] *masculine* macho*, male, manful, manly, mannish, muscular, potent, virile;

CONCEPTS *371,408,648*

he-man [*n*] *masculine man* caveman*, hunk*, macho man*, man's man, strong man, virile man; CONCEPTS *414,419*

hem/hem in [*v*] *enclose, restrict* begird, beset, border, bound, cage, circle, circumscribe, close in, confine, corral, define, edge, encircle, encompass, envelop, environ, fence, fringe, girdle, hedge in, immure, margin, pen, rim, ring, round, shut, shut in, skirt, surround, verge; CONCEPTS *130,758* —*Ant.* let go, release

hemorrhage [*v*] *bleed* drain, extravasate, gush, lose blood, ooze, open vein, outflow, phlebotomize, seep, spill blood; CONCEPT *185*

hence [*adv*] *for that reason; therefore* accordingly, as a deduction, away, consequently, ergo, forward, from here, from now on, henceforth, henceforward, hereinafter, in the future, it follows that, on that account, onward, out, so, then, thence, thereupon, thus, wherefore; CONCEPT *799*

henchman [*n*] *follower* abettor, accessory, accomplice, adherent, adjunct, aide, ally, appointee, apprentice, assistant, attendant, backer, backup*, bodyguard, coadjutant, coadjutor, cohort, collaborator, colleague, companion, deputy, fellow worker, flunky, friend, gal Friday*, girl Friday*, gofer*, hanger-on, hatchet man/woman, help, helper, helpmate, lackey, man Friday*, partner, right-hand man/woman, right-hand person, secretary, servant, sidekick*, stooge*, subordinate, supporter, yes-person*; CONCEPTS *348,423*

henpeck [*v*] *nag* badger, berate, bother, bug*, bully, carp, fuss, give a hard time*, harass, hector, hound, intimidate, irritate, needle, pester, pick on*, ride, scold, torment; CONCEPTS *7,19,52*

herald [*n*] *omen, messenger* adviser, bearer, courier, crier, forerunner, harbinger, indication, outrider, precursor, prophet, reporter, runner, sign, signal, token; CONCEPTS *274,284,423*

herald [*v*] *bring message* advertise, announce, ballyhoo*, broadcast, declare, forerun, foretoken, harbinger, indicate, pave the way*, portend, precede, preindicate, presage, proclaim, publicize, publish, promise, show, tout, trumpet*, usher in*; CONCEPT *60*

herbicide [*n*] *poison* DDT, defoliant, fungicide, insecticide, paraquat, pesticide, weedkiller; CONCEPTS *307,475,674,675*

Herculean [*adj*] *powerful, strong* almighty, backbreaking, colossal, courageous, forceful, gargantuan, gigantic, hard, heroic, huge, impressive, laborious, mighty, strenuous, tough, vigorous; CONCEPTS *489,527,540,574*

herd [*n*] *large group* assemblage, bevy, brood, clan, collection, covey, crowd, crush, drift, drove, flight, flock, gaggle, gathering, hoi polloi*, horde, lot, mass, mob, multitude, nest, pack, people, populace, press, rabble, school, swarm, throng; CONCEPTS *397,432*

herd [*v*] *gather; shepherd* assemble, associate, collect, congregate, corral, drive, flock, force, goad, guide, huddle, lead, muster, poke, punch, rally, round up*, run, scare up*, spur; CONCEPT *109* —*Ant.* disperse, scatter

here [*adv*] *in this place* attendant, attending, available, hereabouts, hither, hitherto, in this direction, on board, on deck, on hand, on-the-spot, on this spot, present, within reach; CONCEPT 583 —*Ant.* there

hereafter [*adv*] *from now on* after this, eventually, hence, henceforth, henceforward, hereupon, in the course of time, in the future, ultimately; CONCEPT 799

hereafter [*n*] *life after death* afterlife, aftertime, afterward, afterworld, by-and-by*, future, future existence, future life, heaven, hell, next world, offing, otherworld, the beyond*, to-be*, underworld, world to come*; CONCEPT 370 —*Ant.* life

hereditary [*adj*] *inherited; transmitted at birth* ancestral, bequeathed, family, genealogical, genetic, handed down, heritable, inborn, inbred, inheritable, inherited, lineal, maternal, paternal, patrimonial, traditional, transmissible, transmitted, willed; CONCEPT 549 —*Ant.* acquired

heredity [*n*] *transmission of traits from parents to offspring* ancestry, congenital traits, constitution, eugenics, genesiology, genetic make-up, genetics, inborn character, inheritance; CONCEPT 648 —*Ant.* acquirement

heresy [*n*] *unorthodox opinion, especially in religious matters* agnosticism, apostasy, atheism, blasphemy, defection, disbelief, dissent, dissidence, divergence, error, fallacy, heterodoxy, iconoclasm, impiety, infidelity, misbelief, nonconformism, nonconformity, paganism, revisionism, schism, sectarianism, secularism, sin; CONCEPT 689 —*Ant.* orthodoxy

heretical [*adj*] *unorthodox* agnostic, apostate, atheistic, differing, disagreeing, dissenting, dissentive, dissident, freethinking, heterodox, iconoclastic, idolatrous, impious, infidel, misbelieving, miscreant, nonconformist, revisionist, schismatic, sectarian, skeptical, unbelieving; CONCEPTS 529,545 —*Ant.* orthodox

heritage [*n*] *person's background, tradition* ancestry, bequest, birthright, convention, culture, custom, dowry, endowment, estate, fashion, heirship, heritance, inheritance, legacy, lot, patrimony, portion, right, share, tradition; CONCEPTS 296,648,678

hermeneutical [*adj*] *interpretive* critical, demonstrative, explanatory, explicative, expository, illustrative, investigative, revealing; CONCEPT 268

hermeneutics [*n*] *the science of searching for hidden meaning in texts* exegetics, exploration, interpretation, investigation, literary criticism, psychoanalytic criticism, revealing, unmasking; CONCEPT 349

hermetic [*adj*] *airtight* completely sealed, impervious, sealed, shut, tight, waterproof, watertight; CONCEPT 483

hermit [*n*] *person who chose to live alone outside of human society* anchoret, anchorite, ascetic, eremite, misanthrope, pillarist, recluse, skeptic, solitaire, solitarian, solitary, stylite; CONCEPTS 361,423

hero [*n*] *submarine sandwich* grinder, hoagie, sub*, submarine*, torpedo; CONCEPTS 457,460

hero/heroine [*n*] *brave person; champion* ace, adventurer, celebrity, combatant, conqueror, daredevil, demigod, diva, exemplar, gallant, god, goddess, great person, heavy, ideal, idol, lead, leading person*, lion, martyr, model, paladin, person of the hour*, popular figure,

prima donna*, principal, protagonist, saint, star, superstar, tin god*, victor, worthy; CONCEPTS 352,416

heroic [*adj*] *brave, champion* bigger than life*, bold, classic, courageous, daring, dauntless, doughty, elevated, epic, exaggerated, fearless, fire-eating*, gallant, grand, grandiose, gritty, gutsy*, gutty*, high-flown, impavid, inflated, intrepid, lion-hearted, mythological, noble, stand tall*, stouthearted, unafraid, undaunted, valiant, valorous; CONCEPTS 401,404 —*Ant.* afraid, cowardly, fearful, meek, timid

heroin [*n*] *smack* big H*, candy*, crap*, diacetylmorphine, doojee*, dope, drug, flea powder*, H*, hard stuff*, horse*, junk*, mojo*, narcotic, opium, scag*, white stuff*; CONCEPT 307

heroism [*n*] *bravery* boldness, courage, courageousness, daring, doughtiness, fearlessness, fortitude, gallantry, intrepidity, nobility, prowess, spirit, strength, valiance, valiancy, valor, valorousness; CONCEPTS 411,633 —*Ant.* cowardice, fear, meekness, timidity

hesitant [*adj*] *uncertain, waiting* afraid, averse, backward, dawdling, delaying, diffident, disinclined, doubtful, doubting, faltering, half-hearted, halting, hanging back, hesitating, indecisive, irresolute, lacking confidence, lazy, loath, reluctant, shy, skeptical, slow, tentative, timid, uneager, unpredictable, unsure, unwilling, vacillating, wavering; CONCEPTS 534,535,542 —*Ant.* certain, definite, resolute, sure, unhesitant, unwavering

hesitate [*v*] *wait; be uncertain* alternate, balance, balk, be irresolute, be reluctant, be unwilling, blow hot and cold*, dally, debate, defer, delay, demur, dillydally*, dither, doubt, equivocate, falter, flounder, fluctuate, fumble, hang*, hang back, hedge, hem and haw*, hold back, hold off, hover, linger, oscillate, pause, ponder, pull back, pussyfoot*, scruple, seesaw*, shift, shrink, shy away, sit on fence*, stammer, stop, straddle, stumble, stutter, swerve, tergiversate, think about, think twice*, vacillate, waffle*, waver, weigh; CONCEPTS 21,121,681 —*Ant.* attack, carry on, continue, go, go ahead, persevere, resolve

hesitation [*n*] *waiting; uncertainty* averseness, dawdling, delay, delaying, demurral, doubt, dubiety, equivocation, faltering, fluctuation, fumbling, hemming and hawing*, hesitancy, indecision, indecisiveness, indisposition, irresolution, misgiving, mistrust, oscillation, pause, procrastination, qualm, reluctance, scruple, skepticism, stammering, stumbling, stuttering, unwillingness, vacillation, wavering; CONCEPTS 21,121,410,681 —*Ant.* certainty, eagerness, go, perseverance, sureness

heterogeneous [*adj*] *assorted, miscellaneous* amalgamate, composite, confused, conglomerate, contrary, contrasted, different, discordant, discrepant, disparate, dissimilar, divergent, diverse, diversified, incongruous, independent, inharmonious, jumbled, mingled, mixed, mongrel, mosaic, motley, multifarious, multiplex, odd, opposed, unallied, unlike, unrelated, variant, varied, variegated; CONCEPT 564 —*Ant.* homogeneous, identical, pure, single, unchanging, uniform

hex [n] *curse, spell* abracadabra*, allure, bewitching, bewitchment, charm, conjuration, double whammy*, enchantment, evil eye, hexing, hocus-pocus*, jinx, magic, magic spell, mumbo jumbo*, sorcery, voodoo*, whammy*; CONCEPTS 370,673,689

heyday [n] *prime* acme, culmination, day, height, high point, high spot, peak, pinnacle, prime time, salad days, time, zenith; CONCEPT 816 —*Ant.* low point

hiatus [n] *pause, interruption* aperture, blank, breach, break, chasm, discontinuity, gap, interim, interval, lacuna, lapse, opening, rift, space; CONCEPT 807 —*Ant.* continuation, continuity

hibernate [v] *lie dormant; sleep through cold weather* hide, hole up, immure, lie torpid, sleep, vegetate, winter; CONCEPT 315

hick [n] *rustic* backwoodsman/woman, boor, bumpkin, clodhopper, cornfed*, country * boy/girl, country cousin*, countryman/woman, farmer, hayseed*, hillbilly, local yokel*, redneck*, rube, rural, yokel*; CONCEPT 413

hidden [adj] *unseen, secret* abstruse, buried, clandestine, cloaked, close, clouded, concealed, covered, covert, cryptic, dark, disguised, eclipsed, esoteric, hermetic, hermetical, imperceivable, indiscernible, in the dark, invisible, latent, masked, mysterious, mystic, mystical, obscure, occult, out of view, private, QT*, recondite, screened, secluded, sequestered, shadowy, shrouded, surreptitious, ulterior, undercover, underground, undetected, undisclosed, unexposed, unknown, unrevealed, veiled, withheld; CONCEPT 576 —*Ant.* bare, exhibited, exposed, open, out, seen, showing, uncovered

hide [v] *conceal; remain unseen* adumbrate, blot out, bury, cache, camouflage, cloak, cover, curtain*, disguise, dissemble, ditch, duck, eclipse, ensconce, go into hiding, go underground, harbor, hold back, hole up*, hush up, keep from, keep secret, lie low*, lock up, mask, not give away, not tell, obscure, plant, protect, put out of the way, reserve, salt away*, screen, secrete, shadow, shelter, shield, shroud, smuggle, squirrel*, stash, stifle, stow away, suppress, take cover, tuck away, veil, withhold; CONCEPTS 17,188 —*Ant.* bare, disclose, divulge, exhibit, expose, lay bare, let out, open, reveal, show, tell, uncover, unmask

hideous [adj] *grotesque, horrible* abominable, animal, appalling, awful, beast, bestial, detestable, disgusting, dreadful, frightful, ghastly, grim, grisly, gross*, gruesome, hateful, horrendous, horrid, loathsome, macabre, monstrous, morbid, nasty, odious, offensive, repellent, repugnant, repulsive, revolting, shocking, sick, sickening, terrible, terrifying, ugly, uncomely, unsightly, weird; CONCEPTS 537,579 —*Ant.* attractive, beautiful, charming, delightful, pleasing

hideout [n] *hiding place* cover, den, hideaway, refuge, safe house, safe place, sanctuary, shelter; CONCEPTS 198,515

hierarchy [n] *order* chain of command*, due order, echelons, grouping, pecking order, placing, position, pyramid, ranking, scale; CONCEPT 727

high [adj1] *tall; at a great distance aloft* aerial, alpine, altitudinous, big, colossal, elevated, eminent, flying, formidable, giant, gigantic, grand, great, high-reaching, high rise, hovering, huge, immense, large, lofty, long, sky-high, sky-scraping, soaring, steep, towering, tremendous, uplifted, upraised; CONCEPTS 779,782 —*Ant.* dwarfed, low, lowly, short, stunted

high [adj2] *extreme* costly, dear, excessive, exorbitant, expensive, extraordinary, extravagant, grand, great, high-priced, intensified, lavish, luxurious, precious, rich, sharp, special, steep, stiff, strong, unusual; CONCEPTS 334, 569 —*Ant.* inferior, mean, worthless

high [adj3] *important* arch, capital, chief, consequential, crucial, distinguished, eminent, essential, exalted, extreme, grave, influential, leading, necessary, noble, powerful, prominent, ruling, serious, significant, superior; CONCEPT 567 —*Ant.* dishonorable, inferior, low, unimportant, worthless

high [adj4] *very happy* boisterous, bouncy, cheerful, elated, excited, exhilarated, exuberant, joyful, lighthearted, merry, psyched*, pumped*; CONCEPT 403 —*Ant.* depressed, down, low, upset

high [adj5] *intoxicated, drugged* delirious, doped, drunk, euphoric, flying*, freaked out*, inebriated, on a trip*, potted*, spaced out*, stoned*, tanked*, tipsy; CONCEPT 314 —*Ant.* sober

high [adj6] *shrill, strong (on the senses)* acute, high-pitched, loud, malodorous, penetrating, piercing, piping, putrid, rancid, rank, reeking, sharp, smelly, soprano, strident, treble; CONCEPTS 406,594,598 —*Ant.* low, soft, weak

high and mighty [adj] *haughty, overbearing* arrogant, cavalier, cocky*, conceited, contemptuous, disdainful, egotistic, egotistical, highfalutin*, high-handed*, hoity-toity*, imperious, lofty, lordly, on high horse*, presumptuous, sniffy, snobbish, snooty*, snotty, stuck-up*, stuffy, superior, uppity*; CONCEPTS 401,404

highbrow [adj] *intellectual* bookish, brainy*, cerebral, cultivated, cultured, erudite, intellective, intelligent, learned, scholarly, studious, wise; CONCEPT 402

highbrow [n] *intellectual, very smart person* academic, academician, bluestocking, brain*, egghead*, Einstein*, genius, illuminato, intelligentsia, literato, longhair, philosopher, sage, savant, scholar, thinker, whiz*; CONCEPT 402

high-class [adj] *first-class, fine* best, choice, classy, deluxe, elite, superior, supreme, upper-class, upper-crust*; CONCEPTS 568,572

highfalutin [adj] *pompous* arrogant, boastful, conceited, flaunting, grandiose, high and mighty*, important, lofty, ostentatious, overbearing, presumptuous, pretentious, puffed up*, puffy, self-centered, stuck-up*, swanky, uppity*, vain; CONCEPTS 267,401,542

high-flown [adj] *exalted, lofty* bombastic, elaborate, exaggerated, extravagant, grandiloquent, grandiose, inflated, showy, turgid; CONCEPT 562

high-handed [adj] *domineering* authoritarian, autocratic, bossy, dictatorial, imperious, ironhanded, oppressive, overbearing, tyrannical; CONCEPTS 319,401

highlight [n] *memorable part* best part, climax, feature, focal point, focus, high point, high spot, main feature, peak; CONCEPT *832*

highly [adv] *very, well* awful, awfully, bloody*, but good*, decidedly, deeply, eminently, exceedingly, exceptionally, extraordinarily, extremely, greatly, hugely, immensely, jolly, mighty, mucho*, notably, parlous, plenty, powerful, profoundly, real, really, remarkably, right, so, so much*, strikingly, supremely, surpassingly, terribly, terrifically, too much*, tremendously, vastly, very much; CONCEPTS *537,569* —**Ant.** little

high-minded [adj] *principled* chivalrous, conscientious, ethical, honest, moral, noble, righteous, upright, virtuous; CONCEPT *545*

high-powered [adj] *powerful* authoritarian, authoritative, commanding, controlling, dominant, dynamic, effective, effectual, forceful, forcible, in control, influential, in the saddle*, mighty, potent, robust, ruling, strong, supreme, weighty; CONCEPTS *489,527,540,574*

high society [n] *cultured class* aristocracy, beau monde, beautiful people*, best people, cream of society, elite, fashionable society, high life, jet set*, polite society, privileged class, smart set, upper class; CONCEPTS *387,388,417*

high-strung [adj] *nervous* all shook up*, choked*, easily upset, edgy, excitable, fidgety, hyper*, impatient, irascible, irritable, jittery, jumpy, nervy, neurotic, on pins and needles*, on ragged edge, restless, sensitive, spooked*, stressed, taut, temperamental, tense, tight*, unrestful, uptight*, wired*, zonkers*; CONCEPTS *401,404* —**Ant.** calm, easy-going, laid-back, peaceful

highway [n] *heavily traveled, capacious road* artery, avenue, boulevard, drag*, four-lane*, freeway, interstate, parking lot*, parkway, path, pike*, roadway, skyway, street, superhighway, super slab*, thoroughfare, toll road, track, turnpike; CONCEPT *501*

hijack [v] *seize control* carjack, commandeer, kidnap, shanghai, skyjack, steal, take hostage; CONCEPTS *90,139*

hijacker [n] *abductor* carjacker, kidnapper, robber, skyjacker, terrorist, thief; CONCEPTS *90,139*

hike [n] *journey by foot* backpack, constitutional, excursion, exploration, march, ramble, tour, traipse, tramp, trek, trip, walk, walkabout; CONCEPTS *149,224,363*

hike [v1] *walk for recreation* backpack, explore, hit the road*, hoof*, leg it*, ramble, rove, stroll, stump, tour, tramp, travel, tromp; CONCEPTS *149,224,363*

hike [v2] *raise, increase* advance, boost, jack, jump, lift, pull up, put up, up*, upgrade; CONCEPTS *236,245* —**Ant.** decrease, lower, reduce

hilarious [adj] *very funny* amusing, comical, convivial, entertaining, exhilarated, frolicsome, gay, gleeful, gut-busting*, happy, humorous, jocular, jolly, jovial, joyful, joyous, laughable, lively, merry, mirthful, noisy, priceless, riot, rollicking, scream, side-splitting*, uproarious, witty; CONCEPT *529* —**Ant.** grave, serious, somber, tragic, unfunny

hill [n] *uprising of earth's surface; pile* acclivity, ascent, bluff, butte, cliff, climb, down, drift,

dune, elevation, eminence, esker, fell, gradient, headland, heap, height, highland, hillock, hilltop, hummock, inclination, incline, knoll, mesa, mound, mount, precipice, prominence, promontory, protuberance, range, ridge, rise, rising ground, shock, slope, stack, summit, talus, tor, upland; CONCEPT *509* —**Ant.** canyon, ditch, gulley

hillbilly [n] *hayseed* backwoodsman/woman, boor*, bumpkin, clodhopper*, country boy/girl, country bumpkin, country cousin*, hick*, rube, rustic, yokel; CONCEPT *413*

hillock [n] *small hill* acclivity, ascent, bluff, butte, cliff, drift, dune, elevation, esker, headland, heap, highland, hilltop, hummock, inclination, incline, knoll, mesa, mound, mount, precipice, prominence, promontory, ridge, rise, slope, summit; CONCEPT *509*

hinder [v] *prevent, slow down* arrest, balk, bar, block, bottleneck, box in, burden, check, choke, clog, contravene, counteract, crab, cramp, crimp, cripple, curb, debar, delay, deter, encumber, fetter, frustrate, get in the way*, hamper, hamstring*, handicap, hog-tie*, hold back, hold up, impede, inhibit, interfere, interrupt, louse up*, muzzle, neutralize, obstruct, offset, oppose, preclude, prohibit, resist, retard, shut out, snafu*, stay, stop, stymie*, terminate, thwart, trammel; CONCEPTS *121,130* —**Ant.** advance, aid, allow, assist, encourage, facilitate, forward, further, help, permit, promote, push

hindrance [n] *obstruction, difficulty* albatross*, baggage*, ball and chain*, bar, barrier, catch, Catch-22*, check, clog, crimp, cumbrance, deterrent, drag, drawback, encumbrance, excess baggage*, foot dragging*, glitch*, gridlock, handicap, hang-up*, hitch, impedance, impediment, interference, interruption, intervention, jam-up*, joker, limitation, lock, millstone*, monkey wrench*, obstacle, restraint, restriction, snag, stoppage, stumbling block*, trammel; CONCEPTS *666,674* —**Ant.** advance, aid, assistance, encouragement, expedition, help, promotion, push

hindsight [n] *retrospect* 20/20 vision*, experience, knowledge, looking back, Monday morning quarterbacking, recollection, remembering, wisdom; CONCEPTS *17,40,410*

hinge [n] *pivot, turning point* articulation, axis, ball-and-socket, butt, elbow, hook, joint, juncture, knee, link, pin, spring, swivel; CONCEPTS *471,498*

hinge [v] *be contingent on* be subject to, be undecided, depend, hang, pend, pivot, rest, revolve around, stand on, turn, turn on; CONCEPT *711*

hint [n] *indication; suggestion* adumbration, advice, allusion, announcement, clue, communication, connotation, denotation, evidence, flea in ear*, glimmering, help, idea, implication, impression, inference, information, inkling, innuendo, insinuation, intimation, iota, lead, mention, notice, notion, observation, omen, pointer, print, reference, reminder, scent, sign, signification, smattering, suspicion, symptom, taste, telltale, tinge, tip, tip-off*, token, trace, warning, whiff*, whisper, wink*, word to wise*, wrinkle*; CONCEPT *274*

hint [v] *suggest; indicate* acquaint, adumbrate,

advise, allude to, angle, apprise, bring up, broach, coax, connote, cue, drop, expose, fish*, foreshadow, give an inkling*, impart, imply, infer, inform, insinuate, intimate, jog memory, leak*, let it be known, let out of bag*, make*, mention, point, prefigure, press, prompt, put flea in ear*, recall, refer to, remind, say in passing, shadow, signify, solicit, spring, tip off*, tip one's hand*, touch on*, whisper, wink*; CONCEPTS 60,74,75

hinterland [n] *backcountry* boondocks*, boonies*, borderland, brush, bush country, frontier, outback, sticks*, wasteland, wilderness, woods; CONCEPTS 513,745

hip [adj] *fashionable, stylish* all the rage*, chic, chichi*, contemporary, cool*, current, faddy*, hot*, in style, in-thing*, in vogue, latest*, latest thing*, mod*, modern, modish*, natty*, new, now, popular, smart, sophisticated, trendsetting, trendy, with it*; CONCEPTS 579,580

hippie [n] *nonconformist* beatnik, Bohemian, drop-out, flower child, freak, free spirit, freethinker, yippie; CONCEPT 423

hire [v] *commission for responsibility, use* add to payroll, appoint, authorize, book, bring in, bring on board, carry, charter, contract for, delegate, draft, employ, empower, engage, enlist, exploit, fill a position, find help, give a break*, give job to, give work, ink*, lease, let, make use of, obtain, occupy, pick, place, pledge, procure, promise, put on*, put to work, rent, retain, secure, select, sign on, sign up*, sublease, sublet, take on, truck with*, utilize; CONCEPT 351 —Ant. discharge, fire, lay off, let go

hiss [n] *buzzing sound; jeer* boo, Bronx cheer*, buzz, catcall, contempt, derision, hoot, sibilance, sibilation; CONCEPTS 278,595

hiss [v] *make buzzing sound; ridicule* blow, boo, catcall, condemn, damn, decry, deride, disapprove, hoot, jeer, mock, rasp, revile, seethe, shout down, shrill, sibilate, siss, spit, wheeze, whirr, whisper, whistle, whiz; CONCEPTS 52,77

historic [adj] *momentous, remarkable* celebrated, consequential, extraordinary, famous, important, memorable, notable, outstanding, red-letter*, significant, well-known; CONCEPTS 548,568 —Ant. unimportant, unremarkable

historical [adj] *recorded as actually having happened* actual, ancient, archival, attested, authentic, chronicled, classical, commemorated, documented, factual, important, in truth, old, past, real, verifiable; CONCEPTS 548,582,820 —Ant. fictional

history [n1] *past events, experiences* ancient times, antiquity, bygone times, days of old*, days of yore*, good old days*, old days*, olden days*, past, yesterday, yesteryear; CONCEPTS 678,807 —Ant. future

history [n2] *chronicle of events* account, annals, autobiography, biography, diary, epic, journal, memoirs, narration, narrative, prehistory, recapitulation, recital, record, relation, report, saga, story, tale, version; CONCEPTS 268,271

histrionic [adj] *overly dramatic* melodramatic, overacting, overplayed, theatrical, thespian; CONCEPTS 537,548

histrionics [n] *theatrics* dramatics, dramatization, performance, performing; CONCEPT 674

hit [n1] *strike, bump* bang, bat, bell-ringer*, belt, blow, bonk, box*, buffet, butt, chop, clash, clip, clout, collision, cuff*, fisticuff, glance, impact, knock, kick*, one-two punch*, paste*, pat, plunk, punch, rap, roundhouse*, shock, shot, slap, slog, smack, smash, sock, spank, stroke, swat, swing, swipe, tap, uppercut, wallop, whammy*, whop, zap*, zinger*; CONCEPTS 189,200

hit [n2] *entertainment success* achievement, bang, click, favorite, knockout, masterstroke, sellout, sensation, smash, SRO*, triumph, winner, wow; CONCEPT 706 —Ant. failure, flop, loss

hit [v1] *strike* bang, bash, bat, batter, beat, belt, blast, blitz, box*, brain*, buffet, bump, clap, clip, clobber, clout, club, crack, cudgel, cuff*, dab, ding*, flail, flax, flog, give a black eye*, hammer*, hook, jab, kick, knock, knock around, knock out, KO*, lace, lambaste, larrup, lather, let fly*, let have it*, lob, nail*, pellet, pelt, percuss, pop, pound, punch, rap, ride roughshod*, slap, smack, sock, stone, swat, tap, thrash, thump, thwack, trash, uppercut, wallop, whack*, whang*; CONCEPTS 189,200

hit [v2] *collide, bump into* bang into, buffet, butt, carom, clash, crash, glance, jostle, knock, light, meet, meet head-on*, pat, rap, run into, scrape, sideswipe, smash, stumble, tap, thud, thump; CONCEPTS 189,208

hit [v3] *accomplish* achieve, affect, arrive at, attain, gain, influence, leave a mark, occur, overwhelm, reach, secure, strike, touch; CONCEPTS 199,706 —Ant. fail, lose

hitch [n] *problem, difficulty* block, bug*, catch, check, delay, discontinuance, drawback, glitch*, hang-up, hindrance, hold-up, impediment, interruption, joker, mishap, snafu*, snag, stoppage, stumbling block, tangle, trouble; CONCEPTS 666,674 —Ant. advantage, benefit, chance, opening, opportunity

hitch [v] *join, fasten* attach, chain, connect, couple, harness, hook, lash, make fast, moor, strap, tether, tie, unite, yoke; CONCEPTS 85,113,160 —Ant. disjoin, unchain, unfasten, unhitch, unlock

hit it off [v] *get along well* be of one mind*, be on the same wavelength*, click, make friends, see eye to eye, take to; CONCEPT 388

hit man [n] *professional killer* assassin, contract killer, executioner, gunman, hatchet man, hired gun*, hired killer, murderer, triggerman; CONCEPT 412

hit-or-miss [adj] *random* accidental, aimless, arbitrary, casual, chance, contingent, fluky, fortuitous, haphazard, incidental, irregular, slipshod, trial-and-error, unplanned, unpremeditated; CONCEPTS 535,548,557

hoard [n] *stockpile* abundance, accumulation, agglomeration, aggregation, amassment, backlog, cache, collection, conglomeration, cumulation, fund, garner, heap, inventory, mass, nest egg*, pile, reserve, reservoir, riches, stock, store, supply, treasure, treasure-trove*, trove, wealth; CONCEPT 712 —Ant. debt

hoard [v] *put away, accumulate* acquire, amass, buy up, cache, collect, deposit, garner, gather, hide, keep, lay away, lay up, pile up, put aside for rainy day*, put by, save, scrimp, sock away*, squirrel*, stash, stockpile, store, stow away, treasure; CONCEPTS 135,710 —*Ant.* expend, spend, squander, throw away, waste

hoarse [*adj*] *raspy in voice* blatant, breathy, cracked, croaking, croaky, croupy, discordant, dry, grating, gravelly, growling, gruff, guttural, harsh, husky, indistinct, jarring, piercing, ragged, raucous, rough, scratching, squawking, stertorous, strident, stridulous, thick, throaty, uneven, whispering; CONCEPT 594 —*Ant.* smooth, soft, soothing

hoary [*adj1*] *ancient* aged, age-old, antiquated, antique, elderly, lot of mileage*, old, older, old-fashioned, oldie*, out-of-date, relic, rusty, time-worn, venerable, very old; CONCEPTS 578,797

hoary [*adj2*] *gray or white* frosty, gray-haired, graying, salt and pepper, silvery, snowy-haired, white-haired, whitish; CONCEPT 618

hoax [*n*] *trick* cock-and-bull story*, con*, con game*, crock*, deceit, deception, dodge, fabrication, fake, falsification, fast one*, fast shuffle*, fib, flimflam*, fraud, gimmick, gyp*, hooey*, humbug*, hustle, imposture, joke, lie, practical joke, prank, put-on, racket, ruse, scam, sell, shift, snow job*, spoof, sting, swindle, whopper*; CONCEPTS 59,63

hoax [*v*] *trick* bamboozle*, bluff, chicane, con, deceive, delude, dupe, fake out, fleece, flim-flam*, fool, frame, gammon, gull, hoodwink*, Murphy*, play games with*, pull one's leg*, rook*, run a game on*, set up*, sting*, swindle, take for a ride*, take in*; CONCEPT 59

hobble [*v1*] *limp* clump, dodder, falter, halt, hitch, scuff, shuffle, stagger, stumble, totter; CONCEPT 151 —*Ant.* go, move, run, walk

hobble [*v2*] *cripple, restrict* clog, cramp, cramp one's style, crimp, curb, entrammel, fasten, fetter, gimp, hamper, hamstring*, hang up*, hinder, hog-tie*, leash, put a crimp in*, shackle, tie, trammel; CONCEPT 130 —*Ant.* free, let go, release

hobby [*n*] *pleasurable pastime* amusement, art, avocation, bag*, craft, craze, distraction, diversion, divertissement, fad*, fancy, favorite occupation, fun, game, interest, kick*, labor of love*, leisure activity, leisure pursuit, obsession, occupation, pet topic, play, quest, relaxation, schtick*, shot, sideline, specialty, sport, thing*, vagary, weakness, whim, whimsy; CONCEPTS 363,364 —*Ant.* profession, vocation, work

hobgoblin [*n*] *mischievous goblin* bogeyman, brownie, elf, fairy, fay, imp, leprechaun, pixie, puck, sprite; CONCEPT 370

hobnob [*v*] *associate with* chum around, consort, fraternize, hang around*, hang out with*, keep company, knock around with*, mingle, mix, pal, pal around, rub elbows*, rub shoulders*, socialize, spend time; CONCEPT 384

hobo [*n*] *homeless person* beggar, bum, derelict, drifter, migrant worker, street person, tramp, transient, vagabond, vagrant, wanderer, wino; CONCEPTS 412,423

hock [*v*] *pawn* borrow, give security, pledge; CONCEPTS 115,330

hocus-pocus [*n*] *deception, magic* abracadabra*, artifice, cant, chant, charm, cheating, chicanery, conjuring, deceit, delusion, flimflam*, fraud, gibberish, gobbledegook*, hoax, humbug, imposture, incantation, jargon,

juggling, legerdemain, mumbo jumbo*, mummery, nonsense, open sesame*, rigmarole*, sleight of hand*, spell, swindle, trick, trickery; CONCEPTS 59,278 —*Ant.* reality, truth

hodgepodge [*n*] *mixture, mess* collection, combination, goulash*, hash, jumble, medley, mélange, miscellany, mishmash*, mixed bag, olio, patchwork, potpourri, salmagundi*; CONCEPTS 260,432 —*Ant.* singularity

hog [*n1*] *pig* boar, cob roller*, oinker*, piggy, piglet, porker*, razorback, shoat, sow, swine, warthog; CONCEPTS 394,400

hog [*n2*] *glutton* cormorant, epicure, gorger*, gormandizer, gourmand, greedy eater, hefty eater, pig*, swine*; CONCEPT 412

hog [*v*] *be selfish* be greedy, gobble up, grab all of, have all to oneself*, monopolize; CONCEPTS 90,190

hogwash [*n*] *nonsense* absurdity, balderdash*, baloney*, BS*, bull*, bunk*, debris, drivel*, foolishness, hokum, hooey*, horsefeathers*, poppycock*, refuse, ridiculousness, rot, rubbish, trash, twaddle*; CONCEPT 278 —*Ant.* sense, truth

hoi polloi [*n*] *the masses* commonality, commoners, common people, rank and file, the herd, the multitude, the proletariat, the working class; CONCEPTS 379,417

hoist [*v*] *lift* elevate, erect, heave, pick up, raise, rear, take up, uphold, uplift, upraise, uprear; CONCEPT 196 —*Ant.* drop, fall, hold down, lower, push

hokey [*adj*] *corny* banal, commonplace, dull*, feeble, hackneyed, mawkish, old-fashioned, old hat*, sentimental, shopworn, stale, trite; CONCEPT 550

hold [*n*] *grasp, possession* authority, clasp, clench, clinch, clout, clutch, control, dominance, dominion, grip, influence, occupancy, occupation, ownership, pull, purchase, retention, sway, tenacity, tenure; CONCEPTS 190,343,710 —*Ant.* dispossession, release

hold [*v1*] *have in one's hands, possession; grasp* adhere, arrest, bind, bottle up, carry, catch, check, cherish, clasp, cleave, clench, clinch, cling, clutch, confine, contain, cork up*, cradle, detain, embrace, enclose, enjoy, fondle, freeze to*, grip, handle, hang on, have, hug, imprison, keep, keep close, keep out, lock up, maintain, not let go, nourish, occupy, own, palm, possess, press, put a lock on, restrain, retain, secure, seize, squeeze, stay put, stick, take, trammel, vise, wield, withhold, wring; CONCEPTS 190,191,200,710 —*Ant.* drop, let go, release

hold [*v2*] *believe* assume, aver, bet bottom dollar*, buy*, consider, credit, cross one's heart*, deem, entertain, esteem, feel, have hunch*, have sneaking suspicion*, judge, lap up, lay money on, maintain, okay, presume, reckon, regard, sense, set store by*, swear by, swear up and down*, take as gospel truth*, take stock in*, think, view; CONCEPT 12 —*Ant.* abandon, disbelieve, forsake

hold [*v3*] *continue, endure* apply, be in effect, be in force, be the case, be valid, exist, have bearing, hold good, hold true, last, operate, persevere, persist, remain, remain true, resist, stand up, stay, stay staunch, wear; CONCEPT 239 —*Ant.* cease, desert, halt, quit, stop

hold [v4] *support* bear, bolster, brace, buttress, carry, lock, prop, shore up, shoulder, stay, sustain, take, underpin, uphold; CONCEPTS *110,190*

hold [v5] *have a capacity for* accommodate, be equipped for, carry, comprise, contain, include, seat, take; CONCEPTS *719,742*

hold [v6] *conduct meeting, function* assemble, call, carry on, celebrate, convene, have, officiate, preside, run, solemnize; CONCEPTS *324, 384* —*Ant.* cancel

hold back/hold off [v] *repress* bit, bridle, check, control, curb, defer, delay, deny, forbear, hold down, hold in, inhibit, keep, keep back, keep out, postpone, prevent, put off, refrain, refuse, restrain, stop, suppress, withhold; CONCEPTS *121,130* —*Ant.* let go, reveal

holdup [n1] *problem* bottleneck*, delay, difficulty, gridlock*, hitch, obstruction, setback, snag, stoppage, traffic jam*, trouble, wait; CONCEPTS *192,674* —*Ant.* aid, assistance, help

holdup [n2] *take goods illegally by force* burglary, crime, mugging, robbery, stickup, theft; CONCEPT *192*

hold up [v1] *postpone* delay, detain, hinder, hold off, impede, interfere, interrupt, pause, prorogue, retard, set back, slow down, stay, stop, suspend, waive; CONCEPTS *121,130* —*Ant.* allow, continue, forward, permit, promote

hold up [v2] *rob* burglarize, mug, steal from, stick up, waylay; CONCEPTS *139,192* —*Ant.* give

hole [n1] *opening in a solid object* aperture, breach, break, burrow, cave, cavern, cavity, chamber, chasm, chink, cistern, cleft, covert, crack, cranny, crater, cut, den, dent, depression, dimple, dip, excavation, eyelet, fissure, foramen, fracture, gap, gash, gorge, hollow, hovel, keyhole, lacuna, lair, leak, mouth, nest, niche, nick, notch, orifice, outlet, passage, peephole, perforation, pit, pocket, pockmark, puncture, rent, retreat, scoop, shaft, shelter, space, split, tear, tunnel, vacuity, vent, void, window; CONCEPT *513* —*Ant.* closure, solid

hole [n2] *predicament* box*, corner*, difficulty, dilemma, emergency, fix, imbroglio, impasse, jam, mess, pickle*, plight, quandary, scrape, spot, tangle; CONCEPT *674* —*Ant.* advantage, benefit, good fortune

holiday [n] *celebratory day; time off* anniversary, break, celebration, day of rest, feast, festival, festivity, fete, few days off*, fiesta, gala, gone fishing*, holy day, jubilee, layoff, leave, liberty, long weekend*, recess, red-letter day*, saint's day, vacation; CONCEPTS *364,802*

holier-than-thou [adj] *self-righteously pious* goody-goody, high-hat, judgmental, pietistic, sanctimonious, smug, snobbish, unctuous; CONCEPT *401*

holiness [n] *religiousness* asceticism, beatitude, blessedness, consecration, devotion, devoutness, divineness, divinity, faith, godliness, grace, humility, inviolability, piety, purity, religiosity, reverence, righteousness, sacredness, saintliness, sanctity, spirituality, unction, venerableness, virtuousness, worship; CONCEPTS *368,645* —*Ant.* agnosticism, atheism, sin, unholiness, wickedness

holistic [adj] *complete, whole* aggregate,

comprehensive, entire, full, integrated, total, universal; CONCEPT *531*

holler [v] *shout, yell* bawl, bellow, call, cheer, complain, cry, hoot, howl, roar, scream, screech, shriek, shrill, squawk, squeal, ululate, vociferate, wail, whoop, yap, yelp; CONCEPTS *47,595*

hollow [adj1] *empty, hollowed out* alveolate, arched, carved out, cavernous, cleft, concave, cupped, cup-shaped, curved, deep-set, depressed, dimpled, excavated, incurved, indented, infundibular, notched, not solid, pitted, striated, sunken, troughlike, unfilled, vacant, vaulted, void; CONCEPTS *483,490* —*Ant.* convex, full, raised, solid

hollow [adj2] *deep, resonant in sound* cavernous, clangorous, dull, echoing, flat, ghostly, low, muffled, mute, muted, resounding, reverberant, ringing, roaring, rumbling, sepulchral, sounding, thunderous, toneless, vibrant, vibrating; CONCEPT *594* —*Ant.* high, light, soft

hollow [adj3] *meaningless* empty, fruitless, futile, idle, nugatory, otiose, pointless, specious, unavailing, useless, vain, worthless; CONCEPT *560* —*Ant.* earnest, meaningful, sincere, substantial

hollow [adj4] *false, artificial* cynical, deceitful, faithless, flimsy, hypocritical, insincere, treacherous, unsound, weak; CONCEPT *267* —*Ant.* frank, genuine, honest, real, sincere, truthful

hollow [n] *empty or dented area* basin, bottom, bowl, cave, cavern, cavity, chamber, channel, cleft, concavity, crater, cup, dale, den, depression, dimple, dip, dish, excavation, groove, gulf, hole, indentation, notch, pit, pocket, sag, scoop, sinkage, sinkhole, socket, trough, vacuity, valley, void; CONCEPTS *740,754* —*Ant.* solid

hollow [v] *empty out; make concave* channel, chase, corrugate, dent, dig, dish, ditch, excavate, furrow, gorge, groove, indent, notch, pit, rabbet, remove, rut, scoop, shovel, trench; CONCEPTS *178,211* —*Ant.* fill, make convex, raise

holocaust [n] *widespread destruction* annihilation, carnage, catastrophe, devastation, extermination, extinction, genocide, immolation, inferno, massacre, mass murder, slaughter; CONCEPT *252*

holy [adj] *religious, sacred* angelic, believing, blessed, chaste, clean, consecrated, dedicated, devoted, devotional, devout, divine, faithful, faultless, glorified, god-fearing, godlike, godly, good, hallowed, humble, immaculate, innocent, just, moral, perfect, pietistic, pious, prayerful, pure, revered, reverent, righteous, sacrosanct, sainted, saintlike, saintly, sanctified, seraphic, spiritual, spotless, sublime, uncorrupt, undefiled, untainted, unworldly, upright, venerable, venerated, virtuous; CONCEPTS *545,567,574* —*Ant.* depraved, evil, immoral, irreligious, irreverent, sacrilegious, sinful, unholy, unsacred, vile, wicked

homage [n] *devotion, admiration* adoration, adulation, allegiance, awe, deference, duty, esteem, faithfulness, fealty, fidelity, genuflection, honor, kneeling, loyalty, obeisance, praise, respect, reverence, service, tribute, worship; CONCEPTS *32,69* —*Ant.* dishonor, disloyalty, disrespect, faithlessness, scorn, treachery

home [adj] *domestic* at ease, at rest, central, down home*, familiar, family, homely, homey, household, inland, in one's element*, internal, in the bosom*, local, national, native; CONCEPT 536 —*Ant.* business, commercial

home [n1] *place where a human lives* abode, address, apartment, asylum, boarding house, bungalow, cabin, castle, cave*, commorancy, condo, condominium, co-op, cottage, crash pad*, diggings*, digs*, domicile, dormitory, dump*, dwelling, farm, fireside*, flat, habitation, hangout*, haunt, hearth, hideout, hole in the wall*, home plate*, homestead, hospital, house, hut, joint*, living quarters, manor, mansion, nest*, orphanage, pad*, palace, parking place*, place, residence, resort, roof*, rooming house, roost*, shanty, shelter, trailer, turf, villa, where the hat is*; CONCEPT 516 —*Ant.* office

home [n2] *birthplace, environment* abode, camping ground*, country, element, family, farm, fireside*, habitat, habitation, haunt, haven, hearth, hills, home ground, homeland, homestead, hometown, household, land, locality, neck of the woods*, neighborhood, range, roof, site, soil, stamping ground*, stomping ground*, territory; CONCEPTS 510,515,648

homeboy [n] *friend* bro*, brother*, buddy, fellow gang member, homie, neighbor; CONCEPT 423

homegrown [adj] *grown at home* domestic, homemade, native; CONCEPT 536

homeless [adj] *displaced* abandoned, banished, deported, derelict, desolate, destitute, disinherited, displaced, dispossessed, down-and-out*, estranged, exiled, forlorn, forsaken, friendless, houseless, itinerant, outcast, refugee, uncared-for, unhoused, unsettled, unwelcome, vagabond, vagrant, wandering, without a roof*; CONCEPT 555 —*Ant.* settled

homely [adj1] *ordinary, comfortable* comfy, cozy, domestic, everyday, familiar, friendly, homelike, homespun, homey, inelaborate, informal, modest, natural, plain, simple, snug, unaffected, unassuming, unostentatious, unpretentious, welcoming; CONCEPTS 579,589

homely [adj2] *unattractive* animal, disgusting, not beautiful, ordinary, plain, ugly, unaesthetic, unalluring; CONCEPT 579 —*Ant.* attractive, beautiful

homemade [adj] *made in the home* do-it-yourself, handcrafted, handmade, homegrown, homespun, natural; CONCEPT 536

homesick [adj] *nostalgic* hankering, heartsick, lonely, longing for home, missing, wistful, yearning; CONCEPTS 403,529

homespun [adj] *spun from home* crude, handcrafted, handmade, homemade, ordinary, plain, rough, rustic, simple, unrefined, unsophisticated; CONCEPT 536

homey [adj] *comfortable* adequate, cared for, cheerful, comfy*, complacent, contented, cozy, delightful, easy, familiar, folksy, friendly, intimate, plain, pleasant, relaxed, rested, restful, simple, snug, snug as a bug in a rug*, soft, soothed, warm; CONCEPT 572

homicidal [adj] *murderous* bloodthirsty, deadly, lethal, maniacal, slaughterous, violent; CONCEPTS 538,548,565

homicide [n] *killing* assassination, big chill*,

bloodshed, bump-off*, butchery, carnage, crime, death, erase*, foul play, hit, manslaughter, murder, offing, ride, rubout*, slaying; CONCEPT 252 —*Ant.* birth

homogenous [adj] *similar, comparable* akin, alike, analogous, cognate, consistent, homologous, identical, kindred, like, uniform, unvarying; CONCEPTS 487,573 —*Ant.* different, discrete, dissimilar, heterogeneous, miscellaneous, varied

homosexual [adj] *sexually attracted to the same sex* gay, homoerotic, homophile, lesbian; CONCEPT 372

hone [v] *sharpen* acuminate, edge, file, grind, make sharp, put an edge on, put a point on, whet; CONCEPTS 137,250

honest [adj] *truthful, candid* above-board, authentic, bona fide*, conscientious, decent, direct, equitable, ethical, fair, fair and square*, forthright, frank, genuine, high-minded*, honorable, impartial, ingenuous, just, law-abiding*, lay it on the line*, like it is*, no lie*, on the level*, on the up and up*, open, outright, plain, proper, real, reliable, reputable, scrupulous, sincere, straight, straightforward, true, true blue*, trustworthy, trusty, undisguised, unfeigned, upfront*, upright, veracious, virtuous, what you see is what you get*; CONCEPTS 267,545 —*Ant.* deceptive, devious, dishonest, false, fraudulent, lying, misleading, treacherous, untrustworthy, untruthful

honest-to-God [adj] *genuine* absolute, accurate, actual, authentic, authenticated, bona fide, certain, certified, factual, for real*, for-sure, honest, honest-to-goodness*, kosher*, legit, legitimate, no buts about it*, official, on the level*, on the up-and-up, positive, real, really-truly*, real stuff*, straight, sure-enough, sure-thing, true, unquestionable, valid; CONCEPT 582

honesty [n] *truthfulness, candidness* bluntness, candor, confidence, conscientiousness, equity, evenhandedness, fairness, faithfulness, fidelity, frankness, genuineness, goodness, honor, impeccability, incorruptibility, integrity, justness, loyalty, morality, openness, outspokenness, plainness, principle, probity, rectitude, reputability, responsibility, right, scrupulousness, self-respect, sincerity, soundness, straightforwardness, straightness, trustiness, trustworthiness, uprightness, veracity, virtue; CONCEPTS 633,645 —*Ant.* artifice, cheating, deceit, deception, dishonesty, duplicity, falsehood, fraud, fraudulence, lying, treachery

honeyed [adj] *sweetened* cajoling, candied, dulcet, flattering, ingratiating, sugarcoated, sugary; CONCEPT 170

honk [v] *toot* beep, blare, blast, blow, blow the horn, sound, sound one's horn, tootle; CONCEPT 65

honor [n1] *respect* account, adoration, adulation, aggrandizement, apotheosis, approbation, attention, canonization, celebration, confidence, consideration, credit, deference, deification, dignity, distinction, elevation, esteem, exaltation, faith, fame, fealty, glorification, glory, greatness, high standing, homage, immortalization, laud, laurel, lionization, notice, obeisance, popularity, praise, prestige, rank, recognition, renown, reputation, repute, reverence, tribute,

trust, veneration, worship, wreath; CONCEPTS
668,689 —*Ant.* debasement, degradation,
denunciation, derision, disgrace, dishonor,
disrespect, humiliation

honor [*n2*] *integrity* character, chastity,
courage, decency, fairness, goodness, honestness, honesty, incorruption, incorruptness, innocence, modesty, morality, morals, principles,
probity, purity, rectitude, righteousness, trustworthiness, truthfulness, uprightness, virtue;
CONCEPTS *411,645* —*Ant.* blemish, disgrace,
dishonor, ill repute, stigma

honor [*n3*] *praise, award* acclaim, accolade,
adoration, badge, bays, commendation, compliment, credit, decoration, deference, distinction,
favor, homage, kudos, laurels, pleasure, privilege, recognition, regard, respect, reverence,
source of pride, tribute, veneration; CONCEPT
278 —*Ant.* censure, condemnation, reproach

honor [*v*] *recognize, treat with respect* acclaim,
admire, adore, aggrandize, appreciate, be faithful, be true, celebrate, commemorate, commend,
compliment, decorate, dignify, distinguish,
ennoble, erect, esteem, exalt, give glad hand*,
give key to city*, glorify, hallow, keep, laud,
lionize, live up to, look up to, magnify, observe,
praise, prize, revere, roll out red carpet*, sanctify, sublime, uprear, value, venerate, worship;
CONCEPTS *10,633* —*Ant.* betray, denounce,
disgrace, dishonor, disrespect, reproach, shame

honorable [*adj*] *reputable* acclaimed, celebrated, chivalrous, conscientious, dependable,
distinguished, eminent, esteemed, ethical,
faithful, forthright, high-principled, honest,
honored, illustrious, just, knightly, law-abiding, noble, notable, of good repute, on the
up-and-up*, principled, reliable, respectable,
righteous, sincere, sterling, straightforward,
trustworthy, truthful, unstained, upright,
virtuous; CONCEPTS *545,567,574*

honorary [*adj*] *honorific* celebratory, congratulatory, titular; CONCEPTS *668,689*

hood/hoodlum [*n*] *gangster* criminal, delinquent, gangster, goon*, hooligan, mobster,
punk, rioter, rowdy, ruffian, thug, troublemaker;
CONCEPT *545*

hoodwink [*v*] *deceive* bamboozle*, beat out of,
bilk, bluff, buffalo*, burn, cheat, con, defraud,
double-cross, dupe, fake, fleece, fool, gull,
gyp*, hoax, hornswoggle, kid, mislead, pull
a fast one*, pull the wool over one's eyes*,
scam, screw, suck in*, swindle, take advantage
of, take for a ride*, take to the cleaners*, trick,
victimize; CONCEPTS *7,19,59*

hook [*n*] *curved fastener* angle, catch, clasp,
crook, curve, grapnel, grapple, hasp, holder,
link, lock, peg; CONCEPTS *260,498*

hook [*v*] *grab, catch* angle, bag, clasp, crook,
curve, enmesh, ensnare, entrap, fasten, fix, hasp,
lasso, net, pin, secure, snare, trap; CONCEPT *190*
—*Ant.* let go, release, unhook, unlatch, unlock

hooked [*adj*] *addicted* absorbed, captivated,
dependent, devoted, enamored, obsessed,
prone, strung out*, under the influence*;
CONCEPT *542*

hooker [*n*] *prostitute* bawd, call girl, concubine,
courtesan, fallen woman*, floozy*, harlot,
hustler, lady of the evening, moll, nymphomaniac*, painted*, pro*, streetwalker, strumpet,

whore, woman of the streets, working girl*;
CONCEPTS *348,412,415,419*

hooligan [*n*] *hoodlum* criminal, delinquent,
gangster, goon*, hood, mobster, punk, rioter,
rowdy, ruffian, thug, troublemaker; CONCEPT
545

hoopla [*n*] *excitement* action, activity,
brouhaha, bustle, buzz*, commotion, drama,
elation, emotion, excitation, feeling, fever,
fireworks*, flurry, frenzy, furor, fuss, heat*,
hubbub*, hullabaloo*, hysteria, passion, racket,
rage, ruckus, rumpus, stir, thrill; CONCEPT *388*

hoot [*v*] *cry* boo, catcall, heckle, hiss, howl,
jeer, razz*, scoff at, scorn, scream, shout
down, whistle; CONCEPTS *44,47*

hop [*n/v*] *jump on one leg* bounce, bound,
caper, dance, hurdle, leap, lop, lope, skip,
skitter, spring, step, trip, vault; CONCEPT *194*

hope [*n*] *longing; dream* achievement, ambition,
anticipation, aspiration, assumption, belief,
bright side*, buoyancy, castles in air*, concern,
confidence, daydream, dependence, desire,
endurance, expectancy, expectation, faith,
fancy, fool's paradise*, fortune, gain, goal,
greedy glutton*, hopefulness, light at end of
tunnel*, optimism, pipe dream*, promise,
promised land*, prospect, reliance, reverie,
reward, rosiness, sanguineness, security, stock,
thing with feathers*, Utopia, wish; CONCEPTS
20,410,709 —*Ant.* despair, disbelief, discouragement, hopelessness, pessimism

hope [*v*] *long for, dream about* anticipate, aspire, assume, await, believe, be sure of, cherish,
contemplate, count on, deem likely, depend on,
desire, expect, feel confident, foresee, hang in*,
have faith, hold, keep fingers crossed*, knock
on wood*, look at sunny side*, look forward to,
pray, presume, promise oneself, rely, suppose,
surmise, suspect, sweat*, sweat it*, sweat it
out*, take heart*, think to, trust, watch for, wish;
CONCEPT *20* —*Ant.* despair, disbelieve, fear

hopeful [*adj1*] *optimistic, expectant* anticipating, anticipative, assured, at ease, blithe, buoyant, calm, cheerful, comfortable, confident,
content, eager, elated, emboldened, enthusiastic, expecting, faithful, forward-looking*,
high, hoping, inspirited, keeping the faith*,
lighthearted, looking forward to, reassured,
rose-colored*, rosy*, sanguine, satisfied,
serene, trustful, trusting, unflagging, upbeat;
CONCEPT *403* —*Ant.* despairing, despondent,
discouraged, fearful, gloomy, hopeless, low,
pessimistic, sad

hopeful [*adj2*] *promising, auspicious* advantageous, arousing, beneficial, bright, cheerful,
cheering, conducive, convenient, elating, encouraging, enlivening, exciting, expeditious,
fair, favorable, fine, fit, flattering, fortifying,
fortunate, golden, good, gracious, halcyon,
heartening, helpful, inspiring, inspiriting, likely,
lucky, opportune, pleasant, pleasing, probable,
promiseful, propitious, providential, reasonable,
reassuring, roseate, rosy*, rousing, stirring,
suitable, sunny, timely, uplifting, well-timed;
CONCEPT *548* —*Ant.* desperate, hopeless,
inauspicious, pointless, unpromising, wretched

hopeless [*adj*] *futile, pessimistic* bad, beyond
recall, cynical, dejected, demoralized, despairing, desperate, despondent, disconsolate,

discouraging, downhearted, fatal, forlorn, gone*, goner*, helpless, ill-fated, impossible, impracticable, incurable, in despair, irredeemable, irreparable, irreversible, irrevocable, lost, menacing, no-win, past hope, pointless, sad, shot down*, sinister, sunk, threatening, tragic, unachievable, unavailing, unfortunate, unmitigable, up the creek*, useless, vain, woebegone, worsening; CONCEPTS 529,548 —*Ant.* auspicious, bright, encouraging, expectant, hopeful, optimistic, promising, propitious, rosy

horde [n] *uncontrolled throng, pack* band, crew, crowd, crush, drove, everybody, gang, gathering, host, jam, mob, multitude, press, push, squash, swarm, troop, turnout, wall-to-wall*; CONCEPTS 397,417

horizon [n] *skyline, extent* border, boundary, compass, field of vision, ken, limit, perspective, prospect, purview, range, reach, realm, scope, sphere, stretch, vista; CONCEPTS 484,509,529

horizontal [adj] *lying flat* accumbent, aligned, even, flush, level, parallel, plane, recumbent, regular, smooth, straight, uniform; CONCEPTS 581,583 —*Ant.* upright, vertical

horny [adj] *sexually aroused* concupiscent, desiring, hard up, hot*, hot to trot*, lascivious, libidinous, lustful, oversexed, passionate, randy, turned on; CONCEPT 372

horoscope [n] *astrological forecast* astrology, crystal gazing, prediction; CONCEPT 70

horrible/horrendous/horrid [adj] *repulsive, very unpleasant* abhorrent, abominable, appalling, awful, beastly, cruel, detestable, disagreeable, disgusting, dreadful, eerie, execrable, fearful, frightful, ghastly, grim, grisly, gross*, gruesome, heinous, hideous, loathsome, lousy, lurid, mean, nasty, obnoxious, offensive, repellent, revolting, scandalous, scary, shameful, shocking, terrible, terrifying, ungodly, unholy, unkind; CONCEPTS 529,537 —*Ant.* agreeable, delightful, magnificent, pleasant, pleasing, wonderful

horrify [v] *scare* affright, alarm, appall, chill off*, consternate, daunt, disgust, dismay, frighten, intimidate, outrage, petrify, scare to death*, shake, shock, sicken, terrify, terrorize; CONCEPTS 7,14,19 —*Ant.* delight, make happy, please

horror [n] *fear, revulsion* abhorrence, abomination, alarm, antipathy, apprehension, aversion, awe, chiller, consternation, detestation, disgust, dislike, dismay, dread, fright, hate, hatred, loathing, monstrosity, panic, repugnance, terror, trepidation; CONCEPTS 27,29,532,690 —*Ant.* beauty, delight, miracle, pleasure, wonder

hors d'oeuvre [n] *appetizer* antipasto, aperitif, canape, cocktail, dip, finger food, finger sandwich, munchies, sample, starter; CONCEPT 457

horse [n] *equine species* bronco, colt, filly, foal, gelding, mare, mustang, nag, plug*, pony, stallion, steed; CONCEPT 394

horse around [v] *fool around* carry on, cavort, cut up, lark, monkey around*, play around; CONCEPTS 114,384

horseplay [n] *rough play* antics, buffoonery, capers, clowning, fooling around, fun and games, hijinks, misbehavior, pranks, roughhousing, rowdiness, shenanigans, tomfoolery; CONCEPT 386

horticulture [n] *gardening* agriculture, arboriculture, cultivation, farming, floriculture, groundskeeping, viniculture, viticulture; CONCEPTS 205,257

hospitable [adj] *sociable, accommodating* accessible, amenable, amicable, bountiful, charitable, companionable, convivial, cooperative, cordial, courteous, friendly, generous, genial, gracious, gregarious, kind, liberal, magnanimous, neighborly, obliging, open, open-minded, philanthropic, receptive, red-carpet treatment*, responsive, tolerant, welcoming; CONCEPTS 542,555 —*Ant.* hostile, inhospitable, isolated, solitary, unaccommodating, uncordial, unfriendly, unkind, unsociable

hospital [n] *place where ill, injured are treated* clinic, emergency room, health service, hospice, infirmary, institution, nursing home, rest home, sanatorium, sanitarium, sick bay*, surgery, ward; CONCEPTS 312,439,449

hospitality [n] *neighborliness* accommodation, affability, amiability, cheer, companionship, comradeship, consideration, conviviality, cordiality, entertainment, friendliness, generosity, geniality, good cheer, heartiness, hospitableness, obligingness, reception, sociability, warmth, welcome; CONCEPTS 388,657 —*Ant.* hostility, inhospitality, unfriendliness, unneighborliness, unsociableness

host [n1] *person who entertains, performs* anchor, anchor person, emcee, entertainer, innkeeper, keeper, manager, moderator, owner, person of the house, presenter, proprietor; CONCEPT 352 —*Ant.* guest, visitor

host [n2] *large group* army, array, cloud, crowd, crush, drove, flock, gathering, horde, legion, multitude, myriad, rout, score, swarm, throng; CONCEPTS 417,432

host [v] *entertain, accommodate* do the honors*, introduce, pick up the check*, present, receive, spread oneself*, throw a party, treat, wine and dine*; CONCEPTS 292,384

hostage [n] *person held captive until captor's demand is met* captive, earnest, guaranty, pawn, pledge, prisoner, sacrificial lamb*, scapegoat*, security, surety, token, victim; CONCEPTS 359, 423 —*Ant.* captor

hostile [adj] *antagonistic, mean* adverse, alien, allergic, anti*, argumentative, bellicose, belligerent, bitter, catty*, chill*, cold*, competitive, contentious, contrary, disapproving, dour, hateful, ill-disposed, inhospitable, inimical, malevolent, malicious, malignant, militant, nasty, opposed, opposite, oppugnant, ornery*, pugnacious, rancorous, scrappy*, sour*, spiteful, surly, unfavorable, unfriendly, unkind, unpropitious, unsociable, unsympathetic, unwelcoming, viperous, virulent, vitriolic, warlike; CONCEPTS 401,542 —*Ant.* agreeable, friendly, gentle, kind, nice, welcoming

hostility [n] *antagonism, meanness* abhorrence, aggression, animosity, animus, antipathy, aversion, bad blood*, bellicosity, belligerence, bitterness, detestation, disaffection, enmity, estrangement, grudge, hatred, ill will, inimicality, malevolence, malice, opposition, rancor, resentment, spite, spleen, unfriendliness, venom, virulence, war, warpath; CONCEPTS

ho
ho

633,657 —*Ant.* agreeableness, friendliness, friendship, gentleness, kindness, niceness

hot [*adj1*] *very high in temperature* baking, blazing, blistering, boiling, broiling, burning, calescent, close, decalescent, febrile, fevered, feverish, feverous, fiery, flaming, heated, humid, igneous, incandescent, like an oven*, on fire, ovenlike, parching, piping, recalescent, red*, roasting, scalding, scorching, searing, sizzling, smoking, steaming, stuffy, sultry, summery, sweltering, sweltry, thermogenic, torrid, tropic, tropical, very warm, warm, white*; CONCEPT *605* —*Ant.* cold, cool, freezing, frigid

hot [*adj2*] *spicy to taste* acrid, biting, peppery, piquant, pungent, racy, sharp, spicy, zestful; CONCEPT *613* —*Ant.* mild, moderate

hot [*adj3*] *passionate, vehement* angry, animated, ardent, aroused, distracted, eager, enthusiastic, excited, fervent, fervid, fierce, fiery, furious, ill-tempered, impassioned, impetuous, indignant, inflamed, intense, irascible, lustful, raging, stormy, temperamental, touchy, violent; CONCEPTS *401,403* —*Ant.* calm, indifferent, unfeeling

hot [*adj4*] *new, in vogue* approved, cool*, dandy, favored, fresh, glorious, groovy*, in demand, just out*, keen, latest*, marvelous, neat*, nifty*, peachy*, popular, recent, sought-after, super, trendy, up-to-the-minute*; CONCEPT *589* —*Ant.* old, old-fashioned, out, unpopular

hot [*adj5*] *sexually excited* aroused, carnal, concupiscent, erotic, lascivious, lewd, libidinous, lustful, passionate, prurient, salacious, sensual; CONCEPTS *372,555* —*Ant.* frigid, turned off

hot dog [*n1*] *frankfurter* foot long*, frank, pigs in a blanket, red-hot, weenie*, wiener; CONCEPTS *399,457,460*

hot dog [*n2*] *showoff* boaster, braggart, crowd-pleaser, granstander, showboat; CONCEPT *412*

hotel [*n*] *place where one pays for accommodation* auberge, boarding house, caravansary, dump*, fleabag*, flophouse*, hospice, hostel, hostelry, house, inn, lodging, motel, motor inn, public house, resort, roadhouse, rooming house, spa, tavern; CONCEPTS *439,449,516*

hotfoot [*v*] *hurry* barrel*, bolt, boogie*, burn rubber*, clip, dart, dash, fly, gallop, go like a bat out of hell*, hightail it*, hurtle, make haste, race, run, scoot*, speed, sprint, streak, tear*, zip*, zoom; CONCEPT *150* —*Ant.* dawdle

hotheaded [*adj*] *quick-tempered* easily provoked, excitable, explosive, hot-tempered, impetuous, passionate, rash, short-fused, touchy, volatile; CONCEPTS *401,542,548*

hound [*n*] *dog* afghan, airedale, akita, basset, beagle, bowwow*, canine, dachshund, man's best friend*, mongrel, mutt, pointer, pooch, poodle, retriever; CONCEPTS *394,400*

hound [*v*] *chase, badger* annoy, bait, be at, beat the bushes*, be on one's back*, be on one's case*, be on one's tail*, bird-dog*, bother, bug, chivy, curdle, dog*, drive, give chase, goad, harass, harry, hassle, heckle, hector, hunt, hunt down, impel, leave no stone unturned*, persecute, pester, prod, provoke, pursue, rag*, rag on*, ride, scout, scratch, scratch around, search high heaven*, tail, take out after*, track down, turn inside out, turn upside down, yap at*; CONCEPTS *7,19,207* —*Ant.* leave alone

house [*n1*] *human habitat* abode, apartment, box*, building, bullpen, castle, cave*, commorancy, condo, condominium, co-op, coop, crash pad*, crib*, cubbyhole*, den, diggings*, digs*, domicile, dump*, dwelling, edifice, flat, flophouse*, habitation, hole in the wall*, home, home plate*, homestead, joint, kennel, layout, lean-to*, mansion, pad, pied-à-terre, pigpen*, pigsty*, rack*, residence, residency, roof, roost*, setup, shack, shanty, turf*; CONCEPT *439*

house [*n2*] *family, ancestry* clan, dynasty, family tree, folk, folks, household, kin, kindred, line, lineage, ménage, race, stock, tradition, tribe; CONCEPT *296*

house [*n3*] *business establishment* company, concern, corporation, firm, organization, outfit, partnership; CONCEPT *325*

house [*n4*] *government body, sometimes elected, responsible for laws* commons, congress, council, legislative body, legislature, parliament; CONCEPT *299*

household [*adj*] *domestic* domiciliary, everyday, family, home, homely, homey, ordinary, plain; CONCEPT *536* —*Ant.* business, commercial, industrial

household [*n*] *domestic establishment* family, family unit, folks, home, house, ménage; CONCEPTS *296,516*

housekeeper [*n*] *domestic* caretaker, chambermaid, house cleaner, housemaid, housewife, maid, servant; CONCEPTS *348,415*

housework [*n*] *cleaning, maintaining a home* administration, bed-making, cooking, domestic art, domestic science, dusting, home economics, homemaking, housecraft, housekeeping, ironing, laundering, management, mopping, sewing, stewardship, sweeping, washing; CONCEPTS *165,170,202*

housing [*n*] *place of accommodation* construction, digs*, dwelling, habitation, home, house, lodgment, quarter, quarterage, residence, roof, shelter, sheltering, stopping place; CONCEPTS *388,516*

hovel [*n*] *tiny unkempt house* burrow, cabin, cottage, den, dump*, hole*, hut, hutch, lean-to, pigpen*, pigsty*, rathole*, rattrap*, shack, shanty, shed, stall, sty*; CONCEPT *516*

hover [*v*] *hang, float over* be suspended, brood over, dance, drift, flicker, flit, flitter, flutter, fly, hang about, linger, poise, wait nearby, waver; CONCEPT *154* —*Ant.* lie, rest, settle

how [*adv*] *in what way or manner* according to what, after what precedent, by means of, by virtue of what, by what means, by what method, by whose help, from what source, through what agency, through what medium, to what degree, whence, whereby, wherewith; CONCEPT *544*

however [*adv*] *still, nevertheless* after all, all the same, anyhow, be that as it may, but, despite, for all that, howbeit, in spite of, nonetheless, notwithstanding, on the other hand, per contra, though, withal, without regard to, yet; CONCEPT *544*

howl [*n/v*] *long, painful cry* bark, bawl, bay, bellow, blubber, clamor, groan, growl, hoot, keen, lament, moan, outcry, quest, roar, scream, shout, shriek, ululate, wail, weep, whimper, whine, yell, yelp, yip, yowl; CONCEPTS *64,77,595*

hub [n] *center, focal point* core, focus, heart, middle, nerve center*, pivot, polestar, seat; CONCEPT 826 —*Ant.* exterior, exteriority, outside

hubbub [n] *commotion, disorder* babel, bedlam, brouhaha*, clamor, confusion, din, disturbance, fuss, hassle, hell broke loose*, hue and cry*, hullabaloo*, hurly-burly*, jangle, noise, pandemonium, racket, riot, rowdydow*, ruckus, ruction, rumpus, to-do*, tumult, turmoil, uproar, whirl; CONCEPTS 230, 384,388 —*Ant.* calm, order, peace

hubris [n] *arrogance* airs, audacity, brass*, cheek*, chutzpah*, cockiness, conceitedness, contemptuousness, disdain, insolence, loftiness, nerve, ostentation, overbearance, pomposity, pompousness, presumption, pretension, pretentiousness, self-importance, vanity; CONCEPTS 411,633

huckster [n] *peddler* colporteur, costermonger, hawker, pitchperson, salesperson, seller, street seller, street vendor; CONCEPTS 347,348

huddle [n] *assemblage, crowd, often disorganized* bunch, chaos, cluster, clutter, confab*, conference, confusion, disarray, discussion, disorder, gathering, group, heap, jumble, mass, meeting, mess*, muddle; CONCEPTS 230,260

huddle [v] *meet, discuss* bunch, cluster, confer, consult, converge, crouch, crowd, cuddle, curl up, draw together, flock, gather, herd, hug, hunch up*, mass, nestle, parley, powwow*, press, press close, snuggle, throng; CONCEPTS 56,114,154 —*Ant.* cancel

hue [n] *color, shade* aspect, cast, chroma, complexion, dye, tincture, tinge, tint, tone, value; CONCEPT 622

hue and cry [n] *public clamor* brouhaha, bugle call, hullabaloo, outcry, protest, rallying cry, uproar; CONCEPTS 46,65,106,674

huff [n] *bad mood* anger, annoyance, dudgeon, miff, offense, passion, perturbation, pet*, pique, rage, snit*, stew*, temper, tiff, umbrage; CONCEPT 410 —*Ant.* delight, good mood, happiness

huff [v] *sigh, breathe out forcefully* blow, expire, gasp, heave, pant, puff; CONCEPT 163 —*Ant.* inhale

huffy [adj] *angry, in a bad mood* angered, annoyed, crabbed, crabby, cross, crotchety, crusty, curt, disgruntled, exasperated, fractious, grumpy, huffish, hurt, insulted, irked, irritable, miffed, moody, moping, nettled, offended, peeved, peevish, pettish, petulant, piqued, provoked, put out*, querulous, resentful, riled, short, snappish, snappy, stewed, sulky, sullen, surly, testy, touchy, vexed, waspish; CONCEPTS 401,403 —*Ant.* cheerful, delighted, happy, joyful

hug [n] *embrace* affection, bear hug*, bunny hug*, caress, clasp, clinch, lock, squeeze, tight grip; CONCEPTS 190,375 —*Ant.* push, release

hug [v] *hold close, cling to* bear hug, be near to, cherish, clasp, clinch, cradle, cuddle, embrace, enbosom, enfold, envelop, fold in arms, follow closely, grasp, hold onto, keep close, lie close, lock, love, nestle, nurse, press, receive, retain, seize, squeeze, stay near, take in one's arms, welcome; CONCEPTS 190,375 —*Ant.* push away, release

huge [adj] *extremely large* behemothic, bulky, colossal, cyclopean, elephantine, enormous, extensive, gargantuan, giant, gigantic, great, gross*, humongous, immeasurable, immense, jumbo, leviathan, lusty, magnificent, mammoth, massive, mighty, mondo*, monster*, monstrous*, monumental, mountainous, outsize, oversize, planetary, prodigious, stupendous, titanic*, towering, tremendous, vast, walloping, whopping*; CONCEPTS 771,773 —*Ant.* dwarf, little, miniature, minute, small, teeny, tiny

hulk [n] *large piece, lump; remains* blob, body, bulk, chunk, clod, clump, frame, hull, hunk, mass, ruins, shambles, shell, shipwreck, skeleton, wreck; CONCEPT 829 —*Ant.* bit

hulking [adj] *massive* big, bulky, clumsy, colossal, cumbersome, elephantine, enormous, extensive, gargantuan, gigantic, grand, great, heavy, hefty, huge, immense, imposing, large, lumbering, mammoth, monumental, solid, titanic, towering, tremendous, unwieldy, weighty; CONCEPTS 773,781

hull [n] *skeleton, body* bark, case, casing, cast, covering, frame, framework, husk, mold, peel, peeling, pod, rind, shell, shuck, skin, structure; CONCEPTS 484,829

hullabaloo [n] *uproar* bedlam, big scene*, brouhaha, chaos, clamor, commotion, confusion, free-for-all*, furor, fuss, hassle, hubbub, hue and cry, mayhem, melee, noise, pandemonium, racket*, riot, row, ruckus, to-do*; CONCEPTS 46,65,106,230,384,388,674

hum [v] *buzz, vibrate* bombilate, bombinate, bum, bumble, croon, drone, moan, murmur, murmur, purr, rustle, sing, sing low, sound, strum, throb, thrum, trill, warble, whir, whisper, zoom; CONCEPTS 55,77

human [adj] *characteristic of people* animal, anthropoid, anthropological, anthropomorphic, biped, bipedal, civilized, creatural, ethnologic, ethological, fallible, fleshly, forgivable, hominal, hominid, hominine, humanistic, individual, mortal, personal, vulnerable; CONCEPTS 406,549 —*Ant.* immortal, inhuman, unmanly

human [n] *person, Homo sapiens* being, biped, body, character, child, creature, individual, life, mortal, personage, soul, wight; CONCEPT 417 —*Ant.* abstract, immortal, inanimate, nonentity, plant

humane [adj] *kind, compassionate* accommodating, altruistic, amiable, approachable, benevolent, benign, benignant, broad-minded, charitable, clement, considerate, cordial, democratic, forbearing, forgiving, friendly, generous, genial, gentle, good, good-natured, gracious, helpful, human, humanitarian, indulgent, kindhearted, kindly, lenient, liberal, magnanimous, merciful, mild, natural, obliging, open-minded, philanthropic, pitying, righteous, sympathetic, tender, tenderhearted, tolerant, understanding, unselfish, warmhearted; CONCEPTS 401,542 —*Ant.* cruel, fierce, inhumane, merciless, uncivilized, uncompassionate, unkind, unsympathetic, violent

humanitarian [adj] *giving, compassionate* altruistic, beneficent, benevolent, charitable, eleemosynary, generous, good, humane, idealistic, kindly, philanthropic, public-spirited; CONCEPT 542 —*Ant.* egoistic, egotistic, inhumanitarian, uncompassionate, ungiving

humanitarian [n] *person who gives generously* altruist, benefactor, bleeding heart*, do-gooder*, Good Samaritan*, good scout*, helper, patron, philanthropist; CONCEPTS 416, 423 —*Ant.* egoist, stingy

humanity [n1] *human race* Homo sapiens, human beings, humankind, humanness, mankind, people, society; CONCEPT 417

humanity [n2] *benevolence* altruism, amity, brotherly love, charity, compassion, empathy, feeling, friendship, generosity, goodness, goodwill, heart, kindheartedness, kindness, mercy, sympathy; CONCEPTS 410,633

humankind [n] *the human race* community, flesh, Homo sapiens, human beings, humanity, human species, mortality, mortals, people, populace, society; CONCEPT 417

humble [adj1] *meek, unassuming* apprehensive, backward, bashful, biddable, blushing, content, courteous, deferential, demure, diffident, docile, fearful, gentle, hesitant, lowly, manageable, mild, modest, obliging, obsequious, ordinary, polite, quiet, reserved, respectful, retiring, reverential, sedate, self-conscious, self-effac-ing, servile, sheepish, shy, simple, soft-spoken, standoffish, submissive, subservient, supplica-tory, tentative, timid, timorous, tractable, unambitious, unobtrusive, unostentatious, unpretentious, withdrawn; CONCEPTS 401,404 —*Ant.* assertive, boasting, brave, conceited, egotistical, insolent, pretentious, proud, showy

humble [adj2] *poor, inferior* base, beggarly, common, commonplace, contemptible, hum-drum, ignoble, inglorious, insignificant, little, low, low-born, lowly, low-ranking, meager, mean, measly, menial, miserable, modest, ob-scure, ordinary, paltry, petty, pitiful, plebeian, proletarian, puny, rough, scrubby, seemly, servile, severe, shabby, simple, small, sordid, trivial, unassuming, uncouth, underprivileged, undistinguished, unfit, unimportant, unpreten-tious, unrefined, vulgar, wretched; CONCEPTS 334,549,589 —*Ant.* luxurious, rich, superior

humble [v] *shame, put down* abase, abash, be-mean, break, bring down*, cast down, chagrin, chasten, confound, confuse, crush*, cut to the quick*, debase, deflate, degrade, demean, de-mote, deny, discomfit, discredit, disgrace, em-barrass, hide, humiliate, lower*, make eat dirt*, make one feel small*, mortify, overcome, pop one's balloon*, pull down*, put away*, put one away*, put to shame, reduce, silence, sink, snub, squash*, squelch, strike dumb, subdue, take down*, take down a peg*, upset; CONCEPTS 14,16,44,52 —*Ant.* build up, praise, promote

humbug [n1] *nonsense* babble, balderdash*, baloney*, BS*, bull*, bunk*, drivel, empty talk, gibberish, hogwash*, hooey*, hot air*, poppycock*, pretense, rubbish, silliness, trash*; CONCEPTS 230,388,633

humbug [n2] *hoax* con*, con game*, deceit, fast one*, flimflam*, fraud, gyp*, hustle, prank, put-on, scam, snow job*, spoof, sting, swindle; CONCEPTS 59,63

humdinger [n] *something extraordinary* ace, beauty, champ, champion, crackerjack*, doozy, hit, hot stuff*, knockout, lulu, pip*, pistol*, smash hit, something, something else, whopper, winner; CONCEPT 668

humdrum [adj] *boring, uneventful* arid, banau-sic, blah, bromidic, common, commonplace, dim, dime a dozen*, drab, dreary, dull, everyday, garden-variety*, insipid, lifeless, monotone, monotonous, mundane, ordinary, pedestrian, plodding, prosy, repetitious, routine, tedious, tiresome, toneless, treadmill, uninter-esting, unvaried, vanilla*, wearisome, white-bread*; CONCEPT 548 —*Ant.* busy, eventful, exciting, lively, unusual

humid [adj] *very damp, referring to weather* boiling, clammy, close, dank, irriguous, moist, mucky, muggy, oppressive, sodden, soggy, steamy, sticky, stifling, stuffy, sultry, sweaty, sweltering, watery, wet; CONCEPTS 525,603 —*Ant.* arid, dry

humidity [n] *very damp weather* clamminess, dampness, dankness, dew, dewiness, evapora-tion, fogginess, heaviness, humectation, humidness, moistness, moisture, mugginess, oppressiveness, sogginess, steam, steaminess, stickiness, sultriness, sweatiness, swelter, thick-ness, vaporization, wet, wetness; CONCEPTS 524,607 —*Ant.* aridity, dryness

humiliate [v] *embarrass, put down* abase, abash, base, bemean, blister, break, bring down*, bring low*, cast down, chagrin, chasten, confound, confuse, conquer, crush*, cut down to size*, debase, degrade, demean, denigrate, deny, depress, discomfit, discounte-nance, disgrace, dishonor, downplay, humble, lower, make a fool of*, make ashamed, mortify, pan, play down, put out of countenance*, put to shame, rip*, run down*, shame, shoot down*, slam*, smear, snub, squash*, subdue, take down*, take down a peg*, tear down*, vanquish, wither; CONCEPTS 14,44,52 —*Ant.* build up, elevate, laud, praise

humiliation [n] *embarrassment* abasement, affront, chagrin, comedown*, comeuppance, condescension, confusion, degradation, discom-fiture, disgrace, dishonor, humbling, ignominy, indignity, loss of face*, mental pain, mortifica-tion, put-down, resignation, self-abasement, shame, submission, submissiveness, touché*; CONCEPTS 388,410 —*Ant.* elevation, flattery, glorification, praise, success, triumph

humility [n] *humbleness, modesty* abasement, bashfulness, demureness, diffidence, docility, fawning, inferiority complex, lack of pride, lowliness, meekness, mortification, nonresis-tance, obedience, obsequiousness, passiveness, reserve, resignation, self-abasement, self-abne-gation, servility, sheepishness, shyness, subjec-tion, submissiveness, subservience, timidity, timorousness, unobtrusiveness, unpretentious-ness; CONCEPTS 633,657 —*Ant.* arrogance, assertiveness, egoism, pretentiousness, pride, self-importance

humor [n1] *comedy, funniness* amusement, bad-inage, banter, buffoonery, clowning, comical-ity, comicalness, drollery, facetiousness, farce, flippancy, fun, gag, gaiety, happiness, high spirits, jest, jesting, jocoseness, jocularity, joke, joking, joyfulness, kidding, levity, lightness, playfulness, pleasantry, raillery, tomfoolery, whimsy, wisecrack, wit, witticism, wittiness; CONCEPT 293 —*Ant.* depression, drama, sadness, seriousness, tragedy, unhappiness

humor [*n2*] *mood, temperament* bee, bent, bias, caprice, character, complexion, conceit, disposition, fancy, frame of mind, individualism, individuality, makeup, mind, nature, notion, personality, propensity, quirk, spirits, strain, temper, tone, vagary, vein, whim; CONCEPT *410*

humorist [*n*] *comedian* card*, clown, comedienne, comic, cutup, entertainer, jester, joker, jokesmith, jokester, satirist, stand-up comic, wisecracker, wit; CONCEPTS *352,423*

humorous [*adj*] *funny, comical* amusing, camp*, campy*, comic, droll, entertaining, facetious, farcical, hilarious, jocose, jocular, jokey, joshing, laughable, ludicrous, merry, playful, pleasant, priceless, ribald, screaming*, side-splitting*, too funny for words*, waggish, whimsical, witty; CONCEPTS *267,529* —*Ant.* depressing, dramatic, gloomy, morose, sad, serious, tragic, uncomical, unfunny

hump [*n*] *swelling, projection* bulge, bump, convexedness, convexity, dune, elevation, eminence, excrescence, gibbosity, hill, hummock, hunch, knap, knob, knurl, kyphosis, mound, prominence, protrusion, protuberance, ridge, swell, tumescence; CONCEPTS *471,513* —*Ant.* depression

hunch [*n*] *feeling, idea* anticipation, apprehension, auguration, augury, boding, clue, expectation, feeling in one's bones*, foreboding, forecast, foreknowledge, forewarning, forewisdom, funny feeling*, glimmer, hint, impression, inkling, instinct, intuition, misgiving, notion, omination, portent, preapprehension, precognition, preconceived notion, premonition, prenotation, prenotice, presage, presagement, prescience, presentiment, qualm, suspicion, thought; CONCEPT *689* —*Ant.* proof, reality, truth

hunch [*v*] *cower, crouch* arch, bend, bow, curve, draw in, draw together, huddle, hump, lean, scrooch down, squat, stoop, tense; CONCEPT *154* —*Ant.* stand, straighten

hunger [*n*] *appetite for food, other desire* ache, appetence, appetency, appetition, a stomach for*, big eyes*, bottomless pit*, craving, desire, emptiness, esurience, eyes for*, famine, famishment, gluttony, greed, greediness, hungriness, longing, lust, mania, munchies*, ravenousness, starvation, sweet tooth*, vacancy, void, voracity, want, yearning, yen; CONCEPTS *20,709* —*Ant.* satiation, satisfaction

hungry [*adj*] *starving; desirous* athirst, avid, carnivorous, could eat a horse*, covetous, craving, eager, edacious, empty, esurient, famished, famishing, flying light*, got the munchies*, greedy, hankering, hoggish, hollow, hungered, insatiate, keen, omnivorous, on empty stomach*, piggish*, rapacious, ravenous, starved, unfilled, unsatisfied, voracious, yearning; CONCEPTS *20,406* —*Ant.* full, replete, satiated, satisfied, stuffed

hunk [*n*] *chunk of solid material* a lot*, batch, bit, block, bulk, bunch, clod, glob, gob*, large piece, loads*, loaf, lump, mass, morsel, nugget, piece, pile, portion, quantity, slab, slice, wad, wedge; CONCEPTS *470,471*

hunt [*n*] *search, chase* coursing, exploration, field sport, following, frisking, game, hounding, hunting, inquest, inquiry, inquisition, interroga-

tion, investigation, look-see*, meddling, probe, prosecution, prying, pursuance, pursuing, pursuit, quest, race, raid, reconnaissance, research, rummage, scrutiny, seeking, sifting, snooping, sporting, steeplechase, study, tracing, trailing; CONCEPTS *207,216*

hunt [*v1*] *chase for killing* beat the bushes*, bird-dog*, capture, course, dog, drag, drive, fish, follow, give chase, grouse, gun*, gun for*, hawk, heel, hound, kill, look for, poach, press, pursue, ride, run, scent, scratch, scratch around, seek, shadow, shoot, snare, stalk, start, track, trail; CONCEPTS *207,216,252,363* —*Ant.* let go

hunt [*v2*] *look, search for* be on the lookout*, cast about, delve, drag, examine, ferret out, fish for, forage, go after, grope, inquire, interrogate, investigate, look all over hell*, look high and low*, nose around*, probe, prowl, quest, question, ransack, rummage, run down, scour, scratch around*, search high heaven*, seek, sift, trace, trail, try to find, winnow; CONCEPT *216* —*Ant.* ignore, neglect

hurdle [*n*] *barrier, obstacle* bar, barricade, blockade, complication, difficulty, fence, hamper, handicap, hedge, hindrance, impediment, interference, mountain, obstruction, rub, snag, stumbling block, traverse, wall; CONCEPTS *470,674* —*Ant.* clear path, opening

hurdle [*v*] *jump over an obstacle* bounce, bound, clear, conquer, down, hop, jump across, leap over, lick, lop, master, negotiate, over, overcome, saltate, scale, spring, surmount, vault; CONCEPT *194*

hurl [*v*] *throw forcefully* bung, cast, chuck, chunk, fire, fling, gun, heave, launch, let fly, lob, peg, pitch, project, propel, send, sling, toss; CONCEPT *222*

hurricane [*n*] *violent windstorm* blow, cyclone, gale, line storm, monsoon, storm, tempest, tornado, tropical cyclone, tropical storm, twister, typhoon, whirlwind; CONCEPTS *524,526*

hurried [*adj*] *quick, rushed* abrupt, breakneck, brief, cursory, fast, hasty, headlong, hectic, impetuous, perfunctory, precipitant, precipitate, precipitous, rushing, short, slapdash, speedy, subitaneous, sudden, superficial, swift; CONCEPTS *548,588,799* —*Ant.* easily, leisurely, slow, unhurried, unrushed

hurry [*n*] *speed in action, motion* bustle, celerity, commotion, dash, dispatch, drive, expedition, expeditiousness, flurry, haste, precipitance, precipitateness, precipitation, promptitude, push, quickness, rush, rustle, scurry, speediness, swiftness, urgency; CONCEPTS *657,748,755* —*Ant.* delay, procrastination, rest, slowness, stall, wait

hurry [*v*] *act, move speedily* accelerate, barrel, beeline*, be quick, bestir, breeze, bullet, burst, bustle, dash, dig in, drive, expedite, fleet, flit, fly, get a move on*, goad, go like lightning*, haste, hasten, hurry up, hustle, jog, lose no time, make haste, make short work of*, make time*, make tracks*, nip, push, quicken, race, rip, rocket, roll, run, rush, sally, scoot, scurry, shake a leg*, smoke, speed, speed up, spur, step on gas*, step on it*, turn on steam*, urge, whirl, whish, whisk, whiz, zip; CONCEPTS *150,234* —*Ant.* dally, dawdle, delay, procrastinate, rest, slow, stall, wait

hurt [*adj*] *physically or mentally injured* aching,

aggrieved, agonized, all torn up*, battered, bleeding, bruised, buffeted, burned, busted up*, contused, crushed, cut, damaged, disfigured, distressed, disturbed, grazed, harmed, hit, impaired, indignant, in pain, lacerated, marred, mauled, miffed, mutilated, nicked, offended, pained, piqued, put away, resentful, rueful, sad, scarred, scraped, scratched, shook, shot, sore, stricken, struck, suffering, tender, tortured, umbrageous, unhappy, warped, wounded; CONCEPTS *314,403* —Ant. comforted, cured, healed, healthy, ok, pleased, remedied, well

hurt [n] *injury; damage* ache, black and blue*, blow, boo-boo*, bruise, chop, detriment, disadvantage, disaster, discomfort, disservice, distress, down, gash, harm, ill, ill-treatment, loss, mark, mischief, misfortune, nick, ouch, outrage, pain, pang, persecution, prejudice, ruin, scratch, sore, soreness, suffering, wound, wrong; CONCEPTS *316,728* —Ant. aid, assist, cure, healing, help, remedy

hurt [v1] *cause physical pain; experience pain* abuse, ache, afflict, ail, belt, be sore, be tender, bite, blemish, bruise, burn, cramp, cut, cut up, damage, disable, do violence, flail, flog, harm, impair, injure, kick, lacerate, lash, maltreat, mar, maul, mess up, nip, pierce, pinch, pommel, prick, pummel, punch, puncture, punish, rough up, shake up, slap, slug, smart, spank, spoil, squeeze, stab, sting, tear, throb, torment, torture, total, trouble, wax, whack, whip, wing, wound, wrack up, wring; CONCEPTS *246,313* —Ant. aid, assist, assuage, cure, heal, help, relieve, remedy, soothe

hurt [v2] *cause mental pain* abuse, afflict, aggrieve, annoy, burn, chafe, constrain, cut to the quick*, discomfit, discommode, displease, distress, excruciate, faze, give no quarter*, go for jugular*, grieve, hit where one lives*, injure, lambaste, lay a bad trip on*, lean on*, martyr, martyrize, prejudice, punish, put down, put out, sadden, sting*, thumb nose at*, torment, torture, try, upset, vex, vitiate, work over*, wound, zing*; CONCEPTS *7,14,19* —Ant. calm, placate, please, relieve, soothe

hurtful [adj] *injurious, cruel* aching, afflictive, bad, cutting, damaging, dangerous, deadly, deleterious, destructive, detrimental, disadvantageous, distressing, evil, harmful, hurting, malicious, mean, mischievous, nasty, nocuous, noxious, ominous, pernicious, poisonous, prejudicial, spiteful, unkind, upsetting, wounding; CONCEPTS *537,542* —Ant. aiding, assisting, harmless, helpful, helping, kind, nice, relieving

hurtle [v] *plunge, charge* bump, collide, fly, lunge, push, race, rush, rush headlong, scoot, scramble, shoot, speed, spurt, tear; CONCEPT *150*

husband [n] *married man* bridegroom, companion, consort, groom, helpmate, hubby, mate, monogamist, monogynist, other half, partner, spouse; CONCEPTS *414,419* —Ant. wife

hush [n] *quiet* calm, lull, peace, peacefulness, quietude, silence, still, stillness, tranquility; CONCEPT *65* —Ant. clamor, yelling

hush [v] *attempt to make quiet* burke, choke, gag, muffle, mute, muzzle, quiet, quieten, shush*, shut up, silence, stifle, still, stop, suppress; CONCEPTS *65,87* —Ant. yell

hush-hush [adj] *secret* clandestine, classified, closet, confidential, covert, dark, private, restricted, sub-rosa*, surreptitious, undercover, under-the-table*; CONCEPT *576* —Ant. known, public, revealed, told

hush up [v] *keep secret* burke, conceal, cover, cover up, keep dark, sit on, smother, squash, stifle, suppress; CONCEPT *266* —Ant. reveal, tell

husk [n] *covering, case* aril, bark, case, chaff, glume, hull, outside, pod, rind, shell, shuck, skin; CONCEPTS *428,484* —Ant. core

husky [adj] *deep, scratchy in sound* croaking, croaky, growling, gruff, guttural, harsh, hoarse, loud, rasping, raucous, rough, throaty; CONCEPT *594* —Ant. low, quiet, soft

husky [adj2] *big, burly* brawny, gigantic, hefty, Herculean*, mighty, muscular, powerful, rugged, sinewy, stalwart, stocky, stout, strapping, strong, sturdy, thickset, well-built; CONCEPT *773* —Ant. little, small, thin

hussy [n] *loose woman* broad, floozy, jade, Jezebel, minx, slut, strumpet, tart*, tramp, trollop, vamp, wench, whore; CONCEPTS *348, 412,415,419*

hustle [v] *hurry; work hurriedly* apply oneself, be conscientious, bulldoze*, bustle, elbow, fly, force, haste, hasten, hotfoot*, impel, jog, press, push, race, rush, shove, speed, thrust, use elbow grease*; CONCEPTS *91,150* —Ant. dally, delay, procrastinate, slow, wait

hustler [n] *con artist; prostitute* call girl, cheater, fast talker, floozy, grifter, hooker, rip-off artist*, scam artist, streetwalker, swindler, whore; CONCEPTS *348,412,415,419*

hut [n] *tiny, often roughly built, house* box*, bungalow, cabana, cabin, camp, chalet, cot, cottage, crib*, den, dugout, dump*, hovel*, hutch, lean-to, lodge, log house, pigeonhole*, rathole*, refuge, shack, shanty, shed, shelter, summer house, tepee, wigwam; CONCEPT *516*

hybrid [n] *composite, mixture* amalgam, bastard, combination, compound, cross, crossbreed, half-blood, half-breed, half-caste, incross, miscegenation, mongrel, mule, outcross; CONCEPTS *260,394,414,429* —Ant. homogeneous, pedigreed, pure, purebred, thoroughbred, unmixed

hygiene [n] *cleanliness* healthful living, hygienics, preventive medicine, public health, regimen, salutariness, sanitation, wholesomeness; CONCEPTS *316,405* —Ant. dirtiness, filth, foulness

hygienic [adj] *clean* aseptic, disinfected, germ-free, good, healthful, healthy, pure, salubrious, salutary, salutiferous, sanitary, sterile, uncontaminated, uninfected, wholesome; CONCEPT *621* —Ant. contaminated, dirty, diseased, filthy, foul, infected, unclean, unpure, unsanitary, unsterile

hymn [n] *religious song* aria, canticle, carol, chant, choral, chorale, descant, ditty, evensong, hosanna, laud, lay, lied, littany, ode, oratorio, paean, psalm, shout, song of praise, worship song; CONCEPTS *262,595*

hype [n] *extensive publicity* advertising, buildup*, plugging*, promotion; CONCEPTS *292,324* —Ant. secrecy

hyperactive [adj] *excessively active* excitable, high-strung, hyper*, overactive, overzealous, uncontrollable, wild; CONCEPTS *401,404*

hyperbole [*n*] *exaggeration* amplification, big talk*, coloring*, distortion, embellishment, embroidering, enlargement, hype*, laying it on thick*, magnification, metaphor, mountain out of molehill*, overstatement, PR*, tall talk*; CONCEPT *268* —*Ant.* understatement

hypercritical [*adj*] *captious* carping, caviling, censorious, critical, demanding, faultfinding, finicky, fussy, hair-splitting, hard to please, niggling, nit-picking, overcritical, persnickety; CONCEPTS *267,404*

hyperinflation [*n*] *extremely high, rising economic inflation* devaluation, overextension, run-away inflation, wheelbarrow economics; CONCEPT *335*

hypermedia [*n*] *system giving access to multimedia information on a single subject* data base, information bank, information retrieval; CONCEPT *274*

hypnotic [*adj*] *spellbinding, sleep-inducing* anesthetic, anodyne, calmative, lenitive, mesmeric, mesmerizing, narcotic, opiate, sleepy, somniferous, somnolent, soothing, soporific, soporose, trance-inducing; CONCEPTS *529,537* —*Ant.* exciting, exhilarating, inciteful, inspiring, stimulating

hypnotize [*v*] *put in trance; spellbind* anesthetize, bring under control, captivate, charm, drug, dull the will, entrance, fascinate, hold under a spell, induce, lull to sleep, magnetize, make drowsy, make sleepy, mesmerize, narcotize, put to sleep, soothe, stupefy, subject to suggestion; CONCEPT *250* —*Ant.* excite, exhilarate, incite, inspire, stimulate

hypochondriac [*adj*] *neurotic* health-obsessed, hypochondriacal, hypochondric, imagining, preoccupied with health, valetudinarian; CONCEPT *403*

hypochondriac [*n*] *neurotic* hypochondriast, valetudinarian; CONCEPT *316*

hypocrisy [*n*] *deceitfulness, pretense* affectation, bad faith*, bigotry, cant, casuistry, deceit, deception, dishonesty, display, dissembling, dissimulation, double-dealing, duplicity, false profession, falsity, fraud, glibness, imposture, insincerity, irreverence, lie, lip service*, mockery, pharisaicalness, pharisaism, phoniness, pietism, quackery, sanctimoniousness, sanctimony, speciousness, unctuousness; CONCEPTS *63,633,657* —*Ant.* forthrightness, honesty, righteousness, sincerity, truth

hypocrite [*n*] *person who pretends, is deceitful* actor, attitudinizer, backslider*, bigot, bluffer, casuist, charlatan, cheat, con artist, crook, deceiver, decoy, dissembler, dissimulator, fake, faker, four-flusher*, fraud, hook*, humbug, impostor, informer, lip server*, malingerer, masquerader, mountebank, Pharisee, phony, playactor*, poser, pretender, quack*, smoothie*, sophist, swindler, trickster, two-face*, two-timer*, wolf in sheep's clothing*; CONCEPT *412*

hypocritical [*adj*] *deceitful, pretending* affected, artificial, assuming, bland, canting, captious, caviling, deceptive, deluding, dissembling, double, double-dealing, duplicitous, faithless, false, feigning, fishy*, fraudulent, glib, hollow, insincere, jivey, left-handed, lying, moralistic, oily, pharisaical, phony,

pietistic, pious, sanctimonious, self-righteous, smooth, smooth-spoken, smooth-tongued*, snide, specious, spurious, two-faced*, unctuous, unnatural, unreliable; CONCEPTS *267,401,542* —*Ant.* actual, authentic, forthright, honest, just, real, reliable, righteous, sincere, truthful, upright

hypothesis [*n*] *theory* antecedent, apriority, assignment, assumption, attribution, axiom, basis, belief, conclusion, condition, conjecture, data, deduction, demonstration, derivation, explanation, foundation, ground, guess, inference, interpretation, layout, lemma, philosophy, plan, position, postulate, premise, presupposition, principle, proposal, proposition, rationale, reason, scheme, shot in the dark*, speculation, starting point, suggestion, supposition, surmise, system, tentative law, term, theorem, thesis; CONCEPTS *661,689* —*Ant.* calcualtion, measurement, proof, reality, truth

hypothetical [*adj*] *guessed, assumed* academic, assumptive, casual, concocted, conditional, conjecturable, conjectural, contestable, contingent, debatable, disputable, doubtful, equivocal, imaginary, imagined, indefinite, indeterminate, postulated, presumptive, presupposed, pretending, problematic, provisory, putative, questionable, refutable, speculative, stochastic, supposed, suppositional, suppositious, suspect, theoretic, theoretical, uncertain, unconfirmed, vague; CONCEPTS *529,552,582* —*Ant.* calculated, confirmed, factual, measured, proven, proven, real, reliable, truthful

hysteria [*n*] *state of extreme upset* agitation, delirium, excitement, feverishness, frenzy, hysterics, madness, mirth, nervousness, panic, unreason; CONCEPT *410* —*Ant.* calm, control, sereneness

hysterical [*adj*] *very upset, excited* agitated, berserk, beside oneself, blazing, carried away*, convulsive, crazed, crazy, delirious, distracted, distraught, emotional, fiery, frantic, frenzied, fuming, furious, impassioned, impetuous, in a fit, incensed, irrepressible, mad, maddened, nervous, neurotic, overwrought, panic-stricken, passionate, possessed, rabid, raging, rampant, raving, seething, spasmodic, tempestuous, turbulent, uncontrollable, uncontrolled, unnerved, unrestrained, uproarious, vehement, violent, wild, worked up*; CONCEPTS *403,542* —*Ant.* calm, controlled, serene

I

ice [*n*] *frozen water* chunk, crystal, cube ice, diamonds*, dry ice, floe, glacier, glaze, hail, hailstone, iceberg, ice cube, icicle, permafrost, sleet; CONCEPTS *470,514* —*Ant.* water

ice-cold [*adj*] *very cold* algid, arctic, biting, bitter, bitterly cold, brumal, chill, cutting, freezing, frozen, gelid, glacial, icy, piercing, polar, raw, Siberian, sub-zero, wintry; CONCEPTS *605,606* —*Ant.* burning hot, hot, warm

icing [*n*] *frosting* cream, glacé, glaze, ornamentation, sugar paste, topping, trimming; CONCEPT *457*

icky [*adj*] *not pleasant* disgusting, horrible, loathsome, nasty, noisome, offensive, repellent,

revolting, sickening, vile; CONCEPT 570
—*Ant.* good, nice, pleasing

icon [n] *image* figure, graphical user interface, graphic image, idol, ikon, likeness, painted image, picture, portrait, portrayal, representation, symbol; CONCEPTS 259,667,716

iconoclast [n] *detractor* critic, cynic, denouncer, dissenter, dissident, heretic, image-breaker, nonbeliever, non-conformist, questioner, radical, rebel, revolutionist, ruiner, sceptic, unbeliever; CONCEPTS 359,423

icy [adj1] *frozen; slippery when frozen* antarctic, arctic, biting, bitter, chill, chilled to the bone*, chilling, chilly, cold, freezing, frigid, frostbound, frosty, frozen over, gelid, glacial, glaring, iced, polar, raw, refrigerated, rimy, shivering, shivery, sleeted, smooth as glass*; CONCEPTS 605,606 —*Ant.* unfrozen, watery

icy [adj2] *aloof* chill, cold, distant, emotionless, forbidding, frigid, frosty, glacial, hostile, indifferent, steely, stony, unemotional, unfriendly, unwelcoming; CONCEPTS 401,404 —*Ant.* friendly, warm

idea [n] *something understood, planned, or believed* abstraction, aim, approximation, belief, brainstorm*, clue, concept, conception, conclusion, conviction, design, doctrine, end, essence, estimate, fancy, feeling, flash*, form, guess, hint, hypothesis, import, impression, inkling, intention, interpretation, intimation, judgment, meaning, notion, object, objective, opinion, pattern, perception, plan, purpose, reason, scheme, sense, significance, solution, suggestion, suspicion, teaching, theory, thought, understanding, view, viewpoint; CONCEPTS 529,660,661,689

ideal [adj1] *model, perfect* absolute, archetypal, classic, classical, complete, consummate, excellent, exemplary, fitting, flawless, have-it-all*, indefectible, optimal, paradigmatic, pie-in-the-sky*, prototypical, quintessential, representative, Shangri-la*, supreme; CONCEPTS 533,574 —*Ant.* flawed, imperfect, incorrect, problematic, wrong

ideal [adj2] *conceptual; impractical* abstract, chimerical, dreamlike, extravagant, fanciful, fictitious, high-flown, hypothetical, imaginary, intellectual, in the clouds*, ivory-tower*, mental, mercurial, notional, out-of-reach*, quixotic, theoretical, transcendent, transcendental, unattainable, unearthly, unreal, Utopian*, visionary; CONCEPTS 529,552 —*Ant.* actual, common, material, practical, pragmatic

ideal [n] *model* archetype, criterion, epitome, example, exemplar, goal, idol, jewel, last word*, mirror, nonesuch, nonpareil, paradigm, paragon, pattern, perfection, prototype, standard; CONCEPTS 671,686 —*Ant.* error, flaw, imperfection, problem, wrong

idealist [n] *person who holds fancies in mind, who believes in perfection* dreamer, enthusiast, escapist, optimist, Platonist, radical, romancer, romantic, romanticist, seer, stargazer, theorizer, transcendentalist, utopian, visionary; CONCEPTS 359,416,423 —*Ant.* pragmatist, realist

idealistic [adj] *visionary* abstracted, chimerical, dreaming, idealized, impractical, optimistic, quixotic, radical, romantic, starry-eyed, unrealistic, utopian; CONCEPTS 529,560,582

ideals [n] *moral beliefs* ethics, goals, principles, standards, values; CONCEPTS 645,689

identical [adj] *alike, equal* carbon copy*, corresponding, dead ringer*, ditto*, double, duplicate, equivalent, exact, identic, indistinguishable, interchangeable, like, like two peas in a pod*, look-alike, matching, same, same difference*, selfsame, spitting image*, tantamount, twin, very, very same, Xerox*; CONCEPTS 487,566, 573 —*Ant.* different, dissimilar, distinct, diverse, opposite, unequal, unlike

identification [n] *labeling; means of labeling* apperception, assimilation, badge, bracelet, cataloging, classifying, credentials, description, dog tag, establishment, ID*, identity bracelet, letter of introduction, letter of recommendation, naming, papers, passport, recognition, tag, testimony; CONCEPTS 268,271

identify [v] *recognize; label* analyze, button down*, card, catalog, classify, describe, determinate, determine, diagnose, diagnosticate, distinguish, establish, find, make out, name, peg*, pick out, pinpoint, place, put one's finger on*, select, separate, single out*, spot, tab*, tag*; CONCEPTS 38,62 —*Ant.* confuse, mistake

identify with [v] *put oneself in the place of another* ally, associate, empathize, feel for*, put in same category*, put oneself in another's shoes*, relate to, respond to, see through someone's eyes*, sympathize, think of in connection*, understand; CONCEPTS 15,39

identity [n1] *person's individuality* character, circumstances, coherence, distinctiveness, existence, identification, integrity, ipseity, name, oneness, particularity, personality, self, selfdom, selfhood, selfness, singleness, singularity, status, uniqueness; CONCEPT 411

identity [n2] *similarity, correspondence* accord, agreement, congruence, congruity, empathy, equality, equivalence, identicalness, likeness, oneness, rapport, resemblance, sameness, selfsameness, semblance, similitude, unanimity, uniformity, unity; CONCEPTS 664,670 —*Ant.* difference, dissimilarity, opposition

ideology [n] *beliefs* articles of faith*, credo, creed, culture, dogma, ideas, outlook, philosophy, principles, system, tenets, theory, view, Weltanschauung*; CONCEPTS 688,689

idiocy [n] *utter stupidity* asininity, cretinism, derangement, fatuity, fatuousness, foolishness, imbecility, inanity, insanity, insipidity, lunacy, madness, senselessness, tomfoolery; CONCEPTS 409,410 —*Ant.* brains, intelligence

idiom [n] *manner of speaking, turn of phrase* argot, colloquialism, dialect, expression, idiosyncrasy, jargon, language, lingo*, localism, locution, parlance, patois, phrase, provincialism, set phrase, street talk*, style, talk, tongue, usage, vernacular, vernacularism, word; CONCEPT 275 —*Ant.* standard

idiosyncrasy [n] *oddity, quirk* affectation, bit, characteristic, distinction, eccentricity, feature, habit, mannerism, peculiarity, singularity, trait, trick; CONCEPTS 411,644

idiot [n] *very stupid person* blockhead, bonehead*, cretin, dimwit, dork, dumbbell, dunce, fool, ignoramus, imbecile, jerk, kook*, moron, nincompoop, ninny*, nitwit, out to lunch*,

pinhead*, simpleton, stupid, tomfool, twit*;
CONCEPT 412 —*Ant.* brain

idiotic [*adj*] *very stupid* asinine, batty*, birdbrained*, crazy, daffy* daft, dull, dumb,
fatuous, foolhardy, foolish, harebrained*,
imbecile, imbecilic, inane, insane, lunatic,
moronic, senseless, silly, squirrelly*, thick-
witted*, unintelligent; CONCEPT 402 —*Ant.*
brainy, intelligent, smart

idle [*adj1*] *not used; out of action* abandoned,
asleep, barren, closed down, dead, deserted,
down, dusty, empty, gathering dust*, inactive,
inert, jobless, laid-off, leisured, mothballed,
motionless, on the bench*, on the shelf*, out
of operation, out of work*, passive, quiet,
redundant, resting, rusty, sleepy, stationary,
still, uncultivated, unemployed, unoccupied,
untouched, unused, vacant, void, waste,
workless; CONCEPTS 542,560 —*Ant.* active,
busy, employed, productive, used, working

idle [*adj2*] *lazy* at rest, indolent, lackadaisical,
resting, shiftless, slothful, sluggish, taking it
easy*; CONCEPTS 401,538 —*Ant.* ambitious,
busy, diligent, hustling, productive

idle [*adj3*] *worthless, ineffective* abortive, bootless, empty, frivolous, fruitless, futile, groundless, hollow, insignificant, irrelevant, not
serious, nugatory, of no avail*, otiose, pointless,
rambling, superficial, trivial, unavailing, unhelpful, unnecessary, unproductive, unsuccessful,
useless, vain; CONCEPTS 267,560 —*Ant.*
effective, important, productive, worthwhile

idleness [*n*] *laziness, inaction* dawdling, dilly-
dallying*, dormancy, droning, goof-off time*,
hibernation, inactivity, indolence, inertia, job-
lessness, laze, lazing, leisure, lethargy, loafing,
loitering, otiosity, own sweet time*, pottering,
shiftlessness, sloth, slothfulness, slouch,
slowness, sluggishness, stupor, time on one's
hands*, time to burn*, time to kill*, time-
wasting, torpidity, torpor, trifling, truancy,
unemployment, vegetating; CONCEPTS 657,
677,681 —*Ant.* action, ambition, busyness,
diligence, employment, hustle, industry, labor,
occupation, work

idol [*n*] *person greatly admired* beloved, darling,
dear, deity, desire, eidolon, false god, favorite,
fetish, god, goddess, golden calf*, graven
image, hero, icon, image, inamorata, pagan symbol, simulacrum, superstar; CONCEPTS 352,423

idolize [*v*] *think of very highly; worship* admire,
adore, apotheosize, bow down, canonize, deify,
dote on, exalt, glorify, look up to*, love, put
on a pedestal*, revere, reverence, venerate;
CONCEPTS 10,32 —*Ant.* despise

idyllic [*adj*] *perfect; extremely pleasant* arcadian, bucolic, charming, comfortable, halcyon,
heavenly, ideal, idealized, out-of-this-world*,
pastoral, peaceful, picturesque, pleasing, rustic,
unspoiled; CONCEPTS 529,572 —*Ant.* bad,
disagreeable, flawed, imperfect

iffy [*adj*] *uncertain* capricious, chancy, conditional, dicey, doubtful, erratic, fluctuant,
incalculable, in lap of gods*, problematic,
undecided, unpredictable, unsettled, up in the
air*, whimsical; CONCEPT 552 —*Ant.* certain,
definite, reliable, sure

ignite [*v*] *set on fire* burn, burst into flames,
catch fire, enkindle, fire, flare up, inflame,

kindle, light, put match to*, set alight, set fire
to, start up, take fire, touch off; CONCEPT 249
—*Ant.* extinguish, put out

ignoble [*adj*] *lowly, unworthy* abject, base,
baseborn, coarse, common, contemptible, corrupt, craven, dastardly, degenerate, degraded,
despicable, disgraceful, dishonorable, heinous,
humble, infamous, inferior, lewd, low, mean,
menial, modest, ordinary, peasant, petty, plain,
plebeian, poor, rotten, scurvy, servile, shabby,
shameful, simple, sordid, unwashed, vile,
vulgar, wicked, wretched, wrong; CONCEPTS
542,545,549 —*Ant.* dignified, grand, high,
honorable, noble, reputable, respectable, worthy

ignorance [*n*] *unintelligence, inexperience*
benightedness, bewilderment, blindness,
callowness, crudeness, darkness, denseness,
disregard, dumbness, empty-headedness*, fog*,
half-knowledge, illiteracy, incapacity, incomprehension, innocence, inscience, insensitivity,
lack of education, mental incapacity, naiveté,
nescience, oblivion, obtuseness, philistinism,
rawness, sciolism, shallowness, simplicity,
unawareness, unconsciousness, uncouthness,
unenlightenment, unfamiliarity, unscholarli-
ness, vagueness; CONCEPTS 409,678 —*Ant.*
competence, cultivation, education, experience,
intelligence, knowledge, literacy, talent,
wisdom

ignorant [*adj*] *unaware, unknowing* apprenticed, benighted, birdbrained*, blind to*,
cretinous, dense, green*, illiterate, imbecilic,
inexperienced, innocent, insensible, in the
dark*, mindless, misinformed, moronic, naive,
nescient, oblivious, obtuse, shallow, thick, unconscious, unconversant, uncultivated, uncultured, uneducated, unenlightened, uninformed,
uninitiated, unintellectual, unknowledgeable,
unlearned, unlettered, unmindful, unread, unschooled, unsuspecting, untaught, untrained,
unwitting, witless; CONCEPTS 402,542 —*Ant.*
aware, competent, educated, intelligent, knowledgeable, literate, talented, wise

ignore [*v*] *disregard on purpose* avoid, be
oblivious to, blink, brush off*, bury one's head
in sand*, cold-shoulder*, discount, disdain,
evade, fail, forget, let it go*, neglect, omit,
overlook, overpass, pass over, pay no attention
to, pay no mind*, pooh-pooh*, reject, scorn,
shut eyes to*, slight, take no notice, tune out*,
turn back on*, turn blind eye*, turn deaf ear;
CONCEPT 30 —*Ant.* acknowledge, heed, look
at, note, notice, pay attention, recognize, regard,
take notice

ilk [*n*] *kind, type* brand, class, classification,
denomination, gender, kin, lot, order, persuasion, race, set, sort, species, variety; CONCEPTS
378,411,673

ill [*adj1*] *sick* afflicted, ailing, a wreck*, below
par*, bummed*, diseased, down, down with,
feeling awful, feeling rotten, feeling terrible,
got the bug*, indisposed, infirm, laid low*, off
one's feet*, on sick list*, out of sorts*, peaked,
poorly, queasy, rotten, run-down, running temperature, sick as a dog*, under the weather*,
unhealthy, unwell, woozy*; CONCEPT 314
—*Ant.* good, healthy, sound, strong, well

ill [*adj2*] *bad, evil* acrimonious, adverse, antagonistic, cantankerous, cross, damaging, deleteri-

ous, detrimental, disrespectful, disturbing, foreboding, foul, harmful, harsh, hateful, hostile, hurtful, ill-mannered, impertinent, inauspicious, inimical, iniquitous, injurious, malevolent, malicious, nocent, nocuous, noxious, ominous, ruinous, sinister, sullen, surly, threatening, unfavorable, unfortunate, unfriendly, ungracious, unhealthy, unkind, unlucky, unpromising, unpropitious, unwholesome, vile, wicked, wrong; CONCEPTS 537,545,570 —*Ant.* good

ill [*n*] *misfortune* abuse, affection, affliction, ailment, badness, complaint, condition, cruelty, damage, depravity, destruction, disease, disorder, evil, harm, hurt, illness, indisposition, infirmity, injury, insult, malady, malaise, malice, mischief, misery, pain, sickness, suffering, syndrome, trial, tribulation, trouble, unpleasantness, wickedness, woe, wrong; CONCEPTS 316, 674,675 —*Ant.* benefit, blessing, fortune, happiness, luck, privilege, profit, prosperity

ill-advised [*adj*] *unwise, not thought out* brash, confused, foolhardy, foolish, half-baked*, hotheaded*, ill-considered, ill-judged, impolitic, imprudent, inappropriate, incautious, inconsiderate, indiscreet, inexpedient, injudicious, madcap*, misguided, off the top of one's head*, overhasty, rash, reckless, short-sighted*, thoughtless, unseemly, wrong; CONCEPTS 544, 548 —*Ant.* reasonable, sensible, well-advised, wise

ill at ease [*adj*] *uncomfortable, nervous* anxious, awkward, discomfited, disquieted, disturbed, doubtful, edgy, faltering, fidgety, hesitant, insecure, on edge*, on pins and needles*, on tenterhooks*, out of place*, restless, self-conscious, shy, suspicious, tense, uneasy, unrelaxed, unsettled, unsure; CONCEPTS 401, 403 —*Ant.* at ease, comfortable, content

illegal [*adj*] *against the law* actionable, banned, black-market*, bootleg*, contraband, criminal, crooked, extralegal, felonious, forbidden, heavy*, hot*, illegitimate, illicit, interdicted, irregular, lawless, not approved, not legal, outlawed, outside the law, prohibited, proscribed, prosecutable, racket, shady, smuggled, sub rosa, taboo, unauthorized, unconstitutional, under the table*, unlawful, unlicensed, unofficial, unwarrantable, unwarranted, verboten, violating, wildcat*, wrongful; CONCEPTS 319, 545 —*Ant.* allowed, authorized, ethical, good, lawful, legal, legitimate, moral, permissible, right

illegible [*adj*] *unreadable* cacographic, crabbed, cramped, difficult to read, faint, hard to make out*, hieroglyphic, indecipherable, indistinct, obscure, scrawled, unclear, undecipherable, unintelligible; CONCEPTS 535,576 —*Ant.* decipherable, legible, readable, understandable

illegitimate [*adj*] *not legal* contraband, illegal, illicit, improper, invalid, misbegotten, spurious, supposititious, unauthorized, unconstitutional, unlawful, unsanctioned, wicked, wrong; CONCEPTS 319,549 —*Ant.* authorized, blessed, ethical, justifiable, legal, legitimate, moral, sanctioned, warranted

ill-fated/ill-starred [*adj*] *doomed* blighted, catastrophic, destroyed, disastrous, hapless, ill-omened, inauspicious, luckless, misfortunate, ruined, star-crossed*, unfortunate,

unhappy, unlucky, untoward; CONCEPTS 537, 548 —*Ant.* happy, lucky

illicit [*adj*] *not legal; forbidden* adulterous, black-market*, bootleg*, clandestine, contraband, contrary to law, criminal, crooked, dirty*, felonious, furtive, guilty, heavy*, illegal, illegitimate, immoral, improper, in violation of law, lawless, out of line* prohibited, racket, unauthorized, unlawful, unlicensed, wrong, wrongful; CONCEPTS 319,545 —*Ant.* blessed, good, legal, legitimate, licit, moral, noble, proper, right

illiterate [*adj*] *unable to read well; lacking education* benighted, catachrestic, ignorant, inerudite, solecistic, uneducated, unenlightened, ungrammatical, uninstructed, unlearned, unlettered, unread, unschooled, untaught, untutored; CONCEPT 402 —*Ant.* able, educated, learned, literate, taught

ill-mannered [*adj*] *badly behaved* bad-mannered, boorish, cheap, churlish, coarse, discourteous, disrespectful, ill-behaved, ill-bred, impertinent, impolite, insolent, loud, loud-mouthed, loutish, raunchy*, raw, rough, roughneck*, rude, tacky*, uncivil, uncouth, ungracious, unmannerly, unrefined, vulgar; CONCEPT 401 —*Ant.* behaved, mannered, mannerly, polite

ill-natured [*adj*] *bad-tempered* catty, churlish, crabbed, crabby, cross, crotchety, cussed*, dirty*, disagreeable, disobliging, dyspeptic, hot-tempered, ill-humored, irritable, malevolent, malicious, mean, nasty, ornery*, perverse, petulant, spiteful, sulky, sullen, surly, temperamental, tempersome, touchy, unfriendly, unkind, unpleasant; CONCEPTS 401,404 —*Ant.* friendly, good-natured, good-tempered, nice, pleasant

illness [*n*] *disease; bad health* affliction, ailing, ailment, attack, breakdown, bug*, collapse, complaint, confinement, convalescence, disability, diseasedness, disorder, disturbance, dose, failing health, fit, flu, ill health, indisposition, infirmity, malady, malaise, poor health, prostration, relapse, seizure, sickness, syndrome, unhealth, virus, what's going around*; CONCEPT 306 —*Ant.* good health, health, well-being, wellness

illogical [*adj*] *not making sense* absurd, casuistic, cockeyed*, fallacious, false, fatuous, faulty, groundless, hollow, implausible, inconclusive, incongruous, inconsequent, inconsistent, incorrect, invalid, irrational, irrelevant, mad, meaningless, not following, nutty*, off the wall*, preposterous, screwy*, self-contradictory, senseless, sophistic, sophistical, specious, spurious, unconnected, unproved, unreasonable, unscientific, unsound, unsubstantial, untenable, wacky, without basis, without foundation; CONCEPTS 267,529 —*Ant.* correct, logical, meaningful, rational, reasonable, right, sensible

ill-suited [*adj*] *inappropriate* bad form, ill-fitted, ill-matched, ill-timed, improper, inapt, incompatible, incorrect, irrelevant, malapropos, mismatched, out of character, out of its element, out of place, unbecoming, unfit, unfitting, unseemly, unsuitable, wrong; CONCEPT 558

ill-tempered [*adj*] *irritable* annoyed, bad-tempered, bearish, cantankerous, choleric, crabby, cross, crotchety, grouchy, grumpy, irascible, moody, nasty, quick-tempered, sharp, snappy, sour, spiteful, surly, testy, touchy, vicious; CONCEPTS 401,403

ill-timed [adj] *not occurring at a suitable time* awkward, badly timed, improper, inappropriate, inconvenient, inept, inopportune, malapropos, mistimed, unbecoming, unbefitting, unfavorable, unseasonable, unseemly, unsuitable, untimely, unwelcome; CONCEPT 548 —*Ant.* appropriate, convenient, opportune, suitable, welcome, well-timed

illuminate [v1] *make light* brighten, fire, flash, floodlight, highlight, hit with a light*, ignite, illume, illumine, irradiate, kindle, light, lighten, light up, limelight*, spot, spotlight; CONCEPT 624 —*Ant.* cloud, darken, obscure

illuminate [v2] *make clear; educate* better, clarify, clear up, construe, define, dramatize, edify, elucidate, enlighten, explain, expound, express, finish, give insight, gloss, illustrate, improve, instruct, interpret, perfect, polish, shed light on*, uplight; CONCEPTS 57,285 —*Ant.* cloud, complicate, dull, involve, obscure

illumination [n1] *light; making light* beam, brightening, brightness, brilliance, flame, flash, gleam, lighting, lights, radiance, ray; CONCEPTS 620,624 —*Ant.* darkness, dimness

illumination [n2] *clear understanding* awareness, clarification, edification, education, enlightenment, information, insight, inspiration, instruction, perception, revelation, teaching; CONCEPTS 274,409 —*Ant.* ignorance, misconception, misunderstanding, obscurity, vagueness

illusion [n] *false appearance; false belief* apparition, bubble*, chimera, confusion, daydream, deception, déjèvu*, delusion, error, fallacy, false impression, fancy, fantasy, figment of imagination*, fool's paradise*, ghost, hallucination, head trip*, hocus-pocus*, idolism, ignus fatuus, image, invention, make-believe, mirage, misapprehension, misbelief, misconception, misimpression, mockery, myth, optical illusion, paramnesia, phantasm, pipe dream*, rainbow*, seeming, semblance, trip*, virtual reality; CONCEPTS 689,716 —*Ant.* certainty, event, fact, reality, truth

illusory/illusive [adj] *deceptive, false* apparent, blue-sky*, chimerical, deceitful, delusive, delusory, fake, fallacious, fanciful, fantastic, fictional, fictitious, fictive, hallucinatory, ideal, imaginary, misleading, mistaken, ostensible, pseudo*, seeming, semblant, sham*, supposititious, unreal, untrue, visionary, whimsical; CONCEPTS 529,552,582 —*Ant.* certain, factual, real, sure, true

illustrate [v1] *demonstrate, exemplify* allegorize, bring home*, clarify, clear, clear up, delineate, depict, disclose, draw a picture*, elucidate, emblematize, embody, emphasize, epitomize, evidence, evince, exhibit, explain, expose, expound, get across*, get over*, highlight, illuminate, imitate, instance, interpret, lay out*, limelight*, make clear, make plain, manifest, mark, mirror, ostend, personify, picture, point up*, portray, proclaim, represent, reveal, show, show and tell*, spotlight*, symbolize, typify, vivify; CONCEPTS 57,97 —*Ant.* hide, obscure

illustrate [v2] *explain by drawing, decorating* adorn, delineate, depict, embellish, illuminate, limn, ornament, paint, picture, portray, represent, sketch; CONCEPTS 57,174

illustration [n1] *demonstration, exemplification* analogy, case, case history, case in point, clarification, elucidation, example, explanation, for instance, instance, interpretation, model, representative, sample, sampling, specimen; CONCEPTS 268,686

illustration [n2] *drawing, artwork that assists explanation* adornment, cartoon, decoration, depiction, design, engraving, etching, figure, frontispiece, halftone, image, line drawing, painting, photo, photograph, picture, plate, sketch, snapshot, tailpiece, vignette; CONCEPT 259

illustrative [adj] *explanatory* allegorical, clarifying, comparative, corroborative, delineative, descriptive, diagrammatic, emblematic, exemplifying, explicatory, expository, fi gurative, graphic, iconographic, illuminative, illustrational, illustratory, imagistic, indicative, interpretive, metaphoric, pictorial, pictoric, representative, revealing, sample, specifying, symbolic, typical; CONCEPT 267 —*Ant.* atypical, complicated, confusing, involved

illustrious [adj] *famous, prominent* big league*, brilliant, celeb*, celebrated, distinguished, eminent, esteemed, exalted, famed, glorious, great, heavy, lofty, monster*, name*, noble, notable, noted, outstanding, remarkable, renowned, resplendent, signal, splendid, star, sublime, superstar, well-known; CONCEPT 568 —*Ant.* infamous, lowly, unimportant, unknown, unremarkable

ill will [n] *hatred; hard feelings* acrimony, animosity, animus, antagonism, antipathy, aversion, bad blood*, bad will, blame, despite, dislike, enmity, envy, feud, grudge, hate, hostility, malevolence, malice, maliciousness, no love lost*, objection, rancor, resentment, spite, spitefulness, spleen, unfriendliness, venom; CONCEPT 29 —*Ant.* friendliness, friendship, good feelings, good will, liking, loving

image [n1] *representation; counterpart* angel*, appearance, carbon*, carbon copy, carved figure, chip off old block*, copy, dead ringer*, double, drawing, effigy, equal, equivalent, facsimile, figure, form, icon, idol, illustration, likeness, match, model, photocopy, photograph, picture, portrait, reflection, replica, reproduction, similitude, simulacre, simulacrum, spitting image*, statue; CONCEPTS 259,667,716

image [n2] *concept* apprehension, conceit, conception, construct, figure, idea, impression, intellection, mental picture, notion, perception, phantasm, thought, trope, vision; CONCEPTS 529,689 —*Ant.* concrete, entity

imaginable [adj] *believable, possible* apprehensible, calculable, comprehensible, conceivable, conjecturable, convincing, credible, likely, plausible, sensible, supposable, thinkable, under the sun*; CONCEPTS 529,552 —*Ant.* impossible, improbable, incomprehensible, unbelieveable, unimaginable, unthinkable

imaginary [adj] *fictitious, invented* abstract, apocryphal, apparitional, assumed, chimerical, deceptive, delusive, dreamed-up*, dreamlike, dreamy, fabulous, fancied, fanciful, fantastic, fictional, figmental, fool's paradise*, hallucinatory, hypothetical, ideal, illusive, illusory, imaginative, imagined, legendary, made-up, mythological, nonexistent, notional, phantasmal, phantasmic, quixotic, shadowy, spectral, supposed, suppositious, theoretical, trumped up*, unreal, unsubstantial, visionary, whimsical; CONCEPTS 529,582 —Ant. existing, factual, genuine, physical, real, substantial, true

imagination [n] *power to create in one's mind* acuteness, artistry, awareness, chimera, cognition, conception, creation, creative thought, creativity, enterprise, fabrication, fancy, fantasy, flight of fancy*, idea, ideality, illusion, image, imagery, ingenuity, insight, inspiration, intelligence, invention, inventiveness, mental agility, notion, originality, perceptibility, realization, resourcefulness, sally, supposition, thought, thoughtfulness, unreality, verve, vision, visualization, wit, wittiness; CONCEPTS 409,410 —Ant. being, entity, existence, material, reality, substance, truth

imaginative [adj] *creative, inventive* artistic, avant-garde, blue-sky*, brain wave, breaking ground, clever, dreamy, enterprising, extravagant, fanciful, fantastic, fertile, fictive, high-flown*, ingenious, inspired, offbeat, original, originative, pie-in-the-sky*, poetic, poetical, productive, quixotic, romantic, utopian, visionary, vivid, way out*, whimsical; CONCEPTS 529,542 —Ant. dull, uncreative, unimaginative, uninventive, unresourceful

imagine [v1] *dream up, conceive* brainstorm, build castles in air*, conceptualize, conjure up, cook up*, create, depict, devise, envisage, envision, fabricate, fancy, fantasize, fantasy, feature, figure, form, frame, harbor, image, invent, make up, nurture, perceive, picture, plan, project, realize, scheme, see in one's mind*, spark, think of, think up, vision, visualize; CONCEPT 43

imagine [v2] *assume, deduce* apprehend, believe, conjecture, deem, expect, fancy, gather, guess, infer, presume, realize, reckon, suppose, surmise, suspect, take for granted, take it, think, understand; CONCEPTS 12,26 —Ant. know

imbecile [adj] *stupid, foolish* asinine, backward, deranged, dim-witted, dull, fatuous, feeble-minded, idiotic, imbecilic, inane, ludicrous, moronic, simple, simple-minded, slow, thick, witless; CONCEPT 402 —Ant. brainy, intelligent, smart

imbecile [n] *very stupid person* birdbrain, dimwit, dolt, dummy, dunce, fool, idiot, jerk, lamebrain*, moron, pinhead*, simpleton; CONCEPT 412 —Ant. brain

imbibe [v] *drink, often heavily* absorb, assimilate, belt*, consume, down, gorge, guzzle*, ingest, ingurgitate, irrigate, partake, put away*, quaff, raise a few*, sip, swallow, swig*, swill*, toss*; CONCEPT 169 —Ant. abstain

imbroglio [n] *misunderstanding; fight* altercation, argument, bickering, brawl, broil*, brouhaha*, complexity, complication, dispute, embarrassment, embroilment, entanglement, falling-out*, flack*, involvement, knock-down-drag-out*, miff*, quandary, quarrel, row, run-in*, soap opera*, spat, squabble; CONCEPTS 46,106 —Ant. agreement, peacemaking

imbue [v] *infuse, saturate* bathe, diffuse, impregnate, inculcate, infix, ingrain, inoculate, instill, invest, leaven, permeate, pervade, steep,

suffuse; CONCEPTS 209,236,245 —Ant. drain, take out

imitate [v] *pretend to be; do an impression of* act like, affect, ape, assume, be like, borrow, burlesque, carbon*, caricature, clone, copy, counterfeit, ditto*, do like*, do likewise, duplicate, echo, emulate, falsify, feign, follow, follow in footsteps*, follow suit*, forge, impersonate, look like, match, mime, mimic, mirror, mock, model after, parallel, parody, pattern after, personate, play a part, pretend, put on*, reduplicate, reflect, repeat, replicate, reproduce, resemble, send up*, sham, simulate, spoof, take off*, travesty, Xerox*; CONCEPTS 87,111,171 —Ant. be original, clash, differ, oppose, reverse

imitation [n] *simulation, substitution* apery, aping, carbon copy, clone, copy, counterfeit, counterfeiting, counterpart, ditto*, dupe*, duplicate, duplication, echoing, ersatz*, fake, forgery, image, impersonation, impression, likeness, match, matching, mime, mimicry, mirroring, mockery, parallel, paralleling, paraphrasing, parody, parroting, patterning, phony, picture, reflection, replica, representing, reproduction, resemblance, ringer, semblance, sham*, simulacrum, takeoff*, transcription, travesty, Xerox*; CONCEPTS 171,180,716 —Ant. difference, opposite, original, reverse

imitative [adj] *simulated, unoriginal* artful, copied, copycat, copying, counterfeit, deceptive, derivative, echoic, emulative, emulous, following, forged, mimetic, mimic, mimicking, mock, onomatopoeic, parrot*, plagiarized, pseudo*, put-on*, reflecting, reflective, secondhand, sham*, simulant; CONCEPT 582 —Ant. different, genuine, original

immaculate [adj1] *very clean; unspoiled* bright, clean, errorless, exquisite, faultless, flawless, impeccable, irreproachable, neat, pure, snowy*, spick-and-span*, spotless, spruce, stainless, taintless, trim, unexceptionable, unsoiled, unsullied; CONCEPT 621 —Ant. dirty, filthy, foul, tainted, unclean, unsterile

immaculate [adj2] *innocent, uncorrupted* above reproach, chaste, clean, decent, faultless, flawless, guiltless, incorrupt, modest, perfect, pure, sinless, spotless, stainless, unblemished, uncontaminated, undefiled, unpolluted, unsullied, untarnished, virtuous; CONCEPTS 404,545 —Ant. corrupt, defiled, immoral, impure, sinful

immaterial [adj1] *irrelevant* extraneous, foreign, impertinent, inapplicable, inapposite, inappropriate, inconsequential, inconsiderable, inconsiderate, inessential, insignificant, irrelative, matter of indifference, meaningless, no big deal*, no never mind*, of no account*, of no consequence*, of no importance*, trifling, trivial, unimportant, unnecessary; CONCEPT 575 —Ant. essential, important, material, meaningful, relevant, substantial

immaterial [adj2] *not existing in physical form* aerial, airy, apparitional, asomatous, bodiless, celestial, disbodied, discarnate, disembodied, dreamlike, dreamy, ethereal, ghostly, heavenly, impalpable, imponderable, incorporate, incorporeal, insensible, intangible, metaphysical, nonmaterial, nonphysical, psychic, shadowy, spectral, spiritlike, spiritual, subjective, supernatural, unearthly, unembodied, unfleshly, unsubstantial, unworldly, wraithlike; CONCEPT 539 —*Ant.* bodily, material, physical, real, solid, substantial

immature [*adj*] *young, inexperienced* adolescent, baby, babyish, callow, childish, crude, green*, half-grown, imperfect, infantile, infantine, jejune, juvenile, kid, kidstuff*, premature, puerile, raw, sophomoric, tender*, tenderfoot*, underdeveloped, undergrown, undeveloped, unfinished, unfledged, unformed, unripe, unseasonable, unseasoned, unsophisticated, untimely, wet behind ears*, youthful; CONCEPTS 485,578, 797 —*Ant.* adult, developed, experienced, grown, mature, old

immeasurable [*adj*] *infinite, incalculable* alive with, bottomless, boundless, countless, crawling with, endless, extensive, illimitable, immense, indefinite, inestimable, inexhaustible, jillion*, large, limitless, measureless, no end of*, no end to*, umpteen*, unbounded, uncountable, unfathomable, unlimited, unmeasurable, unreckonable, vast, zillion*; CONCEPTS 762,773,781 —*Ant.* bounded, calculable, finite, limited, measurable

immediate [*adj1*] *instantaneous; without delay* actual, at once, at present time, at this moment, critical, current, existing, extant, first, hair-trigger*, instant, live, next, now, on hand*, paramount, present, pressing, prompt, up-to-date*, urgent; CONCEPTS 567,585,812,820 —*Ant.* eventually, later, never

immediate [*adj2*] *near, next* adjacent, close, contiguous, direct, firsthand, near-at-hand, nearby, nearest, nigh, primary, proximal, proximate, recent; CONCEPTS 586,778 —*Ant.* away, distant, far

immediately [*adv*] *at once, right away* anon, at short notice, away, directly, double-time*, forthwith, hereupon, in a flash*, in a jiffy*, in a New York minute*, in nothing flat*, instantaneously, instanter, instantly, like now*, now, now or never*, on the dot*, on the double*, on the spot*, PDQ*, promptly, pronto*, rapidly, right now, shortly, soon, soon afterward, straight away*, straight off*, summarily, thereupon, this instant, this minute, tout de suite*, unhesitatingly, urgently, without delay, without hesitation; CONCEPTS 544,820 —*Ant.* eventually, later, never

immemorial [*adj*] *ancient, old* age-old, archaic, fixed, forever, long-standing, of yore, olden, prehistoric, primeval, rooted, time-honored, traditional; CONCEPTS 578,797,799 —*Ant.* current, lately, memorable, new, recent, young

immense [*adj*] *extremely large* barn door*, boundless, Brobdingnagian*, colossal, elephantine, endless, enormous, eternal, extensive, giant, gigantic, great, gross, huge, humongous, illimitable, immeasurable, infinite, interminable, jumbo*, limitless, mammoth, massive,measureless, mighty, monstrous, monumental, prodigious, stupendous, super, titanic*, tremendous, unbounded, vast; CONCEPT 773 —*Ant.* little, miniature, minute, small, teeny, tiny

immerse [*v1*] *submerge in liquid* asperse, baptize, bathe, bury, christen, dip, douse, drench, drown, duck, dunk, merge, plunge, saturate, sink, slop, soak, souse, sprinkle, steep, submerse; CONCEPT 256 —*Ant.* dry, retrieve

immerse [*v2*] *become deeply involved* absorb, busy, engage, engross, interest, involve, occupy, soak, take up; CONCEPTS 17,100 —*Ant.* disinvolve, ignore, neglect

immersed [*adj*] *deeply involved with* absorbed, bound-up*, buried*, busy, consumed, deep, eat sleep and breathe*, engaged, engrossed, intent, into*, mesmerized, occupied, preoccupied, rapt, spellbound, taken up*, tied up*, turned on*, wrapped up*; CONCEPT 542 —*Ant.* ignorant, neglectful, negligent

immigrant [*n*] *person from a foreign land* adoptive citizen, alien, colonist, documented alien, foreigner, incomer, migrant, naturalized citizen, newcomer, outsider, pioneer, settler, undocumented alien; CONCEPT 413 —*Ant.* local, national, native

immigrate [*v*] *enter a foreign area intending to live there* arrive, colonize, come in, go in, migrate, settle; CONCEPT 159 —*Ant.* emigrate, stay

imminent [*adj*] *at hand, on the way* about to happen, approaching, brewing*, close, coming, expectant, fast-approaching, forthcoming, gathering, handwriting-on-the-wall*, immediate, impending, ineluctable, inescapable, inevasible, inevitable, in store*, in the air*, in the cards*, in the offing*, in the wind*, in view*, likely, looming, menacing, near, nearing, next, nigh, on its way, on the horizon, on the verge, overhanging, possible, probable, see it coming*, threatening, to come, unavoidable, unescapable; CONCEPTS 548,820 —*Ant.* distant, doubtful, far, future, later

immobile [*adj*] *motionless, fixed* anchored, at a standstill, at rest, frozen, immobilized, immotile, immovable, nailed, nailed down, pat, quiescent, rigid, riveted, rooted, stable, stagnant, static, stationary, steadfast, stiff, still, stock-still, stolid, unmovable, unmoving; CONCEPTS 488,584 —*Ant.* mobile, movable, moving, unfixed

immoderate [*adj*] *excessive, extreme* dizzying, egregious, enormous, exaggerated, exorbitant, extravagant, inordinate, intemperate, overindulgent, profligate, steep, too much*, too-too*, towering, unbalanced, unbridled, uncalled-for*, unconscionable, uncontrolled, undue, unjustified, unmeasurable, unreasonable, unrestrained, unwarranted, wanton; CONCEPTS 544,569 —*Ant.* calm, justified, mild, moderate, reasonable, restrained

immodest [*adj*] *shameless* bawdy, bold, brazen, coarse, depraved, forward, indecent, lewd, obscene, revealing, risqué, unashamed, unchaste, unseemly; CONCEPTS 401,545

immoral [*adj*] *evil, degenerate* abandoned, bad, corrupt, debauched, depraved, dishonest, dissipated, dissolute, fast*, graceless, impure, indecent, iniquitous, lewd, licentious, loose*, nefarious, obscene, of easy virtue*, pornographic, profligate, rakish, reprobate, saturnalian, shameless, sinful, speedy, unchaste, unclean*, unethical, unprincipled, unscrupulous, vicious, vile, villainous, wicked, wrong, X-rated*; CONCEPT 545 —*Ant.* chaste, good, moral, noble, pure, right, uncorrupt, virtuous

immortal [*adj1*] *death-defying, imperishable* abiding, amaranthine, ceaseless, constant, deathless, endless, enduring, eternal, evergreen, everlasting, incorruptible, indestructible, indissoluble, interminable, lasting, never-ceasing, never-ending, perdurable, perennial, permanent, perpetual, phoenixlike, sempiternal, timeless, undying, unfading; CONCEPTS 539, 798 —Ant. destructible, ephemeral, human, mortal, perishable

immortal [adj2] *famous* celebrated, eminent, epic, genius, glorious, heroic, illustrious, laureate, paragon, storied; CONCEPT 568 —Ant. infamous, insignificant, mortal, unimportant, unknown

immortality [n1] *endless life* athanasia, deathlessness, endurance, eternal life, eternity, everlasting life, perpetuity, timelessness; CONCEPTS 539,798

immortality [n2] *enduring fame* celebrity, fame, famousness, glorification, glory, great-ness, lasting fame, renown; CONCEPTS 388,668

immovable [adj] *fixed, stubborn* adamant, constant, dead set on*, dug in, fast, firm, hard-nosed, immobile, immotile, immutable, impassive, inflexible, intransigent, locked in*, motionless, obdurate, quiescent, resolute, rooted, secure, set, set in concrete*, set in stone*, solid, stable, stand pat*, stationary, steadfast, stick to guns*, stuck, tough nut*, unalterable, unchangeable, uncompromising, unmodifiable, unshakable, unwavering, unyielding; CONCEPTS 404,488,534 —Ant. mobile, movable, moving, unfixed

immune [adj] *invulnerable* allowed, clear, ex-empt, favored, free, hardened to, insusceptible, irresponsible, licensed, not affected, not liable, not subject, privileged, protected, resistant, safe, unaffected, unanswerable, unliable, unsus-ceptible; CONCEPTS 314,552 —Ant. susceptible, unguarded, unprotected, vulnerable

immunity [n] *privilege, exemption* amnesty, charter, exoneration, franchise, freedom, impunity, indemnity, invulnerability, liberty, license, prerogative, protection, release, resis-tance, right; CONCEPTS 316,376,388 —Ant. defenselessness, responsibility, susceptibility, vulnerability

immutable [adj] *unchangeable* abiding, ageless, changeless, constant, enduring, fixed, immovable, inflexible, invariable, permanent, perpetual, sacrosanct, stable, steadfast, unalter-able, unmodifiable; CONCEPT 534 —Ant. alter-able, changeable, flexible, mutable, variable

imp [n] *mischievous child, small person* brat, demon, devil, deviling, devilkin, elf, fiend, gamin, gnome, gremlin, hellion, minx, pixie, puck, rascal, rogue, scamp, sprite, troll, tyke, urchin, villain; CONCEPT 412

impact [n1] *collision, force* appulse, bang, blow, bounce, brunt, buffet, bump, clash, concussion, contact, crash, crunch, crush, encounter, hit, im-pingement, jar, jolt, jounce, kick, knock, meet-ing, percussion, pound, punch, quake, quiver, ram, rap, rock, shake, shock, slap, smash, smashup, strike, stroke, thump, tremble, tremor, wallop; CONCEPTS 189,641

impact [n2] *effect* brunt, burden, consequences, full force, impression, imprint, influence, mark, meaning, power, repercussion, significance, thrust, weight; CONCEPT 230

impact [v] *hit with force* bang into, clash, collide, crack up, crash, crush, jolt, kick,

register, smash, smash up, strike, wrack up*; CONCEPT 189

impair [v] *harm, hinder* blemish, blunt, cheapen, damage, debase, debilitate, decrease, destroy, deteriorate, devaluate, devalue, dimin-ish, ding*, disqualify, enervate, enfeeble, hurt, injure, invalidate, lessen, lose strength, make useless, mar, prejudice, queer, reduce, rough up*, spoil, tarnish, total, tweak, undermine, unfit, vitiate, weaken, worsen; CONCEPTS 130,240,246 —Ant. aid, assist, help

impaired [adj] *injured, faulty* broken, busted, damaged, debilitated, defective, down*, flawed, harmed, hurt, imperfect, kaput*, marred, on the blink*, on the fritz*, spoiled, unsound; CONCEPT 485 —Ant. healthy, perfect, strong

impale [v] *stab* lance, perforate, pierce, prick, punch, puncture, run through, skewer, skiver, spear, spike, stick, transfix; CONCEPT 220

impalpable [adj] *intangible, unsubstantial* airy, delicate, disembodied, fine, imperceptible, imponderable, imprecise, inappreciable, incorporeal, indiscernible, indistinct, insensible, insubstantial, nebulous, shadowy, tenuous, thin, unapparent, unobservable, unperceivable, vague; CONCEPTS 485,529,619 —Ant. believe-able, palpable, perceptible, substantial, tangible, understandable

impart [v1] *make known* admit, announce, break, communicate, convey, disclose, discover, divulge, expose, inform, pass on, publish, relate, reveal, tell, transmit; CONCEPT 60 —Ant. conceal, hide

impart [v2] *give* accord, afford, allow, bestow, cede, confer, contribute, grant, lead, offer, part with, present, relinquish, render, yield; CONCEPT 108 —Ant. keep, take

impartial [adj] *fair, unprejudiced* candid, detached, disinterested, dispassionate, equal, equitable, evenhanded, fair-minded, impersonal, just, middle-of-the-road*, neutral, nondiscriminating, nondiscriminatory, nonpartisan, objective, on-the-fence, open-minded, unbiased, unbigoted, uncolored, unslanted, without favor; CONCEPTS 403,542 —Ant. biased, discriminating, favoring, partial, prejudiced, unfair, unjust

impasse [n] *stalemate* box*, Catch-22*, cessa-tion, corner*, cul-de-sac*, dead end, deadlock, dilemma, fix, gridlock, jam, mire*, morass*, pause, pickle*, plight, predicament, quandary, rest, scrape*, standoff, standstill; CONCEPT 674 —Ant. agreement, breakthrough

impassioned [adj] *excited, vehement* animated, ardent, blazing, burning, deep, fervent, fervid, fierce, fiery, fired up*, flaming, furious, glow-ing, heated*, hot-blooded*, inflamed, inspired, intense, melodramatic, moving, mushy, overe-motional, passionate, perfervid, powerful, pro-found, red-hot*, romantic, rousing, sentimental, starry-eyed*, steamed up*, stirring, torrid, violent, vivid, warm, white-hot*, wild about, worked up*, zealous; CONCEPT 403 —Ant. apathetic, calm, cool, impassive, indifferent, unconcerned, unexcited

impassive [adj] *aloof, cool* apathetic, callous, cold, cold-blooded*, collected, composed, dispassionate, dry, emotionless, hardened, heartless, imperturbable, indifferent, indurated, inexcitable, inexpressive, inscrutable, insensible, insusceptible, matter-of-fact, nonchalant, passionless, phlegmatic, placid, poker-faced*, reserved, reticent, sedate, self-contained, serene, spiritless, stoic, stoical, stolid, taciturn, unconcerned, unemotional, unexcitable, unfeeling, unflappable, unimpressible, unmoved, unruffled, wooden; CONCEPTS *404, 542* —*Ant.* emotional, feeling, passionate, responsive, sensitive, susceptible, warm

impatience [*n*] *inability, unwillingness to wait* agitation, anger, annoyance, ants in pants*, anxiety, avidity, disquietude, eagerness, edginess, excitement, expectancy, fretfulness, haste, hastiness, heat*, impetuosity, intolerance, irritability, irritableness, nervousness, quick temper, rashness, restiveness, restlessness, shortness, snappiness, suspense, uneasiness, vehemence, violence; CONCEPTS *633,657* —*Ant.* control, ease, endurance, forbearance, patience, tolerance, waiting, willingness

impatient [*adj*] *unable, unwilling to wait* abrupt, agog, antsy, anxious, appetent, ardent, athirst, avid, breathless, brusque, chafing, choleric, curt, demanding, dying to*, eager, edgy, feverish, fretful, hasty, having short fuse*, headlong, hot-tempered, hot under collar*, impetuous, indignant, intolerant, irascible, irritable, itchy, keen, on pins and needles*, quick-tempered, racing one's motor*, restless, ripe*, snappy, straining, sudden, testy, thirsty, unforbearing, unindulgent, vehement, violent; CONCEPTS *401,542* —*Ant.* controlled, easy-going, enduring, forbearing, laid-back, patient, tolerant, waiting, willing

impeach [*v*] *denounce, censure* accuse, arraign, blame, bring charges against, call into question, call to account, cast aspersions on, cast doubt on, challenge, charge, criminate, criticize, discredit, disparage, hold at fault, impugn, incriminate, inculpate, indict, query, question, reprehend, reprimand, reprobate, tax, try; CONCEPTS *44,52,317* —*Ant.* elect

impeccable [*adj*] *above suspicion; flawless* accurate, aces, A-okay*, apple-pie*, clean, correct, errorless, exact, exquisite, faultless, fleckless, immaculate, incorrupt, infallible, innocent, irreproachable, nice, note-perfect, on target*, perfect, precise, pure, right, sinless, stainless, ten*, unblemished, unerring, unflawed, unimpeachable; CONCEPTS *535,574,621* —*Ant.* blemished, corrupt, defective, flawed, imperfect, suspicious, wrong

impecunious [*adj*] *poverty-stricken* beggared, broke*, cleaned out*, destitute, dirt poor*, homeless, impoverished, indigent, insolvent, necessitous, needy, penniless, penurious, poor, strapped*, unprosperous; CONCEPT *334* —*Ant.* moneyed, rich, wealthy

impede [*v*] *obstruct, hinder* bar, block, blow whistle on*, brake, check, clog, close off, cramp one's style*, curb, cut off, dam, delay, deter, discomfit, disconcert, disrupt, embarrass, faze, flag one*, freeze, hamper, hang up, hold up, interfere, oppose, rattle, restrain, retard, saddle with*, shut down, shut off, slow, slow down, stonewall*, stop, stymie, thwart; CONCEPTS *121,130* —*Ant.* advance, aid, assist, facilitate, forward, help, support

impediment [*n*] *obstruction, hindrance* bar, barricade, barrier, block, blockage, bottleneck*, burden, catch*, Catch-22*, chain, check, clog, cramp, curb, dead weight*, defect, delay, deterrent, detriment, difficulty, disadvantage, drag*, drawback, encumbrance, fault, flaw, handicap, hazard, hitch, holdup, hurdle, inhibition, load, manacle, millstone*, obstacle, prohibition, red tape*, restraint, restriction, retardation, retardment, road block*, rub*, setback, shackle, snag, stoppage, stricture, stumbling block*, tie, trammel, wall; CONCEPT *666* —*Ant.* aid, assistance, facilitation, furtherance, help, support

impel [*v*] *prompt, incite* actuate, boost, compel, constrain, drive, excite, foment, force, goad, induce, influence, inspire, instigate, jog, lash, mobilize, motivate, move, oblige, poke, power, press, prod, propel, push, require, set in motion, shove, spur, start, stimulate, thrust, urge; CONCEPTS *14,68,221,242* —*Ant.* delay, dissuade, repress, slow, suppress

impending [*adj*] *forthcoming* approaching, at hand, brewing, coming, gathering, handwriting-on-the-wall*, hovering, imminent, in the cards*, in the offing*, in the wind*, looking to*, looming, menacing, near, nearing, ominous, on the horizon*, overhanging, portending, proximate, see it coming*, threatening, waiting to; CONCEPTS *548,820* —*Ant.* distant, later, never, remote

impenetrable [*adj1*] *dense* bulletproof, close, compact, firm, hard, hermetic, impassable, impermeable, impervious, inviolable, solid, substantial, thick, unpiercable; CONCEPTS *483,604* —*Ant.* clear, penetrable, permeable, porous, soft, thin

impenetrable [*adj2*] *incomprehensible* arcane, baffling, cabalistic, dark, Delphic, enigmatic, enigmatical, hidden, incognizable, indiscernible, inexplicable, inscrutable, mysterious, mystic, obscure, sibylline, unaccountable, unfathomable, ungraspable, unintelligible, unknowable; CONCEPTS *529,576* —*Ant.* comprehensible, intelligible, penetrable, understandable

imperative [*adj1*] *necessary* acute, burning, clamant, clamorous, compulsory, critical, crucial, crying, essential, exigent, immediate, important, importunate, indispensable, inescapable, insistent, instant, no turning back*, obligatory, pressing, urgent, vital; CONCEPT *546* —*Ant.* inessential, optional, secondary, unnecessary, voluntary

imperative [*adj2*] *authoritative* aggressive, autocratic, bidding, bossy, commanding, dictatorial, dominant, domineering, harsh, high-handed, imperial, imperious, ordering, overbearing, peremptory, powerful, stern; CONCEPTS *267, 574* —*Ant.* discretionary, free, unrestrained, voluntary

imperceptible [*adj*] *hard to sense; faint* ephemeral, evanescent, fine, gradual, impalpable, imponderable, inappreciable, inaudible, inconsiderable, inconspicuous, indiscernible, indistinct, indistinguishable, infinitesimal, insensible, insignificant, invisible, microscopic, minute, momentary, shadowy, slight, small, subtle, tiny, trivial, undetectable, unnoticeable, vague; CONCEPTS *406,537* —*Ant.* apparent, conspicuous, distinct, evident, noticeable, obvious, perceptible, seeable, striking, unobscured

imperfect [adj] flawed amiss, below par, bottom-of-barrel*, broken, damaged, defective, deficient, disfigured, dud*, faulty, few bugs*, garbage*, immature, impaired, incomplete, inexact, injured, junk*, lemon*, limited, low, marred, minus, partial, patchy, rudimentary, schlocky*, sick, sketchy, two-bit*, undeveloped, unfinished, unsound, vicious, warped; CONCEPTS 570,574,579 —Ant. excellent, faultless, finished, perfect, pure, unblemished, unflawed

imperfection [n] flaw blemish, bug*, catch, defect, deficiency, deformity, demerit, disfigurement, failing, fallibility, fault, foible, frailty, glitch*, gremlin*, inadequacy, incompleteness, infirmity, insufficiency, peccadillo, problem, shortcoming, sin, stain, taint, weakness, weak point; CONCEPTS 230,671,718 —Ant. excellence, flawlessness, perfection, purity

imperil [v] cause to be in danger chance it, compromise, endanger, expose, hazard, jeopard, jeopardize, jeopardy, menace, peril, risk; CONCEPT 240 —Ant. guard, protect, save

imperious [adj] bossy, overbearing arrogant, authoritative, autocratic, commanding, compulsatory, compulsory, despotic, dictatorial, domineering, exacting, haughty, high-handed, imperative, imperial, mandatory, obligatory, oppressive, overweening, peremptory, required, tyrannical, tyrannous; CONCEPTS 267,574 —Ant. fawning, helpless, humble, obedient, servile, subservient, weak

impermeable [adj] impenetrable airtight, dense, hermetic, impassable, impervious, leakproof, nonporous, sealed, waterproof, water-resistant, watertight; CONCEPTS 483,604

impersonal [adj] cold, unfriendly abstract, bureaucratic, businesslike, candid, cold-blooded*, cold turkey*, colorless, cool, detached, disinterested, dispassionate, emotionless, equal, equitable, fair, formal, impartial, indifferent, inhuman, neutral, nondiscriminatory, objective, poker-faced*, remote, straight, strictly business*, unbiased, uncolored, unpassioned; CONCEPTS 401,542,544 —Ant. friendly, informal, personable, personal, warm

impersonate [v] pretend to be another act, act a part, act like, act out, ape, assume character, ditto*, do, do an impression of, double as, dress as, enact, fake, imitate, make like*, masquerade as, mimic, mirror, pass oneself off as*, perform, personate, play, playact, play a role, portray, pose as, put on an act*, represent, take the part of; CONCEPTS 59,292 —Ant. be original, differ, oppose, reverse

impertinence [n] boldness assurance, audacity, backchat, back talk*, brazenness, cheek*, chutzpah*, come-back*, crust*, disrespect, disrespectfulness, effrontery, forwardness, freshness, gall, guff, hardihood, impropriety, impudence, incivility, insolence, insolency, lip*, nerve, pertness, presumption, rudeness, sass*, smart mouth*, wisecrack*, wise guy*; CONCEPT 633 —Ant. humility, manners, politeness

impertinent [adj] bold, disrespectful arrogant, brash, brassy*, brazen, contumelious, discourteous, disgracious, flip*, forward, fresh, ill-mannered, impolite, impudent, inappropriate,

incongruous, inquisitive, insolent, interfering, intrusive, lippy*, meddlesome, meddling, nosy*, off base*, offensive, out of line*, pert, presumptuous, procacious, prying, rude, sassy*, smart, smart alecky*, uncalled-for*, uncivil, ungracious, unmannerly, unsuitable; CONCEPT 401 —Ant. kind, mannered, nice, polite, refined, respectful

imperturbable [adj] calm, collected assured, complacent, composed, cool, cool as cucumber*, disimpassioned, equanimous, hard as nails*, immovable, nerveless, nonchalant, roll with punches*, sedate, self-possessed, self-satisfied, smug, stiff upper lip*, stoical, thick-skinned, tranquil, unaffected, undisturbed, unexcitable, unflappable, unmoved, unruffled, untouched; CONCEPT 404 —Ant. excitable, irritable, jittery, perturbable, touchy

impervious [adj] unable to be penetrated closed to, hermetic, immune, impassable, impassive, impenetrable, impermeable, imperviable, inaccessible, invulnerable, resistant, sealed, tight, unaffected, unapproachable, unmoved, unpierceable, unreceptive, watertight; CONCEPTS 485,534,604 —Ant. exposed, open, penetrable, responsive, sensitive, vulnerable

impetuous [adj] acting without thinking abrupt, ardent, eager, fervid, fierce, furious, going off deep end*, hasty, headlong, hurried, impassioned, impulsive, passionate, precipitant, precipitate, precipitous, rash, restive, rushing, spontaneous, spur-of-the-moment, subitaneous, sudden, swift, unbridled, unexpected, unplanned, unpremeditated, unreflecting, unrestrained, unthinking, vehement, violent; CONCEPTS 404,542 —Ant. calm, cautious, circumspect, considerate, reflective, sensible, thoughtful, wise

impetus [n] stimulus, force catalyst, energy, goad, impulse, impulsion, incentive, incitation, incitement, momentum, motivation, power, pressure, push, spur, stimulant, urge; CONCEPTS 641,661 —Ant. block, check, hindrance

impinge [v] trespass affect, bear upon, disturb, encroach, influence, infringe, intrude, invade, make inroads, meddle, obtrude, pry, touch, violate; CONCEPTS 14,156 —Ant. avoid, dodge

impious [adj] not religious agnostic, apostate, atheistic, blasphemous, canting, contrary, deceitful, defiling, desecrating, desecrative, diabolic, disobedient, disrespectful, godless, hardened, hypocritical, iconoclastic, immoral, iniquitous, irreligious, irreverent, perverted, pietistical, profane, recusant, reprobate, sacrilegious, sanctimonious, satanic, scandalous, sinful, unctuous, undutiful, unethical, unfaithful, ungodly, unhallowed, unholy, unregenerate, unrighteous, unsanctified, wayward, wicked; CONCEPT 545 —Ant. holy, pious, religious

impish [adj] mischievous casual, devilish, devil-may-care*, elfin, elvish, fiendish, flippant, free and easy*, fresh, frolicsome, giddy, jaunty, naughty, offhand, pert, pixieish, playful, prankish, puckish, rascally, saucy*, sportive, waggish; CONCEPT 401 —Ant. behaved, subdued, unmischievous

implacable [adj] merciless, cruel grim, inexorable, inflexible, intractable, ironfisted, mortal, pitiless, rancorous, relentless, remorseless, ruthless, unappeasable, unbending, uncompromising, unflinching, unforgiving, unrelenting, unyielding, vindictive; CONCEPT 542 —Ant. kind, merciful, nice, placable

implausible [adj] not likely doubtful, dubious, farfetched, far out*, fishy*, flimsy, for the birds*, full of holes*, impossible, improbable, inconceivable, incredible, obscure, problematic, puzzling, reachy, suspect, thin*, too much*, unbelievable, unconvincing, unreasonable, unsubstantial, weak, won't hold water*, won't wash*; CONCEPT 552 —Ant. believable, likely, plausible, possibly, probably, reasonable

implement [n] agent, tool apparatus, appliance, contraption, contrivance, device, equipment, gadget, instrument, machine, utensil; CONCEPT 499

implement [v] start, put into action achieve, actualize, bring about, carry out, complete, effect, enable, enforce, execute, fulfill, invoke, make good*, make possible, materialize, perform, provide the means, put into effect, realize, resolve; CONCEPTS 91,99,221 —Ant. cancel, cease, delay, halt, hinder, pause, stop

implicate [v] imply, involve accuse, affect, associate, blame, charge, cite, compromise, concern, connect, embroil, entangle, frame, hint, impute, include, incriminate, inculpate, insinuate, lay at one's door*, link, mean, mire, name, pin on*, point finger at*, relate, stigmatize, suggest, tangle*; CONCEPTS 44,112 —Ant. defend, pardon, support

implication [n] association, suggestion assumption, conclusion, connection, connotation, entanglement, guess, hint, hypothesis, incrimination, indication, inference, innuendo, intimation, involvement, link, meaning, overtone, presumption, ramification, reference, significance, signification, undertone, union; CONCEPTS 28,39

implicit [adj] included without question, inherent, absolute accurate, certain, complete, constant, constructive, contained, definite, entire, firm, fixed, full, implicative, implied, inarticulate, inevitable, inferential, inferred, latent, practical, steadfast, tacit, taken for granted, total, undeclared, understood, unexpressed, unhesitating, unqualified, unquestioned, unreserved, unsaid, unshakable, unspoken, unuttered, virtual, wholehearted; CONCEPTS 267,535,549 —Ant. explicit, specific

implied [adj] hinted at adumbrated, alluded to, allusive, connoted, constructive, figured, foreshadowed, hidden, implicit, indicated, indicative, indirect, inferential, inferred, inherent, insinuated, intended, involved, latent, lurking, meant, occult, parallel, perceptible, potential, significative, signified, suggested, symbolized, tacit, tacitly assumed, undeclared, understood, unexpressed, unsaid, unspoken, unuttered, wordless; CONCEPTS 267,535 —Ant. explicated, expressed, stated

implode [v] collapse inward cave in, fall down, fall in, fold, fold up; CONCEPTS 230,316,410,674

implore [v] beg appeal, beseech, conjure, crave, entreat, go on bended knee*, importune, plead, pray, solicit, supplicate, urge; CONCEPT 48 —Ant. answer

imply [v] indicate, mean betoken, connote, denote, designate, entail, evidence, give a hint,

hint, import, include, insinuate, intend, intimate, involve, mention, point to, presuppose, refer, signify, suggest; CONCEPTS 75,97,682 —Ant. define, explicate, express, state

impolite [adj] having bad manners bad-mannered, boorish, churlish, crude, discourteous, disgracious, disrespectful, ill-bred, ill-mannered, indecorous, indelicate, insolent, irritable, loutish, moody, oafish, rough, rude, sullen, uncivil, ungracious, unmannered, unmannerly, unrefined; CONCEPT 401 —Ant. courteous, mannerly, polite

impolitic [adj] unwise, careless brash, ill-advised, ill-judged, imprudent, inadvisable, inconsiderate, indiscreet, inexpedient, injudicious, maladroit, misguided, rash, stupid, tactless, undiplomatic, untimely; CONCEPTS 401,544 —Ant. careful, cautious, discreet, politic, wise

import [n1] meaning acceptation, bearing, bottom line*, construction, drift*, gist*, heart*, implication, intendment, intention, interpretation, meat*, message, name of the game*, nature of beast*, nuts and bolts*, point, punch line*, purport, score*, sense, significance, significancy, signification, stuff*, thrust, understanding; CONCEPT 682

import [n2] significance, weight consequence, design, emphasis, importance, intent, magnitude, moment, momentousness, object, objective, pith, purpose, signification, stress, substance, value, weightiness, worth; CONCEPTS 346,668 —Ant. insignificance

importance [n1] significance, weight accent, attention, bearing, caliber, concern, concernment, consequence, denotation, distinction, drift*, effect, emphasis, force, gist*, gravity, import, influence, interest, materiality, moment, momentousness, notability, paramountcy, point, precedence, preponderance, preponderancy, priority, purport, relevance, sense, seriousness, signification, standing, stress, substance, tenor, usefulness, value, weightiness; CONCEPTS 346, 668,682 —Ant. insignificance

importance [n2] prominence, standing consequence, conspicuousness, distinction, eminence, esteem, fame, greatness, influence, lionization, mark, notability, note, noteworthiness, rank, reputation, salience, status, usefulness, worth; CONCEPTS 388,671

important [adj1] valuable, substantial big, big-league*, chief, considerable, conspicuous, critical, crucial, decisive, determining, earnest, essential, esteemed, exceptional, exigent, extensive, far-reaching, foremost, front-page*, grave, great, heavy, imperative, importunate, influential, large, marked, material, mattering much, meaningful, momentous, necessary, of moment, of note, of substance, paramount, ponderous, pressing, primary, principal, relevant, salient, serious, signal, significant, something, standout, urgent, vital, weighty; CONCEPT 567 —Ant. inappreciable, insignificant, little, nonessential, small, trivial, unimportant, unsubstantial

important [adj2] eminent, influential, outstanding aristocratic, big-time*, distinctive, distinguished, effective, esteemed, extraordinary, famous, first-class*, foremost, four-star*, front-page*, grand, heavy*, high-level, high

profile, high-ranking, high-up, honored, illustrious, imposing, incomparable, leading, majestic,
major-league*, noble, notable, noted, noteworthy, of note, page-one*, potent, powerful,
preeminent, prominent, remarkable, seminal,
signal, solid, superior, talented, top-drawer*,
top-notch*, upper-class, VIP*, well-known;
CONCEPTS 555,574 —Ant. insignificant,
powerless, unimportant, unknown, worthless

imported [adj] brought in from another place
alien, carried, choice, exotic, ferried, foreign,
introduced, rare, sent, shipped, transported,
trucked; CONCEPT 549 —Ant. exported

importunate [adj] demanding, insistent burning, clamant, clamorous, crying, disturbing,
dogged, earnest, exigent, harassing, imperative,
instant, overly solicitous, persevering, persistent, pertinacious, pressing, solicitous, troublesome, urgent; CONCEPTS 267,401 —Ant.
relaxed, undemanding, unimportant

importune [v] demand, insist appeal, ask, badger, beg, beseech, beset, besiege, con*, crave,
dun, egg on*, entreat, goose*, harass, hound*,
implore, invoke, nag, persuade, pester, plague,
plead, pray, press, sell, solicit, supplicate, urge,
work on*; CONCEPT 53

impose [v] set, dictate appoint, burden, charge,
command, compel, constrain, decree, demand,
encroach, enforce, enjoin, establish, exact, fix,
foist, force, force upon, horn in, inflict, infringe,
institute, introduce, intrude, lade, lay, lay down,
lay down the law, levy, move in on, oblige, obtrude, ordain, order, place, prescribe, presume,
promulgate, put, put foot down*, read riot act*,
require, saddle*, take advantage, trespass, visit,
wish, wreak, wreck; CONCEPTS 18,53,133

imposing [adj] impressive august, big, commanding, dignified, effective, exciting, grand,
grandiose, imperial, magnificent, majestic,
massive, mega*, mind-blowing*, monumental,
moving, noble, ominous, one for the book*,
overblown, overwhelming, pretentious, regal,
royal, something else*, something to write
home about*, stately, stirring, striking, towering; CONCEPTS 537,574,773 —Ant. common,
modest, ordinary, poor, subordinate, trivial,
unimportant, unimposing, unimpressive

imposition [n1] deception artifice, cheating,
con, craftiness, dissimulation, fraud, hoax,
hocus-pocus*, hypocrisy, illusion, imposture,
stratagem, trick, trickery; CONCEPTS 59,645
—Ant. forthrightness, honesty

imposition [n2] burden charge, command,
constraint, demand, drag, duty, encroachment,
encumbrance, intrusion, levy, pain, pain in the
neck*, pressure, presumption, restraint, tax;
CONCEPTS 14,130 —Ant. advantage, aid, benefit,
blessing, help, profit

impossible [adj1] beyond the bounds of possibility absurd, beyond, contrary to reason,
cureless, futile, hardly possible, hopeless,
hundred-to-one*, impassable, impervious,
impracticable, impractical, inaccessible,
inconceivable, inexecutable, infeasible, insurmountable, irrealizable, irreparable, no-go*,
not a prayer*, no-way*, no-win*, out of the
question*, preposterous, too much, unachievable, unattainable, uncorrectable, unfeasible,
unimaginable, unobtainable, unreasonable,

unrecoverable, unthinkable, unworkable,
useless, visionary, way out; CONCEPT 552
—Ant. achievable, believable, obtainable,
possible, reasonable, tenable

impossible [adj2] intolerable, ungovernable
absurd, egregious, hopeless, improper, incongruous, ludicrous, objectionable, offensive,
outrageous, preposterous, unacceptable, unanswerable, undesirable, unreasonable, unsuitable; CONCEPT 401 —Ant. behaving, good,
governable, manageable, tolerable

impostor [n] person pretending to be something
else actor, beguiler, bluffer, charlatan, cheat,
con artist, deceiver, empiric, fake, faker, fourflusher*, fraud, hypocrite, imitator, impersonator, masquerader, mimic, mocker, mountebank,
pettifogger, phony, pretender, pseudo, quack,
scorner, sham, sharper, shyster, trickster;
CONCEPT 412

imposture [n] fraud, trick artifice, cheat, con,
copy, counterfeit, deceit, deception, fabrication,
fake, feint, fiddle, flimflam*, forgery, gambit,
hoax, hocus-pocus*, illusion, imitation, impersonation, imposition, make-believe, maneuver,
masquerade, phony, ploy, pretense, pretension,
put-on*, quackery, ruse, sell*, sham, sleight,
spoof, stratagem, swindle, wile; CONCEPTS
59,192,645,674 —Ant. honesty, reality, truth

impotent [adj] disabled; unable to perform
action barren, crippled, dud, effete, enervated,
enfeebled, feeble, forceless, frail, gutless,
helpless, inadequate, incapable, incapacitated,
incompetent, ineffective, ineffectual, inept,
infecund, infirm, nerveless, paper tiger*,
paralyzed, powerless, prostrate, sterile, unfruitful, unproductive, weak; CONCEPT 485 —Ant.
able, capable, fertile, potent, productive, strong

impound [v] confine cage, coop up, enclose,
fence in, hold, imprison, keep, pen, seize, shut
in, take; CONCEPTS 121,130

impoverished [adj] poor, exhausted bankrupt,
barren, beggared, broke, clean, depleted, destitute, distressed, drained, empty, flat*, flat
broke*, have-not*, hurting, impecunious, indigent, insolvent, necessitous, needy, penurious,
played out*, poverty-stricken, reduced, ruined,
spent, sterile, strapped; CONCEPTS 334,560
—Ant. enriched, full, plentiful, rich

impracticable/impractical [adj] unrealistic
abstract, absurd, chimerical, idealistic, illogical,
impossible, impracticable, improbable, inapplicable, inefficacious, infeasible, inoperable,
irrealizable, ivory-tower*, no-go*, nonfunctional, nonviable, not a prayer*, otherworldly,
out of the question*, quixotic, romantic, speculative, starry-eyed*, theoretical, unattainable,
unbusinesslike, unfeasible, unreal, unserviceable, unusable, unwise, unworkable, useless,
visionary, wild, won't fly*; CONCEPT 552
—Ant. practicable, practical, probable, realistic,
reasonable, tenable, viable

impregnable [adj] unyielding firm, fortified,
impenetrable, indestructible, invincible,
invulnerable, secure, solid, strong, unassailable;
CONCEPTS 489,540,551

impregnate [v] infuse, fill; make pregnant
charge, conceive, drench, fecundate, fertilize,
imbrue, implant, inoculate, inseminate, leaven,
overflow, percolate, permeate, pervade,

procreate, produce, reproduce, saturate, seethe, soak, sodden, souse, steep, suffuse, transfuse; CONCEPTS *179,375* —*Ant.* deplete, take out

impresario [*n*] *manager, producer* director, showperson, sponsor, stage manager; CONCEPT *347*

impress [*v1*] *influence* affect, arouse, awe, be conspicuous, blow away*, buffalo*, bulldoze*, carry, electrify, enforce, enthuse, excite, faze, galvanize, get*, grab, grandstand*, inspire, kill*, knock out*, make a hit*, make an impression, make splash*, move, overawe, pique, provoke, push around*, register, score, show off, slay*, stimulate, stir, strike, sway, thrill, touch*; CONCEPTS *7,19,22,261*

impress [*v2*] *press down to make design* carve, dent, emboss, engrave, etch, imprint, indent, inscribe, mark, print, stamp; CONCEPT *174* —*Ant.* take apart

impress [*v3*] *emphasize* bring home*, drive home*, establish, fix, get into head*, inculcate, instill, press, set, stress; CONCEPT *49* —*Ant.* neglect

impression [*n1*] *influence* consequence, effect, feeling, impact, reaction, response, result, sway; CONCEPT *230*

impression [*n2*] *feeling, idea* apprehension, belief, conceit, concept, conception, conjecture, conviction, fancy, feel, hunch, image, inkling, intellection, memory, notion, opinion, perception, recollection, sensation, sense, supposition, suspicion, theory, thought, view; CONCEPTS *529,689* —*Ant.* materiality, physicality

impression [*n3*] *design made by pressing* brand, cast, dent, depression, dint, fingerprint, footprint, form, hollow, impress, imprint, indentation, mark, matrix, mold, outline, pattern, print, sign, spoor, stamp, stamping, trace, track, vestige; CONCEPTS *284,625*

impression [*n4*] *pretending to be somebody* imitation, impersonation, masquerade, parody, sendup, takeoff; CONCEPT *263*

impressionable [*adj*] *easily taught; gullible* affectable, affected, feeling, impressible, influenceable, ingenuous, open, perceptive, plastic*, receptive, responsive, sensible, sensile, sensitive, sentient, suggestible, susceptible, susceptive, vulnerable, wax-like; CONCEPTS *402,403* —*Ant.* insusceptible, obstinate, stubborn, unimpressionable, unresponsive

impressive [*adj*] *powerful, influential* absorbing, affecting, arresting, august, awe-inspiring, consequential, cool*, deep*, dramatic, effective, eloquent, excited, exciting, extraordinary, forcible, grand, impassioned, important, imposing, inspiring, intense, lavish, luxurious, majestic, massive, momentous, monumental, moving, noble, notable, penetrating, prime*, profound, remarkable, rousing, splendid, stately, stirring, striking, sumptuous, superb, thrilling, touching, towering, vital, well-done; CONCEPTS *574,773* —*Ant.* inconsequential, ineffective, insignificant, unimportant, unimpressive, weak

imprint [*n*] *impression; symbol* banner, dent, design, effect, emblem, heading, impress, indentation, influence, mark, name, print, sign, signature, stamp, trace, trademark; CONCEPTS *284,625*

imprint [*v*] *stamp* designate, engrave, establish,

etch, fix, impress, inscribe, mark, offset, print; CONCEPT *174*

imprison [*v*] *confine; put in jail* apprehend, bastille, bottle up*, cage, check, circumscribe, closet, commit, constrain, curb, detain, fence in, hold, hold captive, hold hostage, hold in custody, ice*, immure, impound, incarcerate, intern, jail, keep, keep captive, keep in custody, limit, lock in, lock up, nab*, occlude, pen, put away, put behind bars, rail in, remand, restrain, send to prison, send up*, shut in, stockade, take prisoner, trammel; CONCEPTS *90,191,317* —*Ant.* free, let go, release

improbable [*adj*] *not likely* doubtful, dubious, fanciful, far-fetched, flimsy*, hundred-to-one*, iffy*, implausible, inconceivable, not expected, outside chance*, questionable, rare, slim, slim and none*, unbelievable, uncertain, unconvincing, unheard of, unimaginable, unlikely, unsubstantial, weak; CONCEPT *552* —*Ant.* believable, likely, ostensible, plausible, possible, probable, tenable

impromptu [*adj/adv*] *unrehearsed, improvised* ad-lib*, dashed off, extemporaneous, extempore, extemporized, fake, faked, improv*, improviso, offhand, off the cuff*, played by ear*, shot from the hip*, spontaneous, spur-of-the-moment, thrown off*, tossed off*, unpremeditated, unprepared, unscripted, unstudied, vamped, whipped up*, winged*; CONCEPT *267* —*Ant.* deliberate, designed, planned, premeditated, rehearsed

improper [*adj1*] *not suitable* abnormal, at odds, awkward, bad form, discordant, discrepant, erroneous, false, ill-advised, ill-timed, imprudent, inaccurate, inadmissible, inadvisable, inapplicable, inapposite, inappropriate, inapt, incongruous, incorrect, inexpedient, infelicitous, inharmonious, inopportune, irregular, ludicrous, malapropos, odd, off-base*, out-of-place*, out-of-season*, preposterous, unapt, unbefitting, uncalled-for*, uncomely, undue, unfit, unfitting, unseasonable, unsuitable, unsuited, untimely, unwarranted, wrong; CONCEPT *558* —*Ant.* appropriate, correct, fitting, proper, right, suitable

improper [*adj2*] *vulgar, immoral* blue*, dirty, impolite, indecent, indecorous, indelicate, lewd, malodorous, naughty, risqué, rough, salacious, suggestive, unbecoming, unconventional, unequitable, unethical, ungodly, unjust, unrighteous, unrightful, unseemly, untoward, wrong, wrongful; CONCEPTS *542,545* —*Ant.* decent, formal, good, moral, proper, uncorrupt

impropriety [*n*] *bad taste, mistake* barbarism, blunder, faux pas, gaffe, gaucherie, goof*, immodesty, impudence, incongruity, incorrectness, indecency, indecorum, inelegance, rudeness, slip*, solecism, unseemliness, unsuitability, vulgarism, vulgarity; CONCEPTS *101,278,674* —*Ant.* correctness, propriety, suitability, tastefulness

improve [*v*] *make or become better* advance, ameliorate, amend, augment, better, boost, civilize, come around*, convalesce, correct, cultivate, develop, doctor up*, edit, elevate, emend, enhance, gain ground*, help, increase, lift, look up*, make strides, meliorate, mend, perk up*, pick up*, polish, progress, promote, purify, raise, rally, recover, rectify, recuperate, refine, reform, revamp, revise, rise, set right*, shape up*, sharpen, skyrocket*, straighten out*, take off*, touch up*, turn the corner*, update, upgrade; CONCEPTS 244,700 —*Ant.* damage, decline, decrease, diminish, harm, hurt, injure, weaken, worsen

improvement [n] *bettering; something bettered* advance, advancement, amelioration, amendment, augmentation, betterment, change, civilization, correction, cultivation, development, elevation, enhancement, enrichment, furtherance, gain, growth, increase, preferment, progress, progression, promotion, rally, reclamation, recovery, rectification, reformation, regeneration, renovation, revision, rise, upbeat, upgrade, upswing; CONCEPTS 230,700 —*Ant.* damage, decline, decrease, diminishing, harm, hurt, injury, weakening, worsening

improvident [adj] *careless, spendthrift* extravagant, heedless, imprudent, inconsiderate, lavish, negligent, prodigal, profligate, profuse, reckless, shiftless, shortsighted, thoughtless, thriftless, uneconomical, unthrifty, wasteful; CONCEPTS 334,542 —*Ant.* careful, miserly, provident, thrifty

improvisation [n] *extemporary speech* ad-libbing, autoschediasm, extemporization, speaking off the cuff, spontaneity, winging it; CONCEPT 266

improvise [v] *make up* ad-lib, brainstorm, coin, concoct, contrive, dash off*, devise, do offhand, do off top of head*, dream up, extemporize, fake, fake it, improv*, improvisate, invent, jam*, knock off*, make do*, slapdash*, spark, speak off the cuff*, throw together*, wing it*; CONCEPTS 173,266 —*Ant.* design, devise, plan, premeditate

improvised [adj] *made-up* ad-lib, autoschediastic, Band-Aid*, extemporaneous, extempore, extemporized, fly-by-night*, hit-or-miss*, impromptu, improviso, makeshift, offhand, spontaneous, spur-of-the-moment*, unprepared, unrehearsed, unstudied; CONCEPT 267 —*Ant.* designed, planned, premeditated, rehearsed

imprudent [adj] *without much thought* brash, careless, foolhardy, foolish, heedless, illadvised, ill-considered, ill-judged, impolitic, improvident, incautious, inconsiderate, indiscreet, inexpedient, injudicious, irresponsible, leaving self wide open*, off the deep end*, overhasty, playing with fire*, rash, reckless, temerarious, thoughtless, unadvisable, unthinking, unwise; CONCEPTS 267,542 —*Ant.* careful, cautious, discreet, prudent, wise

impudent [adj] *bold, shameless* arrant, audacious, barefaced, blatant, boldfaced, brassy, brazen, bumptious, cheeky*, cocky*, contumelious, cool*, flip*, forward, fresh, immodest, impertinent, insolent, nervy*, off-base*, overbold, pert, presumptuous, procacious, rude, sassy*, saucy*, smart*, smart-alecky*, unabashed, unblushing, wise*; CONCEPT 401 —*Ant.* humble, modest, polite, retiring

impugn [v] *criticize, challenge* assail, attack, blast, break, call into question, cast aspersions upon, cast doubt upon, come down on*, contradict, contravene, cross, cut to shreds*, deny, disaffirm, dispute, gainsay, knock*, negate, negative, oppose, pin something on*, put down*, question, resist, run down, skin alive*,

slam*, smear*, stick it to*, swipe at*, tar*, throw doubt on, throw the book at*, thumb nose at*, traduce, trash, traverse, zap*, zing*; CONCEPTS 52,58 —*Ant.* flatter, praise

impulse [n1] *drive, resolve* actuation, appeal, bent, caprice, catalyst, desire, disposition, excitant, extemporization, fancy, feeling, flash*, goad, hunch, impellent, impulsion, incitation, incitement, inclination, influence, inspiration, instinct, itch*, lash, lust, mind, motivation, motive, notion, passion, spontaneity, spur, thought, urge, vagary, whim, whimsy, wish, yen; CONCEPTS 20,410

impulse [n2] *throb, stimulus* augmentation, beat, bump, catalyst, drive, force, impetus, impulsion, lash, momentum, movement, pressure, propulsion, pulsation, pulse, push, rush, shock, shove, stroke, surge, thrust, vibration; CONCEPT 641

impulsive [adj] *tending to act without thought* abrupt, ad-lib*, automatic, careless, devilmay-care*, emotional, extemporaneous, flaky*, gone off deep end*, hasty, headlong, hot-and-cold*, impetuous, instinctive, intuitive, involuntary, jumping the gun*, mad, offhand, passionate, precipitate, quick, rash, spontaneous, sudden, swift, unconsidered, unexpected, unmeditated, unpredictable, unpremeditated, unprompted, up-and-down*, violent, winging it*; CONCEPTS 401,542 —*Ant.* cautious, considering, heedful, premeditative, thoughtful, wise

impunity [n] *freedom* dispensation, exception, exemption, immunity, liberty, license, nonliability, permission, privilege, security; CONCEPT 376 —*Ant.* imprisonment, incarceration

impure [adj] *not clean mentally, physically; mixed* admixed, adulterated, alloyed, carnal, coarse, common, contaminated, corrupt, debased, defiled, desecrated, diluted, dirty, doctored*, filthy, foul, gross*, grubby*, immodest, immoral, indecent, infected, lewd, nasty, not pure, obscene, polluted, profaned, smutty*, squalid, sullied, tainted, unchaste, unclean, unrefined, unwholesome, vile, vitiated, weighted, wicked; CONCEPTS 545,621 —*Ant.* chaste, clean, impeccable, pure, sterile

impurity [n] *contaminant* adulteration, contamination, corruption, defilement, dirt, filth, foreign matter, grime, pestilence, poisoning, pollutant, pollution, scum, stain, taint, uncleanness; CONCEPTS 230,306,674

impute [v] *attribute* accredit, accuse, adduce, ascribe, assign, blame, brand, censure, charge, credit, hang something on*, hint, indict, insinuate, intimate, lay, pin on*, refer, reference, stigmatize; CONCEPTS 44,49 —*Ant.* defend, guard, help, protect

inability [n] *disabling lack of talent, skill* disqualification, failure, frailty, impotence, inadequacy, inaptitude, incapability, incapacitation, incapacity, incompetence, ineffectiveness, inef-fectualness, inefficacy, inefficiency, ineptitude, ineptness, insufficiency, inutility, lack, necessity, powerlessness, shortcoming, unfitness, weakness; CONCEPT 630 —*Ant.* ability, capacity, competence, skill, talent

inaccessible [adj] *out of reach* aloof, away, beyond, distant, elusive, far, faraway, far-off, impassable, impervious, impracticable, insurmountable, not at hand*, out-of-the-way*, remote, unachievable, unapproachable, unattainable, unavailable, unfeasible, ungettable, unobtainable, unreachable, unrealizable, unworkable; CONCEPT 576 —*Ant.* accessible, approachable, reachable

inaccuracy [*n*] *error, erroneousness* blunder, corrigendum, deception, defect, erratum, exaggeration, fault, howler*, imprecision, incorrectness, inexactness, miscalculation, mistake, slip*, solecism, typo*, unfaithfulness, unreliability, wrong; CONCEPTS *101,230* —*Ant.* accuracy, correctness, right

inaccurate [*adj*] *erroneous* all wet*, careless, counterfactual, defective, discrepant, doesn't wash*, fallacious, false, faulty, imprecise, incorrect, in error, inexact, mistaken, off, off base*, out*, specious, unfaithful, unreliable, unsound, untrue, way-off*, wide*, wild*, wrong; CONCEPTS *565,582* —*Ant.* accurate, correct, right

inactive [*adj*] *not engaged in action; inert, lazy* abeyant, asleep, blah*, disengaged, do-nothing*, dormant, down, draggy, dull, idle, immobile, indolent, in holding pattern*, inoperative, jobless, latent, lax, lethargic, limp, low-key, mothballed*, motionless, on hold, ossified, out of action, out of commission*, out of service, out of work*, passive, quiescent, quiet, sedentary, slack, sleepy, slothful, slow, sluggish, somnolent, stable, static, still, torpid, unemployed, unoccupied, unused; CONCEPTS *401,560,584* —*Ant.* active, busy, involved, working

inadequacy [*n*] *shortage, defect, inability* blemish, dearth, defalcation, defectiveness, deficiency, deficit, drawback, failing, faultiness, flaw, imperfection, inadequateness, inaptness, incapacity, incompetence, incompetency, incompleteness, ineffectiveness, ineffectualness, inefficacy, inefficiency, ineptitude, insufficiency, lack, meagerness, paucity, poverty, scantiness, shortcoming, skimpiness, underage, unfitness, unsuitableness, weakness; CONCEPTS *335,674,709* —*Ant.* ability, adequacy, enough, plenty, sufficiency

inadequate [*adj*] *defective, insufficient, incompetent* bare, barren, bush-league*, deficient, depleted, dry, failing, faulty, feeble, found wanting, glitch*, imperfect, impotent, inappreciable, inapt, incapable, incommensurate, incompetent, incomplete, inconsiderable, insubstantial, junk*, lacking, lame*, lemon*, lousy, low, meager, minus, miserly, niggardly, not enough, parsimonious, poor, scanty, scarce, short, shy*, sketchy*, skimpy*, small, spare, sparse, sterile, stinted, stunted*, thin*, too little, unequal, unproductive, unqualified, weak; CONCEPTS *546,570,771* —*Ant.* able, adequate, competent, enough, sufficient

inadmissible [*adj*] *not appropriate* exceptionable, ill-favored, ill-timed, immaterial, improper, inappropriate, inapt, incompetent, inept, irrelevant, malapropos, objectionable, unacceptable, unallowable, unbecoming, undesirable, unfit, unqualified, unreasonable, unsatisfactory, unseemly, unsuited, unwanted, unwelcome; CONCEPTS *319,558* —*Ant.* acceptable, admissible, allowable, appropriate

inadvertent [*adj*] *accidental* careless, chance,

feckless, heedless, irreflective, negligent, not on purpose, reckless, thoughtless, uncaring, unconcerned, undesigned, undevised, unheeding, unintended, unintentional, unmindful, unplanned, unpremeditated, unthinking, unthought, unwitting; CONCEPTS *542,544* —*Ant.* advertent, attentive, deliberate, intentional, planned

inadvisable [*adj*] *not recommended* careless, foolhardy, foolish, harebrained*, ill-advised, impolitic, improper, imprudent, inappropriate, incautious, inconvenient, indiscreet, inexpedient, injudicious, pointless, rash, undesirable, unsensible, unsuitable, unwise, wrong; CONCEPTS *529,558* —*Ant.* advisable, good, ok, recommended, wise

inalienable [*adj*] *absolute, inherent* basic, entailed, inbred, inviolable, natural, nonnegotiable, nontransferable, sacrosanct, unassailable, untransferable; CONCEPT *535* —*Ant.* acquired, alienable, changeable, impermanent, transitory

inane [*adj*] *stupid* absurd, asinine, daft, empty, fatuous, flat, foolish, frivolous, futile, harebrained*, idiotic, illogical, imbecilic, innocuous, insipid, jejune, laughable, meaningless, mindless, pointless, puerile, ridiculous, sappy*, senseless, silly, trifling, unintelligent, vacant, vacuous, vain, vapid, weak, wishy-washy*, worthless; CONCEPTS *542,548* —*Ant.* bright, intelligent, smart

inanimate [*adj*] *not alive, not organic* azoic, cold, dead, defunct, dull, exanimate, extinct, idle, inactive, inert, inoperative, insensate, insentient, lifeless, mineral, motionless, nonanimal, nonvegetable, quiescent, soulless, spiritless; CONCEPT *539* —*Ant.* animate, living

inapplicable [*adj*] *not relevant* extraneous, foreign, garbage*, immaterial, impertinent, inapposite, inappropriate, inappurtenant, inapropos, inapt, inconsistent, irrelative, irrelevant, remote, unsuitable, unsuited; CONCEPT *546* —*Ant.* applicable, related, relevant, suitable

inappropriate [*adj*] *not proper, suitable* bad form, disproportionate, foot-in-mouth*, garbage*, ill-fitted, ill-suited, ill-timed, improper, inapplicable, inapropos, incongruous, inconsonant, incorrect, indecorous, inept, irrelevant, left-field*, malapropos, off*, out of line, out of place, tasteless, unbecoming, unbefitting, undue, unfit, unfitting, unmeet, unseasonable, unseemly, unsuitable, untimely, way off*, wrong, wrong-number*; CONCEPT *558* —*Ant.* appropriate, fitting, ok, proper, suitable

inapt [*adj*] *incompetent; not suitable* awkward, banal, clumsy, dull, flat, gauche, ill-adapted, ill-fitted, ill-suited, improper, inadept, inapposite, inappropriate, incongruous, inept, inexperienced, inexpert, infelicitous, insipid, jejune, maladroit, malapropos, slow, stupid, unable, undexterous, unfacile, unfit, unhandy, unmeet, unproficient, unskilled, unsuitable, unsuited, untimely; CONCEPTS *527,558* —*Ant.* apt, competent, happy, suitable, suited

inarticulate [*adj*] *unable to speak well* blurred, dumb, faltering, halting, hesitant, hesitating, inaudible, incoherent, incomprehensible, indistinct, maundering, muffled, mumbled, mumbling, mute, obscure, reticent, silent, speechless, stammering, tongue-tied, unclear, unintelligible, unspoken, unuttered, unvocal, unvoiced, vague, voiceless; CONCEPT 267 —*Ant.* articulate, communicative

inattentive [*adj*] *negligent, not paying attention* absent, absentminded, apathetic, blind, bored, careless, distracted, distrait, distraught, diverted, dreamy, faraway, heedless, inadvertent, indifferent, inobservant, listless, lost*, musing, neglectful, oblivious, off-guard*, out to lunch*, preoccupied, rapt, regardless, remiss, removed, scatterbrained* thoughtless, unconscious, undiscerning, unheeding, unmindful, unnoticing, unobservant, unobserving, unperceiving, unthinking, unwatchful, vague; CONCEPTS 403,542 —*Ant.* attentive, heedful, looking, noticing, observant

inaudible [*adj*] *silent* closemouthed, faint, hushed, imperceptible, low, muffled, mum, mumbled, mute, muted, noiseless, nonvocal, not talkative, quiet, soundless, still, unclear, uncommunicative, unhearable, voiceless, wordless; CONCEPT 594

inaugurate [*v*] *begin; install* bow, break in, break the ice*, commence, commission, dedicate, get things rolling*, get under way*, induct, initiate, instate, institute, introduce, invest, jump, kick off*, launch, make up, open, ordain, originate, set in motion*, set-up, start, usher in; CONCEPT 221 —*Ant.* adjourn, close, end, stop, uninstall

inauguration [*n*] *installation of newcomers* commencement, inaugural, induction, initiation, institution, investiture, launch, launching, opening, setting up; CONCEPT 386 —*Ant.* adjournment, close, end, finish

inauspicious [*adj*] *ominous, unpromising* bad, baleful, baneful, black, dire, discouraging, evil, fateful, foreboding, ill-boding, ill-omened, impending, inopportune, sinister, threatening, unfavorable, unfortunate, unlucky, unpromising, unpropitious, untimely, untoward; CONCEPTS 548,570 —*Ant.* auspicious, favorable, fortunate, lucky, promising

inborn/inbred [*adj*] *coming from birth; natural* congenital, connate, connatural, constitutional, deep-seated, essential, hereditary, inbred, indigenous, indwelling, ingenerate, ingrained, inherent, inherited, innate, instinctive, intrinsic, intuitive, native, unacquired; CONCEPTS 406,549 —*Ant.* acquired, earned

incalculable [*adj*] *countless, limitless* boundless, capricious, chancy, enormous, erratic, fluctuant, iffy*, immense, incomputable, inestimable, infinite, innumerable, jillion*, measureless, no end of*, no end to*, numberless, uncertain, uncountable, unfixed, unforeseen, unpredictable, unreckonable, untold, vast, whimsical, without number, zillion*; CONCEPTS 535,773,781 —*Ant.* calculable, countable, limited, measurable

incandescent [*adj*] *glowing* beaming, brilliant, effulgent, fulgent, intense, lambent, lucent, luminous, phosphorescent, radiant, red-hot*, refulgent, shining, white-hot*; CONCEPT 617 —*Ant.* dark, dim

incantation [*n*] *spell, magic* abracadabra*, ala kazam*, bewitchment, black magic, chant, charm, conjuration, conjuring, enchantment, formula, hex, hocus-pocus*, hoodoo*, hymn, invocation, mumbo-jumbo*, necromancy, open sesame*, rune, sorcery, voodoo*, witchcraft, wizardry; CONCEPTS 370,689

incapable [*adj*] *not adequate; helpless* butterfingers*, disqualified, feeble, impotent, inadequate, incompetent, ineffective, ineligible, inept, inexperienced, inexpert, inproficient, insufficient, losing, naive, not equal to, not up to*, poor, powerless, unable, uncool*, unequipped, unfit, unqualified, unskilled, unskillful, unsuited, weak; CONCEPT 527 —*Ant.* capable, competent, qualified, strong

incapacitate [*v*] *put out of action* clip wings*, cripple, damage, disable, disarm, disenable, disqualify, hamstring*, hinder, hog-tie*, hurt, immobilize, lame, lay up*, maim, paralyze, prostrate, put out of commission*, take out, undermine, weaken; CONCEPTS 121,246 —*Ant.* allow, facilitate, mobilize, permit

incapacitated [*adj*] *disabled* bedridden, broken-down, confined, crippled, debilitated, handicapped, helpless, hurt, immobilized, impaired, impotent, incapable, infirm, laid-up, lame, maimed, out-of-action*, out of commission*, paralyzed, powerless, sidelined, weak, weakened, wornout; CONCEPTS 314,527

incarcerate [*v*] *put in jail, confinement* bastille, book*, cage*, commit, confine, constrain, coop up*, detain, hold, immure, impound, imprison, intern, jail, lock up, put away, put on ice*, put under lock and key*, railroad*, restrain, restrict, send up the river*, settle, slough, take away, throw book at*; CONCEPTS 90,191,317 —*Ant.* free, let go, release

incarnate [*adj*] *in bodily form* embodied, exteriorized, externalized, human, in human form, in the flesh*, made flesh, manifested, materialized, personified, physical, real, substantiated, tangible, typified; CONCEPTS 490,539

incautious [*adj*] *not careful* any old way*, bold, brash, careless, caught napping*, devil-may-care*, fast-and-loose*, foot-in-mouth*, hasty, heedless, hotheaded*, ill-advised, illjudged, impetuous, improvident, imprudent, impulsive, inconsiderate, indiscreet, injudicious, madcap*, neglectful, negligent, off guard*, pay no mind*, playing with fire*, precipitate, rash, reckless, regardless, sticking one's neck out*, thoughtless, unalert, unguarded, unmindful, unthinking, unvigilant, unwatchful, wary, wide open*; CONCEPTS 542,544 —*Ant.* careful, cautious, discreet, thoughtful

incendiary [*adj*] *causing trouble, damage* dangerous, demagogic, dissentious, inflammatory, malevolent, provocative, rabble-rousing*, seditious, subversive, treacherous, wicked; CONCEPTS 537,570 —*Ant.* peacemaking

incendiary [*n*] *person who causes fire, trouble* agitator, arsonist, criminal, demagogue, demonstrator, firebrand*, insurgent, pyromaniac, rabble-rouser*, rebel, revolutionary, rioter; CONCEPT 412

incense [*n*] *strongly fragrant smoke* aroma, balm, bouquet, burnt offering, essence, flame, frankincense, fuel, myrrh, odor, perfume, punk, redolence, scent, spice; CONCEPTS 599,600

incense [*v*] *make very angry* anger, ask for it*, bother, disgust, egg on*, enrage, exasperate, excite, fire up*, get a rise out of*, get under one's skin*, inflame, infuriate, ire, irritate, mad, madden, make blood boil*, make see red*, provoke, rile, umbrage; CONCEPT 14 —*Ant.* calm, comfort, please

incensed [adj] *very angry* at end of one's rope*, buffaloed*, bugged*, bummed out*, burned up*, dogged, enraged, exasperated, fuming, furious, hacked, hot and bothered*, huffy*, indignant, infuriated, irate, ireful, mad, maddened, miffed, on the warpath*, peeved, riled, rousted, rubbed the wrong way*, steamed up*, up in arms*, uptight*, wrathful; CONCEPT 403 —*Ant.* cheerful, happy, joyous, pleased

incentive [n] *lure, inducement* allurement, bait, carrot*, catalyst, come-on*, consideration, determinant, drive, encouragement, enticement, excuse, exhortation, goad, ground, impetus, impulse, incitement, influence, insistence, inspiration, instigation, motivation, motive, persuasion, provocation, purpose, rationale, reason, reason why, spring, spur, stimulant, stimulation, stimulus, temptation, urge, whip; CONCEPT 661 —*Ant.* block, hindrance, turn-off

inception [n] *beginning* birth, commencement, dawn, derivation, fountain, inauguration, initiation, kickoff, origin, outset, provenance, provenience, rise, root, source, start, well, wellspring; CONCEPTS 648,832 —*Ant.* conclusion, end, ending, finish

incessant [adj] *never-ending, persistent* ceaseless, constant, continual, continuous, day-and-night*, endless, eternal, everlasting, interminable, interminate, monotonous, nonstop, perpetual, relentless, round-the-clock*, timeless, unbroken, unceasing, unending, unrelenting, unremitting; CONCEPTS 534,798 —*Ant.* broken, ceasing, ending, intermittent, interrupted

inch [n] *one-twelfth of a foot/2.54 centimeters measured* fingerbreadth, one thirty-sixth of a yard, square; CONCEPTS 790,791

inchoate [adj] *undeveloped, beginning* amorphous, elementary, embryonic, formless, immature, imperfect, inceptive, just begun, nascent, preliminary, rudimentary, shapeless, unfinished, unformed, unshaped; CONCEPTS 485,578,797 —*Ant.* developed, grown, mature

incident [n] *occurrence* adventure, circumstance, episode, event, fact, happening, matter, milestone, occasion, scene, trip; CONCEPT 2

incidental [adj] *related; minor* accidental, accompanying, adventitious, ancillary, attendant, by-the-way*, casual, chance, circumstantial, coincidental, concomitant, concurrent, contingent, contributing, contributory, fluke*, fortuitous, irregular, nonessential, occasional, odd, random, secondary, subordinate, subsidiary; CONCEPTS 547,548,577 —*Ant.* basic, essential, fundamental, important, vital

incidentally [adv] *by chance* accidentally, as a by-product, as side effect, by the bye*, by the way, casually, fortuitously, in passing, in related manner, not by design, obiter, parenthetically, remotely, subordinately, unexpectedly; CONCEPT 544 —*Ant.* purposely

incinerate [v] *reduce to ashes* blaze, burn, combust, consume, cremate, flame, ignite, light, parch, scald, scorch, set a match to, torch; CONCEPT 249

incinerator [n] *furnace* boiler, burner, cinera-

tor, crematory, heater, heating system, oil burner; CONCEPT 463

incipient [adj] *developing* basic, beginning, commencing, elementary, embryonic, fundamental, inceptive, inchoate, initial, initiative, initiatory, introductory, nascent, originating, start; CONCEPT 585 —*Ant.* developed, grown, mature

incision [n] *cut, slit* carving, cleavage, cleft, dissection, gash, groove, laceration, mark, nick, nip, notch, opening, pierce, slash, stab, wound; CONCEPT 309

incisive [adj1] *intelligent* acute, bright, clever, concise, keen, penetrating, perspicacious, piercing, profound, sharp, trenchant; CONCEPT 402 —*Ant.* incompetent, stupid

incisive [adj2] *sarcastic* acerb, acerbic, acid, biting, caustic, clear-cut, concise, crisp, cutting, drilling, laconic, mordant, penetrating, sardonic, satirical, scathing, severe, sharp, slashing, succinct, tart, terse, trenchant; CONCEPT 267 —*Ant.* gentle, kind, nice

incite [v] *encourage, provoke* abet, activate, actuate, agitate, animate, arouse, coax, craze, drive, egg on*, encourage, excite, exhort, fan the fire*, foment, force, forward, further, get to*, goad, impel, induce, inflame, influence, inspire, inspirit, instigate, juice*, key up*, motivate, persuade, prick, promote, prompt, provoke, psych*, push, put up to*, raise, rouse, set, set off*, solicit, spur, stimulate, stir up*, talk into, taunt, trigger, urge, whip up*, work up*; CONCEPTS 14,221,242 —*Ant.* delay, deter, discourage, prohibit

incivility [n] *discourtesy* bad manners, coarseness, discourteousness, disrespect, impoliteness, rudeness, unmannerliness; CONCEPTS 29,633

inclement [adj1] *bitter, nasty (weather)* brutal, cold, foul, hard, harsh, intemperate, raw, rigorous, rough, rugged, severe, stormy, tempestuous, violent, wintry; CONCEPT 525 —*Ant.* clear, mild, nice, sunny

inclement [adj2] *cruel, merciless* callous, draconian, harsh, intemperate, pitiless, rigorous, ruthless, savage, severe, tyrannical, unfeeling, unkind, unmerciful; CONCEPT 401 —*Ant.* kind, merciful, nice, sympathetic

inclination [n1] *tendency, bent* affection, appetite, aptitude, aptness, attachment, attraction, bias, capability, capacity, cup of tea*, desire, disposition, drift, druthers*, fancy, fondness, groove*, idiosyncrasy, impulse, leaning, liking, mind, movement, partiality, penchant, persuasion, pleasure, predilection, predisposition, preference, prejudice, proclivity, proneness, propensity, slant*, soft spot*, stomach*, susceptibility, taste, temperament, thing*, trend, turn*, type, urge, velleity, weakness, whim, will, wish; CONCEPTS 20,411,630

inclination [n2] *slant, angle* acclivity, bank, bend, bending, bevel, bow, bowing, cant, declivity, deviation, direction, downgrade, grade, gradient, hill, incline, lean, leaning, list, pitch, ramp, slope, tilt; CONCEPT 738

incline [n] *slope* acclivity, approach, ascent, cant, declivity, descent, dip, grade, gradient, inclination, lean, leaning, plane, ramp, rise, slant, tilt; CONCEPT 738

incline [v1] *tend toward* affect, be disposed, bend, be partial, be predisposed, be willing, bias, drive, favor, govern, gravitate toward, impel, induce, influence, lean to, look, make willing, move, not mind, persuade, predispose, prefer, prejudice, prompt, sway, turn, verge; CONCEPT 657

incline [v2] *bend, lean* aim, bevel, bow, cant, cock, deviate, diverge, heel, lay, level, list, lower, nod, point, recline, skew, slant, slope, stoop, tend, tilt, tip, train, turn, veer, yaw; CONCEPT 738

inclined [adj] *having a preference* apt, bent on, disposed, given, in the mood, likely, predisposed, prone, tending, willing; CONCEPT 542

include [v] *contain, involve* accommodate, add, admit, allow for, append, bear, be composed of, be made up of, build, build in, carry, combine, comprehend, comprise, consist of, constitute, count, cover, cut in on, embody, embrace, encircle, enclose, encompass, entail, enter, have, hold, implicate, incorporate, inject, insert, interject, interpolate, introduce, make allowance for, make room for, number, number among, receive, subsume, take in, take into account, teem with, work in; CONCEPTS 112,532,643 —*Ant.* eliminate, exclude, neglect, reject

including [adj] *containing* along with, among other things, as well as, counting, in addition to, inclusive of, in conjunction with, made up of, not to mention, plus, together with, with; CONCEPT 577 —*Ant.* excluding, rejecting

inclusion [n] *addition* admittance, composition, comprisal, embodiment, embracement, encompassment, formation, incorporation, insertion, involvement, subsumption; CONCEPT 642 —*Ant.* exclusion, subtraction

inclusive [adj] *all-encompassing, all-embracing* across-the-board*, all-around, all the options*, all together, ball-of-wax*, blanket*, broad, catchall*, comprehensive, encyclopedic, full, general, global, in toto*, overall, sweeping, umbrella*, wall-to-wall*, whole, without exception; CONCEPT 772 —*Ant.* exclusive, incomprehensive, narrow

incognito [adj] *in disguise* anonymous, bearded, camouflaged, concealed, disguised, hidden, incog*, isolated, masked, masquerading, obscure, under assumed name, unknown, unrecognized; CONCEPTS 576,589 —*Ant.* known, openly, seen, unhidden

incoherent [adj] *unintelligible* breathless, confused, disconnected, discontinuous, discordant, disjointed, disordered, dumb, faltering, inarticulate, incohesive, incomprehensible, incongruous, inconsistent, indistinct, indistinguishable, irrational, jumbled, maundering, muddled, muffled, mumbling, mute, muttered, puzzling, rambling, stammering, stuttering, tongue-tied*, uncommunicative, unconnected, uncoordinated, uneven, unvocal, wandering, wild; CONCEPT 267 —*Ant.* coherent, intelligible, understandable

income [n] *money earned by work or investments* assets, avails, benefits, bottom line*, cash, cash flow, commission, compensation, dividends, drawings, earnings, gains, gravy*, gross, harvest, honorarium, interest, in the black*, livelihood, means, net, pay, payoff, proceeds, profit, receipts, returns, revenue, royalty, salary, take home, wage; CONCEPTS 340,344 —*Ant.* bills, debt, expenses

incoming [adj1] *arriving* approaching, coming, coming in, entering; CONCEPT 159 —*Ant.* outgoing

incoming [adj2] *succeeding* designate, elect, elected, future, new, next, to-be; CONCEPT 585 —*Ant.* outgoing

incomparable [adj] *superlative* beyond compare, excellent, exceptional, ideal, inimitable, matchless, paramount, peerless, perfect, preeminent, second to none, sovereign, superior, supreme, surpassing, towering, transcendent, ultimate, unequalled, unmatchable, unmatched, unparalleled, unrivalled, unsurpassable; CONCEPT 574 —*Ant.* common, inferior, lowly, poor, unimpressive

incompatible [adj] *antagonistic, contradictory* adverse, antipathetic, antipodal, antithetical, clashing, conflicting, contrary, counter, disagreeing, discordant, discrepant, disparate, factious, inadmissible, inappropriate, incoherent, inconformable, incongruous, inconsistent, inconsonant, inconstant, irreconcilable, jarring, marching to a different drummer*, mismatched, night and day*, offbeat*, opposed, opposite, poles apart*, unadapted, uncongenial, unsuitable, unsuited, warring, whale of difference*; CONCEPT 564 —*Ant.* compatible, consonant, harmonious, loving, suited, well-matched

incompetent [adj] *unskillful, unable* amateur, amateurish, awkward, bungling, bush-league*, clumsy, disqualified, floundering, helpless, inadequate, incapable, ineffectual, inefficient, ineligible, inept, inexperienced, inexpert, insufficient, maladroit, not cut out for*, not equal to, not have it*, out to lunch*, raw, unadapted, unequipped, unfit, unfitted, unhandy, uninitiated, unproficient, unqualified, unskilled, untrained, useless; CONCEPT 527 —*Ant.* able, adept, capable, competent, dexterous, effective, efficient, experienced, expert, proficient, skillful

incomplete [adj] *unfinished, wanting* abridged, broken, crude, defective, deficient, expurgated, fractional, fragmentary, garbled, half-done, immature, imperfect, inadequate, incoherent, insufficient, lacking, meager, part, partial, rough, rude, rudimentary, short, sketchy, unaccomplished, unconsummated, under construction, undeveloped, undone, unexecuted, unpolished; CONCEPT 531 —*Ant.* accomplished, complete, finished, perfect

incomprehensible [adj] *not understandable* baffling, beats me*, beyond comprehension, beyond one's grasp*, clear as mud*, cryptic, Delphic*, enigmatic, fathomless, Greek*, impenetrable, incognizable, inconceivable, inscrutable, mysterious, mystifying, obscure, opaque, over one's head*, perplexing, puzzling, sibylline, unclear, unfathomable, ungraspable, unimaginable, unintelligible, unknowable; CONCEPTS 402,529 —*Ant.* comprehensible, fathomable, intelligible, understandable

inconceivable [adj] *beyond reason, belief* extraordinary, fantastic, imcomprehensible, implausible, impossible, improbable, incogitable, incredible, insupposable, mind-boggling*, phony, rare, reachy, staggering, strange, thin*, unbelievable, unconvincing, unheard-of, unimaginable, unknowable, unlikely, unsubstantial, unthinkable, weak*, won't fly*, won't wash*; CONCEPTS *529,552 —Ant.* believable, conceivable, fathomable, imaginable, reasonable

inconclusive [adj] *up in the air* ambiguous, deficient, incomplete, indecisive, indeterminate, lacking, open, uncertain, unconvincing, undecided, uneventful, unfateful, unfinished, unsatisfactory, unsettled, vague; CONCEPTS *537,548 —Ant.* certain, conclusive, decisive, definite, sure

incongruous [adj] *out of place; absurd* alien, bizarre, conflicting, contradictory, disconsonant, discordant, disparate, distorted, divergent, extraneous, fantastic, fitful, foreign, illogical, improper, inappropriate, inapropos, inapt, incoherent, incompatible, incongruent, inconsistent, irreconcilable, irregular, jumbled, lopsided, mismatched, out of keeping*, rambling, shifting, twisted, unavailing, unbalanced, unbecoming, unconnected, uncoordinated, uneven, unintelligible, unpredictable, unrelated, unsuitable, unsuited; CONCEPTS *547,558 —Ant.* compatible, congruous, consistent, corresponding, fitting, harmonious, matched, suitable, uniform

inconsequential/inconsiderable [adj] *of no significance* casual, dinky*, entry-level*, exiguous, immaterial, inadequate, inappreciable, inconsequent, insignificant, insufficient, light, little, measly, minor, negligible, paltry, petty, picayune, puny, runt, scanty, shoestring*, skimpy, small, small potatoes*, small-time*, trifling, trivial, two-bit*, unconsidered, unimportant, wimpy*, worthless; CONCEPT *575 —Ant.* consequential, considerable, important, significant

inconsiderate [adj] *insensitive to others* boorish, brash, careless, discourteous, hasty, impolite, incautious, indelicate, intolerant, reckless, rude, self-centered, selfish, sharp, short, tactless, thoughtless, unceremonious, uncharitable, ungracious, unkind, unthinking; CONCEPT *401 —Ant.* considerate, generous, kind, nice, sensitive, tactful, thoughtful

inconsistent [adj] *contradictory, irregular* at odds, at variance, capricious, changeable, conflicting, contrary, discordant, discrepant, dissonant, erratic, fickle, illogical, incoherent, incompatible, in conflict, incongruent, incongruous, inconstant, irreconcilable, lubricious, mercurial, out of step*, temperamental, uncertain, unpredictable, unstable, variable, warring; CONCEPTS *534,564 —Ant.* consistent, consonant, regular, steady, unchanging

inconsolable [adj] *brokenhearted* comfortless, dejected, desolate, despairing, disconsolate, discouraged, distressed, forlorn, heartbroken, heartsick, sad, unconsolable; CONCEPT *403 —Ant.* consolable, happy, understanding

inconspicuous [adj] *hidden, unnoticeable* camouflaged, concealed, dim, faint, hidden, indistinct, insignificant, low-key*, low-profile*, modest, muted, ordinary, plain, quiet, retiring, secretive, shy, soft-pedalled*, subtle, tenuous, unassuming, unemphatic, unobtrusive, unostentatious; CONCEPTS *485,576 —Ant.* conspicuous, exposed, noticeable, open, unhidden

inconstant [adj] *changeable* capricious, changeful, erratic, fickle, flickering, fluctuating, impulsive, inconsistent, intermittent, irregular, irresolute, mercurial, shifting, uncertain,

undependable, unreliable, unsettled, unstable, vacillating, variable, varying, volatile, waffling, wavering; CONCEPT *534*

incontinent [adj] *lacking control* unchecked, uncontrollable, uncontrolled, ungovernable, unsuppressed; CONCEPT *94 —Ant.* continent, restrained

incontrovertible [adj] *beyond dispute* accurate, authentic, certain, established, incontestable, indisputable, indubitable, irrefutable, nailed down*, no mistake*, no two ways about it*, positive, sure, surefire*, sure thing*, uncontestable, undeniable, unequivocable, unquestionable, unshakable; CONCEPT *535 —Ant.* changeable, controvertible, questionable, uncertain, variable

inconvenience [n] *bother, trouble* aggravation, annoyance, awkwardness, bothersomeness, cumbersomeness, difficulty, disadvantage, disruption, disturbance, drawback, exasperation, fuss, hindrance, nuisance, pain*, stew*, trial, troublesomeness, uneasiness, unfitness, unhandiness, unsuitableness, untimeliness, unwieldiness, upset, vexation; CONCEPT *674 —Ant.* advantage, benefit, convenience, profit

inconvenience [v] *bother, trouble* aggravate, discombobulate, discommode, decompose, disoblige, disrupt, disturb, exasperate, give a hard time*, give trouble*, hang up*, interfere, irk, make it tough*, meddle, put in a spot*, put on the spot*, put to trouble*, try, upset; CONCEPTS *14,242 —Ant.* aid, assist, be convenient, benefit, help

inconvenient [adj] *bothersome, troublesome* annoying, awkward, cumbersome, detrimental, difficult, disadvantageous, discommoding, discommodious, disturbing, embarrassing, incommodious, inexpedient, inopportune, pestiferous, prejudicial, remote, tiresome, troublesome, unhandy, unmanageable, unseasonable, unsuitable, untimely, unwieldy, vexatious; CONCEPTS *537,548 —Ant.* aiding, beneficial, convenient, helpful

incorporate [v] *include, combine* absorb, add to, amalgamate, assimilate, associate, blend, charter, coalesce, consolidate, cover, dub, embody, form, fuse, gang up*, hook in*, imbibe, integrate, join, link, merge, mix, organize, pool, put together, start, subsume, tie in*, unite; CONCEPTS *112,113,324 —Ant.* divide, drop, exclude, separate

incorrect [adj] *wrong* counterfactual, erroneous, false, faulty, flawed, imprecise, improper, inaccurate, inappropriate, inexact, mistaken, not trustworthy, out*, specious, unfitting, unreliable, unseemly, unsound, unsuitable, untrue, way off*, wide of the mark*, wrong number*; CONCEPTS *558,570 —Ant.* correct, right, true

incorrigible [adj] *bad, hopeless* abandoned, beastly, hardened, incurable, intractable, inveterate, irredeemable, irreparable, loser, recidivous, uncorrectable, unreformed, useless, wicked; CONCEPT *570 —Ant.* good, manageable, nice, obedient, reformable

incorruptible [adj] *honest, honorable* above suspicion, imperishable, indestructible, inextinguishable, just, loyal, moral, perpetual, persistent, pure, reliable, straight, trustworthy, unbribable, undestroyable, untouchable, upright; CONCEPTS 485,545 —*Ant.* bad, corruptible, dishonest

increase [n] *addition, growth* access, accession, accretion, accrual, accumulation, aggrandizement, augmentation, boost, breakthrough, burgeoning, cumulation, development, elaboration, enlargement, escalation, exaggeration, expansion, extension, gain, hike, incorporation, increment, inflation, intensification, maximization, merger, multiplication, optimization, raise, rise, spread, step-up, surge, swell, swelling, upgrade, upsurge, upturn, waxing; CONCEPTS 763,780 —*Ant.* decrease, depletion, diminishment, loss, subtraction

increase [v] *add or grow* advance, aggrandize, aggravate, amplify, annex, augment, boost, broaden, build, build up, deepen, develop, dilate, distend, double, enhance, enlarge, escalate, exaggerate, expand, extend, further, heighten, inflate, intensify, lengthen, magnify, mark up, mount, multiply, pad*, progress, proliferate, prolong, protract, pullulate, raise, redouble, reinforce, rise, sharpen, slap on*, snowball*, spread, step up, strengthen, supplement, swarm, swell, tack on*, teem, thicken, triple, wax, widen; CONCEPTS 236,245,780 —*Ant.* decrease, deplete, diminish, lose, subtract

increasingly [adv] *to a greater extent* more, more and more, progressively, with acceleration; CONCEPT 772 —*Ant.* decreasingly, less

incredible [adj1] *beyond belief* absurd, farfetched, fishy*, flimsy*, implausible, impossible, improbable, incogitable, inconceivable, insupposable, outlandish, out of the question*, phony, preposterous, questionable, ridiculous, rings phony*, suspect, thin*, unbelievable, unconvincing, unimaginable, unsubstantial, untenable, unthinkable; CONCEPT 552 —*Ant.* believable, credible, plausible, possible, realistic, tenable

incredible [adj2] *marvellous* ace*, amazing, astonishing, astounding, awe-inspiring, awesome, extraordinary, fabulous, glorious, great, prodigious, superhuman*, unreal*, wonderful; CONCEPTS 529,572 —*Ant.* bad, poor, terrible

incredulous [adj] *unbelieving* disbelieving, distrustful, doubtful, doubting, dubious, hesitant, mistrustful, questioning, quizzical, show-me*, skeptical, suspect, suspicious, uncertain, unconvinced, unsatisfied, wary; CONCEPTS 403,529 —*Ant.* believing, convinced, credulous

increment [n] *small step toward gain* accession, accretion, accrual, accrument, addition, advancement, augmentation, enlargement, increase, profit, raise, rise, supplement; CONCEPTS 763,780 —*Ant.* decrease, loss

incriminate [v] *accuse* allege, attack, attribute, blame, brand, bring charges, charge, cite, finger*, frame, hold accountable, implicate, inculpate, indict, involve, name, pin on*, point the finger at*, prosecute, serve summons; CONCEPT 44

incubus [n] *evil spirit* demon, devil, fiend, goblin, hobgoblin, nightmare, succuba, succubus; CONCEPTS 370,412

inculcate [v] *implant, infuse information* brainwash*, break down, communicate, drill, drum into*, educate, hammer into*, impart, impress,

indoctrinate, inseminate, instill, instruct, plant, program, shape up, teach, work over*; CONCEPTS 14,285

incur [v] *bring upon oneself* acquire, arouse, be subjected to, bring down on*, catch, contract, draw, earn, expose oneself to, gain, get, induce, meet with, obtain, provoke; CONCEPT 93

incurable [adj] *unfixable, unchangeable* cureless, deadly, fatal, hopeless, immedicable, impossible, inoperable, irrecoverable, irremediable, irreparable, nowhere to go*, out of time*, remediless, serious, terminal, uncorrectable, unrecoverable; CONCEPTS 485,548 —*Ant.* curable, healable, medicable, operable

incursion [n] *invasion* aggression, attack, foray, infiltration, inroad, intrusion, irruption, penetration, raid; CONCEPTS 86,320 —*Ant.* retreat

indebted [adj] *under an obligation* accountable, answerable for, appreciative, beholden, bound, bounden, chargeable, duty-bound, grateful, honor-bound, hooked*, in debt, in hock*, liable, obligated, obliged, owed, owing, responsible, thankful; CONCEPTS 334,546 —*Ant.* paid, settled

indecency [n] *obscenity, vulgarity* bawdiness, coarseness, crudity, drunkenness, evil, foulness, grossness, immodesty, impropriety, impurity, incivility, indecorum, indelicacy, lewdness, licentiousness, offense, outrageousness, pornography, ribaldry, smuttiness, unseemliness, vileness; CONCEPTS 633,645 —*Ant.* chastity, cleanness, decency, modesty, purity, virtue

indecent [adj] *obscene, vulgar; offensive* blue*, coarse, crude, dirty*, filthy, foul, foulmouthed, gross*, ill-bred, immodest, immoral, improper, impure, in bad taste, indecorous, indelicate, lewd, licentious, malodorous, off-color*, outrageous, pornographic, raunchy*, raw, ridiculous, rough, salacious, scatological, shameless, shocking, smutty*, tasteless, unbecoming, undecorous, unseemly, untoward, vile, wicked, X-rated*; CONCEPT 545 —*Ant.* chaste, clean, decent, modest, pure, virtuous

indecisive [adj] *uncertain, indefinite* astraddle, changeable, doubtful, faltering, halting, hemming and hawing*, hesitant, hesitating, hot and cold*, inconclusive, indeterminate, irresolute, of two minds*, on the fence*, tentative, unclear, undecided, undetermined, uneventful, unsettled, unstable, vacillating, waffling, wavering, weak-kneed*, wishy-washy*; CONCEPTS 534,535 —*Ant.* certain, decisive, definite, deliberate, determined, sure

indeed [adv] *actually* absolutely, amen*, certainly, doubtlessly, easily, even, for real, in point of fact, in truth, much, naturally, of course, positively, really, strictly, surely, sure thing*, to be sure, truly, undeniably, undoubtedly, verily, veritably, very, very much, well; CONCEPT 535

indefatigable [adj] *untiring* active, assiduous, bound and determined*, dead set on*, determined, diligent, dogged, energetic, hell-bent*, industrious, inexhaustible, ironclad, nose to grindstone*, painstaking, patient, persevering, persistent, pertinacious, relentless, sedulous, steadfast, stop at nothing*, strenuous, tireless, unfaltering, unflagging, unflinching, unremitting, unwavering, unwearied, unwearying, vigorous; CONCEPT 542 —*Ant.* fatigued, tired, weary

indefensible [adj] *inexcusable* bad, faulty, inexpiable, insupportable, unforgivable, unjustifiable, unpardonable, untenable, unwarrantable, wrong; CONCEPTS 545,548 —*Ant.* defensible, excusable, justifiable, justified

indefinite [adj] *ambiguous, vague* broad, confused, doubtful, dubious, equivocal, evasive, general, ill-defined, imprecise, indeterminable, indeterminate, indistinct, inexact, inexhaustible, infinite, innumerable, intangible, loose, obscure, shadowy, uncertain, unclear, undefined, undependable, undetermined, unfixed, unknown, unlimited, unsettled; unspecific, unsure, wide; CONCEPT 535 —*Ant.* certain, definite, distinct, sure

indefinitely [adv] *continually* considerably, endlessly, forever, frequently, regularly, sine die, without end; CONCEPT 798 —*Ant.* definitely, incontinuously

indelible [adj] *not able to be erased, indestructible* enduring, ineffaceable, ineradicable, inerasable, inexpungible, inextirpable, ingrained, lasting, memorable, permanent, rememberable, stirring, unforgettable; CONCEPTS 482,529 —*Ant.* delible, destructible, erasable, impermanent

indelicate [adj] *obscene, vulgar* base, brash, brutish, callow, coarse, crude, earthy, embarrassing, immodest, improper, indecent, indecorous, lewd, low, lowbred, off-color*, offensive, outrageous, risqué, rude, suggestive, tasteless, unbecoming, unblushing, uncouth, unseemly, untactful, untoward; CONCEPTS 544,545 —*Ant.* decent, delicate, inoffensive, nice, pure

indent [v] *make a space; push in slightly* bash, cave in, cut, dent, depress, dint, hollow, jag, mark, nick, notch, pink, pit, rabbet, rut, scallop, score, serrate; CONCEPTS 158,201,208 —*Ant.* flush

independence [n] *liberty, freedom* ability, aptitude, autarchy, autonomy, home rule*, license, qualification, self-determination, self-government, self-reliance, self-rule, self-sufficiency, separation, sovereignty; CONCEPTS 376,691 —*Ant.* dependence, subordination

independent [adj] *liberated, free* absolute, autarchic, autarchical, autonomous, freewheeling, individualistic, nonaligned, nonpartisan, on one's own, self-contained, self-determining, self-governing, self-reliant, self-ruling, self-sufficient, self-supporting, separate, separated, sovereign, unaided, unallied, unconnected, unconstrained, uncontrolled, unregimented; CONCEPT 554 —*Ant.* dependent, subordinate, subservient

independently [adv] *alone* all by one's self, apart, autonomously, by oneself, exclusive of, freely, individually, of one's own volition, one at a time, one by one, on one's own, separately, severally, singly, solo, unaided, unrestrictedly, unsupervised, without regard to, without support; CONCEPT 554 —*Ant.* dependently

indescribable [adj] *beyond words* impossible, incommunicable, indefinable, ineffable, inexpressible, nondescript, sublime, subtle, unspeakable, untellable, unutterable; CONCEPT 267 —*Ant.* definable, describable, explainable

indestructible [adj] *lasting, unable to be destroyed* abiding, deathless, durable, enduring, everlasting, immortal, immutable, imperishable, incorruptible, indelible, indissoluble, inextinguishable, inextinguishable, inextirpable, irrefragable, irrefrangible, nonperishable, permanent, perpetual, unalterable, unbreakable, unchangeable, undestroyable, undying, unfading; CONCEPTS 489,534 —*Ant.* breakable, destructible, perishable

indeterminate [adj] *uncertain, vague* borderless, general, imprecise, inconclusive, indefinite, indistinct, inexact, undefined, undetermined, unfixed, unspecified, unstipulated; CONCEPT 535 —*Ant.* certain, definite, determined, exact, fixed, measurable, sure

index [n] *indication* basis, clue, evidence, formula, guide, hand, indicant, indication, indicator, indicia, mark, model, needle, pointer, ratio, rule, sign, significant, symbol, symptom, token; CONCEPTS 284,290

index [v] *arrange, order* alphabetize, catalogue, docket, file, list, record, tabulate; CONCEPT 84 —*Ant.* disarrange, disorder, disorganize

indicate [v] *signify, display* add up to, announce, argue, attest, augur, bespeak, be symptomatic, betoken, button down*, card, connote, demonstrate, denote, designate, evidence, evince, express, finger, hint, illustrate, imply, import, intimate, make, manifest, mark, mean, name, peg*, pin down*, pinpoint*, point out, point to, prove, read, record, register, reveal, show, sign, signal, slot, specify, suggest, symbolize, tab, tag, testify, witness; CONCEPTS 74,118,266 —*Ant.* conceal, hide, mislead

indication [n] *evidence, clue* adumbration, attestation, augury, auspice, cue, earnest, explanation, expression, forewarning, gesture, hint, implication, index, indicia, inkling, intimation, manifestation, mark, nod, note, notion, omen, pledge, portent, preamble, prefiguration, prognostic, prolegomenon, proof, reminder, show, sign, signal, significant, signifier, suggestion, symptom, telltale, token, trace, vestige, warning, wind*, wink*; CONCEPTS 74,278,284 —*Ant.* misinformation

indicative [adj] *exhibitive* apocalyptic, augural, auspicious, characteristic, connotative, demonstrative, denotative, denotive, designative, diagnostic, emblematic, evidential, evincive, expressive, inauspicious, indicatory, indicial, ominous, pointing to, prognostic, significant, significatory, suggestive, symbolic, symptomatic, testatory, testimonial; CONCEPT 267

indicator [n] *sign* barometer, beacon, clue, dial, gauge, guide, hint, index, mark, meter, omen, pointer, signal, symbol, warning; CONCEPTS 274,529,673,689

indict [v] *accuse* arraign, censure, charge, criminate, face with charges, finger*, frame*, impeach, incriminate, inculpate, prosecute, summon, tax; CONCEPTS 44,317 —*Ant.* absolve, acquit, exonerate

indictment [n] *accusation* allegation, arraignment, bill, blame, censure, charge, citation, detention, findings, impeachment, incrimination, presentment, prosecution, statement, summons, warrant, writ; CONCEPTS 44,317,318 —*Ant.* absolution, acquittal, exoneration

indifference [n] *absence of feeling, interest* alienation, aloofness, apathy, callousness, carelessness, cold-bloodedness, coldness, cold shoulder*, coolness, detachment, disdain, disinterest, disinterestedness, dispassion, disregard, equity, heedlessness, immunity, impartiality, impassiveness, impassivity, inattention, inertia, insensitivity, insouciance, isolationism, lack, lethargy, listlessness, negligence, neutrality, nonchalance, noninterference, objectivity, stoicism, torpor, unconcern, unmindfulness; CONCEPTS 410,657 —Ant. caring, compassion, concern, feeling, interest, involvement, regard, sympathy

indifferent [adj] *unfeeling, uninterested* aloof, apathetic, blasé, callous, cold, cool, detached, diffident, disinterested, dispassionate, distant, equitable, haughty, heartless, heedless, highbrow, impartial, impervious, inattentive, listless, neutral, nonchalant, nonpartisan, objective, passionless, phlegmatic, regardless, scornful, silent, stoical, supercilious, superior, unaroused, unbiased, uncaring, uncommunicative, unconcerned, unemotional, unimpressed, uninvolved, unmoved, unprejudiced, unresponsive, unsocial, unsympathetic; CONCEPTS 403,542 —Ant. caring, compassionate, concerned, feeling, interested, involved, sympathetic

indigenous [adj] *native, inborn* aboriginal, autochthonous, chthonic, congenital, connate, domestic, endemic, homegrown, inbred, inherent, inherited, innate, natural, original, primitive, unacquired; CONCEPT 549 —Ant. alien, foreign

indigent [adj] *poor* beggared, busted, destitute, down and out*, flat broke*, hard up*, homeless, impecunious, impoverished, in want, necessitous, needy, penniless, penurious, povertystricken; CONCEPT 334 —Ant. rich, wealthy

indigestion [n] *upset stomach* acid indigestion, acidosis, digestive upset, dyspepsia, dyspepsy, flatulence, flu, gas, gaseous stomach, heartburn, nausea, pain; CONCEPT 306

indignant [adj] *angry* acrimonious, annoyed, bent out of shape*, boiling*, bugged*, burned up*, disgruntled, displeased, exasperated, fuming, furious, heated, huffy*, in a huff*, incensed, irate, livid, mad, miffed, peeved, piqued, p.o.'d*, provoked, resentful, riled, scornful, seeing red*, up in arms*, upset, wrathful; CONCEPT 403 —Ant. gleeful, happy, pleased

indignation [n] *anger* animus, boiling point*, danger, displeasure, exasperation, fury, huff*, ire, mad, miff*, pique, rage, resentment, rise, scorn, slow burn*, umbrage, wrath; CONCEPTS 29,657 —Ant. glee, happiness, joy

indignity [n] *embarrassment, humiliation* abuse, affront, backhanded compliment*, contumely, discourtesy, dishonor, disrespect, grievance, injury, injustice, insult, obloquy, opprobrium, outrage, put-down*, reproach, slap*, slight, slur, snub, take-down*, taunt; CONCEPTS 278,410 —Ant. dignity, esteem, honor, regard, respect

indirect [adj] *roundabout; unintended* ambiguous, ancillary, circuitous, circular, circumlocutory, collateral, complicated, contingent, crooked, devious, discursive, duplicitous, erratic, eventual, implied, incidental, long, long-drawn-out*, long way home*,

long-winded*, meandering, oblique, obscure, out-of-the-way, périphrastic, rambling, secondary, serpentine*, sidelong, sinister, sinuous, snaking*, sneaking, sneaky, subsidiary, tortuous, twisting, underhand, vagrant, wandering, winding, zigzag; CONCEPTS 544,581 —Ant. direct, straight, straightforward

indiscreet [adj] *injudicious* careless, foolish, hasty, heedless, imprudent, inconsiderate, insensitive, rash, reckless, unthinking; CONCEPT 542

indiscretion [n] *mistake* bumble, crudeness, dropping the ball*, dumb move*, error, excitability, faux pas, folly, foolishness, fool mistake*, foul-up, gaffe, gaucherie, goof*, hastiness, imprudence, indiscreetness, ingenuousness, lapse, miscue, misjudgment, misspeak, naiveté, rashness, recklessness, screw-up*, simple-mindedness, slip*, slip of the tongue*, slip-up*, stumble, stupidity, tactlessness, thoughtlessness, unseemliness; CONCEPTS 101,633,674 —Ant. care, discreetness, discretion, right

indiscriminate [adj] *random, chaotic* aimless, assorted, broad, careless, confused, designless, desultory, extensive, general, haphazard, heterogeneous, hit-or-miss*, imperceptive, jumbled, mingled, miscellaneous, mixed, mongrel, motley*, multifarious, promiscuous, purposeless, shallow, spot, superficial, sweeping, unconsidered, uncritical, undiscriminating, unmethodical, unplanned, unselective, unsystematic, varied, variegated, wholesale*, wide; CONCEPTS 403,542,585,772 —Ant. chosen, critical, definite, discriminatory, methodical, particular, selective, specific, systematic

indispensable [adj] *necessary* basal, basic, cardinal, crucial, essential, fundamental, imperative, key, necessitous, needed, needful, prerequisite, primary, required, requisite, vital; CONCEPT 546 —Ant. dispensable, needless, nonessential, redundant, superfluous, unnecessary

indisposed [adj1] *not well* ailing, below par, confined, down, down with*, feeling rotten*, got a bug*, ill, infirm, laid up*, on sick list*, out of action*, poorly, sick, sickly, under the weather*, unwell; CONCEPT 314 —Ant. healthy, well

indisposed [adj2] *unwilling* afraid, antagonistic, antipathetic, averse, backward, disinclined, hesitant, hostile, inimical, loath, reluctant, uncaring, uneager, uninclined; CONCEPT 542 —Ant. bent, disposed, inclined, tending, willing

indisputable [adj] *beyond doubt* absolute, accurate, actual, certain, double-checked, evident, incontestable, incontrovertible, indubitable, irrefutable, no ifs ands or buts about it*, no mistake*, open and shut*, positive, real, sure, that's a fact*, true, unassailable, undeniable, undoubted, unfalsed, unquestionable, veridical; CONCEPTS 535,582 —Ant. disputable, doubtful, dubious, indefinite, questionable, refutable, uncertain, unreliable, unsure, vague

indistinct [adj] *obscure, ambiguous* bleared, bleary, blurred, confused, dark, dim, doubtful, faint, fuzzy, hazy, ill-defined, inaudible, inconspicuous, indefinite, indeterminate, indiscernible, indistinguishable, inexact, misty, muffled, murky, out of focus, shadowy, unclear, undefined, undetermined, unheard, unintelligible, vague, weak; CONCEPTS 485,535 —**Ant.** apparent, certain, defined, definite, discernible, distinct, evident, explicit, plain, positive, sure

indistinguishable [adj] alike duplicate, equivalent, identic, identical, like, same, tantamount, twin; CONCEPT 566 —**Ant.** different, distinguishable, unalike, unlike

individual [adj] distinctive, exclusive alone, characteristic, definite, diacritic, diagnostic, different, discrete, distinct, especial, express, idiosyncratic, indivisible, lone, odd, only, original, own, particular, peculiar, personal, personalized, proper, reserved, respective, secluded, select, separate, several, single, singular, sole, solitary, special, specific, uncommon, unique, unitary, unusual; CONCEPTS 404,564 —**Ant.** common, general, ordinary

individual [n] singular person, thing being, body, character, child, creature, dude*, entity, existence, human being, man, material, matter, mortal, number, party, person, personage, self, singleton, somebody, something, soul, stuff, substance, type, unit, woman; CONCEPTS 389,433 —**Ant.** group

individuality [n] personality air, character, complexion, difference, discreteness, disposition, dissimilarity, distinction, distinctiveness, eccentricity, habit, humor, identity, idiosyncrasy, independence, individualism, ipseity, makeup, manner, nature, oddity, oneness, originality, particularity, peculiarity, rarity, seity, selfdom, selfhood, selfness, separateness, singleness, singularity, singularness, temper, temperament, uniqueness, unity, unlikeness, way; CONCEPT 411

individually [adv] separately alone, apart, by oneself, distinctively, exclusively, independently, one at a time, one by one, personally, restrictedly, severally, singly, without help; CONCEPT 544 —**Ant.** together

individual retirement account [n] IRA Keogh plan, retirement plan, Roth IRA, self-funded retirement plan, tax-free savings account; CONCEPTS 335,340,446,710

indoctrinate [v] brainwash break down, convince, drill, ground, imbue, implant, inculcate, influence, initiate, instill, instruct, plant, program, school, teach, train, work over; CONCEPTS 14,285 —**Ant.** leave alone, neglect

indolent [adj] lazy drony, easygoing, fainéant, idle, inactive, inert, lackadaisical, languid, lax, lazy, lethargic, listless, resting, shiftless, slothful, slow, slow-going, sluggish, torpid; CONCEPTS 538,542,584 —**Ant.** active, busy, diligent, energetic, enthusiastic, hard-working, industrious, intent

indomitable [adj] steadfast, unyielding dogged, impassable, impregnable, insuperable, insurmountable, invincible, invulnerable, obstinate, pertinacious, resolute, ruthless, staunch, stubborn, unassailable, unbeatable, unconquerable, undefeatable, unflinching, willful; CONCEPTS 404,489,534 —**Ant.** beatable, conquerable, unstable, weak, yielding

indubitably [adv] unquestionably certainly, definitely, for sure, indeed, no question, of course, positively, surely, undoubtedly, without doubt; CONCEPT 535

induce [v] cause to happen; encourage abet, activate, actuate, argue into, breed, bring about, bring around, bulldoze*, cajole, cause, coax, convince, draw, draw in, effect, engender, generate, get*, get up, give rise to, goose*, impel, incite, influence, instigate, lead to, make, motivate, move, occasion, persuade, press, prevail upon, procure, produce, promote, prompt, sell one on*, set in motion, soft-soap*, squeeze, steamroll*, suck in*, sway, sweet-talk*, talk into*, twist one's arm*, urge, wheedle, win over*; CONCEPTS 14,68,242 —**Ant.** discourage, halt, hinder, prevent

inducement [n] incentive, motive attraction, bait, brainwash*, carrot*, cause, come-on*, con*, consideration, desire, encouragement, hard sell*, hook*, impulse, incitement, influence, leader, lure, reward, snow job*, soft soap*, spur, stimulus, sweet talk*, temptation, twist, urge; CONCEPTS 68,661 —**Ant.** discouragement, disincentive, hindrance, prevention

induct [v] take into an organization conscript, draft, enlist, inaugurate, initiate, install, instate, introduce, invest, recruit, sign on, sign up, swear in; CONCEPTS 50,88,320,384 —**Ant.** blackball, expel, reject, turn away

induction [n1] taking in, initiation consecration, draft, entrance, greetings, inaugural, inauguration, installation, instatement, institution, introduction, investiture, ordination, selection; CONCEPTS 320,384,685 —**Ant.** blackballing, expulsion, rejection

induction [n2] inference conclusion, conjecture, deducement, generalization, judgment, logical reasoning, ratiocination, rationalization, reason; CONCEPTS 37,689

indulge [v1] treat oneself or another to allow, baby, cater, coddle, cosset, delight, entertain, favor, foster, give in, give rein to*, go along, go easy on*, gratify, humor, mollycoddle*, nourish, oblige, pamper, pander, pet, please, regale, satiate, satisfy, spoil, spoil rotten*, take care of*, tickle, yield; CONCEPT 110 —**Ant.** disappoint, distress, hurt

indulge [v2] luxuriate in bask in, ego trip*, enjoy, go in for*, live it up*, look out for number one*, revel in, rollick*, take part, wallow in; CONCEPT 20 —**Ant.** abstain, moderate, not use

indulgence [n] luxury; gratification allowance, appeasement, attention, babying*, coddling*, courtesy, endurance, excess, extravagance, favor, favoring, fondling, fondness, forbearance, fulfillment, goodwill, gratifying, hedonism, immoderation, intemperance, intemperateness, kindness, kowtowing*, lenience, leniency, pampering, partiality, patience, permissiveness, petting, placating,pleasing, privilege, profligacy, profligateness, satiation, satisfaction, service, spoiling, toadying*, tolerance, toleration, treating, understanding; CONCEPTS 337,657,712 —**Ant.** abstention, care, moderation, temperance

indulgent [adj] lenient, giving able to live with*, big*, charitable, clement, compassionate, complaisant, compliant, considerate, easy, easygoing, favorable, fond, forbearing, gentle, going along with*, going easy on*, gratifying, kind, kindly, liberal, merciful, mild, overpermissive, permissive, soft-shelled*, tender, tolerant, understanding; CONCEPTS 404,542 —Ant. abstaining, moderate, moderating, strict, tempering

industrial [adj] related to manufacturing automated, business, factory-made, industrialized, in industry, machine-made, manufactured, manufacturing, mechanical, mechanized, modern, smokestack, streamlined, technical; CONCEPT 536 —Ant. domestic

industrious [adj] hardworking active, assiduous, ball of fire*, burning, busy, conscientious, diligent, dynamic, eager, energetic, grind*, in full swing*, intent, involved, jumping, laborious, on the go*, operose, perky*, persevering, persistent, plugging, productive, psyched up on*, purposeful, sedulous, spirited, steady, tireless, zealous; CONCEPT 538 —Ant. idle, inactive, indolent, lackadaisical, lazy, lethargic, slack, unemployed, unproductive

industry [n1] manufacturing big business*, business, commerce, commercial enterprise, corporation, management, manufactory, megacorp*, mob, monopoly, multinational, outfit*, production, trade, traffic; CONCEPTS 323,325

industry [n2] hard work activity, application, assiduity, attention, care, determination, diligence, dynamism, effort, energy, enterprise, intentness, inventiveness, labor, pains, patience, perseverance, persistence, tirelessness, toil, vigor, zeal; CONCEPT 677 —Ant. idleness, indolence, laziness, lethargy, unemployment, worthlessness

inebriated [adj] drunk blind drunk*, bombed, boozy, high*, inebriate, intoxicated, loaded*, plastered*, smashed*, tight*, tipsy, under the influence, wasted*; CONCEPT 314 —Ant. sober, straight

ineffable [adj] too great for words beyond words, celestial, divine, empyreal, empyrean, ethereal, heavenly, holy, ideal, impossible, incommunicable, incredible, indefinable, indescribable, inexpressible, nameless, sacred, spiritual, too sacred for words*, transcendent, transcendental, unspeakable, untellable, unutterable; CONCEPTS 267,574 —Ant. definable, describable, utterable

ineffective/ineffectual [adj] weak, useless abortive, anticlimactic, barren, bootless, defeasible, feckless, feeble, forceless, fruitless, futile, idle, impotent, inadequate, incompetent, indecisive, inefficacious, inefficient, inept, inferior, innocuous, inoperative, invertebrate, lame, limited, neutralized, nugatory, null, null and void*, paltry, powerless, spineless, unable, unavailing, unfruitful, unproductive, unprofitable, unsuccessful, vain, void, withered, worthless; CONCEPTS 537,560 —Ant. competent, effective, effectual, efficient, powerful, strong, useful

inefficient [adj] not working well; wasteful can't hack it*, careless, disorganized, extravagant, faulty, feeble, half-baked*, improficient, improvident, incapable, incompetent, ineffective, ineffectual, inefficacious, inept, inexpert, not cut out for*, prodigal, shooting blanks*, slack, slipshod, sloppy, slovenly, unfit, unprepared, unqualified, unskilled, unskillful, untrained, weak; CONCEPTS 402,527,560 —Ant. able, capable, competent, efficient, expert, useful

inelegant [adj] clumsy, crude awkward, coarse, crass, gauche, graceless, gross, indelicate, labored, oafish, raw, rough, rude, stiff*, uncouth, uncultivated, uncultured, ungainly, ungraceful, unpolished, unrefined, vulgar, wooden*; CONCEPTS 267,542,555 —Ant. elegant, glamorous, graceful, refined, sophisticated

ineligible [adj] not qualified disqualified, inappropriate, incompetent, objectionable, ruled out, unacceptable, unavailable, undesirable, unequipped, unfit, unqualified, unsuitable; CONCEPTS 402,558 —Ant. acceptable, eligible, equipped, qualified, suitable

inept [adj1] clumsy, unskilled; incompetent all thumbs*, artless, awkward, bumbling, bungling, butterfingers*, gauche, halting, inadept, incapable, incompetent, inefficient, inexpert, loser, maladroit, unapt, undexterous, unfacile, ungraceful, unhandy, unproficient, unskillful, wooden*; CONCEPTS 402,527 —Ant. able, adroit, competent, dexterous, fit, skilled, skillful

inept [adj2] not suitable; improper absurd, ill-timed, inappropriate, inapt, infelicitous, malapropos, meaningless, not adapted, out of place*, pointless, ridiculous, undue, unfit, unseasonable, unseemly, unsuitable; CONCEPT 558 —Ant. acceptable, proper, suitable

inequality [n] prejudice; lack of balance asperity, bias, contrast, difference, discrimination, disparity, disproportion, dissimilarity, dissimilitude, diversity, imparity, incommensurateness, injustice, irregularity, one-sidedness, partisanship, preferentiality, roughness, unequivalence, unevenness, unfairness, unjustness, variation; CONCEPT 665 —Ant. balance, equality, evenness, similarity

inequitable [adj] unfair arbitrary, biased, discriminatory, one-sided, partial, partisan, prejudiced, unbalanced, unequal, unethical, uneven, unjust; CONCEPTS 480,544,545,548

inert [adj] not moving; lifeless apathetic, asleep, dead, dormant, down, dull, idle, immobile, impassive, impotent, inactive, inanimate, indolent, languid, languorous, lazy, leaden, listless, motionless, numb, paralyzed, passive, phlegmatic, powerless, quiescent, quiet, slack, sleepy, slothful, sluggard, sluggish, slumberous, static, still, stolid, torpid, unmoving, unreactive, unresponsive; CONCEPTS 542,584 —Ant. active, alive, animated, lively, mobile, moving, working

inertia [n] disinclination to move; lifelessness apathy, deadness, drowsiness, dullness, idleness, immobility, immobilization, inactivity, indolence, languor, lassitude, laziness, lethargy, listlessness, oscitancy, paralysis, passivity, sloth, sluggishness, stillness, stupor, torpidity, torpor, unresponsiveness; CONCEPT 657 —Ant. activity, animation, life, liveliness, moving

inevitable [adj] certain; cannot be avoided all locked up*, assured, binding, compulsory, decided, decreed, destined, determined, doomed, fated, fateful, fixed, for certain, foreordained, imminent, impending, ineluctable, ineludible, inescapable, inexorable, inflexible, in the bag*, irresistible, irrevocable, necessary, no ifs ands or buts*, obligatory, ordained, pat*, prescribed, settled, sure, unalterable, unavoidable, undeniable, unpreventable, without recourse; CONCEPTS 535,552 —Ant. avoidable, doubtful, escapable, fortuitous, preventable, uncertain, unlikely, unsure

inexcusable [adj] *not forgivable* blamable, blameworthy, censurable, criticizable, impermissible, indefensible, inexpiable, intolerable, outrageous, reprehensible, unallowable, unforgivable, unjustifiable, unpardonable, unpermissible, untenable, unwarrantable, wrong; CONCEPTS 545,570 —*Ant.* excusable, forgivable, justifiable

inexhaustible [adj] *unlimited* bountiful, endless, infinite, limitless, never-ending, no end to*, numberless; CONCEPT 772

inexhaustible [adj] *tireless* enduring, indefatigable, unflagging, untiring, unwearying, vigorous; CONCEPTS 538,542

inexorable [adj] *cruel, pitiless* adamant, adamantine, bound, bound and determined*, compulsory, dead set on*, dogged, hard, harsh, hell bent on*, immobile, immovable, implacable, ineluctable, inescapable, inflexible, ironclad, like death and taxes*, locked in*, mean business*, merciless, necessary, no going back*, obdurate, obstinate, relentless, remorseless, resolute, rigid, set in stone*, severe, single-minded, stubborn, unappeasable, unbending, uncompromising, unmovable, unrelenting, unyielding; CONCEPTS 401,534 —*Ant.* flexible, lenient, merciful, remorseful, yielding

inexpensive [adj] *not high priced* bargain, budget, buy, cheap, cost next to nothing*, cut-rate, dime a dozen*, dirt-cheap*, economical, for a song*, half-price, low, low-cost, low-priced, marked down, modest, nominal, popular, popularly priced, real buy*, real steal*, reasonable, reduced, steal, thrifty; CONCEPT 334 —*Ant.* costly, dear, expensive, high-cost, high-priced

inexperienced [adj] *unskilled, unfamiliar* amateur, callow, fresh, green*, ignorant, immature, inept, inexpert, innocent, kid*, naive, new, prentice, raw*, rookie, rude, sophomoric, spring chicken*, tenderfoot*, unaccustomed, unacquainted, unconversant, undisciplined, unfamiliar with, unfledged, unpracticed, unschooled, unseasoned, unsophisticated, untrained, untried, unused, unversed, unworldly, verdant, wet behind ears*, young; CONCEPTS 402,404,527 —*Ant.* educated, experienced, expert, familiar, schooled, seasoned, skilled, trained, versed

inexplicable [adj] *beyond comprehension, explanation* baffling, enigmatic, incomprehensible, indecipherable, indescribable, inexplainable, inscrutable, insoluble, mysterious, mystifying, obscure, odd, peculiar, puzzling, strange, unaccountable, undefinable, unexplainable, unfathomable, unintelligible, unsolvable; CONCEPTS 267,529 —*Ant.* comprehendible, explainable, explicable, intelligible

infallible [adj] *unerring, dependable* acceptable, accurate, agreeable, apodictic, authoritative, certain, correct, effective, effectual, efficacious, efficient, exact, faultless, flawless, foolproof, handy, helpful, impeccable, incontrovertible, inerrable, inerrant, omniscient, perfect, positive, reliable, satisfactory, satisfying, sure, surefire, true, trustworthy, unbeatable, undeceivable, unfailing, unimpeachable, unquestionable, useful; CONCEPTS 535,560,574 —*Ant.* erring, fallible, faulty, imperfect

infamous [adj] *shameful, bad in reputation* abominable, atrocious, base, caitiff, contemptible, corrupt, degenerate, despicable, detestable, disgraceful, dishonorable, disreputable, egregious, evil, flagitious, foul, hateful, heinous, ignominious, ill-famed, iniquitous, loathsome, miscreant, monstrous, nefarious, notorious, odious, offensive, opprobrious, outrageous, perverse, questionable, rotten, scandalous, scurvy, shady, shocking, sorry, unhealthy, vicious, vile, villainous, wicked; CONCEPTS 404,545,570 —*Ant.* dignified, glorious, good, innocent, moral, perfect, principled, pure, respectable, righteous, virtuous

infamy [n] *shameful, bad reputation* abomination, atrocity, disapprobation, discredit, disesteem, disgrace, dishonor, disrepute, enormity, evil, ignominy, immorality, impropriety, notoriety, notoriousness, obloquy, odium, opprobrium, outrageousness, scandal, shame, stigma, villainy, wickedness; CONCEPTS 411,645 —*Ant.* dignity, goodness, innocence, morality, righteousness, virtue

infant [n] *baby* babe, bairn, bambino, bantling, bundle, child, kid, little one, neonate, newborn, small child, suckling, toddler, tot; CONCEPTS 414,424 —*Ant.* adult

infant/infantile [adj] *very young* baby, babyish, callow, childish, childlike, dawning, developing, early, emergent, green*, growing, immature, infantine, initial, juvenile, kid, naive, nascent, newborn, puerile, tender, unfledged, unripe, weak, youthful; CONCEPTS 542,578, 797,820 —*Ant.* adult, grown-up, mature

infatuated [adj] *in love with; obsessed* beguiled, besotted, bewitched, captivated, carried away*, charmed, crazy about*, enamored, enraptured, far gone on*, fascinated, foolish, inflamed, intoxicated, possessed, seduced, silly*, smitten, spellbound, under a spell*; CONCEPTS 32,403 —*Ant.* despising, disenchanted, hating

infect [v] *pollute, contaminate* affect, blight, corrupt, defile, disease, influence, poison, spoil, spread among, spread to, taint, touch, vitiate; CONCEPTS 143,246

infection [n] *contamination* bug*, communicability, contagion, contagiousness, corruption, defilement, disease, epidemic, flu, germs, impurity, insanitation, poison, pollution, septicity, virus, what's going around*; CONCEPTS 230,306 —*Ant.* sanitation, sterility

infectious [adj] *catching, spreading* communicable, contagious, contaminating, corrupting, defiling, diseased, epidemic, infective, mephitic, miasmic, noxious, pestilent, pestilential, poisoning, polluting, toxic, transferable, transmittable, virulent, vitiating; CONCEPTS 314,559 —*Ant.* antiseptic, germless, harmless, non-infectious, uncommunicable, uncontagious

infer [v] *conclude* arrive at, ascertain, assume, believe, collect, conjecture, construe, deduce, derive, draw, draw inference, figure, figure out, gather, glean, guess, induce, interpret, intuit, judge, presume, presuppose, reach conclusion, read between lines*, read into*, reason, reckon, speculate, suppose, surmise, think, understand; CONCEPTS 12,15,37 —*Ant.* misconceive, misunderstand

inference [n] *conclusion, deduction* assumption, conjecture, corollary, guess, hint, interpretation, presumption, reading, reasoning, supposition; CONCEPT 689

inferior [adj1] *less in rank, importance* back seat*, bottom, bottom-rung*, entry-level, junior, less, lesser, lower, menial, minor, minus, nether, peon, second, secondary, second-banana*, second-fiddle*, second-string*, smaller, subjacent, subordinate, subsidiary, under, underneath; CONCEPT 567 —Ant. best, better, extraordinary, first-class, first-rate, foremost, superior

inferior [adj2] *poor, second-rate* average, bad, base, common, déclassé, fair, good-for-nothing*, hack*, imperfect, indifferent, junk*, lemon*, lousy, low-grade, low-rent*, mean, mediocre, middling, ordinary, paltry, poorer, sad, second-class, sorry*, substandard, tawdry, two-bit*, worse, wretched; CONCEPT 574

inferior [n] *person of lesser rank, importance* adherent, attendant, auxiliary, deputy, disciple, follower, hanger-on, hireling, junior, menial, minion, minor, peon, satellite, second banana*, subaltern, subject, subordinate, sycophant, underling; CONCEPTS 348,423 —Ant. superior

infernal [adj] *damned; underworld* accursed, blamed, blasted, chthonian, confounded, cursed, cussed, damnable, demonic, devilish, diabolical, execrable, fiendish, hellish, lower, malevolent, malicious, monstrous, nether, satanic, subterranean, sulphurous, wicked; CONCEPT 536 —Ant. heavenly, otherworldly

inferno [n] *hell* blazes*, bottomless pit*, everlasting fire*, fire and brimstone*, Hades, hellfire, netherworld, purgatory, underworld; CONCEPTS 370,435,674

infertile [adj] *not bearing fruit, young* barren, depleted, drained, effete, exhausted, impotent, impoverished, infecund, nonproductive, sterile, unbearing, unfertile, unfruitful, unproductive; CONCEPTS 406,560 —Ant. fertile, fruitful, potent, productive

infest [adj] *flood, overrun* abound, annoy, assail, beset, crawl, crowd, defile, fill, flock, harass, harry, infect, invade, overspread, overwhelm, pack, penetrate, pester, plague, pollute, press, ravage, swarm, teem, throng, worry; CONCEPTS 14,86,179

infidel [n] *nonbeliever* agnostic, atheist, gentile, heathen, heretic, nonworshiper, pagan, unbeliever; CONCEPT 689

infidelity [n] *disloyalty to an obligation* adultery, affair, bad faith, betrayal, cheating, duplicity, extramarital relations, faithlessness, falseness, falsity, inconstancy, lewdness, perfidiousness, perfidy, treacherousness, treachery, treason, two-timing*, unfaithfulness; CONCEPTS 388,645 —Ant. faithfulness, fidelity, loyalty

infiltrate [v] *creep in* access, crack*, edge in, filter through, foist, impregnate, insinuate, penetrate, percolate*, permeate, pervade, saturate, sneak in, tinge, work into, worm into*; CONCEPTS 159,179

infinite [adj] *limitless, without end* absolute, all-embracing, bottomless, boundless, enduring, enormous, eternal, everlasting, illimitable, immeasurable, immense, incalculable, incessant, inestimable, inexhaustible, interminable, measureless, million, never-ending, no end of, no end to, numberless, perdurable, perpetual, sempiternal, stupendous, supertemporal, supreme,

total, unbounded, uncounted, unending, untold, vast, wide, without limit, without number; CONCEPTS 762,781,798 —Ant. bounded, calculable, confined, countable, definite, ephemeral, finite, fleeting, limited, measurable

infinitesimal [adj] *small* atomic, imperceptible, inappreciable, inconsiderable, insignificant, little, microscopic, miniature, minuscule, minute, negligible, teeny*, tiny, unnoticeable; CONCEPTS 773,789 —Ant. big, huge, large, significant, substantial

infinity [n] *endlessness* beyond, boundlessness, continuity, continuum, endless time, eternity, expanse, extent, immeasurability, immensity, infinitude, limitlessness, myriad, perpetuity, sempiternity, space, ubiquity, unlimited space, vastitude, vastness; CONCEPTS 730,807 —Ant. bounds, definiteness, ending, finiteness, limitation

infirm [adj] *sick, weak* ailing, anemic, anile, debilitated, decrepit, delicate, enfeebled, failing, faint, faltering, feeble, flimsy, fragile, frail, halting, ill, insecure, irresolute, laid low*, lame, sensile, shaky, unsound, unstable, unsubstantial, vacillating, wavering, wobbly; CONCEPTS 314,485,489 —Ant. firm, healthy, hearty, robust, sound, strong

infirmity [n] *weakness, sickness* affliction, ailing, ailment, confinement, debilitation, debility, decay, decrepitude, defect, deficiency, disease, diseasedness, disorder, failing, fault, feebleness, flu, frailty, ill health, imperfection, indisposition, malady, malaise, shortcoming, sickliness, unhealth, unhealthiness, unwellness, vulnerability; CONCEPTS 306,674,732 —Ant. good health, healthiness, robustness, soundness, strength

inflame [v] *anger, aggravate* agitate, annoy, arouse, burn, disturb, embitter, enrage, exacerbate, exasperate, excite, fan, fire, fire up, foment, gall, get*, grate, heat, heat up, ignite, impassion, incense, increase, infuriate, intensify, intoxicate, irritate, kindle, light, madden, provoke, put out*, rile, roil, rouse, steam up, stimulate, vex, worsen; CONCEPTS 7,14,19,22,249 —Ant. alleviate, appease, cool, pacify, placate, put out, quench, soothe, tranquilize

inflammable [adj] *ready to burn* burnable, combustible, dangerous, flammable, hazardous, ignitable, incendiary, risky, unsafe; CONCEPT 485 —Ant. fire-proof, incombustible, nonflammable, non-inflammable

inflammation [n] *redness, swelling* burning, infection, irritation, pain, rash, sore, tenderness; CONCEPTS 306,309

inflammatory [adj] *instigative, angering* anarchic, demagogic, exciting, explosive, fiery, incendiary, incitive, inflaming, insurgent, intemperate, provocative, rabble-rousing*, rabid, rebellious, revolutionary, riotous, seditionary, seditious; CONCEPTS 537,542 —Ant. calming, mitigating, placating, pleasing, tranquilizing

inflate [v] *blow up, increase* aerate, aggrandize, amplify, augment, balloon*, beef up*, bloat, boost, build up, cram*, dilate, distend, enlarge, escalate, exaggerate, exalt, expand, flesh out*, magnify, maximize, overestimate, pad*, puff up*, pump up*, pyramid, raise, spread, stretch, surcharge, swell up*, widen; CONCEPTS 236,245,780 —*Ant.* compress, contract, deflate, let air out, shrink

inflated [*adj*] *exaggerated* aggrandized, amplified, augmented, aureate, bloated, bombastic, diffuse, dilated, distended, dropsical, enlarged, euphuistic, extended, filled, flatulent, flowery, fustian, grandiloquent, grown, magnified, magniloquent, ostentatious, overblown, overestimated, pompous, pretentious, prolix, puffed, pumped up, ranting, rhapsodical, rhetorical, showy, spread, stretched, surcharged, swollen, tumescent, tumid, turgid, verbose, windy, wordy; CONCEPTS 267,773 —*Ant.* deflated, shrunken

inflation [*n*] *increase, swelling* aggrandizement, blowing up, boom, boost, buildup, distension, enhancement, enlargement, escalation, expansion, extension, hike, intensification, prosperity, puffiness, rise, spread, tumefaction; CONCEPTS 335,763,780 —*Ant.* compression, decrease, deflation, shrinkage

inflection [*n*] *accent, intonation* articulation, change, emphasis, enunciation, modulation, pitch, pronunciation, sound, timbre, tonality, tone, tone of voice, variation; CONCEPTS 65,595 —*Ant.* monotone

inflexible [*adj1*] *stubborn* adamant, adamantine, determined, dogged, dyed-in-the-wool*, firm, fixed, hard, hard-and-fast*, immovable, immutable, implacable, indomitable, inexorable, intractable, iron, obdurate, obstinate, relentless, resolute, rigid, rigorous, set, set in one's ways*, single-minded, stand one's ground*, staunch, steadfast, steely, stiff, strict, stringent, unadaptable, unbending, unchangeable, uncompliant, uncompromising, unrelenting, unswayable, unyielding; CONCEPT 404 —*Ant.* flexible, reasonable, willing, yielding

inflexible [*adj2*] *hardened, stiff* hard, immalleable, impliable, inelastic, nonflexible, rigid, set, starched, taut, unbending; CONCEPT 604 —*Ant.* bendable, elastic, flexible, pliable, pliant, resilient, soft

inflict [*v*] *impose something* administer, apply, bring upon, command, deal out, deliver, dispense, exact, expose, extort, force, force upon, give, give it to*, lay down the law*, levy, mete out, require, stick it to*, strike, subject, visit, wreak; CONCEPTS 50,53,88,242

influence [*n*] *power, authority* access, agency, ascendancy, character, clout, command, connections, consequence, control, credit, direction, domination, dominion, drag, effect, esteem, fame, fix, force, grease*, guidance, hold, impact, importance, imprint, in, juice*, leadership, leverage, magnetism, mark, moment, money, monopoly, network, notoriety, predominance, prerogative, pressure, prestige, prominence, pull, repercussion, reputation, ropes*, rule, significance, spell, supremacy, sway, weight*; CONCEPT 687 —*Ant.* impotence, incapacity, inferiority, powerlessness, weakness

influence [*v*] *lead to believe, do* act upon, affect, alter, argue into, arouse, be recognized, bias, brainwash*, bribe, bring to bear, carry weight, change, channel, compel, control, count, determine, direct, dispose, form, get at*, guide, have a part in, impact on, impel,

impress, incite, incline, induce, instigate, manipulate, modify, mold, move, persuade, predispose, prejudice, prevail, prompt, pull strings*, regulate, rouse, rule, seduce, sell, shape, snow*, sway, talk into, train, turn, urge, work upon; CONCEPTS 18,68,242

influential [*adj*] *effective, powerful* affecting, authoritative, big-gun*, big-wheel*, controlling, dominant, efficacious, famous, forcible, governing, guiding, hot-dog*, important, impressive, inspiring, instrumental, leading, major-league*, meaningful, momentous, moving, name, persuasive, potent, prominent, significant, strong, substantial, telling, touching, weighty; CONCEPTS 537,568 —*Ant.* ineffective, ineffectual, unimportant, uninfluential, unmoving, weak

influx [*n*] *flow, rush* arrival, coming in, convergence, entrance, incursion, inflow, inpouring, inrush, introduction, inundation, invasion, penetration; CONCEPTS 159,179,786

infomercial [*n*] *full-length television program existing solely to market a product* advertorial, commercial, demonstration, docutainment, infotainment, paid announcement; CONCEPT 277

inform [*v*] *communicate knowledge, information* acquaint, advise, apprise, betray, blab*, brief, caution, clue, edify, educate, endow, endue, enlighten, familiarize, fill in, forewarn, give a pointer, give a tip, give away, give two cents*, illuminate, inspire, instruct, invest, leak, let in on*, let know, level, make conversant with, notify, post, relate, send word, show the ropes*, snitch, squeal, tattle, teach, tell, tell on, tip, tout, update, warn, wise; CONCEPT 60 —*Ant.* conceal, hide, secret

informal [*adj*] *casual, simple* breezy, colloquial, congenial, cool*, democratic, down home*, easy, easygoing, everyday, extempore, familiar, folksy, frank, free, free-and-easy*, homey, improv*, inconspicuous, intimate, laid back*, loose, low-pressure, mellow, mixed, motley, natural, off-the-cuff*, open, ordinary, relaxed, spontaneous, sporty, straightforward, throwaway*, unceremonious, unconstrained, unconventional, unfussy, unofficial, unrestrained, urbane, without ceremony; CONCEPTS 548,589 —*Ant.* buttoned-up, ceremonious, dressed-up, formal, official, rigid, stiff

informant/informer [*n*] *person who delivers news* accuser, adviser, announcer, betrayer, blabbermouth*, canary*, crier, deep throat*, double-crosser, herald, interviewer, journalist, messenger, newscaster/newsperson, notifier, preacher, propagandist, rat*, reporter, sneak, source, stool pigeon*, tattler, tattletale; CONCEPTS 348,354,423

information [*n*] *facts, news* advice, ammo*, break*, chapter and verse*, clue, confidence, counsel, cue, data, dirt*, dope*, dossier, earful*, enlightenment, erudition, illumination, info*, inside story*, instruction, intelligence, knowledge, leak, learning, lore, lowdown*, material, message, network, notice, notification, orientation, propaganda, report, science, scoop, score, tidings, tip, what's what*, whole story*, wisdom, word*; CONCEPT 274 —*Ant.* ignorance

informative [*adj*] *educational* advisory, chatty, communicative, descriptive, edifying, educative, elucidative, enlightening, explanatory, forthcoming, gossipy, illuminating, informational, instructional, instructive, newsy, revealing, revelatory, significant; CONCEPT 267 —*Ant.* unilluminating, unimportant, uninformative, useless

informed [*adj*] *cognizant, conversant* abreast, acquainted, apprized, au courant*, au fait*, briefed, enlightened, erudite, expert, familiar, in the know*, into*, knowledgeable, know the score*, know what's what*, learned, on top of*, posted*, primed*, reliable, savvy*, tuned in*, up*, up on*, up-to-date, versant, versed, well-read, wise to*; CONCEPT 402 —*Ant.* ignorant, unaware, uninformed, unknowledgeable

infraction [*n*] *violation* breach, breaking, contravention, crime, error, faux pas, infringement, lapse, offense, sin, slip*, transgression, trespass; CONCEPTS 192,645 —*Ant.* obedience

infrastructure [*n*] *foundation* base, footing, framework, groundwork, root, support, underpinning; CONCEPTS 442,826

infrequent [*adj*] *not happening regularly* exceptional, few, few and far between*, isolated, limited, meager, occasional, odd, rare, scant, scanty, scarce, scattered, seldom, semioccasional, sparse, spasmodic, sporadic, stray, uncommon, unusual; CONCEPT 530 —*Ant.* common, frequent, often, usual

infringe [*v*] *violate* borrow, breach, break, contravene, crash, disobey, encroach, entrench, impose, infract, intrude, invade, lift, meddle, obtrude, offend, pirate, presume, steal, transgress, trespass; CONCEPTS 192,384 —*Ant.* comply, discharge, obey, observe

infuriate [*v*] *make angry* aggravate, anger, enrage, exasperate, incense, ire, irritate, madden, make blood boil*, provoke, rile, T-off*, umbrage; CONCEPT 14 —*Ant.* make happy, please

infuse [*v*] *introduce; soak* animate, breathe into, imbue, impart, implant, impregnate, inculcate, indoctrinate, ingrain, inoculate, inspire, instill, intersperse, invest, leaven, permeate, pervade, plant, saturate, steep, suffuse; CONCEPTS 140, 179,187

ingenious [*adj*] *clever; brilliant* able, adroit, artistic, bright, canny, crafty, creative, cunning, deviceful, dexterous, gifted, imaginative, innovational, innovative, innovatory, intelligent, inventive, original, ready, resourceful, shrewd, skillful, sly, subtle; CONCEPT 402 —*Ant.* awkward, dumb, ignorant, incompetent, inept, stupid

ingenuity [*n*] *cleverness* ability, adroitness, astuteness, brains, brightness, brilliance, creativity, cunning, dexterity, flair, genius, gumption, intelligence, inventiveness, resourcefulness, shrewdness, skill, smartness, talent, wisdom, wit; CONCEPT 409

ingenuous [*adj*] *honest, trustful* artless, candid, childlike, frank, green*, guileless, innocent, like a babe in the woods*, naive, natural, open, outspoken, plain, simple, sincere, square, straightforward, trusting, unaffected, unartful, unartificial, undisguised, unreserved, unschooled, unsophisticated, unstudied, up front*; CONCEPTS 267,542,589 —*Ant.* deceitful, dishonest, sly

ingest [*v*] *swallow* absorb, consume, devour, digest, down, drink, eat, inhale; CONCEPT 169

inglorious [*adj*] *disgraceful* blameworthy, contemptible, degrading, detestable, dishonorable, disreputable, ignoble, ignominious, offensive, reprehensible, shameful, unrespectable, unworthy; CONCEPT 555

ingrained [*adj*] *deep-rooted* built-in, chronic, confirmed, congenital, constitutional, deep-seated, fixed, fundamental, hereditary, implanted, inborn, inbred, inbuilt, indelible, indwelling, ineradicable, inherent, innate, in the blood*, intrinsic, inveterate, rooted; CONCEPTS 535,549 —*Ant.* superficial, surface

ingratiate [*v*] *get on the good side of someone* attract, blandish, brownnose*, captivate, charm, crawl, flatter, get in with*, grovel, hand a line*, insinuate oneself, kowtow*, play up to*, seek favor, truckle; CONCEPTS 7,22,68 —*Ant.* deter, disgust, repel

ingratiating [*adj*] *fawning, servile* charming, crawling, deferential, disarming, flattering, humble, insinuating, obsequious, saccharine, serving, silken, smarmy, soft, sycophantic, toadying*, unctuous; CONCEPT 401 —*Ant.* deterring, disgusting, repellent

ingredient [*n*] *component of concoction* additive, constituent, element, factor, fixing, fundamental, innards, integral, integrant, making, part, part and parcel*, piece; CONCEPT 835 —*Ant.* whole

inhabit [*v*] *take up residence in* abide, crash, dwell, indwell, live, locate, lodge, make one's home, occupy, park, people, perch, populate, possess, reside, roost, settle, squat, stay, tenant; CONCEPT 226 —*Ant.* depart, leave, move, vacate

inhabitant [*n*] *person who is resident of habitation* aborigine, addressee, autochthon, boarder, citizen, colonist, denizen, dweller, householder, incumbent, indweller, inmate, lessee, lodger, native, neighbor, occupant, occupier, renter, resider, roomer, settler, squatter, suburbanite, tenant, urbanite; CONCEPTS 354,413

inhale [*v*] *breathe in* drag, draw in, gasp, inspire, insufflate, puff, pull, respire, smell, sniff, snort, suck in; CONCEPTS 163,601 —*Ant.* breathe out, exhale

inherent [*adj*] *basic, hereditary* built-in, characteristic, congenital, connate, constitutional, deep-rooted, deep-seated, distinctive, elementary, essential, fixed, fundamental, genetic, immanent, implicit, inborn, inbred, inbuilt, indigenous, indispensable, individual, indwelling, ingrained, inherited, innate, inner, instinctive, integral, integrated, internal, in the grain, intimate, intrinsic, inward, latent, native, natural, original, part and parcel*, resident, running in the family*, subjective, unalienable; CONCEPTS 404,549 —*Ant.* acquired, added, external, extrinsic, incidental, learned

inherit [*v*] *gain as possession from someone's death* accede, acquire, be bequeathed, be granted, be left, come in for, come into, derive, fall heir, get, obtain, receive, succeed, take over; CONCEPTS 124,317

inheritance [*n*] *possession gained through someone's death* bequest, birthright, devise, estate, gift, heirloom, heritage, heritance, legacy, primogeniture; CONCEPT 337

inherited [*adj*] *hereditary* congenital, connate, genetic, handed down, inborn, inbred, innate, in the blood, in the genes, passed down, rooted; CONCEPT *549*

inhibit [*v*] *restrict, prevent* arrest, avert, bar, bit, bridle, check, constrain, cramp, curb, discourage, enjoin, faze, forbid, frustrate, hang up*, hinder, hog-tie*, hold back, hold down, hold in, impede, interdict, keep in, obstruct, outlaw, prohibit, put on brakes*, repress, restrain, sandbag*, stop, stymie, suppress, taboo*, ward withhold; CONCEPTS *121,130* —*Ant.* aid, allow, approve, assist, free, help

inhibited [*adj*] *shy* bottled up*, cold, constrained, frustrated, guarded, hung up*, passionless, repressed, reserved, reticent, self-conscious, subdued, undemonstrative, unresponsive, uptight, withdrawn; CONCEPTS *404,542* —*Ant.* aggressive, bold, forward, immodest, self-confident

inhibition [*n*] *restriction, hindrance* bar, barrier, blockage, check, embargo, hangup, interdict, interference, obstacle, prevention, prohibition, reserve, restraint, reticence, self-consciousness, shyness, sublimation, suppression; CONCEPTS *411,657* —*Ant.* aid, approval, assistance, freedom, hand, liberation

inhospitable [*adj*] *unfriendly* brusque, cold, cool, hostile, rude, short, uncongenial, unfavorable, ungenerous, unkind, unreceptive, unsociable, unwelcoming; CONCEPT *401* —*Ant.* friendly, generous, hospitable, kind

inhuman/inhumane [*adj*] *animal, savage* barbaric, barbarous, bestial, brutal, cannibalistic, cold-blooded, cruel, devilish, diabolical, fell, ferocious, fiendish, fierce, grim, hateful, heartless, implacable, malicious, malign, malignant, mean, merciless, pitiless, relentless, remorseless, ruthless, truculent, uncompassionate, unfeeling, unkind, unrelenting, unsympathetic, vicious; CONCEPTS *401,545* —*Ant.* animate, human/humane, sensate

inhumanity [*n*] *lack of compassion* atrocity, barbarism, bloodthirstiness, brutality, brutishness, callousness, cold-bloodedness, cruelty, ferocity, heartlessness, maliciousness, ruthlessness, savagery, viciousness, violence; CONCEPTS *29,645*

inimical [*adj*] *antagonistic, contrary* adverse, antipathetic, destructive, disaffected, harmful, hostile, hurtful, ill, ill-disposed, inimicable, injurious, noxious, opposed, oppugnant, pernicious, repugnant, unfavorable, unfriendly, unwelcoming; CONCEPTS *401,537* —*Ant.* friendly, hospitable, kind

inimitable [*adj*] *incomparable* consummate, matchless, nonpareil, peerless, perfect, supreme, unequalled, unexampled, unique, unmatched, unparalleled, unrivalled, unsurpassable; CONCEPT *574* —*Ant.* comparable, indistinctive, matchable

iniquity [*n*] *sin, evil* abomination, baseness, crime, evildoing, heinousness, immorality, infamy, injustice, miscreancy, misdeed, offense, sinfulness, unfairness, unrighteousness, wickedness, wrong, wrongdoing; CONCEPT *645* —*Ant.* good, goodness, virtue

initial [*adj*] *beginning, primary* antecedent, basic, commencing, earliest, early, elementary, embryonic, first, foremost, fundamental, germi-nal, headmost, inaugural, inceptive, inchoate, incipient, infant, initiative, initiatory, introductory, leading, nascent, opening, original, pioneer, virgin; CONCEPTS *585,799,828* —*Ant.* closing, final, last

initiate [*v1*] *start, introduce* admit, begin, break the ice*, come out with, come up with, commence, dream up, enter, get ball rolling*, get feet wet*, get under way, inaugurate, induct, install, instate, institute, intro*, invest, kick off*, launch, make up, open, originate, pioneer, set in motion, set up, take in, take up, trigger, usher in; CONCEPT *221* —*Ant.* close, conclude, end, finish, terminate

initiate [*v2*] *teach* brief, coach, edify, enlighten, familiarize, indoctrinate, induct, inform, instate, instruct, introduce, invest, train; CONCEPT *285* —*Ant.* ignore, neglect

initiation [*n*] *start, introduction* admission, baptism, beginning, commencement, debut, enrollment, entrance, inaugural, inauguration, inception, indoctrination, induction, installation, instatement, investiture, preliminaries; CONCEPTS *221,386* —*Ant.* close, conclusion, end, ending, finish, termination

initiative [*n*] *eagerness to do something* action, ambition, drive, dynamism, energy, enterprise, enthusiasm, get-up-and-go*, gumption*, inventiveness, leadership, moxie*, originality, punch, push, resource, resourcefulness, spunk*, steam*, vigor; CONCEPTS *411,657* —*Ant.* indifference, lethargy

inject [*v1*] *put in, introduce* add, drag in, force into, imbue, implant, impregnate, include, infuse, insert, instill, interjaculate, interject, place into, squeeze in, stick in, throw in; CONCEPTS *187,208,209* —*Ant.* take out

inject [*v2*] *introduce into bloodstream by use of a needle* give a shot, inoculate, jab, mainline*, shoot, vaccinate; CONCEPTS *179,310*

injection [*n*] *introduction into bloodstream* booster, dose, dram, enema, inoculation, needle, vaccine; CONCEPT *311*

injunction [*n*] *decree* admonition, ban, bar, behest, bidding, charge, command, demand, dictate, embargo, enjoinder, exhortation, instruction, mandate, order, precept, prohibition, ruling, word, writ; CONCEPTS *271,318*

injure [*v*] *hurt, harm* abuse, aggrieve, batter, blemish, blight, break, contort, cripple, cut up, damage, deface, deform, disable, disfigure, distort, distress, do in*, draw blood*, foul, foul up, grieve, hack up, impair, maim, maltreat, mangle, mar, mutilate, pain, pique, prejudice, ruin, shake up, spoil, sting, tarnish, torment, torture, total, undermine, vitiate, wax, weaken, wound, wrong; CONCEPT *246* —*Ant.* aid, assist, cure, fix, heal, help, mend

injurious [*adj*] *hurtful* abusive, adverse, bad, baneful, corrupting, damaging, dangerous, deadly, deleterious, destructive, detrimental, disadvantageous, evil, harmful, iniquitous, insulting, libeling, mischievous, nocent, nocuous, noxious, opprobrious, pernicious, poisonous, prejudicial, ruinous, slanderous, unconducive, unhealthy, unjust, wrongful; CONCEPTS *537,570* —*Ant.* aiding, assisting, beneficial, constructive, curing, fixing, good, healing, helpful, mending, nice

injury [n] *hurt, harm* abrasion, abuse, affliction, affront, agony, bad, bite, blemish, boo-boo*, bruise, burn, chop, cramp, cut, damage, deformation, detriment, discomfiture, disservice, distress, evil, fracture, gash, grievance, hemorrhage, ill, impairment, indignity, injustice, insult, laceration, lesion, libel, loss, mischief, misery, mutilation, nick, ouch*, outrage, pang, ruin, scar, scratch, shock, slander, sore, sprain, stab, sting, suffering, swelling, trauma, twinge, wound, wrong; CONCEPTS 309,728 —*Ant.* aid, assistance, benefit, blessing, favor, good, health, help, right

injustice [n] *unfair treatment; bias* abuse, breach, crime, crying shame*, damage, dirty deal*, discrimination, encroachment, favoritism, grievance, inequality, inequity, infraction, infringement, iniquity, malfeasance, malpractice, maltreatment, miscarriage, mischief, negligence, offense, onesidedness, oppression, outrage, partiality, partisanship, prejudice, railroad*, ruin, sellout*, transgression, trespass, unfairness, unjustness, unlawfulness, villainy, violation, wrong, wrongdoing; CONCEPTS 192,645,674 —*Ant.* equality, equity, ethics, fairness, impartiality, justice, lawfulness, morality

inkling [n] *idea, clue* conception, cue, faintest idea*, foggiest idea*, glimmering, hint, hot lead*, hunch*, impression, indication, innuendo, intimation, lead, notion, sneaking suspicion*, suggestion, suspicion, tip, tipoff, whisper; CONCEPT 689

inlet [n] *arm of the sea* basin, bay, bayou, bight, canal, channel, cove, creek, delta, entrance, estuary, firth, fjord, gulf, harbor, ingress, loch, narrows, passage, slew, slough, sound, strait; CONCEPTS 509,514

inn [n] *accommodation for travellers* auberge, hospice, hostel, hostelry, hotel, lodge, motel, public house, resort, roadhouse, saloon, tavern; CONCEPTS 439,449,516

innards [n] *internal organs* bowels, entrails, guts, insides, intestines, numbles, viscera, vital organs; CONCEPT 393

innate [adj] *inherited, native* congenital, connate, connatural, constitutional, deep-seated, elemental, essential, hereditary, inborn, inbred, indigenous, ingrained, inherent, instinctive, intrinsic, intuitive, natural, normal, regular, standard, typical, unacquired; CONCEPTS 406,549 —*Ant.* acquired, extrinsic, learned

inner [adj1] *central, middle physically* close, constitutional, essential, familiar, focal, inherent, innermore, inside, interior, internal, intestinal, intimate, intrinsic, inward, nuclear; CONCEPTS 826,830 —*Ant.* exterior, external, outer, outside

inner [adj2] *mental, private* central, concealed, deep-rooted, deep-seated, emotional, esoteric, essential, focal, gut*, hidden, individual, inherent, innate, inside, interior, internal, intimate, intrinsic, intuitive, inward, personal, psychological, repressed, secret, spiritual, subconscious, unrevealed, visceral, viscerous; CONCEPTS 529,576 —*Ant.* outer, physical

innocence [n1] *blamelessness* chastity, clean hands*, clear conscience*, guiltlessness, immaculateness, impeccability, incorruptibility, incorruption, inculpability, probity, purity, righteousness, sinlessness, stainlessness, uprightness, virtue; CONCEPT 645 —*Ant.* badness, blame, corruption, evil, guilt, sin

innocence [n2] *harmlessness, naiveté* artlessness, candidness, credulousness, forthrightness, frankness, freshness, guilelessness, gullibility, ignorance, inexperience, ingenuousness, innocuousness, innoxiousness, inoffensiveness, lack, nescience, plainness, purity, simplicity, sincerity, unaffectedness, unawareness, unfamiliarity, unknowingness, unsophistication, unworldliness, virtue; CONCEPTS 409,411 —*Ant.* experience, impurity, knowledge, treacherousness, wildness

innocent [adj1] *blameless* above suspicion, angelic, chaste, clean, cleanhanded, clear, crimeless, exemplary, faultless, free of, good, guilt-free, guiltless, honest, immaculate, impeccable, impeccant, inculpable, in the clear*, irreproachable, lawful, legal, legitimate, licit, not guilty, pristine, pure, righteous, safe, sinless, spotless, stainless, unblemished, uncensurable, uncorrupt, unimpeachable, uninvolved, unoffending, unsullied, untainted, upright, virginal, virtuous; CONCEPT 545 —*Ant.* bad, blamable, corrupt, evil, guilty, sinful

innocent [adj2] *harmless, naive* artless, childlike, credulous, frank, fresh, guileless, gullible, hurtless, ignorant, inexperienced, ingenuous, innocuous, innoxious, inobnoxious, inoffensive, offenseless, open, raw, safe, simple, soft, square, unacquainted, unartificial, uncool, unfamiliar, unhurtful, uninjurious, unmalicious, unobjectionable, unoffensive, unschooled, unsophisticated, unstudied, unsuspicious, unworldly, well-intentioned, wellmeant, wide-eyed, youthful; CONCEPTS 404,542 —*Ant.* cunning, experienced, impure, knowledgeable

innocuous [adj] *harmless* banal, bland, flat, innocent, innoxious, inobnoxious, inoffensive, insipid, jejune, kind, painless, safe, sapless, unobjectionable, unoffending, weak; CONCEPTS 401,572 —*Ant.* bad, damaging, destructive, harmful, hurtful, injurious

innovation [n] *change, novelty* addition, alteration, contraption, cutting edge*, departure, deviation, introduction, last word*, latest thing*, leading edge*, modernism, modernization, modification, mutation, newness, notion, permutation, shift, variation, vicissitude, wrinkle*; CONCEPTS 260,529,660,665 —*Ant.* custom, habit, old, old hat, rut, tradition

innovative [adj] *creative* avant-garde, breaking new ground*, contemporary, cutting-edge*, deviceful, ingenious, innovational, innovatory, inventive, just out*, leading-edge*, new, newfangled*, original, originative, state-of-the-art; CONCEPTS 529,578,589,797 —*Ant.* customary, habitual, old, traditional, uncreative, unimaginative

innovator [n] *inventor* avant-garde, creator, discoverer, groundbreaker, pioneer, trailblazer, trendsetter, vanguard; CONCEPTS 348,413

innuendo [n] *suggestion* allusion, aside, aspersion, hint, implication, imputation, insinuation, intimation, overtone, reference, whisper; CONCEPTS 75,278 —*Ant.* evidence, proof

innumerable [adj] *many, infinite* alive with*, beyond number, countless, frequent, incalculable, multitudinous, myriad, numberless, numerous, uncountable, unnumbered, untold; CONCEPT 762 —*Ant.* computable, countable, definite, finite, known, numbered, numerable

inoculation [n] *immunization* injection, prevention, shot, vaccination; CONCEPT 310

inoffensive [adj] *not obnoxious; harmless* calm, clean, friendly, humble, innocent, innocuous, innoxious, mild, neutral, nonprovocative, peaceable, pleasant, quiet, retiring, safe, unobjectionable, unobtrusive, unoffending; CONCEPTS 267,542 —*Ant.* damaging, harmful, malicious, offensive, provocative

inopportune [adj] *not appropriate or suitable* contrary, disadvantageous, disturbing, ill-chosen, ill-timed, inappropriate, inauspicious, inconvenient, malapropos, mistimed, troublesome, unfavorable, unfortunate, unpropitious, unseasonable, unsuitable, untimely; CONCEPT 558 —*Ant.* appropriate, auspicious, ok, opportune, suitable, timely

inordinate [adj] *excessive, extravagant* disproportionate, dizzying, exorbitant, extortionate, extreme, gratuitous, immoderate, intemperate, irrational, outrageous, overindulgent, overmuch, preposterous, supererogatory, superfluous, surplus, too much, towering, uncalled-for, unconscionable, uncurbed, undue, unmeasurable, unreasonable, unrestrained, untempered, unwarranted, wanton, wasteful; CONCEPTS 570,781 —*Ant.* moderate, ok enough, reasonable, warranted

inorganic [adj] *not organic* dead, extinct, inanimate, lifeless, manmade, mineral, not living, not natural; CONCEPT 549 —*Ant.* organic

inquest [n] *investigation* delving, examination, hearing, inquiry, inquisition, probe, probing, quest, research, trial; CONCEPTS 48,290,318 —*Ant.* conclusion, findings

inquire [v] *ask; look into* analyze, catechize, examine, explore, feel out, go over, grill, hit, hit up, inspect, interrogate, investigate, knock, probe, prospect, pry, query, question, request information, roast, scrutinize, search, seek, seek information, sift, study, test the waters*; CONCEPTS 24,48 —*Ant.* answer, respond

inquiring [adj] *wondering, curious* analytical, catechistic, doubtful, examining, fact-finding, heuristic, inquisitive, interested, interrogative, investigative, investigatory, nosy, outward-looking, probing, prying, questioning, quizzical, searching, Socratic, speculative, studious; CONCEPTS 402,542 —*Ant.* disinterested, incurious, unskeptical

inquiry [n] *asking; looking into* analysis, audit, catechizing, check, cross-examination, delving, disquisition, examination, exploration, fishing expedition*, grilling, hearing, inquest, inquisition, inspection, interrogation, interrogatory, investigation, legwork*, poll, probe, probing, pursuit, Q and A*, query, quest, question, questioning, quizzing, request, research, scrutiny, search, study, survey, third degree*, trial balloon*; CONCEPTS 24,48,290 —*Ant.* answer, reply

inquisitive [adj] *curious* big-eyed*, analytical, challenging, forward, impertinent, inquiring, inquisitorial, interested, intrusive, investigative, meddlesome, meddling, nosy, peering,

personal, poking, presumptuous, probing, prying, questioning, scrutinizing, searching, sifting, snooping, speculative; CONCEPT 402 —*Ant.* incurious, indifferent, unconcerned, uninterested

inroad [n] *advance, foray* encroachment, impingement, incursion, intrusion, invasion, irruption, onslaught, raid, trespass; CONCEPTS 86,704

insane [adj] *mentally ill; foolish* batty*, bizarre, cracked*, crazed, crazy, cuckoo*, daft, demented, derailed, deranged, fatuous, frenzied, idiotic, impractical, irrational, irresponsible, loony*, lunatic, mad, maniacal, mental, moonstruck*, nuts*, nutty*, off one's rocker*, of unsound mind, out of one's mind*, paranoid, preposterous, psychopathic, psychotic, rabid, raging, raving, schizophrenic, screwy, senseless, touched, unhinged, unsettled, wild; CONCEPTS 314,403,548 —*Ant.* balanced, healthy, rational, reasonable, sane, sound, well

insanely [adv] *extremely* crazily, ferociously, fiercely, furiously, idiotically, irrationally, stupidly, violently, wildly; CONCEPT 569

insanity [n] *mental illness; foolishness* aberration, absurdity, alienation, craziness, delirium, delusion, dementia, derangement, distraction, dotage, folly, frenzy, hallucination, hysteria, illusion, inanity, irrationality, irresponsibility, lunacy, madness, mania, mental disorder, neurosis, phobia, preposterousness, psychopathy, psychosis, senselessness, unbalance, unreasonableness, witlessness; CONCEPTS 316,410 —*Ant.* balance, sanity, soundness, wellness

insatiable [adj] *voracious, wanting* clamorous, crying, demanding, desiring, exigent, gluttonous, greedy, importunate, insatiate, insistent, intemperate, pressing, quenchless, rapacious, ravenous, unappeasable, unquenchable, unsatisfiable, unsatisfied, urgent, yearning; CONCEPTS 20,403,546 —*Ant.* fulfilled, full, pleased, satiable, satisfied

inscribe [v] *imprint, write* book, carve, cut, engrave, engross, etch, impress, indite, list, record, register, scribe; CONCEPT 79

inscription [n] *message* autograph, caption, dedication, engraving, epitaph, heading, imprint, label, legend, lettering, saying, signature, wording; CONCEPT 283

inscrutable [adj] *hidden, mysterious; blank* ambiguous, arcane, cabalistic, deadpan*, difficult, enigmatic, impenetrable, incomprehensible, inexplicable, mysterial, mystic, poker-faced*, secret, sphinxlike, unaccountable, undiscoverable, unexplainable, unfathomable, unintelligible, unknowable, unreadable; CONCEPTS 529,576 —*Ant.* clear, comprehensible, evident, intelligible, obvious, plain

insect [n] *bug* ant, aphid, bedbug, bee, beetle, bumblebee, butterfly, cockroach, cootie, daddy longlegs, dragonfly, flea, fly, fruit fly, gnat, grasshopper, hornet, ladybug, louse, mite, mosquito, moth, pest, praying mantis, termite, tick, vermin, yellowjacket; CONCEPT 398

insecure [adj] *uncertain, worried* afraid, anxious, apprehensive, choked, Delphic, diffident, hanging by thread*, hesitant, jumpy, on thin ice*, questioning, shaky, touch and go*, touchy*, troubled, unassured, unconfident, unpoised, unsure, up in the air*, uptight*, vague; CONCEPTS 403,542 —Ant. certain, confident, secure, sure

insecure [adj2] dangerous, precarious defenseless, exposed, fluctuant, frail, hazardous, immature, insubstantial, loose, open to attack*, perilous, rickety, rocky, rootless, shaky, unguarded, unprotected, unreliable, unsafe, unshielded, unsound, unstable, unsteady, vacillating, vulnerable, wavering, weak, wobbly; CONCEPTS 488,570 —Ant. guarded, protected, safe, secure, sound

insensitive [adj1] indifferent, callous aloof, bloodless*, coldhearted*, crass, feelingless, hard, hard as nails*, hard-boiled*, hardened, hardhearted*, heartless, imperceptive, incurious, obtuse, stony, tactless, thick-skinned*, tough, uncaring, unconcerned, unfeeling, unkind, unresponsive, unsusceptible; CONCEPT 401 —Ant. caring, concerned, feeling, impressionable, mindful, responsive, sensitive

insensitive [adj2] numb anesthetized, asleep, benumbed, dead, deadened, immune to, impervious to, insensible, nonreactive, senseless, unfeeling; CONCEPT 406 —Ant. aware, feeling, sensate, touched

inseparable [adj] unable to be divided as one, attached, conjoined, connected, entwined, inalienable, indissoluble, indivisible, inseverable, integral, integrated, intertwined, interwoven, molded, secure, tied up, unified, united, whole; CONCEPT 531 —Ant. dividable, separable

insert [v] put, tuck in admit, drag in, embed, enter, fill in, imbed, implant, include, infix, infuse, inject, inlay, insinuate, instill, intercalate, interject, interlope, interpolate, interpose, introduce, intrude, lug in, obtrude, place, pop in*, root, set, shoehorn*, shove in, squeeze in, stick, work in; CONCEPTS 201,209 —Ant. remove, take out, withdraw

inside [adj1] in the middle; interior central, indoors, inner, innermost, internal, intramural, inward, surrounded, under a roof; CONCEPTS 583,830 —Ant. exterior, external, outer, outside

inside [adj2] secret classified, closet, confidential, esoteric, exclusive, hushed, internal, limited, private, restricted; CONCEPTS 529,576 —Ant. known, public

inside [adv] within indoors, under a roof, under cover, within doors, within walls; CONCEPT 583 —Ant. exterior, outside

inside [n] middle, lining belly, bowels, breast, center, contents, gut, heart, innards, inner portion, interior, recess, soul, stuffing, womb; CONCEPT 830 —Ant. exteriority, outside

insidious [adj] sneaky, tricky artful, astute, corrupt, crafty, crooked, cunning, dangerous, deceitful, deceptive, deep, designing, dishonest, disingenuous, duplicitous, ensnaring, false, foxy, guileful, intriguing, like a snake in the grass*, Machiavellian, perfidious, perilous, secret, slick, sly, smooth, snaky*, sneaking, stealthy, subtle, surreptitious, treacherous, wily, wormlike*; CONCEPTS 401,542,545 —Ant. fair, honest, open, sincere

insight [n] intuitiveness, awareness acumen, click*, comprehension, discernment, divination, drift*, intuition, judgment, observation, penetration, perception, perceptivity, perspicacity, sagaciousness, sagacity, sageness, sapience, shrewdness, understanding, vision, wavelength*, wisdom; CONCEPTS 409,410 —Ant. ignorance, stupidity

insightful [adj] perceptive alert, astute, awake, aware, brainy, conscious, cute, discerning, ear to the ground*, intelligent, intuitive, keen, knowing, knowledgeable, knows what's what*, observant, penetrating, penetrative, quick, responsive, savvy, sensitive, sharp, shrewd, smart, tuned in*, understanding, wise; CONCEPTS 402,542

insignia [n] emblem badge, coat of arms, crest, decoration, earmark, ensign, mark, paraphernalia, regalia, symbol; CONCEPTS 259,284

insignificant [adj] not important; of no consequence casual, immaterial, inappreciable, inconsequential, inconsiderable, infinitesimal, irrelevant, lesser, light, lightweight*, little, meager, meaningless, minim, minimal, minor, minuscule, minute, negligible, nondescript, nonessential, not worth mentioning*, nugatory, paltry, petty, pointless, purportless, scanty, secondary, senseless, small, trifling, trivial, unimportant, unsubstantial; CONCEPT 575 —Ant. consequential, important, significant, substantial, valuable

insincere [adj] dishonest, pretended ambidextrous, backhanded, deceitful, deceptive, devious, disingenuous, dissembling, dissimulating, double, double-dealing, duplicitous, evasive, faithless, fake, false, hollow, hypocritical, lying, mendacious, perfidious, phony, pretentious, put-on*, shifty, slick, sly, snide, two-faced*, unfaithful, untrue, untruthful; CONCEPTS 267,542 —Ant. forthright, frank, honest, open, sincere

insinuate [v1] hint, suggest allude, ascribe, connote, imply, impute, indicate, intimate, mention, propose, purport, refer, signify; CONCEPTS 49,75 —Ant. conceal, hide, withhold

insinuate [v2] force one's way into curry favor*, edge in, fill in, foist, get in with*, horn in*, infiltrate, infuse, ingratiate, inject, insert, instill, intercalate, interject, interpose, introduce, muscle in*, slip in, wedge in, work in, worm in*; CONCEPTS 159,208,384 —Ant. leave alone

insipid [adj1] dull, uninteresting anemic, arid, banal, beige, blah*, bland, characterless, colorless, commonplace, dead*, drab, driveling, dry, feeble, flat, ho-hum*, inane, innocuous, jejune, lifeless, limp, mild, mundane, nebbish, nothing, ordinary, plain, pointless, prosaic, prosy, slight, soft*, spiritless, stale, stupid, subdued, tame, tedious, tenuous, thin, tired, trite, unimaginative, vapid, watery, weak, wearful, wearisome, wishy-washy*; CONCEPTS 402,404,537 —Ant. exciting, exhilarating, interesting, pleasing

insipid [adj2] tasteless bland, distasteful, flat, flavorless, jejune, mild, savorless, stale, unappetizing, unpalatable, unsavory, vapid, watered-down, watery; CONCEPT 613 —Ant. appetizing, delicious, tasty, yummy

insist [v] order and expect; claim assert, asseverate, aver, be firm, contend, demand, hold, importune, lay down the law*, maintain, persist, press, reiterate, repeat, request, require, stand firm, swear, take a stand*, urge, vow; CONCEPTS 49,53 —Ant. endure, forget, tolerate

insistent [adj] *demanding* assertive, burning, clamant, clamorous, continuous, crying, dire, dogged, emphatic, exigent, forceful, imperative, imperious, importunate, incessant, obstinate, peremptory, perseverant, persevering, persistent, pressing, reiterative, resolute, resounding, unrelenting, urgent; CONCEPTS 267,534,540 —Ant. disinterested, indifferent, lenient, tolerant

insolence [n] *boldness, disrespect* abuse, arrogance, audacity, back talk, brass*, brazenness, cheek*, chutzpah*, contempt, contemptuousness, contumely, effrontery, gall, guff*, hardihood, impertinence, impudence, incivility, insubordination, lip*, offensiveness, pertness, presumption, rudeness, sass*, sauce*, uncivility; CONCEPT 633 —Ant. humility, modesty, politeness, respect

insolent [adj] *bold, disrespectful* abusive, arrogant, barefaced, brassy*, brazen, breezy, contemptuous, contumelious, dictatorial, discourteous, disdainful, flip*, fresh, imperative, impertinent, impolite, impudent, insubordinate, insulting, magisterial, nervy, off-base*, offensive, out-of-line*, overbearing, peremptory, pert, procacious, put down, rude, sassy*, saucy*, smart, smart-alecky*, uncivil, ungracious; CONCEPTS 267,401 —Ant. cowardly, humble, modest, polite, respectful, servile

insoluble [adj] *mysterious, unable to be solved or answered* baffling, difficult, impenetrable, indecipherable, inexplicable, inextricable, irresolvable, mystifying, obscure, unaccountable, unconcluded, unfathomable, unresolved, unsolvable, unsolved; CONCEPTS 529,576 —Ant. explainable, explicable, obvious, open, solvable

insolvent [adj] *financially ruined* bankrupt, broke*, broken, busted*, failed, foreclosed, in Chapter 11*, in Chapter 13*, indebted, in receivership, in the red*, lost, on the rocks*, out of money, strapped*, taken to the cleaners*, unbalanced, undone, wiped out*; CONCEPT 334 —Ant. moneyed, rich, solvent, wealthy

insomnia [n] *inability to sleep soundly* indisposition, insomnolence, restlessness, sleeplessness, stress, tension, vigil, vigilance, wakefulness; CONCEPT 315 —Ant. sleep

insouciant [adj] *easygoing, casual* airy, breezy, buoyant, carefree, careless, free and easy*, gay, happy-go-lucky*, heedless, jaunty, lighthearted, nonchalant, sunny*, thoughtless, unconcerned, untroubled, unworried; CONCEPTS 404,542 —Ant. anxious, high-strung, nervous

inspect [v] *examine, check* audit, canvass, case, catechize, check out, clock*, eye*, give the once-over*, go over, go through, inquire, interrogate, investigate, kick the tires*, look over, notice, observe, oversee, probe, question, review, scan, scope, scout, scrutinize, search, study, superintend, supervise, survey, vet, view, watch; CONCEPTS 103,623 —Ant. forget, ignore, neglect

inspection [n] *examination, check* analysis, checkup, frisk, inquest, inquiry, inquisition, inventory, investigation, look-over, maneuvers, once-over*, pageant, parade, perlustration, probe, read, research, review, scan, scrutiny, search, superintendence, supervision, surveillance, survey, view; CONCEPTS 103,290 —Ant. ignorance, neglect

inspector [n] *examiner* assessor, auditor, checker, controller, detective, investigator, monitor, overseer, police officer, private eye, reviewer, scrutinizer, sleuth, tester; CONCEPT 348

inspiration [n] *idea, stimulus* afflatus, animus, approach, arousal, awakening, brainchild*, brainstorm*, creativity, deep think*, elevation, encouragement, enthusiasm, exaltation, fancy, flash*, genius, hunch*, illumination, impulse, incentive, inflatus, influence, insight, motivation, motive, muse, notion, revelation, rumble, spark, spur, stimulation, thought, vision, whim; CONCEPTS 529,661

inspire [v] *encourage, stimulate* affect, animate, arouse, be responsible for, carry, cause, commove, elate, embolden, endue, enkindle, enliven, exalt, excite, exhilarate, fire up*, galvanize, get*, give impetus, give one an idea*, give rise to, hearten, imbue, impress, infect, inflame, influence, inform, infuse, inspirit, instill, invigorate, motivate, occasion, produce, provoke, quicken, reassure, set up, spark, spur, start off, stir, strike, sway, touch, trigger, urge, work up; CONCEPTS 7,22,221,242 —Ant. discourage, dissuade

instability [n] *imbalance, inconstancy* alternation, anxiety, capriciousness, changeability, changeableness, disequilibrium, disquiet, fickleness, fitfulness, flightiness, fluctuation, fluidity, frailty, hesitation, immaturity, impermanence, inconsistency, inquietude, insecurity, irregularity, irresolution, mutability, oscillation, pliancy, precariousness, restlessness, shakiness, transience, uncertainty, unfixedness, unpredictability, unreliability, unsteadiness, vacillation, variability, volatility, vulnerability, wavering, weakness; CONCEPTS 410,637,731 —Ant. balance, constancy, soundness, stability, steadfastness

install [v] *set up, establish* build in, ensconce, fix, fix up, furnish, inaugurate, induct, instate, institute, introduce, invest, lay, line, lodge, place, plant, position, put in, settle, station; CONCEPTS 201,221

installation [n1] *establishment, inauguration* accession, coronation, fitting, furnishing, inaugural, induction, installment, instatement, investiture, investment, launching, ordination, placing, positioning, setting up; CONCEPTS 201, 221,832

installation [n2] *equipment* base, establishment, fort, fortification, furnishings, lighting, machinery, plant, post, power, station, system, wiring; CONCEPTS 439,463,496

installment [n] *part, section* chapter, division, earnest, episode, partial payment, payment, portion, repayment, token; CONCEPTS 344,835 —Ant. whole

instance [n] *case, situation* case history, case in point, detail, example, exemplification, exponent, ground, illustration, item, occasion, occurrence, particular, precedent, proof, reason, representative, sample, sampling, specimen, time; CONCEPTS 686,696,815

instance [v] *name* adduce, cite, exemplify, illustrate, mention, quote, refer, show, specify; CONCEPT 73

instant [adj] *immediate, urgent* burning*, clamant, contemporary, crying*, current, dire, direct, exigent, existent, extant, fast, imperative, importunate, insistent, instantaneous, on-the-spot*, present, present-day, pressing, prompt, quick, split-second*; CONCEPTS 544,588,799 —*Ant.* delayed, eventual, late, later

instant [n] *moment* bat of the eye*, breath, crack, flash, jiffy*, juncture, minute, nothing flat*, occasion, point, sec*, second, shake*, short while, split second*, tick, time, trice, twinkling*, while, wink*; CONCEPTS 802,808

instantaneous [adj] *immediate* direct, fast, hair-trigger*, in a flash*, instant, momentary, quick, rapid, spontaneous, transitory; CONCEPT 820 —*Ant.* delayed, eventual, late, later

instantly [adv] *right now* at once, away, directly, double-time*, first off*, forthwith, immediately, in a flash*, instantaneously, instanter, now, on a dime*, PDQ*, pronto*, right, right away, spontaneously, straight away*, there and then*, this minute, tout de suite*, without delay; CONCEPTS 544,588,799 —*Ant.* eventually, later

instead [adv] *alternatively* alternately, alternative, as a substitute, in lieu, in place of, in preference, on behalf of, on second thought, preferably, rather, rather than; CONCEPT 560

instigate [v] *influence, provoke* abet, actuate, add fuel, bring about, egg on*, encourage, fire up*, foment, goad, hint, impel, incite, inflame, initiate, insinuate, kindle, make waves*, move, needle*, persuade, plan, plot, prompt, put up to, rabble-rouse*, raise, rouse, scheme, set on, spur, start, steam up, stimulate, stir up, suggest, turn on, urge, whip up*, work up; CONCEPTS 7,19,22,221,242 —*Ant.* halt, prevent, stop

instigator [n] *troublemaker* agent provocateur, agitator, firebrand, hellion, incendiary, inciter, inflamer, knave, meddler, mischief-maker, nuisance, provocateur*, punk*, rabble-rouser*, ringleader, sparkplug*, wise guy*; CONCEPT 412

instill [v] *implant, introduce* brainwash*, catechize, diffuse, disseminate, engender, engraft, force in, imbue, impart, impregnate, impress, inculcate, indoctrinate, infiltrate, infix, infuse, inject, inoculate, inseminate, insert, insinuate, inspire, interject, intermix, program, propagandize, put in head*, suffuse, transfuse; CONCEPTS 14,221,285 —*Ant.* dislodge, halt, stop, uproot

instinct [n] *gut feeling, idea* aptitude, faculty, feeling, funny feeling*, gift, gut reaction*, hunch, impulse, inclination, intuition, knack, know-how*, nose*, predisposition, proclivity, savvy*, sense, sentiment, sixth sense*, talent, tendency, urge; CONCEPTS 529,689 —*Ant.* knowledge, reason

instinctive [adj] *reflex, automatic* accustomed, by seat of one's pants*, congenital, habitual, impulsive, inborn, ingrained, inherent, innate, instinctual, intrinsic, intuitional, intuitive, involuntary, knee-jerk*, mechanical, native, natural, normal, regular, rooted, second-nature*, spontaneous, typical, unlearned, unmeditated, unpremeditated, unprompted, unthinking, visceral; CONCEPT 544 —*Ant.* conscious, deliberate, meditated, reasonable, sensible

institute [n1] *law; custom* convention, decree, decretum, doctrine, dogma, edict, establishment, fixture, habit, maxim, ordinance, practice, precedent, precept, prescript, principle, regulation, rite, ritual, rule, statute, tenet, tradition; CONCEPTS 318,688

institute [v] *begin; put into operation* appoint, bow, break in, bring into being, come out with, come up with, commence, constitute, create, enact, establish, fix, found, inaugurate, induct, initiate, install, introduce, invest, launch, make up, open, open up, ordain, organize, originate, pioneer, rev*, set in motion, settle, set up, start, usher in*; CONCEPTS 173,221,242 —*Ant.* cease, halt, prevent, stop

institute/institution [n2] *organization, usually educational* academy, association, asylum, business, clinic, college, company, conservatory, establishment, fixture, foundation, guild, hospital, orphanage, school, seminar, seminary, society, system, think tank, university; CONCEPTS 288,381,439

instruct [v1] *inform, teach* acquaint, advise, apprise, brainwash*, break in, break it to, brief, clue in, coach, counsel, discipline, disclose, drill, drum into*, educate, engineer, enlighten, give lessons, ground, guide, keep posted*, lead, lecture, level, notify, pilot, reveal, school, steer, tell, train, tutor, update, wise up*; CONCEPTS 60,285 —*Ant.* learn

instruct [v2] *order, command* assign, bid, charge, define, direct, enjoin, prescribe, tell, warn; CONCEPTS 53,61 —*Ant.* ask

instruction [n1] *education* apprenticeship, chalk talk*, coaching, direction, discipline, drilling, edification, enlightenment, grounding, guidance, information, lesson, preparation, schooling, teaching, training, tuition, tutelage; CONCEPTS 274,285

instruction [n2] *demand, command* advice, briefing, direction, directive, information, injunction, mandate, order, plan, ruling; CONCEPTS 274,278 —*Ant.* question

instructive [adj] *informative* educational, educative, enlightening, explanatory, helpful, illuminating, informational, instructional, useful; CONCEPT 267

instructor [n] *person who educates* adviser, coach, demonstrator, exponent, guide, lecturer, mentor, pedagogue, preceptor, professor, teacher, trainer, tutor; CONCEPT 350 —*Ant.* pupil, student

instrument [n1] *tool, implement* apparatus, appliance, contraption, contrivance, device, doodad*, equipment, gadget, gear, gizmo*, machine, machinery, mechanism, paraphernalia, tackle, utensil; CONCEPTS 463,499

instrument [n2] *means, agent* agency, channel, factor, force, instrumentality, material, mechanism, medium, ministry, organ, vehicle, wherewithal; CONCEPTS 6,687 —*Ant.* end

instrumental [adj] *influential, assisting* active, auxiliary, conducive, contributory, helpful, helping, involved, of help, of service, partly responsible, serviceable, subsidiary, useful; CONCEPT 560 —*Ant.* unhelpful, useless

insubordinate [adj] *rebellious* contrary, contumacious, defiant, disaffected, disobedient, disorderly, dissentious, factious, fractious, insurgent, intractable, mutinous, naughty, perverse, recalcitrant, refractory, riotous, seditious, treacherous, turbulent, uncompliant, uncomplying, undisciplined, ungovernable, unruly; CONCEPT 401 —Ant. behaved, compliant, obedient

insubordination [n] *disobedience* defiance, dereliction, disregard, dissension, indiscipline, infringement, insurrection, mutiny, noncompliance, noncooperation, nonobservance, rebellion, revolt, revolution, riot, sabotage; CONCEPT 633

insubstantial [adj] *weak, imaginary* aerial, airy, chimerical, decrepit, ephemeral, false, fanciful, feeble, flimsy, fly-by-night*, fragile, frail, idle, illusory, immaterial, imponderable, incorporeal, infirm, intangible, metaphysical, petty, poor, puny, slender, slight, tenuous, thin, too little too late*, unreal, unsound, unsubstantial; CONCEPT 485 —Ant. real, strong, substantial

insufferable [adj] *horrible, intolerable* detestable, distressing, dreadful, impossible, insupportable, outrageous, painful, unacceptable, unbearable, unendurable, unspeakable; CONCEPTS 529,537 —Ant. delightful, endurable, happy, pleasant, sufferable, tolerable

insufficient [adj] *not enough; lacking* bereft, defective, deficient, destitute, devoid, drained, dry, failing, faulty, imperfect, inadequate, incapable, incommensurate, incompetent, incomplete, infrequent, meager, minus, out of, poor, rare, scant, scarce, short, short of, shy, thin*, too little too late*, unample, unfinished, unfitted, unqualified, unsatisfactory, wanting; CONCEPTS 546,771 —Ant. adequate, ample, enough, sufficient

insular [adj] *narrow-minded* bigoted, circumscribed, closed, confined, contracted, cut off, detached, illiberal, inward-looking, isolated, limited, narrow, parochial, petty, prejudiced, provincial, restricted, secluded, separate, separated, sequestered; CONCEPTS 403,583 —Ant. broad-minded, unbiased, unprejudiced

insulate [v] *protect; close off* coat, cocoon, cushion, cut off, inlay, island, isolate, keep apart, line, seclude, separate, sequester, set apart, shield, tape, treat, wrap; CONCEPT 172

insult [n] *hateful communication* abuse, affront, aspersion, black eye*, blasphemy, cheap shot*, contempt, contumely, derision, despite, discourtesy, disdainfulness, disgrace, disrespect, ignominy, impertinence, impudence, incivility, indignity, insolence, invective, libel, mockery, obloquy, offense, opprobrium, outrage, put-down, rudeness, scorn, scurrility, shame, slam, slander, slap, slap in the face*, slight, snub, superciliousness, taunt, unpleasantry, vilification, vituperation; CONCEPTS 52,54,278 —Ant. compliment, flattery, praise

insult [v] *abuse, offend* abase, affront, aggravate, annoy, blister, curse, cut to the quick*, debase, degrade, deride, dishonor, disoblige, dump on*, flout, gird, humiliate, injure, irritate, jeer, libel, mock, outrage, pan*, provoke, put down*, revile, ridicule, roast*, scoff, slam*, slander, slight, sneer, snub, step on one's toes*, taunt, tease, underestimate, vex; CONCEPTS 52, 54 —Ant. compliment, flatter, praise

insulting [adj] *abusive* biting, degrading, derogatory, discourteous, disparaging, disrespectful, hurtful, insolent, offensive, repulsive, ridiculing, rude, slighting, uncivil; CONCEPTS 267,529,537

insurance [n] *protection, security* allowance, assurance, backing, cover, coverage, guarantee, indemnification, indemnity, provision, safeguard, support, warrant, warranty; CONCEPTS 318,332

insure [v] *protect, secure* assure, cinch, cover, guarantee, guard, hedge, indemnify, register, safeguard, shield, underwrite, warrant; CONCEPTS 317,330

insurgent [adj] *rebellious* anarchical, contumacious, disobedient, factious, insubordinate, insurrectionary, mutinous, revolting, revolutionary, riotous, seditious; CONCEPT 401 —Ant. obedient, subordinate

insurgent [n] *rebel* agitator, anarch, anarchist, demonstrator, frondeur, insurrectionist, malcontent, mutineer, radical, resister, revolter, revolutionary, revolutionist, rioter; CONCEPTS 359,412

insurmountable [adj] *impossible* forget it, hopeless, impassable, impregnable, inaccessible, indomitable, ineluctable, insuperable, invincible, not a prayer*, no way*, no-win*, overwhelming, unbeatable, unconquerable, unmasterable; CONCEPTS 552,565 —Ant. attainable, beatable, defeatable, possible, surmountable

insurrection [n] *rebellion* coup, disorder, insurgence, insurgency, mutiny, revolt, revolution, riot, rising, sedition, uprising; CONCEPTS 86,320 —Ant. compliance, obedience, subordination

intact [adj] *undamaged; all in one piece* complete, entire, flawless, imperforate, indiscrete, perfect, scatheless, sound, together, unblemished, unbroken, uncut, undefiled, unharmed, unhurt, unimpaired, uninjured, unmarred, unscathed, untouched, unviolated, whole; CONCEPTS 485,531 —Ant. broken, damaged, defective, harmed, hurt, injured, violated

intangible [adj] *indefinite, obscured* abstract, abstruse, airy, dim, eluding, elusive, ethereal, evading, evanescent, evasive, hypothetical, impalpable, imperceptible, imponderable, inappreciable, incorporeal, indeterminate, insensible, invisible, rare, shadowy, slender, slight, unapparent, uncertain, unobservable, unreal, unsubstantial, unsure, vague; CONCEPTS 535,582 —Ant. definite, obvious, palpable, perceptible, tangible

integral [adj1] *necessary, basic* component, constituent, elemental, essential, fundamental, indispensable, intrinsic, requisite; CONCEPT 546 —Ant. extrinsic, secondary, supplemental, unnecessary

integral [adj2] *complete* aggregate, choate, elemental, entire, full, indivisible, intact, part-and-parcel*, perfect, unbroken, undivided, whole; CONCEPT 531 —Ant. accessory, fractional, part, partial, supplementary

integrate [v] *mix, merge* accommodate, amalgamate, arrange, articulate, assimilate, associate, attune, blend, coalesce, combine, come together, compact, concatenate, concentrate, conform, conjoin, consolidate, coordinate, desegregate, embody, fuse, get together, harmonize, incorporate, interface, intermix, join, knit, link, meld with, mesh, orchestrate, organize, proportion, reconcile, reconciliate, symphonize, synthesize, systematize, throw in together, tune, unify, unite, wed; CONCEPTS 113,114 —Ant. divide, separate

integrity [n1] *honor, uprightness* candor, forthrightness, goodness, honestness, honesty, honorableness, incorruptibility, incorruption, principle, probity, purity, rectitude, righteousness, sincerity, straightforwardness, virtue; CONCEPT 411 —*Ant.* corruption, disgrace, dishonesty, dishonor

integrity [n2] *completeness* absoluteness, coherence, cohesion, entireness, perfection, purity, simplicity, soundness, stability, totality, unity, wholeness; CONCEPT 635 —*Ant.* incompleteness

intellect [n] *capability of the mind; someone with capable mind* ability, acumen, brains*, cerebration, comprehension, egghead*, genius, intellectual, intellectuality, intelligence, intuition, judgment, mentality, mind, psyche, pundit, reason, savvy, sense, smarts, thinker, understanding, what it takes*, wits; CONCEPTS 409,416 —*Ant.* ignorance

intellectual [adj] *very smart* bookish, brainy*, cerebral, creative, highbrow*, highbrowed*, intellective, intelligent, inventive, learned, mental, phrenic, psychological, rational, scholarly, studious, subjective, thoughtful; CONCEPT 402 —*Ant.* foolish, ignorant, simple, stupid

intellectual [n] *very smart person* academic, academician, avant-garde, brain*, braintruster*, doctor, egghead*, Einstein*, genius, highbrow*, intelligentsia, philosopher, pundit, sage, scholar, thinker, whiz*, wizard; CONCEPTS 350,416 —*Ant.* ignoramus

intelligence [n1] *ability to perceive, understand* acuity, acumen, agility, alertness, aptitude, brainpower, brains*, brightness, brilliance, capacity, cleverness, comprehension, coruscation, discernment, gray matter*, intellect, IQ*, judgment, luminosity, mentality, mind, penetration, perception, perspicacity, precocity, quickness, quotient, reason, sagacity, savvy, sense, skill, smarts, subtlety, the right stuff*, trenchancy, understanding, what it takes*, wit; CONCEPT 409 —*Ant.* ignorance, inability, ineptness

intelligence [n2] *secret information* advice, clue, data, dirt, disclosure, facts, findings, hot tip*, info*, inside story*, knowledge, leak, lowdown*, news, notice, notification, picture, report, rumor, tidings, tip-off*, word*; CONCEPT 274

intelligent [adj] *very smart* able, acute, alert, alive, all there*, apt, astute, brainy*, bright, brilliant, calculating, capable, clever, comprehending, creative, deep*, discerning, enlightened, exceptional, highbrow*, imaginative, ingenious, instructed, inventive, keen, knowing, knowledgeable, original, penetrating, perceptive, perspicacious, profound, quick, quick-witted, rational, ready, reasonable, resourceful, responsible, sage, sharp, smart, thinking, together*, understanding, well-informed, whiz*, wise, witty; CONCEPT 402 —*Ant.* foolish, idiotic, imbecile, stupid, unintelligent

intelligible [adj] *understandable* apprehensible, clear, comprehensible, distinct, fathomable, graspable, knowable, lucid, luminous, obvious, open, plain, unambiguous, unequivocal, unmistakable; CONCEPT 529 —*Ant.* ambiguous, confusing, equivocal, obscure, perplexing, unintelligible

intend [v] *have in mind; determine* add up, aim, appoint, aspire to, attempt, be determined, be resolved, connote, contemplate, decree, dedicate, denote, design, designate, destine, devote, endeavor, essay, expect, express, figure on, have in mind, hope to, import, indicate, look forward, mean, meditate, ordain, plan, plot, propose, purpose, reserve, resolve, scheme, set apart, set aside, signify, spell, strive, think, try; CONCEPTS 18,36,73,129

intended [adj] *engaged; destined* accidentally on purpose*, advised, affianced, aforethought, asked for, betrothed, calculated, contemplated, contracted, designed, expected, future, intentional, meant, pinned, planned, plighted, prearranged, predestined, predetermined, promised, proposed, set, steady; CONCEPT 552

intense [adj] *forceful, severe; passionate* acute, agonizing, all-consuming, ardent, biting, bitter, burning, close, concentrated, consuming, cutting, deep, diligent, eager, earnest, energetic, exaggerated, exceptional, excessive, exquisite, extraordinary, extreme, fanatical, fervent, fervid, fierce, forcible, full, great, hard, harsh, heightened, impassioned, intensified, intensive, keen, marked, piercing, powerful, profound, protracted, pungent, sharp, shrill, stinging, strained, strong, supreme, undue, vehement, violent, vivid, zealous; CONCEPT 569 —*Ant.* calm, dull, low-key, mild, moderate

intensify [v] *make more forceful, severe* accent, accentuate, add fuel*, add to, aggrandize, aggravate, augment, beef up*, boost, brighten, build up, concentrate, darken, deepen, emphasize, enhance, escalate, exacerbate, exalt, heat up*, heighten, increase, intensate, lighten, magnify, point, pour it on*, quicken, raise, redouble, reinforce, rise, rouse, set off, sharpen, spike*, step up, strengthen, stress, tone up, whet; CONCEPTS 233,250 —*Ant.* calm, lower, slow, soothe, weaken

intensity [n] *passion, force* acuteness, anxiety, ardor, concentration, deepness, depth, earnestness, emotion, emphasis, energy, excess, excitement, extreme, extremity, fanaticism, ferment, ferociousness, ferocity, fervency, fervor, fierceness, fire, force, forcefulness, fury, high pitch*, intenseness, keenness, magnitude, might, nervousness, potency, power, severity, sharpness, strain, strength, tenseness, tension, vehemence, vigor, violence, volume, weightiness, wildness; CONCEPTS 641,669 —*Ant.* apathy, dullness, inactivity, laziness, lethargy, moderation

intensive [adj] *exhaustive* accelerated, all-out*, complete, comprehensive, concentrated, deep, demanding, fast, hard, in-depth, out-and-out*, profound, radical, severe, speeded-up*, thorough, thoroughgoing; CONCEPT 531 —*Ant.* incomplete, incomprehensive, superficial, surface

intent [adj] *determined, resolute* absorbed, alert, attending, attentive, bent, bound, committed, concentrated, concentrating, decided, decisive, deep, eager, earnest, engaged, engrossed, enthusiastic, firm, fixed, hell-bent*, immersed, industrious, intense, minding, occupied, piercing, preoccupied, rapt, resolved, riveted*, set, settled, steadfast, steady, watchful, watching, wrapped up*; CONCEPTS 403,542 —*Ant.* distracted, irresolute

intent/intention [n] *aim, purpose* acceptation, animus, bottom line*, conation, design, desire, drift, end, goal, heart, hope, idea, import, intendment, meaning, meat*, name of the game*, nature, notion, nub, nuts and bolts*, object, objective, plan, point, project, purport, scheme, score, sense, significance, significancy, signification, target, understanding, volition, will, wish; CONCEPT 659

intentional [adj] *deliberate* advised, aforethought, calculated, considered, designed, designful, done on purpose, intended, meant, meditated, planned, prearranged, premeditated, proposed, purposed, studied, unforced, voluntary, willful, willing, witting; CONCEPT 544 —*Ant.* accidental, unintentional, unplanned

intently [adv] *with concentration* attentively, closely, fixedly, hard, keenly, searchingly, sharply, steadily, watchfully; CONCEPTS 403, 544 —*Ant.* distractedly

inter [v] *bury* cover up, entomb, inhume, inurn, lay to rest, plant, put away, sepulcher, sepulture, tomb; CONCEPTS 172,178,367 —*Ant.* dig up, exhume

interact [v] *communicate* collaborate, combine, connect, contact, cooperate, get across*, get the message*, interface, interplay, interreact, join, keep in touch, merge, mesh, network, reach out, relate, touch, touch base*, unite; CONCEPT 266 —*Ant.* not speak

intercede [v] *mediate* advocate, arbitrate, barge in, butt in*, intermediate, interpose, intervene, intrude, mix in, monkey with*, negotiate, plead, reconcile, speak, step in; CONCEPTS 56,110

intercept [v] *head off; interrupt* ambush, appropriate, arrest, block, catch, check, curb, cut in, cut off, deflect, head off at pass*, hijack, hinder, interlope, interpose, make off with, obstruct, prevent, seize, shortstop*, stop, take, take away; CONCEPTS 121,164 —*Ant.* abet, forward, help

interchange [n] *switch, exchange* altering, alternation, barter, change, crossfire, give-and-take*, intersection, junction, mesh, networking, reciprocation, shift, trade, transposition, variation, varying; CONCEPTS 104,697

interchange [v] *switch, exchange* alternate, bandy, barter, commute, connect, contact, convert, interact, interface, mesh, network, reciprocate, relate, reverse, substitute, swap, trade, transpose; CONCEPTS 56,104

interchangeable [adj] *identical, transposable* changeable, commutative, compatible, converse, convertible, correspondent, equivalent, exchangeable, fungible, interconvertible, mutual, reciprocal, reciprocative, same, substitutable, synonymous, workalike; CONCEPTS 487,573 —*Ant.* different, dissimilar

intercourse [n1] *sexual act* carnal knowledge, coition, coitus, copulation, fornication, intimacy, love-making, relations, sex, sexual relations; CONCEPT 375

intercourse [n2] *communication; business exchange* association, commerce, communion, connection, contact, converse, correspondence, dealings, give-and-take, interchange, intercommunication, mesh, networking, team play, teamwork, trade, traffic, transactions; CONCEPTS 266,324 —*Ant.* miscommunication

interest [n1] *attraction, curiosity* absorption, activity, affection, attentiveness, care, case, concern, concernment, consequence, diversion, engrossment, enthusiasm, excitement, game, hobby, importance, interestedness, into, leisure activity, matter, moment, note, notice, passion, pastime, preoccupation, pursuit, racket, recreation, regard, relaxation, relevance, significance, sport, suspicion, sympathy, thing; CONCEPTS 20,532,690 —*Ant.* apathy, boredom, disinterest, indifference

interest [n2] *advantage* benefit, gain, good, profit, prosperity, welfare, well-being; CONCEPT 693 —*Ant.* disadvantage

interest [n3] *share, investment* accrual, authority, bonus, claim, commitment, credit, discount, due, earnings, gain, influence, involvement, participation, percentage, piece, points, portion, premium, right, stake, title; CONCEPTS 332, 344,835

interest [v] *hold the attention of* affect, amuse, appeal, appeal to, arouse, attract, be interesting to, concern, divert, engage, engross, entertain, enthrall, excite, fascinate, grab, hook, intrigue, involve, lure, move, perk up, pique, please, pull, sit up, snare, tantalize, tempt, titillate, touch, turn on; CONCEPTS 7,11,22 —*Ant.* bore, bother, disenchant, disinterest

interested [adj] *concerned, curious* absorbed, affected, attentive, attracted, awakened, biased, caught, drawn, eat sleep and breathe*, engrossed, enticed, excited, fascinated, fired*, gone*, hooked*, implicated, impressed, inspired, inspirited, intent, into*, involved, keen, lured, moved, obsessed, occupied, on the case*, open, partial, partisan, predisposed, prejudiced, responsive, roused, sold, stimulated, stirred, struck, sympathetic, taken, touched; CONCEPT 403 —*Ant.* apathetic, disinterested, incurious, unconcerned

interesting [adj] *appealing, entertaining* absorbing, affecting, alluring, amusing, arresting, attractive, beautiful, captivating, charismatic, compelling, curious, delightful, elegant, enchanting, engaging, engrossing, enthralling, entrancing, exceptional, exotic, fascinating, fine, gracious, gripping, impressive, intriguing, inviting, lovely, magnetic, pleasing, pleasurable, prepossessing, provocative, readable, refreshing, riveting, stimulating, stirring, striking, suspicious, thought-provoking, unusual, winning; CONCEPTS 529,572 —*Ant.* boring, dull, unexciting, unstimulating

interfere [v] *meddle, intervene* baffle, balk, barge in, busybody*, butt in*, conflict, discommode, foil, fool with, frustrate, get in the way*, get involved, hamper, handicap, hang up*, hinder, hold up, horn in*, impede, incommode, inconvenience, inhibit, intercede, interlope, intermeddle, intermit, interpose, intrude, jam, make*, mix in, obstruct, obtrude, oppose, poke nose in*, prevent, remit, step in, stop, suspend, tamper, thwart, trammel, trouble; CONCEPTS 121,384 —*Ant.* aid, assist, help

interference [n] *meddling, impedance* arrest, background, backseat driving*, barging in*, barring, blocking, checking, choking, clashing, clogging, conflict, hampering, hindrance, intermeddling, interposition, intervention, intrusion, meddlesomeness, obstruction, opposition, prying, resistance, retardation, tackling, tampering, trespassing; CONCEPTS 121,384 —*Ant.* aid, assistance, help

interim [*adj*] *temporary* acting, ad interim, caretaker*, improvised, intervening, makeshift, pro tem, pro tempore, provisional, stopgap, thrown-together*; CONCEPT 560 —*Ant.* continual, permanent

interim [*n*] *interval* breach, break, breather, breathing spell, coffee break, cutoff, downtime*, gap, hiatus, interlude, interregnum, interruption, lacuna, layoff, letup*, meantime, meanwhile, pause, take ten*, time*, time-out; CONCEPTS 807,822 —*Ant.* continuation, permanence

interior [*adj*] *inside, central* autogenous, domestic, endogenous, gut, home, in-house, inland, inner, innermost, internal, intimate, inward, private, remote, secret, visceral, viscerous, within; CONCEPTS 583,826,830 —*Ant.* exterior, external, outer, outside

interior [*n*] *center, core* belly, bosom, contents, heart, heartland, innards, inner parts, inside, internals, intrinsicality, lining, marrow, midst, pith, pulp, soul, substance, viscera, within; CONCEPTS 742,826,830 —*Ant.* exterior, exteriority, outside

interject [*v*] *throw in; interrupt* add, fill in, force in, implant, import, include, infiltrate, infuse, ingrain, inject, insert, insinuate, intercalate, interpolate, interpose, intersperse, introduce, intrude, parenthesize, put in, splice, squeeze in; CONCEPTS 14,51

interloper [*n*] *person who intrudes, meddles* alien, busybody, intermeddler, intruder, meddler, obtruder, trespasser, uninvited guest, unwanted visitor; CONCEPTS 412,423

interlude [*n*] *pause, break* breathing space*, delay, episode, halt, hiatus, idyll, interim, intermission, interregnum, interruption, interval, lull, meantime, meanwhile, parenthesis, recess, respite, rest, spell, stop, stoppage, wait; CONCEPT 807 —*Ant.* continuation

intermediary [*n*] *person who negotiates* agent, broker, channel, connection, cutout, delegate, emissary, entrepreneur, fixer, go-between*, influence, instrument, interagent, interceder, intercessor, intermediate, mediator, medium, middle person, negotiator, organ, vehicle; CONCEPTS 348,354

intermediate [*adj*] *middle, in-between* average, between, center, central, common, compromising, fair, halfway, indifferent, intermediary, interposed, intervening, mean, medial, median, mediocre, medium, mid, middling, midway, moderate, neutral, so-so*, standard, transitional; CONCEPTS 585,830 —*Ant.* end, extreme

interment [*n*] *burial* burying, entombment, funeral, inhumation, inurning, obsequy, sepulture; CONCEPT 367

interminable [*adj*] *infinite* boring, boundless, ceaseless, constant, continuous, day-and-night*, dragged out*, dull, endless, eternal, everlasting, immeasurable, incessant, interminate, limitless, long, long-drawn-out*, long-winded, looped, never-ending, no end of*, no end to*, on-a-treadmill*, permanent, perpetual, protracted, spun out*, strung out*, timeless, unbound, unceasing, uninterrupted, unlimited, wearisome; CONCEPT 798 —*Ant.* bounded, ending, finite, terminable

intermingle [*v*] *blend, mix* amalgamate, associate, combine, come together, commingle, commix, fuse, immingle, interblend, interfuse, interlace, intermix, interweave, join, merge, mesh, network, pool, throw in with, throw together, wed; CONCEPTS 113,114 —*Ant.* divide, separate, unmix

intermission [*n*] *break, recess* abeyance, abeyancy, break-off, breather, breathing spell, cessation, doldrums, dormancy, downtime*, interim, interlude, interregnum, interruption, interval, latency, layoff, let-up*, lull, parenthesis, pause, quiescence, quiescency, respite, rest, spell, stop, stoppage, suspense, suspension, time, time-out, wait; CONCEPT 807

intermittent [*adj*] *irregular, sporadic* alternate, arrested, broken, by bits and pieces*, checked, cyclic, cyclical, discontinuing, discontinuous, epochal, every other, fitful, here and there*, hit-or-miss*, infrequent, interrupted, isochronal, isochronous, iterant, iterative, metrical, now and then*, occasional, on and off*, periodic, periodical, punctuated, recurrent, recurring, rhythmic, rhythmical, seasonal, serial, shifting, spasmodic, stop-and-go*; CONCEPTS 482,534,799 —*Ant.* constant, continual, continuing, perpetual, regular

internal [*adj*] *within* centralized, circumscribed, civic, constitutional, domestic, enclosed, gut, home, indigenous, inherent, in-house, innate, inner, innermore, inside, interior, intestine, intimate, intramural, intrinsic, inward, municipal, national, native, private, subjective, visceral, viscerous; CONCEPTS 536,585,826,830 —*Ant.* external, outer

international [*adj*] *worldwide* all-embracing, cosmopolitan, ecumenical, foreign, global, intercontinental, universal, world; CONCEPTS 536,772 —*Ant.* local, national

Internet [*n*] *computer network* ARPANET, cyberspace, hyperspace, infobahn, information highway, information superhighway, national information infrastructure, online network, the Net*, the Web*, W3, World Wide Web, WWW; CONCEPTS 381,388,770

interplay [*n*] *interaction* coaction, exchange, give-and-take*, mesh, meshing, networking, reciprocation, reciprocity, team play*, teamwork, tit for tat*, transaction; CONCEPT 266

interpolate [*v*] *add* admit, annex, append, enter, fill in, include, inject, insert, insinuate, intercalate, interjaculate, interject, interlope, interpose, introduce, intrude, throw in; CONCEPTS 112,201,209 —*Ant.* erase, remove, subtract

interpret [*v*] *make sense of; define* adapt, annotate, clarify, comment, commentate, construe, decipher, decode, delineate, depict, describe, elucidate, enact, exemplify, explain, explicate, expound, gather, gloss, illustrate, image, improvise, limn, make of, mimic, paraphrase, perform, picture, play, portray, read, reenact, render, represent, solve, spell out, take*, throw light on*, translate, understand, view; CONCEPTS 57,292 —*Ant.* misinterpret, misunderstand

interpretation [*n*] *understanding* analysis, apprehension, assimilation, awareness, clarification, comprehension, discernment, explanation, grasp, grip, insight, judgment, knowing, meaning, perception, reading, slant, translation; CONCEPT 409

interrogate [v] *ask pointed questions* catechize, cross-examine, cross-question, examine, give the third degree*, go over*, grill, inquire, investigate, pump, put the screws to*, put through the wringer*, query, question, quiz, roast*, sweat out*, work over*; CONCEPTS 48, 53 —*Ant.* answer, reply

interrupt [v] *bother, interfere* arrest, barge in, break, break in, break off, break train of thought*, bust in*, butt in*, check, chime in*, come between, crash, crowd in, cut, cut in on*, cut off*, cut short*, defer, delay, disconnect, discontinue, disjoin, disturb, disunite, divide, edge in, get in the way, halt, heckle, hinder, hold up, horn in, impede, in, infringe, inject, insinuate, intrude, lay aside, obstruct, prevent, punctuate, put in, separate, sever, shortstop*, stay, stop, suspend, work in; CONCEPTS 51, 121,384

interruption [n] *break; interference* abeyance, abeyancy, arrest, blackout, breach, break-off, cessation, check, cutoff, delay, disconnection, discontinuance, disruption, dissolution, disturbance, disuniting, division, doldrums, dormancy, gap, halt, hiatus, hindrance, hitch, impediment, interim, intermission, interval, intrusion, lacuna, latency, layoff, letup*, obstacle, obstruction, parenthesis, pause, quiescence, rift, rupture, separation, severance, split, stop, stoppage, suspension; CONCEPTS 807,832 —*Ant.* continuation

intersect [v] *cut across; cross at a point* bisect, break in two, come together, converge, crisscross, cross, crosscut, cut, decussate, divide, intercross, join, meet, separate, touch, traverse; CONCEPTS 113,738,749

intersection [n] *crossroads* circle, cloverleaf, crossing, crosswalk, crossway, interchange, junction, stop; CONCEPT 501

intersperse [v] *scatter* bestrew, diffuse, distribute, infuse, interfuse, interlard, intermix, intersow, intersprinkle, pepper, sprinkle; CONCEPTS 201,222 —*Ant.* collect, gather

interstice [n] *opening, crack* aperture, chink, cleft, cranny, crevice, fissure, gap, hole, interval, slit, space; CONCEPT 513 —*Ant.* closing, closure

intertwine/interweave [v] *twist around* associate, braid, connect, convolute, crisscross, cross, entwine, interknit, interlace, intertwist, intervolve, interwind, interwreathe, link, mesh, network, relate, reticulate, tangle, tat, weave; CONCEPTS 113,114 —*Ant.* untwine, untwist

interval [n] *break; pause* breach, breathing space*, comma, delay, distance, downtime, five*, gap, hiatus, interim, interlude, intermission, interregnum, interruption, lacuna, layoff, letup, lull, meantime, opening, parenthesis, pausation, period, playtime, rest, season, space, spell, ten*, term, time, time-out, wait, while; CONCEPTS 807,822 —*Ant.* continuation

intervene [v1] *mediate* arbitrate, barge in, butt in*, come between, divide, horn in*, intercede, interfere, intermediate, interpose, interrupt, intrude, involve, meddle, mix in, muscle in*, negotiate, obtrude, part, put in two cents*, reconcile, separate, settle, sever, step in, take a hand*; CONCEPTS 110,234,266 —*Ant.* ignore, leave alone

intervene [v2] *happen* bedevil, befall, come to pass, ensue, occur, succeed, supervene, take place; CONCEPTS 4,242

interview [n] *questioning and evaluation* account, audience, call, call back, cattle call*, communication, conference, consultation, conversation, dialogue, examination, hearing, meeting, oral, parley, press conference, record, statement, talk; CONCEPTS 48,351

interview [v] *ask questions and evaluate* consult, converse, examine, get for the record, get opinion, give oral examination, hold inquiry, interrogate, question, quiz, sound out, talk, talk to; CONCEPTS 48,351

interviewer [n] *questioner* inquirer, inquistor, interrogator, reporter, talk-show host; CONCEPTS 348,356

intestinal/intestine [adj] *pertaining to digestive organs* abdominal, alimentary, bowel, celiac, duodenal, gut, inner, inside, interior, internal, inward, rectal, stomachic, ventral, visceral; CONCEPT 406

in the bag [adj] *certain* assured, bound, certified, cinched, concluded, decided, definite, ensured, fixed, guaranteed, insured, set, settled, sure; CONCEPT 535

intimacy [n] *closeness between people* acquaintance, affection, affinity, close relationship, communion, confidence, confidentiality, experience, familiarity, friendship, inwardness, understanding; CONCEPT 388 —*Ant.* disagreement, incompatibility

intimate [adj1] *friendly, devoted* affectionate, bosom, buddy-buddy*, cherished, chummy*, close, clubby*, comfy, confidential, cozy, dear, dearest, faithful, fast, fond, loving, mellow, mix, near, nearest, next, nice, regular, roommate, snug, warm; CONCEPT 555 —*Ant.* cool, formal, incompatible, unfriendly

intimate [adj2] *private, personal* confidential, deep, deep-seated, detailed, elemental, essential, exhaustive, experienced, firsthand, guarded, gut*, immediate, inborn, inbred, in-depth, indwelling, ingrained, inherent, inmost, innate, innermost, interior, internal, intrinsic, penetrating, privy, profound, secret, special, thorough, trusted, uptight, visceral, viscerous; CONCEPTS 529,549 —*Ant.* formal, public

intimate [n] *a close friend; familiar person* associate, bosom buddy*, chum, companion, comrade, confidant, confidante, crony, familiar, family, lover, mate, pal; CONCEPTS 416,423 —*Ant.* enemy, foe

intimate [v] *suggest; tip off* affirm, air, allude, announce, assert, aver, avouch, communicate, connote, declare, drop a hint*, expose, express, hint, impart, imply, indicate, infer, insinuate, leak, let cat out of bag*, let it be known, make known, make noise*, profess, remind, spill the beans*, spring, state, utter, vent, voice, warn; CONCEPTS 49,60,75

intimation [n] *clue, hint* allusion, announcement, breath, communication, cue, declaration, implication, indication, inkling, innuendo, insinuation, notice, notion, reminder, shade, shadow, strain, streak, suggestion, suspicion, telltale, tinge, tip, trace, warning, wind; CONCEPTS 274,689

intimidate [v] *frighten, threaten* alarm, appall, awe, badger, bait, bludgeon, bluster, bowl over*, browbeat*, buffalo*, bulldoze*, bully, chill, coerce, compel, constrain, cow*, daunt, dishearten, dismay, dispirit, disquiet, dragoon, enforce, force, hound*, lean on*, oblige, overawe, push around*, ride*, ruffle, scare, showboat, spook, strong-arm, subdue, terrify, terrorize, twist someone's arm*; CONCEPTS 7,14,19 —*Ant.* assist, encourage, help

intimidating [adj] *threatening* aggressive, bullying, frightening, pressuring, terrifying, terrorizing; CONCEPTS 525,548,570

intolerable [adj] *unacceptable; beyond bearing* a bit much, enough already*, excruciating, extreme, impossible, insufferable, insupportable, last straw*, offensive, painful, unbearable, undesirable, unendurable; CONCEPT 529 —*Ant.* acceptable, bearable, tolerable

intolerant [adj] *impatient, prejudiced* antipathetic, averse, biased, bigoted, chauvinistic, communist, conservative, contemptuous, dictatorial, disdainful, dogmatic, fanatical, fractious, hateful, illiberal, indignant, individualistic, inflexible, irate, irritable, jaundiced, narrow, narrow-minded, obdurate, one-sided, outraged, racialist, racist, short-fuse*, small-minded*, snappy, stuffy, tilted, uncharitable, unfair, unforbearing, unindulgent, unsympathetic, unwilling, upset, waspish, worked-up*, xenophobic; CONCEPTS 403,404,542 —*Ant.* fair, impartial, patient, tolerant, unprejudiced

intonation [n] *inflection* accent, articulation, emphasis, enunciation, modulation, pitch, pronunciation, sound, tonality, tone, tone of voice; CONCEPTS 65,595

intoxicated [adj1] *drunk* blind*, bombed*, boozed*, buzzed*, drunken, high*, inebriated, loaded*, looped*, muddled, potted*, sloppy, smashed*, tanked*, three sheets to the wind*, tied one on*, tight*, tipsy, under the influence, unsober; CONCEPT 406 —*Ant.* sober, straight

intoxicated [adj2] *extremely happy* absorbed, affected, beside oneself, captivated, concerned, delirious, dizzy, drunk, ecstatic, elated, enraptured, euphoric, excited, exhilarated, galvanized, high*, infatuated, interested, moved, piqued, quickened, sent*, stimulated, turned-on*; CONCEPT 403 —*Ant.* sad, unhappy

intoxicating [adj] *causing great happiness* exciting, exhilarant, exhilarating, exhilarative, eye-popping, heady, inspiring, provocative, rousing, stimulating, stirring, thrilling; CONCEPT 537 —*Ant.* saddening, sobering

intractable /intransigent [adj] *difficult, stubborn* awkward, bullheaded*, cantankerous, contrary, hang tough*, hard-line*, headstrong, immovable, incompliant, incurable, indocile, indomitable, insoluble, locked in*, mulish, obdurate, obstinate, pat, pertinacious, perverse, pigheaded*, recalcitrant, refractory, resolute, self-willed, set in stone, tenacious, tough, tough-nut*, unbending, uncompromising, uncooperative, undisciplined, ungovernable, unmanageable, unpliable, unruly, unyielding, wayward, wild, willful; CONCEPTS 401,534,542 —*Ant.* amenable, easy, facile, manageable

intrepid [adj] *brave, nervy* audacious, bodacious*, bold, courageous, daring, dauntless, doughty, fearless, gallant, game, gritty, gutsy*, heroic, impavid, lionhearted, nerveless, plucky, resolute, spunky*, stalwart, unafraid, undaunted, unflinching, valiant, valorous; CONCEPT 401 —*Ant.* cowardly, meek, timid

intricate [adj] *complicated, elaborate* abstruse, baroque, Byzantine*, can of worms*, complex, convoluted, Daedal*, difficult, entangled, fancy, hard, high-tech*, involved, labyrinthine, obscure, perplexing, rococo, sophisticated, tangled, tortuous, tricky; CONCEPT 562 —*Ant.* direct, methodical, simple, systematic, understandable

intrigue [n1] *scheme* artifice, cabal, chicanery, collusion, complication, conspiracy, contrivance, deal, design, dodge, double-dealing*, fix, frame-up*, fraud, game, graft, hookup, little game*, machination, maneuver, manipulation, plan, plot, ruse, stratagem, trickery, wile; CONCEPTS 192,660

intrigue [n2] *love affair* affair, amour, attachment, case, flirtation, infatuation, interlude, intimacy, liaison, romance; CONCEPT 388

intrigue [v1] *arouse curiosity* appeal, attract, bait, captivate, charm, con, delight, draw, enchant, entertain, excite, fascinate, grab, hook, interest, lead on*, mousetrap*, pique, please, pull, rivet, tickle, titillate, tout; CONCEPTS 7,11,22 —*Ant.* bore

intrigue [v2] *plot* angle, be in cahoots*, cogitate, collude, connive, conspire, contrive, cook up*, devise, finagle, frame up*, machinate, maneuver, operate, plan, promote, scheme, set up*, work hand in glove*; CONCEPT 36 —*Ant.* forget, neglect

intriguing [adj] *interesting* absorbing, alluring, appealing, arousing, attractive, beguiling, captivating, compelling, curious, enchanting, enthralling, exciting, fascinating, gripping, provocative, puzzling, riveting, stimulating, stirring, thought-provoking; CONCEPTS 529,572

intrinsic [adj] *basic, inborn* built-in, central, congenital, connate, constitutional, constitutive, deep-seated, elemental, essential, fundamental, genuine, hereditary, inbred, indwelling, inherent, inmost, innate, intimate, material, native, natural, particular, peculiar, real, true, underlying; CONCEPTS 404,406,546 —*Ant.* accidental, acquired, extrinsic, incidental, learned

introduce [v1] *make known; present* acquaint, advance, air, announce, bring out, bring up, broach, come out with, do the honors*, familiarize, fix up, get things rolling*, get together, give introduction, harbinger*, herald, kick off, knock down, lead into, lead off, moot, offer, open, open up, originate, pave the way*, precede, preface, propose, put forward, recommend, set forth, spring with, start ball rolling*, submit, suggest, usher, ventilate; CONCEPTS 60,384 —*Ant.* close, end, finish, take away

introduce [v2] *begin, institute* admit, bring forward, bring in, commence, enter, establish, found, inaugurate, induct, initiate, innovate, install, invent, kick off*, launch, organize, pioneer, plan, preface, present, set up, start, unveil, usher in; CONCEPT 221 —*Ant.* close, end, finish

introduce [v3] *add, insert* carry, enter, fill in, freight, import, include, infix, inject, inlay, inlet, inset, insinuate, instill, intercalate, interject, interpolate, interpose, put in, send, ship, throw in, transport, work in; CONCEPTS *112,113, 209* —*Ant.* erase, extract, subtract, take away

introduction [n] *something new; something that begins* addition, admittance, awakening, baptism, basic principles, basic text, beginning, commencement, debut, essentials, establishment, exordium, first acquaintance, first taste, foreword, inauguration, inception, induction, influx, ingress, initiation, insertion, installation, institution, interpolation, intro*, launch, lead, lead-in, opening, opening remarks, overture, pioneering, preamble, preface, preliminaries, prelude, presentation, primer, proem, prolegomenon, prologue, survey; CONCEPTS *270,727, 828* —*Ant.* conclusion, end, ending, finish

introductory [adj] *preliminary, first* anterior, basic, beginning, early, elementary, inaugural, incipient, inductive, initial, initiatory, opening, original, precursory, prefatory, prelusive, preparative, preparatory, primary, prior, proemial, provisional, rudimentary, starting; CONCEPTS *546,585* —*Ant.* concluding, ending, final, finishing, last

introspection [n] *self-analysis* brooding, contemplation, deep thought, egoism, heartsearching, introversion, meditation, reflection, rumination, scrutiny, self-absorption, self-examination, self-observation, self-questioning, soul-searching; CONCEPTS *24,410*

introvert [n] *person who retreats mentally* autist, brooder, egoist, egotist, loner*, narcissist, self-observer, solitary, wallflower*; CONCEPT *423* —*Ant.* extrovert

introverted [adj] *reserved* bashful, cautious, close-mouthed, cold*, collected, cool, demure, introspective, modest, offish, quiet, reclusive, restrained, secretive, shy, soft-spoken, solitary, standoffish, uncommunicative, withdrawn; CONCEPTS *401,404*

intrude [v] *trespass, interrupt* barge in, bother, butt in*, chisel in*, cut in, disturb, encroach, entrench, go beyond, hold up, horn in*, infringe, insinuate, intercalate, interfere, interject, interlope, intermeddle, interpolate, interpose, introduce, invade, meddle, obtrude, overstep, pester, push in, thrust, violate; CONCEPTS *14,159, 208,266* —*Ant.* leave, leave alone, withdraw

intruder [n] *person who trespasses* burglar, criminal, gate-crasher*, infiltrator, interferer, interloper, interrupter, invader, meddler, nuisance, obtruder, prowler, raider, snooper, squatter, thief, trespasser; CONCEPTS *412,423*

intrusive [adj] *obtrusive* forward, interfering, invasive, meddlesome, meddling, nosy*, presumptuous, protruding, prying; CONCEPTS *401,542*

intuition [n] *insight* clairvoyance, discernment, divination, ESP*, feeling*, foreknowledge, gut reaction*, hunch*, innate knowledge, inspiration, instinct, intuitiveness, nose* penetration, perception, perceptivity, premonition, presentiment, second sight*, sixth sense*; CONCEPTS *409,689* —*Ant.* knowledge, reason, reasoning

intuitive [adj] *instinctive* automatic, direct, emotional, habitual, immediate, inherent, innate, instinctual, involuntary, natural, perceptive, spontaneous, understood, unreflecting, untaught, visceral; CONCEPT *402* —*Ant.* calculated, meditated, reasoned, taught

inundate [v] *drown, overwhelm* deluge, dunk, engulf, flood, glut, immerse, overflow, overrun, pour down on, snow*, submerge, swamp, whelm; CONCEPTS *172,179* —*Ant.* underwhelm

inure [v] *accustom* acclimate, familiarize, habituate, harden, make ready, season, toughen, train; CONCEPTS *15,38*

invade [v] *attack and encroach* access, assail, assault, breach, burglarize, burst in, crash, descend upon, entrench, fall on, foray, go in, infect, infest, infringe, inroad, interfere, loot, make inroads*, maraud, meddle, muscle in*, occupy, overrun, overspread, overswarm, penetrate, permeate, pervade, pillage, plunder, raid, ravage, storm, swarm over, trespass, violate; CONCEPTS *86,159,320* —*Ant.* leave alone, surrender, yield

invalid [adj1] *worthless; unfounded* bad, baseless, fallacious, false, ill-founded, illogical, inoperative, irrational, mad, not binding, not working, nugatory, null, null and void*, reasonless, sophistic, unreasonable, unreasoned, unscientific, unsound, untrue, void, wrong; CONCEPTS *552,560* —*Ant.* sound, valid, worthwhile, worthy

invalid [adj2] *sickly* ailing, bedridden, below par, debilitated, disabled, down, feeble, frail, ill, infirm, laid low*, on the sick list*, out of action*, peaked, poorly, run-down, sick, weak; CONCEPT *314* —*Ant.* healthy, well

invalid [n] *sick person* consumptive, convalescent, incurable, patient, shut-in, sufferer; CONCEPT *424*

invalidate [v] *render null and void* abate, abolish, abrogate, annihilate, annul, blow sky-high*, cancel, circumduct, counteract, counterbalance, disannul, discredit, disqualify, impair, negate, negative, neutralize, nix, nullify, offset, overrule, overthrow, quash, refute, revoke, shoot full of holes*, undermine, undo, unfit, weaken, X-out*; CONCEPTS *121,234* —*Ant.* approve, permit, validate

invaluable [adj] *priceless* beyond price, costly, dear, expensive, helpful, inestimable, precious, serviceable, valuable; CONCEPTS *334,568* —*Ant.* worthless

invariable [adj] *not changing* changeless, consistent, constant, fixed, immovable, immutable, inalterable, inflexible, monotonous, perpetual, regular, rigid, same, set, static, unalterable, unchangeable, unchanging, undiversified, unfailing, uniform, unmodifiable, unrelieved, unvarying, unwavering; CONCEPT *534* —*Ant.* changeable, changing, variable, varying

invasion [n] *attack, encroachment* aggression, assault, breach, entrenchment, foray, forced entrance, incursion, infiltration, infraction, infringement, inroad, intrusion, irruption, maraud, offense, offensive, onslaught, overstepping, raid, transgression, trespass, usurpation, violation; CONCEPTS *86,159,320* —*Ant.* retreat, surrender, withdrawal

invective [n] *verbal abuse* accusation, berating, billingsgate, blame, blasphemy, castigation, censure, condemnation, contumely, denunciation, diatribe, epithet, jeremiad, obloquy, philippic, reproach, revilement, sarcasm, scurrility, tirade, tongue-lashing*, vilification, vituperation; CONCEPTS 44,52,54,278 —*Ant.* compliment, flattery, praise

inveigh [v] *blame, denounce* admonish, berate, blast, castigate, censure, condemn, crack down on*, except, expostulate, go after*, have at*, jump down one's throat*, kick, lambaste, lay into, lay out, let have it, object, protest, rail, read out*, recriminate, remonstrate, reproach, rip into, roast, scold, scorch, sound off, tongue-lash, trash*, upbraid, vituperate, work over*; CONCEPTS 44,52,54 —*Ant.* flatter, praise

inveigle [v] *entice, manipulate* allure, bait, bamboozle, beguile, blandish, butter*, cajole, charm, coax, con*, decoy, egg on*, ensnare, entrap, get around*, honey*, hook, influence, jolly, lay it on thick*, lead on*, lure, maneuver, massage, oil*, overdo it, persuade, play up to, rope in*, seduce, snow*, soap*, soften up*, string along*, stroke*, sweet talk*, tempt, toll, urge, wheedle, work over*; CONCEPTS 11,14,59 —*Ant.* disenchant, disgust, turn off

invent [v1] *create, think up* ad-lib, author, bear, bring into being, coin, come upon, come up with, compose, conceive, contrive, cook up*, design, devise, discover, dream up, envision, execute, fake, fashion, find, forge, form, formulate, frame, hatch, imagine, improve, improvise, inaugurate, initiate, jam*, knock off*, make, make up, mint, off-the-cuff*, originate, plan, produce, project, toss off*, turn out, wing*; CONCEPTS 36,173,221 —*Ant.* steal

invent [v2] *fabricate* concoct, conjure up, create out of thin air*, equivocate, fake, falsify, feign, fib, forge, lie, make believe, make up, misrepresent, misstate, pretend, prevaricate, simulate, tell a white lie*, tell untruth, think up, trump up*, vamp; CONCEPTS 59,63 —*Ant.* tell truth

invention [n1] *creation, creativeness* apparatus, black box*, brainchild*, coinage, concoction, contraption, contrivance, creativity, design, development, device, discovery, doodad*, gadget, genius, gimmick, gizmo*, imagination, ingenuity, innovation, inspiration, inventiveness, novelty, opus, original, originality, resourcefulness; CONCEPTS 260,409,660 —*Ant.* steal

invention [n2] *fabrication* lie deceit, fake, falsehood, fancy, fantasy, fib, fiction, figment, forgery, prevarication, sham*, story, tall story*, untruth, yarn*; CONCEPTS 63,278 —*Ant.* truth

inventive [adj] *creative* adroit, artistic, avant-garde, breaking new ground, causative, constructive, demiurgic, deviceful, fertile, forgetive, formative, fruitful, gifted, imaginative, ingenious, innovational, innovative, innovatory, inspired, original, originative, poetical, productive, resourceful, teeming; CONCEPTS 402,542 —*Ant.* stolen, uncreative, uninventive, unoriginal

inventor [n] *discoverer* architect, author, builder, coiner, creator, designer, experimenter, father, founder, innovator, maker, originator, pioneer; CONCEPTS 348,352,361

inventory [n] *list of stock; stock* account, backlog, catalogue, file, fund, hoard, index, itemization, record, register, reserve, reservoir, roll, roster, schedule, stock book, stockpile, store,

summary, supply, table, tabulation; CONCEPTS 283,338

inverse [adj] *opposite* changed, contrary, converse, flipped, inverted, reverse, reversed, reverted, transposed, turned, turned over; CONCEPT 564

invert [v] *reverse; turn upside down* alter, backtrack, capsize, change, convert, double back, evert, flip, flip-flop*, introvert, inverse, modify, overturn, renege, revert, tip, transplace, transpose, turn, turn down, turn inside out, turn over, turn the tables*, upend, upset, upturn; CONCEPTS 213,232

invest [v1] *contribute money to make money* advance, back, bankroll, buy into, buy stock, devote, endow, endue, entrust, get into, go in for, imbue, infuse, lay out, lend, loan, pick up the tab*, plow back into*, plunge, provide, put in, put up dough*, salt away*, sink, spend, stake, supply; CONCEPTS 115,330,341 —*Ant.* divest, take out

invest [v2] *give power or authority* adopt, authorize, bequeath, charge, consecrate, empower, endow, endue, enthrone, establish, honor, inaugurate, induct, initiate, install, instate, license, ordain, sanction, vest; CONCEPTS 50,88 —*Ant.* divest, take away

investigate [v] *check into thoroughly* be all ears*, bug, case*, check out, check over, check up, consider, delve, dig, examine, explore, eyeball*, feel out, frisk, give the once over*, go into, inquire, inquisite, inspect, interrogate, listen in, look into, look over, look-see, make inquiry, muckrake, nose around*, poke, probe, prospect, pry, put to the test*, question, read, reconnoiter, research, review, run down, scout, scrutinize, search, sift, spy, stake out, study, tap, wiretap; CONCEPTS 48,103,216 —*Ant.* ignore

investigation [n] *thorough check* analysis, case, delving, examination, exploration, fact-finding, gander, hearing, hustle, inquest, inquiry, inquisition, inspection, legwork, observation, observing, pike, probe, probing, quest, quiz, research, review, scrutiny, search, sounding, study, survey, surveying; CONCEPTS 48, 103,216,290

investigator [n] *person who checks thoroughly* agent, analyst, attorney, auditor, detective, examiner, gumshoe*, hound*, inquirer, inspector, plainclothes officer, police, private detective, private eye, prosecutor, researcher, reviewer, Sherlock Holmes*, sleuth, snooper, spy, tester, undercover cop; CONCEPTS 348,355

investment [n] *something given, lent for a return* advance, ante, asset, backing, bail, contribution, endowment, expenditure, expense, finance, financing, flutter, grant, hunch, inside, interests, investing, loan, money, piece, plunge, property, purchase, smart money*, spec*, speculation, stab*, stake, transaction, venture, vested interests; CONCEPTS 330,332,340 —*Ant.* divestment

investor [n] *financier* backer, banker, capitalist, lender, shareholder, stockholder, venture capitalist; CONCEPTS 347,348,353

inveterate [adj] *long-standing, established* abiding, accustomed, addicted, chronic, confirmed, continuing, customary, deep-rooted, deep-seated, dyed-in-the-wool*, enduring,

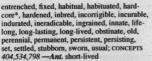

entrenched, fixed, habitual, habituated, hard-core*, hardened, inbred, incorrigible, incurable, indurated, ineradicable, ingrained, innate, life-long, long-lasting, long-lived, obstinate, old, perennial, permanent, persistent, persisting, set, settled, stubborn, sworn, usual; CONCEPTS 404,534,798 —*Ant.* short-lived

invidious [*adj*] *hateful* abominable, calumnious, defamatory, detestable, detracting, detractive, detractory, discriminatory, envious, envying, green-eyed*, jealous, libelous, maligning, obnoxious, odious, offensive, repugnant, scandalous, slanderous, slighting, undesirable, vilifying; CONCEPTS 401,403 —*Ant.* delightful, likeable, lovable

invigorate [*v*] *stimulate* activate, animate, brace, buck up, energize, enliven, excite, exhilarate, fortify, freshen, galvanize, harden, inspirit, liven up, nerve, pep up, perk up, pick up, quicken, rally, refresh, reinforce, rejuvenate, renew, restore, revitalize, rouse, snap up*, stir, strengthen, trigger, turn on*, vitalize, vivify, zap; CONCEPTS 7,14,22,110 —*Ant.* bore, depress, dishearten, dull, enervate

invigorating [*adj*] *stimulating* aesthetic, bracing, brisk, charged, energizing, exhilarating, exhilarative, fascinating, fresh, healthful, high*, hyper*, interesting, lively, quickening, refreshing, rejuvenating, rejuvenative, restorative, salubrious, tonic, uplifting, vitalizing; CONCEPT 537 —*Ant.* boring, depressing, dull, enervating, unstimulating

invincible [*adj*] *indestructible* bulletproof, impassable, impregnable, indomitable, insuperable, inviolable, invulnerable, irresistible, powerful, strong, unassailable, unattackable, unbeatable, unconquerable, undefeatable, unsurmountable, untouchable, unyielding; CONCEPTS 485,540,551 —*Ant.* beatable, breakable, conquerable, destructible

invisible [*adj*] *unable to be seen; hidden* concealed, covert, deceptive, disguised, ethereal, gaseous, ghostly, ideal, impalpable, imperceptible, imponderable, inappreciable, inconspicuous, indiscernible, infinitesimal, insensible, intangible, masked, microscopic, not in sight, obliterated, obscured, occult, out of sight, perdu, screened, supernatural, ulterior, unapparent, undisclosed, ungraspable, unnoticeable, unobservable, unperceivable, unreal, unseeable, unseen, unviewable, vaporous, veiled, wraithlike; CONCEPTS 485,582,619 —*Ant.* detectable, obvious, seen, visible

invitation [*n*] *proposal; asking* allurement, appeal, attraction, begging, bid, bidding, call, challenge, compliments, coquetry, date, encouragement, enticement, feeler*, ground, hit, incitement, inducement, invite, lure, motive, offer, open door*, overture, paper, pass, petition, pressure, proffer, prompting, proposition, provocation, rain check*, reason, request, solicitation, suggestion, summons, supplication, temptation, urge; CONCEPTS 48,384

invite [*v*] *ask to do something socially* allure, appeal to, attract, beg, bid, bring on, call, command, countenance, court, draw, encourage, entice, entreat, give invitation, have in, have over, include as guest, insist, inveigle, invitation, issue, lead, lure, persuade, petition, ply,

pray, press, prevail on, propose, provoke, request, send invitation, solicit, suggest, summon, supplicate, tempt, toll, urge, vamp, welcome, woo; CONCEPTS 48,68,384 —*Ant.* reject

inviting [*adj*] *alluring, captivating* agreeable, appealing, attractive, beguiling, bewitching, charming, cordial, delightful, encouraging, engaging, enticing, fascinating, intriguing, magnetic, mouthwatering, open, persuasive, pleasing, provocative, seductive, tempting, warm, welcoming, winning, winsome; CONCEPTS 404,529,537 —*Ant.* disenchanting, disgusting, uninviting

in vitro [*adj*] *artificial insemination, outside the womb, test-tube*; CONCEPTS 372,723

invocation [*n*] *prayer* abracadabra*, appeal, beseeching, calling, command, conjuration, entreaty, hocus-pocus*, hoodoo*, mumbo jumbo*, petition, rune, summons, supplication, voodoo*; CONCEPTS 48,278,368

invoice [*n*] *itemized bill* account, bill of sale, check, IOU, note, statement; CONCEPTS 329,332

invoke [*v1*] *call upon* adjure, appeal to, beg, beseech, call forth, conjure, crave, entreat, implore, importune, petition, plead, pray, request, send for, solicit, summon, supplicate; CONCEPT 48

invoke [*v2*] *put into effect* apply, call in, effect, enforce, have recourse to, implement, initiate, resort to, use; CONCEPTS 50,88

involuntary [*adj*] *automatic; not done willingly* automatic, begrudging, blind, compulsory, conditioned, forced, grudging, habitual, impulsive, instinctive, instinctual, knee-jerk*, obligatory, reflex, reflexive, reluctant, spontaneous, uncalculated, unconscious, uncontrolled, unintended, unintentional, unmeditated, unpremeditated, unprompted, unthinking, unwilling, unwitting, will-less; CONCEPT 544 —*Ant.* conscious, intentional, unforced, voluntary

involve [*v*] *draw in; include* absorb, affect, argue, associate, bind, catch, commit, complicate, comprehend, comprise, compromise, concern, connect, contain, cover, denote, embrace, embroil, engage, engross, enmesh, entail, entangle, grip, hold, hook, implicate, imply, incorporate, incriminate, inculpate, link, mean, mire, mix up*, necessitate, number, point to, preoccupy, presuppose, prove, relate, require, rivet, rope in, snarl up, suggest, take in, tangle, touch, wrap up in*; CONCEPT 112 —*Ant.* exclude, free, remove

involved [*adj1*] *complicated* Byzantine*, complex, confusing, convoluted, difficult, elaborate, Gordian*, high-tech*, intricate, knotty*, labyrinthine, mazy, muddled, ramified, sophisticated, tangled, tortuous, winding; CONCEPT 562 —*Ant.* easy, simple, uncomplicated

involved [*adj2*] *implicated in action* affected, caught, concerned, eat sleep and breathe*, embarrassed, embroiled, enmeshed, entangled, hooked, immersed in, incriminated, interested, into, knee-deep in*, mixed up in*, mixed up with*, occupied, participating, taking part in, tangled, up to here in*, up to one's neck in*; CONCEPTS 542,545 —*Ant.* blameless, exonerated

invulnerable [*adj*] *invincible* bulletproof, impassable, impenetrable, impregnable, indestructible, powerful, secure, strong, unbeatable, untouchable; CONCEPTS 489,540,551

inward [adj1] ingoing entering, inbound, incoming, infiltrating, inflowing, inpouring, penetrating, through; CONCEPT 581 —Ant. outgoing, outward

inward [adj2] private confidential, hidden, inmost, inner, innermost, inside, intellectual, interior, internal, intimate, personal, privy, psychological, religious, secret, spiritual; CONCEPT 529 —Ant. outward, public

iota [n] small bit atom, crumb, grain, hint, infinitesimal, jot, mite, molecule, nucleus, ounce, particle, ray, scintilla, scrap, smidgen, speck, trace, whit; CONCEPT 831 —Ant. lot

IRA [n] individual retirement account Keogh plan, retirement plan, Roth IRA, self-funded retirement plan, tax-free savings account; CONCEPTS 335,340,446,710

irascible [adj] crabby angry, bearish, bristly, cantankerous, choleric, crabbed, cranky, cross, feisty, fractious, grouchy, hasty, hot-tempered, huffy, ireful, irritable, ogre, passionate, peevish, petulant, querulous, quick-tempered, short-tempered, snappish, surly, testy, thin-skinned*, touchy, uptight; CONCEPT 401 —Ant. cheerful, happy

irate [adj] angry angered, annoyed, blown a gasket*, enraged, exasperated, fuming, furious, incensed, indignant, infuriated, irritated, livid, mad, piqued, provoked, riled, steamed*, ticked off*, up in arms*, worked up*, wrathful, wroth; CONCEPTS 403,542 —Ant. calm, cheerful, happy, pleased

ire [n] anger annoyance, boiling point*, conniption, conniption fit*, displeasure, exasperation, fury, indignation, more heat than light*, passion, rage, slow burn*, wrath; CONCEPT 410 —Ant. cheer, happiness

iridescent [adj] rainbow-colored irised, lustrous, many-colored, nacreous, opalescent, opaline, pearly, polychromatic, prismatic, rainbowlike, shimmering; CONCEPT 618

irk [v] aggravate; rub the wrong way abrade, annoy, bother, bug*, discommode, disturb, eat*, fret, gall, get on nerves*, get to*, give a hard time*, harass, incommode, inconvenience, irritate, make waves*, miff, nettle, peeve, provoke, put out*, rasp, rile, ruffle, trouble, vex; CONCEPTS 7,19 —Ant. delight, please

irksome [adj] annoying aggravating, boring, bothersome, burdensome, irritating, tedious, tiresome, troublesome, troubling, vexing; CONCEPT 529

iron [adj] hard, tough; inflexible adamant, adamantine, cruel, dense, ferric, ferrous, firm, heavy, immovable, implacable, indomitable, inexorable, insensible, obdurate, relentless, rigid, robust, steel, steely, strong, stubborn, thick, unbending, unyielding; CONCEPTS 534,604 —Ant. flexible, soft, weak

iron [n1] hard, ferrous metal cast, coke, pig; CONCEPT 476

iron [n2] restraint made of metal bond, chain, cuffs, fetter, handcuffs, leg irons, manacles, shackles; CONCEPT 476

ironclad [adj] fixed, rigid abiding, agreed, arranged, certain, changeless, confirmed, definite, determinate, enduring, firm, inflexible,

in the bag*, planned, prearranged, settled, stated, stubborn, sure, unalterable, uncompromising, unwavering; CONCEPTS 535,554

ironic/ironical [adj] sarcastic acrid, alert, arrogant, backbiting, biting, bitter, burlesque, caustic, chaffing, clever, contemptuous, contradictory, critical, cutting, cynical, defiant, derisive, disparaging, double-edged, exaggerated, implausible, incisive, incongruous, jibing, keen, mocking, mordant, paradoxical, pungent, quick-witted, ridiculous, sardonic, satiric, satirical, scathing, scoffing, sharp, sneering, spicy, trenchant, twisted, uncomplimentary, witty, wry; CONCEPTS 267,548 —Ant. considerate, deferential

iron out [v] reconcile a situation agree, arbitrate, clear up*, compromise, eliminate, eradicate, erase, expedite, get rid of*, harmonize, negotiate, put right*, reach agreement, resolve, settle, settle differences, simplify, smooth over*, sort out*, straighten out*, unravel; CONCEPT 126 —Ant. make worse, mess up

irony [n] sarcasm banter, burlesque, contempt, contrariness, criticism, derision, humor, incongruity, jibe, mockery, mordancy, paradox, quip, raillery, repartee, reproach, ridicule, sardonicism, satire, taunt, twist, wit; CONCEPTS 230,278 —Ant. consideration, deference

irrational [adj] illogical, senseless aberrant, absurd, brainless, cockamamie*, crazy, delirious, demented, disconnected, disjointed, distraught, fallacious, flaky*, foolish, freaky, incoherent, injudicious, insane, invalid, kooky*, loony*, mad, mindless, nonsensical, nutty*, off-the-wall*, preposterous, raving, reasonless, ridiculous, silly, sophistic, specious, stupid, unreasonable, unreasoning, unsound, unstable, unthinking, unwise, wacky*, wild, wrong; CONCEPTS 402,403,529 —Ant. logical, rational, reasonable, reflective, sensible, sound, stable

irreconcilable [adj] hostile, conflicting clashing, diametrically opposed, discordant, discrepant, dissonant, hard-line, implacable, incompatible, incongruous, inconsistent, inexorable, inflexible, inharmonious, intransigent, opposed, reluctant, unappeasable, uncompromising, unfriendly; CONCEPTS 401,564 —Ant. compromising, friendly, reconcilable

irrefutable [adj] beyond question accurate, apodictic, can bet on it*, certain, double-checked, evident, final, inarguable, incontestable, incontrovertible, indisputable, indubitable, invincible, ironclad, irrebuttable, irrefragable, irresistible, nof ifs ands or buts*, obvious, odds-on*, positive, proven, set, sure, unanswerable, unassailable, undeniable, unimpeachable, unquestionable; CONCEPTS 529,535, 582 —Ant. doubtful, dubious, questionable, refutable, uncertain

irregular [adj1] random, variable aberrant, aimless, capricious, casual, changeable, designless, desultory, disconnected, discontinuous, eccentric, erratic, faltering, fitful, fluctuating, fragmentary, haphazard, hit-or-miss*, inconstant, indiscriminate, infrequent, intermittent, jerky, nonuniform, occasional, out of order, patchy, purposeless, recurrent, shaky, shifting, spasmodic, sporadic, uncertain, unconsidered, uneven, unmethodical, unpunctual, unreliable, unsettled, unsteady, unsystematic, up and down*, weaving; CONCEPTS 534,799 —*Ant.* conventional, methodical, regular, systematic

irregular [adj2] *abnormal, peculiar* aberrant, anomalous, atypical, capricious, deviant, different, disorderly, divergent, eccentric, exceptional, extraordinary, immoderate, improper, inappropriate, inordinate, odd, off-key*, queer, quirky, singular, strange, unconventional, unique, unnatural, unofficial, unorthodox, unsuitable, unusual; CONCEPT 547 —*Ant.* common, conventional, normal, standard, usual

irregular [adj3] *bumpy, uneven* aberrant, amorphous, asymmetrical, bent, broken, cockeyed*, craggy, crooked, devious, disproportionate, eccentric, elliptic, elliptical, hilly, jagged, lopsided, lumpy, meandering, notched, not uniform, off-balance, off-center, out of proportion, pitted, protuberant, rough, scarred, serrate, serrated, unaligned, unbalanced, unequal, unsymmetrical, variable, wobbly, zigzagged; CONCEPTS 490,606 —*Ant.* even, flat, level, smooth

irregularly [adv] *intermittently* anyhow, any which way*, at intervals, by fits and starts*, by turns, disconnectedly, eccentrically, erratically, fitfully, haphazardly, helter-skelter*, infrequently, in snatches*, jerkily, now and again, occasionally, off and on*, out of sequence, periodically, slapdash, spasmodically, sporadically, uncertainly, uncommonly, unevenly, unmethodically, unpunctually, willy-nilly*; CONCEPTS 544,548,799 —*Ant.* evenly, regularly

irrelevant [adj] *beside the point* extraneous, foreign, garbage, immaterial, impertinent, inapplicable, inapposite, inappropriate, inappurtenant, inapropos, inapt, inconsequent, inconsequential, insignificant, not connected with, not germane, not pertaining to, off the point, off the topic, out of order, out of place, outside, pointless, remote, trivial, unapt, unconnected, unimportant, unnecessary, unrelated, without reference; CONCEPTS 560,575 —*Ant.* appropriate, necessary, pertinent, related, relevant

irreligious [adj] *ungodly* agnostic, atheistic, blasphemous, faithless, free-thinking, godless, heathen, iconoclastic, impious, irreverent, pagan, sacrilegious, sinful, unbelieving, undevout, unholy; CONCEPT 545

irreparable [adj] *unable to be fixed* beyond repair, broken, cureless, destroyed, hopeless, impossible, incorrigible, incurable, irrecoverable, irredeemable, irremediable, irremedial, irreplaceable, irretrievable, irreversible, ruined, uncorrectable, unrecoverable; CONCEPTS 314, 485 —*Ant.* fixable, mendable, repairable, reparable

irrepressible [adj] *effervescent, vivacious* boisterous, bubbling, buoyant, ebullient, enthusiastic, insuppressible, rebellious, rhapsodical, tumultous/tumultuous, unconstrained, uncontainable, uncontrollable, unmanageable, unquenchable, unrestrainable, unrestrained, unruly, unstoppable; CONCEPT 401 —*Ant.* depressed, despondent, grave, hopeless, serious

irreproachable [adj] *innocent* beyond reproach, blameless, exemplary, faultless, good, guiltless, impeccable, inculpable, innocent, irreprehensible, irreprovable, perfect,

pure, reproachless, righteous, unblamable, unblemished, unimpeachable, virtuous; CONCEPTS 545,574 —*Ant.* blameable, imperfect

irresistible [adj] *compelling; inescapable* alluring, beckoning, charming, enchanting, fascinating, glamorous, imperative, indomitable, ineluctable, inevitable, inexorable, invincible, lovable, overpowering, overwhelming, potent, powerful, ravishing, scrumptious, seductive, stunning, tempting, unavoidable, unconquerable, urgent; CONCEPTS 529,574,579 —*Ant.* avoidable, escapable, resistible

irresolute [adj] *indecisive* changing, doubtful, doubting, faltering, fearful, fickle, fluctuating, halfhearted*, halting, hesitant, hesitating, hot-and-cold*, infirm, on-the-fence*, shaky, tentative, timid, uncertain, undecided, undetermined, unsettled, unstable, unsteady, vacillating, waffling*, wavering, weak, weak-kneed*, wimpy*, wishy-washy*, wobbly; CONCEPTS 403,535 —*Ant.* definite, determined, obstinate, resolute, stubborn, unyielding, willful

irresponsible [adj] *careless, reckless* capricious, carefree, devil-may-care*, feckless, fickle, flighty, fly-by-night*, giddy, harebrained, ill-considered, immature, immoral, incautious, lax, loose*, no-account*, rash, scatterbrained*, shiftless, thoughtless, unaccountable, unanswerable, uncareful, undependable, unpredictable, unreliable, unstable, untrustworthy, wild; CONCEPTS 404,544 —*Ant.* accountable, careful, liable, reliable, responsible, trustworthy

irreverence [n] *disrespect* blasphemy, cheek, derision, discourtesy, flippancy, heresy, impertinence, impiety, impudence, insult, mockery, profanity, ridicule, rudeness, sauciness*, sin, sinfulness; CONCEPT 633 —*Ant.* regard, respect, reverence

irreverent [adj] *disrespectful* aweless, cheeky*, cocky*, contemptuous, crusty*, derisive, flip*, flippant, fresh, iconoclastic, impertinent, impious, impudent, insolent, irreverential, mocking, out-of-line*, profane, rude, sacrilegious, sassy*, saucy*, tongue-in-cheek*, ungodly, unhallowed, unholy; CONCEPT 401 —*Ant.* religious, respectful, reverent

irrevocable [adj] *fixed, unchangeable* certain, changeless, constant, doomed, established, fated, final, immutable, indelible, inevitable, invariable, irremediable, irretrievable, irreversible, lost, permanent, predestined, predetermined, settled, unalterable, unrepealable, unreversible; CONCEPTS 534,551 —*Ant.* alterable, changeable, reversible, revocable

irritable [adj] *bad-tempered, crabby* annoyed, bearish, brooding, cantankerous, carping, choleric, complaining, contentious, crabbed, cross, crotchety, disputatious, dissatisfied, dyspeptic, easily offended, exasperated, fiery, fractious, fretful, fretting, gloomy, grouchy, grumbling, hasty, hot, huffy, hypercritical, ill-humored, irascible, moody, morose, out of humor, oversensitive, peevish, petulant, plaintive, prickly, querulous, quick-tempered, resentful, sensitive, snappy, snarling, surly, tense, testy, touchy; CONCEPTS 401,403 —*Ant.* cheerful, happy, nice

irritate [v1] *upset, anger* abrade, affront, aggravate, annoy, bother, bug*, burn*, chafe, confuse, distemper, disturb, drive up the wall*, enrage, exasperate, fret, gall, get, get on nerves*, get under skin*, grate, harass, incense, inflame, infuriate, irk, madden, needle*, nettle, offend, pain, peeve, pester, pique, provoke, put out, rankle, rasp, rattle, rile, roil, rub the wrong way*, ruffle, sour, try, vex; CONCEPTS 7,19 —*Ant.* assuage, delight, help, please

irritate [v2] *hurt, chafe* aggravate, burn, erupt, fret, inflame, intensify, itch, pain, redden, rub, sensitize, sharpen, sting, swell; CONCEPT 246 —*Ant.* aid, assist, calm, help, soothe

island [n] *land surrounded by body of water* archipelago, atoll, bar, cay, enclave, haven, isle, islet, key, peninsula, reef, refuge, retreat, sanctuary, shelter; CONCEPT 509

isolate [v] *cut off, set apart* abstract, block off, close off, confine, detach, disconnect, disengage, divide, divorce, insulate, island, keep apart, part, quarantine, remove, seclude, segregate, separate, sequester, sever, sunder; CONCEPTS 188,201 —*Ant.* include, incorporate, integrate, join, mingle

isolated [adj] *unique; private* abandoned, abnormal, alone, anomalous, apart, backwoods*, confined, deserted, detached, exceptional, far-out, forsaken, hidden, incommunicado*, lonely, lonesome, off beaten track*, outlying, out-of-the-way*, random, remote, retired, screened, secluded, segregated, sequestered, single, solitary, special, stranded, unaccompanied, unfrequented, unrelated, untypical, unusual, withdrawn; CONCEPTS 577,583 —*Ant.* included, incorporated, mingling, public

isolation [n] *seclusion* aloneness, aloofness, beleaguerment, concealment, confinement, desolation, detachment, exile, hiding, monkhood, privacy, privateness, quarantine, reclusion, reclusiveness, remoteness, retreat, seclusiveness, segregation, sequestration, solitude, withdrawal; CONCEPTS 135,188,388,631

issue [n1] *point in question* affair, argument, concern, contention, controversy, matter, matter of contention, point, point of departure, problem, puzzle, question, subject, topic; CONCEPTS 278,532

issue [n2] *result* causatum, conclusion, consequence, culmination, effect, end, end product, eventuality, finale, fruit, outcome, payoff, sequel, termination, upshot; CONCEPT 230 —*Ant.* cause, origin, source

issue [n3] *edition of publication* copy, impression, installment, number, printing; CONCEPT 280

issue [n4] *distribution* circulation, delivery, dispersion, dissemination, granting, issuance, issuing, publication, sending out, supply, supplying; CONCEPT 140

issue [n5] *children* brood, descendants, get, heirs, offspring, posterity, progeniture, progeny, scions, seed; CONCEPTS 296,414 —*Ant.* parent

issue [v1] *distribute* air, allot, announce, assign, bring out, broadcast, circulate, consign, declare, deliver, dispatch, dispense, emit, get out, give out, promulgate, publish, put in circulation, put out, release, send, send out, transmit; CONCEPTS 60,140,292 —*Ant.* hold, keep

issue [v2] *emit, emerge; come from* appear, arise, be a consequence, birth, come forth, derive from, emanate, exude, flow, give off,

give out, ooze, originate, proceed, release, rise, send forth, spring, spurt, stem, throw off, vent, well; CONCEPTS 179,648 —*Ant.* hold, keep, repress, retain, suppress

itch [n1] *scratching; tingling* crawling, creeping, irritation, itchiness, prickling, psoriasis, rawness, tickle; CONCEPTS 608,728

itch [n2] *strong desire* aphrodisia, appetite, appetition, concupiscence, craving, eroticism, hankering, hunger, impulse, longing, lust, lustfulness, motive, passion, prurience, restlessness, urge, yearning, yen; CONCEPTS 20,529 —*Ant.* dislike, hate, hatred

itch [v1] *scratch; tingle* crawl, creep, irritate, prick, prickle, sting, tickle, titillate; CONCEPTS 185,313,612

itch [v2] *desire strongly* ache, be impatient, burn, chafe, crave, hanker, have a yen for, hunger, long, lust, pant, pine, sigh, thirst, want, yearn; CONCEPT 20 —*Ant.* dislike, hate

item [n] *part, article* account, aspect, bit, blurb*, bulletin, column, component, consideration, conversation piece, detail, dispatch, element, entry, feature, incidental, information, matter, minor point, minutia, news, note, notice, novelty, paragraph, particular, piece, point, report, scoop*, scrap, specific, story, thing, write-up; CONCEPTS 270,831,835

itemize [v] *keep detailed record* catalog, circumstantiate, cite, count, detail, document, enumerate, individualize, instance, inventory, lay out, list, mention, number, particularize, quote, recite, record, recount, rehearse, relate, set out, specify, spell out, tally; CONCEPTS 57,125

itinerant [adj] *roaming* afoot, ambulant, ambulatory, floating, gypsy, journeying, migratory, moving, nomadic, on foot, peripatetic, ranging, riding the rails*, roving, shifting, travelling, unsettled, vagabond, vagrant, wandering, wayfaring; CONCEPTS 536,584 —*Ant.* permanent, settled

itinerary [n] *plan of travel* beat, circuit, course, guide, guidebook, journey, line, outline, path, program, route, run, schedule, tour, way; CONCEPTS 281,660

J

jab [n/v] *poke* blow, buck, bump, bunt, dig, hit, jog, lunge, nudge, prod, punch, push, stab, tap, thrust; CONCEPT 189

jabber [v] *talk incessantly and trivially* babble, blather*, chatter, drivel, gab, go on and on*, jaw, mumble, murmur, mutter, prate, ramble, run off at mouth*, shoot the breeze*, talk, tattle, utter, yak, yap; CONCEPTS 51,56 —*Ant.* be silent

jacket [n] *covering* case, casing, coat, envelope, folder, fur, hide, parka, pelt, sheath, skin, threads, tunic, wrapper, wrapping; CONCEPTS 451,484

jaded [adj] *exhausted, indifferent* been around, blah*, blasé, bored, cool*, done it all*, dulled, fagged, fatigued, fed up*, had it*, mellow, sated, satiated, sick of*, spent, surfeited, tired, tired-out*, up to here*, wearied, weary, worn, worn-down, worn-out; CONCEPTS 401,406 —*Ant.* fresh, unused

jagged [adj] *ragged, notched* asperous, barbed, broken, cleft, craggy, denticulate, harsh, indented, irregular, pointed, ridged, rough, rugged, scabrous, serrated, snaggy, spiked, toothed, uneven, unlevel, unsmooth; CONCEPTS *490,606* —*Ant.* even, smooth

jail [n] *place for incarceration* bastille, black hole*, brig, bullpen*, can*, cell, clink*, cooler*, detention camp, dungeon, house of correction, inside*, jailhouse, joint*, lockup, pen, penal institution, penitentiary, pound, prison, rack*, reformatory, slammer*, solitary*, stir*, stockade, up the river*; CONCEPTS *439,449,516*

jail [v] *incarcerate* bastille, book, cage, can*, confine, constrain, detain, hold, immure, impound, imprison, lock up, prison, put away*, put behind bars*, put on ice*, railroad*, send up*, sentence, take away*, throw away the keys*, throw in dungeon, throw the book at*; CONCEPT *317* —*Ant.* free, liberate

jailer [n] *prison warden* correctional officer, corrections officer, guard, prison guard, turnkey; CONCEPT *348*

jalopy [n] *old, dilapidated automobile* bucket of bolts*, clunker, heap*, junker*, rattletrap*, tin lizzie*, wreck; CONCEPTS *260,674*

jam [n] *troublesome situation* bind, box, corner, difficulty, dilemma, fix, hole, hot water*, pickle*, plight, predicament, problem, quandary, scrape, spot, strait, trouble; CONCEPT *674* —*Ant.* benefit, boon

jam [v] *squeeze in; compress* bear, bind, block, cease, clog, congest, cram, crowd, crush, elbow, force, halt, jam-pack, jostle, obstruct, pack, press, push, ram, squash, squish, stall, stick, stuff, tamp, throng, wad, wedge; CONCEPTS *121,208*

jamboree [n] *noisy celebration* bash*, blowout*, ceremony, convention, festival, gathering, hoopla, jubilee, party, rally, revelry, shindig, wingding*; CONCEPT *377*

jangle [n] *cacophony of noises* babel, clang, clangor, clash, din, dissonance, hubbub*, hullabaloo*, jar, pandemonium, racket, rattle, reverberation, roar, tumult, uproar; CONCEPT *595*

jangle [v] *make clinking noises* chime, clank, clash, clatter, conflict, disaccord, discord, disharmonize, hit a sour note*, jar, jingle, mismatch, rattle, vibrate; CONCEPT *65*

janitor [n] *person who cleans and maintains* attendant, caretaker, cleaning person, concierge, custodian, doorkeeper, doorperson, gatekeeper, house sitter, porter, sitter, super, superintendent, sweeper, watchperson; CONCEPT *348*

jar [n1] *container* basin, beaker, bottle, burette, can, chalice, crock, cruet, decanter, ewer, flagon, flask, jug, pitcher, pot, tun, urn, vase, vat, vessel; CONCEPT *494*

jar [n2] *shocking hit* bump, clash, collision, concussion, crash, impact, jolt, jounce, rock, smash, succussion, thud, thump; CONCEPT *189*

jar [v1] *shock, jolt* agitate, bang, bounce, bump, clash, convulse, crash, disturb, grate, grind, hit, irritate, jerk; jiggle, jounce, jump, offend, quake, rasp, rattle, rock, shake, slam, thump, tremor, vibrate, wiggle, wobble; CONCEPTS *65,189*

jar [v2] *clash, disharmonize* annoy, bicker, contend, disaccord, disagree, discompose, discord, grate, grind, interfere, irk, irritate, jangle, mismatch, nettle, oppose, outrage, quarrel, shock, wrangle; CONCEPTS *7,19* —*Ant.* agree, harmonize

jargon [n] *specialized language; dialect* abracadabra*, argot, balderdash*, banality, bombast, bunk*, buzzwords*, cant, cliché, colloquialism, commonplace term, doublespeak, drivel, fustian, gibberish, hackneyed term, idiom, insipidity, lexicon, lingo*, mumbo jumbo*, neologism, newspeak, nonsense, overused term, palaver, parlance, patois, patter, rigmarole, shoptalk, slang, slanguage*, speech, stale language, street talk*, tongue, trite language, twaddle*, usage, vernacular, vocabulary; CONCEPTS *275,276* —*Ant.* standard

jaundiced [adj] *tainted, prejudiced* biased, bigoted, bitter, colored, cynical, disapproving, distorted, envious, grudging, hostile, intolerant, jealous, one-sided, opprobrious, partial, partisan, preconceived, prepossessed, resentful, skeptical, spiteful, suspicious, tendentious, unfair, unfriendly, unindifferent, warped, yellow; CONCEPTS *401,403,542* —*Ant.* clean, fresh, unbiased, unprejudiced

jaunt [n] *expedition* adventure, airing, amble, beat, canter, circuit, constitutional, course, cruise, drive, excursion, frolic, gallop, hike, jog, journey, junket, march, outing, patrol, peregrination, picnic, promenade, prowl, ramble, ride, round, roundabout, run, safari, sally, saunter, stroll, tour, tramp, travel, trek, trip, turn, voyage, walk; CONCEPTS *159,195,224*

jaunty [adj] *lively* airy, animated, bold, brash, breezy, buoyant, carefree, careless, cocky, dapper, dashing, debonair, devilish, devil-may-care*, easy, exhilarated, flip*, flippant, forward, free, fresh, frisky, frolicsome, gamesome, gay, high-spirited, hilarious, impetuous, impish, impudent, jocose, joking, jolly, jovial, light, natty, nervy, perky, playful, prankish, provocative, reckless, rollicking, self-confident, showy, smart, sportive, sporty, sprightly, spruce, swaggering, trim, venturesome, vivacious; CONCEPTS *401,404* —*Ant.* depressed, lethargic, lifeless

jaw [n] *bones of chin* bone, chops*, jowl, mandible, maxilla, mouth, muzzle*, orifice; CONCEPT *392*

jaw [v1] *talk a lot* babble, chat, chatter, gab*, gossip, jabber, lecture, orate, prate, prattle, yak; CONCEPTS *51,56* —*Ant.* be quiet

jaw [v2] *criticize* abuse, baste, berate, blame, call on the carpet*, censure, rail, rate, revile, scold, tongue-lash*, upbraid, vituperate; CONCEPT *52* —*Ant.* praise

jazz [n] *style of music* bebop*, blues, boogie*, boogie-woogie*, Dixieland, fusion jazz, hot jazz, improvisational music, jive*, ragtime, swing; CONCEPT *595*

jazzed-up [adj] *souped up* gassed-up, high geared, high performance, high speed, hopped-up*, pepped-up*, pumped-up*, revved-up*, speedy, supercharged; CONCEPTS *401,404*

jazzy [adj] *fancy* animated, exciting, flashy, gaudy, lively, salacious, sexy, smart, snazzy*, spirited, vivacious, wild, zestful, zippy*; CONCEPTS *537,589* —*Ant.* conservative, simple, unfancy

jealous [adj] *desirous; wary* anxious, apprehensive, attentive, begrudging, covetous, demanding, doubting, emulous, envious, envying, grabby, grasping, green-eyed, grudging, guarded, intolerant, invidious, jaundiced, mistrustful, monopolizing, possessive, possessory, protective, questioning, resentful, rival, skeptical, solicitous, suspicious, vigilant, watchful, zealous; CONCEPTS 403,542 —*Ant.* confident, content, satisfied, trusting, unresentful

jealousy [*n*] *envy* backbiting, begrudging, covetousness, enviousness, evil eye*, green-eyed monster*, grudge, grudgingness, jaundiced eye*, resentfulness, resentment, spite; CONCEPT 410

jeans [*n*] *dungarees* blue jeans, chaps, denims, Lees™, Levi's™, pants, trousers, Wranglers™; CONCEPT 451

jeer [*v*] *heckle* banter, comeback, contemn, deride, dig*, fleer, flout, gibe, hector, hoot, jab, jest, laugh at, make a crack*, mock, poke fun, put down, put on, quip, ridicule, scoff, sneer, snipe, taunt; CONCEPT 54

jell [*v*] *coagulate* clot, cohere, come together, condense, congeal, crystallize, finalize, form, freeze, gel, gelate, gelatinize, harden, jellify, jelly, materialize, set, solidify, stick, stiffen, take shape, thicken; CONCEPTS 250,469 —*Ant.* liquidate, melt

jeopardize [*v*] *endanger* be careless, chance, chance it*, gamble, hazard, imperil, lay on the line*, peril, put at risk, put in danger, put in jeopardy, risk, stake, subject to, tempt fate, threaten; CONCEPTS 246,252,384

jeopardy [*n*] *danger, trouble* accident, chance, double-trouble*, endangerment, exposure, hazard, insecurity, liability, on the line*, on the spot*, out on a limb*, peril, precariousness, risk, venture, vulnerability; CONCEPT 675 —*Ant.* protection, safety

jerk [*n*1] *a lurching move* bounce, bump, flick, flop, jolt, pull, quake, quiver, shiver, snag, thrust, tug, tweak, twitch, wiggle, wrench; wriggle, yank; CONCEPTS 80,149,150

jerk [*n*2] *stupid, bumbling person* brute, fool, idiot, nincompoop, ninny, oaf, rascal; CONCEPT 423

jerk [*v*] *move with lurch* bounce, bump, dance, flick, fling, flip, flop, grab, hook, hurtle, jolt, lug, pluck, pull, quake, quiver, seize, shiver, shrug, sling, snag, snatch, throw, thrust, tug, tweak, twitch, vellicate, whisk, wiggle, wrench, wrest, wriggle, wring, yank; CONCEPTS 150,152

jerky [*adj*] *uncontrolled* bouncy, bumpy, convulsive, fitful, jarring, jolting, lurching, paroxysmal, rough, shaking, shaky, spasmodic, tremulous, twitching, twitchy, uncontrollable; CONCEPT 482 —*Ant.* fluid, smooth

jerry-built [*adj*] *flimsy* cheap, defective, insubstantial, jerry-rigged, junky, makeshift, ramshackle, rickety, shoddy, slipshod, unsound, unsubstantial; CONCEPT 267

jest [*n*] *joke* banter, bon mot, crack, fun, funny, gag, game, hoax, jive, jolly, laugh, one-liner*, play, pleasantry, prank, quip, rib, rib-tickler*, ridicule, sally, spoof, sport, wisecrack, witticism; CONCEPT 273

jest [*v*] *joke* banter, chaff, deride, flout, fool, fun*, gibe*, gird*, jeer, jive*, jolly*, josh*, kid, mock, needle*, put on, quip, rag*, razz*, rib*, roast*, scoff, sneer, spoof, tease; CONCEPT 273

jester [*n*] *person who jokes, plays jokes* actor, antic, banterer, buffoon, card*, clown, comedian, comic, cutup*, droll, fool, harlequin, humorist, japer, joker, jokester, larker, life of the party*, madcap*, pantaloon, practical joker, prankster, quipster, standup comic, trickster, wag*, wisecracker*, wit; CONCEPT 423

jet [*adj*] *black* atramentous, coal-black, dark, ebon, ebony, inky, midnight, obsidian, pitch-black, pitch-dark, raven, sable; CONCEPT 618 —*Ant.* white

jet [*n*1] *rush, gush of substance* flow, fountain, spout, spray, spring, spritz, spurt, squirt, stream; CONCEPTS 465,467

jet [*n*2] *vehicle propelled by ejection of pressurized gas or liquid* airbus, airplane, plane, supersonic, supersonic transport, turbo; CONCEPTS 463,503

jet [*v*] *spurt, gush* blow, fly, issue, pour, roll, rush, shoot, soar, spew, spout, spritz, squirt, stream, surge, travel, zoom; CONCEPT 179

jet set [*n*] *high society* beau monde, beautiful people, cream of society, elite, fashionable society, in-crowd, leisured class, moneyed class, polite society, smart set, the well-to-do, upper crust; CONCEPTS 387,388,417

jettison [*v*] *eject; throw overboard* abandon, abdicate, cashier*, cast, cast off, deep-six*, discard, dump, expel, heave, hurl, junk*, maroon, reject, scrap*, shed, slough, throw away, unload*; CONCEPTS 180,222 —*Ant.* take in, take on

jetty [*n*] *pier* barrier, breakwater, dock, groin, landing, quay, seawall, slip, wharf; CONCEPTS 439,443,479

jewel [*n*1] *precious stone* baguette, bauble, bead, bijou, birthstone, brilliant, gem, gemstone, glass, gullion, hardware*, ornament, rock*, sparkler*, stone, trinket; CONCEPTS 446,474,478

jewel [*n*2] *something, someone precious* charm, find, gem, genius, ideal, masterpiece, nonesuch, nonpareil, paragon, pearl*, phenomenon, phoenix*, prize, prodigy, rarity, specialty, treasure, wonder; CONCEPT 671

jewelry [*n*] *precious stones, metals worn as decoration* adornment, anklet, band, bangle, bauble, beads, bijou, bracelet, brass, brooch, cameo, chain, charm, choker, costume, cross, crown, diamonds, earring, finery, frippery, gem, glass*, gold, ice*, jewel, junk*, knickknack, lavaliere, locket, necklace, ornament, pendant, pin, regalia, ring, rock, rosary, silver, solitaire, sparkler, stickpin, stone, tiara, tie pin, treasure, trinket; CONCEPT 446

Jewish [*adj*] *Israelite* Hasidic, Hebrew, Judaistic, Semitic; CONCEPT 369

Jezebel [*n*] *prostitute* broad, fallen woman*, femme fatale, floozy*, harlot, hooker, hussy, jade, loose woman, scarlet, slut, strumpet, tart, trollop, vamp, whore; CONCEPTS 348,412, 415,419

jibe [*v*] *agree* accord, conform, correspond, dovetail, fit, fit in, go, harmonize, match, resemble, square, tally; CONCEPT 664 —*Ant.* clash, disagree

jiffy [*n*] *instant* breath, crack, flash, jiff*, minute, moment, second, shake*, split second*, trice, twinkling*; CONCEPT 808

jiggle [v] *bounce up and down* agitate, bob, fidget, jerk, jig, jigger, jog, joggle, shake, shimmer, shimmy, twitch, vellicate, wiggle; CONCEPTS 150,152

jilt [v] *abandon, betray* break off*, coquette, deceive, desert, disappoint, discard, ditch*, drop*, dump*, forsake, get rid of, leave, leave at the altar*, leave flat*, reject, throw over*; CONCEPTS 195,297,384 —*Ant.* keep, love

jingle [v] *make metallic clinking noise* chime, chink, chinkle, clamor, clang, clatter, clink, ding, jangle, rattle, reverberate, ring, sound, tingle, tinkle, tintannabulate; CONCEPT 65

jinx [n] *curse* black magic, charm, enchantment, evil eye*, hex, hoodoo*, kiss of death*, nemesis, plague, spell, voodoo*; CONCEPTS 230,679 —*Ant.* advantage, benefit, boon, luck

jinx [v] *curse* bedevil, bewitch, cast a spell on, charm, condemn, damn*, enchant, give the evil eye*, hex; CONCEPTS 14,192 —*Ant.* benefit

jitters [n] *nervousness* anxiety, dither, fidgets, heebie-jeebies*, jumps, nerves, shakes, shivers, tenseness, willies*; CONCEPTS 230,410,690 —*Ant.* calmness

jittery [adj] *nervous* antsy*, anxious, apprehensive, edgy, excitable, fidgety, high-strung*, jumpy, on edge*, on pins and needles*, panicky, quivering, restless, shaky, skittish, spooked, tense, trembling, uneasy, uptight; CONCEPT 401

job [n1] *employment* activity, appointment, assignment, berth, billet, business, calling, capacity, career, chore, connection, craft, daily grind*, engagement, faculty, function, gig*, grind*, handicraft, line, livelihood, means, métier, niche, nine-to-five*, occupation, office, opening, operation, place, position, post, posting, profession, pursuit, racket*, rat race*, situation, spot, stint, swindle*, task, trade, vocation, work; CONCEPTS 351,360 —*Ant.* unemployment

job [n2] *task* act, action, affair, assignment, burden, business, care, charge, chore, commission, concern, contribution, deed, devoir, duty, effort, enterprise, errand, function, matter, mission, obligation, office, operation, project, province, pursuit, responsibility, role, stint, task, taskwork, thing*, tour of duty, undertaking, venture, work; CONCEPT 362 —*Ant.* fun

jobless [adj] *unemployed* between jobs*, collecting unemployment benefits, laid off, on the dole*, out of a job, out of work, without employment, without gainful employment, workless; CONCEPT 538

jock [n] *athlete* competitor, letterman/woman, letterperson, player, sportsman/woman, sportsperson; CONCEPT 366

jockey [v] *maneuver* direct, guide, handle, move, navigate, negotiate, pilot, position, ride, steer, turn, twist; CONCEPTS 187,225

jocular/jocose/jocund [adj] *funny, playful* amusing, blithe, camp, cheerful, comic, comical, crazy, daffy, droll, facetious, flaky*, frolicsome, gay, gleeful, happy, humorous, jesting, jokey, joking, jolly, joshing, jovial, joyous, laughable, lighthearted, lively, ludicrous, merry, mischievous, pleasant, roguish, sportive, teasing, wacky, waggish, whimsical, witty; CONCEPTS 267,529 —*Ant.* morose, serious, unfunny

jog [v1] *activate, push* agitate, arouse, bounce, dig, hit, jab, jar, jerk, jiggle, joggle, jolt, jostle, jounce, nudge, press, prod, prompt, punch, remind, rock, shake, shove, stimulate, stir, suggest, whack; CONCEPTS 14,208 —*Ant.* repress

jog [v2] *run for recreation* amble, canter, dash, dogtrot, lope, pace, sprint, trot; CONCEPT 151

John Hancock [n] *signature* autograph, endorsement, inscription, mark, seal, undersignature; CONCEPT 284

joie de vivre [n] *cheerfulness* delight, enjoyment, gaiety, gladsomeness, happiness, high spirits, joviality, joy, joyfulness, joyousness, lightheartedness, love of life, merriment, molliness, spiritedness; CONCEPTS 410,411 —*Ant.* depression, sobriety

join [v1] *unite* accompany, add, adhere, affix, agglutinate, annex, append, assemble, associate, attach, blend, bracket, cement, clamp, clasp, clip, coadunate, coalesce, combine, compound, concrete, conjoin, conjugate, connect, copulate, couple, entwine, fasten, fuse, grapple, hitch on, incorporate, interlace, intermix, juxtapose, knit, leash, link, lock, lump together, marry, mate, melt, mix, pair, put together, slap on, span, splice, stick together, tack on, tag on, tie, tie up, touch, weave, wed, weld, yoke; CONCEPT 113 —*Ant.* disjoin, divide, separate

join [v2] *affiliate with organization* align, associate with, be in, come aboard*, consort, cooperate, enlist, enroll, enter, fall in with*, follow, go to, mingle with, pair with, plug into*, side with, sign on, sign up, take part in, take up with, team up with, throw in with*, tie up with; CONCEPT 114 —*Ant.* leave, resign, withdraw

join [v3] *touch; border on* abut, adjoin, be adjacent to, be at hand, be close to, be contiguous to, bound, butt, communicate, conjoin, extend, fringe, hem, lie beside, lie near, lie next to, line, march, meet, neighbor, open into, parallel, reach, rim, skirt, trench on, verge on; CONCEPT 747 —*Ant.* separate

joint [adj] *shared, combined* collective, common, communal, concerted, conjoint, conjunct, consolidated, cooperative, hand in hand, intermutual, joined, mutual, public, united; CONCEPTS 577,708 —*Ant.* disjoint, separate, single, uncombined, unshared

joint [n1] *intersection, juncture* abutment, articulation, bend, bond, bracket, bridge, concourse, confluence, conjuncture, connection, copula, coupling, crux, elbow, hinge, hyphen, impingement, interconnection, junction, knot, link, meeting, nexus, node, point, seam, splice, suture, swivel, tangency, tie, union, vinculum; CONCEPTS 393,830,831

joint [n2] *cheap hangout* bar, club, dive*, hole in the wall*, honky-tonk*, juke joint*, roadhouse, tavern; CONCEPTS 439,449

jointly [adv] *as one* accordingly, agreeably, alike, arm in arm*, coincidentally, collectively, combined, companionably, concomitantly, concurrently, conjointly, connectedly, cooperatively, en masse, hand in glove*, hand in hand*, harmoniously, in a group, in common, in company with, in concert, in conjunction, inextricably, in league, in partnership, inseparably, intimately, in unison, mutually, reciprocally, side by side*, similarly, simultaneously, synchronically, together, unitedly, with one another; CONCEPT 577 —*Ant.* singly

joke [n1] *fun, quip* antic, bon mot, buffoonery, burlesque, caper, caprice, chestnut*, clowning, drollery, epigram, escapade, farce, frolic, gag, gambol, game, ha-ha*, hoodwinking*, horseplay*, humor, jape, jest, lark, laugh, mischief, monkeyshine*, mummery, one-liner*, parody, payoff, play, pleasantry, prank, pun, put-on, quirk, raillery, repartee, revel, rib, sally, saw, shaggy-dog story*, shenanigan*, snow job*, sport, spree, stunt, tomfoolery, trick, vagary, whimsy, wisecrack, witticism, yarn; CONCEPT 273

joke [n2] *person that is made fun of* buffoon, butt, clown, derision, fool, goat, jackass, jestee, laughingstock, mockery, simpleton, sport, target; CONCEPTS 412,423

joke [v] *kid, tease* banter, chaff, deceive, deride, fool, frolic, fun, gambol, horse around*, jape, jest, jive*, jolly, josh, kid around, laugh, make merry, mock, needle, play, play the clown, play tricks, poke fun*, pull one's leg*, pun, put on, quip, rag, revel, rib, ridicule, roast*, spoof, sport, taunt, trick, wisecrack*; CONCEPT 273
—*Ant.* be serious

joker [n] *person who kids, teases* actor, banana*, buffoon, card*, clown, comedian, comic, cutup*, droll, farceur, fool, funster*, gagster*, humorist, jester, jokesmith, jokester, josher*, kidder, life of the party*, prankster*, punster*, quipster*, second banana*, stand-up comic, stooge, straight person, top banana*, trickster*, wag, wisecracker*, wit; CONCEPTS 352,423

jolly [adj] *laughing, joyful* blithe, blithesome, bouncy, carefree, cheerful, chipper, chirpy, convivial, daffy, delightful, enjoyable, entertaining, festive, frolicsome, funny, gay, gladsome, gleeful, happy, hilarious, jocund, jokey, joshing, jovial, joyous, jubilant, larking, lighthearted, lots of laughs, merry, mirthful, playful, pleasant, sportive, sprightly, zippy*; CONCEPTS 267,542,548 —*Ant.* sad, unhappy

jolt [n] *surprise; sudden push* blow, bombshell*, bounce, bump, clash, collision, concussion, double whammy*, impact, jar, jerk, jog, jounce, jump, kick, lurch, percussion, punch, quiver, reversal, setback, shake, shock, shot, start, surprise, thunderbolt; CONCEPTS 42,208

jolt [v] *surprise; push suddenly* astonish, bowl over*, bump, churn, convulse, discompose, disturb, floor, jar, jerk, jog, jostle, knock, knock over*, lay out*, perturb, rock, shake, shake up*, shock, shove, spring something on*, stagger, start, startle, stun, throw a curve*, upset; CONCEPTS 42,208

jostle [v] *bump, shake* bang into, bulldoze*, bump heads*, butt*, crash, crowd, elbow, hustle, jab, jog, joggle, jolt, nudge, press, push, push around, push aside, rough and tumble*, scramble, shoulder, shove, squeeze, thrust; CONCEPTS 152,189,208

journal [n] *chronicle* account, almanac, annals, annual, calendar, chronology, comic book, daily, daybook, diary, gazette, ledger, log, magazine, memento, memoir, minutes, monthly, newspaper, note, observation, organ, paper, periodical, publication, rag, record, register, reminder, reminiscence, review, scandal sheet*, statement, tabloid, weekly; CONCEPTS 271,280,801

journalism [n] *reporting* broadcast writing, news, newspaper writing, the fourth estate, the press, writing; CONCEPTS 280,349,356

journalist [n] *person who writes about factual events for a living* announcer, broadcaster, columnist, commentator, contributor, correspondent, cub, editor, hack, media person, newspaper person, newsperson, pencil pusher*, press, publicist, reporter, scribe, scrivener, stringer*, television commentator, writer; CONCEPTS 348,356

journey [n] *excursion* adventure, airing, beat, campaign, caravan, circuit, constitutional, course, crossing, drive, expedition, exploration, hike, itinerary, jaunt, junket, march, migration, odyssey, outing, passage, patrol, peregrination, pilgrimage, progress, promenade, quest, ramble, range, roaming, round, route, run, safari, sally, saunter, sojourn, stroll, survey, tour, tramp, transit, transmigration, travel, traveling, traverse, trek, trip, vagabondage, vagrancy, venture, visit, voyage, wandering, wayfaring; CONCEPT 224

journey [v] *travel* circuit, cruise, fare, fly, globe trot*, go, go places, hie, hop, jaunt, jet, junket, knock about*, pass, peregrinate, proceed, process, push on, ramble, range, repair, roam, rove, safari, take a trip, tour, traverse, trek, voyage, wander, wend; CONCEPT 224 —*Ant.* stay, wait

jovial [adj] *happy* affable, airy, amiable, animated, bantering, blithe, blithesome, bouncy, buoyant, chaffing, cheery, chipper, chirpy, companionable, conversable, convivial, cordial, daffy*, delightful, dizzy*, enjoyable, facetious, festal, festive, gay, glad, gleeful, good-natured, hilarious, humorous, jocose, jocund, jokey, jolly, jollying, joshing, jubilant, larking, lighthearted, loony, lots of laughs*, merry, mirthful, nutty*, off-the-wall*, pleasant, sociable; CONCEPTS 401,403 —*Ant.* sad, unhappy

joy [n] *great happiness, pleasure* alleviation, amusement, animation, bliss, charm, cheer, comfort, delectation, delight, diversion, ecstasy, elation, exultation, exulting, felicity, festivity, frolic, fruition, gaiety, gem, gladness, glee, good humor, gratification, hilarity, humor, indulgence, jewel, jubilance, liveliness, luxury, merriment, mirth, pride, pride and joy, prize, rapture, ravishment, refreshment, regalement, rejoicing, revelry, satisfaction, solace, sport, transport, treasure, treat, wonder; CONCEPTS 410,529 —*Ant.* sadness, sorrow, unhappiness, woe

joyful/joyous [adj] *happy* blithesome, cheerful, cheery, delighted, ecstatic, effervescent, elated, enjoyable, enraptured, expansive, festive, flying*, gay, glad, gladsome, gratified, heartening, high*, high as a kite*, jubilant, lighthearted, merry, overjoyed, pleased, pleasurable, popping*, rapturous, satisfied, sunny*, sunny-side up*, transported, upbeat; CONCEPTS 403,542, 548 —*Ant.* sad, sorrowful, unhappy, woeful

joyless [adj] *unhappy* black, bleak, blue, cheerless, dejected, depressant, depressed, depressing, dismal, dispirited, dispiriting, doleful, downcast, down in the mouth*, dragged, dreary, droopy, gloomy, have the blahs*, heavy*, low, melancholic, melancholy, miserable, mopey, mournful, sad, saddening, somber; CONCEPTS 403,542, 548 —*Ant.* cheerful, delighted, happy, joyful

jubilant [*adj*] *happy* celebrating, doing handsprings*, elated, enraptured, euphoric, excited, exuberant, exultant, exulting, flipping, flying*, glad, gleeful, joyous, overjoyed, pleased, rejoicing, rhapsodic, thrilled, tickled*, triumphal, triumphant; CONCEPTS 401,403 —*Ant.* depressed, sad, sorrowful, unhappy

Judas [*n*] *traitor* backstabber, Benedict Arnold, betrayer, conspirator, deceiver, rat, turncoat, two-timer*, weasel; CONCEPT 412

judge [*n*] *person who arbitrates* adjudicator, appraiser, arbiter, assessor, authority, bench, chancellor, conciliator, court, critic, evaluator, expert, honor, inspector, intercessor, intermediary, interpreter, judiciary, justice, justice of peace, legal official, magister, magistrate, marshal, moderator, negotiator, peacemaker, reconciler, referee, umpire, warden; CONCEPT 355

judge [*v*] *make decision from evidence; deduce* act on, adjudge, adjudicate, appraise, appreciate, approximate, arbitrate, arrive, ascertain, assess, check, collect, conclude, condemn, consider, criticize, decide, decree, deduct, derive, determine, discern, distinguish, doom, draw, esteem, estimate, evaluate, examine, find, gather, give a hearing, make, make out, mediate, pass sentence, place, pronounce sentence, put, rate, reckon, referee, resolve, review, rule, sentence, settle, sit, size up, suppose, test, try, umpire, value; CONCEPTS 18,317

judgment [*n1*] *common sense* acumen, acuteness, apprehension, astuteness, awareness, brains, capacity, comprehension, discernment, discrimination, experience, genius, grasp, incisiveness, ingenuity, intelligence, intuition, keenness, knowledge, mentality, penetration, perception, percipience, perspicacity, prudence, quickness, range, rationality, reach, readiness, reason, reasoning, sagacity, sanity, sapience, savvy, sense, sharpness, shrewdness, sophistication, soundness, taste, understanding, wisdom, wit; CONCEPTS 37,409 —*Ant.* ignorance, inanity, misjudgment, stupidity

judgment [*n2*] *decision about blame* analysis, appraisal, appreciation, arbitration, assaying, assessment, award, belief, close study, conclusion, contemplation, conviction, decree, deduction, determination, estimate, estimation, evaluation, examination, exploration, finding, idea, inference, inquest, inquiry, inquisition, inspection, observation, opinion, order, probing, pursuit, quest, reconnaissance, regard, report, research, resolution, result, review, ruling, scrutiny, search, sentence, sifting, summary, verdict, view, weigh-in; CONCEPTS 103,689 —*Ant.* indecision

judgment [*n3*] *doom, fate* affliction, castigation, chastisement, correction, damnation, infliction, manifestation, misfortune, mortification, punishment, retribution, visitation; CONCEPT 679

judicial [*adj*] *legal* administrative, authoritative, constitutional, discriminating, distinguished, equitable, forensic, impartial, judgelike, judiciary, juridical, jurisdictional, juristic, lawful,

legalistic, magisterial, official, pontifical, principled, regular, statutory; CONCEPT 319

judicious [*adj*] *wise, thoughtful* accurate, acute, astute, calculating, careful, cautious, circumspect, clear-sighted, considerate, considered, diplomatic, discerning, discreet, discriminating, efficacious, enlightened, expedient, far-sighted, informed, judicial, keen, perceptive, perspicacious, politic, profound, prudent, quick-witted, rational, reasonable, sagacious, sage, sane, sapient, seasonable, seemly, sensible, sharp, shrewd, skillful, sober, sophisticated, sound, thorough, wary, well-advised, well-judged, worldly-wise; CONCEPTS 402,403,542 —*Ant.* foolish, hasty, idiotic, injudicious, irrational, nonsensical, reckless, senseless, thoughtless, unwise

jug [*n*] *container for liquid* amphora, beaker, bottle, bucket, canteen, carafe, crock, cruet, decanter, ewer, flagon, flask, growler, hooker, jar, pitcher, pot, tub, urn, vase, vessel; CONCEPT 494

juggle [*v*] *mislead, falsify; handle several things at once* alter, beguile, betray, bluff, change, conjure, delude, disguise, doctor*, double-cross, fix, humbug*, illude, maneuver, manipulate, misrepresent, modify, perform magic, prestidigitate, shuffle, take in, tamper with, trim; CONCEPTS 59,63 —*Ant.* be honest

juice [*n*] *liquid squeezed from fruit, plant* abstract, alcohol, aqua vitae, distillation, drink, essence, extract, fluid, liquor, milk, nectar, oil, sap, sauce, secretion, serum, spirit, syrup, water; CONCEPTS 428,467

juicy [*adj1*] *moist* dank, dewy, dripping, humid, liquid, luscious, lush, mellow, oily, oozy, pulpy, sappy, saturated, sauced, slippery, slushy, soaked, sodden, succulent, syrupy, viscid, watery, wet; CONCEPT 603 —*Ant.* dry

juicy [*adj2*] *exciting, interesting* colorful, fascinating, intriguing, piquant, provocative, racy, risqué, sensational, spicy, suggestive, tantalizing, vivid; CONCEPTS 537,548 —*Ant.* unexciting, uninteresting

jumble [*n*] *hodgepodge* assortment, chaos, clutter, confusion, derangement, disarrangement, disarray, disorder, farrago, gallimaufry, garbage, goulash, hash*, litter, medley, mélange, mess, miscellany, mishmash, mixture, muddle, olio, pastiche, patchwork, potpourri, salmagundi, scramble, shuffle, snarl, tangle, tumble; CONCEPT 432 —*Ant.* order, organization

jumble [*v*] *mix up, confuse* clutter, confound, derange, disarrange, disarray, dishevel, disorder, disorganize, disturb, entangle, foul up, mess up, mistake, muddle, rummage, shuffle, snarl, tangle, tumble; CONCEPTS 16,84 —*Ant.* arrange, clear up, order, organize

jumbled [*adj*] *confused, mixed-up* blurred, chaotic, cluttered, disarranged, disordered, disorderly, disorganized, in disarray, messy, misunderstood, out of order, scrambled, tangled, unsettled, unsorted, untidy; CONCEPT 585

jumbo [*adj*] *gigantic* colossal, cyclopean, elephantine, giant, huge, immense, large, mammoth, mighty, oversized, prodigious; CONCEPT 781 —*Ant.* little, mini, miniature, small, tiny

jump [*n1*] *leap* bob, bounce, bound, buck, canter, caper, capriole, dance, dive, drop, fall, gambade, gambol, hop, hopping, hurdle, jar, jerk, jolt, leapfrog, leapfrogging, leaping, lurch, nosedive, plummet, plunge, pounce, rise, saltation, shock, skip, skipping, spring, start, swerve, twitch, upspring, upsurge, vault, wrench; CONCEPT 194

jump [n2] *increase, advantage* advance, ascent, augmentation, boost, handicap, head start, increment, inflation, rise, spurt, start, upper hand, upsurge, upturn; CONCEPTS 704,763 —*Ant.* decline, decrease, disadvantage

jump [n3] *obstacle* bar, barricade, barrier, fence, hurdle, impediment, rail, stretch; CONCEPTS 470,674 —*Ant.* opening

jump [v1] *leap, spring* bail out, barge, bob, bounce, bound, buck, canter, caper, clear, curvet, dive, drop, fall, gambol, hop, hurdle, hurtle, jerk, jiggle, jounce, lollop, lop, lunge, lurch, parachute, plummet, pop, quiver, rattle, ricochet, saltate, shake, skip, sky, somersault, surge, take, top, trip, vault, waver, wobble; CONCEPT 194

jump [v2] *recoil* bob, bolt, bounce, carom, flinch, jerk, jounce, rebound, ricochet, spring, start, startle, wince; CONCEPT 213

jump [v3] *omit, avoid* abandon, cancel, clear out, cover, cross out, digress, evade, leave, miss, nullify, overshoot, pass over, skip, switch; CONCEPT 25 —*Ant.* address, face

jump [v4] *increase* advance, ascend, boost, escalate, gain, hike, jack up, mount, put up, raise, rise, surge, up; CONCEPTS 236,245,763 —*Ant.* decline, decrease

jumpy [adj] *nervous* agitated, antsy*, anxious, apprehensive, creepy*, excitable, excited, fidgety, frisky, high-strung*, jittery, on edge*, on pins and needles*, restless, sensitive, shaky, skittish, spooked, tense, timorous, unrestful; CONCEPTS 401,690 —*Ant.* calm, collected, composed, easy-going, laid-back

junction/juncture [n1] *link, connection* alliance, annexation, articulation, assemblage, attachment, bond, coalition, coherence, collocation, combination, combine, concatenation, concourse, concursion, confluence, conjugation, consolidation, convergence, coupling, crossing, crossroads, dovetail, elbow, gathering, gore, hinge, hookup, interface, intersection, joining, joint, knee, linking, meeting, miter, mortise, node, pivot, plug-in, reunion, seam, splice, terminal, tie-in, tie-up, union, weld; CONCEPTS 746,830

juncture [n2] *turning point* choice, circumstance, condition, contingency, crisis, crossroad, crux, emergency, exigency, instant, meeting point, moment, occasion, pass, pinch, plight, point, position, posture, predicament, quandary, state, status, strait, time, zero hour*; CONCEPTS 388,693,815

jungle [n] *wilderness full of plant and animal life* boscage, bush, chaparral, forest, labyrinth, maze, morass, primeval forest, tangle, undergrowth, wasteland, web, wood, zoo; CONCEPT 517

junior [adj] *subordinate, younger* inferior, lesser, lower, minor, second, secondary, second-string*; CONCEPTS 574,578,797 —*Ant.* elder, older, senior

junk [n] *odds and ends; garbage* clutter, collateral, debris, filth, hogwash*, litter, miscellany,

offal, refuse, rubbish, rubble, rummage, salvage, scrap, trash, waste; CONCEPTS 260,432

jurisdiction [n] *area of authority* administration, arbitration, area, authority, bailiwick, bounds, circuit, command, commission, compass, confines, control, discretion, district, domination, dominion, empire, extent, field, hegemony, influence, inquisition, judicature, limits, magistracy, might, orbit, power, prerogative, province, purview, range, reach, reign, right, rule, say, scope, slot, sovereignty, sphere, stomping grounds*, supervision, sway, territory, turf*, zone; CONCEPTS 198,376,651

jurist [n] *jurisprudent* attorney, barrister, counsel, counsellor, counselor, defender, judge, justice, lawyer, legal adviser, legal expert, legal scholar, magistrate; CONCEPT 355

jury [n] *panel that hears legal matter* board, judges, peers, tribunal; CONCEPTS 299,318

just [adj1] *fair, impartial* aloof, blameless, condign, conscientious, decent, dependable, dispassionate, due, equal, equitable, ethical, evenhanded, fair-minded, good, honest, honorable, lawful, nondiscriminatory, nonpartisan, objective, pure, reliable, right, righteous, rightful, rigid, scrupulous, strict, tried, true, trustworthy, unbiased, uncolored, upright, virtuous; CONCEPTS 319,545 —*Ant.* inequitable, partial, unfair, unjust

just [adj2] *accurate, precise* cogent, correct, exact, faithful, good, justified, normal, proper, regular, right, sound, strict, true, undistorted, veracious, veridical, well-founded, well-grounded; CONCEPTS 535,582 —*Ant.* imprecise, inaccurate, unjust, unjustified, wrong

just [adj3] *suitable, appropriate* apt, befitting, condign, deserved, due, felicitous, fit, fitting, happy, justified, legitimate, meet, merited, proper, reasonable, requisite, right, rightful, well-deserved; CONCEPT 558 —*Ant.* inappropriate, unfitting, unjust, unsuitable, unsuited

just [adv1] *definitely* absolutely, accurately, completely, directly, entirely, exactly, expressly, perfectly, precisely, right, sharp, smack-dab*, square, squarely, unmistakably; CONCEPT 535 —*Ant.* indefinitely

just [adv2] *only now* almost, a moment ago, approximately, at this moment, barely, by very little, hardly, this a while ago, just now, lately, nearly, now, presently, recently, right now, scarce, scarcely; CONCEPTS 544,820

just [adv3] *merely* at most, but, no more than, nothing but, only, plainly, simply, solely; CONCEPT 557

just about [adv] *almost* about, all but, approximately, around, as good as, close to, nearly, nigh, not quite, practically, well-nigh; CONCEPTS 762,771,799

justice [n1] *lawfulness, fairness* amends, appeal, authority, authorization, charter, code, compensation, consideration, constitutionality, correction, credo, creed, decree, due process, equity, evenness, fair play, fair treatment, hearing, honesty, impartiality, integrity, judicatory, judicature, justness, law, legality, legalization, legal process, legitimacy, litigation, penalty, reasonableness, recompense, rectitude, redress, reparation, review, right, rule, sanction, sentence, square deal*, truth; CONCEPTS 376,

645,691 —*Ant.* illegality, injustice, lawlessness, partiality, unethicalness, unfairness

justice [*n2*] *person who oversees court of law* chancellor, court, judge, magistrate, umpire*; CONCEPT 354

justifiable [*adj*] *reasonable, well-founded* acceptable, admissible, allowable, condonable, defensible, excusable, fair, fit, forgivable, lawful, legit*, legitimate, licit, logical, pardonable, probable, proper, reasonable, remissible, right, rightful, sound, suitable, tenable, understandable, valid, vindicable, warrantable; CONCEPTS 545,558 —*Ant.* unjustifiable, unreasonable, unwarranted

justification [*n*] *reason, excuse* absolution, account, acquittal, advocacy, answer, apologia, apology, approval, argument, basis, confirmation, defense, exculpation, exoneration, explanation, extenuation, grounds, idea, mitigation, palliation, palliative, plea, pretext, raison d'être, rationale, rationalization, rebuttal, redemption, reply, response, salvation, sanctification, song and dance*, story, support, validation, vindication, warrant, whatfor*, wherefore*, whitewashing*, whole idea*, why and wherefore*; CONCEPT 661

justify [*v*] *legitimize, substantiate* absolve, acquit, advocate, alibi*, answer for, apologize for, approve, argue for, assert, be answerable for, bear out, brief, claim, clear, condone, confirm, contend, cop a plea*, countenance, crawl, defend, do justice to, establish, exculpate, excuse, exonerate, explain, favor, legalize, maintain, make allowances, make good*, palliate, pardon, plead, rationalize, rebut, show cause, speak in favor, square, stand up for, support, sustain, uphold, validate, verify, vindicate, warrant; CONCEPTS 49,57

justly [*adv*] *fairly* accurately, befittingly, beneficently, benevolently, benignly, candidly, charitably, correctly, decently, decorously, duly, duteously, dutifully, equally, equitably, evenhandedly, fitly, fittingly, frankly, helpfully, honestly, honorably, impartially, lawfully, legally, legitimately, moderately, nicely, piously, properly, reasonably, respectably, righteously, rightfully, rightly, straightforwardly, temperately, tolerantly, unreservedly, uprightly, virtuously, well; CONCEPTS 544,545 —*Ant.* unfairly, unjustly

jut [*v*] *extend* beetle, bulge, elongate, impend, lengthen, overhang, poke, pop, pouch, project, protrude, protuberate, stand out, stick out; CONCEPT 201 —*Ant.* indent, recede

juvenile [*adj*] *childish* adolescent, babyish, beardless, blooming, boyish, budding, callow, childlike, developing, formative, fresh, girlish, green, growing, immature, inexperienced, infant, infantile, jejune, junior, kid stuff*, milk-fed*, naive, pubescent, puerile, teenage, tender, undeveloped, unfledged, unripe, unsophisticated, unweaned, vernal, young, younger, youthful; CONCEPTS 401,578,797 —*Ant.* adult, grown-up, mature

juvenile [*n*] *young person* adolescent, boy, child, girl, infant, kid*, minor, youngster, youth; CONCEPT 424 —*Ant.* adult

juvenile delinquent [*n*] *hooligan, punk* criminal, first offender, gangster, goon*, hood,

hoodlum, punk, rowdy, ruffian, thug, troublemaker; CONCEPT 412

juxtapose [*v*] *place side by side* appose, bring near, bring together, connect, pair, place in proximity, set side by side; CONCEPTS 85, 113,160

K

kaleidoscopic [*adj*] *multicolored* many-colored, motley, multicolor, particolored, polychromatic, prismatic, psychedelic, rainbow, varicolored, variegated; CONCEPT 618 —*Ant.* monochrome

kaput [*adj*] *ruined, wrecked* all washed up*, belly-up*, burned out, cooked*, dead*, destroyed, done for, down and out, down for the count*, down the drain*, down the tubes*, finished, floored, had it, nonfunctioning, on the skids*, out of business, out of circulation, sunk, totaled, washed up, wiped out; CONCEPT 252

keel over [*v*] *fall, faint* black out, capsize, collapse, drop, founder, go down, overturn, pass out, pitch, plunge, slump, swoon, topple, tumble, upset; CONCEPTS 152,181 —*Ant.* stand, straighten

keen [*adj1*] *enthusiastic* agog, alert, animate, animated, anxious, appetent, ardent, athirst, avid, breathless, devoted, dying to*, eager, earnest, ebullient, fervent, fervid, fierce, fond of, gung ho*, impassioned, impatient, intense, intent, interested, lively, perfervid, spirited, sprightly, thirsty, vehement, vivacious, warm, zealous; CONCEPTS 401,403 —*Ant.* reluctant, unenthusiastic, uninterested

keen [*adj2*] *sharp, piercing* acid, acute, caustic, cutting, edged, extreme, fine, honed, incisive, intense, observant, penetrating, perceptive, pointed, quick-witted, razor-sharp*, sardonic, satirical, strong, tart, trenchant, unblunted; CONCEPT 267 —*Ant.* blunt, dull, obtuse, pointless

keen [*adj3*] *intelligent* astute, bright, brilliant, canny, clever, discerning, discriminating, Einstein*, nobody's fool*, perceptive, perspicacious, quick, sagacious, sapient, sensitive, sharp, sharp as a tack*, shrewd, whiz, wise; CONCEPT 402 —*Ant.* idiotic, ignorant, obtuse, stupid

keep [*v1*] *hold, maintain* accumulate, amass, cache, care for, carry, conduct, conserve, control, deal in, deposit, detain, direct, enjoy, garner, grasp, grip, have, heap, hold back, manage, own, pile, place, possess, preserve, put, put up, reserve, retain, save, season, stack, stock, store, trade in, withhold; CONCEPT 710 —*Ant.* consume, disperse, give, give up, hand over, let go, release

keep [*v2*] *tend; provide for* administer, attend, board, care for, carry on, command, conduct, continue, defend, direct, endure, feed, foster, guard, look after, maintain, manage, mind, minister to, nourish, nurture, operate, ordain, protect, provision, run, safeguard, shelter, shield, subsidize, support, sustain, victual, watch over; CONCEPTS 110,140 —*Ant.* abandon, ignore, neglect

keep [*v3*] *prevent* arrest, avert, block, check, constrain, control, curb, delay, detain, deter, hamper, hamstring, hinder, hold back, impede, inhibit, limit, obstruct, restrain, retard, shackle, stall, stop, withhold; CONCEPT *121 —Ant.* let go, let happen

keep [*v4*] *commemorate; pay attention to* adhere to, bless, celebrate, comply with, consecrate, fulfill, hold, honor, laud, obey, observe, perform, praise, regard, respect, ritualize, sanctify, solemnize; CONCEPT *377 —Ant.* dishonor, ignore

keep at [*v*] *continue, endure* be steadfast, carry on, complete, drudge, finish, grind, labor, last, maintain, persevere, persist, remain, slave, stay, stick, toil; CONCEPTS *23,87 —Ant.* discontinue, give in, give up

keeper [*n*] *guardian* archivist, attendant, caretaker, conservator, curator, custodian, defender, guard, jailer, lookout, overseer, protector, sentinel, sentry, steward, superintendent, supervisor, warden; CONCEPTS *414,423*

keep one's cool [*v*] *remain calm* control one's temper, go with the flow*, keep calm, keep cool*, keep one's shirt on*, restrain oneself; CONCEPTS *121,130,191*

keepsake [*n*] *something precious* emblem, favor, memento, memorial, relic, remembrance, reminder, souvenir, symbol, token, trophy; CONCEPT *446*

keep up [*v*] *maintain, sustain* balance, compete, contend, continue, emulate, go on, hold on, keep pace, keep step, match, pace, persevere, preserve, rival, run with, vie; CONCEPTS *23,87,363 —Ant.* let go, neglect

keg [*n*] *barrel* butt, cask, container, drum, firkin, hogshead, pipe, tub, tun, vat; CONCEPT *494*

ken [*n*] *perception* acumen, apprehending, apprehension, attention, attitude, awareness, cognizance, comprehension, concept, consciousness, grasp, idea, impression, insight, judgment, knowledge, light, notion, picture, realizing, recognition, sense, sight, understanding, vision; CONCEPTS *409,410,689*

kernel [*n*] *seed, essence* atom, bit, center, core, crux, fruit, germ, gist, grain, heart, hub, keynote, marrow, matter, meat, morsel, nub, nubbin, nut, part, piece, pith, root, substance, upshot; CONCEPTS *668,826*

kettle [*n*] *metal pot* boiler, cauldron, pot, steamer, teakettle, vat, vessel; CONCEPT *494*

key [*adj*] *essential, important* basic, chief, crucial, decisive, fundamental, indispensable, leading, main, major, material, pivotal, primary, principal, vital; CONCEPT *568 —Ant.* inessential, insignificant, nonessential, unimportant

key [*n1*] *item that unlocks* latchkey, opener, passkey, screw*, skeleton; CONCEPT *499 —Ant.* lock

key [*n2*] *answer, solution* blueprint, brand, cipher, clue, code, core, crux, cue, earmark, explanation, fulcrum, guide, hinge, index, indicator, interpretation, lead, lever, marker, means, nexus, nucleus, passport, password, pivot, pointer, root, sign, symptom, ticket, translation; CONCEPTS *274,668 —Ant.* question

keynote/keystone [*n*] *essence, theme* basic idea, basis, center, core, cornerstone, criterion, crux, gist, heart, idea, kernel, linchpin, mainspring, marrow, measure, motive, nub, pith, principle, root, source, spring, standard, substance;CONCEPTS *532,661,688*

kibosh [*n*] *stop* cancellation, check, curb, end, halt, veto; CONCEPT *119*

kick [*n1*] *thrill, enjoyment* bang*, buzz*, excitement, fun, gratification, hoot*, joy, pleasure, refreshment, sensation, stimulation, wallop*; CONCEPTS *388,410 —Ant.* boredom

kick [*n2*] *power, strength* backlash, blow, boot*, force, intensity, jar, jolt, pep, punch, pungency, snap, sparkle, tang, verve, vitality, zest, zing*; CONCEPTS *641,732 —Ant.* dullness, powerlessness, tastelessness, weakness

kick [*v1*] *hit with foot* boot, calcitrate, dropkick, give the foot, jolt, punt; CONCEPT *189*

kick [*v2*] *complain* anathematize, carp, combat, condemn, criticize, curse, damn, except, execrate, expostulate, fight, fuss, gripe, grumble, inveigh, mumble, object, oppose, protest, rebel, remonstrate, repine, resist, spurn, wail, whine, withstand; CONCEPT *52 —Ant.* compliment, praise

kick [*v3*] *quit a habit* abandon, desist, give up, go cold turkey*, leave off, stop; CONCEPT *234 —Ant.* take up

kickback [*n*] *bribe* cut, gift, graft, money under the table*, oil*, payment, payoff, payola, percentage, recompense, reward, share; CONCEPTS *192,344*

kick back [*v*] *relax* breathe easy*, calm down*, catch one's breath, chill out*, collect oneself, compose oneself, cool off*, feel at home, hang loose*, lie down, loosen up, make oneself at home*, mellow out*, put one's feet up*, recline, rest, settle back, sit around, sit back, take a break*, take a breather*, take a load off*, take it easy*, take ten*, unwind, wind down; CONCEPT *210*

kick in [*v*] *contribute* ante up, chip in, commit, dish out*, dole out*, donate, fork over*, furnish, give, hand out, hand over, pitch in*, pony up*, provide; CONCEPTS *108,140*

kick out [*v*] *get rid of* ax, boot*, bounce*, can*, cashier*, chase, chuck, discharge, dismiss, drop, eject, evict, expel, extrude, fire, oust, out, reject, remove, sack*, throw out, toss out; CONCEPTS *180,351,384 —Ant.* allow, hold, keep

kid [*n*] *young person* baby, bairn, boy, child, daughter, girl, infant, juvenile, lad, lass, little one*, son, teenager, tot, youngster, youth; CONCEPTS *414,424 —Ant.* adult

kid [*v*] *fool, ridicule* bamboozle*, banter, beguile, bother, cozen, delude, dupe, flimflam*, fun*, gull, hoax, hoodwink, jape, jest, joke, jolly, josh, make fun of, make sport of, mock, pretend, rag*, razz, rib, roast, spoof, tease, trick; CONCEPTS *59,273 —Ant.* be serious

kid around [*v*] *tease* annoy, badger, bait, banter, bother, chaff, disturb, dog*, fool around, give a hard time*, goad, harass, josh, lead on*, mock, needle*, nudge, pester, pick on*, rag*, razz*, rib*, ride, ridicule, roast*, taunt; CONCEPTS *7,11,19,22*

kidnap [*v*] *abduct; hold for ransom* body snatch*, bundle off, capture, carry away, carry off, coax, decoy, entice, grab, hijack, impress, inveigh, lay hands on, lure, make off with*, pirate, remove, run away with, seduce, seize, shanghai*, skyjack, snatch, spirit away*, steal, waylay; CONCEPTS *90,139*

kill [*v1*] *deprive of existence; destroy* annihilate,

asphyxiate, assassinate, crucify, dispatch, do away with*, do in*, drown, dump, electrocute, eradicate, erase*, execute, exterminate, extirpate, finish, garrote, get*, guillotine, hang, hit*, immolate, liquidate, lynch, massacre, murder, neutralize, obliterate, off*, poison, polish off*, put away*, put to death, rub out*, sacrifice, slaughter, slay, smother, snuff, strangle, suffocate, waste*, wipe out*, X-out*, zap*; CONCEPT 252 —*Ant.* bear, create, give birth

kill [v2] *turn off; cancel* annul, cease, counteract, deaden, defeat, extinguish, forbid, halt, negative, neutralize, nix*, nullify, prohibit, quash, quell, recant, refuse, revoke, ruin, scotch*, shut off, smother, stifle, still, stop, suppress, turn out, veto; CONCEPTS 121,239 —*Ant.* begin, initiate, start, turn on

killer [n] *murderer* assassin, butcher, cut-throat, executioner, exterminator, gunman/woman, gunperson, hit-man/woman, hit person, hunter, slayer, soldier; CONCEPT 412

killing [n] *murder* assassination, bloodshed, bumping off*, capital punishment, carnage, execution, extermination, homicide, manslaughter, massacre, slaughter, slaying; CONCEPTS 192,252

killjoy [n] *spoilsport* complainer, dampener, doomsdayer, grinch*, grouch*, moaner, partypooper, pessimist, prophet of doom*, stick in the mud*, wet blanket*, whiner; CONCEPT 412

kin [n] *blood relative* affinity, blood, clan, connection, consanguinity, cousin, extraction, family, folk, house, kindred, kinsfolk, kinship, kinsperson, kith, lineage, member, people, race, relation, relationship, sibling, stock, tribe; CONCEPTS 296,414,421

kind [adj] *generous, good* affectionate, all heart*, altruistic, amiable, amicable, beneficent, benevolent, benign, big, bleeding-heart*, bounteous, charitable, clement, compassionate, congenial, considerate, cordial, courteous, eleemosynary, friendly, gentle, good-hearted, gracious, heart in right place*, humane, humanitarian, indulgent, kindhearted, kindly, lenient, loving, mild, neighborly, obliging, philanthropic, propitious, softhearted, soft touch*, sympathetic, tenderhearted, thoughtful, tolerant, understanding; CONCEPTS 401,404,542 —*Ant.* bad, bitter, cruel, inconsiderate, mean, unfriendly, ungenerous, unkind

kind [n1] *class, species* brand, breed, classification, family, genus, ilk, kin, order, race, set, sort, type, variety; CONCEPT 378

kind [n2] *type, character* breed, complexion, connection, denomination, description, designation, essence, fiber, gender, habit, ilk, likes, lot, manner, mold, nature, number, persuasion, set, sort, stamp, stripe, style, temperament, tendency, tribe, variety, way; CONCEPTS 411,673

kindhearted [adj] *compassionate, helpful* altruistic, amiable, amicable, considerate, generous, good, good-natured, gracious, humane, kind, merciful, responsive, softhearted, sympathetic, tender, tenderhearted, warm, warmhearted; CONCEPTS 404,542 —*Ant.* nasty, uncompassionate, unsympathetic

kindle [v1] *start a fire* blaze, burn, fire, flame, flare, glow, ignite, inflame, light, set alight, set fire; CONCEPT 249 —*Ant.* extinguish, put out

kindle [v2] *excite, incite* agitate, animate, arouse, awaken, bestir, burn up*, challenge, egg on*, enkindle, exasperate, fire up*, foment, get smoking*, induce, inflame, inspire, key up*, provoke, rally, rouse, sharpen, stimulate, stir, thrill, turn on*, wake, waken, whet, work up*; CONCEPTS 7,14,22,221 —*Ant.* disenchant, turn off

kindly [adj] *compassionate, helpful* attentive, beneficial, benevolent, benign, benignant, cool, cordial, favorable, friendly, generous, genial, gentle, good, good-hearted, good-natured, gracious, hearty, humane, kind, kindhearted, mellow, merciful, mild, neighborly, pleasant, polite, sociable, sympathetic, thoughtful, warm; CONCEPTS 404,542 —*Ant.* disagreeable, inconsiderate, unkindly, unsympathetic

kindly [adv] *with compassion* affectionately, agreeably, benevolently, benignly, carefully, charitably, compassionately, considerately, cordially, courteously, delicately, generously, genially, good-naturedly, graciously, heedfully, helpfully, humanely, politely, solicitously, sympathetically, tenderly, thoughtfully, tolerantly, understandingly, well; CONCEPTS 542, 544 —*Ant.* disagreeably, inconsiderately, unkindly

kindness [n1] *compassion, generosity* affection, altruism, amiability, beneficence, benevolence, charity, clemency, consideration, cordiality, courtesy, decency, delicacy, fellow feeling, forbearance, gentleness, good intention, goodness, good will, grace, graciousness, heart, helpfulness, hospitality, humanity, indulgence, kindliness, magnanimity, mildness, patience, philanthropy, serviceability, solicitousness, solicitude, sweetness, sympathy, tact, tenderness, thoughtfulness, tolerance, understanding, unselfishness; CONCEPTS 633,657 —*Ant.* cruelty, harshness, meanness

kindness [n2] *helping act; service* accommodation, aid, alms, assistance, benediction, benefaction, benevolence, benison, blessing, boon, boost, bounty, charity, dispensation, favor, generosity, good deed, good turn, help, indulgence, lift, mercy, philanthropy, relief, succor; CONCEPTS 110,657 —*Ant.* barbarousness, cruelty

kindred [adj] *corresponding, matching* affiliated, agnate, akin, alike, allied, analogous, cognate, congeneric, congenial, connate, connatural, consanguine, germane, homogeneous, incident, kin, likable, parallel, related, similar; CONCEPT 563 —*Ant.* irrelevant, noncorresponding, unaffiliated

kindred [n] *blood relative* affinity, blood, clan, connection, consanguinity, cousin, family, flesh, folk, homefolk, house, kin, kinsfolk, kinsperson, lineage, race, relation, relationship, stock, tribe; CONCEPTS 296,414,421

kingdom [n] *historically, an area ruled by a monarch* commonwealth, country, county, crown, division, domain, dominion, dynasty, empire, field, lands, monarchy, nation, possessions, principality, province, realm, reign, rule, scepter, sovereignty, sphere, state, suzerainty, sway, territory, throne, tract; CONCEPTS 508,510

kink [n1] *bend, twist* coil, corkscrew, crimp,

crinkle, curl, curve, entanglement, frizz, knot, loop, tangle, wrinkle; CONCEPT 436 —*Ant.* line

kink [n2] *spasm of muscular tissue* charley horse*, cramp, crick, knot, muscle spasm, pain, pang, pinch, stab, stitch, tweak, twinge; CONCEPTS 185,728

kink [n3] *complication* defect, difficulty, flaw, hitch, impediment, imperfection, knot, tangle; CONCEPT 674 —*Ant.* easiness, simplicity

kink [n4] *person's idiosyncrasy* eccentricity, fetish, foible, notion, peculiarity, quirk, singularity, vagary, whim; CONCEPT 411 —*Ant.* normalcy

kinky [adj1] *twisted* coiled, crimped, curled, curly, frizzled, frizzy, knotted, matted, matty, rolled, tangled; CONCEPT 486 —*Ant.* straight, unkinked, untwisted

kinky [adj2] *bizarre, perverted* degenerated, depraved, deviant, eccentric, far-out, licentious, odd, outlandish, outre, peculiar, queer, quirky, sick, strange, unconventional, unnatural, unusual, warped, weird; CONCEPTS 372,542,589 —*Ant.* clean, decent, ethical, normal, unperverted, usual

kinship [n] *family relationship* affinity, blood, clan, family, flesh, folk, kin, kindred, lineage, relations, tribe; CONCEPTS 296,414,421

kiosk [n] *gazebo* bandstand, booth, rotunda, stall, stand; CONCEPTS 442,443

kismet [n] *fate, fortune* chance, destination, destiny, divine will*, doom, handwriting on the wall*, horoscope, karma, Lady Luck*, lot, luck, portion, predestination, providence; CONCEPT 679

kiss [n] *touching lips to another* butterfly*, caress, embrace, endearment, osculation, peck, salutation, salute, smack*, smooch*; CONCEPTS 185,375

kiss [v] *touch one's lips to another's* blow, brush, butterfly*, French*, glance, graze, greet, lip*, make out*, mush*, neck*, osculate, peck, pucker up*, salute, smack*, smooch*; CONCEPTS 185,375

kit [n] *provisions, equipment* accoutrements, apparatus, assortment, bag, collection, container, effects, gear, impedimenta, implements, material, outfit, pack, paraphernalia, rig, satchel, selection, set, stock, stuff, suitcase, supplies, tackle, things, tools, trappings, utensils; CONCEPTS 494,496

kitchen [n] *room for cooking food* canteen, cookery, cookhouse, cook's room, cuisine, eat-in, gallery, galley, kitchenette, mess, scullery; CONCEPT 448

kittenish [adj] *frisky, playful* childish, coquettish, coy, elvish, flirtatious, frolicsome, fun-loving, impish, jaunty, mischievous, sportive; CONCEPT 401 —*Ant.* lethargic, stiff, unplayful

klutz [n] *clumsy person* bungler, butterfingers*, dolt, dullard, lummox, oaf; CONCEPT 412

knack [n] *ability, talent* adroitness, aptitude, aptness, bent, capacity, command, dexterity, expertise, expertism, expertness, facility, faculty, flair, forte, genius, gift, handiness, hang of it*, head*, ingenuity, know-how, mastership, nose*, propensity, quickness, readiness, savvy*, set, skill, skillfulness, trick, turn; CONCEPTS 409,630 —*Ant.* inability, ineptitude, lack, want

knapsack [n] *backpack* carryall, duffel bag, haversack, kit bag, pack, rucksack, satchel; CONCEPT 446

knead [v] *mix by pressing* aerate, alter, blend, form, manipulate, massage, mold, ply, press, push, rub, shape, squeeze, stroke, twist, work; CONCEPTS 170,208

kneel [v] *get down on one's knees* bow, bow down, curtsey, do obeisance, genuflect, kowtow, prostrate oneself, stoop; CONCEPT 154

knickknack [n] *trinket; decorative piece* bagatelle, bauble, bibelot, bric-a-brac, conversation piece, curio, curiosity, device, embellishment, flummery, frill, furbelow, gadget*, miniature, notion, novelty, objet d'art, ornament, plaything*, showpiece, souvenir, thingamajig*, toy, trapping, trifle, whatnot*, whimsy; CONCEPTS 259,260,446

knife [n] *cutting tool* bayonet, blade, bolo, cutlass, cutter, cutting edge, dagger, edge, lance, lancet, machete, point, ripper, sabre, scalpel, scimitar, scythe, shank, shiv, sickle, skewer, skiver, steel, stiletto, switchblade, sword, tickler; CONCEPTS 495,499

knife [v] *stab with pointed tool* brand, carve, chop down, clip, cut, hurt, impale, jag, kill, lacerate, lance, open up, pierce, shank, shiv, slash, slice, spit, stick, thrust, wound; CONCEPTS 176,220,246

knit [v] *intertwine* affiliate, affix, ally, bind, cable, connect, contract, crochet, fasten, heal, interlace, intermingle, join, link, loop, mend, net, purl, repair, secure, sew, spin, tie, unite, weave, web; CONCEPTS 113,202,218 —*Ant.* unknit

knob [n] *lump, handle* bulge, bulk, bump, bunch, doorknob, hump, knot, knurl, latch, lever, nub, opener, projection, protrusion, protuberance, snag, stud, swell, swelling, trigger, tumor; CONCEPTS 445,471

knock [n1] *pushing, striking* beating, blow, box, clip, conk, cuff, hammering, hit, injury, lick, rap, slap, smack, swat, swipe, thump, whack; CONCEPT 189

knock [n2] *strong criticism* blame, censure, condemnation, defeat, failure, flak, pan, rap, rebuff, rejection, reversal, setback, stricture, swipe; CONCEPTS 52,278 —*Ant.* compliment, praise

knock [v1] *push over; strike* abuse, bash, batter, beat, beat up, bob, bruise, buffet, clap, clout, cuff, damage, deck, drub*, fell, flatten, floor, hit, hurt, KO*, level, maltreat, manhandle, maul, mistreat, pound, punch, rap, roughhouse, slap, smack, tap, thrash, thump, thwack*, total, wallop, whack*, wound; CONCEPT 189

knock [v2] *criticize harshly* abuse, alive*, belittle, blame, carp, cavil, censure, condemn, denounce, denunciate, deprecate, disparage, find fault, lambaste, reprehend, reprobate, run down*, skin*, slam; CONCEPT 52 —*Ant.* compliment, praise

knock about/knock around [v] *roam, wander* drift, ramble, range, rove, traipse, travel, walk; CONCEPTS 151,224 —*Ant.* stay, wait

knock off [v1] *kill* assassinate, do away with*, do in*, dust*, eliminate, execute, finish, liquidate, murder, rub out*, shoot, slay, stab, waste; CONCEPT 252 —*Ant.* bear, create

knock off [v2] *steal* filch, knock over, loot, pilfer, pinch, plunder, purloin, ransack, relieve, rifle, rip off*, rob, thieve; CONCEPTS *139,192* —*Ant.* give

knock off [v3] *stop action; accomplish* achieve, cease, complete, conclude, desist, discontinue, eliminate, finish, give over, halt, leave off, quit, stop work, succeed, surcease, terminate; CONCEPT *119* —*Ant.* continue, pursue, start

knoll [n] *small hill* acclivity, ascent, bluff, butte, cliff, drift, dune, elevation, esker, headland, heap, highland, hillock, hilltop, hummock, inclination, incline, knoll, mesa, mound, mount, precipice, prominence, promontory, ridge, rise, slope, summit; CONCEPT *509*

knot [n1] *bow, loop* bond, braid, bunch, coil, connection, contortion, entanglement, gnarl, helix, hitch, joint, kink, ligament, ligature, link, mat, nexus, perplexity, rosette, screw, snag, snarl, spiral, splice, tangle, tie, twirl, twist, vinculum, warp, whirl, whorl, yoke; CONCEPTS *436,471* —*Ant.* line

knot [n2] *lump; crowd* aggregation, assemblage, assortment, band, bunch, circle, clique, clump, cluster, collection, company, crew, gang, gathering, group, heap, mass, mob, pack, pile, set, squad, swarm, tuft; CONCEPT *432*

knot [v] *weave, complicate* bind, cord, entangle, knit, loop, secure, tat, tether, tie; CONCEPTS *85,113,160* —*Ant.* unknot

knotty [adj] *troublesome* baffling, complex, complicated, difficult, effortful, elaborate, formidable, Gordian*, hard, intricate, involved, labyrinthine, mazy, mystifying, perplexing, problematical, puzzling, ramified, reticular, rough, rugged, sophisticated, sticky*, terrible, thorny*, tough, tricky, uphill*; CONCEPTS *529,565* —*Ant.* simple, uncomplicated, untroublesome

know [v1] *understand information* apperceive, appreciate, apprehend, be acquainted, be cognizant, be conversant in, be informed, be learned, be master of, be read, be schooled, be versed, cognize, comprehend, differentiate, discern, discriminate, distinguish, experience, fathom, feel certain, get the idea*, grasp, have, have down pat*, have information, have knowledge of, keep up on, ken, learn, notice, on top of*, perceive, prize, realize, recognize, see, undergo; CONCEPTS *15,38* —*Ant.* misinterpret, misunderstand

know [v2] *be familiar with* associate, be acquainted with, be friends with, experience, feel, fraternize, get acquainted, have dealings with, identify, savor, see, sustain, taste, undergo; CONCEPT *384* —*Ant.* be ignorant, forget

know-how [n] *skill, talent* ability, adroitness, aptitude, art, background, capability, command, craft, cunning, dexterity, experience, expertise, expertness, faculty, flair, ingenuity, knack, knowledge, proficiency, savoir-faire, wisdom; CONCEPTS *409,630* —*Ant.* ignorance, lack, want

knowing [adj] *experienced, aware* alive, apprehensive, astute, awake, brainy, bright, brilliant, canny, clever, cognizant, competent, conscious, conversant, cool*, crack*, deliberate, discerning, expert, insightful, intelligent, intended, intentional, judicious, knowledgeable, observant, perceptive, percipient, qualified, quick,

quick-witted, sagacious, sage, sensible, sentient, sharp, skillful, slick*, smart, sophic, sophisticated, tuned-in, vigilant, watchful, well-informed, wise, with-it, witting, worldly, worldly-wise; CONCEPT *402* —*Ant.* inexperienced, unaware, uncognizant, unknowing

know-it-all [n] *intellectual, smart aleck* braggart, brain*, smarty-pants*, walking encyclopedia, windbag, wiseacre, wise guy*; CONCEPTS *412,423*

knowledge [n] *person's understanding; information* ability, accomplishments, acquaintance, apprehension, attainments, awareness, cognition, comprehension, consciousness, dirt*, discernment, doctrine, dogma, dope*, education, enlightenment, erudition, expertise, facts, familiarity, goods*, grasp, inside story*, insight, instruction, intelligence, judgment, know-how*, learning, light*, lore, observation, philosophy, picture, power*, principles, proficiency, recognition, scholarship, schooling, science, scoop*, substance, theory, tuition, wisdom; CONCEPTS *274,409,529* —*Ant.* ignorance

knowledgeable [adj] *aware, educated* abreast, acquainted, alert, appreciative, apprised, au courant, au fait, brainy*, bright, brilliant, clever, cognizant, conscious, conversant, discerning, erudite, experienced, familiar, informed, insightful, intelligent, in the know, knowing, learned, lettered, omniscient, perceptive, plugged in*, posted, prescient, privy, quick-witted, sagacious, sage, savvy, scholarly, sensible, sharp, smart, sophic, sophisticated, tuned-in*, understanding, versed, well-informed, well-rounded, wise, with-it; CONCEPT *402* —*Ant.* ignorant, unaware, uneducated, uninformed

known [adj] *famous, popular* accepted, acknowledged, admitted, avowed, celebrated, certified, common, confessed, conscious, down pat*, established, familiar, hackneyed, manifest, noted, notorious, obvious, patent, plain, proverbial, published, received, recognized, well-known; CONCEPTS *529,567,576* —*Ant.* obscure, unknown

knurled [adj] *knotted* bumpy, coarse, gnarled, knobby, knotty, rough; CONCEPTS *485,606*

kook [n] *eccentric person* crackpot, crank, crazy*, dingbat*, flake*, fruitcake*, lamebrain, lunatic, nut, screwball*, wacko*, weirdo; CONCEPTS *412,423*

kosher [adj1] *ritually proper* apropos, clean, decent, ritually pure, undefiled; CONCEPTS *401,404*

kosher [adj2] *legitimate* acceptable, according to law, authentic, genuine, legal, permissible, permitted, proper; CONCEPTS *319,558,582*

kowtow [v] *grovel* bow, brownnose*, cave in*, court, cower, cringe, fawn, flatter, fold, genuflect, give in, go along with, kneel, knuckle under, lie down and roll over*, pander, prostrate, say uncle*, stoop, toe the mark*; CONCEPT *384*

kudos [n] *praise, acclaim* applause, credit, distinction, eminence, esteem, fame, flattery, glory, honor, illustriousness, laudation, notability, pat on the back*, plaudits, plum*, PR*, preeminence, prestige, prominence, puff*, pumping up*, raves*, regard, renown, repute, strokes*; CONCEPTS *69,268* —*Ant.* blame, criticism

L

label [n] *marker, description; brand* characterization, classification, company, design, epithet, hallmark, identification, insignia, logo, mark, number, price mark, stamp, sticker, tag, tally, ticket, trademark; CONCEPTS 268,270,284

label [v] *mark, describe; brand* call, characterize, class, classify, define, designate, identify, name, specify, stamp, sticker, tag, tally; CONCEPTS 62,79

labor [n1] *work, undertaking* activity, chore, daily grind, diligence, drudgery, effort, employment, endeavor, energy, exercise, exertion, grind*, gruntwork*, industry, job, moonlight*, operation, pains*, pull, push, strain, stress, struggle, sweat, toil, travail; CONCEPTS 87,100,351,360,362 —*Ant.* entertainment, fun

labor [n2] *person(s) performing service* apprentice, blue collar, breadwinner, employee, hack*, hand*, hard hat*, help, helper, hireling, instrument, laborer, learner, operative, prentice, proletariat, rank and file*, toiler, worker, work force, working people; CONCEPTS 325,348 —*Ant.* management, manager

labor [n3] *childbirth process* birth, birth pangs, childbearing, contractions, delivery, giving birth, pains, parturition, throes, travail; CONCEPT 374

labor [v] *work very hard* bear down, cultivate, drive, drudge, endeavor, exert oneself, grind, plod, plug away*, pour it on*, slave, strain, strive, struggle, sweat, tend, toil, travail, work oneself to the bone*; CONCEPTS 87,100 —*Ant.* idle, laze, relax

laboratory [n] *testing room* chemistry laboratory, lab, research laboratory, workshop; CONCEPTS 312,439,441,448,449

labored [adj] *difficult to understand, unclear* affected, arduous, awkward, clumsy, contrived, effortful, forced, hard, heavy, inept, maladroit, operose, overdone, overwrought, ponderous, stiff, strained, strenuous, studied, toilsome, unnatural, uphill*, weighty; CONCEPT 538 —*Ant.* easy, facile, natural, relaxed

laborer [n] *worker* blue-collar worker, drudge, farmhand, grunt, hand, hireling, manual worker, migrant worker, peon, unskilled worker, working man/woman, working stiff*; CONCEPT 348

laborious [adj1] *hard, difficult* arduous, backbreaking, burdensome, effortful, fatiguing, forced, heavy, herculean*, labored, onerous, operose, ponderous, rough go*, stiff, strained, strenuous, tiresome, toilsome, tough, tough job*, wearing, wearisome, wicked*; CONCEPTS 538,565 —*Ant.* easy, effortless, facile, simple, trivial

laborious [adj2] *hardworking* active, assiduous, diligent, indefatigable, industrious, operose, painstaking, persevering, sedulous, tireless, unflagging; CONCEPTS 538,550 —*Ant.* idle, lackadaisical, lazy, reticent

labyrinth [n] *maze, complexity* coil, complication, convolution, entanglement, intricacy, jungle, knot, mesh, morass, perplexity, problem, puzzle, riddle, skein, snarl, tangle, web; CONCEPTS 436,663,666

labyrinthine [adj] *mazelike* complex, convoluted, elaborate, intricate, mazy, meandering, serpentine, sinuous, tangled, tortuous, twisting, wandering, winding, zigzag; CONCEPT 436 —*Ant.* simple, straight, straightforward

lace [n1] *netted material* appliqué, banding, border, crochet, edging, filigree, mesh, net, netting, openwork, ornament, tatting, threadwork, tissue, trim, trimming; CONCEPT 473

lace [n2] *string used to connect* band, cord, rope, shoelace, thong, thread, tie; CONCEPT 475

lace [v] *fasten, intertwine* add, attach, bind, close, do up, fortify, interlace, interweave, mix, plat, spike, strap, thread, tie, twine; CONCEPT 113 —*Ant.* unfasten, unlace, untie, untwine

lacerate [v] *tear, cut; wound* claw, gash, harm, hurt, injure, jag, lance, maim, mangle, mutilate, puncture, rend, rip, score, serrate, slash, stab, torment, torture; CONCEPTS 137,176,214,220, 246

laceration [n] *cut, wound* gash, injury, lesion, pierce, rip, slash, slice, slit, stab, tear; CONCEPT 309

lack [n] *deficiency, need* abridgement, absence, curtailment, dearth, decrease, default, defect, deficit, depletion, deprivation, destitution, distress, exigency, exiguity, inadequacy, inferiority, insufficience, insufficiency, loss, meagerness, miss, necessity, paucity, poverty, privation, reduction, retrenchment, scantiness, scarcity, shortage, shortcoming, shortfall, shortness, shrinkage, shrinking, slightness, stint, want; CONCEPTS 707,709 —*Ant.* abundance, enough, excess, extra, lot, plenty, plethora, profusion, surplus

lack [v] *do not have* be deficient in, be short of, be without, have need of, hurting for*, minus, miss, need, not got*, out, require, too little too late*, want; CONCEPTS 20,646 —*Ant.* have

lackadaisical [adj] *careless, indifferent* abstracted, apathetic, daydreaming, disinterested, dreamy, dull, energyless, enervated, faineant, halfhearted, idle, inattentive, incurious, indolent, inert, laid-back, languid, languishing, languorous, lazy, lethargic, limp, listless, moony*, passive, romantic, sentimental, slothful, spiritless, spring fever*, unconcerned; CONCEPTS 403,542,544 —*Ant.* active, careful, caring, energetic, enthusiastic, hard-working

lackey [n] *servant* attendant, butler, domestic, doormat, drudge, factotum, flunkey, retainer, steward, subordinate, toady, underling, valet, yes-person; CONCEPT 348

lacking [adj] *wanting, deficient* can't cut it*, coming up short*, defective, deprived of, flawed, impaired, inadequate, incomplete, minus, missing, needed, needing, not hacking it*, not making it*, sans, short, without; CONCEPTS 546,771 —*Ant.* abundant, enough, having, profuse, sufficient

lackluster [adj] *dull, lifeless* blah*, blind, boring, colorless, dark, dead, dim, drab, draggy*, dry, flat*, ho-hum*, laid-back*, leaden, lusterless, matte, muted, nothing*, obscure, pabulum*, prosaic, sombre, unimaginative, uninspired, vanilla*, vapid, zero*; CONCEPTS 542,548,617 —*Ant.* bright, enthusiastic, lively, shining, shiny, spirited

laconic [adj] *short, to the point* breviloquent, brief, brusque, compact, compendiary, compendious, concise, crisp, curt, pithy, sententious, short and sweet*, succinct, terse; CONCEPTS 267,773,798 —Ant. long-winded, verbose, wordy

lacquer [n] *coating* covering, finish, glaze, lamination, layer, varnish, veneer; CONCEPT 475

lacy [adj] *delicate, netlike* elegant, fancy, filigree, fine, frilly, gauzy, gossamer, lacelike, meshy, open, ornate, patterned, sheer, thin, transparent; CONCEPT 606 —Ant. heavy, thick

lad [n] *young man* boy, buddy, child, fellow, guy, half-pint*, juvenile, kid*, runt*, schoolboy, son, stripling, youngster, youth; CONCEPTS 419,424 —Ant. man

laden [adj] *loaded down* burdened, charged, encumbered, fraught, full, hampered, oppressed, taxed, weighed down, weighted; CONCEPTS 485,538 —Ant. empty, light, unladen, unloaded

lag [v] *move slowly; delay* be behind, dally, dawdle, decrease, dillydally*, diminish, drag, drag one's feet*, ebb, fail, fall off, falter, flag, get no place fast*, hang back, hobble, idle, inch, inch along*, jelly, limp, linger, loiter, lose strength, lounge, plod, poke, procrastinate, put off, retard, saunter, shuffle, slacken, slouch, slow, slow up, stagger, stay, straggle, tail, tarry, tool, trail, trudge, wane; CONCEPTS 151,153 —Ant. run, rush

laggard [n] *straggler* dawdler, idler, lingerer, loafer, lounger, slowpoke, slow starter; CONCEPT 151

lagoon [n] *shallow body of water* bayou, gulf, marsh, pond, pool, shallows, shoal, tidal pond; CONCEPT 514

laid-back [adj] *relaxed* easygoing, lax, low-pressure, mellow, undemanding, unhurried; CONCEPT 404

lair [n] *hideout, habitat* burrow, cave, den, earth, form, hideaway, hole, nest, pen, refuge, resting place, retreat, sanctuary; CONCEPT 515

laissez-faire [n] *free enterprise, for the most part unrestrained by law* free trade, indifference, individualism, live and let live*, neutrality, nonintervention; CONCEPTS 388,691

lake [n] *inland body of water* basin, creek, inland sea, lagoon, lakelet, loch, mere, millpond, mouth, pond, pool, reservoir, sluice, spring, tarn; CONCEPT 514

lambaste [v] *punish, beat* assail, attack, berate, blister, bludgeon, castigate, censure, criticize, cudgel, denounce, excoriate, flay, flog, hammer, hit, lash into*, pan, pelt, pound, pummel, rake - over the coals*, read the riot act*, rebuke, reprimand, rip into, roast, scathe, scold, scorch, scourge, shellac, slam, slap, slash, smear, smother, strike, thrash, trim, upbraid, wallop, whip; CONCEPTS 52,54,86 —Ant. praise, uphold

lame [adj1] *unable to walk properly* bruised, deformed, disabled, game, gimp, gimpy, halt, handicapped, hobbling, limping, pained, raw, sidelined, sore, stiff; CONCEPTS 314,489 —Ant. able, agile, mobile, uncrippled, walking

lame [adj2] *feeble, weak* faltering, faulty, flabby, flimsy, inadequate, ineffective, inefficient, insufficient, poor, thin, unconvincing, unpersuasive, unpleasing, unsatisfactory, unsuitable; CONCEPTS 558,570 —Ant. able, capable, efficient, satisfactory, strong

lament [v] *to mourn or grieve deeply* bawl,

beat one's breast*, bemoan, bewail, bleed, cry, deplore, eat one's heart out*, howl, hurt, kick self*, moan, rain, regret, repine, rue, sing, sob, sorrow, take it hard*, wail, weep; CONCEPTS 52,54 —Ant. celebrate, compliment, laud, praise

lamentable [adj] *upsetting, miserable* afflictive, awful, bad, calamitous, deplorable, dire, dirty, distressing, doleful, dolorous, god-awful, grievous, grim, heartbreaking, hurting, lousy, low, lugubrious, meager, mean, melancholy, mournful, pitiful, plaintive, poor, regretful, rotten, rueful, sad, sorrowful, stinking, tragic, unfavorable, unfortunate, unsatisfactory, woeful, wretched; CONCEPTS 529,537 —Ant. cheering, fortunate, good, lucky, satisfactory

lament/lamentation [n] *grief, complaint* complaining, dirge, elegy, grieving, jeremiad, keen, keening, lament, moan, moaning, mourning, plaint, requiem, sob, sobbing, sorrow, tears, threnody, ululation, wail, wailing, weeping; CONCEPTS 29,278,410 —Ant. celebration, enjoyment, praise

laminate [v] *cover with veneer* coat, exfoliate, face, flake, foil, foliate, layer, overlayer, plate, separate, split, stratify, veneer; CONCEPT 172 —Ant. strip

lamp [n] *lantern* beacon, flashlight, gas lamp, gaslight, hurricane lamp, kerosene lamp, light, searchlight, torch; CONCEPTS 620,624,628,810

lampoon [n] *parody, satire* burlesque, caricature, invective, pasquil, pasquinade, pastiche, ridicule, roast*, send-up*, skit, squib, takedown, takeoff*; CONCEPTS 263,273

lampoon [v] *ridicule, make fun of* burlesque, caricature, jape, mock, parody, pasquinade, put on*, rail, roast*, satirize, send up*, squib, take off*, travesty; CONCEPT 273 —Ant. applaud, approve, praise, support

lance [v] *pierce* bore, cut, cut into, gash, gore, incise, penetrate, prick, puncture, slash, slice, slit, stab, stick into; CONCEPTS 137,159,176,220

land [n] *earth's surface; ownable property* acreage, acres, area, beach, continent, country, countryside, dirt, district, earth, estate, expanse, extent, farming, farmland, field, ground, grounds, holding, home, homeland, loam, mainland, manor, nation, old sod, parcel, plot, province, purlieu, quarry, quinta, ranch, real estate, realty, region, shore, sod, soil, stretch, sweep, terra firma, terrain, territory, tillage, tract; CONCEPTS 508,509, 510,515 —Ant. sea, sky

land [v1] *arrive, come to rest on* alight, berth, bring in, check in, come ashore, come down, come in, come to berth, debark, descend upon, disembark, ditch, dock, drop anchor, flatten out, get down, ground, level off, light on, make land, pilot, put down, put in, set down, set on deck, settle, sit down, splash down, steer, take down, thump, touch down; CONCEPTS 159,181 —Ant. ascend, take off

land [v2] *achieve, acquire* annex, bring in, gain, get, have, obtain, pick up, procure, secure, win; CONCEPTS 120,706 —Ant. fail, lose

landfill [n] *dump* ash heap*, depot, disposal area, dumping ground, garbage lot, hazardous waste dump, junk pile*, junkyard, recycling station, refuse heap, rubbish pile, toxic waste site, transfer station; CONCEPTS 438,449,680

landing [n] *harbor* anchorage, berth, dock, jetty, landing place, marina, pier, platform, quay, slip, wharf; CONCEPT *442*

landlord [n] *owner of property leased* freeholder, hotelier, hotelkeeper, innkeeper, lessor, property owner, proprietor, saw, squire; CONCEPT *347* —*Ant.* boarder, leaser, renter

landmark [n1] *historical or notable sight* battleground, benchmark, bend, blaze, feature, fragment, guide, hill, mark, marker, memorial, milepost, milestone, monument, mountain, museum, promontory, remnant, ruins, souvenir, specimen, stone, survival, trace, tree, vantage point, vestige, waypost; CONCEPTS *198,284,447*

landmark [n2] *turning point* crisis, event, milepost, milestone, stage, watershed, waypost; CONCEPTS *696,817*

landscape [n] *countryside; picture of countryside* mural, outlook, painting, panorama, photograph, prospect, scene, scenery, sketch, view, vista; CONCEPTS *259,509*

landslide [n1] *landslip* avalanche, earthfall, mudslide, rockslide, snowslide; CONCEPTS *509,524,786*

landslide [n2] *great victory* advantage, clean sweep*, conquest, defeat, grand slam*, killing*, overthrow, superiority, sweep, triumph, win; CONCEPTS *95,671,706,832*

lane [n] *road* alley, artery, avenue, back street, boulevard, byway, drive, expressway, highway, parkway, passage, pathway, roadway, route, street, thoroughfare, throughway, thruway, turnpike; CONCEPT *501*

language [n] *system of words for communication* accent, argot, articulation, brogue, cant, communication, conversation, dialect, diction, dictionary, discourse, doublespeak*, expression, gibberish, idiom, interchange, jargon, lexicon, lingua franca, palaver, parlance, patois, phraseology, prose, signal, slang, sound, speech, style, talk, terminology, tongue, utterance, verbalization, vernacular, vocabulary, vocalization, voice, word, wording; CONCEPT *276*

languid [adj] *drooping, dull, listless* apathetic, blah*, blahs*, comatose, dopey, easy, energyless, enervated, faint, feeble, heavy, impassive, inactive, indifferent, inert, infirm, lackadaisical, laid-back, languishing, languorous, lazy, leaden, leisurely, lethargic, limp, moony*, nebbish, phlegmatic, pining, sickly, sleepyhead*, slow, sluggish, snoozy*, spiritless, supine, torpid, unconcerned, unenthusiastic, unhurried, uninterested, weak, weary, wimpy*; CONCEPTS *403, 542,584* —*Ant.* alert, animated, energetic, lively, spirited, vivacious

languish [v] *droop; become dull, listless* be disregarded, be neglected, brood, conk out*, decline, desire, despond, deteriorate, die on vine*, dwindle, ebb, fade, fag, fag out, fail, faint, fizzle out, flag, go soft*, go to pieces*, grieve, hanker, hunger, knock out, long, pine, repine, rot, sicken, sigh, snivel, sorrow, suffer, tucker, waste, waste away, weaken, wilt, wither, yearn; CONCEPTS *20,105,469* —*Ant.* flourish, grow, improve, strengthen

languor [n] *lethargy* apathy, dullness, fatigue, idleness, inaction, inactivity, laziness, listlessness, sluggishness, tiredness, torpor, weakness; CONCEPTS *315,410,633,748*

lanky [adj] *tall and thin* angular, attenuated, beanpole*, beanstalk*, bony, broomstick*, extenuated, gangling, gangly, gaunt, lean, meager, rangy, rawboned, scraggy, scrawny, slender, spare, spindling, spindly, stilt, stringy, twiggy*, weedy; CONCEPTS *491,779* —*Ant.* squat

lantern [n] *lamp* beacon, flashlight, gas lamp, gaslight, hurricane lamp, kerosene lamp, light, searchlight, torch; CONCEPTS *620,624,628,810*

lap [n] *orbit, circuit* circle, course, distance, loop, round, tour; CONCEPTS *364,436*

lap [v1] *slosh, wash against* bathe, bubble, burble, drink, gurgle, lave, lick, lip, plash, purl, ripple, sip, slap, splash, sup, swish; CONCEPT *144*

lap [v2] *overlap* cover, enfold, envelop, fold, imbricate, overlie, override, ride, shingle, swaddle, swathe, turn, twist, wrap; CONCEPTS *172,201*

lapse [n1] *mistake* blunder, breach, bungle, crime, error, failing, failure, fault, flub, foible, frailty, gaff, goof, goof-up*, indiscretion, miscue, negligence, offense, omission, oversight, screw-up*, sin, slip, slip-up, transgression, trespass, trip*, vice, violation; CONCEPTS *101, 674* —*Ant.* achievement, perfection, success

lapse [n2] *break in action* gap, intermission, interruption, interval, lacuna, lull, passage, pause; CONCEPT *807* —*Ant.* continuity

lapse [n3] *backsliding* decadence, declension, decline, degeneration, descent, deterioration, devolution, drop, fall, recession, regression, relapse, retrogradation, retrogression; CONCEPTS *230,316,388* —*Ant.* progress

lapse [v] *become void; fall back into previous pattern* apostatize, backslide, become obsolete, cease, decline, degenerate, descend, deteriorate, die, elapse, end, expire, go by, pass, recede, recidivate, relapse, retrograde, return, revert, run out, slide, slip, subside, terminate, weaken; CONCEPT *119* —*Ant.* continue, go on, restart

larceny [n] *theft* burglary, crime, lift, misappropriation, pilfering, pinch, purloining, robbery, steal, stealing, thievery, thieving, touch*; CONCEPTS *139,192*

larder [n] *provisions* food supply, groceries, pantry, provender, stock, storage, supplies; CONCEPTS *140,712*

large [adj] *big, abundant* ample, barn door*, blimp*, booming, broad, bulky, capacious, colossal, comprehensive, considerable, copious, enormous, excessive, exorbitant, extensive, extravagant, full, generous, giant, gigantic, goodly, grand, grandiose, great, gross, hefty, huge, humongous*, immeasurable, immense, jumbo*, liberal, massive, monumental, mountainous, plentiful, populous, roomy, sizable, spacious, stupendous, substantial, super, sweeping, thumping, tidy, vast, voluminous, whopping*, wide; CONCEPTS *773,781* —*Ant.* little, miniature, small, tiny

largely [adv] *to a great extent* abundantly, as a rule, broadly, by and large, chiefly, commodiously, comprehensively, considerably, copiously, expansively, extensively, extravagantly, generally, generously, grandly, immoderately, imposingly, in a big way, in a grand manner, lavishly, liberally, magnificently, mainly, mostly, on a large scale, overall, predominantly, primarily, principally, prodigally, prodigiously, voluminously, widely; CONCEPTS *544,772*

larger than life [adj] legendary awesome, celebrated, extraordinary, famed, famous, immortal, imposing, impressive, mythical, renowned, towering; CONCEPT 568

largess [adj] generosity aid, alms, altruistic, benefaction, benevolence, charitable, charity, donation, endowment, generous, gift, giving, philanthropy, thoughtful; CONCEPTS 404,542

lascivious [adj] sexually aroused; displaying excessive interest in sex bawdy, blue, bodily, carnal, coarse, crude, evil-minded, fast*, fleshly, gross*, hard-core*, hot*, immoral, incontinent, indecent, lecherous, lewd, libertine, libidinous, licentious, low-down*, lubricious, lustful, nasty, obscene, off-color*, offensive, orgiastic, pornographic, prurient, randy, raunchy*, raw, ribald, rough, salacious, scurrilous, sensual, smutty*, soft-core*, steamy, suggestive, unchaste, voluptuous, vulgar, wanton, X-rated*; CONCEPTS 372,403 —Ant. chaste, decent, moral

lash [v1] beat, whip baste, batter, buffet, chastise, dash, drum, flagellate, flay, flog, hammer, hide, hit, horsewhip, knock, lam, lather, pound, pummel, scourge, smack, strap, strike, thrash, wear out, whale*; CONCEPT 189

lash [v2] criticize harshly abuse, attack, baste, bawl out*, belabor, berate, blister, castigate, censure, chew out*, exprobate, flay, fulminate, jaw, lambaste, lampoon, ridicule, satirize, scold, tear into*, tell off*, tongue-lash*, upbraid; CONCEPT 52 —Ant. compliment, praise

lass [n] young woman colleen, damsel, female, girl, lassie, maid, maiden, miss, missy; CONCEPTS 548,585

lassitude [n] lethargy apathy, dullness, exhaustion, fatigue, idleness, inaction, inactivity, languor, laziness, listlessness, sleepiness, sluggishness, tiredness, torpor, weakness, weariness; CONCEPTS 315,410,633,748

lasso [n] lariat bola, halter, rope, snare; CONCEPT 475

last [adj] final; newest aftermost, antipodal, at the end, bitter end, climactic, closing, concluding, conclusive, crowning, curtains*, definitive, determinate, determinative, end, ending, eventual, extreme, far, far-off, farthest, finishing, furthest, hindmost, lag, latest, least, lowest, meanest, most recent, once and for all*, outermost, rearmost, remotest, supreme, swan song*, terminal, ulterior, ultimate, utmost, uttermost; CONCEPTS 585,778,799 —Ant. beginning, first, front, initial, introductory, oldest, primary, starting

last [n] end close, completion, conclusion, ending, finale, finis, finish, omega, termination; CONCEPT 832 —Ant. beginning, commencement, introduction, lead, start

last-ditch [adj] last-minute desperate, do-or-die, eleventh-hour, final, frantic, last-chance, last-gasp, last-resort; CONCEPT 799

lasting [adj] enduring, unending abiding, constant, continual, continuing, deep-rooted, durable, endless, eternal, everlasting, forever, incessant, indelible, indissoluble, inexhaustible, inexpungible, in for the long haul*, lifelong, longstanding, long-term, old, perdurable, perennial, permanent, perpetual, persisting, stable, till the cows come home*, unceasing, undying,

unremitting; CONCEPTS 551,798 —Ant. ceasing, ending, ephemeral, fleeting, passing, short-lived, temporary, transient

lastly/last [adv] in the end after, after all, all in all, at last, at the end, behind, bringing up rear*, finally, in conclusion, in the rear, to conclude, to sum up, ultimately; CONCEPTS 585,799 —Ant. firstly/first

latch [n] lock bar, bolt, catch, clamp, fastening, hasp, hook, padlock; CONCEPTS 445,499 —Ant. key

latch [v] fasten with lock bar, bolt, cinch, close, close up, lock, make fast, secure; CONCEPT 85 —Ant. loose, loosen, unfasten, unlatch, unlock

late [adj1] not on time backward, behind, behindhand, behind time, belated, blown*, delayed, dilatory, eleventh-hour*, gone, held up, hung up*, in a bind*, in the lurch*, jammed*, lagging, last-minute, missed the boat*, out of luck*, overdue, postponed, put off, remiss, slow, stayed, strapped*, tardy, too late, unpunctual; CONCEPTS 548,799 —Ant. early, on time, prompt, punctual

late [adj2] new advanced, fresh, just out, modern, recent; CONCEPTS 578,797 —Ant. antique, old, old-fashioned

late [adj3] dead asleep, bygone, cold, deceased, defunct, departed, erstwhile, ex-*, exanimate, extinct, former, inanimate, lifeless, old, once, onetime, past, preceding, previous, quondam, sometime; CONCEPT 539 —Ant. live

late [adv] at the last minute backward, behind, behindhand, behind time, belatedly, dilatorily, slowly, tardily, unpunctual; CONCEPT 799 —Ant. early, on time, punctually

lately [adv] new, recently afresh, anew, a short time ago, in recent times, just now, latterly, newly, not long ago, of late; CONCEPT 820 —Ant. in the past, old

latent [adj] dormant, hidden abeyant, between the lines, concealed, contained, covert, idle, immature, implied, in abeyance, inactive, inert, inferential, inferred, inherent, inoperative, intrinsic, invisible, involved, lurking, passive, possible, potential, quiescent, rudimentary, secret, sleeping, smoldering, suppressed, suspended, tacit, torpid, underdeveloped, underlying, undeveloped, unexposed, unexpressed, unrealized, unripe, unseen, veiled, vestigial; CONCEPTS 404,576 —Ant. active, apparent, clear, live, manifest, obvious, open, public

later [adj] coming after downstream, ensuing, following, more recent, next, posterior, postliminary, proximate, subsequent, subsequential, succeeding, ulterior; CONCEPT 799 —Ant. before, earlier

later [adv] happening after after, afterward, again, at another time, behind, by and by*, come Sunday*, down the line*, down the road*, in a while, in time, later on, latterly, more recent, next, subsequently, succeeding, thereafter; CONCEPT 799 —Ant. before, earlier

lateral [adj] sideways crabwise, edgeways, flanking, oblique, side, side-by-side, sidelong, sideward, sidewise, skirting; CONCEPTS 581, 583 —Ant. centered, central

lather [n1] bubbles cream, foam, froth, head, soap, soapsuds, spume, suds, yeast; CONCEPTS 260,437

lather [n2] *commotion, fuss* agitation, bustle, clamor, confusion, dither, fever, flap*, fluster, hassle, hoopla*, hubbub*, hullabaloo*, state, stew*, storm*, sweat*, tizzy*, tumult, turbulence, turmoil, twitter*; CONCEPTS 230,388 —*Ant.* calm, peace

lather [v] *cause to bubble* beat, foam, froth, scrub, soap, wash, whip; CONCEPT 165 —*Ant.* flatten

latitude [n] *freedom, room to move; scope* breadth, compass, elbow room, extent, independence, indulgence, laxity, leeway, liberty, license, margin, play, range, reach, room, run, run of, space, span, spread, sweep, swing, unrestrictedness, width; CONCEPTS 651,739,756,788 —*Ant.* limitation, restriction

latter [adj] *latest, concluding* closing, eventual, final, following, hindmost, lag, last, last-mentioned, later, modern, rearmost, recent, second, terminal; CONCEPTS 585,799 —*Ant.* earliest, former, preceding

lattice [n] *mesh, trellis* filigree, frame, fretwork, grating, grid, grill, latticework, net, network, openwork, reticulation, screen, structure, tracery, web; CONCEPT 259 —*Ant.* solid

laud [v] *acclaim, praise* admire, adore, approve, bless, boost, build up, celebrate, commend, compliment, cry up, eulogize, extol, flatter, glorify, hand it to*, honor, hymn, magnify, panegyrize, pat on the back*, revere, reverence, sing the praises of*, stroke, venerate, worship; CONCEPT 69 —*Ant.* blame, castigate, criticize

laudable [adj] *admirable* commendable, creditable, deserving, estimable, excellent, mean, meritable, meritorious, of note, praisable, praiseworthy, stellar, terrific, thankworthy, worthy; CONCEPT 574 —*Ant.* bad, blameable

laudatory [adj] *complimentary* acclamatory, adulatory, approbative, approbatory, approving, commendatory, encomiastic, eulogistic, flattering, laudative, panegyrical, praiseful; CONCEPT 267 —*Ant.* blaming, castigating, critical

laugh [v] *expressing amusement, happiness with sound* be in stitches*, break up*, burst*, cachinnate, chortle, chuckle, convulsed*, crack up*, crow, die laughing*, fracture*, giggle, grin, guffaw, howl, roar, roll in the aisles*, scream, shriek, snicker, snort, split one's sides*, titter, whoop*; CONCEPTS 77,185 —*Ant.* cry

laughable [adj] *easily made fun of* absurd, amusing, asinine, bizarre, camp, campy, comic, comical, derisive, derisory, diverting, droll, eccentric, entertaining, facetious, fantastic, farcical, funny, gelastic, har-har*, hilarious, humorous, inane, jocose, jocular, jokey, joshing, ludicrous, mirthful, mocking, nonsensical, preposterous, rich, ridiculous, riot, risible, scream, unusual, witty; CONCEPTS 267,550 —*Ant.* grave, serious

laugh at [v] *ridicule* belittle, deride, hoot, jeer, lampoon, make fun of, mock, scoff, taunt; CONCEPT 54

laugh/laughter [n] *audible expression of amusement* amusement, cachinnation, cackle, chortle, chuckle, chuckling, crack-up*, crow, fit, gesture, giggle, giggling, glee, guffaw, hilarity, howling, merriment, mirth, peal, rejoicing, roar, shout, shriek, snicker, snigger, snort, sound, titter, yuck*; CONCEPTS 77,185 —*Ant.* cry

laughing stock [n] *object of ridicule* Aunt Sally, butt, dupe, fair game, fall guy*, fool, goat*, joke, laughingstock, stooge, target, victim; CONCEPT 412

launch [v1] *send off* barrage, bombard, bung, cast, catapult, discharge, dispatch, drive, eject, fire, fling, heave, hurl, lance, pitch, project, propel, send forth, set afloat, set in motion, shoot, sling, throw, toss; CONCEPTS 179,222 —*Ant.* hold, keep

launch [v2] *begin, initiate* bow, break the ice*, break the seal*, commence, embark upon, get show on road*, inaugurate, instigate, institute, introduce, jump, kick off*, open, originate, set going, start, start ball rolling*, usher in*; CONCEPT 221 —*Ant.* cease, end, finish, stop

launder [v] *wash* clean, cleanse, do the laundry*, do the washing*, rinse; CONCEPT 165

laurels [n] *credit, praise* acclaim, accolade, award, badge, bays, blue ribbon, commendation, crown, decoration, distinction, fame, feather in cap*, glory, gold, gold star*, kudos, prestige, recognition, renown, reward; CONCEPTS 69,278,337 —*Ant.* criticism

lavatory [n] *bathroom* latrine, powder room, restroom, shower, toilet, washroom, water closet, WC; CONCEPT 448

lavish [adj] *profuse; splendid* abundant, bountiful, copious, effusive, exaggerated, excessive, extravagant, exuberant, first-class, free, generous, gorgeous, grand, immoderate, impressive, improvident, inordinate, intemperate, liberal, lush, luxuriant, luxurious, munificent, openhanded, opulent, plentiful, plush, posh, prodigal, profligate, profusive, prolific, riotous, ritzy, sumptuous, swanky, thriftless, unreasonable, unrestrained, unsparing, unstinging, wasteful, wild; CONCEPTS 334,589,781 —*Ant.* economical, scanty, scarce, small, spare

lavish [v] *pamper, shower* be generous, be wasteful, deluge, dissipate, expend, fritter, give, go through, heap, pour, run through*, scatter, spend, spend money like water*, squander, thrust upon, waste; CONCEPTS 110,327,341 —*Ant.* economize, hoard, limit, starve

law [n1] *rules of a government, society* act, assize, behest, bidding, bylaw, canon, case, caveat, charge, charter, code, command, commandment, constitution, covenant, decision, decree, decretum, demand, dictate, divestiture, due process, edict, enactment, equity, garnishment, injunction, institute, instruction, jurisprudence, legislation, mandate, measure, notice, order, ordinance, precedent, precept, prescript, prescription, reg, regulation, requirement, ruling, statute, subpoena, summons, warrant, writ; CONCEPT 318 —*Ant.* breaking, lawlessness, transgression, violation

law [n2] *standard, principle of behavior* assumption, axiom, base, canon, cause, criterion, exigency, formula, foundation, fundamental, generalization, ground, guide, maxim, origin, postulate, precept, principium, proposal, proposition, reason, regulation, rule, source, theorem, truth, usage; CONCEPT 688 —*Ant.* transgression, violation

lawbreaker [n] *criminal* blackmailer, black marketeer, con, convict, crook, culprit, delinquent, felon, fugitive, gangster, hood*,

hoodlum, hooligan, jailbird, malefactor, mobster, offender, outlaw, racketeer, scofflaw; CONCEPT 412

law court [n] *place for legal action* court, court of justice, court of law, judicature, tribunal; CONCEPT 299

lawful [adj] *allowable, legitimate* authorized, bona fide, canonical, card-carrying*, commanded, condign, constitutional, decreed, due, enacted, enforced, enjoined, established, innocent, judged, judicial, jural, juridical, jurisprudent, just, justifiable, kosher*, legal, legalized, legislated, legit*, legitimatized, licit, mandated, official, of right, on the level*, on the up and up*, ordained, ordered, passed, permissible, proper, protected, rightful, ruled, statutory, valid, vested, warrantable, warranted; CONCEPTS 319,545 —Ant. illegal, illegitimate, illicit, prohibited, taboo, unlawful

lawless [adj] *reckless, ungoverned* anarchic, anarchical, anarchistic, bad, barbarous, chaotic, contumacious, criminal, despotic, disobedient, disordered, disorderly, evil, fierce, heterodox, infringing, insubordinate, insurgent, mutinous, nihilistic, noncompliant, nonconformist, piratical, rebellious, recusant, revolutionary, riotous, savage, seditious, tempestuous, terrorizing, traitorous, turbulent, tyrannous, uncivilized, uncultivated, unorthodox, unpeaceful, unrestrained, unruly, untamed, violent, warlike, wild; CONCEPTS 319,545 —Ant. governed, lawful, legal, legitimate, licit, proper, rightful, valid

lawn [n] *cultivated area of green grass* backyard, garden, grass, grassplot, green, park, plot, terrace, yard; CONCEPTS 509,513,517

lawsuit [n] *case brought to court* accusation, action, argument, arraignment, assumpsit, bill, cause, claim, contest, dispute, impeachment, indictment, litigation, presentment, proceedings, prosecution, replevin, suit, trial; CONCEPT 318

lawyer [n] *person who is trained to counsel or argue in cases of law* advocate, attorney, attorney-at-law, barrister, counsel, counsellor, counselor, defender, jurisprudent, jurist, legal adviser, legal eagle*, legist, member of the bar, mouthpiece*, pleader, practitioner, proctor, procurator, solicitor; CONCEPT 355

lax [adj] *slack, remiss* any way*, asleep on job*, behindhand, broad, careless, casual, delinquent, derelict, devil-may-care*, disregardful, easygoing, flaccid, forgetful, general, imprecise, inaccurate, indefinite, indifferent, inexact, lenient, neglectful, negligent, nonspecific, oblivious, overindulgent, paying no mind*, regardless, shapeless, slipshod, sloppy, soft, unmindful, vague, yielding; CONCEPTS 401,542,557 —Ant. hard, rigid, strict, tight

laxative [n] *aperient* cathartic, purgative; CONCEPT 307

lay [adj] *amateur, not trained in a religious or other profession* inexpert, nonclerical, nonprofessional, nonspecialist, ordinary, secular, temporal, unsacred; CONCEPT 530 —Ant. ordained, professional

lay [v1] *put, place* arrange, deposit, dispose, establish, fix, leave, locate, order, organize, plant, posit, position, repose, rest, set, set down, set out, settle, spread, stick, systematize; CONCEPTS 158,201 —Ant. lift, take

lay [v2] *produce, advance* adduce, allege, bear, bring forth, bring forward, cite, deposit, generate, lodge, offer, present, put forward, submit, yield; CONCEPTS 66,205

lay [v3] *credit, allocate* accredit, address, aim, allot, apply, ascribe, assess, assign, attribute, burden, cast, charge, direct, encumber, impose, impute, incline, level, point, refer, saddle, tax, train, turn, zero in*; CONCEPTS 49,50,88,187

lay [v4] *design, plan* concoct, contrive, devise, hatch, plot, prepare, work out; CONCEPT 36 —Ant. neglect

lay [v5] *make smooth* allay, alleviate, appease, assuage, calm, even, flatten, flush, iron, level, plane, press, quiet, relieve, steam, still, suppress; CONCEPTS 235,250 —Ant. rough

lay [v6] *bet, wager* gamble, game, give odds, hazard, play, risk, stake; CONCEPT 363

layer [n] *coating, tier* band, bed, blanket, coat, coping, couch, course, cover, covering, film, flag, flap, floor, fold, girdle, lamina, lamination, lap, mantle, overlap, overlay, panel, ply, row, seam, sheet, slab, story, stratum, stripe, substratum, thickness, zone; CONCEPTS 744,835

lay into [v] *criticize, attack* assail, battle, belabor, fire at*, invade, lambaste, let fly at*, set about; CONCEPTS 52,86 —Ant. compliment, praise

layoff [n] *dismissal from job or responsibility* cutback, discharge, early retirement, respite, unemployment; CONCEPT 351 —Ant. employment, hiring

lay off [v1] *stop doing* cease, desist, end, give a rest, give up, halt, leave alone, leave off, let up, lie by, quit, rest, spell; CONCEPTS 119,234 —Ant. begin, start

lay off [v2] *relieve of responsibility* discharge, dismiss, drop, fire, let go, oust, pay off, retire early; CONCEPT 351 —Ant. employ, hire

layout [n] *physical arrangement* blueprint, chart, design, diagram, draft, formation, geography, map, organization, outline, plan, purpose; CONCEPTS 625,660

lay out [v1] *spend money* disburse, expend, give, invest, lend, outlay, pay, put out, put up, shell out*; CONCEPTS 327,341 —Ant. hoard, save

lay out [v2] *design, plan* arrange, chart, diagram, display, exhibit, map, outline, set out, spread out; CONCEPTS 36,158,174 —Ant. neglect

layperson [n] *amateur person, not trained in religious or other profession* believer, dilettante, follower, laic, member, neophyte, nonprofessional, novice, outsider, parishioner, proselyte, recruit, secular; CONCEPTS 361,423 —Ant. minister, ordained, priest, professional, reverend

lay up [v1] *hurt, incapacitate* beat up, confine, disable, harm, hospitalize, injure; CONCEPT 246 —Ant. heal, help

lay up/lay by [v2] *set aside, store* accumulate, amass, build up, bury, conserve, cumulate, garner, hide, hoard, keep, lay in, preserve, put away, roll up, salt away, save, spare, store up, treasure; CONCEPTS 120,134 —Ant. squander, use, waste

laziness [n] *unwillingness to work, be active* apathy, dilatoriness, do-nothingness, dormancy, dreaminess, drowsiness, dullness, faineance, faineacy, heaviness, idleness, inactivity, indolence, inertia, inertness, lackadaisicalness, languidness, languorousness, laxness, leadenness, leisureliness, lethargy, listlessness, neglectfulness, negligence, otioseness, otiosity, passivity, remissness, slackness, sleepiness, sloth, slothfulness, slowness, sluggishness, stolidity, supineness, tardiness, torpescence, torpidness, weariness; CONCEPTS *411,633* —*Ant.* activity, diligence, hard work, industriousness, industry, liveliness

lazy [*adj*] *inactive, sluggish* apathetic, asleep on the job*, careless, comatose, dallying, dilatory, drowsy, dull, flagging, idle, inattentive, indifferent, indolent, inert, lackadaisical, laggard, lagging, languid, languorous, lethargic, lifeless, loafing, neglectful, out of it*, passive, procrastinating, remiss, shiftless, slack, sleepy, slothful, slow, slow-moving, snoozy*, somnolent, supine, tardy, tired, torpid, trifling, unconcerned, unenergetic, unindustrious, unpersevering, unready, weary; CONCEPTS *401,404* —*Ant.* active, diligent, energetic, hard-working, industrious, lively

leach [*v*] *drain, empty* extract, filter, filtrate, lixiviate, percolate, seep, strain, wash away; CONCEPTS *142,211,225*

lead [*n1*] *first place, supremacy* advance, advantage, ahead, bulge, cutting edge*, direction, edge, example, facade, front rank, guidance, head, heavy, leadership, margin, model, over, pilot, point, precedence, primacy, principal, priority, protagonist, spark, star, start, title role, top, top spot, vanguard; CONCEPTS *668,693,828* —*Ant.* last

lead [*n2*] *clue* evidence, guide, hint, indication, proof, sign, suggestion, tip, trace; CONCEPTS *274,284*

lead [*v1*] *guide physically* accompany, attend, be responsible for, chaperone, coerce, compel, conduct, convey, convoy, direct, drive, escort, find a way, force, get, go along with, guard, impel, induce, manage, pass along, persuade, pilot, point out, point the way, precede, prevail, protect, quarterback*, route, safeguard, see, shepherd, show, show around, show in, show the way, span, squire, steer, traverse, usher, watch over; CONCEPT *187* —*Ant.* follow

lead [*v2*] *guide mentally; influence* affect, bring, bring on, call the shots*, cause, command, conduce, contribute, convert, direct, dispose, draw, get the jump on*, go out in front*, govern, head, helm, incline, induce, introduce, manage, motivate, move, persuade, preside over, prevail, produce, prompt, quarterback*, result in, run things*, serve, shepherd, spearhead*, spur, supervise, tend, trail-blaze*; CONCEPTS *68,117, 221* —*Ant.* comply, consent, follow, obey

lead [*v3*] *surpass* be ahead, blaze a trail*, come first*, exceed, excel, outdo, outstrip, precede, preface, transcend, usher; CONCEPT *141* —*Ant.* fall behind, lose

lead (a life) [*v4*] *experience* have, live, pass, spend, undergo; CONCEPT *678*

leader [*n*] *person who guides* boss, captain, chief, chieftain, commander, conductor, controller, counsellor, dean, dignitary, director, doyen, eminence, exec, forerunner, general, governor, guide, harbinger, head, herald, lead, lion*, luminary, manager, mistress, notability, notable, officer, pacesetter, pilot, pioneer, precursor, president, principal, rector, ringleader, ruler, shepherd, skipper, superintendent, superior; CONCEPTS *347,354* —*Ant.* follower

leadership [*n*] *guidance* administration, authority, capacity, command, conduction, control, conveyance, direction, directorship, domination, foresight, hegemony, influence, initiative, management, pilotage, power, preeminence, primacy, skill, superintendency, superiority, supremacy, sway; CONCEPTS *376,687*

leading [*adj*] *chief, superior* arch, best, champion, dominant, dominating, famous, first, foremost, governing, greatest, headmost, highest, inaugural, initial, main, noted, notorious, number one*, outstanding, popular, preeminent, premier, primary, principal, prominent, ruling, stellar, top, well-known; CONCEPTS *574,585* —*Ant.* inferior, last, subordinate, supplementary, unimportant

leaf [*n1*] *green foliage of plant* blade, bract, flag, foliole, frond, leaflet, needle, pad, petal, petiole, scale, stalk, stipule; CONCEPT *428*

leaf [*n2*] *page of document* folio, paper, sheet; CONCEPT *270*

leaf [*v*] *flip through* browse, dip into, glance, riff, riffle, run through, scan, skim, thumb; CONCEPTS *72,623*

leafy [*adj*] *abundant in foliage* abounding, abundant, covered, green, hidden, leafed, leaved, shaded, shady, umbrageous, verdant, wooded; CONCEPTS *485,583* —*Ant.* leafless

league [*n1*] *association, federation* alliance, band, bunch, circle, circuit, club, coalition, combination, combine, compact, company, confederacy, confederation, conference, consortium, crew, gang, group, guild, loop, mob, order, organization, outfit, partnership, pool, ring, society, sodality, union, unit; CONCEPTS *365,381,387*

league [*n2*] *group of a certain ability* category, circle, class, grade, grouping, level, pigeonhole*, rank, status, tier; CONCEPTS *388,630*

league [*v*] *associate* ally, amalgamate, band, coadjute, collaborate, combine, concur, confederate, conjoin, consolidate, cooperate, federate, join forces, unite; CONCEPTS *8,10, 114* —*Ant.* disassociate

leak [*n*] *opening; seepage through opening* aperture, chink, crack, crevice, decrease, destruction, detriment, drip, drop, escape, expenditure, exposure, fissure, flow, hole, leakage, leaking, loss, outgoing, percolation, pit, puncture, short circuit, slip; CONCEPTS *116,513*

leak [*v*] *seep; make known* break, come out, discharge, disclose, divulge, drip, drool, escape, exude, get out, give away, let slip*, make public, ooze, out, pass, pass on, percolate, reveal, slip, spill, spill the beans, tell, transpire, trickle; CONCEPTS *60,116,179*

lean [*adj*] *bare, thin* angular, anorexic, barren, beanpole*, bony, emaciated, gangling, gangly, gaunt, haggard, inadequate, infertile, lank, lanky, meager, no fat, pitiful, poor, rangy, rawboned, scanty, scraggy, scrawny, shadow*, sinewy, skinny, slender, slim, spare, sparse, stick, stilt, stringy, svelte, sylphlike, twiggy*, unfruitful, unproductive, wasted, wiry, wizened, worn; CONCEPTS *485,491* —*Ant.* fat, plump

lean [*v1*] *bend, angle toward* bear on, beetle, be off, be slanted, bow, cant, careen, cock, curve, decline, deflect, dip, divert, drift, droop, fasten on, hang on, heel, incline, jut, list, nod, overhang, pitch, place, prop, put weight on, recline, repose, rest, rest on, roll, sag, sheer, sink, slant, slope, tilt, tip, turn, twist, veer; CONCEPTS *147,201,738* —*Ant.* straighten

lean [*v2*] *be disposed to* prone, be willing, favor, gravitate toward, have propensity, incline, look, not mind, prefer, tend; CONCEPT *20* —*Ant.* dislike, not like

lean [*v3*] *count, depend on* bank on*, believe in, bet bottom dollar*, bet on*, confide, gamble on*, have faith, hinge on*, lay money on*, put faith in, rely, trust; CONCEPTS *12,26* —*Ant.* disregard, forget

leaning [*n*] *tendency, bias* aptitude, bent*, cup of tea*, disposition, drift, favor, favoritism, inclination, inclining, liking, mindset, partiality, penchant, predilection, predisposition, proclivity, proneness, propensity, sentiment, taste, thing, weakness; CONCEPTS *20,32,689*

leap [*n*] *jump; increase* bound, caper, escalation, frisk, hop, rise, skip, spring, surge, upsurge, upswing, vault; CONCEPTS *194,780*

leap [*v*] *jump, jump over; increase* advance, arise, ascend, bounce, bound, caper, cavort, clear, escalate, frisk, hop, hurdle, lop, mount, rise, rocket, saltate, skip, soar, spring, surge, vault; CONCEPTS *194,780*

learn [*v1*] *acquire information* apprentice, attain, become able, become versed, be taught, be trained, brush up on*, burn midnight oil*, commit to memory, con, crack the books*, cram*, determine, drink in*, enroll, gain, get, get down pat*, get the hang of*, get the knack of*, grasp, grind, imbibe, improve mind, lucubrate, major in, master, matriculate, memorize, minor in, peruse, pick up*, pore over, prepare, read, receive, review, soak up*, specialize in, study, take course*, take in, train in, wade through*; CONCEPTS *31,33* —*Ant.* teach

learn [*v2*] *discover, find out* ascertain, catch on, detect, determine, dig up*, discern, gain, gather, hear, see, smoke out*, stumble upon*, trip over, tumble, uncover, understand, unearth; CONCEPTS *34,183* —*Ant.* miss, overlook

learned [*adj*] *well-informed* abstruse, academic, accomplished, bookish, brainy*, conversant, cultivated, cultured, deep*, educated, erudite, esoteric, experienced, expert, grave, grounded, highbrow*, intellectual, in the know*, judicious, lettered, literary, literate, omniscient, pansophic, pedantic, philosophic, philosophical, polymath, posted, professorial, recondite, sage, sapient, scholarly, scientific, sharp, skilled, solemn, solid, sound, studied, studious, versed, well-educated, well-grounded, well-read, well-rounded; CONCEPT *402* —*Ant.* ignorant, stupid, uninformed

learner [*n*] *person who receives education* abecedarian, apprentice, beginner, bookworm, catechumen, disciple, initiate, neophyte, novice, probationer, pupil, scholar, student, trainee; CONCEPT *350* —*Ant.* ignoramus

learning [*n*] *education, knowledge* acquirements,attainments, culture, erudition, information, letters, literature, lore, research, scholarship, schooling, science, study, training, tuition, wisdom; CONCEPTS *274,409* —*Ant.* ignorance

lease [*v*] *rent object, residence* charter, hire, let, loan, rent out, sublease, sublet; CONCEPTS *89,115* —*Ant.* sell

leash [*n*] *rein* bridle, chain, check, control, cord, curb, deterrent, hold, lead, restraint, rope, strap, tether; CONCEPT *475*

leash [*v*] *rein, hold* bridle, check, clog, control, curb, entrammel, fasten, fetter, hamper, hobble, hog-tie*, hold back, restrain, secure, shackle, suppress, tether, tie, tie up, trammel; CONCEPT *191* —*Ant.* let go, release

least [*adj*] *slightest, smallest* atomic, bottom, entry-level, feeblest, fewest, finical, first, gutter, infinitesimal, last, lowest, meanest, microcosmic, microscopic, minimal, minimum, minute, minutest, molecular, most trivial, nadir, next to nothing*, niggling*, piddling*, poorest, second, short-end*, third*, tiniest, trivial, unimportant; CONCEPTS *585,789* —*Ant.* most

leathery [*adj*] *hard, durable* coriaceous, hardened, leatherlike, rough, rugged, strong, tough, wrinkled; CONCEPTS *489,60* —*Ant.* soft, supple

leave [*n1*] *permission* allowance, assent, authorization, concession, consent, dispensation, freedom, go-ahead*, green light*, liberty, okay, permit, sanction, sufferance, tolerance*; CONCEPTS *376,685* —*Ant.* limitation, prohibition, restriction

leave [*n2*] *holiday, time off* adieu, departure, farewell, furlough, goodbye, leave of absence, leave-taking, liberty, parting, retirement, sabbatical, vacation, withdrawal; CONCEPTS *802,807* —*Ant.* workday

leave [*v1*] *depart, abandon physically* abscond, beat it*, break away, clear out*, come away, cut out, decamp, defect, desert, disappear, ditch*, elope, embark, emigrate, escape, exit, flee, flit, fly, forsake, give the slip*, go, go away, go forth, head out*, issue, migrate, move, move out, part, pull out*, push off*, quit, relinquish, remove oneself, retire, ride off*, run along*, sally, say goodbye*, scram, set out, slip out, split*, start, step down, take a hike*, take leave, take off, vacate, vamoose*, vanish, walk out, withdraw; CONCEPT *195* —*Ant.* come, go

leave [*v2*] *abandon, renounce* back out*, cease, cede, desert, desist, drop, drop out*, evacuate, forbear, forsake, give notice, give up*, hand over, knock off, maroon, quit, refrain, relinquish, resign, stop, surrender, terminate, waive, yield; CONCEPT *234* —*Ant.* continue, hold, keep

leave [*v3*] *forget, neglect* allow, drop, have, lay down, leave behind, let, let be, let continue, let go, let stay, mislay, omit, permit, suffer; CONCEPTS *30,83* —*Ant.* care, maintain

leave [*v4*] *give, especially after death* allot, apportion, assign, bequeath, bequest, cede, commit, confide, consign, demise, devise, entrust, give over, hand down, leave behind, legate, refer, transmit, will; CONCEPTS *108,317* —*Ant.* hold

leave off [*v*] *stop* abstain, break off, cease, desist, discontinue, end, give over, give up, halt, knock off*, quit, refrain, surcease; CONCEPT *234* —*Ant.* begin, continue, restart

lecherous [adj] *lustful, lewd* carnal, concupiscent, corrupt, fast*, hot and heavy*, incontinent, lascivious, libertine, libidinous, licentious, low-down*, lubricious, prurient, raunchy*, salacious, satyric, sensual, unchaste, wanton; CONCEPTS 372,401 —Ant. chaste, clean

lechery [n] *lewdness* carnality, debauchery, lasciviousness, libertinism, licentiousness, lust, lustfulness, raunchiness, salaciousness, wantonness; CONCEPTS 20,709

lectern [n] *reading desk* ambo, platform, pulpit, reading stand, rostrum, stand, support; CONCEPTS 440,443

lecture [n1] *lesson, speech* address, allocution, chalk talk*, discourse, disquisition, harangue, instruction, oration, pep talk*, pitch*, soapbox*, spiel*, talk; CONCEPTS 60,278

lecture [n2] *speech of criticism* castigation, censure, chiding, dressing-down*, going-over*, harangue, moralism, preaching, preachment, rebuke, reprimand, reproof, scolding, sermon, talking-to*, telling off*; CONCEPTS 52,54

lecture [v1] *give a lesson, speech* address, declaim, deliver, discourse, expound, get on a soapbox*, give a talk, harangue, hold forth, orate, prelect, recite, speak, spiel*, spout, talk, teach; CONCEPTS 60,266

lecture [v2] *criticize lengthily* admonish, berate, chide, exprobate, flay, give going-over*, give piece of mind*, moralize, preach, rank on, rate, reprimand, reprove, scold, sermonize, tell off; CONCEPT 52 —Ant. praise

ledge [n] *shelf* bar, bench, berm, bracket, console, edge, jut, mantle, offset, path, projection, reef, ridge, rim, route, sill, step, strip, tier, track, trail, walk, way; CONCEPTS 445,513

ledger [n] *account book* books, daybook, journal, record book, register; CONCEPTS 271, 280,801

leech [n] *parasite* barnacle, bloodsucker*, bum*, freeloader, scrounger, sponge*, sycophant; CONCEPTS 394,412

leer [n/v] *look at longingly* eye, eyeball*, gloat, goggle*, ogle, smirk, sneer, squint, stare, wink; CONCEPT 623

leery [adj] *suspicious* careful, cautious, chary, distrustful, doubting, dubious, on one's guard*, shy, skeptical, uncertain, unsure, wary; CONCEPT 529 —Ant. certain, sure, unwary

leeway [n] *room to move, grow* elbow room*, extent, headway, latitude, margin, play, scope, space; CONCEPT 739

left [adj1] *on west side when facing north* hard to left, larboard, near, nigh side, port, portside, sinister, sinistral, south; CONCEPTS 581,583 —Ant. right

left [adj2] *politically radical* leftist, left-wing, liberal, progressive, revolutionary, socialist; CONCEPT 529 —Ant. right

left [adj3] *abandoned* continuing, departed, extra, forsaken, gone out, leftover, marooned, over, remaining, residual, split, staying; CONCEPT 577

leftover [adj] *remaining, excess* extra, residual, surplus, unconsumed, uneaten, untouched, unused, unwanted; CONCEPTS 560,771 —Ant. core, main, principle

leftover [n] *remainder, remains* debris, leavings, legacy, oddments, odds and ends*,

orts, remnants, residue, scraps, surplus, survivor, trash; CONCEPTS 260,457 —Ant. main meal

left-wing [adj] *liberal* communist, leftist, radical, socialist; CONCEPTS 529,542

leg [n] *appendage used for support* brace, column, lap, limb, member, part, pile, pole, portion, post, prop, section, segment, shank, stage, stake, stilt, stretch, stump, support, upright; CONCEPTS 392,471,832

legacy [n] *inheritance, heritage* bequest, birthright, devise, endowment, estate, gift, heirloom, throwback, tradition; CONCEPTS 337,710

legal [adj] *allowable, permissible* acknowledged, allowed, authorized, card-carrying*, chartered, clean*, condign, constitutional, contractual, decreed, due, enforced, enforcible, enjoined, fair, forensic, granted, innocent, judged, judicial, juridical, just, justifiable, justified, lawful, legalized, legit*, legitimate, licit, on the level*, on the up and up*, ordained, passed, precedented, prescribed, proper, protected, right, rightful, sanctioned, sound, statutory, straight, sure enough, valid, warranted, within the law; CONCEPT 319 —Ant. illegal, illegitimate, illicit, unlawful, wrong

legalize [v] *allow, validate* approve, authorize, clean up, codify, constitute, decree, decriminalize, enact, formulate, launder, legislate, legitimate, legitimatize, license, ordain, permit, regulate, sanction; CONCEPTS 298,317 —Ant. deny, prohibit, refuse, veto

legend [n1] *story of the past, often fictitious* fable, fiction, folklore, folk story, folk tale, lore, myth, mythology, mythos, narrative, saga, tale, tradition; CONCEPT 282

legend [n] *brief description in document* cipher, code, device, epigraph, epitaph, head, heading, inscription, key, motto, rubric, table, underline; CONCEPTS 268,270

legendary [adj1] *fictitious but well known* allegorical, apocryphal, created, customary, doubtful, dubious, fabled, fabricated, fabulous, fanciful, figmental, handed-down*, imaginary, imaginative, improbable, invented, mythical, mythological, related, romantic, storied, told, traditional, unhistoric, unhistorical, unreal, unverifiable; CONCEPTS 267,552 —Ant. factual, real, true

legendary [adj2] *famous* celebrated, famed, illustrious, immortal, renowned, well-known; CONCEPT 568 —Ant. infamous, unimportant

legerdemain [n] *sleight of hand* artlessness, chicanery, conjuring, craftiness, cunning, deceit, deception, hocus-pocus, manipulation, trickery; CONCEPTS 59,278

legible [adj] *easy to read* clear, coherent, decipherable, distinct, easily read, intelligible, lucid, neat, plain, readable, sharp, understandable; CONCEPTS 267,535,576 —Ant. illegible, unreadable

legion [adj] *numerous* countless, many, multifarious, multitudinal, multitudinous, myriad, numberless, populous, several, sundry, various, very many, voluminous; CONCEPTS 762,781 —Ant. few, numbered

legion [n] *mass, force of people* army, body, brigade, cloud, company, division, drove, flock, group, horde, host, multitude, myriad, number, phalanx, rout, scores, throng, troop; CONCEPTS *322,387,417*

legislation [n] *law of a government* act, bill, charter, codification, constitution, enactment, lawmaking, measure, prescription, regulation, ruling, statute; CONCEPT *318*

legislative [adj] *lawmaking* congressional, decreeing, enacting, jurisdictive, lawgiving, legislational, legislatorial, ordaining, parliamentarian, parliamentary, senatorial, statute-making, synodical; CONCEPT *319*

legislator [n] *person in government who makes laws* administrator, aldermember, assembly-member, council member, deputy, lawgiver, lawmaker, leader, member, member of Congress, parliamentarian, representative, senator; CONCEPT *354*

legislature [n] *governmental body, most often elected, that makes laws* assembly, body, chamber, congress, council, diet, house, house of representatives, lawmakers, parliament, plenum, senate, voice of the people; CONCEPT *299*

legitimate [adj] *authentic, valid, legal* accepted, accredited, acknowledged, admissible, appropriate, authorized, canonical, certain, cogent, consistent, correct, customary, fair, genuine, innocent, just, justifiable, lawful, licit, logical, natural, normal, official, on the level, on the up and up, orthodox, probable, proper, real, reasonable, received, recognized, regular, reliable, rightful, sanctioned, sensible, sound, statutory, sure, true, typical, usual, verifiable, warranted, well-founded; CONCEPTS *319,558, 582* —Ant. illegal, illegitimate, invalid, unlawful, unwarranted

leisure [n] *free time and its activities* chance, convenience, ease, freedom, holiday, idle hours, intermission, leave of absence, liberty, one's own sweet time*, opportunity, pause, quiet, range, recess, recreation, relaxation, repose, requiescence, respite, rest, retirement, sabbatical, scope, spare moments*, spare time, time, time off*, unemployment, vacant hour*, vacation; CONCEPTS *363,681,807* —Ant. employment, work

leisurely [adj] *casual, unhurried* comfortable, delayed, deliberate, dilatory, easy, free, gentle, laggard, laid-back*, languid, lax, lazy, relaxed, restful, slack, slackened, slow, slow-moving, unhasty; CONCEPTS *550,584,799* —Ant. hectic, hurried

leisurely [adv] *casually, unhurriedly* at one's convenience*, at one's leisure, calmly, comfortably, composedly, deliberately, dilatorily, easily, gradually, inactively, indolently, laggardly, langorously, languidly, lazily, lethargically, lingeringly, listlessly, slowly, sluggishly, taking one's time*, tardily, torpidly, with delay, without haste; CONCEPTS *544,584,799* —Ant. hectically, hurriedly

lemon [n] *dud* failure, flop, junk, piece of junk, reject; CONCEPTS *412,423*

lend [v] *loan, accommodate* add, advance, afford, allow, bestow, confer, contribute, entrust, extend, furnish, give, grant, impart, lay on one, lend-lease, let, loan shark*, oblige, permit, present, provide, shark, stake, supply, trust; CONCEPTS *115,140* —Ant. borrow

length [n] *extent of object, distance, time* breadth, compass, continuance, diameter, dimension, duration, elongation, endlessness, expanse, expansion, extensiveness, height, interval, lastingness, lengthiness, limit, linearity, loftiness, longitude, longness, magnitude, measure, mileage, orbit, panorama, period, piece, portion, protractedness, purview, quantity, radius, range, ranginess, reach, realm, remoteness, season, section, segment, space, spaciousness, span, stretch, stride, tallness, term, unit, width, year; CONCEPTS *651,721,743, 788,804* —Ant. height

lengthen [v] *extend* amplify, augment, continue, dilate, distend, drag out, draw, draw out*, elongate, expand, increase, let out, make longer, pad, proceed, prolong, prolongate, protract, reach, spin out*, stretch, string out*; CONCEPTS *236,239,245* —Ant. abbreviate, cut, shorten

lengthy [adj] *extended* diffuse, dragging, drawn-out, elongate, elongated, interminable, lengthened, long, longish, long-winded, overlong, padded, prolix, prolonged, protracted, tedious, tiresome, verbose, very long, wearisome, windy, wordy; CONCEPTS *267,482,782* —Ant. abbreviated, curtailed, shortened

lenient [adj] *permissive* allowing, amiable, assuaging, assuasive, being big*, benign, benignant, charitable, clement, compassionate, complaisant, compliant, condoning, easy, easygoing, emollient, excusing, favoring, forbearing, forgiving, gentle, going easy on*, good-natured, humoring, indulgent, kind, kindly, letting, live with*, loving, merciful, mild, mollycoddling*, obliging, pampering, pardoning, permitting, soft, softhearted, soft-shell*, sparing, spoiling, sympathetic, tender, tolerant, yielding; CONCEPTS *401,542* —Ant. hard, intolerant, limiting, restrictive, rigorous, severe

leprechaun [n] *elf* brownie, elfin, fairy, fay, gnome, nisse, pixie, sprite; CONCEPT *370*

lesion [n] *injury, wound* abrasion, bruise, contusion, cut, gash, laceration, scrape, scratch, sore; CONCEPT *309*

less [adj] *smaller, inferior* beneath, declined, deficient, depressed, diminished, excepting, fewer, lacking, lesser, limited, lower, minor, minus, negative, not as great, reduced, secondary, shortened, shorter, slighter, subordinate, subtracting, unsubstantial, without; CONCEPTS *574,762,789* —Ant. bigger, more, superior

less [adv] *little* barely, in a lower degree, meagerly, to a smaller extent; CONCEPTS *530, 544* —Ant. more

lessen [v] *lower, reduce* abate, abridge, amputate, attenuate, become smaller, clip, close, contract, crop, curtail, cut, cut back, decline, decrease, de-escalate, degrade, die down, dilute, diminish, downsize, drain, dwindle, ease, erode, grow less, impair, lighten, minify, minimize, mitigate, moderate, narrow, roll back, shrink, slacken, slack up, slow down, soft-pedal*, take the bite out*, take the edge off*, take the sting out*, taper, taper off, thin, truncate, weaken, wind down; CONCEPTS *247,698,776* —Ant. enlarge, extend, increase, raise, strengthen

lesser [adj] *inferior, secondary* a notch under*, bottom, bush, bush-league*, dinky*, insignificant, less important, low, lower, minor, minor-

league*, nether, second-fiddle*, second-string*, slighter, small, small-fry*, small-time*, subjacent, subordinate, third-string*, undersized; CONCEPTS 575,793 —*Ant.* greater, higher, major, superior

lesson [n1] *information taught* assignment, chalk talk*, class, coaching, drill, education, exercise, homework, instruction, lecture, period, practice, quiz, reading, recitation, schooling, study, task, teaching, test, tutoring; CONCEPTS 274,285,287

lesson [n2] *helpful example, communication* admonition, censure, chiding, deterrent, exemplar, helpful word, message, model, moral, noble action, notice, precept, punishment, rebuke, reprimand, reproof, scolding, warning; CONCEPTS 123,661,686

let [v1] *allow* accredit, approve, authorize, be big*, cause, certify, commission, concede, enable, endorse, free up, give, give leave, give okay, give permission, grant, have, hear of, leave, license, live with, make, permit, sanction, sit still for*, suffer, tolerate, warrant; CONCEPTS 50,83,88 —*Ant.* forbid, hinder, hold, impede, inhibit, keep, obstruct, prevent

let [v2] *rent out object, property* charter, hire, lease, sublease, sublet; CONCEPTS 89,115 —*Ant.* buy, sell

letdown [n] *disappointment* anticlimax, balk, bitter pill*, blow, chagrin, comedown, disgruntlement, disillusionment, frustration, setback, washout*; CONCEPTS 410,728 —*Ant.* advantage, benefit, blessing, boon, satisfaction

let down [v] *disappoint* abandon, depress, disenchant, disillusion, dissatisfy, fail, fall short, leave in lurch*, leave stranded*, lower, pull down, take down; CONCEPTS 7,19 —*Ant.* benefit, satisfy

lethal [adj] *deadly* baleful, dangerous, deathly, destructive, devastating, fatal, harmful, hurtful, malignant, mortal, mortiferous, mortuary, murderous, necrotic, noxious, pernicious, pestilent, pestilential, poisonous, virulent; CONCEPT 537 —*Ant.* beneficial, harmless, helpful, life-giving

lethargic [adj] *lazy, sluggish* apathetic, blah*, comatose, debilitated, dilatory, dopey, dormant, draggy*, drowsy, dull, enervated, having spring fever*, heavy, idle, impassive, inactive, indifferent, inert, lackadaisical, laggard, laid-back*, languid, languorous, listless, moony*, nebbish, out of it*, passive, phlegmatic, sleepy, sleepyhead*, slothful, slow, slumberous, snoozy, somnolent, spiritless, stolid, stretchy, stupefied, supine, torpid, wimpy*; CONCEPTS 401,403,584 —*Ant.* active, busy, energetic, lively, vital, vivacious

lethargy [n] *laziness, sluggishness* apathy, coma, disinterest, disregard, drowsiness, dullness, hebetude, heedlessness, idleness, impassivity, inaction, inactivity, inanition, indifference, indolence, inertia, inertness, insouciance, languor, lassitude, listlessness, passiveness, phlegm, sleep, sleepiness, sloth, slowness, slumber, stupor, supineness, torpidity, torpidness, torpor, unconcern, unmindfulness; CONCEPTS 315,410,633,748 —*Ant.* activity, busyness, energy, life, liveliness, vigor, vitality, vivaciousness, vivacity

let off [v] *make not subject to punishment or action* abandon, absolve, discharge, dispense,

drop, excuse, exempt, exonerate, forgive, let go, pardon, privilege from, release, relieve, remove, spare; CONCEPTS 50,83,88,317 —*Ant.* blame, incarcerate, punish

let on [v] *acknowledge, admit* allow, avow, betray, concede, confess, disclose, divulge, give away, grant, hint, imply, indicate, let out, make known, mouth*, own, own up*, reveal, say, spill*, suggest, tell, uncover, unveil; CONCEPTS 57,60 —*Ant.* deny, disacknowledge

letter [n1] *symbol of an alphabet* ABCs*, alphabet, cap, capital, character, majuscule, minuscule, rune, sign, small letter, type, uncial; CONCEPT 284 —*Ant.* number

letter [n2] *written communication* acknowledgment, answer, billet, dispatch, epistle, junk mail*, kite, line, memo, memorandum, message, missive, note, postcard, reply, report, thank you; CONCEPTS 271,278 —*Ant.* speech

letup [n] *pause* abatement, break, cessation, interval, lapse, lessening, let-up, lull, recess, remission, respite, slackening; CONCEPT 807 —*Ant.* continuation

let up [v] *pause* abate, cease, decrease, die down, die out, diminish, ease, ease off, ease up, ebb, fall, moderate, release, relent, slacken, slow down, stop, subside, wane; CONCEPTS 240,698 —*Ant.* continue

levee [n] *embankment* bank, breakwater, dam, earthwork, mound; CONCEPT 509

level [adj] *smooth, balanced* akin, aligned, alike, calm, commensurate, common, comparable, consistent, constant, continuous, equable, equivalent, even, exact, flat, flush, horizontal, identical, in line, leveled, like, lined up, matched, matching, of same height, on a line, on a par, on one plane, parallel, plain, planate, plane, planed, polished, precise, proportionate, regular, rolled, same, stable, steady, straight, trim, trimmed, unbroken, unfluctuating, uniform, uninterrupted; CONCEPTS 401,490,566 —*Ant.* ragged, uneven

level [n1] *horizontal position or thing* altitude, elevation, floor, height, layer, plain, plane, story, stratum, surface, zone; CONCEPTS 738,744

level [n2] *rank, position* achievement, degree, grade, stage, standard, standing, status; CONCEPTS 286,388

level [v1] *make even* equalize, equate, even, even off, even out, flatten, flush, grade, lay, make equal, make flat, mow, plane, press, roll, smooth, smoothen, straighten, surface; CONCEPT 250 —*Ant.* jag, rough up

level [v2] *destroy, demolish* bring down, bulldoze*, devastate, down*, drop, equalize, fell, flatten, floor, ground, knock down, knock over, lay low, mow*, pull down, raze, ruin, smooth, tear down, waste*, wreck; CONCEPTS 208,252 —*Ant.* build, construct

level [v3] *be honest* be above-board, be frank, be on the up and up*, be open, be straight, be straightforward, be up-front*, come clean*, come to terms*, keep nothing back*, talk straight*, tell the truth; CONCEPT 49 —*Ant.* deceive, lie

level [v4] *aim, direct* address, beam, cast, focus, incline, lay, point, slant, train, turn, zero in on; CONCEPT 187 —*Ant.* point away, turn

levelheaded [adj] *reasonable, calm* all there*, balanced, collected, commonsensical, composed, cool, cool as cucumber*, coolheaded*, dependable, discreet, even-tempered, farsighted, in one's right mind*, judicious, practical, prudent, rational, sane, self-possessed, sensible, steady, together, unflappable, wise, with all marbles*; CONCEPTS 403,542 —*Ant.* nervous, unreasonable, upset

leverage [n] *influence* advantage, ascendancy, authority, bargaining chip*, break, clout, drag, edge, grease*, jump on*, power, pull, rank, ropes*, suction, weight; CONCEPTS 687,693

levitate [v] *rise into the air* be suspended, defy gravity, drift, float, fly, hang, hover, rise, soar; CONCEPT 154

levity [n] *funniness, silliness* absurdity, amusement, buoyancy, facetiousness, festivity, fickleness, flightiness, flippancy, folly, foolishness, frivolity, giddiness, happiness, high spirits, hilarity, jocularity, laughs, lightheartedness, mirth, picnic*, pleasantry, repartee, trifling, triviality, volatility, wit; CONCEPTS 273,410 —*Ant.* gravity, seriousness

levy [n] *assessment, tax* burden, collection, custom, duty, exaction, excise, fee, gathering, imposition, impost, muster, tariff, toll; CONCEPT 329

levy [v] *assess, impose* call, call up, charge, collect, demand, exact, extort, gather, lay on, place, put on, raise, set, summon, tax, wrest, wring; CONCEPT 330 —*Ant.* disapprove, veto

lewd [adj] *vulgar, indecent* bawdy, blue, coarse, erotic, fast*, filthy*, foul-mouthed, gross*, hardcore*, immodest, immoral, improper, impure, in bad taste, incontinent, indelicate, lascivious, lecherous, libertine, libidinous, licentious, loose*, lustful, naughty, obscene, off-color*, pornographic, profligate, questionable, racy*, rakish, ribald, risqué, salacious, scandalous, scurrilous, shameless, smutty*, suggestive, taboo, unchaste, unclean, unconventional, unvirtuous, vile, wanton, wicked, X-rated*; CONCEPTS 372,542,545 —*Ant.* clean, decent, moral

lexicon [n] *collection of word meanings, usage* dictionary, glossary, terminology, thesaurus, vocabulary, wordbook, wordlist, word stock; CONCEPTS 276,280

liability [n1] *answerability, responsibility* accountability, accountableness, amenability, amenableness, arrearage, blame, burden, compulsion, culpability, debt, duty, indebtedness, obligation, onus, owing, subjection, susceptibility; CONCEPT 645 —*Ant.* irresponsibility, unaccountability

liability [n2] *burden, debt* account, arrear, arrearage, bad news*, baggage*, balance, bite*, chance, chit*, contingency, contract, damage, debit, disadvantage, drag*, drawback, due*, encumbrance, handicap, hindrance, impediment, inconvenience, indebtedness, indebtment, involvement, IOU*, lease, loan, millstone*, minus, misfortune, mortgage, nuisance, obligation, onus, pledge, possibility, remainder, responsibility, tab; CONCEPTS 332,674 —*Ant.* asset

liability [n3] *chance, probability* exposure, likelihood, openness, proneness, susceptibility,

tendency, vulnerability, vulnerableness; CONCEPTS 650,657

liable [adj1] *answerable, responsible* accountable, amenable, bound, chargeable, obligated, subject, tied; CONCEPT 545 —*Ant.* excusable, freed, irresponsible, unaccountable

liable [adj2] *open, likely* apt, assailable, attackable, beatable, conquerable, disposed, exposed, given, inclined, in danger, penetrable, prone, sensitive, subject, susceptible, tending, verisimilar, vincible, vulnerable; CONCEPTS 542,552 —*Ant.* immune, unlikely

liaison [n1] *person who acts as go-between* communication, connection, contact, fixer, hookup, in, interchange, interface, intermediary, link; CONCEPTS 348,354,423

liaison [n2] *love affair* amour, encounter, entanglement, fling, illicit romance, interlude, intrigue, romance; CONCEPTS 32,388

liar [n] *person who tells falsehood* cheat, con artist, deceiver, deluder, dissimulator, equivocator, fabler, fabricator, fabulist, false witness, falsifier, fibber, maligner, misleader, perjurer, phony, prevaricator, promoter, storyteller, trickster*; CONCEPT 412

libel [n] *purposeful lie about someone, often malicious* aspersion, calumny, defamation, denigration, lying, malicious, obloquy, smear, vituperation; CONCEPTS 63,318 —*Ant.* compliment, praise

libel [v] *purposefully lie about someone* asperse, bad-mouth*, blister, burlesque, calumniate, caricature, crack, defame, denigrate, derogate, drag name through mud*, give a black eye*, knock, malign, mark*, mark wrong, revile, roast, scandalize, scorch, sizzle, slur, smear, tear down, traduce, travesty, vilify; CONCEPTS 63,192 —*Ant.* tell truth

libelous [adj] *derogatory* aspersive, backbiting, calumniatory, calumnious, contumelious, debasing, defamatory, depreciative, detracting, detractory, disparaging, false, injurious, invidious, malevolent, malicious, maligning, opprobrious, pejorative, sarcastic, scurrilous, traducing, untrue, vilifying, vituperative; CONCEPT 267 —*Ant.* complimentary, praising

liberal [adj1] *progressive* advanced, avant-garde, broad, broad-minded, catholic, enlightened, flexible, free, general, high-minded, humanistic, humanitarian, indulgent, intelligent, interested, latitudinarian, left, lenient, libertarian, loose, magnanimous, permissive, radical, rational, reasonable, receiving, receptive, reformist, tolerant, unbiased, unbigoted, unconventional, understanding, unorthodox, unprejudiced; CONCEPTS 529,542 —*Ant.* conservative, narrow, narrow-minded

liberal [adj2] *giving, generous* altruistic, beneficent, benevolent, bighearted*, bounteous, bountiful, casual, charitable, eleemosynary, exuberant, free, free-and-easy, handsome, kind, lavish, loose, munificent, openhanded, openhearted, philanthropic, princely, prodigal, profuse, soft-touch, unselfish, unsparing, unstinging; CONCEPTS 334,401,404 —*Ant.* economical, greedy, mean, thrifty, ungenerous

liberal [adj3] *abundant, profuse* ample, aplenty, bounteous, bountiful, copious, dime a dozen*, galore, generous, handsome, lavish, munificent,

no end, plentiful, plenty, rich; CONCEPT 771
—*Ant.* lacking, poor, wanting

liberate [v] *give freedom* bail one out*, deliver, detach, discharge, disembarrass, emancipate, free, free up*, get out from under*, let loose*, let out*, loose, loosen, manumit, redeem, release, rescue, save, save one's neck*, set free, unbind, unchain, unhook, unshackle; CONCEPTS 83,110 —*Ant.* hold back, limit, prevent, restrain

liberation [n] *freedom* abolition, deliverance, democracy, emancipation, freeing, liberty, release, salvation, setting free, sovereignty, unchaining, unshackling; CONCEPT 691

liberty [n] *freedom* autarchy, authorization, autonomy, birthright, carte blanche, choice, convenience, decision, deliverance, delivery, dispensation, emancipation, enfranchisement, enlightenment, exemption, franchise, free speech, immunity, independence, leave, leisure, liberation, license, opportunity, permission, power of choice, prerogative, privilege, relaxation, release, rest, right, sanction, self-determination, self-government, sovereignty, suffrage, unconstraint; CONCEPTS 388,691 —*Ant.* arrest, imprisonment, incarceration, restraint

libidinous [adj] *lustful* carnal, coarse, concupiscent, debauched, fast, hot*, impure, incontinent, lascivious, lecherous, libertine, loose*, obscene, passionate, prurient, salacious, satyric, sensual, unchaste, wanton, wicked; CONCEPTS 372,545 —*Ant.* clean, decent, moral

libido [n] *sex instinct* eroticism, lust, passion, sex drive, sexual desire, sexuality, sexual urge, the hots*; CONCEPTS 20,709

library [n] *book repository* athenaeum, atheneum, bibliotheca, book collection, book room, information center, media center, reference center, study; CONCEPT 435

license [n1] *authority, permission* authorization, carte blanche, certificate, charter, consent, dispensation, entitlement, exemption, freedom, go-ahead*, grant, green light*, immunity, independence, latitude, leave, liberty, okay*, permit, privilege, right, self-determination, ticket, unconstraint, warrant; CONCEPT 685 —*Ant.* ban, prohibition, refusal, withholding

license [n2] *abandon, indulgence* anarchy, animalism, arrogance, audacity, boldness, complacency, debauchery, disorder, effrontery, excess, forwardness, gluttony, immoderation, impropriety, irresponsibility, lawlessness, laxity, looseness, presumptuousness, prodigality, profligacy, refractoriness, relaxation, relaxedness, sauciness*, self-indulgence, sensuality, slackness, temerity, unrestraint, unruliness, wantonness, wildness; CONCEPTS 633,645 —*Ant.* reason

license [v] *authorize* accredit, allow, certify, commission, empower, enable, let, permit, privilege, sanction, suffer, warrant; CONCEPTS 50,83,88 —*Ant.* ban, prohibit, refuse, withhold

licentious [adj] *immoral, uncontrolled* abandoned, amoral, animal, carnal, corrupt, debauched, depraved, desirous, disorderly, dissolute, fast, fast and loose*, fleshly, impure, incontinent, in the fast lane*, lascivious, lax, lecherous, lewd, libertine, libidinous, lickerish, loose*, lubricious, lustful, oversexed, profligate, promiscuous, relaxed, reprobate, salacious,

satyric, scabrous, sensual, swinging, unconstrained, uncontrollable, uncurbed, unmoral, unprincipled, unruly, wanton; CONCEPTS 372, 401,545 —*Ant.* chaste, controlled, good, innocent, moral

lick [n] *light touch; little amount* bit, brush, cast, dab, dash, hint, sample, smack, speck, stroke, suggestion, taste, tinge, trace, whiff; CONCEPTS 612,831

lick [v1] *touch with tongue* brush, calm, caress, fondle, glance, gloss, graze, lap, lap against, move over, osculate, pass over, play, quiet, ripple, rub, soothe, stroke, sweep, taste, tongue, touch, wash; CONCEPT 185,612

lick [v2] *play over with fire* blaze, burn, dart, flick, flicker, fluctuate, flutter, ignite, kindle, leap, palpitate, quiver, ripple, run over, shoot, touch, tremble, vacillate, vibrate, waver; CONCEPTS 249,612

lick [v3] *defeat, sometimes by hitting* beat, best, clobber, conquer, down, excel, flog, hit, hurdle, lambaste, master, outdo, outstrip, overcome, overwhelm, rout, slap, smear, smother, spank, strike, surmount, surpass, thrash, throw, top, trim, trounce, vanquish, wallop, whip; CONCEPTS 95,141,189 —*Ant.* lose

lid [n] *top covering* cap, cover, hood, roof, top; CONCEPT 836

lie [n] *untruth* aspersion, backbiting, calumniation, calumny, deceit, deception, defamation, detraction, dishonesty, disinformation, distortion, evasion, fable, fabrication, falsehood, falseness, falsification, falsity, fib, fiction, forgery, fraudulence, guile, hyperbole, inaccuracy, invention, libel, mendacity, misrepresentation, misstatement, myth, obloquy, perjury, prevarication, revilement, reviling, slander, subterfuge, tale, tall story*, vilification, white lie*, whopper; CONCEPTS 63,278 —*Ant.* honesty, truth

lie [v1] *tell an untruth* bear false witness, beguile, be untruthful, break promise, BS*, bull*, con, concoct, deceive, delude, dissemble, dissimulate, distort, dupe*, equivocate, exaggerate, fabricate, fake, falsify, fib, forswear, frame, fudge, go back on*, invent, make believe, malign, misguide, misinform, misinstruct, mislead, misrepresent, misspeak, misstate, overdraw, palter, perjure, pervert, phony, plant*, prevaricate, promote, put on*, put up a front*, snow*, soft-soap*, string along*, victimize; CONCEPT 63 —*Ant.* be honest

lie [v2] *be prostrate, flat* be prone, be recumbent, be supine, couch, go to bed*, laze, lie down, loll, lounge, nap, recline, repose, rest, retire, siesta, sleep, sprawl, stretch out, turn in; CONCEPTS 154,201 —*Ant.* be upright, stand, straighten

lie [v3] *be situated* be, be beside, be buried, be established, be even, be fixed, be found, be interred, be level, be located, belong, be on, be placed, be seated, beset, be smooth, exist, extend, have its seat in, occupy, prevail, reach, remain, spread, stretch; CONCEPT 746

life [n1] *animation, spirit* activity, being, breath, brio, dash, élan*, élan vital*, energy, enthusiasm, entity, esprit, essence, excitement, get-up-and-go*, go*, growth, heart, high spirits, impulse, lifeblood, liveliness, oomph*, sentience, soul, sparkle, verve, viability, vigor,

vitality, vivacity, zest*, zing*; CONCEPT 411
—Ant. inanimacy

life [n2] *existence, duration* being, career, continuance, course, cycle, days, endurance, epoch,
era, expectancy, extent, generation, history,
length, life span, lifetime, longevity, orbit,
period, pilgrimage, record, season, span,
survival, time; CONCEPTS 816,817

life [n3] *being* animal, animateness, animation,
body, breath, consciousness, continuance,
creature, endurance, entity, essence, existence,
flesh, flesh and blood*, growth, human, human
being, individual, living, living being, living
thing, man, metabolism, mortal, mortal being,
organism, person, personage, presence, soul,
subsistence, substantiality, survival, symbiosis,
viability, vitality, vital spark*, wildlife, woman;
CONCEPT 389 —Ant. death, inanimacy

life [n4] *history, biography* autobiography, bio,
career, confession, curriculum vitae, journal, life
story, memoir, memorial, story; CONCEPT 271

life [n5] *person's experiences* attainment, behavior, circumstances, conduct, development,
enjoyment, enlightenment, growth, hand one is
dealt*, happiness, human condition, journey,
knowledge, lifestyle, participation, personality,
realization, suffering, trials and tribulations*,
vicissitudes, way of life*, world; CONCEPT 678

life-and-death [adj] *vitally important* critical,
crucial, determining, earth-shaking, essential,
imperative, meaningful, paramount, pivotal,
serious, significant, urgent, vital; CONCEPT 567

lifeless [adj1] *not living, not containing living
things* asleep, bare, barren, brute, cold, comatose, dead, deceased, defunct, departed,
desert, empty, exanimate, extinct, faint, inanimate, inert, inorganic, insensate, insensible,
late, out cold*, sterile, unconscious, uninhabited, waste; CONCEPTS 485,539 —Ant. alive,
animate, living

lifeless [adj2] *dull, spiritless* blah*, cold, colorless, drab, draggy*, flat, hollow, insipid, lackluster, lethargic, listless, lusterless, nothing*,
pabulum*, passive, prosaic, prosy, slothful,
slow*, sluggish, spent, static, stiff*, torpid,
wooden*, zero*; CONCEPTS 401,542,584 —Ant.
energetic, lively, spirited

lifelike [adj] *realistic* authentic, faithful,
graphic, natural, original, real, representational,
representative, true, true to life; CONCEPT 582

lifelong [adj] *lasting* constant, continuing, deep-
rooted, enduring, for life, inveterate, lifetime,
livelong, long-lasting, long-lived, long-standing,
old, perennial, permanent, persistent; CONCEPT
798 —Ant. short-lived, temporary, tenuous

lifestyle [n̄] *way of life* behavior, conduct,
habits, style of living, way of acting; CONCEPT
633

lifetime [n] *span of animate being's existence*
all one's born days*, career, continuance,
course, cradle to grave*, days, endurance,
existence, life, life span, natural life, period,
time; CONCEPT 817

lifework [n] *person's calling* business, career,
interest, mission, occupation, profession,
purpose, pursuit, vocation, work; CONCEPTS
349,360 —Ant. task

lift [n1] *transportation* car ride, drive, journey,
passage, ride, run, transport; CONCEPT 155

lift [n2] *help, aid* assist, assistance, boost,
comfort, encouragement, hand, leg up*, pick-
me-up*, reassurance, relief, secours, shot in
the arm*, succor, support; CONCEPTS 110,700
—Ant. harm, ill will

lift [v1] *move upwards; ascend* arise, aspire,
bear aloft, boost, bring up, build up, buoy up,
climb, come up, disappear, disperse, dissipate,
draw up, elevate, erect, goose*, heft, hike, hike
up, hoist, jack up, jump up, mount, move up,
pick up, put up, raise, raise high, rear, rise, soar,
take up, up, upheave, uphold, uplift, upraise,
uprear, vanish; CONCEPTS 196,200,236,245
—Ant. descend, drop, lower

lift [v2] *repeal, revoke* annul, cancel, countermand, dismantle, end, recall, relax, remove,
rescind, reverse, stop, terminate; CONCEPTS
234,317 —Ant. impose, set down

lift [v3] *steal* abstract, appropriate, cop, copy,
crib, filch, hook, nip, pilfer, pinch, pirate,
plagiarize, pocket, purloin, snitch, swipe, take,
thieve; CONCEPTS 139,200 —Ant. give, receive

lift [v4] *promote, improve* advance, ameliorate,
boost, build up, dignify, elevate, enhance,
exalt, hike, jack up, raise, support, upgrade;
CONCEPTS 110,244 —Ant. demote, depress,
dispirit, weaken

liftoff [n] *rocket launch* blast-off, rocket firing,
rocket ignition, shot, take-off; CONCEPTS 179,222

ligature [n] *link* band, bandage, binding, bond,
connection, knot, ligament, nexus, rope, tie,
yoke; CONCEPTS 471,831

light [adj1] *illuminated* ablaze, aglow, bright,
brilliant, burnished, clear, cloudless, flashing,
fluorescent, glossy, glowing, lambent, lucent,
luminous, lustrous, phosphorescent, polished,
radiant, refulgent, resplendent, rich, scintillant,
shining, shiny, sunny, unclouded, unobscured,
vivid, well-lighted, well-lit; CONCEPTS 617,618
—Ant. black, dark, darkened, dim, gloomy,
obscure

light [adj2] *blond, fair* bleached, faded, fair-
skinned, light-hued, light-skinned, light-toned,
pale, pastel, tow-headed; CONCEPTS 406,618
—Ant. brunette, dark, dusky

light [adj3] *not heavy* agile, airy, atmospheric,
buoyant, crumbly, dainty, delicate, downy,
easy, effervescent, ethereal, featherweight,
feathery, filmy, flimsy, floatable, floating,
fluffy, friable, frothy, gossamery, graceful,
imponderous, inconsequential, insubstantial,
light-footed, lightweight, lithe, little, loose,
meager, nimble, petty, porous, portable, sandy,
sheer, slender, slight, small, spongy, sprightly,
sylphlike, thin, tissuelike, trifling, trivial, un-
heavy, unsubstantial, weightless; CONCEPT 491
—Ant. heavy, weighted

light [adj4] *small in amount, content* casual,
digestible, faint, fractional, fragmentary, frivolous, frugal, gentle, hardly any, hardly enough,
inadequate, inconsequential, inconsiderable, indistinct, insignificant, insufficient, mild, minor,
minuscule, minute, moderate, modest, not many,
not much, not rich, puny, restricted, scanty,
shoestring*, slight, soft, sparse, superficial, thin,
tiny, trifling, trivial, unimportant, unsubstantial,
weak, wee; CONCEPTS 762,789 —Ant. heavy

light [adj5] *simple, easy* effortless, facile,
manageable, moderate, smooth, undemanding,

unexacting, untaxing, untroublesome; CONCEPT 538 —Ant. difficult, heavy, laborious

light [adj6] *funny, cheery* airy, amusing, animated, blithe, carefree, cheerful, chipper*, chirpy, diverting, dizzy, entertaining, fickle, flighty, frivolous, gay, giddy, high, humorous, lighthearted, lively, merry, perky, pleasing, sunny, sunny-side up*, superficial, trifling, trivial, up, upbeat, witty; CONCEPTS 401,542 —Ant. grave, serious, solemn

light [n1] *luminescence from sun or other source* aurora, beacon, blaze, brightness, brilliance, brilliancy, bulb, candle, coruscation, dawn, daybreak, daylight, daytime, effulgence, emanation, flare, flash, fulgor, glare, gleam, glimmer, glint, glitter, glow, illumination, incandescence, irradiation, lambency, lamp, lantern, lighthouse, luminosity, luster, morn, morning, phosphorescence, radiance, radiation, ray, refulgence, scintillation, sheen, shine, sparkle, splendor, star, sun, sunbeam, sunrise, sunshine, taper, torch, window; CONCEPTS 620,624,628, 810 —Ant. dark, darkness, night, obscurity

light [n2] *context; point of view; understanding* angle, approach, aspect, attitude, awareness, comprehension, condition, education, elucidation, enlightenment, example, exemplar, explanation, illustration, information, insight, interpretation, knowledge, model, paragon, slant, standing, vantage point, viewpoint; CONCEPTS 274,409,682,686 —Ant. misconception, misunderstanding

light [v1] *illuminate* animate, brighten, cast, fire, flood, floodlight, furnish with light, highlight, ignite, illume, illumine, inflame, irradiate, kindle, lighten, light up, limelight, make bright, make visible, put on, shine, spot, spotlight, switch on, turn on; CONCEPTS 250,624 —Ant. darken, dull, obscure

light [v2] *start on fire* burn, enkindle, fire, flame, ignite, inflame, kindle, set fire to, set on fire, spark, strike a match; CONCEPT 249 —Ant. drench, extinguish, put out, quench

light [v3] *step down; land* alight, arrive, come down, deplane, detrain, disembark, drop, fly down, get down, perch, rest, roost, set down, settle, settle down, sit, sit down, stop, touch down; CONCEPTS 159,181 —Ant. mount

lighten [v1] *illuminate* become light, brighten, flash, gleam, illume, irradiate, light, light up, make bright, shine; CONCEPT 624 —Ant. blacken, darken, dim, dull

lighten [v2] *reduce weight, load* allay, alleviate, ameliorate, assuage, attenuate, buoy, change, comfort, cut down, decrease, dilute, disburden, disencumber, ease, empty, eradicate, extenuate, facilitate, free, jettison, lessen, levitate, make less, make lighter, mitigate, mollify, pour out, put off, reduce, relieve, remove, shift, take, take a load off*, thin, throw out, unburden, unload, uplift, upraise; CONCEPTS 110,244,250 —Ant. burden, weigh down

lighten [v3] *cheer up; inspire* brighten, buoy up, cheer, elate, encourage, gladden, hearten, lift, perk up, revive, take a load off; CONCEPTS 7,22 —Ant. bring down, burden, depress, upset

light-headed [adj] *silly; feeling faint* changeable, delirious, dizzy, empty, featherbrained*, fickle, flighty, flippant, foolish, frivolous,

gaga*, giddy, harebrained*, hazy, punchy*, reeling, rocky, scatterbrained*, shallow, superficial, swimming, swimmy, tired, trifling, vertiginous, whirling, woozy*; CONCEPTS 314,401 —Ant. healthy, ok, sober

lighthearted [adj] *carefree, untroubled* blithe, blithesome, bright, buoyant, cheerful, effervescent, expansive, feelgood*, frolicsome, gay, glad, gleeful, happy, happy-go-lucky*, high-spirited, insouciant, jocund, jolly, jovial, joyful, joyous, laid-back, lightsome, lively, merry, playful, resilient, spirited, sprightly, sunny, upbeat, vivacious, volatile; CONCEPTS 404,542 —Ant. depressed, heavy-hearted, troubled, upset, worried

lightly [adv] *gently, effortlessly* agilely, airily, breezily, carelessly, casually, daintily, delicately, easily, ethereally, faintly, flippantly, freely, frivolously, gingerly, heedlessly, indifferently, leniently, mildly, moderately, nimbly, peacefully, quietly, readily, simply, slightingly, slightly, smoothly, softly, sparingly, sparsely, subtly, tenderly, tenuously, thinly, thoughtlessly, timidly, unsubstantially, well; CONCEPTS 538,544,584 —Ant. effortfully, heavily

light out [v] *run away* abscond, depart, escape, head, leave, make, make off, quit, set out, strike out, take a hike, take off; CONCEPT 195 —Ant. stay, wait

lightweight [adj] *inconsequential* failing, featherweight, foolish, imponderous, incompetent, insignificant, of no account, paltry, petty, slight, trifling, trivial, unimportant, weightless, worthless; CONCEPTS 491,575 —Ant. big, consequential, heavyweight, important, major

likable [adj] *nice, pleasant* agreeable, amiable, appealing, attractive, charismatic, charming, engaging, enjoyable, friendly, genial, good, good-natured, likeable, pleasing, preferable, relishable, sweet, sweet-natured, sympathetic, winning, winsome; CONCEPT 404 —Ant. bad, disagreeable, hateful, mean, unlikable, unlikeable, unpleasant

like [adj] *similar* according to, agnate, akin, alike, allied, allying, analogous, approximating, approximative, close, coextensive, cognate, commensurate, comparable, compatible, conforming, congeneric, congenerous, consistent, consonant, corresponding, double, equal, equaling, equivalent, homologous, identical, in the manner of, jibing, matching, much the same, near, not far from, not unlike, on the order of, parallel, related, relating, resembling, same, selfsame, such, twin, undifferentiated, uniform; CONCEPTS 487,573 —Ant. different, dissimilar, unlike

like [v1] *enjoy, be fond of* admire, adore, appreciate, approve, be gratified by, be keen on, be partial to, be pleased by, be sweet on, care for, care to, cherish, delight in, derive pleasure from, dig*, dote on, esteem, exclaim, fancy, feast on, find appealing, get a kick out of*, go for*, hanker for, hold dear, indulge in, love, luxuriate in, prize, rejoice in, relish, revel in, savor, stuck on*, take an interest in, take delight in, take satisfaction in, take to; CONCEPT 32 —Ant. despise, dislike, hate

like [v2] *choose, feel inclined* care to, desire, elect, fancy, feel disposed, feel like, have a preference for, incline toward, please, prefer, select, want, will, wish; CONCEPTS 20,41 —*Ant.* dislike, ignore

likelihood [n] *chance of something happening* coin flip*, direction, even break, fair shake, fifty-fifty*, fighting chance*, good chance*, liability, likeliness, long shot*, outside chance*, plausibility, possibility, presumption, probability, prospect, reasonableness, shot at*, strong possibility, tendency, toss-up*, trend; CONCEPT 650 —*Ant.* unlikelihood

likely [adj] *probable, apt, hopeful* acceptable, achievable, anticipated, assuring, attainable, believeable, conceivable, conjecturable, credible, destined, disposed, expected, fair, favorite, feasible, given to, imaginable, inclined, in favor of, inferable, in the cards*, in the habit of*, liable, odds-on*, on the verge of, ostensible, plausible, possible, practicable, predisposed, presumable, promising, prone, rational, reasonable, seeming, subject to, supposable, tending, thinkable, true, up-and-coming*, verisimilar, workable; CONCEPT 552 —*Ant.* implausible, inapt, unforeseeable, unlikely

likely [adv] *probably* assumably, doubtless, doubtlessly, in all likelihood, in all probability, like as not, most likely, no doubt, presumably, presumptively, prima facie, seemingly, to all appearances; CONCEPT 552 —*Ant.* improbably, unlikely

like-minded [adj] *similar* agreeing, compatible, harmonious, in accord, in agreement, in harmony, of one mind, unanimous; CONCEPTS 487,573

liken [v] *compare* allegorize, approach, approximate to, assimilate, balance, bear comparison, be in the same class as*, be on a par with*, come up to, correlate, distinguish between, draw parallel, equal, equate, identify with, link, make like, match, notice similarities, parallel, put alongside, relate, resemble, show correspondence; CONCEPT 39

likeness [n] *correspondence in appearance; something that corresponds* affinity, agreement, alikeness, analogousness, analogy, appearance, carbon, clone, comparableness, comparison, conformity, copy, counterpart, dead ringer*, delineation, depiction, ditto*, double, effigy, equality, equivalence, facsimile, form, guise, identicalness, identity, image, knock-off*, lookalike*, model, parallelism, photocopy, photograph, picture, portrait, replica, representation, reproduction, resemblance, sameness, semblance, similarity, simile, similitude, study, uniformity, Xerox*; CONCEPTS 664,670,716 —*Ant.* difference, dissimilarity, unlikeness

likewise [adv] *also, similarly* additionally, along, as well, besides, correspondingly, further, furthermore, in addition, in like manner, in the same way, more, moreover, so, too, withal; CONCEPT 563 —*Ant.* contrariwise, opposing, opposite, reverse

liking [n] *fondness, taste* affection, affinity, appetite, appreciation, attachment, attraction, bent, bias, desire, devotion, fancy, favoritism, inclination, love, mind, palate, partiality, passion, penchant, pleasure, predilection, preference, proneness, propensity, relish, soft spot*, stomach, sympathy, tendency, tooth,

velleity, weakness, will; CONCEPTS 20,32,529 —*Ant.* dislike, hate, hatred

limb [n] *appendage* arm, bough, branch, extension, extremity, fin, gam*, leg, lobe, member, offshoot, part, pin, pinion, process, projection, spray, sprig, spur, stem, switch, unit, wheel, wing; CONCEPTS 392,428

limber [adj] *flexible* agile, deft, elastic, graceful, lissome, lithe, lithesome, loose, nimble, plastic, pliable, pliant, resilient, springy, spry, supple; CONCEPTS 406,488 —*Ant.* rigid, stiff, straight, unbending

limbo [n] *state of uncertainty* demilitarized zone, left field*, nothingness, nowhere, oblivion, out there*, Siberia*; CONCEPTS 679,705 —*Ant.* certainty, certitude, sureness, surety

limelight [n] *public attention* eminence, exposure, fifteen minutes of fame*, focus of-attention, glare, hype*, media attention, photo opportunity, prominence, public eye, public interest, public notice, public recognition, renown, spotlight; CONCEPT 261 —*Ant.* obscurity

limit [n1] *greatest extent* absolute, bitter end*, border, bottom line*, bound, bourne, breaking point*, brim, brink, cap, ceiling, check, circumscription, conclusion, confinement, confines, curb, cutoff point*, deadline, destination, edge, end, end point, extremity, far out, farthest point, farthest reach, fence, finality, goal, limitation, margin, maximum, obstruction, restraint, restriction, rim, termination, the max*, the most*, tops*, ultimate, utmost, verge; CONCEPTS 529,548,832 —*Ant.* infinity, limitlessness

limit [n2] *physical boundary* border, borderland, compass, confines, edge, end, extent, extreme, extremity, frontier, perimeter, periphery, precinct, purlieu; CONCEPTS 513, 745 —*Ant.* limitlessness

limit [v] *confine, restrict* appoint, assign, bar, bottle up, bound, cap, check, circumscribe, constrict, contract, cork, cramp, curb, define, delimit, delimitate, demarcate, draw the line, fix, hem in, hinder, inhibit, keep the lid on*, lessen, narrow, prescribe, ration, reduce, restrain, set, specify; CONCEPTS 5,130 —*Ant.* free, let go, release, unbound

limitation [n] *restraint, disadvantage* bar, block, check, circumspection, condition, constraint, control, cramp, curb, definition, drawback, impediment, inhibition, injunction, modification, obstruction, qualification, reservation, restriction, snag, stint, stricture, taboo; CONCEPTS 666,674 —*Ant.* advantage, extent, freedom, infinity, range, release

limited [adj1] *restricted, definite* bound, bounded, checked, circumscribed, confined, constrained, controlled, curbed, defined, delimited, determinate, finite, fixed, hampered, hemmed in, local, modified, narrow, particular, precise, qualified, reserved, restrained, sectional, topical; CONCEPTS 554,557 —*Ant.* indefinite, limitless, unbounded, unlimited, unrestricted

limited [adj2] *inadequate, short* cramped, diminished, faulty, ineffectual, insufficient, little, mean, minimal, narrow, paltry, poor, reduced, restricted, set, small, unsatisfactory; CONCEPT 771 —*Ant.* adequate, ok, satisfactory, sufficient

limitless [adj] *never-ending, infinite* bottomless, boundless, countless, endless, illimitable, immeasurable, immense, incomprehensible, indefinite, inexhaustible, innumerable, measureless, no end of*, no end to*, no holds barred*, no strings*, numberless, unbounded, uncalculable, undefined, unending, unfathomable, unlimited, untold, vast, wide-open; CONCEPTS 762,771,798 —*Ant.* calculable, ending, exhaustible, finite, limited, measureable

limp [*adj*] *not stiff; weak* bending, debilitated, drooping, droopy, ductile, enervated, exhausted, feeble, flabby, flaccid, flexible, flexuous, flimsy, floppy, impressible, infirm, languid, languishing, lax, lethargic, limber, listless, loose, plastic, pliable, pliant, relaxed, slack, soft, spent, spiritless, supple, tired, unsubstantial, weakened, wearied, worn out, yielding; CONCEPTS 490,604 —*Ant.* hard, inflexible, rigid, stiff, straight, strong, unbending

limp [*n*] *faltering walk* bad wheel, falter, flat wheel, floppy, gimp, halt, hitch, hobble, lameness; CONCEPT 151

limp [*v*] *walk with faltering step* clump, dodder, falter, flag, gimp, halt, hitch, hobble, hop, lag, scuff, shamble, shuffle, stagger, stumble, teeter, totter, waddle, walk lamely; CONCEPT 151

limpid [*adj*] *clear, comprehensible* bright, comprehensible, crystal-clear, crystalline, definite, distinct, filmy, intelligible, lucid, luculent, obvious, pellucid, perspicuous, pure, see-through, thin, translucent, transparent, transpicuous, unambiguous; CONCEPT 535 —*Ant.* incomprehensible, muddy, obscure, unintelligible, vague

line [*n1*] *mark, stroke; border* band, bar, borderline, boundary, channel, configuration, contour, crease, dash, delineation, demarcation, edge, figuration, figure, frontier, furrow, groove, limit, lineament, lineation, outline, profile, rule, score, scratch, silhouette, streak, stripe, tracing, underline, wrinkle; CONCEPTS 284,436

line [*n2*] *row, succession; course* arrangement, array, axis, band, block, border, catalogue, channel, column, concatenation, crack, direction, division, drain, echelon, file, fissure, formation, furrow, groove, group, lane, length, list, magazine, mark, order, path, progression, queue, rank, ridge, road, route, row, scar, seam, sequence, series, street, string, thread, tier, track, train, trajectory, trench, way; CONCEPTS 501,727,738,744

line [*n3*] *cord, rope* cable, filament, strand, string, thread, wire; CONCEPT 475

line [*n4*] *belief, policy* approach, avenue, course, course of action, ideology, method, polity, position, practice, principle, procedure, program, route, scheme, system; CONCEPTS 688,689

line [*n5*] *person's calling, interest* activity, area, business, department, employment, field, forte, job, occupation, profession, province, pursuit, racket*, specialization, trade, vocation, work; CONCEPTS 349,360 —*Ant.* entertainment, fun

line [*n6*] *ancestry* breed, descent, family, heredity, lineage, pedigree, race, stock, strain, succession; CONCEPT 296

line [*n7*] *written communication* card, letter, message, note, postcard, report, word; CONCEPT 271 —*Ant.* speech

line [*n8*] *hint; influential communication* clue, indication, information, lead, patter, persuasion,

pitch, prepared speech, song and dance*, spiel*; CONCEPT 278

line [*n9*] *merchandise carried by store* commodity, goods, involvement, materials, produce, trade, vendibles, wares; CONCEPT 338

line [*v1*] *border, mark* abut, adjoin, align, allineate, array, bound, butt against, communicate, crease, cut, delineate, draw, edge, fix, follow, fringe, furrow, group, inscribe, join, line up, march, marshal, neighbor, order, ordinate, outline, place, queue, range, rank, rim, rule, score, skirt, touch, trace, underline, verge; CONCEPTS 79,84,753

line [*v2*] *put covering inside object* bush, ceil, cover, encrust, face, fill, incrust, interline, overlay, panel, quilt, reinforce, sheath, stuff, wad, wainscot; CONCEPTS 172,218 —*Ant.* strip, unline

lineage [*n*] *ancestry* birth, blood, breed, clan, descendants, descent, extraction, family, folk, forebears, genealogy, heredity, house, kin, kindred, line, offspring, origin, pedigree, progenitors, progeny, race, stirps, stock, succession, tribe; CONCEPT 296

line-up [*n*] *list of participants* bill, cast, list, listing, program, queue, selection, side, squad, team; CONCEPT 294

linger [*v1*] *loiter, delay* amble, be dilatory, be long, be tardy, crawl, dally, dawdle, dillydally*, drift, falter, fool around*, fritter away*, goof off*, hang around*, hang out*, hesitate, hobble, idle, lag, loll, lumber, mope, mosey, plod, poke, procrastinate, put off, putter, remain, saunter, shuffle, sit around, slouch*, stagger, stay, stick around, stop, stroll, take one's time*, tarry, tool, totter, trail, traipse, trifle, trudge, vacillate, wait, wait around; CONCEPTS 151,681 —*Ant.* go, hurry, leave, rush

linger [*v2*] *continue, endure* abide, bide, cling, hang on, last, persist, remain, stand, stay, stick around, survive, wait; CONCEPTS 23,239 —*Ant.* halt, stop

lingerie [*n*] *women's undergarments* nightclothes, nightwear, underclothes, underclothing, underthings*, underwear, undies*, unmentionables*; CONCEPT 451

lingo [*n*] *dialect spoken by a group* argot, cant, idiom, jargon, language, patois, patter, slang, speech, talk, tongue, vernacular, vocabulary; CONCEPT 276 —*Ant.* standard

liniment [*n*] *ointment* balm, cream, dressing, embrocation, emollient, lenitive, lotion, medicine, salve, unguent; CONCEPTS 311,466

link [*n*] *component, connection* articulation, association, attachment, bond, channel, connective, constituent, contact, copula, coupler, coupling, division, element, fastening, hitch, hookup, in, interconnection, interface, intersection, joining, joint, junction, knot, ligament, ligation, ligature, loop, member, network, nexus, part, piece, relationship, ring, seam, section, splice, tie, tie-up, vinculum, weld, yoke; CONCEPTS 471,835 —*Ant.* whole

link [*v*] *connect* associate, attach, bind, bracket, combine, conjoin, conjugate, couple, fasten, group, hitch on, hook up, identify, incorporate, interface, join, meld with, network, plug into, relate, slap on, tack on, tag along, tag on, team up with, throw in with*, tie, tie in with, unite, yoke; CONCEPTS *113,114,193* —Ant. disconnect, divide, separate, unfasten, unlink

lionize [v] *celebrate* acclaim, adulate, aggrandize, eulogize, exalt, glorify, hero-worship, honor, idolize, immortalize, praise, roll out the red carpet*, show respect, worship; CONCEPT *69*

lip [n1] *edge, brink* border, brim, chops, flange, flare, labium, labrum, margin, nozzle, overlap, portal, projection, rim, spout; CONCEPTS *392,484,513* —Ant. inside, interior, middle

lip [n2] *insolence* back talk, cheek*, effrontery, guff*, impertinence, jaw*, mouth*, rudeness, sass*, sauce*, sauciness*; CONCEPTS *54,278* —Ant. kindness

lip service [n] *empty talk* duplicity, hollow words, insincerity, token agreement, tongue in cheek, unctuousness; CONCEPTS *267,542,545*

liquefy [v] *melt* deliquesce, dissolve, thaw; CONCEPTS *250,255*

liqueur [n] *liquor* alcohol, alcoholic beverage, aperitif, booze*, brandy, cognac, cordial, flavored drink, intoxicant, port, spirits; CONCEPT *455*

liquid [adj1] *fluid, flowing, melting* aqueous, damp, deliquescent, dissolvable, dissolved, dulcet, fluent, fluidic, fusible, ichorous, juicy, liquefied, liquescent, liquiform, luscious, melliflued, mellifluous, mellow, meltable, melted, moist, molten, moving, pulpy, running, runny, sappy, serous, smooth, soft, solvent, splashing, succulent, thawed, thin, uncongealed, viscous, watery, wet; CONCEPTS *485,584,603* —Ant. close, condensed, dense, firm, hard, solid

liquid [adj2] *readily available* convertible, fluid, free, marketable, negotiable, quick, ready, realizable, usable; CONCEPT *334* —Ant. frozen, unavailable

liquid [n] *fluid* aqua, aqueous material, broth, elixir, extract, flow, flux, goo*, goop*, juice, liquor, melted material, nectar, sap, secretion, slop*, solution, swill*; CONCEPT *467* —Ant. solid

liquidate [v1] *pay; change into cash* cash, cash in, cash out, clear, convert, discharge, exchange, honor, pay off, quit, realize, reimburse, repay, satisfy, sell off, sell up, settle, square; CONCEPT *330* —Ant. invest, keep

liquidate [v2] *destroy, dissolve* abolish, annihilate, annul, cancel, dispatch, do away with*, do in*, eliminate, exterminate, finish off*, get rid of*, kill, murder, purge, remove, rub out*, silence, terminate, vaporize, wipe out*; CONCEPT *252* —Ant. build, construct, create

liquor [n] *drink; alcoholic beverage* alcohol, aqua vitae, booze*, broth, decoction, drinkable, elixir, extract, firewater*, fluid, hard stuff*, inebriant, infusion, intoxicant, liquid, moonshine*, poison*, potable, sauce*, solvent, spirits, stock, the bottle*, whiskey; CONCEPT *455*

lissom [adj] *supple* adaptable, agile, bendable, bending, elastic, flexible, graceful, limber, lithe, lithesome, loose, malleable, moldable, pliable, pliant, resilient, rubber, springy, stretchy, wiry; CONCEPTS *488,604*

list [n] *record, tabulation* account, agenda, archive, arrangement, ballot, bill, brief, bulletin, calendar, canon, catalog, catalogue, census, checklist, contents, dictionary, directory, docket, draft, enumeration, file, gazette, index, inventory, invoice, lexicon, lineup, listing, loop, manifest, memorandum, menu, outline, panel, poll, program, prospectus, register, roll, roll call, row, schedule, screed, scroll, series, slate, statistics, syllabus, table, tally, thesaurus, ticket, timetable, vocabulary; CONCEPT *281*

list [v1] *keep a record; tabulate* arrange, bill, book, button down, calender, catalogue, census, chart, chronicle, classify, detail, docket, enroll, enter, enumerate, file, index, inscribe, insert, inventory, invoice, itemize, keep count, manifest, note, numerate, particularize, peg, place, poll, post, put down as, put down for, record, register, run down, schedule, set down, specialize, specify, spell out, tab, tally, tick off, write down; CONCEPTS *79,125* —Ant. forget

list [v2] *lean, slant* cant, careen, heel, incline, pitch, recline, slope, tilt, tip; CONCEPTS *154,201,738* —Ant. straighten

listen [v] *hear and pay attention* accept, admit, adopt, attend, audit, auscult, auscultate, be all ears*, be attentive, catch, concentrate, eavesdrop, entertain, get, get a load of*, give an audience to, give attention, give heed to, hang on words*, hark, harken, hearken, hear out, hear tell, lend an ear*, mind, monitor, obey, observe, overhear, pick up on*, prick up ears*, receive, take advice*, take into consideration*, take notice, take under advisement*, tune in, tune in on*, welcome; CONCEPT *596* —Ant. speak, talk

listless [adj] *spiritless, without energy* absent, abstracted, apathetic, blah*, bored, careless, dormant, dreamy, drowsy, dull, easygoing, energyless, enervated, faint, heavy, heedless, impassive, inanimate, inattentive, indifferent, indolent, inert, insouciant, lackadaisical, lagging, laid-back*, languid, languishing, languorous, leaden, lethargic, lifeless, limp, lukewarm, lymphatic, mopish, out of it*, passive, phlegmatic, slack, sleepy, slow, sluggish, stupid, supine, thoughtless, torpid, uninterested, vacant; CONCEPTS *401,584* —Ant. active, alert, attentive, energetic, lively, untired

litany [n] *recital of items, often part of religious services* account, catalogue, enumeration, invocation, list, petition, prayer, recitation, refrain, repetition, supplication, tale; CONCEPTS *278,368*

literacy [n] *ability to read* articulacy, articulateness, background, cultivation, education, knowledge, learning, proficiency, refinement, scholarship; CONCEPTS *409,630* —Ant. ignorance, illiteracy

literal [adj] *word for word; exact, real* accurate, actual, apparent, authentic, bona fide, close, critical, faithful, genuine, gospel, methodical, natural, not figurative, ordinary, plain, scrupulous, simple, strict, to the letter*, true, undeviating, unerring, unexaggerated, unvarnished, usual, veracious, verbal, verbatim, veritable, written; CONCEPTS *267,557* —Ant. exaggerated, figurative, imaginative, loose

literally [adv] *word for word; exactly* actually, completely, correctly, direct, directly, faithfully, indisputably, letter by letter*, literatim, not figuratively, plainly, precisely, really, rightly, rigorously, sic*, simply, straight, strictly, to the letter*, truly, undeviatingly, undisputably, unerringly, unmistakably, verbatim, veritably; CONCEPTS *267,557* —Ant. figuratively, loosely

literary [*adj*] *concerning books* belletristic, bookish, classical, erudite, formal, learned, lettered, literate, scholarly, well-read; CONCEPTS 267,536 —**Ant.** illiterate

literate [*adj*] *able to read and write* cultivated, cultured, educated, instructed, knowledgeable, learned, lettered, scholarly, schooled; CONCEPT 402

literature [*n*] *written matter, both fictional and nonfictional* abstract, article, belles-lettres, biography, books, brochure, classics, comment, composition, critique, discourse, disquisition, dissertation, drama, essay, exposition, findings, history, humanities, information, leaflet, letters, lit*, literary works, lore, novel, observation, pamphlet, paper, poetry, précis, prose, report, research, story, summary, theme, thesis, tract, treatise, treatment, writings, written work; CONCEPT 280 —**Ant.** speech

lithe [*adj*] *flexible, graceful and slender* agile, lean, lightsome, limber, lissome, loose, nimble, pliable, pliant, slight, slim, spare, supple, thin; CONCEPTS 488,491,584 —**Ant.** awkward, fat, stiff, thick

litigate [*v*] *bring matter before court of law* appeal, contest, dispute, drag into court*, file suit, go to court, go to law, institute legal proceedings, press charges, prosecute, see one in court*, sue, take the law on*; CONCEPT 317

litigation [*n*] *matter coming before court of law* action, case, cause, contention, dispute, lawsuit, process, prosecution, suit, trial; CONCEPT 318

litigious [*adj*] *quarrelsome* argumentative, belligerent, combative, contentious, disputable; CONCEPTS 401,542

litter [*n1*] *mess, debris* clutter, collateral, confusion, detritus, disarray, disorder, garbage, hash, hodgepodge, jumble, jungle, junk, mishmash, muck, muddle, offal, rash, refuse, rubbish, rummage, scattering, scramble, shuffle, trash, untidiness, waste; CONCEPTS 260,432 —**Ant.** cleanliness, sterility

litter [*n2*] *animal offspring* brood, cubs, family, kittens, piglets, progeny, puppies, school, young; CONCEPTS 394,397

litter [*v*] *make a mess* clutter, confuse, derange, dirty, disarrange, disarray, disorder, jumble, mess up, scatter, strew; CONCEPT 254 —**Ant.** clean up, tidy

little [*adj1*] *small in size, amount* babyish, bantam, brief, cramped, diminutive, dinky, elfin, embryonic, fleeting, hardly any, hasty, immature, imperceptible, inappreciable, inconsiderable, infant, infinitesimal, insufficient, junior, light, Lilliputian*, limited, meager, microscopic, mini, miniature, minute, not big, not large, peanut*, petite, scant, short, short-lived, shrimpy*, shriveled, skimpy, slight, snub, sparse, stubby, stunted, teeny, tiny, toy, truncated, undeveloped, wee, wizened, young; CONCEPTS 773,789 —**Ant.** big, enormous, giant, great, huge, immense, large, massive

little [*adj2*] *not important* casual, inconsiderable, insignificant, light, minor, minute, negligible, paltry, petty, shoestring*, small, trifling, trivial, unimportant; CONCEPT 575 —**Ant.** great, important, magnificent

little [*adj3*] *narrow-minded* base, bigoted, cheap, contemptible, hidebound, illiberal, ineffectual, limited, mean, narrow, paltry, petty, provincial, self-centered, selfish, set, small, small-minded, vulgar, wicked; CONCEPT 404 —**Ant.** magnanimous, open, open-minded

little [*adv*] *infrequently, not much* a little, barely, hardly, hardly ever, not many, not often, not quite, only just, rarely, scarcely, seldom, somewhat; CONCEPTS 530,544 —**Ant.** frequently, more, much

little [*n*] *small amount of something* bit, dab, dash, fragment, hint, modicum, particle, pinch, snippet, soupçon, speck, spot, taste, touch, trace, trifle, whit; CONCEPT 835 —**Ant.** lot

liturgy [*n*] *worship, ceremony* celebration, ceremonial, form, formality, formula, observance, rite, ritual, sacrament, service, services; CONCEPT 368

livable [*adj*] *adequate, acceptable* bearable, comfortable, cozy, endurable, fit, habitable, homey, inhabitable, livable, lodgeable, passable, satisfactory, snug, sufferable, supportable, sustainable, tenantable, tolerable, worthwhile; CONCEPTS 485,558 —**Ant.** inadequate, unacceptable, unbearable, unlivable, unsuitable

live [*adj1*] *existent* alive, animate, aware, breathing, conscious, living, vital; CONCEPT 539 —**Ant.** dead, non-existent

live [*adj2*] *energetic, vigorous* active, alert, brisk, burning, controversial, current, dynamic, earnest, effective, effectual, efficacious, efficient, functioning, hot*, lively, operative, pertinent, pressing, prevalent, running, topical, unsettled, vital, vivid, working; CONCEPT 542 —**Ant.** apathetic, dispirited, inactive, lethargic

live [*v1*] *exist* abide, be, be alive, breathe, continue, draw breath, endure, get along, get by, have life, last, lead, maintain, make it, move, pass, persist, prevail, remain, remain alive, subsist, survive; CONCEPT 407 —**Ant.** cease, depart, die

live [*v2*] *inhabit a dwelling* abide, bide, bunk*, crash*, dwell, hang one's hat*, hang out*, locate, lodge, nest, occupy, perch, reside, roost, settle; CONCEPT 226 —**Ant.** not use

live [*v3*] *enjoy being alive* be happy, delight, experience, flourish, love, luxuriate, make the most of, prosper, relish, savor, take pleasure, thrive; CONCEPT 678

live [*v4*] *make money to support living* acquire a livelihood, earn a living, earn money, fare, feed, get along*, get by*, maintain, make ends meet*, make it, profit, subsist, support; CONCEPT 351

livelihood [*n*] *occupation* alimentation, art, bread and butter*, business, circumstances, craft, employment, game*, grind*, income, job, keep*, living, maintenance, means, nine-to-five*, profession, racket*, rat race*, resources, slot, source of income, subsistence, support, sustenance, thing*, trade, vocation, what one is into*, work; CONCEPTS 349,351, 360 —**Ant.** entertainment, fun

lively [*adj*] *energetic, active, busy* agile, alert, animate, animated, astir, blithe, blithesome, bouncy, bright, brisk, buoyant, bustling, buzzing, cheerful, chipper*, chirpy*, complex, dashing, driving, effervescent, enjoyable, enterprising, entertaining, festive, frisky, frolicsome, full of pep*, gay, go-go*, happy, hyper*, industrious, involved, jocund, jumping, keen, merry, nimble, peppy*, perky, pert, provocative, quick, refreshing, rousing, snappy, sparkling, spirited, sprightly, spry, stimulating, stirring, vigorous, vivacious, zippy*; CONCEPTS 401,542,548 —*Ant.* apathetic, dispirited, inactive, lethargic, lifeless, sleepy

livid [*adj1*] *pale, ashen* ashy, blanched, bloodless, colorless, discolored, dusky, gloomy, greyish, grisly, leaden, lurid, murky, pallid, pasty, wan, waxen; CONCEPT 618 —*Ant.* blushing, brilliant, flushed, radiant, rosy

livid [*adj2*] *bruised* black-and-blue, contused, purple; CONCEPT 618

livid [*adj3*] *extremely angry* beside oneself, black*, boiling, enraged, exasperated, flaming, fuming, furious, hot*, incensed, indignant, infuriated, mad, offended, outraged; CONCEPTS 403,542 —*Ant.* cheerful, happy

living [*adj*] *existing, active* alert, alive, animated, around, awake, breathing, brisk, contemporary, continuing, current, developing, dynamic, existent, extant, in use, live, lively, ongoing, operative, persisting, strong, subsisting, ticking, vigorous, vital, warm; CONCEPTS 539,560 —*Ant.* dead, inactive

living [*n*] *lifestyle; source of income* alimentation, bread and butter*, existence, income, job, keep*, livelihood, maintenance, mode, occupation, salt*, subsistence, support, sustainment, sustenance, sustentation, way, work; CONCEPTS 335,351 —*Ant.* entertainment, fun

load [*n1*] *cargo, freight* amount, bale, bundle, capacity, charge, consignment, contents, encumbrance, goods, haul, heft, hindrance, lading, mass, pack, parcel, part, payload, shipment, shot, weight; CONCEPTS 338,432

load [*n2*] *burden, pressure* affliction, albatross, care, charge, cumber, deadweight*, drag, drain, duty, encumbrance, excess baggage*, incubus, liability, millstone*, obligation, onus, oppression, responsibility, task, tax, trouble, trust, weight, worry; CONCEPT 674 —*Ant.* benefit, blessing

load [*v1*] *burden, saddle* arrange, ballast, bear, carry, charge, chock, choke, containerize, cram, fill, flood, freight, glut, gorge, heap, heap up, jam*, lade, lumber, mass, oversupply, pack, pile, pile it on, pile up, place, pour in, put aboard, ram in, stack, store, stow, stuff, surfeit, swamp, top, top off, weigh, weigh down, weight; CONCEPT 209 —*Ant.* aid, assist, benefit, bless, help

load [*v2*] *overburden, pressure* burden, charge, encumber, hamper, lade, oppress, saddle, task, tax, trouble, weigh down, weight, worry; CONCEPT 14 —*Ant.* relieve, unburden

loaf [*n*] *block of something* bun, cake, cube, dough, lump, mass, pastry, roll, slab, twist; CONCEPTS 436,457,460,461

loaf [*v*] *be idle, lazy* be inactive, be indolent, be slothful, be unoccupied, bum*, bum around*, dally, dillydally*, dream, drift, evade, fool around*, fritter away*, goldbrick, hang out*, idle, kill time*, knock around*, laze, let down, lie, loiter, loll, lounge, lounge around, malinger, not lift a finger*, pass time, piddle, relax, saunter, shirk, sit around, slack, slow down,

stall, stand around, stroll, take it easy, trifle, twiddle thumbs*, vegetate, waste time, while away hours*; CONCEPTS 210,681 —*Ant.* achieve, do, energize, labor, work hard

loafer [*n*] *person who is idle, lazy* beachcomber, deadbeat, do-nothing, good-for-nothing*, goof-off*, idler, lazybones*, lounger, malingerer, ne'er-do-well*, shirker, slacker, slouch, sluggard, sponger, wanderer, waster, wastrel; CONCEPT 412 —*Ant.* hard worker

loan [*n*] *money given temporarily* accommodation, advance, allowance, credit, extension, floater, investment, mortgage, time payment, trust; CONCEPT 332

loan [*v*] *give money, possession temporarily* accommodate, advance, allow, credit, lay on one, lend, let out, provide, score, scratch, stake, touch; CONCEPT 115 —*Ant.* borrow

loath [*adj*] *against, averse* afraid, counter, disinclined, hesitant, indisposed, opposed, reluctant, remiss, resisting, uneager, unwilling; CONCEPTS 29,542 —*Ant.* approving, for, unopposed, willing

loathe [*v*] *dislike strongly* abhor, abominate, be allergic to*, be down on, decline, despise, detest, execrate, feel repugnance, find disgusting, hate, have aversion to, have no use for*, refuse, reject, repudiate, revolt, spurn; CONCEPT 29 —*Ant.* like, love

loathing [*n*] *abhorrence* contempt, detestation, disgust, dislike, enmity, hatred, repugnance, revulsion; CONCEPT 29

loathsome [*adj*] *hateful* abhorrent, abominable, beastly, bitchy*, creepy, deplorable, detestable, disgusting, execrable, gross, hideous, horrible, invidious, lousy, nasty, nauseating, obnoxious, odious, offensive, pesky, pestiferous, repellent, repugnant, repulsive, revolting, sleazy*, slimy*, uncool*, vile; CONCEPTS 485,529,570 —*Ant.* liking, lovable, respectful

lob [*v*] *toss* chuck, flip, hurl, launch, loft, pitch, project, propel; CONCEPT 222

lobby [*n*] *entrance hall* antechamber, corridor, doorway, foyer, gateway, hall, hallway, passage, passageway, porch, vestibule, waiting room; CONCEPTS 441,448

lobby [*v*] *press for political action* advance, affect, alter, bill, billboard*, boost, bring pressure to bear*, build up, campaign for, change, drum, exert influence, further, hard sell*, high pressure, hype*, induce, influence, make a pitch for*, modify, persuade, pitch, plug, politick, press, pressure, procure, promote, pull strings*, push, put pressure on, request, sell, sell on*, soft-sell*, soft-soap*, solicit, solicit votes, splash, spot, sway, sweet-talk*, thump, urge; CONCEPTS 68,300

lobbyist [*n*] *special interest representative* activist, influence peddler, mover and shaker, person of influence, powerbroker, pressure group; CONCEPTS 348,354

local [*adj*] *of a community, restricted to immediate area* bounded, civic, confined, district, divisional, geographical, insular, legendary, limited, narrow, neighborhood, parish, parochial, provincial, regional, sectarian, sectional, small-town, territorial, town, vernacular; CONCEPT 536 —*Ant.* foreign, nonnative

local [*n*] *person deeply rooted in community*

character, inhabitant, native, resident; CONCEPTS *413,423* —*Ant.* alien, foreigner, nonnative

locale/locality [n] *physical setting* area, bailiwick, belt, district, domain, haunt, hole, home, location, locus, neck of the woods*, neighborhood, place, position, region, scene, sector, site, sphere, spot, stage, stomping ground*, territory, theater, tract, turf, venue, vicinity, zone; CONCEPT *198*

localize [v] *confine* center, contain, limit, narrow, pinpoint, restrain, restrict, stop from spreading; CONCEPTS *121,130*

locate [v1] *find* come across, come upon, detect, determine, discover, establish, ferret out*, get at, happen upon, hit upon, hook*, lay one's hands on*, light upon*, meet with, pick up on, pin down, pinpoint, place, position, read, search out, smell out, smoke out*, spot, station, strike, stumble on, track down, trip over* uncover, unearth, zero in on*; CONCEPT *183* —*Ant.* lose, miss

locate [v2] *settle* dig in, dispose, dwell, establish, fix, hang one's hat*, inhabit, park, place, put, reside, seat, set, situate, squat, stand; CONCEPT *226* —*Ant.* depart, leave, move

located [adj] *situated* based, occupying, placed, positioned, posted, stationed; CONCEPTS *158,201*

location [n] *place of residence or activity* area, bearings, district, fix*, hole, locale, locality, locus, neck of the woods*, neighborhood, part, point, position, post, region, scene, section, site, situation, spot, station, tract, turf, venue, whereabouts; CONCEPT *198*

lock [n] *device that fastens and bars free passage* bar, bolt, bond, catch, clamp, clasp, clinch, connection, fastening, fixture, grapple, grip, hasp, hook, junction, latch, link, padlock; CONCEPT *499* —*Ant.* key

lock [v] *fasten, clasp* bar, bolt, button, button up, clench, close, clutch, embrace, encircle, enclose, engage, entwine, grapple, grasp, hug, join, latch, link, mesh, press, seal, secure, shut, turn the key, unite; CONCEPTS *85,160* —*Ant.* unclasp, unfasten, unlock

locker [n] *compartment* cabinet, chest, closet, trunk; CONCEPT *440*

locomotion [n] *movement* action, mobileness, mobility, motion, moving, progression, travel, travelling; CONCEPTS *2,145,697*

locution [n] *phrasing* accent, articulation, dialect, diction, expression, inflection, language, phraseology; CONCEPT *77*

lodge [n] *cabin; vacation residence* abode, auberge, burrow, camp, chalet, cottage, couch, country house, den, dormitory, dwelling, gatehouse, haunt, home, hospice, hostel, hostelry, hotel, house, hut, inn, motel, public house, retreat, roadhouse, shack, shanty, shelter, stopover, tavern, villa; CONCEPT *516*

lodge [v1] *become fixed or wedged* abide, catch, come to rest, embed, entrench, fix, imbed, implant, infix, ingrain, install, plant, remain, root, stay, stick; CONCEPT *201* —*Ant.* dislodge, get out

lodge [v2] *stay at temporary residence* abide, accommodate, bestow, board, bunk, canton, crash, domicile, dwell, entertain, harbor, hole up*, hostel, house, locate, nest, park*, perch*, put up, quarter, rent, reside, room, roost*,

shelter, sojourn, squat, station, stay, stay over, stop; CONCEPT *226* —*Ant.* leave

lodging [n] *accommodation for rent* abode, address, apartment, bed and breakfast, boarding house, camp, castle, chambers, cover, domicile, dorm, dwelling, habitation, harbor, home, hostel, hotel, inn, lodge, lodgment, motel, palace, pied-à-terre, place, port, protection, quarters, residence, resort, roof, room, room and board, rooming house, shelter; CONCEPT *516*

loft [n] *room on upper floor* apartment, attic, dormer, garret, storage, studio; CONCEPT *448*

lofty [adj1] *high, elevated* aerial, airy, high-rise, lifted, raised, sky-high, skyscraping, skyward, soaring, spiring, tall, towering; CONCEPT *779* —*Ant.* below, beneath, low

lofty [adj2] *grand, stately* arresting, benevolent, big, chivalrous, commanding, considerate, dignified, distinguished, elevated, exalted, generous, great, illustrious, imposing, magnanimous, majestic, noble, renowned, striking, sublime, superb, superior, utopian, visionary; CONCEPT *574* —*Ant.* below, beneath, humble, low, modest, unobtrusive

lofty [adj3] *arrogant, high and mighty* ambitious, cavalier, condescending, disdainful, grandiose, haughty, high-minded, immodest, insolent, overbearing, patronizing, pretentious, proud, snooty, supercilious; CONCEPT *401* —*Ant.* humble, modest

log [n1] *stump of tree* block, bole, chunk, length, piece, stick, timber, trunk, wood; CONCEPTS *428,479*

log [n2] *record* account, book, chart, daybook, diary, journal, listing, logbook, register, tally; CONCEPT *271*

logic [n] *science of reasoning* antithesis and synthesis, argumentation, coherence, connection, course of thought, deduction, dialectic, good sense, induction, inference, linkage, philosophy, ratiocination, rationale, relationship, sanity, sense, sound judgment, syllogism, syllogistics, thesis, train of thought; CONCEPTS *37,349,689* —*Ant.* unreasonableness

logical [adj] *probable, reasonable* analytic, analytical, clear, cogent, coherent, commonsensical, compelling, congruent, consequent, consistent, convincing, deducible, discerning, discriminating, extensional, fair, germane, holding together, holding water*, inferential, intelligent, judicious, juridicious, justifiable, kosher*, legit*, legitimate, lucid, most likely, necessary, obvious, perceptive, perspicuous, pertinent, plausible, rational, relevant, sensible, sound, subtle, telling, valid, well-organized, wise; CONCEPTS *402,529,552* —*Ant.* illogical, improbable, irrational, unlikely, unreasonable

logistics [n] *management* coordination, engineering, masterminding, organization, planning, plans, strategy, systematization; CONCEPT *660*

logo [n] *trademark* brand, brand name, emblem, identification, imprint, label, logotype, symbol, tag; CONCEPTS *259,284*

loiter [v] *hang around; stroll* amble, dabble, dally*, dawdle, delay, diddle, drag, flag, fritter away, get no place fast*, halt, hover, idle, lag, linger, loaf, loll, lounge, pass time, pause, poke, procrastinate, put off, ramble, saunter, shamble, shuffle, slacken, slough, tarry, trail, traipse, wait, waste time; CONCEPTS *151,210,681* —Ant. hurry, leave, rush, vamoose

loll [v] *lay sprawled* bum, dangle, dawdle, droop, drop, flap, flop, goof off, hang, hang loose, idle, laze, lean, loaf, loiter, lounge, recline, relax, rest, sag, slouch, slump, sprawl; CONCEPTS *154,210* —Ant. sit up straight

lone [adj] *by oneself; only* abandoned, alone, deserted, forsaken, isolated, lonely, lonesome, one, onliest, particular, secluded, separate, separated, single, singular, sole, solitary, solo, stag, unaccompanied, unique; CONCEPT *577* —Ant. accompanied, along, together

loneliness [n] *isolation* alienation, aloneness, desolation, forlornness, friendlessness, heartache, lonesomeness, remoteness, seclusion, solitariness, solitude, withdrawal; CONCEPTS *135,188,388,631*

lonely [adj1] *feeling friendless, forlorn* abandoned, alone, apart, by oneself, comfortless, companionless, deserted, desolate, destitute, disconsolate, down, empty, estranged, forsaken, godforsaken, homeless, isolated, left, lone, lonesome, outcast, reclusive, rejected, renounced, secluded, single, solitary, troglodytic, unattended, unbefriended, uncherished, unsocial, withdrawn; CONCEPTS *403,555* —Ant. befriended, loved, unlonely

lonely [adj2] *out-of-the-way* alone, deserted, desolate, godforsaken, isolated, obscure, off the beaten track*, private, quiet, remote, removed, retired, secluded, secret, sequestered, solitary, unfrequented, uninhabited; CONCEPT *583* —Ant. close, frequented, inhabited

loner [n] *recluse* anomic, hermit, introvert, lone wolf*, outsider, solitary; CONCEPTS *361,423*

lonesome [adj] *forlorn, friendless* alone, cheerless, companionless, deserted, desolate, dreary, gloomy, homesick, isolated, lone, lonely, solitary; CONCEPTS *403,555* —Ant. befriended, loved, unlonesome

long [adj1] *extended in space or time* continued, deep, distant, drawn out, elongate, elongated, enduring, enlarged, expanded, extensive, faraway, far-off, far-reaching, gangling, great, high, lanky, lasting, lengthened, lengthy, lingering, lofty, longish, outstretched, prolonged, protracted, rangy, remote, running, spread out, spun out, stretch, stretched, stretching, stringy, sustained, tall, towering; CONCEPTS *482,779,798* —Ant. abbreviated, abridged, short

long [adj2] *interminable, excessive in length* boundless, delayed, diffuse, diffusive, dilatory, dragging, drawn-out, for ages*, forever and a day*, late, lengthy, limitless, lingering, long-drawn-out*, long-winded*, overlong, prolix, prolonged, protracted, slow, sustained, tardy, unending, verbose, without end, wordy; CONCEPTS *544,798* —Ant. ephemeral, evanescent, fleeting, short

long [v] *desire, crave* ache, aim, aspire, covet, dream of, hanker, have a yen for, hunger, itch, lust, miss, pine, sigh, spoil for, suspire, thirst, want, wish, yearn; CONCEPT *20* —Ant. despise, dislike, hate

longevity [n] *long life* durability, endurance, lastingness, old age; CONCEPTS *411,633*

longing [adj] *desirous* anxious, ardent, avid, craving, eager, hungry, languishing, pining, ravenous, wishful, wistful, yearning; CONCEPT *403* —Ant. despising, hating, loathing

longing [n] *strong desire* ambition, aspiration, coveting, craving, fire in the belly*, hankering, hunger, hungering, itch, pining, thirst, urge, wish, yearning, yen; CONCEPTS *20,709* —Ant. dislike, hate, hatred

long shot [n] *outside chance* fluke, hundred-to-one shot, little chance, lucky shot, no chance, off-chance, one in a million*, slim chance, small chance; CONCEPT *679*

long-standing [adj] *existing for some time* abiding, durable, enduring, established, fixed, lasting, long-established, long-lasting, long-lived, traditional; CONCEPTS *551,798*

long-winded [adj] *wordy* bombastic, chatty*, gabby*, garrulous, loquacious, palaverous, prolix, rambling, talkative, verbose, voluble; CONCEPT *267*

look [n1] *visual examination* attention, beholding, case, cast, contemplation, evil eye*, eye*, flash, gander, gaze, glance, glimpse, gun, inspection, introspection, keeping watch, leer, look-see*, marking, noticing, observation, once-over, peek, reconnaissance, regard, regarding, review, scrutiny, sight, slant, speculation, squint, stare, surveillance, survey, swivel, view, viewing; CONCEPT *623* —Ant. disregard, ignorance

look [n2] *characteristic, stylish appearance* air, aspect, bearing, cast, complexion, countenance, demeanor, effect, expression, face, fashion, guise, manner, mien, mug*, physiognomy, presence, seeming, semblance, visage; CONCEPTS *655,673,716*

look [v1] *examine visually* admire, attend, behold, beware, consider, contemplate, eye, feast one's eyes*, flash, focus, gape, gawk, gaze, get a load of, glance, glower, goggle, heed, inspect, mark, mind, note, notice, observe, ogle, peep, peer, pore over, read, regard, rubberneck*, scan, scout, scrutinize, see, spot, spy, stare, study, survey, take a gander*, take in the sights*, tend, view, watch; CONCEPT *623* —Ant. disregard, ignore, miss, overlook

look [v2] *appear, seem to be* display, evidence, exhibit, express, indicate, look like, make clear, manifest, present, resemble, show, sound, strike as; CONCEPTS *261,716*

look [v3] *expect, anticipate* await, count on, divine, forecast, foretell, hope, hunt, reckon on, search, seek; CONCEPT *26*

look [v4] *face* front, front on, give onto, overlook; CONCEPT *746* —Ant. avoid, dodge

look-alike [n] *double* carbon copy, clone, copy, dead ringer*, duplicate, impersonator, match, replica, ringer*, spitting image*, stand-in*, twin; CONCEPTS *664,716*

look down on [v] *hold in contempt* abhor, contemn, despise, disdain, scorn, scout, sneer, spurn, turn nose up at*; CONCEPT *29* —Ant. approve, honor, laud, look up to, praise

look into [v] *check, research* audit, check out, delve into, dig, examine, explore, follow up, go into, inquire, inspect, investigate, look over, make inquiry, probe, prospect, scrutinize, sift, study; CONCEPT *103* —Ant. disregard, ignore

lookout [n] *guard; place from which to guard* anchor, beacon, belvedere, case, catbird seat*, citadel, crow's nest*, cupola, eagle eye*, hawk, observance, observation, observatory, outlook, overlook, panorama, patrol, post, scene, scout, sentinel, sentry, spotter, station, surveillance, tip, tower, view, vigil, vigilance, ward, watch, watcher, watch person watchtower*, weather eye*; CONCEPTS 198,358,623

look out [v] *be wary* be alert, be careful, be on guard, beware, check out, have a care, heads up*, hearken, keep an eye out*, keep tabs*, listen, mind, notice, pay attention, peg*, pick up on*, scope, shotgun*, size up, spot, spy, watch out; CONCEPTS 35,623 —*Ant.* disregard, ignore, neglect

look up [v1] *research* come upon, confirm, discover, find, hunt for, peruse, scan, search for, seek, seek out, track down; CONCEPTS 72,216 —*Ant.* wing it

look up [v2] *improve* advance, ameliorate, come along, convalesce, gain, get better, mend, perk up, pick up, progress, recuperate, shape up, show improvement; CONCEPTS 303,700 —*Ant.* deciine, worsen

loom [v] *appear, often imposingly* approach, await, be at hand*, become visible, be coming, be forthcoming, be imminent, be in the cards*, be in the wind*, be near, break through, brew, bulk, come forth, come into view, come on, come on the scene*, dawn, dominate, emanate, emerge, figure, gather, hang over, hover, impend, impress, issue, lower*, make up, menace, mount, near, overhang, overshadow, overtop, portend, rear, rise, seem huge, seem large, show, soar, stand out, take shape, threaten, top, tower; CONCEPTS 118,159,261

loony [adj] *crazy* ape, barmy, batty, berserk, bonkers*, cracked, crazed, cuckoo, daffy*, daft, delirious, demented, deranged, flaky, flipped out*, insane, kooky, lunatic, mad, maniacal, mental*, nuts, nutty, out of one's mind*, out to lunch*, psycho*, screwball*, screwy*, silly, touched*, unbalanced, wacky; CONCEPT 403

loony bin [n] *mental health facility* bughouse*, funny farm*, insane asylum, madhouse*, mental hospital, mental institution, nut house*, psychiatric hospital, psychiatric ward, sanatorium; CONCEPTS 312,439,516

loop [n] *circle, spiral* bend, circuit, circumference, coil, convolution, curl, curve, eyelet, hoop, kink, knot, loophole, noose, ring, twirl, twist, whorl, wreath; CONCEPT 436 —*Ant.* line

loop [v] *circle, spiral* arc, arch, begird, bend, bow, braid, coil, compass, connect, crook, curl, curve, curve around, encircle, encompass, fold, gird, girdle, join, knot, ring, roll, surround, tie together, turn, twist, wind around; CONCEPTS 147,201,754 —*Ant.* line

loophole [n] *escape* alternative, escape clause, means of escape, outlet, technicality, way out; CONCEPT 102

loose [adj1] *not tight; unconstrained* apart, asunder, at large, baggy, clear, detached, disconnected, easy, escaped, flabby, flaccid, floating, free, hanging, insecure, lax, liberated, limp, loosened, movable, not fitting, relaxed, released, separate, slack, slackened, sloppy, unattached, unbolted, unbound, unbuttoned, uncaged, unclasped, unconfined, unconnected, undone, unfastened, unfettered, unhinged, unhooked, unlatched, unlocked, unpinned,

unrestrained, unrestricted, unsecured, unshackled, untied, wobbly; CONCEPT 485 —*Ant.* constrained, restricted, taut, tight

loose [adj2] *indefinite, vague* detached, diffuse, disconnected, disordered, ill-defined, imprecise, inaccurate, indistinct, negligent, obscure, rambling, random, remiss; CONCEPTS 267,529 —*Ant.* clear, definite, precise, strict

loose [adj3] *promiscuous* abandoned, capricious, careless, corrupt, debauched, disreputable, dissipated, dissolute, easy, fast, heedless, high living*, immoral, imprudent, inconstant, lax, lewd, libertine, licentious, light, negligent, out of control*, playing, profligate, rash, reckless, speeding, swinging, thoughtless, unchaste, unmindful, unrestrained, wanton; CONCEPTS 372,401 —*Ant.* clean, decent, moral

loose/loosen [v] *set free; unbind* alleviate, become unfastened, break up, deliver, detach, discharge, disconnect, disengage, disenthrall, disjoin, ease, ease off, emancipate, extricate, free, let go, let out, liberate, manumit, mitigate, relax, release, separate, slacken, unbar, unbolt, unbuckle, unbutton, unchain, unclasp, undo, unfasten, unfix, unhitch, unhook, unlace, unlash, unlatch, unleash, unlock, unloose, unpin, unscrew, unsnap, unstick, unstrap, untie, untighten, work free, work loose; CONCEPTS 127,250 —*Ant.* bind, limit, restrict, tighten

loot [n] *stolen goods* booty, dough*, graft, haul, hot goods*, lift*, make*, money, pickings*, pillage, plunder, plunderage, prize, seizure, spoils, squeeze, take*; CONCEPTS 337,340

loot [v] *steal goods* appropriate, boost, burglarize, despoil, grab, gut, liberate, lift, loft, make, moonlight requisition*, pillage, plunder, raid, ransack, ravage, relieve, requisition, rifle, rip off*, rob, sack, salvage, smash and grab*, snatch, snitch*, stick up, swipe, take, thieve, tip over; CONCEPTS 139,192 —*Ant.* give, receive

looter [n] *thief* criminal, marauder, pilferer, pillager, plunderer, raider, ransacker, ravager, spoiler; CONCEPT 412

lop [v] *trim* chop, clip, crop, cut, cut back, cut down, mow, pare, pare down, prune, shear, snip, truncate; CONCEPTS 176,236,247

lope [v] *stride* bound, canter, gallop, run, trot; CONCEPT 149

lopsided [adj] *leaning, falling to one side; larger on one side* askew, asymmetrical, awry, cockeyed, crooked, disproportional, disproportionate, inclinatory, irregular, nonsymmetrical, off-balance, one-sided, out of shape, overbalanced, squint, tilting, top-heavy, unbalanced, unequal, uneven, unsteady, warped; CONCEPT 480 —*Ant.* even, level, straight, unleaning

loquacious [adj] *talkative* babbling, chattering, chatty, fluent, gabby*, garrulous, gossipy, jabbering, long-winded*, loose-lipped*, motormouth*, multiloquent, prolix, verbose, voluble, wordy, yacking*; CONCEPTS 267,401 —*Ant.* quiet, restrained, silent, subdued

lore [n] *myths, traditional wisdom* adage, belief, custom, doctrine, enlightenment, erudition, experience, fable, folklore, information, knowledge, learning, legend, letters, mythology, mythos, saga, saw, saying, scholarship, science, superstition, tale, teaching, tradition; CONCEPTS 274,282,287

lose [v1] *be deprived of; mislay* be careless, become poorer, be impoverished, bereave, be reduced, capitulate, consume, default, deplete, disinherit, displace, dispossess, dissipate, divest, drain, drop, exhaust, expend, fail, fail to keep, fall short, forfeit, forget, give up, lavish, misplace, miss, misspend, oust, pass up, relinquish, rob, sacrifice, squander, suffer, suffer loss, surrender, use up, waste, yield; CONCEPTS *116,156* —*Ant.* hold on to, keep, maintain

lose [v2] *be defeated* be humbled, be outdistanced, be sunk, be taken to cleaners*, be the loser, be worsted*, come up short, decline, drop, drop a bundle*, fall, kiss goodbye*, lose out, miss, succumb, suffer defeat, take a beating*, take the count*, take the heat*, yield; CONCEPTS *384,674* —*Ant.* achieve, succeed, win

lose [v3] *escape, avoid* clear, dodge, duck, elude, evade, give the slip*, leave behind, outrun, rid, shake, shake off*, slip away, stray, throw off*, unburden, wander from; CONCEPTS *30,102* —*Ant.* confront, face, meet

loser [n] *person, thing that fails* also-ran*, deadbeat*, defeated, disadvantaged, down-and-outer*, dud*, failure, flop*, flunkee*, has-been, underdog, underprivileged; CONCEPTS *412,423,433* —*Ant.* achiever, success, winner

loss [n] *misfortune, deficit; something misplaced or lost* accident, bad luck, bereavement, calamity, casualty, cataclysm, catastrophe, cost, damage, death, debit, debt, defeat, deficiency, depletion, deprivation, destitution, destruction, detriment, disadvantage, disappearance, disaster, dispossession, failure, fall, fatality, forfeiture, harm, hurt, impairment, injury, losing, misadventure, mishap, mislaying, misplacing, need, perdition, privation, retardation, ruin, sacrifice, shrinkage, squandering, trial, trouble, undoing, want, waste, wreckage; CONCEPTS *407,674,707* —*Ant.* accomplishment, achievement, success, win

lost [adj1] *missing, off-track* absent, adrift, astray, at sea, cast away, disappeared, disoriented, down the drain*, fallen between cracks*, forfeit, forfeited, gone, gone astray, hidden, invisible, irrecoverable, irretrievable, irrevocable, kiss goodbye*, lacking, minus, mislaid, misplaced, missed, nowhere to be found*, obscured, off-course, out the window*, strayed, unredeemed, vanished, wandering, wayward, without; CONCEPT *576* —*Ant.* accomplishing, found, successful, winning

lost [adj2] *extinct, destroyed* abolished, annihilated, bygone, consumed, dead, demolished, devastated, dissipated, eradicated, exterminated, forgotten, frittered, gone, lapsed, misspent, misused, obliterated, obsolete, out-of-date, past, perished, ruined, squandered, unremembered, wasted, wiped out*, wrecked; CONCEPTS *539, 560* —*Ant.* alive, existent, existing, living

lost [adj3] *distracted, dreaming* absent, absent-minded, absorbed, abstracted, bemused, bewildered, distrait, dreamy, engrossed, entranced, faraway, feeble, going in circles*, ignorant, inconscient, musing, perplexed, preoccupied, rapt, spellbound, taken in*, taken up*, unconscious, wasted; CONCEPT *403* —*Ant.* attentive, aware, cognizant

lot [n1] *piece of property* acreage, allotment, apportionment, area, block, clearing, division, field, frontage, parcel, part, patch, percentage, piece, plat, plot, plottage, portion, property, real estate, tract; CONCEPTS *509,710*

lot [n2] *quantity, often large* abundance, aggregate, aggregation, amplitude, assortment, barrel, batch, body, bunch, bundle, circle, clump, cluster, clutch, collection, conglomerate, conglomeration, consignment, crowd, great deal, group, heap, load, mass, mess*, much, multiplicity, number, ocean, oodles, order, pack, pile, plenitude, plenty, push, reams, requisition, scores, set, stack, stacks; CONCEPTS *432,787* —*Ant.* little

lot [n3] *portion, share* allotment, allowance, bite, cut, parcel, part, percentage, piece, quota, ration, slice, take; CONCEPTS *710,835* —*Ant.* totality, whole

lot [n4] *fate, destiny* accident, break, breaks, chance, circumstance, decree, doom, foreordination, fortune, hand one is dealt*, hazard, karma, kismet, Moirai, plight, portion, predestination, run of luck*, way cookie crumbles*, wheel of fortune*; CONCEPT *679*

lothario [n] *womanizer* Casanova, Don Juan, gigolo, ladies' man, lady-killer, lecher, libertine, lover, philanderer, rake, Romeo, seducer, skirt chaser, stud*, wolf*; CONCEPTS *372,401*

lotion [n] *creamy solution* balm, cosmetic, cream, demulcent, embrocation, lenitive, liniment, medicine, ointment, palliative, preparation, salve, unguent, wash; CONCEPTS *311,446,466*

lottery [n] *drawing* chance, door prize, gambling, game of chance, Lotto, luck of the draw, numbers game, raffle, sweepstake; CONCEPTS *28,363*

loud [adj1] *blaring, noisy* big, blatant, blustering, boisterous, booming, cacophonous, clamorous, crashing, deafening, deep, ear-piercing, ear-splitting, emphatic, forte, full, full-mouthed, fulminating, heavy, high-sounding, intense, loud-voiced, lusty, obstreperous, pealing, piercing, powerful, rambunctious, raucous, resonant, resounding, ringing, roaring, rowdy, sonorous, stentorian, strident, strong, thundering, tumultuous, turbulent, turned up, uproarious, vehement, vociferous, wakes the dead*; CONCEPTS *592,594* —*Ant.* inaudible, low, quiet, soft, subdued

loud [adj2] *offensive, gaudy* brash, brassy, brazen, chintzy, coarse, crass, crude, flamboyant, flashy, garish, glaring, gross, lurid, meretricious, obnoxious, obtrusive, ostentatious, raucous, rude, showy, tasteless, tawdry, vulgar; CONCEPTS *401,542,589* —*Ant.* inoffensive, quiet, soft, tasteful

loudmouthed [adj] *loud-voiced* bellowing, bigmouthed, big-voiced, blustering, boisterous, full-throated, obnoxious, vociferous; CONCEPT *401*

lounge [n] *club, socializing place* bar, barroom, club room, cocktail lounge, dive*, drinkery, hideaway, lobby, mezzanine, parlor, pub, reception, saloon, spot, tap, taproom, watering hole*; CONCEPTS *293,449*

lounge [v] *lie about, waste time* bum*, dawdle, fritter away, goldbrick*, goof off*, idle, kill time*, laze, loaf, loiter, loll*, pass time, recline, relax, repose, saunter, sprawl, take it easy*; CONCEPTS 154,210,681 —Ant. do, hustle

lousy [adj] *very bad* awful, base, contemptible, despicable, dirty, disliked, execrable, faulty, harmful, hateful, horrible, inferior, low, mean, miserable, no good*, outrageous, poor, rotten, second-rate*, shoddy, slovenly, terrible, unpopular, unwelcome, vicious, vile; CONCEPT 571 —Ant. good, great, magnificent, wonderful

lout [n] *boor* barbarian, bear, boob*, brute, buffoon, bumpkin, cad, churl, clod, clodhopper, dolt, dork*, goon*, lummox, oaf, philistine, rube, slob*, vulgarian; CONCEPT 423

loutish [adj] *boorish* bad-mannered, barbaric, bearish, bungling, cantankerous, churlish, cloddish, clodhopping*, clownish, clumsy, coarse, dense, doltish, gross*, gruff, ill-bred, ill-mannered, impolite, loud, oafish, ornery, rough, rude, rustic, swinish, uncivilized, uncouth, uncultured, uneducated, unmannerly, unpolished, unrefined, vulgar; CONCEPT 404

lovable [adj] *very likable; endearing* adorable, agreeable, alluring, amiable, angelic, appealing, attractive, bewitching, captivating, charming, cuddly, delightful, desirable, enchanting, engaging, enthralling, entrancing, fascinating, fetching, friendly, genial, lovely, lovesome, pleasing, ravishing, seductive, sweet, winning, winsome; CONCEPT 404 —Ant. hateable, hateful, unendearing

love [n1] *adoration; very strong liking* adulation, affection, allegiance, amity, amorousness, amour, appreciation, ardency, ardor, attachment, case*, cherishing, crush, delight, devotedness, devotion, emotion, enchantment, enjoyment, fervor, fidelity, flame, fondness, friendship, hankering, idolatry, inclination, infatuation, involvement, like, lust, mad for, partiality, passion, piety, rapture, regard, relish, respect, sentiment, soft spot*, taste, tenderness, weakness, worship, yearning, zeal; CONCEPT 32 —Ant. dislike, hate, hatred

love [n2] *person who is loved by another* admirer, angel, beau, beloved, boyfriend, courter, darling, dear, dearest, dear one, flame, girlfriend, honey, inamorata, inamorato, Juliet*, loved one, lover, paramour, passion, Romeo*, spark, suitor, swain, sweet, sweetheart, truelove, valentine; CONCEPT 423

love [v1] *adore, like very much* admire, adulate, be attached to, be captivated by, be crazy about, be enamored of, be enchanted by, be fascinated with, be fond of, be in love with, canonize, care for, cherish, choose, deify, delight in, dote on, esteem, exalt, fall for, fancy, glorify, go for*, gone on*, have affection for, have it bad*, hold dear, hold high, idolize, long for, lose one's heart to*, prefer, prize, put on pedestal*, think the world of*, thrive with, treasure, venerate, wild for*, worship; CONCEPT 32 —Ant. dislike, hate, scorn

love [v2] *have sexual relations* caress, clasp, cling, cosset, court, cuddle, draw close, embrace, feel, fondle, hold, hug, kiss, lick, look tenderly, make love, neck*, pet*, press, shine, soothe, stroke, take into one's arms, tryst, woo; CONCEPTS 375,384 —Ant. abstain

love affair [n] *sexual relationship outside of* marriage adultery, affair, amour, devotion, extracurricular activity*, flirtation, intrigue, liaison, love, ménage à trois, passion, romance, thing, triangle; CONCEPTS 375,388

love handles [n] *bulging waistline* fat, flab, hate handles*, keg*, middle age spread*, spare tire*; CONCEPTS 723,734

lovelorn [n] *unloved* bereft, crossed in love, dejected, forsaken, jilted, loveless, lovesick, rejected, spurned; CONCEPTS 21,30,384

lovely [adj] *beautiful, charming; agreeable* admirable, adorable, alluring, amiable, attractive, beauteous, bewitching, captivating, comely, dainty, delectable, delicate, delicious, delightful, enchanting, engaging, enjoyable, exquisite, fair, good-looking, gorgeous, graceful, gratifying, handsome, knockout, lovesome, nice, picture, pleasant, pleasing, pretty, pulchritudinous, rare, scrumptious, splendid, stunning, sweet, winning; CONCEPTS 537,579,589 —Ant. awful, disagreeable, drab, homely, ugly, unlovely, unsightly

lovemaking [n] *sexual activity* carnal knowledge, coition, coitus, copulation, coquetting, courting, courtship, cuddling, dalliance, fondling, fooling around, foreplay, hugging, intercourse, intimacy, kissing, mating, screwing, sexual intercourse, sexual relations, smooching*, snuggling, sucking face*; CONCEPT 375

lover [n] *person having sexual relationship* admirer, beau, beloved, boyfriend, companion, courter, darling, dear, dearest, escort, fiancé, fiancée, flame, girlfriend, idolizer, inamorata, inamorato, infatuate, Juliet*, paramour, petitioner, Romeo*, significant other, solicitor, steady, suitor, supplant, swain, sweetheart, truelove, valentine, wooer; CONCEPT 423 —Ant. enemy

lovesick [adj] *longing* desiring, infatuated, languishing, lovelorn, pining, yearning; CONCEPTS 21,30,384

loving [adj] *expressing adoration* admiring, affectionate, amatory, amiable, amorous, anxious, appreciative, ardent, attached, attentive, benevolent, bound up, caring, concerned, considerate, cordial, dear, demonstrative, devoted, doting, earnest, enamored, erotic, expressive, faithful, fervent, fond, friendly, generous, idolatrous, impassioned, infatuated, kind, liking, loyal, passionate, respecting, reverent, reverential, romantic, sentimental, solicitous, tender, thoughtful, valuing, warm, warm-hearted, worshipful, zealous; CONCEPTS 372,401,542 —Ant. disliking, hating, mean

low [adj1] *close to the ground; short* below, beneath, bottom, bottommost, crouched, decumbent, deep, depressed, flat, ground-level, inferior, junior, lesser, level, little, lowering, low-hanging, low-lying, low-set, minor, nether, not high, profound, prostrate, rock-bottom, shallow, small, squat, squatty, stunted, subjacent, subsided, sunken, under, unelevated; CONCEPTS 583,779,782,793 —Ant. above, high, tall

low [adj2] *reduced; mediocre* cheap, cut, cut-rate*, deficient, depleted, economical, inadequate, inexpensive, inferior, insignificant, little, low-grade, marked down, meager, moderate, modest, nominal, paltry, poor, puny, reasonable, scant, second-rate*, shoddy, slashed, small, sparse, substandard, trifling, uncostly, worthless; CONCEPTS 334,574,789 —*Ant.* above, elevated, high, increased, prominent

low [*adj3*] *crude, vulgar* abject, base, blue, coarse, common, contemptible, crass, crumby, dastardly, degraded, depraved, despicable, disgraceful, dishonorable, disreputable, gross*, ignoble, ill-bred, inelegant, mean, menial, miserable, nasty, obscene, off-color*, offensive, raw, rough, rude, scrubby, scruffy*, scurvy, servile, sordid, unbecoming, uncouth, undignified, unrefined, unworthy, vile, woebegone, woeful, wretched; CONCEPTS 404,542 —*Ant.* decent, honest, honorable, moral, respectable, upright

low [*adj4*] *living in, coming from poor circumstances* base, baseborn, humble, ignoble, lowborn, lowly, mean, meek, obscure, plain, plebeian, poor, rude, simple, unpretentious, unwashed; CONCEPT 549 —*Ant.* high, rich

low [*adj5*] *depressed* bad, blue*, crestfallen, dejected, despondent, disheartened, down, down and out*, downcast, downhearted, down in the dumps*, down in the mouth*, dragged, fed up, forlorn, gloomy, glum, in the pits*, lowdown*, miserable, moody, morose, sad, singing the blues*, spiritless, unhappy; CONCEPT 403 —*Ant.* cheerful, gay, happy

low [*adj6*] *not feeling well* ailing, debilitated, dizzy, dying, exhausted, faint, feeble, frail, ill, indisposed, poorly, prostrate, reduced, sick, sickly, sinking, stricken, unwell, weak; CONCEPT 314 —*Ant.* healthy, strong, well

low [*adj7*] *not loud* faint, gentle, hushed, muffled, muted, quiet, soft, subdued, whispered; CONCEPT 594

lowbrowed [*adj*] *uncultivated, vulgar* ignorant, illiterate, uneducated, unlearned, unlettered, unread, unrefined, unschooled, unsophisticated, untaught, untutored; CONCEPT 402

lower [*adj*] *under, inferior* bush-league*, curtailed, decreased, diminished, junior, lessened, lesser, low, lower rung, minor, nether, pared down, reduced, secondary, second-class, second-fiddle*, second-string*, smaller, subjacent, subordinate, under; CONCEPTS 586,772 —*Ant.* higher, important, superior

lower [*v1*] *let down; fall* bring low, cast down, couch, demit, depress, descend, detrude, droop, drop, ground, let down, make lower, push down, reduce, set down, sink, submerge, take down; CONCEPT 181 —*Ant.* elevate, increase, raise

lower [*v2*] *reduce, minimize* abate, clip, curtail, cut, cut back, cut down, decrease, decry, deescalate, deflate, demote, depreciate, devaluate, devalue, diminish, downgrade, downsize, lessen, mark down, moderate, pare, prune, roll back, scale down, shave, slash, soften, tone down, undervalue, write off; CONCEPTS 236,240 —*Ant.* elevate, heighten, increase, rise

lower [*v3*] *belittle, disgrace* abase, bemean, cast down, condescend, debase, degrade, deign, demean, depress, devalue, downgrade, humble, humiliate, stoop; CONCEPTS 7,19 —*Ant.* compliment, laud, praise

low-key [*adj*] *subdued* easygoing, laid-back*, loose, low-pitched, muffled, muted, played down, quiet, relaxed, restrained, sober, softened,

soft-sell*, subtle, toned down, understated; CONCEPTS 542,544,548 —*Ant.* energized, high-key, high-strung, nervous, pumped up

lowly [*adj*] *inferior, plain* average, base, baseborn, cast down, common, commonplace, docile, dutiful, everyday, gentle, humble, ignoble, low, lowborn, mean, meek, menial, mild, modest, mundane, obscure, obsequious, ordinary, plebeian, poor, proletarian, prosaic, retiring, reverential, servile, simple, submissive, subordinate, unassuming, unpretentious, withdrawing; CONCEPTS 404,547,549 —*Ant.* higher, lofty, noble, pretentious, superior

loyal [*adj*] *faithful, dependable* allegiant, ardent, attached, behind one, believing, coming through, constant, devoted, dutiful, dyed-in-the-wool*, firm, on one's side*, patriotic, resolute, staunch, steadfast, tried-and-true*, true, true-blue*, trustworthy, trusty, unfailing, unswerving, unwavering; CONCEPTS 404,545 —*Ant.* disloyal, undependable, unfaithful

loyalty [*n*] *faithfulness, dependability* adherence, allegiance, ardor, attachment, bond, conscientiousness, constancy, devotedness, devotion, duty, earnestness, faith, fealty, fidelity, homage, honesty, honor, incorruptibility, integrity, inviolability, obedience, patriotism, probity, reliability, resolution, scrupulousness, sincerity, single-mindedness, singleness, staunchness, steadfastness, subjection, submission, support, tie, troth, trueheartedness, trueness, trustiness, trustworthiness, truth, truthfulness, uprightness, zeal; CONCEPTS 411,645 —*Ant.* disloyalty, undependability, unfaithfulness

LSD [*n*] *lysergic acid diethylamide* acid, blotter acid*, blue heaven*, California sunshine*, cubes*, dots*, drug, electric Kool-aid*, hallucinogen, instant Zen*, Lucy in the sky with diamonds*, mellow yellows*, microdots*, Owsley, Owsley's acid, purple haze, strawberry fields*, sunshine, tabs*, yellow sunshine*; CONCEPT 307

lubricant [*n*] *lubricator* coating, grease, oil, silicone, wax, WD40™; CONCEPT 606

lubricate [*v*] *make slippery* anoint, cream, grease, lard, lube, make, oil, oil the wheels*, slick, smear, smooth, tallow, wax; CONCEPT 202 —*Ant.* dry

lucid [*adj1*] *evident, obvious* apprehensible, clear, clear-cut, comprehendible, comprehensible, crystal clear, distinct, explicit, fathomable, graspable, intelligible, knowable, limpid, luminous, pellucid, plain, translucent, transparent, transpicuous, unambiguous, unblurred, understandable; CONCEPT 529 —*Ant.* clouded, obscure, unclear, vague

lucid [*adj2*] *brilliant, shining* beaming, bright, effulgent, gleaming, incandescent, lambent, luminous, lustrous, radiant, refulgent, resplendent; CONCEPT 617 —*Ant.* cloudy, dark, gloomy, murky, shadowy

lucid [*adj3*] *clear, transparent* crystalline, diaphanous, gauzy, glassy, limpid, obvious, pellucid, pure, sheer, translucent, transpicuous, unblurred; CONCEPTS 606,619 —*Ant.* foggy, muddied, unclear

lucid [*adj4*] *clearheaded, sensible* all there, compos mentis, cool, got head together*, in right mind, normal, rational, reasonable, right, sane, sober, sound, together; CONCEPTS *402,403* —*Ant.* confused, puzzled, unclear, unreasonable

Lucifer [*n*] *Satan* archangel, beast, Beelzebub, devil, diablo, evil one, fallen angel, Mephistopheles, Prince of Darkness; CONCEPTS *370,412*

luck [*n1*] *good fortune* advantage, big break*, blessing, break*, fluke*, fortunateness, godsend*, good luck, happiness, health, in the cards*, karma*, kismet*, luckiness, lucky break*, occasion, opportunity, profit, prosperity, run of luck*, serendipity, smile*, streak of luck, stroke, success, triumph, victory, weal, wealth, win, windfall; CONCEPT *693* —*Ant.* bad fortune, misfortune

luck [*n2*] *chance* accident, break, destiny, fate, fifty-fifty*, fortuity, fortune, hap*, happenstance, hazard, occasion, occurrence, toss-up*, unforeseen event; CONCEPT *679*

luckily [*adv*] *happily* by chance, favorably, fortuitously, fortunately, opportunely, propitiously, providentially; CONCEPTS *544,572* —*Ant.* unhappily, unluckily

lucky [*adj*] *fortunate, opportune* advantageous, adventitious, all systems go*, auspicious, beneficial, benign, blessed, charmed, coming up roses*, everything going*, favored, felicitous, fortuitous, getting a break*, golden, happy, hit it big*, holding aces*, hopeful, hot*, in the groove*, into something, on a roll*, on a streak, promising, propitious, prosperous, providential, serendipitous, striking it rich*, successful, timely, well; CONCEPTS *537,572* —*Ant.* bad, inopportune, unfortunate, unlucky, unpropitious, unsuccessful

lucrative [*adj*] *productive, well-paid* advantageous, cost effective, fatness, fruitful, gainful, good, high-income*, in the black*, money-making, paying, profitable, remunerative, sweet, worthwhile; CONCEPT *334* —*Ant.* poorly paid, unprofitable

lucre [*n*] *money, profits* capital, cash, earnings, funds, gain, gate*, gravy*, income, proceeds, receipts, resources, revenue, riches, take*, wealth; CONCEPTS *332,340,344,693*

ludicrous [*adj*] *absurd, ridiculous* antic, bizarre, burlesque, comic, comical, crazy, droll, fantastic, farcical, foolish, funny, gelastic, grotesque, incongruous, laughable, nonsensical, odd, outlandish, preposterous, risible, silly, zany; CONCEPT *548* —*Ant.* logical, reasonable, sensible

lug [*v*] *drag something around* bear, buck, carry, convey, draw, ferry, haul, heave, hump, jerk, lift, lurch, pack, pull, rake, schlepp*, snap, tote, tow, transport, trawl, tug, vellicate, yank; CONCEPT *206*

luggage [*n*] *bag, suitcase* baggage, carry-on, case, fortnighter, gear, impedimenta, paraphernalia, suit bag, things*, tote bag, trunk, valise; CONCEPTS *446,494*

lukewarm [*adj1*] *slightly heated* blood-warm, milk-warm, tepid, warm, warmish; CONCEPT *605* —*Ant.* chilly, cool, cooled

lukewarm [*adj2*] *indifferent, unenthusiastic* apathetic, chilly, cold, cool, halfhearted, hesitant, indecisive, irresolute, phlegmatic, tepid, uncertain, uncommitted, unconcerned,

undecided, uninterested, unresolved, unresponsive, wishy-washy*; CONCEPTS *403,542* —*Ant.* enthusiastic, excited, happy, interested, warm

lull [*n*] *pause, calm* abeyance, break, breather, breathing spell, calmness, coffee break, comma*, downtime*, hiatus, hush, layoff, letup, pausation, quiescence, quiet, respite, silence, stillness, stop, time-out*, tranquility; CONCEPT *807* —*Ant.* busyness, continuation, disturbance, energy

lull [*v*] *calm, ease off* abate, allay, balm, becalm, cease, chill out*, compose, cool*, cool off*, decrease, die down, diminish, dwindle, ebb, fall, hush, lay back, let up, lullaby, moderate, pacify, put a lid on*, qualify, quell, quiet, quiet down, settle, slacken, soft-pedal*, soothe, still, stroke, subdue, subside, take it easy*, take the edge*, take the sting out*, temper, tranquilize, wane; CONCEPTS *7,22,210,698* —*Ant.* energize, excite

lumber [*v1*] *walk heavily, clumsily* barge, clump, galumph, lump, plod, shamble, shuffle, slog, stump, trudge, trundle, waddle; CONCEPT *151* —*Ant.* glide

lumber [*v2*] *burden* charge, cumber, encumber, impose upon, lade, land, load, saddle, tax, weigh; CONCEPT *14* —*Ant.* relieve, unburden

lumbering [*adj*] *clumsy, awkward* blundering, bovine, bumbling, clodhopping*, clunking, elephantine, gauche, gawky, halting, heavy, heavy-footed, hulking, inept, klutzy*, lead-footed*, lumpish, maladroit, overgrown, ponderous, splay, two left feet*, ungainly, unhandy, unwieldy, wooden; CONCEPTS *406,584* —*Ant.* agile, gliding, lithe

luminary [*n*] *very important person* big name*, celeb*, celebrity, dignitary, eminence, leader, lion*, name, notability, notable, personage, personality, somebody*, star, superstar, VIP*, worthy; CONCEPTS *352,423*

luminescent [*adj*] *glowing, shining* bright, effulgent, fluorescent, luminous, phosphorescent, radiant; CONCEPT *617* —*Ant.* dull, obscured, unshiny

luminous [*adj1*] *bright, glowing* beaming, brilliant, clear, crystal, effulgent, fulgent, illuminated, incandescent, lambent, lighted, lit, lucent, lucid, luminescent, lustrous, radiant, refulgent, resplendent, shining, translucent, transparent, vivid; CONCEPT *617* —*Ant.* dark, dim, dull, gloomy

luminous [*adj2*] *obvious, understandable* apprehensible, bright, brilliant, clear, comprehendible, comprehensible, evident, fathomable, graspable, intelligible, knowable, lucid, perspicacious, perspicuous; CONCEPT *529* —*Ant.* obscure, unclear, unintelligible, vague

lummox [*n*] *oaf* beast, blunderer, boor, bruiser, brute, bumpkin, chump*, clod, clodhopper, clown, dolt, dumb ox*, dunce, fool, goon*, half-wit*, hayseed, idiot, imbecile, klutz*, loser, lout*, lunkhead, moron, nincompoop*, ox*, sap*, simpleton*, yokel; CONCEPT *412*

lump [*n*] *clump, mass* agglomeration, ball, bit, block, bulge, bulk, bump, bunch, cake, chip, chunk, cluster, crumb, dab, gob, group, growth, handful, hunk, knot, knurl, lot, morsel, mountain, much, nugget, part, peck, piece, pile, portion, protrusion, protuberance, scrap, section, solid, spot, swelling, tumescence, tumor, wad, wedge; CONCEPTS 432,470,471

lump [v] *tolerate, withstand* abide, bear, brook, digest, endure, put up with, stand, stomach, suffer, swallow, take; CONCEPT 23 —*Ant.* change, fight, stand up

lunacy [n] *craziness, madness* aberration, absurdity, alienation, asininity, dementia, derangement, distraction, fatuity, folly, foolhardiness, foolishness, idiocy, imbalance, imbecility, inanity, ineptitude, insanity, mania, psychopathy, psychosis, senselessness, silliness, stupidity; CONCEPTS 410,633 —*Ant.* saneness

lunatic [adj] *crazy, mad* absurd, baked*, balmy*, bananas*, bonkers*, cracked, crazed, daft, demented, deranged, dippy*, flaky*, flipped out*, foolish, freaked out*, fried*, idiotic, insane, irrational, kooky*, loco, maniac, maniacal, nonsensical, nutty*, preposterous, psyched out*, psychotic, schizoid*, screwy*, stupid, unsound, whacko*, zany; CONCEPTS 401,403 —*Ant.* healthy, sane, sensible

lunatic [n] *person who is crazy, mad* crackpot*, crank, cuckoo*, demoniac, flake*, fruitcake*, kook*, lamebrain*, loon*, maniac, neurotic, nut*, paranoid, psycho*, psychopath, psychotic, scatterbrain, schizophrenic, sociopathic; CONCEPTS 412,809 —*Ant.* sane

lunge [n] *pounce* charge, cut, jab, jump, pass, spring, stab, swing, swipe, thrust; CONCEPTS 159,194 —*Ant.* retreat

lunge [v] *pounce, dive for* bound, burst, charge, cut, dash, drive, fall upon, hit, jab, jump, leap, lurch, pitch, plunge, poke, push, set upon, stab, strike, surge, thrust; CONCEPTS 159,194 —*Ant.* retreat

lurch [v] *move toward with jerk* blunder, bumble, careen, dodge, duck, falter, flounder, heave, jerk, lean, list, move to the side, pitch, reel, rock, roll, seesaw, slide, slip, stagger, stumble, sway, swing, teeter, tilt, toss, totter, wallow, weave, wobble, yaw; CONCEPTS 80, 150,152,194 —*Ant.* retreat

lure [n] *bait* allurement, ambush, appeal, attraction, bribe, call, camouflage, carrot*, come-on*, con game*, decoy, delusion, draw, enticement, fake, gimmick, hook, illusion, incentive, inducement, inveiglement, invitation, magnet*, mousetrap*, pull, seducement, seduction, siren song*, sitting duck*, snare, sweetener*, temptation, tout, trap, trick; CONCEPTS 32,529 —*Ant.* deterrent, warning

lure [v] *attract, seduce* allure, bag, bait, beckon, beguile, bewitch, cajole, captivate, capture, catch, charm, come on*, decoy, drag, draw, enchant, ensnare, entice, fascinate, grab, haul, hit on*, hook, inveigle, invite, lead on, pull, rope, steer, suck in*, sweep off one's feet*, tempt, train, turn on; CONCEPT 11 —*Ant.* antagonize, disenchant, disgust, dissuade, repulse, turn off

lurid [adj] *shocking, gruesome* ashen, bloody, deep, disgusting, distinct, exaggerated, extreme, fiery, ghastly, gory*, graphic, grim, grisly, hideous, horrible, horrid, horrifying, livid, low-down, macabre, melodramatic, obscene, off-color*, offensive, purple*, racy, raunchy, revolting, rough, salty, sanguine*, savage, sensational, sinister, startling, terrible, terrify-

ing, violent, vivid, yellow*; CONCEPTS 267,537 —*Ant.* clean, humble, modest

lurk [v] *hide; move stealthily* conceal oneself, creep, crouch, go furtively, gumshoe, lie in wait, prowl, skulk, slide, slink, slip, snake, sneak, snoop, stay hidden, steal, wait; CONCEPTS 151, 188 —*Ant.* come out

luscious [adj] *delicious, delectable* adorable, ambrosial, appetizing, choice, darling, delish, deluxe, distinctive, divine, exquisite, flamboyant, flavorsome, heavenly, honeyed, juicy, lush, luxurious, mellow, mouth-watering, nectarious, opulent, ornate, palatable, palatial, piquant, rare, rich, savory, scrumptious, succulent, sumptuous, sweet, toothsome, voluptuous, yummy*; CONCEPTS 574,613 —*Ant.* nasty, poor, unappetizing, unsavory

lush [adj] *profuse and delightful* abundant, ambrosial, delectable, delicious, deluxe, dense, elaborate, extensive, extravagant, exuberant, flourishing, fresh, grand, green, heavenly, juicy, lavish, luscious, luxuriant, luxurious, opulent, ornate, overgrown, palatial, plush, prodigal, prolific, rank, rich, riotous, ripe, ritzy, scrumptious, sensuous, succulent, sumptuous, teeming, tender, verdant, voluptuous; CONCEPTS 574,589,771 —*Ant.* austere, bare, barren, sparse

lust [n] *appetite, passion* animalism, aphrodisia, appetence, appetition, avidity, carnality, concupiscence, covetousness, craving, cupidity, desire, eroticism, excitement, fervor, greed, hunger, itch, lasciviousness, lechery, lewdness, libido, licentiousness, longing, prurience, pruriency, salaciousness, salacity, sensualism, sensuality, thirst, urge, wantonness, weakness, yen; CONCEPTS 20,709 —*Ant.* chastity, disenchantment, disgust

lust [v] *desire strongly* ache, be consumed with desire, be hot for*, covet, crave, hanker, hunger for, itch, long, need, pine, thirst, want, wish, yearn, yen; CONCEPT 20 —*Ant.* be chaste, be pure, dislike

luster [n] *gloss, shine* afterglow, brightness, brilliance, brilliancy, burnish, candescence, dazzle, effulgence, glaze, gleam, glint, glitter, glow, incandescence, iridescence, lambency, luminousness, opalescence, polish, radiance, refulgence, resplendence, sheen, shimmer, sparkle; CONCEPT 620 —*Ant.* darkness, dullness, matte

lustrous [adj] *glossy, shining* bright, burnished, dazzling, effulgent, fulgent, glacé, gleaming, glinting, glistening, glorious, glowing, incandescent, lambent, lucent, luminous, polished, radiant, refulgent, shimmering, shiny, sparkling, splendid, waxy; CONCEPT 617 —*Ant.* dark, dull, matte, unshiny

lusty [adj] *energetic, healthy* brawny, dynamic, hale, hearty, potent, powerful, red-blooded, robust, rugged, stalwart, stout, strapping, strenuous, strong, sturdy, tough, vigorous, vital; CONCEPTS 314,485,489 —*Ant.* lethargic, unenergetic, unhealthy, weak

luxuriant [adj] *profuse, plush* abundant, ample, copious, deluxe, dense, elaborate, excessive, extravagant, exuberant, fancy, fecund, fertile, flamboyant, flourishing, fruitful, lavish, luscious, lush, opulent, overflowing, palatial, plenteous, plentiful, prodigal, productive, profusive, prolific, rampant, rank, rich, riotous, sumptuous, superabundant, teeming, thriving; CONCEPTS 574,771 —*Ant.* barren, plain, poor

luxuriate [*v*] *indulge, prosper* abound, bask, be in clover*, bloom, burgeon, delight, eat up*, enjoy, feast, flourish, grow, increase, live extravagantly, live high on hog*, live in luxury*, live it up*, love, overdo, relish, revel, riot, roll, rollick, take it easy*, thrive, wallow, wanton; CONCEPTS 539,544,589 —*Ant.* refrain

luxurious [*adj*] *affluent, indulgent* comfortable, costly, deluxe, easy, elaborate, epicurean, expensive, extravagant, fancy, fit for a king/ queen*, gorgeous, grand, grandiose, gratifying, hedonistic, immoderate, imposing, impressive, in the lap of luxury, lavish, luscious, lush, magnificent, majestic, opulent, ostentatious, palatial, pampered, pleasurable, pleasure-loving, plush, plushy, posh, pretentious, rich, ritzy*, self-indulgent, sensual, sensuous, splendid, stately, sumptuous, sybaritic, upscale, voluptuous, well-appointed; CONCEPTS 544,574,589 —*Ant.* austere, frugal, poor

luxury [*n*] *great pleasure, indulgence* affluence, bliss, comfort, delight, enjoyment, exorbitance, extravagance, frill, gratification, hedonism, high living, immoderation, intemperance, leisure, luxuriousness, opulence, rarity, richness, satisfaction, splendor, sumptuousness, treat, well-being; CONCEPTS 337,388,712 —*Ant.* austerity, economy, frugality

lying [*adj*] *dishonest* committing perjury, deceitful, deceptive, delusive, delusory, dissembling, dissimulating, double-crossing*, double-dealing*, equivocating, false, falsifying, fibbing, guileful, inventing, mendacious, misleading, misrepresenting, misstating, perfidious, prevaricating, shifty, treacherous, tricky, two-faced*, two-timing*, unreliable, untruthful, wrong; CONCEPT 267 —*Ant.* direct, frank, honest

lynching [*n*] *hanging* capital punishment, execution, mob justice*, stringing up*, the gallows*, vigilante justice; CONCEPT 252

lyric [*adj*] *musical* choral, coloratura, mellifluous, melodic, melodious, poetic, songful, songlike, tuneful; CONCEPT 594

lyrical [*adj*] *musical* agreeable, blending, chiming, choral, dulcet, emotional, euphonious, expressive, harmonious, lilting, melodic, melodious, operatic, orchestral, passionate, pleasing, poetic, rhapsodic, rhythmic, songful, songlike, soulful, sweet-sounding, symphonic, symphonious, tuneful; CONCEPT 594

lyricist [*n*] *songwriter* composer, lyrist, musician, music writer, poet, songsmith, songwriter; CONCEPT 352

lyrics [*n*] *words of a song* book, libretto, lines, text, theme, verse, words; CONCEPTS 264,595

M

macabre [*adj*] *eerie; deathlike* cadaverous, deathly, dreadful, frightening, frightful, ghastly, ghostly, ghoulish, grim, grisly, gruesome, hideous, horrible, horrid, lurid, morbid, offensive, scary, spookish, spooky, terrible, unearthly, weird; CONCEPTS 537,547 —*Ant.* common, living, normal

macaroni [*n*] *pasta* noodles, penne, shells, spaghetti, tortellini; CONCEPTS 457,460,461

Machiavellian [*adj*] *scheming* artful, astute, calculating, conniving, contriving, crafty, cunning, deceitful, devious, expedient, opportunist, plotting, shrewd, sly, underhanded, unscrupulous, wily; CONCEPTS 401,545

machinate [*v*] *maneuver, plot* cogitate, collude, come up with, connive, conspire, contrive, design, devise, engineer, finagle, hatch, intrigue, invent, plan, play games*, promote, pull strings*, scheme, trump up*, wangle; CONCEPT 36 —*Ant.* leave alone

machination [*n*] *maneuver, plot* artifice, cabal, conspiracy, design, device, dirty work*, dodge*, intrigue, monkey business*, on the make*, ploy, practice, ruse, scheme, sellout, skullduggery*, song and dance*, stratagem, trick; CONCEPT 660

machine [*n1*] *device that performs a task* apparatus, appliance, automaton, automobile, computer, contraption, contrivance, engine, gadget, implement, instrument, mechanism, motor, robot, thingamabob*, tool, vehicle, widget*; CONCEPT 463

machine [*n2*] *well-run political organization* agency, lineup, machinery, movement, party, ring, setup, structure, system; CONCEPT 301

machine [*n3*] *person who acts automatically* agent, automaton, clone, drudge, grind, laborer, mechanical, puppet, robot, zombie*; CONCEPTS 348,423

machinery [*n*] *devices performing work* accoutrement, agency, agent, apparatus, appliance, channel, contraption, contrivance, engine, equipment, gadget, gear, habiliments, implement, instrument, materiel, means, mechanism, medium, method, motor, organ, outfit, paraphernalia, shifts, structure, system, tackle, tool, utensil, vehicle, works; CONCEPTS 463,770

machismo [*n*] *masculinity* macho*, male, manful, manliness, mannish, masculine, muscular, virile; CONCEPTS 371,408,648

macho [*adj*] *masculine* aggressive, cocky, courageous, manful, manly, potent, ultramasculine, virile; CONCEPTS 371,408,648

mad [*adj1*] *crazy, insane* aberrant, absurd, bananas*, batty, crazed, cuckoo*, daft, delirious, demented, deranged, distracted, fantastic, foolhardy, foolish, frantic, frenetic, frenzied, illogical, imprudent, invalid, irrational, kooky*, loony*, ludicrous, lunatic, mental, non compos mentis, nonsensical, nutty*, off one's rocker*, of unsound mind, out of one's mind*, preposterous, psychotic, rabid, raving, senseless, unbalanced, unhinged, unreasonable, unsafe, unsound, unstable, wacky*; CONCEPTS 403,529 —*Ant.* balanced, ok, rational, reasonable, sane, sound

mad [*adj2*] *angry* abandoned, agitated, berserk, distracted, distraught, enraged, exasperated, excited, frantic, frenetic, fuming, furious, incensed, infuriated, irritated, livid, provoked, raging, resentful, seeing red*, uncontrolled, very upset, wild, wrathful; CONCEPT 403 —*Ant.* calm, cheered, collected, happy

mad [adj3] *enthusiastic; in love* ardent, avid, crazy, daft, devoted, enamoured, enthused, fanatical, fond, hooked*, impassioned, infatuated, keen, nuts*, wild, zealous; CONCEPTS 32,403 —Ant. disenchanted, unenthusiastic

madcap [adj] *crazy, impulsive* brash, foolhardy, foolish, frivolous, harebrained*, heedless, hotheaded, ill-advised, imprudent, incautious, inconsiderate, lively, rash, reckless, stupid, thoughtless, wild; CONCEPT 548 —Ant. reasonable, sane

madden [v] *make angry* anger, annoy, bother, craze, derange, distract, drive crazy, drive insane, drive out of mind*, drive to distraction*, enrage, exasperate, frenzy, incense, inflame, infuriate, ire, irritate, make see red*, pester, possess, provoke, shatter, steam up*, umbrage, unbalance, unhinge*, upset, vex; CONCEPTS 7,19 —Ant. gladden, make happy

maddening [adj] *irritating* aggravating, annoying, exasperating, frustrating, infuriating, provoking, riling, troubling, trying, vexatious; CONCEPTS 529,565

made-up [adj] *invented mentally* fabricated, false, fictional, imaginary, make-believe, mythical, prepared, specious, trumped-up, unreal, untrue; CONCEPT 582 —Ant. original, real, true

madhouse [n] *place where mentally ill live; place full of commotion* asylum, bedlam, chaos, insane asylum, loony bin*, mental hospital, mental institution, pandemonium, psychiatric hospital, sanitarium, turmoil, uproar; CONCEPTS 312,449,516,674 —Ant. calm, harmony, peace

madly [adj] *wildly, fiercely* absurdly, crazily, deliriously, dementedly, desperately, devotedly, distractedly, energetically, exceedingly, excessively, excitedly, extremely, foolishly, frantically, frenziedly, furiously, hard, hastily, hurriedly, hysterically, insanely, intensely, irrationally, like mad, ludicrously, nonsensically, passionately, psychotically, quickly, rabidly, rapidly, rashly, recklessly, senselessly, something fierce, speedily, stormily, to distraction, tumultously/tumultuously, turbulently, unreasonably, violently; CONCEPTS 537,540, 544 —Ant. calmly, normally

madness [n] *insanity* aberration, absurdity, craziness, delirium, delusion, dementia, derangement, fanaticism, foolishness, hysteria, irrationality, lunacy, madness, mania, mental disorder, mental illness, neurosis, phobia, psychopathy, psychosis, stupidity, unbalance; CONCEPTS 316,410

mad person [n] *person who is considered mentally ill* bedlamite, crazy person, demented, deranged, idiot, imbecile, loon, lunatic, maniac, mental case*, patient, psycho*, psychopath, psychotic, raver*, schizophrenic, sociopath; CONCEPTS 412,423

maelstrom [n1] *agitation* bedlam, chaos, confusion, disorder, flap*, fuss, pandemonium, turbulence, turmoil, uproar; CONCEPTS 230,674

maelstrom [n2] *whirlpool* eddy, stir, swirl, undercurrent, undertow, vortex, whirl; CONCEPT 514

magazine [n1] *periodic publication* annual, bimonthly, biweekly, booklet, broadside, brochure, circular, daily, digest, gazette, glossy, joint, journal, monthly, monthly, newsletter, newspaper, organ, pamphlet, paper, periodical, pulp*, quarterly, rag*, review, semiweekly, sheet*, slick, throwaway*, weekly; CONCEPT 280

magazine [n2] *arsenal of weapons* ammunition dump, armory, cache, depository, depot, munitions dump, repertory, repository, store, storehouse, warehouse; CONCEPTS 321,500

magic [n] *supernatural power; appearance of impossible feats by tricks* abracadabra*, alchemy, allurement, astrology, augury, bewitchment, black art, conjuring, conjury, devilry, diabolism, divination, enchantment, exorcism, fascination, foreboding, fortune-telling, hocuspocus*, hocuscopy, illusion, incantation, legerdemain, magnetism, necromancy, occultism, power, prediction, presage, prestidigitation, prophecy, rune, sleight of hand, soothsaying, sorcery, sortilege, spell, superstition, taboo, thaumaturgy, trickery, voodoo, voodooism, witchcraft, wizardry; CONCEPTS 370,689

magician [n] *person who performs supernatural feats or tricks* archimage, charmer, conjurer, diabolist, diviner, enchanter, enchantress, exorciser, exorcist, fortune-teller, genie, genius, illusionist, marvel, medicine person, medium, miracle worker, necromancer, prophet, satanist, seer, shaman, siren, soothsayer, sorcerer, spellbinder, thaumaturge, theurgist, trickster, virtuoso, voodoo, warlock, witch, witch doctor, wizard; CONCEPTS 352,361

magic/magical [adj] *bewitching, charming* bewitched, charismatic, clairvoyant, conjuring, demoniac, diabolic, eerie, enchanted, enchanting, ensorcelled, entranced, entrancing, extraordinary, fascinating, fiendish, ghostly, haunted, imaginary, magnetic, marvelous, miraculous, mysterious, mystic, mythical, necromantic, occult, otherworldly, parapsychological, runic, sorcerous, spectral, spellbinding, spellbound, spiritualistic, spooky, telekinetic, thaumaturgic, tranced, uncanny, unusual, weird, witching, witchlike, wizardly, wonderful; CONCEPTS 537, 548,582 —Ant. normal, unmoving

magistrate [n] *civil officer* bailiff, JP, judge, justice, justice of the peace; CONCEPT 354

magnanimous [adj] *giving and kind* all heart, altruistic, beneficent, benevolent, big, bighearted, bountiful, charitable, considerate, forgiving, free, generous, great, greathearted, handsome, has heart in right place*, high-minded, kindly, knightly, liberal, lofty, loose, munificent, noble, openhanded, Santa Claus*, selfless, soft*, soft-touch*, ungrudging, unselfish, unstinting; CONCEPTS 404,542 —Ant. petty, stingy, suspicious

magnate [n] *important person, usually in business* aristocrat, bigwig*, businessperson, capitalist, captain of industry, chief, figure, financier, industrialist, leader, lion*, merchant, mogul, name, noble, notable, peer, personage, plutocrat, tycoon, VIP*; CONCEPT 347 —Ant. lowly

magnetic [adj] drawing, attractive alluring, appealing, arresting, bewitching, captivating, charismatic, charming, enchanting, entrancing, fascinating, hypnotic, inviting, irresistible, mesmerizing, pulling, seductive; CONCEPTS 404,537 —Ant. repellent, repulsive

magnetism [n] charm, attractiveness allure, appeal, attraction, captivatingness, charisma, draw, drawing power, enchantment, fascination, glamour, hypnotism, influence, lure, magic, mesmerism, power, pull, seductiveness, spell, witchcraft, witchery; CONCEPTS 411,676 —Ant. repugnance, repulsion

magnificent [adj] glorious, wonderful arresting, august, brilliant, chivalric, commanding, elegant, elevated, exalted, excellent, fine, glittering, gorgeous, grand, grandiose, high-minded, imperial, imposing, impressive, lavish, lofty, luxurious, magnanimous, magnific, majestic, noble, opulent, outstanding, palatial, plush, pompous, posh, proud, radiant, regal, resplendent, rich, royal, smashing, splendid, standout, stately, striking, sublime, sumptuous, superb, superior, superlative, swanky, towering, transcendent; CONCEPTS 485,572 —Ant. bad, offensive, poor, ugly

magnify [v1] enlarge, intensify aggrandize, aggravate, amplify, augment, bless, blow up, boost, build up, deepen, dignify, dilate, distend, enhance, ennoble, eulogize, exalt, expand, extend, glorify, heighten, hike, hike up, increase, inflate, intensate, jack up, jump up, mount, multiply, pad, pyramid, redouble, rise, rouse, run up, step up, sweeten, swell; CONCEPTS 236,244,245 —Ant. decrease, diminish, lessen, miniaturize, weaken

magnify [v2] exaggerate, blow out of proportion aggrandize, blow up*, boost, color, dramatize, embellish, embroider, enhance, fudge*, inflate, make mountain of molehill*, overcharge, overdo, overdraw, overemphasize, overestimate, overplay, overrate, overstate, overstress, pad*, puff up*, pyramid; CONCEPTS 49,69,266 —Ant. diminish, play down, weaken

magnitude [n1] importance consequence, degree, eminence, grandeur, greatness, import, mark, moment, momentousness, note, pith, significance, signification, weight, weightiness; CONCEPT 668 —Ant. insignificance, unimportant

magnitude [n2] size admeasurement, amount, amplitude, bigness, breadth, bulk, capacity, compass, dimension, dimensions, enormity, enormousness, expanse, extent, greatness, hugeness, immensity, intensity, largeness, mass, measure, measurement, proportion, proportions, quantity, range, reach, sizableness, space, strength, tremendousness, vastness, volume; CONCEPT 730 —Ant. littleness, smallness, tininess

maharishi [n] spiritual leader guru, master, mentor, mystic, spiritual guide, swami, teacher; CONCEPT 350

maiden [adj] earliest beginning, first, fresh, inaugural, initial, initiatory, intact, introductory, new, original, pioneer, primary, prime, un-broached, untapped, untried, unused; CONCEPTS 548,585 —Ant. concluding, final, latest

mail [n] written correspondence; system for sending correspondence air mail, communication, junk mail, letter, package, post, postal service, postcard, post office; CONCEPTS 271,770 —Ant. conversation

mail [v] send through the postal system dispatch, drop, express, forward, post, send by mail, transmit; CONCEPT 217

maim [v] cripple, put out of action batter, blemish, break, castrate, crush, damage, deface, disable, disfigure, dismember, disqualify, gimp*, hack, hamstring*, harm, hog-tie*, hurt, impair, incapacitate, injure, lame, mangle, mar, massacre, maul, mayhem, mutilate, spoil, truncate, warp, wound; CONCEPT 246 —Ant. aid, cure, heal, help, repair

main [adj1] principal, predominant capital, cardinal, central, chief, controlling, critical, crucial, essential, foremost, fundamental, head, leading, major, necessary, outstanding, paramount, particular, preeminent, premier, prevailing, primary, prime, special, star, stellar, supreme, vital; CONCEPTS 546,567,829 —Ant. auxiliary, extra, insignificant, minor, secondary, subordinate, unimportant

main [adj2] absolute, utter brute, direct, downright, entire, mere, only, pure, sheer, simple, undisguised, utmost; CONCEPT 535 —Ant. inessential, nonessential, unnecessary

main [n] pipe for system cable, channel, conduit, duct, line, trough, trunk; CONCEPT 494

mainly [adv] for the most part above all, chiefly, essentially, first and foremost, generally, in general, in the main, largely, mostly, most of all, on the whole, overall, predominantly, primarily, principally, substantially, to the greatest extent, usually; CONCEPTS 530,544

mainstay [n] chief support anchor, backbone, brace, bulwark, buttress, crutch*, good right arm*, linchpin*, maintainer, pillar, prop, right-hand person*, sinew, staff, standby, stay, strength, supporter, sustainer, upholder; CONCEPTS 646,712

mainstream [adj] prevailing accepted, average, common, conventional, current, dominant, established, general, normal, popular, predominant, primary, regular, standard, typical, widespread; CONCEPT 530 —Ant. heterodox

maintain [v1] care for, keep up advance, carry on, conserve, continue, control, cultivate, finance, go on with, guard, keep, keep going, look after, manage, nurture, perpetuate, persevere, preserve, prolong, protect, provide, renew, repair, retain, save, supply, support, sustain, take care of, uphold; CONCEPTS 134, 140 —Ant. ignore, neglect

maintain [v2] assert, claim; argue for advocate, affirm, allege, asseverate, attest, aver, avow, back, champion, contend, correct, declare, defend, emphasize, fight for, hold, insist, justify, persist, plead for, profess, protest, rectify, report, right, say, stand by, state, stress, uphold, vindicate; CONCEPTS 46,49,68 —Ant. condemn, desert, discard, forget

maintenance [n] *perpetuation, support; sustenance* aliment, alimentation, alimony, allowance, bacon*, bread, bread and butter*, care, carrying, conservation, continuance, continuation, food, keep, keeping, livelihood, living, nurture, preservation, prolongation, provision, repairs, resources, retainment, salt*, subsistence, supply, sustaining, sustainment, sustention, upkeep, wherewithal; CONCEPTS *134,340,457,712* —*Ant.* desertion, forsaking, ignorance, neglect

majestic [adj] *impressive, splendid* august, awesome, ceremonious, cool, courtly, dignified, elevated, exalted, fab*, grand, grandiose, imperial, imposing, lofty, magnific, magnificent, marvelous, mind-blowing*, monumental, noble, out of this world*, pompous, regal, royal, smashing, sovereign, stately, stunning, sublime, sumptuous, superb; CONCEPTS *567,572,574* —*Ant.* humble, low, lowly, shabby

major [adj1] *bigger* above, better, big, chief, considerable, dominant, elder, exceeding, extensive, extreme, greater, hefty, higher, large, larger, large-scale, leading, main, most, oversized, primary, senior, sizable, superior, supreme, ultra, upper, uppermost; CONCEPTS *574,773* —*Ant.* lesser, little, minor, small

major [adj2] *important* big, chief, critical, crucial, dangerous, grave, great, grievous, heavyweight, influential, life and death*, main, major-league, meaningful, notable, outstanding, overshadowing, preeminent, principal, radical, serious, significant, star, stellar, top, vital, weighty; CONCEPT *568* —*Ant.* insignificant, minor, unimportant

majority [n1] *plurality, most* best part*, bulk, greater number, greater part, larger part, lion's share*, mass, max*, more, more than half*, preponderance, superiority; CONCEPTS *766, 829,835* —*Ant.* minority, secondary

majority [n2] *adulthood* age of consent, drinking age, estate, full age, legal majority, manhood, maturity, prime, prime of life*, ripe age*, seniority, voting age, womanhood; CONCEPTS *715,817* —*Ant.* adolescence, childhood, minority, underage

make [v1] *create, build* accomplish, adjust, arrange, assemble, beget, brew, bring about, cause, compose, conceive, constitute, construct, cook, cook up*, dash off*, draw on, dream up, effect, engender, fabricate, fashion, forge, form, frame, generate, get ready, give rise to, hatch, initiate, invent, knock off*, lead to, manufacture, mold, occasion, originate, parent, prepare, procreate, produce, put together, secure, shape, spawn, synthesize, tear off, throw together*, whip, whip out*; CONCEPTS *168,173,205,221* —*Ant.* crush, destroy, raze, ruin

make [v2] *induce, compel* bring about, cause, coerce, concuss, constrain, dragoon, drive, effect, force, horn in*, impel, impress, initiate, interfere, meddle, oblige, press, pressurize, prevail upon, require, secure, shotgun, start, tamper; CONCEPTS *14,221* —*Ant.* discourage, dissuade, halt, prevent, stop

make [v3] *designate, appoint* advance, assign, constitute, create, delegate, elect, finger, install, invest, name, nominate, ordain, proffer, select, tap, tender; CONCEPTS *50,88* —*Ant.* demote, renounce

make [v4] *enact, execute* act, carry on, carry out, carry through, conduct, declare, decree, do, draft, draw up, effect, engage in, establish, fix, form, formulate, frame, legislate, pass, perform, practice, prepare, prosecute, wage; CONCEPTS *91,100,242* —*Ant.* deny, disallow, refuse, refute, veto

make [v5] *add up to; constitute* amount to, come to, compose, compound, comprise, construct, embody, equal, fabricate, form, make up, mix, organize, put together, represent, structure, synthesize, texture; CONCEPTS *664,667*

make [v6] *estimate, infer* calculate, collect, conclude, deduce, deduct, derive, dope out, draw, figure, gather, gauge, judge, reckon, suppose, think; CONCEPTS *15,37* —*Ant.* calculate, measure

make [v7] *earn, acquire* bring home bacon*, bring in, clean up*, clear, gain, get, harvest, hustle, net, obtain, pull, pull down*, rate, realize, reap, receive, secure, sock*, take in; CONCEPTS *120,124,351* —*Ant.* lose

make [v8] *arrive, aim at* advance, arrive at, arrive in time, attain, bear, break for, catch, get to, go, head, light out, meet, move, proceed, progress, reach, set out, strike out, take off; CONCEPTS *159,224* —*Ant.* fail

make-believe [adj] *imagined, unreal* acted, dream, false, fantasized, fantasy, fictional, fraudulent, imaginary, made-up, mock, pretend, pretended, sham, simulated; CONCEPTS *529,582* —*Ant.* real, true, unimagined

make-believe [n] *unreality* charade, disguise, dissimulation, dream, fairy tale, fakery, fantasy, imagination, pageant, playacting, pretense, pretension, pretentiousness, sham; CONCEPTS *689,725* —*Ant.* reality, truth

make believe [v] *pretend, dream* act as if, act as though, counterfeit, enact, fantasize, feign, fool, imagine, play, playact*, simulate; CONCEPTS *12,59* —*Ant.* live reality

make off [v] *flee, run away* abscond, bolt*, clear, cut and run, decamp, depart, escape, fly*, go, leave, make away, quit, retire, run, run for it, run off, scamper, scoot, skedaddle*, skip*, withdraw; CONCEPTS *102,150,195* —*Ant.* stay, wait

make out [v1] *see, recognize* detect, discern, discover, distinguish, espy, notice, observe, perceive, remark; CONCEPT *626* —*Ant.* fail

make out [v2] *understand* accept, catch, collect, compass, comprehend, conclude, decipher, deduce, deduct, derive, dig, fathom, follow, gather, grasp, infer, judge, perceive, realize, recognize, see, take in, work out; CONCEPTS *15,18* —*Ant.* misconceive, misunderstand

make out [v3] *get by, succeed* accomplish, achieve, do, do well enough, do with, endure, fare, flourish, get along, get on, manage, muddle through, prosper, score, thrive; CONCEPTS *23,91,140* —*Ant.* fail

makeshift [adj] *temporary* alternative, Band-Aid*, expedient, hit-or-miss*, make-do*, provisional, quick-and-dirty*, slapdash*, stop-gap, substitute, temp, throwaway*; CONCEPTS 551,560 —*Ant.* complete, finished, permanent, ready

makeshift [*n*] *temporary help* expediency, expedient, last resort, pis aller, recourse, refuge, replacement, resort, resource, shift, stopgap, substitute; CONCEPTS 658,712 —*Ant.* permanent

makeup [*n1*] *cosmetics* blush, face*, foundation, greasepaint, lipstick, maquillage, paint, pancake, powder*; CONCEPT 446

makeup [*n2*] *structure, composition* architecture, arrangement, assembly, configuration, constitution, construction, content, contents, design, form, format, formation, layout, order, ordering, organization, plan, scheme, setup, shape, spread, style; CONCEPT 757

makeup [*n3*] *person's character* build, cast, complexion, constitution, disposition, fiber, figure, frame of mind, grain, humor, individualism, individuality, make, mold, nature, personality, stamp, stripe, temper, temperament, vein; CONCEPT 411

make up [*v1*] *create* ad-lib*, blend, coin, combine, compose, compound, concoct, construct, contrive, cook up*, devise, dream up, fabricate, fake it, fashion, fix, formulate, frame, fuse, hatch, improv*, improvise, invent, join, knock off, make, meld, merge, mingle, mix, originate, play by ear*, prepare, pretend, put together, ready, trump up, whip up*, wing it*, write; CONCEPTS 173,202 —*Ant.* be real, tell truth

make up [*v2*] *comprise, constitute* complete, compose, consist, fill, form, furnish, include, make, meet, provide, supply; CONCEPT 643

make up [*v3*] *compensate, reconcile* accommodate, atone, balance, bury the hatchet*, come to terms, compose, conciliate, counterbalance, counterpoise, countervail, forgive and forget, make amends, make peace, mend, offset, outweigh, pacify, recompense, redeem, redress, requite, set off, settle, shake hands; CONCEPTS 126,384 —*Ant.* disagree

maladjusted [*adj*] *maladapted* abnormal, disturbed*, messed up*, muddled, neurotic, unfit, unstable; CONCEPT 547

maladroit [*adj1*] *awkward, clumsy* all thumbs*, blundering, bumbling, bungling, clunky, floundering, gauche, halting, heavy-handed, inept, inexpert, klutzy*, lumbering, stumbling, two left feet*, ungraceful, unhandy, unskillful; CONCEPTS 401,584 —*Ant.* able, capable, skillful

maladroit [*adj2*] *tactless* brash, gauche, impolitic, inconsiderate, inelegant, insensitive, thoughtless, undiplomatic, untactful, untoward; CONCEPT 401 —*Ant.* diplomatic, nice, sensitive, tactful

malady [*n*] *disease* ache, affection, affliction, ailment, attack, blight, bug*, cancer, complaint, condition, contagion, debility, disability, disorder, distemper, epidemic, fever, flu, ill health, illness, infection, infirmity, inflammation, plague, sickness, syndrome, virus; CONCEPT 306

malaise [*n*] *depression, sickness* angst, anxiety, debility, decrepitude, despair, discomfort, disquiet, distress, doldrums, enervation, feebleness,

illness, infirmity, infirmness, lassitude, melancholy, pain, sickliness, unease, uneasiness, unhealthiness, weakness; CONCEPTS 316,410 —*Ant.* good health, healthiness, well being

malapropos [*adj*] *inappropriate* inapposite, inapt, infelicitous, inopportune, tactless, uncalled for, unseemly, unsuitable, untimely; CONCEPT 558

malarky [*n*] *nonsense* absurdity, babble, balderdash*, baloney*, bombast, bull*, bunk*, drivel, foolishness, gibberish, giddiness, hogwash*, hot air*, jive*, poppycock*, prattle, rubbish, silliness, trash*; CONCEPTS 230,388,633

malcontent [*adj*] *dissatisfied* belly-aching, complaining, discontented, disgruntled, unhappy, unsatisfied; CONCEPT 403

male [*adj*] *masculine* macho*, manful, manlike, manly, paternal, potent, virile; CONCEPTS 371, 408 —*Ant.* female

male [*n*] *man* boy, brother, father, fellow, gent*, gentleman, grandfather, guy, he, husband, Mr., sir, son; CONCEPT 419 —*Ant.* female

malediction [*n*] *curse* anathema, commination, curse word, cuss, cuss word, damn, damnation, damning, darn, denunciation, dirty name*, dirty word*, execration, expletive, four-letter word*, imprecation, jinx, no-no*, oath, swear word, whammy*; CONCEPT 278 —*Ant.* blessing

malevolent [*adj*] *hateful* baneful, baleful, catty*, despiteful, dirty, evil, evil-minded, hellish, hostile, lousy, malicious, malign, malignant, murder, murderous, pernicious, poison, rancorous, rough, sinister, spiteful, tough, vengeful, vicious, vindictive, waspish, wicked; CONCEPTS 401,542 —*Ant.* amiable, harmless, kind, liking, loving

malformation [*n*] *deformity* abberation, abnormality, defect, disfigurement, impairment, injury, malconformation, misshape, monstrosity, mutation; CONCEPT 580

malformed [*adj*] *distorted* abnormal, contorted, crooked, deformed, grotesque, irregular, misshapen, twisted, warped; CONCEPT 486 —*Ant.* perfect, regular, shapely, undistorted

malfunction [*n*] *breakdown, failure* bug*, defect, fault, flaw, glitch*, gremlin*, impairment, slip; CONCEPTS 658,674 —*Ant.* perfection, working

malice [*n*] *hate, vengefulness* acerbity, animosity, animus, antipathy, bad blood, bane, bile, bitterness, despite, despitefulness, dirt, dislike, down, enmity, evil, grudge, hatefulness, hatred, hostility, ill will, implacability, malevolence, maliciousness, malignance, malignity, meanness, mordacity, poison, rancor, repugnance, resentment, spite, spitefulness, spleen, umbrage, venom, viciousness, vindictiveness; CONCEPT 29 —*Ant.* benevolence, friendliness, kindness, like, sympathy, thoughtfulness

malicious [*adj*] *hateful* awful, bad-natured, baleful, beastly, bitter, catty*, cussed, deleterious, despiteful, detrimental, envious, evil, evil-minded, green*, green-eyed*, gross*, ill-disposed, injurious, jealous, low, malevolent, malign, malignant, mean, mischievous, nasty, noxious, ornery, pernicious, petty, poisonous,

rancorous, resentful, spiteful, uncool*,
vengeful, venomous, vicious, virulent, wicked;
CONCEPTS 267,401 —*Ant.* benevolent, friendly,
good, kind, likeable, sympathetic, thoughtful

malign [*adj*] *hurtful, injurious* antagonistic,
antipathetic, bad, baleful, baneful, deleterious,
despiteful, destructive, detrimental, evil,
harmful, hateful, hostile, inimical, malefic,
maleficent, malevolent, malignant, noxious,
pernicious, rancorous, sinister, spiteful,
vicious, wicked; CONCEPTS 267,537,542
—*Ant.* aiding, benign, helpful, nice

malign [*v*] *slander, defame* abuse, accuse,
asperse, backbite*, bad-mouth*, befoul,
besmirch, bespatter, blacken, calumniate,
cast aspersion, curse, decry, defile, denigrate,
depreciate, derogate, detract, dirty*, disparage,
harm, injure, insult, misrepresent, mudsling,
opprobriate, pollute, rap, revile, roast*, run
down*, scandalize, slur, smear, soil, spatter*,
speak ill of, stain, sully, taint, take a swipe at*,
tarnish, tear down, traduce, vilify, villainize,
vituperate; CONCEPTS 44—*Ant.* praise, uphold

malignant [*adj*] *diseased* cancerous, deadly,
destructive, fatal, internecine, lethal, mortal,
pestilential, poisonous; CONCEPT 314 —*Ant.*
benign, harmless, uncancerous

malingerer [*n*] *slacker* dodger, goof-off, idler,
loafer, shirker; CONCEPT 412

mall [*n1*] *commercial complex with many
individual retail stores* commercial center,
market, mart, mini-mart, plaza, shopping center,
shopping mall; CONCEPTS 325,439,449

mall [*n2*] *shopping center* marketplace, shopping complex, shopping mall, shopping plaza;
CONCEPTS 323,333,449

mall [*n3*] *promenade* alameda, boardwalk,
boulevard, esplanade, parade, public walk,
walk; CONCEPT 501

malleable [*adj*] *pliable* adaptable, compliant,
ductile, flexible, governable, go-with-the-flow*,
impressionable, manageable, moldable, plastic,
pliant, putty in hands*, rolls with punches*,
soft, submissive, supple, tractable, tractile,
transformable, workable, yielding; CONCEPTS
403,485 —*Ant.* firm, rigid, stiff

malnutrition [*n*] *poor nutrition* anorexia
nervosa, bulimia, dietary deficiency, hunger,
malnourishment, starvation, undernourishment;
CONCEPTS 20,709

malodorous [*adj*] *foul-smelling* bad, decayed,
decomposed, fetid, foul, frowzy, funky*, fusty,
gamy*, high*, infested, lousy, mephitic, musty,
nasty, nauseating, noisome, noxious, off*,
offensive, pestilential, poisonous, polluted,
putrid, rancid, rank, reeking, rotten, smelly,
stale, stenchful, stinking, strong, tainted, vile;
CONCEPT 598 —*Ant.* aromatic, fragrant,
perfumed, savory, sweet

malpractice [*n*] *abuse, misconduct* carelessness,
dereliction, malefaction, misbehavior, misdeed,
mismanagement, negligence, offense, transgression, violation; CONCEPTS 101,156,310,324

mammoth [*adj*] *huge* behemothic, colossal,
elephantine, enormous, gargantuan, giant, gigantic, high, immense, jumbo, large, leviathan,
long, massive, mighty, monstrous, monumental,
mountainous, prodigious, stupendous, titanic,
vast; CONCEPT 773 —*Ant.* little, miniature,
small, tiny

man [*n*] *male human* beau, boyfriend, brother,
father, fellow, gentleman, grandfather, guy, he,
husband, Mr., nephew, papa, sir, son, spouse,
swain*, uncle; CONCEPT 419 —*Ant.* woman

manacle [*n*] *handcuff* bond, bracelet, chain,
fetter, iron, pinion, shackle; CONCEPT 497

manage [*v1*] *be in charge, control* administer,
advocate, boss, call the shots*, call upon,
captain, care for, carry on, command, concert,
conduct, counsel, designate, direct, disburse,
dominate, engage in, engineer, execute, govern,
guide, handle, head, hold down*, influence, instruct, maintain, manipulate, minister, officiate,
operate, oversee, pilot, ply, preside, regulate,
request, rule, run, run the show, steer, superintend, supervise, take care of, take over, take the
helm*, train, use, watch, watch over, wield;
CONCEPTS 94,117 —*Ant.* bumble, mismanage

manage [*v2*] *accomplish* achieve, arrange,
bring about, bring off, carry out, con*, contrive,
cook*, cope with, deal with, doctor*, effect,
engineer, execute, finagle, fix, jockey*, plant*,
play games*, pull strings*, push around, put
one over*, rig*, scam*, succeed, swing, upstage,
wangle*, work; CONCEPTS 91,706 —*Ant.* fail

manage [*v3*] *survive, get by* bear up, carry on,
cope, endure, fare, get along*, get on*, make
do*, make out*, muddle, scrape by*, shift,
stagger; CONCEPTS 23,407

manageable [*adj*] *controllable* amendable,
convenient, docile, easy, feasible, governable,
obedient, submissive, tamable, tractable,
trained, workable; CONCEPTS 401,404

management [*n1*] *persons running an organization* administration, authority, board, bosses,
brass, directorate, directors, employers, execs*,
executive, executives, executive suite, front
office*, head, mainframe*, management, micro
management*, person upstairs*, top brass*,
upstairs*; CONCEPT 325 —*Ant.* employees

management [*n2*] *running an organization*
administration, care, charge, command,
conduct, control, direction, governance,
government, guidance, handling, intendance,
manipulation, operation, oversight, rule,
superintendence, superintendency, supervision;
CONCEPTS 117,324 —*Ant.* mismanagement

manager [*n*] *person who runs organization*
administrator, boss, comptroller, conductor,
controller, director, exec*, executive, governor,
handler, head, head person, officer, official,
organizer, overseer, producer, proprietor,
slavedriver*, straw boss*, superintendent,
supervisor, zookeeper*; CONCEPT 347
—*Ant.* employee

mandate [*n*] *authority, order* authorization,
behest, bidding, blank check*, carte blanche*,
charge, command, commission, decree, dictate,
directive, edict, fiat, go-ahead*, green light*,
imperative, injunction, instruction, okay*,
precept, sanction, warrant, word*; CONCEPTS
318,685 —*Ant.* denial, veto

mandatory [adj] *required, necessary* binding, commanding, compelling, compulsatory, compulsory, de rigueur, essential, forced, imperative, imperious, indispensable, involuntary, irremissible, needful, obligatory, requisite; CONCEPT 546 —*Ant.* optional, unnecessary, voluntary

maneuver [n1] *move, tactic* action, angle, artifice, contrivance, curveball, demarche, device, dodge, fancy footwork*, feint, finesse, gambit, game, gimmick, intrigue, jig*, machination, manipulation, measure, movement, plan, play, plot, ploy, procedure, proceeding, ruse, scheme, shenanigans*, shuffle*, step, stratagem, stunt, subterfuge, trick; CONCEPTS 6,660

maneuver [n2] *military practice, operation* battle, deployment, drill, evolution, exercise, measure, movement, parade, plan, procedure, proceeding, stratagem, tactics, war games; CONCEPT 320

maneuver [v1] *plan, scheme* angle, beguile, cheat, come up with, con*, conspire, contrive, cook, design, devise, doctor, engineer, exploit, fence, finagle, finesse, go around, intrigue, jockey, leave holding the bag*, machinate, manage, manipulate, move, navigate, operate, play, play games*, plot, proceed, pull strings*, push around, put one over*, rig, scam, sham, shift, trick, upstage, wangle, work; CONCEPTS 36,59 —*Ant.* neglect

maneuver [v2] *direct physically* deploy, dispense, drive, exercise, guide, handle, manipulate, move, navigate, negotiate, pilot, ply, steer, swing, wield; CONCEPTS 187,225 —*Ant.* leave alone

mangle [v] *mutilate, deform* batter, break, bruise, butcher, carve, contort, crush, cut, damage, deface, destroy, disfigure, distort, flay, hack, hash, impair, injure, lacerate, maim, mar, maul, rend, ruin, separate, slash, slay, slice, slit, spoil, tear, wound, wreck; CONCEPTS 176,246,252 —*Ant.* cure, heal, help, preserve

mangy [adj] *scruffy* decrepit, dirty, impoverished, indigent, mean, moth-eaten*, poor, ragtag*, shabby, shoddy, sick, sleazy*, squalid, tattered; CONCEPTS 485,621 —*Ant.* kempt, neat

manhood/womanhood [n] *physical maturity and strength of adult male or female* adulthood, coming of age*, fecundity, femininity, fertility, manfulness, manliness, masculinity, mettle, potency, virility, womanliness, womanness; CONCEPTS 633,715 —*Ant.* childhood

mania [n] *fixation, madness* aberration, ax to grind*, bee*, bee in bonnet*, bug*, bug in ear*, compulsion, craving, craze, craziness, delirium, dementia, derangement, desire, disorder, enthusiasm, fad, fancy, fascination, fetish, fixed idea, frenzy, furor, grabber*, hang-up*, idée fixe, infatuation, insanity, lunacy, monomania, obsession, on the brain*, partiality, passion, preoccupation, rage, thing, tiger*, tiger by the tail*; CONCEPTS 20,32,410

maniac [n] *person who is crazy, overenthusiastic* bedlamite, bigot, crackpot*, enthusiast, fan, fanatic, fiend, flake*, freak, fruitcake*, kook*, loon, loony*, lunatic, madperson, nut*, nut-case*, psycho*, psychopath, schizoid*, screwball*, Section 8*, zealot; CONCEPT 412

manic/maniacal [adj] *overexcited, crazy* berserk, crazed, demented, deranged, excited, flipped*, flipped out*, freaked out*, freaky*, frenzied, high*, insane, lunatic, mad, nutty*, psychotic, rabid, raving, turned-out, unbalanced, up*, wild; CONCEPT 403 —*Ant.* balanced, calm, sane

manifest [adj] *clear, obvious* apparent, big as life*, bold, clear-cut*, conspicuous, crystal clear*, disclosed, distinct, divulged, evidenced, evident, evinced, glaring, noticeable, open, palpable, patent, plain, prominent, revealed, shown, straightforward, told, unambiguous, unmistakable, visible; CONCEPTS 529,576 —*Ant.* ambiguous, concealed, obscure, unclear, vague

manifest [v] *exhibit, make plain* confirm, declare, demonstrate, display, embody, establish, evidence, evince, expose, express, exteriorize, externalize, flash, illustrate, incarnate, let it all hang out*, mark, materialize, objectify, ostend, parade, personalize, personify, personize, proclaim, prove, reveal, set forth, show, show and tell*, showcase, signify, sport, strut, substantiate, suggest, utter, vent, voice, wave around*; CONCEPTS 118,261 —*Ant.* bury, conceal, cover, obscure, withhold

manifestation [n] *exhibition, proof* appearance, demonstration, disclosure, display, explanation, exposure, expression, indication, instance, mark, materialization, meaning, phenomenon, revelation, show, sign, symptom, token; CONCEPTS 642,672 —*Ant.* concealment, cover, hiding, obscurity, vagueness

manifesto [n] *public declaration* announcement, notice, platform, policy, proclamation, promulgation, public notice, statement of belief; CONCEPTS 271,274,278

manifold [adj] *abundant, many* assorted, complex, copious, different, diverse, diversified, diversiform, multifarious, multifold, multiform, multiple, multiplied, multitudinous, multivarious, numerous, sundry, varied, various; CONCEPTS 564,762,781 —*Ant.* one, single, sole

manipulate [v1] *maneuver, handle physically* employ, feel, finger*, form, manage, mold, operate, ply, shape, swing, thumb*, use, wield, work; CONCEPTS 225,612 —*Ant.* leave alone

manipulate [v2] *change to suit one's desire* beguile, conduct, control, direct, engineer, exploit, finagle, finesse, guide, handle, influence, jockey, machinate, maneuver, massage, mold, negotiate, play, play games*, pull strings*, pull wires*, push around, shape, steer, upstage, use; CONCEPTS 14,234 —*Ant.* leave alone

manner [n1] *person's behavior, conduct* address, affectation, affectedness, air, appearance, aspect, bearing, comportment, demeanor, deportment, idiosyncrasy, look, mannerism, mien, peculiarity, presence, style, tone, turn, way; CONCEPTS 411,633,644

manner [n2] *method, approach* consuetude, custom, fashion, form, genre, habit, habitude, line, means, mode, modus, practice, procedure, process, routine, style, system, tack, technique, tenor, tone, trick, usage, use, vein, way, wise, wont; CONCEPTS 6,660

manner [n3] *class, category* brand, breed, form, kind, nature, sort, type, variety; CONCEPT 378

mannered [adj] *affected, put-on* airish*, apish*, artificial, artsy, campy*, chichi*, conscious, gone Hollywood*, highfaluting*, posed, pretentious, self-conscious, stilted, stuck up*, unnatural; CONCEPT 401 —*Ant.* natural, unpretentious

mannerism [n] *peculiarity of how someone behaves, acts* affectation, air, characteristic, eccentricity, foible, habit, idiosyncrasy, oddness, pose, pretension, queerness, quirk, singularity, trait, trick; CONCEPT 644

mannerly [adj] *polite, well-behaved* charming, civil, civilized, considerate, courteous, decorous, genteel, gracious, polished, refined, respectful, well-bred, well-mannered; CONCEPT 401 —*Ant.* crass, crude, gross, impolite, misbehaved, rude

manners [n] *polite, refined social behavior* amenities, bearing, behavior, breeding, carriage, ceremony, civilities, comportment, conduct, courtesy, culture, decorum, demeanor, deportment, dignity, elegance, etiquette, formalities, good breeding, good form, mien, mores, polish, politeness, politesse, propriety, protocol, p's and q's*, refinement, social graces, sophistication, taste, urbanity; CONCEPT 633

mansion [n] *very large house* abode, building, castle, chateau, dwelling, estate, habitation, hall, home, manor, palace, residence, seat, villa; CONCEPTS 439,516 —*Ant.* hut

manslaughter [n] *killing without malicious forethought* crime, foul play*, hit*, homicide, killing, murder; CONCEPT 252

manual [adj] *done by hand* hand-operated, human, not automatic, physical, standard; CONCEPT 544 —*Ant.* automated, automatic

manual [n] *book giving instruction* bible, compendium, cookbook, enchiridion, guide, guidebook, handbook, primer, reference book, schoolbook, text, textbook, workbook; CONCEPT 280

manufacture [v1] *build, produce* accomplish, assemble, carve, cast, cobble*, complete, compose, construct, create, execute, fabricate, fashion, forge, form, frame, fudge together*, machine, make, make up, mass-produce, mill, mold, prefab, process, put together, shape, synthesize, throw together, tool, turn out; CONCEPT 205 —*Ant.* destroy, ruin

manufacture [v2] *concoct, invent* contrive, cook up*, create, devise, fabricate, hatch, make up, produce, think up, trump up*; CONCEPTS 35,36

manufacture/manufacturing [n] *production of processed goods* accomplishment, assembling, assembly, casting, completion, composing, composition, construction, creation, doing, erection, fabrication, finishing, forging, formation, making, mass-production, preparing, produce, tooling; CONCEPT 324

manure [n] *fertilizer* buffalo chips*, compost, cow chips*, cowplop*, droppings, dung, excrement, guano, maul*, meadow muffins*, mulch; CONCEPTS 260,399,429

manuscript [n] *book, script* article, composition, document, hard copy, palimpsest, text; CONCEPTS 263,271

many [adj] *profuse, abundant* abounding, alive with, bounteous, bountiful, copious, countless, crowded, divers, frequent, innumerable, legion, lousy with*, manifold, multifarious, multifold, multiplied, multitudinous, myriad, no end of*, numberless, numerous, plentiful, populous, prevalent, rife, several, sundry, teeming, umpteen, uncounted, varied, various; CONCEPTS 762,771 —*Ant.* few, scarce

many [n] *abundance; a lot* gobs*, heaps*, horde, jillion*, large numbers, mass, multitude, oodles*, piles*, plenty, scads*, scores, thousands, throng, tons, umpteen*, whole slew*; CONCEPTS 432,787 —*Ant.* few

map [n] *chart of geographic area* atlas, delineation, design, diagram, draft, drawing, elevation, globe, graph, ground plan, outline, picture, plan, plat, portrayal, print, projection, sketch, topographical depiction, tracing; CONCEPT 625

mapmaker [n] *cartographer* mapper, surveyor, topographer; CONCEPTS 37,103,291

mar [v] *hurt, damage* bend, blemish, blight, blot, break, bruise, deface, deform, detract, ding*, disfigure, foul up, harm, impair, injure, louse up, maim, mangle, mess up*, mutilate, queer*, rough up, ruin, scar, scratch, shake up, spoil, stain, sully, taint, tarnish, tweak, vitiate, warp, wreck; CONCEPT 246 —*Ant.* aid, heal, help

marathon [n] *long-distance race* cross-country race, endurance run, test of endurance; CONCEPT 363

maraud [v] *pillage and plunder* despoil, forage, foray, harass, harry, loot, raid, ransack, ravage, sack; CONCEPTS 86,139 —*Ant.* behave

marauder [n] *pillager, raider* bandit, buccaneer, corsair, freebooter, looter, outlaw, pirate, plunderer, ravager, robber, thief; CONCEPT 412

march [v] *walk with deliberation* advance, boot, debouch, drill, file, forge ahead, go on, hoof it*, journey, mount, move, move out, pace, parade, patrol, pound, pound the pavement*, proceed, progress, promenade, range, space, stalk, step, step out, stomp, stride, strut, traipse, tramp, tread; CONCEPT 150

margin [n] *border; room around something* allowance, bound, boundary, brim, brink, compass, confine, edge, elbowroom*, extra, field, frame, hem, latitude, leeway, limit, lip, perimeter, periphery, play, rim, scope, selvage, shore, side, skirt, space, surplus, trimming, verge; CONCEPTS 270,484,513 —*Ant.* center, core, interior

marginal [adj] *borderline; slight* bordering, insignificant, low, minimal, minor, negligible, on the edge, peripheral, rimming, small, verging; CONCEPTS 513,789 —*Ant.* central, core, interior, internal

marijuana [n] *grass, pot* Acapulco gold*, bhang*, cannabis, Columbian*, doobie*, dope*, ganja*, hash, hashish, hemp, herb*, Jamaican*, joint, loco weed*, maryjane*, Maui wowie*, Mexican*, Panama red*, reefer, roach, sinsemilla, tea*, weed*; CONCEPT 307

marina [n] *dock* berth, boat basin, boatyard, harbor, landing, moorings, pier, port, quay, slip, wharf; CONCEPT 439

marinate [v] *soak* bathe, brine, immerse, marinade, pickle, season, souse, steep; CONCEPT 256

marine/maritime [adj] *concerning the sea* abyssal, aquatic, coastal, deep-sea, hydrographic, littoral, maritime, natatorial, nautical, naval, navigational, Neptunian, oceangoing, oceanic, oceanographic, of the sea, pelagic, saltwater, sea, seafaring, seagoing, seashore, seaside, shore; CONCEPT 536

mariner [n] *person who makes living on the sea* bluejacket*, captain, crew, mate, navigator, sailor, salt*, sea dog*, seafarer, shipmate, swab*, yachtie*; CONCEPTS 348,366

marionette [n] *puppet* doll, dummy, fantoccini, figurine, manikin, moppet; CONCEPTS 423,446

marital [adj] *concerning marriage* conjugal, connubial, married, matrimonial, nuptial, spousal, wedded; CONCEPT 555 —*Ant.* divorce

maritime [adj] *nautical* aquatic, deep-sea, marine, naval, oceangoing, oceanic, pelagic, seafaring, seagoing; CONCEPT 536

mark [n1] *blemish; character* autograph, blaze, blot, blotch, brand, brand name, bruise, check, cross, dent, dot, impression, imprint, ink, John Hancock*, John Henry*, label, line, logo, nick, pock, point, record, register, representation, scar, score, scratch, sign, signature, smudge, splotch, spot, stain, stamp, streak, stroke, symbol, tag, ticket, trace, trademark, underlining, X*; CONCEPTS 79,284

mark [n2] *characteristic, symptom* affection, attribute, badge, blaze, brand, character, device, distinction, earmark, emblem, evidence, feature, hallmark, idiosyncrasy, image, impression, incision, index, indication, indicia, label, marking, note, particularity, peculiarity, print, proof, property, quality, seal, sign, significant, stamp, symbol, token, trait, type, virtue; CONCEPTS 411,644,716

mark [n3] *criterion, standard* gauge, level, measure, norm, yardstick; CONCEPTS 561,783

mark [n4] *goal, target* aim, ambition, bull's eye*, duty, end, function, object, objective, prey, purpose, use; CONCEPT 659

mark [n5] *importance* consequence, dignity, distinction, effect, eminence, fame, influence, manifestation, notability, note, notice, prestige, quality, regard, result, standing, value; CONCEPTS 346,668 —*Ant.* unimportance

mark [v1] *blemish, stain* autograph, blaze, blot, blotch, brand, bruise, chalk, check, dent, dot, impress, imprint, initial, ink, inscribe, label, letter, nick, pinpoint, point, print, scar, score, scratch, seal, sign, smudge, splotch, stamp, streak, trace, underline, write, X*; CONCEPTS 79,250

mark [v2] *characterize* bespeak, betoken, brand, check off, demonstrate, denote, designate, distinguish, earmark, evidence, evince, exemplify, exhibit, feature, identify, illustrate, indicate, individualize, individuate, label, manifest, mark off, ostend, point out, point up*, proclaim, qualify, remark, set apart, show, show up, signalize,

signify, singularize, stake out*, stamp; CONCEPT 261

mark [v3] *see, notice* attend, behold, chronicle, discern, distinguish, eye, hearken, mind, note, observe, pay attention, pay heed, perceive, regard, register, remark, take notice of, view, watch, write down; CONCEPTS 38,626

marked [adj] *apparent, obvious* arresting, clear, considerable, conspicuous, decided, distinct, evident, manifest, notable, noted, noticeable, outstanding, patent, pointed, prominent, pronounced, remarkable, salient, signal, striking; CONCEPTS 485,535,589 —*Ant.* ambiguous, obscure, unapparent, unnoticeable, vague

markedly [adv] *distinctly* clearly, considerably, conspicuously, decidedly, especially, evidently, greatly, manifestly, notably, noticeably, obviously, outstandingly, particularly, patently, remarkably, signally, strikingly, to a great extent; CONCEPTS 535,544 —*Ant.* indistinctly, unmarkedly

market [v] *package and sell goods* advertise, barter, display, exchange, merchandise, offer for sale, retail, vend, wholesale; CONCEPTS 324,345 —*Ant.* buy

marketable [adj] *easily sold; in demand* bankable, commercial, fit, for sale, good, hot*, merchandisable, merchantable, profitable, salable, sellable, selling, sought after, sound, trafficable, vendible, wanted; CONCEPTS 334, 546 —*Ant.* unmarketable

market/mart [n] *place, venue for selling goods* bazaar, bodega, booth, business, chain store, co-op, corner store, deli, delicatessen, department store, dimestore, drugstore, emporium, exchange, fair, general store, grocery store, mall, mart, outlet, shop, shopping mall, showroom, souk, square, stall, stock exchange, store, supermarket, trading post, truck, variety store, warehouse; CONCEPTS 323,333,449

maroon [v] *abandon* beach, cast ashore, cast away, desert, forsake, isolate, leave, leave high and dry*, strand; CONCEPTS 195,384 —*Ant.* care, help, maintain, rescue, save, take care

marriage [n] *legal joining of two people; a union* alliance, amalgamation, association, confederation, conjugality, connubiality, consortium, coupling, espousal, holy matrimony, link, match, mating, matrimony, merger, monogamy, nuptials, pledging, sacrament, spousal, tie, tie that binds*, wedded bliss*, wedded state, wedding, wedding bells*, wedding ceremony, wedlock; CONCEPTS 297,388 —*Ant.* divorce

marrow [n] *heart, essence* bottom, core, cream, essentiality, gist, kernel, meat, pith, quick, quintessence, quintessential, soul, spirit, stuff, substance, virtuality; CONCEPT 826

marry [v] *become husband and wife in legal ceremony* ally, associate, become one, bond, catch*, combine, conjoin, conjugate, contract, couple, drop anchor*, espouse, get hitched*, get married, join, knit, land*, lead to altar, link, match, mate, merge, one, pledge, plight one's troth, promise, relate, settle down*, take vows, tie, tie the knot*, unify, unite, walk down aisle*, wed, yoke; CONCEPT 297 —*Ant.* divorce

marsh [n] *swamp* bog, estuary, everglade, fen, mire, morass, moss, quag, quagmire, slough, swampland, wetland; CONCEPT 509

marshal [v] *organize, guide* align, arrange, array, assemble, collect, conduct, deploy, direct, dispose, distribute, draw up, escort, gather, group, lead, line up, methodize, mobilize, muster, order, rally, rank, shepherd, space, systematize, usher; CONCEPTS 84,117, 187 —Ant. disorganize

marshy [adj] *swampy* boggy, fenny, miry, moory, mucky, paludal, quaggy, soggy; CONCEPT 509

martial [adj] *having to do with armed hostilities* aggressive, bellicose, belligerent, combative, hostile, military, pugnacious, soldierly, warlike; CONCEPT 401 —Ant. civil, peaceful

martinet [n] *disciplinarian* authoritarian, bully, despot, drillmaster, drill sergeant, enforcer, hard master, slavedriver, stickler, taskmaster, tyrant; CONCEPTS 350,354,423

martyrdom [n] *suffering endured for sake of a cause* affliction, agonizing, agony, anguish, crucifixion, devotion, distress, mortification, ordeal, pain, persecution, sacrifice, self-immolation, self-sacrifice, torment, torture, unselfishness; CONCEPTS 410,411 —Ant. contentment, happiness, satisfaction

marvel [n] *wonder* curiosity, genius, miracle, one for the books*, phenomenon, portent, prodigy, sensation, something else*, stunner, whiz; CONCEPTS 529,671 —Ant. expectation

marvel [v] *be amazed* be awed, be surprised, feel surprise, gape, gaze, goggle, stand in awe, stare, wonder; CONCEPT 17 —Ant. expect

marvelous [adj1] *hard to believe; amazing* astonishing, astounding, awe-inspiring, awesome, awful, bewildering, breathtaking, confounding, difficult to believe, extraordinary, fabulous, fantastic, implausible, improbable, incomprehensible, inconceivable, incredible, miraculous, phenomenal, prodigious, remarkable, singular, spectacular, staggering, strange, striking, stunning, stupendous, supernatural, surprising, unbelievable, unimaginable, unlikely, unusual, wonderful, wondrous; CONCEPTS 529,552 —Ant. believable, expected, ordinary, plain, unamazing

marvelous [adj2] *superb, great* agreeable, astonishing, bad*, boss*, colossal, cool*, divine, dreamy*, enjoyable, excellent, fab*, fabulous, fantastic, glorious, greatest, groovy*, hot*, keen, magnificent, neat*, out of this world*, outrageous, peachy, pleasant, pleasurable, prime*, rewarding, satisfying, sensational, smashing, solid*, solid gold*, spectacular, splendid, stupendous, super, supreme, swell, terrific, wonderful; CONCEPT 574 —Ant. inconsiderable, insignificant, paltry, worthless

masculinity/masculine [n/adj] *manly* andric, gender, macho*, male, manful, mannish, potent, virile; CONCEPTS 371,372,408,648 —Ant. feminine

mash [v] *smash, squash* brew, bruise, chew, crush, decoct, grind, hash, infuse, macerate, masticate, mush up, pound, press, pulp,

pulverize, push, reduce, scrunch, squeeze, squish, steep, triturate; CONCEPTS 170,186,208

mask [n] *false face, cover* affectation, air*, appearance, aspect, beard*, blind, camouflage, cloak*, concealment, cover-up, disguise, disguisement, dissembling, dissimulation, domino*, facade, fig leaf*, front, guise, hood, masquerade, pose, posture, pretense, pretext, put-on*, screen, semblance, show*, simulation, veil*, veneer, visage, visor, window dressing*; CONCEPTS 450,716

mask [v] *disguise* beard, camouflage, cloak, conceal, cover, cover up, defend, dissemble, dissimulate, dress up, front, guard, hide, obscure, protect, safeguard, screen, secrete, shield, veil; CONCEPTS 172,188,384 —Ant. reveal, uncover, unmask

masquerade [n] *disguise; social occasion for disguises* carnival, circus, cloak, color, costume, costume ball, cover, cover-up, deception, dissimulation, domino*, facade, festivity, front, guise, impersonation, imposture, Mardi Gras*, mask, masked ball, masking, mummery, personation, pose, pretense, put-on*, revel, screen, show, subterfuge, veil; CONCEPTS 172,188,383, 451

masquerade [v] *disguise* attitudinize, dissemble, dissimulate, frolic, impersonate, mask, pass as, pass for, pass off, pose, posture, pretend, revel; CONCEPT 59 —Ant. reveal, unmask

mass [n1] *body of matter; considerable portion* accumulation, aggregate, assemblage, band, batch, block, bulk, bunch, chunk, clot, coagulation, collection, combination, concretion, conglomeration, core, corpus, crowd, entirety, gob, great deal, greater part, group, heap, horde, host, hunk, knot, lion's share*, load, lot, lump, majority, mob, mound, mountain, much, number, object, peck, piece, pile, plurality, preponderance, pyramid, quantity, shock, stack, staple, stockpile, sum, sum total, throng, totality, troop, volume, wad, whole; CONCEPTS 432,787,835

mass [n2] *bulk, measurement* dimension, extent, greatness, magnitude, size, span, volume; CONCEPT 792

massacre [n] *killing of many* annihilation, assassination, bloodbath, bloodshed, butchery, carnage, decimation, extermination, genocide, internecion, murder, slaughter, slaying; CONCEPT 252

massacre [v] *kill, often in great numbers* annihilate, butcher, decimate, depopulate, exterminate, mass murder, murder, slaughter, slay; CONCEPT 252 —Ant. create, give birth

massage [n] *kneading of body parts* back rub, beating, chirapsia, manipulation, rolfing*, rubbing, rubbing-down, stroking; CONCEPTS 308,310

massage [v] *knead body parts* caress, manipulate, pat, press, push, rolf*, rub, rub down, stimulate, stroke; CONCEPTS 208,308,310

masses [n] *public, crowd* commonalty, common people, great unwashed*, hoi polloi*, lower class, mob, multitude, proletariat, rabble, rank and file*, riffraff*; CONCEPT 417 massive [adj] large big, bulky, colossal, cracking, cumbersome, cumbrous, elephantine, enormous, extensive, gargantuan, gigantic, grand, great, gross, heavy, hefty, huge, hulking, immense, imposing, impressive, mammoth, mighty, monster, monumental, mountainous, ponderous, prodigious, solid, stately, substantial, titanic, towering, tremendous, unwieldy, vast, walloping, weighty, whopping*; CONCEPTS 773,781 —Ant. little, miniature, small, tiny

master [adj1] expert ace*, adept, crack*, crackerjack*, experienced, masterly, proficient, skilled, skillful; CONCEPT 527 —Ant. amateur

master [adj2] main ascendant, chief, controlling, foremost, grand, great, leading, major, original, overbearing, paramount, predominant, predominate, preponderant, prevalent, prime, principal, regnant, sovereign, supreme; CONCEPT 568 —Ant. auxiliary, copy, duplicate, minor, subordinate

master [n1] person in charge, female or male administrator, boss, captain, chief, chieftain, commandant, commander, commanding officer, conqueror, controller, director, employer, general, governor, guide, guru, head, head person, instructor, judge, lord, manager, matriarch, overlord, overseer, owner, patriarch, pedagogue, preceptor, principal, pro, ruler, schoolmaster/ mistress, skipper, slave driver*, spiritual leader, superintendent, supervisor, swami*, taskmaster, teacher, top dog*, tutor, wheel*; CONCEPTS 347,350,354 —Ant. servant

master [n2] expert, skilled person, female or male ace*, adept, artist, artiste, authority, buff*, champion, connoisseur, conqueror, doctor, doyen, doyenne, genius, guru, maestro, maven, old hand*, old pro*, past master, prima donna*, pro, professional, proficient, pundit, real pro*, sage, savant, scientist, shark*, victor, virtuoso, whiz*, whiz-bang*, winner, wizard; CONCEPTS 350,366,423 —Ant. amateur

master [v] learn; become proficient acquire, beat the game*, beat the system*, bone up*, bury yourself in*, comprehend, cram, excel in, gain mastery, get down cold*, get down pat*, get hold of*, get the hang of*, get the knack of*, grasp, grind, hit the books*, learn the ropes*, megastudy*, pick up, study, swamp*, understand; CONCEPTS 31,630 —Ant. be ignorant

masterful [adj] expert, skilled ace, adroit, clever, consummate, crack, crackerjack*, deft, dexterous, excellent, exquisite, fine, finished, first-rate, master, masterly, preeminent, proficient, skillful, superior, superlative, supreme, transcendent; CONCEPT 527 —Ant. amateurish, ignorant, stupid, unproficient, unskilled

masterpiece [n] respected work of art chef d'oeuvre, classic, cream*, cream of the crop*, flower, gem*, jewel*, magnum opus, masterstroke, master work, model, monument, perfection, pièce de résistance*, prize, showpiece, standard, tour de force*, treasure; CONCEPT 259

mastery [n] command, expertise ability, acquirement, adeptness, adroitness, attainment, capacity, cleverness, comprehension, cunning, deftness, dexterity, expertism, expertness,

familiarity, finesse, genius, grasp, grip, ken, knack, know-how, knowledge, mastership, power, proficiency, prowess, skill, understanding, virtuosity, wizardry; CONCEPT 630 —Ant. amateurishness, failure, inefficiency, lack

match [n1] competition bout, contest, engagement, event, game, meet, race, rivalry, sport, test, trial; CONCEPT 363

match [n2] counterpart, equal adversary, analogue, antagonist, approximation, companion, competitor, complement, copy, correlate, countertype, dead ringer*, double, duplicate, equivalent, like, lookalike, mate, opponent, parallel, peer, replica, ringer*, rival, spitting image*, twin; CONCEPTS 664,667,716 —Ant. clash, difference, imbalance

match [n3] couple affiliation, alliance, combination, duet, espousal, marriage, mating, pair, pairing, partnership, union; CONCEPTS 297,388 —Ant. mismatch

matching [adj] corresponding, equal analogous, comparable, coordinating, double, duplicate, equivalent, identical, like, paired, parallel, same, twin; CONCEPT 566 —Ant. different, uncorrespondent, unequal

matchless [adj] unequalled, unique alone, consummate, excellent, exquisite, incomparable, inimitable, nonpareil, only, peerless, perfect, superior, superlative, supreme, unapproached, unmatched, unparalleled, unrivaled; CONCEPT 574 —Ant. common, commonplace, mediocre, regular, usual

mate [n] one of a pair; partner acquaintance, alter ego, analog, assistant, associate, bedmate, bride, buddy*, chum*, classmate, cohort, colleague, companion, compeer, complement, comrade, concomitant, consort, coordinate, counterpart, coworker, crony, double, duplicate, familiar, friend, groom, helper, helpmate, intimate, match, pal*, peer, playmate, reciprocal, roommate, schoolmate, sidekick*, spouse, twin; CONCEPTS 296,423,664

mate [v] marry and breed cohabit, copulate, couple, crossbreed, generate, join, land*, match, merge, pair, procreate, serve, tie, tie the knot*, wed, yoke; CONCEPTS 297,375 —Ant. abstain, uncouple

material [adj1] bodily, tangible actual, animal, appreciable, carnal, concrete, corporeal, earthly, fleshly, incarnate, nonspiritual, objective, palpable, perceptible, phenomenal, physical, real, sensible, sensual, substantial, true, worldly; CONCEPT 485 —Ant. ethereal, incorporeal, intangible, mental

material [adj2] important, relevant ad rem, applicable, appreciable, apposite, apropos, big, cardinal, consequential, considerable, essential, fundamental, germane, grave, indispensable, intrinsic, key, meaningful, momentous, pertinent, pointful, primary, serious, significant, substantial, vital, weighty; CONCEPT 567 —Ant. immaterial, irrelevant, unimportant, unsubstantial

material [n1] matter, fabric being, body, bolt, cloth, component, constituent, crop, element, entity, equipment, gear, goods, habiliments, individual, ingredient, machinery, materiel, object, outfit, paraphernalia, staple, stock, stuff, substance, supply, tackle, textile, thing; CONCEPTS 475,523

material [n2] *written matter* data, evidence, facts, information, notes, reading, text, work; CONCEPTS 271,274

materialistic [adj] *thinking mainly about physical things* acquisitive, banausic, carnal, earthly-minded, earthy, greedy, material, mundane, object-oriented, possessive, profane, secular, sensual, temporal, terrestrial, unspiritual; CONCEPT 542 —*Ant.* spiritual, thrifty, ungreedy

materialize [v] *come into being* actualize, appear, become concrete, become real, become visual, be incarnate, be realized, coalesce, come about, come to pass, corporealize, develop, embody, emerge, entify, evolve, exteriorize, externalize, happen, hypostatize, make real, manifest, metamorphose, objectify, occur, personalize, personify, personize, pragmatize, realize, reify, substantialize, substantiate, symbolize, take form, take place, take shape, turn up, typify, unfold, visualize; CONCEPTS 105,173,184,231,251

maternity [n] *period of being pregnant with child* gestation, maternology, motherhood, parenthood; CONCEPTS 316,817 —*Ant.* paternity

mathematical [adj] *concerning manipulation of numbers* algebraic, algorithmic, analytical, arithmetical, computative, geometrical, math, measurable, numerical, scientific, trigonometric; CONCEPT 762

mathematics [n] *arithmetic* addition, algebra, calculation, calculus, division, figures, geometry, math, multiplication, numbers, subtraction, trigonometry; CONCEPTS 349,764

matriculate [v] *begin, enroll* enter, join, register, sign up for; CONCEPTS 114,119 —*Ant.* graduate

matrimonial [adj] *married* betrothed, conjugal, connubial, engaged, epithalamic, espoused, marital, nuptial, spousal, wedded, wedding; CONCEPT 555 —*Ant.* divorce

matrimony [n] *being joined in marriage* alliance, belief*, conjugality, connubiality, marital rites, marriage, match, nuptials, shotgun wedding*, union, wedding, wedding bells*, wedding ceremony, wedlock; CONCEPT 297 —*Ant.* divorce

matrix [n] *something from which another originates* cast, forge, form, grid, model, mold, origin, pattern, source, womb; CONCEPT 648

matronly [adj] *womanly* dignified, female, honorable, ladylike, mature, motherly, respected, stately; CONCEPTS 404,555,574

matted [adj] *tangled* disordered, kinky, knotted, rumpled, snarled, tousled, twisted, uncombed; CONCEPT 606 —*Ant.* unknotted, untangled

matter [n1] *substance* amount, being, body, constituents, corporeality, corporeity, element, entity, individual, material, materialness, object, phenomenon, physical world, protoplasm, quantity, stuff, substantiality, sum, thing; CONCEPTS 407,433,470 —*Ant.* nothing, nothingness, zero

matter [n2] *concern, issue* affair, bag, business, circumstance, episode, event, goings-on*,

incident, job, lookout, nub, occurrence, proceeding, question, shooting match*, situation, subject, thing, topic, transaction, undertaking; CONCEPTS 532,696

matter [n3] *subject, thesis* argument, context, focus, head, interest, motif, motive, point, purport, resolution, sense, subject matter, substance, text, theme, topic; CONCEPTS 349,529

matter [n4] *significance, meaning* amount, body, burden, consequence, content, core, extent, gist*, import, importance, magnitude, meat, moment, neighborhood, note, order, pith, range, sense, substance, text, tune, upshot, vicinity, weight; CONCEPTS 651,668 —*Ant.* insignificance, meaninglessness

matter [n5] *difficulty, problem* circumstance, complication, distress, grievance, perplexity, predicament, to-do*, trouble, upset, worry; CONCEPTS 666,674

matter [n6] *secretion of a sore* discharge, infection, maturation, purulence, pus, suppuration, ulceration; CONCEPTS 311,467

matter [v] *be of consequence, importance* affect, be important, be of value, be substantive, carry weight, count, cut ice*, express, have influence, imply, import, involve, make a difference, mean, mean something, signify, value, weigh; CONCEPTS 7,19,22,130,682

matter-of-fact [adj] *realistic, unembellished* apathetic, calm, cold, cold-blooded*, deadpan, down-to-earth*, dry, dull, earthy, emotionless, factual, feasible, flat, hard-boiled*, impassive, impersonal, lifeless, mundane, naked*, objective, phlegmatic, plain, practical, pragmatic, prosaic, prosy, serious, sober, stoic, stolid, unaffected, unidealistic, unimaginative, unimpassioned, unsentimental, unvarnished; CONCEPTS 267,582 —*Ant.* emotional, imaginative, lively

mature [adj] *adult, grown-up* complete, cultivated, cultured, developed, fit, full-blown, full-fledged, full-grown, fully grown, grown, in full bloom, in one's prime, matured, mellow, mellowed, of age, perfected, prepared, prime, ready, ripe, ripened, seasoned, settled, sophisticated; CONCEPTS 485,578,797 —*Ant.* green, immature, inexperienced, young, youthful

mature [v] *become adult, fully grown* advance, age, arrive, attain majority, become experienced, become wise, bloom, blossom, come of age, culminate, develop, evolve, fill out, flower*, grow, grow up, maturate, mellow*, mushroom*, perfect, prime, progress, reach adulthood, reach majority, ripen, round, season, settle down*, shoot up*; CONCEPT 704

maturity [n] *adulthood, full growth* ability, advancement, capability, civilization, completion, cultivation, development, experience, fitness, full bloom, fullness, majority, manhood, maturation, matureness, maturescence, mellowness, mentality, perfection, postpubescence, prime, prime of life, readiness, ripeness, sophistication, wisdom, womanhood; CONCEPTS 678,715,720 —*Ant.* childhood, minority, youth

maudlin [adj] *teary, overemotional* bathetic, befuddled, confused, cornball*, drippy*, gushing, insipid, lachrymose, mawkish, mushy*, romantic, schmaltzy*, sentimental, slush*, soap*, soapy*, soppy*, syrupy*, tearful, tear-jerking*, weak, weepy; CONCEPTS 529,542 —*Ant.* calm, matter-of-fact, unimaginative

maul [v] *mangle, abuse* bang, bash, batter, beat, beat up, bludgeon, break face, buffet, claw, clean, drub, flagellate, flail, handle roughly, hit, hurt, ill-treat, knock about*, knock around*, lacerate, lash, lean on*, let have it*, maltreat, molest, mug, muscle, paste*, paw, pelt, pound, pummel, put in the hospital*, rough up, skin, take care of*, thrash, trample, wax, whip, work over*; CONCEPTS 189,246 —*Ant.* guard, maintain, protect, take care

mausoleum [n] *tomb* burial, burial chamber, burial place, catacomb, cemetery, charnel house, coffin, crypt, grave, monument, sepulcher, vault; CONCEPT 305

mauve [adj] *purplish color* lavender, lilac, plum, violaceous, violet; CONCEPT 618

maverick [n] *person who takes chances, departs from accepted course* bohemian, dissenter, extremist, malcontent, nonconformist, radical; CONCEPTS 348,423

mawkish [adj] *sentimental, emotional* bathetic, cloying, feeble, gooey*, gushing, gushy*, lovey-dovey*, maudlin, mushy*, nauseating, romantic, sappy*, schmaltzy*, sickening, sloppy, tear-jerking*, teary; CONCEPTS 401,542 —*Ant.* calm, serious, unemotional

maxim [n] *saying* adage, aphorism, apophthegm, axiom, belief, brocard, byword, canon, commonplace, device, dictum, epithet, formula, law, moral, motto, platitude, precept, prescript, proverb, rule, saw, tenet, theorem, truism; CONCEPTS 278,689

maximum [adj] *highest, utmost* best, biggest, greatest, largest, maximal, most, mostest, outside, paramount, superlative, supreme, top, topmost, ultimate; CONCEPTS 574,762,781 —*Ant.* least, lowest, minimum, smallest

maximum [n] *upper limit, greatest amount* apex, apogee, ceiling, climax, crest, culmination, extremity, height, max*, maxi*, most, nonpareil, peak, pinnacle, preeminence, record, summit, supremacy, the end*, top, utmost, uttermost, zenith; CONCEPTS 706,766,836 —*Ant.* least, low, minimum, smallest

maybe [adv] *possibly* as it may be, can be, conceivable, conceivably, could be, credible, feasible, imaginably, it could be, might be, obtainable, perchance, perhaps, weather permitting; CONCEPT 552 —*Ant.* certainly, definitely, surely

mayhem [n] *chaos, confusion* anarchy, commotion, destruction, disorder, fracas, havoc, pandemonium, trouble, violence; CONCEPTS 106,675 —*Ant.* calm, harmony, peace

maze [n] *labyrinth; confusion* bewilderment, convolution, entanglement, hodgepodge, imbroglio, intricacy, jungle, knot, meander, meandering, mesh, miscellany, morass, muddle, network, perplexity, puzzle, quandary, skein, snarl, tangle, torsion, twist, uncertainty, web, winding; CONCEPTS 436,529,674

meadow [n] *grassy field* bottoms*, carpet*, grassland, heath, lea, mead, pasturage, pasture, plain, prairie, rug*, steppe, veldt; CONCEPT 509

meager [adj1] *small, inadequate; poor* bare, barren, deficient, exiguous, flimsy, inappreciable, inconsiderable, infertile, insubstantial, insufficient, little, mere, minimum, miserable, paltry, puny, scant, scanty, scrimp, scrimpy, shabby, short, skimp, skimpy, slender, slight, spare, sparse, subtle, tenuous, too little too late*, unfinished, unfruitful, unproductive, wanting, weak; CONCEPTS 546,789 —*Ant.* adequate, large, liberal, plenty, substantial, sufficient

meager [adj2] *very thin* angular, bare, beanpole*, beanstalk*, bony, broomstick*, emaciated, gangling, gangly, gaunt, hungry, lacking, lank, lanky, lean, lithe, little, narrow, rattle-boned, rawboned, scraggy, scrawny, skin and bones*, skinny, slender, slim, spare, starved, stinted, stunted, tenuous, underfed, wanting, willowy, withered; CONCEPT 491 —*Ant.* big, fat, full, large, wide

meal [n] *food, often taken by several individuals together* banquet, blue plate*, board, breakfast, brunch, carryout, chow*, chow time*, collation, cookout, dessert, din-din*, dinner, eats*, fare, feast, feed, grub*, lunch, luncheon, mess, munchies*, picnic, potluck, refection, refreshment, regalement, repast, snack, special*, spread, square meal*, supper, table, tea; CONCEPT 459 —*Ant.* snack

mean [adj1] *ungenerous* close, greedy, mercenary, mingy, miserly, niggard, parsimonious, penny-pinching*, penurious, rapacious, scrimpy, selfish, stingy, tight, tight-fisted*; CONCEPT 334 —*Ant.* generous, kind, unselfish

mean [adj2] *hostile, rude* bad-tempered, callous, cantankerous, churlish, contemptible, dangerous, despicable, difficult, dirty*, disagreeable, dishonorable, down*, evil, formidable, hard, hard-nosed*, ignoble, ill-tempered, infamous, knavish, liverish, lousy*, low-down and dirty*, malicious, malign, nasty, perfidious, pesky, rotten, rough, rugged, scurrilous, shameless, sinking, snide, sour, the lowest*, touch, treacherous, troublesome, ugly, unfriendly, unpleasant, unscrupulous, vexatious, vicious, vile; CONCEPTS 267,401,542 —*Ant.* compassionate, kind, nice, noble, polite, sympathetic

mean [adj3] *poor; of or in inferior circumstances* base, beggarly, common, contemptible, déclassé, down-at-heel*, hack, humble, ignoble, ineffectual, inferior, insignificant, limited, low, lowborn, lowly, mediocre, menial, miserable, modest, narrow, obscure, ordinary, paltry, petty, pitiful, plebeian, proletarian, run-down*, scruffy*, second-class*, second-rate, seedy*, servile, shabby*, sordid, squalid, tawdry, undistinguished, unwashed, vulgar, wretched; CONCEPTS 334,485,589

mean [adj4] *average* common, conventional, halfway, intermediate, medial, median, mediocre, medium, middle, middling, normal, popular, standard, traditional; CONCEPTS 547, 585 —*Ant.* extreme

mean [n] *average* balance, center, compromise, happy medium, median, middle, middle course,

midpoint, norm, par; CONCEPTS *727,830*
—*Ant.* extreme

mean [v1] *signify, convey* add up, adumbrate, allude, allude to, argue, attest, augur, betoken, connote, denote, designate, determine, drive at*, express, foreshadow, foretell, herald, hint at, imply, import, indicate, intimate, involve, name, point to, portend, presage, promise, purport, represent, say, speak of, spell, stand for, suggest, symbolize, tell the meaning of, touch on; CONCEPTS *55,73,682*

mean [v2] *have in mind; intend* aim, anticipate, aspire, contemplate, design, desire, destine, direct, expect, fate, fit, make, match, plan, predestine, preordain, propose, purpose, resolve, set out, suit, want, wish; CONCEPTS *26,36*

meander [v] *wander, zigzag* be all over the map*, change, drift, extravagate, gallivant, get sidetracked, peregrinate, ramble, range, recoil, roam, rove, snake, stray, stroll, traipse, turn, twine, twist, vagabond, wind; CONCEPTS *151,738* —*Ant.* go direct, stay on path

meaning [n1] *message, signification* acceptation, allusion, bearing, bottom line*, connotation, content, context, definition, denotation, drift, effect, essence, explanation, force, gist, heart*, hint, implication, import, interpretation, intimation, meat, name of the game*, nature of beast*, nitty-gritty*, nuance, nuts and bolts*, pith, point, purport, sense, significance, spirit, stuff, subject, subject matter, substance, suggestion, symbolization, tenor, thrust, understanding, upshot, use, value, worth; CONCEPTS *278,661*

meaning [n2] *intention, aim* animus, design, end, goal, idea, intent, interest, object, plan, point, purpose, trend; CONCEPT *659*

meaningful [adj] *significant* allusive, big, clear, concise, consequential, considerable, deep, eloquent, essential, exact, explicit, expressive, heavy, important, indicative, intelligible, material, momentous, pointed, pregnant, purposeful, relevant, sententious, serious, substantial, succinct, suggestive, useful, valid, weighty, worthwhile; CONCEPTS *267,567* —*Ant.* insignificant, meaningless, useless, worthless

meaningless [adj] *without use, value, worth* absurd, aimless, blank, doesn't cut it*, doubles-peak*, double-talk*, empty, feckless, fustian, futile, good-for-nothing, hollow, hot air*, inane, inconsequential, insignificant, insubstantial, nonsensical, nothing, nugatory, pointless, purportless, purposeless, senseless, trifling, trivial, unimportant, unmeaning, unpurposed, useless, vacant, vague, vain, valueless, vapid, worthless; CONCEPT *575* —*Ant.* meaningful, significant, useful, valuable, worthwhile

means [n1] *way, method* agency, agent, aid, apparatus, auspices, avenue, channel, course, dodge*, equipment, expedient, factor, fashion, gimmick*, instrument, instrumentality, instrumentation, intermediary, machinery, manner, measure, mechanism, medium, ministry, mode, modus operandi, organ, organization, paraphernalia, path, power, process, road, route, step, stepping-stone, system, tactic, technique, trick, vehicle, ways and means*; CONCEPT *6*

means [n2] *wealth, resources* ace in the hole*, affluence, assets, backing, bankroll, budget, bundle, capital, dough*, estate, finances, fortune, funds, holdings, income, intangibles, kitty*, money, nest egg*, nut*, pocket, possessions, property, purse, rainy day*, reserves, revenue, riches, savings, securities, sock*, stake, stuff, substance, ways and means*, wherewithal; CONCEPTS *332,340* —*Ant.* paucity, poorness, shame

meantime [n/adv] *in the intervening time* at the same time, concurrently, for now, for the duration, for the moment, for then, interim, interregnum, interruption, interval, in the interim, in the interval, in the meanwhile, meanwhile, recess, simultaneously, while; CONCEPTS *799,807*

meanwhile [adv] *at the same time* ad interim, concurrently, during the interval, for now, for the duration, for the moment, for then, for the time being, in the interim, in the interval, in the intervening time, in the meantime, meantime, simultaneously, till, until, up to, when; CONCEPT *799*

measly [adj] *skimpy* beggarly, contemptible, insignificant, meager, mean, miserable, miserly, niggling*, paltry, pathetic, petty, picayune, piddling*, pitiful, poor, puny, scanty, stingy, trifling, trivial, ungenerous, unimportant, valueless, worthless; CONCEPT *789* —*Ant.* abundant, plenty, proficient, satisfactory, sufficient

measurable [adj] *determinable* assessable, calculable, commensurate, computable, fathomable, gaugeable, material, mensurable, perceptible, quantifiable, quantitative, significant, surveyable, weighable; CONCEPT *529* —*Ant.* imperceptible, insignificant, undeterminable, unmeasurable

measure [n1] *portion, scope* admeasurement, admensuration, allotment, allowance, amount, amplification, amplitude, area, bang, breadth, bulk, capacity, degree, depth; dimension, distance, duration, extent, fix, frequency, height, hit, magnitude, mass, meed, mensuration, nip, part, pitch, proportion, quantity, quantum, quota, range, ratio, ration, reach, share, shot, size, slug, span, strength, sum, volume, weight; CONCEPTS *787,792,835*

measure [n2] *standard, rule* benchmark*, canon, criterion, example, gauge, meter, method, model, norm, pattern, scale, system, test, touchstone*, trial, type, yardstick; CONCEPTS *686,688*

measure [n3] *preventive or institutive action* act, action, agency, bounds, control, course, deed, device, effort, expedient, limit, limitation, makeshift, maneuver, means, moderation, move, procedure, proceeding, project, proposal, proposition, resort, resource, restraint, shift, step, stopgap*, strategem; CONCEPT *5* —*Ant.* ignorance, inaction

measure [n4] *bill, law* act, enactment, project, proposal, proposition, resolution, statute; CONCEPT *318*

measure [n5] *beat, rhythm* accent, cadence, cadency, division, melody, meter, rhyme, step, stress, stroke, swing, tempo, throb, time, tune, verse, vibration; CONCEPTS 65,262

measure [v] *calculate, judge* adapt, adjust, align, appraise, assess, average, beat, blend, bound, calibrate, caliper, check, check out, choose, compute, delimit, demarcate, determine, dope out*, estimate, evaluate, even, eye*, figure, fit, gauge, gradate, grade, graduate, level, limit, line, look over, mark, mark out, mete, pace off, peg*, plumb, portion, quantify, rank, rate, read, reckon, regulate, rhyme, rule, scale, shade, size, size up, sound, square, stroke, survey, tailor, take account, time, value, weigh; CONCEPTS 103,197,764 —*Ant.* estimate, guess

measurement [n] *calculation* altitude, amount, amplitude, analysis, appraisal, area, assessment, calibration, capacity, computation, degree, density, depth, determination, dimension, distance, estimation, evaluation, extent, frequency, height, judgment, length, magnitude, mass, measure, mensuration, metage, pitch, quantification, quantity, range, reach, scope, size, survey, thickness, time, valuation, volume, weight, width; CONCEPTS 730,792 —*Ant.* estimate, guess

meat [n1] *flesh of animal consumed as food* aliment, brawn, chow, comestible, eats*, edible, fare, food, foodstuff, grub*, muscle, nourishment, nutriment, provision, ration, subsistence, sustenance, victual; CONCEPTS 399,457,460

meat [n2] *core, gist* burden, essence, heart, kernel, marrow, matter, nub, nucleus, pith, point, sense, short, substance, thrust, upshot; CONCEPTS 682,826 —*Ant.* exterior, exteriority, outside

meat-eating [adj] *carnivorous* cannibalistic, flesh-eating, omophagous, predacious; CONCEPT 401

meaty [adj] *significant* compact, epigrammatic, factual, full of content, interesting, meaningful, pithy, pointed, profound, rich, substantial, weighty; CONCEPT 267 —*Ant.* insignificant, thin

mecca [n] *center, goal* aim, capital, destination, focal point, focus, heart, hub, nerve center, objective, purpose; CONCEPTS 435,438,507,659

mechanical [adj] *done by machine; machine-like* automated, automatic, cold, cursory, emotionless, fixed, habitual, impersonal, instinctive, involuntary, laborsaving, lifeless, machine-driven, matter-of-fact, monotonous, perfunctory, programmed, routine, spiritless, standardized, stereotyped, unchanging, unconscious, unfeeling, unthinking, useful; CONCEPT 544 —*Ant.* by hand, conscious, feeling, manual

mechanism [n1] *machine, device* apparatus, appliance, black box*, components, contrivance, doohickey*, gadget, gears, gimmick, innards, instrument, machinery, motor, structure, system, tool, workings, works; CONCEPT 463

mechanism [n2] *means, method* agency, execution, functioning, medium, operation, performance, procedure, process, system, technique, workings; CONCEPT 6

mechanize [v] *automate* equip, industrialize, motorize, rig; CONCEPTS 538,549

medal [n] *decoration of honor* badge, commemoration, gold, hardware*, laurel, medallion, reward, ribbon, wreath; CONCEPTS 337,476

meddle [v] *intervene, interfere* abuse rights, advance, barge in, break in on, busybody*, butt in*, chime in, come uninvited, crash the gates*, dabble in, encroach, encumber, fool with, hinder, horn in*, impede, impose, infringe, inquire, interlope, intermeddle, interpose, intrude, invade, kibitz*, mess around*, mix in, molest, obtrude, pry, push in, put two cents in*, sidewalk-superintend*, snoop*, stick nose in*, tamper, trespass, worm in*; CONCEPTS 14,384 —*Ant.* avoid, dodge, ignore, stay out of

meddlesome [adj] *interfering* busy, busybody*, chiseling*, curious, encumbering, hindering, impeding, impertinent, intermeddling, interposing, interrupting, intruding, intrusive, kibitzing*, meddling, mischievous, nosy, obstructive, officious, prying, pushy, snooping*, snoopy*, tampering, troublesome; CONCEPT 555 —*Ant.* avoiding, dodging, ignorant

media [n] *communication by publication or broadcast* announcement, announcing, cable, communications, correspondence, disclosure, expression, intelligence, news, publishing, radio, television; CONCEPT 279

median [n/adj] *middle* average, center, centermost, central, equidistant, halfway, intermediary, intermediate, mean, medial, mid, middlemost, midmost, midpoint, midway, par; CONCEPTS 585,727 —*Ant.* extreme, outside

mediate [v] *try to bring to an agreement* act as middle*, arbitrate, bring to terms, conciliate, deal, go fifty-fifty*, intercede, interfere, intermediate, interpose, intervene, make a deal, make peace, meet halfway*, moderate, negotiate, propitiate, reconcile, referee, resolve, restore harmony, settle, step in, strike happy medium*, trade off, umpire; CONCEPTS 126,324,384 —*Ant.* argue, contend, disagree, fight

mediation [n] *attempt to bring to agreement* arbitration, conciliation, intercession, interposition, intervention, negotiation, reconciliation; CONCEPTS 126,324,384 —*Ant.* argument, contention, disagreement, fight

mediator [n] *person who negotiates agreement* advocate, arbiter, arbitrator, broker, conciliator, fixer, go-between*, interagent, interceder, intermediary, intermediator, judge, medium, middle person, moderator, negotiator, peacemaker, ref*, referee, rent-a-judge*, troubleshooter*, umpire; CONCEPTS 348,423 —*Ant.* arguer, fighter

medicine/medication [n] *substance that helps cure, alleviate, or prevent illness* anesthetic, antibiotic, antidote, antiseptic, antitoxin, balm, biologic, capsule, cure, dose, drug, elixir, injection, inoculation, liniment, lotion, medicament, ointment, pharmaceutical, pharmacon, physic, pill, potion, prescription, remedy, salve, sedative, serum, tablet, tincture, tonic, vaccination, vaccine; CONCEPT 307

medieval [adj] *having to do with the Middle Ages; old* antediluvian, antiquated, antique, archaic, feudal, Gothic, old, old-fashioned, primitive, unenlightened; CONCEPTS 549,578,797 —*Ant.* modern

mediocre [adj] *average, commonplace* characterless, colorless, common, conventional, decent, dull, fair, fairish, fair to middling*, humdrum*, indifferent, inferior, insignificant, intermediate, mainstream, mean, medium, middling, moderate, no great shakes*, of poor quality, ordinary, passable, pedestrian, run-of-the-mill*, second-rate, so-so*, standard, tolerable, undistinguished, unexceptional, uninspired, vanilla*; CONCEPTS 533,547 —Ant. exceptional, extraordinary, inferior, superior, unusual

meditate [v] contemplate brood over, cogitate, consider, deliberate, design, devise, dream, entertain idea*, figure, have in mind*, intend, moon*, mull over, muse, plan, ponder, purpose, put on thinking cap*, puzzle over, reflect, revolve, roll, ruminate, say to oneself, scheme, speculate, study, think, think deeply, think over, track, view, weigh; CONCEPT 17 —Ant. dismiss, ignore, neglect

meditation [n] contemplation concentration, deep thought, introspection, pondering, quiet time, reflection, rumination, self-examination; CONCEPTS 17,24

meditative [adj] contemplative awake, aware, cogitative, introspective, lucubratory, musing, pensive, philosophical, prayerful, rapt, reflective, ruminant, ruminative, thinking, thoughtful; CONCEPT 402

medium [adj] midway, average common, commonplace, fair, fairish, intermediate, mean, medial, median, mediocre, middle, middling, moderate, neutral, normal, ordinary, par, passable, popular, run-of-the-mill*, so-so*, standard, tolerable; CONCEPTS 533,547 —Ant. extreme

medium [n1] means, mode agency, agent, avenue, channel, clairvoyant, factor, form, instrument, instrumentality, intermediate, measure, mechanism, ministry, organ, psychic, seer, tool, vehicle, way; CONCEPTS 658,712

medium [n2] atmosphere, setting ambience, ambient, climate, conditions, element, habitat, influences, milieu, surroundings; CONCEPTS 673,696

medium [n3] area of artistic expression art, drama, interpretation, manifestation, mark, music, painting, revelation, sculpture, speech, writing; CONCEPTS 259,263,293

medley [n] miscellany assortment, brew, collection, combo, composition, confusion, conglomeration, farrago, hodgepodge, jumble, mélange, melee, mingling, mishmash, mixed bag, mixture, pasticcio, pastiche, patchwork, potpourri, salmagundi, variety; CONCEPTS 262,432 —Ant. loneness, singularity

meek [adj] shy; compliant acquiescent, deferential, docile, forbearing, gentle, humble, lenient, longanimous, long-suffering, lowly, manageable, mild, milquetoast*, modest, nothing, orderly, pabulum*, passive, patient, peaceful, plain, resigned, serene, soft, spineless, spiritless, subdued, submissive, tame, timid, tolerant, unassuming, unpretentious, unresisting, weak, weak-kneed*, wishy-washy*, yielding, zero*; CONCEPT 401 —Ant. bold, brave, emboldened, immodest, impertinent, uninhibited

meet [adj] fitting accommodated, applicable, appropriate, apt, conformed, equitable, expedient, fair, felicitous, fit, good, happy, just, proper, reconciled, right, suitable, timely; CONCEPT 558 —Ant. improper, inappropriate, unfitting, unseemly

meet [n] sporting event involving several participants athletic event, competition, conflict, contest, event, match, meeting, tournament, tourney; CONCEPT 363

meet [v1] happen on accost, affront, brush against, bump into, chance on, clash, collide, come across, come up against, confront, contact, cross, dig up*, encounter, engage, experience, face, fall in with*, find, front, get together, grapple, greet, hit, light, luck*, make a meet, meet face to face, rendezvous with, rub eyeballs*, run across, run into, run up against, salute, see, strike, stumble, touch shoulders*, tumble, tussle, wrestle; CONCEPTS 183,384,626 —Ant. miss

meet [v2] connect, join abut, adhere, adjoin, border, coincide, connect, converge, cross, intersect, link, link up, reach, touch, unite; CONCEPTS 612,759 —Ant. disconnect, disjoin, divide, separate

meet [v3] perform, carry out answer, approach, come up to, comply, cope with, discharge, equal, execute, fit, fulfill, gratify, handle, match, measure up, rival, satisfy, suffice, tie, touch; CONCEPT 91 —Ant. avoid, dodge

meet [v4] come together, convene appear, assemble, assembly, be introduced, be present, be presented, collect, congregate, converge, enter in, flock, foregather, gather, get together, get to know, join, make acquaintance, muster, open, rally, rendezvous, show, sit; CONCEPTS 114,324 —Ant. cancel

meeting [n1] gathering, conference affair, assemblage, assembly, assignation, audience, bunch, call, cattle call*, company, competition, conclave, concourse, concursion, confab*, conflict, confrontation, congregation, congress, contest, convention, convocation, date, encounter, engagement, gang, get-together, huddle, introduction, meet, one on one*, parley, powwow*, rally, rendezvous, reunion, session, showdown, talk, tryst, turnout*; CONCEPTS 324,363,384

meeting [n2] convergence, intersection abutment, agreement, apposition, concourse, confluence, conjunction, connection, contact, crossing, joining, junction, juxtaposition, unification, union; CONCEPTS 113,684 —Ant. division, separation

melancholy [adj] depressed, sad blue*, dejected, despondent, destroyed, disconsolate, dismal, dispirited, doleful, dolorous, down*, down and out*, downbeat, downcast, downhearted, down in the dumps*, down in the mouth*, dragged, droopy, funereal, gloomy, glum, grim, heavyhearted, in blue funk*, joyless, lachrymose, low, low-spirited, lugubrious, mirthless, miserable, moody, moony*, mournful, pensive, saddened, saddening, somber, sorrowful, sorry*, torn up, trite, unhappy, wet blanket*, wistful, woebegone, woeful; CONCEPT 403 —Ant. cheerful, happy, joyful

melancholy [n] *depression, sadness* blahs*, blue devils*, blue funk*, blues*, boredom, bummer*, dejection, despair, desperation, despondency, dismals, dolefuls, dolor, downer*, down trip*, dumps, ennui, funk, gloom, gloominess, grief, letdown, low spirits, miserableness, misery, mopes*, mournfulness, pensiveness, sorrow, tedium, unhappiness, wistfulness, woe, wretchedness; CONCEPT 410 —*Ant.* cheer, happiness, joy

mélange [n] *mixture* assortment, combo, confusion, farrago, gallimaufry, hodgepodge, jumble, medley, miscellany, mishmash, mix, mixed bag, pasticcio, pastiche, patchwork, potpourri, salmagundi, soup, stew; CONCEPT 432 —*Ant.* singularity

meld [v] *blend, bring together* amalgamate, associate, compound, dissolve, feather in, fuse, interblend, interface, interfuse, intermingle, marry, merge, mingle, mix, unite; CONCEPTS 113,193 —*Ant.* divide, separate

melee [n] *battle, fight* affray, battle royal*, brawl, broil, brouhaha*, brush, clash, donny-brook*, fracas, fray, free-for-all*, knock-down-drag-out*, row, ruckus, ruction, rumpus, scrimmage, scuffle, set-to*, skirmish, to-do*, tussle, words; CONCEPT 106 —*Ant.* agreement, peace

mellifluous [adj] *smooth and sweet sounding* agreeable, dulcet, euphonic, fluid, harmonic, honeyed, mellow, pleasing, resonant, songful, soothing, symphonious, tuned, tuneful; CONCEPT 594

mellow [adj] *ripe, mature; softened* aged, cultured, cured, delicate, developed, dulcet, flavorful, full, full-flavored, fully developed, juicy, matured, mellifluent, mellifluous, melodious, perfect, perfected, rich, ripened, rounded, sapid, savory, seasoned, smooth, soft, soothing, sweet, tuneful; CONCEPTS 462,578,594,797 —*Ant.* hard, immature, sour, tart, unripe

mellow [v] *ripen, mature* age, arrive, develop, grow, grow up, improve, maturate, milden, mollify, perfect, ripe, season, settle down, soften, sweeten; CONCEPTS 678,704

melodious/melodic [adj] *harmonious, musical* accordant, agreeable, assonant, canorous, clear, concordant, dulcet, euphonic, euphonious, harmonic, in tune, mellifluous, mellow, pleasing, resonant, silvery, soft, songful, sweet, sweet-sounding, symphonic, symphonious, tuned, tuneful, well-tuned; CONCEPT 594 —*Ant.* cacophonous, discordant, grating, harsh, inharmonious, unmelodic, unmusical

melodramatic [adj] *extravagant in speech, behavior* artificial, blood-and-thunder*, cliff-hanging*, cloak-and-dagger*, exaggerated, ham*, hammy*, histrionic, hokey*, overdra-matic, overemotional, sensational, spectacular, stagy, theatrical; CONCEPT 542 —*Ant.* calm, normal, untheatrical

melody [n] *harmony, tune* air, aria, assonance, carillon, chant, chime, concord, consonance, descant, diapason, euphony, inflection, lay, lyric, measure, melodiousness, music, musical-ity, refrain, resonance, run, song, strain, theme, tunefulness, unison; CONCEPTS 262,595 —*Ant.* cacophony, disharmony

melt [v1] *liquefy; dissolve* cook, deliquesce, diffuse, disappear, disintegrate, disperse, evanesce, evaporate, fade, flow, flux, fuse, go, heat, merge, pass away, relent, run, smelt, soften, thaw, vanish, warm, waste away; CONCEPTS 250,255 —*Ant.* coagulate, condense, solidify

melt [v2] *give in, yield* become lenient, disarm, forgive, mollify, relax, relent, show mercy, soften, touch; CONCEPT 35 —*Ant.* fight

member [n1] *part of a group* affiliate, associ-ate, branch, chapter, component, comrade, constituent, cut, division, joiner, offshoot, parcel, piece, portion, post, representative, section, segment, unit; CONCEPTS 417,834,835

member [n2] *appendage* arm, component, constituent, element, extremity, feature, frag-ment, leg, limb, organ, part, portion, segment; CONCEPT 392

membership [n] *belonging to organization; those belonging to a group* associates, association, body, club, company, enrollment, fellows, group, members, participation, society; CONCEPTS 381,417

membrane [n] *covering layer* film, lamina, leaf, mucosa, sheath, sheet; CONCEPT 484

memento [n] *souvenir* keepsake, memorial, relic, remembrance, remembrancer, reminder, token, trace, trophy, vestige; CONCEPTS 337,446

memoir [n] *record of experiences* account, anecdote, annal, autobiography, bio*, biogra-phy, chronicle, confessions, diary, discourse, dissertation, essay, journal, life, life story, mem-ory, monograph, narrative, note, recollection, register, reminiscence, thesis, tractate, transac-tions, treatise, vita; CONCEPTS 271,280,282

memorabilia [n] *mementos* annals, archives, collectibles, keepsakes, relics, remembrances, reminders, souvenirs, tokens, trophies; CONCEPTS 337,446

memorable [adj] *noteworthy, significant* A-1*, big-league*, bodacious, catchy, celebrated, critical, crucial, decisive, distinguished, doozie*, enduring, eventful, extraordinary, famous, great, heavy*, heavyweight*, historic, hot*, illustrious, important, impressive, indelible, interesting, lasting, major-league, meaningful, mind-blowing*, momentous, monumental, notable, observable, red-letter*, remarkable, rememberable, rubric, serious, signal, something, standout, striking, super, surpassing, terrible, terrific, top-drawer, unforgettable; CONCEPT 529 —*Ant.* forgettable, insignificant, unimpressive, unnoteworthy

memorandum/memo [n] *written note* announcement, chit, diary, directive, dispatch, epistle, jotting, letter, message, minute, missive, notation, notice, record, reminder, tickler; CONCEPTS 271, 277,278

memorial [adj] *commemorative* canonizing, celebrative, commemoratory, consecrating, con-secrative, dedicatory, deifying, enshrining, in tribute, memorializing, monumental, remember-ing; CONCEPT 537 —*Ant.* abusive, dishonorable

memorial [n] *monument, testimonial in honor, praise* cairn, ceremony, column, headstone, inscription, keepsake, mausoleum, memento, monolith, obelisk, pillar, plaque, record, relic, remembrance, reminder, shaft, slab, souvenir, statue, stele, tablet, token, tombstone, trophy; CONCEPTS 337,386

memorize [v] *remember* commit to memory, cram, fix in the mind, keep forever, know, know by heart, learn, learn by heart, master, nail down, recall, recollect, remind, retain, store; CONCEPT 40

memory [n1] *ability to hold in the mind* anamnesis, awareness, camera-eye*, cognizance, consciousness, dead-eye*, flashback, memorization, mind, mindfulness, mind's eye*, recall, recapture, recognition, recollection, reflection, remembrance, reminiscence, retention, retentiveness, retrospection, subconsciousness, thought; CONCEPT 409 —*Ant.* amnesia, forgetfulness, ignorance

memory [n2] *specific thing remembered* concept, cue, fantasy, hint, image, jog, memo, memoir, mnemonic, picture, prod, prompt, reminder, representation, suggestion, thought, vision; CONCEPTS 529,678

menace [n] *danger; pest* annoyance, caution, commination, hazard, intimidation, jeopardy, nuisance, peril, plague, risk, scare, threat, thunder, trouble, troublemaker, warning; CONCEPTS 412,675 —*Ant.* aid, assistance, help

menace [v] *bother, frighten* alarm, bad-eye*, browbeat, bully, chill, compromise, endanger, hazard, impend, imperil, intimidate, jeopardize, lean on, loom, lower, overhang, peril, portend, push around, put heat on*, risk, scare, scare hell out of*, spook, terrorize, threaten, torment, whip around*; CONCEPTS 7,19 —*Ant.* aid, assist, help

menacing [adj] *intimidating, ominous* alarming, approaching, dangerous, frightening, imminent, impending, intimidatory, looming, louring, lowering, minacious, minatory, overhanging, threatening; CONCEPTS 401,537,548 —*Ant.* aiding, assisting, helping, unthreatening

menagerie [adj] *zoo* aquarium, collection, exhibition, safari park, wildlife park, zoological garden; CONCEPTS 509,513

mend [v] *correct, improve, fix* aid, ameliorate, amend, better, condition, convalesce, cure, darn, doctor, emend, fiddle with, gain, get better, get well, heal, knit, look up, overhaul, patch, perk up, ready, rebuild, recondition, reconstruct, recover, rectify, recuperate, redress, refit, reform, refurbish, rejuvenate, remedy, renew, renovate, repair, restore, retouch, revamp, revise, right, service, sew; CONCEPTS 126,244,303,700 —*Ant.* break, destroy, hurt, ruin, weaken

mendacious [adj] *dishonest* deceitful, deceptive, duplicitous, equivocating, erroneous, fallacious, false, fibbing, fraudulent, insincere, lying, paltering, perfidious, perjured, prevaricating, shifty, spurious, untrue, untruthful, wrong; CONCEPT 267 —*Ant.* frank, honest, sincere, truthful

menial [adj] *lowly, low-status* abject, base, baseborn, boring, common, degrading, demeaning, dull, fawning, grovelling, humble, humdrum, ignoble, ignominious, low, mean, obeisant, obsequious, routine, servile, slavish, sorry, subservient, sycophantic, unskilled, vile; CONCEPTS 574,575 —*Ant.* elevated, skilled, superior, talented

men's movement [n] *men's attempt to redefine gender roles* gender revisionism, male reform, men's liberation, men's studies; CONCEPT 388

mental [adj1] *concerning the mind* brainy*, cerebral, clairvoyant, deep, heavy, ideological, imaginative, immaterial, inner, intellective, intellectual, mysterious, phrenic, psychic, psychical, psychological, rational, reasoning, spiritual, subconscious, subjective, subliminal, telepathic, thinking, thoughtful, unreal; CONCEPTS 402,403 —*Ant.* body, physical

mental [adj2] *insane* deranged, disturbed, fruity, loco*, lunatic, mad, maniac, mentally ill, mindless, non compos mentis, nuts*, nutsy*, psychiatric, psychotic, unbalanced, unstable; CONCEPTS 314,403 —*Ant.* balanced, sane

mental hospital [n] *psychiatric hospital* bughouse*, funny farm*, insane asylum, loony bin*, madhouse*, mental health facility, mental institution, nuthouse*, psychiatric ward, sanatorium; CONCEPTS 312,439,516

mental illness [n] *mental disorder* depression, emotional disorder, emotional instability, insanity, maladjustment, mania, mental sickness, nervous breakdown, neurosis, neurotic disorder, personality disorder, phobia, psychosis, schizophrenia; CONCEPTS 316,410

mentality [n] *state of mind; intelligence* attitude, brainpower, brains, cast, character, comprehension, disposition, frame of mind*, headset*, intellect, intelligence quotient, IQ, makeup, mental age, mind, mindset*, outlook, personality, psychology, rationality, reasoning, routine, sense, turn of mind*, understanding, way of thinking*, wit; CONCEPTS 409,411 —*Ant.* physicality

mention [n] *referral, observation* acknowledgment, allusion, citation, comment, footnote, indication, naming, note, notice, notification, recognition, reference, remark, specifying, tribute, utterance; CONCEPTS 73,278 —*Ant.* quiet, silence

mention [v] *refer to* acknowledge, acquaint, adduce, advert, allude to, bring up, broach, call attention to, cite, communicate, declare, designate, detail, disclose, discuss, divulge, enumerate, hint at, impart, infer, instance, intimate, introduce, make known, name, notice, notify, observe, point out, point to, quote, recount, remark, report, reveal, speak about, speak of, specify, state, suggest, tell, throw out, touch on; CONCEPT 73

mentor [n] *person who advises* adviser, coach, counsellor, guide, instructor, teacher, trainer, tutor; CONCEPT 350

menu [n] *list from which to choose, often to choose food* bill of fare, card, carte, carte du jour, cuisine, food, spread, table; CONCEPT 283

mercenary [adj] *greedy for money* acquisitive, avaricious, bribable, corrupt, covetous, grabby, grasping, miserly, money-grubbing, selfish, sordid, stingy, unethical, unprincipled, unscrupulous, venal; CONCEPT 401 —Ant. generous, unselfish

mercenary [n] *person who fights, kills for money* hireling, legionnaire, merc, professional soldier, slave, soldier of fortune, warrior; CONCEPTS 358,412

merchandise [n] *goods for sale* commodity, effects, job lot, line, material, number, produce, product, seconds, staple, stock, stuff, truck, vendible, wares; CONCEPT 338

merchandise [v] *sell goods* advertise, buy and sell, deal in, distribute, do business in, market, promote, publicize, retail, trade, traffic in, vend, wholesale; CONCEPT 345 —Ant. buy

merchant [n] *person who sells goods* broker, businessperson, consigner, dealer, exporter, handler, jobber, marketer, operator, retailer, salesperson, seller, sender, shipper, shopkeeper, storekeeper, trader, tradesperson, trafficker, tycoon, vendor, wholesaler; CONCEPT 347 —Ant. buyer, customer

merciful [adj] *kind, sparing* all heart*, benefi-cent, benign, benignant, bleeding heart*, charitable, clement, compassionate, condoning, easygoing, feeling, forbearing, forgiving, gener-ous, gentle, gracious, heart in right place*, hu-mane, humanitarian, indulgent, kindly, lenient, liberal, mild, pardoning, pitiful, pitying, soft*, softhearted*, sympathetic, tender, tenderhearted, tolerant; CONCEPTS 401,542 —Ant. cruel, merci-less, unforgiving, unkind, unmerciful

merciless [adj] *mean, heartless* barbarous, callous, compassionless, cruel, cutthroat, dog-eat-dog*, fierce, gratuitous, grim, hard, hard-hearted, harsh, hatchet job*, having a killer instinct*, implacable, inexorable, inhumane, iron-fisted, mean machine*, mortal, pitiless, relentless, ruthless, severe, unappeasable, uncalled-for, unfeeling, unflinching, unforgiv-ing, unmerciful, unpitying, unrelenting, unsparing, unsympathetic, unyielding, wanton; CONCEPTS 401,542 —Ant. giving, kind, merci-ful, nice, sparing, sympathetic

mercurial [adj] *flighty, temperamental* blowing hot and cold*, bubbleheaded*, buoyant, capricious, changeable, effervescent, elastic, erratic, expansive, fickle, flaky, flip*, fluctuating, gaga*, gay, impulsive, inconstant, irregular, irrepressible, lighthearted, lively, lubricious, mad, mobile, movable, quicksilver, resilient, short-fuse*, spirited, sprightly, ticklish, unpre-dictable, unstable, up-and-down*, variable, volatile, yo-yo*; CONCEPTS 401,404 —Ant. calm, tranquil, unchangeable, unperturbable, unvarying

mercy [n] *kindness, compassion* benevolence, benignancy, blessing, boon, charity, clemency, commiseration, favor, forbearance, forgiveness, generosity, gentleness, godsend, goodwill, grace, humanity, kindliness, lenience, leniency, lenity, lifesaver, luck, mildness, pity, quarter, relief, ruth, softheartedness, sympathy, tender-ness, tolerance; CONCEPTS 32,633 —Ant. cruelty, intolerance, meanness, uncompassion

mere [adj] *nothing more; absolute* bald, bare, blunt, common, complete, entire, insignificant, little, minor, plain, poor, pure, pure and simple, sheer, simple, small, stark, unadorned, unadul-terated, unmitigated, unmixed, utter, very; CONCEPTS 535,589

meretricious [adj] *gaudy, flashy* blatant, bogus, brazen, chintzy, counterfeit, garish, glaring, insincere, loud, misleading, ornate, phony, plastic*, put-on*, sham, showy, spurious, superficial, tawdry, tinsel, trashy; CONCEPTS 542,589 —Ant. genuine, real, undecorated, unembellished

merge [v] *bring or come together* absorb, amalgamate, assimilate, become lost in, become partners, be swallowed up*, blend, cement, centralize, coalesce, combine, come aboard*, compound, conglomerate, consolidate, con-verge, deal one in, fuse, hitch on*, hook up*, immerge, incorporate, interface, intermingle, intermix, join, join up, line up, marry, meet, meld, melt into, mingle, mix, network, plug into, pool, slap on, submerge, synthesize, tack on*, tag, team up*, throw in together*, tie in, unite; CONCEPTS 113,193,324 —Ant. divide, part, separate

merger [n] *consolidation* alliance, amalgama-tion, cahoots*, coadunation, coalition, combina-tion, fusion, hookup, incorporation, lineup, melding, mergence, merging, organization, pool, takeover, tie-in, tie-up, unification, union; CONCEPTS 323,324,703 —Ant. division, part-ing, separation

meridian [n] *summit, climax* acme, apex, apogee, crest, culmination, extremity, high noon, high-water mark, peak, pinnacle, zenith; CONCEPTS 832,836

merit [n] *advantage* arete, asset, benefit, caliber, credit, desert, dignity, excellence, excellency, good, goodness, honor, integrity, perfection, quality, stature, strong point, talent, value, virtue, worth, worthiness; CONCEPT 693 —Ant. demerit, disadvantage, fault, weakness

merit [v] *be entitled to* be in line for, be worthy, deserve, earn, get one's comeuppance*, get one's due*, get one's just desserts*, get what is coming*, have a claim, have a right, have com-ing, incur, justify, rate, warrant; CONCEPT 129

meritorious [adj] *honorable, commendable* admirable, boss*, choice, creditable, deserving, estimable, excellent, exemplary, golden, good, laudable, meritable, noble, praisable, praisewor-thy, right, righteous, thankworthy, top drawer*, virtuous, winner, world-beating*, worthy; CONCEPTS 404,548,572 —Ant. corrupt, dishon-orable, immoral, improper, unworthy, wrong

merriment/merrymaking [n] *enjoyment, amusement* brawl, buffoonery, cheerfulness, conviviality, festivity, frolic, fun, fun and games*, gaiety, glee, happiness, hilarity, hoopla*, indulgence, jocularity, jocundity, jollity, joviality, joy, laughs, laughter, levity, liveliness, mirth, picnic, recreation, revel, rev-elry, self-indulgence, shindig, sport, whoopee*, wingding*; CONCEPTS 386,410 —Ant. sadness, sorrow, unhappiness

merry [*adj*] *very happy; festive* amusing, blithe, blithesome, boisterous, boon, carefree, cheerful, comic, comical, convivial, enjoyable, entertaining, facetious, frolicsome, fun-loving, funny, gay, glad, gleeful, grooving*, hilarious, humorous, jocund, jolly, joyful, joyous, jumping, larking, lighthearted, lively, mad, mirthful, perky, pleasant, riotous, rip-roaring*, rocking, rollicking, saturnalian, sportive, sunny, unconstrained, uproarious, vivacious, wild, winsome, zappy*, zingy*, zippy*; CONCEPTS *403,548,572* —*Ant.* grave, sad, serious, sorrowful, unhappy, upset

mesa [*n*] *plateau* butte, elevation, highland, plain, tableland, upland; CONCEPTS *509,744*

mesh [*n*] *netting, entanglement* cobweb, jungle, knot, labyrinth, maze, morass, net, network, plexus, reticulation, screen, skein, snare, snarl, tangle, toils, tracery, trap, web; CONCEPT *473*

mesh [*v*] *entangle, connect* agree, catch, coincide, combine, come together, coordinate, dovetail, engage, enmesh, ensnare, fit, fit together, harmonize, interlock, knit, net, snare, tangle, trap; CONCEPTS *113,193* —*Ant.* disconnect, unmesh, untangle

mesmerize [*v*] *captivate* catch up, control, deaden, drug, ensorcell, enthrall, entrance, fascinate, grip, hold spellbound, hypnotize, magnetize, numb, render unconscious, spellbind, stupefy; CONCEPTS *11,14* —*Ant.* disenchant, turn off

mess [*n1*] *disorder, litter* botch, chaos, clutter, combination, compound, confusion, debris, dirtiness, disarray, discombobulation*, disorganization, every which way*, eyesore, fright, hash, hodgepodge, jumble, mayhem, mishmash, monstrosity, salmagundi, shambles, sight, turmoil, untidiness, wreck, wreckage; CONCEPTS *230,260* —*Ant.* order, organization, tidiness

mess [*n2*] *difficulty, predicament* dilemma, fix, imbroglio, jam, mix-up, muddle, perplexity, pickle*, plight, stew; CONCEPT *674* —*Ant.* benefit, solution

message [*n1*] *communication, often written* bulletin, cannonball, communiqué, directive, dispatch, dope, earful, epistle, information, intelligence, intimation, letter, memo, memorandum, missive, news, note, notice, paper, report, tidings, wire, word; CONCEPTS *271,274*

message [*n2*] *meaning, idea* acceptation, import, intendment, moral, point, purport, sense, significance, significancy, signification, theme, understanding; CONCEPTS *661,682*

mess around [*v*] *fiddle; goof off* amuse oneself, dabble, dawdle, doodle, fool around, loiter, muck around*, play, play around, play the fool*, potter, puddle, putter, tinker, trifle; CONCEPTS *87,363* —*Ant.* labor, toil, work

messenger [*n*] *person carrying information to another* agent, ambassador, bearer, carrier, commissionaire, courier, crier, delegate, delivery person, detachment, detail, dispatcher, emissary, envoy, errand person*, flag-bearer, forerunner, go-between*, gofer*, harbinger, herald, intermediary, mediator, minister, post, precursor, prophet, runner, schlepper*; CONCEPT *348* —*Ant.* receiver

mess up [*v*] *disorder, dirty* befoul, besmirch, bobble, bollix*, botch, bungle, clutter, confuse, damage, derange, destroy, disarrange, discompose, dishevel, disorganize, disturb, foul, goof up*, gum up*, jumble, litter, louse up, muddle, pollute, ruin, rummage, scramble, screw up*, smear, soil, spoil, unsettle, upset; CONCEPTS *158,252,254* —*Ant.* arrange, order, organize, tidy

messy [*adj*] *cluttered, dirty* blotchy*, careless, chaotic, confused, disheveled, disordered, disorganized, grimy, grubby*, littered, muddled, raunchy*, rumpled, slapdash*, slipshod*, sloppy, slovenly, unfastidious, unkempt, untidy; CONCEPTS *485,621* —*Ant.* clean, ordered, organized, uncluttered

metal [*n*] *lustrous chemical element* alloy, casting, deposit, foil, hardware, ingot, leaf, load, mail, mineral, native rock, ore, plate, solder, vein; CONCEPT *476*

metamorphose [*v*] *convert, transform* age, alter, be reborn, change, commute, develop, diverge, mature, mutate, remake, remodel, reshape, ripen, transfigure, translate, transmogrify, transmute, transubstantiate, vary; CONCEPTS *469,697,701* —*Ant.* stagnate

metamorphosis [*n*] *conversion, transformation* alteration, change, changeover, evolution, mutation, rebirth, transfiguration, transfigurement, translation, transmogrification, transmutation, transubstantiation; CONCEPTS *469,697, 701* —*Ant.* stagnation

metaphor [*n*] *figure of speech, implied comparison* allegory, analogy, emblem, hope, image, metonymy, personification, similitude, symbol, trope; CONCEPT *275* —*Ant.* plain speech

metaphorical [*adj*] *figurative* allegorical, denotative, descriptive, emblematic, illustrative, metaphoric, representative, symbolic, tropological; CONCEPTS *267,582*

metaphysical [*adj*] *not physical; without physical presence* abstract, abstruse, bodiless, deep, difficult, discarnate, esoteric, eternal, fundamental, high-flown, ideal, immaterial, impalpable, incorporeal, insubstantial, intangible, intellectual, jesuitic, mystical, nonmaterial, nonphysical, numinous, oversubtle, philosophical, preternatural, profound, recondite, spiritual, superhuman, superior, supermundane, supernatural, suprahuman, supramundane, supranatural, theoretical, transcendental, unearthly, unfleshly, universal, unphysical, unreal, unsubstantial; CONCEPTS *529,582* —*Ant.* concrete, material, objective, physical, real, solid, substantial

mete [*v*] *administer, distribute* admeasure, allocate, allot, allow, apportion, assign, deal, dispense, divide, dole, give, lot, measure, parcel, portion, ration, share; CONCEPTS *98,108*

meteoric [*adj*] *brief, sudden* dazzling, ephemeral, flashing, fleeting, momentary, overnight, rapid, spectacular, speedy, swift, transient; CONCEPTS *548,798,799* —*Ant.* slow

meteorology [*n*] *weather science* aerology, climatology, weather forecasting; CONCEPTS *522,524*

meter [n] *rhythm, beat* cadence, cadency, feet, lilt, measure, mora, music, pattern, poetry, rhyme, structure, swing; CONCEPTS 65,262

method [n1] *means, procedure* adjustment, approach, arrangement, channels, course, custom, design, disposal, disposition, fashion, form, formula, habit, line, manner, mechanism, method, mode, modus, modus operandi, nuts and bolts*, plan, practice, proceeding, process, program, receipt, recipe, red tape*, ritual, rote, routine, rubric, rule, rut, schema, scheme, short-cut, style, system, tack, tactics, technic, technique, tenor, the book*, usage, way, ways and means*, wise, wrinkle*; CONCEPTS 6,660

method [n2] *order, pattern* arrangement, classification, design, form, orderliness, organization, plan, planning, purpose, regularity, structure, system; CONCEPTS 727,770

methodical/methodic [adj] *organized, precise* all together, analytical, businesslike, by the book*, by the numbers, careful, cut-and-dried*, deliberate, disciplined, efficient, exact, fixed, framed, in a groove*, logical, methodized, meticulous, neat, ordered, orderly, painstaking, planned, regular, scrupulous, set-up*, structured, systematic, tidy, together, well-regulated; CONCEPTS 326,542,544,585 —*Ant.* confused, disorderly, disorganized, imprecise, unmethodical/unmethodic

methodology [n] *methods* approach, channels, design, manner, mode, plan, practice, procedure, process, program, style, technique, way; CONCEPTS 6,644

meticulous [adj] *detailed, perfectionist* accurate, cautious, conscientious, conscionable, crossing the t's*, dotting the i's*, exact, fastidious, fussy, heedful, microscopic, nitpicking*, painstaking, particular, persnickety*, picky, precise, punctilious, punctual, scrupulous, stickling, strict, thorough; CONCEPTS 542,544,557 —*Ant.* careless, messy, sloppy, undetailed

métier [n] *occupation* calling, chosen work, craft, day gig*, employment, field, forte, job, line of work, one's specialty, profession, pursuit, racket*, thing*, trade, vocation, walk of life*, work; CONCEPTS 349,351,360

metropolis [n] *major city* capital, downtown, megalopolis, metropolitan area, municipality; CONCEPT 507

metropolitan [adj] *concerning a city* city, cosmopolitan, modern, municipal, urban, urbane; CONCEPT 536 —*Ant.* country

mettle [n] *boldness, strength of character* animation, ardor, backbone, bravery, caliber, courage, daring, dauntlessness, disposition, energy, fire, force, fortitude, gallantry, gameness, grit*, guts*, hardihood, heart*, indomitability, kidney*, life*, makeup, moxie, nature, nerve, pluck, quality, resolution, resolve, spirit, spunk, stamina, stamp*, starch, temper, temperament, valor, vigor, vitality; CONCEPT 411 —*Ant.* weakness

miasma [n] *effluvium* fetor, foul air, fumes, gas, mephitis, odor, pollution, reek, smell, smog, stench, stink, vapor; CONCEPT 465

microbe [n] *bacteria* bacillus, bacterium, bug*, crud, germ, microorganism, pathogen, plague, virus; CONCEPT 306

microorganism [n] *germ* bacterium, bug*, disease, disease-causing agent, microbe, parasite, pathogen, plague, virus; CONCEPTS 306,392

microscopic [adj] *tiny, almost undetectable* atomic, diminutive, imperceptible, infinitesimal, invisible, little, minuscule, minute, negligible, teeny*, wee*; CONCEPTS 773,789 —*Ant.* big, huge, large, macroscopic

microwave [v] *cook* bake, heat, melt, nuke*, warm up, zap*; CONCEPT 170

midday [n] *middle of the day* 12 PM, high noon, lunchtime, noon, noontide, noontime, twelve hundred, twelve noon, twelve o'clock; CONCEPT 802 —*Ant.* 12 AM, midnight

middle [adj] *central* average, between, betwixt and between*, center, centermost, equidistant, halfway, inner, inside, intermediate, intervening, mainstream, mean, medial, median, medium, mezzo*, middlemost, middle of the road*, midmost, smack in the middle, straddling the fence*; CONCEPTS 547,583,830 —*Ant.* border, extreme, outer, outside

middle [n] *center* core, deep, focus, halfway, halfway point, heart, inside, marrow, mean, media, midpoint, midriff, midsection, midst, thick, waist; CONCEPTS 746,761,830,833 —*Ant.* border, margin, outside

middle-of-the-road [adj] *moderate* balanced, cautious, compromising, conservative, controlled, disciplined, even, impartial, indifferent, inexpensive, midway, mild, modest, neutral, noncommittal, nonpartisan, not excessive, on the fence*, reasonable, straight; CONCEPTS 533,575

middle person [n] *person who acts as intermediary* agent, broker, connection, distributor, entrepreneur, fixer, go-between*, influence, interagent, interceder, intercessor, intermediate, intermediator, jobber*, mediator, representative, salesperson, wholesaler; CONCEPT 348

middling [adj] *adequate, okay* all right, average, common, conventional, decent, fair, fairish, good, indifferent, intermediate, mean, mediocre, medium, moderate, modest, okay, ordinary, passable, run-of-the-mill*, so-so*, tolerable, traditional, unexceptional, unremarkable; CONCEPT 547 —*Ant.* exceptional, extraordinary

midget [adj] *short, small* baby, diminutive, knee-high*, Lilliputian, miniature, minikin, pocket, teensy*, teeny*, tiny; CONCEPTS 773,779 —*Ant.* big, giant, huge, large, tall

midget [n] *small person* bantam, gnome, homuncule, homunculus, Lilliputian*, little person, manikin, midge, runt*; CONCEPT 424 —*Ant.* giant

midnight [n] *middle of the night* 12 o'clock at night, bewitching hour*, dead of night*, small hours*, twelve o'clock at night, witching hour*; CONCEPTS 801,802,806

midst [n] *middle, core* betwixt and between*, bosom, center, deep, depths, halfway, heart, hub, interior, mean, medium, midpoint, nucleus, thick; CONCEPT 830 —*Ant.* exterior, exteriority, outside

mien [n] *person's presence, manner* act, address, air, appearance, aspect, aura, bearing, carriage, countenance, demeanor, deportment, expression, front, image, look, mannerism, port, set, style; CONCEPTS 411,644

miff [v] *annoy* aggrieve, bother, displease, hurt, irk, irritate, nettle, offend, pester, pique, provoke, put out, resent, upset, vex; CONCEPTS 7,19 —Ant. appease, mollify, please

miffed [adj] *displeased* annoyed, chagrined, disgruntled, irked, irritated, nettled, offended, pained, peeved*, piqued, put out, resentful, riled, upset, vexed; CONCEPT 570 —Ant. pleased

might [n] *ability, power* adequacy, arm, authority, capability, capacity, clout, command, competence, control, domination, efficacy, efficiency, energy, force, forcefulness, forcibleness, get-up-and-go*, jurisdiction, lustiness, mastery, moxie*, muscle*, potency, powerfulness, prowess, puissance, punch, qualification, qualifiedness, sinew*, steam, strength, strenuousness, strong arm*, sway, valor, vigor, vigorousness; CONCEPTS 411,641,732 —Ant. inability, powerlessness, weakness

mightily [adv1] *very much, extremely* decidedly, exceedingly, greatly, highly, hugely, intensely, mighty, notably, surpassingly, very; CONCEPT 569 —Ant. little

mightily [adv2] *forcefully* arduously, energetically, forcibly, hard, hardly, laboriously, lustily, might and main*, powerfully, strenuously, strongly, vigorously, with all one's strength; CONCEPTS 540,544 —Ant. weakly

mighty [adj1] *forceful, powerful* boss*, doughty, hardy, indomitable, lusty, muscular, omnipotent, potent, powerhouse, puissant, robust, stalwart, steamroller*, stout, strapping, strengthy, strong, strong as ox*, sturdy, vigorous, wieldy; CONCEPTS 489,540 —Ant. delicate, powerless, weak

mighty [adj2] *gigantic, monumental* august, bulky, colossal, considerable, dynamic, eminent, enormous, extensive, extraordinary, grand, great, heroic, high, huge, illustrious, immense, imposing, impressive, intense, irresistible, large, magnificent, majestic, massive, moving, notable, prodigious, renowned, stupendous, titanic, towering, tremendous, vast; CONCEPTS 537,773. —Ant. insignificant, small, tiny, unimportant

migrant [n] *person who moves to a foreign place* departer, drifter, emigrant, evacuee, expatriate, gypsy, immigrant, itinerant, migrator, mover, nomad, rover, tinker, transient, traveler, vagrant, wanderer; CONCEPT 413

migrant/migratory [adj] *moving, traveling* casual, changing, drifting, emigrating, errant, gypsy, immigrant, immigrating, impermanent, itinerant, migrative, migratorial, mobile, nomad, nomadic, on the move, passing over, passing through, peripatetic, ranging, roving, seasonal, shifting, temporary, tramp, transient, transmigratory, unsettled, vagabond, vagrant, wandering; CONCEPT 584 —Ant. staying

migrate [v] *move, travel to another place* drift, emigrate, immigrate, journey, leave, nomadize,

range, roam, rove, shift, transmigrate, trek, voyage, wander; CONCEPTS 198,224 —Ant. stay

mild [adj1] *gentle, temperate, nonirritating* balmy, benign, benignant, blah*, bland, breezy, calm, choice, clear, clement, cool, dainty, delicate, demulcent, easy, emollient, exquisite, faint, fine, flat, genial, ho-hum*, lenient, lenitive, light, lukewarm, medium, mellow, moderate, mollifying, nothing, nothing much*, pabulum, pacific, peaceful, placid, smooth, soft, soothing, sunny, tempered, tepid, untroubled, vanilla*, warm, weak, wimpy*; CONCEPTS 485,525,537 —Ant. fierce, harsh, rough, violent

mild [adj2] *easygoing, pleasant in personality* amiable, balmy, bland, calm, clement, compassionate, complaisant, deferential, docile, dull, easy, equable, feeble, flat, forbearant, forbearing, forgiving, gentle, good-humored, good-natured, good-tempered, humane, indulgent, insipid, jejune, kind, lenient, meek, mellow, merciful, mild-mannered, moderate, obeisant, obliging, pacific, patient, peaceable, placid, serene, smooth, soft, spiritless, subdued, submissive, subservient, tame, temperate, tender, tranquil, unassuming, vapid, warm; CONCEPTS 401,404 —Ant. agitated, flappable, nervous

mile [n] *5, 280 feet/1.609 kilometers measured* nautical, square, statute; CONCEPTS 790,791

milestone [n] *achievement* anniversary, breakthrough, discovery, event, landmark, milepost, occasion, turning point, waypoint; CONCEPTS 2, 706

milieu [n] *environment, atmosphere* ambience, ambient, background, bag, climate, element, locale, location, medium, mise-en-scène, nabe, neighborhood, place, scene, setting, space, sphere, surroundings, turf; CONCEPT 673

militant [adj] *aggressive, combative* active, assertive, assertory, bellicose, belligerent, combating, contending, contentious, embattled, fighting, gladiatorial, in arms, martial, militaristic, military, offensive, pugnacious, pushy, quarrelsome, scrappy, self-assertive, truculent, up in arms, vigorous, warlike, warring; CONCEPT 401 —Ant. compliant, peaceful, peaceloving, submissive, tolerant

militant [n] *person who fights, is aggressive* activist, belligerent, combatant, demonstrator, fighter, objector, partisan, protester, rioter, warrior; CONCEPTS 358,359

military [adj] *soldierlike; concerning the armed forces* aggressive, armed, army, combatant, combative, fighting, martial, militant, militaristic, noncivil, soldierly, warlike, warmongering; CONCEPT 536 —Ant. civilian

military [n] *armed force* air force, army, force, marines, navy, service, servicepeople, soldiery, troop; CONCEPT 322

milk [n] *liquid produced by mammals* buttermilk, chalk*, condensed, cream, evaporated, formula, goat, half-and-half, homogenized, laiche, low fat, moo juice*, pasteurized, powdered, raw, skim, two-percent, whole; CONCEPT 467

milk [v] *tap; exploit* bleed, drain, draw off, elicit, empty, evince, evoke, exhaust, express, extort, extract, fleece, impose on, let out, press, pump, siphon, suck, take advantage, take out, use, wring; CONCEPTS *139,142,156,225* —*Ant.* hoard, save

milksop [*n*] *coward* baby*, caitiff, chicken*, chicken heart*, chicken liver*, cry-baby, deserter, fraidy-cat*, jellyfish*, lily liver, momma's boy*, namby-pamby, pansy, panty-waist, quitter, scaredy cat*, sissy*, weakling, wimp, wuss*, wussy*, yellow, yellow belly*; CONCEPT *423*

milky [*adj*] *white, cloudy* alabaster, clouded, frosted, lacteal, lacteous, lactescent, milk-white, opalescent, opaline, opaque, pearly, whitish; CONCEPT *618* —*Ant.* black, blackish, dark

mill [*n*] *factory* foundry, manufactory, plant, shop, sweatshop, works; CONCEPTS *439,449*

mill [*v*] *grind* comminute, crush, granulate, grate, pound, powder, press, pulverize; CONCEPT *186*

millenium [*n*] *one thousand years* one-thousandth anniversary, turn of the century; CONCEPTS *807,816*

millstone [*n*] *burden* accountability, affliction, albatross*, anxiety, ball and chain*, blame, charge, concern, cross, deadweight, difficulty, encumbrance, grievance, hardship, hindrance, load, mental weight, misfortune, onus, punishment, responsibility, strain, stress, task, thorn in one's side*, trial, trouble, worry; CONCEPTS *532,690*

mimic [*n*] *person who imitates* actor, caricaturist, comedian, copycat, imitator, impersonator, impressionist, mime, mummer, parodist, parrot, performer, playactor, player, thespian, trouper; CONCEPT *352*

mimic [*v*] *imitate, mock* act, ape, burlesque, caricature, copy, copycat, ditto*, do, do like*, echo, enact, fake, go like*, impersonate, look like*, make believe, make fun of, make like*, mime, mirror, pantomime, parody, parrot, perform, personate, play, resemble, ridicule, sham, simulate, take off*, travesty; CONCEPTS *54,59,111,171*

mince [*v1*] *chop up* chip, crumble, cut, dice, divide, grind, hack, hash, whack; CONCEPT *176*

mince [*v2*] *pose, put on airs* attitudinize, flounce, posture, prance, sashay, strut; CONCEPT *59*

mince [*v3*] *euphemize, hold back in communication* alleviate, decrease, diminish, extenuate, lessen, minimize, moderate, palliate, soften, spare, tone down, weaken; CONCEPT *266* —*Ant.* reveal, tell all

mincing [*adj*] *affected, pretentious* artificial, dainty, delicate, effeminate, fastidious, finical, finicky, fussy, genteel, insincere, la-di-da*, nice, particular, persnickety, precious, sissy, squeamish, stilted, too-too*, unnatural; CONCEPTS *401,404* —*Ant.* extroverted, unaffected, unpretentious

mind [*n1*] *intelligence* apperception, attention, brain*, brainpower, brains*, capacity, cognizance, conception, consciousness, creativity, faculty, function, genius, head, imagination, ingenuity, instinct, intellect, intellectual, intellectuality, intuition, judgment, lucidity,

marbles*, mentality, observation, perception, percipience, power, psyche, ratiocination, reason, reasoning, regard, sanity, sense, soul, soundness, spirit, talent, thinker, thought, understanding, wisdom, wits; CONCEPTS *393, 409* —*Ant.* body, corporeality, physicality

mind [*n2*] *memory* attention, cognizance, concentration, head, mark, note, notice, observance, observation, recollection, regard, remark, remembrance, subconscious, thinking, thoughts; CONCEPTS *409,630* —*Ant.* amnesia

mind [*n3*] *inclination, tendency; belief* attitude, bent, conviction, desire, determination, disposition, eye, fancy, feeling, humor, impulse, intention, judgment, leaning, liking, mood, notion, opinion, outlook, persuasion, pleasure, point of view, purpose, sentiment, strain, temper, temperament, thoughts, tone, urge, vein, view, way of thinking, will, wish; CONCEPTS *20,657,689* —*Ant.* disbelief, disinclination

mind [*v1*] *be bothered; care* be affronted, be opposed, complain, deplore, disapprove, dislike, look askance at, object, resent, take offense; CONCEPTS *21,29*

mind [*v2*] *comply, obey* adhere to, attend, behave, do as told, follow, follow orders, heed, keep, listen, mark, note, notice, observe, pay attention, pay heed, regard, respect, take heed, watch; CONCEPTS *23,91* —*Ant.* disobey, disregard, ignore

mind [*v3*] *attend, tend* baby-sit, be attentive, behold, care for, discern, discipline, ensure, give heed to, govern, guard, have charge of, keep an eye on*, listen up, look, make certain, mark, mind the store*, note, notice, observe, oversee, perceive, regard, ride herd on*, see, sit, superintend, supervise, watch; CONCEPTS *110,295,596,623* —*Ant.* ignore, neglect

mind [*v4*] *be careful* be cautious, be concerned, be on guard, be solicitous, be wary, have a care, mind one's p's and q's*, take care, tend, toe the line*, trouble, watch, watch one's step*, watch out*; CONCEPT *34*

mind [*v5*] *remember* bethink, bring to mind, cite, recall, recollect, remind, reminisce, retain; CONCEPT *40* —*Ant.* forget

mind-blowing [*adj*] *amazing, intense* astonishing, eye-opening, hallucinatory, mind-altering, mind-boggling, overwhelming, psychedelic, staggering, stunning, wonderful; CONCEPTS *547,572*

mind-boggling [*adj*] *overwhelming* amazing, astonishing, breathtaking, eye-opening, mind-blowing, spectacular, staggering, startling, stunning, stupendous, surprising, wonderful; CONCEPTS *547,572*

mindful [*adj*] *attentive, aware* alert, alive to, apprehensive, au courant, be up on*, cagey, careful, cautious, chary, cognizant, conscientious, conscious, conversant, heedful, in the know, know all the answers*, knowing, know ins and outs*, knowledgeable, observant, observative, observing, on one's toes*, on the ball*, on the job*, on to*, plugged in*, regardful, respectful, sensible, solicitous, thoughtful, tuned in*, vigilant, wary, watchful,

with eyes peeled*; CONCEPTS 402,403,542
—*Ant.* absent-minded, careless, heedless,
inattentive, unaware

mindless [*adj*] *oblivious, stupid; automatic*
asinine, brutish, careless, daydreaming, foolish,
forgetful, gratuitous, heedless, idiotic, imbecilic, inattentive, mooning, moony, moronic,
neglectful, negligent, nitwitted, obtuse, out,
out of it*, rash, senseless, silly, simple, spaced-
out*, thoughtless, unaware, unintelligent,
unmindful, unthinking, witless; CONCEPTS
403,538 —*Ant.* intelligent, mindful, thinking,
thoughtful

mind reader [*n*] *psychic* augur, channeller,
clairvoyant, diviner, fortune-teller, haruspex,
horoscopist, medium, mentalist, oracle, palm
reader, prophet, seer, soothsayer, telepathis;
CONCEPT 423

mind-set [*n*] *mental attitude* air, approach,
belief, character, demeanor, disposition, frame
of mind, headset, inclination, mental outlook,
mental state, mood, opinion, perspective,
philosophy, point of view, position, sentiment,
stance, stand, standing, standpoint, temperament, view, way of thinking; CONCEPTS 410,689

mine [*n*] *deposit, supply* abundance, bed,
bonanza, ditch, excavation, field, fount, fountain, fund, gold mine, hoard, lode, pit, quarry,
reserve, shaft, source, spring, stock, store,
treasure trove, treasury, trench, vein, wealth,
well, wellspring; CONCEPTS 449,509,712

mine [*v*] *dig up* burrow, delve, dig for, drill,
excavate, extract, hew, pan, quarry, sap,
scoop, shovel, unearth, work; CONCEPT 178
—*Ant.* bury

mingle [*v1*] *physically join* admix, alloy, blend,
coalesce, commingle, compound, intermingle,
intermix, interweave, make up, marry, meld,
merge, mix, unite, wed; CONCEPT 193 —*Ant.*
disjoin

mingle [*v2*] *socialize* associate, circulate, consort, fraternize, gang up*, hang out*, hobnob,
mix, network, pool, rub shoulders*, tie in, work
the room*; CONCEPT 384 —*Ant.* be unsociable

miniature [*adj*] *tiny* baby, diminutive, itsy-
bitsy*, itty-bitty*, Lilliputian*, little, midget,
mini, minikin, minuscule, minute, mite, model,
petite, pint-sized*, pocket, reduced, scaled-
down, small, small-scale, teensy*, teeny*, toy,
wee; CONCEPTS 773,789 —*Ant.* big, giant,
huge, large

miniature [*n*] *tiny thing* baby, insignificancy,
midget, model, pocket edition, toy; CONCEPT
730 —*Ant.* giant

minimal [*adj*] *littlest, slightest* basal, basic,
essential, fundamental, least, least possible,
lowest, minimum, nominal, smallest, token;
CONCEPTS 762,773,789 —*Ant.* maximum, most

minimize [*v*] *make smaller; underrate* abbreviate, attenuate, belittle, cheapen, curtail, cut
down to size, cut rate, decrease, decry, deprecate, depreciate, derogate, detract, diminish,
discount, disparage, downplay*, dwarf*,
knock*, knock down*, lessen, make light of*,
make little of, miniaturize, pan, play down,
pooh-pooh*, poor-mouth*, prune, put down,

reduce, run down, shrink, underestimate,
underplay; CONCEPTS 54,240,247 —*Ant.*
enlarge, maximize, overestimate, overrate

minimum [*adj*] *least, lowest* least possible,
littlest, merest, minimal, slightest, smallest,
tiniest; CONCEPTS 762,789 —*Ant.* largest,
maximum, most

minimum [*n*] *lowest amount* atom, bottom, dab,
depth, dot, gleam, grain, hair, iota, jot, least,
lowest, margin, modicum, molecule, nadir,
narrowest, particle, pittance, point, scintilla,
scruple, shadow, slightest, smallest, smidgen,
soupçon, spark, speck, trifle, whit; CONCEPTS
787,831 —*Ant.* largest, maximum, most

minion [*n*] *sycophant* backscratcher*,
backslapper*, bootlicker*, brownnoser*,
dependent, doormat, fan, fawner, flatterer,
flunky*, follower, groupie, hanger-on*,
lackey, parasite, puppet, slave, stooge*,
subordinate, toady, yes-man/woman, yes-
person; CONCEPTS 352, 366,423

miniscule/minuscule [*adj*] *tiny, very small*
diminutive, dwarf, infinitesimal, itsy-bitsy,
Lilliputian, little, meager, microscopic, mini*,
miniature, minute, pint-sized*, puny*, short,
slight, small-scale, stunted, teensy*, teeny,
trivial, undersized, wee*; CONCEPTS 773,789

minister [*n1*] *person in charge of church* abbot,
archbishop, archdeacon, bishop, chaplain,
clergy, clergyperson, cleric, clerical, clerk, confessor, curate, deacon, dean, diocesan, divine,
ecclesiastic, lecturer, missionary, monk, parson,
pastor, preacher, prelate, priest, pulpiteer, rector, reverend, shepherd, vicar; CONCEPT 361

minister [*n2*] *person high in government* administrator, agent, aide, ambassador, assistant,
cabinet member, consul, delegate, diplomat,
envoy, executive, legate, liaison, lieutenant,
officeholder, official, plenipotentiary, premier,
prime minister, secretary; CONCEPT 354

minister [*v*] *help, serve* accommodate, administer, aid, answer, attend, be solicitous of, cater
to, cure, doctor, do for, foster, heal, nurse,
pander, pander to, remedy, succor, take care of,
tend, treat, wait on, watch over; CONCEPT 110
—*Ant.* hurt, injure

minor [*adj*] *insignificant, small* accessory,
below the mark, bush-league*, casual, dependent, dinky*, inconsequential, inconsiderable,
inferior, junior, lesser, light, low, minus,
negligible, paltry, petty, piddling, secondary,
second-string*, slight, smaller, small-fry*,
small-time, subordinate, subsidiary, tacky,
trifling, trivial, two-bit*, unimportant, younger*;
CONCEPTS 575,773,789 —*Ant.* adult, greater,
large, major, significant

minor [*n*] *person under legal age of maturity*
adolescent, baby, boy, child, girl, infant, junior,
juvenile, lad, little one, schoolboy, schoolgirl,
teenager, underage, youngster, youth; CONCEPT
424 —*Ant.* adult

mint [*adj*] *brand-new* excellent, first-class, fresh,
intact, original, perfect, spanking-new*, spick-
and-span*, unblemished, undamaged, unmarred,
untarnished, virgin; CONCEPTS 574,578,797
—*Ant.* ancient, damaged, imperfect, old, used

mi
mi

mint [n] *a lot of money* boodle, bundle, fortune, heap, million, packet, pile, pot, roll, wad; CONCEPTS 340,787

mint [v] *create, coin* cast, construct, devise, fabricate, fashion, forge, invent, issue, make, make up, mold, monetize, produce, provide, punch, stamp, strike, think up; CONCEPTS 43,173,205,251

minute [adj1] *very small* atomic, diminutive, exact, exiguous, fine, inconsiderable, infinitesimal, insignificant, invisible, little, microbic, microscopic, miniature, minim, minimal, minuscule, molecular, peewee*, piddling, precise, puny, slender, teeny-weeny*, tiny, wee; CONCEPTS 773,789 —Ant. big, giant, gigantic, huge, large, mighty

minute [adj2] *unimportant* immaterial, inconsiderable, insignificant, light, little, minor, negligible, nonessential, paltry, petty, picayune, piddling, puny, slight, small, trifling, trivial; CONCEPT 575 —Ant. consequential, considerable, important, substantial

minute [adj3] *exact, precise* blow-by-blow*, careful, circumstantial, clocklike, close, critical, detailed, elaborate, exhaustive, full, itemized, meticulous, painstaking, particular, particularized, punctilious, scrupulous, specialized, thorough; CONCEPT 557 —Ant. imprecise, inexact, rough

minute [n] *brief time period* bat of an eye*, breath, breathing, crack, flash, instant, jiffy*, min*, mo*, moment, nothing flat*, sec*, second, shake, short time*, sixtieth of hour, sixty seconds, split second, twinkling*; CONCEPTS 803,807,821

minutiae [n] *trivial detail* incidental, minor detail, small detail, trifle, trivia, triviality, trivial matter, unimportant detail, useless information; CONCEPTS 274,543

miracle [n] *wonderful, surprising event or thing* marvel, phenomenon, portent, prodigy, rarity, revelation, sensation, stunner, supernatural occurrence, surprise, thaumaturgy, unusualness, wonder; CONCEPTS 671,689,693 —Ant. normalcy, usualness

miraculous [adj] *surprisingly wonderful* amazing, anomalous, astonishing, astounding, awesome, extraordinary, fabulous, freakish, heavy, incredible, inexplicable, magical, marvelous, monstrous, numinous, phenomenal, preternatural, prodigious, spectacular, staggering, strange, stupefying, stupendous, superhuman, superior, supermundane, supernatural, supranatural, thaumaturgic, the utmost, unaccountable, unbelievable, unearthly, unimaginable, unreal, wonderworking, wondrous; CONCEPTS 529,548, 572 —Ant. normal, usual

mirage [n] *imaginary vision* delusion, fantasy, hallucination, ignis fatuus, illusion, optical illusion, phantasm; CONCEPTS 529,628

mire [n] *muck, morass* bog, dirt, fen, glop*, goo*, gunk*, marsh, moss, mud, ooze*, quagmire, quicksand, slime*, swamp; CONCEPTS 509,674 ·

mire [v] *delay, catch up in* bog down, cling, decelerate, detain, dirty, embroil, enmesh, ensnare, entangle, entrap, flounder, hang up, implicate, involve, retard, set back, sink, slow down, slow up, snare, soil, stick, tangle, trap; CONCEPTS 112,121

mirror [n] *glass that reflects image* cheval glass, gaper, hand glass, imager, looking glass, pier glass, polished metal, reflector, seeing glass, speculum; CONCEPTS 443,470

mirror [v] *copy, reflect* act like, depict, double, echo, embody, emulate, epitomize, exemplify, follow, glass, illustrate, image, imitate, make like*, mimic, personify, represent, show, simulate, symbolize, take off*, typify; CONCEPTS 111,118,171

mirth [n] *great joy* amusement, cheer, cheerfulness, convulsions, entertainment, festivity, frivolity, frolic, fun, gaiety, gladness, glee, happiness, hilarity, hysteria, hysterics, jocularity, jocundity, jollity, joviality, joyousness, kicks*, laughs, laughter, levity, lightheartedness, merriment, merrymaking, pleasure, rejoicing, revelry, sport, whoopee*; CONCEPTS 388,410 —Ant. blues, depression, distress, sadness, unhappiness

mirthful [adj] *merry* amusing, blithe, blithesome, carefree, cheerful, cheery, convivial, enjoyable, entertaining, festive, frolicsome, fun-loving, funny, gay, glad, gleeful, happy, jocund, jolly, joyful, joyous, larking, lighthearted, lively, perky, playful, sunny, vivacious; CONCEPTS 403,548,572

misadventure [n] *bad luck, mishap* accident, adversity, bad break*, blunder, calamity, casualty, cataclysm, catastrophe, debacle, disaster, error, failure, faux pas, ill fortune, lapse, mischance, misfortune, reverse, setback, slip, tragedy, woe; CONCEPT 674 —Ant. blessing, good fortune, good luck, success, triumph

misanthrope [n] *person who hates others* cynic, doubter, egoist, egotist, hater, isolate, loner, misanthropist, recluse, skeptic; CONCEPT 412 —Ant. humanitarian, philanthropist

misanthropic [adj] *unsociable, cynical* antisocial, egoistic, egotistical, eremitic, hating, inhumane, malevolent, misanthropical, reclusive, reserved, sarcastic, selfish, solitary, standoffish, unfriendly; CONCEPT 404 —Ant. humanitarian, philanthropic, sociable

misapprehend [v] *get the wrong idea, impression* blunder, confuse, err, misconceive, misconstrue, misinterpret, misread, miss, mistake, misunderstand; CONCEPT 15 —Ant. apprehend, comprehend, understand

misappropriate [v] *use wrongly; steal* abuse, appropriate, defalcate, embezzle, misapply, misspend, misuse, peculate, plunder, pocket, rob, swindle; CONCEPTS 139,156,341 —Ant. appropriate, use wisely

misbegotten [adj] *illegitimate, illicit* baseborn, bastard, dishonest, disreputable, illegal, natural, poor, shady, spurious, stolen, suppositious, unlawful, unrespectable; CONCEPTS 319,549 —Ant. lawful, legal, legitimate, licit

misbehave [v] *act in inappropriate manner* act up, be at fault, be bad, be dissolute, be guilty, be immoral, be indecorous, be insubordinate, be mischievous, bend the law*, be out of line*, be out of order*, be reprehensible, carry on, cut up, deviate, do evil, do wrong, fail, fool around*, get into mischief, go astray, go wrong, make trouble, misconduct, offend, roughhouse*, sin, sow wild oats*, take a wrong turn*, transgress, trespass; CONCEPTS 633,645 —Ant. behave, obey

misbehavior [n] *naughty act, conduct* acting up*, fault, immorality, impropriety, incivility, indiscipline, insubordination, mischief, misconduct, misdeed, misdemeanor, misdoing, monkey business*, naughtiness, rudeness, shenanigans*, transgression, wrongdoing; CONCEPTS 633,645 —Ant. behavior, good conduct, manners, obedience

miscalculate [v] *make a mistake* blow*, blunder, discount, disregard, drop the ball*, err, get signals crossed*, get wrong, go wrong, mess up*, misconstrue, miscount, misinterpret, misjudge, misread, misreckon, miss by a mile*, misunderstand, mix up, overestimate, overlook, overrate, overvalue, slip up, stumble, underestimate, underrate, undervalue; CONCEPT 101 —Ant. do correctly, figure correctly, succeed

miscarriage [n] *failure* abortion, botch, breakdown, defeat, error, interruption, malfunction, misadventure, mischance, misfire, mishap, miss, mistake, nonsuccess, perversion, undoing; CONCEPTS 230,699 —Ant. carriage, success

miscellaneous [adj] *diversified, various* assorted, confused, conglomerate, different, disordered, disparate, divergent, divers, diverse, heterogeneous, indiscriminate, jumbled, many, mingled, mixed, motley, muddled, multifarious, multiform, odd, promiscuous, scattered, scrambled, sundry, unmatched, unsorted, varied, variegated; CONCEPT 564 —Ant. alone, lone, simple, single, singular

miscellany [n] *varied collection* accumulation, aggregation, anthology, assortment, brew, collectanea, combination, combo, compilation, conglomeration, cumulation, diversity, farrago, gallimaufry, garbage*, hash, hodgepodge, jumble, medley, mélange, melee, mess, mishmash, mix, mixed bag, mixture, muddle, odds and ends*, olio, pasticcio, pastiche, patchwork, potpourri, salad, salmagundi, smorgasbord, stew, variety; CONCEPTS 432,665 —Ant. single

mischief [n] *trouble, damage* atrocity, catastrophe, devilment, devilry, dirty trick*, evil, fault, friskiness, frolicsomeness, funny business*, gag, harm, high jinks*, hurt, ill, impishness, injury, misbehavior, mischievousness, misconduct, misdoing, misfortune, monkey business*, naughtiness, outrage, playfulness, prank, rascality, roguery, roguishness, sabotage, shenanigans, sportiveness, transgression, vandalism, waggery, waggishness, waywardness, wrong, wrongdoing; CONCEPTS 192,633,645 —Ant. behavior, obedience

mischievous [adj] *devilish, wicked* arch, artful, bad, bothersome, damaging, dangerous, deleterious, destructive, detrimental, dickens*, evil, exasperating, foxy*, frolicsome, harmful, hazardous, holy terror*, hurtful, ill, ill-behaved, impish, injurious, insidious, irksome, malicious, malignant, misbehaving, naughty, nocuous, perilous, pernicious, playful, precarious, puckish, rascal, rascally, risky, rude, sinful, sly, spiteful, sportive, teasing, tricky, troublesome, vexatious, vexing, vicious, wayward; CONCEPTS 401,545 —Ant. behaved, good, nice, obedient

misconception [n] *wrong idea, impression* delusion, error, fallacy, fault, misapprehension, misconstruction, misinterpretation, mistake, mistaken belief, misunderstanding; CONCEPTS 409,689 —Ant. comprehension, perception, understanding

misconduct [n] *bad or unethical behavior* delinquency, dereliction, evil, immorality, impropriety, malfeasance, malpractice, malversation, misbehavior, mischief, misdemeanor, misdoing, mismanagement, naughtiness, offense, rudeness, transgression, wrongdoing; CONCEPTS 192,633, 645 —Ant. behavior, manners, obedience

misconstrue [v] *get a wrong or false impression* distort, exaggerate, misapprehend, misconceive, misinterpret, misjudge, misread, mistake, mistranslate, misunderstand, pervert, take the wrong way; CONCEPT 15 —Ant. discern, get, perceive, understand

miscreant [adj] *evil, immoral* corrupt, criminal, degenerate, depraved, flagitious, infamous, iniquitous, nefarious, perverse, rascally, reprehensible, reprobate, unhealthy, unprincipled, vicious, villainous, wicked; CONCEPTS 401,545 —Ant. good, moral, nice

miscreant [n] *person who is very bad, immoral* blackguard, black sheep*, bootlegger, bully, cad, caitiff, convict, criminal, culprit, delinquent, drunkard, evildoer, felon, fink*, heel*, hoodlum, jailbird, loafer, louse*, lowlife*, malefactor, outcast, outlaw, pickpocket, racketeer, rapscallion, rascal, rat*, reprobate, rowdy, ruffian, scalawag, scamp, scoundrel, scum*, sinner, sneak, vagabond, villain, wretch, wrongdoer; CONCEPT 412 —Ant. goody-goody

misdeed/misdemeanor [n] *sin, crime* breach of law, criminality, dirt*, dirty deed*, dirty pool*, fault, infringement, malefaction, misbehavior, misconduct, miscue, offense, peccadillo, slipup, transgression, trespass, villainy, violation, wrong, wrongdoing; CONCEPTS 192,633,645 —Ant. goodness

miser [n] *person who hoards money, possessions* cheapskate*, churl, harpy*, hoarder, moneygrubber*, penny-pincher*, pinchfist*, pinchpenny*, Scrooge*, stiff*, tightwad*; CONCEPTS 348,412,423 —Ant. spender, spendthrift, waster, wastrel

miserable [adj] *unhappy, depressed* afflicted, agonized, ailing, anguished, brokenhearted, crestfallen, dejected, desolate, despairing, despondent, destroyed, disconsolate, discontented, distressed, doleful, dolorous, down, downcast, down in the mouth*, forlorn, gloomy, heartbroken, hopeless, hurt, hurting, ill, injured, in pain, melancholy, mournful, on a downer*, pained, pathetic, pitiable, racked, rueful, ruthful, sad, sick, sickly, sorrowful, strained, suffering, tormented, tortured, tragic, troubled, woebegone, wounded, wretched; CONCEPT 403 —Ant. cheerful, elated, happy, joyful, merry

miserable [adj2] *destitute, shabby* abject, bad, contemptible, deplorable, despicable, detestable, disgraceful, godforsaken, impoverished, indigent, inferior, lamentable, low, meager, mean, needy, paltry, pathetic, penniless, piteous, pitiable, poor, poverty-stricken, sad, scanty, scurvy, shameful, sordid, sorry, squalid, tragic, vile, worthless, wretched; CONCEPTS 485,570 —Ant. generous, rich, wealthy

miserly [adj] *greedy, stingy* abject, avaricious, beggarly, cheapskate*, churlish, close, closefisted, covetous, grasping, ignoble, illiberal, mean, parsimonious, penny-pinching*, penurious, skinflint*, sordid, tightfisted*, ungenerous; CONCEPTS 326,334,401,404 —Ant. generous, giving, liberal

misery [n1] *pain, mental or physical* ache, agony, anguish, anvil chorus, bad news*, blues*, depression, desolation, despair, despondency, discomfort, distress, dolor, gloom, grief, hardship, headache, heartache, hurting, melancholy, pang, passion, sadness, sorrow, squalor, stitch, suffering, throe, torment, torture, twinge, unhappiness, woe, worriment, worry, wretchedness; CONCEPT 728 —Ant. cheer, delight, fun, gladness, happiness, joy, pleasure

misery [n2] *trouble, disaster* adversity, affliction, anxiety, bitter pill*, burden, calamity, catastrophe, curse, destitution, difficulty, grief, indigence, load, misfortune, need, ordeal, penury, poverty, privation, problem, sordidness, sorrow, squalor, trial, tribulation, want, woe; CONCEPTS 335,666,674 —Ant. advantage, benefit, blessing, boon, good fortune, good luck

misfire [v] *fail* abort, backfire, blunder, break down, come to nothing, explode, fall flat*, fall short*, fizzle, fizzle out, fizz out, flop, flounder, go up in smoke*, go wrong, miscarry, miss, peter out, poop out, slip; CONCEPT 699

misfit [n] *nonconformist* beatnik*, bohemian*, different breed*, dissenter, dissident, dropout, eccentric, fish out of water*, freak*, individualist, lone wolf, loser, oddball, odd man out, offbeat, outsider, weirdo*; CONCEPTS 359,423

misfortune/mishap [n] *bad luck; disaster* accident, adversity, affliction, annoyance, anxiety, bad break*, bad news*, blow*, burden, calamity, casuality, cataclysm, catastrophe, contretemps, cross, crunch, debacle, disadvantage, disappointment, discomfort, dole, failure, hard luck*, hardship, harm, inconvenience, infelicity, loss, misadventure, mischance, misery, nuisance, reverse, rotten luck, setback, stroke of bad luck*, tough luck*, tragedy, trial, tribulation, trouble, unpleasantness, visitation, worry; CONCEPTS 674,679 —Ant. advantage, benefit, blessing, fortune, good luck

misgiving [n] *uncertainty* anxiety, apprehension, apprehensiveness, distrust, doubt, fear, foreboding, hesitation, mistrust, premonition, prenotion, presage, presentiment, qualm, reservation,

scruple, suspicion, unbelief, unease, worry; CONCEPTS 21,689,690 —Ant. certainty, confidence, doubtlessness, sureness, trust

misguided [adj] *ill-advised, deluded* bearded, bum-steer*, confused, deceived, disinformed, erroneous, faked-out*, foolish, imprudent, indiscreet, inexpedient, injudicious, led up the garden path*, misled, misplaced, mistaken, stonewalled*, uncalled for, unreasonable, unwarranted, unwise, wrong; CONCEPTS 544, 548,570 —Ant. well-guided

mishandle/mismanage [v] *mess up* abuse, be incompetent, be inefficient, blow, blunder, botch*, bungle, confound, err, flub*, foul up, fumble, goof*, goof up*, gum up*, harm, make a hash of*, make a mess of*, maladminister, misapply, misconduct, misdirect, misemploy, misgovern, mistreat, misuse, muff*, overlook, pervert, prostitute, put foot in*, screw up*, shoot oneself in foot*; CONCEPTS 101,156,384 —Ant. handle, manage

mishap [n] *accident* blow, blunder, calamity, collision, crack-up*, disaster, fender-bender*, fluke*, hazard, ill-fortune, misadventure, misfortune, mistake, pileup*, rear-ender*, setback, smash*, smashup*, stack-up*, total*, wrack-up*; CONCEPT 674

mishmash [n] *hodgepodge* collection, combination, goulash*, hash, jumble, medley, mélange, mess, miscellany, mixed bag, mixture, olio, patchwork, potpourri, salmagundi*; CONCEPTS 260,432

misinform [v] *give wrong information intentionally* bait and switch*, cover up, deceive, disinform, doublespeak*, double-talk*, lead astray, lie, misdirect, misguide, mislead, misstate, mousetrap*, pervert, prevaricate, put on*, put on an act*, put on false front*, put up smoke screen*, signify, string along, wrong steer*; CONCEPT 63 —Ant. inform, tell all

misjudge [v] *get the wrong idea* bark up wrong tree*, be misled, be overcritical, be partial, be unfair, be wrong, come to hasty conclusion, dogmatize, drop the ball*, err, misapprehend, miscalculate, miscomprehend, misconceive, misconjecture, misconstrue, misdeem, misreckon, miss by a mile*, mistake, misthink, misunderstand, overestimate, overrate, prejudge, presume, presuppose, put foot in*, stumble, suppose, underestimate, underrate; CONCEPTS 12,18,101 —Ant. figure, judge well, understand

mislead [v] *give someone the wrong idea, information* bait, beguile, betray, bilk, bluff, bunk, cheat, cozen, deceive, defraud, delude, double-cross*, dupe, enmesh, ensnare, entangle, entice, fool, fudge*, gull, hoax, hoodwink*, hose*, illude, inveigle, juggle, lead astray, lead on*, lie, lure, misdirect, misguide, misinform, misrepresent, outwit, overreach, pervert, pull wool over eyes*, put on*, rip off*, rook, rope in*, scam, seduce, shaft, snow*, take in, tempt, trick, victimize; CONCEPTS 59,63 —Ant. advise, counsel, guard, lead, protect

misleading [adj] *deceptive, confusing* ambiguous, beguiling, bewildering, casuistical, catchy, confounding, deceitful, deceiving, deluding, delusive, delusory, demagogic, disingenuous, distracting, evasive, fallacious, false, inaccurate, perplexing, puzzling, sophistical, specious, spurious, tricky, wrong; CONCEPTS 267,548 —*Ant.* honest, truthful

mismatch [*n*] *disparity* discrepancy, disproportion, dissemblance, dissimilarity, divergence, divergency, diverseness, imbalance, imparity, incongruity, inequality, unevenness; CONCEPT 665

misogynist [*n*] *woman-hater* anti-feminist, male chauvinist, misanthrope, sexist; CONCEPT 689

misplace [*v*] *lose; be unable to find* be unable to lay hands on*, confuse, disarrange, dishevel, disorder, disorganize, displace, disturb, forget whereabouts of, lose track of, misfile, mislay, miss, mix, muss, place unwisely, place wrongly, put in wrong place, remove, scatter, unsettle; CONCEPTS 116,201 —*Ant.* find

misrepresentation [*n*] *falsehood* adulteration, coloring, distortion, exaggeration, fabrication, false light, falsification, lie, misstatement, mutilation, not a true picture*, slant, story*, stretch, tall story*, twist, untruth; CONCEPTS 63,580

misrepresent/misquote [*v*] *lie, distort* adulterate, angle, beard*, belie, build up, cloak, color, con, confuse, cover up, disguise, distort, dress, embellish, embroider, equivocate, exaggerate, falsify, garble, give snow job*, mangle, mask, miscolor, misinterpret, misreport, misstate, overdraw, overstate, palter, pervert, phony up*, pirate*, prevaricate, promote, puff*, skew, slant, snow*, spread it on*, stretch, take out of context*, throw a curve*, trump up*, twist, warp; CONCEPT 63 —*Ant.* be forthright, be honest, explain

miss [*n*] *failure* absence, blunder, default, defect, error, fault, loss, mishap, mistake, omission, oversight, slip, want; CONCEPTS 101, 699 —*Ant.* success, triumph, win

miss [*v1*] *fail, make a mistake* be late for, blow, blunder, botch, disregard, drop, drop the ball*, err, fall flat on face*, fall short, flub*, forget, fumble, ignore, juggle, let go, let slip, lose, miscarry, misfire, mislay, misplace, muff*, neglect, omit, overlook, overshoot, pass over, pass up, skip, slight, slip, trip, trip up, undershoot; CONCEPTS 101,699 —*Ant.* do well, get, succeed

miss [*v2*] *want; feel a loss* crave, desire, long, need, pine, wish, yearn; CONCEPT 20 —*Ant.* don't want

misshapen [*adj*] *deformed* askew, awry, bent, blemished, bowed, buckled, contorted, crooked, curved, damaged, disfigured, disjointed, distorted, grotesque, ill-made, irregular, malformed, mangled, marred, out of shape, twisted, ugly, unshapely, warped; CONCEPTS 485,486

missile [*n*] *projectile weapon* ammunition, arrow, bat, bird*, bolt, bomb, bullet, cartridge, dart, MX*, pellet, projectile, rocket, shot, stealth, trajectile; CONCEPT 500

missing [*adj*] *gone, absent* astray, away, AWOL*, disappeared, lacking, left behind, left out, lost, mislaid, misplaced, not present,

nowhere to be found*, omitted, removed, short, unaccounted for, wanting; CONCEPTS 539,576 —*Ant.* found, here, present

mission [*n*] *person's task, responsibility* aim, assignment, business, calling, charge, commission, duty, end, errand, goal, job, lifework, object, objective, office, operation, profession, purpose, pursuit, quest, sortie, trade, trust, undertaking, vocation, work; CONCEPTS 360, 362,659

missionary [*n*] *person who aids, does religious work* apostle, clergy, clergyperson, converter, evangelist, herald, messenger, minister, missioner, pastor, preacher, promoter, propagandist, proselytizer, revivalist, teacher; CONCEPTS 361,416

missive [*n*] *written communication* dispatch, epistle, letter, line, memo, memorandum, message, note, report, word; CONCEPTS 271,278

misspent [*adj*] *wasted* blown*, dissipated, down the drain*, idle, imprudent, misapplied, prodigal, profitless, squandered, thrown away; CONCEPTS 544,560,570 —*Ant.* profitable, unwasted, used well

misstatement [*n*] *misrepresentation* adulteration, coloring, distortion, exaggeration, fabrication, falsehood, false light, falsification, inaccuracy, lie, misstatement, mutilation, not a true picture*, slant, story*, stretch, tall story*, twist, untruth; CONCEPTS 63,580

misstep [*n*] *mistake, wrong move* bad move*, blunder, bungle, error, failure, false step, faux pas, fluff*, gaffe, indiscretion, lapse, miscue, miss, slip, slipup*, stumble, trip; CONCEPTS 101,674,699 —*Ant.* success

mist [*n*] *film, vapor* brume, cloud, condensation, dew, drizzle, fog, ground clouds, haze, moisture, rain, smog, soup*, spray, steam, visibility zero*; CONCEPT 524

mist [*v*] *cloud, steam up* becloud, befog, blur, dim, drizzle, film, fog, haze, mizzle, murk, obscure, overcast, overcloud, rain, shower, sprinkle, steam; CONCEPT 526 —*Ant.* burn off, uncloud

mistake [*n*] *error, misunderstanding* aberration, blooper*, blunder, boo-boo*, bungle, confusion, delusion, erratum, false move, false step, fault, faux pas, flub*, fluff*, gaffe, illusion, inaccuracy, inadvertence, lapse, misapplication, misapprehension, miscalculation, misconception, misinterpretation, misjudgment, misprint, misstatement, misstep, muddle, neglect, omission, overestimation, oversight, slight, slip, slip of tongue*, slipup*, snafu*, solecism, trip*, typographical error, underestimation; CONCEPTS 101,230,410 —*Ant.* accuracy, calculation, certainty, correction, correctness, proof, success, truth, understanding

mistake [*v*] *mix up, misunderstand* addle, be off the mark*, be wrong, blunder, botch*, bungle, confound, confuse, deceive oneself, err, fail, get wrong, goof*, have wrong impression, jumble, lapse, make a mess*, misapprehend, miscalculate, misconceive, misconstrue, miscount, misdeem, misinterpret, misjudge, misknow, misread, miss, miss the boat*, not know, omit, overestimate, overlook, put foot in*, slip*, slip up*, snarl, take for*, tangle, underestimate; CONCEPTS 15,101 —*Ant.* be certain, be sure, comprehend, interpret, perceive, understand

mistaken [*adj*] *wrong, incorrect* all wet*, at fault, barking up wrong tree*, confounded, confused, confused with, deceived, deluded, duped, erroneous, fallacious, false, faulty, fooled, ill-advised, illogical, inaccurate, inappropriate, misconstrued, misguided, misinformed, misinterpreting, misjudging, misled, misunderstanding, off base*, off track*, tricked, unadvised, under wrong impression, unfounded, unreal, unsound, untrue, warranted, way off*, wide of mark*, wrongly identified, wrong number*; CONCEPTS 402,529 —*Ant.* correct, exact, fair, just, precise, right, sound, true

mistreat [*v*] *treat badly or wrongly* abuse, backbite, bash, brutalize, bung up*, chop, do wrong, dump on*, give black eye*, handle roughly, harm, injure, kick around, knock around, maltreat, maul, mess up, misuse, molest, outrage, push around, rip, roughhouse*, rough up, shake up, total*, trash*, wax*, wound, wrong; CONCEPTS 14,156,246 —*Ant.* coddle, favor, pamper, pet, please, satisfy, treat well

mistrust [*n*] *doubtfulness* apprehension, chariness, concern, distrust, doubt, dubiety, dubiosity, fear, foreboding, incertitude, misgiving, presentiment, scruple, skepticism, suspicion, uncertainty, wariness, wonder; CONCEPTS 21,27,690 —*Ant.* belief, certainty, confidence, faith, trust

mistrust [*v*] *doubt* apprehend, beware, be wary, challenge, disbelieve, dispute, distrust, fear, have doubts, question, scruple, suspect, suspicion; CONCEPT 21 —*Ant.* be certain, believe, have faith, trust

misty [*adj*] *filmy, obscure* bleary, blurred, closed in, clouded, cloudy, dark, dewy, dim, enveloped, foggy, fuzzy, hazy, indistinct, murky, mushy, nebulous, opaque, overcast, shrouded, socked in, soupy*, unclear, vague, vaporous; CONCEPTS 525,603,617

misunderstand [*v*] *get the wrong idea* be at cross purposes*, be bewildered, be confused, be perplexed, confound, confuse, fail, get signals crossed*, get signals mixed*, get wrong, get wrong impression*, misapply, misapprehend, miscalculate, miscomprehend, misconceive, misconstrue, misinterpret, misjudge, misknow, misread, misreckon, miss*, miss the point*, mistake, not register*, take amiss, take wrongly; CONCEPT 15 —*Ant.* comprehend, construe, get, grasp, interpret, perceive, understand

misunderstanding [*n1*] *instance of having the wrong idea* confounding, confusion, delusion, error, false impression, misapprehension, misconception, misconstruction, misinterpretation, misjudgment, misreckoning, mistake, mix-up; CONCEPT 409 —*Ant.* comprehension, understanding

misunderstanding [*n2*] *argument, fight* bad vibes*, blowup*, breach, break, clash, conflict, crossed wires*, debate, difference, difficulty, disagreement, discord, dissension, falling-out*,

feud, fuss, quarrel, rift, row, run-in*, rupture, set-to, sour note*, spat, squabble, tiff*, variance, words*; CONCEPTS 46,106 —*Ant.* agreement, concord, concurrence, harmony, peace

misuse [*n*] *abuse; wrong application* abusage, barbarism, catachresis, corruption, cruel treatment, desecration, dissipation, exploitation, harm, ill-treatment, injury, malapropism, maltreatment, misapplication, misemployment, mistreatment, misusage, perversion, profanation, prostitution, rough handling, solecism, squandering, waste; CONCEPT 156

misuse [*v*] *abuse; apply wrongly* blow*, brutalize, corrupt, cut up, desecrate, dissipate, exploit, go through, handle roughly, ill-treat, maltreat, maul, mess up*, misapply, misemploy, mistreat, molest, outrage, pervert, profane, prostitute, run through*, shake up, squander, waste, wrong; CONCEPT 156 —*Ant.* use correctly

mitigate [*v*] *check, diminish, lighten* abate, allay, alleviate, appease, assuage, blunt, calm, come together, cool*, dull, ease, extenuate, lessen, meet halfway*, moderate, modify, mollify, pacify, palliate, placate, quiet, reduce, relieve, remit, soften, soothe, subdue, take the edge off*, temper, tone down, tranquilize, weaken; CONCEPTS 233,240 —*Ant.* aggravate, incite, increase, intensify, irritate, worsen

mix [*v1*] *combine, join* admix, adulterate, alloy, amalgamate, associate, blend, braid, coalesce, commingle, commix, compound, conjoin, cross, embody, fuse, hybridize, incorporate, infiltrate, infuse, instill, interbreed, intermingle, interweave, jumble, knead, link, lump, make up, merge, mingle, mix up, put together, saturate, stir, suffuse, synthesize, tangle, transfuse, unite, weave, work in; CONCEPTS 113,193 —*Ant.* detach, disconnect, divide, remove, separate, sever, unmix

mix [*v2*] *socialize* associate, come together, consort, get along, hang out, hobnob, join, mingle; CONCEPT 114 —*Ant.* disengage, dissociate, segregate, separate

mixed [*adj*] *assorted, combined* alloyed, amalgamated, assimilated, assorted, blended, brewed, composite, compound, conglomerate, crossbred, crossed, different, disordered, diverse, diversified, embodied, fused, heterogeneous, hybrid, hybridized, incorporated, infused, interbred, interdenominational, joint, kneaded, married, merged, mingled, miscellaneous, mongrel, motley, multifarious, tied, transfused, united, varied, woven; CONCEPTS 485,564, 772 —*Ant.* lone, single, singular, unmixed, uncombined

mixed bag [*n*] *assortment* all shapes and sizes, array, choice, collection, combination, combo*, diversity, hodgepodge, jumble, medley, melange, miscellany, mishmash, mixture, potpourri; CONCEPTS 432,665

mixed-up [*adj*] *confused* baffled, befuddled, bewildered, come apart*, confounded, dazed, discombobulated*, disconcerted, disorganized, disoriented, flummoxed, flustered, lost, muddled, out to lunch*, perplexed, puzzled, stumped, thrown off balance*; CONCEPT 403

mix/mixture [n] *assortment, combination* admixture, adulteration, alloy, amalgam, amalgamation, assimilation, association, batter, blend, brew, combine, combo, commixture, composite, compound, concoction, confection, conglomeration, cross, crossing, dough, fusion, goulash, grab bag*, hodgepodge, hybrid, hybridization, incorporation, infiltration, interfusion, jumble, mash, medley, mélange, merger, mingling, miscellany, mishmash, mixed bag, mosaic, package, patchwork, potpourri, salmagundi, saturation, soup*, stew*, transfusion, union, variety; CONCEPTS 260,432 —Ant. disconnection, division, separation

mix-up [n] *confusion, misunderstanding* botch*, chaos, commotion, disorder, jumble, mess, mistake, muddle, shambles*, tangle, turmoil; CONCEPTS 230,674 —Ant. understanding

mix up [v] *confuse* addle, befuddle, bewilder, confound, derange, disorder, disorganize, disrupt, distract, disturb, dizzy, fluster, foul up*, jumble, mess up*, mistake, muddle, perplex, puzzle, snafu*, upset; CONCEPTS 16,158 —Ant. clear up, explain, explicate

moan [n] *groan, complaint* beef, cry, gripe, grouse, grumble, lament, lamentation, plaint, sigh, sob, wail, whine; CONCEPTS 52,77

moan [v] *groan, complain* bemoan, bewail, carp, deplore, grieve, gripe, grouse, grumble, keen, lament, mourn, sigh, sob, wail, whine; CONCEPTS 52,77

moat [n] *ditch* canal, channel, fosse, gully, trench; CONCEPTS 509,513

mob [n] *large group of people* assemblage, body, cabal, camp, canaille, cattle, circle, clan, class, clique, collection, commonality, company, coterie, crew, crowd, crush, drove, flock, gang, gathering, herd, horde, host, jam, lot, mass, masses, multitude, pack, populace, posse, press, proletariat, rabble, riffraff*, ring, riot, scum, set, swarm, throng, troop; CONCEPT 378

mob [v] *come upon by pushing; surround* attack, cram, crowd, fill, hustle, jam, jostle, overrun, pack, riot, set upon, swarm, throng; CONCEPTS 208,758 —Ant. avoid, ignore, leave alone, shun

mobile [adj] *movable, travelling* adaptable, ambulatory, changeable, fluid, free, itinerant, liquid, locomotive, loose, migrant, migratory, motile, motorized, moving, mutable, nomadic, peripatetic, portable, roaming, roving, unsettled, unstable, unstationary, unsteadfast, unsteady, versatile, wandering; CONCEPTS 576,584 —Ant. fixed, immobile, stable, stationary, unmovable

mobility [n] *ability to move* adjustability, flexibility, maneuverability, motility, movability, moveableness, portability, transportability; CONCEPT 584

mobilize [v] *ready for action, movement* activate, actuate, animate, assemble, call to arms, call up, catalyze, circulate, drive, gather, get ready, impel, make ready, marshal, muster, organize, prepare, propel, put in motion, rally, ready, set in motion, set off; CONCEPTS 148,187, 221,320 —Ant. check, demobilize, end, halt, hold back, stop

mobster [n] *gangster* criminal, crook, godfather, goon, gunman/ woman, hit man/woman, hood, hoodlum, hooligan*, Mafioso*, member of the family*, outlaw, racketeer, soldier*, thug, wiseguy*; CONCEPT 412

mock [adj] *artificial, fake* apish*, bogus*, counterfeit, dummy, ersatz*, faked, false, feigned, forged, fraudulent, hokey*, imitation, imitative, make-believe, mimic, phony, pretended, pseudo*, put-on*, quasi*, sham*, simulated, so-called*, spurious, substitute, unreal; CONCEPTS 566,582 —Ant. authentic, genuine, real

mock [v1] *ridicule* buffoon, burlesque, caricature, chaff, deride, flout, hoot, insult, jape, jeer, kid, laugh at, make fun of, needle, parody, poke fun at*, rally, rib*, scoff, scorn, show contempt, sneer, taunt, tease, thumb nose at*, travesty; CONCEPTS 7,19,49 —Ant. flatter, praise

mock [v2] *mimic* affect, ape, assume, burlesque, caricature, counterfeit, ditto*, do, fake, feign, hoke, imitate, lampoon, mime, mirror, parody, satirize, send up*, simulate, take off*, travesty; CONCEPT 111 —Ant. exalt

mock [v3] *deceive* beguile, belie, betray, challenge, cheat, defeat, defy, delude, disappoint, double-cross*, dupe, elude, foil, fool, frustrate, juggle, let down*, mislead, sell out*, thwart; CONCEPTS 59,63 —Ant. tell truth

mockery [n1] *joke, parody* burlesque, butt*, caricature, deception, farce, imitation, jest, lampoon, laughingstock, mimicry, mock, pretense, send-up*, sham*, spoof, sport*, take-off*, travesty; CONCEPTS 111,278 —Ant. seriousness, solemnity

mockery [n2] *insult, disrespect* contempt, contumely, derision, disdain, disparagement, gibe, jeer, ridicule, scoffing, scorn, sport; CONCEPTS 49,278 —Ant. flattery, praise, respect

mode [n1] *manner, way* approach, book, channels, condition, course, custom, fashion, form, mechanism, method, modus, nuts and bolts*, plan, posture, practice, procedure, process, quality, rule, situation, state, status, style, system, technique, tone, vein, wise; CONCEPTS 6,644

mode [n2] *trend, fad* chic, convention, craze, cry, dernier cri*, fashion, furor, last word*, latest thing*, latest wrinkle*, look, mainstream, now*, rage*, style, thing*, vogue; CONCEPTS 529,655

model [adj] *typical, ideal* archetypal, classic, classical, commendable, copy, dummy, exemplary, facsimile, flawless, illustrative, imitation, miniature, paradigmatic, perfect, prototypical, quintessential, representative, standard, typical, very; CONCEPTS 566,574 —Ant. atypical, imperfect, unusual

model [n1] *imitation, replica* cartoon, clone, copy, copycat, dead ringer*, ditto*, dummy, duplicate, effigy, engraving, facsimile, figure, figurine, game plan, illustration, image, knock-off, layout, look-alike, miniature, mock-up, painting, paste-up, photograph, picture, pocket, portrait, print, relief, representation, ringer*, setup, sketch, spitting image*, statue, statuette, tracing, visual; CONCEPTS 259,625,628,667

model [n2] *example, standard* apotheosis, archetype, beau ideal, criterion, design, emblem, embodiment, epitome, exemplar, gauge, hero, ideal, lodestar, mirror, mold, nonesuch, nonpareil, original, paradigm, paragon, pattern, prototype, quintessence, role model, saint, symbol, touchstone; type; CONCEPTS 686,688

model [n3] *person, thing that poses* dummy, manikin, mannequin, nude, sitter, subject; CONCEPT 348 —*Ant.* photographer

model [n4] *type, version* configuration, design, form, kind, mark, mode, style, variety; CONCEPTS 378,463,505,654

model [v1] *form, shape* base, carve, cast, create, design, fashion, mold, pattern, plan, sculpt; CONCEPT 184

model [v2] *display, pose* parade, represent, set example, show off, sit, sport, wear; CONCEPT 138 —*Ant.* photograph

moderate [adj1] *calm, temperate* abstinent, balanced, bearable, careful, cautious, compromising, conservative, considerate, considered, controlled, cool, deliberate, disciplined, dispassionate, equable, even, gentle, impartial, inconsiderable, inexpensive, judicious, limited, low-key, measured, middle-of-the-road*, midway, mild, modest, monotonous, neutral, nonpartisan, not excessive, pacific, peaceable, pleasant, reasonable, reserved, restrained, sober, soft, steady, straight, tame, tolerable, tolerant, tranquil, untroubled; CONCEPTS 533,563 —*Ant.* excessive, extreme, immoderate, outrageous, uncontrolled, unlimited, unreasonable, unrestrained, violent, wild

moderate [adj2] *fair, average, so-so* bland, fairish*, fair to middling*, inconsequential, inconsiderable, indifferent, intermediate, mean, mediocre, medium, middling*, ordinary, paltry, passable, piddling*, trifling, trivial, unexceptional; CONCEPTS 547,575 —*Ant.* considerable, extravagant, extreme, immoderate, liberal, significant

moderate [v1] *restrain, control* abate, allay, alleviate, appease, assuage, calm, chasten, check, constrain, cool*, cool out*, curb, decline, decrease, die down, diminish, ease off, fall, lessen, let up, meet halfway, mitigate, modify, modulate, mollify, pacify, play down, qualify, quiet, reduce, regulate, relent, relieve, repress, slacken, slow, soften, soft-pedal, subdue, subside, tame, temper, tone down, wane; CONCEPTS 94,130,240 —*Ant.* egg on, free, incite, let go, liberate, unleash

moderate [v2] *mediate, arbitrate* chair, judge, make peace*, negotiate, preside, referee, take the chair*, umpire; CONCEPTS 18,317 —*Ant.* turn over

moderately [adv] *to a degree, to some extent* a little, averagely, enough, fairly, gently, in moderation, in reason, kind of, more or less*, more than not*, not exactly, passably, pretty, quite, quite a bit, rather, reasonably, slightly, some, something, somewhat, sort of, so-so*, temperately, tolerable, tolerably, tolerantly, within limits*, within reason*; CONCEPTS 544,772 —*Ant.* immoderately, unlimitedly

moderation [n] *temperance* balance, calmness, composure, constraint, coolness, dispassionateness, equanimity, fairness, forbearance, golden mean, judiciousness, justice, justness, lenity, measure, mildness, moderateness, patience, poise, quiet, reasonableness, restraint, sedateness, sedation, sobriety, steadiness, toleration; CONCEPTS 633,657 —*Ant.* extreme, indulgence, intemperance, intensity, outrageousness, severity, unlimitedness, violence, wildness

moderator [n] *mitigator* alleviator, mediator, pacifier, peacemaker, referee, soother, stabilizer; CONCEPTS 348,366

modern [adj] *new, up-to-date* avant-garde, coincident, concomitant, concurrent, contempo, contemporary, current, cutting-edge*, fresh, last word*, late, latest, latter-day*, leading-edge*, modernistic, modernized, modish, neoteric, newfangled*, new-fashioned, novel, now, present, present-day, prevailing, prevalent, recent, state-of-the-art*, stylish, today, twenty- first century*, up-to-the-minute, with-it*; CONCEPTS 578,589,797 —*Ant.* ancient, antiquated, obsolete, old, old-fashioned, outdated, passe

modernize [v] *bring up to date; remodel* improve, refresh, regenerate, rejuvenate, remake, renew, renovate, restore, revamp, revive, update; CONCEPTS 168,177,202 —*Ant.* antique, date, outmode, regress, wear

modest [adj1] *shy* bashful, blushing, chaste, coy, demure, diffident, discreet, humble, lowly, meek, moderate, nice, proper, prudent, quiet, reserved, resigned, reticent, retiring, seemly, self-conscious, self-effacing, sheepish, silent, simple, temperate, timid, unassertive, unassuming, unassured, unboastful, unobtrusive, unpresuming, unpretending, unpretentious, withdrawing; CONCEPTS 401,404 —*Ant.* arrogant, assured, bold, brave, conceited, courageous, egotistical, proud, self-confident, unabashed, unashamed

modest [adj2] *limited, ordinary* average, cheap, discreet, dry, economical, fair, humble, inelaborate, inexpensive, middling, moderate, natural, plain, reasonable, simple, small, unadorned, unaffected, unembellished, unembroidered, unexceptional, unexcessive, unextravagant, unextreme, unobtrusive, unornamented, unostentatious, unpretentious, unradical, unstudied; CONCEPTS 334,547,562 —*Ant.* extraordinary, immodest, ostentatious, presumptuous, unlimited

modesty [n] *shyness* bashfulness, celibacy, chastity, constraint, coyness, decency, delicacy, demureness, diffidence, discreetness, humbleness, humility, inhibition, innocence, lack of pretension, meekness, propriety, prudery, purity, quietness, reserve, reticence, self-effacement, simplicity, timidity, unobtrusiveness, unostentatiousness, unpretentiousness, virtue; CONCEPT 633 —*Ant.* arrogance, boldness, braveness, conceit, courage, ego, pride, self-confidence

modicum [n] *bit, small amount* atom, crumb, dash, drop, fraction, fragment, grain, inch, iota, jot, little, minim, mite, molecule, ounce, particle, pinch, scrap, shred, smidge, speck, tinge, touch, trifle, whit; CONCEPT 831 —*Ant.* lot

modify [*v1*] *alter, change* adapt, adjust, become, convert, correct, customize, doctor, mutate, recast, redo, refashion, reform, remodel, reorganize, repair, reshape, revise, rework, shift gears*, switch over, transfigure, transform, transmogrify, transmute, turn, turn one around*, turn over new leaf*, turn the corner*, turn the tables*, tweak*, vary; CONCEPT 232 —*Ant.* leave alone, stagnate

modify [*v2*] *lessen, reduce* abate, curb, decrease, limit, lower, mitigate, moderate, modulate, qualify, relax, remit, restrain, restrict, slacken, soften, temper, tone down; CONCEPTS 236,240, 247 —*Ant.* grow, increase

modish [*adj*] *fashionable* a la mode*, all the rage*, chic, contemporary, current, dashing, exclusive, faddy, fresh, happening, hip*, in*, in-thing*, last-word, latest, mod*, now*, smart, stylish, swank, swish*, trendy, up-to-date, up-to-the-minute, vogue, voguish, with-it*; CONCEPTS 578,589,797 —*Ant.* old-fashioned, unfashionable, unstylish

modulate [*v*] *adjust, harmonize* attune, balance, fine-tune, inflect, regulate, restrain, revamp, switch, temper, tone, transmogrify, tune, tweak, vary; CONCEPT 202 —*Ant.* leave alone

modus operandi [*n*] *mode of operation* manner, method, method of operation, M.O., procedure, process, rule of thumb, technique, way, way of doing things, workings; CONCEPTS 6,630

mogul [*n*] *person who has great power, many possessions* executive, key player*, king, magnate, notable, personage, potentate, prince, princess, queen, royalty, top brass*, tycoon, VIP*; CONCEPTS 347,354

moist [*adj*] *wet, wettish* clammy, damp, dampish, dank, dewy, dripping, drippy, drizzly, humid, irriguous, muggy, not dry, oozy*, rainy, soggy, teary, watery; CONCEPT 603 —*Ant.* dry

moisten [*v*] *make wet, damp* bathe, bedew, dampen, dip, drench, humidify, lick, mist, moisturize, rain on, rinse, saturate, shower, soak, sog, sop, splash, splatter, spray, sprinkle, squirt, steam, steep, wash, water, water down, waterlog, wet; CONCEPT 256 —*Ant.* dry

moisture [*n*] *dampness; liquid* damp, dankness, dew, drizzle, fog, humidity, mist, perspiration, precipitation, rain, sweat, water, wateriness, wet, wetness; CONCEPTS 467,524 —*Ant.* dryness

moisturizer [*n*] *lotion* balm, cream, demulcent, emollient, liniment, oil, ointment, salve, unction, unguent; CONCEPTS 311,446,466,467,468

mold [*n*] *form, pattern* cast, cavity, character, class, depression, description, design, die, frame, image, impression, kind, lot, matrix, model, nature, shape, sort, stamp, type, womb; CONCEPTS 378,411,436

mold [*v*] *form, give shape* build, construct, devise, erect, fashion, forge, form, frame, make, pat, plan, plant, plot, put together, round, scheme, sculpt, whittle; CONCEPTS 173, 175,184, 251 —*Ant.* dismantle

moldy [*adj*] *musty* airless, dirty, funky,

mildewed, mildewy, putrid, rotten, rotting, smelly, stale, stuffy; CONCEPTS 578,598,603,797

mole [*n1*] *blemish* beauty mark, beauty spot, birthmark, blot, freckle, nevus, strawberry mark; CONCEPT 580

mole [*n2*] *spy* agent, double agent, infiltrator, informer, inside man/woman, secret agent; CONCEPTS 348,412

molecule [*n*] *smallest part* bit, fragment, iota, jot, minim, mite, modicum, mote, ounce, particle, ray, speck, unit; CONCEPTS 393,831

molest [*v1*] *physically abuse* accost, assail, attack, disorganize, displace, disturb, encroach, fondle, harm, hinder, hurt, illtreat, injure, interfere, intrude, maltreat, meddle, misuse, rape; CONCEPTS 246,375 —*Ant.* be careful, guard, protect

molest [*v2*] *bother, annoy* abuse, afflict, badger, bait, bedevil, beset, break in, bug*, confuse, discommode, discompose, disquiet, disturb, encroach, frighten, harass, harry, heckle, hector, interrupt, intrude, irk, irritate, obtrude, persecute, perturb, pester, plague, pother, pursue, scare, tease, terrify, torment, trouble, upset, vex, worry; CONCEPTS 7,14,19 —*Ant.* assist, cheer, make happy, please

mollify [*v*] *pacify, soothe* abate, allay, alleviate, ameliorate, appease, assuage, blunt, calm, compose, conciliate, cool, cushion, decrease, diminish, dulcify, ease, fix up, lessen, lighten, lull, mellow, mitigate, moderate, modify, pacify, patch things up*, placate, propitiate, quell, quiet, reduce, relieve, soften, sweeten, take sting out*, temper, tranquilize; CONCEPTS 7,22,244,698 —*Ant.* agitate, depress, exasperate, harass, incite, provoke, trouble, upset, worry

mollycoddle [*v*] *pamper* baby, caress, cater to, coddle, cosset, dandle*, fondle, indulge, overindulge, overprotect, pet, spoil, wait on; CONCEPTS 136,295

molt [*v*] *shed* cast off, decorticate, doff, exuviate, peel, pull off, slough, take off; CONCEPTS 142,176,179,180,992

molten [*adj*] *melted* fused, glowing, igneous, liquefied, smelted; CONCEPTS 250,255

mom [*n*] *mother* child-bearer, grandmother, ma*, mama*, matriarch, matron, mommy*, mum*, mumsy*, parent; CONCEPTS 394, 400,414

moment [*n1*] *brief time period* bit, breathing, crack, date, flash, hour, instant, jiff*, jiffy*, juncture, minute, nothing flat*, no time*, occasion, point, point in time, sec*, second, shake, split second*, stage, three winks*, tick*, time, trice*, twinkle*, twinkling*, while, wink*; CONCEPTS 807,808

moment [*n2*] *importance* advantage, avail, concern, consequence, gravity, import, magnitude, momentousness, note, pith, profit, seriousness, significance, signification, substance, use, value, weight, weightiness, worth; CONCEPT 668 —*Ant.* triviality, unimportance

momentarily [*adv*] *for a short time* briefly, for a little while, for a minute, for a moment, for an instant, for a second, for a short time, for a short while, immediately, instantly, now, right

now, temporarily; CONCEPT 820 —*Ant.*
lengthily, permanently

momentary [adj] *brief, fleeting* cursory,
dreamlike, ephemeral, evanescent, flashing,
flitting*, flying, fugacious, fugitive, gone in
flash*, hasty, impermanent, impulsive, instantaneous, in wink of an eye*, like lightning,
passing, quick, shifting, short, short-lived,
spasmodic, summary, temporary, transient,
transitory, vanishing, volatile; CONCEPT 798
—*Ant.* lasting, long-lasting, permanent, staying

momentous [adj] *important; serious* big, chips
are down*, consequential, considerable, critical,
crucial, decisive, earth-shaking, earth-shattering,
epochal, eventful, far-reaching, fateful, grave,
heavy, heavy number, historic, material, meaningful, memorable, notable, of moment, outstanding, pivotal, significant, substantial, vital,
weighty; CONCEPT 568 —*Ant.* immaterial,
insignificant, trifling, trivial, unimportant

momentum [n] *impetus, push* drive, energy,
force, impulse, power, propulsion, strength,
thrust; CONCEPTS 641,712

monarch [n] *ruler* autocrat, crowned head,
despot, emperor, empress, king, majesty,
potentate, prince, princess, queen, sovereign;
CONCEPTS 354,422

monastery [n] *place where monks live* abbey,
cloister, friary, house, lamasery, priory, religious community; CONCEPTS 368,439,516

monetary [adj] *concerning money, finances*
budgetary, capital, cash, commercial, financial,
fiscal, pecuniary, pocket; CONCEPT 334

money [n] *currency accepted as exchange for
goods, services* almighty dollar*, banknote,
bankroll, bill, bread*, bucks*, capital, cash,
check, chips, coin, coinage, dough*, finances,
fund, funds, gold, gravy*, greenback*, hard
cash*, legal tender, loot*, medium of exchange,
pay, payment, pesos*, property, resources,
riches, roll, salary, silver, specie, treasure, wad*,
wage, wealth, wherewithal*; CONCEPT 340

moneyed [adj] *rich* affluent, fat-cat*, flush*,
leisure-class*, loaded*, opulent, prosperous,
upper-class, upscale, uptown, wealthy, well-
heeled*, well-off*, well-to-do*; CONCEPT 334
—*Ant.* destitute, poor

moneymaking [adj] *producing profit* advantageous, gainful, going, good, lucrative, paying,
profitable, remunerative, successful, thriving,
well-paying; CONCEPT 334 —*Ant.* unprofitable

mongrel [n] *animal of mixed background* bastard, cross, crossbreed, cur, half-blood, half-
breed, hybrid, mixed breed, mixture, mule,
mutt; CONCEPT 394

moniker [n] *nickname* appellation, byname,
denomination, handle*, label, pet name*,
sobriquet, tag*; CONCEPTS 268,683

monitor [n] *person who watches, oversees*
adviser, auditor, counselor, director, eavesdropper, guide, informant, invigilator, listener,
overseer, supervisor, watchdog; CONCEPTS
348,350

monitor [v] *listen, watch carefully* advise, audit,
check, control, counsel, follow, keep an eye
on*, keep track of*, observe, oversee, record,

scan, supervise, survey, track; CONCEPTS 117,
596,623 —*Ant.* forget, ignore, neglect

monk [n] *man who devotes life to contemplation
of god* abbot, anchorite, ascetic, brother,
cenobite, eremite, friar, hermit, monastic,
priest, recluse, religious, solitary; CONCEPT 361

monkey [n] *primate* anthropoid, ape, baboon,
chimpanzee, gorilla, imp, lemur, monk,
orangutan, rascal, scamp, simian; CONCEPT 394

monkey [v] *fiddle, tamper with* busybody,
butt in*, fool, fool around*, fool with*, horn
in*, interfere, interlope, intermeddle, make*,
meddle, mess, play, pry, tinker, trifle;
CONCEPTS 87,612 —*Ant.* leave alone

monkey business [n] *foolishness* absurdity,
absurdness, antics, carrying-on*, craziness,
disobedience, foolery, high jinks, horse
feathers*, horseplay, inanity, insanity, irresponsibility, ludicrousness, lunacy, misbehavior,
mischief-making, nonsense, poppycock*,
silliness, stupidity, tommyrot*; CONCEPT 633

monolithic [adj] *massive* big, bulky, colossal,
consistent, elephantine, enormous, gargantuan,
giant, gigantic, grand, great, huge, hulking,
immense, immovable, imposing, mammoth,
permanent, solid, titanic, towering, uniform,
vast, whopping*; CONCEPTS 773,781

monologue [n] *speech by one person* address,
descant, discourse, disquisition, harangue,
lecture, sermon, soliloquy, speech, stand-up
bit*, talk; CONCEPTS 266,278 —*Ant.* dialogue

monopolize [v] *dominate, control* absorb,
acquire, bogart, consume, copyright, corner,
corner the market*, devour, employ, engross,
exclude, exercise control, have, hog*, hold,
keep to oneself, lock up*, manage, own, own
exclusively, patent, possess, restrain, sew up*,
sit on*, syndicate, take over, take up, use,
utilize; CONCEPTS 94,324,710 —*Ant.* distribute,
scatter, share

monopoly [n] *something held, owned exclusively* cartel, consortium, copyright, corner,
holding, oligopoly, ownership, patent, pool,
possessorship, proprietorship, syndicate,
trust; CONCEPT 710 —*Ant.* distribution, joint-
ownership, scattering, sharing

monotonous [adj] *all the same, remaining the
same* banausic, blah*, boring, colorless, dreary,
droning, dull, dull as dishwater*, flat, flat as
pancake*, ho-hum*, humdrum*, monotone,
nothing, pedestrian, plodding, prosaic, puts one
to sleep*, recurrent, reiterated, repetitious,
repetitive, samely, sing-song*, soporific, tedious,
tiresome, toneless, treadmill, unchanged, unchanging, uniform, uninflected, uninteresting,
unrelieved, unvaried, unvarying, wearisome,
wearying; CONCEPT 529 —*Ant.* changing, ever-
changing, exciting, lively, variable, versatile

monotony [n] *boredom; sameness* colorlessness, continuance, continuity, dreariness,
dryness, dullness, ennui, equability, evenness,
flatness, humdrum*, identicalness, invariability,
levelness, likeness, monotone, monotonousness,
oneness, repetitiousness, repetitiveness, routine,
same old thing*, similarity, tediousness, tedium,
tiresomeness, unchangeableness, uniformity,

mo
mo

wearisomeness; CONCEPTS *410,637,673* —*Ant.*
change, color, excitement, liveliness, variability,
versatility

monster [*n*] *giant animal; supernatural being*
abnormality, barbarian, beast, behemoth, brute,
centaur, colossus, demon, devil, dragon, fiend,
Frankenstein, freak, giant, hellion, horror,
leviathan, lusus naturae, mammoth, miscreation,
monstrosity, mutant, ogre, phoenix, savage,
titan, villain, werewolf, whale; CONCEPT *370*

monstrosity [*n*] *freak* abnormality, atrocity,
deformity, dreadfulness, enormity, eyesore,
freakishness, frightfulness, grotesqueness,
heinousness, hideousness, horror, monster,
mutant, mutation; CONCEPTS *411,657*

monstrous [*adj1*] *unnatural, shocking* aberrant,
abnormal, atrocious, cruel, desperate, devilish,
diabolical, disgraceful, dreadful, egregious,
evil, fiendish, flagitious, foul, freakish, frightful,
grotesque, gruesome, heinous, hellish, hideous,
horrendous, horrible, horrifying, infamous,
inhuman, intolerable, loathsome, macabre,
miscreated, morbid, obscene, odious, ominous,
outrageous, preposterous, rank, satanic, scandalous, teratoid, terrible, uncanny, unusual,
vicious, villainous; CONCEPTS *537, 564,582*
—*Ant.* average, common, expected, natural,
ordinary, standard

monstrous [*adj2*] *very large* colossal, cracking,
elephantine, enormous, fantastic, gargantuan,
giant, gigantic, grandiose, great, huge, immense, impressive, magnificent, mammoth,
massive, monumental, prodigious, stupendous,
titanic, towering, tremendous, vast, whopping;
CONCEPTS *773,781* —*Ant.* little, miniature,
small, tiny

monument [*n*] *memorial, remembrance* cairn,
cenotaph, column, commemoration, erection,
footstone, gravestone, headstone, ledger, magnum opus, marker, masterpiece, mausoleum,
memento, monolith, obelisk, pile, pillar, record,
reminder, shrine, slab, statue, stele, stone, tablet,
testament, token, tomb, tombstone, tower,
tribute, witness; CONCEPTS *259,271, 305,470*

monumental [*adj*] *impressive, overwhelming*
awe-inspiring, awesome, classic, enduring,
enormous, fantastic, gigantic, grand, great,
historic, huge, immense, immortal, important,
lasting, lofty, majestic, mammoth, massive,
memorable, mighty, mortal, mountainous, outstanding, prodigious, significant, stupendous,
towering, tremendous, unforgettable, vast;
CONCEPTS *568,773* —*Ant.* insignificant, trivial,
unimportant, unimposing, unimpressive

mooch [*v*] *cadge* beg, borrow, bum*, bum
off*, freeload, leach off*, scrounge, sponge;
CONCEPT *89*

mood [*n*] *state of mind* affection, air, atmosphere, attitude, aura, bent*, blues*, caprice,
character, color*, condition, crotchet, cue, depression, desire, disposition, doldrums, dumps*,
emotion, fancy, feel*, feeling, frame of mind*,
high spirits, humor, inclination, individuality,
low spirits, melancholy, mind, personality, pleasure, propensity, response, scene, semblance,
soul, spirit, strain, temper, temperament,

tendency, tenor, timbre, vagary, vein, whim,
wish; CONCEPTS *410,411,673* —*Ant.* health

moody [*adj*] *crabby, temperamental* angry,
cantankerous, capricious, changeable, crabbed*,
crestfallen, cross, dismal, doleful, dour, downcast, down in the dumps*, down in the mouth*,
erratic, fickle, fitful, flighty, frowning, gloomy,
glum, huffy, ill-humored, ill-tempered, impulsive, in a huff*, in the doldrums, introspective,
irascible, irritable, lugubrious, melancholy,
mercurial, miserable, moping, morose, offended,
out of sorts*, pensive, petulant, piqued, sad,
saturnine, short-tempered, splenetic, sulky,
sullen, testy, touchy; CONCEPT *403* —*Ant.*
balanced, cheerful, happy, overjoyed

moon [*n*] *Earth's satellite* celestial body, crescent, full moon, half-moon, heavenly body, new
moon, old moon, orb of night*, planetoid, pump-
kin*, quarter-moon, satellite; CONCEPTS *511,809*

moon [*v*] *dream about; desire* daydream,
idle, languish, mope, pine, waste time, yearn;
CONCEPT *20* —*Ant.* abhor, despise, dislike, hate

moonshine [*n*] *illegally distilled alcohol*
bathtub gin*, bootleg, firewater*, home brew,
hooch*, mountain dew*, rotgut*, white
lightning; CONCEPTS *454,467*

moor [*v*] *anchor, fasten securely* berth, catch,
chain, dock, fix, lash, make fast, picket,
secure, tether, tie, tie up; CONCEPTS *85,160*
—*Ant.* loose, push off, unhitch

mooring [*n*] *landing* anchorage, berth, dock,
harbor, marina, pier, port, station, wharf;
CONCEPT *439*

moot [*adj*] *doubtful, arguable* at issue, contestable, controversial, debatable, disputable,
dubious, open, open to debate, problematic,
questionable, suspect, uncertain, undecided,
unresolved, unsettled; CONCEPT *535* —*Ant.*
decided, definite, proven, resolved

mop [*n1*] *tangle of material, often used to
absorb liquid* duster, sponge, squeegee,
swab, sweeper, towel; CONCEPTS *392,499*

mop [*n2*] *thick mass of hair* mane, shock,
tangle, thatch, tresses; CONCEPT *399*

mop [*v*] *clean by using water and cloth* dab,
dust, pat, polish, rub, soak up, sponge, squeegee,
swab, towel off, wash, wipe; CONCEPT *165*

mope [*v*] *pout, be dejected* ache, be apathetic,
be down in the mouth*, be gloomy, be in a
funk*, bleed*, brood, chafe, despair, despond,
droop, eat one's heart out, fret, grieve, grumble,
grump, idle, lament, languish, lose heart, moon,
pine, pine away*, repine, sink, stew
over*, sulk, sweat over*, waste time*, wear
a long face*, yearn; CONCEPTS *20,410* —*Ant.*
be elated, be happy

moral [*adj*] *ethical, honest* aboveboard, blameless, chaste, conscientious, correct, courteous,
decent, decorous, dutiful, elevated, exemplary,
good, high-minded, honorable, immaculate,
incorruptible, innocent, just, kindly, kosher*,
laudable, meet, meritorious, modest, moralistic,
noble, praiseworthy, principled, proper, pure,
respectable, right, righteous, saintly, salt of the
earth*, scrupulous, seemly, square, straight,
true-blue*, trustworthy, truthful, upright,

upstanding, virtuous, worthy; CONCEPT 545
—*Ant.* amoral, bad, corrupt, dishonest, evil, immoral, sinful, unethical, unprincipled, vile

moral [n] *lesson, proverb* adage, aphorism, apophthegm, axiom, dictum, epigram, gnome, maxim, meaning, message, moralism, motto, point, precept, rule, saw, saying, sermon, significance, truism; CONCEPTS 278,283

morale [n] *confidence, self-esteem* assurance, attitude, disposition, drive, esprit, esprit de corps, heart, humor, mettle, mood, outlook, resolve, self-confidence, self-possession, spirit, temper, temperament, turn, vigor; CONCEPTS 410

morality [n] *ethics, honesty* chastity, conduct, decency, ethicality, ethicalness, gentleness, godliness, good habits, goodness, honor, ideals, incorruptibility, incorruption, integrity, justice, manners, moral code, morals, mores, philosophy, principle, principles, probity, purity, rectitude, righteousness, rightness, saintliness, standards, uprightness, virtue, worthiness; CONCEPT 645
—*Ant.* amorality, badness, corruption, dishonesty, evil, immorality, sinfulness, unethicalness

moralize [v] *preach* admonish, edify, lecture, pass judgment, pontificate, pontify, preachify, sermonize, teach; CONCEPTS 51,75

morals [n] *personal principles, standards* behavior, beliefs, conduct, customs, dogmas, ethic, ethics, habits, ideals, integrity, manners, morality, mores, policies, scruples; CONCEPTS 411,645,688 —*Ant.* amorality, disrespectability, immorality, indecency, unethicalness

morass [n] *bog; mess* chaos, confusion, fen, jam, jungle, knot, labyrinth, marsh, maze, mesh, mix-up, muddle, quagmire, skein, snarl, swamp, tangle, web; CONCEPTS 230,509
—*Ant.* order, organization

moratorium [n] *suspension* abeyance, abeyancy, adjournment, ban, break, breather*, breathing spell*, deferment, delay, downtime*, five*, freeze, grace period, halt, pause, postponement, reprieve, respite, stay, truce; CONCEPTS 119, 807,832

morbid [adj] *gloomy, nasty, sickly* aberrant, abnormal, ailing, brooding, dark, deadly, depressed, despondent, diseased, dreadful, frightful, ghastly, ghoulish, grim, grisly, gruesome, hideous, horrid, infected, irascible, macabre, malignant, melancholy, monstrous, moody, pessimistic, saturnine, sick, somber, sullen, unhealthy, unnatural, unsound, unusual, unwholesome; CONCEPTS 314,403,537 —*Ant.* cheerful, happy, healthy, pleased, sound

mordant [adj] *sarcastic* acerb, acerbic, acid, biting, bitter, caustic, cutting, cynical, disparaging, disrespectful, mean, poignant, pointed, sardonic, scathing, sharp; CONCEPT 267

more [adj] *additional, greater* added, aggrandized, also, amassed, and, another, augmented, besides, bounteous, deeper, else, enhanced, exceeding, expanded, extended, extra, farther, fresh, further, heavier, higher, in addition, increased, innumerable, larger, likewise, major, massed, more than that, new, numerous, other, over and above, spare, supplementary, too many, wider; CONCEPTS 762,771 —*Ant.* fewer, less

more [adv] *to a greater extent* additionally, along with, also, as well, besides, better, beyond, further, furthermore, in addition, likewise, longer, moreover, over, too, withal; CONCEPTS 544,772 —*Ant.* fewer, less

more or less [adv] *approximately* about, almost, around, ballpark figure*, bordering on, circa, close to, in the ballpark*, in the neighborhood of, in the vicinity of, just about, not far from, not quite, on average, relatively, roughly, thereabouts, very close; CONCEPT 566

moreover [adv] *additionally* also, as well, besides, by the same token*, further, furthermore, in addition, likewise, more, to boot*, too, what is more*, withal, yet; CONCEPTS 544,772

mores [n] *traditional customs* attitude, codes, established ways, etiquette, formalities, manners, morals, policies, practices, principles, protocol, rites, rituals, routines, rules, social conduct, standards, way of life; CONCEPTS 644,687

morgue [n] *mortuary* charnel house, crematory, funeral home, funeral parlor; CONCEPTS 172,386

moribund [adj] *dying* at death's door*, at the end of the rope*, declining, done for*, doomed, expiring, fading, fated, going, mortal, mortally ill, one foot in the grave*, on one's deathbed, on one's last leg*, passing, perishing; CONCEPT 539

morning [n] *first part of the day* after midnight, AM, ante meridiem, aurora, before lunch, before noon, breakfast time*, break of day, cockcrow*, crack of dawn*, dawn, daybreak, daylight, dayspring, early bright*, first blush*, foreday, forenoon, morn*, morningtide, morrow, prime*, sunrise, sunup, wee hours*; CONCEPTS 801,802,806,810

moron [n] *stupid person* addlepate, blockhead*, boob*, dimwit, dingbat*, dolt, dope*, dork*, dumbbell*, dummy*, dunce, fool, halfwit, idiot, ignoramus, imbecile, lamebrain*, loony*, loser*, mental defective*, nerd*, simpleton; CONCEPT 423 —*Ant.* brain

moronic [adj] *stupid* asinine, brainless, dense, dimwitted, doltish, dopey*, dumb, foolish, half-baked*, idiotic, ill-advised, imbecilic, inane, irresponsible, ludicrous, mindless, nonsensical, pointless, senseless, unintelligent, unthinking; CONCEPTS 402,548

morose [adj] *depressed, pessimistic* acrimonious, blue*, brusque, cantankerous, choleric, churlish, crabbed*, crabby*, cranky*, cross, dolorous, dour, down, down in the dumps*, down in the mouth*, frowning, gloomy, glum, grouchy, gruff, harsh, having blue devils*, having the blahs*, ill-humored, ill-tempered, in a bad mood*, in a blue funk*, irritable, low, melancholy, moody, moping, mournful, perverse, perversive, sad, saturnine, singing the blues*, snappish, sour, splenetic, sulky, sullen, surly, taciturn, testy, troubled, ugly; CONCEPT 403 —*Ant.* cheerful, friendly, happy, light-hearted, optimistic, uplifted

morsel [n] *tiny piece* bait, bit, bite, chunk, crumb, cut, delicacy, drop, fraction, fragment, grain, hunk, lump, mouthful, nibble, nosh, part, sample, scrap, segment, slice, snack, soupçon, taste, tidbit, treat; CONCEPTS *457,458, 831,835 —Ant.* lot

mortal [*adj1*] *deadly* bitter, death-dealing, deathly, destructive, dire, ending, extreme, fatal, grave, great, grievous, grim, intense, killing, last, lethal, malignant, merciless, monstrous, mortiferous, murderous, noxious, pestilent, pestilential, poisonous, relentless, remorseless, ruthless, severe, terminal, terrible, unrelenting; CONCEPT *537 —Ant.* invigorating, lifegiving, permanent, refreshing

mortal [*adj2*] *human* animate, bipedal, corporeal, creatural, earthly, ecce homo, ephemeral, evanescent, fading, finite, frail, fugacious, impermanent, momentary, passing, perishable, precarious, sublunary, temporal, transient, weak, worldly; CONCEPT *549 —Ant.* animal, immortal, inhuman

mortal [*n*] *human being* animal, being, body, character, creature, earthling, human, individual, living soul, man, naked ape, party, person, personage, soul, woman; CONCEPT *417 —Ant.* animal, plant

mortality [*n1*] *death* bloodshed, carnage, deadliness, destruction, dying, extinction, fatality, killing, lethality, loss of life; CONCEPT *407 —Ant.* birth, life

mortality [*n2*] *humanness* being, ephemerality, flesh, Homo sapiens, humanity, humankind, human race, impermanence, temporality, transience; CONCEPTS *417,648 —Ant.* animal life, immortality, inhumanness, plant life

mortally [*adv*] *fatally* badly, critically, gravely, painfully, seriously; CONCEPTS *544,565,568*

mortgage [*n*] *loan agreement* contract, debt, deed, homeowner's loan, pledge, title; CONCEPT *332*

mortician [*n*] *undertaker* embalmer, funeral director; CONCEPT *304*

mortification [*n*] *humiliation* abasement, affront, bring down, chagrin, condescension, degradation, disgrace, dishonor, embarrassment, humbling, ignominy, loss of face*, put-down, resignation, shame; CONCEPTS *388,410*

mortify [*v*] *embarrass* abase, abash, affront, annoy, belittle, chagrin, chasten, confound, control, crush, deflate, deny, disappoint, discipline, discomfit, disgrace, displease, get one's comeuppance*, harass, humble, humiliate, put to shame, ridicule, shame, subdue, take down a peg*, take the wind out*, vex, worry; CONCEPTS *7,19,52,54 —Ant.* compliment, flatter, praise, satisfy

mortuary [*n*] *funeral home* charnel house, crematory, funeral parlor, morgue; CONCEPT *304*

mosaic [*n*] *collage* checker, montage, motley, patchwork, plaid, tessellation, variegation; CONCEPTS *259,625*

mosey [*v*] *saunter* amble, dally, dilly-dally, drift, linger, loiter, meander, mope*, move slowly, ramble, stroll along, take a stroll, take it easy, traipse, walk slowly; CONCEPT *151*

mosque [*n*] *temple* cathedral, chapel, church, holy place, house of God, house of worship,

masjid, place of worship, sanctuary, shrine, synagogue, tabernacle; CONCEPTS *368,439*

mossback [*n*] *old-fashioned person* conservative, fuddy-duddy*, geezer*, old fogy*, old geezer*, square*; CONCEPT *424*

most [*adj*] *best, greatest* better, biggest, greater, highest, largest, lion's share*, max*, maximum, ultimate, utmost, uttermost; CONCEPTS *771,772 —Ant.* least

most [*adv*] *nearly all; extremely* about, all but, almost, approximately, close, eminently, exceedingly, in the majority, mightily, much, nearly, nigh, practically, remarkably, super, surpassingly, too, very, well-nigh; CONCEPTS *544,569,771 —Ant.* least

mostly [*adv*] *generally, mainly* above all, almost entirely, as a rule*, chiefly, customarily, essentially, for the most part*, frequently, in many instances*, largely, many times, most often, often, on the whole*, overall, particularly, predominantly, primarily, principally, regularly, usually; CONCEPTS *544,548,772*

mote [*n*] *speck* atom, bit, crumb, dot, fleck, fragment, grain, iota, particle, small thing, smidgen, speckle, tiny bit, trace; CONCEPT *831*

motel [*n*] *temporary, short-term residence, often for travelers* cabin, court, hotel, inn, lodge, motor court, resort, roadhouse; CONCEPTS *439, 449,516*

moth-eaten [*adj*] *shabby; stale* ancient, antiquated, archaic, dated, decayed, decrepit, dilapidated, moribund, old-fashioned, outdated, ragged, tattered, threadbare, worn-out; CONCEPT *485*

mother [*n*] *female person who has borne children* ancestor, child-bearer, creator, forebearer, mom*, mommy*, origin, parent, predecessor, procreator, progenitor, source; CONCEPTS *394,400,414,415,423 —Ant.* father

motif [*n*] *central theme* concept, design, idea, logo, notion, pattern, structure, subject; CONCEPTS *278,682,689*

motion [*n1*] *movement, action* act, advance, agitation, ambulation, body English*, change, changing, direction, drift, dynamics, flow, fluctuation, flux, full swing*, gesticulation, gesture, high sign*, inclination, kinetics, locomotion, mobility, motility, move, oscillation, passage, passing, progress, sign, signal, stir, stirring, stream, sway, sweep, swing, tendency, travel, wave, wavering; CONCEPT *145 —Ant.* immobility, repose, rest, stagnation, stiffness, stillness

motion [*n2*] *formal suggestion in a meeting* plan, proposal, proposition, recommendation, submission; CONCEPTS *75,278*

motion [*v*] *gesture, direct* beckon, flag, gesticulate, guide, invite, move, nod, sign, signal, signalize, wave; CONCEPT *149 —Ant.* be still

motionless [*adj*] *calm, not moving* apoplectic, at a standstill, at rest, becalmed, dead, deadlocked, deathly, firm, fixed, frozen, halted, immobile, immotile, inanimate, inert, lifeless, numb, palsied, paralyzed, petrified, quiescent, quiet, spellbound, stable, stagnant, stalled, standing, static, stationary, steadfast, still, stock-still, torpid, transfixed, unmovable, unmoved, unmoving; CONCEPTS 488,584 —*Ant.* active, busy, lively, mobile, moving

motion picture [n] *movie* cine, cinema, cinematics, cinematograph, feature film, film, flick*, moving picture, picture show, silver screen*, talkie*, talking picture, videotape; CONCEPTS 263,293

motivate [v] *stimulate, instigate* actuate, arouse, bring, cause, dispose, draw, drive, egg on*, excite, fire, galvanize, give incentive, goad, goose*, impel, incite, incline, induce, innervate, innerve, inspire, inspirit, lead, move, persuade, pique, predetermine, predispose, prevail upon, prompt, propel, provoke, quicken, rouse, set afoot, set astir, sound, spark, spur, suggest, sway, touch off, trigger, whet; CONCEPTS 14,68,242 —*Ant.* depress, disconcert, discourage, dissuade

motivation [n] *ambition, inspiration* action, actuation, angle, catalyst, desire, disposition, drive, encouragement, fire, get up and go*, gimmick, goose*, hunger, impetus, impulse, impulsion, incentive, incitation, incitement, inclination, inducement, instigation, interest, kick*, motive, persuasion, predetermination, predisposition, provocation, push, reason, right stuff*, spur, stimulus, suggestion, wish; CONCEPTS 20,411,689 —*Ant.* depression, discouragement

motive [n] *reason, purpose* aim, antecedent, basis, cause, consideration, design, determinant, drive, emotion, end, feeling, grounds, idea, impulse, incentive, incitement, inducement, influence, inspiration, intent, intention, mainspring, motivation, object, occasion, passion, rationale, root, spring, spur, stimulus, thinking; CONCEPTS 20,661,689 —*Ant.* deterrent, discouragement, hindrance

motley [adj] *mixed, varied* assorted, conglomerate, dappled, discrepant, disparate, dissimilar, diversified, heterogeneous, indiscriminate, kaleidoscopic, mingled, miscellaneous, mixed, mottled, multicolor, multicolored, multiform, multihued, polychromatic, prismatic, rainbow, unlike, varicolored, variegated, various, versicolor; CONCEPTS 564,618 —*Ant.* homogenous, like, same, similar, uniform, unmixed, unvaried

motor [n] *engine* cylinder, diesel, generator, mechanism, piston, power train, transformer, turbine, what's under the hood*; CONCEPT 463

motorcade [n] *procession of motor vehicles* caravan, convoy, parade; CONCEPTS 432,503

motorcycle [n] *motorbike* chopper*, dirt bike, enduro, hog*, minibike, moped, scooter; CONCEPTS 364,505

motor home [n] *recreational vehicle* camper, mobile home, RV; CONCEPT 505

motorized [adj] *power-driven* mechanical, mechanized, powered; CONCEPT 544

mottled [adj] *speckled* blotchy, checkered, dappled, flecked, freckled, maculate, marbled, motley, piebald, pied, skewbald, spotted, streaked, tabby, variegated; CONCEPTS 606, 618 —*Ant.* plain, unflecked

motto [n] *saying, slogan* adage, aphorism, apothegm, battle cry, byword, catchphrase, cry, epigram, formula, maxim, precept, proverb, rallying cry, rule, saw, sentiment, shibboleth, war cry, watchword, word; CONCEPT 278

mound [n] *heap, hill* anthill, bank, drift, dune, embankment, hillock, knoll, mass, molehill, mountain, pile, rise, shock, stack, tumulus; CONCEPTS 432,509 —*Ant.* depression, ditch, valley

mount [v1] *climb* arise, ascend, back, bestride, clamber up, climb onto, climb up on, escalade, escalate, get astride, get up on, go up, jump on, lift, rise, scale, soar, tower, up, vault; CONCEPTS 149,154,166 —*Ant.* alight, dismount, fall

mount [v2] *increase, grow* accumulate, aggravate, augment, build, deepen, enhance, enlarge, escalate, expand, heighten, intensate, intensify, multiply, pile up, redouble, rise, rouse, swell, upsurge, wax; CONCEPTS 704,780 —*Ant.* decline, decrease, drop, fall, slump, subside

mount [v3] *affix, frame* emplace, exhibit, fit, install, place, position, prepare, produce, put in place, put on, set up, show, stage; CONCEPTS 174,261 —*Ant.* dismount, unfix

mountain [n] *very large hill* abundance, alp, bank, bluff, butte, cliff, crag, dome, drift, elevation, eminence, glob, heap, height, hump, mass, mesa, mound, mount, palisade, peak, pike, pile, precipice, pyramid, range, ridge, shock, sierra, stack, ton, tor, volcano; CONCEPTS 432,509 —*Ant.* crevasse, valley

mountaineer [n] *mountain climber* alpinist, backpacker, climber, cragsman, cragswoman, hiker, rock climber; CONCEPTS 149,224,363

mountaineering [n] *mountain climbing* alpinism, backpacking, hiking, hill-climbing, rock-climbing; CONCEPTS 149,224,363

mountainous [adj] *hilly; large* alpine, big, colossal, gigantic, highland, huge, mammoth, tall, towering; CONCEPT 509

mountebank [n] *charlatan* cheat, con man/woman*, grifter, imposter, rip-off artist*, swindler; CONCEPT 412

mourn [v] *be sad over loss* ache, agonize, anguish, be brokenhearted*, bemoan, be sad, bewail, bleed, blubber, carry on, complain, cry, deplore, fret, grieve, hurt, keen, lament, languish, long for, miss, moan, pine, regret, repine, rue, sigh, sob, sorrow, suffer, take it hard*, wail, wear black*, weep, wring hands*, yearn; CONCEPTS 23,410 —*Ant.* be happy, be joyful

mournful [adj] *sorrowful* anguished, bereft, cheerless, depressed, disconsolate, distressing, doleful, dolent, forlorn, full of sorrow, griefstricken, grieving, grievous, heartbroken, in mourning, in pain, in sorrow, lamentable, pitiful, sad, sombre, woeful; CONCEPT 403

mourning [n] *sadness, time of sadness* aching, bereavement, blackness, crying, darkness, grief, grieving, keening, lamentation, lamenting, languishing, moaning, pining, repining, sorrowing, wailing, weeping, woe; CONCEPTS 388,410 —*Ant.* cheer, happiness, joy

mousy [adj] *drab; quiet* bashful, colorless, diffident, dull, indeterminate, ineffectual, pale, plain, self-effacing, shy, timid, timorous, unassertive, unassuming; CONCEPTS 401,618 —Ant. beautiful, extroverted, fancy, fixed-up

mouth [n1] *opening* aperture, beak, box, cavity, chops*, clam, crevice, delta, door, embouchement, entrance, estuary, firth, fly trap, funnel, gate, gills, gob, harbor, inlet, jaws, kisser*, lips, mush*, orifice, portal, rim, trap*, yap*; CONCEPTS 392,513 ˚

mouth [n2] *backtalk* boasting, braggadocio, bragging, cheek, empty talk*, freshness, gas*, guff*, hot air*, idle talk, impudence, insolence, lip*, rudeness, sass*, sauce*; CONCEPTS 54,278

mouth off [v] *talk back* answer back, come back at, sass, sass back, wise off; CONCEPTS 44,52

mouthpiece [n] *spokesperson* agent, delegate, PR person, representative, speaker, spokesman, spokeswoman; CONCEPTS 348,354,359

mouth-watering [adj] *appetizing* aperitive, appealing, cheek, delectable, delicious, divine*, flavorsome, full of flavor, heavenly*, luscious, palatable, piquant, saporous, savory, scrumptious, succulent, tasty, tempting, yummy*; CONCEPT 613

mouthy [adj] *talkative* big-mouthed*, chattering, chatty*, full of hot air*, gabby, garrulous, gossipy, long-winded*, loose-lipped*, loudmouthed*, ranting, talky, vociferous, windy*; CONCEPT 267

movable [adj] *transportable* adaptable, adjustable, ambulatory, conveyable, deployable, detachable, in parts, liftable, loose, mobile, motile, moving, not fastened, not fixed, on wheels, portable, portative, removable, separable, shiftable, transferable, turnable, unattached, unfastened, unstationary, unsteady; CONCEPTS 488,584 —Ant. fixed, immovable, permanent, unmovable, untransportable

move [n] *progress, deed* act, action, alteration, change, maneuver, measure, modification, motion, movement, ploy, procedure, proceeding, shift, step, stir, stirring, stratagem, stroke, turn, variation; CONCEPTS 2,660 —Ant. idleness, inaction, inactivity, regression, stagnation

move [v1] *be in motion, put in motion* actuate, advance, blow, budge, bustle, carry, change, climb, crawl, cross, depart, dislocate, disturb, drift, drive, exit, flow, fly, get away, get going, get off, glide, go, go away, head for, hurry, impel, jump, leap, leave, locomote, march, migrate, off-load, position, proceed, progress, propel, pull out, push, quit, relocate, remove, roll, run, scram, shift, ship, shove, skip out, split, stir, switch, take off, transfer, transport, transpose, travel, traverse, walk, withdraw; CONCEPTS 147,149,198 —Ant. fix, pause, remain, stay, stop

move [v2] *motivate, influence* activate, actuate, advocate, affect, agitate, bring, bring up, budge, carry, cause, convert, draw up, drive, excite, get going, give rise to, impel, impress, incite, induce, inspire, inspirit, instigate, introduce, lead, operate, persuade, play on, prevail upon, prompt, propel, propose, push, put forward, quicken, recommend, rouse, shift, shove, start,

stimulate, stir, strike, submit, suggest, sway, touch, tug at, turn, urge, work on; CONCEPTS 7,19,22,75,242 —Ant. discourage, dishearten, dissuade

movement [n1] *motion, activity* act, action, advance, agitation, alteration, change, changing, deed, development, displacement, dynamism, evolution, evolving, exercise, flight, flow, flux, gesture, journey, journeying, locomotion, maneuver, migration, mobility, motility, movableness, move, moving, operation, operativeness, passage, progress, progression, regression, roaming, shift, shifting, steps, stir, stirring, transferal, transit, translating, transplanting, undertaking, velocity, voyaging, wandering; CONCEPTS 2,145,697 —Ant. cessation, halt, inaction, inactivity, pause, stoppage

movement [n2] *drive, campaign* change, crusade, current, demonstration, displacement, drift, evolution, faction, flight, flow, front, group, grouping, march, mobilization, organization, party, patrol, shift, sweep, swing, tendency, transfer, transition, trend, unrest, withdrawal; CONCEPTS 381,697 —Ant. indifference

mover and shaker [n] *doer* achiever, catalyst, enterprising person, entrepreneur, generator, go-getter*, mover, player*, producer, spark plug*, upstart, wheeler and dealer*; CONCEPT 347

movie [n] *presentation of action on continuous film* cine, cinema, cinematics, cinematograph, feature, film, flick*, motion picture, moving picture, photoplay, picture, screenplay, show, silent*, silver screen*, talkie*, talking picture, videotape; CONCEPTS 263,293

moving [adj1] *affecting, exciting* affective, arousing, awakening, breathless, dynamic, eloquent, emotional, emotive, expressive, facund, far-out*, felt in gut*, grabbed by*, gripping, hairy*, heartbreaking, heartrending, impelling, impressive, inspirational, inspiring, meaningful, mind-bending*, mind-blowing*, motivating, persuasive, poignant, propelling, provoking, quickening, rallying, rousing, sententious, significant, something*, stimulating, stimulative, stirring, stunning, touching, turned on by*; CONCEPTS 529,537 —Ant. unaffecting, unemotional, unexciting, unmoving

moving [adj2] *mobile* advancing, changing, climbing, evolving, flying, going, jumping, motile, movable, nomadic, portable, progressing, roaming, roving, running, shifting, traversing, unfixed, unstable, unsteadfast, unsteady, walking; CONCEPTS 488,584 —Ant. fixed, immobile, permanent, stationary, unmoving

mow [v] *cut* clip, crop, scythe, shear, sickle, trim; CONCEPTS 137,176,236,247

moxie [n] *courage* adventuresomeness, adventurousness, audacity, backbone, boldness, braveness, bravery, daring, dash, dauntlessness, determination, fearlessness, fortitude, gameness, grit, guts, hardihood, mettle, nerve, pluck, prowess, spirit, spunk, stamina, tenacity, toughness, valor; CONCEPTS 411,633

much [adj] *plenty* abundant, adequate, a lot of*, ample, complete, considerable, copious, countless, endless, enough, everywhere, extravagant, full, galore, generous, great, heaps*, immeasurable, jam-packed*, lavish, loads*, lotsa*, many, mega*, mucho*, no end*, plenteous, plentiful, profuse, satisfying, scads*, sizable, substantial, sufficient, very many, voluminous; CONCEPTS 772,781 —*Ant.* little

much [*adv*] *greatly, a lot* again and again, a great deal*, considerably, decidedly, eminently, exceedingly, exceptionally, extremely, frequently, highly, hugely, indeed, notably, oft, often, over and over*, regularly, repeatedly, surpassingly, time and time again*, very; CONCEPTS 530,544,548 —*Ant.* little

much [*n*] *a great deal* abundance, all kinds of*, a lot*, amplitude, appreciable amount, barrel, breadth, completeness, copiousness, excess, exuberance, fullness, gobs*, great quantity, heaps*, loads*, lots*, lump, mass, mess*, mountain, multiplicity, oodles*, overage, oversupply, pack, peck, pile, plentifulness, plenty, plethora, profuseness, riches, scads*, sufficiency, superabundance, superfluity, thousands, tons*, very much, volume, wealth; CONCEPT 771 —*Ant.* little

mud [*n*] *wet dirt* clay, mire, muck, ooze, silt, slab, sludge, slush; CONCEPT 509

muddle [*n*] *confused state* ataxia, awkwardness, botch, chaos, clutter, complexity, complication, confusion, daze, difficulty, dilemma, disarrangement, disarray, disorder, disorganization, emergency, encumbrance, fog, foul-up*, hash, haze, intricacy, involvement, jumble, mess, mess and a half*, mix-up*, muss*, perplexity, plight, predicament, quandary, rat's nest*, screw-up*, shambles*, snarl, struggle, tangle, trouble; CONCEPTS 230,410,666 —*Ant.* enlightenment, order, organization

muddle [*v*] *confuse, disorganize* addle, befuddle, bewilder, blunder, botch, bungle, clutter, complicate, confound, daze, derange, disarrange, discombobulate*, disorder, disorient, disturb, entangle, fluster, foul, foul up*, jumble, louse up, make a mess of*, mess, misarrange, mix, mix up*, muck, mumble, murmur, nonplus, perplex, perturb, psych out*, rattle, ravel, ruffle, scramble, shuffle, snafu*, snarl, spoil, stir up, stumble, stupefy, tangle, throw, throw off, tumble; CONCEPTS 16,84,242 —*Ant.* clear up, educate, enlighten, explain, explicate, order, organize

muddled [*adj*] *confused* addled, befuddled, bewildered, blurred, chaotic, convoluted, dazed, disarranged, disarrayed, disordered, disorderly, disorganized, in disarray, jumbled, messy, mixed up, scrambled, topsy-turvy, untidy; CONCEPT 585

muddy [*adj*] *dark and cloudy* addled, bemired, bespattered, black, blurred, boggy*, caked, confused, dingy, dirty, dull, filthy, flat, foul, fuzzy, gloomy, greasy, grimy, grubby*, gummy*, gunky*, hazy, impure, indistinct, marshy, miry, mucky*, obscure, opaque, roily, sloppy, slushy, smoky, sodden, soggy, soiled, subfuse, swampy, turbid, unclean, unclear; CONCEPTS 485,606,618 —*Ant.* bright, clean, clear

mudslinging [*n*] *smear campaign* character

assassination, defamation, dirty politics, dragging one's name through the mud, negative campaign, slander; CONCEPT 54

muff [*v*] *bungle* blunder, boggle, botch, choke*, drop the ball*, err, flub, foul up, fumble, goof up*, make a mess of, mess up, miscalculate, mishandle, mismanage, screw up*, slip; CONCEPT 101

muffle [*v*] *suppress, make quiet* conceal, cover, cushion, dampen, deaden, decrease, drown, dull, envelop, gag, hide, hush, mellow, mute, muzzle, put the lid on*, quieten, shut down, silence, sit down on*, smother, soften, soft-pedal*, squelch, stifle, subdue, tone down*, wrap*; CONCEPTS 65,121,240 —*Ant.* blab, let loose, tell

muffled [*adj*] *quietened* deadened, dim, dull, faint, flat, indistinct, mute, muted, obscure, silenced, stifled, strangled, subdued, suppressed; CONCEPT 594 —*Ant.* clear, unblocked

mug [*n1*] *drinking cup* coffee cup, demitasse, flagon, jug, stoup, tankard, toby; CONCEPT 494

mug [*n2*] *face* countenance, frown, grimace, kisser*, mask, profile, puss*; CONCEPT 484

mug [*v*] *hold up* assault, hold up*, purse-snatch, rob, steal, stick up*; CONCEPTS 52,86

muggy [*adj*] *humid* clammy*, close, damp, dampish, dank, moist, mucky*, oppressive, soggy, sticky, stuffy, sultry; CONCEPTS 525,603 —*Ant.* dry

mulish [*adj*] *obstinate* adamant, bullheaded, dead set on*, dogged, firm, hardheaded, head-strong, immovable, inflexible, intractable, obdurate, opinionated, persistent, pigheaded*, recalcitrant, relentless, single-minded, steadfast, strong-minded, stubborn, tenacious; CONCEPTS 401,404,542

mull [*v*] *think about seriously* brood over, chaw, consider, contemplate, delay, deliberate, examine, figure, hammer away at*, linger, meditate, moon*, muse on, ponder, pore over, procrastinate, rack one's brains*, reflect, review, revolve, ruminate, stew over*, study, sweat over*, think over, turn over, weigh, woolgather*; CONCEPT 17 —*Ant.* ignore, neglect

multicolored [*adj*] *having various hues* checkered, dappled, flecked, kaleidoscopic, marbled, motley, mottled, multicolor, particolored, piebald, pied, polychrome, prismatic, speckled, spotted, streaked, varicolored, veined, versicolor; CONCEPT 618 —*Ant.* monochrome

multiculturalism [*n*] *doctrine acknowledging contributions and interests of many cultures* cross-culturalism, cultural diversity, diversity, ethnic inclusiveness, ethnic mosaic, multiracialism, pluralism; CONCEPTS 665,689

multifarious [*adj*] *diverse* assorted, divers, diversified, manifold, many, miscellaneous, multiple, multitudinous, myriad, numerous, varied, various; CONCEPT 564 —*Ant.* homogenous

multimedia [*n*] *combined use of several media* interactive media, intermedia, mixed media; CONCEPT 274

multinational [*adj*] *international* continental, global, intercontinental, multicultural, universal, worldwide; CONCEPTS 536,772

multiple/multifarious [adj] *diversified, miscellaneous* assorted, collective, conglomerate, different, diverse, diversiform, heterogeneous, indiscriminate, legion, manifold, many, mixed, motley, multiform, multiplex, multitudinal, multitudinous, numerous, populous, several, sundry, varied, variegated, various, voluminous; CONCEPTS *564,762,772* —*Ant.* single, singular, unvaried

multiply [v] *increase; reproduce* accumulate, add, aggrandize, aggregate, augment, boost, breed, build up, compound, cube, double, enlarge, expand, extend, generate, heighten, magnify, manifold, mount, populate, procreate, produce, proliferate, propagate, raise, repeat, rise, spread, square; CONCEPTS *171,374* —*Ant.* decrease, divide, lessen, reduce

multitude [n] *large group* aggregation, army, assemblage, assembly, collection, commonalty, concourse, congregation, crowd, crush, drove, great number, heap, herd, horde, host, infinitude, infinity, jam*, legion, loads, lot, lots*, majority, mass, mob, much, myriad, number, numbers, ocean*, oodles*, people, plenitude, plurality, populace, proletariat, public, push*, quantity, scores*, sea, slew*, swarm, throng, turnout; CONCEPTS *417,432* —*Ant.* handful, portion, single, zero

multitudinous [adj] *many, considerable* abounding, abundant, copious, countless, great, heaps*, infinite, innumerable, innumerous, legion, manifold, multifarious, myriad, numberless, numerous, populous, profuse, several, sundry, teeming, uncountable, uncounted, unnumbered, untold, various, voluminous; CONCEPTS *762,781* —*Ant.* few, limited

mum [adj] *silent* bashful, buttoned up*, clammed up*, closemouthed, hushed, mute, muted, nonvocal, not forthcoming, not talkative, quiet, reserved, secretive, shy, soundless, speechless, still, tight-lipped, tongue-tied, uncommunicative, unsociable, unspeaking, voiceless, wordless, zipped*; CONCEPT *594*

mumble [v] *say low and inarticulately* grumble, maunder, murmur, mutter, ramble, rumble, say to oneself, speak, stammer, stutter, swallow, talk, utter, verbalize, vocalize, voice, whimper, whine, whisper; CONCEPTS *47,77* —*Ant.* speak clearly

munch [v] *chew, eat* bite, break up, champ, chomp, crunch, crush, grind, mash, masticate, press, reduce, ruminate, scrunch, smash, soften; CONCEPTS *169,185*

mundane [adj] *ordinary* banal, commonplace, day-to-day, earthly, everyday, humdrum*, lowly, normal, prosaic, routine, workaday*, workday, worldly; CONCEPT *547* —*Ant.* exciting, extraordinary, heavenly, supernatural, wonderful

municipal [adj] *concerning cities* borough, burghal, city, civic, civil, community, corporate, domestic, home, incorporated, internal, local, metropolitan, native, public, town, urban; CONCEPT *536* —*Ant.* country, suburban

municipality [n] *city* borough, community, district, metropolis, precinct, town, township, village; CONCEPT *507*

munificent [adj] *giving, generous* beneficent, benevolent, big, big-hearted, bounteous, bountiful, charitable, free, handsome, kind, lavish, liberal, loose, magnanimous, open-handed, philanthropic, rich, unsparing, unstinting; CONCEPTS *334,401* —*Ant.* careful, greedy, mean, selfish, stingy

munitions [n] *ammunition* ammo*, armament, arsenal, bombs, bullets, explosives, grenades, gunpowder, missiles, shells, torpedos, weapons; CONCEPTS *498,500*

murder [n] *killing* annihilation, assassination, blood, bloodshed, butchery, carnage, crime, death, destruction, dispatching, felony, foul play*, hit*, homicide, knifing, liquidation, lynching, manslaughter, massacre, off*, offing*, one-way ticket*, rub out*, shooting, slaying, taking out*, terrorism, the business*, the works*; CONCEPTS *192,252*

murder [v] *kill* abolish, asphyxiate, assassinate, behead, blot out*, bump off*, butcher, chill*, cool*, decapitate, defeat, destroy, dispatch, do in*, drub*, dust off*, electrocute, eliminate, eradicate, execute, exterminate, extinguish, finish, garotte, guillotine, hang, hit*, knife, knock off*, liquidate, lynch, mangle, mar, massacre, misuse, off*, put away*, rub out*, ruin, shoot, slaughter, slay, smother, snuff, spoil, strangle, take a life, take for a ride*, take out*, thrash*, waste*; CONCEPTS *192, 252* —*Ant.* guard, preserve, protect, save

murderer [n] *person who kills* assassin, butcher, criminal, cutthroat, enforcer, executioner, hit-and-run*, hit person*, homicide, killer, manslaughterer, perpetrator, slaughterer, slayer, soldier, trigger person*; CONCEPT *412*

murderous [adj] *difficult* arduous, brutal, criminal, cruel, dangerous, deadly, destroying, destructive, devastating, exhausting, fell, ferocious, harrowing, hellish, killing, lethal, ruinous, sapping, savage, strenuous, unpleasant; CONCEPTS *538,548* —*Ant.* easy, facile, pleasant

murk [n] *darkness* dimness, dusk, gloom, murkiness; CONCEPT *620*

murky [adj] *gloomy, obscure* black, caliginous, cheerless, cloudy, dark, darkened, dim, dingy, dirty, dismal, drab, dreary, dull, dun*, dusk, dusky, filthy, foggy, foul, fuzzy, glowering, gray, grubby*, impenetrable, lowering, misty, mucky, muddy, nasty, nebulous, nubilous, overcast, roily, sad, smoky, somber, squalid, stormy, tenebrous, turbid, unclean; CONCEPTS *617,618* —*Ant.* bright, clear, light, luminous, sparkling, unobscured

murmur [n] *low, continuous sound* babble, buzz, buzzing, drone, grumble, hum, humming, mumble, murmuration, mutter, muttering, purr, rumble, rumor, undertone, whisper, whispering; CONCEPTS *65,595*

murmur [v] *make low, continuous sound* babble, burble, buzz, drip, drone, flow, growl, gurgle, hum, meander, moan, mumble, mutter, purl, purr, ripple, rumble, stage-whisper, stammer, stutter, susurrate, tinkle, trickle, utter, verbalize, vocalize, voice, whisper; CONCEPTS *65,77* —*Ant.* speak clearly

muscle [n1] *large fibers of animal body* beef, brawn, flesh, meat, might, sinew, tendon, thew, tissue; CONCEPTS 393,420

muscle [n2] *power, influence* brawn, clout, energy, force, forcefulness, might, potency, sinew, stamina, strength, strong arm*, sturdiness, weight; CONCEPTS 641,687 —*Ant.* impotence, powerlessness, weakness

muscular [adj] *powerfully built* able-bodied, athletic, brawny, bruising, burly, fibrous, hefty, Herculean*, hulky, husky, lusty, mighty, muscled, powerful, powerhouse*, pumped up*, ripped*, robust, ropy, sinewy, stalwart, stout, strapping, stringy, strong, sturdy, tiger*, tough, vigorous, well-built, wiry; CONCEPTS 485,489 —*Ant.* delicate, flabby, infirm, skinny, weak

muse [v] *think about, dream* be lost in thought*, brood, build castles in air*, chew over*, cogitate, consider, contemplate, deliberate, feel, meditate, moon*, mull over, percolate, ponder, puzzle over, reflect, revolve, roll, ruminate, speculate, think, think over, turn over, weigh; CONCEPT 17 —*Ant.* ignore, neglect

museum [n] *place for viewing artifacts or exhibits* archive, building, depository, exhibition, foundation, gallery, hall, institution, library, menagerie, repository, salon, storehouse, treasury, vault; CONCEPTS 439,449

mushroom [v] *sprout; grow quickly* augment, blow up, boom, burgeon, burst, detonate, expand, explode, flourish, go off, grow, grow rapidly, increase, luxuriate, proliferate, shoot up, spread, spring up; CONCEPTS 179,704 —*Ant.* shrink, shrivel

mushy [adj1] *doughy, soft* gelatinous, jelled, mashy*, muddy, pap*, pastelike, pulpous, pulpy, quaggy, semiliquid, semisolid, slushy, spongy, squashy*, squishy*; CONCEPTS 604, 606 —*Ant.* hard, stiff

mushy [adj2] *romantic, corny* bathetic, effusive, emotional, lovey-dovey*, maudlin, mawkish, saccharine, schmaltzy*, sentimental, sloppy*, slushy*, soppy*, sugary, syrupy, tear-jerking, weepy, wet; CONCEPTS 267,542 —*Ant.* unfeeling, unromantic

music [n] *sounds that are pleasant, harmonized* a cappella, acoustic, air, bebop, bop, chamber, classical, folk, fusion, hard rock, harmony, heavy metal, hymn, instrumental, jazz, measure, melody, modern, opera, piece, plainsong, popular, ragtime, rap, refrain, rock, rock and roll, singing, song, soul, strain, swing, tune; CONCEPTS 263,595 —*Ant.* silence

musical [adj] *harmonic, lyrical* agreeable, blending, chiming, choral, consonant, dulcet, euphonious, harmonious, lilting, mellow, melodic, melodious, operatic, orchestral, pleasing, rhythmic, silvery, songful, sweet, sweet-sounding, symphonic, symphonious, tuned, tuneful, vocal; CONCEPT 594 —*Ant.* cacophonous, discordant, dissonant, inharmonious, unmusical

music hall [n] *concert hall* amphitheater, auditorium, opera house, theater; CONCEPTS 263,293,439,448

musician [n] *person who performs music* artist, artiste, composer, conductor, diva, entertainer, instrumentalist, performer, player, session player, soloist, virtuoso, vocalist; CONCEPT 352

muss [n] *disorder* chaos, confusion, disarrangement, hash, mess, mess-up, mix-up*, muddle, shambles, turmoil; CONCEPTS 230,674 —*Ant.* order, organization

muss [v] *dishevel, disorder* clutter, crumple, disarrange, disarray, disorganize, disrupt, disturb, jumble, mess up, mix up*, muddle, ruffle, rummage, rumple, tangle, tousle, upset, wrinkle; CONCEPT 158 —*Ant.* fix up, order, organize

must [n] *necessity, essential* charge, commitment, committal, condition, devoir, duty, fundamental, imperative, necessary, need, obligation, ought, precondition, prerequisite, requirement, requisite, right, sine qua non; CONCEPTS 646,709

must [v] *ought, should* be compelled, be destined, be directed, be doomed*, be driven*, be made, be necessitated, be obliged, be one's fate, be ordered, be required, got to, have, have got to*, have no choice, have to, must needs*, need, pushed to the wall*; CONCEPT 650

muster [n] *gathering* aggregation, assemblage, assembly, call-up*, collection, company, congeries, convocation, crowd, draft, group, head count*, meeting, mobilization, nose count*, rally, roll, roll call*, roster, roundup*; CONCEPTS 417,432 —*Ant.* division, separation

muster [v] *gather, come together* assemble, call together, call up, collect, congregate, congress, convene, convoke, enroll, enter, group, join up, marshal, meet, mobilize, organize, raise, rally, rendezvous, round up, sign on, sign up, summon; CONCEPT 109 —*Ant.* divide, remove, separate, throw away

musty [adj1] *stuffy, aged* airless, ancient, antediluvian, antique, crumbling, dank, decayed, decrepit, dirty, dried-out*, dry, fetid, filthy, frowzy*, malodorous, mildewed, mildewy, moldy, moth-eaten*, noisome, old, putrid, rotten, smelly, spoiled, squalid, stale, stuffy; CONCEPTS 578,598,603,797 —*Ant.* clean, clear, new, sweet-smelling

musty [adj2] *worn-out, clichéd* ancient, antiquated, banal, common, commonplace, dull, hackneyed, hoary, obsolete, old-fashioned, old hat*, shopworn*, stale, stereotypical, threadbare, timeworn*, tired, trite, warmed-over*, worn; CONCEPTS 267,530,578,797 —*Ant.* new, unused

mutant [n] *mutation* abnormality, deformity, deviation, freak, freak of nature, monster; CONCEPTS 424,580

mutation [n] *metamorphosis* alteration, anomaly, change, deviant, deviation, evolution, innovation, modification, mutant, novelty, permutation, transfiguration, transformation, variation, vicissitude; CONCEPTS 665,697 —*Ant.* inaction, stagnation

mute [adj] *unable to speak* aphasiac, aphasic, aphonic, muffled, mum, quiet, silenced, silent, speechless, tongueless, tongue-tied, unexpressed, unpronounced, unsounded, unspeaking, unspoken, voiceless, wordless; CONCEPT 593 —*Ant.* articulate, speaking, vocal

mute [*v*] *muffle, tone down sound* benumb, bottle up*, cork up*, dampen, deaden, decrease the volume, drown, gag, hush, keep it down*, lower, moderate, muzzle, pipe down*, put damper on*, put the lid on*, reduce, silence, soften, soft-pedal*, subdue, turn down; CONCEPTS 65,240 —*Ant.* articulate, speak, voice

mutilate [*v*] *maim, damage* adulterate, amputate, batter, bowdlerize, butcher, cripple, crush, cut to pieces, cut up, deface, disable, disfigure, dismember, distort, expurgate, hack*, hash up*, hurt, injure, lacerate, lame, mangle, mar, mess up*, ravage, scratch, spoil, weaken; CONCEPTS 176,246 —*Ant.* fix, mend, repair

mutilated [*adj*] *dismembered* amputated, disfigured, maimed, mangled, marred; CONCEPTS 137,246,250

mutinous [*adj*] *rebellious* anarchistic, contumacious, defiant, disloyal, disobedient, disorderly, dissident, factious, iconoclastic, insubordinate, insurgent, insurrectionary, radical, rebel, revolutionary, rioting, riotous, subversive, traitorous, treasonable, ungovernable, unmanageable; CONCEPTS 401,529,542

mutiny [*n*] *defiance, resistance* disobedience, insubordination, insurrection, refusal to obey, revolt, revolution, riot, rising, strike, uprising; CONCEPTS 300,388,633 —*Ant.* obedience, subservience

mutiny [*v*] *defy, revolt* be insubordinate, disobey, insurrect, kick over, rebel, refuse to obey, resist, rise against, rise up, strike; CONCEPTS 300,384 —*Ant.* obey, observe, serve, subject

mutter [*v*] *grumble, mumble* complain, croak, groan, grouch*, grouse, growl, grunt, moan, muddle, murmur, rumble, snarl, sputter, swallow, whisper; CONCEPTS 52,77 —*Ant.* speak clearly

mutual [*adj*] *shared, common* associated, bilateral, collective, communal, conjoint, conjunct, connected, convertible, correlative, dependent, give-and-take*, given and taken*, interactive, interchangeable, interchanged, interdependent, intermutual, joint, partaken, participated, public, reciprocal, reciprocated, related, requited, respective, returned, two-sided*, united; CONCEPTS 563,708 —*Ant.* detached, dissociated, distinct, separate, unshared

mutual fund [*n*] *stock fund* 401(k) fund, bond fund, hedge fund, individual retirement account, investment fund, IRA, money market funds, retirement plan; CONCEPTS 330,332,340

mutually [*adv*] *together* all at once, as a group, by agreement, by contract, commonly, conjointly, cooperatively, en masse, in collaboration, in combination, in conjunction, jointly, reciprocally, respectively; CONCEPTS 544,577 —*Ant.* dissimilarly, distinctly

muzzle [*n*] *covering for control* cage, cover, envelope, gag, guard, sheath, wrap; CONCEPT 172

muzzle [*v*] *gag, quiet* bottle up*, censor, check, choke, clamp down on*, cork, crack down on*, curb, dry up*, dummy up*, hush, ice*, muffle,

prevent, quieten, repress, restrain, restrict, shush, shut down, silence, squash, squelch, stifle, still, stop, suppress, tongue-tie*, trammel; CONCEPTS 121,250 —*Ant.* free, let go, liberate

myopic [*adj*] *able only to see things near at hand* astigmatic, biased, blind, halfsighted, nearsighted, presbyopic, shortsighted; CONCEPT 619 —*Ant.* far-sighted

myriad [*adj*] *innumerable* countless, endless, gobs*, heaping, immeasurable, incalculable, infinite, multiple, multitudinous, no end of*, numberless, thousand-and-one*, uncounted, untold, variable; CONCEPTS 762,781 —*Ant.* calculable, limited, measurable

myriad [*n*] *a lot* army, flood, heap, horde, host, loads*, mint, mountain*, multitude, oodles*, scores, slew, stacks*, swarm, thousands*; CONCEPT 787 —*Ant.* little

mysterious [*adj*] *secret, concealed* abstruse, alchemistic, arcane, astrological, baffling, cabalistic, covert, cryptic, curious, dark, difficult, enigmatic, enigmatical, equivocal, esoteric, furtive, hidden, impenetrable, incomprehensible, inexplicable, inscrutable, insoluble, magical, mystical, mystifying, necromantic, obscure, occult, oracular, perplexing, puzzling, recondite, secretive, sphinxlike, spiritual, strange, subjective, symbolic, transcendental, uncanny, unfathomable, unknowable, unknown, unnatural, veiled, weird; CONCEPTS 529,576 —*Ant.* apparent, known, obvious, plain, public, straightforward, tangible, unmysterious

mystery [*n*] *puzzle, secret* abstruseness, brainteaser*, braintwister*, charade, chiller, cliffhanger*, closed book*, conundrum, crux, cryptogram, difficulty, enigma, grabber, inscrutability, inscrutableness, mindboggler*, mystification, occult, oracle, perplexity, poser, problem, puzzlement, question, rebus, riddle, rune, secrecy, sixty-four-thousand-dollar question*, sphinx, stickler, stumper, subtlety, teaser, thriller, tough nut to crack*, twister, whodunit*, why*; CONCEPTS 282,532,696 —*Ant.* known, understanding

mystic/mystical [*adj*] *secret, esoteric* abstruse, anagogic, arcane, cabalistic, cryptic, enigmatical, hidden, imaginary, impenetrable, inscrutable, magic, magical, metaphysical, mysterial, mysterious, necromantic, nonrational, numinous, occult, otherworldly, paranormal, preternatural, quixotic, sorcerous, spiritual, supernatural, telestic, thaumaturgic, transcendental, unaccountable, unknowable, visionary, wizardly; CONCEPTS 529,549,582 —*Ant.* knowable, natural, palpable, undisguised

mystify [*v*] *bewilder, confuse* baffle, bamboozle*, beat*, befog*, buffalo*, confound, deceive, elude, escape, floor*, fog in*, hoodwink*, lick*, lie, perplex, puzzle, stump*, throw*, trick; CONCEPT 16 —*Ant.* clear up, enlighten, explain, explicate

mystique [*n*] *person's strong impression* attitude, awe, character, charisma, charm, complex, fascination, glamour, magic, nature, spell, temperament; CONCEPT 411

myth [n] *fictitious story, often ancient* allegory, apologue, creation, delusion, fable, fabrication, fairy story, fancy, fantasy, fiction, figment, folk ballad, folk tale, illusion, imagination, invention, legend, lore, mythos, parable, saga, superstition, tale, tall story*, tradition; CONCEPT 282 —*Ant.* fact, non-fiction, truth

mythical/mythological [adj] *make-believe, fairy-tale* allegorical, chimerical, created, fabled, fabricated, fabulous, false, fanciful, fantasy, fictitious, fictive, folkloric, imaginary, invented, legendary, made-up, mythic, nonexistent, pretended, storied, supposititious, traditional, unreal, untrue, visionary, whimsical; CONCEPTS 267,582 —*Ant.* factual, historical, real, true

mythology [n] *folklore* belief, conviction, folk tales, legend, lore, mythicism, mythos, myths, stories, tradition; CONCEPT 282 —*Ant.* actuality, history, reality, truth

N

nab [v] *seize* apprehend, arrest, capture, catch, clutch, cop*, detain, grab, nail*, pick up*, run in*, snatch*, take*, take into custody; CONCEPTS 90,317 —*Ant.* let go, release

nadir [n] *lowest point* all-time low, base, bottom, floor, low point, record low, rock bottom, zero level; CONCEPT 442

nag [v] *harass, bother* annoy, badger, bait, berate, bug*, carp at, dog*, eat*, egg*, find fault, fuss, give a hard time*, goad, harry, heckle, hector, hound, importune, irk, irritate, needle, nudge*, pester, pick at, plague, prod, provoke, ride, scold, take it out on*, tease, torment, upbraid, urge, vex, work on*, worry; CONCEPTS 7,19,52 —*Ant.* assuage, please

nail [v1] *fasten, fix with pointed object* attach, beat, bind, drive, hammer, hit, hold, join, pin, pound, secure, sock*, spike, strike, tack, whack*; CONCEPTS 85,160,189 —*Ant.* unfasten, unnail

nail [v2] *capture, arrest* apprehend, bag, catch, collar*, detain, get*, hook*, nab, pinch*, prehend, secure, seize, take*; CONCEPTS 90,317 —*Ant.* let go, liberate, release

naive [adj] *childlike, trusting* aboveboard, artless, callow, candid, confiding, countrified, credulous, forthright, frank, fresh, green*, guileless, gullible, harmless, ignorant, impulsive, ingenuous, innocent, innocuous, instinctive, jejune, lamb*, like a babe in the woods*, natural, open, original, patsy*, plain, simple, simple-minded, sincere, spontaneous, square, sucker*, unaffected, unjaded, unpretentious, unschooled, unsophisticated, unsuspecting, unsuspicious, untaught, unworldly, virgin, wide-eyed*; CONCEPTS 401,542,678 —*Ant.* experienced, leery, skeptical, wise

naiveté [n] *innocence, gullibility* artlessness, callowness, candor, childishness, credulity, frankness, guilelessness, inexperience, ingenuousness, naturalness, openness, simplicity; CONCEPTS 633,657,678 —*Ant.* experience, leeriness, skepticism, sophistication

naked [adj1] *without covering* au naturel, bald, bare, bared, bare-skinned, barren, defenseless,

denuded, disrobed, divested, exposed, helpless, in birthday suit*, in dishabille*, in the altogether*, in the buff*, in the raw*, leafless, natural, nude, open, peeled*, raw, stark-naked*, stripped, threadbare, unclad, unclothed, unconcealed, uncovered, undraped, undressed, unprotected, unveiled, vulnerable, without a stitch*; CONCEPTS 485,589 —*Ant.* clothed

naked [adj2] *manifest, evident* artless, blatant, disclosed, discovered, dry, matter-of-fact, obvious, open, overt, palpable, patent, plain, pure, revealed, sheer, simple, stark, unadorned, undisguised, unexaggerated, unmistakable, unqualified, unvarnished; CONCEPTS 267,529 —*Ant.* hidden, private, secret

namby-pamby [n] *pansy baby*, caitiff, chicken*, chicken heart*, chicken liver*, coward, cry-baby, fraidy-cat*, jellyfish*, lily liver, milksop, momma's boy*, pantywaist, quitter, scaredy cat*, sissy*, weakling, wimp, wuss*, wussy*, yellow, yellow belly*; CONCEPT 423

name [n1] *title given to something, someone* agname, agnomen, alias, appellation, autograph, autonym, brand, cognomen, compellation, denomination, designation, epithet, eponym, flag*, handle*, head, heading, label, matronymic, moniker, monogram, nickname, nom de guerre, nom de plume, nonem, patronymic, pen name, pet name, place name, prenomen, proper name, pseudonym, rubric, sign, signature, sobriquet, stage name, style, surname, tag, term, trade name; CONCEPTS 268,683

name [n2] *fame, distinction* character, credit, eminence, esteem, honor, note, praise, renown, rep*, report, reputation, repute; CONCEPT 388

name [n3] *celebrity* big name*, celeb*, entertainer, headliner, hero, lion*, luminary, notability, notable, personality, somebody*, star, superstar; CONCEPTS 352,366 —*Ant.* unknown

name [v1] *give a title* baptize, call, characterize, christen, classify, cognominate, define, denominate, designate, dub, entitle, give a handle*, identify, label, nickname, nomenclature, put tag on, style, tag, term, ticket, title; CONCEPT 62

name [v2] *choose, designate* announce, appoint, cite, classify, commission, connote, declare, delegate, denote, elect, identify, index, instance, list, make, mark, mention, nominate, peg*, pin down*, point to, put down for, put finger on*, recognize, refer to, remark, select, signify, single out, slot, specify, suggest, tab, tag, tap; CONCEPTS 41,50,88 —*Ant.* ignore, neglect

name-dropper [n] *snob* social climber, status seeker; CONCEPT 423

nameless [adj] *unknown, anonymous* incognito, inconspicuous, innominate, obscure, pseudonymous, unacknowledged, uncelebrated, undesignated, undistinguished, unfamed, unheardof, unnamed, unnoted, unsung, untitled, whatchamacallit*, X*; CONCEPTS 267,576 —*Ant.* designated, distinguished, eminent, famous, known, named, prominent, renowned

namely [adv] *that is to say* by way of explanation, especially, expressly, id est*, i.e., in other words, in plain English*, particularly, scilicet, specially, specifically, strictly speaking, that is, to wit, videlicet, viz.; CONCEPT 557

nanny [n] *children's nurse* au pair, baby-sitter, governess, nursemaid, wet nurse; CONCEPT 295

nap [*n1*] *short, light sleep* break, catnap, doze, few z's*, forty winks*, interlude, intermission, microsleep*, nod, pause, respite, rest, shuteye*, siesta, snooze*, spot; CONCEPT 315

nap [*n2*] *grain of material* down, feel, fiber, grit, outside, pile, roughness, shag, smoothness, surface, tooth, wale, warp, weave, weft, woof; CONCEPTS 473,611

nap [*v*] *take a short, light sleep* catch forty winks*, catnap, doze, drop off*, drowse, get some shut-eye*, grab some z's*, nod, nod off, rack*, relax, rest, sleep, snooze, take a siesta*, take a snooze*; CONCEPTS 210,315

napkin [*n*] *linen* cloth, doily, moist towelette, serviette, towel, wipe; CONCEPT 473

nappy [*adj*] *fuzzy* downy, frizzy, furry, hairy, kinky, napped, velutinous, woolly; CONCEPT 606

narcissistic [*adj*] *concerned only with oneself* conceited, egotistic, egotistical, self-centered, self-involved, self-loving, stuck-up*, vain, vainglorious; CONCEPTS 401,404 —*Ant.* outgoing, sacrificing, unselfish

narcotic [*adj*] *dulling, painkilling* analgesic, anesthetic, calming, deadening, hypnotic, numbing, opiate, sedative, somnifacient, somnific, somnolent, somnorific, soporiferous, soporific, stupefacient, stupefactive, stupefying; CONCEPT 537

narcotic [*n*] *powerful drug inducing anesthesia or sleep* analgesic, anesthetic, anodyne, dope*, downer*, fix*, hard drug, hard stuff*, heroin, hypnotic, junk*, laudanum, lenitive, merchandise*, nepenthe, opiate, opium, painkiller, sedative, somnifacient, soporific, stuff*, stupefacient, tranquilizer; CONCEPT 307

narrate [*v*] *describe, detail* characterize, chronicle, delineate, depict, descant, disclose, discourse, enumerate, expatiate, give an account of, hold forth, make known, paint, picture, portray, proclaim, recite, recount, rehearse, relate, repeat, report, reveal, set forth, spin, state, tell, tell a story, unfold; CONCEPTS 55,72 —*Ant.* conceal, hide, suppress

narration [*n*] *description, reading* account, anecdote, explanation, narrative, recital, recountal, recounting, rehearsal, relation, report, story, storytelling, tale, telling, voice-over*, yarn*; CONCEPTS 55,72,282 —*Ant.* concealment, suppression

narrative [*adj*] *storylike, chronological* anecdotal, fictional, fictive, historical, narrated, recounted, reported, retold, sequential; CONCEPT 267 —*Ant.* rambling

narrative [*n*] *story, tale* account, anecdote, book, chronicle, chronology, description, detail, fiction, history, line, long and short of it*, narration, plot, potboiler*, recount, report, statement, version, yarn*; CONCEPTS 271,282

narrator [*n*] *storyteller* author, chronicler, describer, novelist, raconteur, reporter, teller of tales, writer, yarn spinner; CONCEPTS 348,356

narrow [*adj1*] *confined, restricted* attenuated, circumscribed, close, compressed, confining, constricted, contracted, cramped, definite, determinate, exclusive, exiguous, fine, fixed, incapacious, limited, linear, meager, near, paltry, pent, pinched, precarious, precise, scant, scanty, select, set, shrunken, slender, slim, small, spare, strait, taper, tapered, tapering, thin, threadlike,

tight; CONCEPTS 554,773 —*Ant.* broad, generous, liberal, unconfined, unrestricted, wide

narrow [*adj2*] *intolerant, small-minded* biased, bigoted, conservative, conventional, dogmatic, hidebound, illiberal, inexorable, inflexible, narrow-minded, obdurate, parochial, partial, prejudiced, reactionary; CONCEPTS 403,542 —*Ant.* accepting, broad-minded, liberal, tolerant

narrow [*adj3*] *cheap, stingy* avaricious, close, mean, mercenary, scrimpy*, tight*, ungenerous; CONCEPT 334 —*Ant.* generous, spendthrift, wasting

narrow [*v*] *reduce, simplify* circumscribe, constrict, contract, diminish, limit, taper, tighten; CONCEPTS 130,236,247 —*Ant.* broaden, complicate, expand, increase, intensify

narrowly [*adv*] *just, closely* almost, barely, by a hair*, by a whisker*, by narrow margin, carefully, close, nearly, only just, painstakingly, scarcely, scrutinizingly; CONCEPTS 544,799 —*Ant.* carelessly, imprecisely

narrow-minded [*adj*] *biased, intolerant* bigoted, conservative, conventional, hidebound, illiberal, insular, narrow, opinionated, parochial, petty, prejudiced, provincial, reactionary, short-sighted, small-minded, strait-laced, unenlarged; CONCEPTS 403,542 —*Ant.* broad-minded, liberal, tolerant, unbiased

nasty [*adj1*] *disgusting, offensive* awful, beastly, bum*, dirty, disagreeable, fierce, filthy, foul, gross, grubby, hellish, horrible, horrid, icky*, impure, loathsome, lousy, malodorous, mephitic, murderous*, nauseating, noisome, noxious, objectionable, obnoxious, obscene, odious, ornery, outrageous, poison, polluted, raunchy*, repellent, repugnant, repulsive, revolting, rough, sickening, soiled, squalid, stinking, tough, unappetizing, unclean, uncleanly, ungodly, unholy, unpleasant, vile, vulgar, yucky*; CONCEPTS 485,548,571 —*Ant.* great, magnificent, pleasing, wonderful

nasty [*adj2*] *indecent, smutty* blue*, coarse, dirty, filthy, foul, gross, immodest, immoral, improper, impure, indecorous, indelicate, lascivious, lewd, licentious, obscene, pornographic, raunchy*, ribald, scatological, shameful, unseemly, vulgar, wicked, X-rated*; CONCEPTS 372,545 —*Ant.* clean, decent, moral

nasty [*adj3*] *bad-tempered, mean* abusive, annoying, beastly, critical, cruel, despicable, disagreeable, distasteful, evil, fierce, hateful, malevolent, malicious, malign, malignant, ornery, ruthless, sarcastic, sordid, spiteful, squalid, unkind, unpleasant, vicious, vile, wicked; CONCEPT 401 —*Ant.* agreeable, friendly, happy, kind, pleasant

nasty [*adj4*] *injurious, dangerous* bad, critical, damaging, harmful, noxious, painful, poisonous, serious, severe, ugly; CONCEPT 537 —*Ant.* aiding, assisting, helpful, helping, safe

nation [*n*] *country with its own government* body politic, commonwealth, community, democracy, domain, dominion, empire, land, monarchy, people, populace, population, principality, public, race, realm, republic, society, sovereignty, state, tribe, union; CONCEPT 510

national [*adj*] *concerning a country with a government* civic, civil, communal, country-wide, domestic, ethnic, federal, general,

governmental, home, imperial, inland, internal, interstate, nationwide, native, politic, political, public, royal, social, societal, sovereign, state, sweeping, vernacular, widespread; CONCEPT 536 —*Ant.* local

nationality [n] *place of birth* allegiance, body politic, citizenship, community, country, ethnic group, nation, native land, origin, political home, race, society; CONCEPTS 380,510

native [adj1] *innate, inherent* built-in, congenital, connate, connatural, constitutional, endemic, essential, fundamental, genuine, hereditary, implanted, inborn, inbred, indigenous, ingrained, inherited, instinctive, intrinsic, inveterate, inwrought, natal, natural, original, real, unacquired, wild; CONCEPTS 404,549 —*Ant.* alien, foreign, outside

native [adj2] *domestic, home* aboriginal, autochthonous, belonging, endemic, from, home-grown, homemade, indigenous, inland, internal, local, municipal, national, original, primary, primeval, primitive, regional, related, vernacular; CONCEPT 536 —*Ant.* foreign, outside

native [n] *person born in the country in which he/she dwells* aboriginal, aborigine, ancient, autochthon, citizen, dweller, home towner, indigene, inhabitant, local, national; CONCEPT 413 —*Ant.* alien, foreigner, immigrant, stranger

native land [n] *homeland* fatherland, God's country, home, mother country, motherland, native soil, the old country*; CONCEPTS 510,515

natty [adj] *dapper* chic, chichi, classy, clean, dainty, dashing, dressed to kill*, dressed to the nines*, elegant, fashionable, neat, prim, sharp, slick, smart, snazzy*, spiffy*, spruce, spruced up, stylish, swanky, trim, well-groomed; CONCEPT 579

natural [adj1] *normal, everyday* accustomed, anticipated, characteristic, common, commonplace, congenital, connatural, consistent, constant, counted on, customary, essential, familiar, general, habitual, inborn, indigenous, ingenerate, inherent, innate, instinctive, intuitive, involuntary, legitimate, logical, looked for, matter-of-course, natal, native, ordinary, prevailing, prevalent, probable, reasonable, regular, relied on, spontaneous, typic, typical, unacquired, uncontrolled, uniform, universal, usual; CONCEPTS 530,547 —*Ant.* abnormal, different, uncommon, unnatural

natural [adj2] *open, unaffected* artless, being oneself, candid, childlike, credulous, direct, easy, folksy, forthright, frank, genuine, homey*, ignorant, impulsive, inartificial, ingenuous, innocent, instinctive, laid-back*, naive, plain, primitive, provincial, real, rustic, simple, simple-hearted, sincere, spontaneous, straightforward, trusting, unassumed, uncontrived, undesigning, unembarrassed, unfeigned, unforced, unlabored, unpolished, unpretentious, unschooled, unsophisticated, unstudied, unworldly, up-front*; CONCEPTS 267,401,404 —*Ant.* affected, artificial, pretended, unnatural

natural [adj3] *organic, unrefined* agrarian, agrestal, crude, native, plain, pure, raw, unbleached, uncultivated, undomesticated, unmixed, unpolished, unprocessed, whole, wild; CONCEPTS 462,485 —*Ant.* artificial, fixed, modified, refined, unnatural

naturalist [n] *wildlife expert* biologist, botanist, conservationist, ecologist, environmentalist, life scientist, natural historian, preservationist, zoologist; CONCEPT 349

naturally [adv] *as anticipated* artlessly, but of course*, by birth, by nature, candidly, casually, characteristically, commonly, consistently, customarily, easily, freely, generally, genuinely, habitually, impulsively, informally, innocently, instinctively, normally, openly, ordinarily, readily, simply, spontaneously, typically, unaffectedly, uniformly, unpretentiously, usually; CONCEPT 544 —*Ant.* affectedly, unnaturally

natural selection [n] *Darwinism* Darwinian theory, evolution, evolutionism, social Darwinism, survival of the fittest; CONCEPT 704

nature [n1] *character, disposition* attributes, being, bottom line*, complexion, constitution, description, drift, essence, essentiality, features, heart*, humor, individualism, individuality, like, makeup, meat*, mood, name of game*, name of tune*, nature of beast*, outlook, personality, point, quality, score, stuff, temper, temperament, texture, traits, type; CONCEPTS 411,682

nature [n2] *type, kind* anatomy, brand, cast, category, character, color, conformation, description, figure, framework, ilk, shape, sort, species, stripe*, structure, style, variety, way; CONCEPT 378

nature [n3] *earth, creation* cosmos, country, countryside, environment, forest, generation, landscape, macrocosm, megacosm, natural history, outdoors, scenery, seascape, setting, universe, view, world; CONCEPTS 407,429,509,511

naughty [adj1] *bad, misbehaved* annoying, badly behaved*, contrary, disobedient, disorderly, evil, exasperating, fiendish, fractious, froward, headstrong, impish, indecorous, insubordinate, intractable, mischievous, obstreperous, perverse, playful, rascally, raunchy, recalcitrant, refractory, rough, rowdy, sinful, teasing, tough, ungovernable, unmanageable, unruly, wanton, wayward, wicked, willful, worthless, wrong; CONCEPT 401 —*Ant.* behaved, controlled, good, obedient

naughty [adj2] *obscene, vulgar* adult, bawdy, blue*, dirty*, hot*, improper, lascivious, lewd, loose*, off-color*, pornographic, purple*, ribald, risqué, steamy*; CONCEPTS 372,545 —*Ant.* clean, good, moral, pure

nausea [n] *sickness in stomach; revulsion* abhorrence, aversion, biliousness, disgust, hatred, loathing, offense, qualm, qualms, queasiness, regurgitation, rejection, repugnance, retching, squeamishness, vomiting; CONCEPTS 316,410

nauseate [v] *make sick; disgust* bother, disturb, horrify, offend, reluct, repel, repulse, revolt, sicken; CONCEPTS 14,308 —*Ant.* please, soothe

nauseating [adj] *nauseous* abhorrent, detestable, disgusting, distasteful, fulsome, loathsome, offensive, repugnant, repulsive, revolting, sickening; CONCEPTS 314,529

nauseous [adj] *disgusting* abhorrent, brackish, detestable, distasteful, ill, loathsome, nauseated, nauseating, offensive, queasy, repugnant, repulsive, revolting, rocky*, seasick, sick, sick as dog*, sickening, squeamish; CONCEPTS 314,529 —*Ant.* nice, pleasing, soothing

nautical/naval [adj] *concerning ships, sea* abyssal, aquatic, boating, cruising, deep-sea, marine, maritime, navigating, navigational, oceangoing, oceanic, oceanographic, pelagic, rowing, sailing, sailorly, salty, seafaring, seagoing, sea-loving, thalassic, yachting; CONCEPT 536

navigate [v] *guide along route, often over water* captain*, cross, cruise, direct, drive, handle, head out for*, helm, journey, lay the course*, maneuver, operate, pilot, plan, plot, ride out, sail, skipper*, steer, voyage; CONCEPTS 148,187,224 —Ant. get lost

navigation [n] *traveling, guiding along route, often over water* aeronautics, boating, cruising, exploration, flying, helmsmanship, nautics, navigating, ocean travel, pilotage, piloting, plotting a course, sailing, seafaring, seamanship, shipping, steerage, steering, voyage, voyaging, yachting; CONCEPTS 155,187,224

navigator [n] *course plotter* helmsman, pilot, steersman, wheelman; CONCEPT 348

navy [n] *fleet* argosy, armada, flotilla, marine defense, merchant marine, naval force, sea force, sea power, vessels, warships; CONCEPTS 322,432,506

naysayer [n] *pessimist* complainer, cynic, defeatist, downer, gloomy, killjoy*, misanthrope, party pooper*, prophet of doom*, sourpuss*, wet blanket*; CONCEPTS 412,423

near [adj1] *close by physically* abreast, abutting, adjacent, adjoining, alongside, along toward, approximal, around, at close quarters, available, beside, bordering, burning, close, close-at-hand, close-by, close shave*, conterminous, contiguous, convenient, hair's breadth*, handy, immediate, in close proximity*; near-at-hand*, nearby, neighboring, next door*, nigh*, not remote, practically, proximal, proximate, ready, side-by-side, touching, vincinal, warm*, within stone's throw*; CONCEPTS 586,778 —Ant. away, distant, far, remote

near [adj2] *close in time; forthcoming* approaching, approximate, at hand, coming, comparative, expected, imminent, impending, in the offing*, looming, near-at-hand*, next, relative; CONCEPTS 812,820 —Ant. deferred, distant, expired, far, postponed, remote

near [adj3] *familiar* affecting, akin*, allied, attached, close, connected, dear, friendly, intimate, related, touching; CONCEPT 555 —Ant. far, gone, past, unfamiliar

nearby [adj] *adjoining* adjacent, close, close-at-hand, close-by, contiguous, convenient, handy, immediate, neighboring, proximate, ready; CONCEPTS 586,778 —Ant. far, faraway

nearby [adv] *within reach* about, at close quarters, close, close at hand, hard, near, near-at-hand*, nigh*, not far away; CONCEPTS 586,778 —Ant. far, faraway

nearing [adj] *approaching* advancing, approximating, coming, forthcoming, imminent, impending, oncoming, threatening, upcoming; CONCEPTS 548,820 —Ant. departing, gone, leaving, past

nearly [adv] *almost* about, all but*, approaching, approximately, as good as*, circa*, close but no cigar*, closely, give or take a little*, in effect, in essence, in substance, in the

ballpark*, in the neighborhood*, just about, more or less, most, much, nearabout, not quite, practically, pretty near, roughly, round, roundly, some, somewhere, upwards of*, virtually, well-nigh*, within a little*; CONCEPT 566

near miss [n] *close call* close shave, narrow escape, near hit; CONCEPT 747

nearsighted [adj] *myopic* blind as a bat*, purblind, shortsighted; CONCEPT 619

neat [adj1] *arranged well, uncluttered* accurate, apple-pie order*, chic*, correct, dainty, dapper, elegant, exact, fastidious, finical, finicky, immaculate, in good order, in good shape, methodical, natty, neat as a pin*, nice, orderly, precise, prim, proper, regular, shipshape*, sleek, slick, smart, spick-and-span*, spotless, spruce, systematic, tidy, trim, well-groomed, well-kept; CONCEPTS 485,539,621 —Ant. disorderly, messed up, sloppy, slovenly, unkempt

neat [adj2] *clever, practiced* able, adept, adroit, agile, apt, artful, deft, dexterous, efficient, effortless, elegant, expert, finished, graceful, handy, nimble, precise, proficient, quick, ready, skillful, speedy, stylish, well-judged; CONCEPTS 527,542 —Ant. disorganized, unpracticed

neaten [v] *tidy* arrange, clean, clear the decks*, fix up, groom, order, put in good shape, put in order, shape up, spruce up*, straighten up, whip into shape*; CONCEPT 250

neatly [adv] *tidily* accurately, adeptly, adroitly, aptly, cleanly, efficiently, expertly, fastidiously, handily, methodically, nicely, orderly, precisely, skillfully, sprucely; CONCEPTS 326,485,585,589

nebulous [adj] *confused, obscure* ambiguous, amorphous, cloudy, dark, dim, hazy, imprecise, indefinite, indeterminate, indistinct, misty, murky, shadowy, shapeless, uncertain, unclear, unformed, vague; CONCEPTS 535,617 —Ant. apparent, definite, obvious, plain

necessarily [adv] *inevitably, certainly* accordingly, as a matter of course*, automatically, axiomatically, beyond one's control*, by definition, by its own nature*, cardinally, come what may*, compulsorily, consequently, exigently, from within*, fundamentally, incontrovertibly, indubitably, ineluctably, inescapably, inexorably, irresistibly, naturally, no doubt, of course, of necessity, perforce, positively, pressingly, significantly, undoubtedly, unpreventably, unquestionably, vitally, willy-nilly*, without fail*; CONCEPTS 535,544 —Ant. unnecessarily

necessary [adj1] *essential* all-important, basic, binding, bottom-line*, cardinal, chief, compelling, compulsory, crucial, decisive, de rigueur*, elementary, exigent, expedient, fundamental, imperative, incumbent on, indispensable, mandatory, momentous, name of game*, needed, needful, obligatory, paramount, prerequisite, pressing, prime, principal, quintessential, required, requisite, significant, specified, unavoidable, urgent, vital, wanted; CONCEPTS 546,568 —Ant. inessential, unimportant, unnecessary, useless

necessary [adj2] *inevitable* assured, certain, fated, imminent, ineluctable, ineludible, inerrant, inescapable, inevasible, inexorable, infallible, returnless, unavoidable, undeniable, unescapable; CONCEPTS 535,548 —Ant. contingent, needless, optional, voluntary

necessitate [v] *call for, make necessary* ask, behoove, cause, coerce, command, compel, constrain, crave, demand, drive, entail, force, impel, make, oblige, postulate, require, take; CONCEPTS 53,242,646

necessity [n] *need, essentiality* call, cause, claim, compulsion, demand, desideratum, duress, essence, essential, exaction, exigency, fundamental, godsend*, imperative, indispensability, inevitability, inexorableness, life or death*, must, necessary, needfulness, no alternative, no choice, obligation, pinch, precondition, prerequisite, privation, requirement, requisite, sine qua non, stress, undeniability, urgency, vital part, vitals, want; CONCEPTS 646,709 —*Ant.* desire, want

necking [n] *kissing* canoodling, caressing, cuddling, embracing, fondling, lovemaking, making love*, making out*, parking*, petting, smooching, sucking face*; CONCEPTS 185,375

necklace [n] *chain* beads, carcanet, choker, jewelry, lavalliere, locket, pearls, pendant, riviere, strand, string; CONCEPT 446

necromancy [n] *sorcery* abracadabra*, alchemy, bewitchment, black art, black magic, charm, conjuring, devilry, divination, enchantment, evil eye, hocus-pocus*, incantation, jinx, magic, mumbo jumbo*, mysticism, occultism, spell, thaumaturgy, voodoo, witchcraft, witchery, witching, wizardry; CONCEPTS 370,689

necropolis [n] *cemetery* boot hill*, catacomb, charnel, charnel house, churchyard, city of the dead*, crypt, funerary grounds, God's acre*, graveyard, potter's field, sepulcher, tomb, vault; CONCEPTS 305,368

need [n1] *want, requirement* charge, commitment, committal, compulsion, demand, desideratum, devoir, duty, essential, exigency, extremity, longing, must, obligation, occasion, ought, requisite, right, the urge, urgency, use, weakness, wish; CONCEPTS 20,709 —*Ant.* have

need [n2] *poverty* deprivation, destitution, distress, extremity, impecuniousness, impoverishment, inadequacy, indigence, insufficiency, lack, neediness, paucity, pennilessness, penury, poorness, privation, shortage, want; CONCEPTS 335,709 —*Ant.* luxury, riches, wealth

need [n3] *emergency; pressing lack* deficiency, exigency, inadequacy, insufficiency, necessity, obligation, shortage, urgency, want; CONCEPTS 646,709 —*Ant.* comfort, fortune, have, plenty

need [v] *want something* be deficient, be deprived, be down and out*, be hard up*, be inadequate, be in need of, be in want, be needy, be poor, be short, be without, call for, claim, covet, crave, demand, desire, die for*, do without, drive for*, exact, feel a dearth of*, feel the necessity for, feel the pinch*, go hungry*, hanker, have occasion for, have occasion to, have use for*, hunger, hurt for, lack, long, lust, miss, necessitate, pine, require, suffer privation, thirst, wish, yearn, yen for; CONCEPTS 20,646 —*Ant.* do not want, have

needle [v] *tease, annoy* aggravate, badger, bait, bedevil, bother, examine, gnaw, goad, harass, hector, irk, irritate, nag, nettle, pester, plague, prick, prod, provoke, question, quiz, ride*, rile, ruffle, spur, sting, taunt, tweak*, worry; CONCEPTS 7,19,54 —*Ant.* praise

needless [adj] *unnecessary, groundless* causeless, dispensable, excessive, expendable, gratuitous, inessential, nonessential, pointless, redundant, superfluous, uncalled-for, undesired, unrequired, unwanted, useless; CONCEPTS 546,575 —*Ant.* affluent, necessary, needed

needlework [n] *needlepoint* crocheting, darning, embroidery, knitting, lace, quilting, sewing, stitchery, stitching, tatting; CONCEPT 128

needy [adj] *deprived, impoverished* beggared, dead broke*, destitute, dirt poor*, disadvantaged, down-and-out*, down at heel*, down to last cent*, flat*, impecunious, indigent, necessitous, penniless, penurious, poor, poverty-stricken, underprivileged, unprosperous; CONCEPT 334 —*Ant.* affluent, rich, wealthy

ne' er-do-well [n] *irresponsible person* bum*, good-for-nothing, idler, lazybones*, loafer, sloucher, wastrel; CONCEPT 412

nefarious [adj] *bad, sinful* abominable, atrocious, base, corrupt, criminal, degenerate, depraved, detestable, dreadful, evil, execrable, flagitious, flagrant, foul, glaring, gross, heinous, horrible, infamous, infernal, iniquitous, miscreant, monstrous, odious, opprobrious, outrageous, perverse, putrid, rank, rotten, shameful, treacherous, vicious, vile, villainous, wicked; CONCEPTS 401,545,548 —*Ant.* good, honorable, respectable, virtuous, worthy

negate [v] *contradict, countermand* abate, abolish, abrogate, annihilate, annul, belie, blackball*, break with*, cancel, cancel out, controvert, countercheck, cross*, deny, ding*, disaffirm, disallow, disprove, dump*, fly in the face of*, frustrate, gainsay, impugn, invalidate, kill, negative, neutralize, nullify, oppose, put down, quash*, rebut, redress, refute, repeal, rescind, retract, reverse, revoke, stonewall*, traverse, turn down, turn thumbs down*, undo, vitiate, void; CONCEPTS 46,50,88,121 —*Ant.* allow, approve, permit

negation [n] *contradiction, denial* antithesis, antonym, blank, cancellation, contrary, converse, counterpart, disavowal, disclaimer, forget it*, gainsaying, inverse, negatory, neutralization, no, nonexistence, nothingness, nullification, nullity, opposite, opposition, proscription, refusal, rejection, renunciation, repudiation, reverse, vacuity, veto, void; CONCEPTS 121,278 ,685 —*Ant.* allowance, approval, permission

negative [adj] *bad, contradictory* abrogating, adverse, against, annulling, antagonistic, anti, balky, colorless, con, contrary, contravening, counteractive, cynical, denying, detrimental, disallowing, disavowing, dissentient, dissenting, gainsaying, gloomy, impugning, invalidating, jaundiced, naysaying, neutralizing, nugatory, nullifying, opposing, pessimistic, privative, recusant, refusing, rejecting, removed, repugnant, resisting, resistive, unaffirmative, unenthusiastic, unfavorable, uninterested, unwilling, weak; CONCEPTS 267,403,570 —*Ant.* good, positive

negative [n] *contradiction* denial, disavowal, nay, refusal, refutation; CONCEPT 278 —*Ant.* positive

negative attitude [n] *pessimism* chip on one's shoulder*, cynicism, dim view*, expectation of the worst, gloomy outlook, hopelessness, lack of confidence, low spirits, negativism; CONCEPTS *410,689*

neglect [*n1*] *disregard* carelessness, coolness, delinquency, disdain, disregardance, disrespect, heedlessness, inadvertence, inattention, inconsideration, indifference, laxity, laxness, oversight, scorn, slight, thoughtlessness, unconcern; CONCEPTS *410,657* —*Ant.* care, obedience, observance, regard, respect, watchfulness

neglect [*n2*] *failure, default* carelessness, chaos, delay, delinquency, dereliction, dilapidation, forgetfulness, lapse, laxity, laxness, limbo, neglectfulness, negligence, omission, oversight, pretermission, remissness, slackness, slovenliness; CONCEPTS *674,699* —*Ant.* accomplishment, achievement, completion, finish, success

neglect [*v1*] *be indifferent, leave alone* affront, brush aside, brush off, condemn, depreciate, despise, detest, discount, disdain, dismiss, disregard, have nothing to do with*, ignore, keep at arm's length*, keep one's distance*, laugh off*, let go*, live with*, make light of*, not care for*, overlook, pass by, pass over, pass up, pay no attention to, pay no mind*, pretermit, rebuff, reject, scant, scorn, shrug off*, slight, slur, spurn, tune out*, underestimate; CONCEPTS *30,681* —*Ant.* cherish, concern, guard, nurture, protect, take care of, watch

neglect [*v2*] *fail to do; forget* be careless, be derelict, be irresponsible, be negligent, be remiss, bypass, defer, discard, dismiss, disregard, elide, evade, gloss over*, let pass*, let slide*, look the other way*, lose sight of*, miss, not trouble oneself*, omit, overleap, overlook, overpass, pass over, postpone, procrastinate, shirk, skimp, skip, suspend, think little of*, trifle; CONCEPTS *101,699* —*Ant.* accomplish, achieve, complete, do, finish, succeed

neglectful [*adj*] *careless, failing* behindhand, delinquent, derelict, disregardful, heedless, inattentive, indifferent, lax, lazy, negligent, regardless, remiss, slack, thoughtless, uncaring, unmindful; CONCEPTS *401,542* —*Ant.* attentive, careful, caring, mindful, successful

negligee [*n*] *nightgown* camisole, dishabille, nightdress, nightie, peignoir, robe, teddy, wrap, wrapper; CONCEPT *451*

negligence [*n*] *carelessness* disregard, failure, forgetfulness, heedlessness, inattention, inattentiveness, laxity, laxness, neglect, neglectfulness, oversight, thoughtlessness, unpreparedness; CONCEPTS *30,633*

negligent [*adj*] *careless, indifferent* asleep at switch*, behindhand, cursory, delinquent, derelict, discinct, disregardful, forgetful, heedless, inadvertent, inattentive, inconsiderate, incurious, lax, neglectful, nonchalant, offhand, regardless, remiss, slack, slapdash*, slipshod*, sloppy*, slovenly, thoughtless, unconcerned, unheedful, unmindful, unthinking; CONCEPTS *401,542* —*Ant.* attentive, careful, caring, mindful, successful

negligible [*adj*] *insignificant* imperceptible, inconsequential, minor, minute, off*, outside, petty, remote, slender, slight, slim, small, trifling, trivial, unimportant; CONCEPTS *552,575, 789* —*Ant.* important, major, significant

negotiate [*v1*] *bargain, discuss* accommodate, adjudicate, adjust, agree, arbitrate, arrange,

bring to terms*, bury the hatchet*, come across with*, compose, concert, conciliate, confer, connect, consult, contract, covenant, cut a deal*, deal, debate, dicker*, haggle, hammer out a deal*, handle, horse trade*, intercede, make a deal, make peace*, make terms*, manage, mediate, moderate, network, parley*, referee, settle, step in*, stipulate, swap, transact, treat, umpire*, work out*, work out a deal; CONCEPTS *8,56,68*

negotiate [*v2*] *traverse, cross* clear, get around, get over, get past, hurdle, leap over, overleap, pass, pass through, surmount, vault; CONCEPTS *149,224* —*Ant.* remain, stay

negotiation [*n*] *bargaining* agreement, arbitration, colloquy, compromise, conference, consultation, debate, diplomacy, discussion, intervention, mediation, meeting, transaction; CONCEPTS *56,68,684*

negotiator [*n*] *person who bargains, controls discussion* adjudicator, ambassador, arbitrator, broker, delegate, diplomat, fixer*, go-between*, interagent, intermediary, intermedium, judge, mediator, middleperson, moderator; CONCEPTS *348,354,423*

neighbor [*n*] *person who lives close by* acquaintance, bystander, friend, homebody*, nearby resident, next-door neighbor; CONCEPT *423*

neighbor [*v*] *be next to* abut, adjoin, be adjacent, be contiguous, be near, be nearby, border, butt against, communicate, connect, join, line, march, surround, touch, verge; CONCEPT *759*

neighborhood [*n*] *community, surroundings* adjacency, area, block, closeness, confines, contiguity, district, environs, ghetto, hood, jungle*, locale, locality, nearness, neck of the woods*, parish, part, precinct, propinquity, proximity, purlieus, quarter, region, section, slum, stomping ground*, street, suburb, territory, tract, turf, vicinage, vicinity, ward, zone, zoo*; CONCEPTS *198,379,516*

neighborly [*adj*] *friendly* amiable, civil, companionable, considerate, cooperative, cordial, genial, gracious, gregarious, harmonious, helpful, hospitable, kind, obliging, sociable, social, well-disposed; CONCEPT *401* —*Ant.* cold, distant, unfriendly, unneighborly, unsociable

neither here nor there [*adj*] *irrelevant* beside the point, extraneous, immaterial, impertinent, inconsequential, not connected with, not germane, not pertaining to, off the point, off the topic, pointless, trivial, unconnected, unimportant; CONCEPTS *560,575*

nemesis [*n*] *bane* adversary, affliction, bête noire, curse, infliction, opponent, plague, rival, ruination, scourge, torment; CONCEPTS *529,674*

neologism [*n*] *new word* buzz word*, coinage, neology, new phrase, slang, synthetic word*, vogue word*; CONCEPT *275* —*Ant.* time-worn

neophyte [*n*] *beginner* abecedarian, amateur, apprentice, colt*, fledgling, freshman, greenhorn, new boy/girl, newcomer, new kid on the block*, novice, recruit, rookie*, tenderfoot*, trainee, tyro*; CONCEPTS *423,424*

nepotism [*n*] *favoritism* bias, discrimination, inequity, one-sidedness, partiality, partisanship, preference, preferential treatment; CONCEPTS *41,388,645*

ne
ne

nerd [n] *geek* dolt, dork*, dweeb*, fool, goober*, goofball*, jerk*, oaf, techie*, trekkie*, weirdo; CONCEPTS 564,570

nerve [n] *daring, boldness* assumption, assurance, audacity, backbone, brass*, bravery, brazenness, cheek*, chutzpah*, confidence, coolness, courage, crust*, determination, effrontery, endurance, energy, face*, fearlessness, firmness, force, fortitude, gall*, gameness, grit*, guts*, hardihood, hardiness, heart*, impertinence, impudence, insolence, intestinal fortitude, intrepidity, mettle, might, moxie*, pluck*, presumption, resolution, sauce*, spirit, spunk*, starch*, steadfastness, stomach*, temerity, vigor, will; CONCEPTS 411 —*Ant.* fear, modesty, shyness, timidity

nerve [v] *strengthen, hearten* animate, brace, cheer, embolden, encourage, enhearten, fortify, inspirit, invigorate, steel; CONCEPTS 7,14,22 —*Ant.* discourage, dishearten, fear, weaken

nerve center [n] *control center* command post, core, focal point, focus, headquarters, heart, HQ, hub; CONCEPTS 532,826,829

nerveless [adj] *calm, cool* collected, composed, controlled, imperturbable, intrepid, patient, self-possessed, tranquil, unemotional; CONCEPT 542 —*Ant.* disconcerted, nervous

nerveless [adj2] *scared to death* awkwardly, debilitated, enervated, fearful, feeble, nervous, petrified, spineless*, timid, weak, yellow-bellied*; CONCEPTS 401,403 —*Ant.* brave, courageous, nervy, unafraid

nerve-racking [adj] *distressing* aggravating, annoying, disquieting, disturbing, exasperating, irksome, irritating, maddening, stressful, taxing, tense, trying, upsetting; CONCEPTS 548,565

nerves [n] *extreme anxiety* fretfulness, hysteria, imbalance, irritation, nervousness, neurasthenia, sleeplessness, strain, stress, tenseness, tension; CONCEPT 410 —*Ant.* calm, coolness

nervous [adj] *anxious, fearful* afraid, agitated, annoyed, apprehensive, basket case*, bothered, concerned, distressed, disturbed, edgy, excitable, fidgety, fitful, flustered, fussy*, hesitant, high-strung*, hysterical, irritable, jittery*, jumpy*, nervy*, neurotic, on edge*, overwrought, querulous, restive, ruffled, sensitive, shaky*, shrinking, shy, skittish, snappish, solicitous, spooked*, taut, tense, timid, timorous, troubled, twitchy*, uneasy, unrestful, unstrung*, upset, uptight, volatile, weak, wired*, worried; CONCEPTS 403,542 —*Ant.* brave, calm, unafraid, unnervous, unworried

nervous breakdown [n] *mental collapse* burnout*, crackup*, depression, emotional collapse, nervous exhaustion, nervous prostration, shattered nerves; CONCEPT 410

nervousness [n] *anxious state* agitation, all-overs*, anger, animation, butterflies*, cold sweat*, creeps*, delirium, discomfiture, disquiet, disquietude, dithers*, excitability, feverishness, fidgets*, flap*, fluster*, fuss*, impatience, jitters*, jumps*, moodiness, neurasthenia, neuroticism, perturbation, quivers, sensitivity, shakes, stage fright, stimulation, stress, tension, timidity, tizzy*, to-do*, touchiness, trembles*, tremulousness, turbulence, uneasiness, willies*, worry; CONCEPTS 410,657 —*Ant.* calm, calmness, collectedness

nervy [adj] *bold, pushy* cheeky*, crass, crude, forward, fresh*, impudent, inconsiderate, pert, plucky*, rude, sassy*, smart, smart-alecky*, wise; CONCEPT 401 —*Ant.* afraid, modest, shy, timid, unwilling

nest [n] *home* aerie, breeding ground, burrow, den, haunt, hideaway, lair, refuge, roost; CONCEPTS 198,515

nest egg [n] *savings* backup, cache, funds, investment, life savings, mad money*, means, money in the bank, piggy bank, provisions, rainy day fund*, reserves, resources, savings account, stash*, stockpile; CONCEPTS 335,340,446,710

nestle [v] *curl up* bundle, burrow, cuddle, huddle, lie against, lie close, make snug*, move close, nuzzle, settle down, snug*, snuggle, take shelter; CONCEPTS 154,612

net [adj] *profiting* after deductions, after taxes, clear, excluding, exclusive, final, irreducible, pure, remaining, take-home, undeductible; CONCEPT 334 —*Ant.* unprofitable

net [n] *mesh, web* cloth, fabric, lace, lacework, lattice, netting, network, openwork, reticulum, screen, tracery; CONCEPTS 473,770

net [v1] *capture* bag*, catch, enmesh, ensnare, entangle, hook*, lasso*, nab*, trap; CONCEPT 90 —*Ant.* free, let go, release

net [v2] *gain after expenses* accumulate, bring in, clean up, clear, earn, make, profit, realize, reap; CONCEPT 330 —*Ant.* gross

nettle [v] *provoke, upset* annoy, chafe, disgust, disturb, exasperate, fret, get*, goad, harass, huff, incense, insult, irritate, miff, peeve*, pester, pet, pique, put out*, rile, roil, ruffle, snit*, stew*, sting*, tease, tiff*, vex; CONCEPTS 7,14,19 —*Ant.* appease, mollify, please

nettlesome [adj] *irritating* aggravating, annoying, bothersome, burdensome, distressing, disturbing, exasperating, irksome, nagging, troublesome, trying, vexatious, vexing; CONCEPTS 529,537

network [n] *system of connections* arrangement, artery, chain, checkerboard*, circuitry, complex, convolution, crisscross*, fabric, fiber, grid, grill*, grillwork, hookup, interconnections, jungle, labyrinth, maze, mesh, net, netting, nexus, organization, patchwork*, plexus, reticulation, reticule, screening, structure, system, tessellation, tracks, wattle, weave, web, wiring; CONCEPTS 381,388,770

network [v] *to socialize for professional or personal gain* associate, circulate, hobnob, make contacts, meet, meet and greet*, mingle, rub elbows*, schmooze*; CONCEPT 384

neurosis [n] *mental disturbance, disorder* aberration, abnormality, affliction, breakdown, compulsion, crack-up*, derangement, deviation, hysteria, inhibition, insanity, instability, madness, maladjustment, mental illness, neurasthenia, obsession, personality disorder, phobia, psychological disorder, psychopathy; CONCEPTS 316,410 —*Ant.* adjustment, balance, sanity

neurotic [adj] *mentally maladjusted* aberrant, abnormal, anxious, basket case*, bundle of nerves*, choked*, clutched*, compulsive, deviant, disordered, disoriented, distraught, disturbed, erratic, hung up*, hysteric, inhibited, manic, nervous, nervous wreck*, obsessive, overwrought, psychoneurotic, unhealthy, unstable, upset, uptight, wired*; CONCEPTS 314,403 —Ant. adjusted, balanced, sane, stable

neuter [v] *remove sex organs* alter, castrate, change, desexualize, doctor, dress, fix, geld, make barren, make impotent, make infertile, make sexless, mutilate, spay, sterilize, unsex; CONCEPTS 157,250

neutral [adj1] *impartial, noncommittal* aloof, bystanding, calm, clinical, collected, cool, detached, disengaged, disinterested, dispassionate, easy, evenhanded, fair-minded, impersonal, inactive, indifferent, inert, middle-of-road*, nonaligned, nonbelligerent, nonchalant, non-combatant, nonparticipating, nonpartisan, on sidelines*, on the fence*, pacifistic, poker-faced*, relaxed, unaligned, unbiased, uncommitted, unconcerned, undecided, uninvolved, unprejudiced; CONCEPTS 403,542 —Ant. biased, committal, partial, predisposed, prejudiced

neutral [adj2] *flat, dull to senses* abstract, achromatic, colorless, drab, expressionless, indeterminate, indistinct, indistinguishable, intermediate, toneless, undefined, vague, vanilla; CONCEPTS 485,537,618 —Ant. bright, loud, strong

neutralize [v] *counteract* abrogate, annul, balance, cancel, compensate for, conquer, counterbalance, countercheck, counterpoise, countervail, defeat, frustrate, invalidate, negate, negative, nullify, offset, overcome, override, overrule, redress, subdue, undo; CONCEPTS 121,232

never [adv] *not at any time* at no time, don't hold your breath*, forget it, nevermore, not at all, not ever, not in any way, not in the least, not on your life*, not under any condition, no way*; CONCEPT 799 —Ant. always, forever

never-ending [adj] *continual, unceasing* amaranthine, boundless, ceaseless, constant, continuous, endless, eternal, everlasting, immortal, incessant, interminable, nonstop, perpetual, persistent, relentless, timeless, unbroken, unchanging, uninterrupted, unremitting; CONCEPTS 482,798 —Ant. ceasing, ending, halting, intermittent, interrupted

nevertheless [adv] *however* after all, although, but, even so, even though, howbeit, nonetheless, not the less, notwithstanding, regardless, still, still and all, though, withal, yet; CONCEPT 544

new [adj1] *recent, fresh* advanced, au courant, brand-new, contemporary, current, cutting-edge*, dewy, different, dissimilar, distinct, fashionable, inexperienced, just out*, late, latest, modern, modernistic, modish*, neoteric, newfangled*, novel, now*, original, recent, spick-and-span*, state-of-the-art, strange, topical, ultramodern, unaccustomed, uncontaminated, unfamiliar, unique, unknown, unlike, unseasoned, unskilled, unspoiled, untouched, untrained, untried, untrodden, unused, unusual, up-to-date, virgin, youthful; CONCEPTS 564,578, 797 —Ant. deteriorated, old, old-fashioned, outdated, worn

new [adj2] *additional* added, another, else, extra, farther, fresh, further, increased, more, other, supplementary; CONCEPTS 771,824 —Ant. common, existent, existing, usual

new [adj3] *modernized, restored* altered, changed, improved, redesigned, refreshed, regenerated, renewed, revived; CONCEPT 589 —Ant. old, old-fashioned, outdated, out-of-date, unstylish

new [adv] *recently* afresh, anew, freshly, lately, newly, of late; CONCEPT 820 —Ant. old, past

new age [adj] *of a broad-ranging consciousness-raising movement* Age of Aquarius*, alternative, astrological, balanced, crystal healing, holistic, mystic, occult, planetary, spiritual, supernaturalist; CONCEPTS 403,529

newborn [n] *infant* babe, baby, bairn, bambino, bantling, bundle, child, kid, little one, neonate, nursling, small child, suckling, tot; CONCEPTS 414,424

newcomer [n] *person who has just arrived in area* alien, arrival, beginner, blow-in*, colt*, foreigner, greenhorn*, immigrant, incomer, Johnny-come-lately*, late arrival, latecomer, maverick, neophyte, new kid on the block*, novice, novitiate, outsider, rookie, settler, stranger, tenderfoot*; CONCEPTS 413,423 —Ant. native, old hack

newfangled [adj] *quite recent* contemporary, fashionable, fresh, gimmicky*, in vogue, modern, modernistic, neoteric, new, new-fashioned, novel, popular, unique; CONCEPTS 578,589,797 —Ant. old, old-fashioned, old hack, outmoded

newly [adv] *recently* anew, freshly, just, lately, latterly, of late; CONCEPT 820 —Ant. past

news [n] *information, revelation* account, advice, announcement, broadcast, bulletin, cable, cognizance, communication, communiqué, copy, data, description, disclosure, discovery, dispatch, enlightenment, exposé, eye-opener*, front-page news*, headlines, hearsay, intelligence, itemization, knowledge, leak, lowdown, message, narration, news flash, particularization, recital, recognition, release, report, rumor, scandal, scoop*, specification, statement, story, telecast, telegram, telling, the goods*, tidings*, word*; CONCEPTS 268,274,293 —Ant. history

newscaster [n] *broadcaster* anchor, anchor man/woman, anchor person, announcer, commentator, news anchor, news commentator, reporter; CONCEPTS 348,356

newsletter [n] *special interest publication* bulletin, journal, magazine, pamphlet, report; CONCEPTS 279,280

newsman/newswoman [n] *reporter* anchor, anchor man/woman, anchor person, announcer, columnist, copy editor, correspondent, cub*, editor, foreign correspondent, ink slinger*, interviewer, investigative reporter, journalist, legman/woman*, newscaster, newshound, newspaperman/woman, newswriter, pressman/woman, stringer, war correspondent, writer; CONCEPTS 348,356

newspaper [n] *regular, continuous publication containing information* biweekly, bulldog*, community, daily, extra, gazette, journal, magazine, metropolitan, organ, paper, periodical, press, rag*, record, review, scandal sheet*, sheet, tabloid, trade, weekly; CONCEPTS 279,280

newsworthy [adj] *important* consequential, critical, crucial, essential, far-reaching, front-page*, great, influential, material, meaningful, momentous, of note, of substance, paramount, relevant, serious, significant, urgent, vital; CONCEPT 567

next [*adj*] *coming immediately after in space, time, order* abutting, adjacent, adjoining, after, alongside, attached, back-to-back, beside, close, closest, coming, consequent, coterminous, ensuing, following, hard by*, later, meeting, nearest, neighboring, on the side, proximate, side-by-side, subsequent, succeeding, touching; CONCEPTS 585,586,799 —*Ant.* earlier, preceding, previous

next [*adv*] *immediately after in time, space, order* after, afterward, afterwhile, behind, by and by, closely, coming up, following, later, latterly, next off, subsequently, thereafter; CONCEPTS 585,586,799 —*Ant.* earlier, preceding, previous

nibble [*n*] *morsel, bite* crumb, peck, snack, soupçon, taste, tidbit; CONCEPTS 458,831 —*Ant.* mouthful

nibble [*v*] *bite, pick at* crop, eat, eat like a bird*, gnaw, munch, nip*, nosh on*, peck*, snack; CONCEPT 169 —*Ant.* gorge

nice [*adj*] *likable, agreeable* admirable, amiable, approved, attractive, becoming, charming, commendable, considerate, copacetic, cordial, courteous, decorous, delightful, ducky, fair, favorable, fine and dandy*, friendly, genial, gentle, good, gracious, helpful, ingratiating, inviting, kind, kindly, lovely, nifty*, obliging, okay*, peachy*, pleasant, pleasurable, polite, prepossessing, seemly, simpatico, superior, swell, unpresumptuous, welcome, well-mannered, winning, winsome; CONCEPTS 404,548, 572 —*Ant.* bad, disagreeable, horrible, nasty, repulsive, unlikable, unpleasant

nice [*adj2*] *precise, neat, refined* accurate, becoming, befitting, careful, choosy, conforming, correct, critical, cultured, dainty, decent, delicate, discerning, discriminating, distinguishing, exact, exacting, fastidious, fine, finespun, finical, finicking, finicky*, fussy*, genteel, hairsplitting*, meticulous, minute, particular, persnickety*, picky*, proper, respectable, right, rigorous, scrupulous, seemly, squeamish, strict, subtle, tidy, trim, trivial*, virtuous, well-bred; CONCEPTS 542,557,558 —*Ant.* disordered, imprecise, unmannerly, unrefined

nicety [*n*] *fine point* detail, exactness, fine distinction, meticulousness, nuance, precision, refinement, rigor, rigorousness, shade, subtlety; CONCEPT 638

niche [*n*] *place all one's own* alcove, byplace, calling, compartment, corner, cranny*, cubbyhole*, hole, hollow, indentation, nook, opening, pigeonhole*, position, recess, slot, vocation; CONCEPTS 440,513,630

nick [*n/v*] *chip, scratch* cut, damage, dent, dint, indent, jag, knock, mark, mill, notch, scar, score, slit; CONCEPTS 137,176,208

nickname [*n*] *informal title* appellation, byname, byword, denomination, diminutive, epithet, familiar name, handle*, label, moniker, pet name*, sobriquet, style, tag*; CONCEPTS 268,683

nifty [*adj*] *marvelous* chic, clever, cool*, dandy, enjoyable, excellent, groovy*, keen, neat, peachy*, pleasing, quick, sharp, smart, spruce, stylish, super, swell, terrific; CONCEPT 572 —*Ant.* bad, displeasing, unhandy, unpleasant

niggle [*v*] *nitpick* argue, carp, cavil, complain,

find fault, fuss, grouse, grumble, moan, nag, object; CONCEPT 46

night [*n*] *part of day after sundown and before sunrise* after dark, after hours*, bedtime, before dawn, black*, blackness, dark, dark hours, darkness, dead of night*, dim, duskiness, dusk to dawn, evening, eventide, gloom, midnight, nightfall, nighttide, nighttime, obscurity*, pitch dark, twilight, witching hour*; CONCEPTS 620, 801,806,810 —*Ant.* day

nightclub [*n*] *place for evening entertainment* bar, bistro, cabaret, café, casino, disco*, discotheque, dive*, hideaway*, honky-tonk*, joint*, nightery, night spot, nitery, restaurant, roadhouse, saloon, speakeasy*, spot, supper club, tavern, theatre, watering hole*; CONCEPTS 293,439,449

nightfall [*n*] *beginning of darkness* black*, crepuscule, dim, dusk, eve, eventide, sundown, sunset, twilight, vespers; CONCEPT 810 —*Ant.* daybreak

nightgown [*n*] *dress in which to sleep* bedgown, lingerie, negligee, nightdress, nightie*, nightrobe, nightshirt, pajamas, PJs*, sleeper*; CONCEPT 451

nightly [*adj/adv*] *each evening; after dark* at night, by night, every night, in the night, night after night, nights, nighttime, nocturnal, nocturnally; CONCEPTS 541,799,801 —*Ant.* daily

nightmare [*n*] *bad dream or experience* dream, fancy, fantasy, hallucination, horror, illusion, incubus, ordeal, phantasm, succubus, torment, trial, tribulation, vision; CONCEPTS 315,674 —*Ant.* daymare

nightmarish [*adj*] *frightening* alarming, awful, chilling, creepy, dire, direful, disquieting, dreadful, eerie, fearful, fearsome, ghastly, ghoulish, grim, grisly, hair-raising, hellish, horrible, horrid, horrifying, macabre, morbid, ominous, petrifying, scary, spooky, terrible, terrifying, traumatic, unnerving; CONCEPTS 529,537

night stick [*n*] *billy club* billy*, blackjack, cudgel, police officer's club, shillelagh; CONCEPTS 470,499

nihilism [*n*] *refusal to believe* abnegation, agnosticism, anarchy, atheism, denial, disbelief, disorder, lawlessness, mob rule*, nonbelief, rejection, renunciation, repudiation, skepticism, terrorism; CONCEPT 689 —*Ant.* belief, faith, obedience, optimism

nil [*adj*] *nonexistent* naught, nihil, nix*, none, nothing, nought, zero; CONCEPTS 539,762,771 —*Ant.* existent, existing

nimble [*adj*] *dexterous, smart* active, adept, adroit, agile, alert, bright, brisk, clever, deft, handy, light, lissome, lithe, lively, proficient, prompt, quick, quick-witted, ready, skillful, sprightly, spry, swift, vigilant, wide-awake; CONCEPTS 402,527,584 —*Ant.* awkward, clumsy, lumbering, slow, undexterous, unhandy

nip [*n*] *swallow, taste* bite, catch, dram, drop, finger, jolt, morsel, mouthful, nibble, pinch, portion, shot*, sip, slug*, snifter, soupçon, toothful; CONCEPTS 458,831 —*Ant.* mouthful

nip [*v*] *bite; take small part* catch, clip, compress, grip, munch, nab at*, nibble, pinch, sink teeth into*, snag, snap*, snip*, squeeze*, take a chunk out of*, tweak, twinge, twitch; CONCEPTS 142,169,190 —*Ant.* gorge

nip [v2] *stop, thwart* arrest, balk, blight, check, dash, end, frustrate; CONCEPTS *121,234* —*Ant.* allow, encourage, permit

nirvana [n] *enlightenment* awakening, bliss, cloud nine*, ecstasy, happiness, heaven, joy, paradise, peace, serenity, tranquillity; CONCEPT *409*

nitty-gritty [n] *heart of the matter* basics, bottom line*, chief part, chief thing, core, essential part, focus, fundamentals, gist, important matter, nuts and bolts*, root, the facts*; CONCEPTS *442,668,826*

nitwit [n] *idiot* blockhead, bonehead*, cretin, dimwit, dork, dumbbell, dummy, dunce, fool, halfwit, ignoramus, imbecile, jerk, moron, nincompoop, ninny*, numskull, pinhead*, simpleton, stupid person; CONCEPT *412*

nobility [n] *aristocracy; eminence* dignity, elevation, elite, ennoblement, exaltation, excellence, generosity, gentry, glorification, grandeur, greatness, high society, honor, illustriousness, incorruptibility, integrity, loftiness, magnanimity, magnificence, majesty, nobleness, patricians, peerage, royalty, ruling class, society, stateliness, sublimity, superiority, upper class, uprightness, virtue, worthiness; CONCEPTS *378,388,668*

noble [adj1] *aristocratic* gentle, highborn, imperial, kingly, patrician, queenly, titled, wellborn; CONCEPTS *549,555* —*Ant.* ignoble, lowly, servile, unaristocratic, unsophisticated

noble [adj2] *dignified, excellent* august, beneficent, benevolent, benign, big, bounteous, brilliant, charitable, courtly, cultivated, dignified, distinguished, elevated, eminent, extraordinary, first-rate, generous, gracious, grand, great, great-hearted, high-minded, honorable, humane, imposing, impressive, liberal, lofty, magnanimous, magnificent, meritorious, preeminent, refined, remarkable, reputable, splendid, stately, sublime, supreme, sympathetic, tolerant, upright, virtuous, worthy; CONCEPTS *401,404,572* —*Ant.* ignoble, undignified, unrefined, unsophisticated

noble [n] *member of royal or important family* archduchess, archduke, aristocrat, blue blood*, count, countess, duchess, duke, emperor, empress, gentleman, gentlewoman, lady, lord, patrician, peer, prince, princess, royalty, silk stocking*; CONCEPTS *422,423*

nobody/nonentity [n] *person of little importance* cipher, insignificancy, lightweight*, menial, nix*, nothing, parvenu*, small potato*, squirt*, upstart, wimp*, zero*, zip; CONCEPT *423* —*Ant.* somebody

nocturnal [adj] *happening at night* after dark, late, night, night-loving, nightly, nighttime; CONCEPTS *799,801*

nod [n] *gesture of the head* acceptance, acknowledgment, affirmative, beckon, bow, dip, greeting, inclination, indication, permission, salute, sign, signal, yes; CONCEPTS *74,185,685*

nod [v1] *gesture with head* acknowledge, acquiesce, agree, approve, assent, beckon, bend, bow, concur, consent, curtsy, dip, duck, greet, indicate, recognize, respond, salute, say yes, sign, signal; CONCEPTS *10,50,74,88,185*

nod [v2] *fall asleep* become inattentive, be sleepy, doze, drift, drift off, droop, drowse, nap, sleep, slump; CONCEPTS *210,315,681*

node/nodule [n] *knot, growth* bud, bulge, bump, burl, clot, knob, lump, protuberance, swelling, tumor; CONCEPTS *471,831*

noise [n] *sound that is loud or not harmonious* babble, babel, bang, bedlam, bellow, bewailing, blare, blast, boisterousness, boom, buzz, cacophony, caterwauling, clamor, clang, clatter, commotion, crash, cry, detonation, din, discord, disquiet, disquietude, drumming, eruption, explosion, fanfare, fireworks, fracas*, fuss*, hoo-ha*, hubbub*, hullabaloo*, jangle, lamentation, outcry, pandemonium, peal, racket, ring, roar, row, shot, shouting, sonance, squawk, stridency, talk, thud, tumult, turbulence, uproar, uproariousness, yelling, yelp; CONCEPTS *521,595* —*Ant.* silence

noiseless [adj] *quiet* hushed, hushful, inaudible, mute, muted, silent, soundless, speechless, still, voiceless, wordless; CONCEPT *594* —*Ant.* clamorous, noisy

noiseproof [adj] *soundproof* insulated, nonresonant, silent; CONCEPT *594*

noisome [adj] *immoral, bad, offensive* baneful, dangerous, deadly, deleterious, disgusting, fetid, foul, harmful, horrid, hurtful, injurious, insalubrious, insalutary, loathsome, malodorous, mephitic, mischievous, nauseating, noxious, pernicious, pestiferous, pestilential, poisonous, putrid, rank, reeking, repulsive, sickening, sickly, smelly, stinking, unhealthful, unhealthy, unwholesome, vile, yucky*; CONCEPTS *537,571,598* —*Ant.* good, just, moral, upright

noisy [adj] *very loud and unharmonious in sound* blatant, blusterous, boisterous, booming, cacophonous, chattering, clamorous, clangorous, clattery, deafening, disorderly, ear-popping*, ear-splitting*, jumping, loudmouth, obstreperous, piercing, rackety, raising Cain*, raising the roof*, rambunctious, raspy, riotous, rowdy, screaming, strepitous, strident, tumultous/tumultuous, turbulent, turned up, uproarious, vociferous; CONCEPTS *592,594* —*Ant.* noiseless, quiet, silent, still

nomad [n] *person who wanders from place to place* hobo, itinerant, migrant, pilgrim, rambler, roamer, rover, vagabond, wanderer, wayfarer; CONCEPT *413*

nomadic [adj] *itinerant* drifting, gypsy, itinerate, migrant, migratory, pastoral, perambulant, perambulatory, peripatetic, roaming, roving, traveling, vagabond, vagrant, wandering, wayfaring; CONCEPTS *401,536,584* —*Ant.* native, settled

nom de plume [n] *pen name* AKA*, alias, anonym, assumed name, nickname, nom de guerre, professional name, pseudonym; CONCEPTS *268,683*

nomenclature [n] *vocabulary* classification, codification, glossary, locution, phraseology, taxonomy, terminology; CONCEPTS *275,276,683*

nominal [adj1] *supposed, theoretical* alleged, apparent, as advertised, formal, given, honorary, in effect only, in name only, mentioned, named, ostensible, pretended, professed, puppet, purported, seeming, self-styled, simple, so-called, stated, suggested, titular; CONCEPT *582* —*Ant.* actual, real, true

nominal [adj2] *insignificant* cheap, inconsiderable, inexpensive, low, low-priced, meaningless, minimal, small, symbolic, token, trifling, trivial, unnecessary; CONCEPTS *334,575,789* —*Ant.* important, significant

nominate [*v*] *designate, select* appoint, assign, call, choose, cognominate, commission, decide, denominate, draft, elect, elevate, empower, intend, make, mean, name, offer, present, proffer, propose, purpose, put down for, put up, recommend, slate, slot, specify, submit, suggest, tab, tap, tender, term; CONCEPTS *41,50,75,88,300* —*Ant.* ignore, pass over

nomination [*n*] *appointment for responsibility* choice, designation, election, naming, proposal, recommendation, selection, suggestion; CONCEPTS *41,50,75,88,300*

nominee [*n*] *candidate* applicant, appointee, aspirant, contender, contestant, entrant, hopeful*, office-seeker, runner, seeker; CONCEPT *359*

nonagression [*n*] *pacifism* nonviolence, passivity, peaceableness; CONCEPTS *7,22,250*

nonchalant [*adj*] *easygoing, laid back* airy, aloof, apathetic, blasé, calm, careless, casual, cold, collected, composed, cool, detached, disimpassioned, disinterested, dispassionate, easy, effortless, happy, impassive, imperturbable, incurious, indifferent, insouciant, lackadaisical, light, listless, loose, lukewarm, mellow, neglectful, negligent, neutral, offhand, placid, serene, smooth, trifling, uncaring, unconcerned, unemotional, unexcited, unfeeling, unflappable, unimpressible, unperturbed, unruffled, untroubled; CONCEPTS *401,404,542* —*Ant.* intense, jumpy, nervous, unnerved

noncommittal [*adj*] *unwilling to decide* ambiguous, buttoned up*, careful, cautious, circumspect, clammed up*, constrained, discreet, equivocal, evasive, even-steven*, guarded, hush-hush*, incommunicable, indefinite, judicious, middle-ground*, middle-of-the-road*, neutral, on-the-fence*, politic, reserved, restrained, tactful, temporizing, tentative, unrevealing, vague, wary, zipped*; CONCEPTS *267,403,542* —*Ant.* committal, decisive, definite, judgemental, willing

noncompliant [*adj*] *unwilling to go along with something* belligerent, contumacious, declinatory, declining, divergent, impatient, irregular, negative, objecting, rebellious, recalcitrant, refractory, refusing, restive, truculent; CONCEPTS *401,542* —*Ant.* compliant, obedient, subservient, willing

nonconforming [*adj*] *nonobservant* independent, individualistic, marching to the beat of a different drummer*, nonadhering, noncompliant, one's own sweet way*, radical, unorthodox; CONCEPT *554*

nonconformist [*adj*] *unwilling to behave, believe as most do* beatnik*, bohemian*, dissident, freak*, heretical, heterodox, hippie*, iconoclastic, maverick, oddball*, offbeat, original, rebel, schismatic*, sectarian, swinger, unorthodox, weird*; CONCEPTS *401,542* —*Ant.* conforming, conformist, obeying, orthodox

nonconformist [*n*] *person who goes against normal behavior, beliefs* beatnik*, bohemian*, demonstrator, different breed*, dissenter, dissentient, dissident, dropout, eccentric, fish out of water*, freak*, heretic, iconoclast, individualist, liberal, malcontent, maverick,

misbeliever, night person, oddball, offbeat, original, protester, radical, rebel, sectary, separatist, swinger, weirdo*; CONCEPTS *359, 423* —*Ant.* conformist, orthodox

nonconformity [*n*] *belief, behavior different from most* bohemianism, breach, contumaciousness, denial, disaffection, disagreement, disapprobation, disapproval, discordance, disobedience, dissent, eccentricity, exception, heresy, heterodoxy, iconoclasm, insubordination, lawlessness, mutinousness, negation, nonacceptance, nonagreement, noncompliance, nonconsent, objection, opposition, originality, recalcitrance, recusance, recusancy, rejection, strangeness, transgressiveness, unconventionality, uniqueness, unorthodoxy, unruliness, veto, violation; CONCEPTS *633,657,689* —*Ant.* compliance, conformity, obedience, orthodoxy

nondescript [*adj*] *undistinguished, commonplace* characterless, colorless, common, dull, empty, featureless, garden*, indescribable, indeterminate, mousy*, ordinary, unclassifiable, unclassified, unexceptional, uninspiring, uninteresting, unmemorable, unremarkable, vague; CONCEPTS *529,537,547* —*Ant.* describable, different, distinguished, illustrative, remarkable, superior, uncommon

none [*pron*] *not one thing* nil, nobody, no one, no one at all, no part, not a bit, not any, not anyone, not anything, not a soul, not a thing, nothing, not one, zero, zilch*; CONCEPT *407* —*Ant.* some

nonessential [*adj*] *not needed or important* deadwood*, dispensable, excess baggage*, excessive, expendable, extraneous, inessential, insignificant, peripheral, petty, superfl uous, trivial, unimportant, unnecessary; CONCEPTS *546,575* —*Ant.* essential, important, necessary, needed-

nonexistent [*adj*] *fictional, not real* absent, airy, baseless, blank, chimerical, dead, defunct, departed, dreamlike, dreamy, empty, ethereal, extinct, extinguished, fancied, flimsy, gone, gossamery, groundless, hallucinatory, hypothetical, illusory, imaginary, imagined, immaterial, imponderable, insubstantial, legendary, lost, missing, mythical, negative, null, null and void*, passed away, passed on, perished, shadowy, tenuous, ungrounded, unreal, unsubstantial, vacant, vague, vaporous, void, without foundation; CONCEPTS *539,582* —*Ant.* actual, existent, existing, real, true

nonpartisan [*adj*] *impartial; not political* detached, equitable, fair, free-wheeling*, independent, indifferent, just, middle-of-the-road*, neutral, nonaligned, nondiscriminatory, objective, on one's own*, on-the-fence*, playing it cool*, unaffected, unaffiliated, unbiased, unbigoted, uncolored, unimplicated, uninfluenced, uninvolved, unprejudiced; CONCEPT *542* —*Ant.* biased, decided, partial, partisan, political, prejudiced

nonplus [*v*] *confuse, perplex* astonish, astound, baffle, balk, beat, bewilder, boggle, buffalo*, confound, daze, discomfit, disconcert, discountenance, dismay, dumbfound, embarrass, faze, floor*, flurry, fluster, frustrate, get*, mess with one's head*, muddle, mystify, overcome, paralyze, puzzle, rattle, rattle one's cage*, stagger,

stick, stump, stun, stymie*; take aback, throw*, throw into tizzy*, thwart; CONCEPTS *14,16*
—*Ant.* clear up, educate, enlighten, explain

nonsense [*n*] *craziness, ridiculousness* absurdity, babble, balderdash*, baloney*, bananas*, bombast, bull*, bunk*, claptrap*, drivel, fatuity, flightiness, folly, foolishness, fun, gibberish, giddiness, hogwash*, hooey*, hot air*, imprudence, inanity, irrationality, jazz, jest, jive*, joke, ludicrousness, madness, mumbo jumbo*, palaver, poppycock*, prattle, pretense, ranting, rashness, rot, rubbish, scrawl, scribble, senselessness, silliness, soft soap*, stupidity, thoughtlessness, trash*, tripe*; CONCEPTS *230,388,633*
—*Ant.* clarity, common sense, fact, intelligibility, sense, truth, understanding

nonstop [*adj*] *continuous, direct* ceaseless, constant, endless, incessant, interminable, relentless, round-the-clock*, steady, unbroken, unending, unfaltering, uninterrupted, unremitting; CONCEPTS *482,584,798* —*Ant.* incontinuous, indirect, intermittent, stopping, terminating

nonviolence [*n*] *abstention from violence* nonaggression, pacification, pacifism, passiveness, passivity, peaceableness; CONCEPTS *388,691*

nonviolent [*adj*] *peaceful* irenic, nonbelligerent, pacifist, passive, peaceable, quiet, resistant, without violence; CONCEPT *401* —*Ant.* hateful, mean, violent, wicked, wild

nook [*n*] *corner, cubbyhole* alcove, byplace, cavity, compartment, cranny, crevice, den, hideout, hole, inglenook, niche, opening, quoin, recess, retreat; CONCEPTS *440,513*

noon [*n*] *the middle of a day* apex, high noon, meridian, midday, noonday, noontide, noontime, twelve noon, twelve o'clock; CONCEPTS *801,802,806* —*Ant.* midnight

norm [*n*] *average, standard* barometer, benchmark*, criterion, gauge, mean, measure, median, medium, model, par, pattern, rule, scale, touchstone*, type, yardstick; CONCEPTS *647,686,688* —*Ant.* end, exception, extreme

normal [*adj1*] *common, usual* accustomed, acknowledged, average, commonplace, conventional, customary, general, habitual, mean, median, methodical, natural, orderly, ordinary, popular, prevalent, regular, routine, run-of-the-mill*, standard, traditional, typic, typical, unexceptional; CONCEPT *547* —*Ant.* abnormal, irregular, odd, strange, uncommon, unconventional, unusual

normal [*adj2*] *sane, rational* all there*, compos mentis*, cool*, healthy, in good health, in one's right mind*, lucid, reasonable, right, right-minded, sound, together, well-adjusted, whole, wholesome; CONCEPTS *314,403* —*Ant.* abnormal, eccentric, insane, irrational, irregular, odd, unbalanced

normally [*adv*] *usually* as a rule, commonly, habitually, ordinarily, regularly, typically; CONCEPT *547* —*Ant.* abnormally, never

north [*adj/adv*] *toward the top pole of the earth* arctic, boreal, cold, frozen, hyperborean, northbound, northerly, northern, northmost, northward, polar, septentrional, toward North Pole, tundra; CONCEPTS *581,583* —*Ant.* south

nose [*n*] *smelling organ of animate being* adenoids, beak*, bill*, horn*, muzzle*, nares, nostrils, olfactory nerves, proboscis, schnoz*,

smeller*, sneezer*, sniffer*, snoot*, snout*, snuffer*, whiffer*; CONCEPTS *392,601*

nose [*v*] *detect, search* busybody*, examine, inspect, meddle, mouse*, pry, scent, smell, sniff, snoop*; CONCEPTS *103,216*

nosh [*n*] *snack* bite, bite to eat*, break, goodies*, grub, light meal, midnight snack, pickings, refreshment, tidbit, tiny meal; CONCEPTS *457,459*

nosh [*v*] *snack* eat between meals, munch, nibble, pick at, taste; CONCEPT *169*

nostalgia [*n*] *pleasant remembrances* fond memories*, hearts and flowers*, homesickness, longing, pining, reminiscence, remorse, schmaltz*, sentimentality, tear-jerker*, wistfulness, yearning; CONCEPTS *20,410*

nostalgic [*adj*] *longingly remembering* cornball*, down memory lane*, drippy*, homesick, like yesterday*, lonesome, longing, mushy*, regretful, sappy*, sentimental, sloppy, syrupy*, wistful, yearning; CONCEPTS *403,529*

nostrum [*n*] *cure-all, often ineffective* catholicon, cure, drug, elixir, fix, formula, home remedy, medicine, panacea, patent medicine, potion, quack medicine*, quick fix*, remedy, treatment; CONCEPTS *307,311*

nosy [*adj*] *curious; prying* eavesdropping, inquisitive, inquisitorial, inquisitory, interested, interfering, intermeddling, intrusive, meddlesome, personal, searching, snooping, snoopy; CONCEPT *401* —*Ant.* indifferent, uncaring, unconcerned, uninterested

notable [*adj*] *important; famous* big-league*, bodacious*, celebrated, celebrious, conspicuous, distingué, distinguished, eminent, eventful, evident, extraordinary, famed, great, heavy*, high-profile*, illustrious, major-league*, manifest, marked, memorable, momentous, nameable, noteworthy, noticeable, notorious, observable, outstanding, preeminent, prominent, pronounced, rare, red-letter*, remarkable, renowned, rubric, serious, something else*, striking, top-drawer*, uncommon, unusual, well-known; CONCEPT *568* —*Ant.* commonplace, inconsequential, insignificant, ordinary, unimportant, unnoticeable, unremarkable

notable [*n*] *person who is famous, important* big name*, big shot*, big-time operator*, big wheel*, celebrity, chief, dignitary, eminence, executive, figure*, heavyweight*, high-up, hotdog*, leader, lion*, luminary, magnate, mogul, name, notability, personage, personality, pooh-bah*, power, somebody*, star, superstar, VIP*, worthy; CONCEPTS *347,352,423* —*Ant.* lowlife, unknown

notably [*adv*] *especially* conspicuously, distinctly, exceedingly, exceptionally, extremely, greatly, highly, hugely, markedly, noticeably, outstandingly, particularly, prominently, remarkably, reputably, signally, strikingly, uncommonly, very; CONCEPT *569* —*Ant.* insignificantly, unnotably, unremarkably

notarize [*v*] *certify* attest, authenticate, document, endorse, register, sign and seal, swear, validate, verify, witness; CONCEPTS *50,88*

notary [*n*] *notary public* certifier, commissioner for oaths, court clerk, endorser, public official, recorder, registrar, scrivener, signatory, witness; CONCEPTS *355,423*

notation [n] *written remarks* characters, chit, code, documentation, figures, jotting, memo, memorandum, note, noting, record, representation, script, signs, symbols, system; CONCEPTS 268,284

not born yesterday [adj] *experienced* battle-scarred, been around, canny, cunning, on the ball*, savvy, seasoned, trained, unbelieving, wise, worldly; CONCEPTS 402,527

notch [n1] *indentation* cleft, cut, gap, gash, groove, incision, indent, indenture, mark, mill, nick, nock, rabbet, rut, score, scratch; CONCEPT 513

notch [n2] *level within classification* cut, degree, grade, rung, stage, step; CONCEPTS 388,744

notch [v] *indent* chisel, cleave, crenelate, crimp, cut, dent, gash, incise, jag, mark, mill, nick, scallop, score, scratch; CONCEPTS 137,176,208 —*Ant.* flush

note [n1] *symbol, often used in reference to music* character, degree, figure, flat, indication, interval, key, lick*, mark, natural, pitch, representation, scale, sharp, sign, step, token, tone; CONCEPTS 262,284

note [n2] *attention, heed* cognizance, mark, mind, notice, observance, observation, regard, remark; CONCEPT 529 —*Ant.* heedlessness, ignorance, neglect, unobservance

note [v] *observe, perceive* catch, clock, denote, descry, designate, dig, discern, discover, distinguish, document, enter, get a load of*, get an eyeful*, heed, indicate, jot down, mark, mention, notice, pick up on*, put down, record, register, remark, see, set down, spot, take in*, transcribe, view, write, write down; CONCEPTS 34,626 —*Ant.* ignore, neglect

notebook [n] *writing tablet* binder, blotter, daybook, diary, exercise book, journal, log, loose-leaf notebook, memo book, pad, scratch pad, spiral notebook, workbook; CONCEPT 271

noted [adj] *famous, eminent* acclaimed, celeb, celebrated, conspicuous, distinguished, esteemed, illustrious, leading, name, notable, notorious, of note, popular, prominent, recognized, redoubted, renowned, somebody, star, well-known; CONCEPT 568 —*Ant.* insignificant, unimportant, unknown

note/notes [n3] *written communication* agenda, annotation, calendar, comment, commentary, datum, definition, diary, dispatch, entry, epistle, gloss, inscription, jotting, journal, letter, line, marginalia, mark, memo, memorandum, message, minute, missive, obiter dictum, observation, record, remark, reminder, scratch, scrawl, scribble, summary, thank-you, word; CONCEPT 271

notes [n] *outline* annotation, draft, impressions, jottings, marginalia, record, report, rough draft, summary, synopsis; CONCEPT 268

noteworthy [adj] *important* boss*, conspicuous, cool*, evident, exceptional, extraordinary, heavy*, high-profile*, hot*, major-league*, manifest, meaningful, memorable, mind-blowing*, murder, nameable, notable, noticeable, observable, outstanding, patent, prominent, red-letter*, remarkable, serious, significant, something else*, splash*, stand-out*, super, terrific, the end*, underlined*, unique, unusual, utmost; CONCEPTS 567,568 —*Ant.* common,

inconsequential, insignificant, ordinary, unimportant

nothingness [n1] *insignificance* pettiness, smallness, unimportance, worthlessness; CONCEPT 668 —*Ant.* eminence, importance, significance

nothing/nothingness [n2] *emptiness, nonexistence* annihilation, aught, blank, cipher, extinction, fly speck*, insignificancy, naught, nihility, nobody, nonbeing, nonentity, not anything, nought, nullity, obliteration, oblivion, shutout*, trifle, void, wind*, zero*, zilch*, zip; CONCEPTS 407,707 —*Ant.* capacity, fullness

nothing to it [adj] *effortless* a breeze*, child's play*, duck soup*, easy, easy as ABC*, easy as pie*, no problem*, no sweat*, painless, piece of cake*, simple, snap*, uncomplicated; CONCEPT 565

notice [n1] *observation* apprehension, attention, care, cognizance, concern, consideration, ear, grasp, heed, mark, mind, note, observance, regard, remark, respect, thought, understanding; CONCEPTS 34,532 —*Ant.* heedlessness, ignorance, neglect

notice [n2] *announcement, information* admonition, advertisement, advice, caution, caveat, circular, clue, comment, comments, communication, criticism, critique, cue, declaration, directive, enlightenment, goods*, handbill, info*, instruction, intelligence, intimation, know*, lowdown*, manifesto, memo, memorandum, news, note, notification, order, picture, poster, proclamation, remark, review, score, sign, squib*, story, tip, warning, whole story*, write-up; CONCEPTS 271,274,278

notice [v] *observe, perceive* acknowledge, advert, allude, catch, clock, descry, detect, dig*, discern, distinguish, espy, flash on*, get a load of*, heed, look at, make out*, mark, mind, note, pick up on, recognize, refer, regard, remark, see, spot, take in; CONCEPTS 34,626 —*Ant.* ignore, miss, neglect, overlook

noticeable [adj] *conspicuous, evident* apparent, appreciable, arresting, arrestive, big as life*, can't miss it*, clear, distinct, eye-catching, manifest, marked, notable, noteworthy, observable, obvious, open and shut*, outstanding, palpable, patent, perceptible, plain, pointed, prominent, remarkable, salient, sensational, signal, spectacular, striking, under one's nose*, unmistakable; CONCEPTS 529,537, 567 —*Ant.* forgotten, inconspicuous, obscure, overlooked, unnoticeable

notification [n] *announcement* advertisement, advisory, alert, bulletin, communication, communique, declaration, information, message, news, notice, proclamation, release, report, statement, warning; CONCEPTS 49,274

notify [v] *inform* acquaint, advise, air, alert, announce, apprise, assert, blazon, brief, broadcast, cable, caution, circulate, clue in, convey, cue, debrief, declare, disclose, disseminate, divulge, enlighten, express, fill in, give, herald, hint, let in on, let know, make known, mention, pass out, post, proclaim, promulgate, publish, radio, report, reveal, send word, speak, spread, state, suggest, talk, teach, telephone, tell, tip off, vent, warn, wire, wise up*, write; CONCEPTS 60,79 —*Ant.* conceal, hide, suppress

notion [n1] *belief, idea* angle, apprehension, approach, assumption, awareness, clue, comprehension, conceit, concept, conception, consciousness, consideration, cue, discernment, flash, hint, image, imagination, impression, inclination, indication, inkling, insight, intellection, intimation, intuition, judgment, knowledge, opinion, penetration, perception, sentiment, slant, spark, suggestion, telltale, thought, twist, understanding, view, wind, wrinkle; CONCEPTS 529,532,689

notion [n2] *whim, desire* caprice, conceit, fancy, humor, imagination, impulse, inclination, wish; CONCEPT 20 —*Ant.* need

notoriety [n] *reputation* ballyhoo*, celebrity, center stage*, dishonor, disrepute, éclat*, fame, flak*, infamy, ink*, name*, obloquy, opprobrium, renown, rep*, scandal, splash*, spotlight*, wise*; CONCEPTS 388,411

notorious [adj] *known for a trait, often an unadmirable one* belled, blatant, dishonorable, disreputable, flagrant, glaring, ill-famed, infamous, leading, noted, obvious, opprobrious, overt, patent, popular, prominent, questionable, scandalous, shady, shameful, undisputed, wanted, well-known, wicked; CONCEPT 404

notwithstanding [adv/prep] *although, however* after all, against, at any rate, but, despite, for all that, howbeit, in any case, in any event, in spite of, nevertheless, nonetheless, on the other hand, regardless of, though, to the contrary, withal, yet; CONCEPT 544

nourish [v] *feed, care for* attend, cherish, comfort, cultivate, encourage, foster, furnish, maintain, nurse, nurture, promote, provide, supply, support, sustain, tend; CONCEPTS 140,295 —*Ant.* abandon, deprive, neglect, starve

nourishing [adj] *healthful* alimentative, beneficial, health-giving, healthy, nutrient, nutrimental, nutritious, nutritive, wholesome; CONCEPTS 462,537 —*Ant.* bad, unhealthy, unwholesome

nourishment [n] *food* aliment, diet, feed, foodstuff, home cooking*, maintenance, nutriment, nutrition, pabulum, pap*, provender, support, sustenance, viands, victuals, vittles*; CONCEPT 457 —*Ant.* deprivation, starvation

nouveau riche [n] *new rich* DINK*, parvenu, social climber, upstart, vulgarian, yuppie*; CONCEPT 423

novel [adj] *new, original* at cutting edge*, atypical, avant-garde, breaking new ground*, contemporary, different, far cry*, fresh, funky*, innovative, just out*, modernistic, neoteric, newfangled, new-fashioned, now*, odd, offbeat, peculiar, rare, recent, singular, strange, uncommon, unfamiliar, unique, unusual; CONCEPTS 564,578,797 —*Ant.* common, customary, familiar, old, ordinary, overused, used, usual, worn

novel [n] *fictional book* best-seller, cliff-hanger, fiction, narrative, novelette, novella, paperback, potboiler*, prose, romance, story, tale, yarn*; CONCEPT 280

novelty [n1] *newness, originality* change, crazy*, creation, dernier cri*, freshness, innovation, last word*, modernity, mutation, newfangled contraption, oddball, oddity, original, origination, permutation, recentness, sport*, strangeness, surprise, unfamiliarity, uniqueness, vicissitude, weird*; CONCEPTS 665,697,715

novelty [n2] *trinket, gadget* bagatelle*, bauble, bibelot*, conversation piece, curio, curiosity, gewgaw*, gimcrack*, gimmick, item, knickknack, memento, objet d'art*, oddity, souvenir, trifle, whatnot*; CONCEPTS 260,446

novice [n] *person just learning something* amateur, apprentice, beginner, colt*, convert*, cub*, first of May*, fledgling, greenhorn, gremlin, know from nothing*, learner, mark*, neophyte, newcomer, new kid on the block*, novitiate, plebe, postulant, prentice, probationer, proselyte, punk*, pupil, recruit, rookie, starter, student, tenderfoot*, trainee; CONCEPTS 348,350,423 —*Ant.* expert, professional

now [adv] *presently* any more, at once, at the moment, at this moment, at this time, away, directly, first off, forthwith, here and now, immediately, in a minute, in a moment, in nothing flat, instanter, instantly, just now, like now*, momentarily, nowadays, on the double*, PDQ*, promptly, pronto*, right away, right now, soon, straightaway, these days, this day, today; CONCEPTS 812,820 —*Ant.* future, later, past

now and then [adv] *once in a while* at intervals, at times, every now and then, every once in a while, every so often, from time to time, hardly, infrequently, intermittently, irregularly, now and again, occasionally, off and on, once in a blue moon*, on occasion, periodically, sometimes, sporadically; CONCEPTS 530,541

noxious [adj] *deadly, injurious* baneful, corrupting, dangerous, deleterious, destructive, detrimental, fetid, foul, harmful, hurtful, insalubrious, insalutary, noisome, pernicious, pestiferous, pestilent, pestilential, poisonous, putrid, sickly, spoiled, stinking, toxic, unhealthful, unhealthy, unwholesome, venomous, virulent; CONCEPTS 485,537 —*Ant.* curing, good, healthy, helpful, hygienic, pure, sterile, wholesome

nozzle [n] *spout* cock, faucet, spigot, tap; CONCEPTS 445,464,499

nuance [n] *slight difference; shading* dash, degree, distinction, gradation, hint, implication, nicety, refinement, shade, shadow, soupçon, subtlety, suggestion, suspicion, tinge, touch, trace; CONCEPT 665

nub [n1] *core, gist* basic, bottom line*, crux, essence, heart*, kernel, meat*, meat and potatoes*, nitty-gritty*, nubbin, nucleus, pith, point, short, substance, upshot; CONCEPTS 661,682,826 —*Ant.* exterior, outside

nub [n2] *bump, knot* bulge, knob, lump, node, protuberance, swelling; CONCEPT 471

nuclear energy [n] *nuclear power* atomic energy, atomic power, nuclear fission power, nuclear fusion power, thermonuclear power; CONCEPT 520

nuclear reactor [n] *atomic reactor* atomic pile, atomic power plant, breeder reactor, core reactor, nuclear power plant, thermonuclear reactor; CONCEPT 520

nuclear weapon [n] *explosive driven by nuclear energy* A-bomb, atomic bomb, atomic weapon, doomsday machine*, H-bomb, hydrogen bomb, mininuke*, mirv*, MX*, neutron bomb, nuke*; CONCEPT 500

nucleus [n] *core; basis for something's beginning* bud, center, crux, embryo, focus, foundation, germ, heart, hub, kernel, matter, nub, pivot, premise, principle, seed, spark; CONCEPTS 393,826,828 —Ant. exterior, exteriority, outside

nude [adj] *without clothes, covering* au naturel*, bald, bare, bare-skinned, buck naked*, dishabille*, disrobed, exposed, garmentless, in birthday suit, in one's skin*, in the altogether*, naked, peeled*, raw, skin, stark, stark-naked*, stripped, unattired, unclad, unclothed, uncovered, undraped, undressed, wearing only a smile*, without a stitch*; CONCEPT 485 —Ant. clothed, covered

nudge [n/v] *bump, elbow* dig, jab, jog, poke, prod, punch, push, shove, tap, touch; CONCEPTS 208,612

nudity [n] *nakedness* bareness, birthday suit*, natural state, naturism, nudism, the buff*, the nude, the raw*, undress; CONCEPT 453

nugget [n] *lump, solid piece; often of metal ore* asset, bullion, chunk, clod, clump, gold, hunk, ingot, mass, plum, rock, treasure, wad*; CONCEPT 471

nuisance [n] *annoyance; annoying person* besetment, blister, bore, bother, botheration, botherment, bum*, creep, drag*, drip*, exasperation, frump, gadfly, headache*, inconvenience, infliction, insect*, irritant, irritation, louse, nag*, nudge*, offense, pain, pain in the neck*, pest, pester, pesterer, pill*, plague, poor excuse*, problem, terror, trouble, vexation; CONCEPTS 412,674 —Ant. delight, happiness, pleasantry, pleasure

nuke [n] *nuclear weapon* A-bomb, atomic bomb, atomic weapon, doomsday machine*, H-bomb, hydrogen bomb, neutron bomb; CONCEPT 500

nuke [v1] *attack with nuclear weapons* annihilate, bomb, destroy, eliminate, incinerate, kill, obliterate, wipe out; CONCEPTS 86,252

nuke [v2] *cook* bake, brown, heat, microwave, warm up, zap; CONCEPT 170

null [adj] *ineffectual, valueless* absent, bad, barren, characterless, imaginary, ineffective, inefficacious, inoperative, invalid, negative, nonexistent, nothing, null and void*, powerless, unavailing, unreal, unsanctioned, useless, vain, void, worthless; CONCEPT 560 —Ant. effective, effectual, valid, valuable, worthwhile, worthy

nullify [v] *cancel, revoke* abate, abolish, abrogate, annihilate, annul, ax, blue pencil*, bring to naught*, call all bets off*, compensate, confine, counteract, counterbalance, countervail, disannul, forget it*, invalidate, kill*, limit, negate, neutralize, nig*, offset, quash*, render null and void*, renege, renig*, repeal, rescind, restrict, scratch*, scrub*, squash*, stamp out*, take out*, torpedo*, trash*, undo, veto, vitiate, void, wash out*, wipe out*, zap*; CONCEPTS 50,88, 121,234 —Ant. affirm, pass, sanctify, validate

numb [adj] *deadened, insensitive* aloof, anesthetized, apathetic, asleep, benumbed, callous, casual, comatose, dazed, dead, detached, disinterested, frozen, immobilized, incurious, indifferent, insensate, insensible, insentient, lethargic, listless, numbed, paralyzed, phlegmatic, remote, senseless, stupefied, stuporous, torpid, unconcerned, unconscious, uncurious, unfeeling, uninterested; CONCEPTS 403,609 —Ant. lively, responsive, sensitive

numb [v] *deaden* anesthetize, benumb, blunt, chill, desensitize, dull, freeze, frost, immobilize, obtund, paralyze, stun, stupefy; CONCEPTS 250,255 —Ant. enliven

number [n1] *unit of the mathematical system* cardinal, character, chiffer, cipher, count, decimal, denominator, digit, emblem, figure, folio, fraction, googol, integer, numeral, numerator, ordinal, prime, representation, sign, statistic, sum, symbol, total, whole number; CONCEPTS 765,784 —Ant. letter

number [n2] *aggregate, bunch* abundance, amount, caboodle*, collection, company, conglomeration, crowd, estimate, flock, horde, jillion*, lot, manifoldness, many, multitude, plenitude, plenty, product, quantity, slew*, sum, throng, total, totality, umpteen*, volume, whole, zillion*; CONCEPTS 432,787 —Ant. one

number [v] *count, calculate* account, add, add up, aggregate, amount, come, computer, count heads*, count noses*, count off, enumerate, estimate, figure in, figure out, include, keep tabs, numerate, reckon, run, run down, run into, run to, sum, take account of, tale, tally, tell, tick off*, total, tote*, tote up*; CONCEPT 764 —Ant. estimate, guess

numbered [adj] *limited in number* categorized, checked, contained, counted, designated, doomed, enumerated, fated, fixed, included, indicated, marked, specified, told, totalled; CONCEPT 554 —Ant. infinite, unlimited, unnumbered

numberless [adj] *infinite* countless, endless, heaps*, incalculable, innumerable, jillion, many, multitudinous, myriad, no end of*, no end to*, numerous, umpteen*, uncountable, uncounted, unnumbered, untold, zillion*; CONCEPTS 482,762,781 —Ant. counted, finite, limited, numbered

numskull [n] *idiot* blockhead, bonehead*, buffoon, cretin, dimwit, dolt, dork, dumbbell, dummy, dunce, fathead*, fool, halfwit, ignoramus, imbecile, jerk, moron, nincompoop, ninny*, nitwit, pinhead*, simpleton, stupid person; CONCEPT 412

numeral [n] *symbol of mathematical system* character, chiffer, cipher, digit, figure, integer, number; CONCEPTS 284,784 —Ant. letter

numeric/numerical [adj] *concerning mathematics* algebraic, algorithmic, arithmetic, arithmetical, binary, differential, digital, exponent, exponential, fraction, fractional, integral, logarithm, logarithmic, mathematical, numeral, numerary, statistical; CONCEPT 762 —Ant. alphabetic, alphabetical

numerous [adj] *many, abundant* big, copious, diverse, great, infinite, large, legion, lousy with*, multifarious, multitudinal, multitudinous, plentiful, populous, profuse, rife, scads*, several, sundry, thick, umpteen*, various, voluminous, zillion*; CONCEPTS 762,781 —Ant. deficient, few, lacking, little, small

nun [n] *woman in religious order* abbess, anchorite, canoness, mother superior, postulant, prioress, religious woman, sister, vestal; CONCEPT 361 —Ant. monk

nunnery [n] *convent* abbey, cloister, monastery, priory, religious community, retreat; CONCEPTS 368,516

nuptial [adj] *concerning marriage* bridal, conjugal, connubial, espousal, marital, married, matrimonial, spousal, wedded, wedding; CONCEPT 555 —**Ant.** divorce

nuptials [n] *marriage ceremony* bridal, espousal, marriage, matrimony, spousal, wedding; CONCEPT 297 —**Ant.** divorce

nurse [n] *person who tends to sick, cares for someone* assistant, attendant, baby sitter, caretaker, foster parent, medic, minder, nurse practitioner, practical nurse, registered nurse, RN, sitter, therapist, wet nurse; CONCEPTS 357,414

nurse [v] *care for, tend* advance, aid, attend, baby-sit, cherish, cradle, cultivate, encourage, father, feed, forward, foster, further, harbor, humor, immunize, indulge, inoculate, irradiate, keep alive, keep an eye on*, keep tabs on*, look after, medicate, minister to, mother, nourish, nurture, pamper, preserve, promote, see to, serve, sit, succor, support, take care of, treat, vaccinate, wait on, watch out for, watch over; CONCEPTS 110,140 —**Ant.** ignore, neglect

nurse [v2] *give milk, usually from breast* bottle-feed, breast-feed, cradle, dry-nurse, feed, give suck, lactate, nourish, nurture, suck, suckle, wet-nurse; CONCEPTS 140,295

nursemaid [n] *nanny* au pair, baby-sitter, governess, nurserymaid, wet nurse; CONCEPT 295

nursing home [n] *convalescent home* old folks home*, old people's home, rest home, retirement home; CONCEPT 312

nurture [n] *development, nourishment* breeding, care, diet, discipline, edibles, education, feed, food, instruction, nutriment, provender, provisions, rearing, subsistence, sustenance, training, upbringing, viands, victuals; CONCEPTS 457,712 —**Ant.** deprivation, ignorance, neglect, starvation

nurture [v] *feed, care for* back, bolster, bring up, cherish, cultivate, develop, discipline, educate, foster, instruct, nourish, nurse, nursle, provide, raise, rear, school, support, sustain, tend, train, uphold; CONCEPTS 110,140,295 —**Ant.** deprive, ignore, neglect, starve

nut [n1] *seed of fruit, vegetable* achene, caryopsis, kernel, stone, utricle; CONCEPT 428

nut [n2] *crazy, overenthusiastic person* bedlamite, bigot, crackpot, crank, dement, eccentric, fanatic, fiend, freak, harebrain*, loony*, lunatic, maniac, non compos mentis, screwball*, zealot; CONCEPTS 412,423 —**Ant.** sane person

nut house [n] *mental health facility* bughouse*, funny farm*, insane asylum, loony bin, madhouse*, mental hospital, mental institution, psychiatric hospital, psychiatric ward, sanatorium; CONCEPTS 312,439,516

nutrient [n] *source of nourishment* fiber, food, health food, mineral, nutriment, supplements, vitamin; CONCEPT 457

nutrition [n] *food* diet, menu, nourishment, nutriment, subsistence, sustenance, victuals; CONCEPT 457 —**Ant.** deprivation, starvation

nutritious [adj] *healthy* alimental, alimentative, balanced, beneficial, good, healthful, health-giving, invigorating, nourishing, nutrient, nutrimental, nutritive, salubrious, salutary, strengthening, wholesome; CONCEPT 462 —**Ant.** bad, insubstantial, unhealthful, unhealthy, unwholesome

nuts/nutty [adj] *mentally deranged* absurd, batty*, bedlamite, cracked*, crazy, daffy, daft, demented, eccentric, enthusiastic, foolish, gung ho*, harebrained*, insane, irrational, keen, kooky, loony, lunatic, mad, out of one's mind*, ridiculous, touched, unusual, wacky*, warm, zealous; CONCEPT 403 —**Ant.** balanced, calm, sane, well

nuts and bolts [n] *practical details* basic details, basics, brass tacks*, essentials, fundamentals, mechanics, nitty-gritty*, practicalities; CONCEPT 546

nuzzle [v] *cuddle* bundle, burrow, caress, fondle, nestle, nudge, pet, snug, snuggle; CONCEPTS 190,612

nylons [n] *stockings* hose, hosiery, panty hose, tights; CONCEPT 451

nymph [n] *female nature spirit* dryad, fairy, goddess, mermaid, naiad, nymphet, spirit, sprite, sylph; CONCEPTS 415,424

O

oaf [n] *person who is clumsy, stupid* beast, blunderer, bruiser, brute, chump*, clod, clown, dolt, dumb ox*, dunce, fool, goon*, idiot, imbecile, klutz*, loser, lout*, moron, nincompoop*, ox*, sap*, simpleton; CONCEPT 412 —**Ant.** handyman

oafish [adj] *clumsy, stupid* all thumbs*, blundering, blunderous, bumbling, bungling, butterfingered*, dumb, gawkish, gawky, graceless, half-witted*, heavy-handed, idiotic, ignorant, inelegant, inept, klutzy*, lubberly, lumbering, lumpish, moronic, simple, simpleminded, slow, stumbling, uncoordinated, undexterous, ungainly, unintelligent; CONCEPTS 401,402, 548,584

oasis [n1] *spring* fountain, watering hole, well, wellspring; CONCEPT 514

oasis [n2] *refuge* asylum, cover, escape, harbor, haven, hideaway, resting place, retreat, safe place, sanctuary, sanctum, shelter; CONCEPTS 198,515

oath [n1] *promise* adjuration, affidavit, affirmation, avowal, bond, contract, deposition, pledge, profession, sworn declaration, sworn statement, testimony, vow, word, word of honor; CONCEPTS 71,278 —**Ant.** break

oath [n2] *curse* blasphemy, cuss*, cuss word*, dirty name*, dirty word*, expletive, four-letter word*, imprecation, malediction, no-no*, profanity, strong language, swearword; CONCEPTS 54,278 —**Ant.** kindness, pleasantry

obdurate [adj] *pigheaded, stubborn* adamant, bullhead*, callous, cold fish*, dogged, firm, fixed, hanging tough*, hard, hard-boiled*, hard-hearted*, hard-nosed*, harsh, heartless, immovable, implacable, indurate, inexorable, inflexible, iron*, mean, mulish*, obstinate, perverse, relentless, rigid, set in stone*, stiff-necked*, thick-skinned*, tough, tough nut to crack*, unbending, uncompassionate, uncompromising, uncooperative, unemotional, unfeeling, unimpressible, unrelenting, unshakable, unsympathetic, unyielding; CONCEPTS 401,542 —**Ant.** amenable, gentle, submissive, susceptible, yielding

obedience [n] *good behavior; submissiveness* accordance, acquiescence, agreement, compliance, conformability, conformity, deference, docility, duteousness, dutifulness, duty, manageability, meekness, observance, orderliness, quietness, respect, reverence, servility, submission, subservience, tameness, tractability, willingness; CONCEPTS *411,633* —*Ant.* bad behavior, disobedience, misbehavior, mischief, mutiny, rebellion

obedient [adj] *well-behaved; submissive* acquiescent, amenable, at one's beck and call*, attentive, biddable, complaisant, compliant, controllable, deferential, devoted, docile, · docious, duteous, dutiful, faithful, governable, honoring, in one's clutches*, in one's pocket*, in one's power*, law-abiding, loyal, obeisant, obliging, observant, on a string*, pliant, regardful, resigned, respectful, reverential, sheeplike*, subservient, tame, tractable, under control, venerating, well-trained, willing, wrapped around finger*, yielding; CONCEPTS *401,404* —*Ant.* contrary, disobedient, insolent, misbehaving, mutinous, obstinate, rebellious

obeisance [n] *salutation* allegiance, bending of the knee*, bow, curtsy, deference, fealty, genuflection, homage, honor, kowtow*, loyalty, praise, respect, reverence, salaam*; CONCEPTS *154,384* —*Ant.* bad manners, disobedience, disregard, disrespect

obeisant [adj] *showing respect* courtly, deferential, dutiful, regarding, respectful, respecting, reverent, reverential, servile, standing; CONCEPT *401*

obese [adj] *very overweight* adipose, avoirdupois, corpulent, fat, fleshy*, gross*, heavy, outsize, paunchy, plump, porcine, portly, pudgy, rotund, stout; CONCEPT *491* —*Ant.* emaciated, skinny, underweight

obesity [n] *corpulence* bulk, chubbiness, chunkiness, fatness, overweight, paunchiness, plumpness, portliness, rotundness, stoutness; CONCEPT *734*

obey [v] *conform, give in* abide by, accede, accept, accord, acquiesce, act upon, adhere to, agree, answer, assent, be loyal to, be ruled by, bow to*, carry out, comply, concur, discharge, do as one says, do one's bidding, do one's duty, do what is expected, do what one is told, embrace, execute, follow, fulfill, get in line*, give way*, heed, hold fast*, keep, knuckle under*, live by, mind, observe, perform, play second fiddle*, respond, serve, submit, surrender, take orders, toe the line*; CONCEPTS *91,136* —*Ant.* disobey, mutiny, rebel

obfuscate [v] *confuse* baffle, becloud, befuddle, bewilder, cloud, complicate, conceal, confound, darken, fog, fuddle, muddle, obscure, perplex, puzzle, rattle; CONCEPT *16*

obituary [n] *notice of person's death* announcement, death notice, eulogy, mortuary tribute, necrology, obit, register; CONCEPTS *268,270* —*Ant.* birth announcement

object [n1] *thing able to be seen/felt/perceived* article, body, bulk, commodity, doodad*, doohickey*, entity, fact, gadget, gizmo*, item, mass, matter, phenomenon, reality, something, substance, thingamajig*, volume, whatchamacallit*, widget*; CONCEPT *433*

object [n2] *purpose, use* aim, design, duty, end, end in view, end purpose, function, goal, idea, intent, intention, mark, mission, motive, objective, point, reason, target, view, wish; CONCEPT *659*

object [n3] *aim, recipient* butt*, focus, ground zero*, receiver, target, victim, zero*; CONCEPTS *124,532* —*Ant.* subject

object [v] *disagree, argue against* balk, be displeased, challenge, complain, crab*, criticize, cross, demur, deprecate, disapprove, disavow, discommend, discountenance, disesteem, dispute, dissent, except, expostulate, frown, go-one-on-one*, gripe, grouse, inveigh, kick*, make a stink*, mix it up with*, oppose, protest, rail, raise objection, rant, rave, remonstrate, sound off*, spurn, squawk*, storm, take exception, take on, tangle*; CONCEPTS *12,21,46* —*Ant.* accept, agree, concur, consent, go along

objection [n] *argument, disagreement* cavil, censure, challenge, counter-argument, criticism, declination, demur, demurral, demurring, difficulty, disapprobation, disapproval, discontent, disesteem, disinclination, dislike, displeasure, dissatisfaction, doubt, exception, grievance, gripe, hesitation, kick, niggle*, odium, opposition, protest, protestation, question, rejection, reluctance, remonstrance, remonstration, repugnancy, revilement, scruple, shrinking, squawk*, stink*, unwillingness; CONCEPTS *21,46,410,689* —*Ant.* acceptance, agreement, concurrence, consent

objectionable [adj] *not nice; unpleasant* abhorrent, censurable, deplorable, disagreeable, dislikable, displeasing, distasteful, exceptionable, ill-favored, inadmissible, indecorous, inexpedient, insufferable, intolerable, invidious, loathsome, lousy, murder, noxious, obnoxious, offensive, opprobrious, poison, regrettable, repellent, reprehensible, repugnant, repulsive, revolting, unacceptable, undesirable, unfit, unpalatable, unsatisfactory, unseemly, unsuitable, unwanted, unwelcome; CONCEPTS *548, 558,570* —*Ant.* good, nice, pleasant, welcome

objective [adj] *fair, impartial* cold, cool, detached, disinterested, dispassionate, equitable, evenhanded, impersonal, judicial, just, like it is*, nondiscriminatory, nonpartisan, open-minded*, straight, strictly business*, unbiased, uncolored, unemotional, uninvolved, unprejudiced, unprepossessed; CONCEPTS *403,542* —*Ant.* partial, prejudiced, subjective, unfair

objective [n] *aim, goal* ambition, aspiration, design, end, end in view*, ground zero*, intention, mark, mission, object, purpose, target, zero*; CONCEPT *659*

objectively [adv] *impartially* considerately, detachedly, disinterestedly, dispassionately, equitably, evenhandedly, indifferently, justly, neutrally, on the up and up*, open-mindedly*, soberly, squarely, with an open mind*, with impartiality, with objectivity, without favor, without prejudice; CONCEPTS *542,544* —*Ant.* emotionally, subjectively

objectivity [n] *impartiality* detachment, disinterest, disinterestedness, dispassion, equality, equitableness, indifference, neutrality, open-mindedness; CONCEPTS *403,542*

objet d'art [n] *work of art* bibelot, bric-a-brac,

collector's item, collector's piece, curio, knick-knack; CONCEPT 446

objurgate [v] *berate* bawl out, castigate, censure, chastise, chew out*, chide, give one hell*, jump all over*, rake over the coals*, rebuke, reprimand, reproach, scold, upbraid; CONCEPT 52

obligate [v] *require* astrict, bind, constrain, force, indebt, make indebted, oblige, restrain, restrict; CONCEPTS 53,130,646 —*Ant.* let off

obligated [adj] *bound* bounden, called by duty, committed, compelled, contracted, duty-bound, enslaved, forced, indebted, indentured, obliged, pledged, required, tied, under obligation, urged; CONCEPT 554

obligation [n] *responsibility* accountability, accountableness, agreement, bond, burden, business, call, cause, charge, chit*, commitment, committal, compulsion, conscience, constraint, contract, debit, debt, devoir, due bill, dues, duty, engagement, IOU*, liability, must, necessity, need, occasion, onus, ought, part, place, promise, requirement, restraint, right, trust, understanding; CONCEPTS 329,335,388,645

obligatory [adj] *essential, required* binding, coercive, compulsory, compulsory, de rigueur, enforced, imperative, imperious, mandatory, necessary, requisite, unavoidable; CONCEPT 546 —*Ant.* nonessential, optional, unrequired, voluntary

oblige [v1] *require* bind, coerce, command, compel, constrain, force, impel, make, necessitate, obligate, shotgun*; CONCEPTS 14,242,646 —*Ant.* let off

oblige [v2] *do a favor or kindness* accommodate, aid, assist, avail, bend over backward*, benefit, come around, contribute, convenience, don't make waves*, favor, fill the bill*, fit in, go fifty-fifty*, gratify, grin and bear it*, help, indulge, make a deal*, make room*, meet halfway*, please, profit, put oneself out*, roll with it*, serve, swim with the tide*, take it*, toe the mark*; CONCEPTS 110,136,384 —*Ant.* be mean

obliged [adj] *bound* bounden, called by duty, committed, compelled, contracted, duty-bound, enslaved, forced, indebted, indentured, obligated, pledged, required, tied, under obligation, urged; CONCEPT 554

obliging [adj] *friendly, helpful* accommodating, agreeable, amiable, cheerful, civil, complaisant, considerate, cooperative, courteous, eager to please, easy, easygoing, good-humored, good-natured, hospitable, kind, lenient, mild, polite, willing; CONCEPTS 401,404 —*Ant.* disobliging, inconsiderate, mean, uncooperative, unfriendly, unhelpful

oblique [adj1] *slanting; at an angle* angled, askance, askew, aslant, asymmetrical, awry, bent, cater-cornered, crooked, diagonal, distorted, diverging, inclined, inclining, leaning, on the bias, pitched, pitching, sideways, skew, slanted, sloped, sloping, strained, tilted, tilting, tipped, tipping, turned, twisted; CONCEPT 490

oblique [adj2] *indirect, evasive* backhanded, circuitous, circular, circumlocutory, collateral, devious, implied, obliquitous, obscure, round-about, sidelong, vague; CONCEPT 267 —*Ant.* direct, forthright, straightforward

obliterate [v] *destroy* annihilate, ax*, black out*, blot out*, blue pencil*, bog, cancel, cover, cut, defeat, delete, do in*, efface, eliminate, eradicate, erase, expunge, exterminate, extirpate, finish, finish off*, kill, knock off*, knock out*, KO*, level*, liquidate, mark out, nix*, obscure, off, ravage, root out*, rub off*, rub out*, scratch, scrub, shoot down, sink, smash, squash, take apart, take out*, torpedo*, total*, trash*, wash out*, waste, wipe off face of earth*, wipe out*, X-out*, zap*; CONCEPT 252 —*Ant.* build, construct, create

oblivion [n1] *mental blankness* abeyance, amnesia, carelessness, disregard, forgetfulness, inadvertence, indifference, insensibility, insensibleness, Lethe*, neglect, nirvana*, obliviousness, unawareness, unconcern, unconsciousness, unmindfulness; CONCEPTS 410,633 —*Ant.* awareness, consciousness, understanding

oblivion [n2] *nothingness, obscurity* blackness, darkness, eclipse, emptiness, extinction, limbo, nihility, nirvana*, nonexistence, nothing, nowhere*, nullity, out there*, void; CONCEPTS 407,672,679

oblivious [adj] *unaware, ignorant* absent, absentminded, absorbed, abstracted, amnesic, blind*, blundering, careless, deaf*, disregardful, distracted, dreamy, forgetful, forgetting, gone, heedless, inattentive, incognizant, inconversant, insensible, neglectful, negligent, not all there*, out to lunch*, overlooking, preoccupied, regardless, spacey*, strung out*, unacquainted, unconcerned, unconscious, undiscerning, unfamiliar, uninformed, uninstructed, unknowing, unmindful, unnoticing, unobservant, unrecognizing, unwitting, zonked*; CONCEPTS 402,403,542 —*Ant.* aware, concerned, conscious, mindful, sensitive

oblong [adj] *elongated and rounded* egg-shaped, ellipsoidal, elliptical, elongate, long, oval, ovaliform, ovaloid, ovate, ovated, ovoid, rectangular; CONCEPT 486

obloquy [n] *calumny* abuse, animadversion, aspersion, bad press, censure, criticism, defamation, disgrace, humiliation, ignominy, insult, invective, reproach, slander, vituperation; CONCEPTS 271,277,278

obnoxious [adj] *offensive, repulsive* abhorrent, abominable, annoying, awful, beastly*, big mouth*, detestable, disagreeable, disgusting, dislikable, displeasing, foul, gross*, hateable, hateful, heel, horrid, insufferable, invidious, loathsome, mean, nasty, nauseating, objectionable, odious, off-color*, ornery, pain in the neck*, pesky*, pestiferous, pill*, repellent, reprehensible, repugnant, revolting, rotten, sickening, stinking, unpleasant; CONCEPTS 267,401,542 —*Ant.* agreeable, delightful, kind, likeable, nice, pleasant, soft

obscene [adj] *indecent, offensive, immoral* atrocious, barnyard*, bawdy, blue*, coarse, crude, dirty*, disgusting, evil, filthy, foul, gross, heinous, hideous, horrible, immodest, improper, impure, lascivious, lewd, licentious, loathsome, loose*, lustful, nasty, noisome, outrageous, porno*, pornographical, profane, prurient, rank*, raunchy*, raw, repellent, repugnant, ribald, salacious, scabrous, scatological, scurrilous, shameless, shocking, sickening, smutty*, suggestive, unchaste, unclean, unwholesome, vile, wanton, wicked, X-rated*; CONCEPTS 267,372,545 —*Ant.* clean, decent, innocent, moral, pure, upright

obscenity [n] *indecency, immorality; vulgarism* abomination, affront, atrocity, bawdiness, blight, blueness*, coarseness, curse, dirtiness, dirty name*, dirty word*, evil, filthiness, foulness, four-letter word*, immodesty, impropriety, impurity, indecency, indelicacy, lewdness, licentiousness, lubricity, offense, outrage, porn*, pornography, profanity, prurience, salacity, scatology, scurrility, sleaze*, smut*, smuttiness, suggestiveness, swearword, vileness, vulgarity, wrong, X-rating*; CONCEPTS 278,645 —*Ant.* cleanness, decency, innocence, morality, propriety, purity, uprightness

obscure [adj1] *not easily understood* abstruse, ambiguous, arcane, clear as mud*, complicated, concealed, confusing, cryptic, dark, deep, dim, doubtful, enigmatic, enigmatical, esoteric, far-out, hazy, hidden, illegible, illogical, impenetrable, incomprehensible, inconceivable, incredible, indecisive, indefinite, indeterminate, indistinct, inexplicable, inscrutable, insoluble, intricate, involved, mysterious, occult, opaque, recondite, unaccountable, unbelievable, unclear, undefined, unfathomable, unintelligible, vague; CONCEPT 529 —*Ant.* apparent, clear, explicit, obvious, perceptible, understood

obscure [adj2] *cloudy, shadowy* blurred, caliginous, clouded, dark, dense, dim, dusk, dusky, faint, fuliginous, gloomy, indistinct, lightless, murky, obfuscated, shady, somber, tenebrous, umbrageous, unilluminated, unlit, veiled; CONCEPT 617 —*Ant.* bright, clear, visible

obscure [adj3] *out-of-the-way, little-known* abstruse, arcane, blind, cabalistic, close, covered, cryptic, dark, deep, devious, distant, enigmatic, esoteric, far, far-off, hidden, humble, inaccessible, inconspicuous, inglorious, invisible, irrelevant, lonesome, lowly, minor, mysterious, nameless, odd, oracular, orphic, rare, recondite, remote, removed, reticent, retired, secluded, secret, secretive, seldom seen, sequestered, solitary, undisclosed, undistinguished, unheard-of, unhonored, unimportant, unknown, unnoted, unseen, unsung; CONCEPT 576 —*Ant.* distinguished, famous, known

obscure [v] *conceal, hide* adumbrate, becloud, bedim, befog, belie, blear, blind, block, block out, blur, camouflage, cloak, cloud, cloud the issue*, con, confuse, cover, cover up, darken, dim, disguise, double-talk*, eclipse, equivocate, falsify, fog, fuzz, gloom, gray, haze, mask, misrepresent, mist, muddy, muddy the waters*, murk, obfuscate, overcast, overcloud, overshadow, pettifog*, screen, shade, shadow, shroud, stonewall*, throw up smoke screen*, veil, wrap; CONCEPTS 16,63,172,188 —*Ant.* illuminate, loose, reveal

obsequious [adj] *groveling, submissive* abject, beggarly, brownnosing*, complacent, compliable, compliant, cringing, crouching, deferential, enslaved, fawning, flattering, ingratiating, kowtowing*, menial, obeisant, oily*, parasitic, parasitical, prostrate, respectful, servile, slavish, sneaking, sniveling, spineless*, stipendiary, subject, submissive, subordinate, subservient,

sycophantic, toadying*, unctuous; CONCEPTS 401,404 —*Ant.* arrogant, assertive, brazen, confident, presumptuous

obsequy [n] *funeral ceremony* eulogy, funeral rite, funeral service; CONCEPTS 69,278

observable [adj] *apparent* appreciable, clear, detectable, discernible, discoverable, evident, noticeable, obvious, open, palpable, patent, perceivable, perceptible, recognizable, sensible, tangible, visible; CONCEPTS 529,576 —*Ant.* hidden, imperceptible, unrecognizable

observance [n1] *attention to, knowledge of something* acknowledgment, acquittal, acquittance, adherence, awareness, carrying out, celebration, cognizance, compliance, discharge, fidelity, fulfillment, heed, heeding, honoring, keeping, mark, mind, note, notice, obedience, observation, performance, regard, remark, satisfaction; CONCEPTS 409,410,633 —*Ant.* carelessness, heedlessness, neglect, thoughtlessness

observance [n2] *ceremony, rite* celebration, ceremonial, custom, fashion, form, formality, liturgy, performance, practice, ritual, rule, service, tradition; CONCEPTS 377,384,688 —*Ant.* unorthodoxy

observant [adj] *alert, watchful* advertent, alive, attentive, bright, clear-sighted*, comprehending, considering, contemplating, correct, deducing, detecting, discerning, discovering, discriminating, eager, eagle-eyed*, heedful, intelligent, intentive, interested, keen, mindful, not missing a trick*, obedient, observative, on one's toes*, on the ball*, penetrating, perceptive, questioning, quick, regardful, searching, sensitive, sharp, sharp-eyed*, surveying, understanding, vigilant, wide-awake*; CONCEPTS 402,403 —*Ant.* careless, inattentive, indifferent, thoughtless, unaware, unmindful, unobservant, unwatchful

observation [n1] *attention, scrutiny* ascertainment, check, cognition, cognizance, conclusion, consideration, detection, estimation, examination, experience, heedfulness, information, inspection, investigation, knowledge, mark, measurement, mind, monitoring, note, notice, noticing, once-over*, overlook, perception, probe, recognizing, regard, remark, research, review, search, study, supervision, surveillance, view, watching; CONCEPTS 409,410 —*Ant.* heedlessness, inattention, indifference, neglect, thoughtlessness

observation [n2] *comment on something scrutinized* annotation, catch phrase, comeback, commentary, crack*, finding, mention, mouthful*, note, obiter dictum, opinion, pronouncement, reflection, remark, saying, say so*, thought, utterance, wisecrack; CONCEPTS 51, 278 —*Ant.* no comment

observe [v1] *see, notice* beam, behold, catch, contemplate, detect, dig, discern, discover, distinguish, eagle-eye*, espy, examine, eyeball*, flash*, get a load of*, get an eyeful of*, inspect, keep one's eye on*, lamp*, look at, make out*, mark, mind, monitor, note, pay attention to, perceive, pick up on*, read, recognize, regard, scrutinize, spot, spy, study, survey, take in*, view, watch, witness; CONCEPTS 24,34,103,265,626 —*Ant.* ignore, miss, overlook

observe [v2] *comment, remark* animadvert, commentate, declare, mention, mouth off*, note, opine, say, state, wisecrack; CONCEPT *51* —*Ant.* be quiet, forget

observe [v3] *celebrate, commemorate* dedicate, hold, honor, keep, remember, respect, revere, reverence, solemnize, venerate; CONCEPT *377* —*Ant.* forget, miss

observe [v4] *abide by, obey* adhere, adopt, comply, comply with, conform, follow, fulfill, heed, honor, keep, mind, perform, respect; CONCEPTS *91,384* —*Ant.* break, violate

observer [n] *spectator* beholder, bystander, eyewitness, gaper, gazer, looker, looker-on, onlooker, viewer, watcher, witness; CONCEPTS *366,423*

obsess [v] *preoccupy* beset, consume, dominate, engross, grip, harass, haunt, hold, infatuate, possess, torment; CONCEPT *403*

obsessed [adj] *consumed, driven about belief, desire* bedeviled, beset, bewitched, captivated, controlled, dogged*, dominated, eat sleep and breathe*, engrossed, fiendish, fixated, gripped, harassed, haunted, have on the brain*, held, hooked, hung up on*, immersed in, infatuated, into*, overpowered, plagued*, possessed, preoccupied, prepossessed, really into*, seized, taken over, tied up*, tormented, troubled, turned on, up to here in*, wound up with*, wrapped up in*; CONCEPTS *403,404* —*Ant.* indifferent, unconcerned

obsession [n] *fixation; consumption with belief, desire* attraction, ax to grind*, bug in ear*, case*, complex, compulsion, concrete idea, craze*, crush, delusion, enthusiasm, fancy, fascination, fetish, hang-up*, idée fixe, infatuation, mania, monkey*, must, neurosis, one-track mind*, passion, phantom, phobia, preoccupation, something on the brain*, thing*, tiger by the tail*; CONCEPTS *20,410,529, 689,690* —*Ant.* indifference

obsolete [adj] *no longer in use, in vogue* anachronistic, ancient, antediluvian, antiquated, antique, archaic, bygone, dated, dead, dead and gone*, dinosaur*, discarded, disused, done for*, dusty, extinct, fossil, gone, had it*, has-been*, horse and buggy*, kaput*, moldy*, moth-eaten*, old, old-fashioned, old-hat, old-school, out*, outmoded, out-of-date, out-of-fashion, outworn, passé, stale, superannuated, superseded, timeworn, unfashionable; CONCEPTS *539,560,589* —*Ant.* contemporary, current, in vogue, modern, new, present, up-to-date

obstacle [n] *impediment, barrier* bar, block, booby trap*, bump*, catch, Catch-22*, check, clog*, crimp*, difficulty, disincentive, encumbrance, hamper, handicap, hang-up*, hardship, hindrance, hitch*, hurdle, interference, interruption, joker*, monkey wrench*, mountain, obstruction, restriction, rub*, snag, stumbling block*, traverse, vicissitude; CONCEPTS *470,532,666,674* —*Ant.* advantage, assistance, blessing, clearance, help

obstinate [adj] *stubborn, determined* adamant, cantankerous, contradictory, contrary, contumacious, convinced, dead set on*, dogged, dogmatic, firm, hard, hardened, headstrong, heady, immovable, indomitable, inflexible, intractable, intransigent, locked in*, mulish*, obdurate, opinionated, opinionative, persistent, pertinacious, perverse, pigheaded*, recalcitrant, refractory, relentless, resolved, restive, self-willed, steadfast, strong-minded, tenacious, unalterable, unflinching, unmanageable, unyielding, willful; CONCEPTS *401,542* —*Ant.* agreeable, amenable, cooperative, flexible, helpful, submissive, willing, yielding

obstreperous [adj] *noisy* blusterous, boisterous, booming, clamorous, disorderly, loud, out of hand, piercing, raising Cain*, raising the roof*, rambunctious, riotous, rowdy, screaming, strepitous, tumultuous, unmanageable, unruly, uproarious, vociferous, wild; CONCEPTS *592,594*

obstruct [v] *restrict, restrain* arrest, bar, barricade, block, check, choke, clog, close, congest, crab, curb, cut off, drag one's feet*, fill, foul up, frustrate, get in the way*, hamper, hamstring*, hang up*, hide, hinder, hold up, impede, inhibit, interfere, interrupt, mask, monkey with*, obscure, occlude, plug, restrain, retard, sandbag*, shield, shut off, slow down, stall, stonewall*, stop, stopper, stymie*, terminate, throttle, thwart, trammel, weigh down; CONCEPTS *5,121,130* —*Ant.* abet, aid, assist, boost, clear, help, promote, support

obstruction [n] *obstacle, impediment* bar, barricade, barrier, block, blockage, blocking, booby trap*, check, checkmate*, circumvention, difficulty, gridlock*, hamper, hindrance, hurdle, interference, jam*, lock, monkey wrench*, mountain*, restraint, roadblock*, snag, stop, stoppage, stumbling block*, trammel, trouble, wall; CONCEPTS *532,674* —*Ant.* aid, assistance, boost, help, promotion, support

obtain [v] *get, acquire* access, accomplish, achieve, annex, attain, beg borrow or steal*, capture, chalk up*, collect, come by, compass, cop*, corral, drum up*, earn, effect, fetch, gain, gather, get at, get hold of*, get one's hands on*, glean, gobble up*, grab, have, hoard, inherit, invade, lay up, make use of, nab*, occupy, pick up, pocket*, procure, purchase, reach, realize, reap, receive, recover, retrieve, salvage, save, score, scrape together, scrape up, secure, seize, snag, take, wangle, win; CONCEPT *120* —*Ant.* forfeit, forsake, lose, sacrifice

obtainable [adj] *achievable, available* at hand*, attainable, derivable, duck soup*, gettable, in stock, no problem*, no sweat*, on deck*, on offer*, on tap*, piece of cake*, procurable, purchasable, pushover, ready, realizable, securable, there for the taking*, to be had*; CONCEPTS *528,576* —*Ant.* unachievable, unavailable, unobtainable

obtrusive [adj] *pushy, obvious* bulging, busy, forward, impertinent, importunate, interfering, intrusive, jutting, meddlesome, meddling, nosy, noticeable, officious, presumptuous, projecting, prominent, protruding, protuberant, prying, sticking out*; CONCEPTS *401,542* —*Ant.* modest, shy, unobtrusive

obtuse [adj1] *slow to understand* dense, dopey*, dull*, dumb, imperceptive, insensitive, opaque, slow on uptake*, stolid, thick, uncomprehending, unintelligent; CONCEPT *402* —*Ant.* bright, intelligent, quick, smart

obtuse [adj2] *blunt, not sharp* round, rounded; CONCEPTS *485,486* —*Ant.* pointed, sharp

obviate [v] *make unnecessary* anticipate, avert, block, counter, counteract, deter, do away with, forestall, forfend, hinder, interfere, interpose, intervene, preclude, prevent, remove, restrain, rule out, stave off, ward; CONCEPT *121* —*Ant.* allow, help, permit

obvious [adj] *apparent, understandable* accessible, barefaced, bright, clear, clear as a bell*, conclusive, conspicuous, discernible, distinct, distinguishable, evident, explicit, exposed, glaring, indisputable, in evidence, lucid, manifest, noticeable, observable, open, overt, palpable, patent, perceivable, perceptible, plain, precise, prominent, pronounced, public, recognizable, self-evident, self-explanatory, standing out, straightforward, transparent, unconcealed, undeniable, undisguised, unmistakable, unsubtle, visible; CONCEPTS *485,529* —*Ant.* ambiguous, indefinite, obscure, unclear, vague

obviously [adv] *unmistakably* apparently, certainly, clearly, definitely, distinctly, evidently, incontestably, noticeably, of course, openly, plainly, seemingly, surely, undeniably, undoubtedly, unquestionably, visibly, without doubt; CONCEPTS *535,552*

occasion [n1] *chance* break*, convenience, demand, excuse, incident, instant, moment, need, occurrence, opening, opportunity, possibility, season, shot*, show, time, use; CONCEPT *693*

occasion [n2] *reason, cause* antecedent, basis, call, circumstance, determinant, excuse, foundation, ground, grounds, incident, inducement, influence, justification, motivation, motive, necessity, obligation, prompting, provocation, purpose, right, warrant; CONCEPT *661*

occasion [n3] *event, happening* affair, celebration, circumstance, episode, experience, go*, goings-on*, happening, incident, instant, milepost*, milestone, moment, occurrence, scene, thing*, time, while; CONCEPTS *2,386*

occasion [v] *make happen, bring about* breed, cause, create, do, effect, elicit, engender, evoke, generate, give rise to, hatch, induce, influence, inspire, lead to, move, muster, originate, persuade, produce, prompt, provoke, work up; CONCEPTS *68,242*

occasional [adj] *irregular, sporadic* casual, desultory, especial, exceptional, exclusive, few, incidental, infrequent, intermittent, not habitual, odd, off and on*, particular, random, rare, scarce, seldom, special, specific, uncommon, unfrequent, unusual; CONCEPTS *530,541* —*Ant.* constant, frequent, regular, steady, usual

occasionally [adv] *every now and then* at intervals, at random, at times, every so often, from time to time, hardly, infrequently, irregularly, now and again, once in a blue moon*, once in a while, once or twice*, on occasion, periodically, seldom, sometimes, sporadically, uncommonly; CONCEPTS *530,541* —*Ant.* always, constantly, frequently, regularly, steadily, usually

occlude [v] *block, prevent* choke, clog, close, close out, congest, curb, fill, hinder, impede, leave out, lock out, obstruct, plug, seal, shut, stopper, stop up, throttle; CONCEPTS *121,201* —*Ant.* allow, help, permit

occlusion [n] *obstruction* barricade, barrier, block, blockage, blocking, closure, stoppage; CONCEPTS *470,532,666,674*

occult [adj] *mysterious, secret; supernatural* abstruse, acroamatic, arcane, cabalistic, concealed, deep, eerie, esoteric, hermetic, hidden, invisible, magic, magical, mystic, mystical, obscure, orphic, preternatural, profound, psychic, recondite, transmundane, unearthly, unknown, unrevealed, veiled, weird; CONCEPTS *576,582* —*Ant.* known, natural

occupancy [n] *residence of place* control, deed, habitation, holding, inhabitance, inhabitancy, occupation, ownership, possession, retention, settlement, tenancy, tenure, term, title, use; CONCEPTS *518,710*

occupant [n] *person who resides in a place* addressee, denizen, dweller, holder, householder, incumbent, indweller, inhabitant, lessee, occupier, possessor, renter, resident, resider, tenant, user; CONCEPT *414* —*Ant.* displaced person

occupation [n1] *profession, business* activity, affair, calling, chosen work, craft, daily grind*, day gig*, do, dodge*, employment, game*, grindstone*, hang*, job, lick*, line, line of work, métier, moonlight*, nine-to-five*, play*, post, pursuit, racket*, rat race*, slot*, thing*, trade, vocation, walk of life*, what one is into*, work; CONCEPTS *349,351,360* —*Ant.* entertainment, fun, hobby, pastime

occupation [n2] *control, possession* habitation, holding, inhabitancy, inhabitation, occupancy, ownership, residence, settlement, tenancy, tenure, title, use; CONCEPTS *518,710*

occupation [n3] *seizure, takeover* attack, capture, conquest, entering, foreign rule, invasion, subjugation; CONCEPTS *86,90,320* —*Ant.* giving up, surrender, yielding

occupational [adj] *pertaining to work* business, career, employment, job-related, professional, vocational, work; CONCEPT *360*

occupied [adj1] *busy* active, clocked up*, employed, engaged, engrossed, head over heels*, tied up*, too much on plate*, working; CONCEPT *542* —*Ant.* idle, inactive, not busy, unoccupied

occupied [adj2] *inhabited; in use* busy, engaged, full, leased, lived-in*, peopled*, populated, populous, rented, settled, taken, unavailable, utilized; CONCEPT *560* —*Ant.* empty, free, uninhabited, unoccupied, vacant

occupy [v1] *be busy with* absorb, amuse, attend, be active with, be concerned with, busy, divert, employ, engage, engross, entertain, fill, hold attention, immerse, interest, involve, keep busy, monopolize, preoccupy, soak, take up, tie up, utilize; CONCEPTS *7,17,19,22* —*Ant.* be inactive, be lazy, idle

occupy [v2] *reside; use* be established, be in command, be in residence, cover, dwell, ensconce, establish, fill, hold, inhabit, involve, keep, live in, maintain, own, people, permeate, pervade, populate, possess, remain, sit, stay, take up, tenant, utilize; CONCEPTS *225,226* —*Ant.* not use

occupy [v3] *seize, take over* capture, conquer, garrison, hold, invade, keep, obtain, overrun, take possession; CONCEPTS *86,90,320* —*Ant.* surrender, yield

occur [v1] *take place, happen* action, appear, arise, befall, be found, be present, betide, chance, come about, come off*, come to pass, cook*, crop up, develop, ensue, eventualize, eventuate, exist, follow, go, jell*, manifest, materialize, obtain, present itself, result, shake*, show, smoke*, take place, transpire, turn out, turn up; CONCEPTS 4,242

occur [v2] *come to mind* come to one's*, cross one's mind*, dawn on*, expose, flash*, go through one's head*, hit, offer itself, present itself, reveal, spring to mind*, strike, suggest itself; CONCEPTS 34,43

occurrence [n] *happening, development* accident, adventure, affair, appearance, circumstance, condition, contingency, emergency, episode, event, exigency, existence, incidence, incident, instance, juncture, manifestation, materialization, occasion, pass, piece, proceeding, routine, scene, situation, state, thing*, transaction, transpiration; CONCEPTS 3,4,230,696

ocean [n] *very large body of water* blue*, bounding main*, brine, briny*, briny deep*, Davy Jones's locker*, deep, drink*, high seas*, main, pond, puddle, salt water, sea, seaway, Seven Seas, sink, tide; CONCEPT 514

oceanic [adj] *marine* aquatic, coastal, maritime, nautical, naval, oceangoing, oceanographic, of the sea, pelagic, seafaring, seagoing; CONCEPT 536

odd/oddball [adj1] *unusual, abnormal* atypical, avant-garde, bizarre, character, crazy, curious, deviant, different, eccentric, erratic, exceptional, extraordinary, fantastic, flaky*, freak*, freakish*, freaky*, funny, idiosyncratic, irregular, kinky*, kooky*, offbeat, off-the-wall*, outlandish, out of the ordinary, peculiar, quaint, queer, rare, remarkable, singular, spacey*, strange, uncanny, uncommon, unconventional, unique, way out*, weird, weirdo*, whimsical; CONCEPTS 404,542,564 —Ant. common, conventional, habitual, normal, ordinary, regular, standard, usual

odd [adj2] *miscellaneous, various* accidental, casual, chance, contingent, different, fluky*, fortuitous, fragmentary, incidental, irregular, occasional, odd-lot*, periodic, random, seasonal, sundry, varied; CONCEPT 552 —Ant. like, similar, unvaried

odd [adj3] *single, unmatched; uneven* additional, alone, exceeding, individual, irregular, left, leftover, lone, lonely, over, over and above, remaining, singular, sole, solitary, spare, surplus, unconsumed, unitary, unpaired; CONCEPTS 480,577 —Ant. matched

oddity [n1] *abnormality* anomaly, bizarreness, characteristic, conversation piece, curiosity, eccentricity, extraordinariness, freak, freakishness, idiosyncrasy, incongruity, irregularity, kink, oddness, outlandishness, peculiarity, phenomenon, queerness, quirk, rarity, singularity, strangeness, unconventionality, unnaturalness; CONCEPTS 260,411,665 —Ant. convention, habit, norm, normality, regularity, standard, usualness

oddity/oddball [n2] *person who is very different* case*, character, duck*, eccentric, fish out of water*, maverick, misfit, odd bird*, original*, rara avis, screwball*, weirdo*; CONCEPT 423 —Ant. conservative, normal

odds [n1] *advantage* allowance, benefit, bulge, difference, disparity, dissimilarity, distinction, draw, edge, handicap, head start, lead, overlay,

start, superiority, vantage; CONCEPT 693 —Ant. disadvantage

odds [n2] *probability* balance, chances, favor, likelihood, superiority, toss-up; CONCEPT 650 —Ant. improbability, unlikelihood

odds and ends [n] *miscellaneous paraphernalia* assortment, bits, bits and pieces*, debris, etcetera*, hodgepodge, jumble, leavings, litter, medley, mélange, melee, miscellany, motley, oddments, olio, particles, potpourri, remnants, rest, rubbish, rummage, scraps, sundry items, this and that*; CONCEPTS 260,432,446

odds-on-favorite [n] *front-runner* best bet, contender, favorite, first choice, top seed; CONCEPTS 423,446

ode [n] *poem* ballad, composition, epode, limerick, lyric, poesy, rhyme, song, sonnet, verse; CONCEPTS 268,282

odious [adj] *hateful, horrible* abhorrent, abominable, creepy*, detestable, disgusting, execrable, foul, hateable, horrid, loathsome, mean, obnoxious, offensive, ornery, pain in the neck*, repellent, repugnant, repulsive, revolting, unpleasant, vile; CONCEPTS 401,404 —Ant. agreeable, delightful, great, likeable, loveable, pleasing

odium [n] *shame, dishonor* abhorrence, antipathy, aversion, bar sinister*, black eye*, blame, blot, blur, brand, censure, condemnation, detestation, disapproval, discredit, disesteem, disfavor, disgrace, dislike, disprobation, disrepute, enmity, execration, hate, hatred, ignominy, infamy, malice, obloquy, onus, opprobrium, rebuke, reprobation, resentment, slur, spot, stain, stigma; CONCEPTS 29,388 —Ant. approval, honor, regard, respect

odor [n] *scent* air, aroma, bouquet, effluvium, efflux, emanation, essence, exhalation, flavor, fragrance, musk, perfume, pungence, pungency, redolence, smell, snuff, stench, stink, tang, tincture, trail, whiff; CONCEPT 599

odorless [adj] *without fragrance* deodorant, deodorizing, flat, inodorous, odor-free, unaromatic, unfragrant, unperfumed, unscented, unsmelling; CONCEPT 598 —Ant. aromatic, odorous, perfumed, scented, smelly

odorous [adj] *having fragrance* aromatic, balmy, dank, effluvious, fetid, flavorsome, flowery, foul, fragrant, heady, honeyed, loud, malodorous, mephitic, miasmic, moldy, musty, nauseous, odoriferant, odoriferous, offensive, olfactive, olfactory, perfumatory, perfumed, perfumy, pungent, putrid, redolent, reeking, rotten, savorous, savory, scented, scentful, scent-laden, skunky*, smelly, spicy, stagnant, stale, stinking, strong, sweet, sweet-scented, sweet-smelling, tumaceous, unsavory, whiffy*; CONCEPT 598 —Ant. odorless

odyssey [n] *journey* adventure, excursion, expedition, exploration, pilgrimage, quest, sojourn, tour, travels, trek, trip, voyage, wanderings; CONCEPT 224

of course [adv] *as expected* by all means, certainly, definitely, indeed, indubitably, naturally, obviously, surely, undoubtedly, without a doubt; CONCEPT 544

off [adj1] *gone; remote* absent, canceled, finished, inoperative, negligible, not employed, not on duty, on vacation, outside, postponed,

slender, slight, slim, small, unavailable;
CONCEPT 552 —*Ant.* here, present

off [adj2] *inferior; spoiled* bad, decomposed,
disappointing, disheartening, displeasing,
low-quality, mortifying, not up to par*, not up
to snuff*, poor, putrid, quiet, rancid, rotten,
slack, sour, substandard, turned, unrewarding,
unsatisfactory; CONCEPT 570 —*Ant.* on

off [adv] *apart, away* above, absent, afar, ahead,
aside, away from, behind, below, beneath, beside, disappearing, divergent, elsewhere, far,
farther away, gone away, in the distance, not
here, out, over, removed, to one side, turning
aside, up front, vanishing; CONCEPTS 583,778
—*Ant.* close, here, present

off and on [adv] *intermittently* alternately, at
intervals, at times, every once in a while, every
so often, fluctuating, from time to time, irregularly, now and then, occasionally, once in a
while, on occasion, sometimes, sporadically,
vacillating, variably; CONCEPTS 530,541

offbeat [adj] *strange, very different* bizarre,
bohemian*, eccentric, far-out, freaky, fresh,
idiosyncratic, novel, oddball, outré, uncommon,
unconventional, unique, unorthodox, unusual,
way-out*, weird; CONCEPT 564 —*Ant.* expected,
normal, usual

off-center [adj] *wide* adrift, askew, astray,
far-off, inaccurate, off-course, off-target, off
the mark, stray; CONCEPTS 581,583

off-color [adj] *risqué* blue*, indelicate, purple*,
racy*, salty*, shady, suggestive, vulgar,
wicked; CONCEPT 545 —*Ant.* clean, nice

off-course [adj] *strayed* astray, confused,
disoriented, lost, lost one's bearing, off-track,
roaming, roving; CONCEPTS 576,583

offend [v] *displease, insult* affront, aggrieve,
anger, annoy, antagonize, be disagreeable,
disgruntle, disgust, disoblige, distress, disturb,
exasperate, fret, gall, horrify, hurt, irritate, jar,
miff, nauseate, nettle, outrage, pain, pique,
provoke, repel, repulse, rile, shock, sicken,
sin, slight, slur, snub, sting, transgress, trespass,
turn one off*, upset, vex, wound, zing*;
CONCEPTS 7,14,19 —*Ant.* compliment, please

offender [n] *perpetrator* con*, convict, criminal, crook, culprit, delinquent, felon, guilty
party, guilty person, jailbird*, lawbreaker,
malefactor, sinner, suspect, transgressor,
wrongdoer; CONCEPT 91

offense [n1] *violation, trespass* breach, crime,
delinquency, fault, infraction, lapse, malfeasance, misdeed, misdemeanor, peccadillo,
sin, transgression, wrong, wrongdoing;
CONCEPTS 192,691 —*Ant.* obedience

offense [n2] *insult, displeasure* affront, aggression, assailment, assault, attack, battery, black
eye*, blitz*, blitzkrieg*, dig*, dirty dig*,
harm, hit*, hurt, indignation, indignity, injury,
injustice, left-handed compliment*, mugging,
onset, onslaught, outrage, push*, put-down*,
slam*, slap in the face*, slight, snub, zinger*;
CONCEPT 52 —*Ant.* kindness, pleasure

offense [n3] *anger, hard feelings* annoyance,
conniption*, displeasure, explosion, fit,
flare-up*, huff, indignation, ire, miff, needle*,
outburst, pique, resentment, scene, tantrum,
tizzy*, umbrage, wounded feelings, wrath;
CONCEPT 410 —*Ant.* happiness, pleasure

offensive [adj1] *disrespectful, insulting; displeasing* abhorrent, abusive, annoying, biting,
cutting, detestable, disagreeable, discourteous,
distasteful, dreadful, embarrassing, evil, foul,
ghastly, grisly, gross, hideous, horrible, horrid,
impertinent, insolent, invidious, irritating,
nauseating, objectionable, obnoxious, odious,
off-color*, offending, opprobrious, outrageous,
repellent, reprehensible, repugnant, repulsive,
revolting, rotten, rude, shocking, stinking*,
terrible, uncivil, unmannerly; CONCEPTS 267,
529,537 —*Ant.* agreeable, kind, nice, pleasing,
respectful

offensive [adj2] *attacking* aggressive, assailing, assaulting, belligerent, invading; CONCEPT
548 —*Ant.* defending, defensive, guarding

offensive [n] *attack* aggression, assailment,
assault, drive, invasion, onset, onslaught, push;
CONCEPTS 86,320 —*Ant.* defending, defensive

offer [n] *proposal, suggestion* action, attempt,
bid, endeavor, essay, feeler*, hit*, overture,
pass*, pitch*, presentation, proposition, pro-
poundment, rendition, submission, tender;
CONCEPTS 66,67,278 —*Ant.* refusal, taking,
withdrawal

offer [v1] *present, propose for acceptance*
accord, advance, afford, allow, award, be at
service, bid, come forward, display, donate,
exhibit, extend, furnish, give, grant, hold out,
lay at one's feet*, make available, move, place
at disposal*, ply, pose, press, proffer, propound,
provide, put forth, put forward, put on the
market, put up, put up for sale, sacrifice, show,
submit, suggest, tender, volunteer; CONCEPT
67 —*Ant.* take, take back, withdraw, withhold

offer [v2] *propose* adduce, advance, advise,
allege, cite, make a motion, make a pitch*,
present, proposition, submit, suggest; CONCEPT
66 —*Ant.* deny, refuse, withhold

offer [v3] *try* assay, attempt, endeavor, essay,
seek, strive, struggle, undertake; CONCEPT 87

offering [n] *donation* alms, atonement, benefaction, beneficence, charity, contribution,
expiation, gift, oblation, present, sacrifice,
subscription; CONCEPTS 337,340 —*Ant.* withdrawal

off-guard [adj] *unprepared* asleep, asleep on
the job*, daydreaming, flat-footed*, inattentive,
napping, spaced out*, unalert, unready, unsuspecting, unvigilant, unwatchful, zoned out*;
CONCEPTS 403,542

offhand [adj1] *abrupt, careless* aloof, breezy,
brusque, casual, cavalier, cool*, curt, easygoing,
folksy, glib, informal, laid-back, mellow, perfunctory, unceremonious, unconcerned, uninterested; CONCEPTS 267,401,542 —*Ant.* calculated,
careful, considered, deliberate, planned

offhand [adj2/adv] *ad-lib, extemporaneous* extemporary, extempore, impromptu, improvised,
informal, off the cuff*, off the hip*, off the top
of head*, spontaneous, spur-of-the-moment*,
throwaway*, unpremeditated, unprepared,
unrehearsed, unstudied, without preparation;
CONCEPT 267 —*Ant.* planned, practiced

office [n1] *business, responsibility* appointment,
berth, billet, capacity, charge, commission,
connection, duty, employment, function, job,
obligation, occupation, performance, place,
post, province, responsibility, role, service,

situation, spot, station, trust, work; CONCEPTS *351,362,376*

office [n2] *place of business* agency, building, bureau, cave*, center, department, facility, factory, foundry, room, salt mines*, setup, shop, store, suite, warehouse, workstation; CONCEPTS *312,439,441,448,449* —*Ant.* home

officer [n1] *person who has high position in organization* administrator, agent, appointee, bureaucrat, chief, civil servant, deputy, dignitary, director, executive, functionary, head, leader, magistrate, manager, officeholder, official, president, public servant, representative; CONCEPT *347*

officer [n2] *person in law enforcement* arm*, badge*, black and white*, captain, cop*, deputy, detective, flatfoot*, mounty, police, police officer, sergeant, sheriff; CONCEPTS *354,355,358*

official [adj] *authorized, legitimate* accredited, approved, authentic, authenticated, authoritative, bona fide, canonical, cathedral, ceremonious, certified, cleared, conclusive, correct, customary, decided, decisive, definite, endorsed, established, ex cathedra, ex officio, fitting, formal, legitimate, licensed, okay*, ordered, orthodox, positive, precise, proper, real, recognized, rightful, sanctioned, suitable, true, valid; CONCEPT *535* —*Ant.* unauthorized, unofficial, unsanctioned

official [n] *person representing organization* administrator, agent, big shot*, boss, brains*, brass*, bureaucrat, CEO*, chancellor, civil servant, commissioner, comptroller, dignitary, director, exec*, executive, front office*, functionary, governor, head person, higher-up*, incumbent, leader, magistrate, manager, marshal, mayor, minister, officeholder, officer, panjandrum, premier, president, representative, secretary, top*, top brass*, top dog*, top drawer*, treasurer; CONCEPTS *347,354*

officiate [v] *oversee, manage* act, boss, chair, command, conduct, direct, do the honors*, emcee, function, govern, handle, preside, run, serve, superintend, umpire; CONCEPT *117* —*Ant.* follow

officious [adj] *self-important, dictatorial* busy, forward, impertinent, inquisitive, interfering, intrusive, meddlesome, meddling, obtrusive, opinionated, overzealous, pragmatic, pushy, rude; CONCEPT *404* —*Ant.* modest, shy, timid

off-key [adj] *not harmonious* abnormal, anomalous, clinker*, deviant, discordant, dissonant, divergent, inharmonious, irregular, jarring, out of keeping*, out of tune*, sour*, sour note*, unnatural; CONCEPT *594* —*Ant.* concordant, harmonious, on-key

off-limits [adj] *prohibited* against the law, banned, barred, forbidden, illegal, illicit, no-no*, not allowed, outlawed, out of bounds*, restricted, taboo, unlawful, verboten; CONCEPTS *554,576*

offset [v] *counterbalance, compensate* account, allow for, atone for, balance, be equivalent, cancel out, charge, counteract, counterpoise, counterpose, countervail, equal, equalize, equipoise, make amends, make up for, negate, neutralize, outweigh, recompense, redeem, require, set off; CONCEPTS *126,232*

offshoot [n] *development, product* adjunct,

appendage, branch, by-product, derivative, descendant, limb, outgrowth, spin-off, sprout; CONCEPTS *260,824* —*Ant.* origin, source

offspring [n] *child, children* baby, bambino*, brood, chip off old block*, cub, descendant, family, generation, heir, heredity, issue, kid*, lineage, offshoot, posterity, produce, progeniture, progeny, pup*, scion, seed, spawn, succession, successor, young; CONCEPTS *296,414* —*Ant.* parent

off the cuff [adj] *impromptu* ad-lib, extemporaneous, improv*, improvised, improviso, off-hand, played by ear*, shot from the hip*, spontaneous, spur-of-the-moment, unpremeditated, unprepared, unrehearsed, unscripted, whipped up*, winged*; CONCEPT *267*

off the record [adj] *confidential* arcane, backdoor, classified, hushed, hush-hush*, in private, inside, not for publication, not public, on the QT, private, privy, secret, unofficial; CONCEPTS *267,576*

often [adv] *frequently* again and again, a number of times, generally, many a time, much, oftentimes, ofttimes, over and over, recurrently, regularly, repeatedly, time after time, time and again, usually; CONCEPT *541* —*Ant.* infrequently, rarely, seldom

ogle [v] *stare* eagle eye*, eye, eyeball*, fix, focus, gape at, gawk, gaze, glare, goggle*, lay eyes on*, leer, look, look fixedly, make eyes at, peer, rivet, rubberneck*, watch; CONCEPT *623*

ogre [n] *nasty person* demon, devil, fiend, giant, monster, monstrosity, specter, troll; CONCEPT *412* —*Ant.* humanitarian, philanthropist

oil [v] *lubricate* anoint, coat, grease, lard, lube, pomade, slick, smear; CONCEPTS *172,256* —*Ant.* dry

oily [adj1] *fatty, greasy* adipose, buttery, creamy, lardy, lubricant, lubricative, lubricous, lustrous, oiled, oil-soaked, oleaginous, polished, rich, saponaceous, sleek, slippery, smeary, smooth, soapy, soothing, swimming, unctuous, waxy; CONCEPTS *603,606* —*Ant.* dry

oily [adj2] *flattering* bland*, cajoling, coaxing, compliant, fulsome, glib, gushing*, hypocritical, ingratiating, insinuating, obsequious, plausible, servile, slick, smarmy*, smooth, smooth-tongued*, suave, supple, unctuous; CONCEPTS *267,401* —*Ant.* hateful

ointment [n] *cream for treatment* balm, cerate, demulcent, dressing, embrocation, emollient, lenitive, liniment, lotion, medicine, salve, unguent; CONCEPTS *311,466*

okay [adj] *acceptable, satisfactory* accurate, adequate, all right, approved, convenient, correct, fair, fine, good, in order, middling, not bad, ok, passable, permitted, so-so*, surely, tolerable; CONCEPT *558* —*Ant.* bad, incorrect, intolerable, unacceptable, unsatisfactory, unsuitable, wrong

okay [n] *agreement* acceptance, affirmation, approbation, approval, assent, authorization, benediction, blessing, consent, endorsement, favor, go-ahead*, green light*, ok, permission, sanction, say-so*, seal of approval*, yes; CONCEPT *684* —*Ant.* denial, disagreement, refusal, veto

okay [v] *agree to* accept, accredit, approve, authorize, certify, condone, confirm, consent to, endorse, give one's consent, give the go-ahead*, give the green light*, notarize, ok, pass, rubber-

stamp*, sanction, say yes to; CONCEPTS *10,50,88*
—*Ant.* deny, disagree, refuse, reject, veto

old [*adj1*] *advanced in age* aged, along in years*, ancient, broken down*, debilitated, decrepit, elderly, enfeebled, exhausted, experienced, fossil*, geriatric, getting on*, gray, gray-haired*, grizzled*, hoary*, impaired, inactive, infirm, mature, matured, not young, olden, oldish, over the hill*, past one's prime*, seasoned, senile, senior, skilled, superannuated, tired, venerable, versed, veteran, wasted*; CONCEPTS *578,797* —*Ant.* fresh, new, young, youthful

old [*adj2*] *obsolete, outdated* aboriginal, age-old, antediluvian, antiquated, antique, archaic, bygone, cast-off, crumbling, dated, decayed, demode, done, early, erstwhile, former, hackneyed*, immemorial, late, moth-eaten*, of old, of yore, olden, oldfangled, old-fashioned, old-time, once, onetime, original, outmoded, out-of-date, passé, past, primeval, primitive, primordial, pristine, quondam, relic, remote, rusty, sometime, stale, superannuated, time-worn, traditional, unfashionable, unoriginal, venerable, worn-out; CONCEPTS *558,560,799* —*Ant.* contemporary, current, fresh, late, modern, new, recent, up-to-date

old [*adj3*] *traditional, long-established* age-old, constant, continuing, enduring, established, experienced, familiar, firm, hardened, inveterate, lifelong, long-lasting, long-lived, of long standing, perennial, perpetual, practiced, skilled, solid, staying, steady, time-honored, versed, veteran, vintage; CONCEPTS *482,530,798* —*Ant.* contemporary, current, modern, new

old age [*n*] *latter part of animate life* advancing years*, age, agedness, autumn of life*, caducity, debility, declining years*, decrepitude, dotage, elderliness, evening of life*, feebleness, golden age*, golden years*, infirmity, second childhood*, senectitude, senescence, senility, years; CONCEPTS *715,817* —*Ant.* adolescence, childhood, infancy, youth

old country [*n*] *native land* fatherland, homeland, mother country, motherland, the old country*; CONCEPT *516*

older [*adj*] *most senior* earlier, elder, eldest, first, first-born, former, lower, of a former period, of an earlier time, preceding, prior, senior; CONCEPTS *578,585,797* —*Ant.* younger

old-fashioned [*adj*] *outmoded, obsolete* ancient, antiquated, antique, archaic, behind the times*, bygone, corny*, dated, dead*, démodé, demoded, disapproved, dowdy*, extinct, grown old, moldy*, musty, neglected, not current, not modern, not with it*, obsolescent, odd*, of old, of olden days*, of the old school*, olden, old-fangled*, old-hat*, old-time, out*, outdated, passé*, past, primitive, rococo*, superannuated, unfashionable, unstylish, vintage; CONCEPTS *578,589,797,799* —*Ant.* contemporary, current, in vogue, modern, new

old hand [*n*] *person experienced in something* expert, knowing, old guard*, old school*, old-timer*, pro*, vet*, veteran; CONCEPT *423* —*Ant.* amateur, greenhorn, rookie

old school [*adj*] *traditional* acceptable, accustomed, classic, classical, conservative, conven-

tional, customary, habitual, long-established, old, old line, popular, regular, rooted, time-honored; CONCEPTS *530,533*

old-timer [*n*] *elderly person* fossil*, geezer*, golden-ager*, gramps*, mossback, old dog*, old hand, old soldier, senior, veteran, war-horse; CONCEPT *424*

old wives' tale [*n*] *superstition* fairy story, fallacy, false belief, folklore, folk tale, legend, lore, myth, notion, tall story, tall tale; CONCEPTS *282,689*

oligarchic [*adj*] *governed by small group* cabalistic, cliquey*, elite, exclusive, select; CONCEPTS *554,568*

omen [*n*] *sign of something to come* augury, auspice, bodement, boding, foreboding, foretoken, harbinger, indication, portent, premonition, presage, prognostic, prognostication, prophecy, straw, warning, writing on the wall*; CONCEPTS *74,278,689*

ominous [*adj*] *menacing, foreboding* apocalyptic, augural, baleful, baneful, clouded, dangerous, dark, dire, direful, dismal, doomed, doomful, fateful, fearful, forbidding, gloomy, grim, haunting, hostile, ill-boding, ill-fated, impending, inauspicious, inhospitable, lowering, malefic, malificent, malign, minatory, perilous, portentous, precursive, premonitory, presaging, prescient, prophetic, sinister, suggestive, threatening, unfriendly, unlucky, unpromising, unpropitious; CONCEPT *548* —*Ant.* auspicious, happy, lucky, promising, propitious

omission [*n*] *something forgotten or excluded* blank, breach, break, cancellation, carelessness, chasm, cutting out, default, disregard, disregardance, elimination, elision, excluding, exclusion, failing, failure, forgetfulness, gap, hiatus, ignoring, inadvertence, inadvertency, lack, lacuna, lapse, leaving out, missing, neglect, noninclusion, overlook, overlooking, oversight, passing over, preclusion, preterition, pretermission, prohibition, repudiation, skip, slighting, slip, withholding; CONCEPTS *25,116,699* —*Ant.* addition, inclusion, insertion, remembrance

omit [*v*] *exclude, forget* bar, blink at*, bypass, cancel, cast aside, count out, cut, cut out, delete, discard, dismiss, disregard, drop, edit, eliminate, evade, except, fail, ignore, knock off, leave out, leave undone, let go, let slide*, miss, miss out, neglect, overlook, overpass, pass by, pass over, preclude, prohibit, reject, repudiate, skip, slight, snip, trim, void, withhold, X-out*; CONCEPTS *25,121,211* —*Ant.* add, enter, include, inject, insert, remember

omitted [*adj*] *excluded* absent, deleted, erased, expunged, forgotten, left out, missing, neglected, overlooked, precluded; CONCEPTS *121,211*

omnipotent [*adj*] *all-powerful* almighty, divine, godlike, mighty, supreme, unlimited, unrestricted; CONCEPT *574* —*Ant.* impotent, weak

omnipresent [*adj*] *all-present* everywhere, infinite, pervading, pervasive, ubiquitary, ubiquitous, universal; CONCEPT *583*

omniscient [*adj*] *all-knowing* all-seeing, almighty, infinite, knowledgeable, pansophical, preeminent, wise; CONCEPT *402* —*Ant.* stupid, unknowing

on [adv] *in contact; ahead of* about, above, adjacent, against, approaching, at, beside, close to, covering, from, forward, held, leaning on, near, next, on top of, onward, over, resting on, situated on, supported, touching, toward, upon, with; CONCEPTS 585,586,750 —*Ant.* off

on and off [adv] *intermittently* at intervals, at times, discontinuously, every now and then, every once in a while, every so often, from time to time, hardly, infrequently, intermittently, irregularly, now and again, now and then, occasionally, off and on, once in a blue moon*, once in a while, on occasion, periodically, sometimes, sporadically; CONCEPTS 530,541

on and on [adv] *continuously* ad nauseam, constantly, forever, never-ending, perpetually, relentlessly, repeatedly, steadily, unceasingly, unremittingly; CONCEPTS 534,798

on call [adj] *standing by* accessible, at hand, at one's fingertip, night call, on alert, on the spot, prepared, within reach; CONCEPT 576

once [adj/adv] *in the past; occurred one time only* already, a single time, at one time, away back, back, back when, before, but once, by-gone, earlier, erstwhile, formerly, heretofore, in the old days, in the olden days, in times gone by, in times past, late, long ago, old, once only, once upon a time, one, one time before, one time previously, only one time, on one occasion, previously, quondam, sometime, this time, time was, whilom; CONCEPTS 799,820 —*Ant.* never

once and for all [adv] *finally* after all, at last, at long last*, at the end, conclusively, in conclusion, in the end, it's about time*, sooner or later*; CONCEPT 799

once in a while [adv] *occasionally* at intervals, at times, every now and then, every so often, from time to time, hardly, infrequently, irregularly, now and again, once in a blue moon*, on occasion, periodically, rarely, seldom, sometimes, sporadically; CONCEPTS 530,541

oncoming [adj] *impending* advancing, approaching, coming, expected, forthcoming, imminent, looming, nearing, onrushing, upcoming; CONCEPTS 548,799 —*Ant.* past, preceding

on duty [adj] *working* busy, clocked in*, engaged, in a job, in gear, laboring, obliged, on the job, punched in*; CONCEPTS 538,560

one [adj] *individual* alone, definite, different, lone, odd, one and only, only, particular, peculiar, precise, separate, single, singular, sole, solitary, special, specific, uncommon, unique; CONCEPTS 577,762,789 —*Ant.* none

one by one [adv] *in succession* gradually, individually, little by little, one at a time, singly, step by step; CONCEPTS 544,588,799

on edge [adj] *tense* agitated, anxious, apprehensive, beside oneself*, bundle of nerves*, edgy, excited, fidgety, high-strung*, hyper*, impatient, in a tizzy*, jittery, jumpy, keyed up*, nerve-racking, nervous, nervous wreck*, overanxious, restless, stressful, unnerved, uptight, wired*, worried, wound up*; CONCEPTS 401,403,548

onerous [adj] *difficult; requiring hard labor* arduous, austere, backbreaking, burdensome, crushing, cumbersome, demanding, difficult, distressing, embittering, exacting, excessive, exhausting, exigent, fatiguing, formidable, galling, grave, grinding, grueling, hard*, harsh, headache, heavy*, intolerable, irksome, laborious, merciless, oppressive, overpowering, overtaxing, painful, plodding, ponderous, pressing, responsible, rigorous, serious, severe, strenuous, taxing, tiresome, tiring, toilsome, troublesome, vexatious, weighty; CONCEPTS 538,565 —*Ant.* common, easy, light, trivial

one-sided [adj] *biased* colored, discriminatory, favorably, inclined, influenced, partisan, predisposed, prejudiced, unequal, unfair, unjust; CONCEPTS 403,542

one-track mind [n] *obsession* attraction, compulsion, fascination, fixation, hang-up*, infatuation, passion, preoccupation, tunnel vision; CONCEPTS 20,410,529,689,690

ongoing [adj] *continuous* advancing, continuing, current, developing, evolving, extant, growing, heading, in process, in progress, marching, open-ended, progressing, successful, unfinished, unfolding; CONCEPTS 482,798 —*Ant.* incontinuous, infrequent, intermittent, stopping

on guard [adj] *defensive* alert, averting, cautious, checking, defending, expectant, guarding, preservative, preventive, protecting, safeguarding, vigilant, warding off, watchful, withstanding; CONCEPTS 401,550

on-line [adj] *electronically connected* accessible by computer, installed, linked, networked, on stream*, operative, plugged in, ready for use, wired; CONCEPT 274

onlooker [n] *person observing an event* beholder, bystander, eyewitness, looker-on, observer, sightseer, spectator, viewer, watcher, witness; CONCEPT 423 —*Ant.* participant

only [adj] *singular* alone, apart, by oneself, exclusive, individual, isolated, lone, matchless, once in a lifetime, one, one and only, one shot, onliest, particular, peerless, single, sole, solitary, solo, unaccompanied, unequaled, unique, unparalleled, unrivaled; CONCEPT 577

only [adv] *barely; exclusively* alone, at most, but, entirely, hardly, just, merely, nothing but, particularly, plainly, purely, simply, solely, totally, uniquely, utterly, wholly; CONCEPTS 535,772

on paper [adv] *in theory* abstractly, conceivably, hypothetically, theoretically; CONCEPT 529

on purpose [adv] *deliberately* after consideration, by design, calculatingly, consciously, designed, freely, in cold blood, intentionally, knowingly, premeditatively, purposely, purposively, voluntarily, willfully, with eyes wide open*, wittingly; CONCEPTS 401,542

onrush [n] *rush* attack, avalanche, blitz, charge, dash, deluge, flood, flow, flux, haste, hastiness, hurriedness, hurry, onslaught, push, race, scramble, stampede, storm, stream, surge, swiftness; CONCEPTS 145,748,818

onset [n] *beginning; attack* access, aggression, assailment, assault, birth, charge, commencement, dawn, dawning, encounter, inception, incipience, kickoff*, offense, offensive, onfall, onrush, onslaught, opening, origin, outbreak, outset, outstart, rush, seizure, start; CONCEPTS 86,221 —*Ant.* conclusion, end, ending, finish

onslaught [n] *attack* aggression, assailment, assault, blitz, charge, incursion, invasion, offense, offensive, onfall, onrush, onset; CONCEPT 86 —*Ant.* defense

on the ball [adj] *alert* active, all ears*, attentive, bright, cagey*, careful, clever, good hands*, heads up*, intelligent, lively, observant, on guard*, on one's toes*, on the job*, on the lookout*, on the stick*, perceptive, quick, ready, sharp, spirited, vigilant, watchful, wise, with it*; CONCEPTS 402,403

on the blink [adj] *broken* busted, defective, disabled, down, fallen apart, faulty, gone to pieces*, haywire, in disrepair, in need of repair, inoperable, in the shop*, kaput*, not functioning, not working, on the fritz*, on the shelf*, out, out of commission*, out of kilter*, out of order, out of whack*, run-down, shot, spent, wrecked; CONCEPTS 485,560

on the double [adv] *quickly* chop-chop*, expeditiously, fast, flat-out*, fleetly, full tilt*, hastily, hurriedly, in a flash*, in haste, lickety-split*, like a shot*, like greased lightning*, like wildfire*, promptly, pronto, quick, rapidly, swift, swiftly; CONCEPTS 588,799

on the fence [adj] *undecided* ambivalent, betwixt and between*, blowing hot and cold*, borderline, debatable, divided, hemming and hawing*, hesitant, iffy*, impartial, indecisive, in the middle*, irresolute, neutral, not definite, not sure, of two minds*, open, running hot and cold*, tentative, torn, uncertain, unclear, uncommitted, undetermined, unsure, up in the air*, waffling, wavering, wishy-washy*; CONCEPTS 403,529

on the house [adj] *free* chargeless, complimentary, compliments of the house, costless, for nothing, for the asking, freebie*, free of cost, free ride*, gratis, gratuitous, no charge, on the cuff*; CONCEPT 334

on the level [adj] *legitimate* aboveboard, accepted, accredited, authentic, authorized, for real*, honest, lawful, official, on the up and up, proper, sanctioned, straight, true, valid, verifiable; CONCEPTS 319,558,582

on the wagon [adj] *sober* abstaining, abstemious, abstinent, cold sober*, dry, drying out, nonindulgent, not drinking, not drunk, not partaking of alcohol, restrained, took the pledge*; CONCEPT 401

onus [n] *burden* bar sinister*, black eye*, blame, blot, blur, brand, charge, culpability, deadweight*, duty, encumbrance, fault, guilt, incubus, liability, load, millstone*, obligation, odium, oppression, responsibility, slur, spot, stain, stigma, task, tax, weight; CONCEPTS 388,674 —*Ant.* aid, benefit, blessing, help

onward/onwards [adv] *ahead, beyond* alee, along, forth, forward, in front, in front of, moving on, on, on ahead; CONCEPTS 585,778 —*Ant.* backward, backwards

oodles [n] *a lot* abundance, billions, gobs*, heaps*, large number, loads, lots, many, masses, millions, piles*, plenty, scads*, thousands, tons, zillions; CONCEPTS 432,786

oomph [n] *energy* animation, ardor, birr, dash, drive, effectiveness, endurance, exertion, fire, force, forcefulness, fortitude, get-up-and-go*, go, hardihood, initiative, intensity, juice, life, liveliness, might, moxie*, muscle, pep, pizzazz, pluck, potency, power, punch, spirit, stamina, steam, strength, vigor, vim, virility, vitality, zeal, zest, zing, zip; CONCEPT 411

ooze [n] *liquid emitted* alluvium, fluid, glop*, goo*, gook*, gunk*, mire, muck*, mud, silt, slime*, sludge; CONCEPTS 466,467

ooze [v] *emit liquid* bleed, discharge, drain, dribble, drip, drop, escape, exude, filter, flow, issue, leach, leak, overflow, percolate, perspire, seep, spurt, strain, sweat, swelter, trickle, weep, well; CONCEPT 179

opaque [adj1] *clouded, muddy* blurred, cloudy, dark, darkened, dim, dirty, dull, dusky, filmy, foggy, frosty, fuliginous, gloomy, hazy, impenetrable, lusterless, misty, muddied, murky, nontranslucent, nontransparent, nubilous, obfuscated, shady, smoky, sooty, thick, turbid; CONCEPTS 606,617,618 —*Ant.* clear, lucid, translucent, transparent, unclouded

opaque [adj2] *hard to understand* abstruse, amphibological, arcane, baffling, concealed, cryptic, difficult, enigmatic, equivocal, imperceptive, incomprehensible, nubilous, obscure, obtuse, perplexing, purblind, tenebrous, uncertain, unclear, unfathomable, unintelligible, vague; CONCEPT 529 —*Ant.* clear, crystal-clear, easy, unambiguous, understandable

open [adj1] *unfastened, unclosed* accessible, agape, airy, ajar, bare, clear, cleared, dehiscent, disclosed, emptied, expanded, expansive, exposed, extended, extensive, free, gaping, made passable, naked, navigable, passable, patent, patulous, peeled, removed, rent, revealed, ringent, rolling, spacious, spread out, stripped, susceptible, unbarred, unblocked, unbolted, unburdened, uncluttered, uncovered, unfolded, unfurled, unimpeded, unlocked, unobstructed, unplugged, unsealed, unshut, unstopped, vacated, wide, yawning; CONCEPTS 485,576 —*Ant.* closed, fastened, locked, shut

open [adj2] *accessible; not forbidden* admissible, agreeable, allowable, approachable, appropriate, attainable, available, employable, fit, free, general, getable*, nondiscriminatory, not posted, obtainable, on deck*, on tap*, open-door*, operative, permitted, practicable, proper, public, reachable, securable, suitable, to be had*, unconditional, unoccupied, unqualified, unrestricted, usable, vacant, welcoming, within reach; CONCEPTS 560,576 —*Ant.* blocked, closed, inaccessible, obstructed, shut, unavailable

open [adj3] *clear, obvious* apparent, avowed, barefaced, blatant, conspicuous, downright, evident, flagrant, frank, manifest, noticeable, overt, plain, unconcealed, undisguised, visible, well-known; CONCEPTS 267,535 —*Ant.* ambiguous, closed, deceitful, unclear, vague

open [adj4] *undecided* ambiguous, arguable, controversial, debatable, doubtful, dubious, dubitable, equivocal, indecisive, in question, moot, problematic, questionable, uncertain, unresolved, unsettled, up for discussion*, up in the air*, yet to be decided*; CONCEPTS 267, 529 —*Ant.* certain, decided, definite, sure

open [adj5] *honest, objective* artless, candid, disinterested, fair, frank, free, guileless, impartial, ingenuous, innocent, lay it on the line*, mellow, natural, objective, on the level*, open-and-shut*, openhearted*, plain, receptive, sincere, straightforward, talking turkey*, transparent, unbiased, uncommitted, unconcealed, undisguised, undissembled, unprejudiced, unreserved, up-front*; CONCEPTS 267,542 —*Ant.* deceitful, deceptive, dishonest, lying, shifty, subjective

open [v1] *begin* begin business, bow, commence, convene, embark, get things rolling*, inaugurate, initiate, jump, kick off, launch, meet, raise the curtain*, ring in*, set in motion, set up shop*, sit, start, start the ball rolling*; CONCEPT 221 —*Ant.* close, conclude, end, finish, shut

open [v2] *clear, expose; spread* bare, break in, break out, broach, burst, bust in, come apart, crack, disclose, display, disrupt, expand, fissure, free, gap, gape, hole, jimmy, kick in, lacerate, lance, penetrate, perforate, pierce, pop, puncture, release, reveal, rupture, separate, sever, slit, slot, split, tap, throw wide, unbar, unblock, unbolt, unclose, unclothe, uncork, uncover, undo, unfasten, unfold, unfurl, unlatch, unlock, unroll, unseal, unshut, unstop, untie, unwrap, vent, ventilate, yawn, yawp; CONCEPTS 135,250,469 —*Ant.* block, bury, cover, exclude, hide, hinder, shut

open-and-shut [adj] *obvious* apparent, cinched, clear, clear as a bell*, conclusive, cut and dried, distinguishable, easy, evident, explicit, glaring, indisputable, ordinary, plain, routine, self-evident, self-explanatory, simple, straightforward, undeniable, undisguised, unmistakable; CONCEPTS 485,529

openhanded [adj1] *generous* altruistic, benevolent, big, big-hearted, bountiful, charitable, considerate, giving, helpful, hospitable, kind, kindhearted, kindly, liberal, magnanimous, philanthropic, thoughtful, unselfish; CONCEPT 404

openhearted [adj1] *frank* aboveboard, bare-faced*, blunt, candid, direct, downright, forthright, from the hip*, honest, lay it on the line*, like it is*, matter-of-fact, open, plain, plainspoken, saying what one thinks*, sincere, straight, straightforward, truthful, up front*; CONCEPTS 267,582

openhearted [adj2] *kindly* benevolent, compassionate, friendly, generous, good, good-hearted, gracious, humane, kind, kindhearted, neighborly, sympathetic, thoughtful; CONCEPTS 404,542

opening [n1] *gap, hole* aperture, breach, break, cavity, chink, cleft, crack, cranny, crevice, cut, discontinuity, door, fissure, hatch, interstice, mouth, orifice, outlet, perforation, recess, rent, rift, rupture, scuttle, slit, slot, space, split, spout, tear, vent, window; CONCEPT 513 —*Ant.* closing, closure, solid

opening [n2] *chance* availability, big break*, connection, cut*, fling*, go*, go-at*, in the running*, iron in the fire*, look-in*, occasion, opportunity, place, possibility, run, scope, shot*, show, squeak*, time, vacancy, whack*; CONCEPT 693 —*Ant.* misfortune

opening [n3] *beginning* birth, coming out, commencement, curtain-raiser*, dawn, inauguration, inception, initiation, kickoff, launch, launching, onset, opener, outset, start; CONCEPT 832 —*Ant.* closing, conclusion, ending, finish

openly [adv] *honestly* aboveboard, artlessly, blatantly, brazenly, candidly, face to face, flagrantly, forthrightly, frankly, fully, honestly, in broad daylight, in full view, ingenuously, in public, in the open, naively, naturally, plainly, publicly, readily, shamelessly, simply, straight, unabashedly, unashamedly, under one's nose*, unhesitatingly, unreservedly, wantonly, warts and all*, willingly, without pretense, without reserve; CONCEPTS 267,544 —*Ant.* secretly, shamefully

open-minded [adj] *receptive* acceptant, acceptive, approachable, broad-minded, impartial, interested, observant, open to suggestions, perceptive, persuadable, swayable, tolerant, unbiased, understanding; CONCEPT 404

operable [adj] *possible* achievable, conceivable, doable, feasible, obtainable, practicable, realizable, serviceable, viable, workable; CONCEPTS 528,552,576

operate [v1] *perform, function* accomplish, achieve, act, act on, advance, behave, be in action, bend, benefit, bring about, burn, carry on, click*, compel, complete, concern, conduct, contact, contrive, convey, cook*, determine, direct, do, enforce, engage, exert, finish, fulfill, get results, go, hit*, hum, influence, keep, lift, move, ordain, percolate, proceed, produce, produce a result, progress, promote, react, revolve, roll, run, serve, spin, take, tick, transport, turn, work; CONCEPTS 91,680,706

operate [v2] *manage, use* administer, be in charge, be in driver's seat*, be in saddle*, call the play*, call the shots*, call the signals*, carry on, command, conduct, drive, handle, hold the reins*, keep, make go*, maneuver, manipulate, ordain, pilot, play, ply, pull the strings*, pull the wires*, run, run the show*, run things*, sit on top of*, steer, wield, work; CONCEPTS 94,117,148

operate [v3] *perform surgery* amputate, carve up, cut, excise, explore, open up, remove, set, transplant, treat; CONCEPT 310

operation [n1] *movement, working* act, action, activity, affair, agency, application, ballgame*, bit, carrying on, conveyance, course, deal, deed, doing, effect, effort, employment, engagement, enterprise, exercise, exercising, exertion, exploitation, force, handiwork, happening, influence, instrumentality, labor, manipulation, motion, movement, performance, play, procedure, proceeding, process, progress, progression, scene, service, transaction, transference, trip, undertaking, use, work, workmanship; CONCEPTS 658,680 —*Ant.* idleness, inaction, inutility, uselessness

operation [n2] *business concern* affair, deal, enterprise, proceeding, transaction, undertaking; CONCEPTS 324,325

operation [n3] *surgical procedure* biopsy, excision, surgery; CONCEPT 310

operational [adj] *functional* fit, in service, in working order, operative, practicable, practical, prepared, ready, serviceable, usable, useful, viable, workable, working; CONCEPT 560

operative [adj] *active, functioning; influential* accessible, active, crucial, current, dynamic, effective, efficient, employable, functional, important, indicative, in force, in operation, key, live, open, operational, practicable, relevant, running, serviceable, significant, standing, usable, workable, working; CONCEPTS 560,567 —*Ant.* inactive, ineffective, ineffectual, inoperative, unfunctional, unworking, useless, worthless

opine [v] *think* believe, conceive, conclude, declare, express an opinion, feel, guess, imagine, judge, presume, say, suggest, suppose, surmise, venture; CONCEPTS 12,26

opinion [n] *belief* assessment, assumption, attitude, conception, conclusion, conjecture, estimate, estimation, eye*, fancy, feeling, guess, hypothesis, idea, imagining, impression, inclination, inference, judgment, mind, notion, persuasion, point of view, postulate, presumption, presupposition, reaction, say-so*, sentiment, slant, speculation, supposition, surmise, suspicion, take*, theorem, theory, thesis, think*, thought, view, viewpoint; CONCEPT 689 —*Ant.* reality, truth

opinionated [adj] *believing very strongly and conveying it* adamant, arbitrary, assertive, biased, bigoted, bossy, bullheaded*, cocksure*, cocky*, conceited, dictatorial, doctrinaire, dogmatic, hard-line*, high-handed, inflexible, intransigent, locked in*, obdurate, obstinate, one-sided, oracular, overbearing, pigheaded*, positive, pragmatic, pragmatical, prejudiced, self-assertive, set in stone*, set-on, single-minded, stubborn, tilted, uncompromising, unyielding, weighted; CONCEPTS 267,404 —*Ant.* compromising, indifferent, open-minded

opium [n] *narcotic* brown stuff*, codeine, dope, drug, heroin, hypnotic, morphine, opiate, papaverine, poppy, sleep-inducer, soporific, tar; CONCEPT 307

opponent [n] *person with whom one competes* adversary, antagonist, anti*, aspirant, assailant, bandit*, bidder, candidate, challenger, competitor, con, contestant, counteragent, dark horse*, disputant, dissentient, enemy, entrant, foe, litigant, match, opposer, opposition, oppugnant, player, rival; CONCEPT 366 —*Ant.* ally, associate, colleague, helper

opportune [adj] *advantageous, lucky* appropriate, apt, auspicious, convenient, favorable, felicitous, fit, fitting, fortuitous, fortunate, happy, helpful, pat, proper, propitious, seasonable, suitable, timely, timeous, well-timed; CONCEPTS 548,572 —*Ant.* disadvantageous, inauspicious, inopportune, unlucky, unsuitable

opportunity [n] *lucky chance; favorable circumstances* befalling, break*, connection, contingency, convenience, cut*, event, excuse, fair shake*, fighting chance*, fitness, fling*, fortuity, freedom, go*, good fortune, good luck, happening, hope, hour, iron in the fire*, juncture, leisure, liberty, moment, occasion, one's move*, one's say*, one's turn*, opening, pass, prayer*, probability, relief, room, run, scope, shot*, show, space, spell, squeak, stab, the hunt*, the running*, time, turn, whack*; CONCEPT 693 —*Ant.* bad luck, misfortune

oppose [v1] *fight, obstruct* argue, assail, assault, attack, bar, battle, bombard, call in question, check, combat, confront, contradict, controvert, counter, counterattack, cross, debate, defy, deny, disagree, disapprove, dispute, encounter, expose, face, face down*, fight, fly in the face of*, frown at, gainsay, hinder, neutralize, not countenance, prevent, protest, resist, reverse, run counter to, search out, speak against, stand up to, take a stand, take issue, take on, taunt, thwart, turn the tables*, withstand; CONCEPTS 21,54,106 —*Ant.* aid, assist, favor, help, support

oppose [v2] *compare, play off* array, confront, contrast, counter, counterbalance, face, match, pit, set against, vie; CONCEPTS 73,363 —*Ant.* join, participate

opposed/opposing [adj] *antagonistic, against* against the grain*, allergic*, anti*, antipathetic, antithetical, antonymous, at cross-purposes, at odds, averse, battling, clashing, combating, conflicting, confronting, contrary, controverting, counter, crossing, defending, defensive, denying, disagreeing, disputed, disputing, dissentient, enemy, exposing, facing, gainsaying, hostile, incompatible, inimical, in opposition, irreconcilable, objecting, obstructive, opposite, protesting, repelling, restrictive, rival, up against, warring; CONCEPTS 403,542,564 —*Ant.* aiding, assisting, compatible, helping, similar

opposite [adj] *unlike, conflicting; completely different* adverse, antagonistic, antipodal, antipodean, antithetical, contradictory, contrapositive, contrary, contrasted, corresponding, counter, crosswise, diametric, diametrically opposed, different, differing, dissimilar, diverse, facing, flip-side*, fronting, hostile, inconsistent, independent, inimical, inverse, irreconcilable, obverse, opposed, ornery*, paradoxical, polar, repugnant, retrograde, reverse, reversed, separate, unlike, unconnected, unrelated, unsimilar, violative, vis-á-vis; CONCEPT 564 —*Ant.* compatible, like, similar

opposite [n] *something completely unlike another* adverse, antilogy, antipode, antipole, antithesis, antonym, contra*, contradiction, contrary, contrast, converse, counterpart, foil, inverse, obverse, opposition, other extreme*, other side*, other side of coin*, paradox, reverse, vice versa; CONCEPT 665 —*Ant.* likeness, same, similarity

opposition [n1] *obstruction, antagonism* action, antinomy, antithesis, aversion, brush, civil disobedience, clash, combat, competition, con, conflict, confronting, contention, contest, contradistinction, contraposition, contrariety, counteraction, counterattack, defense, defiance, disapproval, duel, encounter, engagement, fray, grapple, hostility, negativism, obstructiveness, opposure, oppugnancy, prevention, repugnance, repulsion, resistance, rivalry, skirmish, strife, struggle, unfriendliness, violation, war, warfare; CONCEPTS 29,92,106,665 —*Ant.* compatibility, harmony, peace

opposition [n2] *person, people competing* adversary, antagonist, disputant, enemy, foe, iconoclast, opponent, other side, rebel, rival; CONCEPTS 348,366 —*Ant.* team, teammates

oppress [v] *depress, subdue* abuse, afflict, aggrieve, annoy, beat down*, burden, crush, despotize, dishearten, dispirit, distress, encumber, force, handicap, harass, harry, hound*, keep down, maltreat, outrage, overcome, overload, overpower, overthrow, overwhelm, persecute, pick on, plague, press, prey on, put down, put screws to*, put the squeeze on*, put upon, ride, rule, sadden, saddle*, smother, strain, subjugate, suppress, tax, torment, torture, trample, trouble, tyrannize, vex, weigh heavy upon, worry, wrong; CONCEPTS 7,14,19,133 —*Ant.* aid, boost, delight, gladden, help, make happy

oppressed [adj] downtrodden abject, abused, a slave to*, at one's feet*, at one's mercy*, burdened, destitute, distressed, enslaved, exploited, have-not, helpless, maltreated, mistreated, persecuted, subservient, suppressed, tormented, tyrannized, underfoot*, under one's thumb*; CONCEPT 542

oppression [n] misery, hardship abuse, abusiveness, autocracy, brutality, calamity, coercion, compulsion, conquering, control, cruelty, despotism, dictatorship, domination, fascism, force, forcibleness, hardness, harshness, injury, injustice, iron hand*, maltreatment, martial law, overthrowing, persecution, severity, subduing, subjection, suffering, torment, tyranny; CONCEPTS 14,320,674 —*Ant.* cheer, delight, happiness, joy

oppressive [adj1] overwhelming, repressive backbreaking*, bleak, brutal, burdensome, confining, cruel, demanding, depressing, depressive, despotic, dictatorial, discouraging, disheartening, dismal, dispiriting, exacting, exigent, gloomy, grievous, grinding, harsh, headache*, heavy, heavy-handed*, hefty, inhuman, ironhanded*, mean, onerous, overbearing, rough going*, severe, somber, superincumbent, taxing, tough, troublesome, tyrannical, unjust, weighty; CONCEPTS 537,548 —*Ant.* calm, gentle, relieving

oppressive [adj2] hot and humid airless, close, heavy, muggy, overpowering, steam bath*, steamy, sticky, stifling, stuffy, suffocating, sultry, sweat box*, torrid; CONCEPT 525 —*Ant.* cool, mild, temperate

oppressor [n] tyrant absolute ruler, authoritarian, autocrat, bully, despot, dictator, martinet, persecutor, slave driver, taskmaster; CONCEPTS 354,412

opprobrious [adj] abusive, hateful abasing, calumniatory, contemptuous, contumelious, damaging, debasing, defamatory, defaming, denigrating, depreciative, derogative, despicable, despiteful, detractive, disgracing, dishonoring, disparaging, humiliating, hurting, injuring, injurious, insolent, insulting, invective, libeling, malevolent, malign, malignant, maligning, notorious, offending, offensive, pejorative, reproaching, reviling, scandalous, scurrilous, shaming, spiteful, truculent, vile, vitriolic, vituperative, vulgar; CONCEPTS 267,404,542 —*Ant.* complimentary, flattering, kind, nice, praising

opprobrium [n] disgrace black eye*, blemish, debasement, debasing, degradation, discredit, dishonor, disrepute, disrespect, humiliation, ignominy, ill repute, infamy, loss of honor, obloquy, shame, stain, stigma, tarnish; CONCEPT 388

oppugn [v] oppose argue, attack, call into question, contradict, controvert, criticize, debate, shoot down, take issue; CONCEPTS 21,54,106

opt [v] choose cull, decide, elect, exercise choice, go for*, make a selection, mark, pick, prefer, select, single out*, take; CONCEPT 41

optimal [adj] optimum 24-carat*, A1*, ace, best, capital, choice, choicest, excellent, flaw-

less, gilt-edge*, greatest, highest, ideal, matchless, maximum, most advantageous, most favorable, peak, peerless, perfect, select, solid gold*, superlative, top, world class*; CONCEPT 574

optimism [n] state of having positive beliefs anticipation, assurance, brightness, buoyancy, calmness, certainty, cheer, cheerfulness, confidence, easiness, elation, encouragement, enthusiasm, exhilaration, expectation, good cheer, happiness, hopefulness, idealism, looking on bright side*, positivism, rose-colored glasses*, sanguineness, sureness, trust; CONCEPTS 410,689 —*Ant.* doubt, gloom, hopelessness, pessimism

optimist [n] positive thinker dreamer, hoper, idealist, Pollyanna; CONCEPT 529

optimistic [adj] believing positively assured, bright, buoyant, cheerful, cheering, confident, encouraged, expectant, happy, high, hopeful, hoping, idealistic, keeping the faith, merry, on cloud nine*, on top of world*, positive, promising, ray of sunshine*, rose-colored*, rosy, sanguine, sunny*, trusting, upbeat, Utopian; CONCEPTS 404,542 —*Ant.* dejected, depressed, doubtful, gloomy, hopeless, pessimistic, sorrowful

optimum [adj] best A1*, ace, capital, -carat*, choice, choicest, excellent, flawless, gilt-edge*, greatest, highest, ideal, matchless, maximum, most advantageous, most favorable, optimal, peak, peerless, perfect, select, solid gold*, superlative, world class*; CONCEPT 574 —*Ant.* least, poorest, worst

option [n] alternative advantage, benefit, choice, claim, dibs*, dilemma, discretion, druthers, election, flipside*, franchise, free will*, grant, license, opportunity, other side of coin*, pickup, preference, prerogative, privilege, right, selection, take it or leave it*; CONCEPTS 376,712

optional [adj] possible; available as choice alternative, arbitrary, discretional, discretionary, elective, extra, facultative, free, noncompulsory, nonobligatory, no strings attached*, not required, open, unforced, unrestricted, up to the individual, volitional, voluntary; CONCEPTS 552,576 —*Ant.* compulsory, forced, required

opulence [n] wealth abundance, affluence, belongings, excess, fortune, goods, lap of luxury, lavishness, luxury, means, money, plenitude, possessions, property, prosperity, prosperousness, riches, stocks and bonds, substance, substantiality; CONCEPTS 340,710

opulent [adj] rich, luxurious, profuse abundant, affluent, copious, deluxe, extravagant, exuberant, frilly*, lavish, luscious, luxuriant, moneyed, ostentatious, palatial, plentiful, plush, pretentious, prodigal, profusive, prolific, prosperous, rich, riotous, showy, sumptuous, swank, upholstered*, velvet*, wealthy, well-heeled*, well-off*, well-to-do*; CONCEPTS 334,589,781 —*Ant.* depressed, destitute, poor

opus [n] great work of writing or music composition, creation, magnum opus, music, oeuvre, piece, product, production; CONCEPTS 263,271

oracle [n] prophecy answer, apocalypse, augury, canon, commandment, divination, edict, fortune, law, prediction, prognostication, revelation, vision; CONCEPTS 70,278,689

op
or

oracular |adj| *prophetic* ambiguous, anticipating, apocalyptic, arcane, auguring, auspicious, authoritative, cabalistic, clairvoyant, cryptic, Delphian, discovering, divining, divulging, dogmatic, fatidic, foreboding, forecasting, foretelling, imperious, interpretive, mantic, mysterious, mystical, obscure, occult, ominous, peremptory, portending, portentous, positive, predicting, presaging, prescient, proclaiming, prognosticating, prophesying, sage, secret, sibylline, significant, soothsaying, vague, vatic, venerable, wise; CONCEPT 267

oral |adj| *spoken* articulate, ejaculatory, lingual, narrated, phonated, phonetic, phonic, recounted, related, said, sonant, sounded, told, unwritten, uttered, verbal, viva voce, vocal, voiced, word-of-mouth; CONCEPT 267 —*Ant.* printed, written

orange |n/adj| *combination of red and yellow* apricot, bittersweet, cantaloupe, carrot, coral, peach, red-yellow, salmon, tangerine, titian; CONCEPTS 618,622

orate |v| *speak* address, expound, grandstand, lecture, moralize, pontificate, preach, sermonize, talk, vociferate; CONCEPTS 60,285

oration |n| *speech* address, chalk talk*, declamation, discourse, harangue, homily, lecture, pep talk*, pitch*, sermon, soapbox*, spiel*; CONCEPTS 266,278 —*Ant.* print, writing

orator |n| *speaker* declaimer, lector, lecturer, pontificator, preacher, public speaker, reciter, rhetorician, sermonizer; CONCEPTS 60,285

oratory |n| *public speaking* articulation, declamation, diction, elocution, eloquence, grandiloquence, rhetoric, speaking, speech, speechifying, speechmaking; CONCEPTS 60,285

orb |n| *globe* ball, circle, eye*, lamp, ring, rondure, round, sphere; CONCEPT 436

orbit |n1| *circuit, revolution* apogee, circle, circumgyration, course, curve, cycle, ellipse, lap, locus, path, pattern, perigee, rotation, round, track, trajectory; CONCEPTS 436,738

orbit |n2| *influence, domain* ambit, area, arena, boundary, bounds, career, circle, circumference, compass, course, department, dominion, extension, extent, field, jurisdiction, limit, pilgrimage, precinct, province, purview, radius, range, reach, realm, scope, sphere, sweep; CONCEPTS 349,673,687

orchard |n| *fruit farm* fruit garden, garden, grove, plantation, vineyard; CONCEPTS 449, 509,517

orchestra |n| *symphony* band, ensemble, group, sinfonietta; CONCEPT 294

orchestrate |v| *organize; cause to happen* arrange, blend, compose, concert, coordinate, harmonize, integrate, manage, present, put together, score, set up, symphonize, synthesize, unify; CONCEPTS 117,242 —*Ant.* disorganize, ignore

ordain |v| *establish, install* anoint, appoint, bless, call, commission, consecrate, constitute, deal, deal with, decree, delegate, destine, dictate, elect, enact, enjoin, fix, frock, impose, institute, invest, lay down the law*, legislate, nominate, order, prescribe, pronounce, put foot down*, rule, set, walk heavy*, will; CONCEPTS 18,50,88,317 —*Ant.* cancel, disallow, retract, void

ordeal |n| *trouble, suffering* affliction, agony, anguish, calamity, calvary, cross, crucible, difficulty, distress, nightmare, test, torment, torture, trial, tribulation, visitation; CONCEPTS 674,728 —*Ant.* happiness, pleasure

order |n1| *arrangement, organization* adjustment, aligning, array, assortment, cast, categorization, classification, codification, composition, computation, disposal, disposition, distribution, establishment, form, grouping, harmony, layout, line, lineup, management, method, neatness, ordering, orderliness, pattern, placement, plan, procedure, procession, progression, propriety, regularity, regulation, rule, scale, scheme, sequence, series, setup, standardization, structure, succession, symmetry, system, tidiness, uniformity; CONCEPT 727 —*Ant.* confusion, disorder, disorganization, mess, muddle

order |n2| *lawfulness* calm, control, decorousness, decorum, discipline, goodness, integrity, law, law and order, niceness, orderliness, peace, peacefulness, probity, properness, propriety, quiet, rectitude, rightness, seemliness, suitability, tranquility, uprightness; CONCEPTS 633,691 —*Ant.* lawlessness, liberty, license

order |n3| *class, status* bracket, branch, breed, cast, caste, degree, description, estate, family, feather, genre, genus, grade, hierarchy, ilk, kidney, kind, line, nature, pecking order*, pigeonhole*, place, position, rank, set, slot, sort, species, station, stripe, subclass, taxonomic group, type; CONCEPT 378

order |n4| *command* authorization, behest, bidding, charge, commandment, decree, dictate, direction, directive, injunction, instruction, law, mandate, ordinance, permission, precept, regulation, rule, say-so*, stipulation, ukase, word*; CONCEPTS 53,278,685 —*Ant.* answer

order |n5| *request; purchase* agreement amount, application, booking, bulk, commission, engagement, goods, materials, purchase, quantity, requisition, reservation, reserve, shipment, stipulation; CONCEPTS 332,338,684

order |n6| *organization* association, brotherhood, club, community, company, fraternity, guild, league, lodge, sect, sisterhood, society, sodality, sorority, union; CONCEPT 387

order |v1| *command, authorize* adjure, apply for, bid, book, buy, call for, call the shots*, call the signals*, charge, contract for, decree, dictate, direct, enact, engage, enjoin, hire, instruct, obtain, ordain, prescribe, pull strings*, request, require, reserve, rule the roost*, secure, send away for, tell, warn; CONCEPTS 50,53,88,327 —*Ant.* disallow, prevent, rescind

order |v2| *arrange, organize* adapt, adjust, align, alphabetize, array, assign, catalogue, class, classify, codify, conduct, control, dispose, distribute, establish, file, fix, formalize, furnish, group, index, lay out, line, line up, locate, manage, marshal, methodize, neaten, normalize, pattern, place, plan, put away, put to rights*, range, regiment, regularize, regulate, right, routine, set guidelines, set in order, settle, sort out, space, standardize, streamline, systematize, tabulate, tidy; CONCEPTS 84,158 —*Ant.* disorder, disorganize, mess up, mix up, muddle

order about |v| *dominate* boss, bully, call the shots*, command, control, dictate, direct, influence, keep under one's thumb*, manage, master, run the show*; CONCEPTS 94,117,298

ordered [adj] *orderly* all together, arranged, businesslike, controlled, disciplined, in good shape, in order, law-abiding, methodical, neat, organized, peaceable, precise, shipshape*, systematic, systematized, tidy, well-behaved, well-organized; CONCEPTS 326,485,585,589

orderly [adj1] *methodical, organized* alike, all together, arranged, businesslike, careful, clean, conventional, correct, exact, fixed, formal, framed, in apple-pie order*, in good shape, in order, in shape, methodic, neat, neat as button*, neat as pin*, precise, regular, regulated, scientific, set-up, shipshape*, slick, spick-and-span*, systematic, systematized, thorough, tidy, together, to rights*, trim, uncluttered, uniform; CONCEPTS 326,485,585,589 —Ant. complicated, disorderly, disorganized, unmethodical, unsystematic, untidy

orderly [adj2] *well-behaved* at peace, calm, controlled, decorous, disciplined, docile, law-abiding, manageable, nonviolent, obedient, peaceable, quiet, restrained, submissive, tranquil, well-mannered; CONCEPT 401 —Ant. bad, misbehaving, unruly

ordinance [n] *law, rule* authorization, canon, code, command, decree, dictum, direction, edict, enactment, fiat, mandate, order, precept, prescript, reg, regulation, ruling, statute, ukase; CONCEPT 318

ordinarily [adv] *usually* as a rule, commonly, customarily, frequently, generally, habitually, in general, normally, regularly; CONCEPT 530 —Ant. infrequently, rarely, sometimes

ordinary [adj1] *common, regular* accustomed, customary, established, everyday, familiar, frequent, general, habitual, humdrum*, natural, normal, popular, prevailing, public, quotidian, routine, run-of-the-mill*, settled, standard, stock, traditional, typical, usual, wonted; CONCEPTS 533,547 —Ant. abnormal, extraordinary, irregular, uncommon

ordinary [adj2] *average; not distinctive* characterless, common, commonplace, conventional, dull, fair, familiar, garden*, garden variety*, generic, habitual, homespun, household, humble, indifferent, inferior, mean, mediocre, modest, no great shakes*, normal, pedestrian, plain, plastic, prosaic, quotidian, routine, run-of-the-mill*, second-rate, simple, so-so*, stereotyped, undistinguished, uneventful, unexceptional, uninspired, unmemorable, unnoteworthy, unpretentious, unremarkable, usual, vanilla*, white-bread*, workaday; CONCEPTS 530,575 —Ant. different, distinctive, remarkable, special

ordnance [n] *artillery* arms, big guns*, bombs, heavy stuff*, missiles, munitions, weapons; CONCEPTS 322,500

organ [n] *means, tool* agency, agent, channel, device, element, forum, implement, instrument, journal, magazine, medium, member, ministry, mouthpiece, newspaper, paper, part, periodical, process, publication, review, structure, unit, vehicle, voice, way; CONCEPTS 280,499,712

organic [adj] *basic, natural* amoebic, anatomical, animate, basal, biological, biotic, cellular, constitutional, elemental, essential, fundamental,

inherent, innate, integral, live, living, necessary, nuclear, original, plasmic, primary, prime, primitive, principal, structural, vital; CONCEPT 549 —Ant. inorganic, man-made, unnatural

organism [n] *living thing* animal, being, body, creature, entity, morphon, person, plant, structure; CONCEPTS 389,429 —Ant. concept, inanimate

organization [n1] *arrangement, arranging* alignment, assembling, assembly, chemistry, composition, configuration, conformation, constitution, construction, coordination, design, disposal, format, formation, forming, formulation, framework, grouping, harmony, institution, make-up, making, management, method, methodology, organism, organizing, pattern, plan, planning, regulation, running, situation, standard, standardization, structure, structuring, symmetry, system, unity, whole; CONCEPTS 84,117,727 —Ant. disorganization

organization [n2] *group bound by interest/work/goal* affiliation, aggregation, alliance, association, band, body, business, cartel, circle, clique, club, coalition, combination, combine, company, concern, concord, confederation, consortium, cooperative, corporation, coterie, crew, establishment, federation, fraternity, guild, house, industry, institute, institution, league, lodge, machine, monopoly, order, outfit, party, profession, set, society, sodality, sorority, squad, syndicate, team, trade, troupe, trust, union; CONCEPT 381

organize [v] *arrange, systematize* adapt, adjust, be responsible for, catalogue, classify, codify, combine, compose, constitute, construct, coordinate, correlate, create, dispose, establish, fashion, fit, form, formulate, frame, get going*, get together, group, harmonize, lick into shape*, line up, look after, marshal, methodize, mold, pigeonhole*, put in order, put together, range, regulate, run, see to, settle, set up, shape, standardize, straighten, straighten out, tabulate, tailor, take care of, whip into shape*; CONCEPTS 36,84,158 —Ant. destroy, disarrange, disorder, disorganize

organized [adj] *arranged, systematized* catalogued, classified, coordinated, correlated, formed, formulated, grouped, methodized, standardized, straightened out, tabulated; CONCEPTS 84,94

organized crime [n] *the underworld* Cosa Nostra, gangland, Mafia, mob, organized crime family, the syndicate; CONCEPTS 412,645

organizer [n] *planner* arranger, coordinator, designer, developer, facilitator, promoter; CONCEPT 347

orgasm [n] *climax* ejaculation, frenzy, peak, spasm; CONCEPTS 706,836

orgy [n] *celebration devoted to sensual enjoyment* bacchanal, bacchanalia, bender*, binge*, blowout*, bout*, carousal, circus*, debauch, dissipation, excess, feast, fling*, indulgence, jag*, merrymaking, overindulgence, party, rampage*, revel, revelry, saturnalia, splurge, spree, surfeit, tear*; CONCEPTS 377,383

orient [v] *familiarize* acclimatize, adapt, adjust, align, conform, determine, direct, get one's bearings*, locate, orientate, turn; CONCEPTS 35,202 —Ant. disorient

orientation [n] *introduction, adjustment* acclimatization, adaptation, assimilation, bearings, breaking in*, coordination, direction, familiarization, fix*, lay of the land*, location, position, sense of direction, settling in*; CONCEPTS 31,832 —*Ant.* disorientation, mix-up

orifice [n] *opening* aperture, cavity, crack, hole, mouth, outlet, slit, spout, vent, window; CONCEPT 513

origin [n1] *cause, basis* agent, ancestor, ancestry, antecedent, author, base, causality, causation, connection, creator, derivation, determinant, egg*, element, embryo, fountain, generator, germ, horse's mouth*, impulse, inception, inducement, influence, inspiration, mainspring, motive, nucleus, occasion, parent, parentage, principle, producer, progenitor, provenance, provenience, root, roots, seed, source, spring, stock, well, wellspring; CONCEPTS 229,648,661 —*Ant.* consequence, destiny, effect, goal, outcome, outgrowth, result

origin [n2] *beginning, inception* alpha, birth, blast off, commencement, creation, dawn, dawning, day one*, early stage, embarkation, emergence, entrance, entry, forging, foundation, genesis, git go*, inauguration, ingress, initiation, introduction, launch, nativity, opener, origination, outbreak, outset, rise, square one*, start, starting point*; CONCEPT 832 —*Ant.* close, closing, conclusion, death, end, finale, termination

origin [n3] *family, heritage* ancestry, beginnings, birth, blood, descent, extraction, lineage, maternity, parentage, paternity, pedigree, stock; CONCEPT 296

original [adj1] *earliest* aboriginal, archetypal, authentic, autochthonous, beginning, commencing, early, elementary, embryonic, first, first-hand, genuine, inceptive, infant, initial, introductory, opening, pioneer, primary, prime, primeval, primitive, primordial, pristine, prototypal, rudimental, rudimentary, starting, underivative, underived; CONCEPTS 549,585 —*Ant.* derivative, latest, newest

original [adj2] *fresh, new* avant garde, breaking new ground*, causal, causative, conceiving, creative, demiurgic, devising, envisioning, fertile, formative, generative, imaginative, ingenious, innovational, innovative, innovatory, inspiring, inventive, novel, originative, productive, quick, ready, resourceful, seminal, sensitive, unconventional, unprecedented, untried, unusual; CONCEPTS 549,585,797 —*Ant.* borrowed, hackneyed, old, used, worn

original [n1] *standard, prototype* archetype, coinage, creation, exemplar, forerunner, invention, model, novelty, paradigm, pattern, precedent, precursor, type; CONCEPTS 260,686 —*Ant.* creation, derivative, offshoot

original [n2] *person who is eccentric* anomaly, card*, case*, character, eccentric, nonconformist, oddball, oddity, queer, weirdo*; CONCEPT 412

originality [n] *creativeness* boldness, brilliance, cleverness, creative spirit, creativity, daring, freshness, imagination, imaginativeness, individuality, ingeniousness, ingenuity, innovation, innovativeness, invention, inventiveness, modernity, new idea, newness, nonconformity,

novelty, resourcefulness, spirit, unconventionality, unorthodoxy; CONCEPTS 409,410 —*Ant.* orthodoxy

originally [adv] *initially* at first, at the outset, at the start, basically, by birth, by origin, first, formerly, incipiently, in the beginning, in the first place, primarily, primitively, to begin with; CONCEPTS 578,585,797,799 —*Ant.* secondarily

originate [v1] *begin; spring* arise, be born, birth, come, come from, come into existence, commence, dawn, derive, emanate, emerge, flow, hail from, issue, proceed, result, rise, start, stem; CONCEPTS 105,221 —*Ant.* end, finish, terminate

originate [v2] *create, introduce* break the ice*, bring about, cause, coin, come up with, compose, conceive, develop, discover, evolve, form, formulate, found, generate, give birth to, hatch, inaugurate, initiate, innovate, institute, invent, launch, make, open up, parent, pioneer, procreate, produce, set in motion, set up, spark, spawn, start, think up, usher in; CONCEPTS 43, 173,251 —*Ant.* effect, result

origination [n] *origin* beginning, birth, commencement, conception, creation, dawn, dawning, discovery, genesis, innovation, introduction, launch, source, start, starting point*; CONCEPT 832

originator [n] *creator* architect, author, begetter, designer, discoverer, father, founder, initiator, innovator, inventor, maker, mastermind, mother, pioneer, producer; CONCEPTS 348,352,361

ornament [n] *decoration* accessory, adornment, art, bauble, beautification, design, doodad*, embellishment, embroidery, flower, frill, frou frou*, garnish, gewgaw*, gimcrack*, gingerbread*, honor, jewel, knickknack*, pride, treasure, trimming, trinket; CONCEPTS 259,476

ornament [v] *decorate* adorn, array, beautify, bedeck, bedizen, brighten, deck, dress, dress up*, embellish, embroider, enrich, festoon, fix up*, garnish, gild, grace, ornamentalize, polish, prank, prettify, primp, prink, smarten*, spruce up*, trim; CONCEPTS 162,167,177 —*Ant.* leave alone

ornamental [adj] *decorative* accessory, adorning, attractive, beautiful, beautifying, decking, decorating, delicate, dressy, elaborate, embellishing, enhancing, exquisite, fancy, festooned, florid, for show*, furbishing, garnishing, heightening, luxurious, ornate, setting off*, showy; CONCEPTS 579,589 —*Ant.* plain, unembellished

ornate [adj] *fancily decorated* adorned, aureate, baroque, beautiful, bedecked, bright, brilliant, busy, colored, convoluted, dazzling, elaborate, elegant, embroidered, fancy, fine, flamboyant, flashy, flaunting, florid, flowery, fussy, gaudy, gilded, glamorous, glitzy, glossy, high-wrought, jeweled, lavish, luscious, magnificent, meretricious, opulent, ornamented, ostentatious, overdone, overelaborate, pretentious, resplendent, rich, rococo, showy, sparkling, splashy, sumptuous, superficial, tawdry, variegated; CONCEPTS 579,589 —*Ant.* plain, simple

ornery [adj] *mean* cantankerous, contemptible, crabby, cranky, crusty*, difficult, disagreeable, grouchy*, grumpy*, hard-nosed*, ignoble, ill-tempered, irritable, nasty, obstinate, quarrelsome, rotten, sour, surly, testy, un-friendly, vicious; CONCEPTS 267,401,542

orphan [n] *child without parents* foundling, ragamuffin*, stray, waif; CONCEPT 414

orthodox [adj] *accepted, traditional* according to the book*, acknowledged, admitted, approved, authoritative, buttoned-down*, by the numbers*, canonical, conformist, conservative, conventional, correct, customary, devout, die-hard, doctrinal, established, in line*, legitimate, official, old-line*, pious, proper, punctilious, re-actionary, received, recognized, religious, right, rightful, sanctioned, sound, square, standard, straight, straight arrow, traditionalistic, true, well-established; CONCEPT 533 —*Ant.* hetero-dox, unconventional, unorthodox, untraditional

oscillate [v] *change back and forth* be unsteady, dangle, fishtail, flicker, fluctuate, librate, lurch, palpitate, pendulate, pitch, pivot, reel, ripple, rock, roll, seesaw, stagger, sway, swing, switch, swivel, teeter, teeter-totter*, thrash, toss, totter, undulate, vacillate, vary, vibrate, waddle, wag, waggle, waltz, wave, waver, whirl, wiggle, wob-ble; CONCEPTS 13,147,697 —*Ant.* remain, stay

ossified [adj] *bony* fossilized, hard, hardened, petrified, rigid; CONCEPTS 404,542

ossify [v] *become hard from aging* congeal, fossilize, freeze, harden, indurate, petrify, solidify, stiffen, thicken, turn to bone; CONCEPT 469 —*Ant.* melt, soften

ossuary [n] *urn* container, receptacle, vault, vessel; CONCEPT 494

ostensible [adj] *alleged, supposed* apparent, avowed, colorable, demonstrative, exhibited, illusive, illusory, likely, manifest, notable, outward, plausible, pretended, professed, purported, quasi, seeming, semblant, so-called*, specious, superficial; CONCEPTS 552, 582 —*Ant.* improbable, obscure, unlikely, vague

ostensibly [adv] *apparently* at first blush*, evidently, externally, for all intents and pur-poses*, for show*, officially, on the face*, on the surface*, outwardly, professedly, seemingly, sensibly, superficially, supposedly, to the eye*; CONCEPT 582 —*Ant.* improbably, obscurely, unlikely

ostentation [n] *exhibitionism, flashiness* affec-tation, array, boast, boasting, brag, braggado-cio*, bragging, bravado, demonstration, display, exhibition, false front*, flamboyance, flash*, flaunting, flourish, fuss, garishness, grandstand play*, magnificence, pageant, pageantry, parade, parading, pomp, pomposity, pompousness, pretending, pretension, pretentiousness, put-on, shine*, show, showiness, showing off*, showoff*, spectacle, splendor, splurge, swag-ger*, swaggering, swank*, vainglory, vaunt*, vaunting*, window-dressing; CONCEPTS 633,655 —*Ant.* modesty, plainness, quiet, reservation

ostentatious [adj] *flashy, showy* boastful, chichi*, classy, conspicuous, crass*, dashing, egotistic, exhibitionistic, extravagant, flamboy-ant, flatulent, flaunted, fussy, garish, gaudy, gay, glittery, grandiose, highfaluting*, jaunty, loud, obtrusive, peacocky, pompous, preten-tious, spectacular, splashy, splurgy, sporty, swank, swanky*, theatrical, tinsel*, tony*, uptown*, vain, vulgar; CONCEPT 589 —*Ant.* modest, plain, quiet, reserved

ostracism [n] *banishment* avoidance, black-balling, boycott, cold-shouldering, exclusion, excommunication, exile, expulsion, isolation, rejection, shunning; CONCEPTS 25,130

ostracize [v] *exile, banish* avoid, blackball*, blacklist*, boycott, cast out, cold-shoulder*, cut, deport, displace, drop, exclude, excommunicate, expatriate, expel, expulse, leave in the cold, oust, reject, shun, shut out, snub, throw out; CONCEPTS 25,384 —*Ant.* embrace, welcome

other [adj1] *additional, added* alternative, another, auxiliary, else, extra, farther, fresh, further, more, new, spare, supplementary; CONCEPT 771 —*Ant.* included, related

other [adj2] *different* contrasting, disparate, dissimilar, distant, distinct, divergent, diverse, opposite, otherwise, remaining, separate, unalike, unequal, unlike, unrelated, variant; CONCEPT 564 —*Ant.* coinciding, same, similar

otherwise [adv] *in another way; alternatively* any other way, contrarily, differently, diversely, elseways, if not, in different circumstances, on the other hand, or else, or then, under other conditions, variously; CONCEPT 544

otherworldly [adj] *extraterrestrial; psychic* alien, ethereal, heavenly, magical, mystical, out of this world, spiritual, supernatural, transcendental, uncanny, unearthly, unworldly, visionary; CONCEPTS 529,549,582

ounce [n] *one-sixteenth of a pound/28.35 grams of weight* avoirdupois, troy, uncia; CONCEPT 795

oust [v] *expel, get rid of* banish, bereave, boot out*, bounce*, bundle off*, cast out, chase, depose, deprive, dethrone, discharge, disinherit, dislodge, displace, dispossess, divest, drive out, eject, evict, expulse, fire, force out, give the 1-2-3*, kick out, lay off, let go, lose, ostracize, pack off, pink slip*, relegate, remove, rob, sack, send packing*, show the door*, throw out, topple, transport, turn out, unseat; CONCEPTS 25,211,351 —*Ant.* hold, keep, retain

ouster [n] *ejection* banishment, disbarment, discharge, dismissal, eviction, expulsion, loss of right, overthrow, removal, sack, the heave-ho*; CONCEPTS 179,222

out [adj] *not possible; gone* absent, antiquated, at an end, away, behind the times*, cold, dated, dead, demode, doused, ended, exhausted, ex-pired, extinguished, finished, impossible, not allowed, not on, old-fashioned, old-hat*, out-moded, outside, passé, ruled out, unacceptable, unfashionable, used up; CONCEPTS 539,552,576 —*Ant.* here, in, possible

out [adv] *outside, outdoors* out of doors, outward, without; CONCEPT 583 —*Ant.* in, indoors, inside

out-and-out [adj] *complete* absolute, arrant, consummate, downright, full, outright, perfect, thorough, thoroughgoing, through-and-through, total, uncompromising, undiminished, unmiti-gated, unqualified, utter, whole; CONCEPT 531

outbreak [n] *sudden happening* beginning, blowup, brawl, break, breaking, burst, bursting, commencement, commotion, convulsion, crack, crash, dawn, detonation, discharge, disorder, disruption, ebullition, effervescence, epidemic, eruption, explosion, fit, flare-up, flash, fury, gush, gushing, insurrection, irruption, mutiny, onset, outburst, outpouring, paroxysm, plague, rebellion, rending, revolution, roar, sally, sortie, spasm, spurt, storm, sundering, surge, thunder, tumult, uprising, volley; CONCEPTS 2,86,179,832 —*Ant.* conclusion, end, finale

outburst [n] *fit of temper* access, attack, blow, burst, conniption*, discharge, eruption, explosion, flare, flare-up, frenzy, gush, gust, outbreak, outpouring, paroxysm, rapture, scene, spasm, storm, surge, tantrum, transport, upheaval; CONCEPT 633 —*Ant.* harmony, order, peace

outcast [n] *person who is unwanted, not accepted* bum*, castaway, deportee, derelict, displaced person, exile, expatriate, fugitive, gypsy, hobo*, persona non grata*, rascal, refugee, reprobate, tramp, untouchable, vagabond, vagrant, wretch; CONCEPT 423 —*Ant.* favorite, friend, idol

outclass [v] *surpass* beat, best, better, cap, dominate, eclipse, exceed, excel, go beyond, go one better*, improve upon, outdistance, outdo, outhussle, outmatch, outpace, outperform, outplay, outrank, outrival, outrun, outshine, outstrip, pass, put to shame*, rise above, surmount, top, tower, win the race; CONCEPT 141

out cold [adj] *unconscious* benumbed, blacked out*, comatose, dead to the world*, down for the count*, drowsy, feeling no pain*, flattened*, in a trance, numb, on the canvas*, out, out like a light*, passed out*, put away*, senseless, zonked*; CONCEPTS 314,539

outcome [n] *consequence, effect* aftereffect, aftermath, blowoff, causatum, chain reaction*, conclusion, end, end result*, event, fallout, issue, payback*, payoff*, reaction, result, score, sequel, upshot*; CONCEPT 230 —*Ant.* beginning, cause, origin, source

outcry [n] *scream, exclamation* clamor, commotion, complaint, convulsion, cry, ferment, flak*, hoo-ha*, howl, hubba-hubba*, hullabaloo*, noise, objection, outburst, protest, screech, tumult, uproar, upturn, yell; CONCEPTS 77,278 —*Ant.* quiet, silence

outdated/out-of-date [adj] *old-fashioned* anachronous, antiquated, antique, archaic, back number*, behind the times*, dated, démodé, dusty, has-been*, moth-eaten*, musty, not with it*, obsolete, old, old-hat*, out, outmoded, out-of-style*, passé, square, tired, unfashionable, vintage; CONCEPTS 578,589,797 —*Ant.* current, fashionable, modern, new, popular, up-to-date

outdistance [v] *outrun* beat, best, better, exceed, go beyond, go one better*, leave behind, outclass, outdo, outhussle, outpace, outperform, outplay, overtake, pass, surpass, top, win the race; CONCEPT 141

outdo [v] *better, overcome* beat, best, blow out of water*, bulldoze*, bury*, cook*, cream*, defeat, do in*, down*, eclipse, exceed, excel, fake out*, go one better*, leave behind*, lick*, outclass, outdistance, outfox, outgun, outjockey, outmaneuver, outrival, outshine, outsmart, outstrip, pull a fast one*, shake off*, shoot ahead*, snow*, surpass, top, transcend, trash*; CONCEPTS 95,141 —*Ant.* fail, lose

outdoor [adj/adv] *in the open air* alfresco, casual, free, garden, healthful, hilltop, informal, in the open, invigorating, mountain, natural, nature-loving, out-of-doors, out of the house,

outside, patio, picnic, rustic, unrestricted, woods, yard; CONCEPT 583 —*Ant.* indoor

outdoors [n] *open air; nature* bucolic surroundings, country, countryside, environment, fresh air, garden, green earth*, hill, mountain, open, out-of-doors, patio, without, woods, yard; CONCEPT 198 —*Ant.* indoors

outer [adj] *external, exposed* alien, beyond, exoteric, exterior, extraneous, extrinsic, outermost, outlying, outmost, outside, outward, over, peripheral, remote, superficial, surface, without; CONCEPTS 484,583 —*Ant.* central, inner, interior

outermost [adj] *outer* beyond, distant, fringe, furthermost, outlying, outmost, outward, peripheral, remote; CONCEPTS 484,583

outfit [n1] *set of clothes or equipment* accoutrements, apparatus, appliances, clothing, costume, ensemble, garb, gear, get-up*, guise, kit, machinery, materiel, outlay, paraphernalia, provisions, rig, rigging, suit, supplies, tackle, togs, trappings*, wardrobe; CONCEPTS 451,496

outfit [n2] *large group; business* band, clique, company, concern, corps, coterie, crew, enterprise, establishment, firm, house, organization, party, set, squad, team, troop, troupe, unit; CONCEPTS 325,417

outfit [v] *clothe, equip* accoutre, appoint, arm, deck out*, drape, fit out*, furnish, gear, prepare, provide, provision, rig up*, stock, suit, supply, tog*, turn out*; CONCEPTS 167, 182 —*Ant.* bare, unclothe

outflank [v] *outmaneuver* beat, best, better, defeat, excel, outclass, outdo, outfox, outperform, outplay, outshine, outsmart, outwit, surpass, top; CONCEPT 141

outflow [n] *efflux* discharge, drainage, effluence, effluent, effluvium, effusion, emergence, gush, gushing outpouring, rush, spout, stream, streaming; CONCEPTS 179,748

outfox [v] *outsmart* best, defeat, excel, outclass, outdo, outperform, outplay, outwit, surpass, top; CONCEPT 141

outgoing [adj1] *demonstrative, extroverted* approachable, civil, communicative, cordial, easy, expansive, extrovert, friendly, genial, gregarious, informal, kind, open, sociable, sympathetic, unconstrained, unreserved, unrestrained, warm; CONCEPT 404 —*Ant.* introverted, reclusive, shy

outgoing [adj2] *leaving* departing, ex-*, former, last, migratory, outbound, outward-bound, past, retiring, withdrawing; CONCEPTS 581,584 —*Ant.* arriving, entering, incoming

outgrowth [n1] *projection* bulge, enlargement, excrescence, jut, node, offshoot, outcrop, process, prolongation, prominence, protuberance, shoot, sprout, swelling; CONCEPTS 471,824 —*Ant.* ingrowth

outgrowth [n2] *product, consequence* aftereffect, branch, by-product*, derivative, descendant, development, effect, emergence, end, end result*, issue, member, offshoot, offspring, outcome, result, spin-off*, yield; CONCEPTS 230,260

outhouse [n] *toilet* bathroom, latrine, lavatory, outbuilding, privy, washroom, water closet, WC; CONCEPT 448

outing [n] *short trip* airing, drive, excursion, expedition, jaunt, junket, long weekend, picnic, pleasure trip, roundabout, spin*, vacation, weekend; CONCEPTS 224,386

outing [n2] *politically motivated exposure of another's secrets* announcement, declaration, demystification, disclosure, proclamation, revealing, tossing, uncloseting, unmasking; CONCEPT 60

outlandish [adj] *bizarre, strange* alien, awkward, barbaric, barbarous, boorish, clumsy, curious, droll, eccentric, erratic, exotic, extravagant, fantastic, far-out*, foreign, freakish, gauche, graceless, grotesque, kinky*, odd, outrageous, outré, peculiar, preposterous, quaint, queer, ridiculous, rude, singular, tasteless, ultra, unconventional, uncouth, unheard-of*, unorthodox, unusual, weird, whimsical, wild; CONCEPTS 401,548 —*Ant.* common, familiar, normal, ordinary, usual

outlast [v] *endure beyond another* hang on, outlive, outstay, outwear, remain, survive; CONCEPT 407 —*Ant.* fail, fall apart, lose, peter out, shoot, succumb

outlaw [n] *person who is running from the law* bandit, brigand, con, criminal, crook, desperado, drifter, ex-con, fugitive, gangster, gunslinger*, hood*, hoodlum, hooligan*, jailbird, marauder, mobster, mug*, outcast, pariah, racketeer, robber, wrong number*; CONCEPT 412

outlaw [v] *prohibit; make illegal* ban, banish, bar, condemn, damn, disallow, embargo, enjoin, exclude, forbid, illegalize, inhibit, interdict, prevent, proscribe, stop, taboo; CONCEPTS 121,317 —*Ant.* allow, legalize, permit

outlay [n] *expenses* bite*, bottom line*, charge, cost, damage, disbursement, expenditure, expense, highway robbery*, investment, price tag, score*, setback*, spending, tab*, throw*, tune*; CONCEPT 344 —*Ant.* income, pay

outlet [n1] *place or means of escape, release* aperture, avenue, break, channel, crack, duct, egress, escape, exit, hole, nozzle, opening, orifice, porthole, release, safety valve, spout, tear, vent, way out; CONCEPTS 513,693 —*Ant.* egress, entrance

outlet [n2] *store that sells discounted items* factory store, market, mill store, seconds store, shop, showroom; CONCEPTS 439,448,449

outline [n1] *plan, sketch* bare facts*, blueprint, diagram, draft, drawing, floor plan, frame, framework, ground plan, layout, main features, recapitulation, résumé, rough draft, rough idea, rundown, skeleton, summary, synopsis, thumbnail sketch*, tracing; CONCEPT 268

outline [n2] *form, tracing of an object* configuration, conformation, contour, delineation, figuration, figure, profile, shape, silhouette; CONCEPTS 436,625 —*Ant.* inside

outline [v] *sketch out; plan* adumbrate, block out, characterize, chart, delineate, describe, draft, lay out, paint, plot, recapitulate, rough out, skeleton, skeletonize, summarize, tell about, trace; CONCEPTS 36,55,174

outlive [v] *outlast* continue, endure, hang on, outstay, prevail, remain, survive; CONCEPT 407

outlook [n1] *point of view* angle*, attitude, direction, frame of mind*, headset*, mind-set*, perspective, routine, scope, side, size of it*, slant*, standpoint, viewpoint, views, vision; CONCEPTS 410,689 —*Ant.* indifference

outlook [n2] *probable future* appearances, chance, expectation, forecast, law of averages*, likelihood, normal course, opening, opportunity, possibility, probability, prospect, prospects, risk; CONCEPT 679 —*Ant.* past

outlook [n3] *scene, view* aspect, lookout, panorama, perspective, prospect, scape, sight, vista; CONCEPTS 509,628

outlying [adj] *in rural area; remote* afar, backwoods, distant, external, faraway, far-flung*, far-off, off-lying, outer, out-of-the-way*, peripheral, provincial, removed; CONCEPT 583 —*Ant.* central, inner, middle

outmoded [adj] *obsolete, old-fashioned* anachronistic, antediluvian, antiquated, antique, archaic, behind the times*, bent, bygone, dated, dead, démodé, dinosaur*, disused, extinct, fossilized, has-been*, horse and buggy*, moldy*, moth-eaten*, musty*, obsolescent, obsolete, olden, old-hat*, old-time, out, out-of-date, out-of-style, outworn, passé*, superannuated, superseded, tired, unfashionable, unstylish, unusable, vintage; CONCEPTS 560, 578,589,797 —*Ant.* current, modern, new, new-fangled, popular, up-to-date

out of the closet [adj] *open* brought to light, candid, disclosed, divulged, exposed, open and aboveboard, open to view, out in the open, revealed, unveiled; CONCEPT 60

out of the way [adj] *secluded* backwoods, distant, faraway, far-flung, godforsaken, inaccessible, isolated, lonely, obscure, off the beaten track, outer, outermost, outlying, peripheral, remote, sequestered; CONCEPT 586 —*Ant.* accessible, handy, near

out of work [adj] *not employed* between jobs, collecting unemployment, idle, jobless, laid off, on the dole, out of a job, unemployed; CONCEPT 351 —*Ant.* employed

outpouring [n] *outflow* cascade, deluge, discharge, effluence, effusion, flood, flow, gush, issue, jet, leakage, outburst, rush, spurt*, stream, torrent; CONCEPT 179

output [n] *something produced* achievement, amount, crop, harvest, making, manufacture, manufacturing, producing, product, production, productivity, profit, take, turnout, yield; CONCEPTS 205,260 —*Ant.* input

outrage [n1] *atrocity, evil* abuse, affront, barbarism, damage, desecration, enormity, evildoing, harm, hurt, indignity, inhumanity, injury, insult, mischief, misdoing, offense, profanation, rape, rapine, ravishing, ruin, shock, violation, violence, wrongdoing; CONCEPTS 192,645,674 —*Ant.* delight, happiness

outrage [n2] *anger* blowup, flare-up*, fury, huff*, hurt, indignation, resentment, ruckus*, shock*, stew*, storm*, wrath; CONCEPT 29 —*Ant.* cheer, glee, happiness, joy

outrage [v] *wrong, offend, abuse* affront, aggrieve, boil over*, burn up*, defile, deflower, desecrate, do violence to, fire up*, force, illtreat, incense, infuriate, injure, insult, jar*, kick up a row*, madden, make hit the ceiling*, maltreat, mistreat, misuse, oppress, persecute, raise Cain*, rape, ravage, ravish, reach boiling point*, scandalize, shock, spoil, violate, whip up*; CONCEPTS 7,19,29,246 —*Ant.* delight, make happy, please

outrageous [adj1] very bad abominable, atrocious, barbaric, beastly, brazen, contemptible, contumelious, corrupt, criminal, debasing, debauching, degenerate, depraving, disgraceful, disgracing, egregious, flagitious, flagrant, gross, heinous, horrendous, horrible, ignoble, infamous, inhuman, iniquitous, malevolent, monstrous, nefarious, notorious, odious, opprobrious, scandalous, scurrilous, shameless, shaming, shocking, sinful, unbearable, ungodly, unspeakable, villainous, violent, wanton, wicked; CONCEPT 571 —Ant. delightful, good, magnificent, pleasing, wonderful

outrageous [adj2] beyond reasonable limits barbarous, crazy*, excessive, exorbitant, extortionate, extravagant, immoderate, inordinate, last straw*, offensive, out of bounds*, preposterous, scandalous, shocking, steep*, too much*, uncivilized, unconscionable, unreasonable; CONCEPTS 569,771 —Ant. acceptable, mild, reasonable, sensible

outright [adj] complete, unconditional absolute, all, arrant, consummate, definite, direct, downright, entire, flat, gross, out-and-out*, perfect, positive, pure, straightforward, thorough, thoroughgoing, total, undeniable, unequivocal, unmitigated, unqualified, utter, whole, wholesale; CONCEPTS 531,535 —Ant. ambiguous, conditional, hesitating, incomplete, indefinite, provisional

outside [adj1] external alfresco, alien, apart from, away from, exterior, extramural, extraneous, extreme, farther, farthest, foreign, furthest, open-air, out, outdoor, outer, outermost, outward, over, surface; CONCEPTS 484,583 —Ant. central, inside, internal, middle

outside [adj2] slight, slim distant, faint, far, marginal, negligible, off, remote, slender, small, unlikely; CONCEPTS 552,789 —Ant. certain, definite, good, likely, sure

outside [n] exterior; out-of-doors appearance, covering, facade, face, front, integument, open, open air, outdoors, seeming, sheath, skin, surface, topside, without; CONCEPTS 198,484 —Ant. center, indoors, inside, interior, middle

outsider [n] person who is foreign to something alien, floater*, foreigner, incomer*, interloper, intruder, newcomer, odd one out*, outlander, refugee, stranger; CONCEPTS 413,423 —Ant. insider

outskirts [n] edge of a geographic area bedroom community*, border, boundary, edge, environs, limit, outpost, periphery, purlieu, purlieus, sticks*, suburb, suburbia, vicinity; CONCEPTS 508,513 —Ant. center, downtown

outspoken [adj] explicit, unreserved abrupt, artless, blunt, calling spade a spade*, candid, direct, forthright, frank, free, laying it on the line*, open, plain, plain-spoken, point-blank*, round, square, straightforward, strident, talking turkey*, unceremonious, unequivocal, unreticent, up front*, vocal; CONCEPTS 267,404 —Ant. cautious, diplomatic, introverted, reserved, retiring, shy, tactful

outstanding [adj1] superior, excellent A-1*, ace*, A-number-1*, bad*, boss*, capital*, celebrated, chief, cool*, crack*, distinguished, dominant, eminent, eventful, exceptional, famous, far-out*, great, greatest, hundred-proof*, important, impressive, magnificent, main, major, meritorious, momentous, mostest, number one*, out-of-sight*, out-of-this-world*, phenomenal, predominant, preeminent, primo*, principal, special, standout, star, steller, super, superior, superlative, tops*, well-known, world-class; CONCEPTS 568,574 —Ant. average, bad, inferior, ordinary, poor, regular, unexceptional, unremarkable

outstanding [adj2] noticeable, striking arresting, arrestive, conspicuous, distinguished, eye-catching, important, leading, marked, memorable, notable, noteworthy, prominent, pronounced, remarkable, salient, signal; CONCEPTS 485,537 —Ant. inconspicuous, ordinary, unnoticeable, unstriking

outstanding [adj3] referring to an unpaid debt due, mature, ongoing, open, overdue, owing, payable, pending, remaining, uncollected, unresolved, unsettled; CONCEPT 334 —Ant. paid, resolved, settled

outward [adj] visible; for appearances apparent, evident, exterior, external, from within, noticeable, observable, obvious, on the surface, open, ostensible, out, outer, outside, over, perceptible, superficial, surface, to the eye, toward the edge; CONCEPTS 576,581,583 —Ant. invisible, inward

outwardly [adv] to all appearances apparently, as far as one can see, evidently, externally, for all intents and purposes*, in appearance, officially, on the face of it, on the surface, ostensibly, professedly, seemingly, superficially, to the eye; CONCEPTS 544,576 —Ant. inside, internally, inwardly, privately

outweigh [v] override, dominate atone for, balance, cancel out, compensate, counterbalance, counterpoise, countervail, eclipse, exceed, excel, make up for, offset, outbalance, outrival, outrun, overcome, overshadow, predominate, preponderate, prevail, set off, surpass, take precedence, tip the scales; CONCEPT 141

outwit/outsmart [v] get the better of; figure out before another baffle, bamboozle*, beat*, bewilder, cap, cheat, circumvent, con*, confuse, deceive, defeat, defraud, dupe, end-run*, fake out*, finagle*, fox*, goose*, gull*, have*, hoax, hoodwink, lead astray*, make a fool of*, make a monkey of*, mislead, outdo, outfox, outgeneral, outguess, outjockey, outmaneuver, outthink, overreach, pull a fast one on*, put one over on*, run circles around*, swindle, take in*, top*, trick, worst*; CONCEPTS 15,59

oval [adj] long and rounded in shape egg-shaped, ellipsoidal, elliptic, elliptical, oblong, ooid, ovaloid, ovate, oviform, ovoid; CONCEPT 486

ovation [n] clapping and cheers acclaim, acclamation, applause, big hand*, bravos, cheering, hand, laudation, plaudits, praise, salvo, testimonial, tribute; CONCEPTS 69,264 —Ant. silence

oven [n] kitchen stove kiln, kitchen range, microwave, microwave oven, range, roaster, stove, tandoor; CONCEPT 463

over [adj1] accomplished ancient history, at an end, by, bygone, closed, completed, concluded, done, done with, ended, finished, gone, past, settled, up; CONCEPTS 531,548 —Ant. failed, incomplete, unfinished

over [adj2/adv1] *in addition* additionally, beyond, ever, excessively, extra, extremely, immensely, in excess, inordinately, left over, more, over and above, overly, overmuch, remaining, superfluous, surplus, too, unduly, unused; CONCEPTS 544,771 —*Ant.* fewer, less

over [adj2] *above* aloft, beyond, covering, farther up, higher than, in heaven, in the sky, off, on high, on top of, overhead, overtop, straight up, traversely, upstairs; CONCEPTS 583, 793 —*Ant.* under

overabundance [n] *excess* embarrassment of riches*, glut, nimiety, overflow, overkill, overmuch, oversupply, plethora, profusion, superabundance, superfluity, surfeit, surplus, surplusage, too much*; CONCEPTS 767,787 —*Ant.* lack, need, scarcity, want

overall [adj] *complete, general* all-embracing, blanket, comprehensive, global, inclusive, long-range, long-term, sweeping, thorough, total, umbrella; CONCEPT 772 —*Ant.* incomplete, narrow, specific

overall [adv] *in general* all over, chiefly, everyplace, everywhere, generally speaking, in the long run, largely, mainly, mostly, on the whole, predominantly, primarily, principally, throughout; CONCEPT 772 —*Ant.* incomplete, narrow

overbearing [adj] *arrogant, domineering* ascendant, autocratic, bossy, cavalier, cocky*, despotic, dictatorial, disdainful, dogmatic, egotistic, haughty, high-and-mighty*, high-handed*, imperative, imperial, imperious, insolent, magisterial, officious, oppressive, overweening, paramount, peremptory, predominant, preponderant, prevalent, proud, regnant, sniffy*, snotty*, sovereign, stuffy, supercilious, superior, tyrannical, uppity*; CONCEPTS 401,404 —*Ant.* kind, modest, nice, unassertive

overblown [adj] *excessive, too much* aureate, bombastic, disproportionate, euphuistic, flowery, fulsome, grandiloquent, hyped up*, immoderate, inflated, magniloquent, oratorical, overdone, pompous, pretentious, profuse, rhetorical, sonorous, superfluous, turgid, undue, verbose, windy; CONCEPTS 267,548 —*Ant.* underrated, undervalued

overcast [adj] *cloudy, darkened* clouded, clouded over, dark, dismal, dreary, dull, gray, hazy, leaden, lowering, murky, nebulous, not clear, not fair, oppressive, somber, sunless, threatening; CONCEPT 525 —*Ant.* bright, clear, sunny

overcome [adj] *overwhelmed; visibly moved* affected, at a loss for words, beaten, blown-away*, bowled-over*, buried*, conquered, defeated, overthrown, run-over*, speechless, swamped, swept off one's feet*, taken*, unable to continue; CONCEPT 403 —*Ant.* indifferent, unbothered, unconcerned, unflappable, unmoved

overcome [v] *beat, defeat best*, be victorious, come out on top*, conquer, crush, down*, drown, get around*, get the better of*, hurdle, knock over*, knock socks off*, lick*, master, outlive, overpower, overthrow, overwhelm, prevail, prostrate, reduce, render, rise above*, shock, stun, subdue, subjugate, surmount, survive, throw*, triumph over, vanquish, weather*, whelm*, win, worst*; CONCEPT 95 —*Ant.* give in, surrender, yield

ou
ov

overconfident [adj] *overly sure of oneself* brash, careless, cocksure*, cocky*, foolhardy, heading for a fall*, heedless, hubristic, impudent, overweening, presuming, presumptuous, pushy*, rash, reckless, self-assertive; CONCEPTS 401,542 —*Ant.* cautious, pessimistic

overdo [v] *go to extremes; carry too far* amplify, be intemperate, belabor, bite off too much*, do to death, drive oneself, exaggerate, fatigue, go overboard*, go too far*, hype, lay it on*, magnify, make federal case*, not know when to stop*, overburden, overestimate, overindulge, overload, overplay, overrate, overreach, overstate, overtax, overtire, overuse, overvalue, overwork, pile on*, pressure, puff*, run into the ground*, run riot*, strain oneself, stretch, talk big*, wear down*, wear oneself out*; CONCEPT 156 —*Ant.* ignore, neglect

overdue [adj] *late, behind schedule* behind-hand, behind time, belated, delinquent, due, held up*, hung up*, jammed*, long delayed, mature, not punctual, outstanding, owing, payable, tardy, unpaid, unpunctual, unsettled; CONCEPTS 334,548,799 —*Ant.* early, paid

overeat [v] *eat too much* binge*, eat like a horse*, feast, gluttonize, gorge, gourmandize, overindulge, pack it away, pig*, pig out*, put it away, scarf*, stuff oneself*, stuff one's face*, surfeit; CONCEPT 316 —*Ant.* diet, fast

overflow [n] *flood, inundation* advance, cataclysm, cataract, congestion, deluge, discharge, encroachment, enforcement, engorgement, excess, exuberance, flash flood, flooding, infringement, niagara, overabundance, overcrowding, overkill, overmuch, overproduction, plethora, pour, propulsion, push, redundancy, spate, spill, spillover, submergence, submersion, superfluity, surfeit, surplus, torrent; CONCEPT 740

overflow [v] *pour out, flood* brim, bubble over, cascade, cover, deluge, discharge, drain, drown, engulf, fall over, gush, inundate, irrupt, issue, jet, leak, overbrim, overrun, overtop, pour, run over, rush, shed, shower, slop, slosh, soak, spill, spill over, spout, spray, spurt, squirt, submerge, surge, swamp, water, wave, well, well over, wet, whelm; CONCEPTS 179,256,740

overhang [v] *bulge, hang over* beetle, be imminent, be suspended, cast a shadow, command, dangle over, droop over, endanger, extend, flap over, impend, jut, loom, menace, overtop, poke, portend, pouch, project, protrude, rise above, stand out, stick out, swing over, threaten, tower above; CONCEPT 752

overhaul [v] *redo, restore* check, debug, doctor*, do up*, examine, fiddle with*, fix, give facelift*, improve, inspect, mend, modernize, patch, rebuild, recondition, reconstruct, reexamine, renew, repair, retread, revamp, service, survey; CONCEPTS 126,202, 212

overhead [adj/adv] *up above* above, aerial, aloft, atop, hanging, in the sky, on high, over, overhanging, roof, skyward, upper, upward; CONCEPT 586 —*Ant.* below, underfoot

overhead [n] *general, continuing costs of operation* budget, burden, cost, depreciation, expense, expenses, insurance, outlay, rent, upkeep, utilities; CONCEPTS 329,332

overjoyed [adj] *extremely happy* charmed, delighted, deliriously happy, elated, euphoric, happy as a clam*, happy as a lark*, joyful, jubilant, on cloud nine*, only too happy*, over the moon*, rapturous, ravished, thrilled, tickled pink*, transported; CONCEPT 403 —Ant. disappointed, sad, sorrowful, upset

overlap [v] *lie over something else* extend along, flap, fold over, go beyond, imbricate, lap over, overhang, overlay, overlie, overrun, project, protrude, ride, run over, shingle; CONCEPT 759 —Ant. divide, separate

overlook [v1] *disregard, neglect* discount, disdain, fail to notice, forget, ignore, leave out, leave undone, let fall between the cracks*, let go, let slide*, make light of*, miss, omit, overpass, pass, pass by, pay no attention, slight, slip up*; CONCEPTS 30,101,699 —Ant. attend, heed, honor, look at, notice, regard, respect

overlook [v2] *make allowances for* bear with*, blink at*, condone, disregard, excuse, forgive, go along with, grin and bear it*, handle, ignore, let bygones be bygones*, let go, let pass*, live with*, look the other way, pay no mind*, play past*, put up with*, roll with punches*, stand for, stomach, swim with the tide*, take, tune out*, turn blind eye to*, whitewash*, wink at*, wipe slate clean*; CONCEPTS 10,83 —Ant. deny, prevent, refuse, veto

overlook [v3] *have a view of something* afford a view, command, command a view, dominate, front on, give on, give upon, have a prospect of, inspect, look down, look out, look out on, look over, mount, oversee, overtop, soar above, surmount, survey, top, tower over, view, watch over; CONCEPT 752

overlook [v4] *supervise* boss, chaperon, control, oversee, quarterback*, superintend, survey; CONCEPTS 94,117 —Ant. follow, serve

overly [adv] *excessively* ever, exceedingly, extremely, immensely, immoderately, inordinately, over, overfull, overmuch, too, too much, too-too*, unduly, very much; CONCEPT 544 —Ant. inadequately, insufficiently

overplay [v] *be dramatic* accent, accentuate, blow out of proportion*, dramatize, exaggerate, get carried away*, ham it up*, hyperbolize, labor at, lay it on thick*, magnify, maximize, mug*, overact, overdo, overdraw, overemphasize, overstate, overstress, overuse, overwork, point up*, show off*; stretch; CONCEPTS 59,87,292 —Ant. play down

overpower [v] *beat; get the upper hand* bear down, beat down, blank, blow away*, bulldoze*, bury, clobber, conquer, cream*, crush, defeat, drown, drub*, immobilize, knock out*, lay one out*, murder*, overcome, overthrow, overwhelm, prostrate, put away*, quell, reduce, roll over*, rout, shellack*, shut off*, smash*, subdue, subjugate, swamp*, take care of*, take out*, torpedo*, total*, trash*, trounce, vanquish, waste*, wax*, whelm*; CONCEPTS 95,191 —Ant. surrender, yield

overrate [v] *assign too much value, importance* assess too highly, build up, exaggerate, exceed, expect too much of, magnify, make too much of*, overassess, overesteem, overestimate, overpraise, overprize, overreckon, oversell, overvalue, rate too highly, think too highly of*,

think too much of*; CONCEPTS 12,49 —Ant. underrate, undervalue

overrated [adj] *overvalued* exaggerated, hyped-up, overestimated, overpaid, overpriced, overpromoted, puffed up, pumped up*; CONCEPTS 267,542,562

override/overrule [v] *cancel, reverse a decision* alter, annul, bend to one's will*, control, countermand, direct, disallow, disregard, dominate, govern, ignore, influence, invalidate, make null and void*, make void, not heed, nullify, outvote, outweigh, overturn, prevail over, quash, recall, repeal, rescind, revoke, ride roughshod*, rule against, set aside, supersede, sway, take no account of*, thwart, trample, upset, vanquish, veto; CONCEPTS 50,88,121, 298,317 —Ant. allow, approve, permit, support

overriding [adj] *central, most important* cardinal, compelling, determining, dominant, final, main, major, number one*, overruling, paramount, pivotal, predominant, prevailing, primary, prime, principal, ruling, supreme, ultimate; CONCEPT 568 —Ant. insignificant, least, unimportant

overrule [v] *repeal* abrogate, annul, cancel, disallow, invalidate, negate, nullify, override, overturn, quash, rescind, reverse, revoke, rule down, veto, void; CONCEPTS 50,88,121,234

overrun [v1] *defeat, invade* beat, clobber, drub*, foray, inroad, lambaste, lick*, massacre, occupy, overwhelm, put to flight, raid, rout, swamp*, thrash, trim, whip; CONCEPTS 86,95 —Ant. lose, surrender

overrun [v2] *infest, spread over; exceed* beset, choke, deluge, go beyond, inundate, invade, overflow, overgrow, overshoot, overspread, overstep, overwhelm, permeate, ravage, run on, run over, spill, spread like wildfire*, surge, surpass, swarm, well over; CONCEPTS 172,179, 651 —Ant. evacuate, retreat

overseas [adj] *across an ocean* abroad, across, away, foreign, in foreign land, transatlantic, transoceanic, transpacific; CONCEPT 583 —Ant. at home

oversee [v] *manage, supervise* baby-sit*, be in driver's seat*, boss, call the shots*, captain, chaperon, command, eye*, herd, inspect, keep one's eye on*, look after, overlook, quarterback*, ride herd on*, run the show*, shepherd, sit on top of*, skipper, superintend, survey, watch; CONCEPT 117 —Ant. follow, obey

overseer [n] *person who supervises others' work* executive, head, head honcho*, manager, pit boss*, straw boss*, superintendent, supervisor; CONCEPT 347

overshadow [v] *make obscure, dim, vague* adumbrate, becloud, bedim, cloud, command, darken, dim, dominate, dwarf, eclipse, excel, govern, haze, leave in the shade*, obfuscate, outshine, outweigh, overcast, overcloud, overweigh, preponderate, rise above*, rule, shadow, steal spotlight*, surpass, take precedence, tower above*, veil; CONCEPTS 620,668

oversight [n1] *failure, omission* blank*, blunder, carelessness, chasm, default, delinquency, dereliction, disregard, error, fault, inattention, lapse, laxity, miscue, mistake, neglect, overlook, overlooking, preterition, pretermission, skip, slip, slipup*; CONCEPT 101 —Ant. attention, care, recollection, remembrance, success

oversight [n2] *care, supervision* administration, aegis, charge, check, control, custody, direction, guard, guardianship, handling, inspection, intendance, keep, keeping, maintenance, management, superintendence, surveillance, tutelage; CONCEPT 117 —Ant. ignorance, neglect

overstate [v] *exaggerate* amplify, blow out of proportion*, boast, boost, brag, build up, embellish, embroider, emphasize, enlarge, exalt, expand, fabricate, fudge*, heighten, hike, inflate, lay it on thick*, lie, magnify, misquote, misreport, misrepresent, overdo, overemphasize, overestimate, pad*, play up, puff; CONCEPT 63

overt [adj] *obvious, unconcealed* apparent, clear, definite, manifest, observable, open, patent, plain, public, undisguised, visible; CONCEPT 535 —Ant. concealed, hidden, private, secret

overtake [v] *catch; pass* beat, befall, better, catch up with, come upon, engulf, gain on, get past, get to, happen, hit, leave behind, outdistance, outdo, outstrip, overhaul, overwhelm, reach, strike, take by surprise; CONCEPTS 95, 141 —Ant. fall behind

overthrow [v] *defeat, destroy* abolish, beat, bring down, bring to ruin, conquer, crush, demolish, depose, dethrone, do away with, eradicate, exterminate, knock down, knock over, level, liquidate, oust, overcome, overpower, overrun, overturn, overwhelm, purge, put an end to, raze, ruin, subdue, subjugate, subvert, terminate, tip, topple, tumble, unseat, upend, upset, vanquish; CONCEPTS 95,252,320 —Ant. give in, surrender, yield

overtone [n] *implication, hint* association, connotation, flavor, inference, innuendo, intimation, meaning, nuance, sense, suggestion, tone, undercurrent, undertone; CONCEPT 278

overture [n] *introduction, approach* advance, bid, conciliatory move, exordium, foreword, invitation, offer, opening, preamble, preface, prelude, prelusion, presentation, proem, prologue, proposal, proposition, signal, suggestion, tender; CONCEPTS 278,384,828,832 —Ant. conclusion, finish

overturn [v] *flip over* annul, bring down, capsize, countermand, down, invalidate, invert, keel over, knock down, knock over, nullify, overbalance, prostrate, repeal, rescind, reverse, roll, set aside, spill, tip over, topple, tumble, turn over, turn upside down, upend, upset, upturn, void; CONCEPTS 147,232

overview [n] *survey* analysis, aperçu, audit, capsulization, critique, examination, inquiry, inspection, outline, pandect, précis, review, scrutiny, sketch, study, syllabus, synopsis, thumbnail, view; CONCEPTS 37,103,197,271,291

overweight [adj] *heavier than average* ample, bulky, corpulent, fat, fleshy, gross, heavy, hefty, huge, massive, obese, outsize, overfed, overstuffed, plump, portly, pudgy, rotund, stout, upholstered*, weighty; CONCEPT 491 —Ant. skinny, thin, underweight

overwhelm [v1] *flood, beat physically* bury, conquer, crush, defeat, deluge, destroy, drown, drub*, engulf, inundate, massacre, overcome, overflow, overpower, overrun, overthrow, rout, smother, submerge, swamp, thrash, total*, whip*, win*; CONCEPTS 86,95 —Ant. underwhelm

overwhelm [v2] *astonish, devastate* bewilder, blow out of the water*, bowl over*, confound, confuse, demoralize, destroy, disturb, do in*, downgrade*, drown, dumbfound, floor*, kill*, overcome, overpower, prostrate, puzzle, render speechless*, run circles around, shatter, shock, stagger, steamroller*, stun, subordinate, surprise, swamp, upset, wreck; CONCEPTS 16,42 —Ant. not impress, underwhelm

overwhelming [adj] *overpowering* amazing, astounding, breathtaking, crushing, devastating, exciting, eye-opening, mind-boggling, overcoming, paralyzing, shattering, staggering, stunning, vast; CONCEPT 42

overworked [adj] *worn out* burned out*, exhausted, fatigued, overburdened, overloaded, overtaxed, strained, stressed, stressed out*, tense, under stress; CONCEPT 485

overwrought [adj] *exhausted and excited* affected, agitated, all shook up*, beside oneself*, crazy, distracted, emotional, excitable, fired-up*, flipped out*, frantic, freaked-out*, high*, hot-and-bothered*, hot under collar*, hyper*, in a state*, keyed-up*, nervous, neurotic, on edge*, overexcited, overstrung, overworked, spent, steamed up*, stirred*, strung-out*, tense, tired, uneasy, unstrung*, uptight*, weary, wired, worked-up, worn, wound-up; CONCEPTS 401,403,542 —Ant. calm, collected, cool, rested, unruffled

owe [v] *have an obligation* be beholden, be bound, be contracted, behind, be in arrears, be in debt, be indebted, be into one for, be obligated, be under obligation, feel bound, get on credit, have borrowed, incur, in hock*, lost, on the tab*, ought to, run up a bill*; CONCEPT 335 —Ant. pay, resolve, settle

owing [adj] *unpaid* attributable, comeuppance, due, in debt, mature, matured, outstanding, overdue, owed, payable, unsettled; CONCEPT 334 —Ant. paid, resolved, settled

own [adj] *belonging to individual* endemic, hers, his, individual, inherent, intrinsic, its, mine, owned, particular, peculiar, personal, private, resident, theirs, very own, yours; CONCEPT 710

own [v1] *possess; be responsible for* be in possession of, be possessed of, boast, control, dominate, enjoy, fall heir to, have, have in hand, have rights, have title, hold, inherit, keep, occupy, reserve, retain; CONCEPT 710 —Ant. dispossess, lack, lose, need, not have, sell

own [v2] *acknowledge, admit* allow, assent to, avow, come clean*, concede, confess, declare, disclose, grant, let on*, make clean breast of*, own up, recognize, tell the truth; CONCEPT 57 —Ant. deny, disavow, reject

owner [n] *person who has possession of something* buyer, governor, heir, heir-apparent, heiress, heritor, holder, keeper, landowner, legatee, partner, possessor, proprietor, purchaser, sharer, squire, titleholder; CONCEPTS 343,347,414 —Ant. leaser, renter

ownership [n] *possession of property* buying, claim, control, cut, deed, dominion, end, hand, having, holding, occupancy, partnership, piece, possessorship, property, proprietary rights, proprietorship, purchase, purchasing, residence, slice, takeover, tenancy, tenure, title, use; CONCEPT 710 —*Ant.* lease, renting

P

pace [n1] *steps in walking* clip, footstep, gait, getalong, lick*, measure, step, stride, tread, walk; CONCEPT 149

pace [n2] *speed, tempo of motion* beat, bounce, celerity, clip, downbeat, lick*, momentum, motion, movement, progress, quickness, rapidity, rapidness, rate, swiftness, time, velocity; CONCEPTS 755,818

pace [v1] *walk back and forth* ambulate, canter, foot it*, gallop, hoof*, march, patrol, pound*, step, stride, traipse, tread, troop, trot, walk up and down; CONCEPT 149 —*Ant.* sit, stay

pace [v2] *measure by footsteps* count, determine, mark out, step, step off*; CONCEPTS 291,764

pacesetter [n] *pacemaker* bellwether, forerunner, leader, pacer, pioneer; CONCEPTS 347,354

pacific [adj] *appeasing, peaceful* amicable, at peace, calm, conciliatory, diplomatic, friendly, gentle, neutral, peaceable, peace-loving, peacemaking, placatory, placid, quiet, serene, tranquil, untroubled; CONCEPTS 485,542

pacifist [n] *peace-lover* antiwar demonstrator, conscientious objector, dove, passive resister, peacemaker, peacemonger, peacenik; CONCEPTS 354,416

pacify [v] *make peaceful; appease* allay, ameliorate, assuage, bury the hatchet*, butter up*, calm, chasten, compose, con, conciliate, cool, dulcify, fix up, grease*, kiss and make up*, lay back, lull, make peace, mitigate, moderate, mollify, pacificate, placate, propitiate, put the lid on*, qualify, quell, quiet, relieve, repress, silence, smooth over, soften, soft-pedal*, soothe, square, still, stroke, subdue, sweeten*, take the edge off*, tame, temper, tranquilize; CONCEPTS 7,22,250 —*Ant.* agitate, incite, irritate, upset

pack [n1] *kit, package* backpack, baggage, bale, bundle, burden, equipment, haversack, knapsack, load, luggage, outfit, parcel, rucksack, truss; CONCEPTS 260,446,496

pack [n2] *group, bunch* assemblage, band, barrel, bundle, circle, collection, company, crew, crowd, deck, drove, flock, gang, great deal, heap, herd, horde, lot, lump, mess, mob, much, multiplicity, number, peck, pile, press, set, swarm, throng, troop; CONCEPTS 397,417

pack [v1] *make ready for transport* batch, bind, brace, bunch, bundle, burden, collect, dispose, fasten, gather, get ready, load, package, put in order, store, stow, tie, warehouse; CONCEPT 202 —*Ant.* dismantle, unpack, untie

pack [v2] *fill, compact* arrange, bind, charge, chock, choke, compress, condense, contract, cram, crowd, drive in, heap, insert, jam, jam-pack*, lade, load, mob, pile, press, push, put away, ram, ram in*, sardine*, squeeze, stuff, tamp, throng, thrust in, top off, wedge; CONCEPT 209 —*Ant.* allocate, disperse, dispose, distribute, unpack

pack [v3] *transport, carry* bear, buck, convey, ferry, freight, gun, haul, heel, hump, jag, journey, lug, piggyback*, ride, shlep*, shoulder, tote, trek, truck; CONCEPTS 148,217 —*Ant.* keep, maintain

package [n] *bundle; whole* amalgamation, assortment, bag, baggage, bale, batch, biddle, bottle, box, bunch, burden, can, carton, combination, container, crate, entity, kit, load, lot, luggage, pack, packet, parcel, pile, sack, sheaf, stack, suitcase, tin, trunk, unit; CONCEPTS 432,494

packed [adj] *full* arranged, awash, brimful, brimming, bundled, chock, chock-full*, compact, compressed, congested, consigned, crammed, crowded, filled, full to the gills*, jammed, jam-packed*, loaded, mobbed, overflowing, overloaded, packed like sardines*, seething, serried, stuffed, swarming, to the roof*, tumid, up to the hilt*, up to the rafters*, wall-to-wall*, wrapped; CONCEPTS 481,483, 740,774 —*Ant.* deserted, empty

packet [n] *small, often flat, bundle* bag, carton, container, envelope, file, folder, package, parcel, wrapper, wrapping; CONCEPT 494

pact [n] *agreement* alliance, arrangement, bargain, bond, compact, concord, concordat, contract, convention, covenant, deal, league, paper, piece of paper, protocol, settlement, transaction, treaty, understanding; CONCEPTS 271,684 —*Ant.* disagreement

pad/padding [n1] *protection* buffer, cushion, filling, packing, stuffing, wad, wadding, waste; CONCEPTS 473,475

pad [n2] *tablet of paper* block, jotter, memorandum, notebook, notepad, paper, parchment, quire, ream, scratch, scratch pad, slips; CONCEPTS 260,475

pad [n3] *dwelling, room* abode, coop*, crib*, digs*, hangout*, hideout*, hive*, house, layout*, lodging, quarters, residence, residency, setup*; CONCEPT 516

pad [v1] *protect with cushioning* cushion, fill, fill out, line, pack, protect, shape, stuff; CONCEPTS 134,202

pad [v2] *elaborate, amplify* augment, bulk, embellish, embroider, enlarge, exaggerate, expand, fill out, flesh out*, fudge*, increase, inflate, lengthen, magnify, overdraw, overstate, protract, spin, stretch; CONCEPTS 63,244 —*Ant.* simplify, uncomplicate

pad [v3] *walk quietly; walk ploddingly* creep, go barefoot, hike, march, patter*, pitter-patter*, plod, pussyfoot*, sneak, steal, traipse, tramp, trek, trudge; CONCEPT 149

paddle [n] *item used for propelling object* oar, paddlewheel, pole, propeller, pull, scull, sweep; CONCEPTS 479,499

paddle [v] *propel with arms or tool* boat, cruise, cut water*, drift, drive, navigate, oar, pull, row, run rapids*, scull, sky an oar*, slop, splash, stir, sweep, thrash, wade; CONCEPT 147

pagan [adj] *irreligious* agnostic, atheistic, heathen, idolatrous, impious, infidel, polytheistic, profane; CONCEPT 542 —*Ant.* believing, religious

pagan [n] *person who does not believe in an orthodox religion* agnostic, atheist, doubter, freethinker, heathen, heretic, iconoclast, idolater, idolist, infidel, paganist, pantheist, polytheist, scoffer, preconize, skeptic, unbeliever; CONCEPT 361 —*Ant.* believer, Christian, Jew

page [*n1*] *sheet of paper* folio, leaf, recto, side, signature, surface, verso; CONCEPT 475

page [*n2*] *person who serves others* attendant, bellhop, equerry, errand runner, servant, youth; CONCEPTS 348,354

page [*v1*] *call for over communications system* announce, beep, call, call out, call the name of, hunt for, preconize, seek, send for, summon; CONCEPTS 74,78 —*Ant.* answer

page [*v2*] *mark sheets of document* check, count, foliate, number, paginate; CONCEPTS 79,764

pageant [*n*] *spectacle or contest* celebration, charade, display, exhibition, exposition, extravaganza, fair, make-believe, motorcade, parade, pomp, procession, ritual, show, tableau; CONCEPTS 292,377

pageantry [*n*] *flashy display* affectation, array, ceremonial, ceremony, extravagance, fanfare, flourish, formality, glitter, grandeur, grandiosity, magnificence, ostentation, pageant, panoply, parade, pomp, pomposity, show, spectacle, splash, splendor; CONCEPTS 335,377,655

pain [*n1*] *physical suffering* ache, affliction, agony, burn, catch, convulsion, cramp, crick, discomfort, distress, fever, gripe, hurt, illness, injury, irritation, laceration, malady, misery, pang, paroxysm, prick, sickness, smarting, soreness, spasm, sting, stitch, strain, tenderness, throb, throe, tingle, torment, torture, trouble, twinge, wound; CONCEPTS 316,728 —*Ant.* comfort, good health, health, well-being

pain [*n2*] *mental suffering* affliction, agony, anguish, anxiety, bitterness, despondency, distress, grief, heartache, hurt, malaise, martyrdom, misery, rack, sadness, shock, suffering, torment, torture, travail, tribulation, woe, worry, wretchedness; CONCEPTS 410,728 —*Ant.* cheer, happiness, joy, pleasure, well-being

pain [*n3*] *problem* aggravation, annoyance, bore, bother, drag, effort, exertion, irritation, nuisance, pest, trouble, vexation; CONCEPT 532 —*Ant.* irritation

pain [*v*] *bother, trouble* ache, afflict, aggrieve, agonize, ail, anguish, annoy, bite, chafe, chasten, constrain, convulse, cut to the quick*, discomfort, disquiet, distress, exasperate, excruciate, gall, grieve, gripe, harass, harm, harrow, hit where one lives*, hurt, inflame, injure, irk, irritate, nick, prick, punish, rack, rile, sadden, smart, sting, strain, stress, suffer, throb, tingle, torment, torture, upset, vex, worry, wound; CONCEPTS 7,19,246 —*Ant.* aid, assist, assuage, help, please

painful [*adj*] *physically or mentally agonizing* aching, afflictive, agonizing, arduous, awful, biting, burning, caustic, difficult, dire, disagreeable, distasteful, distressing, dreadful, excruciating, extreme, extremely bad, grievous, hard, harrowing, hurtful, hurting, inflamed, irritated, laborious, piercing, raw, saddening, sensitive, severe, sharp, smarting, sore, stinging, tedious, tender, terrible, throbbing, tormenting, troublesome, trying, uncomfortable, unpleasant, vexatious; CONCEPTS 529,537 —*Ant.* delightful, easy, painless, pleasant

painkiller [*n*] *anesthetic* alleviative, analgesic, anodyne, aspirin, dope*, drug, medicine, morphine, ointment, opiate, pain reliever, sedative, tranquilizer; CONCEPT 307

painstaking [*adj*] *meticulous, thorough* assiduous, by the book*, by the numbers*, careful, conscientious, conscionable, diligent, earnest, exact, exacting, finicky, fussbudget*, fussy, hard-working, heedful, industrious, particular, persevering, persnickety*, picky, punctilious, punctual, scrupulous, sedulous, stickler*, strenuous, thoroughgoing; CONCEPTS 326,538 —*Ant.* careless, easy, half-baked, half-done, thoughtless, unmindful, unthorough

paint [*n*] *tinted covering* acrylic, chroma, color, coloring, cosmetic, dye, emulsion, enamel, flat, gloss, greasepaint, latex, makeup, oil, overlay, pigment, rouge, stain, tempera, varnish, veneer, wax; CONCEPTS 467,475

paint [*v*] *apply colored tint, often to make design* brush, catch a likeness, coat, color, compose, cover, cover up, daub, decorate, delineate, depict, design, draft, draw, dye, figure, fresco, gloss over, limn, ornament, outline, picture, portray, put on coats*, represent, shade, sketch, slap on*, slather, stipple, swab, tint, touch up, wash; CONCEPTS 172,174 —*Ant.* strip

pair [*n*] *two of something* brace, combination, combine, combo, couple, deuce, doublet, duality, duo, dyad, match, mates, span, team, twins, two, two of a kind, twosome, yoke; CONCEPTS 432,784 —*Ant.* one, single

pair [*v*] *make, become a twosome* brace, bracket, combine, couple, join, marry, match, match up, mate, pair off, put together, team, twin, unite, wed, yoke; CONCEPT 113 —*Ant.* divide, separate, sever

pajamas [*n*] *sleeping clothes* jamas*, jammies*, jams*, loungewear, lounging robe, nightdress, nightie*, nightshirt, nightwear, PJ's*, sleeper, sleeping suit; CONCEPT 451

pal [*n*] *person's friend* amiga, amigo, associate, boon companion*, bosom buddy*, bro*, brother, buddy, chum, companion, comrade, connate, crony, cuz, good buddy*, homeboy, homegirl, mate, sidekick, sis*, sister; CONCEPT 423 —*Ant.* enemy, foe

palace [*n*] *royal or enormous home* alcazar, castle, chateau, dwelling, hall, manor, mansion, official residence, royal residence; CONCEPT 516

palatable [*adj*] *delicious, agreeable* acceptable, A-OK*, aperitive, appetizing, attractive, cool, copacetic, delectable, delightful, divine, enjoyable, fair, flavorsome, good-tasting, heavenly, home-cooking*, luscious, mellow, mouthwatering, peachy, pleasant, relishing, sapid, saporific, saporous, satisfactory, savory, scrumptious, sugar-coated*, sweetened, tasteful, tasty, tempting, toothsome, toothy*, yummy*; CONCEPTS 529,613 —*Ant.* bitter, disagreeable, distasteful, sour, unsavory, untasty

palatial [*adj*] *grand, opulent* deluxe, grandiose, illustrious, imposing, impressive, lush, luxuriant, luxurious, magnificent, majestic, monumental, noble, plush, regal, rich, silken, spacious, splendid, stately, sumptuous, upholstered; CONCEPTS 334,485,589 —*Ant.* cramped, minor, small, tiny

pale [*adj*] *light in color or effect* anemic, ashen,

ashy, blanched, bleached, bloodless, cadaverous, colorless, deathlike, dim, doughy, dull, faded, faint, feeble, ghastly, gray, haggard, inadequate, ineffective, ineffectual, insubstantial, livid, lurid, pallid, pasty, poor, sallow, sick, sickly, spectral, thin, unsubstantial, wan, washed-out, waxen, waxlike, weak, white, whitish; CONCEPTS 537,618 —Ant. bright, colorful, glowing, radiant

pale [v] *become, make lighter or weakened* blanch, decrease, dim, diminish, dull, fade, faint, go white, grow dull, lessen, lose color, lose luster, muddy, tarnish, whiten; CONCEPTS 240,250 —Ant. brighten, darken, glow, radiate

pall [n] *cloud, gloom* cloak, cloth, covering, damp, damper, dismay, mantle, melancholy, shadow, shroud, veil; CONCEPTS 620,674 —Ant. brightness, excitement, happiness

pall [v] *bore, tire* become dull, become tedious, cloy, disgust, fill, glut, gorge, jade, sate, satiate, sicken, surfeit, weary; CONCEPTS 7,19 —Ant. brighten, excite, make happy

palliate [v] *gloss over; cover up* abate, allay, alleviate, apologize for, assuage, camouflage, cloak, conceal, condone, cover, diminish, disguise, dissemble, ease, exculpate, excuse, extenuate, gloze, hide, hush up*, justify, lessen, lighten, make light of*, mask, minimize, mitigate, moderate, mollify, prettify, put on a Band-Aid*, qualify, quick fix*, relieve, screen, soften, soothe, sugarcoat*, temper, varnish, veil, veneer, vindicate, white, whiten, whitewash*; CONCEPTS 57,59,172,188 —Ant. accuse, blame, condemn

pallid [adj] *pale* anemic, ashen, ashy, blanched, bloodless, colorless, dull, faded, feeble, ghastly, gray, lackluster, lifeless, pasty, sallow, sickly, spiritless, uninspired, wan, weak, whitish; CONCEPTS 537,618

pallor [n] *paleness* achromatic, bloodlessness, cadaverousness, colorlessness, etiolation, pallidity, pastiness, sallowness, wanness, whiteness; CONCEPTS 537,618

palpable [adj1] *clear, obvious* apparent, appreciable, arresting, believable, blatant, certain, colorable, conspicuous, credible, detectable, discernible, distinct, evident, manifest, noticeable, observable, open, ostensible, patent, perceivable, perceptible, plain, plausible, positive, remarkable, seeming, sensible, straightforward, striking, sure, tangible, unequivocal, unmistakable, visible; CONCEPTS 529,535 —Ant. hidden, obscure, unclear, vague

palpable [adj2] *concrete, real* material, sensible, solid, substantial, tactile, tangible, touchable; CONCEPT 582 —Ant. abstract, doubtful, dubious, inferential, questionable, unreal

palpitate [v] *beat at a rapid pace, like a heart* flutter, pitpat*, pitter-patter*, pound, pulsate, pulse, quiver, shiver, throb, tremble, vibrate; CONCEPTS 152,308 —Ant. be still

palsied [adj] *crippled* arthritic, atonic, debilitated, disabled, diseased, helpless, neurasthenic, paralytic, paralyzed, rheumatic, sclerotic, shaking, shaky, sick, spastic, trembling, tremorous, weak; CONCEPTS 314,485 —Ant. healthy, steady, walking

palsy-walsy [adj] *very friendly* affectionate, buddy-buddy*, chummy*, close, clubby, confiding, fond, intimate, kissy-huggy*, lovey-dovey*, neighborly, pally, thick; CONCEPT 555

paltry [adj] *poor; worthless* base, beggarly, cheap, common, contemptible, derisory, despicable, inconsiderable, ineffectual, insignificant, limited, low, low-down*, meager, mean, measly, minor, miserable, narrow, petty, picayune, piddling, pitiful, puny, set, shabby, shoddy, sleazy*, slight, small, sorry*, trashy, trifling, trivial, unconsequential, unimportant, vile, wretched; CONCEPTS 334,485 —Ant. important, rich, significant, substantial, wealthy, worthy

pamper [v] *serve one's every need, whim* baby, caress, cater to, coddle, cosset, dandle*, fondle, gratify, humor, indulge, mollycoddle*, overindulge, pet, please, regale, satisfy, spare the rod*, spoil, spoil rotten*, tickle, yield; CONCEPTS 136,295 —Ant. be mean, hurt, ignore, neglect, withhold

pamphlet [n] *booklet* announcement, broadside, brochure, bulletin, circular, compilation, flyer*, folder, handout, leaflet, throwaway*, tract, tractate; CONCEPTS 271,280

pan [n] *container for cooking food* bucket, casserole, double boiler, frying pan, kettle, pail, pannikin, pot, roaster, saucepan, sheet, skillet, vessel; CONCEPTS 493,494

pan [v1] *look, search for over a wide area* follow, move, scan, separate, sift, sweep, swing, track, traverse, wash; CONCEPT 216

pan [v2] *criticize strongly* blame, censure, condemn, cut up, denounce, denunciate, disparage, flay, hammer, jeer at, knock, rap, reprehend, review unfavorably, roast, slam; CONCEPT 52 —Ant. praise

panacea [n] *cure-all* catholicon, cure, elixir, nostrum, patent medicine, relief, remedy; CONCEPTS 307,311

panache [n] *person's flamboyant spirit* brio, charisma, dash, élan, flair, flamboyance, flourish, style, swagger, verve, vigor; CONCEPT 411 —Ant. spiritlessness

pancake [n] *flat, round breakfast cake* batter cake, blanket*, cake, crepe, flapjack, griddle cake, hotcake, johnnycake, jonnycake, sourdough, waffle, wheat*, wheat cake; CONCEPTS 457,461

pandemonium [n] *craziness, commotion* anarchy, babel, bedlam, bluster, brouhaha*, chaos, clamor, clatter, confusion, din, hassle, hubbub*, hue and cry*, hullabaloo*, jangle, noise, racket, riot, ruckus*, rumpus, tumult, turbulence, turmoil, uproar; CONCEPTS 388,674 —Ant. calm, peace

pander [v] *cater to, indulge* brownnose*, cajole, fall all over*, gratify, lay it on*, massage, play the game*, play up to*, please, politic, satisfy, snow*, soap*, soften up, stroke, suck up to*; CONCEPTS 59,136,384 —Ant. deny, dissatisfy, refuse

panel [n] *committee* board, bureau, cabinet, commission, consultants, council, forum, group, jury, representatives, task force, tribunal; CONCEPT 381

pang [n] *ache, twinge* agony, anguish, bite, discomfort, distress, gripe, misery, pain, prick, spasm, stab, sting, stitch, throb, throe, wrench; CONCEPT 728 —Ant. tingle

panhandle [v] *beg ask alms, bum*, cadge*, freeload*, hit up*, hold out one's hand*, hustle, live hand to mouth*, mooch*, pass the hat*, scrounge, solicit charity, sponge*; CONCEPT 53*

panic [n1] *extreme fright* agitation, alarm, cold feet*, confusion, consternation, crush, dismay, dread, fear, frenzy, horror, hysteria, jam, rush, scare, stampede, terror, trepidation; CONCEPTS 27,410,690 —*Ant.* calm, collectedness, confidence, contentment, security

panic [n2] *sudden drop in value in financial markets* Black Monday*, bust, crash, depression, rainy day*, slump; CONCEPT 335

panic [v] *become, make afraid or distressed* alarm, become hysterical, be terror-stricken, chicken out*, clutch, come apart, freeze up*, go to pieces*, have a fit*, lose it*, lose nerve*, overreact, push panic button*, run scared*, scare, shake in boots*, stampede, startle, terrify, unnerve; CONCEPTS 14,27 —*Ant.* be calm, be content

panorama [n] *scene, horizon* bird's-eye view*, compass, dimension, diorama, extent, orbit, overview, perspective, picture, prospect, purview, radius, range, reach, scenery, scenic view, scope, spectacle, survey, sweep, view, vista; CONCEPTS 529,628,651

panoramic [adj] *sweeping* all-around, all-embracing, all-encompassing, all-inclusive, bird's-eye*, blanket, broad, complete, comprehensive, far-reaching, full, panned, scenic, wide-ranging; CONCEPTS 531,772

pan out [v] *come to pass; succeed* click*, come out*, culminate, eventuate, go, go over*, happen, net*, prove out, result, turn out, work out, yield; CONCEPT 706 —*Ant.* fail, not happen

pant [v1] *gasp for air* be out of breath, blow, breathe, chuff, gulp, heave, huff, palpitate, puff, snort, throb, wheeze, whiff, wind; CONCEPT 163

pant [v2] *long for* ache, aim, aspire, covet, crave, desire, hunger, lust, pine, sigh, thirst, want, wish, yearn; CONCEPT 20 —*Ant.* despise

panties [n] *women's underwear* bikini, briefs, intimate things, lingerie, underclothes, undergarment, underpants, undies; CONCEPT 451

pantry [n] *kitchen storage room* buttery, cellar, chamber, closet, cupboard, larder, store room; CONCEPT 448

pants [n] *clothing for legs, lower half of body* Bermudas*, bloomers, blue jeans, boxer shorts, breeches, briefs, britches*, chaps*, chinos, clam diggers*, cords*, corduroys, denims, drawers, dungarees, jeans, jodhpurs, knickers, overalls, pantaloons*, panties*, pedal pushers*, shorts, slacks, trousers, underpants; CONCEPT 451

pantywaist [n] *sissy* baby*, chicken*, coward, cry-baby, fraidy-cat*, milksop, momma's boy*, namby-pamby, pansy, scaredy cat*, weakling, wimp*, wuss*, wussy*; CONCEPT 423

paparazzi [n] *photographers* cameraperson, celebrity photographer, freelance photographer, paparazzo, shutterbug; CONCEPT 352

paper [adj] *thin, flimsy* cardboard, disposable, insubstantial, paper-thin, papery, wafer-thin; CONCEPT 606 —*Ant.* thick

paper [n2] *newspaper* daily, gazette, journal, news, organ, rag*, weekly; CONCEPT 280

paper [n3] *thesis, article* analysis, assignment, composition, critique, dissertation, essay,

examination, monograph, report, script, study, theme, treatise; CONCEPTS 271,280

paper [n4] *material upon which one writes* card, filing card, letterhead, newsprint, note, note card, note pad, onion skin, pad, papyrus, parchment, poster, rag, sheet, stationery, tissue, vellum; CONCEPTS 260,475

paper [v] *line with material* cover, hang, paste up, plaster, wallpaper; CONCEPTS 172,177 —*Ant.* peal, strip, unline

paper/papers [n] *legal document* affidavit, archive, bill, certificate, certification, citation, contract, credentials, data, deed, diaries, diploma, documentation, dossier, file, grant, ID*, identification papers, indictment, instrument, letter, letters, order, passport, plea, record, subpoena, summons, testimony, token, visa, voucher, warrant, will, writ, writings; CONCEPTS 271,318

par [n] *average, equilibrium* adequation, balance, coequality, criterion, equal footing, equality, equatability, equivalence, equivalency, level, mean, median, model, norm, parity, sameness, standard, usual; CONCEPTS 636,667 —*Ant.* extreme

parable [n] *moral story* allegory, fable, legend, lesson, tale, teaching; CONCEPT 282

parade [n] *pageant, display* array, autocade, cavalcade, ceremony, column, demonstration, exhibition, fanfare, flaunting, line, march, ostentation, panoply, pomp, procession, review, ritual, shine, show, spectacle, train, vaunting; CONCEPTS 377,386

parade [v] *show off; march* advertise, air, boast, brag, brandish, declare, demonstrate, disclose, display, disport, divulge, exhibit, expose, flash, flaunt, march in review, prance, proclaim, publish, reveal, sport, strut, swagger, trot out*, vaunt; CONCEPT 261 —*Ant.* conceal, hide

paradigm [n] *example* archetype, beau ideal*, chart, criterion, ensample, exemplar, ideal, mirror, model, original, pattern, prototype, sample, standard; CONCEPT 686

paradise [n] *land, feeling of great pleasure; absence of evil* Arcadia*, ballpark, bliss, cloud nine*, delight, divine abode*, Eden*, felicity, happy hunting ground*, heaven, heavenly kingdom, kingdom come*, next world*, pearly gates*, promised land, Shangri-la*, Utopia*, wonderland, Zion*; CONCEPT 515 —*Ant.* hell

paradox [n] *contradiction, puzzle* absurdity, ambiguity, anomaly, catch, Catch-22*, enigma, error, inconsistency, mistake, mystery, nonsense, oddity, opposite, reverse; CONCEPT 532

paragon [n] *outstanding example* apotheosis, archetype, beau ideal*, beauty, best, champ, champion, crackerjack*, cream*, criterion, cynosure, epitome, essence, exemplar, gem, ideal, jewel*, love, lovely, model, nonesuch, nonpareil, original, paradigm, pattern, peach*, perfection, pick, prototype, quintessence, standard, sublimation, tops*, trump*, ultimate; CONCEPTS 671,686

parallel [adj1] *aligned, side-by-side* alongside, coextending, coextensive, coordinate, equidistant, extending equally, in the same direction, lateral, laterally, never meeting, running alongside; CONCEPTS 581,586 —*Ant.* crooked, separate, skewed, zigzag

parallel |adj2| *akin, similar* agnate, alike, analogous, comparable, complementary, conforming, consonant, correspondent, corresponding, equal, identical, like, matching, resembling, uniform; CONCEPTS 487,573 —*Ant.* different, dissimilar, divergent

parallel |n| *complement, correlation* analogue, analogy, comparison, corollary, correlate, correspondence, correspondent, counterpart, countertype, double, duplicate, duplication, equal, equivalent, homologue, kin*, likeness, match, parallelism, resemblance, similarity, twin; CONCEPTS 667,670 —*Ant.* difference, divergence, opposite, reverse

parallel |v| *be alike* agree, assimilate, collimate, collocate, compare, complement, conform, copy, correlate, correspond, equal, equate, imitate, keep pace, liken, match, paragon, parallelize; CONCEPTS 111,171,667 —*Ant.* differ, distort, diverge, separate, skew

paralytic |adj| *impaired in movement* diplegic, disabled, immobile, immobilized, inactive, incapacitated, insensible, lame, numb, palsied, palsified, paralyzed, paraplegic, powerless, quadriplegic; CONCEPTS 314,485 —*Ant.* healthy, uncrippled

paralyze |v| *immobilize* anesthetize, appall, arrest, astound, bemuse, benumb, bring to grinding halt*, close, daunt, daze, deaden, debilitate, demolish, destroy, disable, disarm, enfeeble, freeze, halt, incapacitate, knock out, lame, make inert, make nerveless, nonplus, numb, palsy, petrify, prostrate, shut down*, stop dead*, stun, stupefy, transfix, weaken; CONCEPTS 14,121, 246,252 —*Ant.* incite, mobilize, stimulate

paramedic |n| *emergency medical technician* ambulance attendant, EMT, medical assistant, nurse; CONCEPTS 357,414

parameter |n| *limit* constant, criterion, framework, guideline, limitation, restriction, specification; CONCEPT 688

paramount |adj| *principal, superior* ascendant, capital, cardinal, chief, commanding, controlling, crowning, dominant, eminent, first, foremost, headmost, leading, main, outstanding, overbearing, predominant, predominate, preeminent, premier, preponderant, prevalent, primary, prime, regnant, sovereign, supreme; CONCEPTS 568,574 —*Ant.* inferior, last, least, less, lesser, lowest, minor, secondary, smallest, trivial

paramour |n| *lover* admirer, beau, boyfriend, concubine, courter, courtesan, doxy, escort, fiancé, fiancée, girlfriend, inamorata, inamorato, kept woman, mistress, steady, sweetheart; CONCEPTS 415,423

paranormal |adj| *supernatural* abnormal, celestial, ghostly, metaphysical, mysterious, mystic, occult, phenomenal, preternatural, psychic, spectral, transcendental, uncomprehensible, unearthly; CONCEPT 582

parapet |n| *bulwark* barricade, barrier, bastion, buffet, buttress, defense, embankment, fortification, partition, protection, protective wall, rampart, safeguard; CONCEPTS 96,729

paraphernalia |n| *equipment, belongings* accoutrements, apparatus, appurtenances, baggage, effects, equipage, gear, habiliments, impedimenta, impediments, machinery,

material, materiel, outfit, regalia, stuff, tackle, things, trappings; CONCEPTS 446,496

paraphrase |n| *translation, interpretation* digest, explanation, rehash, rendering, rendition, rephrasing, restatement, rewording, summary, version; CONCEPTS 55,57,268 —*Ant.* quotation

paraphrase |v| *interpret, translate* express in other words, express in own words, recapitulate, rehash, render, rephrase, restate, reword, summarize, transcribe; CONCEPTS 55,57 —*Ant.* quote

parasite |n| *something that exists by taking from or depending on another* barnacle, bloodsucker*, bootlicker*, deadbeat*, dependent, flunky, freeloader*, groupie*, hanger-on*, idler, leech, scrounger, sponge*, stooge*, sucker*, sycophant, taker*; CONCEPTS 394,412 —*Ant.* blessing

parcel |n1| *container prepared to be sent* bindle, bundle, carton, load, pack, package, packet; CONCEPT 494

parcel |n2| *group, bunch* array, band, batch, body, clot, clump, cluster, clutch, collection, company, crew, crowd, gang, lot, pack; CONCEPT 432 —*Ant.* none, one

parcel |n3| *piece of land* acreage, plat, plot, property, tract; CONCEPTS 509,513

parcel |n4| *part, piece* bite, chunk, cut, division, lion's share*, member, moiety, piece of the action*, portion, rake-off*, section, segment, slice; CONCEPTS 829,835 —*Ant.* whole

parch |v| *dry, burn* blister, brown, dehydrate, desiccate, dry up, evaporate, exsiccate, make thirsty, scorch, sear, shrivel, stale, wither; CONCEPTS 249,255 —*Ant.* dampen, moisten, wet

parched |adj| *dry* arid, burned, cotton-mouth*, dehydrated, dried out, dried up*, dry as dust*, scorched, shriveled, thirsty, waterless, withered; CONCEPT 603 —*Ant.* damp, moist, wet

pardon |n| *forgiveness* absolution, acquittal, allowance, amnesty, anchor, clemency, commute, conciliation, condonation, discharge, exculpation, excuse, exoneration, forbearance, freeing, grace, indemnification, indemnity, indulgence, justification, kindness, lifeboat*, lifesaver*, mercy, release, remission, reprieve, vindication; CONCEPTS 10,318,685 —*Ant.* chastisement, condemnation, damning, ostracization, penalty, punishment

pardon |v| *forgive* absolve, accept, acquit, amnesty, blink at*, bury the hatchet*, clear, condone, discharge, exculpate, excuse, exonerate, free, give absolution, grant amnesty, justify, let off*, let off easy*, liberate, lifeboat*, overlook, release, remit, reprieve, rescue, spring*, suspend charges, tolerate, wink at*, wipe slate clean*, write off*; CONCEPTS 10, 50,88,317 —*Ant.* chastise, condemn, damn, ostracize, penalize, punish

pare |v| *peel, trim* carve, clip, crop, cut, cut back, cut down, decorticate, decrease, dock, flay, knock off, lop, lower, mark down, prune, reduce, scalp, scrape, shave, shear, skin, skive, slash, strip, thin, uncover; CONCEPTS 176,202, 236,247 —*Ant.* cover

parent |n| *person, source of product* ancestor, architect, author, begetter, cause, center, creator, father, folks, forerunner, fountainhead, guardian, mother, origin, originator, procreator, progenitor, prototype, root, source, wellspring; CONCEPTS 414,648 —*Ant.* child

parental [*adj*] *having the quality or nature of a parent* affectionate, benevolent, benign, caring, comforting, devoted, fatherly, fond, forbearing, gentle, indulgent, kind, loving, maternal, matriarchal, motherly, paternal, patriarchal, protective, sheltering, supportive, tender, warm, watchful; CONCEPTS 401,542

parenthetical [*adj*] *incidental* bracketed, by the way, episodic, explanatory, extraneous, extrinsic, incidental, in parenthesis, inserted, intermediate, interposed, qualifying, related, subordinate; CONCEPTS 544,577 —*Ant.* basic, consequential, important

pariah [*n*] *social outcast* bum*, castaway, deportee, derelict, displaced person, exile, expatriate, fugitive, hobo*, leper, outsider, persona non grata*, rascal, refugee, tramp, undesirable, vagabond, vagrant, waif; CONCEPT 423

parish [*n*] *congregation of a church* archdiocese, bethel, church, churchgoers, community, flock*, fold*, parishioners, territory; CONCEPT 369

parity [*n*] *equality, balance* adequation, affinity, agreement, analogy, approximation, closeness, coequality, conformity, congruity, consistency, correspondence, equal terms, equivalence, equivalency, likeness, nearness, par, parallelism, paraphernalia, resemblance, sameness, similarity, similitude, uniformity, unity; CONCEPT 670 —*Ant.* dissimilitude, imbalance, inequality

park [*n*] *land that is reserved for pleasure, recreation* esplanade, estate, forest, garden, grass, green, grounds, lawn, lot, meadow, parkland, place, playground, plaza, pleasure garden, recreation area, square, tract, village green, woodland; CONCEPTS 509,513

park [*v*] *place vehicle in a position* deposit, leave, line up, maneuver, order, position, put, seat, stand, station, store; CONCEPTS 148,201 —*Ant.* back out, depart

parlance [*n*] *idiom* argot, colloquialism, dialect, diction, expression, idiosyncrasy, jargon, language, lingo*, localism, locution, patois, phrase, provincialism, set phrase, speech, street talk*, talk, tongue, vernacular; CONCEPT 275

parlay [*v*] *bet; maneuver* engineer, gamble, jockey, lay down, manage, move, plan, play, risk, speculate, venture, wager; CONCEPTS 36,59,292,330

parlor [*n*] *sitting room* drawing room, front room, guest room, living room, lounge, reception, salon, waiting room; CONCEPT 448

parochial [*adj*] *narrow-minded, restricted* biased, bigoted, conservative, conventional, insular, inward-looking, limited, local, narrow, petty, prejudiced, provincial, regional, sectarian, sectional, shallow, small-minded, small-town; CONCEPT 542 —*Ant.* broad, liberal, unrestricted

parody [*n*] *imitation, spoof* apology, burlesque, caricature, cartoon, copy, derision, farce, irony, jest, joke, lampoon, mime, mimicry, misrepresentation, mockery, mock-heroic*, pastiche, play-on*, raillery, rib*, ridicule, roast*, satire, send-up*, skit, takeoff*, travesty; CONCEPTS 59,273,292 —*Ant.* reality, truth

parody [*v*] *imitate, spoof* ape, burlesque, caricature, copy, deride, disparage, distort,

do a takeoff of*, exaggerate, impersonate, jeer, jest, joke, lampoon, laugh at, mime, mimic, mock, poke fun at, put on*, ridicule, roast, satirize, send up, sheik*, take off*, travesty; CONCEPTS 59,111,273 —*Ant.* be truthful

paroxysm [*n*] *seizure, spasm* agitation, anger, attack, convulsion, eruption, excitement, explosion, fit, flare-up*, frenzy, frothing, fuming, furor, fury, hysterics, outbreak, outburst, passion, rage, violence; CONCEPTS 308,316,410

parrot [*v*] *repeat* ape, chant, copy, copycat, echo, imitate, mime, mimic, quote, recite, reiterate; CONCEPTS 47,77,171

parry [*v*] *ward off, circumvent* anticipate, avoid, block, bypass, deflect, dodge, duck*, elude, evade, fence*, fend off, forestall, hold at bay*, preclude, prevent, rebuff, rebuke, repel, repulse, resist, shirk, shun, sidestep, stave off; CONCEPTS 25,30,121 —*Ant.* deal with, face, meet

parsimonious [*adj*] *penny-pinching* avaricious, chintzy*, close, frugal, greedy, illiberal, mean, miserly, penurious, prudent, saving, scrimpy, selfish, skinflint*, sparing, stingy*, tight*, tightfisted*, tightwad*; CONCEPTS 334,401 —*Ant.* generous, lavish, liberal

parson [*n*] *cleric* chaplain, churchman/woman, clergyman/woman, ecclesiastic, minister, padre, pastor, preacher, priest, rector, reverend, vicar; CONCEPT 361

part [*n1*] *piece, portion of something* allotment, any, apportionment, articulation, atom, bit, bite, branch, chip, chunk, component, constituent, cut, department, detail, division, element, extra, factor, fraction, fragment, helping, hunk, ingredient, installment, item, limb, lot, lump, measure, meed, member, module, moiety, molecule, organ, parcel, particle, partition, piece, quantum, quota, ration, scrap, section, sector, segment, share, side, slab, slice, sliver, splinter, subdivision, unit; CONCEPT 834 —*Ant.* whole

part [*n2*] *person or group's interest, concern* behalf, bit, business, capacity, cause, charge, duty, faction, function, involvement, office, party, place, responsibility, role, say, share, side, task, work; CONCEPTS 362,532

part [*n3*] *theatrical role* antagonist, bit, bit part, cameo, character, dialogue, hero, lead, leading role, lines, minor role, piece, principal character, protagonist, romantic lead, silent bit, stock character, straight part, supporting role, title role, villain, walk-on; CONCEPT 263

part [*v1*] *break, disconnect* articulate, break up, cleave, come apart, detach, dichotomize, disjoin, dismantle, dissever, disunite, divide, factor, itemize, particularize, partition, portion, rend, section, segment, separate, sever, slice, split, strip, subdivide, sunder, tear; CONCEPTS 98,135 —*Ant.* connect, join

part [*v2*] *leave, go away from someone* break, break off, break up, clear out*, cut and run*, dedomicile, depart, ease out, go, go separate ways*, hit the road*, leave flat*, part company, pull out*, push off, quit, quit the scene*, say goodbye, separate, ship out*, shove off*, split, split up*, take a hike*, take leave, take off, walk out on, withdraw; CONCEPTS 195,297,384 —*Ant.* arrive, come

partake [v] *eat, share* be a party to, be in on, be into, consume, devour, divide, engage, enter into, feed, get in the act, have a finger in, ingest, participate, receive, sample, savor, sip, sit in, sit in on, take, take part, tune in; CONCEPTS *169,225* —*Ant.* abstain, refrain

partial [adj1] *incomplete* fractional, fragmentary, half done, halfway, imperfect, limited, part, sectional, uncompleted, unfinished, unperformed; CONCEPT *531* —*Ant.* complete, entire, total, whole

partial [adj2] *biased, prejudiced* colored, discriminatory, disposed, favorably inclined, influenced, interested, jaundiced, minded, one-sided, partisan, predisposed, prepossessed, tendentious, unfair, unindifferent, unjust, warped; CONCEPTS *403,542* —*Ant.* fair, just, unbiased, unprejudiced

partiality [n] *favoritism, fondness* affinity, bias, cup of tea*, dish, druthers*, flash, inclination, inclining, leaning, liking, love, partisanship, penchant, predilection, predisposition, preference, prejudice, proclivity, propensity, taste, tendency, thing*, type, weakness; CONCEPTS *32,709*—*Ant.* disinterest, fairness, impartiality, justice

partially [adv] *incompletely* by degrees, by installments, fractionally, halfway, in part, in some measure, little by little, moderately, not wholly, partly, piece by piece, piecemeal, somewhat, to a certain degree, to a certain extent; CONCEPTS *531,544* —*Ant.* completely, totally, wholly

participant [n] *person who takes part in activity* actor, aide, a party to, assistant, associate, attendant, colleague, contributor, helper, in, member, partaker, participator, partner, party, player, shareholder, sharer; CONCEPTS *352,366,423* —*Ant.* fan, spectator

participate [v] *take part in activity* aid, associate with, be a participant, be a party to, be into*, chip in*, come in, compete, concur, cooperate, engage, engage in, enter into, get in on*, get in on the act*, go into, have a hand in*, have to do with, join in, latch on*, lend a hand, partake, perform, play, share, sit in*, sit in on*, strive, take an interest in, tune in*; CONCEPT *100* —*Ant.* observe, watch

particle [n] *atom, piece* bit, crumb, dot, dribble, drop, fleck, fragment, grain, hoot*, iota, jot, minim, mite, modicum, molecule, morsel, mote, ounce, ray, scrap, scruple, seed, shred, smidgen, smithereen, speck, spot, stitch, whit; CONCEPT *831*

particular [adj1] *exact, specific* accurate, appropriate, blow-by-blow*, circumstantial, clocklike, detailed, distinct, especial, express, full, individual, intrinsic, itemized, limited, local, meticulous, minute, painstaking, particularized, peculiar, precise, scrupulous, selective, singular, special, thorough, topical; CONCEPT *557*—*Ant.* general, imprecise, indefinite, inexact

particular [adj2] *notable, uncommon* especial, exceptional, exclusive, lone, marked, noteworthy, odd, one, only, peculiar, personal, remarkable, respective, separate, single, singular, sole, solitary, unique, unusual; CONCEPT *564* —*Ant.* common, general, ordinary, unimportant, usual

particular [adj3] *finicky, demanding* careful, choicy, choosy, critical, dainty, discriminating, exacting, fastidious, finical, fussbudget*, fussy, hard to please, meticulous, nice, nit-picking*, persnickety*, picky*, rough, stickler*, tough; CONCEPTS *404,542* —*Ant.* indifferent, nonchalant, undemanding, undiscriminating

particular [n] *detail* ABC's*, article, bottom line*, brass tacks*, case, chapter and verse*, circumstance, clue, cue, element, fact, facts of life, feature, gospel, item, know*, lowdown*, nitty-gritty*, nuts and bolts*, picture, point, rundown*, scoop*, score*, speciality, specific, specification, story, thing*, what's what*, whole story*; CONCEPTS *274,532,832* —*Ant.* generality

particularly [adv] *specifically* decidedly, distinctly, especially, exceptionally, explicitly, expressly, individually, in particular, markedly, notably, outstandingly, peculiarly, principally, singularly, specially, surprisingly, uncommonly, unusually; CONCEPT *557* —*Ant.* commonly, generally, usually

parting [adj] *farewell* departing, final, goodbye, last, valedictory; CONCEPT *267* —*Ant.* greeting, introductory

parting [n] *goodbye, separation* adieu, bisection, break, breaking, breakup, crossroads*, departure, detachment, divergence, division, farewell, going, leave-taking, on the rocks*, partition, rift, rupture, severance, split, split-up, valediction; CONCEPTS *195,297,384* —*Ant.* greeting, hello, introduction

partisan [adj] *interested, factional* accessory, adhering, biased, bigoted, blind, cliquish, colored, conspiratorial, denominational, devoted, diehard*, exclusive, fanatic, jaundiced, one-sided, overzealous, partial, prejudiced, prepossessed, sectarian, sympathetic, tendentious, unjust, unreasoning, warped, zealous; CONCEPTS *401,542,548* —*Ant.* disinterested

partisan [n] *person devoted to another or cause* accessory, adherent, backer, champion, cohort, defender, devotee, disciple, follower, satellite, stalwart, supporter, sycophant, sympathizer, upholder, votary, zealot; CONCEPTS *359,423*

partition [n] *divider, division* allotment, apportionment, barrier, detachment, disconnection, dissolution, distribution, disunion, dividing, hindrance, obstruction, parting, portion, rationing, rupture, screen, segregation, separation, severance, share, splitting, wall; CONCEPTS *98,440,443,470* —*Ant.* attachment, juncture, union, unity

partition [v] *divide, separate* apportion, cut, cut in, cut into, cut up, deal, disburse, dispense, disperse, distribute, divvy up*, dole out*, fence off*, measure out, parcel out, portion, screen, section, segment, separate, share, size into, slice, split, split up, subdivide, wall off*; CONCEPTS *98,135* —*Ant.* attach, combine, join, unite

partly [adv] *not completely* at best, at least, at most, at worst, bit by bit, by degrees, carelessly, halfway, inadequately, in a general way, in bits and pieces*, incompletely, in part, in some measure, in some ways, insufficiently, little by little, measurably, notably, not entirely, not fully, noticeably, not strictly speaking, not wholly, partially, piece by piece, piecemeal, relatively, slightly, so far as possible, somewhat, to a certain degree, to a certain extent, up to a certain point, within limits*; CONCEPT 531 —*Ant.* completely, totally, wholly

partner [n] *person who takes part with another* accomplice, ally, assistant, associate, buddy, chum*, cohort, collaborator, colleague, companion, comrade, confederate, consort, coworker, crony*, date, friend, helper, helpmate, husband, mate, pal*, participant, playmate, sidekick*, spouse, teammate, wife; CONCEPTS 348,414,423 —*Ant.* enemy, foe

partnership [n] *alliance; participation* affiliation, assistance, association, band, body, brotherhood, business, cahoots*, cartel, chumminess, clique, club, combination, combine, community, companionship, company, conglomerate, conjunction, connection, consociation, cooperation, cooperative, corporation, coterie, crew, faction, firm, fraternity, friendship, gang, help, hookup, house, interest, joining, lodge, mob, organization, ownership, party, ring, sharing, sisterhood, society, sorority, tie-up, togetherness, union; CONCEPTS 325,381,388

party [n1] *social gathering* affair, amusement, at-home*, ball, banquet, barbecue, bash*, blowout*, carousal, carousing*, celebration, cocktails, coffee klatch, coming-out, dinner, diversion*, do*, entertainment, feast, festive occasion, festivity, fete, fun, function, gala, get-together, luncheon, movable feast*, orgy*, prom, reception, riot, shindig*, social, soiree, splurge*, spree*, tea; CONCEPT 383

party [n2] *gang, group* assembly, band, bevy, body, bunch, cluster, company, corps, covey, crew, crowd, detachment, force, gathering, mob, multitude, outfit, squad, team, troop, troupe, unit; CONCEPTS 417,432

party [n3] *group supporting certain beliefs* alliance, association, bloc, body, cabal, clique, coalition, combination, combine, confederacy, coterie, electorate, faction, grouping, junta, league, ring, sect, set, side, union; CONCEPTS 301,381

party [n4] *individual being, body, character, creature, human, man, mortal, part, person, personage, somebody, someone, woman;* CONCEPT 417

party [n5] *person(s) involved in legal action* actor, agent, cojuror, compurgator, confederate, contractor, defendant, litigant, partaker, participant, participator, plaintiff, plotter, sharer; CONCEPT 355

pass [n1] *opening through solid* canyon, cut, gap, gorge, passage, passageway, path, ravine; CONCEPTS 509,513 —*Ant.* closing, closure

pass [n2] *authorization, permission* admission, chit*, comp, free ride*, furlough, identification, license, order, paper, passport, permit, safe-conduct*, ticket, visa, warrant; CONCEPTS 271, 685 —*Ant.* denial, grounding, refusal, veto

pass [n3] *sexual proposition* advance, approach, overture, play, suggestion; CONCEPTS 375,384

pass [n4] *predicament* condition, contingency, crisis, crossroads*, emergency, exigency, juncture, pinch, plight, situation, stage, state, strait, turning point*, zero hour*; CONCEPT 674

pass [v1] *go by, elapse; move onward* befall, blow past, catch, come off, come to pass, come

up, crawl, cross, cruise, depart, develop, drag, fall out, fare, flow, fly, fly by, get ahead, give, glide, glide by, go, go past, happen, hie, journey, lapse, leave, linger, move, occur, pass away, pass by, proceed, progress, push on, reach, repair, rise, roll, run, run by, run out, slip away, take place, transpire, travel, wend; CONCEPTS 2,149,242 —*Ant.* get, take, use

pass [v2] *surpass, beat* exceed, excel, go beyond, go by, leave behind, outdistance, outdo, outgo, outrace, outshine, outstrip, shoot ahead of, surmount, top, transcend; CONCEPT 141 —*Ant.* fall behind, lose

pass [v3] *succeed, graduate* answer, do, get through, matriculate, pass muster, qualify, suffice, suit; CONCEPT 706 —*Ant.* fail, fall behind

pass [v4] *give, transfer* buck, convey, deliver, exchange, hand, hand over, kick, let have, reach, relinquish, send, shoot, throw, transmit; CONCEPTS 108,217 —*Ant.* receive, take

pass [v5] *cease* blow over*, cash in*, close, decease, demise, depart, die, disappear, discontinue, dissolve, drop, dwindle, ebb, end, evaporate, expire, fade, go, melt away, pass away, perish, peter out*, stop, succumb, terminate, vanish, wane; CONCEPTS 105,119 —*Ant.* live

pass [v6] *enact, legislate* accept, adopt, approve, authorize, become law, become ratified, become valid, be established, be ordained, be sanctioned, carry, decree, engage, establish, ordain, pledge, promise, ratify, sanction, undertake, validate, vote in; CONCEPTS 298,317 —*Ant.* deny, refuse, veto

pass [v7] *express formally* claim, declare, deliver, pronounce, state, utter; CONCEPTS 49,60

pass [v8] *decide not to do* decline, discount, disregard, fail, forget, ignore, miss, neglect, not heed, omit, overlook, pass on, pass up, refuse, skip, slight; CONCEPTS 25,30 —*Ant.* accept, be willing

pass [v9] *rid of waste* defecate, discharge, eliminate, emit, empty, evacuate, excrete, expel, exude, give off, send forth, void; CONCEPT 179

passable [adj1] *acceptable, admissible* adequate, allowable, all right, average, common, fair, fair enough, mediocre, middling, moderate, not too bad*, ordinary, presentable, respectable, so-so*, tolerable, unexceptional; CONCEPT 558 —*Ant.* excellent, exceptional, superior

passable [adj2] *clear and able to be traveled* accessible, attainable, beaten, broad, crossable, easy, fair, graded, motorable, navigable, open, penetrable, reachable, travelable, traveled, traversable, unblocked, unobstructed; CONCEPTS 559,576 —*Ant.* blocked, obstructed

passage/passageway [n1] *path for travel* access, alley, alleyway, avenue, channel, corridor, course, doorway, entrance, entrance hall, exit, gap, hall, hallway, lane, line, lobby, opening, pathway, road, route, shaft, subway, thoroughfare, tunnel, vestibule, way; CONCEPTS 440,501 —*Ant.* blockage, stop

passage [n2] *excerpt from document* clause, extract, paragraph, piece, portion, quotation, reading, section, sentence, text, transition, verse; CONCEPT 270 —*Ant.* whole

passage [n3] *travel* advance, change, conversion, crossing, flow, journey, motion, movement, passing, progress, progression, tour, traject, transfer, transference, transit, transition, transmission, transmittal, transmittance, traverse, traversing, trek, trip, voyage; CONCEPTS 145,217,224,704 —Ant. idleness, inaction, wait

passage [n4] *authorization; enactment* acceptance, allowance, establishment, freedom, legalization, legislation, passing, passport, permission, ratification, right, safe-conduct, visa, warrant; CONCEPTS 318,685 —Ant. denial, refusal, veto

passageway [n] *corridor* aisle, alley, couloir, entrance hall, entranceway, hall, hallway, ingress, lobby, passage, path, walkway; CONCEPT 440

pass away [v] *die* decease, demise, depart, drop, expire, pass on, perish, succumb; CONCEPT 304 —Ant. be born, live

pass by [v] *neglect, forget* abandon, disregard, fail, ignore, leave, miss, not choose, omit, overlook, overpass, pass over; CONCEPTS 25,30 —Ant. attend, heed, take care of

passé [adj] *old-fashioned* antiquated, belated, dated, dead, démodé, disused, extinct, has-been*, obsolete, outdated, outmoded, out-of-date, outworn, superseded, unfashionable, yesterday; CONCEPTS 578,589,797 —Ant. current, fashionable, in, in vogue, modern, new

passenger [n] *person who rides in vehicle conducted by another* commuter, customer, excursionist, fare*, hitchhiker, patron, pilgrim, rider, tourist, traveler, voyager, wanderer, wayfarer; CONCEPT 423 —Ant. driver

passing [adj] *brief, casual* cursory, ephemeral, evanescent, fleeting, fugacious, fugitive, glancing, hasty, impermanent, momentary, quick, shallow, short, short-lived, slight, superficial, temporary, transient, transitory; CONCEPTS 551,798 —Ant. lasting, long-lasting, permanent

passing [n] *death* decease, defunction, demise, dissolution, end, finish, loss, silence, sleep, termination; CONCEPT 304 —Ant. birth, living

passion [n1] *strong emotion* affection, affectivity, agony, anger, animation, ardor, dedication, devotion, distress, dolor, eagerness, ecstasy, excitement, feeling, fervor, fire, fit, flare-up, frenzy, fury, heat, hurrah, indignation, intensity, ire, joy, misery, outbreak, outburst, paroxysm, rage, rapture, resentment, sentiment, spirit, storm, suffering, temper, transport, vehemence, warmth, wrath, zeal, zest; CONCEPT 410 —Ant. calm, calmness

passion [n2] *adoration, love* affection, amorousness, amour, appetite, ardor, attachment, concupiscence, craving, crush*, desire, emoting, eroticism, excitement, fondness, infatuation, keenness, lust, prurience, urge, weakness, yen; CONCEPTS 32,372 —Ant. dislike, hate, hatred

passion [n3] *strong interest* craving, craze, drive, enthusiasm, fad*, fancy, fascination, idol, infatuation, jazz*, mania, obsession; CONCEPTS 349,532,690 —Ant. indifference

passionate [adj1] *sensual, desirous* amorous, ardent, aroused, concupiscent, desirous, erotic, heavy*, hot*, lascivious, libidinous, loving, lustful, prurient, romantic, sexy, steamy*, stimulated, sultry, turned-on*, wanton, wistful; CONCEPT 372 —Ant. cold, cool, frigid, indifferent, uncaring, unpassionate

passionate [adj2] *excited; enthusiastic* affecting, animated, ardent, blazing, burning, deep, dramatic, eager, eloquent, emotional, expressive, fervent, fervid, fierce, fiery, flaming, forceful, frenzied, glowing, headlong, heartfelt, heated, high-powered, high-pressure, hot*, hotblooded*, impassioned, impetuous, impulsive, inspiring, intense, melodramatic, moving, poignant, precipitate, quickened, spirited, steamed up*, stimulated, stirring, strong, thrilling, vehement, violent, warm, wild, zealous; CONCEPTS 401,542 —Ant. apathetic, dull, unenthusiastic, unexcited, unpassionate

passionate [adj3] *angry* all shook up*, choleric, enraged, fiery, frantic, furious, hotheaded*, hottempered*, inflamed, irascible, irritable, mean, peppery, quick-tempered, shaken, steamed-up*, stormy, tempestuous, testy, touchy*, vehement, violent; CONCEPTS 401,542 —Ant. happy

passive [adj] *lifeless, inactive* acquiescent, apathetic, asleep, bearing, compliant, cool, docile, enduring, flat, forbearing, going through motions*, hands off*, idle, indifferent, inert, laid-back*, latent, long-suffering, moony, motionless, nonresistant, nonviolent, patient, phlegmatic, poker-faced*, quiescent, quiet, receptive, resigned, sleepy, static, stolid, submissive, tractable, unassertive, unflappable, uninvolved, unresisting, walking through it*, yielding; CONCEPTS 542,584 —Ant. active, dynamic, lively

pass off [v] *give because one does not want it* eject, foist, make a pretense of*, palm, palm off*, send forth, work off; CONCEPT 108 —Ant. keep, maintain

pass out [v] *become unconscious, usually from abusing a substance* black out*, drop, faint, keel over*, lose consciousness, swoon; CONCEPT 308

pass over [v] *ignore, disregard* dismiss, fail, forget, miss, neglect, not dwell on, omit, overlook, overpass, pass, pass by, skip, take no notice of*; CONCEPTS 25,30 —Ant. attend, heed, take care, tap

passport [n] *identification of origin, country* authorization, credentials, key, license, pass, permit, safe-conduct*, ticket, travel permit, visa, warrant; CONCEPTS 271,685

password [n] *secret word given for entry* countersign, identification, key, key word, open sesame*, parole, phrase, signal, ticket, watchword, word; CONCEPT 278

past [adj1] *preceding, done* accomplished, ago, antecedent, anterior, completed, elapsed, ended, extinct, finished, foregoing, forgotten, former, gone, gone by, over, over and done, precedent, previous, prior, spent; CONCEPTS 531,585 —Ant. current, future, present

past [adj2] *olden, former* ages ago*, ancient, ancient history*, back when*, behind one*, bygone, bypast, down memory lane*, earlier, early, erstwhile, ex-*, foregoing, gone-by*, good old days*, late, latter, latter-day, long-ago, old, olden days*, once, one-time, over, preceding, previous, prior, quondam, recent, retired, sometime, time was*, way back*, way back when*; CONCEPT 820 —Ant. current, future, present

past [n1] *time gone by* antiquity, days gone by*, former times, good old days*, history, long ago, olden days*, old lang syne, old times*, time immemorial*, times past*, years ago*, yesterday, yesteryear, yore; CONCEPTS 807,811,816,818 —*Ant.* future, present

paste [n/v] *glue, adhesive* cement, fasten, fix, gum, mucilage, patch, plaster, spit, stick, stickum*; CONCEPTS 85,160,466

pastel [adj] *muted in color* delicate, light, pale, soft-hued, toned; CONCEPT 618 —*Ant.* bright, loud, vivid

pastiche [n] *work of art formed from disparate sources* assortment, collage, collection, compilation, copy, hodgepodge, imitation, mishmosh*, paste-up, patchwork, potpourri, reappropriation, reproduction, synthesis; CONCEPT 260

pastime [n] *leisure activity* amusement, distraction, diversion, entertainment, fun, fun and games*, game, hobby, play, recreation, relaxation, sport; CONCEPT 363 —*Ant.* profession, task, work

pastor [n] *person who conducts church services* cleric, divine, ecclesiastic, minister, parson, preacher, priest, rector, reverend, shepherd, vicar; CONCEPT 361

pastoral [adj] *peaceful, especially referring to the countryside* agrarian, agrestic, Arcadian, bucolic, countrified, country, idyllic, outland, provincial, rural, rustic, simple, sylvan; CONCEPT 583 —*Ant.* agitated, bustling, busy, urban

pastry [n] *baked product made with flour* bread, cake, croissant, danish, Danish, delicacy, doughnut, éclair, panettone, patisserie, phyllo, pie, strudel, sweet roll, tart, turnover; CONCEPTS 457,461

pasty [adj1] *sticky* adhesive, doughy, gelatinous, gluelike, gluey, glutinous, gooey, mucilaginous, starchy; CONCEPT 606 —*Ant.* smooth, unsticky

pasty [adj2] *pale* anemic, ashen, bloodless, dull, pallid, sallow, sickly, unhealthy, wan, waxen; CONCEPT 618 —*Ant.* blushing, flushed, healthy, vivid

pat [adj] *relevant, suitable* apposite, apropos, apt, auspicious, felicitous, fitting, happy, neat, opportune, pertinent, propitious, rehearsed, timely, to the point; CONCEPT 558 —*Ant.* imprecise, inexact, irrelevant, unacceptable, unsuitable, wrong

pat [adv] *exactly, fittingly* aptly, faultlessly, flawlessly, just right, opportunely, perfectly, plumb, precisely, relevantly, seasonably; CONCEPTS 535,557 —*Ant.* wrongly

pat [n1/v] *tap, touch* beat, caress, dab, fondle, form, hit, massage, mold, pet, punch, rub, slap, stroke, tip, whittle; CONCEPT 184 —*Ant.* hit

pat [n2] *small slice or slab* cake, dab, lump, piece, portion; CONCEPTS 458,835 —*Ant.* lot

patch [n1] *piece, spot, area* bit, blob, chunk, fix, ground, hunk, land, lot, plat, plot, scrap, shred, stretch, strip, tract; CONCEPTS 452,471,513

patch [n2] *piece applied to cover a gap or lack* application, appliqué, Band-Aid*, mend, reinforcement; CONCEPTS 452,831

patch [v] *fix, mend* cobble, cover, darn, do up, fiddle with, overhaul, rebuild, recondition, reconstruct, reinforce, repair, retread, revamp, sew; CONCEPTS 212,218 —*Ant.* break, damage, rend, tear

patch up [v] *settle differences* adjust, appease, bury the hatchet*, compensate, conciliate, make friends*, mediate, negotiate, placate, restore, settle*, smooth; CONCEPT 384 —*Ant.* argue, bicker, disagree, fight

patchwork [n] *mixture, hodgepodge* check, confusion, disorder, hash*, jumble, medley, miscellany, mishmash, muddle, olio, pastiche, plaid, salad*, salmagundi, stew*, tartan; CONCEPTS 260,432,475

patchy [adj] *spotty, not consistent* erratic, fitful, irregular, random, sketchy, uneven, variable, varying; CONCEPT 482 —*Ant.* consistent, continuous, regular, unspotted

patent [adj] *unconcealed, conspicuous* apparent, barefaced*, blatant, clear, clear-cut, controlled, crystal clear*, distinct, downright, evident, exclusive, flagrant, glaring, gross*, indisputable, limited, manifest, obvious, open, open and shut*, palpable, plain, prominent, rank, straightforward, transparent, unequivocal, unmistakable; CONCEPT 576 —*Ant.* concealed, hidden, inconspicuous

patent [n] *copyright on an invention* charter, concession, control, franchise, license, limitation, privilege, protection; CONCEPTS 271,318,685

path [n] *course, way* aisle, artery, avenue, beat, beaten path, boulevard, byway, crosscut, direction, drag, footpath, groove, highway, lane, line, pass, passage, pathway, procedure, rail, road, roadway, route, rut, shortcut, street, stroll, terrace, thoroughfare, track, trail, walk, walkway; CONCEPTS 6,501 —*Ant.* blockage

pathetic [adj] *sad, affecting* commiserable, deplorable, distressing, feeble, heartbreaking, heartrending*, inadequate, lamentable, meager, melting, miserable, moving, paltry, petty, piteous, pitiable, pitiful, plaintive, poignant, poor, puny, rueful, sorry*, tender, touching, useless, woeful, worthless, wretched; CONCEPTS 485,529 —*Ant.* cheerful, happy, useful, worthwhile

pathos [n] *deep sadness* desolation, emotion, feeling, passion, pitiableness, pitifulness, plaintiveness, poignance, poignancy, sentiment; CONCEPT 410 —*Ant.* cheer, glee, happiness, joy

patience [n] *capacity, willingness to endure* backbone*, bearing, calmness, composure, constancy, cool*, diligence, endurance, equanimity, even temper, forbearance, fortitude, grit*, guts*, gutsiness, heart, humility, imperturbability, intestinal fortitude*, legs*, leniency, longanimity, long-suffering, moderation, moxie*, nonresistance, passiveness, passivity, perseverance, persistence, poise, resignation, restraint, self-control, serenity, starch*, staying power*, stoicism, submission, sufferance, tolerance, toleration, yielding; CONCEPTS 411,657 —*Ant.* agitation, frustration, impatience, intolerance

patient [adj] *capable, willing to endure* accommodating, calm, composed, easy-going, enduring, even-tempered, forbearing, forgiving, gentle, imperturbable, indulgent, lenient, longsuffering, meek, mild, mild-tempered, persevering, persistent, philosophic, philosophical, quiet, resigned, self-possessed, serene, stoical, submissive, tolerant, tranquil, uncomplaining, understanding, unruffled, untiring; CONCEPTS

404,542 —Ant. agitated, frustrated, impatient, intolerant, unwilling

patient [n] *person being treated for medical problem* case, convalescent, emergency, inmate, invalid, outpatient, shut-in, sick person, subject, sufferer, victim; CONCEPT 357 —Ant. doctor

patio [n] *porch* balcony, courtyard, deck, veranda; CONCEPTS 509,513

patrician [adj] *upper-class* aristocratic, blue-blooded*, gentle, grand, highborn, high-class, noble, royal, wellborn; CONCEPTS 334,549 —Ant. common, lower-class

patrician [n] *person born to upper class* aristocrat, blue blood*, gentleperson, noble, nobleperson, peer, silk stocking*, upper cruster*; CONCEPT 423 —Ant. commoner

patriot [n] *person who loves his or her country* flag-waver*, good citizen, jingoist*, loyalist, nationalist, partisan, patrioteer, statesperson, ultranationalist, volunteer; CONCEPT 413 —Ant. expatriot, traitor

patriotism [n] *love of one's country* allegiance, chauvinism, flag-waving, loyalty, nationalism, public spirit; CONCEPT 689

patrol [n] *guarding; guard* convoying, defending, escorting, garrison, lookout, patroler, policing, protecting, protection, rounds, safeguarding, scouting, sentinel, spy, vigilance, watch, watchdog, watchperson; CONCEPTS 134, 354,358

patrol [v] *guard, protect* cruise, inspect, keep guard, keep watch, make the rounds*, mount, police, pound, range, ride shotgun, safeguard, shotgun, walk the beat*, watch; CONCEPTS 134,623 —Ant. ignore, neglect

patron [n1] *person who supports a cause* advocate, angel*, backer, benefactor, booster, champion, defender, encourager, fairy godparent*, fan, financer, friend, front*, guarantor, guardian, guide, head, helper, leader, partisan, patron saint*, philanthropist, protector, sponsor, supporter, surety, sympathizer, well-wisher; CONCEPTS 348,359,423 —Ant. detractor, enemy, opponent, opposition

patron [n2] *person who does business at establishment* buyer, client, customer, frequenter, habitué, purchaser, shopper; CONCEPT 348 —Ant. employee, manager, owner

patronage [n1] *support of a cause* advocacy, aegis, aid, assistance, auspices, backing, benefaction, championship, encouragement, financing, grant, guardianship, help, promotion, protection, recommendation, sponsorship, subsidy, support; CONCEPTS 110,332,341 —Ant. antagonism, detraction, opposition

patronage [n2] *business done at an establishment* buying, clientage, clientele, commerce, custom, shopping, trade, trading, traffic; CONCEPTS 323,324 —Ant. competition

patronage [n3] *condescension* civility, cronyism, deference, deigning, disdain, insolence, patronization, patronizing, stooping, sufferance, toleration; CONCEPTS 83,300 —Ant. humility, modesty

patronize [v1] *condescend* be gracious to, be lofty, be overbearing, deign, favor, indulge, look down on*, pat on the back*, snub, stoop, talk down to*, toss a few crumbs*, treat as inferior, treat badly, treat like a child*; CONCEPT 384 —Ant. be humble, be modest

patronize [v2] *support a cause* assist, back, befriend, foster, fund, help, maintain, promote, sponsor, subscribe to; CONCEPTS 110,341 —Ant. antagonize, contend, oppose

patronize [v3] *do business at an establishment* be a client, be a customer, buy, buy from, deal with, frequent, give business to, habituate, purchase from, shop at, shop with, trade with; CONCEPT 324 —Ant. ignore, use competition

patsy [n] *fall guy* boob*, chump, doormat*, dupe, easy mark*, fool, goat*, gull*, pigeon*, pushover*, sap*, scapegoat, schmuck*, sitting duck*, stooge, sucker, victim, weakling; CONCEPT 412

patter [n1/v1] *light walk; soft beat* chatter, pad, pat, pelt, pitapat*, pitter-patter*, rat-a-tat*, rattle, scurry, scuttle, skip, tap, tiptoe, trip; CONCEPTS 65,149

patter [n2] *casual talk* argot, cant, chatter, dialect, jabber*, jargon, jive*, line*, lingo, monologue, patois, pitch*, prattle*, slant*, spiel*, vernacular; CONCEPTS 276,278 —Ant. quiet, silence

patter [v2] *gab, chatter* babble, blab*, clack*, hold forth*, jabber, jaw*, prate, prattle, rattle, spiel*, spout, tattle, yak*, yakety-yak*; CONCEPT 266 —Ant. be silent

pattern [n1] *design, motif* arrangement, decoration, device, diagram, figure, guide, impression, instruction, markings, mold, motive, original, ornament, patterning, plan, stencil, template, trim; CONCEPTS 259,625 —Ant. plainness

pattern [n2] *arrangement, order* constellation, kind, method, orderliness, plan, sequence, shape, sort, style, system, type, variety; CONCEPTS 6,727,770 —Ant. disorder, disorganization, plainness

pattern [n3] *model, example* archetype, beau ideal*, copy, criterion, cynosure, ensample, exemplar, guide, mirror, norm, original, paradigm, paragon, prototype, sample, specimen, standard; CONCEPT 686

pattern [v] *copy, imitate; decorate* design, emulate, follow, form, model, mold, order, shape, style, trim; CONCEPTS 111,171 —Ant. be original

paucity [n] *lack, scarcity* absence, dearth, deficiency, famine, fewness, insufficiency, insufficiency, meagerness, paltriness, poverty, rarity, scantiness, scarceness, shortage, slenderness, slightness, smallness, sparseness, sparsity; CONCEPTS 335,646,767 —Ant. abundance, affluence, plenty

paunch [n] *large stomach* abdomen, belly, bulge, epigastrium, fat, gut, potbelly*, spare tire*, tummy*; CONCEPT 399 —Ant. sleekness

pauper [n] *person who is poor* almsperson, bankrupt, beggar, bum, dependent, destitute, down-and-out*, have-not*, homeless person, indigent, insolvent, in the gutter*, lazarus*, mendicant, poor person, supplicant; CONCEPT 423 —Ant. rich, wealthy

pause [n] *wait, delay* abeyance, break, break-off*, breathing space*, breathing spell*, caesura, cessation, coffee break*, comma*, cutoff, deadlock, discontinuance, downtime*, freeze*, gap, gridlock*, halt, happy hour*, hesitancy, hesitation, hiatus, hitch*, hush*, interim, interlude, intermission, interregnum, interruption, interval, lacuna, lapse, layoff, letup*, lull, pausation, recess, respite, rest, rest period, stand, standstill, stay, stillness, stopover, stoppage, suspension, time out*; CONCEPT 807 —Ant. continuation, persistence

pause [v] *wait, delay* break it up*, call time*, catch one's breath*, cease, come to standstill*, deliberate, desist, discontinue, drop, halt, hesitate, hold back, interrupt, put on hold, reflect, rest, shake, sideline, stop briefly, suspend, take a break*, take a breather*, take five*, take ten*, think twice*, waver; CONCEPTS 119,121,234 —Ant. continue, persist, restart

pave [v] *cover with asphalt, concrete* brick, cobblestone, flagstone, gravel, lay asphalt, lay concrete, macadamize, surface, tar, tile; CONCEPTS 168,172 —Ant. dig up, strip

pavement [n] *blacktop* asphalt, concrete, flagstone, road, sidewalk, tar; CONCEPT 604

pavilion [n] *domed building or tent* awning, canopy, cover, covering, dome, structure; CONCEPT 439

paw [v] *touch roughly* clap, claw, clutch, dig, feel, finger, fondle, grab, grate, grope, handle, hit, maul, molest, palpate, pat, rake, rasp, rub, scratch, search, slap, smite, stroke; CONCEPTS 375,612 —Ant. manhandle

pawn [n1] *security for a loan* assurance, bond, collateral, earnest, forfeit, gage, gambit, guarantee, guaranty, pledge, security, token, warrant; CONCEPT 332

pawn [n2] *person who is a fool* creature, dupe*, instrument, mark*, patsy*, pigeon*, puppet, stooge*, sucker*, tool, toy, victim; CONCEPT 412

pawn [v] *give as security for a loan* deposit, give in earnest, hazard, hock*, hook*, mortgage, pledge; CONCEPTS 115,330

pay [n] *earnings from employment* allowance, bacon*, bread*, commission, compensation, consideration, defrayment, emoluments, fee, hire*, honorarium, income, indemnity, meed, payment, perquisite, pittance, proceeds, profit, reckoning, recompensation, recompense, redress, reimbursement, remuneration, reparation, requital, return, reward, salary, satisfaction, scale, settlement, stipend, stipendium, take-home*, takings*, wage, wages; CONCEPTS 329, 332,340,344

pay [v1] *give money for goods, services* adjust, bear the cost, bear the expense, bequeath, bestow, chip in*, clear, come through, compensate, confer, cough up*, defray, dig up*, disburse, discharge, extend, foot*, foot the bill*, grant, handle, hand over*, honor, kick in*, liquidate, make payment, meet, offer, plunk down*, prepay, present, proffer, put up*, recompense, recoup, refund, reimburse, remit, remunerate, render, repay, requite, reward, satisfy, settle, stake, take care of*; CONCEPTS 327,341,351 —Ant. earn

pay [v2] *be advantageous* benefit, be worthwhile, repay, serve; CONCEPT 700

pay [v3] *make amends* answer, atone, be punished, compensate, get just desserts*, suffer, suffer consequences; CONCEPT 23

pay [v4] *profit, yield* be profitable, be remunerative, bring in, kick back*, make a return, make money, pay dividends, pay off*, pay out*, produce, provide a living, return, show gain, show profit, sweeten*, yield profit; CONCEPT 330 —Ant. lose

pay [v5] *get revenge* avenge oneself, get even, make up for, pay back*, pay one's dues*, punish, reciprocate, recompense, repay, requite, retaliate, settle a score*, square, square things*; CONCEPT 122

payable [adj] *to be paid* due, mature, maturing, obligatory, outstanding, overdue, owed, owing, receivable, unpaid, unsettled; CONCEPT 334 —Ant. paid, settled

payback [n] *return* accrual, accruement, compensation, gain, gate, income, interest, proceeds, profit, reciprocation, recompense, reimbursement, reparation, repayment, reward, take, yield; CONCEPTS 340,710

pay dirt [n] *profit* accumulation, benefit, bottom line*, cleanup, earnings, gate*, goods*, gravy*, harvest, killing*, net, payoff, proceeds, receipts, return, revenue, score*, split*, surplus, take*, winnings; CONCEPTS 332,344,693

payment [n] *fee; installment of fee* acquittal, advance, alimony, amends, amortization, amount, annuity, award, bounty, cash, defrayal, defrayment, deposit, disbursement, discharge, down, fee, hire, indemnification, outlay, part, paying, pay-off, pension, portion, premium, quittance, reckoning, recompense, redress, refund, reimbursement, remittance, remuneration, reparation, repayment, requital, restitution, retaliation, return, reward, salary, settlement, subsidy, sum, support, wage; CONCEPT 344

payoff [n] *conclusion, climax* adjustment, clincher*, consequence, culmination, day of reckoning*, finale, final reckoning*, judgment, moment of truth*, outcome, pay, payment, punch line*, result, retribution, reward, settlement, upshot*; CONCEPTS 230,679 —Ant. introduction, start

peace [n1] *harmony, agreement* accord, amity, armistice, cessation, conciliation, concord, friendship, love, neutrality, order, pacification, pacifism, reconciliation, treaty, truce, unanimity, union, unity; CONCEPTS 388,691 —Ant. disagreement, disharmony, fighting, war

peace [n2] *calm, serenity* amity, calmness, composure, concord, congeniality, contentment, equanimity, harmony, hush, lull, peacefulness, placidity, quiet, quietude, relaxation, repose, reserve, rest, silence, stillness, sympathy, tranquility; CONCEPTS 410,705,720 —Ant. agitation, distress, frustration, upset, worry

peaceable [adj] *friendly, serene* amiable, amicable, calm, complacent, conciliatory, gentle, irenic, mild, neighborly, nonviolent, pacific, pacificatory, pacifist, peaceful, peace-loving, placid, quiet, restful, still, tranquil; CONCEPT 548 —Ant. belligerent, cold, cool, mean, unfriendly

peaceful [adj] *friendly, serene* all quiet, amicable, at peace, bloodless, calm, collected, composed, constant, easeful, equable, free from strife*, gentle, halcyon, harmonious, irenic, level, mellow, neutral, neutralist, nonbelligerent, nonviolent, on friendly terms*, on good terms*, pacifistic, peaceable, peace-loving, placatory, placid, quiet, restful, smooth, sociable, steady, still, tranquil, undisturbed, unruffled, untroubled, without hostility; CONCEPTS 485,542 —*Ant.* clamorous, disturbed, excited, noisy, turbulent, unfriendly, violent

peacemaker [*n*] *person who settles problem* appeaser, arbitrator, conciliator, diplomat, make-peace, mediator, negotiator, pacificator, pacifier, pacifist, peacekeeper, peacemonger*, placater, statesperson; CONCEPTS 354,416 —*Ant.* agitator, instigator

peak [*n1*] *top of something* aiguille, alp, apex, brow, bump, cope, crest, crown, hill, mount, mountain, pinnacle, point, roof, spike, summit, tip, vertex; CONCEPTS 509,836 —*Ant.* base, bottom, nadir

peak [*n2*] *maximum, zenith* acme, apex, apogee, capstone, climax, crown, culmination, greatest, height, high point, meridian, ne plus ultra, pinnacle, summit, tip, tòp; CONCEPTS 668,766, 767,832 —*Ant.* base, nadir

peak [*v*] *reach highest point* be at height, climax, come to a head*, crest, culminate, reach the top, reach the zenith, top out*;CONCEPTS 763,780 —*Ant.* fall, hit bottom, plunge

peaked [*adj*] *pale, sick* ailing, bilious, emaciated, ill, in bad shape*, peaky, poorly, sickly, under the weather*, wan; CONCEPTS 314,618 —*Ant.* blushing, colorful, flushed, healthy

peal [*n*] *chime, clang* blast, carillon, clamor, clap, crash, resounding, reverberation, ring, ringing, roar, rumble, sound, thunder, tintinnabulation*; CONCEPT 595

peal [*v*] *chime, clang* bell, bong, crack, crash, knell, resonate, resound, reverberate, ring, ring out, roar, roll, rumble, sound, strike, thunder, tintinnabulate*; toll; CONCEPT 65

pearly [*adj*] *opalescent* fair, frosted, iridescent, ivory, milky, nacreous, off-white, opaline, pearl, silver; CONCEPT 618

peasant [*n*] *farmer* boor, bumpkin, countryman/woman, cropper, farmhand, hayseed*, hick*, hired hand, laborer, peon, planter, provincial, rube, rustic, serf, sharecropper, villein; CONCEPTS 347,348,423

peccadillo [*n*] *small fault* bad habit, faux pas, impropriety, indiscretion, minor fault, minor infraction, minor sin, misdemeanor, petty offense, slight transgression, small infraction, small sin, venial sin, vice; CONCEPTS 372,645

peck [*n/v*] *bite* beak, dig, hit, jab, kiss, mark, nibble, pick, pinch, poke, prick, rap, strike, tap; CONCEPTS 169,189

pecking order [*n*] *hierarchy* chain of command*, corporate ladder, due order, echelons, grouping, order, placing, position, ranking, scale; CONCEPT 727

peculiar [*adj1*] *characteristic, distinguishing* appropriate, diacritic, diagnostic, distinct, distinctive, endemic, exclusive, idiosyncratic, individual, intrinsic, local, particular, personal, private, proper, restricted, special, specific, typical, unique; CONCEPTS 404,557 —*Ant.* abnormal, uncharacteristic

peculiar [*adj2*] *bizarre, odd* abnormal, bent*, creepy*, curious, eccentric, exceptional, extraordinary, flaky*, freakish, freaky, funny, idiosyncratic, kinky*, kooky*, oddball, offbeat, off-the-wall*, outlandish, quaint, queer, singular, strange, uncommon, unconventional,

uncustomary, unusual, wacky*, way-out*, weird, wonderful; CONCEPTS 404,564 —*Ant.* normal, ordinary, regular, standard, usual

peculiarity [*n*] *characteristic; oddity* abnormality, affectation, attribute, bizarreness, character, distinctiveness, eccentricity, feature, foible, freakishness, gimmick, idiosyncrasy, kink*, mannerism, mark, odd trait, particularity, property, quality, queerness, quirk, savor, schtick*, singularity, slant*, specialty, trait, twist*, unusualness; CONCEPTS 411,665 —*Ant.* normality, usualness

pecuniary [*adj*] *financial* banking, budgeting, business, economic, fiscal, monetary; CONCEPT 334

pedagogic [*adj*] *educational* academic, dogmatic, instructive, lèarned, professorial, profound, scholastic, teaching; CONCEPTS 529,536

pedantic [*adj*] *bookish, precise* abstruse, academic, arid, didactic, doctrinaire, donnish, dry, dull, egotistical, erudite, formal, fussy, hairsplitting*, learned, nit-picking, ostentatious, overnice, particular, pedagogic, pompous, priggish*, punctilious, scholastic, schoolish, sententious, stilted; CONCEPTS 401,529 —*Ant.* imprecise, informal

peddle [*v*] *sell door to door* canvas*, hawk*, huckster*, market, monger*, push, shove, solicit, trade, vend; CONCEPT 345 —*Ant.* buy

peddler [*n*] *hawker* huckster, salesperson, street vendor, vendor; CONCEPT 348

pedestal [*n*] *support for something* base, bed, bottom, foot, foundation, mounting, platform, plinth, podium, stand, substructure, support; CONCEPT 442

pedestrian [*adj*] *everyday, dull* banal, banausic, blah*, boring, commonplace, dim, dreary, flat, humdrum*, inane, jejune, mediocre, monotone, monotonous, mundane, ordinary, platitudinous, plodding, prosaic, run-of-the-mill*, stodgy, truistic, unimaginative, uninspired, uninteresting, wishy-washy*; CONCEPTS 530, 547 —*Ant.* different, exceptional, extraordinary, interesting

pedestrian [*n*] *person traveling on foot* ambler, hiker, jaywalker*, passerby, stroller, walker; CONCEPT 366

pedigree [*adj*] *purebred* full-blooded, pedigreed, pure-blood, thoroughbred; CONCEPT 549 —*Ant.* base-born, lowly

pedigree [*n*] *ancestry, heritage* blood, breed, clan, derivation, descent, extraction, family, family tree, genealogy, heredity, line, lineage, origin, race, stirps, stock; CONCEPT 296

peek/peep [*n*] *sneaked look* blink, gander*, glance, glimpse, look-see, sight; CONCEPT 623

peek/peep [*v*] *sneak a look* blink, glance, glimpse, have a gander*, look, peer, snatch, snoop, spy, squint, stare, take a look; CONCEPT 623

peel [*n*] *skin, covering* bark, cover, epicarp, exocarp, husk, peeling, pellicle, rind, shell, shuck; CONCEPTS 428,484 —*Ant.* innards, insides

peel [*v*] *take off outer covering* decorticate, delaminate, desquamate, excorticate, exfoliate, flake, flay, pare, pull off, scale, shave, skin, strip, tear off, uncover; CONCEPTS 142,176,211 —*Ant.* cover

peep [n1/v1] *chirp* chatter, cheep, chirrup, chuck, churr, coo, cry, hoot, pipe, squeak, tweet, twitter; CONCEPT 64

peep/peer [v2] *appear briefly* become visible, crop up, emerge, open to view, peep out, peer out, show partially; CONCEPT 261

peer [n] *person who is another's equal* associate, coequal, companion, compeer, like, match, rival; CONCEPT 423 —*Ant.* inferior, superior

peer [v1] *scan, scrutinize* bore, eagle eye*, eye*, eyeball*, focus, gape, gawk, gaze, get a load of, glare, glim, gloat, inspect, look, peep, pin*, pry, rubberneck*, snoop, spy, squint, stare; CONCEPTS 103,623

peerless [adj] *having no equal; superior* aces*, all-time, alone, best, beyond compare, champion, excellent, faultless, gilt-edge*, greatest, incomparable, matchless, most, nonpareil*, only, outstanding, perfect, second to none*, solid-gold*, super, superlative, supreme, tops*, unequaled, unexampled, unique, unmatched, unparagoned, unparalleled, unrivaled, unsurpassed, world class*; CONCEPT 574 —*Ant.* imperfect, inferior, lowly, mediocre, secondary, subordinate

peeve [n] *something strongly disliked* annoyance, bother, gripe, nuisance, pest, sore point*, vexation; CONCEPTS 532,690 —*Ant.* attraction, desire, like, love, want

peeve [v] *bother, annoy* aggravate, anger, bug*, bum*, burn*, disturb, drive up the wall*, exasperate, gall, get, get one's goat*, hack*, irk, irritate, miff*, nettle, pique, provoke, put out, rile, roil, rub the wrong way*, steam*, T-off*, vex; CONCEPTS 7,19 —*Ant.* attract, charm, enchant, please

peevish [adj] *irritable, testy* acrimonious, angry, bad-tempered, cantankerous, captious, carping, caviling, childish, churlish, complaining, crabbed*, cranky, critical, cross, crotchety*, crusty*, cussed, fault-finding, fractious, fretful, fretting, grouchy, grousing, growling, grumpy, huffy, ill-natured, mean, morose, obstinate, ogre, ornery, out-of-sorts*, pertinacious, petulant, querulous, short-tempered, snappy, splenetic, sulky, sullen, surly, tetchy, touchy, ugly, waspish, waspy, whining; CONCEPT 401 —*Ant.* accepting, friendly, happy, pleasant

peg [v] *attach* clinch, fasten, fix, join, make fast, pin, secure, tighten; CONCEPTS 85,160 —*Ant.* detach, unfasten

pejorative [adj] *negative, belittling* debasing, deprecatory, depreciatory, derisive, derogatory, detracting, detractive, detractory, disadvantageous, disparaging, irreverent, rude, slighting, uncomplimentary, unpleasant; CONCEPT 267 —*Ant.* complimentary, positive, praising

pell-dull [adj] *disordered* chaotic, confused, disarrayed, disorganized, haphazard, muddled, tumultous/tumultuous; CONCEPTS 562,585 —*Ant.* ordered, organized

pell-mell [adv] *hurriedly and carelessly* foolishly, full tilt*, hastily, headlong, heedlessly, helter-skelter, impetuously, incontinently, indiscreetly, posthaste, precipitiously, rashly, recklessly, thoughtlessly; CONCEPTS 544,799 —*Ant.* carefully, cautiously

pell-mell [n] *disorder* anarchy, ataxia, chaos, clutter, confusion, disarray, ferment, helter-

skelter, huddle, muddle, pandemonium, snarl, tumult, turmoil, upheaval; CONCEPT 674 —*Ant.* order, organization

pelt [n] *animal fur* coat, epidermis, fell, hair, hide, jacket, skin, slough, wool; CONCEPT 399

pelt [v] *beat; throw hard* assail, batter, belabor, belt, bombard, career, cast, charge, dash, hammer, hurl, knock, lapidate, pepper, pound, pour, pummel, rain, rush, shoot, shower, sling, speed, stone, strike, swat, tear, thrash, wallop; CONCEPTS 189,222

pen [n1] *enclosure* cage, coop, corral, fence, fold, hedge, hutch, jail, penitentiary, prison, sty, wall*; CONCEPTS 439,443 —*Ant.* open space

pen [n2] *writing instrument* ball point, felt-tip, fountain pen, marker, nib, quill, reed, stick, stylograph; CONCEPTS 277,499 —*Ant.* pencil

pen [v1] *enclose* box, cage, case, close in, confine, coop, corral, fence in, hedge, hem in, mew*, shut in; CONCEPTS 191,758 —*Ant.* free, let go, release

pen [v2] *write* autograph, commit to paper, compose, draft, draw up, engross, indict, jot down; CONCEPT 79 —*Ant.* speak

penal [adj] *disciplinary* chastening, corrective, penalizing, punishing, punitive, punitory, reformatory, retributive; CONCEPTS 548,583

penalize [v] *punish* amerce, castigate, chasten, chastise, condemn, correct, discipline, dock*, fine, handicap, hit with*, impose penalty, inflict handicap, judge, mulct, put at disadvantage, scold, slap with*, throw the book at*; CONCEPT 122 —*Ant.* excuse, forgive, pardon, reward

penalty [n] *punishment* amends, amercement, cost, damages, disadvantage, discipline, dues, fall, fine, forfeit, forfeiture, handicap, mortification, mulct, price, rap*, retribution; CONCEPTS 344,679 —*Ant.* award, forgiveness, pardon, reward

penance [n] *reparation for wrong* absolution, atonement, attrition, compensation, compunction, confession, contrition, expiation, forgiveness, hair shirt*, mortification, penalty, penitence, punishment, purgation, remorse, remorsefulness, repentance, retribution, rue, ruth, sackcloth and ashes*, self-flagellation*, shrift, sorrow, suffering; CONCEPTS 126,367, 384,410

penchant [n] *fondness, inclination* affection, affinity, attachment, bias, disposition, druthers*, inclining, itch*, leaning, liking, partiality, predilection, predisposition, proclivity, proneness, propensity, taste, tendency, tilt*, turn*, weakness, yen; CONCEPTS 20,32,411, 709 —*Ant.* dislike, hate, hatred, indifference

pending [adj] *about to happen* awaiting, continuing, dependent, forthcoming, hanging, imminent, impending, indeterminate, in line*, in the balance*, in the offing*, in the works*, ominous, on board*, on line*, pensile, undecided, undetermined, unsettled, up in the air*; CONCEPT 548 —*Ant.* improbable, unlikely

pendulous/pendent [adj] *hanging* dangling, dependent, drooping, pending, pendulant, pensile, suspended, swinging; CONCEPTS 485,584

penetrate [v1] *pierce; get through physically* access, barge in, bayonet, blow in, bore, break in, breeze in, bust in, charge, come, crack, diffuse, drill, drive, eat through, encroach, enter, filter in, force, get in, gore, go through, impale, infiltrate, ingress, insert, insinuate, introduce, invade, jab, knife, make a hole, make an entrance, pass through, percolate, perforate, permeate, pervade, pop in, prick, probe, puncture, ream, run into, saturate, seep, sink into, spear, stab, stick into, suffuse, thrust, trespass; CONCEPTS 159,179,220 —*Ant.* exit, take out, withdraw

penetrate [v2] *understand or be understood* affect, become clear, come across*, comprehend, decipher, discern, fathom, figure out, get across*, get over*, get through*, get to the bottom*, grasp, impress, perceive, put over*, see through*, sink in*, soak in*, touch, unravel, work out; CONCEPT 15 —*Ant.* misconstrue, misinterpret, misunderstand

penetrating [adj1] *stinging, harsh* biting, carrying, clear-cut, crisp, cutting, edged, entering, forcing, going through, infiltrating, ingoing, intrusive, passing through, penetrant, permeating, pervasive, piercing, pointed, puncturing, pungent, sharp, shrill, strong, trenchant; CONCEPTS 267,537 —*Ant.* blunt, dull

penetrating [adj2] *intelligent* acute, astute, critical, discerning, discriminating, incisive, keen, penetrative, perceptive, perspicacious, profound, quick, quick-witted, sagacious, searching, sharp, sharp-witted, shrewd; CONCEPT 402 —*Ant.* idiotic, senseless, stupid, unintelligent

penitence [n] *shame, sorrow* anguish, attrition, compunction, contriteness, contrition, debasement, degradation, distress, grief, humbling, humiliation, penance, qualm, regret, remorse, remorsefulness, repentance, rue, ruefulness, ruth, sadness, scruple, self-castigation, self-condemnation, self-flagellation, self-punishment, self-reproach; CONCEPT 410 —*Ant.* shamelessness

penitent [adj] *shamed, sorrowful* abject, apologetic, atoning, attritional, compunctious, conscience-stricken, contrite, penitential, regretful, remorseful, repentant, rueful, sorry; CONCEPTS 403,542 —*Ant.* happy, unashamed, unrepentent

penitentiary [n] *jail* big house*, campus, can*, college, cooler*, correctional institution, inside*, joint*, lockup*, pen*, penal institution, prison, reformatory, slammer*, stockade; CONCEPTS 439,449,516

pen name [n] *pseudonym* AKA*, alias, anonym, assumed name, nickname, nom de guerre, nom de plume, professional name, pseudonym; CONCEPTS 268,683

pennant [n] *flag, banner* banderole, bunting, burgee, color, decoration, emblem, ensign, jack, pennon, screamer, standard, streamer; CONCEPTS 260,473

penniless [adj] *without any money* bankrupt, broke*, clean*, cleaned out*, dead broke*, destitute, dirt poor*, down to last penny*, flat*, flat broke*, impecunious, impoverished, indigent, in the gutter*, lacking, moneyless, necessitous, needy, on last leg*, over a barrel*, penurious, poor, poverty-stricken, ruined, strapped*, tapped out*, without a dime*; CONCEPT 334 —*Ant.* affluent, rich, wealthy

pension [n] *benefits paid after retirement* allowance, annuity, gift, grant, IRA*, payment, premium, retirement account, reward, social security, subsidy, subvention, superannuation, support; CONCEPTS 332,344

pensive [adj] *meditative, solemn* absorbed, abstracted, attentive, cogitative, contemplative, dreamy, grave, musing, pondering, preoccupied, reflecting, reflective, ruminating, ruminative, serious, sober, speculative, thinking, thoughtful, wistful, withdrawn; CONCEPT 403 —*Ant.* ignorant, shallow

pent-up [adj] *held within* bottled-up, bridled, checked, constrained, curbed, held-back, held in check, inhibited, repressed, restrained, restricted, smothered, stifled, suppressed; CONCEPTS 401,403 —*Ant.* public, released

penurious [adj] *stingy* avaricious, cheap, chintzy*, close-fisted, costive, curmudgeonly, economical, frugal, greedy, hoarding, miserly, parsimonious, penny-pinching, pennywise*, pinchpenny*, saving, scrimping, sparing, thrifty, tightfisted, uncharitable, ungenerous, ungiving; CONCEPTS 326,334,401

peon [n] *menial worker* drudge, farmhand, farm worker, gopher, laborer, peasant, serf, servant, slave, unskilled laborer; CONCEPT 348

people [n] *human beings* bodies, body politic*, bourgeois, cats*, citizens, clan, commonality, common people, community, crowd, family, folk, folks, general public, heads*, herd, hoi polloi*, horde, humanity, humankind, human race, humans, inhabitants, John/Jane Q. Public*, kin, masses, mob, mortals, multitude, nation, nationality, person in the street*, persons, plebeians, populace, population, proletariat, public, rabble, race, rank and file*, riffraff*, society, tribe; CONCEPTS 296,379, 380,417 —*Ant.* animals, plants

pep [n] *vim, vigor* animation, bang, birr, energy, get-up-and-go*, go, gusto, hardihood, high spirits, life, liveliness, moxie*, potency, punch*, push, snap*, spirit, starch*, tuck*, verve, vitality, vivacity, zip*; CONCEPTS 411,633 —*Ant.* apathy, inactivity, lethargy, lifelessness

peppery [adj1] *highly seasoned* fiery, hot, piquant, poignant, pungent, racy, snappy, spicy, zestful, zesty; CONCEPT 613

peppery [adj2] *irritable; sarcastic* acute, angry, astringent, biting, caustic, choleric, cranky, cross, fiery, hot-tempered, incisive, irascible, keen, lively, passionate, quick-tempered, sharp, sharp-tempered, snappish, spirited, spunky, stinging, testy, touchy, trenchant, waspish; CONCEPTS 267,401,542 —*Ant.* cheerful, happy

peppy [adj] *lively, vigorous* active, alert, animate, animated, bright, gay, keen, perky, sparkling, spirited, sprightly, vivacious; CONCEPTS 401,404 —*Ant.* apathetic, inactive, lethargic, tired

pep up [v] *invigorate, inspire* animate, enliven, exhilarate, jazz up*, quicken, stimulate, vitalize, vivify; CONCEPTS 7,22 —*Ant.* discourage, tire, wear

perceive [v1] *notice, see* apperceive, apprehend, be aware of, behold, descry, discern, discover, distinguish, divine, espy, feel, grasp, identify, look, make out, mark, mind, note, observe, realize, recognize, regard, remark, seize, sense, spot, spy, take; CONCEPTS 38,626 —*Ant.* miss, neglect, overlook

perceive [v2] *understand* appreciate, apprehend, comprehend, conclude, copy, deduce, distinguish, feature, feel, flash*, gather, get, get the message*, get the picture*, grasp, know, learn, pin*, read, realize, recognize, see, sense, track; CONCEPT 15 —*Ant.* misinterpret, misunderstand

percentage [n] *portion, allotment* allowance, bite, bonus, chunk, commission, corner*, cut, discount, division, duty, fee, holdout, interest, juice*, payoff, percent, piece, piece of the action*, points*, proportion, quota, rate, ratio, section, slice*, split*, taste*, winnings; CONCEPTS 766,784,835 —*Ant.* whole

perceptible [adj] *noticeable, obvious* apparent, appreciable, audible, clear, cognizable, conspicuous, detectable, discernible, distinct, distinguishable, evident, lucid, observable, palpable, perceivable, perspicuous, recognizable, sensible, signal, tangible, understandable, visible; CONCEPTS 529,576 —*Ant.* ambiguous, imperceptible, invisible, obscure, silent, unnoticeable, vague

perception [n] *understanding, idea* acumen, apprehending, apprehension, approach, attention, attitude, awareness, big idea*, brainchild*, brain wave*, conceit, concept, conception, consciousness, discernment, feeling, flash, grasp, image, impression, insight, intellection, judgment, knowledge, light, notion, observation, opinion, perspicacity, picture, plan, realizing, recognition, sagacity, sensation, sense, study, taste, thought, viewpoint; CONCEPTS 409, 410,689

perceptive [adj] *alert, sensitive* acute, astute, awake, aware, brainy*, conscious, discerning, discreet, ear to the ground*, gnostic, incisive, insighted, insightful, intuitive, judicious, keen, knowing, knowledgeable, knows what's what*, observant, penetrating, penetrative, percipient, perspicacious, quick, rational, responsive, sagacious, sage, savvy*, sharp, sophic, tuned in*, wise, wise to*; CONCEPTS 402,542 —*Ant.* dense, insensitive, unaware, unobservant

perch [n] *object placed high for sitting on* branch, landing place, lounge, pole, post, resting place, roost, seat; CONCEPTS 443,479

perch [v] *sit atop of* alight, balance, land, light, rest, roost, set down, settle, sit on, squat, touch down; CONCEPT 154 —*Ant.* lower

percolate [v] *seep, drip (liquid)* bleed, bubble, charge, drain, exude, filter, filtrate, impregnate, leach, ooze, pass through, penetrate, perk, permeate, pervade, saturate, strain, sweat, transfuse, transude, weep; CONCEPTS 179,181

perdition [n] *hell* Abaddon*, abyss, affliction, bottomless pit*, condemnation, damnation, everlasting fire*, fire and brimstone*, Gehenna*, Hades, infernal regions, inferno, loss of the soul, lower world, nether world, pit, place of torment, punishment, purgatory, ruin, suffering, underworld; CONCEPTS 370,435,674

peremptory [adj] *overbearing, authoritative* absolute, arbitrary, assertive, autocratic, binding, bossy, categorical, certain, commanding, compelling, decided, decisive, dictatorial, dogmatic, domineering, final, finished, firm, fixed, high-handed, imperative, imperial, imperious, incontrovertible, intolerant, irrefutable, magisterial,

obligatory, obstinate, positive, rigorous, severe, stringent, tyrannical, uncompromising, undeniable; CONCEPTS 535,537,542 —*Ant.* easy-going, indulgent, laid-back, lax, lenient, mild, moderate

perennial [adj] *enduring, perpetual* abiding, annual, ceaseless, chronic, constant, continual, continuing, deathless, durable, eternal, everlasting, immortal, imperishable, incessant, inveterate, lasting, lifelong, long-lasting, long-lived, longstanding, never-ending, old, perdurable, permanent, persistent, recurrent, seasonal, sustained, unceasing, unchanging, undying, unfailing, uninterrupted, yearlong, yearly; CONCEPTS 539,798 —*Ant.* changing, intermittent, interrupted

perfect [adj1] *flawless, superlative* absolute, accomplished, aces*, adept, A-OK*, beyond compare, blameless, classical, consummate, crowning, culminating, defectless, excellent, excelling, experienced, expert, faultless, finished, foolproof, ideal, immaculate, impeccable, indefectible, matchless, out-of-this-world*, paradisiac, paradisiacal, peerless, pure, skilled, skillful, sound, splendid, spotless, stainless, sublime, superb, supreme, ten*, unblemished, unequaled, unmarred, untainted, untarnished, utopian; CONCEPT 574 —*Ant.* flawed, imperfect, inferior, second-rate, unbroken

perfect [adj2] *whole, intact* absolute, choate, complete, completed, consummate, downright, entire, finished, flawless, full, gross, integral, out-and-out*, outright, positive, rank, sheer, simple, sound, unadulterated, unalloyed, unblemished, unbroken, undamaged, unimpaired, unmitigated, unmixed, unqualified, utter; CONCEPTS 482,485 —*Ant.* broken, imperfect, incomplete, part, unfinished

perfect [adj3] *accurate, correct* appropriate, bull's-eye*, certain, close, dead-on*, definite, distinct, exact, express, faithful, fit, ideal, model, needed, on target*, on the button*, on the money*, precise, proper, required, requisite, right, sharp, strict, suitable, textbook, to a T*, to a turn*, true, unerring, very; CONCEPTS 535,557,558 —*Ant.* imperfect, imprecise, inaccurate, wrong

perfect [v] *polish; achieve* accomplish, ameliorate, carry out, complete, consummate, crown, cultivate, develop, effect, elaborate, finish, fulfill, hone, idealize, improve, perform, put finishing touch on, realize, refine, round, slick, smooth; CONCEPTS 91,244,706 —*Ant.* destroy, ruin

perfection [n] *achievement, completeness* accomplishment, achieving, acme, arete, completion, consummation, crown, ending, entireness, evolution, exactness, excellence, excellency, exquisiteness, faultlessness, finish, finishing, fulfillment, ideal, idealism, impeccability, integrity, maturity, merit, paragon, perfectness, phoenix, precision, purity, quality, realization, ripeness, sublimity, superiority, supremacy, transcendence, virtue, wholeness; CONCEPTS 671,706 —*Ant.* damage, deficiency, flaw, imperfection, incompleteness, uselessness, worthlessness

perfectionist [n] *stickler* formalist, fussbudget, fusspot, idealist, nit-picker, purist, quibbler; CONCEPTS 359,416,423

perfectly [*adv1*] *absolutely* altogether, completely, consummately, entirely, fully, quite, thoroughly, totally, utterly, well, wholly; CONCEPTS 531,544 —*Ant.* imperfectly, partially

perfectly [*adv2*] *without flaw* admirably, correctly, excellently, exquisitely, faultlessly, fitly, flawlessly, ideally, impeccably, superbly, superlatively, supremely, to perfection, wonderfully; CONCEPT 574 —*Ant.* flawed, imperfectly

perfidious [*adj*] *treacherous* betraying, deceitful, deceptive, double-crossing*, double-dealing*, faithless, false, insidious, misleading, recreant, shifty*, slick*, snake in the grass*, traitorous, two-faced*, two-timing*, undependable, unfaithful, unloyal, unreliable, untrustworthy; CONCEPTS 401,404

perforate [*v*] *make a hole in* bore, drill, drive, hole, honeycomb*, penetrate, permeate, pierce, pit, poke full of holes*, probe, punch, puncture, shoot full of holes*, slit, stab; CONCEPT 220 —*Ant.* close up

perform [*v1*] *carry out, accomplish* achieve, act, be engaged in, behave, bring about, bring off, carry through, carry to completion, complete, comply, deliver the goods*, discharge, dispose of, do, do justice to*, do to a turn*, effect, end, enforce, execute, finish, fulfill, function, go that route*, implement, meet, move, observe, operate, percolate, perk, pull off*, put through, react, realize, run with the ball*, satisfy, take, take care of business*, tick, transact, wind up, work; CONCEPTS 91,199 —*Ant.* fail, halt, prevent, stop

perform [*v2*] *act, depict as entertainment* act out, appear as, be on, bring down the house*, discourse, display, do a number*, do a turn*, dramatize, emote, enact, execute, exhibit, give, go on, ham*, ham it up*, impersonate, offer, personate, play, playact, present, produce, put on, render, represent, show, stage, tread the boards*; CONCEPT 292 —*Ant.* direct

performance [*n1*] *accomplishment* achievement, act, administration, attainment, carrying out, completion, conduct, consummation, discharge, doing, enforcement, execution, exploit, feat, fruition, fulfillment, pursuance, realization, work; CONCEPT 706 —*Ant.* failure

performance [*n2*] *acting, depiction* act, appearance, ballet, behavior, burlesque, business, ceremony, concert, custom, dance, display, drama, exhibition, gig*, interpretation, matinee, offering, opera, pageant, play, portrayal, presentation, production, recital, rehearsal, representation, review, revue, rigmarole, rite, set, show, special, spectacle, stage show, stunt, to-do*; CONCEPT 263 —*Ant.* direction

performance [*n3*] *efficiency* action, conduct, effectiveness, efficacy, exercise, functioning, operation, practice, pursuit, running, working; CONCEPT 630 —*Ant.* ineffectualness, inefficiency

perfume [*n*] *scent, often manufactured and packaged for personal use* aroma, attar, balm, balminess, bouquet, cologne, eau de cologne, essence, fragrance, incense, odor, oil, redolence, sachet, smell, spice, sweetness; CONCEPTS 599, 600 —*Ant.* odor, stench, stink

perfunctory [*adj*] *automatic, unthinking* apathetic, careless, cool, cursory, disinterested, going through the motions*, heedless, impersonal, inattentive, indifferent, involuntary, lackadaisical, laid-back*, mechanical, negligent, offhand, phoning it in*, routine, sketchy, slipshod*, slovenly, standard, stereotyped, stock, superficial, unaware, unconcerned, uninterested, usual, walking through it*, wooden*; CONCEPTS 542,544 —*Ant.* careful, precise, thoughtful

perhaps [*adv*] *possibly* as it may be, as the case may be, conceivably, feasibly, for all one knows, imaginably, it may be, maybe, perchance, reasonably; CONCEPT 552 —*Ant.* improbably, never, unlikely

peril [*n*] *danger, risk* cause for alarm*, double trouble*, endangerment, exposure, hazard, insecurity, jeopardy, liability, menace, openness, pitfall, risky business*, uncertainty, vulnerability; CONCEPT 675 —*Ant.* safeness, safety, security

perilous [*adj*] *dangerous* chancy, delicate, dicey*, dynamite, exposed, hairy*, hazardous, insecure, loaded*, on thin ice*, playing with fire*, precarious, risky, rugged, Russian roulette*, shaky, threatening, ticklish, touch and go*, touchy, treacherous, uncertain, unhealthy, unsafe, unsound, unstable, unsteady, unsure, vulnerable, wicked*; CONCEPTS 548,587 —*Ant.* ok, safe, secure

perimeter [*n*] *circumference, border* ambit, borderline, boundary, bounds, brim, brink, circuit, compass, confines, edge, fringe, hem, limit, margin, outline, periphery, skirt, verge; CONCEPTS 484,745,792 —*Ant.* center, inside, interior, middle

period [*n1*] *extent of time* aeon, age, course, cycle, date, days, duration, epoch, era, generation, interval, measure, season, space, span, spell, stage, stretch, term, time, while, years; CONCEPTS 807,822

period [*n2*] *ending* cessation, close, closing, closure, conclusion, discontinuance, end, limit, stop, termination; CONCEPT 832

periodic [*adj*] *at fixed intervals* alternate, annual, at various times, centennial, cyclic, cyclical, daily, epochal, every once in a while, every so often, fluctuating, hourly, infrequent, intermittent, isochronal, isochronous, monthly, occasional, on-again-off-again*, on certain occasions, orbital, perennial, periodical, recurrent, recurring, regular, repeated, rhythmic, routine, seasonal, serial, spasmodic, sporadic, weekly, yearly; CONCEPTS 541,799 —*Ant.* constant, continual, irregular, lasting, permanent, sporadic, variable

periodical [*n*] *regular publication* journal, mag*, magazine, monthly, newspaper, number, paper, quarterly, rag*, review, serial, sheet*, slick*, throwaway*, weekly; CONCEPT 280

peripatetic [*adj*] *constantly traveling* ambulant, itinerant, itinerate, migrant, mobile, nomadic, perambulant, roaming, roving, vagabond, vagrant, wandering, wayfaring; CONCEPTS 401, 584 —*Ant.* fixed, settled

peripheral [*adj*] *minor, outside* beside the point, borderline, exterior, external, incidental, inessential, irrelevant, minor, outer, outermost, perimetric, secondary, superficial, surface, tangential, unimportant; CONCEPTS 575,583,831 —*Ant.* central, crucial, internal, major

periphery [*n*] *outskirts, outer edge* ambit,

pe
pe

border, boundary, brim, brink, circuit, circumference, compass, covering, edge, fringe, hem, margin, outside, perimeter, rim, skirt, verge; CONCEPTS 484,745 —Ant. center

perish [v] *die, decline, decay* be destroyed, be killed, be lost, bite the dust*, break down, buy the farm*, cease, check out*, collapse, corrupt, croak, crumble, decease, decompose, demise, depart, disappear, disintegrate, end, expire, fall, give up the ghost*, go, go under, kick the bucket*, lose life, OD*, pass, pass away, pass on, rot, succumb, vanish, waste*, wither; CONCEPTS 13,105,304 —Ant. give birth, revive

perishable [adj] *liable to spoil, rot* decaying, decomposable, destructible, easily spoiled, short-lived, unstable; CONCEPTS 462,485 —Ant. continuation, endurance

perjure [v] *give false testimony* bear false witness*, commit perjury, deceive, delude, equivocate, falsify, forswear, lie, lie under oath, mislead, prevaricate, swear falsely, trick; CONCEPTS 63,317 —Ant. attest, certify, prove

perjury [n] *lying while under oath* deceitfulness, deception, dishonesty, falsehood, false oath, false swearing, false testimony, falsification, untruth, untruthfulness; CONCEPTS 63,278

perk [n] *benefit* advantage, bonus, dividend, extra, fringe benefit, gratuity, gravy*, lagniappe, largess, perquisite, plus, tip; CONCEPT 344 —Ant. disadvantage

perk up [v] *cheer* ameliorate, be refreshed, brighten, buck up*, cheer up, convalesce, gain, improve, invigorate, liven up, look up, mend, pep up, rally, recover, recuperate, refresh, renew, revive, shake, take heart*; CONCEPTS 7,22,244,308 —Ant. depress

perky [adj] *animated, happy* active, alert, aware, bouncy, bright, bright-eyed and bushy-tailed*, brisk, bubbly, buoyant, cheerful, cheery, gay, in fine fettle*, jaunty, lively, spirited, sprightly, sunny, vivacious; CONCEPTS 401,404 —Ant. depressed, gloomy

permanent [adj] *constant, lasting* abiding, changeless, continual, diurnal, durable, enduring, everlasting, fixed, forever, forever and a day*, for keeps*, immutable, imperishable, indestructible, in for the long haul*, invariable, long-lasting, perdurable, perduring, perennial, perpetual, persistent, set, set in concrete*, set in stone*, stable, steadfast, unchanging, unfading; CONCEPTS 551,649,798 —Ant. ephemeral, temporary

permeable [adj] *absorbent, penetrable* absorptive, accessible, enterable, passable, pervious, porose, porous, spongelike, spongy; CONCEPTS 576,604,606 —Ant. inpenetrable, unpermeable

permeate [v] *filter, spread throughout* charge, diffuse, drench, fill, go through, imbue, impregnate, infiltrate, infuse, ingrain, interfuse, invade, pass through, penetrate, percolate, pervade, pierce, saturate, seep, soak, stab, stalk, steep, suffuse, transfuse; CONCEPTS 159,179,256

permissible [adj] *allowable, legal* acceptable, admissible, all right, approved, authorized, bearable, endorsed, kosher*, lawful, legalized, legit*, legitimate, licit, okay*, on the up and up*, permitted, proper, sanctioned, tolerable, tolerated, unforbidden, unprohibited; CONCEPT 319 —Ant. illegal, prohibited, unpermissible

permission [n] *authorization, consent* acceptance, acknowledgment, acquiescence, admission, agreement, allowance, approbation, approval, assent, avowal, canonization, carte blanche*, concession, concurrence, condonance, condonation, dispensation, empowerment, endorsement, freedom, imprimatur, indulgence, leave, letting, liberty, license, okay, permit, privilege, promise, recognition, rubber stamp*, sanctification, sanction, stamp of approval*, sufferance, tolerance, toleration, verification, warrant; CONCEPTS 50,83,88,376, 685 —Ant. denial, prohibition, veto

permissive [adj] *lenient* acquiescent, agreeable, allowing, approving, easy-going, forbearing, free, indulgent, latitudinarian, lax, liberal, open-minded, permitting, susceptible, tolerant; CONCEPT 401 —Ant. intolerant, mean, strict

permit [n] *authorization* admittance, allowance, charter, concession, consent, empowering, favor, franchise, go-ahead*, grant, green light*, indulgence, leave, legalization, liberty, license, pass, passport, patent, permission, privilege, safe-conduct, sanction, sufferance, toleration, visa, warrant; CONCEPTS 271,376,685 —Ant. grounding, prohibition

permit [v] *allow participation* abet, accede, accept, acquiesce, admit, agree, authorize, bless, blink at*, boost, buy, charter, concede, concur, condone, consent, empower, enable, endorse, endure, franchise, give leave, give permission, go for, grant, have, humor, indulge, leave, let, let pass, license, okay, pass, privilege, sanctify, sanction, say yes, shake on*, sign, sign off on*, suffer, take kindly to*, thumbs up*, tolerate, warrant, wink at*; CONCEPTS 50,83,88 —Ant. deny, disallow, refuse, reject

pernicious [adj] *bad, hurtful* baleful, damaging, dangerous, deadly, deleterious, destructive, detrimental, devastating, evil, fatal, harmful, iniquitous, injurious, killing, lethal, maleficent, malevolent, malicious, malign, malignant, miasmatic, miasmic, mortal, nefarious, noisome, noxious, offensive, pestiferous, pestilent, pestilential, poisonous, prejudicial, ruinous, sinister, toxic, venomous, virulent, wicked; CONCEPTS 537,548,571 —Ant. helpful, innocuous, kind, lovable, loving

perpendicular [adj] *at right angles to* erect, horizontal, on end, plumb, sheer, standing, stand-up, steep, straight, straight-up, upright, vertical; CONCEPT 581 —Ant. horizontal, level

perpetrate [v] *be responsible for* act, bring about, carry out, commit, do, effect, enact, execute, inflict, perform, pull, up and do*, wreak; CONCEPT 91 —Ant. abstain

perpetual [adj] *continual, lasting* abiding, ceaseless, constant, continued, continuous, endless, enduring, eternal, everlasting, going on, immortal, imperishable, incessant, infinite, interminable, intermittent, never-ceasing, never-ending, perdurable, perennial, permanent, persistent, recurrent, recurring, reoccurring, repeated, repeating, repetitious, returning, sempiternal, unceasing, unchanging, undying, unending, unfailing, uninterrupted, unremitting, without end; CONCEPTS 551,649,798,799 —Ant. brief, ephemeral, fleeting, momentary, temporary, transient

perpetuate [v] *keep going* bolster, conserve, continue, eternalize, eternize, immortalize, keep, keep alive, keep in existence, keep up, maintain, preserve, secure, support, sustain; CONCEPT 239 —*Ant.* cease, halt, prevent, stop

perplex [v] *confuse, mix up* astonish, astound, baffle, balk, befuddle, beset, bewilder, buffalo*, complicate, confound, discombobulate*, discompose, dumbfound, encumber, entangle, fog, get to*, involve, jumble, muck, muddle, muddy the waters*, mystify, nonplus, perturb, pose, puzzle, rattle, ravel, snarl up, stumble, stump, surprise, tangle, thicken, thwart; CONCEPTS 16,84 —*Ant.* clarify, clear up, enlighten, explain

perplexing [adj] *difficult to understand* baffling, beyond one, complicated, confusing, convoluted, disconcerting, impenetrable, intricate, involved, knotty, mind-bending, mysterious, mystifying, paradoxical, puzzling, taxing, thorny, worrying; CONCEPT 529

perquisite [n] *fringe benefit* advantage, bonus, dividend, extra, gratuity, gravy*, lagniappe, largess, perk*, plus, reward, tip; CONCEPT 344

per se [adv] *essentially* alone, as such, by and of itself, by definition, by itself, by its very nature, fundamentally, independently, in essence, in itself, intrinsically, of itself, singularly, solely, virtually; CONCEPTS 544,577

persecute [v] *wrong, torment* afflict, aggrieve, annoy, badger, bait, beat, be on one's case*, bother, crucify, distress, dog*, dragoon, drive up the wall*, exile, expel, harass, hector, hound*, hunt, ill-treat, injure, maltreat, martyr, molest, oppress, outrage, pester, pick on, plague, pursue, tease, torture, tyrannize, vex, victimize, worry; CONCEPTS 7,19,44,246 —*Ant.* comfort, commend, console, reward, soothe

perseverance [n] *diligence, hard work* backbone*, constancy, continuance, cool, dedication, determination, doggedness, drive, endurance, grit*, guts*, immovability, indefatigability, moxie*, persistence, pertinacity, pluck*, prolonging, purposefulness, pursuance, resolution, sedulity, spunk, stamina, steadfastness, stick-to-itiveness*, tenacity; CONCEPTS 411,633 —*Ant.* apathy, idleness, indolence, laziness, lethargy

persevere [v] *keep at; work hard* be determined, be resolved, be stubborn, carry on, continue, endure, go for broke*, go for it*, go on, hang in*, hang tough*, hold fast*, hold on, keep driving*, keep going, keep on, leave no stone unturned*, maintain, persist, plug away*, press on, proceed, pursue, remain, see it through*, stand firm*, stay the course*, stick with it*; CONCEPTS 87,239 —*Ant.* be lazy, give up, idle, leave, quit, stop

persist [v] *carry on, carry through* abide, be resolute, be stubborn, continue, endure, follow through*, follow up*, go all the way*, go on, go the limit*, grind, hold on, insist, keep up*, last, leave no stone unturned*, linger, obtain, perdure, persevere, persevere, prevail, pursue, recur, remain, repeat, see through, stick it out*, stick to guns*, strive, tough it out*; CONCEPTS 23,87,91,239 —*Ant.* cease, give up, leave, quit, stop

persistent [adj] *determined; continuous* assiduous, bound, bound and determined*, bulldogged*, constant, continual, dogged, endless, enduring, firm, fixed, immovable, incessant, indefatigable, in for long haul*, insistent, interminable, like bad penny*, never-ending, obdurate, obstinate, perpetual, perseverant, persevering, persisting, pertinacious, relentless, repeated, resolute, steadfast, steady, sticky*, stubborn, tenacious, tireless, unflagging, unrelenting, unremitting, unshakable; CONCEPTS 326,401,404,538 —*Ant.* lazy, relenting, surrendering, yielding

persnickety [adj] *fussy, particular* careful, choosy, fastidious, finicky, nice, picky; CONCEPT 404 —*Ant.* open, unconcerned, unfussy

person [n] *human being* being, body, character, creature, customer, gal, guy, human, identity, individual, individuality, joker*, life, living soul, man, mortal, party, personage, personality, self, somebody, soul, specimen, spirit, unit*, woman; CONCEPT 417 —*Ant.* animal, plant

personable [adj] *friendly, sociable* aces*, affable, agreeable, all heart*, all right*, amiable, attractive, charming, easygoing, good egg*, gregarious, likable, nice, okay, pleasant, pleasing, presentable, sweetheart*, white-hat*, winning; CONCEPT 404 —*Ant.* disagreeable, unfriendly, unsociable

personage/personality [n/n2] *celebrity, notable* big shot*, bigwig*, brass*, celeb*, chief, cynosure, dignitary, distinguished person, eminence, face*, hot shot*, individual, luminary, monster*, name*, public figure, somebody, star, superstar, top dog*, VIP*, worthy; CONCEPTS 352,354,423 —*Ant.* lowlife

personal [adj] *private, individual* claimed, exclusive, intimate, own, particular, peculiar, privy, retired, secluded, secret, special; CONCEPT 536 —*Ant.* general, public

personal computer [n] *computer* clone, desktop computer, home computer, IBM PC, laptop*, MAC, Macintosh, microcomputer, minicomputer, PC; CONCEPTS 269,463

personality [n1] *person's character, traits* charisma, charm, complexion, disposition, dynamism, emotions, identity, individuality, likableness, magnetism, makeup, nature, psyche, self, seldom, selfhood, singularity, temper, temperament; CONCEPT 411

personally [adv] *independently* alone, by oneself, directly, for oneself, for one's part, individualistically, individually, in one's own view, in person, in the flesh, narrowly, on one's own, privately, solely, specially, subjectively; CONCEPT 544 —*Ant.* generally, objectively

personify [v] *represent some other being, character* act out, body forth, contain, copy, emblematize, embody, epitomize, exemplify, express, exteriorize, externalize, hominify, humanize, illustrate, image, imitate, impersonate, incarnate, live as, make human, manifest, materialize, mirror, objectify, personize, substantiate, symbolize, typify; CONCEPTS 261,716

personnel [n] *employees of business or other enterprise* cadre, corps, crew, faculty, group, helpers, human resources, members, men and women, office, organization, people, shop, staff, troop, troops, workers, work force; CONCEPTS 325,417

perspective [n] *view, outlook* angle, aspect, attitude, broad view, context, frame of reference*, headset*, landscape, mindset*, objectivity, overview, panorama, proportion, prospect, relation, relative importance, relativity, scene, size of it*, viewpoint, vista, way of looking; CONCEPTS 410,629,689

perspicacious [adj] *observant, perceptive*
acute, alert, astute, aware, clear-sighted, clever, discerning, heady*, judicious, keen, penetrating, percipient, sagacious, savvy*, sharp, sharp-witted, shrewd; CONCEPT 402 —Ant. ignorant, unobservant, unperceptive

perspicuous [adj] *clear, obvious* apparent, clear-cut, comprehensible, crystal*, crystal-clear*, distinct, easily understood, explicit, intelligible, limpid, lucent, lucid, luminous, pellucid, plain, self-evident, straightforward, transparent, unambiguous, unblurred, understandable; CONCEPT 529 —Ant. obscure, unclear, vague

perspire [v] *become wet with sweat* be damp, be wet, break a sweat*, drip, exude, get in a lather*, glow, lather, pour, secrete, swelter; CONCEPTS 185,469 —Ant. dry

persuade [v] *cause to believe; convince to do* actuate, advise, affect, allure, argue into, assure, blandish, brainwash*, bring around, bring to senses, cajole, coax, convert, counsel, draw, enlist, entice, exhort, gain confidence of, get, impel, impress, incite, incline, induce, influence, inveigle, lead, lead to believe, lead to do, move, prevail upon, prompt, propagandize, proselyte, proselytize, reason, satisfy, seduce, sell, stroke, sway, talk into, touch, turn on to, urge, wear down*, wheedle, win argument, win over, woo, work over; CONCEPT 68 —Ant. discourage, dissuade, hinder, prevent, repress, stop, suppress

persuasion [n1] *influencing to do, believe* alignment, alluring, arm-twist*, blandishment, brainwashing*, cajolery, cogency, con*, conversion, enticement, exhortation, force, goose*, hard sell*, hook*, inducement, inveiglement, persuasiveness, potency, power, promote, pull*, seduction, sell*, snow job*, soft soap*, squeeze*, sweet talk*, wheedling, winning over, working over; CONCEPTS 68,687 —Ant. discouragement, dissuasion, hindrance, prevention

persuasion [n2] *belief, religion* bias, camp, certitude, church, communion, connection, conviction, credo, creed, cult, denomination, eye, faction, faith, feeling, mind*, opinion, partiality, party, predilection, prejudice, school, school of thought*, sect, sentiment, side, tenet, view; CONCEPT 689 —Ant. atheism, disbelief

persuasive [adj] *effective, influential* actuating, alluring, cogent, compelling, conclusive, convictive, convincing, credible, effectual, efficacious, efficient, eloquent, energetic, enticing, forceful, forcible, impelling, impressive, inducing, inspiring, inveigling, logical, luring, moving, plausible, pointed, potent, powerful, seductive, slick, smooth, sound, stimulating, stringent, strong, swaying, telling, touching, unctuous, valid, weighty, wheedling, winning; CONCEPTS 267,537,542 —Ant. dampening, discouraging, disheartening, dissuasive, ineffective, ineffectual

pert [adj] *lively, bold* animated, audacious, brash, brazen, breezy, bright, brisk, cheeky*, dapper, daring, dashing, disrespectful, flip*, flippant, forward, fresh, gay, impertinent, impudent, insolent, jaunty, keen, nervy, perky, presumptuous, sassy*, saucy*, smart, smart-alecky*, spirited, sprightly, vivacious, wise; CONCEPTS 401,404 —Ant. dull, humble, lifeless

pertain [v] *be relevant to* affect, appertain, apply, associate, be appropriate, bear on, befit, belong, be part of, be pertinent, combine, concern, connect, inhere with, join, refer, regard, relate, touch, vest; CONCEPT 532

pertinent [adj] *relevant, suitable* admissible, ad rem, applicable, apposite, appropriate, apropos, apt, connected, fit, fitting, germane, kosher*, legit*, material, on target*, on the button*, on the nose*, opportune, pat*, pertaining, proper, related, right on, to the point, to the purpose; CONCEPT 558 —Ant. inappropriate, irrelevant, unsuitable

perturb [v] *upset, unsettle* agitate, alarm, annoy, bewilder, bother, bug*, confound, confuse, disarrange, discompose, disconcert, discountenance, dismay, disorder, disquiet, disturb, flurry, fluster, irritate, make a scene*, make waves*, muddle, needle, perplex, pester, ruffle, stir up*, trouble, vex, worry; CONCEPTS 7,16,19 —Ant. calm, please, soothe

peruse [v] *check out; examine* analyze, browse, glance over, inspect, look through, pore over, read, scan, scrutinize, skim, study; CONCEPTS 72,103 —Ant. neglect, overlook

pervade [v] *affect strongly; spread through* charge, diffuse, extend, fill, imbue, impregnate, infuse, overspread, penetrate, percolate, permeate, suffuse, transfuse; CONCEPTS 172,179

pervasive [adj] *extensive all over the place*, can't get away from*, common, general, inescapable, omnipresent, permeating, pervading, prevalent, rife, ubiquitous, universal, wall-to-wall*, widespread; CONCEPT 772 —Ant. light, limited, narrow

perverse [adj] *mean, ornery; troublesome* abnormal, bad-tempered, cantankerous, capricious, contradictory, contrary, contumacious, corrupt, crabby*, cross, degenerate, delinquent, depraved, deviant, disobedient, dogged*, erring, fractious, hard-nosed*, headstrong, intractable, intransigent, irritable, miscreant, mulish*, nefarious, obdurate, obstinate, petulant, pigheaded*, rebellious, refractory, rotten*, self-willed, spiteful, stubborn, unhealthy, unmanageable, unreasonable, unyielding, villainous, wayward, wicked, willful; CONCEPTS 401,542,571 —Ant. agreeable, compliant, happy, nice, reasonable, willing

perversion [n] *sexual abnormality* aberration, anomaly, corruption, debauchery, deviance, fetish, immorality, kink*, kinkiness, sexual deviation; CONCEPT 545

pervert [n] *person who lacks morals* debauchee, degenerate, deviant, deviate, freak, weirdo*; CONCEPT 412

pervert [v] *twist, turn away from what is acceptable or correct* abuse, adulterate, alloy, animalize, brainwash, color, corrupt, cut*, debase, debauch, demoralize, deprave, desecrate, distort, divert, doctor, doctor up*, fake, falsify, fudge*, garble, misconstrue, misinterpret, misrepresent, misstate, mistreat, misuse, outrage, phony up*, prostitute, ruin, salt*, seduce, spike,

vitiate, warp, water*; CONCEPTS *14,63,156,252*
—*Ant.* leave alone, straighten

perverted [*adj*] *immoral, evil* abandoned, aberrant, abnormal, abused, contorted, corrupt, corrupted, debased, debauched, defiled, depraved, deviant, deviating, distorted, foreign, grotesque, impaired, kinky*, misguided, misused, monstrous, outraged, polluted, queer, sick, tainted, twisted, unhealthy, unnatural, vicious, vitiate, vitiated, warped, wicked; CONCEPTS *485,545*
—*Ant.* clean, good, healthy, moral

pesky [*adj*] *bothersome* annoying, disturbing, irksome, mean, nettlesome, peeving, provoking, troublesome, ugly, vexatious, vexing, wicked; CONCEPTS *529,537* —*Ant.* pleasing, untroubling

pessimism [*n*] *belief in bad outcome* cynicism, dark side*, dejection, depression, despair, despondency, dim view*, distrust, dyspepsia, expectation of worst, gloom, gloominess, gloomy outlook, glumness, grief, hopelessness, low spirits, melancholy, sadness, unhappiness; CONCEPTS *410,689* —*Ant.* confidence, optimism, trust

pessimist [*n*] *person who expects bad outcome* complainer, crepehanger*, cynic, defeatist, depreciator, downer, gloomy, killjoy*, misanthrope, party pooper*, prophet of doom*, sourpuss*, wet blanket*, worrier, worrywart*; CONCEPTS *412,423* —*Ant.* optimist

pessimistic [*adj*] *expecting bad outcome* bleak, cynical, dark, dejected, depressed, despairing, despondent, discouraged, distrustful, downhearted, fatalistic, foreboding, gloomy, glum, hopeless, melancholy, misanthropic, morbid, morose, resigned, sad, sullen, troubled, worried; CONCEPTS *403,548* —*Ant.* confident, optimistic, trusting

pest [*n*] *person or thing that presents problem* annoyance, badgerer, bane, besetment, blight, blister, bore, bother, botheration, bug*, contagion, crashing bore*, creep, curse, drag, drip, epidemic, exasperation, headache*, infection, irritant, irritation, nag, nuisance, pain*, pain in the neck*, pesterer, pestilence, pill*, plague*, scourge*, tease*, thorn in side*, tormentor, trial*, trouble, vexation, virus*; CONCEPTS *306,398,412,674*

pester [*v*] *bother, harass* annoy, badger, be at, bedevil, beleaguer, bug*, disturb, dog*, drive crazy, drive up the wall*, fret, get at*, get in one's hair*, get on one's nerves*, get to*, harry, hassle, hector, hound, importune, insist, irk, mess with*, nag, nudge, pick at*, plague, provoke, remind, ride*, tantalize, tease, torment, work on*, worry; CONCEPTS *7,19,48* —*Ant.* delight, make happy, please

pestilence [*n*] *epidemic* contagion, disease, endemic, infection, outbreak, plague, rash, scourge, sickness, virus; CONCEPTS *306,316*

pestilent/pestilential [*adj*] *dangerous, harmful* baneful, contagious, contaminating, corrupting, deadly, deleterious, destructive, detrimental, diseased, evil, fatal, infectious, injurious, lethal, mortal, noxious, pernicious, pestiferous, ruinous, tainting, troublesome, vicious; CONCEPTS *314,537* —*Ant.* clean, healthy, hygienic, safe, sanitary

pet [*adj*] *favorite* affectionate, cherished, darling, dear, dearest, endearing, favored, loved, precious, preferred, special; CONCEPTS *568,574* —*Ant.* disfavored, hated

pet [*n*] *favorite thing, person* apple of eye*, beloved, cat, darling, dear, dog, evergreen*, idol, jewel*, love, lover, persona grata*, treasure*; CONCEPTS *394,416*

pet [*v*] *stroke, kiss* baby, caress, coddle, cosset, cuddle, dandle, embrace, fondle, grab, hug, love, make love, neck*, pamper, pat, smooch*, spoil, spoon*, touch; CONCEPTS *375,612*

peter out [*v*] *dwindle, decrease* abate, come to nothing*, die out*, diminish, drain, ebb, evaporate, fade, fail, give out, lessen, pall, rebate, recede, run dry, run out, stop, taper off, wane; CONCEPTS *105,698* —*Ant.* develop, grow, increase

petite [*adj*] *small* baby, bantam, dainty, delicate, diminutive, elfin, little, miniature, minikin*, slight, smallish, tiny, wee*; CONCEPTS *773,779,789* —*Ant.* extra-large, huge, tall

petition [*n*] *appeal, plea* address, application, entreaty, imploration, imprecation, invocation, memorial, prayer, request, round robin, solicitation, suit, supplication; CONCEPTS *271,662*

petition [*v*] *plead, appeal for* adjure, ask, beg, beseech, call upon, entreat, impetrate, implore, pray, press, put in for, request, seek, solicit, sue, supplicate, urge; CONCEPTS *48,53*

petrified [*adj1*] *hardened* calcified, fossilized, frozen, ossified, solidified; CONCEPTS *483,604*

petrified [*adj2*] *terrified* afraid, alarmed, anxious, dazed, fearful, frightened, frozen, have cold feet*, immobilized, in a cold sweat*, in a panic*, numb, panicky, pushing the panic button*, scared, scared stiff*, shocked, speechless, spooked, startled, stunned, terrorized, terror-stricken, unnerved; CONCEPTS *403,690*

petrify [*v1*] *make hard* calcify, clarify, fossilize, harden, lapidify, mineralize, set, solidify, turn to stone; CONCEPT *250* —*Ant.* melt, soften

petrify [*v2*] *frighten* alarm, amaze, appall, astonish, astound, benumb, chill, confound, daze, dismay, dumbfound, horrify, immobilize, numb, paralyze, put chill on*, scare, scare silly*, scare stiff*, spook*, startle, stun, stupefy, terrify, transfix; CONCEPTS *7,14,19,42* —*Ant.* calm, comfort, please, soothe

petroleum [*n*] *oil* crude oil, fossil fuel, fuel, gas, gasoline, kerosene, naphtha, natural gas, petrol; CONCEPTS *467,520,523,661*

petty [*adj*] *trivial, insignificant* base, casual, cheap, contemptible, frivolous, inconsequent, inconsiderable, inessential, inferior, irrelevant, junior, lesser, light, little, lower, measly, minor, narrow-minded, negligible, nickel-and-dime*, niggling*, paltry, peanut*, penny-ante*, pettifogging*, picayune, piddling*, scratch, secondary, shabby, shallow, shoestring*, slight, small, small-minded, subordinate, trifling, two-bit*, unimportant; CONCEPTS *403,575* —*Ant.* consequential, important, major, necessary, prominent, significant, useful

petulant [*adj*] *crabby, moody* bad-tempered, captious, caviling, complaining, cranky*, cross, crybaby*, displeased, fault-finding, fractious, fretful, grouchy, grumbling, huffy, ill-humored, impatient, irritable, mean, peevish, perverse, pouting, querulous, snappish, sour, sulky, sullen, testy, touchy, ungracious, uptight*,

waspish, whining, whiny; CONCEPTS *401,542*
—*Ant.* good-natured, happy, pleasant

phantom [*n*] *ghost; figment of the imagination*
apparition, chimera, daydream, delusion,
dream, eidolon, figment, hallucination, haunt,
ignis fatuus, illusion, mirage, nightmare,
phantasm, revenant, shade, shadow, specter,
spirit, spook, vision, wraith; CONCEPTS *370,
529* —*Ant.* reality

pharmacist [*n*] *druggist* apothecary, pharmacologist; CONCEPT *357*

phase [*n*] *period in life of something* appearance, aspect, chapter, condition, development,
facet, juncture, point, position, posture, stage,
state, step, time; CONCEPTS *816,834*

phenomenal [*adj*] *astounding, exceptional*
extraordinary, fantastic, marvelous, miraculous,
outstanding, preternatural, prodigious, rare,
remarkable, sensational, singular, substantial,
uncommon, unique, unparalleled, unusual, unwonted, wondrous; CONCEPTS *564,574* —*Ant.*
normal, regular, unexceptional

phenomenology [*n*] *study of subject and
objects of a person's experience* intentionality,
life-world, lived experience, meaning-making;
CONCEPTS *282,349*

phenomenon [*n*] *rare occurrence; wonder*
abnormality, actuality, anomaly, appearance,
aspect, circumstance, curiosity, episode, event,
exception, experience, fact, happening, incident,
marvel, miracle, nonpareil, one for the books*,
paradox, peculiarity, portent, prodigy, rara
avis*, rarity, reality, sensation, sight, something
else*, spectacle, stunner*, uniqueness; CONCEPTS
230,529,678 —*Ant.* normality, regularity

philanderer [*n*] *person who has many love
affairs* adulterer, chaser, cruiser, dallier,
debaucher, flirt, gallant, lover, operator*,
swinger; CONCEPT *423* —*Ant.* faithful

philanthropic [*adj*] *charitable, giving* altruistic,
beneficent, benevolent, benignant, big-hearted,
bountiful, contributing, donating, eleemosynary, generous, good, gracious, helpful, humane,
humanitarian, kind, kindhearted, liberal, magnanimous, munificent, openhanded, patriotic,
public- spirited; CONCEPTS *404,542* —*Ant.*
misanthropic, miserly, stingy, uncharitable

philanthropist [*n*] *humanitarian* altruist,
benefactor, bleeding heart*, contributor,
do-gooder*, donor, Good Samaritan*, good
scout*, helper, patron; CONCEPTS *416,423*

philanthropy [*n*] *humanitarianism* alms, alms-
giving, altruism, assistance, benefaction, beneficence, charity, contribution, dole, donation,
endowment, fund, generosity, gifting, good
works, helping hand*; relief; CONCEPTS *337,657*

philosopher [*n*] *deep thinker* logician, sage,
savant, sophist, theorist, wise person; CONCEPTS
349,687,689

philosophical/philosophic [*adj1*] *thinking
deeply, rationally* abstract, cogitative, deep,
erudite, judicious, learned, logical, pensive,
profound, rational, reflective, sagacious, sapient, theoretical, thoughtful, wise; CONCEPT *402*
—*Ant.* irrational, narrow-minded, thoughtless,
unreasonable

philosophical/philosophic [*adj2*] *calm,
serene* collected, commonsensical, composed,
cool*, as cool as cucumber*, enduring, impassive,

imperturbable, patient, resigned, stoical,
tranquil, unagitated, unflappable, unmoved,
unruffled; CONCEPT *401* —*Ant.* excited,
imprudent, rash

philosophy [*n*] *principles, knowledge* aesthet-
ics,attitude, axiom, beliefs, conception,
convictions, doctrine, idea, ideology, logic,
metaphysics, ontology, outlook, rationalism,
reason, reasoning, system, tenet, theory, thinking, thought, truth, values, view, viewpoint,
wisdom; CONCEPTS *349,688,689*

phlegmatic [*adj*] *unemotional* along for the
ride*, apathetic, blah*, cold, cool, deadpan,
desensitized, disinterested, dispassionate, dull,
emotionless, flat, frigid, groggy, indifferent,
lethargic, lifeless, listless, passionless, passive,
sluggish, uncompassionate, undemonstrative,
unexcitable, unfeeling, uninvolved, unresponsive; CONCEPTS *401,403*

phobia [*n*] *fear* anxiety, aversion, avoidance,
awe, detestation, disgust, dislike, distaste, dread,
fear, hang-up*, hatred, horror, irrationality,
loathing, neurosis, obsession, repulsion, resentment, revulsion, terror, thing*, thing about*;
CONCEPTS *27,29,529* —*Ant.* liking, love

phobic [*adj*] *fearful* afraid, anxious, apprehensive, discomposed, disquieted, disturbed,
frightened, have cold feet*, irrational, jittery,
jumpy, nervous, neurotic, panicky, scared,
shy, skittish, tense, worried; CONCEPT *401*

phony [*adj*] *fake, false* affected, artificial,
assumed, bogus, counterfeit, forged, imitation,
pseudo, put-on*, sham*, spurious, trick;
CONCEPT *582* —*Ant.* genuine, real, sincere

photocopy [*n/v*] *mechanical image produced
from a copier; making the image* copy, duplicate, reproduce, stat, velox, Xerox; CONCEPT
269

photograph [*n*] *a still picture taken with a
camera* blowup, close-up, image, Kodachrome*,
Kodak*, likeness, microfilm, mug*, negative,
photo, photostat, pic*, picture, pinup*, pix*,
Polaroid*, portrait, positive, print, shot*, slide,
snap, snapshot, transparency; CONCEPT *265*

photograph [*v*] *take a picture with a camera*
capture*, capture on film*, cinematize, close-
up*, copy, film, get, get a likeness*, get a shot*,
illustrate, lens*, make a picture*, microfilm,
mug*, photo, photoengrave, photostat, picture,
print, record, reproduce, roll, shoot, snap*,
snapshot, take*, turn*, X-ray*; CONCEPT *174*

photographer [*n*] *cameraperson* freelance
photographer, paparazzo, photojournalist,
shutterbug; CONCEPT *352*

photographic [*adj*] *exact, retentive in detail*
accurate, cinematic, detailed, faithful, filmic,
graphic, lifelike, minute, natural, pictorial,
picturesque, precise, realistic, true-to-life*,
visual, vivid; CONCEPT *557*

phrase [*n*] *group of words; way of speaking*
byword, catchphrase, catchword, diction,
expression, idiom, locution, maxim, motto,
parlance, phraseology, phrasing, remark,
saying, shibboleth, slogan, styling, tag, terminology, utterance, verbalism, verbiage, watchword, wordage, wording; CONCEPTS *275,278*

phrase [*v*] *express in words carefully* couch,
formulate, frame, present, put, put into words,
say, term, utter, voice, word; CONCEPT *55*

physical [adj1] *tangible, material* concrete, corporeal, environmental, gross, materialistic, natural, objective, palpable, phenomenal, ponderable, real, sensible, solid, somatic, substantial, visible; CONCEPT 582 —*Ant.* immaterial, mental, spiritual

physical [adj2] *concerning the body* bodily, brute, carnal, corporal, corporeal, earthly, fleshly, incarnate, mortal, personal, somatic, unspiritual, visceral; CONCEPT 485 —*Ant.* mental, psychological

physician [n] *person trained in medical science* bones*, doc*, doctor, general practitioner, healer, intern, MD*, medic, medical practitioner, quack*, sawbones*, specialist, surgeon; CONCEPT 357 —*Ant.* patient

physique [n] *build of human body* anatomy, body, built, character, configuration, corpus, figure, form, frame, habit, habitus, makeup, muscles, nature, shape, structure, type; CONCEPTS 405,757

picayune [adj] *trivial* diminutive, everyday, frivolous, immaterial, incidental, inconsequential, inconsiderable, insignificant, irrelevant, little, meager, mean, meaningless, minor, minute, negligible, nonessential, of no account*, paltry, petty, piddling*, puny, slight, small, superficial, trifling, trite, unimportant; CONCEPT 575

pick [n] *a chosen option, usually the choicest* aces, bag, best, choice, choosing, cream*, crème de la crème*, cup of tea*, decision, druthers*, elect, elite, flower*, preference, pride, prime, prize, select, selection, top, tops; CONCEPTS 529,671 —*Ant.* rejection

pick [v1] *choose, select* cull, decide upon, elect, finger*, fix upon, go down the line*, hand-pick, mark, name, optate, opt for, pick and choose, pick out, prefer, say so, separate, settle on, sift out*, single out, slot, sort out, tab, tag, take, take it or leave it*, tap, winnow; CONCEPT 41 —*Ant.* refuse, reject

pick [v2] *gather, harvest* accumulate, choose, collect, cull, cut, draw, pluck, pull; CONCEPTS 41,109,206 —*Ant.* grow, plant

pick [v3] *break into something closed, locked* break open, crack, dent, force, hit, indent, jimmy, open, pry, strike; CONCEPT 192

pick at/pick on [v] *nag, provoke* badger, bait, blame, bully, carp, cavil, criticize, find fault, foment, get at*, get to*, goad, hector, incite, instigate, quibble, start, tease, torment; CONCEPTS 7,19,52 —*Ant.* compliment, praise

picket [n1] *post of structure* pale, paling, palisade, panel, peg, pillar, rail, stake, stanchion, upright; CONCEPTS 445,479

picket [n2] *person who demonstrates for cause* demonstrator, picketer, protester, striker; CONCEPTS 348,359

picket [n3] *person acting as guard* guard, lookout, patrol, scout, sentinel, sentry, spotter, ward, watch, watchperson; CONCEPT 348

picket [v] *protest against, for cause* blockade, boycott, demonstrate, hit the bricks*, strike, walk out; CONCEPTS 300,351

pickle [n] *sticky situation* bind, box*, corner*, difficulty, dilemma, disorder, fix, hole*, hot water*, jam*, predicament, quandary, scrape, spot*, tight spot*; CONCEPT 674 —*Ant.* boon, pleasure

pickle [v] *preserve fruit or vegetable* can, cure, keep, marinade, salt, souse, steep; CONCEPT 170

pick-me-up [n] *stimulant* analeptic, catalyst, drug, energizer, incentive, motivation, motive, restorative, reviver, shot in the arm*, spark plug*, spur, stimulus, tonic, upper; CONCEPTS 240,307,661

pickpocket [n] *petty thief* bag snatcher, cutpurse, dipper, finger, pocket picker, purse snatcher, sneak thief, thief, wallet lifter; CONCEPT 412

pick up [v1] *lift, raise* elevate, gather, grasp, hoist, rear, take up, uphold, uplift, upraise, uprear; CONCEPT 196 —*Ant.* drop, lower

pick up [v2] *obtain, find* acquire, annex, buy, chalk up*, come across, compass, cull, extract, gain, garner, gather, get, get the hang of*, glean, happen upon*, have, learn, procure, purchase, score, secure, take; CONCEPTS 31,120,183 —*Ant.* have, spend, throw away

pick up [v3] *improve* continue, gain, gain ground*, get better, get well, increase, make a comeback*, mend, perk up*, rally, recommence, recover, renew, reopen, restart, resume, swell, take up; CONCEPTS 234,700 —*Ant.* weaken, worsen

pick up [v4] *call for socially* accompany, collect, drop in for*, get*, give a lift*, go for*, go to get*, invite, offer, proposition, stop for*; CONCEPTS 224,384

pick up [v5] *arrest for crime* apprehend, book*, bust*, collar*, detain, nab, pinch*, pull in*, run in*, take into custody; CONCEPT 317 —*Ant.* free, release

picky [adj] *choosy, finicky* captious, critical, dainty, fastidious, fault-finding, fussy, nice, particular, persnickety; CONCEPT 404 —*Ant.* accepting

picnic [n1] *outdoor meal* barbecue, clambake, cookout, dining alfresco, excursion, fish fry, outing, weiner roast; CONCEPTS 386,459

picnic [n2] *easy undertaking* breeze*, child's play*, cinch, duck soup*, kid stuff*, lark*, light work, no trouble, piece of cake*, pushover*, setup*, smooth sailing*, snap, sure thing, walkover*; CONCEPTS 362,693 —*Ant.* difficulty, drudgery

picture [n1] *illustration, likeness of something* account, art, blueprint, canvas, cartoon, copy, delineation, depiction, description, doodle, double, draft, drawing, duplicate, effigy, engraving, figure, icon, image, impression, lookalike, outline, painting, panorama, photo, photograph, piece, portrait, portrayal, presentment, print, re-creation, replica, report, representation, ringer*, similitude, simulacrum, sketch, spectacle, spitting image*, statue, tableau, twin; CONCEPTS 259,625

picture [n2] *perfect example* archetype, embodiment, epitome, essence, idea, personification; CONCEPT 686

picture [n3] *entertainment film* cartoon, cinema, flick*, motion picture, movie, moving picture, photoplay, picture show, show; CONCEPT 293

picture [v1] *depict, describe* delineate, draw, illustrate, image, interpret, limn, paint, photograph, portray, render, represent, show, sketch; CONCEPTS 79,174

picture [v2] *form vision in one's mind* conceive

of, create, daydream, dream, envision, fancy, fantasize, imagine, portray, see, see in the mind's eye*, visualize; CONCEPTS *17,43*

picturesque [*adj*] *attractive, referring to scenery* arresting, artistic, beautiful, charming, colorful, graphic, photographic, pictorial, pleasant, pretty, quaint, scenic, striking, vivid; CONCEPT *579* —*Ant.* hideous, ugly, unsightly

piddling [*adj*] *insignificant* derisory, little, measly*, niggling*, paltry, peanut*, pettifogging*, petty, picayune, puny, trifling, trivial, unimportant, useless, worthless; CONCEPTS *575,789* —*Ant.* important, major, significant

piddly [*adj*] *meager, trivial* barren, deficient, diddly*, flimsy, inconsiderable, insubstantial, insufficient, little, measly*, mere, microscopic, minute, negligible, paltry, petty, puny, rinkydink*, scant, scrimpy, short, skimpy, slight, small, sparse, superficial, too little too late*, two-bit*, unproductive, worthless; CONCEPTS *546,789*

piece [*n1*] *part* allotment, bit, bite, chunk, cut, division, dole, end, example, fraction, fragment, gob, half, hunk, instance, interest, iota, item, length, lot, lump, member, moiety, morsel, parcel, percentage, portion, quantity, quota, sample, scrap, section, segment, share, shred, slice, smithereen*, specimen; CONCEPTS *834, 835* —*Ant.* whole

piece [*n2*] *work of art, music, writing* arrangement, article, bit, composition, creation, discourse, dissertation, engraving, exposition, icon, item, lines, painting, paper, part, photograph, print, production, sketch, song, statue, study, theme, thesis, treatise, treatment, vignette, work; CONCEPTS *259,262,263,271*

piece [*v*] *put together* assemble, combine, compose, create, fix, join, make, mend, patch, repair, restore, unite; CONCEPTS *113,173,193,251* —*Ant.* divide, separate

piece de resistance [*n1*] *outstanding accomplishment* achievement, chef d'oeuvre, feat, great performance, jewel, magnum opus, masterpiece, master work, prize, showpiece, tour de force*; CONCEPT *259*

piecemeal [*adj/adv*] *bit by bit* at intervals, by degrees, by fits and starts*, fitfully, fragmentary, gradual, gradually, intermittent, intermittently, interrupted, little by little*, partial, partially, patchy, spotty, step by step*; CONCEPTS *531,544* —*Ant.* all, completely, totally, wholly

pier [*n*] *support; place for boats* berth, buttress, column, dam, dock, jetty, landing, levee, mole, pierage, pilaster, pile, piling, pillar, post, promenade, quay, slip, upright, wharf; CONCEPTS *439,443,479*

pierce [*v*] *cut, penetrate* bore, break, break in, break through, cleave, crack, crack open, drill, enter, gash, incise, intrude, pass through, perforate, plow, prick, probe, puncture, run through, slash, slice, slit, spike, stab, stick into, transfix; CONCEPTS *137,159,176,220* —*Ant.* sew up

piercing [*adj*] *intense to the senses* acute, agonizing, arctic, biting, bitter, blaring, cold, deafening, earsplitting, excruciating, exquisite, fierce, freezing, frosty, high, high-pitched, keen, knifelike, loud, numbing, painful, penetrating, powerful, racking, raw, roaring, severe, sharp,

shattering, shooting, shrill, stabbing, stentorian, stentorious, thin, treble, wintry; CONCEPTS *406, 537,592,594* —*Ant.* low, soft, weak

piety [*n*] *devotion, religiousness* allegiance, application, ardor, belief, devoutness, docility, dutifulness, duty, faith, fealty, fervor, fidelity, godliness, grace, holiness, loyalty, obedience, passion, religion, religiosity, reverence, sanctity, veneration, zeal; CONCEPTS *633,689* —*Ant.* impiety, irreverence

piffle [*n*] *nonsense* balderdash*, baloney*, bull*, bunk*, drivel, empty talk, foolishness, futile talk, gibberish, hogwash*, hooey*, hot air*, jive*, palaver, poppycock*, prattle, rubbish, silliness, trash*, useless words; CONCEPTS *230, 388,633*

pig [*n*] *animal of swine family* boar, cob roller*, hog, piggy*, piglet, porker*, porky, shoat, sow, swine; CONCEPTS *394,400*

pigeonhole [*n*] *compartment* box, carrel, chamber, corner, cranny, cubbyhole, cubicle, hole, niche, nook, place, pocket, recess, section, slot, stall; CONCEPT *434*

pigeonhole [*v*] *categorize; shelve* assort, class, classify, defer, dismiss, file, group, hold, hold off, hold up, label, lay aside, peg*, postpone, put aside, put down as, put off, put on hold, put on ice*, put on the back burner*, rank, sideline, sort, tab, table, type cast; CONCEPTS *39,121*

pigheaded [*adj*] *stubborn* bullheaded, contrary, dense*, forward, headstrong, inflexible, insistent, intractable, mulish*, obstinate, perverse, recalcitrant, self-willed, stiff-necked, stupid*, unyielding, willful; CONCEPTS *404,542* —*Ant.* flexible, reasonable, submissive, willing

pigment [*n*] *color, shade* colorant, coloring, coloring matter, dye, dyestuff, oil, paint, stain, tincture, tint; CONCEPTS *259,622* —*Ant.* colorlessness

pig out [*v*] *overeat* binge, blimp out*, devour, dive in*, eat like a horse*, eat to excess, feed, gluttonize, gobble, gorge, gormandize, gulp, guzzle, hoover*, overindulge, pork out*, scarf out*, shovel it in*, stuff oneself, wolf*; CONCEPT *169*

pile [*n1*] *heap, collection* accumulation, aggregate, aggregation, amassment, assemblage, assortment, bank, barrel, buildup, chunk, conglomeration, drift, gob, great deal, hill, hoard, hunk, jumble, lump, mass, mound, mountain, much, ocean, oodles*, pack, peck, pyramid, quantity, shock, stack, stockpile; CONCEPTS *432,787* —*Ant.* ditch, hole

pile [*n2*] *wealth* affluence, boodle*, bundle*, dough*, fortune, mint*, money, pot*, riches, wad*; CONCEPTS *335,340* —*Ant.* poverty

pile [*v*] *gather, pack; put on top of another* accumulate, amass, assemble, bank, bunch, collect, crowd, crush, fill, flock, heap, hill, hoard, jam, load, mass, mound, rush, stack, store; CONCEPTS *84,109,201,750* —*Ant.* dissipate, scatter, separate

pilfer [*v*] *steal, embezzle* annex, appropriate, borrow, cop*, crib*, filch*, liberate*, lift*, moonlight*, palm*, pinch*, pluck*, purloin, requisition, rip off*, rob, scrounge, snare, snatch, swipe, take, thieve, walk off with*; CONCEPTS *139,142,192* —*Ant.* give, receive

ph
pi

pilgrimage [n] *long journey* crusade, excursion, expedition, mission, tour, travel, trip, wayfaring; CONCEPT 224 —*Ant.* jaunt

pill [n1] *capsule of medicine* bolus, dose, lozenge, medicine, pellet, pilule, tablet, troche; CONCEPTS 307,470

pill [n2] *person who is annoying* bore, drag*, nuisance, pain*, pain in the neck*, pest, trial*; CONCEPTS 412,423

pillage [v] *plunder, destroy* appropriate, arrogate, confiscate, depredate, desecrate, desolate, despoil, devastate, devour, gut, invade, lay waste*, lift*, loot, maraud, nab*, pilfer, pinch*, purloin, raid, ransack, ravage, rifle*, rob, ruin, sack, spoil, spoliate, steal, strip, thieve, trespass, waste; CONCEPTS 86,139,252 —*Ant.* protect, safeguard

pillar [n1] *column of building, or freestanding column* colonnade, mast, obelisk, pedestal, pier, pilaster, piling, post, prop, shaft, stanchion, support, tower, upright; CONCEPT 440

pillar [n2] *mainstay; source of strength* backbone*, guider, leader, light*, rock*, sinew, supporter, tower of strength*, upholder, worthy; CONCEPTS 423,712

pilot [n] *person who guides aircraft, ship, or other vehicle* ace*, aerialist, aeronaut, aviator, bellwether*, captain, conductor, coxswain, dean, director, doyen/doyenne, eagle*, flier*, flyer, guide, helmsperson, jockey*, lead, leader, navigator, one at the controls, one at the wheel, scout*, steerer, steersperson, wheelperson; CONCEPT 348

pimple [n] *small swelling on the skin* abscess, acne, beauty spot, blackhead, blemish, blister, boil, bump, carbuncle, caruncle, excrescence, furuncle, hickey*, inflammation, lump, papula, papule, pustule, spot, whitehead, zit*; CONCEPT 306

pin [v] *attach, hold in place* affix, bind, clasp, close, fasten, fix, hold down, hold fast, immobilize, join, pinion, press, restrain, secure; CONCEPTS 85,160,190 —*Ant.* detach, unfasten, unlatch, unpin

pinch [n1] *tight pressing* compression, confinement, contraction, cramp, grasp, grasping, hurt, limitation, nip, nipping, pressure, squeeze, torment, tweak, twinge; CONCEPT 728

pinch [n2] *small amount* bit, dash, drop, jot, mite, small quantity, soupçon, speck, splash, splatter, taste; CONCEPT 831 —*Ant.* lot

pinch [n3] *predicament* box*, clutch, contingency, crisis, crunch*, difficulty, emergency, exigency, hardship, juncture, necessity, oppression, pass, plight, pressure, strait, stress, tight spot*, tight squeeze*, turning point*, zero hour*; CONCEPT 674 —*Ant.* advantage, blessing, good fortune

pinch [v1] *press tightly* chafe, compress, confine, cramp, crush, grasp, hurt, nip, pain, squeeze, tweak, twinge, wrench, wrest, wring; CONCEPTS 219,313

pinch [v2] *be stingy* afflict, distress, economize, oppress, pinch pennies*, press, scrape, scrimp, skimp, spare, stint; CONCEPT 330 —*Ant.* be generous, give, offer

pinch [v3] *steal* cop*, crib*, filch*, knock off*, lift*, nab*, pilfer, purloin, rob, snatch, swipe, take; CONCEPT 139 —*Ant.* give, receive

pinch [v4] *arrest* apprehend, bust*, collar*, detain, hold, nab*, pick up*, pull in*, run in*, take into custody; CONCEPTS 90,317 —*Ant.* free, release

pine [v] *long for* ache, agonize, brood, carry a torch*, covet, crave, desire, dream, fret, grieve, hanker, languish for, lust after, mope*, mourn, sigh, spoil for*, thirst for, want, wish, yearn, yen for; CONCEPT 20 —*Ant.* despise, dislike, hate

pink [n1/adj] *rose color* blush, coral, flush, fuchsia, rose, roseate, salmon; CONCEPT 622

pink [n2] *best condition* acme*, best, bloom*, fitness, good health, height*, peak, perfection, prime, summit, trim*; verdure; CONCEPTS 316,388 —*Ant.* poor health, sickness

pink [v] *cut in zigzag* incise, notch, perforate, prick, punch, scallop, score; CONCEPT 176

pinnacle [n] *top, crest* acme, apex, apogee, climax, cone, crown, culmination, greatest, height, max*, most*, needle*, obelisk, peak, pyramid, spire, steeple, summit, tops, tower, vertex, zenith; CONCEPTS 706,836 —*Ant.* base, bottom, nadir

pinpoint [v] *define, locate* determinate, diagnose, distinguish, finger*, get a fix on*, home in on*, identify, place, recognize, spot; CONCEPTS 38,183 —*Ant.* be ambiguous, lose

pioneer [adj] *early, first* avant-garde, brave, experimental, head, inaugural, initial, lead, original, primary, prime; CONCEPT 585 —*Ant.* following, last, late, later

pioneer [n] *person who finds a new place, founds something* colonist, colonizer, developer, explorer, founder, frontier settler, guide, homesteader, immigrant, innovator, leader, pathfinder, pilgrim, scout, settler, squatter, trailblazer; CONCEPTS 348,413

pioneer [v] *invent; lay the groundwork* begin, colonize, create, develop, discover, establish, explore, found, go out in front*, initiate, instigate, institute, launch, map out, open up, originate, prepare, show the way, spearhead*, start, take the lead, trailblaze*; CONCEPTS 173, 221,324

pious [adj] *dedicated, religious* born-again*, clerical, devoted, devout, divine, ecclesiastical, godly, goody-goody*, orthodox, prayerful, priestly, reverent, righteous, sacred, saintly, sanctimonious, spiritual; CONCEPT 401 —*Ant.* atheist, impious, irreligious, sinful, wicked

pipe [n] *passage, tube* aqueduct, canal, channel, conduit, conveyer, duct, hose, line, main, pipeline, sewer, spout, trough, vent, vessel; CONCEPTS 475,499

pipe [v1] *conduct through tube, passage* bring in, carry, channel, convey, funnel, siphon, supply, traject, transmit; CONCEPT 217

pipe [v2] *make a sound; peep* blubber*, boohoo*, cheep*, cry, play, say, shout, sing, sob, sound, speak, talk, toot*, trill, tweet, twitter, wail, warble, weep, whistle; CONCEPTS 47,65,77

pipe dream [n] *fantasy* air castle, airy hope, castle in the sky*, chimera, daydream, fantastic notion, fool's paradise*, unreal hope, wishful thinking; CONCEPTS 20,529,689

pipsqueak [n] *nonentity* nobody, runt, shrimp, squirt, twerp, whippersnapper; CONCEPT 424

piquant [adj] *flavorful, biting* highly-seasoned,

interesting, lively, peppery, poignant, provocative, pungent, racy, savory, sharp, snappy, sparkling, spicy, spirited, stimulating, stinging, tangy, tart, well-flavored, with a kick*, zestful, zesty; CONCEPTS 529,613 —*Ant.* bland, dull

pique [n] *anger, irritation* annoyance, blowup*, conniption*, dander*, displeasure, flare-up, grudge, huff, hurt, irk, miff*, offense, peeve, pet*, provocation, resentment, rise, ruckus*, slow burn*, snit, sore*, stew*, storm*, tiff*, umbrage, vexation; CONCEPTS 29,410 —*Ant.* cheer, happiness, joy

pique [v] *offend, provoke* absorb, affront, annoy, arouse, bother, bug*, displease, egg on*, exasperate, excite, fire up*, gall, galvanize, get*, get a rise out of*, get under skin*, give a hard time*, give the business*, goad, goose*, grab, ignite, incense, irk, irritate, kindle, make waves*, miff*, mortify, motivate, move, nettle, offend, peeve, prick, put out*, quicken, rile, rouse, spur, stimulate, sting*, stir, vex, whet, work up*, wound; CONCEPTS 7,14,19,22 —*Ant.* delight, please

piracy [n] *robbery* bootlegging, buccaneering, commandeering, copying, freebooting, hijacking, infringement, marauding, pirating, plagiarism, rapine, stealing, swashbuckling, theft; CONCEPTS 139,192

pirate [n] *buccaneer* corsair, filibuster, freebooter, marauder, picaroon, privateer, raider, rover, sea rover; CONCEPT 412

pissed off [adj] *angry* affronted, annoyed, bent out of shape*, boiling*, cross, displeased, enraged, fighting mad*, fit to be tied*, fuming, furious, hopping mad*, hot, huffy*, in a tizzy*, incensed, inflamed, infuriated, irate, irritated, livid, mad, maddened, offended, outraged, peed*, peeved off*, provoked, raging, riled, sore, steamed, steamed up*, steaming, storming, t'd off*, tee'd off*, ticked off*; CONCEPT 403

pistol [n] *revolver* firearm, forty-five*, gun, handgun, piece*, rod*, Saturday night special*, six-shooter, thirty-eight*; CONCEPT 500

pit [n] *hole, cavity* abyss, chasm, crater, dent, depression, dimple, excavation, grave, gulf, hell, hollow, indentation, mine, perforation, pockmark, pothole, puncture, shaft, tomb, trench, well; CONCEPTS 509,513 —*Ant.* mountain

pit [v] *oppose, play off* contend, counter, match, put in opposition, set against, vie; CONCEPTS 92,363 —*Ant.* agree, go along

pitch [n1] *tilt* angle, cant, degree, dip, gradient, height, incline, level, point, slant, slope, steepness; CONCEPTS 692,738

pitch [n2] *tone of sound* frequency, harmonic, modulation, rate, sound, timbre; CONCEPT 65

pitch [n3] *talk to convince* patter*, persuasion, sales talk, song and dance*, spiel*; CONCEPTS 68,278

pitch [v1] *throw, hurl* bung, cast, chuck*, fire, fling, gun, heave, launch, lob, peg, sling, toss, unseat; CONCEPT 222

pitch [v2] *put up, erect* fix, locate, place, plant, raise, settle, set up, station; CONCEPT 168 —*Ant.* destroy, raze

pitch [v3] *dive, roll* ascend, bend, bicker, careen, descend, dip, drive, drop, fall, flounder, go down, heave, lean, lunge, lurch, plunge, rise, rock, seesaw, slope, slump, stagger, tilt, topple,

toss, tumble, vault, wallow, welter, yaw; CONCEPTS 147,181,201

pitcher [n1] *jug* amphora, bottle, canteen, carafe, container, crock, cruet, decanter, ewer, flagon, flask, jar, vase, vessel; CONCEPT 494

pitcher [n2] *baseball pitcher* ace*, baseball player, closer, hurler, knuckleballer, middle reliever, reliever; CONCEPT 366

pitch in [v] *help; get busy* aid, attack, begin, buckle down*, chip in*, come through, commence, contribute, cooperate, do, do one's bit*, fall to*, get cracking*, get going, go to it*, hop to it*, join in, jump in*, launch, lend a hand*, participate, plunge into*, set about, set to, subscribe, tackle, tee off*, volunteer, wade in; CONCEPTS 100,110 —*Ant.* hinder, prevent

piteous [adj] *miserable, pathetic* beseeching, commiserable, deplorable, distressing, doleful, dolorous, entreating, grievous, heartbreaking, heartrending, imploring, lamentable, melancholy, mournful, moving, pitiable, pitiful, plaintive, poignant, poor, rueful, ruined, sad, sorrowful, supplicating, woeful, wretched; CONCEPTS 485,529 —*Ant.* cheerful, happy

pitfall [n] *hazard, trap* booby trap*, catch*, danger, deadfall*, difficulty, downfall, drawback, entanglement, hook*, mesh*, mousetrap*, peril, pit*, quicksand*, risk, setup*, snag*, snare, swindle*, toil, web; CONCEPTS 674,679 —*Ant.* advantage, blessing, good luck

pithy [adj] *brief, to the point* cogent, compact, concise, crisp, curt, down to brass tacks*, effective, epigrammatic, expressive, honed, laconic, meaningful, meaty*, pointed, short, short-and-sweet*, significant, succinct, terse, trenchant; CONCEPT 267 —*Ant.* long-winded, verbose, wordy

pitiful [adj] *in bad shape; poor* abject, affecting, afflicted, arousing, base, beggarly, cheap, cheerless, comfortless, commiserative, compassionate, contemptible, deplorable, despicable, dismal, distressed, distressing, grievous, heartbreaking, heartrending, inadequate, insignificant, joyless, lamentable, low, mean, miserable, mournful, moving, paltry, pathetic, piteous, pitiable, sad, scurvy, shabby, sorrowful, sorry, stirring, suffering, tearful, touching, vile, woeful, worthless, wretched; CONCEPTS 485,529 —*Ant.* excellent, happy, superb, superior, wonderful, worthwhile

pitiless [adj] *without mercy or care* austere, barbarous, brutal, callous, cold*, coldblooded*, coldhearted*, cruel, cutthroat*, dog-eat-dog*, frigid, hardhearted*, harsh, hatchetjob*, heartless, implacable, indifferent, inexorable, inhuman, inhumane, insensible, killer instinct*, mean, merciless, obdurate, relentless, remorseless, ruthless, satanic, savage, soulless*, stony*; CONCEPT 401 —*Ant.* charitable, kind, merciful, sympathetic

pittance [n] *small amount* allowance, bit, chicken feed*, dribble*, drop*, drop in the bucket*, inadequacy, insufficiency, mite, modicum, peanuts*, pension, portion, ration, scrap*, slave wages*, smidgen, trace, trifle; CONCEPTS 344,787 —*Ant.* generosity, lot, plenty

pity [n1] *feeling of mercy toward another* benevolence, charity, clemency, comfort, commiseration, compassion, compunction, condolement, condolence, dejection, distress, empathy, favor, forbearance, goodness, grace, humanity, kindliness, kindness, lenity, melancholy, mercy, philanthropy, quarter, rue, ruth, sadness, solace, sorrow, sympathy, tenderness, understanding, warmth; CONCEPTS 410,657 —*Ant.* disdain, malevolence, mercilessness

pity [n2] *sad situation* bad luck, catastrophe, crime, crisis, crying shame*, disaster, mischance, misfortune, mishap, regret, shame, sin; CONCEPT 674 —*Ant.* advantage, blessing, good fortune

pity [v] *feel sorry for; spare* ache*, be sorry for, be sympathetic, bleed for*, comfort, commiserate, condole, console, feel for, feel with, forgive, give quarter*, grant amnesty, grieve with, have compassion, have mercy on, identify with, lament with, pardon, put out of one's misery*, relent, reprieve, show forgiveness*, show sympathy*, solace, soothe, sympathize, take pity on*, understand, weep for*; CONCEPTS 10, 34,83 —*Ant.* disdain, scorn

pivot [n] *center point about which something revolves* axis, axle, center, focal point, fulcrum, heart, hinge, hub, kingpin, shaft, spindle, swivel, turning point; CONCEPTS 445,464,498,830 —*Ant.* exterior, exteriority, outside

pivot [v] *revolve around center point* be contingent, depend, hang, hinge, rely, rotate, sheer, spin, swivel, turn, twirl, veer, volte-face, wheel, whip, whirl; CONCEPTS 147,532

pivotal [adj] *important* cardinal, central, climactic, critical, crucial, decisive, determining, essential, focal, middle, momentous, overriding, overruling, principal, ruling, vital; CONCEPT 568 —*Ant.* inconsequential, unimportant, unsubstantial

pixie [n] *fairy* bogie, brownie, elf, fay, gnome, goblin, gremlin, hob, imp, leprechaun, nisse, puck, spirit, sprite; CONCEPT 370

pizzazz [n] *energy; flamboyance* ability, animation, aptitude, bounce, dash, drive, effectiveness, élan, fire, force, forcefulness, get-up-and-go*, gift, hustle, intensity, juice, knack, life, liveliness, moxie*, muscle, oomph*, panache, pep, pluck, potency, power, presence, punch, push, shine*, spirit, splash*, spunk, stamina, vim, virility, vitality, vivacity, zeal, zest, zing, zip*; CONCEPTS 411,630,706

placard [n] *sign, notice* advertisement, announcement, banner, bill, billboard, handbill, marquee, poster, public notice, signboard; CONCEPTS 271,284

placate [v] *soothe, pacify* appease, assuage, calm, cheer, comfort, conciliate, humor, make peace*, make up*, mollify, pacify, play up to*, pour oil on*, propitiate, reconcile, satisfy, softpedal*, soothe, stroke*, sweeten, tranquilize, win over*; CONCEPTS 7,22,126 —*Ant.* agitate, upset, worry

place [n1] *location with purpose, function* abode, accommodation, apartment, area, berth, city, community, compass, corner, country, distance, district, domicile, dwelling, field, habitat, hamlet, hangout, hole*, home, house, joint, latitude, lay, locale, locality, locus, longitude, neighborhood, niche, nook, pad*, part, plant, point, position, property, quarter, region, reservation, residence, room, seat, section, site, situation, spot, station, stead, suburb, town, venue, vicinity, village, volume, whereabouts, zone; CONCEPTS 435,515

place [n2] *position, rank* capacity, character, footing, grade, pecking order*, slot, standing, state, station, status; CONCEPT 388

place [n3] *job, employment* appointment, berth, connection, occupation, office, position, post, profession, situation, spot, trade; CONCEPT 360 —*Ant.* unemployment

place [n4] *duty, role* affair, charge, concern, function, prerogative, responsibility, right; CONCEPT 532

place [v1] *locate, situate* allocate, allot, assign, deposit, distribute, establish, finger, fix, install, lay, lodge, nail, park, peg, plant, position, put, quarter, repose, rest, set, settle, spot, stand, station, stick, store, stow; CONCEPT 201 —*Ant.* dislodge, displace, empty, lose, misplace, remove

place [v2] *order, sort* allocate, appoint, approximate, arrange, assign, call, charge, class, classify, commission, constitute, delegate, deputize, designate, entrust, estimate, fix, give, grade, group, judge, name, nominate, ordain, put, rank, reckon; CONCEPTS 50,84,88,98 —*Ant.* disarrange, discompose, disorder

place [v3] *identify, recognize* associate, determinate, determine, diagnose, distinguish, figure out*, finger*, indicate, know, nail*, peg*, pinpoint, put one's finger on*, remember, set in context, spot, tell; CONCEPT 38 —*Ant.* forget, overlook

placebo [n] *fake pill* inactive drug, inactive medicine, inactive substance, sugar pill, test substance; CONCEPTS 260,412

placid [adj] *calm, mild* collected, composed, cool*, cool as a cucumber*, detached, easygoing, equable, even, even-tempered, gentle, halcyon, hushed, imperturbable, irenic, peaceful, poised, quiet, restful, self-possessed, serene, still, tranquil; CONCEPTS 401,485 —*Ant.* agitated, excited

plagiarism [n] *copying of another's written work* appropriation, borrowing, counterfeiting, cribbing, falsification, fraud, infringement, lifting, literary theft, piracy, stealing, theft; CONCEPTS 139,192 —*Ant.* original, originality

plague [n1] *disease that is widespread* affliction, contagion, curse, epidemic, hydra, infection, infestation, influenza, invasion, outbreak, pandemic, pestilence, rash, ravage, scourge; CONCEPT 306

plague [n2] *annoyance, curse* affliction, aggravation, bane, besetment, blast, blight, bother, botheration, calamity, cancer, evil, exasperation, hydra, irritant, nuisance, pain, pest, problem, scourge, thorn in side, torment, trial, vexation; CONCEPTS 674,679 —*Ant.* advantage, good fortune, good luck

plague [v] *annoy, disturb* afflict, badger, bedevil, beleaguer, bother, chafe, fret, gall, gnaw, harass, harry, hassle, haunt, hector, hound, infest, irk, molest, pain, persecute, pester, pursue, ride, tease, torment, torture, trouble, vex, worry; CONCEPTS 7,14,19 —*Ant.* aid, assist, help, please

plaid [adj] *checkered* checked, tartan, variegated; CONCEPTS 259,625

plain [*adj1*] *clear, obvious* apparent, audible, big as life*, broad, comprehensible, definite, distinct, evident, legible, lucid, manifest, open, open-and-shut*, palpable, patent, talking turkey*, transparent, understandable, visible; CONCEPTS 529,535,576 —*Ant.* complex, complicated, hidden, intricate, obscured, unclear, vague

plain [*adj2*] *straightforward in speech* abrupt, artless, blunt, candid, direct, forthright, frank, guileless, honest, impolite, ingenuous, open, outspoken, rude, sincere; CONCEPT 267 —*Ant.* abstruse, ambiguous, incomprehensible, imperceptible, obscure, unclear, vague

plain [*adj3*] *normal, everyday* average, common, commonplace, conventional, dull, homely, lowly, modest, ordinary, quotidian, routine, simple, traditional, usual, vanilla*, white-bread*, workaday; CONCEPT 547 —*Ant.* abnormal, complex, difficult, extraordinary, uncommon

plain [*adj4*] *unembellished, basic* austere, bare, bare bones*, clean, discreet, dry, modest, muted, pure, restrained, severe, simple, spartan, stark, stripped down, unvarnished, vanilla*; CONCEPTS 485,589 —*Ant.* decorated, dressed-up, embellished, formal, ornate

plain [*adj5*] *ugly* deformed, hard on the eyes*, homely, not beautiful, ordinary, plain-featured; CONCEPT 579 —*Ant.* attractive, beautiful, pretty

plain [*n*] *level land* champaign, expanse, field, flat, flatland, grassland, heath, level, meadow, moor, moorland, open country, plateau, prairie, steppe, tundra; CONCEPT 509

plaintive [*adj*] *pathetic, woebegone* beefing*, bellyaching*, cantankerous, crabby*, cranky*, disconsolate, doleful, grief-stricken, grievous, grousing, grumpy*, heartrending, lamenting, lugubrious, melancholy, mournful, out of sorts*, pathetic, piteous, pitiful, rueful, sad, saddening, sorrowful, wailing, wistful, woeful; CONCEPTS 401,529 —*Ant.* cheerful, happy

plan [*n1*] *scheme, design, way of doing things* aim, angle, animus, arrangement, big picture*, contrivance, course of action, deal, device, disposition, expedient, game plan, gimmick, ground plan, idea, intent, intention, layout, machination, meaning, means, method, orderliness, outline, pattern, picture, platform, plot, policy, procedure, program, project, projection, proposal, proposition, purpose, scenario, stratagem, strategy, suggestion, system, tactics, treatment, trick, undertaking; CONCEPT 660

plan [*n2*] *written description; diagram* agenda, agendum, blueprint, chart, delineation, draft, drawing, form, illustration, layout, map, projection, prospectus, representation, road map, rough draft, scale drawing, sketch, time line, view; CONCEPTS 268,271,625

plan [*v1*] *think out; prepare in advance* arrange, bargain for, block out, blueprint, brainstorm*, calculate, concoct, conspire, contemplate, contrive, cook up*, craft, design, devise, draft, engineer, figure on, figure out, fix to, form, formulate, frame, hatch*, intrigue, invent, lay in provisions, line up*, make arrangements, map, meditate, organize, outline, plot, project, quarterback*, ready, reckon on, represent, rough in*, scheme, set out, shape, sketch, steer, trace, work out; CONCEPT 36 —*Ant.* forget, ignore, neglect

plan [*v2*] *intend, mean* aim, bargain for*, contemplate, count on, design, envisage, foresee, have every intention*, mind, propose, purpose, reckon on*; CONCEPTS 26,35

plane [*adj*] *level, horizontal* even, flat, flush, plain, planate, regular, smooth, uniform; CONCEPTS 490,581 —*Ant.* upright, vertical

plane [*n1*] *flat surface; level* condition, degree, extension, face, facet, footing, grade, horizontal, obverse, position, sphere, stratum; CONCEPTS 744,757

plane [*n2*] *aircraft* airbus, airplane, airship, bird*, craft, crate, jet, ship, twin-engine; CONCEPT 504

planet [*n*] *celestial body orbiting a star* apple*, asteroid, earth, globe, heavenly body, luminous body, marble, orb*, planetoid, sphere, terrene, wandering star*, world; CONCEPT 511

plant [*n1*] *organism belonging to the vegetable kingdom* annual, biennial, bush, creeper*, cutting*, flower, grass, greenery, herb, perennial, seedling, shoot, shrub, slip, sprout, tree, vine, weed; CONCEPT 429 —*Ant.* animal

plant [*n2*] *factory and its buildings, equipment* apparatus, forge, foundry, gear, machinery, manufactory, mill, shop, works, yard; CONCEPTS 439,449,463,496

plant [*v1*] *put in the ground for growing* bury, cover, farm, grow, implant, pitch, pot, raise, scatter, seed, seed down, set out, sow, start, stock, transplant; CONCEPTS 178,253 —*Ant.* harvest, reap

plant [*v2*] *establish, set* deposit, fix, found, imbed, insert, install, institute, lodge, park, plank, plank down, plop, plunk, root, settle, station; CONCEPTS 18,201,221 —*Ant.* disestablish, disorder, disorganize, unsettle, upset

plantation [*n*] *large farm* estate, hacienda, homestead, orchard, ranch, vineyard; CONCEPTS 258,449,509,517

plaster [*n*] *thick, gooey material that hardens* adhesive, binding, cement, coat, dressing, glue, gum, gypsum, lime, mortar, mucilage, paste, plaster of Paris, stucco; CONCEPTS 466,475

plaster [*v*] *spread, smear* adhere, bedaub, besmear, bind, cement, coat, cover, daub, glue, gum, overlay, paste, smudge; CONCEPT 202

plastered [*adj*] *drunk* bashed, blitzed*, bombed*, boozed up*, buzzed*, crocked*, dead drunk*, dead to the world*, drinking, drunk as a skunk*, drunken, feeling good*, feeling no pain*, flushed*, flying*, fried*, gone*, groggy, half-crocked*, half in the bag*, high*, hooched up*, inebriated, juiced*, liquored up*, lit*, loaded*, pissed*, polluted*, potted*, sauced*, schnockered*, seeing double*, sloshed*, stewed*, stoned*, tanked*, three sheets to the wind*, tipsy, totaled*, under the influence, under the table*, wasted*, woozy*, zonked*; CONCEPTS 314,545

plastic [*adj1*] *flexible, soft; made of manufactured, treated compounds* bending, ductile, elastic, fictile, formable, moldable, molded, pliable, pliant, resilient, shapeable, supple, workable; CONCEPT 604 —*Ant.* hard, inflexible, stiff

plastic [*adj2*] *easily influenced* amenable, bending, compliant, docile, ductile, flexible, giving, impressionable, influenceable, malleable, manageable, moldable, pliable, pliant,

receptive, responsive, suggestible, supple, susceptible, tractable, yielding; CONCEPT 542
—*Ant.* inflexible, unflappable

plastic [*adj3*] *artificial; made of manufactured compounds* cast, chemical, ersatz, false, manufactured, phony, pseudo*, substitute, synthetic, unnatural; CONCEPT 582

plastic surgery [*n*] *cosmetic surgery* blepharoplasty, breast implant, breast reduction, collagen injections, dermabrasion, dermatoplasty, eyelift, face-lift, face-lifting, liposuction, mammaplasty, mammoplasty, nose job, reconstructive surgery, rhinoplasty, skin grafting, suction lipectomy, tummy tuck; CONCEPT 310

plate [*n1*] *dish or meal served* bowl, casserole, course, helping, platter, portion, service, serving, trencher; CONCEPTS 459,493

plate [*n2*] *sheet, panel* coat, disc, flake, foil, lamella, lamina, layer, leaf, plane, print, scale, slab, slice, spangle, stratum; CONCEPT 475

plate [*v*] *coat with metallic material* anodize, bronze, chrome, cover, electroplate, enamel, encrust, face, flake, foil, gild, laminate, layer, nickel, overlay, platinize, scale, silver, stratify; CONCEPTS 172,202

plateau [*n*] *level; flat, often high, land* elevation, highland, mesa, plain, stage, table, tableland, upland; CONCEPTS 509,744

platform [*n1*] *stand or stage* belvedere, dais, floor, podium, pulpit, rostrum, scaffold, scaffolding, staging, terrace; CONCEPTS 440,443

platform [*n2*] *political stance, promises* manifesto, objectives, party line*, plank, policy, principle, program, soapbox*, stump*, tenets; CONCEPTS 278,689

platitude [*n*] *dull, overused saying* banality, boiler plate*, bromide*, buzzword, chestnut*, cliché, commonplace, corn*, evenness, familiar tune*, flatness, hackneyed saying, high camp*, hokum*, inanity, insipidity, monotony, motto, old chestnut*, old story*, potboiler*, prosaicism, proverb, saw*, shibboleth, stereotype, tag*, triteness, trite remark, triviality, truism, vapidity, verbiage; CONCEPTS 278,388 —*Ant.* coinage, nuance

platonic [*adj*] *expressing nonphysical love* ideal, idealistic, intellectual, quixotic, spiritual, transcendent, Utopian, visionary; CONCEPTS 403,555 —*Ant.* physical

platoon [*n*] *group of military people* army, array, batch, battery, bunch, clump, cluster, company, detachment, lot, outfit, parcel, patrol, set, squad, squadron, team, troop, unit; CONCEPTS 322,417

plaudits [*n*] *applause* acclaim, acclamation, accolade, big hand, cheering, cheers, clapping, commendation, hand, hurrahs, kudos, laudation, ovation, praise, raves, rooting, stamping, standing ovation; CONCEPTS 69,189

plausible [*adj*] *reasonable, believable* conceivable, credible, creditable, like enough*, likely, logical, persuasive, possible, presumable, probable, smooth, sound, supposable, tenable, valid, very likely; CONCEPT 552 —*Ant.* implausible, improbable, unbelievable, unlikely, unreasonable

play [*n1*] *theater piece* comedy, curtain-raiser*, drama, entertainment, farce, flop*, hit*, mask*, musical, one-act*, opera, performance, pot-

boiler*, show, smash*, smash hit*, stage show, theatrical, tragedy, turkey*; CONCEPT 263

play [*n2*] *amusement, entertainment* caper, dalliance, delight, disport, diversion, foolery, frisk, frolic, fun, gambol, game, gaming, happiness, humor, jest, joking, lark, match, pastime, pleasure, prank, recreation, relaxation, romp, sport, sportiveness, teasing; CONCEPTS 292,363 —*Ant.* work

play [*n3*] *latitude, range* action, activity, elbowroom*, exercise, give, leeway, margin, motion, movement, operation, room, scope, space, sweep, swing, working*; CONCEPTS 651,745 —*Ant.* extreme

play [*v1*] *have fun* amuse oneself, be life of party*, caper, carouse, carry on, cavort, clown, cut capers, cut up*, dally, dance, disport, divert, entertain oneself, fool around, frisk, frolic, gambol, go on a spree*, horse around*, idle away, joke, jump, kibitz*, kick up heels*, let go*, let loose*, let one's hair down*, make merry, mess around*, rejoice, revel, romp, show off, skip, sport, toy, trifle; CONCEPTS 292,384 —*Ant.* work

play [*v2*] *compete in sport* be on a team, challenge, contend, contest, disport, engage in, participate, recreate, rival, sport, take on, take part, vie; CONCEPTS 92,363 —*Ant.* watch

play [*v3*] *act; take the part of* act the part of, discourse, do*, enact, execute, ham*, ham it up*, impersonate, lay an egg*, perform, personate, playact, play a gig*, portray, present, read a part, represent, take the role of, tread the boards*; CONCEPT 292 —*Ant.* direct

play [*v4*] *gamble, risk* bet, chance, exploit, finesse, game, hazard, jockey*, lay money on*, maneuver, manipulate, put, set, speculate, stake, take, wager; CONCEPTS 341,363

play [*v5*] *produce music* blow, bow, drum, execute, fiddle, fidget, finger, operate, pedal, perform, render, tickle, work; CONCEPT 65 —*Ant.* listen

play ball [*v*] *cooperate* agree, be in cahoots, collaborate, comply with, conspire, go along with, join forces, join in, participate, play the game*, pull together, stick together, work together; CONCEPTS 110,112

play dirty [*v*] *cheat* bamboozle*, beguile, bend the rules*, bilk, burn, caboodle, chisel, con, deceive, defraud, do a number on*, double-cross, double-deal, dupe, finagle, fleece, flimflam, fudge*, hit below the belt*, hoodwink, hose, mislead, pull something funny*, rip off*, rook*, sandbag, scam, screw, shaft, stack the cards*, stretch the rules*, sucker, swindle, trick, victimize; CONCEPTS 59,139,192

play down [*v*] *pretend as if something were unimportant* belittle, deemphasize, gloss over*, hold back*, make light of*, make little of*, minimize, mute, restrain, soften, soft-pedal*, underplay, underrate; CONCEPTS 49,59,63 —*Ant.* blow up, build up, explode, play up

player [*n1*] *person participating in sport* amateur, athlete, champ, competitor, contestant, jock*, member, opponent, participant, pro, professional, rookie, sportsperson, superjock*, sweat*, team player; CONCEPT 366 —*Ant.* fan, spectator

player [*n2*] *person who acts in performance*

actor, bit player, entertainer, extra, ham*, hambone*, impersonator, lead, mime, mimic, performer, playactor, scene stealer*, stand-in, star, thespian, trouper, understudy, walk-on; CONCEPT 352 —*Ant.* director

player [n3] *person who produces music* artist, instrumentalist, musician, music maker, performer, rocker, soloist, virtuoso; CONCEPT 352 —*Ant.* conductor

playful [adj] *funny, fun-loving* antic, blithe, cheerful, coltish*, comical, elvish*, feeling one's oats*, flirtatious, frisky, frolicsome, full of pep*, gamesome, gay, good-natured, impish, jaunty, jesting, jocund, joking, joyous, light-hearted, lively, merry, mirthful, mischievous, prankish, puckish, rollicking, snappy, spirited, sportive, sprightly, teasing, tongue-in-cheek*, vivacious, waggish, whimsical, zippy*; CONCEPT 542 —*Ant.* humorless, serious, working

playground [n] *recreation area* jungle gym, park, playing field; CONCEPTS 509,513

play it safe [v] *be cautious* avoid risk, be on the safe side, hedge one's bets*, take no chances, take precautions; CONCEPTS 401,403

plaything [n] *toy* amusement, bauble, doll, gadget, game, gimcrack, pastime, trifle, trinket; CONCEPT 446 —*Ant.* tool

play up [v] *emphasize* accentuate, bring to the fore*, call attention to, feature, highlight, italicize*, magnify, make a production of*, point up, stress, turn spotlight on*, underline, underscore; CONCEPT 49 —*Ant.* deemphasize, play down, underrate, undervalue

playwright [n] *person who writes for the theater* author, dramatist, dramaturge, dramaturgist, librettist, scenarist, scripter, tragedian, writer; CONCEPT 348

plaza [n] *central location, spot* common, court, green, park, square, village green; CONCEPTS 509,513

plea [n1] *begging request* appeal, application, entreaty, imploration, imprecation, intercession, orison, overture, petition, prayer, round robin*, solicitation, suit, supplication; CONCEPT 662 —*Ant.* answer, reply

plea [n2] *excuse, defense* action, alibi, allegation, apology, argument, cause, claim, cop-out*, explanation, extenuation, fish tale*, justification, mitigation, out, palliation, pleading, pretext, rationalization, right, song and dance*, story, vindication, whitewash*; CONCEPTS 57,278,318 —*Ant.* decision, sentence

plead [v1] *beg, request* appeal, ask, beseech, cop a plea*, crave, crawl, entreat, entreaty, implore, importune, make up for, petition, pray, solicit, square things*, supplicate; CONCEPT 48 —*Ant.* answer, reply

plead [v2] *present a defense* adduce, advocate, allege, answer charges, argue, assert, avouch, cite, cop a plea*, declare, give evidence, maintain, plea bargain, present, put forward, respond, use as excuse, vouch; CONCEPTS 49,317 —*Ant.* decide, punish, sentence

pleasant [adj] *acceptable; friendly* affable, agreeable, amiable, amusing, bland, charming, cheerful, civil, civilized, congenial, convivial, cool*, copacetic, cordial, delectable, delightful, diplomatic, enchanting, engaging, enjoyable, fine, fine and dandy*, fun, genial, good-

humored, gracious, gratifying, homey, jolly, jovial, kindly, likable, lovely, mild, mild-mannered, nice, obliging, pleasing, pleasurable, polite, refreshing, satisfying, social, soft, sweet, sympathetic, urbane, welcome; CONCEPTS 542,548,572 —*Ant.* bothersome, disagreeable, hateful, nasty, troubling, unacceptable, unfriendly, unhappy, unpleasant, worrisome

pleasantry [n] *nice remark* badinage, banter, bon mot*, humor, jest, joke, joking, levity, merriment, quip, quirk, repartee, sally*, squib*, wit, witticism; CONCEPTS 273,278 —*Ant.* criticism

please [v1] *delight, make happy* amuse, charm, cheer, content, enchant, entertain, fill the bill*, gladden, go over big*, grab, gratify, hit the spot*, humor, indulge, kill*, make the grade*, overjoy, satisfy, score, suit, sweep off feet*, tickle*, tickle pink*, titillate, turn on*, wow*; CONCEPTS 7,22 —*Ant.* anger, annoy, depress, displease, disturb, upset, worry

please [v2] *will, elect to do* be inclined, choose, command, demand, desire, like, opt, prefer, see fit, want, wish; CONCEPT 20 —*Ant.* be unwilling, deny, refuse

pleasing/pleasurable [adj] *welcome, nice* agreeable, amiable, amusing, charming, congenial, delightful, enchanting, engaging, enjoyable, entertaining, favorable, good, grateful, gratifying, likable, luscious, musical, palatable, pleasant, polite, satisfactory, satisfying, savory, suitable, sweet, winning; CONCEPTS 537,572 —*Ant.* bad, disagreeable, dismal, displeasing, grim, hurtful, troublesome, unpleasant, unwelcome, upsetting

pleasure [n1] *delight, happiness* amusement, bliss, buzz*, comfort, contentment, delectation, diversion, ease, enjoyment, entertainment, felicity, flash*, fruition, game, gladness, gluttony, gratification, gusto, hobby, indulgence, joie de vivre, joy, joyride*, kick*, kicks*, luxury, primrose path*, recreation, relish, revelry, satisfaction, seasoning, self-indulgence, solace, spice, thrill, titillation, turn-on*, velvet*, zest; CONCEPT 388 —*Ant.* gloom, melancholy, pain, sadness, sorrow, trouble, unhappiness, worry

pleasure [n2] *will, inclination* choice, command, desire, fancy, liking, mind, option, preference, purpose, velleity, want, wish; CONCEPTS 20,659 —*Ant.* dislike, hate, hatred

plebeian [adj] *base, lower-class* banal, coarse, common, conventional, humble, ignoble, low, lowborn, lowly, mean, ordinary, pedestrian, popular, proletarian, traditional, uncultivated, unrefined, unsophisticated, unwashed*, vulgar, working-class; CONCEPT 549 —*Ant.* aristocratic, noble, rich, upper-class, wealthy

plebeian [n] *person of lower class* commonality, commoner, common people, peasant, person in the street*, pleb*, plebe*, proletarian, rank and file*; CONCEPTS 413,423 —*Ant.* aristocrat, noble, patrician, rich, wealthy

pledge [n1] *word of honor* agreement, assurance, covenant, guarantee, health, oath, promise, toast, undertaking, vow, warrant, word; CONCEPTS 71,278 —*Ant.* break

pledge [n2] *sign of good faith* bail, bond, collateral, deposit, earnest, gage, guarantee, guaranty, pawn, security, surety, token, warrant, warranty; CONCEPTS 318,332,446 —*Ant.* break

pledge [v] *guarantee; give word of honor* contract, engage, give word*, hock*, hook*, mortgage, pawn, plight, promise, sign for, soak*, swear, undertake, vouch, vow; CONCEPT 71 —*Ant.* break, disobey, falsify

plenary [adj] *entire, whole* absolute, complete, full, general, inclusive, open, sweeping, thorough; CONCEPT 531 —*Ant.* incomplete, limited, part, partial, restricted

plentiful/plenty [adj] *abundant, productive* abounding, ample, bounteous, bountiful, bumper*, chock-full*, complete, copious, enough, excessive, extravagant, exuberant, fertile, flowing, flush*, fruitful, full, fulsome, generous, improvident, infinite, large, lavish, liberal, lousy with*, lush, luxuriant, overflowing, plenteous, prodigal, profuse, prolific, replete, rife, sufficient, superabundant, superfluous, swarming, swimming, teeming; CONCEPTS 762,781 —*Ant.* few, lacking, little, needing, rare, scarce, wanting

plenty [n] *much, abundance* affluence, avalanche*, capacity, copiousness, cornucopia, deluge*, enough, flood*, fruitfulness, full house*, fund, good deal*, great deal*, heaps*, loads*, lots, luxury, mass, masses*, mine*, mountains*, oodles*, opulence, peck*, piles*, plethora, profusion, prosperity, quantity, stacks*, store, sufficiency, torrent*, volume, wealth; CONCEPTS 767,787 —*Ant.* few, lack, little, need, scarcity, want

plethora [n] *excess* deluge, flood, glut, many, much, overabundance, overflow, overkill, overmuch, plenty, profusion, superabundance, superfluity, surfeit, surplus; CONCEPTS 767,787 —*Ant.* few, lack, little, need, rarity, scarcity, want

pliable [adj] *bendable, adaptable* compliant, docile, ductile, easily led, easy, flexible, impressionable, limber, lithe, malleable, manageable, manipulable, moldable, obedient, plastic, pliant, putty*, receptive, responsive, rolling with the punches*, spongy, submissive, supple, susceptible,tractable, yielding; CONCEPTS 404,488 —*Ant.* inflexible, rigid, stiff, unadaptable, unbendable, unpliable, unpliant, unyielding

plight [n] *dilemma, difficulty; situation* bad news*, circumstances, condition, corner*, double trouble*, extremity, fix*, hole*, impasse, jam, perplexity, pickle*, pinch*, predicament, quandary, scrape*, spot*, state*, straits, tight situation, trouble; CONCEPTS 666, 674 —*Ant.* blessing, boon, good fortune

plod [v1] *walk heavily* clump*, drag, flounder, hike, lumber*, plug, schlepp*, slog*, stamp, stomp, toil, tramp, trample, tread, tromp, trudge, wallow; CONCEPT 151 —*Ant.* tiptoe, walk lightly

plod [v2] *work slowly and under duress* bear down*, buckle down*, drudge, grind, knuckle down*, labor, persevere, plough through*, plug away*, scratch*, slave, sweat*, toil; CONCEPTS 87,677 —*Ant.* breeze

plot [n1] *plan, scheme* artifice, booby trap*, cabal, collusion, complicity, connivance, conniving, conspiracy, contrivance, covin, design, device, fix, frame, frame-up*, game, intrigue, little game*, machination, maneuver, practice, ruse, scam, setup, stratagem, trick;CONCEPT 660

plot [n2] *story line* action, design, development, enactment, events, incidents, movement, narrative, outline, picture, progress, scenario, scene, scheme, story, structure, subject, suspense, theme, thread, unfolding; CONCEPTS 264,282

plot [n3] *tract of land* acreage, allotment, area, division, ground, land, lot, parcel, patch, piece, plat, spread; CONCEPTS 509,513

plot [v1] *plan, scheme* angle, brew*, cabal, cogitate, collude, conceive, concoct, connive, conspire, contrive, cook up*, design, devise, draft, finagle, frame, hatch*, imagine, intrigue, lay*, machinate, maneuver, operate, outline, project, promote, rough out*, set up, sketch, wangle; CONCEPT 36 —*Ant.* forget, neglect

plot [v2] *map out; draw* calculate, chart, compute, draft, lay out, locate, mark, outline, put forward; CONCEPTS 36,79,174

plow [v] *dig up ground for cultivation* break, break ground, bulldoze, cultivate, farm, furrow, harrow, harvest, list, push, rake, reap, ridge, rush, shove, smash, till, trench, turn, turn over; CONCEPT 178 —*Ant.* fill

ploy [n] *game, trick* artifice, contrivance, device, dodge, feint, gambit, maneuver, move, play, ruse, scheme, stratagem, subterfuge, tactic, wile; CONCEPT 59

pluck [n] *person's resolution, courage* backbone*, boldness, bravery, dauntlessness, determination, grit, guts*, hardihood, heart*, intestinal fortitude*, intrepidity, mettle, moxie*, nerve, resolution, spirit, spunk; CONCEPT 411 —*Ant.* cowardice, dispiritedness, irresolution

pluck [v] *grab, pull out; pick at* catch, clutch, collect, cull, draw, finger, gather, harvest, jerk, plunk, pull at, snatch, strum, tug, tweak, yank; CONCEPT 206 —*Ant.* insert

plucky [adj] *brave* adventurous, bold, confident, courageous, daring, determined, fearless, game, gritty, gutsy, heroic, lionhearted, nervy, persevering, spirited, sporting, spunky, stalwart, tenacious, unafraid, undaunted, unfearful, valiant; CONCEPT 401

plug [n1] *stopper* bung, connection, cork, filling, fitting, occlusion, river, spigot, stopple, tampon, wedge; CONCEPTS 471,836 —*Ant.* mouth, opening

plug [n2] *publicity* advertisement, blurb*, good word*, hype*, mention, push*, write-up; CONCEPT 274

plug [v1] *stop up* block, bung, choke, clog, close, congest, cork, cover, drive in, fill, obstruct, occlude, pack, ram, seal, secure, stop, stopper, stopple, stuff; CONCEPT 209 —*Ant.* uncork, unplug, unstopper

plug [v2] *publicize* advertise, boost*, build up*, hype*, mention, promote, push*, write up; CONCEPTS 49,60 —*Ant.* conceal, hide, withhold

plum [n] *reward, prize* asset, bonus, carrot*, catch*, cream*, dividend, find, meed, nugget*, pick, premium, treasure; CONCEPTS 337,712 —*Ant.* penalty, punishment

plumb [adj] *vertical* erect, perpendicular, sheer, straight, straight up, up and down, upright; CONCEPT 581 —*Ant.* flat, horizontal, level

plumb [v] *probe, go into* delve, explore, fathom, gauge, get to the bottom of*, measure, penetrate, search, sound, take soundings, unravel; CONCEPTS 181,216,291 —*Ant.* leave alone

plummet [v] *fall hard and fast* collapse, crash, decline, decrease, descend, dip, dive, downturn, drop, drop down, dump, fall, nose-dive, plunge, precipitate, sink, skid, stoop, swoop, tumble; CONCEPTS *181,698,763* —*Ant.* ascend, rise, shoot up

plump [adj] *chubby, fat* beefy*, burly, buxom, chunky*, corpulent, filled, fleshy, full, obese, portly, pudgy*, rotund, round, stout, tubby*; CONCEPT *491* —*Ant.* lean, skinny, thin

plunder [n] *something stolen* booty, goods*, graft, hot goods*, loot, make*, pickings*, pillage, plunderage, prey, prize, quarry, rapine, raven, spoil, stuff*, take*, trappings*, winnings*; CONCEPT *710* —*Ant.* gift

plunder [v] *ravage, steal* appropriate, burn, depredate, despoil, devastate, fleece, forage, foray, grab, gut, kip, knock off*, knock over*, lay waste, liberate, lift, loft, loot, maraud, moonlight requisition*, pillage, prey, prowl, raid, ransack, relieve, requisition, rifle, rip off*, rob, sack, salvage, smash and grab*, snatch, spoil, stick up*, strip; CONCEPTS *86,139,252* —*Ant.* give, receive

plunge [n] *quick drop; enthusiastic attempt* belly flop*, descent, dive, duck, dunk, fall, high dive, immersion, investment, jump, nose-dive, spree, submergence, submersion, swoop, venture; CONCEPTS *100,150,152,181,194* —*Ant.* ascent, increase, rise

plunge [v] *dive or fall fast* belly-flop*, career, cast, charge, dash, descend, dip, drive, drop, duck, fling, go down, go the limit, go whole hog*, hurtle, immerge, immerse, jump, keel, lunge, lurch, nose-dive, pitch, plummet, plunk, propel, rush, shoot the works*, sink, sound, submerge, submerse, swoop, take a flyer*, take a header*, tear, throw, throw oneself, thrust, topple, tumble; CONCEPTS *100,150,152,181,194* —*Ant.* ascend, increase, rise

plunk [v] *throw down* drop, dump, plonk, plop, plump, unload; CONCEPTS *181,200*

plural [adj] *more than one* dual, many, multiple, not alone, not singular, numerous; CONCEPTS *564,762,772*

plurality [n] *large part of a group* advantage, bulk, greater part, lead, majority, mass, most, multiplicity, nearly all, numerousness, preponderance, profusion, variety; CONCEPTS *382,829* —*Ant.* minority

plus [adj] *added, extra* additional, augmented, boosted, enlarged, expanded, increased, positive, supplementary, surplus; CONCEPTS *762,771* —*Ant.* detrimental, minus, negative

plus [n] *asset; something added* advantage, benefit, bonus, extra, gain, good point, overage, overstock, oversupply, perk, surplus; CONCEPT *693* —*Ant.* detriment, disadvantage, minus

plush [adj] *luxurious, rich* costly, deluxe, elegant, lavish, luscious, lush, luxury, opulent, palatial, ritzy, silken, sumptuous; CONCEPTS *334,589* —*Ant.* barren, destitute, poor

ply [v] *use, work at* carry on, dispense, employ, exercise, exert, follow, function, handle, maneuver, manipulate, practice, pursue, put out, swing, throw, utilize, wield; CONCEPTS *100, 225* —*Ant.* be lazy, idle

poach [v] *infringe upon; trespass* appropriate, encroach, filch, fish illegally, hunt illegally,

intrude, pilfer, plunder, rob, smuggle, steal; CONCEPTS *139,192* —*Ant.* keep off

pocket [adj] *small, portable* abridged, canned, capsule, compact, concise, condensed, diminutive, epitomized, itsy-bitsy*, little, midget, miniature, minute, peewee*, pint-sized*, potted, tiny, wee*; CONCEPT *773* —*Ant.* big, huge, large

pocket [n] *cavity, pouch* bag, chamber, compartment, hole, hollow, opening, receptacle, sack, socket; CONCEPTS *452,513* —*Ant.* mound, mountain

pocket [v] *help oneself to something* abstract, appropriate, conceal, enclose, filch, hide, lift, nab, pilfer, pinch, purloin, shoplift, steal, swipe, take; CONCEPTS *139,142* —*Ant.* give

pocketbook [n] *accessory for carrying personal items* bag, clutch, frame, handbag, hide, leather, pouch, purse, reticule, suitcase, wallet; CONCEPTS *446,450*

pockmark [n] *pitlike scar* blemish, cavity, crater, dent, dimple, pimple, welt, zit; CONCEPT *580*

pod [n/v] *encasement of vegetable seeds* capsule, case, covering, hull, husk, sheath, sheathing, shell, shuck, skin, vessel; CONCEPTS *428,484*

podium [n] *structure from which speakers orate* dais, platform, pulpit, rostrum, soapbox*, stage, stump*; CONCEPT *443*

poem [n] *highly expressive, rhythmical literary piece* ballad, beat, blank verse, composition, creation, epic, free verse, haiku, limerick, lines, lyric, ode, poesy, poetry, quatrain, rhyme, rime, rune, sestina, song, sonnet, verse, villanelle, words, writing; CONCEPTS *268,282* —*Ant.* prose

poet [n] *person who writes expressive, rhythmic verse* artist, author, balladist, bard, dilettante, dramatist, librettist, lyricist, lyrist, maker, metrist, odist, parodist, poetaster, rhapsodist, rhymer, rimer, sonnetist, versifier, writer; CONCEPTS *348,423*

poetic [adj] *with rhythm and beauty; related to poetic composition* anapestic, dactylic, dramatic, elegiac, epic, epical, epodic, iambic, idyllic, imaginative, lyric, lyrical, melodious, metrical, odic, rhythmical, romantic, songlike, tuneful; CONCEPT *267* —*Ant.* prosaic

poetry [n] *expressive, rhythmic literary work* balladry, doggerel, metrical composition, paean, poems, poesy, rhyme, rhyming, rime, rune, song, stanza, verse, versification; CONCEPTS *268,282,349* —*Ant.* prose

poignant [adj1] *affecting, painful* agitating, agonizing, bitter, distressing, disturbing, emotional, heartbreaking, heartrending, impressive, intense, moving, passionate, pathetic, perturbing, piteous, pitiful, sad, sentimental, sorrowful, touching, upsetting; CONCEPTS *529,548* —*Ant.* calm, numb, pleasant, soothing, unaffecting

poignant [adj2] *sharp, bitter* acrid, acute, biting, caustic, keen, penetrating, peppery, piercing, piquant, pointed, pungent, racy, sarcastic, severe, snappy, spicy, stinging, tangy, zesty; CONCEPTS *267,613* —*Ant.* blah, blunt, dull

point [n1] *speck* bit, count, dot, fleck, flyspeck, full stop, iota, mark, minim, mite, mote, notch, particle, period, scrap, stop, tittle, trace; CONCEPTS *79,831*

point [n2] *specific location* locality, locus,

place, position, site, situation, spot, stage, station, where; CONCEPT 198

point [n3] *sharp end, top, end of extension* apex, awn, barb, beak, bill, cape, claw, cusp, dagger, foreland, head, headland, jag, nib, pin point, prick, prickler, promontory, prong, snag, spike, spine, spire, spur, sticker, stiletto, summit, sword, thorn, tine, tip, tooth; CONCEPTS 827,836 —*Ant.* bluntness, dullness

point [n4] *circumstance, stage; limited time* brink, condition, date, degree, duration, edge, extent, instant, juncture, limit, moment, period, point in time, position, threshold, time, verge, very minute; CONCEPTS 696,815

point [n5] *goal, aim* appeal, attraction, bottom line*, charm, cogency, design, effectiveness, end, fascination, intent, intention, interest, motive, name of the game*, nitty-gritty*, nub, nuts and bolts*, object, objective, punch*, purpose, reason, significance, use, usefulness, utility, validity, validness; CONCEPT 659

point [n6] *meaning, essence* argument, bottom line*, burden, core, crux, drift, force, gist, head, heart, idea, import, kicker*, main idea, marrow, matter, meat*, motif, motive, name of the game*, nitty-gritty*, nub, nuts and bolts*, pith, pointer, proposition, punch line*, question, score, stuff, subject, subject matter, text, theme, thrust, tip, tip-off*, topic; CONCEPTS 274,682

point [n7] *aspect, characteristic* attribute, case, circumstance, circumstantial, constituent, detail, element, facet, feature, instance, item, material, nicety, part, particular, peculiarity, property, quality, respect, side, thing*, trait; CONCEPTS 274,411,654 —*Ant.* personality, whole

point [n8] *scoring unit of sport competition* count, mark, notch, score, tally; CONCEPTS 364,784

point [v1] *show as probable; call attention* bespeak, button down*, denote, designate, direct, finger*, hint, imply, indicate, lead, make*, name, offer, peg*, pin down*, put down for*, put finger on*, signify, suggest, tab*, tag*; CONCEPTS 118,138

point [v2] *direct, aim* beam*, bring to bear, cast, face, guide, head, influence, lay, level, look, slant, steer, tend, train, turn, zero in*; CONCEPTS 187,201,623

pointed [adj1] *having a sharp end or part* acicular, aciculate, acuminate, acuminous, acute, barbed, cornered, cuspidate, edged, fine, keen, mucronate, peaked, piked, pointy, pronged, sharp, sharp-cornered, spiked; CONCEPTS 490,606 —*Ant.* blunt, dull

pointed [adj2] *penetrating, biting* accurate, acid, acute, barbed, boiled down, calling a spade a spade*, cutting, in a nutshell*, incisive, insinuating, keen, laid on the line*, legit, meaty*, on the button*, on the nose*, pertinent, pregnant, right-on*, right to it*, sarcastic, sharp, short-and-sweet*, tart, telling, trenchant; CONCEPT 267 —*Ant.* calming, mild, nice, soothing

pointer [n1] *indicator* arrow, dial, director, gauge, guide, hand, index, mark, needle, register, rod, signal; CONCEPTS 464,498

pointer [n2] *hint, suggestion* advice, caution, clue, information, recommendation, steer, tip, tip-off, warning; CONCEPTS 75,274

pointless [adj] *ridiculous, senseless* absurd, aimless, around in circles*, fruitless, futile, going nowhere*, impotent, inane, inconsequential, ineffective, ineffectual, insignificant, in vicious circle*, irrelevant, meaningless, needle in haystack*, nongermane, nonsensical, not pertinent, on treadmill*, powerless, purportless, remote, silly, stupid, trivial, unavailing, uninteresting, unnecessary, unproductive, unprofitable, useless, vague, vain, worthless; CONCEPTS 529,548 —*Ant.* beneficial, meaningful, pointed, profitable, sensible

point out [v] *call attention to* advert, allude, bring up, denote, designate, identify, indicate, mention, refer, remind, reveal, show, specify; CONCEPTS 49,73,261 —*Ant.* distract

poise [n] *self-composure, dignity* address, aplomb, assurance, balance, bearing, calmness, confidence, cool, coolness, delicatesse, diplomacy, elegance, equability, equanimity, equilibrium, grace, gravity, polish, presence, presence of mind, sangfroid, savoir faire, self-assurance, self-possession, serenity, stasis, tact, tactfulness, tranquility; CONCEPTS 633,717 —*Ant.* excitedness

poise [v] *balance, suspend* ballast, be ready, brood, float, hang, hold, hover, position, stabilize, stand, steady, support, wait; CONCEPT 154 —*Ant.* drop, fall

poison [n] *substance that causes harm, death* adulteration, bacteria, bane, blight, cancer, contagion, contamination, corruption, germ, infection, malignancy, miasma, toxicant, toxin, toxoid, venin, venom, virus; CONCEPTS 307,475,674,675 —*Ant.* antidote

poison [v] *contaminate, pollute* adulterate, corrupt, debase, defile, deprave, destroy, envenom, fester, harm, infect, injure, kill, make ill, murder, pervert, stain, subvert, taint, undermine, vitiate, warp; CONCEPTS 14,246,252 —*Ant.* purify, sterilize

poison/poisonous [adj] *harmful* bad, baleful, baneful, corrupt, corruptive, dangerous, deadly, deleterious, destructive, detrimental, evil, fatal, hurtful, infective, lethal, malicious, malignant, mephitic, miasmatic, morbid, mortal, nocuous, noisome, noxious, peccant, pernicious, pestiferous, pestilential, septic, toxic, toxicant, toxiferous, venomous, vicious, viperous, virulent; CONCEPT 537 —*Ant.* aiding, antidotal, assisting, curing, healing, helpful

poke [n] *push, thrust* blow, boost, bunt, butt, dig, hit, jab, nudge, prod, punch, shove, stab; CONCEPTS 189,208

poke [v1] *push at; thrust* arouse, awaken, bulge, butt*, crowd, dig, elbow*, goose*, hit, jab, jostle, jut, nudge*, overhang, prod, project, protrude, provoke, punch, ram, rouse, shoulder*, shove, stab, stand out, stick, stick out, stimulate, stir; CONCEPTS 189,208,723

poke [v2] *interfere, snoop* busybody*, butt in*, intrude, meddle, nose*, peek, pry, tamper; CONCEPT 384 —*Ant.* leave alone

poke [v3] *move along slowly* dally, dawdle, delay, drag, get no place fast*, idle, lag, loiter, mosey*, procrastinate, put off*, schlepp along*, tarry, toddle*, trail; CONCEPT 151 —*Ant.* rush

poker [n] *card game* blind poker, draw poker, five-card stud poker, seven-card stud poker, straight poker, strip poker, stud poker; CONCEPTS 260,271

polar [adj1] *cold* arctic, extreme, farthest, freezing, frigid, frozen, glacial, icy, north, south, terminal; CONCEPTS 583,605 —*Ant.* tropic, tropical

polar [adj2] *opposite, opposed* antagonistic, antipodal, antipodean, antithetical, contradictory, contrary, converse, counter, diametric, reverse; CONCEPT 564 —*Ant.* same, similar

pole [n] *bar, post* beam, extremity, flagpole, flagstaff, leg, mast, pile, plank, rod, shaft, spar, staff, stake, standard, stave, stick, stilt, stud, terminus; CONCEPTS 440,470,475,479

police/police officer [n] *person, people hired to uphold the laws* arm of the law*, badge*, bear*, beat cop, black and white*, blue*, bluecoat*, bobby, constable, constabulary, cop*, copper*, corps*, detective, fed*, flatfoot*, force, gendarme, heat*, law, law enforcement, narc*, patrol; CONCEPTS 299,354 —*Ant.* criminal

policy [n] *procedure, tactics* action, administration, approach, arrangement, behavior, channels, code, course, custom, design, guideline, line, management, method, order, organization, plan, polity, practice, program, protocol, red tape*, rule, scheme, stratagem, strategy, tenet, the book*, the numbers*, theory; CONCEPTS 6,271,660,688

polish [n1] *shine, brightness* brilliance, burnish, finish, glaze, glint, gloss, luster, sheen, smoothness, sparkle, varnish, veneer, wax; CONCEPTS 492,611,620 —*Ant.* dullness

polish [n2] *cultivated look, performance* breeding, class, cultivation, culture, elegance, finesse, finish, grace, politesse, refinement, style, suavity, urbanity; CONCEPTS 388,633,655

polish [v1] *shine, buff* brighten, burnish, clean, finish, furbish, glaze, gloss, rub, scour, scrub, sleek, slick, smooth, wax; CONCEPTS 202,215 —*Ant.* dull, roughen

polish [v2] *improve performance, look* amend, better, brush up, correct, cultivate, emend, enhance, finish, furbish, make improvement, mature, mend, perfect, refine, round, sleek, slick, smooth, touch up; CONCEPT 244 —*Ant.* deface, ruin, spoil

polish off [v] *finish using* consume, devour, dispatch, dispose of, do away with*, down*, eat, eat up, eliminate, get rid of*, liquidate, put away*, swill*, use up, wolf*;CONCEPTS 169,225 —*Ant.* hoard, save

polite [adj] *mannerly, civilized* affable, amenable, amiable, attentive, bland, civil, complaisant, concerned, conciliatory, condescending, considerate, cordial, courteous, courtly, cultured, deferential, diplomatic, elegant, friendly, genteel, gentle, good-natured, gracious, mild, neighborly, nice, obliging, obsequious, pleasant, polished, politic, punctilious, refined, respectful, smooth, sociable, solicitous, sympathetic, thoughtful, urbane, well-behaved, well-bred, well-mannered; CONCEPT 401 —*Ant.* impolite, rude, uncivil, uncivilized, unmannerly, unrefined, unsophisticated

politic [adj] *wise, tactful* adroit, advisable, canny*, cool, diplomatic, discreet, expedient, in one's best interests*, judicious, on the lookout*, perspicacious, prudent, sagacious, sensible, sharp, shrewd, smooth, tactical, tuned in*, urbane; CONCEPT 401 —*Ant.* impolitic, indiscreet, injudicious, tactless, unwise

political [adj] *governmental* bureaucratic, civic, constitutional, economical, legislative, official; CONCEPT 535

politically correct [adj] *sensitive to other political views* bias-free, considerate, diplomatic, gender-free, inclusive, inoffensive, liberal, multicultural, nondiscriminatory, nonracist, nonsexist, PC*, respectful, sensitive; CONCEPTS 529,542

politician [n] *person pursuing or occupying elective office* baby-kisser*, boss, chieftain, congressperson, democrat, grandstander*, handshaker*, lawmaker, leader, legislator, member of Congress, member of parliament, officeholder, office seeker, orator, partisan, party member, president, public servant, republican, senator, speaker, statesperson, whistle-stopper*; CONCEPT 359

politics [n] *art and science of administration of government* affairs of state, backroom*, campaigning, civics, domestic affairs, electioneering, foreign affairs, government, government policy, hat in the ring*, internal affairs, jungle*, legislature, matters of state, political science, polity, smoke-filled room*, statecraft, stateship, zoo*; CONCEPTS 300,301

poll [n] *census; tally of answers to questions of opinion* ballot, canvass, count, figures, opinion, returns, sampling, survey, vote, voting; CONCEPTS 48,300

poll [v] *take census; question* ballot, canvass, enroll, examine, interview, list, register, sample, send up a balloon*, survey, tally, test the waters*, vote; CONCEPTS 48,300

pollster [n] *polltaker* canvasser, market researcher, public opinion gatherer, sampler, survey taker; CONCEPTS 37,103,197,291

pollutant [n] *contaminant* hazardous waste, poison, pollution, toxic waste, toxin; CONCEPT 720

pollute [v] *make dirty; corrupt* adulterate, alloy, befoul, besmirch, contaminate, debase, debauch, defile, deprave, desecrate, dirty, dishonor, foul, infect, make filthy, mar, poison, profane, soil, spoil, stain, sully, taint, violate; CONCEPTS 246,254 —*Ant.* clean, cleanse, purify

pollution [n] *dirtiness, contamination* abuse, adulteration, besmearing, besmirching, blight, corruption, decomposition, defilement, desecration, deterioration, dirtying, fouling, foulness, impairment, impurity, infection, misuse, polluting, profanation, rottenness, soiling, spoliation, taint, tainting, uncleanness, vitiation; CONCEPT 720 —*Ant.* cleanliness, purification

Pollyanna [n] *optimist* dreamer, hoper, idealist, positive thinker; CONCEPTS 410,689

poltergeist [n] *ghost* apparition, appearance, banshee, demon, doppelganger, haunter, kelpie, phantasm, phantom, revenant, specter, spirit, spook, vision, visitor; CONCEPT 370

polygamy [n] *plural marriage* bigamy, polyandry, polygyny; CONCEPTS 297,388

pomp [n] *pageantry, display* affectation, array, ceremonial, ceremony, fanfare, flourish, formality, grandeur, grandiosity, magnificence, ostentation, pageant, panoply, parade, pomposity, ritual, shine, show, solemnity, splendor, state, vainglory; CONCEPTS *335,377,655* —*Ant.* dullness, plainness, simplicity

pompous [*adj*] *arrogant, egotistic* affected, bloated, boastful, bombastic, conceited, flatulent, flaunting, flowery, fustian, grandiloquent, grandiose, high and mighty*, highfaluting*, high-flown*, imperious, important, inflated, magisterial, magniloquent, narcissistic, orotund, ostentatious, overbearing, overblown, pontifical, portentous, presumptuous, pretentious, puffed up*, puffy*, rhetorical, self-centered, self-important, selfish, showy, sonorous, stuck-up*, supercilious, turgid, uppity*, vain, vainglorious, windy*; CONCEPTS *267,401,542* —*Ant.* dull, modest, plain, simple, unassuming

poncho [*n*] *cloak* cape, capote, coat, manteau, mantle, raincoat, shawl, wrap; CONCEPTS *451,475,680*

pond [*n*] *small body of water* basin, dew, duck pond, lagoon, lily pond, millpond, pool, puddle, small lake, splash; CONCEPT *514*

ponder [*v*] *think about seriously* appraise, brood, build castles in air*, cerebrate, cogitate, consider, contemplate, daydream, debate, deliberate, dwell, evaluate, examine, excogitate, figure, give thought to, meditate, mind, moon*, mull, mull over, muse, noodle around*, perpend, pipe dream*, put on thinking cap*, puzzle over, reason, reflect, revolve, roll, ruminate, speculate, study, think out, think over, turn over, weigh, woolgather*; CONCEPTS *17,24* —*Ant.* forget, ignore, neglect

ponderous [*adj1*] *heavy, cumbersome* awkward, bulky, burdensome, clumsy, cumbrous, dull, elephantine, graceless, hefty, huge, laborious, lifeless, lumbering, massive, onerous, oppressive, substantial, troublesome, unhandy, unwieldy, weighty; CONCEPTS *491,565* —*Ant.* airy, buoyant, delicate, light, unburdensome

ponderous [*adj2*] *dreary, tedious* arid, barren, cardboard*, dry, dull, heavy, humdrum*, labored, lifeless, long-winded*, monotonous, pedantic, pedestrian, plodding, prolix, stiff*, stilted, stodgy, stuffy*, vapid, verbose, wooden*; CONCEPTS *267,529,542* —*Ant.* fun, light

pontificate [*v*] *sermonize* address, admonish, dogmatize, evangelize, get on a soapbox*, give sermon, harangue, lecture, minister, moralize, preach, pulpiteer, teach; CONCEPTS *51,75,285, 367*

pooh-pooh [*v*] *dismiss* belittle, brush aside, discount, disregard, make light of, play down, rebuff, reject, repudiate, scoff at, sneer at, treat with contempt, wave aside; CONCEPTS *35,54*

pool [*n1*] *collection of liquid* basin, bath, lagoon, lake, mere, millpond, mud puddle, natatorium, pond, puddle, splash, swimming pool, tank, tarn; CONCEPTS *364,514*

pool [*n2*] *supply of money, goods* bank, combine, conglomerate, equipment, funds, group, jackpot, kitty*, pot, provisions, stakes; CONCEPTS *340, 432* —*Ant.* lack, want

pool [*v*] *combine* amalgamate, blend, join forces, league, merge, put together, share; CONCEPTS *113,193* —*Ant.* divide, separate

pooped [*adj*] *tired* beat*, burned out*, bushed*, collapsing, dead on one's feet*, dog-tired*, done for*, done in*, drained, drooping, drowsy,

enervated, exhausted, fatigued, fried*, out of gas*, overworked, played out*, run-down, run ragged, shot*, sleepy, spent, tuckered out, wasted, weary, worn out; CONCEPTS *314,403,406*

poor [*adj1*] *lacking sufficient money* bad off*, bankrupt, beggared, beggarly, behind eight ball*, broke*, destitute, dirt poor*, down-and-out*, empty-handed*, flat*, flat broke*, fortuneless, hard up*, impecunious, impoverished, indigent, in need, insolvent, in want, low, meager, moneyless, necessitous, needy, pauperized, penniless, penurious, pinched*, poverty-stricken, reduced*, scanty*, stone broke*, strapped*, suffering, truly needy, underprivileged, unprosperous; CONCEPT *334* —*Ant.* affluent, rich, wealthy

poor [*adj2*] *deficient, inadequate* base, below par, common, contemptible, crude, diminutive, dwarfed, exiguous, faulty, feeble, humble, imperfect, incomplete, inferior, insignificant, insufficient, lacking, low-grade, lowly, meager, mean, mediocre, miserable, modest, niggardly*, ordinary, paltry, pitiable, pitiful, plain, reduced, rotten, scanty, second-rate*, shabby, shoddy, skimpy, slight, sorry*, sparse, subnormal, subpar, substandard, trifling, trivial, unsatisfactory, valueless, weak, worthless; CONCEPTS *570,574* —*Ant.* adequate, sufficient, superior

poor [*adj3*] *weak, unfertile* bare, barren, depleted, exhausted, feeble, fruitless, impaired, imperfect, impoverished, indisposed, infertile, infirm, puny, sick, sterile, unfruitful, unproductive, worthless; CONCEPT *314* —*Ant.* fertile, potent, strong

poor [*adj4*] *unfortunate, unhappy* commiserable, hapless, ill-fated, luckless, miserable, pathetic, piteous, pitiable, pitiful, rueful, unlucky, wretched; CONCEPTS *542,548* —*Ant.* fortunate, great, happy, lucky

poorly [*adj*] *not well* ailing, below par, failing, ill, indisposed, low, mean, out of sorts*, rotten*, sick, sickly, under the weather*, unwell; CONCEPT *314* —*Ant.* healthy, well

poorly [*adv*] *unsatisfactorily* badly, crudely, defectively, inadequately, incompetently, inexpertly, inferiorly, insufficiently, meanly, shabbily, unsuccessfully; CONCEPTS *544,571,574* —*Ant.* satisfactorily, well

pop [*n*] *bang* burst, crack, explosion, jump, leap, report, snap, strike, thrust, whack; CONCEPT *595*

pop [*v*] *jump, burst* appear, bang, blow, crack, dart, explode, go, go off, hit, insert, leap, protrude, push, put, report, rise, shove, snap, sock, stick, strike, thrust, whack; CONCEPT *145*

poppycock [*n*] *nonsense* babble, balderdash*, baloney*, bull*, bunk*, drivel, empty talk, foolery, foolishness, gibberish, hogwash*, hooey*, hot air*, jive*, malarkey, mumbo jumbo*, palaver, prattle, rubbish, silliness, trash*; CONCEPTS *230,388,633*

popular [*adj1*] *well-known, favorite* accepted, approved, attractive, beloved, caught on*, celebrated, crowd-pleasing*, faddish*, famous, fashionable, favored, in*, in demand, in favor, in the mainstream*, in vogue, leading, likable, liked, lovable, noted, notorious, now*, okay*, pleasing, praised, preferred, prevailing, prominent, promoted, right stuff*, run-after*, selling, social, societal, sought, sought-after, stylish, suitable, the rage*, thing*, trendy, well-liked, well-received; CONCEPTS *555,589* —*Ant.* disliked, unknown, unpopular

popular [*adj2*] *common, standard* accepted, accessible, adopted, approved, conventional, current, demanded, embraced, familiar, general, in demand, in use, ordinary, prevailing, prevalent, proletarian, public, rampant, regnant, rife, ruling, stock, ubiquitous, universal, widespread; CONCEPT *530* —*Ant.* different, uncommon, unusual

popularity [*n*] *recognition, celebrity* acceptance, acclaim, adoration, approval, currency, demand, esteem, fame, fashion, fashionableness, favor, following, heyday, idolization, lionization, prevalence, regard, renown, reputation, repute, universality, vogue; CONCEPTS *388,655* —*Ant.* dislike, unpopularity

popularize [*v*] *make widely popular, accessible* catch on, disseminate, familiarize, generalize, give currency, make available, promote, restore, resurrect, revive, simplify, spread, universalize; CONCEPTS *324,384* —*Ant.* discredit, shun

population [*n*] *inhabitants of a place* citizenry, community, culture, denizens, dwellers, folk, natives, people, populace, public, residents, society, state; CONCEPT *379*

populous [*adj*] *packed with inhabitants* crawling, crowded, dense, heavily populated, jammed, legion, many, multifarious, multitudinal, multitudinous, numerous, occupied, overpopulated, peopled, populated, settled, several, swarming, teeming, thick, thronged, various, voluminous; CONCEPT *583* —*Ant.* deserted

porch [*n*] *patio* balcony, deck, portico, steps, stoop, veranda; CONCEPTS *509,513*

pore [*n*] *small aperture in skin* foramen, opening, orifice, outlet, stoma, sweat gland, vesicle; CONCEPT *418*

pore [*v*] *go over carefully* brood, contemplate, dwell on, examine, look over, muse, peruse, ponder, read, regard, scan, scrutinize, study; CONCEPTS *24,72,103* —*Ant.* flip through, scan

pornographic [*adj*] *obscene* adult, immoral, indecent, lewd, off-color, offensive, porn*, porno*, prurient, purple*, raunchy*, rough, salacious, sexy, smutty*, steamy*, X-rated*; CONCEPTS *267,372,545* —*Ant.* clean, moral

pornography [*n*] *obscenity* adult material, adult movie, bawdiness, dirt, dirty movie, erotica, filth, girlie magazine, hard-core pornography, indecency, obscene materials, porn, porno, porno film, sexploitation, sexually explicit material, skin flick, smut, soft-core pornography, stag film, X-rated material, X-rated movie; CONCEPTS *372,545*

porous [*adj*] *having holes; absorbent* absorptive, penetrable, permeable, pervious, spongelike, spongy; CONCEPT *606* —*Ant.* impermeable

port [*n*] *place for boat docking, traffic, and storage* anchorage, boatyard, dockage, docks, dockyard, gate, harbor, harborage, haven, landing, piers, refuge, retreat, roads, roadstead, sanctuary, seaport, shelter, wharf; CONCEPTS *449,509*

portable [*adj*] *easily transported* carriageable, cartable, compact, convenient, conveyable, easily carried, handy, haulable, light, lightweight, manageable, movable, portative, transportable,

wieldy; CONCEPTS *491,584,773* —*Ant.* clumsy, cumbersome

portal [*n*] *hole or door in vessel* doorway, entrance, entry, entryway, gate, gateway, ingress, opening, way in; CONCEPT *502*

portend [*v*] *foreshadow, indicate* adumbrate, augur, be in the cards*, bespeak, betoken, bode, call*, crystal-ball*, forebode, forecast, foreshow, foretell, foretoken, forewarn, harbinger, have a hunch, herald, hint, omen, point to, predict, premonish, presage, prognosticate, promise, prophesy, read, see coming*, threaten, warn of; CONCEPTS *71,78,261*

portent [*n1*] *indication, forewarning* augury, bodement, boding, caution, clue, foreboding, foreshadowing, foretoken, funny feeling*, handwriting on the wall*, harbinger, hunch, omen, premonition, presage, presentiment, prognostic, prognostication, sign, sinking feeling*, threat, vibes*, warning; CONCEPT *278*

portent [*n2*] *miracle* marvel, phenomenon, prodigy, sensation, stunner, wonder; CONCEPTS *230,529* —*Ant.* doom

portentous [*adj*] *exciting; foreboding* alarming, amazing, apocalyptic, astounding, augural, destined, doomed, exhilarating, extraordinary, fated, fateful, haunting, ill-boding, ill-fated, impending, important, inauspicious, inspiring, intriguing, ominous, phenomenal, premonitory, prophetic, remarkable, suggestive, threatening, thrilling; CONCEPTS *529,542,548*

porter [*n*] *person who serves as attendant, caretaker* baggage carrier, bearer, bellhop, carrier, concierge, doorkeeper, doorperson, gatekeeper, janitor, redcap*, skycap*, transporter; CONCEPT *348*

portfolio [*n*] *flat case for transporting papers* attaché case, bag, brief bag, briefcase, case, container, envelope, folder, notebook, valise; CONCEPT *494*

portion [*n1*] *share, cut, ration* allocation, allotment, allowance, apportionment, bang, bit, chunk, division, divvy*, drag*, dram, excerpt, extract, fix, fraction, fragment, gob, helping, hit, hunk, lagniappe, lion's share*, lot, lump, measure, meed, member, moiety, morsel, parcel, part, piece, piece of action*, plum, quantity, quantum, quota, scrap, section, segment, serving, shot*, slug*, smithereen*, taste; CONCEPT *835* —*Ant.* all, entirety, whole

portion [*n2*] *fate, destiny* circumstance, cup*, doom, fortune, kismet*, lot*, luck; CONCEPT *679*

portion [*v*] *divide into pieces* administer, allocate, allot, apportion, assign, deal, dispense, distribute, divvy up*, dole out*, mete out*, parcel, part, partition, piece, prorate, quota, ration, section, share, shift; CONCEPTS *98,140* —*Ant.* collect, combine, gather, join

portly [*adj*] *bulky, fat* ample, avoirdupois, beefy*, broad, burly, corpulent, fleshy, heavy, hefty, husky, large, obese, overweight, plump, rotund, stout; CONCEPT *491* —*Ant.* skinny, slender, thin

portrait [*n*] *drawn representation; description* account, characterization, depiction, figure, image, likeness, model, painting, photograph, picture, portraiture, portrayal, profile, silhou-

ette, simulacrum, sketch, snapshot, spitting
image*, vignette; CONCEPTS 259,268,625

portray [v] *represent, imitate* act like, characterize, copy, delineate, depict, describe, draw,
duplicate, figure, illustrate, image, impersonate,
interpret, limn, mimic, paint, parody, photograph, picture, render, reproduce, simulate,
sketch; CONCEPTS 55,174,265

pose [n] *artificial position* act, affectation, air,
attitude, attitudinizing, bearing, carriage, facade, fake, false show, front, guise, mannerism,
masquerade, mien, positure, posture, posturing,
pretense, pretension, role, stance, stand;
CONCEPTS 633,716 —*Ant.* movement

pose [v1] *sit, stand in place* arrange, model,
peacock, poise, position, posture, sit for, strike
a pose, strut; CONCEPTS 154,174 —*Ant.* go,
move

pose [v2] *pretend, fake* act, affect, attitudinize,
feign, grandstand*, impersonate, make believe,
make out like*, masquerade, pass off*, peacock*, playact, posture, profess, purport, put on
airs*, put up a front*, sham*, show off*, strike
an attitude*, take off as*; CONCEPTS 59,63,633
—*Ant.* be genuine

pose [v3] *offer, put forward idea* advance, ask,
extend, give, hold out, posit, prefer, present,
proffer, propose, proposition, propound, put,
query, question, set, state, submit, suggest,
tender; CONCEPTS 66,67,75 —*Ant.* withhold

posh [adj] *luxurious, upper-class* chic, classy,
deluxe, elegant, exclusive, fashionable, grand,
high-class, la-di-da*, luxury, modish*, opulent,
rich, ritzy*, smart, swank, swanky*, swish*,
trendy; CONCEPTS 334,589 —*Ant.* destitute,
lower-class, poor

position [n1] *physical place* area, bearings,
district, environment, fix, geography, ground,
locale, locality, location, locus, point, post, reference, region, scene, seat, setting, site, situation, space, spot, stand, station, surroundings,
topography, tract, whereabouts*; CONCEPT 198

position [n2] *posture, stance* arrangement,
attitude, ballgame*, bearing, carriage, circumstances, condition, deportment, disposition,
form, habit, how things stack up*, like it is*,
manner, mien, pass, plight, port, pose, predicament, situation, spot, stand, state, status, strait,
the size of it*; CONCEPT 696

position [n3] *belief, point of view* angle, attitude, color, judgment, opinion, outlook, slant,
stance, stand, standpoint, view, viewpoint;
CONCEPT 689

position [n4] *class, stature* cachet, capacity,
caste, character, consequence, dignity, footing,
importance, place, prestige, rank, reputation,
situation, sphere, standing, station, status;
CONCEPTS 378,388

position [n5] *responsibility in business or other
enterprise* berth, billet, capacity, connection,
do*, duty, employment, function, job, nine-to-
five*, occupation, office, place, post, profession,
role, situation, slot*, spot*, trade; CONCEPTS
324,349,360 —*Ant.* unemployment

position [v] *place physically in location*
arrange, array, dispose, fix, lay out, locate,
put, set, settle, stand, stick; CONCEPTS 158,201
—*Ant.* displace, lose

positive [adj1] *definite, certain* absolute, actual,

affirmative, assured, categorical, clear, clear-
cut, cocksure*, cold*, complete, conclusive,
concrete, confident, consummate, convinced,
decided, decisive, direct, downright, explicit,
express, factual, firm, forceful, forcible, genuine, hard, inarguable, incontestable, incontrovertible, indisputable, indubitable, irrefutable,
out-and-out*, outright, perfect, rank, real, specific, sure, thorough, thoroughgoing, unambiguous, undeniable, unequivocal, unmistakable,
unmitigated; CONCEPTS 535,582 —*Ant.* doubtful, indefinite, negative, uncertain, unsure

positive [adj2] *beneficial, helpful* affirmative,
constructive, effective, efficacious, forward-
looking, good, practical, productive, progressive, reasonable, sound, useful; CONCEPT 572
—*Ant.* disadvantageous, negative, unhelpful

positively [adv] *absolutely, definitely* amen*,
assuredly, categorically, certainly, doubtless,
doubtlessly, easily, emphatically, firmly, flat*,
flat out*, for a fact*, indubitably, no catch*, no
holds barred*, no ifs ands or buts*, no kicker*,
no strings attached*, on the money*, on the
nose*, really truly*, right on*, sure, surely, the
ticket*, to a tee*, undeniably, undoubtedly,
unequivocally, unmistakably, unquestionably,
with certainty, without qualification; CONCEPTS
535,544,582 —*Ant.* doubtfully, questionably

possess [v] *have or obtain* acquire, bear, be
blessed with, be born with, be endowed with,
carry, control, corner*, corner the market*,
dominate, enjoy, get hands on*, get hold of*,
grab, have to name*, hog*, hold, latch on to,
lock up, maintain, occupy, own, retain, seize,
sit on, take over, take possession; CONCEPTS
120,710 —*Ant.* dispossess, lose, miss, not have

possessed [adj] *bewitched; under a spell* bedeviled, berserk*, consumed, crazed*, cursed,
demented, enchanted, enthralled, fiendish,
frenetic, frenzied, gone*, haunted, hooked*,
insane, into*, mad*, obsessed, raving*, taken
over*, violent; CONCEPT 401 —*Ant.* normal

possession [n1] *control, ownership* custody,
dominion, hold, occupancy, occupation,
possessorship, proprietary, proprietary rights,
proprietorship, retention, tenancy, tenure, title;
CONCEPTS 343,710 —*Ant.* lack, need, want

possession [n2] *something owned; property*
accessories, appointments, appurtenances,
assets, baggage, belongings, chattels, effects,
equipment, estate, fixtures, furnishings,
furniture, goods, impedimenta, paraphernalia,
province, real estate, settlement, tangibles,
territory, things, trappings, tricks, wealth;
CONCEPTS 446,710

possessive [adj] *greedy* acquisitive, avaricious,
controlling, craving, desirous, dominating,
grabby, grasping, hoggish*, selfish; CONCEPTS
326,403,542

possibilities [n] *potential* capabilities, potentiality, promise, prospects, talent; CONCEPTS
411,650 —*Ant.* impossible

possibility [n] *feasibility, likelihood; chance*
achievability, action, attainableness, break,
circumstance, contingency, fair shake*,
fifty-fifty*, fling*, fluke*, fortuity, happening,
hazard, hope, incident, instance, liability,
likeliness, occasion, occurrence, odds*, opportunity, outside chance*, plausibility, play*,

potentiality, practicability, prayer*, probability, prospect, risk*, shot*, stab*, toss-up*, work-ableness; CONCEPTS 650,693 —*Ant.* impossibil-ity, impossible, unfeasibility, unlikelihood

possible [*adj*] *likely, attainable* accessible, achievable, adventitious, advisable, available, breeze*, can do*, cinch, conceivable, credible, dependent, desirable, doable, dormant, duck soup*, easy as pie*, expedient, feasible, fortu-itous, hopeful, hypothetical, imaginable, inde-terminate, latent, no sweat*, obtainable, piece of cake*, potential, practicable, probable, promising, pushover*, realizable, setup, simple as ABC*, snap, thinkable, uncertain, viable, welcome, within reach, workable; CONCEPTS 528,552,576 —*Ant.* impossible, unattainable, ungettable, unlikely, unrealizable

possibly [*adv*] *by chance; in some way* at all, by any chance, by any means, conceivably, could be, God willing*, if possible, in any way, likely, maybe, not impossibly, peradventure, perchance, perhaps, probably, within realm of possibility; CONCEPTS 544,552 —*Ant.* impossi-bly, unlikely

post [*n1*] *upright support* column, doorpost, leg, mast, newel, pale, palisade, panel, pedestal, picket, pile, pillar, pole, prop, rail, shaft, stake, standard, stilt, stock, stud; CONCEPTS 440,445, 470,479

post [*n2*] *job, employment* appointment, assign-ment, berth, billet, office, place, position, situa-tion; CONCEPTS 351,362 —*Ant.* unemployment

post [*n3*] *lookout, station* beat, locus, place, position, whereabouts; CONCEPTS 198,321,439

post [*n4*] *mail service* collection, delivery, mail, PO*, postal service, post office; CONCEPTS 299,770

post [*v1*] *situate, position* assign, establish, locate, place, put, set, station; CONCEPT 201 —*Ant.* displace

post [*v2*] *advise, inform* acquaint, apprive, brief, clue, fill in, notify, put wise to, report, tell, warn, wise up; CONCEPT 60 —*Ant.* withhold

poster [*n*] *large paper advertisement* affiche, announcement, banner, bill, billboard, broad-side, handbill, notice, placard, public notice, sheet, sign, signboard, sticker; CONCEPT 271

posterior [*adj1*] *rear* after, back, behind, dor-sal, hind, hinder, hindmost, in back of, last, re-tral; CONCEPTS 583,827 —*Ant.* anterior, front

posterior [*adj2*] *subsequent* after, coming after, ensuing, following, later, latter, next, postlimi-nary, subsequential, succeeding; CONCEPTS 585,799 —*Ant.* front, preceding, previous

posterior [*n*] *behind of animate being* back, backside, bottom, butt*, buttocks, can*, cheeks*, derriere, duff*, fanny*, hind part, keester*, moon*, rear, rear end, rump, seat, tail, tail end, tuchis*, tush*; CONCEPT 392 —*Ant.* anterior, front

posterity [*n*] *future generations* breed, brood, children, descendants, family, heirs, issue, lineage, next generation, offspring, progeniture, progeny, scions, seed, stock, succeeding gener-ations, successors, unborn; CONCEPT 296 —*Ant.* past

posthaste [*adj/adv*] *fast* at once, breakneck*, directly, double-quick*, expeditious, flat-out*, fleet, fleetly, full tilt*, hastily, hasty, headlong,

lickety-split*, pell-mell*, promptly, pronto, quick, quickly, rapid, rapidly, speedily, speedy, straightaway, swift, swiftly; CONCEPTS 544,588,799 —*Ant.* eventually, slow, slowly

postmortem [*adj*] *following death* future, later, posthumous, postmundane, post-obit, post-obituary; CONCEPT 799

postmortem [*n*] *analysis after death* autopsy, coroner's report, dissection, examination, necropsy, post*; CONCEPTS 103,310

postpone [*v*] *put off till later time* adjourn, cool it*, defer, delay, give a rain check*, hang fire*, hold off, hold over, hold up, lay over, pigeon-hole*, prorogue, put back, put on back burner*, put on hold, shelve, suspend, table; CONCEPT 130 —*Ant.* carry out, continue, do, expedite, forward, maintain, persevere

postulate [*v*] *suppose, figure* advance, affirm, assert, assume, aver, estimate, guess, hypothe-size, posit, predicate, premise, presuppose, propose, put forward, speculate, suppose, take for granted, theorize; CONCEPTS 12,26 —*Ant.* calculate

posture [*n1*] *stance, circumstance* aspect, attitude, bearing, brace, carriage, condition, demeanor, deportment, disposition, mien, mode, phase, port, pose, position, positure, presence, set, situation, stance; CONCEPTS 657,723

posture [*n2*] *beliefs* attitude, disposition, feel-ing, frame of mind, inclination, mood, outlook, point of view, sentiment, stance, standpoint; CONCEPT 410

posture [*v*] *display an attitude* affect, attitudi-nize, display, do a bit*, do for effect*, fake, fake it, make a show*, masquerade, pass for, pass off, playact, pose, put on airs*, put up a front*, show off*; CONCEPTS 59,261 —*Ant.* be truthful

pot [*n1*] *container, cauldron* basin, bowl, bucket, can, canister, crock, crucible, cup, jar, jug, kettle, mug, pan, pitcher, receptacle, saucepan, tankard, urn, vessel; CONCEPT 494

pot [*n2*] *marijuana* cannabis, grass*, hashish, maryjane*, weed*; CONCEPT 307

potable [*adj*] *drinkable* edible, palatable, safe to drink; CONCEPT 169

potable [*n*] *beverage* alcoholic beverage, cooler, draft, drink, libation, liquor; CONCEPT 454

potbelly [*n*] *large stomach* bay window*, beer belly, beer gut*, belly, corporation, fat stomach, gut, middle-age spread, paunch, pot*, pot belly, spare tire*, tummy; CONCEPT 393

potency [*n*] *effectiveness* authority, birr, capa-bility, capacity, command, control, dominion, efficacy, efficiency, energy, force, go*, hardi-hood, influence, juice*, kick*, might, moxie*, muscle*, pep, potential, power, puissance, punch, sinew*, snap, sock*, steam*, strength, sway, vigor, virtue, what it takes*, zap*, zing*, zip*; CONCEPTS 411,676,732 —*Ant.* disability, impotency, ineffectiveness, weakness

potent [*adj*] *effective, powerful, forceful* almighty, authoritative, ball of fire*, cogent, commanding, compelling, convincing, dominant, dynamic, efficacious, forcible, full-bodied, go-getter*, great, gutsy*, impressive, influential, lusty, mighty, persuasive, power-house, puissant, punchy, robust, spanking, stiff, strong, sturdy, telling, trenchant, useful, vigorous; CONCEPTS *372,489,540* —*Ant.* disabled, fragile, helpless, impotent, incapable, ineffective, weak

potentate [*n*] *monarch* autocrat, chief, chieftain, crowned head, despot, dictator, emperor, empress, head of state, king, leader, majesty, prince, princess, queen, royalty, ruler, sovereign; CONCEPTS *354,422*

potential [*adj*] *promising* abeyant, budding, conceivable, dormant, embryonic, future, hidden, imaginable, implied, inherent, latent, likely, lurking, plausible, possible, prepotent, probable, quiescent, thinkable, undeveloped, unrealized, within realm of possibility; CONCEPTS *528,552* —*Ant.* helpless, impossible, lacking, unpromising

potential [*n*] *possibility for achievement* ability, aptitude, capability, capacity, potentiality, power, the makings*, what it takes*, wherewithal; CONCEPTS *650,706* —*Ant.* impossible, lack

pothole [*n*] *chuckhole* cavity, crater, depression, dip, fracture, gap, hole, pit, pocket, rut, split; CONCEPT *513*

potion [*n*] *concoction prepared for mental or physical effect* aromatic, brew, cordial, cup, dose, draft, dram, draught, drink, elixir, libation, liquid, liquor, medicine, mixture, nip, philter, remedy, restorative, spirits, stimulant, tonic; CONCEPTS *307,467*

potpourri [*n*] *miscellany* assortment, blend, collection, combination, combo, gallimaufry, goulash, hash, hodgepodge, medley, mélange, mishmash, mixed bag, mixture, motley, olio*, pastiche*, patchwork, salmagundi*, soup, stew; CONCEPTS *260,432* —*Ant.* ingredient, singular

pottery [*n*] *containers made from clay; clay art* ceramics, crockery, earthenware, firing, glazing, porcelain, porcelainware, stoneware, terra cotta; CONCEPTS *174,259,494*

pouch [*n*] *soft container, often made of cloth or skin* bag, pocket, poke, purse, receptacle, sac, sack; CONCEPTS *446,450,494*

pounce [*n/v*] *leap at; take by surprise* ambush, attack, bound, dart, dash, dive, drop, fall upon, jump, snatch, spring, strike, surge, swoop, take unawares; CONCEPTS *86,159,194*

pound [*n*] *sixteen ounces/.454 kilograms of weight* avoirdupois, pint, troy; CONCEPT *795*

pound [*v1*] *crush; beat rhythmically* batter, belabor, bruise, buffet, clobber, comminute, drub, hammer, hit, malleate, palpitate, pelt, pestle, powder, pulsate, pulse, pulverize, pummel, stomp, strike, thrash, throb, thump, tramp, triturate, wallop; CONCEPTS *150,186,189*

pound [*v2*] *impress; make someone listen* din, drive, drub, drum, grave, hammer, stamp; CONCEPTS *14,49* —*Ant.* give up

pour [*v*] *be or make flowing* cascade, cataract, course, crowd, decant, deluge, discharge, drain, drench, emit, flood, flow, give off, gush, inundate, issue, jet, let flow, proceed, rain, rill, roll, run, rush, sheet, shower, sluice, spew, spill, splash, spout, spring, stream, surge, swarm, teem, throng; CONCEPTS *146,179,209*

pout [*n*] *sad face* frown, glower, long face, moue, sullen look; CONCEPT *716* —*Ant.* grin, smile

pout [*v*] *make a sad face; be sad* be cross, be in bad mood*, be moody, be petulant, be sullen, frown, grouch, grump*, make a long face*, make a moue, mope, stick one's lip out*, sulk; CONCEPTS *261,410* —*Ant.* grin, smile

poverty [*n*] *want; extreme need, often financial* abjection, aridity, bankruptcy, barrenness, beggary, dearth, debt, deficiency, deficit, depletion, destitution, difficulty, distress, emptiness, exiguity, famine, hardship, impecuniousness, impoverishment, inadequacy, indigence, insolvency, insufficiency, lack, meagerness, necessitousness, necessity, pass, paucity, pauperism, penniless, penury, pinch, poorness, privation, reduction, scarcity, shortage, starvation, straits, underdevelopment, vacancy; CONCEPTS *335,709* —*Ant.* abundance, affluence, luxury, richness, wealth

poverty-stricken [*adj*] *in great need; financially poor* bad off*, bankrupt, beggared, beggarly, broke*, destitute, dirt poor*, distressed, down-and-out*, hard up*, impecunious, impoverished, indigent, in dire circumstances, in want, moneyless, necessitous, needful, needy, penniless, penurious, short*, stone broke*, stranded*, strapped*, unmoneyed, wanting; CONCEPT *334* —*Ant.* rich, wealthy

powder [*n*] *fine, loose grains made by crushing a solid* crumb, dust, film, grain, grit, meal, particle, pounce, pulverization, seed, talc; CONCEPTS *471,831* —*Ant.* solid

powder [*v*] *crush into fine grains; sprinkle fine grains* abrade, bray, comminute, cover, crumble, crunch, dredge, dust, file, flour, granulate, grate, grind, pestle, pound, pulverize, rasp, reduce, scatter, scrape, smash, strew, triturate; CONCEPTS *186,222* —*Ant.* solidify

powder room [*n*] *bathroom* comfort station, ladies', ladies' room, lavatory, loo, restroom, toilet, washroom; CONCEPT *448*

powdery [*adj*] *consisting of fine, loose grains* arenaceous, arenose, branny, chalky, crumbling, crumbly, dry, dusty, fine, floury, friable, grainy, granular, gravelly, gritty, impalpable, loose, mealy, pulverized, pulverulent, sandy; CONCEPT *606* —*Ant.* solid

power [*n1*] *ability, competence* aptitude, bent, capability, capacity, competency, dynamism, effectiveness, efficacy, endowment, faculty, function, gift, influence, potential, potentiality, qualification, skill, talent, turn, virtue; CONCEPT *630* —*Ant.* inability, incapacity, incompetence, weakness

power [*n2*] *physical ability, capacity* applied force, arm*, brawn, dynamism, energy, force, forcefulness, horsepower, intensity, mechanical energy, might, muscle*, omnipotence, potency, potential, puissance, sinew*, strength, vigor, vim, virtue, voltage, weight; CONCEPTS *520, 641,732* —*Ant.* debility, disability, impairment, impotence, infirmity, weakness

power [*n3*] *control; dominance* ascendancy, authority, authorization, birthright, clout, command, connection, diadem, direction, domination, dominion, hegemony, imperium, influence, inside track*, jurisdiction, law, leadership, license, management, might, moxie*, omnipotence, paramountcy, predominance, prerogative, prestige, privilege, regency, right, rule, say-so*, sovereignty, steam, strength, strings*, superiority, supremacy, sway, warrant, weight*, wire*; CONCEPTS 376,671 —Ant. inefficiency, subservience, surrender, weakness, yielding

powerful |adj| *strong, effective* able, all-powerful, almighty, authoritarian, authoritative, capable, cogent, commanding, compelling, competent, controlling, convincing, dominant, dynamic, effectual, efficacious, energetic, forceful, forcible, impressive, in control, influential, in the saddle*, mighty, omnipotent, overruling, paramount, persuasive, potent, preeminent, prevailing, puissant, robust, ruling, sovereign, stalwart, strapping*, strengthy, sturdy, supreme, telling, upper hand*, vigorous, weighty, wicked*, wieldy; CONCEPT 489,—Ant. impotent, incapable, ineffective, unable, weak

powerfully |adv| *with energy, authority* effectively, energetically, forcefully, forcibly, hard, intensely, mightily, severely, strongly, vigorously, with might and main; CONCEPTS 540,544,569 —Ant. softly, weakly

powerless |adj| *weak; unable* blank, chicken*, debilitated, defenseless, dependent, disabled, disenfranchised, etiolated, feeble, frail, gutless, helpless, impotent, incapable, incapacitated, ineffective, ineffectual, inert, infirm, out of gas*, paralyzed, passive, prostrate, subject, supine, tied, unarmed, unfit, vulnerable, wimp*, wishy-washy*; CONCEPTS 489,527 —Ant. able, dominant, potent, powerful, strong

powwow |n| *discussion* confab*, confabulation, conference, consultation, council, get-together, huddle, meeting, palaver, parley, talk; CONCEPTS 56,324,384 —Ant. quiet

powwow |v| *discuss* advise, confab*, confabulate, confer, consult, get together, go into a huddle*, huddle, meet, palaver, parley, talk, treat; CONCEPT 56

practicable |adj| *within the realm of possibility* accessible, achievable, applicable, attainable, doable, employable, feasible, functional, handy, open, operative, performable, possible, practical, serviceable, usable, useful, utile, utilizable, viable, workable; CONCEPT 560 —Ant. impossible, impracticable, unattainable, unreasonable, unworkable

practical |adj1| *realistic, useful* applied, both feet on the ground*, businesslike, commonsensical, constructive, doable, down-to-earth, efficient, empirical, experimental, factual, functional, handy, hard-boiled*, implicit, in action, in operation, matter-of-fact*, nuts and bolts*, operative, orderly, possible, practicable, pragmatic, rational, reasonable, sane, sensible, serviceable, sober, solid, sound, systematic, unidealistic, unromantic, usable, utile, utilitarian, virtual, workable, workaday, working; CONCEPTS 533,542,560 —Ant. impossible, impractical, unfeasible, unrealistic, unserviceable, unworkable, useless, worthless

practical |adj2| *experienced, proficient* accomplished, cosmopolitan, effective, efficient, qualified, seasoned, skilled, sophisticated, trained, versed, vet*, veteran, working, worldly, worldly-wise; CONCEPTS 326,527,528,678 —Ant. incapable, inefficient, inexperienced, unproficient, unseasoned, unskilled, untrained, useless

practically |adj| *almost; nearly* about, all but, approximately, as good as, as much as, basically, close to, essentially, for all intents and purposes*, fundamentally, in effect, in essence, morally, most, much, nearly, nigh, virtually, well-nigh; CONCEPTS 531,772 —Ant. far, not close

practice |n1| *routine, usual procedure* convenance, convention, custom, fashion, form, habit, habitude, manner, method, mode, praxis, proceeding, process, rule, system, tradition, trick, usage, use, usefulness, utility, way, wont; CONCEPT 688 —Ant. abstention, refrain

practice |n2| *exercise, application* action, assignment, background, discipline, drill, drilling, effect, experience, homework, iteration, operation, preparation, prepping, recitation, recounting, rehearsal, relating, repetition, seasoning, study, training, tune-up, use, work-out; CONCEPTS 87,100,658 —Ant. ignorance, neglect

practice |n3| *business; clientele of business* career, clients, patients, profession, vocation, work; CONCEPTS 325,417

practice |v1| *repeat action to improve* become seasoned, build up, discipline, do again, dress, dress rehearse*, drill, dry run*, exercise, go over, habituate, hone, iterate, polish, prepare, recite, rehearse, run through, shake-down*, sharpen, study, train, try out, tune up, walk through, warm up, work, work out; CONCEPTS 87,100

practice |v2| *carry out; undertake* apply, carry on, do, engage in, execute, follow, fulfill, function, live up to, observe, perform, ply, pursue, put into effect, specialize in, work at; CONCEPTS 91,310,317,324 —Ant. cease, forget, halt, neglect, stop

practitioner |n| *expert* doctor, master, pro, professional, specialist; CONCEPTS 348,350,416

pragmatic |adj| *sensible* businesslike, commonsensical, down-to-earth, efficient, hard, hard-boiled*, hardheaded*, logical, matter-of-fact, practical, realistic, sober, unidealistic, utilitarian; CONCEPTS 401,542 —Ant. idealistic, unreasonable

prairie |n| *grassland* grassy field, meadow, pasturage, pasture, plain, savanna, steppe, veldt; CONCEPT 509

praise |n| *congratulations; adoration* acclaim, acclamation, accolade, applause, appreciation, approbation, approval, big hand*, boost, bravo, celebration, cheer, cheering, citation, commendation, compliment, cry, devotion, encomium, esteem, eulogy, exaltation, extolment, flattery, glorification, glory, good word*, homage, hurrah, hymn, kudos*, laudation, obeisance, ovation, panegyric, pat on the back*, plaudit, puff*, rave, recognition, recommendation, regard, sycophancy, thanks, tribute, worship; CONCEPTS 69,278 —Ant. blame, censure, condemnation, criticism

praise |v| *congratulate; adore* acclaim, admire, adulate, advocate, aggrandize, applaud, appreciate, approve, bless, boost, bow down*, build up*, cajole, celebrate, cheer, cite, clap, commend, compliment, cry up*, dignify, distinguish, elevate, endorse, ennoble, eulogize, exalt, extol, flatter, give thanks, glorify, hail, honor, laud, make much of*, panegyrize, pay homage, pay tribute, proclaim, puff*, rave over, recommend, resound, reverence, root*, sanction, sing the praises*, smile on*, stroke*, tout, worship; CONCEPT 69 —*Ant.* accuse, blame, censure, condemn, denounce, reproach

praiseworthy [*adj*] *deserving congratulations, adoration* admirable, commendable, creditable, estimable, excellent, exemplary, fine, gnarly, gone, honorable, keen, laudable, meritable, meritorious, pillar, salt of earth*, select, slick, stellar, swell, thankworthy, tough, worthy; CONCEPTS 568,574 —*Ant.* dishonorable, disliked, disrespected, unworthy

prance [*v*] *cavort; show off* bound, caper, dance, flounce, foot it*, frisk, gambol, hoof it*, jump, leap, mince, parade, romp, sashay, skip, spring, stalk, step, strut, swagger, sweep, tread; CONCEPTS 150,292,384

prank [*n*] *practical joke; frivolity* antic, caper, caprice, escapade, fancy, fooling, frolic, gag, gambol, high jinks*, horseplay*, hotfoot*, lark, levity, lightness, monkeyshines*, play, put-on, rib*, rollick, roughhouse*, roughhousing*, rowdiness, shenanigans, shine*, skylarking*, spoof, sport, tomfoolery, trick, whim; CONCEPTS 59,384

prattle [*n*] *babble* blubbering, burble, chatter, chit-chat, drivel, gab, gabble, gibberish, gossip, hot air*, idle talk, jabber, jabbering, jargon, murmur, ranting, small talk, tattling, trivial talk, twaddle; CONCEPTS 266,278

pray [*v*] *plead; call upon for help, answer* adjure, appeal, ask, beseech, brace, commune with, crave, cry for, entreat, implore, importune, invocate, invoke, petition, recite, request, say, solicit, sue, supplicate, urge; CONCEPTS 48,367

prayer [*n*] *pleading, especially with a deity; request for help, answer* adoration, appeal, application, begging, benediction, beseeching, communion, devotion, entreaty, grace, imploration, imploring, imprecation, invocation, litany, orison, petition, plea, pleading, request, rogation, service, suit, supplication, worship; CONCEPTS 48,367,662

preach [*v1*] *speak publicly about beliefs* address, deliver, deliver sermon, evangelize, exhort, give sermon, homilize, inform, minister, mission, missionary, orate, prophesy, pulpiteer, sermonize, talk, teach; CONCEPTS 51,285,367

preach [*v2*] *lecture, moralize* admonish, advocate, blow, exhort, get on a soapbox*, harangue, pile it on*, preachify, sermonize, talk big*, urge; CONCEPTS 51,75

preacher [*n*] *person who gives religious instruction* clergy, cleric, clerical, divine, ecclesiastic, evangelist, evangelizer, minister, missionary, parson, pulpiter, reverend, revivalist, sermonizer; CONCEPT 361

precarious [*adj*] *tricky, doubtful* ambiguous, borderline, chancy, contingent, dangerous, delicate, dicey*, dubious, dynamite, equivocal, hairy*, hanging by a thread*, hazardous, iffy*, impugnable, indecisive, insecure, loaded, on thin ice*, open, out on a limb*, perilous, problematic, risky, rocky, rugged*, sensitive, shaky, slippery, ticklish, touch and go*, touchy, uncertain, unhealthy, unreliable, unsafe, unsettled, unstable, unsteady, unsure; CONCEPTS 535,587

—*Ant.* certain, definite, firm, stable, strong, sure, undoubted

precaution [*n*] *carefulness; preventative measure* anticipation, canniness, care, caution, circumspection, discreetness, discretion, foresight, forethought, insurance, protection, providence, provision, prudence, regard, safeguard, safety measure, wariness; CONCEPTS 410,633, 729 —*Ant.* carelessness

precede [*v*] *go ahead of* antecede, antedate, anticipate, be ahead of, come first, forerun, foreshadow, go before, go in advance, guide, harbinger, have a head start*, head, head up, herald, in space, introduce, lead, light the way*, outrank, pace, pave the way*, pioneer, predate, preexist, preface, presage, rank, ring in*, run ahead, scout, take precedence, time, usher; CONCEPTS 727,747,813,818 —*Ant.* follow, go after

precedence [*n*] *highest in rank; first in order* antecedence, anteposition, earliness, lead, precedency, precession, preeminence, preexistence, preference, prevenience, previousness, primary, priority, rank, seniority, superiority, supremacy; CONCEPTS 671,727,747,818 —*Ant.* inferiority, last, lowest

precedent [*n*] *authoritative example* antecedent, authority, criterion, exemplar, instance, model, paradigm; CONCEPT 686

preceding [*adj*] *earlier, above* above-mentioned, above-named, aforeknown, aforementioned, aforesaid, ahead of, antecedent, anterior, before, erstwhile, foregoing, forerunning, former, forward, front, head, heretofore, introductory, lead, leading, one time, other, past, pioneer, pioneering, precedent, precursive, precursory, preexistent, prefatory, preliminary, preparatory, prevenient, previous, prior, supra; CONCEPTS 585,586,799,811,818 —*Ant.* after, below, following, later

precept [*n*] *law, rule of behavior, action* axiom, behest, bidding, byword, canon, command, commandment, decree, decretum, direction, doctrine, dogma, edict, formula, fundamental, guideline, injunction, instruction, law, mandate, maxim, motto, order, ordinance, prescript, principle, regulation, rule, saying, statute, tenet; CONCEPTS 318,688

precinct [*n*] *subdivision* area, community, department, development, district, division, neighborhood, province, quarter, section, tract, ward, zone; CONCEPTS 513,835

precious [*adj1*] *favorite, valued* adored, beloved, cherished, darling, dear, dearest, idolized, inestimable, loved, pet, prized, treasured; CONCEPTS 529,567 —*Ant.* disfavored, useless, valueless, worthless

precious [*adj2*] *expensive; rare* choice, costly, dear, exquisite, fine, high-priced, inestimable, invaluable, priceless, prizable, prized, recherché, rich, treasurable, valuable, worth a king's ransom*, worth eyeteeth*, worth one's weight in gold*; CONCEPT 334 —*Ant.* cheap, common, inexpensive

precious [*adj3*] *extremely sophisticated and picky* affected, alembicated, artful, artificial, chichi*, choosy, dainty, delicate, fastidious, finicky, fragile, fussy, la-di-da*, nice, ostentatious, overnice, overrefined, particular, persnickety*, precieux, pretentious, refined, showy, stagy, studied; CONCEPT *401* —*Ant.* defective, deficient, impaired

precipice [*n*] *face or brink of a rock, mountain* bluff, cliff, crag, height, sheer drop, steep; CONCEPTS *509,513*

precipitate [*v*] *hurry, speed* accelerate, advance, bring on, cast, discharge, dispatch, expedite, fling, further, hasten, hurl, launch, let fly, press, push forward, quicken, send forth, speed up, throw, trigger; CONCEPTS *152,242, 704* —*Ant.* check, slow, wait

precipitation [*n*] *moisture in air or falling from sky* cloudburst, condensation, drizzle, hail, hailstorm, heavy dew, precip*, rain, rainfall, rainstorm, sleet, snow, storm, wetness; CONCEPTS *467,524,526* —*Ant.* dryness

precipitous [*adj1*] *steep, falling sharply* abrupt, arduous, craggy, dizzy, dizzying, high, perpendicular, precipitate, sharp, sheer; CONCEPTS *490,583,779* —*Ant.* gradual

precipitous/precipitate [*adj2*] *fast, sudden; impulsive; initial* abrupt, breakneck*, brief, frantic, gone off half-cocked*, harum-scarum*, hasty, headlong, heedless, hurried, ill-advised, impatient, impetuous, indiscreet, jump the gun*, madcap, off the hip*, off the top of head*, plunging, precipitant, quick, rapid, rash, reckless, refractory, rushing, subitaneous, swift, unanticipated, uncontrolled, unexpected, unforeseen, violent, willful, without warning; CONCEPTS *229,401,542,588,799* —*Ant.* careful, cautious, slow

précis [*n*] *abridgment* abstract, aperçu, compendium, condensation, digest, outline, pandect, résumé, rundown, sketch, summary, survey, syllabus, synopsis; CONCEPT *283* —*Ant.* expansion

precise [*adj1*] *exact, accurate* absolute, actual, categorical, circumscribed, clear-cut, correct, decisive, definite, determinate, explicit, express, fixed, individual, limited, literal, narrow, nice, on the button*, on the money*, on the nose*, particular, proper, restricted, right, rigid, rigorous, specific, strict, stringent, unequivocal, very, well-defined; CONCEPTS *535,557,653* —*Ant.* ambiguous, false, imprecise, inaccurate, inexact, questionable

precise [*adj2*] *meticulous, fastidious* careful, ceremonious, choosy, exact, finicky, formal, fussy, genteel, inflexible, nice, particular, persnickety*, picky, priggish, prim, prissy, punctilious, rigid, scrupulous, stickling, stiff*, strict, stuffy, uncompromising; CONCEPTS *401,542* —*Ant.* careless, loose, negligent, slipshod

precisely [*adv*] *exactly, just* absolutely, accurately, as well, correctly, definitely, even, expressly, for a fact, for sure, just so, literally, no ifs ands or buts*, no mistake*, on the button*, on the money*, on the nose*, plumb, right, sharp, smack*, smack-dab*, specifically, square, squarely, strictly, sure, sure thing*, the ticket*, the very thing*, to a tee*; yes; CONCEPTS *535,557* —*Ant.* imprecisely, questionably, unsure

precision [*n*] *accuracy* attention, care, carefulness, correctness, definiteness, definitiveness, definitude, exactitude, exactness, fidelity, heed, meticulousness, nicety, particularity, precise-

ness, rigor, sureness; CONCEPTS *638,654* —*Ant.* imprecision, inaccuracy, inexactness

preclude [*v*] *inhibit; make impossible* avert, cease, check, debar, deter, discontinue, exclude, forestall, forfend, hinder, impede, interrupt, make impracticable, obviate, prevent, prohibit, put a stop to, quit, restrain, rule out, stave off, stop, ward; CONCEPTS *121,234* —*Ant.* allow, permit, support

precocious [*adj*] *exceptionally smart, ahead of age in understanding* advanced, aggressive, ahead of time*, beforehand, bold, brassy*, bright, cheeky*, cocky*, developed, early, flip*, flippant, forward, fresh, intelligent, mature, nervy, premature, presumptuous, pushy, quick, sassy*, smart-alecky*; CONCEPT *402* —*Ant.* stupid

precognition [*n*] *clairvoyance* acumen, discernment, ESP, extra sensory perception, feeling, foreknowledge, foresight, fortune-telling, insight, intuition, omen, penetration, perception, prediction, premonition, prophecy, psyche, second sight, sixth sense*, telepathy; CONCEPTS *409,410*

preconception [*n*] *idea formed before event occurs or facts are received* assumption, bias, delusion, illusion, inclination, notion, preconceived idea, predisposition, prejudgment, prejudice, prepossession, presumption, presupposition; CONCEPT *689* —*Ant.* ignorance

precursor [*n1*] *something that indicates outcome or event beforehand* forerunner, harbinger, herald, messenger, outrider, usher, vanguard; CONCEPTS *70,278*

precursor [*n2*] *something that precedes another* ancestor, antecedent, antecessor, forebear, foregoer, forerunner, original, originator, parent, pioneer, predecessor, prototype; CONCEPTS *648,727,828*

predator [*n*] *hunter, killer* animal of prey, beast of prey, carnivore, meat-eater; CONCEPT *252*

predatory [*adj*] *eating, destroying for sustenance or without conscience* bloodthirsty, carnivorous, depredatory, despoiling, greedy, hungry, hunting, marauding, pillaging, plundering, predacious, predative, preying, rapacious, raptorial, ravaging, ravening, thieving, voracious, vulturine, vulturous, wolfish; CONCEPTS *401,406*

predecessor [*n*] *something, someone that comes before* ancestor, antecedent, antecessor, forebear, foregoer, forerunner, former, precursor, previous, prior, prototype; CONCEPTS *414,828* —*Ant.* derivative, descendant, successor

predestination [*n*] *destiny* course of events, divine decree, fate, foreordination, fortune, God's will, inevitability, karma, kismet*, ordinance, portion, predetermination, way the ball bounces*, way the cookie crumbles*, what is written*; CONCEPT *679*

predetermined [*adj*] *decided in advance* agreed, arranged, calculated, cut and dried*, deliberate, destined, determined, doomed, fated, fixed, foredestined, foreordained, forethought, planned, prearranged, precogitated, predestined, premeditated, preordained, preplanned, proposed, set, settled, set up; CONCEPT *548* —*Ant.* unarranged, undetermined, unplanned, unsettled

predicament [*n*] *difficult situation* asperity, bad

news*, bind*, Catch-22*, circumstance, clutch, condition, corner*, crisis, deadlock, deep water*, dilemma, drag*, emergency, exigency, fix*, hang-up*, hardship, hole, hot water*, imbroglio, impasse, jam*, juncture, large order*, lot, mess*, muddle, pass, perplexity, pickle*, pinch, plight, position, posture, puzzle, quagmire,quandary, rigor, rough go*, scrape*, soup*, spot*, state*, strait, tall order* ticklish spot* tight situation* trouble, vicissitude; CONCEPT 674 —*Ant.* fix, good fortune, solution

predict [v] *express an outcome in advance* adumbrate, anticipate, augur, be afraid, call, call it, conclude, conjecture, croak, crystal-ball* divine, envision, figure, figure out, forebode, forecast, foresee, forespeak, foretell, gather, guess, have a hunch*, hazard a guess*, infer, judge, make book*, omen, portend, presage, presume, prognosticate, prophesy, psych out*, read, see coming*, see handwriting on wall*, size up*, soothsay, suppose, surmise, telegraph*,think, vaticinate; CONCEPT 70

predictable [adj] *easy to foretell* anticipated, calculable, certain, expected, foreseeable, foreseen, likely, prepared, sure, sure-fire*; CONCEPTS 404,542,548 —*Ant.* improbable, unexpected, unforeseen, unpredictable

prediction [n] *declaration made in advance of event* anticipation, augury, cast, conjecture, crystal gazing*, divination, dope, forecast, forecasting, foresight, foretelling, fortune-telling, guess, horoscope, hunch*, indicator, omen, palmistry, presage, prevision, prognosis, prognostication, prophecy, soothsaying, surmising, tip, vaticination, zodiac; CONCEPTS 70,278, 689

predilection [n] *inclination, preference toward something* bent*, bias, cup of tea*, dish*, druthers*, fancy, flash, fondness, groove, inclining, leaning, liking, love, mindset*, partiality, penchant, predisposition, proclivity, proneness, propensity, taste*, tendency, thing*, type, weakness; CONCEPTS 20,32,709 —*Ant.* antipathy, disinterest, dislike, hate

predispose [v] *influence to believe something* activate, affect, animate, bend*, bias, cultivate, dispose, govern, impress, incline, indoctrinate, induce, inspire, lead, make expectant, make of a mind to*, prejudice, prepare, prime, prompt, stimulate, strike, sway, teach, urge; CONCEPTS 12,14,26,68 —*Ant.* discourage, dissuade

predisposed [adj] *willing, inclined* agreeable, amenable, biased, eager, enthusiastic, fain, given to, liable, likely, minded, partial, prone, ready, subject, susceptible; CONCEPT 403 —*Ant.* disagreeing, disinclined, unprepared, unwilling

predisposition [n] *willingness, inclination* bent*, bias, choice, cup of tea*, dish*, disposition, druthers*, flash, groove, leaning, likelihood, liking, option, partiality, penchant, potentiality, predilection, preference, proclivity, proneness, propensity, susceptibility, tendency, thing*, type, weakness;CONCEPTS 20,32,410,709 —*Ant.* disinclination, unwillingness

predominant [adj] *ruling; most important* absolute, all-powerful, almighty, arbitrary, ascendant, authoritative, capital, chief, controlling, directing, dominant, dominating, effective, efficacious, governing, holding the reins*,

imperious, influential; leading, main, mighty, official, omnipotent, overbearing, overpowering, paramount, potent, predominate, preponderant, prevailing, prevalent, primary, prime, principal, prominent, reigning, sovereign, superior, superlative, supervisory, supreme, surpassing, transcendent, weighty; CONCEPTS 568,574 —*Ant.* inconsequential, minor, trivial, unimportant

predominate [v] *be the most important, noticeable* carry weight*, command, dominate, domineer, get the upper hand*, govern, hold sway*, manage, outweigh, overrule, overshadow, preponderate, prevail, reign, rule, tell; CONCEPTS 94,117,141

preeminent [adj] *most important; superior* capital, chief, consummate, distinguished, dominant, excellent, foremost, incomparable, main, major, matchless, number one*, outstanding, paramount, peerless, predominant, principal, renowned, stellar, supreme, surpassing, towering, transcendent, ultimate, unequalled, unmatchable, unrivaled, unsurpassable, unsurpassed; CONCEPTS 568,574 —*Ant.* inferior, low, unimportant, unknown

preempt [v] *take over in place of another* accroach, acquire, annex, anticipate, appropriate, arrogate, assume, bump, commandeer, confiscate, expropriate, obtain, seize, sequester, take, usurp; CONCEPTS 121,142,234

preen [v] *admire and clean oneself* beautify, clean, doll up, groom, prettify, pretty, primp, prink, spruce up, tidy; CONCEPT 161

preface [n] *introduction* beginning, exordium, explanation, foreword, overture, preamble, preliminary, prelude, prelusion, proem, prolegomenon, prologue; CONCEPT 270 —*Ant.* appendix, conclusion, ending, epilogue, finish

preface [v] *introduce* begin, commence, launch, lead, lead up to, open, precede, prefix, usher; CONCEPTS 57,221 —*Ant.* conclude, end, finish

prefer [v] *favor; single out* adopt, advance, aggrandize, be partial to, be turned on to, choose, cull, desire, elect, elevate, fancy, finger, fix upon, go for, incline, like better, mark, optate, opt for, pick, place, pose, present, promote, propone, proposition, propound, put, put forward, raise, select, suggest, tag, take, tap, upgrade, wish, would rather*; would sooner*; CONCEPTS 20,41 —*Ant.* dislike, hate, reject, spurn

preference [n1] *first choice* alternative, choice, cup of tea*, desire, druthers*, election, favorite, flash*, groove, inclination, option, partiality, pick, predilection, prepossession, propensity, say, say so*, selection, top, weakness; CONCEPTS 20,529,709 —*Ant.* dislike, hate, hatred, last choice, rejection

preference [n2] *favorable treatment* advancement, advantage, elevation, favoritism, first place, precedence, preferment, prelation, pride of place, priority, promotion, upgrading; CONCEPT 693 —*Ant.* disfavor, equality, rejection

preferred [adj] *favorite, chosen* adopted, approved, culled, decided upon, elected, endorsed, fancied, favored, handpicked, liked, named, picked, popular, sanctioned, selected, set apart, settled upon, singled out, taken, well-liked; CONCEPTS 555,574 —*Ant.* ill-favored, rejected, undesirable

pregnancy [n] *gestation* child-bearing, fertilization, germination, gravidity, gravidness, impregnation, parturiency, propagation;CONCEPT 427

pregnant [adj1] *carrying developing offspring within the body* abundant, anticipating, carrying a child, enceinte, expectant, expecting*, fecund, fertile, fraught, fruitful, gestating, gravid, heavy, hopeful, in family way*, parous, parturient, preggers*, productive, prolific, replete, teeming, with child*; CONCEPTS 406,485

pregnant [adj2] *significant, meaningful* charged, cogent, consequential, creative, eloquent, expressive, fecund, imaginative, important, inventive, loaded, momentous, original, pointed, redolent, rich, seminal, sententious, suggestive, telling, weighty; CONCEPTS 267,567 —Ant. insignificant, trivial, unmeaningful

prehistoric [adj] *before recorded history* ancient, antediluvian, antiquated, archaic, earliest, early, old, olden, primeval, primitive, primordial; CONCEPTS 558,560,799

prejudice [n] *belief without basis, information; intolerance* ageism, animosity, antipathy, apartheid, aversion, bad opinion, bias, bigotry, chauvinism, contemptuousness, detriment, discrimination, disgust, dislike, displeasure, disrelish, enmity, foregone conclusion, illiberality, injustice, jaundiced eye, mindset*, misjudgment, narrow-mindedness, one-sidedness, partiality, pique, preconceived notion, preconception, prejudgment, prepossession, racism, repugnance, revulsion, sexism, slant, spleen, tilt, twist, umbrage, unfairness, warp, xenophobia; CONCEPT 689 —Ant. fairness, justice, regard, respect, tolerance

prejudice [v] *influence another's beliefs without basis, information* angle*, bend*, bias, blemish*, color*, damage, dispose, distort, harm, hinder, hurt, impair, incline, indoctrinate, injure, jaundice, mar, poison*, predispose, prejudge, prepossess, skew*, slant*, spoil, sway*, twist*, undermine, vitiate, warp*; CONCEPTS 7,14,19 —Ant. approve, be fair, be just, regard, respect, tolerate

prejudicial [adj] *harmful, undermining* bad, biased, bigoted, counterproductive, damaging, deleterious, detrimental, differential, disadvantageous, discriminatory, evil, hurtful, inimical, injurious, mischievous, nocuous, unfavorable, unjust; CONCEPTS 537,545,570 —Ant. approving, fair, just, unbiased

preliminary [adj] *introductory, initial* basic, elemental, elementary, exploratory, first, fundamental, inductive, initiatory, opening, pilot, preceding, precursory, prefatory, preparing, primal, primary, prior, qualifying, readying, test, trial; CONCEPTS 549,585,799 —Ant. closing, concluding, final

preliminary [n] *introductory event; beginning* first round, foundation, groundwork, initiation, introduction, opening, preamble, preface, prelims*, prelude, preparation, start; CONCEPTS 828,832 —Ant. closing, conclusion, finale

prelude [n] *beginning of event* commencement, curtain-raiser*, exordium, foreword, intro*, introduction, overture, preamble, preface, preliminary, prelusion, preparation, proem, prolegomenon, prologue, start; CONCEPTS 264, 832 —Ant. ending, epilogue, postlude

premature [adj1] *earlier in occurrence than anticipated* a bit previous, abortive, early on, embryonic, forward, green*, immature, incomplete, inopportune, overearly, oversoon, precipitate, predeveloped, previous, raw*, soon, unanticipated, undeveloped, unfledged, unripe, untimely; CONCEPTS 485,549 —Ant. backward, delayed, late, mature, overdue

premature [adj2] *rash, impulsive* half-baked*, half-cocked*, hasty, ill-considered, inopportune, jumping the gun*, overhasty, precipitate, previous, too soon, untimely;CONCEPTS 401, 542 —Ant. careful, cautious, prepared, slow

premeditated [adj] *planned, intended* advised, aforethought, calculated, conscious, considered, contrived, deliberate, designed, fixed, framed up, intentional, laid-out*, prepense, purposed, rigged*, set-up*, sewn-up*, stacked deck*, studied, thought-out, willful; CONCEPTS 542, 548 —Ant. accidental, casual, spontaneous

premier [adj] *leading; original* arch, beginning, champion, chief, earliest, first, foremost, head, highest, inaugural, initial, main, opening, primary, prime, principal; CONCEPTS 568,585 —Ant. inferior, minor

premiere [n] *original production* beginning, debut, first night, first performance, first showing, opening, opening night; CONCEPTS 263,832 —Ant. closing

premise [n] *hypothesis, argument* apriorism, assertion, assumption, basis, evidence, ground, posit, postulate, postulation, presumption, presupposition, proof, proposition, supposition, thesis; CONCEPTS 529,689 —Ant. fact, reality, truth

premise [v] *hypothesize* announce, assume, begin, commence, introduce, posit, postulate, predicate, presume, presuppose, start, state, suppose; CONCEPTS 18,37 —Ant. be factual

premises [n] *grounds and buildings* bounds, campus, digs, establishment, fix, flat, hangout*, home, house, joint*, land, lay, layout, limits, neck of the woods*, office, pad, place, plant, property, real estate*, roof, scene, site, spot, terrace, turf, zone; CONCEPTS 198,515

premium [adj] *excellent* choice, exceptional, prime, select, selected, superior; CONCEPT 574 —Ant. inferior, low, low-class, poor

premium [n] *bonus, prize* appreciation, boon, bounty, carrot*, dividend, extra, fee*, gravy*, guerdon, meed, percentage, perk*, perquisite, plum*, recompense, regard, remuneration, reward, spiff*, stock, store, value; CONCEPTS 337,344 —Ant. lowness, paucity

premonition [n] *feeling that an event is about to occur* apprehension, apprehensiveness, feeling, feeling in bones*, foreboding, forewarning, funny feeling, handwriting on wall*, hunch, idea, intuition, misgiving, omen, portent, prenotion, presage, presentiment, sign, sinking feeling, suspicion, vibes, vibrations, warning, wind change*, winds*, winds of change*, worriment; CONCEPTS 410,529,689,692

preoccupied [adj] *busy; mentally caught up in something* absent, absent-minded, absorbed, abstracted, airheaded*, asleep*, bemused, bugged*, daydreaming, deep*, distracted, distrait, engaged, engrossed, faraway, fascinated, forgetful, have on the brain*, heedless, hung up*, immersed, inconscient, intent, lost, lost in thought*, mooning*, moony*, oblivious, obsessed, rapt, removed, spellbound, spread out*, taken up, unaware, woolgathering*, wrapped-up*; CONCEPT 403 —Ant. observant, thoughtful, unoccupied

preparation [n1] *development, readiness* alertness, anticipation, arrangement, background, base, basis, build-up*, construction, dry run*, education, establishment, evolution, expectation, fitting, foresight, formation, foundation, gestation, getting ready, groundwork, homework, incubation, lead time*, making ready, manufacture, measure, plan, precaution, preparedness, preparing, provision, putting in order, qualification, readying, rehearsal, rundown, safeguard, schoolwork, study, substructure, training, tryout, workout; CONCEPTS 35,202,285 —Ant. unreadiness

preparation [n2] *something concocted, put together* arrangement, blend, brew, composition, compound, concoction, confection, decoction, medicine, mixture, product, tincture; CONCEPT 260 —Ant. ingredient

preparatory [adj] *introductory, basic* before, elementary, in advance of, in anticipation of, inductive, opening, precautionary, prefatory, preliminary, prelusive, prep*, preparative, previous, primary, prior to; CONCEPTS 546,585 —Ant. auxiliary, supplementary

prepare [v] *make or get ready* adapt, adjust, anticipate, appoint, arrange, assemble, brace, build up, coach, concoct, construct, contrive, cook, develop, dispose, draw up, endow, equip, fabricate, fashion, fill in, fit, fit out, fix, form, formulate, fortify, furnish, gird, groom, lay the groundwork, make, make provision, make up, outfit, perfect, plan, practice, prime, produce, provide, put in order, put together, qualify, ready, settle, smooth the way*, steel*, strengthen, supply, train, turn out, warm up; CONCEPTS 35,202 —Ant. disorganize, ignore, neglect

prepared [adj] *ready in body or mind* able, adapted, adjusted, all bases covered*, all set*, all systems go*, arranged, available, disposed, fit, fixed, framed, gaffed, groomed, handy, inclined, in order, in readiness, minded, of a mind, on guard*, planned, predisposed, prepped, primed, processed, psyched-up*, put up, qualified, rehearsed, rigged*, set, set-up, sewed-up, stacked, up*, up on*, willing, wired; CONCEPTS 403,485,560 —Ant. ignorant, neglectful, unprepared, unready

preponderance [n] *great numbers; supremacy* advantage, ascendancy, bigger half*, bulk, command, dominance, domination, dominion, extensiveness, greater part, lion's share*, mass, max*, mostest, power, predominance, prevalence, superiority, sway, weight; CONCEPTS 671,687, 767 —Ant. inferiority

prepossessed [adj] *made partial by initial impression* biased, colored, inclined, jaundiced, one-sided, opinionated, partisan, predisposed, prejudiced, tendentious, unindifferent, warped; CONCEPTS 403,542 —Ant. total, whole

prepossessing [adj] *attractive, handsome* alluring, amiable, appealing, attracting, beautiful, bewitching, captivating, charming, drawing, enchanting, engaging, fair, fascinating, fetch-

ing, good-looking, inviting, likable, lovable, magnetic, pleasant, pleasing, striking, taking, winning; CONCEPTS 404,537 —Ant. homely, repulsive, ugly, unattractive, unprepossessing

preposterous [adj] *ridiculous, bizarre* absurd, asinine, crazy, excessive, exorbitant, extravagant, extreme, fantastic, far-out*, foolish, harebrained*, impossible, incredible, insane, irrational, laughable, ludicrous, monstrous, nonsensical, out of the question*, outrageous, senseless, shocking, silly, stupid, taking the cake*, thick*, too much*, unbelievable, unreasonable, unthinkable, unusual, wacky*, wild; CONCEPTS 529,548,552 —Ant. reasonable, sensible

prerequisite [adj] *necessary* called for, essential, expedient, imperative, important, indispensable, mandatory, necessitous, needful, obligatory, of the essence, required, requisite, vital; CONCEPT 546 —Ant. optional, unnecessary, voluntary

prerequisite [n] *condition, necessity* essential, imperative, must, need, postulate, precondition, qualification, requirement, requisite, sine qua non; CONCEPTS 646,709 —Ant. extra, option

prerogative [n] *right, privilege* advantage, appanage, authority, birthright, choice, claim, droit, due, exemption, immunity, liberty, perquisite, sanction, title; CONCEPT 376 —Ant. duty, obligation

presage [n] *prediction, indication* apprehension, apprehensiveness, augury, auspice, bodement, boding, forecast, foretoken, forewarning, harbinger, intimation, misgiving, omen, portent, premonition, prenotion, presentiment, prognostic, prognostication, prophecy, sign, warning; CONCEPTS 410,529,689

presage [v] *predict or have a feeling* adumbrate, announce, augur, betoken, bode, divine, feel, forebode, forecast, forerun, foresee, foreshadow, foreshow, foretell, foretoken, forewarn, harbinger, herald, intuit, omen, point to, portend, preindicate, prognosticate, promise, prophesy, sense, signify, soothsay, vaticinate, warn; CONCEPTS 34,70,118

preschool [n] *nursery school* day care center, kindergarten, playgroup, pre-K; CONCEPT 287

prescribe [v] *stipulate action to be taken* appoint, assign, choose, command, decide, decree, define, designate, determine, dictate, direct, enjoin, establish, fix, guide, impose, lay down, ordain, order, pick out, require, rule, select, set, settle, specify, write prescription; CONCEPTS 50,60,61,88

prescription [n] *formula, medicine* decree, direction, drug, edict, instruction, law, mixture, ordinance, preparation, prescript, recipe, regulation, remedy, rule; CONCEPTS 274,307,311,318

presence [n1] *occupancy, attendance* being, companionship, company, existence, habitation, inhabitance, latency, occupation, omnipresence, potentiality, residence, subsistence, ubiety, ubiquity, whereabouts; CONCEPTS 407,518,710 —Ant. absence

presence [n2] *appearance, demeanor* address, air, aspect, aura, bearing, behavior, carriage, comportment, deportment, ease, look, mien, personality, poise, port, seeming, self-assurance, set; CONCEPTS 411,673,716

presence [n3] *closeness, vicinity* immediate circle, nearness, neighborhood, propinquity, proximity; CONCEPT 747 —*Ant.* distance

presence [n4] *ghost* apparition, manifestation, shade, specter, spirit, supernatural being, wraith; CONCEPT 370 —*Ant.* reality

presence [n5] *composure of mind* acumen, alertness, aplomb, calmness, cool, coolness, imperturbability, levelheadedness, quickness, sangfroid, self-assurance, self-command, self-composure, self-possession, sensibility, sobriety, watchfulness, wits; CONCEPTS 410,657 —*Ant.* agitation, confusion, distress, upset

presence of mind [n] *coolheadedness* calm, clearheadedness, coolness, patience; CONCEPTS 388,411,720

present [adj1] *existing; at this time* ad hoc, already, at this moment, begun, being, coeval, commenced, contemporaneous, contemporary, current, even now, existent, extant, for the time being, going on, immediate, in duration, in process, instant, just now, modern, nowadays, present-day, prompt, started, today, topical, under consideration, up-to-date; CONCEPT 820 —*Ant.* absent, former, future, past, previous

present [adj2] *nearby, here* accounted for, at hand, attendant, available, existent, in attendance, in view, made the scene*, near, on board, on deck, on hand, on-the-spot, ready, show up, there, there with bells on*, within reach; CONCEPTS 539,583 —*Ant.* absent, away, distant, far

present [n1] *existing time* here and now, instant, nonce, now, present moment, the time being, this day, this time, today; CONCEPTS 802,807,815 —*Ant.* future, past

present [n2] *gift* benefaction, benevolence, boon, bounty, compliment, donation, endowment, favor, gifting, giveaway, goodie*, grant, gratuity, handout, largess, lump, offering, stake, write-off; CONCEPT 337

present [v1] *introduce; demonstrate* acquaint, adduce, advance, allege, cite, declare, display, do, do the honors, exhibit, expose, expound, extend, fix up, get together, give, give an introduction, hold out, imply, infer, intimate, lay, make a pitch*, make known, manifest, mount, offer, open to view, perform, pitch, pose, produce, proffer, proposition, put forward, put ·on, raise, recount, relate, roll out, show, stage, state, submit, suggest, tender, trot out; CONCEPTS 66,261 —*Ant.* refrain, subdue, withhold

present [v2] *give, hand over* award, bestow, come up with, confer, devote, donate, entrust, furnish, gift, give away, grant, hand out, kick in*, lay on*, offer, proffer, put at disposal, put forth; CONCEPTS 67,108 —*Ant.* take

presentable [adj] *respectable; fit to be seen* acceptable, attractive, becoming, decent, fit, good enough*, not bad*, okay*, passable, prepared, proper, satisfactory, suitable, tolerable; CONCEPTS 558,579 —*Ant.* ugly, unacceptable, unfit, unpresentable

presentation [n] *performance; something given, displayed* act, appearance, arrangement, award, bestowal, coming out, conferral, debut, delivering, delivery, demonstration, display, dog and pony show*, donation, exhibition, exposition, giving, introduction, investiture,

knockdown*, launch, launching, offering, overture, pitch, present, production, proposal, proposition, reception, remembrance, rendition, representation, sales pitch*, show, staging, submission; CONCEPTS 261,263,337

presentiment [n] *anticipation, expectation* apprehension, apprehensiveness, discomposure, disquietude, disturbance, fear, feeling, feeling in bones*, foreboding, forecast, forethought, funny feeling*, handwriting on wall*, hunch, intuition, misgiving, perturbation, premonition, prenotion, presage, sinking feeling, vibes*, worriment; CONCEPTS 410,532,689

presently [adv] *in a short while* anon, before long, before you know it, by and by, directly, down the line*, down the pike*, down the road*, immediately, in a minute, in a moment, in a short time, now, nowadays, pretty soon, shortly, soon, today, without delay; CONCEPT 820 —*Ant.* eventually, later, never

preservation [n] *maintenance, protection* canning, care, conservancy, conservation, curing, defense, evaporation, freezing, guard, guardianship, keeping, perpetuation, pickling, preserval, refrigeration, safeguard, safeguarding, safekeeping, safety, salvation, saving, security, shield, storage, support, sustentation, tanning, upholding, ward; CONCEPTS 134,170,202,257 —*Ant.* destruction, ruin

preserve [v] *care for, maintain; continue* bottle, can, conserve, cure, defend, evaporate, freeze, guard, keep, keep up, mothball*, mummify, perpetuate, pickle, process, protect, put up, refrigerate, retain, safeguard, save, season, secure, shelter, shield, store, sustain, uphold; CONCEPTS 134,170 —*Ant.* destroy, hurt, ruin

preserves [n] *thickened fruit prepared for storage and use as a condiment* confection, confiture, conserve, extract, gelatin, jam, jell, jelly, marmalade, pectin, spread, sweet; CONCEPTS 457,461

preside [v] *be in authority* administer, advise, be at the head of*, be in driver's seat*, call the signals*, carry on, chair, conduct, control, direct, do the honors, govern, handle, head, head up, keep, lead, manage, officiate, operate, ordain, oversee, pull the strings*, run, run the show*, sit on top of*, supervise; CONCEPTS 94,117 —*Ant.* follow, serve

president [n] *chief executive* boss, CEO, chief executive officer, chief of state, commander in chief, head of state, leader, person in charge, premier, prime minister; CONCEPT 347

press [n1] *people or person working in communications* columnist, correspondent, editor, fourth estate*, interviewer, journalism, journalist, magazine, media, newspaper, newsperson, paper, periodical, photographer, publicist, publisher, reporter, writer; CONCEPTS 280,349,356

press [n2] *horde, large group* bunch, crowd, crush, drove, flock, herd, host, mob, multitude, pack, push, swarm, throng; CONCEPT 432

press [n3] *strain, pressure* bustle, confusion, demand, hassle, haste, hurry, rush, stress, urgency; CONCEPTS 230,674 —*Ant.* calm, harmony, peace

press [v1] *push on with force* bear down, bear heavily, bulldoze*, clasp, compress, condense, constrain, crowd, crush, cumber, depress, embrace, enfold, express, finish, flatten, force down, hold, hug, impel, iron, jam, level, mangle, mash, mass, move, pack, pile, pin down, ram, reduce, scrunch, shove, smooth, squash, squeeze, squish, steam, stuff, thrust, unwrinkle, weigh; CONCEPTS 191,208 —Ant. pull

press [v2] *pressure, trouble* afflict, assail, beg, beset, besiege, buttonhole*, come at, compel, constrain, demand, depress, disquiet, enjoin, entreat, exhort, force, harass, implore, importune, insist on, lean on, oppress, petition, plague, plead, pressurize, push, railroad*, sadden, sell, squeeze, sue, supplicate, torment, urge, vex, weigh down, work on, worry; CONCEPT 14 —Ant. leave alone

pressing [adj] *important; urgent* acute, burning, claiming, clamant, clamorous, compelling, constraining, critical, crucial, crying, demanding, dire, distressing, exacting, exigent, forcing, heat-on*, high-priority, hurry-up*, immediate, imperative, importunate, insistent, instant, life-and-death*, obliging, requiring, serious, vital; CONCEPTS 548,568 —Ant. insignificant, trivial, unimportant

pressure [n1] *physical force, weight* burden, compressing, compression, crushing, encumbrance, heaviness, load, mass, shear, squeeze, squeezing, strain, strength, stress, tension, thrust; CONCEPTS 641,734

pressure [n2] *demand, difficulty* adversity, affliction, albatross*, burden, choke, clout, coercion, compulsion, confinement, constraint, crunch, discipline, distress, drag, duress, exigency, force, full court press*, hardship, hassle, heat, hurry, influence, inside track*, load, misfortune, necessity, obligation, persuasion, power, press, pressure cooker*, pull, requirement, strain, stress, sway, tension, trouble, unnaturalness, urgency, weight; CONCEPTS 14,666,674,687 —Ant. ease, facility, peace

pressure [v] *bother, urge* come at, compel, constrain, drive, impel, insist, lean on*, politick, press, push, push around*, rush, sell, squeeze, twist arm*, work over*; CONCEPTS 7,14,19,22 —Ant. leave alone

prestige [n] *fame, influence* authority, cachet, celebrity, consequence, control, credit, dignity, distinction, éclat*, eminence, esteem, illustriousness, importance, kudos*, position, power, preeminence, prominence, prominency, rank, regard, renown, reputation, repute, standing, state, stature, status, sway, weight; CONCEPTS 388,668 —Ant. humility, lowliness

prestigious [adj] *famous, influential* celebrated, distinguished, eminent, esteemed, exalted, famed, great, illustrious, important, imposing, impressive, notable, prominent, renowned, reputable, respected; CONCEPTS 555,568 —Ant. humble, insignificant, modest, unimportant, unprestigious

presumably [adv] *likely, reasonably* apparently, assumably, credible, doubtless, doubtlessly, hypothetically, in all likelihood, in all probability, indubitably, it would seem, most likely, on the face of it, presumptively, probably, seemingly, supposedly, surely, theoretically, unquestionably; CONCEPTS 544, 552 —Ant. doubtfully, unlikely

presume [v1] *make assumption; believe* assume,

bank on*, be afraid, conclude, conjecture, consider, count on, depend, figure, gather, guess, infer, jump the gun*, posit, postulate, predicate, premise, presuppose, pretend, rely, speculate, suppose, surmise, take for granted, take it, think, trust; CONCEPTS 12,26,28 —Ant. disbelieve

presume [v2] *dare; take the liberty* go so far, have the audacity, impose, infringe, intrude, make bold, undertake, venture; CONCEPT 87 —Ant. abstain

presumption [n1] *belief, hypothesis* anticipation, apriorism, assumption, basis, chance, conjecture, grounds, guess, likelihood, opinion, plausibility, posit, postulate, postulation, premise, presupposition, probability, reason, shot, shot in the dark*, sneaking suspicion*, stab, supposition, surmise, suspicion, thesis; CONCEPT 689 —Ant. reality, truth

presumption [n2] *forwardness, daring* arrogance, assurance, audacity, boldness, brashness, brass, cheek*, chutzpah*, confidence, contumely, effrontery, gall, impudence, insolence, nerve, presumptuousness, rudeness, temerity; CONCEPT 633 —Ant. humility

presumptuous [adj] *self-confident* arrogant, audacious, bold, cheeky*, conceited, confident, contumelious, egotistic, foolhardy, forward, fresh, insolent, overconfident, overfamiliar, overweening, pompous, presuming, pretentious, pushy, rash, rude, self-assertive, self-assured, self-satisfied, smug, supercilious, uppity*; CONCEPTS 401,542 —Ant. humble, modest

pretend [v1] *fake, falsify* act, affect, allege, assume, be deceitful, beguile, be hypocritical, bluff, cheat, claim, claim falsely, counterfeit, cozen, deceive, delude, dissemble, dissimulate, dupe, fake out*, feign, fish*, fool, fudge*, hoodwink*, impersonate, jazz*, jive*, lay claim*, let on*, make out*, malinger, masquerade, mislead, pass off*, pass oneself off as*, profess, purport, put on*, put up a front*, sham*, shuck and jive*, simulate, stonewall*, sucker*, whitewash*; CONCEPTS 59,63 —Ant. tell truth

pretend [v2] *play the part of* act, assume the role, imagine, imitate, impersonate, make as if, make believe, make out like, make up, masquerade, mimic, play, playact, portray, pose, purport, put on a front*, put on airs*, put on an act*, represent, reproduce, suppose; CONCEPTS 111,171,292,384 —Ant. be honest

pretended [adj] *alleged; imaginary* affected, artificial, assumed, avowed, bluffing, bogus, charlatan, cheating, concealed, counterfeit, covered, dissimulated, factitious, fake, false, falsified, feigned, fictitious, impostrous, imposturous, lying, make-believe, masked, mock, ostensible, phony, pretend, professed, pseudo*, purported, put-on*, quack*, sham*, shammed*, simulated, so-called, spurious, supposed; CONCEPTS 545,582 —Ant. genuine, real, sincere

pretense [n] *falsehood, affected show; cover* act, acting, affectation, appearance, artifice, charade, claim, cloak, deceit, deception, display, dissimulation, double-dealing*, dumb act*, evasion, excuse, fabrication, facade, fakery, faking, falsification, feigning, gag, guise, insincerity, invention, make-believe, mask, masquerade, misrepresentation, misstatement, ostentation, posing, posturing, pretentiousness, pretext, routine, ruse, schtick*, semblance, sham*, shuffling, simulation, stall, stunt, subterfuge, trickery, veil, veneer, wile; CONCEPTS 59,63,633, 716 —*Ant.* honesty, openness, reality, truth

pretension [n1] *airs, snobbishness* affectation, big talk*, charade, conceit, disguise, fake*, false front*, front, hypocrisy, ostentation, phony, pomposity, pretentiousness, put-on*, self-importance, show, showboat*, showiness, showoff, snobbery, splash*, vainglory, vanity; CONCEPT 633 —*Ant.* honesty, humility

pretension [n2] *false claim, assertion of importance* allegation, ambition, ambitiousness, aspiration, assumption, charade, declaration, demand, disguise, maintenance, make-believe, pageant, pretense, pretext, profession, title; CONCEPTS 278,657 —*Ant.* honesty, truth

pretentious [adj] *snobbish, conceited* affected, arty, assuming, aureate, big*, bombastic, chichi*, conspicuous, euphuistic, exaggerated, extravagant, feigned, flamboyant, flashy, flaunting, flowery, gaudy, grandiloquent, grandiose, highfaluting*, high-flown*, high-sounding*, hollow, imposing, inflated, jazzy*, la-di-da*, lofty, magniloquent, mincing, ornate, ostentatious, overambitious, overblown, pompous, puffed up*, put-on*, rhetorical, showy, specious, splashy, stilted, swank, too-too*, tumid, turgid, utopian, vainglorious; CONCEPTS 401, 542,589 —*Ant.* humble, modest, unconceited

preternatural [adj] *unusual, abnormal* aberrant, anomalous, atypical, deviant, deviative, extraordinary, ghostly, inexplicable, irregular, marvelous, miraculous, mysterious, odd, peculiar, strange, superhuman, superior, supermundane, supernatural, unaccountable, unearthly, unnatural, unrepresentative, untypical; CONCEPT 564 —*Ant.* common, natural, normal, regular, usual

pretext [n] *disguise; alleged reason* affectation, alibi, appearance, bluff, cleanup, cloak, color*, coloring*, cop-out*, cover, cover story*, cover-up*, device, excuse, face, feint, fig leaf*, front, guise, mask, masquerade, plea, ploy, pretense, red herring*, routine, ruse, semblance, show, simulation, song and dance*, stall, stratagem, subterfuge, veil*; CONCEPTS 59,661,716 —*Ant.* reality, truth

pretty [adj] *attractive* appealing, beauteous, beautiful, boss*, charming, cheerful, cher*, comely, cute, dainty, darling, delicate, delightful, dishy*, dreamboat*, elegant, eyeful*, fair, fine, foxy*, good-looking, graceful, handsome, looker, lovely, neat, nice, picture, pleasant, pleasing, pulchritudinous, tasteful; CONCEPT 579 —*Ant.* disgusting, ugly

pretty [adv] *considerable; somewhat* a little, ample, fairly, kind of, large, moderately, more or less, much, notable, pretty much, quite, rather, reasonably, sizable, some, something, sort of, tolerably; CONCEPTS 531,569

prevail [v] *dominate, control* abound, beat, be common, be current, be prevalent, best, be usual, be victorious, be widespread, carry, come out on top*, command, conquer, domineer, exist generally, gain, get there, go great guns*, go places*, hit pay dirt*, luck out*, make it, make out, master, move out, obtain, overcome, overrule, predominate, preponderate, prove,

reign, succeed, take off, triumph, win; CONCEPTS 94,95,141 —*Ant.* lose, surrender

prevailing [adj] *general, dominant* all-embracing, by the numbers*, catholic, common, comprehensive, current, customary, ecumenical, established, familiar, fashionable, influential, in style, in vogue, main, operative, ordinary, popular, predominant, predominating, preponderating, prevalent, principal, rampant, regnant, regular, rife, ruling, set, steady, sweeping, universal, usual, widespread, worldwide; CONCEPT 530 —*Ant.* individual, minor, peculiar, private, unimportant

prevail upon/prevail on [v] *persuade, influence* affect, argue into, bring around, convince, crack, dispose, draw, get, get around, impress, incline, induce, promote, prompt, put across, ram down throat*, sell*, suck in*, sway, talk into, win over; CONCEPT 68 —*Ant.* discourage, dissuade, leave alone

prevalent [adj1] *accepted, widespread* accustomed, common, commonplace, current, customary, established, everyday, extensive, faddy, frequent, general, habitual, in use, latest*, latest word*, leading edge*, natural, new, normal, now*, ongoing, popular, prevailing, rampant, regnant, regular, rife, run-of-the-mill*, state-of-the-art*, stylish, swinging, trendy, typic, typical, ubiquitous, universal, up-to-date, usual, with it*, wonted; CONCEPTS 530,547,589 —*Ant.* isolated, limited, uncommon

prevalent [adj2] *governing, superior* ascendant, compelling, dominant, overbearing, paramount, powerful, predominant, predominate, preponderant, prevailing, regnant, ruling, sovereign, successful; CONCEPTS 536,574 —*Ant.* inferior, subservient

prevaricate [v] *deceive; stretch the truth* beat around the bush*, beg the question*, belie, cavil, con, distort, dodge, equivocate, evade, exaggerate, fabricate, falsify, fib, garble, hedge, invent, jive*, lie*, misrepresent, misspeak, palter, phony up*, put on*, quibble, shift, shuffle, tergiversate; CONCEPT 63 —*Ant.* tell truth

prevent [v] *keep from happening or continuing* anticipate, arrest, avert, avoid, baffle, balk, bar, block, check, chill*, cool, cork, counter, counteract, dam, debar, defend against, foil, forbid, forestall, forfend, frustrate, halt, hamper, head off, hinder, hold back, hold off, impede, inhibit, intercept, interdict, interrupt, keep lid on*, limit, nip in the bud*, obstruct, obviate, preclude, prohibit, put an end to, put a stop to, repress, restrain, restrict, retard, rule out, shut out, stave off, stop, thwart, turn aside, ward off; CONCEPT 121 —*Ant.* aid, allow, assist, cause, help, let go

prevention [n] *stop* avoidance, blockage, deterence, determent, forestalling, halt, hindrance, impediment, inhibitor, interception, interruption, obstacle, obstruction, prohibition, stoppage, thwarting; CONCEPTS 240,832

preview [n] *preliminary showing* examination, preliminary study, research, show, sneak, sneak peek*, survey, viewing; CONCEPTS 263,292,832 —*Ant.* criticism

previous [adj1] *former, prior* antecedent, anterior, earlier, erstwhile, ex, foregoing, one-time, past, precedent, preceding, quondam,

pr
pr

sometime; CONCEPTS *585,811,818,820* —**Ant.** current, future, later, present

previous [*adj2*] *premature* ahead of, early, inopportune, overearly, oversoon, precipitate, soon, too early, too soon, unfounded, untimely, unwarranted; CONCEPTS *558,799* —**Ant.** on time, timely, well-timed

previously [*adv*] *earlier* ahead, already, ante, antecedently, at one time, away back, a while ago, back, back when, before, beforehand, erstwhile, fore, formerly, forward, heretofore, hitherto, in advance, in anticipation, in days gone by, in the past, long ago, once, one-shot, precedently, then, time was, until now; CONCEPT *820* —**Ant.** currently, future, later, presently

prey [*n*] *target of attack* casualty, chased*, dupe*, game, kill, loot, mark, martyr, mug*, pillage, quarry, quest, raven, spoil, sufferer, underdog, victim; CONCEPTS *394,423* —**Ant.** attacker

prey on [*v*] *attack, terrorize* blackmail, bleed, bully, burden, consume, depredate, devour, distress, eat, exploit, feed on, fleece, haunt, hunt, intimidate, live off, load, oppress, plunder, raid, seize, take advantage of, tax, trouble, victimize, weigh, worry; CONCEPTS *14,86,169* —**Ant.** guard, protect, save

price [*n1*] *financial value* amount, appraisal, appraisement, asking price, assessment, barter, bill, bounty, ceiling, charge, compensation, consideration, cost, damage, demand, disbursement, discount, dues, estimate, exaction, expenditure, expense, face value, fare, fee, figure, hire, outlay, output, pay, payment, premium, prize, quotation, ransom, rate, reckoning, retail, return, reward, score, sticker*, tab, tariff, ticket, toll, tune*, valuation, wages, wholesale, worth; CONCEPT *329*

price [*n2*] *consequences of action* cost, expense, penalty, sacrifice, toll; CONCEPT *230* —**Ant.** cause

price [*v*] *assess financial value* appraise, cost, estimate, evaluate, fix, mark down, mark up, put a price on, rate, reduce, sticker, value; CONCEPT *330*

priceless [*adj1*] *precious, irreplaceable* beyond price, cherished, collectible, costly, dear, expensive, incalculable, incomparable, inestimable, invaluable, out-of-bounds*, out-of-sight*, prized, rare, rich, treasured, valuable, valued, without price, worth a king's ransom*, worth its weight in gold*; CONCEPTS *334,568* —**Ant.** cheap, replaceable, useless, worthless

priceless [*adj2*] *extremely funny* absurd, amusing, comic, droll, hilarious, humorous, killing, rib-tickling*, ridiculous, riotous, scream, sidesplitting; CONCEPT *267* —**Ant.** grave, serious

prick [*n*] *small hole made by stab* cut, gash, jab, jag, perforation, pinhole, prickle, puncture, stab, wound; CONCEPT *309*

prick [*v*] *stab, perforate* bore, cut, drill, enter, hurt, jab, lance, pierce, pink, punch, puncture, slash, slit, smart, spur, sting; CONCEPT *220*

prickly [*adj1*] *thorny or difficult* annoying, barbed, bothersome, brambly, briery, bristly, complicated, echinated, intricate, involved, knotty, nettlesome, pointed, sharp, spiny,

stimulating, ticklish, tricky, troublesome, trying; CONCEPTS *485,565* —**Ant.** smooth

prickly [*adj2*] *irritable, bad-tempered* cantankerous, edgy, fractious, fretful, grumpy, irritable, peevish, petulant, snappish, touchy, waspish; CONCEPT *401* —**Ant.** happy, pleasant

pride [*n1*] *self-esteem* amour-propre, delight, dignity, ego, egoism, egotism, ego trip, face, gratification, happiness, honor, joy, pleasure, pridefulness, repletion, satisfaction, self-admiration, self-confidence, self-glorification, self-love, self-regard, self-respect, self-satisfaction, self-sufficiency, self-trust, self-worth, sufficiency; CONCEPT *411* —**Ant.** humility

pride [*n2*] *arrogance, self-importance* airs, assumption, big-headedness*, cockiness*, conceit, condescension, contumely, disdain, disdainfulness, egoism, egotism, haughtiness, hauteur, hubris, huff, immodesty, insolence, loftiness, narcissism, overconfidence, patronage, pragmatism, presumption, pretension, pretentiousness, proud flesh*, self-exaltation, self-love, smugness, snobbery, superbity, superciliousness, swagger, swelled head*, vainglory, vanity; CONCEPT *633* —**Ant.** humility, modesty, shyness, timidity

pride [*n3*] *treasure; best* boast, choice, cream, elite, fat, flower*, gem*, glory, jewel*, pick, pride and joy*, prime, prize, top*; CONCEPTS *446,668,689* —**Ant.** disgrace

pride [*v*] *take pleasure in accomplishment* be proud, boast, brag, congratulate, crow, exult, felicitate, flatter oneself, gasconade, glory in, hold head high, overbear, pique*, plume*, prance, preen, presume, puff up*, revel in, strut, swagger, swell, vaunt; CONCEPTS *10,633* —**Ant.** humble

priest [*n*] *man who is minister in Roman or Orthodox Catholic church* clergyperson, cleric, curate, divine, ecclesiastic, elder, father, father confessor, friar, holy man, lama, man of God, man of the cloth*, monk, padre, pontiff, preacher, rector, vicar; CONCEPT *361*

priesthood [*n*] *clergy* canonicate, canonry, cardinalate, deaconry, diaconate, ecclesiastics, ministry, pastorate, rabbinate, the cloth, the pulpit; CONCEPT *369*

prim [*adj*] *particular, fussy* blue-nose*, ceremonial, ceremonious, choosy, cleanly, conventional, correct, dapper*, decorous, demure, fastidious, formal, genteel, good, goody-goody*, nice, nit-picking*, orderly, overmodest, polite, precise, priggish, prissy, proper, prudish, puritanical, rigid, shipshape*, spic-and-span*, spruce, stickling, stiff, straight, strait-laced, stuffy*, tidy, uncluttered, upright, Victorian, well-groomed, wooden*; CONCEPTS *401,404* —**Ant.** informal, rumpled

prima donna [*n1*] *star* diva, first lady, headliner, leading lady, lead vocalist, opera singer, singer, soloist, superstar, topliner*; CONCEPTS *352,366*

prima donna [*n2*] *temperamental person* conceited person, crybaby, egotist, narcissist, princess, self-centered person, spoiled brat, vain person; CONCEPT *411*

primal [*adj*] *primeval; primary* aboriginal, ancient, central, chief, earliest, early, first, fundamental, highest, old, original, paramount, past, prehistoric, primitive, primordial, principal, pristine; CONCEPT 799

primarily [adv1] *generally; for the most part* above all, basically, chiefly, especially, essentially, fundamentally, generally, largely, mainly, mostly, on the whole, overall, predominantly, principally; CONCEPTS 531,544,772 —*Ant.* secondarily

primarily [adv2] *in the beginning* at first, at the start, first and foremost, from the start, initially, in the first place, originally, primitively; CONCEPTS 548,799 —*Ant.* finally

primary/prime [adj1] *best, principal* capital, cardinal, chief, crackerjack*, dominant, excellent, fab*, first, first-class*, greatest, heavy, highest, hot*, leading, main, number one*, paramount, primo*, state-of-the-art*, stellar, top, top-of-the-line*, tough*, world-class*; CONCEPTS 567,574 —*Ant.* inferior, least, minor, secondary, second-rate, subordinate, worst

primary/prime [adj2] *earliest* aboriginal, beginning, direct, first, firsthand, immediate, initial, original, pioneer, primal, primeval, primitive, primordial, pristine; CONCEPTS 585,799 —*Ant.* final, latest

primary/prime [adj3] *basic, fundamental* basal, beginning, bottom, central, elemental, elementary, essential, first, foundational, introductory, meat-and-potatoes*, original, primitive, principal, radical, rudimentary, simple, three R's*, ultimate, underivative, underived, underlying; CONCEPTS 549,585 —*Ant.* auxiliary, secondary, supplemental

prime [n1] *best part of existence* best, best days*, bloom, choice, cream*, elite, fat*, flower*, flowering*, height, heyday, maturity, peak, perfection, pink*, prize, spring, springtime, top, verdure, vitality, zenith; CONCEPT 816 —*Ant.* downfall

prime [n2] *beginning; spring* adolescence, aurora, dawn, daybreak, dew, greenness*, juvenility, morn*, morning, opening, puberty, pubescence, springtime, start, sunrise, sunup, tender years*, vitality, youth, youthfulness; CONCEPTS 817,832 —*Ant.* conclusion, end

prime [v] *get ready; prepare* break in, brief, clue*, coach, cram, excite, fill in, fit, galvanize, groom, inform, innervate, make ready, motivate, move, notify, prep*, provoke, rehearse, stimulate, tell, train; CONCEPTS 7,19,22,35,202 —*Ant.* forget, neglect

prime minister [n] *premier* chancellor, chief executive, chief of state, commander in chief, head of state, leader, person in charge, president; CONCEPTS 347,354

primeval [adj] *ancient* earliest, early, first, old, original, prehistoric, primal, primary, primitive, primordial, pristine; CONCEPT 799 —*Ant.* modern, new

primitive [adj1] *ancient, original* archaic, basic, earliest, early, elementary, essential, first, fundamental, old, primal, primary, primeval, primordial, pristine, substratal, underivative, underived, underlying, undeveloped, unevolved; CONCEPT 799 —*Ant.* current, modern, new, present

primitive [adj2] *barbaric, crude* animal, atavistic, austere, barbarian, barbarous, brutish, childlike, fierce, ignorant, naive, natural, non-literate, preliterate, raw, rough, rude, rudimentary, savage, simple, uncivilized, uncultivated, uncultured, underdeveloped, undeveloped, undomesticated, unlearned, unrefined, unsophisticated, untamed, untaught, untrained, untutored, vestigial, wild; CONCEPTS 406,485 —*Ant.* cultured, modern, sophisticated

primordial [adj] *earliest* basic, early, elemental, first, fundamental, original, prehistoric, primal, primary, prime, primeval, primitive, pristine, radical; CONCEPT 799 —*Ant.* last, latest

primp [v] *beautify and dress nicely* deck out*, dress up, fix up, get dressed up, groom, gussy up*, preen, prepare, slick*, smarten, spiff, spruce, titivate; CONCEPT 202 —*Ant.* mess up, uglify

principal [adj] *most important* arch, capital, cardinal, champion, chief, controlling, crowning, dominant, essential, first, foremost, greatest, head, highest, incomparable, key, leading, main, mainline, major, matchless, maximum, outstanding, paramount, peerless, predominant, preeminent, premier, prevailing, primary, prime, prominent, second-to-none, sovereign, star, stellar, strongest, supereminent, superior, supreme, transcendent, unapproachable, unequaled, unparalleled, unrivaled; CONCEPTS 568,574 —*Ant.* auxiliary, extra, least, lesser, minor, secondary, trivial, unimportant

principal [n1] *person in charge of organization, often an educational one* administrator, boss, chief, dean, director, exec*, head, key player*, lead, leader, preceptor, protagonist, rector, ruler, star, superintendent; CONCEPTS 347,350

principal [n2] *original amount of property either owned or owed* assets, capital, capital funds, money; CONCEPT 332 —*Ant.* interest

principally [adv] *mainly* above all, basically, before anything else, cardinally, chiefly, dominantly, eminently, especially, essentially, first and foremost, first of all, for the most part, fundamentally, generally, importantly, in the first place, in the main, largely, materially, mostly, notably, particularly, peculiarly, predominantly, preeminently, prevailingly, prevalently, primarily, to a great degree, universally, vitally; CONCEPTS 531,544,772 —*Ant.* secondarily, trivially

principle [n1] *law, standard* assumption, axiom, basis, canon, convention, criterion, dictum, doctrine, dogma, ethic, form, formula, foundation, fundamental, golden rule*, ground, maxim, origin, postulate, precept, prescript, principium, proposition, regulation, rule, source, theorem, truth, usage, verity; CONCEPTS 318,688

principle/principles [n2] *belief, morality; morals* attitude, character, code, conduct, conscience, credo, ethic, ethics, faith, ideals, integrity, opinion, policy, probity, rectitude, scruples, sense of duty, sense of honor, system, teaching, tenet, uprightness; CONCEPTS 645,689 —*Ant.* immorality, unethicalness

print [n] *publication; something impressed* black-and-white*, book, characters, composition, copy, edition, engraving, face, font, impress, impression, imprint, indentation, issue, lettering, letters, lithograph, magazine, newspaper, newsprint, periodical, photograph, printed matter, stamp, type, typeface, typescript, typesetting, writing; CONCEPTS 259,265,280

print [v] *produce writing, impression; reproduce publication* calligraph, compose, disseminate, engrave, go to press, impress, imprint, issue, let roll, letter, mark, offset, publish, put to bed*, reissue, reprint, run off, set, set type, stamp, strike off; CONCEPTS 174,203,205

printer [n1] *typesetter* compositor, pressperson, publisher, typographer; CONCEPTS 174,203,205

printer [n2] *computer peripheral device* ball printer, character printer, color printer, daisy-wheel printer, dot-matrix printer, graphics printer, ink-jet printer, laser printer, LCD printer, LED printer, line printer, thermal printer; CONCEPT 463

prior [adj] *earlier* above-mentioned, aforementioned, ahead, antecedent, anterior, before, foregoing, former, forward, past, precedent, preceding, preexistent, preexisting, previous; CONCEPTS 811,812,818,820 —Ant. after, later

priority [n] *first concern* antecedence, arrangement, crash project*, greatest importance, lead, order, precedence, preeminence, preference, prerogative, previousness, rank, right of way*, seniority, superiority, supremacy, transcendence; CONCEPT727 —Ant. unimportance

prison [n] *residence for incarcerating criminals* bastille, can*, clink*, confinement, cooler*, dungeon, G*, guardhouse, jail, keep, lockup, pen*, penal institution, penitentiary, reformatory, slammer*, statesville*, stockade, up the river*; CONCEPTS 439,449,516

prisoner [n] *person jailed for crime; person kept against his or her will* captive, chain gang member, con, convict, culprit, detainee, hostage, internee, jailbird*, lag*, lifer*, loser*, tough*, yardbird*; CONCEPT 412

prissy [adj] *particular and fussy* epicene, fastidious, finicky, genteel, goody-goody*, goody-two-shoes*, overnice, pansified, persnickety, picky, precious, prim, prim and proper*, prudish, puritanical, sissified, sissy, squeamish, stickling, strait-laced, stuffy*, tight-laced*, Victorian; CONCEPTS 401,404 —Ant. informal, unconcerned

pristine [adj] *clean, pure; primeval* earliest, early, first, immaculate, intact, natural, original, primal, purified, refined, sanitary, snowy, spotless, stainless, sterile, sterilized, taintless, unadulterated, uncorrupted, undebased, unpolluted, unsoiled, unspotted, unstained, unsullied, untainted, untarnished, untouched, virginal, wholesome; CONCEPTS 621,799

privacy [n] *solitude, secrecy* aloofness, clandestineness, concealment, confidentiality, isolation, one's space, penetralia, privateness, quiet, retirement, retreat, seclusion, separateness, separation, sequestration, solitude; CONCEPTS 388,631,714 —Ant. publicity, publicness, sociableness

private [adj1] *personal, intimate* behind the scenes*, clandestine, closet*, close to one's chest*, confidential, discreet, exclusive, hushed, hush-hush*, independent, individual, inside, nonpublic, not open, off the record*, own, particular, privy*, reserved, secret, separate, special, under one's hat*, unofficial; CONCEPTS 267,406 —Ant. open, public, sociable

private [adj2] *hidden, isolated* concealed, discreet, quiet, removed, retired, secluded, secret, separate, sequestered, solitary, withdrawn; CONCEPTS 576,583 —Ant. open, revealed, unconcealed

private [n] *lowest rank of person enlisted in armed service* enlisted person, first-class*, GI, infantry, private soldier, sailor, second-class*, soldier; CONCEPT 358

private eye [n] *private detective* agent, bird dog*, bloodhound*, cop, dick*, peeper*, P.I.*, private investigator, sleuth, snoop*, tail*; CONCEPT 348

privation [n] *deprivation* destitution, disadvantage, hardship, indigence, lack, necessity, need, neediness, poverty, want; CONCEPTS 121,142,709

privilege [n] *right, due* advantage, allowance, appanage, appurtenance, authority, authorization, benefit, birthright, boon, chance, charter, claim, concession, entitlement, event, exemption, favor, franchise, freedom, grant, immunity, liberty, license, opportunity, perquisite, prerogative, right, sanction; CONCEPT 376 —Ant. detriment, disadvantage

privileged [adj1] *favored, elite* advantaged, entitled, honored, indulged, powerful, ruling, special; CONCEPTS 334,574 —Ant. disadvantageous, poor, underprivileged

privileged [adj2] *allowed, exempt* authorized, chartered, eligible, empowered, entitled, excused, franchised, free, furnished, granted, immune, kosher*, legit*, licensed, okay*, okayed*, palatine, qualified, sanctioned, special, vested; CONCEPT 548 —Ant. prevented, unexempt

privileged [adj3] *confidential, secret* exceptional, for eyes only*, inside, not for publication, off the record*, on the QT*, privy, special, top secret, under one's hat*; CONCEPT 267 —Ant. known, open, public

privy [adj1] *secret* buried, concealed, confidential, covert, hidden, hush-hush*, obscured, off the record*, personal, private, separate, shrouded, ulterior; CONCEPTS 267,576 —Ant. known, public, revealed

privy [adj2] *aware* acquainted, apprised, cognizant, conscious, informed, in on*, in the know*, private, privileged, wise; CONCEPT 402 —Ant. unaware, unknowing

prize [adj] *best* award-winning, champion, choice, cream*, elite, fat*, first-class*, first-rate*, outstanding, pick, prime, top, topnotch, winning; CONCEPT 574 —Ant. worst

prize [n1] *award, winnings* accolade, acquirement, acquisition, advantage, blue ribbon*, bonus, bounty, cake*, capture, carrot*, championship, citation, crown, decoration, dividend, feather in cap*, first place*, gold*, gold star*, gravy*, guerdon, haul, honor, inducement, jackpot, laurel, loot*, medal, meed, payoff, pickings*, pillage, plum*, plunder*, possession, premium, privilege, purse, recompense, requital, reward, scholarship, spoil, spoils, stakes, strokes*, swag*, title, trophy, windfall; CONCEPTS 337,710 —Ant. blame, punishment

prize [n2] *goal; best* aim, ambition, choice, conquest, cream*, desire, elite, fat, flower*, gain, gold*, hope, pick, pride, prime, top*; CONCEPTS 659,709

prize [v] *value highly* appreciate, apprize, cherish, count, enshrine, esteem, guard, hold dear, rate, regard highly, set store by*, treasure; CONCEPTS *10,32* —*Ant.* despise, dislike, hate, not care

probability [n] *likelihood of something happening* anticipation, chance, chances, conceivability, contingency, credibility, expectation, feasibility, hazard, liability, likeliness, odds, outside chance*, plausibility, possibility, practicability, prayer, presumption, promise, prospect, reasonableness, shot, snowball's chance*, toss-up*; CONCEPT *650* —*Ant.* improbability, unlikelihood

probable [adj] *likely to happen* apparent, believable, credible, earthly, feasible, illusory, in the cards*, mortal, most likely, odds-on*, ostensible, plausible, possible, presumable, presumed, rational, reasonable, seeming; CONCEPT *552* —*Ant.* improbable, unlikely

probably [adv] *likely to happen* apparently, as likely as not, assumably, as the case may be, believably, dollars to doughnuts*, doubtless, expediently, feasibly, imaginably, in all likelihood, in all probability, like enough, maybe, most likely, no doubt, one can assume, perchance, perhaps, plausibly, possibly, practicably, presumably, presumptively, reasonably, seemingly, to all appearances; CONCEPT *552* —*Ant.* improbably, unlikely

probation [n] *trial period* apprenticeship, noviciate, test period, trial; CONCEPTS *87,290,291*

probe [n] *investigation* delving, detection, examination, exploration, fishing expedition*, inquest, inquiry, inquisition, legwork*, probing, quest, research, scrutiny, study, third degree*; CONCEPTS *31,103,216,290*

probe [v] *explore, investigate* ask, catechize, check, check out, check over, check up, delve into, dig, examine, eye, feel around, feel out, go into, inquire, interrogate, look into, look-see, penetrate, pierce, poke, prod, prospect, put out a feeler*, query, quiz, scrutinize, search, sift, sound, sound out, study, test, test the waters*, verify; CONCEPTS *31,103,216*

probity [n] *fairness, honesty* equity, fidelity, goodness, honor, integrity, justice, morality, rectitude, righteousness, rightness, sincerity, trustworthiness, truthfulness, uprightness, virtue, worth; CONCEPTS *411,645* —*Ant.* deceit, dishonesty, unfairness

problem [n1] *difficulty; bad situation* botheration, box*, can of worms*, complication, count*, crunch*, dilemma, disagreement, dispute, disputed point, doubt, headache*, hitch*, hot water*, issue, mess*, obstacle, pickle*, point at issue*, predicament, quandary, question, scrape*, squeeze*, trouble, worriment; CONCEPTS *666,674* —*Ant.* good situation, solution

problem [n2] *puzzle, question* brainteaser*, bugaboo*, cliff-hanger*, conundrum, enigma, example, grabber*, illustration, intricacy, mind-boggler*, mystery, poser*, puzzler, query, riddle, sixty-four thousand dollar question*, stickler, stumper, teaser, twister; CONCEPTS *529,532* —*Ant.* solution

problematic [adj] *open to doubt* ambiguous, arguable, chancy, debatable, disputable, doubtful, dubious, dubitable, enigmatic, iffy*, indecisive, moot, open, precarious, problematical, puzzling, questionable, suspect, tricky, uncertain, unsettled, up for grabs*; CONCEPT *529* —*Ant.* certain, fixable, settled, solvable, sure

procedure [n] *process, system for accomplishing something* action, agenda, agendum, channels, conduct, course, custom, daily grind*, fashion, form, formula, game plan*, gimmick, grind, idea, layout, line, maneuver, measure, method, mode, modus operandi, move, nuts and bolts*, operation, performance, plan, policy, polity, practice, proceeding, program, red tape*, routine, scheme, setup, step, strategy, style, the book*, the numbers*, transaction; CONCEPT *6*

proceed [v1] *physically or mentally carry on, carry out* advance, continue, fare, get, get going, get on with, get under way*, go ahead, go on, hie, journey, make a start, march, move on, move out, pass, press on, progress, push on, repair, set in motion, travel, wend; CONCEPTS *43,91* —*Ant.* cease, halt, stop, wait

proceed [v2] *flow from; originate* arise, come, derive, emanate, ensue, extend, follow, head, issue, pass, result, rise, spring, stem; CONCEPTS *179,230,676* —*Ant.* return

proceeding [n] *undertaking, course of action* act, action, adventure, casualty, circumstance, come off, deed, exercise, experiment, go-down*, goings-on*, happening, incident, maneuver, measure, move, movement, occurrence, operation, performance, procedure, process, step, transaction, venture; CONCEPTS *2,3*

proceedings [n] *account, report of event* affairs, annals, archives, business, dealings, documents, doings*, matters, minutes, records, transactions; CONCEPT *271*

proceeds [n] *earnings from business* gain, gate, handle, income, interest, lucre, produce, product, profit, receipts, result, returns, revenue, reward, split, take, takings, till, yield; CONCEPT *344* —*Ant.* loss

process [n] *method; series of actions to achieve result* action, advance, case, channels*, course, course of action*, development, evolution, fashion, formation, growth, manner, means, measure, mechanism, mode, modus operandi, movement, operation, outgrowth, performance, practice, procedure, proceeding, progress, progression, red tape*, routine, rule, stage, step, suit, system, technique, transaction, trial, unfolding, way, wise, working; CONCEPT *6*

process [v] *subject to series of actions to achieve result* alter, concoct, convert, deal with, dispose of, fulfill, handle, make ready, prepare, refine, take care of, transform, treat; CONCEPT *204* —*Ant.* forget, neglect

procession [n] *parade, sequence* advance, autocade, cavalcade, column, consecution, cortege, course, cycle, file, march, motorcade, movement, order, process, run, series, string, succession, train; CONCEPTS *155,727*

proclaim [v] *advertise, make known* affirm, announce, annunciate, blast, blaze, blazon, broadcast, call, circulate, declare, demonstrate, disseminate, enunciate, evidence, evince, exhibit, expound, get on a soapbox*, give out, herald, illustrate, indicate, manifest, mark, ostend, pass the word*, profess, promulgate, publish, shoot off mouth*, shout out, show, sound off, spiel*, spout, spread it around*, stump*, trumpet*, utter, vent, ventilate, voice; CONCEPTS 49,60 —*Ant.* conceal, hide

proclamation [n] *advertisement, announcement* broadcast, declaration, decree, edict, manifesto, notice, notification, promulgation, pronouncement, pronunciamento*, publication; CONCEPTS 271,278 —*Ant.* secret

proclivity [n] *inclination, tendency* bent*, bias, cup of tea*, disposition, druthers, facility, flash*, groove*, inclining, leaning, liableness, penchant, predilection, predisposition, proneness, propensity, thing for*, type, weakness; CONCEPTS 20,32,411 —*Ant.* disinclination

procrastinate [v] *delay, put off doing* adjourn, be dilatory, cool*, dally, dawdle, defer, drag, drag one's feet*, give the run around*, goldbrick*, hang fire*, hesitate, hold off, lag*, let slide, linger, loiter, pause, play a waiting game*, play for time*, poke*, postpone, prolong, protract, retard, shilly-shally*, stall, stay, suspend, tarry, temporize, wait; CONCEPTS 121,237,681 —*Ant.* accelerate, advance, complete, do, finish, go ahead, quicken

procreate [v] *reproduce* beget, breed, conceive, create, engender, father, generate, get, give birth to, hatch, impregnate, make, mother, multiply, originate, parent, produce, progenerate, proliferate, propagate, sire, spawn; CONCEPTS 173,251,374 —*Ant.* kill

procure [v] *acquire, obtain* annex, appropriate, bring around, buy, buy out, buy up, come by, compass, cop*, corral, draw, earn, effect, find, gain, get, get hold of, grab, have, induce, land*, latch on to, lay hands on, make a haul*, manage to get*, persuade, pick up, prevail upon, promote, purchase, score, secure, solicit, wangle, win; CONCEPTS 68,120,327 —*Ant.* give away, have, lose

prod [v] *poke at* crowd, dig, drive, elbow, goose, jab, jog, nudge, press, prick, punch, push, shove; CONCEPT 208

prod [v] *urge, incite* crowd*, egg on*, excite, exhort, goad, goose*, impel, instigate, jog memory, motivate, move, pique, prick, prompt, propel, provoke, push, remind, rouse, sic*, sound, spark, spur, stimulate, stir up, trigger, turn on; CONCEPTS 7,19,22,242 —*Ant.* discourage, dissuade

prodigal [adj1] *wasteful* dissipated, excessive, extravagant, immoderate, improvident, intemperate, lavish, profligate, reckless, spendthrift, squandering, wanton; CONCEPTS 401,560 —*Ant.* careful, thrifty

prodigal [adj2] *luxurious, profuse* abundant, bounteous, bountiful, copious, exuberant, lavish, lush, luxuriant, moneyed, munificent, opulent, riotous, sumptuous, superabundant, teeming; CONCEPTS 334,781 —*Ant.* modest, poor

prodigal [n] *person who spends a lot* big spender*, compulsive shopper*, deep pockets*, dissipator, high roller*, profligate, spender, spendthrift, sport, squanderer, waster, wastrel; CONCEPTS 348,412

prodigious [adj1] *huge, enormous* big, colossal*, fantastic, giant, gigantic, gross, Herculean*, immeasurable, immense, inordinate, jumbo*, king-size*, large, mammoth, massive, mighty, monstrous, monumental, mortal, stupendous, towering, tremendous, vast; CONCEPTS 773,781 —*Ant.* little, small, tiny

prodigious [adj2] *extraordinary, fabulous* abnormal, amazing, astonishing, astounding, bad, exceptional, fab*, fantastic, heavy, impressive, marvelous, miraculous, out-of-this-world*, phenomenal, preternatural, remarkable, spectacular, staggering, startling, state-of-the-art*, striking, stupendous, surprising, unreal, unusual, utmost, wonderful; CONCEPTS 567,572,574 —*Ant.* common, insignificant, ordinary, unremarkable

prodigy [n] *person or thing that is extraordinary* brain*, child genius, curiosity, enormity, freak*, genius, intellect, marvel, mastermind, miracle, monster, natural, one in a million*, phenomenon, portent, rare bird*, rarity, sensation, spectacle, stunner, talent, whiz*, whiz kid*, wizard, wonder, wonder child, wunderkind; CONCEPTS 416,671,706

produce [n] *fruit and vegetables* crop, fruitage, goods, greengrocery, harvest, income, outgrowth, outturn, production, yield; CONCEPTS 426,429,431,457,461

produce [v1] *generate, create* afford, assemble, author, bear, beget, blossom, breed, bring forth, bring out, build, come through, compose, conceive, construct, contribute, cultivate, deliver, design, develop, devise, effectuate, engender, erect, fabricate, fetch, flower, form, frame, furnish, give, give birth, give forth, imagine, invent, make, manufacture, multiply, offer, originate, parent, present, procreate, propagate, provide, put together, render, reproduce, return, show fruit, supply, turn out, write, yield; CONCEPTS 173,205,251,374 —*Ant.* consume, destroy, ruin

produce [v2] *cause, effect* beget, breed, bring about, draw on, engender, generate, get up, give rise to, hatch, induce, make, make for*, muster, occasion, provoke, result in, secure, set off, work up; CONCEPT 242 —*Ant.* result

produce [v3] *demonstrate, show* advance, bring forward, bring to light, display, exhibit, offer, present, put forward, set forth, unfold; CONCEPT 261

produce [v4] *put on a public performance* act, come through, direct, do, exhibit, make, mount, percolate, perform, perk, play, present, pull off*, show, stage; CONCEPTS 292,324 —*Ant.* act, play

product [n] *result or goods created* aftermath, amount, artifact, blend, brand, brew, by-product, commodity, compound, concoction, confection, consequence, contrivance, creation, crop, decoction, device, effect, emolument, fabrication, fruit, gain, handiwork, invention, issue, legacy, line, manufacture, merchandise, offshoot, outcome, outgrowth, output, preparation, produce, production, profit, realization, result, returns, spinoff, stock, synthetic, yield, work, yield; CONCEPTS 230,338 —*Ant.* cause, resource

production [n] *creating of goods, result* assembly, authoring, bearing, blossoming, construction, creation, direction, elongation, engendering, extention, fabrication, formulation, fructification, generation, giving, lengthening, making, management, manufacture, manufacturing, origination, preparation, presentation, producing, prolongation, protraction, provision, rendering, reproduction, return, staging, yielding; CONCEPT 205 —*Ant.* destruction, ruin

productive [*adj*] *fruitful, creative* advantageous, beneficial, constructive, dynamic, effective, energetic, fecund, fertile, gainful, generative, gratifying, inventive, plentiful, producing, profitable, prolific, rewarding, rich, teeming, useful, valuable, vigorous, worthwhile; CONCEPTS 537,542,560 —*Ant.* fruitless, impotent, unfruitful, unproductive

productivity [*n*] *output, work rate* abundance, capacity, fecundity, fertility, mass production, potency, production, productiveness, richness, yield; CONCEPT 630 —*Ant.* idleness, unproductivity

profane [*adj*] *immoral, crude, disrespectful of religion* abusive, atheistic, blasphemous, coarse, dirty*, filthy*, foul, godless, heathen, idolatrous, impious, impure, indecent, infidel, irreligious, irreverent, irreverential, mundane, nasty, obscene, pagan, profanatory, raunchy, sacrilegious, sinful, smutty*, temporal, transient, transitory, unconsecrated, ungodly, unhallowed, unholy, unsanctified, vulgar, wicked, worldly; CONCEPTS 267,401,545 —*Ant.* clean, moral, sacred

profane [*v*] *defile, desecrate* abuse, be evil, befoul, blaspheme, commit sacrilege, commit sin, contaminate, curse, cuss, damn, darn, debase, despoil, do wrong, flame, hoodoo*, misuse, mock, mudsling*, pervert, pollute, prostitute, put double whammy on*, revile, scorn, swear, talk dirty*, tar, trash, vice, violate, vitiate, voodoo*; CONCEPTS 44,52,58,63 —*Ant.* cleanse, purify

profanity [*n*] *foul language* abuse, blasphemy, curse, cursing, cuss, cuss word, dirty language*, dirty name*, dirty word*, execration, four-letter word*, impiety, imprecation, irreverence, malediction, no-no*, obscenity, profaneness, sacrilege, swearing, swearword, taboo; CONCEPTS 278,645 —*Ant.* clean language

profess [*v*] *declare, assert* acknowledge, act as if, admit, affirm, allege, announce, asseverate, aver, avouch, avow, blow hot air*, certify, claim, come out*, confess, confirm, constate, croon, cross heart*, depose, dissemble, fake, feign, get off chest*, get on soapbox*, maintain, make out, open up*, own, own up*, predicate, pretend, proclaim, purport, say so*, sing*, soapbox*, spiel*, spout*, state, stump*, swear on bible*, swear up and down*, talk big*, vouch; CONCEPTS 49,63 —*Ant.* conceal, hide

profession [*n1*] *line of work requiring academic or practical preparation* art, avocation, berth, billet, biz*, business, calling, career, chosen work, concern, craft, dodge*, employment, engagement, field, game*, handicraft, lifework, line*, line of work*, métier, occupation, office, position, post, pursuit, rat race*, role, service, situation, slot*, specialty, sphere, thing*, trade, undertaking, vocation, walk of life*; CONCEPT 360 —*Ant.* avocation, entertainment, fun, hobby

profession [*n2*] *declaration* acknowledgment, affirmation, assertion, attestation, avowal, claim, confession, pretense, statement, testimony, vow; CONCEPT 278 —*Ant.* quiet, silence

professional [*adj*] *skilled, trained* able, ace, acknowledged, adept, competent, crackerjack*, efficient, experienced, expert, finished, knowing one's stuff*, known, learned, licensed, on the ball*, polished, practiced, proficient, qualified, sharp, skillful, slick*, there*, up to speed*, well-qualified; CONCEPTS 326,402,527,528 —*Ant.* amateur, rookie, unprofessional, unskilled, untrained

professional [*n*] *person prepared for work by extended study or practice* adept, artist, artiste, authority, brain*, egghead*, expert, hotshot*, old hand*, old pro*, old war-horse*, phenom, powerhouse, pro, proficient, pundit, shark, specialist, star, superstar, virtuoso, whiz*, whiz kid*, wizard; CONCEPTS 347,348 —*Ant.* amateur, apprentice, greenhorn, rookie

professor [*n*] *person who teaches college courses* assistant, brain*, educator, egghead*, faculty member, fellow, instructor, lecturer, pedagogue, principal, prof*, pundit, quant*, rocket scientist*, sage, savant, teacher, tutor; CONCEPT 350 —*Ant.* pupil, student

proffer [*v*] *suggest, offer* extend, gift, give, hand, hit on, hold out, make a pitch*, pose, present, propose, proposition, propound, submit, tender, volunteer; CONCEPTS 66,67,75 —*Ant.* discourage, dissuade, take back

proficiency [*n*] *ability, skillfulness* accomplishment, advance, advancement, aptitude, chops, competence, dexterity, efficiency, expertise, expertness, facility, formula, green thumb*, headway*, knack*, know-how*, knowledge, learning, makings, mastery, moxie*, oil*, progress, right stuff*, savvy*, skill, stuff, talent, what it takes*; CONCEPTS 409,630,706 —*Ant.* clumsiness, inability, incompetence, ineptness

proficient [*adj*] *able, skilled* accomplished, adept, apt, capable, clever, competent, consummate, conversant, crack*, crackerjack*, drilled, effective, effectual, efficient, exercised, experienced, expert, finished, gifted, on the beam*, phenom, pro, qualified, savvy*, sharp, skillful, slick*, talented, trained, up to speed*, versed, whiz*, with it*; CONCEPTS 402,527,528 —*Ant.* clumsy, incompetent, inept, unable, unskilled

profile [*n1*] *drawing of outline* contour, delineation, figuration, figure, form, likeness, line, lineament, lineation, portrait, shadow, shape, side view, silhouette, sketch; CONCEPTS 259,625

profile [*n2*] *description, characterization* analysis, biography, character sketch, chart, diagram, review, sketch, study, survey, thumbnail sketch, vignette, vita; CONCEPTS 268,283

profit [*n*] *gain* accumulation, acquisition, advancement, advantage, aggrandizement, augmentation, avail, benefit, bottom line*, cleanup, earnings, emoluments, gain*, goods*, gravy*, gross, harvest, income, interest, killing, lucre, net, output, outturn, percentage, proceeds, product, production, receipt, receipts, remuneration, return, revenue, saving, skim*, split*, surplus, take*, takings*, turnout, use, value, velvet*, winnings, yield; CONCEPTS 332,344,693 —*Ant.* loss

profit [*v*] *gain; get or give an advantage* aid, avail, benefit, be of advantage, better, capitalize on, cash in on, clean up, clear, contribute, earn, exploit, help, improve, learn from, make a haul*, make a killing*, make capital, make good use of*, make it big*, make money, make the most of*, pay, pay off, promote, prosper, put to good use*, realize, reap the benefit*, recover, score, serve*, stand in good stead*, take advantage of, thrive, turn to advantage, use, utilize, work for; CONCEPTS 110,124,330, 693 —Ant. lose

profitable [adj] advantageous; money-making
assisting, beneficial, commercial, conducive, contributive, cost-effective, effective, effectual, favorable, fruitful, gainful, going*, good, instrumental, in the black*, lucrative, paid off, paying, paying well, practical, pragmatic, productive, remunerative, rewarding, self-sustaining, serviceable, successful, sustaining, sweet*, useful, valuable, well-paying, worthwhile; CONCEPTS 334,537,572 —Ant. disadvantageous, unprofitable

profligate [adj1] immoral, corrupt abandoned, debauched, degenerate, depraved, dissipated, dissolute, iniquitous, lax, lewd, libertine, licentious, loose, promiscuous, reprobate, shameless, unprincipled, vicious, vitiated, wanton, wicked, wild; CONCEPT 545 —Ant. good, moral, nice

profligate [adj2] wasteful extravagant, immoderate, improvident, lavish, prodigal, reckless, spendthrift, squandering; CONCEPTS 334,401 —Ant. careful, saving

profligate [n] person who is immoral debauchee, degenerate, dissipater, good-for-nothing*, lecher, libertine, nighthawk*, no-good*, old goat*, operator*, prodigal, rake, reprobate, roué, swinger, waster, wastrel; CONCEPT 412

profound [adj1] intellectual, thoughtful abstruse, acroamatic, deep, difficult, discerning, enlightened, erudite, esoteric, heavy*, hermetic, informed, intellectual, intelligent, knowing, knowledgeable, learned, mysterious, occult, Orphic, penetrating, philosophical, recondite, reflective, sagacious, sage, scholarly, secret, serious, shrewd, skilled, subtle, thorough, weighty, wise; CONCEPTS 402,529 —Ant. ignorant, stupid

profound [adj2] bottomless abysmal, buried, cavernous, deep, fathomless, subterranean, yawning; CONCEPT 777 —Ant. shallow, slight

profound [adj3] intense; emotional abject, absolute, acute, consummate, deep, deeply felt, deep-seated, exhaustive, extensive, extreme, far-reaching, great, hard, heartfelt, heartrending, hearty, keen, out-and-out*, pronounced, sincere, thorough, total, utter; CONCEPTS 403,531,569 —Ant. mild, moderate, unemotional

profuse [adj] abundant, excessive abounding, alive with*, ample, aplenty, bounteous, bountiful, copious, crawling with*, dime a dozen*, extravagant, extreme, exuberant, fulsome, galore, generous, immoderate, lavish, liberal, lush, luxuriant, no end*, openhanded, opulent, overflowing, plentiful, plenty, prodigal, profusive, prolific, riotous, sumptuous, superfluous, swarming, teeming, thick with*, unstinting; CONCEPTS 762,781 —Ant. lacking, sparse, wanting

profusion [n] abundance ampleness, copiousness, excess, extravagance, flood, glut, great quantity, opulence, outpouring, overflow, plenitude, plenty, prosperity, prosperousness, surplus, wealth; CONCEPTS 710,767

progeny [n] offspring begats, breed, children, descendants, family, get*, issue, kids*, lineage, posterity, progeniture, race, scions, seed, stock, young; CONCEPTS 296,414 —Ant. parent

prognosis [n] forecast cast, diagnosis, expectation, foretelling, guess, prediction, prevision, prognostication, projection, prophecy, speculation, surmise; CONCEPTS 274,689

prognosticate [v] predict, foretell adumbrate, augur, betoken, call it*, crystal-ball*, divine, forebode, forecast, foreshadow, harbinger, have a hunch*, herald, make book*, point to, portend, presage, prophesy, read, see coming*, soothsay, vaticinate; CONCEPT 70

prognosticator [n] forecaster augur, channeller, diviner, fortune-teller, medium, oracle, prophet, seer, soothsayer, telepathist, visionary; CONCEPT 423

program [n1] agenda, list affairs, appointments, arrangements, bill, bulletin, business, calendar, card, catalog, chores, curriculum, details, docket, happenings, index, lineup, listing, meetings, memoranda, necessary acts*, order of business*, order of events*, order of the day*, plan, plans, preparations, record, schedule, series of events, slate, syllabus, things to do*, timetable; CONCEPTS 281,283

program [n2] scheme, plan course, design, instructions, line, order, plan of action, policy, polity, procedure, project, sequence; CONCEPTS 274,660

program [n3] performance in medium broadcast, presentation, production, show; CONCEPT 263

program [v] plan out; supply instructions arrange, bill, book, budget, calculate, compile, compute, design, draft, edit, engage, enter, estimate, feed, figure, formulate, get on line*, itemize, lay on, lay out, line up, list, map out, pencil in*, poll, prearrange, prioritize, process, register, schedule, set, set up, slate, work out; CONCEPTS 36,60,84,384 —Ant. forget, neglect

progress [n] advancement, gain advance, amelioration, anabasis, betterment, boost, break, breakthrough, buildup, course, dash, development, evolution, evolvement, expedition, flowering, growth, headway, hike, impetus, improvement, increase, journey, lunge, march, momentum, motion, movement, ongoing, pace, passage, process, procession, proficiency, progression, promotion, rate, rise, step forward, stride, tour, unfolding, voyage, way; CONCEPTS 704,706 —Ant. decline, decrease, deterioration, retreat, retrogression

progress [v1] move forward advance, continue, cover ground*, dash, edge, forge ahead, gain ground, get along, get on, go forward, keep going, lunge, make headway*, make strides*, move on, proceed, shoot, speed, travel; CONCEPTS 149,159 —Ant. back up, decline, retreat, stop

progress [v2] improve, advance ameliorate, become better, better, blossom, boost, develop, gain, grow, increase, make first rate, mature, shape up, straighten up, truck, turn over new leaf*, upgrade; CONCEPT 700 —Ant. decline, decrease, deteriorate, retrogress

progression [n] progress advance, advancement, amelioration, betterment, boost, break, breakthrough, development, evolution, evolvement, forward march, furtherance, getting ahead, giant strides, going forward, growth, headway, improvement, promotion, step forward; CONCEPTS 704,706

progressive [adj] *liberal; growing* accelerating, advanced, advancing, avant-garde*, bleeding-heart*, broad, broad-minded, continuing, continuous, developing, dynamic, enlightened, enterprising, escalating, forward-looking, go-ahead*, gradual, graduated, increasing, intensifying, left*, left of center*, lenient, modern, ongoing, onward, open-minded, radical, reformist, revolutionary, tolerant, up-and-coming*, up-to-date, wide; CONCEPTS 542,544 —*Ant.* conservative, moderate

prohibit [v] *make impossible; stop* ban, block, bottle up*, box in*, bring to screeching halt*, constrain, cool*, cork*, debar, disallow, enjoin, forbid, forfend, freeze*, gridlock, halt, hamper, hang up*, hinder, hold up, impede, inhibit, interdict, jam up*, keep lid on*, kill, lock up, nix, obstruct, outlaw, pass on*, preclude, prevent, proscribe, put a lock on*, put a stopper in*, put chill on*, put down, put half nelson on*, restrain, restrict, rule out, shut out, spike*, stymie*, taboo*, throw cold water on*, tie up*, veto, zing*; CONCEPTS 50,88,121,130,317 —*Ant.* conserve, favor, permit, push

prohibited [adj] *forbidden* banned, barred, closed down, contraband, crooked*, illegal, illicit, no-no*, not allowed, not approved, off limits*, out of bounds*, out of line*, proscribed, refused, restricted, shady*, taboo, verboten, vetoed, wildcat*; CONCEPTS 554,576 —*Ant.* allowed, permitted

prohibition [n] *ban, forbiddance* bar, constraint, disallowance, don't*, embargo, exclusion, injunction, interdict, interdiction, negation, no-no*, obstruction, off limits*, out of bounds*, prevention, proscription, refusal, repudiation, restriction, taboo, temperance, veto; CONCEPTS 121,130,652,691 —*Ant.* allowance, clearance, permission

prohibitive [adj] *restrictive; beyond one's financial means* conditional, excessive, exorbitant, expensive, extortionate, forbidding, high-priced, limiting, preposterous, preventing, prohibiting, proscriptive, repressive, restraining, sky-high*, steep*, suppressive; CONCEPTS 334,524 —*Ant.* reasonable, unlimited, unrestrictive

project [n] *undertaking, work* activity, adventure, affair, aim, assignment, baby*, blueprint*, business, concern, deal, design, enterprise, exploit, feat, game plan, intention, job, matter, occupation, outline, pet*, plan, program, proposal, proposition, scheme, setup, strategy, task, thing*, venture; CONCEPTS 324,349,362

project [v1] *plan* arrange, blueprint, calculate, cast, chart, conceive, contemplate, contrive, delineate, design, devise, diagram, draft, envisage, envision, estimate, extrapolate, feature, forecast, frame, gauge, image, imagine, intend, map out, outline, predetermine, predict, propose, purpose, reckon, scheme, see, think, vision, visualize; CONCEPTS 28,36,37,70

project [v2] *bulge, hang out* be conspicuous, beetle, be prominent, extend, hang over, jut, lengthen, overhang, poke, pop out, pout,

prolong, protrude, protuberate, push out, stand out, stick out, stretch out, thrust out; CONCEPT 747 —*Ant.* cave in

project [v3] *throw, discharge* cast, fling, heave, hurl, launch, pitch, propel, shoot, transmit; CONCEPTS 179,222 —*Ant.* keep

projection [n1] *bulge, overhang* bump, bunch, eaves, extension, hook, jut, knob, ledge, outthrust, point, prolongation, prominence, protrusion, protuberance, ridge, rim, shelf, sill, spine, spur, step, swelling; CONCEPTS 471,509,513 —*Ant.* depression

projection [n2] *prediction* calculation, computation, estimate, estimation, extrapolation, forecast, guess, prognostication, reckoning; CONCEPTS 28,278

proletariat [n] *working class* blue-collar workers, bourgeoisie, commoners, common people, hoi polloi, lower class, peasant, plebians, proletarian, rank and file, working stiff; CONCEPTS 413,423

proliferate [v] *increase quickly* breed, burgeon, engender, escalate, expand, generate, grow rapidly, multiply, mushroom*, procreate, propagate, reproduce, run riot*, snowball*; CONCEPT 780 —*Ant.* decline, decrease, fall off

prolific [adj] *fruitful, productive* abounding, abundant, bountiful, breeding, copious, creative, fecund, fertile, generating, generative, luxuriant, profuse, proliferant, rank, reproducing, reproductive, rich, spawning, swarming, teeming, yielding; CONCEPTS 485,542 —*Ant.* barren, fruitless, impotent, unfruitful, unproductive

prologue [n] *preface* beginning, exordium, explanation, foreword, introduction, opening, overture, preamble, prelude, proem, prolegomenon; CONCEPT 270

prolong [v] *extend, draw out* carry on, continue, delay, drag one's feet*, drag out*, hold, hold up, increase, lengthen, let it ride*, make longer, pad*, perpetuate, protract, spin out*, stall, stretch, stretch out; CONCEPTS 239,250 —*Ant.* abbreviate, shorten

prominence [n1] *something that sticks out* bulge, bump, cliff, conspicuousness, crag, crest, elevation, eminence, headland, height, high point, jutting, markedness, mound, pinnacle, projection, promontory, protrusion, protuberance, rise, spur, swelling, tor; CONCEPTS 513,836 —*Ant.* depression

prominence [n2] *distinction, outstandingness* celebrity, eminence, fame, greatness, illustriousness, importance, influence, kudos*, name, notability, precedence, preeminence, prestige, rank, renown, reputation, salience, specialness, standing, top billing*, weight; CONCEPT 668 —*Ant.* obscurity, unimportance

prominent [adj1] *sticking out; conspicuous* arresting, beetling, bulging, easily seen, embossed, extended, extrusive, eye-catching, flashy, hanging out, hilly, in the foreground, jutting, marked, noticeable, obtrusive, obvious, outstanding, projecting, pronounced, protruding, protrusive, protuberant, raised, relieved, remarkable, rough, rugged, salient, shooting out, signal, standing out, striking, to the fore, unmistakable; CONCEPTS 485,583,619 —*Ant.* depressed, inconspicuous, invisible, obscured, sunken

prominent [adj2] *important; famous*

big-league*, big-name*, big-shot*, celebrated, chief, distinguished, eminent, famed, foremost, great, high-profile*, leading, main, notable, noted, notorious, outstanding, popular, preeminent, renowned, respected, top, underlined, VIP*, well-known, well-thought-of, world-class*; CONCEPT 568 —Ant. common, obscure, ordinary, unimportant, unknown

promiscuous [adj] *indiscriminately sexually active* abandoned, debauched, dissipated, dissolute, easy*, fast*, immoral, indiscriminate, lax, libertine, licentious, loose*, of easy virtue, oversexed, profligate, pushover, unbridled, unchaste, undiscriminating, unrestricted, wanton, wild; CONCEPTS 372,545 —Ant. chaste, cold, cool, frigid

promise [n1] *one's word that something will be done* affiance, affirmation, agreement, asseveration, assurance, avowal, betrothal, bond, commitment, compact, consent, contract, covenant, earnest, engagement, espousal, guarantee, insurance, marriage, oath, obligation, pact, parole, pawn, pledge, plight, profession, promissory note, sacred word, security, stipulation, swear, swearing, token, troth, undertaking, vow, warrant, warranty, word, word of honor; CONCEPTS 71,278 —Ant. break, renege

promise [n2] *hope, possibility* ability, aptitude, capability, capacity, encouragement, flair, good omen, outlook, potential, talent; CONCEPTS 630,650 —Ant. hopelessness, impossibility

promise [v1] *give word that something will be done* accede, affiance, affirm, agree, answer for, assent, asseverate, assure, bargain, betroth, bind, commit, compact, consent, contract, covenant, cross heart*, declare, engage, ensure, espouse, guarantee, hock*, insure, live up to*, mortgage, obligate, pass, pawn*, pledge, plight, profess, say so*, secure, stipulate, string along*, subscribe, swear, swear on bible*, swear up and down*, take an oath, undertake, underwrite, vouch, vow, warrant; CONCEPT 71 —Ant. break, renege

promise [v2] *bring hope, possibility* augur, bespeak, betoken, bode, denote, encourage, forebode, foreshadow, foretoken, give hope, hint, hold out hope*, hold probability, indicate, lead to expect, like, look, omen, portend, presage, seem likely, show signs of*, suggest; CONCEPTS 118,650 —Ant. discourage

promising [adj] *hopeful* able, assuring, auspicious, bright, encouraging, favorable, gifted, happy, likely, lucky, propitious, reassuring, rising, roseate, rosy, talented, up-and-coming; CONCEPTS 406,548 —Ant. hopeless, unpromising

promontory [n] *headland* bluff, cape, cheronese, foreland, jetty, jutty, peninsula, point, ridge; CONCEPTS 509,514

promote [v1] *help, advance* advertise, advocate, aid, assist, avail, back, befriend, benefit, bolster, boost, build up*, call attention to, champion, contribute, cooperate, cry*, develop, encourage, endorse, espouse, forward, foster, further, get behind, hype*, improve, nourish, nurture, patronize, plug*, popularize, propagandize, publicize, puff*, push, push for, recommend, sell, serve, speak for, speed, sponsor, stimulate, subsidize, succor, support,

uphold, urge, work for; CONCEPTS 49,110,324 —Ant. condemn, discredit, dishonor, hurt

promote [v2] *give a higher position in organization* advance, aggrandize, ascend, better, dignify, elevate, ennoble, exalt, favor, graduate, honor, increase, kick upstairs*, magnify, move up, prefer, raise, skip, up*, upgrade; CONCEPT 351 —Ant. degrade, demote, discredit

promoter [n] *supporter* advertiser, advocate, ally, backer, booster, endorser, follower, organizer, publicist, sponsor; CONCEPT 423

promotion [n1] *higher position in organization* advance, advancement, advocacy, aggrandizement, backing, betterment, boost, break, breakthrough, buildup, bump, elevation, encouragement, ennoblement, exaltation, favoring, furtherance, go-ahead*, hike, honor, improvement, jump, jump up, lift, move up, preference, preferment, prelation, progress, raise, rise, step up, support, upgrade, upgrading; CONCEPT 351 —Ant. demotion

promotion [n2] *publicity* advertising, advertising campaign, ballyhoo*, blurb*, buildup*, hard sell*, hoopla*, hype*, notice, pitch, pizzazz*, plug*, PR*, press*, press-agentry, promo*, propaganda, publicity, public relations, puff*, puffery*, pushing, squib*; CONCEPTS 49,110,271,324 —Ant. silence

prompt [adj] *early, responsive* alert, apt, brisk, eager, efficient, expeditious, immediate, instant, instantaneous, on the ball*, on the button*, on the dot*, on the nose*, on time, precise, punctual, quick, rapid, ready, smart, speedy, swift, timely, unhesitating, vigilant, watchful, wide-awake, willing; CONCEPTS 401,799 —Ant. late, negligent, slow, tardy

prompt [n] *hint* cue, help, jog, jolt, mnemonic, prod, reminder, spur, stimulus, twit; CONCEPT 274

prompt [v] *incite, cue* advise, aid, arouse, assist, bring up, call forth, cause, convince, draw, egg on*, elicit, evoke, exhort, get, give rise to, goad, help, help out, hint, impel, imply, indicate, induce, inspire, instigate, jog, mention, motivate, move, occasion, persuade, prick*, prod, propel, propose, provoke, refresh, remind, sic*, spur, stimulate, suggest, talk into, urge, win over; CONCEPTS 68,242 —Ant. halt, prevent, stop

promptly [adv] *immediately* at once, directly, expeditiously, fast, flat-out*, fleetly, hastily, in nothing flat*, instantly, lickety-split*, like a shot*, now, on the dot*, on the double*, on time, PDQ*, posthaste, pronto, punctually, quickly, rapidly, right away, sharp, speedily, straightaway, swiftly, unhesitatingly; CONCEPTS 544,799 —Ant. late, negligently

promulgate [v] *make known* advertise, announce, annunciate, broadcast, call, circulate, communicate, declare, decree, disseminate, drum, issue, make public, notify, pass the word*, proclaim, promote, publish, sound, spread, toot, trumpet; CONCEPT 60 —Ant. conceal, hide

prone [adj1] *lying down* decumbent, face down, flat, horizontal, level, procumbent, prostrate, reclining, recumbent, resupine, supine; CONCEPT 583 —Ant. sitting, straight, upright

prone [adj2] *liable, likely* apt, bent, devoted,

disposed, exposed, fain, given, inclined, minded, open, predisposed, ready, sensitive, subject, susceptible, tending, willing; CONCEPTS 542, 552 —*Ant.* improbably, unlikely

pronounce [v1] *produce words vocally* accent, articulate, enunciate, phonate, say, sound, speak, stress, utter, verbalize, vocalize, voice; CONCEPT 47 —*Ant.* mumble

pronounce [v2] *announce, declare* affirm, assert, blast, call, decree, deliver, drum, judge, mouth, proclaim, say, sound off, spread around, trumpet, verbalize; CONCEPT 49 —*Ant.* conceal, hide

pronounced [adj] *distinct, evident* arresting, assured, broad, clear, clear-cut, conspicuous, decided, definite, marked, notable, noticeable, obvious, outstanding, striking, strong, unmistakable; CONCEPTS 535,576,619 —*Ant.* indistinct, obscure, unpronounced, vague

pronouncement [n] *declaration, statement* advertisement, announcement, broadcast, decree, dictum, edict, judgment, manifesto, notification, proclamation, promulgation, pronunciamento*, publication, report, ukase; CONCEPTS 271,274,278 —*Ant.* concealment

proof [n1] *evidence, authentication* affidavit, argument, attestation, averment, case, certification, chapter and verse*, clincher*, clue, confirmation, corroboration, credentials, criterion, cue*, data, demonstration, deposition, documents, establishment, exhibit, facts, goods*, grabber*, grounds, information, lowdown*, nitty-gritty*, paper trail*, picture, reason, reasons, record, scoop*, score*, skinny*, smoking gun*, straight stuff*, substantiation, testament, testimony, trace, validation, verification, warrant, wherefore*, why*, whyfor*, witness; CONCEPT 274 —*Ant.* hypothesis, theory

proof [n2] *photographic print* galley, galley proof, impression, page proof, pass, pull, repro, revise, slip, stereo, trial, trial print, trial proof; CONCEPT 265

proofread [v] *copyedit* analyze, blue-pencil*, check, correct, cut, delete, edit, go over, rearrange, refine, remove errors, rephrase, revise, strike out; CONCEPTS 79,126,203

prop [n] *support* aid, assistance, brace, buttress, column, mainstay, post, shore, stanchion, stay, strengthener, strut, truss, underpinning; CONCEPTS 440,470

prop [v] *hold up or lean against* bear up, bolster, brace, buoy, buttress, carry, maintain, rest, set, shore, stand, stay, strengthen, support, sustain, truss, underprop, uphold; CONCEPTS 190,201 —*Ant.* drop, fall

propaganda [n] *information that is designed to mislead or persuade* advertising, agitprop, announcement, brainwashing*, disinformation, doctrine, evangelism, handout, hogwash*, hype*, implantation, inculcation, indoctrination, newspeak, promotion, promulgation, proselytism, publication, publicity; CONCEPT 278 —*Ant.* truth

propagate [v1] *breed, reproduce* bear, beget, engender, father, fecundate, fertilize, generate, grow, impregnate, increase, inseminate, make pregnant, mother, multiply, originate, procreate, produce, proliferate, raise, sire; CONCEPT 374 —*Ant.* destroy, kill

propagate [v2] *spread, make known* broadcast, circulate, develop, diffuse, disperse, disseminate, distribute, proclaim, promulgate, publicize, publish, radiate, scatter, strew, transmit; CONCEPTS 60,222 —*Ant.* conceal, hide

propel [v] *throw; release into air* actuate, drive, force, impel, launch, mobilize, move, press, push, send, set going, set in motion, shoot, shove, start, thrust; CONCEPTS 208,221, 222 —*Ant.* hinder, hold, keep

propensity [n] *inclination, weakness* ability, aptness, bent*, bias, capacity, competence, disposition, flash, inclining, leaning, liability, partiality, penchant, predilection, predisposition, proclivity, proneness, susceptibility, sweet tooth*, talent, tendency, thing*, tilt*, yen; CONCEPTS 20,411,630,709 —*Ant.* antipathy, disinclination, dislike, hate

proper [adj1] *suitable* able, applicable, appropriate, apt, au fait, becoming, befitting, capable, competent, convenient, decent, desired, felicitous, fit, fitting, good, happy, just, legitimate, meet, qualified, right, suited, true, useful; CONCEPT 558 —*Ant.* improper, unacceptable, unsuitable

proper [adj2] *mannerly, decent* becoming, befitting, by the book*, by the numbers*, comely, comme il faut*, conforming, correct, decorous, demure, de rigueur*, genteel, in line, kosher*, moral, nice, polite, precise, priggish, prim, prissy, prudish, punctilious, puritanical, refined, respectable, right, seemly, solid, square*, stone, straight*, strait-laced*, stuffy*; CONCEPTS 401,404 —*Ant.* crass, crude, misbehaving, objectionable

proper [adj3] *conventional, correct* absolute, accepted, accurate, arrant, complete, consummate, customary, decorous, established, exact, formal, free of error, on target*, on the button*, on the nose*, on the right track*, orthodox, out-and-out*, precise, right, unmistaken, usual, utter; CONCEPTS 326,533 —*Ant.* incorrect, substandard, unconventional

proper [adj4] *individual, personal* characteristic, distinctive, idiosyncratic, own, particular, peculiar, private, respective, special, specific; CONCEPTS 549,557 —*Ant.* general

property [n1] *possessions, real estate* acreage, acres, assets, belongings, buildings, capital, chattels, claim, dominion, effects, equity, estate, farm, freehold, goods, holdings, home, house, inheritance, land, means, ownership, plot, possessorship, premises, proprietary, proprietorship, realty, resources, riches, substance, title, tract, wealth, worth; CONCEPTS 446,509,515,710

property [n2] *characteristic, feature* ability, affection, attribute, character, hallmark, idiosyncrasy, mark, peculiarity, quality, trait, virtue; CONCEPTS 411,654

prophecy [n] *prediction* apocalypse, augury, cast, divination, forecast, foretelling, oracle, presage, prevision, prognosis, prognostication, revelation, second sight, soothsaying, vision; CONCEPTS 70,278,689

prophesy [v] *predict, warn* adumbrate, augur, call*, call the turn*, crystal-ball*, divine, forecast, foresee, foretell, forewarn, have a hunch*, make book*, portend, predict, presage, prognosticate, psych it out*, see coming*, soothsay, vaticinate; CONCEPT 70

prophet [n] *person, thing that predicts future* astrologer, augur, auspex, bard, clairvoyant, diviner, druid, evocator, forecaster, fortuneteller, haruspex, horoscopist, magus, medium, meteorologist, oracle, ovate, palmist, predictor, prognosticator, prophesier, reader, seer, seeress, sibyl, soothsayer, sorcerer, tealeaf reader, witch, wizard; CONCEPTS 361,423

prophetic [adj] *telling of the future* apocalyptic, augural, Delphian*, divinatory, fatidic, foreshadowing, mantic, occult, oracular, predictive, presaging, prescient, prognostic, prophetical, pythonic, sibylline, vaticinal, veiled; CONCEPT 267

propitious [adj1] *full of promise; good, favorable* advantageous, auspicious, beneficial, benign, brave, bright, dexter, encouraging, favoring, fortunate, happy, hopeful, lucky, opportune, pat*, promising, prosperous, rosy, seasonable, timely, toward, useful, well-timed; CONCEPTS 548,560,572 —Ant. inauspicious, unfavorable, unpromising

propitious [adj2] *friendly* benevolent, benign, favorably inclined, gracious, kind, nice, well-disposed; CONCEPT 401 —Ant. cold, cool, unfriendly

proponent [n] *person who advocates, supports cause* advocate, backer, champion, defender, enthusiast, exponent, expounder, friend, partisan, patron, protector, second, seconder, spokesperson, subscriber, supporter, upholder, vindicator; CONCEPTS 355,359,423 —Ant. enemy, foe, opponent

proportion [n1] *relative amount, size of part to whole* admeasurement, amplitude, apportionment, breadth, bulk, capacity, cut, degree, dimension, distribution, division, equation, expanse, extent, fraction, magnitude, measure, measurement, part, percentage, portion, quota, rate, ratio, relationship, scale, scope, segment, share, volume; CONCEPTS 730,783

proportion [n2] *balance between parts of whole* agreement, congruity, correspondence, harmony, symmetry; CONCEPTS 664,717 —Ant. disproportion, imbalance, unevenness

proportionate/proportional [adj] *balanced, corresponding* commensurable, commensurate, comparable, comparative, compatible, consistent, contingent, correlative, correspondent, corresponding, dependent, equal, equitable, equivalent, even, in proportion, just, reciprocal, relative, symmetrical, uniform; CONCEPTS 480, 563 —Ant. disproportionate, imbalanced, irrelevant

proportions [n] *measurements* amount, area, breadth, compass, depth, diameter, dimensions, expanse, extent, height, length, magnitude, range, scope, size, volume, width; CONCEPTS 730,792

proposal [n] *suggestion, presentation for action* angle, bid, big idea*, brain child*, design, feeler*, game plan*, idea, layout, motion, offer, outline, overture, pass, picture, pitch, plan, proffer, program, project, proposition, recommendation, scenario, scheme, setup, tender, terms; CONCEPTS 271,324,662

propose [v1] *suggest, present for action* adduce,

advance, advise, affirm, ask, assert, broach, come up with*, contend, counsel, hit on*, hold out, introduce, invite, kibitz*, lay before*, lay on the line*, make a motion, make a pitch*, move for, name, nominate, offer, pose, prefer, press, proffer, propone, proposition, propound, put forward, put to, put up, recommend, request, set forth, solicit, speak one's piece*, spitball*, state, submit, tender, urge, volunteer; CONCEPTS 66,75 —Ant. condemn, deny, oppose, refuse, reject

propose [v2] *intend; have in mind* aim, contemplate, design, have every intention, mean, mind, plan, purpose, scheme; CONCEPTS 26,36 —Ant. disbelieve, repulse

propose [v3] *ask for hand in marriage* ask in marriage, fire the question*, get down on one knee*, make a proposal, offer marriage, pop the question*, press one's suit*; CONCEPTS 48,297

proposition [n] *suggestion; scheme* hypothesis, invitation, motion, overture, plan, premise, presentation, proffer, program, project, proposal, recommendation; CONCEPTS 384,662 —Ant. condemnation, denial, opposition, refusal, rejection

proposition [v] *make suggestion, often improper* accost, approach, ask, pose, prefer, propose, propound, put, solicit, suggest; CONCEPTS 48,375

proprietor [n] *person who owns something* freeholder*, front office, holder, land owner, meal ticket*, owner, possessor, proprietary, titleholder; CONCEPTS 343,347 —Ant. customer

propriety [n1] *suitableness, appropriateness* accordance, advisability, agreeableness, appositeness, aptness, becomingness, compatibility, concord, congruity, consonance, convenience, correctness, correspondence, decorum, ethicality, expedience, fitness, harmony, justice, legitimacy, meetness, morality, order, pleasantness, properness, recommendability, rectitude, respectability, rightness, seemliness, suitability; CONCEPT 656 —Ant. immorality, impropriety, inappropriateness, unsuitableness, wrong

propriety [n2] *good manners* accepted conduct, amenities, breeding, civilities, correctness, courtesy, decency, decorum, delicacy, dignity, etiquette, good behavior, good form, modesty, mores*, niceties, politeness, politesse, protocol, punctilio, rectitude, refinement, respectability, rules of conduct, seemliness, social conventions, social grace, the done thing*; CONCEPTS 633,644 —Ant. bad manners, impropriety, misbehavior, misconduct

propulsion [n] *force* drive, effort, energy, full head of steam*, horsepower, impulse, momentum, muscle, power, pressure, punch, push, speed, steam, strength, stress, tension, thrust, velocity; CONCEPTS 641,724

pro rata [adv] *in proportion* correlatively, proportionally, respectively; CONCEPTS 480,563

prosaic [adj] *unimaginative* actual, banal, blah*, boring, clean, colorless, common, commonplace, dead*, diddly*, drab, dry, dull, everyday, factual, flat*, garden-variety*, hackneyed, ho-hum*, humdrum*, irksome, lackluster, lifeless, literal, lowly, lusterless, matter-of-fact, monotonous, mundane, nothing, nowhere, ordinary, pabulum*, pedestrian, platitudinous, plebeian, practicable, practical, prose, prosy, routine, square, stale, tame, tedious, trite, uneventful, unexceptional, uninspiring, vanilla*, vapid, workaday, yawn*, zero*; CONCEPTS 267,537, 547 —*Ant.* creative, imaginative, interesting, thinking

proscribe [v] *condemn, exclude* ban, banish, blackball*, boycott, censure, damn, denounce, deport, doom*, embargo, excommunicate, exile, expatriate, expel, forbid, interdict, ostracize, outlaw, prohibit, reject, sentence; CONCEPTS 25,121,317 —*Ant.* admit, allow, include, praise, welcome

prose [n] *written, nonrhythmic literature* book, composition, essay, exposition, fiction, nonfiction, speech, story, talk, text, tongue*, writing; CONCEPTS 268,271 —*Ant.* poem, poetry

prosecute [v1] *bring action against in court* arraign, bring suit, bring to trial, contest, do, haul into court*, indict, involve in litigation, law, litigate, prefer charges, pull up, put away*, put on docket, put on trial, see in court*, seek redress, sue, summon, take to court, try, turn on the heat*; CONCEPT 317 —*Ant.* exonerate, free, liberate, pardon

prosecute [v2] *follow through, persevere* carry on, carry through, conduct, continue, direct, discharge, engage in, execute, follow up, manage, perform, persist, practice, pursue, put through, see through, wage, work at; CONCEPT 91 —*Ant.* cease, halt, stop

proselytize [v] *convert, espouse* accept, adopt, advocate, alter conviction, approve, be born again*, cause to adopt, change belief, convince, defend, embrace, get into*, persuade, stand behind*, sway, uphold; CONCEPTS 10,12,14,35

prospect [n1] *outlook for future* anticipation, calculation, chance, contemplation, expectancy, expectation, forecast, future, hope, in the cards*, irons in the fire*, likelihood, odds, opening, plan, possibility, presumption, probability, promise, proposal, thought; CONCEPTS 689,693

prospect [n2] *landscape, vista* lookout, outlook, overlook, panorama, perspective, scape, scene, sight, spectacle, view, vision; CONCEPTS 509,628

prospect [v] *look for; seek* delve, dig, explore, go after, go into, inquire, investigate, look, look into, probe, search, sift, survey; CONCEPT 216 —*Ant.* miss, overlook

prospective [adj] *anticipated, potential* about to be, approaching, awaited, coming, considered, destined, eventual, expected, forthcoming, future, hoped-for, imminent, impending, intended, likely, looked-for, planned, possible, promised, proposed, soon-to-be, to be*, to come; CONCEPTS 548,552 —*Ant.* agreed, concurred

prospectus [n] *details, outline of event* announcement, catalogue, conspectus, design, list, plan, program, scheme, syllabus, synopsis; CONCEPT 283

prosper [v] *be fortunate; succeed* advance, arrive, augment, batten, bear, bear fruit, become rich, become wealthy, be enriched, benefit, bloom, blossom, catch on*, do well, do wonders*, fare well, fatten*, feather nest*, flourish, flower, gain, get on*, get there*, go places*, go to town*, grow rich, hit it big, hit the jackpot*,

increase, make a killing*, make good*, make it*, make mark*, make money, make out*, multiply, produce, progress, rise, score*, strike it rich*, thrive, turn out well, yield; CONCEPT 706 —*Ant.* fail, lose

prosperity [n] *affluence, good fortune* abundance, accomplishment, advantage, arrival, bed of roses*, benefit, boom, clover, do, ease*, easy street*, exorbitance, expansion, flying colors*, fortune, good, good times, gravy train*, growth, high on the hog*, increase, inflation, interest, life of luxury*, luxury, opulence, plenteousness, plenty, prosperousness, riches, success, successfulness, the good life*, thriving, velvet, victory, wealth, welfare, well-being; CONCEPTS 335,706 —*Ant.* failure, loss, poorness, poverty

prosperous [adj] *successful, thriving* affluent, blooming, booming, comfortable, doing well, easy, flourishing, fortunate, halcyon, in clover*, in the money*, lousy rich, lucky, main-line*, moneyed, money to burn*, on top of heap*, opulent, palmy, prospering, rich, roaring, robust, sitting pretty*, snug, substantial, upper-class*, uptown, wealthy, well, well-heeled*, well-off, well-to-do; CONCEPTS 334,528 —*Ant.* failing, losing, poor, unprosperous, unsuccessful

prosperous [adj2] *promising, advantageous* appropriate, auspicious, bright, convenient, desirable, favorable, felicitous, fortunate, good, happy, lucky, opportune, profitable, propitious, seasonable, timely, well-timed; CONCEPTS 548,572 —*Ant.* disadvantageous, hopeless, unpromising, unprosperous

prostitute [n] *person who sells own abilities, talent, or name for inferior purpose* betrayer, cheater, deceiver, gigolo, hustler, seducer; CONCEPT 412

prostitute [v] *to put one's talent to an unworthy use* abuse, cheapen, corrupt, debase, debauch, degrade, demean, deprave, devalue, misapply, misemploy, misuse, pervert, profane, vitiate; CONCEPTS 156,645

prostrate [adj1] *flat, horizontal* abject, bowed low, procumbent, prone, reclining, recumbent, supine; CONCEPT 583 —*Ant.* erect, straight, upright, vertical

prostrate [adj2] *helpless* beaten, defenseless, disarmed, impotent, open, overcome, overpowered, overwhelmed, paralyzed, powerless, reduced, weak; CONCEPT 542 —*Ant.* happy, self-sufficient, strong, successful

prostrate [adj3] *tired, worn* crippled, dejected, depressed, disarmed, drained, drowned, exhausted, fagged*, fallen, frazzled*, immobilized, incapacitated, inconsolable, knocked over*, obedient, overcome, paralyzed, pooped*, spent*, submissive, subservient, tuckered*, wearied, worn out; CONCEPTS 406,485 —*Ant.* hale, healthy, strong

prostrate [v1] *fall on knees; submit* abase, bow, bow down, cast before, cringe, fall at feet, give in, grovel, kneel, kowtow*, obey, surrender; CONCEPT 384 —*Ant.* erect, stand, straighten

prostrate [v2] *overwhelm; wear out* bring low, cripple, debilitate, defeat, destroy, disable, disarm, drain, drown, exhaust, fatigue, fell, floor, frazzle*, immobilize, impair,

pr
pr

incapacitate, knock over, level, mow*, over-come, overpower, overthrow, overtire, overturn, paralyze, reduce, ruin, sap, tire, tucker out*, weary, whelm, wreck; CONCEPTS 95,250,252 —*Ant.* aid, assist, assuage, help, please, soothe

protagonist [n] *person who takes the lead; central figure of narrative* advocate, central character, champion, combatant, exemplar, exponent, hero, idol, lead, lead character, leader, mainstay, prime mover, principal, standard-bearer, warrior; CONCEPTS 352,359,423 —*Ant.* antagonist

protect [v] *take care of; guard from harm* assure, bulwark, care for, champion, chaperon, conserve, cover, cover all bases*, cover up, cushion, defend, fend, foster, give refuge, give sanctuary*, go to bat for*, harbor, hedge, insulate, keep, keep safe, look after, preserve, ride shotgun for*, safeguard, save, screen, secure, sentinel, shade, shelter, shield, shotgun*, stand guard, stonewall*, support, take under wing*, watch, watch over; CONCEPTS 96,134 —*Ant.* attack, harm, hurt, injure

protection [n] *care, guardianship* aegis, armament, armor, assurance, barrier, buffer, bulwark, camouflage, certainty, charge, conservation, cover, custody, defense, fix, guard, guarding, insurance, invulnerability, preservation, protecting, reassurance, refuge, safeguard, safekeeping, safety, salvation, screen, security, self-defense, shelter, shield, stability, strength, surety, tutelage, umbrella*, ward, wardship; CONCEPTS 712,729 —*Ant.* attack, harm, hurt, injury, threat

protective [adj] *guarding, securing* careful, conservational, conservative, covering, custodial, defensive, emergency, guardian, insulating, jealous, possessive, preservative, protecting, safeguarding, sheltering, shielding, vigilant, warm, watchful; CONCEPTS 542,550 —*Ant.* attacking, harmful, hurtful, injurious, threatening

protégé [n] *dependent, pupil* apprentice, charge, discovery, star student, student, ward; CONCEPTS 348,423

protest [n] *complaint, disapproval* bellyache*, big stink*, blackball*, challenge, clamor, declaration, demonstration, demur, demurral, difficulty, dissent, flak*, formal complaint, grievance, gripe, grouse*, holler*, howl, kick*, knock*, march, moratorium, nix, objection, outcry, protestation, question, rally, remonstrance, remonstration, revolt, riot, stink*, tumult, turmoil; CONCEPTS 52,54,300 —*Ant.* acceptance, approval, praise

protest [v] *complain, disapprove; argue against* affirm, assert, asseverate, attest, avouch, avow, back-talk*, be against, be displeased by, blast*, buck, combat, constate, contend, cry out, declare, demonstrate, demur, disagree, except, expostulate, fight, holler, howl, insist, inveigh against, kick*, maintain, make a stink*, object, oppose, predicate, profess, put up a fight*, rebel, remonstrate, resist, revolt, say no*, sound off*, squawk*, take exception*, testify, thumbs down*; CONCEPTS 46,52,54,300 —*Ant.* accept, approve, praise

protocol [n] *rules of conduct, behavior in certain situation* agreement, code, compact, concordat, contract, conventions, courtesy, covenant, custom, decorum, etiquette,

formalities, good form, manners, obligation, order, pact, politesse, propriety, p's and q's*, treaty; CONCEPTS 684,688 —*Ant.* bad manners, crudeness, impropriety

prototype [n] *original, example* ancestor, antecedent, antecessor, archetype, criterion, first, forerunner, ideal, mock-up*, model, norm, paradigm, pattern, precedent, precursor, predecessor, standard, type; CONCEPT 686

protract [v] *extend, draw out* continue, cool*, defer, delay, drag on*, drag out*, draw, elongate, hold off, hold up, keep going, lengthen, pad*, postpone, procrastinate, prolong, prolongate, put off, put on hold, spin out*, stall, stretch, stretch out; CONCEPTS 237,239, 250 —*Ant.* abbreviate, curtail, shorten

protrude [v] *stick out* beetle, bulge, butt out, come through, distend, extend, extrude, jut, jut out, obtrude, overhang, point, poke, pop, pouch, pout, project, shoot out, stand out, start, stick up, swell; CONCEPTS 208,746 —*Ant.* depress, sink

protuberance [n] *lump, outgrowth* bulge, bump, excrescence, jut, jutting, knob, outthrust, process, projection, prominence, protrusion, swelling, tumor; CONCEPTS 471,824 —*Ant.* depression, ingrowth, sinkage

proud [adj1] *pleased, pleasing* appreciative, august, content, contented, dignified, eminent, fiery, fine, glad, glorious, gorgeous, grand, gratified, gratifying, great, great-hearted, honored, illustrious, imposing, impressive, magnificent, majestic, memorable, noble, red-letter*, rewarding, satisfied, satisfying, self-respecting, spirited, splendid, stately, sublime, superb, valiant, vigorous, well-pleased; CONCEPTS 403,572,574 —*Ant.* sad, sorry

proud [adj2] *arrogant, self-important* bloated, boastful, cavalier, cocky*, conceited, contemptuous, cool*, disdainful, dismissive, domineering, egotistic, egotistical, haughty, high-and-mighty*, high-handed*, huffy*, imperious, insolent, lofty, narcissistic, ostentatious, overbearing, pompous, presumptuous, pretentious, puffed up*, scornful, self-satisfied, sniffy*, snobbish, snooty*, stuck-up*, supercilious, superior, vain, vainglorious; CONCEPTS 401,542 —*Ant.* humble, meek, modest

prove [v] *establish facts; put to a test* add up, affirm, analyze, ascertain, assay, attest, authenticate, back, bear out, certify, check, confirm, convince, corroborate, declare, demonstrate, determine, document, end up, evidence, evince, examine, experiment, explain, find, fix, have a case*, justify, make evident, manifest, pan out*, result, settle, show, show clearly, show once and for all*, substantiate, sustain, test, testify, trial, try, turn out, uphold, validate, verify, warrant, witness; CONCEPTS 57,118, 138 —*Ant.* discredit, disprove, hypothesize, theorize

proverb [n] *saying referring to common fact, knowledge* adage, aphorism, apophthegm, axiom, byword, catch phrase, daffodil*, dictum, epigram, folk wisdom, gnome, maxim, moral, motto, platitude, precept, repartee, saw*, text, truism, witticism, word; CONCEPTS 275,278

proverbial [adj] *conventional, traditional* accepted, acknowledged, archetypal, axiomatic, current, customary, famed, familiar, famous, general, legendary, notorious, self-evident, time-honored, typical, unquestioned, well-known; CONCEPT 530 —*Ant.* abnormal, atypical, different, unconventional, unknown, untraditional

provide [*v1*] *supply, support* accommodate, add, administer, afford, arrange, bestow, bring, care, cater, contribute, dispense, equip, favor, feather*, feed, fit, fit out, fix up, fix up with, furnish, give, grant, hand over, heel*, impart, implement, indulge, keep, lend, line, look after, maintain, minister, outfit, prepare, present, procure, produce, proffer, provision, ration, ready, render, replenish, serve, stake, stock, stock up*, store, sustain, take care of, transfer, turn out, yield; CONCEPTS *108,110,136,140* —*Ant.* deprive, remove, take

provide [*v2*] *determine, specify* condition, lay down, postulate, require, state, stipulate; CONCEPTS *18,646*

provident [*adj*] *careful, frugal* canny, cautious, discreet, economical, expedient, far-sighted, foresighted, judicious, penny-pinching*, politic, prepared, prudent, sagacious, saving, shrewd, sparing, thrifty, tight, unwasteful, vigilant, well-prepared, wise; CONCEPTS *334,401* —*Ant.* careless, improvident, spendthrift, wasteful

providing/provided [*conj*] *as long as; with the understanding* contingent upon, given, if, if and only if, in case, in the case that, in the event, on condition, on the assumption, on these terms, subject to, supposing, with the proviso; CONCEPTS *544,546*

province [*n*] *area of rule, responsibility* arena, bailiwick, business, calling, canton, capacity, champaign, charge, colony, concern, county, demesne, department, dependency, district, division, domain, dominion, duty, employment, field, function, jurisdiction, line, office, orbit, part, post, pursuit, realm, region, role, section, shire, sphere, terrain, territory, tract, walk, work, zone; CONCEPTS *198,349,362, 508,532*

provincial [*adj*] *countrified; limited* bigoted, bucolic, country, hidebound, homegrown, homespun, insular, inward-looking, local, narrow, narrow-minded, parochial, pastoral, petty, rude, rural, rustic, sectarian, small-minded, small-town, uninformed, unpolished, unsophisticated; CONCEPTS *403,549,589* —*Ant.* citified, liberal, metropolitan, modern

provision [*n1*] *supplies, supplying* accouterment, arrangement, catering, emergency, equipping, fitting out, foundation, furnishing, groundwork, outline, plan, prearrangement, precaution, preparation, procurement, providing, stock, store, supplying; CONCEPTS *140,712* —*Ant.* removal, taking

provisional [*adj*] *contingent, tentative* conditional, dependent, ephemeral, experimental, interim, limited, makeshift, passing, pro tem, provisionary, provisory, qualified, rough-and-ready*, stopgap*, temporary, test, transient, transitional; CONCEPTS *546,554,711* —*Ant.* certain, definite, permanent

provision/proviso [*n2*] *stipulation, condition of agreement* agreement, catch*, Catch-22*, clause, demand, fine print*, joker*, kicker*, limitation, prerequisite, qualification,

requirement, reservation, restriction, rider, small print*, specification, stipulation, strings*, term, terms; CONCEPTS *270,684,711*

provocation [*n*] *incitement, stimulus* affront, annoyance, bothering, brickbat*, casus belli, cause, challenge, dare, defy, grabber*, grievance, grounds, harassment, incentive, indignity, inducement, injury, instigation, insult, irking, justification, motivation, offense, provoking, reason, taunt, vexation, vexing; CONCEPTS *14,240,532* —*Ant.* prevention, repression, suppression

provocative [*adj1*] *aggravating* annoying, challenging, disturbing, exciting, galling, goading, heady, incensing, inciting, influential, inspirational, insulting, intoxicating, offensive, outrageous, provoking, pushing, spurring, stimulant, stimulating; CONCEPT *529* —*Ant.* repressive, suppressive, unprovocative

provocative [*adj2*] *sexually stimulating* alluring, arousing, enchanting, erotic, exciting, heady, interesting, intoxicating, intriguing, inviting, seductive, sexy, stimulating, suggestive, tantalizing, tempting; CONCEPTS *372, 537* —*Ant.* unexciting, unprovocative, unstimulating

provoke [*v1*] *make angry* abet, abrade, affront, aggravate, anger, annoy, bother, bug*, chafe, enrage, exasperate, exercise, foment, fret, gall*, get*, get on one's nerves*, get under one's skin*, grate, hit where one lives*, incense, incite, inflame, infuriate, insult, irk, irritate, madden, make blood boil*, make waves*, nag, offend, perturb, pique, put out, raise, rile, roil, ruffle, set*, set on*, try one's patience*, upset, vex, whip up*, work into lather*, work up*; CONCEPTS *7,19* —*Ant.* delight, make happy, please

provoke [*v2*] *start, evoke; stimulate* animate, arouse, awaken, begin, bestir, bring about, bring down, bring on, bring to one's feet*, build up, call forth, cause, challenge, draw forth, electrify, elicit, enthuse, excite, fire, fire up*, galvanize, generate, give rise to, incite, induce, inflame, innervate, inperve, inspire, instigate, kindle, lead to, make, motivate, move, occasion, pique, precipitate, prime, produce, promote, prompt, quicken, rally, rouse, roust, stir, suscitate, thrill, titillate, titivate, waken, whet; CONCEPTS *7,19,22,221,242* —*Ant.* end, halt, prevent, stop

prowess [*n1*] *ability, skill* accomplishment, address, adeptness, adroitness, aptitude, attainment, command, deftness, dexterity, excellence, expertise, expertness, facility, genius, mastery, readiness, sleight, talent; CONCEPT *630* —*Ant.* inability, weakness

prowess [*n2*] *bravery* backbone*, boldness, courage, daring, dauntlessness, fearlessness, gallantry, grit*, guts*, heart*, heroism, intrepidity, mettle, moxie*, nerve, pluck, right stuff*, spunk, starch*, stomach*, stuff*, true grit*, valiance, valiancy, valor, valorousness, what it takes*; CONCEPTS *411,633* —*Ant.* cowardice, weakness

prowl [*v*] *move stealthily* cruise, hunt, lurk, nose around*, patrol, range, roam, rove, scavenge, skulk, slink, snake, sneak, stalk, steal, stroll, tramp; CONCEPT *151* —*Ant.* rush

pr
pr

prowler [n] *thief* burglar, crook, housebreaker, lurker, pilferer*, robber, sneakthief*; CONCEPT 412

proximity [n] *nearness to something* adjacency, appropinquity, closeness, concurrence, contiguity, contiguousness, immediacy, juxtaposition, propinquity, togetherness; CONCEPT 747 —*Ant.* distance, remoteness

proxy [n] *agent* alternate, ambassador, assignee, attorney, backup, broker, delegate, deputy, emissary, envoy, executor, intermediary, lawyer, mediary, negotiator, representative, stand-in, substitute, surrogate; CONCEPT 348

prude [n] *prig* goody-goody, goody two-shoes*, Mrs. Grundy, old maid, puritan, Victorian; CONCEPT 416

prudent [adj] *wise, sensible in action and thought* advisable, canny, careful, cautious, circumspect, discerning, discreet, economical, far-sighted, frugal, hedging one's bets*, judgmatic, judicious, leery, playing safe*, politic, provident, reasonable, sagacious, sage, sane, sapient, shrewd, sound, sparing, tactical, thinking twice*, thrifty, vigilant, wary; CONCEPTS 401,542 —*Ant.* careless, imprudent, incautious, unwise

prudish [adj] *shy and strict in behavior* affected, artificial, austere, bigoted, conventional, demure, fastidious, finicky*, genteel, illiberal, mincing, narrow, narrow-minded, offish, overexact, overmodest, overnice, precise, pretentious, priggish*, prim, prissy*, proper, puritanical, rigid, rigorous, scrupulous, severe, simpering, square, squeamish*, starchy*, stern, stiff*, stilted, straitlaced, stuffy, uptight*, Victorian*; CONCEPT 401 —*Ant.* bold, brave, extroverted, outgoing

prune [v] *trim; cut short* clip, cut back, dock, eliminate, exclude, gut, knock off, lop, pare down, reduce, shape, shave, shear, shorten, skive, snip, thin; CONCEPTS 137,176,236,247

prurient [adj] *lascivious* bawdy, carnal, crude, desirous, erotic, fleshly, horny, hot*, lecherous, lewd, libertine, libidinous, licentious, lustful, obscene, offensive, orgiastic, pornographic, raunchy*, salacious, sensual, sexual, smutty*, suggestive, unchaste, vulgar; CONCEPTS 372, 403

pry [v1] *interfere in someone else's business* be a busybody*, be all ears*, be curious, be inquisitive, be nosy, bug*, ferret out, gape, gaze, hunt, inquire, intrude, investigate, listen in, meddle, nose, peek, peep, peer, poke, poke nose into*, ransack, reconnoiter, rubberneck*, search, snoop, spy, stare, tap, tune in on*, wiretap; CONCEPTS 216,384,623 —*Ant.* leave alone

pry [v2] *force or break open* disengage, disjoin, divide, elevate, elicit, extort, extract, heave, hoist, jimmy, lever, lift, move, pick up, press, prize, pull, push, raise, rear, separate, take up, tear, tilt, turn, turn out, twist, uplift, upraise, uprear, wrest, wring; CONCEPTS 196,206,211 —*Ant.* close

psalm [n] *song of praise* canticle, celebration, chant, chorale, eulogy, hymn, paean, shout, verse; CONCEPT 595

pseudo [adj] *artificial, fake* bogus, counterfeit, ersatz, false, imitation, mock, not genuine, not kosher*, not legit*, not real, phony, pirate, pretend, pretended, quasi*, sham*, simulated, spurious, wrong; CONCEPT 582 —*Ant.* genuine, real, true

pseudonym [n] *false name* AKA*, alias, ananym, anonym, assumed name, handle*, incognito*, nickname, nom de guerre, nom de plume, pen name, professional name, stage name, summer name*; CONCEPTS 268,683 —*Ant.* name

psyche [n] *innermost self; personality* anima, animus, character, ego, élan vital, essential nature, individuality, inner child, inner self, mind, pneuma, self, soul, spirit, spirituality, subconscious, true being; CONCEPTS 410,411 —*Ant.* body, physicality

psyched [adj] *excited* animated, aroused, awakened, beside oneself*, charged, delighted, eager, enthusiastic, feverish, fired up*, high*, inspired, juiced up*, keyed up*, moved, on fire*, passionate, pumped, stimulated, stirred, thrilled, wild, worked up; CONCEPTS 401,403

psychedelic [adj] *affecting the mind so as to produce vivid visions* consciousness-expanding, crazy*, experimental, freaky*, hallucinatory, hallucinogenic, kaleidoscopic, mind-bending*, mind-blowing*, mind-changing, mind-expanding*, multicolored*, psychoactive, psychotomimetic, psychotropic, trip*; CONCEPTS 529,537 —*Ant.* normal

psychiatrist [n] *person who treats mental disorders* analyst, clinician, doctor, psychoanalyst, psychologist, psychotherapist, shrink*, therapist; CONCEPT 357

psychic [adj] *extrasensory in perception* analytic, cerebral, clairvoyant, immaterial, impressible, impressionable, intellective, intellectual, mental, metaphysical, mystic, occult, preternatural, psychal, psychical, psychogenic, psychological, responsive, sensible, sensile, sensitive, sentient, spiritual, supernatural, supersensible, supersensitive, supersensory, supersensual, susceptible, susceptive, telekinetic, telepathic, transmundane, unworldly; CONCEPTS 402,403

psychobabble [n] *rhetoric using psychological terms* argot, buzzword, jargon, patter, pop psych*, psychospeak, self-help; CONCEPT 275

psychological [adj] *concerning the mind* cerebral, cognitive, emotional, experimental, imaginary, intellective, intellectual, in the mind, mental, psychical, subconscious, subjective, unconscious; CONCEPTS 403,536 —*Ant.* body, physical

psychology [n] *study of the mind; emotional and mental constitution* attitude, behaviorism, medicine, mental make-up, mental processes, personality study, psych*, science of the mind, therapy, way of thinking*, where head is at*; CONCEPTS 349,360,410

psychopath [n] *person who is mentally deranged, often prone to hurt others* antisocial personality, insane person, lunatic, mad person, maniac, mental case*, nutcase*, psycho*, psychotic, schizoid*, sociopath, unstable personality; CONCEPT 412

psychotic [adj] *mentally deranged* certifiable*, crazy, demented, distracted, flipped-out*, insane, lunatic, mad, manic-depressive, mental, non compos mentis, nuts*, off one's rocker*, over the edge*, psycho*, psychopathic, schizophrenic, sick, unbalanced, unhinged*; CONCEPT 403

pub [*n*] *business where liquor and food are served* after-hours joint*, ale house*, bar, barroom, beer joint*, drinkery, drinking establishment, gin mill*, inn, joint*, lounge, public house, roadhouse, saloon, taproom, tavern; CONCEPTS 439,448,449

puberty [*n*] *young adulthood* adolescence, awkward stage*, boyhood, girlhood, greenness*, high-school years, juvenescence, juvenility, potency, preadolescence, pubescence, spring*, springtide*, springtime*, teenage years, teens, youth, youthfulness; CONCEPT 817 —*Ant.* adulthood

public [*adj1*] *community, general* accessible, city, civic, civil, common, communal, conjoint, conjunct, country, federal, free, free to all, government, governmental, intermutual, metropolitan, municipal, mutual, national, not private, open, open-door, popular, social, state, universal, unrestricted, urban, widespread, without charge; CONCEPTS 536,576 —*Ant.* particular, private, specific

public [*adj2*] *known, acknowledged* exposed, general, in circulation, notorious, obvious, open, overt, patent, plain, popular, prevalent, published, recognized, social, societal, usual, vulgar, widespread; CONCEPTS 267,530 —*Ant.* private, unknown

public [*n*] *people of community; people interested in something* audience, bodies*, buyers, citizens, clientele, commonalty, community, country, electorate, everyone, followers, following, heads, masses, men and women, mob, multitude, nation, patrons, people, populace, population, society, suite, supporters, voters; CONCEPTS 379,417

publication [*n1*] *printing of written or visual material* advertisement, airing, announcement, appearance, broadcast, broadcasting, communication, declaration, disclosure, discovery, dissemination, divulgation, issuance, issuing, notification, proclamation, promulgation, pronunciamento, publicity, public relations, publishing, reporting, revelation, statement, ventilation, writing; CONCEPTS 60,274,292

publication [*n2*] *something printed for reading* annual, book, booklet, brochure, handbill, information, issue, leaflet, magazine, news, newsletter, newspaper, pamphlet, periodical; CONCEPT 280

publicity [*n*] *promotion of something, someone* advertising, announcement, announcing, attention, ballyhoo*, big noise*, billing, blurb*, boost*, broadcasting, build-up*, clout*, commercial, currency, distribution, fame, handout, hoopla*, hype*, ink*, limelight*, noise*, notoriety, pitch, plug*, PR*, press, press-agentry, promo*, promulgation, propaganda, public notice, public relations, puff*, puffery*, pushing, réclame, release, report, scratch*, spotlight*, spread, write-up; CONCEPTS 274,280, 293 —*Ant.* secret

publicize [*v*] *make widely known; promote* advance, advertise, announce, bill, billboard, boost*, broadcast, build up*, cry, drum*, extol, hard sell*, headline, hype*, immortalize, make

a pitch for, pitch, play up*, plug*, press-agent, promulgate, propagandize, puff*, push, put on the map*, skywrite*, soft-sell*, splash, spot*, spotlight*, spread, tout, trumpet*, write up; CONCEPTS 60,292,324 —*Ant.* conceal, hide, secret

publish [*v*] *have printed, issue* announce, bring out, broadcast, circulate, communicate, declare, disclose, distribute, divulge, let it be known*, print, proclaim, produce, promulgate, publicize, put in print, put out, report, spotlight; CONCEPTS 60,140,292

pucker [*n*] *wrinkle* crease, crinkle, crumple, fold, furrow, plait, ruck, ruckle; CONCEPT 754 —*Ant.* smoothness

pucker [*v*] *draw together; wrinkle* cockle, compress, condense, contract, crease, crinkle, crumple, fold, furrow, gather, knit, purse, ruckle, ruck up, ruffle, screw up, squeeze, tighten; CONCEPTS 185,219 —*Ant.* open, smooth

pudgy [*adj*] *slightly fat* chubby*, hefty, plump, plumpish, rotund, round, stout, thick-bodied, tubby*; CONCEPTS 491,773 —*Ant.* skinny, slight, thin

puerile [*adj*] *childish* babyish, babylike, callow, foolish, green*, immature, inane, inexperienced, infantile, irresponsible, jejune, juvenile, naive, petty, ridiculous, silly, trivial, unfledged, ungrown, weak, young; CONCEPTS 401,578,797 —*Ant.* adult, mature

puff [*n1*] *blast of air* breath, draft, drag, draught, draw, emanation, flatus, flurry, gust, pull, smoke, waft, whiff, wind, wisp; CONCEPTS 437,524

puff [*n2*] *advertisement* advertising, blurb*, boost*, buildup*, commendation, favorable mention, good word, hype*, laudation, plug*, praise, press-agentry, promo*, promotion, publicity, puffery*, push*, sales talk, write-up; CONCEPTS 69,278,324

puff [*v1*] *inhale or exhale air* blow, breathe, distend, drag, draw, enlarge, fill, gasp, gulp, heave, huff, huff and puff*, inflate, pant, pull at, pull on, smoke, suck, swell, wheeze, whiff; CONCEPTS 163,185,526

puff [*v2*] *publicize* admire, advertise, ballyhoo*, blow up*, build, commend, congratulate, cry*, flatter, hype*, overpraise, plug*, praise, press-agent*, promote, push; CONCEPTS 49,69 —*Ant.* conceal, hide, secret

puffy [*adj*] *swollen* billowy, bloated, blown, bulgy, distended, distent, enlarged, expanded, full, increased, inflamed, inflated, puffed up; CONCEPT 485 —*Ant.* flat, tight, unswollen

pugnacious [*adj*] *belligerent* aggressive, antagonistic, argumentative, bellicose, brawling, cantankerous, chip on shoulder*, choleric, combative, contentious, defiant, disputatious, have a bone to pick*, hot-tempered, irascible, irritable, itching to fight*, militant, petulant, pushing, pushy*, quarrelsome, ready to fight, rebellious, salty*, scrappy*, self-assertive, truculent, warlike; CONCEPTS 401,542 —*Ant.* easy-going, kind, laid-back, nice

puke [*v*] *vomit* barf*, be sick, bring up, chunder, cough up, do the technicolor yawn*, gag, get sick, heave, hurl*, regurgitate, retch, spew, spit

up, throw up, toss one's cookies*, upchuck*;
CONCEPT 179

pulchritude [n] *beauty* adorableness, allure,
allurement, attraction, elegance, exquisiteness,
glamor, good looks, handsomeness, loveliness,
physical attractiveness, prettiness, shapeliness;
CONCEPT 718

pull [v1] *drawing something with force* cull,
dislocate, drag, evolve, extract, gather, haul,
heave, jerk, lug, paddle, pick, pluck, remove,
rend, rip, row, schlepp*, sprain, strain, stretch,
take out, tear, tow, trail, truck, tug, twitch,
uproot, weed*, wrench, yank; CONCEPT 206
—*Ant.* push

pull [v2] *attract* draw, entice, get, lure, magnetize, obtain, pick up, secure, win; CONCEPT 11
—*Ant.* deter, repel, repulse

pull down [v] *destroy; knock over* annihilate,
bulldoze, decimate, demolish, destruct, dismantle, let down, lower, raze, remove, ruin, take
down, tear down, wreck; CONCEPT 252 —*Ant.*
build, construct

pull in [v1] *arrest* apprehend, bust, collar, detain, nab, nail, pick up, pinch, run in, take into
custody; CONCEPTS 90,317 —*Ant.* exonerate,
free, let go

pull in [v2] *attract, obtain* absorb, bring in,
clear, draw, draw in, earn, gain, gross, make,
net, pocket, suck, take home*; CONCEPT 120
—*Ant.* repel, throw away

pull off [v] *accomplish* achieve, bring off, carry
out, manage, score, score a success, secure,
succeed, win; CONCEPTS 91,706 —*Ant.* fail

pull out [v] *quit* abandon, depart, evacuate,
exit, get off, go, leave, retire, retreat, shove
off, stop, stop participating, take off, withdraw;
CONCEPTS 119,121,195 —*Ant.* continue, persevere, start

pull through [v] *recover* come through, get
better, get over, improve, rally, ride out*,
survive, triumph, weather*; CONCEPTS 303,
700,706 —*Ant.* die, fail, lose

pull up [v] *stop, halt* arrive, brake, bring up,
come to a halt, come to a stop, draw up, fetch
up, get there, haul up, pause, reach a standstill;
CONCEPTS 119,121,159 —*Ant.* continue, go

pulp [adj] *cheap, vulgar, especially regarding
reading material* lurid, mushy, rubbish, sensational, trash, trashy; CONCEPT 267 —*Ant.* clean,
moral, nice

pulp [n] *flesh of plant, animal* batter, curd,
dough, grume, jam, marrow, mash, mush, pap,
paste, pomace, poultice, sarcocarp, semisolid,
soft part, sponge, triturate; CONCEPTS 399,428

pulp [v] *mash, pulverize* bruise, coagulate,
crush, gelatinate, macerate, squash, triturate;
CONCEPTS 208,219

pulpit [n] *structure from which sermon is given*
desk, lectern, platform, podium, rostrum,
soapbox*, stage, stump*; CONCEPTS 368,443

pulsate/pulse [v] *quiver, beat* drum, fluctuate,
hammer, oscillate, palpitate, pound, pump,
roar, throb, thrum, thud, thump, tick, vibrate;
CONCEPTS 147,185

pulse [n] *rhythm, beat* beating, oscillation,
pulsation, stroke, throb, throbbing, vibration;
CONCEPTS 147,185

pulverize [v1] *smash by beating, crushing*
abrade, atomize, beat, bray, break up, buck,

comminute, contriturate, crumble, crunch,
crush, flour, fragment, fragmentalize, fragmentize, granulate, grate, grind, levigate, micronize,
mill, mull, pestle, pound, powder, shatter,
splinter, triturate; CONCEPTS 186,219

pulverize [v2] *destroy* annihilate, crush,
decimate, defeat, demolish, destruct, dynamite,
flatten, rub out*, ruin, shatter, smash, tear
down*, vanquish, vaporize, wax, wreck;
CONCEPT 252 —*Ant.* build, construct, create

pummel [v] *beat, pommel* bash, batter, belt,
clout, club, crush, cudgel, flog, hammer, hit,
knock, lash, let one have it*, lick, mash, maul,
pelt, pound, punch, ram, slug, smack, strike,
swat, thrash, trounce, wallop, whale, wham,
whip; CONCEPTS 189,246

pump [v1] *draw or push out* bail out, blow
up, dilate, distend, draft, drain, draw, draw
off, drive, drive out, elevate, empty, force,
force out, inflate, inject, pour, push, send,
siphon, supply, swell, tap; CONCEPTS 142,
206,208

pump [v2] *question relentlessly* cross-examine,
draw out, give the third degree*, grill, interrogate, probe, query, question, quiz, worm out
of*; CONCEPTS 48,53 —*Ant.* answer, reply

pumped [adj] *excited* animated, aroused, awakened, beside oneself*, charged, cranked up,
delighted, eager, enthusiastic, feverish, fired
up*, geared up, high*, inspired, juiced up*,
keyed up*, moved, on fire*, passionate, psyched, rarin' to go*, stimulated, stirred, thrilled,
wild, worked up; CONCEPTS 401,403

pun [n] *play on words* ambiguity, calembour,
conceit, double entendre, double meaning,
equivoque, joke, paronomasia, quibble, quip,
witticism; CONCEPTS 273,278

punch [n1/v1] *hit* bash, belt, biff, blow, bop,
box, buffet, clip, clout, cuff, dig, jab, jog,
knock, lollop, nudge, one-two*, plug, plunk*,
poke, prod, pummel, rap, shot, slam, slap,
slug, smack, smash, sock, strike, stroke, thrust,
thump, wallop; CONCEPT 189

punch [n2] *energy, vigor* bite, cogency, drive,
effectiveness, force, forcefulness, impact, point,
validity, validness, verve; CONCEPTS 676,682
—*Ant.* idleness, lethargy, unenthusiasm

punch [v2] *perforate, prick* bore, cut, drill, jab,
pierce, poke, puncture, stab, stamp; CONCEPT
220 —*Ant.* close

punch-drunk [adj] *dazed* agog, baffled, befuddled, confused, dazzled, dizzy, dumbfounded,
dumbstruck, flustered, lost, muddled, perplexed,
punchy*, puzzled, rattled, slap-happy, staggered;
CONCEPTS 402,403

punctilio [n] *etiquette* ceremony, civility, code,
convention, courtesy, customs, decorum, dignity, form, formalities, formality, mores, nicety,
politesse, proper behavior, protocol, p's and
q's*, refinement, rules, social graces; CONCEPT
633

punctilious [adj] *careful, finicky* ceremonious,
conscientious, conscionable, conventional,
exact, formal, formalistic, fussy, good eye*,
heedful, meticulous, nice, observant, overcon-
scientious, overscrupulous, painstaking, particular, persnickety, precise, proper, punctual, right
on*, scrupulous, strict; CONCEPTS 401,542,557
—*Ant.* careless, easy-going, informal, uncaring

punctual [adj] *on time* accurate, careful, conscientious, conscionable, constant, cyclic, dependable, early, exact, expeditious, fussy, heedful, in good time*, meticulous, on schedule, on the button*, on the dot*, on the nose*, painstaking, particular, periodic, precise, prompt, punctilious, quick, ready, recurrent, regular, reliable, scrupulous, seasonable, steady, strict, timely, under the wire*; CONCEPTS 544,550,799 —*Ant.* late, tardy

punctuate [v] *lay stress on* accent, accentuate, break, divide, emphasize, interject, interrupt, intersect, intersperse, mark, pepper*, point, point up*, separate, sprinkle, stress, underline; CONCEPTS 49,79,98,266

puncture [n] *hole, rupture* break, cut, damage, flat, flat tire*, jab, leak, nick, opening, perforation, prick, slit, stab; CONCEPTS 309,513,674

puncture [v1] *poke hole in* bore, cut, cut through, deflate, drill, go down, go flat, knife, lacerate, lance, nick, open, penetrate, perforate, pierce, prick, punch, riddle, rupture; CONCEPTS 137,220 —*Ant.* close, sew

puncture [v2] *deflate someone's idea, feelings* blow sky high*, discourage, discredit, disillusion, disprove, explode, flatten*, humble, knock bottom out*, knock props from under*, poke full of holes*, shoot full of holes*, take down a peg*, take wind out of sails*; CONCEPTS 7,19, 54 —*Ant.* build up

pundit [n] *person who is authority* auger, bookworm, brain*, buff, cereb*, cognoscenti, egghead*, expert, intellectual, learned one, philosopher, professor, savant, scholar, solon, teacher, thinker; CONCEPT 423 —*Ant.* amateur

pungent [adj1] *highly flavored* acid, acrid, aromatic, bitter, effluvious, hot, nosey*, odoriferous, peppery, piquant, poignant, racy, rich, salty, seasoned, sharp, snappy, sour, spicy, stinging, stinking*, strong, tangy, tart, whiffy*, zesty; CONCEPT 613 —*Ant.* blah, bland, dull, flavorless, tasteless

pungent [adj2] *sharp, stinging in speech* acrimonious, acute, barbed, biting, bitter, caustic, cutting, exciting, hot, incisive, keen, mordant, penetrating, peppery, piercing, poignant, pointed, provocative, racy, salt, salty, sarcastic, scathing, snappy, spicy, stimulating, stringent, telling, trenchant, zesty; CONCEPT 267 —*Ant.* dull, mild

punish [v] *penalize for wrongdoing* abuse, attend to, batter, beat, beat up, blacklist, castigate, chasten, chastise, correct, crack down on*, cuff, debar, defrock, discipline, dismiss, do in, execute, exile, expel, fine, flog, give a going over*, give the works*, harm, hurt, immure, incarcerate, injure, knock about, lash, lecture, maltreat, misuse, oppress, paddle, rap knuckles*, reprove, rough up, scourge, sentence, slap wrist, spank, switch, teach a lesson, throw the book at*, train, whip; CONCEPT 122 —*Ant.* award, exonerate, let go, praise, protect, reward

punishment [n] *penalty* abuse, amercement, beating, castigation, chastening, chastisement, comeuppance, confiscation, correction, deprivation, disciplinary action, discipline, forfeit, forfeiture, gallows, hard work, infliction, just desserts*, lumps, maltreatment, mortification, mulct, ostracism, pain, penance, proof, punitive measures, purgatory, reparation, retribution, rod, rough treatment, sanction, sequestration, short shrift*, slave labor*, suffering, torture, trial, unhappiness, victimization, what for*; CONCEPT 123 —*Ant.* encouragement, exoneration, praise, protection, reward

punitive [adj] *concerning punishment* castigating, correctional, disciplinary, in reprisal, in retaliation, penal, punishing, punitory, retaliative, retaliatory, revengeful, vindictive; CONCEPT 319 —*Ant.* beneficial, rewarding

punk [n] *hoodlum* bully, criminal, delinquent, gangster, goon*, hood, hooligan, mobster, rioter, rowdy, ruffian, thug, troublemaker; CONCEPT 412

puny [adj] *small, insignificant* diminutive, feeble, fragile, frail, half-pint*, inconsequential, inferior, infirm, little, measly*, minor, niggling*, nothing, paltry, peanut*, peewee*, petty, picayune, piddling*, pint-sized*, runt, shrimp*, small-fry*, small time*, stunted, tiny, trifling, trivial, two-bit*, unconsequential, underfed, undersized, undeveloped, unsound, unsubstantial, weak, weakly, wee*, worthless, zero*, zilch*; CONCEPTS 489,575,773 —*Ant.* big, giant, huge, large

pupil [n] *person who is learning something* adherent, attendant, beginner, bookworm*, brain*, catechumen, disciple, first-year student, follower, graduate student, junior, learner, neophyte, novice, satellite, scholar, schoolboy/girl, senior, sophomore, student, tenderfoot*, undergraduate; CONCEPT 350 —*Ant.* professor, teacher

puppet [n] *person or toy manipulated by another* creature, doll, dupe*, figurehead, figurine, instrument, jerk*, manikin, marionette, moppet, mouthpiece*, patsy*, pawn, pushover, schlemiel*, servant, soft touch*, stooge*, tool*, victim; CONCEPTS 423,446

purchase [n] *possession obtained with money* acquirement, acquisition, asset, bargain, booty*, buy, gain, investment, property, steal; CONCEPTS 446,710 —*Ant.* sale, sell

purchase [v] *buy, obtain* achieve, acquire, attain, come by, cop*, deal in, earn, gain, get hold of, go shopping, invest, make a buy, make a purchase, market, patronize, pay for, pick up, procure, realize, redeem, secure, shop, shop for, take, take up, truck*, win; CONCEPT 327 —*Ant.* sell

pure [adj1] *unmixed, genuine* authentic, bright, classic, clear, complete, fair, flawless, kosher*, limpid, lucid, natural, neat, out-and-out*, pellucid, perfect, plain, plenary, pure and simple, real, simple, straight, total, transparent, true, twenty-four carat*, unadulterated, unalloyed, unclouded, undiluted, unmingled; CONCEPT 485 —*Ant.* impure, mixed, ungenuine

pure [adj2] *clean, uncontaminated* disinfected, germ-free, immaculate, intemerate, pasteurized, pristine, purified, refined, sanitary, snowy, spotless, stainless, sterile, sterilized, taintless, unadulterated, unblemished, undebased, unpolluted, unsoiled, unspotted, unstained, unsullied, untainted, untarnished, wholesome; CONCEPT 621 —*Ant.* contaminated, dirty, polluted, tainted

pure [adj3] *virginal, chaste* babe in woods*, blameless, celibate, clean, continent, decent, exemplary, fresh, good, guileless, honest, immaculate, inculpable, innocent, inviolate, irreproachable, kid, lily white*, maidenly, modest, pure as driven snow*, righteous, sinless, spotless, stainless, true, unblemished, unblighted, uncorrupted, undefiled, unprofaned, unspotted, unstained, upright, virgin, virtuous, wet behind ears*, wide-eyed; CONCEPT 372 —Ant. corrupt, dirty, immodest, indecent, obscene, unchaste, vulgar

pure [adj4] absolute, utter blasted*, blessed*, complete, confounded, infernal*, mere, out-and-out, sheer, thorough, unmitigated, unqualified; CONCEPTS 531,535 —Ant. indefinite, uncertain

pure [adj5] theoretical abstract, academic, philosophical, speculative, tentative, unproved; CONCEPT 529 —Ant. applied

purely [adv] simply, absolutely all, all in all, altogether, barely, completely, entirely, essentially, exactly, exclusively, in toto*, just, merely, only, plainly, quite, solely, totally, utterly, wholly; CONCEPTS 531,544 —Ant. indefinitely

purgatory [n] hell Abaddon*, abyss, bottomless pit*, everlasting fire*, fire and brimstone*, Gehenna, Hades, infernal regions, limbo, lower world, nether world, perdition, pit, place of torment, suffering, underworld; CONCEPTS 370,435,674

purge [n] elimination, removal abolition, abstersion, catharsis, clarification, cleaning, cleanup, coup, crushing, disposal, disposition, ejection, eradication, evacuation, excretion,expulsion, expurgation, extermination, extirpation, liquidation, murder, purification, reign of terror*, suppression, witch hunt; CONCEPTS 165,211,252 —Ant. holding, keeping, maintenance

purge [v] rid of; clean out abolish, absolve, clarify, cleanse, clear, depurate, disabuse, dismiss, dispose of, do away with*, eject, eradicate, erase, excrete, exonerate, expel, expiate, expunge, exterminate, forgive, kill, liquidate, oust, pardon, prevent, purify, remove, rout out, shake out*, sweep out, unload, wash, wipe off map*, wipe out; CONCEPTS 165,211, 252 —Ant. hold, keep, maintain

purification [n] freeing, cleansing ablution, absolution, atonement, baptism, bathing, catharsis, depuration, disinfection, distillation, expiation, expurgation, forgiveness, grace, lavation, laving, lustration, purgation, purge, purifying, rarefaction, rebirth, redemption, refinement, regeneration, salvation, sanctification, washing; CONCEPTS 165,367 —Ant. adulteration, corruption, dirtying, pollution

purify [v] free; make clean absolve, aerate, aerify, atone, chasten, clarify, clean, cleanse, clear, decontaminate, deodorize, depurate, deterge, disinfect, edulcorate, elutriate, exculpate, exonerate, expiate, filter, fumigate, lustrate, oxygenate, purge, rarify, redeem, refine, remit, sanctify, sanitize, shrive, sublimate, wash; CONCEPTS 165,367 —Ant. adulterate, corrupt, dirty, pollute

puritanical [adj] proper, straitlaced abstinent, austere, conforming, moral, priggish, prim, prissy, prudish, rigid, stern, strict, stuffy; CONCEPTS 401,404

purloin [v] steal appropriate, burglarize, cheat, defraud, embezzle, filch, heist, lift*, make off with*, misappropriate, pilfer, pillage, pinch*, plunder, poach, rip off*, shoplift, snitch, swindle, take, thieve; CONCEPT 139

purple [n/adj] blue and red colors mixed together amaranthine, amethyst, bluish red, color, heliotrope, lavender, lilac, magenta, mauve, mulberry, orchid, perse, plum, pomegranate, reddish blue, violaceous, violet, wine; CONCEPTS 618,622

purport [n] meaning, implication acceptation, aim, bearing, burden, connotation, core, design, drift, gist, heart, idea, import, intendment, intent, intention, matter, meat, message, nub, object, objective, pith, plan, point, purpose, score, sense, significance, significancy, signification, spirit, stuff, substance, tendency, tenor, thrust, understanding, upshot; CONCEPTS 20,659,660,689

purport [v] assert, mean allege, betoken, claim, convey, declare, denote, express, imply, import, indicate, intend, maintain, point to, pose as, pretend, proclaim, profess, signify, suggest; CONCEPTS 49,682

purpose [n] intention, meaning, aim ambition, animus, aspiration, big idea*, bourn, calculation, design, desire, destination, determination, direction, dream, drift, end, expectation, function, goal, hope, idea, intendment, intent, mecca, mission, object, objective, plan, point, premeditation, principle, project, proposal, proposition, prospect, reason, resolve, scheme, scope, target, ulterior motive, view, whatfor*, where one's headed*, whole idea*, why and wherefore*, whyfor*, will, wish; CONCEPTS 20,659,660,689

purpose [n2] persistence, resolve confidence, constancy, determination, faith, firmness, resolution, single-mindedness, steadfastness, tenacity, will; CONCEPTS 633,644

purpose [n3] use advantage, avail, benefit, duty, effect, function, gain, goal, good, mark, mission, object, objective, outcome, profit, result, return, target, utility; CONCEPTS 658,694

purpose [v] intend, set sights on aim, aspire, bid for, commit, conclude, consider, contemplate, decide, design, determine, have a mind to*, have in view, make up one's mind*, mean, meditate, mind, plan, ponder, propose, pursue, resolve, think to, work for, work toward; CONCEPTS 18,36,87

purposeful [adj] resolved to do something bent, be out for blood*, bound, calculated, dead set on*, decided, deliberate, determined, firm, fixed, intense, intent, mean business*, obstinate, persistent, playing hard ball*, positive, purposive, resolute, settled, single-minded, stalwart, staunch, steadfast, steady, strong-willed, stubborn, teleological, tenacious, undeviating, unfaltering, unwavering; CONCEPTS 326,403, 542 —Ant. aimless, thoughtless, undetermined, unplanned, wanton

purposeless [adj] useless, insignificant aimless, designless, desultory, drifting, empty, feckless, floundering, fustian, goalless, good-for-nothing*, haphazard, hit-or-miss*, indiscriminate, irregular, meaningless, motiveless, needless, nonsensical, pointless, purportless, random, senseless, uncalled for, undirected, unhelpful, unnecessary, unplanned, unprofitable, unpurposed, vacuous, wanton, worthless; CONCEPTS 544,560 —*Ant.* decided, deliberate, determined, planned, purposeful, significant, useful

purposely [*adv*] *intentionally* advisedly, by design, calculatedly, consciously, deliberately, designedly, explicitly, expressly, knowingly, on purpose, prepensely, purposedly, willfully, with intent; CONCEPTS 529,544 —*Ant.* impulsively, spontaneously, unintentionally

purse [*n1*] *tote for carrying personal items* bag, billfold, bursa, carryall, clutch, frame, handbag, hide, leather, lizard, moneybag, pocket, pocketbook, poke, pouch, receptacle, reticule, sack, wallet; CONCEPTS 339,446,450,494

purse [*n2*] *award; winnings* coffers, exchequer, funds, gift, means, money, present, prize, resources, reward, stake, treasury, wealth, wherewithal; CONCEPTS 337,344 —*Ant.* loss

purse [*v*] *press together* close, cockle, contract, crease, knit, pucker, ruffle, tighten, wrinkle; CONCEPTS 185,208 —*Ant.* open

pursue [*v1*] *chase, follow* accompany, attend, badger, bait, bird-dog*, bug, camp on the doorstep of*, chivy, dog*, fish*, give chase, go after, harass, harry, haunt, hound, hunt, hunt down, move behind, nose around*, persevere, persist, plague, play catch up*, poke around, prowl after, ride, run after, run down, scout out, search for, search high heaven*, search out, seek, shadow, stalk, tag, tail*, take out after*, trace, track, track down, trail; CONCEPT 207 —*Ant.* retreat, run away

pursue [*v2*] *have as one's goal* aim for, aspire to, attempt, desire, go in for, go out for, have a go at, purpose, seek, strive for, try for, work for, work toward; CONCEPTS 20,36 —*Ant.* eschew, ignore, shun

pursue [*v3*] *persist, persevere* adhere, apply oneself, carry on, conduct, continue, cultivate, engage in, hold to, keep on, maintain, perform, ply, practice, proceed, prosecute, see through, tackle, wage, work at; CONCEPTS 87,100,239 —*Ant.* discontinue, give up, stop

pursue [*v4*] *seek social alliance with* address, call, chase, chase after, court, date, go after, go for, pay attention, pay court*, play up to, rush*, spark, sue, sweetheart*, woo; CONCEPT 384 —*Ant.* ignore

pursuit [*n1*] *chase, search* following, going all out, hunt, hunting, inquiry, pursual, pursuance, pursuing, quest, reaching, seeking, stalk, tracking, trail, trailing; CONCEPT 207 —*Ant.* retreat, surrender

pursuit [*n2*] *occupation, interest of person* accomplishing, accomplishment, activity, biz*, business, calling, career, do*, employment, game*, go*, hang*, hobby, job, line*, occupation, pastime, pleasure, racket, thing*, undertaking, venture, vocation, work; CONCEPT 349

push [*n1*] *physical force* advance, assault, attack, bearing, blow, butt, charge, drive, driving, effort, energy, exerting, exertion, forcing, impact, jolt, lean, mass, nudge, offensive, onset, poke, prod, propulsion, shove, shoving, straining, thrust, thrusting, weight; CONCEPTS 200,208,641,724 —*Ant.* pull

push [*n2*] *mental determination* ambition, drive, dynamism, energy, enterprise, get-up-and-go*, go*, gumption*, guts*, initiative, pep, punch,

snap, spunk, starch, vigor, vitality; CONCEPTS 410,411 —*Ant.* discouragement, disinterest

push [*v1*] *thrust, press with force* accelerate, bear down, budge, bulldoze*, bump, butt, crowd, crush against, depress, dig, drive, elbow, exert, force, gore, high pressure*, hustle, impel, jam, jostle, launch, lie on, make one's way*, move, muscle, nudge, poke, pour it on*, pressure, propel, put the arm on*, railroad*, ram*, rest on, shift, shoulder, shove, squash, squeeze, squish, steamroll*, stir, strain, strongarm*; CONCEPTS 200,208,243 —*Ant.* pull

push [*v2*] *incite, urge* bear down, browbeat, bulldoze*, coerce, constrain, dragoon, egg on*, encourage, exert influence, expedite, fire up*, goad, goose*, go to town on*, hurry, impel, influence, inspire, jolly, key up*, kid, lean on*, motivate, oblige, overpress, persuade, pour it on*, press, pressure, prod, push around, put the screws to*, put up to*, railroad*, sell on*, speed, speed up, spur, squeeze, steamroll*, strong-arm*, turn on*; CONCEPTS 14,68,243 —*Ant.* discourage, dissuade, repress, suppress

push [*v3*] *advertise, promote* advance, boost, cry up*, hype*, make known, plug*, propagandize, publicize, puff*; CONCEPTS 49,324 —*Ant.* conceal, hide

push off/push on [*v*] *leave; go to another place* beat it*, continue, depart, exit, fare, get away, get lost*, go, go away, hie, hit the road*, journey, keep going, launch, light out, make oneself scarce*, make progress, pass, proceed, process, pull out, quit, repair, shove off, start, take off, travel, wend, withdraw; CONCEPTS 195,704 —*Ant.* arrive, come

pushover [*n*] *something or someone easily influenced* breeze, child's play*, chump*, cinch, duck soup*, easy game*, easy mark*, easy pickings*, fool, kid stuff*, picnic*, piece of cake*, setup, snap, soft touch*, stooge*, sucker, victim, walkover; CONCEPTS 423,693

pushy [*adj*] *aggressive, offensive* ambitious, assertive, bold, brash, bumptious, forceful, loud, militant, obnoxious, obtrusive, officious, presumptuous, pushful, pushing, self-assertive; CONCEPTS 401,404 —*Ant.* modest, quiet, shy, unassuming

pussyfoot [*v*] *be cautious* avoid, beat around the bush*, be noncommittal, creep, dodge, duck the issues, equivocate, evade, glide, hedge, hem and haw*, lurk, play it close to the vest*, prevaricate, prowl, shuffle, sidestep, sit on the fence*, skirt*, skulk, slide, slink, slip, sneak, steal, tergiversate, tergiverse, tiptoe, tread warily, watch one's step*, weasel*; CONCEPTS 151,410 —*Ant.* plod

put [*v1*] *position* bring, concenter, concentrate, deposit, embed, establish, fasten, fix, fixate, focus, insert, install, invest, lay, nail, park, peg, place, plank, plank down, plant, plop, plunk, plunk down, quarter, repose, rest, rivet, seat, set, settle, situate, stick; CONCEPT 201 —*Ant.* remove, take

put [*v2*] *propose; express in words* advance, air, bring forward, couch, express, formulate, forward, give, offer, phrase, pose, posit, prefer, present, propone, proposition, propound, render, set, set before, state, submit, suggest, tender, translate, transpose, turn, utter, vent, ventilate, word; CONCEPTS 47,66,67

put [v3] *commit, assign* condemn, consign, constrain, doom, employ, enjoin, force, impose, induce, inflict, levy, make, oblige, require, set, subject, subject to; CONCEPTS 14,242 —*Ant.* change, displace, transfer

putative [adj] *commonly believed* accepted, alleged, assumed, conjectural, hypothetical, imputed, presumed, presumptive, reported, reputed, supposed, suppositional, suppositious; CONCEPT 529 —*Ant.* proven, real, true

put away [v2] *incarcerate* certify, commit, confine, institutionalize, jail, lock up; CONCEPT 317 —*Ant.* free, liberate

put away [v3] *consume* devour, eat up, gobble*, gulp down, polish off*, punish, put down, shift, swill, wolf down*; CONCEPT 169 —*Ant.* abstain, refrain

put away [v4] *kill* assassinate, bury, cool*, cut off, destroy, dispatch, do away with, do in*, dust off*, execute, finish, inter, knock off*, liquidate, murder, plant, put down*, put out of its misery*, put to sleep*, slay, tomb; CONCEPT 252 —*Ant.* give birth

put away/put aside/put by [v1/v] *keep in reserve* cache, deposit, keep, lay aside, lay away, lay by, lay in, put by, put out of the way, salt away*, save, set aside, squirrel away*, stockpile, store, store away*, stow away; CONCEPTS 129,134 —*Ant.* spend, use up, waste

put-down [n] *nasty commentary* cut*, dig*, disparagement, gibe*, humiliation, indignity, insult, jibe*, knock*, pan*, rebuff, sarcasm, slight, sneer*, snub, suppression; CONCEPTS 54,278 —*Ant.* flattery, praise

put down [v1] *write into record* enter, inscribe, jot down, log, record, set down, take down, transcribe, write down; CONCEPT 79 —*Ant.* erase, extract

put down [v2] *subdue* annihilate, crush, defeat, dismiss, extinguish, quash*, quell, reject, repress, silence, squash*, stamp out*, suppress; CONCEPTS 95,252 —*Ant.* boost, build up

put down [v3] *comment negatively* belittle, condemn, crush, decry, deflate, derogate, discount, dismiss, disparage, downcry, humiliate, minimize, mortify, opprobriate, reject, run down, shame, slight, snub, write off; CONCEPT 54 —*Ant.* build up, compliment, flatter, praise

put off [v] *defer, delay* adjourn, dally, dawdle, dillydally*, drag one's feet*, hold off, hold over, lag*, lay over, linger, loiter, poke*, postpone, prorogue, put back, reschedule, retard, shelve, stay, suspend, tarry, trail; CONCEPTS 121,234 —*Ant.* accomplish, achieve, carry out, do, succeed

put on [v1] *pretend* act, affect, assume, bluff, confound, confuse, counterfeit, deceive, don, fake, feign, make believe, masquerade, playact, pose, pull, put on a front, put on an act, sham, simulate, strike, take on, trick; CONCEPT 59 —*Ant.* be truthful

put on [v2] *stage a performance* do, mount, present, produce, show; CONCEPT 292

put out [v1] *upset, irritate; inconvenience* aggravate, anger, annoy, bother, burn, confound,

discomfit, discommode, discompose, disconcert, discountenance, disoblige, displease, dissatisfy, disturb, embarrass, exasperate, gall, get*, grate, harass, impose upon, incommode, inflame, irk, nettle, perturb, provoke, put on the spot*, rile, roil, trouble, vex; CONCEPTS 7,14,19 —*Ant.* assuage, help, please

put out [v2] *extinguish fire* blow out, douse, out, quench, smother, snuff out, stamp out; CONCEPT 252 —*Ant.* start

putrefy [v] *rot* break down, corrupt, crumble, decay, decompose, deteriorate, disintegrate, go bad*, molder, putresce, spoil, stink, taint, turn; CONCEPT 469

putrid [adj] *rotten, stinking* bad, contaminated, corrupt, decayed, decomposed, fetid, foul, high, malodorous, moldered, nidorous, noisome, off, putrefied, rancid, rank, reeking, rotting, smelly, spoiled, strong, tainted, whiffy*; CONCEPTS 485,598 —*Ant.* fresh, perfumed, sweet

putter [v] *dawdle* doodle, fiddle, fritter, goof around*, loiter, mess, mess around*, niggle, poke*, potter*, puddle*, shuffle around, tinker*; CONCEPTS 87,210 —*Ant.* execute

put up [v1] *accommodate guest* bestow, billet, board, bunk, domicile, entertain, give lodging, harbor, house, lodge, make welcome, provide, quarter, take in; CONCEPTS 324,384 —*Ant.* turn away

put up [v2] *build, erect* construct, fabricate, forge, make, put together, raise, rear, shape, uprear; CONCEPT 168 —*Ant.* destroy, ruin

puzzle [v1] *baffle, confuse* addle, amaze, bamboozle*, beat, befog, befuddle, bemuse, bewilder, buffalo*, complicate, confound, discombobulate*, disconcert, distract, disturb, dumbfound, flabbergast, floor*, flummox, foil, frustrate, get to*, mystify, nonplus, obscure, perplex, pose, profundicate, psych out*, put off, rattle, snow*, stir, stumble, stump, throw; CONCEPT 16 —*Ant.* clarify, elucidate, explain, illustrate, unravel

puzzle [v2] *wonder about* ask oneself, brood, cudgel, marvel, mull over, muse, ponder, rack one's brains*, study, think about, think hard; CONCEPT 17 —*Ant.* not care

puzzled [adj] *confused* at a loss*, at sea*, baffled, bewildered, bollixed, clueless, come apart, come unzipped*, discombobulated*, dopey*, doubtful, floored*, foggy, fouled up*, hung up*, in a fog*, lost, loused up*, messed up*, mind-blown*, mixed up*, mucked up*, mystified, nonplussed, perplexed, rattled, screwed up*, shook, shook up, spaced out*, stuck, stumped, thrown, unglued*, without a clue; CONCEPTS 403,690 —*Ant.* aware, certain, cognizant, sure

puzzling [adj] *confusing* abstruse, ambiguous, baffling, bewildering, beyond one, difficult, enigmatic, hard, incomprehensible, inexplicable, involved, knotty, labyrinthine, misleading, mystifying, obscure, perplexing, surprising, unaccountable, unclear, unfathomable; CONCEPT 529 —*Ant.* comprehendible, intelligible, understandable

pyramid [n] *monument* cairn, cenotaph, edifice, mastaba, memorial, monolith, obelisk, shrine, tomb, tribute; CONCEPTS 259,271,305,470

Q

quack [adj] counterfeit bum*, dishonest, dissembling, fake, false, fraudulent, phony, pretended, pretentious, pseudo*, sham*, simulated, unprincipled; CONCEPT 582 —Ant. genuine, original, real

quack [n] person who pretends to be an expert actor, bum*, bunco artist, charlatan, cheat, con artist, counterfeit, counterfeiter, fake, faker, flimflammer*, four-flusher*, fraud, hoser*, humbug, impostor, mountebank, phony, playactor, pretender, pseudo*, put-on*, quacksalver*, sham, shammer*, shark*, sharp*, simulator, slicker*, whip*; CONCEPT 412

quaff [v] drink down down, gulp, guzzle, imbibe, ingurgitate, partake, sip, sup, swallow, swig, swill, toss; CONCEPT 169 —Ant. eject

quagmire [n1] bad situation box*, corner*, difficulty, dilemma, entanglement, fix, hole*, imbroglio, impasse, involvement, jam, mire, morass, muddle, pass, perplexity, pickle*, pinch*, plight, predicament, quandary, scrape, trouble; CONCEPTS 666,674 —Ant. blessing, solution, success

quagmire [n2] bog fen, marsh, marshland, mire, morass, moss, quag, quicksand, slough, swamp; CONCEPT 509

quail [v] cower, shrink blanch, blench, cringe, droop, faint, falter, flinch, have cold feet*, quake, recoil, shake, shudder, start, tremble, wince; CONCEPTS 35,149,195 —Ant. face, meet

quaint [adj1] strange, odd bizarre, curious, droll, eccentric, erratic, fanciful, fantastic, freakish, freaky*, funny, idiosyncratic, laughable, oddball, offbeat, off the beaten track*, original, outlandish, peculiar, queer, singular, special, unusual, weird*, whimsical; CONCEPTS 564,589 —Ant. common, conventional, regular, usual

quaint [adj2] old-fashioned; nostalgically attractive affected, ancient, antiquated, antique, archaic, artful, baroque, captivating, charming, colonial, curious, cute, enchanting, fanciful, Gothic*, ingenious, old-world, picturesque, pleasing, Victorian*, whimsical; CONCEPT 578 —Ant. current, new, new-fangled, up-to-date

quake [n] earthquake aftershock, convulsion, quaker, seism, shake, shock, temblor, tremblor, tremor; CONCEPT 526

quake [v] shake, vibrate convulse, cower, fluctuate, jar, jitter, move, pulsate, quail, quiver, rock, shiver, shrink, shudder, throb, totter, tremble, tremor, twitter, waver, wobble; CONCEPT 152 —Ant. be still

qualification [n1] ability, aptitude accomplishment, adequacy, attainment, attribute, capability, capacity, competence, eligibility, endowment, experience, fitness, goods, makings, might, qualifiedness, quality, skill, stuff, suitability, suitableness, what it takes*; CONCEPT 630 —Ant. disqualification, inability, inaptitude, lack

qualification [n2] requirement, restriction allowance, caveat, condition, contingency, criterion, essential, exception, exemption, limitation, modification, need, objection, postulate, prerequisite, provision, proviso, requisite, reservation, stipulation; CONCEPTS 646,652

qualified [adj1] able, skillful accomplished, adept, adequate, all around, au fait, capable, catechized, certified, competent, disciplined, efficient, equipped, examined, experienced, expert, fit, fitted, good, instructed, knowledgeable, licensed, practiced, pro*, proficient, proper, proved, quizzed, talented, tested, trained, tried, up to snuff*, up to speed*, vet*, veteran, war-horse*, wicked*; CONCEPT 527 —Ant. incapable, unable, unproficient, unqualified, unskilled, untalented

qualified [adj2] limited, restricted bounded, circumscribed, conditional, confined, contingent, definite, determined, equivocal, fixed, guarded, modified, partial, provisional, reserved; CONCEPT 554 —Ant. open, unlimited, unrestricted

qualify [v1] make or become ready, prepared authorize, capacitate, certify, check out, come up to snuff*, commission, condition, cut it*, earn one's wings*, empower, enable, endow, entitle, equip, fill the bill*, fit, get by*, ground, hack it*, make it*, make the cut*, make the grade*, measure up, meet, pass, pass muster*, permit, ready, sanction, score, suffice, suit, train; CONCEPTS 99,630 —Ant. be unprepared, disqualify

qualify [v2] lessen, restrict abate, adapt, alter, assuage, change, circumscribe, diminish, ease, limit, mitigate, moderate, modify, modulate, reduce, regulate, restrain, soften, temper, vary, weaken; CONCEPTS 240,698 —Ant. allow, be lenient

qualify [v3] characterize, distinguish ascribe, assign, attribute, describe, designate, impute, individualize, individuate, mark, name, predicate, signalize, singularize; CONCEPT 411

quality [n1] characteristic, feature affection, affirmation, aspect, attribute, character, condition, constitution, description, element, endowment, essence, factor, genius, individuality, kind, make, mark, name of tune*, nature, nature of beast*, parameter, peculiarity, predication, property, savor, sort, trait, virtue, way of it*; CONCEPT 543

quality [n2] value, status arete, caliber, capacity, character, class, condition, distinction, excellence, excellency, footing, grade, group, kind, merit, perfection, place, position, preeminence, rank, repute, standing, state, station, stature, step, superbness, superiority, variety, virtue, worth; CONCEPTS 346,378,668

qualm [n] nagging doubt agitation, anxiety, apprehension, compunction, conscience, demur, disquiet, foreboding, hesitation, indecision, insecurity, misdoubt, misgiving, mistrust, nervousness, objection, pang, perturbation, presentiment, regret, reluctance, remonstrance, remorse, scruple, suspicion, twinge, uncertainty, unease, uneasiness; CONCEPTS 410,532 —Ant. approval, comfort, contentedness

quandary [n] delicate situation bewilderment, bind, Catch-22*, clutch, corner*, difficulty, dilemma, double trouble*, doubt, embarrassment, hang-up*, impasse, mire, perplexity, pickle*, plight, predicament, puzzle, spot*, strait, uncertainty, up a tree*; CONCEPTS 532, 674,690 —Ant. advantage, certainty, solution

quantify [v] *measure* appraise, assess, calibrate, check, compute, count, determine, estimate, evaluate, figure, gauge, look over, rank, rate, size, specify, value, weigh; CONCEPTS 103,197,764

quantity [n] *number or amount* abundance, aggregate, allotment, amplitude, batch, body, budget, bulk, capacity, deal, expanse, extent, figure, greatness, length, load, lot, magnitude, mass, measure, multitude, part, pile, portion, profusion, quota, size, sum, total, variety, volume; CONCEPT 787

quantum leap [n] *abrupt change* advance, breakthrough, giant strides, jump, leaps and bounds, radical change; CONCEPTS 230,260,701

quarantine [n] *isolation* detention, lazaretto, seclusion, segregation, separation, sequestration; CONCEPTS 135,188,388,631

quarantine [v] *isolate* block off, close off, confine, cordon, detach, insulate, keep apart, remove, restrict, seal off, seclude, segregate, separate, sequester; CONCEPTS 188,201

quarrel [n] *disagreement* affray, altercation, argument, battle royal*, beef*, bickering*, brannigan*, brawl, breach, broil*, catfight*, combat, commotion, complaint, contention, controversy, difference, difference of opinion, difficulty, disapproval, discord, disputation, dispute, dissension, dissidence, disturbance, dust*, falling-out*, feud, fight, fisticuffs*, fracas, fray, fuss, hassle, misunderstanding, objection, rhubarb*, row, ruckus*, run-in, scrap, set-to*, spat, squabble, strife, struggle, tiff, tumult, vendetta, wrangle; CONCEPTS 46,106 —Ant. agreement, peace

quarrel [v] *disagree* altercate, argue, battle, be at loggerheads*, bicker, brawl, break with, bump, carp, caterwaul, cavil, charge, clash, collide, complain, contend, contest, cross swords*, differ, disapprove, dispute, dissent, divide, embroil, fall out*, feud, fight, find fault, get tough with*, hassle, have it out*, have words*, lock horns*, mix it up*, object to, row, scrap, set to, spar, spat, squabble, strive, take exception, take on, tangle, vary, war, wrangle; CONCEPTS 46,106 —Ant. agree, make peace

quarrelsome [adj] *being disagreeable* argumentative, bad-tempered, bellicose, belligerent, brawling, cantankerous, cat-and-dog*, choleric, churlish, combative, contentious, crabby*, cross, disputatious, dissentious, excitable, fiery, fractious, gladiatorial, hasty, have chip on shoulder*, hotheaded*, huffy, impassioned, irascible, irritable, litigious, ornery, passionate, peevish, pettish, petulant, pugnacious, querulous, ructious, snappy, tempestuous, thin-skinned*, touchy, truculent, turbulent, unruly, violent, war; CONCEPTS 401,542 —Ant. agreeable, forgiving, friendly, good-natured, happy, patient

quarry [n] *goal* aim, chase, game, objective, prey, prize, quest, ravin, victim; CONCEPT 659

quarter [n1] *one of four equal parts* division, farthing, fourth, one-fourth, part, portion, quad, quadrant, quartern, section, semester, span, term, two bits*; CONCEPT 835

quarter [n2] *area, neighborhood* barrio, bearing, direction, district, division, domain, ghetto, inner city, locality, location, neck of the woods*, old town, part, place, point, position, precinct, province, region, section, sector, side, skid row, slum, spot, station, stomping ground*, territory, turf, zone, zoo*; CONCEPTS 508,512

quarter [n3] *forgiveness* clemency, compassion, favor, grace, leniency, lenity, mercy, pity; CONCEPTS 410,633 —Ant. disfavor, mercilessness

quarter [v1] *divide into four equal parts* cleave, cut, cut up, dismember, fourth; CONCEPT 98

quarter [v2] *provide lodging* accommodate, billet, board, bunk, canton, domicile, domiciliate, entertain, establish, harbor, house, install, lodge, place, post, put up, settle, shelter, station; CONCEPT 140 —Ant. turn away

quarters [n] *place to live or sleep* abode, accommodation, apartment, barracks, billet, cabin, cantonment, chambers, condo, cottage, digs*, domicile, dorm, dwelling, flat, fraternity, habitat, habitation, home, house, lodge, lodging, place, post, ranch, residence, room, roost*, shelter, sorority, station, tent; CONCEPT 516

quash [v1] *destroy, defeat* annihilate, beat, crush, extinguish, extirpate, overcome, overthrow, put down, quell, quench, repress, scrunch*, snow under*, squash*, squish*, subdue, suppress, trash; CONCEPTS 95,252 —Ant. aid, assist, help, rebuild

quash [v2] *nullify, cancel* abrogate, annul, black out*, bottle up*, clamp down on, cork up*, crack down on*, declare null and void*, discharge, dissolve, hush up*, invalidate, kill, negate, overrule, overthrow, put damper on*, put the lid on*, repeal, rescind, reverse, revoke, set aside, shut down, squelch, undo, vacate, veto, vitiate, void, watergate*; CONCEPTS 121,234,266 —Ant. allow, permit, sanction, start, support

quasi [adj] *almost; to a certain extent* apparent, apparently, fake, mock, near, nominal, partly, pretended, pseudo-*, seeming, seemingly, semi-, sham*, so-called, supposedly, synthetic, virtual, would-be*; CONCEPT 582 —Ant. entire, total, whole

queasy [adj] *not feeling well; not comfortable* anxious, bilious, concerned, fidgety, green around gills*, groggy, ill, ill at ease, indisposed, nauseated, pukish, qualmish, queer, restless, rocky*, sick, sick as a dog*, sickly, squeamish, troubled, uncertain, uncomfortable, under the weather*, uneasy, unwell, upset, worried; CONCEPTS 314,403 —Ant. comfortable, healthy, satisfied

queer [adj1] *odd; abnormal* anomalous, atypical, bizarre, crazy, curious, demented, disquieting, doubtful, droll, dubious, eccentric, eerie, erratic, extraordinary, fishy*, flaky*, fly ball*, freaky*, funny, idiosyncratic, irrational, irregular, kinky*, kooky*, mad, mysterious, oddball, off the wall*, outlandish, outré, peculiar, puzzling, quaint, questionable, remarkable, shady, singular, strange, suspicious, touched, unbalanced, uncanny, uncommon, unconventional, unhinged, unnatural, unorthodox, unusual, wacky*, weird; CONCEPTS 404,548,564 —Ant. normal, regular, typical, usual

queer [adj2] *not feeling well* dizzy, faint, giddy, green*, ill, lightheaded, pukish*, qualmish, qualmy*, queasy*, reeling, sick, squeamish*, uneasy; CONCEPT 314 —Ant. healthy, well

quell [v1] *defeat, suppress* annihilate, conquer, crush, extinguish, hush up*, kill, overcome, overpower, put down, put the lid on*, queer, quench, shut down, silence, sit on, stamp out*, stifle, stop, subdue, subjugate, vanquish; CONCEPTS 95,121,234 —*Ant.* succeed, win

quell [v2] *alleviate, calm* allay, appease, assuage, check, compose, deaden, dull, ease, mitigate, moderate, mollify, pacify, quiet, reduce, silence, soothe, still; CONCEPTS 7,22,110 —*Ant.* aggravate, agitate, disturb, irritate, perturb

quench [v1] *destroy, extinguish* annihilate, check, choke, crush, dampen, decimate, demolish, destruct, dismantle, douse, end, kill, knock down, moisten, put down, put out, quash*, quell, raze, ruin, shatter, smother, snuff out*, stifle, suppress, wreck; CONCEPTS 234,252 —*Ant.* set, start

quench [v2] *satisfy, especially thirst* allay, alleviate, appease, assuage, content, cool*, glut, gorge, gratify, lighten, mitigate, moisten, relieve, sate, satiate, slake; CONCEPTS 136,244 —*Ant.* dissatisfy

querulous [adj] *grouchy, hard to please* bearish, bemoaning, cantankerous, captious, carping, censorious, complaining, critical, cross, crying, deploring, discontented, dissatisfied, edgy, fault-finding, fretful, grousing, grumbling, grumbly, huffy* irascible, irritable, lamenting, out of sorts* peevish, petulant, plaintive, scrappy, snappy, sour, testy, thin-skinned* touchy, uptight, wailing, waspish, waspy, whimpering, whining, whiny; CONCEPTS 401,542 —*Ant.* cheerful, easy-going, happy

query [n] *demand for answers* concern, doubt, dubiety, inquiry, interrogation, interrogatory, mistrust, objection, problem, question, questioning, reservation, skepticism, suspicion, uncertainty; CONCEPTS 21,48,53,662 —*Ant.* answer, reply

query [v] *ask* catechize, challenge, disbelieve, dispute, distrust, doubt, enquire, examine, hit up, impeach, impugn, inquire, interrogate, knock, mistrust, put out a feeler* question, quiz, suspect, test the waters*; CONCEPTS 21,48,53 —*Ant.* answer, reply

quest [n] *search, exploration* adventure, chase, crusade, delving, enterprise, examination, expedition, hunt, inquest, inquiry, inquisition, investigation, journey, mission, pilgrimmage, prey, probe, probing, pursual, pursuit, quarry, research, seeking, voyage; CONCEPTS 48,103,216

question [n1] *asking for answer* catechism, examination, inquest, inquiring, inquiry, inquisition, interrogation, interrogatory, investigation, poll, Q and A*, query, questioning, third degree*, wringer*; CONCEPTS 48,53 —*Ant.* answer, reply

question [n2] *controversy, doubt* argument, challenge, confusion, contention, debate, demur, demurral, difficulty, dispute, dubiety, enigma, misgiving, mystery, objection, problem, protest, puzzle, query, remonstrance, remonstration, uncertainty; CONCEPTS 666,674 —*Ant.* concord, harmony

question [n3] *issue, point at issue* discussion, motion, point, problem, proposal, subject, theme, topic; CONCEPTS 532,690 —*Ant.* agreement

question [v1] *ask for answer* ask about, catechize, challenge, cross-examine, enquire, examine, give the third degree*, go over, grill, hit*, hit up*, hold out for, inquire, interrogate, interview, investigate, knock*, make inquiry, petition, pick one's brains*, probe, pry, pump, put through the wringer*, put to the question*, query, quest, quiz, raise question, roast*, search, seek, show curiosity, solicit, sound out*, sweat it out of*, work over*; CONCEPTS 48,53 —*Ant.* answer, reply

question [v2] *doubt* call into question, cast doubt upon, challenge, controvert, disbelieve, dispute, distrust, hesitate, impeach, impugn, mistrust, oppose, puzzle over, query, suspect, suspicion, wonder about; CONCEPT 21 —*Ant.* certainty, doubtlessness, sureness, surety

questionable [adj] *doubtful, uncertain* ambiguous, apocryphal, arguable, contingent, controversial, controvertible, cryptic, debatable, disputable, dubious, dubitable, enigmatic, equivocal, fishy*, hard to believe, hypothetical, iffy*, indecisive, indefinite, indeterminate, moot, mysterious, obscure, occult, open to doubt, open to question, oracular, paradoxical, problematic, problematical, provisional, shady, suspect, suspicious, unconfirmed, undefined, under advisement, under examination, unproven, unreliable, unsettled, vague; CONCEPTS 529,535 —*Ant.* certain, definite, indisputable, proven, sure, undoubted, unquestionable

queue [n] *sequence* chain, concatenation, echelon, file, line, order, progression, rank, row, series, string, succession, tail, tier, train; CONCEPTS 432,727 —*Ant.* disorganization

quibble [n] *objection, complaint* artifice, cavil, criticism, dodge, duplicity, equivocation, evasion, hair-splitter*, nicety, niggle*, nit-picker*, pretense, prevarication, protest, quiddity, quirk, shift, sophism, subterfuge, subtlety; CONCEPTS 46,52 —*Ant.* agreement, approval, concurrence

quibble [v] *disagree over minor issues* altercate, argue over, argufy, avoid, bicker, blow hot and cold*, carp, catch at straws*, cavil, chicane, criticize, dispute, equivocate, evade, fence*, flip-flop*, hassle, have at it*, hem and haw*, hypercriticize*, make a big thing about*, nit-pick*, paralogize, pettifog*, pretend, prevaricate, put up an argument, set to, shift, spar, split hairs*, squabble, talk back, waffle, wrangle; CONCEPTS 46,52 —*Ant.* agree, approve, concur

quick [adj1] *fast, speedy* abrupt, accelerated, active, agile, alert, a move on*, animated, ASAP*, breakneck*, brief, brisk, cursory, curt, double time*, energetic, expeditious, expeditive, express, fleet, flying, going, harefooted*, hasty, headlong, hurried, immediate, impatient, impetuous, instantaneous, keen, lively, mercurial, move it, nimble, on the double*, perfunctory, posthaste, prompt, pronto*, rapid, snappy, spirited, sprightly, spry, sudden, swift, the lead out*, winged*; CONCEPTS 544,588 —*Ant.* lazy, slow, sluggish

quick [adj2] *smart* able, active, acute, adept, adroit, all there, apt, astute, bright, canny, capable, clever, competent, deft, dexterous, discerning, effective, effectual, intelligent, keen, knowing, nimble-witted, on the ball*, perceptive, perspicacious, prompt, quick on the draw, quick on the trigger*, quick on the uptake*, quick-witted, ready, receptive, savvy*, sharp, sharp as a tack*, shrewd, skillful, slick, smart as a whip*, vigorous, whiz*, wired*, wise; CONCEPT 402 —Ant. ignorant, slow, stupid, uneducated

quicken [v] make faster; invigorate accelerate, activate, actuate, animate, arouse, awaken, dispatch, energize, excite, expedite, galvanize, goad, grow, hasten, hurry, impel, incite, increase, innervate, innerve, inspire, kindle, liven, make haste, motivate, move, pique, precipitate, promote, refresh, revitalize, revive, rouse, shake up, speed, spring, spur, step up, stimulate, stir, strengthen, urge, vitalize, vivificate, vivify; CONCEPTS 7,19,22,250 —Ant. dull, retard, slow, weaken

quickly [adv] fast apace, briskly, chop-chop*, expeditiously, flat-out*, fleetly, full tilt*, hastily, hurriedly, immediately, in a flash*, in haste, in nothing flat*, in short order*, instantaneously, instantly, lickety-split*, like a bat out of hell*, like a flash*, like a shot*, promptly, pronto, quick, rapidly, speedily, swift, swiftly; CONCEPTS 588,799

quick-tempered [adj] easily upset, angered choleric, cranky, cross, excitable, fiery, hot-tempered, impatient, impulsive, inflammable, irascible, irritable, passionate, peppery, petulant, quarrelsome, ratty, sensitive, short-tempered, shrewish, splenetic, temperamental, testy, waspish; CONCEPTS 401,404 —Ant. calm, cool, easy-going, even-tempered, laid-back

quick-witted [adj] smart acute, agile, alert, apt, astute, brainy, bright, brilliant, canny, clever, facetious, humorous, intelligent, keen, knowing, nimble-witted, on the ball*, penetrating, penetrative, perceptive, prompt, quick, quick on the draw*, quick on the uptake*, ready, savvy*, sharp, sharp as a tack*, sharp-sighted, sharp-witted, shrewd, slick*, whiz*, wired*, wise, witty; CONCEPTS 267,402 —Ant. slow, slow-witted, stupid, uneducated

quiescent [adj] inactive asleep, at rest, deactivated, dormant, fallow, idle, immobile, in abeyance, inert, inoperative, latent, motionless, passive, quiet, slumbering, stagnant, still; CONCEPT 584 —Ant. active

quiet [adj1] without or with little sound buttoned up*, clammed up*, close, close-mouthed, could hear a pin drop*, dumb, hushed, hushful, inaudible, low, low-pitched, muffled, mute, muted, noiseless, not saying boo*, peaceful, quiescent, quieted, reserved, reticent, secretive, silent, soft, soundless, speechless, still, stilled, taciturn, tight-lipped*, uncommunicative, unexpressed, unspeaking, unuttered, whist; CONCEPTS 592,594 —Ant. boisterous, clamorous, loud, noisy

quiet [adj2] calm, peaceful collected, contented, docile, fixed, gentle, halcyon, hushed, inactive, isolated, level, meek, mild, motionless, pacific, placid, private, remote, reserved, restful, retired, secluded, secret, sedate, sequestered, serene, shy, smooth, stable, stagnant, still, tranquil, unanxious, undisturbed, unexcited, unfrequented, unruffled, untroubled; CONCEPTS 401,583,584,705 —Ant. agitated, troubled

quiet [adj3] simple, unobtrusive conservative, homely, inobtrusive, modest, plain, restrained, sober, subdued, tasteful, unassuming, unpretentious; CONCEPT 589 —Ant. complex, complicated, intricate, obtrusive

quiet [n] calmness, silence calm, cessation, dead air*, ease, hush, lull, noiselessness, peace, quietness, quietude, relaxation, repose, rest, serenity, soundlessness, speechlessness, still, stillness, stop, termination, tranquillity; CONCEPTS 65,315,592,673,705 —Ant. clamor, clangor, loudness, noise

quiet [v] make silent, calm allay, ameliorate, appease, assuage, becalm, button one's lip*, calm down, can it, choke, clam up*, compose, console, cool it*, cool out*, dummy up*, fix up, gag, gratify, hold it down, hush, ice*, inactivate, lull, moderate, mollify, muffle, muzzle, pacify, palliate, patch things up*, please, quieten, reconcile, relax, satisfy, settle, shush, shut up, silence, slack, smooth, soften, soft-pedal*, soothe, square, squash, squelch, still, stroke, subdue, take the bite out of*, tranquilize; CONCEPTS 126,244,266 —Ant. turn up

quietly [adv1] silently faintly, in a low voice, inaudibly, in a whisper, in low tones, in silence, murmuring, noiselessly, softly, sotto voce, soundlessly, tacitly, under one's breath, weakly; CONCEPTS 592,594 —Ant. audibly, loudly

quietly [adv2] discreetly confidentially, conservatively, off the record, privately, secretly, unobtrusively, unofficially; CONCEPT 589 —Ant. loudly, publicly

quietly [adv3] calmly patiently, placidly, serenely, unassumingly; CONCEPTS 401,583,584,705

quilt [n] thick bedcovering made of patches batt, bedspread, blanket, comforter, counterpane, cover, coverlet, down, duvet, eiderdown, pad, patchwork, pouf, puff; CONCEPTS 445,451,473

quintessence [n] essence, core apotheosis, bottom, distillation, epitome, essentiality, extract, gist, heart, kernel, last word, lifeblood, marrow, pith, quiddity, soul, spirit, stuff, substance, ultimate, virtuality; CONCEPTS 682, 826 —Ant. extra

quip [n] witty communication, often verbal badinage, banter, bon mot, crack, drollery, gag, gibe, insult, jeer, jest, joke, mockery, offense, pleasantry, pun, repartee, retort, riposte, sally, satire, spoof, wisecrack, witticism; CONCEPTS 273,278

quirk [n] oddity of personality, way of doing something aberration, caprice, characteristic, conceit, crotchet, eccentricity, equivocation, fancy, fetish, foible, habit, humor, idée fixe, idiosyncrasy, irregularity, kink, knack, mannerism, peculiarity, quibble, singularity, subterfuge, trait, turn, twist, vagary, whim, whimsy; CONCEPTS 411,644

quirky [adj] eccentric bizarre, far out*, freakish, freaky*, idiosyncratic, in left field*, kinky*, odd, off-the-wall*, out of the ordinary, outre, peculiar, strange, unconventional, unorthodox, unusual, wacky*, way-out*, weird; CONCEPT 401 —Ant. conventional

quisling [n] traitor back-stabber, betrayer, collaborator, colluder, defector, deserter, double-crosser, double-dealer, Judas, snake in the grass*, sympathizer, turncoat, two-timer*; CONCEPT 412

quit [v1] *abandon, leave* abdicate, blow*, book*, bow out, check out, cut out*, decamp, depart, desert, drop, drop out, evacuate, exit, forsake, get off, give up, go, go away from, hang it up*, leave flat*, leave hanging*, pull out, push off*, relinquish, renounce, resign, retire, run out on, surrender, take a walk*, take off, throw over*, vacate, walk out on, withdraw, yield; CONCEPT 195 —*Ant.* come, remain, stay

quit [v2] *stop doing something* abandon, break off, call it a day*, call it quits*, cease, conclude, cut it out*, desist, discontinue, drop, end, get on the wagon*, give notice, give over*, give up, halt, hang it up*, kick over*, kick the habit*, knock off*, leave, leave off*, pack in*, quit cold, resign, retire, secede, sew up*, surcease, suspend, take the cure*, terminate, wind up*, withdraw, wrap up*; CONCEPTS 119,234 —*Ant.* complete, continue, do, finish, persevere

quite [adv1] *completely* absolutely, actually, all, all in all, all told, altogether, considerably, entirely, fully, in all respects, in fact, in reality, in toto, in truth, just, largely, perfectly, positively, precisely, purely, really, thoroughly, totally, truly, utterly, well, wholly, without reservation; CONCEPTS 531,582 —*Ant.* incompletely

quite [adv2] *to a certain extent* considerably, fairly, far, moderately, more or less, pretty, rather, reasonably, relatively, significantly, somewhat, to some degree, very; CONCEPT 569

quiver [n] *shaking, vibration* convulsion, flash, glimmer, glitter, oscillation, palpitation, pulsation, shake, shimmer, shiver, shudder, sparkle, spasm, throb, tic, tremble, tremor, twinkle; CONCEPT 152 —*Ant.* quiet, stillness

quiver [v] *shake, vibrate* agitate, beat, convulse, dither, jitter, oscillate, palpitate, pulsate, pulse, quake, quaver, shiver, shudder, thrill, throb, tremble, tremor, twitter; CONCEPT 152 —*Ant.* be still

quixotic [adj] *idealistic* chimerical, chivalrous, dreaming, dreamy, foolish, impetuous, impractical, impulsive, romantic, starry-eyed, unrealistic, utopian, visionary; CONCEPTS 529,560,582

quiz [n] *questioning, often in an organized academic setting* blue book*, check, exam, examination, investigation, query, shotgun*, test; CONCEPT 290 —*Ant.* answer, reply

quiz [v] *question* ask, catechize, check, cross-examine, examine, give the third degree*, grill*, inquire, interrogate, investigate, pick one's brains*, pump*, query, test; CONCEPT 48 —*Ant.* answer, reply

quizzical [adj] *appearing confused or curious* amusing, aporetic, arch, bantering, derisive, disbelieving, eccentric, incredulous, inquiring, inquisitive, mocking, odd, probing, quaint, queer, questioning, sardonic, searching, showme*, skeptical, supercilious, suspicious, teasing, unbelieving, unusual; CONCEPTS 267,485 —*Ant.* certain, understanding

quota [n] *portion allotted to something* allocation, allotment, allowance, apportionment, assignment, bite, chunk, cut, division, divvy*, end, lot, measure, meed, part, partage, percentage, piece, piece of action*, proportion, quantum, ration, share, slice, split; CONCEPTS 768,835

quotation/quote [n1] *repetition of something spoken or written by someone* citation, citing, cutting, excerpt, extract, passage, quote, recitation, reference, saying, selection; CONCEPTS 274,278

quotation/quote [n2] *financial estimate* bid, bid price, charge, cost, current price, figure, market price, price, price named, published price, quote, rate, stated price, tender; CONCEPTS 274,332,784

quote [v] *repeat something spoken, written by another* adduce, attest, cite, detail, excerpt, extract, instance, name, paraphrase, parrot, proclaim, recall, recite, recollect, reference, refer to, retell; CONCEPTS 79,171

R

rabble [n] *mob* commonality, commoners, crowd, drove, flock, gang, gathering, herd, hoi polloi, horde, lower class, mass, masses, multitude, pack, proletariat, rank and file, riffraff, ring, riot, scum, throng; CONCEPTS 378,417,432

rabid [adj] *very angry; maniacal* berserk, bigoted, bitten, corybantic, crazed*, crazy, delirious, deranged, enthusiastic, extreme, extremist, fanatical, fervent, flipped*, foaming at the mouth*, frantic, freaked out*, frenetic, frenzied, furious, hot*, infuriated, insane, intemperate, intolerant, irrational, keen, mad, mad-dog*, narrow-minded, nutty*, obsessed, overboard, poisoned, radical, raging, revolutionary, sick*, sizzling, smoking*, steamed up*, ultra, ultraist, violent, virulent, wild, zealous; CONCEPT 403 —*Ant.* delighted, happy, pleased

race [n1] *pursuit; running, speeding* chase, clash, clip, competition, contention, contest, course, dash, engagement, event, go, marathon, match, meet, relay, rivalry, run, rush, scurry, sprint, spurt; CONCEPT 363

race [n2] *ethnic group* blood, breed, clan, color, cultural group, culture, family, folk, house, issue, kin, kind, kindred, line, lineage, nation, nationality, offspring, people, progeny, seed, species, stock, strain, tribe, type, variety; CONCEPT 380

race [n3] *stream, river* branch, brook, creek, duct, gill, raceway, rill, rindle, rivulet, run, runnel, sluice, tide; CONCEPT 514

race [v] *run, speed in competition* boil, bolt, bustle, career, chase, compete, contest, course, dart, dash, fling, fly, gallop, haste, hasten, hie, hurry, hustle, lash, outstrip, plunge ahead, post, pursue, rush, scamper, scramble, scud, scuttle, shoot, skim, sprint, spurt, swoop, tear, whisk, wing; CONCEPTS 150,363

racial [adj] *ethnic* ancestral, ethnological, folk, genealogical, genetic, hereditary, lineal, national, phyletic, phylogenetic, tribal; CONCEPT 549

racism [n] *prejudice against an ethnic group* apartheid, bias, bigotry, discrimination, illiberality, one-sidedness, partiality, racialism, sectarianism, segregation, unfairness; CONCEPT 689

racist [adj] *bigoted* anti-Semitic, biased, illiberal, intolerant, narrow-minded, opinionated, partial, prejudiced, sectarian, small-minded, xenophobic; CONCEPTS 403,555

racist [n] *bigot* anti-Semite, black supremacist, chauvinist, diehard, doctrinaire, fanatic, klansperson, opinionated person, prejudiced person, sectarian, segregationist, sexist person, white supremacist, xenophobe; CONCEPTS 359, 423

rack [n] *frame, framework* arbor, bed, box, bracket, counter, furniture, holder, ledge, perch, receptacle, shelf, stand, structure, trestle; CONCEPTS 443,479

rack [v] *torture; strain* afflict, agonize, crucify, distress, excruciate, force, harass, harrow, martyr, oppress, pain, persecute, pull, shake, stress, stretch, tear, torment, try, wrench, wring; CONCEPTS 7,19 —*Ant.* please, pleasure, soothe

racket [n1] *commotion; fight* agitation, babel, battle, blare, brawl, clamor, clangor, clash, clatter, din, disturbance, fracas, free-for-all*, fuss, hoo-ha*, hubbub*, jangle, noise, outcry, pandemonium, riot, roar, row, ruction, rumpus*, shouting, shuffle, squabble, squall, stir, to-do*, tumult, turbulence, turmoil, uproar, vociferation, wrangle; CONCEPTS 65,106,230 —*Ant.* harmony, peace

racket [n2] *criminal activity* cheating, confidence game, con game, conspiracy, corruption, crime, dirty pool*, dishonesty, dodge, extortion, fraud, game, graft, illegality, illicit scheme, intrigue, lawlessness, lay, plot, push, scheme, shakedown, squeeze*, swindle, swindling, theft, trick, underworld; CONCEPT 192

rack up [v] *achieve, gain* accomplish, acquire, actualize, attain, carry out, do, earn, get done, obtain, produce, reach, realize, score, wind up; CONCEPT 706

racy [adj1] *energetic, zestful* animated, bright, buoyant, clever, distinctive, entertaining, exciting, exhilarating, fiery, forceful, forcible, gingery, heady, keen, lively, mettlesome, peppery, piquant, playful, poignant, pungent, rich, salty, saucy*, sharp, snappy, sparkling, spicy, spirited, sportive, sprightly, stimulating, strong, tangy, tart, tasty, vigorous, vivacious, witty, zesty; CONCEPTS 401,613 —*Ant.* dull, idle, languid, lazy

racy [adj2] *risqué, vulgar* bawdy, blue*, broad, erotic, immodest, indecent, indelicate, lewd, lurid, naughty, off-color*, purple*, shady*, smutty*, spicy*, suggestive, wicked; CONCEPTS 267,545 —*Ant.* clean, modest, moral, upright

radar [n] *radio detecting and ranging* direction finding, scanning system, sonar, tracking system; CONCEPT 279

radiance [n1] *brightness, luminescence* brilliance, effulgence, glare, gleam, glitter, glow, incandescence, light, luminosity, luster, resplendence, shine; CONCEPT 620 —*Ant.* cloudiness, dark, dimness, dullness

radiance [n2] *happiness* delight, gaiety, joy, pleasure, rapture, warmth; CONCEPT 633 —*Ant.* sadness

radiant [adj1] *bright, luminous* beaming, brilliant, effulgent, gleaming, glittering, glorious, glowing, incandescent, lambent, lucent, lustrous, radiating, refulgent, resplendent, shining, sparkling, sunny; CONCEPT 617 —*Ant.* cloudy, dark, dim, dull

radiant [adj2] *happy in appearance* beaming, beatific, blissful, bright, cheerful, cheery,

delighted, ecstatic, gay, glad, glowing, joyful, joyous, rapturous; CONCEPT 401 —*Ant.* sad

radiate [v] *give off; scatter* afford, beam, branch out, broadcast, circulate, diffuse, disseminate, distribute, diverge, emanate, emit, expand, give out, gleam, glitter, illumine, irradiate, issue, light up, pour, proliferate, propagate, ramble, ramify, send out, shed, shine, shoot out, spread, spread out, sprinkle, strew, throw out, transmit, yield; CONCEPTS 118,217, 620,716 —*Ant.* collect, gather

radical [adj1] *fundamental, basic* basal, bottom, cardinal, constitutional, deep-seated, essential, foundational, inherent, innate, intrinsic, meat-and-potatoes*, native, natural, organic, original, primal, primary, primitive, profound, thoroughgoing, underlying, vital; CONCEPTS 546,549 —*Ant.* extrinsic, nonessential, superficial

radical [adj2] *deviating by extremes* advanced, anarchistic, complete, entire, excessive, extremist, fanatical, far-out*, freethinking, iconoclastic, immoderate, insubordinate, insurgent, insurrectionary, intransigent, lawless, leftist, militant, mutinous, nihilistic, progressive, rabid, rebellious, recalcitrant, recusant, refractory, restive, revolutionary, riotous, seditious, severe, sweeping, thorough, ultra, ultraist, uncompromising, violent, way out*; CONCEPTS 403,529,542 —*Ant.* conservative, moderate

radical [n] *person who advocates significant, often extreme change* agitator, anarchist, avant-garde, extremist, fanatic, firebrand, freethinker, iconoclast, insurgent, insurrectionist, leftist, left-winger, militant, mutineer, nihilist, nonconformist, objector, pacifist, progressive, rebel, reformer, renegade, revolter, revolutionary, rioter, secessionist, subversive, ultraist; CONCEPT 359 —*Ant.* conservative, moderate

radio [n] *communication by electronic air waves* AM-FM, CB, Marconi, radionics, radiotelegraph, radiotelegraphy, radiotelephone, radiotelephonics, receiver, shortwave, telegraphy, telephony, transmission, Walkman, wireless; CONCEPT 279

radius [n] *range, sweep* ambit, boundary, compass, expanse, extension, extent, interval, limit, orbit, purview, reach, semidiameter, space, span, spoke; CONCEPT 651

raffish [adj] *unmindful of social conventions* bohemian*, careless, casual, coarse, dashing, devil-may-care*, disreputable, fast*, gay, jaunty, rakish, sporty, tasteless, tawdry, unconventional, uncouth, vulgar, wild; CONCEPT 401 —*Ant.* behaved, couth, proper

raffle [n] *lottery for a prize* bet, betting, disposition, draw, drawing, flier*, gambling, game of chance, gaming, long odds*, lots*, numbers*, numbers game*, pool, random shot, speculation, stake, sweep, sweepstake, tossup*, wager, wagering; CONCEPTS 363,364

ragamuffin [n] *person who is poor, tattered* beggar, bum*, gamin, guttersnipe*, hobo, loafer, orphan, scarecrow, street person, tatterdemalion*, tramp, urchin, vagabond, vagrant, waif, wastrel; CONCEPTS 412,423 —*Ant.* sophisticate

rage [n1] *extreme anger* acerbity, acrimony, agitation, animosity, apoplexy, asperity, bitterness, blowup*, bluster, choler, convulsion, dander, eruption, exasperation, excitement, explosion, ferment, ferocity, fireworks, frenzy, furor, fury, gall, heat*, hemorrhage, huff*, hysterics, indignation, ire, irritation, madness, mania, obsession, outburst, paroxysm, passion, rampage, raving, resentment, spasm, spleen, squall, storm, tantrum, temper, umbrage, uproar, upset, vehemence, violence, wingding*, wrath; CONCEPTS 410,657 —Ant. glee, happiness

rage [n2] *something in vogue; popular notion* caprice, chic, conceit, craze, crotchet, cry, dernier cri, enthusiasm, fad, fancy, fashion, freak, furor, happening, hot spot*, in*, in-spot*, in-thing*, last word*, latest*, latest thing*, latest wrinkle*, mania, mode, newest wrinkle*, now*, passion, style, thing*, up to the minute*, vagary, whim; CONCEPTS 388,655

rage [v] *be angry* be beside oneself*, be furious, be uncontrollable, blow a fuse*, blow one's top*, blow up*, boil over*, bristle, chafe, champ at bit*, erupt, fly off the handle*, foam at the mouth*, fret, fulminate, fume, go berserk, have a fit, have a tantrum, let off steam*, look daggers*, make a fuss over, overflow, rail at, rampage, rant, rant and rave*, rave, roar, scold, scream, seethe, snap at, splutter, steam, storm, surge, tear, throw a fit*, work oneself into sweat*, yell; CONCEPTS 29, 410 —Ant. be happy

ragged [adj] *worn-out; in shreds* badly dressed, badly worn, battered, broken, contemptible, crude, desultory, dilapidated, dingy, disorganized, down at the heel*, fragmented, frayed, frazzled, full of holes*, in holes*, in rags, in tatters*, irregular, jagged, mean, moth-eaten, notched, patched, poor, poorly made, rent, rough, rugged, scraggy, seedy, serrated, shabby, shaggy, shoddy, shredded, tacky*, tattered, tatty*, threadbare, torn, uneven, unfinished, unkempt, unpressed, worse for wear*; CONCEPT 485 —Ant. even, kempt, new, smooth

raging [adj] *violent; mad* angry, at boiling point*, bent*, bent out of shape*, beside oneself*, blowing a gasket*, blowing one's top*, blustering, blustery, boiling mad*, boiling over*, enraged, fit to be tied*, frenzied, fuming, furious, going ape*, incensed, infuriated, irate, mad as a hornet*, on the warpath*, rabid*, ranting and raving*, raving, raving mad, rough, seeing red*, seething, stormy, tempestuous, throwing a fit, turbulent, wild; CONCEPTS 403,542 —Ant. delighted, giddy, gleeful, happy

raid [n] *attack, seizure* arrest, assault, break-in, bust, capture, descent, foray, forced entrance, hit-and-run*, incursion, inroad, invasion, irruption, onset, onslaught, pull, reconnaissance, roundup, sally*, shootup*, sortie*, surprise attack, sweep, tipover*; CONCEPTS 86,317

raid [v] *attack, pillage* assail, assault, blockade, bomb, bombard, breach, break in, charge, descend on, despoil, devastate, fall upon, fire on, forage, foray, harass, harry, inroad, invade, knock off*, knock over*, lean against, lean on, loot, maraud, march on, overrun, pirate, plunder, rake, ransack, rifle, rob, sack, sally, sally forth, shell, slough, spoliate, storm, strafe, strike, sweep, swoop, tip over*, torpedo, waste; CONCEPT 86 —Ant. aid, assist, guard, help, protect

rail [v] *criticize harshly* abuse, attack, bawl out*, berate, blast, castigate, censure, chew out*, complain, fulminate, fume, inveigh, jaw, objurate, rant, rate, revile, scold, thunder, tongue-lash*, upbraid, vituperate, vociferate, whip; CONCEPT 52 —Ant. compliment, praise

rail/railing [n] *post, pole along an edge* balustrade, banister, bar, barrier, fence, paling, rails, rest, siding; CONCEPTS 443,479

railroad [n] *train line* elevated railway, line, metro, monorail, rail line, railway, streetcar line, subway, tracks, trolley line, tube, underground railway; CONCEPTS 155,503

rain [n] *downpour of water or other substance* cat-and-dog weather*, cloudburst, condensation, deluge, drencher, drizzle, fall, flood, flurry, hail, heavy dew, liquid sunshine*, mist, monsoon, pour, pouring, precip*, precipitation, raindrops, rainfall, rainstorm, sheets, shower, showers, sleet, spate, spit, sprinkle, sprinkling, stream, sun shower*, torrent, volley*, wet stuff*, window washer*; CONCEPT 526 —Ant. aridity, dryness

rain [v] *drop water or other substance* bestow, bucket, come down in buckets*, deposit, drizzle, fall, hail, lavish, mist, patter, pour, shower, sleet, sprinkle, storm; CONCEPT 526

rainbow [n] *color spectrum* arc, band of color, bow, crescent, curve, prism, variegation; CONCEPT 436

raise [n] *increase in salary or position* accession, accretion, addition, advance, augmentation, boost, bump, hike, hold-up*, increment, jump, jump-up*, leg*, leg-up*, move-up*, promotion, raising, rise, step-up*; CONCEPTS 344,351,763 —Ant. decrease, drop, reduction

raise [v1] *lift; build from the ground* boost, bring up, construct, elevate, erect, establish, exalt, heave, hoist, hold up, lever, lift, lift up, mount, move up, place up, promote, pry, pull up, put on its end, put up, rear, run up, set up, set upright, shove, stand up, take up, throw up, upcast, upheave, uplift, upraise, uprear; CONCEPTS 168,196 —Ant. demolish, destroy, drop, lower, raze

raise [v2] *increase, augment* advance, aggravate, amplify, assemble, boost, build up, collect, congregate, congress, dignify, enhance, enlarge, escalate, exaggerate, exalt, fetch up, forgather, form, gather, get, goose*, goose up*, heighten, hike, hike up*, honor, inflate, intensify, jack up, jump, jump up, levy, look up, magnify, mass, mobilize, mushroom*, muster, obtain, perk up, pick up, promote, put up, pyramid, rally, recruit, reinforce, rendezvous, run up*, send through the roof*, shoot up, snowball*, strengthen, up; CONCEPTS 236,244,245 —Ant. decrease, depress, diminish, lessen, lower, reduce

raise [v3] *start up, motivate; introduce* abet, activate, advance, arouse, awaken, bring up, broach, cause, evoke, excite, foment, foster, incite, instigate, kindle, moot, motivate, provoke, put forward, resurrect, set, set on, stir up, suggest, whip up; CONCEPTS 75,221 —Ant. conclude, finish, stop

raise [v4] *nurture, care for* breed, bring up, cultivate, develop, drag up, fetch up, foster, group, grow, nourish, nurse, plant, produce, propagate, provide, rear, sow, suckle, support, train, wean; CONCEPTS 253,257,295 —Ant. abandon, ignore, neglect, repress, suppress

raison d'etre [n] *reason for being* basis, justification for existing, rationale, reason for existing, reason why; CONCEPT 661

rake [v] *scrape up, hoe* break up, clean up, clear, clear up, collect, comb, enfilade, examine, fine-comb, fine-tooth-comb*, gather, grade, graze, grub, harrow, hunt, ransack, rasp, remove, rummage, scan, scour, scrape, scratch, scrutinize, search, smooth, sweep, weed; CONCEPTS 109,165,178,216

rakish [adj] *charming and immoral* abandoned, chic, dashing, debauched, depraved, devil-may-care*, dissipated, dissolute, fashionable, fast*, flashy, gay, jaunty, lecherous, licentious, loose*, natty, prodigal, profligate, raffish, saucy, sinful, smart, sporty, wanton, wild; CONCEPTS 401,545 —Ant. clean, moral, upright

rally [n1] *celebratory meeting* assemblage, assembly, celebration, clambake*, convention, convocation, get-together, mass meeting, meet, pep rally, pow-wow*, session; CONCEPT 377

rally [n2] *turn for the better* comeback, improvement, recovery, recuperation, renewal, resurgence, revival, turning point; CONCEPT 700 —Ant. regression, remission, weakening

rally [v1] *reorganize, unite* arouse, assemble, awaken, bestir, bond together, bring together, bring to order, call to arms*, challenge, charge, collect, come about, come together, come to order, convene, counterattack, encourage, fire, gather, get together, inspirit, kindle, marshal, mobilize, muster, organize, reassemble, redouble, reform, refresh, regroup, rejuvenate, renew, restore, resurrect, resuscitate, revive, round up, rouse, summon, surge, urge, wake, waken, whet, wreak havoc*; CONCEPTS 7,22,117,320 —Ant. disperse, divide, scatter

rally [v2] *revive; take a turn for the better* bounce back, brace up, come along, come around, come from behind, enliven, get act together*, get back in shape*, get better, get second wind*, grow stronger, improve, invigorate, make a comeback, perk up, pick up, pull through, recover, recuperate, refresh, regain strength, shape up, snap out of it, surge, turn around, turn things around*; CONCEPT 700 —Ant. lose, regress, weaken

ram [v] *bang into; pack forcibly* beat, butt, collide with, cram, crash, crowd, dash, dig, drive, drum, force, hammer, hit, hook, impact, jack, jam-pack, pack, plunge, poke, pound, run, run into, sink, slam, smash, stab, stick, strike, strike head-on, stuff, tamp, thrust, wedge; CONCEPTS 189,208,209 —Ant. tap

ramble [n] *aimless walk* constitutional, excursion, hike, perambulation, peregrination, roaming, roving, saunter, stroll, tour, traipse, trip, turn; CONCEPTS 151,224

ramble [v1] *wander about; travel aimlessly* amble, bat around*, be all over the map*, branch off, clamber, climb, cruise, depart, digress, divagate, diverge, drift, excurse, extend, fork, gad, gallivant, get sidetracked*, knock about*, knock around*, meander, perambulate, percolate, peregrinate, promenade, range, roam, rove, saunter, scramble, snake, sprangle, sprawl, spread, spread-eagle, straddle, straggle, stray, stroll, trail, traipse, turn, twist, walk, wind, zigzag; CONCEPTS 151, 154,581,692 —Ant. be direct, stay

ramble [v2] *talk aimlessly, endlessly* amplify, babble, beat around bush*, be diffuse, blather, chatter, depart, descant, digress, divagate, diverge, drift, drivel, dwell on, enlarge, excurse, expatiate, get off the subject*, go astray, go off on tangent*, go on and on*, gossip, harp on, lose the thread*, maunder, meander, prose, protract, rant and rave*, rattle on*, stray, talk nonsense, talk off top of head*, talk randomly, wander; CONCEPT 51 —Ant. be direct

rambling [adj1] *disconnected, wordy* circuitous, confused, desultory, diffuse, digressive, discursive, disjointed, incoherent, incongruous, irregular, long-winded, periphrastic, prolix; CONCEPT 267 —Ant. connected, direct, straightforward

rambling [adj2] *sprawling, spread out* at length, covering, gangling, here and there, irregular, random, scattered, spreading, straggling, strewn, trailing, unplanned; CONCEPTS 485,772 —Ant. direct, straight

rambunctious [adj] *loud, energetic* boisterous, noisy, raucous, rough, rowdy, rude, termagant, tumultous/tumultuous, turbulent, unruly; CONCEPT 542 —Ant. introverted, meek, quiet, shy

ramification [n] *consequence, development* bifurcation, branch, branching, breaking, complication, consequence, divarication, division, excrescence, extension, forking, offshoot, outgrowth, partition, radiation, result, sequel, subdividing, subdivision, upshot; CONCEPTS 98,230,824 —Ant. cause

ramp [n] *incline* access, adit, grade, gradient, hill, inclination, inclined plane, rise, slope; CONCEPTS 443,757

rampage [n] *storm, violence* binge, blowup, boiling point*, destruction, disturbance, ferment, fling, frenzy, fury, mad*, more heat than light*, orgy, rage, ruckus, splurge, spree, tear, tempest, tumult, turmoil, uproar, wingding; CONCEPT 86 —Ant. calm, harmony, peace

rampage [v] *go crazy; storm* go berserk, rage, run amuck, run riot, run wild, tear; CONCEPTS 86,384 —Ant. be calm

rampant [adj] *uncontrolled, out of hand* aggressive, blustering, boisterous, clamorous, dominant, epidemic, exceeding bounds, excessive, extravagant, exuberant, fanatical, flagrant, furious, growing, impetuous, impulsive, luxuriant, on the rampage, out of control, outrageous, pandemic, predominant, prevalent, profuse, raging, rampaging, rank, rife, riotous, spreading, tumultous/tumultuous, turbulent, unbridled, unchecked, uncontrollable, ungovernable, unrestrained, unruly, vehement, violent, wanton, widespread, wild; CONCEPTS 544,554,772 —Ant. checked, controlled, limited, restrained

rampart [n] *fortification, stronghold* barricade, barrier, bastion, breastwork, bulwark, defense, earthwork, elevation, embankment, fence, fort, guard, hill, mound, parapet, protection, ridge, security, support, vallation, wall; CONCEPTS 321,439,509

ramshackle [adj] *falling apart; in poor condition* broken-down, crumbling, decrepit, derelict, dilapidated, flimsy, jerry-built*, rickety, shabby, shaky, tottering, tumble-down, unfirm, unsafe, unsteady; CONCEPTS 485,488 —*Ant.* good, nice, repaired, stable

ranch [*n*] *farm* acreage, cattle farm, dairy farm, estate, farmstead, hacienda, homestead, land, plantation; CONCEPTS 258,449,517

rancid [*adj*] *rotten, strong-smelling* bad, carious, contaminated, curdled, decomposing, disagreeable, disgusting, evil-smelling, feculent, fetid, foul, frowzy, fusty, gamy, high, impure, loathsome, malodorous, moldy, musty, nasty, nidorous, noisome, noxious, off, offensive, olid, polluted, putrefactive, putrefied, putrescent, putrid, rank, reeky, repulsive, sharp, smelly, sour, soured, stale, stinking, strong, tainted, turned, unhealthy, whiffy; CONCEPTS 462,570,598,613 —*Ant.* perfumed, sweet

rancor [*n*] *bitterness, hatefulness* acerbity, acrimony, animosity, animus, antagonism, antipathy, aversion, bad blood*, bile*, dudgeon, enmity, grudge, hardness of heart*, harshness, hate, hatred, hostility, ill feeling, ill will, malevolence, malice, malignity, mordacity, pique, resentfulness, resentment, retaliation, revengefulness, ruthlessness, spite, spitefulness, spleen, umbrage, uncharitableness, unfriendliness, variance, vengeance, vengefulness, venom, vindictiveness, virulence; CONCEPTS 29,410, 633 —*Ant.* kindness, love, respect, sympathy

random [*adj*] *haphazard, chance* accidental, adventitious, aimless, arbitrary, casual, contingent, designless, desultory, driftless, fluky, fortuitous, hit-or-miss*, incidental, indiscriminate, irregular, objectless, odd, promiscuous, purposeless, slapdash*, spot, stray, unaimed, unconsidered, unplanned, unpremeditated; CONCEPTS 535,548,557 —*Ant.* definite, methodical, particular, specific, systematic

range [*n1*] *sphere, distance, extent* ambit, amplitude, area, bounds, circle, compass, confines, diapason, dimension, dimensions, domain, earshot*, elbowroom*, expanse, extension, extensivity, field, gamut, hearing, ken, latitude, leeway, length, limits, magnitude, matter, neighborhood, orbit, order, panorama, parameters, play, province, purview, radius, reach, realm, run, run of, scope, space, span, spectrum, sphere, spread, stretch, sweep, swing, territory, tune, vicinity, width; CONCEPTS 651,743,745, 756,760,960 —*Ant.* extreme

range [*n2*] *order, series* assortment, chain, class, collection, file, gamut, kind, line, lot, rank, row, selection, sequence, sort, string, tier, variety; CONCEPTS 727,769 —*Ant.* part

range [*v1*] *order, categorize* align, allineate, arrange, array, assort, bias, bracket, catalogue, categorize, class, classify, dispose, draw up, file, grade, group, incline, line, line up, pigeonhole*, predispose, rank; CONCEPTS 84,158 —*Ant.* disorder, disorganize

range [*v2*] *wander, roam* circumambulate, cover, cross, cruise, drift, encompass, explore, float, follow one's nose*, gallivant, globe-trot*, hit the road*, hit the trail*, make circuit, meander, pass over, ply, prowl, ramble, reach, reconnoiter, rove, scour, search, spread, straggle, stray, stroll, sweep, traipse, tramp, travel, traverse, trek; CONCEPTS 151,224 —*Ant.* be direct

range [*v3*] *extend; change within limits* differ, diverge from, fluctuate, go, reach, run, stretch, vary, vary between; CONCEPT 697 —*Ant.* limit, restrict

rangy [*adj*] *long and lean* gangling, gangly, lanky, leggy, long-legged, long-limbed, reedy, skinny, spindling, spindly, thin, weedy; CONCEPT 779 —*Ant.* chubby, dumpy, fat, thick

rank [*adj1*] *stinking, foul* bad, dank, disagreeable, disgusting, evil-smelling, feculent, fetid, funky*, fusty*, gamy*, graveolent, gross*, high, humid, loathsome, mephitic, moldy, musty, nasty, nauseating, noisome, noxious, obnoxious, off, offensive, olid, pungent, putrescent, putrid, rancid, reeking, repulsive, revolting, smelly, sour, stale, strong, strong-smelling, tainted, turned; CONCEPT 598 —*Ant.* aromatic, perfumed, sweet

rank [*adj2*] *abundant, luxurious* coarse, dense, excessive, extreme, exuberant, fertile, flourishing, fructiferous, grown, high-growing, junglelike, lavish, lush, luxuriant, overabundant, overgrown, productive, profuse, prolific, rampant, rich, semitropical, tropical, vigorous, wild; CONCEPT 485 —*Ant.* rare, scarce, sparse

rank [*adj3*] *utter, absolute* arrant, blatant, capital, complete, conspicuous, consummate, downright, egregious, excessive, extravagant, flagrant, glaring, gross, noticeable, outright, outstanding, perfect, positive, rampant, sheer, thorough, total, undisguised, unmitigated; CONCEPTS 531,535 —*Ant.* indefinite

rank [*adj4*] *obscene, vulgar* abusive, atrocious, coarse, crass, dirty, filthy, foul, gross, indecent, nasty, outrageous, raunchy, scurrilous, shocking, smutty, wicked; CONCEPT 545 —*Ant.* clean, moral

rank [*n1*] *standing in a system, often a social one* ancestry, authority, birth, blood, cachet, capacity, caste, circumstance, class, classification, condition, consequence, degree, dignity, distinction, division, echelon, estate, esteem, family, footing, grade, hierarchy, level, nobility, note, order, paramountcy, parentage, pecking order, pedigree, place, position, primacy, privilege, quality, reputation, seniority, situation, slot, sort, sovereignty, sphere, state, station, stature, status, stock, stratum, supremacy, type; CONCEPTS 296,378,388,744

rank [*n2*] *column, tier of individuals* echelon, file, formation, group, hierarchy, line, queue, range, row, series, string; CONCEPT 727

rank [*v1*] *line up; classify in system* align, arrange, array, assign, assort, button down*, class, dispose, establish, estimate, evaluate, fix*, give precedence, grade, include, judge, list, locate, marshal, order, peg, pigeonhole*, place, place in formation, position, put, put away, put down as, put down for, put in line, range, rate, regard, settle, size up, sort, tab, typecast, valuate, value; CONCEPTS 37,84,158 —*Ant.* disorder, scatter

rank [*v2*] *be worthwhile; have supremacy* antecede, be classed, belong, be worth, come first, count among, forerun, go ahead of, go before, have the advantage, outrank, precede, stand, take the lead; CONCEPTS 388,671

rankle [*v*] *annoy, irritate* aggravate, anger, bother, chafe, embitter, exasperate, fester, fret, gall, get one's goat*, harass, hurt, inflame, irk, mortify, nettle, obsess, pain, pester, plague, rile, torment, vex; CONCEPTS 7,14,19 —*Ant.* delight, make happy, please

ransack [v] *turn inside out in search; ravage* appropriate, comb, despoil, explore, ferret, filch, go over with a fine-tooth comb*, go through, gut*, hunt, investigate, lay waste, leave no stone unturned*, lift, look all over for*, look high and low*, look into, loot, make off with*, maraud, overhaul, peer, pilfer, pillage, pinch, plunder, poach, probe, pry, purloin, raid, rake, rape, ravish, rifle, rob, rummage, rustle, sack, scan, scour, scrutinize, search, seek, seize, shake down*, sound, spoil, spy, steal, strip, take away, thieve; CONCEPTS 103, 139,142,216 —*Ant.* care for, clean, neaten, tidy

ransom [n] *blackmail money paid for return of possession or person* bribe, compensation, deliverance, expiation, liberation money, payment, payoff, price, redemption, release, rescue; CONCEPT 344

ransom [v] *pay blackmail money for return of possession or person* buy freedom of, buy out, deliver, emancipate, extricate, free, liberate, manumit, obtain release of, pay for release of, recover, redeem, regain, release, reprise, repurchase, rescue, save, set free, unchain, unfetter; CONCEPTS 127,131,341

rant [n] *yelling, raving* bluster, bombast, diatribe, fustian, harangue, oration, philippic, rhapsody, rhetoric, rodomontade, tirade, vociferation; CONCEPTS 44,49,52 —*Ant.* calm, quiet

rant [v] *yell, rave* bellow, bloviate, blow one's top*, bluster, carry on, clamor, cry, declaim, fume, harangue, mouth, objurgate, orate, perorate, rage, rail, roar, scold, shout, sizzle*, soapbox*, sound off*, spiel*, spout*, storm*, stump*, take on*, vociferate; CONCEPTS 44,49, 52 —*Ant.* be quiet

rap [n1/v1] *hit quickly and lightly* beat, blow, conk, crack, knock, lick, pat, strike, swat, swipe, tap, whack; CONCEPT 189

rap [n2] *conversation* causerie, chat, chin*, colloquy, confabulation, conference, deliberation, dialogue, discourse, discussion, prose, talk, ventilation, yarn; CONCEPTS 56,266 —*Ant.* silence

rap [n3] *blame; criticism* admonishment, admonition, censure, chiding, flak, knock, pan*, punishment, rebuke, reprimand, reproach, reproof, responsibility, sentence, swipe; CONCEPTS 52, 123,317 —*Ant.* approval, flattery, praise

rap [v2] *talk casually; speak abruptly* babble, bark, chat, chatter, chitchat, confabulate, converse, discourse, jabber, palaver, run off at the mouth*, spit, talk; CONCEPTS 56,266

rap [v3] *criticize* blame, castigate, censure, condemn, denounce, denunciate, knock*, pan*, reprehend, reprimand, reprobate, scold, skin, tick off*; CONCEPT 52 —*Ant.* praise

rapacious [adj] *plundering* avaricious, ferocious, furious, greedy, marauding, murderous, predatory, preying, ravening, ravenous, savage, voracious; CONCEPTS 326,403,406,542

rape [n] *defilement; a forced sexual assault* abduction, abuse, criminal attack, depredation, despoilment, despoliation, forcible violation, maltreatment, molestation, pillage, plunder,

plundering, rapine, spoliation, statutory offense, violation; CONCEPTS 192,375

rape [v] *sexual assault by force; act of plunder* abuse, attack, betray, compromise, corrupt, deceive, despoil, force, loot, molest, pillage, plunder, ransack, ruin, sack, seize, spoliate, violate; CONCEPTS 192,375

rapid [adj] *very quick* accelerated, active, agile, breakneck, brisk, double time, expeditious, expeditive, express, fast, fleet, fleet of foot*, flying, hasty, hurried, in nothing flat*, lightfooted*, like a house on fire*, lively, mercurial, nimble, on the double*, precipitate, prompt, quick as a wink*, quickened, ready, really rolling*, screaming*, speedy, spry, swift, winged; CONCEPTS 541,588,799 —*Ant.* languishing, leisurely, slack, slow

rapidity [n] *quickness* acceleration, alacrity, bat, briskness, celerity, dispatch, expedition, fleetness, gait, haste, hurry, pace, precipitateness, promptitude, promptness, rapidness, rush, speed, speediness, swiftness, velocity; CONCEPTS 755,805 —*Ant.* languidity, slowness

rapidly [adv] *very quickly* at speed, briskly, expeditiously, fast, flat out*, full tilt*, hastily, hurriedly, immediately, in a hurry, in a rush, in haste, lickety-split*, like a shot*, posthaste, precipitately, promptly, speedily, swiftly, with dispatch; CONCEPTS 544,588,799 —*Ant.* leisurely, slowly

rapport [n] *understanding between people* affinity, agreement, bond, compatibility, concord, cotton, empathy, good vibes*, good vibrations, groove, harmony, hitting it off*, interrelationship, link, relationship, same wavelength*, simpatico*, soul, sympathy, the groove*, togetherness, unity; CONCEPT 388 —*Ant.* coldness, unfriendliness

rapprochement [n] *restoration of harmony* agreement, cordiality, detente, friendliness, friendship, harmonization, harmony, reconcilement, reconciliation, reunion, softening; CONCEPTS 384,388 —*Ant.* disagreement, trouble, upset

rapt [adj] *absorbed, fascinated* absent, absentminded, abstracted, beguiled, bewitched, blissful, busy, captivated, carried away*, caught up in*, charmed, daydreaming, deep*, delighted, dreaming, ecstatic, employed, enamored, engaged, engrossed, enraptured, enthralled, entranced, gripped, happy, held, hung up*, hypnotized, immersed, inattentive, intent, involved, lost, oblivious, occupied, overwhelmed, preoccupied, rapturous, ravished, spellbound, taken*, transported, unconscious, wrapped*, wrapped up*; CONCEPT 403 —*Ant.* disenchanted, repulsed, turned off

rapture [n] *extreme happiness and delight in something* at-oneness*, beatitude, bliss, buoyancy, cheer, cloud nine*, communion, contentment, cool*, delectation, ecstasy, elation, elysium, enchantment, enjoyment, enthusiasm, euphoria, exaltation, exhilaration, felicity, gaiety, gladness, glory, good spirits, gratification, heaven, inspiration, joy, jubilation, nirvana, paradise, passion, pleasure, ravishment, rhapsody, satisfaction, seventh heaven*, spell, transport, well-being; CONCEPTS 32,410 —*Ant.* dislike, hate, hatred

rare [adj1] *exceptional, infrequent* attenuate, attenuated, deficient, extraordinary, few, few and far between*, flimsy, inconceivable, isolated, light, limited, occasional, out of the ordinary, rarefied, recherché, scanty, scarce, scattered, seldom, semioccasional, short, singular, sparse, sporadic, strange, subtile, subtle, tenuous, thin, uncommon, unfrequent, unheard of, unimaginable, unique, unlikely, unthinkable, unusual, unwonted; CONCEPTS 530,576 —Ant. common, frequent, regular, typical, usual

rare [adj2] *precious, excellent* admirable, choice, dainty, delicate, elegant, exquisite; extreme, fine, great, incomparable, invaluable, matchless, peerless, priceless, recherché, rich, select, superb, superlative, unique; CONCEPT 574 —Ant. cheap, ordinary, worthless

rare [adj3] *not fully cooked* bloody, half-cooked, half-raw, moderately done, nearly raw, not done, rarely done, red, undercooked, underdone; CONCEPT 462 —Ant. well-done

rarefied [adj] *exclusive* cliquish, elevated, esoteric, exalted, lofty, private, select; CONCEPT 554 —Ant. commonplace

rarely [adv] *not often; exceptionally* almost never, barely, extra, extraordinarily, extremely, finely, hardly, hardly ever, infrequently, little, notably, now and then, once in a while, once in blue moon*, on rare occasions, remarkably, scarcely ever, seldom, singularly, uncommon, uncommonly, unfrequently, unoften, unusually; CONCEPTS 530,541 —Ant. frequently, regularly

raring [adj] *eager* champing at the bit*, enthusiastic, itching*, keen, longing, ready, willing; CONCEPT 401 —Ant. reluctant

rascal [n] *person who is unprincipled, does not work hard* beggar, blackguard, black sheep*, bully, bum, cad, cardsharp*, charlatan, cheat, delinquent, devil, disgrace, felon, fraud, good-for-nothing*, grafter, hooligan*, hypocrite, idler, imp, liar, loafer, mischief-maker, miscreant, opportunist, pretender, prodigal, profligate, recreant, reprobate, robber, rowdy, ruffian, scamp, scoundrel, sinner, skunk*, sneak*, swindler, tough*, tramp, trickster, varmint*, villain, wastrel, wretch; CONCEPT 412

rash [adj] *careless, impulsive* adventurous, audacious, bold, brash, daring, determined, devil-may-care*, fiery, foolhardy, frenzied, furious, harebrained, hasty, headlong, headstrong, heedless, hotheaded, ill-advised, ill-considered, immature, impetuous, imprudent, incautious, indiscreet, injudicious, insuppressible, irrational, jumping to conclusions*, madcap, overhasty, passionate, precipitant, precipitate, premature, reckless, thoughtless, unguarded, unthinking, unwary, venturesome, venturous, wild; CONCEPT 401 —Ant. careful, cautious, planned, thoughtful

rash [n] *outbreak of disease or condition* breakout, epidemic, eruption, flood, hives, pandemic, plague, series, spate, succession, wave; CONCEPTS 230,306

rasp [v] *grind, rub* abrade, bray, excoriate, file, grate, irk, irritate, jar, pound, raze, rub, sand, scour, scrape, scratch, vex, wear; CONCEPTS 7,19

raspy [adj] *rough* cracked, croaky, dry, grating, gravelly, gruff, harsh, hoarse, husky, scratchy, thick, throaty; CONCEPT 594

rat [n] *informer* backstabber, betrayer, blabbermouth*, canary*, deep throat*, double-crosser, fink, informant, sneak, snitch, source, squealer, stoolie, stool pigeon*, tattler, tattletale, turncoat, whistle-blower; CONCEPTS 348,354,423

rate [n1] *ratio, proportion* amount, comparison, degree, estimate, percentage, progression, quota, relation, relationship, relative, scale, standard, weight; CONCEPT 768 —Ant. whole

rate [n2] *fee charged for service, privilege, goods* allowance, charge, cost, dues, duty, estimate, figure, hire, price, price tag, quotation, tab, tariff, tax, toll, valuation; CONCEPTS 329,766

rate [n3] *speed, pace* clip, dash, flow, gait, gallop, hop, measure, motion, movement, pace, spurt, tempo, time, tread, velocity; CONCEPT 755

rate [v1] *judge, classify* adjudge, admire, appraise, apprise, assay, assess, button down*, calculate, class, consider, count, deem, determine, esteem, estimate, evaluate, fix, grade, guess at, measure, peg, pigeonhole*, price, put away, put down as*, put down for*, rank, reckon, redline*, regard, relate to standard, respect, score, set at, size up*, stand in with, survey, tab*, tag, take one's measure, think highly of, typecast*, valuate, value, weigh; CONCEPTS 12,37

rate [v2] *be entitled to* be accepted, be favorite, be welcome, be worthy, deserve, earn, merit, prosper, succeed, triumph; CONCEPTS 129,376,388 —Ant. disqualify

rather [adv1] *moderately* a bit, a little, averagely, comparatively, enough, fairly, in a certain degree, kind of, more or less, passably, pretty, quite, ratherish, reasonably, relatively, slightly, some, something, somewhat, sort of, so-so*, tolerably, to some degree, to some extent; CONCEPTS 544,548 —Ant. extremely, violently

rather [adv2] *significantly* a good bit, considerably, noticeably, quite, somewhat, very, well; CONCEPTS 544,772 —Ant. insignificantly, little

rather [adv3] *preferably; instead* alternately, alternatively, as a matter of choice, by choice, by preference, first, in lieu of, in preference, just as soon, more readily, more willingly, much sooner, sooner, willingly; CONCEPT 529

ratify [v] *affirm, authorize* accredit, approve, authenticate, bear out, bind, bless, certify, commission, confirm, consent, corroborate, endorse, establish, give stamp of approval*, go for*, license, okay*, rubber stamp*, sanction, sign, substantiate, uphold, validate; CONCEPTS 50,88 —Ant. deny, disaffirm, disagree, renounce, revoke, veto

rating [n] *grade* appraisal, assessment, category, class, classification, degree, judgment, level, mark, order, rank, score, standard, tier, valuation; CONCEPTS 286,378,665,727,744

ratio [n] *percentage, relation of part to whole* arrangement, correlation, correspondence, equation, fraction, proportion, proportionality, quota, quotient, rate, relationship, scale; CONCEPT 768 —Ant. whole

ration [n] *allotment of limited supply* allowance, apportionment, assignment, bit, consignment, cut, distribution, division, dole, drag, food, helping, measure, meed, part, piece of action*, portion, provender, provision, quantum, quota, share, store, supply; CONCEPT 835 —Ant. whole

ra
ra

ration [v] *divide something into portions* allocate, allot, apportion, assign, budget, conserve, control, deal, distribute, divvy*, divvy up*, dole, give out, issue, limit, measure out, mete, mete out, parcel, parcel out, proportion, prorate, quota, restrict, save, share; CONCEPTS *98,140* —*Ant.* collect, gather

rational [adj] *realistic; of sound mind* all there*, analytical, balanced, calm, cerebral, circumspect, cognitive, collected, cool*, deductive, deliberate, discerning, discriminating, enlightened, far-sighted, impartial, intellectual, intelligent, judicious, knowing, levelheaded, logical, lucid, normal, objective, perspicacious, philosophic, prudent, ratiocinative, reasonable, reasoning, reflective, sagacious, sane, sensible, sober, sound, stable, synthetic, thinking, thoughtful, together, well-advised, wise; CONCEPT *402* —*Ant.* irrational, ridiculous, unrealistic, unreasonable, unsound

rationale [n] *logic for belief, action* account, excuse, explanation, exposition, grounds, hypothesis, justification, motivation, motive, philosophy, principle, raison d'être, rationalization, reason, reasons, song and dance*, sour grapes*, story*, the big idea*, theory, the whole idea*, whatfor*, why and wherefore*, whyfor*; CONCEPT *661*

rationalize [v] *make excuse; justify* account for, apply logic, cop a plea*, cop out*, deliberate, elucidate, excise, excuse, explain away, extenuate, give alibi*, intellectualize, justify, make allowance, reason, reason out, reconcile, resolve, think, think through, vindicate; CONCEPT *57*

rattle [v1] *bang, jiggle* bicker, bounce, clack, clatter, drum, jangle, jar, jolt, jounce, knock, shake, shatter, sound, vibrate; CONCEPTS *65,152*

rattle [v2] *talk aimlessly, endlessly* babble, cackle, chat, chatter, clack, gab, gabble, gush, jabber, jaw, list, prate, prattle, reel off, run on, run through, yak; CONCEPT *51*

rattle [v3] *disconcert, upset someone* abash, addle, bewilder, bother, confound, confuse, discombobulate, discomfit, discompose, discountenance, distract, disturb, embarrass, faze, flummox, frighten, get to*, muddle, nonplus, perplex, perturb, psych out*, put off, put out, put out of countenance, rattle one's cage*, scare, shake, throw, unnerve; CONCEPT *16* —*Ant.* appease, placate, soothe

raucous [adj1] *noisy, rough* absonant, acute, atonal, blaring, blatant, braying, brusque, cacophonous, discordant, dissonant, dry, ear-piercing, grating, grinding, gruff, harsh, hoarse, husky, inharmonious, jarring, loud, piercing, rasping, sharp, squawking, stertorous, strident, thick, unharmonious, unmusical; CONCEPTS *592,594* —*Ant.* calm, quiet, soft, subdued

raucous [adj2] *rowdy* boisterous, disorderly, intemperate, rambunctious, tumultuous/tumultuous, turbulent, unruly; CONCEPT *401* —*Ant.* calm, quiet, subdued

raunchy [adj] *lewd, obscene* bawdy, dirty, erotic, filthy*, foul-mouthed, gross*, hard-core*, improper, in bad taste, lascivious, lecherous, lustful, naughty, off-color*, pornographic, racy*, risqué, sexually explicit, smutty, suggestive, taboo, vulgar, wicked, X-rated*; CONCEPTS *372,542,545*

ravage [v] *destroy, ransack* annihilate, break up, capture, consume, cream*, crush, damage, demolish, desecrate, desolate, despoil, devastate, dismantle, disorganize, disrupt, exterminate, extinguish, forage, foray, gut, harry, impair, lay waste, leave in ruins, loot, overrun, overthrow, overwhelm, pillage, pirate, plunder, prey, prostrate, pull down, raid, rape, raze, rob, ruin, sack, seize, shatter, sink, smash, spoil, spoliate, stamp out, strip, sweep away, total*, trample, trash, waste, wreak havoc, wreck, wrest; CONCEPTS *86, 252* —*Ant.* aid, assist, help, protect

rave [v1] *talk endlessly* babble, be delirious, bloviate, blow one's top*, carry on*, come unglued*, declaim, flip one's lid*, freak out*, fume, gabble, go ape*, go bananas*, go crazy, go mad, harangue, jabber, make a to-do*, mouth, orate, perorate, prate, prattle, rage, rail, rant, rattle on, roar, run amuck*, splutter, storm, talk wildly, thunder, wander; CONCEPTS *51,54*

rave [v2] *be very enthusiastic* be delighted, be excited, be mad about, be wild about, bubble*, carry on about*, cry up*, effervesce, enthuse, fall all over*, go on about*, gush, make a to-do*, praise, rhapsodize; CONCEPTS *49,410* —*Ant.* denounce, discourage

ravel [v] *come apart; unwind* disentangle, free, loosen, reel, smooth out, unbraid, unravel, unsnarl, untangle, untwine, untwist, unweave, unwind, weave out; CONCEPTS *250, 469* —*Ant.* put together, twist

ravenous [adj] *very hungry; desirous* avaricious, could eat a horse*, covetous, devouring, edacious, empty, famished, ferocious, gluttonous, grasping, greedy, insatiable, insatiate, omnivorous, predatory, rapacious, ravening, starved, starved to death*, starving, voracious, wolfish; CONCEPT *406* —*Ant.* full, satisfied

ravine [n] *gap in earth's surface* abyss, arroyo, break, canyon, chasm, clove, coulee, crevasse, crevice, cut, defile, ditch, fissure, flume, gorge, gulch, gulf, gully, notch, pass, valley, wash; CONCEPTS *509,513* —*Ant.* plain

ravish [v1] *enchant* allure, attract, bewitch, captivate, charm, delight, draw, enrapture, enthrall, entrance, fascinate, hold, hypnotize, magnetize, mesmerize, overjoy, please, spellbind, trance, transport; CONCEPT *11* —*Ant.* disenchant, repulse, turn off

ravish [v2] *sexually assault* abduct, abuse, force, rape, violate; CONCEPTS *192,375*

ravishing [adj] *attractive* adorable, alluring, appealing, beautiful, bewitching, captivating, charming, dazzling, enchanting, enticing, glamorous, good-looking, gorgeous, handsome, inviting, lovely, luring, pleasing, pretty, radiant, seductive, stunning, tantalizing; CONCEPTS *529,579*

raw [adj1] *not cooked, prepared* basic, bloody, callow, coarse, crude, fibrous, fresh, green, hard, immature, impure, native, natural, organic, rough, rough-hewn, rude, unbaked, uncooked, undercooked, underdone, undressed, unfashioned, unformed, unfried, ungraded, unpasteurized, unprepared, unprocessed, unrefined, unripe, unsorted, unstained, untreated; CONCEPT *462* —*Ant.* cooked, done, well-done

raw [adj2] *exposed, tender, referring to skin* abraded, au naturel, blistered, bruised, chafed, cut, dressed, galled, grazed, naked, nude, open, pared, peeled, scraped, scratched, sensitive, skinned, sore, unclad, unclothed, uncovered, wounded; CONCEPTS *406,485* —*Ant.* healed, healthy

raw [adj3] *inexperienced* callow, fresh, green, ignorant, immature, inexperienced, new, unconversant, undisciplined, unpracticed, unseasoned, unskilled, untaught, untrained, untried, unversed, young; CONCEPT *527* —*Ant.* experienced, sophisticated

raw [adj4] *vulgar, nasty* coarse, crass, crude, dirty, filthy, foul, gross, indecent, inelegant, low, mean, obscene, pornographic, rank, rough, rude, smutty, uncouth, unrefined, unscrupulous; CONCEPTS *372,545* —*Ant.* clean, good, moral

raw [adj5] *harsh, unpleasant, referring to weather* biting, bitter, bleak, breezy, chill, chilly, cold, damp, freezing, piercing, wet, wind-swept, windy; CONCEPT *525* —*Ant.* clement, pleasant, warm

ray [n] *beam; indication* bar, blaze, blink, emanation, flash, flicker, gleam, glimmer, glint, glitter, hint, incandescence, irradiation, light, moonbeam, patch, pencil, radiance, radiation, scintilla, shaft, shine, spark, sparkle, streak, stream, sunbeam, trace, wave; CONCEPTS *624, 628*

raze [v] *flatten, knock down; wipe out* batter, blow down, bomb, break down, bulldoze, capsize, cast down, crash, decimate, delete, demolish, destroy, dynamite, efface, erase, expunge, extinguish, extirpate, fell, level, mow down, obliterate, overthrow, overturn, pull down, reduce, remove, rub out*, ruin, scatter, scratch out, smash, spill, strike out, subvert, tear down, tear up, throw down, topple, total, unbuild, undo, unmake, upset, wipe out, wrack, wreck, zap*; CONCEPT *252* —*Ant.* build, construct

reach [n] *extent, range; stretch* ability, ambit, capacity, command, compass, distance, extension, gamut, grasp, horizon, influence, jurisdiction, ken, latitude, magnitude, mastery, orbit, play, power, purview, radius, scope, spread, sweep, swing; CONCEPTS *651,756* —*Ant.* limitation

reach [v1] *arrive at* arrive, attain, catch up to, check in, clock in*, come, come to, enter, gain on*, get as far as, get in, get to, hit, hit town*, land, make, make it, make the scene*, overtake, ring in*, roll in, show, show up, sign in, turn up, wind up at; CONCEPT *159* —*Ant.* depart, go, leave

reach [v2] *stretch to; touch* approach, attain, buck, carry to, come at, come up to, contact, continue to, encompass, end, equal, extend to, feel for, get a hold of, get hold of, get to, go, go as far as, go on, go to, grasp, hand, hold out, join, lead, lunge, make, make contact with, overtake, pass, pass along, put out, roll on, seize, shake hands, shoot, span, spread, stand, strain, strike; CONCEPTS *108,612,756*

reach [v3] *attain; rise* accomplish, achieve, amount to, arrive at, climb to, come to, drop, fall, gain, move, rack up*, realize, score, sink, win; CONCEPTS *706,763,780* —*Ant.* fail, lose

reach [v4] *communicate with* affect, approach, contact, get, get in touch, get through, get to,

influence, keep in contact, keep in touch, maintain, move, sway, touch; CONCEPTS *7,19, 22,266* —*Ant.* miss

react [v] *respond; conduct oneself* acknowledge, act, answer, answer back, backfire, be affected, behave, boomerang*, bounce back*, counter, echo, feel, function, get back at, give a snappy comeback*, give back, have a funny feeling*, have vibes*, operate, perform, proceed, rebound, reciprocate, recoil, recur, reply, return, revert, talk, talk back, turn back, work; CONCEPTS *45,633*

reaction [n1] *response* acknowledgment, answer, attitude, backfire, backlash, back talk*, boomerang*, comeback, compensation, counteraction, counterbalance, counterpoise, double-take*, echo, feedback, feeling, hit, kick, kickback, knee-jerk*, lip*, opinion, reagency, rebound, reception, receptivity, reciprocation, recoil, reflection, reflex, rejoinder, repercussion, reply, retort, return, reverberation, revulsion, sass*, snappy comeback*, take*, vibes*, wise-crack; CONCEPTS *45,633* —*Ant.* cause, question

reaction [n2] *political conservatism* backlash, backsliding, counterrevolution, obscurantism, regression, relapse, retreat, retrenchment, retrogression, right, right wing, status quo, Toryism, withdrawal; CONCEPTS *300,689*

reactionary [adj] *conservative* counterrevolutionary, die-hard*, obscurantist, old-line*, orthodox, regressive, retrogressive, right, rightist*, rigid, standpat*, tory*, traditional, traditionalistic; CONCEPTS *529,542* —*Ant.* liberal, progressive, radical

reactionary [n] *person who is politically conservative* bitter-ender*, counterrevolutionary, diehard*, hard hat*, intransigent, obscurantist, reactionist, rightist*, right-winger, royalist, standpatter*, Tory*, traditionalist, ultraconservative; CONCEPT *359* —*Ant.* liberal, progressive, radical

read [v1] *look at and understand written word* apprehend, bury oneself in*, comprehend, construe, decipher, dip into*, discover, flip through*, gather, glance, go over, go through, interpret, know, leaf through*, learn, make out*, perceive, peruse, pore over*, refer to, scan, scratch the surface*, see, skim, study, translate, unravel, view; CONCEPT *72* —*Ant.* write

read [v2] *express, state* affirm, announce, assert, declaim, deliver, display, explain, expound, hold, indicate, mark, paraphrase, pronounce, recite, record, register, render, restate, say, show, speak, utter; CONCEPT *266*

readable [adj1] *understandable, legible* clear, coherent, comprehensible, decipherable, distinct, explicit, flowing, fluent, graphic, intelligible, lucid, orderly, plain, precise, regular, simple, smooth, straightforward, tidy, unequivocal, unmistakable; CONCEPTS *272,529* —*Ant.* illegible, unintelligible, unreadable

readable [adj2] *pleasurable to peruse* absorbing, amusing, appealing, brilliant, clever, easy, eloquent, engaging, engrossing, enjoyable, entertaining, enthralling, exciting, fascinating, gratifying, gripping, ingenious, interesting, inviting, pleasant, pleasing, relaxing, rewarding, satisfying, smooth, stimulating, well-written, worthwhile; CONCEPT *272* —*Ant.* disgusting

ra
re

readily [adv] *quickly; effortlessly* at once, at the drop of a hat*, cheerfully, eagerly, easily, facilely, freely, gladly, hands down*, immediately, in a jiffy*, in no time*, lightly, no sweat*, nothing to it*, piece of cake*, promptly, quick as a wink*, right away, slick as whistle*, smoothly, speedily, straight away, swimmingly, unhesitatingly, well, willingly, without delay, without demur, without difficulty, without hesitation; CONCEPTS 544,820 —*Ant.* unwillingly

readiness [n] *skill; eagerness* address, adroitness, alacrity, aptness, deftness, dexterity, dispatch, ease, eloquence, expedience, expedition, facility, fitness, fluency, good will, handiness, inclination, keenness, maturity, preparation, preparedness, promptitude, promptness, prowess, quickness, rapidity, ripeness, sleight, volubility, willingness; CONCEPTS 630,633,678 —*Ant.* discouragement, unpreparedness

reading [n] *interpretation of written word* account, book-learning, commentary, conception, construction, edification, education, erudition, examination, grasp, impression, inspection, knowledge, learning, lesson, paraphrase, perusal, rendering, rendition, review, scholarship, scrutiny, study, translation, treatment, understanding, version; CONCEPTS 72,271,274 —*Ant.* writing

ready [adj1] *prepared; available* accessible, adjusted, all set, all systems go*, anticipating, apt, arranged, at beck and call*, at fingertips*, at hand, at the ready, champing at bit*, close to hand, completed, convenient, covered, equal to, equipped, expectant, fit, fixed for, handy, in line, in order, in place, in position, in readiness, in the saddle*, near, on call, on hand, on tap*, on the brink*, open to, organized, primed, qualified, ripe, set, waiting, wired*; CONCEPTS 560,576,799 —*Ant.* immature, slow, unavailable, unprepared, unready, unripe, unsuitable

ready [adj2] *willing, inclined* agreeable, apt, ardent, disposed, eager, enthusiastic, fain, game, game for, glad, happy, keen, minded, predisposed, prompt, prone, psyched up*, wired*, zealous; CONCEPTS 401,542 —*Ant.* disinclined, unprepared, unwilling

ready [adj3] *skillful, intelligent* active, acute, adept, adroit, alert, apt, astute, bright, brilliant, clever, deft, dexterous, dynamic, expert, handy, keen, live, masterly, perceptive, proficient, prompt, quick, quick-witted, rapid, resourceful, sharp, skilled, smart; CONCEPTS 402,527 —*Ant.* immature, slow, uneducated, unprepared, unskilled, untrained

ready [v] *prepare* arrange, brace, brief, clear the decks*, equip, fill in, fit, fit out, fix, fortify, gear up*, get, get ready, get set, gird, keep posted*, let in on*, make, make ready, make up, order, organize, pave the way*, post, prep, provide, psych up*, put on to*, set, strengthen, warm up, wise up*; CONCEPTS 35,60,202 —*Ant.* hold back, retard, slow

real [adj] *genuine in existence* absolute, actual, authentic, bodily, bona fide, certain, concrete, corporal, corporeal, de facto, embodied, essential, evident, existent, existing, factual, firm, heartfelt, honest, incarnate, indubitable, in the flesh*, intrinsic, irrefutable, legitimate, live, material, original, palpable, perceptible,

physical, positive, present, right, rightful, sensible, sincere, solid, sound, stable, substantial, substantive, tangible, true, unaffected, undeniable, undoubted, unfeigned, valid, veritable; CONCEPT 582 —*Ant.* dishonest, fake, false, feigned, imaginary, invalid, untrue

realistic [adj1] *sensible, matter-of-fact* astute, businesslike, commonsense, down-to-earth, earthy, hard, hard-boiled*, levelheaded, practical, pragmatic, pragmatical, prudent, rational, real, reasonable, sane, sensible, shrewd, sober, sound, unfantastic, unidealistic, unromantic, unsentimental, utilitarian; CONCEPTS 403,542, 548 —*Ant.* impractical, irrational, unrealistic

realistic [adj2] *genuine* authentic, faithful, graphic, lifelike, natural, original, representational, representative, true, true to life, truthful; CONCEPT 582 —*Ant.* fanciful, insincere

reality [n] *facts of existence* absoluteness, actuality, authenticity, being, bottom line*, brass tacks*, certainty, concreteness, corporeality, deed, entity, existence, genuineness, how things are*, like it is*, materiality, matter, name of the game*, nuts and bolts*, object, palpability, perceptibility, phenomenon, presence, realism, realness, real world*, sensibility, solidity, substance, substantiality, substantive, tangibility, truth, validity, verisimilitude, verity, way of it*, what's what*; CONCEPTS 689,725 —*Ant.* belief, fantasy, hypothesis, imagination, theory

realize [v1] *appreciate, become aware of* apprehend, be cognizant of, become conscious of, catch, catch on*, comprehend, conceive, discern, envisage, envision, fancy*, feature*, get, get it*, get the idea*, get the picture*, get through one's head*, grasp, image, imagine, know, pick up*, recognize, see daylight*, take in*, think, understand, vision, visualize; CONCEPT 15 —*Ant.* ignore, neglect

realize [v2] *accomplish* actualize, bring about, bring off*, bring to fruition, carry out, carry through, complete, consummate, corporealize, do, effect, effectuate, fulfill, make concrete, make good*, make happen, materialize, perfect, perform, reify; CONCEPT 91 —*Ant.* fail

realize [v3] *gain, earn* accomplish, achieve, acquire, attain, bring in, clear, get, go for*, make, make a profit, net, obtain, produce, rack up*, reach, receive, score*, sell for, take in, win; CONCEPTS 120,124,330 —*Ant.* lose

really [adv] *without a doubt* absolutely, actually, admittedly, as a matter of fact, assuredly, authentically, beyond doubt, categorically, certainly, de facto, easily, for real*, genuinely, honestly, in actuality, indeed, indubitably, in effect, in fact, in point of fact, in reality, legitimately, literally, no ifs ands or buts*, nothing else but, of course, positively, precisely, surely, truly, undoubtedly, unmistakably, unquestionably, verily, well; CONCEPTS 535, 582 —*Ant.* doubtfully

realm [n] *area of responsibility or rule* branch, compass, country, department, dimension, domain, dominion, empire, expanse, extent, field, ground, kingdom, land, monarchy, neck of the woods*, neighborhood, orbit, place, principality, province, purview, radius, range, reach, region, scope, sphere, state, stomping grounds*, sweep, territory, turf*, world, zone; CONCEPTS 349,362,512,651

reap [v] *collect, harvest* acquire, bring in, come to have, crop, cull, cut, derive, draw, gain, garner, gather, get, get as a result, glean, ingather, mow, obtain, pick, pick up, pluck, procure, produce, profit, realize, receive, recover, retrieve, secure, strip, take in, win; CONCEPTS 109,120,124,257 —Ant. plant, sow

rear [adj] *back, end* aft, after, astern, backward, behind, dorsal, following, hind, hinder, hindermost, hindmost, last, mizzen, posterior, postern, rearmost, rearward, retral, reverse, stern, tail; CONCEPT 583 —Ant. beginning, front

rear [n] *back or end part* afterpart, back, back door*, back end, back seat*, backside, behind, bottom, butt, buttocks, end, heel, hind, hind part, hindquarters, posterior, postern, rear end, rear guard, rearward, reverse, rump, seat, stern, tail, tail end, tailpiece, tush*; CONCEPTS 825, 827 —Ant. beginning, front

rear [v1] *raise young* breed, bring up, care for, cultivate, educate, foster, grow, nurse, nurture, propagate, train; CONCEPT 295 —Ant. abandon, neglect

rear [v2] *lift, rise* bring up, elevate, hoist, hold up, jump, leap, loom, pick up, raise, set upright, soar, spring up, support, take up, tower, turn up, uphold, uplift, upraise; CONCEPTS 194,196,741 —Ant. drop, fall

rear [v3] *build* construct, erect, fabricate, put up, raise, set up, uprear; CONCEPT 168 —Ant. destroy

reason [n1] *mental analysis* acumen, apprehension, argumentation, bounds, brain*, brains*, comprehension, deduction, dialectics, discernment, generalization, induction, inference, intellect, intellection, judgment, limits, logic, lucidity, marbles*, mentality, mind, moderation, propriety, ratiocination, rationalism, rationality, rationalization, reasonableness, reasoning, saneness, sanity, sense, senses*, sensibleness, sound mind, soundness, speculation, understanding, wisdom, wit; CONCEPTS 37,409

reason [n2] *intention, aim* antecedent, argument, basis, cause, consideration, design, determinant, end, goal, grounds, idea, impetus, incentive, inducement, motivation, motive, object, occasion, proof, purpose, rationale, root, spring, target, ulterior motive, warrant, wherefore*, why, why and wherefore*, whyfor*; CONCEPT 659

reason [n3] *explanation for an action* account, apologia, apology, argument, case, cover, defense, excuse, exposition, ground, idea, justification, notion, proof, rationale, rationalization, song and dance*, sour grapes*, the whole idea*, vindication, whatfor*, wherefore*, why*, why and wherefore*, whyfor*; CONCEPT 661

reason [v1] *mentally analyze* adduce, cerebrate, cogitate, conclude, contemplate, decide, deduce, deduct, deliberate, draw conclusion, draw from, examine, figure out, gather, generalize, infer, make out, philosophize, ratiocinate, rationalize, reflect, resolve, solve, speculate, study, suppose, syllogize, think, think through, thresh out, work out; CONCEPT 37

reason [v2] *argue, persuade* bring around, contend, debate, demonstrate, discourse, discuss, dispute, dissuade, establish, expostulate, justify, move, point out, prevail upon, prove, remonstrate, show error of ways*, talk into, talk out of, urge, win over; CONCEPTS 46,56,68 —Ant. agree, go along

reasonable [adj1] *moderate, tolerable* acceptable, analytical, average, cheap, circumspect, conservative, controlled, discreet, equitable, fair, feasible, fit, honest, humane, impartial, inexpensive, judicious, just, justifiable, knowing, legit, legitimate, low-cost, low-priced, making sense, modest, objective, okay, plausible, politic, proper, prudent, rational, reflective, restrained, right, sane, sapient, sensible, sound, standing to reason*, temperate, understandable, unexcessive, unextreme, valid, within reason; CONCEPTS 547,558 —Ant. expensive, intolerable, outrageous, unreasonable

reasonable [adj2] *intelligent, practical* advisable, all there*, arguable, believable, cerebral, clear-cut, cognitive, commonsensical, conscious, consequent, consistent, cool*, credible, in one's right mind*, judicious, justifiable, levelheaded, logical, perceiving, percipient, plausible, ratiocinative, rational, reasoned, reasoning, reflective, sane, sensible, sober, sound, tenable, thoughtful, thought-out, together*, tolerant, unbiased, unprejudiced, well-advised, wise; CONCEPT 402 —Ant. implausible, impractical, nonsensical, stupid, unreasonable

reasoning [n] *logic, interpretation* acumen, analysis, apriority, argument, case, cogitation, concluding, corollary, deduction, dialectics, exposition, generalization, hypothesis, illation, induction, inference, interpretation, logistics, premise, proof, proposition, ratiocination, rationale, rationalizing, reason, syllogism, syllogization, thinking, thought, train of thought; CONCEPTS 37,529 —Ant. irrationality, nonsense

reassure [v] *restore confidence to* assure, bolster, brace, buoy, cheer, comfort, console, convince, encourage, give a lift*, give confidence, guarantee, hearten, inspire, inspirit, perk up, pick up*, put one's mind to rest*, relieve, snap one out of it*; CONCEPTS 7,22 —Ant. discourage, dishearten, unnerve

rebate [n] *refund given to purchaser* abatement, allowance, bonus, deduction, discount, kickback, payback, reduction, reimbursement, remission, repayment, subtraction; CONCEPT 344

rebel [adj] *not obeying* insubordinate, insurgent, insurrectionary, mutinous, rebellious, revolutionary; CONCEPT 401 —Ant. complaisant, compliant, obedient

rebel [n] *person who does not obey* agitator, anarchist, antagonist, apostate, demagogue, deserter, disectarian, dissenter, experientialist, experimenter, frondeur, guerrilla, heretic, iconoclast, independent, individualist, innovator, insurgent, insurrectionary, malcontent, mutineer, nihilist, nonconformist, opponent, overthrower, recreant, renegade, resistance, revolter, revolutionary, revolutionist, rioter, schismatic, secessionist, seditionist, separatist, subverter, traitor, turncoat; CONCEPTS 359,412,423

rebel [v] *refuse to obey* be insubordinate, boycott, break with*, censure, combat, come out against*, criticize, defy, denounce, disobey, dissent, drop out*, fight, get out of line*, insurrect, make waves*, mutiny, oppose, opt out*, overthrow, overturn, remonstrate, renounce, resist, revolt, riot, rise up*, rock the boat*, run amok*, secede, strike, take up arms, turn against, upset; CONCEPTS 106,633 —*Ant.* agree, comply, obey

rebellion [n] *disobedience; revolt* apostasy, defiance, disobedience, dissent, heresy, insubordination, insurgence, insurgency, insurrection, nonconformity, revolution, rising, schism, uprising; CONCEPTS 106,300, 320,633 —*Ant.* calm, harmony, peace

rebellious [adj] *disobedient, unmanageable* alienated, anarchistic, attacking, bellicose, contumacious, defiant, difficult, disaffected, disloyal, disobedient, disorderly, dissident, factious, fractious, iconoclastic, incorrigible, individualistic, insurgent, insurrectionary, intractable, mutinous, obstinate, pugnacious, quarrelsome, radical, rebel, recalcitrant, refractory, resistant, restless, revolutionary, rioting, riotous, sabotaging, seditious, threatening, treasonable, turbulent, ungovernable, unruly, warring; CONCEPTS 401,529,542 —*Ant.* compliant, governable, manageable, obedient

rebound [v] *bounce back; ricochet* backfire, boomerang, convalesce, get back on one's feet*, get better, get in shape, get well, heal, kick back, make a comeback*, mend, overcome, pick up, pull through, rally, recoil, recuperate, regain one's health, rejuvenate*, return, return to form, revive, snap back*, spring back, start anew; CONCEPTS 150,194,195,303,700

rebuff [n] *turning away; ignoring* brushoff*, check, cold shoulder*, cut, defeat, denial, discouragement, go-by*, hard time*, insult, kick in the teeth*, nix*, nothing doing*, opposition, rebuke, refusal, rejection, reprimand, repulse, slight, snub, thumbs down*, turndown; CONCEPTS 30,278 —*Ant.* inclusion, welcome

rebuff [v] *turn away; give the cold shoulder* beat off, brush off, check, chide, cross, cut, decline, deny, disallow, discourage, dismiss, disregard, fend off, hold off, ignore, keep at a distance*, keep at arm's length*, keep at bay, lash out at, neglect, not hear of, oppose, pass up, push back, put in one's place*, put off, rebuke, refuse, reject, repel, reprove, repudiate, repulse, resist, send away, slight, snub, spurn, stave off, tell off*, turn down, ward off; CONCEPTS 30,54 —*Ant.* hug, include, take in, welcome

rebuke [n] *reprimand; harsh criticism* admonishment, admonition, affliction, bawling-out*, berating, blame, castigation, censure, chewing-out*, chiding, comeuppance, condemnation, correction, disapproval, dressing-down*, earful*, expostulation, going-over*, hard time*, kick in the teeth*, lecture, lesson, objurgation, ostracism, punishment, put-down*, rap*, rating, rebuff, refusal, remonstrance, reprehension, reproach, reproof, reproval, repulse, row, scolding, slap in the face*, snub, talking-to*, telling-off*, tongue-lashing*, upbraiding; CONCEPTS 44,52,278 —*Ant.* compliment, flattery, praise

rebuke [v] *reprimand; criticize harshly* admonish, bawl out*, berate, blame, call on the carpet*, carp on, castigate, censure, chew out*, chide, climb all over*, dress down*, fry*, go after*, jawbone*, jump down one's throat*, jump on*, lay into*, lean on*, lecture, lesson,

monish, oppose, pay, rake, read*, reprehend, reprimand, reproach, reprove, rip*, scold, sit on*, sound off*, take to task*, tear apart*, tell off*, tick off*, upbraid, zap*; CONCEPTS 44,52 —*Ant.* compliment, flatter, praise

rebut [v] *argue against; prove wrong* break, come back at, confound, confute, controvert, cross, defeat, deny, disconfirm, disprove, evert, fend off, get back at, hold off, invalidate, keep off, negate, negative, overturn, prove false, quash, refute, repel, repulse, stave off, take on, top, ward off; CONCEPTS 46,54 —*Ant.* agree, approve, back down, concede

rebuttal [n] *counterstatement* answer, confutation, counteraccusation, counterargument, countercharge, counterclaim, defense, rejoinder, reply; CONCEPTS 274,278

recalcitrant [adj] *disobedient, uncontrollable* contrary, contumacious, defiant, fractious, indomitable, insubmissive, insubordinate, intractable, obstinate, opposing, radical, rebellious, refractory, resistant, resisting, stubborn, undisciplinable, undisciplined, ungovernable, unmanageable, unruly, untoward, unwilling, wayward, wild, willful, withstanding; CONCEPT 401 —*Ant.* amenable, obedient, passive

recall [n1] *remembrance* anamnesis, memory, recollection, reminiscence; CONCEPT 529 —*Ant.* forgetfulness

recall [n2] *request for return* annulment, cancellation, nullification, recision, repeal, rescindment, rescission, retraction, revocation, withdrawal; CONCEPTS 662,685 —*Ant.* restoration

recall [v1] *remember* arouse, awaken, bethink, bring to mind, call to mind, call up, cite, come to one, educe, elicit, evoke, extract, flash, flash on*, look back, mind, nail it down*, recollect, reestablish, reinstate, reintroduce, remind, reminisce, renew, retain, retrospect, revive, ring a bell*, rouse, stir, strike a note*, summon, think back*, think of, waken; CONCEPT 40 —*Ant.* forget

recall [v2] *ask for return of offending thing* abjure, annul, call back, call in, cancel, countermand, discharge, dismantle, dismiss, disqualify, forswear, lift, nullify, palinode, recant, repeal, rescind, retract, reverse, revoke, suspend, take back, unsay, withdraw; CONCEPTS 50,88,131, 143 —*Ant.* restore

recant [v] *take back something said* abjure, abnegate, abrogate, annul, apostatize, back down, back off, back out, backtrack*, call back, cancel, contradict, countermand, deny, disavow, disclaim, disown, eat one's words*, forswear, go back on one's word*, nullify, recall, renege, renounce, repeal, repudiate, rescind, retract, revoke, take back, unsay, void, weasel out*, welsh*, withdraw, worm out of*; CONCEPTS 25,266 —*Ant.* confirm, emphasize, recapitulate

recapitulate [v] *go over something again* epitomize, go over same ground*, go the same round*, outline, paraphrase, recap*, recount, rehash, reiterate, repeat, rephrase, replay, restate, review, reword, run over*, run through again*, summarize, sum up; CONCEPT 266 —*Ant.* take back

recede [v] *withdraw; diminish* abate, back, close, decline, decrease, depart, die off, diminish, drain away, draw back, drop, dwindle, ebb, fade, fall back, flow back, go away, go back, lessen, reduce, regress, retire, retract, retreat, retrocede, retrograde, retrogress, return, shrink, sink, subside, taper, wane; CONCEPTS 195,698, 776 —*Ant.* advance, forge, forward, increase

receipt [n1] *acknowledgment of delivery* cancellation, certificate, chit, counterfoil, declaration, discharge, letter, notice, proof of purchase, quittance, release, sales slip, slip, stub, voucher; CONCEPTS 271,332

receipt [n2] *delivery of goods* acceptance, accession, acquiring, acquisition, admission, admitting, arrival, getting, intaking, receiving, reception, recipience, taking; CONCEPT 124

receipts [n] *money earned in business venture* bottom line*, cash flow, comings in*, earnings, gain, gate, get*, gross, handle*, income, net, proceeds, profit, return, revenue, revenue stream, royalty, take*, take-in*, taking*; CONCEPT 344 —*Ant.* loss, losses

receive [v1] *accept delivery of something* accept, acquire, admit, apprehend, appropriate, arrogate, assume, be given, be informed, be in receipt of, be told, catch, collect, come by, come into, cop*, corral*, derive, draw, earn, gain, gather, get, get from, get hands on*, get hold of*, grab, hear, hold, inherit, latch on to*, make, obtain, perceive, pick up, pocket*, procure, pull, pull down*, reap, redeem, secure, seize, snag*, take, take in, take possession, win; CONCEPT 124 —*Ant.* deliver, donate, give, offer

receive [v2] *endure, sustain* bear, be subjected to, encounter, experience, go through, meet with, suffer, undergo; CONCEPT 23

receive [v3] *take in guest or member* accept, accommodate, admit, allow entrance, bring in, entertain, greet, host, induct, initiate, install, introduce, invite, let in, let through, make comfortable, make welcome, meet, permit, roll out red carpet*, shake hands*, show in, take in, usher in, welcome; CONCEPTS 50,83,88, 140 —*Ant.* turn away

recent [adj] *current* contempo*, contemporary, fresh, hot off the fire*, hot off the press*, just out*, late, latter, latter-day, modern, modernistic, neoteric, new, newborn, newfangled, novel, present-day, the latest*, today, up-to-date, young; CONCEPTS 578,797,820 —*Ant.* earlier, future, old, past

recently [adv] *currently* afresh, anew, freshly, in recent past, in recent times, just a while ago, just now, lately, latterly, new, newly, not long ago, of late, short while ago, the other day; CONCEPT 820 —*Ant.* before, later

receptacle [n] *container for disposal, storage* bowl, box, holder, hopper, repository, vessel, wastebasket; CONCEPT 494

reception [n1] *acceptance; acknowledgment* accession, acquisition, admission, disposition, encounter, gathering, greeting, induction, introduction, meeting, reaction, receipt, receiving, recipience, recognition, response, salutation, treatment, welcome; CONCEPTS 83,124,384 —*Ant.* disacknowledgment

reception [n2] *celebratory party* buffet, dinner, do*, entertainment, function, gathering, levee,

matinee, soiree, supper, tea; CONCEPT 383

receptive [adj] *open to new ideas* acceptant, acceptive, accessible, alert, amenable, approachable, bright, favorable, friendly, hospitable, influenceable, interested, observant, open, open-minded, open to suggestions, perceptive, persuadable, pushover*, quick on the uptake*, ready, recipient, responsive, sensitive, suggestible, susceptible, swayable, sympathetic, welcoming, well-disposed; CONCEPT 404 —*Ant.* unfriendly, unreceptive

recess [n1] *niche, corner* alcove, ambush, angle, apse, bay, break, carrel, cavity, cell, closet, cove, cranny, crutch, crypt, cubicle, dent, depression, depths, embrasure, fork, heart, hiding place, hole, hollow, indentation, mouth, nook, opening, oriel, penetralia, reaches, retreat, secret place, slot, socket; CONCEPTS 440,513

recess [n2] *break, interval in action* break-off, breather*, breathing spell*, cessation, closure, coffee break*, cutoff, downtime*, halt, happy hour*, hiatus, holiday, interlude, intermission, interregnum, layoff, letup, lull, pause, respite, rest, stop, suspension, ten*, time-out, vacation; CONCEPT 807 —*Ant.* continuation

recess [v] *stop action* adjourn, break off*, break up*, call time*, dissolve, drop, drop it, pigeonhole*, prorogate, prorogue, put on hold, rise, shake, sideline*, take a break, take a breather*, take five*, take ten*, terminate; CONCEPTS 119,121 —*Ant.* continue

recession [n] *reversal of action; reduction of business activity* bad times*, bankruptcy, big trouble*, bottom-out*, bust, collapse, decline, deflation, depression, downturn, hard times*, inflation, rainy days*, shakeout*, slide, slump, stagnation, unemployment; CONCEPT 335 —*Ant.* advance, inflation

recharge [v] *revitalize* bounce back*, breathe new life into*, bring back to life*, come to life, energize, invigorate, reenergize, refresh, regenerate, rejuvenate, renew, restore, resuscitate, revive; CONCEPTS 13,221,469,697

recipe [n] *directions, formula* compound, ingredients, instructions, method, modus operandi, prescription, procedure, process, program, receipt, technique; CONCEPT 274 —*Ant.* ingredient

reciprocal [adj] *exchanged, alternate* changeable, companion, complementary, convertible, coordinate, correlative, corresponding, dependent, double, duplicate, equivalent, exchangeable, fellow, give-and-take*, interchangeable, interdependent, matching, mutual, reciprocative, reciprocatory, twin; CONCEPTS 566,577 —*Ant.* independent, singular

reciprocate [v] *exchange, alternate; equal* barter, be equivalent, correspond, feel in return, interchange, make up for*, match, pay one's dues*, recompense, render, repay, reply, requite, respond, retaliate, retort, return, return the compliment*, scratch one's back*, serve out, share, square, swap, swing, tit for tat*, trade, vacillate; CONCEPTS 45,104,384 —*Ant.* deny, refuse

recital [n] *narrative, rendering* account, concert, description, detailing, enumeration, fable, musical, musicale, narration, performance, portrayal, presentation, reading, recapitulation, recitation, recountal, recounting, rehearsal, relation, repetition, report, statement, story, tale, telling; CONCEPTS 263,264

recitation [n] *reading to audience* address, appeal, declaiming, delivery, discourse, discoursing, discussion, exercise, holding forth, lecture, monologue, narrating, narration, oration, passage, performance, piece, playing, proclamation, recital, recounting, rehearsal, rendering, report, selection, soliloquizing, speaking, talk, telling; CONCEPTS 72,263,266

recite [v] *read out loud; narrate* account for, address, answer, chant, communicate, convey, declaim, delineate, deliver, describe, detail, discourse, dramatize, enact, enlarge, enumerate, expatiate, explain, give an account, give a report, give verbal account, hold forth, impart, interpret, itemize, mention, parrot*, perform, picture, portray, quote, recapitulate, recount, reel off*, rehearse, relate, render, repeat, reply, report, retell, soliloquize, speak, state, tell, utter; CONCEPTS 55,57,72,266

reckless [adj] *irresponsible in thought, deed* adventuresome, adventurous, any which way*, audacious, brash, breakneck, carefree, careless, daredevil, daring, desperate, devil-may-care*, fast and loose*, feckless, foolhardy, harebrained, hasty, headlong, heedless, helter-skelter, hopeless, hotheaded*, ill-advised, imprudent, inattentive, incautious, inconsiderate, indiscreet, kooky*, madcap, mindless, negligent, overventuresome, playing with fire*, precipitate, rash, regardless, temerarious, thoughtless, uncareful, venturesome, venturous, wild; CONCEPTS 401,542 —*Ant.* careful, cautious, responsible, wary

reckon [v1] *add up; evaluate* account, appraise, approximate, calculate, call, cast, cipher, compute, conjecture, consider, count, count heads*, count noses*, deem, enumerate, esteem, estimate, figure, figure out, foot, gauge, guess, hold, judge, keep tabs*, look upon, number, place, put, rate, regard, run down, square, sum, surmise, take account of, tally, think of, tick off*, tot, total, tote*, tote up*, tot up, view; CONCEPTS 37,764 —*Ant.* neglect, subtract

reckon [v2] *suppose, imagine* assume, bank on, bargain for, believe, be of the opinion, build on, conjecture, count on, depend on, expect, fancy, gather, guess, plan on, rely on, surmise, suspect, take, think, trust in, understand; CONCEPTS 12,26 —*Ant.* disbelieve

reckoning [n] *computation, account* adding, addition, arithmetic, bad news*, bill, calculation, charge, check, ciphering, cost, count, counting, debt, due, estimate, estimation, fee, figuring, grunt*, invoice, IOU*, score, settlement, statement, summation, tab, working; CONCEPT 331

recline [v] *lie down* be recumbent, cant, heel, lay down, lean, lie, list, loll, lounge, repose, rest, slant, slope, sprawl, stretch, stretch out, tilt, tip; CONCEPTS 154,201 —*Ant.* sit up, straighten

recluse [n] *person who does not want social contact* anchorite, ascetic, cenobite, eremite, hermit, monk, nun, solitaire, solitary, troglodyte; CONCEPT 423 —*Ant.* extrovert

recluse/reclusive [adj] *hermitlike, unsociable* antisocial, ascetic, cloistered, eremetic, hermetic,

isolated, misanthropic, monastic, reserved, retiring, secluded, secluse, seclusive, sequestered, solitary, standoffish, withdrawn; CONCEPTS 404, 555 —*Ant.* extroverted, friendly, sociable

recognition [n1] *identification, acknowledgment* acceptance, acknowledging, admission, allowance, apperception, appreciation, apprehending, assimilation, avowal, awareness, cognizance, concession, confession, consciousness, detection, discovery, double take*, high sign*, identifying, memory, notice, noticing, perceiving, perception, realization, recall, recalling, recognizance, recollection, recurrence, remembering, remembrance, respect, salute, sensibility, tumble*, understanding, verifying; CONCEPT 38 —*Ant.* forgetfulness, ignorance

recognition [n2] *appreciation given* acceptance, acknowledgment, approval, attention, credit, esteem, gratitude, greeting, honor, notice, pat on back*, pat on head*, plum*, puff*, puffing up*, pumping up*, rave, regard, renown, salute, strokes*; CONCEPTS 10,337,689 —*Ant.* abuse, disclaimer, dishonor

recognize [v1] *identify* admit, be familiar, button down*, descry, determinate, diagnose, diagnosticate, distinguish, espy, finger*, flash on*, know, know again, make*, make out, nail*, note, notice, observe, peg*, perceive, pinpoint, place, recall, recollect, remark, remember, ring a bell*, see, sight, spot, tab, tag, verify; CONCEPT 38 —*Ant.* miss

recognize [v2] *acknowledge, understand; approve* accept, admit, agree, allow, appreciate, assent, avow, be aware of, comprehend, concede, confess, grant, greet, honor, make, own, perceive, realize, respect, salute, sanction, see; CONCEPT 15 —*Ant.* disapprove, misunderstand

recoil [v] *shrink away* backfire, balk, blanch, blench, blink, carom, cringe, demur, dodge, draw back, duck, falter, flinch, hesitate, jerk, kick, pull back, quail, quake, react, rebound, reel, resile, shake, shirk, shrink, shudder, shy away, spring, start, step back, stick, stickle, swerve, tremble, turn away, waver, wince, withdraw; CONCEPTS 150,194,195 —*Ant.* face, meet

recollect [v] *remember* arouse, awaken, bethink, bring to mind, call to mind, cite, come to one, flash, flash on*, look back on, mind, place, recall, recognize, remind, reminisce, retain, retrospect, revive, rouse, stir, summon, waken; CONCEPT 40 —*Ant.* forget

recommend [v] *advise, approve* acclaim, advance, advocate, applaud, back, be all for*, be satisfied with, celebrate, commend, compliment, confirm, counsel, endorse, enjoin, esteem, eulogize, exalt, exhort, extol, favor, front for*, glorify, go on record for*, hold up, justify, laud, magnify, plug*, praise, prescribe, prize, propose, put forward, put in a good word*, put on to*, sanction, second, speak highly of, speak well of, stand by, steer, suggest, think highly of, uphold, urge, value, vouch for; CONCEPTS 10,75 —*Ant.* disapprove, discourage, dissuade

recommendation [n] *advice, approval* advocacy, approbation, blessing, certificate, character reference, charge, commendation, counsel, direction, endorsement, eulogy, favorable mention, good word*, guidance, injunction, instruction, judgment, letter of support, order, pass, plug*, praise, proposal, proposition, reference, sanction, steer*, suggestion, support, testimonial, tip, tribute, two cents' worth*, urging; CONCEPTS 274,278 —*Ant.* condemnation, disapproval, discouragement

recompense [n] *something returned, paid back* amends, atonement, bus fare*, compensation, cue, damages, emolument, expiation, gravy*, indemnification, indemnity, overcompensation, pay, payment, propitiation, quittance, recoupment, recovery, redemption, redress, remuneration, reparation, repayment, requital, restitution, retrieval, retrievement, return, reward, salvo, satisfaction, solatium, sweetener*, tip, wages; CONCEPTS 340,344 —*Ant.* take

recompense [v] *pay back, make restitution* ante up*, atone, atone for, balance, comp*, compensate, cough up*, counterbalance, counterpoise, countervail, do business*, equalize, expiate, fix, give satisfaction, grease*, indemnify, make amends, make good*, make up for, offset, overcompensate, pay, pay for, propitiate, put out*, reciprocate, recoup, recover, redress, reimburse, remunerate, repay, requite, retaliate, retrieve, return, reward, satisfy, spring for, square*, sweeten the pot*, swing for*, take care of; CONCEPTS 126,341 —*Ant.* disagree, refuse

reconcile [v1] *make peace; adjust* accommodate, accord, accustom, appease, arbitrate, arrange, assuage, attune, bring together, bring to terms, bury the hatchet*, come together, compose, conciliate, conform, cool*, coordinate, fit, fix up, get together on, harmonize, integrate, intercede, kiss and make up*, make matters up, make up, mediate, mitigate, pacify, patch things up*, patch up*, placate, propitiate, proportion, reconciliate, rectify, re-establish, regulate, resolve, restore harmony, reunite, settle, suit, tune, win over; CONCEPTS 384,697 —*Ant.* disagree, refuse

reconcile [v2] *resign oneself to something* accept, accommodate, get used to*, make the best of*, put up with*, resign, submit, yield; CONCEPT 23 —*Ant.* divorce, estrange

recondite [adj] *mysterious, obscure* abstruse, academic, acroamatic, arcane, cabalistic, concealed, cryptic, dark, deep, difficult, esoteric, hard, heavy*, hermetic, hidden, involved, little-known, mystic, mystical, occult, orphic, pedantic, profound, scholarly, secret; CONCEPTS 529,576 —*Ant.* obvious, plain, simple, straightforward

reconnaissance [n] *inspection* exploration, investigation, maneuvers, probe, recon, reconnoiter, review, scan, scrutiny, search, surveillance, survey; CONCEPTS 103,290

reconsider [v] *think about again* amend, change one's mind, consider again, correct, emend, go over, have second thoughts*, polish, rearrange, reassess, recheck, reevaluate, reexamine, rehash, replan, rethink, retrace, review, revise, reweigh, rework, run through, see in a new light*, sleep on, take another look, think better of*, think over, think twice*, work over; CONCEPT 17 —*Ant.* ignore, refuse

reconstruct [v] *reorganize, build up* copy, deduce, doctor*, do up*, fix, fix up, make over,

modernize, overhaul, patch, piece together, reassemble, rebuild, recast, recondition, reconstitute, recreate, reestablish, refashion, reform, regenerate, rehabilitate, rejuvenate, remake, remodel, remold, renovate, reorient, repair, replace, reproduce, reshuffle, restore, retool, revamp, rework; CONCEPTS 84,168,171 —*Ant.* destroy, raze, ruin

record [n1] *account of event or proceedings* almanac, annals, archive, archives, chronicle, comic book*, diary, directory, document, documentation, entry, evidence, file, history, inscription, jacket, journal, legend, log, manuscript, memo, memoir, memorandum, memorial, minutes, monument, note, paper trail*, register, registry, remembrance, report, script, scroll, story, swindle sheet*, testimony, trace, track record*, transcript, transcription, witness, writing, written material; CONCEPTS 271,281

record [n2] *background, experience* accomplishment, administration, career, case history, conduct, curriculum vitae, history, past behavior, performance, reign, studies, track record*, way of life*, work; CONCEPT 678

record [n3] *achievement* ceiling, maximum; CONCEPT 706 —*Ant.* loss

record [v1] *write down; store information* book, can*, catalog, chalk up*, chronicle, copy, cut, cut a track*, document, dub*, enroll, enter, enumerate, file, indite, inscribe, insert, jot down, keep account, lay down, list, log, make a recording, mark, mark down, matriculate, note, post, preserve, put down, put in writing, put on file*, put on paper*, put on tape*, register, report, set down, tabulate, take down, tape, tape-record, transcribe, video*, videotape, wax*, write in; CONCEPT 125

record [v2] *give evidence of* contain, designate, explain, indicate, mark, point out, point to, read, register, say, show; CONCEPT 261

recount [v] *tell a story* break a story*, convey, delineate, depict, describe, detail, echo, enumerate, give an account of, itemize, narrate, picture, play back, portray, recap*, recapitulate, recite, rehash, rehearse, relate, repeat, report, run by again*, run down*, run through*, say again, state, tell, track, unload, verbalize; CONCEPTS 55,266 —*Ant.* conceal, repress

recoup [v] *recover, make up for* compensate, get back, get out from under*, get well, make good, make redress for, make well, redeem, refund, regain, reimburse, remunerate, repay, repossess, requite, retrieve, satisfy, win back; CONCEPTS 124,126,342,700 —*Ant.* downslide, lose, worsen

recourse [n] *alternative* aid, appeal, choice, expediency, expedient, help, makeshift, option, refuge, remedy, resort, resource, shift, stand-by, stopgap, substitute, support, way out; CONCEPTS 693,712

recover [v1] *find again* balance, bring back, catch up, compensate, get back, make good, obtain again, offset, reacquire, recapture, reclaim, recoup, recruit, redeem, rediscover, regain, reoccupy, repair, replevin, replevy, repossess, rescue, restore, resume, retake, retrieve, salvage, take back, win back; CONCEPTS 120,183 —*Ant.* lose, mislay, miss

recover [v2] *improve in health* be out of woods*, better, bounce back*, come around, convalesce, feel oneself again*, forge ahead, gain, get back on feet*, get better, get in shape, get out from under*, get over, get well, grow, heal, increase, make a comeback*, mend, overcome, perk up*, pick up, pull through, rally, rebound, recuperate, refresh, regain one's health, regain one's strength, rejuvenate, renew, restore, return to form, revive, snap back*, sober up*, start anew, take turn for better; CONCEPTS *303, 700* —*Ant.* decline, deteriorate, wane

recreation [n] *sports, games, special interests* amusement, avocation, ball*, disport, dissipation, distraction, diversion, divertissement, ease, enjoyment, entertainment, exercise, festivity, field day*, frolic, fun, fun and games*, game, hilarity, hobby, holiday, jollity, laughs*, leisure activity, mirth, pastime, picnic, play, playtime, pleasure, R and R*, rec, refreshment, relaxation, relief, repose, rollick, sport, vacation; CONCEPTS *363,364* —*Ant.* labor, profession, work

recruit [n] *person beginning service* apprentice, beginner, convert, draftee, enlisted person, fledgling, GI*, greenhorn*, helper, initiate, learner, neophyte, newcomer, new person, novice, novitiate, plebe*, proselyte, rookie, sailor, selectee, serviceperson, soldier, tenderfoot*, trainee, volunteer; CONCEPTS *348,358*

recruit [v] *gather resources* augment, better, build up, call to arms, call up, deliver, draft, engage, enlist, enroll, fill up, find human resources, gain, impress, improve, induct, levy, mobilize, muster, obtain, procure, proselytize, raise, reanimate, recoup, recover, recuperate, refresh, regain, reinforce, renew, repair, replenish, repossess, restore, retrieve, revive, round up, select, sign on, sign up, store up, strengthen, supply, take in, take on, win over; CONCEPTS *41,109,120,320*

rectify [v] *correct a situation; make something right* adjust, amend, clean up, clean up act*, debug, dial back*, doctor, emend, fix, fix up, go over, improve, launder, make good*, make up for*, mend, pay one's dues*, pick up, put right, recalibrate, redress, reform, remedy, repair, revise, right, scrub, shape up, square, straighten out, straighten up, turn things around*; CONCEPT *126* —*Ant.* damage, ruin, worsen

recumbent [adj] *lying down* decumbent, flat, horizontal, level, procumbent, prostrate, reclining, resupine, sprawling, supine; CONCEPT *583*

recuperate [v] *improve in health* ameliorate, be on the mend*, be out of the woods*, bounce back*, convalesce, gain, get back on one's feet*, get better, get well, heal, look up, make a comeback*, mend, perk up*, pick up, pull out of it*, pull through, rally, recover, regain health, snap out of it*, turn the corner*; CONCEPTS *303,700* —*Ant.* decline, deteriorate, fail, worsen

recur [v] *happen again; repeat in one's mind* be remembered, be repeated, come again, come and go, come back, crop up again*, haunt thoughts*, iterate, persist, reappear, recrudesce, reiterate, repeat, return, return to mind, revert, run through one's mind*, turn back; CONCEPTS *3,242* —*Ant.* halt, stop

recurrent [adj] *repeating* alternate, chain, continued, cyclical, frequent, habitual, intermittent, isochronal, isochronous, periodic, periodical, recurring, regular, reoccurring, repeated, repetitive, rolling; CONCEPTS *541,544* —*Ant.* halted, infrequent, permanent, prevented, stopped

recycle [v] *reuse* convert, reclaim, recover, reprocess, salvage, save; CONCEPT *134*

red [n/adj] *color of blood; shade resembling such a color* bittersweet, bloodshot, blooming, blush, brick, burgundy, cardinal, carmine, cerise, cherry, chestnut, claret, copper, coral, crimson, dahlia, flaming, florid, flushed, fuchsia, garnet, geranium, glowing, healthy, inflamed, infrared, magenta, maroon, pink, puce, rose, roseate, rosy, rubicund, ruby, ruddy, rufescent, russet, rust, salmon, sanguine, scarlet, titian, vermilion, wine; CONCEPTS *618,622*

redden [v] *blush, make rosy* bloody, color, crimson, dye, flush, glow, go red, incarnadine, mantle, paint, pink, pinken, rose, rouge, rubify, rubric, rubricate, ruby, ruddle, ruddy, rust, suffuse, tint, turn red; CONCEPTS *250,469* —*Ant.* lighten, pale

redeem [v1] *recover possession* buy back, buy off, call in, cash, cash in, change, cover, defray, discharge, exchange, get back, make good, pay off, purchase, ransom, recapture, reclaim, recoup, regain, reinstate, repay, replevin, replevy, repossess, repurchase, restore, retrieve, settle, take in, trade in, win back; CONCEPTS *104,131,327* —*Ant.* forfeit, lose

redeem [v2] *free; buy the freedom of* deliver, disenthrall, disimprison, emancipate, extricate, liberate, loose, manumit, pay ransom, ransom, release, rescue, save, set free, unbind, unchain, unfetter; CONCEPTS *127,327* —*Ant.* abandon, forfeit

redeem [v3] *atone for; compensate* abide by, absolve, acquit, adhere to, balance, carry out, compensate, counterbalance, counterpoise, countervail, defray, discharge, fulfill, hold to, keep, keep the faith*, make amends, make good, make up for, meet, offset, outweigh, perform, redress, rehabilitate, reinstate, restore, satisfy, save, set off; CONCEPTS *91,126* —*Ant.* disregard, ignore

redeeming [adj] *offsetting* compensating, compensatory, extenuating, extenuatory, qualifying, redemptive, saving; CONCEPT *537*

red herring [n] *distraction* attention-grabber, bait, commotion, deviation, disturbance, diversion, gimmick, interruption, maneuver, ploy, smoke screen, wild-goose chase*; CONCEPTS *293,410,532,690*

redneck [n] *hick* backwoodsman/woman, boor, bumpkin, clodhopper, cornfed*, country boy/girl, country cousin*, countryman/woman, farmer, good old boy*, hayseed*, hillbilly, local yokel*, rube, rural, rustic, yokel*; CONCEPT *413*

redolent [adj] *aromatic; suggestive* ambrosial, balmy, evocative, fragrant, odoriferous, perfumed, pungent, remindful, reminiscent, scented, sweet-smelling; CONCEPTS *267,529,598*

redress [n] *help, compensation* aid, amendment, amends, assistance, atonement, balancing, change, conciliation, correction, cure, ease, indemnity, justice, offsetting, payment, quittance, recompense, rectification, reestablishment, reformation, rehabilitation, relief, remedy, remission, remodeling, renewal, repair, reparation, reprisal, requital, restitution, retribution, return, revision, reward, reworking, satisfaction, vengeance; CONCEPTS 344,712 —*Ant.* hurt, injury

redress [*v*] *change, rectify* adjust, amend, annul, balance, cancel, compensate, correct, counteract, countercheck, dial back*, ease, even out, frustrate, make amends, make reparation, make restitution, make up for, mend, negate, negative, neutralize, pay for, pay one's dues*, put right*, recalibrate, recompense, reform, regulate, relieve, remedy, repair, restore, revise, square, turn around, turn over new leaf*, turn things around*, vindicate; CONCEPTS 126,697 —*Ant.* worsen

red tape [*n*] *bureaucracy* authority, city hall*, government, management, officialdom, officialism, powers that be*, proper channels, regulatory commission, the Establishment*, the system*; CONCEPTS 325,770

reduce [*v1*] *make less; decrease* abate, abridge, bankrupt, bant, break, cheapen, chop, clip, contract, curtail, cut, cut back, cut down, debase, deflate, depreciate, depress, diet, dilute, diminish, discount, drain, dwindle, go on a diet*, impair, impoverish, lessen, lose weight, lower, mark down, moderate, nutshell, pare, pauperize, rebate, recede, roll back, ruin, scale down, shave, shorten, slash, slim, slow down, step down, take off weight, taper, taper off, tone down, trim, truncate, turn down, weaken, wind down; CONCEPTS 137,236,240,247,698 —*Ant.* expand, extend, grow, increase, raise, upgrade

reduce [*v2*] *defeat* bear down, beat down, break, bring, conquer, cripple, crush, disable, drive, enfeeble, force, master, overcome, overpower, ruin, subdue, subjugate, undermine, vanquish, weaken; CONCEPT 95 —*Ant.* win

reduce [*v3*] *humble, humiliate* abase, break, bring low, bump*, bust*, declass, degrade, demerit, demote, disgrade, disrate, downgrade, lower, take down a peg*; CONCEPTS 7,19,384 —*Ant.* invigorate, raise, strengthen

redundant [*adj*] *excessive; repetitious* bombastic, de trop*, diffuse, extra, extravagant, inessential, inordinate, iterating, long-winded*, loquacious, oratorical, padded*, palaverous, periphrastic, pleonastic, prolix, reiterating, spare, supererogatory, superfluous, supernumerary, surplus, tautological, unnecessary, unwanted, verbose, wordy; CONCEPTS 553,781 —*Ant.* concise, essential, single, singular

reef [*n*] *underwater or partially submerged ledge* atoll, bank, bar, beach, cay, coral reef, ridge, rock, rock barrier, sand bar, shoal, skerry; CONCEPT 509

reek [*n*] *strong odor* effluvium, fetor, mephitis, smell, stench, stink; CONCEPT 600

reek [*v*] *smell of; be characterized by* be permeated by, be redolent of, emit, fume, give off odor, have an odor, smell, smoke, steam, stench, stink; CONCEPT 600

reel [*v*] *wobble; spin around* bob, careen, falter, feel giddy, go around, lurch, pitch, revolve, rock, roll, shake, stagger, stumble, sway, swim, swing, swirl, teeter, titubate, totter, turn, twirl, waver, weave, wheel, whirl; CONCEPTS 151,153

refer [*v1*] *mention* accredit, adduce, advert, allude, ascribe, assign, associate, attribute,

bring up, charge, cite, credit, designate, direct attention, excerpt, exemplify, extract, give as example, glance, hint, impute, indicate, insert, instance, interpolate, introduce, invoke, lay, make allusion, make mention of, make reference, name, notice, point, point out, put down to, quote, speak about, speak of, specify, touch on; CONCEPT 73

refer [*v2*] *direct, guide* commit, consign, deliver, hand in, hand over, introduce, pass on, point, put in touch, recommend, relegate, send, submit, transfer, turn over; CONCEPTS 143,187 —*Ant.* hold back

refer [*v3*] *concern, apply* answer, appertain, be about, be a matter of, bear upon, be directed to, belong, be relevant, connect, correspond with, cover, deal with, encompass, have a bearing on, have reference, have relation, have to do with, hold, include, incorporate, involve, pertain, point, regard, relate, take in, touch; CONCEPT 532

refer [*v4*] *seek information* advise, apply, commune, confer, consult, go, have recourse, look up, recur, repair, resort, run, turn, turn to; CONCEPTS 72,216

referee [*n*] *person who mediates, judges* adjudicator, arbiter, arbitrator, conciliator, judge, ref*, umpire; CONCEPTS 348,366

referee [*v*] *judge, mediate* adjudge, adjudicate, arbitrate, umpire; CONCEPT 18

reference [*n1*] *remark, citation* advertence, allusion, associating, attributing, bringing up, connecting, hint, implication, indicating, innuendo, insinuation, mention, mentioning, note, plug*, pointing out, quotation, relating, resource, source, stating; CONCEPT 278

reference [*n2*] *testimonial of good character* certificate, certification, character, credentials, endorsement, good word, recommendation, tribute; CONCEPTS 69,274

reference [*n3*] *printed matter with information* archives, cyclopedia, dictionary, encyclopedia, evidence, source, thesaurus, writing; CONCEPTS 271,280

refine [*v1*] *purify* clarify, cleanse, distill, filter, process, rarefy, strain; CONCEPT 165 —*Ant.* corrupt, dirty, pollute

refine [*v2*] *perfect, polish* better, civilize, clarify, cultivate, elevate, explain, hone, improve, make clear, round, sleek, slick, smooth, temper; CONCEPT 244 —*Ant.* damage, ruin

refined [*adj1*] *cultured, civilized* aesthetic, civil, classy*, courteous, courtly, cultivated, delicate, discerning, discriminating, elegant, enlightened, exact, fastidious, fine, finespun, genteel, gracious, high-brow*, high-minded, nice, plush, polished, polite, posh, precise, punctilious, restrained, ritzy*, sensitive, snazzy*, sophisticated, spiffy*, suave, sublime, subtle, swanky*, tasteful, urbane, well-bred, well-mannered; CONCEPTS 401,555,589 —*Ant.* uncivilized, uncultured, unrefined, unsophisticated

refined [*adj2*] *cleaned of impurities* aerated, boiled down, clarified, clean, cleansed, distilled, drained, expurgated, filtered, processed, pure, purified, rarefied, strained, washed; CONCEPT 621 —*Ant.* corrupt, dirtied, polluted

refinement [*n1*] *cleansing* clarification, cleaning, depuration, detersion, distillation, draining, filtering, processing, purification, rarefaction, rectification; CONCEPT 165 —*Ant.* corruption, dirtying, pollution

refinement [n2] *cultivation, civilization* affability, civility, courtesy, courtliness, delicacy, dignity, discrimination, elegance, enlightenment, erudition, fastidiousness, fineness, fine point*, finesse, fine tuning*, finish, gentility, gentleness, good breeding, good manners, grace, graciousness, knowledge, lore, nicety, nuance, polish, politeness, politesse, precision, sophistication, style, suavity, subtlety, tact, taste, urbanity; CONCEPTS 388,633,655 —*Ant.* bad manners, crudeness, rudeness

reflect [v1] *give back* cast, catch, copy, echo, emulate, flash, follow, give forth, imitate, match, mirror, rebound, repeat, repercuss, reply, reproduce, resonate, resound, return, reverberate, reverse, revert, shine, take after, throw back; CONCEPTS 65,171,624

reflect [v2] *think about* cerebrate, chew*, cogitate, consider, contemplate, deliberate, meditate, mull over, muse, ponder, reason, ruminate, speculate, stew*, study, think, weigh, wonder; CONCEPTS 17,24 —*Ant.* disregard, ignore

reflect [v3] *demonstrate, indicate* bear out, bespeak, communicate, display, evince, exhibit, express, indicate, manifest, reveal, show; CONCEPT 261

reflection [n1] *thought, thinking* absorption, brainwork, cerebration, cogitation, consideration, contemplation, deliberation, idea, imagination, impression, meditation, musing, observation, opinion, pensiveness, pondering, rumination, speculation, study, view; CONCEPTS 17,24

reflection [n2] *mirror image* appearance, counterpart, duplicate, echo, idea, image, impression, light, likeness, picture, representation, reproduction, shadow; CONCEPT 628

reflection [n3] *criticism* animadversion, aspersion, blame, censure, derogation, discredit, disesteem, imputation, obloquy, reproach, slam, slur, stricture; CONCEPT 52 —*Ant.* praise

reflective [adj] *thoughtful* cogitating, contemplative, deliberate, meditative, pensive, pondering, reasoning, ruminative, speculative, studious; CONCEPT 403 —*Ant.* ignorant, unthoughtful

reform [v] *correct, rectify* ameliorate, amend, better, bring up to code*, change one's ways*, clean up, clean up one's act*, convert, correct, cure, emend, go straight*, improve, make amends, make over, mend, rearrange, rebuild, reclaim, reconstitute, reconstruct, redeem, refashion, regenerate, rehabilitate, remake, remedy, remodel, renew, renovate, reorganize, repair, resolve, restore, revise, revolutionize, rework, shape up, standardize, swear off, transform, turn over a new leaf*, uplift; CONCEPTS 35,110,126,202 —*Ant.* hurt, impair, worsen

reformatory [n] *reform school* boot camp*, cooler*, correctional facility, correctional institution, jail, penal institution, penitentiary, prison, training school; CONCEPTS 439,449,516

refrain [n] *chorus of musical piece* burden, melody, music, song, strain, theme, tune, undersong; CONCEPTS 264,595

refrain [v] *do without; keep from doing* abstain,

arrest, avoid, be temperate, cease, check, curb, desist, eschew, forbear, forgo, give up, go on the wagon*, halt, inhibit, interrupt, keep, leave off, not do, pass, pass up, quit, renounce, resist, restrain, sit out*, stop, take the cure*, take the pledge*, withhold; CONCEPT 121,681 —*Ant.* do, go ahead, jump in

refresh [v] *make like new; give new life* brace, breathe new life into, bring around, brush up, cheer, cool, enliven, exhilarate, freshen, inspirit, jog, modernize, prod, prompt, quicken, reanimate, recreate, regain, reinvigorate, rejuvenate, renovate, repair, replenish, restore, resuscitate, revitalize, revive, revivify, stimulate, update, vivify; CONCEPTS 35,202,697 —*Ant.* damage, ruin

refreshing [adj] *new; rejuvenating* bracing, cooling, different, energizing, exhilarating, fresh, invigorating, novel, original, restorative, restoring, revitalizing, revivifying, stimulating, thirst-quenching, unique; CONCEPTS 564,578, 797

refreshment [n] *small amount of food or drink* bite, pick-me-up*, snack, spread, tidbit; CONCEPT 457

refrigerate [v] *chill, usually in storage* air-condition, air-cool, cool, freeze, ice, keep cold, make cold; CONCEPTS 202,255 —*Ant.* heat, warm

refuge [n] *place to hide, have privacy* ambush, anchorage, asylum, cover, covert, den, escape, exit, expedient, fortress, harbor, harborage, haven, hideaway, hideout, hiding place, hole, home, immunity, ivory tower*, makeshift, opening, outlet, port, preserve, protection, recourse, resort, resource, retreat, safe place, sanctuary, security, shelter, shield, stopgap*, stronghold, way out*; CONCEPTS 198,515

refugee [n] *person running from something, often oppression* alien, boat person*, castaway, defector, derelict, deserter, displaced person, DP*, emigrant, émigré, escapee, evacuee, exile, expatriate, expellee, foreigner, foundling, fugitive, homeless person, leper, maroon, outcast, outlaw, prodigal, renegade, runaway, stateless person; CONCEPTS 359,413

refund [n] *returned money* acquittance, allowance, compensation, consolation, discharge, discount, give-back*, give-up*, kickback, money back, payment, rebate, reimbursement, remuneration, repayment, restitution, retribution, return, satisfaction, settlement; CONCEPTS 340,344

refund [v] *return money; rebate* adjust, balance, compensate, give back, honor a claim, indemnify, make amends, make good*, make repayment, make up for, pay back, recompense, recoup, redeem, redress, reimburse, relinquish, remit, remunerate, repay, restore, reward, settle; CONCEPT 341

refurbish [v] *spruce up* clean up, do up*, fix up, gussy up*, mend, modernize, overhaul, recondition, redo, reequip, refit, refresh, rehab, rehabilitate, rejuvenate, remodel, renew, renovate, repair, restore, retread, revamp, set to rights, spruce, update; CONCEPTS 177, 202 —*Ant.* destroy, ruin

refusal [n] *denial of responsibility; unwillingness* abnegation, ban, choice, cold shoulder*, declension, declination, defiance, disallowance, disapproval, disavowal, disclaimer, discountenancing, disfavor, dissent, enjoinment, exclusion, forbidding, interdiction, knockback*, negation, nix*, no, nonacceptance, noncompliance, nonconsent, option, pass*, prohibition, proscription, rebuff, refutation, regrets, rejection, renouncement, renunciation, repudiation, repulse, repulsion, reversal, thumbs down*, turndown, veto, withholding, writ; CONCEPTS 278,633 —Ant. approval, grant, offer, ok, sanction

refuse [n] garbage debris, dregs, dross, dump, dust, hogwash*, junk, leavings, litter, muck, offal, rejectamenta*, remains, residue, rubbish, scraps, scum*, sediment, slop*, sweepings, swill, trash, waste, waste matter; CONCEPT 260 —Ant. assets, possessions, property

refuse [v] deny; say no beg off, brush off*, decline, demur, desist, disaccord, disallow, disapprove, dispense with, dissent, dodge, evade, give thumbs down to*, hold back, hold off, hold out, ignore, make excuses, nix*, not budge, not budget, not buy*, not care to*, pass up, protest, rebuff, refuse to receive, regret, reject, repel, reprobate, repudiate, send regrets*, set aside*, shun, spurn, turn away, turn deaf ear to*, turn down, turn from, turn one's back on*, withdraw, withhold; CONCEPTS 30,49,266 —Ant. accept, allow, approve, consent, grant, offer, ok, sanction

refute [v] prove false; discredit abnegate, argue against, blow sky high*, break, burn, burn down, cancel, cancel out, confute, contend, contradict, contravene, convict, counter, crush, debate, demolish, disclaim, disconfirm, dispose of, disprove, dispute, evert, explode, expose, gainsay, give the lie to*, give thumbs down to*, invalidate, negate, oppose, overthrow, parry, quash, rebut, reply to, repudiate, shoot down, shoot full of holes*, show up, silence, squelch, take a stand against, tear down*, top*; CONCEPT 54 —Ant. endorse, prove, ratify, sanction, support

regain [v] get back, get back to achieve, attain, compass, gain, get out from under, get well, make well, reach, reach again, reacquire, reattain, recapture, reclaim, recoup, recover, recruit, redeem, repossess, retake, retrieve, return to, save, take back, win back; CONCEPTS 120,124,131 —Ant. forfeit, lose

regal [adj] fit for royalty august, glorious, imposing, kingly, magnificent, majestic, monarchial, monarchical, noble, proud, queenly, resplendent, royal, sovereign, splendid, stately, sublime; CONCEPT 589 —Ant. common

regale [v] throw a party; have fun amuse, delight, divert, entertain, feast, fracture, give a party, grab, gratify, have a get-together, laugh it up, nurture, party, please, ply, refresh, satisfy, serve, toss a party; CONCEPTS 292,384

regard [n1] attention, look care, carefulness, cognizance, concern, consciousness, curiosity, gaze, glance, heed, interest, interestedness, mark, mind, note, notice, observance, observation, once-over*, remark, scrutiny, stare, view; CONCEPTS 596,623,626,690 —Ant. disregard, ignorance, neglect

regard [n2] affection, good opinion account,

appreciation, approbation, approval, attachment, care, cherishing, concern, consideration, curiosity, deference, devotion, esteem, estimation, favor, fondness, homage, honor, interest, interestedness, liking, love, note, opinion, prizing, reputation, repute, respect, reverence, satisfaction, store, sympathy, thought, value, valuing, veneration, worship; CONCEPTS 10, 532, 689 —Ant. dislike, disregard, disrespect, hate

regard [n3] feature, detail aspect, bearing, concern, connection, item, matter, particular, point, reference, relation, relevance, respect; CONCEPTS 532,644

regard [v1] look at; listen to advertise, attend, beam, behold, contemplate, eye, eyeball*, flash, gaze, get a load of*, give attention, heed, look on, mark, mind, note, notice, observe, overlook, pay attention, pipe*, pore over*, read, remark, respect, scan, scrutinize, see, spy, stare at, take into consideration, take notice of, view, watch, witness; CONCEPTS 596,623,626 —Ant. disregard, ignore, look away

regard [v2] believe, judge account, adjudge, admire, assay, assess, consider, deem, esteem, estimate, look upon, rate, reckon, respect, revere, see, suppose, surmise, think, treat, value, view; CONCEPTS 10,12 —Ant. disbelieve, disregard

regard [v3] have something to do with apply to, bear upon, be relevant to, concern, have a bearing on, have to do with*, interest, pertain to, refer to, relate to; CONCEPT 532

regardful [adj] attentive, observant advertent, arrect, aware, careful, considerate, deferential, duteous, dutiful, heedful, intentive, mindful, observative, observing, respectful, thoughtful, watchful; CONCEPT 401 —Ant. disregarding, ignorant, inattentive, unobservant

regardless [adj] indifferent, unconcerned behindhand, blind, careless, coarse, crude, deaf, delinquent, derelict, disregarding, heedless, inadvertent, inattentive, inconsiderate, insensitive, lax, listless, mindless, neglectful, negligent, nonobservant, rash, reckless, remiss, rude, slack, unfeeling, unheeding, uninterested, unmindful; CONCEPT 401 —Ant. attentive, concerned, heedful

regardless [adv] despite everything against, although, anyway, aside from, at any cost, but, come what may, despite, distinct from, for all that, in any case, in spite of everything, leaving aside, nevertheless, no matter what, nonetheless, notwithstanding, without considering, without regard to; CONCEPTS 544,548 —Ant. irregardless

regards [n] best wishes commendations, compliments, deference, devoirs, good wishes, greeting, love, love and kisses*, remembrances, respects, salutation, salutations; CONCEPT 278

regenerate [v] breathe new life into change, exhilarate, inspirit, invigorate, produce, raise from the dead*, reanimate, reawaken, reconstruct, recreate, reestablish, refresh, reinvigorate, rejuvenate, renew, renovate, reproduce, restore, revive, revivify, uplift; CONCEPTS 7,22,173,202,251 —Ant. destroy, kill, ruin

regime [n] leadership of organization administration, dynasty, establishment, government, incumbency, management, pecking order*, reign, rule, system, tenure; CONCEPTS 299,325

regimented [*adj*] *strictly regulated* controlled, disciplined, ordered, orderly, organized, strict, systematic, uniform; CONCEPTS 94,117 —*Ant.* free, varied

region [*n*] *area, domain; scope* arena, bailiwick, belt, block, clearing, country, demesne, district, division, domain, dominion, environs, expanse, field, ghetto, ground, inner city, jungle, land, locale, locality, neck of woods*, neighborhood, part, place, precinct, province, quarter, range, realm, scene, section, sector, shire, sphere, stomping ground*, suburb, terrain, territory, tract, turf*, vicinity, walk, ward, world, zone; CONCEPTS 198,508,512

register [*n*] *list, record* annals, archives, book, catalog, catalogue, chronicle, diary, entry, file, ledger, log, memorandum, registry, roll, roll call, roster, schedule, scroll; CONCEPT 281

register [*v1*] *enter in list, record* catalogue, check in, chronicle, enlist, enroll, file, inscribe, join, list, note, record, schedule, set down, sign on, sign up, sign up for, subscribe, take down, weigh in; CONCEPTS 79,114,125 —*Ant.* eradicate, erase

register [*v2*] *indicate, reveal* be shown, bespeak, betray, disclose, display, exhibit, express, manifest, mark, point out, point to, read, record, reflect, say, show; CONCEPT 261

register [*v3*] *make an impression* come home to, dawn on, get through to, have an effect on, impress, sink in, tell; CONCEPTS 7,19,22

regress [*v*] *return to earlier way of doing things* backslide, degenerate, deteriorate, ebb, fall away, fall back, fall off, go back, lapse, lose ground, recede, relapse, retreat, retrogress, revert, roll back, sink, throw back, turn back; CONCEPTS 633,698 —*Ant.* develop, grow, progress

regret [*n*] *upset over past action* affliction, anguish, annoyance, apologies, apology, bitterness, care, compunction, conscience, conscience, contrition, demur, disappointment, discomfort, dissatisfaction, dole, grief, heartache, heartbreak, lamentation, misgiving, nostalgia, pang, penitence, qualm, regretfulness, remorse, repentance, ruefulness, scruple, self-accusation, self-condemnation, self-disgust, self-reproach, sorrow, uneasiness, woe, worry; CONCEPTS 21,410 —*Ant.* contentedness, happiness, satisfaction

regret [*v*] *be upset about* apologize, be disturbed, bemoan, be sorry for, bewail, cry over*, cry over spilled milk*, deplore, deprecate, disapprove, feel remorse, feel sorry, feel uneasy, grieve, have compunctions*, have qualms*, kick oneself*, lament, look back, miss, moan, mourn, repent, repine, rue, weep, weep over; CONCEPTS 21,410 —*Ant.* be content, be satisfied

regretful [*adj*] *sad, sorry* apologetic, ashamed, attritional, compunctious, contrite, disappointed, mournful, penitent, remorseful, repentant, rueful, sorrowful; CONCEPT 403 —*Ant.* content, happy, not guilty, satisfied

regrettable [*adj*] *unfortunate, wrong* afflictive, calamitous, deplorable, dire, disappointing, distressing, dreadful, grievous, heartbreaking, ill-advised, lamentable, pitiable, pitiful, sad,

shameful, unfavorable, unhappy, woeful; CONCEPTS 548,571 —*Ant.* blessed, fortunate, happy, lucky, right

regular [*adj1*] *normal, common* approved, bona fide, classic, commonplace, correct, customary, daily, established, everyday, formal, general, habitual, lawful, legitimate, natural, official, ordinary, orthodox, prevailing, prevalent, proper, routine, run-of-the-mill*, sanctioned, standard, time-honored, traditional, typic, typical, unexceptional, unvarying, usual; CONCEPTS 530,533,547 —*Ant.* abnormal, anomalous, eccentric, extraordinary, irregular, rare, uncommon, unusual

regular [*adj2*] *orderly, consistent, balanced* accordant, alternating, arranged, automatic, classified, congruous, consonant, constant, cyclic, dependable, efficient, established, even, exact, expected, fixed, flat, formal, harmonious, in order, invariable, level, measured, mechanical, methodical, momentary, ordered, organized, patterned, periodic, precise, probable, punctual, rational, recurrent, regulated, rhythmic, routine, serial, set, smooth, standardized, stated, steady, straight, successive, symmetrical, systematic, uniform; CONCEPTS 326,544, 566,585 —*Ant.* changing, disorderly, imbalanced, inconsistent, infrequent, irregular, unsteady, variable

regulate [*v*] *manage, organize* adapt, adjust, administer, allocate, arrange, balance, classify, conduct, control, coordinate, correct, determine, direct, dispose, fit, fix, govern, guide, handle, improve, legislate, measure, methodize, moderate, modulate, monitor, order, oversee, pull things together*, put in order, readjust, reconcile, rectify, rule, run, set, settle, shape up*, square, standardize, straighten up, superintend, supervise, systematize, temper, time, true, tune, tune up*; CONCEPTS 94,117 —*Ant.* deregulate, disorganize, mismanage

regulation [*n1*] *managing, organizing* adjustment, administration, arrangement, classification, codification, control, coordination, direction, governance, governing, government, guidance, handling, management, moderation, modulation, reconciliation, regimentation, reorganization, settlement, standardization, superintendence, supervision, systematization, tuning; CONCEPTS 94,117 —*Ant.* deregulation, disorganization, mismanagement

regulation [*n2*] *rule, requirement* bible, book, canon, chapter and verse*, code, commandment, decree, decretum, dictate, direction, edict, law, no-nos*, numbers, order, ordinance, precept, prescript, principle, procedure, reg*, standing order, statute; CONCEPTS 318,688 —*Ant.* lawlessness

regurgitate [*v*] *vomit* be seasick*, be sick, boff*, drive the bus*, dry heave*, eject, emit, expel, gag*, heave*, hurl*, lose one's lunch*, pray to the porcelain god*, puke*, ralph*, retch, spew, spit up, throw up, toss one's cookies*, upchuck*, urp*; CONCEPTS 179, 185,308

rehabilitate [*v*] *renovate, adjust* change, clear, convert, fix up, furbish, improve, make good*, mend, rebuild, reclaim, recondition, reconstitute, reconstruct, recover, redeem, reestablish, reform, refurbish, rehab*, reinstate, reintegrate, reinvigorate, rejuvenate, renew, restitute, restore, save; CONCEPTS *35,126,134,202* —*Ant.* destroy, hurt, ruin

rehash [v] *talk over again* change, discuss, reiterate, repeat, rephrase, restate, reuse, rework, rewrite, say again, state differently; CONCEPT *56* —*Ant.* deny, refuse

rehearsal [n] *preparation for performance* call, description, drill, dry run*, experiment, going-over, practice, practice session, prep*, reading, readying, recital, recitation, recounting, rehearsing, relation, retelling, run-through, shakedown*, test flight*, trial balloon*, trial performance, tryout, workout; CONCEPTS *264, 292,363* —*Ant.* cold turkey

rehearse [v] *prepare for performance* act, depict, describe, do over, drill, dry run*, experiment, go over, go through, hold a reading*, hone, iterate, learn one's part, narrate, practice, ready, recapitulate, recite, recount, reenact, reiterate, relate, repeat, review, run lines, run through, study, take from the top*, tell, test, train, try out, tune up, walk through*, warm up, work out; CONCEPTS *266,292,363* —*Ant.* go cold turkey

reign [n] *rule, dominion* administration, ascendancy, command, control, dynasty, empire, hegemony, incumbency, influence, monarchy, power, regime, sovereignty, supremacy, sway, tenure; CONCEPTS *198,376*

reign [v] *have power over; prevail* administer, be in power, be in the driver's seat*, be supreme, boss, command, dominate, domineer, govern, head up, helm, hold power, hold sway*, influence, manage, obtain, occupy, overrule, predominate, preponderate, rule, rule the roost*, run the show*, run things*, sit, superabound, wear the crown*; CONCEPTS *117,298* —*Ant.* serve, submit

reimburse [v] *pay back something owed* balance, compensate, indemnify, make reparations, make up for, offset, pay, recompense, recover, refund, remunerate, repay, requite, restore, return, square, square up; CONCEPT *341* —*Ant.* take

rein [n] *restraint, control* bit, brake, bridle, check, curb, deterrent, governor, halter, harness, hold, line, restriction, strap; CONCEPT *499*

rein [v] *restrain, control* bridle, check, collect, compose, cool, curb, halt, hold, hold back, limit, repress, restrict, simmer down, slow down, smother, suppress; CONCEPT *130* —*Ant.* free, let go

reinforce [v] *strengthen, augment* add fuel to fire*, add to, back up, beef up*, bolster, boost, build up, buttress, carry, emphasize, energize, enlarge, fortify, harden, heat up, hype, increase, lend a hand, multiply, pick up, pillar, prop, prop up, punch up, shore up, soup up*, stand up for, stiffen, stress, stroke, supplement, support, sustain, toughen, underline; CONCEPTS *5,236,245,250* —*Ant.* subtract, take away, undermine, weaken

reinstate [v] *give back responsibility* bring back, put back, put in power again, recall, redeem, reelect, reestablish, rehabilitate, rehire, reintroduce, reinvest, renew, replace, restore, return, revive; CONCEPTS *351,384* —*Ant.* fire, let go

reiterate [v] *say or do again* come again, ditto*, double-check, echo, go over again, ingeminate, iterate, play back, recap*, recapitulate, recheck, rehash, renew, repeat, reprise, resay, restate, retell, rewarn, say again; CONCEPTS *100,171,266* —*Ant.* take back

reject [v] *say no to* burn*, cashier*, cast aside, cast off, cast out, chuck, decline, deny, despise, disallow, disbelieve, discard, discount, discredit, disdain, dismiss, eliminate, exclude*, give thumbs down to*, jettison, jilt, kill*, nix*, not buy*, pass by, pass on, pass up, put down, rebuff, refuse, renounce, repel, reprobate, repudiate, repulse, scoff, scorn, scout, scrap, second, shed, shoot down*, shun, slough, spurn, throw away, throw out, turn down, veto; CONCEPTS *21,30,180* —*Ant.* accept, allow, approve, choose, ratify, sanction

rejection [n] *denial, refusal* bounce, brush-off*, cold shoulder*, disallowance, dismissal, elimination, exclusion, hard time*, kick in teeth*, nix*, no dice*, no go*, nothing doing*, no way*, pass*, rebuff, renunciation, repudiation, slap in the face*, thumbs down*, turndown, veto; CONCEPTS *21,30,180* —*Ant.* acceptance, allowance, approval, choice, ratification, sanction

rejoice [v] *be very happy about something* be glad, be overjoyed, celebrate, delight, enjoy, exult, feel happy, glory, joy, jump for joy, make merry, revel, triumph; CONCEPT *410* —*Ant.* be sad

rejoinder [n] *answer, reply* comeback, confutation, counteraccusation, counterargument, countercharge, counterclaim, counterstatement, defense, rebuttal, repartee, response, retort, return, wisecrack; CONCEPTS *274,278*

rejuvenate [v] *make new again* breathe new life into*, do, do up*, exhilarate, give face lift to*, give new life to, make young again, modernize, reanimate, reclaim, recondition, reconstruct, recover, refresh, refurbish, regenerate, rehab, reinvigorate, renew, renovate, restitute, restore, retread, revitalize, revivify, spruce, spruce up*, update; CONCEPTS *35,202* —*Ant.* destroy, kill, ruin

relapse [n] *deterioration, weakening* backsliding, fall, fall from grace*, lapse, loss, recidivism, recurrence, regression, repetition, retrogression, return, reversion, setback, turn for the worse*, worsening; CONCEPT *698* —*Ant.* healing, progress, strengthening

relapse [v] *deteriorate, weaken* backslide, be overcome, be overtaken, degenerate, fade, fail, fall, fall back, lapse, recidivate, regress, retrogress, revert, sicken, sink, slide back, slip back, suffer, turn back, worsen; CONCEPT *698* —*Ant.* get better, heal, progress, strengthen

relate [v/] *give an account of* break a story*, chronicle, clue one in*, depict, describe, detail, disclose, divulge, express, get off one's chest*, give the word*, impart, itemize, lay it on the line*, let one's hair down*, narrate, particularize, picture, present, recite, recount, rehearse, report, retell, reveal, run down, run through, set forth, shoot the breeze*, sling*, spill, spill the beans*, spin a yarn*, state, tell, track, verbalize; CONCEPT *55* —*Ant.* conceal, hide

relate [v2] *correlate, pertain* affect, ally, appertain, apply, ascribe, assign, associate, bear upon, be joined with, be relevant to, bracket, combine, compare, concern, conjoin, connect, consociate, coordinate, correspond to, couple, credit, have reference to, have to do with, identify with, impute, interconnect, interdepend, interrelate, join, link, orient, orientate, pertain, refer, tie in with, touch, unite, yoke; CONCEPT 532 —*Ant.* dissociate

related [adj] *connected, accompanying* affiliated, agnate, akin, alike, allied, analogous, associated, cognate, complementary, concomitant, connate, connatural, consanguine, convertible, correlated, correspondent, dependent, enmeshed, fraternal, germane, incident, interchangeable, interconnected, interdependent, interrelated, intertwined, interwoven, in the same category, in touch with, joint, knit together*, like, linked, mutual, of that ilk, parallel, pertinent, reciprocal, relevant, similar, tied up; CONCEPTS 487,573,577 —*Ant.* alien, different, disassociated, disconnected, dissimilar, foreign, unrelated

relation [n] *connection, family connection* affiliation, affinity, alliance, association, consanguinity, kin, kindred, kinship, kinsperson, liaison, propinquity, relationship, relative, sibling, similarity; CONCEPTS 296,414,421,714

relationship [n] *connection; friendship* accord, affair, affiliation, affinity, alliance, analogy, appositeness, association, bond, communication, conjunction, consanguinity, consociation, contact, contingency, correlation, dependence, dependency, exchange, homogeneity, hookup, interconnection, interrelation, interrelationship, kinship, liaison, likeness, link, marriage, nearness, network, parallel, pertinence, pertinency, proportion, rapport, ratio, relation, relativity, relevance, similarity, tie, tie-in, tie-up; CONCEPTS 388,714

relative [adj1] *comparative, respective* about, allied, analogous, approximate, associated, concerning, conditional, connected, contingent, corresponding, dependent, in regard to, near, parallel, proportionate, reciprocal, referring, related, relating to, reliant, with respect to; CONCEPT 563 —*Ant.* disproportionate, irrelevant, irrespective, unequal

relative [adj2] *pertinent, applicable* apposite, appropriate, appurtenant, apropos, contingent, dependent, germane, pertaining, referring, related, relevant; CONCEPT 558 —*Ant.* irrelevant, separate, unrelated

relative [n] *member of a family* agnate, aunt, blood, brother-in-law, clansperson, cognate, connection, cousin, father, father-in-law, folk, folks, grandparents, great-grandparents, in-laws, kinsperson, mother, mother-in-law, nephew, niece, relation, sib*, sibling, sister-in-law, stepbrother, stepparent, stepsister, uncle; CONCEPT 414

relatively [adv] *in or by comparison* almost, approximately, comparably, comparatively, nearly, proportionately, rather, somewhat, to some extent; CONCEPTS 544,772

relax [v1] *be or feel at ease* breathe easy*, calm, calm down*, collect oneself, compose oneself, cool off*, ease off, feel at home, hang loose*, knock off*, laze, let oneself go*, lie down,

loosen up, make oneself at home*, put one's feet up*, recline, repose, rest, settle back, simmer down*, sit around, sit back, soften, stop work, take a break*, take a breather*, take it easy*, take one's time*, take ten*, take time out*, tranquilize, unbend, unlax*, unwind; CONCEPT 210 —*Ant.* agitate, excite, tense, worry

relax [v2] *diminish, lessen* abate, ease, ease off, ebb, lax, let up, loose, loosen, lose speed, lower, mitigate, moderate, modify, modulate, reduce, relieve, remit, slack, slacken, slow, slow down, untighten, weaken; CONCEPTS 240,698 —*Ant.* grow, increase

relaxation [n] *entertainment; resting or recovering* alleviation, amusement, assuagement, diversion, enjoyment, fun, leisure, loosening, mitigation, pleasure, reclining, recreation, refreshment, relief, repose, requiescence, rest; CONCEPTS 210,292,363 —*Ant.* intensification, labor, work

relay [v] *pass on, transmit* broadcast, carry, communicate, deliver, hand down, hand on, hand over, send, send forth, spread, transfer, turn over; CONCEPT 143 —*Ant.* check, hold on, keep

release [n1] *delivery; dispensation* absolution, acquittal, acquittance, charge, clemency, commute, deliverance, discharge, emancipation, exemption, exoneration, floater, freedom, freeing, let-off*, liberation, liberty, lifeboat, lifesaver, manumission, relief, spring, turnout, walkout; CONCEPTS 127,685 —*Ant.* check, collection, gathering, hold

release [n2] *publication* announcement, flash*, handout, issue, leak, news, notice, offering, proclamation, propaganda, publicity, story; CONCEPTS 271,280

release [v] *let go, let out* absolve, acquit, bail out, cast loose, clear, commute, deliver, discharge, disengage, dispense, drop, emancipate, exculpate, excuse, exempt, exonerate, extricate, free, give off, give out, go easy on, issue, leak, let off, let off steam*, let loose*, liberate, loose, loosen, manumit, open up, set at large, set free, set loose, spring, surrender, take out, turn loose, turn out, unbind, unchain, undo, unfasten, unfetter, unleash, unloose, unshackle, unite, vent, wipe slate clean*, yield; CONCEPTS 50,60, 88, 127,143 —*Ant.* collect, gather, hold, keep, maintain

relegate [v1] *assign, transfer* accredit, charge, commend, commit, confide, consign, credit, delegate, entrust, hand over, pass on, refer, turn over; CONCEPTS 41,143 —*Ant.* assume, hold, keep

relegate [v2] *banish, downgrade* demote, deport, dismiss, displace, eject, exile, expatriate, expel, expulse, lag, ostracize, remove, throw out, transport; CONCEPTS 30, 121,211 —*Ant.* promote, upgrade

relent [v] *die down; let up* acquiesce, be merciful, capitulate, cave in*, change one's mind, come around, comply, cool it*, cry uncle*, die away, drop, ease, ease off, ease up on*, ebb, fall, fold, forbear, give in, give quarter*, give some slack*, give up, give way, go along with, go easy on*, have mercy, have pity, lay back, let go, let it happen*, lighten up*, mellow out*, melt, moderate, quit, relax, say uncle*, show mercy, slacken, slow, soften, subside, wane, weaken, yield; CONCEPTS *35,698,776* —*Ant.* build, increase, rise

relentless [*adj1*] *cruel, merciless* adamant, bound, bound and determined, dead set on*, determined, dogged, ferocious, fierce, go for broke*, grim, hang in*, hang-tough*, hard, harsh, implacable, inexorable, inflexible, inhuman, mortal, obdurate, pitiless, remorseless, rigid, rigorous, ruthless, single-minded, stiff, stop at nothing, strict, stringent, unappeasable, unbending, uncompromising, undeviating, unflinching, unforgiving, unrelenting, unstoppable, unyielding, vindictive; CONCEPT *401* —*Ant.* kind, merciful, sympathetic, understanding

relentless [*adj2*] *continuous, neverending* incessant, nonstop, persistent, pertinacious, punishing, sustained, tenacious, unabated, unbroken, unfaltering, unflagging, unrelenting, unrelieved, unremitting, unstoppable; CONCEPTS *326,534* —*Ant.* ending, intermittent, stopping

relevant [*adj*] *appropriate; to the purpose* accordant, admissible, ad rem, allowable, applicable, applicatory, apposite, appurtenant, apt, becoming, cognate, compatible, concerning, conformant, conforming, congruent, congruous, consistent, consonant, correlated, correspondent, fit, fitting, germane, harmonious, having direct bearing on, having to do with, important, material, on the button*, on the nose*, pat*, pertaining to, pertinent, pointful, proper, referring, related, relative, significant, suitable, suited, to the point, weighty; CONCEPT *558* —*Ant.* inappropriate, irrelevant, unsuitable

reliable [*adj*] *trustworthy* candid, careful, certain, conscientious, constant, decent, decisive, definite, dependable, determined, devoted, faithful, firm, good, high-principled, honest, honorable, impeccable, incorrupt, loyal, okay, positive, predictable, proved, reputable, respectable, responsible, righteous, safe, sincere, solid, sound, stable, staunch, steadfast, steady, sterling, strong, sure, there, tried, tried-and-true*, true, true-blue*, true-hearted, trusty, unequivocal, unfailing, unimpeachable, upright, veracious; CONCEPTS *535,542,544* —*Ant.* deceptive, irresponsible, unreliable, untrustworthy

reliance [*n*] *confidence* assurance, belief, credence, credit, dependence, faith, hope, interdependence, interdependency, stock, trust; CONCEPT *689* —*Ant.* disbelief, independence

relic [*n*] *something saved from the past* antique, antiquity, archaism, artifact, curio, curiosity, evidence, fragment, heirloom, keepsake, memento, memorial, monument, remains, remembrance, remembrancer, reminder, remnant, residue, ruins, scrap, souvenir, survival, testimonial, token, trace, trophy, vestige; CONCEPT *446*

relief [*n*] *remedy, aid; relaxation* abatement, allayment, alleviation, amelioration, appeasement, assistance, assuagement, balm, break, breather, cheer, comfort, comforting, consolation, contentment, cure, deliverance, diversion, ease, easement, extrication, fix, hand, happiness, help, letup, lift, lightening, load off one's mind*, maintenance, mitigation, mollification, palliative, quick fix*, refreshment, release, remission, reprieve, respite, rest, restfulness, satisfaction, softening, solace, succor, support, sustenance; CONCEPTS *681,712* —*Ant.* damage, hurt, injury, pain

relieve [*v1*] *make less painful; let up on* abate, allay, alleviate, appease, assuage, break, brighten, calm, comfort, console, cure, decrease, diminish, divert, dull, ease, free, interrupt, lighten, mitigate, moderate, mollify, palliate, qualify, quiet, relax, salve, slacken, soften, solace, soothe, subdue, take load off one's chest*, take load off one's mind*, temper, vary; CONCEPTS *244,700* —*Ant.* harm, hurt, injure, pain

relieve [*v2*] *help; give assistance* aid, assist, bring aid, give a break*, give a hand*, give a rest, spell, stand in for, substitute for, succor, support, sustain, take over from, take the place of; CONCEPT *110* —*Ant.* burden, discourage, hurt, trouble, upset, worry

relieve [*v3*] *remove blame, responsibility* absolve, deliver, discharge, disembarrass, disencumber, dismiss, dispense, excuse, exempt, force to resign, free, let off, privilege, pull, release, spare, throw out, unburden, yank*; CONCEPTS *50,88,351* —*Ant.* accuse, blame, condemn

religion [*n*] *belief in divinity; system of beliefs* church, communion, creed, cult, denomination, devotion, doctrine, higher power, morality, myth, mythology, observance, orthodoxy, pietism, piety, prayer, preference, religiosity, rites, ritual, sacrifice, sanctification, sect, spirituality, spiritual-mindedness, standards, superstition, theology, veneration; CONCEPTS *368,689* —*Ant.* agnosticism, atheism, disbelief

religious [*adj1*] *concerning belief in divinity* believing, born-again*, canonical, churchgoing, churchly, clerical, deistic, devotional, devout, divine, doctrinal, ecclesiastical, god-fearing, godly, holy, ministerial, moral, orthodox, pietistic, pious, pontifical, prayerful, priestly, pure, reverent, righteous, sacerdotal, sacred, sacrosanct, saintlike, saintly, scriptural, sectarian, spiritual, supernatural, theistic, theological; CONCEPTS *536,545* —*Ant.* agnostic, atheistic, irreligious, ungodly

religious [*adj2*] *conscientious, scrupulous* exact, faithful, fastidious, meticulous, punctilious, rigid, rigorous, steadfast, unerring, unswerving; CONCEPT *538* —*Ant.* careless, erring, indolent, lazy, undetailed

relinquish [*v*] *give up, let go* abandon, abdicate, abnegate, back down, cast, cast off, cede, cut loose*, desert, discard, ditch*, drop, drop like hot potato*, drop out, dump*, forbear, forgo, forsake, forswear, hand over, kick, kiss goodbye*, lay aside, leave, opt out, quit, quit cold turkey*, release, renounce, repudiate, resign, retire from, sacrifice, shed, stand down, surrender, swear off*, take the oath*, take the pledge*, vacate, waive, withdraw, yield; CONCEPTS *119,127,234* —*Ant.* hold, keep, take

relish [*n*] *great appreciation of something* appetite, bias, delectation, diversion, enjoying, enjoyment, fancy, flair, flavor, fondness, gusto, heart, leaning, liking, love, loving, palate, partiality, penchant, pleasure, predilection, prejudice, propensity, sapidity, sapor, savor, smack, stomach, tang, taste, zest; CONCEPTS *20,32* —*Ant.* dislike, hate, hatred

re
re

relish [v] *look forward to; appreciate* admire, be fond of, cherish, delight in, dig*, enjoy, fancy, go, go for*, like, luxuriate in, mind, prefer, revel in, savor, taste; CONCEPT *32 —Ant.* dislike, hate

reluctant [adj] *unenthusiastic, unwilling* afraid, averse, backward, calculating, cautious, chary, circumspect, demurring, diffident, discouraged, disheartened, disinclined, grudging, hanging back, hesitant, hesitating, indisposed, involuntary, laggard, loath, opposed, queasy, recalcitrant, remiss, shy, slack, slow, squeamish, tardy, uncertain, uneager, wary; CONCEPT *401 —Ant.* anxious, eager, enthusiastic, ready, willing

rely [v] *have confidence in* await, bank, be confident of, believe in, be sure of, bet, bet bottom dollar on*, build, calculate, commit, confide, count, depend, entrust, expect, gamble on, have faith in, hope, lay money on*, lean, look, reckon, ride on coattails*, swear by*, trust; CONCEPTS *12,26 —Ant.* be independent, distrust, doubt

remain [v] *stay, wait* abide, be left, bide, bivouac, bunk*, cling, continue, delay, dwell, endure, freeze, go on, halt, hang, hang out, hold over, hold the fort*, hover, inhabit, keep on, last, linger, live, lodge, make camp, nest, outlast, outlive, pause, perch, persist, prevail, put on hold, remain standing, reside, rest, roost, sit out, sit through, sit tight*, sojourn, squat, stand, stay behind, stay in, stay over, stay put, stick around, stop, survive, tarry, visit, wait; CONCEPTS *23,239,681,804 —Ant.* depart, forge, go, leave, move

remainder [n] *balance, residue* bottom of barrel*, butt, carry-over, detritus, dregs, excess, fragment, garbage, hangover*, heel, junk, leavings, leftover, obverse, oddment, odds and ends*, overplus, refuse, relic, remains, remnant, residuum, rest, ruins, salvage, scrap, stump, surplus, trace, vestige, waste, wreck, wreckage; CONCEPTS *260,835 —Ant.* base, core

remains [n] *remaining part* debris, detritus, leavings, leftovers, remainder, remnant, remnants, residue, rest, scraps; CONCEPT *260*

remark [n] *comment, observation* acknowledgment, annotation, assertion, attention, back talk, bon mot*, cognizance, comeback, commentary, conclusion, consideration, crack*, declaration, elucidation, exegesis, explanation, explication, exposition, expression, gloss, heed, illustration, interpretation, mention, mind, note, notice, obiter dictum, observance, opinion, point, recognition, reflection, regard, saying, statement, talk, thought, two cents' worth*, utterance, wisecrack, witticism, word; CONCEPTS *51,278 —Ant.* silence

remark [v] *notice and comment* animadvert, behold, catch, commentate, crack*, declare, descry, espy, heed, make out, mark, mention, mouth off*, note, observe, pass comment, perceive, pick up on, reflect, regard, say, see, speak, spot, state, take note, take notice, utter, wisecrack; CONCEPTS *38,51,626 —Ant.* hold back, suppress

remarkable [adj] *extraordinary, unusual* arresting, arrestive, conspicuous, curious, distinguished, exceptional, famous, gilt-edged*, greatest, important, impressive, marked, miraculous, momentous, notable, noteworthy,

noticeable, odd, outstanding, peculiar, phenomenal, preeminent, primo*, prominent, rare, salient, signal, significant, singular, smashing, solid, splashy*, strange, striking, super, surprising, uncommon, uncustomary, unique, unordinary, unwonted, weighty, wicked*, wonderful, world class*, zero cool*; CONCEPT *574 —Ant.* normal, ordinary, unremarkable, usual

remedial [adj] *healing, restorative* alleviative, antidotal, antiseptic, corrective, curative, curing, healthful, health-giving, invigorating, medicating, medicinal, purifying, recuperative, reformative, remedying, repairing, restitutive, sanative, sanatory, solving, soothing, therapeutic, tonic, treating, vulnerary, wholesome; CONCEPT *537 —Ant.* damaging, harmful, hurtful, injurious

remedy [n] *cure, solution* antidote, assistance, biologic, corrective, counteractant, counteraction, counteractive, counteragent, countermeasure, counterstep, cure-all*, drug, elixir, fix, improvement, medicament, medicant, medicine, panacea, pharmaceutical, pharmacon, physic, pill, quick fix*, redress, relief, restorative, support, therapy, treatment; CONCEPTS *307,311, 693,712 —Ant.* disease, injury, pain

remedy [v] *fix, cure* aid, alleviate, ameliorate, amend, assuage, attend, change, clean up, clean up one's act*, control, correct, debug*, doctor, ease, fiddle with, fix up, go over, heal, help, launder, make up for, mitigate, palliate, pick up, put right, recalibrate, rectify, redress, reform, relieve, renew, repair, restore, revise, right, scrub, set right, set to rights*, shape up, solve, soothe, square*, square up*, straighten out, treat, upgrade; CONCEPTS *126,212,310 —Ant.* get sick, harm, hurt, injure, worsen

remember [v] *keep in mind; summon into mind* bear in mind, bethink, brood over, call to mind, call up, cite, commemorate, conjure up, dig into the past*, dwell upon, educe, elicit, enshrine, extract, fix in the mind, flash on*, get, go back, have memories, hold dear*, keep forever, know by heart*, learn, look back, memorialize, memorize, mind, nail down*, recall, recognize, recollect, refresh memory, relive, remind, reminisce, retain, retrospect, revive, revoke, ring a bell*, strike a note*, summon up, think back, treasure; CONCEPT *40 —Ant.* disregard, forget

remembrance [n1] *memory, recollection* afterthought, anamnesis, flash*, flashback*, hindsight*, mental image, mind, recall, recognition, reconstruction, regard, reminiscence, retrospect, thought; CONCEPTS *40,529 —Ant.* forgotten

remembrance [n2] *gift, testimonial* commemoration, favor, keepsake, memento, memorial, monument, present, relic, remembrancer, reminder, reward, souvenir, token, trophy; CONCEPT *337*

remind [v] *awaken memories of something* admonish, advise, bethink, bring back to, bring to mind, call attention, call to mind, call up, caution, cite, emphasize, give a cue*, hint, imply, intimate, jog one's memory*, make one remember, make one think, mention, note, point out, prod, prompt, put in mind, recall, recollect, refresh memory, remember, reminisce, retain, retrospect, revive, stir up, stress, suggest, warn; CONCEPTS *7,19,22,40,78 —Ant.* forget

reminder [n] *warning, notice; keepsake* admonition, expression, gesture, hint, indication, intimation, memento, memo, memorandum, memorial, note, relic, remembrance, remembrancer, sign, souvenir, suggestion, token, trinket, trophy; CONCEPTS 271,278,529 —*Ant.* forgetfulness

reminisce [v] *go over in one's memory* bethink, call up, cite, hark back, live in the past, look back, mind, muse over, recall, recollect, remember, remind, retain, retrospect, review, revive, think back; CONCEPT 17 —*Ant.* forget, repress

reminiscent [adj] *suggestive of something in the past* bringing to mind, evocative, implicative, mnemonic, nostalgic, recollective, redolent, remindful, similar; CONCEPT 529 —*Ant.* forgetful, oblivious

remiss [adj] *careless, thoughtless* any old way*, any which way*, asleep at switch*, asleep on job*, behindhand, culpable, daydreaming, defaultant, delinquent, derelict, dilatory, disregardful, fainéant, forgetful, heedless, inattentive, indifferent, indolent, lackadaisical, lax, lazy, neglectful, negligent, regardless, slack, slapdash, slipshod, sloppy, slothful, slow, tardy, uninterested, unmindful, woolgathering*; CONCEPT 401 —*Ant.* careful, mindful, scrupulous, thorough, thoughtful

remission [n1] *acquittal, pardon* absolution, amnesty, discharge, excuse, exemption, exoneration, forgiveness, indulgence, mercy, release, reprieve; CONCEPT 685 —*Ant.* accusation, blame

remission [n2] *pause; lessening* abatement, abeyance, alleviation, amelioration, break, decrease, delay, diminution, ebb, interruption, letup, lull, moderation, reduction, relaxation, release, respite, suspension; CONCEPTS 303,698,807 —*Ant.* increase, rise, worsening

remit [v1] *send, transfer* address, consign, dispatch, forward, mail, make payment, pay, post, route, settle, ship, square, transmit; CONCEPTS 217,341 —*Ant.* hold, keep

remit [v2] *stop, postpone* abate, alleviate, amnesty, cancel, condone, decrease, defer, delay, desist, diminish, dwindle, ease up, excuse, exonerate, fall away, forbear, forgive, halt, hold off, hold up, intermit, mitigate, moderate, modify, modulate, pardon, prorogue, put off, reduce, relax, release, repeal, reprieve, rescind, respite, shelve, sink, slack, slacken, soften, stay, suspend, wane, weaken; CONCEPTS 234,698 —*Ant.* encourage, forge, forward

remnant [n] *leftover part* balance, bit, dregs, dross, end, end piece, excess, fragment, hangover*, heel, leavings, lees, leftovers, odds and ends*, orts, part, particle, piece, portion, remainder, remains, residual, residue, residuum, rest, rump, scrap, shred, strip, surplus, survival, vestige; CONCEPTS 260,835 —*Ant.* whole

remodel [v] *reconstruct* do up*, fix, fix up, make over, modernize, overhaul, reassemble, rebuild, recast, recondition, recreate, redesign, refurbish, rehabilitate, rejuvenate, remake, renovate, repair, restore, revamp, upgrade; CONCEPTS 84,168,171

remonstrate [v] *argue against* animadvert, blame, censure, challenge, combat, criticize, decry, demur, deprecate, disapprove, disparage, dispute, dissent, except, expostulate, fight, find fault, frown upon, inveigh, kick*, nag, object, oppose, pick at, protest, rain, recriminate, resist, scold, sound off*, take exception, take issue, withstand; CONCEPTS 46, 52,54 —*Ant.* agree, concede, give in

remorse [n] *guilty or bad conscience* anguish, attrition, compassion, compunction, contriteness, contrition, grief, guilt, pangs of conscience*, penance, penitence, penitency, pity, regret, remorsefulness, repentance, rue, ruefulness, self-reproach, shame, sorrow; CONCEPTS 410,728 —*Ant.* good conscience, happiness, remorselessness, satisfaction

remorseful [adj] *guilty, ashamed* apologetic, attritional, chastened, compunctious, conscience-stricken, contrite, guilt-ridden, mournful, penitent, penitential, regretful, repentant, rueful, sad, self-reproachful, sorrowful, sorry; CONCEPT 401 —*Ant.* callous, merciless, remorseless, ruthless, unashamed, unmerciful

remorseless [adj] *without guilt in spite of wrongdoing* avaricious, barbarous, bloody, callous, cruel, fierce, forbidding, greedy, grim, hard, hard-bitten, hardened, hard-hearted, harsh, impenitent, implacable, inexorable, inhuman, inhumane, insensitive, intolerant, merciless, murderous, obdurate, pitiless, relentless, rigorous, ruthless, savage, shameless, sour, tough, tyrannical, uncompassionate, uncontrite, unforgiving, unmerciful, unregenerate, unrelenting, unremitting, unrepenting, unyielding, vindictive; CONCEPT 401 —*Ant.* ashamed, guilty, remorseful, sad, sorry

remote [adj1] *out-of-the-way; in the distance* alien, back, backwoods, beyond, boondocks*, devious, distant, far, faraway, far-flung, far-off, foreign, frontier, godforsaken*, god-knows-where*, in a backwater*, inaccessible, isolated, lonely, lonesome, middle of nowhere*, obscure, off-lying, off the beaten path*, outlandish, outlying, private, removed, retired, secluded, secret, undiscovered, unknown, unsettled, wild; CONCEPT 583 —*Ant.* close, convenient, near, nearby

remote [adj2] *irrelevant, unrelated* abstracted, alien, alone, apart, detached, exclusive, extraneous, extrinsic, farfetched, foreign, immaterial, inappropriate, indirect, nongermane, obscure, outside, pointless, removed, strange, unconnected; CONCEPTS 564,575 —*Ant.* close, related, relevant

remote [adj3] *unlikely, improbable* doubtful, dubious, faint, implausible, inconsiderable, meager, negligible, off, outside, poor, slender, slight, slim, small; CONCEPT 552 —*Ant.* close, likely, possible, probable

remote [adj4] *cold, detached; unapproachable* abstracted, aloof, casual, cool*, disinterested, distant, faraway, icy, incurious, indifferent, introspective, introverted, laid-back*, offish, putting on airs, removed, reserved, standoffish, stuck up, uncommunicative, unconcerned, uninterested, uninvolved, uppity, withdrawn; CONCEPTS 401,404 —*Ant.* approachable, friendly, gentle, warm

remove [v1] *lift or move object; take off, away* abolish, abstract, amputate, carry away, carry off, cart off, clear away, cut out, delete, depose, detach, dethrone, dig out, discard, discharge, dislodge, dismiss, displace, disturb, do away with, doff, efface, eject, eliminate, erase, evacuate, expel, expunge, extract, get rid of, junk*, oust, pull out, purge, raise, relegate, rip out, separate, shed, ship, skim, strike out, take down, take out, tear out, throw out, transfer, transport, unload, unseat, uproot, wipe out*, withdraw; CONCEPT 211 —*Ant.* fix, place, remain, stay

remove [*v2*] *do away with; kill* assassinate, blot out*, clear away, dispose of, do in*, drag, drag down, eliminate, eradicate, erase, exclude, execute, expunge, exterminate, extirpate, get rid of, liquidate, murder, obliterate, purge, scratch, sterilize, take down, take out, waste*, wipe out*; CONCEPTS 121,252 —*Ant.* give birth, plant, sow

remunerate [*v*] *compensate, reward* accord, ante up*, award, dish out*, do business*, grant, guerdon, indemnify, pay, pay off, pay up, post, recompense, redress, reimburse, repay, requite, shell out*, spring for*, vouchsafe; CONCEPT 341 —*Ant.* charge, seize, take, withhold

renaissance [*n*] *rebirth* awakening, invigoration, new dawn, reawakening, regeneration, rejuvenation, renascence, renewal, resurgence, revitalization, revival; CONCEPTS 119,221

render [*v1*] *contribute* cede, deliver, distribute, exchange, furnish, give, give back, give up, hand over, impart, make available, make restitution, minister, part with, pay, pay back, present, provide, relinquish, repay, restore, return, show, submit, supply, surrender, swap, tender, trade, turn over, yield; CONCEPTS 108, 140 —*Ant.* remove, take

render [*v2*] *show; execute* act, administer, administrate, carry out, delineate, depict, display, do, evince, exhibit, give, govern, image, interpret, limn, manifest, perform, picture, play, portray, present, represent; CONCEPTS 91,261 —*Ant.* conceal, fail, suppress

render [*v3*] *translate, explain* construe, deliver, interpret, paraphrase, pass, put, reproduce, restate, reword, state, transcribe, transliterate, transpose, turn; CONCEPTS 57,266 —*Ant.* cloud, confuse, obscure

rendezvous [*n1*] *get-together* affair, appointment, assignation, blind date, double date, engagement, heavy date*, matinee, meet, meeting, one night stand*, tête-à-tête, tryst; CONCEPT 384

rendezvous [*n2*] *place for get-together* gathering point, hangout*, haunt, lonke nest*, meeting place, purlieu, resort, spot, stomping ground*, venue, watering hole*; CONCEPT 198

rendezvous [*v*] *meet, often secretly* assemble, be closeted, be reunited, collect, come together, congregate, congress, converge, forgather, gather, get together, join up, meet behind closed doors*, meet privately, muster, raise, rally; CONCEPT 384

rendition [*n*] *explanation; interpretation* arrangement, construction, delivery, depiction, execution, interpretation, performance, portrayal, presentation, reading, rendering, transcription, translation, version; CONCEPTS 263,278 —*Ant.* obscurity, vagueness

renegade [*adj*] *rebellious* apostate, backsliding, disloyal, dissident, heterodox, mutinous, outlaw, radical, reactionary, rebel, recreant,

revolutionary, runaway, schismatic, traitorous, unfaithful, untraditional; CONCEPTS 401,542 —*Ant.* obedient, passive, submissive

renegade [*n*] *person who is rebellious* abandoner, apostate, backslider, betrayer, defector, deserter, dissident, double-crosser*, escapee, exile, forsaker, fugitive, heretic, iconoclast, insurgent, mutineer, outlaw, rebel, recreant, refugee, runaway, schismatic, snake*, snake in the grass*, tergiversator, traitor, turnabout, turncoat; CONCEPTS 359,412 —*Ant.* adherent, follower, passivist

renege [*v*] *go back on one's word* break one's promise, cop out*, default, reverse, weasel out*, welsh; CONCEPTS 59,63,330

renew [*v*] *start over; refurbish* begin again, brace, breathe new life into*, bring up to date*, continue, exhilarate, extend, fix up, freshen, gentrify, go over, mend, modernize, overhaul, prolong, reaffirm, reawaken, recommence, recondition, recreate, reestablish, refit, refresh, regenerate, rehabilitate, reinvigorate, rejuvenate, remodel, renovate, reopen, repair, repeat, replace, replenish, restate, restock, restore, resume, resuscitate, retread, revitalize, revive, spruce, stimulate, transform; CONCEPTS 35,202,221 —*Ant.* finish, halt, kill, stop

renounce [*v*] *abandon, reject* abdicate, abjure, abnegate, abstain from, apostacize, arrogate, cast off, decline, defect, demit, deny, desert, disavow, discard, disclaim, disown, divorce oneself from*, drop out, dump*, eschew, forgo, forsake, forswear, give up, leave flat*, leave off, opt out, quit, rat*, recant, relinquish, repudiate, resign, sell out*, spurn, swear off, take the pledge*, tergiversate, tergiverse, throw off, throw over, toss over, turn, waive, walk out on, wash hands of*; CONCEPTS 30,54,195 —*Ant.* allow, approve, condone

renovate [*v*] *fix up, modernize* clean, cleanse, do*, do up*, face-lift*, gussy up*, make over, overhaul, reactivate, recondition, reconstitute, recreate, refit, reform, refresh, refurbish, rehabilitate, rekindle, remake, remodel, renew, repair, restore, resurrect, resuscitate, retread, retrieve, revamp, revitalize, revive, revivify, spruce, spruce up*, update; CONCEPTS 168,177, 202 —*Ant.* demolish, destroy, ruin

renown [*adj*] *fame* acclaim, celebrity, distinction, éclat, eminence, glory, honor, illustriousness, kudos, luster, mark, note, notoriety, preeminence, prestige, prominence, prominency, rep*, reputation, repute, stardom; CONCEPT 668 —*Ant.* anonymity, obscurity, unimportance

renowned [*adj*] *famous* acclaimed, celebrated, celebrious, distinguished, eminent, esteemed, extolled, famed, great, illustrious, in the limelight*, lauded, monster*, name*, notable, noted, of note, outstanding, praised, prominent, redoubted, signal, splashy, star, superstar, well-known; CONCEPTS 568,574 —*Ant.* anonymous, obscure, unimportant, unknown

rent [*n1*] *fee paid for use, service, or privilege* hire, lease, payment, rental, tariff; CONCEPT 329 —*Ant.* purchase

rent [*n2*] *opening, split* breach, break, chink, cleavage, crack, discord, dissension, division, faction, fissure, flaw, fracture, gash, hole, perforation, rift, rip, rupture, schism, slash, slit, tatter, tear; CONCEPTS 513,665 —*Ant.* closed

rent [v] *pay or charge fee for use, service, or privilege* allow the use of, borrow, charter, contract, engage, hire, lease, lend, let, loan, make available, put on loan, sublet, take it; CONCEPTS 89,115 —*Ant.* buy, purchase

renunciation [n] *abandonment, rejection* abdication, abjuration, abnegation, abstention, cancellation, denial, disavowal, disclaimer, eschewal, eschewing, forbearing, forswearing, giving up, rebuff, refusal, relinquishment, remission, renouncement, repeal, repudiation, resignation, sacrifice, self-abnegation, self-denial, self-sacrifice, spurning, surrender, veto, waiver, yielding; CONCEPTS 30,54,195 —*Ant.* allowance, approval, condonation

repair [n] *restoration, fixing* adjustment, darn, improvement, mend, new part, overhaul, patch, reconstruction, reformation, rehabilitation, replacement, substitution; CONCEPTS 513,700,824 —*Ant.* breaking, damage, destruction, harm, hurt, injury, neglect, wrecking

repair [v1] *fix, restore* compensate for, correct, darn, debug*, doctor*, do up*, emend, fiddle with, give a face-lift*, heal, improve, make good, make up for, mend, overhaul, patch, patch up, put back together, put in order, put right, rebuild, recondition, recover, rectify, redress, reform, refresh, refurbish, rejuvenate, remedy, renew, renovate, retread, retrieve, revamp, revive, right, settle, sew, square*, touch up; CONCEPT 212 —*Ant.* break, damage, destroy, hurt, injure, ruin, spoil, wreck

repair [v2] *leave; retire* apply, betake oneself, fare, go, head for, hie, journey, move, pass, proceed, process, push on, recur, refer, remove, resort, run, set off for, travel, turn, wend, withdraw; CONCEPT 195 —*Ant.* maintain, remain, stay

reparation [n] *compensation, amends* adjustment, apology, atonement, damages, dues, emolument, expiation, indemnification, indemnity, making good, payment, penance, propitiation, quittance, recompense, redemption, redress, remuneration, renewal, repair, repayment, reprisal, requital, restitution, retribution, reward, satisfaction, settlement, squaring things*; CONCEPTS 337,344,712 —*Ant.* extortion, penalty, theft

repartee [n] *pleasant conversation* answer, badinage, banter, bon mot*, comeback, humor, irony, persiflage, pleasantry, quip, raillery, rejoinder, reply, response, retort, riposte, sally, sarcasm, satire, wit, witticism, wittiness, wordplay; CONCEPTS 45,56,266 —*Ant.* argument, disagreement, fight

repast [n] *meal* banquet, chow*, eats*, fare, feast, feed, food, grub*, mess, refection, refreshment, snack, spread, victuals; CONCEPT 459

repay [v1] *give back money or possession* accord, award, balance, compensate, indemnify, make amends, make restitution, make up for, offset, pay back, pay dues, rebate, recompense, refund, reimburse, remunerate, requite, restore, return, reward, settle up, square*; CONCEPTS 131,341 —*Ant.* deprive, extort, penalize, seize, steal, take

repay [v2] *get even; obtain restitution for past*

injustice avenge, even the score, get back at, get revenge, make reprisal, pay back, reciprocate, requite, retaliate, return, return the compliment*, revenge, settle the score*, square accounts*; CONCEPTS 7,19,246,384 —*Ant.* leave alone

repeal [n] *cancellation* abolition, abrogation, annulment, invalidation, nullification, rescinding, rescindment, rescission, revocation, withdrawal; CONCEPTS 121,318,685 —*Ant.* approval, enactment, passage, sanction, validation

repeal [v] *declare null and void* abolish, abrogate, annul, back out, backpedal*, blow, call off*, cancel, countermand, dismantle, invalidate, kill*, KO*, lift, nix*, nullify, opt out, recall, renig, rescind, reverse, revoke, scrub, set aside, shoot down, stand down, throw over, vacate, void, wash out, weasel out*, wipe out, withdraw, worm out*, X-out*, zap*; CONCEPTS 50,88,121,317 —*Ant.* approve, enact, pass, sanction, validate

repeat [n] *something done over; duplicate* echo, recapitulation, reiteration, repetition, replay, reproduction, rerun, reshowing; CONCEPT 695 —*Ant.* original

repeat [v] *duplicate, do again* chime, come again, din, ditto*, drum into*, echo, go over again, hold over, imitate, ingeminate, iterate, make like*, occur again, play back, play over, quote, read back, reappear, recapitulate, recast, reciprocate, recite, reconstruct, recrudesce, recur, redo, refashion, reform, rehash*, rehearse, reissue, reiterate, relate, remake, renew, reoccur, replay, reprise, reproduce, rerun, resay, reshow, restate, retell, return, revert, revolve, rework*, run over, sing same old song*; CONCEPTS 91, 111,171

repeatedly [adv] *over and over again* again, again and again, frequently, many a time, many times, much, oft, often, oftentimes, ofttimes, regularly, time after time, time and again; CONCEPT 553 —*Ant.* never

repel [v1] *push away; repulse* beat back, beat off, brush off, buck, cast aside, chase away, check, confront, cool*, cut, decline, dismiss, disown, dispute, drive away, drive back, drive off, duel, fend off, fight, force back, force off, give cold shoulder to*, hold back, hold off, keep at arm's length*, keep at bay*, keep off, kick, knock down, oppose, parry, push back, put down, put to flight, rebuff, rebut, refuse, reject, resist, stand up against, stave off, traverse, turn down, ward off, withstand; CONCEPTS 30, 208 —*Ant.* attract, draw

repel [v2] *induce aversion* disgust, give a pain in neck*, make sick*, offend, put off*, reluct, repulse, revolt, sicken, turn off*, turn one's stomach*; CONCEPTS 7,19,303 —*Ant.* attract, draw

repent [v] *ask forgiveness* apologize, atone, be ashamed, be contrite, be sorry, bewail, deplore, feel remorse, have qualms, lament, reform, regret, relent, reproach oneself, rue, see error of ways*, show penitence, sorrow; CONCEPTS 48,410

repentance [n] *feeling bad for past action* attrition, compunction, conscience, contriteness, contrition, grief, guilt, penitence, penitency, regret, remorse, rue, ruth, self-reproach, sorriness, sorrow; CONCEPTS 410,728 —*Ant.* happiness

repercussion [n] *consequence* backlash, chain reaction, echo, effect, fallout, feedback, flak*, follow-through*, follow-up, impact, imprint, influence, kickback*, mark, reaction, rebound, recoil, re-echo, result, reverberation, side effect, spinoff*, waves*; CONCEPT 230 —*Ant.* cause

repertoire [n] *collection* range, repertory, repository, reserve, stock, stockpile, store, supply; CONCEPTS 263,432,712

repertory [n] *collection* bit, cache, depot, list, range, rep*, repertoire, repository, routine, schtick*, stock, stockroom, store, storehouse, stunt*, supply; CONCEPTS 263,432,712

repetition [n] *duplication; doing again* alliteration, broken record*, chant, chorus, copy, echo, encore, ingemination, iteracy, iterance, iteration, litany, paraphrase, periodicity, perseveration, practice, reappearance, recapitulation, recital, recurrence, redundancy, rehearsal, reiteration, relation, renewal, reoccurrence, repeat, repetitiousness, replication, report, reproduction, restatement, return, rhythm, rote, tautology; CONCEPT 695 —*Ant.* instance

repetitious [adj] *wordy, tedious* alliterative, boring, dull, echoic, iterant, iterative, long-winded, plangent, pleonastic, prolix, recapitulatory, redundant, reiterative, repeating, repetitive, resonant, tautological, verbose, windy; CONCEPT 553 —*Ant.* concise, simple

rephrase [v] *say in another way* express differently, paraphrase, put another way, put differently, put in other words, recast, reword; CONCEPT 57

replace [v] *take the place of; put in place of* alter, back up, change, compensate, displace, fill in, follow, front for*, give back, mend, oust, outplace, patch, pinch hit for*, put back, reconstitute, recoup, recover, redeem, redress, repay, restitute, restore, retrieve, ring, ring in, shift, sit in, stand in, stand in lieu of, step into shoes of*, sub*, substitute, succeed, supersede, supplant, supply, swap places, take out, take over, take over from; CONCEPTS 104,128,211,697 —*Ant.* leave alone

replenish [v] *fill, stock* furnish, make up, provide, provision, refill, refresh, reload, renew, replace, restock, restore, top; CONCEPTS 140,209 —*Ant.* deplete, use up, waste

replete [adj] *full, well-stocked* abounding, abundant, alive, awash, brimful, brimming, charged, chock-full*, complete, crammed, crowded, filled, full up*, glutted, gorged, jammed, jam-packed, lavish, loaded, luxurious, overfed, overflowing, packed, plenteous, rife, sated, satiated, stuffed, swarming, teeming, thronged, well-provided; CONCEPTS 483,740 —*Ant.* empty, needy, wanting

replica [n] *duplicate* carbon, carbon copy, chip off old block*, clone, copy, ditto*, dupe*, facsimile, flimsy*, imitation, likeness, look-alike, mimeo, mimic, miniature, model, photocopy, reduplication, repeat, replication, repro, reproduction, stat, Xerox*; CONCEPTS 260,670,686 —*Ant.* original

reply [n] *answer* acknowledgment, antiphon, back talk*, comeback, counter, echo, feedback, knee-jerk reaction*, lip*, reaction, reciprocation, rejoinder, respond, response, retaliation,

retort, return, riposte, sass*, snappy comeback*, vibes*, wisecrack; CONCEPT 278 —*Ant.* question, request

reply [v] *answer* acknowledge, be in touch*, come back*, counter, echo, feedback, field the question*, get back to, react, reciprocate, rejoin, respond, retaliate, retort, return, riposte, shoot back*, squelch*, top*, write back; CONCEPT 45 —*Ant.* question, request

report [n1] *account, story* address, announcement, article, blow by blow*, brief, broadcast, cable, chronicle, communication, communique, declaration, description, detail, digest, dispatch, handout, history, hot wire*, information, message, narration, narrative, news, note, opinion, outline, paper, picture, piece, précis, proclamation, pronouncement, recital, record, relation, release, résumé, rundown, scoop*, statement, summary, tale, telegram, tidings, version, wire, word*, write-up; CONCEPTS 274,282,283

report [n2] *gossip, talk* advice, blow by blow*, buzz*, canard, chat, chatter, chitchat, comment, conversation, cry*, dirt*, earful, grapevine*, hash*, hearsay, intelligence, murmur, news, prating, rumble*, rumor, scandal, scuttlebutt*, small talk*, speech, tattle, the latest*, tidings, whispering, word*; CONCEPTS 51,278

report [n3] *loud noise* bang, blast, boom, crack, crash, detonation, discharge, explosion, reverberation, sound; CONCEPT 595 —*Ant.* quiet, silence

report [n4] *reputation* character, esteem, fame, name, regard, rep*, repute; CONCEPT 388

report [v1] *communicate information, knowledge* account for, advise, air, announce, bring word, broadcast, cable, circulate, cover, declare, describe, detail, disclose, document, enunciate, give an account of, give the facts, impart, inform, inscribe, itemize, list, make known, make public, mention, narrate, note, notify, pass on, present, proclaim, promulgate, provide details, publish, recite, record, recount, rehearse, relate, relay, retail, reveal, set forth, spread, state, summarize, telephone, tell, trumpet, wire, write up; CONCEPT 60 —*Ant.* conceal, suppress

report [v2] *present oneself* appear, arrive, be at hand, be present, clock in*, come, get to, reach, show, show up, turn up*; CONCEPT 159

reporter [n] *person who informs* anchor, anchorperson, announcer, columnist, correspondent, cub*, editor, ink slinger*, interviewer, journalist, legperson*, newscaster, newshound*, newsperson, newswriter, press person, scribe, scrivener, stringer, writer; CONCEPTS 348,356

repose [n] *restfulness; calm* ease, inaction, inactivity, leisure, peace, quiet, quietness, quietude, refreshment, relaxation, relaxing, renewal, requiescence, respite, rest, restoration, sleep, slumber, stillness, tranquillity; CONCEPTS 410,681,720 —*Ant.* agitation, disturbance, upset, worry

repose [v] *relax; recline* deposit, lay down, lie, lie down, loaf, loll, lounge, place, rest, settle, settle down, slant, sleep, slumber, stretch, stretch out, take it easy, tilt; CONCEPTS 154,210 —*Ant.* be active, be busy, energize

repository [n] *warehouse* archive, depository, depot, magazine, safe, stockroom, storage place, storehouse, store room, vault; CONCEPTS 435,439,449

repossess [v] *take back* get back, obtain again, reacquire, recapture, reclaim, recover, retake, retrieve; CONCEPTS 120,183

reprehensible [adj] *very bad; shameful* amiss, blamable, blameworthy, censurable, condemnable, culpable, delinquent, demeritorious, discreditable, disgraceful, errant, erring, guilty, ignoble, objectionable, opprobrious, remiss, sinful, unholy, unworthy, wicked; CONCEPT 571 —Ant. creditable, good, kind, respectable

represent [v1] *present image of; symbolize* act as, act as broker, act for, act in place of, appear as, assume the role of, be, be agent for, be attorney for, be proxy for, betoken, body, buy for, copy, correspond to, do business for, emblematize, embody, enact, epitomize, equal, equate, exemplify, exhibit, express, factor, hold office, imitate, impersonate, mean, perform, personify, play the part, produce, put on, reproduce, sell for, serve, serve as, show, speak for, stage, stand for, steward, substitute, typify; CONCEPTS 87,317,682,716

represent [v2] *depict, show* body forth, delineate, denote, describe, design, designate, display, draft, enact, evoke, exhibit, express, hint, illustrate, interpret, limn, narrate, outline, picture, portray, realize, relate, render, reproduce, run down, run through, sketch, suggest, track; CONCEPTS 138,261

representative [adj] *characteristic, typical* adumbrative, archetypal, classic, classical, delineative, depictive, emblematic, evocative, exemplary, ideal, illustrative, model, presentational, prototypal, prototypical, quintessential, rep*, symbolic, symbolical; CONCEPTS 487, 573 —Ant. atypical, different, uncharacteristic, unrepresentative

representative [n1] *person who acts in the stead of another* agent, assemblyperson, attorney, commissioner, congressperson, councilor, councilperson, counselor, delegate, deputy, lawyer, legislator, member, messenger, proxy, rep*, salesperson, senator, spokesperson; CONCEPTS 348,354

representative [n2] *typical example* archetype, case, case history, embodiment, epitome, exemplar, illustration, instance, personification, sample, sampling, specimen, type; CONCEPT 686 —Ant. atypical

repress [v] *hold back, hold in* black out*, bottle, chasten, check, collect, compose, control, cool*, cork*, crush, curb, gridlock*, hinder, hold back, inhibit, jam up, keep in, keep in check, keep under wraps*, kill*, lock, master, muffle, overcome, overpower, quash, quelch, quell, rein, restrain, shush, silence, simmer down*, smother, squelch, stifle, subdue, subjugate, suppress, swallow, throw cold water on*, tie up*; CONCEPTS 121,130 —Ant. allow, let go, permit

reprieve [n] *relief of blame, responsibility* abatement, abeyance, absolution, acquittal, alleviation, amnesty, anchor*, clearance, clemency, commute, deferment, freeing, let-up*, lifeboat*, lifesaver*, mitigation, palliation, pardon, postponement, release, remission, respite, spring*, stay, suspension, truce; CONCEPTS 318,685

reprieve [v] *relieve of blame, responsibility* abate, absolve, allay, alleviate, amnesty, excuse, forgive, grant a stay, let go, let off, let off the hook*, let off this time*, let up on*, mitigate, palliate, pardon, postpone, remit, respite; CONCEPTS 50,88,317 —Ant. accusation, blame

reprimand [n] *oral punishment* admonishment, admonition, bawling out*, blame, calling down*, castigation, censure, chiding, comeuppance, dressing-down*, going over*, grooming, hard time*, lecture, piece of one's mind*, ragging*, rap*, rebuke, reprehension, reproof, scolding, slap on wrist*, talking-to, telling-off, tongue-lashing, what for*; CONCEPTS 123,278 —Ant. forgiveness, praise, reward

reprimand [v] *blame, scold* admonish, call on the carpet*, castigate, censure, check, chew out*, chide, come down on*, criticize, denounce, dress down*, give piece of one's mind*, give the dickens*, lecture, lesson, light into*, lower the boom*, monish, rap, rebuke, reprehend, reproach, reprove, take to task*, tell off, tick off*, upbraid; CONCEPTS 44,52 —Ant. exonerate, forgive, reward

reprisal [n] *revenge* avengement, avenging, counterblow, counterstroke, eye for an eye*, paying back, requital, retaliation, retribution, vengeance; CONCEPT 384 —Ant. kindness, sympathy

reproach [n] *strong criticism; dishonor* abuse, admonishment, admonition, blame, blemish, censure, chiding, condemnation, contempt, disapproval, discredit, disgrace, disrepute, ignominy, indignity, obloquy, odium, opprobrium, rap*, rebuke, reprehension, reprimand, reproof, scorn, shame, slight, slur, stain, stigma; CONCEPTS 44,52,123,388 —Ant. approval, honor, praise, respect

reproach [v] *find fault with* abuse, admonish, blame, call down, call to task*, cavil, censure, chide, condemn, criticize, defame, discredit, disparage, give comeuppance*, give the devil*, jawbone*, lay on*, lesson, rake, ream, rebuke, reprehend, reprimand, reprove, scold, sit on*, take to task, trim, upbraid; CONCEPTS 44,52 —Ant. approve, praise

reprobate [adj] *shameless* bad, corrupt, degenerate, foul, immoral, improper, incorrigible, lewd, rude, sinful, unprincipled, vile, wanton, wicked; CONCEPTS 401,545

reproduce [v1] *make more copies of* carbon*, clone, copy, do again, dupe*, duplicate, echo, emulate, engross, follow, imitate, knock off, manifold, match, mimeo*, mimeograph, mirror, parallel, photocopy, photograph, photostat, pirate, portray, print, reawaken, recount, recreate, redo, reduplicate, reenact, reflect, relive, remake, repeat, replicate, represent, reprint, restamp, revive, transcribe, type, Xerox*; CONCEPTS 111,171 —Ant. abort, destroy, stop

reproduce [v2] *make something new; give birth* bear, beget, breed, engender, father, fecundate, generate, hatch, impregnate, mother, multiply, procreate, produce young, progenerate, proliferate, propagate, repopulate, sire, spawn; CONCEPTS 173,251,374 —Ant. abort, kill

reproduction [n] *something duplicated; duplication* breeding, carbon*, carbon copy, chip off old block*, clone, copy, ditto*, dupe*, facsimile, fake, flimsy, generation, imitation, increase, look-alike, mimeo*, mimeograph, mirror image*, multiplication, offprint, photocopy, photograph, Photostat, pic*, picture, portrayal, print, procreation, proliferation, propagation, recreation, reduplication, reenactment, renewal, replica, replication, reprinting, repro*, revival, stat, transcription, twin, Xerox*, X-ray*; CONCEPTS 173,625,670,716 —*Ant.* original

reprove [v] *rebuke* admonish, bawl out*, berate, castigate, censure, chew out*, chide, condemn, jump down one's throat*, lambaste, lay into*, lecture, read the riot act*, reprimand, reproach, scold, take to task*, upbraid; CONCEPTS 44,52

repudiate [v] *reject; turn one's back on* abandon, abjure, apostatize, banish, be against, break with, cast, cast off, cut off, decline, default, defect, demur, deny, desert, disacknowledge, disapprove, disavow, discard, disclaim, dishonor, disinherit, dismiss, disown, dump, flush*, fly in the face of*, forsake, nix*, oust, rat*, recant, refuse, renounce, repeal, reprobate, rescind, retract, reverse, revoke, spurn, tergiversate, tergiverse, turn, turn down, wash one's hands of*; CONCEPTS 13,21,30 —*Ant.* admit, approve

repugnant [adj] *bad, obnoxious; hostile* abhorrent, abominable, adverse, against, alien, antagonistic, antipathetic, averse, conflicting, contradictory, counter, creepy*, different, disagreeable, disgusting, distasteful, extraneous, extrinsic, foreign, foul, hateful, horrid, incompatible, inconsistent, inconsonant, inimical, in opposition, invidious, loathsome, nasty, nauseating, noisome, objectionable, odious, offensive, opposed, opposite, repellent, revolting, revulsive, sickening, unconformable, unfitted, unfriendly, vile; CONCEPTS 401,564,571 —*Ant.* friendly, good, nice, pleasant

repulse [n] *snub; rejection* brush-off*, check, cold shoulder*, defeat, disappointment, failure, nix*, nothing doing*, rebuff, refusal, reverse, slap in the face*, spurning, thumbs down*, turndown; CONCEPTS 388,674 —*Ant.* attraction, enchantment

repulse [v1] *push away* beat off, brush off*, check, defeat, drive back, fend off, fight off, heave-ho*, hold off, keep off, kick in the teeth*, nix*, overthrow, push back, put down, rebuff, rebut, reject, repel, resist, set back, stave off, throw back, ward off; CONCEPTS 96,208 —*Ant.* attract, enchant

repulse [v2] *make sick* disdain, disgust, disregard, give a pain*, rebuff, refuse, reject, reluct, repel, revolt, sicken, snub, spurn, turn down, turn off; CONCEPTS 21,410 —*Ant.* please, soothe

repulsion [n] *hatred, disgust* abhorrence, abomination, antipathy, aversion, denial, detestation, disrelish, distaste, hate, horror, loathing, malice, rebuff, refusal, repugnance, repugnancy, resentment, revolt, revulsion, snub; CONCEPT 29 —*Ant.* attraction, liking, love

repulsive [adj] *very disgusting, offensive* abhorrent, abominable, animal*, creepy*, disagreeable, distasteful, forbidding, foul, gross, hateful, hideous, horrid, loathsome, nasty, nauseating, noisome, objectionable, obnoxious, odious, off-putting, pugnacious, repellent, revolting,

sickening, sleazy*, ugly, undesirable, unpleasant, unsightly, vile; CONCEPTS 529,571,579 —*Ant.* attractive, enchanting, inviting, pleasing

reputable [adj] *worthy of respect* acclaimed, celebrated, conscientious, constant, creditable, dependable, distinguished, eminent, esteemed, estimable, excellent, fair, faithful, famed, famous, favored, good, high-principled, high-ranking, honest, honorable, honored, illustrious, in high favor, just, legitimate, notable, of good repute, popular, prominent, redoubted, reliable, renowned, respectable, righteous, salt of the earth*, sincere, straightforward, trustworthy, truthful, upright, well-known, well-thought-of; CONCEPTS 545,567,574 —*Ant.* disreputable, notorious, unrespected, untrustworthy

reputation [n] *commonly held opinion of person's character* acceptability, account, approval, authority, character, credit, dependability, distinction, éclat, eminence, esteem, estimation, fame, favor, honor, influence, mark*, name*, notoriety, opinion, position, prestige, privilege, prominence, rank, regard, reliability, renown, rep*, report, repute, respectability, standing, stature, trustworthiness, weight; CONCEPTS 388,411,689 —*Ant.* disreputableness, ill repute, notoriety

reputed [adj] *believed* accounted, alleged, assumed, conjectural, considered, deemed, estimated, gossiped, held, hypothetical, ostensible, putative, reckoned, regarded, reported, rumored, said, seeming, supposed, suppositional, supposititious, suppositious, suppositive, suppository, thought; CONCEPT 529 —*Ant.* actual, real, true

request [n] *question or petition* appeal, application, asking, begging, call, commercial, demand, desire, entreaty, inquiry, invitation, offer, prayer, recourse, requisition, solicitation, suit, supplication; CONCEPT 662 —*Ant.* answer, reply

request [v] *ask for* appeal, apply, beg, beseech, bespeak, call for, demand, desire, entreat, hit, hit up for*, hold out for*, hustle*, inquire, petition, pray, promote, put in for*, requisition, seek, solicit, sponge*, sue, supplicate, touch; CONCEPT 53 —*Ant.* answer, reply

requiem [n] *hymn, mass* canticle, ceremony, chant, death song, dirge, elegy, eulogy, funeral hymn, liturgy, memorial service, monody, psalm, religious song, ritual, sermon, threnody, worship; CONCEPTS 262,368,595

require [v1] *need, want* crave, depend upon, desire, feel necessity for, have need, hurting for, lack, miss, stand in need, wish; CONCEPTS 20,646 —*Ant.* dislike, have, not want

require [v2] *ask, demand; necessitate* assert oneself, beg, beseech, bid, call for, call upon, cause, challenge, claim, command, compel, constrain, crave, demand, direct, enjoin, entail, exact, expect, insist upon, instruct, involve, look for, obligate, oblige, order, postulate, push for, request, requisition, solicit, take; CONCEPTS 53,646

required/requisite [adj] *necessary* appropriate, called for, compulsory, compulsory, condign, demanded, deserved, due, enforced, essential, imperative, imperious, indispensable, just, mandatory, needed, needful, obligatory, prerequisite, prescribed, recommended, right, rightful, set, suitable, unavoidable, vital;

CONCEPT 546 —*Ant.* nonessential, optional, unnecessary

requirement/requisite [*n*] *necessity, want* claim, compulsion, concern, condition, demand, desideratum, element, engrossment, essential, exaction, exigency, extremity, fulfillment, fundamental, imperative, lack, must, need, obligation, obsession, pinch, precondition, preliminary, preoccupation, prepossession, prerequisite, prescription, provision, proviso, qualification, sine qua non, specification, stipulation, terms, urgency, vital part; CONCEPTS 646,709 —*Ant.* desire, option, wish

requisition [*n*] *demand; application for need* appropriation, call, commandeering, occupation, request, seizure, summons, takeover; CONCEPT 662

requisition [*v*] *ask for; apply for something needed* buy, call for, challenge, claim, demand, exact, order, postulate, put dibs on*, put in for, request, require, solicit; CONCEPTS 48,53 —*Ant.* answer, reply

requite [*v*] *compensate, give in return* indemnify, make, make amends, make good, pay, pay off, quit, reciprocate, recompense, redeem, redress, reimburse, remunerate, repay, respond, restitution, retaliate, return, revenge, reward, satisfy, settle; CONCEPTS 126,131,341,384 —*Ant.* dissatisfy, refuse

rescind [*v*] *declare null and void* abolish, abrogate, annul, back out of, backpedal*, backwater*, call off, cancel, countermand, crawl out of*, dismantle, forget, invalidate, lift, nix*, overturn, pull the plug*, quash, recall, remove, renege, repeal, retract, reverse, revoke, scrub*, set aside, void, wangle out*, weasel out*, X-out*; CONCEPTS 121,234,317 —*Ant.* allow, approve, permit

rescue [*n*] *saving from danger* deliverance, delivery, disembarrassment, disentanglement, emancipation, exploit, extrication, feat, heroics, heroism, liberation, performance, ransom, reclaiming, reclamation, recovering, recovery, redemption, release, relief, salvage, salvation, saving; CONCEPT 134 —*Ant.* danger, peril

rescue [*v*] *save from danger* bail one out*, conserve, deliver, disembarrass, disentangle, emancipate, extricate, free, get off the hook*, get out, get out of hock*, give a break, hold over, keep, liberate, manumit, preserve, protect, pull out of the fire*, ransom, recapture, recover, redeem, regain, release, retain, retrieve, safeguard, salvage, save life of, set free, spring*, unleash, unloose; CONCEPT 134 —*Ant.* harm, hurt, imperil, injure

research [*n*] *examination, study* analysis, delving, experimentation, exploration, fact-finding, fishing expedition*, groundwork, inquest, inquiry, inquisition, investigation, legwork*, probe, probing, quest, R and D*, scrutiny; CONCEPTS 349,362 —*Ant.* ignorance

research [*v*] *examine, study* analyze, consult, do tests, experiment, explore, inquire, investigate, look into, look up, play around with*, probe, read up on, scrutinize; CONCEPTS 31,103 —*Ant.* ignore, neglect

researcher [*n*] *research worker* analyst, analyzer, clinician, experimenter, investigator, scientist, tester; CONCEPTS 348,357

resemblance [*n*] *correspondence, similarity* affinity, alikeness, analogy, birds of a feather*, carbon*, carbon copy, clone, closeness, coincidence, comparability, comparison, conformity, counterpart, double, facsimile, image, kinship, likeness, like of, look-alike, parallel, parity, peas in a pod*, ringer*, sameness, semblance, simile, similitude, spitting image*, two of a kind*, Xerox*; CONCEPTS 664,670,716 —*Ant.* contrast, difference, dissimilarity, diversity

resemble [*v*] *look or be like* appear like, approximate, bear resemblance to, be similar to, be the very picture of*, bring to mind, coincide, come close to, come near, correspond to, double, duplicate, echo, favor, feature, follow, have earmarks of*, have signs of, match, mirror, parallel, pass for, relate, remind one of, seem like, simulate, smack of*, sound like, take after; CONCEPTS 664,670,716 —*Ant.* contradict, contrast, deviate, differ, disagree

resent [*v*] *be angry about* bear a grudge, begrudge, be in a huff*, be insulted, be offended by, be put off by*, be rubbed wrong way*, be vexed, dislike, feel bitter, feel sore*, frown at, get nose out of joint*, grudge, harbor a grudge*, have hard feelings*, object to, take amiss, take as an insult, take exception, take offense, take umbrage; CONCEPTS 29,410 —*Ant.* be happy, like, love

resentment [*n*] *hate, anger* acerbity, acrimony, animosity, animus, annoyance, antagonism, bad feeling, bitterness, choler, cynicism, displeasure, dudgeon, exacerbation, exasperation, fog, fury, grudge, huff, hurt, ill feeling, ill will, indignation, ire, irritation, malice, malignity, miff, offense, outrage, passion, perturbation, pique, rage, rancor, rise, spite, umbrage, vehemence, vexation, wrath; CONCEPTS 29,410 —*Ant.* affection, happiness, liking, love, pleasure

reservation [*n1*] *condition, stipulation* catch, circumscription, demur, doubt, fine print*, grain of salt*, hesitancy, kicker*, provision, proviso, qualification, restriction, scruple, skepticism, string*, strings*, terms; CONCEPTS 646,711 —*Ant.* openness

reservation [*n2*] *the act of holding something, or thing held for future use* bespeaking, booking, exclusive possession, place, restriction, retaining, retainment, setting aside, withholding; CONCEPT 710

reservation [*n3*] *habitat for large group* enclave, homeland, preserve, reserve, sanctuary, territory, tract; CONCEPTS 512,516

reserve [*n1*] *supply* ace in hole*, assets, backlog, cache, capital, drop, emergency fund*, fund, hoard, insurance, inventory, nest egg*, plant, provisions, rainy day fund*, reservoir, resources, savings, stash*, stock, stockpile, store, wealth; CONCEPTS 340,710,712 —*Ant.* emptiness, nothing

reserve [*n2*] *coolness of manner* aloofness, backwardness, calmness, caution, coldness, constraint, coyness, demureness, diffidence, formality, inhibition, modesty, quietness, reluctance, repression, reservation, restraint, reticence, secretiveness, self-restraint, shyness, silence, suppression, taciturnity, uncommunicativeness, unresponsiveness; CONCEPT 633 —Ant. friendliness, warmth

reserve [v1] *keep, hold back* conserve, defer, delay, duck*, have, hoard, hold, keep back, keep out, lay up, maintain, plant, possess, postpone, preserve, put away, put by, put off, retain, save, set aside, squirrel*, squirrel away*, stash, stockpile, store, store up, stow away, withhold; CONCEPT 129 —Ant. distribute, give, let go, offer

reserve [v2] *hold for future use* bespeak, book, contract, engage, prearrange, preengage, retain, schedule, secure; CONCEPT 53 —Ant. spend, use, waste

reserved [adj1] *silent, unsociable; constrained* aloof, backward, bashful, cautious, ceremonious, close, close-mouthed, cold*, collected, composed, conventional, cool, demure, diffident, distant, eremitic, formal, frigid, gentle, icy*, mild, misanthropic, modest, noncommittal, offish, peaceful, placid, prim, quiet, reclusive, restrained, reticent, retiring, secretive, sedate, self-contained, serene, shy, soft-spoken, solitary, standoffish, taciturn, unapproachable, uncommunicative, uncompanionable, undemonstrative, unresponsive, withdrawn; CONCEPTS 401,404 —Ant. extroverted, friendly, outgoing, sociable

reserved [adj2] *held for future use* appropriated, arrogated, booked, claimed, engaged, kept, laid away, limited, preempted, private, qualified, restricted, retained, roped off, set apart, set aside, spoken for, taken; CONCEPTS 576,710 —Ant. given, offered, unreserved

reservoir [n] *accumulation, repository* backlog, basin, cistern, container, fund, holder, lake, nest egg*, pond, pool, receptacle, reserve, source, spring, stock, stockpile, storage, store, supply, tank, tarn; CONCEPTS 514,712 —Ant. nothingness, zilch

reside [v] *live or exist in* abide, be intrinsic to, be vested, bide, consist, continue, crash*, dig*, dwell, endure, hang one's hat*, inhabit, inhere, lie, locate, lodge, nest, occupy, park*, people, perch, populate, remain, rest with, roost, settle, sojourn, squat, stay, take up residence, tenant; CONCEPTS 226,407

residence [n] *place for living* abode, address, apartment, condo, co-op, domicile, dwelling, habitation, hall, headquarters, hole, home, homeplate*, house, household, inhabitancy, inhabitation, living quarters, lodging, manor, mansion, occupancy, occupation, palace, rack*, roof*, roost*, seat, settlement, villa; CONCEPT 516 —Ant. business, industry, office

resident [n] *person living in a particular place* citizen, denizen, dweller, habitant, householder, indweller, inhabitant, inmate, liver, local, lodger, native, occupant, resider, squatter, suburbanite, tenant, urbanite; CONCEPT 413

residual [adj] *leftover* balance, continuing, enduring, extra, lingering, net, remaining, surplus, unconsumed, unused, vestigial; CONCEPTS 560,771 —Ant. base, core

residue [n] *leftover part* balance, debris, dregs, dross, excess, extra, garbage, heel, junk, leavings, leftovers, orts, parings, remainder, remains, remnant, residual, residuum, rest, scourings, scum, sewage, shavings, silt, slag, surplus, trash; CONCEPTS 260,432 —Ant. base, core

resign [v] *give up responsibility* abandon, abdicate, bail out, bow out, capitulate, cease work, cede, demit, divorce oneself from, drop, drop out, end service, fold, forgo, forsake, give notice, give up the ship*, hand in resignation, hand over, hang it up*, leave, quit, relinquish, renounce, retire, secede, separate oneself from, sign off, stand aside, stand down, step down, surrender, terminate, throw in the towel*, turn over, vacate, waive, walk out, wash hands of*, yield; CONCEPTS 119,195,351 —Ant. agree, take on

resignation [n1] *relinquishment of responsibility* abandonment, abdication, departure, giving up, leaving, notice, quitting, renunciation, retirement, surrender, tendering, termination, vacating, withdrawal; CONCEPTS 119,195,351 —Ant. agreement, taking on

resignation [n2] *endurance, passivity* acceptance, acquiescence, compliance, conformity, deference, docility, forbearing, fortitude, humbleness, humility, longanimity, lowliness, meekness, modesty, nonresistance, patience, patientness, resignedness, submission, submissiveness, sufferance; CONCEPTS 410,657 —Ant. impatience, intolerance, resistance

resigned [adj] *enduring, passive* accommodated, acquiescent, adapted, adjusted, agreeable, amenable, biddable, calm, compliant, cordial, deferential, docile, genial, gentle, long-suffering, manageable, nonresisting, obedient, patient, peaceable, philosophical, pliant, quiescent, quiet, ready, reconciled, relinquishing, renouncing, satisfied, stoical, subdued, submissive, subservient, tame, tolerant, tractable, unassertive, unprotesting, unresisting, well-disposed, willing, yielding; CONCEPTS 401,542 —Ant. intolerant

resilient [adj] *bouncy, flexible* airy, buoyant, effervescent, elastic, expansive, hardy, irrepressible, plastic, pliable, quick to recover, rebounding, rolling with punches*, rubbery, snapping back, springy, stretchy, strong, supple, tough, volatile; CONCEPTS 488,489 —Ant. hard, inflexible, rigid, stiff

resist [v] *withstand, oppose* abide, abstain from, antagonize, assail, assault, battle, bear, brook, buck, check, combat, confront, contend, continue, counteract, countervail, curb, defy, die hard, dispute, duel, endure, fight back, forbear, forgo, hinder, hold, hold off, hold out against, keep from, leave alone, maintain, persevere, persist, prevent, put up a fight, refrain, refuse, remain, remain firm, repel, stand up to, stay, stonewall*, struggle against, suffer, thwart, traverse, turn down, weather; CONCEPTS 23,35, 96,106 —Ant. comply, conform, go along

resistance [n] *fighting, opposition* battle, blocking, check, combat, contention, counteraction, cover, defiance, detention, fight, friction, halting, hindrance, holding, impedance, impediment, impeding, intransigence, obstruction, parrying, protecting, protection, rebuff, refusal, retardation, safeguard, screen, shield, stand, striking back, struggle, support, warding off, watch, withstanding; CONCEPTS 23,96, 106,410 —Ant. compliance, conforming, cooperation, submission

resolute [adj] *determined, strong-willed* adamant, bold, constant, courageous, dead set on*, decided, dogged, faithful, firm, fixed, immutable, inflexible, intent upon, intrepid, loyal, meaning business*, obstinate, persevering, persistent, persisting, purposeful, relentless, resolved, serious, set, settled, staunch, steadfast, steady, strong, stubborn, tenacious, true, unbending, unchanging, uncompromising, undaunted, unfaltering, unflagging, unflinching, unshakable, unshaken, unwavering, unyielding, valiant; CONCEPTS 403,542 —*Ant.* afraid, cautious, cowardly, irresolute, weak

resolution [n1] *determination, strong will* aim, boldness, constancy, courage, dauntlessness, decidedness, decision, declaration, dedication, doggedness, earnestness, energy, firmness, fixed purpose, fortitude, guts*, heart*, immovability, intent, intention, judgment, mettle, moxie*, obstinacy, perseverance, pluck, purpose, purposefulness, purposiveness, relentlessness, resoluteness, resolve, settlement, sincerity, spirit, spunk, staunchness, staying power, steadfastness, stubbornness, tenacity, verdict, willpower; CONCEPTS 410,657 —*Ant.* compliance, indecision, weakness

resolution [n2] *answer, judgment* analysis, assertion, breakdown, call, conclusion, decision, declaration, determination, dissection, elucidation, end, exposition, finding, interpretation, motion, nod, outcome, pay dirt*, presentation, proposal, proposition, quick fix*, recitation, recommendation, resolve, settlement, solution, solving, sorting out, ticket*, unravelling, upshot, verdict, working out; CONCEPTS 18,230,274 —*Ant.* problem, question, trouble

resolve [n] *decision, determination* boldness, conclusion, courage, decidedness, design, earnestness, firmness, fixed purpose, intention, objective, project, purpose, purposefulness, purposiveness, resoluteness, resolution, steadfastness, undertaking, will, willpower; CONCEPTS 410,659,689 —*Ant.* indecision, question, wavering

resolve [v] *make up one's mind; find solution* agree, analyze, anatomize, answer, break, break down, choose, clear up, clinch*, conclude, deal with, decide, decipher, decree, design, determine, dissect, dissolve, elect, elucidate, fathom, figure, fix, intend, iron out*, lick, make a point of, pan out*, pass upon, propose, purpose, puzzle out, remain firm, rule, settle, solve, take a stand, undertake, unfold, unravel, untangle, unzip*, will, work, work out, work through; CONCEPTS 15,18,24 —*Ant.* mull, question, waver, wonder

resonant [adj] *vibrant in sound* beating, booming, clangorous, consonant, deep, deep-toned, earsplitting, echoing, electrifying, enhanced, full, heightened, intensified, loud, mellow, noisy, orotund, plangent, powerful, profound, pulsating, pulsing, resounding, reverberant, reverberating, rich, ringing, roaring, round, sonorant, sonorous, stentorian, strident, thrilling, throbbing, thundering, thunderous; CONCEPT 594 —*Ant.* faint, quiet

resonate [v] *resound* echo, oscillate, reproduce, reverberate, ring, sound, vibrate; CONCEPTS 65,91,171

resort [n1] *vacation place* camp, fat farm*, hangout, harbor, haunt, haven, hideaway, hideout, holiday spot, hotel, hot spring*, inn, lodge, mineral spring, motel, nest, park, purlieu, refuge, rendezvous, retreat, spa, spot, spring, stomping ground*, tourist center, tourist trap*; CONCEPTS 198,516

resort [n2] *alternative, recourse* chance, course, device, expediency, expedient, hope, makeshift, opportunity, possibility, reference, refuge, relief, resource, shift, stopgap, substitute, surrogate; CONCEPTS 693,712

resort [v] *have recourse to; make use of* address, affect, apply, avail oneself of, benefit by, bring into play, devote, direct, employ, exercise, fall back on, frequent, go, go to, haunt, head for, look to, make use of, put to use, recur, recur to, refer to, repair, run, take up, try, turn, turn to, use, utilize, visit; CONCEPT 225 —*Ant.* avoid, dodge

resound [v] *resonate* boom, bounce back, echo, reproduce, reverberate, ring, sound, vibrate; CONCEPTS 65,91,171

resource [n] *supply drawn upon, either material or nonmaterial* ability, appliance, artifice, assets, capability, capital, cleverness, contraption, contrivance, course, creation, device, expedient, fortune, hoard, ingenuity, initiative, inventiveness, makeshift, means, measure, method, mode, nest egg*, property, quick-wittedness, recourse, refuge, relief, reserve, resourcefulness, riches, shift, source, step, stock, stockpile, store, stratagem, substance, substitute, support, surrogate, system, talent, way, wealth, worth; CONCEPTS 340,523,658,710,712 —*Ant.* product

resourceful [adj] *imaginative* able, active, adventurous, aggressive, bright, capable, clever, creative, enterprising, ingenious, intelligent, inventive, original, quick-witted, sharp, talented, venturesome; CONCEPT 402 —*Ant.* dull, uncreative, unimaginative, unresourceful

resources [n] *money, possessions, natural resources* ace in hole*, assets, backing, bankroll, basics, belongings, budget, capital, collateral, effects, funds, holdings, income, kitty*, material goods, means, nest egg*, nut*, property, reserves, revenue, riches, savings, sock*, stuff, supplies, the goods*, ways and means*, wealth, wherewithal*; CONCEPTS 340,446,523,710,712 —*Ant.* debt

respect [n1] *admiration given by others* account, adoration, appreciation, approbation, awe, consideration, courtesy, deference, dignity, esteem, estimation, favor, fear, homage, honor, obeisance, ovation, recognition, regard, repute, reverence, testimonial, tribute, veneration, worship; CONCEPT 689 —*Ant.* disdain, dishonor, disrespect

respect [n2] *way, sense* aspect, bearing, character, connection, detail, facet, feature, matter, particular, point, reference, regard, relation; CONCEPT 682

respect [v] *admire; obey* abide by, adhere to, adore, appreciate, attend, be awed by, be kind to, comply with, defer to, esteem, follow, have good opinion of, have high opinion, heed, honor, look up to, note, notice, observe of, pay attention, recognize, regard, revere, reverence, set store by, show consideration, show courtesy, spare, take into account, think highly of, uphold, value, venerate; CONCEPTS 10,32 —Ant. condemn, disobey, disrespect, scorn

respectable [adj1] good, honest admirable, appropriate, august, becoming, befitting, comely, conforming, correct, creditable, decent, decorous, dignified, done, estimable, fair, honorable, mediocre, moderate, modest, nice, ordinary, passable, presentable, proper, redoubtable, redoubted, reputable, reputed, respected, satisfactory, seemly, sublime, suitable, tolerable, upright, venerable, virtuous, well-thought-of, worthy; CONCEPTS 572 —Ant. bad, corrupt, dishonest, dishonorable, unrespectable, unworthy

respectable [adj2] substantial, ample appreciable, considerable, decent, fair, fairly good, good, goodly, presentable, reasonable, sensible, sizable, tidy, tolerable; CONCEPT 771 —Ant. cheap, inadequate, miserly

respectful [adj] courteous, mannerly admiring, appreciative, civil, considerate, courtly, deferential, duteous, dutiful, gracious, humble, obedient, obeisant, polite, recognizing, regardful, regarding, reverent, reverential, self-effacing, solicitous, submissive, upholding, venerating, well-mannered; CONCEPT 401 —Ant. discourteous, mean, unmannerly

respective [adj] particular, specific corresponding, each, individual, own, personal, relevant, separate, several, singular, various; CONCEPT 556 —Ant. indefinite

respects [n] good wishes best wishes, compliments, courtesies, deference, devoirs, greetings, kind wishes, regards, salaam*, salutations; CONCEPT 278

respite [n] pause, suspension in activity acquittal, adjournment, break, breath*, breather*, breathing space*, cessation, coffee break*, deadlock, deferment, delay, deliverance, discharge, downtime*, ease, exculpation, five*, forgiveness, halt, hiatus, immunity, intermission, interregnum, interruption, interval, layoff, leisure, letup*, lull, moratorium, pardon, postponement, protraction, recess, relaxation, release, relief, reprieve, rest, stay, stop, ten*, time, time out*, truce; CONCEPTS 121,681,807 —Ant. continuation

resplendent [adj] bright, radiant beaming, blazing, brilliant, dazzling, effulgent, flaming, gleaming, glittering, glorious, glossy, glowing, gorgeous, irradiant, luminous, lustrous, magnificent, proud, refulgent, shining, shiny, splendid, splendiferous, splendorous, sublime, superb; CONCEPTS 579,589,617 —Ant. cloudy, dull, gloomy, withering

respond [v] act in answer to something acknowledge, act in response, answer, answer back, behave, be in touch with, come back, come back at, come in, counter, feedback, feel for, field the question*, get back to*, get in touch, react, reciprocate, rejoin, reply, retort, return, talk back; CONCEPTS 45,384 —Ant. ask, question, request

response [n] answer, reaction acknowledgment, antiphon, back talk*, comeback, counter, double-take*, echo, feedback, hit, kickback*, knee-jerk reaction*, lip*, rejoinder, reply, respond, retort, return, reverberation, riposte,

sass*, snappy comeback*, vibes*, wisecrack; CONCEPT 278 —Ant. asking, question, request

responsibility [n1] accountability, blame albatross*, amenability, answerability, authority, boundness, burden, care, charge, constraint, contract, culpability, duty, encumbrance, engagement, fault, guilt, holding the bag*, importance, incubus, incumbency, liability, obligation, obligatoriness, onus, pledge, power, rap, restraint, subjection, trust; CONCEPT 645 —Ant. exemption, freedom, immunity, irresponsibility

responsibility [n2] maturity, trustworthiness ability, capableness, capacity, competency, conscientiousness, dependability, dependableness, efficiency, faithfulness, firmness, honesty, levelheadedness, loyalty, rationality, reliability, sensibleness, soberness, stability, steadfastness, trustiness, uprightness; CONCEPTS 411,633 —Ant. distrust, immaturity, irresponsibility

responsible [adj1] accountable, in charge answerable, at fault, at the helm, authoritative, bonded, bound, bound to, carrying the load, censurable, chargeable, compelled, constrained, contracted, culpable, decision-making, devolving on, duty-bound, engaged, executive, exposed, fettered, guilty, hampered, held, high, important, in authority, in control, incumbent, liable, minding the store*, obligated, obliged, on the hook*, open, pledged, subject, susceptive, sworn to, tied, to blame, under contract, under obligation; CONCEPT 545 —Ant. excused, exempt, free, immune, irresponsible

responsible [adj2] trustworthy, mature able, adult, capable, competent, conscientious, dependable, dutiful, effective, efficient, faithful, firm, levelheaded, loyal, qualified, rational, reliable, self-reliant, sensible, sober, sound, stable, steadfast, steady, tried, trusty, upright; CONCEPTS 401,404 —Ant. immature, irresponsible, untrustworthy

responsive [adj] quick to react acknowledging, active, alive, answering, awake, aware, compassionate, conscious, forthcoming, impressionable, influenceable, kindhearted, open, passionate, perceptive, persuadable, reactive, receptive, replying, respondent, sensible, sensile, sensitive, sentient, sharp, softhearted, susceptible, susceptive, sympathetic, tender, warm, warmhearted; CONCEPTS 401,542 —Ant. insensitive, unresponsive, unsusceptible

rest [n1] inactivity break, breather*, breathing space*, calm, calmness, cessation, coffee break*, comfort, composure, cutoff, downtime*, doze, dreaminess, ease, forty winks*, halt, holiday, hush, idleness, interlude, intermission, interval, leisure, letup*, lull, motionlessness, nap, pause, peace, quiescence, quiet, quietude, recess, recreation, refreshment, relaxation, relief, repose, respite, siesta, silence, sleep, slumber, somnolence, stand still, stay, stillness, stop, time off, tranquillity, vacation; CONCEPTS 315,681,807 —Ant. action, activity, energy

rest [n2] remainder of something balance, bottom of barrel*, dregs, dross, excess, heel, leavings, leftovers, odds and ends*, orts, others, overplus, remains, remnant, residual, residue, residum, rump, superfluity, surplus; CONCEPTS 260,835 —Ant. base, core rest [n3] *base, foundation* basis, bed, bottom, footing, ground, groundwork, holder, pedestal, pediment, pillar, prop, seat, seating, shelf, stand, stay, support, trestle; CONCEPTS *442,825*

rest [v1] *be calm; sleep* be at ease, be comfortable, breathe, compose oneself, doze, dream, drowse, ease off, ease up, idle, laze, lean, let down, let up, lie by, lie down, lie still, loaf, loll, lounge, nap, nod, put feet up*, recline, refresh oneself, relax, repose, sit down, slack, slacken, slack off, slumber, snooze, spell, stretch out, take a break, take a nap, take five*, take it easy*, take life easy*, take ten*, take time out, unbend, unlax*, unwind, wind down; CONCEPTS *210,315,681* —Ant. activate, be active, carry out, do, energize

rest [v2] *lie, recline* be quiet, be supported, lay, lean, lie still, loll, lounge, pause, prop, repose, roost, settle, sit, stand, stand still, stretch out; CONCEPTS *154,681* —Ant. move, stand, walk

rest [v3] *depend, hinge* base, be based, be contingent, be dependent, be founded, be seated on, be supported, be upheld, bottom, count, establish, found, ground, hang, lie, predicate, rely, reside, stay, turn; CONCEPT *711*

restaurant [n] *business establishment serving food and drink* bar, café, cafeteria, canteen, chophouse*, coffee shop, diner, dining room, dive*, doughnut shop, drive-in, eatery, eating house, eating place, fast-food place, greasy spoon*, grill, hamburger stand, hashery*, hideaway*, hotdog stand, inn, joint*, luncheonette, lunchroom, night club, outlet*, pizzeria, saloon, soda fountain, watering hole*; CONCEPTS *439, 448,449*

restful [adj] *quiet* calm, comfortable, contented, hushed, inactive, motionless, pacific, peaceful, placid, relaxed, relaxing, retired, sedate, serene, soothing, still, tranquil, unanxious, unexcited, untroubled; CONCEPTS *401,583,705*

restitution [n] *compensation, repayment* amends, dues, indemnification, indemnity, payment, quittance, rebate, recompense, redress, refund, reimbursement, remuneration, reparation, reprisal, requital, restoration, return, satisfaction, squaring things*; CONCEPT *344* —Ant. dissatisfaction, fee, penalty, taking

restive [adj] *impatient, nervous* agitated, balky, contrary, edgy, fidgety, fractious, fretful, froward, ill at ease, jittery, jumpy, nervy, obstinate, on edge, ornery*, perverse, recalcitrant, refractory, restless, stubborn, tense, uneasy, unruly, unyielding, uptight; CONCEPTS *401,542* —Ant. calm, collected, patient, relaxed

restless [adj] *not content; moving about* active, agitated, antsy*, anxious, bundle of nerves*, bustling, changeable, disturbed, edgy, fidgeting, fidgety, fitful, footloose*, fretful, hurried, ill at ease, inconstant, intermittent, irresolute, itchy*, jumpy, nervous, nomadic, on edge, perturbed, restive, roving, sleepless, spasmodic, strung out*, tossing and turning*, transient, troubled, turbulent, uneasy, unpeaceful, unquiet, unrestful, unruly, unsettled, unstable, unsteady, wandering, worried; CONCEPTS *403,542,584* —Ant. agitated, jumpy, nervous, restive

restlessness [n] *constant motion; discontent* activity, agitation, ailment, ants*, antsiness*, anxiety, bustle, disquiet, disquietude, disturbance,

edginess, excitability, ferment, fitfulness, fretfulness, hurry, inconstancy, inquietude, insomnia, instability, jitters, jumpiness, movement, nervousness, restiveness, transience, turbulence, turmoil, uneasiness, unrest, unsettledness, worriedness; CONCEPTS *410,657,748* —Ant. calm, contentedness, relaxation, restfulness

restore [v1] *fix, make new* bring back, build up, cure, heal, improve, make healthy, make restitution, mend, modernize, reanimate, rebuild, recall, recondition, reconstitute, reconstruct, recover, redeem, reinforce, reerect, reestablish, refresh, refurbish, rehabilitate, reimpose, reinstate, reintroduce, rejuvenate, renew, renovate, repair, replace, rescue, retouch, revitalize, revive, revivify, set to rights, strengthen, touch up, update, win back; CONCEPTS *126,212,244* —Ant. break, damage, destroy, hurt

restore [v2] *give back* hand back, put back, replace, return, send back; CONCEPTS *131,232*

restrain [v] *keep under control; hold back* arrest, bind, bottle up, box up, bridle, chain, check, choke back, circumscribe, confine, constrain, contain, control, cool*, cork*, crack down*, curb, curtail, debar, delimit, detain, deter, direct, fetter, gag, govern, guide, hamper, handicap, harness, hem in, hinder, hogtie*, hold, impound, imprison, inhibit, jail, keep, keep down, keep in line*, kill*, limit, lock up, manacle, muzzle, pinion, prevent, proscribe, pull back, repress, restrict, sit on, stay, subdue, suppress, tie down, tie up; CONCEPTS *121,130,191* —Ant. free, liberate, release

restrained [adj] *calm, quiet* bottled up, calm and collected, chilled, conservative, controlled, cool, corked up, discreet, in charge, in check, inobtrusive, laid-back*, mild, moderate, muted, on a leash*, plain, reasonable, reticent, retiring, self-controlled, shrinking, soft, steady, subdued, tasteful, temperate, unaffable, undemonstrative, under control, under wraps*, unexcessive, unexpansive, unextreme, unobtrusive, uptight, withdrawn; CONCEPTS *401,542* —Ant. assured, bold, confident, extroverted, outgoing

restraint [n1] *self-control* abstemiousness, abstinence, caution, coercion, command, compulsion, confines, constraint, control, coolness, curtailment, economy, forbearance, grip, hindrance, hold, inhibition, limitation, moderation, prevention, repression, reserve, restriction, secretiveness, self-denial, self-discipline, self-government, self-possession, self-restraint, silence, suppression, unnaturalness, withholding; CONCEPT *633* —Ant. agitation, arousal, wildness

restraint [n2] *limitation; something that holds* abridgment, arrest, ban, bar, barrier, bondage, bridle, captivity, chains, check, command, confinement, constraint, cramp, curb, decrease, deprivation, detention, determent, deterrence, embargo, fetters, hindrance, impediment, imprisonment, instruction, interdict, limit, manacles, obstacle, obstruction, order, pinions, prohibition, reduction, rein, repression, restriction, rope, stop, stoppage, straitjacket, string*, taboo, weight; CONCEPTS *5,666,674* —Ant. freedom, liberation

restrict [v] *confine, limit situation or ability to participate* bind, bottle up, bound, chain, check, circumscribe, come down on, constrict, contain, contract, cool down, cramp, curb, decrease, define, delimit, delimitate, demarcate, demark, diminish, encircle, enclose, hamper, handicap, hang up, hem in, hold back, hold down, impede, inclose, inhibit, keep within bounds, keep within limits, moderate, modify, narrow, pin down, prelimit, put away, put on ice*, qualify, reduce, regulate, restrain, send up, shorten, shrink, shut in, surround, temper, tether, tie;CONCEPT *130* —*Ant.* enlarge, expand, free, let go, release

restriction [*n*] *limit* ball and chain*, bounds, brake, catch, check, circumscription, condition, confinement, constraint, containment, contraction, control, cramp, curb, custody, demarcation, excess baggage*, fine print*, glitch*, grain of salt*, handicap, hang-up*, inhibition, limitation, limits, lock*, no-no*, qualification, regulation, reservation, restraint, rule, small difficulty, stint, stipulation, stricture, string*, stumbling block*; CONCEPTS *666,674* —*Ant.* enlargement, expansion, freedom, release

result [*n*] *effect brought about by something* aftereffect, aftermath, arrangement, backwash*, by-product, close, completion, conclusion, consequence, consummation, corollary, creature, crop, decision, denouement, determination, development, emanation, end, ensual, event, eventuality, execution, finish, fruit*, fruition, harvest, issue, offshoot*, outcome, outcropping, outgrowth, payoff, proceeds, product, production, reaction, repercussion, returns, sequel, sequence, settlement, termination, upshot; CONCEPT *230* —*Ant.* cause, source

result [*v*] *happen, develop* accrue, appear, arise, attend, become of, be due to, come about, come forth, come from, come of, come out, conclude, culminate, derive, effect, emanate, emerge, end, ensue, eventualize, eventuate, finish, flow, follow, fruit, germinate, grow, issue, occur, originate, pan out, proceed, produce, rise, spring, stem, terminate, turn out, wind up, work out; CONCEPTS *4,119,242* —*Ant.* cause

résumé [*n*] *outline of experience* abstract, bio*, biography, curriculum vitae, CV*, digest, epitome, précis, recapitulation, review, rundown, sum, summary, summation, summing-up, synopsis, vita, work history; CONCEPTS *271,283*

resume [*v*] *begin again* assume again, carry on, come back, continue, go on, go on with, keep on, keep up, occupy again, pick up, proceed, reassume, recapitulate, recommence, recoup, regain, reinstitute, reoccupy, reopen, repossess, restart, retake, return to, take back, take up; CONCEPTS *221,239* —*Ant.* finish, halt, stop

resurgence [*n*] *revival* comeback, reawakening, rebirth, rebound, recovery, rejuvenation, renaissance, renascence, renewal, restoration, resurrection, return, revitalization, triumph; CONCEPTS *119,221,706*

resurrection [*n*] *awakening from the dead* reappearance, reawakening, rebirth, restoration, resurgence, return to life, revival; CONCEPT *221*

resuscitate [*v*] *revive* arouse, awaken, breathe new life into*, bring back to life, bring to*, come to life, energize, enkindle, enliven, give mouth-to-mouth resuscitation, invigorate, perform CPR, rejuvenate, renovate, restore, resurrect, revitalize, save, wake up; CONCEPTS *13,221,469,697*

retain [*v1*] *hold on to physically or mentally* absorb, bear in mind, cling to, clutch, contain, detain, enjoy, grasp, hand onto, have, hold, hold fast, husband, keep, keep in mind, keep possession, maintain, memorize, mind, own, possess, preserve, put away, recall, recognize, recollect, remember, reminisce, reserve, restrain, retrospect, save, withhold; CONCEPTS *40,190,710* —*Ant.* free, let go, lose, release, spend

retain [*v2*] *hire* commission, contract, employ, engage, maintain, pay, reserve; CONCEPT *351* —*Ant.* fire, let go, pass up

retaliate [*v*] *get even with someone* even the score*, exact retribution, get, get back at, give and take*, make reprisal, pay, pay back, reciprocate, recompense, repay, requite, retrospect, return, return the compliment, revenge, revive, settle, square accounts*, strike back, take an eye for an eye*, take revenge, turn the tables on*, turn upon, wreak vengeance; CONCEPTS *126,384* —*Ant.* forgive, pardon, sympathize

retard [*v*] *hinder, obstruct* arrest, back off, baffle, balk, bog, bog down, brake, bring to screeching halt*, check, choke, choke off, clog, close off, crimp, dawdle, decelerate, decrease, defer, delay, detain, down, encumber, falter, fetter, flag, hamper, handicap, hang up, hesitate, hold back, hold up, impede, lessen, let up, loaf, loiter, mire, poke, postpone, reduce, retardate, set back, shut down, shut off, slacken, slow down, slow up, stall, take down; CONCEPTS *121,130,190,240* —*Ant.* advance, help, push

reticent [*adj*] *secretive, quiet* bashful, clammed up*, close, close-mouthed, dried up*, dummied up*, hesitant, mum, reserved, restrained, shy, silent, taciturn, tight-lipped, uncommunicative, unforthcoming, unspeaking, uptight*; CONCEPTS *267,401* —*Ant.* communicative, forward, unrestrained

retire [*v*] *leave a place or responsibility* absent oneself, decamp, deny oneself, depart, draw back, ebb, exit, fall back, get away, get off, give ground, give up work, give way, go, go away, go to bed, go to one's room*, go to sleep, hand over, hit the sack*, leave service, make vacant, part, pull back, pull out, recede, regress, relinquish, remove, repeal, rescind, resign, retreat, revoke, run along, rusticate, secede, seclude oneself, separate, sever connections, stop working, surrender, take off, turn in, withdraw, yield; CONCEPTS *195,234,351* —*Ant.* begin, enter, join

retiring [*adj*] *shy, undemonstrative* backward, bashful, coy, demure, diffident, humble, meek, modest, nongregarious, not forward, quiet, rabity, recessive, reclusive, reserved, restrained, reticent, self-effacing, shrinking, timid, timorous, unaffable, unassertive, unassuming, unexpansive, unsociable, withdrawing, withdrawn; CONCEPT *401* —*Ant.* demonstrative, extroverted, outgoing, self-confident

retort [*n*] *snappy answer* antiphon, back answer, back talk, comeback, cooler, counter, crack*, gag*, jape, jest, joke, lip*, parting shot*, quip, rejoinder, repartee, reply, reprisal, respond, response, retaliation, return, revenge, riposte, sally, snappy comeback*, topper*, wisecrack, witticism; CONCEPT *278* —*Ant.* question, request

retort [v] *answer* answer back, come back at*, counter, crack*, rebut, rejoin, repay, reply, requite, respond, retaliate, return, riposte, sass*, shoot back*, snap back*, squelch*, talk back, top*; CONCEPT 45 —*Ant.* question, request

retract [v] *take back; renege on* abjure, back, back down, back off, back out of, call off, cancel, change one's mind, countermand, deny, disavow, disclaim, disown, draw in, eat one's words*, eliminate, exclude, fall back, forget it, forswear, go back, have change of heart*, nig*, pull back, pull in, recall, recant, recede, reel in*, renege, renounce, repeal, repudiate, rescind, retreat, retrocede, retrograde, reverse, revoke, rule out, sheathe, suspend, take back, take in, unsay, welsh*, withdraw; CONCEPTS 25,49,119,697 —*Ant.* corroborate, emphasize, reaffirm, repeat

retreat [n1] *departure* ebb, evacuation, flight, retirement, withdrawal; CONCEPTS 30,195 —*Ant.* advance, arrival, coming

retreat [n2] *place one goes for peace* adytum, ark, asylum, cell, cloister, convent, cover, covert, defense, den, habitat, harbor, haunt, haven, hermitage, hideaway, hiding place, ivory tower*, port, privacy, refuge, resort, retirement, safe house, safe place, sanctuary, seclusion, security, shelter, solitude; CONCEPT 516

retreat [v] *pull back, go away* abandon, avoid, back, back away, back down, back off, back out, backtrack, beat it, cave in, decamp, depart, disengage, draw back, ebb, elude, escape, evacuate, evade, fall back, fold, give ground, go, go along with, go back, hand over, hide, keep aloof, keep apart, lay down, leave, move back, opt out*, pull out, quail, quit, recede, recoil, reel, regress, relinquish, resign, retire, retrocede, retrograde, reverse, run, seclude oneself, sequester, shrink, start back, turn tail*, vacate, withdraw; CONCEPT 195 —*Ant.* advance, face, forge, meet

retribution [n] *payback for another's action* avengement, avenging, comeuppance, compensation, counterblow, eye for an eye*, just desserts*, justice, punishment, reckoning, recompense, redress, repayment, reprisal, requital, retaliation, revanche, revenge, reward, satisfaction, vengeance, what for*; CONCEPTS 123,126,384 —*Ant.* forgiveness, pardon, sympathy

retrieve [v] *get back* bring back, fetch, reacquire, recall, recapture, reclaim, recoup, recover, recruit, redeem, regain, repair, repossess, rescue, restore, salvage, save, win back; CONCEPTS 120,131 —*Ant.* give, offer, relinquish

retro [adj] *from yesteryear* dated, evocative, in period style, nostalgic, old-fashioned, old world, out-of-date, passe, period; CONCEPT 578 —*Ant.* modern

retrospect [n] *afterthought* hindsight, recollection, reconsideration, reexamination, remembering, remembrance, reminiscence, retrospection, review, revision, survey; CONCEPTS 17,40,410 —*Ant.* forethought, prophesy, prospect

return [n1] *coming again* acknowledgment, answer, appearance, arrival, coming, entrance, entry, homecoming, occurrence, reaction, reappearance, rebound, recoil, recoiling, recompense, recompensing, recovery, recrudescence, recurrence, reestablishment, reinstatement,

rejoinder, reoccurrence, replacement, repossession, restitution, restoration, restoring, retreat, reversion, revisitation; CONCEPTS 4,695 —*Ant.* departure, leave

return [n2] *earnings, benefit* accrual, accruement, advantage, avail, compensation, gain, gate, income, interest, lucre, proceeds, profit, reciprocation, recompense, reimbursement, reparation, repayment, requital, results, retaliation, revenue, reward, take*, takings, yield; CONCEPTS 340,710 —*Ant.* debt, payment

return [n3] *answer* antiphon, comeback, rejoinder, reply, respond, response, retort, riposte; CONCEPT 278 —*Ant.* question, request

return [n4] *summary* account, form, list, record, report, statement, tabulation; CONCEPTS 283,331

return [v1] *go back, turn back* back up, bounce back, circle back, come again, come back, double back, go again, hark back to, move back, react, reappear, rebound, recoil, reconsider, recrudesce, recur, reel back, reenter, reexamine, reoccur, repair, repeat, retire, retrace steps, retreat, revert, revisit, revolve, rotate, turn, CONCEPTS 159,242 —*Ant.* depart, leave

return [v2] *give back, send back* bestow, carry back, convey, give, hand back, make restitution, pay back, put back, react, rebate, reciprocate, recompense, reestablish, refund, reimburse, reinsert, reinstate, remit, render, repay, replace, requite, reseat, restitute, restore, retaliate, roll back, send, take back, thrust back, toss back, transmit; CONCEPTS 108,131,217 —*Ant.* keep, take

return [v3] *earn* bring in, cash in on*, clean up*, clear*, make, make a killing*, net, pay, pay dividend, pay off, repay, score, show profit, yield; CONCEPT 330 —*Ant.* pay

return [v4] *answer* announce, arrive at, bring in, come back, come in, come to, communicate, declare, deliver, pass, rejoin, render, reply, report, respond, retort, state, submit; CONCEPT 45 —*Ant.* ask, request

reunion [n] *social gathering* assembly, get-together, homecoming, making up*, reconciliation, reuniting; CONCEPTS 109,113

revamp [v] *renovate* clean, do up*, face-lift*, make over, overhaul, recondition, refresh, refurbish, rehabilitate, remake, remodel, renew, repair, restore, resurrect, retread, revitalize, revive, spruce up*, update; CONCEPTS 168,177,202

reveal [v1] *disclose, tell* acknowledge, admit, affirm, announce, avow, betray, break the news*, bring out into open*, bring to light*, broadcast, come out with, communicate, concede, confess, declare, divulge, explain, expose, get out of system*, give away, give out, give the low-down*, impart, inform, leak, let cat out of the bag*, let fall, let on, let out, let slip*, make known, make plain, make public, notify, proclaim, publish, put cards on table*, report, talk, tell, unfold, utter; CONCEPT 60 —*Ant.* conceal, hide, suppress

reveal [v2] *show, uncover* bare, disclose, display, exhibit, expose, flash, lay bare, manifest, open, unclothe, unearth, unmask, unveil; CONCEPT 138 —*Ant.* cover, hide

revel [n] *celebration, merrymaking* bacchanal, carousal, carouse, debauch, festivity, frolic, gaiety, gala, high jinks*, jollification, jollity, merriment, party, reveling, revelment, saturnalia, skylarking*, spree, wassail, whoopee*; CONCEPTS 292,377

revel [v] *take pleasure; celebrate* bask, blow off steam*, carouse, carry on, crow, cut loose*, delight, enjoy, fool around*, frolic, gloat, go on a spree*, indulge, kick up heels*, kid around*, lap up*, lark, let go*, let loose*, live it up*, luxuriate, make merry, paint the town*, rejoice, relish, riot, roister, roll, rollick, run around, savor, step out, thrive, wallow, whoop it up*; CONCEPTS 292,377,384 —*Ant.* dislike, hate

revelation [n] *disclosure, telling* adumbration, announcement, apocalypse, betrayal, blow by blow*, break, broadcasting, clue, communication, cue, discovery, display, divination, divulgement, earful, exhibition, expose, exposition, exposure, eye-opener*, flash, foreshadowing, inspiration, leak, lightning bolt*, manifestation, news, oracle, proclamation, prophecy, publication, scoop*, showing, sign, the latest*, tip, uncovering, unearthing, unveiling, vision; CONCEPTS 60,274 —*Ant.* secret

revelry [n] *merrymaking* carousal, carouse, celebration, debauch, debauchery, entertainment, festival, festivity, fun, gaiety, high jinks*, jollification, jollity, party, reveling, revelment, saturnalia, spree, whoop-de-do*, whoopla*; CONCEPTS 377,384 —*Ant.* mourning, sadness, sobriety

revenge [n] *retaliation for wrong, grievance* animus, attack, avenging, avengment, counterblow, counterinsurgency, counterplay, eye for an eye*, fight, getting even*, ill will, implacability, malevolence, measure for measure, rancor, repayment, reprisal, requital, retribution, return, ruthlessness, satisfaction, sortie, spitefulness, tit for tat*, vengeance, vengefulness, vindictiveness; CONCEPTS 86,122,384 —*Ant.* forgiveness, pardon, sympathy

revenge [v] *retaliate for wrong, grievance* avenge, be out for blood*, defend, even the score*, fight back, fix, fix one's wagon*, get, get back at, get even, give comeuppance, give just desserts*, hit back, justify, kick back, make reprisal, match, pay back, pay back in spades*, pay off, punish, reciprocate, redress, repay, requite, retort, return, return the compliment*, score, settle up, settle with, square, stick it to, take an eye for an eye*, turn the tables on*, venge, vindicate; CONCEPTS 86,122,384 —*Ant.* forgive, pardon, sympathize

revenue [n] *income, profit* acquirement, annuity, bottom line*, cash flow, credit, dividend, earnings, emolument, fruits*, fund, gain, gate*, get*, gravy*, handle*, interest, means, net, pay, payoff, perquisite, proceeds, receipt, resources, return, reward, salary, split*, stock, strength, take*, takings*, wages, wealth, yield; CONCEPTS 329,332,344 —*Ant.* debt, payment

reverberate [v] *vibrate in sound* echo, react, rebound, recoil, redound, reecho, resound, ring; CONCEPT 65 —*Ant.* quieten

reverence [n] *high opinion of something* admiration, adoration, apotheosis, approbation, approval, awe, bow, deference, deification, devotion, devoutness, esteem, fealty, fear, genuflection, high esteem, homage, honor,

love, loyalty, obeisance, obsequiousness, piety, praise, prostration, religiousness, respect, veneration, worship; CONCEPTS 10,32 —*Ant.* disdain, disregard, disrespect, scorn

reverent [adj] *respectful* admiring, appreciative, deferential, devout, dutiful, gracious, humble, obedient, obeisant, pious, polite, regardful, reverential, solemn, upholding, worshipping; CONCEPT 401

revere/reverence [v] *have a high opinion of* admire, adore, apotheosize, appreciate, be in awe of, cherish, defer to, deify, enjoy, esteem, exalt, hold in awe, honor, look up to*, love, magnify, pay homage, prize, put on pedestal*, regard, respect, think highly of, treasure, value, venerate, worship; CONCEPTS 10,32 —*Ant.* despise, disregard

reverie [n] *daydream* absent-mindedness, absorption, abstraction, castle-building*, castles in the air*, contemplation, detachment, dreaminess, dreaming, fantasy, fool's paradise*, head trip*, inattention, meditation, mind trip*, muse, musing, pensiveness, phantasy, pipe dream*, preoccupation, study, thought, trance, trip*, woolgathering*; CONCEPTS 529,532 —*Ant.* nightmare

reversal [n] *about-face* annulment, backpedaling, cancellation, change in direction, doubleback, repeal, rescinding, retraction, switch, turnabout, turnaround, U-turn, volte-face; CONCEPT 697

reverse [n1] *opposite* about-face, antipode, antipole, antithesis, back, bottom, change of mind, contra, contradiction, contradictory, contrary, converse, counter, counterpole, flip-flop*, flip side*, inverse, other side, overturning, rear, regression, retrogression, retroversion, reversal, reversement, reversion, switch, turn, turnabout, turn around, turning, underside, verso, volte-face, wrong side; CONCEPTS 665,697,738 —*Ant.* identical, same

reverse [n2] *bad luck; failure* adversity, affliction, bath, blow, catastrophe, check, conquering, defeat, disappointment, hardship, misadventure, misfortune, mishap, repulse, reversal, setback, trial, turnabout, vanquishment, vicissitude; CONCEPTS 674,679 —*Ant.* good fortune, good luck, progress, success

reverse [v1] *turn upside down or backwards* about-face*, back, backpedal*, backtrack, back up, capsize, double back*, evaginate, evert, exchange, flip-flop*, go back, go backwards, interchange, inverse, invert, move backwards, overturn, rearrange, retreat, revert, shift, switch, transfer, transplace, transpose, turn around, turn back, turn over, upend, upset; CONCEPTS 158,213,697

reverse [v2] *cancel, change* alter, annul, backpedal*, backtrack, convert, countermand, declare null and void*, dismantle, double back*, flip-flop*, invalidate, lift, modify, negate, nullify, overrule, overset, overthrow, overturn, quash, recall, renege, repeal, rescind, retract, revoke, set aside, turn around, turn the tables*, undo, upset; CONCEPTS 13,234,697 —*Ant.* do, enforce, go ahead, meet, reserve

revert [v] *return to an earlier, less-developed condition* about-face*, backslide, change, come back, decline, degenerate, deteriorate, fall off

the wagon*, flip-flop*, go back, hark back,
inverse, invert, lapse, react, recrudesce, recur,
regress, relapse, resume, retrograde, retrogress,
return, take up where left off*, throw back,
transpose, turn, turn back; CONCEPTS
13,385,698 —*Ant.* develop, grow, progress

review [n1] *examination, study* analysis, another look*, audit, check, checkup, drill, file,
fresh look*, inspection, march past*, once-
over*, parade, procession, reassessment, recapitulation, reconsideration, reflection, report,
rethink, retrospect, revision, scan, scrutiny,
second look, second thought, survey, view;
CONCEPTS 24,103

review [n2] *critique; summary* abstract, analysis, appraisal, article, assessment, blurb, book
review, canvass, column, comment, commentary, criticism, discourse, discussion, dissertation, essay, evaluation, exposition, inspection,
investigation, journal, judgment, magazine,
mention, monograph, notice, organ, outline,
pan*, periodical, recapitulation, redraft, reviewal, revision, study, synopsis, theme, thesis,
treatise, write-up; CONCEPTS 280,283

review [v1] *go over again* analyze, brush up*,
call to mind, check out, check thoroughly, debrief, go over, hash over*, look at again, look
back on, polish up, reassess, recall, recap*, recapitulate, recollect, reconsider, reevaluate, reexamine, reflect on, rehash*, remember, rethink,
revise, revisit, run over, run through, run up
flagpole*, summon up, take another look, think
over; CONCEPT 103 —*Ant.* ignore, neglect

review [v2] *criticize, scrutinize* assess, bad-
mouth*, correct, discuss, evaluate, examine,
give one's opinion, inspect, judge, knock*,
pan*, put down*, rave, read through, reedit,
revise, rip, skin alive*, slam*, study, swipe at*,
take down*, trash*, weigh, write a critique,
zap*; CONCEPTS 49,52 —*Ant.* approve, praise

reviewer [n] *critic* analyst, appraiser, commentator, connoisseur, evaluator, expert, interpreter,
judge, reporter; CONCEPT 348

revile [v] *scold* abuse, admonish, berate, blame,
castigate, censure, chide, criticize, denigrate,
denounce, disparage, give a talking to*, lambaste, lay down the law*, lecture, rake over the
coals*, ream, reprimand, reproach, reprobate,
reprove, scorn, tongue-lash, vilify, vituperate;
CONCEPTS 44,52,54

revise [v] *correct, edit* alter, amend, blue-
pencil*, change, clean up, compare, cut, debug,
develop, emend, go over, improve, launder,
look over, modify, overhaul, perfect, polish,
recalibrate, recast, reconsider, redo, redraft,
redraw, reexamine, rehash, reorganize, restyle,
revamp, review, rework, rewrite, run through,
scan, scrub, scrutinize, study, tighten, update,
upgrade; CONCEPTS 79,126,244

revision [n] *change; rewriting* afterlight, alteration, amendment, correction, editing, emendation, homework, improvement, modification,
overhauling, polish, recension, reconsideration,
rectification, rectifying, redaction, redraft,
reediting, reexamination, rescript, restyling,
retrospect, retrospection, review, revisal, revise,
updating; CONCEPTS 79,126,244,700

revival [n] *rebirth, reawakening* awakening,
cheering, consolation, enkindling, freshening,

invigoration, quickening, reanimation, recovery, recrudescence, regeneration, rejuvenation,
renaissance, renascence, renewal, restoration,
resurgence, resurrection, resuscitation, revitalization, revivification, risorgimento; CONCEPTS
119,221 —*Ant.* destruction, killing, suppression

revive [v] *start again; bring back to life* animate, arouse, awaken, bounce back*, breathe
new life into*, brighten, bring around*, bring
to*, cheer, come around*, come to life, comfort, console, encourage, energize, enkindle,
enliven, exhilarate, gladden, inspirit, invigorate,
make whole*, overcome, please, quicken, rally,
reanimate, recondition, recover, refresh, rejuvenate, rekindle, relieve, renew, renovate, repair,
restore, resurrect, resuscitate, revitalize, rouse,
snap out of it*, solace, spring up*, strengthen,
touch up*, wake up; CONCEPTS 13,221,469,697
—*Ant.* destroy, kill, suppress

revoke [v] *take back; cancel* abjure, abolish,
abrogate, annul, back out of*, backpedal*, call
back, call off, countermand, counterorder, declare null and void*, deny, disclaim, dismantle,
dismiss, disown, erase, expunge, forswear,
invalidate, lift, negate, nix*, nullify, obliterate,
quash*, recall, recant, remove, renounce,
repeal, repudiate, rescind, retract, reverse, rub
out*, scrub*, set aside, vacate, void, wipe out*,
withdraw; CONCEPTS 50,88,121,234 —*Ant.*
approve, authorize, enforce

revolt [n] *uprising* defection, displeasure, insurgency, insurrection, mutiny, rebellion, revolution, rising, sedition; CONCEPTS 106,300,320
—*Ant.* calm, harmony, peace

revolt [v1] *rebel, rise up against* arise, boycott,
break, defect, defy, drop out, get out of line*,
insurrect, make waves*, mutiny, oppose, opt
out, overthrow, overturn, renounce, resist,
riot, rock the boat*, strike, take up arms,
turn against; CONCEPTS 106,300,320 —*Ant.*
comply, harmonize, obey, submit

revolt [v2] *disgust, nauseate* crawl*, gross out*,
make flesh crawl*, make sick, offend, pain,
reluct, repel, repulse, shock, sicken, turn off*,
turn stomach*; CONCEPTS 7,19 —*Ant.* delight,
make happy, please

revolting [adj] *disgusting, nauseating* abhorrent, abominable, appalling, awful, distasteful,
foul, gross, horrible, horrid, loathsome, nasty,
nauseous, noisome, obnoxious, obscene, offensive, repellent, repugnant, repulsive, rotten,
shocking, sickening, sleazy*, vile; CONCEPT 529
—*Ant.* delightful, good, nice, pleasant, pleasing

revolution [n1] *drastic action or change, often
in politics* anarchy, bloodshed, cabal, coup, coup
d'état, crime, debacle, destruction, disorder,
foment, golpe, guerrilla activity, innovation,
insubordination, insurgency, metamorphosis,
mutiny, outbreak, overthrow, overturn, plot,
radical change, rebellion, reformation, reversal,
revolt, rising, row, shake-up, shift, strife, strike,
subversion, transformation, tumult, turbulence,
turmoil, turnover, underground activity, unrest,
upheaval, uprising, uproar, upset, violence;
CONCEPTS 106,300,320,697 —*Ant.* stagnation,
submission

revolution [n2] *circuit around something*
circle, circumvolution, cycle, gyration, gyre,
lap, orbit, pirouette, reel, revolve, revolving,

roll, rotation, round, spin, swirl, turn, turning, twirl, wheel, whirl; CONCEPTS 436,484,738,792

revolutionary [adj1] *rebellious* anarchistic, defiant, disobedient, disorderly, factious, insubordinate, insurgent, mutinous, radical, rebel, rioting, riotous, subversive, warring; CONCEPTS 401,529,542

revolutionary [adj2] *new, progressive* advanced, advancing, avant-garde*, contemporary, cutting edge*, developing, forward-looking, innovative, just out*, latest, left, modern, novel, open-minded, radical, state-of-the-art*, up-and-coming*; CONCEPTS 542,544,564,578,797

revolve [v1] *turn, circle* circumduct, go around, gyrate, gyre, orbit, roll, rotate, spin, turn around, twist, wheel, whirl; CONCEPTS 147,738

revolve [v2] *think about* consider, deliberate, meditate, mull over, muse, ponder, reflect, roll, ruminate, study, think over, turn over in mind; CONCEPT 17 —Ant. ignore, neglect

revulsion [n] *disgust, hatred* abhorrence, abomination, aversion, detestation, dislike, distaste, hate, horror, loathing, recoil, repugnance, repulsion; CONCEPT 29 —Ant. like, liking, love, loving

reward [n] *payment, prize* accolade, award, benefit, bonus, bounty, carrot*, comeuppance, compensation, crown*, cue, dividend, feather in cap*, fringe benefit, gain, garland, goodies*, gravy*, grease*, guerdon, honor, just deserts*, meed, merit, perks*, plum*, premium, profit, punishment, recompense, remuneration, repayment, requital, retribution, return, salve, strokes*, sweetener*, tip, wages; CONCEPTS 337,344 —Ant. penalty, punishment

reward [v] *pay; give prize* compensate, honor, recompense, remunerate, repay, requite, stroke*, sugarcoat*, take care of*, tip; CONCEPTS 108,132,341 —Ant. penalize, punish, take away

rewarding [adj] *beneficial, pleasing* advantageous, edifying, fruitful, fulfilling, gainful, gratifying, productive, profitable, remunerative, satisfying, valuable, worthwhile; CONCEPTS 548,572 —Ant. troubling, upsetting

rhetoric [n] *wordiness; long speech* address, balderdash*, big talk*, bombast, composition, discourse, elocution, eloquence, flowery language, fustian, grandiloquence, hot air*, hyperbole, magniloquence, oration, oratory, pomposity, rant, verbosity; CONCEPTS 51,277, 278 —Ant. conciseness

rhetorical [adj] *wordy; flowery in speech* articulate, aureate, bombastic, declamatory, eloquent, embellished, euphuistic, exaggerated, flamboyant, flashy*, florid, fluent, glib*, grand, grandiloquent, grandiose, high-flown, hyperbolic, imposing, inflated, magniloquent, mouthy, oratorical, ornate, ostentatious, overblown, overdone, overwrought, pompous, pretentious, showy, silver-tongued, sonorous, stilted, swollen, tumescent, tumid, turgid, verbose, vocal, voluble, windy*; CONCEPT 267 —Ant. concise

rhyme [n] *poetry in which lines end with like sounds* alliteration, beat, cadence, couplet, doggerel, half-rhyme, harmony, iambic pentameter, measure, meter, nursery rhyme, ode, poem, poesy, poetry, rhythm, rune, slant rhyme, song, tune, verse, vowel-chime; CONCEPTS 278,595

rhythm [n] *beat, accent of sound, music* bounce, cadence, cadency, downbeat, flow, lilt, measure, meter, metre, movement, pattern, periodicity, pulse, regularity, rhyme, rise and fall, swing, tempo, time, uniformity; CONCEPT 595

ribald [adj] *vulgar, obscene* base, bawdy, blue*, coarse, devilish, earthy, fast*, filthy*, foul-mouthed, gross*, indecent, indecorous, juicy, lascivious, lewd, licentious, low-down and dirty, naughty, off-color, out of line*, purple*, racy, rascally, raunchy, raw*, risqué*, rogue, rough, rude, salacious, salty, scabrous, scurrilous, sly, smutty, spicy*, unbecoming; CONCEPTS 267,401 —Ant. chaste, clean, decent

rich [adj1] *having a lot of money* affluent, bloated, comfortable, easy, fat, filthy rich*, flush, gilded, in clover*, independent, in the money*, loaded*, made of money*, moneyed, opulent, plush, propertied, prosperous, rolling in it*, swimming, upscale, uptown, wealthy, well-heeled*, well-off*, well provided for*, well-to-do*, worth a million*; CONCEPT 334 —Ant. poor

rich [adj2] *abundant, well-supplied* abounding, ample, chic, classy, copious, costly, deluxe, elaborate, elegant, embellished, expensive, exquisite, extravagant, exuberant, fancy, fecund, fertile, fine, fruitful, full, gorgeous, grand, high-class, lavish, lush, luxurious, magnificent, ornate, palatial, plenteous, plentiful, plush, posh, precious, priceless, productive, prolific, resplendent, ritzy*, smart, snazzy*, spiffy, splendid, stylish, sumptuous, superb, swank*, swanky*, swell*, valuable, well-endowed; CONCEPTS 334,589,771 —Ant. depleted, impoverished, needy

rich [adj3] *flavorful* creamy, delicious, fatty, full-bodied, heavy, highly flavored, juicy, luscious, nourishing, nutritious, oily, satisfying, savory, spicy, succulent, sustaining, sweet, tasty; CONCEPT 613 —Ant. bland, tasteless

rich [adj4] *full in color or sound* bright, canorous, deep, dulcet, eloquent, expressive, intense, mellifluous, mellow, resonant, rotund, significant, silvery, sonorous, strong, vibrant, vivid, warm; CONCEPTS 406,594,618 —Ant. low, weak

rich [adj5] *very funny* absurd, amusing, comical, diverting, droll, entertaining, farcical, foolish, hilarious, humorous, incongruous, laughable, ludicrous, odd, preposterous, queer, ridiculous, risible, side-splitting*, slaying*, splitting*, strange; CONCEPTS 267,529 —Ant. serious

rich [n] *wealthy people or institutions* bountiful, haves*, landed, monied, nouveau riche, old money, upper class, upper crust*, well-to-do*; CONCEPT 423 —Ant. poor

riches [n] *money and possessions* abundance, affluence, assets, clover, fortune, gold, lap of luxury*, means, opulence, plenty, property, resources, richness, substance, treasure, wealth, worth; CONCEPTS 335,340,446,710 —Ant. debt

rickety [adj] *unsound, broken-down* broken, decrepit, derelict, dilapidated, feeble, flimsy, fragile, frail, imperfect, infirm, insecure, jerry-built*, precarious, ramshackle, rattletrap*, rocky, shaky, tottering, tottery*, tumble-down, unsteady, wavering, weak, wobbly; CONCEPT 488 —Ant. sound, stable

ricochet [v] *rebound* backfire, boomerang, bounce back, deflect, kick back, recoil, return, snap back*, spring back; CONCEPTS 150,194, 195,303,700

rid [v] *do away with; free* abolish, clear, deliver, disabuse, disburden, disembarrass, disencumber, dump*, eject, eliminate, eradicate, expel, exterminate, extinguish, extirpate, fire, give the brush*, heave-ho*, junk*, kiss goodbye*, liberate, make free, purge, release, relieve, remove, roust, scrap, send packing*, shake off, shed, throw away, throw out, toss out, unburden, unload, uproot; CONCEPTS 180,211 —*Ant.* get

riddle [n] *brain-teaser* bewilderment, braintwister*, charade, closed book*, complexity, complication, confusion, conundrum, cryptogram, dilemma, distraction, doubt, embarrassment, enigma, entanglement, intricacy, knotty question*, labyrinth, maze, mindboggler*, mystery, mystification, perplexity, plight, poser, predicament, problem, puzzle, puzzlement, quandary, question, rebus, sixty-four dollar question*, stickler*, strait, stumper*, teaser, tough nut to crack*, tough proposition, twister*; CONCEPT 532

riddle [v] *perforate, permeate* bore, corrupt, damage, honeycomb*, impair, infest, mar, pepper, pervade, pierce, pit, puncture, spoil; CONCEPTS 156,220

ride [n] *journey, trip in vehicle* airing, commute, drive, excursion, expedition, hitch, jaunt, joyride*, lift, outing, pick up*, run, spin, Sunday drive, tour, transportation, turn, whirl; CONCEPT 224

ride [v1] *carry or be carried* be supported, control, cruise, curb, direct, drift, drive, float, go, go with, guide, handle, hitch a ride*, hitchhike, journey, manage, motor, move, post, progress, restrain, roll, sit, sit on, thumb a ride*, tool around*, tour, travel; CONCEPTS 94,148,224

ride [v2] *dominate, oppress* afflict, annoy, badger, bait, be arbitrary, be autocratic, berate, disparage, domineer, enslave, grip, harass, harry, haunt, hector, hound, override, persecute, rate, reproach, revile, scold, torment, torture, tyrannize, upbraid; CONCEPTS 7,14,19 —*Ant.* free, release

rider [n1] *equestrian; commuter* cowboy, driver, gaucho, horseback rider, horseman/woman, passenger, straphanger*, suburbanite, traveler; CONCEPT 348

rider [n2] *amendment, clause* addendum, addition, adjunct, alteration, attachment, clarification, codicil, measure, modification, revision, supplement; CONCEPT 270

ridge [n] *raised part of solid* backbone, chine, corrugation, crease, crinkle, elevation, esker, fold, furrow, hill, hogback, moraine, parapet, plica, pole, range, rib, rim, rimple, rivel, ruck, seam, spine, upland, wrinkle; CONCEPTS 471,509,513 —*Ant.* flat, plain

ridicule [n] *contemptuous laughter at someone or something* badinage, banter, buffoonery, burlesque, caricature, chaff, comeback, contempt, derision, dig*, disdain, disparagement, farce, foolery, gibe, irony, jab*, jeer, laughter, leer, mockery, mordancy, needling, parody, parting shot*, persiflage, putdown*, put-on*, raillery, rally, razz*, rib*, roast*, sarcasm,

sardonicism, satire, scorn, slam*, sneer*, swipe*, taunt, taunting, travesty; CONCEPTS 54,59 —*Ant.* flattery, praise

ridicule [v] *make contemptuous fun of something or someone* banter, caricature, cartoon, chaff, deflate, deride, expose, fleer, gibe, haze, humiliate, jape, jeer, jive, jolly, josh*, kid, lampoon, laugh at, make a fool of*, make a game of*, make a laughing-stock*, make fun of, mimic, mock, needle, pan*, parody, poke fun at*, pooh-pooh*, pull one's leg*, put down*, quiz, rag, rail at, rally, raz*, rib*, ride*, roast*, run down*, satirize, scoff, scorn, send up*, show up, sneer, takeoff, taunt, travesty, twit, unmask; CONCEPTS 54,59 —*Ant.* flatter, praise

ridiculous [adj] *stupid, funny* absurd, antic, bizarre, comic, comical, contemptible, daffy*, derisory, droll, fantastic, farcical, foolheaded*, foolish, gelastic, goofy*, grotesque, harebrained*, hilarious, impossible, incredible, jerky*, laughable, ludicrous, nonsensical, nutty*, outrageous, preposterous, risible, sappy*, silly, slaphappy*, unbelievable, wacky*; CONCEPTS 529,548,552 —*Ant.* believable, reasonable, sensible, serious

rife [adj] *overflowing* abounding, abundant, alive, common, current, epidemic, extensive, frequent, general, many, multitudinous, numerous, pandemic, plentiful, popular, prevailing, prevalent, profuse, raging, rampant, regnant, replete, ruling, swarming, teeming, thronged, ubiquitous, universal, widespread; CONCEPTS 771,772 —*Ant.* low, scarce

riffraff [n] *rabble* commonality, commoners, dregs of society*, gang, gathering, hoi polloi, lower class, mob, one-percenters, outcast, rank and file, ring, scum, trash, undesirables, vermin; CONCEPTS 378,417,432

rifle [v] *ransack* burglarize, burgle, despoil, go through, grab, gut, loot, pillage, plunder, rip, rip off*, rob, rummage, sack, smash and grab*, strip, take, tip over*, trash*, waste*; CONCEPT 139 —*Ant.* order, organize

rift [n1] *break, crack* breach, chink, cleavage, cleft, cranny, crevice, fault, fissure, flaw, fracture, gap, hiatus, interruption, interval, opening, parting, rent, rima, rime, space, split; CONCEPT 513 —*Ant.* closing, closure

rift [n2] *difference of opinion* alienation, breach, break, clash, disagreement, division, estrangement, falling out*, misunderstanding, quarrel, rupture, schism, separation, split; CONCEPTS 46,106,388 —*Ant.* agreement, concordance

rig [n] *equipment* accouterments, apparatus, equipage, fittings, fixtures, gear, machinery, outfit, paraphernalia, tackle; CONCEPT 496

rig [v1] *outfit, supply* accouter, appoint, arm, array, attire, clothe, costume, dress, equip, fit out, furnish, gear, kit, provision, set up, turn out; CONCEPTS 140,167,182

rig [v2] *arrange for certain outcome* doctor, engineer, fake, falsify, fiddle with*, fix, gerrymander*, juggle, manipulate, tamper with, trump up*; CONCEPTS 202,697

right [adj1] *fair, just* appropriate, condign, conscientious, deserved, due, equitable, ethical, fitting, good, honest, honorable, justifiable, lawful, legal, legitimate, merited, moral, proper, requisite, righteous, rightful, scrupulous, stand-up*, suitable, true, upright, virtuous; CONCEPT 545 —Ant. corrupt, immoral, inequitable, unfair, unjust, wrong

right [adj2] *accurate, precise* absolute, admissible, amen, authentic, bona fide, complete, correct, exact, factual, faithful, free of error, genuine, immaculate, indubitable, inerrant, infallible, just, nice, on the money*, on the nose*, out-and-out*, perfect, proper, punctilious, real, right as rain*, righteous, right on*, rigorous, satisfactory, solemn, sound, strict, sure, thoroughgoing, true, undistorted, undoubted, unerring, unmistaken, utter, valid, veracious, veridical, veritable, watertight*; CONCEPTS 535,557,582 —Ant. imprecise, inaccurate, inadmissible, wrong

right [adj3] *appropriate, fitting* acceptable, adequate, advantageous, all right, becoming, befitting, comely, comme il faut, common, condign, convenient, correct, decent, decorous, deserved, desirable, done*, due, favorable, felicitous, fit, good, happy, ideal, merited, nice, opportune, proper, propitious, requisite, rightful, satisfactory, seemly, sufficient, suitable, tolerable; CONCEPTS 558,572 —Ant. inappropriate, unfitting, unsuitable, unsuited, wrong

right [adj4] *sane, healthy* all there, balanced, circumspect, compos mentis, discerning, discreet, enlightened, far-sighted, fine, fit, hale, in good health*, in the pink*, judicious, lucid, normal, penetrating, rational, reasonable, sound, unimpaired, up to par*, well, wise; CONCEPTS 314,403 —Ant. insane, mad, unfit, unhealthy

right [adj5] *conservative politically* die-hard*, old-line*, orthodox, reactionary, right wing, traditionalistic; CONCEPTS 529,689 —Ant. left

right [adj6] *opposite of left* clockwise, dexter, dextral, right-handed; CONCEPT 581 —Ant. left

right [adv1] *accurately, precisely* absolutely, all the way, altogether, bang*, clear, completely, correctly, entirely, exactly, factually, fully, genuinely, just, perfectly, quite, sharp, slap, smack-dab*, square, squarely, thoroughly, totally, truly, utterly, well, wholly; CONCEPTS 531,557,582 —Ant. inaccurately, incorrectly, wrongly

right [adv2] *appropriately, suitably* acceptably, adequately, amply, aptly, becomingly, befittingly, fittingly, properly, satisfactorily, well; CONCEPTS 558,572 —Ant. inappropriately, unsuitably, wrongly

right [adv3] *fairly, justly* conscientiously, decently, dispassionately, equitably, ethically, evenly, honestly, honorably, impartially, lawfully, legitimately, morally, objectively, properly, reliably, righteously, sincerely, squarely, virtuously, without bias, without prejudice; CONCEPT 545 —Ant. unfairly, unjustly, wrongly

right [adv4] *beneficially* advantageous, exceedingly, extremely, favorably, for the better, fortunately, highly, notably, perfectly, remarkably, to advantage, very, well; CONCEPTS 537,572 —Ant. unfairly

right [adv5] *directly, without delay* at once, away, direct, due, first off, forthwith, immediately, instanter, instantly, now, promptly, quickly, right away, straight, straight away, straightly, undeviatingly; CONCEPT 799 —Ant. indirectly

right [n1] *privilege* advantage, appanage, authority, benefit, birthright, business, claim, comeuppance, desert, deserving, due, exemption, favor, franchise, freedom, immunity, interest, liberty, license, merit, permission, perquisite, power, preference, prerogative, priority, title; CONCEPT 376

right [n2] *justice, morality* correctness, emancipation, enfranchisement, equity, freedom, good, goodness, honor, independence, integrity, lawfulness, legality, liberty, properness, propriety, reason, rectitude, right, righteousness, rightness, straight, truth, uprightness, virtue; CONCEPT 645 —Ant. corruption, immorality, injustice, unfairness, unjustness, wrong

right [v] *fix, correct* adjust, amend, balance, clean up, compensate for, debug*, dial back*, doctor*, do justice, emend, fiddle with*, fix up, go straight, launder, make up for, mend, overhaul, patch, pick up, put in place, put right, recalibrate, recompense, recondition, reconstruct, rectify, redress, repair, restore, reward, scrub, set straight, settle, set upright, shape up, sort out, square, straighten, straighten out, turn around, vindicate; CONCEPTS 126,212 —Ant. break, upset, wrong

righteous [adj] *good, honest* angelic, blameless, charitable, commendable, conscientious, creditable, deserving, devoted, devout, dutiful, equitable, ethical, exemplary, fair, faithful, godlike, guiltless, holy, honorable, impartial, innocent, irreproachable, just, laudable, law-abiding, matchless, meritorious, moral, noble, peerless, philanthropic, philanthropical, praiseworthy, punctilious, pure, reverent, right-minded, saintly, scrupulous, sinless, spiritual, sterling, trustworthy, upright, virtuous, worthy; CONCEPT 545 —Ant. bad, corrupt, dishonest, immoral, unfair

rightful [adj] *legitimate* applicable, appropriate, apt, authorized, befitting, bona fide, canonical, card-carrying*, condign, deserved, due, ethical, fair, fit, fitting, holding water, honest, just, kosher*, lawful, legal, legit*, merited, moral, moralistic, noble, official, on the level*, on the up and up*, orthodox, permitted, principled, proper, real, requisite, right, right-minded, suitable, true, twenty-four carat*, valid, virtuous; CONCEPTS 545,558 —Ant. illegal, illegitimate, incorrect, wrongful

right stuff [n] *essential qualities* abilities, bravery, courage, credentials, dependability, drive, experience, guts, knowledge, power, self-confidence, skills, talent, what it takes; CONCEPT 630

right-wing [adj] *conservative politically* conservative, conventional, reactionary, rightist, ultra-conservative, unprogressive; CONCEPT 542 —Ant. left-wing, radical

rigid [adj] *stiff, strict, severe* adamant, adamantine, austere, bullheaded, changeless, chiseled*, dead set*, definite, determined, exact, firm, fixed, hard, hard-line*, harsh, incompliant, inelastic, inexorable, inflexible, intransigent, invariable, locked in*, obdurate, rigorous, set, set in stone*, single-minded, solid, static, stern, strait-laced*, stringent, tough nut to crack*, unalterable, unbending, unbreakable, unchanging, uncompromising, undeviating, unmoving, unpermissive, unrelenting, unyielding; CONCEPTS

403,534,535 —*Ant.* bending, flexible, lenient, limber, pliable, pliant, soft, yielding

rigmarole [n] *nonsense* babble, balderdash*, baloney, blather, bull, bunk*, drivel, foolishness, gibberish, gobbledygook*, hogwash*, hot air*, jargon, jive*, madness, mumbo jumbo*, palaver, poppycock*, prattle, rubbish, senselessness, silliness, trash*; CONCEPTS 230, 388,633

rigor [n] *strictness, exactness* accuracy, affliction, asperity, austerity, conscientiousness, conventionalism, difficulty, exactitude, firmness, hardness, hardship, harshness, inclemency, inflexibility, intolerance, meticulousness, obduracy, ordeal, preciseness, precision, privation, punctiliousness, rigidity, roughness, severity, sternness, stiffness, stringency, suffering, tenacity, thoroughness, traditionalism, trial, tribulation, vicissitude, visitation; CONCEPTS 638,654, 666 —*Ant.* ease, elasticity, flexibility, leniency, pliability

rigorous [adj] *severe; exact* accurate, ascetic, austere, bitter, brutal, burdensome, correct, definite, dogmatic, exacting, hard, harsh, inclement, inflexible, intemperate, ironhanded, meticulous, nice, onerous, oppressive, precise, proper, punctilious, right, rigid, rugged, scrupulous, stern, stiff, strict, stringent, uncompromising, unpermissive; CONCEPTS 535,557,565 —*Ant.* easy, easy-going, lax, lenient, loose, mild

rile [v] *anger, upset* acerbate, aggravate, annoy, bother, bug*, disturb, exasperate, gall, get one's goat*, get under skin*, grate, inflame, irk, irritate, nettle, peeve, pique, provoke, put out*, roil, rub one the wrong way*, try one's patience*, vex; CONCEPTS 7,19 —*Ant.* make happy, please

rim [n] *border; top edge* band, brim, brink, brow, circumference, confine, curb, end, fringe, hem, ledge, limit, line, lip, margin, outline, perimeter, periphery, ring, skirt, strip, terminus, top, verge; CONCEPTS 484,836 —*Ant.* center, middle

ring [n1] *circle; circular object* arena, band, brim, circlet, circuit, circus, enclosure, eye, girdle, halo, hoop, loop, ringlet, rink, round; CONCEPTS 436,446

ring [n2] *group participating together* association, band, bloc, bunch, cabal, camp, cartel, cell, circle, clan, clique, coalition, combination, combine, corner, coterie, crew, crowd, faction, gang, in-group, junta, junto, knot, Mafia, mob, monopoly, organization, outfit, party, pool, push, racket, syndicate, troop, troupe, trust; CONCEPTS 325,381

ring [n3] *chime, bell-like noise* buzz, call, clangor, clank, jangle, jingle, knell, peal, reverberation, tinkle, toll, vibration; CONCEPT 595

ring [v1] *encircle* begird, belt, circle, circumscribe, compass, confine, enclose, encompass, gird, girdle, hem in, inclose, loop, move around, rim, round, seal off, surround; CONCEPT 758 —*Ant.* free

ring [v2] *chime; make bell-like noise* bang, beat, bong, buzz, clang, clap, clang, jangle, jingle, knell, peal, play, pull, punch, resonate, resound, reverberate, sound, strike, tinkle, tintinnabulate, toll, vibrate; CONCEPT 595

ringleader [n] *leader* agitator, boss, brains*, captain, chief, chieftain, commander, general,

head, head honcho*, inciter, instigator, mastermind, orchestrator, president, ruler, skipper, spokesperson, troublemaker; CONCEPTS 347,354

rinse [v] *wash off, out* bathe, clean, cleanse, dip, flush, soak, splash, wash, water, wet; CONCEPTS 165,256

riot [n1] *uprising, disorder* anarchism, anarchy, brannigan*, brawl, burst, commotion, confusion, distemper, disturbance, flap, fray, free-for-all*, fuss, hassle, lawlessness, misrule, mix-up, mob violence, protest, quarrel, racket, row, ruckus, ruction, rumble, rumpus, run-in, scene, shivaree, shower, snarl, stir, storm, street fighting, strife, to-do*, trouble, tumult, turbulence, turmoil, uproar, wingding*; CONCEPTS 106,300 —*Ant.* calm, peace

riot [n2] *very funny happening* boisterousness, carousal, confusion, excess, extravaganza, festivity, flourish, frolic, high jinks*, howl*, jollification, lark, merrymaking, panic*, revelry, romp, scream*, sensation, show, sidesplitter*, skylark*, smash*, splash*, tumult, uproar, wow*; CONCEPTS 384,386 —*Ant.* seriousness, solemnity

riot [v] *protest; cause an uproar* arise, debauch, dissipate, fight, go on rampage, racket, rampage, rebel, revolt, rise, run riot*, stir up trouble*, take to the streets*; CONCEPTS 106,300 —*Ant.* comply, cooperate, make peace

riotous [adj] *chaotic, wild* anarchic, deranged, disordered, disorderly, disorganized, helter-skelter*, insurrectionary, lawless, mutinous, out of control, rampageous, rebellious, rowdy, tumultuous, turbid, turbulent, uncontrolled, unruly, violent; CONCEPT 548

rip [n] *tear, cut* cleavage, gash, hole, laceration, rent, slash, slit, split; CONCEPTS 309,513 —*Ant.* closure

rip [v] *tear, cut* burst, claw, cleave, fray, frazzle, gash, hack, lacerate, rend, rive, score, shred, slash, slit, split; CONCEPT 214 —*Ant.* close, sew

ripe [adj1] *fully developed; experienced* accomplished, adult, aged, completed, conditioned, consummate, enlightened, enriched, filled out, finished, fit, full, full-blown, full-fledged, fully grown, grown, grown-up, increased, informed, in readiness, judicious, learned, mature, matured, mellow, overdue, perfected, plump, prepared, prime, ready, ripened, sagacious, seasoned, skilled, skillful, sound, timely, usable, versed, well-timed, wise; CONCEPTS 462,560,578,797 —*Ant.* immature, inexperienced, undeveloped, unripe

ripe [adj2] *favorable, ideal* auspicious, opportune, right, suitable, timely; CONCEPT 558 —*Ant.* inopportune, unfavorable, untimely

rip-off [n] *trick; robbery* cheat, con*, exploitation, fraud, gyp*, larceny, lift*, pinch*, purloining, racket*, steal, stealing, swindle, theft, thievery, thieving; CONCEPTS 139,192 —*Ant.* gift, giving, offering

rip off [v] *rob; trick* abuse, appropriate, bleed*, cheat, con*, cop*, defraud, dupe, exploit, filch*, fleece*, heist, impose on*, lift*, nab*, pilfer, pinch, plunder, ransack, relieve, rifle, skin*, soak*, stick*, swindle, swipe, thieve, use; CONCEPTS 139,192 —*Ant.* give, offer

ripple [n] *wave; wrinkle* billow, breaker, crest, curl, fold, furrow, line, rippling, rush, surge, swell, tide, undulation, whitecap; CONCEPTS 147,436,514

ripple [v] *wave* coil, curl, flow, fluctuate, flutter, motion, oscillate, palpitate, pulsate, quiver, splash, stir, surge, sway, swell, swish, undulate, vacillate, vibrate; CONCEPTS 74,147,149

rise [n1] *increase, improvement* acceleration, accession, accretion, addition, advance, advancement, aggrandizement, ascent, augmentation, boost, breakthrough, climb, distention, doubling, enlargement, growth, heightening, hike, increment, inflation, intensification, intensifying, multiplication, piling up, progress, promotion, raise, stacking up, step-up, surge, swell, upgrade, upsurge, upswing, upturn, waxing; CONCEPTS 700,780 —*Ant.* decline, decrease, drop, fall, slump, worsening

rise [n2] *movement upward; upward slope* acclivity, ascension, ascent, climb, elevation, eminence, highland, hillock, incline, lift, mount, rising, rising ground, soaring, surge, towering, upland, upsurge; CONCEPTS 166,738,752 —*Ant.* decline, drop, fall

rise [v1] *get up; ascend* arise, arouse, aspire, awake, be erect, be located, be situated, blast off*, bob up*, climb, come up, get out of bed, get steeper, get to one's feet*, go uphill, grow, have foundation, levitate, lift, mount, move up, pile out*, push up, reach up, rise and shine*, rise up, rocket, roll out*, rouse, scale, sit up, slope upwards, soar, sprout, stand up, straighten up, surface, surge, surmount, sweep upward, tower, turn out, up*, upspring; CONCEPTS 154,166,738 —*Ant.* descend, lower

rise [v2] *increase, grow* accelerate, add to, advance, aggravate, arise, ascend, augment, billow, build, bulge, climb, deepen, distend, double, enhance, enlarge, expand, go through the roof*, go up, heighten, improve, inflate, intensate, intensify, levitate, lift, magnify, mount, move up, multiply, perk up, pick up, pile up, raise, redouble, rouse, soar, speed up, spread, stack up, swell, take off, upsurge, wax; CONCEPTS 700,780 —*Ant.* decline, decrease, lessen, lower, recede

rise [v3] *progress in business* advance, be elevated, be promoted, better oneself, climb the ladder*, flourish, get on, get somewhere*, go places*, progress, prosper, succeed, thrive, work one's way up*; CONCEPTS 351,704 —*Ant.* decline, drop, fall, slump

rise [v4] *become apparent* appear, arise, befall, begin, betide, chance, come, crop up, dawn, derive, develop, emanate, emerge, eventuate, fall out*, flare up, flow, go, happen, head, issue, loom, occur, originate, proceed, spring, stem, surface, transpire, turn up*; CONCEPTS 4,716 —*Ant.* decline, recede, regress

rise [v5] *rebel* insurrect, mount, mutiny, resist, revolt, riot, take up arms; CONCEPT 106 —*Ant.* comply, cooperate, give in, go along

risk [n] *chance taken* accident, contingency, danger, exposedness, exposure, flyer*, fortuity, fortune, gamble, hazard, header, jeopardy, liability, liableness, luck, openness, opportunity, peril, plunge, possibility, prospect, shot in the dark*, speculation, stab*, uncertainty, venture, wager; CONCEPTS 675,693 —*Ant.* certainty, safety, sureness, surety

risk [v] *take a chance* adventure, beard, be caught short*, brave, chance, compromise, confront, dare, defy, defy danger, encounter, endanger, expose to danger, face, gamble, go out of one's depth*, hang by a thread*, hazard, imperil, jeopardize, jeopardy, leap before looking*, leave to luck*, meet, menace, peril, play with fire*, plunge, put in jeopardy, run the chance, run the risk, skate on thin ice*, speculate, tackle, take a flyer*, take a header*, take a plunge*, take on*, take the liberty*, venture, wager; CONCEPTS 87,100 —*Ant.* be certain

risky [adj] *dangerous* chancy, delicate, dicey*, endangered, fraught with danger*, going for broke*, hairy*, hanging by a thread*, hazardous, iffy*, insecure, jeopardous, long shot*, not a prayer*, off the deep end*, on slippery ground*, on the spot*, on thin ice*, out on a limb*, perilous, playing with fire*, precarious, rocky*, sensitive, speculative, ticklish, touch-and-go*, touchy, treacherous, tricky, uncertain, unhealthy, unsafe, unsound, venturesome, wicked, wide-open; CONCEPT 548 —*Ant.* assured, certain, safe, sure

risqué [adj] *improper, referring to sex* amoral, bawdy*, blue*, breezy, crude, daring, dirty, earthy, erotic, filthy*, foul, grossy*, hot*, immodest, immoral, indecent, indecorous, indelicate, indiscreet, inelegant, lewd, lurid, naughty, obscene, off-base*, off-color, offensive, out-of-line, provocative, purple*, racy, raw, ribald, salacious, salty, shady, sizzling, smart, smutty, spicy*, suggestive, unrefined, vulgar, wanton, warm, wicked, X-rated*; CONCEPTS 267,545,548 —*Ant.* acceptable, decent, moral, proper

rite [n] *ceremony, tradition* act, celebration, ceremonial, communion, custom, form, formality, liturgy, observance, occasion, ordinance, practice, procedure, ritual, sacrament, service, solemnity; CONCEPTS 377,386

ritual [n] *ceremony, tradition* act, ceremonial, communion, convention, custom, form, formality, habit, liturgy, observance, ordinance, practice, prescription, procedure, protocol, red tape*, rite, routine, sacrament, service, solemnity, stereotype, usage; CONCEPTS 386,634,688

ritzy [adj] *elegant, luxurious* aristocratic, chic, choice, classy, cultivated, dignified, elaborate, expensive, exquisite, fancy, fine, grand, grandiose, handsome, lavish, lush, opulent, ornamented, ornate, ostentatious, overdone, plush, posh, refined, rich, snazzy, stately, stuffy, sumptuous, swank; CONCEPTS 544,574,579,589

rival [adj] *opposing* battling, combatant, combating, competing, competitive, conflicting, contending, contesting, cutthroat, disputing, emulating, emulous, equal, opposed, striving, vying; CONCEPTS 542,564 —*Ant.* assisting, associate, supporting

rival [n] *person who opposes in competition* adversary, antagonist, bandit, buddy, challenger, competition, competitor, contender, contestant, emulator, entrant, equal, equivalent, match, opponent, opposite number, peer; CONCEPTS 348,366,423 —*Ant.* associate, cohort, companion

rival [v] *oppose; be a match for* amount, approach, approximate, bear comparison with*, come near to*, come up to*, compare with, compete, contend, contest, correspond, emulate, equal, go after, go for, jockey for position*, match, measure up to, meet, near, partake, resemble, rivalize, scramble for, seek to displace, tie, touch, vie with; CONCEPTS 92,667 —*Ant.* aid, assist, cooperate, help, support

rivalry [n] *competition* antagonism, athletic event, bout, candidacy, clash, conflict, contest, duel, emulation, encounter, engagement, event, fight, game, jealousy, match, matchup, one on one*, opposition, race, sport, strife, struggle, tournament, tug-of-war; CONCEPTS 92,363

river [n] *waterway* beck, branch, brook, course, creek, estuary, rill, rivulet, run, runnel, stream, tributary, watercourse; CONCEPT 514

riveting [adj] *fascinating, gripping* absorbing, alluring, appealing, bewitching, captivating, compelling, enchanting, engaging, engrossing, enthralling, enticing, hypnotic, intriguing, irresistible, magnetic, mesmerizing, seducing, seductive, spellbinding; CONCEPT 529

road [n] *path upon which travel occurs* alley, artery, asphalt, avenue, back street, boulevard, byway, cobblestone, concrete, course, crossroad, direction, drag*, dragway, drive, expressway, highway, lane, line, main drag*, parking lot*, parkway, passage, pathway, pavement, pike, roadway, route, street, subway, terrace, thoroughfare, throughway, thruway, track, trail, turnpike, viaduct, way; CONCEPT 501

roam [v] *wander about* bum*, bum around*, drift, gad, gallivant, hike, hit the road*, knock around*, meander, peregrinate, prowl, ramble, range, rove, saunter, straggle, stray, stroll, struggle along, traipse, tramp, travel, traverse, trek, vagabond, walk; CONCEPTS 151,224

roar [n1] *growl, howl* barrage, bawl, bay, bellow, blast, bluster, boom, clamor, clash, crash, cry, detonation, din, drum, explosion, holler, outcry, reverberation, rumble, shout, thunder, uproar, yell; CONCEPTS 77,595

roar [n2/v2] *laugh loudly* belly laugh, guffaw, hoot, howl, scream; CONCEPT 77

roar [v1] *growl, howl* bark, bawl, bay, bellow, blast, bluster, boom, brawl, bray, clamor, crash, cry, detonate, din, drum, explode, holler, rebound, reecho, repercuss, resound, reverberate, roll, rout, rumble, shout, sound, thunder, trumpet, vociferate, yell; CONCEPTS 64,77

rob [v] *steal, deprive* abscond, appropriate, bereave, break into, burglarize, burgle, cheat, con, cop*, defalcate, defraud, despoil, disinherit, dispossess, divest, do out of*, embezzle, filch*, heist, hijack, hold up*, hustle, liberate, lift*, loot, lose, mug, oust, peculate, pilfer, pillage, pinch, plunder, promote, purloin, raid, ransack, relieve, requisition, rifle, rip off*, roll*, sack*, scrounge, snitch*, stick up, strip, strong-arm*, swindle, swipe, take, thieve, withhold; CONCEPTS 139,142,192 —*Ant.* give, offer

robber [n] *person who steals* bandit, brigand, buccaneer, burglar, cardsharper*, cat burglar, cattle thief*, cheat*, chiseler*, con artist, corsair, crook, desperado, despoiler, fence, forager, fraud, grafter, hijacker, holdup artist*, housebreaker, looter, marauder, mugger, operator, pickpocket, pilferer, pillager, pirate, plunderer, prowler, punk*, raider, rustler, safecracker, sandbagger*, second-story

operator*, shoplifter, stealer, stickup, swindler, thief, thug; CONCEPT 412

robbery [n] *stealing* break-in, burglary, caper, embezzlement, felony, heist*, hit, holdup*, job, larceny, looting, mortal sin, mugging, purse-snatching, stickup*, theft, thievery, unlawful act, wrongdoing; CONCEPT 192

robe [n] *gown, often for wearing at home* bathrobe, cape, costume, covering, dress, dressing gown, frock, garment, habit, housecoat, kimono, mantle, muumuu, negligee, outfit, peignoir, vestment, wrapper; CONCEPT 451

robot [n] *android, machine* automation, bionic person, cyborg, mechanical person; CONCEPT 463

robust [adj] *healthy, strong* able-bodied, athletic, boisterous, booming, brawny, built, concentrated, fit, fit as fiddle*, flourishing, full-bodied, hale, hardy, hearty, hefty, husky, in fine fettle*, in good health, in good shape, in the pink*, live, lusty, muscular, peppy, potent, powerful, powerhouse, prospering, prosperous, roaring, rough, rugged, sinewy, snappy, sound, stout, strapping, sturdy, thriving, tiger*, tough, vigorous, well, wicked*, zappy*, zippy*; CONCEPTS 314,489,613 —*Ant.* flabby, infirm, soft, unhealthy, weak

rock [n1] *stone* bedrock, boulder, cobblestone, crag, crust, earth, gravel, lava, lodge, mass, metal, mineral, ore, pebble, promontory, quarry, reef, rubble, shelf, slab, slag; CONCEPTS 470,474,477,478,508,990

rock [n2] *foundation* anchor, bulwark, cornerstone, defense, mainstay, protection, Rock of Gibraltar*, strength, support; CONCEPTS 442,712

rock [v] *move back and forth* agitate, billow, careen, concuss, convulse, falter, heave, jiggle, jog, jolt, jounce, lurch, move, oscillate, pitch, push and pull, quake, quaver, quiver, reel, roll, roll about, shake, shock, stagger, sway, swing, toss, totter, tremble, undulate, vibrate, wobble; CONCEPTS 147,149 —*Ant.* hold, stabilize

rocket [n] *projectile* booster, firework, guided missile, ICBM, intercontinental ballistic missile, missile, spacecraft, spaceship, torpedo, weapon; CONCEPT 500

rocket [v] *shoot up* ascend, climb, escalate, go through the ceiling, grow, lift, rise, sail, skyrocket, soar, take off*, tower, zoom; CONCEPTS 148,150

rock the boat [v] *cause trouble* complain, disagree, disturb, make a stink*, make waves*, not conform*, object, protest, stir things up*, upset the apple cart*; CONCEPTS 46,52,54,300

rocky [adj1] *rugged, stony* bouldered, craggy, flinty, hard, inflexible, jagged, lapidarian, lithic, pebbly, petrified, petrous, rockbound, rock-ribbed, rough, solid, stonelike; CONCEPTS 485,604 —*Ant.* flat, smooth

rocky [adj2] *unyielding, inflexible* adamant, bloodless, firm, flinty, hard, impassible, insensate, insensible, insensitive, obdurate, pitiless, rocklike, rough, rugged, solid, steady, tough; CONCEPT 401 —*Ant.* flexible, steady, yielding

rocky [adj3] *doubtful, undependable* dizzy, ill, rickety, shaky, sick, sickly, staggering, ticklish, tottering, tricky, uncertain, unreliable, unstable, unsteady, unwell, weak, wobbly; CONCEPTS 314,488,489 —*Ant.* dependable, happy, healthy

ri
ro

rod [n] *bar, pole* baton, billet, birch, cane, cylinder, dowel, ingot, mace, pin, rodule, scepter, sceptre, shaft, slab, spike, staff, stave, stick, strip, switch, wand; CONCEPTS 436,470,479

rogue [n] *person who deceives, swindles* bad egg*, bad news*, blackguard*, black sheep*, charlatan, cheat, cheater, con artist, criminal, crook, defrauder, devil, fraud, heel*, hooligan*, lowlife*, mischief, miscreant, monstrosity, ne'er-do-well*, outlaw, problem*, rapscallion, rascal, reprobate, scalawag, scamp, scoundrel, swindler, trickster, villain; CONCEPT 412

roguish [adj] *deceitful; mischievous* beguiling, crafty, crooked, cunning, deceiving, deceptive, devilish, dishonest, fraudulent, impish, knavish, lying, naughty, playful, puckish, rascally, shifty, slick, sly, sneaky, tricky, underhand, underhanded, unprincipled, untruthful; CONCEPTS 401,545

role [n1] *impersonation of a character* act, acting, appearance, aspect, bit, character, clothing, execution, extra, guise, hero, ingenue, lead, look, part, performance, personification, piece, player, portrayal, presentation, representation, seeming, semblance, show, star, stint, super, title, walk-on; CONCEPTS 263,716

role [n2] *duty, function* act, bit, business, capacity, execution, game*, guise, job, office, part, piece, pose, position, post, posture, province, stint, task, what one is into*; CONCEPTS 362,694

roll [n1] *revolving, turning* cycle, gyration, reel, revolution, rotation, run, spin, trundling, turn, twirl, undulation, whirl; CONCEPTS 147,201

roll [n2] *cylindrical object* ball, barrel, bobbin, cartouche, coil, cone, convolution, cornucopia, cylinder, fold, reel, rundle, scroll, shell, spiral, spool, trundle, volute, wheel, whorl; CONCEPT 436

roll [n3] *list, roster* annals, catalog, census, chronicle, directory, head count, index, muster, nose count*, register, roll call, schedule, scroll, table; CONCEPT 281

roll [n4] *growl, reverberation* barrage, boom, booming, clangor, drone, drumbeat, drumming, echoing, grumble, quaver, racket, rat-a-tat*, resonance, roar, rumble, rumbling, thunder; CONCEPT 595

roll [v1] *revolve, turn; proceed smoothly* alternate, be in sequence, bowl, circle, circumduct, coil, curve, drape, drive, eddy, elapse, enfold, entwine, envelop, flow, fold, follow, furl, go around, go past, gyrate, gyre, impel, pass, pirouette, pivot, propel, reel, rock, rotate, run, spin, spiral, succeed, swaddle, swathe, swing around, swirl, swivel, trundle, twirl, twist, undulate, wheel, whirl, wind, wrap; CONCEPTS 147,201

roll [v2] *spread out* even, flatten, grind, level, press, pulverize, smooth; CONCEPTS 137,208,250 —Ant. collect, gather, pile

roll [v3] *thunder, reverberate* bombinate, boom, cannonade, drum, echo, growl, grumble, hum, pattern, quaver, rattle, re-echo, resound, roar, ruffle, rumble, rustle, sound, trill, whirr; CONCEPT 65

roll [v4] *rock, sway* billow, drift, flow, glide, heave, incline, jibe, lean, lumber, lurch, pitch, ramble, range, reel, roam, rove, run, stagger, stray, surge, swagger, swing, toss, tumble, undulate, waddle, wallow, wave, welter, yaw; CONCEPTS 147,149 —Ant. stabilize, steady

rollicking [adj] *fun-loving, lively* antic, boisterous, carefree, cavorting, cheerful, devil-may-care*, exuberant, frisky, frolicsome, glad, happy, hearty, jaunty, jovial, joyful, joyous, lighthearted, merry, playful, rip-roaring*, romping, spirited, sportive, sprightly; CONCEPTS 401,548 —Ant. serious, solemn

roly-poly [adj] *pudgy* buxom, chubby*, dumpy, fat, hefty, obese, overweight, plump, plumpish, rotund, round, stout, thick-bodied, tubby*; CONCEPTS 491,773

romance [n1] *love affair* affair, affair of the heart*, amour, attachment, courtship, enchantment, fascination, fling, flirtation, intrigue, liaison, love, love story, passion, relationship; CONCEPTS 375,384

romance [n2] *fanciful story or narrative* ballad, fairy tale, fantasy, fiction, idealization, idyll, legend, love story, lyric, melodrama, novel, story, tale, tear-jerker*; CONCEPT 280

romance [n3] *adventure, flight of fancy* charm, color, excitement, exoticness, fairy tale, fancy, fantasy, fascination, glamour, hazard, idealization, idyll, mystery, nostalgia, risk, sentiment, venture; CONCEPT 673

romantic [adj] *sentimental, idealistic* adventurous, amorous, bathetic, charming, chimerical, chivalrous, colorful, corny*, daring, dreamy, enchanting, erotic, exciting, exotic, extravagant, fairy-tale, fanciful, fantastic, fascinating, fond, glamorous, idyllic, impractical, lovey-dovey*, loving, maudlin, mushy*, mysterious, nostalgic, passionate, picturesque, poetic, quixotic, sloppy*, soppy*, starry-eyed, syrupy, tear-jerking*, tender, unrealistic, utopian, visionary, whimsical, wild; CONCEPTS 403,542,548 —Ant. pragmatic, realistic, unromantic

romp [n] *fun; caper* cakewalk*, cavort, dance, escapade, frisk, frolic, gambol, hop, lark, leap, play, rollick, rout, skip, sport; CONCEPTS 292,384 —Ant. seriousness

romp [v] *have fun, enjoy oneself* caper, cavort, celebrate, cut capers*, cut up*, fool around*, frisk, frolic, gambol, go on the town*, kid around*, lark, let loose*, make merry, play, prance, revel, roister, rollic, skip, skylark, sport, whoop it up*; CONCEPTS 292,384

rookie [n] *novice* amateur, apprentice, beginner, colt*, cub*, fledgling, freshman/woman, greenhorn, neophyte, newcomer, new kid on the block*, tenderfoot*, trainee; CONCEPTS 348, 350,423

room [n1] *space, range* allowance, area, capacity, chance, clearance, compass, elbowroom, expanse, extent, latitude, leeway, license, margin, occasion, opening, opportunity, place, play, range, reach, rein, rope, scope, sway, sweep, territory, vastness, volume; CONCEPTS 651,756

room [n2] *enclosed section of building designed for specific purpose* accommodation, alcove, apartment, cabin, cave*, chamber, cubbyhole, cubicle, den, flat, flop*, joint*, lodging, niche, office, setup*, suite, turf, vault; CONCEPT 448

roomy [adj] *having ample space* ample, broad, capacious, commodious, extensive, generous, large, sizable, spacious, wide; CONCEPT 583 —Ant. cluttered, cramped, narrow

root [*n*] *base, core* basis, bedrock, beginnings, bottom, cause, center, crux, derivation, essence, essentiality, footing, foundation, fountain, fountainhead, fundamental, germ, ground, groundwork, heart, inception, infrastructure, mainspring, marrow, motive, nub, nucleus, occasion, origin, pith, provenance, provenience, quick, quintessence, radicle, radix, reason, rhizome, rock bottom*, seat, seed, soul, source, starting point, stem, stuff, substance, substratum, tuber, underpinning, well; CONCEPTS *442,648,661,826,829* —*Ant.* derivation, derivative, sprout

root [*v*] *dig and search* burrow, delve, embed, ferret, forage, grub, grub up, hunt, ingrain, lodge, nose, place, poke, pry, rummage; CONCEPT *178* —*Ant.* cover

rootin'-tootin [*adj*] *rowdy* boisterous, disorderly, loud, loudmouthed, mischievous, noisy, rambunctious, raucous, unruly, uproarious, vigorous, wild; CONCEPT *401*

roots [*n*] *ancestry* background, birthplace, blood, breed, descent, family history, family tree, genealogy, heritage, kindred, line, lineage, origin, parentage, pedigree, race; CONCEPTS *414,648*

rope [*n*] *cord, line* braiding, cable, cordage, hawser, lace, lanyard, lariat, lasso, strand, string, tape, thread, twine; CONCEPT *475*

roster [*n*] *list of items, names* agenda, catalog, head count, index, inventory, listing, muster, nose count*, program, record, register, roll, roll call, rota, schedule, scroll, table; CONCEPTS *281,283*

rosy [*adj1*] *pink, reddish in color* aflush, blooming, blushing, colored, coral, deep pink, fresh, glowing, healthy-looking, high-colored, incarnadine, pale red, peach, red, red-complexioned, red-faced, roseate, rose-colored, rubicund, ruddy; CONCEPT *618* —*Ant.* pale

rosy [*adj2*] *cheerful, hopeful* alluring, auspicious, bright, encouraging, favorable, glowing, likely, optimistic, pleasing, promising, reassuring, roseate, rose-colored, sunny; CONCEPTS *529,548* —*Ant.* depressing, hopeless, sad

rot [*n1*] *corrosion, disintegration* blight, canker, decay, decomposition, deterioration, mold, putrefaction, putrescence; CONCEPTS *469,698* —*Ant.* building, development, growth

rot [*n2*] *garbage, nonsense* balderdash, bilge, bunk, claptrap, drivel, foolishness, guff, hogwash, hooey*, moonshine*, poppycock, rubbish, silliness, stuff and nonsense*, tommyrot; CONCEPTS *278,529* —*Ant.* truth

rot [*v*] *corrode, deteriorate* break down, corrupt, crumble, debase, debauch, decay, decline, decompose, degenerate, demoralize, deprave, descend, disimprove, disintegrate, fester, go bad*, go downhill*, go to pot*, languish, molder, perish, pervert, putrefy, retrograde, sink, spoil, stain, taint, turn, warp, waste away, wither, worsen; CONCEPTS *240,469,698* —*Ant.* build, flourish, grow

rotary [*adj*] *turning* encircling, gyral, gyratory, revolving, rotating, rotational, rotatory, spinning, vertiginous, vorticular, whirligig, whirling; CONCEPTS *581,584*

rotate [*v1*] *go around in circle* circle, circumduct, circumvolve, gyrate, gyre, move, pirouette, pivot, reel, revolve, roll, spin, swivel, troll, trundle, turn, twirl, twist, waltz, wheel, whirl, whirligig, whirr; CONCEPTS *147,738*

rotate [*v2*] *alternate* bandy, ensue, exchange, follow, follow in sequence, interchange, relieve, spell, succeed, switch, take turns; CONCEPTS *104,697* —*Ant.* stay

rotten [*adj1*] *decayed, decaying* bad, badsmelling, corroded, corrupt, crumbled, crumbling, decomposed, decomposing, disgusting, disintegrated, disintegrating, fecal, feculent, festering, fetid, foul, gross, infected, loathsome, loud, mephitic, moldering, moldy, noisome, noxious, offensive, overripe, perished, polluted, purulent, pustular, putrescent, putrid, putrified, rancid, rank, rotting, smelling, sour, spoiled, stale, stinking, strong, tainted, touched, unsound; CONCEPTS *462,485* —*Ant.* fresh, good, new, pleasant, undecayed

rotten [*adj2*] *dishonest, immoral* bent, bribable, contaminated, corrupt, crooked, debauched, deceitful, defiled, degenerate, depraved, dirtied, dishonorable, disloyal, faithless, filthy, flagitious, impure, mercenary, nefarious, perfidious, perverse, polluted, soiled, sullied, tainted, treacherous, unclean, untrustworthy, venal, vicious, villainous, vitiated; CONCEPTS *404,545* —*Ant.* decent, good, honest, moral, trustworthy, uncorrupt

rotten [*adj3*] *despicable, inferior, bad* amiss, base, below par*, bruised, bum*, contemptible, crummy*, defective, deplorable, dirty, disagreeable, disappointing, diseased, displeasing, dissatisfactory, filthy, impaired, inadequate, injured, lousy*, low-grade, mean, nasty, poor, punk*, regrettable, rough, scurrilous, shaky, sorry, sour, substandard, unacceptable, unfortunate, unhappy, unlucky, unpleasant, unsatisfactory, unsound, vile, wasted, wicked, withering, wrong; CONCEPTS *570,571,574* —*Ant.* good, kind, nice, superior

rotund [*adj1*] *fat* beefy*, big, broad, burly, chunky*, dumpy, elephantine, fleshy, heavy, heavyset, hefty, husky, obese, overweight, plump, plumpish, portly, pudgy*, roly-poly*, round, solid, stout, tubby*, weighty; CONCEPT *491*

rotund [*adj2*] *sonorous* booming, loud, resonant, resounding; CONCEPTS *592,594*

rough [*adj1*] *uneven, irregular* asperous, bearded, brambly, bristly, broken, bumpy, bushy, chapped, choppy, coarse, cragged, craggy, cross-grained, disheveled, fuzzy, hairy, harsh, jagged, knobby, knotty, nappy, nodular, not smooth, nodded, rocky, ruffled, rugged, scabrous, scraggy, shaggy, sharp, stony, tangled, tousled, tufted, unequal, unfinished, unlevel, unshaven, unshorn, woolly, wrinkled, wrinkly; CONCEPTS *485,606* —*Ant.* even, level, polished, regular, smooth

rough [*adj2*] *stormy; not quiet* agitated, blustering, blustery, boisterous, buffeting, cacophonous, choppy, coarse, discordant, dry, furious, grating, gruff, harsh, hoarse, husky, inclement, inharmonious, jarring, raging, rasping, raucous, rugged, squally, stridulent, tempestuous, tumultuous/tumultuous, turbulent, unmusical, wild; CONCEPTS *525,592,594* —*Ant.* calm, mild, moderate, temperate

rough [adj3] *rude, impolite* bearish, bluff, blunt, boisterous, boorish, brief, brusque, churlish, coarse, crass, crude, cruel, crusty, curt, discourteous, drastic, extreme, gross*, hairy*, hard, harsh, ill-mannered, improper, inconsiderate, indecorous, indelicate, inelegant, loud, loutish, mean, nasty, raw, rowdy, severe, sharp, short, tough, unceremonious, uncivil, uncouth, uncultivated, uncultured, unfeeling, ungracious, unjust, unmannerly, unpleasant, unpolished, unrefined, untutored, violent, vulgar; CONCEPTS 267,401 —*Ant.* courteous, nice, polite, refined, sophisticated

rough [adj4] *basic, incomplete* austere, crude, cursory, formless, hard, imperfect, raw, rough-and-ready*, roughhewn, rudimentary, shapeless, sketchy, spartan, uncompleted, uncut, undressed, unfashioned, unfinished, unformed, unhewn, unpolished, unprocessed, unrefined, unwrought; CONCEPT 531 —*Ant.* accurate, complete, definite, precise

rough [adj5] *approximate* amorphous, estimated, foggy, general, hazy, imprecise, inexact, proximate, rude, sketchy, uncertain, unprecise, vague; CONCEPT 557 —*Ant.* accurate, complete, definite, precise

roughly [adv] *about* approximately, around, in the ball park*, in the neighborhood, more or less, practically, pretty near, somewhere around; CONCEPT 583

rough out [v] *do preliminary design* adumbrate, block out, chalk, characterize, delineate, draft, outline, plan, skeleton, sketch, suggest; CONCEPTS 36,79,174

rough up [v] *beat up* bash, batter, hit, knock about, knock around, maltreat, mishandle, mistreat, roughhouse, slap around, thrash; CONCEPTS 189,246 —*Ant.* aid, help, protect

round [adj1] *ball-shaped; semicircular area* annular, arced, arched, arciform, bent, bowed, bulbous, circular, coiled, curled, curved, curvilinear, cylindrical, discoid, disk-shaped, domical, egg-shaped, elliptical, globose, globular, looped, orbed, orbicular, orbiculate, oval, ringed, rotund, rounded, spherical, spheroid, spiral; CONCEPT 486

round [adj2] *complete* accomplished, done, entire, finished, full, rounded, solid, unbroken, undivided, whole; CONCEPT 531 —*Ant.* incomplete, lacking, unfinished

round [adj3] *full-bodied, ample in size* chubby, expansive, fleshy, generous, large, plump, plumpish, pudgy*, roly-poly*, rotund, rounded, tubby; CONCEPTS 491,773 —*Ant.* inadequate, small, tiny

round [adj4] *resonant, rich in sound* consonant, full, mellifluous, orotund, plangent, resounding, ringing, rotund, sonorous, vibrant; CONCEPT 594 —*Ant.* low, soft, weak

round [adj5] *honest, direct* blunt, candid, frank, free, outspoken, plain, straightforward, unmodified, vocal; CONCEPT 267 —*Ant.* deceitful, dishonest, indirect

round [adv] *approximate* about, all but, almost, around, as good as, close to, in the neighborhood of, just about, most, near, nearly, practically, roughly; CONCEPT 762 —*Ant.* definite, exact, precise

round [n1] *globe, ball; semicircular area* arc, arch, band, bend, bow, circle, circlet, curvation, curvature, curve, disc, disk, equator, eye, gyre, hoop, loop, orb, orbit, ring, ringlet, sphere, wheel; CONCEPT 436

round [n2] *cycle, stage* ambit, beat, bout, circuit, circulation, circumvolution, compass, course, division, gyration, lap, level, performance, period, revolution, rotation, round trip, routine, schedule, sequence, series, session, succession, tour, turn, wheel, whirl; CONCEPTS 364,727,807

round [n3] *unit of ammunition* bullet, cartridge, charge, discharge, load, shell, shot; CONCEPTS 498,500

round [v1] *turn; encircle* begird, bypass, circle, circulate, circumnavigate, compass, encompass, flank, gird, girdle, go around, gyrate, hem, pivot, revolve, ring, roll, rotate, skirt, spin, surround, wheel, whirl; CONCEPTS 147,149,187

round [v2] *make curved; remove angles* arch, bend, bow, coil, convolute, crook, curl, curve, form, loop, mold, perfect, polish, recurve, refine, shape, sleek, slick, smooth, whorl; CONCEPTS 184,202

roundabout [adj] *indirect* ambiguous, circuitous, circular, circumlocutory, collateral, deviating, devious, discursive, evasive, meandering, oblique, obliquitous, periphrastic, taking the long way*, tortuous; CONCEPTS 559,581,584 —*Ant.* direct, honest, straightforward

round off [v] *finish* bring to a close, cap, climax, close, complete, conclude, crown, culminate, finish off, settle, top off; CONCEPT 234 —*Ant.* start

roundup [n] *collection, collation* assembly, branding, gathering, herding, marshalling, muster, rally, summary, survey; CONCEPTS 257,397 —*Ant.* dispersal, scattering

round up [v] *collect, gather* assemble, bring in, bring together, cluster, drive, group, herd, marshal, muster, rally; CONCEPTS 109,257 —*Ant.* disperse, scatter

rouse [v1] *wake* arouse, awake, awaken, call, get up, raise, rise, stir, wake up; CONCEPT 250 —*Ant.* nap, sleep

rouse [v2] *stimulate, excite* aggravate, agitate, anger, animate, arouse, ask for it*, awaken, bestir, bug*, challenge, craze, deepen, disturb, enhance, enliven, exhilarate, fire up*, foment, galvanize, get going, heighten, incite, inflame, innervate, innerve, instigate, intensate, intensify, key up*, kindle, magnify, make waves*, mount, move, needle, pep up*, pique, provoke, quicken, rally, redouble, rile, rise, startle, steam up*, stir, trigger, urge, vivify, wake, waken, wake up, whet, whip up*, work up; CONCEPTS 7,22,244 —*Ant.* calm, disenchant, dull

rousing [adj] *stirring* active, alert, animated, astir, bouncy, bright, brisk, buoyant, bustling, busy, buzzing, chirpy, dashing, energetic, enthusiastic, frisky, full of pep*, hyper*, industrious, jumping, lively, peppy*, perky, refreshing, snappy, spirited, spry, stimulating, vigorous, zippy*; CONCEPTS 401,542,548

rout [n] *overwhelming defeat* beating, clobbering*, comedown, confusion, debacle, disaster, drubbing*, embarrassment, flight, hiding, overthrow, retreat, romp, ruin, shambles, shutout, thrashing, trashing*, upset, vanquishment, walkover*, washout*, waxing*, whipping; CONCEPTS 95,119,363

rout [v] *defeat overwhelmingly* bash, beat, blow out of water*, bulldoze*, bury*, chase, clean up on*, clobber, conquer, cream*, crush, cut to pieces*, destroy, discomfit, dispel, drive off, expel, finish*, hunt, kill*, lambaste*, larrup*, murder*, outmaneuver, overpower, overthrow, put to flight*, repulse, scatter, scuttle, shut out*, skunk*, subdue, subjugate, swamp*, torpedo*, total*, trounce, vanquish, wallop, wax*, whip, wipe off map*, wipe out*, worst, zap*; CONCEPT 95 —*Ant.* win

route [n] *path over which someone or something travels* avenue, beat, beeline, byway, circuit, course, detour, digression, direction, divergence, itinerary, journey, line, meandering, passage, pavement, pike, plot, program, rambling, range, road, round, rounds, run, short cut, tack, track, trail, wandering, way; CONCEPTS 501,660

route [v] *send along a path* address, conduct, consign, convey, direct, dispatch, escort, forward, guide, lead, pilot, remit, see, shepherd, ship, show, steer, transmit; CONCEPTS 187,217 —*Ant.* hold, keep

routine [adj] *habitual* accepted, accustomed, chronic, conventional, customary, everyday, familiar, general, methodical, normal, ordinary, periodic, plain, quotidian, regular, seasonal, standard, typical, unremarkable, usual, wonted, workaday; CONCEPTS 530,547 —*Ant.* breaking, different, original, untraditional, unusual

routine [n] *habitual activity* act, beaten path*, bit, channels, custom, cycle, daily grind*, drill, formula, grind*, groove*, habit, line, method, order, pace, pattern, piece, practice, procedure, program, rat race*, rote, round, rut, schtick*, spiel*, system, tack, technique, treadmill, usage, way, wont; CONCEPTS 6,362,770 —*Ant.* break, excitement, unusual

row [n1] *sequence, series* bank, chain, column, consecution, echelon, file, line, order, progression, queue, range, rank, string, succession, tier, train; CONCEPTS 432,727,744

row [n2] *fight, ruckus* affray, altercation, bickering, brawl, castigation, commotion, controversy, dispute, disturbance, falling-out*, fracas, fray, fuss, knock-down-drag-out*, lecture, melee, noise, quarrel, racket, reprimand, reproof, riot, rumpus, run-in*, scrap*, set-to*, shouting match*, squabble, talking-to*, telling-off*, tiff, tongue-lashing*, trouble, tumult, uproar, words*, wrangle; CONCEPTS 46,52,106 —*Ant.* agreement, peace

row [v1] *move boat with paddle* drag, oar, paddle, pull, punt, sail, scud, scull, sky an oar, swim*; CONCEPT 187

row [v2] *argue, fight* bawl out, berate, bicker, brawl, call on the carpet*, dispute, jaw, quarrel, ream, scold, scrap, spat, squabble, tiff, tonguelash*, wrangle; CONCEPTS 46,106 —*Ant.* agree, concur

rowdy [adj] *boisterous, noisy* disorderly, lawless, loud, loudmouthed, loutish, mischievous, obstreperous, rambunctious, raucous, rebellious, rough, roughhouse, rude, turbulent, unruly, uproarious, wild; CONCEPT 401 —*Ant.* calm, moderate, quiet, restrained

rowdy [n] *person who is boisterous, noisy* brawler, bully, hellion, hooligan, lout, punk, roughneck, ruffian, terror*, troublemaker; CONCEPT 412

royal [adj] *monarchical, grand* aristocratic, august, authoritative, baronial, commanding, dignified, elevated, eminent, grandiose, high, highborn, honorable, illustrious, imperial, imposing, impressive, kingly, lofty, magnificent, majestic, noble, queenly, regal, regnant, reigning, renowned, resplendent, ruling, sovereign, splendid, stately, superb, superior, supreme, worthy; CONCEPTS 549,574 —*Ant.* common

rub [n1] *stroke, massage* abrasion, attrition, brushing, caress, friction, grinding, kneading, pat, polish, rasping, scouring, scraping, shine, smear, smoothing, stroking, swab, swipe, wear, wipe; CONCEPT 215

rub [n2] *difficulty, problem* bar, catch, crimp, dilemma, drawback, hamper, hindrance, hitch, hurdle, impediment, obstacle, predicament, snag, stumbling block*, traverse, trouble; CONCEPT 666 —*Ant.* blessing, boon, solution

rub [v] *stroke, massage* abrade, anoint, apply, bark, brush, buff, burnish, caress, chafe, clean, coat, cover, curry, daub, erase, erode, excoriate, file, fray, fret, furbish, glance, glaze, gloss, grate, graze, grind, knead, mop, paint, pat, plaster, polish, put, rasp, scour, scrape, scrub, shine, slather, smear, smooth, spread, swab, triturate, wear, wear down, wipe; CONCEPT 215

rubberneck [v] *stare* eagle eye*, eye, eyeball*, focus, gawk, gaze, glare, goggle*, lay eyes on*, look, ogle, peer, rivet; CONCEPT 623

rubbish [n1] *garbage* debris, dregs, dross, junk, litter, lumber, offal, refuse, rubble, rummage, scrap, sweepings, trash, waste; CONCEPT 260 —*Ant.* possessions, property

rubbish [n2] *nonsense* balderdash, bilge*, bunkum, drivel, gibberish, hogwash, hooey*, poppycock, rot*, stuff and nonsense*, tommyrot; CONCEPTS 230,278 —*Ant.* sense, truth

rubdown [n] *massage* back rub, chirapsia, kneading, manipulation, stroking; CONCEPTS 308,310

rub the wrong way [v] *irritate* aggravate, anger, annoy, bother, bug*, disturb, drive up the wall*, enrage, get on one's nerves*, get to, get under one's skin*, infuriate, irk, needle*, pester, rattle, ruffle one's feathers*; CONCEPTS 7,19

ruckus [n] *disturbance* big scene*, big stink*, bother, brawl, brouhaha*, commotion, disorder, disruption, distraction, explosion, fisticuffs, fracas, fray, fuss, hubbub*, hullabaloo*, interruption, quarrel, racket, rampage, riot, rumble, rumpus, stink*, stir, turmoil, upheaval, uprising, uproar; CONCEPTS 388,410,674,720

ruddy [adj] *pinkish, blushing* blooming, blowsy, bronzed, crimson, florid, flush, flushed, fresh, full-blooded, glowing, healthy, pink, red, red-complexioned, reddish, roseate, rosy, rubicund, ruby, sanguine, scarlet; CONCEPT 618 —*Ant.* pale

rude [adj1] *disrespectful, rough* abrupt, abusive, bad-mannered, barbarian, barbaric, barbarous, blunt, boorish, brusque, brutish, cheeky, churlish, coarse, crabbed, crude, curt, discourteous, graceless, gross, gruff, ignorant, illiterate, impertinent, impolite, impudent, inconsiderate, insolent, insulting, intrusive, loutish, low, obscene, offhand, peremptory, raw, savage, scurrilous, short, surly, uncivil, uncivilized, uncouth, uncultured, uneducated, ungracious, unmannerly, unpolished, unrefined, vulgar, wild; CONCEPTS 267,401 —Ant. kind, mannerly, nice, polite, respectful

rude [adj2] *crude, primitive* angular, artless, barbarous, callow, coarse; formless, fresh, green, ignorant, inartistic, inelegant, inexperienced, inexpert, makeshift, primal, raw, rough, roughhewn, roughly made, rudimental, rudimentary, shapeless, simple, uncivilized, unconversant, uncultivated, unfashioned, unfinished, unformed, unhewn, unpolished, unprocessed, unrefined, wild; CONCEPTS 490,531 —Ant. polished, refined, sophisticated

rude [adj3] *sudden; approximate* abrupt, guessed, harsh, imperfect, imprecise, inexact, in the ballpark*, proximate, rough, sharp, startling, stormy, surmised, turbulent, unpleasant, unprecise, violent; CONCEPTS 557,799 —Ant. exact, gradual, smooth

rudimentary [adj] *basic, fundamental* abecedarian, basal, beginning, early, elemental, elementary, embryonic, immature, initial, introductory, larval, nuts-and-bolts*, primary, primitive, simple, simplest, uncompleted, undeveloped, vestigial; CONCEPTS 546,549 —Ant. additional, advanced, derivative, developed, extra, nonessential

rudiments [n] *fundamentals* ABCs*, basics, beginnings, elements, essentials, first principles, foundation, guts*, heart, nitty-gritty, principles; CONCEPTS 668,687,826,829

rue [v] *regret* apologize, be sorry for, cry over*, deplore, feel remorse, feel sorry, grieve, kick oneself*, lament, mourn, weep over*; CONCEPTS 21,410

rueful [adj] *regretful* apologetic, ashamed, deplorable, lamentable, mournful, remorseful, repentant, sad, sorrowful, sorry; CONCEPT 403

ruffian [n] *hoodlum* brute, bully, criminal, delinquent, gangster, goon*, hood, hooligan, mobster, punk, rioter, rowdy, thug, tough guy*, troublemaker; CONCEPT 412

ruffle [v1] *mess up* cockle, confuse, crease, crinkle, crumple, crush, derange, disarrange, discompose, dishevel, disorder, pucker, purse, rifle, rumple, tangle, tousle, wrinkle; CONCEPT 158 —Ant. smooth

ruffle [v2] *upset, irritate* abrade, agitate, anger, annoy, bluster, bother, browbeat, bully, chafe, confuse, cow*, disconcert, disquiet, disturb, excite, floor*, flummox, flurry, fluster, fret, fuddle, gall, get to*, harass, intimidate, irk, nettle, peeve, perturb, provoke, put off, put out, rattle, rattle one's cage*, shake up*, stir, stump, throw into tizzy*, torment, trouble, unsettle, vex, wear, worry; CONCEPTS 7,14,19 —Ant. calm, soothe

rug [n1] *carpet* carpeting, floor covering, mat, matting, runner, shag*, tapestry, throw rug, wall-to-wall carpeting; CONCEPT 473

rug [n2] *hairpiece* false hair, hair extension, hair implant, hair weaving, toupee, wig; CONCEPT 392

rugged [adj1] *bumpy, weathered* asperous, broken, coarse, craggy, difficult, furrowed,

harsh, hilly, irregular, jagged, leathery, lumpy, mountainous, ragged, rocky, rough, roughhewn, scabrous, scraggy, stark, uneven, unlevel, unpolished, unrefined, unsmooth, weather-beaten, worn, wrinkled; CONCEPTS 490,606 —Ant. even, flat, level, smooth

rugged [adj2] *severe, violent* bitter, brutal, difficult, hard, harsh, inclement, intemperate, rigorous, rough, stormy, tempestuous, turbulent; CONCEPTS 525,537 —Ant. calm, gentle, mild, moderate

rugged [adj3] *uncouth, crude* barbarous, blunt, boorish, churlish, graceless, ill-bred, loutish, rude, uncultured, unpolished, unrefined; CONCEPT 401 —Ant. courteous, nice, refined, sophisticated

rugged [adj4] *difficult, rigorous* arduous, demanding, exacting, formidable, hairy*, hard, harsh, heavy*, heavy sledding*, knotty*, laborious, large order*, mean, murder*, no picnic*, operose, rough, stern, strenuous, taxing, tough, trying, uncompromising, uphill*; CONCEPTS 538,565 —Ant. easy, facile

rugged [adj5] *big, strong* able-bodied, athletic, brawny, energetic, forceful, hale, hardy, healthy, husky, indefatigable, lusty, muscular, robust, sturdy, tough, unflagging, vigorous, well-built; CONCEPTS 314,489 —Ant. small, tiny, weak

ruin [n] *situation of devastation* atrophy, bane, bankruptcy, bath, breakdown, collapse, confusion, crackup, crash, crumbling, damage, decay, defeat, degeneracy, degeneration, demolition, destitution, destruction, deterioration, dilapidation, disintegration, disrepair, dissolution, downfall, downgrade, extinction, failure, fall, havoc, insolvency, loss, nemesis, overthrow, ruination, skids*, subversion, the end*, undoing, waste, waterloo, wreck, wreckage; CONCEPT 674 —Ant. building, construction, creation, development, growth

ruin [v] *devastate, destroy* bankrupt, beggar, botch, break, bring down, bring to ruin, bust, clean out, crush, decimate, deface, defeat, defile, demolish, deplete, deplore, depredate, desecrate, despoil, devour, dilapidate, disfigure, do in*, drain, exhaust, fleece, impoverish, injure, lay waste, maim, make a shambles of, mangle, mar, mutilate, overthrow, overturn, overwhelm, pauperize, pillage, rape, ravish, raze, reduce, sack, shatter, smash, spoil, spoilate, total, use up, wipe out*, wrack, wreak havoc on, wreck; CONCEPTS 234,246,252 —Ant. build, construct, create, develop, grow

ruinous [adj] *disastrous, devastating* annihilative, baleful, baneful, calamitous, cataclysmic, catastrophic, crippling, damaging, deadly, deleterious, depleting, dire, draining, exhausting, extravagant, fatal, fateful, harmful, hurtful, immoderate, impoverishing, injurious, murderous, noxious, pernicious, shattering, suicidal, unfortunate, wasteful, withering, wrackful; CONCEPTS 537,548,570 —Ant. advantageous, assisting, beneficial, helpful

ruins [n] *buildings that are dilapidated* ashes, debris, destruction, detritus, foundation, relics, remains, remnants, residue, rubble, traces, vestiges, wreck, wreckage; CONCEPTS 234,733

rule [n1] *standard, principle of behavior* aphorism, apothegm, assize, axiom, basis, brocard, canon, chapter and verse*, command, commandment, criterion, decorum, decree, decretion, dictum, direction, edict, etiquette, formula, fundamental, gnome, guide, guideline, keynote, keystone, law, maxim, model, moral, no-no's*, order, ordinance, precedent, precept, prescription, propriety, regimen, regulation, ruling, statute, tenet, test, the book*, the numbers*, truism; CONCEPT 688

rule [n2] *leadership of organization* administration, ascendancy, authority, command, control, direction, domination, dominion, empire, government, influence, jurisdiction, power, regime, regnancy, reign, sovereignty, supremacy, sway; CONCEPTS 299,376

rule [n3] *method, way* course, custom, formula, habit, normalcy, normality, order of things, policy, practice, procedure, routine; CONCEPTS 6,647

rule [v1] *govern, manage* administer, be in authority, be in driver's seat*, be in power, bridle, command, conduct, control, crack the whip*, curb, decree, dictate, direct, dominate, domineer, guide, hold sway*, hold the reins*, keep under one's thumb*, lay down the law*, lead, order, overrule, predominate, preponderate, preside, prevail, regulate, reign, restrain, rule the roost*, run, run the show*, sit on top of*, sway, take over; CONCEPTS 117,133,298 —Ant. serve, submit

rule [v2] *judge, decide* adjudge, adjudicate, conclude, decree, deduce, determine, establish, figure, find, fix, gather, hold, infer, lay down, pass upon, postulate, prescribe, pronounce, resolve, settle, theorize; CONCEPTS 18,81 —Ant. plead

rule out [v] *exclude, reject* abolish, avert, ban, bate, cancel, count out, debar, deter, dismiss, eliminate, except, forbid, forestall, forfend, leave out, not consider, obviate, preclude, prevent, prohibit, proscribe, recant, revoke, stave off, suspend, ward off; CONCEPTS 25,121 —Ant. add, include, keep

ruler [n1] *historically, person who ruled an area* baron, baroness, caesar, caliph, contessa, count, countess, crowned head, czar, czarina, dame, duchess, duke, dynast, emperor, empress, gerent, imperator, kaiser, khan, king, lady, lord, magnate, maharajah, maharani, majesty, mikado, mogul, monarch, oligarch, overlord, pasha, potentate, prince, princess, queen, rajah, rani, rex, royal, shah, sovereign, sultan, sultana, tycoon; CONCEPT 422 —Ant. commoner, subject

ruler [n2] *tool for measuring or calculating length* folding rule, measure, measuring stick, rule, slide rule, straightedge, T-square, yardstick; CONCEPT 499

ruling [adj1] *dominant, governing* cardinal, central, commanding, controlling, leading, overriding, overruling, pivotal, regnant, reigning, sovereign, supreme, upper; CONCEPT 574 —Ant. inferior, subjective, submissive, yielding

ruling [adj2] *prevailing, main* chief, current, dominant, pivotal, popular, predominant, preeminent, preponderant, prevalent, principal, rampant, rife, widespread; CONCEPT 568 —Ant. inferior, minor, subordinate

ruling [n] *judgment, decree* adjudication, decision, directive, edict, finding, law, order,

precept, pronouncement, resolution, rule, ukase, verdict; CONCEPT 318 —Ant. plea

rumble [v] *growl, thunder* boom, grumble, resound, roar, roll; CONCEPT 65

ruminate [v] *think about seriously* brainstorm*, brood, chew over, cogitate, consider, contemplate, deliberate, excogitate, figure, meditate, mull over, muse, ponder, rack one's brains*, reflect, revolve, stew about*, think, turn over, use one's head*, weigh; CONCEPT 24 —Ant. ignore, neglect

rummage [v] *ransack, search* beat the bushes*, comb, delve, dig out, disarrange, disarray, disorder, disorganize, disrupt, disturb, examine, explore, ferret out, fish, forage, grub, hunt, jumble, leave no stone unturned*, look high and low*, mess up, mix up, poke, rake, root, scour, search high heaven*, seek, shake, shake down, spy, toss, turn inside out*, turn upside down*; CONCEPTS 158,216 —Ant. order, organize

rumor [n] *talk about supposed truth* back-fence talk*, breeze*, bruit, canard, comment, cry, dispatch, earful*, fabrication, falsehood, fame, fiction, gossip, grapevine*, hearsay, hoax, innuendo, intelligence, invention, lie, news, notoriety, report, repute, rumble, scandal, scuttlebutt*, story, suggestion, supposition, tale, tattle, tidings, whisper, wire*, word; CONCEPTS 274,277,278 —Ant. truth

rumor [v] *tell a supposed truth* bruit, buzz*, circulate, gossip, noise about*, pass around, publish, report, say, talk, tattle, whisper; CONCEPTS 49,54 —Ant. tell truth

rump [n] *bottom, posterior of animal or human* back, backside, beam, behind, breech, bum*, butt, butt end, buttocks, can*, croup, derrière, duff*, fanny*, haunches, hind end, hindquarters, keister*, moon*, prat, rear, rear end, sacrum, seat, tail*, tail end, tush*; CONCEPTS 392,825

rumple [v] *crush, wrinkle* bedraggle, cockle, crease, crimp, crinkle, crumple, derange, dishevel, disorder, fold, muss, muss up, pucker, ruck up, ruffle, screw up, scrunch, seam, tousle, wreathe; CONCEPTS 137,219,250 —Ant. flatten, iron, smooth

rumpus [n] *clamor* brouhaha*, commotion, discord, disturbance, donnybrook, fracas, fuss, hassle, hubba-hubba*, hubbub, hullabaloo*, noise, outcry, pandemonium, racket, rhubarb, ruckus, tumult, turmoil, upheaval, uproar; CONCEPTS 386,595,674

run [n1] *fast moving on foot* amble, bound, break, canter, dart, dash, drop, escape, fall, flight, gallop, jog, lope, pace, race, rush, scamper, scuttle, spring, sprint, spurt, tear, trot, whisk; CONCEPT 150 —Ant. standing, walking

run [n2] *journey* drive, excursion, jaunt, joy ride*, lift, outing, ride, round, spin, tour, travel, trip; CONCEPT 224

run [n3] *sequence, course* bearing, chain, continuance, continuation, continuity, current, cycle, drift, duration, endurance, field, flow, line, motion, movement, passage, path, period, persistence, progress, prolongation, round, route, season, series, spell, streak, stream, stretch, string, succession, swing, tendency, tenor, tide, trend, way; CONCEPTS 721,727,738

run [v1] *move fast on foot* abscond, amble, barrel, beat it*, bolt, bound, bustle, canter, career, clear out, course, cut and run*, dart, dash, decamp, depart, dog it*, escape, flee, flit, fly, gallop, go like lightning*, hasten, hie, hotfoot*, hurry, hustle, jog, leg it*, light out*, lope, make a break*, make off, make tracks*, pace, race, rush, scamper, scoot, scorch, scramble, scud, scurry, shag, shoot, skedaddle*, skip, skitter, smoke*, speed, spring, sprint, spurt, take flight, take off, tear, tear out, travel, trot, whisk; CONCEPTS 150,195 —Ant. stand, walk

run [v2] *move rapidly, flowingly* bleed, cascade, course, deliquesce, diffuse, discharge, dissolve, drop, fall, flow, flux, fuse, glide, go, go soft, gush, issue, leak, leap, liquefy, melt, pass, pour, proceed, roll, sail, scud, skim, slide, spill, spin, spout, spread, stream, thaw, tumble, turn to liquid, whirl, whiz; CONCEPT 146 —Ant. cease, halt, stop

run [v3] *operate, drive* act, bear, carry, command, control, convey, go, govern, handle, manage, maneuver, move, perform, ply, propel, tick, transport, use, work; CONCEPTS 225,680

run [v4] *manage, supervise* administer, be in charge, be in driver's seat*, be in saddle*, boss, carry on, conduct, control, coordinate, direct, head, head up*, helm*, keep, lead, look after, operate, ordain, oversee, own, pull the strings*, regulate, ride herd on*, superintend, take care of*; CONCEPT 117 —Ant. obey, serve

run [v5] *continue, range* be current, circulate, cover, encompass, extend, go, go around, go on, last, lie, move past, persevere, proceed, reach, spread, stretch, trail, vary; CONCEPTS 651,721 —Ant. cease, halt, stop

run [v6] *attempt to be elected to public office* be a candidate, challenge, compete, contend, contest, hit the campaign trail*, kiss babies*, oppose, politick, race, ring doorbells*, shake hands*, stand, stump, whistlestop*; CONCEPT 300

run-around [n] *avoidance* come-off, delay, detour, difficulty, diversion, elusion, escape, escaping, eschewal, evasion, inertia, postponement, roundabout, shunning; CONCEPTS 30,121 —Ant. challenge, facing, meeting

runaway [adj] *out of control* delinquent, disorderly, escaped, fleeing, fugitive, loose, out of hand*, running, uncontrolled, wild; CONCEPT 401 —Ant. controlled, stable, staying, steady

runaway [n] *person who is trying to escape* absconder, delinquent, deserter, escapee, escaper, fugitive, lawbreaker, maroon, offender, truant, wanted person; CONCEPT 412

run-down [adj] *shabby, in bad shape* abandoned, beat-up, below par, broken-down, crumbling, debilitated, decrepit, derelict, deserted, desolate, dilapidated, dingy, dog-eared*, down-at-the-heel*, drained, enervated, exhausted, fatigued, forsaken, frowzy*, in a bad way*, neglected, old, out of condition, peaked, ramshackle, ratty*, rickety, seedy, tacky, tattered, tired, tumble-down, uncared-for, under the weather*, unhealthy, untended, used up, weak, weary, worn-out; CONCEPTS 314,485, 570 —Ant. fresh, good, healthy, ok

rundown [n] *summary* briefing, outline, précis, recap*, recapitulation, report, résumé, review, run-through, sketch, synopsis; CONCEPT 283

run down [v] *ridicule* belittle, criticize, decry,

defame, denigrate, depreciate, derogate, detract, diminish, disparage, dispraise, downcry, knock*, make fun of, opprobriate, revile, speak ill of, vilify; CONCEPTS 52,54 —Ant. praise

rung [n] *notch, step* bar, board, crossbar, crosspiece, degree, grade, level, rod, round, rundle, stage, tread; CONCEPTS 471,744

run-in [n] *argument* altercation, bickering, brush, confrontation, contretemps, dispute, encounter, falling-out*, fight, hassle, quarrel, row, set-to*, skirmish, tussle; CONCEPTS 46, 106 —Ant. agreement, harmony, peace

run in [v] *arrest* apprehend, bust, collar, cop*, detain, handcuff, jail, nab, pick up, pinch*, pull in, put the cuffs on*, take into custody, throw in jail*; CONCEPTS 298,317 —Ant. exonerate, free, let go

running [adj] *continuous, flowing, operating* active, alive, constant, cursive, dynamic, easy, effortless, executing, fluent, functioning, going, in action, incessant, in operation, in succession, live, moving, operative, perpetual, proceeding, producing, smooth, together, unbroken, unceasing, uninterrupted, working; CONCEPT 538, 560,584 —Ant. broken, discontinuous, intermittent, occasional

running [adv] *continually* consecutively, continuously, night and day*, successively, together, unintermittedly, uninterruptedly; CONCEPTS 482,798 —Ant. broken, intermittently, occasionally

running [n] *management of organization* administration, care, charge, conduct, control, coordination, direction, functioning, handling, intendance, leadership, maintenance, operation, organization, oversight, performance, regulation, superintendency, supervision, working; CONCEPT 117

run-of-the-mill [adj] *average* common, commonplace, customary, dime a dozen, everyday, fair, fair to middling*, garden-variety*, humdrum, intermediate, mainstream, mediocre, medium, middle of the road*, middling, ordinary, regular, routine, so-so*, undistinguished, unexceptional, usual; CONCEPT 547

run out [v] *fail, be exhausted* be cleaned out*, be out of, cease, close, come to a close, depart, dissipate, dry up, end, exhaust, expire, finish, give out, go, have no more, have none left, lose, peter out*, stop, terminate, tire, waste, waste away, weaken, wear out; CONCEPTS 105,699 —Ant. get, have, succeed, supply

runt [n] *very small person* half-pint*, homunculus, Lilliputian, midget, peewee*, punk*, shrimp*; CONCEPT 424

run through [v] *use up; waste* blow, consume, dissipate, exhaust, expend, finish, fritter away, lose, spend, squander, throw away, wash up; CONCEPT 156 —Ant. hoard, save

rupture [n1] *break, split* breach, burst, cleavage, cleft, crack, division, fissure, fracture, hernia, herniation, parting, rent, schism, tear; CONCEPTS 309,513 —Ant. closing, closure

rupture [n2] *disagreement, dissolution* altercation, breach, break, break-up, bustup*, clash, contention, detachment, disruption, disunion, division, divorce, divorcement, estrangement, falling-out, feud, hostility, misunderstanding, parting, partition, quarrel,

rift, schism, separation, split, split-up*;
CONCEPTS 46,388 —Ant. agreement, harmony,
peace

rupture [v1] *break open* breach, burst, cleave,
crack, disrupt, divide, erupt, fracture, hold,
open, part, puncture, rend, rive, separate, sever,
shatter, split, sunder, tear; CONCEPTS 98,246,
308 —Ant. close, join, mend

rupture [v2] *disagree; dissolve union* break
off, break up, come between, disjoin, disrupt,
dissect, dissever, disunite, divide, divorce, part,
separate, split, split up, sunder; CONCEPTS 297,
384 —Ant. agree, join, marry

rural [adj] *country, not urban* agrarian,
agricultural, agronomic, Arcadian, backwoods,
bucolic, countrified, farm, georgic, idyllic,
natural, outland, pastoral, provincial, ranch,
rustic, rustical, simple, sylvan, unsophisticated;
CONCEPT 583 —Ant. city, metropolitan, suburban, urban

ruse [n] *trick, deception* angle, artifice, blind,
booby trap*, curveball*, deceit, device, dodge,
feint, gambit, game, game plan*, gimmick,
hoax, imposture, jig*, maneuver, ploy, scenario,
sham, shenanigans*, shift, stratagem, stunt, subterfuge, switch*, twist*, wile; CONCEPTS 59,674

rush [n1] *hurry, speed* blitz, dispatch,
dispatch, expedition, flood, flow, flux, haste,
hastiness, hurriedness, precipitance, precipitancy, precipitation, race, scramble, stream,
surge, swiftness, urgency; CONCEPTS
145,748,818 —Ant. retardation, slowness

rush [n2] *attack* assault, blitz, charge, onslaught,
push, storm, surge, violence; CONCEPT 86
—Ant. guarding, protection

rush [v1] *hurry, speed* accelerate, barrel, bolt,
break, career, charge, chase, course, dart,
dash, dispatch, expedite, fire up*, fleet, fling,
flit, fly, get cracking*, get the lead out*, go like
lightning*, hasten, hasten, hotfoot*, hurry up,
hustle, lose no time*, make haste, make short
work of*, press, push, quicken, race, roll, run,
scramble, scud, scurry, shake a leg*, shoot,
speed up, sprint, step on gas*, streak, surge,
tear, whiz*, zip*, zoom*; CONCEPTS 91,150,
152 —Ant. retard, slow

rush [v2] *charge, attack* capture, overcome,
storm, surge, take by storm*; CONCEPT 86
—Ant. guard, protect

rust [n] *corrosion* blight, corruption, decay,
decomposition, dilapidation, mold, oxidation,
rot, wear; CONCEPTS 309,720

rust [v] *corrode* decay, decline, degenerate,
deteriorate, oxidize, stale, tarnish, wither;
CONCEPT 469

rustic [adj1] *country, rural* agrarian, agricultural, Arcadian, artless, austere, bucolic, countrified, homely, homespun, homey, honest,
natural, outland, pastoral, picturesque, plain,
primitive, provincial, simple, sylvan, unaffected, unpolished, unrefined, unsophisticated,
verdant; CONCEPTS 583,589 —Ant. city, metropolitan, suburban, urban

rustic [adj2] *crude, uncouth* awkward, boorish,
churlish, clodhopping, clownish, coarse, countrified, dull, foolish, graceless, ignorant, inelegant, loutish, maladroit, rough, rude, stupid,
uncultured, uneducated, ungainly, unmannerly,
unpolished, unsophisticated; CONCEPT 401

—Ant. couth, cultured, polished, refined,
sophisticated

rustic [n] *person from the country, with little
experience* backwoodsperson, boor, country
cousin*, countryperson, farmer, hayseed*,
hick*, hillbilly, mountaineer, peasant, provincial, redneck*, rural, yokel*; CONCEPT 413
—Ant. city boy

rustle [n] *whisper, swish* crackle, crepitation,
crinkling, friction, noise, patter, ripple, rustling,
sound, stir; CONCEPT 595

rustle [v] *swish, whisper* crackle, crepitate,
crinkle, hum, murmur, patter, sigh, stir, tap,
whir, whish, whoosh; CONCEPT 65

rustle up [v] *provide* accommodate, arrange,
assemble, bring, cater, cook, furnish, get ready,
give, hand over, indulge, make, prepare,
present, produce, put together, ready, render,
scrape up, serve, supply, take care of, turn out;
CONCEPTS 35,108,110,136,140,200

rusty [adj1] *corroded* decayed, oxidized,
rust-covered, rusted; CONCEPT 485

rusty [adj2] *out of practice; inexperienced*
deficient, impaired, neglected, not what it was*,
sluggish, soft, stale, unpracticed, unqualified,
weak; CONCEPT 527 —Ant. experienced,
practiced, talented

rut [n1] *groove, indentation* furrow, gouge,
hollow, pothole, rabbet, score, track, trench,
trough; CONCEPT 513 —Ant. closing

rut [n2] *routine of daily life* circle, circuit,
course, custom, daily grind*, dead end*,
grind*, groove, habit, humdrum*, pace,
pattern, performance, practice, procedure,
rote, round, system, treadmill, usage, wont;
CONCEPTS 6,647 —Ant. break, difference

ruthless [adj] *mean, heartless* adamant, barbarous, brutal, callous, cold, cold-blooded,
cruel, cutthroat, dog-eat-dog*, feral, ferocious,
fierce, grim, hard, hard-hearted, harsh, implacable, inexorable, inhuman, ironfisted, killer,
malevolent, merciless, mortal, obdurate, pitiless,
rancorous, relentless, remorseless, revengeful,
sadistic, savage, severe, stern, stony, surly,
unappeasable, unfeeling, unforgiving, unmerciful, unrelenting, unsympathetic, unyielding,
vicious, vindictive, without pity; CONCEPTS
401,404 —Ant. compassionate, considerate,
gentle, giving, kind, nice, sympathetic

S

sabbatical [n] *leave* break, furlough, holiday,
leave of absence, liberty, recess, time off,
vacation; CONCEPTS 802,807

sable [adj] *very dark in color* black, dark,
dusky, dusty, ebon, ebony, gloomy, inky, jet,
jetty, murky, pitch-black, pitch-dark, raven,
somber; CONCEPT 618

sabotage [n] *damage* demolition, destruction,
disruption, impairment, injury, mischief, overthrow, subversion, subversiveness, treachery,
treason, undermining, vandalism, wreckage,
wrecking; CONCEPTS 86,246,252 —Ant. aiding,
assistance, fix, help

sabotage [v] *incapacitate, damage* attack,
block, bollix, break up, cripple, deep six*,
destroy, disable, disrupt, do*, do in*, foul up*,

frustrate, hamper, hinder, louse up*, mess up*, obstruct, put out of action, put out of commission*, screw up*, subvert, take out*, throw a monkey wrench into*, torpedo*, undermine, vandalize, wreck; CONCEPTS 86,246,252 —Ant. abet, aid, fix, help

sack [v1] *remove from position of responsibility* ax*, bounce*, can*, cashier, discharge, dismiss, drop, expel, fire, give a pink slip*, give marching orders*, give the boot*, kick out, send packing*, ship, terminate; CONCEPT 351 —Ant. employ, hire

sack [v2] *raid, plunder* demolish, depredate, desecrate, desolate, despoil, destroy, devastate, devour, fleece, gut, lay waste, loot, maraud, pillage, ravage, rifle, rob, ruin, spoil, spoliate, strip, waste; CONCEPTS 139,252 —Ant. guard, protect, save

sacrament [n] *rite* baptism, celebration, ceremony, communion, confession, confirmation, custom, holy orders, liturgy, marriage, matrimony, oath, observance, practice, ritual, service, vow; CONCEPTS 377,386

sacred [adj1] *holy, blessed* angelic, cherished, consecrated, divine, enshrined, godly, hallowed, numinous, pious, pure, religious, revered, sacramental, saintly, sanctified, solemn, spiritual, unprofane, venerable; CONCEPT 574 —Ant. irreligious, lay, profane, ungodly, unholy, unsacred

sacred [adj2] *protected* dedicated, defended, guarded, immune, inviolable, inviolate, invulnerable, sacrosanct, secure, shielded, untouchable; CONCEPT 587 —Ant. open, unprotected, vulnerable

sacrifice [v] *give up, let go* cede, drop, endure, eschew, forfeit, forgo, immolate, kiss goodbye*, lose, offer, offer up, part with, renounce, resign oneself to, spare, suffer, surrender, waive, yield; CONCEPTS 108,116 —Ant. hold, refuse

sacrilege [n] *irreverence* blasphemy, crime, curse, desecration, heresy, impiety, mockery, offense, profanation, profaneness, profanity, sin, violation; CONCEPT 645 —Ant. piety, respect, reverence

sacrilegious [adj] *profane* atheistic, blasphemous, desecrating, dirty*, filthy*, foul, godless, heathen, impious, indecent, infidel, irreligious, irreverent, irreverential, obscene, pagan, sinful, ungodly, unhallowed, unholy, violating; CONCEPTS 267,401,545

sacrosanct [adj] *sacred* blessed, consecrated, divine, godly, hallowed, holy, pious, pure, religious, revered, sacramental, saintly, sanctified, spiritual, unprofane, venerated; CONCEPT 574

sad [adj1] *unhappy, depressed* bereaved, bitter, blue*, cheerless, dejected, despairing, despondent, disconsolate, dismal, distressed, doleful, down, downcast, down in dumps*, down in mouth*, forlorn, gloomy, glum, grief-stricken, grieved, heartbroken, heartsick, heavyhearted, hurting, in doldrums*, in grief, in the dumps*, languishing, low, low-spirited, lugubrious, melancholy, morbid, morose, mournful, out of sorts*, pensive, pessimistic, sick at heart*, somber, sorrowful, sorry, troubled, weeping, wistful, woebegone; CONCEPT 403 —Ant. cheerful, glad, happy, joyful

sad [adj2] *unfortunate, distressing* bad, calamitous, dark, dejecting, deplorable, depressing, disastrous, discomposing, discouraging, disheartening, dismal, dispiriting, dreary, funereal, grave, grievous, hapless, heart-rending, joyless, lachrymose, lamentable, lugubrious, melancholic, miserable, moving, oppressive, pathetic, pitiable, pitiful, poignant, regrettable, saddening, serious, shabby, sorry, tearful, tear-jerking*, tragic, unhappy, unsatisfactory, upsetting, wretched; CONCEPTS 529,548 —Ant. fortunate, great, happy, lucky

sadden [v] *upset, depress* break one's heart*, bring one down*, bum out*, cast down, dampen spirits, dash, deject, deplore, desolate, discourage, dishearten, dispirit, distress, down, drag down*, grieve, make blue*, oppress, press, put a damper on*, put into a funk*, throw cold water on*, turn one off*, weigh down*; CONCEPTS 7,19 —Ant. cheer, delight, gladden, make happy

sadistic [adj] *cruel, perverted* barbarous, brutal, fiendish, perverse, ruthless, vicious; CONCEPTS 542,545 —Ant. humane, kind, merciful

sadness [n] *unhappiness, depression* anguish, blahs*, bleakness, blue devils*, blue funk*, broken heart*, bummer, cheerlessness, dejection, despondency, disconsolateness, dismals*, dispiritedness, distress, dolefulness, dolor, downcastness, downer*, dysphoria, forlornness, funk, gloominess, grief, grieving, heartache, heartbreak, heavy heart*, hopelessness, letdown, listlessness, melancholy, misery, moodiness, mopes*, mournfulness, mourning, poignancy, sorrow, sorrowfulness, the blues*, the dumps*, tribulation, woe; CONCEPT 410 —Ant. cheer, gladness, happiness, joy

safari [n] *hunting expedition* hunt, journey, quest, trek, trip; CONCEPT 224

safe [adj1] *free from harm* buttoned up*, cherished, free from danger, guarded, home-free*, impervious, impregnable, in safety, intact, inviolable, invulnerable, maintained, okay*, out of danger, out of harm's way*, preserved, protected, safe and sound*, safeguarded, secure, sheltered, shielded, sitting pretty*, snug, tended, unassailable, undamaged, under lock and key*, under one's wing*, unharmed, unhurt, uninjured, unmolested, unscathed, unthreatened, vindicated, watched; CONCEPT 587 —Ant. exposed, unguarded, unprotected, unsafe, vulnerable

safe [adj2] *not dangerous* certain, checked, clear, competent, decontaminated, dependable, harmless, healthy, innocent, innocuous, innoxious, inoffensive, neutralized, nonpoisonous, nontoxic, pure, reliable, risk-free, riskless, secure, sound, tame, trustworthy, uninjurious, unpolluted, wholesome; CONCEPTS 314,537,548 —Ant. dangerous, harmful, poisonous, unsafe

safe [adj3] *cautious, conservative* calculating, careful, chary, circumspect, competent, considerate, dependable, discreet, gingerly, guarded, on safe side*, prudent, realistic, reliable, sure, tried and true*, trustworthy, unadventurous, wary; CONCEPTS 401,542 —Ant. incautious, risky, unthoughtful

safeguard [n] *protection* aegis, armament, armor, buffer, bulwark, convoy, defense, escort, guard, screen, security, shield, surety, ward; CONCEPT 712 —Ant. endangerment, harm, hurt, injury

safeguard [v] *protect* assure, bulwark, conserve, cover, defend, ensure, fend, guard, insure, look after, preserve, ride shotgun*, save, screen, secure, shield, watch over; CONCEPT 96 —*Ant.* endanger, harm, hurt, injure, lay open

safekeeping [n] *protection* aegis, assurance, care, certainty, cover, custody, guardianship, guarding, insurance, preservation, protecting, reassurance, refuge, safeguard, security, shelter, supervision, trust; CONCEPTS 712,729

safety [n] *protection from harm* assurance, asylum, cover, defense, freedom, immunity, impregnability, inviolability, invulnerability, refuge, safeness, sanctuary, security, shelter; CONCEPT 729 —*Ant.* danger, exposure, jeopardy, vulnerability

safety net [n] *level of economic security guaranteed by government* benefits, buffer, government aid, insurance, precaution, protective umbrella, safeguard, subsidy; CONCEPT 344

sag [n] *drop, decline* basin, cant, concavity, depression, dip, distortion, downslide•, downswing*, downtrend, downturn, droop, fall, fall-off, hollow, list, settling, sink, sinkage, sinkhole, sinking, slant, slip, slump, tilt; CONCEPTS 181,698,776 —*Ant.* increase, rise

sag [v] *droop* bag, bend, bow, bulge, cave in, curve, dangle, decline, dip, drop, drop off, fail, fall, fall away, fall off, flag, flap, flop, give way, hang, hang down, languish, lean, settle, sink, slide, slip, slump, swag, wilt; CONCEPTS 181,698,776 —*Ant.* bulge, draw up, tighten

saga [n] *story, often long* adventure, chronicle, epic, legend, narrative, soap opera*, tale, yarn; CONCEPT 282

sagacious [adj] *smart, judicious* acute, apt, astucious, astute, cagey, canny, clear-sighted, clever, cool*, discerning, discriminating, far-sighted, foxy*, gnostic, heady, hip*, insightful, intelligent, keen, knowing, knowledgeable, perceptive, perspicacious, prudent, rational, sage, sapient, savvy*, sensible, sharp, shrewd, smooth, sophic, wise, witty; CONCEPT 402 —*Ant.* careless, foolish, ignorant, stupid

sagacity [n] *wisdom* acumen, astuteness, brains*, clear thinking, common sense, comprehension, discernment, discrimination, enlightenment, experience, foresight, good judgment, insight, intelligence, judgment, knowledge, levelheadedness, perceptiveness, perspicacity, practicality, prudence, sageness, sapience, sense, shrewdness, understanding; CONCEPT 409

sage [adj] *wise* astute, aware, careful, clever, contemplative, cunning, discerning, educated, enlightened, experienced, foresighted, informed, insightful, intelligent, intuitive, judicious, knowing, knowledgeable, learned, perceptive, reflective, sagacious, sapient, scholarly, sensible, sharp, shrewd, smart, sound, thoughtful, understanding; CONCEPT 402

sage [n] *wise person* guide, guru, intellect, intellectual, learned person, mahatma, master, mentor, philosopher, pundit, savant, teacher, thinker, wise man/woman; CONCEPTS 350,409,416

sail [v] *travel through water, air; glide* boat, captain, cast anchor, cast off, cross, cruise, dart, drift, embark, flit, float, fly, get under way*, leave, make headway, motor, move, navigate, pilot, put to sea*, reach, run, scud, set sail, shoot, skim, skipper, skirr, soar, steer, sweep, tack, voyage, weigh anchor, wing; CONCEPT 224

sailboat [n] *a boat propelled with wind by sailcloth* bark, brig, brigantine, catamaran, clipper, craft, cutter, dory, gaff-rigged sailboat, galleon, galley, jack, ketch, pinnace, ragboat*, schooner, ship, skiff, sloop, Sunfish, tall ship, vessel, windjammer, wooden boat, yacht, yawl; CONCEPT 506

sailor [n] *person who travels by sea* able-bodied sailor, bluejacket*, boater, cadet, circumnavigator, deck hand, diver, hearty*, jack*, lascar*, marine, mariner, mate, middy, midshipman/woman, navigator, old salt*, pilot, pirate, salt*, sea dog*, seafarer, sea person, shellback*, shipmate, swab, swabber*, swabbie*, tar*, tarpaulin*, water dog*, windjammer*, yachter; CONCEPTS 348,358,366

saint [n] *holy person* angel, glorified soul, good person, holy being, loved one, martyr, pietist; CONCEPTS 361,370

saintly [adj] *good, righteous* angelic, beatific, blameless, blessed, devout, divine, god-fearing, godly, holy, pious, pure, religious, sainted, saintlike, seraph, sinless, upright, upstanding, virtuous, worthy; CONCEPT 404 —*Ant.* bad, sinful, unholy, unrighteous, wicked

salacious [adj] *lascivious* bawdy, carnal, erotic, fast*, horny, hot*, indecent, lecherous, lewd, libertine, libidinous, licentious, lubricious, lustful, nasty, obscene, orgiastic, prurient, raunchy, sensual, smutty*, steamy, suggestive, voluptuous, wanton; CONCEPTS 372,403

salad [n] *dish of vegetables* coleslaw, fruit salad, greens, mixed greens, potato salad, tossed salad, Waldorf salad; CONCEPT 431

salary [n] *money paid for work done* bacon*, bread*, earnings, emolument, fee, hire, income, pay, payroll, recompense, remuneration, scale, stipend, take, take-home*, wage, wages; CONCEPT 344 —*Ant.* debt

sale [n] *exchange of object for money* auction, barter, business, buying, clearance, closeout, commerce, consuming, deal, demand, disposal, dumping, enterprise, marketing, negotiation, purchase, purchasing, reduction, selling, trade, transaction, unloading, vending, vendition; CONCEPTS 324,345

salesperson [n] *salesman/woman* businessperson, clerk, dealer, peddler, rep, sales assistant, salesclerk, salesgirl, sales rep, sales representative, seller, store clerk, traveling salesperson, vendor; CONCEPT 348

salient [adj] *noticeable, important* arresting, arrestive, conspicuous, famous, impressive, intrusive, jutting, marked, moving, notable, obtrusive, obvious, outstanding, pertinent, projecting, prominent, pronounced, protruding, remarkable, signal, significant, striking, weighty; CONCEPT 567 —*Ant.* inconspicuous, unimportant, unnoticeable

saliva [n] *spit* dribble, drool, froth, slaver, slobber, spittle, sputum; CONCEPT 467

sallow [adj] *pale, unhealthy* anemic, ashen, ashy, bilious, colorless, dull, greenish-yellow, jaundiced, muddy, pallid, pasty, wan, waxy, yellowish; CONCEPT 618 —*Ant.* colorful, dark, flushed, healthy

saloon [n] *business establishment that primarily serves liquor* alehouse, bar, barroom, beer joint*, cocktail lounge, dive*, drinkery, gin mill*, hangout*, joint*, nightclub, pub, public house, speakeasy, taproom, tavern, watering hole*; CONCEPTS 439,448,449

salt away [v] *save, store up* accumulate, amass, bank, cache, hide, hoard, invest, lay aside, lay away, put away, put by, put in the bank, save for rainy day*, set aside, spare, stash, stockpile; CONCEPT 330 —*Ant.* spend, throw away, waste

salty [adj1] *flavored with sodium chloride* acrid, alkaline, brackish, briny, highly flavored, over-salted, pungent, saliferous, saline, salt, salted, saltish, sour; CONCEPTS 462,613 —*Ant.* bland, unsalted, unsalty

salty [adj2] *spicy, colorful* humorous, lively, piquant, pungent, racy, sharp, snappy, tangy, tart, witty, zestful; CONCEPTS 401,589 —*Ant.* blah, bland, dull

salubrious [adj] *health-giving* beneficial, good, healthful, healthy, hygienic, invigorating, salutary, sanitary, wholesome; CONCEPTS 560,572 —*Ant.* insalubrious, unhealthy, unwholesome

salutary [adj] *healthy* aiding, beneficial, fit, good, healing, healthful, nourishing, nutritious, restorative, salubrious, sound, tonic, well, wholesome; CONCEPTS 314,462,537,545

salute [v] *greet; honor* accost, acknowledge, address, bow, call to, congratulate, hail, pay homage, pay respects, pay tribute, present arms, receive, recognize, snap to attention*, speak, take hat off to*, welcome; CONCEPTS 38,69,320

salute/salutation [n] *greeting, recognition* address, bow, howdy*, kiss, obeisance, tribute, welcome; CONCEPT 38 —*Ant.* farewell, goodbye

salvage [v] *save, rescue* deliver, get back, glean, ransom, reclaim, recover, redeem, regain, restore, retrieve, salve; CONCEPT 134 —*Ant.* endanger, harm, hurt, injure, lose, waste

salvation [n] *rescue, saving* conservancy, conservation, deliverance, emancipation, escape, exemption, extrication, keeping, liberation, lifeline, pardon, preserval, preservation, redemption, release, reprieve, restoration, safekeeping, sustentation; CONCEPT 134 —*Ant.* endangerment, harm, hurt, injury, loss, waste

salve [n] *ointment for relief of pain or illness* aid, balm, cerate, counterirritant, cream, cure, dressing, emolient, help, liniment, lotion, lubricant, medication, medicine, remedy, unction, unguent; CONCEPTS 311,466

salve [v] *soothe* alleviate, ally, assuage, balm, becalm, calm, calm down, cool off*, ease, heal, mollify, pacify, pour oil on*, quiet, relieve, settle, smooth down, soften, still, take the edge off*, take the sting out of*, unburden, untrouble; CONCEPTS 7,22,110,384

same [adj1] *alike, identical* aforementioned, aforesaid, carbon*, carbon-copy*, clone, co-equal, comparable, compatible, corresponding, ditto*, double, dupe*, duplicate, equal, equivalent, indistinguishable, interchangeable, in the same manner, like, likewise, look-alike, related, same difference, selfsame, similar, similarly, synonymous, tantamount, twin, very, Xerox*; CONCEPTS 487,566,573 —*Ant.* different, inconsistent, polar, unlike

same [adj2] *unchanging* changeless, consistent, constant, invariable, perpetual, unaltered, unchanged, unfailing, uniform, unvarying; CONCEPT 534 —*Ant.* changing, inconsistent, variable, wavering

sameness [n] *likeness, similarity* adequation, alikeness, analogy, equality, equivalency, identicalness, identity, indistinguishability, monotony, no difference, oneness, par, parity, predictability, repetition, resemblance, self-sameness, standardization, tedium, uniformity, unison, unity, unvariedness; CONCEPTS 667,670 —*Ant.* difference, dissimilarity, variableness, variety

sample [n] *example, model* bit, bite, case, case history, constituent, cross section, element, exemplification, fragment, illustration, indication, individual, instance, morsel, part, pattern, piece, portion, representative, sampling, segment, sign, specimen, typification, unit; CONCEPTS 686,835

sample [v] *taste, try* examine, experience, experiment, inspect, partake, savor, sip, test; CONCEPTS 103,616

sanctify [v] *hold in highest esteem* absolve, anoint, bless, cleanse, consecrate, dedicate, deify, enshrine, glorify, hallow, purify, set apart, worship; CONCEPTS 10,12 —*Ant.* desecrate, dishonor, disrespect

sanctimonious [adj] *self-righteous* bigoted, canting, deceiving, false, goody-goody*, holier-than-thou*, hypocritical, insincere, pharisaical, pietistic, pious, preachy, self-satisfied, smug, stuffy, unctuous; CONCEPTS 401,404 —*Ant.* humble, meek, modest

sanction [n1] *authorization* acquiescence, allowance, approbation, approval, assent, authority, backing, confirmation, consent, countenance, encouragement, endorsement, fiat, go-ahead*, green light*, leave, nod, okay*, permission, permit, ratification, recommendation, seal of approval*, stamp of approval*, sufferance, support, word; CONCEPT 685 —*Ant.* disapproval, prevention, refusal, veto

sanction [n2] *embargo, punishment* ban, boycott, coercive measure, command, decree, injunction, penalty, punitive measure, sentence, writ; CONCEPT 123 —*Ant.* award, honor, reward

sanction [v] *authorize, confirm* accredit, allow, approve, back, bless, certify, commission, countenance, empower, endorse, get behind*, give the go-ahead*, give the green light*, give the nod*, go for*, license, okay*, permit, ratify, support, vouch for, warrant; CONCEPTS 50,88 —*Ant.* disapprove, prevent, refuse, veto

sanctioned [adj] *authorized* accepted, accredited, allowed, approved, confirmed, empowered, licensed, okayed, permitted, warranted; CONCEPTS 542,798

sanctity [n] *holiness* asceticism, blessedness, consecration, devotion, devoutness, divineness, divinity, faith, godliness, goodness, grace, hallowedness, inviolability, mercy, piety, purity, religiousness, reverence, righteousness, sacredness, saintliness, solemnity, spirituality, venerableness; CONCEPTS 368,645

sanctuary [n1] *church; holiest room or area in religious building* altar, chancel, holy place, sanctorium, sanctum, shrine, temple; CONCEPTS 368,439,448

sanctuary [n2] *place to hide, be safe* asylum, church, convent, cover, covert, defense, den, harbor, harborage, haven, hideaway, hideout, hole, hole-up*, ivory tower*, oasis, port, protection, refuge, resort, retreat, safe house, screen, shelter, shield; CONCEPTS 515,516

sanctuary [n3] *safe place for wildlife* asylum, conservation area, game refuge, harborage, national park, nature preserve, park, preserve, refuge, reserve, retreat, shelter; CONCEPT 517

sandwich [n] *grinder* BLT, club sandwich, Dagwood*, hero*, hoagie, open-faced sandwich, Reuben, sub, submarine sandwich; CONCEPTS 457,460,461

sane [adj] *mentally sound; reasonable* all there*, balanced, both oars in water*, commonsensical, compos mentis, discerning, fairminded, fit, having all marbles*, healthy, in one's right mind*, intelligent, judicious, levelheaded, logical, lucid, moderate, normal, of sound mind, oriented, playing with full deck*, prudent, rational, right, right-minded, sagacious, sage, sapient, self-possessed, sensible, sober, sound, steady, together*, well, wise; CONCEPTS 314,402,403 —*Ant.* crazy, insane, unreasonable, unsound, unstable

sanguine [adj1] *happy; optimistic* animated, assured, buoyant, cheerful, confident, enthusiastic, expectant, hopeful, lively, positive, secure, self-assured, self-confident, spirited, undoubtful, upbeat; CONCEPTS 403,542 —*Ant.* depressed, pessimistic, sad, unhappy

sanguine [adj2] *reddish; flushed* bloody, florid, flush, glowing, red, rubicund, ruddy, scarlet; CONCEPT 618 —*Ant.* pale, pallid, sallow

sanitary [adj] *clean, germ-free* healthful, healthy, hygienic, prophylactic, purified, salubrious, sanative, sterile, uncontaminated, uninfected, unpolluted, unsullied, wholesome; CONCEPT 621 —*Ant.* dirty, diseased, polluted, unsanitary

sanitize [v] *sterilize* antisepticize, clean, decontaminate, disinfect, freshen, fumigate, make sanitary, purify; CONCEPTS 231,250

sanity [n] *mental health; soundness of judgment* acumen, balance, clear mind, common sense, comprehension, good judgment, healthy mind, intelligence, judiciousness, levelheadedness, lucidity, lucidness, marbles*, normality, prudence, rationality, reason, reasonableness, right mind*, sagacity, saneness, sense, sound mind, soundness, stability, understanding, wit; CONCEPTS 409,410 —*Ant.* craziness, insanity, instability, madness, unsoundness

sap [n] *stupid person* chump, dolt, dupe, fool, idiot, jerk, nitwit, patsy*, pigeon*, simpleton, sucker*, weakling; CONCEPT 412

sap [v] *squeeze out; weaken* attenuate, bleed, blunt, cripple, debilitate, deplete, destroy, devitalize, disable, drain, enervate, enfeeble, erode, exhaust, impair, prostrate, rob, ruin, subvert, undermine, vitiate, wear down, wreck;

CONCEPTS 142,156,240,246 —*Ant.* build, help, increase, put in, strengthen

sapient [adj] *sagacious* acute, astucious, astute, cagey*, canny, clear-sighted, clever, contemplative, discerning, discriminating, educated, enlightened, experienced, farsighted, foxy*, informed, insightful, intelligent, judicious, keen, knowing, knowledgeable, perceptive, reflective, sage, scholarly, sensible, sharp, shrewd, smart, thoughtful, wise; CONCEPT 402

sappy [adj] *foolish, sentimental* absurd, balmy, bathetic, crazy*, drippy*, idiotic, illogical, insane, loony*, maudlin, mushy*, preposterous, silly, slushy*, soppy*, sticky*, stupid; CONCEPTS 403,542 —*Ant.* realistic, serious

sarcasm [n] *mocking remark* acrimony, aspersion, banter, bitterness, burlesque, causticness, censure, comeback, contempt, corrosiveness, criticism, cut*, cynicism, derision, dig*, disparagement, flouting, invective, irony, lampooning, mockery, mordancy, put-down*, raillery, rancor, ridicule, satire, scoffing, scorn, sharpness, sneering, superciliousness, wisecrack; CONCEPTS 52,54,277,278

sarcastic [adj] *nasty, mocking in speech* acerb, acerbic, acid, acrimonious, arrogant, austere, backhanded, biting, bitter, brusque, captious, carping, caustic, chaffing, contemptuous, contumelious, corrosive, cussed*, cutting, cynical, derisive, disillusioned, disparaging, disrespectful, evil, hostile, irascible, ironical, mean, mordant, needling, offensive, ornery*, salty, sardonic, satirical, saucy*, scorching, scornful, scurrilous, severe, sharp, smart-alecky*, snarling, sneering, taunting, trenchant, twitting, weisenheiming*; CONCEPT 267 —*Ant.* kind, nice

sardonic [adj] *sarcastic* acerbic, arrogant, biting, bitter, carping, caustic, cynical, derisive, disrespectful, evil, irascible, mean, mocking, mordant, nasty, offensive, salty*, satirical, scorching, scornful, sharp, smart-alecky*, sneering, taunting, wise*; CONCEPT 267

sass [n] *back talk* answer, cheek, guff, lip, mouth, nasty reply, retort, sauce; CONCEPTS 46

sass [v] *talk back* answer back, give lip*, mouth off*, wise off*; CONCEPT 401

sassy [adj] *impudent* arrant, audacious, bold, brassy, brazen, cheeky*, discourteous, disrespectful, flip*, flippant, fresh, insolent, mouthy*, overbold, rude, saucy*, smart-alecky*, smartmouthed, wise; CONCEPT 401

Satan [n] *the Devil* Angel of Darkness, Antichrist, Apollyon, archfiend, Beelzebub, demon, Diabolus, King of Hell, Lucifer, Mephistopheles, Prince of Darkness, the Evil Spirit; CONCEPTS 370,412

satanic [adj] *demonic* crazed, cruel, devilish, diabolic, diabolical, evil, fiendish, frenetic, hellish, infernal, mad, maniacal, possessed, unhallowed, vicious, wicked; CONCEPTS 404,545

satchel [n] *small bag* attaché, backpack, briefcase, carryall, carry-on, duffel bag, garment bag, handbag, haversack, knapsack, overnight bag, pack, pouch, rucksack, saddlebag, suitcase, tote, travel bag; CONCEPTS 339,450,494

satiate [v] *stuff, satisfy completely or excessively* cloy, content, feed to gills*, fill, glut, gorge, gratify, indulge, jade, nauseate, overdose, overfill, pall, sate, saturate, slake, surfeit;

CONCEPTS *169,740* —*Ant.* deprive, dissatisfy, leave wanting

satire [n] *ridicule intended to expose truth* banter, burlesque, caricature, causticity, chaffing, irony, lampoon, lampoonery, mockery, parody, pasquinade, persiflage, play-on, put-on*, raillery, sarcasm, send-up*, skit, spoof, squib*, takeoff*, travesty, wit, witticism; CONCEPTS *263,271,280*

satirical/satiric [adj] *mocking* abusive, bantering, biting, bitter, burlesque, caustic, censorious, chaffing, cutting, cynical, farcical, incisive, ironical, lampooning, mordant, paradoxical, parodying, pungent, ridiculing, sarcastic, sardonic, spoofing, taunting; CONCEPT *267*

satirize [v] *ridicule* banter, burlesque, caricature, caricaturize, cartoon, deride, haze, humiliate, jape, jeer, jive, josh, kid, lampoon, laugh at, make a fool of*, make fun of, mimic, mock, needle, pan*, parody, poke fun at*, pull one's leg, raz*, rib*, ride*, roast*, spoof; CONCEPT *54*

satisfaction [n] *giving or enjoying a state of comfort, content* achievement, amends, amusement, atonement, bliss, cheerfulness, comfort, compensation, complacency, conciliation, contentedness, contentment, delight, ease, enjoyment, fulfillment, gladness, good fortune, gratification, happiness, indemnification, indulgence, joy, justice, peace of mind, pleasure, pride, propitiation, recompense, redress, refreshment, reimbursement, relief, reparation, repletion, resolution, reward, satiety, serenity, settlement, vindication, well-being; CONCEPTS *344,410,720* —*Ant.* discontent, dissatisfaction, need, unhappiness, want

satisfactory [adj] *acceptable, sufficient* adequate, all right, ample, A-OK*, appeasing, assuaging, assuasive, average, cogent, comfortable, competent, cool*, decent, delighting, enough, fair, fulfilling, good, good enough, gratifying, groovy*, passable, peachy*, pleasing, satisfying, solid, sound, sufficing, suitable, tolerable, unexceptional, up to snuff*, valid; CONCEPTS *529,558, 560* —*Ant.* inadequate, insufficient, unacceptable, unfit, unsatisfactory, unsuitable

satisfy [v1] *please, content* amuse, animate, appease, assuage, befriend, brighten up, captivate, capture, cheer, cloy, comfort, conciliate, delight, do the trick*, elate, enliven, entertain, enthrall, exhilarate, fascinate, fill, fill the bill*, flatter, get by, gladden, glut, gorge, gratify, hit the spot*, humor, indulge, make merry, make the grade*, meet, mollify, pacify, placate, propitiate, quench, rejoice, sate, satiate, score, sell, sell on, slake, suit, surfeit; CONCEPTS *7,22* —*Ant.* anger, disappoint, discontent, dissatisfy, upset

satisfy [v2] *answer, persuade* accomplish, appease, assuage, assure, avail, be adequate, be enough, be sufficient, come up to, complete, comply with, conform to, convince, dispel doubt, do, equip, fill, fulfill, furnish, get by, induce, inveigle, keep promise, make good, make the grade*, meet, observe, pass muster*, perform, provide, put mind at ease*, qualify, quiet, reassure, score, sell, serve, serve the purpose*, suffice, tide over*, win over; CONCEPTS *108,140,656* —*Ant.* dissuade, fail, frustrate

satisfy [v3] *pay, compensate* answer, atone, clear up, disburse, discharge, indemnify, liquidate, make good*, make reparation, meet, pay off, quit, recompense, remunerate, repay, requite, reward, settle, square*; CONCEPTS *126,341* —*Ant.* dissatisfy, fail

satisfying [adj] *fulfilling* delightful, enjoyable, favorable, gratifying, hitting the spot, pleasant, pleasing, pleasurable, refreshing, rewarding, satiating, satisfactory, savory, sweet; CONCEPTS *537,572*

saturate [v] *drench, wet through* bathe, douche, douse, imbue, immerse, impregnate, infuse, overfill, penetrate, percolate, permeate, pervade, sate, satiate, soak, sop, souse, steep, suffuse, surfeit, transfuse, wash, waterlog; CONCEPT *256* —*Ant.* dehydrate, dry

saturnine [adj] *gloomy* blue*, cheerless, dejected, depressed, desolate, despondent, dispirited, dour, down, down in the dumps*, forlorn, glum, grave, hopeless, in low spirits*, in the dumps*, low, melancholy, miserable, moping, morose, sad, solemn, sorrowful, sulky, sullen, unhappy, woebegone, woeful; CONCEPT *403*

sauce [n] *condiment* coulis, dip, dressing, flavoring, gravy, jus, relish, topping; CONCEPT *457*

saucy [adj] *disrespectful* arch, audacious, bold, brash, brazen, cheeky*, combative, contumelious, flip*, flippant, forward, fresh, impertinent, impudent, insolent, intrusive, meddlesome, nervy, obtrusive, pert, presumptuous, rude, sassy, smart, smart-alecky*, smug, snippy*, volatile, weisenheiming*, wise; CONCEPTS *267,401* —*Ant.* kind, polite, respectful

saunter [n] *stroll* airing, amble, constitutional, promenade, ramble, turn, walk; CONCEPT *151* —*Ant.* run

saunter [v] *stroll along* amble, ankle, dally, drift, linger, loiter, meander, mope*, mosey*, ooze*, percolate, promenade, ramble, roam, rove, sashay, stump, tarry, toddle, traipse, trill, wander; CONCEPT *151* —*Ant.* run

savage [adj1] *wild, untamed* aboriginal, ancient, archaic, barbarian, barbaric, bestial, brutal, brute, crude, earliest, feral, ferocious, fierce, first, fundamental, harsh, in a state of nature, lupine, native, natural, nonliterate, original, primary, primeval, primitive, primordial, pristine, rough, rude, rugged, rustic, simple, turbulent, unbroken, uncivilized, uncultivated, uncultured, undomesticated, unmodified, unrestrained, unspoiled, vicious; CONCEPTS *401,485* —*Ant.* calm, civilized, domesticated, tame

savage [adj2] *cruel, vicious* atrocious, barbarous, beastly, bestial, bloodthirsty, bloody, brutal, brutish, cold-blooded, crazed, demoniac, destructive, devilish, diabolical, fell, feral, ferine, ferocious, fierce, frantic, furious, grim, harsh, heartless, hellish, infernal, inhuman, inhumane, malevolent, malicious, merciless, murderous, pitiless, rabid, raging, rapacious, ravening, relentless, remorseless, ruthless, sadistic, truculent, unrelenting, violent, wolfish; CONCEPTS *401,540* —*Ant.* benign, kind, nice

savanna/savannah [n] *grassland* grassy field, llano, meadow, pasturage, pasture, plain, prairie, steppe, veldt; CONCEPT *509*

savant [n] *scholar* academic, bookworm, brain*, egghead*, expert, intellect, intellectual, learned person, learner, master, philosopher, pundit, sage, wise person; CONCEPT 350

save [v1] *rescue* bail out, come to rescue, defend, deliver, emancipate, extricate, free, get off the hook*, get out of hock*, give a break, liberate, pull out of fire*, ransom, recover, redeem, salvage, save one's neck*, set free, spring, unchain, unshackle; CONCEPTS 127,134 —*Ant.* endanger, harm, hurt

save [v2] *economize; set money aside for later use* amass, be frugal, be thrifty, cache, collect, conserve, cut corners*, deposit, feather nest*, gather, hide away, hoard, hold, keep, lay aside, lay away, maintain, make ends meet*, manage, pile up, pinch pennies*, put by, reserve, retrench, roll back*, salt away*, save for rainy day*, scrimp, skimp, sock away*, spare, squirrel*, stash, stockpile, store, stow away, tighten belt*, treasure; CONCEPTS 120, 129 —*Ant.* squander, throw away, waste

save [v3] *guard, protect* conserve, defend, keep safe, keep up, look after, maintain, preserve, safeguard, screen, shield, sustain, take care of; CONCEPTS 96,117 —*Ant.* endanger, leave open, make vulnerable

savings [n] *provision for future* accumulation, ace in hole*, cache, fund, funds, gleanings, harvest, hoard, investment, kitty*, mattress full*, means, money in the bank, nest egg*, property, provision, provisions, rainy day fund*, reserve, reserves, resources, riches, sock, stake, stockpile, store; CONCEPTS 335,340,446,710 —*Ant.* loss

savior [n] *person who redeems, aids in time of difficulty* conservator, defender, deliverer, friend in need*, Good Samaritan*, guardian, guardian angel, hero, liberator, preserver, protector, rescuer, salvager, salvation; CONCEPTS 370,416 —*Ant.* enemy, foe, satan

savor [n1] *taste, flavor* odor, piquancy, relish, salt, sapidity, sapor, scent, smack, smell, spice, tang, tinge, zest; CONCEPT 614

savor [n2] *distinctive quality* affection, attribute, character, characteristic, excitement, feature, flavor, interest, mark, property, salt, spice, trait, virtue, zest; CONCEPTS 411,543

savor [v] *delight in, enjoy* appreciate, experience, feel, gloat, know, like, luxuriate in, partake, relish, revel in, sample, sip, smack, smell, taste; CONCEPTS 32,616 —*Ant.* dislike, refuse, shun

savory [adj] *pleasing, delicious in flavor* agreeable, ambrosial, aperitive, appetizing, aromatic, dainty, decent, delectable, exquisite, fragrant, full-flavored, good, luscious, mellow, mouth-watering, palatable, perfumed, piquant, pungent, redolent, relishing, respectable, rich, sapid, savorous, scrumptious, spicy, sweet, tangy, tasty, tempting, toothsome, wholesome; CONCEPT 613 —*Ant.* bland, displeasing, distasteful, offensive, tasteless, unappetizing

savvy [adj] *shrewd* acute, astute, brainy*, cagey*, calculating, canny, clever, crafty, cunning, discerning, experienced, farsighted, foxy*, heady*, ingenious, intelligent, in the know*, judicious, keen, knowing, on the ball*, perceptive, sagacious, sensible, sharp, slick*, sly, smart, smooth, streetwise, wise; CONCEPTS 401,402

savvy [n] *shrewdness* acumen, awareness, comprehension, discernment, experience, grasp, grip, insight, intellect, intelligence, judgment, know-how, knowing, knowledge, mastery, perception, perceptiveness, sense, sharpness, smarts*, understanding; CONCEPT 409

say [v] *make declaration* add, affirm, allege, announce, answer, assert, break silence*, claim, come out with, communicate, conjecture, convey, declare, deliver, disclose, divulge, do, estimate, express, flap*, gab*, give voice*, guess, imagine, imply, jaw, judge, lip*, maintain, make known, mention, opine, orate, perform, pronounce, put forth, put into words, rap*, read, recite, rehearse, relate, remark, render, repeat, reply, report, respond, reveal, rumor, speak, spiel*, state, suggest, tell, utter, verbalize, voice, yak*; CONCEPTS 51,266 —*Ant.* ask, question, request

saying [n] *maxim, proverb* adage, aphorism, apophthegm, axiom, byword, dictum, epigram, motto, precept, saw, statement, truism; CONCEPT 278

scads [n] *large quantity* bags*, barrels*, bunches, bundles*, gobs*, heaps*, jillion*, large number, loads, lots, many and then some*, oodles*, piles, plenty, scores, stacks, tons, zillions; CONCEPTS 432,787

scale [n1] *graduated system* calibration, computation, degrees, extent, gamut, gradation, hierarchy, ladder, order, pecking order*, progression, proportion, range, ranking, rate, ratio, reach, register, rule, scope, sequence, series, spectrum, spread, steps, system, way; CONCEPTS 651,744,770,788

scale [n2] *thin covering, skin* film, flake, incrustation, lamina, layer, plate, scurf; CONCEPTS 399,484

scale [v1] *ascend, climb* clamber, escalade, escalate, go up, mount, surmount; CONCEPT 166 —*Ant.* descend

scale [v2] *measure* adjust, balance, calibrate, compare, compute, estimate, gauge, graduate, proportion, prorate, regulate, size; CONCEPT 764

scam [n] *swindle* blackmail, cheating, con, con game, crooked deal*, deceit, deception, dirty pool*, double-cross*, double-dealing*, extortion, fast one*, flimflam*, fraud, hoax, hosing*, hustle, racket*, rip-off*, shady deal*, shake-down, sham, shell game*, snow job*, sting, sucker game*; CONCEPTS 59,139,192

scamp [n] *rascal* cheat, cheater, delinquent, fraud, hooligan*, liar, mischief-maker, prankster, rapscallion, reprobate, rogue, rowdy, ruffian, scalawag, scallywag, scoundrel, shyster, sneak, swindler, trickster, troublemaker, villain, whippersnapper; CONCEPT 412

scamper [v] *run, dash* bolt, dart, flee, fly, hasten, hie, hurry, light out, make off, race, romp, rush off, scoot, scurry, scuttle, shoot, skedaddle*, skip, speed, speed away, sprint, tear, trot, whip, zip*; CONCEPT 150 —*Ant.* stroll

scan [v] *look over, scrutinize lightly* browse, check, consider, contemplate, dip into*, examine, flash*, flip through, give the once-over*, glance at, glance over, have a look-see*, inquire, investigate, leaf through*, look, look through, look up and down*, overlook, regard, riff, riffle, rumble, run over, run through, scour, search, size up, skim, study, survey, sweep, take a gander*, take stock of*, thumb through*; CONCEPTS 103,623

scandal [n] *public embarrassment* aspersion, backbiting, backstabbing, belittlement, calumny, crime, defamation, depreciation, detraction, dirty linen*, discredit, disgrace, dishonor, disparagement, disrepute, dynamite, eavesdropping, gossip, hearsay, idle rumor, ignominy, infamy, mud, obloquy, opprobrium, reproach, rumor, scorcher, shame, sin, skeleton in closet*, slander, tale, talk, turpitude, wrongdoing; CONCEPTS 278,645,674

scandalous [adj] *disreputable* atrocious, backbiting, calumnious, crying, defamatory, desperate, detracting, detractive, disgraceful, gossiping, heinous, ignominious, infamous, libelous, maligning, monstrous, odious, opprobrious, outrageous, red hot*, scurrilous, shameful, shocking, slanderous, traducing, unseemly, untrue, vilifying; CONCEPTS 545 —*Ant.* proper, reputable, respected

scant/scanty [adj] *inadequate* bare, barely sufficient, close, deficient, exiguous, failing, insufficient, limited, little, meager, minimal, narrow, poor, rare, restricted, scrimpy, short, shy, skimpy, slender, spare, sparing, sparse, stingy, thin, tight, wanting; CONCEPTS 766,767, 789 —*Ant.* abundant, adequate, ample, covering, limited, plentiful, sufficient

scapegoat [n] *person who takes blame for another's action* boob*, chump, doormat*, dupe, easy mark*, fall guy*, fool, goat*, gull*, mark*, patsy, pigeon*, pushover*, sacrifice, sap*, schmuck*, sitting duck*, stooge, sucker, victim, weakling; CONCEPT 412

scar [n] *blemish from previous injury or illness* blister, cicatrice, cicatrix, crater, defect, discoloration, disfigurement, flaw, hurt, mark, pockmark, scab, track, wound; CONCEPT 580 —*Ant.* perfection

scar [v] *mark, hurt* beat, blemish, brand, cut, damage, deface, disfigure, flaw, injure, maim, mar, pinch, score, scratch, slash, stab, traumatize; CONCEPTS 7,19 —*Ant.* perfect, smooth

scarce [adj] *insufficient, infrequent* at a premium, deficient, failing, few, few and far between*, in short supply, limited, occasional, rare, scant, scanty, seldom, seldom met with, semioccasional, short, shortened, shy, sparse, sporadic, truncated, uncommon, unusual, wanting; CONCEPTS 541,789 —*Ant.* abundant, frequent, plentiful, sufficient

scarcely [adv] *barely* hardly, imperceptibly, infrequently, just, just barely, only just, rarely, scantily, seldom, slightly; CONCEPTS 541,789 —*Ant.* adequately, commonly, sufficiently

scare [n] *frightened state* alarm, alert, fright, panic, shock, start, terror; CONCEPTS 230,410 —*Ant.* calmness, comfort, ease

scare [v] *frighten someone* affright, alarm, awe, chill, daunt, dismay, freeze, give a fright, give a turn*, intimidate, panic, paralyze, petrify, scare silly*, scare stiff*, scare the pants off*, shake up*, shock, spook, startle, strike terror in, terrify, terrorize; CONCEPTS 7,19,42 —*Ant.* calm, comfort, reassure, soothe

scared [adj] *frightened* afraid, aghast, anxious, fearful, having cold feet*, panicked, panicky,

panic-stricken, petrified, shaken, startled, terrified, terror-stricken; CONCEPT 403 —*Ant.* confident, encouraged, unafraid

scarf [n] *muffler* ascot, bandanna, boa, kerchief, neckwear, shawl, stole, wrapping; CONCEPT 451

scary [adj] *frightening, terrifying* alarming, bloodcurdling, chilling, creepy, eerie, hair-raising, hairy*, horrendous, horrifying, intimidating, shocking, spine-chilling, spooky, unnerving; CONCEPTS 529,548 —*Ant.* calming, encouraging, soothing

scathing [adj] *nasty, critical in remarks* belittling, biting, brutal, burning, caustic, cruel, cutting, harsh, mordacious, mordant, salty, sarcastic, scorching, scornful, searing, severe, sulphurous, trenchant, withering; CONCEPT 267 —*Ant.* generous, kind, nice, praising

scatter [v] *strew, disperse* besprinkle, broadcast, cast, derange, diffuse, disband, discard, disject, dispel, disseminate, dissipate, distribute, disunite, diverge, divide, expend, fling, intersperse, litter, migrate, part, pour, put to flight*, run away, scramble, separate, set, set asunder, sever, shatter, shed, shower, sow, spend, split up, spray, spread, sprinkle, sunder, take off in all directions*, throw around, throw out; CONCEPTS 179,217,222 —*Ant.* collect, gather

scatterbrained [adj] *not thinking clearly* birdbrained*, careless, dizzy, empty-headed*, featherbrained*, flighty, forgetful, frivolous, giddy, harebrained*, illogical, inattentive, irrational, irresponsible, madcap, silly, slaphappy*, stupid, thoughtless; CONCEPT 402 —*Ant.* aware, careful, sensible, thoughtful

scenario [n] *master plan; sequence of events* book, outline, pages, plot, résumé, rundown, scheme, sides, sketch, story line, summary, synopsis; CONCEPTS 282,283,660

scene [n1] *setting of a performance or event* arena, backdrop, background, blackout, display, exhibition, flat, flats, landscape, locale, locality, location, mise en scène, outlook, pageant, picture, place, representation, scenery, seascape, set, setting, show, sight, site, spectacle, spot, stage, tableau, theater, view; CONCEPTS 263,625,628

scene [n2] *part of a dramatic performance* act, bit, episode, incident, part, piece, routine, schtick, spot; CONCEPT 264

scene [n3] *display of emotion* carrying-on*, commotion, confrontation, exhibition, fit, fuss, performance, row, tantrum, temper tantrum, to-do*, upset; CONCEPT 633 —*Ant.* composure

scene [n4] *field of interest* arena, business, compass, culture, environment, field, milieu, setting, sphere, world; CONCEPT 349

scenery [n] *surroundings* backdrop, decor, flat, flats, furnishings, furniture, landscape, mise en scène, neighborhood, properties, props, prospect, set, setting, spectacle, sphere, stage set, stage setting, terrain, view, vista; CONCEPTS 263,628

scenic [adj] *beautiful, picturesque* breathtaking, dramatic, grand, impressive, panoramic, spectacular, striking; CONCEPTS 485,579 —*Ant.* despicable, dreary, gloomy, ugly

scent [n] *smell, aroma* aura, balm, bouquet, essence, fragrance, incense, odor, perfume,

SC
SC

redolence, spice, tang, track, trail, whiff; CONCEPT 599 —**Ant.** odor, stench, stink

scent [v] *detect, smell* be on the track of*, be on the trail of*, discern, get wind of*, nose, nose out*, recognize, sense, sniff; CONCEPTS 601,602

scented [adj] *fragrant* ambrosial, aromal, aromatic, balmy, delectable, odoriferous, odorous, perfumed, perfumy, redolent, smelling, spicy, sweet-smelling; CONCEPT 598

schedule [n] *plan for one's time* agenda, appointments, calendar, catalog, chart, diagram, docket, inventory, itinerary, lineup*, list, order of business, program, record, registry, roll, roster, sked*, table, timetable; CONCEPTS 271,283,660 —**Ant.** disorganization

schedule [v] *plan one's time* appoint, arrange, be due, book, card, catalog, engage, get on line*, line up*, list, note, organize, pencil in*, program, record, register, reserve, set, set up, sew up*, slate, time, write in one's book*; CONCEPTS 36,125 —**Ant.** disorder, disorganize

schematic [adj] *diagrammatic* delineative, graphic, illustrative, representational, simplified, symbolic; CONCEPT 625

scheme [n1] *course of action* arrangement, blueprint, chart, codification, contrivance, design, device, diagram, disposition, expedient, game plan, layout, order, ordering, outline, pattern, plan, presentation, program, project, proposal, proposition, purpose, schedule, schema, strategy, suggestion, system, tactics, theory; CONCEPTS 271,625,660

scheme [n2] *plot, maneuver to get result* action, angle*, brainchild*, cabal, conspiracy, covin, dodge*, frame-up*, game, game plan*, gimmick, hookup*, hustle, hype*, intrigue, layout, machination, picture*, pitch, ploy, practice, proposition, put-up job*, ruse, scenario, scene, setup*, shift*, story, stratagem, subterfuge, tactics, trick*, twist*; CONCEPTS 59,645,660

scheming [adj] *deceitful, sly* artful, calculating, conniving, crafty, cunning, designing, duplicitous, foxy, slippery, tricky, underhand, wily; CONCEPT 542 —**Ant.** aboveboard, honest, open

schism [n] *separation* alienation, break, breakup, difference, disagreement, discord, dissension, disunion, division, divorce, faction, fissure, fracture, gap, parting, rift, rupture, secession, splinter group, split; CONCEPTS 135,195,297,388

schlemiel [n] *dolt* blockhead*, boob*, bungler, dimwit*, dope, dork*, dumbbell*, dunce, fool, goof*, goon*, idiot, ignoramus, jerk, lunkhead*, meathead*, nincompoop*, ninny*, nitwit*, sap*, schmuck, simpleton, stooge*, stupid; CONCEPTS 412,423

schlepp [v] *lug* carry, drag, haul, heave, lift, lurch, pull, tote, tow, tug, yank; CONCEPT 206

scholar [n] *person who is very involved in education and learning* academic, augur, bookish person, bookworm*, brain*, critic, disciple, doctor, egghead*, gnome*, grind*, intellectual, learned person, learner, litterateur, person of letters, philosopher, professor, pupil, sage, savant, schoolchild, scientist, student, teacher, tool, wise person; CONCEPT 350

scholarly [adj] *academic* bookish, cultured, educated, erudite, intellectual, learned, lettered, literate, longhair*, scholastic, schooled, studious,

taught, trained, well-read; CONCEPT 402 —**Ant.** uneducated, unscholarly

scholarship [n1] *knowledge* ability, awareness, cognition, comprehension, discernment, education, erudition, expertise, grasp, insight, instruction, intelligence, know-how*, learnedness, learning, lore, philosophy, schooling, wisdom; CONCEPTS 274,409,529

scholarship [n2] *grant* assistance, award, bursary, charity, donation, fellowship, financial aid, reward; CONCEPTS 337,344

school [n1] *place, system for educating* academy, alma mater, blackboard*, college, department, discipline, establishment, faculty, hall, halls of ivy*, institute, institution, jail*, schoolhouse, seminary, university; CONCEPTS 287,289

school [n2] *persons receiving education* academy, adherents, circle, class, clique, denomination, devotees, disciples, faction, followers, following, group, party, pupils, sect, set; CONCEPTS 288,350

school [n3] *body of philosophy on subject* belief, creed, faith, outlook, persuasion, school of thought, stamp*, way, way of life; CONCEPTS 349,689

school [v] *teach* advance, coach, control, cultivate, direct, discipline, drill, educate, guide, indoctrinate, inform, instruct, lead, manage, prepare, prime, show, train, tutor, verse; CONCEPT 285 —**Ant.** learn

science [n] *methodical study of part of material world* art, body of knowledge, branch, discipline, education, erudition, information, learning, lore, scholarship, skill, system, technique, wisdom; CONCEPTS 274,349,360 —**Ant.** art

scientific [adj] *systematic; discovered through experimentation* accurate, clear, controlled, deductive, exact, experimental, logical, mathematical, methodical, objective, precise, sound; CONCEPT 535 —**Ant.** artistic

scientist [n] *researcher* analyst, chemist, examiner, expert, lab technician, physicist, prober, tester; CONCEPTS 349,362

scintilla [n] *small bit, trace* atom, crumb, dab, dash, drop, flash, hint, iota, particle, pinch, ray, shade, shred, small quantity, smidgen, soupçon, sparkle, speck, spot, whiff, whisper; CONCEPTS 529,831

scintillating [adj] *bright, stimulating* animated, brilliant, clever, dazzling, ebullient, exciting, flashing, gleaming, glimmering, glinting, glittering, lively, shining, smart, sparkling, sprightly, twinkling, witty; CONCEPTS 401,529, 617 —**Ant.** blah, dull

scion [n] *offshoot, descendant* begotten, branch, brood, child, chip off old block*, graft, heir, heiress, issue, junior, offspring, progeny, seed, shoot, slip, sprout, successor, twig; CONCEPTS 414,428 —**Ant.** cause, root, source

scoff [v] *make fun of; despise* belittle, boo*, contemn, deride, dig at*, disbelieve, discount, discredit, disdain, flout, gibe, jeer, knock*, laugh at, make light of*, mock, pan*, poke fun at, pooh-pooh*, rag*, rally, reject, revile, ride, ridicule, scorn, show contempt, sneer, tease; CONCEPT 54 —**Ant.** be nice, praise

scold [v] *find fault with* abuse, admonish, asperse, berate, blame, castigate, cavil, censure, chasten, chide, criticize, denounce, disparage, dress down*, expostulate, give a talking-to*, jump on*, keep aft*, lay down the law*, lecture, light into*, nag, objurate, preach, put down, rail, rake over the coals*, rate, ream, rebuke, recriminate, reprimand, reproach, reprobate, reprove, revile, take to task*, taunt, tell off*, upbraid, vilify, vituperate; CONCEPTS 44,52,54 —Ant. compliment, flatter, praise

scoop [n1] *utensil, tool for shovelling* bail, dipper, ladle, shovel, spade, spoon, trowel; CONCEPTS 493,499

scoop [n2] *previously secret information that is suddenly public* beat, exclusive, exposé, inside story*, news, revelation, sensation; CONCEPT 274

scoop [v] *dig up; shovel* bail, clear away, dig, dig out, dip, empty, excavate, gather, gouge, grub, hollow, lade, ladle, lift, pick up, remove, scrape, spade, sweep away, sweep up, take up; CONCEPT 178

scoot [v] *hurry* accelerate, beeline*, be quick, bolt, clear out, dart, dash, expedite, fly, get a move on*, go like lightning, hasten, hurry up, hustle, make haste, make time*, make tracks*, move, move fast, race, run, rush, scamper, scurry, shake a leg*, skedaddle, speed, split, spur, step on it*, vamoose, whiz, zip; CONCEPTS 150,234

scope [n] *extent or range of something* ambit, amplitude, area, breadth, capacity, compass, comprehensiveness, confines, elbow room*, extension, field, field of reference, freedom, fullness, latitude, leeway, liberty, margin, opportunity, orbit, outlook, play, purview, radius, reach, room, run, space, span, sphere, wideness; CONCEPTS 651,739,788

scorch [v] *burn* bake, blacken, blister, broil, char, cook, melt, parch, roast, scald, sear, seethe, shrivel, simmer, singe, stale, stew, swelter, wither; CONCEPTS 249,255 —Ant. freeze

score [n1] *total, points* account, addition, aggregate, amount, average, count, final count, grade, mark, number, outcome, rate, reckoning, record, result, stock, sum, summary, summation, tab, tally; CONCEPTS 364,784

score/scores [n2] *large group; a great number* army, cloud, crowd, drove, flock, host, hundred, legion, lot, mass, million, multitude, myriad, rout, swarm, throng, very many; CONCEPT 432 —Ant. none

score [n3] *musical arrangement* charts, composition, music, orchestration, transcript; CONCEPT 262

score [n4] *obligation; account payable* account, amount due, bill, charge, debt, grievance, grudge, injury, injustice, invoice, reckoning, statement, tab, tally, total; CONCEPTS 332,645

score [v1] *keep count* add, calculate, chalk up, count, enumerate, keep tally, rack up*, reckon, record, register, tally, total; CONCEPTS 125,764

score [v2] *achieve, succeed* accomplish, amass, arrive, attain, chalk up*, connect, flourish, gain, gain advantage, get*, hit pay dirt*, impress, luck out*, make a killing*, make an impression*, make the grade*, notch, procure, prosper, pull off*, put over*, rack up*, reach, realize, secure, take the cake*, thrive, triumph, win; CONCEPTS 704,706 —Ant. fail, lose

score [v3] *cut, nick* cleave, crosshatch, deface, furrow, gash, gouge, graze, groove, indent, line, mark, mill, notch, scrape, scratch, serrate, slash, slit; CONCEPTS 137,176 —Ant. mend, smooth

score [v4] *write a musical arrangement* adapt, arrange, compose, orchestrate, set; CONCEPTS 79,292

scorn [n] *contempt toward something* contemptuousness, contumely, derision, despisal, despisement, despite, disdain, disparagement, disregard, jeering, mockery, ridicule, sarcasm, scoffing, scornfulness, slight, sneer, sport, taunting, teasing; CONCEPTS 29,54 —Ant. approval, delight, pleasure

scorn [v] *hold in contempt; look down on* abhor, avoid, be above, confute, consider beneath one*, contemn, defy, deride, despise, disdain, disregard, flout, gibe, hate, ignore, make fun of, mock, put down, refuse, refute, reject, renounce, repudiate, ridicule, run down*, scoff at, shun, slight, sneer, spurn, taunt, trash*, turn back on*, turn nose up at*; CONCEPTS 21,30,52,54 —Ant. admire, approve, like, love

scoundrel [n] *person who is deceptive and uncaring of others* bad egg*, bad news*, blackguard*, black sheep*, caitiff, cheat, creep, crook, dastard, good-for-nothing*, heel, imp, incorrigible, lowlife*, maggot*, mischiefmaker, miscreant, ne'er-do-well*, rascal, reprobate, scalawag, scamp, thief, vagabond, villain, wretch; CONCEPT 412

scour [v1] *clean, polish thoroughly* abrade, brush, buff, burnish, cleanse, flush, furbish, mop, pumice, purge, rub, sand, scrub, wash, whiten; CONCEPT 165 —Ant. dirty, rust

scour [v2] *search thoroughly* beat, comb, ferret out, find, forage, go over with a finetooth comb*, grub, hunt, inquire, leave no stone unturned*, look for, look high and low*, look up and down*, rake, ransack, rout, rummage, seek, track down, turn inside out*, turn upside down*; CONCEPT 216 —Ant. ignore, overlook

scourge [n] *plague, torment* affliction, bane, correction, curse, infliction, misfortune, penalty, pest, pestilence, punishment, terror, visitation; CONCEPTS 674,675 —Ant. advantage, benefit, blessing, boon, delight, happiness

scourge [v] *beat, punish often physically* afflict, belt, cane*, castigate, chastise, curse, discipline, excoriate, flail, flog, harass, hit, horsewhip*, lambaste*, lash, penalize, plague, scathe, scorch*, tan*, terrorize, thrash, torment, trounce, wallop*, whale*, whip; CONCEPTS 14,52,122, 189 —Ant. guard, protect

scout [n] *person who is searching, investigating* advance, adventurer, detective, escort, explorer, guard, lookout, outpost, outrider, patrol, picket, pioneer, precursor, reconnoiterer, recruiter, runner, sleuth, spotter, spy, vanguard; CONCEPTS 348,358 —Ant. target

scout [v] *investigate, check out* case, examine, explore, ferret, have a look-see*, hunt, inspect, look for, observe, probe, reconnoiter, run reconnaissance, rustle up*, search, seek, set eyes on*, spot, spy, stake out, survey, take in, track down, watch; CONCEPTS 103,216,623 —Ant. ignore, overlook, shun

SC
SC

scowl [n] *frown* black look*, dirty look*, evil eye*, glower, grimace; CONCEPTS 185,716 —*Ant.* grin, smile

scowl [v] *frown* disapprove, glare, gloom, glower, grimace, look daggers at*, lour, lower, make a face*; CONCEPT 185 —*Ant.* grin, smile

scraggly [adj] *ragged* badly dressed, badly worn, bedraggled, dilapidated, dingy, dirty, disheveled, frayed, frazzled, full of holes*, grubby*, grungy*, in tatters*, messy, moth-eaten, scruffy, shabby, sloppy, tacky*, tattered, threadbare, torn, unclean, uncombed, ungroomed, unkempt, worse for wear*; CONCEPTS 485,621

scram [v] *leave quickly* beat it*, clear out*, decamp, depart, disappear, get lost*, go away, hightail*, make oneself scarce*, make tracks*, scoot*, skedaddle*, take off, vamoose*; CONCEPT 195 —*Ant.* dally, wait

scramble [n] *mix-up, confusion* clutter, commotion, competition, conglomeration, free-for-all*, hash*, hassle, hustle, jumble, jungle, litter, melee, mishmash, muddle, race, rat race*, rush, shuffle, struggle, tumble, tussle; CONCEPTS 230,388,432 —*Ant.* order, organization

scramble [v] *race; get into position clumsily* clamber, climb, contend, crawl, hasten, jockey for position*, jostle, look alive*, make haste, move, push, run, rush, scrabble, scurry, scuttle, strive, struggle, swarm, trek, vie; CONCEPTS 87,150

scrap [n1] *tiny bit of something* atom, bite, bits and pieces*, butt, castoff, chip, chunk, crumb, cutting, discard, end, fragment, glob, gob, grain, hunk, iota, jot, junk, leaving, leftover*, lump, mite, modicum, morsel, mouthful, odds and ends*, orts, part, particle, piece, portion, remains, shred, slice, sliver, smithereen*, snatch, snippet, speck, stump, trace, waste; CONCEPTS 831,835 —*Ant.* load, lot

scrap [n2] *argument, fight* affray, battle, brawl, broil*, disagreement, dispute, fracas, fray, quarrel, row, scuffle, set-to*, squabble, tiff*, wrangle; CONCEPTS 46,106 —*Ant.* agreement, harmony, peace

scrap [v1] *abandon; throw away* break up, cast, chuck, consign to scrap heap*, demolish, discard, dismiss, dispense with, ditch, do away with*, drop, forsake, get rid of, jettison, junk, put out to pasture*, reject, retire, shed, slough, throw out, toss out, write off; CONCEPTS 121, 180 —*Ant.* hoard, keep, save, store

scrap [v2] *fight, argue* battle, bicker, caterwaul, come to blows*, fall out, have shouting match*, have words*, quarrel, row, spat, squabble, tiff, wrangle; CONCEPTS 46,106 —*Ant.* agree, harmonize, make peace

scrape [n] *bad or embarrassing situation* awkward situation, corner*, difficulty, dilemma, discomfort, distress, embarrassment, fix*, hole*, jam*, mess*, pickle*, plight, predicament, tight spot*, trouble; CONCEPT 674 —*Ant.* resolution, solution

scrape [v1] *scratch, remove outer layer* abrade, bark, bray, chafe, clean, erase, file, grate, graze, grind, irritate, pare, peel, rasp, rub, scour, scuff, shave, skin, squeak, thin, triturate; CONCEPTS 165,186,215 —*Ant.* smoothe

scrape [v2] *be very frugal* cut it close*, get

along, get by, pinch, save, scrimp, shave, skimp, stint, struggle; CONCEPT 330 —*Ant.* spend, squander, waste

scratch [n] *small cut or mark* blemish, claw mark, gash, graze, hurt, laceration, score, scrape; CONCEPTS 309,513 —*Ant.* perfection

scratch [v1] *cut; make a mark on* claw, damage, etch, grate, graze, incise, lacerate, mark, prick, rasp, rub, scarify, score, scrape, scrawl, scribble; CONCEPTS 79,176 —*Ant.* heal, mend, smooth

scratch [v2] *cancel* annul, delete, eliminate, erase, pull, pull out, strike, withdraw; CONCEPT 121 —*Ant.* schedule, set up

scrawl [v] *write erratically* doodle, inscribe, scrabble, scratch, scribble, squiggle; CONCEPT 79

scrawny [adj] *unhealthily thin* angular, bony, gaunt, lank, lanky, lean, rawboned, scraggy, skeletal, skin-and-bones*, skinny, spare, under-nourished, underweight; CONCEPTS 490,491,773 —*Ant.* chubby, fat, healthy, plump

scream [n1] *outcry* cry, high-pitched shout, holler*, howl, screech, shriek, wail, yell, yelp; CONCEPT 595

scream [n2] *person or thing that is very funny* card*, character*, comedian, comedienne, comic, entertainer, guffaw*, hoot*, howl*, joker, laugh, panic*, riot, sensation, sidesplitter*, wit; CONCEPTS 423,529 —*Ant.* seriousness

scream [v] *cry out* bawl, bellow, blare, caterwaul, holler*, howl, jar, roar, screak, screech, shout, shriek, shrill, sing out, squeal, voice, wail, yell, yip, yowl; CONCEPT 77 —*Ant.* be quiet

screen [n] *protection used in or as furniture, motion picture display* awning, canopy, cloak, concealment, cover, covering, curtain, divider, envelope, guard, hedge, mantle, mask, net, partition, security, shade, shelter, shield, shroud, veil; CONCEPTS 277,440,443,445,473

screen [v1] *hide, protect* adumbrate, blind, block out, bulwark, bury, cache, camouflage, cloak, close, conceal, cover, cover up, defend, disguise, ensconce, fend, guard, mask, obscure, obstruct, safeguard, seclude, secrete, secure, separate, shade, shadow, shelter, shield, shroud, shut off, shut out, shutter, stash, umbrage, veil, wall off; CONCEPTS 96,188 —*Ant.* lay open, open, reveal, uncover

screen [v2] *examine and choose* cull, eliminate, evaluate, extract, filter, gauge, grade, pick out, process, riddle, scan, select, separate, sieve, sift, sort, winnow; CONCEPT 41

screw [v1] *twist* in spiral, tighten, turn, twine, wind, work; CONCEPTS 85,160 —*Ant.* unscrew, untwist

screw [v2] *twist, contort* contract, crimp, crinkle, crumple, distort, pucker, rimple, ruck up, rumple, scrunch, wrinkle; CONCEPT 219 —*Ant.* unscrew, untwist

screw [v3] *pressure* bilk, bleed, cheat, chisel, coerce, constrain, defraud, do*, exact, extort, extract, force, hold a knife to*, oppress, pinch*, pressurize, put screws to*, ream*, shake down*, squeeze, wrench, wrest, wring; CONCEPTS 14,192 —*Ant.* help

screw up [v] *make a mess of* blow, bobble, bollix*, botch, bungle, confuse, flub*, foul up, goof*, goof up*, louse, make hash of*, mess, mess up, mishandle, mismanage, muck up*, muddle, muff, queer, snafu*, spoil; CONCEPT 101 —*Ant.* succeed

screwy [*adj*] *eccentric* abnormal, batty, bizarre, crazy, daft, dotty, far out*, flaky, funky*, irregular, kooky, mad, nutty, odd, oddball, offbeat, off-center, off the wall*, out in left field*, outlandish, peculiar, queer, quirky, strange, uncommon, unconventional, weird; CONCEPTS 547,564

scribble [*v*] *write illegibly* doodle, jot, scratch, scrawl, squiggle, write badly, write erratically; CONCEPT 79

scrimp [*v*] *economize* be cheap, be economical, be frugal, be prudent, be sparing, conserve, curtail, cut back, cut corners*, make ends meet*, pinch pennies*, run a tight ship*, save, skimp, stretch a dollar*, tighten one's belt*; CONCEPT 330

script [*n1*] *handwriting* calligraphy, characters, chirography, fist, hand, letters, longhand, penmanship, writing; CONCEPTS 79,284

script [*n2*] *story for a performance* article, book, copy, dialogue, libretto, lines, manuscript, playbook, scenario, text, typescript, words; CONCEPTS 263,271

Scrooge [*n*] *skinflint* cheapskate, meanie, misanthrope, misanthropist, miser, moneygrubber, niggard, penny-pincher, tightwad; CONCEPT 412

scrounge [*v*] *beg, forage for* bum, freeload, hunt, sponge, wheedle; CONCEPTS 48,216 —*Ant.* give, offer

scrub [*v1*] *clean with force* abrade, brush, buff, cleanse, mop, polish, rub, scour, wash; CONCEPT 165 —*Ant.* dirty

scrub [*v2*] *cancel* abandon, abolish, abort, call off, delete, discontinue, do away with, drop, forget about, give up; CONCEPTS 121,234 —*Ant.* organize, schedule, set up

scruffy [*adj*] *rough, bedraggled* badly groomed, frowzy*, mangy*, messy, ragged, run-down, seedy, shabby, slovenly, tacky*, tattered, threadbare, ungroomed, unkempt, untidy; CONCEPTS 485,589 —*Ant.* kempt, smooth, tidy

scrumptious [*adj*] *delicious* ambrosial, appetizing, delectable, delightful, exquisite, heavenly, inviting, luscious, lush, magnificent, mouthwatering, rich, succulent, tasty, yummy; CONCEPTS 529,613 —*Ant.* unappetizing, untasty

scrunch [*v*] *crumple* compress, crumple up, crunch, rumple, squash, squeeze; CONCEPT 184

scruple [*n*] *misgiving, doubt* anxiety, caution, censor, compunction, conscience, demur, difficulty, faltering, hesitancy, hesitation, pause, perplexity, qualm, reconsideration, reluctance, reluctancy, second thought*, squeamishness, superego, twinge, uneasiness; CONCEPTS 532,690 —*Ant.* ignorance, negligence, unconcern

scruple [*v*] *balk, have misgivings* be loath, be reluctant, be unwilling, boggle, demur, doubt, falter, fret, gag, have qualms, hesitate, question, shy, stick, stickle, stumble, think twice about*, vacillate, waver, worry; CONCEPT 21 —*Ant.* not care

scrupulous [*adj*] *extremely careful* conscientious, conscionable, critical, exact, fastidious, fussy, heedful, honest, honorable, just, meticulous, minute, moral, nice, painstaking, particular, precise, principled, punctilious, punctual, right, rigorous, strict, thinking twice*, true,

upright; CONCEPTS 401,538,542 —*Ant.* careless, negligent, unscrupulous

scrutinize [*v*] *examine closely* analyze, burn up, candle, canvass, case, check, check out, check over, comb*, consider, contemplate, dig, dissect, explore, eyeball*, get a load of*, go over with a fine-tooth comb*, inquire into, inspect, investigate, look over, overlook, peg*, penetrate, perlustrate, peruse, pierce, pore over, probe, put under a microscope*, scan, scope, scrutinate, search, sift, smoke*, stare, study, survey, take the measure of, view, watch, weigh; CONCEPTS 24,103,623

scrutiny [*n*] *close examination* analysis, audit, close-up, eagle eye*, exploration, inquiry, inspection, investigation, long hard look*, perlustration, perusal, review, scan, search, sifting, study, surveillance, survey, tab*, the eye*, view; CONCEPTS 24,103,623

scuttle [*n*] *fight* affray, brawl, broil, commotion, disturbance, fracas, fray, fuss*, go*, jump, mix-up, row, ruckus, ruction, rumpus, scrap, set-to*, shuffle, strife, tussle, wrangle; CONCEPT 106 —*Ant.* agreement, peace

scuffle [*v*] *fight* clash, come to blows, contend, cuff, grapple, jostle, skirmish, struggle, tussle, wrestle; CONCEPT 106 —*Ant.* make peace

sculpture [*v*] *form a three-dimensional art object* carve, cast, chisel, cut, engrave, fashion, hew, model, mold, sculp, sculpt, shape; CONCEPTS 137,174,184

scum [*n1*] *superficial impurities, dirt* algae, crust, dross, film, froth, residue, scruff, spume, waste; CONCEPT 260 —*Ant.* cleanliness

scum [*n2*] *people who are bad, despicable* curs*, dregs, lowest, mass, mob, proletariat, rabble, riffraff, rubbish*, scum of the earth*, trash*, unwashed, vermin; CONCEPT 412

scurrilous [*adj*] *foul-mouthed, vulgar* abusive, coarse, contumelious, defamatory, dirty, filthy, foul, gross, indecent, infamous, insulting, invective, lewd, low, nasty, obscene, offending, offensive, opprobrious, outrageous, raunchy, ribald, salacious, scabrous, scandalous, shameless, slanderous, smutty*, truculent, vituperative, vituperatory, vituperous; CONCEPTS 267, 542,545 —*Ant.* clean, polite, upright

scurry [*v*] *move along swiftly* barrel, bustle, dart, dash, dust, fly, hasten, hop along, hurry, race, rip, run, rush, scamper, scoot, scud, scutter, scuttle, shoot, skim, sprint, step along, tear, whirl, whisk, zip*; CONCEPT 150 —*Ant.* dawdle, loaf, walk

scuttlebutt [*n*] *gossip* babble, back-fence talk*, blather, chatter, chitchat, dirty laundry*, grapevine*, hearsay, meddling, prattle, rumor, talk; CONCEPTS 274,278

sea [*n*] *large body of water; large mass* abundance, blue*, bounding main*, brine, briny*, briny deep*, Davy Jones's locker*, deep, drink*, expanse, lake, main, multitude, number, ocean, plethora, pond, profusion, sheet, splash*, surf, swell, waves; CONCEPT 514 —*Ant.* land

seafarer [*n*] *sailor* bluejacket, boater, boatman/woman, deck hand, mariner, mate, middy, midshipman/woman, old salt*, pirate, sailorman/woman, sea dog*, seaman/woman, swabbie*, yachtsman/woman; CONCEPTS 348, 358,366

seal [n] *authentication; stamp* allowance, assurance, attestation, authorization, cachet, confirmation, imprimatur, insignia, notification, permission, permit, ratification, signet, sticker, tape, tie; CONCEPTS 284,685 —*Ant.* disapproval, refusal

seal [v1] *make airtight* close, cork, enclose, fasten, gum, isolate, paste, plaster, plug, quarantine, secure, segregate, shut, stop, stopper, stop up, waterproof; CONCEPTS 85,160 —*Ant.* loosen, open, unseal

seal [v2] *ensure, finalize* assure, attest, authenticate, clinch, conclude, confirm, consummate, establish, ratify, settle, shake hands on*, stamp, validate; CONCEPTS 234,324 —*Ant.* delay, put off, refuse

seam [n] *line where two objects are connected* bond, closure, connection, coupling, gore, gusset, hem, joint, junction, juncture, pleat, stitching, suture, tuck, union; CONCEPTS 452,471

seaman/woman [n] *sailor* bluejacket, boater, boatman/woman, deck hand, mariner, mate, middy, midshipman/woman, old salt*, pirate, sailorman/woman, sea dog*, seafarer, swabbie*, yachtsman/woman; CONCEPTS 348,358, 366

seamy [adj] *corrupt, unwholesome* bad, dark, degraded, disagreeable, disappointing, disreputable, disturbing, low, nasty, rough, sordid, squalid, unpleasant; CONCEPT 545 —*Ant.* respectable, upright, wholesome

sear [v] *dry, burn* blight, brand, brown, burn up, cauterize, cook, dehydrate, desiccate, dry out, dry up, exsiccate, harden, parch, scorch, seal, shrivel, sizzle, tan, toast, wilt, wither; CONCEPTS 170,249 —*Ant.* freeze

search [n] *seeking to find something* chase, examination, exploration, fishing expedition*, frisking*, going-over*, hunt, inquest, inquiry, inspection, investigation, legwork*, perquisition, pursual, pursuance, pursuing, pursuit, quest, research, rummage, scrutiny, shakedown*, wild-goose chase*, witch hunt*; CONCEPT 216 —*Ant.* finding

search [v] *seek to find something* beat, beat about, cast about, chase after, check, comb, examine, explore, ferret, forage, frisk, go in quest of, go over with a fine-tooth comb*, go through, grope, grub, gun for*, hunt, hunt for, inquire, inspect, investigate, leave no stone unturned*, look, look for, look high and low*, look over, poke into, probe, prospect, pry, quest, rake, ransack, rifle through, root, rummage, run down, scan, scour, scout, scrutinize, seek, shake down, sift, smell around, study, track down, turn inside out*, turn upside down*; CONCEPT 216 —*Ant.* find

searching [adj] *probing* curious, experimental, exploratory, fact-finding, inquiring, inquisitive, penetrating, seeking, sharp, studious; CONCEPT 402

seashore [n] *beach* bank, coast, littoral, oceanfront, seaboard, seafront, seaside, shingle, shore, strand, waterfront; CONCEPTS 509,514

season [n] *time of year governed by annual equinoxes* autumn, division, fall, interval, juncture, occasion, opportunity, period, spell, spring, summer, term, time, while, winter; CONCEPT 814

season [v1] *flavor food* color, enliven, lace, leaven, pep, pepper, salt, spice; CONCEPT 170 —*Ant.* cook plain

season [v2] *acclimatize, prepare* acclimate, accustom, anneal, climatize, discipline, fit, habituate, harden, inure, mature, qualify, school, steel, temper, toughen, train; CONCEPTS 35,202

seasonable [adj] *timely, appropriate* apropos, apt, auspicious, convenient, favorable, fit, opportune, pertinent, propitious, prosperous, providential, relevant, seasonal, suitable, timeous, towardly, welcome, well-timed; CONCEPT 558 —*Ant.* inappropriate, inclement, unfitting, unseasonable, unsuitable, untimely

seasoned [adj] *experienced* accomplished, adept, battle-scarred, been around*, been there*, competent, expert, familiar, hardened, instructed, knowledgeable, matured, old hand*, practiced, prepared, pro, professional, qualified, skillful, tested, toughened, trained, tried, vet, veteran, weathered, wise, worldly, worldly wise*; CONCEPTS 402,527

seasoning [n] *flavoring for food* condiment, dressing, gravy, herb, pepper, pungency, relish, salt, sauce, spice, zest; CONCEPTS 457,461

seat [n1] *furniture for sitting, reclining* bench, chair, chaise lounge, chesterfield, couch, davenport, lounge, loveseat, pew, recliner, settee, settle, stall, stool, swing chair; CONCEPT 443

seat [n2] *central location of organization* abode, axis, capital, center, cradle, focal point, fulcrum, headquarters, heart, house, hub, location, mansion, nerve center, place, polestar, post, residence, site, situation, source, spot, station; CONCEPT 198 —*Ant.* annex, offshoot

seat [n3] *base, foundation* basement, basis, bed, bottom, cause, fitting, footing, ground, groundwork, rest, seating, support; CONCEPT 442

seat [n4] *rear end of animate being* backside, behind, bottom, breech, derrière, duff*, fanny*, fundament*, keister*, posterior, rear, rear end, rump, tush*; CONCEPTS 392,825,827

seat [v] *place in furniture, position* accommodate, deposit, establish, fix, hold, install, locate, lounge, nestle, perch, plant, put, roost, set, settle, sit, squat, take; CONCEPTS 154,201,384 —*Ant.* displace, move, remove

secede [v] *pull away; split from* abdicate, apostatize, break with, disaffiliate, leave, quit, resign, retire, retract, retreat, separate, withdraw; CONCEPTS 119,298,384 —*Ant.* combine, come in, join, unite

secession [n] *withdrawal* breakaway, breakup, defection, disaffiliation, dissension, disunion, division, exiting, parting, rift, rupture, schism, separation, splinter group, split; CONCEPTS 135,195,211,297,388,000

seclude [v] *isolate, hide* blockade, boycott, cloister, closet, conceal, confine, cover, embargo, enclose, evict, immure, ostracize, quarantine, retire, screen, segregate, separate, sequester, shut off, withdraw; CONCEPTS 121,135,188 —*Ant.* join, mingle, socialize

secluded [adj] *isolated, sheltered* abandoned, alone, aloof, beleaguered, blockaded, cloistered, close, closet, confidential, covert, cut off, deserted, hermetic, hidden, incommunicado, insular, isolate, lonely, lonesome, off the beaten track*, out-of-the-way*, personal, private, quarantined, quiet, reclusive, remote, removed, reserved, retired, screened, secluse, seclusive, secret, segregated, sequestered, shut off, shy, singular, solitary, tucked away*, unapproachable, unfrequented, uninhabited, unsociable, withdrawn; CONCEPTS 401,576,583 —*Ant.* joining, mingling, open, public, sociable, socializing

seclusion [n] *isolation* aloneness, aloofness, beleaguerment, blockade, concealment, desolation, detachment, hiding, privacy, privateness, quarantine, reclusion, reclusiveness, remoteness, retirement, retreat, seclusiveness, separateness, separation, sequestration, shelter, solitude, withdrawal; CONCEPTS 135,188,388,631 —*Ant.* open, public

second [adj] *next; subordinate* additional, alternative, another, double, duplicate, extra, following, further, inferior, lesser, lower, next in order, other, place, repeated, reproduction, runner-up, secondary, subsequent, succeeding, supporting, twin, unimportant; CONCEPTS 575,585

second [n1] *shortest interval of time* bat of an eye*, flash, instant, jiffy*, moment, nothing flat*, sec*, shake*, split second, twinkling*, wink; CONCEPTS 803,821

second [n2] *support; duplicate* assistant, backer, double, exponent, helper, placer, proponent, reproduction, runner-up, supporter, twin; CONCEPTS 423,670

second [v] *support, advance a suggestion* aid, approve, assist, back, back up, encourage, endorse, forward, further, give moral support, go along with, promote, stand by, uphold; CONCEPTS 298,324,384 —*Ant.* move

secondary [adj1] *subordinate; less important* accessory, alternate, auxiliary, backup, bush-league*, collateral, consequential, contingent, dependent, dinky*, extra, inconsiderable, inferior, insignificant, lesser, lower, minor, minor-league*, petty, relief, reserve, second, second-rate, small, small-fry*, small-time*, subject, subservient, subsidiary, substract, supporting, tributary, trivial, under, unimportant; CONCEPTS 574,575 —*Ant.* first-class, first-rate, important, primary, superior

secondary [adj2] *derivative* auxiliary, borrowed, consequent, dependent, derivate, derivational, derived, developed, eventual, indirect, proximate, resultant, resulting, second-hand, subordinate, subsequent, subsidiary, vicarious; CONCEPT 549 —*Ant.* causative, primary, source

secondhand [adj] *used* handed down, hand-me-down, not new, old, pre-owned, previously owned, unnew; CONCEPTS 578,797

second-rate/second-class [adj] *inferior, cheap* cheap and dirty*, common, commonplace, déclassé, hack*, low-grade, low-quality, mean, mediocre, poor, shoddy*, substandard, tacky*, tawdry; CONCEPTS 334,567,574 —*Ant.* excellent, first-class, first-rate, great, superior, wonderful

secrecy [n] *concealment* clandestineness, confidence, confidentiality, covertness, dark, darkness, furtiveness, hiding, hush, isolation, mystery, privacy, reticence, retirement, seclusion, secretiveness, secretness, silence, solitude, stealth, suppression, surreptitiousness; CONCEPT 631 —*Ant.* forthrightness, honesty, openness, publicity, revelation

secret [adj1] *hidden, unrevealed* abstruse, ambiguous, arcane, backdoor, camouflaged, classified, cloak-and-dagger*, close, closet, clouded, conspiratorial, covered, covert, cryptic, dark, deep, disguised, enigmatical, esoteric, furtive, hush-hush*, mysterious, mystic, mystical, obscure, occult, on the QT*, out-of-the-way*, private, recondite, reticent, retired, secluded, shrouded, strange, undercover, underground, under wraps*, undisclosed, unenlightened, unfrequented, unintelligible, unknown, unpublished, unseen, veiled; CONCEPTS 529,576 —*Ant.* clear, defined, explicit, forthright, honest, open, public, revealed, unconcealed

secret [adj2] *underhand, clandestine* backdoor, backstairs, camouflaged, classified, close, confidential, covert, cryptic, discreet, disguised, dissembled, dissimulated, furtive, hush-hush*, in ambush, incognito, inside, restricted, secretive, sly, sneak, sneaky, stealthy, sub-rosa, surreptitious, top secret, unacknowledged, under false pretense*, underhanded, under-the-table*; CONCEPTS 545,576 —*Ant.* aboveboard, known, legal, legitimate, public

secret [n] *something kept hidden, unrevealed* cipher, classified information, code, confidence, confidential information, enigma, formula, key, magic number*, mystery, occult, oracle, password, privileged information, puzzle, skeleton in cupboard*, unknown; CONCEPTS 274,631 —*Ant.* known, public knowledge, revelation

secretary [n1] *office worker* assistant, clerk, executive secretary, receptionist, typist, word processor; CONCEPT 348

secretary [n2] *desk* bureau, davenport, escritoire, secretaire, writing desk, writing table; CONCEPT 443

secrete [v1] *hide* bury, cache, conceal, cover, cover up, deposit, disguise, ditch, ensconce, finesse, harbor, hide out, keep quiet, keep secret, keep to oneself, keep under wraps*, palm*, paper, plant, screen, seclude, secure, shroud, squirrel*, stash, stash away, stonewall*, stow, sweep under rug*, veil, whitewash*, withhold; CONCEPTS 188,266 —*Ant.* lay bare, reveal, tell, uncover

secrete [v2] *give off, emit* discharge, emanate, excrete, extravasate, extrude, exude, perspire, produce, sweat; CONCEPTS 146,179 —*Ant.* fill, pour in

secretive [adj] *uncommunicative* backstairs, buttoned up*, cagey, clammed up*, close, close-mouthed*, covert, cryptic, enigmatic, feline, furtive, hushed, in chambers*, in privacy*, in private, in the background*, in the dark*, on the QT*, reserved, reticent, silent, taciturn, tight-lipped*, undercover, unforthcoming, withdrawn, zipped*; CONCEPTS 267,548 —*Ant.* communicative, forthright, honest, open

secretly [adv] *in hidden manner* behind closed doors*, behind someone's back*, by stealth, clandestinely, confidentially, covertly, furtively, hush-hush*, in camera*, in confidence, in holes and corners*, in secret, insidiously, in strict confidence*, intimately, obscurely, on the QT*, on the quiet*, on the sly*, personally, privately, privily, quietly, slyly, stealthily, sub rosa, surreptitiously, underhandedly, under the table*, unobserved; CONCEPTS 267,548 —Ant. openly, publicly

sect [n] *school of thought* camp, church, communion, connection, creed, crew, cult, denomination, division, faction, faith, following, group, order, party, persuasion, religion, school, splinter group, team, wing; CONCEPTS 381,382

sectarian [adj] *narrow-minded, exclusive* bigoted, clannish, cliquish, dissident, doctrinaire, dogmatic, factional, fanatic, fanatical, hidebound, insular, limited, local, nonconforming, nonconformist, parochial, partisan, provincial, rigid, schismatic, skeptical, small-town*, splinter; CONCEPT 403 —Ant. broad, broad-minded, liberal, nonsectarian

sectarian [n] *person who is narrow-minded* adherent, bigot, cohort, disciple, dissenter, dissident, dogmatist, extremist, fanatic, heretic, maverick, misbeliever, nonconformist, partisan, radical, rebel, revolutionary, satellite, schismatic, separatist, supporter, true believer, zealot; CONCEPTS 359,423 —Ant. liberal, nonsectarian

section [n] *division, portion* area, belt, bite, branch, category, chunk, classification, component, cross section, cut, department, district, drag, end, field, fraction, fragment, hunk, installment, locality, lump, member, moiety, parcel, part, passage, piece, precinct, quarter, region, sample, sector, segment, share, slice, slot, sphere, split, subdivision, territory, tier, tract, vicinity, zone; CONCEPT 835 —Ant. whole

sectional [adj] *localized, divided* exclusive, factional, local, narrow, partial, regional, selfish, separate, separatist; CONCEPTS 557,785 —Ant. general, universal, widespread

sector [n] *area, subdivision* category, district, division, part, precinct, quarter, region, stratum, zone; CONCEPTS 508,835 —Ant. whole

secular [adj] *not spiritual or religious* civil, earthly, laic, lavical, lay, material, materialistic, nonclerical, nonreligious, of this world*, profane, temporal, unsacred, worldly; CONCEPTS 529,549 —Ant. godly, holy, religious, spiritual

secure [adj1] *safe* defended, guarded, immune, impregnable, out of harm's way, protected, riskless, sheltered, shielded, unassailable, undamaged, unharmed; CONCEPT 587 —Ant. endangered, insecure, unprotected, unsafe

secure [adj2] *fastened, stable* adjusted, anchored, bound, buttoned down*, fast, firm, fixed, fortified, immovable, iron, locked, nailed, safe and sound*, set, solid, solid as a rock*, sound, staunch, steady, strong, sure, tenacious, tight; CONCEPT 488 —Ant. loose, moving, unfastened, unfixed, unsecure, unstable

secure [adj3] *certain, definite* able, absolute, assured, at ease, balanced, carefree, cinch, conclusive, confident, determined, easy, established, firm, hopeful, in the bag*, locked on*, nailed down*, on ice*, reassured, reliable, resolute, sanguine, self-assured, self-confident, settled, shoo-in*, solid, sound, stable, steadfast, steady, strong, sure, sure thing*, tried and true*, unanxious, undoubtful, well-founded; CONCEPTS 403,535 —Ant. indefinite, insecure, uncertain, undecided, unsure

secure [v1] *obtain* access, achieve, acquire, annex, assure, bag*, buy, capture, catch, chalk up*, cinch, come by, ensure, gain, get, get hold

of, grasp, guarantee, have, hook, insure, land, lock, lock up, make sure, pick up, procure, rack up*, take, win; CONCEPT 120 —Ant. forfeit, give up, lose

secure [v2] *attach, tie up* adjust, anchor, batten down, bind, bolt, button, button down, catch, cement, chain, clamp, clinch, close, fasten, fix, hitch, hook on, lash, lock, lock up, make fast, moor, nail, padlock, pinion, rivet, settle, tack, tie, tie down, tighten; CONCEPTS 85,160 —Ant. let go, loose, loosen, unfasten, untie

secure [v3] *protect, make safe* assure, bulwark, cover, defend, ensure, fend, guarantee, guard, insure, safeguard, screen, shield; CONCEPT 96 —Ant. endanger, harm, hurt, injure

security [n1] *safety, protection* aegis, agreement, armament, armor, asylum, bail, bond, care, collateral, compact, contract, covenant, cover, custody, defense, earnest, freedom, guarantee, guard, immunity, insurance, pact, pawn, pledge, precaution, preservation, promise, redemption, refuge, retreat, safeguard, safekeeping, safeness, safety measure, salvation, sanctuary, shelter, shield, surety, surveillance, token, ward, warrant; CONCEPTS 712,729 —Ant. danger, insecurity, peril, trouble

security [n2] *peace of mind* assurance, calm, certainty, confidence, conviction, ease, freedom, positiveness, reliance, soundness, sureness, surety; CONCEPT 410 —Ant. insecurity, uncertainty, worry

sedate [adj] *calm, collected* cold sober*, composed, cool, cool as cucumber*, decorous, deliberate, demure, dignified, dispassionate, earnest, grave, imperturbable, laid-back*, no-nonsense, placid, proper, quiet, seemly, serene, serious, sober, solemn, somber, staid, steady, tranquil, unflappable, unruffled; CONCEPTS 404,542 —Ant. agitated, excitable, excited, lively, upset

sedative [adj] *soothing* allaying, anodyne, calmative, calming, lenitive, relaxing, sleepinducing, soporific, tranquillizing; CONCEPT 537 —Ant. agitating, excitative, upsetting

sedative [n] *soothing agent, medicine* analgesic, anodyne, barbiturate, calmant, calmative, depressant, dope*, downer, drug, hypnotic, knockout pill, medication, narcotic, nerve medicine, opiate, pacifier, pain-killer, pain pill*, quietive, sleeping pill, tranquillizer; CONCEPT 307 —Ant. antidepressant

sedentary [adj] *motionless, lazy* desk, deskbound, idle, inactive, seated, settled, sitting, sluggish, stationary, torpid; CONCEPTS 542, 584 —Ant. activated, active, energetic, mobile, moving

sediment [n] *solid residue from liquid solution* debris, deposit, dregs, dross, gook*, grounds, gunk*, lees, matter, powder, precipitate, precipitation, residuum, settling, silt, slag, solids, trash, waste; CONCEPT 260 —Ant. whole

sedition [n] *rebellion* agitation, defiance, disobedience, dissent, insubordination, insurgence, insurgency, insurrection, mutiny, revolt, revolution, treason, uprising; CONCEPTS 106,300,320,633

seditious [adj] *rebellious* anarchistic, bellicose, defiant, disloyal, disobedient, disorderly, dissident, factious, iconoclastic, insurgent, insurrectionary, mutinous, radical, rebel, resistant, revolutionary, riotous, subversive, treasonable, warring; CONCEPTS *401,529,542*

seduce |v1| *tempt, ensnare* bait, beguile, betray, bribe, coax, deceive, decoy, delude, draw, entice, entrap, hook, induce, inveigle, invite, lead astray*, lead on*, lure, mislead, mousetrap*, persuade, pull, rope in, steer, string along*, sucker*, wheedle; CONCEPT *11* —*Ant.* disenchant, turn off

seduce |v2| *entice sexually* allure, attract, beguile, captivate, charm, come on to*, enamour, entrance, sweep off one's feet*, tempt; CONCEPT *375*

seduction |n| *enticement* allurement, attraction, cajolery, come-on*, inducement, lure, persuasion, tantalizing, temptation; CONCEPTS *7,19, 22,68*

seductive |adj| *alluring, sexy* attracting, attractive, beguiling, bewitching, captivating, charming, come-hither*, desirable, drawing, enchanting, enticing, fascinating, flirtatious, inviting, irresistible, magnetic, provocative, ravishing, siren, specious, tempting; CONCEPTS *372,579* —*Ant.* distasteful, ugly, unpleasing

sedulous |adj| *assiduous* active, busy, determined, diligent, hard-working, industrious, laborious, persevering, plugging, tireless; CONCEPTS *538,542*

see |v1| *perceive with eyes* beam, be apprised of, behold, catch a glimpse of, catch sight of, clock*, contemplate, descry, detect, discern, distinguish, espy, examine, eye, flash, gape, gawk, gaze, get a load of*, glare, glimpse, heed, identify, inspect, lay eyes on*, look, look at, make out, mark, mind, note, notice, observe, pay attention to, peek, peep, peer, peg*, penetrate, pierce, recognize, regard, remark, scan, scope, scrutinize, sight, spot, spy, stare, survey, take notice, view, watch, witness; CONCEPTS *590,626* —*Ant.* be blind

see |v2| *appreciate, comprehend* appraise, ascertain, behold, catch, catch on, conceive, descry, determine, discern, discover, distinguish, envisage, envision, espy, experience, fancy, fathom, feature, feel, find out, follow, get, get the drift*, get the hang of*, grasp, have, hear, imagine, investigate, know, learn, make out, mark, mind, note, notice, observe, perceive, ponder, realize, recognize, remark, study, suffer, sustain, take in, think, tumble, undergo, understand, unearth, view, visualize, weigh; CONCEPTS *15,31,43* —*Ant.* ignore, neglect, overlook

see |v3| *accompany, guide* associate with, attend, bear company, call, come by, come over, conduct, consort with, date, direct, drop by, drop in, encounter, escort, go out with, go with, keep company with, lead, look up, meet, pilot, pop in, receive, route, run into, shepherd, show, speak to, steer, stop by, stop in, take out, usher, visit, walk; CONCEPTS *187,227,384* —*Ant.* turn loose

see |v4| *visualize* anticipate, conceive, divine, envisage, envision, fancy, feature, foresee, foretell, imagine, picture, realize, think, vision; CONCEPT *12*

seed |n1| *beginning, source* berry, bud, cell, conceit, concept, conception, core, corn, ear,

egg, embryo, germ, grain, image, impression, inkling, kernel, notion, nucleus, nut, ovule, ovum, particle, rudiment, semen, spark, sperm, spore, start, suspicion; CONCEPTS *393,428,648* —*Ant.* effect, end, ending, result

seed |n2| *children* brood, descendants, heirs, issue, offspring, posterity, progeniture, progeny, race, scions, spawn, successors; CONCEPT *414* —*Ant.* ancestor, parent

seedy |adj| *run-down, dilapidated* ailing, beat up, bedraggled, crummy*, decaying, decrepit, dingy, dog-eared*, down-at-the-heel*, drooping, droopy, faded, flagging, frowzy, gone to seed*, grubby, in a bad way*, mangy, messy, neglected, old, overgrown, poor, poorly, ragged, ratty, sagging, scruffy, shabby, sickly, sleazy*, slovenly, squalid, tacky, tattered, threadbare, tired, torn, unkempt, untidy, unwell, used up, wilted, wilting, worn; CONCEPTS *485, 570* —*Ant.* luxurious, neat, posh

seek |v1| *look for* be after, beat the bushes*, bird-dog*, bob for, cast about, chase, comb, delve, delve for, dig for, dragnet, explore, fan, ferret out, fish, fish for*, follow, go after, gun for*, hunt, inquire, investigate, leave no stone unturned*, look about, look around, look high and low*, mouse*, nose*, prowl, pursue, quest, ransack, root, run after, scout, scratch, search for, search out, sniff out*, track down; CONCEPT *216* —*Ant.* find

seek |v2| *try, attempt* aim, aspire to, assay, endeavor, essay, have a go at*, offer, pursue, strive, struggle, undertake; CONCEPT *87* —*Ant.* neglect

seek |v3| *ask, inquire* beg, entreat, find out, invite, petition, query, request, solicit; CONCEPT *48* —*Ant.* answer, reply

seem |v| *appear; give the impression* assume, be suggestive of, convey the impression, create the impression, give the feeling of*, give the idea of*, have the appearance of, have the aspects of, have the earmarks of*, have the features of, have the qualities of, hint, imply, insinuate, intimate, look, look as if, look like, look to be, make a show of, pretend, resemble, show, show every sign of, sound, sound like, strike one as being, suggest; CONCEPT *543* —*Ant.* be real

seeming |adj| *apparent* appearing, illusive, illusory, ostensible, outward, professed, quasi-, semblant, specious, surface; CONCEPTS *487,573* —*Ant.* real, true

seemly |adj| *appropriate, suitable* becoming, befitting, comme il faut, compatible, conforming, congenial, congruous, consistent, consonant, correct, decent, decorous, fit, fitting, in good taste, meet, nice, pleasing, proper, suited, timely; CONCEPT *558* —*Ant.* inappropriate, unseemly, unsuitable

seep |v| *leak* bleed, drain, drip, exude, flow, ooze, percolate, permeate, soak, sweat, transude, trickle, weep, well; CONCEPTS *146, 179* —*Ant.* pour

seer |n| *clairvoyant* augur, channeller, crystal ball gazer, diviner, forecaster, fortune-teller, medium, oracle, palm reader, prophet, psychic, soothsayer; CONCEPT *423*

seethe |v| *be very angry* be furious, be incensed, be livid, be mad, be on the warpath*, blow one's stack*, blow up*, boil, breathe fire*, bristle, burn, ferment, flare, flip, foam, foam at mouth*, froth, fume, hit the ceiling*, rage, see red*, simmer, smolder, spark, stew*, storm; CONCEPTS 29,34 —Ant. be happy

segment [n] part of something articulation, bit, compartment, cut, division, member, moiety, parcel, piece, portion, section, sector, slice, subdivision, wedge; CONCEPT 835 —Ant. whole

segregate [v] discriminate and separate choose, close off, cut off, disconnect, dissociate, divide, insulate, island, isolate, quarantine, select, sequester, set apart, sever, single out, split up; CONCEPTS 21,135,645 —Ant. combine, desegregate, gather, join, unite

segregation [n] separation apartheid, discrimination, dissociation, disunion, division, exlusion, isolation, partition, seclusion, splitting up; CONCEPTS 135,195,297,388

seize [v1] grab, take appropriate, catch, catch hold of, clasp, clinch, clinch, clutch, compass, embrace, enclose, enfold, envelope, fasten, grapple, grasp, grip, hang onto, hold fast, lay hands on*, lay hold of*, pinch, pluck, snag, snatch, squeeze, take hold of; CONCEPTS 142,164,190 —Ant. give, let go, offer, release

seize [v2] abduct; take by force ambush, annex, apprehend, appropriate, arrest, arrogate, bag, bust, capture, carry off, catch, claw, clutch, commandeer, confiscate, conquer, exact, force, gain, get, grab, grasp, hijack, hook, impound, incorporate, kidnap, lift, nab, nail*, occupy, overcome, overpower, overrun, overwhelm, pick up, pounce, secure, snag, snare, spirit away*, subdue, take, take by storm*, take captive, take over, take possession of, throttle, trap, usurp, wrench; CONCEPT 90 —Ant. free, liberate, release

seizure [n1] convulsive attack access, breakdown, convulsion, fit, illness, paroxysm, spasm, spell, stroke, throe, turn; CONCEPT 308

seizure [n2] capture, taking abduction, annexation, apprehension, arrest, bust*, collar*, commandeering, confiscation, drop, grab, grabbing, hook*, pinch*, seizing, snatch; CONCEPT 90 —Ant. letting go, liberation, release

seldom [adv] infrequently a few times, every now and then, from time to time, hardly, hardly ever, in a few cases, inhabitually, irregularly, little, not often, not very often, occasionally, on and off, once in a blue moon*, once in a while, rarely, scarcely, scarcely ever, semioccasionally, sometimes, sporadically, uncommonly, unoften, unusually, whimsically; CONCEPT 541 —Ant. frequently, often, usually

select [adj] excellent, elite, preferable best, blue-chip*, boss*, choice, chosen, cool*, cream*, culled, delicate, discriminating, eclectic, elect, elegant, exclusive, exquisite, favored, first-class*, first-rate*, handpicked, limited, number one*, pick, picked, posh, preferred, prime, privileged, rare, recherché, screened, selected, selective, special, superior, top, topnotch, tops*, weeded*, winner, winnowed, world-class*; CONCEPTS 574,653 —Ant. inferior, poor, second-rate

select [v] pick out, prefer from among choices choose, cull, decide, elect, make, make a choice, make a selection, mark, name, opt,

optate, opt for, peg*, pick, pin down, say so*, single out, slot*, sort out, tab*, tag*, take, tap*, winnow; CONCEPT 41 —Ant. refuse, reject

selection [n] preference from among choices alternative, choice, choosing, collection, culling, draft, druthers*, election, excerpt, option, pick, picking; CONCEPT 529 —Ant. refusal, rejection

selective [adj] discriminating careful, choicy, choosy, discerning, discriminatory, eclectic, fussy, judicious, particular, persnickety*, picky, scrupulous, select; CONCEPTS 404,542 —Ant. open, uncaring, undiscriminating, unselective

self-assured [adj] confident assured, believing, bold, brave, cocksure*, cocky, courageous, expectant, expecting, fearless, overconfident, positive, puffed up*, secure, sure, unafraid; CONCEPTS 403,404

self-centered [adj] absorbed with oneself egocentric, egoistic, egomaniacal, egotistic, egotistical, grandstanding, having a swelled head*, independent, inward-looking, know-it-all*, narcissistic, on an ego trip*, self-absorbed, self-indulgent, self-interested, self-involved, selfish, self-seeking, self-serving, self-sufficient, stuck on oneself*, wrapped up with oneself*; CONCEPT 404 —Ant. benevolent, giving, unselfish

self-confident [adj] secure with oneself assured, fearless, hotdog*, hotshot*, know-it-all*, poised, sanguine, self-assured, self-reliant, sure of oneself, undoubtful; CONCEPT 404 —Ant. humble, insecure, meek, unselfconfident, unsure

self-conscious [adj] insecure with oneself affected, anxious, artificial, awkward, bashful, diffident, discomfited, embarrassed, ill-at-ease, mannered, nervous, out of countenance, shamefaced, sheepish, shy, stiff, stilted, uncertain, uncomfortable, uneasy, unsure; CONCEPTS 401,404 —Ant. assured, secure, sure, unselfconscious

self-control [n] willpower over one's actions abstemiousness, aplomb, balance, constraint, dignity, discipline, discretion, poise, repression, reserve, restraint, reticence, self-constraint, self-discipline, self-government, sobriety, stability, stoicism, strength of character; CONCEPT 633 —Ant. agitation, rashness

self-evident/self-explanatory [adj] obvious apparent, axiomatic, clear, comprehensible, incontrovertible, inescapable, manifest, patently true, plain, prima facie, undeniable, understandable, unmistakable, unquestionable, visible; CONCEPTS 529,548 —Ant. obscure, questionable

self-important [adj] conceited arrogant, big-headed*, cocky, egotistical, full of hot air*, immodest, know-it-all, overbearing, pompous, puffed up*, smug, stuck up*, swollen-headed*, vain, vainglorious; CONCEPT 404

selfish [adj] thinking only of oneself egocentric, egoistic, egoistical, egomaniacal, egotistic, egotistical, greedy*, hoggish*, mean, mercenary, miserly, narcissistic, narrow, narrow-minded, out for number one*, parsimonious, prejudiced, self-centered, self-indulgent, self-interested, self-seeking, stingy, ungenerous, wrapped up in oneself*; CONCEPTS 404,542 —Ant. caring, kind, unselfish

se
se

self-reliant [*adj*] *independent* autonomous, on one's own, self-contained, self-governing, self-sufficient, self-supporting, self-sustaining, unaided, unallied; CONCEPT 554

self-respect/self-esteem [*n*] *pride in oneself* amour-propre, conceit, confidence, dignity, egotism, faith in oneself, morale, narcissism, self-assurance, self-content, self-regard, self-satisfaction, vanity, worth; CONCEPTS 411,689 —*Ant.* self-doubt, uncertainty

self-righteous [*adj*] *smug* affected, canting, complacent, egotistical, goody-goody*, holier-than-thou*, hypocritical, noble, pharisaic, pietistic, pious, preachy, sanctimonious, self-satisfied, superior; CONCEPTS 401,542 —*Ant.* caring, humble, thoughtful, understanding

self-satisfaction [*n*] *pride, contentment* complacency, conceit, glow, peace of mind, self-approbation, self-approval, self-pleasure, smugness; CONCEPTS 410,689 —*Ant.* humility, meekness, self-doubt

self-satisfied [*adj*] *proud, content* complacent, conceited, egotistic, flushed, pleased, puffed up*, self-congratulatory, smug, vain; CONCEPTS 404,542 —*Ant.* humble, meek, unsure

self-sufficient [*adj*] *able to take care of oneself* arrogant, closed, competent, conceited, confident, doing one's own thing*, efficient, egotistic, haughty, independent, individual, on one's own, out for number one*, self-confident, self-dependent, self-sufficing, self-supported, self-supporting, self-sustained, self-sustaining, smug, unit; CONCEPTS 334,404 —*Ant.* incapable, needy, unable

sell [*v1*] *exchange an object for money* advertise, auction, bargain, barter, be in business*, boost, clinch the deal, close, close the deal, contract, deal in, dispose, drum, dump, exchange, handle, hawk, hustle, market, merchandise, move, peddle, persuade, pitch, plug, puff*, push, put across, put up for sale, retail, retain, snow, soft sell*, soft soap*, spiel*, stock, sweet talk*, trade, traffic, unload, vend, wholesale; CONCEPT 345 —*Ant.* buy

seller [*n*] *person who gives object in exchange for money* agent, auctioneer, businessperson, dealer, marketer, merchant, peddler, representative, retailer, sales help, salesperson, shopkeeper, storekeeper, trader, tradesperson, vendor; CONCEPTS 347,348 —*Ant.* buyer

sell/sell out [*v2*] *betray* beguile, break faith, bunk, cross, deceive, deliver up, delude, disappoint, double-cross*, fail, four-flush*, give away, give up, mislead, play false, rat on*, sell down the river*, stab in the back*, surrender, take in, violate; CONCEPTS 14,63 —*Ant.* guard, protect

semblance [*n*] *aura, appearance* affinity, air, alikeness, analogy, aspect, bearing, comparison, facade, face, false front*, feel, feeling, figure, form, front, guise, image, likeness, mask, mien, mood, pose, pretense, resemblance, seeming, show, showing, similarity, simile, similitude, simulacrum, veil, veneer; CONCEPTS 673,716

semester [*n*] *term* course, period, quarter, session; CONCEPTS 807,822

seminar [*n*] *conference* convention, discussion, forum, group discussion, meeting, open discussion, palaver, powwow*, rap session, round table, symposium, workshop; CONCEPTS 56, 324,386

semiotics [*n*] *study of signs as elements of communication* langue, parole, pragmatics, semantics, sign systems, symbolism, syntactics; CONCEPT 349

send [*v1*] *transmit, transfer through a system* accelerate, address, advance, assign, broadcast, cast, circulate, commission, commit, communicate, consign, convey, delegate, deliver, detail, direct, dispatch, drop, emit, expedite, express, fire, fling, forward, freight, get under way, give off, grant, hasten, hurl, hurry off, impart, issue, let fly, mail, post, propel, put out, radiate, relay, remit, route, rush off, ship, shoot, televise, troll, wire; CONCEPTS 217,223 —*Ant.* receive

send [*v2*] *please* charm, delight, electrify, enrapture, enthrall, enthuse, excite, intoxicate, move, ravish, stir, thrill, titillate, turn on; CONCEPTS 7,11,22 —*Ant.* displease

senile [*adj*] *failing in physical and mental capabilities due to old age* aged, ancient, anile, decrepit, doddering, doting, enfeebled, feeble, imbecile, infirm, in second childhood*, old, senescent, shattered, sick, weak; CONCEPTS 314,402,403 —*Ant.* alert, well, young

senior [*adj*] *older or of higher rank* chief, elder, higher, leading, major, more advanced, next higher, superior; CONCEPTS 574,578,585,797 —*Ant.* behind, inferior, junior

senior [*n*] *older person* ancient, doyen, doyenne, elder, elderly person, first-born, golden-ager*, grandfather, grandmother, head, matriarch, old folk*, oldster*, old-timer*, patriarch, pensioner, retired person, senior citizen; CONCEPTS 414,424 —*Ant.* inferior, junior, younger

seniority [*n*] *rank in organization due to length of service* advantage, antiquity, eldership, precedence, preference, priority, rank, ranking, standing, station, superiority; CONCEPTS 671,727

sensation [*n1*] *feeling, perception* awareness, consciousness, emotion, gut reaction*, impression, passion, response, sense, sensibility, sensitiveness, sensitivity, sentiment, susceptibility, thought, tingle, vibes*; CONCEPTS 34,410,529

sensation [*n2*] *something wonderful or awe-inspiring* agitation, bomb*, bombshell*, commotion, excitement, flash, furor, hit, marvel, miracle, phenomenon, portent, prodigy, scandal, stir, stunner, surprise, thrill, wonder, wow*; CONCEPTS 293,529

sensational [*adj1*] *startling, exaggerated* amazing, arresting, astounding, breathtaking, coarse, colored, conspicuous, dramatic, electrifying, emotional, excessive, exciting, extravagant, hair-raising, horrifying, juicy*, livid, lurid, marked, melodramatic, noticeable, outstanding, piquant, pointed, prominent, pungent, remarkable, revealing, rough, salient, scandalous, sensationalistic, shocking, signal, spectacular, staggering, stimulating, sultry, tabloid*, thrilling, vulgar, X-rated*; CONCEPTS 267,537,545 —*Ant.* ordinary, run-of-the-mill, unexceptional, usual

sensational [*adj2*] *excellent, superb* agitating, astonishing, breathtaking, cool*, dandy*, divine, dramatic, eloquent, exceptional, exciting,

fabulous, first-class*, glorious, impressive,
incredible, keen, marvelous, mind-blowing,
most*, moving, out of this world*, smashing,
spectacular, stirring, surprising, thrilling, zero
cool*; CONCEPT 574 —*Ant.* bad, inferior, poor

sensationalism [n] *exaggeration* aggrandizement, boasting, excess, fabrication, fish story*,
hype, hyperbole, overemphasis, puffery, tabloid
journalism, tall story*, whopper*, yellow
journalism*; CONCEPTS 63,278,663

sense [n1] *feeling of animate being* faculty,
feel, function, hearing, impression, kinesthesia,
sensation, sensibility, sensitivity, sight, smell,
taste, touch; CONCEPT 405

sense [n2] *awareness, perception* ability,
appreciation, atmosphere, aura, brains, capacity, clear-headedness, cleverness, cognizance,
common sense, consciousness, discernment,
discrimination, feel, feeling, gumption*,
imagination, impression, insight, intellect,
intelligence, intuition, judgment, knowledge,
mentality, mind, premonition, presentiment,
prudence, quickness, reason, reasoning, recognition, sagacity, sanity, sentiment, sharpness,
smarts*, soul, spirit, tact, thought, understanding, wisdom, wit; CONCEPTS 33,409

sense [n3] *point, meaning* acceptation, advantage, bottom line*, burden, core, definition,
denotatiton, drift, gist, good, heart, implication,
import, intendment, interpretation, logic, matter, meat*, meat and potatoes*, message, name
of the game*, nature of the beast*, nitty-gritty*,
nuance, nub, nuts and bolts*, punch line*,
purport, purpose, reason, short, significance,
significancy, signification, stuff, substance,
thrust, understanding, upshot, use, value, worth;
CONCEPTS 668,682

sense [v] *become aware of* anticipate, apperceive, appreciate, apprehend, believe, be with
it, catch, catch on, catch the drift*, consider,
credit, deem, dig*, discern, divine, feel, feel
in bones*, feel in gut*, get the drift*, get the
idea*, get the impression*, get the picture*, get
vibes*, grasp, have a feeling*, have a hunch*,
hold, know, notice, observe, perceive, pick up,
read, realize, savvy*, suspect, take in, think,
understand; CONCEPT 34 —*Ant.* be numb, be
unaware, overlook

senseless [adj] *silly, meaningless* absurd, asinine, batty, crazy, daft, doublespeak*, double
talk*, fatuous, flaky, foolish, idiotic, illogical,
imbecilic, inane, incongruous, inconsistent, insignificant, irrational, ludicrous, mad, mindless,
moronic, nonsensical, nutty, pointless, purportless, purposeless, ridiculous, simple, stupid,
trivial, unimportant, unintelligent, unmeaning,
unreasonable, unsound, unwise, wacky*, without rhyme or reason*; CONCEPTS 548,558
—*Ant.* feeling, intelligent, rational, reasonable,
sensible, wise

sensibility [n] *responsiveness; ability to feel*
affection, appreciation, awareness, discernment,
emotion, feeling, gut reaction*, heart*, insight,
intuition, judgment, keenness, perceptiveness,
rationale, sensation, sense, sensitiveness, sensitivity, sentiment, susceptibility, taste, vibes*;
CONCEPTS 409,410 —*Ant.* apathy, indifference,
insensibility, lethargy

sensible [adj] *realistic, reasonable* all there*,

astute, attentive, au courant, aware, canny,
cognizant, commonsensical, conscious, consequent, conversant, cool*, discerning, discreet,
discriminating, down-to-earth, far-sighted, having all one's marbles*, informed, in right mind,
intelligent, judicious, knowing, logical, matter-
of-fact, practical, prudent, rational, sagacious,
sage, sane, sentient, shrewd, sober, sound,
together, well-reasoned, well-thought-out, wise,
witting; CONCEPTS 402,542 —*Ant.* indiscreet,
senseless, unrealistic, unreasonable, unwise

sensitive [adj1] *impressionable* acute, cognizant, conscious, delicate, easily affected,
emotionable, emotional, feeling, fine, high-
strung, hung up*, hypersensitive, impressible,
irritable, keen, knowing, nervous, oversensitive,
perceiving, perceptive, precarious, precise,
psychic, reactive, receptive, responsive, seeing,
sensatory, sensile, sensorial, sensory, sentient,
supersensitive, susceptible, tense, ticklish,
touchy, touchy feely*, tricky, tuned in*, turned
on to*, umbrageous, understanding, unstable,
wired*; CONCEPT 403 —*Ant.* impassive,
insensitive, thick-skinned, unsusceptible

sensitive [adj2] *easily hurt* delicate, easily
harmed, painful, sore, tender; CONCEPT 406
—*Ant.* heartless, indifferent, insensitive, numb,
unfeeling

sensitivity [n] *responsiveness to stimuli* acuteness, affectibility, awareness, consciousness,
delicacy, feeling, impressionability, nervousness, reactiveness, reactivity, receptiveness,
sensation, sense, sensitiveness, subtlety, susceptibility, sympathy; CONCEPTS 405,410 —*Ant.*
apathy, impassivity, insensitivity, numbness

sensory [adj] *affecting animate nerve organs*
acoustic, afferent, audible, audiovisual, auditory, aural, auricular, clear, discernible, distinct,
gustative, gustatory, hearable, lingual, neural,
neurological, ocular, olfactive, olfactory,
ophthalmic, optic, perceptible, phonic, plain,
receptive, sensational, sensatory, sensible,
sensual, sonic, tactile, visual; CONCEPT 406

sensual [adj] *physical, erotic* animal, animalistic, arousing, bodily, carnal, debauched, delightful, epicurean, exciting, fleshly, heavy*,
hedonic, hot*, lascivious, lecherous, lewd,
libidinous, licentious, lustful, moving, pleasing,
rough, sensuous, sexual, sexy, sharpened,
steamy, stimulating, stirring, tactile, unchaste,
unspiritual, voluptuous, X-rated*; CONCEPTS
372,401 —*Ant.* abstemious, chaste, mental

sensuous [adj] *gratifying to senses* carnal,
epicurean, exciting, fleshly, fleshy, hedonistic,
luscious, lush, luxurious, passionate, physical,
pleasurable, pleasure-loving, pleasure-seeking,
primrose, rich, self-indulgent, sensory, sensual,
sensualistic, sumptuous, sybaritic, voluptuous;
CONCEPTS 372,537 —*Ant.* despicable, distasteful

sentence [n] *punishing decree* book, censure,
clock, condemnation, considered opinion,
decision, determination, dictum, doom, edict,
fall, getup*, hitch, jolt, judgment, knock, order,
penalty, pronouncement, punishment, rap*,
ruling, sending up the river*, sleep, stretch,
term, time, trick, vacation, verdict; CONCEPT
318 —*Ant.* accusation, charge

sentence [v] *decide punishment* adjudge,
adjudicate, blame, condemn, confine, convict,

se
se

damn, denounce, devote, doom, impound, imprison, incarcerate, jail, judge, mete out, ordain, pass judgment, penalize, proscribe, punish, put away*, put on ice*, railroad*, rule, send to prison, send up the river*, settle, take the fall*, throw the book at*; CONCEPTS *122,317* —*Ant.* accuse, blame, charge

sentient [*adj*] *conscious* able to recognize, alert, apperceptive, attentive, awake, aware, cognizant, feeling, informed, in on*, in the right mind, knowing, noticing, observing, perceiving, receptive, recognizing, responsive, seeing, sensitive to, understanding, watchful; CONCEPTS *402,539*

sentiment [*n*] *emotion, belief* affect, affectivity, attitude, bias, conception, conviction, disposition, emotionalism, eye, feeling, hearts and flowers*, idea, inclination, inclining, judgment, leaning, mind, opinion, overemotionalism, partiality, passion, penchant, persuasion, position, posture, predilection, propensity, romanticism, sensibility, sentimentality, slant, softheartedness, tendency, tender feeling, tenderness, thought, view, way of thinking; CONCEPTS *32, 410,689*

sentimental [*adj*] *emotional, romantic* affected, affectionate, corny*, demonstrative, dewy-eyed, dreamy, effusive, gushing, gushy, idealistic, impressionable, inane, insipid, jejune, languishing, lovey-dovey*, loving, maudlin, moonstruck*, mushy*, nostalgic, overacted, overemotional, passionate, pathetic, rosewater*, saccharine*, sappy*, schmaltzy*, silly, simpering, sloppy*, slushy*, soapy*, soft, softhearted*, sugary*, sweet, syrupy*, tearful, tear-jerking*, tender, touching, vapid, visionary, weepy; CONCEPTS *267,401,542* —*Ant.* hard-hearted, indifferent, pragmatic, unemotional, unromantic, unsentimental

sentinel [*n*] *sentry* guard, keeper, lookout, picket, protector, watchman/woman, watchperson; CONCEPT *348*

separate [*adj1*] *disconnected* abstracted, apart, apportioned, asunder, cut apart, cut in two, detached, disassociated, discrete, disembodied, disjointed, distant, distributed, disunited, divergent, divided, divorced, far between, free, independent, in halves, isolated, loose, marked, parted, partitioned, put asunder, removed, scattered, set apart, set asunder, severed, sovereign, sundered, unattached, unconnected; CONCEPT *577* —*Ant.* combined, connected, joined, mixed, together, united

separate [*adj2*] *alone, individual* apart, autonomous, detached, different, discrete, distinct, distinctive, diverse, free, independent, lone, one, only, particular, peculiar, several, single, sole, solitary, unique, various; CONCEPTS *557,564* —*Ant.* associated, together, united

separate [*v1*] *remove something from group; keep or set apart* break, break off, cleave, come apart, come away, come between, detach, dichotomize, disconnect, disentangle, disjoin, disjoint, dissect, dissever, distribute, divide, divorce, intersect, part, rupture, sever, split, split up, sunder, uncombine, uncouple, undo; CONCEPT *135* —*Ant.* combine, join, mix, unite

separate [*v2*] *isolate, segregate* assign, break up, classify, close off, comb, compartment, compartmentalize, cut off, discriminate, distribute, draw apart, group, insulate, interval, intervene, island, order, put on one side, rope off, seclude, sequester, sift, single out, sort, space, split up, stand between, winnow; CONCEPTS *158,201* —*Ant.* desegregate, join, unite

separate [*v3*] *part company in a romantic relationship or marriage* alienate, bifurcate, break it off*, break off, break up, dedomicile, depart, discontinue, disunify, disunite, diverge, divorce, drop, estrange, go away, go different ways*, go separate ways*, leave, part, pull out, split up, take leave, uncouple, unlink, untie the knot*; CONCEPTS *297,384* —*Ant.* marry

separately [*adv*] *alone, individually* apart, clearly, definitely, disjointly, distinctly, independently, one at a time, one by one, personally, severally, singly, solely; CONCEPTS *544,577* —*Ant.* together

separation [*n*] *being apart; break-up* break, dedomiciling, departure, detachment, disconnection, disengagement, disjunction, disrelation, dissociation, dissolution, disunion, division, divorce, divorcement, embarkation, estrangement, farewell, gap, leave-taking*, parting, parting of the ways*, partition, pffft*, rift, rupture, segregation, severance, split, split-up*; CONCEPTS *135,195,297,388* —*Ant.* togetherness

sepulchral [*adj*] *gloomy* black, bleak, cheerless, dark, deathly, dismal, dreary, forlorn, funereal, grave, hollow, morbid, mournful, obscure, somber; CONCEPTS *525,617,618*

sequel [*n*] *follow-up* aftereffect, aftermath, alternation, causatum, chain, close, closing, conclusion, consecution, consequence, continuation, development, effect, end, ending, epilogue, eventuality, finish, finishing, issue, order, outcome, part two*, payoff, progression, result, row, sequence, sequent, series, spin-off*, termination, train, upshot; CONCEPTS *271,293, 824,832* —*Ant.* original

sequence [*n*] *series, order* arrangement, array, catenation, chain, classification, concatenation, consecution, consecutiveness, continuance, continuity, continuousness, course, cycle, disposition, distribution, flow, graduation, grouping, ordering, pecking order*, perpetuity, placement, procession, progression, row, run, sequel, skein, streak, string, subsequence, succession, successiveness, track, train; CONCEPTS *721,727*

sequential [*adj*] *occurring in an order* consecutive, constant, continuous, following, incessant, later, next, persistent, regular, sequent, serial, steady, subsequent, subsequential, succedent, succeeding, successive; CONCEPTS *482,548,585* —*Ant.* nonsequential

sequester [*v*] *isolate, seclude* cloister, close off, cut off, draw back, enisle, hide, insulate, island, secrete, segregate, separate, set apart, set off, withdraw; CONCEPTS *90,188* —*Ant.* bring out, make public, reveal, uncover

serendipity [*n*] *accidental discovery* blessing, break*, dumb luck*, fluke*, good luck, happenstance, happy chance, luck, lucky break*, stumbling upon, tripping over; CONCEPT *693*

serene [*adj*] *calm, undisturbed* at peace, clear, collected, comfortable, composed, content, cool*, cool as a cucumber*, dispassionate, easy, easygoing, fair, halcyon, imperturbable, laid-back*, limpid, patient, peaceful, pellucid, phlegmatic, placid, poised, quiescent, quiet, reconciled, resting, satisfied, sedate, self-possessed, smooth, still, stoical, tranquil, unflappable, unruffled, untroubled; CONCEPTS 401,485 —*Ant.* agitated, disturbed, excited, troubled

serenity [n] *calm, peacefulness* calmness, composure, cool, patience, peace, peace of mind, placidity, quietness, quietude, stillness, tranquility; CONCEPTS 633,673 —*Ant.* agitation, disruption, disturbance, excitement, trouble

serf [n] *slave* bondservant, bondsman/woman, chattel, laborer, peon, servant, vassal, villain, villein; CONCEPT 348

serial [adj] *in continuing order* consecutive, continual, continued, continuing, ensuing, following, going on, sequent, sequential, succedent, succeeding, successional, successive; CONCEPTS 482,585 —*Ant.* disordered

series [n] *order, succession* alternation, arrangement, array, category, chain, classification, column, consecution, continuity, course, file, gradation, group, line, list, procession, progression, range, row, run, scale, sequel, sequence, set, skein, streak, string, suit, suite, tier, train; CONCEPTS 721,727,769 —*Ant.* disorder, disorganization

serious [adj1] *somber, humorless* austere, bound, bound and determined*, businesslike, cold sober*, contemplative, deadpan*, deliberate, determined, downbeat*, earnest, funereal, genuine, go for broke*, grave, grim, honest, intent, long-faced*, meditative, no-nonsense*, pensive, pokerfaced*, reflective, resolute, resolved, sedate, set, severe, sincere, sober, solemn, staid, steady, stern, thoughtful, unhumorous, unsmiling, weighty; CONCEPTS 403, 542 —*Ant.* flippant, funny, happy, light

serious [adj2] *crucial, weighty* arduous, dangerous, deep, difficult, far-reaching, fateful, fell, formidable, grave, grievous, grim, hard, heavy, important, laborious, major, meaning business*, meaningful, menacing, momentous, no joke*, no laughing matter*, of consequence, operose, out for blood*, playing hard ball*, pressing, severe, significant, smoking*, sobering, strenuous, strictly business*, threatening, tough, ugly, unamusing, unhumorous, urgent, worrying; CONCEPTS 538,565,568 —*Ant.* light, minor, trivial, unimportant, unserious

seriously [adv1] *not humorously* actively, all joking aside*, cool it*, cut the comedy*, determinedly, down, earnestly, fervently, for real*, gravely, in all conscience, in all seriousness, in earnest, intently, passionately, purposefully, resolutely, sedately, simmer down*, sincerely, soberly, solemnly, sternly, straighten out, thoughtfully, vigorously, with a straight face*, with forethought, with sobriety, zealously; CONCEPTS 535,542,544 —*Ant.* funnily, lightly

seriously [adv2] *dangerously, critically* acutely, badly, decidedly, deplorably, distressingly, gravely, grievously, harmfully, intensely, menacingly, perilously, precariously, quite, regrettably, severely, sorely, threateningly, very; CONCEPT 544 —*Ant.* casually, minor, trivially

seriousness [n1] *humorlessness* calmness, coolness, earnest, earnestness, gravity, intentness, sedateness, serious-mindedness, sincerity, sober-mindedness, sobriety, solemnity, staidness, sternness, thoughtfulness; CONCEPTS 410,657 —*Ant.* funniness, humor, lightness

seriousness [n2] *danger; criticalness* enormity, gravity, importance, moment, significance, urgency, weight; CONCEPTS 668,675 —*Ant.* triviality, unimportance

sermon [n] *instructive speech with a moral* address, advice, discourse, doctrine, exhortation, harangue, homily, lecture, lesson, moralism, pastoral, preach, preaching, preachment, tirade; CONCEPTS 278,368

serpentine [adj] *winding; sly* anfractuous, artful, cagey, circuitous, clever, coiling, convoluted, crafty, cunning, curved, curvy, foxy, indirect, mazy, meandering, meandrous, shrewd, sinuous, slick, slinky, snakelike, snaky*, subtle, supple, twisting, twisting and turning*, wily; CONCEPTS 401,542,581

serrated [adj] *jagged* denticulate, indented, notched, ragged, sawlike, sawtooth, saw-toothed, scored, serrate, serried, serriform, serrulate, toothed; CONCEPT 486 —*Ant.* smooth

servant [n] *person who waits on another* assistant, attendant, cleaning person, dependent, domestic, drudge, help, helper, hireling, live-in, menial, minion, retainer, serf, server, slave; CONCEPT 348 —*Ant.* master

serve [v1] *aid, help; supply* arrange, assist, attend to, be of assistance, be of use, care for, deal, deliver, dish up*, distribute, do for, give, handle, hit, minister to, nurse, oblige, play, present, provide, provision, set out, succor, wait on, work for; CONCEPTS 110,136,140 —*Ant.* receive, take

serve [v2] *act, do* accept, agree, attend, be employed by, carry on, complete, discharge, follow, fulfill, function, go through, hearken, labor, obey, observe, officiate, pass, perform, subserve, toil, work; CONCEPT 91 —*Ant.* refrain, refuse

serve [v3] *suffice; do the work of* advantage, answer, answer the purpose, apply, avail, be acceptable, be adequate, be good enough, benefit, be of use, be useful, content, do, do duty as, fill the bill*, fit, function, make, profit, satisfy, service, suit, work, work for; CONCEPTS 656,658

service [n1] *aid, help* account, advantage, applicability, appropriateness, assistance, avail, benefit, business, check, courtesy, dispensation, duty, employ, employment, favor, fitness, indulgence, kindness, labor, maintenance, ministration, office, overhaul, relevance, serviceability, servicing, supply, use, usefulness, utility, value, work; CONCEPTS 110,324,658 —*Ant.* damage, disservice, hurt, injury

service [n2] *rite of a church* ceremonial, ceremony, formality, function, liturgy, observance, ritual, sermon, worship; CONCEPT 368

service [n3] *time in military operation* action, active duty, combat, duty, fighting, sting; CONCEPTS 320,321

serviceable [adj] *useful, functional* advantageous, aiding, assistive, beneficial, convenient, dependable, durable, efficient, handy, hard-wearing, helpful, invaluable, operative, practical, profitable, usable, utile, utilitarian, valuable;

CONCEPT 560 —Ant. unhelpful, unprofitable, unserviceable, useless, weak, worthless

servile [adj] grovelling, subservient abject, base, beggarly, bootlicking, craven, cringing, despicable, eating humble pie*, eating crow*, fawning, humble, ignoble, low, mean, obedient, obeisant, obsequious, passive, slavish, submissive, sycophantic, toadying, unctuous, unresisting; CONCEPTS 401,404 —Ant. aggressive, dominant

servitude [n] slavery bondage, bonds, chains, confinement, enslavement, obedience, peonage, serfdom, serfhood, subjection, subjugation, thrall, thralldom, vassalage, yoke; CONCEPTS 388,410 —Ant. mastery

session [n] meeting, gathering affair, assembly, concourse, conference, discussion, get-together, hearing, huddle, jam session*, meet, period, showdown, sitting, term; CONCEPTS 114,324

set [adj1] decided agreed, appointed, arranged, bent, certain, concluded, confirmed, customary, dead set on*, decisive, definite, determined, entrenched, established, firm, fixed, hanging tough*, immovable, intent, inveterate, ironclad, locked in*, obstinate, pat, pigheaded*, prearranged, predetermined, prescribed, regular, resolute, resolved, rigid, rooted, scheduled, set in stone*, settled, solid as a rock*, specified, stated, steadfast, stiff-necked, stipulated, stubborn, unflappable, usual, well-set; CONCEPTS 535,542 —Ant. indefinite, undecided, unfixed

set [adj2] firm, hardened; inflexible entrenched, fixed, hard and fast, hidebound, immovable, jelled, located, placed, positioned, rigid, settled, sited, situate, situated, solid, stable, stiff, strict, stubborn, unyielding; CONCEPT 488 —Ant. flexible, movable, soft, unfixed

set [n1] physical bearing address, air, attitude, carriage, comportment, demeanor, deportment, fit, hang, inclination, mien, port, position, posture, presence, turn; CONCEPT 757

set [n2] stage setting flats, mise en scène, scene, scenery, setting, stage set; CONCEPT 263

set [n3] group, assortment array, assemblage, band, batch, body, bunch, bundle, camp, circle, clan, class, clique, clump, cluster, clutch, collection, company, compendium, coterie, crew, crowd, faction, gaggle, gang, kit, lot, mob, organization, outfit, pack, push, rat pack*, sect, series; CONCEPTS 417,432,769 —Ant. individual, single

set [v1] position, place affix, aim, anchor, apply, arrange, bestow, cast, deposit, direct, embed, ensconce, establish, fasten, fix, head, insert, install, introduce, lay, level, locate, lock, lodge, make fast, make ready, mount, park, plank, plant, plop, plunk, point, post, prepare, put, rest, seat, settle, situate, spread, station, stick, train, turn, wedge, zero in*; CONCEPTS 201,202 —Ant. displace, remove

set [v2] decide upon agree upon, allocate, allot, appoint, arrange, assign, conclude, decree, designate, determine, dictate, direct, establish, estimate, fix, fix price, impose, instruct, lay down, make, name, ordain, prescribe, price, rate, regulate, resolve, schedule, settle, specify, stipulate, value; CONCEPT 18

set [v3] harden become firm, cake, clot, coagulate, condense, congeal, crystallize, fix, gel, gelate, gelatinize, jell, jellify, jelly,

solidify, stiffen, thicken; CONCEPT 250 —Ant. liquefy, soften

set [v4] decline descend, dip, disappear, drop, go down, sink, subside, vanish; CONCEPT 181 —Ant. ascend, go up, rise

set [v5] start, incite abet, begin, commence, foment, initiate, instigate, provoke, put in motion, raise, set on*, stir up*, whip up*; CONCEPT 221 —Ant. discourage, dissuade, end, finish, halt, hinder

setback [n] disappointment about-face*, backset, bath*, blow, bottom, check, comedown, defeat, delay, difficulty, drawing board*, flip-flop*, hindrance, hitch*, hold-up, impediment, misfortune, obstacle, rebuff, regress, regression, reversal, reversal of fortune, reverse, slow-down, stumbling block*, trouble, upset, whole new ballgame*; CONCEPTS 388,674,679 —Ant. achievement, advance, blessing, boon, boost, success

set back [v] delay, hinder bog down*, decelerate, defeat, detain, embog, hang up*, hold up, impede, mire, retard, reverse, slow, slow down, slow up; CONCEPT 130 —Ant. advance, forward

setting [n] scene, background ambience, backdrop, context, distance, environment, frame, framework, horizon, jungle, locale, location, mise en scène, mounting, perspective, set, shade, shadow, site, stage set, stage setting, surroundings; CONCEPTS 198,263

settle [v1] straighten out, resolve achieve, adjudicate, adjust, appoint, arrange, call the shots*, choose, cinch, clean up, clear, clear up, clinch, come to a conclusion, come to a decision, come to an agreement, complete, concert, conclude, confirm, decide, determine, discharge, dispose, end, establish, figure, fix, form judgment, judge, make a decision, make certain, mediate, nail down*, negotiate, order, pay, put an end to, put into order, reconcile, regulate, rule, satisfy, seal, set to rights, square, verify, work out; CONCEPTS 18,126,341 —Ant. confuse, mix up, unsettle

settle [v2] calm, relieve allay, assure, becalm, compose, lull, pacify, quell, quiet, quieten, reassure, relax, sedate, soothe, still, tranquilize; CONCEPTS 7,22,469 —Ant. confuse, trouble, upset, worry

settle [v3] come to rest; fall alight, bed down, decline, descend, flop, immerse, land, lay, light, lodge, perch, place, plop, plunge, put, repose, roost, seat, set down, settle down, sink, sit, submerge, submerse, subside, touch down; CONCEPT 181 —Ant. move

settle [v4] make one's home abide, colonize, dwell, establish, hang up one's hat*, inhabit, keep house, live, locate, lodge, move to, park, put down roots*, reside, set up home, squat, take root*, take up residence; CONCEPT 226 —Ant. depart, leave, move

settlement [n1] decision, conclusion adjustment, agreement, arrangement, clearance, compact, compensation, completion, conclusion, confirmation, contract, covenant, deal, defrayal, determination, discharge, disposition, establishment, happy medium*, liquidation, pay, payment, payoff, quietus, reimbursement, remuneration, resolution, satisfaction, showdown, termination, trade-off, working out; CONCEPTS 230,684 —Ant. confusion, indecision

settlement [n2] *community* colonization, colony, encampment, establishment, foundation, habitation, hamlet, inhabitancy, occupancy, occupation, outpost, plantation, principality, residence; CONCEPTS 512,515

set up [v] *start* arrange, assemble, back, begin, build, build up, compose, constitute, construct, create, elevate, erect, establish, excite, exhilarate, found, inaugurate, initiate, inspire, install, institute, introduce, launch, make provision for, open, organize, originate, prearrange, prepare, put together, put up, raise, rear, stimulate, strengthen, subsidize, usher in; CONCEPT 221 —*Ant.* conclude, end, finish

sever [v1] *cut apart* bisect, carve, cleave, cut, cut in two, detach, disconnect, disjoin, dissect, dissever, dissociate, disunite, divide, part, rend, rive, separate, slice, split, sunder; CONCEPTS 98,176 —*Ant.* combine, join, unite

sever [v2] *dissociate* abandon, break off, disjoint, dissolve, divide, divorce, put an end to, separate, terminate; CONCEPTS 297,384 —*Ant.* associate, unite

several [adj] *assorted, various* a few, a lot, any, certain, considerable, definite, different, disparate, distinct, divers, diverse, handful, hardly any, indefinite, individual, infrequent, manifold, many, not many, numerous, only a few, particular, personal, plural, proportionate, quite a few, rare, respective, scant, scanty, scarce, scarcely any, separate, single, small number, some, sparse, special, specific, sundry; CONCEPTS 564,762 —*Ant.* individual, none, one, single

severe [adj1] *uncompromising, stern* astringent, austere, biting, caustic, close, cold, cruel, cutting, disapproving, dour, earnest, firm, flinty, forbidding, grave, grim, hard, hard-nosed*, harsh, inconsiderate, inexorable, inflexible, iron-handed, obdurate, oppressive, peremptory, pitiless, relentless, resolute, resolved, rigid, satirical, scathing, serious, sober, stern, stiff*, strait-laced*, strict, tight-lipped*, unalterable, unbending, unchanging, unfeeling, unrelenting, unsmiling, unsparing; CONCEPTS 401,534,542 —*Ant.* amenable, compromising, easy-going, friendly, willing

severe [adj2] *difficult, harsh* acute, arduous, ascetic, austere, bitter, bleak, consequential, critical, dangerous, dear, demanding, despotic, distressing, domineering, drastic, effortful, exacting, extreme, fierce, forbidding, grave, grim, grinding, hard, heavy, hefty, implacable, inclement, intemperate, intense, mordant, oppressive, overbearing, pitiless, punishing, rigorous, rugged, serious, sharp, sore, strenuous, stringent, taxing, toilsome, tough, tyrannical, unpleasant, unrelenting, violent, weighty, wicked; CONCEPTS 565,569 —*Ant.* calm, easy, facile, mild, temperate

severely [adv] *harshly* acutely, badly, critically, dangerously, extremely, firmly, gravely, hard, hardly, intensely, markedly, painfully, rigorously, roughly, seriously, sharply, sorely, sternly, strictly, with an iron hand; CONCEPT 569 —*Ant.* compassionately, lightly

sew [v] *prepare fabric for clothing, covering* baste, bind, embroider, fasten, piece, seam, stitch, tack, tailor, work; CONCEPT 218 —*Ant.* rip, tear

sewage [n] *waste* discharge, excess, excrement, garbage, junk, leavings, rubbish, runoff, slop, trash; CONCEPT 260

sex [n1] *male or female gender* femininity, manhood, manliness, masculinity, sexuality, womanhood, womanliness; CONCEPT 648

sex [n2] *intercourse between animate beings* birds and the bees*, coition, coitus, copulation, facts of life*, fornication, generation, intimacy, lovemaking, magnetism, procreation, relations, reproduction, sensuality, sexuality; CONCEPT 375 —*Ant.* abstention, chastity

sex appeal [n] *magnetism* allure, appeal, attraction, attractiveness, charisma, charm, drawing power, enchantment, glamour, it*, lure, pull, seductiveness; CONCEPTS 411,676

sexism [n] *sex discrimination* bias, bigotry, chauvinism, inequality, inequity, partiality, prejudice; CONCEPTS 29,689

sexual [adj] *concerning reproduction, intercourse* animal, animalistic, bestial, carnal, erotic, fleshly, generative, genital, genitive, intimate, loving, passionate, procreative, reproductive, sensual, sharing, venereal, voluptuous, wanton; CONCEPT 372 —*Ant.* asexual, nonsexual

sexual assault [n] *violation* date rape, grope, molestation, rape, ravishment, sex crime, sexual abuse; CONCEPTS 192,375

sexual harassment [n] *unwanted sexual advances* inappropriate behavior, sexual abuse, sexual pressure, suggestive comments, unprofessional behavior, victimization; CONCEPT 246

sexually transmitted disease [n] *STD* acquired immune deficiency syndrome, AIDS, chancroid, chlamydia, crab louse, crabs, genital herpes, genital warts, gonorrhea, herpes, herpes simplex, HIV, scabies, SIDA, social disease, syphilis, tabes dorsalis, VD, venereal disease; CONCEPT 306

sexy [adj] *being erotically attractive to another* arousing, come-hither*, cuddly, flirtatious, hot*, inviting, kissable, libidinous, mature, provocative, provoking, racy, risqué, seductive, sensual, sensuous, slinky*, spicy*, steamy*, suggestive, titillating, voluptuous; CONCEPT 372 —*Ant.* disgusting, unattractive, unsexy

shabby [adj1] *broken-down; in poor shape* bare, bedraggled, crummy, decayed, decaying, decrepit, degenerated, desolate, deteriorated, deteriorating, dilapidated, dingy, disfigured, disreputable, dog-eared*, faded, frayed, gone to seed*, mangy, meager, mean, miserable, moth-eaten, neglected, pitiful, poor, poverty-stricken, ragged, ramshackle, ratty, rickety, ruined, ruinous, run-down, scrubby, scruffy, seedy, shoddy, sleazy, slipshod, squalid, tacky, tattered, threadbare, tired, worn, worn-out, worse for wear*, wretched; CONCEPT 485 —*Ant.* good, nice

shabby [adj2] *despicable* beggarly, cheap, contemptible, despisable, dirty, disgraceful, dishonorable, disreputable, ignoble, ignominious, inconsiderate, inglorious, low, low-down, mean, mercenary, miserly, rotten, scummy, selfish, shady, shameful, shoddy, sordid, sorry, stingy, thoughtless, unkind, unworthy; CONCEPTS 401,404 —*Ant.* honorable, respectable

shack [n] *shanty* cabin, camp, cottage, hut,

lean-to, shed, shelter, small house, tiny house; CONCEPT 516

shackle [n] *restraint* bracelet, chain, cuff, electronic ankle bracelet, fetter, handcuff, irons, leg-iron, manacle, rope, trammel; CONCEPTS 130,191,500

shackle [v] *restrain* bind, chain, confine, cuff, fetter, handcuff, hog-tie*, hold, hold captive, manacle, put a straitjacket on*, secure, tie up, trammel; CONCEPTS 130,191

shade [n1] *dimness* adumbration, blackness, coolness, cover, darkness, dusk, gloominess, obscuration, obscurity, penumbra, screen, semi-darkness, shadiness, shadow, shadows, umbra, umbrage; CONCEPT 620 —*Ant.* brightness, light

shade [n2] *blind, shield* awning, canopy, cover, covering, curtain, screen, veil; CONCEPT 445

shade [n3] *color, hue* brilliance, cast, saturation, stain, tinge, tint, tone; CONCEPTS 620,622

shade [n4] *slight difference* amount, cast, dash, degree, distinction, gradation, hint, nuance, proposal, semblance, soupçon, spice, streak, suggestion, suspicion, tincture, tinge, trace, variation, variety; CONCEPT 665 —*Ant.* gap

shade [n5] *ghost* apparition, bogey, haunt, manes, phantasm, phantom, revenant, shadow, specter, spirit, umbra, wraith; CONCEPT 370

shade [v] *shut out the light* adumbrate, be overcast, blacken, cast a shadow, cloud, cloud over, cloud up, conceal, cover, darken, deepen, dim, eclipse, gray, hide, inumbrate, mute, obscure, overshadow, protect, screen, shadow, shelter, shield, shutter, tone down, umbrage, veil; CONCEPTS 250,526 —*Ant.* open

shadow [n1] *darkness* adumbration, cover, dark, dimness, dusk, gloom, obscuration, obscurity, penumbra, protection, shade, shelter, umbra, umbrage; CONCEPTS 620,622 —*Ant.* brightness, light

shadow [n2] *hint, suggestion* breath, intimation, memento, relic, smack, suspicion, tincture, tinge, touch, trace, vestige; CONCEPT 278 —*Ant.* information

shadow [v1] *make dark* adumbrate, becloud, bedim, cast a shadow, cloud, darken, dim, gray, haze, inumbrate, obscure, overcast, overcloud, overhang, overshadow, screen, shade, shelter, shield, umbrage, veil; CONCEPT 250 —*Ant.* brighten, lighten

shadow [v2] *follow secretly* dog, keep in sight, pursue, spy on, stalk, tag, tail, trail, watch; CONCEPT 207

shady [adj1] *dark, covered* adumbral, bosky, cloudy, cool, dim, dusky, indistinct, leafy, out of the sun*, screened, shaded, shadowed, shadowy, sheltered, umbrageous, umbrous, under a cloud, vague; CONCEPTS 485,617 —*Ant.* bright, light, open

shady [adj2] *disreputable, suspicious* crooked, disgraceful, dishonest, dishonorable, dubious, fishy, ignominious, infamous, inglorious, notorious, questionable, scandalous, shabby, shameful, shifty, shoddy, slippery, suspect, underhanded, unethical, unrespectable, unscrupulous, untrustworthy; CONCEPT 545 —*Ant.* aboveboard, honorable, reputable, respectable

shaggy [adj] *hairy, unkempt* furry, hirsute, long-haired, ragged, rough, ruffled, rugged,

uncombed, unshorn; CONCEPT 485 —*Ant.* kempt, shaven, smooth

shake [v1] *quiver, tremble* agitate, brandish, bump, chatter, churn, commove, concuss, convulse, discompose, disquiet, dither, dodder, flap, flicker, flit, flitter, flourish, fluctuate, flutter, jar, jerk, jog, joggle, jolt, jounce, move, oscillate, palpitate, perturb, quail, quake, quaver, rattle, reel, rock, roil, ruffle, set in motion, shimmer, shimmy, shiver, shudder, stagger, stir up, succuss, sway, swing, totter, tremor, twitter, upset, vibrate, waggle, water, wave, whip, wobble; CONCEPTS 150,152

shake [v2] *upset deeply* appall, bother, consternate, daunt, discompose, dismay, distress, disturb, frighten, horrify, impair, intimidate, jar, knock props out*, make waves*, move, rattle, throw, throw a curve*, undermine, unnerve, unsettle, unstring, upset, weaken, worry; CONCEPTS 7,19 —*Ant.* calm, placate, soothe

shake off [v] *lose by getting away* clear, dislodge, drop, elude, get away from, get rid of, give the slip*, leave behind, remove, rid oneself of, throw off, unburden; CONCEPTS 102,195 —*Ant.* appear, present

shake up [v] *upset, unsettle* agitate, break with past*, cause revolution*, churn up*, clean out, clean up, clear out, disturb, liquidate, make a clean sweep*, mix, overturn, purge, remove, reorganize, rid, shock, stir up, turn upside down*; CONCEPTS 14,324 —*Ant.* calm, placate, soothe

shaky [adj1] *trembling* all aquiver*, aquake, aquiver, ashake, faltering, fluctuant, infirm, insecure, jellylike, jerry-built*, jittery, nervous, not set, precarious, quaking, quivery, rattletrap, rickety, rocky, rootless, shaking, tottering, tottery, tremorous, tremulous, tumbledown, unfirm, unsettled, unsound, unstable, unsteady, unsure, vacillating, wavering, weak, wobbly, yielding; CONCEPT 488 —*Ant.* firm, steady, unshaky, unwavering

shaky [adj2] *doubtful* dubious, indecisive, not dependable, not reliable, precarious, problematic, questionable, suspect, uncertain, unclear, independable, unreliable, unsettled, unsound, unsteady, unsupported, unsure; CONCEPT 535 —*Ant.* certain, firm, indubious, sure

shallow [adj1] *not deep* cursory, depthless, empty, flat, hollow, inconsiderable, sand bar, shelf, shoal, slight, superficial, surface, trifling, trivial, unsound; CONCEPTS 737,777 —*Ant.* deep

shallow [adj2] *unintelligent, ignorant* cursory, empty, empty-headed, farcical, featherbrained, flighty, flimsy, foolish, frivolous, frothy, half-baked*, hollow, idle, inane, lightweight, meaningless, paltry, petty, piddling, puerile, simple, sketchy, skin-deep*, slight, superficial, surface, trifling, trivial, uncritical, unthinking, vain, wishy-washy*; CONCEPT 402 —*Ant.* aware, considered, deep, intelligent, thoughtful

sham [adj] *artificial, counterfeit* adulterated, affected, assumed, bogus*, dummy, ersatz*, fake, false, feigned, fictitious, forged, fraudulent, imitation, lying, make-believe, misleading, mock, phony, plaster*, pretend, pretended, pseudo*, simulated, so-called, spurious, substitute, synthetic, untrue; CONCEPT 582 —*Ant.* real, true

sham [n] *hoax, trick* burlesque, cant, caricature,

cheat, counterfeit, cover-up, deceit, deception, facade, fake, fakery, false front, farce, feint, flimflam*, forgery, fraud, hypocrisy, hypocriticalness, imitation, impostor, imposture, jive*, mock, mockery, pharisaism, phoniness, pretend, pretense, pretext, pseudo*, put-on, sell, smoke*, snow job*, spoof, travesty, whitewash*; CONCEPTS 59,192

sham [v] *trick; pull a hoax* act, affect, ape, assume, bluff, copy, counterfeit, create, do a number*, fake, fake it, feign, imitate, invent, lie, make like, mislead, mock, play possum*, pretend, put on, put up a front*, shuck and jive*, simulate, sucker*; CONCEPTS 59,111, 171 —Ant. tell truth

shaman [n] *religious specialist* healer, medicine man, priest, sorcerer, witch doctor; CONCEPT 361

shambles [n] *a mess* anarchy, babel, bedlam, botch, chaos, confusion, disarray, disorder, disorganization, hash, havoc, hodge-podge, madhouse, maelstrom, mess-up, mix-up, muddle; CONCEPTS 230,674 —Ant. order, organization

shame [n] *disgrace, embarrassment* abashment, bad conscience*, blot, chagrin, compunction, confusion, contempt, contrition, degradation, derision, discomposure, discredit, disesteem, dishonor, disrepute, guilt, humiliation, ignominy, ill repute, infamy, irritation, loss of face*, mortification, obloquy, odium, opprobrium, pang, pudency, remorse, reproach, scandal, self-disgust, self-reproach, self-reproof, shamefacedness, skeleton in the cupboard*, smear, stigma, stupefaction, treachery; CONCEPTS 388,410 —Ant. honor, pride, respect

shame [v] *disgrace, embarrass* abash, blot, confound, cut down to size*, debase, defile, degrade, disconcert, discredit, dishonor, give a black eye*, humble, humiliate, mortify, reproach, ridicule, shoot down*, smear, stain, take down*, take down a peg*; CONCEPTS 7,14,19 —Ant. be proud, honor, regard, respect

shamefaced [adj] *embarrassed* abashed, chagrined, disgraced, guilty, humble, humbled, humiliated, mortified, regretful, shamed, sorry; CONCEPT 550

shameful [adj] *atrocious; disreputable* base, carnal, contemptible, corrupt, dastardly, debauched, degrading, diabolical, disgraceful, dishonorable, drunken, embarrassing, flagrant, heinous, humiliating, ignominious, immodest, immoral, impure, indecent, infamous, intemperate, lewd, low, mean, mortifying, notorious, obscene, opprobrious, outrageous, profligate, reprehensible, reprobate, ribald, scandalous, shaming, shocking, sinful, unbecoming, unclean, unworthy, vile, villainous, vulgar, wicked; CONCEPTS 401,545,571 —Ant. good, reputable, respectable

shameless [adj] *corrupt, indecent* abandoned, arrant, audacious, barefaced, bold, brash, brassy, brazen, cheeky*, depraved, dissolute, flagrant, forward, hardened, high-handed*, immodest, immoral, improper, impudent, incorrigible, insolent, lewd, outrageous, overbold, presumptuous, profligate, reprobate, rude, unabashed, unashamed, unblushing, unchaste, unprincipled, wanton; CONCEPTS 401,545 —Ant. decent, good, moral

shanghai [v] *kidnap* abduct, capture, carry away, carry off, grab, hijack, hold for ransom, pirate, run away with, seize, skyjack, snatch; CONCEPTS 90,139

Shangri-la [n] *utopia* Arcadia, bliss, Eden, Elysian Fields*, Erewhon*, Garden of Eden, heaven, paradise, promised land*, seventh heaven, Xanadu; CONCEPTS 370,689

shanty [n] *shack* cabin, camp, cottage, hut, lean-to, shed, shelter, small house, tiny house; CONCEPT 516

shape [n1] *form, structure* appearance, architecture, aspect, body, build, cast, chassis, circumscription, configuration, conformation, constitution, construction, contour, cut, embodiment, figure, format, frame, guise, likeness, lineation, lines, look, make, metamorphosis, model, mold, outline, pattern, profile, semblance, shadow, silhouette, simulacrum, stamp, symmetry; CONCEPTS 436,754,757

shape [n2] *condition, health* case, estate, fettle, fitness, kilter, order, repair, state, trim, whack*; CONCEPTS 316,720

shape [v1] *form, create* assemble, block out, bring together, build, carve, cast, chisel, construct, crystallize, cut, embody, fabricate, fashion, forge, frame, hew, knead, make, mint, model, mold, pat, pattern, produce, roughhew, sculpture, sketch, stamp, streamline, throw together*, trim, whittle; CONCEPTS 137,184 —Ant. deform, destroy

shape [v2] *devise, plan* accommodate, adapt, become, define, develop, form, frame, grow, guide, modify, prepare, regulate, remodel, tailor, take form, work up; CONCEPT 36 —Ant. neglect

shapeless [adj] *formless* abnormal, amorphic, amorphous, anomalous, asymmetrical, baggy, deformed, disfigured, embryonic, ill-formed, inchoate, indefinite, indeterminate, indistinct, invisible, irregular, malformed, misshapen, mutilated, nebulous, undeveloped, unformed, ungraceful, unmade, unshapely, unstructured, unsymmetrical, vague, without character, without form; CONCEPTS 486,589 —Ant. formed, proportioned, shapely, symmetrical

shapely [adj] *well-proportioned* balanced, beautiful, built, comely, curvaceous, elegant, full-figured, graceful, neat, pleasing, proportioned, regular, rounded, sightly, statuesque, sylphlike, symmetrical, trim, well-formed, well-turned; CONCEPTS 406,490 —Ant. deformed, disfigured, disproportioned, formless, shapeless, unshapely

share [n] *portion, allotment* allowance, apportionment, bite, chunk, claim, commission, contribution, cut, cut in, cut up, divide, dividend, division, divvy*, dose, drag*, due, end, fifty-fifty*, fraction, fragment, halver, helping, heritage, interest, lagniappe, lot, measure, meed, parcel, part, partage, percentage, piece, pittance, plum, points, proportion, quantum, quota, quotient, quotum, rake-off*, ration, segment, serving, slice, split, stake, taste, whack*; CONCEPTS 710,835 —Ant. whole

share [v] *use in common with others* accord, administer, allot, apportion, assign, be a party to, bestow, cut the pie*, deal, dispense, distribute, divide, divide with, divvy*, divvy up*, dole out, experience, give and take, give out, go Dutch*, go fifty-fifty*, go halves*, go in with, have a hand in, have a portion of, mete out, parcel out, part, partake, participate, partition, pay half, piece up, prorate, quota, ration, receive, shift, slice, slice up, split, split up, take a part of, yield; CONCEPTS 98,100,384 —Ant. be selfish, hold, keep

sharp [adj1] knifelike, cutting aciculate, acuate, acuminate, acuminous, acute, apical, barbed, briery, cuspate, cuspidate, edged, fine, ground fine, honed, horned, jagged, keen, keen-edged, knife-edged, needlelike, needle-pointed, peaked, pointed, pointy, prickly, pronged, razor-sharp, salient, serrated, sharp-edged, sharpened, spiked, spiky, spiny, splintery, stinging, tapered, tapering, thorny, tined, tipped, unblunted, whetted; CONCEPTS 486 —Ant. blunt, dull

sharp [adj2] sudden abrupt, distinct, extreme, intense, marked; CONCEPTS 581,799 —Ant. lazy, slow

sharp [adj3] perceptive, quick-witted acute, adroit, alert, apt, astute, brainy, bright, brilliant, canny, clever, critical, cute, discerning, discriminating, fast, foxy*, having smarts*, ingenious, intelligent, keen, knowing, nimble, nobody's fool*, not born yesterday*, observant, on the ball*, original, penetrating, penetrative, quick, quick on the trigger*, quick on the uptake*, ready, resourceful, savvy*, sensitive, slick, smart, smart as a tack*, subtle, wise; CONCEPT 402 —Ant. ignorant, stupid, unintelligent

sharp [adj4] dishonest, deceitful artful, bent, crafty, cunning, designing, ornery, salty, shady, shrewd, slick, slippery, sly, smart, snaky, two-faced*, underhand, unethical, unscrupulous, wily; CONCEPT 545 —Ant. aboveboard, forthright, frank, honest

sharp [adj5] severe, intense acute, agonizing, biting, cutting, distinct, distressing, drilling, excruciating, fierce, keen, knifelike, painful, paralyzing, penetrating, piercing, shooting, smart, sore, stabbing, stinging, violent; CONCEPTS 537,569 —Ant. calm, mild, moderate

sharp [adj6] distinct, well-defined audible, clear, clear-cut, crisp, definite, explicit, obvious, visible; CONCEPT 535 —Ant. indefinite, indistinct, undefined

sharp [adj7] stylish chic, classy, dashing, distinctive, dressy, excellent, fashionable, fine, first-class*, fly*, in style, smart, snappy*, swank*, tony*, trendy; CONCEPT 589 —Ant. boring, old-fashioned, unstylish

sharp [adj8] hurtful, bitter in speech acrimonious, angry, barbed, biting, caustic, cutting, double-edged, harsh, incisive, inconsiderate, penetrating, peppery, piercing, pointed, pungent, sarcastic, sardonic, scathing, severe, short, stabbing, stinging, tart, thoughtless, trenchant, unceremonious, ungracious, virulent, vitriolic; CONCEPT 267 —Ant. benevolent, kind, nice

sharp [adj9] having strong affect on animate senses acerbic, acid, acrid, active, astringent, austere, bitter, brisk, burning, harsh, hot, lively, odorous, piquant, pungent, sour, strong-smelling, suffocating, tart, vigorous, vinegary; CONCEPTS 537,598,613 —Ant. bland, calm, dull, flat, low, mild, moderate, tasteless

sharp [adv] on time abruptly, accurately, bang,

exactly, just, on the button*, on the dot*, precisely, promptly, punctually, right, smack-dab*, square, squarely, suddenly; CONCEPT 799 —Ant. late

sharpen [v] make knifelike acuminate, dress, edge, file, grind, hone, make acute, make sharp, put an edge on, put a point on, sharp, stroke, strop, taper, whet; CONCEPTS 137,250 —Ant. blunt, dull

sharp-tongued [adj] critical belittling, biting, carping, censuring, condemning, cursing, cutting, cynical, demeaning, derogatory, harsh, hypercritical, mean, nasty, sarcastic, satirical; CONCEPT 267

shatter [v1] break into small pieces blast, blight, burst, crack, crash, crunch, crush, dash, demolish, destroy, disable, exhaust, explode, fracture, fragment, fragmentalize, fragmentize, impair, implode, overturn, pulverize, rend, rive, ruin, scrunch, shiver, smash, smash to smithereens*, smatter, snap, splinter, splinterize*, split, torpedo*, total*, wrack up*, wreck; CONCEPTS 246,252 —Ant. fix, mend

shatter [v2] hurt someone badly break a heart*, crush, destroy, devastate, dumbfound, rattle, ruin, upset; CONCEPTS 7,19 —Ant. aid, assist, help

shave [v] cut outer covering off barber, brush, clip, crop, cut, cut back, cut down, decorticate, graze, kiss, make bare, pare, peel, plane, prune, shear, shingle, shred, skim, skin, slash, slice thin, sliver, strip, touch, trim; CONCEPTS 137, 162,176,202

shear [v] clip, cut crop, cut back, fleece, groom, mow, pare, prune, shave, shorten, snip, trim; CONCEPTS 137,176

shed [v] cast off afford, beam, cashier, cast, diffuse, disburden, discard, doff, drop, emit, exude, exuviate, give, give forth, jettison, junk, let fall, molt, pour forth, radiate, reject, scatter, scrap, send forth, shower, slip, slough, spill, sprinkle, take off, throw, throw away, throw out, yield; CONCEPTS 179,180,181,211 —Ant. put on

sheen [n] brightness, shine burnish, finish, glaze, gleam, glint, gloss, luster, patina, polish, shimmer, shininess, wax; CONCEPT 620 —Ant. darkness, dullness

sheepish [adj] shy, embarrassed abashed, ashamed, chagrined, diffident, docile, foolish, guilty, mortified, retiring, self-conscious, shamefaced, silly, tame, timid, timorous, uncomfortable; CONCEPT 401 —Ant. aggressive, bold, unashamed, unembarrassed

sheer [adj1] abrupt, steep arduous, erect, headlong, perpendicular, precipitate, precipitous, sideling, upright; CONCEPTS 490,581 —Ant. moderate, slow

sheer [adj2] utter, absolute altogether, arrant, blasted, blessed, complete, confounded, downright, gross, infernal, out-and-out*, outright, perfect, pure, quite, rank, simple, single, thoroughgoing, total, unadulterated, unalloyed, undiluted, unmitigated, unmixed, unqualified; CONCEPTS 531,535,544 —Ant. indefinite, uncertain

sheer [adj3] see-through, thin airy, chiffon, clear, cobwebby, delicate, diaphanous, filmy, fine, flimsy, fragile, gauzy, gossamer, lacy, limpid, lucid, pellucid, pure, slight, smooth, soft, tiffany, translucent, transparent; CONCEPT 606 —*Ant.* heavy, impermeable, thick

sheet [*n*] *coating, covering; page* area, blanket, coat, expanse, film, foil, folio, folio, lamina, layer, leaf, membrane, overlay, pane, panel, piece, plate, ply, slab, stratum, stretch, surface, sweep, veneer; CONCEPTS 172,270,475,484

shelf [*n*] *jutting, flat area or piece* bank, bracket, console, counter, cupboard, ledge, mantelpiece, mantle, rack, reef, ridge, rock, shallow, shoal; CONCEPTS 445,509,513

shell [*n*] *structure; covering* carapace, case, chassis, crust, frame, framework, hull, husk, integument, nut, pericarp, plastron, pod, scale, shard, shuck, skeleton, skin; CONCEPTS 399,428, 484 —*Ant.* center, inside, interior, middle

shell out [*v*] *give* ante up, disburse, expend, fork over*, hand over, lay out, outlay, pay, pay for, pay out, spend; CONCEPT 341 —*Ant.* receive, take

shelter [*n*] *protection, habitat* apartment, asylum, cave, condo, co-op, cover, covert, crib*, defense, den, digs*, dwelling, guard, guardian, harbor, harborage, haven, hermitage, hide, hideaway, hideout, hole in the wall*, home, homeplate*, house, housing, hut, joint*, lodging, pad*, pen, port, preserve, protector, quarterage, rack, refuge, retirement, retreat, roof, roof over head*, roost*, safety, sanctuary, screen, security, shack, shade, shadow, shed, shield, tent, tower, turf, umbrella; CONCEPTS 515,712

shelter [*v*] *provide safety, cover* chamber, conceal, cover, cover up, defend, enclose, guard, harbor, haven, hide, house, lodge, preserve, protect, roof, safeguard, screen, secure, shield, surround, take care of, take in, ward, watch over; CONCEPTS 134,188 —*Ant.* turn away

shelve [*v*] *defer, postpone* delay, dismiss, drop, freeze*, give up, hang up, hold, hold off, hold over, hold up, lay aside, mothball*, pigeonhole*, prolong, prorogue, put aside, put off, put on back burner*, put on hold, put on ice*, scrub*, sideline, slow up, stay, suspend, table, tie up, waive; CONCEPT 121 —*Ant.* carry out, do, go ahead

shenanigans [*n*] *mischief* antics, capers, dirty trick*, fooling around, frolicsomeness, funny business*, gag, hanky-panky*, high jinks*, horseplay, horsing around, misbehavior, mischievousness, monkey business*, naughtiness, nonsense, prank, trouble, vandalism; CONCEPTS 192,633,645

shield [*n*] *protection* absorber, aegis, armament, armor, buckler, buffer, bulwark, bumper, cover, defense, escutcheon, guard, mail, rampart, safeguard, screen, security, shelter, ward; CONCEPTS 712,729

shield [*v*] *protect* bulwark, chamber, conceal, cover, cover all bases*, cover up, defend, fend, give cover, give shelter, go to bat for*, guard, harbor, haven, house, ride shotgun*, roof, safeguard, screen, secure, shelter, shotgun*, stonewall*, take under one's wing*, ward off; CONCEPTS 96,134 —*Ant.* endanger, lay bare, open, uncover

shift [*n1*] *switch, fluctuation* about-face*, alteration, bend, change, changeover, conversion, deflection, deviation, displacement, double,

fault, modification, move, passage, permutation, rearrangement, removal, shifting, substitution, tack, transfer, transference,transformation, transit, translocation, turn, variation, veering, yaw; CONCEPTS 213,697 —*Ant.* deactivation, maintenance, stagnation

shift [*n2*] *trick, stratagem* artifice, contrivance, craft, device, dodge, equivocation, evasion, expediency, expedient, gambit, hoax, makeshift, maneuver, move, ploy, recourse, refuge, resort, resource, ruse, stopgap*, strategy, substitute, subterfuge, wile; CONCEPTS 59,660

shift [*n3*] *time served doing work* bout, go, period, spell, stint, time, tour, trick, turn, working time; CONCEPT 802

shift [*v*] *switch, fluctuate* about-face*, alter, blow hot and cold*, bottom out*, budge, change, change gears, cook*, deviate, dial back*, dislocate, displace, disturb, do up*, drift, exchange, fault, flip-flop*, hem and haw*, move, move around, move over, rearrange, recalibrate, relocate, remove, replace, reposition, ship, shuffle, slip, stir, substitute, swap places, swerve, switch over, tack, transfer, transmogrify, transpose, turn, turn around, turn the corner*, turn the tables*, vacillate, vary, veer, waffle, yo-yo*; CONCEPTS 213,232,697 —*Ant.* deactivate, remain, stagnate

shiftless [*adj*] *lazy* apathetic, dallying, directionless, good-for-nothing, idle, inattentive, incompetent, indolent, lackadaisical, laggard, lagging, lethargic, lifeless, loafing, procrastinating, slack, slothful, unambitious, unenergetic, unindustrious, unmotivated; CONCEPTS 401,404

shifty [*adj*] *deceitful, untrustworthy* cagey, collusive, conniving, contriving, crafty, crooked, cunning, devious, dishonest, dodging, duplicitous, elusive, equivocating, evasive, fly-by-night*, foxy, fraudulent, furtive, insidious, lying, mendacious, prevaricative, prevaricatory, roguish, scheming, shady, shrewd, shuffling, slick, slimy*, slippery, sly, sneaky, treacherous, tricky, underhand, unhonest, unprincipled, untruthful, wily; CONCEPTS 401,404 —*Ant.* forthright, frank, honest, trustworthy

shimmer [*n*] *gleam* blinking, coruscation, diffused light, flash, glimmer, glint, glisten, glitter, gloss, glow, incandescence, iridescence, luster, phosphorescence, scintillation, sheen, spangle, spark, sparkle, twinkle; CONCEPTS 620,624 —*Ant.* dullness

shimmer [*v*] *glisten* blaze, coruscate, dance, flare, flash, gleam, glint, glow, jiggle, phosphoresce, scintillate, shimmy, shine, sparkle, twinkle; CONCEPT 624

shindig [*n*] *party* affair, ball, banquet, barbecue, bash*, blowout*, celebration, dance, dinner, feast, festivity, function, gala, get-together, reception, shindy, social gathering; CONCEPT 383

shine [*n*] *brightness; polish* flash, glare, glaze, gleam, glint, glitz, gloss, lambency, light, luminosity, luster, patina, radiance, rub, sheen, shimmer, show, sparkle; CONCEPT 620 —*Ant.* darkness, dullness

shine [*v1*] *give off or reflect light* beam, bedazzle, blaze, blink, burn, dazzle, deflect, emit light, flare, flash, flicker, give light, glare, gleam, glimmer, glisten, glitter, glow, illuminate, illumine, incandesce, irradiate, luminesce, mirror, radiate, scintillate, shimmer, sparkle, twinkle; CONCEPT 624 —*Ant.* dull

shine [v2] *polish, burnish* brush, buff, buff up, finish, furbish, give a sheen, glance, glaze, gloss, make brilliant, put a finish on, put a gloss on, rub, scour, sleek, wax; CONCEPT 202 —*Ant.* dull

shiny [adj] *bright, glistening* agleam, burnished, clear, gleaming, glossy, lustrous, polished, satiny, sheeny, slick, sparkling, sunny; CONCEPT 617 —*Ant.* dark, dull

ship [v] *send, transport* address, consign, direct, dispatch, drop, embark, export, forward, freight, go aboard, haul, move, put on board, remit, route, shift, ship out, smuggle, transfer, transmit; CONCEPTS 148,217 —*Ant.* hold, keep

shipshape [adj] *tidy* businesslike, chipper, clean, in good shape, in tip-top condition, neat, ordered, orderly, spick-and-span*, trim, uncluttered, well-groomed, well-kept; CONCEPTS 485,585,621

shirk [v] *avoid, get out of responsibility* bypass, cheat, creep, dodge, dog*, duck, elude, eschew, evade, fence, get around, goldbrick*, lie down on job*, lurk, malinger, parry, pussyfoot*, quit, shuffle off, shun, sidestep, skulk, slack, slink, slip, slough off, snake, sneak, steal; CONCEPTS 30,59,681 —*Ant.* do, face, meet

shirker [n] *slacker* avoider, bum, deadbeat*, goldbrick, good-for-nothing, goof-off*, idler, loafer, quitter, slouch; CONCEPTS 412,423

shiver [v1] *shake, tremble* be cold, dither, flutter, freeze, have the quivers, have the shakes, palpitate, quake, quaver, quiver, shudder, tremor, twitter, vibrate, wave; CONCEPTS 152,185 —*Ant.* steady

shiver [v2] *shatter; break into small pieces* burst, crack, fragment, fragmentalize, pash, rive, smash, smash to smithereens*, smatter, splinter, splinterize*; CONCEPTS 246,252 —*Ant.* fix, mend

shock [n] *complete surprise; blow* awe, bombshell*, breakdown, bump, clash, collapse, collision, concussion, confusion, consternation, crash, distress, disturbance, double whammy*, earthquake, encounter, excitement, eye-opener*, hysteria, impact, injury, jarring, jolt, percussion, prostration, ram, scare, start, stroke, stupefaction, stupor, trauma, traumatism, turn, upset, whammy*, wreck; CONCEPTS 33,309,529 —*Ant.* expectation

shock [v] *completely surprise* abash, agitate, anger, antagonize, appall, astound, awe, bowl over*, daze, disgust, dismay, displease, disquiet, disturb, electrify, flabbergast, flood, floor*, give a turn*, hit like ton of bricks*, horrify, insult, jar, jolt, knock out*, nauseate, numb, offend, outrage, overcome, overwhelm, paralyze, revolt, rock, scandalize, shake, shake up, sicken, stagger, startle, stun, stupefy, throw a curve*, traumatize, unsettle; CONCEPT 42

shocking [adj] *outrageous; very surprising* abominable, appalling, atrocious, awful, burning, crying, desperate, detestable, direful, disgraceful, disgusting, disquieting, distressing, dreadful, fearful, formidable, foul, frightful, ghastly, glaring, hateful, heinous, hideous, horrible, horrific, horrifying, loathsome, monstrous, nauseating, odious, offensive, repulsive,

revolting, scandalous, shameful, sickening, stupefying, terrible, ugly, unspeakable; CONCEPTS 548,571 —*Ant.* calming, comforting, soothing

shoddy [adj] *in bad shape* base, broken-down, cheap, cheesy*, common, dilapidated, dingy, discreditable, disgraceful, dishonorable, disreputable, gaudy, ignominious, inferior, inglorious, junky, makeshift, mean, not up to snuff*, paltry, plastic, poor, pretentious, run-down, scruffy*, second-rate*, seedy, shabby, shady, shameful, sleazy*, slipshod, tacky*, tawdry, trashy, unrespectable; CONCEPTS 485,571 —*Ant.* fine, good, nice

shoe [n] *footwear* basketball shoe, boat shoe, boot, cleat, clog, cowboy boot, flip-flops*, footgear, golf shoe, high heels, hightops*, loafer, moccasin, penny loafer, platform shoe, pump, running shoe, sandals, slipper, sneaker, tennis shoe, wing-tip, work shoe; CONCEPT 451

shoot [v1] *discharge a projectile, often to injure or kill* bag*, barrage, blast, bombard, bring down, catapult, dispatch, drop the hammer*, emit, execute, expel, explode, fire, fling, gun, hit, hurl, ignite, kill, launch, let fly, let go with, loose, murder, open fire*, open up*, pick off*, plug, pop*, project, propel, pull the trigger, pump*, set off, throw lead*, torpedo, trigger, zap*; CONCEPTS 179,246,252 —*Ant.* backfire

shoot [v2] *dash* boil, bolt, charge, chase, dart, flash, fling, fly, gallop, hotfoot*, hurry, hurtle, lash, pass, race, reach, run, rush, scoot, skirr, speed, spring, spurt, streak, tear, whisk, whiz; CONCEPTS 150,152 —*Ant.* walk

shoot the breeze [v] *chat, converse* BS*, chatter, chew the fat*, gab*, palaver, prate, prattle*, run off at the mouth*, schmooze*, shoot the bull*, yack*, yap*; CONCEPT 266

shop [n] *place of retail business* boutique, chain, deli, department store, emporium, five-and-dime, market, mill, outlet, showroom, stand, store, supermarket; CONCEPTS 439,441,448,449

shop [v] *look for merchandise to buy* buy, go shopping, hunt for, look for, market, purchase, try to buy; CONCEPTS 327,330 —*Ant.* sell

shopkeeper [n] *merchant* businessperson, dealer, entrepreneur, proprietor, retailer, salesperson, seller, storekeeper, store owner, vendor, wholesaler; CONCEPT 347

shoplift [v] *steal* burglarize, carry off, defraud, embezzle, heist, hold up, lift*, loot, make off with*, pilfer, pillage, pinch*, rip off*, run off with*, snatch*, stick up*, swipe, take, walk off with*; CONCEPT 139

shopper [n] *customer* browser, buyer, client, clientele, consumer, patron, prospect, purchaser, window-shopper; CONCEPT 348

shopping [n] *buying* browsing, e-commerce, electronic commerce, purchasing, spending; CONCEPT 327

shopping center [n] *concentrated area for shopping* agora, arcade, bazaar, emporium, fair, flea market, galleria, mall, marketplace, mart, piazza, shopping complex, shopping mall, shopping plaza, strip mall; CONCEPT 333

shore [n] *waterside* bank, beach, border, brim, brink, coast, coastland, embankment, lakeshore, lakeside, littoral, margin, riverbank, riverside, sand, sands, seaboard, seacoast,

seashore, shingle, strand, waterfront; CONCEPT
509 —*Ant.* inland

shore [v] *reinforce* bear up, bolster, brace,
bulwark, buttress, carry, hold, prop, strengthen,
support, sustain, underpin, upbear, uphold;
CONCEPT 110—*Ant.* discourage, dissuade, ruin

short [adj1] *abridged* abbreviate, abbreviated,
aphoristic, bare, boiled down, breviloquent,
brief, compendiary, compendious, compressed,
concise, condensed, curtailed, curtate, cut
short, cut to the bone*, decreased, decurtate,
diminished, epigrammatic, fleeting, in a nutshell*, laconic, lessened, little, momentary, not
protracted, pithy, pointed, precise, sententious,
short and sweet*, shortened, short-lived,
short-term, succinct, summarized, summary,
terse, undersized, unprolonged, unsustained;
CONCEPTS 267,272,798 —*Ant.* large, lengthy,
long, unabridged

short [adj2] *not tall* abbreviated, chunky, close
to the ground, compact, diminutive, little, low,
not long, petite, pint-sized*, pocket, pocket-
sized*, runty, sawed-off*, skimpy, slight, small,
squat, squatty, stocky, stubby, stunted, thick,
thickset, tiny, undersized, wee; CONCEPTS
773,779,782 —*Ant.* high, lengthy, long, tall

short [adj3] *insufficient* deficient, exiguous,
failing, inadequate, lacking, limited, low on,
meager, needing, niggardly, poor, scant, scanty,
scarce, short-handed*, shy, skimpy, slender,
slim, sparse, tight, wanting; CONCEPTS 527,
560,762 —*Ant.* adequate, enough, sufficient

short [adj4] *abrupt, discourteous* bad-tempered,
blunt, breviloquent, brief, brusque, curt, direct,
gruff, impolite, inconsiderate, irascible, offhand,
rude, sharp, short-spoken, short-tempered,
snappy*, snippety*, snippy*, straight, terse,
testy, thoughtless, unceremonious, uncivil, ungracious; CONCEPTS 267,401 —*Ant.* courteous,
kind, polite

short [adj5] *crumbly* brittle, crisp, crunchy, delicate, fragile, friable; CONCEPT 462 —*Ant.* thick

short [adv] *abruptly* aback, by surprise, forthwith, sudden, suddenly, unanticipatedly, unaware, unawares, without delay, without
hesitation, without warning; CONCEPT
799 —*Ant.* long

shortage [n] *deficiency* curtailment, dearth,
defalcation, deficit, failure, inadequacy,
insufficiency, lack, lapse, leanness, paucity,
pinch, poverty, scantiness, scarcity, shortfall,
tightness, underage, want, weakness; CONCEPTS
646,709,767 —*Ant.* abundance, ample,
enough, sufficiency

shortchange [v] *cheat* bamboozle*, bilk,
deceive, defraud, double-deal, dupe, finagle,
fleece, flimflam, gyp*, hose, mislead, rip off*,
rook*, sandbag, scam, screw, shaft, stiff,
swindle, take, trick; CONCEPTS 59,139,192

shortcoming [n] *weak point* bug*, catch*,
defect, deficiency, demerit, drawback, failing,
fault, flaw, frailty, imperfection, infirmity, lack,
lapse, sin, weakness; CONCEPTS 411,666,674,
679 —*Ant.* advantage, strong point, success

shorten [v] *diminish, decrease* abbreviate,
abridge, blue pencil*, bob, boil down*, chop,
clip, compress, condense, contract, curtail, cut,
cut back, cut down, cut to the bone* dock, edit,
elide, excerpt, lessen, lop, make a long story

short*, minimize, put in a nutshell*, reduce,
retrench, shrink, slash, snip, trim; CONCEPTS
137,236,240,247 —*Ant.* amplify, elongate,
enlarge, grow, increase, lengthen

shortfall [n] *deficit; imperfection* arrears,
default, defectiveness, deficiency, flaw,
inadequacy, incompleteness, insufficiency,
insufficiency, in the hole*, in the red, lack,
loss, red ink*, shortage, shortcoming, underage;
CONCEPTS 230,335,646,671,718

short-lived [adj] *temporary* brief, ephemeral,
evanescent, fleeting, fugacious, fugitive,
impermanent, momentary, passing, short,
short-haul*, short-run, short-term, transient,
transitory; CONCEPT 798 —*Ant.* enduring,
ethereal, lasting, lengthy, long-lived, permanent

shortly [adv] *right away* any minute
now, before long, by and by, in a little while,
presently, proximately, quickly, soon; CONCEPT
820 —*Ant.* later

shortsighted [adj] *unmindful of future consequences* astigmatic, blind, careless, foolish,
headlong, ill-advised, ill-considered, imperceptive, impolitic, impractical, improvident, imprudent, injudicious, myopic, nearsighted, rash,
stupid, unsagacious, unwary; CONCEPTS 401,542
—*Ant.* careful, longsighted, prudent, thoughtful,
wise

shot [n1] *try, chance* attempt, break, conjecture,
effort, endeavor, fling*, go*, guess, occasion,
opening, opportunity, pop*, show, slap*, stab*,
surmise, time, turn, whack*, whirl*; CONCEPT
693

shot [n2] *discharge; ammunition* ball, buckshot,
bullet, dart, lead, lob, missile, pellet, projectile,
slug, throw; CONCEPT 498 —*Ant.* backfire

shoulder [v1] *be responsible for* accept, assume, bear, carry, take on, take upon oneself;
CONCEPT 23 —*Ant.* deny, refuse

shoulder [v2] *push, jostle* bulldoze*, elbow,
hustle, nudge, press, push aside, shove, thrust;
CONCEPT 208

shout [n] *loud outcry* bark, bawl, bellow, call,
cheer, clamor, cry, howl, hue, roar, salvo,
scream, screech, shriek, squall, squawk, tumult,
vociferation, whoop*, yammer*, yap*, yawp*,
yell; CONCEPTS 77,595 —*Ant.* whimper

shout [v] *cry out loudly* bawl, bay, bellow, call
out, cheer, clamor, exclaim, holler*, raise voice,
roar, scream, screech, shriek, squall, squawk,
vociferate, whoop*, yammer*, yap*, yawp*,
yell; CONCEPT 77 —*Ant.* whimper

shove [v] *push without gentleness* boost, buck,
bulldoze*, cram, crowd, dig, drive, elbow,
hustle, impel, jab, jam, jostle, nudge, poke,
press, prod, propel, shoulder, thrust; CONCEPT
208 —*Ant.* pull

shove off [v] *leave quickly* blow, clear out,
depart, exit, get off, go, go away, pull out,
push off, quit, run along, start out, take off,
vamoose*; CONCEPT 195 —*Ant.* arrive, come

show [n1] *demonstration, exhibition* appearance, array, display, expo*, exposition, fair,
fanfare, fireworks, grandstand, manifestation,
occurrence, pageant, pageantry, panoply,
parade, pomp, presentation, program, representation, shine*, showboat*, showing, sight,
spectacle, splash*, view; CONCEPT 261
—*Ant.* concealment, hiding

show [n2] *entertainment event* act, appearance, burlesque, carnival, cinema, comedy, drama, entertainment, film, flick*, motion picture, movie, pageant, picture, play, presentation, production, showing, spectacle; CONCEPTS 263,293

show [n3] *false front; appearance given* affectation, air, display, effect, face*, front, grandstand play*, guise, illusion, impression, likeness, make-believe*, ostentation, parade, pose, pretense, pretext, profession, seeming, semblance, sham, shine*, showboat*, showing, simulacrum, splash*; CONCEPTS 633,716 —Ant. reality, truth

show [v1] *actively exhibit something* afford, air, arrive, attend, bare, blazon, brandish, deal in, demonstrate, display, disport, exhibit, expose, flash, flaunt, flourish, lay bare, lay out, mount, offer, parade, present, produce, proffer, put on, reveal, sell, set out, showcase, show off, sport, spread, stage, streak, submit, supply, trot out, unfold, unfurl, unveil, vaunt, wave; CONCEPT 138 —Ant. conceal, hide

show [v2] *passively exhibit something* appear, arrive, assert, be visible, blow in, clarify, come, demonstrate, determine, disclose, discover, display, divulge, elucidate, emerge, establish, evidence, evince, explain, get, get in, illustrate, indicate, instruct, lay out, loom, make known, make out, make the scene*, manifest, mark, materialize, note, ostend, point, present, proclaim, project, prove, put in appearance, reach, register, reveal, show one's face*, show up, teach, testify to, turn up, unveil; CONCEPT 261 —Ant. conceal, hide

show [v3] *grant* accord, act with, bestow, confer, dispense, give; CONCEPT 108 —Ant. deny, refuse, veto

show [v4] *accompany* attend, conduct, direct, escort, guide, lead, pilot, route, see, shepherd, steer; CONCEPTS 187,384 —Ant. abandon, leave alone

show business [n] *entertainment industry* Broadway, Hollywood, motion picture industry, movie industry, show biz, the stage, the theater; CONCEPTS 383,384,386,388

showdown [n] *confrontation* breaking point, clash, climax, crisis, culmination, exposé, moment of truth, unfolding; CONCEPTS 388,674 —Ant. agreement, peacemaking

shower [n] *precipitation* cloudburst, deluge, downpour, drizzle, flood, hail, rain, rainstorm, sleet, storm, thunderstorm; CONCEPTS 524, 526

shower [v1] *rain come down in buckets*, downpour, drench, drizzle, fall, hail, mist, patter, pour, sleet, spray, sprinkle, storm; CONCEPT 526

shower [v2] *lavish* be generous, deluge, give, pamper; CONCEPTS 110,327,341

showoff [n] *person who brags about him- or herself* boaster, braggadocio, braggart, egotist, exhibitionist, swaggerer, vulgarian; CONCEPT 412 —Ant. introvert

show off [v] *flaunt; brag* advertise, boast, brandish, demonstrate, display, disport, exhibit, expose, flash*, hand a line*, make a spectacle of, parade, spread out, swagger, trot out*; CONCEPTS 49,261 —Ant. be modest, cower, shy away

showpiece [n] *exhibit* display, masterpiece, model, work of art; CONCEPTS 259,261

show up [v1] *arrive, attend* appear, be conspicuous, be visible, blow in*, come, get, get in, make an appearance, put in appearance, reach, show, stand out, turn up; CONCEPT 159 —Ant. be absent, depart, leave, miss

show up [v2] *expose, embarrass* belittle, convict, debunk, defeat, discover, discredit, highlight, invalidate, lay bare, let down, mortify, pinpoint, put spotlight on*, put to shame*, reveal, shame, show in bad light*, uncloak, undress, unmask, unshroud, worst; CONCEPTS 54,60 —Ant. conceal, hide, secrete

showy [adj] *flamboyant, flashy* classy, dashing, flash, garish, gaudy, glaring, histrionic, jazzy*, loud, luxurious, meretricious, opulent, ornate, ostentatious, overdone, overwrought, peacocky, pompous, pretentious, resplendent, screaming, sensational, snazzy*, splashy, splendiferous, sumptuous, swank*, tawdry, tinsel*, tony*; CONCEPT 589 —Ant. dismal, drab, gloomy, moderate, restrained

shred [n] *tiny piece* atom, bit, cantlet, crumb, fragment, grain, iota, jot, modicum, ounce, part, particle, rag, ray, ribbon, scintilla, scrap, shadow, sliver, smidgen, snippet, speck, stitch, tatter, trace, whit; CONCEPT 831 —Ant. lot

shred [v] *cut into ribbons* cut, fray, frazzle, make ragged, reduce, shave, sliver, strip, tatter, tear; CONCEPT 176 —Ant. mend, sew

shrewd [adj] *clever, intelligent* acute, argute, artful, astucious, astute, brainy*, cagey, calculating, canny, crafty, cunning, cutting*, deep*, discerning, discriminating, farsighted, foxy*, heady*, ingenious, inside, in the know*, judicious, keen, knowing, on the inside*, on top of*, penetrating, perceptive, perspicacious, piercing, probing, profound, prudent, quick-witted, sagacious, savvy*, sensible, shark, sharp, slick*, slippery*, sly, smart, smooth, streetwise, tricky, underhand, up on*, wily, wise, wised up*; CONCEPTS 401,402 —Ant. foolish, frivolous, naive, stupid, unthinking

shriek [n/v] *high-pitched scream* blare, cry, howl, screech, shout, shrill, squawk, squeal, wail, whoop, yell; CONCEPTS 77,595 —Ant. peep

shrill [adj] *high-pitched, harsh in sound* acute, argute, blaring, blatant, cacophonous, clanging, clangorous, deafening, discordant, ear-piercing, earsplitting, high, metallic, noisy, penetrating, piercing, piping, raucous, screeching, sharp, strident, thin, treble; CONCEPTS 592,594 —Ant. low, soft

shrine [n] *tribute to a god, idol, or spirit* altar, chapel, church, enshrinement, grave, hallowed place, holy place, mausoleum, reliquary, sacred place, sanctorium, sanctuary, sanctum, sepulcher, temple; CONCEPTS 368,439,448

shrink [v1] *become smaller* compress, concentrate, condense, constrict, contract, decrease, deflate, diminish, drop off, dwindle, fail, fall off, fall short, grow smaller, lessen, narrow, reduce, shorten, shrivel, wane, waste, waste away, weaken, wither, wrinkle; CONCEPTS 137,698,776 —Ant. develop, enlarge, expand, grow, stretch

shrink [v2] *recoil, shy away* blench, boggle, contract, cower, cringe, crouch, demur, draw back, flinch, hang back, huddle, quail, recede, refuse, retire, retreat, scruple, shudder, slink,

sh
si

wince, withdraw; CONCEPTS *188,195*
—*Ant.* face, meet, take on

shrivel [*v*] *dehydrate, dry up* burn, contract, desiccate, dwindle, fossilize, mummify, mummy, parch, scorch, sear, shrink, stale, welter, wilt, wither, wizen, wrinkle; CONCEPTS *137,250,255* —*Ant.* enlarge, expand, grow, unwrinkle

shudder [*v*] *shake, quiver* convulse, dither, gyrate, jitter, quake, shimmy, shiver, tremble, tremor, twitter, wave; CONCEPTS *34,150,152* —*Ant.* steady

shuffle [*v1*] *move along lazily* drag, limp, muddle, pad, scrape, scuff, scuffle, shamble, straggle, stumble, trail; CONCEPT *151* —*Ant.* run

shuffle [*v2*] *rearrange, mix up* break the deck*, change, change the order, confuse, disarrange, disarray, discompose, dislocate, disorder, disorganize, disrupt, disturb, intermix, jumble, mess up*, shift; CONCEPTS *158,363* —*Ant.* arrange, order, organize

shun [*v*] *avoid, ignore* bilk, cold-shoulder*, cut, decline, despise, disdain, ditch*, dodge, double, duck, elude, escape, eschew, evade, get around, give a wide berth*, give the runaround*, have no part of*, have nothing to do with*, hide out, keep away from, keep clear of, neglect, palm off*, pass up, refuse, reject, scorn, shake, shake off, shy, snub, stall, stand aloof from, stay shy of, steer clear of*, turn back on*; CONCEPTS *30,384* —*Ant.* accept, face, meet

shut [*v*] *close* bar, batten down*, cage, close down, close up, confine, draw, drop the curtain*, enclose, exclude, fasten, fold, fold up, imprison, lock, push, put to, seal, secure, shut down, slam, wall off; CONCEPTS *85,121,160,206,208,304* —*Ant.* open

shut off/shut out [*v*] *exclude; screen* bar, beleaguer, blockade, block out, close, conceal, cover, debar, discontinue, evict, fence off, hide, keep out, lock out, mask, obstruct, ostracize, refuse, seclude, shroud, veil; CONCEPTS *25,121, 188* —*Ant.* include, welcome

shuttle [*n*] *space shuttle* airplane, plane, shuttle bus, spacecraft, spaceport, train, transporter; CONCEPT *504*

shuttle [*v*] *travel back and forth* commute, drive back and forth, go back and forth, transport to and fro, travel; CONCEPT *224*

shut up [*v*] *be or make quiet* bottle up*, choke, dry up*, dummy up*, fall silent, gag, hold tongue*, hush, keep trap shut*, muzzle, pipe down*, quiet, quieten, quit chattering, shush*, silence, soft-pedal*, still, stop talking; CONCEPT *77* —*Ant.* speak, talk

shy [*adj1*] *quiet and self-conscious* afraid, apprehensive, averse, backward, bashful, cautious, chary, circumspect, conscious, coy, demure, diffident, disinclined, distrustful, fearful, hesitant, humble, indisposed, introvert, introverted, loath, loner, modest, nervous, recessive, reluctant, reserved, reticent, retiring, self-effacing, shamefaced, sheepish, shrinking, skittish, suspicious, timid, unassertive, unassured, uneager, uneffusive, unresponsive, unsocial, unwilling, wary; CONCEPTS *401,404* —*Ant.* confident, extroverted, unashamed, unreserved, unshy

shy [*adj2*] *lacking, failing* deficient, inadequate, insufficient, scant, scanty, scarce, short, unsuffi-

cient, wanting; CONCEPTS *546,762,789*
—*Ant.* adequate, enough, sufficient

shyster [*n*] *unscrupulous lawyer; swindler* ambulance chaser, cheater, chiseler, crooked lawyer, mouthpiece*, pettifogger, scammer, trickster, unethical lawyer; CONCEPT *412*

sick [*adj1*] *not healthy, not feeling well* ailing, bedridden, broken down, confined, debilitated, declining, defective, delicate, diseased, disordered, down, feeble, feverish, frail, funny*, green*, hospitalized, ill, impaired, imperfect, in a bad way*, incurable, indisposed, infected, infirm, in poor health, invalid, laid-up, lousy, mean, nauseated, not so hot*, peaked, poorly, qualmish, queasy, rickety, rocky, rotten, run down, sick as a dog*, suffering, tottering, under medication, under the weather*, unhealthy, unwell, weak, wobbly; CONCEPT *314*
—*Ant.* healthy, undiseased, well

sick [*adj2*] *morbid, gross* black, ghoulish, macabre, morose, sadistic, sickly; CONCEPTS *537,571* —*Ant.* clean, gentle, moral, nice

sick [*adj3*] *fed up, displeased* blasé, bored, disgusted, jaded, revolted, satiated, tired, up to here with*, weary; CONCEPT *403*
—*Ant.* content, happy, pleased, satisfied

sicken [*v*] *revolt, make ill* affect, afflict, derange, disgust, disorder, gross out*, nauseate, offend, reluct, repel, repulse, turn, turn one's stomach*, unhinge, unsettle, upset; CONCEPTS *14,246*
—*Ant.* cure, heal, help, make well, mend

sickening [*adj*] *disgusting, awful* diseased, distasteful, foul, gross*, icky*, loathsome, nasty, nauseating, nauseous, noisome, offensive, putrid, repugnant, repulsive, revolting, rotten, stinking, stomach-turning, tainted; CONCEPTS *529,571* —*Ant.* delightful, mild, nice, pleasing

sickly [*adj1*] *not healthy* ailing, below par, bilious, cranky, delicate, diseased, down, dragging, faint, feeble, indisposed, infirm, in poor health, lackluster, laid-low, languid, low, mean, off-color*, out of action*, out of shape*, pallid, peaked, peaky, pining, poorly, rocky, run-down, seedy, sickish, unhealthy, wan, weak; CONCEPT *314* —*Ant.* fine, healthy, hearty, well, wholesome

sickly [*adj2*] *revolting* bilious, cloying, insalubrious, mawkish, morbid, morose, nauseating, noisome, noxious, sick, unwholesome; CONCEPTS *537,571* —*Ant.* gentle, nice

sickness [*n*] *ill or abnormal condition* affection, affliction, ailment, bug*, complaint, condition, disease, diseasedness, disorder, ill, ill health, illness, indisposition, infirmity, malady, nausea, queasiness, syndrome, unhealth, unhealthfulness, unwellness; CONCEPT *306* —*Ant.* good health, health, wholesomeness

side [*adj*] *minor; flanking* ancillary, incidental, indirect, lateral, lesser, marginal, not the main, oblique, off-center, postern, roundabout, secondary, sidelong, sideward, sideways, sidewise, skirting, subordinate, subsidiary, superficial; CONCEPT *575* —*Ant.* important, major, serious

side [*n1*] *edge, exteriority of object* aspect, attitude, border, bottom, boundary, direction, disposition, division, elevation, face, facet, flank, front, hand, haunch, jamb, lee, limit, loin, margin, part, perimeter, periphery, posture, quarter, rear, rim, sector, stance, stand, surface, top, verge, view, wing; CONCEPTS *513,835* —*Ant.* extremity, inside, middle, torso

side [n2] *point of view* angle, appearance, aspect, belief, direction, facet, hand, light, opinion, outlook, phase, position, slant, stand, standpoint, viewpoint; CONCEPT 689

side [n3] *opposing person or view* behalf, belligerent, camp, cause, combatant, competition, contestant, crew, enemy, faction, foe, interest, part, party, rival, sect, team; CONCEPTS *301,365*

sidekick [n] *companion* accompaniment, accomplice, aide, ally, amigo, assistant, associate, buddy, chum, cohort, colleague, comrade, consort, coworker, crony, friend, pal, partner, playmate; CONCEPT 423

sideline [n] *secondary occupation* distraction, diversion, hobby, leisure activity, leisure pursuit, moonlighting, recreation, second job, side job, side project, subsidiary; CONCEPT 360

sidesplitting [adj] *extremely funny* amusing, entertaining, farcical, good-humored, hilarious, hysterical, joking, knee-slapper*, silly, slapstick, uproarious, witty; CONCEPTS *267,529,537*

sidestep [v] *dodge* avoid, bypass, dance around*, ditch, duck, elude, escape, evade, fudge*, get around, get out of, give the slip*, go around, juke, pussyfoot*, put the move on*, shake, shake off*, shirk, skip out on*, skirt, weasel*; CONCEPTS *59,102*

sidetrack [v] *divert* alter, avert, change, deflect, digress, redirect, swerve, switch, veer; CONCEPTS *187,213*

sideways [adv] *to the edge, exteriority* alongside, aside, aslant, aslope, athwart, broadside, crabwise, edgeways, indirectly, laterally, obliquely, side by side, sidelong, sidewards, slanting, slantingly, slantwise, sloping, to the side; CONCEPTS *581,583*

sift [v] *take out residue; remove impurities* analyze, clean, colander, comb, delve into, dig into, drain, evaluate, examine, explore, fathom, filter, go into, go through, grade, inquire, investigate, look into, pan, part, pore over, probe, prospect, purify, riddle, screen, scrutinize, search, separate, sieve, size, sort, strain, winnow; CONCEPTS *103,165* —*Ant.* put in

sigh [v1] *breathe out heavily* blow, complain, cry, exhale, gasp, grieve, groan, howl, lament, moan, murmur, pant, respire, roar, sob, sorrow, sough, suspire, wheeze, whine, whisper, whistle; CONCEPT 163

sigh [v2] *long for* ache, crave, dream, hanker, hunger, languish, lust, mourn, pine, suspire, thirst, yearn; CONCEPT 20 —*Ant.* dislike, hate

sight [n1] *ability to perceive with eyes* afterimage, appearance, apperception, apprehension, eye, eyes, eyeshot, eyesight, field of vision, ken, perception, range of vision, seeing, view, viewing, visibility, vision; CONCEPT 629 —*Ant.* blindness

sight [n2] *spectacle* display, exhibit, exhibition, outlook, pageant, parade, point of interest, scene, show, view, vista; CONCEPTS *261,293*

sight [n3] *horrifying person or thing* blot, eyesore, fright, mess, monstrosity, ogre, ogress, scarecrow, slob, spectacle, tramp; CONCEPTS *412,513* —*Ant.* beauty

sight [v] *see* behold, discern, distinguish, eyeball*, make out*, observe, perceive, spot, view, witness; CONCEPT 626 —*Ant.* be blind

sign [n1] *indication, evidence* assurance, augury, auspice, badge, beacon, bell, caution, clue, divination, flag, flash, foreboding, foreknowledge, foreshadowing, foretoken, forewarning, gesture, giveaway, handwriting on wall*, harbinger, herald, high sign*, hint, light, manifestation, mark, nod, note, omen, portent, precursor, prediction, premonition, presage, presentiment, prognostic, proof, signal, suggestion, symbol, symptom, token, trace, vestige, warning, wave, whistle, wink; CONCEPTS *274,529,673,689*

sign [n2] *document with information; symbol* badge, board, character, cipher, crest, device, emblem, ensign, guidepost, insignia, logo, mark, notice, placard, proof, representation, signboard, signpost, symbolization, token, type, warning; CONCEPTS *271,284*

sign [v1] *write name* acknowledge, authorize, autograph, confirm, endorse, initial, ink, inscribe, put John Hancock on*, put John Henry on*, rubber-stamp*, set one's hand to*, signature, subscribe, witness; CONCEPT 79

sign [v2] *motion to another* beckon, express, flag, gesticulate, gesture, indicate, motion, signal, signalize, signify, use sign language, wave; CONCEPT 74

signal [adj] *extraordinary, outstanding* arresting, arrestive, characteristic, conspicuous, distinctive, distinguished, eminent, exceptional, eye-catching, famous, illustrious, individual, marked, memorable, momentous, notable, noteworthy, noticeable, peculiar, prominent, pronounced, remarkable, renowned, salient, significant, striking; CONCEPTS *568,574* —*Ant.* insignificant, unexceptional, unimpressive, unnoteworthy

signal [n] *indication; authorization* alarm, alert, beacon, bleep, blinker, cue, flag, flare, gesture, go-ahead*, green light*, high sign*, indicator, mark, Mayday*, movement, nod, okay*, omen, sign, SOS*, tocsin, token, wink; CONCEPTS *74,284,529,685*

signal [v] *indicate; give a sign to* beckon, communicate, flag, flash, gesticulate, gesture, motion, nod, semaphore, sign, signalize, warn, wave, wink; CONCEPT 74

significance [n1] *meaning* acceptation, bottom line*, connotation, drift, force, heart, implication, import, intendment, kicker*, meat*, message, name of the game*, nature of the beast*, nitty-gritty*, nub, nuts and bolts*, point, punch line*, purport, score, sense, significancy, signification, stuff, understanding; CONCEPT 682 —*Ant.* insignificance, meaninglessness, unimportance

significance [n2] *importance* authority, consequence, consideration, credit, excellence, gravity, import, impressiveness, influence, magnitude, matter, merit, moment, momentousness, perfection, pith, prestige, relevance, signification, virtue, weight, weightiness; CONCEPT 668 —*Ant.* insignificance, triviality, unimportance

significant [adj1] *telling, meaningful* cogent, compelling, convincing, denoting, eloquent, expressing, expressive, facund, forceful, heavy,

important, indicative, knowing, meaning, momentous, powerful, pregnant, representative,
rich, sententious, serious, sound, suggestive,
symbolic, valid, weighty; CONCEPTS 267,567
—Ant. insignificant, meaningless, unimportant

significant [adj2] important, critical big, carrying a lot of weight*, consequential, considerable, heavy, material, meaningful, momentous,
notable, noteworthy, serious, substantial, vital,
weighty; CONCEPT 568 —Ant. minor, trivial,
unimportant

signify [v1] mean, indicate add up to, announce,
bear, be a sign of, bespeak, betoken, carry, communicate, connote, convey, denote, disclose,
evidence, evince, exhibit, express, flash, imply,
import, insinuate, intend, intimate, manifest,
matter, portend, proclaim, purport, represent,
show, sign, spell, stand for, suggest, symbolize,
talk, tell, wink; CONCEPTS 55,266,682

signify [v2] be of importance be of consequence,
be of significance, carry weight, count, import,
matter, mean, weigh; CONCEPT 668

silence [n] absence of sound, speech blackout,
calm, censorship, dead air, death, dumbness,
hush, hush-hush*, inarticulateness, iron curtain*, laconism, lull, muteness, noiselessness,
peace, quiescence, quiet, quietness, quietude,
quietus, reserve, reticence, saturninity, secrecy,
sleep, speechlessness, still, stillness, sulk,
sullenness, taciturnity, uncommunicativeness;
CONCEPT 65 —Ant. clamor, communication,
noise, talk

silence [v] make or be quiet choke off*, clam,
clam up*, close up, cool it*, cut off, cut short,
dampen, deaden, decrease the volume, dry up*,
dull, dumb, dummy up*, extinguish, gag, hold
one's tongue*, hush, hush-hush*, hush one's
mouth*, keep it down*, lull, muffle, mute,
muzzle, overawe, pipe down*, quash, quell,
quiet, quiet down, quieten, say nothing, shush*,
shut up, sit on*, soft-pedal*, squelch, stifle,
still, strike dumb*, subdue, suppress, tongue-
tie*; CONCEPT 266 —Ant. be noisy, communicate, talk

silent [adj1] quiet; speechless bashful, buttoned
up*, checked, clammed up*, close, closed up,
closemouthed, curbed, dumb, dummied up*,
faint, hush, hushed, iced*, inarticulate, incoherent, inconversable, indistinct, inhibited, laconic,
mousy, mum, mute, muted, noiseless, nonvocal,
not talkative, reserved, restrained, reticent,
shy, silentious, soundless, still, struck dumb,
taciturn, tongue-tied, unclear, uncommunicative, unheard, unsociable, unspeaking, voiceless, wordless, zipped*; CONCEPT 594 —Ant.
clamorous, communicative, noisy, talkative

silent [adj2] understood, implied aphonic,
implicit, indescribable, inexpressible, nameless,
tacit, unexpressed, unpronounced, unspoken,
unuttered, unvoiced, wordless; CONCEPT 267
—Ant. explicit, tangible

silhouette [n] outline contour, delineation, etching, figuration, form, likeness, line, lineament,
lineation, portrait, profile, shade, shadow, shape;
CONCEPTS 259,625 —Ant. body

silky [adj] very smooth; like satin cottony, delicate, glossy, like silk, luxurious, plush, satiny,
silk, silken, sleek, soft, tender, velvety; CONCEPT
606 —Ant. rough

silly [adj] absurd, giddy, foolish asinine, balmy,
brainless, childish, crazy, dippy*, dizzy*,
empty, empty-headed*, fatuous, featherbrained*, flighty, foolhardy, frivolous, harebrained*, idiotic, ignorant, illogical, immature,
imprudent, inane, inappropriate, inconsistent,
irrational, irresponsible, ludicrous, meaningless,
muddle-headed*, nitwitted, nonsensical, pointless, preposterous, puerile, ridiculous, senseless,
sheepheaded*, simple, simpleminded, stupid,
unintelligent, unreasonable, unwise, vacuous,
witless; CONCEPTS 401,403,542 —Ant. mature,
mundane, practical, sensible, serious, wise

silver [adj] shiny gray in color argent, argentate,
bright, lustrous, pale, pearly, plated, resplendent, silvered, silvery, sterling, white; CONCEPT
618

similar [adj] very much alike agnate, akin,
allied, analogous, coincident, coincidental,
coinciding, collateral, companion, comparable,
complementary, congruent, congruous, consonant, consubstantial, correlative, corresponding,
homogeneous, identical, in agreement, kin,
kindred, like, matching, much the same, parallel, reciprocal, related, resembling, same, twin,
uniform; CONCEPTS 487,573 —Ant. alien,
different, dissimilar, opposite, unalike, unlike

similarity [n] likeness, correspondence affinity,
agreement, alikeness, analogy, approximation,
association, closeness, coincidence, collation,
community, comparability, comparison, concordance, concurrence, conformity, congruence, congruity, connection, correlation, dead
ringer*, harmony, homogeneity, identity, interrelation, kinship, likes of, look-alike, parallel,
parallelism, parity, peas in a pod*, proportion,
reciprocity, relation, relationship, resemblance,
sameness, semblance, simile, similitude, syn-
onymity, two of a kind*; CONCEPT 670 —Ant.
difference, dissimilarity, opposition, unlikeness

simmer [v] boil, smolder be agitated, be angry,
be tense, be uptight*, bubble, burn, churn, cook,
effervesce, ferment, fizz, fret, fricassee, fume,
parboil, rage, seethe, smart, sparkle, stew, stir,
warm; CONCEPTS 35,170,410 —Ant. freeze

simple [adj1] clear, understandable; easy
child's play*, cinch*, clean, easy as pie*,
effortless, elementary, facile, incomplex, intelli-
gible, light, lucid, manageable, mild, no problem*, no sweat*, not difficult, picnic*, piece
of cake*, plain, quiet, self-explanatory, simple
as ABC*, smooth, snap*, straightforward, transparent, uncomplicated, uninvolved, unmistakable, untroublesome, walkover*; CONCEPT 529
—Ant. complex, complicated, convoluted, difficult, exacting, intricate, unclear, unintelligible

simple [adj2] uncluttered, natural absolute,
austere, classic, clean, discreet, elementary,
folksy, homely, homey, humble, inelaborate,
lowly, mere, modest, not complex, open and
shut*, plain, pure, pure and simple*, rustic,
sheer, single, Spartan, unadorned, unadulterated, unaffected, unalloyed, unblended,
uncombined, uncomplicated, uncompounded,
undecorated, unelaborate, unembellished,
unfussy, unmitigated, unmixed, unornamented,
unostentatious, unpretentious, unqualified,
vanilla*; CONCEPTS 562,589 —Ant. cluttered,
decorated, embellished, jumbled, ornate

simple [adj3] *childlike, innocent* amateur, artless, bald, basic, childish, direct, frank, green, guileless, honest, ingenuous, naive, naked, natural, plain, sincere, square, stark, trusting, unaffected, unartificial, undeniable, unexperienced, unpretentious, unschooled, unsophisticated, unstudied, unvarnished; CONCEPTS 267,401,542 —*Ant.* mature, older, sophisticated

simple [adj4] *feeble-minded; not intelligent* amateur, asinine, backward, brainless, credulous, dense, dimwitted, dull, dumb, fat, feeble, foolish, green*, gullible, half-witted, idiotic, ignorant, illiterate, imbecile, inane, inexperienced, inexpert, insensate, mindless, moronic, nitwitted, obtuse, senseless, shallow, silly, simple-minded, slow, soft, soft-headed*, stupid, thick, uneducated, unintelligent, witless; CONCEPT 402 —*Ant.* aware, intelligent, on-the-ball, smart

simpleminded [adj] *unsophisticated* brainless, childlike, clueless, crude, dumb, feeble-minded, idiotic, ignorant, moronic, naive, slow, stupid, uncomplicated, unschooled, unstudied, untutored, unworldly; CONCEPTS 401,548,562

simpleton [n] *fool* birdbrain*, blockhead*, bonehead*, boob*, buffoon, clod*, clown, dimwit*, dolt*, dope*, dunce, dunderhead*, fathead*, idiot, ignoramus, imbecile, jerk*, lamebrain*, lunkhead*, moron, nitwit, numskull*, oaf, stooge*; CONCEPTS 412,423

simplicity [n] *absence of complication, sophistication* artlessness, candor, chastity, clarity, classicality, clean lines, clearness, directness, ease, easiness, elementariness, guilelessness, homogeneity, ingenuousness, innocence, integrity, lack of adornment, modesty, monotony, naiveté, naturalness, obviousness, openness, plainness, primitiveness, purity, restraint, severity, singleness, straightforwardness, uniformity, unity; CONCEPTS 633,655,663 —*Ant.* complexity, complication, difficultness, difficulty

simplify [v] *make easy, intelligible* abridge, analyze, boil down, break down, break it down, chasten, clarify, clean it up*, clean up, clear up, cut down, cut the frills*, decipher, disentangle, disinvolve, draw a picture*, elucidate, explain, facilitate, get down to basics*, get to the meat*, hit the high spots*, interpret, lay out, let daylight in*, let sunlight in*, make clear, make perfectly clear, make plain, order, put in a nutshell*, put one straight*, reduce, shorten, spell out, streamline, unscramble; CONCEPTS 57,110,261 —*Ant.* complicate, confuse, make difficult

simply [adv1] *plainly, clearly* artlessly, candidly, commonly, directly, easily, frankly, guilelessly, honestly, ingenuously, intelligibly, matter-of-factly, modestly, naturally, openly, ordinarily, quietly, sincerely, straightforwardly, unaffectedly, unpretentiously, without any elaboration; CONCEPTS 544,562 —*Ant.* difficultly

simply [adv2] *merely* barely, but, just, only, purely, solely, utterly; CONCEPTS 544,557

simply [adv3] *absolutely, completely* in fact, altogether, really, totally, unreservedly, utterly, wholly; CONCEPT 531 —*Ant.* incompletely, indefinitely

simulate [v] *pretend, imitate* act, act like, affect, ape, assume, bluff, borrow, cheat, concoct, copy, counterfeit, crib*, deceive, disguise, dissemble, do, do a take-off*, do like*, equivocate, exaggerate, fabricate, fake, favor, feature, feign, fence, gloss over, invent, knock off*, lie, lift, make believe, mimic, mirror, misrepresent, phony, pirate, play, playact, pose, prevaricate, put on*, put on an act*, replicate, reproduce, resemble, steal; CONCEPTS 59,63,111,171 —*Ant.* be real

simulation [n] *imitation* carbon copy, clone, copy, counterfeit, duplicate, duplication, facsimile, fake, image, likeness, match, mirroring, paralleling, reflection, replica, reproduction, sham; CONCEPTS 171,260,716

simultaneous [adj] *happening at about the same time* accompanying, agreeing, at the same time, coetaneous, coeval, coexistent, coexisting, coincident, coinciding, concurrent, concurring, contemporaneous, contemporary, dead heat*, in sync*, synchronal, synchronic, synchronous, with the beat*; CONCEPTS 548,799 —*Ant.* asynchronous, different, divided, following, preceding, separate

sin [n] *illegal or immoral action* anger, covetousness, crime, damnation, debt, deficiency, demerit, disobedience, envy, error, evil, evil-doing, fault, gluttony, guilt, immorality, imperfection, iniquity, lust, misdeed, offense, peccability, peccadillo, peccancy, pride, shortcoming, sinfulness, sloth, tort, transgression, trespass, ungodliness, unrighteousness, veniality, vice, violation, wickedness, wrong, wrongdoing, wrongness; CONCEPTS 101,645 —*Ant.* behavior, goodness, morality

sin [v] *commit illegal or immoral action* backslide*, break commandment, break law, cheat, commit crime, deviate, do wrong, err, fall, fall from grace*, go astray*, lapse, live in sin, misbehave, misconduct, offend, sow wild oats*, stray, take the primrose path*, transgress, trespass, wallow in the mire*, wander; CONCEPTS 101,375,645 —*Ant.* behave, comply, obey

sincere [adj] *straightforward, honest* aboveboard, actual, artless, bona fide, candid, dead-level*, dear, devout, earnest, faithful, forthright, frank, genuine, guileless, heartfelt, honest to God*, like it is*, meant, natural, no fooling*, no-nonsense*, on the level*, on the line*, on up and up*, open, outspoken, plain, pretensionless, real, regular, righteous, saintly, serious, square*, sure enough, true, true-blue*, trustworthy, twenty-four carat*, unaffected, undesigning, undissembled, unfeigned, unpretentious, up-front*, wholehearted; CONCEPTS 267,401,542 —*Ant.* dishonest, insincere, tricky, untrustworthy

sincerely [adv] *seriously, honestly* aboveboard, candidly, deeply, earnestly, frankly, from bottom of heart, genuinely, in all conscience, in all sincerity, ingenuously, in good faith, naturally, profoundly, really, truly, truthfully, wholeheartedly, without equivocation; CONCEPTS 267,582 —*Ant.* dishonestly, untruthfully

sincerity [n] *straightforwardness, honesty* artlessness, bona fides, candor, earnestness, frankness, genuineness, good faith, goodwill, guilelessness, heart, honor, impartiality, innocence, justice, openness, probity, reliability, seriousness, sincereness, singleness, trustworthiness, truth, truthfulness, veracity, wholeheartedness; CONCEPTS *633,657* —*Ant.* dishonesty, insincerity, untrustworthiness

sinewy [adj] *stringy, tough* athletic, brawny, fibrous, firm, hard, leathery, muscular, powerful, strong, sturdy, vigorous; CONCEPTS *314, 485,489,490*

sinful [adj] *immoral, criminal* amiss, bad, base, blamable, blameful, blameworthy, censurable, corrupt, culpable, damnable, demeritorious, depraved, disgraceful, erring, evil, guilty, iniquitous, irreligious, low, morally wrong, reprehensible, reprobate, shameful, ungodly, unholy, unregenerate, unrighteous, vicious, vile, wicked, wrong; CONCEPTS *545,548* —*Ant.* honest, moral, righteous, upright

sing [v1] *carry a tune with one's voice* belt out*, burst into song*, buzz*, canary*, cantillate, carol, chant, chirp, choir, croon, descant, duet, groan*, harmonize, hum, hymn, intone, lift up a voice*, line out*, lullaby, make melody*, mouth, pipe, purr*, resound, roar, serenade, shout, singsong, solo, trill, troll, tune, vocalize, wait, warble, whine, whistle, yodel; CONCEPTS *47,77,292* —*Ant.* be quiet

sing [v2] *tattle on someone* betray, blow the whistle*, fink*, inform, peach*, rat*, snitch*, spill the beans*, talk, turn in; CONCEPTS *60,317* —*Ant.* conceal

singe [v] *burn* blacken, blaze, brand, brown, cauterize, char, cook, flame, ignite, incinerate, parch, scald, scorch, sear, toast, torch; CONCEPT *249*

singer [n] *person who can carry a tune* accompanist, artist, artiste, chanter, chanteuse, choralist, chorister, crooner, diva, intoner, melodist, minstrel, musician, nightingale, serenader, soloist, songbird, songster, troubadour, vocalist, voice, warbler, yodeler; CONCEPT *352*

single [adj] *alone, distinct* distinguished, especial, exceptional, exclusive, individual, indivisible, isolated, lone, loner, not general, not public, odd, one, only, original, particular, peerless, personal, private, rare, restricted, secluded, separate, separated, simple, singled-out, singular, sole, solitary, special, specific, strange, unalloyed, unblended, uncommon, uncompounded, undivided, unique, unitary, unmixed, unrivaled, unshared, unusual, without equal; CONCEPTS *564,577,762* —*Ant.* combined, double, mixed, together, united

single [adj2] *not married* bachelor, companionless, divorced, eligible, free, living alone, loner, separated, sole, solo, spouseless, unattached, unfettered, unmarried, unwed; CONCEPT *555* —*Ant.* married, together, wed, wedded

single-handed [adj] *unassisted* alone, by oneself, independent, on one's own, solitary, solo, unaided; CONCEPTS *577,583*

singles bar [n] *dating bar* bar, club, cocktail lounge, lounge, meat market*, nightclub, pickup joint*, pub; CONCEPTS *325,439*

singly [adv] *individually* apart, independently, one at a time, one by one, particularly, respectively, separately, severally; CONCEPT *577* —*Ant.* together

singular [adj] *unique, odd* atypical, avant-garde, bizarre, breaking new ground*, conspicuous, cool*, curious, eccentric, eminent, exceptional, extraordinary, loner, noteworthy, original, outlandish, out-of-the-way, outstanding, peculiar, prodigious, puzzling, queer, rare, remarkable, special, strange, uncommon, unimaginable, unordinary, unparalleled, unprecedented, unthinkable, unusual, unwonted, weird; CONCEPT *564* —*Ant.* normal, ordinary, regular, usual

singular [adj2] *alone, separate* certain, definite, discrete, exclusive, individual, one, only, particular, respective, single, sole, solitary, solo, unique, unrepeatable; CONCEPT *577* —*Ant.* attached, combined, mixed, together

sinister [adj] *nasty, menacing* adverse, apocalyptic, bad, baleful, baneful, blackhearted, corrupt, deleterious, dire, disastrous, dishonest, disquieting, doomful, evil, foreboding, harmful, hurtful, ill-boding, inauspicious, injurious, lowering, malefic, malevolent, malign, malignant, mischievous, obnoxious, ominous, pernicious, perverse, poisonous, portentous, threatening, unfavorable, unfortunate, unlucky, unpropitious, woeful; CONCEPTS *401,548,571* —*Ant.* benevolent, kind, nice

sink [v1] *fall in, go under* bore, bring down, capsize, cast down, cave in, couch, decline, demit, depress, descend, dig, dip, disappear, drill, drive, droop, drop, drown, ebb, engulf, excavate, fall, flounder, force down, founder, go down, go to the bottom, immerse, lay, let down, lower, overturn, overwhelm, plummet, plunge, put down, ram, regress, run, sag, scuttle, set, settle, shipwreck, slope, slump, stab, stick, stoop, submerge, subside, swamp, thrust, tip over, touch bottom, wreck; CONCEPTS *181,213* —*Ant.* float, rise

sink [v2] *fall, decrease* abate, collapse, diminish, drop, lapse, lessen, relapse, retrogress, slip, slump, subside, wane; CONCEPTS *698,776* —*Ant.* grow, increase, rise

sink [v3] *deteriorate* decay, decline, decrease, degenerate, depreciate, descend, die, diminish, disimprove, disintegrate, dwindle, fade, fail, flag, go downhill*, lessen, retrograde, rot, spoil, waste, weaken, worsen; CONCEPTS *469, 698* —*Ant.* increase, rise, strengthen

sink [v4] *be humble or humbled* abase, bemean, be reduced to, cast down, debase, degrade, demean, humiliate, lower, stoop, succumb; CONCEPTS *7,19,35* —*Ant.* brave, fight

sinuous [adj] *winding, twisting* anfractuous, circuitous, coiling, convoluted, crooked, curved, curvy, deviative, devious, flexuous, indirect, meandering, meandrous, serpentine, snaky*, supple, tortuous, twisting and turning*, undulating, vagrant; CONCEPT *581* —*Ant.* straight, untwisted, unwinding

sip [v] *drink slowly* drink in, extract, imbibe, partake, quaff, sample, savor, sup, swallow, taste, toss; CONCEPT *169* —*Ant.* down, slurp

sissy [n] *weakling* baby, chicken*, coward, cream puff*, crybaby, daisy*, jellyfish*, milksop, momma's boy*, namby-pamby, pansy, pantywaist*, pushover, wimp*, wuss*, yellow belly*; CONCEPTS *412,423*

sister [n] *female sibling* blood sister, kin, kinsperson, relation, relative, twin; CONCEPTS *414,415*

sit [v1] *rest on one's behind* bear on, be seated, cover, ensconce, give feet a rest*, grab a chair*, have a place, have a seat, hunker*, install, lie, park*, perch*, plop down*, pose, posture, put it there*, relax, remain, rest, seat, seat oneself, settle, squat, take a load off*, take a place, take a seat; CONCEPTS 154,201 —Ant. stand

sit [v2] *hold a meeting* assemble, be in session, come together, convene, deliberate, hold an assembly, meet, officiate, open, preside; CONCEPTS 324,384 —Ant. cancel

site [n] *place of activity* fix, ground, habitat, hangout, haunt, home, lay, layout, locale, locality, location, locus, mise en scène, plot, point, position, post, range, scene, section, situation, slot, spot, station, wherever, X marks the spot*; CONCEPT 198

sit-in [n] *protest* complaint, demonstration, fast, grievance, love-in*, march, peace march, rally, revolt, riot, strike, walkout; CONCEPTS 52,54, 261,300

sit tight [v] *be patient, wait* anticipate, bide one's time*, cool it*, fill time, hang around*, hang out, hold on, hold the phone*, keep your shirt on*, lie in wait*, lie low*, linger, mark time*, put on hold*, stall, stand by, stay put*, stick around*; CONCEPTS 210,681

situate [v] *locate* establish, fix, park, place, position, put, put in place, set, settle, stand; CONCEPT 226

situated [adj] *located* established, fixed, occupying, parked, placed, planted, positioned, set, settled, stationed; CONCEPT 488

situation [n1] *place of activity* bearings, direction, footing, latitude, locale, locality, location, locus, longitude, position, post, seat, setting, site, spot, stage, station, where, whereabouts; CONCEPT 198

situation [n2] *circumstances, status* ballgame*, bargain, capacity, case, character, condition, footing*, how things stack up*, like it is*, mode, picture, place, plight, position, posture, rank, scene, size of it*, sphere, stage, standing, standpoint, state, state of affairs, station, status quo*; CONCEPTS 388,696

situation [n3] *employment status* appointment, berth, billet, capacity, connection, employment, engagement, hire, job, office, place, placement, position, post, profession, spot, trade; CONCEPTS 351,360,668

sixth sense [n] *intuition* clairvoyance, divination, ESP*, extrasensory perception, feeling, foreknowledge, gut feeling*, instinct, perception, premonition, second sight*, vibes; CONCEPTS 409,689

sizable [adj] *considerable, large* ample, big, burly, capacious, comprehensive, decent, decent-sized, extensive, good, goodly, great, gross, hefty, husky, jumbo*, largish, major, massive, ponderous, respectable, sensible, spacious, strapping, substantial, tidy, voluminous, whopping*; CONCEPT 781 —Ant. inadequate, inconsiderable, insufficient, little, short, small, tiny

size [n] *extent or bulk of some dimension* admeasurement, amount, amplitude, area, bigness, body, breadth, caliber, capaciousness, capacity, content, diameter, dimensions, enormity, extension, extent, greatness, height, highness, hugeness, immensity, intensity, largeness, length, magnitude, mass, measurement, proportion, proportions, range, scope, spread, stature,

stretch, substance, substantiality, tonnage, vastness, volume, voluminosity, width; CONCEPTS 730,792

sizzle [v] *hiss, fry* broil, brown, buzz, cook, crackle, fizz, fizzle, frizzle, grill, roast, sear, sibilate, spit, sputter, swish, wheeze, whisper, whiz; CONCEPTS 65,170

skate [v] *slide* coast, flow, glide, glissade, ice skate, roller skate, sail along, skim; CONCEPTS 150,152

skedaddle [v] *flee* blow*, bolt, clear out, dart, dash, decamp, expedite, fly, fly the coop*, get a move on*, go like lightning, hasten, hightail it*, hurry, hurry up, hustle, leave, make haste, make oneself scarce*, make time*, make tracks*, move, move fast, race, run, rush, scamper, scat, scoot, scurry, shake a leg*, speed, split, spur, step on it*, take off, vamoose, whiz, zip; CONCEPTS 102,150,195, 234

skeleton [n] *structure of bones in animate being or supports in an object* bones, bony structure, cage, design, draft, frame, framework, osteology, outline, scaffolding, sketch, support; CONCEPTS 393,733 —Ant. carcass

skeptic [n] *person who is leery, unbelieving* agnostic, apostate, atheist, cynic, disbeliever, dissenter, doubter, doubting Thomas*, freethinker, heathen, heretic, infidel, materialist, misanthrope, misbeliever, nihilist, pagan, pessimist, profaner, questioner, rationalist, scoffer, unbeliever; CONCEPTS 361,423 —Ant. believer, devotee, disciple

skeptical [adj] *disbelieving, leery* agnostic, aporetic, cynical, dissenting, doubtful, doubting, dubious, freethinking, hesitating, incredulous, mistrustful, questioning, quizzical, scoffing, show-me*, suspicious, unbelieving, unconvinced; CONCEPT 403 —Ant. believing, devoted, undoubting

skepticism [n] *doubt* agnosticism, apprehension, disbelief, distrust, dubiety, dubiousness, faithlessness, hesitation, indecision, lack of confidence, leeriness, questioning, suspicion, uncertainty; CONCEPTS 21,410,689, 690

sketch [n] *drawing, outline* account, adumbration, aperçu, blueprint, cartoon, chart, compendium, configuration, copy, delineation, depiction, description, design, diagram, digest, doodle, draft, figuration, figure, form, illustration, likeness, monograph, painting, picture, piece, plan, portrayal, précis, report, representation, rough, shape, skeleton, summary, survey, syllabus, version, vignette; CONCEPTS 268, 283,625

sketch [v] *draw, outline* adumbrate, block out*, blueprint*, chalk, characterize, chart, delineate, depict, describe, design, detail, develop, diagram, doodle, draft, lay out*, line, map out, paint, plan, plot, portray, represent, rough out*, skeleton, skeletonize, trace; CONCEPTS 36,174

sketchy [adj] *rough, incomplete* coarse, crude, cursory, defective, depthless, faulty, imperfect, inadequate, insufficient, introductory, outline, perfunctory, preliminary, scrappy, shallow, skimpy, slight, superficial, uncritical, unfinished, vague; CONCEPT 531 —Ant. complete, detailed, finished, full

si
sk

skew [v] *distort* alter, bend, bias, change, color, contort, curve, doctor*, fake, falsify, fudge*, misrepresent, misshape, slant, throw off balance, twist, warp; CONCEPTS *63,137,232,250*

skid [v] *slide against will* drift, glide, go into skid, move, sheer, skew, slip, slue, swerve, veer; CONCEPT *152*

skill [n] *ability, talent to do something* accomplishment, address, adroitness, aptitude, art, artistry, cleverness, clout, command, competence, craft, cunning, deftness, dexterity, dodge*, ease, experience, expertise, expertism, expertness, facility, finesse, goods*, handiness, ingenuity, intelligence, job, knack*, know-how*, line, makings, moxie*, one's thing*, profession, proficiency, prowess, quickness, readiness, right stuff*, savvy*, skillfulness, sleight, smarts*, stuff*, technique, trade, what it takes*; CONCEPTS *409,630* —*Ant.* ignorance, inability, incapability, incapacity, inexperience

skillful [adj] *able, talented* accomplished, adept, adroit, a hand at*, apt, brainy, clever, competent, cool*, crack*, crackerjack*, dexterous, experienced, expert, good, handy, into*, learned, old*, on the ball*, practical, practiced, prepared, pretty, primed, pro*, professional, proficient, quick, ready, really into*, savvy*, seasoned, sharp, skilled, smart, smooth, there*, trained, tuned in*, versant, versed, vet*, veteran, well-versed, whiz, wicked*, wised up*; CONCEPTS *402,527* —*Ant.* green, ignorant, incapable, incapacitated, inexperienced, unable, unskilled, unskillful, untalented

skim [v1] *remove the top part* brush, cream, dip, get the cream, glance, graze, ladle, ream, scoop, separate, shave, top; CONCEPT *211* —*Ant.* pour

skim [v2] *glide over quickly, lightly* brush, carom, coast, dart, float, fly, graze, kiss, ricochet, sail, scud, shoot, skate, skip, skirr, skitter, smooth along, soar, trip; CONCEPTS *150,152* —*Ant.* pour

skim [v3] *look through cursorily* browse, brush over, dip, examine, flip through, get the cream*, give the once-over*, glance, glance over, go once over lightly*, hit the high spots*, leaf through*, read, read swiftly, riff, riffle, run eye over*, scan, skip, thumb through*, turn the pages*; CONCEPTS *72,103,623* —*Ant.* pour

skimp [v] *be cheap or frugal about* be mean with, be sparing, cut corners*, make ends meet*, pinch, pinch pennies*, roll back, save, scamp, scant, scrape, screw, scrimp, slight, spare, stint, tighten one's belt*, withhold; CONCEPT *330* —*Ant.* spend, use, waste

skimpy [adj] *sparse, inadequate* deficient, exiguous, failing, insufficient, meager, miserly, niggardly, poor, scant, scanty, scrimp, scrimpy, short, shy, spare, stingy, thin, tight, unsufficient, wanting; CONCEPTS *334,762,789* —*Ant.* adequate, enough, generous, sufficient

skin [n] *outer covering, especially of animate being* bark, carapace, case, casing, coating, crust, cutis, derma, dermis, epidermis, fell, film, fur, hide, hull, husk, integument, jacket, membrane, outside, parchment, peel, pelt, rind, sheath, sheathing, shell, shuck, slough, surface, tegument, vellum; CONCEPTS *392,428,484* —*Ant.* body, core, interior, middle

skin [v] *remove outer covering* abrade, bare, bark, cast, cut off, decorticate, excoriate, exuviate, flay, gall, graze, hull, husk, lay bare, pare, peel, pull off, remove, rind, scale, scalp, scrape, shave, shed, shuck, slough, strip, trim; CONCEPTS *176,211* —*Ant.* cover

skin-deep [adj] *superficial* apparent, casual, cursory, empty, flimsy, meaningless, one-dimensional, on the surface, shallow, trivial; CONCEPTS *557,777*

skinflint [n] *cheapskate* hoarder, miser, moneygrubber*, penny-pincher*, pinchfist*, pinchpenny*, Scrooge*, tightwad; CONCEPTS *348,412,423*

skinny [adj] *very thin* angular, bony, emaciated, gaunt, lank, lanky, lean, like a rail*, malnourished, rawboned, scraggy, scrawny, skeletal, skin-and-bone*, slender, spare, twiggy, undernourished, underweight; CONCEPTS *490,491* —*Ant.* chubby, fat, heavy, large, overweight, plump, thick

skip [v1] *bounce or jump over* bob, bolt, bound, buck, canter, caper, carom, cavort, dance, flee, flit, fly, frisk, gambol, glance, graze, hippety-hop*, hop, leap, lope, make off, prance, ricochet, run, scamper, scoot, skedaddle*, skim, skirr, skitter, spring, step, tiptoe, trip; CONCEPTS *150,194*

skip [v2] *avoid, miss* cut, desert, disregard, escape, eschew, flee, leave out, miss out, neglect, omit, pass over, pass up, play hooky*, run away, skim over, split; CONCEPTS *30,681* —*Ant.* face, meet, take on

skirmish [n] *fight* altercation, argument, battle, bout, brawl, brush, clash, combat, conflict, confrontation, disagreement, dispute, encounter, engagement, feud, fisticuffs*, fracas, fray, melee, quarrel, row, ruckus, rumble, run-in*, scrap*, scuffle, strife, tiff, tussle, war; CONCEPT *106*

skirmish [v] *fight* altercate, argue, battle, bicker, brawl, clash, combat, conflict, cross swords, dispute, do battle, engage, feud, go to war, grapple, mix it up*, quarrel, scrap, scuffle, spar, struggle, tussle, wage war, war, wrangle, wrestle; CONCEPT *106*

skirt [n1] *border, edge* brim, brink, fringe, hem, margin, outskirts, perimeter, periphery, purlieus, rim, skirting, verge; CONCEPTS *484,825* —*Ant.* center, inside, interior, middle

skirt [n2] *ladies' garment that hangs from waist* culottes, dirndl, dress, hoop, kilt, midi, mini, pannier, petticoat, sarong, tutu; CONCEPT *451*

skirt [v1] *border; be on the edge* bound, define, edge, flank, fringe, hem, lie along, lie alongside, margin, rim, surround, verge; CONCEPT *751* —*Ant.* center

skirt [v2] *avoid; get around* burke, bypass, circumnavigate, circumvent, detour, dodge, duck, elude, equivocate, escape, evade, hedge, ignore, sidestep, skip, steer clear of; CONCEPTS *30,102,147* —*Ant.* face, meet, take on

skit [n] *sketch* act, parody, performance, play, satire, spoof, takeoff; CONCEPT *263*

skittish [adj] *very nervous* agitable, alarmable, capricious, changeable, combustible, dizzy*, edgy, excitable, excited, fearful, fickle, fidgety, flighty, frivolous, giddy, harebrained, high-strung*, irresponsible, jumpy, lighteaded, lively, peppy, playful, restive, scatterbrained*, sensitive, spirited, undependable, unreliable,

volative, whimsical, zippy*; CONCEPT *401*
—*Ant.* calm, collected, easy-going, laid-back,
unworried

skulk [v] *lurk; shirk* avoid, bypass, conceal
oneself, creep, crouch, dodge, elude, evade,
hide, lie in wait, prowl, pussyfoot*, sidestep,
slack, slink, snake, sneak, snoop, steal;
CONCEPTS *30,59,151,188,681*

sky [n] *Earth's atmosphere* azure, celestial
sphere, empyrean, firmament, heavens, lid*,
the blue*, upper atmosphere, vault, vault of
heaven*, welkin, wild blue yonder*; CONCEPT
437 —*Ant.* earth

skyrocket [v] *soar* arise, ascend, catapult,
escalate, go through the ceiling*, go through
the roof*, lift, rise, rocket, shoot, shoot up, take
off, tower, vault up, zoom; CONCEPTS *148,150*

skyscraper [n] *tall building* high-rise, high-
rise building, superstructure, tower; CONCEPTS
439,441

slab [n] *chunk of solid object* bar, billet, bit,
board, boulder, chip, cut, cutting, hunk, ingot,
lump, muck, piece, plate, portion, rod, slice,
stave, stick, stone, strip, wedge; CONCEPTS
471,835

slack [adj1] *loose, baggy; inactive* dull, easy,
feeble, flabby, flaccid, flexible, flimsy, inert,
infirm, laggard, lax, leisurely, limp, not taut,
passive, quaggy, quiet, relaxed, sloppy, slow,
slow-moving, sluggish, soft, supine, unsteady,
weak; CONCEPTS *485,584,589* —*Ant.* rigid,
stiff, taut, tight

slack [adj2] *lazy, negligent* asleep on the job*,
behindhand, careless, delinquent, derelict,
dilatory, disregardful, dormant, dull, easy-
going, faineant, idle, inactive, inattentive,
indolent, inert, lackadaisical, lax, lethargic,
neglectful, not busy, permissive, quiescent,
quiet, regardless, remiss, slothful, slow, slow-
moving, sluggish, stagnant, tardy; CONCEPT
538 —*Ant.* active, alert, disciplined

slack [n] *looseness, excess* give, leeway,
play, room, slackening, slowdown, slow-up;
CONCEPTS *513,807* —*Ant.* rigidity, stiffness,
tautness, tightness

slacker [n] *shirker* avoider, bum, deadbeat*,
goldbrick, good-for-nothing, goof-off*, idler,
loafer, quitter, slouch; CONCEPTS *412,423*

slack/slacken [v] *do little or nothing; loosen*
abate, decrease, diminish, dodge, drop off,
dwindle, ease, ease off, featherbed*, flag, goldbrick*, goof off*, idle, lax, lay back, lessen, let
up, lie down on job*, loose, moderate, neglect,
reduce, relax, release, shirk, slack off, slow
down, taper, tire, untighten, wane; CONCEPTS
210,681,698 —*Ant.* stiffen, tighten

slam [n1] *loud noise from impact* bang, bash,
blast, blow, boom, burst, clap, crack, crash,
ding, pound, smack, smash, whack, wham;
CONCEPTS *189,595*

slam [n2] *harsh criticism* animadversion,
aspersion, jab, obloquy, potshot*, slap*,
slur*, stricture, swipe*; CONCEPTS *52,278*
—*Ant.* compliment, flattery, praise

slam [v1] *throw or push very hard* bang, bat,
batter, beat, belt, blast, clobber, close, crash,
cudgel, dash, fling, hammer, hit, hurl, knock,
pound, shut, slap, slug, smash, strike, swat,
thump, thwack, wallop; CONCEPTS *189,208,222*

slam [v2] *criticize very harshly* attack, castigate,
damn, excoriate, flay, lambaste*, lash into*,
pan, scathe, scourge, shoot down, slap, slash,
vilify; CONCEPTS *52,54* —*Ant.* flatter, praise

slander [n] *scandalous remark* aspersion,
backbiting*, backstabbing*, belittlement,
black eye*, calumny, defamation, depreciation,
detraction, dirt*, dirty linen*, disparagement,
hit*, libel, lie, misrepresentation, muckraking,
mud*, mud-slinging*, obloquy, rap*, scandal,
slam*, slime*, smear*, tale; CONCEPTS
54,192,278 —*Ant.* glorification, nicety, praise

slander [v] *make a scandalous remark* asperse,
assail, attack, backbite*, bad-mouth*, belie,
belittle, besmirch, blacken name*, blaspheme,
blister, blot, calumniate, cast a slur on, curse,
damage, decry, defame, defile, denigrate, depreciate, derogate, detract, dishonor, disparage,
give a bad name*, hit*, hurt, injure, libel, malign, muckrake, pan*, plaster, revile, roast*, run
smear campaign*, scandalize, scorch, slam*,
sling mud*, slur, smear, smirch, sneer, strumpet,
sully, tarnish, tear down, traduce, vilify; CON-
CEPTS *54,192* —*Ant.* flatter, glorify, praise

slang [n] *casual dialect* argot, cant, colloquialism, informal speech, jargon, lingo, neologism,
patois, patter, pidgin, shoptalk, slanguage*,
street talk, vernacular, vulgarism, vulgarity;
CONCEPT *276* —*Ant.* standard

slant [n1] *angle, slope* camber, cant, declination, diagonal, grade, gradient, inclination,
incline, lean, leaning, pitch, rake, ramp, tilt;
CONCEPT *738* —*Ant.* evenness, level

slant [n2] *particular opinion* angle, attitude,
bias, direction, emphasis, judgment, leaning,
one-sidedness, outlook, point of view, predilection, predisposition, prejudice, prepossession,
sentiment, side, standpoint, view, viewpoint;
CONCEPT *689*

slant [v1] *angle off, slope* aim, bank, beam,
bend, bevel, cant, decline, descend, deviate,
direct, diverge, grade, heel, incline, lean, level,
lie obliquely, list, point, skew, splay, swerve,
tilt, tip, train, veer; CONCEPTS *201,738* —*Ant.*
even, level

slant [v2] *change to suit; distort* aim, angle,
bias, color, concentrate, direct, focus, influence,
orient, point, prejudice, train, twist, warp,
weight; CONCEPTS *63,266* —*Ant.* leave alone,
maintain

slap [n/v] *hard hit, often with hand* bang, bash,
blip, blow, box, buffet, bust, chop, clap, clout,
crack, cuff, pat, percuss, poke, potch, punch,
slam, smack, sock, spank, strike, swat, wallop,
whack, wham; CONCEPT *189*

slapdash [adj] *careless* clumsy, haphazard,
hasty, heedless, improvident, irresponsible,
lackadaisical, lax, messy, negligent, nonchalant,
reckless, slipshod, sloppy; CONCEPT *542*

slaphappy [adj] *dazed* befuddled, bewildered,
dazzled, gaga*, giddy, groggy*, hazy, punch-
drunk*, punchy*, puzzled, senile, silly, staggered, staggering, tipsy, unsteady, weak in
the knees*, weak-kneed*, wobbly, woozy;
CONCEPTS *314,480*

slash [v1] *cut* carve, chop, gash, hack, incise,
injure, lacerate, open up, pierce, rend, rip,
score, sever, slice, slit, wound; CONCEPTS *137,
176* —*Ant.* fix, mend, sew

slash [v2] *reduce greatly* abbreviate, abridge, clip, curtail, cut, cut back, cut down, drop, hack, lower, mark down, pare, retrench, shave, shorten; CONCEPTS 236,240,247 —*Ant.* increase, raise

slaughter [n] *killing* annihilation, bloodbath, bloodshed, butchery, carnage, destruction, extermination, liquidation, massacre, murder, slaying; CONCEPT 252 —*Ant.* birth

slaughter [v] *kill* butcher, crush, decimate, defeat, destroy, do in* exterminate, finish, liquidate, maim, mangle, massacre, murder, mutilate, overwhelm, rout, slay, stick, thrash, torture, total* trounce, vanquish, waste, wipe out*; CONCEPT 252 —*Ant.* bear, create, give birth

slave [n] *person who serves, often under duress* bondservant, captive, chattel, drudge, help, laborer, menial, peon, retainer, serf, servant, skivvy, subservient, thrall, toiler, vassal, victim, worker, workhorse; CONCEPT 348 —*Ant.* master

slave [v] *work very hard* be servile, drudge, grind, grovel, grub, muck, plod, skivvy, slog, toil, work fingers to bone*; CONCEPT 87 —*Ant.* be lazy

slavery [n] *state of working under duress or without freedom* bondage, bullwork, captivity, chains* constraint, drudge, drudgery, enslavement, enthrallment, feudalism, grind, helotry, indenture, labor, menial labor, moil, peonage, restraint, serfdom, serfhood, servitude, subjection, subjugation, thrall, thralldom, toil, vassalage, work; CONCEPTS 324,388 —*Ant.* mastery

slay [v] *kill* annihilate, assassinate, butcher, cut off, destroy, dispatch, do* do away with, do in*, down*, eliminate, erase, execute, exterminate, finish, hit, knock off*, liquidate, massacre, murder, neutralize, put away*, rub out*, slaughter, snuff*, waste*; CONCEPT 252 —*Ant.* bear, create, give birth

sleazebag [n] *creep* crud*, degenerate, deviant, dip*, dirtbag*, dirtball*, pervert, pig*, scum*, scumbag*, scuzzbag*, sleaze*, sleazeball*, slimebag*, slimeball*, slimebucket*, slob*, weirdo*; CONCEPT 412

sleazy [adj] *disreputable* base, broken-down, cheap, common, dilapidated, flimsy, limp, low, mean, paltry, poor, run-down, seedy, shabby, shoddy, sordid, squalid, tacky*, trashy, unsubstantial; CONCEPTS 334,485,589 —*Ant.* fine, good, nice, reputable, respectable

sled [n] *sleigh* bobsled, dogsled, horse sleigh, luge, sledge, toboggan; CONCEPTS 187,217

sleek [adj] *smooth, glossy* glassy, glistening, lustrous, polished, satin, shiny, silken, silky; CONCEPT 606 —*Ant.* dull, raised, rough, ungroomed, unkempt

sleep [n] *suspension of consciousness* bedtime, catnap, coma, dormancy, doze, dream, dullness, few z's*, forty winks*, hibernation, lethargy, nap, nod, repose, rest, sack time*, sandman*, shuteye*, siesta, slumber, slumberland*, snooze, torpidity, torpor, trance; CONCEPT 315 —*Ant.* awakening, consciousness, wakefulness

sleep [v] *suspend consciousness* bed down*, bunk*, catch a wink*, catch forty winks*, catnap, conk out*, cop some z's*, crash*, doze, dream, drop off*, drowse, fall asleep, fall out*, flop*, hibernate, hit the hay*, hit the sack*, languish, nap, nod, nod off, oversleep, relax, repose, rest, retire, sack out*, saw wood*, slumber, snooze, snore, take a nap, turn in*, yawn, zonk out*, zzz*; CONCEPT 315 —*Ant.* wake, waken

sleepless [adj] *insomniac, restless* active, alert, antsy*, anxious, bustling, edgy, fidgeting, fidgety, jumpy, nervous, on edge, strung out*, tossing and turning*, troubled, unsettled, wakeful, wide-awake, wired*, worried; CONCEPTS 403,542,584

sleepy [adj] *tired, dull* asleep, blah*, comatose, dopey*, dozy, draggy, drowsy, heavy, hypnotic, inactive, lethargic, listless, out* of it*, quiet, sleeping, sleepyhead*, slow, sluggish, slumberous, slumbersome, snoozy*, somnolent, soporific, torpid, yawning; CONCEPTS 315,539 —*Ant.* animated, awake, energetic, unsleepy

sleigh [n] *sled* bobsled, dogsled, horse sleigh, luge, sledge, toboggan; CONCEPTS 187,217

slender/slim [adj1] *thin, not heavy* attenuate, beanpole*, beanstalk*, fine, insubstantial, lean, lithe, narrow, reedy, skeleton, skinny, slight, spare, stalky, stick, svelte, sylphlike, tenuous, threadlike, trim, twiggy, willowy; CONCEPTS 490,491 —*Ant.* chubby, fat, heavy, overweight, plump, thick

slender/slim [adj2] *inadequate, flimsy* bare, deficient, faint, feeble, fragile, inconsiderable, insufficient, little, meager, poor, remote, scant, scanty, scarce, short, shy, slight, small, spare, tenuous, thin, wanting, weak; CONCEPTS 552,771 —*Ant.* adequate, reasonable, sensible, sufficient

sleuth [n] *detective* agent, bloodhound*, cop, dick*, eavesdropper, flatfoot*, gumshoe*, investigator, P.I.*, police officer, private detective, private eye, private investigator, sleuthhound, spy, tail*, tracker; CONCEPT 348

slice [n] *piece; share* allotment, allowance, bite, chop, cut, helping, lot, part, piece of pie*, portion, quota, segment, sliver, thin piece, triangle, wedge; CONCEPT 835 —*Ant.* whole

slice [v] *cut into portions, shares* carve, chiv, cleave, dissect, dissever, divide, gash, hack, incise, pierce, segment, sever, shave, shred, slash, slit, split, strip, subdivide, sunder; CONCEPTS 98,137,176 —*Ant.* combine, unite

slick [adj1] *smooth, polished* glossy, greasy, icy, lubricious, oily, oleaginous, shiny, sleek, sleeky, slippery, slithery, soapy; CONCEPT 606 —*Ant.* coarse, rough, unpolished

slick [adj2] *smart, clever* adroit, cagey, canny, deft, dextrous, foxy, glib, knowing, meretricious, plausible, professional, quick, sharp, shrewd, skillful, sly, smooth, smooth-spoken, sophisticated, specious, streetwise*, unctuous, urbane, wise; CONCEPTS 401,402 —*Ant.* amateurish, clumsy, stupid, unclever, unintelligent

slide [v] *move smoothly; move down* accelerate, coast, drift, drive, drop, fall, fall off, flow, glide, glissade, launch, move, move along, move over, propel, sag, scooch*, shift, shove, skate, skid, skim, slip, slither, slump, smooth along, spill, stream, thrust, toboggan, tumble, veer; CONCEPTS 150,152

slight [adj1] *insignificant, small* fat, feeble, inconsiderable, insubstantial, meager, minor, modest, negligible, off, outside, paltry, petty, piddling, remote, scanty, slender, slim, sparse, superficial, trifling, trivial, unessential, unimportant, weak; CONCEPTS 575,762,789 —*Ant.* big, great, important, large, significant

slight [adj2] *thin, small in build* attenuate, broomstick*, dainty, delicate, feeble, flimsy, fragile, frail, light, reedy, shadow, skeleton, skinny, slender, slim, spare, stick, twiggy; CONCEPTS 490,491 —*Ant.* chubby, fat, large, tall, thick

slight [n] *insult, disrespect* affront, brush-off, call-down, cold shoulder*, contempt, cut, discourtesy, disdain, disregard, inattention, indifference, kick, neglect, put-down*, rebuff, rejection, slap in the face*, snub; CONCEPTS 30,384,529 —*Ant.* compliment, praise, respect

slight [v] *offend, insult* affront, blink at, brush off, chill, contemn, cool*, cut*, despise, discount, disdain, disparage, disregard, fail, flout, forget, give the brush*, give the cold shoulder to*, ignore, make light of, neglect, not give time of day*, omit, overlook, pooh-pooh*, reject, scoff, scorn, show disrespect, shrug off, skip, slur, sneeze at*, snub, treat with contempt, turn deaf ear to*, upstage; CONCEPTS 7,19,30,384 —*Ant.* compliment, flatter, praise

slightly [adv] *a little* hardly, hardly at all, hardly noticeable, imperceptibly, inappreciably, inconsiderably, insignificantly, kind of, lightly, marginally, more or less, on a small scale, pretty, scarcely any, somewhat, to some degree, to some extent; CONCEPTS 544,772 —*Ant.* a lot, considerably, greatly

slim [v] *lose weight* diet, reduce, slenderize; CONCEPT 202 —*Ant.* gain

slime [n] *muck, gelled waste* fungus, glop*, goo*, gunk*, mire, mucus, mud, ooze, scum, sludge; CONCEPT 260

slimy [adj] *oozy, gooey* clammy, glutinous, miry, mucky, mucous, muculent, muddy, scummy, viscous, yukky*; CONCEPTS 485,621 —*Ant.* dry

sling [v] *throw or hang over* bung, cast, catapult, chuck, dangle, fire, fling, heave, hoist, hurl, launch, lob, peg, pitch, raise, send, shoot, suspend, swing, toss, weight; CONCEPTS 181,222

slink/slither [v] *creep by* coast, cower, glide, glissade, go stealthily, gumshoe*, lurk, meander, pass quietly, prowl, pussyfoot*, shirk, sidle, skitter, skulk, slick, slide, slip, snake, sneak, steal, undulate; CONCEPT 151

slip [n1] *error, goof* blooper*, blunder, bungle, failure, fault, flub*, fluff*, foul-up*, gaff, howler*, imprudence, indiscretion, lapse, misdeed, misstep, mistake, muff*, omission, oversight, screw-up*, slip of the tongue*, slip-up*, trip; CONCEPT 101 —*Ant.* correction, perfection, success

slip [n2] *piece of paper* label, leaf, page, sheet, sliver, strip, tag, ticket; CONCEPTS 270,475

slip [v1] *fall; glide* drop, glissade, lose balance, lose footing, lurch, move, shift, skate, skid, slick, slide, slither, smooth along, totter, trip; CONCEPTS 150,152

slip [v2] *err* blunder, drop the ball*, flub*, fluff*, goof*, go wrong, make a mistake, miscalculate, misjudge, mistake, muff*, put foot in mouth*, slip up, stumble, trip; CONCEPT 101 —*Ant.* correct, perfect

slippery [adj1] *smooth, slick* glacé, glassy, glazed, glistening, greasy, icy, like a skating rink*, lubricious, lustrous, perilous, polished, satiny, silky, sleek, slimy, soapy, unctuous, unsafe, unstable, unsteady, waxy, wet; CONCEPT 606 —*Ant.* dry, unslippery

slippery [adj2] *uncertain, unreliable* cagey, changeable, crafty, cunning, devious, dishonest, duplicitous, elusive, evasive, false, fly-by-night*, foxy, inconstant, insecure, mutable, shifty, slick, slithery, smooth, sneaky, treacherous, tricky, two-faced*, unpredictable, unsafe, unstable, unsteady, untrustworthy, variable; CONCEPTS 401,534,535 —*Ant.* certain, definite, reliable, stable

slipshod [adj] *careless; not well done* bedraggled, botched*, disheveled, faulty, fly-by-night*, fouled-up*, haphazard, imperfect, inaccurate, inexact, junky*, loose, messed-up, messy, neglected, negligent, raunchy, screwed-up*, scrubby*, scruffy*, shabby*, shoddy*, slapdash*, sloppy, slovenly, tacky*, tattered, threadbare, unkempt, unmeticulous, unsystematic, unthorough, untidy; CONCEPTS 485,570,589 —*Ant.* careful, neat, polished, refined, well-done

slipup [n] *error* blooper, blunder, boner*, boo-boo*, bungle, faux pas, flaw, glitch, goof*, lapse, miscalculation, miscue, misjudgment, misstep, mistake, misunderstanding, oversight, screwup, slight, stumble, transgression; CONCEPTS 101,230,674,699

slit [n] *small opening, cut* aperture, breach, cleavage, cleft, crack, crevice, fissure, gash, hole, incision, rent, split, tear; CONCEPT 513 —*Ant.* closure

slit [v] *cut open* gash, incise, knife, lance, pierce, rip, sever, slash, slice, slot, split open, tear; CONCEPT 176 —*Ant.* close, mend, sew

slither [v] *slide* coast, crawl, glide, glissade, move, skate, skid, slink, slip, snake*, sneak, wriggle; CONCEPTS 150,152

sliver [n] *tiny piece, usually of wood or metal* bit, flake, fragment, paring, shaving, shred, slice, slip, snip, snippet, splinter, thorn; CONCEPTS 471,831

slobber [v] *drool* dribble, drip, drivel, froth, salivate, slabber, slaver, water at the mouth; CONCEPT 185

slog [v] *plod* bear down*, buckle down*, drag, drudge, flounder, grind, labor, lumber*, plough through*, plug, schlepp*, slave, stomp, sweat*, toil, tramp, trample, trudge; CONCEPTS 87,151

slogan [n] *motto* byword, catchphrase, catchword, expression, idiom, jingle, phrase, proverb, rallying cry*, saying, shibboleth*, trademark*, war cry*, watchword; CONCEPT 278

slop [v] *splash; make a mess* dash, drip, flounder, let run out, let run over, overflow, slosh, smear, smudge, spatter, spill, splatter, spray, wallow; CONCEPT 250 —*Ant.* clean up

slope [n] *slant, tilt* abruptness, bank, bend, bevel, bias, cant, declination, declivity, deflection, descent, deviation, diagonal, downgrade, gradient, hill, inclination, incline, lean, leaning, obliqueness, obliquity, pitch, ramp, rise, rising ground, shelf, skew, steepness, swag, sway, tip; CONCEPTS 738,757 —*Ant.* evenness, level

slope [v] *slant, tilt* angle, ascend, bank, bevel, cant, descend, dip, drop, drop away, fall, heel, incline, lean, list, pitch, rake, recline, rise,

shelve, skew, splay, tip; CONCEPTS 201,738
—*Ant.* even, level

sloppy [*adj*] *messy* awkward, bedraggled, botched, careless, clumsy, dingy, dirty, disheveled, inattentive, mediocre, muddy, not clean, poor, slapdash, slipshod, slovenly, sludgy*, slushy*, splashy*, tacky*, unkempt, unthorough, untidy, watery, wet; CONCEPTS 531,603,621 —*Ant.* clean, neat, orderly, tidy

slot [*n*] *opening, place* aperture, channel, cut, groove, hole, niche, position, recess, slit, socket, space, time, vacancy; CONCEPT 513

sloth [*n*] *laziness* do-nothingness, idleness, inactivity, indolence, inertia, lackadaisicalness, languidness, laxness, lethargy, listlessness, slackness, slothfulness, slowness, sluggishness, supineness; CONCEPTS 411,633

slothful [*adj*] *lazy* comatose, dallying, dull, idle, inactive, inattentive, indolent, inert, lack-adaisical, laggard, lagging, languid, lethargic, lifeless, listless, loafing, passive, procrastinating, slack, slow, sluggish, snoozy*, supine, tired, unenergetic; CONCEPTS 401,404

slouch [*v*] *slump over* be lazy, bend, bow, crouch, droop, lean, loaf, loll, lounge, sag, stoop, wilt; CONCEPTS 154,201 —*Ant.* straighten

slovenly [*adj*] *dirty, disordered* bedraggled, botched, careless, dingy, disheveled, disorderly, dowdy, down-at-the-heel*, frowzy*, frumpy*, grody*, grubby, grungy*, heedless, icky*, loose, messed up*, messy, mussy, negligent, pigpen*, raunchy, seedy, slack, slapdash, sleazy*, slipshod, sloppy, tacky, topsy-turvy, unfastidious, unkempt, unthorough, untidy; CONCEPTS 485,621 —*Ant.* clean, ordered, organized

slow [*adj1*] *unhurried, lazy* apathetic, crawling, creeping, dawdling, delaying, deliberate, dilatory, disinclined, dreamy, drowsy, easy, gradual, heavy, idle, imperceptible, inactive, indolent, inert, lackadaisical, laggard, lagging, leaden, leisurely, lethargic, listless, loitering, measured, moderate, negligent, passive, phlegmatic, plodding, ponderous, postponing, procrastinating, quiet, reluctant, remiss, slack, sleepy, slothful, slow-moving, sluggish, snail-like, stagnant, supine, tardy, torpid, tortoiselike; CONCEPTS 538,584,588 —*Ant.* active, busy, fast, hurried, quick, rapid

slow [*adj2*] *behind, late* backward, behindhand, belated, conservative, dead, delayed, detained, dilatory, down, draggy*, dull, gradual, hindered, impeded, inactive, lingering, long-delayed, long-drawn-out*, low, moderate, off, overdue, prolonged, protracted, reduced, slack, sleepy, sluggish, stagnant, stiff, tame, tardy, tedious, time-consuming, uneventful, unproductive, unprogressive, unpunctual; CONCEPTS 529,537, 548 —*Ant.* on cue, on time, ready, waiting

slow [*adj3*] *unintelligent* awkward, dense, dim, dimwitted, dull, dumb, dunce, imbecile, limited, moronic, obtuse, simple, slow on the uptake*, stupid, thick, unresponsive; CONCEPT 402 —*Ant.* cognizant, intelligent, smart

slow [*v*] *delay, restrict* abate, anchor it, back-water*, bog down, brake, check, choke, curb, curtail, cut back, cut down, decelerate, decrease, detain, diminish, ease off, ease up, embog, handicap, hinder, hit the brakes*, hold back, hold up, impede, keep waiting, lag, lessen, let

down flaps*, loiter, lose speed, lose steam*, mire, moderate, postpone, procrastinate, qualify, quiet, reduce, reduce speed, reef, regulate, rein in, relax, retard, retardate, set back, slacken, stall, stunt, temper, wind down; CONCEPTS 130,234,250 —*Ant.* advance, forward, push

slowdown [*n*] *slacking off; gradual decrease* arrest, deceleration, decline, delay, downtrend, downturn, drop, drop-off, falloff, freeze, inactivity, retardation, slack, slackening, slow-up, stagnation, stoppage, strike; CONCEPTS 121,130 —*Ant.* breakthrough, increase, rise, speed-up

slowpoke [*n*] *laggard* dawdler, dilly-dallyer, idler, plodder, procrastinator, slug, sluggard, snail, straggler; CONCEPTS 121,237,681

sludge [*n*] *mud* glop*, goo*, goop*, grease, gunk*, mire, muck, oil, ooze, scum, sediment, silt, slime, slop; CONCEPT 260

slug [*v*] *hit* bang, bash, bat, batter, beat, belt, box*, bump, clobber, clock*, clout, club, crack, flail, flog, hammer*, jab, knock, KO*, lambaste, let have it*, nail*, pelt, pop, pound, punch, slam, slap, smack, sock, swat, thrash, thwack, wallop, whack*, whale; CONCEPTS 189,200

slugfest [*n*] *fight* altercation, argument, battle, battle royal*, bout, brawl, clash, conflict, dispute, dogfight, donnybrook, engagement, feud, fisticuffs*, fracas, fray, free-for-all*, melee, riot, ruckus, rumble, struggle, tussle, war; CONCEPT 106

sluggish [*adj*] *dull, slow-moving* apathetic, blah*, comatose, dopey*, down, dragging, draggy*, drippy*, heavy, hebetudinous, inactive, indolent, inert, laid-back*, languid, languorous, leaden, lethargic, lifeless, listless, lumpish, mooney*, off, phlegmatic, pokey*, slack, sleepyheaded*, slothful, slow, sluggard, slumberous, stagnant, stiff, sullen, torpid, unresponsive; CONCEPTS 401,584 —*Ant.* active, alert, energetic, fast, lively, spirited

slum [*n*] *ghetto* blighted area, public squalor, run-down neighborhood, shanty town, skid row, tenement housing; CONCEPTS 335,709

slumber [*n*] *sleep* coma, dormancy, doze, drowse, forty winks*, inactivity, languor, lethargy, nap, repose, rest, sack time*, shut-eye*, snooze, stupor, torpor; CONCEPT 315 —*Ant.* awakening, consciousness, wakefulness

slump [*n*] *decline, failure* bad period, bad times, blight, blue devils*, blue funk*, bottom, bust, collapse, crash, depreciation, depression, descent, dip, downer*, downslide*, downswing*, downtrend, downturn, drop, dumps*, fall, falling-off*, funk, hard times*, letdown*, low, rainy days*, recession, reverse, rut, sag, slide, slip, stagnation, the skids*, trough; CONCEPTS 335,410,674 —*Ant.* blessing, boon, increase, success

slump [*v*] *decline, sink* bend, blight, cave in, collapse, crash, decay, deteriorate, droop, drop, fall, fall off*, go down, go downhill*, go to ruin*, hunch, keel over, loll, pitch, plummet, plunge, reach new low*, sag, slide, slip, slouch, topple, tumble; CONCEPTS 181,698,699,763 —*Ant.* ascend, increase, rise

slur [*n*] *insult* accusation, affront, animadversion, aspersion, bar sinister*, black eye*, blemish, blot, blur, brand, brickbat*, calumny, dirty dig*, discredit, disgrace, dump, expose, hit, innuendo, insinuation, knock, obloquy, odium, onus, put-down*, rap*, reflection, reproach, slam, smear, stain, stigma, stricture, zinger*; CONCEPTS 44,54,278 —*Ant.* compliment, flattery, praise

slur [v1] *insult* blacken, blemish, blister, blot, blow off*, brand, calumniate, cap, chop*, cut to the quick*, cut up*, defame, denigrate, detract, discredit, disgrace, dump on*, give a black eye*, hit where one lives*, insinuate, kick in the teeth*, libel, malign, miff, offend, push, put down*, reproach, roast*, scorch*, skin alive*, slander, slap in the face*, slight, smear*, snub, spatter, stain, tear down, traduce, vilify, zing*; CONCEPTS 7,19,44,54 —*Ant.* compliment, flatter, praise

slur [v2] *mumble words* garble, mispronounce, miss, skip, stutter; CONCEPT 47 —*Ant.* enunciate, pronounce

sly [adj] *clever, devious* arch, artful, astute, bluffing, cagey, calculating, canny, captious, conniving, covert, crafty, crooked, cunning, deceitful, deceptive, delusive, designing, dishonest, dishonorable, dissembling, double-dealing, elusive, foxy, furtive, guileful, illusory, impish, ingenious, insidious, intriguing, mean, mischievous, plotting, roguish, scheming, secret, sharp, shifty, shrewd, slick, smart, smooth, sneaking, stealthy, subtle, traitorous, treacherous, tricky, underhand, unscrupulous, wily; CONCEPTS 401,542 —*Ant.* honest, open, simple, straight, straightforward, unclever

smack [adv] *directly, exactly* accurately, bang*, clearly, just, plumb, point-blank*, precisely, right, sharp, square, squarely, straight; CONCEPT 557 —*Ant.* indirectly, inexactly, off

smack [n/v] *strike, often with hand* bang, blip, blow, box, buffet, chop, clap, clout, crack, cuff, hit, pat, punch, slap, snap, sock, spank, tap; CONCEPT 189

small [adj1] *tiny in size, quantity* baby, bantam, bitty*, cramped, diminutive, humble, immature, inadequate, inconsequential, inconsiderable, insufficient, limited, little, meager, microscopic, mini*, miniature, minuscule, minute, modest, narrow, paltry, petite, petty, picayune, piddling*, pint-sized*, pitiful, pocket-sized*, poor, puny*, runty*, scanty, scrubby, short, shrimp*, slight, small-scale, stunted, teensy*, teeny, toy, trifling, trivial, undersized, unpretentious, wee*, young; CONCEPTS 773,789 —*Ant.* big, enormous, generous, huge, immense, large

small [adj2] *unimportant* bush-league*, inadequate, inconsiderable, ineffectual, inferior, insignificant, lesser, light, limited, lower, mean, minor, minor-league*, minute, narrow, negligible, paltry, petty, secondary, set, small-fry*, small-time*, trifling, trivial, unessential; CONCEPT 575 —*Ant.* distinguished, excellent, famous, fine, important, untrivial

small [adj3] *narrow-minded, nasty* base, grudging, ignoble, illiberal, limited, little, mean, narrow, petty, selfish, set, vulgar; CONCEPT 401 —*Ant.* benevolent, broad-minded, considerate, giving, kind

small-minded [adj] *narrow-minded* biased, bigoted, conservative, illiberal, intolerant, opinionated, petty, prejudiced, selfish, short-sighted; CONCEPTS 403,542

small talk [n] *casual conversation* babble, blab*, blather, chatter, chitchat*, gossip, idle chatter, idle talk, jabber*, prattle, yakking*; CONCEPTS 274,278

small-time [adj] *minor* bush-league*, dinky*, inconsequential, inconsiderable, insignificant, low, petty, piddling, secondary, second-string*, trivial, two-bit*, unimportant; CONCEPTS 575, 773,789

smart [adj1] *intelligent* acute, adept, agile, alert, apt, astute, bold, brainy*, bright, brilliant, brisk, canny, clever, crafty, effective, eggheaded*, fresh, genius, good, impertinent, ingenious, keen, knowing, long-haired*, nervy, nimble, on the ball*, pert, pointed, quick, quick-witted, ready, resourceful, sassy, sharp, shrewd, skull, slick*, whiz*, wise; CONCEPT 402 —*Ant.* dull, stupid, unintelligent

smart [adj2] *stylish, fashionable* chic, dapper, dashing, dressed to kill*, elegant, exclusive, fine, fly*, in fashion, last word*, latest thing*, modish, natty, neat, snappy, spruce, swank, trendy, trim, well turned-out, with it*; CONCEPT 589 —*Ant.* dowdy, old, unfashionable, unstylish, worn

smart [adj3] *brisk, lively* active, bold, brazen, cracking, energetic, forward, good, jaunty, nervy, pert, quick, saucy, scintillating, spanking, spirited, sprightly, vigorous; CONCEPTS 401,542 —*Ant.* apathetic, lethargic, slow

smart [v] *hurt, pain* ache, be painful, bite, burn, prick, prickle, sting, suffer, throb, tingle; CONCEPTS 246,728 —*Ant.* assuage, help, soothe

smart-aleck [n] *wise guy* bigmouth*, know-it-all*, smart ass*, smarty-pants*, wiseacre, wiseass, wisenheimer; CONCEPT 412

smarts [n] *intelligence* acuity, acumen, alertness, aptitude, brainpower, brains*, brightness, brilliance, cleverness, competence, comprehension, gray matter*, intellect, IQ*, judgment, know-how, mind, perception, perspicacity, precocity, reason, savvy, sense, the right stuff*, understanding, what it takes*; CONCEPT 409

smash [n1] *collision; defeat* accident, bang, bash, blast, blow, boom, breakdown, breaking, breakup, burst, clap, collapse, crack, crack-up, crash, debacle, destruction, disaster, downfall, failure, pile-up, ruin, shattering, slam, smash-up, sock, wallop, welt, whack, wham, wreck; CONCEPTS 674,675

smash [n2] *great success* hit, knockout, sensation, wow*; CONCEPT 706 —*Ant.* failure, loss

smash [v1] *break into pieces* bang, belt, blast, break to smithereens*, burst, clobber, collide, crack, crash, crush, demolish, disintegrate, fracture, fragment, hit, make mincemeat of*, pound, powder, pulverize, rive, scrunch, shatter, shiver, slam, slug, splinter, squash, squish, trash, wallop; CONCEPTS 246,252 —*Ant.* fix, mend

smash [v2] *defeat, destroy* annihilate, break up, decimate, demolish, destruct, disrupt, lay in ruins*, lay waste*, overthrow, overturn, put out of action*, put out of commission*, raze, ruin, shatter, tear down, topple, trash, tumble, wreck; CONCEPTS 95,252 —*Ant.* fail, lose

smashup [n] *wreck* accident, collision, crack-up*, crash, fender bender, impact, jolt, mess, pile-up*, rear-ender*, sideswipe, total, wreckage; CONCEPTS 189,260,674

smattering [n] *small amount* basics, bit, elements, little, modicum, rudiments, smidge*, smidgen*, soupçon, tad*; CONCEPT 831

smear [v1] *rub on, spread over* apply, bedaub, besmirch, blur, coat, cover, dab, daub, defile, dirty, discolor, overlay, overspread, patch, plaster, slop, smudge, soil, spatter, spray, sprinkle, stain, sully, taint, tar, tarnish; CONCEPTS 172, 202,215

smear [v2] *tarnish a reputation* asperse, bad-mouth*, befoul, besmirch, blacken, black-guard*, blister, calumniate, defame, defile, denigrate, discolor, drag through mud*, give a black eye*, hit*, libel, malign, pan*, poor-mouth*, rap*, rip up*, scorch*, slam*, slander, sling mud*, slur, sully, taint, traduce, vilify; CONCEPTS 54,63 —Ant. honor, laud, upgrade

smear campaign [n] *mudslinging* character assassination, defamation of character, dragging one's name through the mud*, slander, whispering campaign; CONCEPTS 54,192,278

smell [n] *odor* aroma, bouquet, emanation, essence, flavor, fragrance, incense, perfume, redolence, savor, scent, spice, stench, stink, tang, trace, trail, whiff; CONCEPTS 590,599

smell [v1] *perceive with the nose* breathe, detect, discover, find, get a whiff*, identify, inhale, nose, scent, sniff, snuff; CONCEPTS 590,601,602

smell [v2] *have an odor* be malodorous, funk*, reek, smell to high heaven*, stench, stink, whiff; CONCEPT 600

smelly [adj] *having a bad odor* evil-smelling, fetid, foul, foul-smelling, funky*, high, malodorous, mephitic, noisome, olid, putrid, rancid, rank, reeking, stinking, strong, strong-smelling, whiffy*; CONCEPT 598 —Ant. good-smelling, perfumed

smidgen [n] *tiny amount* atom, chicken feed*, crumb, dab, dash, drop, fraction, fragment, grain, iota, little bit, mite, morsel, particle, pinch, scintilla, scrap, shard, shaving, shred, sliver, small amount, small bit, small quantity, speck, tad, taste, trace, wee bit*, whiff, whisper; CONCEPTS 529,831,835

smile [v] *put on a happy expression* beam, be gracious, express friendliness, express tenderness, grin, laugh, look amused, look delighted, look happy, look pleased, simper, smirk; CONCEPT 185 —Ant. frown, glower

smirk [n] *sly smile* beam, grin, leer, simper, smug look, sneer; CONCEPT 185

smog [n] *air pollution* acid rain, carbon dioxide, fog, haze, smoke, soot; CONCEPT 720

smoke [n] *fume; cigarette* butt*, cig*, exhaust, fog, gas, mist, pollution, smog, soot, vapor; CONCEPT 720

smoke detector [n] *smoke alarm* danger signal, emergency alarm, fire alarm, fire bell, heat sensor, siren; CONCEPTS 269,463

smoky [adj] *hazy, sooty* begrimed, black, burning, caliginous, dingy, fumy, gray, grimy, messy, murky, reeking, silvery, smoke-colored, smoldering, thick, vaporous; CONCEPTS 485,618 —Ant. clean, clear, unpolluted

smolder [v] *burn, simmer* boil, bubble, churn, consume, erupt, explode, ferment, fester, fulminate, fume, seethe, smoke, steam, stir; CONCEPTS 35,249 —Ant. freeze

smooch [v] *kiss* butterfly*, French*, greet, lip*, make out*, mush*, neck*, park*, peck, pucker up*, smack; CONCEPTS 185,375

smooth [adj1] *level, unwrinkled; flowing* bland, continuous, creamy, easy, effortless, equable, even, flat, fluent, fluid, flush, frictionless, gentle, glassy, glossy, hairless, horizontal, invariable, lustrous, mild, mirrorlike, monotonous, peaceful, plain, planate, plane, polished, quiet, regular, rhythmic, rippleless, serene, shaven, shiny, silky, sleek, soft, soothing, stable, steady, still, tranquil, unbroken, undeviating, undisturbed, uneventful, uniform, uninterrupted, unruffled, untroubled, unvarying, velvety; CONCEPTS 406,480,606 —Ant. broken, coarse, intermittent, irregular, rough, uneven, wrinkled

smooth [adj2] *suave in behavior* agreeable, bland, civilized, courteous, courtly, facile, genial, glib, ingratiating, mellow, mild, persuasive, pleasant, polite, slick, smarmy*, unctuous, urbane; CONCEPT 401 —Ant. coarse, rough, uncool

smooth [v1] *make level* burnish, clear, even, flatten, flush, glaze, gloss, grade, iron, lay, level, make uniform, perfect, plane, polish, press, refine, round, sand, sleek, slick, varnish; CONCEPTS 137,250 —Ant. coarsen, roughen, wrinkle

smooth [v2] *make peace* allay, alleviate, appease, assuage, calm, comfort, cool*, ease, extenuate, facilitate, iron out, mellow, mitigate, mollify, palliate, pat, pave the way*, soften, stroke, take the edge off*, take the sting out*; CONCEPTS 7,22 —Ant. aggravate, agitate, incite, irritate, upset

smother [v] *extinguish; cover, hide* asphyxiate, choke, collect, compose, conceal, control, cool, cork, douse, envelop, heap, hush up*, inundate, keep back, kill, muffle, overwhelm, quash, quell, quench, rein, repress, restrain, shower, shroud, simmer down, snuff, squelch, stamp out, stifle, strangle, suffocate, suppress, surround, throttle; CONCEPTS 130,172,188,234 —Ant. light, start, uncover

smudge [n] *dirt smear* blemish, blot, blur, macule, smut, smutch, soiled spot, spot; CONCEPT 723 —Ant. cleanliness

smudge [v] *smear, dirty* begrime, blacken, blotch, blur, daub, defile, foul, grime, mark, plaster, slop, smirch, soil, spatter, sully, taint, tarnish; CONCEPT 254 —Ant. clean

smug [adj] *pleased with oneself* complacent, conceited, egoistic, egotistical, holier-than-thou*, hotshot*, pompous, priggish, puffed-up*, self-contented, self-righteous, self-satisfied, snobbish, stuck on oneself*, stuck-up*, stuffy, superior, vainglorious; CONCEPTS 404,542 —Ant. modest, unhappy, unself-confident, unsure

smuggle [v] *transfer illegal goods* bootleg, deal, export, hide, moonshine*, pirate, push, run, run contraband*, run rum*, snake in*; CONCEPT 192

smut [n] *pornography* adult material, adult movie, bawdiness, dirt, dirty movie, erotica, filth, girlie magazine, hard-core pornography, indecency, indecent material, obscene materials, obscenity, porn, porno, porno film, sexploitation, sexually explicit material, skin flick, smut, soft-core pornography, stag film, X-rated material, X-rated movie; CONCEPTS 267,372,545

smutty [adj] obscene, vulgar bawdy, blue*, coarse, crude, dirty, filthy, foul, immoral, improper, indecent, indelicate, lewd, nasty, off-color, pornographic, prurient, racy, raunchy, raw, risqué, rough, salacious, salty, scatological, suggestive, X-rated*; CONCEPTS 267,372,545 —Ant. clean, decent, moral

snack [n] tiny meal bite, bite to eat*, break, eats*, goodies*, grub*, light meal, lunch, luncheon, midnight snack, morsel, munch*, nibble, nosh*, pickings, piece, refreshment, tea, tidbit; CONCEPTS 457,459 —Ant. meal

snafu [n] mistake blooper*, blunder, bungle, confusion, error, false step, faux pas, flub*, foul-up, goof-up, mess, miscalculation, misjudgment, misunderstanding, mix-up, oversight, screwup*, slip, slipup*; CONCEPTS 101,230,410

snag [n] complication in situation bar, barrier, blockade, brake, bug*, catch, Catch-22, clog, crimp, cropper, crunch, curb, difficulty, disadvantage, drag*, drawback, fix*, glitch, hamper, hitch, holdup*, hole*, hurdle, impediment, inconvenience, knot, obstacle, obstruction, pickle*, problem, puzzler, scrape, spot, stumbling block, the rub*, tight spot*; CONCEPTS 666,674 —Ant. advantage, convenience

snag [v] catch on something hole, nail, rip, run into, tear; CONCEPT 214

snaky [adj1] winding anfractuous, convoluted, entwined, flexuous, indirect, meandering, meandrous, serpentine, sinuous, tortuous, twisted, twisting, writhing, zigzag; CONCEPT 581 —Ant. straight, unwinding

snaky [adj2] devious, sly crafty, insidious, lurking, perfidious, slinking, sneaky, subtle, treacherous, venomous, vipery, virulent; CONCEPT 401 —Ant. forthright, honest, upfront

snap [n] easy thing to accomplish breeze*, child's play*, cinch, duck soup*, ease, easy as pie*, kid stuff*, no problem, picnic*, pie*, smooth sailing*, soft touch*, walkover*; CONCEPT 693 —Ant. difficulty

snap [v1] separate, break click, come apart, crack, crackle, fracture, give way, pop; CONCEPTS 98,246 —Ant. combine, fix

snap [v2] bite, seize bite at, catch, clutch, grab, grasp, grip, jerk, lurch, nip, snatch, twitch, yank; CONCEPTS 90,191 —Ant. free, liberate, loose

snap [v3] speak sharply bark, flare, flash, fly off the handle*, get angry, growl, grumble, grunt, jump down throat*, lash out, retort, roar, snarl, snort, take it out on*, vent, yell; CONCEPT 54

snappy [adj1] nasty, irritable cross, disagreeable, edgy, fractious, hasty, huffy, petulant, quick-tempered, snappish, tart, testy, touchy, waspish; CONCEPTS 267,401 —Ant. happy, nice, pleasant

snappy [adj2] fashionable chic, classy, dapper, dashing, fly*, in good taste, modish, natty, sharp, smart, stylish, swank*, tony*, trendy, up-to-the-minute, with style; CONCEPT 589 —Ant. old, old-fashioned, outdated, unfashionable

snappy [adj3] fast abrupt, breakneck, expeditious, fleet, harefooted, hasty, immediate, instant, on-the-spot, quick, rapid, speedy, sudden, swift, unpremeditated; CONCEPTS 588,799 —Ant. delayed, slow, sluggish

snare [n] trap allurement, bait, booby trap*, catch, come-on*, deception, decoy, enticement,

entrapment, inveiglement, lure, net, noose, pitfall, quicksand, seducement, temptation, trick, wire*; CONCEPTS 529,674 —Ant. freedom, liberation

snare [v] catch, trap arrest, bag*, corral*, decoy, enmesh, entangle, entrap, get hands on*, involve, land, lure, net, pull in, round up, seduce, seize, tempt, wire*; CONCEPTS 11,90 —Ant. free, let go, liberate, loosen

snarl [n] complication, mess chaos, clutter, complexity, confusion, disarray, disorder, entanglement, intricacy, intricateness, jam, jungle, knot, labyrinth, maze, mishmash, morass, muddle, muss, skein, swarm, tangle, web; CONCEPTS 663,666,674 —Ant. ease, order, organization, simplification

snarl [v1] grumble abuse, bark, bluster, bully, complain, fulminate, gnarl, gnash teeth, growl, mumble, murmur, mutter, quarrel, show teeth, snap, threaten, thunder, yelp; CONCEPT 77 —Ant. laugh

snarl [v2] complicate, mess up confuse, embroil, enmesh, ensnarl, entangle, entwine, involve, muck, muddle, perplex, ravel, tangle; CONCEPTS 16,158 —Ant. fix, simplify, uncomplicate

snatch [n] small part bit, fragment, piece, smattering, snippet, spell; CONCEPTS 264,832 —Ant. whole

snatch [v] grab away abduct, catch, clap hands on, clutch, collar*, gain, get fingers on*, grapple, grasp, grip, jerk, jump, kidnap, make off with, nab, nail*, pluck, pull, rescue, seize, snag, spirit away, steal, take, win, wrench, wrest, yank; CONCEPTS 90,191 —Ant. give, receive

snazzy [adj] stylish attractive, beautiful, chic, chichi*, classy, dapper, dashing, dressed to kill*, dressy, fashionable, flashy, in vogue, jazzy, nifty, now*, ritzy, sharp, slick*, smart, snappy, sophisticated, swank*, trendy, upscale, uptown, voguish; CONCEPTS 579,589

sneak [n] person who is very dishonest cheater, con artist, coward, cur, dastard, heel*, informer, louse, rascal, reptile, scoundrel, skunk*, slink*, snake*, snake in grass*, toad*, weasel*, wretch; CONCEPT 412

sneak [v] move stealthily ambush, case, cheat, cower, crawl, creep, deceive, delude, evade, glide, gumshoe*, hide, lurk, mooch, move secretly, ooze, pad, pass, prowl, pussyfoot*, secrete, shirk, sidle, skulk, slide, slink, slip, slither, sly, smuggle, snake, snook, spirit, steal, worm; CONCEPTS 151,188

sneaker [n] running shoe basketball shoe, cleat, footgear, footwear, gym shoe, hightop*, rubber-soled shoe, shoe, sneak, tennis shoe; CONCEPT 451

sneaky [adj] underhanded, dishonest base, contemptible, cowardly, deceitful, devious, disingenuous, double-dealing*, duplicitous, furtive, guileful, indirect, low, malicious, mean, nasty, recreant, secretive, shifty, slippery, sly, sneaking, snide, stealthy, surreptitious, tricky, underhand, unreliable, unscrupulous, untrustworthy, yellow*; CONCEPTS 267,401, 542 —Ant. aboveboard, candid, forthright, frank, honest

sneer [v] mock, condemn affront, belittle, burlesque, caricature, crack, curl one's lip at*, decry, deride, detract, disdain, disparage, dump, fleer, flout, gibe, gird, give Bronx cheer, grin, hold in contempt*, hold up to ridicule*, insult, jeer, jest, lampoon, laugh at, leer, look down on, put down, quip at, rally, rank out, ridicule, satirize, scoff, scorn, slam, slight, smile, sneeze at*, sniff at*, snigger, swipe, taunt, travesty, turn up one's nose*, twit, underrate; CONCEPTS 30,52,54 —Ant. compliment, praise

sneeze at [v] *disregard* blink at*, brush aside, brush away, brush off, discount, have no use for*, laugh off*, let pass*, look the other way*, overlook, pass over, pay no attention to, pay no heed to, pay no mind*, shut eyes to*, slight, snub, take lightly, take no notice of, turn a blind eye*, turn a deaf ear*; CONCEPT 30

snicker/snigger/sniggle [v] *laugh at mockingly* chortle, chuckle, giggle, guffaw, hee-haw, smirk, sneer, teehee, titter; CONCEPT 77

snide [adj] *hateful, nasty* base, cynical, disparaging, hurtful, insinuating, malicious, mean, sarcastic, scornful, sneering, spiteful, unkind; CONCEPT 401 —Ant. gentle, kind, lovable, loving, nice

sniff [v] *breathe in* detect, inhale, inspire, nose, scent, smell, snift, snuff, snuffle; CONCEPTS 601,602 —Ant. hold nose

snippy [adj] *curt* abrupt, blunt, brief, brusque, churlish, gruff, impertinent, rude, sharp, sharp-tongued, snappish, snippety; CONCEPT 267

snitch [n] *informer* betrayer, blabbermouth*, canary*, deep throat*, double-crosser, fink*, informant, narc*, nark*, rat*, sneak, snitcher, source, squealer*, stoolie*, stool pigeon*, tattler, tattletale, tipster*, turncoat, weasel*, whistle-blower; CONCEPTS 348,354,423

snitch [v1] *steal* burglarize, carry off, defraud, embezzle, heist, hold up, keep, lift*, loot, make off with*, pickpocket, pilfer, pillage, pinch*, plunder, poach, remove, rip off*, shoplift, swipe, take, walk off with*; CONCEPT 139

snitch [v2] *inform* betray, blab*, confess, give away, leak, rat on*, squeal, tattle, tell, tell on, tip, turn in; CONCEPT 60

snob [n] *person who looks down on others* braggart, highbrow, name-dropper, parvenu, pretender, smarty pants*, stiff neck*, upstart; CONCEPT 423

snobbish [adj] *stuck-up, conceited* aloof, arrogant, condescending, egotistic, haughty, high-and-mighty*, high-flown*, high-hat*, ostentatious, overbearing, patronizing, persnickety*, pompous, pretentious, putting on airs*, remote, sniffy*, snippy*, snooty*, snotty*, supercilious, superior, swanky, tony*, uppish, uppity*; CONCEPT 401 —Ant. accepting, benevolent, friendly, generous, sociable, welcoming

snoop [n] *person who noses around* busybody, butt-in*, detective, eavesdropper, ferret, gumshoe*, meddler, peeping Tom*, pragmatist, pry, pryer, quidnunc, rubberneck*, scout, sleuth, snooper; CONCEPTS 348,423

snoop [v] *nose around* busybody*, interfere, intrude, meddle, mess with, mouse*, nose, peek, peep, peer, poke, poke nose in*, pry, snook, spy, stare; CONCEPTS 216,384,623 —Ant. ignore, neglect

snooty [adj] *haughty* arrogant, cavalier*, conceited, condescending, egotistic, egotistical,

high and mighty*, hoity-toity, la-di-da*, lofty, on a high horse*, pompous, pretentious, snobbish, snotty*, stuck-up*, superior, uppity*; CONCEPT 401

snooze [n] *light sleep* catnap, doze, forty winks*, nap, siesta, slumber; CONCEPT 315 —Ant. awakening, consciousness, wakefulness

snooze [v] *sleep lightly* catnap, doze, drop off, drowse, nap, nod off*, siesta, slumber, take forty winks*; CONCEPTS 210,315 —Ant. awaken, wake up

snore [v] *make sounds when sleeping* breathe heavily, saw logs*, saw wood*, sleep, snort, snuffle, wheeze; CONCEPTS 77,315

snotty [adj] *arrogant* cheeky, cocky, conceited, fresh, haughty, high and mighty*, highfalutin'*, impertinent, know-it-all*, la-de-da*, pompous, pretentious, puffed up*, sassy, self-important, smart-alecky, smug, snippy*, snobby, snooty, stuck-up*, uppity*; CONCEPTS 401,404

snub [v] *give someone the cold shoulder* act cool*, boycott, brush off*, burr, censure, chill, cool, cut, cut dead*, disdain, disregard, duck, give the brush*, humble, humiliate, ice*, ice out*, ignore, look coldly upon, look right through*, mortify, neglect, not give time of day*, offend, ostracize, pass up, put down, put the chill on*, rebuff, scold, scorn, scratch, shame, shun, slight, slur, snob, swank, upstage; CONCEPTS 30,54,384 —Ant. be friendly, include, socialize, welcome

snug [adj] *cozy, warm* close, comfortable, comfy, compact, convenient, cushy, easeful, easy, homelike, homely, intimate, neat, restful, sheltered, snug as a bug in a rug*, soft, substantial, tight, trim, well-off; CONCEPT 485 —Ant. cold, cool, uncomfortable, uncozy

snuggle [v] *cuddle* bundle, burrow, curl up, grasp, huddle, hug, nestle, nuzzle, snug, spoon; CONCEPTS 190,201 —Ant. separate, stay away

soak [v] *drench, wet* absorb, assimilate, bathe, damp, dip, drink, drown, dunk, flood, imbrue, immerge, immerse, impregnate, infiltrate, infuse, macerate, marinate, merge, moisten, penetrate, percolate, permeate, pour into, pour on, saturate, seethe, soften, sop, souse, steep, submerge, take in, wash, water, waterlog; CONCEPT 256 —Ant. dehydrate, dry

soaked [adj] *saturated* dank, drenched, dripping, drowned, soaking, sodden, soggy, sopping, soppy, soused, water-logged, wet, wringing-wet; CONCEPT 603

soar [v] *climb, fly* arise, ascend, aspire, escalate, glide, lift, mount, rise, rocket, sail, shoot, shoot up, skyrocket, top, tower, up, uprear, wing; CONCEPTS 148,150 —Ant. land

soaring [adj] *high* aerial, ascending, climbing, elevated, flying, going through the ceiling*, going through the roof*, high-reaching, lofty, sky-high, steep, towering; CONCEPTS 779,782

sob [v] *cry hard* bawl, blub, blubber, boohoo*, break down, cry a river*, cry convulsively, cry eyes out*, howl, lament, shed tears, snivel, turn on waterworks*, wail, weep, whimper; CONCEPTS 185,410

sober [adj] *not partaking of alcohol* abstaining, abstemious, abstinent, ascetic, calm, clear-headed, cold sober*, continent, controlled, dry, moderate, nonindulgent, not drunk, on the wagon*, restrained, sedate, self-possessed, serious, steady, temperate, took the pledge*; CONCEPT 401 —*Ant.* drunk, inebriated

sober [*adj2*] *calm, peaceful; dull* abnegating, abstaining, clear-headed, cold, collected, composed, constrained, cool, dark, disciplined, dispassionate, down-to-earth*, drab, earnest, eschewing, forgoing, grave, hard-boiled*, imperturbable, inhibited, levelheaded, low-key, lucid, no-nonsense, pacific, plain, practical, quiet, rational, realistic, reasonable, reserved, restrained, sedate, serene, serious, severe, soft, solemn, somber, sound, staid, steady, subdued, toned down, unexcited, unimpassioned, unruffled; CONCEPTS 401,542 —*Ant.* excited, immoderate, irrational

sobriety [*n*] *abstinence* abstaining, abstemiousness, continence, moderation, refraining, self-restraint, soberness, teetotalism, temperance; CONCEPT 633

sobriquet [*n*] *nickname* AKA*, alias, anonym, appellation, assumed name, byname, handle*, label, moniker, nom de guerre, nom de plume, nomenclature, pen name, pet name*, professional name, pseudonym, tag*; CONCEPT 268

so-called [*adj*] *supposed* alleged, allegedly, commonly named, formal, nominal, ostensible, pretended, professed, purported, self-named, self-styled, soi-disant, itular, wrongly named; CONCEPT 552

sociable [*adj*] *friendly, outgoing* accessible, affable, approachable, close, clubby*, companionable, conversable, convivial, cordial, familiar, genial, good-natured, gregarious, intimate, neighborly, regular, social, warm; CONCEPTS 401,555 —*Ant.* introverted, snobbish, unfriendly, unkind, unsociable

social [*adj*] *public, friendly* amusing, civil, collective, common, communal, communicative, community, companionable, convivial, cordial, diverting, entertaining, familiar, general, gracious, gregarious, group, hospitable, informative, mannerly, neighborly, nice, organized, pleasant, pleasurable, polished, polite, popular, sociable, societal; CONCEPTS 536,555 —*Ant.* hermetical, private, secluded, unfriendly, unsocial

socialism [*n*] *socialist government* Bolshevism, collective ownership, collectivism, communism, Fabianism, Leninism, Maoism, Marxism, state ownerhsip; CONCEPT 301

socialite [*n*] *aristocrat* blueblood, Brahmin, deb*, debutante, gentleperson, lace curtain*, member of the upper class, noble, patrician, silk stocking, upper cruster; CONCEPT 423

socialize [*v*] *be friendly at gatherings* associate, chum with*, club*, consort, entertain, fraternize, get about, get around, get together, go out, hang around with*, hang out, hobnob, join, keep company, league, make advances, make the rounds*, mingle, mix, pal around*, run with*, tie up with*; CONCEPT 384 —*Ant.* exclude, shun

society [*n1*] *humankind, people* association, camaraderie, civilization, commonality, commonwealth, community, companionship, company, comradeship, culture, friendship, general public, humanity, jungle*, nation, population, public, rat race*, social order, world, zoo*; CONCEPTS 379,417

society [*n2*] *organization, institution* alliance, association, circle, clan, clique, club, companionship, comradeship, corporation, coterie, gang, group, guild, hookup, institute, league, network, order, outfit, ring, sodality, syndicate, tie-in*, tie-up*; union; CONCEPTS 381,387

society [*n3*] *upper class of people* aristocracy, beau monde*, beautiful people*, country set*, elite, flower*, gentry, glitterati*, haut monde, high society, jet set*, main line, patriciate, polite society, quality, smart set*, top drawer*, upper crust*, who's who*; CONCEPTS 387,388,417

sociopath [*n*] *psychopath* antisocial personality, crazy person, deranged person, insane person, lunatic, mad person, maniac, psycho*, psychotic, schizoid*; CONCEPT 412

sock [*n/v*] *hit hard* beat, belt, bop, buffet, chop, clout, cuff, ding, nail, paste, punch, slap, smack, smash, soak, whack; CONCEPT 189 —*Ant.* tap

sofa [*n*] *couch* chaise longue, chesterfield, convertible couch, davenport, daybed, divan, futon, love seat, ottoman, settee, sofa bed, window seat; CONCEPT 443

soft [*adj1*] *cushioned, squishy* bendable, comfortable, comfy, cottony, cozy, creamy, cushiony, cushy, delicate, doughy, downy, ductile, easeful, easy, elastic, feathery, fine, flabby, fleecy, fleshy, flexible, flimsy, flocculent, flowing, fluffy, fluid, formless, furry, gelatinous, impressible, limp, malleable, moldable, mushy, pappy, pithy, plastic, pliable, pulpy, quaggy, rounded, satiny, silken, silky, smooth, snug, spongy, squashy, supple, thin, velvety, yielding; CONCEPTS 488,606 —*Ant.* hard, rigid, unyielding

soft [*adj2*] *faint, temperate* ashen, balmy, bland, caressing, comfortable, cool, cushy, delicate, diffuse, dim, dimmed, dulcet, dull, dusky, gentle, hazy, lenient, light, low, low-key, mellifluous, mellow, melodious, mild, misty, murmured, muted, pale, pallid, pastel, pleasing, quiet, restful, shaded, smooth, sober, soothing, subdued, sweet, tinted, toned down, twilight, understated, wan, whispered; CONCEPTS 525,537,592,618 —*Ant.* harsh, loud, rough, severe

soft [*adj3*] *compassionate* affectionate, amiable, benign, courteous, easy, easy-going, effortless, gentle, gracious, indulgent, kind, kindly, lax, lenient, liberal, manageable, overindulgent, permissive, pitying, sensitive, sentimental, simple, spineless, sympathetic, tender, tender-hearted, undemanding, weak; CONCEPT 401 —*Ant.* callous, severe, stern, strict, uncompassionate

soft [*adj4*] *out of condition* doughy, fat, flabby, flaccid, fleshy, formless, gone to seed*, limp, out of shape*, overindulged, pampered, untrained, weak; CONCEPTS 314,485 —*Ant.* firm, healthy, strong, well

soft [*adj5*] *stupid* daft, fatuous, feeble-minded, foolish, silly, simple, witless; CONCEPT 402 —*Ant.* intelligent, smart

soften [*v*] *calm, soothe* abate, allay, alleviate, appease, assuage, become tender, bend, cushion, diminish, disintegrate, dissolve, ease, enfeeble, give, knead, lessen, lighten, lower, mash, mellow, melt, mitigate, moderate, modify, moisten, mollify, palliate, qualify, quell, relax, relent, still, subdue, temper, tenderize, thaw, tone down, turn down, weaken, yield; CONCEPT 250 —Ant. irritate, trouble, upset, worry

softhearted [adj] *tender* all heart*, benevolent, big-hearted, bleeding-heart*, caring, charitable, compassionate, considerate, emotional, forgiving, generous, gentle, kind, lenient, merciful, moving, sensitive, sentimental, soft, sympathetic, tenderhearted, warm, warmhearted; CONCEPTS 401,542

softly [adv] *lightly* agilely, airily, breezily, carelessly, daintily, delicately, faintly, gently, gingerly, gradually, nimbly, quietly, smoothly, tenderly; CONCEPTS 538,544,584

soft-spoken [adj] *quiet* close-mouthed, gentle, hushed, hushful, low, low-keyed, low-pitched, mild, muffled, peaceful, reserved, silent, soft, still; CONCEPTS 592,594

software [n] *computer program* application software, bundled software, courseware, file management system, freeware, groupware, operating system, presentation software, productivity software, program, shareware, spreadsheet, systems software, vaporware; CONCEPTS 269,463

soggy [adj] *damp or soaking* clammy, dank, dripping, heavy, humid, moist, mucky, muggy, mushy, pasty, pulpy, saturated, soaked, sodden, soft, sopping, spongy, sticky, sultry, water-logged; CONCEPT 603 —Ant. dehydrated, dry

soil [n1] *earth, dirt* clay, dry land, dust, grime, ground, land, loam, soot, terra firma; CONCEPT 509

soil [n2] *land where one lives* country, home, homeland, homestead, region, spread, terra firma; CONCEPTS 198,510,511

soil [v] *make dirty* bedraggle, befoul, begrime, besmirch, contaminate, crumb, debase, defile, degrade, dirty, discolor, disgrace, foul, grime, maculate, mess, mess up, muck*, muck up*, muddy, muss*, muss up*, pollute, shame, smear, smudge, spatter, spoil, spot, stain, sully, taint, tar, tarnish; CONCEPT 254 —Ant. clean

sojourn [n] *brief travel; visit* layover, residence, rest, stay, stop, stopover, tarriance, vacation; CONCEPTS 224,226,227

sojourn [v] *travel briefly; visit* abide, dwell, inhabit, linger, lodge, nest, perch, reside, rest, roost, squat, stay, stay over, stop, tarry, vacation; CONCEPTS 224,226,227

solace [n] *comfort, peace* alleviation, assuagement, condolement, condolence, consolation, pity, relief; CONCEPTS 7,22,410 —Ant. discord, disharmony

solace [v] *give comfort, peace* allay, alleviate, buck up, cheer, comfort, condole with, console, mitigate, soften, soothe, upraise; CONCEPTS 7,22 —Ant. trouble, upset, worry

soldier [n] *person serving in military* airforce member, cadet, cavalryperson, commando, conscript, draftee, enlisted person, fighter, GI*, Green Beret, guard, guerrilla, gunner, infantry, infantryperson, marine, mercenary, military person, musketeer, officer, paratrooper, pilot, private, rank, recruit, scout, selectee, serviceperson, soldier, soldier-at-arms, trooper, veteran, volunteer, warmonger, warrior; CONCEPT 358

sole [adj] *alone, singular* ace, exclusive, individual, lone, one, one and only, onliest, only, only one, particular, remaining, separate, single, solitary, solo, unique, unshared; CONCEPTS 555, 564,577 —Ant. shared, together

solely [adv] *only, alone* barely, but, completely, entirely, exclusively, individually, merely, onliest, purely, simply, single-handedly, singly, singularly, totally, undividedly, wholly; CONCEPTS 544,577 —Ant. shared, together

solemn [adj1] *quiet, serious* austere, brooding, cold sober*, deliberate, dignified, downbeat, earnest, funereal, glum, grave, heavy, intense, matter of life and death*, moody, no fooling*, no-nonsense*, pensive, portentous, reflective, sedate, sober, somber, staid, stern, thoughtful, weighty; CONCEPTS 403,542 —Ant. frivolous, funny, laughing, light

solemn [adj2] *impressive, sacred* august, awe-inspiring, ceremonial, ceremonious, conventional, devotional, dignified, divine, formal, full, grand, grave, hallowed, holy, imposing, magnificent, majestic, momentous, ostentatious, overwhelming, plenary, religious, reverential, ritual, sanctified, stately, venerable; CONCEPT 574 —Ant. insignificant, ordinary, unimpressive, unsacred, usual

solicit [v] *plead for; try to sell* accost, apply, approach, ask, beg, beseech, bespeak, bum, cadge, call, canvass, challenge, claim, come on to*, crave, demand, desire, drum*, drum up*, entreat, exact, go, hawk, hit on*, hit up*, hustle, implore, importune, inquire, mooch, panhandle, pass the hat*, peddle, petition, postulate, pray, promote, proposition, query, question, refer, request, require, requisition, resort, seduce, seek, sponge, steer, sue for, supplicate, touch, tout, turn, whistle for*; CONCEPT 345 —Ant. disapprove, refuse, reject

solicitous [adj] *worried* anxious, appetent, apprehensive, ardent, athirst, attentive, avid, beside oneself, careful, caring, concerned, devoted, eager, earnest, heedful, impatient, keen, loving, mindful, raring, regardful, tender, thirsty, troubled, uneasy, worried sick*, worried stiff*, zealous; CONCEPT 403 —Ant. easygoing, laid-back, unafraid, unworried

solicitude [n] *worry, anxiety* attention, attentiveness, care, compunction, concern, concernment, considerateness, consideration, disquiet, disquietude, heed, presentiment, qualm, regard, scruple, tender loving care*, TLC*, unease, uneasiness, watchfulness; CONCEPT 410 —Ant. calm, contentedness, ease, peacefulness

solid [adj1] *hard, dimensional* brick wall*, close, compact, compacted, concentrated, concrete, consolidated, dense, firm, fixed, heavy, hefty, hulk, hunk, husky, massed, material, physical, rock, rocklike, rooted, secure, set, sound, stable, strong, sturdy, substantial, thick, tight, unshakable; CONCEPTS 483,604 —Ant. fluid, gaseous, insubstantial, liquid, soft, vaporous

solid [adj2] *continuous, complete* agreed, brick wall*, consecutive, consentient, continued, firm, like a rock, regular, set in stone*, stable, steady, unalloyed, unanimous, unbroken, undivided, uninterrupted, united, unmixed; CONCEPTS 482, 488,531 —Ant. broken, divided, incomplete, incontinuous, intermittent

solid [adj3] *dependable, reliable* cogent, constant, decent, estimable, genuine, good, law-abiding, levelheaded, pure, real, satisfactory, satisfying, sensible, serious, sober, sound, stalwart, steadfast, trustworthy, trusty, upright, upstanding, valid, worthy; CONCEPTS 401,534 —*Ant.* tenuous, undependable, unreliable, untrustworthy, vulnerable

solidarity [n] *unity* accord, agreement, alliance, comradeship, confederation, consensus, federation, fellowship, harmony, indivisibility, oneness, sameness, support, teamwork, unanimity, undividedness, unification, uniformity, union; CONCEPTS 664,714,837

solidify [v] *harden* amalgamate, anneal, bake, cake, cement, clot, coagulate, cohere, congeal, crystallize, densify, dry, firm, freeze, jell, petrify, set, stiffen, strengthen, thicken; CONCEPTS 250,469

solitary [adj] *alone, single; unsociable* aloof, antisocial, cloistered, companionless, deserted, desolate, distant, eremetic, forsaken, friendless, hermitical, hidden, individual, introverted, isolated, lone, lonely, lonesome, lorn, misanthropic, offish, only, out-of-the-way*, particular, reclusive, remote, reserved, retired, secluded, separate, sequestered, singular, sole, solo, stag, standoffish, unaccompanied, unapproachable, unattended, uncompanionable, unfrequented, unique, unsocial, withdrawn; CONCEPTS 555, 577,583 —*Ant.* accompanied, combined, sociable, together

solitude [n] *aloneness* confinement, desert, detachment, emptiness, isolation, loneliness, loneness, lonesomeness, peace and quiet*, privacy, quarantine, reclusiveness, retirement, seclusion, separateness, silence, solitariness, waste, wasteland, wilderness, withdrawal; CONCEPTS 388,673,714 —*Ant.* companionship, friendship, togetherness

solo [adj] *alone* by oneself, companionless, friendless, individual, in solitary*, me and my shadow*, me myself and I*, on one's own, single, solitary, stag, unaccompanied, unaided, unassisted, unescorted, unmarried; CONCEPTS 577,583

solution [n1] *answer, resolution* Band-Aid*, clarification, elucidation, explanation, explication, key, pay dirt*, quick fix*, result, solving, the ticket*, unfolding, unraveling, unravelment; CONCEPTS 230,661,712 —*Ant.* doubt, problem, quandary, question, trouble

solution [n2] *mixture of liquid and another substance* blend, compound, dissolvent, elixir, emulsion, extract, fluid, juice, mix, sap, solvent, suspension; CONCEPTS 260,467 —*Ant.* chemical, element

solve [v] *answer, resolve* break*, clarify, clear up, construe, crack*, deal with, decide, decipher, decode, determine, disentangle, divine, do, elucidate, enlighten, explain, expound, fathom, figure out, find out, fix, get, get right, get to the bottom*, have, hit, hit upon*, illuminate, interpret, iron out*, lick*, make a dent*, make out*, pan out*, put two and two together*, puzzle, reason, settle, think out, unfold, unlock, unravel, unriddle, untangle, work, work out; CONCEPTS 15,18,37 —*Ant.* pose, question, search, wonder

solvent [adj] *financially sound* able to pay, financially stable, firm, fit, in the pink*, out of the red*, solid, stable; CONCEPTS 314,488

somber [adj] *sad, depressing* black, bleak, blue*, caliginous, cloudy, dark, depressive, dim, dingy, dire, dismal, dispiriting, doleful, down, drab, dragged, dreary, dull, dusky, earnest, funereal, gloomy, grave, grim, hurting, joyless, lugubrious, melancholy, mournful, murky, no-nonsense, obscure, sedate, sepulchral, serious, shadowy, shady, sober, solemn, sourpuss, staid, tenebrous, weighty; CONCEPTS 403,485,529 —*Ant.* cheerful, happy, joyful

somebody [n] *person of fame, importance* celebrity, dignitary, heavyweight*, household name*, luminary, name*, notable, one, personage, person of note, public figure, so-and-so*, someone*, some person*, star, superstar, VIP*, whoever*; CONCEPT 423 —*Ant.* nobody

someday [adv] *eventually* after a while, anytime, at a future time, finally, in a time to come, on a day, one day, one fine day*, one of these days, one time, one time or another, sometime, sooner or later, subsequently, ultimately, yet; CONCEPTS 548,820 —*Ant.* never

somehow [adv] *by some means* after a fashion, anyhow, anyway, anywise, by hook or crook*, come what may*, in one way or another, in some such way, in some way, one way or another, somehow or another, somehow or other; CONCEPT 544 —*Ant.* no way

something [n] *entity* article, being, commodity, existence, existent, individual, object, substance, thing; CONCEPT 433 —*Ant.* nothing

sometimes [adv] *every now and then* at intervals, at times, consistently, constantly, ever and again, every so often, frequently, from time to time, here and there, intermittently, now and again, now and then, occasionally, off and on, once in a blue moon*, once in a while, on occasion, periodically, recurrently; CONCEPT 805 —*Ant.* never

somewhat [adv] *to some extent* adequately, a little, bearably, considerably, fairly, far, incompletely, in part, insignificantly, kind of, moderately, more or less, not much, partially, pretty, quite, rather, ratherish, significantly, slightly, some, something, sort of, to a degree, tolerably, well; CONCEPTS 548,569,772 —*Ant.* not at all

somewhere [adv] *in, or at some place* about, any old place, around, around somewhere, elsewhere, here and there, in one place or another, kicking around*, parts unknown*, scattered, someplace, someplace or another, someplace or other, somewheres; CONCEPT 583 —*Ant.* nowhere

somnolent [adj] *sleepy* asleep, dozy, drowsy, listless, nodding off, out of it*, sleeping, snoozy*, soporific, tired; CONCEPTS 315,539

song [n] *melody sung or played with musical instrument* air, anthem, aria, ballad, canticle, carol, chant, chorale, chorus, ditty, expression, golden oldie*, hymn, lay, lullaby, lyric, melody, number, oldie*, opera, piece, poem, psalm, refrain, rock, rock and roll, round, shanty, strain, tune, verse, vocal; CONCEPT 262

sonorous [adj] *resonant* booming, full-voiced, loud, loud-voiced, powerful, resounding, reverberating, rich, ringing, rotund, thundering; CONCEPTS 592,594

soon [adv] *in the near future* anon, any minute now, before long, betimes, by and by, coming down the pike*, directly, early, ere long, expeditiously, fast, fleetly, forthwith, hastily, in a little while, in a minute, in a second, in a short time, in due time, in short order, instantly, in time, lickety-split*, on time, posthaste, presently, promptly, pronto, quick, quickly, rapidly, short, shortly, speedily; CONCEPTS 548,798,820 —*Ant.* distant, far, later, never

soothe [v] *calm, ease* allay, alleviate, appease, assuage, balm, becalm, butter up*, calm down, cheer, compose, console, cool, cool off*, dulcify, help, hush, lighten, lull, make nice*, make up, mitigate, mollify, pacify, patch things up*, play up to*, pour oil on*, quiet, quieten, relieve, settle, smooth down, soften, square, still, stroke, subdue, take the edge off*, take the sting out*, tranquilize, unburden, untrouble; CONCEPTS 7,22,110,384 —*Ant.* agitate, distress, upset, worry

soothing [adj] *comforting* alleviating, calming, consolatory, consoling, easing, mollifying, pacifying, palliative, reassuring, relaxing, relieving, remedying, softening, tranquilizing, warming; CONCEPT 529

soothsayer [n] *seer* augur, channeller, clairvoyant, crystal ball gazer, diviner, forecaster, fortune-teller, medium, oracle, palm reader, prophet, psychic, soothsayer; CONCEPT 423

sophisticated [adj1] *cosmopolitan, cultured* adult, artificial, been around, blasé, bored, citified, cool*, couth, cultivated, cynical, disenchanted, disillusioned, experienced, in, in the know*, into*, jaded, jet-set*, knowing, laid-back*, mature, mondaine, on to*, practical, practiced, refined, schooled, seasoned, sharp, skeptical, smooth, stagy*, streetwise, studied, suave, svelte, switched on*, uptown*, urbane, well-bred, wised up*, wise to*, with it*, worldly, worldly wise, world-weary; CONCEPTS 401,404,589 —*Ant.* naive, uncultivated, uncultured, unrefined, unsophisticated

sophisticated [adj2] *complex, advanced* complicated, delicate, elaborate, highly developed, intricate, involved, knotty, labyrinthine, modern, multifaceted, refined, subtle; CONCEPT 562 —*Ant.* easy, simple, slow, unsophisticated

sophistication [n] *culture, style* composure, elegance, finesse, poise, refinement, savoir faire, savoir vivre, social grace, tact, urbanity, worldliness, worldly wisdom; CONCEPTS 388,633,655 —*Ant.* ingenuousness, naiveté, simplicity

sophomoric [adj] *inexperienced* brash, foolish, naive, reckless, young; CONCEPT 401 —*Ant.* experienced, expert, knowledgeable, professional

soporific [adj] *sleepy; sleep-inducing* anesthetic, balmy, calming, deadening, dozy*, drowsy, dull, hypnotic, mesmerizing, narcotic, nodding, numbing, opiate, quietening, sedative, slumberous, snoozy*, somniferous, somnolent, soothing, tranquilizing; CONCEPTS 537,539 —*Ant.* awake, conscious, exciting, invigorating, stimulating

sopping [adj] *wet* dank, drenched, dripping, drowned, saturated, soaked, soaking, sodden, soggy, soppy, soused, water-logged, wringing-wet; CONCEPT 603

sorcerer [n] *wizard* alchemist, augurer, charmer, clairvoyant, conjurer, diviner, enchanter, fortune-teller, magician, medium, necromancer, occultist, seer, shaman, soothsayer, sorceress, thaumaturge, warlock, witch; CONCEPT 361

sorcery [n] *black magic, witchcraft* abracadabra*, alchemy, bewitchment, black art, charm, conjuring, devilry, divination, enchantment, evil eye, hocus-pocus*, hoodoo*, incantation, jinx, magic, mumbo jumbo*, necromancy, spell, thaumaturgy, voodoo, witchery, witching, wizardry; CONCEPTS 370,689 —*Ant.* reality

sordid [adj] *dirty, bad, low* abject, avaricious, base, black, calculated, corrupt, covetous, debauched, degenerate, degraded, despicable, disreputable, dowdy, filthy, foul, grasping, grubby, ignoble, impure, low-down, mean, mercenary, miserable, miserly, nasty, poor, scurvy, seedy, selfish, self-seeking, servile, shabby, shameful, sleazy, slovenly, slum, slummy, small, small-minded, squalid, unclean, uncleanly, ungenerous, venal, vicious, vile, wretched; CONCEPTS 334,545,571 —*Ant.* good, honorable, reputable, wonderful

sore [adj1] *hurt physically* abscessed, aching, acute, afflicted, annoying, bruised, burned, burning, chafed, critical, distressing, extreme, hurtful, hurting, inflamed, irritated, pained, painful, raw, reddened, sensitive, severe, sharp, smarting, tender, ulcerated, uncomfortable, unpleasant, vexatious; CONCEPT 314 —*Ant.* good, well

sore [adj2] *angry; hurt mentally* afflicted, aggrieved, annoyed, annoying, critical, distressing, grieved, grieving, indignant, irked, irritated, pained, peeved, pressing, resentful, sensitive, smarting, stung, troubled, upset, urgent, vexed, weighty; CONCEPT 403 —*Ant.* delighted, happy, pleased

sorrow [n] *extreme upset, grief* affliction, agony, anguish, bad news*, big trouble*, blow, blues*, care, catastrophe, dejection, depression, distress, dolor, grieving, hardship, heartache, heartbreak, lamenting, melancholy, misery, misfortune, mourning, pain, rain*, regret, remorse, repentance, rue, sadness, suffering, trial, tribulation, trouble, unhappiness, weeping, woe, worry, wretchedness; CONCEPT 410 —*Ant.* happiness, joy, relief

sorrow [v] *be very upset, grieved* agonize, bemoan, be sad, bewail, carry on, cry a river*, deplore, eat heart out*, grieve, groan, hang crepe*, lament, moan, mourn, regret, sing the blues*, sob, take on*, weep; CONCEPTS 34,410 —*Ant.* be happy, be joyful, delight, relieve

sorrowful [adj] *very upset; grieving* affecting, afflicted, dejected, depressed, disconsolate, distressing, doleful, dolent, full of sorrow, grievous, heartbroken, heartrending, heavy-hearted, hurting, in mourning, in pain, in sorrow, lamentable, lugubrious, melancholy, miserable, mournful, painful, piteous, plaintive, rueful, ruthful, sad, sick at heart*, singing the blues*, sorry, tearful, tear-jerking*, unhappy, woebegone, woeful, wretched; CONCEPT 403 —*Ant.* delighted, happy, joyful

sorry [adj1] *remorseful, regretful* apologetic, attritional, compunctious, conscience-stricken, contrite, guilt-ridden, melted, penitent, penitential, repentant, self-accusing, self-condemnatory, self-reproachful, shamefaced, softened, touched; CONCEPTS 403,545 —*Ant.* glad, happy, unremorseful, unsorry

sorry [adj2] *sad, heartbroken* bad, disconsolate, distressed, grieved, heavyhearted, melancholy, mournful, pitiful, rueful, saddened, sorrowful, unhappy; CONCEPT 403 —*Ant.* happy, heartened, joyful

sorry [adj3] *despicable, pathetic* abject, base, beggarly, cheap, contemptible, deplorable, despisable, disgraceful, dismal, distressing, inadequate, insignificant, mean, miserable, paltry, piteous, pitiable, pitiful, poor, sad, scruffy*, scummy*, scurvy, shabby, shoddy, small, trifling, trivial, unimportant, vile, worthless, wretched; CONCEPTS 485,529 —*Ant.* good, hopeful, nice

sort [n] *type, variety* array, batch, battery, body, brand, breed, category, character, class, clutch, denomination, description, family, genus, group, ilk, kind, likes, likes of*, lot, make, nature, number, order, parcel, quality, race, set, species, stamp, stripe, style, suite; CONCEPT 378

sort [v] *place in order* arrange, assort, button down*, catalogue, categorize, choose, class, classify, comb, cull, distribute, divide, file, grade, group, order, peg, pick, pigeonhole*, put down as, put down for, put in order, put in shape, put to rights*, rank, riddle, screen, select, separate, sift, size up, systematize, tab, typecast, winnow; CONCEPTS 84,158 —*Ant.* disorder, disorganize

sortie [n] *armed attack* assault, charge, invasion, mission, offense, raid, rush, sally*, strike; CONCEPTS 86,317

so-so [adj] *adequate, passable* average, enough, fair, fairish, fair to middling*, indifferent, mediocre, medium, middling*, moderate, not bad*, okay*, ordinary, respectable, run-of-the-mill*, tolerable, undistinguished; CONCEPTS 533,575 —*Ant.* different, distinguished, excellent, exceptional

soul [n1] *psyche, inspiration, energy* anima, animating principle, animation, animus, ardor, bosom, bottom, breast, breath of life, cause, conscience, courage, disposition, ego, elan vital, essence, feeling, fervor, force, genius, heart, individuality, intellect, intelligence, life, marrow, mind, nobility, noumenon, personality, pith, pneuma, principle, quintessence, reason, recesses of heart*, secret self*, spirit, spiritual being, stuff, substance, thought, vital force, vitality, vivacity; CONCEPTS 409,410,411 —*Ant.* body

soul [n2] *being* body, character, creature, ghost, human being, individual, living soul*, man, mortal, person, personage, phantom, shadow, spirit, umbra, woman; CONCEPT 389

soulful [adj] *emotional* ardent, deep, expressive, feeling, fervent, fervid, fiery, impassioned, meaningful, moving, passionate, stirred, stirring, tender, touching; CONCEPTS 403,542

soul-searching [n] *introspection* contemplation, deep thought, heart-searching, meditation, reflection, rumination, self-analysis, self-examination, self-questioning; CONCEPTS 24,410

sound [adj1] *complete, healthy* alive and kicking*, effectual, entire, firm, fit, flawless, hale, hearty, intact, in the pink*, perfect, right, right

as rain*, robust, safe, sane, solid, stable, sturdy, substantial, thorough, total, unblemished, undamaged, undecayed, unhurt, unimpaired, uninjured, up to snuff*, vibrant, vigorous, vital, well, well-constructed, whole, wholesome, wrapped tight*; CONCEPTS 314,488 —*Ant.* incomplete, infirm, unfit, unhealthy, unsound

sound [adj2] *logical, reasonable* accurate, advisable, all there*, cogent, commonsensical, consequent, convincing, cool*, correct, deep, exact, fair, faultless, flawless, got it together*, impeccable, intellectual, judicious, just, levelheaded, orthodox, precise, profound, proper, prudent, rational, reliable, responsible, right, right-minded, right-thinking, satisfactory, satisfying, sensible, sober, solid, telling, thoughtful, together*, true, trustworthy, valid, well-advised, well-founded, well-grounded, wise; CONCEPTS 403,529,558 —*Ant.* illogical, unbelievable, unfathomable, unreasonable, unsound

sound [adj3] *accepted, established* all there*, authoritative, canonical, dependable, fair, faithful, fly*, go*, hanging together*, holding together*, holding up*, holding up in wash*, holding water*, kosher*, legal, legit*, loyal, orthodox, proper, proven, received, recognized, reliable, reputable, safe, sanctioned, secure, significant, solid, solvent, stable, standing up*, tried-and-true*, true, valid, washing; CONCEPTS 535,552,582 —*Ant.* distrusted, refused, rejected

sound [n] *something heard or audible* accent, din, harmony, intonation, loudness, melody, modulation, music, noise, note, pitch, racket, report, resonance, reverberation, ringing, softness, sonance, sonancy, sonority, sonorousness, static, tenor, tonality, tone, vibration, voice; CONCEPT 595 —*Ant.* silence

sound [v1] *produce noise* babble, bang, bark, blare, blow, boom, burst, buzz, cackle, chatter, clack, clang, clank, clap, clatter, clink, crash, creak, detonate, echo, emit, explode, hum, jabber, jangle, jar, moan, murmur, patter, play, rattle, reflect, resonate, resound, reverberate, ring, roar, rumble, shout, shriek, shrill, sing, slam, smash, snort, squawk, thud, thump, thunder, toot, trumpet, vibrate, whine, whisper; CONCEPT 65 —*Ant.* quiet

sound [v2] *give the impression* appear, appear to be, look, seem, strike as being; CONCEPTS 543,716

sound bite [n] *very brief broadcast statement* blurb*, buzzword, clip, excerpt, fifteen minutes of fame*, newsbreak, news item, notation, note, one-liner, outtake, passage, photo opportunity, piece, quotation, quote, saying, selection, slogan, snippet, spot news; CONCEPT 277

soundproof [adj] *silent* hushed, insulated, noiseless, quiet, soundless; CONCEPT 594

soupçon [n] *small amount* atom, crumb, dab, dash, drop, flash, hint, iota, particle, pinch, ray, scintilla, shade, shred, small bit, small quantity, smidgen, sparkle, speck, spot, suggestion, tinge, trace, whiff, whisper; CONCEPTS 829,831

sour [adj1] *bad-tasting; gone bad* acerb, acetic, acetose, acetous, acid, acidic, acidulated, acrid, astringent, bad, biting, bitter, briny, caustic, curdled, cutting, dry, fermented, green, keen, musty, peppery, piquant, pungent, rancid, salty, sharp, soured, sourish, stinging, tart, turned, unpleasant, unripe, unsavory, unwholesome, vinegary, with a kick*; CONCEPTS 462,613 —*Ant.* good, pleasant, sweet, tasty

sour [adj2] *in a bad mood* acid, acrid, acrimonious, bitter, churlish, crabby, cynical, disagreeable, discontented, displeasing, embittered, grouchy, grudging, ill-natured, ill-tempered, irritable, jaundiced, on edge*, peevish, rotten, tart, ungenerous, unhappy, unpleasant, waspish; CONCEPTS 403,542 —*Ant.* cheerful, cordial, friendly, happy

sour [v] *alienate* acidify, curdle, disenchant, embitter, envenom, exacerbate, exasperate, make sour, spoil, turn, turn off; CONCEPTS 14,250 —*Ant.* encourage, excite, incite

source [n] *beginning; point of supply* antecedent, author, authority, authorship, begetter, birthplace, cause, commencement, connection, dawn, dawning, derivation, determinant, expert, father, fount, fountain, fountainhead, horse's mouth*, inception, informant, maternity, mother, onset, opening, origin, origination, originator, parent; paternity, provenance, provenience, rise, rising, root, specialist, spring, start, starting point, wellspring; CONCEPT 648 —*Ant.* effect, end, result

sourpuss [n] *grouch* bellyacher*, crab, crank, crosspatch, curmudgeon, faultfinder, griper, growler, grumbler, grump*, killjoy, moaner, sorehead*, sulker, whiner; CONCEPTS 412,423

souse [v] *make very wet* brine, deluge, dip, douse, drench, drown, duck, dunk, immerse, impregnate, marinate, pickle, preserve, seethe, soak, sop, steep, submerge, submerse, waterlog, wet; CONCEPT 256 —*Ant.* dehydrate, dry

soused [adj] *drunk* bashed, boozed up*, buzzed*, crocked*, feeling no pain*, flushed*, flying*, groggy, high*, inebriated, intoxicated, juiced*, laced*, liquored up*, lit*, plastered*, potted*, seeing double*, sloshed*, smashed*, stewed*, stoned*, tanked*, three sheets to the wind*, tipsy, totaled*, under the influence, under the table*, wasted*; CONCEPTS 314,545

souvenir [n] *keepsake from event* gift, memento, memorial, relic, remembrance, remembrancer, reminder, token, trophy; CONCEPTS 337,446

sovereign [adj] *dominant, effective* absolute, ascendant, autonomous, chief, commanding, directing, effectual, efficacious, excellent, guiding, highest, imperial, independent, lofty, majestic, monarchal, monarchical, overbearing, paramount, predominant, predominate, preponderant, prevalent, principal, regal, regnant, reigning, royal, ruling, self-governed, supreme, unlimited; CONCEPTS 536,568 —*Ant.* inferior, submissive, subservient

sovereign [n] *supreme ruler* autocrat, chief, czar, emperor, empress, king, leader, majesty, monarch, potentate, prince, princess, queen, ruler; CONCEPT 354 —*Ant.* servant

sovereignty [n] *domination* ascendancy, ascendant, dominance, dominion, jurisdiction, preeminence, prepotence, prepotency, primacy, supremacy, supreme power, sway; CONCEPT 299 —*Ant.* submission

sow [v] *plant* broadcast, disject, disseminate, drill, fling, grow, implant, inseminate, lodge, pitch, propagate, put in, raise, scatter, seed,

strew, toss; CONCEPTS 253,257 —*Ant.* dig, harvest, reap

spa [n] *resort* day spa, fat farm*, health club, health facility, holiday spot, hotel, hot spring*, lodge, mineral spring resort, sanitarium, sauna, whirlpool; CONCEPTS 198,516

space [n1] *room, scope* amplitude, area, arena, blank, breadth, capacity, compass, distance, elbowroom, expanse, expansion, extension, extent, field, gap, headroom, headway, infinity, interval, lacuna, leeway, location, margin, omission, play, range, reach, slot, spaciousness, sphere, spot, spread, stretch, territory, tract, turf, volume, zone; CONCEPTS 739,746,756

space [n2] *time interval* bit, duration, period, season, span, spell, stretch, term, time, while; CONCEPT 807

spacecraft [n] *spaceship* flying saucer, rocket, rocket ship, satellite, shuttle, space capsule, space probe, space shuttle, UFO, unidentified flying object; CONCEPT 504

spacey/spacy [adj] *eccentric* beat*, bizarre, crazy, dizzy, erratic, far out*, flaky, flighty, freakish, kooky, nutty, odd, oddball, offbeat, off-center, off the wall*, out in left field, out to lunch*, peculiar, quirky, spaced out*, strange, way out*, weird; CONCEPTS 547,564

spacious [adj] *extensive, expansive* ample, big, boundless, broad, capacious, cavernous, comfortable, commodious, endless, enormous, extended, generous, great, huge, immense, infinite, large, limitless, roomy, sizable, uncrowded, vast, voluminous, wide, widespread; CONCEPTS 481,482,774 —*Ant.* cramped, crowded, small

span [n] *distance, duration* amount, compass, extent, interval, length, measure, period, reach, space, spell, spread, stretch, term, time; CONCEPTS 756,807,822 —*Ant.* extreme

span [v] *stretch over* arch, bridge, connect, cover, cross, extend, ford, go across, link, pass over, range, reach, traverse, vault; CONCEPT 756 —*Ant.* compress, concentrate, condense, shorten

spank [v] *slap, usually on bottom* belt, blip, box, buffet, cane, chastise, clobber, clout, cuff, flax, flog, hide, larrup*, lash, lather*, leather*, lick, paddle, punch, punish, put over one's knee*, smack, sock, tan*, tan one's hide*, thrash, trim, wallop, welt, whip, whup*; CONCEPT 189

spare [adj1] *extra, reserve* additional, backup, de trop, emergency, free, in excess, in reserve, in store, lagniappe, leftover, more than enough*, odd, option, over, supererogatory, superfluous, supernumerary, surplus, unoccupied, unused, unwanted; CONCEPTS 771,824 —*Ant.* necessary

spare [adj2] *thin; sparse* angular, bony, economical, exiguous, frugal, gaunt, lank, lanky, lean, meager, modest, poor, rangy, rawboned, scant, scanty, scraggy, scrawny, shadow, skimpy, skinny, slender, slight, sparing, stick, stilt, stingy, wiry; CONCEPTS 490,491,771 —*Ant.* fat, thick

spare [v1] *do or manage without* afford, allow, bestow, dispense with, give, grant, part with, pinch, provide, put by, relinquish, salt away*, save, scrape, scrimp, short, skimp, stint, supply; CONCEPT 129 —*Ant.* need

spare [v2] *forgive; have mercy upon* absolve, bail out, be lenient, be merciful, discharge, dispense, excuse, exempt, forbear, get off the hook*, get out of hock*, give a break*, give quarter to, go easy on*, leave, let go, let off*, pardon, pity, privilege from, pull out of the fire*, refrain from, release, relent, relieve from, save bacon*, save from, save neck*, spring; CONCEPTS 50,88,134

sparing [adj] *careful, economical* avaricious, canny, chary, close, cost-conscious, frugal, humane, mean, money-conscious, parsimonious, provident, prudent, saving, stewardly, stingy, thrifty, tight, tight-fisted, tolerant, ungiving, unwasteful, wary; CONCEPTS 334,401 —Ant. careless, lavish, spendthrift, uncareful

spark [n] *flash, trace* atom, beam, fire, flare, flicker, gleam, glint, glitter, glow, hint, jot, nucleus, ray, scintilla, scintillation, scrap, sparkle, spit, vestige; CONCEPTS 519,624,828

spark [v] *start, inspire* animate, excite, kindle, precipitate, provoke, set in motion, set off, stimulate, stir, touch off, trigger; CONCEPT 221 —Ant. cease, halt, stop

sparkle [n] *glitter, shine* animation, brilliance, coruscation, dash, dazzle, élan, flash, flicker, gaiety, gleam, glimmer, glint, glitz, glow, life, panache, radiance, scintillation, shimmer, show, spark, spirit, twinkle, vim, vitality, vivacity, zap*, zip*; CONCEPTS 411,624,628 —Ant. dullness

sparkle [v] *glitter, shine* beam, bubble, coruscate, dance, effervesce, fizz, fizzle, flash, flicker, gleam, glimmer, glint, glisten, glow, scintillate, shimmer, spark, twinkle, wink; CONCEPT 624 —Ant. darken, dull

sparse [adj] *very few and scattered* dispersed, exiguous, few and far between, inadequate, infrequent, meager, occasional, poor, rare, scant, scanty, scarce, scrimpy, skimpy, spare, sporadic, thin, uncommon; CONCEPTS 762,789 —Ant. full, lush, plentiful

spasm [n] *twitch, fit* access, attack, burst, contraction, convulsion, eruption, frenzy, jerk, outburst, pain, paroxysm, seizure, throe, yank; CONCEPTS 185,728

spasmodic [adj] *twitching, erratic* bits and pieces*, changeable, choppy, convulsive, desultory, fitful, fits and starts*, intermittent, irregular, jerky, on-again-off-again*, periodic, shaky, spastic, sporadic, spotty, spurtive, uncertain; CONCEPTS 482,530,541 —Ant. resting, uninterrupted

spat [n] *dispute, quarrel* altercation, argument, beef*, bickering, brouhaha, conflict, difference of opinion, disagreement, discord, dissension, embroilment, falling-out, feud, flare-up, fracas, friction, fuss, hubbub, miff*, misunderstanding, row, rumpus*, run-in*, squabble, strife, tiff, words; CONCEPTS 46,106,278

spate [n] *series* deluge, flood, flurry, outpouring, run, rush, string, succession, torrent, wave; CONCEPT 6

spatter [v] *splash, sprinkle* bespatter, bestrew, broadcast, dash, daub, dirty, discharge, disperse, dot, douse, dribble, mottle, polka-dot, scatter, shower, slop, smudge, soil, spangle, speck, speckle, splutter, spot, spray, sputter, stipple, strew, swash, wet; CONCEPTS 172,179,256

spawn [v] *produce* bring forth, create, father, generate, give rise to, hatch, issue, make, mother, originate, parent, procreate, reproduce, sire; CONCEPTS 173,251,374 —Ant. destroy

speak [v1] *talk* allege, articulate, assert, aver, blab*, break silence, chat, chew*, communicate, converse, convey, declare, deliver, descant, discourse, drawl, enunciate, expatiate, express, gab*, gas*, go*, jaw*, lip*, make known, make public, modulate, mouth, mumble, murmur, mutter, open one's mouth, perorate, pop off*, pronounce, put into words, rap*, say, shout, sound, speak one's piece*, spiel*, spill, state, tell, utter, verbalize, vocalize, voice, whisper, yak*, yakkety-yak*, yammer; CONCEPTS 47,266 —Ant. be quiet, listen

speak [v2] *address; give a lecture* argue, declaim, descant, discourse, get across, harangue, hold forth, orate, pitch, plead, prelect, recite, sermonize, spiel*, spout*, stump, talk; CONCEPTS 60,285 —Ant. listen

speaker [n] *talker* after-dinner speaker, announcer, elocutionist, keynoter, lecturer, mouthpiece, orator, public speaker, rhetorician, speechmaker, spokesperson; CONCEPT 348

speak out/speak up [v] *make one's position known* assert, come out with, declare, have one's say*, insist, let voice be heard*, make oneself heard, make plain, say loud and clear*, sound off*, speak loudly, speak one's mind*, stand up for; CONCEPTS 49,57 —Ant. be quiet, shut up

spearhead [v] *lead, start* bring, bring on, cause, direct, get the jump on*, go out in front*, guide, head, helm, influence, initiate, introduce, launch, motivate, move, originate, persuade, pioneer, produce, prompt, quarterback*, run things*, shepherd, spur, trail-blaze*; CONCEPTS 68,117,221

special [adj] *distinguished, distinctive; important in own way* appropriate, best, certain, characteristic, chief, choice, defined, definite, designated, determinate, different, earmarked, especial, exceptional, exclusive, express, extraordinary, festive, first, gala, individual, limited, main, major, marked, memorable, momentous, out of the ordinary, particular, peculiar, personal, primary, proper, rare, red-letter*, reserved, restricted, select, set, significant, smashing*, sole, specialized, specific, uncommon, unique, unreal*, unusual; CONCEPTS 557,564,567 —Ant. common, commonplace, indistinctive, normal, ordinary, undistinguished, unimportant, usual

specialist [n] *person who is an expert in a field* ace, adept, authority, connoisseur, consultant, devotee, doctor, guru*, old hand*, old pro*, pro*, professional, pundit, sage, savant, scholar, technician, veteran, virtuoso; CONCEPTS 347,357 —Ant. general practitioner

specialize [v] *concentrate on specific area* be into, develop oneself in, do one's thing*, go in for, have a weakness for*, limit oneself to, practice, practice exclusively, pursue, study intensively, train, work in; CONCEPTS 91,324 —Ant. broaden

specially [adv] *particularly* distinctively, especially, expressly, in specie, specifically, uniquely; CONCEPT 557 —Ant. broadly

specialty [n] *distinctive feature; concentration* career, claim to fame, cup of tea*, distinguishing feature, field of concentration, forte, game*, hobby, job, long suit*, magnum opus, major, masterpiece, minor, number, object of attention, object of study, occupation, pièce de résistance*, practice, profession, pursuit, racket*, special, speciality, special project, thing*, vocation, weakness, work; CONCEPT 349 —*Ant.* generalization

species [n] *class, variety* breed, category, collection, description, division, group, kind, likes*, lot, nature, number, order, sort, stripe*, type; CONCEPT 378

specific [adj] *particular, distinguishing* bull's eye*, categorical, characteristic, clean-cut, clear-cut, cut fine*, dead on*, definite, definitive, different, distinct, downright, drawn fine, especial, exact, explicit, express, flat out*, hit nail on head*, individual, limited, on target, outright, peculiar, precise, reserved, restricted, right on, set, sole, special, specialized, straight-out, unambiguous, unequivocal, unique; CONCEPTS 535,557,564 —*Ant.* general, indefinite, uncertain, vague

specifically [adv] *expressly, particularly* accurately, categorically, characteristically, clearly, concretely, correctly, definitely, distinctively, especially, exactly, explicitly, in detail, indicatively, individually, in specie, minutely, peculiarly, pointedly, precisely, respectively, specially; CONCEPTS 557,564 —*Ant.* broadly, generally

specification [n] *requirement, qualification* blueprint, condition, designation, detail, item, particular, particularization, spec*, stipulation, term; CONCEPTS 270,646 —*Ant.* generalization, uncertainty, vagueness

specify [v] *designate; decide definitely* be specific, blueprint*, button down*, cite, come to the point, condition, define, detail, determine, draw a picture*, enumerate, establish, finger*, fix, get down to brass tacks*, get to the point*, go into detail, indicate, individualize, instance, inventory, itemize, lay out, limit, list, make, mention, name, particularize, peg, pin down, point out, precise, put down, put finger on*, set, settle, show clearly, slot, specialize, specificate, specificize, spell out, stipulate, tab, tag, tick off; CONCEPTS 18,57 —*Ant.* generalize

specimen [n] *example, sample* case, case history, copy, cross section, embodiment, exemplar, exemplification, exhibit, illustration, individual, instance, model, part, pattern, proof, representation, representative, sampling, sort, species, type, unit, variety; CONCEPTS 686,831

specious [adj] *misleading* apparent, apparently right, beguiling, captious, casuistic, colorable, credible, deceptive, delusive, empty, erroneous, fallacious, false, flattering, hollow, idle, illogical, inaccurate, incorrect, likely, nugatory, ostensible, ostentatious, plausible, presumable, presumptive, pretentious, probable, seeming, sophistic, sophistical, sophisticated, spurious, unsound, untrue, vain, wrong; CONCEPTS 552,582 —*Ant.* real, true, valid

speck [n] *tiny bit* atom, blemish, blot, crumb, defect, dot, fault, flaw, fleck, flyspeck, grain, iota, jot, mark, mite, modicum, molecule, mote,

particle, point, shred, smidgen, speckle, splotch, spot, stain, trace, whit; CONCEPT 831 —*Ant.* lot

speckled [adj] *dotted* brindled, dappled, flaked, flecked, freckled, mosaic, motley, mottled, particolored, patchy, peppered, punctate, spotted, spotty, sprinkled, stippled, studded, variegated; CONCEPTS 485,618 —*Ant.* plain, unspeckled

spectacle [n] *something showy; exhibition* comedy, curiosity, demonstration, display, drama, event, exposition, extravaganza, marvel, movie, pageant, parade, performance, phenomenon, play, production, representation, scene, show, sight, spectacular, tableau, view, wonder; CONCEPT 529 —*Ant.* normality, ordinariness

spectacles [n] *eyeglasses* bifocals, blinkers*, contact lenses, contacts, glasses, goggles, lorgnette, monocle, pair of glasses, pince-nez, reading glasses, shades*, specs*, sunglasses, trifocals; CONCEPT 446

spectacular [adj] *wonderful, impressive* amazing, astonishing, astounding, breathtaking, daring, dazzling, dramatic, eye-catching, fabulous, fantastic, grand, histrionic, magnificent, marked, marvelous, miraculous, prodigious, razzle-dazzle*, remarkable, sensational, splendid, staggering, striking, stunning, stupendous, theatrical, thrilling, wondrous; CONCEPTS 529, 537,574 —*Ant.* normal, ordinary, regular, unspectacular, usual

spectator [n] *person who watches event* beholder, bystander, clapper, eyewitness, fan, gaper*, gazer, kibitzer*, looker, looker-on, moviegoer, observer, onlooker, perceiver, playgoer, seer, showgoer, sports fan, standee, stander-by, theatergoer, viewer, watcher, witness; CONCEPTS 366,423 —*Ant.* participant

specter [n] *ghost* apparition, appearance, demon, doppelganger, phantasm, phantom, poltergeist, presence, shadow, spirit, spook, vision; CONCEPT 370

spectral [adj] *ghostly* apparitional, eerie, haunted, illusory, phantasmal, phantom, scary, shadowy, spiritual, spooky, supernatural; CONCEPTS 485,537

speculate [v1] *think about deeply and theorize* beat one's brains*, brainstorm*, build castles in air*, call it, call the turn, cerebrate, chew over*, cogitate, conjecture, consider, contemplate, deliberate, dope*, dope out*, excogitate, figure, figure out*, guess, guesstimate*, have a hunch*, hazard a guess, head trip*, hypothesize, kick around*, meditate, muse, pipedream*, psych out*, read, read between lines*, reason, reflect, review, ruminate, run it up flagpole*, scheme, size up, study, suppose, surmise, suspect, weigh, wonder; CONCEPTS 17,24,28,37 —*Ant.* ignore, neglect

speculate [v2] *gamble, risk* dare, hazard, make book*, margin up*, play, play the market*, plunge, pour money into*, spec*, stick neck out*, take a chance, take a flier*, take a fling*, venture, wildcat; CONCEPTS 28,330,363 —*Ant.* abstain

speculation [n1] *theory, guess* belief, brainwork*, cerebration, cogitation, conjecture, consideration, contemplation, deliberation, excogitation, guesstimate*, guesswork, hunch, hypothesis, meditation, opinion, reflection, review, shot, shot in the dark*, sneaking suspicion*, stab, stab in the dark*, studying, supposition, surmise, thinking, thought, weighing; CONCEPTS 24,28,529,689 —*Ant.* fact, information, reality, truth

speculation [*n2*] *risk, gamble* backing, flier*, flutter, gambling, hazard, hunch, piece, plunge, right money*, risky business*, risky venture, shot, shot in the dark*, smart money*, spec*, speculative enterprise, stab*, venture, wager; CONCEPTS 192,330,363 —*Ant.* abstention

speculative [*adj*] *theoretical* abstract, analytical, assumed, conceptive, dangerous, dicey, experimental, formularized, hairy, hazardous, hypothetical, ideal, idealized, ideological, iffy, intellectual, in theory, logical, notional, philosophical, presumed, risky, uncertain, unproved, unproven, unsubstantiated; CONCEPT 529

speech [*n1*] *talk* accent, articulation, communication, conversation, dialect, dialogue, diction, discussion, doublespeak*, double talk*, elocution, enunciation, expressing, expression, idiom, intercourse, jargon, language, lingo, locution, mother tongue, native tongue, oral communication, palaver, parlance, prattle, pronunciation, prose, speaking, spiel, tone, utterance, verbalization, vernacular, vocal expression, vocalization, vocalizing, voice, voicing; CONCEPTS 47,266,266 —*Ant.* listening, quiet, silence

speech [*n2*] *formal talk to audience* address, allocution, appeal, bombast, chalk talk*, commentary, debate, declamation, diatribe, discourse, disquisition, dissertation, eulogy, exhortation, harangue, homily, invocation, keynote, lecture, opus, oration, oratory, panegyric, paper, parlance, parley, pep talk*, pitch, prelection, recitation, rhetoric, salutation, sermon, spiel*, stump* tirade, valedictory; CONCEPTS 60,285 —*Ant.* listening

speechless [*adj*] *without ability to talk* aghast, amazed, aphonic, astounded, buttoned up*, clammed up*, close-mouthed, cool*, cool as cucumber*, dazed, dumb, dumbfounded, dumbstruck, inarticulate, mum, mute, not saying boo*, reserved, shocked, silent, taciturn, thunderstruck*, tight-lipped*, tongue-tied*, uncommunicative, unflappable, voiceless, wordless; CONCEPT 267 —*Ant.* articulate, communicative, responsive

speed [*n*] *rate of motion, often a high rate* acceleration, activity, agility, alacrity, breeze, briskness, celerity, clip, dispatch, eagerness, expedition, fleetness, gait, haste, headway, hurry, hustle, legerity, lick, liveliness, momentum, pace, precipitancy, precipitation, promptitude, promptness, quickness, rapidity, rapidness, readiness, rush, rustle, snap, steam, swiftness, urgency, velocity; CONCEPT 755

speed [*v*] *move along quickly* advance, aid, assist, barrel, belt, bomb, boost, bowl over, career, cover ground*, cut along, dispatch, expedite, facilitate, flash, fly, further, gallop, gather momentum, gear up*, get a move on*, get moving, get under way, go all out*, go fast, go like the wind*, hasten, help, hightail*, hurry, impel, lose no time*, make haste, open up throttle*, press on, promote, quicken, race, ride, run, rush, sail, spring, step on it*, tear, urge, whiz, zoom; CONCEPTS 110,150,152 —*Ant.* delay, halt, slow

speedy [*adj*] *fast, quick* accelerated, agile,

alacritous, breakneck, brisk, expeditious, express, fleet, harefooted, hasty, headlong, hurried, immediate, lissome, lively, nimble, precipitate, prompt, quick-fire, rapid, rapid-fire, ready, snappy, summary, supersonic, swift, ultrasonic, winged; CONCEPTS 548,584,588 —*Ant.* delayed, halted, slowed, tardy

spell [*n1*] *interval, period* bit, bout, course, go, hitch, interlude, intermission, patch, relay, season, shift, space, stint, streak, stretch, term, time, tour, tour of duty, trick, turn, while; CONCEPTS 807,817,822

spell [*n2*] *magical aura over an entity* abracadabra*, allure, amulet, bewitching, bewitchment, charm, conjuration, enchanting, enchantment, exorcism, fascination, glamour, hex, hexing, hocus-pocus*, incantation, jinx, magic, mumbo jumbo*, rune, sorcery, talisman, trance, voodoo*, whack*, whammy*, witchery; CONCEPTS 370,673,689

spell [*n3*] *seizure* access, attack, fit, illness, jag, paroxysm, spasm, stroke, throe, turn; CONCEPTS 306,308

spell [*v1*] *mean, imply* add up to, amount to, augur, connote, denote, express, herald, import, indicate, intend, point to, portend, presage, promise, signify, suggest; CONCEPTS 55,74,75

spell [*v2*] *give rest, relief* allow, breathe, free, lay off, lie by, release, relieve, stand in for, take over, take the place of; CONCEPTS 83,110 —*Ant.* abuse, run ragged, use

spellbound [*adj*] *enchanted, fascinated* agape, amazed, bemused, bewildered, bewitched, breathless, captivated, caught up, charmed, enthralled, gripped, held, hooked, mesmerized, open-mouthed, petrified, possessed, rapt, transfixed, transported, under a spell; CONCEPT 403 —*Ant.* disenchanted, disinterested

spell out [*v*] *clarify, explain* break down, brief, clear up, clue in, decipher, decode, define, describe, diagram, draw a map*, expound, fill someone in*, get across*, go into detail, illustrate, interpret, justify, make plain*, point out, put across, put in plain English*, teach, tell, throw light upon*, translate, unfold, unravel, untangle; CONCEPT 57

spend [*v1*] *give, pay out* absorb, allocate, ante up*, apply, bestow, blow*, cast away, come across, come through, concentrate, confer, consume, contribute, cough up*, defray, deplete, disburse, dispense, dissipate, donate, drain, drop, employ, empty, evote, exhaust, expend, foot the bill*, fritter, give, hand out, invest, lavish, lay out, liquidate, misspend, outlay, pay down, pay up, put in, run through, settle, shell out*, spring for*, squander, throw away, use, use up, waste; CONCEPTS 156,169,225,341 —*Ant.* earn, get, receive

spend [*v2*] *use time; occupy* consume, devote, drift, employ, fill, fool around*, fritter, go, idle, kill, laze, let pass, misuse, pass; put in, squander, waste, while away*; CONCEPT 100 —*Ant.* be lazy

spendthrift [*n*] *person careless with money* big spender*, dissipater, high-roller*, improvident, imprudent, prodigal, profligate, spender, sport, squanderer, waster, wastrel; CONCEPTS 348,353, 423 —*Ant.* miser, saver

spent [*adj*] *used up, gone; tired out* all in*,

sp
sp

bleary, blown, burnt-out*, bushed, consumed, dead*, debilitated, depleted, disbursed, dissipated, dog-tired*, done-in*, down the drain*, drained, effete, enervated, exhausted, expended, fagged, far-gone*, finished, had it*, limp, lost, played-out*, prostrate, ready to drop*, shattered, shot, thrown away, used, washed-up*, wasted, weakened, wearied, weary, worn out; CONCEPTS 314,560,771 —Ant. hoarded, retained, saved

spew [v] *spit out* belch, bring up, cascade, disgorge, eject, eruct, erupt, expel, flood, gush, heave, irrupt, puke*, regurgitate, scatter, spit, spit up, spread, spritz, throw up, urp*, vomit; CONCEPTS 179,308

sphere [n1] *globular object* apple*, ball, big blue marble*, circle, Earth, globe, globule, orb, pellet, pill, planet, rondure, round; CONCEPTS 436,511

sphere [n2] *domain of influence* bailiwick, capacity, champaign, circle, class, compass, demesne, department, dominion, employment, field, function, ground, jungle, jurisdiction, level, neck of the woods*, orbit, pale, position, precinct, province, range, rank, realm, scope, station, stomping ground*, stratum, terrain, territory, turf*, walk of life, zone; CONCEPTS 349,388,687

spice [n] *flavor, zest* aroma, color, excitement, fragrance, gusto, guts*, kick, pep, piquancy, pungency, relish, salt, savor, scent, seasoning, tang, zap*, zip*; CONCEPTS 614,673 —Ant. blandness, dullness

spick-and-span [adj] *spotless* clean, fresh, gleaming, hygienic, immaculate, neat, polished, pure, sanitary, shining, shipshape, tidy, unsoiled, unstained, untarnished, very clean; CONCEPTS 404,621

spicy [adj1] *pungent, flavorful* ambrosial, appetizing, aromal, aromatic, distinctive, fiery, flavorsome, fragrant, fresh, herbaceous, highly seasoned, hot, keen, odoriferous, peppery, perfumed, piquant, poignant, racy, redolent, savory, scented, seasoned, snappy, spirited, sweet, tangy, tasty, zesty, zippy*; CONCEPT 613 —Ant. bland, dull, flavorless, tasteless

spicy [adj2] *off-color, vulgar* breezy, broad, erotic, hot*, indelicate, racy, red hot*, ribald, risqué*, salty*, scandalous, sensational, sophisticated, suggestive, titillating, unseemly, wicked, X-rated*; CONCEPTS 267,372,545 —Ant. clean, decent, moral

spiel [n] *patter, sales pitch* chatter, empty talk, jabber*, jive*, line*, pitch*, sales talk, song and dance*; CONCEPTS 276,278

spiffy [adj] *stylish* a la mode*, beautiful, chic, chichi*, classy, dandy, dapper, dashing, dressed to kill*, fashionable, high-class*, in fashion, in vogue, jazzy*, mod*, now*, ritzy, sharp, showy, sleek, slick*, smart, snappy*, snazzy*, stunning, swank*, upscale, uptown, voguish; CONCEPTS 579,589

spike [v] *pierce* fasten, impale, lance, make fast, nail, pin, prick, skewer, spear, spit, stick, transfix; CONCEPT 220

spill [v1] *slop, drop* discharge, disgorge, dribble, drip, empty, flow, lose, overfill, overflow, overrun, overturn, pour, run, run out, run over, scatter, shed, spill over, splash, splatter, spray, sprinkle, spurt, squirt, stream, throw off, upset,

well over; CONCEPTS 179,181 —Ant. clean up, pick up

spill [v2] *reveal* betray, blab, blow, disclose, divulge, give away, inform, let the cat out of the bag*, mouth, squeal, tattle, tell; CONCEPT 60 —Ant. conceal, hide

spin [n] *circular motion* circuit, gyration, revolution, roll, rotation, spiral, turn, twist, whirl; CONCEPT 748 —Ant. immobility, inaction, inactivity

spin [v] *go around, make go around* gyrate, gyre, oscillate, pendulate, pirouette, purl, reel, revolve, rotate, spiral, swim, turn, twirl, twist, wheel, whirl; CONCEPTS 150,152,218 —Ant. stand, steady

spine [n] *backbone* back, bone, chine, rachis, ridge, spinal column, vertebrae, vertebral column; CONCEPTS 393,420

spineless [adj] *cowardly* amoebalike*, fainthearted, fearful, feeble, forceless, frightened, gutless*, impotent, inadequate, ineffective, ineffectual, invertebrate, irresolute, lily-livered*, nerveless, pithless, soft, spiritless, squeamish, submissive, timid, vacillating, weak, weak-kneed, weak-willed, yellow*, yellow-bellied*; CONCEPTS 401,542 —Ant. bold, brave, strong

spin-off [n] *offshoot* adjunct, branch, by-product, derivative, descendant, division, offspring, outgrowth, sequel; CONCEPTS 260,824

spiral [adj] *curling, winding* circling, circular, circumvoluted, cochlear, coiled, corkscrew, curled, helical, helicoid, radial, rolled, screw-shaped, scrolled, tendrillar, tortile, voluted, whorled, wound; CONCEPT 486 —Ant. straight, uncurling, unwinding

spiral [n] *curled shape* coil, corkscrew, curlicue, flourish, gyration, gyre, helix, quirk, screw, volute, whorl; CONCEPT 436

spirit [n1] *soul, attitude* air, animation, ardor, backbone*, boldness, breath, character, complexion, courage, dauntlessness, disposition, earnestness, energy, enterprise, enthusiasm, essence, fire, force, frame of mind, gameness, grit*, guts*, heart, humor, jazz*, life, life force, liveliness, mettle, mood, morale, motivation, nerve, oomph*, outlook, psyche, quality, resolution, resolve, sparkle, spunk*, stoutheartedness, substance, temper, temperament, tenor, vigor, vitality, vital spark, warmth, will, willpower, zest; CONCEPTS 407,411

spirit [n2] *atmosphere, essence* feeling, genius, gist, humor, intent, intention, meaning, purport, purpose, quality, sense, substance, temper, tenor, timbre, tone; CONCEPTS 673,682

spirit [n3] *ghost* apparition, eidolon, phantasm, phantom, poltergeist, shade, shadow, soul, specter, spook, sprite, supernatural being, umbra, vision, wraith; CONCEPT 370 —Ant. being, reality

spirited [adj] *lively, vivacious* active, alert, animate, animated, ardent, audacious, avid, bold, bouncy, brave, bright, burning, chirpy, courageous, dauntless, eager, effervescent, energetic, enthusiastic, fearless, fiery, full of life, game, gingery*, gritty, gutsy*, high-spirited, hot, hyper*, intrepid, jumping, keen, mettlesome, nervy, passionate, peppery, peppy, plucky, resolute, rocking, sharp, snappy, sparkling, sprightly, spunky, vigorous, zappy*,

zealous, zesty, zingy*, zippy*; CONCEPTS
404,542 —*Ant.* apathetic, depressed, dispirited,
lazy, lethargic, unhappy, unlively

spiritless [*adj*] *depressed* apathetic, blah*,
blue*, broken, cast down, dejected, despondent, disconsolate, dispirited, dopey*, down,
downcast, downhearted, down in the dumps*,
down in the mouth*, draggy, drippy, droopy,
dull, enervated, flat*, flat tire*, inanimate,
indifferent, lackadaisical, lackluster, languid,
languishing, languorous, lifeless, limp, listless,
low, melancholic, melancholy, mopy, slothful,
subdued, submissive, tame, torpid, unconcerned,
unenthusiastic, unmoved, zero*; CONCEPT 403,
—*Ant.* energetic, happy, lively, spirited, uplifted

spiritual [*adj*] *religious, otherworldly* airy, asomatous, devotional, discarnate, disembodied,
divine, ethereal, extramundane, ghostly, holy,
immaterial, incorporeal, intangible, metaphysical, nonmaterial, nonphysical, platonic, pure,
rarefied, refined, sacred, supernal, unfleshly,
unphysical; CONCEPTS 536,582 —*Ant.* bodily,
irreligious, irreverent, physical, unspiritual

spit [*n*] *saliva* discharge, dribble, drool, slaver,
spittle, sputum, water; CONCEPT 467

spit [*v*] *eject saliva or substance* discharge,
drool, expectorate, hawk, hiss, sibilate, sizz,
slobber, spatter, spew, splutter, spritz, sputter,
throw out; CONCEPTS 179,185 —*Ant.* swallow

spite [*n*] *hateful feeling* animosity, antipathy,
bad blood*, contempt, despite, enmity, gall,
grudge, harsh feeling, hate, hatred, ill will,
malevolence, malice, maliciousness, malignity,
peeve, pique, rancor, resentment, revenge,
spitefulness, spleen, umbrage, vengeance,
vengefulness, venom, vindictiveness; CONCEPT
29 —*Ant.* liking, love, loving

spite [*v*] *offend, hurt* annoy, begrudge, beset,
crab*, cramp style*, discomfit, gall, get even*,
grudge, hang up*, harass, harm, injure, louse
up*, needle, nettle, persecute, pique, provoke,
put out*, upset the apple cart*, vex; CONCEPTS
7,19,121 —*Ant.* forgive, help, love, please

spiteful [*adj*] *hurtful, nasty* accidentally on
purpose*, angry, barbed, catty*, cruel, cussed*,
despiteful, dirty, evil, hateful, ill-disposed, ill-
natured, malevolent, malicious, malign, malignant, mean, ornery*, rancorous, snide, spleenful,
splenetic, venomous, vicious, vindictive,
waspish, wicked; CONCEPTS 401,542 —*Ant.*
affectionate, forgiving, helpful, loving, pleasing

spitting image [*n*] *look-alike* carbon copy,
clone, double, duplicate, exact likeness, likeness, match, replica, ringer*, twin, very image;
CONCEPTS 414,664,670

splash [*n*] *spattering, impact* burst, dash, display,
effect, patch, sensation, splurge, stir, touch;
CONCEPT 676

splash [*v*] *throw liquid* bathe, bespatter, broadcast, dabble, dash, douse, drench, drown, get
wet, moisten, paddle, plash, plunge, shower,
slop, slosh, soak, sop, spatter, splatter, spray,
spread, sprinkle, squirt, strew, throw, wade,
wallow, wet; CONCEPTS 222,256

splatter [*v*] *splash* bespatter, douse, drench,
drown, get wet, moisten, plunge, shower, slosh,
soak, sop, spatter, spray, sprinkle, squirt, wet;
CONCEPTS 222,256

splendid [*adj1*] *luxurious, expensive* baroque,

beaming, beautiful, bright, brilliant, costly,
dazzling, elegant, fab*, fat*, flamboyant,
glittering, glowing, gorgeous, grand, grandiose,
imposing, impressive, lavish, lustrous, mad*,
magnificent, magnifico, marvelous, ornate,
plush, posh, radiant, refulgent, resplendent,
rich, solid gold*, splashy, splendiferous, splen-
drous, sumptuous, superb, swanky*; CONCEPTS
334,485,589 —*Ant.* drab, poor, shabby, shoddy

splendid [*adj2*] *excellent, illustrious* admirable,
brilliant, celebrated, distinguished, divine,
eminent, exceptional, exquisite, fantastic, fine,
first-class, glorious, gorgeous, grand, great,
heroic, impressive, magnificent, marvelous,
matchless, outstanding, peerless, premium,
proud, rare, remarkable, renowned, resplendent,
royal, splendiferous, splendorous, sterling,
sublime, superb, superlative, supreme, transcendent, unparalleled, unsurpassed, very good,
wonderful; CONCEPTS 568,574 —*Ant.* humble,
insignificant, ordinary, regular, usual

splendor [*n*] *radiance, glory* brightness, brilliance, ceremony, dazzle, display, effulgence,
gorgeousness, grandeur, luster, magnificence,
majesty, pageant, pomp, refulgence, renown,
resplendence, richness, show, solemnity, spectacle, stateliness, sumptuousness; CONCEPTS
620,655,673 —*Ant.* dullness, insignificance,
ordinariness, poorness

splice [*v*] *join, interweave* braid, entwine,
graft, hitch, interlace, intertwine, intertwist,
knit, marry, mate, mesh, plait, tie, unite,
weave, wed, yoke; CONCEPT 193 —*Ant.*
divide, separate, sever

splinter [*n*] *thin piece of solid* bit, chip, flake,
fragment, needle, paring, shaving, sliver, wood;
CONCEPTS 471,479,831

splinter [*v*] *break into thin, small pieces* break
to smithereens*, burst, disintegrate, fracture,
fragment, pash, rive, shatter, shiver, smash,
split; CONCEPT 246 —*Ant.* combine, fix, mend

split [*n1*] *opening* breach, chasm, chink, cleavage, cleft, crack, damage, division, fissure, gap,
rent, rift, rima, rimation, rime, rip, rupture,
separation, slash, slit, tear; CONCEPT 513
—*Ant.* closing, closure

split [*n2*] *difference, disunion* alienation, breach,
break, break-up, discord, disruption, dissension,
divergence, division, estrangement, fissure,
fracture, partition, rent, rift, rupture, schism;
CONCEPT 388 —*Ant.* juncture, marriage, union

split [*v1*] *break up, pull apart* bifurcate, branch,
break, burst, cleave, come apart, come undone,
crack, dichotomize, disband, disjoin, dissever,
disunite, diverge, divide, divorce, fork, gape,
give way, go separate ways, hack, isolate, open,
part, part company, put asunder, rend, rip, rive,
separate, sever, slash, slit, snap, splinter, sunder, tear, whack; CONCEPTS 135,176,297 —*Ant.*
combine, join, pull together

split [*v2*] *divide into parts* allocate, allot,
apportion, carve up, distribute, divvy*,
divvy up*, dole, go even-steven*, go fifty-
fifty*, halve, mete out, parcel out, partition,
share, slice, slice the pie*, slice up; CONCEPT 98
—*Ant.* combine, join

split up [*v*] *keep apart; segregate; separate*
break off, break up, come apart, detach, disband, disconnect, divide, divorce, go separate

ways, group, part, part company, rope off, seclude, sever, sort, stand between, undo; CONCEPTS *135,158,201,297,384*

splurge [v] *spend lavishly* be extravagant, binge, celebrate, fling, give a party*, rampage, spread; CONCEPTS *327,377* —*Ant.* hoard, save

spoil [v1] *ruin, hurt* blemish, damage, debase, deface, defile, demolish, depredate, desecrate, desolate, despoil, destroy, devastate, disfigure, disgrace, harm, impair, injure, make useless, mar, mess up*, muck up*, pillage, plunder, prejudice, ravage, sack, smash, spoliate, squash, take apart, tarnish, trash*, undo, upset, vitiate, waste, wreck; CONCEPTS *246,252* —*Ant.* help

spoil [v2] *baby, indulge* accommodate, cater to, coddle, cosset, favor, humor, kill with kindness*, mollycoddle*, oblige, overindulge, pamper, spoon-feed*; CONCEPTS *14,136* —*Ant.* be indifferent, ignore, neglect

spoil [v3] *decay, turn bad* addle, become tainted, become useless, break down, crumble, curdle, decompose, deteriorate, disintegrate, go bad, go off, mildew, molder, putrefy, rot, taint, turn; CONCEPTS *456,469* —*Ant.* grow

spoils [n] *possessions stolen or gained* booty*, cut*, gain, goods, graft, hot goods/loot, make*, pickings, pillage, plunder, prey, prize, squeeze, swag, take; CONCEPTS *337,710*

spoken [adj] *by word of mouth* announced, articulate, communicated, expressed, lingual, mentioned, oral, phonetic, phonic, put into words, said, sonant, told, traditional, unwritten, uttered, verbal, viva voce, voiced; CONCEPT *267* —*Ant.* heard, written

spokesperson [n] *person who communicates for another* agent, champion, delegate, deputy, mediator, mouth, mouthpiece*, prolocutor, prophet, protagonist, representative, speaker, stand-in, substitute, talker; CONCEPTS *348,354*

sponge [n] *moocher* bum*, cadger, deadbeat*, freeloader*, hanger-on, leech*, panhandler, parasite, scrounger; CONCEPTS *412,423*

sponge [v] *mooch* beg, bum*, cadge, chisel*, freeload*, hit up*, hustle, live off of, panhandle, scrounge; CONCEPT *53*

spongy [adj] *cushioned, absorbent* absorptive, cushiony, elastic, light, mushy, pappy, porous, pulpous, pulpy, resilient, rubbery, soft, springy, squishy, yielding; CONCEPT *606* —*Ant.* hard, impermeable, inflexible

sponsor [n] *person who helps, promotes another* adherent, advocate, angel*, backer, benefactor, godparent, grubstaker, guarantor, mainstay, patron, promoter, supporter, surety, sustainer, underwriter; CONCEPTS *348,423*

sponsor [v] *help, promote* answer for, back, bankroll, be responsible for, finance, fund, grubstake, guarantee, patronize, put up money, stake, subsidize, vouch for; CONCEPTS *110,341* —*Ant.* disapprove, discourage, hurt

spontaneous [adj] *impulsive, willing* ad-lib*, automatic, break loose, casual, down, extemporaneous, extempore, free, free spirited, from the hip*, impetuous, impromptu, improvised, inevitable, instinctive, involuntary, irresistible, natural, offhand, off-the-cuff*, off top of head*, simple, unartful, unavoidable, unbidden, uncompelled, unconscious, unconstrained, uncontrived, uncontrolled, unforced, uninten-

tional, unplanned, unpremediated, unprompted, unsophisticated, unstudied, up front, voluntary; CONCEPTS *401,542,548* —*Ant.* deliberate, intended, planned, premeditated

spoof [n] *trick, mockery* bluff, bon mot, burlesque, caricature, cheat, deceit, deception, fake, flim-flam*, game, hoax, imposture, jest, joke, lampoon, parody, phony, prank, put-on, quip, satire, sell, send-up*, sham, take-off, travesty, trickery, wisecrack; CONCEPTS *59,273*

spook [v] *frighten, scare* alarm, curdle the blood*, discomfort, horrify, make one's blood run cold*, make one's teeth chatter*, panic, petrify, scare away, scare stiff*, scare the pants off of*, scare to death*, startle, strike terror into*, terrify, unnerve; CONCEPTS *7,14,19,42*

spooky [adj] *frightening* chilling, creepy, eerie, ghostly, mysterious, ominous, scary, spine-chilling, supernatural, uncanny, unearthly, weird; CONCEPTS *529,537* —*Ant.* natural, unfrightening

spoon-feed [v] *pamper* baby, cater to, coddle, give in, indulge, mollycoddle*, overindulge, spoil, spoil rotten*; CONCEPTS *136,295*

sporadic [adj] *on and off* bits and pieces*, desultory, few, fitful, fits and starts*, hit-or-miss*, infrequent, intermittent, irregular, isolated, occasional, on-again-off-again*, random, rare, scarce, scattered, seldom, semioccasional, spasmodic, spotty, uncommon, unfrequent; CONCEPT *541* —*Ant.* constant, continuous, dependable

sport [n1] *recreational activity; entertainment* action, amusement, athletics, ball, disport, diversion, exercise, frolic, fun, fun and games*, gaiety, game, games, pastime, physical activity, picnic, play, pleasure, recreation; CONCEPT *363* —*Ant.* vocation, work

sport [n2] *fun, joking* badinage, banter, derision, drollery, escapade, frolic, horseplay, jest, jesting, joke, jollification, jollity, kidding, laughter, merriment, mirth, mockery, mummery, nonsense, pleasantry, practical joke, raillery, scorn, teasing, tomfoolery, trifling; CONCEPTS *59,273* —*Ant.* seriousness

sport [n3] *person who takes kidding* buffoon, butt, jestee, joke, laughingstock, mock, mockery, object of derision, object of ridicule, plaything, target; CONCEPT *423*

sport [v] *display, wear* be dressed in, don, exhibit, have on, model, show off; CONCEPTS *167,261*

sporting/sportive [adj] *playful and fair* antic, coltish, considerate, devil-may-care*, frisky, frolicsome, full of fun*, game, gamesome, gay, generous, impish, jaunty, joyous, larkish, lively, merry, mischievous, reasonable, roguish, rollicking, sportspersonlike, sprightly, square, wild; CONCEPT *401* —*Ant.* unfair, unplayful, unsporting

sportsmanship [n] *integrity* fairness, forthrightness, gamesmanship, goodness, honesty, honor, honorableness, principle, righteousness, sincerity, virtue; CONCEPT *417*

sporty [adj] *casual; flashy* brazen, flamboyant, flaunting, gaudy, glittering, glittery, glitzy, informal, jazzy*, loud, natty, ornate, showy, snazzy; CONCEPTS *401,542,589*

spot [n1] *mark, stain* atom, blemish, blot, blotch, daub, discoloration, dollop, dram, drop, flaw, iota, jot, little bit, mite, molecule, mote, nip, particle, pimple, pinch, shot, smidgen, smudge, snort, speck, taint, whit; CONCEPTS 284,831 —*Ant.* plainness

spot [*n2*] *location* hangout*, hole*, joint*, layout, locality, locus, office, pad, place, plant, point, position, post, roof, scene, seat, section, sector, site, situation, slot, station, wherever*, X*, X marks the spot*; CONCEPT 198

spot [*n3*] *bad situation* box*, corner*, difficulty, dilemma, fix, hole*, jam, mess, pickle*, plight, predicament, quandary, scrape, trouble; CONCEPT 666 —*Ant.* benefit, boon, success

spot [*n4*] *position in organization* appointment, berth, billet, connection, job, office, place, post, responsibility, situation, station, work; CONCEPTS 351,362

spot [*v1*] *mark, stain* besmirch, bespatter, blot, blotch, dapple, dirty, dot, fleck, maculate, marble, mottle, pepper, pimple, soil, spatter, speck, speckle, splash, splotch, stipple, streak, stripe, stud, sully, taint, tarnish; CONCEPTS 79,179 —*Ant.* clean, unspot

spot [*v2*] *see, recognize* catch, catch sight of, descry, detect, determinate, diagnose, discern, discover, distinguish, encounter, espy, ferret out, find, identify, locate, make out, meet with, observe, pick out, pinpoint, place, point out, sight, trace, track, turn up; CONCEPTS 38,183,626 —*Ant.* overlook

spotless [*adj*] *very clean; innocent* above reproach, blameless, chaste, clean, decent, faultless, flawless, gleaming, hygienic, immaculate, irreproachable, modest, pure, sanitary, shining, snowy, stainless, unblemished, undefiled, unimpeachable, unsoiled, unstained, unsullied, untarnished; CONCEPTS 404,621 —*Ant.* dirty, soiled, spotted, stained

spotlight [*n*] *attention; bright beam of light* center stage, fame, flashlight, floodlight, interest, light, limelight, notoriety, public attention, public eye, publicity; CONCEPTS 388,624,668 —*Ant.* obscurity

spotlight [*v*] *focus attention on* accentuate, draw attention, feature, floodlight*, give prominence, highlight, illuminate, limelight*, point up, publicize, put on center stage*; CONCEPTS 261,292 —*Ant.* turn aside

spotted [*adj*] *speckled* blotched, dappled, dotted, flaked, flecked, freckled, mosaic, motley, patchy, pied, spotty, sprinkled; CONCEPTS 485, 618

spotty [*adj*] *blotchy, irregular* desultory, erratic, flickering, fluctuating, not uniform, on-again-off-again*, patchy, pimply, spasmodic, sporadic, unequal, uneven; CONCEPT 534 —*Ant.* constant, regular, unbroken

spouse [*n*] *one of a married couple* better half*, bride, companion, groom, helpmate, husband, man, mate, partner, roommate, wife, woman; CONCEPT 414

spout [*v1*] *spurt, emit* cascade, discharge, eject, erupt, expel, exude, gush, jet, pour, roll, shoot, spill, spray, squirt, stream, surge; CONCEPT 179 —*Ant.* drain

spout [*v2*] *talk forcefully* boast, brag, chatter, declaim, expatiate, go on, gush, harangue, hold forth, orate, pontificate, ramble, rant, sermonize, shoot off one's mouth*, speechify, spellbind,

spiel, vapor, yell; CONCEPTS 49,51 —*Ant.* be quiet

sprawl [*v*] *sit or lie spread out* drape, extend, flop, lie, lie spread-eagle*, loll, lounge, ramble, recline, sit, slouch, slump, spread, straddle, straggle, stretch, trail; CONCEPT 201 —*Ant.* straighten

spray [*n*] *fine mist* aerosol, atomizer, drizzle, droplets, duster, fog, froth, moisture, spindrift, splash, sprayer, sprinkler, vaporizer; CONCEPTS 514,680

spray [*v*] *sprinkle, diffuse* atomize, drizzle, dust, scatter, shoot, shower, smear, spatter, splash, spritz, squirt, throw around; CONCEPTS 179,256 —*Ant.* collect, gather

spread [*n1*] *expansion, development; extent* advance, advancement, compass, diffusion, dispersion, dissemination, enlargement, escalation, expanse, extension, increase, period, profusion, proliferation, radiation, ramification, range, reach, scope, span, spreading, stretch, suffusion, sweep, term, transfusion, transmission; CONCEPTS 651,704,721,788 —*Ant.* stagnation, suppression

spread [*n2*] *outlay of food, meal* array, banquet, blowout, dinner, feast, lunch, regale, repast; CONCEPT 459

spread [*v1*] *open or fan out* arrange, array, be displayed, be distributed, bloat, branch off, broaden, cast, circulate, coat, cover, daub, develop, diffuse, dilate, disperse, diverge, enlarge, escalate, even out, expand, extend, flatten, flow, gloss, increase, lay, lengthen, level, lie, multiply, mushroom, open, outstretch, overlay, paint, pervade, prepare, proliferate, radiate, reach, roll out, set, settle, smear, sprawl, spray, stretch, strew, suffuse, swell, uncoil, unfold, unfurl, unroll, untwist, unwind, widen; CONCEPTS 158,172,201 —*Ant.* close, collect, compress, gather

spread [*v2*] *publicize* advertise, blazon, broadcast, cast, circulate, declare, diffuse, disseminate, distribute, make known, make public, proclaim, promulgate, propagate, publish, radiate, scatter, shed, sow, strew, transmit; CONCEPT 60 —*Ant.* conceal, hide

spree [*n*] *wild activity* bacchanalia, ball, bash, binge, caper, carousal, carouse, carousing, celebration, field day*, fling, frolic, high jinks*, high time*, jag, jamboree, junket, lark, merry-go-round*, orgy, party, rampage, revel, rip*, spending expedition, splurge, tear*; CONCEPTS 327,377,384 —*Ant.* care, thriftiness

sprightly [*adj*] *fun, vivacious* active, agile, airy, alert, animate, animated, blithe, bouncy, breezy, bright, brisk, cheerful, cheery, chipper, chirpy, clever, dapper, dashing, energetic, fairylike, frolicsome, gay, good, grooving, hyper, jaunty, jolly, joyous, jumping, keen, keen-witted, light, lively, nimble, peppy, perky, playful, quick, quick-witted, saucy, scintillating, smart, snappy, spirited, sportive, spry, swinging, zappy*, zingy*,zippy*; CONCEPTS 401,404,542 —*Ant.* dull, inactive, lazy, lethargic

spring [*n1*] *jump, skip* bounce, bounciness, bound, buck, buoyancy, elasticity, flexibility, give, hop, leap, recoil, resilience, saltation, springiness, vault; CONCEPTS 194,731

spring [*n2*] *season following winter* blackberry

winter*, budding, budtime, flowering, prime, seedtime, springtide, springtime, vernal equinox, vernal season; CONCEPT *814*

spring [n3] *origin* beginning, cause, consideration, fount, fountain, fountainhead, impetus, motive, root, source, stimulus, well, wellspring, whence; CONCEPTS *648,661* —Ant. end, result

spring [n4] *body of rushing waters* artesian well, baths, fountain, geyser, hot spring, hydrolysate, spa, thermal spring, watering place, wells; CONCEPT *514*

spring [v1] *jump, skip* bolt, bounce, bound, hippety hop*, hop, hurdle, leap, lop, lope, rebound, recoil, skitter, start, startle, trip, vault; CONCEPT *194*

spring [v2] *originate, emerge* appear, arise, arrive, be derived, be descended, begin, birth, burgeon, come, come into being, come into existence, come out, commence, derive, descend, develop, emanate, flow, grow, hatch, head, issue, loom, mushroom, proceed, rise, shoot up, start, stem, upspring; CONCEPTS *105,302,373*

springy [adj] *elastic* adaptable, bouncy, flexible, limber, malleable, pliable, pliant, resilient, rubberlike, rubbery, stretchable, stretchy; CONCEPTS *490,606*

sprinkle [v] *scatter, disseminate* baptize, christen, dampen, dot, dredge, dust, freckle, mist, moisten, pepper, powder, rain, shake, shower, smear, speck, speckle, spit, spot, spray, spritz, squirt, strew, stud; CONCEPTS *179,222,256* —Ant. collect, gather

sprinkling [n] *hint, dash* admixture, dust, dusting, few, handful, lick, mixture, powdering, scattering, several, smattering, sprinkle, strain, taste, tinge, touch, trace; CONCEPT *831* —Ant. lot

sprint [v] *run very fast* dart, dash, go at top speed, hotfoot*, race, rush, scamper, scoot, scurry, shoot, tear, whiz; CONCEPT *150* —Ant. walk

sprout [v] *develop* bud, burgeon, germinate, grow, push, shoot, shoot up, spring, take root, vegetate; CONCEPT *257* —Ant. die, shrink, shrivel

spruce [adj] *stylish, neat* classy, clean, dainty, dapper, elegant, prim, smart, tidy, trim, well-groomed; CONCEPT *589* —Ant. unkempt, unstylish, untidy

spruce up [v] *make neat, well-groomed* brush, deck out*, dress up, fix up, groom, prim, primp, sleek, slick, smarten, tidy, titivate, wash; CONCEPTS *162,167,202* —Ant. dirty, mess up

spry [adj] *active, vivacious* agile, alert, brisk, energetic, fleet, full of pep, healthy, in full swing*, lithe, nimble, on the go*, prompt, quick, quick on the draw*, ready, robust, rocking, sound, spirited, sprightly, supple, vigorous; CONCEPT *401* —Ant. inactive, lethargic, old, unaware, unenergetic

spunk [n] *courage, nerve* backbone, determination, doggedness, fortitude, gameness, grit*, gumption*, guts*, intestinal fortitude*, mettle, moxie*, pluck, resolution, spirit, toughness, true grit*; CONCEPTS *411,633* —Ant. cowardice

spunky [adj] *spirited* active, alert, animated, bold, bouncy, brave, chirpy, courageous, eager, energetic, enthusiastic, fearless, fiery, full of life, full of spirit, game, gritty, gutsy*, high-

spirited, peppy, plucky, snappy, sprightly, tough, vigorous, zesty; zippy*; CONCEPTS *404,542*

spur [n] *incitement, stimulus* activation, actuation, catalyst, excitant, goad, goose*, impetus, impulse, incentive, incitation, inducement, motivation, motive, needle*, prick, stimulant, trigger, turn-on*, urge; CONCEPT *661* —Ant. curb, hindrance

spur [v] *incite, prompt* animate, arouse, awaken, countenance, drive, egg on*, exhort, favor, fire up*, goad, goose*, impel, instigate, key up, press, prick, prod, propel, push, put up to, rally, rouse, sic*, spark, stimulate, stir, trigger, turn on, urge, work up; CONCEPTS *14,68* —Ant. disapprove, discourage

spurious [adj] *counterfeit, fake* affected, apocryphal, artificial, assumed, bastard*, bent, bogus, bum, contrived, deceitful, deceptive, dummy*, ersatz, faked, false, feigned, forged, framed, illegitimate, imitation, make-believe, mock, phony, pirate, pretend, pretended, pseudo*, put-on*, sham*, simulated, specious, substitute, unauthentic, ungenuine, unreal; CONCEPT *582* —Ant. authentic, genuine, real, true

spurn [v] *turn away; ignore* air, contemn, cut, decline, despise, disapprove, disdain, dismiss, disregard, drop, dump, flout, flush*, give the cold shoulder*, hold in contempt, look down on*, nix*, not hear of*, pass by, rebuff, refuse, reject, reprobate, repudiate, repulse, scoff, scorn, slight, sneer, sneeze at*, snub, steer clear*, turn down, turn nose up at*; CONCEPTS *21,30,384* —Ant. embrace, want, welcome

spurt [n] *burst of activity* access, commotion, discharge, eruption, explosion, fit, jet, outburst, rush, spate, spritz, squirt, stream, surge; CONCEPTS *1,119,179* —Ant. continuity

spurt [v] *erupt* burst, emerge, flow, flow out, gush, issue, jet, ooze, pour out, shoot, spew, spout, spritz, squirt, stream, surge, well; CONCEPT *179*

spy [n] *person who secretly finds out another's business* agent, detective, double agent, emissary, espionage agent, foreign agent, informer, inside agent, intelligencer, investigator, lookout, mole*, observer, operative, patrol, picket, plant*, scout, secret agent, secret service, sleeper, sleuth, snoop, spook, spotter, undercover agent, watcher; CONCEPTS *348,412*

spy [v] *secretly follow, watch another's actions* case, catch sight of, discover, examine, eyeball*, fish out*, get a load of*, glimpse, keep under surveillance, look for, meddle, notice, observe, peep, pry, recon*, reconnoiter, scout, scrutinize, search, set eyes on, shadow, sleuth, snoop, spot, stag, stake out, tail, take in, take note, trail, view, watch; CONCEPTS *103,623*

squabble [n] *argument* altercation, bickering, controversy, difference of opinion, disagreement, dispute, feud, fight, flap*, fuss*, hassle, quarrel, row*, scene*, scrap*, set-to*, spat*, tiff*, words*, wrangle; CONCEPT *46* —Ant. agreement, concurrence

squabble [v] *argue* argufy, bicker, brawl, clash, disagree, dispute, encounter, fall out*, fight, hassle, have words*, quarrel, quibble, row, scrap, spat, tiff*, wrangle; CONCEPT *46* —Ant. agree, concur

squad [n] *team, crew* band, battalion, company, division, force, gang, group, regiment, squadron, troop; CONCEPTS *322,365,417*

squalid [adj] *poor, run-down* abominable, base, broken-down, decayed, despicable, dingy, dirty, disgusting, disheveled, fetid, filthy, foul, grimy, gruesome, horrible, horrid, ignoble, impure, low, mean, miry, moldy, muddy, musty, nasty, odorous, offensive, poverty-stricken, ramshackle, reeking, repellent, repulsive, scurvy, seedy, shabby, shoddy, sloppy, slovenly, soiled, sordid, ugly, unclean, unkempt, vile, wretched; CONCEPTS *334,485, 570* —Ant. clean, good, kept-up, rich

squalor [n] *filth, poverty* decay, destitution, dirtiness, foulness, grunginess, impoverishment, indigence, poorness, seediness, starvation, wretchedness; CONCEPTS *335,709*

squander [v] *fritter away, use up* be prodigal with, be wasteful, blow*, cash out*, consume, dissipate, expend, frivol, frivol away, go through, lavish, misspend, misuse, prodigalize, put out*, run through, scatter, spend, spend like water*, spring for*, throw away, throw money around*, trifle, waste; CONCEPTS *156,225,327* —Ant. hoard, save, set aside

square [adj1] *honest, genuine* aboveboard, decent, equal, equitable, ethical, even, fair, fair-and-square, impartial, impersonal, just, nonpartisan, objective, on-the-level, sporting, sportspersonlike, straight, straightforward, unbiased, unprejudiced, upright; CONCEPTS *267,542* —Ant. deceiving, dishonest, fake

square [adj2] *four-sided* boxlike, boxy, equal-sided, equilateral, foursquare, orthogonal, quadrate, quadratic, quadratical, rectangular, rectilinear, right-angled, squared, squarish; CONCEPT *486*

square [adj3] *old-fashioned, conventional* behind the times, bourgeois, button-down*, conservative, dated, orthodox, out-of-date, straight*, strait-laced*, stuffy*; CONCEPTS *401,404* —Ant. current, in vogue, new, popular, stylish

square [n1] *person who is old-fashioned, conventional* antediluvian, conservative, diehard*, fuddy-duddy*, reactionary, stick-in-the-mud*, traditionalist; CONCEPT *423*

square [n2] *municipal park* area, center, circle, common, green, plaza, space, village green; CONCEPT *509*

square [v1] *correspond, agree* accord, balance, check out, coincide, conform, dovetail*, fit, fit in, gee, harmonize, jibe, match, reconcile, tally; CONCEPT *664* —Ant. disagree

square [v2] *pay off, satisfy* balance, bribe, buy, buy off, clear, clear off, clear up, corrupt, discharge, fix, have, liquidate, make even, pay, pay up, quit, rig, settle, tamper with; CONCEPT *341* —Ant. owe

square [v3] *adapt, regulate* accommodate, adjust, align, conform, even up, fit, level, quadrate, reconcile, suit, tailor, tailor-make*, true; CONCEPTS *126,202*

squash [v] *compress* annihilate, bear, bruise, crowd, crush, distort, extinguish, flatten, jam, kill, macerate, mash, pound, press, pulp, push, put down, quash, quell, scrunch, shut down, sit on, smash, squeeze, squish, stamp on,

suppress, trample, triturate; CONCEPTS *121,208, 219* —Ant. fan, open, uncompress

squat [adj] *short and stocky* broad, chunky, dumpy*, fat, heavy, heavyset, splay, thick, thick-bodied, thickset; CONCEPTS *491,773,779* —Ant. lanky, skinny, slender, tall, thin

squat [v] *lower body by bending knees* bow, cower, crouch, hunch, hunker down, perch, roost, settle, sit, stoop; CONCEPT *201* —Ant. straighten, stretch

squawk [v1] *make high-pitched, animal-like sound* cackle, caw, crow, cry, hoot, screech, yap, yawp, yelp; CONCEPTS *64,77*

squawk [v2] *gripe* bellyache*, complain, kick up a fuss*, protest, raise Cain*, squeal, yammer; CONCEPTS *52,54* —Ant. compliment, praise

squeak [v] *make sharp, high-pitched sound* cheep, creak, cry, grate, peep, pipe, scream, screech, scritch, shrill, sing, sound, squeal, talk, whine, yelp; CONCEPTS *64,65*

squeal [n/v1] *yell in a loud and high-pitched manner* bleat, cheep, creak, grate, howl, peep, rasp, scream, scream bloody murder*, screech, shout, shriek, shrill, squawk, wail, yelp, yip, yowl; CONCEPTS *64,77*

squeal [v2] *inform on* betray, blab*, complain, protest, rat on*, sell down the river*, sing*, snitch*, squawk*, talk, tattle, tattletale*, tell; CONCEPTS *54,60* —Ant. conceal, hide

squeamish [adj] *nauseated; finicky* annoyed, captious, delicate, disgusted, dizzy, exacting, fastidious, fussy, hypercritical, mincing, particular, prim, prudish, puritanical, qualmish, queasy, queer, scrupulous, shaky, sick, sickly, sick to one's stomach*, strait-laced, unsettled, upset, vertiginous; CONCEPTS *314,401,404* —Ant. ready, unpicky, willing

squeeze [n] *pressure, crushing* clasp, clutch, congestion, crowd, crunch, crush, embrace, force, handclasp, hold, hug, influence, jam, press, restraint, squash; CONCEPTS *219,674,687* —Ant. opening

squeeze [v1] *exert pressure on sides, parts of something* bear, choke, clasp, clip, clutch, compress, contract, cram, crowd, crush, cuddle, embrace, enfold, force, grip, hold tight, hug, jam, jostle, nip, pack, pinch, press, quash, ram, scrunch, squash, squish, strangle, stuff, throttle, thrust, wedge, wring; CONCEPT *219* —Ant. expand, uncompress

squeeze [v2] *try to get money out of* bleed*, bring pressure to bear, eke out, extort, extract, lean on*, milk*, oppress, pinch*, pressure, pressurize*, put screws to*, shake down*, wrench, wring; CONCEPTS *53,192,342* —Ant. donate, give

squelch [v] *suppress, restrain* black out, censure, crush, extinguish, kill, muffle, oppress, quelch, quench, repress, settle, shush, sit on, smother, squash, stifle, strangle, thwart; CONCEPT *130* —Ant. allow, release

squint [v] *scrunch up eyes when viewing* cock the eye, look, look askance, look cross-eyed, peek, peep, screw up eyes, squinch*; CONCEPTS *185,623* —Ant. open

squire [v] *accompany* assist, attend, chaperon, companion, date, escort, serve; CONCEPTS *384,714* —Ant. abandon, leave

squirm [v] *wiggle, fidget* agonize, flounder,

shift, skew, squiggle, toss, twist, wind, worm, wriggle, writhe; CONCEPT 213 —*Ant.* sit still

squirt [v] *squeeze out liquid* eject, emit, flow, jet, pour, spatter, spit, splash, splur, spray, sprinkle, spritz, spurt, stream, surge; CONCEPTS 179,256

squish [v] *squash* crush, flatten, jam, mash, pound, press, scrunch, sit on, smash, squeeze, stamp on, trample; CONCEPTS 121,208,219

stab [n1] *piercing cut* ache, blow, gash, hurt, incision, jab, jag, pang, piercing, prick, puncture, rent, stick, thrust, transfixion, twinge, wound; CONCEPT 309

stab [n2] *attempt* crack*, endeavor, essay, fling*, go*, one's best*, shot*, try, venture, whack*, whirl*; CONCEPT 87

stab [v] *puncture, pierce with sharp, pointed object* bayonet, brand, carve, chop, cleave, clip, cut, drive, gore, hit, hurt, injure, jab, jag, knife, open up, penetrate, pierce, plow, plunge, prick, prong, punch, ram, run through, saber, shank, sink, slice, spear, stick, thrust, transfix, wound; CONCEPT 220

stability [n] *resistance of some degree* adherence, aplomb, assurance, backbone, balance, cohesion, constancy, dependability, determination, durability, endurance, establishment, firmness, immobility, immovability, maturity, permanence, perseverance, resoluteness, security, solidity, solidness, soundness, stableness, steadfastness, steadiness, strength, substantiality, support, toughness; CONCEPTS 411,731 —*Ant.* insecurity, instability, unsteadiness, variability, wavering

stabilize [v] *make or keep in steady state; make resistant to change* balance, ballast, bolt, brace, buttress, counterbalance, counterpoise, equalize, fasten, firm, firm up*, fix, freeze*, maintain, ossify, poise, preserve, prop, secure, set, settle, stabilitate, steady, stiffen, support, sustain, uphold; CONCEPTS 110,250 —*Ant.* change, shake, vary, weaken, wobble

stab in the back [v] *betray* abandon, be disloyal, be unfaithful, break promise, commit treason, cross, deceive, double-cross, finger*, go back on, inform on, play Judas*, sell down the river*, sell out, trick, turn in, turn informer, turn traitor; CONCEPT 384

stable [adj] *constant, fixed; resistant* abiding, anchored, balanced, brick-wall*, calm, deep-rooted, durable, enduring, equable, established, even, fast, firm, immutable, invariable, lasting, nailed, perdurable, permanent, poised, reliable, resolute, safe, secure, set, set in stone*, solid, solid as a rock*, sound, stabile, stalwart, stationary, staunch, staying put, steadfast, steady, stout, strong, sturdy, substantial, sure, together, tough, unalterable, unchangeable, unfluctuating, uniform, unvarying, unwavering, well-built, well-founded; CONCEPTS 404,488 —*Ant.* inconstant, shaky, unfixed, unstable, wobbly

stack [n] *pile* assemblage, bank, bundle, cock, drift, heap, hill, hoard, load, mass, mound, mountain, pack, pyramid, sheaf; CONCEPTS 432,440,509

stack [v] *pile up* accumulate, amass, bank up, cock, drift, heap, hill, load, mound, pile, rick, stockpile; CONCEPTS 109,158 —*Ant.* unstack

stadium [n] *arena for recreation or spectating* amphitheater, athletic field, bowl, coliseum, diamond, field, garden, gridiron, gymnasium, pit, ring, stade, strand; CONCEPT 438

staff [n1] *employees of organization* agents, assistants, cadre, cast, crew, deputies, faculty, force, help, officers, operatives, organization, personnel, servants, shop, teachers, team, workers, work force; CONCEPT 325

staff [n2] *stick, usually for walking* cane, club, pikestaff, pole, prop, rod, stave, walking stick, wand; CONCEPTS 311,479

stage [n1] *level, period within structure or system* date, degree, division, footing, grade, juncture, lap, leg, length, moment, node, notch, phase, plane, point, point in time, rung, standing, status, step; CONCEPTS 727, 744,816

stage [n2] *theater platform; theater life* arena, boards*, Broadway, dais, drama, footlights, frame, legit*, limelight*, mise-en-scène, off-Broadway, play, scaffold, scaffolding, scene, scenery, set, setting, show biz*, show business, spotlight, stage set, staging, theater; CONCEPTS 263,349,438,439,448

stage [v] *arrange, produce* bring out, do, engineer, execute, give, mount, open, orchestrate, organize, perform, play, present, put on, show; CONCEPTS 94,292 —*Ant.* close

stagger [v1] *walk falteringly* alternate, careen, dither, falter, halt, hesitate, lurch, overlap, pitch, reel, shake, stammer, step, sway, swing, teeter, titubate, topple, totter, vacillate, waver, wheel, whiffle, wobble, zigzag; CONCEPT 151

stagger [v2] *astound, shock* amaze, astonish, boggle, bowl over*, confound, consternate, devastate, dumbfound, flabbergast, floor*, give a shock, nonplus, overpower, overwhelm, paralyze, perplex, puzzle, shake, shatter, startle, strike dumb*, stump, stun, stupefy, surprise, take aback, take breath away*, throw off balance*; CONCEPTS 7,19,42

staggering [adj] *overwhelming* amazing, astonishing, astounding, distressing, mind-blowing, mind-boggling, shocking, stunning; CONCEPTS 548,571

stagnant [adj] *motionless, dirty* brackish, dead, dormant, filthy, foul, idle, immobile, inactive, inert, lifeless, listless, passive, putrid, quiet, sluggish, stale, standing, static, stationary, still, unmoving; CONCEPTS 584,621 —*Ant.* moving

stagnate [v] *deteriorate by lack of action* constipate, decay, decline, fester, go to seed*, hibernate, idle, languish, lie fallow, not move, putrefy, rot, rust, stall, stand, stand still, stifle, stultify, trammel, vegetate; CONCEPTS 698,748 —*Ant.* grow, strengthen

staid [adj] *restrained, set* calm, cold sober*, collected, composed, cool, decorous, demure, dignified, earnest, formal, grave, no-nonsense*, quiet, sedate, self-restrained, serious, settled, sober, solemn, somber, starchy, steady, stuffy, weighty; CONCEPTS 401,404 —*Ant.* adventurous, frivolous, fun, sporting, willing

stain [n] *spot of dirt, blot, bar* black eye*, blemish, blotch, blur, brand, color, discoloration, disgrace, dishonor, drip, dye, infamy, ink spot, mottle, odium, onus, reproach, shame, sinister*, slur, smirch, smudge, spatter, speck, splotch,

spot, stigma, tint; CONCEPTS *230,622* —*Ant.*
blank, cleanliness

stain [v] *dirty, taint* animalize, bastardize,
besmirch, bestialize, blacken, blemish, blot,
brutalize, color, contaminate, corrupt, daub,
debase, debauch, defile, demoralize, deprave,
discolor, disgrace, drag through the mud*, dye,
mark, pervert, smear, smudge, soil, spot, sully,
tar, tarnish, tinge, tint; CONCEPTS *54,250,254*
—*Ant.* clean

stake [n1] *pole* pale, paling, picket, post, rod,
spike, stave, stick; CONCEPTS *471,479*

stake [n2] *bet, wager* ante, chance, hazard,
peril, pledge, pot, risk, venture; CONCEPT *329*

stake [n3] *share, investment* award, claim,
concern, interest, involvement, prize, purse;
CONCEPTS *344,710,835* —*Ant.* whole

stake [v] *bet, wager* back, bankroll*, capitalize,
chance, finance, gamble, game, grubstake*,
hazard, imperil, jeopardize, lay, play, pledge,
put, put on, risk, set, stake down, venture;
CONCEPTS *330,363*

stale [adj1] *old, decayed* dried, dry, faded, fetid,
flat, fusty, hard, insipid, malodorous, musty,
noisome, parched, rank, reeking, smelly, sour,
spoiled, stagnant, stenchy, stinking, tasteless,
watery, weak, zestless; CONCEPTS *462,485,598*
—*Ant.* fresh, new

stale [adj2] *overused, out-of-date* antiquated,
banal, bent, cliché, clichéd, cliché-ridden, common, commonplace, corny*, dead, drab, dull,
dusty, effete, flat, fusty, hackneyed, insipid,
like a dinosaur*, mawkish, moth-eaten*, out*,
passé, past, platitudinous, repetitious, shopworn, stereotyped, threadbare, timeworn, tired,
trite, unoriginal, well-worn, worn-out, yesterday's*, zestless; CONCEPTS *267,578,589,797*
—*Ant.* current, fresh, new, underused

stalemate [n] *deadlock* arrest, Catch-22*,
check, delay, draw, gridlock, impasse, pause,
standoff, standstill, tie; CONCEPTS *230,807,832*
—*Ant.* headway, progress

stalk [n] *stem of plant* axis, bent, helm, pedicel,
pedicle, reed, shaft, spike, spire, support, trunk,
twig, upright; CONCEPT *428*

stalk [v] *follow, creep up on* ambush, approach,
chase, drive, flush out, haunt, hunt, pace, pursue, shadow, striddle, stride, tail, track, trail,
walk up to; CONCEPTS *149,159,749*

stall [v] *delay for own purposes* arrest, avoid
the issue*, beat around the bush*, brake,
check, die, drag one's feet*, equivocate, fence,
filibuster, halt, hamper, hedge, hinder, hold off,
interrupt, not move, play for time*, postpone,
prevaricate, put off, quibble, shut down, slow,
slow down, stand, stand off, stand still, stay,
still, stonewall*, stop, suspend, take one's
time*, tarry, temporize; CONCEPTS *121,234*
—*Ant.* advance, allow, further, help

stalwart [adj] *strong, valiant* athletic, bold,
bound, bound and determined*, brave, brawny,
brick-wall*, courageous, daring, dauntless,
dead set on*, dependable, fearless, forceful,
gutsy*, hanging tough*, hefty, husky, indomitable, intrepid, lusty, muscular, nervy*,
powerhouse*, redoubtable, robust, rugged,
sinewy, solid, spunky*, staunch, steamroller*,
stout, stouthearted, strapping, sturdy, substantial, tenacious, tough, unafraid, undaunted,

valorous, vigorous; CONCEPTS *404,489*
—*Ant.* cowardly, meek, weak

stamina [n] *strength, vigor* backbone*,
endurance, energy, force, fortitude, grit*, guts*,
gutsiness, heart, indefatigability, intestinal
fortitude*, legs*, lustiness, moxie*, power,
power of endurance, resilience, resistance,
starch*, staying power, tolerance, toleration,
vim, vitality, zip*; CONCEPTS *411,732* —*Ant.*
apathy, lack, laziness, lethargy, weakness

stammer [v] *stutter in speech* falter, halt,
hammer, hem and haw*, hesitate, jabber,
lurch, pause, repeat, splutter, sputter, stop,
stumble, wobble; CONCEPTS *47,266* —*Ant.*
enunciate, pronounce

stamp [n1] *impression, symbol, seal* brand,
cast, earmark, emblem, hallmark, impress,
imprint, indentation, mark, mold, print,
signature, sticker; CONCEPTS *259,284*

stamp [n2] *character* breed, cast, cut, description, fashion, form, ilk, kind, lot, mold, sort,
stripe, type; CONCEPT *411*

stamp [v1] *step on hard* beat, clomp, clump,
crush, stomp, stump, tramp, trample, tromp;
CONCEPT *149*

stamp [v2] *imprint; press mark on* brand, cast,
drive, engrave, etch, fix, grave, hammer, impress, infix, inscribe, letter, mark, mold, offset,
pound, print; CONCEPTS *79,174*

stampede [n] *rush of animals* charge, chase,
crash, dash, flight, fling, hurry, panic, rout, run,
scattering, shoot, smash, tear; CONCEPT *152*

stamp out [v] *extinguish* abolish, blot out*,
crush, destroy, eliminate, end, eradicate, expunge, exterminate, kill, put down, quell, snuff
out, suppress, wipe out*; CONCEPTS *95,252*

stance [n] *position, posture* attitude, bearing,
carriage, color, deportment, posture, say-so*,
slant, stand, standpoint, viewpoint; CONCEPTS
689,757

stand [n1] *position, opinion* angle, attitude,
belief, carriage, determination, notion, poise,
pose, sentiment, slant, sound, stance, standpoint, twist, two cents' worth*, view; CONCEPT
689

stand [n2] *base, stage* board, booth, bracket,
counter, dais, frame, gantry, grandstand, place,
platform, rack, rank, staging, stall, station,
support, table; CONCEPTS *442,443*

stand [v1] *be or get upright* be erect, be on feet,
be vertical, cock, dispose, erect, jump up, locate,
mount, place, poise, position, put, rank, rise,
set, settle; CONCEPT *201* —*Ant.* lay, lie, sit

stand [v3] *be in force, exist* be located, belong,
be situated, be valid, continue, endure, fill, halt,
hold, last, obtain, occupy, pause, prevail,
remain, rest, stay, stop, take up; CONCEPT *407*
—*Ant.* refuse, reject, veto

standard [adj] *regular, approved* accepted, authoritative, average, basic, boilerplate*, canonical, classic, common, customary, definitive,
established, everyday, garden variety*, general,
normal, official, orthodox, popular, prevailing,
recognized, regulation, run-of-the-mill*, set, staple, stock, typical, usual, vanilla*; CONCEPT *533*
—*Ant.* abnormal, different, irregular, unusual

standard [n1] *guideline, principle* archetype,
average, axiom, barometer, beau ideal, belief,
benchmark, canon, code, criterion, ethics,

example, exemplar, fundamental, gauge, grade, guide, ideal, ideals, law, mean, measure, median, mirror, model, morals, norm, par, paradigm, pattern, requirement, rule, rule of thumb*, sample, specification, test, touchstone, type, yardstick; CONCEPT 688

standard [n2] *flag* banderole, banner, bannerol, color, colors, emblem, ensign, figure, insignia, jack, pennant, streamer, symbol; CONCEPT 475

standardize [v] *make regular, similar* assimilate, bring into line, homogenize, institute, institutionalize, mass produce, normalize, order, regiment, stereotype, systematize; CONCEPT 126 —*Ant.* change, differ, differentiate, vary, waver

standby [n] *substitute* assistant, backup, deputy, double, fill-in, pinch-hitter*, relief, replacement, reserve, stalwart, stand-in, sub*, successor, temp*, temporary, understudy; CONCEPTS 423,712

stand for [v] *signify, mean* answer for, appear for, betoken, denote, exemplify, imply, indicate, represent, suggest, symbol, symbolize; CONCEPT 682

standing [adj] *permanent* continuing, existing, fixed, perpetual, regular, repeated; CONCEPT 551 —*Ant.* fleeting, impermanent, temporary

standing [n] *position, rank* cachet, capacity, character, condition, consequence, credit, dignity, eminence, estimation, footing, place, prestige, reputation, repute, scene, situation, slot, state, station, stature, status, term; CONCEPTS 388,727

standoff [n] *draw, tie* dead heat*, deadlock, drawn battle*, even game, impasse, level, Mexican standoff*, stalemate, toss-up, wash; CONCEPTS 364,667

standoffish [adj] *cold, distant* aloof, antisocial, cool, eremitic, haughty, indifferent, misanthropic, reclusive, remote, reserved, solitary, unapproachable, uncompanionable, unsociable, withdrawn; CONCEPTS 401,404 —*Ant.* friendly, sociable, warm

stand out [v] *be conspicuous, prominent* attract attention, be distinct, beetle, be highlighted, be striking, bulge, bulk, catch the eye, emerge, jut, loom, overhang, poke, pouch, project, protrude, stick out; CONCEPT 716 —*Ant.* obscure

standpoint [n] *belief, position* angle, attitude, judgment, opinion, outlook, point of view, stance, stand, view, viewpoint; CONCEPT 689

stand/stand for [v2] *endure, bear* abide, allow, bear with, brook, cope, countenance, experience, handle, hang on, hold, last, live with, put up with, resign oneself to, stay the course*, stomach*, submit, suffer, support, sustain, swallow, take, tolerate, undergo, wear, weather, withstand; CONCEPT 23 —*Ant.* disobey, forget, overlook

standstill [n] *stop* arrest, cessation, check, checkmate, corner*, dead end*, deadlock, dead stop*, delay, gridlock, halt, hole, impasse, inaction, pause, stalemate, standoff, wait; CONCEPTS 119,832 —*Ant.* advance, progress

staple [adj] *necessary, basic* chief, essential, fundamental, important, in demand, key, main, popular, predominant, primary, principal, standard; CONCEPT 546 —*Ant.* auxiliary, extra, minor, secondary, unnecessary

star [adj] *famous, illustrious* brilliant, capital, celebrated, chief, dominant, leading, main, major, outstanding, paramount, predominant, preeminent, principal, prominent, talented, well-known; CONCEPT 568 —*Ant.* minor, unimportant, unknown

star [n] *person who is famous* celebrity, draw*, favorite, headliner, hero, idol, lead, leading role, luminary, name, starlet, superstar, topliner*; CONCEPTS 352,366 —*Ant.* commoner

starchy [adj] *formal, stiff* ceremonious, conventional, inflexible, mannered, prim, reserved, rigid, starched*, stilted, strait-laced, strict, stuffy*; CONCEPT 401

star-crossed [adj] *doomed* catastrophic, cursed, damned, disastrous, ill-fated, ill-omened, ill-starred, jinxed, luckless, misfortunate, unfortunate, unlucky; CONCEPTS 537,548

stardom [n] *fame* acclaim, celebrity, distinction, éclat, eminence, esteem, glory, greatness, honor, illustriousness, immortality, nobility, notoriety, popularity, preeminence, prestige, prominence, public esteem, recognition, renown, standing; CONCEPTS 388,668

stare [v] *gape, watch* beam*, bore*, eagle eye*, eye, eyeball*, fix, focus, gawk, gaze, glare, glim*, goggle*, lay eyes on*, look, look fixedly, ogle, peer, rivet, rubberneck*, take in; CONCEPT 623 —*Ant.* ignore

stark [adj1] *utter, absolute* abrupt, arrant, bald, bare, blasted, blessed, blunt, complete, confounded, consummate, downright, entire, firm, flagrant, gross, infernal, out-and-out*, outright, palpable, patent, pure, rank, severe, sheer, simple, stiff, unalloyed, unmitigated; CONCEPTS 531,569 —*Ant.* indefinite

stark [adj2] *bare, unadorned* au naturel, austere, bald, barren, bleak, chaste, clear, cold, depressing, desolate, dreary, empty, forsaken, grim, harsh, naked, nude, plain, raw, severe, solitary, stripped, unclad, unclothed, uncovered, undraped, vacant, vacuous, void; CONCEPT 485 —*Ant.* clothed, covered

starry-eyed [adj] *unrealistic* dreaming, half-baked*, hoping, impossible, improbable, ivory-tower*, nonrealistic, not sensible, on cloud nine*, optimistic, romantic, silly; CONCEPTS 552,560

start [n1] *beginning* alpha*, birth, bow, commencement, countdown, dawn, dawning, day one*, derivation, embarkation, exit, first step, flying start*, foundation, inauguration, inception, initiation, jump-off, kickoff*, leaving, onset, opening, origin, outset, running start, setting out, source, spring, square one*, start-off, takeoff; CONCEPTS 648,832 —*Ant.* completion, conclusion, death, end, ending, finish, stop

start [n2] *advantage* allowance, backing, break, bulge, chance, draw, edge, handicap, head start, helping hand, introduction, lead, odds, opening, opportunity, sponsorship, vantage; CONCEPT 693 —*Ant.* disadvantage

start [n3] *flinch* convulsion, jar, jump, scare, shock, spasm, turn, twitch; CONCEPTS 150,194

start [v1] *begin; come into existence* activate, appear, arise, arouse, come into being, commence, create, depart, embark, engender, enter upon, establish, found, get going, get under way*, go ahead, hit the road*, inaugurate, incite, initiate, instigate, institute, introduce, issue, launch, lay foundation, leave, light, make a beginning, open, originate, pioneer, rise, rouse, sally forth, see light, set in motion, set out, set up, spring, take first step*, take the plunge*, turn on; CONCEPTS 221,241 —*Ant.* complete, conclude, die, end, finish, stop

start [v2] *flinch* blanch, blench, bolt, bounce, bound, buck, dart, draw back, jerk, jump, jump the gun*, leap, quail, recoil, shrink, shy, spring, squinch, startle, twitch, wince; CONCEPTS 150,194 —*Ant.* ignore

startle [v] *frighten, surprise* affright, agitate, alarm, amaze, astonish, astound, awe, bolt, consternate, floor, fright, give a turn*, jump, make jump, rock, scare, scare to death*, shake up, shock, spook, spring, spring something on*, stagger, start, stun, take aback, terrify, terrorize; CONCEPTS 7,19,42 —*Ant.* calm, comfort, compose, expect

starving/starved [adj] *deprived of food* could eat a horse*, craving, dehydrated, drawn, dying, emaciated, empty, faint, famished, haggard, hungering, hungry, malnourished, peaked, peckish, perishing, pinched, ravenous, skinny, thin, underfed, undernourished, weakened; CONCEPTS 406,546 —*Ant.* fed, full, satisfied

state [n1] *condition or mode of being* accompaniment, attitude, capacity, case, category, chances, character, circumstance, circumstances, contingency, element, environment, essential, estate, event, eventuality, fix, footing, form, frame of mind, humor, imperative, juncture, limitation, mood, nature, occasion, occurrence, outlook, pass, phase, plight, position, posture, predicament, prerequisite, proviso, reputation, requirement, shape, situation, spirits, stand, standing, state of affairs, station, status, stipulation, time, welfare; CONCEPTS 410,639,696, 701,720

state [n2] *dignity, grandeur* cachet, ceremony, consequence, display, glory, majesty, pomp, position, prestige, rank, splendor, standing, stature, status, style; CONCEPT 388

state [n3] *government, country* body politic, commonwealth, community, federation, land, nation, republic, sovereignty, territory, union; CONCEPTS 508,510

state [v] *declare, assert* affirm, air, articulate, asseverate, aver, bring out, chime in*, come out with, deliver, describe, elucidate, enounce, enumerate, enunciate, explain, expound, express, give, give blow-by-blow*, give rundown*, interpret, narrate, pitch, present, pronounce, propound, put, recite, recount, rehearse, relate, report, say; set forth, speak, specify, spiel*, tell, throw out*, utter, vent, ventilate; voice; CONCEPTS 49,51,55 —*Ant.* ask, question

stately [adj] *dignified, impressive* august, ceremonial, ceremonious, conventional, courtly, deliberate, elegant, elevated, formal, gallant, gracious, grand, grandiose, haughty, high, high-faluting*, high-minded*, imperial, imperious, imposing, kingly, large, lofty, luxurious, magnificent, majestic, massive, measured, monumental, noble, opulent, palatial, pompous, portly, proud, queenly, regal, royal, solemn, stiff, sumptuous, superb, towering; CONCEPTS 401,574,589 —*Ant.* common, ignoble, informal, undignified, unimpressive, unstately

statement [n1] *declaration, assertion* ABCs*, account, acknowledgment, affidavit, affirmation, allegation, announcement, articulation, aside, asseveration, assurance, averment, avowal, blow-by-blow*, charge, comment, communication, communiqué, description, dictum, ejaculation, explanation, make*, manifesto, mention, narrative, observation, picture, presentation, presentment, proclamation, profession, protestation, recital, recitation, relation, remark, report, rundown, testimony, utterance, ventilation, verbalization, vocalization, voice, word; CONCEPTS 271,274,278 —*Ant.* question, request

statement [n2] *account of finances* affidavit, audit, bill, budget, charge, invoice, reckoning, record, report, score, tab; CONCEPT 331

state-of-the-art [adj] *up-to-date* advanced, all the rage*, au courant, avant-garde, brand-new, contemporary, cutting edge*, fashionable, in, in-thing*, leading edge, modernistic, new, newest, newfangled, red-hot*, stylish, trendsetting, trendy, ultramodern, up-to-the-minute; CONCEPTS 578,589,797,799

static [adj] *motionless, changeless* at a standstill, constant, deadlocked, fixed, format, gridlocked, immobile, immovable, inactive, inert, latent, passive, rigid, stabile, stable, stagnant, stalled, standing still, stationary, sticky, still, stopped, stuck, unchanging, unfluctuating, unmoving, unvarying; CONCEPTS 534,584 —*Ant.* active, changeable, continuous, mobile, moving, variable

station [n1] *headquarters, base* base of operations, depot, home office, house, location, locus, main office, place, position, post, seat, site, situation, spot, stop, terminal, whereabouts; CONCEPT 198

station [n2] *social or occupational status* appointment, business, calling, capacity, caste, character, class, duty, employment, estate, footing, grade, level, occupation, order, place, position, post, rank, service, situation, sphere, standing, state, stratum; CONCEPTS 349,376,388

station [v] *place at a location* allot, appoint, assign, base, commission, establish, fix, garrison, install, lodge, park, plant, post, put, set; CONCEPTS 50,88,201,320,351 —*Ant.* displace, move, remove

stationary [adj] *not moving; fixed* anchored, at a standstill, immobile, immovable, inert, moored, motionless, nailed*, nailed down*, parked*, pat*, permanent, stable, stagnant, standing, static, stock-still, unmoving; CONCEPTS 488,551 —*Ant.* mobile, moving, restless, unfixed, unsteady

stationery [n] *writing materials* envelopes, letterhead, office supplies, pen and paper, writing paper; CONCEPTS 260,475

statue [n] *trophy or memorial* bronze, bust, cast, effigy, figure, icon, image, ivory, likeness, marble, piece, representation, sculpture, simulacrum, statuary, statuette, torso; CONCEPT 259

statuesque [adj] *tall and dignified* beautiful, graceful, grand, imposing, majestic, regal, shapely, stately, trim, well-proportioned; CONCEPTS 579,589,779 —*Ant.* short, small

stature [n] *importance* ability, cachet, caliber, capacity, competence, consequence, development, dignity, elevation, eminence, growth, merit, position, prestige, prominence, qualification, quality, rank, size, standing, state, station, status, tallness, value, virtue, worth; CONCEPTS *668,741* —*Ant.* insignificance, unimportance

status [n] *rank* cachet, capacity, character, condition, consequence, degree, dignity, distinction, eminence, footing, grade, merit, mode, place, position, prestige, prominence, quality, rating, renown, situation, stage, standing, state, station, stature, worth; CONCEPTS *388,668*

status quo [n] *existing conditions* circumstances, how things stand, no change, state, state of affairs; CONCEPTS *410,639,696,701,720*

statute [n] *rule, law* act, assize, bill, canon, decree, decretum, edict, enactment, measure, ordinance, precept, regulation; CONCEPT *318*

staunch [adj] *resolute, dependable* allegiant, ardent, constant, faithful, fast, firm, inflexible, liege, loyal, reliable, secure, sound, stable, stalwart, steadfast, stiff, stout, strong, sure, tough, tried-and-true, true, true-blue, trustworthy, trusty; CONCEPTS *401,534,542* —*Ant.* irresolute, undependable, unreliable, weak

stay [n1] *visit* break, halt, holiday, sojourn, stop, stopover, vacation; CONCEPT *227*

stay [n2] *hold, delay* deferment, halt, pause, postponement, remission, reprieve, standstill, stop, stopping, suspension; CONCEPTS *121,832* —*Ant.* abet, advance, assist, go, help, leave

stay [n3] *support, underpinning* brace, buttress, column, hold, prop, reinforcement, shore, shoring, stanchion, truss, underpropping; CONCEPTS *440,445*

stay [v1] *wait* abide, bide, bunk, continue, dally, delay, endure, establish oneself, halt, hang, hang about, hang around, hang in, hang out, hold the fort*, hover, lag, last, linger, loiter, nest, outstay, pause, perch, procrastinate, put down roots*, remain, reprieve, reside, respite, roost*, settle, sit tight*, sojourn, squat, stand, stay out, stay put, stick around*, stop, sweat*, sweat it out*, tarry; CONCEPTS *210,681* —*Ant.* advance, go, leave

stay [v2] *visit* be accommodated, bide, dwell, live, lodge, put up, sojourn, stop, stop over, tarry; CONCEPTS *226,227*

stay [v3] *hold in abeyance* adjourn, arrest, check, curb, defer, delay, detain, discontinue, halt, hinder, hold, hold over, impede, intermit, interrupt, obstruct, postpone, prevent, prorogue, put off, shelve, stall, stop, suspend, ward off; CONCEPT *121*

staying power [n] *stamina* backbone*, endurance, fortitude, grit*, guts*, gutsiness, heart, intestinal fortitude*, legs*, power of endurance, resilience, tolerance, vitality; CONCEPTS *411,732*

steadfast [adj] *loyal, steady* abiding, adamant, allegiant, ardent, bound, changeless, constant, dedicated, dependable, enduring, established, faithful, fast, firm, fixed, immobile, immovable, inexorable, inflexible, intense, intent, liege, never-failing, obdurate, persevering, relentless, reliable, resolute, rigid, single-minded, stable, staunch, stubborn, sure, tried-and-true*, true, true-blue*, unbending, unfaltering, unflinching, unmovable, unqualified, unquestioning, unswerving, unwavering, unyielding, wholehearted; CONCEPTS *401,534,542* —*Ant.* disloyal, unreliable, untrustworthy

steady [adj1] *stable, fixed* abiding, brick-wall*, certain, changeless, constant, durable, enduring, equable, even, firm, immovable, never-failing, patterned, regular, reliable, safe, set, set in stone*, solid, solid as a rock*, stabile, steadfast, steady-going, substantial, sure, unchangeable, unchanging, unfaltering, unfluctuating, uniform, unqualified, unquestioning, unshaken, unvarying, unwavering; CONCEPTS *488,534* —*Ant.* unfixed, unstable, unsteady, weak, wobbly

steady [adj2] *continuing* ceaseless, confirmed, consistent, constant, continuous, equable, eternal, even, faithful, habitual, incessant, never-ending, nonstop, persistent, regular, rhythmic, stabile, stable, steady-going, unbroken, unfaltering, unfluctuating, uniform, uninterrupted, unremitting, unvarying, unwavering; CONCEPT *798* —*Ant.* broken, discontinuous, intermittent

steady [adj3] *balanced, faithful in mind* allegiant, ardent, calm, constant, cool, dependable, equable, fast, imperturbable, intense, level-headed, liege, loyal, poised, reliable, reserved, resolute, sedate, self-possessed, sensible, serene, serious-minded, settled, single-minded, sober, staid, staunch, steadfast, unswerving, unwavering, wholehearted; CONCEPTS *403,542* —*Ant.* imbalanced, unfaithful, untrustworthy

steal [v1] *take something without permission* abduct, appropriate, blackmail, burglarize, carry off, cheat, cozen, defraud, despoil, divert, embezzle, heist, hold for ransom, hold up, housebreak*, keep, kidnap, lift*, loot, make off with*, misappropriate, peculate, pilfer, pillage, pinch*, pirate, plagiarize, plunder, poach, purloin, ransack, remove, rifle, rip off*, run off with*, sack*, shoplift, snitch*, spirit away*, stick up*, strip, swindle, swipe, take, take possession of, thieve, walk off with*, withdraw; CONCEPT *139* —*Ant.* give, receive

steal [v2] *sneak around* creep, flit, glide, go stealthily, insinuate, lurk, pass quietly, skulk, slide, slink, slip, snake, tiptoe; CONCEPTS *151,207*

stealthy [adj] *quiet and secretive* catlike, catty*, clandestine, covert, crafty, cunning, enigmatic, feline, furtive, hush-hush*, noiseless, private, secret, shifty, silent, skulking, slinking, sly, sneak, sneaking, sneaky, sub-rosa*, surreptitious, undercover, underhand, under wraps*, wily; CONCEPTS *401,576* —*Ant.* open, public

steam [n] *energy* beef, force, might, muscle, potency, power, puissance, sinew, strength, vigor, vim; CONCEPT *633*

steel [v] *prepare oneself* animate, brace, buck up*, cheer, embolden, encourage, fortify, gird, grit teeth*, harden, hearten, inspirit, make up one's mind*, prepare, rally, ready, reinforce, strengthen; CONCEPT *35* —*Ant.* fail, weaken

steep [adj1] *extreme in direction, course* abrupt, arduous, breakneck, declivitous, elevated, erect, headlong, high, hilly, lifted, lofty, perpendicular, precipitate, precipitous, prerupt, raised, sharp, sheer, straight-up; CONCEPT *581* —*Ant.* gentle, mild, moderate

steep [adj2] *very expensive* dizzying, excessive, exorbitant, extortionate, extreme, high, immoderate, inordinate, overpriced, stiff, towering,

st
st

uncalled-for, undue, unmeasurable, unreasonable; CONCEPTS 334,762 —Ant. cheap, inexpensive, moderate

steep [v] *let soak* bathe, damp, drench, fill, imbue, immerse, impregnate, infuse, ingrain, invest, macerate, marinate, moisten, permeate, pervade, saturate, soak, sodden, sop, souse, submerge, suffuse, waterlog; CONCEPT 256 —Ant. dehydrate, dry

steer [v] *guide, direct on a course* beacon, be in the driver's seat*, captain, conduct, control, drive, escort, govern, head for, helm, herd, lead, pilot, point, route, run, run things, see, shepherd, show, skipper*, take over, take the helm, take the reins; CONCEPTS 94,187

stem [n] *stalk of plant* axis, branch, pedicel, pedicle, peduncle, petiole, shoot, stock, trunk; CONCEPT 428 —Ant. root

stem [v1] *come from* arise, be bred, be brought about, be caused, be generated, derive, develop, emanate, flow, head, issue, originate, proceed, rise, spring; CONCEPT 648 —Ant. cause

stem [v2] *prevent, stop* arrest, bring to a standstill, check, contain, control, curb, dam, hinder, hold back, oppose, resist, restrain, stay, withstand; CONCEPT 121 —Ant. abet, aid, encourage, help

stench [n] *foul odor* fetor, funk*, malodor, mephitis, noisomeness, redolence, smell, stink*; CONCEPTS 599,600 —Ant. perfume, sweetness

step [n1] *pace of feet in walking* footfall, footprint, footstep, gait, impression, mark, print, spoor, stepping, stride, trace, track, trail, tread, vestige, walk; CONCEPT 149

step [n2] *action, move* act, advance, advancement, deed, degree, expedient, gradation, grade, level, maneuver, means, measure, motion, notch, phase, point, procedure, proceeding, process, progression, rank, remove, rung, stage, start; CONCEPTS 1,832

step [n3] *one level of stairs* doorstep, gradation, notch, rest, round, run, rung, stair, tread; CONCEPTS 440,445

step [v] *move foot to walk* advance, ambulate, ascend, dance, descend, go backward, go down, go forward, go up, hoof, mince, move backward, move forward, pace, prance, skip, stride, tiptoe, traipse, tread, trip, troop, walk; CONCEPT 149

step down [v] *resign* abandon, abdicate, bow out, cease work, drop out, give notice, hand in resignation, hang it up*, leave, quit, retire, sign off, terminate, throw in the towel*, walk out; CONCEPTS 119,195,351

step in [v] *become involved* arrive, be invited, chip in*, come, enter, intercede, interfere, intermediate, interpose, intervene, lend a hand*, mediate, negotiate, take action; CONCEPTS 100, 324,384 —Ant. abandon, leave, wash hands

step up [v] *accelerate* augment, boost, escalate, hasten, hurry, improve, increase, intensify, lift, quicken, raise, shake up, speed, speed up; CONCEPTS 236,244,245 —Ant. decelerate, halt, hinder, slow

stereotype [n] *idea held as standard, example* average, boilerplate*, convention, custom, fashion, formula, institution, mold, pattern, received idea; CONCEPT 686 —Ant. difference

stereotype [v] *categorize as being example,*

standard catalogue, conventionalize, define, dub, institutionalize, methodize, normalize, pigeonhole*, regulate, standardize, systematize, take to be, typecast*; CONCEPTS 38,49 —Ant. differentiate, dissimilate

stereotyped [adj] *standard, conventional* banal, clichéd, cliché-ridden, commonplace, corny*, dull, hackneyed, mass-produced, ordinary, overused, platitudinous, played out*, stale, standardized, stock, threadbare*, tired*, trite, unoriginal, well-worn, worn-out, worn thin; CONCEPT 530 —Ant. different, dissimilar, unconventional, unlike

sterile [adj] *unproductive, clean* antiseptic, arid, aseptic, bare, barren, bleak, dead, decontaminated, desert, desolate, disinfected, dry, effete, empty, fallow, fruitless, futile, gaunt, germ-free, hygienic, impotent, infecund, infertile, pasteurized, sanitary, septic, sterilized, unfruitful, uninfected, unprofitable, unprolific, vain, waste, without issue; CONCEPTS 485,621 —Ant. dirty, fruitful, productive

sterilize [v] *make clean or unproductive* alter, antisepticize, autoclave, castrate, change, clean, decontaminate, desexualize, disinfect, emasculate, fix, fumigate, incapacitate, make sterile, neuter, pasteurize, purify, sanitize, spay; CONCEPTS 231,250 —Ant. dirty

sterling [adj] *high-quality* admirable, choice, excellent, exquisite, fine, first-rate, grand, magnificent, marvelous, outstanding, pure, splendid, stunning, superior, the best, very best; CONCEPT 574

stern [adj] *serious, authoritarian* ascetic, astringent, austere, bitter, bullheaded, by the book*, cruel, disciplinary, dyed-in-the-wool*, flinty, forbidding, frowning, grim, hang-tough*, hard, hard-boiled*, hard-core*, hardheaded*, hard-line*, hard-nosed*, hard-shell*, harsh, implacable, inexorable, inflexible, mortified, mulish, relentless, rigid, rigorous, rough, severe, steely, stiff-necked*, strict, stubborn, tough, unrelenting, unsparing, unyielding; CONCEPTS 401,542 —Ant. cheerful, funny, lenient, light, smiling, tolerant

stew [n1] *mixture, miscellany* brew, goulash*, hash, jumble, medley, mélange, mishmash, mulligan*, olio*, pasticcio*, pie*, potpourri, salmagundi*, soup; CONCEPTS 432,457,460,461 —Ant. element

stew [n2] *commotion; mental upset* agitation, confusion, dither, flap, fretting, fuming, fuss, lather, pother, snit, sweat, tizzy, tumult, turbulence, turmoil, worry; CONCEPT 410 —Ant. calm, control, ease, happiness

stew [v] *worry; steam* boil, chafe, cook, fret, fume, fuss, pother, seethe, simmer; CONCEPT 35 —Ant. not care

stick [n] *pole, often wooden* bar, bat, baton, billet, birch, bludgeon, board, branch, cane, club, cudgel, drumstick, ferrule, ingot, mast, rod, rule, ruler, shoot, slab, slat, staff, stake, stalk, stave, stem, strip, switch, timber, twig, wand, wedge; CONCEPTS 470,479

stick [v1] *adhere, affix* attach, be bogged down, become embedded, become immobilized, bind, bond, braze, catch, cement, clasp, cleave, cling, cling like ivy*, clog, cohere, fasten, fix, freeze to, fuse, glue, hold, hold fast, hold on, hug, jam, join, linger, lodge, paste, persist, remain, snag, solder, stay, stay put, stick like barnacle*, stick together, unite, weld; CONCEPTS 85,160 —Ant. loosen, unfasten, unfix, unstick

stick [v2] *poke with pointed object* dig, drive, gore, impale, insert, jab, penetrate, pierce, pin, plunge, prod, puncture, ram, run, sink, spear, stab, thrust, transfix; CONCEPT 220

stick [v3] *position, lay* deposit, drop, establish, fix, install, place, plant, plonk, plunk, put, set, settle, store, stuff; CONCEPT 201 —Ant. displace, remove

stick [v4] *endure* abide, bear, bear up under, brook, get on with, go, grin and bear it*, last, persist, put up with, see through, stand, stay, stomach*, suffer, support, take, take it, tolerate, weather; CONCEPT 23 —Ant. disobey, forget, refuse

stick-in-the-mud [n] *person set in ways* antediluvian, conservative, diehard*, fossil*, mossback*, old fogy*, reactionary; CONCEPT 423 —Ant. adventurer

stick out [v] *bulge* beetle, come through, extend, extrude, jut, obtrude, outthrust, overhang, poke, pouch, pout, project, protend, protrude, push, show, stand out; CONCEPT 751 —Ant. depress

stickup [n] *holdup* armed robbery, burglary, crime, mugging, robbery, stealing, theft; CONCEPT 192

sticky [adj1] *gummy, adhesive* agglutinative, clinging, gluey, glutinous, ropy, syrupy, tacky, tenacious, viscid, viscous; CONCEPT 606 —Ant. dry, smooth, unsticky

sticky [adj2] *humid and hot* clammy, close, dank, mucky, muggy, oppressive, soggy, sultry, sweltering; CONCEPT 525 —Ant. cool, dry

sticky [adj3] *difficult, embarrassing* awkward, delicate, discomforting, formidable, hairy*, hard, heavy*, knotty, laborious, nasty, operose, painful, rough, rugged, strenuous, thorny, tricky, unpleasant; CONCEPT 565 —Ant. easy, facile, pleasant

stiff [adj1] *hard, inflexible* annealed, arthritic, benumbed, brittle, buckram, cemented, chilled, congealed, contracted, creaky, firm, fixed, frozen, graceless, hardened, immalleable, impliable, incompliant, indurate, inelastic, jelled, mechanical, numbed, ossified, petrified, refractory, resistant, rheumatic, rigid, set, solid, solidified, starched, starchy, stark, steely, stiff as a board*, stony, taut, tense, thick, thickened, tight, unbending, unflexible, ungraceful, unsupple, unyielding, wooden; CONCEPT 604 —Ant. flexible, pliable, pliant, soft

stiff [adj2] *formal, standoffish* angular, artificial, austere, ceremonious, cold, constrained, forced, hardheaded, headstrong, inflexible, intractable, labored, mannered, obstinate, pertinacious, pompous, priggish, prim, punctilious, relentless, starchy, stilted, strong, stubborn, uneasy, ungainly, ungraceful, unnatural, unrelaxed, unrelenting, wooden; CONCEPT 401 —Ant. casual, graceful, informal

stiff [adj3] *difficult* arduous, exacting, fatiguing, formidable, hard, laborious, tough, trying, uphill; CONCEPT 565 —Ant. easy

stiff [adj4] *extreme, severe* austere, brisk, cruel, drastic, exact, excessive, exorbitant, extravagant, great, hard, harsh, heavy, immoderate,

inexorable, inordinate, oppressive, pitiless, potent, powerful, rigorous, sharp, steep, strict, stringent, strong, towering, unconscionable, undue, vigorous; CONCEPTS 540,569 —Ant. calm, moderate, normal

stiffen [v] *make or become harder* anneal, benumb, brace, cake, candy, cement, chill, clot, coagulate, condense, congeal, crystallize, curdle, firm, fix, freeze, gel, harden, inflate, inspissate, jell, jelly, ossify, petrify, precipitate, prop, reinforce, set, solidify, stabilize, starch, steady, strengthen, tauten, tense, thicken; CONCEPTS 137,250,469 —Ant. liquefy, loosen, melt

stifle [v] *prevent, restrain* asphyxiate, black out, bring to screeching halt*, burke, check, choke, choke back, clamp down*, clam up*, constipate, cork, cover up, crack down*, curb, dry up*, extinguish, gag, hold it down, hush, hush up, kill*, muffle, muzzle, put the lid on*, repress, shut up, silence, sit on*, smother, spike, squash, squelch, stagnate, stop, strangle, stultify, suffocate, suppress, torpedo*, trammel; CONCEPTS 121,130,191 —Ant. encourage, help, persuade

stigma [n] *shame* bar sinister*, besmirchment, black mark*, blame, blemish, blot, brand, disfigurement, disgrace, dishonor, imputation, lost face*, mark, odium, onus, reproach, scar, slur, spot, stain, taint; CONCEPTS 230,388,689 —Ant. credit, pride

stigmatize [v] *brand, label* characterize, class, classify, defame, denounce, designate, disgrace, mark, stamp, tag; CONCEPTS 62,79

still [adj] *calm, motionless, quiet* at rest, buttoned up*, clammed up*, closed, closemouthed, deathlike, deathly, deathly quiet, deathly still, fixed, halcyon, hushed, hushful, inert, lifeless, noiseless, pacific, peaceful, placid, restful, sealed, serene, silent, smooth, soundless, stable, stagnant, static, stationary, stock-still, tranquil, undisturbed, unruffled, unstirring, untroubled, whist; CONCEPTS 584,594 —Ant. agitated, moving, stirred, unquiet

still [conj] *however* after all, besides, but, even, for all that, furthermore, howbeit, nevertheless, nonetheless, notwithstanding, still and all, though, withal, yet; CONCEPT 544

still [n] *quiet* hush, noiselessness, peace, quietness, quietude, silence, soundlessness, stillness, tranquillity; CONCEPTS 65,748 —Ant. commotion, disturbance, noise

still [v] *make quiet, motionless, calm* allay, alleviate, appease, arrest, balm, becalm, calm, choke, compose, decrease volume, fix, gag, hush, lull, muffle, muzzle, pacify, quiet, quieten, settle, shush*, shut down, shut up, silence, slack, smooth, smooth over, soothe, squash, squelch, stall, stop, subdue, tranquilize; CONCEPTS 7,22,65,121 —Ant. agitate, disturb, irritate, move

stillness [n] *silence* calm, calmness, hush, inaction, inactivity, lull, noiselessness, peace, placidity, quiet, quietness, quietude, serenity, still, tranquility; CONCEPTS 65,388,411,720

stilted [adj] *artificial, pretentious* affected, angular, aureate, bombastic, constrained, decorous, egotistic, euphuistic, flowery, forced, formal, genteel, grandiloquent, high-flown, high-sounding, inflated, labored, magniloquent, mincing, overblown, pedantic, pompous, prim, rhetorical, sonorous, stiff, unnatural, wooden; CONCEPTS 267,401 —Ant. genuine, honest, true

stimulant [n] *substance that invigorates* analeptic, bracer, catalyst, drug, energizer, excitant, goad, impetus, impulse, incentive, incitation, incitement, motivation, motive, pick-me-up*, restorative, reviver, shot in the arm*, spark plug*, spur, stimulus, tonic, upper; CONCEPTS 240,307,661 —Ant. depressant

stimulate [v] *excite, provoke* activate, animate, arouse, build a fire under*, commove, dynamize, elate, encourage, energize, enliven, exhilarate, fan, fire, fire up*, foment, foster, galvanize, get one going*, get one started*, goad, grab, hook, impel, incite, inflame, innervate, innerve, inspire, instigate, jazz*, juice*, key up*, motivate, move, perk, pique, prod, prompt, quicken, rouse, send, set up, spark, spirit, spur, steam up*, stir up*, support, trigger, turn on*, urge, vitalize, vivify, wake up*, whet, work up*; CONCEPTS 14,242 —Ant. calm, depress, discourage

stimulating [adj] *exciting* adrenalizing, appealing, arousing, bracing, breathtaking, challenging, electrifying, energizing, exhilarating, gripping, hair-raising*, hectic, inspiring, interesting, invigorating, lively, moving, provocative, rousing, spine-tingling*, stirring, thought-provoking, thrilling, titillating; CONCEPTS 529,542,548

stimulus [n] *provocation* bang*, boost, catalyst, cause, charge, encouragement, eye-opener*, fillip, fireworks*, flash*, goad, impetus, impulse, incentive, incitation, incitement, inducement, instigation, invitation, kick*, motivation, motive, piquing, propellant, push, shot in the arm*, spur, stimulant, stimulation, sting*, turn-on*, urging; CONCEPTS 240,307,661 —Ant. discouragement, hindrance, tranquilizer

sting [v] *prick, pain* bite, burn, electrify, hurt, injure, inspire, needle, pique, poke, prickle, smart, tingle, wound; CONCEPTS 220,246,313, 728

stingy [adj] *penny-pinching, averse to spending money* acquisitive, avaricious, chary, cheap, chintzy*, churlish, close, close-fisted, costive, covetous, curmudgeonly, economical, extortionate, frugal, grasping, greedy, grudging, ignoble, illiberal, ironfisted, mean, miserly, narrow, near, parsimonious, pennywise*, penurious, petty, pinchpenny*, rapacious, saving, scrimping, scurvy, selfish, skimping, sordid, sparing, thrifty, tightfisted, uncharitable, ungenerous, ungiving; CONCEPTS 326,334,401 —Ant. generous, spendthrift, wasteful

stink [n] *bad smell* fetor, foulness, foul odor, malodor, noisomeness, offensive smell, stench; CONCEPTS 599,600 —Ant. perfume, sweetness

stink [v1] *smell badly* be offensive, be rotten, funk*, have an odor, offend, reek*, smell up, stink to high heaven*; CONCEPT 600 —Ant. perfume

stink [v2] *be lousy, bad* be abhorrent, be detestable, be held in disrepute, be no good, be offensive, be rotten, have a bad name*, smell; CONCEPTS 230,388 —Ant. be excellent, be good

stinking [adj] *smelly* fetid, foul, foul-smelling, funky*, malodorous, mephitic, noisome, odiferous, offensive, putrid, rancid, rank, reeking, stenchy, strong-smelling; CONCEPT 598

stint [n] *period of responsibility* assignment, bit, chore, consignment, duty, job, participation, quota, share, shift, spell, stretch, task, term, time, tour, turn, work; CONCEPTS 362,807,822

stint [v] *economize; hold back* be frugal, begrudge, be parsimonious, be sparing, be stingy, confine, cut corners*, define, go easy on, grudge, limit, make ends meet*, penny-pinch*, pinch, restrain, roll back*, save, save for rainy day*, scrape, scrimp, skimp on*, sock away*, spare, squirrel*, stash, tighten belt*, withhold; CONCEPT 330 —Ant. spend

stipend [n] *payment for services* allowance, award, consideration, emolument, fee, gratuity, hire, pay, pension, salary, take, wage; CONCEPT 344

stipulate [v] *decide on conditions* agree, arrange, bargain, condition, contract, covenant, designate, detail, engage, guarantee, impose, insist upon, lay down, lay finger on, make, make a point, name, particularize, pin down, pledge, postulate, promise, provide, put down for, require, settle, slot, specificate, specificize, specify, spell out, state; CONCEPTS 8,18,60 —Ant. imply, wish

stipulation [n] *condition of agreement* agreement, arrangement, circumscription, clause, contract, designation, engagement, fine print*, limit, obligation, precondition, prerequisite, provision, proviso, qualification, requirement, reservation, restriction, settlement, sine qua non, small print*, specification, string attached*, term, terms; CONCEPTS 270,318,684 —Ant. implication, request, wish

stir [n] *commotion, excitement* activity, ado, agitation, backwash*, bustle, din, disorder, disquiet, disturbance, ferment, flap*, flurry, furor, fuss, movement, pandemonium, pother, racket, row, scene, to-do*, tumult, turmoil, uproar, whirl, whirlwind; CONCEPTS 230,388 —Ant. calm, calmness, moderation, peace

stir [v1] *mix up, agitate* beat, blend, disturb, flutter, mix, move, move about, quiver, rustle, shake, toss, tremble, whip, whisk; CONCEPTS 158,170—Ant. leave alone

stir [v2] *incite, stimulate* abet, actuate, add fuel to fire*, adjy*, affect, agitate, animate, arouse, awaken, bestir, challenge, craze, drive, electrify, energize, excite, feed the fire*, foment, galvanize, impel, inflame, inspire, kindle, make waves*, motivate, move, prompt, provoke, psych*, quicken, raise, rally, rile, rouse, roust, rout, set, spark, spook*, spur, stir embers*, stir up, switch on, thrill, touch, trigger, urge, vitalize, wake, waken, whet, whip up*, work up*; CONCEPTS 14,221 —Ant. calm, discourage

stir [v3] *get up and going* awake, awaken, bestir, be up and about, budge, exert, get a move on*, get moving, hasten, look alive, make an effort, mill about, move, rouse, shake a leg*, wake, waken; CONCEPT 149 —Ant. laze, rest, wait

stirring [adj] *moving, rousing* awakening, dynamic, electrifying, emotional, exhilarating, gripping, heartbreaking, heartrending, inspirational, inspiring, motivating, provoking, stimulating, touching; CONCEPTS *529,537*

stock [*adj*] *commonplace* banal, basic, common, conventional, customary, dull, established, formal, hackneyed, normal, ordinary, overused, regular, routine, run-of-the-mill*, set, standard, staple, stereotyped, traditional, trite, typical, usual, worn-out; CONCEPTS *530,547* —*Ant.* different, original, unusual

stock [*n1*] *merchandise* accumulation, array, articles, assets, assortment, backlog, cache, choice, commodities, fund, goods, hoard, inventory, nest egg*, produce, range, reserve, reservoir, selection, stockpile, store, supply, variety, wares; CONCEPT *338*

stock [*n2*] *animals raised on a farm* animals, beasts, cattle, cows, domestic, farm animals, flock, fowl, herd, hogs, horses, livestock, pigs, sheep, swine; CONCEPTS *394,397*

stock [*n3*] *ancestry* background, breed, clan, descent, extraction, family, folk, forebears, house, kin, kindred, line, lineage, line of descent, parentage, pedigree, race, species, strain, tribe, type, variety; CONCEPTS *296,378*

stock [*n4*] *investment in company* assets, blue chips, bonds, capital, convertible, funds, over-the-counter*, paper, property, share; CONCEPT *332*

stock [*n5*] *estimation, faith* appraisal, appraisement, assessment, confidence, count, dependence, estimate, evaluation, figure, hope, inventory, judgment, reliance, review, trust; CONCEPTS *37,689,764* —*Ant.* fact, truth

stock [*v*] *supply with merchandise* accumulate, amass, carry, deal in, equip, fill, furnish, gather, handle, have, hoard, keep, keep on hand, lay in, provide, provision, put away, reserve, save, sell, stockpile, store, stow away, trade in; CONCEPTS *140,182,324* —*Ant.* deplete, use up, waste

stockade [*n*] *enclosure; jail* barrier, cage, camp, can*, cell, clink*, cooler*, coop, corral, detention camp, dungeon, fence, jailhouse, joint*, pen, penal institution, penitentiary, pound, prison, protection, slammer*, sty; CONCEPTS *439,448,449,513,516*

stock market [*n*] *stock exchange* American Stock Exchange, AMEX, Big Board, Chicago Board of Trade, commodities exchange, Dow Jones, futures exchange, NASDAQ, National Association of Securities Dealers Automated Quotations, New York Stock Exchange, Wall Street; CONCEPTS *323,333,449*

stockpile [*n*] *supply* accumulation, buildup, cache, hoard, inventory, nest egg, reserve, source, stash, stock, store, surplus; CONCEPT *712*

stockpile [*v*] *stock* accumulate, amass, build up, gather, hoard, keep on hand, put away, reserve, save, squirrel away, stash, stock up, store, stow away; CONCEPTS *140,182,324*

stocky [*adj*] *short and overweight; short and muscular* chunky, corpulent, fat, heavyset, plump, solid, squat, stout, stubby, sturdy, thick, thickset; CONCEPTS *491,773* —*Ant.* lanky, skinny, tall, thin, underweight

stodgy [*adj*] *dull, stuffy* banausic, boring, dim, dreary, formal, heavy, labored, monotonous, pedantic, pedestrian, plodding, ponderous, staid, tedious, turgid, unexciting, unimaginative, uninspired, uninteresting, weighty; CONCEPTS

401,404 —*Ant.* adventurous, exciting, ready, willing

stoic/stoical [*adj*] *philosophic, calm* aloof, apathetic, cool, cool as cucumber*, detached, dispassionate, dry, enduring, impassive, imperturbable, indifferent, indomitable, long-suffering, matter-of-fact, patient, phlegmatic, resigned, rolling with punches*, self-controlled, sober, stolid, unconcerned, unemotional, unflappable, unmoved; CONCEPTS *401,404* —*Ant.* anxious, depressed, stressed, upset

stolid [*adj*] *apathetic, stupid* blunt, bovine, dense, doltish, dry, dull, dumb, heavy, impassive, inactive, indifferent, inert, lumpish, matter-of-fact, obtuse, passive, phlegmatic, slow, stoic, supine, unemotional, unexcitable, wooden; CONCEPTS *401,402* —*Ant.* aware, intelligent, interested

stomach [*n1*] *digestive organ of animate being; exterior* abdomen, abdominal region, belly, below the belt*, breadbasket*, gut, inside, insides, maw*, paunch, pot*, potbelly*, solar plexus, spare tire*, tummy*; CONCEPTS *393,420*

stomach [*n2*] *appetite* appetence, desire, inclination, mind, relish, taste, tooth; CONCEPT *20*

stomach [*v*] *endure, tolerate* abide, bear, bear with, bite the bullet*, brook, digest, grin and bear it*, live with*, put up with, reconcile oneself, resign oneself, stand, submit to, suffer, swallow, sweat, take, tolerate; CONCEPT *23* —*Ant.* refuse, reject

stone [*n*] *hard piece of earth's surface* boulder, crag, crystal, gem, grain, gravel, jewel, metal, mineral, ore, pebble, rock; CONCEPTS *474,477*

stoned [*adj*] *high on alcohol or drugs* baked*, bombed*, boozed up*, buzzed*, doped, drugged, drunk, feeling no pain*, flying*, fried, inebriated, intoxicated, loaded, on a trip*, plastered*, ripped*, sloshed*, smashed*, spaced out*, stewed*, strung out*, tanked*, tipsy, totaled*, tripping*, wasted*; CONCEPT *314*

stony [*adj*] *hard, icy in appearance; response* adamant, blank, callous, chilly, cold, cold-blooded, coldhearted, cruel, expressionless, firm, frigid, hard-boiled*, hardened, heartless, hostile, indifferent, inexorable, inflexible, merciless, obdurate, pitiless, rough, tough, uncompassionate, unfeeling, unforgiving, unrelenting, unresponsive, unsympathetic; CONCEPTS *401,485* —*Ant.* friendly, smiling, soft, warm

stooge [*n*] *dupe* chump*, easy mark*, fall guy, flunky, fool, lackey, patsy*, pawn, pigeon*, puppet, pushover*, sap*, sucker, victim; CONCEPT *423*

stool pigeon [*n*] *informer* betrayer, blabbermouth*, canary*, decoy, deep throat*, double-crosser, fink*, informant, narc*, nark*, rat*, sneak, snitch, snitcher, source, squealer*, stoolie*, tattler, tattletale, tipster*, turncoat, weasel*, whistle-blower; CONCEPTS *348,354,423*

stoop [*n*] *slouched posture* droop, round shoulders, sag, slouch, slump; CONCEPT *757* —*Ant.* straightening

stoop [*v1*] *bow down* be bowed, bend, be servile, bow, cringe, crouch, descend, dip, duck, hunch, incline, kneel, lean, nose, sink, slant, squat; CONCEPTS *181,201* —*Ant.* straighten

stoop [v2] *condescend; lower oneself to another* accommodate, act beneath oneself, concede, debase oneself, deign, demean oneself, descend, favor, oblige, patronize, relax, resort, sink, thaw, unbend, vouchsafe; CONCEPTS 35, 384 —*Ant.* rise above

stop [n1] *end, halt; impediment* bar, barricade, blank wall*, block, blockade, break, break off, brick wall*, cease, cessation, check, close, closing, conclusion, control, cutoff, desistance, discontinuation, ending; fence, finish, freeze*, grinding halt*, hindrance, layoff, letup, lull, pause, plug, roadblock*, screeching halt*, standstill, stay, stoppage, termination, wall; CONCEPTS 240,832 —*Ant.* beginning, continuation, go, start

stop [n2] *visit; place of rest* break, depot, destination, halt, rest, sojourn, stage, station, stay, stopover, termination, terminus; CONCEPTS 198,227

stop [v1] *bring or come to a halt or end* be over, blow off*, break, break off, call it a day*, cease, close, cold turkey*, come to a standstill*, conclude, cool it*, cut out*, cut short, desist, discontinue, draw up, drop, end, finish, halt, hang it up*, hold, kill, pause, pull up, put an end to, quit, quit cold*, refrain, run its course*, scrub*, shut down, sign off*, stall, stand, stay, tarry, terminate, wind up*, wrap up*; CONCEPTS 119,234,237 —*Ant.* advance, begin, continue, go, start

stop [v2] *prevent, hold back* arrest, avoid, bar, block, bottle, break, check, choke, choke off, clog, close, congest, cut off*, disrupt, fill, fix, forestall, frustrate, gag, hinder, hush, impede, intercept, interrupt, muzzle, obstruct, occlude, plug, put a stop to, rein in, repress, restrain, seal, shut down, shut off, shut out, silence, stall, staunch, stay, stem, still, stopper, suspend, throw over, turn off, ward off; CONCEPT 121 —*Ant.* allow, continue, encourage

stopgap [adj] *temporarily helping* Band-Aid*, emergency, expedient, impromptu, improvised, makeshift, practical, provisional, rough-and-ready*, rough-and-tumble*, substitute, temp, temporary, throwaway*; CONCEPTS 551,560 —*Ant.* completed, finished, permanent, solved

stopgap [n] *temporary help* Band-Aid*, expediency, expedient, improvisation, makeshift, pis aller*, recourse, refuge, resort, resource, shift, substitute, temporary expedient; CONCEPT 712 —*Ant.* permanency, permanent, solution

stoppage [n] *halt, curtailment* abeyance, arrest, blockage, check, close, closure, cutoff, deduction, discontinuance, down, downtime*, hindrance, interruption, layoff, lockout, obstruction, occlusion, shutdown, sit-down, standstill, stopping, walkout; CONCEPT 832 —*Ant.* beginning, continuation, go, start

store [n1] *collection, supply* abundance, accumulation, backlog, cache, fount, fountain, fund, hoard, inventory, lode, lot, mine, nest egg*, plenty, plethora, provision, quantity, reserve, reservoir, savings, spring, stock, stockpile, treasure, wares, wealth, well; CONCEPTS 432, 710 —*Ant.* debt, need

store [n2] *place for keeping supply* arsenal, bank, barn, box, cache, conservatory, depository, depot, magazine, pantry, repository, reservoir,

stable, storehouse, storeroom, tank, treasury, vault, warehouse; CONCEPTS 439,441, 448,494

store [n3] *business establishment that sells goods* boutique, chain store, convenience store, deli, department store, discount house, discount store, drugstore, emporium, five-and-dime*, five-and-ten*, grocery store, market, mart, outlet, repository, shop, shopping center, showroom, specialty shop, stand, storehouse, super*, superette*, supermarket; CONCEPTS 325,439, 448,449

store [v] *collect and put aside* accumulate, amass, bank, bin, bottle, bury, cache, can, cumulate, deposit, freeze, garner, hide, hive, hoard, hutch, keep, keep in reserve, lay away, lay up*, lock away, lock up, mothball*, pack, pack away, park, plant, put, put away, put by, put in storage, reserve, roll up, salt away*, save, save for rainy day*, sock away*, squirrel*, stash, stock, stockpile, treasure, victual, warehouse; CONCEPTS 109,129 —*Ant.* squander, use, waste

storekeeper [n] *shopkeeper* businessperson, dealer, entrepreneur, grocer, merchant, proprietor, retailer, salesperson, seller, store owner, vendor, wholesaler; CONCEPT 347

storeroom [n] *repository* archive, arsenal, cellar, depository, depot, granary, magazine, safe, silo, stockroom, storage place, storehouse, vault, warehouse; CONCEPTS 435,439,449

storm [n1] *strong weather* blast, blizzard, blow, cloudburst, cyclone, disturbance, downpour, gale, gust, hurricane, monsoon, precip*, precipitation, raining cats and dogs*, snowstorm, squall, tempest, tornado, twister, whirlwind, windstorm; CONCEPT 526 —*Ant.* calm, clearness

storm [n2] *commotion, turmoil* agitation, anger, annoyance, assault, attack, barrage, blitz, blitzkrieg, bluster, bomb, bombardment, broadside, burst, bustle, cannonade, clamor, clatter, convulsion, disturbance, drumfire, furor, fury, fusillade, hail, hassle, hysteria, offensive, onset, onslaught, outbreak, outburst, outcry, passion, perturbation, pother, rabidity, racket, rage, rampancy, roar, row, ruction, rumpus, rush, salvo, squall, stir, strife, temper, tumult, upheaval, violence, volley; CONCEPTS 86,230, 674 —*Ant.* calm, peace

storm [v] *attack, rush* aggress, assail, assault, beset, blow violently, bluster, breathe fire*, burn up, carry on*, charge, come at*, complain, drizzle, drop, fly, fume, go on, howl, pour, rage, rain, rant, rave, rip, roar, scold, set in, sizzle, sound off, spit, squall, stalk, steam up*, stomp, strike, take by storm*, take on*, tear, thunder*; CONCEPTS 52,86,150,526

stormy [adj] *rough (referring to weather)* bitter, blowy, blustering, blustery, boisterous, cold, coming down*, damp, dirty, foul, frigid, furious, gusty, howling, menacing, murky, pouring, raging, raining cats and dogs*, rainy, riproaring*, roaring, savage, squally, stormful, storming, tempestuous, threatening, torrid, turbulent, violent, wet, wild, windy; CONCEPT 525 —*Ant.* calm, clear, clement

story [n1] *account, news* adventure, allegory, anecdote, apologue, article, autobiography, beat, biography, book, chronicle, cliffhanger*, comedy, conte, description, drama, epic, fable, fairy tale, fantasy, feature, fiction, folktale, gag, history, information, legend, long and short of it*, memoir, myth, narration, narrative, news item, nonfiction, novel, old saw*, parable, potboiler*, recital, record, relation, report, romance, saga, scoop*, sequel, serial, spiel*, tale, tragedy, version, yarn*; CONCEPTS 270, 274,282

story [n2] *lie* canard, cock-and-bull story*, fabrication, falsehood, falsity, fib, fiction, misrepresentation, prevarication, tale, untruism, untruth, white lie*; CONCEPTS 278,282 —*Ant.* truth

stout [adj1] *overweight* big, bulky, burly, corpulent, fat, fleshy, heavy, obese, plenitudinous, plump, porcine, portly, rotund, substantial, thick-bodied, tubby, upholstered, weighty, zaftig*; CONCEPTS 491,773 —*Ant.* skinny, thin, underweight

stout [adj2] *strong, brawny* able-bodied, athletic, hard, hardy, hulking, husky, indomitable, invincible, lusty, muscular, robust, stable, stalwart, staunch, strapping, sturdy, substantial, tenacious, tough, vigorous; CONCEPTS 489,490 —*Ant.* weak

stout [adj3] *courageous* bold, brave, dauntless, fearless, gallant, heroic, intrepid, lionhearted, plucky, resolute, stalwart, undaunted, valiant, valorous; CONCEPTS 403,542 —*Ant.* afraid, timid, weak

stouthearted [adj] *brave, courageous* adventurous, bold, daring, dashing, fearless, gallant, game, gritty, gutsy, hardy, heroic, lionhearted, plucky, spunky, stalwart, unafraid, undaunted, unfearful, valiant; CONCEPT 401

stove [n] *range; furnace* boiler, convection oven, cooker, electric stove, heater, kiln, microwave, oven, toaster oven, warmer, wood stove; CONCEPT 463

stow [v] *reserve, store* bundle, deposit, load, pack, pack like sardines*, put away, secrete, stash, stuff, top off, tuck, warehouse*; CONCEPT 209 —*Ant.* throw overboard, use, waste

straggle [v] *wander, stray* be late, dawdle, drift, lag, loiter, maunder, meander, poke, poke around, ramble, range, roam, rove, scramble, spread, straddle, string out, tail, trail; CONCEPT 151 —*Ant.* hurry, run, rush

straight [adj1] *aligned; not curved* beeline*, collinear, consecutive, continuous, direct, erect, even, horizontal, in a line, in a row, inflexible, in line, invariable, level, like an arrow*, lineal, linear, near, nonstop, perpendicular, plumb, precipitous, rectilineal, rectilinear, right, running, sheer, short, smooth, solid, square, straightforward, successive, through, true, unbent, unbroken, uncurled, undeviating, undistorted, uninterrupted, unrelieved, unswerving, upright, vertical; CONCEPTS 482,486,581 —*Ant.* curved, indirect, twisted

straight [adj2] *honest, fair* aboveboard, accurate, authentic, bald, blunt, candid, categorical, decent, equitable, fair and square*, forthright, frank, good, honorable, just, law-abiding, moral, outright, plain, point-blank*, reliable, respectable, straightforward, summary, trustworthy, unqualified, upright; CONCEPTS 267, 542 —*Ant.* corrupt, dishonest, unfair, unjust

straight [adj3] *orderly* arranged, correct, exact,

in order, neat, organized, put to rights, right, shipshape*, sorted, tidy; CONCEPTS 535,585 —*Ant.* disordered, disorderly, disorganized

straight [adj4] *unmixed* concentrated, neat, out-and-out*, plain, pure, strong, thoroughgoing, unadulterated, undiluted, unmodified, unqualified; CONCEPTS 462,621 —*Ant.* diluted, mixed

straight [adj5] *conventional, square* bourgeois, buttoned-down*, conservative, orthodox, traditional; CONCEPT 404 —*Ant.* different, unconventional, untraditional

straight [adv1] *immediately, directly* as the crow flies*, at once, away, dead*, direct, due, exactly, first off, forthwith, in direct line, instanter, instantly, lineally, now, point-blank*, right, right away, straightaway, straightforwardly, straightly, undeviatingly; CONCEPTS 581,820 —*Ant.* later

straight [adv2] *honestly* candidly, frankly, in plain English*, no holds barred*, no punches*, point-blank*; CONCEPTS 267,544 —*Ant.* dishonestly, indirectly

straighten [v] *put in neat or aligned order* align, arrange, compose, correct, even, level, make plumb, make straight, neaten, order, put in order, put perpendicular, put straight, put to rights, put upright, put vertical, rectify, set to rights, smarten up*, spruce up*, tidy, unbend, uncoil, uncurl, unfold, unravel, unsnarl, untwist; CONCEPTS 158,202,231 —*Ant.* bend, curve, move, twist

straightforward [adj1] *honest* aboveboard, barefaced*, candid, direct, forthright, frank, genuine, guileless, honorable, just, laid on the line*, level, like it is*, mellow*, open, outspoken, plain, plain-dealing*, pretenseless, right-on*, sincere, square-shooting*, straight, straight-arrow*, talking turkey*, truthful, unconcealed, undisguised, undissembled, undissembling, unequivocal, unvarnished, up front*, upright, upstanding, veracious; CONCEPT 267 —*Ant.* deceitful, devious, dishonest

straightforward [adj2] *simple, easy* apparent, clear, clear-cut, direct, distinct, elementary, evident, manifest, palpable, patent, plain, routine, straight, through, unambiguous, uncomplicated, undemanding, unequivocal, uninterrupted; CONCEPTS 535,538 —*Ant.* complicated, difficult, hard, indirect, involved

strain [n1] *pain, due to exertion* ache, anxiety, bruise, brunt, burden, constriction, effort, endeavor, exertion, force, injury, jerk, pressure, pull, sprain, stress, stretch, struggle, tautness, tension, tensity, twist, wrench; CONCEPT 728 —*Ant.* health, wellness

strain [n2] *ancestry* blood, breed, descent, extraction, family, lineage, pedigree, race, species, stock; CONCEPTS 296,380

strain [n3] *suggestion, hint* humor, manner, mind, shade, soupçon, spirit, streak, style, suspicion, temper, tendency, tinge, tone, touch, trace, trait, vein, way; CONCEPTS 410,529,682

strain [n4] *melody* air, descant, diapason, lay, measure, song, tune, warble; CONCEPTS 262,595

strain [v1] *stretch, often to limit* constrict, distend, distort, draw tight, drive, exert, extend, fatigue, injure, overexert, overtax, overwork, pull, push, push to the limit, rack, sprain, task, tauten, tax, tear, tighten, tire, weaken, strain [v2] *work very hard* bear down, endeavor, exert, go all out*, go for broke*, grind, hammer, hustle, labor, moil, peg away*, plug, push, strive, struggle, sweat, toil, try; CONCEPT 87 —*Ant.* idle, laze, rest

strain [v3] *filter* exude, percolate, purify, refine, riddle, screen, seep, separate, sieve, sift; CONCEPTS 135,202

strain [v4] *cause mental stress* distress, harass, hassle, irk, pain, pick at, push, stress, trouble, try; CONCEPTS 7,19 —*Ant.* calm, placate, soothe

strained [adj] *forced, pretended* artificial, at end of rope*, awkward, choked, constrained, difficult, embarrassed, false, farfetched, hard put*, in a state*, labored, nervous wreck*, put, self-conscious, stiff, strung out*, taut, tense, tight, uncomfortable, uneasy, unglued, unnatural, unrelaxed, uptight, wired*, wreck*; CONCEPTS 267,401 —*Ant.* genuine, unforced

strait [n1] *crisis, difficulty* bewilderment, bind, bottleneck*, choke point*, contingency, crossroad, dilemma, distress, embarrassment, emergency, exigency, extremity, hardship, hole*, mess*, mystification, pass, perplexity, pinch*, plight, predicament, rigor, squeeze*, turning point*, vicissitude, zero hour*; CONCEPT 674 —*Ant.* advantage, solution, success

strait [n2] *water channel* inlet, narrows, sound; CONCEPT 514

strait-laced [adj] *prudish* old-maidish, priggish*, prim, prissy*, proper, puritanical, rigid, square, starchy, stiff*, strict, stuffy, uptight*, Victorian*; CONCEPT 401

strand [n] *fine thread* fiber, filament, length, lock, rope, string, tress; CONCEPTS 392,452,475 —*Ant.* hunk

stranded [adj] *marooned, abandoned* aground, ashore, beached, cast away, godforsaken*, grounded, helpless, high and dry*, homeless, left at the altar*, left in the lurch*, on the rocks*, out in left field*, passed up, penniless, run aground, shipwrecked, sidelined, sidetracked*, wrecked; CONCEPT 577 —*Ant.* found

strange [adj1] *deviating, unfamiliar* aberrant, abnormal, astonishing, astounding, atypical, bizarre, curious, different, eccentric, erratic, exceptional, extraordinary, fantastic, far-out*, funny, idiosyncratic, ignorant, inexperienced, irregular, marvelous, mystifying, new, newfangled*, odd, oddball*, off, offbeat*, outlandish, out-of-the-way*, peculiar, perplexing, quaint, queer, rare, remarkable, singular, unaccountable, unaccustomed, uncanny, uncommon, unheard of, unseasoned, unusual, weird, wonderful; CONCEPT 564 —*Ant.* common, familiar, normal, regular, standard, usual

strange [adj2] *exotic, foreign* alien, apart, awkward, detached, external, faraway, irrelevant, isolated, lost, new, novel, out of place, outside, remote, romanesque, romantic, unexplored, unfamiliar, unknown, unrelated, untried; CONCEPTS 549,576 —*Ant.* common, native

stranger [n] *person who is unfamiliar* alien, drifter, foreign body, foreigner, guest, immigrant, incomer, interloper, intruder, itinerant person, migrant, migratory worker, new arrival, newcomer, outcomer, outlander, out-of-stater*, outsider, party crasher*, perfect stranger*, squatter*, transient, uninvited person, unknown, unknown person, visitor, wanderer; CONCEPTS 413,423 —*Ant.* acquaintance, friend, local, native

strangle [v] *choke, stifle* asphyxiate, gag, garrote/garrotte, inhibit, kill, muffle, quelch, repress, restrain, shush, smother, squelch, strangulate, subdue, suffocate, suppress, throttle; CONCEPTS 130,191,252 —*Ant.* free, let go, loose

strap [n] *long piece of material* band, belt, harness, leash, strop, switch, thong, tie, whip; CONCEPTS 471,475

strapped [adj] *destitute* beggared, broke*, dirt poor*, flat*, fortuneless, impoverished, out of money, penniless, penurious, poor, stonebroke*; CONCEPT 334 —*Ant.* rich, wealthy

strapping [adj] *big and strong* brawny, burly, hefty, hulk, hulking, hunk, husky, ox, powerful, powerhouse, robust, stalwart, stout, sturdy, tall, vigorous, well-built; CONCEPTS 489,773 —*Ant.* attenuated, skinny, slight, small, thin

stratagem [n] *trick* action, angle, artifice, bit*, booby trap*, brainchild*, con, deception, device, dodge, feint, gambit, game, game plan*, gimmick, grift, intrigue, layout, maneuver, method, pitch, plan, play, plot, ploy, pretext, proposition, racket, ruse, scenario, scene, scheme, setup, shift, slant, stall, story, subterfuge, switch, twist, wile; CONCEPTS 59,660

strategic [adj1] *crucial* cardinal, critical, decisive, imperative, important, key, necessary, vital; CONCEPTS 546,567 —*Ant.* unimportant, unnecessary

strategic [adj2] *clever, calculated* cunning, deliberate, diplomatic, dishonest, planned, politic, tricky; CONCEPT 544 —*Ant.* loose, unplanned

strategy [n] *plan of action* action, angle, approach, artifice, blueprint*, brainchild*, craft, cunning, design, game, game plan*, gimmick, grand design, layout, maneuvering, method, plan, planning, policy, procedure, program, project, proposition, racket*, scenario, scene, scheme, setup, slant, story, subtlety, system, tactics; CONCEPT 660

stratum [n] *layer* bed, gradation, grade, lamina, level, lode, seam, sheet, stratification, thickness, vein; CONCEPT 744

stray [adj] *abandoned, wandering* devious, erratic, homeless, lost, roaming, roving, vagrant; CONCEPT 583

stray [v1] *deviate, err* circumlocute, depart, digress, divagate, diverge, do wrong, excurse, get off the subject*, get off the track*, get sidetracked*, go off on a tangent*, ramble, sin, wander; CONCEPTS 101,266 —*Ant.* remain, stay

stray [v2] *wander; get lost* be abandoned, be lost, deviate, drift, err, gad*, gallivant, go all over the map*, go amiss, go astray, lose one's way, meander, ramble, range, roam, rove, straggle, swerve, traipse, turn, wander away, wander off; CONCEPT 149 —*Ant.* go direct

streak [n] *vein, line; small part* band, bar, beam, dash, element, hint, intimation, layer, ray, ridge, rule, shade, slash, smear, strain, stream, strip, stripe, stroke, suggestion, suspicion, touch, trace; CONCEPTS 436,628,657,727

streak [v] *make a line on* band, dapple, daub,

st
st

fleck, marble, slash, smear, spot, strake, striate, stripe, variegate, vein; CONCEPT 250

stream [n] *small river* beck, branch, brook, burn, course, creek, current, drift, flood, flow, freshet, race, rill, rindle, rivulet, run, runnel, rush, spate, spritz, surge, tide, torrent, tributary, watercourse; CONCEPT 514

stream [v] *flow from* cascade, continue, course, emerge, emit, flood, glide, gush, issue, move past, pour, roll, run, shed, sluice, spill, spout, spritz, spurt, surge; CONCEPTS 146,179 —Ant. flow into

street [n] *path upon which travel occurs* artery, avenue, back alley*, boulevard, byway, court, dead end*, drag*, drive, highway, lane, parkway, passage, pavement, place, road, roadway, route, row, stroll, terrace, thoroughfare, track, trail, turf*, way; CONCEPT 501

street person [n] *homeless person* bag lady, beggar, bum, derelict, drifter, hobo, vagabond, vagrant, wino; CONCEPT 539

street smart [adj] *shrewd* artful, astute, cagey, calculating, canny, clever, crafty, cunning, experienced, foxy*, ingenious, intelligent, perceptive, quick-witted, savvy*, seasoned, sharp, slick*, sly, smart, smooth, streetwise, wily, wise; CONCEPTS 401,402

strength [n1] *stamina, mental or physical* backbone, body, brawn, brawniness, brute force*, clout, courage, durability, energy, firmness, force, fortitude, hardiness, health, healthiness, lustiness, might, muscle, nerve, physique, pith, potency, pow*, power, powerhouse*, robustness, security, sinew, sock*, soundness, stability, stableness, stalwartness, steadiness, steamroller, stoutness, strong arm*, sturdiness, substance, tenacity, toughness, verdure, vigor, vim, vitality, zip*; CONCEPTS 410,732 —Ant. lack, weakness

strength [n2] *intensity* clout, cogency, concentration, depth, effectiveness, efficacy, energy, extremity, fervor, force, juice*, kick*, potency, power, resolution, spirit, vehemence, vigor, virtue; CONCEPT 669 —Ant. enervation, lethargy, weakness

strength [n3] *advantage, substance* anchor, asset, body, burden, connection, core, gist, guts, in, intestinal fortitude, license, mainstay, meat, pith, purport, security, sense, strong point, succor, upper hand, weight, wire; CONCEPTS 682,693 —Ant. disadvantage, weakness

strengthen [v1] *make more forceful, powerful* add, add fuel to fire*, anneal, ascend, bolster, brace, build up, buttress, confirm, corroborate, empower, enhance, enlarge, establish, extend, fortify, harden, heighten, increase, intensify, invigorate, justify, make firm, mount, multiply, regenerate, reinforce, rejuvenate, renew, restore, rise, set up, sinew*, steel, step up, substantiate, support, sustain, temper, tone, tone up, toughen, wax*; CONCEPTS 244,250 —Ant. break down, hurt, weaken

strengthen [v2] *encourage, hearten* animate, back, back up, bear out, bloom, brace, brace up, burgeon, carry weight, cheer, consolidate, embolden, enhearten, enliven, flourish, flower, fortify, gather resources, gird, give weight, harden, inspirit, invigorate, nerve, nourish, prepare, prosper, rally, ready, refresh, rejuvenate,

restore, steel, substantiate, temper, thrive, toughen, uphold; CONCEPTS 7,22,35 —Ant. discourage, dishearten, dissuade, weaken

strenuous [adj1] *difficult; requiring hard work* arduous, demanding, effortful, energy-consuming, exhausting, hard, Herculean, laborious, mean, operose, taxing, toilful, toilsome, tough, tough going*, uphill*, wicked; CONCEPT 538 —Ant. easy, effortless, facile

strenuous [adj2] *energetic, zealous* active, aggressive, ardent, bold, determined, dynamic, eager, earnest, lusty, persistent, red-blooded, resolute, spirited, strong, tireless, vigorous, vital; CONCEPTS 401,542 —Ant. apathetic, enervated, lethargic, unenthusiastic

stress [n1] *emphasis* accent, accentuation, beat, force, import, importance, significance, urgency, weight; CONCEPTS 65,668 —Ant. ignorance, unimportance

stress [n2] *physical or mental pressure* affliction, agony, alarm, albatross*, anxiety, apprehensiveness, burden, clutch, crunch, disquiet, disquietude, distention, draw, dread, expectancy, extension, fear, fearfulness, ferment, flutter, force, hardship, hassle, heat, impatience, intensity, misgiving, mistrust, nervousness, nervous tension, oppression, overextension, passion, protraction, pull, restlessness, spring, strain, stretch, tautness, tenseness, tension, tensity, tightness, traction, trauma, trepidation, trial, urgency, worry; CONCEPTS 410,720,728 —Ant. indifference, relaxation

stress [v1] *accentuate, emphasize* accent, belabor, dwell on, feature, harp on*, headline*, italicize*, lay emphasis on, make emphatic, play up, point up, repeat, rub in*, spot, spotlight*, underline*, underscore*; CONCEPTS 49,68 —Ant. attenuate, reduce, relax

stress [v2] *put under physical or mental pressure* afflict, burden, crunch, distend, force, fret, hassle, overdo, overextend, pull, put in traction*, put on trial*, spring, strain, stretch, tense, tense up*, traumatize, worry; CONCEPTS 7,19,246,313

stretch [n1] *expanse* amplitude, area, branch, breadth, bridge, compass, dimension, distance, expansion, extension, extent, gamut, length, orbit, proliferation, purview, radius, range, reach, region, scope, space, span, spread, sweep, tract, wing; CONCEPTS 651,721,746

stretch [n2] *period of time* bit, continuance, duration, extent, length, run, space, span, spell, stint, term, time, while; CONCEPTS 807,822

stretch [v] *extend, elongate* amplify, branch out, bridge, burst forth, cover, crane, develop, distend, drag out, draw, draw out, expand, fill, go, grow, inflate, lengthen, lie out, magnify, make, make taut, make tense, open, overlap, pad, prolong, prolongate, protract, pull, pull out, pyramid, rack, range, reach, recline, repose, run, shoot up, span, spin out, spread, spread out, spring up, strain, string out, swell, tauten, tighten, unfold, unroll, widen; CONCEPTS 137,250 —Ant. compress, concentrate

strict [adj1] *authoritarian* austere, dead set*, disciplinary, dour, draconian*, exacting, firm, forbidding, grim, hard, hard-boiled*, harsh, iron-fisted*, no-nonsense*, oppressive, picky, prudish, punctilious, puritanical, rigid, rigorous, scrupulous, set, severe, square, stern, stickling, straight, strait-laced*, stringent, stuffy*, tough, unpermissive, unsparing, uptight*; CONCEPTS *401,542* —Ant. amenable, easy-going, flexible, lenient, tolerant, tractable, yielding

strict [adj2] *accurate, absolute* close, complete, exact, faithful, just, meticulous, particular, perfect, precise, religious, right, scrupulous, total, true, undistorted, utter, veracious, veridical; CONCEPTS *535,557* —Ant. inaccurate, indefinite, uncertain

stride [v] *walk purposefully* clump, drill, march, pace, parade, pound, stalk, stamp, stomp, striddle, stump, traipse, tramp, tromp; CONCEPT *149*

strident [adj] *harsh, shrill* blatant, boisterous, clamorous, clashing, discordant, grating, hoarse, jangling, jarring, loud, noisy, obstreperous, rasping, raucous, screeching, squawky, squeaky, stentorian, stertorous, stridulant, stridulous, unmusical, vociferant, vociferous; CONCEPTS *592,594* —Ant. low, mild, moderate, soft

strife [n] *struggle, battle* affray, altercation, animosity, argument, bickering, blowup, brawl, clash, combat, competition, conflict, contention, contest, controversy, difference, disagreement, discord, dispute, dissension, dissent, dissidence, disunity, emulation, faction, factionalism, fighting, friction, fuss, hassle, quarrel, rivalry, spat, squabble, squabbling, static, striving, tug of war*, variance, warfare, words*, wrangle, wrangling; CONCEPTS *46,106,674* —Ant. success, victory

strike [v1] *hit hard* bang, bash, beat, boff, bonk, box, buffet, bump into, chastise, clash, clobber, clout, collide, conk*, crash, cuff*, drive, force, hammer, impel, knock, percuss, plant*, pop*, pound, pummel, punch, punish, run into, slap, slug, smack, smash into, sock, swat, thrust, thump, touch, wallop, whop*; CONCEPT *189* —Ant. tap

strike [v2] *make an impact* affect, be plausible, carry, come to mind*, dawn on*, get*, have semblance, hit*, impress, influence, inspire, look, move, occur to, reach, register*, seem, sway, touch; CONCEPTS *7,19,22,716*

strike [v3] *find, discover* achieve, arrive at, attain, catch, chance upon*, come across, come upon, dig up*, effect, encounter, happen upon*, hit upon*, lay bare*, light upon, open up, reach, seize, stumble across*, take, turn up*, uncover, unearth; CONCEPTS *120,183* —Ant. lose, miss

strike [v4] *devastate, affect* afflict, aggress, assail, assault, attack, beset, deal a blow, excruciate, fall upon, harrow, hit, invade, martyr, rack, set upon, smite, storm, torment, torture, try, wring; CONCEPTS *7,19* —Ant. not touch, pass up

strike [v5] *walk out of job in protest* arbitrate, be on strike, boycott, go on strike, hit the bricks*, hold out, mediate, mutiny, negotiate, picket, quit, refuse to work, resist, revolt, sit down*, sit in*, slow down, stick out, stop, tie up; CONCEPT *351*

strike out [v] *leave to begin new venture* bear, begin, get under way*, head, initiate, light out*, make, set out, start, start out, take off*; CONCEPT *195* —Ant. remain, stay

striking [adj] *extraordinary; beautiful* arresting, arrestive, astonishing, attractive, bizarre, charming, cogent, commanding, compelling, confounding, conspicuous, dazzling, distinguished, dynamite, electrifying, eye-catching, fascinating, forceful, forcible, handsome, impressive, jazzy*, lofty, marked, memorable, noteworthy, noticeable, out of the ordinary*, outstanding, powerful, prominent, remarkable, salient, showy, signal, singular, staggering, startling, stunning, surprising, telling, unusual, wonderful, wondrous; CONCEPTS *574,579* —Ant. homely, horrifying, ugly, unimpressive

string [n1] *long fiber* cord, rope, strand, twine, twist; CONCEPT *475*

string [n2] *succession, series* chain, consecution, echelon, file, line, order, procession, queue, rank, row, sequel, sequence, strand, tier, train; CONCEPTS *727,769* —Ant. individual

string along [v] *play with; keep dangling* bluff, coquet, dally, deceive, dupe, flirt, fool, hoax, lead on*, put one over on*, take for a ride*, toy, trifle, wanton; CONCEPT *59* —Ant. let go, release

stringent [adj] *rigid, tight* acrimonious, binding, brick-wall*, by the book*, by the numbers*, compelling, confining, convincing, dead set on*, demanding, draconian, drawing, dyed-in-the-wool*, exacting, forceful, hard, hard-nosed*, harsh, inflexible, ironclad, iron-fisted, picky, poignant, powerful, rigorous, rough, set, severe, stiff, strict, tough, unpermissive, valid; CONCEPTS *401,535,569* —Ant. flexible, inexact, tolerant

stringy [adj] *long, thin* fibrous, gangling, gristly, lank, lanky, muscular, reedy, ropy, sinewy, spindling, spindly, threadlike, tough, wiry; CONCEPT *490*

strip [n] *thin piece of material* band, banding, bar, belt, billet, bit, fillet, ingot, layer, ribbon, rod, section, segment, shred, slab, slip, stick, stripe, swathe, tape, tongue; CONCEPTS *471,834* —Ant. whole

strip [v] *bare, uncover* decorticate, denude, deprive, despoil, dismantle, displace, disrobe, divest, empty, excorticate, expose, gut, hull, husk, lay bare, lift, peel, pillage, plunder, ransack, ravage, remove, rob, scale, shave, shed, shuck, skin, slip out of, spoil, take off, tear, unclothe, undress, withdraw; CONCEPT *211* —Ant. clothe, cover

stripe [n] *line, strip* band, banding, bar, border, decoration, division, fillet, layer, ribbon, rule, streak, striation, stroke; CONCEPTS *284,622*

strive [v] *try for, exert oneself* aim, assay, attempt, bear down, bend over backward*, break one's neck*, compete, contend, do one's best*, do one's utmost*, drive, endeavor, essay, fight, go after, go all out*, go for broke*, go for the jugular*, go the limit*, hassle, jockey*, knock oneself out*, labor, leave no stone unturned*, make every effort, moil, offer, push, scramble, seek, shoot for*, strain, struggle, sweat, tackle, take on, toil, try hard, tug*, work; CONCEPT *87* —Ant. forget, skip

stroke [n1] *accomplishment* achievement, blow*, feat, flourish, hit*, move, movement; CONCEPT *706* —Ant. failure, loss

stroke [n2] *seizure* apoplexy, attack, collapse, convulsion, fit, shock; CONCEPTS *33,308*

stroke [v] *pat lengthwise* brush, caress, chuck, comfort, fondle, pet, rub, smooth, soothe, tickle; CONCEPT *612*

stroll [n] *lazy walk* airing, breath of fresh air*, constitutional, cruise, excursion, promenade, ramble, saunter, turn; CONCEPT *151* —*Ant.* run

stroll [v] *walk along lazily* amble, cruise, drift, gallivant, linger, make one's way*, mope*, mosey*, promenade, ramble, roam, rove, sashay*, saunter, toddle, traipse, tramp, wander; CONCEPT *151* —*Ant.* run

strong [adj1] *healthy, powerful* able, able-bodied, active, athletic, big, capable, durable, enduring, energetic, firm, fixed, forceful, forcible, hale, hard as nails*, hardy, hearty, heavy, heavy-duty*, in fine feather*, mighty, muscular, reinforced, robust, rugged, secure, sinewy, solid, sound, stable, stalwart, stark, staunch, steady, stout, strapping, sturdy, substantial, tenacious, tough, unyielding, vigorous, well-built, well-founded, well-made; CONCEPTS *314,489,540* —*Ant.* feeble, infirm, unhealthy, unpowerful, weak

strong [adj2] *determined, resolute* aggressive, brave, clear, eager, courageous, dedicated, deep, eager, fervent, fervid, fierce, firm, forceful, gutsy*, handful*, hard-nosed*, independent, intelligent, intense, iron-willed, keen, mean, perceptive, plucky, potent, pushy, resilient, resourceful, sagacious, self-assertive, severe, staunch, steadfast, take charge*, tenacious, tough, unbending, uncompromising, unyielding, vehement, violent, wicked*, zealous; CONCEPTS *403,542* —*Ant.* agreeable, complacent, easygoing, irresolute, laid-back, uncaring, weak

strong [adj3] *distinct, unmistakable* clear, clear-cut, cogent, compelling, convincing, effective, fast, firm, forceful, formidable, great, hard, influential, marked, mighty, overpowering, persuasive, potent, powerful, redoubtable, secure, sharp, sound, stiff, stimulating, telling, trenchant, urgent, weighty, well-established, well-founded; CONCEPTS *535,537* —*Ant.* indistinct, mistakable, obscure, vague

strong [adj4] *extreme* acute, draconian, drastic, forceful, intense, keen, severe, sharp, strict; CONCEPT *569* —*Ant.* mild, moderate

strong [adj5] *forceful on the senses* biting, bold, bright, brilliant, concentrated, dazzling, effective, fetid, full-bodied, glaring, hard, heady, high, highly flavored, highly seasoned, hot, inebriating, intoxicating, loud, malodorous, noisome, piquant, potent, powerful, pungent, pure, rancid, rank, rich, robust, sharp, spicy, stark, stimulating, stinking, straight, strong-flavored, undiluted, unmixed; CONCEPTS *462,598,618* —*Ant.* delicate, low, mild, moderate, pale, soft

stronghold [n] *refuge* bastion, bulwark, castle, citadel, fastness, fort, fortification, fortress, garrison, keep, presidio, redoubt; CONCEPTS *439,712*

structure [n1] *makeup, form* anatomy, architecture, arrangement, build, complex, configuration, conformation, construction, design, fabric, fabrication, format, formation, frame, framework, interrelation, make, morphology, network, order, organization, skeleton, system, texture; CONCEPT *733*

structure [n2] *building* cage, construction, edifice, erection, fabric, house, pile, pile of bricks*, rockpile, skyscraper; CONCEPT *439*

struggle [n] *hard try; fight to win* attempt, battle, brush, clash, combat, conflict, contest, effort, encounter, endeavor, essay, exertion, free-for-all*, grind, hassle, jam, jump, labor, long haul*, pains*, roughhouse*, row, scramble, set-to*, skirmish, strife, striving, toil, trial, tussle, undertaking, work, wrangle; CONCEPTS *87,106,674* —*Ant.* giving in

struggle [v1] *labor, work* assay, attempt, bend over backwards*, break one's back*, break one's neck*, cope, dig, endeavor, exert oneself, give it one's best shot*, give the old college try*, go all out*, grind, hassle, have one's nose to grindstone*, hustle, make every effort*, offer, plug, plug away*, scratch, seek, slave, strain, strive, sweat, tackle, take a crack*, take a stab*, take on, toil, try, try one's hardest*, undertake, work like a dog*; CONCEPT *87* —*Ant.* idle, laze, rest

struggle [v2] *fight, wrestle* battle, brawl, buck, bump heads*, compete, contend, contest, cross swords*, go up against*, grapple, hassle, lock horns*, put up a fight*, romp, rough-house*, row, scrap, scuffle, shuffle, slug, smack, tangle; CONCEPT *106* —*Ant.* surrender, yield

strumpet [n] *prostitute* call girl*, harlot, hooker, hussy, lady of the evening*, slut, streetwalker, whore, woman of the street*; CONCEPT *412*

strut [v] *walk pompously* flaunt, flounce, grandstand*, mince, parade, peacock*, play to audience, prance, put on airs*, sashay*, show off, stalk, stride, swagger, swank, sweep; CONCEPTS *149,261*

stub [n] *stumpy end* butt, counterfoil, dock, remainder, remnant, root, short end*, snag, stump, tag, tail, tail end*; CONCEPTS *825,827*

stubborn [adj] *obstinate, unyielding* adamant, balky, bullheaded, cantankerous, contumacious, cussed*, determined, dogged, firm, fixed, hard-headed, headstrong, inexorable, inflexible, insubordinate, intractable, mulish, obdurate, opinionated, ornery*, persevering, persistent, pertinacious, perverse, pigheaded*, rebellious, recalcitrant, refractory, relentless, rigid, self-willed, set in one's ways*, single-minded, steadfast, stiff-necked*, tenacious, tough, unbending, unmanageable, unreasonable, unshakable, untoward, willful; CONCEPTS *401,404* —*Ant.* broad-minded, complacent, compliant, giving, willing, yielding

stubby [adj] *short and thick* fat, heavyset, squat, stocky, stout, stumpy, thick-bodied, thickset; CONCEPTS *491,773,779* —*Ant.* lanky, long, thin

stuck-up [adj] *snobbish* arrogant, big-headed, cocky, conceited, condescending, egotistic, haughty, high-and-mighty*, hoity-toity, nose in the air*, ostentatious, patronizing, pompous, pretentious, puffed up, snippy*, snooty*, snotty*, too big for one's britches*, uppity*, vain; CONCEPT *401*

student [n] *person actively learning* apprentice, disciple, docent, first-year student, grad, graduate, junior, learner, novice, observer, pupil, registrant, scholar, schoolchild, skill, sophomore, undergrad*, undergraduate; CONCEPT *350* —*Ant.* professor, teacher

studied [adj] *intentional* advised, affected, aforethought, calculated, conscious, considered, deliberate, designed, examined, gone into, investigated, planned, plotted, premeditated, prepared, prepense, purposeful, reviewed, studious, thought-about, thoughtful, thought-out, thought-through, voluntary, well-considered, willful, willing; CONCEPTS 538,548 —Ant. natural, spontaneous, unintentional, unplanned

studious [adj] scholarly, attentive academic, assiduous, bookish*, bookworm*, busy, careful, contemplative, diligent, eager, earnest, grubbing, hard-working, industrious, intellectual, learned, lettered, meditative, reflective, sedulous, serious, thoughtful, well-informed, well-read; CONCEPTS 402,538 —Ant. ignorant, inattentive, lazy, unscholarly

study [n] learning, analysis abstraction, academic work, analyzing, application, attention, class, cogitation, comparison, concentration, consideration, contemplation, course, cramming, debate, deliberation, examination, exercise, inquiry, inspection, investigation, lesson, meditation, memorizing, muse, musing, pondering, questioning, reading, reasoning, reflection, research, reverie, review, rumination, schoolwork, scrutiny, subject, survey, thought, trance, weighing; CONCEPTS 31,103

study [v1] contemplate, learn apply oneself, bone up*, brood over, burn midnight oil*, bury oneself in*, coach, cogitate, consider, crack the books*, cram, dig*, dive into*, examine, excogitate, go into, go over, grind*, hit the books*, inquire, learn, learn the ropes*, lucubrate, meditate, mind, mull over, perpend, peruse, plug*, plunge, polish up*, ponder, pore over*, read, read up, refresh, think, think out, think over, tutor, weigh; CONCEPT 31 —Ant. forget, ignore, neglect

study [v2] examine, analyze brainstorm*, canvass, case, check out, check over, check up, compare, deliberate, do research, figure, give the eagle eye*, inspect, investigate, keep tabs*, look into, peruse, read, research, scope, scrutinize, sort out, survey, view; CONCEPT 103

stuff [n1] personal belongings being, effects, equipment, gear, goods, impedimenta, individual, junk*, kit, luggage, objects, paraphernalia, possessions, substance, tackle, things, trappings; CONCEPTS 432,446

stuff [n2] essence, substance bottom, bottom line*, essentiality, heart, marrow*, matter, meat*, nitty-gritty*, nuts and bolts*, pith, principle, quintessence, soul, staple, virtuality; CONCEPTS 668,682

stuff [n3] fabric cloth, material, raw material, textile, woven material; CONCEPT 167

stuff [v] load with choke up, clog up, compress, congest, cram, crowd, fill, fill to overflowing, fill to the brim, force, glut, gobble, gorge, gormandize, guzzle, jam, jam-pack*, overfill, overindulge, overstuff, pack, pad, push, ram, sate, satiate, shove, squeeze, stow, wad, wedge; CONCEPTS 169,209 —Ant. unload, unstuff

stuffed [adj] crammed bursting, crowded, filled, full, glutted, gorged, jammed, jam-packed*, loaded, overflowing, packed, packed like sardines*, running over, satisfied, saturated, tight; CONCEPTS 481,483,773,774,786

stuffy [adj1] close, oppressive airless, breathless, confined, fetid, heavy, humid, muggy, stagnant, stale, stifling, suffocating, sultry, thick, unventilated; CONCEPT 525 —Ant. airy, breezy, open, ventilated

stuffy [adj2] old-fashioned, prim arrogant, bloated, conventional, dreary, dull, fusty, genteel, humorless, important, magisterial, musty, narrow-minded, pompous, priggish, prim and proper*, prissy, prudish, puffy, puritanical, self-important, staid, stilted, stodgy, straitlaced*, uninteresting, Victorian*; CONCEPTS 401,404 —Ant. current, informal, modern, new

stumble [v1] slip, stagger blunder, bumble, careen, err, fall, fall down, falter, flounder, hesitate, limp, lose balance, lumber, lurch, muddle, pitch, reel, shuffle, stammer, swing, tilt, topple, totter, trip, wallow, waver, wobble; CONCEPTS 101,181

stumble [v2] happen upon blunder upon*, bump, chance, chance upon*, come across, come up against, discover, encounter, fall upon, find, hit, light, light upon*, luck*, meet, run across, stub toe on*, tumble, turn up; CONCEPTS 183,693 —Ant. lose, overlook

stumbling block [n] impediment barricade, barrier, blockage, catch*, Catch-22*, clog, delay, difficulty, drag*, drawback, handicap, hindrance, holdup, hurdle, obstacle, obstruction, road block*, setback, snag; CONCEPT 666

stump [n] end piece butt, end, projection, stub, tail end, tip; CONCEPTS 825,827

stump [v1] confuse, bewilder baffle, bring up short, confound, dumbfound, foil, mystify, nonplus, outwit, perplex, puzzle, stagger, stick, stop, stymie; CONCEPT 16 —Ant. explain, explicate, help

stump [v2] walk with deliberation barge, clomp, clump, galumph, lumber, plod, stamp, stomp, stumble, trudge; CONCEPT 149

stunned [adj] dazed aghast, amazed, astonished, astounded, bewildered, blown away*, bowled over*, breathless, confounded, confused, dismayed, dumbfounded, flabbergasted, floored, frozen, numb, overcome, overwhelmed, shocked, speechless, startled, stumped, stupefied, surprised, taken aback; CONCEPT 403

stunning [adj] beautiful, marvelous beauteous, bonny, brilliant, comely, dazzling, devastating, excellent, fair, famous, fine, first-class*, first-rate*, gorgeous, great, handsome, heavenly, impressive, lovely, number one*, out of this world*, pretty, ravishing, remarkable, royal, sensational, smashing, spectacular, striking, superior, top, wonderful; CONCEPTS 574,579 —Ant. homely, ugly

stun/stupefy [v] amaze, shock astonish, astound, bemuse, bewilder, blow away*, bowl over*, confound, confuse, daze, dumbfound, flabbergast, floor*, fog*, give a turn*, hit like ton of bricks*, knock out*, knock over*, knock unconscious, muddle, overcome, overpower, overwhelm, paralyze, petrify, rock*, shake up*, stagger, strike dumb*, surprise, take breath away*, throw a curve*; CONCEPT 42 —Ant. expect

stunt [n] deed, trick achievement, act, antic, caper, exploit, feat, feature, performance, sketch, skit, tour de force; CONCEPTS 264,384

st
su

stunted [adj] *kept from growing* bantam, diminutive, dwarf, dwarfed, dwarfish, half-pint*, little, measly, mite, peanut*, peewee*, pint-sized*, runted, runtish, runty, scrub, short, shot, shrimp*, small, small fry*, tiny, under-grown, undersized, wee*, yea big*, yea high*; CONCEPTS 773,779 —*Ant.* developing, growing

stupefied [adj] *dazed* amazed, astonished, astounded, bewildered, blown away*, bowled over*, breathless, confounded, confused, dismayed, dumbfounded, flabbergasted, floored, frozen, numb, overcome, overwhelmed, puzzled, shocked, speechless, startled, stumped, stunned, surprised, taken aback; CONCEPT 403

stupendous [adj] *wonderful, amazing* astonishing, astounding, breathtaking, colossal, dynamite, enormous, fab*, fabulous, fantastic, fat*, gigantic, great, huge, marvelous, mind-blowing*, mind-boggling*, miraculous, monster, monumental, overwhelming, phenomenal, prodigious, radical*, smashing, spectacular, staggering, stunning, super, superb, surprising, terrific, titantic, too much*, tremendous, unreal*, utmost*, vast, wondrous; CONCEPTS 574,781 —*Ant.* terrible, unimportant, unimpressive

stupid [adj] *not intelligent; irresponsible* brainless, dazed, deficient, dense, dim, doltish, dopey*, dull, dumb, dummy*, foolish, futile, gullible, half-baked*, half-witted*, idiotic, ill-advised, imbecilic, inane, indiscreet, insensate, irrelevant, laughable, loser*, ludicrous, meaningless, mindless, moronic, naive, nonsensical, obtuse, out to lunch*, pointless, puerile, rash, senseless, shortsighted, simple, simpleminded, slow, sluggish, stolid, stupefied, thick, thick-headed*, trivial, unintelligent, unthinking, witless; CONCEPTS 402,548 —*Ant.* cognizant, intelligent, responsible, smart

stupor [n] *daze, unconsciousness* amazement, anesthesia, apathy, asphyxia, bewilderment, coma, dullness, fainting, hebetude, hypnosis, inertia, inertness, insensibility, languor, lassitude, lethargy, narcosis, numbness, petrifaction, sleep, slumber, somnolence, sopor, stupefaction, suspended animation, swoon, swooning, torpor, trance; CONCEPTS 315,316 —*Ant.* consciousness, sensibility

sturdy [adj] *solid, durable* athletic, built to last*, bulky, determined, firm, flourishing, hardy, hearty, hefty, hulking, husky, lusty, muscular, powerful, powerhouse*, resolute, robust, rugged, secure, sound, stalwart, staunch, steadfast, stiff, stout, stouthearted, strapping, strong, strong-arm*, substantial, tenacious, tough, unyielding, vigorous, well-built, well-made; CONCEPTS 314,488,489 —*Ant.* unstable, weak, wobbly

stutter [v] *speak haltingly* dribble, falter, hesitate, splutter, sputter, stammer, stumble; CONCEPT 77 —*Ant.* continue

style [n1] *fashion, manner* appearance, approach, bearing, behavior, carriage, characteristic, cup of tea*, custom, cut*, description, design, druthers*, flash*, form, genre, groove*, habit, hand, idiosyncrasy, kind, method, mode, number, pattern, peculiarity, rage*, sort, spirit, strain, technique, tenor, thing*, tone, trait, trend, type, variety, vein, vogue, way; CONCEPT 411

style [n2] *fashionableness* chichi*, comfort, cosmopolitanism, craze, dash, delicacy, dernier cri, dressiness, ease, élan, elegance, fad, flair, grace, grandeur, luxury, mode, panache, polish, rage, refinement, savoir-faire, smartness, sophistication, stylishness, taste, thing*, urbanity, vogue; CONCEPTS 655,668 —*Ant.* unstylishness

style [n3] *way of speaking, writing, expressing oneself* diction, expression, mode of expression, phraseology, phrasing, treatment, turn of phrase*, vein, wording; CONCEPT 276

style [v] *name, title* address, baptize, call, christen, denominate, designate, dub, entitle, label, term; CONCEPT 62

stylish [adj] *fashionable* a la mode*, beautiful, chic, chichi*, classy, dap, dapper, dashing, dressed to kill*, dressed to the teeth*, dressy, fly*, groovy*, high-class*, in, in fashion, in the mainstream*, in vogue, jazzy*, latest, mod*, modernistic, new, nifty, now*, ostentatious, polished, pretentious, rakish, ritzy, sassy*, sharp, showy, sleek, slick*, smart, snappy*, snazzy*, swank*, swell, tony*, trendy, upscale, up-to-date, uptown, urbane, voguish; CONCEPTS 579,589 —*Ant.* old-fashioned, unfashionable, unstylish

stymie [v] *frustrate, hinder* balk, block, choke off, confound, corner, crab*, cramp, cramp one's style*, crimp, cut off, dead-end*, defeat, foil, give the run around*, hang fire*, hang up*, hold off, hold up, impede, mystify, nonplus, obstruct, pigeonhole*, prevent, put on back burner*, put on hold, puzzle, shelve, snooker*, stall, stonewall*, stump, throw a monkey wrench into*, thwart; CONCEPTS 121,130 —*Ant.* aid, assist, encourage, help

suave [adj] *charming, smooth* affable, agreeable, bland, civilized, cordial, courteous, courtly, cultivated, cultured, diplomatic, distingué, fulsome, genial, glib, gracious, ingratiating, obliging, oily*, pleasant, pleasing, polished, polite, politic, refined, smooth-tongued*, sociable, soft*, soft-spoken, sophisticated, unctuous, urbane, well-bred, worldly; CONCEPTS 401,404 —*Ant.* awkward, clumsy, unpolished, unsophisticated

subconscious [adj] *innermost in thought* hidden, inmost, inner, intuitive, latent, mental, repressed, subliminal, suppressed, unconscious; CONCEPT 529 —*Ant.* conscious, outer

subconscious [n] *inner thoughts* essence, mind, psyche, soul, subconsciousness, subliminal, subliminal self, submerged mind, underconsciousness, undersense; CONCEPT 410 —*Ant.* conscious, consciousness

subdivision [n] *smaller entity of whole* class, community, development, group, lower group, minor group, subclass, subsidiary, tract; CONCEPTS 513,835 —*Ant.* whole

subdue [v] *keep under control; moderate* bear down, beat down, break, break in, check, conquer, control, crush, defeat, discipline, dominate, drop, extinguish, gentle, get the better of*, get the upper hand*, get under control, humble, mellow, overcome, overpower, overrun, put down, quash, quell, quench, quiet, quieten, reduce, repress, restrain, shut down, soften, squelch, subjugate, suppress, tame, temper, tone down, trample, triumph over, vanquish;

CONCEPTS 121,130,252 —Ant. arouse, incite, release, rouse, start

subdued [adj] *quiet, controlled* chastened, crestfallen, dejected, dim, domestic, domesticated, downcast, down in the mouth*, grave, hushed, inobtrusive, low-key*, mellow*, moderated, muted, neutral, out of spirits*, repentant, repressed, restrained, sad, serious, shaded, sober, soft, softened, solemn, submissive, subtle, tasteful, tempered, toned down, unobtrusive; CONCEPTS 401,403,594 —Ant. aroused, boisterous, communicative, excited, roused, talkative, uncontrolled

subject [adj] *at the mercy of; answerable* accountable, apt, at one's feet*, bound by, captive, collateral, conditional, contingent, controlled, dependent, directed, disposed, enslaved, exposed, governed, in danger of, inferior, liable, likely, obedient, open, prone, provisional, ruled, satellite, secondary, sensitive, servile, slavish, sub*, subaltern, subjugated, submissive, subordinate, subservient, substract, susceptible, tentative, tributary, under, vulnerable; CONCEPTS 552,575 —Ant. master

subject [n1] *issue, matter* affair, argument, business, case, chapter, class, core, course, discussion, field of reference, gist, head, idea, item, material, matter at hand, meat*, motif, motion, motive, object, point, principal object, problem, proposal, question, resolution, study, subject matter, substance, text, theme, theorem, thesis, thought, topic; CONCEPTS 529,532,689

subject [n2] *one under authority of another* case, client, customer, dependent, guinea pig*, liege, national, patient, serf, subordinate, vassal; CONCEPTS 413,423 —Ant. master

subjective [adj] *emotional; based on inner experience rather than fact* abstract, biased, fanciful, idiosyncratic, illusory, individual, instinctive, introspective, introverted, intuitive, nonobjective, nonrepresentative, personal, prejudiced, unobjective; CONCEPTS 529,542 —Ant. objective, unbiased, unemotional, unprejudiced

subjugate [v] *overpower, defeat* bear down, beat down, bring to heel*, bring to knees*, coerce, compel, conquer, crush, enslave, enthrall, force, hold sway, keep under thumb*, kick around*, overcome, overthrow, put down, quell, reduce, reel back in*, rule, rule over, subdue, suppress, tame, triumph, vanquish; CONCEPTS 95,117,133 —Ant. free, liberate

sublime [adj] *great, magnificent* abstract, august, divine, dynamite, elevated, eminent, exalted, glorious, gorgeous, grand, heavenly, high, holy, ideal, imposing, lofty, majestic, noble, outrageous, proud, resplendent, sacred, spiritual, splendiferous, splendorous, stately, super, superb, the most*, too much*, transcendent, transcendental; CONCEPT 574 —Ant. lowly, poor, secondary, second-rate

submarine [n1] *sub* nuclear submarine, submersible, U-boat, underwater craft, underwater robot; CONCEPT 506

submarine [n2] *sandwich* grinder, hero, hoagie, sub*, torpedo; CONCEPTS 457,460,461

submerge [v] *dunk in liquid* deluge, descend, dip, douse, drench, drown, duck, engulf, flood, go down, go under, immerse, impregnate, inundate, overflow, overwhelm, plunge, sink,

sound, souse, submerse, subside, swamp, whelm; CONCEPTS 181,256 —Ant. dry, surface

submission [n] *compliance* acquiescence, appeasement, assent, backing down, bowing, capitulation, cringing, defeatism, deference, docility, giving in, humbleness, humility, malleability, meekness, nonresistance, obedience, passivism, passivity, pliabilty, prostration, recreancy, resignation, servility, subjection, submissiveness, submitting, surrender, tractability, unassertiveness, yielding; CONCEPT 633 —Ant. fight, resistance

submissive [adj] *compliant* abject, accommodating, acquiescent, amenable, bowing down, comfortable, complying, deferential, docile, domesticated, dutiful, giving-in*, humble, ingratiating, lowly, malleable, meek, menial, nonresistant, nonresisting, obedient, obeisant, obeying, obsequious, passive, patient, pliable, pliant, resigned, servile, slavish, subdued, tame, tractable, uncomplaining, unresisting, yes*, yielding; CONCEPT 401 —Ant. disobedient, fighting, intractable, resistant, unyielding

submit [v1] *comply, endure* abide, accede, acknowledge, acquiesce, agree, appease, bend, be submissive, bow, buckle, capitulate, cave, cede, concede, defer, eat crow*, fold, give away, give ground, give in, give way, go with the flow*, grin and bear it*, humor, indulge, knuckle, knuckle under*, kowtow*, lay down arms, obey, put up with, quit, relent, relinquish, resign oneself, say uncle*, stoop, succumb, surrender, throw in the towel*, toe the line*, tolerate, truckle, withstand, yield; CONCEPT 23 —Ant. disobey, fight, resist

submit [v2] *present, offer; argue for* advance, advise, affirm, argue, assert, claim, commit, contend, hand in, make a pitch*, move, proffer, propose, proposition, propound, put, put forward, refer, state, suggest, table, tender, theorize, urge, volunteer; CONCEPT 66 —Ant. conceal, dissuade, hide

subordinate [adj] *lesser, supplementary* accessory, adjuvant, ancillary, auxiliary, baser, below par, collateral, contributory, dependent, inferior, insignificant, junior, low, lower, minor, paltry, satellite, secondary, second-fiddle*, secondstring*, smaller, sub, subaltern, subalternate, subject, submissive, subnormal, subservient, subsidiary, substract, tributary, under, underaverage, unequal; CONCEPT 575 —Ant. chief, important, major, necessary, superior, vital

subordinate [n] *person that serves another* aide, assistant, attendant, dependent, deputy, flunky*, gofer*, helper, inferior, junior, peon, poor relation*, scrub*, second, second fiddle*, second string*, serf, servant, slave, subaltern, third string*, underling; CONCEPTS 348,423 —Ant. boss, chief, leader, major, manager, master, superior

subpoena [n] *writ* command, court order, decree, mandate, summons, warrant, written order; CONCEPT 318

subpoena [v] *issue a writ* cite, order to testify, serve a court order, serve notice, summon; CONCEPT 318

subscribe [v1] *pay for use; contribute* advocate, ante up*, buy, chip in*, come through*, consent, donate, do one's part*, endorse, enroll, give, grant, ink*, make a deal*, offer, pitch in*, pledge, promise, put up*, register, second, set, sign, signature, sign up*; support; CONCEPTS *129,341*

subscribe [*v2*] *agree* accede, acquiesce, advocate, approve, assent, autograph*, back, bless, boost, consent, cosign, countenance, ditto*, endorse, favor, get behind*, give stamp of approval* give the go-ahead*, go along with*, hold with*, ink*, obey, okay*, put John Hancock on*, rubber-stamp*, sanction, sign, signature, support, take, undersign, underwrite, yes*; CONCEPTS *10,50,88* —*Ant.* disagree

subsequent [*adj*] *after* consecutive, consequent, consequential, ensuing, following, later, next, posterior, postliminary, proximate, resultant, resulting, sequent, sequential, serial, subsequential, succeeding, successional, successive; CONCEPTS *585,820* —*Ant.* antecedent, earlier, former, previous, prior

subsequently [*adv*] *afterward* after, afterwards, after while, at a later date, behind, by and by, consequently, finally, infra, in the aftermath, in the end, later, latterly, next; CONCEPTS *585,820* —*Ant.* earlier, former, prior

subservient [*adj1*] *extremely compliant* abject, acquiescent, a slave to*, at one's beck and call*, at one's mercy*, bootlicking, cowering, cringing, dancing, deferential, docile, fawning, ignoble, inferior, in one's clutches*, in one's pocket*, in one's power*, mean, menial, obeisant, obsequious, resigned, servile, slavish, subject, submissive, sycophantic, under one's thumb*; CONCEPTS *401,404* —*Ant.* controlling, domineering

subservient [*adj2*] *secondary, useful* accessory, adjuvant, ancillary, appurtenant, auxiliary, bush-league*, collateral, conducive, contributory, flunky, helpful, inferior, instrumental, minor, serviceable, subordinate, subsidiary, supplemental, supplementary; CONCEPTS *560,575* —*Ant.* unhelpful, unnecessary, useless

subside [*v*] *die down; decrease* abate, cave in, collapse, decline, de-escalate, descend, die away, diminish, drop, dwindle, ease, ease off, ebb, fall, let up, level off, lower, lull, melt, moderate, peter out*, quieten, recede, settle, sink, slacken, taper, wane; CONCEPTS *181,698,776* —*Ant.* grow, increase, rise

subsidiary [*adj*] *secondary, helpful* accessory, adjuvant, aiding, ancillary, appurtenant, assistant, assisting, auxiliary, backup branch, collateral, contributory, cooperative, lesser, minor, serviceable, subject, subordinate, subservient, supplemental, supplementary, tributary, useful; CONCEPTS *560,575* —*Ant.* chief, important, necessary

subsidize [*v*] *give money to get started* angel*, back, bankroll*, contribute, endow, finance, fund, grubstake*, help, juice*, pick up the check*, pick up the tab*, prime the pump*, promote, put up the money for, sponsor, stake, support, underwrite; CONCEPTS *110,341*

subsidy [*n*] *money given to help another* aid, alimony, allowance, appropriation, assistance, bequest, bonus, bounty, contribution, endowment, fellowship, financial aid, gift, grant, gratuity, help, honorarium, indemnity, payment, pension, premium, reward, scholarship,

subsidization, subvention, support, tribute; CONCEPTS *337,344*

subsist [*v*] *keep going, living* barely exist*, be, breathe, continue, eke out a living*, eke out an existence*, endure, exist, get along*, get by*, hang in*, hang on*, hang tough*, just make it*, last, live, make ends meet*, make it*, manage, move, remain, remain alive, ride out*, scrape by*, stay alive, stick it out*, stick with it*, survive, sustain; CONCEPTS *23,330,407*

subsistence [*n*] *provisions for survival* affluence, aliment, alimentation, bread*, bread and butter*, capital, circumstances, competence, earnings, existence, food, fortune, gratuity, income, independence, keep, legacy, livelihood, living, maintenance, means, money, necessities, nurture, pension, property, provision, ration, resources, riches, salary, salt*, substance, support, sustenance, upkeep, victuals, wages, wealth, wherewithal; CONCEPTS *446, 457,646,710*

substance [*n1*] *entity, element* actuality, animal, being, body, bulk, concreteness, core, corpus, fabric, force, hunk, individual, item, mass, material, matter, object, person, phenomenon, reality, something, staple, stuff, texture, thing; CONCEPTS *433,478,523*

substance [*n2*] *essence, meaning* ABCs*, amount, basis, body, bottom, bottom line*, brass tacks*, burden, center, core, corpus, crux, drift, effect, essentiality, focus, general meaning, gist, gravamen, guts*, heart, import, innards, kernel, marrow, mass, matter, meat*, name of the game*, nitty-gritty*, nub, nuts and bolts*, pith, point, purport, quintessence, sense, significance, soul, staple, strength, stuff, subject, sum total*, tenor, theme, thrust, upshot, virtuality, way of it*; CONCEPTS *682,689*

substance [*n3*] *wealth* affluence, assets, estate, fortune, means, property, resources, riches, worth; CONCEPT *335* —*Ant.* poverty

substance abuse [*n*] *chemical abuse* addiction, alcoholic addiction, alcoholism, drug abuse, drug dependence, habit; CONCEPTS *20,316,709*

substandard [*adj*] *inferior* bad, base, below average, below par, below standard, cheap, inadequate, junk*, lemon*, lousy, low-grade, poor, second-rate, shoddy, subpar, unacceptable; CONCEPT *574*

substantial [*adj1*] *important, ample* abundant, big, big-deal*, bulky, consequential, considerable, durable, extraordinary, firm, generous, goodly, heavy, heavyweight, hefty, key, large, major-league*, massive, material, meaningful, momentous, plentiful, principal, serious, significant, sizable, solid, sound, stable, steady, stout, strong, sturdy, superabundant, tidy, valuable, vast, weighty, well-built, worthwhile; CONCEPTS *568,773,781* —*Ant.* insignificant, little, minor, small, unimportant, unsubstantial

substantial [*adj2*] *material, real* actual, card-carrying*, concrete, corporeal, existent, for real*, honest-to-god*, legit*, objective, phenomenal, physical, positive, righteous, sensible, solid, sure enough*, tangible, true, twenty-four-carat*, valid, visible, weighty; CONCEPT *582* —*Ant.* ethereal, mental, spiritual

substantial [*adj3*] *rich* affluent, comfortable, easy, opulent, prosperous, snug, solid, solvent, wealthy, well, well-heeled, well-off, well-to-do; CONCEPT 334 —*Ant.* impoverished, poor

substantially [*adv*] *to a large extent* considerably, essentially, extensively, heavily, in essence, in fact, in reality, in substance, in the main, largely, mainly, materially, much, really; CONCEPTS 569,772 —*Ant.* insignificantly, slightly

substantiate [*v*] *back up a statement, idea* actualize, affirm, approve, attest to, authenticate, bear out, check out, check up, complete, confirm, corroborate, debunk, demonstrate, establish, incarnate, justify, manifest, materialize, objectify, personify, prove, ratify, realize, reify, support, test, try, try on, try out, validate, verify; CONCEPTS 49,138,317 —*Ant.* break, disprove

substitute [*adj*] *alternative* acting, additional, alternate, another, artificial, backup, counterfeit, dummy, ersatz*, experimental, false, imitation, makeshift, mock, near, other, provisional, proxy, pseudo*, replacement, representative, reserve, second, sham, simulated, spurious, stopgap*, substitutive, supplemental, supplementary, supposititious, surrogate, symbolic, temporary, tentative, vicarial, vicarious; CONCEPTS 560,575

substitute [*n*] *someone or something that takes the place of another* agent, alternate, assistant, auxiliary, backup, changeling, delegate, deputy, dernier ressort*, double, dummy, equivalent, expediency, expedient, fill-in, ghost, ghost writer, locum, locum tenens, makeshift, pinch-hitter*, procurator, proxy, recourse, refuge, relay, relief, replacement, representative, reserve, resort, resource, standby, stand-in, stopgap*, sub*, succedaneum, successor, supplanter, supply, surrogate, symbol, temp*, temporary, temporary expedient, understudy, vicar; CONCEPTS 423,712 —*Ant.* permanent

substitute [*v*] *interchange, exchange* act for, alternate, answer for, back up, be in place of, change, commute, cover for, deputize, displace, do the work of, double for, fill in for, fill one's position, go as, proxy, relieve, replace, serve in one's stead, spell, stand for, stand in for, sub*, supersede, supplant, swap, swap places with*, switch, take another's place, take over; CONCEPTS 87,104

subterranean [*adj*] *hidden, underground* below ground, buried, covered, covert, hush-hush*, on the QT*, private, secret, subterrestrial, subversive, sunken, underfoot, under wraps*; CONCEPT 583

subtle [*adj1*] *nice, quiet, delicate* attenuate, attenuated, deep, discriminating, ethereal, exquisite, faint, fine, finespun, hairline, hairsplitting, illusive, implied, inconspicuous, indirect, indistinct, inferred, ingenious, insinuated, mental, penetrating, profound, refined, slight, sophisticated, suggestive, tenuous, thin, understated; CONCEPTS 537,544 —*Ant.* hard, harsh, noisy, unsubtle

subtle [*adj2*] *clever, cunning* analytic, analytical, artful, astute, complex, crafty, deep, designing, detailed, devious, dexterous, exacting, foxy, guileful, insidious, intriguing, keen, penetrating, perceptive, precise, ratiocinative, scheming, shrewd, skillful, sly, wily; CONCEPT 402 —*Ant.* forthright, honest, open

subtract [*v*] *take away* decrease, deduct, detract, diminish, discount, draw back, knock off, remove, take, take from, take off, take out, withdraw, withhold; CONCEPTS 211,764 —*Ant.* add

suburb [*n*] *neighborhood outside of but reliant on nearby large city* bedroom community*, burb*, country, countryside, environs, fringe, hamlet, hinterland, outlying area, outpost, outskirts, precinct, purlieu, residential area, slub, suburbia, village; CONCEPTS 508,512 —*Ant.* center, metropolis

subversive [*adj*] *rebellious, destructive* incendiary, inflammatory, insurgent, insurrectionary, overthrowing, perversive, riotous, ruinous, seditious, treasonous, underground, undermining; CONCEPT 401 —*Ant.* loyal, obedient

subvert [*v*] *rebel, destroy* capsize, contaminate, corrupt, debase, defeat, demolish, deprave, depress, extinguish, invalidate, invert, level, overthrow, overturn, pervert, poison, pull down, raze, reverse, ruin, sabotage, supersede, supplant, suppress, topple, tumble, undermine, upset, vitiate, wreck; CONCEPTS 86,95,252 —*Ant.* be loyal, comply, obey, uphold

succeed [*v1*] *attain good outcome* accomplish, achieve, acquire, arrive, avail, benefit, be successful, carry off*, come off*, conquer, distance, do all right*, do the trick*, earn, flourish, fulfill, gain, get, get to the top*, grow famous, hit*, make a fortune*, make good*, make it*, make out*, obtain, outdistance, outwit, overcome, possess, prevail, profit, prosper, pull off*, realize, reap, receive, recover, retrieve, score, secure, surmount, thrive, triumph, turn out*, vanquish, win, work, worst; CONCEPTS 141,706 —*Ant.* fail

succeed [*v2*] *come after; take the place of* accede, assume, be subsequent, come into, come into possession, come next, displace, ensue, enter upon, follow, follow after, follow in order, go next, inherit, postdate, replace, result, supersede, supervene, supplant, take over; CONCEPTS 727,749,813 —*Ant.* precede

succeeding/successive [*adj*] *following* alternating, consecutive, ensuing, following after, in a row, in line, next, next in line for, next in order, next off, next up, rotating, sequent, sequential, serial, seriate, subsequent, subsequential, succedent, successional; CONCEPTS 585,811,812,818,820 —*Ant.* antecedent, antedating, preceding, previous

success [*n*] *favorable outcome* accomplishment, achievement, advance, arrival, ascendancy, attainment, bed of roses*, benefit, big hit*, boom*, clover*, consummation, do well, Easy Street*, éclat, eminence, fame, flying colors*, fortune, fruition, gain, good luck*, good times*, grand slam*, gravy train*, happiness, happy days*, hit, killing, lap of luxury*, laugher*, maturation, profit, progress, prosperity, realization, reward, savvy, sensation, snap, strike, successfulness, triumph, victory, walkaway*, walkover*, win; CONCEPTS 693,706 —*Ant.* failure, loss

successful [*adj*] *favorable, profitable* acknowledged, advantageous, ahead of the game*, at the top*, at top of ladder*, auspicious, bestselling, blooming, blossoming, booming, champion, crowned, efficacious, extraordinary, flourishing, fortuitous, fortunate, fruitful, happy, lucky, lucrative, moneymaking, notable, noteworthy, on track*, out in front*, outstanding, paying, prosperous, rewarding, rolling, strong, thriving, top, triumphant, unbeaten, undefeated, victorious, wealthy; CONCEPT *528* —*Ant.* forfeiting, losing, unfavorable, unprofitable, unsuccessful

successor [n] *heir* beneficiary, descendant, follower, heritor, inheritor, next in line, replacement, scion; CONCEPTS *355,414*

succinct [adj] *brief, to the point* blunt, boiled down*, breviloquent, brusque, compact, compendiary, compendious, concise, condensed, curt, cut to the bone*, in a nutshell*, in few words*, laconic, pithy, short, summary, terse; CONCEPT *267* —*Ant.* lengthy, long-winded, wordy

succulent [adj] *juicy, delicious* divine, heavenly, luscious, lush, mellow, moist, mouthwatering, pulpy, rich, sappy, tasty, yummy*; CONCEPTS *462,613* —*Ant.* dry, unjuicy

succumb [v] *die or surrender* accede, bow, break down, buckle, capitulate, cave, cave in*, cease, collapse, croak, decease, defer, demise, depart, drop, eat crow*, expire, fall, fall victim to, flake out*, fold, give in, give in to, give out, give up the ghost*, give way, go, go down, go under, knuckle, knuckle under*, meet waterloo*, pack it in*, pass, pass away, perish, quit, show white flag*, submit, take the count*, throw in the towel*, wilt, yield; CONCEPTS *35, 105,385* —*Ant.* conquer, create, overcome, win

such [adv/pron] *aforementioned, specific* aforesaid, akin, alike, analogous, comparable, corresponding, equivalent, like, parallel, said, similar, such a one, such a person, such a thing, suchlike, that, the like, this; CONCEPT *557*

sudden [adj] *unexpected; happening quickly* abrupt, accelerated, acute, expeditious, fast, flash, fleet, hasty, headlong, hurried, immediate, impetuous, impromptu, impulsive, out of the blue*, precipitant, precipitate, precipitous, quick, quickened, rapid, rash, rushing, spasmodic, speeded, subito, swift, unforeseen, unusual; CONCEPT *799* —*Ant.* expected, slow

suddenly [adv] *unexpectedly* aback, abruptly, all at once, all of a sudden, asudden, forthwith, on spur of moment*, quickly, short, sudden, swiftly, unanticipatedly, unaware, unawares, without warning; CONCEPT *799* —*Ant.* expectedly, slowly

sue [v] *bring legal charges against* accuse, appeal, beg, beseech, bring an action, charge, claim, claim damages, contest, demand, drag into court, enter a plea, entreat, file, file a claim, file suit, follow up, haul into court, have the law on, have up, indict, institute legal proceedings, litigate, petition, plead, prefer charges against, prosecute, pull up, put away, see in court, solicit, summon, supplicate, take out after, take to court; CONCEPT *317*

suffer [v1] *be in pain* ache, agonize, ail, be affected, be at disadvantage, be convulsed, be handicapped, be impaired, be racked, be wounded, brave, complain of, deteriorate, droop, endure, experience, fall off, feel wretched, flag, get, go through, grieve, have

a bad time*, hurt, languish, pain, sicken, smart, undergo, writhe; CONCEPTS *308,313* —*Ant.* aid, alleviate, assist, comfort, help, relieve

suffer [v2] *endure, permit* abide, accept, acquiesce, admit, allow, bear, bear with, bleed, bow, brave, brook, carry the torch*, concede, countenance, encounter, experience, feel, go through, have, hurt, indulge, know, let, license, live with, put up with, receive, sanction, see, sit and take it, stand, stomach*, submit, support, sustain, swallow*, sweat*, take*, take it*, tolerate, undergo, wait out, yield; CONCEPTS *23,83* —*Ant.* disallow, fight, refuse, reject

suffering [n] *pain, agony* adversity, affliction, anguish, difficulty, discomfort, distress, dolor, hardship, martyrdom, misery, misfortune, ordeal, passion, torment, torture; CONCEPT *728* —*Ant.* happiness, health, joy

suffice [v] *be adequate, enough* answer, avail, be good enough, be sufficient, be the ticket*, content, do, do the trick*, fill the bill*, get by, go over big*, hack it*, hit the spot*, make a hit*, make the grade*, meet, meet requirement, satisfy, serve, suit; CONCEPT *713* —*Ant.* dissatisfy

sufficient [adj] *enough, adequate* acceptable, agreeable, all right*, ample, aplenty, appreciate, comfortable, commensurable, commensurate, common, competent, copious, decent, due, galore, pleasing, plenteous, plentiful, plenty, proportionate, satisfactory, sufficing, tolerable, unexceptionable, unexceptional, unobjectionable; CONCEPTS *558,560,771* —*Ant.* deficient, inadequate, insufficient, lacking, poor, wanting

suffocate [v] *choke* asphyxiate, drown, smother, stifle, strangle; CONCEPTS *163,246* —*Ant.* free, let go, loose

sugarcoat [v] *sweeten* add sugar, add sweetening, alleviate, candy-coat, make more appealing, make sweet, mollify, pacify, soften up, soothe; CONCEPTS *7,22,170*

suggest [v1] *convey advice, plan, desire* advance, advise, advocate, broach, commend, conjecture, exhort, give a tip*, move, offer, plug*, pose, prefer, propone, propose, proposition, propound, put, put forward, put in two cents*, put on to something*, recommend, steer, submit, theorize, tip, tip off*, tout; CONCEPT *75* —*Ant.* declare, demand, order, tell

suggest [v2] *imply; bring to mind* adumbrate, advert, allude, be a sign of, connote, cross the mind, denote, evoke, hint, indicate, infer, insinuate, intimate, lead to believe, occur, point, point in direction of, promise, put in mind of, refer, represent, shadow, signify, symbolize, typify; CONCEPTS *74,682*

suggestion [n1] *advice, plan* advancement, angle, approach, bid, big idea*, bit*, brainchild*, charge, commendation, exhortation, game plan*, gimmick, hot lead*, idea, injunction, instruction, invitation, lead, motion, opinion, outline, pitch, presentation, proffer, proposal, proposition, recommendation, reminder, resolution, scheme, setup, sneaking suspicion*, steer*, submission, telltale, tender, testimonial, thesis, tip, tip-off*; CONCEPTS *278, 689* —*Ant.* declaration, demand, order, telling

suggestion [n2] *hint, implication* allusion, association, autosuggestion, breath, clue, connotation, cue, indication, inkling, innuendo, insinuation, intimation, notion, overtone, reminder, self-suggestion, shade, signification, smack, soupçon, strain, suspicion, symbol, symbolism, symbolization, symbology, telltale, thought, tinge, trace, undertone, vein, whisper, wind; CONCEPT 529

suggestive [adj1] *signifying* evocative, evocatory, expressive, giving an inkling*, indicative, intriguing, pregnant, redolent, remindful, reminiscent, significative, symbolic, symptomatic; CONCEPTS 267,529 —*Ant.* meaningless, simple

suggestive [adj2] *dirty, vulgar* bawdy, blue*, broad, erotic, immodest, improper, indecent, indelicate, obscene, off-color*, provocative, prurient, racy, ribald, risqué, rude, seductive, sexy, shady, tempting, titillating, unseemly, wicked; CONCEPTS 372,545 —*Ant.* clean, moral, unprovocative

suit [n1] *matching top and bottom clothing* clothing, costume, dress, ensemble, getup*, gray flannel*, habit, livery, outfit, threads*, tuxedo, uniform, wardrobe; CONCEPT 451

suit [n2] *legal action* case, cause, lawsuit, litigation, proceeding, prosecution, trial; CONCEPT 318

suit [n3] *appeal, request* address, application, asking, attention, court, courtship, entreaty, imploration, imprecation, invocation, petition, plea, prayer, requesting, solicitation, soliciting, supplication, wooing; CONCEPT 662 —*Ant.* demand, order

suit [v1] *be acceptable, appropriate* accord, agree, answer, answer a need, become, befit, benefit, be proper for, beseem, be seemly, check, check out, conform, correspond, cut the mustard*, do, enhance, fill the bill*, fit, fit in, flatter, fulfill, get by, go, go together, go with, gratify, harmonize, make the grade*, match, pass muster*, please, satisfy, serve, square, suffice, tally; CONCEPT 656 —*Ant.* disagree, displease, dissatisfy

suit [v2] *adapt, tailor* accommodate, adjust, amuse, change, conform, entertain, fashion, fill, fit, fit in, gratify, modify, please, proportion, quadrate, readjust, reconcile, revise, satisfy, tailor-make*, toe the mark*; CONCEPTS 126,697 —*Ant.* refuse, reject

suitable [adj] *appropriate, acceptable* advisable, applicable, apposite, apt, becoming, befitting, commodious, condign, convenient, copacetic, correct, cut out for*, deserved, due, expedient, felicitous, fit, fitting, good, good enough*, handy, happy, in character, in keeping*, just, kosher*, legit*, meet, merited, nice, okay*, opportune, peachy, pertinent, politic, presentable, proper, reasonable, relevant, requisite, right, righteous, rightful, satisfactory, seemly, sufficient, suited, swell, up to snuff*, useful, user friendly; CONCEPT 558 —*Ant.* improper, inappropriate, irrelevant, unacceptable, unfitting, unsuitable

suite [n1] *set of rooms or furniture* apartment, array, batch, body, chambers, collection, flat, group, lodging, lot, parcel, rental, series, set, tenement; CONCEPTS 441,516

suite [n2] *entourage of people* array, attendants,

batch, body, clutch, cortege, court, escort, faculty, followers, group, lot, retainers, retinue, servants, set, staff, train; CONCEPT 417

suite [n3] *series* chain, concatenation, consecution, line, order, progression, row, scale, sequel, sequence, string, succession, train; CONCEPT 727

suitor [n] *person who desires another* admirer, beau, boyfriend, cavalier*, courter, date, follower, girlfriend, lover, man, paramour, supplicant, swain, woman, wooer; CONCEPT 423

sulk [v] *pout* be down in the mouth*, be in a huff*, be morose, be out of sorts*, be silent, brood, frown, gloom, glower, gripe, grouse, grump*, look sullen, lower, moon*, mope*, scowl, take on; CONCEPTS 35,52 —*Ant.* be happy, grin, smile

sulky [adj] *sullen* brooding, cheerless, crabby*, depressed, dismal, dour, fretful, frowning, gloomy, glum, gruff, grumpy*, ill-humored, irritable, mean, moody, moping, morose, obstinate, ornery*, pouting, pouty, sour, sour-pussed*, sulking, withdrawn; CONCEPT 403

sullen [adj] *brooding, upset* bad-tempered, cheerless, churlish, crabbed*, crabby*, cross, cynical, dismal, dour, dull, fretful, frowning, gloomy, glowering, glum, gruff, grumpy*, heavy, hostile, ill-humored, inert, irritable, malevolent, malicious, malign, mean, moody, morose, obstinate, ornery*, out of sorts*, peevish, perverse, pessimistic, petulant, pouting, pouty, querulous, saturnine, silent, somber, sour, sourpussed*, stubborn, sulking, sulky, surly, tenebrific, tenebrous, ugly, unsociable, uptight*; CONCEPT 403 —*Ant.* bright, cheerful, grinning, happy

sully [v] *soil, stain* besmirch, blacken, blot, contaminate, corrupt, debase, debauch, defile, dirty, discolor, disgrace, dishonor, drag through the mud*, make unclean, mark, smear, smudge, spot, taint, tar, tarnish; CONCEPTS 54,250,254

sultry [adj1] *hot and humid* baking, broiling, burning, close, hot, mucky, muggy, oppressive, red-hot*, scorching, sizzling, smothering, soggy, sticky, stifling, stuffy, suffocating, sweltering, sweltry, torrid, wet; CONCEPTS 525, 605 —*Ant.* cool, dry

sultry [adj2] *sensuous* desirable, erotic, heavy*, hot*, lurid, passionate, provocative, seductive, sexy, steamy*, voluptuous, X-rated*; CONCEPT 372 —*Ant.* cold, cool, frigid, ugly, unappealing

sum [n] *total* aggregate, all, amount, body, bulk, entirety, entity, epitome, gross, integral, mass, quantity, reckoning, résumé, score, structure, summary, summation, sum total*, synopsis, system, tally, totality, value, whole, works*, worth; CONCEPTS 432,784,787 —*Ant.* fraction, part

summarily [adv] *without delay* arbitrarily, at short notice, expeditiously, forthwith, immediately, on the spot, peremptorily, promptly, readily, speedily, swiftly, without waste; CONCEPTS 544,799 —*Ant.* slowly

summarize [v] *give a rundown* abridge, abstract, boil down*, cipher, compile, condense, cut, cut back, cut down, digest, encapsulate, epitomize, get to meat*, give main points, inventory, outline, pare, précis, prune*, put in a nutshell*, recap*, recapitulate, rehash*, retrograde, review, run down*, run through*, shorten, skim, snip, sum, summate, sum up,

synopsize, trim; CONCEPTS 55,236,247
—*Ant.* break down

summary [adj] *concise, to the point* arbitrary, boiled down*, breviloquent, brief, compact, compacted, compendiary, compendious, condensed, cursory, curt, hasty, in a nutshell*, laconic, perfunctory, pithy*, recapped, rehashed, run-down, run-through, short, short and sweet*, succinct, terse; CONCEPTS 267,272 —*Ant.* lengthy, long, long-winded, unabridged, wordy

summary [n] *short statement of main points* abbreviation, abridgment, abstract, analysis, aperçu, brief, capitulation, case, compendium, condensation, conspectus, core, digest, epitome, essence, extract, inventory, long and short of it*, nutshell*, outline, pandect, précis, prospectus, recap*, recapitulation, reduction, rehash*, report, résumé, review, roundup, rundown, run-through, sense, skeleton*, sketch, sum and substance*, summing-up*, survey, syllabus, synopsis, version, wrap-up*; CONCEPT 283 —*Ant.* detail, dissertation, thesis

summer [n] *hot season of the year* daylight savings time*, dog days*, heat, midsummer, picnic days*, riot time*, summer solstice, summertide, summertime, sunny season, vacation; CONCEPT 814 —*Ant.* winter

summit [n] *top, crowning point* acme, apex, apogee, capstone, climax, crest, crown, culmination, head, height, max, meridian, most, peak, pinnacle, roof, vertex, zenith; CONCEPT 836 —*Ant.* base, bottom, nadir

summon [v] *call to a place* arouse, ask, assemble, beckon, beep, bid, call, call back, call for, call forth, call in, call into action, call together, call upon, charge, cite, command, conjure, convene, convoke, direct, draft, draw on, enjoin, gather, hail, invite, invoke, mobilize, motion, muster, order, petition, rally, recall, request, ring, rouse, send for, sign, signal, subpoena, toll; CONCEPT 53 —*Ant.* dismiss, send away

sumptuous [adj] *luxurious, splendid* awe-inspiring, beautiful, costly, dear, deluxe, elegant, expensive, extravagant, gorgeous, grand, grandiose, imposing, impressive, lavish, luscious, luxuriant, magnificent, opulent, out of this world, palatial, plush, pompous, posh, prodigal, profuse, rich, ritzy*, splendiferous, superb, swank*, ultra*, upholstered; CONCEPTS 334,485,574 —*Ant.* mean, poor, wanting

sum up [v] *form an opinion of; summarize* close, conclude, condense, digest, epitomize, estimate, examine, get the measure of, inventory, put in a nutshell*, recapitulate, review, size up, sum, synopsize, total; CONCEPT 55

sunder [v] *separate, sever* break, break apart, break off, come apart, cut in two, detach, disconnect, disjoin, divide, part, rend, slice, split, split up, uncouple, undo, wedge apart; CONCEPT 135

sundry [adj] *miscellaneous* assorted, different, divers, manifold, many, quite a few, several, some, varied, various; CONCEPTS 564,772 —*Ant.* dissimilar, individual, single, singular

sunken [adj] *depressed, hollowed; submerged* buried, caved-in, concave, fallen-in, immersed, indented, recessed; CONCEPT 490

sunny [adj1] *bright, clear (referring to weather)* brilliant, clarion, cloudless, fine, light, luminous, pleasant, radiant, rainless, shining, shiny, summery, sunlit, sunshiny, unclouded, undarkened; CONCEPTS 525,617 —*Ant.* cloudy, gloomy, rainy, stormy

sunny [adj2] *happy* beaming, blithe, buoyant, cheerful, cheery, chirpy, genial, joyful, lighthearted, lightsome, optimistic, pleasant, smiling, sunbeamy; CONCEPTS 401,542 —*Ant.* gloomy, sorrowful, sullen, unhappy, upset

sunrise [n] *rise of sun above horizon* aurora, break of day*, bright, cockcrow*, dawn, dawning, daybreak, daylight, early bright*, light, morn, morning, sunup; CONCEPT 810 —*Ant.* sunset

sunscreen [n] *sunblock* skin protection, sunblocker, sun cream, suntan lotion; CONCEPTS 466,467,468

sunset [n] *fall of sun below horizon* close of day, crepuscular light, dusk, eve, evening, eventide, gloaming, nightfall, sundown, twilight; CONCEPT 810 —*Ant.* sunrise

super [adj] *excellent* cool*, divine, glorious, great, groovy*, hot*, incomparable, keen, magnificent, marvelous, matchless, neat, outstanding, peerless, sensational, smashing*, superb, terrific, topnotch, wonderful; CONCEPT 574 —*Ant.* bad, inferior, poor, second-rate

superabundance [n] *overabundance* excess, glut, great quantity, more than enough, overflow, overmuch, oversupply, plenty, plethora, superfluity, surfeit, surplus, too much*; CONCEPTS 767,787

superb [adj] *excellent, first-rate* admirable, august, best, breathtaking, choice, elegant, elevated, exalted, exquisite, fine, glorious, gorgeous, grand, great, lofty, magnificent, majestic, marvelous, matchless, noble, optimal, optimum, outstanding, peerless, prime, proud, resplendent, solid, splendid, splendiferous, splendorous, standout, state-of-the-art*, stunning, sublime, super, superior, superlative, unrivaled, very best; CONCEPT 574 —*Ant.* bad, inferior, poor, second-rate

supercilious [adj] *arrogant, stuck-up* bossy, cavalier, cocky*, condescending, contemptuous, disdainful, egotistic, haughty, high-and-mighty*, imperious, insolent, lofty, nervy*, overbearing, patronizing, proud, putting on airs*, scornful, snobby, superior, uppity*, vainglorious; CONCEPT 401 —*Ant.* humble, modest

superficial [adj] *without depth, detail* apparent, casual, cosmetic, cursory, depthless, desultory, empty, evident, exterior, external, flash, flimsy, frivolous, general, glib, half-baked*, hasty, hurried, ignorant, inattentive, lightweight, nodding, one-dimensional*, on the surface*, ostensible, outward, partial, passing, perfunctory, peripheral, quick-fix*, seeming, shallow, shoal, silly, sketchy, skin-deep*, slapdash*, slight, smattery, summary, surface, tip of the iceberg*, trivial, uncritical, warped; CONCEPTS 557,777 —*Ant.* analytical, careful, deep, detailed, genuine, thorough

superficially [adv] *lightly; without care* apparently, at first glance, carelessly, casually, externally, extraneously, flimsily, frivolously, hastily, ignorantly, not profoundly, not thoroughly, once over lightly*, on the surface*, ostensibly, outwardly, partially, skim, to the casual eye*; CONCEPTS *531,544* —*Ant.* carefully, deeply, thoroughly

superfluous [*adj*] *extra, unnecessary* abounding, de trop, dispensable, excess, excessive, exorbitant, expendable, extravagant, extreme, gratuitous, inessential, in excess, inordinate, lavish, leftover, needless, nonessential, overflowing, overmuch, pleonastic, profuse, redundant, remaining, residuary, spare, superabundant, supererogatory, superfluent, supernumerary, surplus, unasked, uncalled-for, unneeded, unrequired, unwanted, useless; CONCEPTS *546,560* —*Ant.* important, necessary, needed

superintendent [*n*] *person who oversees organization* administrator, boss, caretaker, chief, conductor, controller, curator, custodian, director, foreperson, governor, head, head person, inspector, manager, overseer, sitter, slave driver*, straw boss*, super*, supervisor, zookeeper*; CONCEPT *347*

superior [*adj1*] *better, greater, higher; excellent* above, a cut above*, admirable, capital, choice, dandy, deluxe, distinguished, exceeding, exceptional, exclusive, expert, famous, fine, finer, first-class, first-rate, first-string*, five-star*, good, good quality, grander, high-caliber, high-class, major, more advanced, more skillful, noteworthy, of higher rank, over, overlying, paramount, predominant, preferable, preferred, premium, prevailing, primary, remarkable, senior, superhuman, superincumbent, surpassing, unrivalled; CONCEPT *574* —*Ant.* bad, below, inferior, lower, minor, poor

superior [*adj2*] *arrogant, haughty* airy, bossy, cavalier, cocky*, condescending, cool, disdainful, high-and-mighty*, high-hat*, insolent, lofty, overbearing, patronizing, pretentious, proud, snobbish, stuck-up*, supercilious, uppity*, upstage*, wiseguy*; CONCEPT *401* —*Ant.* humble, meek

superior [*n*] *person higher or highest in rank* boss, brass*, CEO*, chief, chieftain, director, elder, exec*, executive, head, head honcho*, heavyweight*, higher-up*, key player*, leader, manager, principal, ruler, senior, supervisor, VIP*; CONCEPT *347* —*Ant.* inferior, servant

superiority [*n*] *advantage, predominance* ahead, ascendancy, authority, better, bulge, dominance, edge, eminence, excellence, influence, lead, meliority, nobility, perfection, position, power, predomination, preeminence, preponderance, prestige, prevalence, pull, rank, spark, supremacy, top, transcendence, upper hand*, vantage, victory, whip hand*; CONCEPT *671* —*Ant.* disadvantage, inferiority, subservience

superlative [*adj*] *excellent, first-class* A-1*, accomplished, all-time*, best, capital, consummate, crack, effusive, exaggerated, excessive, extreme, finished, gilt-edge*, greatest, highest, hundred-proof*, inflated, magnificent, matchless, of highest order*, optimum, outstanding, peerless, standout*, superb, supreme, surpassing, tops*, transcendent, unexcelled, unparalleled, unrivaled, unsurpassed, winning, world-class*; CONCEPT *574* —*Ant.* low, lowest, poor, second-class

supernal [*adj*] *celestial* angelic, astral, elevated, empyreal, empyrean, ethereal, heavenly, lofty, otherworldly, seraphic, uplifted; CONCEPTS *536,673*

supernatural [*adj*] *mysterious, not of this world* abnormal, celestial, concealed, dark, fabulous, fairy, ghostly, heavenly, hidden, impenetrable, invisible, legendary, metaphysical, miraculous, mystic, mythical, mythological, numinous, obscure, occult, paranormal, phantom, phenomenal, preternatural, psychic, rare, secret, spectral, superhuman, superior, supermundane, superordinary, supranatural, transcendental, uncanny, uncomprehensible, unearthly, unfathomable, unintelligible, unknowable, unknown, unnatural, unrevealed, unusual; CONCEPT *582* —*Ant.* earthly, existent, genuine, natural, real, true

supersede [*v*] *take the place of; override* abandon, annul, desert, discard, displace, forsake, oust, outmode, outplace, overrule, reject, remove, replace, repudiate, set aside, succeed, supplant, supplement, suspend, take over, usurp; CONCEPTS *128,141* —*Ant.* accept, lower, submit

superstition [*n*] *belief in sign of things to come* false belief, fear, irrationality, notion, shibboleth*, unfounded fear; CONCEPT *689* —*Ant.* fact, reality, truth

supervise [*v*] *manage people, project* administer, be in charge*, be in driver's seat*, be in the saddle, be on duty, be responsible for, boss, call the play*, call the shots*, chaperon, conduct, control, crack the whip*, deal with, direct, handle, inspect, keep an eye on*, look after, overlook, oversee, preside over, quarterback*, ride herd on*, run, run the show*, run things*, sit on top of*, superintend, survey, take care of; CONCEPT *117* —*Ant.* serve

supervision [*n*] *management of people, project* administration, auspices, care, charge, conduct, control, direction, guidance, handling, instruction, intendance, oversight, running, superintendence, superintendency, surveillance; CONCEPT *117* —*Ant.* serve, work

supervisor [*n*] *person who manages people, project* administrator, boss, brass hat*, caretaker, chief, curator, custodian, director, executive, foreperson, head, inspector, manager, overseer, slave driver*, straw boss*, super*, superintendent, zookeeper*; CONCEPT *347* —*Ant.* employee, worker

supine [*adj1*] *lying down* decumbent, flat, flat on one's back, horizontal, level, procumbent, prone, prostrate, reclining, recumbent, stretched out; CONCEPT *583*

supine [*adj2*] *inactive* do-nothing*, dormant, dull, idle, indolent, inert, lackadaisical, lax, lazy, lethargic, listless, motionless, passive, quiet, sedentary, slack, sleepy, slothful, sluggish, unoccupied, unresponsive; CONCEPTS *401,560,584*

supplant [*v*] *displace, replace* back up, bounce, cast out, crowd, cut out, eject, expel, fill in, force, force out, front for, oust, outplace, overthrow, remove, ring, ring in, sit in, stand in, substitute, succeed, supersede, swap places with, take out, take over, take the place of, transfer, undermine, unseat, usurp; CONCEPT *128*

supple [*adj*] *bendable* adaptable, agile, bending, ductile, elastic, flexible, graceful, limber, lissome, lithe, lithesome, malleable, moldable, plastic, pliable, pliant, resilient, rubber, springy, stretch, stretchy, svelte, willowy, wiry, yielding; CONCEPTS 488,604 —Ant. hard, rigid, stiff, unflexible

supplement [n] *something added* added feature*, addendum, addition, additive, appendix, bell*, bells and whistles*, codicil, complement, continuation, extra, insert, option, postscript, pullout, rider, sequel, spin-off*, subsidiary; CONCEPTS 270,824 —Ant. base, core

supplement [v] *add to* add fuel to fire*, augment, beef up*, build up, buttress, complement, complete, enhance, enrich, extend, fill out, fill up, fortify, heat up*, improve, increase, jazz up*, pad*, punch up*, reinforce, step up, strengthen, subsidize, supply, top; CONCEPTS 236,244,245 —Ant. subtract

supplementary [adj] *additional* accompanying, added, ancillary, appended, augmenting, auxiliary, extra, increased, more; CONCEPT 771

supplicate [v] *ask for, pray for* appeal, beg, beseech, desire, petition, pray, put in for*, seek, solicit; CONCEPT 53

supplies [n] *equipment, provisions* food, foodstuffs, items, material, materials, necessities, provender, rations, raw materials, replenishments, stock, store, stores; CONCEPTS 446, 451,457

supply [n] *reserve of goods* accumulation, amount, backlog, cache, fund, hoard, inventory, number, quantity, reservoir, source, stock, stockpile, store, surplus; CONCEPT 712 —Ant. debt, lack

supply [v] *furnish, provide, give a resource* afford, cater, cater to, come across with*, come through*, come up with, contribute, deliver, dispense, drop, endow, equip, feed, fill, find, fix up, fulfill, give with, grant, hand, hand over, heel*, kick in*, minister, outfit, pony up*, produce, provision, purvey, put out, put up, replenish, satisfy, stake, stock, store, transfer, turn over, victual, yield; CONCEPTS 107,140 —Ant. seize, take

support [n1] *something that holds up structure* abutment, agency, back, backing, base, bed, bedding, block, brace, buttress, collar, column, cornerstone, device, flotation, foothold, footing, foundation, fulcrum, groundwork, guide, hold, lining, means, medium, pillar, platform, pole, post, prop, rampart, reinforcement, rest, rib, rod, shore, stake, stanchion, stave, stay, stiffener, stilt, substratum, substructure, sustentation, timber, underpinning; CONCEPTS 440,442, 445,471

support [n2] *help, approval* aid, assist, assistance, backing, blessing, championship, comfort, encouragement, friendship, furtherance, hand, lift, loyalty, moral support, patronage, protection, relief, succor, sustenance; CONCEPTS 10,110,388,712 —Ant. block, disapproval, discouragement, frustration, opposition, stop

support [n3] *food, money, possessions for staying alive* alimentation, alimony, allowance, care, keep, livelihood, living, maintenance, necessities, nutriment, payment, provision, relief, responsibility, stock, stores, subsidy, subsistence, sustenance, upkeep, victuals; CONCEPTS 340,446,457,712

support/supporter [n4] *person who helps*

another adherent, advocate, ally, angel*, apologist, backbone, backer, benefactor, champion, cohort, comforter, confederate, coworker, defender, disciple, endorser, espouser, exponent, expounder, fan, follower, friend, helper, mainstay, maintainer, partisan, patron, pillar, preserver, prop, proponent, satellite*, second, sponsor, stalwart, stay, subscriber, supporter, sustainer, tower of strength*, upholder, well-wisher*; CONCEPT 423 —Ant. enemy, foe

support [v1] *hold up* base, be a foundation for, bear, bed, bolster, bottom, brace, buttress, carry, cradle, crutch, embed, found, ground, hold, keep from falling, keep up, mainstay, poise, prop, reinforce, shore, shore up, shoulder, stand, stay, strut, sustain, undergird, upbear, uphold; CONCEPT 190 —Ant. let down, let go, release

support [v2] *take care of, provide for* angel*, attend to, back, bankroll*, be a source of strength*, bring up, buoy up, care for, chaperon, cherish, earn one's keep, encourage, feed, finance, fortify, foster, fund, give a leg up*, guard, keep, keep an eye on*, look after, maintain, make a living, nourish, nurse, pay expenses of, pay for, pick up the check*, prop, put up money for*, raise, set up, sponsor, stake, stiffen, strengthen, stroke, subsidize, succor, sustain, underwrite, uphold; CONCEPTS 7,19, 22,140,295,341 —Ant. let go, neglect, refuse, reject

support [v3] *defend, advocate belief* abet, advance, agree with, aid, approve, assist, back, bear out, bolster, boost, boost morale, carry, champion, cheer, comfort, countenance, endorse, establish, forward, foster, get behind*, go along with, go to bat for*, help, hold, justify, keep up, maintain, plead for, promote, pull for, put forward, rally round, second, side with, stand behind, stand up for, stay, stick by*, stick up for*, substantiate, sustain, take one's side*, take the part of*, throw in one's lot with*, throw in with*, uphold, verify; CONCEPTS 10,49,110 —Ant. contradict, disapprove, oppose

support [v4] *endure* abide, bear, bear with, brook, carry on, continue, countenance, go, go through, handle, keep up, live with*, maintain, put up with*, stand, stand for*, stay the course*, stick it out*, stomach*, submit, suffer, swallow*, sweat out*, take, tolerate, undergo, wait out; CONCEPT 23 —Ant. refuse, reject

suppose [v1] *assume, guess* accept, admit, brainstorm, calculate, conjecture, cook up*, dare-say*, deem, divine, dream, estimate, expect, figure, go out on a limb*, grant, guesstimate*, hazard a guess*, hypothesize, imagine, infer, judge, opine, posit, predicate, presume, presuppose, pretend, spark, speculate, surmise, suspect, take, take for granted, theorize, think, understand; CONCEPT 28 —Ant. calculate, know, measure

suppose [v2] *believe* assume, be afraid, conceive, conclude, conjecture, consider, deem, dream, expect, fancy, feel, gather, have a hunch*, have sneaking suspicion*, hypothesize, imagine, judge, postulate, pretend, reckon, regard, suspect, swear by, take, take as gospel truth*, take stock in*, think, understand, view; CONCEPT 12 —Ant. disbelieve, know

supposition [n] *guess, belief* apriorism, assumption, condition, conjecture, doubt, guessing, guesstimate*, guesswork, hunch, hypothesis, idea, likelihood, notion, opinion, posit, postulate, postulation, premise, presumption, presupposition, rough guess*, shot in the dark*, sneaking suspicion*, speculation, stab in the dark*, suppose, surmise, suspicion, theory, thesis, view; CONCEPT 689 —Ant. fact, knowledge, proof, reality

suppress [v] *restrain, hold in check* abolish, annihilate, beat down, bottle, bring to naught, burke, censor, check, clamp, conceal, conquer, contain, cover up, crack down on, crush, curb, cut off, extinguish, hold back, hold down, hold in, interrupt, keep in, keep secret, muffle, muzzle, overcome, overpower, overthrow, put an end to, put down, put kibosh on*, put lid on*, quash, quell, quench, repress, shush*, silence, sit on*, smother, snuff out*, spike, squash*, stamp out*, stifle, stop, subdue, trample, withhold; CONCEPTS 121,130,252 —Ant. encourage, let go, release

supremacy [n] *total domination* absolute rule, ascendancy, authority, command, control, dominance, dominion, driver's seat*, paramountcy, power, predominance, preeminence, preponderance, prepotence, primacy, principality, sovereignty, superiority, supreme authority, sway, transcendence; CONCEPTS 133,376 —Ant. subservience

supreme [adj] *greatest, principal* absolute, best, cardinal, chief, closing, crowning, culminating, excellent, extreme, final, first, foremost, head, highest, incomparable, last, leading, marvelous, matchless, maximum, paramount, peerless, perfect, predominant, preeminent, prevailing, prime, sovereign, superb, superlative, surpassing, terminal, top, top-drawer*, towering, transcendent, ultimate, unequaled, unmatched, unparalleled, unsurpassable, unsurpassed, utmost, overtops; CONCEPTS 568,574 —Ant. inferior, least, littlest, lowly, minor, poor, serving

surcharge [n] *fee* additional charge, cost, expense, extra, overcharge, overload, payment, price, surtax, tax; CONCEPTS 329,344

sure [adj1] *certain, definite* abiding, assured, changeless, clear, confident, constant, convinced, convincing, decided, doubtless, enduring, firm, fixed, for a fact, free from doubt*, genuine, incontestable, incontrovertible, indisputable, indubitable, never-failing, persuaded, positive, real, satisfied, set, steadfast, steady, telling, unchangeable, unchanging, uncompromising, undeniable, unequivocal, unfailing, unfaltering, unqualified, unquestionable, unquestioning, unshakable, unshaken, unvarying, unwavering, valid; CONCEPT 535 —Ant. doubtful, dubious, indefinite, uncertain, unsure, variable, wavering

sure [adj2] *physically stable* fast, firm, fixed, safe, secure, solid, staunch, steady, strong; CONCEPT 488 —Ant. swerving, unsteady, unsure, wavering, wobbly

sure [adj3] *inevitable* assured, bound, certain, guaranteed, indisputable, ineluctable, inerrant, inescapable, infallible, irrevocable, surefire, unavoidable, unerring, unfailing; CONCEPT 548 —Ant. doubted, doubtful, dubious, unsure

sure [adj4] *self-confident* arrogant, assured, certain, composed, confident, decided, decisive, positive, self-assured, self-possessed; CONCEPT 401 —Ant. humbled, uncertain, unconfident, unself-confident, unsure

surely [adv] *without doubt* absolutely, admittedly, assuredly, beyond doubt, beyond shadow of doubt*, certainly, clearly, come what may*, conclusively, decidedly, definitely, distinctly, doubtlessly, evidently, explicitly, fixedly, for certain, for real, indeed, indubitably, inevitably, inexorably, infallibly, irrefutably, manifestly, nothing else but, plainly, positively, rain or shine*, to be sure, undoubtedly, unequivocally, unerringly, unfailingly, unmistakably, unquestionably, unshakably, with certainty, without fail; CONCEPT 535 —Ant. doubtfully, questionably, uncertain

sure thing [n] *certainty* all sewn up*, belief, cinch, definiteness, foregone conclusion, lock*, open and shut case*, positiveness, rain or shine*, safe bet, shoo-in*, small risk, sure bet*, surefire*, surety; CONCEPTS 638,725

surface [adj] *external* apparent, covering, depthless, exterior, facial, outer, outside, outward, shallow, shoal, superficial, top; CONCEPTS 485,583 —Ant. central, core, inside, interior, middle

surface [n] *external part of something* area, cover, covering, expanse, exterior, exteriority, externality, facade, face, facet, level, obverse, outside, peel, periphery, plane, rind, side, skin, stretch, superficiality, superficies, top, veneer; CONCEPT 484 —Ant. core, inside, interior, middle

surface [v] *come to the top of* appear, arise, come to light, come up, crop up, emerge, flare up, materialize, rise, transpire; CONCEPTS 166,716 —Ant. dive, drop, fall, sink, submerge

surfeit [n] *excess* bellyful*, glut*, overabundance, overflow, overfullness, overindulgence, overkill, overmuch, overplus, plenitude, plethora, profusion, remainder, repletion, satiety, satisfaction, saturation, superabundance, superfluity, surplus, up to here*; CONCEPT 740 —Ant. base, core, lack, main, necessity, need, want

surfeit [v] *overfill* cloy, cram, eat, fill, glut, gorge, jade, overfeed, overindulge, pall, sate, satiate, satisfy, stuff; CONCEPTS 209,740 —Ant. deplete, use up

surge [n] *rush, usually of liquid* billow, breaker, deluge, efflux, flood, flow, growth, gush, intensification, outpouring, rise, roll, surf, swell, upsurge, wave; CONCEPTS 432,467,787

surge [v] *rush, usually in liquid form* arise, billow, climb, deluge, eddy, flow, grow, gush, heave, mount, pour, ripple, rise, roll, sluice, stream, swell, swirl, tower, undulate, well forth; CONCEPTS 146,179

surly [adj] *gruff, bearish* boorish, brusque, churlish, cross, crusty, curmudgeonly, discourteous, dour, fractious, glum, grouchy, ill-mannered, ill-natured, irritable, morose, perverse, rude, saturnine, sulky, sullen, testy, ugly, uncivil, ungracious; CONCEPT 401 —Ant. gentle, pleasant

surmise [n] *guess, conclusion* assumption, attempt, conjecture, deduction, guesstimate*, guesswork, hunch, hypothesis, idea, inference, notion, opinion, possibility, presumption, sneaking suspicion*, speculation, supposition, suspicion, theory, thought; CONCEPTS 529,689 —*Ant.* calculation, knowledge, measurement

surmise [v] *come to a conclusion* assume, conclude, conjecture, consider, deduce, fancy, guess, guesstimate*, hazard a guess*, hypothesize, imagine, infer, opine, presume, pretend, regard, risk assuming, speculate, suppose, suspect, take a shot*, take a stab*, theorize, think, venture a guess; CONCEPTS 18,28 —*Ant.* question, wonder

surmount [v] *overcome, triumph over* best, better, cap, clear, conquer, crest, crown, defeat, down, exceed, hurdle, leap, lick*, negotiate, outdo, outstrip, over, overpower, overtop, pass, prevail over, rise above, subdue, surpass, throw*, top*, vanquish, vault; CONCEPTS 95, 141 —*Ant.* give in, surrender, yield

surname [n] *family name* cognomen, last name, matronymic, metronymic, patronymic; CONCEPTS 268,683

surpass [v] *outdo something or someone* beat, best, better, cap, eclipse, exceed, excel, go beyond, go one better*, improve upon, outdistance, outdo, outmatch, outpace, outperform, outrank, outrival, outrun, outshine, outstep, outstrip, outweigh, override, overshadow, overstep, pass, put to shame*, rank*, surmount, top, tower, tower above*, transcend, trump*; CONCEPT 141 —*Ant.* fail, fall behind, lose

surplus [adj] *extra* de trop, excess, in excess, leftover, odd*, over, remaining, spare, superfluent, superfluous, supernumerary, too much, unused; CONCEPTS 560,781,824 —*Ant.* essential, lacking, necessary, needing, wanting

surplus [n] *extra material* balance, excess, overage, overflow, overkill, overmuch, overrun, overstock, oversupply, plethora, plus, remainder, residue, something extra, superabundance, superfluity, surfeit, surplusage, the limit, too much; CONCEPTS 260,658,824 —*Ant.* lack, necessity, need, want

surprise [n] *something amazing; state of amazement* abruptness, amazement, astonishment, astoundment, attack, awe, bewilderment, bombshell*, consternation, curiosity, curveball*, disappointment, disillusion, eye-opener*, fortune, godsend*, incredulity, jolt*, kick*, marvel, miracle, miscalculation, phenomenon, portent, precipitance, precipitation, precipitousness, prodigy, rarity, revelation, shock, start, stupefaction, suddenness, thunderbolt*, unexpected, unforeseen, whammy*, wonder, wonderment; CONCEPTS 410,529 —*Ant.* expectation

surprise [v1] *astonish; cause amazement* amaze, astound, awe, bewilder, blow away*, bowl over*, cause wonder, confound, confuse, consternate, daze, dazzle, discomfit, disconcert, dismay, dumbfound, electrify, flabbergast, floor, jar, jolt, leave aghast, leave openmouthed, nonplus, overwhelm, perplex, petrify, rattle, rock, shake up, shock, spring something on, stagger, startle, strike dumb*, strike with awe, stun, stupefy, take aback, take one's breath away*, throw a curve*, unsettle; CONCEPT 42 —*Ant.* expect

surprise [v2] *sneak up on; catch* ambush, burst

in on, bushwhack*, capture, catch in the act*, catch off-balance*, catch off-guard*, catch red-handed*, catch unawares*, come down on, discover, drop in on, grab, grasp, lay for, lie in wait*, nab, seize, spring on, startle, take, take by surprise, waylay; CONCEPTS 42,86 —*Ant.* expect

surprising [adj] *unexpected* accidental, amazing, astonishing, chance, electrifying, extraordinary, fortuitous, from left field*, impulsive, out of the blue*, remarkable, shocking, startling, stunning, sudden, unanticipated, unforeseen, unpredictable, unpredicted, without warning, wonderful; CONCEPTS 544,548

surrender [n] *giving up; resignation* abandonment, abdication, acquiescence, appeasement, capitulation, cessation, dedition, delivery, giving way, relenting, relinquishment, renunciation, submission, succumbing, white flag*, yielding; CONCEPTS 67,108,119,320 —*Ant.* fight, fighting, victory, win

surrender [v] *give up; resign* abandon, buckle under*, capitulate, cave in*, cede, commit, concede, consign, cry uncle*, deliver up, eat crow*, eat humble pie*, entrust, fall, fold, forego, give in, go along with, go down, go under, hand over, knuckle, knuckle under*, leave, let go, pack it in*, part with, play dead*, put up white flag*, quit, relinquish, renounce, roll over*, submit, succumb, throw in the towel*, toss it in*, waive, yield; CONCEPTS 67,108,119 —*Ant.* conquer, fight, surpass, win

surreptitious [adj] *sneaky, secret* clandestine, covert, fraudulent, furtive, hidden, hole-and-corner*, hush-hush*, on the QT*, on the sly*, private, skulking, slinking, sly, sneaking, stealthy, sub-rosa, unauthorized, undercover, underhand, under-the-table*, under wraps*, veiled; CONCEPT 548 —*Ant.* aboveboard, authorized, honest, open

surrogate [n] *person or thing that acts as substitute* agent, alternate, backup, delegate, deputy, expediency, expedient, fill-in, makeshift, pinch hitter*, proxy, recourse, refuge, replacement, representative, resort, resource, stand-in, stopgap*, sub*; CONCEPTS 348,414,423 —*Ant.* real

surround [v] *enclose, encircle something* beleaguer, beset, besiege, blockade, border, bound, box in, circle, circumscribe, circumvent, close around, close in, close in on, compass, confine, edge, enclave, encompass, envelop, environ, fence in, fringe, gird, girdle, go around, hem in, inundate, invest, lay siege to, limit, loop, margin, outline, rim, ring, round, shut in, skirt, verge; CONCEPT 758 —*Ant.* free, let go, release

surroundings [n] *environment* ambience, atmosphere, background, climate, community, environs, home, location, medium, milieu, neighborhood, setting, vicinity; CONCEPTS 198, 673

surveillance [n] *close observation, following* body mike*, bug*, bugging*, care, control, direction, eagle eye*, examination, eye, inspection, lookout, peeled eye*, scrutiny, spying, stakeout, superintendence, supervision, surveyance, tab*, tail*, tap*, track*, vigil, vigilance, watch, wiretap; CONCEPTS 103,298, 749 —*Ant.* indifference, unobservance

survey [n] *scrutiny, examination* analysis, aperçu, audit, check, compendium, critique, digest, inquiry, inspection, outline, overview, pandect, perlustration, perusal, précis, review, sample, scan, sketch, study, syllabus, view; CONCEPTS 37,103,197,271,291 —*Ant.* ignorance, neglect, negligence

survey [v] *scrutinize, take stock of* appraise, assay, assess, canvass, case, check, check out, check over, check up on, contemplate, estimate, evaluate, examine, give the once over*, inspect, look over, look upon, measure, observe, overlook, oversee, plan, plot, prospect, rate, read, reconnoiter, research, review, scan, scope, set at, size, size up, stake out, study, summarize, superintend, supervise, test the waters*, valuate, value, view; CONCEPTS 37,48,103,197, 291 —*Ant.* ignore, neglect

survive [v] *continue to live* bear, be extant, be left, carry on, carry through, come through, cut it, endure, exist, get on, get through, go all the way*, go the limit*, handle, hold out, keep, keep afloat, last, live, live down, live on, live out, live through, make a comeback*, make the cut*, outlast, outlive, outwear, persevere, persist, pull out of it*, pull through, recover, remain, remain alive, revive, ride out*, see through, stand up, subsist, suffer, sustain, tough it out*, weather, withstand; CONCEPTS 23,239,407 —*Ant.* cease, die

susceptible [adj] *exposed, naive* affected, aroused, be taken in, disposed, easily moved, easy, fall for, given, gullible, impressed, impressible, impressionable, inclined, influenced, liable, mark, movable, nonresistant, obnoxious, open, out on a limb*, persuadable, predisposed, prone, pushover, ready, receptive, responsive, roused, sensible, sensile, sensitive, sentient, sitting duck*, soft, stirred, subject, sucker*, suggestible, susceptive, swallow, swayed, tender, touched, tumble for*, vulnerable, wide open; CONCEPTS 403,542 —*Ant.* resistant, resisting, unsusceptible

suspect [adj] *doubtful* doubtable, dubious, fishy*, incredible, open, problematic, pseudo*, questionable, ridiculous, shaky*, suspected, suspicious, thick*, thin*, unbelievable, uncertain, unclear, unlikely, unsure; CONCEPTS 529,582 —*Ant.* innocent, known, trusted, trustworthy

suspect [v] *distrust; guess* assume, be afraid, believe, conceive, conclude, conjecture, consider, disbelieve, doubt, expect, feel, gather, harbor suspicion*, have a hunch*, have doubt, have sneaking suspicion*, hazard a guess*, hold, imagine, mistrust, presume, reckon, smell a rat*, speculate, suppose, surmise, think, think probable, understand, wonder; CONCEPTS 21,28 —*Ant.* know, trust

suspend [v1] *hang from above* append, attach, be pendent, dangle, depend, hang, hang down, hang up, hook up, sling, swing, wave; CONCEPTS 181,190 —*Ant.* rise

suspend [v2] *delay, hold off* adjourn, arrest, bar, break up, can, cease, check, count out, cut short, debar, defer, discontinue, eject, eliminate, exclude, file, halt, hang, hang fire*, hang up, hold up, inactivate, intermit, interrupt, lay aside, lay off, lay on the table*, lay over, omit, pigeonhole*, pink-slip*, postpone,

procrastinate, prorogue, protract, put an end to, put a stop to, put off, put on back burner*, put on hold, put on ice*, put on the shelf*, reject, retard, rule out, shelve, stave off, stay, waive, withhold; CONCEPTS 119,121,130,351 —*Ant.* complete, continue, finish, go, persist, sustain

suspense [n] *anticipation* anxiety, apprehension, chiller*, cliff-hanger*, cloak and dagger*, confusion, dilemma, doubt, eagerness, expectancy, expectation, grabber*, hesitancy, hesitation, impatience, indecision, indecisiveness, insecurity, irresolution, page-turner*, perplexity, potboiler*, tension, thriller*, uncertainty, wavering; CONCEPTS 410,679 —*Ant.* knowledge

suspension [n] *delay* abeyance, abeyancy, adjournment, break, breather*, breathing spell*, cessation, coffee break*, concluding, conclusion, cutoff, deferment, disbarment, discontinuation, discontinuing, doldrums, dormancy, downtime*, end, ending, finish, five*, freeze, halt, heave-ho*, intermission, interruption, latency, layoff, letup, moratorium, pause, period, postponement, quiescence, quiescency, remission, respite, stay, stoppage, suspense, ten*, termination, time-out; CONCEPTS 119,807,832 —*Ant.* completion, continuation, finish, persistence

suspicion [n1] *doubt* bad vibes*, chariness, conjecture, cynicism, distrust, dubiety, dubiosity, funny feeling*, guess, guesswork, gut feeling*, hunch, idea, impression, incertitude, incredulity, jealousy, lack of confidence, misgiving, mistrust, nonbelief, notion, qualm, skepticism, sneaking suspicion*, supposition, surmise, uncertainty, wariness, wonder; CONCEPTS 532,689,690 —*Ant.* trust

suspicion [n2] *hint, trace* cast, glimmer, intimation, shade, shadow, smell, soupçon, strain, streak, suggestion, tinge, touch, whiff; CONCEPTS 529,831 —*Ant.* information, knowledge

suspicious [adj1] *distrustful* apprehensive, cagey, careful, cautious, doubtful, green-eyed*, incredulous, in doubt, jealous, leery, mistrustful, not born yesterday* on the lookout*, questioning, quizzical, skeptical, suspect, suspecting, unbelieving, uptight*, wary, watchful, without belief, without faith, wondering; CONCEPTS 403,542 —*Ant.* innocent, trustworthy, trusty

suspicious [adj2] *doubtful, fishy* borderline, debatable, different, disputable, doubtable, dubious, equivocal, farfetched, funny*, irregular, not kosher*, open, open to doubt, open to question, out of line*, overt, peculiar, phony, problematic, queer, questionable, reaching, rings untrue*, shady, shaky*, suspect, too much*, uncertain, uncommon, unsure, unusual, won't wash*; CONCEPTS 529,564 —*Ant.* believable, indubious, palpable, undoubted, unquestionable

sustain [v] *keep up, maintain* aid, approve, assist, back, bankroll, bear, befriend, bolster, brace, buoy, buttress, carry, comfort, confirm, continue, convey, defend, endorse, favor, feed, foster, go for, help, keep alive, keep from falling, keep going, lend a hand*, lug, nourish, nurse, nurture, pack, preserve, prolong, prop, protract, provide for, ratify, relieve, save, shore up, stand by, stick up for, supply, support, tote, transfer, transport, uphold, validate, verify;

CONCEPTS *110,140,190* —*Ant.* discontinue, halt, stop

sustain [*v2*] *endure, experience* abide, bear, bear up under, bear with, brook, digest, encounter, feel, go, hang in, have, know, live with*, put up with*, see, stand*, stand up to, stomach*, suffer, take it, tolerate, undergo, withstand; CONCEPTS *23,678* —*Ant.* abstain, discontinue, stop

sustenance [*n*] *necessities for existence* aid, aliment, bacon*, bread*, bread and butter*, comestible, daily bread*, eatables, edibles, food, keep, livelihood, maintenance, nourishment, nutrition, pap*, provender, provision, ration, refreshment, salt*, subsistence, support, victual, wherewithal; CONCEPTS *340,446,457,709* —*Ant.* extras

svelte [*adj*] *thin and well-built* graceful, lean, lissom, lithe, slender, slinky, smooth, sylphlike, willowy; CONCEPTS *490,491* —*Ant.* chubby, corpulent, fat, thick

swagger [*v*] *show off; walk pompously* bluster, boast, brag, brandish, bully, cock, flourish, gasconade, gloat, grandstand*, hector, look big*, lord, parade, parade one's wares*, peacock*, play to the crowd*, pontificate, prance, put on, put on airs*, sashay*, saunter, strut, swank*, swashbuckle*, sway, sweep, swell; CONCEPTS *49,149,716*

swallow [*v1*] *consume* absorb, belt*, bolt*, chugalug*, devour, dispatch, dispose, down, drink, drop, eat, gobble, gulp, imbibe, ingest, ingurgitate, inhale, put away, quaff, sip, slurp, swig, swill, take, toss, wash down*, wolf; CONCEPT *169* —*Ant.* expel, regurgitate, spit out

swallow [*v2*] *believe without much thought* accept, be naive, buy, fall for; CONCEPT *12* —*Ant.* disbelieve, doubt

swami [*n*] *religious teacher* guiding light*, guru, master, mentor, mystic, sage, teacher, yogi; CONCEPT *350*

swamp [*n*] *wet land covered with vegetation* bog, bottoms, everglade, fen, glade, holm, marsh, marshland, mire, moor, morass, mud, muskeg, peat bog, polder, quag, quagmire, slough, swale, swampland; CONCEPT *509*

swamp [*v*] *overwhelm, flood* beset, besiege, crowd, drench, drown, engulf, inundate, overcrowd, overflow, overload, satiate, saturate, sink, snow*, submerge, submerse, surfeit, swallow up, upset, wash, waterlog, whelm; CONCEPTS *146,179,641* —*Ant.* pass up, underwhelm

swank/swanky [*adj*] *plush, stylish* chichi*, classy, deluxe, exclusive, expensive, fancy, fashionable, flamboyant, flashy, glamorous, grand, lavish, luxurious, ostentatious, peacocky, plushy*, posh, pretentious, rich, ritzy*, sharp, showy, smart, snappy, splashy, sumptuous, tony*, trendy, with-it*; CONCEPT *589* —*Ant.* modest, poor

swan song [*n*] *final appearance or performance* adieu, climax, closer*, conclusion, crowning achievement, crowning glory*, culmination, end piece, finis, goodbye, last act, last hurrah, peroration, windup*; CONCEPT *832*

swap/swop [*v*] *exchange* bandy, bargain, barter, change, interchange, substitute, switch, trade, traffic, truck; CONCEPT *104* —*Ant.* keep, maintain

swarm [*n*] *large, moving group* army, bevy, blowout, concourse, covey, crowd, crush, drove, flock, herd, horde, host, jam, mass, mob, multitude, myriad, pack, press, push, school, shoal, throng, troop, turnout; CONCEPTS *397,417,432*

swarm [*v*] *move forward as a group* abound, be alive, be numerous, cluster, congregate, crawl, crowd, flock, flow, gather, gather like bees*, jam, mass, mob, move in a crowd, overrun, pullulate, rush together, stream, teem, throng; CONCEPTS *113,114,159* —*Ant.* retreat

swarthy [*adj*] *dark-complexioned* black, brown, brunet, dark, dark-hued, darkish, dark-skinned, dusky, swart, tan, tawny; CONCEPT *618* —*Ant.* blonde, fair, light, pale

swat [*v*] *hit* beat, belt, biff, box, buffet, clobber, clout, cuff, ding, knock, slap, slug, smack, smash, sock, strike, wallop, whack; CONCEPT *189*

sway [*n*] *strong influence* amplitude, authority, clout, command, control, dominion, empire, expanse, government, jurisdiction, mastery, might, power, predominance, range, reach, regime, reign, rule, run, scope, sovereignty, spread, stretch, sweep; CONCEPTS *376,687*

sway [*v1*] *move back and forth* bend, blow hot and cold*, careen, fluctuate, hem and haw*, incline, lean, lurch, oscillate, pendulate, pulsate, rock, roll, stagger, swagger, swing, undulate, vibrate, wave, waver, weave, wobble, yo-yo*; CONCEPTS *13,145,151* —*Ant.* stay, steady

sway [*v2*] *influence, affect* bias, brainwash, carry, conduct, control, crack*, direct, dispose, dominate, get*, govern, guide, hold sway over, hook, impact on, impress, incline, induce, inspire, lead by the nose*, manage, move, overrule, persuade, predispose, prevail on, put across, reign, rule, rule over, sell*, soften up*, strike, suck in*, touch, turn one's head*, twist one's arm*, whitewash*, win over, work on; CONCEPTS *14,68,117* —*Ant.* leave alone

swear [*v1*] *declare under oath* affirm, assert, attest, avow, covenant, cross one's heart*, depend on, depose, give one's word*, give witness, have confidence in, maintain, make an affidavit, pledge oneself, plight, promise, rely on, say so*, state, state under oath, swear by, swear to God*, swear up and down*, take an oath, testify, trust, vouch, vow, warrant; CONCEPT *49*

swear [*v2*] *speak profanely; be vulgar* bedamn, be foul-mouthed, blaspheme, curse, cuss*, execrate, flame*, imprecate, take name in vain*, talk dirty*, use bad language*, utter profanity; CONCEPTS *52,54*

swear by [*v*] *be certain, recommend* advocate, back, bank on, believe in, be satisfied with, compliment, depend on it, endorse, go on the record for*, have faith in, plug*, praise, put in a good word*, speak highly of, speak well of, stand by, suggest, think highly of, vouch for; CONCEPTS *10,75*

swearing [*n*] *foul language* bad language*, blasphemy, cursing, cuss*, cussing*, dirty language*, dirty name*, dirty talk*, dirty word*, execration, expletives, four-letter word*, imprecation, malediction, no-no*, profanity, swearword; CONCEPTS *54,276,278*

su
sw

sweat [n1] *body's perspiring* diaphoresis, excretion, exudation, perspiration, steam, transudation; CONCEPTS 185,467

sweat [n2] *hard work* backbreaker*, chore, drudgery, effort, grind, labor, moil, slavery, task, toil, travail, work; CONCEPTS 362,677 —*Ant.* entertainment, recreation

sweat [v1] *perspire* break out in a sweat, drip, eject, exude, glow, ooze, secrete, seep, spout, swelter, transude, wilt; CONCEPT 185

sweat [v2] *worry about; bear* abide, agonize, be on pins and needles*, be on tenterhooks*, brook, chafe, endure, exert, fret, go, labor, lose sleep over*, stand, stay the course*, stick it out*, stomach*, suffer, take, toil, tolerate, torture, work hard; CONCEPTS 23,35 —*Ant.* be calm, ignore

sweaty [adj] *damp with perspiration* bathed, clammy, covered with sweat, drenched, dripping, drippy, glowing, hot, moist, perspiring, perspiry, soaked, sticky, stinky, sweating, wet; CONCEPT 406 —*Ant.* dry

sweep [n1] *range, extent* ambit, breadth, compass, extension, latitude, length, orbit, purview, radius, reach, region, scope, span, stretch, vista; CONCEPTS 651,756,788

sweep [n2] *movement* arc, bend, course, curve, gesture, move, play, progress, stroke, swing; CONCEPTS 145,748

sweep [v1] *brush off, away* broom, brush, brush up, clean, clear, clear up, mop, ready, remove, scrub, tidy, vacuum; CONCEPT 165

sweep [v2] *fly, glide* career, fleet, flit, flounce, glance, hurtle, pass, sail, scud, skim, tear, wing, zoom; CONCEPTS 150,152

sweeping [adj] *wide-ranging* across-the-board, all-around, all-embracing, all-encompassing, all-inclusive, all-out, bird's-eye*, blanket, broad, complete, comprehensive, exaggerated, exhaustive, extensive, full, general, global, inclusive, indiscriminate, out-and-out*, overall, overdrawn, overstated, radical, thorough, thorough-going, unqualified, vast, wall-to-wall*, whole-hog*, wholesale*, wide; CONCEPTS 531,772 —*Ant.* exclusive, narrow

sweet [adj1] *sugary* candied, candy-coated, cloying, delicious, honeyed, like candy, like honey, luscious, nectareous, saccharine, sugar-coated, sugared, sweetened, syrupy, toothsome; CONCEPT 462 —*Ant.* acid, bitter, salty, sour

sweet [adj2] *friendly, kind* affectionate, agreeable, amiable, angelic, appealing, attractive, beautiful, beloved, charming, cherished, companionable, considerate, darling, dear, dearest, delectable, delicious, delightful, dulcet, engaging, fair, generous, gentle, good-humored, good-natured, heavenly, lovable, loving, luscious, mild, mushy, patient, pet, pleasant, pleasing, precious, reasonable, saccharine, sweet-tempered, sympathetic, taking, tender, thoughtful, treasured, unselfish, winning, winsome; CONCEPTS 401,404,542 —*Ant.* mean, unfriendly, unpleasant

sweet [adj3] *nice-smelling* ambrosial, aromal, aromatic, balmy, clean, fragrant, fresh, new, perfumed, perfumy, pure, redolent, savory, scented, spicy, sweet-smelling, wholesome; CONCEPT 598 —*Ant.* malodorous, stinking, stinky, unpleasant

sweet [adj4] *nice-sounding* dulcet, euphonic, euphonious, harmonious, mellifluous, mellow, melodic, melodious, musical, orotund, rich, rotund, silver-tongued, silvery, smooth, soft, sonorous, soothing, sweet-sounding, tuneful; CONCEPT 594 —*Ant.* cacophonous, discordant, ugly

sweet [n] *sugary food* bonbon, candy, chocolate, confection, confectionery, confiture, delight, dessert, enjoyment, final course, gratification, joy, pleasure, pudding, snack, sugarplum, sweetmeat; CONCEPTS 457,461

sweeten [v1] *add sugar* add sweetening, candy, candy-coat, honey, make sweet, make toothsome, mull, sugar, sugar-coat; CONCEPT 170 —*Ant.* salt, sour

sweeten [v2] *make happy; appease* alleviate, assuage, conciliate, mollify, pacify, placate, propitiate, soften up, soothe; CONCEPTS 7,22 —*Ant.* displease, disrupt, trouble, worry

sweetheart [n] *person whom another loves* admirer, beau, beloved, boyfriend, companion, darling, dear, dear one, flame, girlfriend, heartthrob, honey*, inamorata, inamorato, love, lovebird*, lover, one and only*, paramour, pet, significant other, steady*, suitor, swain, sweet, treasure*, truelove, valentine; CONCEPTS 414,423 —*Ant.* enemy, foe

swell [adj] *wonderful* awesome, cool*, dandy*, deluxe, desirable, excellent, exclusive, fashionable, fine, fly*, grand, groovy*, keen, marvelous, neat, nifty, plush, posh, ritzy*, smart, stylish, super, terrific; CONCEPTS 548, 574 —*Ant.* bad, horrible, shabby

swell [n] *large increase, flow* billow, crescendo, growth, ripple, rise, seat, surf, surge, undulation, uprise, wave; CONCEPT 780 —*Ant.* decline, decrease

swell [v] *become larger* accumulate, add to, aggravate, amplify, augment, balloon, become bloated, become distended, become swollen, be inflated, belly, billow, blister, bloat, bulge, distend, enhance, enlarge, expand, extend, fatten, fill out, grow, grow larger, heighten, increase, intensity, mount, plump, pouch, pout, protrude, puff, puff up, rise, round out, surge, tumefy, uprise, well up; CONCEPTS 236,245,780 —*Ant.* compress, concentrate, contract, shrink

swelling [n] *physical growth; lump* abscess, blister, boil, bruise, bulge, bump, bunion, carbuncle, contusion, corn, dilation, distention, enlargement, hump, increase, inflammation, injury, knob, knurl, node, nodule, pimple, pock, protuberance, puff, puffiness, pustule, ridge, sore, tumescence, tumor, wale, wart, weal, welt; CONCEPTS 306,309 —*Ant.* depression

sweltering [adj] *very hot* airless, baking, broiling, burning, close, fiery, humid, oppressive, perspiring, scorching, sizzling, stewing, sticky, stifling, stuffy, sultry, sweaty, sweltry, torrid; CONCEPT 605 —*Ant.* cold, cool, freezing

swerve [v] *turn aside, often to avoid collision* bend, deflect, depart, depart from, deviate, dip, diverge, err, get off course, go off course, incline, lurch, move, sheer, sheer off, shift, sideslip, sidestep, skew, skid, slue, stray, swing, tack, train off, turn, veer, wander, waver, wind; CONCEPTS 150,195,201 —*Ant.* straighten

swift [adj] *very fast* abrupt, alacritous, barreling, breakneck, cracking*, double-quick*, expeditious, express, fleet, fleet-footed*, flying, hasty, headlong, hurried, in nothing flat*, like crazy*, like mad*, nimble, on the double*, precipitate, prompt, pronto, quick, rapid, ready, screaming, shaking a leg*, short, short-lived, snappy*, spanking*, speedball*, speedy, sudden, supersonic, unexpected, winged; CONCEPTS 588,799 —*Ant.* delayed, slow, sluggish

swiftly/swift [adv] *very fast* apace, double-quick*, expeditiously, flat-out*, fleetly, full tilt*, hastily, hurriedly, in no time*, posthaste, promptly, quick, quickly, rapidly, speedily, without losing time*, without warning*; CONCEPTS 588,799 —*Ant.* slowly, sluggishly

swim [v] *make way through water using arms, legs* bathe, breast-stroke, crawl, dive, dog-paddle, float, freestyle, glide, go for a swim, go swimming, go wading, high-dive, move, paddle, practice, race, skinny-dip*, slip, stroke, submerge, take a dip, wade; CONCEPT 363

swimmingly [adv] *very well* as planned, cosily, easily, effectively, effortlessly, favorably, fortunately, happily, like a dream*, like clockwork*, prosperously, quickly, satisfyingly, smoothly, successfully, well, with flying colors*, with no trouble, without a hitch*; CONCEPTS 528,544 —*Ant.* lousy

swimsuit [n] *bathing suit* bathing costume, beach costume, beachwear, bikini, jams, maillot, one-piece, swimwear, thong, trunks, two-piece; CONCEPT 451

swindle [n] *cheating, stealing* blackmail, cheat, con, crooked deal*, deceit, deception, dirty pool*, double cross*, double-dealing*, extortion, fake, fast one*, fast shuffle*, frame-up, fraud, hoax, hustle, imposition, imposture, knavery, racket*, rip-off*, scam, sell, shady deal*, shakedown, sham, sharp practice*, shell game*, sting, trick, trickery; CONCEPTS 59,139,192 —*Ant.* benevolence, donation, gift

swindle [v] *cheat, steal* bamboozle, beat*, bilk, clip*, con*, cozen, deceive, defraud, diddle*, do*, dupe, extort, fleece*, flimflam*, fool, frame*, fudge*, gouge*, gull*, hoodwink, overcharge, pluck, pull a fast one*, put one over on*, rip off*, rook, run a game on*, sandbag, scam, sell a bill of goods*, set up, shaft, stiff*, sting*, sucker, take for a ride*, take to the cleaners*, trick, trim*, victimize; CONCEPTS 59,139,192 —*Ant.* donate, give

swindler [n] *person who cheats another* absconder, charlatan, cheat, cheater, chiseler, clip, con artist, confidence artist, counterfeiter, crook, deceiver, defrauder, dodger, double-dealer, falsifier, forger, four-flusher*, fraud, gouger, grifter, impostor, mechanic, mountebank, operator, rascal, rook, scammer, scoundrel, shark, sharp, sharper, slicker, thief, trickster; CONCEPT 412 —*Ant.* philanthropist

swing [n] *moving back and forth* beat, cadence, cadency, fluctuation, lilt, measure, meter, motion, oscillation, rhythm, stroke, sway, swaying, tempo, undulation, vibration; CONCEPTS 65,748

swing [v] *move back and forth; be suspended* avert, away, be pendent, curve, dangle, deflect, divert, flap, fluctuate, hang, lurch, oscillate, palpitate, pendulate, pitch, pivot, reel, revolve,

rock, roll, rotate, sheer, shunt, suspend, sway, swerve, swivel, turn, turn about, turn on an axis, twirl, undulate, vary, veer, vibrate, volte-face, wag, waggle, wave, wheel, whirl, wiggle, wobble; CONCEPT 145

swipe [n/v1] *hit* bash, blow, clip, clout, clump, cuff, knock, lash out, lick, rap, slap, smack, sock, strike, swat, wallop, wipe; CONCEPT 189

swipe [v2] *steal* appropriate, cop, filch, heist, hook, lift, make off with, nab, nick, pilfer, pinch, purloin, sneak, snitch; CONCEPT 139

swirl [v] *spin around* agitate, boil, churn, coil, crimp, crisp, curl, eddy, purl, roil, roll, snake, surge, swoosh*, twirl, whirl, whirlpool, whorl, wriggle; CONCEPTS 145,738

swish [adj] *fashionable, elegant* classy, deluxe, exclusive, grand, in, plush, posh, ritzy*, smart, stylish, sumptuous, swank, swell, tony*, trendy, with-it*; CONCEPT 589 —*Ant.* inelegant, unfashionable, unstylish

switch [n] *change, exchange* about-face, alteration, change of direction, reversal, shift, substitution, swap, transformation; CONCEPT 697 —*Ant.* inactivity, stagnation

switch [v] *change, exchange* change course, convert, deflect, deviate, divert, interchange, rearrange, replace, shift, shunt, sidetrack, substitute, swap, trade, turn, turnabout, turn aside, veer; CONCEPTS 104,232,697

swivel [v] *spin around axis* hinge, pirouette, pivot, revolve, rotate, swing around, turn, whirl; CONCEPT 145

swollen [adj] *enlarged* bloated, bulgy, distended, distent, inflamed, inflated, puffed, puffy, tumescent, tumid; CONCEPT 485 —*Ant.* compressed, contracted, shrunken

swoon [v] *faint* become unconscious, be overcome, black out, collapse, drop, feel giddy, feel lightheaded, go out like a light*, keel over, lose consciousness, pass out, weaken; CONCEPTS 303,308

swoop [v] *descend quickly* dive, fall, plummet, plunge, pounce, rush, slide, stoop, sweep; CONCEPTS 150,181 —*Ant.* ascend

sycophant [n] *person who caters to another* adulator, backscratcher*, backslapper*, bootlicker*, brownnoser*, doormat*, fan, fawner, flatterer, flunky*, groupie*, groveler, handshaker*, hanger-on*, lackey, minion, parasite, politician, puppet, slave; CONCEPT 423

syllabus [n] *summary* aperçu, capitulation, conspectus, curriculum, outline, program, review, rundown, schedule, sketch, synopsis; CONCEPT 283

symbol [n] *letter, character, sign of written communication* attribute, badge, denotation, design, device, emblem, figure, image, indication, logo, mark, motif, note, numeral, pattern, regalia, representation, stamp, token, type; CONCEPT 284

symbolic [adj] *representative* allegorical, characteristic, denotative, emblematic, figurative, indicative, indicatory, significant, suggestive, symptomatic, token, typical; CONCEPT 267

symbolize [v] *represent; stand for* betoken, body forth, connote, denote, emblematize, embody, epitomize, exemplify, express, illustrate, indicate, mean, mirror, personify, show, signify, suggest, symbol, typify; CONCEPTS 74,138,682

symmetrical [*adj*] *well-proportioned* balanced, commensurable, commensurate, equal, in proportion, proportional, regular, shapely, well-formed; CONCEPTS 480,485,579 —*Ant.* asymmetrical, different, disproportioned, irregular, uneven, unsymmetrical

symmetry [*n*] *proportion* agreement, arrangement, balance, centrality, conformity, correspondence, equality, equilibrium, equipoise, equivalence, evenness, finish, form, harmony, order, proportionality, regularity, rhythm, shapeliness, similarity; CONCEPTS 716,717 —*Ant.* asymmetry, difference, disproportion, imbalance, irregularity, unevenness

sympathetic [*adj*1] *concerned, feeling* affectionate, all heart*, appreciating, benign, benignant, caring, commiserating, compassionate, comprehending, condoling, considerate, having heart in right place*, interested, kind, kindhearted, kindly, loving, pitying, responsive, sensitive, soft, softhearted, supportive, sympathizing, tender, thoughtful, understanding, vicarious, warm, warmhearted; CONCEPT 542 —*Ant.* callous, merciless, uncaring, unconcerned, unfeeling, unsympathetic

sympathetic [*adj*2] *agreeable, friendly* amenable, appreciative, approving, companionable, compatible, congenial, congruous, consistent, consonant, cool, down, encouraging, favorably disposed, having a heart*, in sympathy with, like-minded, on same wavelength*, open, open-minded, pro*, receptive, responsive, simpatico, tuned in*, vicarious, well-disposed, well-intentioned; CONCEPTS 401,542,563 —*Ant.* cold, cool, disagreeable, unfriendly, unsociable, unsympathetic

sympathize [*v*] *feel for, be compassionate* ache, agree, appreciate, be in accord, be in sympathy, be kind to, be there for*, be understanding, bleed for*, comfort, commiserate, compassionate, comprehend, condole, emphathize, feel heart go out to*, go along with, grieve with, have compassion, identify with, love, offer consolation, pick up on, pity, relate to*, share another's sorrow, show kindliness, show mercy, show tenderness, side with*, tune in*, understand; CONCEPTS 34,110 —*Ant.* disapprove, disregard, ignore

sympathy [*n*1] *shared feeling* accord, affinity, agreement, alliance, attraction, benignancy, close relation, commiseration, compassion, concord, congeniality, connection, correspondence, empathy, feelings, fellow feeling, harmony, heart, kindliness, kindness, mutual attraction, mutual fondness, rapport, responsiveness, sensitivity, tenderness, understanding, union, unity, warmheartedness, warmth; CONCEPTS 388,410,664 —*Ant.* disdain, incompatibility, indifference

sympathy [*n*2] *pity* aid, cheer, comfort, commiseration, compassion, condolence, consolation, empathy, encouragement, reassurance, rue, ruth, solace, tenderness, thoughtfulness, understanding; CONCEPTS 410,633 —*Ant.* callousness, indifference, mercilessness

symposium [*n*] *conference* colloquium, convention, discussion, discussion group, forum, gabfest*, huddle, meeting, panel discussion, parley, powwow, rap session, round table, seminar, talk; CONCEPTS 56,324,386

symptom [*n*] *sign of illness or problem* evidence, expression, index, indication, indicia, manifestation, mark, note, significant, syndrome, token, warning; CONCEPTS 306,316

symptomatic [*adj*] *indicative* associated, characteristic, demonstrative, denotative, denotive, designative, emblematic, evidential, indicating, pointing to, significant, suggestive, symbolic; CONCEPT 267

synagogue [*n*] *church* abbey, cathedral, chapel, house of God, house of prayer, house of worship, mosque, parish, shrine, shul, tabernacle, temple; CONCEPTS 368,449

synchronize [*v*] *coordinate* adjust, agree, atune, harmonize, integrate, keep time with, match, mesh, organize, pool, proportion, pull together, put in sync*, set; CONCEPTS 36,84,158

syndicate [*n*] *group of business entities* association, board, bunch, cabinet, cartel, chain, chamber, combine, committee, company, conglomerate, council, crew, gang, group, megacorp*, mob, multinational*, organization, outfit, partnership, pool, ring, trust, union; CONCEPTS 323,325

syndrome [*n*] *disease, condition* affection, ailment, complaint, complex, diagnostics, disorder, infirmity, malady, problem, prognostics, sickness, sign, symptoms; CONCEPTS 306,674

synergy [*n*] *collaboration, cooperation* alliance, coaction, combined effort, harmony, symbiosis, synergism, team effort, teaming, teamwork, union, unity, working together; CONCEPTS 110,112,388,677

synonymous [*adj*] *equivalent* alike, apposite, coincident, compatible, convertible, correspondent, corresponding, equal, identical, identified, interchangeable, like, one and the same, same, similar, synonymic, tantamount; CONCEPTS 487,573 —*Ant.* different, dissimilar, opposite, polar, unequal

synopsis [*n*] *digest, summary* abridgment, abstract, aperçu, breviary, brief, capsule, compendium, condensation, conspectus, epitome, outline, précis, recap*, résumé, review, rundown, run-through, sketch; CONCEPT 283

synthesis [*n*] *combining; combination* amalgam, amalgamation, blend, building a whole, coalescence, composite, compound, constructing, construction, entirety, forming, fusion, integrating, integration, making one, organism, organization, structure, unification, union, unit, welding, whole; CONCEPTS 113,837 —*Ant.* division, separation

synthesize [*v*] *combine; make whole* amalgamate, arrange, blend, harmonize, incorporate, integrate, manufacture, orchestrate, symphonize, unify; CONCEPTS 113,205 —*Ant.* divide, separate

synthetic [*adj*] *artificial* constructed, counterfeit, ersatz*, fabricated, factitious, fake, false, hokey*, made, makeshift, manufactured, mock, phony, plastic, unnatural; CONCEPTS 485,582 —*Ant.* genuine, natural, real

system [*n*1] *order, whole* arrangement, classification, combination, complex, conformity, coordination, entity, fixed order, frame of reference, ideology, integral, integrate, logical order, orderliness, organization, philosophy, red tape*, regularity, rule, scheme, setup, structure, sum, theory, totality; CONCEPTS 770, 837 —*Ant.* cog, part

system [*n2*] *method, plan* arrangement, artifice, course of action, custom, definite plan, fashion, logical process, manner, methodicalness, methodology, mode, modus, modus operandi, operation, orderliness, orderly process, pattern, policy, practice, procedure, proceeding, process, regularity, routine, scheme, strategy, structure, systematic process, systematization, tactics, technique, theory, usage, way, wise; CONCEPT 6 —*Ant.* disorder, disorganization

systematic [*adj*] *orderly* analytical, arranged, businesslike, complete, efficient, logical, methodic, methodical, ordered, organized, out-and-out*, precise, regular, standardized, systematized, thoroughgoing, well-ordered; CONCEPT 557 —*Ant.* chaotic, confused, disorderly, mixed up, unmethodical, unsystematic

systematize [*v*] *put in order* arrange, array, contrive, design, devise, dispose, establish, frame, get act together, institute, make uniform, marshal, methodize, order, organize, plan, project, pull together, rationalize, regulate, schematize, shape up, standardize, straighten up, systemize, tighten up; CONCEPTS 84,94 —*Ant.* confuse, disorder, disorganize, mix up

T

tab [*n1*] *ticket, label* bookmark, clip, flag, flap, holder, logo, loop, marker, slip, sticker, stop, strip, tag; CONCEPTS 270,475

tab [*n2*] *bill for service* account, charge, check, cost, invoice, price, price tag, rate, reckoning, score, statement, tariff; CONCEPT 329

table [*n1*] *furniture upon which to work, eat* bar, bench, board, buffet, bureau, console, counter, desk, dining table, dinner table, dresser, lectern, pulpit, sideboard, sink, slab, stand, wagon; CONCEPT 443

table [*n2*] *meal* bill of fare, board, cuisine, diet, fare, food, meat and drink, menu, spread, victuals; CONCEPT 459

table [*n3*] *flatland* flat, mesa, plain, plateau, tableland, upland; CONCEPT 509

table [*n4*] *diagram with columns of information* agenda, appendix, canon, catalogue, chart, compendium, digest, graph, illustration, index, inventory, list, plan, record, register, roll, schedule, statistics, summary, synopsis, table of contents, tabulation; CONCEPTS 283,625

table [*v*] *postpone a proposition* cool*, defer, delay, enter, hang*, hold off, hold up, move, pigeonhole*, propose, put aside, put forward, put off, put on back burner*, put on hold*, put on ice*, put on the shelf*, shelve, submit, suggest; CONCEPTS 121,324 —*Ant.* decide, vote

tableau [*n*] *scene, often painted* illustration, picture, representation, spectacle, view; CONCEPTS 625,716

tablet [*n1*] *sheaf of papers that are connected* book, folder, memo pad, notebook, pad, quire, ream, scratch, scratch pad, sheets; CONCEPT 475

tablet [*n2*] *encapsulated medicine* cake, cap-

sule, dose, lozenge, medicine, pellet, pill, square, troche; CONCEPT 307

tableware [*n*] *flatware* dishes, forks, glasses, glassware, knives, silverware, spoons, utensils; CONCEPTS 433,499

tabloid [*n*] *newspaper* paper, rag*, scandal sheet*, sheet; CONCEPTS 279,280

taboo [*adj*] *not allowed, permitted* anathema, banned, beyond the pale*, disapproved, forbidden, frowned on*, illegal, off limits*, outlawed, out of bounds*, prohibited, proscribed, reserved, restricted, ruled out, unacceptable, unmentionable, unthinkable; CONCEPT 548 —*Ant.* acceptable, allowed, mentionable, ok

taboo [*n*] *something not allowed, permitted* anathema, ban, disapproval, don't*, forbiddance, inhibition, interdict, law, limitation, no-no*, prohibition, proscription, regulation, religious convention, reservation, restraint, restriction, sanction, social convention, stricture, superstition, thou-shalt-not*; CONCEPTS 532,688 —*Ant.* allowance, mentionable

tabulate [*v*] *figure, classify* alphabetize, arrange, catalogue, categorize, chart, codify, digest, enumerate, formulate, grade, index, list, methodize, order, range, register, systematize, tabularize; CONCEPTS 84,764 —*Ant.* estimate, guess

tacit [*adj*] *taken for granted; not said aloud* alluded to, allusive, assumed, hinted at, implicit, implied, inarticulate, indirect, inferred, intimated, silent, suggested, undeclared, understood, unexpressed, unsaid, unspoken, unstated, unvoiced, wordless; CONCEPTS 529, 548 —*Ant.* explicit, express

taciturn [*adj*] *uncommunicative* aloof, antisocial, brooding, clammed up*, close, close-mouthed*, cold, curt, distant, dour, dried-up*, dumb, laconic, mum, mute, quiet, reserved, reticent, sententious, silent, sparing, speechless, tight-lipped*, unexpressive, unforthcoming, withdrawn; CONCEPTS 267,401 —*Ant.* communicative, fluent, talkative, wordy

tack [*n1*] *course of movement* aim, alteration, approach, bearing, bend, deflection, deviation, digression, direction, double, echelon, heading, line, method, oblique course, path, plan, point of sail, procedure, set, shift, siding, sidling, sweep, swerve, switch, tactic, tangent, turn, variation, way, yaw, zigzag; CONCEPTS 692,738

tack [*n2*] *short pin for attaching* brad, nail, point, pushpin, staple, thumbtack; CONCEPT 475

tack [*v*] *attach* add, affix, annex, append, baste, fasten, fix, hem, mount, nail, paste, pin, sew, staple, stitch, tag, tie; CONCEPTS 85,160,218 —*Ant.* detach, separate, unfasten, untack

tackle [*n*] *equipment for activity* accouterment, apparatus, appliance, gear, goods, habiliments, hook, impedimenta, implements, line, machinery, materiel, outfit, paraphernalia, rig, rigging, tools, trappings; CONCEPT 496

tackle [*v1*] *make an effort* accept, apply oneself, attack, attempt, bang away at*, begin, come to grips with*, deal with, devote oneself to, embark upon, engage in, essay, give a try*, give a whirl*, go for it*, launch, make a run at*, pitch into, set about, square off*, start the ball rolling*, take a shot at*, take in hand*, take on, take up, try, try on for size*, turn one's hand to*, turn to, undertake, work on; CONCEPTS 87,100 —*Ant.* avoid, dodge, forget, idle, neglect

tackle [v2] *jump on and grab* attack, block, bring down, bring to the ground*, catch, challenge, clutch, confront, down, grapple, grasp, halt, intercept, nail, put the freeze on*, sack, seize, smear, stop, take, take hold of, throw, throw down, upset; CONCEPTS 90,164, 191 —*Ant.* avoid, dodge

tacky [adj] *cheap, tasteless* broken-down, crude, dilapidated, dingy, dowdy, down-at-heel*, faded, frumpy*, gaudy, inelegant, mangy*, messy, nasty*, outmoded, out-of-date, poky*, ratty, run-down, seedy, shabby, shoddy, sleazy*, sloppy*, slovenly, stodgy, threadbare, unbecoming, unkempt, unstylish, unsuitable, untidy, vulgar; CONCEPTS 485,589 —*Ant.* classy, expensive, tasteful

tact [n] *finesse, thoughtfulness* acumen, acuteness,address, adroitness, amenity, aptness, care, common sense, consideration, control, courtesy, delicacy, delicatesse, diplomacy, discernment, discretion, discrimination, gallantry, good taste, head, horse sense*, intelligence, judgment, penetration, perception, perspicacity, poise, policy, politicness, presence, prudence, refinement, repose, savoir faire, sensitivity, skill, smoothness, suavity, subtlety, tactfulness, understanding,urbanity; CONCEPT 633 —*Ant.* carelessness, indiscretion, tactlessness, thoughtlessness

tactful [adj] *thoughtful, careful* adroit, aware, cautious, civil, considerate, courteous, deft, delicate, diplomatic, discreet, gentle, judicious, observant, perceptive, poised, polished, polite, politic, prudent, sensitive, skilled, skillful, suave, subtle, sympathetic, tactical, understanding, urbane, wise; CONCEPT 401 —*Ant.* careless, indiscreet, tactless, unthoughtful

tactical [adj] *strategic* calculated, clever, cunning, deliberate, diplomatic, planned, politic, prudent, skillful, smart, well-planned; CONCEPT 544

tactics [n] *strategy* approach, campaign, channels,course, defense, device, disposition, generalship, line, maneuver, maneuvering, means, method, move, plan, plan of attack, ploy, policy, procedure, red tape*, scheme, stratagem, system, tack, technique, trick, way;CONCEPT 660

tactile [adj] *touchable* material, palpable, physical, solid, tactual, tangible; CONCEPTS 529,582

tactless [adj] *unthinking, careless* awkward, blundering, boorish, brash, bungling, clumsy, crude, discourteous, gauche, gruff, harsh, hasty, impolite, impolitic, imprudent, inconsiderate, indelicate, indiscreet, inept, injudicious, insensitive, maladroit, misunderstanding, rash, rough, rude, sharp, stupid, thoughtless, uncivil, unconsiderate, undiplomatic, unfeeling, unkind, unperceptive, unpolished, unsubtle, unsympathetic, untactful, vulgar; CONCEPT 401 —*Ant.* careful, discreet, tactful, thoughtful

tag [n] *label, ticket* badge, button, card, check, chip, docket, emblem, flap, ID*, identification, inscription, insignia, logo, mark, marker, motto, note, pin, slip, stamp, sticker, stub, tab, tally, trademark, voucher; CONCEPTS 270,284,475

tag [v1] *label; attach label* add, adjoin, affix, annex, append, call, check, christen, designate, docket, dub, earmark, fasten, hold, identify, mark, name, nickname, style, tack, tally, tap, term, ticket, title, touch; CONCEPTS 62,85,160

tag [v2] *follow* accompany, attend, bedog, chase, dog, heel, hunt, pursue, shadow, tail, trace, track, track down, trail; CONCEPT 207 —*Ant.* run away

tail [n] *end piece, part* appendage, behind, butt*, buttocks, caudal appendage, conclusion, empennage, end, extremity, fag end*, hind end, hindmost part, hind part, last part, posterior, rear, rear end, reverse, rudder, rump*, stub, tag, tag end, tailpiece, train, tush*, wagger*; CONCEPTS 392,825,827 —*Ant.* front, head

tail [v] *follow* bedog, dog, eye*, hound, keep an eye on, pursue, shadow, stalk, tag, track, trail; CONCEPT 207 —*Ant.* run away

tailor [n] *person who sews clothing* clothier, costumier, couturier, dressmaker, garment maker, needle worker*, outfitter, suit maker; CONCEPT 348

tailor [v] *make to fit; adjust* accommodate, adapt, alter, conform, convert, custom-make, cut, cut to fit, dovetail*, fashion, fit, make to order, modify, mold, quadrate, reconcile, shape, shape up, square, style, suit, tailor-make*; CONCEPTS 126,202,218

tailor-made [adj] *custom-made* comfortable, custom-built, custom-fit, fitted, made-to-measure, made to order, perfect, snug, suitable, suited, tailored; CONCEPT 558

taint [n] *contamination, corruption* black mark, blemish, blot, contagion, defect, disgrace, dishonor, fault, flaw, infection, pollution, shame, smear, spot, stain, stigma; CONCEPTS 230,388 —*Ant.* cleanliness, perfection

taint [v] *dirty, contaminate; ruin* adulterate, besmirch, blacken, blemish, blight, blot, blur, brand, break down, cast a slur, cloud, cook, corrupt, crud up*, crumble, cut, damage, debase, decay, decompose, defile, deprave, discolor, discredit, disgrace, dishonor, disintegrate, doctor, foul, give a bad name*, harm, hurt, infect, muddy, poison, pollute, putrefy, rot, shame, smear, soil, spike, spoil, stain, stigmatize, sully, tar, tarnish, trash*, turn, water, water down; CONCEPTS 246,254,384 —*Ant.* clean, right

take [n] *profit* booty*, catch, catching, cut, gate, haul*, holding, part, proceeds, receipts, return, returns, revenue, share, takings, yield; CONCEPT 344 —*Ant.* debt, loss

take [v1] *get; help oneself to* abduct, accept, acquire, arrest, attain, capture, carry off, carve out, catch, clasp, clutch, collar*, collect, earn, ensnare, entrap, gain possession, gather up, get hold of, grab, grasp, grip, handle, haul in, have, hold, lay hold of, obtain, overtake, pick up, prehend, pull in, reach, reap, receive, secure, seize, snag, snatch, strike, take hold of, take in, win; CONCEPTS 120,142 —*Ant.* give, receive

take [v2] *steal* abduct, abstract, accroach, annex, appropriate, arrogate, borrow, carry off, commandeer, confiscate, expropriate, filch*, haul in, liberate, lift*, misappropriate, nab*, nail*, nip*, pick up, pinch*, pluck, pocket*, preempt, pull in, purloin, rip off*, run off with*, salvage, seize, sequester, snag, snare, snatch*, snitch*, swipe*, take in; CONCEPT 139 —*Ant.* give, offer

take [*v3*] *buy; reserve* book, borrow, charter, choose, cull, decide on, derive, draw, elect, engage, gain, get, hire, lease, mark, obtain, optate, opt for, pay for, pick, prefer, procure, purchase, rent, select, single out; CONCEPTS 41,327 —*Ant.* refuse, reject

take [*v4*] *endure* abide, accept, accommodate, bear, bear with, brave, brook, contain, give access, go, go through, grin and bear it*, hack*, hang in*, hang on*, hang tough*, hold, let in, live with, put up with, receive, ride out*, stand, stand for, stick it out*, stomach, submit to, suffer, swallow, take it, take it lying down*, take it on the chin*, tolerate, undergo, weather, welcome, withstand; CONCEPT 23 —*Ant.* avoid, discontinue, dodge, refuse, reject, stop

take [*v5*] *consume* devour, down, drink, eat, feed, feed on, imbibe, ingest, inhale, meal, partake of, swallow; CONCEPT 169 —*Ant.* abstain

take [*v6*] *accept, adopt; use* accommodate, admit, appropriate, assume, be aware of, behave, bring, deal with, delight in, do, effect, enjoy, enter upon, execute, exercise, exert, experience, function, give access, have, include, let in, like, luxuriate in, make, observe, operate, perform, play, practice, put in practice, react, receive, relish, sense, serve, take in, treat, undertake, utilize, welcome, work; CONCEPTS 100,124,225 —*Ant.* disallow, refuse, reject

take [*v7*] *understand* accept, apprehend, assume, be aware of, believe, catch, compass, comprehend, consider, deem, expect, experience, feel, follow, gather, grasp, hold, imagine, interpret as, know, look upon, observe, perceive, presume, receive, reckon*, regard, see, see as, sense, suppose, suspect, take in, think, think of as; CONCEPT 15 —*Ant.* misconceive, misunderstand

take [*v8*] *win; be successful* beat, be efficacious, do the trick, have effect, operate, prevail, succeed, triumph, work; CONCEPT 706 —*Ant.* fail, lose

take [*v9*] *carry, transport; accompany* attend, back, bear, bring, buck, cart, conduct, convey, convoy, drive, escort, ferry, fetch, go with, guide, gun, haul, heel, jag, journey, lead, lug, move, pack, piggyback*, pilot, ride, schlepp*, shoulder, steer, tote, tour, trek, truck, usher; CONCEPTS 114,187 —*Ant.* hold, keep, maintain

take [*v10*] *captivate, enchant* allure, attract, become popular, bewitch, charm, delight, draw, entertain, fascinate, magnetize, overwhelm, please, wile, win favor; CONCEPT 11 —*Ant.* disenchant, repulse

take [*v11*] *require* ask, call for, crave, demand, necessitate, need; CONCEPT 646

take [*v12*] *subtract* deduct, discount, draw back, eliminate, knock off, remove, take away, take off, take out; CONCEPTS 211,236, 247 —*Ant.* add

take [*v13*] *cheat, deceive* bamboozle*, beat*, bilk, con, cozen, defraud, do*, dupe, fiddle, flimflam*, gull, hoodwink, pull a fast one*, swindle, take for a ride*, trick; CONCEPTS 59, 192 —*Ant.* be honest

take [*v14*] *contract, catch* be seized, come down with*, derive, draw, get, sicken with, take sick with; CONCEPT 308 —*Ant.* be immune

take a crack at [*v*] *try* attempt, do one's best*, drive for, give a go*, give a whirl*, go after, go

all out*, go for, have a crack*, have a go*, have a rip*, have a shot*, have a stab*, have a whack*, make an attempt, make an effort, make a pass at*, make a stab*, risk, shoot for*, tackle, undertake, vie for; CONCEPT 87

take after [*v*] *emulate* act like, be like, copy, ditto*, do like*, follow, follow in the footsteps of*, follow suit*, follow the example of*, imitate, inherit, look like, make like*, mimic, mirror, pattern after*, rival; CONCEPTS 87,171

take back [*v*] *retract* abjure, back down, backpedal, call off, cancel, change one's mind, eat one's words*, forget it, go back on, have change of heart*, recall, recant, reclaim, renege, repeal, repossess, repudiate, rescind, revoke, withdraw; CONCEPTS 25,49,119,697

take down [*v1*] *write down* inscribe, jot down, make a note of, minute, note, note down, put on record, record, set down, transcribe; CONCEPT 125

take down [*v2*] *humble* deflate, humiliate, let down, lower, mortify, pull down, put down, take apart; CONCEPTS 7,19,52 —*Ant.* build up

take in [*v1*] *deceive, fool* beguile, betray, bilk, bluff, cheat, con, defraud, do*, double-cross*, dupe, flimflam*, four-flush*, gull, hoodwink, lie, mislead, pull wool over eyes*, swindle, trick; CONCEPT 59

take in [*v2*] *understand* absorb, assimilate, comprehend, digest, get, grasp, perceive, receive, savvy, see, soak up, take; CONCEPT 15 —*Ant.* misconceive, misunderstand

take it [*v*] *accept, endure* acknowledge, agree, bear with, bite the bullet, capitulate, don't make waves*, don't rock the boat*, face the music*, go along with, grin and bear it*, hang tough, live with, play the game*, put up with, sit still for*, stand for, stick it out, stomach, submit to, suffer, swallow, take, take one's lumps*, take one's medicine*, tolerate; CONCEPT 23

takeoff [*n1*] *leaving* ascent, climb, departure, hop, jump, launch, liftoff, rise, upward flight; CONCEPT 148 —*Ant.* arrival, coming, landing

takeoff [*n2*] *mockery, satire* burlesque, caricature, cartoon, comedy, imitation, lampoon, mocking, parody, ridicule, send-up, spoof, travesty; CONCEPTS 111,263,292

take off [*v1*] *leave; leave the ground* ascend, bear, beat it, become airborne, begone, blast off, blow*, clear out*, decamp, depart, disappear, exit, get off, get out, go, go away, head, hightail*, hit the road*, hit the trail*, lift off, light out*, make tracks*, pull out, quit, scram*, set out*, shove off*, soar, split, take to the air*, vamoose*, withdraw; CONCEPTS 148,195,224 —*Ant.* arrive, come, stay

take off [*v2*] *mock, satirize* ape, burlesque, caricature, imitate, lampoon, mimic, parody, ridicule, send up, spoof, travesty; CONCEPTS 111,273,292

take on [*v1*] *assume, accept* acquire, add, address oneself to, adopt, agree to do, annex, append, attempt, become, begin, come to have, commence, develop, embrace, employ, endeavor, engage, enlist, enroll, espouse, handle, have a go at*, hire, launch, put on, retain, set about, tackle, take in hand*, take up, take upon oneself*, try, turn, undertake, venture; CONCEPTS 87,221 —*Ant.* refuse, reject

take on [v2] *compete* attack, battle, contend, contest, encounter, engage, face, fight, match, meet, oppose, pit, vie; CONCEPT 92

take on [v3] *challenge, oppose* brave, buck*, call out, confront, dare, defy, denounce, dispute, face off, go eyeball to eyeball with*, go one on one with*, go toe to toe with*, go up against, hang in*, insist upon, investigate, invite competition, make a stand, object to, question, stand up to, throw down the gauntlet*; CONCEPT 53

take up [v] *begin or start again* adopt, assume, become involved in, carry on, commence, continue, embrace, engage in, enter, espouse, follow through, get off, go on, initiate, kick off, open, pick up, proceed, recommence, renew, reopen, restart, resume, set to, start, tackle, take on, tee off, undertake; CONCEPTS 221,239 —Ant. complete, conclude, end, finish

tale [n1] *story* account, anecdote, fable, fairy tale, fiction, folk tale, legend, myth, narration, narrative, novel, relation, report, romance, saga, short story, yarn; CONCEPT 282

tale [n2] *made-up story* canard, chestnut*, clothesline*, cock-and-bull story*, defamation, detraction, exaggeration, fabrication, falsehood, falsity, fib, fiction, lie, misrepresentation, prevarication, rigmarole*, rumor, scandal, slander, spiel*, tall story*, untruism, untruth, yarn*; CONCEPTS 278,282 —Ant. non-fiction

talent [n] *ability* aptitude, aptness, art, a way with*, bent*, capability, capacity, craft, endowment, expertise, facility, faculty, flair, forte, genius, gift, green thumb*, head*, inventiveness, knack*, know-how*, nose*, power, savvy*, set, skill, smarts*, the formula*, the goods*, the right stuff*, thing*, turn*, what it takes*; CONCEPT 630 —Ant. inability, incapacity, lack, weakness

talented [adj] *gifted* able, accomplished, adept, adroit, artistic, brilliant, capable, clever, cut out for, endowed, expert, having a knack*, ingenious, intelligent, masterly, proficient, shining at*, skilled, smart; CONCEPTS 402,527,528

talisman [n] *charm* fetish, good-luck piece, juju, lucky piece, phylactery, rabbit's foot; CONCEPTS 260,284,446

talk [n1] *speech, address to group* allocution, chalk talk*, declamation, descant, discourse, disquisition, dissertation, epilogue, exhortation, expatiation, harangue, homily, lecture, monologue, oration, peroration, prelection, recitation, screed, sermon, spiel*; CONCEPTS 60,285 —Ant. listening

talk [n2] *gossip* allusion, badinage, banter, blather*, bombast, bunk*, buzz*, cant, chat, chatter, chitchat, conversation, cry, gab, grapevine*, hearsay, hint, hot air*, idle talk, innuendo, insinuation, jaw*, jive*, lip*, noise, nonsense*, palaver, persiflage, prose, racket*, raillery, report, rot*, rubbish*, rumble*, rumor, scuttlebutt*, small talk, tête-à-tête, trash*, yarn*; CONCEPTS 51,278

talk [n3] *discussion* argument, colloquy, conclave, confabulation, conference, consultation, conversation, deliberation, dialogue, earful, encounter, eyeball-to-eyeball*, huddle*, interlocution, interview, meeting, negotiation, palaver, parlance, parley, powwow*, seminar,

spiel*, straight talk, symposium, ventilation, visit; CONCEPT 56 —Ant. silence

talk [n4] *communication with language* argot, chatter, dialect, discourse, jargon, lingo, locution, parlance, patois, slang, speaking, speech, utterance, verbalization, vocalization, words; CONCEPTS 47,65 —Ant. silence

talk [v1] *produce words; inform* articulate, babble, broach, chant, chat, chatter, comment on, communicate, confess, converse, describe, divulge, drawl, drone, express, flap one's tongue*, gab, gabble*, give voice to, gossip, influence, intone, notify, palaver, parley, patter, persuade, prate, prattle, pronounce, reveal, rhapsodize, run on*, say, sing*, soliloquize, speak, spill the beans*, spout, squawk*, squeal*, talk one's leg off*, tell, tell all*, use, utter, ventriloquize, verbalize, voice, yak*; CONCEPTS 60,266 —Ant. listen

talk [v2] *discuss with another* argue, be in contact, canvass, carry on conversation, chew*, collogue, commune, confabulate, confer, confide, consult, contact, deliberate, dialogue, engage in conversation, exchange, go into a huddle*, groupthink*, have a meet*, hold discussion, huddle*, interact, interface, interview, join in conversation, keep in touch*, negotiate, network*, palaver, parley, reach out, reason, relate, thrash out*, touch*, touch base*, vent, visit; CONCEPT 56 —Ant. refrain, refuse

talk [v3] *address group* accost, deliver a speech, discourse, give a talk, give speech, harangue, hold forth, induce, influence, lecture, orate, persuade, pitch, prelect, sermonize, speak, spiel*, spout*, stump*, sway*; CONCEPTS 60,285 —Ant. listen

talkative [adj] *excessively communicative* articulate, big-mouthed*, chattering, chatty*, effusive, eloquent, fluent, full of hot air*, gabby*, garrulous, glib, gossipy, long-winded*, loose-lipped*, loquacious, loudmouthed*, mouthy*, multiloquent, prolix, rattling, slick*, smooth*, talky, verbal, verbose, vocal, voluble, windy*, wordy; CONCEPT 267 —Ant. quiet, reserved, silent, uncommunicative

tall [adj1] *high in stature, length* alpine, altitudinous, beanstalk*, big, elevated, giant, great, high-reaching, lank, lanky, lofty, rangy, sizable, sky-high, skyscraping, soaring, statuesque, towering; CONCEPTS 779,782 —Ant. little, low, short, small

tall [adj2] *exaggerated, unreasonable* absurd, demanding, difficult, embellished, exorbitant, farfetched, hard, implausible, impossible, outlandish, overblown, preposterous, steep, unbelievable; CONCEPTS 529,565 —Ant. believable, reasonable, sensible

tally [n] *count, record* account, mark, poll, reckoning, running total, score, summation, tab, total; CONCEPTS 283,787

tally [v] *add up; count, record* catalog, compute, enumerate, inventory, itemize, keep score, mark, mark down, number, numerate, reckon, register, sum, tale, tell, total, write down; CONCEPTS 125,764 —Ant. subtract

tame [adj1] *domesticated, compliant* acclimatized, amenable, biddable, bridled, broken, busted, civilized, cultivated, disciplined, docile, domestic, fearless, gentle, gentle as a lamb*, habituated, harmless, harnessed, housebroken, kindly, manageable, meek, mild, muzzled, obedient, overcome, pliable, pliant, subdued, submissive, tractable, trained, unafraid, unresisting, yoked*; CONCEPT 401 —*Ant.* unmanageable, untamed, violent, wild

tame [*adj2*] *dull, uninteresting* bland, bloodless, boiled down*, boring, conventional, diluted, feeble, flat*, halfhearted, humdrum*, insipid, lifeless, limp, mild, monotonous, prosaic, routine, spiritless, tedious, unexciting, uninspiring, vapid, weak, wearisome, white-bread*, without punch*; CONCEPTS 529,542,548 —*Ant.* bright, exciting, interesting

tame [*v*] *domesticate, make compliant* break, break in, break the spirit*, bridle, bring to heel*, bust, check, conquer, curb, discipline, domesticize, domiciliate, enslave, gentle, housebreak, house-train, humble, mitigate, mute, pacify, repress, restrain, soften, subdue, subjugate, suppress, temper, tone down, train, vanquish, water down*; CONCEPTS 14,250

tamper [*v1*] *interfere, alter* busybody*, butt in*, change, cook, cut, damage, destroy, diversify, doctor, fiddle with*, fool, horn in*, interlope, interpose, intrude, irrigate, manipulate, meddle, mess around with*, monkey around*, muck about*, phony up*, plant*, poke nose into*, spike*, tinker, vary, water*; CONCEPT 232 —*Ant.* leave alone

tamper [*v2*] *bribe* buy, buy off, corrupt, fix, get to, have, influence, lubricate, manipulate, reach, rig, square*; CONCEPT 192

tan [*n/adj*] *light brown* beige, biscuit, bronze, brown, brownish, buff, cream, drab, ecru, gold, khaki, leather-colored, natural, olive, olive-brown, saddle, sand, suntan, tawny, umber, yellowish; CONCEPTS 618,622

tan [*v*] *flog, whip* baste, beat, belt, cane, dust someone's britches*, flay, hide, hit, lambaste, lash, leather, paddle, paddlewhack, punish, spank, strap, strike, switch, tan one's hide*, thrash, warm someone's seat*, wax, whack, whale*, whomp*; CONCEPT 189

tang [*n*] *biting taste or odor* aroma, bite, flavor, guts*, kick*, nip, piquancy, pungency, reek, relish, sapidity, sapor, savor, scent, smack*, smell, spiciness, tanginess, thrill, twang, zest, zip*; CONCEPTS 599,600,614 —*Ant.* blandness, dullness

tangible [*adj*] *real, concrete* actual, appreciable, corporeal, definite, detectable, discernible, distinct, embodied, evident, factual, gross, incarnated, manifest, material, objective, observable, obvious, palpable, patent, perceivable, perceptible, phenomenal, physical, plain, positive, sensible, solid, stable, substantial, tactile, touchable, verifiable, visible, well-grounded; CONCEPTS 529,582 —*Ant.* abstract, conceptual, imperceptible, intangible, unreal

tangle [*n*] *knot, confusion* coil, complication, entanglement, jam, jungle, labyrinth, mass, mat, maze, mesh, mess, mix-up, morass, muddle, rummage, skein, snag, snarl, twist, web; CONCEPTS 230,674,720 —*Ant.* line, order, peace

tangle [*v*] *knot, complicate* catch, coil, confuse, derange, discompose, disorganize, drag into, embroil, enmesh, ensnare, entangle, entrap, foul up*, hamper, implicate, interlace, interlock,

intertwist, interweave, involve, jam, kink, make a party to*, mat, mesh, mess up*, mix up*, muck up*, obstruct, perplex, ravel, snarl, tie up, trap, twist, unbalance, upset; CONCEPTS 112,190 —*Ant.* straighten, uncomplicate, untangle, untwist

tangy [*adj*] *sharp, spicy* appetizing, aromatic, biting, bitter, fiery, flavorful, flavorsome, harsh, highly seasoned, hot, peppery, piquant, pungent, salty, seasoned, sweet, tart, tasty, vinegary, zesty, zippy*; CONCEPTS 537,598,613

tantalize [*v*] *provoke, tease* annoy, badger, baffle, bait, bedevil, beleaguer, charm, entice, fascinate, frustrate, gnaw, harass, harry, keep hanging*, lead on, make mouth water*, pester, plague, taunt, thwart, titillate, torment, torture, worry; CONCEPTS 7,11,19,22 —*Ant.* disenchant, repulse, turn off

tantamount [*adj*] *same* alike, as good as, commensurate, duplicate, equal, equivalent, identical, indistinguishable, like, parallel, same as, selfsame, synonymous, uniform, very; CONCEPTS 487,573 —*Ant.* different, opposite, polar, reverse

tantrum [*n*] *fit* anger, animosity, conniption, dander*, flare-up, hemorrhage* huff*, hysterics, outburst, storm*, temper, temper tantrum, wax; CONCEPTS 306,384 —*Ant.* calm, contentment, peace

tap [*n*] *faucet* bibcock, cock, egress, hydrant, nozzle, petcock, spigot, spout, stopcock, valve; CONCEPTS 445,464

tap [*v1*] *hit lightly* beat, bob, dab, drum, knock, palpate, pat, percuss, rap, strike, tag, thud, thump, tip, touch; CONCEPT 189

tap [*v2*] *pierce to drain* bleed, bore, broach, draft, drain, draw, draw forth, draw off, draw out, drill, empty, lance, milk, mine, open, penetrate, perforate, pump, riddle, siphon, spear, spike, stab, unplug, unstopper, use, utilize; CONCEPTS 142,220

tape [*n*] *ribbon of material* band, braid, edging, line, rope, strip; CONCEPT 475

tape [*v1*] *stick together with material* bandage, bind, bond, fasten, hold together, rope, seal, secure, support, swathe, tie, tie up, truss, wire, wrap; CONCEPTS 85,160 —*Ant.* loosen, unfasten, unglue, unstick, untape

tape [*v2*] *record sounds, sights* audiotape, make a tape, register, tape-record, video, videotape; CONCEPTS 125,292

taper/taper off [*v*] *decrease to a point* abate, bate, close, come to a point, die away, die out, diminish, drain, dwindle, fade, lessen, narrow, recede, reduce, rescind, subside, thin, thin out, wane, weaken, wind down; CONCEPTS 137,698, 776 —*Ant.* go up, increase, rise

tardy [*adj*] *late* backward, behindhand, belated, dawdling, delayed, delinquent, detained, dilatory, held up, hung up*, in a bind, jammed, laggard, loitering, not arrived, not done, overdue, procrastinating, retarded, slack, slow, sluggish, strapped for time*, too late, unpunctual; CONCEPTS 542,548,799 —*Ant.* early, on time, prompt, punctual, ready

target [*n1*] *aim, goal* ambition, bull's-eye*, destination, duty, end, function, ground zero*, intention, mark, object, objective, point, purpose, spot, use; CONCEPT 659

target [n2] *person as object of ridicule* butt*, byword, game, mark*, pigeon*, prey, quarry, scapegoat*, scorn, sitting duck*, sport, victim; CONCEPT 423

tariff [n] *tax or fee* assessment, charge, cost, duty, excise, impost, levy, price, price tag, rate, tab, tax, toll; CONCEPT 329

tarnish [v] *dirty, corrupt* befoul, begrime, blacken, blemish, blot, contaminate, damage, darken, defame, defile, dim, discolor, disgrace, dull, embarrass, grime, harm, hurt, impair, injure, lose luster, lose shine, mar, muddy, pale, pollute, rust, slander, smear, smudge, soil, spoil, spot, stain, sully, taint, tar, vitiate; CONCEPT 246 —*Ant.* clean, fix, polish, uncorrupt

tarry [v] *dawdle, delay* abide, bide, dally, drag, drag one's feet*, dwell, filibuster, get no place fast*, goof around*, hang around*, hold the phone*, lag, linger, lodge, loiter, lose time, pause, poke, procrastinate, put off, remain, rest, sojourn, stall, stay, stick around, stop, stop over, tail, take one's time*, temporize, tool*, trail, visit, wait, warm a chair*; CONCEPTS 35, 151 —*Ant.* carry on, complete, finish, go

tart [adj] *bitter, sour in taste or effect* acerb, acerbic, acetose, acid, acidulous, acrimonious, astringent, barbed, biting, caustic, cutting, dry, harsh, nasty, piquant, pungent, scathing, sharp, short, snappish, snappy, snippy, tangy, testy, trenchant, vinegary, wounding; CONCEPTS 267,613 —*Ant.* sweet

tart [n] *pastry* bun, Danish, eclair, fruit tart, pie, popover, roll, turnover; CONCEPT 457

task [n] *job or chore, often assigned* assignment, bother, burden, business, calling, charge, daily grind*, deadweight*, duty, effort, employment, enterprise, errand, exercise, fun and games*, function, gig*, grind*, grindstone*, headache*, labor, load, long row to hoe*, millstone*, mission, nuisance, occupation, office, onus, pain, project, province, responsibility, stint, strain, tax, toil, trouble, undertaking, vocation, work; CONCEPTS 362,666 —*Ant.* entertainment, fun, pastime

task [v] *assign, burden* charge, encumber, entrust, exhaust, lade, load, oppress, overload, push, saddle, strain, tax, test, weary, weigh, weight; CONCEPTS 14,112,666 —*Ant.* unburden

taskmaster [n] *slave driver* boss, director, disciplinarian, dominator, employer, foreperson, head honcho*, manager, overseer, owner, person in charge, supervisor, taskperson, tyrant; CONCEPT 347

taste [n1] *flavor of some quality* aftertaste, aroma, bang*, bitter, drive, ginger, jolt, kick*, oomph*, palatableness, piquancy, punch*, relish, salt, sapidity, sapor, savor, savoriness, smack, sour, sting*, suggestion, sweet, tang*, wallop, zest, zing*, zip*; CONCEPT 614

taste [n2] *tiny sample* appetizer, bit, bite, canapé, chaw, dash, delicacy, drop, fragment, hint, hors d'oeuvre, morsel, mouthful, nip, sampling, sip, soupçon, spoonful, sprinkling, suggestion, swallow, tidbit, tincture, tinge, titbit, touch, trifle, whiff*, wink*; CONCEPTS 458,835 —*Ant.* lot

taste [n3] *inclination, preference* affection, appetence, appetite, attachment, bent*, comprehension, cup of tea*, desire, disposition,

druthers*, fancy, fondness, gusto, heart, leaning, liking, palate, partiality, penchant, predilection, predisposition, prepossession, relish, soft spot*, stomach*, tendency, thing*, type, understanding, weakness, zest; CONCEPTS 20,32,529,659 —*Ant.* disinclination, dislike, hate, hatred

taste [n4] *capacity to sense flavor* appetence, appetite, gout, gustation, palate, stomach, taste buds, tongue; CONCEPTS 590,615

taste [n5] *judgment, propriety* acumen, acuteness, aestheticism, appreciation, correctness, cultivation, culture, decorum, delicacy, discernment, discretion, discrimination, distinction, elegance, feeling, finesse, good taste, grace, nicety, penetration, perception, polish, politeness, refinement, restraint, style, susceptibility, tact, tactfulness, tastefulness; CONCEPTS 388,411

taste [v1] *judge, try* assay, bite, chew, criticize, differentiate, discern, distinguish, eat, enjoy, lick, nibble, partake, perceive, relish, sample, savor, sense, sip, test, touch, try the flavor of; CONCEPTS 169,616 —*Ant.* abstain

taste [v2] *experience* appreciate, be exposed to, come up against, encounter, feel, have knowledge of, know, meet with, partake of, perceive, run up against, savor, undergo; CONCEPT 678 —*Ant.* abstain, refrain

tasteful [adj] *nice, refined* aesthetically pleasing, artistic, beautiful, charming, chaste, classical, classy, cultivated, cultured, delectable, delicate, discriminating, elegant, esthetic, exquisite, fastidious, fine, graceful, gratifying, handsome, harmonious, in good taste, pleasing, plush, polished, posh, precise, pure, quiet, restrained, rich, savory, smart, snazzy*, spiffy*, splendiferous, stylish, subdued, swank*, tasty, unaffected, unobtrusive, uptown*; CONCEPTS 529,574,589 —*Ant.* tasteless, unrefined, unsophisticated, unstylish

tasteless [adj1] *without flavor* big zero*, blah*, bland, boring, distasteful, dull, flat, flavorless, insipid, mild, nowhere*, pabulum*, plain, plain vanilla*, savorless, stale, tame, thin, unappetizing, uninspired, uninteresting, unpalatable, unpleasurable, unsavory, unseasoned, vanilla*, vapid, watered-down, watery, weak, without spice, zero*; CONCEPT 613 —*Ant.* appetizing, flavorful, savory, tasty

tasteless [adj2] *cheap, vulgar* artificial, barbaric, barbarous, coarse, crass, crude, flashy, foolish, garish, gaudy, graceless, hideous, impolite, improper, indecorous, indelicate, indiscreet, inelegant, loud, low, low-down, low-down-and-dirty*, makeshift*, off-color*, ornate, ostentatious, outlandish, pretentious, raunchy*, rough, rude, showy, stupid, tacky, tactless, tawdry, trivial, uncouth, unlovely, unpolished, unrefined, unseemly, unsightly, useless, wild; CONCEPTS 401,570, 589 —*Ant.* couth, moral, nice, tasteful

tasty [adj] *delicious* appetizing, delectable, delish*, divine, flavorful, flavorsome, flavory, full-flavored, good-tasting, heavenly, luscious, mellow, palatable, piquant, pungent, sapid, savory, scrumptious, spicy, sugar-coated, sweetened, tasteful, toothsome, toothy, yummy, zestful; CONCEPT 613 —*Ant.* tasteless, unappetizing

tattered [*adj*] *shredded* badly dressed, badly worn, battered, broken, dilapidated, frayed, frazzled, full of holes*, in rags, in shreds, in tatters*, moth-eaten, poorly made, ripped, rugged, scraggy, seedy, shabby, shaggy, shoddy, threadbare, torn, torn to pieces, unkempt; CONCEPT 485

tattle [*v*] *gossip; tell rumor* babble, blab*, chat, chatter, give away, give the show away*, gossip, have a big mouth*, jabber, leak, noise, prate, prattle*, rumor, snitch, spill, spill the beans*, spread rumor*, squeal, talk, talk idly, tell on, tell tale*, yak*; CONCEPTS 54,60 —*Ant.* conceal, hide

tattletale/tattler [*n*] *person who gossips, tells rumors* bigmouth*, blabberer, blabbermouth*, busybody, canary*, fat mouth*, fink*, gossip, informer, rat*, rumormonger, scandalmonger, snitch*, squealer*, stool pigeon*, talebearer, taleteller, telltale*, tipster, troublemaker, whistleblower, windbag*; CONCEPTS 412,423

taunt [*n*] *provocation; teasing* backhanded compliment*, barb, brickbat*, censure, comeback, crack, cut, derision, dig, dirty dig*, dump, gibe, insult, jab, jeer, mockery, outrage, parting shot*, put-down*, reproach, ridicule, sarcasm, slam*, slap*, snappy comeback*, swipe*; CONCEPTS 7,19,266 —*Ant.* compliment, praise, respect

taunt [*v*] *provoke, reproach; tease* affront, bother, deride, dig*, disdain, dump on*, flout, insult, jab*, jeer, lout, mock, offend, outrage, put down, quiz, rally, revile, ridicule, scoff at, scorn, scout, slam*, slap*, sneer, swipe at, tantalize, torment, twitter, upbraid; CONCEPTS 7,19,54 —*Ant.* compliment, praise, respect

taut [*adj*] *rigid, tight* close, firm, flexed, snug, stiff, strained, stressed, stretched, tense, tightly drawn, trim, unyielding; CONCEPTS 488,604 —*Ant.* droopy, flabby, loose, slack

tavern [*n*] *business establishment for serving drink, food* alehouse, bar, barroom, beer joint*, dive*, drinkery, gin mill*, grog shop*, honky tonk*, hostelry, hotel, inn, joint*, lodge, lounge, night spot, nineteenth hole*, pub, public house, roadhouse, saloon, speakeasy*, suds*, taphouse*, taproom, watering hole*; CONCEPTS 439,448,449

tawdry [*adj*] *cheap, tasteless* blatant, brazen, chintzy*, common, crude, dirty, flaring, flashy, flaunting, garish, gaudy, gimcrack, glaring, glittering, glitzy, jazzy, junky*, loud, meretricious, obtrusive, offensive, plastic, poor, raffish, screaming, showy, sleazy*, sporty, tacky*, tinsel, vulgar; CONCEPTS 334,589 —*Ant.* nice, sophisticated, tasteful

tax [*n1*] *charge levied by government on property, income* assessment, bite*, brokerage, capitation, contribution, cost, custom, dues, duty, excise, expense, fine, giveaway*, imposition, impost, levy, obligation, pork barrel*, price, rate, salvage, tariff, tithe, toll, towage, tribute; CONCEPT 329

tax [*n2*] *burden* albatross*, charge, deadweight*, demand, difficulty, drain, duty, imposition, load, millstone*, onus, pressure, strain, task, weight; CONCEPTS 388,666

tax [*v1*] *levy charge on property, income* assess, charge, charge duty, demand, demand toll,

enact, exact, exact tribute, extract, impose, lay an impost, rate, require contribution, tithe; CONCEPT 298

tax [*v2*] *burden* charge, cumber, drain, encumber, enervate, exhaust, lade, load, make demands on, oppress, overburden, overtax, overuse, overwork, press hard on, pressure, prey on, push, put pressure on, saddle, sap, strain, stress, stretch, task, tire, try, weaken, wear out, weary, weigh, weigh down, weigh heavily on, weight; CONCEPTS 14,208,240 —*Ant.* unburden

tax [*v3*] *accuse* arraign, blame, censure, charge, criminate, impeach, impugn, impute, incriminate, inculpate, indict, reproach, reprove; CONCEPT 44 —*Ant.* exonerate, release

taxing [*adj*] *burdensome* demanding, difficult, disturbing, enervating, exacting, exigent, grievous, heavy, onerous, oppressive, punishing, sapping, stressful, tedious, tiring, tough, troublesome, trying, wearing, wearisome, weighty; CONCEPT 565 —*Ant.* easy, untroubling

teach [*v*] *educate; instill knowledge* advise, brainwash*, break in*, brief, catechize, coach, communicate, cram, demonstrate, develop, direct, discipline, drill, edify, enlighten, exercise, explain, expound, fit, form, give instruction, give lessons, give the facts, ground, guide, illustrate, imbue, impart, implant, improve mind, inculcate, indoctrinate, inform, initiate, instruct, interpret, lecture, nurture, open eyes*, polish up*, pound into*, prepare, profess, rear, school, sharpen, show, show the ropes*, train, tutor; CONCEPT 285 —*Ant.* learn

teacher [*n*] *person who educates* abecedary, adviser, assistant, coach, disciplinarian, educator, faculty member, guide, instructor, lecturer, mentor, pedagogue, preceptor, professor, pundit, scholar, schoolteacher, supervisor, teach*, trainer, tutor; CONCEPT 350 —*Ant.* pupil, student

teaching [*n*] *education* apprenticeship, book learning*, coaching, cultivation, culture, discipline, drilling, enlightenment, guidance, instruction, learning, reading, schooling, training, tutelage, tutoring; CONCEPTS 285,287,409

team [*n*] *group, crew* aggregation, band, body, bunch, club, company, contingent, duo, faction, foursome, gang, lineup, organization, outfit, pair, partners, party, rig, sect, set, side, span, squad, stable, string, tandem, trio, troop, troupe, unit, workers, yoke; CONCEPTS 365,397,417 —*Ant.* individual, teammate

teamwork [*n*] *collaboration, cooperation* alliance, assistance, coalition, combined effort, confederacy, confederation, doing business with, esprit de corps, federation, harmony, help, joint effort, partisanship, partnership, pulling together, symbiosis, synergism, synergy, team effort, teaming, union, unity, working together; CONCEPTS 110,112,388,677

tear [*n1*] *rip, cut* breach, break, crack, damage, fissure, gash, hole, imperfection, laceration, mutilation, rent, run, rupture, scratch, split, tatter; CONCEPT 513 —*Ant.* perfection

tear/tears [*n2*] *droplets from eyes, often caused by emotion* blubbering*, crying, discharge, distress, drops, grieving, lachryma, lamentation, lamenting, moisture, mourning, pain, regret, sadness, sob, sob act*, sobbing, sorrow, teardrop, wailing, water, waterworks*, weep, weeping, weeps*, whimpering, woe; CONCEPTS 185,467

tear [n3] *wild action* bender, binge, bust, carousal, carouse, drunk, spree, wassail; CONCEPTS 383,384

tear [v1] *cut, rip an object* break, claw, cleave, crack, damage, divide, evulse, extract, fray, frazzle, gash, grab, impair, incise, injure, lacerate, mangle, mutilate, pluck, pull, pull apart, rend, ribbon, rift, rive, run, rupture, scratch, seize, separate, sever, shred, slash, slit, snatch, split, sunder, wrench, wrest, yank; CONCEPTS 206,214 —*Ant.* fix, mend, sew

tear [v2] *move very fast* boil, bolt, career, charge, chase, course, dart, dash, fling, fly, gallop, hurry, lash, race, run, rush, shoot, speed, spring, zoom; CONCEPTS 150,152 —*Ant.* idle, wait

tear down [v] *demolish, raze* annihilate, bulldoze, crush, decimate, devastate, devour, dilapidate, disassemble, dismantle, flatten, knock down, level, obliterate, pulverize, ruin, smash, take apart, total*, trash*, wipe off the map*, wreck; CONCEPTS 169,252

tearful [adj] *crying, very upset* bawling*, blubbering*, blubbery*, distressed, dolorous, in tears, lachrymose, lamentable, lamenting, moist, mournful, pathetic, pitiable, pitiful, poignant, sad, sniveling*, sobbing, sorrowful, teary, watery, weeping, weepy, wet, whimpering, woeful; CONCEPTS 401,403 —*Ant.* cheerful, happy

tease [v] *aggravate, provoke* annoy, badger, bait, banter, be at, bedevil, beleaguer, bother, chaff, devil, disturb, dog*, gibe, give a hard time*, gnaw, goad, harass, harry, hector, importune, jive*, josh, lead on*, mock, needle*, nudge, pester, pick on*, plague, put down*, rag*, rally, razz*, rib*, ride, ridicule, roast*, send up*, slam, snap, sound, spoof, swipe at, tantalize, taunt, torment, vex, worry; CONCEPTS 7,11,19,22

technical [adj] *concerning details, mechanics* abstruse, high-tech*, industrial, mechanical, methodological, occupational, professional, restricted, scholarly, scientific, special, specialized, technological, vocational; CONCEPT 536 —*Ant.* unmechanical, untechnical

technicality [n] *loophole; minor detail* escape clause, formality, minor point, nothing to speak of, nothing to write home about; CONCEPT 633

technique [n] *method* address, approach, art, artistry, capability, capacity, course, craft, delivery, execution, facility, fashion, knack*, know-how*, manner, means, mode, modus, modus operandi, performance, procedure, proficiency, routine, skill, style, system, tactics,technic, touch, usage, way, wise; CONCEPTS 6,630

technology [n] *electronics, science* applied science, automation, computers, electronic components, high tech*, hi tech*, industrial science, machinery, mechanics, mechanization, robotics, scientific know-how, scientific knowledge, technical knowledge, telecommunications; CONCEPTS 463,499

tedious [adj] *dull, monotonous* annoying, arid, banal, boring, bromidic, drab, dragging,

draggy*, dreary, drudging, dry, dull as dishwater*, dusty*, endless, enervating, exhausting, fatiguing, ho-hum*, humdrum, insipid, irksome, laborious, lifeless, long-drawn-out*, mortal, pabulum*, poky*, prosaic, prosy, slow, snooze*, soporific, tiresome, tiring, unexciting, uninteresting, vapid, weariful, wearisome; CONCEPTS 529, 548 —*Ant.* entertaining, exciting, interesting

tedium [n] *dullness, monotony* banality, boredom, deadness*, doldrums, drabness, dreariness, ennui, irksomeness, lack of interest, lifelessness, routine, sameness, tediousness, tiresomeness, wearisomeness, yawn*;CONCEPTS 388,410,668 —*Ant.* diversion, entertainment, excitement

teem [v] *be abundant, full* abound, bear, be crawling with, be full of, be numerous, be plentiful, be prolific, brim, bristle, burst, burst at seams*, bustle, crawl, crowd, flow, grow, jam, overflow, overrun, pack, pour, pour out, produce, prosper, pullulate, rain, roll in, shower, superabound, swarm, swell, swim in, wallow in; CONCEPTS 146,179,740 —*Ant.* lack, need, want

teeming [adj] *abundant, full* alive, brimful, brimming, bristling, bursting, chock-full, crammed, crawling, filled, fruitful, multitudinous, numerous, overflowing, packed, plentiful, populous, pregnant, replete, rife, swarming, thick, thronged; CONCEPTS 481,483,774 —*Ant.* empty, lacking, needing, wanting

teenager [n] *adolescent* juvenile, minor, stripling, sweet sixteen*, teen, teenybopper*, youngster, youth; CONCEPT 424

teeny/teensy [adj] *very small* diminutive, Lilliputian, microscopic, miniature, minuscule, minute, teensy-weensy*, teeny-weeny*, tiny, wee, weeny*; CONCEPTS 773,789 —*Ant.* big, enormous, huge, large

teeter [v] *wobble back and forth* balance, dangle, falter, flutter, lurch, pivot, quiver, reel, rock, seesaw, stagger, stammer, stumble, sway, teeter-totter*, topple, totter, tremble, tremble precariously, waver, weave, wiggle; CONCEPT 145 —*Ant.* stabilize, steady

telecast [n] *broadcast* air time, newscast, program, show, simulcast, transmission; CONCEPTS 274,293

telegram [n] *message sent by coded radio signals* buzzer, cable, cablegram, call, coded message, flash, radiogram, report, signal, summons, telegraph, telegraphic message, teletype, telex, wire; CONCEPTS 269,271

telepathy [n] *ability to know another's thoughts* clairvoyance, ESP*, extrasensory perception, insight, mind-reading, parapsychology, premonition, presentiment, second sight*, sixth sense*, spiritualism, telepathic transmission, telesthesia, thought transference; CONCEPTS 410,630

telephone [v] *communicate through telephone system* buzz*, call, call up, contact, dial, get back to*, get on the horn*, get on the line*, give a call, give a jingle*, give a ring*, make a call, phone, pick up*, put a call through*, ring, ring up, touch base with*; CONCEPTS 225, 266,269

televise [v] *broadcast* air, announce, beam,

be on the air, communicate, go on the air, go on the airwaves, put on television, put on the air, show, simulcast, transmit; CONCEPTS 60,292

television [n] *visual and audio entertainment transmitted via radio waves* audio, baby-sitter*, boob tube*, box*, eye*, idiot box*, receiver, small screen, station, telly*, tube, TV, TV set, vid*, video; CONCEPTS 277,279,293,463

tell [v1] *communicate* acquaint, advise, announce, apprise, authorize, bid, break the news*, call upon, clue in*, command, confess, declare, direct, disclose, divulge, enjoin, explain, express, fill in*, give facts, give out, impart, inform, instruct, keep posted*, lay open*, leak, leave word, let in on*, let know, let slip*, level, make known, mention, notify, open up, order, proclaim, put before, recite, reel off*, report, represent, require, reveal, say, speak, spit it out*, state, summon, utter; CONCEPT 266 —Ant. listen

tell [v2] *narrate, describe* chronicle, depict, express, give an account of, portray, recount, rehearse, relate, report, set forth, speak, state; CONCEPT 55 —Ant. listen

tell [v3] *understand, discern* ascertain, be sure, clinch, comprehend, deduce, determine, differentiate, discover, discriminate, distinguish, divine, find out, identify, know, know for certain, learn, make out, perceive, recognize, see; CONCEPT 15 —Ant. misunderstand

tell [v4] *carry weight* count, have effect, have force, make presence felt, make presence known, militate, register, take effect, take its toll*, weigh; CONCEPT 676

tell [v5] *calculate* compute, count, count one by one, enumerate, number, numerate, reckon, tale, tally; CONCEPT 764 —Ant. estimate, figure, guess

telling [adj] *effective, significant* cogent, considerable, conspicuous, convincing, crucial, decisive, devastating, effectual, forceful, forcible, important, impressive, influential, marked, operative, potent, powerful, satisfactory, satisfying, solid, sound, striking, trenchant, valid, weighty; CONCEPTS 537 567 —Ant. ineffective, insignificant, secondary, unimportant

tell off [v] *reprimand; criticize harshly* berate, censure, chide, give piece of one's mind*, give tongue-lashing*, lecture, rail, rake over the coals*, rebuke, reproach, reprove, revile, scold, take to task*, tick off*, upbraid, vituperate; CONCEPTS 44,52 —Ant. compliment, praise

telltale [adj] *revealing* disclosing, evidential, giveaway, indicatory, informative, meaningful, pointing to, prognostic, significant, significatory, suggestive; CONCEPT 267

temerity [n] *nerve, audacity* assurance, boldness, brass*, carelessness, daring, effrontery, foolhardiness, forwardness, gall, hardihood, hastiness, heedlessness, impertinence, impetuosity, imprudence, impudence, impulsiveness, indiscretion, intrepidity, intrusiveness, overconfidence, pluck, precipitancy, precipitateness, precipitation, presumption, rashness, recklessness, rudeness, thoughtlessness, venturesomeness; CONCEPTS 411,633 —Ant. care, caution, cowardice, forethought, hesitation

temper [n1] *state of mind* atmosphere, attitude, attribute, aura, character, climate, complexion,

condition, constitution, disposition, drift, frame of mind, humor, individualism, individuality, leaning, makeup, mind, mood, nature, orientation, outlook, peculiarity, personality, posture, property, quality, scene, soul, spirit, state, strain, style, temperament, tendency, tenor, thing*, timbre, tone, trend, type, vein, way; CONCEPTS 410,411

temper [n2] *angriness; bad mood* acerbity, anger, annoyance, bad humor, cantankerousness, crossness, dander*, excitability, fit, fretfulness, furor, fury, grouchiness, heat*, hotheadedness, huffiness, ill-humor, impatience, irascibility, ire, irritability, irritation, miff, outburst, passion, peevishness, petulance, pugnacity, rage, resentment, sensitivity, short fuse*, slow burn*, snit, sourness, stew*, sullenness, surliness, tantrum, tartness, tear*, tiff, tizzy*, touchiness, wax; CONCEPTS 29, 410 —Ant. happiness

temper [n3] *calmness* calm, composure, cool, coolness, equanimity, good humor, moderation, poise, self-control, tranquility; CONCEPTS 32, 410 —Ant. upset, wrath

temper [v1] *calm, moderate* abate, adjust, admix, allay, alleviate, assuage, chill out*, cool, cool out*, curb, dilute, ease, fine tune, lessen, make reasonable, mitigate, modulate, mollify, monkey around with*, pacify, palliate, relieve, restrain, revamp, soften, soft-pedal*, soothe, switch, take the bite out of*, take the edge off*, take the sting out of*, tone down, transmogrify, weaken; CONCEPTS 7,22,110,126 —Ant. aggravate, agitate, excite, infuriate, upset

temper [v2] *harden* anneal, bake, braze, cement, chill, congeal, dry, indurate, mold, petrify, set, solidify, starch, steel, stiffen, strengthen, toughen, toughen up; CONCEPTS 250,726 —Ant. bend, flex, soften

temperament [n] *disposition, personality* attitude, bent, capacity, cast, character, complexion, constitution, distinctiveness, ego, emotions, frame of mind, humor, idiosyncrasy, inclination, individualism, individuality, inner nature, intellect, kind, makeup, mentality, mettle, mood, nature, outlook, peculiarity, quality, soul, spirit, stamp, structure, susceptibility, temperament, tendency, turn, type, way; CONCEPTS 410,411

temperamental [adj] *angry most of the time; moody* capricious, changeable, cussed*, easily upset, emotional, erratic, excitable, explosive, fickle, fiery, froward, headstrong, high-strung*, hotheaded*, hyper*, hypersensitive, impatient, in bad mood, inconsistent, irritable, mean, mercurial, neurotic, ornery, passionate, petulant, sensitive, thin-skinned*, ticklish, touchy, uncertain, undependable, unpredictable, unreliable, unstable, variable, volatile, willful; CONCEPT 403 —Ant. easygoing, happy, laid-back, peaceful, pleased

temperance [n] *self-restraint; abstinence* abnegation, abstemiousness, asceticism, astringency, austerity, conservatism, constraint, continence, control, discretion, eschewal, forbearance, forgoing, frugality, golden mean*, happy medium*, measure, moderateness, moderation, moderatism, mortification, prohibition, prudence, reasonableness, refrainment, restraint, sacrifice, self-control, self-denial, self-deprivation, self-discipline, soberness, sobriety, stoicism, teetotalism, uninebriation, unintoxication; CONCEPTS *410,633* —Ant. excess, intemperance, wildness

temperate [adj1] *calm, moderate* agreeable, balmy, checked, clement, collected, composed, conservative, constant, cool, curbed, discreet, dispassionate, equable, even, even-tempered, fair, gentle, levelheaded, medium, mild, modest, pleasant, reasonable, regulated, restrained, self-controlled, self-restrained, sensible, sober, soft, stable, steady, unexcessive, unextreme, unimpassioned, warm; CONCEPTS *525,542,547* —Ant. immoderate, stormy, violent

temperate [adj2] *controlled, sober* abstemious, abstentious, abstinent, continent, moderate, restrained, self-restraining; CONCEPT *401* —Ant. drunk, excessive, inebriated, uncontrolled

temperature [n] *hotness, coldness of some degree* body heat, calefaction, climate, cold, condition, degrees, febricity, feverishness, heat, incalescence, pyrexia, thermal reading, warmth; CONCEPT *610*

tempest [n] *wild storm; commotion* blizzard, bluster, chaos, convulsion, cyclone, disturbance, ferment, furor, gale, hurricane, squall, tornado, tumult, typhoon, upheaval, uproar, wildness, windstorm; CONCEPTS *230,526* —Ant. calm

tempestuous [adj] *wild, stormy* agitated, blustering, blustery, boisterous, breezy, coarse, emotional, excited, feverish, furious, gusty, heated, hysterical, impassioned, intense, passionate, raging, rough, rugged, squally, storming, tumultuous/tumultous, turbulent, unbridled, uncontrolled, unrestrained, violent, windy; CONCEPTS *401,525,542* —Ant. calm, gentle, mild, moderate

temple [n] *house of worship* cathedral, chapel, church, holy place, house, house of God*, house of prayer*, mosque, pagoda, pantheon, place of worship, sanctuary, shrine, synagogue, tabernacle; CONCEPTS *368,439*

tempo [n] *beat, rhythm* bounce, cadence, downbeat, measure, meter, momentum, pace, pulse, rate, speed, time, velocity; CONCEPT *65*

temporal [adj1] *material, worldly* banausic, carnal, civil, earthly, earthy, fleshly, lay, materialistic, mortal, mundane, nonsacred, nonspiritual, physical, profane, secular, sensual, subcelestial, sublunary, terrestrial, unhallowed, unsacred, unsanctified, unspiritual; CONCEPT *582* —Ant. mental, otherworldly, spiritual

temporal [adj2] *momentary* chronological, ephemeral, evanescent, fleeting, fugacious, fugitive, impermanent, of time, passing, short-lived, temporary, transient, transitory; CONCEPT *799* —Ant. endless, lasting, permanent, perpetual, persistent

temporary [adj] *lasting only a short while* acting, ad hoc, ad interim, alternate, Band-Aid*, brief, changeable, ephemeral, evanescent, fleeting, for the time being*, fugacious, fugitive, impermanent, interim, limited, make-do*, makeshift*, momentary, mortal, overnight, passing, perishable, pro tem, pro tempore, provisional, provisory, shifting, short, short-lived, slapdash*, stopgap*, substitute, summary,

supply, temp*, transient, transitory, unfixed, unstable, volatile; CONCEPTS *551,798*

tempt [v] *lure, entice* allure, appeal to, attract, bait, butter up*, captivate, charm, coax, court, dare, decoy, draw, draw out, entrap, fascinate, honey*, hook*, incite, induce, influence, instigate, intrigue, inveigle, invite, lead on, make mouth water*, motivate, mousetrap*, move, oil, persuade, play up to, promote, provoke, risk, rouse, seduce, solicit, stimulate, tantalize, test, train, try, turn one's head*, wheedle, whet, woo*; CONCEPTS *11,68* —Ant. discourage, repulse, turn off

temptation [n] *lure, attraction* allurement, appeal, attractiveness, bait, blandishment, coaxing, come-on*, decoy, draw, enticement, fancy, fascination, hankering, inducement, inveiglement, invitation, provocation, pull, seducement, seduction, snare, tantalization, trap*, yen; CONCEPTS *20,529,532,690,709* —Ant. discouragement, dislike, repulsion

tempting [adj] *alluring, inviting* appetizing, attractive, charming, divine, enticing, fascinating, fetching, heavenly, intriguing, luring, magnetic, mouth-watering*, provoking, rousing, scrumptious, seductive, tantalizing, yummy*; CONCEPTS *462,529* —Ant. disenchanting, repulsive, revolting, unattractive

tenable [adj] *reasonable* arguable, believable, condonable, credible, defendable, defensible, excusable, impregnable, justifiable, maintainable, plausible, rational, reliable, secure, sound, strong, trustworthy, viable, vindicable, warrantable; CONCEPTS *552,558* —Ant. irrational, unbelievable, unjustifiable, unreasonable, untenable

tenacious [adj1] *strong, unyielding* adamant, bound, clinging, coherent, cohesive, determined, dogged, fast, firm, forceful, inflexible, intransigent, iron, meaning business*, mulish, obdurate, obstinate, persevering, persistent, persisting, pertinacious, possessive, purposeful, relentless, resolute, retentive, set, solid, spunky, stalwart, staunch, steadfast, stout, strong-willed, stubborn, sturdy, sure, tight, tough, true, unforgetful, unshakable, unswerving; CONCEPTS *326,401,489,542* —Ant. surrendering, weak, yielding

tenacious [adj2] *sticky* adhesive, clinging, clingy, fast, firm, fixed, glutinous, gummy, inseparable, mucilaginous, resisting, retentive, secure, set, tacky, tight, viscid, viscose, viscous, waxy; CONCEPTS *488,606* —Ant. loose, slack, unattached

tenacity [n] *diligence, stubbornness* application, backbone, chutzpah*, clock*, courage, determination, doggedness, firmness, grit, guts*, gutsiness*, guttiness*, heart*, inflexibility, intestinal fortitude*, intransigence, moxie*, nerve, obduracy, obstinacy, perseverance, persistence, pertinacity, resoluteness, resolution,resolve, spunk, starch*, staunchness, steadfastness, stick-to-itiveness*, stomach*, strength of purpose, true grit*, what it takes*, willfulness; CONCEPTS *411,657* —Ant. indifference, irresolution, slackness, weakness

tenant [n] *person who leases a place* addressee, boarder, dweller, holder, householder, indweller, inhabitant, leaseholder, lessee, lodger, occupant, occupier, possessor, renter, rent payer, resident, roomer; CONCEPTS 348,423 —*Ant.* landlord

tend [*v1*] *be apt, likely* aim, bear, be biased, be conducive, be disposed, be inclined, be in the habit of, be liable, bend, be predisposed, be prejudiced, conduce, contribute, dispose, drift, favor, go, gravitate, have an inclination, have a tendency, head, impel, incline, influence, lead, lean, look, make for, move, move toward, point, redound, result in, serve to, trend, turn, verge on; CONCEPTS 411,650

tend [*v2*] *care for* accomplish, administer, attend, baby-sit, cater to, cherish, control, corral, cultivate, defend, direct, do, do for, feed, foster, guard, handle, keep, keep an eye on*, keep tabs on*, look after, maintain, manage, mind, minister to, nurse, nurture, oversee, perform, protect, ride herd on*, safeguard, see after, see to, serve, shepherd, shield, sit, superintend, supervise, take care of, take under wing*, wait on, watch, watch out for, watch over; CONCEPTS 136,257, 295 —*Ant.* abandon, ignore, neglect

tendency [*n1*] *inclination to think or do in a certain way* addiction, affection, bent*, bias, current, custom, disposition, drift, habit, impulse, inclining, leaning, liability, mind, mindset*, partiality, penchant, predilection, predisposition, proclivity, proneness, propensity, readiness, run, set, shift, slant, susceptibility, temperament, thing*, trend, turn, type, usage, way*, weakness; CONCEPT 657

tendency [*n2*] *direction of movement* aim, bearing, bent, bias, course, current, curve, drift, drive, heading, inclination, leaning, movement, purport, run, shift, tenor, trend, turn, turning, way; CONCEPTS 692,738

tender [*adj1*] *fragile, soft* breakable, dainty, delicate, effete, feeble, frail, supple, weak; CONCEPTS 604,606 —*Ant.* hard, rough, tough

tender [*adj2*] *young, inexperienced* callow, childish, childlike, green*, immature, impressionable, new, raw*, rookie*, sensitive, unripe, vernal, vulnerable, wet behind the ears*, youthful; CONCEPTS 578,797 —*Ant.* experienced, mature, older

tender [*adj3*] *affectionate, loving* all heart*, amorous, benevolent, bleeding-heart*, caring, charitable, commiserative, compassionate, considerate, demonstrative, emotional, evocative, fond, forgiving, gentle, humane, kind, lenient, lovey-dovey*, merciful, mild, moving, mushy*, poignant, responsive, romantic, sensitive, sentimental, soft, softhearted, solicitous, sympathetic, tenderhearted, thoughtful, ticklish, tolerant, touching, touchy, warm, warmhearted, yielding; CONCEPTS 401,542 —*Ant.* callous, uncaring, unfeeling, unloving

tender [*adj4*] *painful, sore* aching, acute, bruised, delicate, hypersensitive, inflamed, irritated, oversensitive, raw, sensitive, smarting, thin-skinned, ticklish, touchy; CONCEPTS 314,403,548 —*Ant.* healthy, ok, unpained

tenderfoot [*n*] *newcomer* amateur, beginner, colt*, greenhorn*, Johnny-come-lately*, neophyte, new kid on the block*, novice, novitiate, rookie, tyro; CONCEPTS 413,423

tenderhearted [*adj*] *tender* affectionate, all heart*, benevolent, bleeding heart*, caring, charitable, compassionate, considerate,

emotional, forgiving, gentle, humane, kind, kindhearted, lenient, loving, merciful, mushy*, sensitive, sentimental, soft, softhearted, sweet, sympathetic, thoughtful, understanding, warm, warmhearted; CONCEPTS 401,542

tenebrous [*adj*] *dark, ominous* ambiguous, amphibological, caliginous, dim, dingy, dusk, dusky, equivocal, gloomy, lightless, murky, obscure, shadowy, shady, somber, sunless, uncertain, unclear, unexplicit, unilluminated, unintelligible, unlit, vague; CONCEPTS 535,617 —*Ant.* inviting, light

tenement [*n*] *apartment house* apartment complex, boarding house, coop, cooperative, den*, digs*, dump*, flat, high-rise, high-rise apartment building, living quarters, pad*, project housing, rental, slum; CONCEPTS 448,516

tenet [*n*] *belief, principle* article of faith, assumption, canon, conception, conviction, credo, creed, doctrine, dogma, faith, impression, maxim, opinion, persuasion, position, precept, presumption, profession, rule, self-conviction, system, teaching, thesis, trust, view; CONCEPTS 688,689

tenor [*n1*] *meaning, intent* aim, body, burden, core, course, course of thought, current, direction, drift, evolution, gist, inclination, meat, mood, path, pith, purport, purpose, run, sense, stuff, substance, tendency, theme, tone, trend, way; CONCEPTS 529,682

tenor [*n2*] *high male voice* alto, countertenor, falsetto; CONCEPT 65 —*Ant.* bass

tense [*adj1*] *tight, stretched* close, firm, rigid, stiff, strained, taut; CONCEPTS 485,604 —*Ant.* limp, limpid, loose, relaxed, slack

tense [*adj2*] *under stress, pressure* agitated, anxious, apprehensive, beside oneself*, bundle of nerves*, choked, clutched, concerned, edgy, excited, fidgety, fluttery, high-strung*, hung up*, hyper*, in a tizzy*, jittery, jumpy, keyed up*, moved, moving, nerve-racking, nervous, nervous wreck*, on edge, overanxious, overwrought, queasy, restive, restless, shaky, shot*, shot to pieces*, strained, stressful, strung out*, uneasy, unnerved, unquiet, up the wall*, uptight*, white knuckled*, wired*, worried, worrying, wound up*, wreck*; CONCEPTS 401,403,548 —*Ant.* calm, easy-going, laid-back, relaxed, uncaring

tension [*n1*] *tightness* astriction, balance, constriction, force, pressure, rigidity, stiffness, strain, straining, stress, stretching, tautness, tenseness, tensity; CONCEPTS 723,726 —*Ant.* limpness, looseness, relaxation, slack

tension [*n2*] *mental stress* agitation, antsiness*, ants in pants*, anxiety, apprehension, bad feeling*, brunt, concern, discomfort, disquiet, edginess, hostility, jitters*, jumps*, nail-biting*, nerves, nervousness, pins and needles*, pressure, restlessness, shakes*, strain, suspense, unease, uneasiness, worriment, worry; CONCEPT 410 —*Ant.* calmness, contentedness, ease, peace, relaxation

tent [*n*] *portable canvas shelter* big top*, canvas, pavilion, tabernacle, teepee, tupik, wigwam, yurt; CONCEPTS 515,712

tentative [*adj1*] *conditional, experimental* acting, ad interim, conjectural, contingent, dependent, iffy*, indefinite, makeshift, not final, not settled, on trial, open for consideration, probationary, provisional, provisionary, provisory, speculative, subject to change, temporary, test, trial, unconfirmed, undecided, unsettled; CONCEPTS 551,552 —Ant. certain, decisive, definite, final, sure

tentative [adj2] indefinite, uncertain backward, cautious, diffident, disinclined, doubtful, faltering, halting, hesitant, irresolute, reluctant, timid, undecided, unsure, vacillating, vacillatory, wobbly; CONCEPTS 534,535,542 —Ant. certain, conclusive, definite, sure

tenuous [adj] weak, thin aerial, airy, attenuate, attenuated, delicate, doubtful, dubious, ethereal, fine, flimsy, gossamer, insignificant, insubstantial, light, narrow, nebulous, questionable, rare, rarefied, reedy, shaky, sketchy, slender, slight, slim, subtle, twiggy; CONCEPTS 489,491,575 —Ant. healthy, significant, stable, strong, substantial, thick

tenure [n] time in position of responsibility administration, clamp, clasp, clench, clinch, clutch, dynasty, grasp, grip, hold, holding, incumbency, occupancy, occupation, ownership, possession, proprietorship, regime, reign, residence, security, tenancy, term; CONCEPTS 287,816

tepid [adj] lukewarm apathetic, cool, disinterested, dull, halfhearted, indifferent, languid, lifeless, mild, milk-warm, moderate, slightly warm, spiritless, temperate, unenthusiastic, unlively, warm, warmish; CONCEPTS 542,605 —Ant. cold, hot

term [n1] description of a concept appellation, article, caption, denomination, designation, expression, head, indication, language, locution, moniker*, name, nomenclature, phrase, style, terminology, title, vocable, word; CONCEPTS 275,683

term [n2] time period course, cycle, duration, go*, hitch*, interval, phase, quarter, season, semester, session, space, span, spell, standing, stretch, time, tour, turn, while; CONCEPTS 807,822

term [n3] limit bound, boundary, close, conclusion, confine, confines, culmination, end, finish, fruition, limitation, terminus; CONCEPTS 745,832

term [v] name something baptize, call, christen, denominate, describe, designate, dub, entitle, label, style, subtitle, tag, title; CONCEPT 62

terminal [adj] final, deadly bounding, check out*, closing, concluding, eventual, extreme, fatal, hindmost, incurable, killing, lag, last, latest, lethal, limiting, mortal, on way out*, period, ultimate, utmost; CONCEPTS 314, 548 —Ant. beginning, initial, opening, reviving, starting

terminal [n1] end of road; limit boundary, depot, end, end of the line, extremity, station, termination, terminus; CONCEPTS 198,745

terminal [n2] computer screen, computer input/output device cathode ray tube, CRT*, display, input device, monitor, screen, VDT*, video display; CONCEPT 463

terminate [v] stop, finish abolish, abort, achieve, adjourn, annul, bounce, bound, bring to an end, cancel, cease, close, come to an end, complete, conclude, confine, cut off, define,

desist, determine, discharge, discontinue, dismiss, dissolve, drop, eliminate, end, expire, extinguish, fire, halt, issue, lapse, limit, perfect, prorogate, prorogue, put an end to, recess, restrict, result, run out, sack, scratch, scrub*, tether, ultimate, wind down, wind up*, wrap*, wrap up*; CONCEPTS 119,121,234 —Ant. begin, initiate, open, start

termination [n] end abortion, ballgame*, cease, cessation, close, completion, conclusion, consequence, curtains*, cut-off*, desistance, discontinuation, effect, ending, end of the line*, expiry, finale, finis, finish, issue, kiss-off*, outcome, payoff*, period, result, stop, terminus, windup*, wrap-up*; CONCEPTS 119,832 —Ant. beginning, initiation, opening, start

terminology [n] wording choice of words, diction, jargon, language, lingo, locution, nomenclature, onomastics, phraseology, phrasing, turn of phrase, vocabulary, wordage, words; CONCEPTS 278,682

terms [n1] conditions, agreement charge, circumstances, conclusion, condition, details, fee, fine print*, items, nitty-gritty*, particulars, payment, points, premise, premises, price, provision, provisions, proviso, provisos, qualifications, rate, reservation, size of it*, small print*, specifications, stipulation, stipulations, strings*, treaty, understanding, what it is*; CONCEPTS 270,318,684

terms [n2] status of relationship balance, equality, equivalence, footing, par, parity, position, relations, relationship, standing; CONCEPT 388

terrain [n] landscape area, bailiwick, contour, country, domain, dominion, field, form, ground, land, profile, province, region, shape, soil, sphere, territory, topography, turf; CONCEPTS 508,509 —Ant. sky

terrestrial [adj] earthly earthbound, earthlike, earthy, global, mundane, physical, profane, prosaic, secular, sublunary, subsolar, telluric, temporal, terrene, uncelestial, unspiritual, worldly; CONCEPT 536 —Ant. cosmic, heavenly, otherworldly

terrible [adj] bad, horrible abhorrent, appalling, atrocious, awe-inspiring, awesome, awful, beastly, dangerous, desperate, dire, disastrous, disturbing, dread, dreaded, dreadful, extreme, fearful, frightful, ghastly, gruesome, harrowing, hateful, hideous, horrendous, horrid, horrifying, inconvenient, loathsome, monstrous, obnoxious, odious, offensive, petrifying, poor, repulsive, revolting, rotten, serious, severe, shocking, unfortunate, unnerving, unpleasant, unwelcome, vile; CONCEPT 571 —Ant. good, great, nice, wonderful

terribly [adv] very awfully, badly, decidedly, desperately, discouragingly, disturbingly, drastically, dreadfully, exceedingly, extremely, fearfully, frightfully, gravely, greatly, highly, horribly, intensely, markedly, mightily, much, notoriously, remarkably, seriously, staggeringly, thoroughly, unbelievably, unfortunately, unhappily; CONCEPTS 569,570 —Ant. little

terrific [adj1] intense agitating, appalling, awesome, awful, deafening, disquieting, dreadful, enormous, excessive, extreme, fearful, fierce, formidable, frightful, gigantic, great, harsh, horrible, horrific, huge, immense, large, monstrous, severe, shocking, terrible, terrorizing, thunderous, tremendous, upsetting; CONCEPT 569 —*Ant.* calm, moderate

terrific [*adj2*] *wonderful* ace*, amazing, breathtaking, divine, excellent, fabulous, fantastic, fine, glorious, great, groovy*, hot*, keen*, magnificent, marvelous, outstanding, sensational, smashing*, stupendous, super, superb, swell, very good; CONCEPT 572 —*Ant.* bad, inferior, low, nasty, poor

terrify [*v*] *scare* alarm, appall, awe, chill, dismay, freeze, fright, frighten, horrify, intimidate, paralyze, petrify, scare stiff*, scare the pants off*, scare to death*, shock, spook, startle, strike fear into*, stun, stupefy, terrorize; CONCEPTS 7,19,42 —*Ant.* calm, delight, please

territory [*n*] *domain, region* area, belt, block, boundary, colony, commonwealth, country, district, dominion, empire, enclave, exclave, expanse, extent, field, land, mandate, nation, neck of the woods*, neighborhood, province, quarter, section, sector, sphere, state, stomping grounds*, street, terrain, terrene, township, tract, turf*, walk, zone; CONCEPTS 198,349,508

terror [*n*] *intense fear* alarm, anxiety, awe, consternation, dismay, dread, fearfulness, fright, horror, intimidation, panic, shock, trepidation, trepidity; CONCEPTS 27,690 —*Ant.* cheer, glee, happiness, joy

terrorize [*v*] *upset, threaten* alarm, appall, awe, bludgeon, browbeat, bulldoze*, bully, coerce, cow, dismay, dragoon, fright, frighten, hector, horrify, intimidate, menace, oppress, petrify, scare, scare to death*, shock, spook, startle, strike terror into*, strong-arm*, terrify; CONCEPT 7 —*Ant.* assuage, calm, help, please

terse [*adj*] *brief, short* abrupt, aphoristic, boiled down*, breviloquent, brusque, clear-cut, clipped, close, compact, compendiary, compendious, concise, condensed, crisp, cryptic, curt, cut to the bone*, elliptical, epigrammatic, exact, gnomic, in a nutshell*, incisive, laconic, lean, neat, pithy, pointed, precise, sententious, short and sweet*, snappy, succinct, summary, taut, to the point, trenchant; CONCEPTS 267,272 —*Ant.* lengthy, long-winded, prolix, wordy

test [*n*] *examination, quiz* analysis, approval, assessment, attempt, blue book*, catechism, check, comp*, confirmation, corroboration, countdown, criterion, dry run*, elimination, essay, evaluation, exam, experiment, final, fling*, go*, inquest, inquiry, inspection, investigation, lick*, oral*, ordeal, pop quiz, preliminary, probation, probing, proof, questionnaire, scrutiny, search, shibboleth, standard, substantiation, touchstone*, trial, trial and error*, trial run, try, tryout, verification, yardstick*; CONCEPTS 5,290

test [*v*] *examine, quiz* analyze, assay, assess, check, confirm, demonstrate, experiment, experimentalize, give a tryout, inquire, investigate, look into, make a trial run, match up, prove, prove out, put to the test*, question, run idea by someone*, run it up a flagpole*, see how it flies*, see how wind blows*, send up a balloon*, shake down*, stack up, substantiate, try, try on, try on for size*, try out, validate, verify; CONCEPTS 5,103,291

testament [*n*] *tribute; last wishes* attestation,

colloquy, confirmation, covenant, demonstration, earnest, evidence, exemplification, instrument, proof, testimonial, testimony, will, witness; CONCEPT 318

tested [*adj*] *proven* approved, certified, creditworthy, dependable, loyal, proved, reliable, safe, tried-and-true*, trustworthy, trusty; CONCEPT 535

testify [*v*] *vouch for; give testimony* affirm, announce, argue, assert, attest, bear witness, bespeak, betoken, certify, corroborate, cross one's heart*, declare, demonstrate, depone, depose, evince, give evidence, give facts, give one's word*, indicate, make evident, mount, point to, prove, say so*, show, sing*, stand up for, state, swear, swear to, swear up and down*, token, warrant, witness; CONCEPTS 49,317

testimonial [*n*] *tribute* affidavit, appreciation, attestation, certificate, character, commemoration, commendation, confirmation, credential, degree, endorsement, evidence, homage, honor, indication, manifestation, memorial, memorialization, monument, ovation, plug*, proof, recommendation, reference, remembrance, salute, salvo, say-so*, show, sign, symbol, testament, testimony, token, voucher, witness; CONCEPTS 49,278,318

testimony [*n*] *declaration about truth; proof* affidavit, affirmation, attestation, avowal, confirmation, corroboration, data, demonstration, deposition, documentation, evidence, facts, grounds, illustration, indication, information, manifestation, profession, statement, submission, substantiation, support, testament, verification, witness; CONCEPTS 49,278,318

testy [*adj*] *irritable, touchy* annoyed, bad-tempered, cantankerous, captious, choleric, crabbed, cranky*, cross, crotchety, edgy, exasperated, fretful, grouchy, grumpy*, impatient, irascible, mean, ornery*, out of sorts, peevish, peppery, petulant, quarrelsome, quick-tempered, short-tempered, snappy*, splenetic, sullen, thin-skinned*, uptight*, waspish; CONCEPTS 401,403,542 —*Ant.* happy, pleasant

tête-è-tête [*n*] *conversation* chat, colloquy, confabulation, confidential discussion, consultation, cozy chat, dialogue, discussion, exchange, face-to-face talk, fireside chat, friendly chat, heart-to-heart talk, intimate discussion, one-on-one talk, pillow talk*, powwow*, talk; CONCEPT 266

tether [*n*] *fastening* binding, bond, chain, cord, fetter, halter, harness, lead, leash, picket, restraint, rope, shackle; CONCEPT 475

tether [*v*] *fasten* batten, bind, chain, fetter, leash, manacle, moor, picket, restrain, rope, secure, shackle, tie; CONCEPTS 85,160 —*Ant.* unchain, unfasten, unshackle

text [*n1*] *subject matter of document* argument, body, consideration, content, contents, context, document, extract, fundamentals, head, idea, issue, line, lines, main body, matter, motify, motive, paragraph, passage, point, quotation, sentence, stanza, subject, theme, thesis, topic, verse, vocabulary, wording, words; CONCEPTS 270,682

text [*n2*] *book used in education* assignment, class book, course book, handbook, manual, reader, reference, reference book, required reading, schoolbook, source, syllabus, textbook, workbook; CONCEPTS *280,287*

textbook [*n*] *text* assigned text, class book, course book, primer, reader, required reading, schoolbook, workbook; CONCEPTS *280,287*

texture [*n*] *characteristics of a surface* arrangement, balance, being, character, coarseness, composition, consistency, constitution, disposition, essence, essentiality, fabric, feel, feeling, fiber, fineness, flexibility, form, framework, grain, intermixture, make, makeup, nap, nature, organization, pattern, quality, roughness, scheme, sense, smoothness, stiffness, strategy, structure, surface, taste, tissue, touch, warp, weave, web, woof; CONCEPTS *611,673, 682*

thank [*v*] *express gratitude* acknowledge, be grateful, be indebted, be obligated, be obliged, bless, bow down*, give thanks, kiss*, praise, say thank you, show appreciation, show courtesy, show gratitude, smile on*; CONCEPTS *60, 69,76*

thankful [*adj*] *appreciative* beholden, content, contented, grateful, gratified, indebted, much obliged, obliged, overwhelmed, pleased, relieved, satisfied; CONCEPTS *401,403* —*Ant.* critical, thankless, unappreciative, ungrateful, unthankful

thankless [*adj1*] *unappreciated* barren, disagreeable, distasteful, fruitless, futile, miserable, not worth it*, ungrateful, unpleasant, unprofitable, unrecognized, unrequited, unreturned, unrewarding, useless, vain, wretched; CONCEPTS *538,548* —*Ant.* appreciated, contented, grateful, rewarded, satisfied, thankful

thankless [*adj2*] *unappreciative, inconsiderate (in behavior)* careless, cruel, heedless, inappreciative, rude, self-centered, thoughtless, ungracious, ungrateful, unmindful, unthankful; CONCEPT *401* —*Ant.* appreciative, considerate, grateful, thankful

thanks [*n*] *spoken or written appreciation* acknowledgment, benediction, blessing, credit, grace, gramercy, gratefulness, gratitude, praise, recognition, thankfulness, thanksgiving, thank you note; CONCEPTS *60,69,278* —*Ant.* criticism

thaw [*v*] *unfreeze, warm* become liquid, become soft, defrost, deliquesce, dissolve, flow, flux, fuse, liquefy, loosen, melt, mollify, open up, relax, relent, run, soften, unbend, warm up; CONCEPTS *13,255,469* —*Ant.* freeze

theater/theatre [*n*] *stage, building for performance* amphitheater, arena, assembly hall, auditorium, barn, boards*, cinema, coliseum, concert hall, deck, drama, drive-in, footlights, hall, hippodrome, house, locale, movie, movie house, oak*, odeum, opera house, playhouse, room, scene, show hall, site; CONCEPTS *263,293,439,448*

theatrical [*adj*] *dramatic* affected, amateur, artificial, campy*, ceremonious, comic, dramaturgic, exaggerated, ham*, hammy*, histrionic, legitimate, mannered, melodramatic, meretricious, operatic, ostentatious, pompous, schmaltzy*, show, showy, staged, stilted, superficial, theatric, thespian, tragic, unnatural, unreal, vaudeville; CONCEPTS *401,536* —*Ant.* comedic, real, undramatic, untheatrical

theft [*n*] *stealing* annexation, appropriation,

break-in, burglary, caper, cheating, crime, defrauding, deprivation, embezzlement, extortion, filch, fleece*, fraud, grab*, heist, holdup, hustle*, job*, larceny, lift*, looting, mugging, peculation, pilferage, pilfering, pillage, pinch*, piracy, plunder, purloining, racket*, rapacity, rip-off*, robbery, robbing, score*, shoplifting, snatch*, snitch*, steal, stickup, swindle, swindling, swiping*, thievery, thieving, touch*, vandalism; CONCEPTS *139,192* —*Ant.* return

theme [*n1*] *idea, subject matter* affair, argument, burden, business, case, head, keynote, leitmotif, line, matter, matter in hand, motif, motive, point, point at issue, problem, proposition, question, stuff, subject, text, thesis, thought, topic; CONCEPTS *278,682,689*

theme [*n2*] *written composition* article, description, dissertation, essay, exercise, exposition, manuscript, paper, report, statement, thesis; CONCEPT *271*

then [*adv1*] *before; at another time* again, all at once, anon, at that instant, at that moment, at that point, at that time, before long, formerly, later, next, on that occasion, soon after, suddenly, thereupon, when, years ago; CONCEPT *799*

then [*adv2*] *therefore* accordingly, consequently, ergo, from that time, from then on, from there on, hence, so, thence, thenceforth, thereupon, thus, whence; CONCEPT *548*

theological [*adj*] *religious, concerning a god-centered philosophy* apostolic, canonical, churchly, deistic, divine, doctrinal, ecclesiastical, metaphysical, scriptural, theistic; CONCEPT *536* —*Ant.* irreligious

theorem [*n*] *explanation based on hypothesis and experiments* assumption, axiom, belief, deduction, dictum, doctrine, formula, fundamental, law, postulate, principium, principle, proposition, rule, statement, theory, thesis; CONCEPTS *529,688,689* —*Ant.* fact, proof

theoretical [*adj*] *hypothetical* abstract, academic, analytical, as a premise, assumed, codified, conjectural, contingent, formalistic, formularized, general, ideal, idealized, ideational, ideological, imaginative, impractical, instanced, intellectual, in the abstract, in theory, logical, metaphysical, notional, on paper*, pedantic, philosophical, postulated, presumed, problematical, pure, quixotic, speculative, suppositional, tentative, transcendent, transcendental, unearthly, unproved, unsubstantiated, vague; CONCEPT *529* —*Ant.* certain, definite, factual, proven, real

theorize [*v*] *hypothesize* conjecture, formulate, guess, project, propound, speculate, submit, suggest, suppose, think; CONCEPT *43* —*Ant.* prove

theory [*n*] *hypothesis, belief* approach, argument, assumption, base, basis, code, codification, concept, conditions, conjecture, doctrine, dogma, feeling, formularization, foundation, grounds, guess, guesswork, hunch, idea, ideology, impression, method, outlook, philosophy, plan, position, postulate, premise, presentiment, presumption, proposal, provision, rationale, scheme, shot*, speculation, stab*, supposal, suppose, supposition, surmise, suspicion, system, systemization, theorem, thesis, understanding; CONCEPTS 529,689 —*Ant.* certainty, fact, proof, reality

therapeutic [*adj*] *healing* ameliorative, analeptic, beneficial, corrective, curative, good, remedial, restorative, salubrious, salutary, sanative; CONCEPT 537 —*Ant.* damaging, harmful, hurtful, injurious, untherapeutic

therapist [*n*] *counselor* adviser, analyst, clinician, doctor, physician, psychiatrist, psychoanalyst, psychologist, psychotherapist, shrink*; CONCEPT 357

therapy [*n*] *healing treatment* analysis, cure, healing, medicine, remedial treatment, remedy, therapeutics; CONCEPT 310 —*Ant.* damage, harm, hurt, injury

thereabout [*adv*] *about there* almost, approximately, around, close at hand, in the neighborhood, in the vicinity, just about, near, nearby, nearly, roughly; CONCEPTS 581,586

thereafter [*adv*] *from that time forward* after that, consequently, following, forever after, from that day forward, from that day on, from there on, hereafter, thenceforth, thenceforward; CONCEPT 799

therefore [*adv*] *as a result; for that reason* accordingly, and so, consequently, ergo, for, forasmuch as, for this reason, hence, inasmuch as, in consequence, in that event, on account of, on the grounds, since, so, then, thence, therefrom, thereupon, thus, to that end, whence, wherefore; CONCEPTS 230,676

thermal [*adj*] *warm* heated, hot, lukewarm, melting, roasting, scorching, sizzling, snug, summery, sweltering, thermic, toasty; CONCEPT 605

thesaurus [*n*] *dictionary of synonyms and antonyms* glossary, language reference book, lexicon, onomasticon, reference book, sourcebook, storehouse of words, terminology, treasury of words, vocabulary, word list; CONCEPT 280

thesis [*n1*] *belief, assumption to be tested* apriorism, contention, contestation, hypothesis, idea, line, opinion, point, posit, position, postulate, postulation, premise, presumption, presupposition, principle, proposal, proposition, sentiment, statement, supposition, surmise, theory, view; CONCEPTS 529,689 —*Ant.* certainty, fact, proof, reality

thesis [*n2*] *written dissertation* argument, argumentation, composition, discourse, disquisition, essay, exposition, memoir, monograph, monography, paper, research, theme, tractate, treatise; CONCEPTS 271,287

thespian [*n*] *actor, actress* artist, bit player, character, entertainer, extra, ham*, headliner, idol, lead, performer, play-actor, player, star, straight person, thesp*, understudy; CONCEPT 352

thick [*adj1*] *deep, bulky* blubbery, broad, burly, chunky, compact, concrete, consolidated, fat, firm, hard, heavy, high, husky, massive, obese, pudgy, solid, squat, stocky, stubby, stumpy, substantial, thickset, wide; CONCEPTS 491,773 —*Ant.* attenuated, slight, thin

thick [*adj2*] *concentrated, dense* caked, clabbered, close, clotted, coagulated, compact, compressed, concrete, condensed, congealed, consolidated, crowded, curdled, deep, firm, fixed, gelatinous, gloppy*, gooey, gummous, gummy, gunky*, heavy, impenetrable, impervious, jelled, jellied, opaque, ossified, ropy, set, sloppy, solid, solidified, stiff, syrupy, thickened, turbid, viscid, viscous, vitrified; CONCEPTS 483,606 —*Ant.* diluted, loose, thin, watery

thick [*adj3*] *crowded, packed* abundant, brimming, bristling, bursting, chock-full*, close, compact, compressed, concentrated, condensed, considerable, covered, crammed, crawling with*, dense, frequent, full, great, heaped, impenetrable, impervious, inspissated, like sardines*, localized, multitudinous, numerous, populated, populous, profuse, rank, replete, several, solid, swarming, teeming, tight; CONCEPT 771 —*Ant.* thin, uncrowded

thick [*adj4*] *stupid* blockheaded, boneheaded, brainless, dense, dim-witted, doltish, dopey*, dull, dumb, ignorant, insensitive, moronic, numbskulled, obtuse, slow, slow-witted, thick-headed; CONCEPT 402 —*Ant.* intelligent, smart

thick [*adj5*] *dense (referring to weather)* cloudy, dull, foggy, heavy, impenetrable, indistinct, muddy, obscure, soupy*, turbid; CONCEPT 525 —*Ant.* clear

thick [*adj6*] *friendly* chummy*, close, confidential, cordial, devoted, familiar, hand in glove*, inseparable, intimate, on good terms; CONCEPT 555 —*Ant.* unfriendly, unsociable

thick [*adj7*] *unreasonable* excessive, flimsy*, implausible, improbable, inconceivable, incredible, thin*, too much*, unbelievable, unconvincing, unfair, unjust, unsubstantial; CONCEPTS 529,548 —*Ant.* reasonable, sensible, wise

thicken [*v*] *set; make more dense* add, buttress, cake, clabber, clot, coagulate, condense, congeal, curdle, deepen, enlarge, expand, freeze, gel, grow thick, harden, inspissate, jell, jelly, ossify, petrify, reinforce, solidify, stiffen, swell, widen; CONCEPTS 137,250,469 —*Ant.* dilute, liquefy, melt, thin, water down

thick-skinned [*adj*] *hardened* benumbed, callous, coldhearted*, hard-as-nails*, hardhearted*, insensitive, seasoned, tough, toughened, unbending, unfeeling; CONCEPTS 404,542

thief [*n*] *person who steals* bandit, burglar, cat burglar, cheat, clip*, criminal, crook, defalcator, embezzler, heister*, highway robber, hijacker, holdup artist, housebreaker, kleptomaniac, larcener, larcenist, lifter*, moonlighter*, mugger, owl*, pickpocket, pilferer, pirate, plunderer, porch climber*, prowler, punk*, purloiner, robber, scrounger, shoplifter, sniper, spider*, stealer, stickup artist*, swindler; CONCEPT 412

thieving/thievish [*adj*] *criminal* crooked, cunning, dishonest, fraudulent, furtive, kleptomaniacal*, larcenous, light-fingered*, pilfering, piratic*, plunderous, predatory, rapacious, secretive, sly, spoliative, stealthy, sticky-fingered*; CONCEPT 401 —*Ant.* benevolent, philanthropic

thin [*adj1*] *fine, light, slender* attenuate, attenuated, beanpole*, beanstalk*, bony*, cadaverous, delicate, emaciated, ethereal, featherweight, fragile, gangling, gangly, gaunt, haggard, lank, lanky, lean, lightweight, meager, narrow, peaked, pinched, pole*, puny*, rangy, rarefied, rawboned, reedy, rickety, scraggy*, scrawny, shadow, shriveled, skeletal, skinny, slight, slim, slinky, small, spare, spindly, stalky*, starved, stick*, stilt*, subtle, thread-like, twiggy*, twiglike, undernourished, under-weight, wan, wasted, wizened; CONCEPT 491 —*Ant.* dense, fat, heavy, inflated, obese, thick

thin [*adj2*] *transparent, fine* attenuate, attenu-ated, delicate, diaphanous, filmy, flimsy, gossamer, paper-thin, permeable, rare, rarefied, refined, see-through, sheer, slight, slim, subtile, subtle, tenuous, translucent, unsubstantial, wafer-thin, wispy; CONCEPT 606 —*Ant.* dense, solid, thick

thin [*adj3*] *deficient, weak* diluted, feeble*, flat*, flimsy*, implausible, improbable, inade-quate, inconceivable, incredible, insubstantial, insufficient, lame, meager, poor, questionable, scant, scanty, scarce, scattered, shallow, sketchy, skimpy*, slight, sparse, stretched, superficial, thick*, transparent, unbelievable, unconvincing, unpersuasive, unsubstantial, untenable, vapid, weak-kneed*; CONCEPT 771 —*Ant.* efficient, solid, strong

thin [*adj4*] *diluted* diffuse, dilute, dispersed, fine, light, rarefied, refined, runny, subtle, watery, weak, wishy-washy*; CONCEPT 485 —*Ant.* concentrated, thick, undiluted

thin [*v*] *make diluted or less dense* attenuate, cook, cut, cut back, decrease, delete, diminish, disperse, doctor, edit, emaciate, expand, extenu-ate, irrigate, lace*, needle*, prune, rarefy, re-duce, refine, shave, spike, trim, water, water down, weaken, weed out; CONCEPTS 137,250 —*Ant.* beef up, thicken

thing [*n1*] *something felt, seen, perceived* affair, anything, apparatus, article, being, body, busi-ness, circumstance, commodity, concept, con-cern, configuration, contrivance, corporeality, creature, device, element, entity, everything, existence, existent, fact, figure, form, gadget, goods, implement, individual, information, in-strument, item, machine, materiality, matter, means, mechanism, object, part, person, phenomenon, piece, point, portion, shape, situation, stuff, subject, substance, tool, word; CONCEPT 433

thing [*n2*] *act* accomplishment, action, circum-stance, deed, doing, duty, episode, event, even-tuality, exploit, feat, happening, incident, job, movement, obligation, occasion, occurrence, phenomenon, proceeding, stunt, task, work; CONCEPT 3

thing [*n3*] *aspect, characteristic* article, attribute, detail, element, facet, factor, feature, item, particular, point, property, quality, state-ment, thought, trait; CONCEPTS 411,657,834

thing [*n4*] *idea, obsession* attitude, bee in bon-net*, craze, fad, fetish, fixation, hang-up*, idée fixe, impression, mania, notion, opinion, phobia, preoccupation, quirk, style, thought; CONCEPT 529 —*Ant.* dislike, hate, hatred

thing/things [*n5*] *personal possessions* ap-parel, attire, baggage, belongings, chattels, clothes, clothing, duds*, effects, equipment, gear, goods, habiliments, impedimenta, lug-gage, odds and ends*, paraphernalia, personal effects, personals*, property, raiment, stuff, trappings, tricks; CONCEPTS 446,451

think [*v1*] *believe; anticipate* assume, be

convinced, comprehend, conceive, conclude, consider, credit, deem, determine, envisage, envision, esteem, estimate, expect, fancy, feature, feel, foresee, gather, guess, hold, image, imagine, judge, plan for, presume, project, realize, reckon, regard, see, sense, suppose, surmise, suspect, take, understand, vision, visualize; CONCEPTS 12,26 —*Ant.* disbelieve, disregard, excogitate

think [*v2*] *contemplate* analyze, appraise, appre-ciate, brood, cerebrate, cogitate, comprehend, conceive, consider, deduce, deliberate, estimate, evaluate, examine, figure out, have in mind, ideate, imagine, infer, intellectualize, judge, logicalize, meditate, mull, mull over, muse, ponder, rack one's brains*, rationalize, reason, reflect, resolve, revolve, ruminate, sort out, speculate, stew*, stop to consider, study, take under consideration, turn over, use one's head*, weigh; CONCEPTS 17,33,43 —*Ant.* forget, ignore, neglect

think [*v3*] *remember* call to mind, recall, recollect, reminisce; CONCEPT 40 —*Ant.* forget

thinkable [*adj*] *believable, feasible* cogitable, comprehendible, comprehensible, conceivable, convincing, imaginable, likely, possible, practicable, practical, presumable, reasonable, supposable, within realm of possibility*, within the limits; CONCEPT 529 —*Ant.* impossible, inconceivable, unbelievable, unfeasible, unlikely, unthinkable

thin-skinned [*adj*] *sensitive* delicate, easily hurt, hypersensitive, oversensitive, soft, touchy, vulnerable; CONCEPT 406

third world [*n*] *underdeveloped countries* developing countries, developing nations, economically developing countries, economi-cally developing nations, emergent nations, underdeveloped nations; CONCEPTS 378,391

thirst [*n*] *craving (especially for liquid)* appetite, aridity, desire, drought, dryness, eagerness, hankering, hunger, keenness, longing, lust, passion, thirstiness, yearning, yen; CONCEPTS 20,709

thirsty [*adj*] *dry, desirous (especially for liquid)* agog*, anxious, appetent, ardent, arid, athirst, avid, bone-dry*, breathless, burning, cotton-mouthed*, craving, crazy for*, dehydrated, droughty, dry as dust*, dying for*, eager, greedy, hankering, hungry, impatient, inclined, itching for*, juiceless, keen, longing, lusting, parched, partial to, sapless, thirsting, waterless, wild for*, yearning; CONCEPTS 403,603 —*Ant.* moist, quenched, satisfied, wet

thorny [*adj1*] *sharp, pointed* barbed, briery, bristling, bristly, prickly, spiked, spiky, spinous, spiny, stinging, thistly; CONCEPT 485 —*Ant.* dull, smooth, unpointed

thorny [*adj2*] *difficult, problematic* awkward, baffling, bothersome, formidable, harassing, hard, irksome, nettlesome, perplexing, prickly, severe, sticky, ticklish, tough, tricky, trouble-some, trying, unpleasant, upsetting, vexatious, worrying; CONCEPT 565 —*Ant.* easy, solvable, untroublesome

thoroughbred [*adj*] *pure, unmixed* blood, full-blooded, graded, papered, pedigree, pedigreed, pure-blooded, purebred; CONCEPT 549 —*Ant.* half-breed, impure, mixed

thoroughly [adv1] *exhaustively* all, assiduously, carefully, completely, comprehensively, conscientiously, earnestly, efficiently, exceedingly, exceptionally, extremely, flat out*, from A to Z*, from top to bottom*, fully, hard, highly, hugely, in and out*, in detail, inside out*, intensely, intensively, meticulously, notably, painstakingly, remarkably, scrupulously, strikingly, sweepingly, through and through*, throughout, unremittingly, up and down*, very, whole hog*, wholly; CONCEPTS 531,538 —*Ant.* incompletely, inexhaustively, partially, superficially

thoroughly [adv2] *utterly* absolutely, altogether, completely, downright, entirely, fully, perfectly, plumb, quite, totally, to the full, well, wholly, without reservation; CONCEPTS 531, 535,557 —*Ant.* deficiently, inadequately

thorough/thoroughgoing [adj1] *exhaustive* absolute, all-embracing, all-inclusive, all-out*, all the way*, assiduous, blow-by-blow*, careful, circumstantial, clocklike, complete, comprehensive, conscientious, detailed, efficient, exact, from A to Z*, full, full-dress*, in-depth, intensive, itemized, meticulous, minute, painstaking, particular, particularized, plenty, royal, scrupulous, slam-bang*, soup to nuts*, sweeping, tough, whole-hog*; CONCEPTS 531,538 —*Ant.* incomplete, inexhaustive, partial, superficial, unfinished

thorough/thoroughgoing [adj2] *absolute, utter* arrant, complete, consummate, downright, entire, out-and-out*, outright, perfect, pure, rank, sheer, straight-out*, total, unmitigated, unqualified; CONCEPTS 531,535,557 —*Ant.* deficient, imperfect, inadequate

though [adv] *however* after all, all the same, for all that, howbeit, nevertheless, nonetheless, notwithstanding, still, still and all, withal, yet; CONCEPT 544

though [conj] *while* albeit, allowing, although, but, despite, despite the fact, even if, even supposing, even though, granted, howbeit, if, much as, notwithstanding, when, whereas; CONCEPT 544

thought [n1] *formation of mental objects* anticipation, apprehending, attention, brainwork, cerebration, cogitation, cognition, concluding, consideration, considering, contemplation, deducing, deduction, deliberation, deriving, discerning, heed, hope, ideation, inducing, inferring, introspection, intuition, judging, knowing, logic, meditation, musing, perceiving, rationalization, rationalizing, realizing, reasoning, reflection, regard, rumination, scrutiny, seeing, speculation, study, theorization, thinking, understanding; CONCEPTS 17,43,409,410 —*Ant.* vacancy, vacuity

thought [n2] *idea, concept* aim, anxiety, appreciation, aspiration, assessment, assumption, attentiveness, belief, brainchild*, brainstorm*, caring, compassion, conception, concern, conclusion, conjecture, conviction, design, dream, drift, estimation, expectation, fancy, feeling, guess, hope, hypothesis, image, inference, intention, intuition, judgment, kindness, knowledge, notion, object, opinion, plan, premise, prospect, purpose, regard, reverie, solicitude, supposition, sympathy, theory, thinking, understanding, view, worry; CONCEPT 529 —*Ant.* concrete, thing

thoughtful [adj1] *caring, mindful* anxious, astute, attentive, aware, benign, canny, careful, cautious, charitable, chivalrous, circumspect, civil, concerned, considerate, cooperative, courteous, deliberate, diplomatic, discreet, friendly, gallant, gracious, heedful, helpful, indulgent, kind, kindly, neighborly, obliging, observant, observative, observing, polite, prudent, regardful, responsive, sensitive, social, solicitous, tactful, unselfish, wary, well-bred, well thought-out; CONCEPTS 401,555 —*Ant.* careless, heedless, inattentive, inconsiderate, uncaring, unmindful, unthoughtful

thoughtful [adj2] *contemplative, introspective* absorbed, analytical, attentive, brainy*, calculating, cerebral, cogitative, deep, deliberative, discerning, earnest, engrossed, farsighted, grave, intellectual, intent, keen, levelheaded, logical, lost in thought*, meditative, melancholy, museful, musing, pensive, philosophic, pondering, preoccupied, rapt, rational, reasonable, reasoning, reflecting, reflective, retrospective, ruminative, serious, sober, studious, subjective, thinking, wise, wistful; CONCEPTS 402,403,542 —*Ant.* idiotic, negligent, obtuse, remiss, stupid, thoughtless

thoughtless [adj1] *inconsiderate* antisocial, apathetic, asocial, blind, boorish, brash, deaf, discourteous, egocentric, hasty, heedless, hot-headed, impolite, inattentive, incautious, indelicate, indifferent, indiscreet, insensitive, listless, madcap, neglectful, negligent, primitive, rash, reckless, rude, self-centered, selfish, sharp, short, tactless, uncaring, unceremonious, unconcerned, undiplomatic, ungracious, unheeding, unkind, unmindful, unrefined; CONCEPTS 401,555 —*Ant.* considerate, kind, thinking, thoughtful, unselfish

thoughtless [adj2] *absent-minded, unobservant* bovine, careless, confused, doltish, dull, empty-headed, flighty, foolish, heedless, ill-advised, ill-considered, imprudent, inadvertent, inane, inattentive, incomprehensible, inept, injudicious, irrational, irreflective, lamebrained*, loony*, mindless, neglectful, negligent, obtuse, puerile, rash, reckless, regardless, remiss, senseless, silly, stupid, undiscerning, unheeding, unmindful, unreasonable, unreasoning, unreflective, unthinking, vacuous, witless; CONCEPTS 402, 403,542 —*Ant.* attentive, heeding, mindful, observant, thoughtful

thought-provoking [adj] *stimulating* absorbing, captivating, exciting, fascinating, gripping, inspirational, interesting, intriguing, inviting, provocative, refreshing, riveting, stirring; CONCEPTS 372,529,537,572

thrash [v] *flail about; beat soundly* beat, beat up, belabor, belt, birch, buffet, bury, cane, chasten, chastise, clobber, crush, defeat, flagellate, flog, jerk, kill, lambaste*, lick, maul, murder, overwhelm, paste, pelt, pitch, pound, pummel, punish, rout, rush, scourge, seesaw, slaughter, spank, stir, strike, surge, tan, tan one's hide*, thresh, toss, toss and turn*, trash, trim, trounce, wallop, wax*, whip, work over*, writhe; CONCEPTS 95,189 —*Ant.* be still

threadbare [adj1] *worn, frayed* beat up*,

damaged, dilapidated, dingy, dog-eared, down-at-the-heel*, faded, frowzy*, impaired, injured, old, ragged, ratty*, run-down, scruffy, seedy, shabby, shopworn, tacky, tattered, timeworn, used, used-up, worn-out, worse for wear*; CONCEPTS 485,606 —Ant. fresh, new, unused

threadbare [adj2] trite, corny banal, bathetic, cliché, clichéd, cliché-ridden, common, commonplace, conventional, dull, everyday, familiar, hackneyed, imitative, moth-eaten*, musty, overused, poor, set, stale, stereotyped, stock, tedious, tired, uncreative, well-worn, worn-out; CONCEPT 267 —Ant. fresh, unused, unworn

threads [n] clothes, clothing accouterment, apparel, attire, civvies*, costume, dress, duds*, finery, garb, garments, gear, habiliment, outfit, personal attire, rags*, raiment, Sunday best*, wardrobe, weeds*; CONCEPT 451

threat [n] warning; danger blackmail, bluff, commination, fix, foreboding, foreshadowing, fulmination, hazard, impendence, intimidation, menace, omen, peril, portent, presage, risk, thunder, writing on the wall*; CONCEPT 278

threaten [v1] warn, pressure abuse, admonish, augur, blackmail, bluster, browbeat, bully, caution, comminate, cow, enforce, flex muscles*, forebode, forewarn, fulminate, growl, intimidate, look daggers*, make threat, menace, portend, presage, pressurize, push around*, scare, scowl, shake fist at*, snarl, spook, terrorize, torment, walk heavy*; CONCEPTS 7,19,78 —Ant. alleviate, help, protect, relieve

threaten [v2] endanger advance, approach, be dangerous, be gathering, be imminent, be in the air*, be in the offing*, be on the horizon*, brewing, come on, forebode, foreshadow, frighten, hang over*, impend, imperil, jeopardize, loom, overhang, portend, presage, put at risk, put in jeopardy, warn; CONCEPTS 231,407 —Ant. guard, protect, save

threatening [adj] menacing, ominous aggressive, alarming, apocalyptic, at hand, baleful, baneful, black, bullying, cautionary, close, comminatory, dangerous, dire, fateful, forthcoming, grim, ill-boding, imminent, impendent, impending, inauspicious, intimidatory, looming, loury, lowering, lowery, minacious, minatory, near, overhanging, portending, portentous, scowling, sinister, terrorizing, ugly, unlucky, unpropitious, unsafe, upcoming, warning; CONCEPTS 525,548,570 —Ant. nice, pleasant

threshold [n] opening; beginning brink, dawn, door, doorstep, doorway, edge, entrance, gate, inception, origin, outset, point, point of departure, sill, start, starting point, verge, vestibule; CONCEPTS 440,513,648,832

thrift [n] economy austerity, carefulness, economizing, frugality, parsimony, providence, prudence, saving, stinginess, thriftiness; CONCEPT 335 —Ant. extravagance, spending, waste

thrifty [adj] economical canny, careful, chary, cheap, chintzy*, close*, close-fisted, conserving, frugal, mean, parsimonious, penny-pinching, preserving, provident, prudent, saving, scrimpy*, sparing, steal, stingy*, tight*, unwasteful; CONCEPTS 334,401 —Ant. extravagant, spendthrift, uneconomical, wasteful

thrill [n] sudden excitement adventure, bang*, blast, charge*, circus, fireworks, flash*, flush*, fun, good feeling, inspiration, kicks*, lift*, pleasure, refreshment, response, sensation, stimulation, tingle*, titillation, turn-on*, twitter*, upper*, wallop*; CONCEPTS 32,529 —Ant. calm, depression

thrill [v] excite, stimulate animate, arouse, blow away*, delight, electrify, enchant, enthuse, fire up*, flush, flutter, galvanize, glow, go over big*, grab*, inspire, juice*, key up*, knock one's socks off*, move, palpitate, quicken, quiver, race one's motor*, rally, rouse, score, send, stir, stir up, tickle*, tingle*, titillate, tremble, turn on*, wow*; CONCEPTS 7,22 —Ant. bring down, depress, discourage, dishearten

thrilling [adj] exciting blood-tingling*, boss*, breathtaking, electrifying, enchanting, exquisite, fab*, fabulous, frantic, gripping, hair-raising*, large, mad, magnificent, mind-bending*, mind-blowing*, miraculous, overwhelming, rip-roaring*, riveting, rousing, sensational, shivering, stimulating, stirring, swinging, trembling, wild, wondrous, zero cool*; CONCEPTS 548,572 —Ant. depressing, discouraging, upsetting

thrive [v] do well advance, arrive, batten, bear fruit, bloom, blossom, boom, burgeon, develop, flourish, get ahead*, get fat*, get on*, get places*, get there*, grow, grow rich, increase, make a go*, mushroom*, progress, prosper, radiate, rise, score*, shine, shoot up, succeed, turn out well, wax; CONCEPTS 704,706 —Ant. decline, fail, languish, lose

thriving [adj] successful advancing, arrived, blooming, booming, burgeoning, cooking*, developing, doing well, flourishing, going strong*, growing, have it made*, have the wherewithal*, healthy, home free*, on top of heap*, progressing, prolific, prospering, prosperous, rich, roaring, robust, rolling*, sitting pretty*, wealthy; CONCEPTS 334,528 —Ant. declining, failing, languishing, losing

throb [v] pulsate, beat flutter, palpitate, pitpat, pound, pulse, resonate, thrill, thump, tingle, tremble, twitter, vibrate; CONCEPTS 152,185

throng [n] large crowd assemblage, assembly, bunch, collection, concourse, congregation, crush, drove, everybody, flock, gathering, horde, host, jam, mass, mob, multitude, pack, press, push, sellout, swarm; CONCEPTS 417,432

throttle [v] choke burke, control, gag, inhibit, silence, smother, stifle, strangle, strangulate, suppress; CONCEPT 191 —Ant. free, release

through [adj1] done buttoned up*, complete, completed, concluded, ended, finis*, finished, in the bag*, over, terminated, wound up*, wrapped up*; CONCEPTS 531,548 —Ant. incomplete, unfinished

through [adj2] direct constant, free, nonstop, one-way, opened, rapid, regular, straight, straightforward, unbroken, unhindered, uninterrupted; CONCEPTS 482,581 —Ant. indirect, stopping

through [prep1] by way of as a consequence, as a result, at the hand of, because of, by, by dint of, by means of, by reason, by the agency of, by virtue of, for, in consequence of, in virtue of, per, through the medium of, using, via, with, with the help of; CONCEPT 544

through [prep2] between, during about, by,

clear, for the period, from beginning to end, in, in and out, in the middle, into, past, round, straight, throughout, within; CONCEPTS 583, 798 —Ant. around

throughout [adj] during the whole of all over, all the time, all through, around, at full length, completely, during, every bit, everyplace, everywhere, far and near, far and wide, for the duration, from beginning to end, from end to end, from one end to the other, from start to finish, from the start, from the word go*, high and low, in all respects, in every place, in everything, inside and out, on all accounts*, over, overall, right through, round, the whole time, through the whole of, to the end, up and down; CONCEPTS 482,531,798

throw [v1] propel something through the air bandy, barrage, bombard, buck, bunt, butt, cant, cast, catapult, chuck, dash, deliver, discharge, dislodge, drive, fell, fire, flick, fling, fling off, flip, floor, force, heave, hurl, impel, lapidate, launch, let fly*, let go, lift, lob, overturn, overwhelm, peg, pellet, pelt, pepper, pitch, precipitate, project, push, put, scatter, send, shove, shower, shy, sling, splatter, spray, sprinkle, start, stone, strew, thrust, toss, tumble, unhorse, unseat, upset, volley, waft; CONCEPT 222 —Ant. catch, receive

throw [v2] confuse addle, astonish, baffle, befuddle, bewilder, confound, disconcert, distract, disturb, dizzy, dumbfound, fluster, mix up*, throw off*, unsettle, upset; CONCEPT 16 —Ant. explain, help

throw away [v1] dispose of abandon, cast, cast off, chase, clear, discard, dismiss, dispense with, ditch*, drop*, dump*, eject, eliminate, evict, extrude, free oneself of, get rid of, jettison, junk*, lose, refuse, reject, rid oneself of, scrap*, shake off*, shed, shuck, slip, throw off, throw out, turn down, unburden; CONCEPT 180 —Ant. hold, keep

throw away [v2] waste be wasteful, blow, consume, dissipate, fail to exploit, fritter, lose, refuse, reject, squander, trifle, turn down; CONCEPT 156 —Ant. hoard, save

throw off [v] elude, escape abuse, deceive, evade, get away from, give the slip*, leave behind, lose, outdistance, outrun, shake off, trick; CONCEPT 102 —Ant. face, meet

throw out [v] comment bring forward, bring to light*, bring up, chime in*, come out with, declare, deliver, produce, reveal, say, state, suggest, tell, utter; CONCEPT 51 —Ant. be quiet

throw over [v] abandon, leave break up with, break with, desert, discard, drop, eighty-six*, finish with, forsake, jilt*, quit, renounce, split up with, walk out on*; CONCEPTS 195,384 —Ant. accompany, join, take on, unite

throw up [v1] vomit, be nauseous be sick, bring up, disgorge, heave, puke*, regurgitate, retch, spew, spit up, upchuck*; CONCEPTS 179,308

throw up [v2] build quickly build overnight*, jerrybuild*, knock together*, patch, put together, roughcast, roughhew, run up*, slap together*, throw together; CONCEPT 168 —Ant. destroy, raze, tear down

thrust [n1] point of communication burden, core, effect, gist, meaning, meat*, pith*,

purport, sense, short, substance, upshot; CONCEPT 682

thrust [n2] forward movement advance, blitz, boost, drive, impetus, impulsion, jump, lunge, momentum, onset, onslaught, poke, pressure, prod, propulsion, punch, push, shove, stab, whack, wham; CONCEPTS 208,222 —Ant. pull

thrust [v] push hard advance, assail, assault, attack, bear down, boost, buck, butt, chuck, chunk, clip, clout, crowd, cut, dig, drive, elbow*, embed, fire, force, heave, hump, impale, impel, interject, jab, jam, jostle, lob, lunge, nick, nudge, peg, pierce, pitch, plunge, poke, pour it on*, press, prod, propel, punch, push forward, put, railroad*, ram, run, shove, sink, sling, smack, stab*, stick, toss, transfix, urge, wham*; CONCEPTS 208,222 —Ant. pull

thud/thump [n/v] dull crash; dull sound bang, beat, blow, clonk, clout, clump, clunk, fall, flutter, hammer, hit, knock, plop, poke, pound, pounding, pulse, rap, slap, smack, strike, throb, thunk*, thwack*, wallop*, whack*; CONCEPTS 65,181,189

thug [n] hoodlum assassin, bandit, bully, criminal, delinquent, gang member, gangster, goon*, gorilla*, gunman, hired killer, hood, hooligan, killer, mobster, murderer, professional killer, punk, rioter, rowdy, ruffian, troublemaker; CONCEPT 412

thumbnail [adj] condensed abbreviated, abridged, brief, compact, concise, contracted, curtailed, epigrammatic, short, short and sweet*, succinct, summary, to the point, truncated; CONCEPT 773

thunder [n] crashing sound barrage, blast, boom, booming, cannonade, clap, cracking, crash, crashing, detonation, discharge, drumfire, explosion, fulmination, outburst, peal, pealing, roar, rumble, rumbling, thunderbolt, thundercrack, uproar; CONCEPTS 524,595

thunder [v1] boom, crash blast, clamor, clap, crack, deafen, detonate, drum, explode, peal, resound, reverberate, roar, rumble, storm; CONCEPTS 65,521,526

thunder [v2] yell at bark, bellow, curse, declaim, denounce, fulminate, gnarl, growl, rail, roar, shout, snarl, threaten, utter threat; CONCEPTS 52,54

thunderstruck [adj] amazed, astonished agape, aghast, astounded, awestruck, bowled over*, confounded, dazed, dismayed, dumbfounded, flabbergasted, floored, overwhelmed, petrified, shocked, staggered, startled, stunned; CONCEPTS 403,690

thus [adv1] in this manner along these lines, as follows, hence, in kind, in such a way, in this fashion, in this way, just like that, like so, like this, so, thus and so, thus and thus, thusly, to such a degree; CONCEPT 544

thus [adv2] accordingly consequently, ergo, for this reason, hence, on that account, so, then, therefore, thereupon; CONCEPT 544

thwart [v] stop, hinder baffle, balk, beat, bilk, check, circumvent, confuse, counter, crab*, cramp, crimp, cross, curb, dash, defeat, disappoint, ditch, dodge, double-cross*, duck, foil, foul up*, frustrate, give the slip*, hold up, impede, louse up*, match, obstruct, oppose, outwit, pit, play off, prevent, queer*, restrain, ruin, scotch*, skin, snafu*, stymie, take down, take wind out of*, trammel, upset, upset one's apple cart*; CONCEPTS *121,130* —*Ant.* aid, assist, encourage, forward, help

tiara [*n*] *crown* chaplet, circlet, coronal, coronet, crown jewels, diadem, garland, headband, headdress, miter, royal crown, wreath; CONCEPT *452*

tic [*n*] *spasm* contraction, fit, jerk, twitch; CONCEPT *308*

tick [*n1*] *clicking sound; one beat* beat, blow, clack, click, clicking, flash, instant, metallic sound, minute, moment, pulsation, pulse, rap, second, shake, tap, tapping, throb, ticktock, twinkling, wink; CONCEPTS *595,808,810*

tick [*n2*] *checkmark* check, cross, dash, flick, indication, line, mark, stroke, X*; CONCEPT *284*

tick [*v*] *click* beat, clack, pulsate, tap, thump, ticktock; CONCEPTS *65,189*

ticket [*n*] *authorization on paper* admission, badge, board, card, certificate, check, chit, coupon, credential, docket, document, invite, key, label, license, marker, note, notice, open sesame, paper, pass, passage, passport, password, permit, raincheck, receipt, record, slip, sticker, stub, tab, tag, token, voucher; CONCEPTS *271,685*

tickle [*v*] *make laugh* amuse, brush, caress, convulse, delight, divert, enchant, entertain, excite, gratify, itch, pat, pet, please, stimulate, stroke, thrill, tingle, titillate, touch, vellicate; CONCEPTS *7,22,612*

ticklish [*adj*] *difficult, tricky* awkward, capricious, chancy, changeable, critical, dangerous, delicate, fickle, inconstant, mercurial, nice, precarious, risky, rocky, temperamental, thorny, touchy, trying, uncertain, unstable, unsteady, variable, volatile; CONCEPTS *548,565* —*Ant.* easy, straightforward, unproblematic

tidbit [*n*] *tiny portion* bit, bite, delicacy, goody*, morsel, mouthful, snack, soupçon, titbit, treat; CONCEPTS *458,835* —*Ant.* lot

tide [*n*] *flow, current* course, direction, drag, drift, ebb, eddy, flood, flux, movement, race, run, rush, sluice, spate, stream, tendency, torrent, trend, undercurrent, undertow, vortex, wave, whirlpool; CONCEPT *514*

tide over [*v*] *help along* aid, assist, bridge the gap*, keep head above water*, keep one going, see through; CONCEPT *110* —*Ant.* hinder, hurt

tidings [*n*] *greetings, news* advice, bulletin, communication, dirt, information, intelligence, message, report, word; CONCEPT *274*

tidy [*adj1*] *clean, neat* apple-pie order*, businesslike, chipper*, cleanly, in good shape, methodical, neat as a pin*, ordered, orderly, shipshape*, sleek, snug, spick-and-span*, spruce, systematic, to rights*, trim, uncluttered, well-groomed, well-kept, well-ordered; CONCEPTS *485,585,621* —*Ant.* chaotic, dirty, disordered, disorganized, littered, messy, sloppy, slovenly, unclean, untidy

tidy [*adj2*] *considerable* ample, fair, generous, good, goodly, handsome, healthy, large, largish, respectable, sizable, substantial, vast; CONCEPTS *762,781* —*Ant.* inconsequential, inconsiderable, little, small, unsubstantial

tidy [*v*] *make neat and orderly* clean, clear the decks*, fix up, frame*, get act together*,

groom, neaten, order, police, pull together, put in good shape, put in order, put in shape, put to rights*, shape up, spruce, spruce up*, straighten, straighten up, tauten, whip into shape*; CONCEPT *250* —*Ant.* dirty, dishevel, disorder, disorganize, jumble, litter

tie [*n1*] *fastening* attachment, band, bandage, bond, brace, connection, cord, fastener, fetter, gag, hookup, joint, knot, ligament, ligature, link, network, nexus, outfit, rope, strap, string, tackle, tie-in, tie-up, yoke, zipper; CONCEPT *680*

tie [*n2*] *deadlock* dead heat*, draw, drawn battle*, equivalence, even game, level, photo finish*, push, stalemate, standoff; CONCEPTS *364,667* —*Ant.* loss, win

tie [*n3*] *relationship* affiliation, allegiance, association, bond, commitment, connection, duty, hookup, kinship, liaison, network, obligation, outfit, tie-in; CONCEPT *388* —*Ant.* break, divorce

tie [*v1*] *connect, interlace* anchor, attach, band, bind, cinch, clinch, do up, fasten, gird, join, knot, lash, link, make a bow, make a hitch, make a knot, make fast, marry, moor, rivet, rope, secure, splice, tether, tie up, tighten, truss, unite, wed; CONCEPTS *85,160,193* —*Ant.* detach, disconnect, loose, loosen, unfasten, unlace, untie

tie [*v2*] *equal* balance, be even, be neck and neck*, be on a par, break even*, deadlock*, draw, even up, keep up with, match, measure up, meet, parallel, rival, touch; CONCEPTS *92,667* —*Ant.* fail, fall behind, go ahead, lose, succeed, surpass

tie/tie up [*v3*] *hamper, hinder* bind, clog, confine, curb, delay, entrammel, fetter, hog-tie*, hold, leash, limit, lock up, obstruct, restrain, restrict, shackle, stop, tie one's hands*, trammel; CONCEPT *130* —*Ant.* aid, assist, encourage, free, help

tier [*n*] *level* bank, category, class, course, echelon, file, grade, group, grouping, layer, league, line, order, pigeonhole*, queue, range, rank, row, series, story, stratum, string; CONCEPTS *378,727,744*

tiff [*n*] *argument* altercation, bad mood, bickering, difference, disagreement, dispute, falling-out*, fit, huff*, miff*, pet, quarrel, row*, run-in*, scrap, spat, squabble, sulk, tantrum, temper, words*, wrangle; CONCEPTS *46,674* —*Ant.* agreement, harmony

tight [*adj1*] *close, snug* bound, clasped, close-fitting, compact, constricted, contracted, cramped, crowded, dense, drawn, enduring, established, fast, firm, fixed, hidebound, inflexible, invulnerable, narrow, quick, rigid, secure, set, skintight, solid, stable, steady, stiff, strained, stretched, strong, sturdy, taut, tenacious, tense, thick, tightened, unbending, unyielding; CONCEPTS *483,485* —*Ant.* comfortable, free, loose, open, slack

tight [*adj2*] *sealed* airtight, blind, blocked, bolted, choking, clumped, cramping, crushing, cutting, fast, fastened, firm, fixed, hermetic, hermetically sealed, impenetrable, impermeable, impervious, locked, nailed, obstructed, padlocked, pinching, plugged, proof, secure, short, shrunken, shut, skintight, slammed, smothering, snapped, sound, stopped up, tied,

tied up, uncomfortable, watertight; CONCEPTS 489,576 —*Ant.* loose, open, unsealed, wide

tight [*adj3*] *stingy* cheap, close, grasping, mean, miserly, parsimonious, penny-pinching*, penurious, sparing, tightfisted; CONCEPTS 334, 401 —*Ant.* free, giving

tight [*adj4*] *difficult, troublesome* arduous, close, critical, dangerous, distressing, disturbing, exacting, hazardous, near, perilous, precarious, punishing, rough, sticky, tense, ticklish, tough, tricky, trying, upsetting, worrisome; CONCEPTS 548,565 —*Ant.* easy, untroubled

tight [*adj5*] *intoxicated* boozy*, buzzed*, drunk, drunken, high*, inebriated, loaded*, pickled*, plastered*, smashed*, stewed*, stoned*, tipsy, under the influence; CONCEPTS 401,406 —*Ant.* sober

tighten [*v*] *constrict* bind, clench, close, compress, condense, congeal, contract, cramp, crush, fasten, fix, grip, harden, narrow, pinch, pressure, rigidify, screw, secure, squeeze, stiffen, strain, strangle, stretch, tauten, tense, toughen; CONCEPTS 250,469,697 —*Ant.* free, let go, loose, loosen, relax, release

tightfisted [*adj*] *cheap* chintzy*, closefisted, economical, frugal, greedy, mean, mingy, miserly, money-conscious, parsimonious, penny-pinching, pennywise*, penurious, pinchpenny*, saving, scrimping, stingy, thrifty, tight*, tightwad*, ungenerous; CONCEPTS 326, 332,334,401

tight-lipped [*adj*] *silent* buttoned up*, clammed up*, closemouthed, dumb, hushed, mum, mute, muted, not talkative, quiet, reserved, restrained, reticent, secretive, taciturn, tongue-tied, zipped; CONCEPT 594

tightwad [*n*] *miser* cheapskate*, churl, hoarder, moneygrubber*, penny-pincher*, pinchfist*, pinchpenny*, Scrooge*, skinflint, stiff; CONCEPTS 348,412,423

till [*n*] *cash box* box, cash drawer, cash register, kitty*, money box, safe, tray, treasury, vault; CONCEPT 339

till [*v*] *cultivate land* dig, dress, farm, grow, harrow, hoe, labor, mulch, plant, plough, plow, prepare, raise crops, sow, tend, turn, turn over, work; CONCEPTS 253,257 —*Ant.* plant, sow

tilt [*n1*] *lean, slope* angle, cant, dip, drop, fall, grade, gradient, inclination, incline, leaning, list, pitch, rake, slant, slide; CONCEPT 738

tilt [*n2*] *fight* attack, bout, clash, collision, combat, conflict, contest, duel, encounter, fracas, joust, meet, scrimmage, scuffle, set-to, skirmish, struggle, tournament, tourney, tussle; CONCEPT 106 —*Ant.* agreement, surrender

tilt [*v1*] *lean, slant* bend, cant, careen, dip, heel, incline, list, lurch, pitch, rake, recline, seesaw, set at an angle, shift, slope, slouch, swag, sway, tip, turn, yaw; CONCEPT 147 —*Ant.* straighten

tilt [*v2*] *attack, fight* break, charge, clash, combat, contend, cross swords*, duel, encounter, joust, overthrow, spar, thrust; CONCEPT 106 —*Ant.* surrender, yield

timber [*n*] *trees, wood* balk, beam, board, boom, club, forest, frame, girder, grove, hardwood, log, mast, plank, pole, rafter, rib, stake, timberland, weald, woodland, woodlot, woods; CONCEPTS 430,479

time [*n1*] *temporal length of event or entity's* existence, period age, allotment, bit, bout, chronology, clock, continuance, date, day, duration, epoch, era, eternity, extent, future, generation, go*, hour, infinity, instance, instant, interval, juncture, lastingness, life, life span, lifetime, many a moon*, moment, month, occasion, pace, past, point, present, season, second, shift, space, span, spell, stage, stint, stretch, tempo, term, tide, tour, turn, week, while, year; CONCEPTS 801,806,809,819,823

time [*n2*] *opportunity* break, chance, heyday, look-in*, occasion, opening, peak, shot, show, squeak*; CONCEPT 693

time-honored [*adj*] *traditional* accustomed, ancestral, classic, classical, conventional, customary, fixed, folk, historic, long-established, old, popular, regular, rooted, standard, taken for granted, universal, usual, vintage, widespread; CONCEPTS 530,533,547

timeless [*adj*] *eternal* abiding, ageless, always, amaranthine, constant, continual, continued, dateless, deathless, endless, enduring, everlasting, forever, illimitable, immemorial, immortal, indefinite, infinite, lasting, never-ending, perennial, permanent, perpetual, persistent, undying, unending, without end; CONCEPTS 482,798

timely [*adj*] *at the right time* appropriate, auspicious, convenient, favorable, fit, fitting, in good time*, in the nick of time*, judicious, likely, meet, modern, now, opportune, pat, promising, prompt, proper, propitious, prosperous, punctual, seasonable, suitable, timeous, towardly, up-to-date, up-to-the-minute, well-timed, with it*; CONCEPTS 558,799 —*Ant.* inappropriate, inopportune, unsuitable, untimely

timetable [*n*] *schedule* agenda, appointments, calendar, chart, chronology, docket, itinerary, list, order of business, plan, program, record; CONCEPTS 271,283,660

timid [*adj*] *shy* afraid, ambivalent, apprehensive, badgered, bashful, browbeaten, bullied, capricious, cowardly, cowed, cowering, coy, daunted, demure, diffident, fainthearted, fearful, feeble, frightened, gentle, having cold feet*, humble, intimidated, irresolute, milquetoast, modest, mousy, nervous, pusillanimous, retiring, shaky, shrinking, soft, spineless, spiritless, submissive, timid, timorous, trembling, unassertive, unassured, unnerved, vacillating, wavering, weak, yellow*; CONCEPT 401 —*Ant.* bold, brave, daring, extroverted, fearless

tinge [*n1*] *color* cast, colorant, coloration, coloring, dye, dyestuff, hue, nib, pigment, shade, stain, tincture, tint, tone, wash; CONCEPT 622 —*Ant.* white

tinge [*n2*] *hint* bit, dash, drop, intimation, nib, pinch, shade, smack, smattering, soupçon, sprinkling, strain, streak, suggestion, tincture, touch, trace; CONCEPTS 529,831 —*Ant.* information

tinge [*v*] *color* complexion, dye, imbue, impregnate, infiltrate, saturate, shade, stain, streak, suffuse, tincture, tint; CONCEPT 250 —*Ant.* pale, whiten

tingle [*v*] *feel tickled, itchy* creep, get excited, have goose bumps*, itch, prickle, shiver, sting, thrill, throb, tickle, twitter; CONCEPT 612

tinker [*v*] *fiddle with* dabble, doodle*, fix, mess*, mess with*, monkey*, muck about*, niggle*, play, play with, puddle, putter, repair, take apart, toy, trifle with; CONCEPTS 87,212 —*Ant.* leave alone

tinkle [v] *jingle, ring* chime, chink, chinkle, clink, ding, jangle, make bell sound, plink, sound, ting, tingle, tintinnabulate; CONCEPT 65

tint [n] *shade of color* cast, chroma, color, coloration, complexion, dash, dye, flush, glow, hint, hue, luminosity, pigmentation, rinse, stain, suggestion, taint, tinct, tincture, tinge, tone, touch, trace, wash; CONCEPT 622 —*Ant.* white

tint [v] *color with a certain shade* affect, complexion, dye, influence, rinse, shade, stain, taint, tincture, tinge, touch, wash; CONCEPT 250 —*Ant.* pale, whiten

tiny [adj] *very small* bitsy*, bitty, diminutive, infinitesimal, insignificant, itsy-bitsy*, itty-bitty*, Lilliputian, little, microscopic, midget, mini*, miniature, minikin, minimum, minuscular, minuscule, minute, negligible, pee-wee*, petite, pint-sized*, pocket, pocket-size*, puny, slight, teensy*, teensy-weensy*, teeny*, trifling, wee, yea big*; CONCEPTS 762,773,789 —*Ant.* big, enormous, gigantic, great, huge, large, vast

tip/tipoff [n1] *inside information* bang*, bug*, buzz*, clue, cue, dope*, forecast, hint, in*, information, inkling, inside wire, knowledge, news, point, pointer, prediction, prompt, secret information, steer*, suggestion, two cents' worth*, warning, whisper, word, word of advice, word to the wise*; CONCEPT 274 —*Ant.* silence

tip [n2] *very top* apex, cap, crown, cusp, edge, end, extremity, head, nip, peak, point, stub, summit, tiptop, vertex; CONCEPT 836 —*Ant.* bottom, nadir

tip [n3] *gratuity paid* compensation, cue, fee, gift, handout, lagniappe, money, one-way*, perk, perquisite, pourboire, reward, small change, something*, sweetener; CONCEPT 344

tip [v1] *knock over; cause to lean* bend, cant, capsize, careen, dump, empty, heel, incline, lean, list, overset, overturn, pour, recline, shift, slant, slope, spill, tilt, topple, topple over, turn over, unload, upend, upset, upturn; CONCEPTS 189,201,208 —*Ant.* straighten

tip [v2] *give inside information* advise, caution, clue, cue, forewarn, give a clue, give a hint, give the low-down*, hint, prompt, steer, suggest, tip off, warn; CONCEPT 60 —*Ant.* conceal, hide

tipsy [adj] *inebriated* addled, dazed, drunk, drunken, fuddled, happy, high*, intoxicated, irrigated*, lit*, loaded*, mellow, merry, stewed*, tight, unsteady, woozy; CONCEPTS 401,406 —*Ant.* sober

tirade [n] *abuse, outburst* anger, berating, censure, condemnation, denunciation, diatribe, dispute, fulmination, harangue, invective, jeremiad*, lecture, malediction, philippic*, ranting, revilement, screed, sermon, tonguelashing*, vituperation; CONCEPTS 44,54,278 —*Ant.* calm, harmony, peace

tire [v] *exhaust, weary* annoy, bore, burn out*, bush*, collapse, crawl, debilitate, deject, depress, disgust, dishearten, dispirit, displease, distress, drain, droop, drop, enervate, ennui, exasperate, fag, fail, faint, fatigue, flag, fold,

give out, go stale, grow weary, harass, irk, irritate, jade, nauseate, overburden, overstrain, overtax, overwork, pain, pall, peter out*, poop out*, prostrate, put to sleep, sap, sicken, sink, strain, tax, vex, weaken, wear, wear down, wear out, wilt, worry, yawn*; CONCEPTS 13, 14,469 —*Ant.* activate, energize, fire up, invigorate, refresh

tired [adj] *exhausted, weary* all in*, annoyed, asleep, beat*, bored, broken-down, burned out*, collapsing, consumed, dead on one's feet*, distressed, dog-tired*, done for*, done in*, drained, drooping, droopy, drowsy, empty, enervated, exasperated, fagged, faint, fatigued, fed up*, finished, flagging, haggard, irked, irritated, jaded, narcoleptic, overtaxed, overworked, petered out*, played out*, pooped*, prostrated, run-down, sick of, sleepy, spent, stale, tuckered out*, wasted, worn, worn out; CONCEPTS 314,403,406 —*Ant.* activated, active, energized, fired up, fresh, invigorated, refreshed, rested

tireless [adj] *determined* active, ball of fire*, eager, energetic, enthusiastic, grind, hard-working*, hyper*, incessant, indefatigable, industrious, jumping, on the go*, perky, persevering, resolute, steadfast, strenuous, unflagging, untiring, unwearied, unwearying, vigorous; CONCEPTS 538,542 —*Ant.* beat, tired, unenthusiastic, weary, worn out

tiresome [adj] *irritating, exasperating* a bit much*, annoying, arduous, boresome, boring, burdensome, demanding, difficult, drag, dragging, drudging, dull, enervative, exacting, exhausting, fatiguing, flat, hard, heavy, hefty, ho-hum*, humdrum, irksome, jading, laborious, monotonous, nowhere, onerous, oppressive, strenuous, tedious, tired, tiring, too much*, tough, trying, uncool*, uninteresting, unrelieved, vexatious, wearing, wearisome, wearying, yawn*; CONCEPTS 529,537,538 —*Ant.* easy, facile, fun, nice, stimulating

titanic [adj] *gigantic, very large* Brobdingnagian*, colossal, elephantine, enormous, epic, gargantuan, giant, Herculean*, huge, immense, jumbo*, larger-than-life, mammoth, massive, monstrous, monumental, titan, towering, tremendous, vast; CONCEPTS 491,773,779,781

titillate [v] *excite, stimulate* amuse, arouse, entertain, grab, grapple, hook, interest, palpate, provoke, switch on, tantalize, tease, thrill, tickle, tickle pink*, turn on; CONCEPTS 7,11,22 —*Ant.* disenchant, repulse, turn off

title [n1] *heading, label* appellation, banner, caption, close, description, head, headline, inscription, legend, name, rubric, salutation, sign, streamer, style, subtitle; CONCEPT 283

title [n2] *name* appellation, appellative, brand, cognomen, denomination, designation, epithet, handle*, honorific, label, moniker*, nom de plume, nomen, pseudonym, sobriquet, style, tab*, tag*, term; CONCEPT 683

title [n3] *possession, laurel* authority, championship, claim, commission, crest, crown, decoration, deed, degree, desert, dibs*, due, entitlement, holding, justification, license, medal, merit, ownership, power, prerogative, pretense, pretension, privilege, proof, ribbon, right; CONCEPTS 376,710

title [v] *name* baptize, call, christen, denominate, designate, dub, entitle, label, style, term; CONCEPT 62

toady [n] *sycophant* adulator, apple polisher, ass-kisser*, backscratcher*, backslapper*, bootlicker*, brownnoser*, doormat, doter, fan, fawner, flatterer, flunky, groupie*, hanger-on*, kiss-up*, lackey, minion, teacher's pet, yes-person*; CONCEPT 423

toady [v] *fawn* apple-polish*, be servile, bootlick*, brownnose*, butter up*, cajole, fall all over, fall on one's knees*, flatter, honey up*, kiss one's feet*, kiss-up*, kowtow*, lay it on*, lick boots*, massage*, oil*, pay court*, play up to*, scratch one's back*, stroke*, suck up to*, truckle, woo*; CONCEPTS 110,384

toast [n] *salutation when drinking alcohol* acknowledgment, celebration, ceremony, commemoration, compliment, down, drink, health, honor, pledge, proposal, salute, sentiment, shingle, thanksgiving, tribute; CONCEPT 278

toast [v] *brown with heat* cook, crisp, dry, grill, heat, parch, roast, warm; CONCEPT 170

toddler [n] *baby* child, infant, kid, little one*, preschooler, rug rat*, tot, youngster; CONCEPTS 414,424

to-do [n] *commotion, excitement* agitation, bother, brouhaha*, bustle, clamor, disorder, disturbance, flap*, furor, fuss, hassle, hoo-ha*, hoopla*, hubbub*, hurly-burly*, hurrah, performance, pother, quarrel, racket, ruction, rumpus, stir, tumult, turmoil, unrest, uproar, whirl; CONCEPTS 230,674 —*Ant.* peace, rest

together [adj] *composed* calm, cool*, in sync*, stable, well-adjusted, well-balanced, well-organized; CONCEPT 542 —*Ant.* imbalanced, unstable, upset, worried

together [adv1] *as a group; all at once* all together, as one, at one fell swoop*, closely, co-incidentally, collectively, combined, commonly, concertedly, concomitantly, concurrently, conjointly, contemporaneously, en masse, hand in glove*, hand in hand*, in a body, in concert, in cooperation, in one breath*, in sync*, in unison, jointly, mutually, on the beat*, side by side, simultaneously, synchronically, unanimously, unitedly, with one accord, with one voice, with the beat; CONCEPTS 538,544, 548 —*Ant.* apart, individually, separately

together [adv2] *in a row* consecutively, continually, continuously, in succession, night and day, one after the other, on end, running, successively, unintermittedly, without a break, without interruption; CONCEPTS 482, 585 —*Ant.* separately

toil [n] *hard work* application, drudgery, effort, exertion, industry, labor, moil, nine-to-five*, occupation, pains*, sweat, travail; CONCEPTS 100,362,677 —*Ant.* entertainment, fun, pastime

toil [v] *work hard* drive, drudge, grind, knock oneself out*, labor, moil, peg away*, plod, plug, push oneself, slave, strain, strive, struggle, sweat, tug, work, work like a dog*; CONCEPTS 100,677 —*Ant.* idle, laze, neglect

toilsome [adj] *laborious* arduous, backbreaking, burdensome, demanding, difficult, exhausting, hard, labored, onerous, operose, rough, strenuous, taxing, tiresome, uphill*; CONCEPT 538

token [n] *indication, remembrance* badge, clue, demonstration, earnest, evidence, expression, favor, gift, index, indicia, keepsake, manifestation, mark, memento, memorial, note, omen, pawn, pledge, presage, proof, relic, reminder, representation, sample, security, sign, significant, souvenir, symbol, symptom, trophy, warning, warrant; CONCEPTS 284,337,529

tolerable [adj] *acceptable, good enough* adequate, allowable, all right, average, bearable, better than nothing*, common, decent, durable, fair, fairly good, fair to middling*, goodish*, indifferent, livable, mediocre, middling*, not bad*, okay*, ordinary, passable, presentable, respectable, run-of-the-mill*, satisfactory, so-so*, sufferable, sufficient, supportable, sustainable, tidy, unexceptionable, unexceptional, unimpeachable; CONCEPTS 529,548 —*Ant.* bad, intolerable, unacceptable, unbearable

tolerance [n1] *open-mindedness* altruism, benevolence, broad-mindedness, charity, clemency, compassion, concession, endurance, forbearance, freedom, good will, grace, humanity, indulgence, kindness, lenience, leniency, lenity, liberalism, liberality, liberalness, license, magnanimity, mercifulness, mercy, patience, permission, permissiveness, sensitivity, sufferance, sympathy, toleration, understanding; CONCEPTS 410,657 —*Ant.* bias, disapproval, intolerance, narrow-mindedness, prejudice

tolerance [n2] *fortitude, grit* endurance, guts*, hardiness, hardness, opposition, patience, resilience, resistance, stamina, staying power*, steadfastness, steadiness, strength, sufferance, toughness, vigor; CONCEPT 732 —*Ant.* intolerance, weakness

tolerant [adj] *open-minded, easygoing* advanced, benevolent, big, broad, broad-minded, catholic, charitable, clement, complaisant, condoning, easy on, easy with, excusing, fair, forbearing, forgiving, free and easy*, humane, indulgent, kindhearted*, lax, lenient, liberal, long-suffering*, magnanimous, merciful, patient, permissive, progressive, radical, receptive, soft, sophisticated, sympathetic, understanding, unprejudiced, wide; CONCEPTS 403,542 —*Ant.* biased, disapproving, intolerant, narrow-minded, prejudiced

tolerate [v] *allow, indulge* abide, accept, admit, authorize, bear, bear with, blink at*, brook, condone, consent to, countenance, endure, go, go along with, have, hear, humor, live with, permit, pocket, put up with, receive, sanction, sit and take it*, sit still for*, stand, stand for, stay the course*, stomach, string along, submit to, suffer, sustain, swallow*, take, tough out*, undergo, wink at*; CONCEPTS 23,83 —*Ant.* check, disallow, disapprove, halt, stop, veto

toll [n1] *fee* assessment, charge, cost, customs, demand, duty, exaction, expense, impost, levy, payment, price, rate, tariff, tax, tribute; CONCEPT 329

toll [n2] *damage, deaths* casualties, cost, expense, inroad, loss, losses, penalty, price; CONCEPT 230

toll [v] *ring out* announce, bell, bong, call, chime, clang, knell, peal, signal, sound, strike, summon, warn; CONCEPT 65

tomb [n] *burial place* box, burial, burial chamber, catacomb, coffin, crypt, grave, mausoleum, monument, pit, sepulcher, trough, vault; CONCEPT 305

tome [n] *large, scholarly book* classic, great work, magnum opus, novel, opus, publication, reference book, schoolbook, textbook, title, tradebook, volume, work, writing; CONCEPT 280

tomfoolery [n] *nonsense* absurdity, antics, bunk, carrying-on*, clowning, craziness, folly, foolery, fooling around, foolishness, fun, funny business, giddiness, high jinks, horseplay, insanity, irresponsibility, joking, kidding around, ludicrousness, lunacy, madness, ridiculousness, senselessness, shenanigans*, silliness; CONCEPTS 230,388,633

tone [n1] *pitch, volume* accent, emphasis, force, inflection, intonation, modulation, resonance, strength, stress, timbre, tonality; CONCEPT 65

tone [n2] *attitude, spirit* air, approach, aspect, character, condition, current, drift, effect, expression, fashion, feel, frame, grain, habit, humor, manner, mind, mode, mood, movement, nature, note, quality, state of things, strain, style, temper, tenor, trend, vein; CONCEPTS 655, 673,682

tone [n3] *color* blend, cast, coloration, hue, shade, tinge, tint, value; CONCEPT 622

tone [n4] *condition of the body* elasticity, health, healthiness, resiliency, strength, tonicity, tonus, vigor; CONCEPT 316

tone down [v] *moderate* chill out*, cloud, dampen, darken, deaden, deepen, dim, mitigate, modulate, play down, reduce, restrain, shade, sober, soften, soft-pedal*, subdue, temper; CONCEPT 240 —Ant. aggravate, increase, raise

tongue [n] *language* argot, articulation, dialect, discourse, expression, idiom, lingo, parlance, patois, speech, talk, utterance, vernacular, voice; CONCEPT 276

tongue-in-cheek [adj] *facetious* amusing, blithe, clever, comic, comical, dry, farcical, flip*, flippant, funny, humorous, in fun, in jest, ironic, ironical, irreverent, jesting, jocular, joking, joshing, laughable, not serious, playful, pulling one's leg*, putting one on*, sarcastic, satirical, smart, whimsical, wisecracking, witty; CONCEPT 267

tongue-tied [adj] *speechless* aghast, amazed, astounded, at a loss for words, bashful, choked up, dazed, dumbfounded, dumbstruck, inarticulate, mum, mute, shocked, shy, silent, stammering, uncommunicative, voiceless; CONCEPT 267

tonic [n] *restorative drink, medicine* analeptic, boost, bracer, conditioner, cordial, drug, fillip, invigorator, livener, pick-me-up*, pickup, refresher, restorative, roborant, shot in the arm*, stimulant, strengthener; CONCEPT 307

too [adv1] *also* additionally, along, as well, besides, further, furthermore, in addition, into the bargain, likewise, more, moreover, to boot, withal; CONCEPTS 544,771

too [adv2] *excessively* awfully, beyond, ever, exceptionally, exorbitantly, extremely, greatly, highly, immensely, immoderately, in excess, inordinately, notably, over, over and above, overly, overmuch, remarkably, strikingly, unconsciously, unduly, unreasonably, very; CONCEPTS 569,772 —Ant. little

tool [n1] *instrument used to shape, form, finish* apparatus, appliance, contraption, contrivance, device, engine, gadget, gizmo*, implement, job, machine, means, mechanism, utensil, weapon, whatchamacallit*; CONCEPT 499

tool [n2] *person who allows himself to be used* accessory, accomplice, agent, auxiliary, chump*, creature, dupe, easy mark*, figurehead, flunky*, go-between, greenhorn*, hireling, idiot, intermediary, jackal, lackey, mark*, medium, messenger, minion, patsy*, pawn, peon, puppet, stooge, stool pigeon*, sucker*; CONCEPTS 348,412,423

toothsome [adj] *delicious* adorable, ambrosial, appetizing, delectable, delightful, divine, flavorful, good, heavenly, luscious, lush, mouthwatering, nectarous, nice, palatable, pleasant, pleasing, rich, savory, scrumptious, sweet, tasteful, tasty, titillating, yummy*; CONCEPTS 572,613

top [adj] *best, most important; highest* apical, capital, chief, crack, crowning, culminating, dominant, elite, excellent, fine, finest, first, first-class, first-rate, five-star*, foremost, greatest, head, lead, leading, loftiest, maximal, maximum, outside, paramount, preeminent, primary, supreme, prime, principal, ruling, sovereign, superior, supreme, tiptop*, top-drawer*, topmost, top-notch, upper, uppermost; CONCEPTS 567,574,583 —Ant. least, low, lower, lowest, second-rate, unimportant

top [n1] *highest point* acme, apex, apogee, cap, capital, ceiling, climax, cork, cover, crest, crown, culmination, cusp, face, fastigium, finial, head, height, high point, lid, limit, maximum, meridian, peak, pinnacle, point, roof, spire, stopper, summit, superficies, surface, tip, utmost, vertex, zenith; CONCEPT 836 —Ant. base, bottom, foot, lowest, nadir

top [n2] *highest rank* best, captain, chief, choice, cream, elite, first place, flower, head, lead, leader, pick, pride, prime, prize, utmost; CONCEPT 668 —Ant. bottom, lowest

top [v1] *place on or reach highest part* ascend, cap, climb, cloak, clothe, cover, crest, crown, face, finish, garnish, piggyback*, protect, reinforce, roof, scale, spread over, superimpose, surmount, tip; CONCEPTS 172,201,750 —Ant. descend, drop, fall, lower

top [v2] *surpass* beat, beat, be first, best, better, blow away*, clobber*, eclipse, exceed, excel, fake out*, finagle*, fox*, go beyond, goose*, outdo, outfox, outshine, outstrip, overrun, run circles around*, shut out*, total*, transcend; CONCEPTS 95,141 —Ant. fall behind, lose

top [v3] *remove the upper part* amputate, cream, crop, curtail, cut off, decapitate, detruncate, dock, file off, lop off, pare, pollard, prune, ream, scrape off, shave off, shear, shorten, skim, trim, truncate; CONCEPT 211 —Ant. add, replace

topic [n] *subject matter* affair, argument, business, case, division, field, head, issue, material, matter, matter in hand, moot point, motif, motion, motive, point, point in question, problem, proposition, question, resolution, subject, text, theme, theorem, thesis; CONCEPT 532

topical [adj1] *current* contemporary, modern, newsworthy, nominal, popular, subjective, thematic, up-to-date; CONCEPT *820* —*Ant.* irrelevant, old, past

topical [*adj2*] *restricted, local* confined, insular, limited, parochial, particular, regional, sectional; CONCEPTS *557,583* —*Ant.* general, unrestricted

top-level [*adj*] *high-ranking, important* aristocratic, distinguished, esteemed, famous, first-class*, foremost, four-star*, front-page*, grand, high-level, high-profile, high-up, honored, illustrious, leading, majestic, major-league*, noble, notable, noted, noteworthy, powerful, preeminent, prominent, top-drawer*, top-notch*, upper-class, VIP*, well-known; CONCEPTS *555,574*

top-notch [*adj*] *first-rate* A-1, ace, blue-chip*, choice, excellent, fine, first-class, first-string*, five-star, highest quality, in a class all by itself*, prime*, sound, superior, supreme, tiptop*, top-level, uppermost, very best, very good; CONCEPT *574*

topple [*v*] *fall or knock over; overthrow* bring down, capsize, collapse, do a pratfall*, fall, falter, founder, go belly up*, go down, hit the dirt*, keel over, knock down, land, lose it*, lurch, nose-dive, oust, overbalance, overturn, pitch, plunge, slump, stagger, stumble, take a header*, teeter, tip over, totter, tumble, turn over, unhorse, unseat, upset; CONCEPTS *95,147,181,208* —*Ant.* place, put, straighten

topsy-turvy [*adj*] *mixed-up* chaotic, cluttered, cockeyed, confused, disarranged, disheveled, disjointed, dislocated, disordered, disorderly, disorganized, downside-up*, inside-out, inverted, jumbled, littered, messy, muddled, overturned, pell-mell*, riotous, tangled, tumultous/tumultuous, unhinged, untidy, upended, upside-down, upturned; CONCEPTS *485,548,585* —*Ant.* ordered, organized, straight

torment [*n*] *severe mental distress* affliction, agony, anguish, annoyance, bane, bother, excruciation, harassment, hell, irritation, misery, nag, nagging, nuisance, pain, pain in the neck*, persecution, pest, plague, provocation, rack, scourge, suffering, torture, trouble, vexation, worry; CONCEPTS *410,728* —*Ant.* contentment, glee, happiness, joy

torment [*v*] *be or make very upset* abuse, afflict, agonize, annoy, bait, bedevil, bone, bother, break, crucify, devil, distress, drive bananas*, drive up the wall*, excruciate, give a hard time*, harass, harrow, harry, heckle, hound, hurt, irritate, mistreat, molest, nag, pain, persecute, pester, plague, play cat and mouse*, provoke, punish, put through wringer*, rack, rub salt in wound*, smite, tease, torture, trouble, try, vex, worry, wring; CONCEPTS *7,19, 313* —*Ant.* delight, make happy, please

torn [*adj1*] *cut open* broken, burst, cleaved, cracked, damaged, divided, fractured, gashed, impaired, lacerated, mangled, ragged, rent, ripped, ruptured, severed, shabby, slashed, sliced, slit, snapped, split, wrenched; CONCEPT *485* —*Ant.* fixed, healed, mended, perfect

torn [*adj2*] *undecided* divided, irresolute, of two minds*, split, uncertain, unsure, vacillating, wavering; CONCEPTS *403,542* —*Ant.* certain, decided, resolute, sure

torpid [*adj*] *lazy, slow* apathetic, benumbed, comatose, dopey*, dormant, drowsy, dull,

faineant, heavy, hebetudinous, idle, inactive, indifferent, indolent, inert, lackadaisical, languid, languorous, latent, leaden, lethargic, listless, lymphatic, motionless, numb, paralyzed, passive, slothful, slow-moving, sluggish, slumberous, sodden, somnolent, stagnant, static, stupid, stuporous; CONCEPTS *401,538* —*Ant.* active, energetic, lively, moving, quick

torpor [*n*] *lethargy* apathy, disinterest, dormancy, drowsiness, dullness, idleness, impassivity, inaction, inactivity, languor, laziness, lifelessness, listlessness, passiveness, sleepiness, sloth, slowness, sluggishness, slumber, stupor, torpidity, torpidness; CONCEPTS *315,410,633,748*

torrent [*n*] *heavy flow* cascade, cataclysm, cataract, cloudburst, deluge, downpour, effusion, flood, flooding, flux, gush, inundation, niagara, outburst, overflow, pour, rush, shower, spate, stream, tide, waterfall; CONCEPTS *146, 179,526* —*Ant.* drip

torrid [*adj1*] *very hot* arid, austral, blazing, blistering, boiling, broiling, burning, dried, dry, fiery, heated, parched, parching, red-hot*, scalding, scorched, scorching, sizzling, stifling, sultry, sweltering, tropic, tropical; CONCEPT *605* —*Ant.* arctic, cold, freezing

torrid [*adj2*] *sensuous* ardent, blazing, burning, erotic, fervent, flaming, hot*, hot-blooded*, impassioned, intense, passionate, red-hot*, sexy, steamy*, sultry, white-hot*; CONCEPT *372* —*Ant.* cold, cool, frigid, unsensual

tortuous [*adj1*] *very twisted* anfractuous, bent, circuitous, convoluted, crooked, curved, flexuous, indirect, involute, labyrinthine, mazy, meandering, meandrous, roundabout, serpentine, sinuous, snaky, twisting, vermiculate, winding, zigzag; CONCEPT *581* —*Ant.* direct, straight, untwisted

tortuous [*adj2*] *complicated* ambiguous, convoluted, cunning, deceptive, devious, indirect, involute, involved, misleading, perverse, roundabout, tricky; CONCEPT *562* —*Ant.* easy, straightforward, uncomplicated, uninvolved

torture [*n*] *severe mental or physical pain* ache, affliction, agony, anguish, crucifixion, distress, dolor, excruciation, impalement, laceration, martyrdom, misery, pang, persecution, rack, suffering, third degree*, torment, tribulation, twinge; CONCEPTS *410,728* —*Ant.* alleviation, contentment, happiness, relief

torture [*v*] *upset or hurt severely* abuse, afflict, agonize, annoy, beat, bother, crucify, distress, disturb, excruciate, grill, harrow, impale, injure, irritate, lacerate, maim, mangle, martyr, martyrize, mistreat, mutilate, oppress, pain, persecute, rack, smite, torment, try, whip, wound, wring, wrong; CONCEPTS *7,19,246,313* —*Ant.* alleviate, make happy, please, relieve

toss [*n/v1*] *throw* bung, cast, chuck, chunk, fire, fling, flip, heave, hurl, launch, lob, peg, pitch, project, propel, sling, twirl, wing; CONCEPT *222* —*Ant.* catch

toss [*v2*] *move back and forth* agitate, agonize, bob, buffet, disturb, flounder, heave, jiggle, joggle, jolt, labor, lurch, move restlessly, oscillate, pitch, rise and fall, rock, roll, seesaw, shake, squirm, stir, sway, swing, thrash, tumble, undulate, wallow, wave, wobble, wriggle, writhe; CONCEPT 147 —*Ant.* lie still

total [*adj*] *complete, thorough* absolute, all-out, comprehensive, consummate, downright, entire, every, full, full-blown, full-scale, gross, inclusive, integral, out-and-out, outright, overall, perfect, plenary, positive, sheer, sweeping, thoroughgoing, totalitarian, unconditional, undisputed, undivided, unlimited, unmitigated, unqualified, unreserved, unrestricted, utter, whole; CONCEPTS 531,762 —*Ant.* incomplete, partial, unfinished

total [*n*] *whole* aggregate, all, amount, body, budget, bulk, entirety, flat out*, full amount, gross, jackpot*, mass, quantity, quantum, result, sum, sum total*, tale, the works*, totality; CONCEPTS 787,837 —*Ant.* part

total [*v*] *add up* add, aggregate, amount to, calculate, cast, come, come to, comprise, consist of, equal, figure, foot, mount up to, number, pile up, reach, reckon, result in, ring up*, run into, run to, stack up, summate, sum up, totalize, tote*, yield; CONCEPT 764 —*Ant.* subtract, take away

totalitarian [*adj*] *dictatorial* absolute, authoritarian, autocratic, communist*, despotic, fascistic, monolithic, Nazi*, one-party, oppressive, total, totalistic, tyrannical, undemocratic; CONCEPT 536 —*Ant.* democratic

totally [*adv*] *completely* absolutely, all, all in all, altogether, comprehensively, consummately, entirely, exactly, exclusively, flat out*, full blast*, fully, in toto*, just, perfectly, quite, thoroughly, top to bottom*, unconditionally, unmitigatedly, utterly, wholeheartedly, wholly; CONCEPT 531 —*Ant.* incompletely, partially

totter [*v*] *move falteringly* blunder, careen, dodder, falter, flounder, hesitate, lurch, quake, quiver, reel, rock, roll, seesaw, shake, shimmy, slide, slip, stagger, stammer, stumble, sway, teeter, topple, tremble, trip, walk unsteadily, waver, weave, wheel, wobble, zigzag; CONCEPT 151

touch [*n1*] *physical contact* blow, brush, caress, collision, communication, contact, contingence, crash, cuddling, embrace, feel, feeling, fondling, graze, grope, handling, hit, hug, impact, junction, kiss, lick, manipulation, nudge, palpation, pat, peck, perception, percussion, petting, push, rub, rubbing, scratch, shock, stroke, stroking, tactility, taction, tap, taste, touching; CONCEPTS 590,608,612

touch [*n2*] *tiny amount* bit, dash, detail, drop, hint, inkling, intimation, jot, pinch, scent, shade, smack, small amount, smattering, soupçon, speck, spot, streak, suggestion, suspicion, taste, tincture, tinge, trace, whiff; CONCEPTS 529,831,832 —*Ant.* lot

touch [*n3*] *manner, method* ability, adeptness, adroitness, approach, art, artistry, awareness, characteristic, command, communication, contact, deftness, direction, effect, facility, faculty, familiarity, finish, flair, hand, handiwork, influence, knack, mastery, skill, style, talent, technique, trademark, understanding, virtuosity, way; CONCEPTS 6,630,655

touch [*v1*] *make physical contact* abut, adjoin, be in contact, border, brush, butt on, caress,

come together, communicate, contact, converge, dab, examine, feel, feel up*, finger, fondle, frisk, glance, graze, grope, handle, hit, impinge upon, inspect, join, kiss, lay a finger on*, lick, line, manipulate, march, massage, meet, neighbor, osculate, palm, palpate, partake, pat, paw, percuss, pet, probe, push, reach, rub, scrutinize, sip, smooth, strike, stroke, suck, sweep, tag, tap, taste, thumb, tickle, tip, toy, verge; CONCEPT 612 —*Ant.* cower, shrink, shy away

touch [*v2*] *have an effect on* affect, arouse, carry, disturb, excite, feel out, get through to*, get to*, grab, impress, influence, inspire, make an impression*, mark, melt, move, quicken, soften, stimulate, stir, strike, strike a chord*, stroke, sway, tug at the heart*, upset; CONCEPTS 7,19,22

touch [*v3*] *have to do with; regard* affect, be a party to, bear on, bear upon, be associated with, belong to, center upon, concern, concern oneself with, consume, deal with, drink, eat, get involved in, handle, interest, involve, partake of, pertain to, refer to, use, utilize; CONCEPT 532

touch [*v4*] *make mention* allude to, bring in, cover, deal with, discuss, go over, mention, note, refer to, speak of, treat; CONCEPT 51 —*Ant.* secrete

touch [*v5*] *compare with; correspond to* amount, approach, be a match for*, be in the same league*, be on a par*, come near, come to, come up to, equal, hold a candle to*, match, measure up, meet, parallel, partake of, rival, tie, verge on; CONCEPT 561

touched [*adj1*] *deeply moved emotionally* affected, disturbed, grabbed*, impressed, melted*, softened, stirred, swayed, turned on by*, turned on to*, upset; CONCEPTS 403,542 —*Ant.* unemotional, unmoved, untouched

touched [*adj2*] *crazy* batty*, bizarre, bonkers*, cuckoo*, daft, eccentric, fanatic, flighty, insane, neurotic, not all there*, not right*, nuts*, nutty*, obsessed, out of one's mind*, peculiar, pixilated, queer, unhinged; CONCEPTS 402,403 —*Ant.* ok, sane, well

touching [*adj1*] *affecting, moving emotionally* compassionate, emotive, heartbreaking, heart-rending, impressive, melting, mind-blowing*, pathetic, piteous, pitiable, pitiful, poignant, responsive, sad, stirring, stunning, sympathetic, tear-jerking, tender, wistful; CONCEPTS 529,537 —*Ant.* unaffecting, unmoving

touch up [*v*] *fix up; improve* amend, brush up, do up, enhance, finish off, give a face-lift*, gloss, make improvements, modify, patch up, perfect, polish, put finishing touches on*, remodel, renew, renovate, repair, retouch, revamp, rework, round off, tease*; CONCEPTS 212,244 —*Ant.* break, damage, harm, hurt

touchy [*adj*] *easily offended* bad-tempered, bundle of nerves*, cantankerous, captious, choleric, crabbed, cranky, cross, delicate, dicey*, grouchy, grumpy, hazardous, hypersensitive, irascible, irritable, jumpy*, mean, ornery*, oversensitive, peevish, perturbable, pettish, petulant, precarious, querulous, quick-tempered, risky, sensitive, splenetic, surly, temperamental, testy, thin-skinned*, ticklish*, tricky, unpredictable, unsafe, uptight*, volatile, wired up*, wound up*; CONCEPTS *401,542,548* —*Ant.* calm, easygoing, laid-back, unflappable

tough [*adj1*] *sturdy, strong* brawny, cohesive, conditioned, dense, durable, fibrous, firm, fit, flinty, hard, hard as nails*, hard-bitten*, hardened, hardy, healthy, indigestible, inflexible, leathery, lusty, mighty, molded, resilient, resistant, rigid, robust, rugged, seasoned, sinewy, solid, stalwart, steeled, stiff, stout, strapping, tenacious, tight, tough as nails*, unbreakable, unyielding, vigorous, withstanding; CONCEPTS *314,489* —*Ant.* delicate, fragile, unstable, vulnerable, weak, wobbly

tough [*adj2*] *obstinate, rough* adamant, arbitrary, callous, confirmed, cruel, desperate, drastic, exacting, ferocious, fierce, firm, fixed, hard, hard-bitten*, hard-boiled*, hard-line*, hard-nosed*, hard-shelled*, harsh, headstrong, immutable, inflexible, intractable, merciless, narrow, obdurate, pugnacious, refractory, resolute, ruffianly, ruthless, savage, severe, stern, stiff, strict, stubborn, taut, terrible, unalterable, unbending, uncompromising, uncontrollable, unforgiving, unmanageable, unyielding, vicious, violent; CONCEPTS *403,542* —*Ant.* gentle, kind, nice, tender

tough [*adj3*] *difficult, laborious* arduous, backbreaking*, baffling, burdensome, demanding, effortful, exacting, exhausting, exigent, grievous, hairy*, handful*, hard, heavy, intractable, intricate, irksome, knotty*, labored, mean, no piece of cake*, onerous, oppressive, perplexing, puzzling, resisting, severe, stiff, strenuous, taxing, thorny, toilsome, troublesome, trying, unyielding, uphill*, weighty*, wicked; CONCEPTS *538,565* —*Ant.* controllable, easy, facile

tough [*n*] *person who is rowdy, mean* bruiser, brute, bully, criminal, gangster, goon*, hood*, hoodlum, hooligan, punk*, rough*, roughneck, rowdy, ruffian, thug, villain; CONCEPT *412*

toughen [*v*] *harden* acclimate, acclimatize, anneal, brutalize, climatize, develop, inure, make difficult, season, strengthen, temper; CONCEPTS *202,250* —*Ant.* flex, soften, tenderize

toupee [*n*] *wig* false hair, hair extension, hair implant, hairpiece, hair weaving, periwig, peruke, postiche, rug*; CONCEPT *392*

tour [*n*] *journey; stint* bout*, circle tour*, circuit, course, cruise, excursion, expedition, getaway*, go*, hitch*, hop*, jaunt*, junket, outing, overnight*, peregrination, progress, road, round*, roundabout*, round trip, run, shift, spell, stretch, stump*, swing* time, travel, trek, trick*, trip, turn, voyage, weekend, whistle-stop*; CONCEPTS *81,224,807*

tour [*v*] *visit, journey* barnstorm*, cruise, explore, globe-trot*, go on the road*, holiday*, hop*, jaunt, jet, junket, peregrinate, sightsee, stump*, swing*, take a trip, travel, vacation, voyage; CONCEPTS *224,227*

tour de force [*n*] *great achievement* accomplishment, attainment, conquest, deed, exploit, masterpiece, performance, stroke of genius, success, triumph, victory; CONCEPTS *1,706*

tourist [*n*] *person who visits a place* daytripper, excursionist, globetrotter, jet-setter, journeyer, rubberneck*, sightseer, stranger, traveler, tripper*, vacationist, visitor, voyager,

wayfarer; CONCEPT *423* —*Ant.* inhabitant, local, native

tournament [*n*] *sporting competition* clash, contest, duel, event, fight, games, joust, match, meet, meeting, series, sport, test, tilt, tourney; CONCEPT *363*

tousled [*adj*] *disarrayed* beat-up*, dirty, disarranged, disheveled, disordered, grubby*, messed-up*, messy, mussed-up*, ruffled, rumpled, sloppy, tangled, uncombed, unkempt; CONCEPTS *485,589* —*Ant.* kempt, neat, ordered

tout [*v*] *brag about, show off* acclaim, ballyhoo*, boost, give a boost*, herald, laud, plug*, praise, proclaim, promote, publicize, push, steer, tip, tip off*, trumpet; CONCEPTS *69,138* —*Ant.* conceal, hide

tow [*v*] *pull along* drag, draw, ferry, haul, lug, propel, push, trail, trawl, tug, yank; CONCEPT *206* —*Ant.* push

toward/towards [*prep1*] *on the way to; near* against, almost, approaching, close to, coming up, contra, en route, facing, for, fronting, headed for, in relation to, in the direction of, in the vicinity, just before, moving, nearing, nearly, not quite, on the road to, over against, pointing to, proceeding, shortly before, to, via, vis-à-vis; CONCEPT *586*

toward/towards [*prep2*] *concerning* about, against, anent, apropos, as for, as to, for, in re, re, regarding, with regard to, with respect to; CONCEPT *532*

tower [*n*] *very high building or building part* belfry, castle, citadel, cloud buster*, column, fort, fortification, fortress, high rise*, keep, lookout, mast, minaret, monolith, obelisk, pillar, refuge, skyscraper, spire, steeple, stronghold, turret; CONCEPTS *439,440*

tower [*v*] *rise above* ascend, be above, dominate, exceed, extend above, look down, look over, loom, mount, overlook, overtop, rear, soar, surmount, surpass, top, transcend; CONCEPTS *141,752*

towering [*adj*] *huge, excessive* aerial, airy, colossal, elevated, extraordinary, extravagant, extreme, fantastic, gigantic, great, high, immoderate, imperial, imposing, impressive, inordinate, intense, lofty, magnificent, massive, mighty, monumental, outstanding, paramount, preeminent, prodigious, skyscraping, soaring, spiring, stately, stupendous, sublime, superior, supreme, surpassing, tall, towery, transcendent, tremendous, ultimate, undue, unmatchable, unmeasurable; CONCEPTS *567,779* —*Ant.* dwarfed, little, minor, short, small, tiny

town [*n*] *incorporated community* apple*, boondocks, borough, burg*, city, hamlet, metropolis, municipality, seat, sticks*, township, whistle-stop*; CONCEPTS *507,508*

toxic [*adj*] *poisonous* baneful, deadly, harmful, lethal, mephitic, noxious, pernicious, pestiltial, poison, septic, toxicant, venomous, virulent; CONCEPT *537* —*Ant.* harmless, nonpoisonous

toxin [*n*] *poison* blight, cancer, contagion, contamination, germ, infection, noxious substance, poisonous substance, toxicant, toxoid, venom, virus; CONCEPTS *307,475,674,675*

toy [*n*] *entertainment article* bauble, curio, doll, game, knickknack, novelty, plaything, trifle, trinket; CONCEPT *446*

toy [v] *play with* amuse oneself, coquet, cosset, dally, dandle, fiddle, flirt, fool, fool around*, jest, lead on, mess around*, pet, play, play around, play games, sport, string along*, tease, trifle, wanton; CONCEPT 384 —*Ant.* work

trace [n] *evidence; small bit* breath, crumb, dab, dash, drop, element, footmark, footprint, fragment, hint, indication, intimation, iota, jot, mark, memento, minimum, nib, nuance, particle, pinch, proof, record, relic, remains, remnant, scintilla, shade, shadow, shred, sign, slot, smell, smidgen, snippet, soupçon, speck, spoor, spot, sprinkling, strain, streak, suggestion, survival, suspicion, taste, tincture, tinge, tittle, token, touch, track, trail, tread, trifle, vestige, whiff, whisper; CONCEPTS 529,831 —*Ant.* lot

trace [v1] *seek, follow* ascertain, detect, determine, discern, discover, ferret out, find, hunt, perceive, pursue, run down, search for, shadow, smell out, spoor, spot, stalk, track, trail, unearth; CONCEPTS 207,216 —*Ant.* ignore, run away

trace [v2] *draw around* chart, copy, delineate, depict, duplicate, map, mark out, outline, record, reproduce, show, sketch; CONCEPTS 79,174

track [n1] *mark, print made by something* clue, footmark, footprint, footstep, groove, impress, impression, imprint, indication, memorial, monument, path, print, record, remains, remnant, rut, scent, sign, slot, spoor, step, symbol, token, trace, tract, trail, tread, vestige, wake; CONCEPTS 513,628

track [n2] *path, way* alley, artery, avenue, beaten path*, boulevard, clearing, course, cut*, drag*, footpath, highway, lane, line, orbit, passage, pathway, rail, rails, road, roadway, route, street, thoroughfare, trackway, trail, trajectory, walk; CONCEPT 501

track/track down [v] *follow, pursue* apprehend, beat the bushes*, be hot on the trail*, bird-dog*, bring to light*, capture, catch, chase, cover, dig up, discover, do, dog*, dog footsteps of*, draw an inference, expose, ferret out, find, go after, hunt, piece together, put together, run down, scout, shadow, smell out*, sniff out*, stalk, stick to, tail, trace, trail, travel, traverse, unearth; CONCEPTS 183,207, 216 —*Ant.* run away

tract [n] *area, lot* amplitude, belt, district, estate, expanse, extent, field, parcel, part, piece, plat, plot, portion, quarter, region, section, sector, spread, stretch, zone; CONCEPTS 508,513

tractable [adj] *manageable* acquiescent, amenable, biddable, complaisant, compliant, controllable, docile, ductile, facile, flexible, game, going along with*, governable, hanging loose*, malleable, meek, obedient, persuadable, plastic, pliable, pliant, putty in hands*, rolling with punches*, subdued, submissive, tame, tractile, willing, workable, yielding; CONCEPTS 401,408,542 —*Ant.* intractable, obstinate, stubborn, uncontrollable, unmanageable, unruly

traction [n] *physical resistance, friction* absorption, adherence, adhesion, constriction, contraction, drag, draught, drawing, grip, haulage, pull, pulling, purchase, resorption, strain, stress, stretch, suck, suction, towage; CONCEPTS 731, 748 —*Ant.* slipperiness

trade [n1] *buying and selling* barter, business, clientele, commerce, contract, custom, customers, deal, dealing, enterprise, exchange, industry, interchange, market, merchantry, patronage, public, sales, swap, traffic, transaction, truck; CONCEPTS 324,327,330,345

trade [n2] *profession, work* art, avocation, business, calling, craft, employment, game, handicraft, job, line, line of work, métier, nine-to-five*, occupation, position, pursuit, skill, thing*, vocation; CONCEPTS 349,360 —*Ant.* entertainment, fun, pastime

trademark [n] *logo, symbol* brand, brand name, identification, initials, label, logotype, mark, stamp, tag; CONCEPTS 259,284

tradition [n] *established practice* attitude, belief, birthright, conclusion, convention, culture, custom, customs, ethic, ethics, fable, folklore, form, habit, heritage, idea, inheritance, institution, law, legend, lore, mores, myth, mythology, mythos, opinion, practice, praxis, ritual, unwritten law, usage, wisdom; CONCEPT 688

traditional [adj] *usual, established* acceptable, accustomed, acknowledged, ancestral, classic, classical, common, conventional, customary, doctrinal, fixed, folk, habitual, historic, immemorial, long-established, old, oral, popular, prescribed, regular, rooted, sanctioned, taken for granted, time-honored, transmitted, universal, unwritten, widely used, widespread; CONCEPTS 530,533 —*Ant.* fresh, new, unestablished, unfixed, untraditional, unusual

traffic [n1] *coming and going* cartage, flux, freight, gridlock, influx, jam, movement, parking lot*, passage, passengers, rush hour, service, shipment, transfer, transit, transport, transportation, travel, truckage, vehicles; CONCEPTS 224,505,770

traffic [n2] *buying and selling* barter, business, closeness, commerce, communication, communion, connection, custom, dealing, dealings*, doings*, exchange, familiarity, industry, interchange, intercourse, intimacy, merchantry, patronage, peddling, relations, relationship, soliciting, trade, transactions, truck*; CONCEPTS 330,335

traffic [v] *buy and sell; do business* bargain, barter, black-market*, bootleg*, connect with, contact, deal, deal in*, dicker, exchange, fence, handle, have dealings, have transaction, horse trade*, interact, interface, make a deal, market, moonshine*, negotiate, network, peddle, push, reach out, relate, shove, swap, touch, touch base*, trade, truck*, work out; CONCEPTS 324, 327,330,345

tragedy [n] *disaster* adversity, affliction, bad fortune, bad luck, blight, blow, calamity, cataclysm, catastrophe, contretemps, curse, curtains*, dole, dolor, doom, downer*, failure, hard knocks*, hardship, humiliation, lot, misadventure, mischance, misfortune, mishap, reverse, shock, struggle, the worst*, unluckiness, waterloo*, woe; CONCEPTS 674, 675 —*Ant.* advantage, blessing, boon, success, victory

tragic [adj] *catastrophic, very bad* adverse, anguished, appalling, awful, calamitous, cataclysmic, crushing, deadly, deathly, deplorable, desolate, destructive, dire, disastrous, doleful,

dreadful, fatal, fateful, forlorn, grievous, grim, hapless, harrowing, heartbreaking, heart-rending, ill-fated, ill-starred, lamentable, miserable, mournful, painful, pathetic, pitiable, pitiful, ruinous, sad, shocking, sorrowful, terrible, unfortunate, unhappy, woeful, wretched; CONCEPTS 548,571 —*Ant.* advantageous, blessed, good, happy, successful

trail [n] *path, track* aisle, beaten track*, byway, footpath, footprints, footsteps, groove*, mark, marks, pathway, road, route, rut, scent, spoor, stream, stroll, tail, trace, train, wake, way; CONCEPT 501

trail [v] *lag behind, follow* bedog, bring up the rear*, chase, dally, dangle, dawdle, delay, dog*, drag, draggle, draw, droop, drop back, extend, fall back, fall behind, falter, flag, follow a scent*, halt, hang, hang back, hang down, haul, hunt, lag, linger, loiter, nose out*, plod, poke, poke along*, procrastinate, pull, pursue, shadow, shag, spook*, spoor, stalk, straggle, stream, string along*, tag along*, tail, take out after, tarry, tow, trace, track, traipse, trudge; CONCEPTS 207,727,753 —*Ant.* lead

train [n] *series* alternation, appendage, caravan, chain, column, concatenation, consecution, convoy, cortege, course, court, entourage, file, following, gradation, line, order, procession, progression, retinue, row, run, scale, sequel, sequence, set, string, succession, suite, tail, thread, tier, track, trail, wake; CONCEPTS 432, 727

train [v1] *prepare* accustom, brainwash*, break in, care for, coach, cultivate, develop, discipline, drill, drum into, dry run*, educate, enlighten, equip, exercise, get a workout, get in shape, ground, grow strong, guide, habituate, harden, hone, improve, instruct, inure, make ready, mold, prime, qualify, rear, rehearse, run through, school, season, shape, sharpen, show the ropes*, study, tame, teach, tutor, update, warm up*, whip into shape*, wise up*, work out; CONCEPTS 35,202,285 —*Ant.* forget, neglect

train [v2] *aim at* beam, bring to bear, cast, cock, direct, draw a bead*, focus, get in one's sights*, head, incline, lay, level, line up, point, slant, turn, zero in*; CONCEPT 201

trainee [n] *beginner* abecedarian, amateur, apprentice, buckwheater*, cadet, colt*, greenhorn, learner, neophyte, newcomer, new kid on the block*, novice, noviciate, pupil, recruit, rookie, starter, student, tenderfoot*, tyro; CONCEPTS 423,424

trainer [n] *instructor, teacher* adviser, breeder, coach, demonstrator, drill sergeant, guide, handler, lecturer, mentor, professor, tutor; CONCEPT 350

training [n] *preparation* background, basics, buildup, chalk talk*, coaching, cultivation, discipline, domestication, drill, education, exercise, foundation, grounding, groundwork, guidance, indoctrination, instruction, practice, preliminaries, principles, readying, schooling, seasoning, sharpening, teaching, tuition, tuneup*, tutelage, upbringing, warm-up*, workout*; CONCEPTS 202,285,678

traipse [v] *walk* amble, ambulate, gad, go on foot*, hike, knock about*, lumber, march,

meander, pace, parade, plod, prance, promenade, roam, rove, shuffle, step, stride, stroll, strut, take a walk, tour, travel on foot, traverse, trek, troop, trudge, wander; CONCEPT 149

trait [n] *characteristic* affection, attribute, birthmark, cast, character, custom, denominator, feature, habit, idiosyncrasy, lineament, manner, mannerism, mark, nature of the beast*, oddity, peculiarity, point, property, quality, quirk, savor, thing*, trick, virtue; CONCEPTS 411,644,834

traitor [n] *person who is disloyal* apostate, backslider*, back-stabber*, Benedict Arnold*, betrayer, conspirator, deceiver, defector, deserter, double-crosser*, fink*, hypocrite, impostor, informer, intriguer, Judas*, miscreant, quisling, rebel, renegade, snake*, sneak*, snitch*, snitcher*, spy, squealer*, stool pigeon*, tattletale, traducer, treasonist, turncoat, two-timer*, whistle-blower*, wolf*; CONCEPT 412 —*Ant.* loyalist

traitorous [adj] *disloyal* apostate, betraying, double-crossing, faithless, perfidious, recreant, subversive, treacherous, treasonable, treasonous, two-faced*, two-timing, undutiful, unfaithful, unpatriotic, untrue, wormlike; CONCEPT 401

trajectory [n] *course* curve, direction, flight, flow, line, movement, orbit, path, range, route, track, trail; CONCEPTS 501,514

tramp [n1] *person who is poor, desperate* beggar, bum, derelict, down-and-out*, drifter, floater, hitchhiker, hobo, homeless person, loafer, outcast, panhandler, vagabond, vagrant, wanderer; CONCEPT 412

tramp [n2] *heavy walk* cruise, excursion, expedition, footfall, footstep, hike, jaunt, march, ramble, saunter, slog, stomp, stroll, tour, traipse, tread, trek, turn, walking trip; CONCEPTS 151,224 —*Ant.* tiptoeing

tramp [v] *walk heavily* crush, footslog, gallop, hike, hop, march, navigate, plod, pound, ramble, range, roam, rove, slog, stamp, stodge, stomp, stroll, stump, thud, toil, tour, traipse, trample, tread, trek, trip, tromp, trudge, walk over; CONCEPTS 151,224 —*Ant.* tiptoe

trample [v] *walk forcibly over* bruise, crush, encroach, flatten, grind, hurt, infringe, injure, override, overwhelm, pound, ride roughshod over*, run over, squash, stamp, step on, stomp, tramp, tread, tromp, violate; CONCEPTS 137,208

trance [n] *hypnotic state* abstraction, coma, daze, dream, ecstasy, glaze, insensibility, muse, petrifaction, rapture, reverie, spell, study, stupor, transfixion, transfixture, unconsciousness; CONCEPT 410 —*Ant.* consciousness

tranquil [adj] *quiet, peaceful* agreeable, amicable, at ease, at peace, balmy, calm, collected, comforting, composed, cool, easy, easygoing, even, even-tempered, gentle, halcyon, hushed, lenient, low, measured, mild, moderate, murmuring, pacific, paradisiacal, pastoral, patient, placid, pleasing, poised, possessed, reasonable, restful, sedate, sedative, serene, smooth, sober, soft, soothing, stable, still, tame, temperate, undisturbed, unexcitable, unexcited, unperturbed, unruffled, untroubled, whispering; CONCEPTS 525,542,594 —*Ant.* chaotic, loud, noisy, turbulent, unpeaceful, violent, wild

tranquility [n] *peace, quiet* ataraxia, calm, calmness, composure, coolness, equanimity, hush, imperturbability, imperturbation, law and order, order, peacefulness, placidity, quietness, quietude, repose, rest, restfulness, sedateness, serenity, stillness; CONCEPTS 65,673 —Ant. chaos, disturbance, loudness, noise, turbulence, violence, wildness

tranquilize [v] *make calm, quiet* balm, calm, calm down, compose, hush, lull, pacify, put at rest, quell, quiet, quieten, relax, sedate, settle one's nerves*, soothe, still, subdue, unruffle; CONCEPTS 7,22,310 —Ant. aggravate, agitate, incite, stir up, upset

transact [v] *do business, carry out* accomplish, button down*, button up*, buy, carry on, clinch, close, conclude, conduct, discharge, do*, effectuate, enact, execute, finish, handle, jell, manage, move, negotiate, operate, perform, prosecute, pull off, run with the ball*, see to, sell, settle, sew up*, take care of, TCB*, work out a deal*, wrap up*; CONCEPTS 91,223,324,330,706 —Ant. deny, refuse

transaction [n] *business dealing; undertaking* act, action, activity, affair, agreement, bargain, bond, business, buying, compact, contract, convention, coup, covenant, deal, deed, disposal, doings*, enterprise, event, execution, goings-on*, happening, intercourse, matter, negotiation, occurrence, pact, performance, play, proceeding, purchase, purchasing, sale, selling, step; CONCEPTS 223,324,330,684 —Ant. denial, refusal, rejection

transcend [v] *go beyond; surpass* beat, best, be superior, better, eclipse, exceed, excel, go above, leave behind, leave in the dust*, outdo, outrival, outshine, outstrip, outvie, overstep, overtop, rise above, top, transform; CONCEPT 141 —Ant. fail, lose

transcendent/transcendental [adj] *extraordinary, superior* absolute, abstract, accomplished, beyond grasp, boundless, consummate, entire, eternal, exceeding, fantastic, finished, hypothetical, ideal, incomparable, infinite, innate, intact, intellectual, intuitive, matchless, obscure, original, otherworldly, peerless, perfect, preeminent, primordial, second to none*, sublime, supernatural, supreme, surpassing, theoretical, towering, transcending, transmundane, ultimate, unequalable, unequalled, unique, unparalleled, unrivalled, whole; CONCEPT 574 —Ant. inferior, ordinary, simple

transcribe [v] *transfer to another medium* copy out, decipher, duplicate, engross, interpret, note, record, render, reprint, reproduce, rewrite, set out, take down, tape, tape-record, transfer, translate, transliterate, write out; CONCEPTS 79, 125,171

transcript [n] *copy* carbon copy*, ditto*, duplicate, facsimile, hard copy, imprint, manuscript, mimeograph, minutes, notes, print, record, recorded material, recording, reprint, reproduction, transcription, translation; CONCEPTS 269,667,716

transfer [n] *change of possession* alteration, assignment, conduction, convection, deportation, displacement, move, relegation, relocation, removal, shift, substitution, transference, translation, transmission, transmittal, transposition,

variation; CONCEPTS 108,143,217,223 —Ant. hold, keeping

transfer [v] *pass possession to* assign, bear, bring, carry, cart, cede, change, consign, convert, convey, deed, delegate, deliver, dislocate, dispatch, dispense, displace, disturb, express, feed, ferry, find, forward, give, hand, hand over, haul, lug, mail, make over, metamorphose, move, pass on, pass the buck*, post, provide, relegate, relocate, remove, sell, send, shift, ship, shoulder, sign over, supply, taxi, tote, transfigure, translate, transmit, transmogrify, transmute, transplant, transport, transpose, turn over; CONCEPTS 108,143,217,223 —Ant. hold, keep

transfix [v1] *hold one's attention* bewitch, captivate, enchant, engross, fascinate, hold, hypnotize, mesmerize, palsy, paralyze, petrify, rivet, root, spellbind, stop in one's tracks*, stop one dead*, stun; CONCEPTS 11,14 —Ant. bore, look away

transfix [v2] *pierce* fix, impale, lance, nail down, penetrate, pin down, puncture, run through, skewer, skiver, spear, spike, spit, stick, transpierce; CONCEPT 220

transform [v] *change completely* alter, commute, convert, cook, denature, doctor, make over, metamorphose, mold, mutate, reconstruct, remodel, renew, revamp, revolutionize, shift gears*, sing different tune*, switch, switch over, transfer, transfigure, translate, transmogrify, transmute, transpose, turn around, turn over new leaf*, turn the corner*, turn the tables*; CONCEPTS 232,697 —Ant. leave alone, preserve, stagnate

transformation [n] *complete change* about-face*, alteration, changeover, conversion, flip-flop*, metamorphosis, radical change, renewal, revolution, shift, switch, transfiguration, transmogrification, transmutation; CONCEPT 697 —Ant. preservation, sameness, stagnation

transgression [n] *violation, misbehavior* breach, breaking of the law, contravention, crime, defiance, disobedience, encroachment, erring, error, fault, infraction, infringement, iniquity, lapse, misdeed, misdemeanor, offense, overstepping, sin, slip, trespass, vice, wrong, wrongdoing; CONCEPTS 101,192,645 —Ant. behavior, good manners, obedience, right

transient/transitory [adj] *temporary, brief* changeable, deciduous, emigrating, ephemeral, evanescent, flash, fleeting, flitting, fly-by-night*, flying, fugacious, fugitive, going by, impermanent, insubstantial, migrating, momentary, moving, passing, provisional, short, short-lived, short-term, temporal, transmigratory, unstable, vacating, volatile; CONCEPT 798 —Ant. enduring, incessant, lasting, long-lasting, neverending, permanent, persistent, undying

transit [n] *transportation* alteration, carriage, carrying, conveyance, crossing, infiltration, motion, movement, osmosis, passage, penetration, permeation, portage, shift, shipment, transfer, transference, transport, transporting, travel, traverse; CONCEPTS 155,224

transition [n] *change, often major* alteration, changeover, conversion, development, evolution, flux, growth, metamorphosis, metastasis, passage, passing, progress, progression,

realignment, shift, transformation, transit, transmutation, turn, turning point, upheaval; CONCEPT
697 —*Ant.* beginning, conclusion, end, finish,
introduction, sameness, stagnation, start

translate [*v1*] *interpret, explain* construe,
convert, decipher, decode, do into, elucidate,
explicate, gloss, make clear, metaphrase,
paraphrase, put, render, reword, simplify,
spell out, transcribe, transliterate, transpose,
turn; CONCEPTS 55,57

translate [*v2*] *change* alter, commute, convert,
metamorphose, transfigure, transform, transmogrify, transmute, transpose, turn; CONCEPT 232
—*Ant.* stagnate

translation [*n*] *rewording; interpretation*
adaptation, construction, crib*, decoding,
elucidation, explanation, gloss, key,
metaphrase, paraphrase, reading, rendering,
rendition, rephrasing, restatement, simplification, transcription, transliteration, version;
CONCEPTS 268,277,278

translator [*n*] *interpreter* adapter, cryptogra-
pher, cryptologist, decoder, dragoman,
explainer, glossator, linguist, polyglot;
CONCEPTS 57,292

translucent [*adj*] *clear* clear-cut, crystal,
crystalline, diaphanous, glassy, limpid, lucent,
lucid, luminous, pellucid, see-through, semi-
opaque, semitransparent, translucid, unblurred;
CONCEPT 618 —*Ant.* blocked, cloudy, opaque

transmit [*v*] *communicate, send* address, bear,
bequeath, break, broadcast, carry, channel,
conduct, consign, convey, diffuse, dispatch,
disseminate, drop a line*, drop a note*, forward, funnel, give a call*, give a ring*, hand
down, hand on, impart, instill, issue, mail, pass
on, pipe, put on the air*, radio, relay, remit,
route, send out, ship, siphon, spread, take,
traject, transfer, transfuse, translate, transport;
CONCEPTS 217,266,292 —*Ant.* get, receive, take

transparent [*adj1*] *see-through* cellophane,
clear, crystal-clear, crystalline, diaphanous,
filmy, gauzy, glassy, gossamer, hyaline, limpid,
lucent, lucid, pellucid, permeable, plain, sheer,
thin, tiffany, translucent, transpicuous, vitreous;
CONCEPTS 606,618 —*Ant.* blocked, cloudy,
dark, opaque

transparent [*adj2*] *obvious, understandable*
apparent, articulate, artless, candid, clear-cut,
direct, distinct, distinguishable, easily seen,
easy, evident, explicit, forthright, frank, guileless, honest, ingenuous, manifest, open, patent,
perspicuous, plain, plain-spoken, recognizable,
self-explanatory, sincere, straight, straightforward, unambiguous, undisguised, unequivocal,
unmistakable, unsophisticated, visible; CONCEPT
267 —*Ant.* cloudy, questionable, unclear,
unintelligible, vague

transpire [*v1*] *occur, happen* arise, befall,
betide, chance, come about, come to pass,
develop, ensue, eventuate, fall out*, gel, go,
result, shake, take place, turn up; CONCEPT 3

transpire [*v2*] *become known* be disclosed, be
discovered, be made public, break, come out,
come to light, emerge, get out, leak; CONCEPTS
261,266

transplant [*v*] *relocate* displace, emigrate,
graft, immigrate, move, readapt, recondition,
remove, reorient, reset, resettle, revamp, shift,

transfer, transpose, uproot; CONCEPTS 213,310
—*Ant.* preserve, save

transport [*n1*] *move, transfer* carriage, carrier,
carrying, carting, conveyance, conveying,
conveyor, freightage, hauling, lift, movement,
mover, moving, passage, removal, shipment,
shipping, transference, transferring, transit,
transportation, transporting, transshipment,
truckage, vehicle; CONCEPTS 155,503 —*Ant.*
idle, remain, stay

transport [*n2*] *delight* ardor, bliss, cloud nine*,
ecstasy, enchantment, enthusiasm, euphoria,
fervor, happiness, heaven, passion, rapture, ravishment, rhapsody, seventh heaven*; CONCEPTS
32,410 —*Ant.* boredom, dislike, indifference

transport [*v1*] *move, transfer* back, bear, bring,
carry, conduct, convey, ferry, fetch, haul, heel*,
jag, lug, pack, piggyback*, remove, ride, run,
schlepp*, ship, shoulder, take, tote, truck;
CONCEPTS 147,187,217 —*Ant.* hold, keep

transport [*v2*] *exile* banish, cast out, deport,
displace, expel, expulse, oust, relegate,
sentence; CONCEPTS 211,317 —*Ant.* remain

transport [*v3*] *captivate, delight* agitate, carry
away, electrify, elevate, enchant, enrapture,
entrance, excite, inflame, move, provoke,
quicken, ravish, send, slay, spellbind, stimulate,
stir, thrill, trance, uplight, wow; CONCEPTS 7,22
—*Ant.* disenchant, repulse, turn off

transpose [*v*] *swap, switch* alter, backtrack*,
change, commute, convert, double back, exchange, flip-flop*, interchange, inverse, invert,
metamorphose, move, put, rearrange, relocate,
render, reorder, reverse, revert, shift, substitute,
transfer, transfigure, transform, translate, transmogrify, transmute, turn, turn the tables*;
CONCEPTS 104,232,697 —*Ant.* leave alone

trap [*n*] *snare, trick* allurement, ambuscade,
ambush, artifice, bait, booby trap*, come-on*,
conspiracy, deception, decoy, device, dragnet,
enticement, feint, gambit, hook*, intrigue, inveiglement, lasso*, lure, machination, maneuver,
net, noose, pitfall, plot, ploy, prank, quagmire,
quicksand, ruse, seducement, snag*, stratagem,
subterfuge, temptation, wile; CONCEPT 674

trap [*v*] *catch, snare; trick* ambuscade, ambush,
beguile, box in*, circumvent, collar*, corner*,
corral*, deceive, decoy, dupe, enmesh, ensnare,
entangle, entrap, fool, grab, hook, inveigle,
land*, mousetrap*, nab, nail*, net, overtake,
rope in*, seduce, snag, suck in*, surprise, take,
tangle, trammel, trip up*; CONCEPTS 59,90
—*Ant.* let go, release

trappings [*n*] *paraphernalia, equipment*
accouterment, adornment, apparel, appointment,
decoration, dress, embellishment, finery, fitting,
fixture, furnishing, gear, livery, ornament,
panoply, personal effects, raiment, rigging,
things, trimming; CONCEPTS 446,451,496

trash [*n1*] *garbage* debris, dregs, droppings,
dross, excess, filth, fragments, junk, leavings,
litter, oddments, odds and ends*, offal, pieces,
refuse, residue, rubbish, rubble, rummage,
scourings, scrap, scraps, scum*, sediment,
shavings, sweepings, waste; CONCEPTS 260,
834 —*Ant.* assets, possessions, valuables

trash [*n2*] *ridiculous communication* balderdash, bilge*, drivel, foolish talk, hogwash,
inanity, malarkey*, nonsense, rot, rubbish,

tripe, twaddle; CONCEPT 278 —Ant. information, sense

trashy [adj] worthless abandoned, barren, bogus, cheap, cheesy, crappy*, cruddy*, crummy*, despicable, empty, flimsy, garbage, good-for-nothing*, grungy, inferior, junky, lousy, low in quality, no-good*, ratty, raunchy, shabby, shoddy, sleazy, tawdry, useless, valueless; CONCEPTS 560,570,575,589

trauma [n] severe mental or physical pain agony, anguish, blow, collapse, confusion, damage, derangement, disturbance, hurt, injury, jolt, ordeal, outburst, shock, strain, stress, suffering, torture, traumatization, upheaval, upset, wound; CONCEPT 728 —Ant. alleviation, healing, help, relief

travel [n] journey biking, commutation, cruising, drive, driving, excursion, expedition, flying, globe-trotting*, hop*, junket, movement, navigation, overnight, passage, peregrination, ramble, ride, riding, sailing, seafaring, sightseeing, swing, tour, touring, transit, trek, trekking, trip, voyage, voyaging, walk, wandering, wanderlust, wayfaring, weekend; CONCEPT 224

travel [v] journey on a trip or tour adventure, carry, cover, cover ground, cross, cruise, drive, explore, fly, get through, go, go abroad, go camping, go into orbit*, go riding, hop*, jaunt, jet*, junket*, knock around, make a journey, make one's way, migrate, motor, move, overnight*, proceed, progress, ramble, roam, rove, sail, scour, set forth, set out, sightsee, take a boat, take a plane, take a train, take a trip, tour, transmit, traverse, trek, vacation, visit, voyage, walk, wander, weekend*, wend; CONCEPT 224 —Ant. remain, stay

traveler [n] person who journeys adventurer, barnstormer*, bum*, commuter, displaced person, drifter, excursionist, expeditionist, explorer, floater, gadabout*, globetrotter, gypsy, haj, hiker, hobo, itinerant, jet-setter, journeyer, junketer, migrant, navigator, nomad, passenger, peddler, pilgrim, rambler, roamer, rover, sailor, seafarer, sightseer, tourist, tramp, transmigrant, trekker, tripper, trouper, truant, vagabond, vagrant, voyager, wanderer, wayfarer; CONCEPT 348,423

traverse [v1] cross over; travel bisect, bridge, cover, crisscross, cross, cut across, decussate, do, go across, go over, intersect, move over, negotiate, pace, peregrinate, ply, quarter, range, roam, span, track, transverse, travel over, tread, walk, wander; CONCEPTS 147,201,692,750

traverse [v2] resist, contradict balk, buck, check, combat, contest, contravene, counter, counteract, cross, deny, disaffirm, dispute, duel, fight, frustrate, gainsay, go against, hinder, impede, impugn, negate, negative, obstruct, oppose, repel, thwart, withstand; CONCEPTS 54,121 —Ant. back up, confirm

travesty [n] spoof, ridicule burlesque, caricature, distortion, exaggeration, farce, lampoon, lampoonery, mimicry, mock, mockery, parody, perversion, play, put-on*, roast*, satire, send-up*, sham*, takeoff*; CONCEPTS 273,292 —Ant. seriousness, solemnity

travesty [v] ridicule, spoof ape, burlesque, caricature, deride, distort, imitate, lampoon,

make a mockery of, make fun of, mimic, mock, parody, pervert, play on*, put on*, satirize, send up*, sham*, take off*; CONCEPTS 273,292 —Ant. be serious

treacherous [adj1] disloyal, dishonest betraying, catchy, deceitful, deceptive, double-crossing*, double-dealing*, duplicitous, faithless, false, false-hearted, fly-by-night*, insidious, misleading, perfidious, recreant, shifty*, slick*, slippery*, snake in the grass*, traitorous, treasonable, tricky, two-faced*, two-timing*, undependable, unfaithful, unloyal, unreliable, untrue, untrustworthy; CONCEPTS 401,404 —Ant. forthright, honest, loyal, true

treacherous [adj2] dangerous alarming, chancy, deceptive, difficult, dissembled, faulty, hairy*, hazardous, icy*, insecure, jeopardous, menacing, misleading, ominous, perilous, precarious, risky, shaky, slippery, ticklish, tricky, undependable, unhealthy, unreliable, unsafe, unsound, unstable, wicked; CONCEPTS 565,587 —Ant. harmless, untreacherous

treachery [n] disloyalty, dishonesty betrayal, bunco, corruption, dirty dealing*, dirty pool*, dirty trick*, dirty work*, disaffection, dodge, double-cross*, double-dealing*, duplicity, faithlessness, fake, falseness, fast shuffle*, flimflam*, grift, gyp*, infidelity, perfidiousness, perfidy, put-on*, racket*, recreancy, scam*, sellout, shell game*, skin game*, spoof, stab in the back*, sweet talk*, treacherousness, treason, two-timing*, whitewash*; CONCEPTS 633,645 —Ant. constancy, devotion, faithfulness, fidelity, honesty, love, loyalty

tread [n] walk footstep, footsteps, gait, march, pace, step, stride, trace, track, tramp; CONCEPTS 149,284

tread [v] walk; bear down ambulate, crush, foot, hike, hoof, march, oppress, pace, plod, quell, repress, squash, stamp, stamp on, step, step on, stride, subdue, subjugate, suppress, traipse, tramp, trample, troop, trudge; CONCEPT 149

treason [n] disloyalty breach of faith, crime, deceit, deceitfulness, deception, disaffection, dishonesty, duplicity, faithlessness, lèse-majesté, mutiny, perfidy, revolt, revolutionary, sedition, seditious act, seditiousness, subversion, traitorousness, treachery; CONCEPTS 192,645 —Ant. allegiance, devotion, faithfulness, fidelity, loyalty

treasonous [adj] disloyal apostate, betraying, double-crossing, faithless, insubordinate, mutinous, perfidious, recreant, subversive, traitorous, treacherous, treasonable, two-faced*, two-timing, undutiful, unfaithful, unpatriotic, untrue, wormlike; CONCEPT 401

treasure [n] prized possession or entity abundance, apple of one's eye*, cache, capital, cash, catch*, darling, find, fortune, funds, gem, gold, hoard, jewel, money, nest egg*, nonpareil, paragon, pearl*, pile*, plum*, pride and joy*, prize, reserve, riches, richness, store, treasure trove, valuable, wealth; CONCEPTS 332,337, 446,710

treasure [v] hold dear adore, appreciate, apprize, cherish, conserve, dote on, esteem, guard, idiolize, love, preserve, prize, revere, reverence, save, value, venerate, worship; CONCEPT 32 —Ant. dislike, disparage, hate

treasury [n] *place where money, valuables are kept* archive, bank, bursar, bursary, cache, chest, coffer, damper, depository, exchange, exchequer, Fort Knox*, gallery, hoard, museum, register, repository, safe, storage, store, storehouse, strongbox, treasure house, vault; CONCEPTS 339,439,449

treat [n] *pleasing entity or occurrence* amusement, banquet, celebration, dainty, delicacy, delight, enjoyment, entertainment, feast, fun, gift, goody*, gratification, joy, party, pleasure, refreshment, serve, take, use, value, wield; thrill, tidbit; CONCEPTS 457,529,693 —*Ant.* bad fortune

treat [v1] *act, behave towards* account, act with regard to, appraise, conduct, conduct oneself toward, consider, deal with*, employ, estimate, evaluate, handle, have business with*, have recourse to*, have to do with*, hold, look upon, manage, negotiate, play, rate, react toward, regard, respect, serve, take, use, value, wield; CONCEPT 633

treat [v2] *doctor, medicate* administer, apply treatment, attend, care for, cure, dose, dress, heal, medicament, minister to, nurse, operate, prescribe; CONCEPT 310 —*Ant.* harm, hurt, injure

treat [v3] *pay the bill for someone else* amuse, blow, buy for, divert, entertain, escort, feast, foot the bill*, give, indulge, pay for, pick up the check*, pick up the tab*, play host*, provide, regale, satisfy, set up, spring for*, stake, stand*, take out, wine and dine*; CONCEPTS 327,384

treat [v4] *be concerned with; discuss* advise, approach, arrange, comment, confabulate, confer, consider, consult, contain, criticize, deal with, deliberate, discourse on, enlarge upon, explain, go into, interpret, manipulate, reason, review, speak about, study, tackle, talk about, think, touch upon, weigh, write about; CONCEPTS 17,56 —*Ant.* ignore, neglect

treatise [n] *written study of a subject* argument, book, commentary, composition, discourse, discussion, disquisition, dissertation, essay, exposition, memoir, monograph, pamphlet, paper, review, script, thesis, tract, tractate, work, writing; CONCEPTS 271,280

treatment [n1] *medical care* analysis, cure, diet, doctoring, healing, hospitalization, medication, medicine, operation, prescription, regimen, remedy, surgery, therapeutics, therapy; CONCEPT 310 —*Ant.* harm, hurt, injury

treatment [n2] *handling of entity, situation* action towards, angle, approach, behavior towards, conduct, custom, dealing, employment, execution, habit, line, management, manipulation, manner, method, mode, modus operandi, practice, procedure, proceeding, processing, reception, strategy, usage, way; CONCEPTS 117,633

treaty [n] *agreement, contract* accord, alliance, arrangement, bargain, bond, cartel, charter, compact, concord, concordat, convention, covenant, deal, entente, league, negotiation, pact, reconciliation, sanction, settlement, understanding; CONCEPTS 684,685 —*Ant.* disagreement

tree [n] *large plant enclosed in bark and shedding leaves* forest, hardwood, pulp,

sapling, seedling, shrub, softwood, stock, timber, wood, woods; CONCEPT 430

trek [n] *long journey* expedition, footslog, hegira, hike, long haul, march, odyssey, peregrination, slog, tramp, travel, trip; CONCEPT 224

trek [v] *journey* be on the move*, be on the trail*, foot, hike, hit the road*, march, migrate, plod, range, roam, rove, slog, traipse, tramp, travel, trudge, walk; CONCEPT 224 —*Ant.* stay

tremble [v] *shake, vibrate* flutter, have the shakes*, jar, jitter, oscillate, palpitate, quake, quaver, quiver, rock, shiver, shudder, teeter, throb, totter, tremor, wobble; CONCEPT 152 —*Ant.* be calm, calm, steady

tremendous [adj] *huge, overwhelming* amazing, appalling, astounding, awesome, awful, blimp, colossal, cracking, deafening, dreadful, enormous, excellent, exceptional, extraordinary, fabulous, fantastic, fearful, formidable, frightful, gargantuan, gigantic, great, great big*, humongous, immense, incredible, jumbo*, large, mammoth, marvelous, massive, mondo*, monstrous, monumental, prodigious, stupendous, super, terrible, terrific, titanic, towering, vast, whale*, whopper, whopping, wonderful; CONCEPTS 574,773,781 —*Ant.* insignificant, little, small, tiny, underwhelming, unimportant

tremor [n] *shaking, shock* agitation, earthquake, flutter, quake, quaking, quaver, quiver, quivering, ripple, shake, shiver, shivering, tremble, trembling, trepidation, upheaval, vibration, wobble; CONCEPTS 145,526 —*Ant.* stillness

trench [n] *ditch, channel dug in earth* arroyo, canal, cut, depression, dike, drain, drill, dugout, earthwork, entrenchment, excavation, fosse, foxhole, furrow, gorge, gulch, gully, gutter, hollow, main, moat, pit, rut, sink, trough, tube, waterway; CONCEPTS 509,513

trenchant [adj] *sarcastic, scathing* acerbic, acid, acidulous, acute, astringent, biting, caustic, clear, clear-cut, crisp, critical, crushing, cutting, distinct, driving, dynamic, effective, effectual, emphatic, energetic, explicit, forceful, forcible, graphic, hurtful, impressive, incisive, intense, keen, mordant, penetrating, piquant, pointed, potent, powerful, pungent, razor-sharp*, salient, salty*, sardonic, sententious, severe, sharp, significant, strong, tart, to the point, unequivocal, unsparing, vigorous, weighty, well-defined; CONCEPTS 267,537 —*Ant.* frivolous, gentle, impotent, kind, nice, weak

trend [n1] *flow, current* aim, bearing, bent, bias, course, direction, drift, inclination, leaning, movement, orientation, progression, run, swing, tendency, tenor, wind; CONCEPTS 230,657,738

trend [n2] *style, fashion that is in favor* craze, cry, fad, furor, in-thing*, latest thing*, look, mode, newest wrinkle*, rage, thing*, vogue; CONCEPT 655

trendy [adj] *in fashion, style à la mode*, contemporary, fashionable, fly*, in, in vogue, latest, modish*, now*, popular, stylish, swank*, tony*, up-to-the-minute, voguish, with-it*; CONCEPT 589 —*Ant.* old-fashioned, unfashionable, unstyly, unstylish

trepidation [n] *anxiety, worry* agitation, alarm, apprehension, blue funk*, butterflies*, cold feet*, cold sweat*, consternation, creeps*, dismay, disquiet, disturbance, dread, emotion, excitement, fear, fright, goose bumps*, horror, jitters, nervousness, palpitation, panic, perturbation, shock, terror, trepidity, uneasiness, worriment; CONCEPT 27 —*Ant.* calm, contentment, happiness

trespass [*n*] *invasion, offense* breach, contravention, crime, delinquency, encroachment, entrenchment, error, evildoing, fault, infraction, infringement, iniquity, injury, intrusion, misbehavior, misconduct, misdeed, misdemeanor, obtrusion, poaching, sin, transgression, unlawful entry, violation, wrongdoing, wrongful entry; CONCEPTS *101,192,645,691* —*Ant.* retreat

trespass [*v*] *infringe, offend* butt in*, chisel in*, crash, crash the gates*, deviate, displease, do wrong by, encroach, entrench, err, horn in*, interlope, intrude, invade, kibitz*, lapse, meddle, misbehave, mix in, muscle in*, nose in*, obtrude, overstep, penetrate, poach, poke, sin, stick nose in*, transgress, violate, wrong; CONCEPTS *101,159,192,384* —*Ant.* retreat

trial [*adj*] *experimental* balloon, exploratory, pilot, preliminary, probationary, provisional, tentative, test, testing; CONCEPTS *548,560* —*Ant.* definite, known, proven

trial [*n1*] *test* analysis, assay, attempt, audition, check, crack*, dry run*, effort, endeavor, essay, examination, experience, experiment, experimentation, fling*, go*, hassle*, investigation, lick*, probation, proof, R and D*, research and development, shakedown*, shot*, showcase*, stab*, striving, struggle, testing, test run, trial and error*, trial run, try, try on*, tryout, undertaking, venture, whack*, workout; CONCEPTS *87,290,291*

trial [*n2*] *legal proceeding* action, arraignment, case, citation, claim, contest, counterclaim, court action, court martial, cross-examination, habeas corpus, hearing, impeachment, indictment, lawsuit, litigation, prosecution, rap*, seizure, suit, tribunal; CONCEPTS *317,691*

trial [*n3*] *trouble, big problem* adversity, affliction, albatross*, anguish, annoyance, bane, blow, bother, burden, calvary, care, complication, cross to bear*, crucible*, difficulty, distress, drag*, grief, hardship, hard time*, hassle*, heartbreak, inconvenience, irritation, load, misery, misfortune, nightmare, nuisance, ordeal, pain, pain in the neck*, pest, plague, rigor, severe test, sorrow, suffering, thorn, tribulation, trying time*, unhappiness, vexation, vicissitude, visitation, woe, wretchedness; CONCEPTS *674,728* —*Ant.* happiness, peace

tribe [*n*] *ethnic group; family* association, blood, caste, clan, class, division, dynasty, horde, house, ilk, kin, kind, kindred, lineage, people, race, seed, society, sort, stock, type; CONCEPTS *296,380,421*

tribulation [*n*] *pain, unhappiness* adversity, affliction, albatross*, bad luck*, blow*, bummer*, burden, care, cross to bear*, crucible*, curse, difficulty, distress, double whammy*, downer*, drag*, grief, hard knock*, hard time*, headache*, heartache*, misery, misfortune, oppression, ordeal, persecution, rainy day*, reverse, sorrow, suffering, trial, trouble, vexation, visitation, woe, worry, wretchedness,

wronging; CONCEPTS *666,728* —*Ant.* calm, comfort, happiness, peace

tribunal [*n*] *court* bar, bench, board, committee, council, court of justice, forum, judge, judiciary, justice, law court, magistrate, seat of judgment; CONCEPTS *299,318*

tributary [*adj*] *secondary; branch* accessory, dependent, feeding, minor, satellite, shoot, side, sub, subject, subordinate, under; CONCEPT *560* —*Ant.* original, primary, source

tribute [*n*] *testimonial, praise* accolade, acknowledgment, applause, appreciation, citation, commendation, compliment, encomium, esteem, eulogy, gift, gratitude, honor, laudation, memorial, offering, panegyric, recognition, recommendation, respect, salutation, salvo; CONCEPTS *69,278* —*Ant.* accusation, blame, criticism

trick [*n1*] *deceit* ambush, artifice, blind, bluff, casuistry, cheat, chicanery, circumvention, con*, concealment, conspiracy, conundrum, cover, deception, decoy, delusion, device, disguise, distortion, dodge*, double-dealing, duplicity, equivocation, evasion, fabrication, fake, falsehood, feint, forgery, fraud, game, gimmick, hoax, illusion, imposition, imposture, intrigue, invention, machination, maneuver, perjury, plot, ploy, pretense, ruse, snare, stratagem, subterfuge, swindle, trap, treachery, wile; CONCEPT *645* —*Ant.* frankness, honesty

trick [*n2*] *prank, joke* accomplishment, antic, caper, catch, device, escapade, feat, frolic, funny business, gag*, gambol, jape, jest, lark, monkeyshine*, practical joke, put-on*, shenanigan*, sleight of hand, sport, stunt, tomfoolery; CONCEPTS *59,273,384* —*Ant.* seriousness

trick [*n3*] *expertise, know-how* ability, art, command, craft, device, facility, gift, hang, knack, method, secret, skill, swing, technique; CONCEPT *630* —*Ant.* ignorance, misunderstanding

trick [*n4*] *characteristic, habit* crotchet, custom, foible, habitude, idiosyncrasy, manner, mannerism, peculiarity, practice, praxis, quirk, trait, usage, use, way, wont; CONCEPTS *411,657*

trick [*n5*] *time working at something* bout, go*, hitch, shift, spell, stint, tour, turn; CONCEPT *807*

trick [*v*] *fool; play joke on* bamboozle, catch*, cheat, con, deceive, defraud, delude, disinform, double deal*, dupe, fake, flimflam*, gull, hoax, hocus-pocus*, hoodwink, impose upon, jive*, mislead, outwit, play for a fool*, pull wool over*, put one over on*, rook*, screw*, set up*, swindle, take for a ride*, take in*, throw, trap, victimize; CONCEPT *59* —*Ant.* be serious

trickery [*n*] *deception, joke* bait and switch*, cheat, cheating, chicane, chicanery, con, deceit, dishonesty, dodge, double-cross*, double-dealing*, dupery, fast shuffle*, flimflam*, fourberie, fraud, funny business*, guile, hoax, imposture, pretense, quackery, razzle-dazzle*, scam, sharp practice, shell game*, shenanigans*, snow job*, sting*, stunt, swindling, underhandedness; CONCEPTS *59,645*

trickle [*v*] *run out* crawl, creep, distill, dribble, drip, drop, exude, flow, issue, leak, ooze, percolate, seep, stream, trill, weep; CONCEPTS *146, 179* —*Ant.* flow

tricky [*adj1*] *complicated, difficult* catchy, complex, critical, delicate, intricate, involved, knotty*, perplexing, precarious, problematic, quirky, risky, rocky, sensitive, sticky, thorny, ticklish, touch-and-go*, touchy, undependable, unstable; CONCEPT 562 —Ant. easy, uncomplicated

tricky [adj2] *deceptive, sly* artful, astute, cagey, catchy, clever, crafty, cunning, deceitful, deep, delusive, delusory, devious, dishonest, foxy, greasy*, guileful, insidious, intelligent, keen, misleading, scheming, shady, sharp, shifty, shrewd, slick*, slippery*, smooth, streetwise*, subtle, treacherous, wily, witted, wry; CONCEPT 401 —Ant. aboveboard, frank, honest

tried [adj] *reliable* approved, certified, constant, demonstrated, dependable, faithful, proved, secure, staunch, steadfast, tested, tried-and-true*, true-blue*, trustworthy, trusty, used; CONCEPT 535 —Ant. unreliable, untried

tried-and-true [adj] *tested* approved, certified, creditworthy, dependable, loyal, proven, proven, reliable, safe, tried, trustworthy, trusty; CONCEPT 535

trifle [n1] *novelty item* bagatelle, bauble, bibelot, curio, gewgaw*, knickknack, nothing*, novelty, objet d'art, plaything, toy, trinket, triviality, whatnot*; CONCEPT 446

trifle [n2] *very small amout* bit, dash, diddly*, drop, eyelash*, fly speck*, fraction, hint, jot, little, no big deal*, particle, picayune*, piece, pinch, shade, smack, soupçon, speck, spice, spot, squat, suggestion, suspicion, touch, trace; CONCEPTS 668,831 —Ant. lot

trifle [v] *toy with; mess around* amuse oneself, be insincere, coquet, dabble, dally, dawdle, dilly-dally*, doodle, fidget, flirt, fool, fool around*, fool with*, fribble*, fritter, futz around*, horse around*, idle, indulge in, lead on, loiter, lollygag*, lounge, mess with*, misuse, monkey, monkey with*, palter, philander, play, play games with*, play with, potter, putter, squander, string along*, toy, twiddle, use up, wanton, waste, waste time, wink at*; CONCEPTS 210,292,363

trifling [adj] *insignificant, worthless* banal, dinky*, empty, forget it*, frivolous, hollow, idle, idling, inane, inconsequential, inconsiderable, insipid, jejune, loitering, measly, minuscule, negligible, niggling*, no big deal*, no big thing*, nugatory, paltry, petty, picayune, piddling, puny, shallow, silly, slight, small, tiny, trivial, unimportant, vain, valueless, vapid; CONCEPTS 575,789 —Ant. important, significant, useful, worthwhile

trigger [v] *cause to happen* activate, bring about, cause, elicit, generate, give rise to, produce, prompt, provoke, set in motion, set off, spark, start; CONCEPT 242 —Ant. block, check, halt, stop

trim [adj1] *neat, orderly* apple-pie order*, clean, clean-cut, compact, dapper, fit, in good shape, neat as a pin*, nice, shipshape*, slick, smart, snug, spick-and-span*, spruce, streamlined, symmetrical, tidy, to rights*, uncluttered, well-groomed; CONCEPTS 485,621 —Ant. disorderly, rough, sloppy, unkempt

trim [adj2] *shapely* beautiful, clean, comely, fit, graceful, in fine fettle*, in good shape, sleek, slender, slick, slim, statuesque, streamlined, svelte, well-balanced, well-proportioned,

willowy; CONCEPTS 314,490,491 —Ant. chubby, fat, overweight

trim [n1] *decoration* adornment, border, edging, embellishment, frill, fringe, garnish, gingerbread*, ornamentation, piping, trimming; CONCEPTS 475,824

trim [n2] *condition, health* commission, fettle*, fitness, form, kilter*, order, repair, shape, situation, state, whack*; CONCEPT 316

trim [v1] *cut shorter* abbreviate, barber, blue pencil*, bob, boil down*, clip, crop, curtail, cut, cut back, cut down, dock, edit, even up, lop, mow, pare, pare down, plane, prune, put in a nutshell*, shave, shear, shorten, slice off, snip, tidy, truncate, whittle down*; CONCEPTS 176,236,247 —Ant. develop, let grow

trim [v2] *decorate* adorn, array, beautify, bedeck, beribbon, deck, dress, dress up, embellish, emblazon, embroider, garnish, ornament, prank, pretty up*, prink*, spangle, spruce up*; CONCEPTS 162,177

trim [v3] *beat, defeat* clobber, drub, lambaste, lick, smother, thrash, trounce, wax*, whip; CONCEPT 95 —Ant. lose

trimmings [n] *accessories, extras* accent, accompaniments, additions, clippings, decorations, fixings, frills, garnish, ornaments, supplements, trappings; CONCEPT 834

trinket [n] *knickknack* bagatelle, bauble, bead, bibelot, curio, doodad*, gadget, gewgaw*, gimcrack*, glass*, hardware, jewel, jewelry, junk, nothing*, novelty, objet d'art, ornament, plaything, rock*, sparkler*, stone, toy, trifle, whatnot*; CONCEPT 446

trio/triple [n] *three of something* leash, set of three, ternion, threesome, trey, triad, triangle, trilogy, trine, trinity, triplet, triplicate, triptych, triumvirate, triune, troika; CONCEPTS 784,792

trip [n1] *journey, excursion* cruise, errand, expedition, foray, hop*, jaunt, junket, outing, overnight, peregrination, ramble*, run, swing*, tour, travel, trek, voyage, weekend; CONCEPT 224

trip [n2] *error, blunder* bungle, fall, false move, false step, faux pas*, indiscretion, lapse, misstep, mistake, slip, stumble; CONCEPTS 101,230 —Ant. correction, fix

trip [v] *fall, err* buck, canter, confuse, disconcert, fall over, founder, frolic, go headlong*, go wrong, hop, lapse, lope, lose balance, lose footing, lurch, make a faux pas*, miscalculate, misstep, pitch, play, plunge, skip, slide, slip, slip on, slip up, sprawl, spring, stumble, throw off, topple, tumble, unsettle; CONCEPTS 101,149 —Ant. correct, fix

tripe [n] *nonsense, rubbish* balderdash, baloney*, bilge, bosh, BS*, bull*, bunk*, drivel, garbage, gibberish, hogwash, hooey*, hot air*, poppycock, trash; CONCEPTS 230,278

trite [adj] *silly, commonplace* banal, bathetic, bromidic, chain, cliché, clichéd, common, cornball*, corny*, drained, dull, exhausted, familiar tune*, flat, hackneyed, hokey*, jejune, mildewed*, moth-eaten*, musty*, old hat*, ordinary, pedestrian, platitudinous, prosaic, ready-made, routine, run-of-the-mill*, set, shopworn, stale, stereotyped, stock, threadbare, timeworn, tired, uninspired, unoriginal, used-up, vapid, warmed-over*, well-worn, worn,

triumph [n1] *extreme happiness* celebration, elation, exultance, exultation, festivity, joy, jubilance, jubilation, jubilee, merriment, pride, rejoicing, reveling; CONCEPT 410 —*Ant.* sadness, sorrow, unhappiness

triumph [n2] *victory, achievement* accomplishment, ascendancy, attainment, big hit*, big win*, cinch, clean sweep*, conquest, coup, feat, feather in cap*, gain, grand slam*, hit, hole in one*, homer*, pushover*, riot, score, sell, sensation, shoo-in*, smash-hit*, splash, success, sure bet*, sure thing*, surmounting, takeover, the gold*, tour de force*, vanquishing, vanquishment, walkover*, win; CONCEPT 706 —*Ant.* disaster, failure, forfeit, loss

triumph [v1] *be very happy* celebrate, crow, delight, exult, gloat, glory, jubilate, rejoice, revel, swagger; CONCEPT 32 —*Ant.* be sad

triumph [v2] *achieve, succeed* beat the game*, beat the system*, best, blow away*, carry the day*, come out on top*, conquer, dominate, flourish, get last laugh*, overcome, overwhelm, prevail, prosper, sink, strike it big*, subdue, sweep, take it all*, take the cake*, thrive, trounce, vanquish, win, win hands down*, win out*; CONCEPTS 95,141,706 —*Ant.* fail, forfeit, lose

triumphant [adj] *successful* boastful, celebratory, champion, conquering, dominant, elated, exultant, glorious, happy, in the lead*, jubilant, looking good, lucky, on top, out front*, prizewinning, proud, rejoicing, swaggering, triumphal, unbeaten, undefeated, victorious, winning; CONCEPT 528 —*Ant.* defeated, failing, losing, unsuccessful

trivia [n] *details* fine points, memorabilia, minutiae, trifles, trivialities; CONCEPTS 274,543 —*Ant.* generality, importance, significance, weight

trivial [adj] *not important* atomic, beside the point*, commonplace, diminutive, evanescent, everyday, flimsy, frivolous, immaterial, inappreciable, incidental, inconsequential, inconsiderable, insignificant, irrelevant, little, meager, mean, meaningless, microscopic, minor, minute, momentary, negligible, nonessential, nugatory, of no account, paltry, petty, piddling*, puny, scanty, skin-deep*, slight, small, superficial, trifling, trite, unimportant, valueless, vanishing, worthless; CONCEPT 575 —*Ant.* consequential, important, significant, useful, valuable, weighty, worthwhile

troll [n] *elf* demon, dwarf, giant, gnome, goblin, hobgoblin, kobold, leprechaun, monster, mythical creature, ogre; CONCEPT 412

troop/troops [n] *group, often military* armed forces, army, assemblage, assembly, band, body, bunch, collection, combatants, company, contingent, corps, crew, crowd, delegation, drove, fighting forces, flock, forces, gang, gathering, herd, horde, host, legion, military, multitude, number, outfit, pack, party, personnel, service personnel, soldiers, soldiery, squad, swarm, team, throng, troopers, troupe, unit; CONCEPTS 322,417

trophy [n] *physical award* blue ribbon*, booty,

citation, crown, cup, decoration, gold*, gold star*, guerdon, keepsake, laurels, medal, memento, memorial, palm, prize, reminder, ribbon, souvenir, spoils*; token; CONCEPT 337

tropical [adj] *warm and humid* close, equatorial, hot, lush, steamy, sticky, stifling, sultry, sweaty, sweltering, torrid, tropic; CONCEPTS 525,605 —*Ant.* arctic, freezing, frigid, polar

trot [v] *move along briskly* amble, canter, go, hurry, jog, lope, pad, rack, ride, run, scamper, step lively; CONCEPT 150

trot out [v] *bring forward* brandish, bring up, come out with, display, disport, drag up, exhibit, expose, flash, flaunt, parade, recite, rehearse, reiterate, relate, repeat, represent, show, show off; CONCEPT 138 —*Ant.* conceal, hide

troubadour [n] *singer* accompanist, artist, balladeer, bard, crooner, jongleur, minnesinger, minstrel, musician, poet, serenader, songster, songwriter, trouveur, vocalist; CONCEPT 352

trouble [n1] *annoyance, worry* agitation, anxiety, bad news*, bind, bother, commotion, concern, danger, difficulty, dilemma, dire straits, discontent, discord, disorder, disquiet, dissatisfaction, distress, disturbance, grief, hang-up*, heartache, hindrance, hot water*, inconvenience, irritation, mess, misfortune, nuisance, pain, pest, pickle*, predicament, problem, puzzle, row, scrape, sorrow, spot, strain, stress, strife, struggle, suffering, task, torment, tribulation, tumult, unrest, vexation, woe; CONCEPTS 532,674,675,690,728 —*Ant.* contentment, happiness, peace

trouble [n2] *something requiring great effort* ado, attention, bother, bustle, care, concern, difficulty, effort, exertion, flurry, fuss, hardship, inconvenience, labor, pains, pother, rigor, strain, stress, struggle, thought, trial, while, work, worry; CONCEPTS 666,677 —*Ant.* advantage, aid, assistance, blessing, help

trouble [n3] *bad health* affliction, ailment, complaint, curse, defect, disability, disease, disorder, failure, illness, malady, malfunction, upset; CONCEPT 316 —*Ant.* fitness, good health

trouble [v1] *bother, worry* afflict, agitate, ail, annoy, bug*, burden, burn up*, concern, discommode, discompose, disconcert, disoblige, disquiet, distress, disturb, drive up the wall*, flip out*, fret, get to, give a bad time*, give a hard time*, grieve, harass, harry, impose on, inconvenience, irk, irritate, make a fuss*, make a scene*, make waves*, pain, perplex, perturb, pester, plague, psych*, put out*, sadden, spook*, stir up, strain, stress, torment, try, upset, vex; CONCEPTS 7,19 —*Ant.* be content, be happy

trouble [v2] *make an effort* be concerned with, exert, go to the effort of, take pains*, take the time*; CONCEPT 100 —*Ant.* aid, assist, help

troublemaker [n] *person who causes a problem* agent provocateur, agitator, bad actor*, firebrand*, gremlin*, heel*, hellion, incendiary, inciter, inflamer, instigator, loose cannon*, meddler, mischief-maker, nuisance, phony*, punk*, rabble-rouser*, rascal, recreant, smart aleck*, snake*, stormy petrel*, weasel*; CONCEPT 412 —*Ant.* peacemaker

troubleshooter [n] *fixer, repair person* maintenance person, mender, Mr. Fixit*, service person, technician; CONCEPTS 126,212

troublesome [*adj*] *bothersome, worrisome*
alarming, annoying, arduous, burdensome,
damaging, dangerous, demanding, difficult,
disquieting, harassing, hard, heavy, importunate, inconvenient, infestive, intractable,
irksome, irritating, laborious, mean, messy,
murder, oppressive, painful, pesky, pestiferous,
pestilential, problematic, refractory, repressive,
rough, taxing, tiresome, tough, tricky, troublous,
trying, ugly, ungovernable, unruly, uphill,
upsetting, vexatious, vexing, wearisome,
wicked, worrying; CONCEPTS 529,565 —*Ant.*
easy, helpful, nice, useful

trough [*n*] *gutter, depression* canal, channel,
crib, cup, dike, dip, ditch, duct, flume, furrow,
gully, hollow, manger, moat, trench, watercourse; CONCEPTS 509,513

trounce [*v*] *defeat overwhelmingly* bash, beat,
blank, bury, bust*, cap, clobber, conquer, cook
one's goose*, crush, drub, dust*, fix one's
wagon*, flog, hammer*, lambaste*, lather*,
lick*, make mincemeat of*, murder, overcome,
overwhelm, paste*, pommel*, put away*, rout,
swamp, thrash*, total*, trash*, walk over*,
wallop*, waste*, wax*, whip, win, wipe off
the mat*; CONCEPT 95 —*Ant.* fail, forfeit, lose

troupe [*n*] *company* acting company, actors,
association, band, cast, crew, ensemble, gang*,
group, party, performers, repertory company,
stock company, team, troop; CONCEPT 417

trousers [*n*] *pants* bloomers, blue jeans,
breeches, britches*, chaps*, chinos, cords*,
corduroys, denims, dungarees, jeans, knickers,
overalls, pantaloons, rompers, slacks; CONCEPT
451

truant [*adj*] *absent* absent without leave, astray,
away, AWOL*, cutting class*, gone, hooky*,
missing, no-show*, not present, playing
hooky*, skipping school*; CONCEPT 583

truant [*n*] *absentee* delinquent, deserter, draft
dodger, hooky player, malingerer, no-show*,
runaway, shirker; CONCEPTS 358,412,423

truce [*n*] *peaceful solution* accord, agreement,
amnesty, armistice, break, breather*, cease-
fire, cessation, de-escalation, detente, halt,
intermission, interval, letup, lull, moratorium,
olive branch*, pause, peace, reconciliation,
reprieve, respite, rest, stay, suspension,
temporary peace, terms, treaty, white flag*,
wind-down*; CONCEPTS 230,298,684 —*Ant.*
disagreement, fight, war

truck [*n1*] *commerce, merchandise* barter,
business, buying and selling, commercial
goods, commodities, communication, communion, connection, contact, dealings, exchange,
goods*, intercourse, relations, stock, stuff*,
trade, traffic, wares*; CONCEPTS 324,330,338

truck [*n2*] *wheeled vehicle for hauling* buggy*,
car, carryall, crate*, dump, eighteen-wheeler*,
four by eight*, four by four*, four-wheel
drive*, freighter, jeep, lorry, pickup, rig*,
semi*, van, wagon, wheels*; CONCEPT 505

truck [*v*] *buy and sell* bargain, barter, deal,
deal in*, do business, exchange, handle, have
dealings, negotiate, peddle, retail, swap, trade,
traffic, transact, wholesale*; CONCEPTS 324,327

truckle [*v*] *fawn* apple-polish*, be servile,
bootlick*, brownnose*, butter up*, cajole, fall
all over, fall on one's knees*, flatter, grovel,

honey up*, kiss one's feet*, kiss-up*, kowtow*,
lay it on*, lick boots*, massage*, oil*, pay
court*, play up to*, scratch one's back*,
stroke*, suck up to*, toady, woo*; CONCEPTS
110,384

truculent [*adj*] *belligerent, hateful* abusive,
aggressive, antagonistic, bad-tempered,
barbarous, bellicose, browbeating, brutal,
bullying, caustic, combative, contentious,
contumelious, cowing, cross, defiant, ferocious,
fierce, frightening, harsh, hostile, inhuman,
inhumane, intimidating, invective, mean,
militant, mordacious, mordant, obstreperous,
opprobrious, ornery*, pugnacious, quarrelsome,
rude, savage, scathing, scrappy, scurrilous,
sharp, sullen, terrifying, terrorizing, trenchant,
violent, vituperative, vituperous; CONCEPTS 267,
401 —*Ant.* cooperative, gentle, mild, nice, tame

trudge [*v*] *walk heavily* clump, drag oneself*,
footslog, hike, lumber, march, plod, plug
along*, schlepp*, slog, step, stumble, stump,
traipse, tramp, tread, trek, wade; CONCEPT 151
—*Ant.* tiptoe

true [*adj1*] *real, valid; concordant with facts*
accurate, actual, appropriate, authentic, authoritative, bona fide, correct, dependable, direct,
exact, factual, fitting, genuine, honest, indubitable, kosher*, lawful, legal, legitimate,
natural, normal, on target*, perfect, precise,
proper, pure, regular, right, rightful, sincere,
straight, sure-enough*, trustworthy, truthful,
typical, undeniable, undesigning, undoubted,
unerring, unfaked, unfeigned, unquestionable,
veracious, veridical, veritable, very, wash*;
CONCEPTS 267,535,582 —*Ant.* corrupt, counterfeit, deceitful, false, fraudulent, invalid, unreal

true [*adj2*] *loyal* allegiant, ardent, confirmed,
conscientious, constant, creditable, dedicated,
dependable, devoted, dutiful, estimable, faithful, fast, firm, high-principled, honest, honorable, just, liege, no lie*, on the up and up*,
pure, reliable, resolute, right, right-minded,
scrupulous, sincere, square, staunch, steadfast,
steady, straight, strict, sure, true-blue*,
truehearted, trustworthy, trusty, unaffected,
undistorted, unfeigned, unswerving, up front*,
upright, veracious, veridical, wholehearted,
worthy; CONCEPTS 267,401,542 —*Ant.*
cheating, dishonest, disloyal, evil, faithless,
hateful, untrustworthy

true [*adv*] *honestly, accurately* correctly, on
target, perfectly, precisely, properly, rightly,
truthfully, unerringly, veraciously, veritably;
CONCEPTS 267,535,544 —*Ant.* dishonestly,
inaccurately, wrongly

true-blue [*adj*] *faithful, loyal* allegiant, ardent,
behind one, dedicated, dependable, devoted,
die-hard, dutiful, firm, genuine, hard-core*,
honorable, patriotic, staunch, steadfast, sure,
tried, tried-and-true*, trustworthy, truthful,
upright; CONCEPTS 401,545

truly [*adv*] *really, doubtlessly* absolutely, accurately, actually, authentically, beyond doubt,
beyond question, confirmedly, constantly,
correctly, de facto, definitely, devotedly,
exactly, factually, faithfully, firmly, genuinely,
honestly, honorably, in actuality, in fact, in
reality, in truth, legitimately, loyally, positively,
precisely, reliably, righteously, rightly, sincerely,

staunchly, steadily, surely, truthfully, unequivocally, veraciously, veritably, very, with all one's heart*, with devotion, without a doubt; CONCEPTS 267,535,582 —*Ant.* doubtfully, dubiously, indefinite

trumped up [*adj*] *false* bogus, concocted, cooked-up*, deceitful, dishonest, fabricated, fake, falsified, fictitious, fishy, framed, fraudulent, imaginary, incorrect, invalid, invented, lying, made up, misleading, phony, sham, unfounded, unsound, untrue; CONCEPTS 267,570,582

truncate [*v*] *shorten* abbreviate, abridge, clip, crop, curtail, cut, cut off, cut short, lop, pare, prune, shear, top, trim; CONCEPTS 137,236,247 —*Ant.* elongate, expand, lengthen, stretch

trunk [*n1*] *body, core* block, bole, butt, column, log, soma, stalk, stem, stock, thorax, torso; CONCEPTS 392,428,826 —*Ant.* extremities

trunk [*n2*] *long nose of animal* beak, proboscis, prow, snoot*, snout; CONCEPT 399

trunk [*n3*] *container, box* bag, baggage, bin, case, chest, coffer, coffin, crate, foot locker, locker, luggage, portmanteau, suitcase, wardrobe; CONCEPTS 494,502

trust [*n1*] *belief in something as true, trustworthy* assurance, certainty, certitude, confidence, conviction, credence, credit, dependence, entrustment, expectation, faith, gospel truth*, hope, positiveness, reliance, stock, store, sureness; CONCEPT 689 —*Ant.* disbelief, distrust, mistrust

trust [*n2*] *responsibility, custody* account, care, charge, duty, guard, guardianship, keeping, liability, moment, obligation, protection, safekeeping, trusteeship, ward; CONCEPTS 376,645

trust [*n3*] *large company* bunch, business, cartel, chain, combine, conglomerate, corporation, crew, crowd, gang, group, institution, megacorp*, mob, monopoly, multinational organization, outfit, pool, ring, syndicate; CONCEPTS 323,325

trust [*v1*] *believe, place confidence in* accredit, assume, bank on, be convinced, bet bottom dollar on*, bet on, build on, calculate on, confide in, count on, depend on, expect, gamble on, have faith in, hope, imagine, lay money on*, lean on, look to, place confidence in, place trust in, presume, reckon on, rely upon, suppose, surmise, swear by, take, take at face value*, think likely; CONCEPT 12 —*Ant.* disbelieve, distrust, mistrust

trust [*v2*] *give to for safekeeping* advance, aid, assign, command, commission, commit, confer, confide, consign, delegate, entrust, give over, grant, lend, let, let out, loan, make trustee, patronize, put into hands of, sign over, store, transfer, turn over; CONCEPT 115 —*Ant.* hold, keep

trustee [*n*] *administrator* agent, custodian, executor, executrix, fiduciary, guardian, keeper, warden; CONCEPTS 414,423

trusting [*adj*] *trustful* believing, confiding, credulous, gullible, innocent, naive, undoubting, unquestioning, unsuspecting, unsuspicious; CONCEPTS 401,542,678

trustworthy/trusty [*adj*] *reliable, believable* accurate, always there*, authentic, authoritative, convincing, credible, dependable, ethical, exact, honest, honorable, kosher*, levelheaded, mature, on the level*, on up and up*, open, plausible, principled, realistic, responsible, righteous, rock solid*, saintly, secure, sensible, solid, square, steadfast, straight, there*, to be trusted, tried, tried-and-true*, true, true-blue*, trustable, truthful, unfailing, up-front*, upright, valid, veracious; CONCEPTS 267,404,535 —*Ant.* corrupt, unbelievable, undependable, unreliable, untrustworthy

truth [*n1*] *reality, validity* accuracy, actuality, authenticity, axiom, case, certainty, correctness, dope*, exactitude, exactness, fact, facts, factualism, factuality, factualness, genuineness, gospel*, gospel truth*, honest truth*, infallibility, inside track*, legitimacy, maxim, naked truth*, nitty-gritty*, perfection, picture, plain talk, precision, principle, rectitude, rightness, scoop, score, trueness, truism, truthfulness, unvarnished truth, veracity, verisimilitude, verity, whole story*; CONCEPTS 278,638,725 —*Ant.* falsehood, invention, untruth

truth [*n2*] *honesty, loyalty* authenticity, candor, constancy, dedication, devotion, dutifulness, faith, faithfulness, fidelity, frankness, integrity, openness, realism, revelation, sincerity, uprightness, veridicality, verity; CONCEPT 657 —*Ant.* dishonesty, disloyalty, falsehood, lie, misrepresentation

truthful [*adj*] *accurate, honest* believable, candid, correct, exact, factual, faithful, forthright, frank, guileless, ingenuous, just, kosher*, legit*, like it is*, literal, on the level*, on the up and up*, open, outspoken, plainspoken, precise, real, realistic, reliable, righteous, scrupulous, sincere, square, straight, straightforward, true, true-blue*, trustworthy, truth-telling, unfeigned, unreserved, veracious, veritable; CONCEPTS 267,542 —*Ant.* dishonest, hypocritical, inaccurate, lying, untruthful

try [*n*] *attempt* all one's got*, best shot*, bid, crack*, dab, effort, endeavor, essay, fling*, go*, jab*, pop*, shot*, slap*, stab*, striving, struggle, trial, undertaking, whack*, whirl*; CONCEPTS 87,677 —*Ant.* abstention

try [*v1*] *attempt* aim, aspire, attack, bear down, chip away at*, compete, contend, contest, do one's best*, drive for, endeavor, essay, exert oneself, go after, go all out*, go for, have a crack*, have a go*, have a shot*, have a stab*, have a whack*, knock oneself out*, labor, lift a finger*, make a bid, make an attempt, make an effort, make a pass at*, propose, put oneself out*, risk, seek, shoot for*, speculate, strive, struggle, tackle, undertake, venture, vie for, work, wrangle; CONCEPT 87 —*Ant.* abstain

try [*v2*] *experiment, test* appraise, assay, check, check out, evaluate, examine, inspect, investigate, judge, prove, put to the proof*, put to the test*, sample, scrutinize, taste, try out, weigh; CONCEPTS 103,291 —*Ant.* abstain

try [*v3*] *bother, afflict* agonize, annoy, crucify, distress, excruciate, harass, inconvenience, irk, irritate, martyr, pain, plague, rack, strain, stress, tax, tire, torment, torture, trouble, upset, vex, weary, wring; CONCEPT 7 —*Ant.* delight, please

try [*v4*] *bring before a judge* adjudge, adjudicate, arbitrate, decide, examine, give a hearing, hear, judge, referee, sit in judgment; CONCEPT 317

trying [adj] *difficult, bothersome* aggravating, annoying, arduous, demanding, exacting, exasperating, exigent, fatiguing, hard, irksome, irritating, onerous, oppressive, pestilent, provocative, rough, severe, sticky, strenuous, stressful, taxing, tight, tiresome, tough, tricky, troublesome, upsetting, vexing, wearisome, weighty; CONCEPTS 548,565 —*Ant.* easy, facile, mild, moderate, unstressful

try on/try out [v] *evaluate, test* appraise, audition, check out, demonstrate, experiment, fit, give a try, have a dry run*, have a fitting*, inspect, practice, probe, prove, put into practice, put to the test, sample, scrutinize, taste, try for size, wear; CONCEPTS 103,167 —*Ant.* abstain

tryst [n] *meeting during a love affair* appointment, assignation, date, engagement, meet, meeting, rendezvous, union; CONCEPTS 375,384

tubby [adj] *fat* beefy*, big, brawny, broad, bulging, bulky, burly, chubby*, chunky*, dumpy, elephantine, fleshy, gargantuan, gross, heavy, heavyset*, hefty, husky, large, obese, oversize, overweight, plump, portly, potbellied, pudgy*, roly-poly*, stout, weighty; CONCEPT 491

tuck [v] *fold together* constrict, contract, draw together, enfold, gather, hem, insert, make snug, pinch, plait, pleat, push, put in, seam, squeeze in, swaddle, wrap; CONCEPTS 193,218

tuckered out [adj] *tired* asleep, beat*, burned out*, collapsing, dead on one's feet*, dog-tired*, done for*, done in*, drained, drooping, droopy, drowsy, enervated, exasperated, exhausted, fatigued, finished, overworked, played out*, pooped*, run-down, sleepy, spent, wasted, weary, worn out; CONCEPTS 314, 403

tuft [n] *clump of strands of something* bunch, cluster, collection, cowlick, feathers, group, knot, plumage, ruff, shock, topknot, tussock; CONCEPTS 392,432,471

tug [n/v] *quick pull* drag, draw, haul, heave, jerk, lug, strain, toil, tow, traction, wrench, yank; CONCEPT 206 —*Ant.* push

tuition [n] *education; education costs* charge, expenditure, fee, instruction, lessons, price, schooling, teaching, training, tutelage, tutoring; CONCEPT 287

tumble [v] *fall or make fall awkwardly* bowl down, bring down, descend, dip, disarrange, disarray, disorder, disturb, do a pratfall, down, drop, fall headlong*, flatten, floor, flop, go belly up*, go down, hit the dirt*, jumble, keel, keel over, knock down, knock over, level, lose footing, lose it*, mess up, nose-dive, pitch, plummet, plunge, roll, sag, skid, slip, slump, spill, stumble, take a header*, tip over, topple, toss, trip, upset; CONCEPTS 147,149,181

tumescent [adj] *swollen* bloated, bulging, bulgy, bursting, distended, distent, enlarged, expanding, inflated, puffed, puffy, tumid; CONCEPT 485

tummy [n] *stomach* abdomen, belly, below the belt*, breadbasket*, gut, insides, paunch, pot*, solar plexus, spare tire*; CONCEPTS 393,420

tumor [n] *abnormal growth in animate being* bump, cancer, carcinoma, cyst, lump, neoplasm, sarcoma, swelling, tumefaction; CONCEPT 316

tumult [n] *uproar, confusion* ado, affray, agitation, altercation, babel, bedlam, brawl, clamor,

commotion, convulsion, din, disorder, disturbance, dither, excitement, ferment, fight, fracas, fuss, hassle*, jangle, lather*, maelstrom, noise, outbreak, outcry, pandemonium, paroxysm, pother, quarrel, racket, riot, row, ruction, seething, stir, strife, turbulence, turmoil, unrest, unsettlement, upheaval, upturn, wildness; CONCEPT 674 —*Ant.* calmness, order, peace

tumultous/tumultuous [adj] *confused; in an uproar* agitated, boisterous, clamorous, disorderly, disturbed, excited, fierce, hectic, irregular, lawless, noisy, obstreperous, passionate, raging, rambunctious, raucous, restless, riotous, rowdy, rowdydowdy, rumbunctious, stormy, termagant, turbulent, unrestrained, unruly, uproarious, violent, vociferous, wild; CONCEPT 548 —*Ant.* calm, orderly, peaceful

tundra [n] *plain* expanse, field, flat, flatland, open country, plateau, prairie, steppe, wasteland; CONCEPT 509

tune [n1] *melody, harmony* air, aria, carol, chorus, composition, concert, consonance, descant, diapason, ditty*, harmony, jingle, lay, measure, melodia, motif, number, piece, song, strain, theme, warble; CONCEPTS 264, 595 —*Ant.* silence

tune [n2] *agreement* accord, chime, chorus, concert, concord, concordance, consonance, euphony, harmony, pitch, sympathy, unison; CONCEPTS 670,714 —*Ant.* disagreement

tuneful [adj] *melodic, melodious* canorous, catchy*, dulcet, euphonic, euphonious, harmonic, harmonious, in tune, musical, pleasing, pleasing to the ear, resonant, songful, sonorous, sweet-sounding, symphonic, symphonious, tuned, well-tuned; CONCEPT 594

tune/tune up [v] *bring into harmony* accommodate, adapt, adjust, attune, conform, coordinate, dial, fix, harmonize, integrate, modulate, pitch, proportion, reconcile, regulate, set, string, tighten; CONCEPTS 65,126 —*Ant.* break, destroy, harm, hurt

tunnel [n] *covered passageway* adit, burrow, channel, crawl space, crawlway, crosscut, drift, hole, hole in the wall*, mine, passage, pit, shaft, subway, tube, underpass; CONCEPTS 509,513

tunnel [v] *dig a passage through* burrow, excavate, mine, penetrate, sap, scoop out, undermine; CONCEPT 178

turbulent [adj] *unsettled, raging (referring to weather)* agitated, bitter, blustering, blustery, boiling, bumpy, choppy, coarse, confused, destructive, disordered, disturbed, fierce, foaming, furious, howling, inclement, moiling, noisy, restless, riotous, roaring, rough, ruffled, rugged, stirred up, stormful, storming, stormy, swirling, tempestuous, thunderous, tremulous, tumultous/tumultuous, unstable, violent, wild; CONCEPT 525 —*Ant.* calm, mild, moderate, settled

turbulent [adj2] *rebellious, unmanageable* agitated, anarchic, angry, bitter, boisterous, chaotic, demonstrative, destructive, disorderly, excited, fierce, fiery, foaming, insubordinate, lawless, mutinous, obstreperous, passionate, perturbed, quarrelsome, rabid, rambunctious, rampant, raucous, refractory, riotous, rough, roughhouse*, rowdy, rude, seditious, shaking, stern, storming, termagant, tumultous/tumultuous, unbridled, uncontrolled, undisciplined, ungovernable, unruly, untamed, uproarious, vehement, violent, vociferous, wild; CONCEPT 401 —Ant. calm, manageable, moderate, obedient, stable

turmoil [n] *chaos* agitation, ailment, anxiety, anxiousness, bedlam, bustle, commotion, confusion, disorder, disquiet, disquietude, distress, disturbance, dither, ferment, flap*, flurry, free-for-all*, fuss, hassle*, hectic, hubbub*, lather*, mix-up, noise, pandemonium, pother, restiveness, restlessness, riot, row, ruckus, stir, strife, to-do*, topsy-turvy, trouble, tumult, turbulence, unrest, uproar, violence, whirl; CONCEPTS 230,674 —Ant. calm, harmony, order, peace

turn [n1] *revolution, curving* about-face, angle, bend, bias, bow, branch, change, changeabout, circle, circuit, circulation, circumvolution, corner, curve, cycle, departure, detour, deviation, direction, drift, flection, flexure, fork, gyration, gyre, heading, hook, pirouette, pivot, quirk, retroversion, reversal, reverse, reversion, right-about, roll, rotation, round, shift, spin, spiral, swing, tack, tendency, trend, turnabout, turning, twist, twisting, wheel, whirl, wind, winding, yaw; CONCEPTS 198,738,754

turn [n2] *sudden change* alteration, bend, branch, crotch, deflection, departure, detour, deviation, digression, distortion, divarication, double, fork, modification, mutation, shift, tack, twist, variation, warp, yaw; CONCEPT 697 —Ant. stagnation

turn [n3] *chance, opportunity* accomplishment, act, action, bit, bout, crack*, deed, favor, fling*, gesture, go*, go around*, move, period, round, routine, say*, service, shift, shot*, spell, stint, succession, time, tour, trick, try; CONCEPT 693 —Ant. failure, miss

turn [n4] *walk, outing* airing, circuit, constitutional, drive, excursion, jaunt, promenade, ramble, ride, saunter, spin, stroll; CONCEPTS 147,224,363

turn [n5] *aptitude, knack* affinity, aptness, bent, bias, bump, disposition, faculty, flair, genius, gift, head, inclination, leaning, predisposition, propensity, talent; CONCEPTS 411,630 —Ant. inability

turn [n6] *scare* attack, blow, fit, fright, jolt, seizure, shock, spell, start, surprise; CONCEPTS 230,410

turn [v1] *revolve, curve* arc, bend, circle, circulate, circumduct, come around, corner, cut, eddy, go around, go round, ground, gyrate, gyre, hang a left*, hang a right*, incline, loop, make a left, make a right, move in a circle, negotiate, orbit, oscillate, pass, pass around, pirouette, pivot, roll, rotate, round, sway, swing, swivel, take a bend*, twirl, twist, vibrate, weave, wheel, whirl, wind, yaw; CONCEPTS 147,201,738,748

turn [v2] *reverse; change course* about-face, aim, alter, alternate, backslide, call off, capsize, change, change position, convert, curve, depart, detour, detract, deviate, digress, direct, diverge, double back, face about, go back, incline, inverse, invert, loop, move, pivot, rechannel, recoil, redirect, regress, relapse, retrace, return, revert, sheer, shift, shunt, shy away, sidetrack, subvert, sway, swerve, swing, swirl, switch, tack, transform, twist, upset, vary, veer, volte-

face, wheel, whip, whirl, zigzag; CONCEPTS 195,198,213

turn [v3] *adapt, fit* alter, become, change, change into, come, convert, divert, fashion, form, get, go, grow into, metamorphose, modify, mold, mutate, pass into, put, refashion, remake, remodel, render, run, shape, transfigure, transform, translate, transmute, transpose, vary, wax; CONCEPTS 232,697

turn [v4] *become sour or tainted* acidify, become rancid, break down, crumble, curdle, decay, decompose, disintegrate, dull, ferment, go bad, molder, putrefy, rot, sour, spoil, taint; CONCEPTS 456,469

turn [v5] *use; resort to* address, appeal, apply, approach, bend, be predisposed to, devote, direct, employ, favor, give, go, have recourse, incline, lend, look, prefer, recur, repair, run, tend, throw, turn one's energies to*, turn one's hand to*, undertake, utilize; CONCEPTS 100,225

turn [v6] *sicken* derange, discompose, disgust, disorder, make one sick*, nauseate, revolt, unbalance, undo, unhinge*, unsettle, upset; CONCEPTS 7,19,250 —Ant. make well

turn [v7] *change one's mind; defect* apostatize, bring round, change sides, desert, go over, influence, persuade, prejudice, prevail upon, rat*, renege, renounce, repudiate, retract, talk into, tergiversate, tergiverse; CONCEPTS 21,41,54

turn [v8] *twist a body part* bruise, crick, dislocate, hurt, sprain, strain, wrench; CONCEPT 246

turnabout [n] *about-face* changeabout, change of direction, doubleback, flip-flop, reversal, reverse, shift, turnaround, U-turn, volte-face; CONCEPT 697

turncoat [n] *traitor* apostate, back-stabber*, Benedict Arnold*, betrayer, conspirator, deceiver, defector, deserter, double-crosser*, fink*, informer, Judas*, quisling, rat*, rebel, renegade, snake*, sneak*, snitch*, spy, squealer*, stool pigeon*, tattletale, tergiversator, treasonist, two-timer*, whistle-blower*; CONCEPT 412

turn down [v] *reject* decline, disapprove, dismiss, rebuff, refuse, reprobate, repudiate, say no, scorn, spurn, throw out; CONCEPTS 18, 54 —Ant. accept, ok, take

turn in [v] *go to bed* bed, catch some z's*, flop*, go to sleep, hit the hay*, hit the sack*, lie down, nap, pile in, rest, retire, roll in; CONCEPT 210 —Ant. awaken, get up, wake

turning point [n] *crucial occurrence* axis, change, climacteric, climax, contingency, crisis, critical moment, critical period, crossing, crossroads, crux, culmination, decisive moment, development, emergency, exigency, hinge, juncture, moment of truth*, pass, peak, pinch, pivot, shift, strait, transition, twist, zero hour*; CONCEPTS 679,832

turn off [v1] *disgust* alienate, bore, disenchant, disinterest, displease, irritate, lose one's interest, make one sick*, nauseate, offend, put off, repel, sicken; CONCEPTS 7,19 —Ant. appeal, cheer, delight, enchant, fascinate

turn off [v2] *stop from operating* close, cut, cut out, douse, extinguish, halt, hit the switch*, kill*, log off, put out, shut, shut down, shut off, switch off, turn out, unplug; CONCEPTS 121,234 —Ant. begin, open, start, turn on

turn on [v1] *excite, please* arouse, attract, captivate, enchant, get started, initiate, introduce, show, stimulate, stir up, thrill, titillate, work up; CONCEPT *11* —*Ant.* disenchant, disgust, displease, turn off

turn on [v2] *start the operation of* activate, begin, energize, get started, ignite, initiate, introduce, log on, put in gear, put on, set in motion, start up, switch on; CONCEPT *221* —*Ant.* close, end, finish, shut down, turn off

turnout [n1] *group assembling for event* assemblage, assembly, attendance, audience, congregation, crowd, gate, gathering, number, throng; CONCEPT *417*

turnout [n2] *amount produced* aggregate, output, outturn, product, production, productivity, quota, turnover, volume, yield; CONCEPTS *338,787* —*Ant.* origin, resource, source

turn out [v1] *equip; produce* accouter, appoint, arm, bear, bring out, build, clothe, dress, fabricate, finish, fit, fit out*, furnish, make, manufacture, outfit, process, put out, rig*, rig out*, yield; CONCEPTS *167,205,234*

turn out [v2] *get out of bed* appear, arise, come, emerge, get up, pile out*, rise, rise and shine*, roll out*, show up, uprise, wake, wake up; CONCEPT *159* —*Ant.* nap, sleep

turn over [v1] *give, transfer* assign, come across with, commend, commit, confer, confide, consign, convey, delegate, deliver, entrust, feed, find, furnish, give over, give up, hand, hand over, pass on, provide, relegate, relinquish, render, supply, surrender, yield; CONCEPTS *108, 143* —*Ant.* receive, take

turn over [v2] *think about or seriously* consider, contemplate, deliberate, give thought to, meditate, mull over, muse, ponder, reflect on, revolve, roll, ruminate, think over, wonder about; CONCEPTS *17,24* —*Ant.* ignore

turnpike [n] *highway* expressway, four-lane*, freeway, interstate, parkway, pike*, roadway, state highway, superhighway, toll road; CONCEPT *501*

turn up [v1] *come, arrive* appear, attend, blow in*, come in, enter, get, get in, make an appearance*, materialize, pop in*, punch in*, put in an appearance*, reach, roll in*, show, show up*, weigh in*; CONCEPT *159* —*Ant.* abandon, go, leave

turn up [v2] *discover or be discovered* become known, be found, bring to light*, catch, come across, come to light*, come to pass, crop up, descry, detect, dig up*, disclose, encounter, espy, expose, find, hit upon*, learn, meet, meet with*, pop up*, reveal, see, spot, track, track down*, transpire, uncover, unearth; CONCEPTS *31,183* —*Ant.* lose, miss

turpitude [n] *depravity* baseness, corruption, criminality, debasement, debauchery, degradation, evil, immorality, improbity, lewdness, licentiousness, perversion, sinfulness, vice, viciousness, vileness, wickedness; CONCEPT *645*

tussle [n] *struggle* battle, brawl, brush, clash, combat, conflict, contest, donnybrook, encounter, fight, fray, free-for-all*, grind, hassle, jam, roughhouse, row, rumble*, scramble, scrap*, scuffle, skirmish, strife, undertaking; CONCEPTS *87,106,674*

tussle [v] *struggle* battle, box, brawl, bump

heads*, conflict, contest, fight, go up against*, grapple, hassle, lock horns*, put up a fight*, romp, rough-house*, row, scrap, scuffle, tangle, wrestle; CONCEPT *106*

tutelage [n] *guardianship; teaching* apprenticeship, care, coaching, custody, drilling, education, guidance, instruction, lesson, preparation, protection, schooling, supervision, training, tutoring; CONCEPTS *274,285*

tutor [n] *person who teaches another privately* coach, educator, governor, grind, guardian, guide, instructor, lecturer, mentor, preceptor, private teacher, prof*, teach*, teacher; CONCEPT *350* —*Ant.* pupil, student

tutor [v] *teach someone privately* clue, coach, direct, discipline, drill, drum into*, edify, educate, guide, instruct, lay it out for*, lecture, let in on*, ready, school, train, tutate, update; CONCEPT *285* —*Ant.* learn

TV [n] *visual and audio entertainment transmitted via radio waves* audio, baby-sitter*, boob tube*, box*, eye*, idiot box*, receiver, small screen, station, television set, telly*, tube, TV set, vid*, video; CONCEPTS *277,279,293,463*

twaddle [n] *nonsense* babble, balderdash*, baloney*, BS*, bull, bunk*, chatter, crap*, drivel, foolishness, gibberish, hogwash*, hooey*, hot air*, idle talk, jive*, mumbo jumbo*, palaver, poppycock*, prattle, rubbish, silliness, trash*, tripe; CONCEPTS *230,388,633*

twilight [n] *onset of darkness at end of day* afterglow, afterlight, crepuscular light, decline, dimness, dusk, early evening, ebb, end, evening, eventide, gloaming, half-light, last phase*, late-afternoon, night, nightfall, sundown, sunset; CONCEPTS *810,832* —*Ant.* daybreak, sunrise

twin [adj] *duplicate, similar* accompanying, bifold, binary, copied, corresponding, coupled, double, dual, duplicating, geminate, identical, joint, like, matched, matching, paired, parallel, same, second, selfsame, twofold, very same; CONCEPTS *487,563,573* —*Ant.* dissimilar, individual, singular, unlike

twin [n] *something exactly like another* clone, companion, coordinate, corollary, counterpart, doppelganger, double, duplicate, fraternal twin, identical twin, likeness, look-alike, match, mate, reciprocal, ringer*, Siamese twin; CONCEPT *414*

twine [n] *rope, cord* braid, coil, convolution, cordage, knot, snarl, string, tangle, thread, twist, whorl, yarn; CONCEPT *475*

twine [v] *coil, twist together* bend, braid, corkscrew, curl, encircle, enmesh, entangle, entwine, interlace, interweave, knit, loop, meander, plait, spiral, splice, surround, tangle, twist, undulate, weave, wind, wrap, wreathe; CONCEPTS *147,201,742* —*Ant.* straighten, untwist

twinge [n] *sharp pain* ache, bite, gripe, lancination, misery, pang, pinch, prick, shiver, smart, spasm, stab, stitch, throb, throe, tic, tweak, twist, twitch; CONCEPT *728*

twinkle [v] *glimmer, shine* blink, coruscate, flash, flicker, gleam, glint, glisten, glitter, glow, illuminate, light, light up, scintillate, shimmer, sparkle, wink; CONCEPT *624*

twirl [v] *turn around circularly* gyrate, gyre, pirouette, pivot, purl, revolve, rotate, spin, turn, twist, wheel, whirl, whirligig, wind; CONCEPTS *150,152* —*Ant.* straight, untwirl, untwist

twist [n1] *curl, spin* arc, bend, braid, coil, convolution, curlicue, curve, flourish, hank, helix, jerk, meander, plug, ply, pull, roll, spiral, swivel, torsion, turn, twine, undulation, warp, wind, wrench, yank, zigzag; CONCEPTS 738,754

twist [n2] *sudden development; oddity* aberration, bent, change, characteristic, confusion, crotchet, eccentricity, entanglement, foible, idiosyncrasy, kink, knot, mess, mix-up, peculiarity, proclivity, quirk, revelation, screw-up*, slant, snarl, surprise, tangle, trait, turn, variation; CONCEPTS 411,832

twist [v1] *curl, spin* coil, contort, corkscrew, encircle, entwine, intertwine, rick, screw, spiral, sprain, squirm, swivel, turn, turn around, twine, twirl, warp, weave, wiggle, wind, wrap, wrap around, wreathe, wrench, wriggle, wring, writhe, zigzag; CONCEPTS 80,147,184,201,206, 704 —*Ant.* straighten, uncurl, untwist

twist [v2] *misrepresent* alter, belie, change, color, contort, distort, falsify, garble, misquote, misstate, pervert, warp; CONCEPT 63 —*Ant.* explain, explicate

twitch [v] *have a spasm* beat, blink, clasp, clutch, flutter, grab, grasp, grip, jerk, jiggle, jump, kick, lug, lurch, nip, pain, palpitate, pluck, pull, seize, shiver, shudder, snap, snatch, squirm, tic, tremble, tug, twinge, vellicate, yank; CONCEPTS 185,206

two-bit [adj] *cheap, worth very little* base, catchpenny, cheesy, crappy*, cruddy, garbage, gaudy, inferior, junky*, lousy, no good, piddling, poor, ratty, rinky-dink*, second-rate, shoddy, sleazy, small-time*, tatty, trashy, valueless, worthless; CONCEPT 589

two-faced [adj] *deceitful* artful, backstabbing, beguiling, crafty, cunning, deceiving, deceptive, dishonest, double-dealing, foxy, fraudulent, guileful, hypocritical, insincere, knavish, lying, misleading, shifty, sly, sneaky, tricky, underhanded, untruthful; CONCEPT 401

two-time [v] *deceive* backstab, be dishonest, be disloyal, betray, be unfaithful, burn, cheat, con, defraud, double-cross, dupe, mislead, take advantage of, trick, victimize; CONCEPTS 7,19,59

tycoon [n] *person who has a lot of money, power* administrator, big shot*, boss, business person, capitalist, captain of industry*, director, entrepreneur, executive, fat cat*, financier, industrialist, investor, magnate, mogul, wealthy person; CONCEPT 347 —*Ant.* pauper

type [n1] *class, kind* blazon, brand, breed, cast, category, character, classification, cut, description, feather, form, genre, group, ilk, likes, lot, mold, nature, number, order, persuasion, rubric, sample, sort, species, specimen, stamp, standard, strain, subdivision, variety, way; CONCEPTS 378, 411

type [n2] *example, model* archetype, epitome, essence, exemplar, original, paradigm, pattern, personification, prototype, quintessence, representative, sample, specimen, standard; CONCEPT 686

type [n3] *printed characters* case, emblem, face, figure, font, point size, print, printing, sign, symbol; CONCEPTS 79,284

type [v1] *classify* arrange, button down*, categorize, class, peg, pigeonhole*, put away, put down as, sort, standardize, stereotype, tab*, typecast; CONCEPTS 18,84

type [v2] *hit keys on machine to print document* copy, dash off*, enter data, hunt-and-peck*, teletype, touch, touch-type, transcribe, type-write, write; CONCEPTS 79,199,203

typical [adj] *usual, conventional* archetypal, archetypical, average, characteristic, classic, classical, common, commonplace, emblematic, essential, everyday, exemplary, expected, general, habitual, ideal, illustrative, in character*, indicative, in keeping, matter-of-course*, model, natural, normal, old hat*, ordinary, orthodox, paradigmatic, patterned, prevalent, prototypal, prototypical, quintessential, regular, representative, standard, standardized, stock, suggestive, symbolic, typic, unexceptional; CONCEPTS 530,533,547 —*Ant.* atypical, different, rare, unconventional, unorthodox, unusual

typify [v] *represent, characterize* body forth, describe, emblematize, embody, epitomize, exemplify, feature, illustrate, incarnate, mean, mirror, model, personify, stand for, sum up, symbolize; CONCEPTS 55,261,682

tyrannical [adj] *despotic, oppressive* authoritarian, autocratic, brutal, cruel, demanding, dictatorial, domineering, harsh, heavy-handed*, ironhanded*, mean, overbearing, repressive, ruthless, totalitarian, tough, unjust; CONCEPTS 537,548

tyranny [n] *dictatorship* absolutism, authoritarianism, autocracy, coercion, cruelty, despotism, domination, fascism, high-handedness, imperiousness, monocracy, oligarchy, oppression, peremptoriness, reign of terror*, severity, terrorism, totalitarianism, totality, unreasonableness; CONCEPTS 299,301 —*Ant.* democracy

tyrant [n] *person who dictates, oppresses* absolute ruler, absolutist, authoritarian, autocrat, bully, despot, dictator, Hitler*, inquisitor, martinet, oppressor, slave driver*, Stalin*; CONCEPTS 354,412 —*Ant.* democrat

tyro [n] *beginner* abecedarian, amateur, apprentice, buckwheater*, cadet, colt*, greenhorn, learner, neophyte, newcomer, new kid on the block*, novice, novitiate, pupil, recruit, rookie, starter, student, tenderfoot*, trainee; CONCEPTS 423,424

U

ubiquitous [adj] *ever-present* all-over, everywhere, omnipresent, pervasive, ubiquitary, universal, wall-to-wall*; CONCEPT 530 —*Ant.* rare, scarce

UFO [n] *unidentified flying object* extraterrestrial spacecraft, flying saucer, rocket, rocketship, spaceship; CONCEPT 504

ugly [adj1] *unattractive* animal, appalling, awful, bad-looking, beastly, deformed, disfigured, foul, frightful, grisly, gross, grotesque, hard-featured, hideous, homely, horrid, ill-favored, loathsome, misshapen, monstrous, not much to look at*, plain, repelling, repugnant, repulsive, revolting, unbeautiful, uncomely, uninviting, unlovely, unprepossessing, unseemly, unsightly; CONCEPT 579 —*Ant.* attractive, beautiful, lovely, pleasing

ugly [adj2] *unpleasant, disagreeable* base,

despicable, dirty, disgusting, distasteful, filthy, foul, frightful, hideous, horrid, ignoble, low, low-down, mean, messy, monstrous, nasty, nauseous, noisome, objectionable, odious, offensive, pesky, repellent, repugnant, repulsive, revolting, scandalous, servile, shocking, sickening, sordid, sorry, terrible, troublesome, troublous, vexatious, vile, wicked, wretched; CONCEPTS 403,571 —*Ant.* agreeable, good, kind, nice, pleasant, pleasing

ugly [adj3] *dangerous, threatening* angry, bellicose, black, cantankerous, crabbed, crabby, dark, disagreeable, dour, evil, fell, forbidding, formidable, gloomy, glum, grave, grievous, major, malevolent, menacing, morose, nasty, obnoxious, ominous, pugnacious, quarrelsome, rough, saturnine, scowling, serious, sinister, spiteful, sullen, surly, treacherous, truculent, vicious, violent, wicked; CONCEPTS 401,548 —*Ant.* delicate, gentle, safe

ulterior [adj] *secret; pertaining to a hidden goal* ambiguous, buried, concealed, covert, cryptic, dark, enigmatic, equivocal, guarded, hidden, implied, obscure, obscured, personal, privy, remote, secondary, selfish, shrouded, under cover, under wraps*, undisclosed, undivulged, unexpressed, unsaid; CONCEPTS 544,576 —*Ant.* expressed, known, overt, public

ultimate [adj1] *last, final* capping, chips down*, closing, concluding, conclusive, decisive, end, eventual, extreme, far out*, farthermost, farthest, final curtain*, furthermost, furthest, hindmost, latest, latter, lattermost, most distant, terminal; CONCEPTS 799,820 —*Ant.* beginning, first, introductory, opening

ultimate [adj2] *best, greatest* extreme, highest, incomparable, max*, maxi*, maximum, most, paramount, preeminent, significant, superlative, supreme, surpassing, the most, topmost, towering, transcendent, unequalable, unmatchable, unsurpassable, utmost; CONCEPTS 568,574 —*Ant.* least, lowest, worst

ultimate [adj3] *fundamental* absolute, basic, categorical, elemental, empyreal, empyrean, primary, radical, sublime, transcendental; CONCEPTS 535,546 —*Ant.* auxiliary, extra, inessential, secondary, unnecessary

ultimately [adv] *eventually* after all, after a while, as a conclusion, at last, at long last, at the close, basically, by and by, climactically, conclusively, finally, fundamentally, hereafter, in conclusion, in consummation, in due time, in future, in the end, in the sequel, presently, sequentially, someday, sometime, somewhere, sooner or later, yet; CONCEPT 820 —*Ant.* never

ultimatum [n] *final offer* conditions, demand, final notice, final proposal, final terms, final warning, final word, last chance, last offer, last word, sticking point, warning; CONCEPT 662

ultra [adj] *extreme* all out*, drastic, excessive, extremist, fanatical, far-out*, gone*, immoderate, outlandish, out of bounds*, outré*, rabid*, radical, revolutionary, too much*; CONCEPTS 562,569 —*Ant.* middle, moderate

ultramodern [adj] *up-to-date* advanced, ahead of its time, avant-garde, contemporary, current, cutting-edge*, fresh, futuristic, latest, leading-edge*, modernistic, modish, new, new-fashioned, nontraditional, now, present-day, revolutionary, state-of-the-art*, stylish, today, twenty-first century*, up-to-the-minute; CONCEPTS 168,177,202

umbrage [n] *personal displeasure* anger, annoyance, chagrin, exasperation, fury, grudge, high dudgeon*, huff, indignation, injury, ire, irking, irritation, miff*, nettling*, offense, pique, provoking, rage, resentment, sense of injury, vexation, wrath; CONCEPTS 29,410 —*Ant.* happiness, like, love, pleasure

umpire [n] *person who settles dispute* adjudicator, arbiter, arbitrator, assessor, compromiser, inspector, judge, justice, mediator, moderator, negotiator, peacemaker, proprietor, ref*, referee, settler, ump*; CONCEPTS 348,366,423

unable [adj] *not having talent, skill* can't cut it*, can't hack it*, can't make the grade*, clumsy, helpless, hog-tied*, impotent, impuissant, inadequate, incapable, incapacitated, incompetent, ineffectual, inefficacious, inefficient, inept, inoperative, no can do*, no good*, not able, not cut out for*, not equal to*, not up to*, out of commission*, powerless, sidelined*, unfit, unfitted, unqualified, unskilled, weak; CONCEPT 527 —*Ant.* able, adequate, capable, competent, fit, qualified, skillful, talented

unabridged [adj] *not shortened* complete, entire, full-length, intact, total, unabbreviated, uncondensed, uncut, unexpurgated, unshortened, whole; CONCEPTS 267,531 —*Ant.* abridged, condensed, incomplete, part, partial, shortened, unfinished

unacceptable [adj] *not suitable or satisfactory* below par*, damaged, disagreeable, displeasing, distasteful, exceptionable, half-baked*, ill-favored, improper, inadmissible, insupportable, lousy*, not up to snuff*, objectionable, obnoxious, offensive, reject, repugnant, unappealing, undesirable, uninviting, unpleasant, unsatisfactory, unwanted, unwelcome, won't do*; CONCEPTS 529,558 —*Ant.* acceptable, desirable, ok, satisfactory, suitable

unaccompanied [adj] *alone* abandoned, a cappella*, apart, by oneself, deserted, detached, hermit, individual, isolate, isolated, lone, loner, odd, on one's own, removed, single, solitary, solo, stag, traveling light*, unattended, unescorted; CONCEPTS 555,577 —*Ant.* accompanied, together

unaccountable [adj] *not explainable; mysterious* arcane, astonishing, baffling, extraordinary, impenetrable, incomprehensible, inexplicable, inscrutable, mystic, odd, peculiar, puzzling, strange, uncommon, unexplainable, unfathomable, unheard-of, unintelligible, unknowable, unusual, unwonted; CONCEPTS 529,564 —*Ant.* accountable, comprehensible, explainable, responsible

unaccustomed [adj1] *not prepared, ready; new* ignorant, incompetent, inexperienced, newcome, not given to*, not used to, novice, too green*, unacquainted, unfamiliar with, uninformed, uninstructed, unpracticed, unseasoned, unskilled, untaught, untrained, unused to, unversed in; CONCEPTS 527,678 —*Ant.* accustomed, prepared, ready

unaccustomed [adj2] *new, strange* alien, altered, bizarre, different, eccentric, exceptional, exotic, foreign, imported, novel, outlandish, out of the ordinary, quaint, remarkable, singular, special, surprising, uncommon, unconventional, uncustomary, unexpected, unfamiliar, unknown, unorthodox, unprecedented, unusual, unwonted, variant; CONCEPTS 547,564 —Ant. customary, normal, usual

unadorned [adj] plain, simple austere, bare, basic, modest, stark, stripped down, undecorated, unembellished; CONCEPTS 485,589

unadulterated [adj] clean, pure; unmixed immaculate, purified, refined, sanitary, spotless, stainless, sterile, sterilized, unblemished, uncontaminated, uncorrupted, undebased, undefiled, undiluted, unpolluted, unsoiled, unstained, unsullied, untainted, untarnished, untouched, wholesome; CONCEPT 621

unadvised [adj] not smart; careless brash, hasty, heedless, hot-headed, ignorant, ill-advised, imprudent, inadvisable, incautious, inconsiderate, indiscreet, injudicious, in the dark*, rash, reckless, thoughtless, unaware, unconsidered, uninformed, unknowing, unsuspecting, unwarned, unwary, unwise; CONCEPTS 403,548 —Ant. advised, wise

unaffected [adj1] honest, unsophisticated artless, candid, direct, folksy*, forthright, frank, genuine, guileless, homey*, ingenuous, modest, naive, natural, plain, simple, sincere, single, spontaneous, straightforward, true, unartificial, unassuming, unpretentious, unschooled, unspoilt, unstudied, up front*; CONCEPTS 401,404 —Ant. refined, sophisticated, unnatural

unaffected [adj2] unchanged, unmoved aloof, callous, calm, casual, cold fish*, cool, easy-going, hard-boiled*, hard-hearted*, impassive, impervious, laid-back*, not influenced, proof, steady, thick-skinned*, unaltered, unconcerned, unexcited, unimpressed, uninfluenced, unresponsive, unruffled, unstirred, untouched; CONCEPTS 542,548 —Ant. affected, changed, moved, unnatural

unafraid [adj] fearless assured, ballsy*, bold, brassy, brave, cheeky, cocky, confident, courageous, daring, dashing, dauntless, gallant, game, gritty, gutsy, having nerves of steel*, heroic, nervy, plucky, spunky, sure, undaunted, unfearing, unfrightened, unscared, unshakable, valiant; CONCEPT 401

unanimous [adj] in agreement; uncontested accepted, accordant, agreed, agreeing, as one, assenting, collective, combined, common, communal, concerted, concordant, concurrent, consensual, consentient, consistent, consonant, harmonious, homogeneous, in complete accord, like-minded, of one mind, popular, public, shared, single, solid, universal, undisputed, undivided, unified, united, unquestioned, with one voice*; CONCEPTS 8,267,563 —Ant. split

unappetizing [adj] distasteful flat, flavorless, grody*, gross, icky*, insipid, savorless, stinky, tasteless, unappealing, unattractive, uninteresting, uninviting, unpalatable, unpleasant, unsavory, vapid, yucky*; CONCEPTS 462,529 —Ant. appetizing, attractive, delicious, savory, tasty

unapproachable [adj1] unfriendly aloof, chilly*, cold, cool, distant, frigid, hesitant, inaccessible, remote, reserved, standoffish, uncommunicative, unsociable, withdrawn;

CONCEPTS 404,555 —Ant. approachable, friendly

unapproachable [adj2] difficult to get to inaccessible, out of reach, out-of-the-way, remote, unattainable, unobtainable, unreachable; CONCEPT 576 —Ant. approachable, easy

unarmed [adj] disarmed exposed, hands tied*, helpless, indefensible, like a sitting duck*, naked*, open, powerless, unguarded, unprotected, unshielded, vulnerable, weaponless, wide open*; CONCEPTS 555,576

unasked [adj] voluntary arrogant, gratuitous, impudent, not asked, of one's own accord, overbearing, presumptuous, spontaneous, supererogatory, unbidden, uncalled-for, undemanded, undesired, uninvited, unprompted, unrequested, unsought, unwanted, unwelcome, voluntarily, willing, without prompting; CONCEPTS 401,558 —Ant. asked, invited, involuntary, solicited

unassuming [adj] shy backward, bashful, diffident, humble, lowly, meek, modest, mousy*, plain, prim, quiet, reserved, retiring, self-effacing, simple, unambitious, unassertive, unobtrusive, unostentatious, unpretending, unpretentious; CONCEPTS 401,404 —Ant. bold, brave, confident, presumptuous

unattached [adj] disconnected, free apart, at liberty, autonomous, available, detached, fancy-free*, footloose*, independent, off the hook*, on one's own*, separate, single, unaffiliated, uncommitted, unconnected, uninvolved, unmarried; CONCEPTS 267,401,482,542

unattractive [adj] ugly bad-looking, beastly, deformed, disfigured, disgusting, frightful, gross, grotesque, hideous, homely, horrid, monstrous, not much to look at*, plain, repelling, repugnant, repulsive, revolting, unalluring, unappealing, unsightly; CONCEPT 579

unauthorized [adj] not sanctioned, permitted crooked*, dirty*, illegal, illegitimate, no-no*, off base*, out of bounds*, out of line*, over the line*, pirated, shady*, unapproved, unconstitutional, under the table*, unjustified, unlawful, unofficial, unsanctioned, unwarranted, wildcat*; wrongful; CONCEPTS 319,548 —Ant. allowable, authorized, official, permitted

unavailing [adj] futile barren, empty, exhausted, fruitless, idle, impractical, ineffective, ineffectual, in vain, on a treadmill*, save one's breath*, to no avail*, to no effect*, to no purpose*, trifling, trivial, unproductive, unprofitable, unsuccessful, useless, vain, valueless, worthless; CONCEPTS 528,548,560

unavoidable [adj] bound to happen certain, compulsory, fated, impending, ineluctable, ineludible, inescapable, inevasible, inevitable, inexorable, locked up*, necessary, obligatory, open and shut*, set, sure, unescapable; CONCEPT 535 —Ant. avoidable, escapable

unaware [adj] ignorant blind, careless, caught napping*, daydreaming, deaf, deaf to*, doped*, forgetful, heedless, in a daze*, inattentive, incognizant, inconversant,insensible, mooning, negligent, nescient, not all there*, not cognizant, oblivious, out cold*, out of it*, out to lunch*, spacey*, unacquainted, unconcerned, unconscious, unenlightened, unfamiliar, uninformed, uninstructed, unknowing, unmindful,

unsuspecting, unwitting; CONCEPT 402
—*Ant.* aware, cognizant, informed, knowing,
suspicious

unawares [*adv*] *without warning; suddenly*
aback, abruptly, accidentally, by accident, by
mistake, by surprise, carelessly, ignorantly,
inadvertently, mistakenly, off guard, short, sudden, surprisingly, unconsciously, unexpectedly,
unintentionally, unknowingly, unprepared,
unready, unwittingly; CONCEPTS 544,548,799
—*Ant.* consciously, knowingly

unbalanced [*adj1*] *not even, stable* asymmetric, asymmetrical, disproportionate, irregular,
lopsided, not balanced, off-balance, shaky,
top-heavy, treacherous, unequal, uneven,
unstable, unsteady, unsymmetrical, wobbly;
CONCEPT 480 —*Ant.* balanced, even, fair,
just, sound, stable

unbalanced [*adj2*] *crazy; mentally disturbed*
batty*, daft, demented, deranged, eccentric,
erratic, flaky*, freaky*, insane, irrational,
kinky*, kooky*, lunatic, mad, nobody home*,
non compos mentis*, not all there*, nutty*,
out to lunch*, psychotic, touched, troubled,
unglued*, unhinged*, unscrewed*, unsound,
unstable; CONCEPT 403 —*Ant.* balanced,
sane, well

unbearable [*adj*] *very bad; too much* a bit
much*, enough, heavy-handed*, inadmissible,
insufferable, insupportable, intolerable, last
straw*, oppressive, unacceptable, unendurable,
unsurpassable; CONCEPTS 537,571 —*Ant.*
acceptable, bearable, good, tolerable

unbecoming [*adj*] *improper, unsuitable* awkward, clumsy, discreditable, gauche, ill-suited,
inappropriate, inapt, incongruous, indecent,
indecorous, indelicate, inept, maladroit, malapropos, offensive, rough, salacious, tacky*,
tasteless, unattractive, unbefitting, uncomely,
undue, unfair, unfit, unfitting, unflattering,
ungodly, unhandsome, unlovely, unseasonable,
unseemly, unsightly, unsuited, untimely, untoward, unworthy; CONCEPTS 558,579,589 —*Ant.*
acceptable, becoming, fitting, proper, seemly,
suitable

unbelievable [*adj*] *beyond the imagination*
astonishing, beyond belief, cockamamie*,
cockeyed*, doubtful, dubious, far-fetched,
fishy*, flaky*, flimsy*, for the birds*, full
of holes*, harebrained*, implausible, impossible,
improbable, incogitable, inconceivable, incredible, kooky*, lamebrained*, open to doubt,
outlandish, past belief, phony, preposterous,
questionable, reaching, scatterbrained*, screwy*,
staggering, suspect, thick*, thin*, too much*,
unconvincing, unimaginable, unsubstantial,
unthinkable, weak, won't hold water*, won't
wash*; CONCEPTS 529,548 —*Ant.* believable,
credible, plausible, real

unbelieving [*adj*] *skeptical* agnostic, cynical,
disbelieving, distrustful, doubtful, doubting,
dubious, freethinking, leery, mistrustful,
nonbelieving, not born yesterday*, questioning,
show-me*, suspicious, unconvinced; CONCEPT
403

unbending [*adj*] *rigid, tough* aloof, crisp, distant, do or die*, dug in*, firm, formal, hard as
nails*, hard-line*, hold one's ground*, hold
the fort*, hold the line*, incompliant, inelastic,

inexorable, inflexible, intractable, locked in*,
obdurate, obstinate, relentless, reserved, resolute,
set in stone*, severe, single-minded, standing
one's ground*, standing pat*, sticking to one's
guns*, stiff, strict, stubborn, uncompromising,
unflexible, unrelenting, unswayable, unyielding, uptight; CONCEPTS 401,534,604 —*Ant.*
bending, flexible, pliable, pliant, relaxed, soft

unbiased [*adj*] *not prejudiced* aloof, cold,
disinterested, dispassionate, equal, equitable,
even-handed, fair, honest, impartial, just,
neutral, nondiscriminatory, nonpartisan,
objective, on the fence*, open-minded, straight,
unbigoted, uncolored, uninterested, unprejudiced; CONCEPT 542 —*Ant.* biased, fair, just,
prejudiced, subjective

unblemished [*adj*] *not flawed* chaste, clean,
decent, faultless, flawless, immaculate, intact,
modest, perfect, pure, sound, spotless, stainless,
undamaged, undefiled, unflawed, unhurt, unimpaired, uninjured, unmarked, unmarred, unspotted, unstained, unsullied, untarnished, whole;
CONCEPTS 485,621 —*Ant.* blemished, flawed,
imperfect

unbreakable [*adj*] *strong, tough* adamantine,
armored, brass-bound, durable, everlasting,
firm, incorruptible, indestructible, infrangible,
invulnerable, lasting, nonbreakable, perdurable,
resistant, rugged, shatterproof, solid, tight,
toughened, unbreakable, unyielding; CONCEPT
488 —*Ant.* breakable, delicate, fragile, weak

unbridled [*adj*] *unrestrained* berserk, chaotic,
crazed, crazy, enthusiastic, hysterical, madcap,
noisy, rabid, riotous, turbulent, unchecked,
unconstrained, uncontrolled, uncurbed, undisciplined, ungovernable, unmanageable, violent,
wild; CONCEPT 401

unbroken [v] *continuous, whole* ceaseless,
constant, deep, endless, entire, even, fast,
incessant, intact, perfect, perpetual, profound,
progressive, regular, solid, sound, successive,
total, undisturbed, unimpaired, uninterrupted,
unremitting, unruffled, untroubled; CONCEPTS
482,485,798 —*Ant.* broken, discontinuous,
inconstant, intermittent, partial

unburden [*adj*] *get rid of* clear, confess, confide, disburden, discharge, disclose, disencumber, dispose of, divulge, dump, ease, empty,
get off one's chest*, lay bare*, let hair down*,
lighten, lose, out with it*, own, relieve, relinquish, reveal, shake, shake off*, tell all*, throw
off, unbosom, unload; CONCEPTS 60,211,244
—*Ant.* conceal, hide

uncalled-for [*adj*] *unnecessary* accidental,
avoidable, fortuitous, futile, inappropriate,
inessential, needless, nonessential, not required,
optional, unessential, uninvited, unneeded, unrequired, unwanted, unwarranted, unwelcome,
useless; CONCEPT 546

uncanny [*adj*] *very strange, unusual* astonishing, astounding, creepy, devilish, eerie, exceptional, extraordinary, fantastic, ghostly,
ghoulish, incredible, inexplainable, inspired,
magical, miraculous, mysterious, mystifying,
preternatural, prodigious, queer, remarkable,
scary, secret, singular, spooky, superhuman,
supernatural, supernormal, supranormal, unearthly, unheard-of, unnatural, weird; CONCEPTS
537,564 —*Ant.* common, earthly, natural, usual

uncaring [*adj*] *indifferent* aloof, blasé, callous, cold, cool, detached, disinterested, dispassionate, heartless, impervious, listless, nonchalant, passionless, unaroused, unconcerned, unemotional, uninvolved, unmoved, unsympathetic; CONCEPTS 403,542

unceasing [*adj*] *incessant* ceaseless, constant, continual, continuous, day-and-night*, endless, eternal, everlasting, lasting, never-ending, nonstop, permanent, perpetual, persistent, relentless, round-the-clock*, steady, unending, uninterrupted, unyielding; CONCEPTS 534,798

uncertain [*adj*] *doubtful, changeable* ambiguous, ambivalent, chancy, conjectural, dubious, erratic, fitful, hanging by a thread*, hazy, hesitant, iffy*, incalculable, inconstant, indefinite, indeterminate, indistinct, insecure, irregular, irresolute, on thin ice*, precarious, questionable, risky, speculative, touch and go*, unclear, unconfirmed, undecided, undetermined, unfixed, unforeseeable, unpredictable, unreliable, unresolved, unsettled, unsure, up for grabs*, up in the air*, vacillating, vague, variable, wavering; CONCEPTS 529,534,535 —*Ant.* certain, clear, definite, determined, foreseeable, secure, sure, unchanging

uncertainty [*n*] *doubt, changeableness* ambiguity, ambivalence, anxiety, bewilderment, concern, confusion, conjecture, contingency, dilemma, disquiet, distrust, doubtfulness, dubiety, guesswork, hesitancy, hesitation, incertitude, inconclusiveness, indecision, irresolution, lack of confidence, misgiving, mistrust, mystification, oscillation, perplexity, puzzle, puzzlement, qualm, quandary, query, questionableness, reserve, scruple, skepticism, suspicion, trouble, uneasiness, unpredictability, vagueness, wonder, worry; CONCEPTS 388, 410,696 —*Ant.* certainty, definiteness, security, sureness

unchangeable [*adj*] *constant, steadfast* changeless, continuing, firm, fixed, immovable, immutable, inalterable, inevitable, inflexible, invariable, irreversible, permanent, resolute, stable, strong, unalterable, unmodifiable, unmovable; CONCEPT 534 —*Ant.* changeable, changing, inconstant, intermittent, temporary

unchanging [*adj*] *constant, permanent* abiding, changeless, consistent, continuing, enduring, equable, eternal, even, fixed, immutable, imperishable, invariable, lasting, perpetual, rigid, same, stabile, static, unchanged, unfading, unfailing, unfluctuating, uniform, unvarying; CONCEPTS 534,551,649 —*Ant.* changeable, changing, inconstant, intermittent, temporary

uncharted [*adj*] *unknown* alien, concealed, distant, exotic, faraway, far-off, foreign, hidden, little known, remote, undiscovered, unexplored, unheard-of, unidentified, unmapped, unnamed; CONCEPT 576

uncivil [*adj*] *rude* abrupt, bad-mannered, barbaric, blunt, boorish, coarse, curt, discourteous, gross, gruff, ill-mannered, impolite, inconsiderate, insulting, mannerless, uncivilized, uncouth, uncultured, unfriendly, ungentlemanly, unmannerly, unpolished, unrefined, vulgar; CONCEPTS 267,401

uncivilized [*adj*] *wild, uncultured* barbarian, barbaric, barbarous, boorish, brutish, churlish, coarse, crass, crude, discourteous, disrespectful, gross, ill-bred, impertinent, impolite, loutish, mannerless, outrageous, philistine, primitive, rude, rugged, savage, unconscionable, uncontrolled, uncouth, uncultivated, uneducated, ungodly, unholy, unmannered, unpolished, unrefined, unsophisticated, vulgar, wicked; CONCEPT 401 —*Ant.* civilized, cultured, domesticated, polished, refined, sophisticated

unclean [*adj*] *dirty* bedraggled, befouled, besmirched, black, blurred, common, contaminated, corrupt, decayed, defiled, desecrated, dusty, evil, feculent, fetid, filthy, foul, grimy, impure, messy, muddy, nasty, polluted, profaned, putrescent, putrid, rancid, rank, rotten, sloppy, slovenly, smeared, smudged, soiled, sooty, sordid, spotted, squalid, stable, stained, stale, stinking, sullied, tainted, tarnished, unhealthful, vile; CONCEPT 621 —*Ant.* clean, hygienic, uncontaminated, unpolluted

uncomfortable [*adj1*] *painful, rough* afflictive, agonizing, annoying, awkward, bitter, cramped, difficult, disagreeable, distressing, dolorous, excruciating, galling, grievous, hard, harsh, ill-fitting, incommodious, irritating, thorny, torturing, troublesome, vexatious, wearisome; CONCEPTS 529,537,583 —*Ant.* comfortable, easy, painless

uncomfortable [*adj2*] *distressed, upset* aching, angry, anguished, annoyed, awkward, chafed, cheerless, comfortless, confused, discomfited, discomposed, disquieted, disturbed, embarrassed, exhausted, fatigued, galled, harsh, hurt, ill at ease, in pain, miserable, nervous, pained, restless, self-conscious, smarting, sore, stiff, strained, suffering, tired, troubled, uneasy, vexed, weary, worn, wracked, wretched; CONCEPT 403 —*Ant.* comfortable, content, happy

uncommitted [*adj*] *free; not involved* cut loose*, don't care*, fence-sitting*, floating, free-spirited, laid-back*, middle ground*, middle of the road*, neutral, nonaligned, nonpartisan, on the fence*, restrained, unaffiliated, unattached, uninvolved, unpledged; CONCEPTS 403,542 —*Ant.* aligned, attached, committed, involved, united

uncommon [*adj1*] *very different* aberrant, abnormal, anomalous, arcane, bizarre, curious, eccentric, egregious, exceptional, exotic, extraordinary, extreme, fantastic, few, freakish, infrequent, irregular, nondescript, noteworthy, novel, odd, original, out of the ordinary, out of the way*, outré, peculiar, prodigious, queer, rare, remarkable, scarce, seldom, singular, sporadic, startling, strange, surprising, unaccustomed, unconventional, uncustomary, unfamiliar, unheard of, unique, unorthodox, unusual, weird; CONCEPT 564 —*Ant.* common, familiar, normal, regular, usual

uncommon [*adj2*] *wonderful, exceptional* distinctive, extraordinary, incomparable, inimitable, notable, noteworthy, outstanding, rare, remarkable, singular, special, superior, unimaginable, unique, unparalleled, unprecedented, unthinkable, unwonted; CONCEPT 574 —*Ant.* bad, imperfect, poor

uncommonly [*adv*] *infrequently* exceptionally, extra, extremely, hardly ever, in few instances, irregularly, not often, now and then, occasionally, oddly, on occasion, particularly, peculiarly, rarely, remarkably, scarcely ever, seldom, sporadically, strangely, unusually, very; CONCEPT 541 —*Ant.* commonly, frequently

uncommunicative [*adj*] *shy, silent* aloof, buttoned up*, clammed up*, close, close-mouthed*, curt, distant, dried up*, evasive, guarded, hush-hush*, offish*, on the QT*, quiet, reserved, reticent, retiring, secretive, short, standoffish, taciturn, tight-lipped*, unapproachable, unresponsive, unsociable; CONCEPT 267 —*Ant.* communicative, confident, extroverted, responsive

uncomplicated [*adj*] *easy* apparent, basic, child's play*, cinch, clear, easily done, effortless, elementary, evident, manageable, no bother*, no problem*, no sweat*, not burdensome, not difficult, nothing to it*, simple, simple as ABC*, snap, straightforward, uninvolved; CONCEPT 565

uncompromising [*adj*] *stubborn* brick-wall*, decided, determined, firm, hard-core*, hard-line*, inexorable, inflexible, intransigent, locked, obdurate, obstinate, pigheaded*, relentless, resolute, rigid, set in stone*, single-minded, steadfast, stiff-necked*, strict, strong, tough, unbending; CONCEPTS 401,542 —*Ant.* compromising, cooperative, flexible, open, willing

unconcerned [*adj*] *carefree; apathetic* aloof, blind, blithe, callous, careless, cold, cool, deaf, detached, dispassionate, distant, easy, feckless, forgetful, hardened, hard-hearted, heedless, impassive, inattentive, incurious, indifferent, insensible, insensitive, insouciant, lackadaisical, lukewarm, negligent, neutral, nonchalant, oblivious, phlegmatic, relaxed, reserved, self-centered, serene, stony, supine, unbothered, uninterested, uninvolved, unmoved, unperturbed, unruffled, unsympathetic, untroubled, unworried; CONCEPTS 403,542 —*Ant.* caring, concerned, curious, interested

unconditional [*adj*] *absolute, total* actual, all out, assured, categorical, certain, clear, complete, decisive, definite, determinate, downright, entire, explicit, final, flat out, full, genuine, indubitable, no catch*, no fine print*, no holds barred*, no ifs ands or buts*, no kicker*, no strings*, open, out-and-out*, outright, plenary, positive, straight out, thorough, thoroughgoing, unconstrained, unequivocal, unlimited, unmistakable, unmitigated, unqualified, unquestionable, unreserved, unrestricted, utter, whole, wide; CONCEPTS 531,535,544 —*Ant.* conditional, incomplete, limited, qualified, unfinished

unconscionable [*adj*] *immoral, immoderate* amoral, barbarous, conscienceless, criminal, dishonest, excessive, exorbitant, extravagant, extreme, inordinate, knavish, outrageous, preposterous, sneaky, too much*, uncivilized, undue, unethical, unfair, ungodly, unholy, unjust, unprincipled, unreasonable, unscrupulous, wanton, wicked; CONCEPTS 545,569 —*Ant.* decent, good, moral, principled

unconscious [*adj1*] *not awake; out cold* benumbed, blacked out*, bombed*, cold*, comatose, dead to the world*, drowsy, entranced, feeling no pain*, flattened*, inanimate, in a trance, inert, insensate, insensible, knocked*, lethargic, numb, on the canvas*, out, out like a light*, palsied, paralyzed, passed out*, put away*, raving, senseless, stunned, stupefied, swooning, torpid, tranced, zonked*; CONCEPTS 314,539 —*Ant.* awake, aware, conscious

unconscious [*adj2*] *ignorant; automatic* accidental, gut*, inadvertent, inattentive, inherent, innate, instinctive, involuntary, latent, lost, reflex, repressed, subconscious, subliminal, suppressed, unaware, uncalculated, undeliberate, unheeding, unintended, unintentional, unmindful, unpremeditated, unrealized, unwitting; CONCEPTS 542,544 —*Ant.* aware, conscious, decided, intended, intentional, knowing

unconstitutional [*adj*] *illegal* against the law, banned, criminal, felonious, forbidden, illegitimate, illicit, lawless, not legal, outlawed, prohibited, prosecutable, unauthorized, unlawful, violating, wrongful; CONCEPTS 319,545

uncontrollable [*adj*] *wild; carried away* beside oneself, disorderly, excited, fractious, frantic, freaked, furious, headstrong, indocile, indomitable, insuppressible, insurgent, intractable, irrepressible, irresistible, lawless, like a loose cannon*, mad, obdurate, obstinate, recalcitrant, strong, stubborn, uncontainable, undisciplinable, undisciplined, ungovernable, unmanageable, unrestrainable, unruly, violent; CONCEPT 401 —*Ant.* controllable, controlled, manageable, mild, moderate

unconventional [*adj*] *very different; odd* anarchistic, atypical, avant-garde, beat, bizarre, crazy, eccentric, far-out*, freakish, freaky, free and easy*, idiosyncratic, individual, individualistic, informal, irregular, kinky*, kooky*, nonconformist, oddball*, offbeat, off the beaten track*, off the wall*, original, out in left field*, out of the ordinary, unceremonious, uncommon, uncustomary, unique, unorthodox, unusual, way-out*, weirdo*; CONCEPT 564 —*Ant.* conventional, formal, normal, standard, usual

uncoordinated [*adj*] *awkward, clumsy* all thumbs*, bumbling, bungling, butterfingered*, gawkish, gawky, graceless, heavy-handed, klutzy*, like a bull in a china shop*, lumbering, not agile, stumbling, unadept, ungainly, ungraceful, unhandy, unskillful; CONCEPTS 401,402,584

uncouth [*adj*] *clumsy, uncultivated* awkward, barbaric, boorish, cheap, clownish, coarse, crass, crude, discourteous, disgracious, gawky, graceless, gross, heavy-handed, ill-bred, ill-mannered, impertinent, impolite, inelegant, loud, loud-mouthed, loutish, oafish, raunchy, raw, rough, rude, rustic, strange, tacky*, uncalled-for*, uncivil, uncivilized, ungainly, ungenteel, ungentlemanly, unpolished, unrefined, unseemly, vulgar; CONCEPT 401 —*Ant.* agile, couth, cultivated, polished, refined, sophisticated

uncover [*v*] *reveal, disclose* bare, betray, break, bring to light*, crack, denude, dig up*, discover, display, divulge, expose, give away, hit upon, lay bare, lay open, leak, make known, open, open up, show, strike, strip, stumble on, subject, tap, tell, tip one's hand*, unclothe, unearth, unmask, unveil, unwrap; CONCEPTS 60,183,261 —Ant. conceal, cover, hide, suppress

uncovered [adj] exposed bare, brought to light*, caught, disclosed, discovered, divulged, dug up*, found out, laid bare*, made public, naked, nude, on display, on view, revealed, shown, solved, stripped, unconcealed, unmasked, unprotected, unveiled, visible, vulnerable, weakened; CONCEPT 576

uncritical [adj] casual, unfussy careless, cursory, easily pleased, imperceptive, imprecise, imprudent, inaccurate, indiscriminate, offhand, perfunctory, shallow, slipshod, superficial, undiscerning, undiscriminating, unexacting, uniformed, unperceptive, unselective, unthinking; CONCEPT 542 —Ant. critical, discriminating, formal, fussy, important

undaunted [adj] brave, bold audacious, coming on strong*, courageous, dauntless, fearless, fire-eating*, gallant, icy*, indomitable, intrepid, not discouraged, not put off*, resolute, spunky, steadfast, unafraid, unalarmed, unapprehensive, undeterred, undiscouraged, undismayed, unfaltering, unflinching, unshrinking, valiant, valorous; CONCEPT 401 —Ant. cowardly, shrinking

undecided [adj] not sure, not definite ambivalent, betwixt and between*, blowing hot and cold*, borderline, debatable, dithering*, doubtful, dubious, equivocal, hemming and hawing*, hesitant, iffy*, indecisive, indefinite, in the middle*, irresolute, moot, of two minds*, on the fence*, open, pendent, pending, running hot and cold*, tentative, torn, uncertain, unclear, uncommitted, undetermined, unfinished, unsettled, unsure, up in the air*, vague, waffling, wavering, wishy-washy*; CONCEPTS 403,529 —Ant. certain, decided, definite, determined, settled, sure, undoubted

undeniable [adj] definite, proven actual, beyond doubt, beyond question, binding, certain, clear, compulsory, evident, for sure*, inarguable, incontestable, incontrovertible, indisputable, indubitable, irrefutable, manifest, necessary, no ifs and or buts*, obligatory, obvious, open and shut*, patent, positive, real, sound, sure, sure thing*, true, unanswerable, unassailable, undoubted, unquestionable; CONCEPT 535 —Ant. contestable, disputable, doubted, indefinite, unproven

undependable [adj] irresponsible bum, capricious, careless, changeable, dubious, erratic, fickle, fly-by-night*, inconsistent, inconstant, indefinite, indeterminate, loose*, no bargain*, no-good*, treacherous, trick, tricky, trustless, unassured, uncertain, unpredictable, unreliable, unsafe, unsound, unstable, unsure, untrustworthy, variable; CONCEPTS 401,535 —Ant. dependable, reliable, responsible, trustworthy

under [adv1/prep1] below beneath, bottom, concealed by, covered by, down, downward, held down, inferior, lower, nether, on the bottom, on the nether side, on the underside, pinned, pressed down, supporting, to the bottom, underneath; CONCEPTS 586,735,793 —Ant. above, higher, more, over, up, upward

under [adv2/prep2] secondary amenable, belonging, collateral, consequent, corollary, dependent, directed, following, governed, included, inferior, in the power of, junior, lesser, low, lower, obedient, obeying, reporting, sub, subject, subjugated, subordinate, subsequent, subservient, subsidiary, substract, subsumed; CONCEPTS 560,575,577 —Ant. major, primary

undercover [adj] secret, spy clandestine, concealed, confidential, covert, creep, furtive, hidden, hole-and-corner*, hush-hush*, incognito*, intelligence, on the QT*, private, stealth, stealthy, sub-rosa*, surreptitious, underground, underhand, underneath, under wraps*; CONCEPTS 544,576 —Ant. known, open, public

undercurrent [n] drift, pull atmosphere, aura, crosscurrent, direction, eddy, feeling, flavor, hint, inclination, indication, insinuation, intimation, murmur, overtone, propensity, riptide, sense, suggestion, tendency, tenor, tinge, trace, trend, underflow, undertone, undertow, vibes*, vibrations; CONCEPTS 673,738

underdog [n] unlikely winner in a contest or struggle bottom dog, dark horse, longshot, out-of-towner; CONCEPTS 366,423 —Ant. favorite

underestimate [v] minimize; rate too low belittle, deprecate, depreciate, disesteem, disparage, make light of*, miscalculate, miscarry, not do justice*, put down*, sell short*, slight, think too little of*, underrate, undervalue; CONCEPTS 12,54,764 —Ant. exaggerate, maximize, overestimate

undergo [v] be subjected to abide, bear, bear up, bow, defer, encounter, endure, experience, feel, go through, have, know, meet with, put up with, see, share, stand, submit to, suffer, support, sustain, tolerate, weather, withstand, yield; CONCEPT 23 —Ant. commit, do, execute

underground [adj1] below the surface below ground, buried, covered, in the recesses, subterranean, subterrestrial, sunken, underfoot; CONCEPT 583 —Ant. aboveground, ground, sky

underground [adj2] secret, subversive alternative, avant-garde, clandestine, concealed, covert, experimental, hidden, hush-hush*, on the QT*, on the sly*, private, radical, resistant, resistive, revolutionary, surreptitious, unbowed, unconventional, undercover, under wraps*, unusual; CONCEPTS 564,576 —Ant. authorized, condoned, known, legal, public

underhand [adj] deceitful clandestine, concealed, crafty, crooked, cunning, deceptive, devious, dirty-dealing*, dishonest, dishonorable, double-crossing*, duplicitous, fraudulent, furtive, guileful, hush-hush*, indirect, insidious, oblique, on the QT*, on the quiet*, secret, secretive, shady, shifty, slippery*, sly*, sneaking, sneaky, stealthy, sub-rosa, surreptitious, treacherous, tricky, two-faced*, two-timing*, undercover, underhanded, under wraps*, unethical, unfair, unjust, unscrupulous, wily; CONCEPTS 401,544 —Ant. aboveboard, forthright, frank, honest

underline [v] emphasize; mark accentuate, bracket, call attention to, caption, check off, draw attention to, feature, give emphasis, highlight, indicate, interlineate, italicize, play up, point to, point up, rule, stress, underscore; CONCEPTS 49,79

underling [n] subordinate aide, assistant, attendant, deputy, flunky*, gofer*, helper, inferior, lackey*, minion, peon, scrub*, second, second fiddle*, second stringer*, serf, servant, slave; CONCEPTS 348,423

underlying [adj] *fundamental, latent* basal, basic, bottom, bottom-line*, cardinal, concealed, critical, crucial, elemental, elementary, essential, hidden, indispensable, intrinsic, lurking, necessary, needful, nitty-gritty*, nub, primary, prime, primitive, radical, root, substratal, veiled, vital; CONCEPTS 546,549 —*Ant.* secondary

undermine [v] *weaken* attenuate, blunt, clip one's wings*, corrode, cripple, debilitate, dig, dig out*, disable, eat away*, enfeeble, erode, excavate, foil, frustrate, hollow out, hurt, impair, knock the bottom out of*, mine, poke full of holes*, ruin, sabotage, sandbag*, sap, soften, subvert, threaten, thwart, torpedo*, tunnel, undercut, wear, whittle away, wreck; CONCEPTS 14,240 —*Ant.* strengthen

underneath [adv/prep] *below* beneath, bottom, covered, lower, neath, nether, under; CONCEPTS 586,735 —*Ant.* above, over, up

underprivileged [adj] *poor* badly off*, depressed, deprived, destitute, disadvantaged, down and out*, handicapped, hapless, hard up*, have-not*, ill-fated, ill-starred, impoverished, indigent, in dire straits, in need, in want, needy, unfortunate, unlucky; CONCEPT 334 —*Ant.* privileged, rich, wealthy

underscore [v] *underline, emphasize* accent, accentuate, call attention to, caption, draw attention to, feature, give emphasis, highlight, indicate, italicize, mark, point to, stress; CONCEPTS 49,79

understand [v1] *appreciate, comprehend* accept, apprehend, be aware, be conscious of, be with it*, catch, catch on, conceive, deduce, discern, distinguish, explain, fathom, figure out, find out, follow, get*, get the hang of*, get the idea*, get the picture*, get the point*, grasp, have knowledge of, identify with, infer, interpret, ken*, know, learn, make out*, make sense of, master, note, penetrate, perceive, possess, read, realize, recognize, register, savvy*, see, seize, sense, sympathize, take in*, take meaning, tolerate; CONCEPT 15 —*Ant.* misinterpret, misunderstand

understand [v2] *think, believe* accept, assume, be informed, concede, conceive, conclude, conjecture, consider, count on, deduce, expect, fancy, feel for, gather, guess, hear, imagine, infer, learn, presume, reckon, suppose, surmise, suspect, take for granted, take it; CONCEPT 12 —*Ant.* disbelieve, mistake

understanding [adj] *accepting, tolerant* compassionate, considerate, discerning, empathetic, forbearing, forgiving, generous, kind, kindly, patient, perceptive, responsive, sensitive, sympathetic; CONCEPTS 401,542 —*Ant.* intolerant, unaccepting

understanding [n1] *comprehension, appreciation* acumen, apperception, apprehension, assimilation, awareness, decipherment, discernment, discrimination, grasp, grip, insight, intellect, intelligence, intuition, judgment, ken, knowing, knowledge, mastery, penetration, perception, perceptiveness, perceptivity, percipience, perspicacity, prehension, realization, reason, recognition, savvy, sense, sharpness,

wit; CONCEPT 409 —*Ant.* misinterpretation, misunderstanding

understanding [n2] *belief* acceptation, conception, conclusion, estimation, idea, import, impression, inkling, intendment, interpretation, judgment, knowledge, meaning, message, notion, opinion, perception, purport, sense, significance, significancy, signification, sympathy, view, viewpoint; CONCEPTS 682,689 —*Ant.* disbelief, mistake

understanding [n3] *informal agreement* accord, common view, concord, deal, handshake*, harmony, meeting of minds*, pact; CONCEPT 684 —*Ant.* disagreement

understood [adj] *assumed, implicit* accepted, appreciated, axiomatic, down pat*, implied, inferential, inferred, known, on to*, pat, presumed, roger*, tacit, taken for granted, undeclared, unexpressed, unsaid, unspoken, unstated, wise to, wordless; CONCEPT 529 —*Ant.* explained, explicit, spoken, written

understudy [n] *substitute* alternate, backup, double, fill-in, pinch hitter*, replacement, reserve, stand-by, stand-in, sub*, successor; CONCEPTS 423,712

undertake [v] *attempt, engage in* address oneself, agree, answer for, bargain, begin, commence, commit, commit oneself, contract, covenant, devote, embark, endeavor, enter upon, fall into, go about, go for, go in for, go into, guarantee, have a hand in*, have a try, hazard, initiate, launch, make a run at*, move, offer, pitch in, pledge, promise, set about, set in motion, set out, shoulder, stake, stipulate, tackle, take on, take the plunge*, take upon oneself, try, try out, venture, volunteer; CONCEPTS 87,100 —*Ant.* abstain, forego, forget

undertaker [n] *funeral director* embalmer, grave digger, mortician; CONCEPT 304

undertaking [n] *endeavor, attempt* adventure, affair, business, deal, effort, engagement, enterprise, essay, experiment, game, happening, hassle, hazard, job, move, operation, outfit, play, project, proposition, pursuit, shop, striving, struggle, task, thing*, trial, try, venture, what one is into*, work; CONCEPTS 87,324,349,362 —*Ant.* abstention

undertone [n] *suggestion, whisper* association, atmosphere, buzz, connotation, feeling, flavor, hint, hum, implication, low tone, mumble, murmur, mutter, overtone, rumor, tinge, touch, trace, undercurrent; CONCEPTS 65,682

underwater [adj] *under the water's surface* immersed, subaquatic, subaqueous, submarine, submerged, sunken, undersea; CONCEPTS 467, 514,603

underwear [n] *clothing worn under outerwear* bikini, boxers*, boxer shorts, bra, briefs, BVDs*, corset, drawers*, intimate things, jockeys, jockey shorts, lingerie, long johns, panties, shorts, skivvies*, smallclothes, underclothes, underclothing, undergarment, underpants, undershirt, underthings, undies; CONCEPT 451

underweight [adj] *thin* angular, anorectic, bony, gangly, malnourished, puny, scrawny, shadow, skeleton*, skin and bones*, skinny, starved, undernourished, undersized; CONCEPT 491 —*Ant.* chubby, fat, overweight, plump, thick

underworld [n] *criminal activity, element* abyss, Cosa Nostra, criminals, felonry, gangland, gangsters, Mafia, mob*, organized crime, racket*, riffraff*, syndicate; CONCEPTS 412,645

underwrite [v] *endorse, insure* accede, agree to, angel*, approve, back, bankroll*, collateral, consent, countersign, endow, finance, float, fund, guarantee, help, initial, okay*, pay, provide, provide financing, sanction, seal, secure, sign, sponsor, stake, subscribe, subsidize, support; CONCEPTS 50,88,110,341 —*Ant.* disapprove, invalidate, refuse, reject

undesirable [adj] *offensive, unacceptable* abominable, annoying, bothersome, defective, disagreeable, disliked, displeasing, distasteful, dreaded, icky, inadmissible, incommodious, inconvenient, inexpedient, insufferable, loathed, loathsome, objectionable, obnoxious, outcast, out of place, rejected, repellent, repugnant, scorned, shunned, to be avoided, troublesome, unattractive, unlikable, unpleasing, unpopular, unsatisfactory, unsavory, unsought, unsuitable, unwanted, unwelcome, unwished for, useless; CONCEPTS 529,570 —*Ant.* acceptable, appealing, desirable, pleasing, savory

undeveloped [adj] *immature* abortive, backward, behindhand, embryonic, half-baked, ignored, inchoate, incipient, inexperienced, latent, potential, primitive, primordial, unactualized, underdeveloped, unevolved, unprogressive, untaught, untrained; CONCEPTS 485,578, 797 —*Ant.* adult, developed, grown, mature

undisciplined [adj] *uncontrolled* defiant, disorderly, headstrong, inconsistent, insubordinate, lacking self-control, mischievous, naughty, noncompliant, ungoverned, unrestrained, unruly, untrained, wayward; CONCEPT 401

undisputed/undisputable [adj] *positive, accepted* acknowledged, admitted, arbitrary, assured, authoritative, beyond question, certain, conclusive, decided, dogmatic, final, incontestable, incontrovertible, indisputable, indubitable, irrefutable, not disputed, recognized, sure, tyrannous, unchallenged, uncontested, undeniable, undoubted, unequivocal, unerring, unquestioned; CONCEPT 535 —*Ant.* disputable, disputed, doubtful, dubious, negative, uncertain, unsure

undistinguished [adj] *ordinary* average, characterless, common, commonplace, dull, everyday, fair, garden-variety*, generic, mean, mediocre, modest, no great shakes*, normal, nothing special, nothing to write home about*, pedestrian, plain, prosaic, routine, run-of-the-mill*, second-rate, so-so*, typical, uneventful, unexceptional, unexciting, uninspired, unmemorable, unnoteworthy, unremarkable, usual; CONCEPTS 530,575

undivided [adj] *whole* absorbed, circumspect, collective, combined, complete, concentrated, concerted, continued, deliberate, detailed, diligent, engrossed, entire, exclusive, fast, fixed, full, intense, intent, joined, lock stock and barrel*, minute, rigid, scrupulous, single, solid, steady, thorough, unanimous, unbroken, uncut, undistracted, unflagging, united, unswerving, vigilant, wholehearted; CONCEPTS 482,531 —*Ant.* divided, partial, separate

undo [v1] *open* disengage, disentangle, free, loose, loosen, release, unbind, unblock, unbutton, unclose, unfasten, unfix, unlock, unloose, unloosen, unravel, unshut, unstop, untie, unwrap; CONCEPT 135 —*Ant.* close, do, fasten

undo [v2] *nullify, invalidate* abate, abolish, abrogate, annihilate, annul, break, bring down, bring to naught*, cancel, cramp*, craze, crimp*, decimate, defeat, demolish, destroy, have*, impoverish, injure, make waves*, mar, negate, neutralize, offset, outfox, outmaneuver, outsmart, overreach, overthrow, overturn, quash, queer*, raze, reverse, ruin, screw up*, shatter, skin*, smash, spoil, stymie*, subvert, unbuild, undermine, unsettle, upset, vitiate, wipe out*, wrack, wreck; CONCEPTS 7,19,121,252 —*Ant.* approve, permit, validate

undoing [n] *destruction, misfortune* accident, adversity, affliction, bad luck, bad omen, bane, blight, blow, blunder, calamity, casualty, catastrophe, collapse, curse, defeat, destroyer, difficulty, disgrace, doom, downfall, error, failure, fault, faux pas, flaw, fumble, grief, humiliation, last straw*, misadventure, miscalculation, mischance, mishap, misstep, omission, overthrow, overturn, reversal, reverse, ruin, ruination, shame, slip, smash, stumble, subversion, trial, trip, trouble, visitation, weakness, wreck; CONCEPTS 230,674,679 —*Ant.* building, creation, doing, good fortune

undoubtedly [adv] *certainly* assuredly, beyond question, beyond shadow of a doubt*, definitely, doubtless, easily, indeed, of course, really, surely, truly, undeniably, unmistakably, unquestionably, well, without doubt; CONCEPT 535 —*Ant.* doubtfully, indefinite, questionably

undress [v] *take off clothes* denude, disarray, dismantle, disrobe, divest oneself, doff, get off, get out of, husk, peel, shed, shock, slip off, slip out of, strip, unattire, uncloak, unclothe, unmask; CONCEPTS 211,453 —*Ant.* clothe, dress

undue [adj] *excessive, unnecessary* disproportionate, exceeding, exorbitant, extravagant, extreme, forbidden, illegal, ill-timed, immoderate, improper, inappropriate, inapt, indecorous, inept, inordinate, intemperate, needless, overmuch, sinister, too great, too much, unapt, uncalled-for, unconscionable, underhanded, undeserved, unfair, unfitting, unjust, unjustifiable, unjustified, unmeasurable, unreasonable, unseasonable, unseemly, unsuitable, untimely, unwarrantable, unwarranted; CONCEPTS 546, 558,569 —*Ant.* moderate, reasonable, sensible

undulate [v] *rise and fall* billow, flow, heave, oscillate, ripple, roll, surge, swell, swing, wave, wobble; CONCEPT 146

unduly [adv] *excessively* disproportionately, ever, extravagantly, extremely, illegally, immensely, immoderately, improperly, indecorously, inordinately, out of proportion, over, overfull, overly, overmuch, too, underhandedly, unfairly, unjustifiably, unjustly, unnecessarily, unreasonably; CONCEPTS 544,546,569 —*Ant.* moderately, reasonably, sensibly

undying [adj] *never-ending* constant, continuing, deathless, eternal, everlasting, immortal, imperishable, indestructible, inextinguishable, infinite, interminable, perennial, permanent, perpetual, persistent, unceasing, undiminished,

unended, unending, unfading; CONCEPT 798
—*Ant.* ending, impermanent, mortal

unearned [*adj*] *undeserved* not deserved, not earned, not merited, not warranted, unmerited, unwarranted; CONCEPTS 545,548,558

unearth [*v*] *dig up* ascertain, bring to light*, catch on*, delve, determine, discover, disinter, dredge up, excavate, exhibit, exhume, expose, ferret, find, find out, hear, hit upon, learn, reveal, root, see, see the light, show, spark, spotlight*, strike, stumble on, turn up, unbury, uncover, uproot; CONCEPTS 178,183 —*Ant.* bury

unearthly [*adj*] *supernatural; very strange* abnormal, absurd, appalling, demonic, devilish, eerie, ethereal, extraordinary, fiendish, frightening, funereal, ghastly, ghostly, ghoulish, hair-raising, haunted, heavenly, hyperphysical, miraculous, nightmarish, not of this world, phantom, preternatural, ridiculous, scary, sepulchral, spectral, spooky*, sublime, superhuman, uncanny, ungodly, unholy, unreasonable, weird; CONCEPTS 536,564,582 —*Ant.* earthly, natural, physical

uneasy [*adj*] *awkward, uncomfortable* afraid, agitated, alarmed, all nerves*, anguished, anxious, apprehensive, bothered, constrained, discomposed, dismayed, disquieted, disturbed, edgy, fearful, fidgety, fretful, harassed, ill at ease, impatient, insecure, in turmoil, irascible, irritable, jittery, jumpy, nervous, on edge, on the qui vive, palpitant, peevish, perplexed, perturbed, precarious, restive, restless, shaken, shaky, strained, suspicious, tense, tormented, troubled, unquiet, unsettled, unstable, upset, vexed, worried, wrung; CONCEPTS 403,548,690 —*Ant.* comfortable, composed, easy-going, laid-back

uneducated [*adj*] *lacking knowledge* benighted, empty-headed, ignoramus, ignorant, illiterate, inerudite, know-nothing*, lowbrow*, uncultivated, uncultured, uninstructed, unlearned, unlettered, unread, unrefined, unschooled, untaught, untutored; CONCEPT 402 —*Ant.* educated, intelligent, learned, lettered, taught

unemotional [*adj*] *not responsive* along for the ride*, apathetic, blah*, callous, chill*, cold, coldhearted*, cool, deadpan, dispassionate, emotionless, flat, frigid, glacial, going with the flow*, hard-boiled*, hard-hearted*, heartless, impassive, indifferent, insensitive, laid-back*, listless, marble*, obdurate, passionless, phlegmatic, quiet, reserved, reticent, rolling with the punches*, thick-skinned*, uncompassionate, undemonstrative, unexcitable, unfeeling, unimpressionable, unresponsive, unsympathetic; CONCEPTS 401,403 —*Ant.* caring, emotional, excitable, feeling, responsive

unemployed [*adj*] *without a job* at liberty*, between jobs*, closed down*, disengaged, down, fired, free, idle, inactive, jobless, laid off, leisured, loafing*, on layoff, on the bench*, on the dole*, on the shelf*, out of action*, out of a job, out of work, resting, unapplied, underemployed, unengaged, unexercised, unoccupied, unused, without gainful employment, workless; CONCEPT 538 —*Ant.* employed, occupied

unending [*adj*] *continuing* amaranthine, ceaseless, constant, continual, continuous, endless,

eternal, everlasting, immortal, incessant, infinite, interminable, never-ending, perpetual, steady, unceasing, uninterrupted, unremitting; CONCEPTS 482,798 —*Ant.* completed, discontinuous, ending, finished, intermittent, transient

unequal [*adj1*] *different* differing, disparate, dissimilar, distant, divergent, diverse, incommensurate, like night and day*, mismatched, not uniform, odd, poles apart*, unalike, unequivalent, uneven, unlike, unmatched, unsimilar, variable, various, varying, weird*; CONCEPT 564 —*Ant.* equal, identical, matched, same, similar

unequal [*adj2*] *not balanced; lopsided* asymmetrical, disproportionate, ill-matched, inequitable, irregular, nonsymmetrical, offbalance, one-sided, overbalanced, unbalanced, uneven, unproportionate, unsymmetrical; CONCEPT 480 —*Ant.* balanced, equal, even, level, same

unequaled [*adj*] *supreme, pre-eminent* alone, beyond compare, incomparable, inimitable, matchless, nonpareil, only, paramount, peerless, second to none*, surpassing, towering, transcendent, ultimate, unique, unmatched, unparagoned, unparalleled, unrivaled, unsurpassed, without equal; CONCEPT 574 —*Ant.* inferior, minor, second-rate

unequivocal [*adj*] *definite, positive* absolute, apparent, categorical, certain, clear, clear-cut, decided, decisive, direct, distinct, downright, evident, explicit, flat out*, incontestable, incontrovertible, indisputable, indubitable, manifest, no catch*, no fine print*, no holds barred*, no ifs ands or buts*, no strings attached*, obvious, open and shut*, palpable, patent, plain, straight, straightforward, straight out, unambiguous, uncontestable, undeniable, undisputable, univocal, unmistakable, unquestionable; CONCEPT 535 —*Ant.* ambiguous, equivocal, indefinite, obscured, uncertain, unsure, vague

unerring [*adj*] *accurate* certain, errorless, exact, faultless, impeccable, inerrable, inerrant, infallible, invariable, just, perfect, reliable, sure, true, trustworthy, unfailing; CONCEPTS 535,574 —*Ant.* erring, imperfect, inaccurate, mistaken

unessential [*adj*] *unnecessary* avoidable, beside the point*, dispensable, expendable, futile, inessential, irrelevant, needless, nonessential, optional, uncalled-for, unimportant, unneeded, unrequired, useless, worthless; CONCEPT 546

unethical [*adj*] *dishonest, immoral* cheating, corrupt, crooked, dirty*, dirty-dealing*, dishonorable, disreputable, double-crossing*, fake, fishy*, flimflam*, fly-by-night*, illegal, improper, mercenary, scam*, shady*, sharp*, slick*, slippery*, sneaky*, two-faced*, two-timing*, underhand, unfair, unprincipled, unprofessional, unscrupulous, wrong; CONCEPT 545 —*Ant.* ethical, good, honest, moral, right, upright

uneven [*adj*] *not smooth or balanced* asperous, asymmetrical, broken, bumpy, changeable, craggy, differing, discrepant, disparate, disproportionate, fitful, fluctuating, harsh, ill-matched, intermittent, irregular, jagged, jerky, leftover, lopsided, nonsymmetrical, notched, not flat, not level, not parallel, odd, off-balance, one-sided, overbalanced, patchy, remaining, rough, rugged, scabrous, scraggy, serrate, spasmodic, spotty, unbalanced, unequal, unfair, unlevel, unsmooth, unsteady, unsymmetrical, variable; CONCEPTS 480,566,606 —Ant. balanced, continuous, even, level, smooth

uneventful [adj] monotonous, dull boring, common, commonplace, humdrum, inconclusive, indecisive, ordinary, prosaic, quiet, routine, tedious, unexceptional, unexciting, unfateful, uninteresting, unmemorable, unnoteworthy, unremarkable, unvaried; CONCEPT 548 —Ant. eventful, exciting, extraordinary, memorable

unexceptional [adj] ordinary average, characterless, common, commonplace, conventional, dull, everyday, fair, garden-variety*, insignificant, mediocre, modest, no great shakes*, normal, nothing special, nothing to write home about*, pedestrian, plain, prosaic, routine, run-of-the-mill*, second-rate, so-so*, typical, undistinguished, uneventful, unexciting, unimpressive, uninspired, unmemorable, unnoteworthy, unremarkable, usual; CONCEPT 530

unexciting [adj] dull big yawn*, blah, boring, common, dead, dreary, familiar, ho hum*, humdrum*, long-winded, monotonous, ordinary, plain, prosaic, routine, run-of-the-mill*, uneventful, unimaginative, uninspiring, uninteresting, usual, usual thing; CONCEPTS 529,530

unexpected [adj] surprising abrupt, accidental, amazing, astonishing, chance, electrifying, eye-opening*, fortuitous, from left field*, impetuous, impulsive, instantaneous, not bargained for*, not in the cards*, out of the blue*, payback, prodigious, staggering, startling, stunning, sudden, swift, unanticipated, unforeseen, unheralded, unlooked-for, unpredictable, unpredicted, wonderful; CONCEPTS 544,548 —Ant. expected

unfailing [adj] certain, unchanging absolute, assiduous, bottomless, boundless, ceaseless, come-through*, consistent, constant, continual, continuing, continuous, counted on, delivering, dependable, diligent, dyed-in-the-wool*, endless, eternal, faithful, inexhaustible, infallible, invariable, loyal, never-failing, persistent, reliable, rock solid*, same, solid, staunch, steadfast, straight, sure, surefire, there*, tried-and-true*, true, trustworthy, unflagging, unlimited, unrelenting; CONCEPTS 534,535,538 —Ant. failing, impermanent, uncertain, unsure

unfair [adj] prejudiced, wrongful arbitrary, bad, base, biased, bigoted, blameworthy, cheating, criminal, crooked, cruel, culpable, discreditable, discriminatory, dishonest, dishonorable, foul, grievous, illegal, immoral, improper, inequitable, inexcusable, iniquitous, injurious, low, mean, one-sided, partial, partisan, petty, shameful, shameless, uncalled-for, undue, unethical, unjust, unjustifiable, unlawful, unprincipled, unreasonable, unrightful, unscrupulous, unsporting, unwarranted, vicious, vile, wicked, wrong; CONCEPTS 544,545,548 —Ant. fair, honest, just, unprejudiced

unfaithful [adj] disloyal, adulterous adulterine, cheating, deceitful, double-crossing*, faithless, false, false-hearted, fickle, foresworn, inconstant, incontinent, moonlighting*, not true to, of bad faith, perfidious, philandering, recreant, shifty*, snaky*, sneaking, traitorous, treacher-

ous, treasonable, two-faced*, two-timing*, unchaste, unreliable, untrue, untrustworthy, wicked; CONCEPT 545 —Ant. faithful, loyal, trustworthy

unfaltering [adj] steadfast abiding, bent on, bound, bound and determined*, dead set on*, enduring, firm, going all the way*, indefatigable, meaning business*, mulish*, never-failing, persevering, pigheaded, resolute, set, steady, stiff-necked*, stubborn, sure, tireless, unailing, unflagging, unflappable, unflinching, unqualified, unquestioning, unswerving, untiring, unwavering, wholehearted; CONCEPTS 403,535,538 —Ant. faltering, unsettled, unstable, unsteady

unfamiliar [adj] different, strange alien, anomalous, bizarre, curious, exotic, extraordinary, fantastic, foreign, little known, new, novel, obscure, original, outlandish, out-of-the-way*, peculiar, recondite, remarkable, remote, unaccustomed, uncommon, unexpected, unexplored, uninvestigated, unknown, unusual; CONCEPT 564 —Ant. familiar, known, usual

unfamiliar [adj2] inexperienced; not knowing about ignorant, incognizant, inconversant, not associated, not versed in, oblivious, out of contact, unaccustomed, unacquainted, unaware, unconversant, uninformed, uninitiated, uninstructed, unknowing, unknown, unpracticed, unskilled, unversed, unwitting; CONCEPTS 402,678 —Ant. experienced, familiar, knowing, versed

unfathomable [adj1] bottomless abysmal, boundless, deep, eternal, immeasurable, infinite, soundless, unending, unmeasured, unplumbed; CONCEPTS 482,777 —Ant. comprehensible, explainable, explicable, fathomable

unfathomable [adj2] hard to believe; difficult to understand abstruse, baffling, clear as mud*, deep, enigmatic, esoteric, heavy, impenetrable, incognizable, incomprehensible, indecipherable, inexplicable, obscure, profound, too deep*, uncomprehensible, ungraspable, unintelligible, unknowable; CONCEPT 529 —Ant. believable, comprehensible, fathomable

unfavorable [adj] very bad adverse, antagonistic, calamitous, contrary, damaging, destructive, disadvantageous, discommodious, hostile, ill, ill-advised, improper, inadvisable, inauspicious, inconvenient, inexpedient, infelicitous, inimical, inopportune, late, low, malapropos, negative, objectionable, ominous, opposed, poor, regrettable, tardy, threatening, troublesome, unfit, unfortunate, unfriendly, unlucky, unpromising, unpropitious, unseasonable, unseemly, unsuited, untimely, untoward, wrong; CONCEPTS 529,571 —Ant. favorable, friendly, good, nice

unfeeling [adj] hard-hearted, numb anesthetized, apathetic, asleep, benumbed, brutal, callous, cantankerous, churlish, cold, cold-blooded, cold fish*, cold-hearted, crotchety, cruel, deadened, exacting, feelingless, hard, hardened, heartless, icy, inanimate, inhuman, insensate, insensible, insensitive, iron-hearted, merciless, obdurate, pitiless, ruthless, sensationless, senseless, severe, stony, surly, thick-skinned*, tough, unamiable, uncaring, uncompassionate, uncordial, unemotional, unkind, unsympathetic; CONCEPT 314 —Ant. caring, concerned, feeling, loving, sensitive

unfinished [adj] *not completed* amateurish,
bare, crude, cut short, dabbling, defective,
deficient, dilettante, faulty, formless, found
wanting, fragmentary, half-baked*, half-done*,
immature, imperfect, incomplete, in the making,
in the rough*, lacking, natural, not done, plain,
raw, rough, roughhewn, shapeless, sketchy,
tentative, unaccomplished, unadorned, unassembled, uncompleted, unconcluded, under construction, undeveloped, undone, unexecuted,
unfashioned, unfulfilled, unperfected, unpolished, unrefined, wanting;CONCEPT 485 —**Ant.**
completed, finished, polished, refined, whole

unfit [adj1] *not appropriate or suited* below
par*, can't make the grade*, debilitated,
decrepit, discordant, down, dragging, feeble,
flimsy, ill-adapted, ill-equipped, ill-suited,
improper, inadequate, inapplicable, inappropriate, incompatible, incongruous, incorrect, ineffective, inexpedient, infelicitous, inharmonious,
laid low*, mistaken, not fit, out of element*,
out of place, out of shape, poorly, rocky*,
unbecoming, uncongenial, uncool, unhealthy,
unlikely, unmeet, unpromising, unsuitable,
unsuited, useless, valueless; CONCEPT 558
—**Ant.** appropriate, fit, suitable

unfit [adj2] *not ready* amateur, awkward, blundering, bungling, bush league*, butter-fingered*,
clumsy, debilitated, disqualified, feeble, heavy-
handed, ill-equipped, impotent, inadequate, incapable, incapacitated, incompetent, ineffective,
inefficient, ineligible, inept, inexperienced,
inexpert, maladjusted, maladroit, no good*,
not cut out for*, not equal to, not up to*, unable,
unapt, unfitted, unhandy, unpracticed, unprepared, unproficient, unqualified, unskilled,
unskillful, untrained, useless, weak; CONCEPT
527 —**Ant.** able, fit, qualified, ready, willing

unflagging [adj] *persistent* active, assiduous,
constant, diligent, dynamic, energetic, fixed, indefatigable, inexhaustible, persevering, staunch,
steady, tireless, unceasing, undeviating, unfailing, unfaltering, unrelenting, unremitting, unre-
tiring, untiring, unwearied; CONCEPTS 538,798
—**Ant.** changing, inconstant, variable, wavering

unflappable [adj] *cool and calm* collected,
composed, deliberate, disimpassioned, easy,
impassive, imperturbable, level-headed, nonchalant, relaxed, self-possessed, unruffled;
CONCEPTS 401,542 —**Ant.** disconcerted,
nervous, upset, worried

unfold [v1] *spread out* disentangle, display,
expand, extend, fan, fan out, flatten, loosen,
open, outspread, outstretch, reel out, release,
shake out, spread, straighten, stretch out, unbend, uncoil, uncrease, uncurl, undo, unfurl,
unravel, unroll, untwist, unwind, unwrap;
CONCEPT 201 —**Ant.** fold, wrap

unfold [v2] *make known* announce, clarify,
clear up, decipher, describe, disclose, discover,
display, divulge, dope out, elucidate, explain,
explicate, expose, figure out, illustrate, present,
publish, resolve, reveal, show, solve, uncover,
unravel; CONCEPTS 55,261 —**Ant.** conceal,
hide, withhold

unfold [v3] *develop* bear fruit, demonstrate,
elaborate, evidence, evince, evolve, expand,
grow, manifest, mature; CONCEPT 704 —**Ant.**
block, check, stagnate, stop

unforeseeable [adj] *unpredictable* capricious,
chance, chancy, changeable, fluky*, from left
field*, incalculable, random, uncertain, unexpected, unknowable; CONCEPT 534

unforeseen [adj] *surprising* abrupt, accidental,
from left field*, not bargained for*, out of the
blue*, startling, sudden, surprise, unanticipated,
uncalculated, unexpected, unlooked-for;
CONCEPTS 544,548 —**Ant.** expected, foreseen,
predictable, predicted

unforgettable [adj] *memorable* catchy, distinguished, enduring, eventful, exceptional, extraordinary, famous, great, historic, illustrious,
important, lasting, meaningful, monumental,
notable, noteworthy, not to be forgotten,
remarkable, rememberable, remembered,
significant, super; CONCEPTS 529,548

unforgivable [adj] *inexcusable* blameworthy,
contemptible, deplorable, disgraceful, indefensible, inexpiable, not forgivable, outrageous,
reprehensible, shameful, unallowable,
unconscionable, unjustifiable, unpardonable,
unpermissible, untenable, wrong; CONCEPTS
545,570

unfortunate [adj] *unlucky, bad* adverse,
afflicted, broken, burdened, calamitous, cursed,
damaging, deplorable, desperate, destitute,
disastrous, doomed, forsaken, hapless,
hopeless, ill-fated, ill-starred, in a bad way*,
inappropriate, infelicitous, inopportune, jinxed,
lamentable, luckless, out of luck*, pained,
poor, regrettable, ruined, ruinous, shattered,
star-crossed*, stricken, troubled, unbecoming,
unfavorable, unhappy, unpropitious, unprosperous, unsuccessful, unsuitable, untoward,
wretched; CONCEPTS 334,548,570 —**Ant.**
fortunate, good, happy, lucky, timely

unfounded [adj] *not based on fact* baseless,
bottomless, deceptive, fabricated, fallacious,
false, foundationless, gratuitous, groundless,
idle, illogical, mendacious, misleading, off-
base, spurious, trumped up*, uncalled-for,
unjustified, unproven, unreal, unsubstantiated,
untrue, untruthful, unwarranted, vain, without
basis, without foundation; CONCEPTS 267,582
—**Ant.** founded, justified, proven, substantiated,
supported

unfriendly [adj] *nasty, hostile* acrimonious,
against, alien, aloof, antagonistic, antisocial,
censorious, chilly, cold, combative, competitive,
conflicting, contrary, disaffected, disagreeable,
distant, estranged, grouchy, grudging, gruff,
hateful, ill-disposed, inauspicious, inhospitable,
inimical, malicious, malignant, misanthropic,
not on speaking terms*, opposed, opposite,
quarrelsome, sour, spiteful, surly, uncharitable,
uncongenial, unfavorable, unneighborly,
unpropitious, unsociable, vengeful, warlike;
CONCEPTS 401,548 —**Ant.** approachable,
friendly, kind, nice, sociable

ungodly [adj1] *not accepting a religious doctrine; impious* atheistic, blasphemous, corrupt,
depraved, godless, improper, indecent, indecorous, indelicate, irreligious, malevolent, profane,
rough, sinful, undecorous, unhallowed, unholy,
unseemly, vile, wicked;CONCEPTS 542,545
—**Ant.** clean, godly, moral, pious, religious

ungodly [adj2] *outrageous* atrocious, barbarous,
dreadful, horrendous, horrid, intolerable, nasty,

shocking, unbelievable, uncivilized, unconscionable, unearthly, unreasonable, unseemly; CONCEPTS 529,548,570 —Ant. reasonable, sensible

ungrateful [adj] *not appreciative* careless, demanding, dissatisfied, faultfinding, forgetful, grasping, grumbling, heedless, ingrate, insensible, oblivious, self-centered, selfish, thankless, unappreciative, unmindful, unnatural, unthankful; CONCEPT 401 —Ant. appreciative, grateful, thankful

unguarded [adj] *thoughtless; unwary* accessible, artless, candid, careless, casual, direct, foolhardy, frank, headlong, heedless, honest, ill-considered, impolitic, imprudent, impulsive, incautious, indiscreet, ingenuous, naive, offhand, rash, spontaneous, straightforward, unalert, uncircumspect, unconscious, undiplomatic, unpremeditated, unreflective, unthinking, unvigilant, unwatchful, unwise, vulnerable, weak; CONCEPT 401 —Ant. careful, cautious, thoughtful

unhappy [adj1] *sad* bleak, bleeding*, blue*, bummed out*, cheerless, crestfallen, dejected, depressed, despondent, destroyed, disconsolate, dismal, dispirited, down*, down and out*, downbeat, downcast, down in the mouth*, dragged, dreary, gloomy, grim, heavy-hearted, hurting, in a blue funk*, in pain, in the dumps*, let-down*, long-faced, low, melancholy, mirthless, miserable, mournful, oppressive, put away*, ripped*, saddened, sorrowful, sorry, teary, troubled; CONCEPT 403 —Ant. cheerful, glad, happy, joyous

unhappy [adj2] *unfortunate, unlucky* afflicted, cursed, hapless, ill-fated, ill-starred, luckless, misfortunate, troubled, untoward, wretched; CONCEPT 548 —Ant. fortunate, happy, lucky, timely

unharmed [adj] *unhurt* all right, free from danger, in one piece*, intact, not hurt, okay*, out of danger, out of harm's way*, protected, safe, safe and sound*, sound, undamaged, uninjured, unscarred, unscathed, unscratched, untouched; CONCEPTS 314,587

unhealthy [adj1] *sick* ailing, below par, debilitated, delicate, diseased, down, dragging, feeble, frail, ill, in a decline, infirm, in ill health, in poor health, invalid, laid low*, out of action*, out of shape, peaked, poorly, run-down, shaky, sickly, unsound, unwell, weak; CONCEPT 314 —Ant. healthy, strong, well

unhealthy [adj2] *very bad in effect on well-being* baneful, chancy, corrupt, corrupting, dangerous, degenerate, degrading, deleterious, demoralizing, detrimental, harmful, hazardous, insalubrious, jeopardious, morbid, nefarious, negative, noisome, noxious, perilous, perverse, poisonous, risky, rotten, treacherous, undesirable, unhealthful, unsanitary, unsound, unwholesome, villainous, virulent, wicked; CONCEPTS 537,571 —Ant. good, healthy

unheard-of [adj] *unique, obscure* exceptional, inconceivable, little-known, nameless, new, novel, outlandish, preposterous, rare, shocking, singular, unbelievable, undiscovered, unfamiliar, unknown, unlikely, unprecedented, unrenowned, unsung, unusual; CONCEPTS 564,576 —Ant. familiar, normal, usual

unhinged [adj] *demented* bananas*, batty*, berserk, bonkers*, confused, crazed, crazy*, deranged, disturbed, insane, loopy*, lunatic, mad, maniac, manic, mental*, out of one's mind, out to lunch*, touched*, unbalanced; CONCEPTS 314,403 —Ant. sane, stable

unholy [adj1] *sacrilegious* base, blameful, corrupt, culpable, depraved, dishonest, evil, godless, guilty, heinous, immoral, impious, iniquitous, irreligious, irreverent, irreverential, profane, sinful, ungodly, unhallowed, unsanctified, vile, wicked; CONCEPTS 542,548 —Ant. godly, holy, pious, religious

unholy [adj2] *outrageous* appalling, awful, barbarous, dreadful, horrendous, shocking, uncivilized, unearthly, ungodly, unnatural, unreasonable; CONCEPT 537 —Ant. reasonable, sensible

unidentified [adj] *secret* anonymous, mysterious, nameless, not known, pseudonymous, unclassified, unfamiliar, unknown, unmarked, unnamed, unrecognized, unrevealed; CONCEPT 576 —Ant. identified, known, public

unification [n] *joining together* affinity, alliance, amalgamation, coalescence, coalition, combination, concurrence, confederation, connection, consolidation, coupling, federation, fusion, hookup, interlocking, linkage, melding, merger, merging, union, uniting; CONCEPTS 230,388 —Ant. division, segregation, separation

unified [adj] *united* affiliated, allied, banded, collective, combined, consolidated, cooperative, incorporated, joined up, leagued, linked, one, pooled, tied in, together, undivided; CONCEPTS 563,577

uniform [adj1] *consistent* compatible, consonant, constant, equable, even, fated, fateful, fixed, habitual, homogeneous, immutable, incorrigible, inflexible, invariable, irreversible, level, methodical, monolithic, normal, of a piece*, ordered, orderly, ossified, plumb, regular, reliable, rigid, smooth, stable, static, steady, straight, symmetrical, systematic, true, unalterable, unbroken, unchanging, undeviating, undiversified, unfluctuating, unmodifiable, unvarying, well-balanced, well-proportioned; CONCEPT 534 —Ant. changing, different, divergent, inconsistent, varied

uniform [adj2] *alike* agnate, akin, analogous, comparable, consistent, consonant, correspondent, ditto*, double, equal, identical, like, mated, monotonous, parallel, same, same difference*, selfsame, similar, treadmill*, undifferentiated, unvaried; CONCEPTS 487, 573 —Ant. deviating, different, dissimilar, divergent, unalike, unlike

uniform [n] *coordinated outfit* attire, costume, dress, garb, gown, habit, khaki*, livery, monkey suit*, OD*, olive drab*, regalia, regimentals, robe, stripes*, suit; CONCEPT 451

unify [v] *unite* affiliate, ally, associate, band, become one, bring together, combine, connect, consolidate, cooperate, couple, gather together, hook up with, join, join forces, link, marry, merge, pool, pull together, stick together, wed; CONCEPTS 113,193

unimaginable [adj] *mind-boggling* beyond wildest dreams*, doubtful, exceptional, extraordinary, fantastic, impossible, improbable, inapprehensible, incogitable, incomprehensible, inconceivable, incredible, indescribable, ineffable, not understandable, rare, singular, unbelievable, uncommon, unheard-of, unique, unknowable, unordinary, unthinkable; CONCEPTS 529,548 —Ant. believable, describable, imaginable

unimaginative [adj] *dull, predictable* banal, barren, bromidic, common, commonplace, derivative, dime a dozen*, dry, dull as dishwater*, flat, hackneyed, ho hum*, lifeless, matter-of-fact, ordinary, pabulum, pedestrian, prosaic, routine, square*, tame, tedious, trite, uncreative, uninspired, unoriginal, unromantic, usual, vanilla*, well-worn, zero*; CONCEPTS 542,547, 548 —Ant. creative, imaginative, original

unimportant [adj] *of no real worth, value* beside the point*, casual, frivolous, frothy, immaterial, inconsequential, inconsiderable, indifferent, insignificant, irrelevant, little, low-ranking, meaningless, minor, minute, negligible, nonessential, nothing*, nugatory, null, of no account, of no consequence, paltry, petty, picayune, second-rate*, shoestring*, slight, trifling, trivial, unnecessary, useless, worthless, zero*, zilch*, zip*; CONCEPT 575 —Ant. big, important, relevant, serious, useful, worthwhile

uninformed [adj] *unaware* blind, caught napping*, daydreaming, deaf, ignorant, inattentive, in the dark*, negligent, not informed, not told, oblivious, out of it*, out to lunch*, unbriefed, unconscious, uneducated, unenlightened, uninstructed, unknowing, unschooled; CONCEPT 402

uninhibited [adj] *free and easy; without restraint* audacious, candid, cut loose*, expansive, fancy-free*, footloose*, frank, free, hanging out*, informal, instinctive, liberated, natural, no holds barred*, off the cuff*, open, relaxed, spontaneous, unbridled, unchecked, unconstrained, uncontrolled, uncurbed, ungoverned, unhampered, unrepressed, unreserved, unrestrained, unrestricted, unselfconscious, unsuppressed; CONCEPTS 267,401 —Ant. careful, inhibited, modest, shy

uninspired [adj] *dull, unoriginal* bromidic, commonplace, corny*, everyday, heavy-handed, humdrum, indifferent, old hat*, ordinary, phoned in*, ponderous, prosaic, stale, sterile, stock, uncreative, unexciting, unimaginative, unimpressed, uninspiring, uninteresting, uninventive, unmoved, yawn*; CONCEPTS 542,547,548 —Ant. creative, inspired, original

unintelligent [adj] *stupid* brainless, deficient, dense, doltish, dumb, empty-headed*, foolish, half-witted*, idiotic, imbecilic, inane, meaningless, mentally deficient, mentally handicapped, mindless, moronic, not intelligent, pointless, senseless, simple, simpleminded, slow, thick-headed*, unthinking, witless; CONCEPTS 402,548

unintelligible [adj] *not understandable* ambiguous, equivocal, fathomless, Greek*, illegible, impenetrable, inarticulate, incognizable, incoherent, incomprehensible, indecipherable, indistinct, inexplicit, jumbled, meaningless, muddled, obscure, opaque, tenebrous, uncertain, unclear, unexplicit, unfathomable, ungraspable, unknowable, unreadable, vague; CONCEPT 267 —Ant. comprehensible, intelligible, meaningful, understandable

unintentional/unintended [adj] *not planned* accidental, aimless, casual, chance, erratic, extemporaneous, fortuitous, haphazard, inadvertent, involuntary, purposeless, random, unconscious, undesigned, undevised, unexpected, unforeseen, unintended, unplanned, unpremeditated, unthinking, unthought, unwitting; CONCEPTS 401,548 —Ant. definite, deliberate, intended, intentional, planned

uninterested [adj] *oblivious to* aloof, apathetic, blasé, bored, bored stiff*, casual, could care less*, detached, disinterested, distant, going through motions*, hard-hearted*, impassive, incurious, indifferent, listless, remote, thick-skinned*, turned off*, unconcerned, uncurious, uninvolved, unresponsive, weary, withdrawn; CONCEPTS 401,403 —Ant. caring, concerned, enthusiastic, feeling, interested

uninteresting [adj] *boring, uneventful* arid, banal, big yawn*, bromidic, common, commonplace, depressing, dismal, drab, dreary, dry, dull, dusty*, fatiguing, flat, ho hum*, humdrum, insipid, irksome, jejune, monotonous, nothing*, nowhere*, pedestrian, prosaic, prosy, soporific, stale, stupid, tedious, tired, tiresome, trite, unenjoyable, unentertaining, unexciting, uninspiring, wearisome; CONCEPTS 529,548 —Ant. eventful, exciting, interesting

uninterrupted [adj] *continuing; unbroken* ceaseless, consecutive, constant, continual, continuous, direct, endless, interminable, nonstop, peaceful, perpetual, steady, straight, straightforward, sustained, through, unceasing, undisturbed, unending, unremitting; CONCEPTS 482,798 —Ant. broken, discontinuous, intermittent, interrupted

uninvited [adj] *unwanted* blackballed*, excluded, inadmissible, left out in the cold*, not in the picture*, not wanted, rejected, shut out, unasked, undesired, unpopular, unsolicited, unwelcome; CONCEPTS 529,555,570

uninviting [adj] *disagreeable, not pleasant* awful, bad, disgusting, displeasing, distasteful, nasty, nauseating, offensive, repulsive, rotten, sickening, sour, unappealing, unappetizing, unpalatable, unpleasant; CONCEPTS 537,548

union [n1] *merger, joining* abutment, accord, agglutination, agreement, amalgam, amalgamation, blend, centralization, coadunation, combination, coming together, commixture, compound, concatenation, conciliation, concord, concurrence, confluence, congregation, conjunction, consolidation, correlation, coupling, fusion, harmony, hookup, incorporation, intercourse, joint, junction, juncture, meeting, melding, merging, mixture, seam, symbiosis, synthesis, tie-in, tie-up, unanimity, unification, unison, uniting, unity; CONCEPTS 113,664,714 —Ant. division, divorce, separation

union [n2] *group with shared interest, cause* alliance, association, brotherhood, club, coalition, confederacy, confederation, congress, employees, federation, guild, labor union, league, local, order, sisterhood, society, sodality, syndicate, trade union; CONCEPTS 325, 381 —Ant. management

unique [adj] *alone, singular* different, exclusive, individual, lone, one, one and only*, onliest*, only, particular, rare, separate, single,

un
un

solitary, solo, sui generis, uncommon, unexampled; CONCEPTS 564,577 —*Ant.* common, commonplace, normal, usual

unique [adj2] *one-of-a-kind; without equal* anomalous, best, exceptional, extraordinary, far-out*, incomparable, inimitable, matchless, most, nonpareil, novel, only, peerless, primo*, rare, singular, something else*, special, standout, strange, uncommon, unequaled, unexampled, unimaginable, unmatched, unparagoned, unparalleled, unprecedented, unreal, unrivaled, utmost, weird*; CONCEPTS 564,574 —*Ant.* like, similar, standard, trite

unison [n] *harmony* accord, accordance, agreement, alliance, community, concert, concord, concordance, conjunction, consent, consonance, cooperation, federation, league, reciprocity, sympathy, unanimity, union, unity; CONCEPT 664 —*Ant.* discord, disharmony

unit [n1] *whole* assemblage, assembly, bunch, complement, crew, crowd, detachment, entirety, entity, gang, group, mob, one, outfit, ring, section, system, total, totality; CONCEPTS 432,837 —*Ant.* part, piece

unit [n2] *part* arm, block, component, constituent, detachment, detail, digit, element, factor, feature, fraction, ingredient, integer, item, joint, layer, length, link, member, module, piece, portion, section, segment, square, wing; CONCEPT 834 —*Ant.* whole

unite [v] *combine; join together* affiliate, ally, amalgamate, associate, band, band together, become one, blend, close ranks*, coadjute, coalesce, commingle, concur, confederate, conjoin, connect, consolidate, cooperate, couple, embody, fuse, gather together, hang together*, harden, hook up with, incorporate, intertwine, join, join forces, keep together, league, link, marry, meet, merge, mix, pool, pull together, relate, solidify, stay together, stick together, strengthen, throw in with*, unify, wed; CONCEPTS 113,193 —*Ant.* divide, separate

united [adj] *combined; in agreement* affiliated, agreed, allied, amalgamated, assembled, associated, banded, coadunate, cognate, collective, concerted, concordant, confederated, congruent, conjoint, conjugate, conjunctive, consolidated, cooperative, corporate, federal, homogeneous, hooked up*, in accord, in cahoots*, incorporated, integrated, joined up, leagued, likeminded*, lined up*, linked, of one mind, of the same opinion, one, plugged in*, pooled, tied in, unanimous, undivided, unified, unitary; CONCEPTS 563,577 —*Ant.* divided, separated

unity [n] *wholeness* accord, agreement, alliance, coadunation, combination, concord, concurrence, confederation, consensus, consent, consonance, entity, federation, harmony, homogeneity, homogeneousness, identity, individuality, indivisibility, integral, integrality, integrity, interconnection, oneness, peace, rapport, sameness, singleness, singularity, soleness, solidarity, synthesis, totality, unanimity, undividedness, unification, uniformity, union, unison; CONCEPTS 664,714,837 —*Ant.* partiality

universal [adj] *worldwide, entire* accepted, all, all-embracing, all-inclusive, all-over, astronomical, broad, catholic, celestial, common, comprehensive, cosmic, cosmopolitan, customary,

diffuse, ecumenical, empyrean, extensive, general, generic, global, multinational, mundane, omnipresent, planetary, prevalent, regular, stellar, sweeping, terrestrial, total, ubiquitous, undisputed, unlimited, unrestricted, usual, whole, widespread, worldly; CONCEPTS 536,772 —*Ant.* confined, local, partial, particular

universe [n] *everything in creation* cosmos, everything, macrocosm, natural world, nature, world; CONCEPTS 370,511 —*Ant.* locality

unjust [adj] *not fair* below the belt*, biased, fixed*, inequitable, influenced, low-down*, one-sided, partial, partisan, prejudiced, shabby*, underhand, undeserved, unfair, unforgivable, unjustified, unmerited, unrighteous, wrong, wrongful; CONCEPT 545 —*Ant.* equitable, fair, just, unbiased, unprejudiced

unjustifiable [adj] *unwarranted* baseless, foundationless, groundless, indefensible, inexcusable, uncalled-for, unconscionable, unforgivable, unfounded, ungrounded, unjust, unjustified, unmerited, unpardonable, wrong; CONCEPTS 545,548,558

unkempt [adj] *shabby, sloppy* bedraggled, coarse, crude, dilapidated, dirty, disarranged, disarrayed, disheveled, disordered, grubby*, grungy*, messed up, messy, mussed up*, neglected, rough, rumpled, scruffy, shaggy, slipshod, slovenly, tousled, unclean, uncombed, unfastidious, ungroomed, unimproved, unneat, unpolished, untidy, vulgar; CONCEPTS 485,621 —*Ant.* kempt, neat, tidy, trim

unkind [adj] *not nice* barbarous, brutal, cold-blooded, coldhearted, cruel, hard-hearted, harsh, hateful, heartless, inconsiderate, inhuman, inhumane, insensitive, malevolent, malicious, malignant, mean, nasty, sadistic, savage, spiteful, thoughtless, uncaring, uncharitable, unfeeling, unfriendly, unsympathetic; CONCEPT 401 —*Ant.* considerate, friendly, giving, kind, nice

unknowing [adj] *unaware* blank, blind, caught napping*, daydreaming, deaf, ignorant, inattentive, in the dark*, negligent, not informed, not knowing, not told, oblivious, out of it*, out to lunch*, unbriefed, unconscious, uneducated, unenlightened, uninformed, uninstructed, unschooled; CONCEPT 402

unknown [adj] *obscure, mysterious* alien, anonymous, concealed, dark, desolate, distant, exotic, far, faraway, far-off, foreign, hidden, humble, incog*, incognito, little known, nameless, new, remote, secret, so-and-so*, strange, such-and-such*, unapprehended, unascertained, uncelebrated, uncharted, undiscovered, undistinguished, unexplained, unexplored, unfamiliar, unheard-of, unidentified, unnamed, unnoted, unperceived, unrecognized, unrenowned, unrevealed, unsung, untold, X*; CONCEPT 576 —*Ant.* familiar, identified, known

unlawful [adj] *against the law* actionable, banned, bootleg*, criminal, flagitious, forbidden, illegal, illegitimate, illicit, improper, iniquitous, lawless, nefarious, outlawed, prohibited, taboo, unauthorized, under-the-counter*, unlicensed, wrongful; CONCEPT 319 —*Ant.* authorized, lawful, legal, right

unlike [adj] *different* apples and oranges*, clashing, conflicting, contradictory, contrary, contrasted, discordant, disharmonious, disparate,

un
un

dissimilar, dissonant, distant, distinct, divergent, diverse, far cry from*, heterogeneous, hostile, incompatible, incongruous, inconsistent, mismatched, not alike, offbeat, opposed, opposite, poles apart*, separate, unalike, unequal, unrelated, variant, various, weird; CONCEPT 564 —Ant. alike, like, related, same, similar

unlikely [adj] not probable absurd, contrary, doubtful, dubious, faint, implausible, improbable, inconceivable, incredible, not likely, out of the ordinary, outside chance, questionable, rare, remote, slight, strange, unbelievable, unconvincing, unheard-of, unimaginable, untoward; CONCEPT 552 —Ant. imaginable, likely, probably

unlimited [adj] extensive, complete absolute, all-encompassing, all-out*, boundless, countless, endless, full, full-blown*, full-out*, full-scale, great, illimitable, immeasurable, immense, incalculable, incomprehensible, indefinite, interminable, limitless, measureless, no end of*, no end to*, no strings*, numberless, total, totalitarian, unbounded, unconditional, unconfined, unconstrained, unfathomed, unfettered, universal, unqualified, unrestrained, unrestricted, untold, vast, wide open; CONCEPT 772 —Ant. bounded, incomplete, limited, restricted

unload [v] take off; empty break bulk, cast, clear out, disburden, discharge, discommode, disencumber, disgorge, dump, get rid of, jettison, lighten, off-load, relieve, remove, rid, slough, take a load off, unburden, unlade, unpack, void; CONCEPTS 180,211 —Ant. fill, load, put on

unlock [v] open; solve break in, crack, decipher, free, jimmy, liberate, open the door*, pop, release, set free, unbolt, unbutton, uncork, undo, unfasten, unhook, unlatch, unravel, unseal, unshut; CONCEPTS 135,250,469

unlucky [adj] unfortunate, doomed afflicted, bad break*, behind eight ball*, black, calamitous, cataclysmic, catastrophic, cursed, dire, disastrous, down on luck*, hapless, hard luck, ill-fated, ill-starred, inauspicious, luckless, miserable, ominous, out of luck, star-crossed*, tough luck, tragic, unfavorable, unhappy, unsuccessful, untimely, untoward; CONCEPTS 529,548 —Ant. fortunate, happy, lucky

unmanageable [adj] unruly, wild awkward, berserk, chaotic, crazy, disobedient, disorderly, hysterical, lawless, madcap, nuts, out of control, outrageous, riotous, rowdy, turbulent, unbridled, uncontrollable, uncontrolled, undisciplined, ungovernable, unrestrained, violent; CONCEPT 401

unmarried [adj] not presently wed bachelor, eligible, husbandless, single, sole, spouseless, unattached, uncoupled, unwed, unwedded, widowed, wifeless; CONCEPT 555 —Ant. married, wed

unmask [v] reveal acknowledge, admit, announce, bare, bring out into the open*, bring to light*, come out with, confess, disclose, display, divulge, exhibit, expose, leak, let cat out of the bag*, make known, make public, show, tell, unclothe, uncover, unearth, unveil; CONCEPTS 60,138

unmerciful [adj] cruel bestial, bloodthirsty, brutal, coldhearted, hard, heartless, hurtful, implacable, inhumane, merciless, monstrous, pitiless, relentless, remorseless, ruthless, tyrannous, uncaring, unfeeling, unpitying, unrelenting, unsparing, vengeful, vindictive; CONCEPT 401 —Ant. generous, kind, merciful, nice

unmistakable [adj] certain, definite apparent, clear, conspicuous, decided, distinct, evident, explicit, for certain, glaring, indisputable, manifest, no ifs ands or buts*, obvious, open and shut*, palpable, patent, plain, positive, pronounced, self-explanatory, straightforward, sure, transparent, unambiguous, unequivocal, univocal; CONCEPT 535 —Ant. doubtful, indefinite, indistinct, mistakable, uncertain, unsure

unmitigated [adj] absolute, pure arrant, austere, clear-cut, complete, consummate, damned, downright, gross, intense, oppressive, out-and-out*, outright, perfect, persistent, rank, relentless, rigid, severe, sheer, simple, straight-out*, thorough, thoroughgoing, unabated, unabridged, unadulterated, unalleviated, unbending, unbroken, undiluted, unmixed, unqualified, unrelieved, utter; CONCEPTS 531,535,569 —Ant. imperfect, mixed

unmotivated [adj] uninspired apathetic, dull, everyday, humdrum, indifferent, lazy, old hat*, ordinary, prosaic, stale, unambitious, uncreative, unexciting, unimaginative, uninspiring, uninteresting, unmoved; CONCEPTS 542,547,548

unnatural [adj] not regular; artificial aberrant, abnormal, affected, anomalous, assumed, bizarre, concocted, contrary, contrived, ersatz*, extraordinary, fabricated, factitious, false, feigned, forced, freakish, freaky, imitation, incredible, insincere, irregular, labored, made-up*, make-believe*, odd, outlandish, outrageous, perverse, perverted, phony, preposterous, pseudo*, put-on*, queer, staged, stiff, stilted*, strained, strange, studied, supernatural, synthetic, theatrical, unaccountable, uncanny, unconforming, unorthodox, unusual; CONCEPTS 564,582 —Ant. acceptable, genuine, natural, real

unnecessary [adj] not required accidental, additional, avoidable, beside the point*, casual, causeless, chance, dispensable, excess, exorbitant, expendable, extraneous, extrinsic, fortuitous, futile, gratuitous, haphazard, inessential, irrelevant, lavish, needless, noncompulsory, nonessential, optional, prodigal, profuse, random, redundant, supererogatory, superfluous, surplus, uncalled-for, uncritical, undesirable, unessential, unneeded, unrequired, useless, wanton, worthless; CONCEPT 546 —Ant. indispensable, necessary, needed, required

unnerve [v] upset, intimidate agitate, bewilder, bowl over*, buffalo*, chill*, confound, daunt, demoralize, disarm, discombobulate, disconcert, discourage, dishearten, dismay, dispirit, distract, enervate, enfeeble, floor*, fluster, frighten, get to*, give a turn*, needle*, perturb, psych out*, rattle, ride, sap*, shake, spook, throw, throw off*, uncalm, undermine, unhinge, unsettle, weaken; CONCEPTS 7,14,19 —Ant. encourage, nerve, steel, strengthen

unnoticed [adj] ignored disregarded, glossed over, hidden, inconspicuous, neglected, overlooked, passed by, pushed aside, secret, unconsidered, undiscovered, unheeded, unobserved, unobtrusive, unperceived, unrecognized, unremarked, unremembered, unrespected, unseen, winked at; CONCEPT 529 —*Ant.* noted, noticed, seen

unobtrusive [*adj*] *keeping a low profile*
humble, inconspicuous, low-key, low-profile, meek, modest, quiet, reserved, restrained, retiring, self-effacing, soft-pedaled*, subdued, tasteful, unassuming, unnoticeable, unostentatious, unpretentious; CONCEPTS 401,548 —*Ant.* flaunting, noticeable, obtrusive

unorganized [*adj*] *disorderly, disorganized*
all over the place*, chaotic, cluttered, confused, dislocated, disordered, jumbled, messed up, messy, mixed up, scattered, scrambled, sloppy, unarranged, unkempt, unsystematic, untidy; CONCEPTS 485,535

unorthodox [*adj*] *abnormal; other than accepted* beatnik*, crazy*, different, dissident, eccentric, far-out, flaky*, heretical, heterodox, irregular, kinky*, nonconformist, off the beaten path*, schismatic, sectarian, unconventional, uncustomary, unusual, unwonted, way-out*, weird*; CONCEPT 564 —*Ant.* conventional, normal, orthodox, standard

unpaid [*adj1*] *free, voluntary* contributed, donated, due, freewilled, gratuitous, honorary, unindemnified, unrewarded, unsalaried, volunteer; CONCEPT 538 —*Ant.* paid

unpaid [*adj2*] *not settled; taken without remuneration* delinquent, due, in arrears, mature, not discharged, outstanding, overdue, owing, past due, payable, undefrayed, unliquidated, unsettled; CONCEPT 334 —*Ant.* paid, settled

unparalleled [*adj*] *superlative* all-time*, alone, beyond compare, champ*, champion, consummate, exceptional, greatest, incomparable, matchless, most, nonpareil, only, peerless, rare, single, singular, solid gold*, ten*, tops*, unequaled, unique, unmatched, unprecedented, unrivaled, unsurpassed, winner, without equal, world-class*; CONCEPT 574 —*Ant.* inferior, lower, second-rate, surpassable

unpleasant [*adj*] *bad* abhorrent, bad news*, bad scene*, disagreeable, displeasing, distasteful, fierce, grody*, gross, hard-time*, icky*, irksome, lousy, nasty, objectionable, obnoxious, poisonous, repulsive, rotten, sour, troublesome, unacceptable, unattractive, uncool*, undesirable, unhappy, unlikable, unlovely, unpalatable, yucky*; CONCEPTS 529,570 —*Ant.* agreeable, delightful, good, great, pleasant, pleasing, wonderful

unpopular [*adj*] *not liked or sought after* abhorred, avoided, creepy*, despised, detested, disesteemed, disfavored, disliked, drip*, dumpy*, execrated, gross*, loathed, loser*, lousy, nerdy*, obnoxious, ostracized, out, out of favor, rejected, scorned, shunned, unaccepted, unattractive, uncared for, undesirable, unloved, unvalued, unwanted, unwelcome, weird, wimpy*; CONCEPTS 529,555 —*Ant.* delightful, desirable, fashionable, liked, popular, wanted

unprecedented [*adj*] *exceptional, original* aberrant, abnormal, anomalous, bizarre, eccentric, exotic, extraordinary, fantastic, freakish, idiosyncratic, marvelous, miraculous, modern, new, newfangled, novel, odd, outlandish, out-of-the-way*, outré, preternatural, prodigious, remarkable, signal, singular, sui generis,

uncommon, unexampled, unheard-of, unique, unparalleled, unrivaled, unusual; CONCEPTS 549,564,574 —*Ant.* known, unexceptional, unremarkable, usual

unpredictable [*adj*] *changeable* capricious, chance, chancy, dicey*, doubtful, erratic, fickle, fluctuating, fluky*, from left field*, hanging by a thread*, iffy*, incalculable, inconstant, random, touch and go*, touchy, uncertain, unforeseeable, unreliable, unstable, up for grabs*, variable, whimsical; CONCEPT 534 —*Ant.* constant, predictable, unchanging, unvarying

unprejudiced [*adj*] *fair* balanced, dispassionate, equal, equitable, even-handed, fair-minded, impartial, just, liberal, nondiscriminatory, nonpartisan, objective, open-minded, straight, unbiased, unbigoted, uncolored, uninfluenced; CONCEPTS 319,401,542 —*Ant.* biased, prejudiced, unfair, unjust

unprepared [*adj*] *not ready* ad-lib*, caught off guard*, ill-considered, impromptu, improvised, napping, not prepared, offhand, off the cuff*, off the top of one's head*, played by ear*, spontaneous, surprised, taken off guard*, unaware, unexpected, unplanned, unready, unrehearsed, unschooled, unskilled, untrained, vulnerable, winged*; CONCEPT 267

unpretentious [*adj*] *simple, honest* discreet, down, down home*, easy-going, folksy*, free-spirited, homey*, humble, inelaborate, laid-back*, lowly, modest, plain, prosaic, straightforward, unaffected, unambitious, unassuming, unbeautified, uncomplex, unembellished, unimposing, unobtrusive, unostentatious, unpresumptuous, unspoiled, up front; CONCEPTS 401,404 —*Ant.* affected, dishonest, flaunting, pretending, pretentious

unprincipled [*adj*] *corrupt* abandoned, amoral, bent*, cheating, conscienceless, crooked, deceitful, devious, dirty-dealing*, dishonest, dissolute, double-crossing*, double-dealing*, immoral, licentious, mercenary, praetorian, profligate, reprobate, shady, sly, stop-at-nothing*, tricky, two-faced*, two-timing*, unconscionable, underhand, unethical, unprofessional, unscrupulous, venal, wanton; CONCEPT 545 —*Ant.* ethical, moral, principled

unproductive [*adj*] *idle, nonproductive* barren, empty, fruitless, futile, ineffective, infertile, pointless, sterile, trivial, unprofitable, useless, worthless; CONCEPTS 267,560

unprofessional [*adj*] *not done well or skillfully* amateur, amateurish, ignorant, improper, inadequate, incompetent, inefficient, inexperienced, inexpert, lax, negligent, nonexpert, unethical, unfitting, unsuitable, untrained, unworthy; CONCEPTS 527,538 —*Ant.* experienced, expert, professional, skilled

unprotected [*adj*] *defenseless* caught, endangered, exposed, helpless, indefensible, in the line of fire*, like a sitting duck*, naked*, open, out on a limb*, powerless, pregnable, unarmed, unguarded, unsafe, vulnerable, weak, wide open*; CONCEPTS 555,576

unqualified [*adj1*] *not prepared, incompetent* amateur, bush, bush-league*, disqualified, ill-equipped, inadequate, incapable, ineligible, inexperienced, not equal to, not up to*, unequipped, unfit, unfitted, unprepared, unskilled; CONCEPT 527 —*Ant.* competent, prepared, qualified, ready

unqualified [*adj2*] *outright, absolute* abiding, blasted, blessed, categorical, certain, clear, complete, confounded, consummate, downright, enduring, entire, explicit, express, firm, flat out*, infernal, never-failing, no catch*, no ifs ands or buts*, out-and-out*, perfect, positive, rank, sheer, simple, steadfast, steady, sure, thorough, thoroughgoing, total, unadulterated, unalloyed, unconditional, unfaltering, unlimited, unmitigated, unreserved, unrestrained, unrestricted, utter, wholehearted, without reservation; CONCEPTS 531,535 —*Ant.* conditional, indefinite, temporary, tentative

unquestionable [*adj*] *definite; beyond doubt* absolute, accurate, authentic, bona fide*, certain, clear, cold, conclusive, dependable, down pat*, downright, established, faultless, flat*, flawless, for certain, genuine, incontestable, incontrovertible, indisputable, indubitable, irrefutable, manifest, no ifs ands or buts*, obvious, pat, patent, perfect, positive, real, reliable, self-evident, superior, sure, sure-enough, true, undeniable, undisputable, undoubted, unequivocal, unimpeachable, unmistakable, veritable, well-founded, well-grounded; CONCEPTS 529,535 —*Ant.* doubtful, indefinite, questionable, uncertain, unsure

unreadable [*adj*] *illegible* cacographic, crabbed, difficult to read, hard to make out*, incomprehensible, indecipherable, scrawled, scribbled, unclear, undecipherable; CONCEPTS 535,576

unreal [*adj*] *fake, make-believe; hypothetical* aerial, artificial, chimerical, delusive, dreamlike, fabled, fabulous, false, fanciful, fictitious, fictive, figmental, hallucinatory, ideal, illusory, imaginary, imagined, immaterial, impalpable, insincere, insubstantial, intangible, invented, legendary, misleading, mock, mythical, nebulous, nonexistent, notional, ostensible, phantasmagoric*, pretended, reachy, romantic, seeming, sham*, storybook*, supposititious, suppositious, theoretical, unbelievable, unsubstantial, visionary; CONCEPT 582 —*Ant.* authentic, genuine, real

unrealistic [*adj*] *not believable or practical* blue sky*, floating, gone*, half-baked*, impossible, impracticable, impractical, improbable, ivory-tower*, nonrealistic, nonsensical, not applicable, not sensible, on cloud nine*, quixotic, reachy, romantic, silly, starry-eyed, theoretical, unreal, unworkable; CONCEPTS 552, 560 —*Ant.* believable, practical, pragmatic, realistic, reasonable, sensible

unreasonable [*adj1*] *not logical or sensible* absurd, all wet*, arbitrary, biased, capricious, contradictory, erratic, fallacious, far-fetched, foolish, full of hot air*, headstrong, illogical, incoherent, incongruous, inconsequential, inconsistent, invalid, irrational, loose, mad, nonsensical, off the wall*, opinionated, preposterous, quirky, reasonless, senseless, silly, stupid, thoughtless, unreasoned, vacant, wrong; CONCEPTS 401,548 —*Ant.* logical, practical, pragmatic, realistic, reasonable, sensible

unreasonable [*adj2*] *extravagant; beyond normal limits* absonant, arbitrary, costing an arm and a leg*, dear, excessive, exorbitant, extortionate, extreme, far-out*, illegitimate, immoderate, improper, inordinate, intemperate, out of bounds*, overkill*, overmuch, peremptory, posh, pricey*, senseless, steep*, stiff*, too great, too much, too-too*, uncalled-for*, unconscionable, undue, unfair, unjust, unjustifiable, unlawful, unrightful, unwarrantable, unwarranted, up to here*, way out*, wrongful; CONCEPTS 334,762,771 —*Ant.* cheap, economical, low, plain, reasonable

unrehearsed [*adj*] *spontaneous* ad-lib*, extemporaneous, from the hip*, impromptu, improvised, impulsive, not rehearsed, off the cuff*, off the top of one's head*, spur of the moment, unpracticed, unprepared; CONCEPTS 401,542,548

unrelated [*adj*] *independent; different* beside the point*, dissimilar, extraneous, inapplicable, inappropriate, irrelative, irrelevant, mismatched, nongermane, not germane, not kin, not kindred, not related, separate, unassociated, unattached, unconnected, unlike; CONCEPTS 563,564 —*Ant.* dependent, related, relevant

unrelenting [*adj*] *merciless* bound, bound and determined, brick-wall*, ceaseless, constant, continual, continuous, cruel, dead set on*, endless, grim, hanging tough*, hard-headed*, implacable, incessant, inexorable, intransigent, iron-fisted, mortal, perpetual, persistent, pitiless, relentless, remorseless, rigid, ruthless, set, steady, stern, stiff, stiff-necked*, tenacious, tough, unabated, unbending, unbroken, unflinching, unremitting, unsparing, unwavering, unyielding; CONCEPTS 401,548,798 —*Ant.* compassionate, flexible, merciful, relenting, sympathetic

unreliable [*adj*] *not trustworthy, not true* capricious, deceitful, deceptive, delusive, disreputable, dubious, erroneous, fake, fallible, false, fickle, fly-by-night*, furtive, hallucinatory, hollow, implausible, inaccurate, inconstant, irresponsible, makeshift, meretricious, mistaken, pretended, pseudo*, questionable, sham, shifty, specious, treacherous, tricky, uncertain, unconvincing, undependable, underhand, underhanded, unfaithful, unsound, unstable, unsure, untrue, untrustworthy, vacillating, wavering, weak; CONCEPTS 542,552,587 —*Ant.* honest, reliable, responsible, true, trustworthy

unresolved [*adj*] *uncertain; not settled* betwixt and between*, changing, doubtful, faltering, hesitant, hesitating, hot and cold*, incomplete, indecisive, irresolute, moot, open to question*, pending, problematical, pussyfooting*, unanswered, unconcluded, undecided, undetermined, unfinished, unsettled, unsolved, up in the air*, vacillating, vague, waffling; CONCEPTS 529,534 —*Ant.* certain, definite, resolved, settled, solved, sure

unrest [*n*] *state of agitation; disturbance* altercation, anarchy, annoyance, anxiety, bickering, bother, chagrin, change, confusion, contention, controversy, crisis, debate, disaffection, discontent, discord, disease, disquiet, dissatisfaction, dissension, distress, dither*, ennui, grief, insurrection, irritation, malaise, moodiness, mortification, perplexity, perturbation, protest, quarrel, rebellion, restlessness, sedition, sorrow, strife, tension, tizzy*, trouble, tumult, turmoil, unease, uneasiness, uproar, upset, vexation, worry; CONCEPTS *410,674* —Ant. calm, harmony, peace, rest

unrestricted [adj] *free* able, allowed, at liberty, free-spirited, independent, lax, liberal, liberated, on one's own*, open, relaxed, unbounded, uncommitted, unconditional, unconstrained, unlimited, unregulated; CONCEPTS *401,542*

unrivaled [adj] *peerless* best, beyond compare, champion, excellent, faultless, greatest, incomparable, matchless, outstanding, perfect, second to none*, super, superior, supreme, tops*, unequaled, unmatched, unparalleled, unsurpassed, without equal; CONCEPT *574*

unruly [adj] *disobedient* assertive, bawdy, disorderly, drunken, forward, fractious, headstrong, heedless, impervious, impetuous, imprudent, impulsive, incorrigible, inexorable, insubordinate, intemperate, intractable, lawless, mean, mutinous, obstreperous, opinionated, ornery, out of control, out of line*, perverse, quarrelsome, rash, rebellious, recalcitrant, reckless, refractory, restive, riotous, rowdy, turbulent, uncontrollable, ungovernable, unmanageable, unyielding, violent, wayward, wild, willful; CONCEPT *401* —Ant. compliant, obedient, yielding

unsafe [adj] *dangerous* alarming, chancy, erratic, explosive, fearsome, hanging by a thread*, hazardous, insecure, on a limb*, on thin ice*, perilous, precarious, risky, shaky, slippery, threatening, ticklish*, touch and go*, touchy*, treacherous, uncertain, undependable, unreliable, unsound, unstable, untrustworthy; CONCEPT *587* —Ant. harmless, protected, safe, secure

unsaid [adj] *not expressed or partially expressed* implicit, implied, inferred, left to the imagination*, silenced, tacit, undeclared, understood, unexpressed, unspoken, unstated, unuttered, unvoiced, wordless; CONCEPT *267* —Ant. expressed, said, stated

unsanitary [adj] *dirty, unclean* contaminated, dusty, filthy, foul, grimy, messy, muddy, polluted, rancid, rank, rotten, sloppy, soiled, stained, stinking, sullied, tarnished, unhealthful, unhealthy, unhygienic; CONCEPT *621*

unsatisfactory [adj] *insufficient, inadequate* amiss, bad, damaged, deficient, disappointing, disconcerting, displeasing, disquieting, distressing, disturbing, for the birds*, junky*, lame, mediocre, no good, not good enough, not up to par*, offensive, poor, regrettable, rotten, schlocky*, second, thin, unacceptable, undesirable, unsuitable, unwelcome, unworthy, upsetting, vexing, weak, wrong; CONCEPTS *529,558, 570* —Ant. acceptable, adequate, ok, satisfactory, sufficient

unsavory [adj] *revolting, sickening* acid, bitter, bland, disagreeable, distasteful, dull, flavorless, gross*, icky*, insipid, lousy, nasty, nauseating, no good*, objectionable, obnoxious, offensive, rancid, rank, raunchy*, repellent, repugnant, repulsive, rough, sad, shady, sharp, shifty, sour, stinking, tart, tasteless, tough, unappetizing, unpalatable, unpleasant, wrong; CONCEPTS *462,571* —Ant. appetizing, attractive, savory

unscathed [adj] *not hurt* in one piece*, safe,

sound, unharmed, unhurt, uninjured, unmarked, unscarred, unscratched, untouched, whole; CONCEPT *314* —Ant. harmed, hurt, injured

unscrupulous [adj] *immoral* arrant, base, casuistic, conscienceless, corrupt, crafty, crooked, deceitful, degraded, degrading, disgraceful, dishonest, dishonorable, exploitative, illegal, improper, low-down*, mercenary, perfidious, petty, questionable, recreant, ruthless, scandalous, scheming, selfish, self-seeking, shady, shameless, shifty, sinister, slippery, sly, two-faced*, unconscientious, unconscionable, underhand, underhanded, unethical, unfair, unprincipled, unworthy, venal, wicked, wrongful; CONCEPTS *401,545* —Ant. ethical, good, moral, principled, scrupulous

unseemly [adj] *improper; in bad taste* cheap, coarse, crude, discreditable, disreputable, inappropriate, inapt, incorrect, indecent, indecorous, indelicate, inept, in poor taste, malapropos, malodorous, out of keeping, out of place, poor, raffish, rough, rowdy, rude, ruffian, tawdry, unapt, unbecoming, unbefitting, undignified, ungodly, unrefined, unsuitable, untoward, vulgar, wrong; CONCEPTS *401,558* —Ant. appropriate, due, fitting, proper, seemly, suited

unseen [adj] *hidden* concealed, curtained, dark, imaginary, imagined, impalpable, impenetrable, imperceptible, inconspicuous, invisible, lurking, not in sight, obscure, occult, out of sight, shrouded, undetected, undiscovered, unnoticed, unobserved, unobtrusive, unperceived, unsuspected, veiled; CONCEPT *576* —Ant. open, seen, visible

unselfish [adj] *kind, giving* altruistic, benevolent, charitable, chivalrous, denying, devoted, disinterested, extroverted, generous, helpful, humanitarian, incorruptible, indulgent, liberal, loving, magnanimous, noble, open-handed, self-effacing, self-forgetting, selfless, self-sacrificing; CONCEPTS *401,404* —Ant. greedy, selfish, uncharitable

unsettle [v] *bother, upset* agitate, confuse, dement, derange, disarrange, disarray, discommode, discompose, disconcert, disorder, disorganize, displace, disquiet, disrupt, disturb, down, flurry, fluster, fuddle, get to*, jumble, needle, perturb, psych out*, put off, rattle, ruffle, rummage, sicken, spook, throw, throw off*, trouble, turn, unbalance, unhinge*, unnerve; CONCEPTS *7,19,242* —Ant. balance, compose, order, settle

unsettled [adj1] *bothered, upset* active, agitated, antsy*, anxious, busy, changeable, changeful, changing, complex, complicated, confused, disorderly, disturbed, explosive, fidgety, fluid, flustered, inconstant, insecure, kinetic, mobile, mutable, on edge*, perilous, perturbed, precarious, rattled, restive, restless, shaken, shaky, shifting, shook up*, tense, thrown, ticklish, troubled, unbalanced, uncertain, uneasy, unnerved, unpeaceful, unpredictable, unquiet, unrestful, unstable, unsteady, variable, wavering, wobbling; CONCEPTS *401,403* —Ant. calmed, content, happy, settled

unsettled [adj2] *not decided, taken care of* betwixt and between*, clouded*, debatable, doubtful, dubious, dubitable, due, immature, in arrears, moot, open, outstanding, overdue, owing, payable, pendent, pending, problematic, uncertain, unclear, undecided, undetermined, unfixed, unpaid, unresolved, up for grabs*, waffling; CONCEPTS *334,535* —Ant. certain, decided, definite, settled, sure

unsightly [*adj*] *not pretty* deformed, disagreeable, drab, dull, hideous, homely, horrid, lackluster, repulsive, revolting, ugly, unattractive, unpleasant, unprepossessing, unshapely; CONCEPT *579* —Ant. beautiful, nice, pleasing, pretty, sightly

unskilled [*adj*] *untrained* awkward, green*, inadequate, incompetent, inept, inexperienced, inexpert, inproficient, not up to*, raw*, unable, undeveloped, uneducated, unequipped, unhandy, unqualified, unschooled, untalented; CONCEPT *527*

unsociable [*adj*] *unfriendly* aloof, antagonistic, brooding, cold, cool, distant, easy-going, hostile, inaccessible, inhospitable, introverted, laidback*, nongregarious, recessive, reclusive, reserved, retiring, secretive, sensitive, shy, standoffish*, stuck-up*, timid, unapproachable, unbending, uncommunicative, uncongenial, unforthcoming, unneighborly, unsocial, uppity*, withdrawn; CONCEPTS *401,555* —Ant. approachable, friendly, nice, sociable, social

unsolicited [*adj*] *unasked for* free, freewilled, gratis*, gratuitous, offered, spontaneous, uncalled-for*, undesirable, undesired, unforced, uninvited, unrequested, unsought, unwelcome, voluntary, volunteered; CONCEPT *538* —Ant. asked, invited, requested, solicited

unsophisticated [*adj*] *natural, simple* artless, authentic, bush-league*, callow, childlike, clean, cornball*, corny*, crude, folksy, genuine, green*, guileless, homey*, inexperienced, ingenuous, innocent, kid*, naive, plain, pure, raw, rookie, straightforward, unadulterated, unaffected, unartificial, uncomplicated, uninvolved, unrefined, unschooled, unstudied, untutored, unworldly, wide-eyed*; CONCEPTS *401,548,562* —Ant. cultured, experienced, refined, sophisticated, upper-class, worldly

unsound [*adj*] *not well; flimsy* ailing, crazed, dangerous, decrepit, defective, delicate, demented, deranged, diseased, erroneous, fallacious, false, faulty, flawed, fragile, frail, ill, illogical, inaccurate, incongruous, incorrect, infirm, in poor health, insane, insecure, insubstantial, invalid, lunatic, mad, not solid, rickety, shaky, specious, tottering, unbacked, unbalanced, unhealthy, unhinged, unreliable, unsafe, unstable, unsteady, unsubstantial, unwell, weak, wobbly; CONCEPTS *314,403,587* —Ant. safe, sound, stable, strong, well

unspeakable [*adj*] *very bad; beyond description* abominable, alarming, appalling, atrocious, awful, beastly, beyond words, calamitous, detestable, dire, disgusting, dreadful, evil, execrable, fearful, frightening, frightful, heinous, horrible, horrid, incommunicable, inconceivable, indefinable, indescribable, ineffable, inexpressible, inhuman, loathsome, monstrous, nameless, obnoxious, odious, offensive, outrageous, overwhelming, preternatural, repellent, repugnant, repulsive, revolting, shocking, unbelievable, unimaginable, unutterable; CONCEPTS *548,571* —Ant. good, nice

unspoiled [*adj*] *fresh* clean, clear, crisp, just out*, latest, natural, new, original, pristine, pure, recent, refreshing, sparkling, uncontaminated, unpolluted, unprocessed, untainted, untouched, whole, young; CONCEPTS *537,578,797*

unstable/unsteady [*adj*] *doubtful, weak* ambiguous, borderline, capricious, changeable, dizzy, dubious, erratic, fickle, fitful, fluctuating, giddy, inconsistent, inconstant, insecure, irrational, lubricious, mercurial, mobile, movable, moving, mutable, not fixed, precarious, rickety, risky, rocky, sensitive, shaky, shifty, slippery, suspect, teetering, temperamental, ticklish, tricky, uncertain, unpredictable, unsettled, unsteady, untrustworthy, vacillating, variable, volatile, wavering, weaving, wiggly, wobbly; CONCEPTS *488,534,542* —Ant. stable, steady, strong

unsubstantiated [*adj*] *questionable, unproven* arguable, controversial, debatable, disputable, doubtful, dubious, dubitable, fishy*, hard to believe, iffy*, indefinite, open to doubt, open to question, suspect, suspicious, uncertain, unconfirmed, uncorroborated, unsupported; CONCEPTS *529,535*

unsuccessful [*adj*] *failing* abortive, defeated, disastrous, doomed, failed, foiled, fruitless, futile, ill-fated, ineffective, ineffectual, losing, thwarted, unlucky, useless, vain; CONCEPTS *485,489*

unsuitable [*adj*] *not proper, inappropriate* clashing, disagreeable, discordant, discrepant, disparate, disproportionate, dissident, dissonant, ill-suited, improper, inadequate, inadmissible, inapposite, inapt, incompatible, incongruous, inconsistent, ineligible, infelicitous, inharmonious, interfering, irrelevant, jarring, malapropos, out of character*, out of keeping, out of place, senseless, unacceptable, unbecoming, unbefitting, uncalled-for, undue, unfit, unfitting, unmatched, unseasonable, unseemly, unsuited; CONCEPT *558* —Ant. appropriate, proper, suitable

unsung [*adj*] *uncelebrated* anonymous, disregarded, forgotten, nameless, neglected, overlooked, unacclaimed, unacknowledged, undistinguished, unfamed, unglorified, unhailed, unhonored, unknown, unnamed, unrecognized, unrenowned; CONCEPTS *267,576*

unsure [*adj*] *doubtful, insecure* betwixt and between*, borderline, distrustful, dubious, fluctuant, fly-by-night*, hesitant, iffy*, in a quandary, indecisive, indeterminate, irresolute, lacking, mistrustful, open, problematic, rootless, shaky, skeptical, suspicious, touch and go*, unassured, uncertain, unclear, unconfident, unconvinced, undecided, undependable, unreliable, unstable, untrustworthy, untrusty, up for grabs*, vacillating, wavering, weak, wimpy*, wobbly; CONCEPT *535* —Ant. certain, definite, secure, sure, undoubted

unsurpassed [*adj*] *supreme* absolute, best, culminating, excellent, final, first, foremost, greatest, highest, incomparable, leading, matchless, paramount, peerless, perfect, prevailing, superior, top, ultimate, unequaled, unmatched, unparalleled, unrivaled; CONCEPTS *568,574*

unsuspecting [*adj*] *gullible* confiding, credulous, easy, inexperienced, ingenuous, innocent, naive, off guard*, simple, swallowing, taken in*, trustful, trusting, unconscious, undoubting, unsuspicious, unwarned, unwary; CONCEPTS 401,404 —Ant. conscious, expecting, knowing, realizing, suspecting

unsympathetic [adj] *without agreement in feeling* aloof, antipathetic, apathetic, aversive, callous, cold, cold-blooded, cool, cruel, disinterested, frigid, halfhearted, hard, harsh, heartless, icy, indifferent, insensitive, lukewarm*, mean, nasty, obdurate, repellent, repugnant, stony, tough, uncompassionate, unconcerned, uncongenial, unemotional, unfeeling, unkind, unmoved, unpitying, unpleasant, unresponsive; CONCEPTS 401,542 —Ant. kind, merciful, sympathetic

untamed [adj] *wild* barbarian, barbaric, barbarous, feral, ferocious, fierce, native, overgrown, overrun, rampant, savage, uncivilized, uncontrollable, uncultivated, undomesticated, uninhabited, unmanageable, vicious; CONCEPTS 406,583

untangle [v] *straighten out* clear up, disembroil, disencumber, disentangle, explain, extricate, put in order, solve, unravel, unscramble, unsnarl, untwist, unweave; CONCEPT 126 —Ant. tangle, twist

unthinkable [adj] *incredible, unusual* absurd, beyond belief, beyond possibility, exceptional, extraordinary, illogical, implausible, impossible, improbable, incogitable, inconceivable, insupportable, outlandish, out of the question*, preposterous, rare, singular, unbelievable, uncommon, unimaginable, unique, unlikely, unordinary, unreasonable; CONCEPTS 564,582 —Ant. believable, conceivable, credible

unthinking [adj] *careless* blundering, brutish, feckless, foolish, heedless, impulsive, inadvertent, inconsiderate, indelicate, insensitive, instinctive, mechanical, napping, negligent, oblivious, outrageous, rash, rude, selfish, senseless, tactless, thoughtless, uncaring, unconscious, undiplomatic, unheeding, unintended, unmeant, unmindful, unpremeditated, unreasoning, untactful, unwise, vacant, witless; CONCEPT 401 —Ant. careful, cautious, thoughtful

untidy [adj] *dirty, disorderly* bedraggled, careless, chaotic, cluttered, disarranged, disarrayed, disheveled, dowdy*, frowzy*, in disorder, jumbled, littered, mess, messy, mixed up*, muddled, rumpled, slapdash*, slipshod*, sloppy, slovenly, snarled, tacky*, tangled, topsy-turvy, tousled, uncombed, unfastidious, unkempt, unneat, unorderly, unsettled, upset; CONCEPTS 589,621 —Ant. clean, neat, orderly, tidy

until [prep] *just before* as far as, before, before the coming, continuously, down to, in advance of, in expectation, prior to, till, to, up till, up to; CONCEPT 820

untimely [adj] *inappropriate* a bit previous*, abortive, anachronistic, awkward, badly timed, bright and early*, disagreeable, early, early bird*, early on, ill-timed, improper, inauspicious, inconvenient, inexpedient, inopportune, intrusive, malapropos, mistimed, out-of-date, overearly, oversoon, premature, previous, soon, too early, too late, undue, unfavorable, unfit, unfortunate, unlucky, unpropitious, unseasonable, unseemly, unsuitable, unsuited, wrong;

CONCEPTS 548,799 —Ant. appropriate, opportune, timely

untiring [adj] *determined, persevering* constant, continued, continuing, dedicated, devoted, dogged, eager beaver*, fireball*, firm, go-go*, grind*, hyper*, incessant, indefatigable, indomitable, inexhaustible, jumping, patient, perky, persistent, pertinacious, plodding, plugging, resolute, staunch, steady, strong, tenacious, tireless, unceasing, undeterred, unfailing, unfaltering, unflagging, unflinching, unremitting, unstinted, unswerving, unwavering, unwearied; CONCEPT 538 —Ant. failing, irresolute, tiring, unpersevering

untold [adj] *very many; enormous* beyond measure, countless, gigantic, hidden, huge, immense, incalculable, indescribable, inexpressible, innumerable, innumerous, mammoth, manifold, many, measureless, mighty, monstrous, multiple, multitudinous, myriad, numberless, private, prodigious, staggering, suppressed, titanic, uncountable, uncounted, undreamed of, unexpressed, unimaginable, unknown, unnumberable, unnumbered, unspeakable; unthinkable, vast; CONCEPTS 529,762,781 —Ant. few, little, small, tiny

untouched [adj] *whole; not spoiled* clear, entire, flawless, fresh, good, immaculate, incorrupt, indifferent, in good condition, intact, out of danger, perfect, pure, safe and sound*, sanitary, secure, shipshape, sound, spotless, unaffected, unblemished, unbroken, unconcerned, undamaged, unharmed, unhurt, unimpressed, uninjured, unmarred, unmoved, unscathed, unstained, unstirred, untried, untouched, virgin, virginal, without a scratch*; CONCEPTS 403,485,621 —Ant. affected, partial, spoiled, touched

untoward [adj1] *troublesome* adverse, annoying, awkward, contrary, disastrous, disturbing, fractious, hapless, ill-starred, inauspicious, inconvenient, indocile, inimical, inopportune, intractable, irritating, luckless, misfortunate, perverse, recalcitrant, refractory, star-crossed, undisciplined, unfavorable, unfortunate, ungovernable, unhappy, unlucky, unmanageable, unpliable, unpropitious, unruly, untimely, unyielding, vexatious, wild; CONCEPTS 542,548,570 —Ant. auspicious, happy, lucky

untoward [adj2] *improper; not suitable* improprietous, inappropriate, indecent, indecorous, indelicate, malodorous, out of place*, rough*, unbecoming, uncouth, unfitting, ungodly*, unseemly; CONCEPTS 401,558 —Ant. acceptable, proper, suitable

untroubled [adj] *calm, peaceful* composed, cool, halcyon, hushed, placid, quiet, serene, steady, still, tranquil, unagitated, unconcerned, undisturbed, unflappable, unflustered, unperturbed, unruffled, unstirred, unworried; CONCEPTS 403,548,594 —Ant. anxious, disturbed, troubled, unnerved

untrue [adj] *dishonest* apocryphal, cheating, counterfactual, deceitful, deceptive, delusive, deviant, disloyal, dissembling, distorted, erroneous, faithless, fallacious, false, fictitious, forsworn, hollow, imprecise, inaccurate, inconstant, incorrect, inexact, lying, meretricious, misleading, mistaken, off*, out of line*, perfidious, perjured, prevaricating, recreant, sham*, specious, spurious, traitorous, treacherous, two-faced*, unfaithful, unloyal, unsound, untrustworthy, untruthful, wide, wrong; CONCEPTS 267,545 —Ant. faithful, honest, true

untrustworthy [adj] not dependable, unfaithful capricious, conniving, crooked, deceitful, devious, dishonest, disloyal, dubious, fair-weather*, faithless, false, fickle, fink*, fly-by-night*, guileful, irresponsible, questionable, shady, sharp, shifty*, slippery, sneaky, treacherous, tricky, trustless, two-faced*, two-timing*, unassured, undependable, unreliable, unsafe, unsure, untrue, untrusty; CONCEPTS 401,542, 545 —Ant. dependable, faithful, honest, reliable, trustworthy

untruthful [adj] dishonest bluffing, cheating, corrupt, crooked, deceitful, deceiving, deceptive, disreputable, double-crossing, double-dealing, false, fraudulent, lying, misleading, shady, shifty, sneaking, sneaky, tricky, two-faced*, two-timing*, underhanded, untrustworthy; CONCEPT 267

unusual [adj] different abnormal, amazing, astonishing, atypical, awe-inspiring, awesome, bizarre, conspicuous, curious, distinguished, eminent, exceptional, extraordinary, far-out*, inconceivable, incredible, memorable, noteworthy, odd, out of the ordinary*, outstanding, phenomenal, prodigious, prominent, queer, rare, refreshing, remarkable, significant, singular, something else*, special, strange, surprising, uncommon, unconventional, unexpected, unfamiliar, unique, unparalleled, unwonted, weird*; CONCEPT 564 —Ant. common, familiar, normal, regular, standard, usual

unusually [adv] extremely almighty*, awful*, awfully, curiously, especially, extra, extraordinarily, mighty, oddly, peculiarly, plenty, powerful, rarely, real, really, remarkably, right, so, so much, strangely, surprisingly, terribly, terrifically, too much, uncommon, uncommonly, very; CONCEPTS 544,569 —Ant. normally, usually

unvarnished [adj] plain, honest bare, candid, clean, folksy*, for real*, frank, genuine, homey*, naked, open, open and shut*, pure, pure and simple*, simple, sincere, stark, straight, straightforward, unadorned, unconcealed, undisguised, undissembled, unembellished, vanilla*; CONCEPTS 267,582 —Ant. dishonest, falsified

unveil [v] reveal bare, betray, bring to light*, come out, disclose, discover, display, divulge, expose, give away, lay bare*, lay open*, let it all hang out*, make known, make public, open, open up, show, spring, tell, tip one's hand*, unbosom, uncover; CONCEPTS 60,138 —Ant. conceal, hide, veil

unwarranted [adj] not reasonable or right baseless, bottomless, foundationless, gratuitous, groundless, indefensible, inexcusable, uncalled-for, unconscionable, undue, unfair, unfounded, ungrounded, unjust, unjustifiable, unjustified, unprovoked, unreasonable, unwarrantable, wrong; CONCEPTS 545,548,558 —Ant. called-for, justifiable, reasonable, warranted

unwary [adj] thoughtless, heedless brash, careless, credulous, hasty, ignorant, ill-advised,

impetuous, imprudent, incautious, inconsiderate, indiscreet, negligent, rash, reckless, unadvised, unalert, uncircumspect, unguarded, unprepared, unsuspecting, unsuspicious, unvigilant, unwatchful; CONCEPTS 401,403 —Ant. cautious, heeding, mindful, thoughtful, wary

unwavering [adj] consistent, unchanging abiding, brick-wall*, dead set on*, dedicated, determined, enduring, firm, fixed, intense, never-failing, pat, regular, resolute, set, set in stone*, single-minded, solid, staunch, steadfast, steady, sure, undeviating, unfaltering, unflagging, unflappable, unqualified, unshakable, unshaken, unswerving, untiring; CONCEPTS 488,535,542 —Ant. changeable, changing, inconsistent, varying, wavering

unwelcome [adj] not wanted, desired blackballed*, disagreeable, displeasing, distasteful, exceptionable, excess baggage*, excluded, ill-favored, inadmissible, left out in cold*, lousy, not in the picture*, objectionable, obnoxious, rejected, repellent, shut out, thankless, unacceptable, unasked, undesirable, uninvited, unpleasant, unpopular, unsought, unwanted, unwished-for; CONCEPTS 529,555,570 —Ant. desirable, wanted, welcome

unwell [adj] sick ailing, bedridden, broken down, debilitated, diseased, feeble, feverish, frail, hospitalized, ill, impaired, incurable, infected, infirm, in poor health, invalid, laid-up, nauseated, not feeling well, run down, sick as a dog*, sickly, suffering, under medication, under the weather*, unhealthy, weak; CONCEPT 314

unwieldy [adj] awkward, bulky burdensome, clumsy, cumbersome, cumbrous, encumbering, gross, hefty, inconvenient, lumbering, massive, onerous, ponderous, uncontrollable, ungainly, unhandy, unmanageable, weighty; CONCEPTS 562,781 —Ant. convenient, handy

unwilling [adj] not in the mood afraid, against, against the grain*, averse, backward, begrudging, compelled, contrary, demurring, disinclined, disobliging, evasive, forced, grudging, hesitating, indisposed, indocile, involuntary, laggard, loath, malcontent, opposed, recalcitrant, refractory, reluctant, remiss, resistant, shrinking, shy, slack, slow, unaccommodating, uncheerful, uncooperative, uneager, unenthusiastic, uninclined, unobliging, unready, unwishful, wayward; CONCEPTS 401,542 —Ant. prepared, ready, willing

unwind [v1] undo, untangle disentangle, free, loose, loosen, ravel, separate, slacken, unbend, uncoil, unfurl, unravel, unreel, unroll, untwine, untwist, unwrap; CONCEPT 158 —Ant. tangle, twist, wind

unwind [v2] relax calm down*, ease off*, loosen up*, quiet down*, quieten, recline, rest, sit back*, slow down*, take a break*, take it easy*, wind down*; CONCEPT 210 —Ant. agitate, prepare, ready

unwise [adj] stupid, irresponsible childish, foolhardy, foolish, ill-advised, ill-considered, immature, impolitic, improvident, imprudent, inadvisable, inane, inappropriate, indiscreet, inept, injudicious, misguided, naive, rash, reckless, senseless, short-sighted, silly, thoughtless, undesirable, unfortunate, unintelligent,

unsound, witless; CONCEPTS 401,402,548
—*Ant.* responsible, sagacious, thoughtful, wise

unwitting [*adj*] *without fully realizing* accidental, aimless, chance, comatose, forgetful, haphazard, ignorant, inadvertent, incognizant, inconversant, innocent, involuntary, numb, oblivious, senseless, unacquainted, unaware, unconscious, undesigned, unfamiliar, uninformed, uninstructed, unintended, unintentional, unknowing, unmeant, unmindful, unplanned, unsuspecting, unthinking; CONCEPTS 401,544,548 —*Ant.* conscious, intentional, realizing, witting

unworldly [*adj1*] *spiritual* abstract, astral, celestial, daydreaming, daydreamy, dreamy, ethereal, extraterrestrial, fantastic, incorporeal, metaphysical, nonmaterialistic, otherworldly, religious, supersensory, transcendental, unearthly, unreal, visionary; CONCEPTS 536,582 —*Ant.* earthly, material, worldly

unworldly [*adj2*] *not sophisticated; inexperienced* artless, babe in woods*, clean, corn-fed*, country, folksy*, green*, idealistic, ingenuous, innocent, naive, natural, raw*, simple, trusting, unaffected, unartificial, uncool, unschooled, unsophisticated, unstudied, wide-eyed*; CONCEPTS 401,555,589 —*Ant.* cultured, experienced, refined, sophisticated, worldly

unworthy [*adj*] *not of value* base, beneath, blamable, contemptible, degrading, disgraceful, dishonorable, disreputable, good-for-nothing, ignoble, improper, inappropriate, ineligible, inexcusable, no-account*, no-good*, not deserving, not fit, not good enough, nothing, not worth, offensive, out of place*, recreant, reprehensible, shameful, unbecoming, unbefitting, undeserving, unfit, unmerited, unseemly, unsuitable, valueless, vile, wretched, wrong; CONCEPTS 404,558,571 —*Ant.* honorable, useful, valuable, worthwhile, worthy

unwritten [*adj*] *understood* accepted, conventional, customary, oral, spoken, tacit, traditional, unformulated, unrecorded, unsaid, verbal, vocal, word-of-mouth; CONCEPTS 267,533 —*Ant.* explained, explicated, stated, written

unyielding [*adj*] *steadfast, resolute* adamant, dead set on*, determined, firm, fixed, hard, hard-core*, hardheaded, hard-line*, hard-nosed*, headstrong*, immalleable, immovable, implacable, impliable, inexorable, inflexible, intractable, locked in, merciless, mulish, obdurate, obstinate, pertinacious, pigheaded*, refractory, relentless, rigid, ruthless, single-minded, solid, staunch, stiff, stiff-necked, stubborn, tough, unbending, uncompliant, uncompromising, unmovable, unrelenting, unswayable, unwavering; CONCEPT 401 —*Ant.* flexible, irresolute, surrendering, yielding

up-and-coming [*adj*] *rising* ambitious, climbing, coming on strong*, determined, eager, enterprising, get up and go*, go-getter*, high-reaching, hungry, promising, soaring, striving, succeeding; CONCEPTS 326,542

upbeat [*adj*] *cheerful* buoyant, cheery, encouraging, favorable, fond, happy, heartening, hopeful, optimistic, positive, promising, rosy, sanguine; CONCEPTS 403,572 —*Ant.* depressed, down, sad

upbraid [*v*] *scold* admonish, berate, blame, castigate, censure, chasten, chastise, chew out*,

chide, criticize, give a talking-to*, jump on*, lay down the law*, lecture, light into*, put down, rake over the coals*, ream, reprimand, reproach, take to task*, tell off*; CONCEPT 44

update [*v*] *bring up to date* amend, modernize, refresh, refurbish, rejuvenate, renew, renovate, restore, revise; CONCEPT 244 —*Ant.* antique, make old

upgrade [*v*] *improve* advance, better, boost, elevate, enhance, increase, lift, make better, make strides, move up, progress, promote, raise; CONCEPTS 244,700

upheaval [*n*] *major change* about-face*, alteration, cataclysm, catastrophe, clamor, commotion, convulsion, disaster, disorder, disruption, disturbance, eruption, explosion, ferment, flip-flop*, new ball-game*, new deal*, outbreak, outburst, outcry, overthrow, revolution, shakeout*, stirring, switch, temblor, tremor, tumult, turmoil, turnaround, upturn; CONCEPT 230 —*Ant.* stagnation

uphill [*adj1*] *going up* acclivous, ascending, climbing, mounting, rising, skyward, sloping upward, toward summit, up, uprising; CONCEPT 581 —*Ant.* downhill

uphill [*adj2*] *difficult, laborious* arduous, effortful, exhausting, grueling, hard, labored, operose, punishing, rugged, strenuous, taxing, toilsome, tough, wearisome; CONCEPTS 538, 565 —*Ant.* downhill, easy, facile

uphold [*v*] *maintain, support* advocate, aid, assist, back, back up, bolster, boost, brace, buoy up, buttress, carry, champion, confirm, countenance, defend, elevate, encourage, endorse, help, hoist, hold to, hold up, hold up one's end*, justify, pick up, promote, prop, raise, rear, second, shore up, side with, stand by, stick by, stick up for*, sustain, take up, upbear, uplift, upraise, uprear, vindicate; CONCEPT 110 —*Ant.* weaken

upkeep [*n*] *maintenance* budget, conservation, costs, expenditure, expenses, keep, outlay, overhead, preservation, price, repair, running, subsistence, support, sustenance, sustentation; CONCEPTS 117,344 —*Ant.* neglect, negligence

uplift [*v*] *elevate, inspire* boost, brighten, bring up, cheer, elate, excite, exhilarate, improve, lift up*, perk up*, raise spirits; CONCEPTS 7,22

upper [*adj1*] *above* high, higher, loftier, more elevated, overhead, top, topmost, uppermost, upward; CONCEPT 583 —*Ant.* below, lower, under

upper [*adj2*] *superior* beautiful, elevated, elite, eminent, greater, important, more important; CONCEPT 555 —*Ant.* inferior, junior, lower

upper hand [*n*] *advantage* benefit, break, control, dominance, edge, favor, gain, help, improvement, leverage, rule, superiority, supremacy; CONCEPT 574

uppermost [*adj1*] *top* apical, culminating, highest, loftiest, most elevated, topmost, upmost; CONCEPT 583 —*Ant.* bottom, lower, lowest

uppermost [*adj2*] *most important; chief* best, big, boss, dominant, executive, foremost, greatest, high-up*, leading, main, paramount, predominant, preeminent, primary, principal, supreme, the most*, tops*, winner, world-class*; CONCEPTS 568,632 —*Ant.* lowest, trivial

uppity [*adj*] *arrogant* audacious, bossy, bragging, cavalier, cheeky, cocky, conceited,

egotistic, haughty, high and mighty*, high falutin'*, know-it-all*, overbearing, pompous,
presumptuous, pretentious, puffed up*, self-
important, smug, snobbish, snooty*, snotty*,
stuck up*, superior, vain; CONCEPTS 401,404

upright [adj1] straight-up cocked, end on, end
up, erect, on end, perpendicular, plumb, raised,
sheer, standing, stand-up, steep, straight, upended, upstanding, upward, vertical; CONCEPTS
581,583 —Ant. fallen, lying, prone

upright [adj2] honorable, honest aboveboard,
blameless, circumspect, conscientious, correct,
equitable, ethical, exemplary, fair, faithful,
good, high-minded, impartial, incorruptible,
just, kosher*, legit*, moral, noble, principled,
punctilious, pure, right, righteous, square,
straight, straightforward, true, true-blue*, trustworthy, unimpeachable, up front*, virtuous;
CONCEPTS 404,545 —Ant. dishonest, dishonorable, disreputable, unrespected

uprising [n] disturbance insurgence, insurrection, mutiny, outbreak, rebellion, revolt, revolution, riot, upheaval; CONCEPTS 106,674 —Ant.
calm, peace

uproar [n] commotion, pandemonium ado,
babble, babel, bedlam, bickering, big scene*,
brawl, broil*, bustle, chaos, clamor, clangor,
clatter, confusion, din, disorder, flap*, fracas*,
free-for-all*, furor, fuss, hassle, jangle, mayhem, melee, noise, outcry, racket, riot, roughhouse*, row, ruction, shivaree*, stink*, stir,
strife, to-do*, turbulence, turmoil, violence;
CONCEPTS 46,65,106,674 —Ant. calm, peace

uproot [v] destroy; rip out of a place abate,
abolish, annihilate, blot out, demolish, deracinate, dig up, displace, do away with*, eliminate, eradicate, excavate, exile, exterminate,
extirpate, extract, move, overthrow, overturn,
pull up, remove, root out, tear up, weed, weed
out, wipe out; CONCEPTS 147,178,211,252
—Ant. plant, settle, sow

upset [adj] disturbed, bothered agitated, all
torn up*, amazed, antsy*, apprehensive,
blue*, broken up*, bummed out*, capsized,
chaotic, come apart*, confused, disconcerted,
dismayed, disordered, disquieted, distressed,
dragged*, frantic, grieved, hurt, ill, in disarray,
jittery, jumpy, low, muddled, overturned,
overwrought, psyched out*, rattled, ruffled*,
shocked, shook up*, sick, spilled, thrown,
tipped over, toppled, troubled, tumbled,
unglued*, unsettled, unzipped*, upside-down,
worried; CONCEPTS 403,485,570 —Ant. happy,
undisturbed, unworried

upset [n] problem agitation, bother, complaint,
defeat, destruction, disorder, disquiet, distress,
disturbance, free-for-all*, goulash*, hassle,
illness, malady, overthrow, queasiness, reverse,
reversion, screw-up*, shake-up*, shock,
sickness, stew*, subversion, surprise, tizzy*,
trouble, turmoil, worry; CONCEPT 674 —Ant.
calm, happiness, peace, solution

upset [v1] disorder; knock over capsize,
change, derange, disarray, disorganize, disturb,
invert, jumble, keel over, mess up*, mix up,
muddle, overset, overturn, pitch, put out of
order, reverse, rummage, spill, spoil, subvert,
tilt, tip over, topple, tumble, turn, turn inside-
out*, turn topsy-turvy*, turn upside-down*,

unsettle, upend, upturn; CONCEPTS 147,208,
213 —Ant. hold, order, place, straighten

upset [v2] bother, trouble adjy*, afflict, agitate,
ail, bewilder, bug*, confound, cramp, craze,
debilitate, derange, discombobulate*, discompose, disconcert, dismay, disquiet, distract,
distress, disturb, egg on*, fire up*, flip*, flip
out*, floor*, flurry, fluster, get to*, give a hard
time*, grieve, incapacitate, indispose, key up*,
lay up, make a scene*, make waves*, perturb,
pick on*, pother, psych*, rattle, rock the
boat*, ruffle, sicken, spook, stir up, throw off
balance*, turn, turn on, unhinge*, unnerve,
unsettle; CONCEPTS 7,19 —Ant. delight, make
happy, please

upset [v3] defeat beat, be victorious, conquer,
get the better of*, outplay, overcome, overpower, overthrow, overturn, topple, triumph
over, win; CONCEPT 95 —Ant. fail, lose

upshot [n] end result aftereffect, aftermath,
burden, climax, completion, conclusion,
consequence, core, culmination, denouement,
development, effect, end, ending, event, eventuality, finale, finish, gist, issue, meaning, meat*,
outcome, payoff, pith*, purport, result, sense,
sequel, substance, termination, thrust; CONCEPTS
230,682 —Ant. cause, origin, source

upside-down [adj] overturned, inverted backward, bottom-side-up, bottom up, confused,
disordered, downside-up*, haywire*, helter-
skelter*, in chaos, in disarray, jumbled, mixed-
up, on head, reversed, tangled, topsy-turvy*,
upended, wrong-side-up, wrong way; CONCEPT
583 —Ant. right-side-up

upstanding [adj] honorable ethical, good,
honest, incorruptible, moral, principled,
straightforward, true, trustworthy, upright;
CONCEPT 545 —Ant. bad, corrupted, dishonorable, disreputable

upstart [n] newly rich name-dropper, nouveau
riche, parvenu, social climber, status seeker;
CONCEPT 347

uptight [adj] nervous anxious, apprehensive,
cautious, concerned, conventional, edgy, nervy,
old-fashioned, on edge*, on the defensive*,
restive, strict, tense, troubled, uneasy, withdrawn, worried; CONCEPT 401 —Ant. calm,
collected, cool

up-to-date [adj] current, modern abreast, advanced, à la mode*, all the rage*, au courant,
avant-garde, brand-new, contemporary, cutting
edge*, dashing, expedient, faddish*, fashionable, fitting, hot*, in, in fashion, in-thing*, in
vogue, modernistic, modish, neoteric, new,
newest, newfangled, now*, opportune, popular,
red-hot*, state-of-the-art*, stylish, suitable,
timely, today*, trendy, up*, up-to-the-minute,
with it*; CONCEPTS 578,589,797,799 —Ant.
old, outdated, out-of-date, past

urban [adj] city burghal, central, citified, civic,
civil, downtown, inner-city, metropolitan,
municipal, nonrural, oppidan, popular, public,
town, village; CONCEPT 536 —Ant. country,
rural, suburban

urbane [adj] civilized affable, balanced, bland,
civil, cosmopolitan, courteous, cultivated, cultured, debonair, elegant, genteel, gracious, mannerly, metropolitan, obliging, poised, polished,
polite, refined, smooth, sophisticated, suave,

well-bred, well-mannered; CONCEPT *401*
—*Ant.* uncivilized, uncouth, unsophisticated

urchin [n] *mischievious youngster* brat*, cub,
dickens*, gamin, imp, juvenile delinquent,
punk*, pup*, ragamuffin, waif; CONCEPT *423*

urge [n] *very strong desire* appetite, appetition,
compulsion, craving, drive, druthers, fancy, fire
in belly*, goad, impetus, impulse, incentive,
itch*, longing, lust, motive, passion, pressure,
stimulant, stimulus, sweet tooth*, weakness,
wish, yearning, yen; CONCEPTS *20,532*
—*Ant.* dislike, hate

urge [v] *beg, push for, encourage* adjure, advance, advise, advocate, appeal to, ask, attract,
beseech, champion, charge, commend, compel,
conjure, counsel, countenance, drive, egg on*,
endorse, entreat, exhort, favor, fire up*, force,
further, goad, hasten, impel, implore, incite,
induce, influence, insist on, inspire, instigate,
maneuver, move, plead, press, promote, prompt,
propel, propose, push, put up to*, rationalize,
recommend, request, sanction, solicit, speak
for, spur, stimulate, support, tempt, wheedle;
CONCEPTS *68,75* —*Ant.* discourage, dissuade

urgent [adj] *needing immediate attention* burning*, called-for, capital, chief, clamant, clamorous, compelling, critical, crucial, crying*,
demanded, demanding, driving, essential, exigent, foremost, heavy*, hurry-up, immediate,
impelling, imperative, important, importunate,
indispensable, insistent, instant, leading, life and
death*, momentous, necessary, paramount, persuasive, pressing, primary, principal, required,
salient, serious, top-priority, touch and go*,
touchy*, vital, wanted, weighty*; CONCEPT *548*
—*Ant.* moderate, unimportant, unnecessary

usable [adj] *available, working* accessible,
adaptable, advantageous, applicable, at disposal,
at hand, beneficial, consumable, convenient,
current, employable, exhaustible, expendable,
exploitable, fit, functional, good, helpful, in
order, instrumental, open, operative, practicable,
practical, profitable, ready, running, serviceable,
subservient, unused, useful, utile, utilizable,
valid, valuable, wieldy; CONCEPTS *560,576*
—*Ant.* unusable, useless

usage [n] *habit, custom* acceptance, control,
convention, currency, form, formula, habitude,
handling, management, matter of course,
method, mode, operation, practice, praxis,
procedure, regime, regulation, rote, routine,
rule, running, tradition, treatment, trick, use,
way, wont; CONCEPTS *6,658*

use [n] *application; employment* account,
adoption, advantage, appliance, applicability,
appropriateness, avail, benefit, call, capitaliza-
tion, cause, convenience, custom, end, exercise,
exercising, exertion, fitness, good, habit, handling, help, helpfulness, mileage, mobilization,
necessity, need, object, occasion, operation,
point, practice, profit, purpose, reason, relevance, service, serviceability, treatment, usabil-
ity, usage, usefulness, utility, value, way, wear
and tear*, wont, worth; CONCEPTS *225,658,923*

use [v] *work with; consume* accept, adopt,
apply, avail oneself of, bestow, bring into
play*, bring to bear*, capitalize, control, do
with, draw on, employ, exercise, exert, exhaust,
expend, exploit, find a use, govern, handle,

make do with*, make the most of*, make use,
manage, manipulate, operate, play on, ply,
practice, press into service*, put forth*, put into
action, put to use, put to work, regulate, relate,
run, run through, set in motion, spend, take
advantage of*, turn to account, utilize, waste,
wield, work; CONCEPTS *169,225* —*Ant.* abstain,
leave alone

used [adj] *secondhand* hand-me-down, nearly
new, not new, passed down, pre-owned,
recycled, worn; CONCEPTS *334,567,574*

used to [adj] *familiar with* acclimated, accustomed, at home with*, common, commonplace,
customary, everyday, knowing, known, old
hat*, ordinary, plain, recognizable, routine,
well-known; CONCEPTS *530,547*

useful [adj] *beneficial, valuable* advantageous,
all-purpose, applied, appropriate, brave,
commodious, convenient, effective, favorable,
fit, fruitful, functional, good, handy, helpful,
instrumental, meet, of assistance, of service,
of use, practicable, practical, pragmatic,
profitable, proper, propitious, purposive,
salutary, serviceable, subsidiary, suitable,
suited, toward, utile; CONCEPT —*Ant.*
unusable, unvaluable, useless, worthless

useless [adj] *not working; not valuable*
abortive, bootless, counterproductive,
disadvantageous, dysfunctional, expendable,
feckless, fruitless, futile, good-for-nothing*,
hopeless, idle, impracticable, impractical,
incompetent, ineffective, ineffectual, inept,
inoperative, inutile, meaningless, no good,
nonfunctional, of no use, pointless, profitless,
purposeless, scrap, stupid*, unavailable,
unavailing, unfunctional, unproductive,
unprofitable, unpurposed, unusable, unworkable, vain, valueless, waste, weak, worthless;
CONCEPT *560* —*Ant.* helpful, usable, useful,
valuable, working, worthwhile

user-friendly [adj] *easily operated* accessible,
adaptable, convenient, easy to use, feasible,
foolproof, handy, manageable, practical,
simple, straightforward, uncomplicated,
useful, wieldy; CONCEPTS *560,576*

usher [n] *person who guides others to place*
attendant, conductor, doorkeeper, doorperson,
escort, guide, herald, lead, leader, page, pilot,
precursor; CONCEPT *352*

usher [v] *guide* bring in, conduct, direct, escort,
herald, inaugurate, initiate, institute, introduce,
launch, lead, marshal, open the door, originate,
pave the way*, pilot, precede, preface, receive,
set up, show around, show in, show out, steer;
CONCEPTS *187,221*

usual [adj] *common, typical* accepted, accustomed, average, chronic, commonplace,
constant, conventional, current, customary,
cut-and-dried*, everyday, expected, familiar,
fixed, frequent, garden variety*, general, grind,
habitual, mainstream, matter-of-course, natural,
normal, ordinary, plain, plastic, prevailing,
prevalent, quotidian, regular, rife, routine,
run-of-the-mill*, so-so*, standard, stock, typic,
unremarkable, vanilla*, white-bread*, wonted,
workaday; CONCEPTS *530,547* —*Ant.* abnormal,
atypical, irregular, uncommon, unusual

usually [adv] *for the most part* as a rule, as is
the custom, as is usual, as usual, by and large,

commonly, consistently, customarily, frequently, generally, habitually, in the main, mainly, more often than not, mostly, most often, normally, now and again, now and then, occasionally, once and again, on the whole, ordinarily, regularly, routinely, sometimes; CONCEPTS 530,541 —*Ant.* exceptionally, unusually

usurp [v] *take over* accroach, annex, appropriate, arrogate, assume, barge in*, butt in*, clap hands on*, commandeer, cut out, displace, elbow in*, get hands on*, grab, grab hold of, highjack*, infringe upon, lay hold of, muscle in*, preempt, seize, squeeze in, supplant, swipe, take, work in, worm in*, wrest; CONCEPTS 142, 384 —*Ant.* give in, relinquish, surrender

utensil [n] *tool, usually for eating* apparatus, appliance, contrivance, convenience, device, equipment, fork, gadget, implement, instrument, knife, silverware, spoon, tableware, ware; CONCEPTS 493,499

utilitarian [adj] *practical* commonsensical, down-to-earth, effective, efficient, functional, hard, hardheaded, matter-of-fact, nuts and bolts*, pragmatic, pragmatical, realistic, sensible, serviceable, unidealistic, unromantic, useful; CONCEPT 560 —*Ant.* impractical, unnecessary

utility [n] *serviceableness* account, adequacy, advantage, advantageousness, applicability, appropriateness, avail, benefit, convenience, efficacy, efficiency, expediency, favor, fitness, function, point, practicality, productiveness, profit, relevance, service, serviceability, use, usefulness; CONCEPT 658

utilize [v] *make use of* advance, apply, appropriate, avail oneself of, bestow, employ, exercise, exploit, forward, further, handle, have recourse to, profit by, promote, put to use, resort to, take advantage of, turn to account, use; CONCEPT 225

utmost [adj] *extreme, maximum* absolute, allout*, chief, complete, entire, exhaustive, farthest, final, full, furthermost, greatest, highest, last, last straw*, maximal, most, most distant, outermost, out of bounds*, outside, paramount, plenary, preeminent, remotest, sheer, supreme, thorough, thoroughgoing, too much*, too-too*, top, topmost, total, ultimate, ultra*, unconditional, undiminished, unlimited, unmitigated, unqualified, unreserved, uttermost, whole, worst case*; CONCEPTS 531, 574,772 —*Ant.* middle, moderate

utopia [n] *ideal place and life* Arcadia, bliss, dreamland, dreamworld, Eden, Elysian Fields*, Erewhon*, fairyland, Garden of Eden, heaven, land of milk and honey*, never-never land*, paradise, perfection, pie in the sky*, promised land*, seventh heaven*, Shangri-La*, wonderland; CONCEPTS 370,689 —*Ant.* hell

utopian [adj] *imaginary, ideal* abstract, airy, ambitious, arcadian, chimerical, dream, fanciful, fantasy, grandiose, hopeful, idealist, idealistic, ideological, illusory, impossible, impractical, lofty, otherworldly, perfect, pie-in-the-sky*, pretentious, quixotic, romantic, transcendental, unfeasible, visionary; CONCEPTS 572,574,582 —*Ant.* real

utter [adj] *outright, absolute* all-fired*, arrant, blasted*, blessed*, blooming*, complete,

confounded, consummate, downright, entire, flat-out*, infernal, out-and-out*, perfect, pure, sheer, stark, straight-out*, thorough, thoroughgoing, total, unmitigated, unqualified; CONCEPTS 531,535 —*Ant.* incomplete, uncertain

utter [v] *say, reveal* affirm, air, announce, articulate, assert, asseverate, blurt, bring out, chime, chin*, come out with*, declaim, declare, deliver, disclose, divulge, ejaculate, enunciate, exclaim, express, give words to*, go, jaw*, lip*, make known, modulate, mouth*, mutter, proclaim, promulgate, pronounce, publish, put into words, recite, shout, speak, spiel*, state, talk, throw out, verbalize, vocalize, voice, whisper; CONCEPTS 47,55 —*Ant.* conceal, hide

utterance [n] *revelation* announcement, articulation, assertion, asseveration, declaration, delivery, discourse, ejaculation, expression, opinion, oration, peroration, pronouncement, rant, recitation, remark, reply, response, saying, sentence, speaking, speech, spiel, statement, talk, vent, verbalization, vocalization, vociferation, voice, word, words; CONCEPTS 47,278 —*Ant.* silence

utterly [adv] *completely* absolutely, all, all in all, altogether, entirely, exactly, extremely, fully, in toto, just, perfectly, plumb*, purely, quite, thoroughly, totally, to the core*, to the nth degree*, well, wholly; CONCEPT 531 —*Ant.* incompletely, uncertain

uttermost [adj] *extreme* farthest, final, furthermost, furthest, last, outermost, outmost, remotest, utmost; CONCEPTS 585,778 —*Ant.* middle, moderate

U-turn [n] *about-face* backtracking, change of heart, change of mind, change of plan, eating one's words*, one-eighty*, retraction, reversal, sea change, turnaround, U-ey*, volte-face; CONCEPTS 201,213

V

vacancy [n] *opening* abstraction, blankness, desertedness, emptiness, gap, job, lack, opportunity, position, post, room, situation, space, vacuity, vacuousness, vacuum, void, voidness; CONCEPTS 513,516,693 —*Ant.* fill, overflow

vacant [adj1] *empty; unoccupied* abandoned, available, bare, clear, deserted, devoid, disengaged, free, idle, not in use, stark, tenantless, to let, unemployed, unengaged, unfilled, uninhabited, unlived in, untaken, untenanted, unused, void, without contents; CONCEPTS 481,560,740, 774 —*Ant.* full, occupied, overflowing

vacant [adj2] *absent-minded; expressionless* abstracted, blank, daydreaming, deadpan, dreaming, dreamy, empty-headed*, foolish, idle, inane, incurious, inexpressive, silly, stupid, thoughtless, unexpressive, unintelligent, unthinking, vacuous, vapid, witless; CONCEPT 402 —*Ant.* aware, cognizant, comprehending

vacate [v] *leave empty* abandon, abrogate, annul, clear, depart, discharge, dissolve, empty, evacuate, give up, go away, leave, move out, move out of, part with, quash, quit, relinquish, renounce, rescind, retract, reverse, revoke, void, withdraw; CONCEPTS 195,234 —*Ant.* fill, occupy, overflow

ur
va

vacation [n] *planned time spent not working* break, breathing space*, day of rest, few days off*, fiesta, furlough, holiday, intermission, layoff, leave, leave of absence, liberty, long weekend*, R and R*, recess, recreation, respite, rest, sabbatical, spell, time off, two weeks with pay*; CONCEPTS 363,807 —*Ant.* work

vaccinate [v] *give a shot to treat or prevent disease* immunize, inject, inoculate, mitigate, prevent, protect, treat, variolate; CONCEPT 310

vaccination [n] *immunization* inoculation, shot*; CONCEPT 307

vacillate [v] *go back and forth* alternate, be indecisive, be irresolute, change, change mind, dither, fence-straddle*, fluctuate, hedge, hem and haw*, hesitate, hover, oscillate, pause, pussyfoot around*, reel, rock, run hot and cold*, seesaw*, shilly-shally*, stagger, straddle, sway, swing, waffle, waver, whiffle*, yo-yo*; CONCEPT 13 —*Ant.* remain, stay

vacuous [adj] *empty; unintelligent* airheaded*, birdbrained*, blank, drained, dull, dumb, emptied, foolish, half-baked*, inane, lamebrained*, minus*, shallow, silly*, stupid, superficial, uncomprehending, unreasoning, vacant, void; CONCEPT 402 —*Ant.* aware, filled, full, intelligent

vacuum [n] *emptiness* exhaustion, free space, gap, nothingness, rarefaction, space, vacuity, void; CONCEPTS 513,740 —*Ant.* fullness

vagabond [adj] *unsettled; vagrant* aimless, destitute, down-and-out*, drifting, errant, fancy-free*, fly-by-night*, footloose*, idle, itinerant, itinerate, journeying, mendicant, migratory, moving, nomadic, perambulant, perambulatory, peripatetic, prodigal, rambling, roaming, rootless, roving, sauntering, shifting, shiftless, straggling, stray, strolling, transient, travelling, unsettled, wandering, wayfaring, wayward; CONCEPT 539 —*Ant.* inhabiting, settled

vagabond [n] *person who leads an unsettled life; traveler* explorer, gypsy, haji, pathfinder, pilgrim, pioneer, rambler, rover, tourist, trailblazer, trekker, wanderer, wayfarer; CONCEPT 423 —*Ant.* inhabitant

vagary [n] *caprice* crotchet, fancy, fool notion*, humor, idea, impulse, inconsistency, inconstancy, notion, quirk, whim, whimsy; CONCEPTS 13,410

vagrant [n] *person with no permanent home and often with no means of support* drifter, floater, homeless person, itinerant, rolling stone*, street person, transient, wanderer; CONCEPT 423

vague [adj] *not definite or clear* ambiguous, amorphous, amphibological, bewildering, bleary, blurred, cloudy, dark, dim, doubtful, dreamlike, dubious, enigmatic, equivocal, faint, fuzzy, generalized, hazy, ill-defined, impalpable, imprecise, indefinite, indeterminate, indistinct, inexplicable, lax, loose, misunderstood, muddy, nebulous, obscure, perplexing, problematic, puzzling, questionable, shadowy, superficial, tenebrous, uncertain, unclear, undetermined, unexplicit, unintelligible, unknown, unsettled, unspecified, unsure; CONCEPTS 267,485,529 —*Ant.* certain, clear, definite, sure

vain [adj1] *egotistical* arrogant, big-headed*, boastful, cocky*, conceited, egocentric, egoistic, haughty, high-and-mighty*, inflated, narcissistic, ostentatious, overweening, pleased with oneself*, proud, puffed up*, self-important, stuck-up*, swaggering*, swollen-headed*, vainglorious; CONCEPTS 401,404 —*Ant.* modest, shy

vain [adj2] *futile, useless* abortive, barren, bootless, delusive, delusory, empty, frivolous, fruitless, going nowhere*, hollow, idle, inefficacious, insignificant, in vicious circle*, misleading, not a prayer*, no-win*, nugatory, on a treadmill*, otiose, paltry, petty, pointless, profitless, puny, senseless, shuck, slight, sterile, time-wasting, trifling, trivial, unavailing, unimportant, unnotable, unproductive, unprofitable, valueless, void, worthless; CONCEPTS 552,575 —*Ant.* possible

vainglorious [adj] *boastful, proud* arrogant, blowing one's own horn*, boasting, bragging, cavalier, cocky*, conceited, egotistical, egotistical, haughty, high-and-mighty*, high-handed*, huffy*, overbearing, pompous, presumptuous, pretentious, puffed up*, self-important, snobbish, snooty*, strutting, stuck-up*, swaggering, vain; CONCEPTS 401,542

vainglory [n] *pride* arrogance, big-headedness*, boastfulness, bragging, cockiness*, conceit, condescension, egoism, egotism, haughtiness, huff, overconfidence, patronage, presumption, pretension, self-importance, smugness, snobbery, strutting, swagger, swelled head*, vanity; CONCEPT 633

valedictory [adj] *farewell* departing, final, goodbye, last, parting, terminal; CONCEPT 267 —*Ant.* welcoming

valetudinarian [n] *hypochondriac* morbid person, neurotic, obsessive person, valetudinary; CONCEPT 316

valiant [adj] *brave* adventurous, assertive, audacious, bold, chivalrous, courageous, dauntless, fearless, fire-eating*, gallant, game, grand, great, gritty*, gutsy*, gutty*, heroic, high-spirited, indomitable, intrepid, lion-hearted, magnanimous, nervy*, noble, plucky*, powerful, puissant, redoubtable, self-reliant, spunky*, stalwart, steadfast, stout, stouthearted, strong-willed, unafraid, undaunted, undismayed, valorous, venturesome, venturous, vigorous, worthy; CONCEPTS 401,404,538 —*Ant.* afraid, cowardly

valid [adj] *right, genuine* accurate, attested, authentic, authoritative, binding, bona fide, cogent, compelling, conclusive, confirmed, convincing, credible, determinative, efficacious, efficient, good, in force, irrefutable, just, kosher*, lawful, legal, legit*, legitimate, logical, official, original, persuasive, potent, powerful, proven, pure, solid, sound, stringent, strong, substantial, telling, tested, true, trustworthy, ultimate, unadulterated, unanswerable, uncorrupted, weighty, well-founded, well-grounded; CONCEPTS 319,545,582 —*Ant.* invalid, unacceptable, unreal, unsound, wrong

validate [v] *ascertain the truth, authenticity of something* approve, authenticate, authorize, bear out, certify, confirm, constitute, corroborate, endorse, give stamp of approval*, give the go-ahead*, give the green light*, give the nod*, John Hancock*, justify, legalize, legitimize,

va
va

make binding*, make legal*, make stick*, okay*, ratify, rubber-stamp*, sanction, set seal on*, sign off on*, substantiate, verify; CONCEPTS 50,88,317 —Ant. refuse, reject, veto

validity [n] *genuineness, lawfulness* authority, cogency, effectiveness, efficacy, force, foundation, gravity, grounds, legality, legitimacy, persuasiveness, point, potency, power, punch, right, soundness, strength, substance, validness, weight; CONCEPT 645 —Ant. invalidity

valley [n] *hollow in the land* basin, bottom, canyon, channel, coulee, dale, dell, depression, dingle, glen, gorge, lowland, notch, plain, swale, trough, vale; CONCEPTS 509,513

valor [n] *bravery* backbone*, boldness, courage, dash*, defiance, derring-do*, determination, fearlessness, fight, firmness, fortitude, gallantry, grit*, guts*, hardihood, heart, heroism, indomitableness, intestinal fortitude*, intrepidity, invincibility, mettle, moxie*, nerve, pluck, prowess, resolution, sand*, spirit, spunk, starch*, stomach*, tenacity, valiance, valiancy; CONCEPTS 411,633 —Ant. cowardice

valorous [adj] *courageous* adventuresome, adventurous, bold, brave, chivalrous, daredevil, daring, dauntless, fearless, gallant, game, gritty*, gutsy*, heroic, lionhearted, nervy, plucky*, Spartan, stalwart, stouthearted, strong, tough, unafraid, undaunted, valiant, venturous; CONCEPTS 401,404

valuable [adj] *very important; priceless* admired, appreciated, beneficial, cherished, collectible, costly, dear, esteemed, estimable, expensive, heirloom, held dear, helpful, high-priced, hot*, hot property*, important, in demand, inestimable, invaluable, of value, precious, prized, profitable, relevant, respected, scarce, serviceable, treasured, useful, valued, worthwhile, worthy; CONCEPTS 334,560 —Ant. unimportant, useless, valueless, worthless

valuable [n] *prized possession* advantage, antique, asset, benefit, collectible, commodity, heirloom, nugget*, plum*, treasure; CONCEPT 446 —Ant. garbage, trash

value [n1] *financial worth* amount, appraisal, assessment, charge, cost, equivalent, expense, market price, monetary worth, price, profit, rate; CONCEPTS 335,336

value [n2] *advantage, worth* account, bearing, benefit, caliber, condition, connotation, consequence, content, denotation, desirability, distinction, drift, eminence, esteem, estimation, excellence, finish, force, goodness, grade, help, implication, import, importance, interpretation, mark, marketability, meaning, merit, power, preference, profit, purpose, quality, regard, repute, sense, serviceableness, significance, state, stature, substance, superiority, use, usefulness, utility, valuation; CONCEPTS 346,658,668,682 —Ant. detriment, disadvantage

valued [adj] *costly; treasured* admired, appreciated, beloved, cherished, dear, esteemed, expensive, fancy, highly regarded, high-priced, loved, precious, priceless, prized, respected, valuable; CONCEPTS 334,555,567

values [n] *principles* attitude, beliefs, character, code, conduct, conscience, ethics, ideals, integrity, morals, mores, scruples, sense of duty, sense of honor, standards; CONCEPTS 645,689

valve [n] *on-and-off device* cock, faucet, flap, gate, hydrant, lid, pipe, plug, shutoff, spigot, stopper, tap; CONCEPTS 445,464,499

vandal [n] *person who defiles property* defacer, despoiler, destroyer, hoodlum, looter, mischief-maker, pillager, pirate, plunderer, ravager, thief; CONCEPT 412

vandalism [n] *destruction* defacing, grafitti, mischief, ravaging, ruin, sacking, smashing, trashing, wreckage, wrecking; CONCEPTS 230,252

vandalize [v] *destroy* annihilate, damage, deface, demolish, despoil, disfigure, impair, mar, ravage, ravish, raze, ruin, smash, spray paint, trash*, wreck; CONCEPTS 246,252

vanilla [adj] *simple, unadorned* austere, clean, elementary, folksy, homely, humble, inelaborate, modest, plain, pure and simple*, rustic, uncluttered, uncomplicated, undecorated, unelaborate, unembellished, unornamented, unostentatious, unpretentious, your basic; CONCEPTS 562,589

vanish [v] *disappear* become invisible, be lost, clear, dematerialize, die, die out, dissolve, evanesce, evaporate, exit, fade, fade away, go away, melt; CONCEPT 105 —Ant. appear, arrive, come

vanity [n] *conceit, egotism* affectation, airs, arrogance, big-headedness*, conceitedness, display, ego trip*, narcissism, ostentation, pretension, pride, self-admiration, self-love, self-worship, show*, showing off*, smugness, vainglory; CONCEPT 410 —Ant. modesty

vanquish [v] *defeat soundly* bear down, beat, conquer, crush, humble, overcome, overpower, overturn, overwhelm, put down, quell, reduce, repress, rout, subdue, subjugate, subvert, surmount, trample, triumph over; CONCEPT 95 —Ant. fail, lose, surrender

vapid [adj] *flat, dull* bland, boring, colorless, dead*, driveling, flat tire*, flavorless, inane, innocuous, insipid, jejune, least, lifeless, limp, milk-and-water*, milquetoast*, nothing, nowhere, stale, tame, tasteless, tedious, tiresome, unimaginative, uninspiring, uninteresting, unpalatable, vacant, vacuous, watery, weak, wishy-washy*, zero*; CONCEPTS 529, 537,575 —Ant. lively, pungent, sharp, spicy, strong

vapor [n] *fumes, mist* breath, condensation, dampness, dew, effluvium, exhalation, fog, gas, haze, miasma, moisture, reek, smog, smoke, steam; CONCEPTS 437,524

variable [adj] *changing, changeable* capricious, changeful, fickle, fitful, flexible, fluctuating, fluid, iffy*, inconstant, irregular, mercurial, mobile, mutable, protean, shifting, shifty, slippery*, spasmodic, temperamental, ticklish, uncertain, unequable, unsettled, unstable, unsteady, vacillating, volatile, waffling, wavering, yo-yo*; CONCEPT 534 —Ant. invariable, unchangeable, unchanging, unvarying

variance [n] *difference* about-face*, argument, change, conflict, contention, deviation, difference of opinion, different strokes*, disaccord, disagreement, discord, discrepancy, dissension, dissent, dissidence, disunity, divergence, diversity, division, flip-flop*, fluctuation, incongruity, inconsistency, mid-course correction*,

mutation, separation, severing, strife, sundering, switch, transmogrification, unharmoniousness, variation, variety; CONCEPTS 388,665,697
—*Ant.* agreement

variant [adj] *different* alternative, derived, differing, divergent, exceptional, modified, various, varying; CONCEPT 564 —*Ant.* agreeing, same, similar

variant [n] *derived form* alternative, branch, development, exception, irregularity, modification, result, spinoff, variation, version; CONCEPT 665 —*Ant.* base, root

variation [n] *difference; alternative* aberration, abnormality, adaptation, alteration, bend, break, change, contradistinction, contrast, curve, deflection, departure, departure from the norm*, deviation, digression, discrepancy, disparity, displacement, dissimilarity, dissimilitude, distinction, divergence, diversification, diversity, exception, fluctuation, inequality, innovation, modification, mutation, novelty, shift, swerve, turn, unconformity, variety; CONCEPTS 665,697 —*Ant.* agreement, root, similarity, source

varied [adj] *different* assorted, conglomerate, discrete, diverse, heterogeneous, indiscriminate, miscellaneous, mixed, motley, multifarious, separate, sundry, variform; CONCEPT 564 —*Ant.* like, same, similar, unvaried

variegated [adj] *diversified; varicolored* assorted, changeable, checkered, diverse, kaleidoscopic, mixed, motley, mottled, multicolor, multicolored, particolored, patched, spotted, streaked, striped, varied, versicolor; CONCEPTS 564,618,772

variety [n1] *difference* array, assortment, change, collection, combo*, conglomeration, cross section, departure, discrepancy, disparateness, divergency, diversification, diversity, fluctuation, heterogeneity, incongruity, intermixture, many-sidedness, medley, mélange, miscellany, mishmash, mixed bag*, mixture, modification, multifariousness, multiplicity, potpourri, range, shift, soup, stew, variance, variation; CONCEPTS 432,665 —*Ant.* uniformity

variety [n2] *type, sort* assortment, brand, breed, category, character, class, classification, description, division, family, genus, grade, ilk, kidney, kind, make, nature, order, quality, race, rank, species, strain, stripe, tribe; CONCEPT 378

various [adj] *miscellaneous, differing* all manner of*, assorted, changeable, changing, different, discrete, disparate, distinct, distinctive, diverse, diversified, heterogeneous, individual, legion, manifold, many, many-sided, multifarious, multitudinal, multitudinous, numerous, omnifarious, peculiar, populous, separate, several, sundry, unalike, unequal, unlike, variant, varied, variegated; CONCEPTS 564,771 —*Ant.* individual, same, similar, uniform

varnish [v] *add a layer to; embellish* adorn, coat, cover, decorate, enamel, finish, gild, glaze, gloss, japan, lacquer, luster, paint, polish, shellac, surface, veneer, wash, wax; CONCEPTS 172,177 —*Ant.* strip

vary [v] *change* alter, alternate, assort, be unlike, blow hot and cold*, convert, depart, deviate, differ, digress, disagree, displace, dissent, divaricate, diverge, diversify, divide, fluctuate, hem and haw*, inflect, interchange, modify,

mutate, part, permutate, range, separate, shilly-shally*, swerve, take turns, transform, turn, variegate, yo-yo*; CONCEPT 697 —*Ant.* remain, stay

varying [adj] *variable* alternating, changeable, changing, deviating, differing, flexible, fluctuating, inconstant, irregular, shifting, uncertain, unstable, unsteady, vacillating, volatile, waffling, wavering; CONCEPT 534

vast [adj] *very large; wide in range* all-inclusive, ample, astronomical, big, boundless, broad, capacious, colossal, comprehensive, detailed, endless, enormous, eternal, expanded, extensive, far-flung, far-reaching, forever, giant, gigantic, great, huge, illimitable, immeasurable, immense, infinite, limitless, mammoth, massive, measureless, monstrous, monumental, never-ending, prodigious, prolonged, spacious, spread-out, stretched-out, sweeping, titanic, tremendous, unbounded, unlimited, voluminous, widespread; CONCEPTS 772,773,781 —*Ant.* bounded, limited, little, narrow, small

vault [n] *depository* basement, box, can, catacomb, cavern, cellar, crib*, crypt, dungeon, grave, mausoleum, pit, repository, safe, safe-deposit box, sepulcher, strong room, tomb; CONCEPT 494

vault [v] *jump over; span* arch, ascend, bend, bounce, bound, bow, clear, curve, hop, hurdle, leap, mount, negotiate, over, overleap, rise, soar, spring, surmount; CONCEPTS 194,752

veer [v] *change direction* angle off, avert, bear, be deflected, bend, change, change course, curve, cut, deflect, depart, deviate, digress, dip, divagate, diverge, divert, drift, get around, make a left*, make a right*, pivot, sheer, shift, skew, skid, swerve, swing, swivel, tack, train off, turn, twist, volte-face*, wheel, whip, whirl; CONCEPTS 148,150,213 —*Ant.* go direct, stay

vegetable [n] *edible part of plant* edible, green, greens, herb, herbaceous plant, legume, produce, root, salad, truck, yellow; CONCEPT 431

vegetate [v1] *be very passive* be inert, decay, deteriorate, exist, go to pot*, go to seed*, hibernate, idle, languish, loaf*, pass time, stagnate, weaken; CONCEPTS 210,698 —*Ant.* activate, carry out, do

vegetate [v2] *grow, sprout* bloom, blossom, bud, burgeon, germinate, shoot, spring, swell; CONCEPTS 253,257 —*Ant.* die, go to seed

vehement [adj] *passionate, opinionated* angry, ardent, concentrated, delirious, desperate, eager, earnest, emphatic, enthusiastic, exquisite, fervent, fervid, fierce, fiery, forceful, forcible, frantic, furious, hearty, heated, hopped up*, hot*, hyper*, impassioned, impetuous, inflamed, intense, lively, on the make*, potent, powerful, pronounced, rabid, strong, terrible, vicious, violent, wild, zealous; CONCEPTS 401,542 —*Ant.* apathetic, indifferent, unpassionate

vehicle [n1] *machine used for transportation* agent, automobile, bicycle, boat, buggy, bus, cab, car, carrier, chariot, conveyance, crate*, jalopy*, jeep, mechanism, motorcycle, taxi, transport, truck, van, vector, wagon, wheels; CONCEPT 503

vehicle [n2] *means of attaining end* agency, agent, apparatus, channel, expedient, implement, instrument, instrumentality, intermediary, means of expression, mechanism, medium, ministry, organ, tool, vector, way, ways and means*; CONCEPTS 6,277,278,694,712 —*Ant.* end, goal

veil [n] *disguise* blind, cloak, coloring, cover, curtain, facade, false front, film, front, guise, mantilla, mask, screen, shade, shroud, veiling; CONCEPTS 451,673

veil [v] *hide* beard*, blanket, camouflage, cloak, conceal, cover, cover up, curtain*, dim, disguise, drape, enclose, enfold, enshroud, envelop, finesse, invest, launder, mantle, mask, obscure, put up a front*, screen, secrete, shield, shroud, stonewall*, whitewash*, wrap; CONCEPT 172 —*Ant.* reveal

veiled [adj] *disguised* camouflaged, cloaked, concealed, covered, hidden, hooded, invisible, masked, screened, secret, shielded, shrouded, undercover, unexposed, unrecognizable, unrevealed; CONCEPTS 547,576,619

vein [n1] *mood, tone* attitude, bent, character, characteristic, complexion, dash, disposition, faculty, fashion, fettle, hint, humor, line, manner, mind, mode, nature, note, spice, spirit, strain, streak, style, suggestion, suspicion, tang, temper, temperament, tenor, tinge, touch, trace, turn, wave, way; CONCEPTS 411,673,682

vein [n2] *blood vessel* capillary, course, current, duct, follicle, hair, lode, nerve, seam, stratum, streak, stripe, thread, venation; CONCEPT 393

velocity [n] *speed* acceleration, celerity, dispatch, expedition, fleetness, gait, haste, headway, hurry, impetus, momentum, pace, quickness, rapidity, rapidness, rate, swiftness, tempo; CONCEPTS 755,792

venal [adj] *bribable, corruptible* amoral, bent*, buyable, conscienceless, corrupt, crooked, dishonest, double-dealing, immoral, mercenary, on the take*, padded*, purchasable, unethical, unprincipled, unprofessional, unscrupulous; CONCEPT 545

vendetta [n] *feud* argument, bad blood*, bickering, conflict, disagreement, discord, dispute, dissension, falling out*, family feud, fight, fracas, grudge, hostility, quarrel, revenge, rivalry, row, squabble, strife; CONCEPTS 46,106,388

vendor [n] *person who sells wares* businessperson, dealer, hawker, huckster*, merchant, outcrier, peddler, pitcher, traveler, traveling salesperson; CONCEPT 348 —*Ant.* customer

veneer [n] *pretense, front* appearance, coating, cover, covering, disguise, exterior, facade, face, finish, gloss, guise, layer, leaf, mask, overlay, semblance, show, surface, window dressing*; CONCEPTS 633,673,716 —*Ant.* reality

veneer [v] *cover, overlay* blanch, coat, extenuate, face, finish, gloss, palliate, plate, shellac, sugarcoat, surface, varnish, whiten, whitewash*; CONCEPT 172 —*Ant.* strip, uncover

venerable [adj] *respected* admirable, aged, august, dignified, esteemed, estimable, experienced, grand, grave, honorable, honored, imposing, matriarchal, noble, patriarchal, philosophical, revered, reverenced, reverend, sacred, sage, sedate, serious, stately, venerated, wise, worshipful, worshipped; CONCEPT 574 —*Ant.* unrespected

venerate [v] *revere* admire, adore, apotheosize, appreciate, be in awe of, cherish, deify, esteem, exalt, hallow, hold in awe, honor, idolize, look up to*, love, put on a pedestal*, regard, respect, reverence, think highly of, treasure, value, worship; CONCEPTS 10,32

vengeance [n] *retaliation for another's act* avengement, avenging, counterblow, evening of score*, eye for an eye*, getting even*, repayment, reprisal, requital, retribution, return, revenge, settling of score*, tit for tat*, vengefulness, wrath; CONCEPTS 29,384 —*Ant.* forgiveness, pardon

vengeful [adj] *retaliating; hating* antagonistic, avenging, hostile, implacable, inimical, punitive, rancorous, relentless, retaliatory, revengeful, spiteful, unforgiving, vindictive; CONCEPTS 401,542 —*Ant.* condoning, forgiving, liking, pardoning

venial [adj] *pardonable* allowable, all right, defensible, excusable, explainable, forgivable, justifiable, minor, not serious*, not too bad*, okay, permissible, slight, tolerable, trivial, understandable; CONCEPT 558

venom [n] *poison; hating* acidity, acrimony, anger, bane, bitterness, contagion, gall, grudge, hate, hatred, ill will, infection, malevolence, malice, maliciousness, malignity, rancor, spite, spitefulness, spleen, taint, toxin, virulence, virus; CONCEPTS 29,399

venomous [adj] *poisonous; hateful* accidentally on purpose*, antagonistic, baleful, baneful, catty*, cussed*, deadly, destructive, dirty, evil, hostile, lethal, malefic, malevolent, malicious, malign, malignant, mean, mephitic, noxious, ornery*, rancorous, savage, spiteful, toxic, toxicant, vicious, vindictive, viperish, viperous, virulent, waspish; CONCEPTS 537,542 —*Ant.* kind, praising, unpoisonous

vent [n] *outlet* aperture, avenue, chimney, drain, duct, exit, flue, hole, opening, orifice, pipe, split, spout, ventilator; CONCEPTS 440, 464 —*Ant.* closure, door

vent [v] *let out; express* air, assert, come out with, declare, discharge, drive out, emit, empty, give, give off, give out, issue, loose, pour out, provide escape, put, release, state, take out on*, throw off*, unleash, utter, ventilate, verbalize, voice; CONCEPTS 49,51,179

ventilate [v] *air out; make known* advertise, air, bring into the open, bring up, broach*, broadcast, circulate, debate, deliberate, discourse, discuss, examine, express, free, give, go into, introduce, moot, publish, put, scrutinize, sift, state, take up, talk about, talk of, talk over, thresh out, vent, verbalize; CONCEPTS 51,60 —*Ant.* close

venture [n] *gamble, attempt* adventure, baby*, chance, deal, endeavor, enterprise, essay, experiment, exploit, feat*, hazard, header, investment, jeopardy, peril, pet project*, project, proposition, pursuit, risk, setup*, shot*, spec*, speculation, stab*, stake, test, thing*, trial, undertaking, wager; CONCEPTS 87,675

venture [v] *take a chance* advance, assay, attempt, bet, brave, challenge, chance, dare, dare say*, defy, endanger, essay, experiment, expose, feel, front*, gamble, get down*, go out on a limb*, grope, have a fling at*, hazard, imperil, jeopardize, lay open, make a stab at*, make bold, operate, play for, play the market*, presume, put in jeopardy*, put up*, risk,

va
ve

speculate, stake, stick one's neck out*, take a
crack at*, take a flyer*, take a plunge*, try, try
out, volunteer, wager; CONCEPTS 87,330,363

venturesome [adj] courageous adventurous,
aggressive, audacious, bold, brave, daredevil,
daring, enterprising, fearless, foolhardy, gutsy,
intrepid, overbold, plucky, pushy, rash, reckless,
resourceful, risky, spirited, spunky, stalwart,
stout, sturdy, temerarious, venturous; CONCEPTS
401,548 —Ant. afraid, cowardly

veracious [adj] true accurate, credible,
dependable, direct, ethical, factual, faithful,
frank, genuine, high-principled, honest, just,
kosher*, legit*, like it is*, on the level*, on
the line*, on the up and up*, open, reliable,
right, righteous, straight-arrow*, straightforward, strict, true-blue*, trustworthy, truthful,
undeceptive, up front*, valid, veridical;
CONCEPTS 267,545,582 —Ant. false, untrue

veracity [n] truth accuracy, actuality,
authenticity, candor, correctness, credibility,
exactitude, exactness, fact, fairness, fidelity,
frankness, genuineness, gospel*, honest-to-god
truth*, honesty, honor, impartiality, integrity,
like it is*, openness, precision, probity, reality,
real McCoy*, rectitude, rightness, sincerity,
straight stuff*, trueness, truism, trustworthiness,
truthfulness, uprightness, verisimilitude, verity,
word*; CONCEPTS 278,645 —Ant. falsehood,
falsity

verbal [adj] spoken exact, expressed, lingual,
literal, oral, rhetorical, said, stated, told,
unwritten, verbatim, word-for-word*, word-
of-mouth*; CONCEPT 267

verbalize [v] speak articulate, blab*, break
silence, chat, communicate, converse, enunciate,
express, gab*, make known, mouth, mumble,
open one's mouth, pronounce, put into words,
rap*, say, shout, sound, state, talk, tell, utter,
vocalize, voice, whisper, yak*, yammer;
CONCEPTS 47,266

verbatim [adj] exactly accurately, direct,
directly, literally, literatim, precisely, sic, to
the letter*, word-for-word*; CONCEPTS 267,
535 —Ant. different

verbiage [n] repetition, wordiness circumlocution, expansiveness, floridity, long-windedness,
loquacity, periphrase, periphrasis, pleonasm,
prolixity, redundancy, tautology, verbosity;
CONCEPTS 278,695 —Ant. conciseness

verbose [adj] wordy, long-winded bombastic,
circumlocutory, diffuse, flowery, full of air*,
fustian, gabby*, garrulous, grandiloquent,
involved, loquacious, magniloquent, palaverous, periphrastic, pleonastic, prolix, redundant,
repeating, repetitious, repetitive, rhetorical,
talkative, talky*, tautological, tautologous,
tedious, tortuous, windy*, yacking*; CONCEPT
267 —Ant. concise, succinct

verbosity [n] wordiness garrulous, logorrhea,
long-windedness, loquaciousness, loquacity,
prolixity, talkativeness, verbiage, verboseness;
CONCEPT 267

verdant [adj] green, blooming flourishing,
fresh, grassy, leafy, lush, verdurous; CONCEPTS
485,618 —Ant. dying

verdict [n] law judgment adjudication, answer,
arbitrament, award, conclusion, decision,
decree, deduction, determination, finding,

opinion, ruling, sentence; CONCEPT 318
—Ant. accusation

verge [n] extremity, limit border, borderline,
boundary, brim, brink, edge, extreme, fringe,
hem, lip, margin, point, rim, selvage, skirt, terminus, threshold; CONCEPT 484 —Ant. middle

verge [v] come near abut, adjoin, approach, be
on the edge*, border, bound, brink on, butt on*,
communicate, edge, end, fringe, gravitate
toward, hem, incline, join, lean, line, march,
margin, neighbor, outline, rim, skirt, surround,
tend, touch, trench, trend; CONCEPTS 657,749
—Ant. retreat

verification [n] proof affidavit, attestation,
authentication, averment, certification,
confirmation, credentials, deposition,
documents, endorsement, evidence, facts,
information, record, scoop*, seal, signature,
stamp, substantiation, testament, testimony;
CONCEPT 274

verify [v] confirm, validate add up*, attest,
authenticate, bear out, certify, check, check
out, check up, check up on*, corroborate,
debunk, demonstrate, document, double-check,
establish, eye*, eyeball*, find out, hold up,
justify, make certain, make sure, pan out*,
peg*, prove, settle, size*, size up*, stand up*,
substantiate, support, test, try; CONCEPTS 291,
317 —Ant. discredit, disprove, invalidate

verisimilitude [n] authenticity color, credibility,
genuineness, likeliness, likeness, plausibility,
realism, resemblance, semblance, show,
similarity, virtual reality; CONCEPT 725
—Ant. falseness, impossibility

veritable [adj] authentic actual, bona fide,
factual, for real*, genuine, indubitable, kosher*,
legit*, real, true, undoubted, unquestionable,
very; CONCEPT 582 —Ant. fake, false, unreal

vernacular [adj] native, colloquial common,
dialectal, domesticated, idiomatic, indigenous,
informal, ingrained, inherent, local, natural,
ordinary, plebian, popular, vulgar; CONCEPTS
267,549

vernacular [n] native language argot, cant,
dialect, idiom, jargon, jive talk*, language,
lingo*, lingua franca, native tongue, parlance,
patois, patter, phraseology, slang, speech,
street talk*, tongue; CONCEPT 276

versatile [adj] adjustable, flexible able,
accomplished, adaptable, adroit, all-around,
all-purpose, ambidextrous, conversant,
dexterous, elastic, facile, functional, gifted,
handy, ingenious, many-sided, mobile,
multifaceted, plastic, pliable, protean, putty-
like*, ready, resourceful, skilled, skillful,
talented, variable, varied; CONCEPTS 527,542
—Ant. inflexible, limited, unadjustable

verse [n] written composition ballad, epic,
jingle, lay, lyric, ode, poem, poesy, poetry,
rhyme, rune, song, sonnet, stanza; CONCEPT 282

versed [adj] experienced, informed abreast,
accomplished, acquainted, au courant*,
au fait*, competent, conversant, familiar,
in the know*, knowledgeable, learned,
practical, practiced, proficient, qualified,
savvy, seasoned, skilled, trained, tuned in*,
up*, up on*, versant, veteran, well-informed;
CONCEPTS 402,403,527 —Ant. green, immature,
inexperienced

version [n] *account of a happening* adaptation, chronicle, clarification, condensation, construction, exercise, form, history, interpretation, narrative, paraphrase, portrayal, reading, redaction, rendering, rendition, report, restatement, rewording, side, simplification, sketch, statement, story, tale, transcription, translation, variant; CONCEPT 282

vertex [n] *top* acme, apex, apogee, cap, cope, crest, crown, culmination, extremity, fastigium, height, peak, pinnacle, roof, summit, tip, upper extremity, zenith; CONCEPT 836 —*Ant.* bottom, nadir

vertical [adj] *upright* bolt upright, cocked, erect, on end, perpendicular, plumb, sheer, steep, straight-up, up-and-down, upward; CONCEPTS 581,583 —*Ant.* horizontal, prone

vertigo [n] *dizziness* disequilibrium, giddiness, lightheadedness, loss of balance, loss of equilibrium, shakiness, spinning head, unsteadiness, wobbliness, wooziness; CONCEPTS 314,480

verve [n] *energy, enthusiasm* activity, ardor, dash, drive, élan, endurance, fire, force, forcefulness, get-up-and-go*, go, gumption, gusto, hardihood, intensity, juice, liveliness, moxie*, passion, pep, pizzazz, pluck, power, punch, sparkle, spirit, spunk, stamina, steam, strength, toughness, vigor, vim, virility, vitality, zeal, zest, zing, zip*; CONCEPT 411

very [adj] *real, exact* actual, appropriate, authentic, bare, bona fide, correct, especial, express, genuine, ideal, identical, indubitable, mere, model, perfect, plain, precise, pure, right, same, selfsame, sheer, simple, special, sure-enough, true, undoubted, unqualified, unquestionable, veritable, very same; CONCEPTS 535,557 —*Ant.* inexact

very [adv] *much, really; to a high degree* absolutely, acutely, amply, astonishingly, awfully, certainly, considerably, dearly, decidedly, deeply, eminently, emphatically, exaggeratedly, exceedingly, excessively, extensively, extraordinarily, extremely, greatly, highly, incredibly, indispensably, largely, notably, noticeably, particularly, positively, powerfully, pressingly, pretty, prodigiously, profoundly, remarkably, substantially, superlatively, surpassingly, surprisingly, terribly, truly, uncommonly, unusually, vastly, wonderfully; CONCEPTS 544,569, 772 —*Ant.* little

vessel [n1] *ship* barge, bark, bateau, boat, bottom, bucket*, can*, craft, liner, ocean liner, steamer, tanker, tub*; CONCEPT 506

vessel [n2] *container, bowl* basin, kettle, pitcher, pot, receptacle, urn, utensil; CONCEPT 494

vest [v] *authorize, entrust* belong, bestow, confer, consign, empower, endow, furnish, invest, lodge, pertain, place, put in the hands of*, settle; CONCEPTS 50,88 —*Ant.* disapprove

vestibule [n] *small room for arrivals* antechamber, anteroom, doorway, entrance, entrance hall, entry, entryway, foyer, gateway, hall, hallway, lobby, narthex, porch, portal, portico; CONCEPT 448

vestige [n] *sign, indication* evidence, glimmer, hint, memento, print, relic, remainder, remains, remnant, residue, scrap, shadow, suspicion, token, trace, track; CONCEPTS 260,284,673

veteran [adj] *experienced, seasoned* adept,

battle-scarred*, been around*, disciplined, exercised, expert, from way back*, hardened, inured, knows one's stuff*, long-serving, long-time, not born yesterday*, of the old school*, old, old-time, practical, practiced, pro*, proficient, skilled, sophisticated, steady, trained, up to speed*, versed, vet*, weathered, wise, wise to ways*, worldly; CONCEPTS 402,527,678 —*Ant.* amateur, green, inexperienced

veteran [n] *person with much experience; particularly in war* expert, GI*, old guard*, old hand*, old pro*, old salt*, old soldier*, old-timer*, pro, shellback*, sourdough*, trouper, vet*, warhorse*; CONCEPTS 358 —*Ant.* rookie

veto [n] *refusal of permission* ban, blackball*, declination, denial, embargo, interdict, interdiction, negative, nonconsent, prohibition; CONCEPTS 81,121,298,685 —*Ant.* allowance, approval, ok, permission, ratification, sanction

veto [v] *refuse permission* ban, blackball*, burn, cut, decline, defeat, deny, disallow, disapprove, discountenance, forbid, give thumbs down*, interdict, kill, negate, negative, nix*, not go for*, pass, pass by, pass on, prohibit, put down, refuse, reject, rule out*, shoot down*, turn away*, throw out*, thumbs down*, turn down; CONCEPTS 50,81,88,121,298 —*Ant.* allow, approve, ok, permit, ratify, sanction

vex [v] *distress, bother* abrade, afflict, aggravate, agitate, anger, annoy, be at, chafe, depress, displease, disquiet, disturb, eat*, embarrass, exasperate, fret, gall*, get in one's hair*, get under one's skin*, give a bad time*, give a hard time*, grate on*, harass, harry, hassle, infuriate, irk, irritate, molest, needle, nettle, offend, peeve, perplex, pester, pique, plague, provoke, put out*, rasp, ride, rile, tease, tick off*, torment, trouble, turn off*, upset, worry; CONCEPTS 7,19 —*Ant.* aid, assist, help, please, soothe

vexatious [adj] *distressing, bothersome* afflicting, aggravating, annoying, burdensome, disagreeable, disappointing, disturbing, exasperating, irksome, irritating, mean, nagging, pesky*, provoking, teasing, tormenting, troublesome, troublous, trying, ugly, unpleasant, upsetting, wicked, worrisome, worrying; CONCEPTS 529,537 —*Ant.* aiding, assisting, helpful, pleasing, soothing

via [prep] *by way of* along, as a means, by, by dint of, by means of, by this route, by virtue of, on the way, over, per, through, through the medium of, through this medium, with; CONCEPT 544

viable [adj] *reasonable, practicable* applicable, doable, feasible, operable, possible, usable, within possibility, workable; CONCEPTS 552,560 —*Ant.* impossible, unachievable, unpractical, unreasonable

vibrant [adj1] *alive, colorful* active, animated, dynamic, electrifying, energetic, lively, peppy, responsive, sensitive, sound, sparkling, spirited, vigorous, virile, vital, vivacious, vivid, zesty*, zippy*; CONCEPTS 401,618 —*Ant.* colorless, dull, pale

vibrant [adj2] *throbbing* aquiver, consonant, oscillating, palpitating, pulsating, pulsing, quaking, quivering, resonant, resounding, reverberant, ringing, sonorant, sonorous, trembling; CONCEPT 584 —*Ant.* quiet

vibrate [v] *shake, quiver* beat, echo, fluctuate, flutter, jar, oscillate, palpitate, pulsate, pulse, quake, resonate, resound, reverberate, ripple, shiver, sway, swing, throb, tremble, tremor, undulate, wave, waver; CONCEPTS 152,748 —*Ant.* be still

vibration [n] *shaking, quivering* beating, fluctuation, judder, oscillation, pulsation, pulse, quake, quiver, resonance, reverberation, shake, shimmy, throb, throbbing, trembling, tremor, vacillation, wave, wavering; CONCEPTS 152,748 —*Ant.* stillness

vicarious [adj] *done or felt for, or on behalf of, another* by proxy, commissioned, delegated, deputed, empathetic, eventual, imagined, indirect, pretended, secondary, substituted, substitutional, surrogate, sympathetic; CONCEPTS 401,538

vice [n1] *bad habit; sin* carnality, corruption, debasement, debauchery, decay, degeneration, depravity, evil, evildoing, ill, immorality, indecency, iniquity, lechery, lewdness, libidinousness, licentiousness, looseness, lubricity, lust, maleficence, malignance, offense, perversion, profligacy, rot, sensuality, squalor, transgression, trespass, venality, wickedness, wrong; CONCEPTS 372,645 —*Ant.* good point, propriety, virtue

vice [n2] *weakness* blemish, defect, demerit, failing, fault, flaw, foible, frailty, imperfection, mar, shortcoming, weak point; CONCEPTS 411,657,666 —*Ant.* good point, strength

vice versa [adv] *contrary, oppositely* about-face*, again, contra, contrariwise*, conversely, far from it*, in reverse, on the contrary, the other way around*, turn about; CONCEPTS 544,564

vicinity [n] *local area* around*, ballpark*, district, environment, environs, hood, locality, nearness, neck of the woods*, neighborhood, precinct, pretty near*, propinquity, proximity, purlieus, range, region, surroundings, territory, turf*, vicinage; CONCEPTS 198,747 —*Ant.* faraway

vicious [adj1] *corrupt, wrong* abandoned, abhorrent, atrocious, bad, barbarous, base, contaminated, cruel, dangerous, debased, degenerate, degraded, demoralized, depraved, diabolical, faulty, ferocious, fiendish, flagitious, foul, heinous, immoral, impious, impure, indecent, infamous, iniquitous, insubordinate, lewd, libidinous, licentious, miscreant, monstrous, nefarious, perverse, profligate, putrid, reprehensible, reprobate, rotten, savage, sinful, unprincipled, untamed, vile, villainous, violent, wicked, wild, worthless; CONCEPTS 401,545,571 —*Ant.* gentle, good, nice, right

vicious [adj2] *nasty, hateful* backbiting*, beastly, bloodthirsty, brutal, cruel, cussed*, defamatory, despiteful, dirty*, evil, fierce, frightful, furious, horrid, intense, lousy*, malevolent, malicious, malign, mean, murderous, ornery*, poisonous, rancorous, rough, savage, slanderous, spiteful, tough, vehement, venomous, vindictive, violent, wicked; CONCEPTS 267,401,542 —*Ant.* friendly, kind, nice, pleasant

vicissitude [n] *change* about-face*, alteration, alternation, diversity, flip-flop*, fluctuation, innovation, mid-course correction*, mutability, mutation, novelty, permutation, progression, reversal, revolution, shift, sport, switch, switchover, transposition, turnaround, uncertainty, ups and downs*, variation, variety; CONCEPT 697 —*Ant.* stability, stagnation

victim [n] *someone or something sacrificed, preyed upon* babe in woods*, butt, casualty, clown, dupe, easy make*, easy mark*, fatality, fool, gambit, gopher*, gudgeon*, gull, hireling, hunted, immolation, injured party, innocent, mark, martyr, patsy, pawn, pigeon*, prey, pushover*, quarry, sacrifice, scapegoat, sitting duck*, sitting target*, soft touch*, stooge*, sucker*, sufferer, underdog, wretch; CONCEPTS 423,659 —*Ant.* criminal, culprit

victimize [v] *cheat, fool* bamboozle*, burn*, chisel*, clip*, con, cozen, deceive, defraud, discriminate against, dupe, exploit, fleece, flimflam*, gull, have it in for*, hoax, hoodwink, immolate, persecute, pick on, pigeon*, prey on, rope in*, screw*, set up*, snow*, stack the deck*, stiff*, sting*, sucker*, swindle, take advantage of, trick, use; CONCEPTS 14,59,192 —*Ant.* aid, assist, help, protect

victor [n] *person who wins* champ, champion, conquering hero*, conqueror, defeater, first*, gold medalist, greatest, hero, king, medalist, prizewinner, queen, subjugator, title holder, top*, top dog*, vanquisher, winner; CONCEPTS 366,416 —*Ant.* loser

Victorian [adj] *prudish* conservative, conventional, demure, genteel, priggish*, prim, prissy*, proper, puritanical, respectable, rigid, smug, square, starchy*, stiff*, straitlaced, stuffy, uptight*; CONCEPT 401

victorious [adj] *successful, winning* arrived, champion, conquering, on top, prizewinning, triumphant, vanquishing; CONCEPT 528 —*Ant.* failing, losing, unsuccessful

victory [n] *win, success* achievement, advantage, ascendancy, bull's-eye*, clean sweep*, conquest, control, defeat, defeating, destruction, dominion, feather in cap*, gain, grand slam*, hit, hole in one*, killing*, laurels, mission accomplished*, overthrow, prize, subjugation, superiority, supremacy, sweep, the gold*, triumph, upper hand*, upset, winning; CONCEPTS 95,671,706,832 —*Ant.* defeat, failure, forfeit, loss

victuals [n] *food supplies* aliment, bread, chow*, comestibles, eatables, eats, edibles, fare, feed, foodstuff, goodies*, groceries*, grub, larder, meal, nourishment, provender, provisions, rations, refreshments, snack, supplies, viands, vittles; CONCEPTS 457,460,461

video [n/adj] *related to the televised image* broadcast, canned*, music video, prerecorded, program, promotional film, recorded, taped, telegenic, television, TV; CONCEPTS 277,293

videocassette [n] *magnetic tape on which video image is recorded* cartridge, flick*, movie, recording, rental, vid*, videotape; CONCEPTS 277,293,464

vie [v] *compete* be rivals, buck, challenge, contend, contest, counter, go for*, go for broke*, go for the gold*, go for the jugular*, jockey for position*, match, oppose, pit, play, play off, push, rival, scramble for, strive, struggle, sweat; CONCEPTS 92,363

view [n1] *something that is seen* appearance, aspect, composition, contour, design, field of vision, glimpse, illustration, landscape, look, opening, outline, outlook, panorama, perspective, picture, prospect, range of vision, representation, scene, seascape, show, sight, spectacle, stretch, tableau, vision, vista, way; CONCEPT 628

view [n2] *examination* analysis, audit, check, contemplation, display, eyeball*, flash*, gander*, inspection, lamp*, look, look-see, perlustration, review, scan, scrutiny, sight, slant, squint*, survey, viewing; CONCEPTS 24,103

view [n3] *belief* attitude, close-up, concept, conception, consideration, conviction, deduction, eye*, feeling, impression, inference, judgment, judgment call*, mind, notion, opinion, persuasion, point of view, say-so*, sentiment, slant*, thought, twist, two cents' worth*, value judgment*, way of thinking; CONCEPT 689

view [v1] *look at* beam, behold, canvass, check out*, check over, consider, contemplate, descry, dig*, discern, distinguish, eagle eye*, espy, examine, explore, eye*, feast eyes on*, flash*, gaze, get a load of*, inspect, lay eyes on, mark, notice, observe, perceive, pipe*, read, regard, rubberneck*, scan, scope, scrutinize, see, set eyes on, spot, spy, stare, survey, take in*, watch, witness; CONCEPTS 623,626 —Ant. ignore

view [v2] *believe* account, consider, deem, judge, look on, reckon, regard, think about; CONCEPT 12 —Ant. disbelieve, mistrust

viewpoint [n] *way of thinking* angle, aspect, attitude, direction, estimation, eye*, frame of reference, ground, light, long view, outlook, perspective, point of observation, point of view, position, posture, respect, side, slant, stance, stand, standpoint, twist, two cents' worth*, vantage point, view; CONCEPT 689

vigil [n] *watch* attention, awareness, duty, eagle eye*, guard, lookout, monitoring, nightwatch, notice, observance, observation, patrol, stakeout, surveillance, vigilance, watchfulness; CONCEPTS 134,623

vigilance [n] *carefulness* acuity, alertness, attention, attentiveness, caution, circumspection, diligence, lookout, observance, surveillance, vigil, watch, watchfulness; CONCEPTS 644,657 —Ant. carelessness, impulsiveness, indiscretion, negligence

vigilant [adj] *careful, watchful* acute, agog, alert, anxious, attentive, aware, cautious, circumspect, guarded, keen, looking for, looking to, observant, on alert, on guard, on the ball*, on the job*, on the lookout, on the qui vive, on toes*, open-eyed*, sharp, sleepless, unsleeping, waiting on, wakeful, wary, wide-awake, with eyes peeled*, with weather eye open*; CONCEPTS 401,542,576 —Ant. careless, impulsive, inattentive, indiscreet, negligent

vigor [n] *power, energy* ability, action, activity, agility, alertness, bang*, birr, bounce, capability, capacity, dash, drive, dynamism, endurance, enterprise, exercise, force, force, get-up-and-go*, go*, hardiness, healthiness, intensity, juice*, kick*, liveliness, lustiness, might, motion, moxie*, muscle*, nimbleness, pep*, pith, potency, puissance, punch*, push, quickness, snap*, sock, soundness, starch*, steam*, strength, tuck*, urgency, vehemence, vim, vitality, well-being, zing*, zip*; CONCEPTS 316,411,732 —Ant. enervation, idleness, inactivity, lethargy, weakness

vigorous [adj] *energetic, powerful* active, athletic, ball of fire*, bouncing, brisk, dashing, driving, dynamic, effective, efficient, enterprising, exuberant, flourishing, forceful, forcible, hale, hard-driving, hardy, healthy, hearty, intense, lively, lusty, mettlesome, peppy, persuasive, potent, red-blooded*, robust, rugged, snappy, sound, spanking, spirited, steamroller*, strapping, strenuous, strong, strong as an ox*, sturdy, take-charge*, take-over*, tough, vital, zealous, zippy*; CONCEPTS 314,404,489 —Ant. enervated, idle, impotent, inactive, lethargic, weak

vile [adj] *offensive, horrible* abandoned, abject, appalling, bad, base, coarse, contemptible, corrupt, debased, degenerate, depraved, despicable, dirty, disgraceful, disgusting, evil, filthy, foul, horrid, humiliating, ignoble, immoral, impure, iniquitous, loathsome, low, mean, miserable, nasty, nauseating, nefarious, noxious, perverted, repellent, repugnant, repulsive, revolting, shocking, sickening, sinful, sleazy*, stinking*, ugly, vicious, vulgar, wicked, worthless, wretched; CONCEPTS 529,545,571 —Ant. gentle, kind, nice

vilify [v] *criticize very harshly* abuse, asperse, assail, attack, bad-mouth*, berate, blister, call down*, calumniate, censure, curse, cuss*, damn, debase, decry, defame, denigrate, denounce, dig*, disparage, dress down*, dump on*, give a black eye*, jinx, knock*, libel, malign, mistreat, mudsling*, pan*, put a whammy on*, put down*, rag on*, rap*, revile, rip up*, roast*, run down, scorch, skin alive*, slam*, slander, slur, smear*, speak ill of, tear down*, tear into*, traduce, vituperate, voodoo*; CONCEPTS 44,52 —Ant. compliment, praise

villa [n] *country estate* chateau, country house, large house, manor, mansion, summer house, vacation home; CONCEPTS 439,516

village [n] *small town* center, crossroads, hamlet, suburb; CONCEPT 507

villain [n] *evil person* antihero, blackguard*, brute, caitiff, creep*, criminal, devil, enfant terrible*, evildoer, heel, libertine, lowlife*, malefactor, mischief-maker*, miscreant, offender, profligate, rapscallion, rascal, reprobate, scoundrel, sinner, wretch; CONCEPT 412 —Ant. hero, heroine

villainous [adj] *criminal* atrocious, bad, corrupt, crooked, cruel, culpable, deplorable, depraved, diabolical, dirty, evil, felonious, hateful, ignoble, illegal, illicit, immoral, iniquitous, knavish, lawless, low, mean, nefarious, peccant, reprehensible, scandalous, shady*, sinful, unlawful, vile, wicked; CONCEPT 545

vindicate [v] *prove one's innocence* absolve, acquit, advocate, argue, assert, bear out, claim, clear, confute, contend, corroborate, defend, disculpate, disprove, do justice to, establish, exculpate, excuse, exonerate, free, free from blame, guard, justify, maintain, plead for, protect, prove, rationalize, refute, rehabilitate, second, shield, substantiate, support, uphold, warrant, whitewash*; CONCEPTS 49,57,317 —Ant. accuse, blame, convict, punish, sentence

vindictive [adj] *hateful, revengeful* avenging, cruel, grim, grudging, implacable, malicious, malignant, merciless, rancorous, relentless, resentful, retaliatory, ruthless, spiteful, unforgiving, unrelenting, vengeful, venomous, wreakful; CONCEPTS 401,542 —Ant. forgiving, helpful, kind, nice

vintage [adj] *superior* best, choice, classic, classical, excellent, mature, old, prime, rare, ripe, select, selected, venerable; CONCEPTS 574, 578,797 —Ant. inferior, minor, unimportant

vintage [n] *crop, especially of wine* collection, epoch, era, generation, grapes, harvest, origin, wine, year; CONCEPT 429

violate [v1] *break a law, agreement* breach, contaminate, contravene, defy, disobey, disregard, disrupt, encroach, err, infract, infringe, meddle, offend, oppose, outrage, profane, resist, sacrilege, sin, tamper with, trample on, transgress, trespass, withstand; CONCEPTS 101,192 —Ant. obey, observe

violate [v2] *rape, defile* abuse, assault, befoul, debauch, defile, desecrate, force, invade, outrage, pollute, profane, ravish, spoil; CONCEPTS 246,375

violation [n1] *breach; breaking of the law* abuse, break, breaking, contravention, encroachment, illegality, infraction, infringement, misbehavior, misdemeanor, negligence, nonobservance, offense, rupture, transgressing, transgression, trespass, trespassing, violating, wrong; CONCEPTS 101,192 —Ant. obedience, observance

violation [n2] *rape, defilement* assault, blasphemy, debasement, defacement, defacing, degradation, desecration, destruction, devastation, dishonor, invasion, mistreatment, outrage, pollution, profanation, rapine, ravishment, ruin, sacrilege, spoliation; CONCEPTS 246,252,375

violence [n] *extreme force, intensity* abandon, acuteness, assault, attack, bestiality, bloodshed, blowup, brutality, brute force, clash, coercion, compulsion, confusion, constraint, cruelty, destructiveness, disorder, disturbance, duress, ferocity, fervor, fierceness, fighting, flap, foul play, frenzy, fury, fuss, harshness, murderousness, onslaught, passion, power, raging, rampage, roughness, ruckus, rumble, savagery, severity, sharpness, storm, storminess, struggle, terrorism, tumult, turbulence, uproar, vehemence, wildness; CONCEPTS 29,641,669,675 —Ant. passivity, peace, peacefulness

violent [adj1] *destructive* agitated, aroused, berserk, bloodthirsty, brutal, coercive, crazy, cruel, demoniac, desperate, distraught, disturbed, enraged, fierce, fiery, forceful, forcible, frantic, fuming, furious, great, headstrong, homicidal, hotheaded*, hysterical, impassioned, impetuous, inflamed, intemperate, mad, maddened, maniacal, mighty, murderous, passionate, potent, powerful, raging, riotous, rough, savage, strong, uncontrollable, ungovernable, unrestrained, urgent, vehement, vicious, wild; CONCEPTS 401,540,544 —Ant. gentle, passive, peaceful

violent [adj2] *severe, extreme* acute, agonizing, biting, blustery, coercive, concentrated, devastating, excruciating, exquisite, forceful, forcible, gale force*, great, harsh, immoderate, inordinate, intense, mighty, outrageous, painful, potent, powerful, raging, rough, ruinous, sharp, strong, tempestuous, terrible, tumultuous/tumultous, turbulent, wild; CONCEPTS 525, 569 —Ant. calm, gentle, mild, moderate

VIP [n] *very important person* big cheese*, big enchilada*, big kahuna*, big name, celebrity, dignitary, famous person, heavyweight*, high muckamuck, luminary, mogul, notable, personality, public figure, star, superstar, top banana*, worthy; CONCEPT 416 —Ant. nobody, nonentity

viperous [adj] *malicious, venomous* bad-natured, baleful, bitter, evil, evil-minded, green-eyed*, jealous, malevolent, mean, nasty, ornery, poisonous, rancorous, resentful, spiteful, vengeful, vicious, vindictive, wicked; CONCEPTS 267,401,542

virginity [n] *celibacy, chastity* abstinence, chasteness, cleanness, continence, honor, immaculacy, innocence, integrity, maidenhood, purity, restraint, sinlessness, spotlessness, virtue; CONCEPT 633

virgin/virginal [adj] *brand-new, unused* first, fresh, idle, immaculate, initial, innocent, intact, modest, natural, new, original, primeval, pristine, pure, spotless, uncorrupted, undefiled, undisturbed, unmarred, unspoiled, unsullied, untapped, untested, untouched, untried, vestal; CONCEPTS 372,560,578,797 —Ant. defiled, sullied, used

virile [adj] *potent, powerful* driving, energetic, forceful, generative, lusty, macho*, procreative, red-blooded*, reproductive, robust, sound, strong, vibrant, vigorous, vital; CONCEPTS 372, 401,404 —Ant. effeminate, impotent, unmanly

virility [n] *masculinity* forceful, machismo, macho*, maleness, manhood, manliness, muscularity, potency, power, ruggedness, strength, vigor; CONCEPTS 371,372,408,648

virtual [adj] *in essence* basic, constructive, essential, fundamental, implicit, implied, in all but name*, in conduct, indirect, in effect, in practice, potential, practical, pragmatic, tacit, unacknowledged; CONCEPTS 487,537,544,573 —Ant. actual, authentic, real

virtually [adv] *for all practical purposes* around, as good as, basically, effectually, essentially, for all intents and purposes*, fundamentally, give or take a little*, guesstimate*, implicitly, in all but name*, in effect, in essence, in substance, in the ballpark*, in the neighborhood*, morally, nearly, not absolutely, not actually, practically, something like*, upwards of*; CONCEPTS 487,544,573

virtue [n] *honor, integrity* advantage, asset, character, charity, chastity, consideration, credit, ethic, ethicality, ethicalness, excellence, faith, faithfulness, fineness, fortitude, generosity, goodness, good point*, high-mindedness, hope, ideal, incorruptibility, innocence, justice, kindness, love, merit, morality, plus*, probity, prudence, purity, quality, rectitude, respectability, righteousness, temper, temperance, trustworthiness, uprightness, value, worth, worthiness; CONCEPTS 411,645 —Ant. dishonor, evil, immorality, vice

virtuoso [n] *person who is an expert* ace, adept, artist, artiste, authority, big league*, brain*, celebrity, champ*, champion, crackerjack*, dillettante, egghead, genius, hotshot*, hot stuff*, intelligent, magician, musician, natural*, no slouch*, old hand*, old pro*, performer, pro*, prodigy, professional, pundit, sharp*, star, superstar, whiz*, wizard; CONCEPTS 348,352,416 —Ant. amateur, greenhorn, rookie

virtuous [adj] *good, ethical; innocent* blameless, celibate, chaste, clean-living, effective, effectual, efficient, excellent, exemplary, faithful, guiltless, high-principled, honest, honorable, incorruptible, inculpable, in the clear*, irreprehensible, kosher*, legit*, moral, moralistic, noble, on the level*, on the up and up*, praiseworthy, principled, pure, regular, righteous, right-minded, spotless, straight, true-blue*, unsullied, untainted, untarnished, up front*, upright, wholesome, without reproach, worthy; CONCEPTS 401,545 —Ant. bad, sinful, unethical, vile, wicked

virulent [adj1] *poisonous, lethal* baneful, deadly, destructive, fatal, harmful, infective, injurious, malign, malignant, mephitic, pernicious, poison, septic, toxic, toxicant, unhealthy, unwholesome, venomous; CONCEPTS 537,571 —Ant. harmless, healthy, nonpoisonous

virulent [adj2] *hostile* acrimonious, antagonistic, bitter, cutting, hateful, malevolent, malicious, rancorous, resentful, scathing, sharp, spiteful, splenetic, stabbing, unfriendly, venomous, vicious, vindictive, vitriolic; CONCEPTS 267, 542 —Ant. gentle, kind, nice

virus [n] *bacterium, bug* ailment, bacillus, disease, germ, illness, infection, microbe, microorganism, pathogen, sickness; CONCEPT 306

visceral [adj] *instinctive* accustomed, automatic, congenital, habitual, inborn, ingrained, inherent, innate, instinctual, intrinsic, intuitional, intuitive, knee-jerk*, natural, reflex, rooted, second-nature*; CONCEPT 544

viscous [adj] *sticky, gummy* adhesive, clammy, gelatinous, gluey*, glutinous, gooey*, mucilaginous, ropy, slimy, stiff, syrupy, tenacious, thick, tough, viscid; CONCEPT 606 —Ant. unsticky, watery

visible [adj] *apparent, seeable* arresting, big as life*, bold, clear, conspicuous, detectable, discernible, discoverable, distinguishable, evident, inescapable, in sight, in view, macroscopic, manifest, marked, not hidden, noticeable, observable, obtrusive, obvious, ocular, open, out in the open*, outstanding, palpable, patent, perceivable, perceptible, plain, pointed, pronounced, revealed, salient, seen, signal, striking, to be seen, unconcealed, under one's nose*, unhidden, unmistakable, viewable, visual; CONCEPTS 529,576,619 —Ant. concealed, hidden, invisible, obscured, unseeable

vision [n1] *ability to perceive with eyes* eyes*, eyesight, faculty, optics, perceiving, perception, range of view, seeing, sight, view; CONCEPT 629 —Ant. blindness, sightlessness

vision [n2] *mental image, concept* angle, aspect, astuteness, breadth of view, castles in the air*, conception, daydream, discernment, divination, dream, facet, fancy, fantasy, farsightedness, foreknowledge, foresight, head trip*, idea, ideal, ideality, imagination, insight, intuition, keenness, mental picture, muse, nightmare, outlook, penetration, perspective, phantasm,

pie in the sky*, pipe dream*, point of view, prescience, retrospect, slant, standpoint, trip, understanding, view; CONCEPTS 529,532,689

vision [n3] *apparition* apocalypse, chimera, delusion, ecstasy, fantasy, ghost, hallucination, haunt, illusion, mirage, nightmare, oracle, phantasm, phantom, phenomenon, presence, prophecy, revelation, specter, spirit, spook, trance, warlock, wraith; CONCEPTS 370,529 —Ant. actuality, fact, reality

vision [n4] *very beautiful thing or person* angel*, dazzler, dream, eyeful*, feast for the eyes*, perfect picture*, picture, sight, sight for sore eyes*, spectacle, stunner*; CONCEPTS 424,529

visionary [adj] *idealized, romantic* abstracted, ambitious, astral, chimerical, daydreaming, delusory, dreaming, dreamy, exalted, fanciful, fantastic, grandiose, ideal, idealist, idealistic, illusory, imaginary, impractical, in the clouds*, introspective, lofty, musing, noble, otherworldly, pretentious, prophetic, quixotic, radical, speculative, starry-eyed*, unreal, unrealistic, unworkable, unworldly, utopian; CONCEPTS 529,560,582 —Ant. practical, real, realistic, unromantic

visionary [n] *person who dreams, is idealistic* castle-builder*, daydreamer, Don Quixote*, dreamer, enthusiast, idealist, mystic, prophet, romancer, romantic, seer, stargazer, theorist, utopian, zealot; CONCEPT 361 —Ant. realist

visit [n] *social call upon another* appointment, call, evening, holiday, interview, sojourn, stay, stop, stopover, talk, tarriance, vacation, visitation, weekend; CONCEPTS 226,227

visit [v1] *be a guest of* call, call on, chat, come around, come by, converse, crash, drop by, drop in, drop over, dwell, frequent, go over to*, go to see*, hit, inspect, look around, look in on, look up, pay a call*, pay a visit to, play, pop in*, reside, see, sojourn, stay at, stay with, step in, stop by*, stop off*, swing by*, take in, talk, tarry, tour; CONCEPTS 226,227

visit [v2] *bother, haunt* afflict, assail, attack, avenge, befall, bring down on, descend upon, force upon, impose, inflict, pain, punish, smite, trouble, wreak, wreck; CONCEPTS 7,14,19

visitor [n] *person temporarily in a foreign location* caller, company, foreigner, guest, habitué, inspector, invitee, out-of-towner, transient, visitant; CONCEPT 423 —Ant. host

vista [n] *view* field of vision, glimpse, landscape, look, outline, panorama, perspective, scene, scenery, seascape, sight, vision; CONCEPT 628

visual [adj] *able to be seen with eyes* beheld, discernible, imaged, observable, observed, ocular, optic, optical, perceptible, seeable, seen, viewable, viewed, visible, visional; CONCEPTS 485,576,619

visualize [v] *make a picture of in the mind* anticipate, apprehend, bring to mind, call to mind, call up, conceive of, conjure up, create, divine, dream up, envisage, envision, fancy, feature, foresee, get the picture*, image, imagine, object, picture, reflect, see, see in the mind's eye*, think, view, vision; CONCEPTS 17,34

vital [adj1] *essential* basic, bottom-line*, cardinal, coal-and-ice*, constitutive, critical, crucial, decisive, fundamental, heavy*, imperative, important, indispensable, integral, key, life-or-death*, meaningful, meat-and-potatoes*, name, name-of-the-game*, necessary, needed, nitty-gritty*, prerequisite, required, requisite, significant, underlined, urgent; CONCEPTS 546,567 —Ant. inessential, insignficant, trivial, unimportant

vital [adj2] *lively* animated, dynamic, energetic, forceful, lusty, red-blooded, spirited, strenuous, vibrant, vigorous, vivacious, zestful; CONCEPT 401 —Ant. dull, sluggish

vital [adj3] *alive* animate, animated, breathing, generative, invigorative, life-giving, live, living, quickening; CONCEPT 539 —Ant. dead

vitality [n] *energy, spirit* animation, ardor, audacity, bang, being, bloom, bounce, clout, continuity, drive, endurance, existence, exuberance, fervor, force, get-up-and-go*, go, guts*, intensity, life, liveliness, lustiness, pep, pizzazz*, power, pulse, punch, robustness, snap, sparkle, spunk*, stamina, starch*, steam, strength, stuff*, venturesomeness, verve, vigor, vim, vivaciousness, vivacity, zest, zing*, zip*; CONCEPTS 407,411,633 —Ant. apathy, lethargy

vitiate [v1] *cancel* abate, abolish, abrogate, annihilate, annul, delete, deny, invalidate, negate, nullify, quash, recant, revoke, undermine, undo; CONCEPTS 121,317 —Ant. schedule, set up

vitiate [v2] *hurt, corrupt* blemish, blight, brutalize, contaminate, damage, debase, debauch, defile, deprave, deteriorate, devalue, harm, impair, injure, mar, pervert, pollute, prejudice, spoil, sully, taint, tarnish, violate, warp, water down, weaken; CONCEPTS 246,250 —Ant. aid, assist, help, protect, save

vitriol [n] *bitterness* acrimoniousness, contempt, disdain, hatefulness, hostility, malevolence, maliciousness, nastiness, sarcasm, venom, virulence; CONCEPTS 410,633

vittles [n] *food* chow*, comestibles, eatables, eats, edibles, fare, foodstuff, goodies*, groceries*, grub, larder, meal, nourishment, provender, provisions, refreshments, snack, viands, victuals; CONCEPTS 457,460,461

vituperate [v] *criticize harshly* abuse, accuse, asperse, bark at*, bawl out*, berate, blame, calumniate, castigate, censure, chew out*, condemn, curse, denounce, find fault, growl, insult, lambaste*, lash, malign, rail, rate, reproach, revile, rip into*, run down*, scold, smear, tear into*, tongue-lash*, traduce, upbraid, vilify, yell at*; CONCEPTS 44,52,54 —Ant. compliment, praise

vituperation [n] *verbal attack* bad-mouthing*, berating, blame, castigation, censure, criticism, defamation, insults, libel, obloquy, reprimand, reproach, scolding, slander, tirade, upbraiding, verbal abuse; CONCEPT 54

vivacious [adj] *lively, spirited* active, alert, animate, animated, bouncy, brash, breezy, bubbling, cheerful, ebullient, effervescent, exuberant, frolicsome, full of life*, gay, happy, high-spirited, jolly, jumping, keen, lighthearted, merry, playful, rocking, scintillating, sparkling, sportive, spritghtly, swinging, upbeat, vibrant, vital, zesty; CONCEPTS 401,404 —Ant. boring, dispirited, dull, unattractive, unhappy

vivid [adj] *intense, powerful* active, animated, bright, brilliant, clear, colorful, definite, distinct, dramatic, dynamic, eloquent, energetic, expressive, flamboyant, gay, glowing, graphic, highly colored, lifelike, lively, lucid, meaningful, memorable, picturesque, realistic, resplendent, rich, sharp, shining, spirited, stirring, striking, strong, telling, theatrical, true-to-life, vigorous; CONCEPTS 537,569,618 —Ant. dull, weak

vixen [n] *foxy person* cat, dragon, harpy, harridan, hellcat, she-devil, shrew, termagant, virago, witch, Xanthippe; CONCEPT 412

vocabulary [n] *language of a person or people* cant, dictionary, glossary, jargon, lexicon, palaver, phraseology, terminology, thesaurus, wordbook, word-hoard*, words, word-stock*; CONCEPTS 276,280

vocal [adj1] *spoken* articulate, articulated, choral, expressed, intonated, lyric, modulated, operatic, oral, phonetic, phonic, pronounced, put into words*, said, singing, sonant, sung, uttered, verbal, viva voce, vocalic, vocalized, voiced, vowel; CONCEPTS 267,594 —Ant. written

vocal [adj2] *extroverted about opinion* articulate, blunt, clamorous, eloquent, expressive, facile, fluent, forthright, frank, free, free-spoken, glib, noisy, outspoken, plainspoken, round, smooth-spoken, stentorian, strident, venting, vociferous; CONCEPTS 267,404 —Ant. introverted, modest, quiet, shy

vocalize [v] *put into words or song* belt out*, canary*, chant, chirp, communicate, convey, croon, emit, enunciate, express, give out*, groan, impart, let out*, moan, pronounce, say, shout, sing, sound, speak, talk, utter, vent, verbalize, voice, warble, yodel; CONCEPT 77

vocation [n] *life's work* art, business, calling, career, craft, do*, dodge*, duty, employment, field, game, handicraft, job, lifework, line*, line of business*, métier, mission, nine-to-five*, occupation, office, post, profession, pursuit, racket*, role, thing*, trade, undertaking; CONCEPTS 349,360 —Ant. entertainment, fun, pastime

vociferous [adj] *loud, insistent* boisterous, clamant, clamorous, distracting, loud-mouthed, noisy, obstreperous, ranting, shouting, shrill, strident, uproarious, vehement, vociferant; CONCEPTS 267,592,594 —Ant. quiet, silent

vogue [adj] *fashionable* faddy*, in*, latest, mod*, modish, now, popular, prevalent, rage*, state-of-the-art*, trendy, up-to-the-minute*, with it*; CONCEPT 589 —Ant. out, unfashionable, unpopular, unstylish

vogue [n] *fashion; current practice* chic, craze*, currency, custom, dernier cri, fad*, fashionableness, favor, in thing*, last word*, latest, mode, popularity, practice, prevalence, rage*, style, stylishness, thing*, trend, usage, use, way; CONCEPT 655 —Ant. disuse, out

voice [n1] *expression, language* articulation, call, cry, delivery, exclamation, inflection, intonation, modulation, murmur, mutter, roar, shout, song, sound, speech, statement, tone, tongue, utterance, vent, vocalization, vociferation, words, yell; CONCEPTS 77,276

voice [n2] *opinion* approval, choice, decision, expression, option, part, participation, preference, representation, right of free speech, say,

say-so*, suffrage, vent, view, vote, vox populi, will, wish; CONCEPTS 278,376

voice [v] *express opinion; put into words* air, announce, articulate, assert, come out with*, cry, declare, deliver, divulge, emphasize, enunciate, give expression, give utterance, inflect, intonate, modulate, present, proclaim, pronounce, put, recount, say, sound, speak, talk, tell, utter, vent, verbalize, vocalize; CONCEPTS 49,51 —*Ant.* be quiet

void [adj1] *empty* abandoned, bare, barren, bereft, clear, deprived, destitute, devoid, drained, emptied, free, lacking, scant, short, shy, tenantless, unfilled, unoccupied, vacant, vacuous, without; CONCEPTS 481,583,740,774 —*Ant.* filled, full, occupied

void [adj2] *nullified, meaningless* avoided, bad, dead, forceless, fruitless, ineffective, ineffectual, inoperative, invalid, negated, not viable, nugatory, null, null and void, set aside, sterile, unconfirmed, unenforceable, unfruitful, unratified, unsanctioned, unsuccessful, useless, vain, voided, worthless; CONCEPT 560 —*Ant.* full, meaningful, valid

void [n] *emptiness, want* blank, blankness, cavity, gap, hole, hollow, lack, nihility, nothingness, nullity, opening, space, vacuity, vacuum; CONCEPTS 513,646,709 —*Ant.* fullness

void [v1] *get rid of; empty* clear, deplete, discharge, dispose, drain, dump, eject, eliminate, emit, evacuate, flow, go, go pour, relieve, remove, throw out, vacate; CONCEPTS 179,180 —*Ant.* keep

void [v2] *nullify, cancel* abnegate, abrogate, annul, black out*, bleep*, blue pencil*, clean up, cut, declare null and void*, discharge, dissolve, drop*, gut*, invalidate, launder, rescind, sanitize, sterilize, take out, trim, vacate; CONCEPTS 50,88,121,211 —*Ant.* allow, permit, sanction, validate

volatile [adj] *explosive, changeable* airy, buoyant, capricious, effervescent, elastic, elusive, ephemeral, erratic, expansive, fickle, fleeting, flighty, flippant, frivolous, fugacious, fugitive, gaseous, gay, giddy, impermanent, imponderable, inconsistent, inconstant, light, lively, lubricious, mercurial, momentary, playful, resilient, short-lived, sprightly, subtle, temperamental, ticklish, transient, transitory, unsettled, unstable, unsteady, up-and-down, vaporous, variable, whimsical; CONCEPTS 401, 534 —*Ant.* calm, firm, stable, steadfast

volition [n] *free will* accord, choice, choosing, conation, desire, determination, discretion, election, option, preference, purpose, resolution, selection, will, willingness, wish; CONCEPTS 20,41

volley [n] *barrage* battery, bombardment, burst, cannonade, crossfire, enfilade, firing, fussilade, gunfire, hail, round, salvo, shelling, shower, storm; CONCEPT 320

voluble [adj] *talkative* articulate, bigmouthed*, chattering, chatty*, fluent, full of hot air*, gabby, garrulous, long-winded*, loquacious, mouthy*, multiloquent, prolix, rambling, running on*, slick*, smooth*, talky, verbal, windy*, wordy; CONCEPT 267

volume [n1] *capacity, measure of capacity* aggregate, amount, body, bulk, compass, content, contents, cubic measure, dimensions, extent, figure, mass, number, object, quantity, size, total; CONCEPTS 719,740,794

volume [n2] *loudness of a sound* amplification, degree, intensity, power, sonority, strength; CONCEPTS 65,792

volume [n3] *book* album, edition, publication, tome, treatise, version; CONCEPT 280

voluminous [adj] *big, vast* abundant, ample, billowing, bulky, capacious, cavernous, comprehensive, convoluted, copious, covering, expansive, extensive, full, great, large, legion, many, massive, multifarious, multitudinous, numerous, prolific, roomy, several, simple, spacious, sundry, swelling, various; CONCEPTS 773,781 —*Ant.* little, slight, small, tiny

voluntarily [adv] *of one's own free will* at one's discretion, by choice, by preference, deliberately, freely, intentionally, of one's own accord*, on one's own, on one's own initiative*, optionally, spontaneously, willingly, with all one's heart*, without being asked, without prompting; CONCEPTS 538,544 —*Ant.* forced, involuntarily, obligatory

voluntary [adj] *willing* autonomous, chosen, deliberate, designful, discretional, elected, free, freely, free-willed, gratuitous, honorary, independent, intended, intentional, opted, optional, spontaneous, unasked, unbidden, uncompelled, unconstrained, unforced, unpaid, unprescribed, volitional, volunteer, willed, willful, wished, witting; CONCEPTS 538,544 —*Ant.* forced, involuntary, obligatory, unwilling

volunteer [v] *offer to do something* advance, bring forward, chip in*, come forward, do on one's own volition*, enlist, go in*, let oneself in for*, offer services, present, proffer, propose, put at one's disposal*, put forward, sign up, speak up, stand up, step forward, submit oneself, suggest, take bull by the horns*, take initiative*, take the plunge*, take upon oneself*, tender; CONCEPTS 66,67 —*Ant.* compel, force, obligate

voluptuous [adj] *given to sensual pleasure; pleasurable to the senses* appealing, attractive, delightful, desirable, enticing, erotic, fleshly, hedonist, hedonistic, indulgent, lubricious, luxurious, pleasing, salacious, self-indulgent, sensuous, sexy, sybaritic, wanton; CONCEPTS 372,485 —*Ant.* flat, underdeveloped

vomit [v] *disgorge* be seasick*, be sick, bring up*, dry heave*, eject, emit, expel, gag*, heave*, hurl*, puke*, regurgitate, retch, ruminate, spew, spit up, throw up, upchuck*; CONCEPTS 179,185,308

voodoo [n] *black magic* abracadabra*, alchemy, black art, charm, conjuring, devilry, divination, enchantment, evil eye, hocus-pocus*, hoodoo, jinx, mumbo jumbo*, necromancy, obeah, obi, sorcery, spell, witchcraft, witchery, wizardry; CONCEPTS 370,689

voracious [adj] *very hungry, greedy* avid, covetous, devouring, dog-hungry*, edacious, empty, gluttonous, gorging, grasping, gross, insatiable, omnivorous, piggy*, prodigious, rapacious, ravening, ravenous, sating, starved, starved to death*, starving, uncontrolled, unquenchable; CONCEPTS 20,401 —*Ant.* quenched, satisfied

vote [n] *decision or right to decide* representation

aye*, ballot, choice, franchise, majority, nay*,
plebiscite, poll, referendum, secret ballot, show
of hands*, suffrage, tally, ticket, will, wish,
yea*, yes or no*; CONCEPTS 300,376

vote [v] *decide on representation* ballot, cast
ballot, cast vote, choose, confer, declare,
determine, effect, elect, enact, enfranchise,
establish, go to the polls*, grant, judge, opt,
pronounce, propose, put in office*, recommend, return, second, suggest; CONCEPTS
41,300 —*Ant.* abstain

vouch [v] *give assurance* act as a witness,
affirm, answer for, assert, asseverate, assure,
attest to, avert, avow, back, bear testimony,
be responsible for, certify, confirm, contend,
corroborate, cosign, declare, get behind*,
give an affidavit, guarantee, maintain, okay*,
predicate, profess, prove, put forth, rubber-
stamp*, say so*, sign for, sponsor, stand up
for*, substantiate, support, swear to, swear
up and down*, testify, uphold, verify, vow,
warrant, witness; CONCEPTS 49,71,317
—*Ant.* deny, disavow, refute, reject, renounce

voucher [n] *receipt* certificate, check, chit,
coupon, credential, debenture, IOU*, note,
notice, proof of purchase, release, sales slip,
slip, stub, ticket, token; CONCEPTS 271,332

vow [n] *promise* affiance, assertion, asseveration, oath, pledge, profession, troth, word of
honor; CONCEPTS 278,689 —*Ant.* breach, break

vow [v] *make a solemn promise* affirm, assure,
consecrate, covenant, cross one's heart*,
declare, dedicate, devote, give word of
honor*, pledge, plight, promise, swear, swear
up and down*, testify, undertake solemnly*,
vouch, warrant; CONCEPTS 71,297 —*Ant.*
disavow

voyage [n] *journey, often by water* boating,
crossing, cruise, excursion, hop, jaunt, junket,
overnight, passage, sail, swing, tour, travel,
travels, trek, trip, weekend; CONCEPTS 155,
224

vulgar [adj1] *rude, offensive* base, blue*,
boorish, cheap, coarse, common, contemptible,
crude, dirty, disgusting, dishonorable, filthy,
fractious, gross*, hard-core*, ignoble, impolite,
improper, indecent, indecorous, indelicate, inferior, low, malicious, nasty, naughty, obscene,
odious, off-color, profane, raw, repulsive,
ribald, risqué, rough, scatological, slippery,
smutty, sneaking, soft-core*, sordid, suggestive, tasteless, tawdry, uncouth, unmannerly,
unrefined, unworthy, villainous, X-rated*;
CONCEPTS 267,372,545 —*Ant.* decent, inoffensive, nice, polite, refined

vulgar [adj2] *common, general* colloquial,
conversational, dime a dozen*, everyday,
familiar, garden variety*, low, native, ordinary,
plastic, plebeian, popular, public, run-of-the-
mill*, unrefined, vernacular; CONCEPT 530
—*Ant.* aesthetic, artistic, fashionable

vulnerable [adj] *open to attack* accessible,
assailable, defenseless, exposed, liable, naked,
on the line*, on the spot*, out on a limb*,
ready, sensitive, sitting duck*, sucker*, susceptible, tender, thin-skinned*, unguarded, unprotected, unsafe, weak, wide open*; CONCEPTS
403,587 —*Ant.* closed, guarded, protected,
safe, secure

W

wacky [adj] *acting crazy* absurd, balmy, crazed,
crazy, daft, demented, deranged, eccentric,
erratic, foolish, hare-brained, insane, irrational,
loony*, lunatic, mad, nuts*, nutty*, odd,
preposterous, screwy*, silly, unpredictable,
wild, zany*; CONCEPTS 401,403 —*Ant.* calm,
collected

wad [n] *ball of something* back, block, boodle,
bunch, bundle, chunk, clump, cushion, fortune,
gathering, heap, hunk, lining, lump, mass, mint,
nugget, packet, pad, pile, plug, pot, ream, roll,
slew, stuff, tuft, wadding; CONCEPTS 432,436

waddle [v] *walk like a duck* rock, shuffle, sway,
toddle, totter, wiggle, wobble; CONCEPT 151

wade [v] *plod, often through water* attack, attempt, bathe, drudge, fall to, ford, get feet wet*,
get stuck in*, go for, initiate, jump in, labor,
launch, light into, paddle, pitch in, set about,
set to, splash, start, stumble, tackle, tear into*,
toil, trek, walk, work through; CONCEPTS 87,151

waffle [v] *waver* change, change one's mind,
equivocate, flip-flop*, vacillate, yo-yo*;
CONCEPT 46

waft [v] *carry* bear, be carried, blow, convey,
drift, float, ride, transmit, transport; CONCEPTS
147,217

wag [n] *person who is very funny* a million
laughs*, card*, clown, comedian, comic,
cutup*, droll*, farceur*, funny person, funster*,
humorist, jester*, joker, jokester, kibitzer*,
kidder, life of the party*, madcap*, prankster,
punster, quipster, show-off*, trickster, wisecracker, wit, zany; CONCEPTS 416,423

wag [v] *wiggle back and forth* beat, bob, fishtail*, flutter, lash, move side to side, nod,
oscillate, quiver, rock, shake, shimmy, stir,
sway, swing, switch, twitch, vibrate, waggle,
wave; CONCEPTS 150,152

wage [v] *carry on* carry out, conduct, do,
engage in, fulfill, make, practice, proceed
with, prosecute, pursue, undertake; CONCEPTS
91,100 —*Ant.* cease, halt, stop

wager [n] *money or something gambled* action,
ante*, bet, challenge, chunk, fifty-fifty*, fighting chance*, flyer*, gamble, handle, hazard,
hedge, hunch, long shot*, odds on*, outside
chance*, parlay, play, pledge, plunge, pot*,
risk, stake, toss-up, venture; CONCEPTS 329,
363,364

wager [v] *bet money or something else in a
gamble* adventure, chance, gamble, game,
hazard, hedge, hustle, lay, lay a wager, parlay,
play, play the market*, pledge, plunge, put
on*, put on the line*, put up, risk, set*, shoot*,
shoot the works*, spec*, speculate, stake, take
action, venture; CONCEPTS 28,363

wage/wages [n] *earnings for work* allowance,
bacon*, bacon and eggs*, bread*, compensation, cut, emolument, fee, hire, pay, payment,
price, receipts, recompense, remuneration,
return, returns, reward, salary, share, stipend,
sugar*, take*, take-home*; CONCEPT 344

waggish [adj] *playful* amusing, blithe, bubbly,
cheerful, clowning, comical, frolicsome, funny,
gamesome, gay, humorous, jaunty, jesting,
jocular, jocund, joking, jolly, joyous, kittenish,

lighthearted, lively, merry, mirthful, snappy, spirited, teasing, whimsical, witty; CONCEPTS 401,542

waggle [v] *shake* bobble, flourish, flutter, jerk, jiggle, joggle, quiver, twitch, wag, wave, wiggle; CONCEPT 150

waif [n] *lost or unclaimed person or thing* castaway, dogie, drop*, fetch*, flotsam, foundling, homeless one, jetsam, orphan, ragamuffin, stray, urchin; CONCEPT 423

wail [v] *cry loudly* bawl, bay, bemoan, bewail, carry on*, complain, cry the blues*, deplore, fuss, grieve, howl, jowl, keen, kick, lament, moan, mourn, repine, sob, squall, ululate, weep, whimper, whine; CONCEPTS 77,185 —*Ant.* whimper

wait [n] *pause, delay* down, downtime*, halt, hold*, hold-up, interim, interval, on hold*, rest, stay, time wasted*; CONCEPT 807 —*Ant.* act, continuation, doing

wait [v] *pause, rest* abide, anticipate, await, bide, bide one's time*, cool it*, dally, delay, expect, fill time, foresee, hang*, hang around*, hang onto your hat*, hang out, hold back, hold everything*, hold on, hold the phone*, hole up*, keep shirt on*, lie in wait*, lie low*, linger, look for, look forward to, mark time*, put on hold*, remain, save it*, sit tight*, sit up for*, stall, stand by, stay, stay up for, stick around*, sweat it*, tarry, watch; CONCEPTS 210,681 —*Ant.* carry out, do, forge, forward, go, go ahead

wait on [v] *serve* arrange, attend, care for, deal, deliver, help, minister, nurse, portion, ready, set, tend; CONCEPTS 136,324

waitperson [n] *server* attendant, butler, carhop, host, hostess, maître d', maître d'hôtel, servant, steward, stewardess, waiter, waitress; CONCEPT 348

waive [v] *give up; let go* abandon, allow, cede, defer, delay, disclaim, disown, dispense with, forgo, grant, hand over, hold off, hold up, leave, neglect, postpone, prorogue, put off, refrain from, reject, relinquish, remit, remove, renege, renounce, reserve, resign, set aside, shelve, stay, surrender, suspend, table, turn over, yield; CONCEPTS 121,234,317 —*Ant.* claim

waiver [n] *giving up; letting go* abandonment, abdication, disclaimer, foregoing, postponement, refusal, rejection, relinquishment, remission, renunciation, reservation, resignation, setting aside, surrender, tabling; CONCEPTS 121,318,685 —*Ant.* accept, claim, face

wake [n1] *formal observance of a body before funeral* deathwatch, funeral service, last rites, obsequies, rites, vigil, watch; CONCEPTS 367,377

wake [n2] *trail behind something* aftermath, backwash, furrow, path, track, train, wash, wave; CONCEPTS 753,824

wakeful [adj] *alert, restless* alive, astir, attentive, careful, heedful, insomniac, insomnious, observant, on guard, on the alert, on the lookout, on the qui vive, sleepless, unsleeping, vigilant, waking, wary, watchful, wide-awake; CONCEPTS 539,542 —*Ant.* sleepy, unaware

wake/waken [v1] *stop sleeping* arise, awake, awaken, be roused, bestir, bring to life*, call, come to, get out of bed*, get up, nudge, open one's eyes*, prod, rise, rise and shine*, roll out,

rouse, shake, stir, stretch, tumble out*, turn out, wake up; CONCEPT 105 —*Ant.* nap, sleep

wake/waken [v2] *excite, stimulate* activate, animate, arouse, awaken, challenge, enliven, fire, fire up*, freshen, galvanize, grasp, jazz up*, key up*, kindle, notice, pep up*, provoke, quicken, rally, renew, rouse, see, steam up*, stir up, switch on*, understand, whet, zip up*; CONCEPTS 7,14,22 —*Ant.* discourage, dissuade

walk [n1] *brief travel on foot* airing, carriage, circuit, constitutional, gait, hike, jaunt, march, pace, parade, perambulation, peregrination, promenade, ramble, saunter, schlepp*, step, stretch, stride, stroll, tour, traipse, tramp, tread, turn; CONCEPTS 149,224

walk [n2] *pathway* aisle, alley, avenue, boardwalk, boulevard, bricks, bypath, byway, catwalk, cloister, course, court, crossing, esplanade, footpath, gangway, lane, mall, passage, path, pavement, pier, platform, promenade, road, sidewalk, street, track, trail; CONCEPT 501

walk [n3] *discipline* area, arena, bailiwick, calling, career, course, domain, dominion, field, line, metier, profession, province, sphere, terrain, territory, trade, vocation; CONCEPT 349

walk [v] *move along on foot* advance, amble, ambulate, canter, escort, exercise, file, foot, go, go on foot*, hike, hit the road*, hoof it, knock about*, lead, leg*, locomote, lumber, march, meander, pace, pad, parade, patrol, perambulate, plod, prance, promenade, race, roam, rove, run, saunter, scuff, shamble, shuffle, slog, stalk, step, stride, stroll, strut, stump, take a walk, toddle, tour, traipse, tramp, travel on foot, traverse, tread, trek, troop, trudge, wander, wend one's way*; CONCEPT 149 —*Ant.* run

wall [n] *obstruction, divider* bank, bar, barricade, barrier, block, blockade, bulwark, curb, dam, embankment, enclosure, facade, fence, fortification, hindrance, hurdle, impediment, levee, limitation, palisade, panel, paneling, parapet, partition, rampart, restriction, retainer, roadblock, screen, side, stockade, stop, surface; CONCEPTS 440,666

wallop [n] *strong hit* bash, belt, blow, bop, bump, clash, collision, crash, haymaker*, impact, jar, jolt, kick, percussion, punch, shock, slam, slug, smack, smash, thump, thwack*, whack; CONCEPT 189

wallop [v1] *beat, hit* bam, bash, batter, belt, blast, boff, bop, buffet, bushwhack*, clobber*, drub*, hide, lambaste*, paste, pelt, plant one*, pound, pummel, punch, slam, slog, slug, smack, smash, sock, strike, swat, take out, tan*, thrash, thump, whack, wham, whomp, zap*; CONCEPT 189

wallop [v2] *defeat soundly* beat, best, clobber*, crush*, drub*, lambaste*, lick*, rout, shellac*, thrash*, trim*, trounce, vanquish, whip*; CONCEPT 95 —*Ant.* fail, lose, surrender

wallow [v1] *slosh around in* bathe in, be immersed, blunder, flounder, get stuck, immerse, lie, loll, lurch, move around in, reel, roll, roll about, roll around in, splash around, sprawl, stagger, stumble, sway, toss, totter, tumble, wade, welter; CONCEPTS 149,201

wallow [v2] *become very involved in* bask, delight, enjoy, glory, grovel, humor, indulge oneself, luxuriate, pamper, relish, revel, roll, rollick, spoil, take pleasure; CONCEPT 384

wan [adj] *colorless, weak* anemic, ashen, ashy, bilious, blanched, bleached, bloodless, cadaverous, dim, discolored, faint, feeble, forceless, ghastly, haggard, ineffective, ineffectual, livid, pale, pallid, pasty, peaked, sickly, washed-out, waxen, white, worn; CONCEPTS 314,618 —*Ant.* colorful, flushed, strong

wand [n] *rod* baton, caduceus, scepter, sprig, staff, stick, twig; CONCEPTS 470,499

wander [v1] *move about aimlessly* aberrate, amble, circumambulate, circumlocute, circumnutate, cruise, deviate, divagate, diverge, drift, float, follow one's nose*, gad*, gallivant*, globe-trot, hike, hopscotch*, jaunt, maunder, meander, peregrinate, ramble, range, roam, roll, rove, saunter, straggle, stray, stroll, take to the road*, trail, traipse, tramp, trek, vagabond, walk the tracks*; CONCEPTS 151,224 —*Ant.* stay

wander [v2] *digress; get lost* babble, depart, deviate, divagate, diverge, err, get off the track*, get sidetracked*, go astray*, go off on a tangent*, lose one's way, lose train of thought*, ramble, rave, shift, stray, swerve, talk nonsense*, veer; CONCEPTS 101,266,665 —*Ant.* go direct, stay

wanderer [n] *person who travels aimlessly* adventurer, beachcomber, bum, drifter, explorer, floater, gad*, gadabout, gallivanter, globe-trotter, gypsy, itinerant, meanderer, nomad, pilgrim, rambler, ranger, roamer, rolling stone*, rover, straggler, stray, stroller, traveler, vagabond, vagrant, voyager; CONCEPT 423

wane [v] *diminish, lessen* abate, atrophy, decline, decrease, die away, die down, die out, dim, draw to a close*, drop, dwindle, ease off, ebb, fade, fade away, fail, fall, fall short, let up, moderate, peter out*, relent, shrink, sink, slacken, slack off, subside, taper off, waste away, weaken, wind down*; CONCEPTS 698,776 —*Ant.* grow, increase, raise, rise

want [n1] *desire* appetite, craving, demand, fancy, hankering, hunger, longing, necessity, need, requirement, thirst, wish, yearning, yen; CONCEPT 20 —*Ant.* disinterest, dislike, hate

want [n2] *lack, need* absence, dearth, default, defect, deficiency, destitution, exigency, exiguousness, famine, impecuniousness, impoverishment, inadequacy, indigence, insufficiency, meagerness, neediness, paucity, pauperism, penury, poorness, poverty, privation, scantiness, scarcity, shortage, skimpiness; CONCEPTS 646,709 —*Ant.* abundance, plenty

want [v1] *desire* ache, aspire, be greedy, choose, could do with*, covet, crave, desiderate, fancy, feel a need, hanker*, have ambition, have an urge for*, have a passion for*, have a yen for*, have eyes for*, hunger, incline toward*, itch for*, long, lust, need, pine, prefer, require, spoil for*, thirst, wish, yearn; CONCEPT 20 —*Ant.* despise, dislike, hate

want [v2] *lack, need* be deficient, be deprived of, be found wanting, be insufficient, be poor, be short of, be without, call for, demand, fall short in, have need of, miss, require, stand in need of, starve; CONCEPT 646 —*Ant.* have

wanting [adj] *lacking, inadequate* absent, away, bankrupt, bereft, burned out*, cooked*, cut off, defective, deficient, deprived, destitute, devoid, disappointing, empty, failing, faulty, gone, half-baked*, imperfect, incomplete, in default, inferior, less, minus, missing, needed, not good enough, not up to par*, omitted, out of gas*, patchy, poor, scant, scanty, scarce, short, shy, sketchy, substandard, too little too late*, unfulfilled, unsound; CONCEPTS 531, 546,560 —*Ant.* adequate, perfect, satisfactory, sufficient

wanton [adj1] *extravagant, lustful* abandoned, fast*, lax, lewd, libertine, libidinous, licentious, outrageous, profligate, promiscuous, shameless, speedy*, unprincipled, unscrupulous, wayward, X-rated*; CONCEPTS 372,401,545 —*Ant.* clean, decent, moral, righteous

wanton [adj2] *cruel, malicious* accidentally on purpose*, arbitrary, contrary, double-crossing*, evil, gratuitous, groundless, inconsiderate, malevolent, mean, merciless, motiveless, needless, ornery, perverse, senseless, spiteful, unasked, uncalled-for*, unfair, unjust, unjustifiable, unjustified, unprovoked, vicious, wayward, wicked, willful; CONCEPT 401 —*Ant.* gentle, kind, nice

wanton [adj3] *careless* capricious, changeable, devil-may-care*, extravagant, fanciful, fickle, fitful, fluctuating, free, frivolous, heedless, hot and cold*, immoderate, inconstant, intemperate, lavish, outrageous, prodigal, profuse, rash, reckless, spendthrift, spoiled, thriftless, unfettered, unreserved, unrestrained, up and down*, variable, volatile, wasteful, whimsical, wild; CONCEPTS 534,542 —*Ant.* careful, observant, thoughtful, wise

wanton [n] *profligate person* debauchee, libertine, rake; CONCEPTS 412,415,419

war [n] *armed conflict* battle, bloodshed, cold war, combat, conflict, contention, contest, enmity, fighting, hostilities, hostility, police action, strife, strike, struggle, warfare; CONCEPT 320 —*Ant.* ceasefire, peace

war [v] *fight, battle* attack, attempt, bombard, campaign against, challenge, clash, combat, contend, contest, differ, disagree, endeavor, engage in combat, go to war, kill, make war, march against, meet, murder, oppugn, shell, shoot, strive, struggle, take on, take the field against, take up arms, tug, wage war; CONCEPTS 106,320 —*Ant.* agree, ceasefire, make peace

ward [n1] *district* area, canton, department, diocese, division, parish, precinct, quarter, territory, zone; CONCEPTS 508,513

ward [n2] *custody; person in one's custody* adopted child, care, charge, child, client, dependent, foster child, godchild, guardianship, keeping, minor, orphan, pensioner, protection, protégé, protégée, pupil, safekeeping, trust; CONCEPTS 414,691

warden [n] *person who guards and manages* administrator, bodyguard, caretaker, curator, custodian, deacon, dogcatcher, gamekeeper, governor, guard, guardian, jailer/jailor, janitor, keeper, officer, overseer, prison head, ranger, skipper, superintendent, watchdog, watchkeeper; CONCEPT 347 —*Ant.* prisoner

wardrobe [n] *clothes or furniture for storing clothes* apparel, attire, buffet, bureau, chest, chiffonier, closet, clothing, commode, costumes, cupboard, drapes*, dresser, dry goods, duds*, ensembles, garments, locker, outfits, rags*, suits, threads*, toggery, togs, trousseau, trunk, vestments, weeds*; CONCEPTS 443,451

ward/ward off [v] *defend, guard* avert, avoid, beat off, block, check, deflect, deter, divert, fend, foil, forestall, frustrate, halt, hold off, interrupt, keep at arm's length*, keep at bay*, keep off, obviate, parry, preclude, prevent, rebuff, rebut, repel, repulse, rule out, stave off, stop, stymie*, thwart, turn, turn aside, turn away; CONCEPTS 96,134 —*Ant.* lay bare, make vulnerable, open

warehouse [n] *storage place* barn, bin, depository, depot, distribution center, establishment, repository, shed, stash house, stockpile, stockroom, store, storehouse; CONCEPTS 439,449

wares [n] *merchandise for sale* articles, commodities, goods, line, lines, manufactures, material, produce, product, products, range, seconds, stock, stuff, vendibles; CONCEPT 338

warfare [n] *armed conflict* armed struggle, arms, battle, blows, campaigning, clash, combat, competition, contest, counterinsurgency, discord, emulation, fighting, hostilities, military operation, passage of arms, rivalry, strategy, strife, striving, struggle, tug-of-war*, war; CONCEPT 320 —*Ant.* harmony, peace

wariness [n] *caution* alertness, attention, care, carefulness, deliberation, discretion, guardedness, heed, heedfulness, prudence, vigilance, watchfulness; CONCEPT 410

warlike [adj] *hostile, battling* aggressive, attacking, bellicose, belligerent, bloodthirsty, combative, contending, contentious, contrary, fighting, gladiatorial, hawkish, inimical, martial, militant, militaristic, military, offensive, pugnacious, quarrelsome, ructious, soldierly, truculent, unfriendly, warmongering, warring; CONCEPTS 401,548 —*Ant.* harmonizing, peaceful

warlock [n] *sorcerer, wizard* astrologer, augurer, clairvoyant, conjurer, diviner, enchanter, fortune-teller, magician, medium, necromancer, occultist, seer, soothsayer, thaumaturge, witch; CONCEPT 361

warm [adj1] *moderately hot* balmy, broiling, clement, close, flushed, glowing, heated, hot, lukewarm, melting, mild, perspiring, pleasant, roasting, scorching, sizzling, snug, summery, sunny, sweating, sweaty, sweltering, temperate, tepid, thermal, toasty, warmish; CONCEPT 605 —*Ant.* cold, cool

warm [adj2] *friendly, kind* affable, affectionate, amiable, amorous, ardent, cheerful, compassionate, cordial, empathetic, fervent, genial, gracious, happy, heartfelt, hearty, hospitable, kindhearted, kindly, loving, pleasant, responsive, sincere, softhearted, sympathetic, tender, warmhearted, wholehearted; CONCEPTS 267,401,404 —*Ant.* aloof, cold, cool, uncaring, unfeeling, unfriendly, unkind

warm [adj3] *enthusiastic* amorous, angry, animated, ardent, earnest, effusive, emotional, excitable, excited, fervent, fervid, glowing, gung-ho*, heated, hot*, intense, irascible, keen, lively, nutty*, passionate, spirited, stormy, vehement, vigorous, violent, zealous; CONCEPTS 401,542 —*Ant.* cool, indifferent, unenthusiastic, uninterested

warm [v] *heat up* bake, chafe, cook, fix, heat, melt, microwave, prepare, put on the fire, thaw, toast, warm over, warm up; CONCEPTS 170,255 —*Ant.* chill, cool, freeze

warmhearted [adj] *compassionate, kindly* all heart, benevolent, charitable, cordial, friendly, generous, genial, gentle, good-hearted, good-natured, gracious, hearty, kind, kindhearted, merciful, neighborly, pleasant, polite, softhearted, sympathetic, tenderhearted, thoughtful, warm; CONCEPTS 401,403,404,542

warmonger [n] *militarist* combatant, fighter, hawk*, jingoist, militant; CONCEPTS 358,359

warn [v] *give notice of possible occurrence* acquaint, address, admonish, advise, advocate, alert, apprise, caution, clue, clue in*, counsel, cry wolf*, deprecate, direct, dissuade, enjoin, exhort, fill in, forbid, forearm, forewarn, give fair warning, give the high sign*, give warning, guide, hint, inform, instruct, lay it out*, make aware, notify, order, post, predict, prepare, prescribe, prompt, put on guard, recommend, remind, remonstrate, reprove, signal, suggest, summon, tell, threaten, tip, tip off*, urge, wise up*; CONCEPT 78

warning [adj] *cautionary* admonishing, admonitory, cautioning, exemplary, exhortatory, monitorial, monitory, ominous, premonitory, threatening; CONCEPT 267

warning [n] *notice of possible occurrence* admonition, advice, alarm, alert, augury, caution, caveat, distress signal, example, exhortation, fore, foretoken, forewarning, guidance, handwriting on wall*, heads up*, hint, indication, information, injunction, intimation, lesson, look out*, Mayday*, notification, omen, portent, prediction, premonition, presage, recommendation, sign, signal, SOS*, suggestion, threat, tip, tip-off*, token, watch-it*, wink, word, word to the wise*; CONCEPTS 78,274

warp [v] *bend, distort* bastardize*, brutalize, color, contort, corrupt, crook, curve, debase, debauch, deform, deprave, deviate, misrepresent, misshape, pervert, swerve, torture, turn, twist, vitiate, wind; CONCEPTS 63,137,213,250 —*Ant.* straighten

warrant [n] *authorization* accreditation, assurance, authentication, authority, basis, carte blanche, certificate, commission, credential, credentials, ducat, earnest, foundation, go-ahead*, green light*, guarantee, license, official document, okay*, pass, passport, pawn, permission, permit, pledge, right, sanction, security, shingle*, sticker, subpoena, summons, tag, testimonial, ticket, token, verification, warranty, word; CONCEPTS 376, 685 —*Ant.* breach, break

warrant [v] *guarantee, justify, authorize* affirm, answer for, approve, argue, assert, assure, attest, avouch, back, bear out, call for, certify, claim, commission, contend, declare, defend, delegate, demand, empower, endorse, ensure, entitle, excuse, explain, give grounds for, guaranty, insure, license, maintain, necessitate, permit, pledge, privilege, promise, require, sanction, secure, sponsor, stand behind, state, stipulate, swear, take an oath*, undertake, underwrite, uphold, vindicate, vouch for, vow; CONCEPTS 50,57,71,88

warranty [n] *promise* assurance, bail, bond, certificate, contract, covenant, guarantee, guaranty, pledge, security, surety, written promise; CONCEPTS 684,685 —*Ant.* breach, break

warrior [n] *person who fights in combat* battler, champion, combatant, conscript, enlisted person, fighter, fighting person, GI*, hero, serviceperson, soldier, trooper; CONCEPT 358

wary [adj] *careful, cautious* alert, attentive, cagey, calculating, canny, chary, circumspect, considerate, discreet, distrustful, doubting, frugal, gingerly, guarded, handling with kid gloves*, heedful, keeping on one's toes*, leery, on guard, on the lookout*, on the qui vive, provident, prudent, safe, saving, sly, sparing, suspicious, thinking twice*, thrifty, unwasteful, vigilant, walking on eggs*, watchful, watching one's step*, watching out, wide-awake; CONCEPTS 401,403 —*Ant.* careless, foolish, heedless, incautious, indiscreet, rash, reckless

wash [n1] *laundry, bath* ablution, bathe, cleaning, cleansing, dirty clothes, laundering, rinse, scrub, shampoo, shower, washing; CONCEPTS 451,514

wash [n2] *wave; water movement* ebb and flow, eddy, flow, gush, heave, lapping, murmur, roll, rush, spurt, surge, surging, sweep, swell, swirl, swishing, undulation; CONCEPT 748

wash [n3] *coloring* coat, coating, film, layer, overlay, rinse, stain, suffusion, swab; CONCEPT 475

wash [v1] *bathe, clean* bath, brush up, bubble, cleanse, clean up, dip, do the dishes*, do the laundry*, douse, drench, float, freshen up*, fresh up*, hose, imbue, immerse, lap, launder, lave, moisten, rinse, scour, scrub, shampoo, shine, shower, slosh, soak, soap, sponge, starch, swab, take a bath*, take a shower*, tub, wash up*, wet, wipe; CONCEPT 165 —*Ant.* dirty

wash [v2] *be convincing* be acceptable, bear scrutiny, be plausible, be reasonable, carry weight, convince, endure, hold up, hold water*, stand up*, stick*; CONCEPT 676

washed-out [adj] *faded* bleached, colorless, discolored, drained, drawn, dull, etiolated, fatigued, lusterless, not shiny, pale, pallid, run-down, shopworn, tattered, threadbare, tired, worn; CONCEPTS 560,617,618

washed-up [adj] *finished* broken down, come to an end, concluded, done, done for, done with, ended, over and done*, over the hill*, shot*, through, useless; CONCEPTS 528,531

wassail [n] *celebration* bash*, blast*, blowout*, carousal, ceremony, festival, festivity, frolic, gala, hoopla, hullabaloo*, joviality, jubilee, merriment, merrymaking, party, revelry, shindig*, spree, wingding*; CONCEPT 377

wassail [v] *celebrate, toast* applaud, carouse, clink glasses, drink to, extol, feast, get drunk, honor, jubilate, let loose*, live it up*, make merry, party, pledge, raise one's glass to*, revel, salute; CONCEPT 377

waste [n1] *spending, use without thought* decay, desolation, destruction, devastation, dilapidation, dissipation, disuse, exhaustion, expenditure, extravagance, fritter*, havoc, improvidence, lavishness, loss, lost opportunity*, misapplication, misuse, overdoing, prodigality, ravage, ruin, squander, squandering, unthrifti-ness, wastage, wastefulness; CONCEPTS 156,252 —*Ant.* hoarding, saving

waste [n2] *land that is uncultivated* badlands, barren, bog, brush, brushland, bush, desert, dust bowl, fen, jungle, marsh, marshland, moor, quagmire, solitude, swamp, tundra, void, wasteland, wild, wilderness, wilds; CONCEPT 509 —*Ant.* development

waste [n3] *garbage, refuse* debris, dreck, dregs, dross, excess, hogwash*, junk, leavings, leftovers, litter, offal, offscourings, rubbish, rubble, ruins, rummage, scrap, slop, sweepings, swill, trash; CONCEPT 260 —*Ant.* possessions

waste [v1] *spend or use without thought; dwindle* atrophy, be of no avail*, blow, burn up, consume, corrode, crumble, debilitate, decay, decline, decrease, deplete, disable, disappear, dissipate, divert, drain, droop, eat away, ebb, emaciate, empty, enfeeble, exhaust, fade, fritter away*, frivol away*, gamble away, gnaw, go to waste, lavish, lose, misapply, misemploy, misuse, perish, pour down the drain*, run dry, run through*, sap, sink, splurge, squander, thin, throw away, trifle away, undermine, wane, wear, wear out, wilt, wither; CONCEPT 156 —*Ant.* hoard, save

waste [v2] *ruin, destroy* depredate, desecrate, desolate, despoil, devastate, devour, lay waste, pillage, rape, ravage, raze, reduce, sack, spoil, spoliate, wreak havoc; CONCEPT 252 —*Ant.* build, create, preserve

wasted [adj1] *emaciated* anorexic, atrophied, attenuated, bony, famished, gaunt, haggard, lank, lean, scrawny, shrivelled, skeletal, skin-and-bones*, skinny, starved, thin, underfed, undernourished, withered; CONCEPTS 490,491

wasted [adj2] *high on drugs* baked*, bombed*, boozed up*, buzzed*, doped, drugged, drunk, feeling no pain*, flying*, fried, inebriated, intoxicated, loaded, on a trip*, plastered, ripped*, sloshed*, smashed*, spaced out*, stewed*, stoned*, strung out*, tanked*, tipsy, totaled*, tripping*; CONCEPT 314

wasteful [adj] *not economical* careless, cavalier, destructive, dissipative, extravagant, immoderate, improvident, incontinent, lavish, liberal, overdone, overgenerous, pound-foolish*, prodigal, profligate, profuse, reckless, ruinous, spendthrift, squandering, thriftless, uneconomical, unthrifty, wanton, wild; CONCEPT 401 —*Ant.* economical, thrifty, unwasteful

watch [n1] *clock worn on body* analog watch, chronometer, digital watch, pocket watch, stopwatch, ticker*, timepiece, timer, wristwatch; CONCEPT 463

watch [n2] *lookout* alertness, attention, awareness, duty, eagle eye*, eye*, gander, guard, hawk, heed, inspection, notice, observance, observation, patrol, picket, scrutiny, sentinel, sentry, supervision, surveillance, tab, tout, vigil, vigilance, watchfulness, weather eye*; CONCEPTS 134,623

watch [v1] *look at* attend, case, check out, concentrate, contemplate, eagle-eye*, examine, eye*, eyeball*, focus, follow, gaze, get a load of*, give the once over*, have a look-see*, inspect, keep an eye on*, keep tabs on*, listen, look, mark, mind, note, observe, pay attention, peer, pipe*, regard, rubberneck*, scan, scope, scrutinize, see, spy, stare, take in, take notice, view, wait; CONCEPT 623 —*Ant.* ignore, overlook, pass by

watch [*v2*] *guard, protect* attend, be on alert*, be on the lookout*, be vigilant*, be wary, be watchful, care for, keep, keep eyes open*, keep eyes peeled*, keep watch over, look after, look out, mind, oversee, patrol, pick up on, police, ride shotgun for*, superintend, take care of, take heed*, tend, wait; CONCEPTS *134,623* —*Ant.* harm, hurt, neglect

watchful [*adj*] *on the lookout* alert, all ears*, attentive, careful, cautious, chary, circumspect, glued*, guarded, heedful, hooked*, keen, not missing a trick*, observant, on guard, on one's toes*, on the ball*, on the job*, on the qui vive, on the watch, open-eyed, prepared, ready, see after, see to, suspicious, unsleeping, vigilant, wakeful, wary, wide-awake, with eyes peeled*; CONCEPT 401 —*Ant.* inattentive, negligent

watchkeeper [*n*] *person who guards, is on lookout* caretaker, curator, custodian, detective, flagger, guard, keeper, lookout, observer, patrol, picket, police officer, ranger, scout, security guard, security officer, sentinel, sentry, signaller, spotter, spy, ward, warden, watch, watcher; CONCEPT 348

water [*n*] *pure liquid hydrogen and oxygen* Adam's ale*, aqua, aqua pura*, drink, H_2O, rain, rainwater, saliva, tears; CONCEPT 467

water [*v*] *dampen; put water in* baptize, bathe, damp, dilute, doctor, douse, drench, drool, flood, hose, imbue, inundate, irrigate, moisten, saturate, soak, sodden, souse, spatter, spray, sprinkle, steep, thin, wash, weaken, wet; CONCEPT 256 —*Ant.* dehydrate, dry

waterfall [*n*] *cascade* cataract, chute, fall, rapids, shoot, weir; CONCEPTS *514,787*

waterlogged [*adj*] *saturated* dank, drenched, dripping, drowned, soaked, soaking, sodden, soggy, sopping, soppy, soused, wet, wringing-wet; CONCEPT 603

waterloo [*n*] *final defeat, total defeat* annihilation, beating, collapse, conquest, crushing defeat, drubbing*, failure, fall, licking, massacre, overthrow, rout, shellacking*, slaughter, thrashing, trashing, trouncing, vanquishment, waxing, whipping, whitewashing; CONCEPT 95

watery [*adj*] *liquid, diluted* adulterated, anemic, aqueous, bloodless, colorless, damp, dilute, doused, flavorless, fluid, humid, insipid, marshy, moist, pale, runny, serous, sodden, soggy, tasteless, thin, washed, watered-down, waterlike, water-logged, weak, wet; CONCEPTS *485,603,618* —*Ant.* concentrated, dehydrated, dry, solid

wave [*n*] *sea surf, current* bending, billow, breaker, coil, comber, convolution, corkscrew, crest, crush, curl, curlicue, drift, flood, foam, ground swell, gush, heave, influx, loop, movement, outbreak, rash, ridge, ripple, rippling, rocking, roll, roller, rush, scroll, sign, signal, stream, surge, sweep, swell, tendency, tide, tube, twirl, twist, undulation, unevenness, uprising, upsurge, whitecap, winding; CONCEPTS *147,436,514*

wave [*v*] *move back and forth; gesture* beckon, billow, brandish, coil, curl, direct, falter, flap, flourish, flow, fluctuate, flutter, fly, gesticulate,

indicate, motion, move to and fro, oscillate, palpitate, pulsate, pulse, quaver, quiver, reel, ripple, seesaw, shake, sign, signal, stir, stream, surge, sway, swell, swing, swirl, swish, switch, tremble, twirl, twist, undulate, vacillate, vibrate, wag, waggle, waver, whirl, wield, wigwag*, wobble; CONCEPTS *74,147,149*

waver [*v*] *shift back and forth; be indecisive* be irresolute, be unable to decide*, blow hot and cold*, change, deliberate, dilly-dally*, dither, falter, flicker, fluctuate, halt, hedge, hem and haw*, hesitate, oscillate, palter, pause, pussyfoot around*, quiver, reel, run hot and cold*, seesaw*, shake, stagger, sway, teeter, totter, tremble, trim, undulate, vacillate, vary, waffle, wave, weave, whiffle, wobble, yo-yo*; CONCEPTS *18,147,410*

wax [*v*] *become large, fuller* augment, become, build, come, develop, dilate, enlarge, expand, fill out, get bigger, get to, grow, grow full, heighten, increase, magnify, mount, multiply, rise, run, swell, turn, upsurge; CONCEPTS *704,780* —*Ant.* shrink

way [*n1*] *method, technique* action, approach, contrivance, course, course of action, custom, design, expedient, fashion, form, groove*, habit, habitude, hang-up*, hook*, idea, instrument, kick, manner, means, measure, mode, modus, move, outline, plan, plot, policy, practice, procedure, process, scheme, shot, step, stroke, style, system, tack, thing*, usage, use, vehicle, wise, wont; CONCEPT 6

way [*n2*] *direction, route* access, admission, admittance, advance, alternative, approach, artery, avenue, bearing, boulevard, byway, channel, course, distance, door, drag*, elbow-room, entrance, entrée, entry, extent, forward motion, gate, gateway, headway, highway, ingress, journey, lane, length, line, march, movement, opening, orbit, passage, path, pathway, progress, progression, ride, road, room, row, space, stone's throw*, street, stretch, tendency, thataway*, thoroughfare, track, trail, trend, walk; CONCEPTS *501,738,739*

way [*n3*] *characteristic, habit* aspect, behavior, circumstance, condition, conduct, consuetude, custom, detail, fashion, feature, fettle, form, gait, groove, guise, hook, idiosyncrasy, kick*, manner, nature, particular, personality, point, practice, praxis, respect, sense, shape, shot, situation, state, status, style, thing*, tone, trait, trick, usage, use, wont; CONCEPT 411

wayfarer [*n*] *traveler* adventurer, barnstormer*, bum*, drifter, excursionist, explorer, gad-about*, globe-trotter, gypsy, hiker, hitchhiker, hobo, itinerant, journeyer, nomad, peddler, pilgrim, rambler, roamer, rover, trekker, vagabond, vagrant, walker, wanderer; CONCEPTS *348,423*

wayfaring [*adj*] *traveling* drifting, gadabout, globe-trotting, itinerant, itinerate, jet-setting*, journeying, nomadic, perambulant, perambulatory, peripatetic, rambling, roving, rubbernecking*, vagabond, vagrant, voyaging, walking, wandering; CONCEPT 401 —*Ant.* unmoving

waylay [*v*] *intercept, ambush* accost, ambuscade, assail, attack, box*, bushwhack*, catch, hold up, jump, lay for*, lie in wait, lurk, pounce on, prowl, set upon, skulk, slink, surprise, swoop down on*; CONCEPTS 86,121 —*Ant.* allow, forward

wayward [adj] *contrary, unmanageable* aberrant, arbitrary, balky, capricious, changeable, contumacious, cross-grained, delinquent, disobedient, disorderly, errant, erratic, fickle, flighty, fractious, froward, headstrong, immoral, inconstant, incorrigible, insubordinate, intractable, mulish, obdurate, obstinate, ornery*, perverse, rebellious, recalcitrant, refractory, restive, self-indulgent, self-willed, stubborn, uncompliant, undependable, ungovernable, unpredictable, unruly, unstable, variable, whimsical, willful; CONCEPT 401 —*Ant.* controllable, manageable, obedient

weak [adj1] *not strong* anemic, debilitated, decrepit, delicate, effete, enervated, exhausted, faint, feeble, flaccid, flimsy, forceless, fragile, frail, hesitant, impuissant, infirm, insubstantial, irresolute, lackadaisical*, languid, languorous, limp, makeshift, out of gas*, powerless, prostrate, puny, rickety, rocky*, rotten, senile, shaky, sickly, sluggish, spent, spindly, supine, tender, torpid, uncertain, undependable, unsound, unsteady, unsubstantial, wasted, wavering, weakened, weakly, wobbly; CONCEPTS 314,488,489 —*Ant.* firm, potent, strong

weak [adj2] *cowardly* faint-hearted, fluctuant, frightened, hesitant, impotent, indecisive, ineffectual, infirm, insecure, irresolute, laid-back*, nerveless, nervous, palsied, powerless, shaky, soft, spineless, tender, timorous, uncertain, undependable, unreliable, unstable, unsure, vacillating, wavering, weak-kneed*, wimpy*, wishy-washy*, wobbly, zero*; CONCEPTS 402,403,542 —*Ant.* bold, brave, confident

weak [adj3] *faint, soft* bated, dim, distant, dull, feeble, gentle, imperceptible, inaudible, indistinct, low, muffled, pale, poor, quiet, reedy, slight, small, stifled, thin, unaccented, unstressed, whispered; CONCEPT 594 —*Ant.* loud, noisy, potent, strong

weak [adj4] *deficient, feeble* faulty, flabby, flimsy, forceless, green*, handicapped, hollow, immature, implausible, impotent, improbable, inadequate, incompetent, incomplete, inconceivable, inconclusive, incredible, ineffective, ineffectual, inept, invalid, lacking, lame, limited, pathetic, poor, raw, shaky, shallow, slight, slim, small, spineless, substandard, thick, thin, unbelievable, unconvincing, unprepared, unqualified, unsatisfactory, unsubstantial, unsure, untrained, wanting; CONCEPTS 537,558,570 —*Ant.* able, capable, fit, sufficient

weak [adj5] *exposed, vulnerable* accessible, assailable, defenseless, helpless, indefensible, unguarded, unprotected, unsafe, untenable, wide-open*, woundable; CONCEPTS 576,587 —*Ant.* guarded, protected, safe, secure

weak [adj6] *watered-down* diluted, insipid, milk-and-water*, runny, tasteless, thin, washy, waterish, watery, wishy-washy*; CONCEPTS 462,485 —*Ant.* concentrated, strong, thick

weaken [v] *reduce the strength of* abate, adulterate, break up, cripple, crumble, cut, debase, debilitate, decline, decrease, depress, devitalize, dilute, diminish, droop, dwindle, ease up, enervate, exhaust, fade, fail, faint, flag, give way,

halt, impair, impoverish, invalidate, languish, lessen, limp, lose, lose spirit, lower, minimize, mitigate, moderate, reduce, relapse, relax, sap, slow down, soften, temper, thin, thin out, tire, totter, tremble, undermine, vitiate, wane, water down, wilt; CONCEPTS 240,698 —*Ant.* build up, strengthen

weakling [n] *person who has no strength* baby, chicken*, chicken heart*, coward, cream puff*, crybaby, dotard, invertebrate, jellyfish*, misfit, pushover, wimp*, yellow belly*; CONCEPTS 412,423 —*Ant.* strongman

weak-minded [adj] *indecisive* astraddle, changeable, hemming and hawing*, hesitant, hesitating, indeterminate, irresolute, on the fence*, spineless, tentative, uncertain, undecided, undetermined, waffling, wavering, weak-kneed*, wishy-washy*, without guts*, yellow-bellied*; CONCEPTS 534,535

weakness [n] *defect, proneness* Achilles heel*, appetite*, blemish, chink in armor*, debility, decrepitude, deficiency, delicacy, enervation, failing, faintness, fault, feebleness, flaw, fondness, fragility, frailty, gap, impairment, imperfection, impotence, inclination, inconstancy, indecision, infirmity, instability, invalidity, irresolution, lack, languor, lapse, liking, passion, penchant, powerlessness, predilection, proclivity, prostration, senility, shortcoming, soft spot*, sore point*, taste*, vice, vitiation, vulnerability; CONCEPTS 411,674,732 —*Ant.* strength, strong point

wealth [n] *money, resources* abundance, affluence, assets, belongings, bounty, cache, capital, cash, clover*, commodities, copiousness, cornucopia, dough*, estate, fortune, funds, gold, goods, hoard, holdings, lap of luxury*, long green*, lucre, luxuriance, luxury, means, opulence, pelf, plenitude, plenty, possessions, profusion, property, prosperity, prosperousness, revenue, riches, richness, security, stocks and bonds, store, substance, substantiality, treasure, velvet*, worth; CONCEPTS 340,710 —*Ant.* lack, need, poverty, want

wealthy [adj] *rich; having a lot of money* affluent, booming, comfortable, having it made*, independent, in the money*, loaded, made of money*, moneyed, of independent means, opulent, pecunious, prosperous, rolling in it*, substantial, upscale, well-heeled*, well-off*, well-to-do*; CONCEPT 334 —*Ant.* deprived, lacking, needy, poor, poverty-stricken, wanting

weapon [n] *arm, armament* ammunition, anlace, arbalest, archery, arrow, assegai, atlatl, ax, axe, backsword, ballista, banderilla, barong, bat, baton, battle-ax, bayonet, bazooka, billy club, blackjack, blade, blowgun, bludgeon, bomb, boomerang, bow and arrow, bowie knife, brass knuckles, cannon, catapult, cleaver, club, crossbow, cudgel, cutlass, dagger, dart, dirk, firearm, flamethrower, gun, harpoon, hatchet, howitzer, hunting knife, knife, lance, machete, machine gun, missile, musket, nerve gas, nuclear bomb, nunchaku, pistol, revolver, rifle, saber, scythe, shotgun, slingshot, spear, spike, stiletto, switchblade, sword, tear gas; CONCEPT 500

wear [n] *use, corrosion* abrasion, attrition, damage, depreciation, deterioration, dilapidation,

wa
we

diminution, disappearance, employment, erosion, friction, impairment, inroads, loss, mileage, service, usefulness, utility, waste, wear and tear; CONCEPTS 658,698

wear [v1] *be clothed in* array, attire, bear, be dressed in, carry, clothe oneself, cover, display, don, draw on, dress in, effect, exhibit, fit out, get into, get on, harness, have on, put on, show, slip on, sport, suit up*, turn out*, wrap; CONCEPTS 167,453 —*Ant.* disrobe, take off

wear [v2] *corrode, use* abrade, become thread-bare, become worn, be worthless, chafe, consume, crumble, cut down, decay, decline, decrease, deteriorate, diminish, drain, dwindle, erode, exhaust, fade, fatigue, fray, gall, go to seed*, graze, grind, impair, jade, overuse, over-work, rub, scrape, scrape off, scuff, shrink, tax, tire, use up, wash away, waste, wear out, wear thin, weary, weather; CONCEPTS 156,225,240, 698 —*Ant.* freshen, rebuild, refresh

wear [v3] *bother, undermine* annoy, drain, enervate, exasperate, exhaust, fatigue, get the better of, harass, irk, pester, reduce, tax, vex, weaken, wear down, weary; CONCEPTS 7,19 —*Ant.* cheer, delight, please

wear [v4] *endure* bear up, be durable, hold up, last, remain, stand, stand up; CONCEPT 23 —*Ant.* refuse, reject

weary [adj] *tired* all in*, beat*, bone-tired*, bored, burned out*, bushed, dead*, dead tired*, discontented, disgusted, dog-tired*, done in*, drained, drooping, drowsy, enervated, ex-hausted, fagged, fatigued, fed up, flagging, had it*, impatient, indifferent, jaded, knocked out, out of gas*, overworked, pooped*, punchy*, ready to drop*, sick, sick and tired*, sleepy, spent*, taxed, wearied, wearing, wiped out*, worn out, zonked*; CONCEPTS 314,403,485 —*Ant.* activated, energetic, fresh, lively, untired

weary [v] *make tired* annoy, bore, burden, cause ennui, cloy, debilitate, depress, disgust, dis-hearten, distress, drain, droop, drowse, enervate, enfeeble, exasperate, exhaust, fade, fag, fail, fall off, fatigue, flag, glut, grow tired, harass, have had enough*, irk, jade, leave one cold*, lose interest, make discontented, nauseate, oppress, overwork, pain, plague, sap, sicken, sink, strain, take it out of*, tax, tire, tire out, try the patience of*, tucker out*, vex, weaken, wear down, wear out, weigh; CONCEPTS 13,250,303 —*Ant.* activate, energize, enliven

weasel [n] *sneak* betrayer, blabbermouth*, canary*, deceiver, deep throat*, double-crosser, fink*, informant, informer, narc*, nark*, rat*, sneak, snitch, snitcher, source, squealer*, stoolie*, stool pigeon*, tattler, tattletale, tipster*, turncoat, whistle-blower; CONCEPTS 348,354,423

weasel [v] *avoid, evade* balk, beat around the bush*, circumvent, cop out, dance around an issue*, dodge, duck, elude, equivocate, eschew, flee, get around, give the runaround*, hedge, hem and haw*, lay low*, pussyfoot, put off, renege, shirk, shuck, sidestep, slip out, sneak away*, tap dance*, waffle*, welsh, worm one's way out of*; CONCEPTS 30,102

weather [n] *atmospheric conditions* climate, clime, elements; CONCEPTS 522,524

weather [v] *endure* acclimate, bear the brunt of*, bear up against*, become toughened, brave, come through, expose, get through, grow hardened, grow strong, harden, make it, overcome, pull through, resist, ride out*, rise above*, season, stand, stick it out*, suffer, surmount, survive, toughen, withstand; CONCEPTS 23,35,202 —*Ant.* refuse, reject

weatherperson [n] *meteorologist* climatolo-gist, storm chaser, weathercaster, weather-fore-caster, weatherman/woman; CONCEPTS 60,292

weave [v] *blend, unite; contrive* braid, build, careen, complect, complicate, compose, con-struct, create, criss-cross, crochet, cue, entwine, fabricate, fold, fuse, incorporate, interfold, interlace, interlink, intermingle, intertwine, introduce, knit, knot, loop, lurch, make, make up, manufacture, mat, merge, mesh, move in and out, net, piece together, plait, ply, put together, reticulate, sew, snake, spin, splice, twine, twist, twist and turn, whip through, wind, wreathe, writhe, zigzag; CONCEPTS 147, 158 —*Ant.* divide, separate

web [n] *netting* cobweb, complexity, entangle-ment, fabric, fiber, filigree, gossamer, intercon-nection, interlacing, involvement, labyrinth, lacework, lattice, mat, matting, maze, mesh, meshwork, morass, net, network, plait, reticula-tion, screen, skein, snarl, tangle, texture, tissue, toil, trellis, warp, weave, webbing, weft, wicker, woof; CONCEPTS 260,473

wed [v1] *marry* become husband and wife, be married, couple, espouse, get hitched*, get mar-ried, join, lead to the altar, make one*, receive in marriage, say I do*, take in marriage, tie*, tie the knot*, unite; CONCEPT 297 —*Ant.* divorce

wed [v2] *join, unite* ally, associate, blend, coalesce, cojoin, combine, commingle, connect, couple, dedicate, fuse, interweave, link, marry, merge, relate, unify, yoke; CONCEPTS 113,193 —*Ant.* divide, separate

wedding [n] *marriage rite* bells*, bridal, espousal, hook, marriage, marriage ceremony, matrimony, nuptial rite, nuptials, spousal, union, wedlock; CONCEPT 297 —*Ant.* divorce

wedge [n] *solid piece, often triangular* block, chock, chunk, cleat, cotter, cusp, keystone, lump, prong, quoin, shim, spire, taper; CONCEPTS 471,499 —*Ant.* whole

wedlock [n] *marriage* alliance, association, conjugality, connubiality, coupling, espousal, holy matrimony, mating, matrimony, nuptials, spousal, union, wedded bliss*, wedding; CONCEPTS 297,388

wee [adj] *very small, tiny* bitsy*, bitty, diminu-tive, infinitesimal, insignificant, itsy-bitsy*, itty-bitty*, Lilliputian, little, microscopic, miniature, minuscular, minuscule, minute, negligible, pee-wee*, petite, pint-sized*, pocket-size*, puny, slight, teensy*, teensy-weensy*, teeny*; CONCEPTS 762,773,789

weep [v] *cry* bawl, bemoan, bewail, blubber*, boohoo*, break down*, burst into tears*, complain, deplore, drip, grieve, howl, keen, lament, let go*, let it out*, mewl, moan, mourn, shed tears, snivel, sob, squall, ululate, wail, whimper, yowl; CONCEPTS 49,185

weigh [v1] *measure heaviness* counterbalance, have a weight of, heft, measure, put in the

balance, put on the scale, scale, tip the scales at;
CONCEPT 103

weigh [v2] *consider, contemplate* analyze,
appraise, balance, brainstorm*, deliberate,
estimate, evaluate, examine, excogitate, give
thought to, hash over*, meditate, mind, mull
over, perpend, ponder, rate, reflect upon, rehash
sort out, study, sweat*, think about, think out,
think over, track; CONCEPT 24 —*Ant.* ignore,
neglect

weigh [v3] *have influence* be heavy, be important, be influential, be something, burden, carry
weight, charge, count, cumber, cut, cut some
ice, import, impress, lade, matter, mean, militate, press, pull, register, saddle, show, stack
stack up against*, tax, tell; CONCEPTS 7,19,22

weigh down [v] *depress* bear down, burden,
cumber, get down, hold down, oppress, overburden, overload, press, press down, prey on,
pull down, sadden, task, trouble, weight, weigh
upon, worry; CONCEPTS 7,19 —*Ant.* cheer,
delight, please

weight [n1] *heaviness* adiposity, avoirdupois,
ballast, burden, density, G-factor*, gravity,
gross, heft, heftiness, load, mass, measurement,
net, ponderosity, ponderousness, poundage,
pressure, substance, tonnage; CONCEPT 795

weight [n2] *something used to measure
heaviness* anchor, ballast, bob, counterbalance,
counterpoise, counterweight, mass, pendulum,
plumb, plumb bob, poundage, pressure, rock,
sandbag, sinker, stone; CONCEPTS 290,470

weight [n3] *importance* access, authority, clout,
connection, consequence, consideration, credit,
effectiveness, efficacy, emphasis, forcefulness,
forcibleness, impact, import, influence, magnitude, moment, momentousness, persuasiveness,
pith, potency, power, powerfulness, prestige,
pull, significance, signification, substance,
sway, value, weightiness; CONCEPTS 668,682
—*Ant.* triviality, unimportance

weight [n4] *burden* albatross*, ball and chain*,
charge, cumber, cumbrance, deadweight*, duty,
encumbrance, excess baggage*, load, millstone*, onus, oppression, pressure, responsibility, strain, task, tax; CONCEPTS 532,674,679,690
—*Ant.* advantage, benefit, pleasure, solution

weighty [adj1] *heavy* burdensome, cumbersome, cumbrous, dense, fat, fleshy, hefty, massive, obese, overweight, ponderous, porcine,
portly, stout; CONCEPT 491 —*Ant.* light, small,
thin, unsubstantial

weighty [adj2] *serious, important* big, big
deal*, consequential, considerable, critical,
crucial, earnest, forcible, grave, heavy*, heavyweight, life and death*, material, meaningful,
momentous, no-nonsense*, portentous, sedate,
severe, significant, sober, solemn, somber, staid,
substantial, underlined; CONCEPTS 548,568
—*Ant.* inconsequential, trivial, unimportant,
unsubstantial

weighty [adj3] *troublesome, difficult* backbreaking, burdensome, crushing, demanding,
exacting, exigent, grievous, onerous, oppressive,
superincumbent, taxing, tough, worrisome,
worrying; CONCEPTS 538,540 —*Ant.* easy,
facile, solvable

weird [adj] *odd, bizarre* awe-inspiring, awful,
creepy*, curious, dreadful, eccentric, eerie*,

far-out*, fearful, flaky*, freaky*, funky*,
ghastly, ghostly, grotesque, haunting, horrific,
inscrutable, kinky*, kooky*, magical, mysterious, occult, oddball*, ominous, outlandish,
peculiar, preternatural, queer, secret, singular,
spooky*, strange, supernal, supernatural,
uncanny, uncouth, unearthly, unnatural;
CONCEPTS 564,570 —*Ant.* normal, regular, usual

weirdo [n] *freak, oddball* case*, character,
crackpot*, eccentric, flake*, fruitcake*, geek*,
misfit, nutcase, odd bird*, screwball*, strange
bird*; CONCEPT 423

welcome [adj] *gladly received* acceptable,
accepted, agreeable, appreciated, cherished,
congenial, contenting, cordial, delightful,
desirable, desired, esteemed, favorable, genial,
good, grateful, gratifying, honored, invited,
nice, pleasant, pleasing, pleasurable, refreshing,
satisfying, sympathetic, wanted; CONCEPTS
555,572 —*Ant.* displeasing, unacceptable,
unwelcome

welcome [n] *greeting* acceptance, entertainment, entrée, friendliness, handshake, hello,
hospitality, howdy*, key to the city*, ovation,
reception, red carpet*, rumble*, salutation,
salute, tumble*; CONCEPT 278 —*Ant.* goodbye

welcome [v] *receive gladly* accept, accept
gladly, accost, admit, bid welcome, embrace,
entertain, flag*, greet, hail, hug, meet, offer
hospitality, receive, roll out red carpet*, salute,
show in, take in, tumble*, usher in; CONCEPTS
266,384 —*Ant.* reject, turn away

weld [v] *bind, connect* bond, braze, cement,
combine, fix, fuse, join, link, solder, unite;
CONCEPT 193 —*Ant.* disconnect, separate

welfare/well-being [n] *health and prosperity*
abundance, advantage, benefit, contentment,
ease, easy street*, euphoria, felicity, good,
good fortune, happiness, interest, luck, profit,
progress, satisfaction, success, thriving;
CONCEPTS 316,693,706

well [adj1] *healthy* able-bodied, alive and kicking*, blooming, bright-eyed*, bushy-tailed*,
chipper*, fine, fit, flourishing, fresh, great, hale,
hardy, hearty, husky, in good health, in the
pink*, right, right as rain*, robust, sane, solid
as a rock*, sound, strong, strong as an ox*,
together, trim, up to par*, vigorous, whole,
wholesome, wrapped tight*; CONCEPT 314
—*Ant.* diseased, ill, sick, unhealthy

well [adj2] *lucky, fortunate* advisable, agreeable, bright, comfortable, fine, fitting, flourishing, good, happy, pleasing, profitable, proper,
prosperous, providential, prudent, right, satisfactory, thriving, useful; CONCEPTS 548,572
—*Ant.* unfortunate, unhappy, unlucky

well [adv1] *happily, pleasantly; capably* ably,
accurately, adeptly, adequately, admirably,
agreeably, attentively, capitally, carefully,
closely, commendably, competently, completely, conscientiously, correctly, effectively,
efficiently, excellently, expertly, famously,
favorably, fully, in a satisfactory manner,
irreproachably, nicely, proficiently, profoundly,
properly, rightly, satisfactorily, skillfully,
smoothly, soundly, splendidly, strongly,
successfully, suitably, thoroughly, with skill;
CONCEPTS 527,528,544 —*Ant.* badly, incapably,
unpleasantly

well [adv2] *sufficiently* abundantly, adequately, amply, appropriately, becomingly, by a wide margin, completely, considerably, easily, effortlessly, entirely, extremely, far, fittingly, freely, fully, greatly, heartily, highly, luxuriantly, plentifully, properly, quite, rather, readily, right, satisfactorily, smoothly, somewhat, substantially, suitably, thoroughly, very much, wholly; CONCEPTS 558,772 —*Ant.* badly, insufficiently

well [n] *water hole* abyss, bore, chasm, depression, derivation, fount, fountain, fountainhead, geyser, hole, inception, mine, mouth, origin, pit, pool, repository, reservoir, root, shaft, source, spa, spout, spring, springs, watering place, wellspring; CONCEPTS 509,513,514

well-balanced [adj] *sensible; equal* all there*, astute, aware, cognizant, discriminating, graceful, having all one's marbles*, informed, intelligent, knowing, level-headed, logical, mentally stable, practical, proportional, prudent, rational, reasonable, sane, sound, symmetrical, together, well-thought-out, wise; CONCEPTS 402,542

well-bred [adj] *mannerly* aristocratic, blue-blooded*, civil, considerate, courteous, courtly, cultivated, cultured, gallant, genteel, gentle, noble, patrician, polished, polite, refined, taught, trained, upper-crust*, urbane, well-behaved, well-mannered; CONCEPTS 334,401 —*Ant.* ignoble, unmannered, unrefined, unsophisticated

well-defined [adj] *clear* apparent, audible, clear-cut, comprehensible, distinct, explicit, graspable, intelligible, legible, lucent, lucid, obvious, plain, precise, sharp, spelled out*, straightforward, transparent, unambiguous, unblurred, understandable, well-marked; CONCEPTS 402,562

well-known [adj] *familiar, famous* acclaimed, big, big name*, celeb*, celebrated, common, conspicuous, eminent, illustrious, important, infamous, in the limelight*, in the public eye*, known, large, leading, name, notable, notorious, outstanding, popular, prominent, public, recognized, renowned, reputable, somebody, splashy, star, superstar, VIP*, widely known, WK*; CONCEPT 568 —*Ant.* unfamiliar, unknown

well-off [adj] *successful, wealthy* affluent, comfortable, easy, flourishing, flush, fortunate, loaded, lucky, moneyed, prosperous, rich, snug, substantial, thriving, well, well-to-do; CONCEPT 334 —*Ant.* destitute, failing, poor, unsuccessful

well-preserved [adj] *well-kept* boyish, childish, fresh, full of life, girlish, tender, unspoiled, young; CONCEPTS 542,578,797

well-to-do [adj] *well-off* affluent, comfortable, flourishing, loaded, moneyed, prosperous, rich, rolling in it*, set for life*, snug, successful, wealthy; CONCEPT 334

welsh [v] *renege, swindle* bamboozle, beat around the bush*, bilk, cheat, con, cop out, deceive, defraud, dodge, duck, dupe, fleece*, flimflam, fool, gull*, hoodwink, pull a fast one*, rip off*, sandbag, scam, shaft, slip out, stiff*, sting*, take for a ride*, take to the cleaners*, trick, weasel*, worm one's way out of*; CONCEPTS 59,139,192

welt [n] *red mark* bruise, contusion, injury, mouse, ridge, scar, streak, stripe, wale, weal, wheal, wound; CONCEPT 309

wet [adj] *damp, moist* aqueous, clammy, dank, dewy, drenched, dripping, drizzling, foggy, humid, misty, moistened, muggy, pouring, raining, rainy, saturate, saturated, showery, slimy, slippery, slushy, snowy, soaked, soaking, sodden, soggy, sopping, soppy, soused, stormy, teary, teeming, water-logged, watery, wringing-wet; CONCEPT 603 —*Ant.* dehydrated, dry

wet [n] *dampness, moisture* clamminess, condensation, damp, drizzle, humidity, liquid, rain, rains, water, wetness; CONCEPT 607 —*Ant.* dehydration, dryness

wet [v] *cause to become damp, moist* bathe, damp, dampen, deluge, dip, douse, drench, drown, hose, humidify, imbue, irrigate, moisten, rinse, saturate, soak, sop, souse, splash, spray, sprinkle, steep, wash, water; CONCEPTS 161,256 —*Ant.* dehydrate, dry

whack [n1/v] *hit* bang, bash, bat, beat, belt, biff, box, buffet, clobber, clout, crack, cuff, ding*, lambaste*, nail, rap, slap, slug, smack, smash, sock, strike, thrash, thump, thwack*, wallop, wham*; CONCEPT 189

whack [n2] *try, attempt* bash, crack, fling, go, pop, shot, slap, stab, turn, whirl; CONCEPT 87

whammy [n] *spell* abracadabra*, charm, conjuration, curse, double whammy*, evil eye, hex, hexing, hocus-pocus*, jinx, magic, mumbo-jumbo*, triple whammy*, voodoo; CONCEPTS 370,673,689

wharf [n] *boat storage* berth, breakwater, dock, jetty, landing, landing stage, levee, pier, quay, slip; CONCEPT 439

wheedle [v] *talk into* banter, blandish, butter up*, cajole, charm, coax, con, court, draw, entice, finagle, flatter, inveigle, kowtow*, lay it on*, oil*, persuade, seduce, snow*, soap*, soften up*, soft-soap*, spread it on*, sweeten up*, sweet-talk*, work on*, worm*; CONCEPT 68

wheel [n] *circle, revolution* caster, circuit, circulation, circumvolution, cycle, disk, drum, gyration, gyre, hoop, pivot, pulley, ratchet, ring, roll, roller, rotation, round, spin, trolley, turn, twirl, whirl; CONCEPTS 436,464,502

wheel [v] *turn, rotate* circle, gyrate, orbit, pirouette, pivot, reel, revolve, roll, spin, swing, swivel, trundle, twirl, whirl; CONCEPT 147

wheeze [v] *breathe roughly, heavily* buzz, catch one's breath, cough, gasp, hiss, murmur, pant, puff, rasp, sibilate, snore, whisper, whistle; CONCEPTS 163,308

when [conj] *though* albeit, although, at, at the same time, during, howbeit, immediately upon, just after, just as, meanwhile, much as, whereas, while; CONCEPT 799

where [n] *place* location, locus, point, position, site, situation, spot, station; CONCEPT 198

where/wherever [adv] *at which point* anywhere, everywhere, in whatever place, in which, to what end, to which, whereabouts, whither; CONCEPT 583

whet [v1] *make sharp* edge, file, finish, grind, hone, sharpen, strop; CONCEPTS 137,250 —*Ant.* blunt, dull

whet [v2] *arouse, excite* animate, awaken, challenge, enhance, incite, increase, kindle, pique, provoke, quicken, rally, rouse, stimulate, stir, wake, waken; CONCEPTS *7,11,22* —*Ant.* blunt, dampen, dishearten

whiff [*n*] *smell of an odor* aroma, blast, breath, dash, draught, flatus, fume, gust, hint, inhalation, odor, puff, scent, shade, smack, sniff, snuff, soupçon, trace, trifle, waft; CONCEPTS *599,601, 602*

while [*conj1*] *as long as* although, at the same time, during, during the time, in the time, throughout the time, whilst; CONCEPT *799*

while [*conj2*] *even though* albeit, although, howbeit, much as, though, when, whereas; CONCEPT *544*

while [*n*] *time interval* bit, instant, interim, meantime, moment, occasion, period, space, spell, stretch, time; CONCEPTS *807,822*

whim [*n*] *sudden idea* caprice, conceit, craze, desire, disposition, dream, fad, fancy, fantasy, freak, humor, impulse, inclination, notion, passing thought, quirk, sport, thought, urge, vagary, vision, whimsy; CONCEPTS *529,661* —*Ant.* plan

whimper [*v*] *cry softly* bleat, blubber, complain, fuss, mewl, moan, object, pule, snivel, sob, weep, whine; CONCEPTS *77,185* —*Ant.* bawl

whimsical [*adj*] *playful, fanciful* amusing, arbitrary, capricious, chancy, chimerical, comical, curious, dicey, droll, eccentric, erratic, fantastic, flaky*, freakish, funny, kinky*, mischievous, odd, peculiar, quaint, queer*, quizzical, singular, uncertain, unpredictable, unusual, waggish, wayward, weird*; CONCEPTS *401,548* —*Ant.* behaving, reasonable, sensible

whine [*n*] *complaint, cry* gripe, grouse, grumble, moan, plaintive cry, sob, wail, whimper; CONCEPTS *54,77* —*Ant.* happiness, pleasure

whine [*v*] *complain, cry* bellyache, carp, drone, fuss, gripe, grouse, grumble, howl, kick, mewl, moan, murmur, pule, repine, snivel, sob, wail, whimper, yowl; CONCEPTS *54,77*

whip [*n*] *length of material for hitting* bat, belt, birch, bullwhip, cane, cat-o'-nine-tails, crop, goad, horsewhip, knout, lash, prod, push, rawhide, rod, ruler, scourge, strap, switch, thong; CONCEPT *499*

whip [*v1*] *hit repeatedly* bash, beat, birch, bludgeon, cane, castigate, chastise, cudgel, drub, ferule, flagellate, flog, hide, larrup*, lash, lather*, punish, scourge, spank, strap, strike, switch, tan, thrash, trash, wallop, whale, whomp*; CONCEPT *189*

whip [*v2*] *defeat soundly* beat, best, blast, clobber, conquer, drub, hammer*, kill*, lambaste, lick*, mop up*, outdo, overcome, overpower, overrun, overwhelm, put away*, rout, run circles around*, settle, steamroller*, subdue, take apart*, thrash, top, trim*, trounce, vanquish, wallop, wax*, whomp*, worst*; CONCEPT *95* —*Ant.* lose, surrender

whip [*v3*] *dash, dart* avert, deflect, dive, divert, flash, flit, fly, jerk, pivot, pull, rush, seize, sheer, shoot, snatch, surge, tear, turn, veer, wheel, whirl, whisk; CONCEPTS *150,152*

whip [*v4*] *agitate, stir up* beat, blend, mix, whisk, work up; CONCEPTS *152,170*

whipping [*n*] *beating* caning, flogging, licking, pasting, pounding, pummeling, punishment, spanking, tanning, thrashing, trouncing, walloping; CONCEPT *123*

whipping boy [*n*] *scapegoat* dupe, fall guy*,

goat*, mark*, patsy*, sacrifice, sucker, target, victim; CONCEPT *412*

whip up [*v*] *incite, excite* abet, agitate, arouse, compel, disturb, drive, foment, goad, hound, inflame, instigate, kindle, prick, prod, provoke, push, raise, set, set on, spur, start, stir, stir up, urge, work up; CONCEPTS *14,221* —*Ant.* discourage, dissuade

whirl [*n1*] *spin, revolution* circle, circuit, circulation, circumvolution, flurry, gyration, gyre, pirouette, reel, roll, rotation, round, surge, swirl, turn, twirl, twist, wheel, whir, whirlpool; CONCEPTS *152,738*

whirl [*n2*] *commotion, confusion* ado*, agitation, bustle, clatter, daze, dither, ferment, flurry, fluster, flutter, furor, fuss, hubbub*, hurly-burly*, hurry, merry-go-round*, moil, pother, round, ruction, rush, series, spin, stir, storm, succession, tempest, tumult, turbulence, uproar, whirlwind; CONCEPTS *230,388* —*Ant.* calm, peace

whirl [*n3*] *attempt* bash, crack, fling, go, pop, shot, slap, stab, try, whack*; CONCEPT *87*

whirl [*v*] *spin around* circle, eddy, gyrate, gyre, pirouette, pivot, purl, reel, revolve, roll, rotate, swirl, swoosh, turn, turn around, twirl, twist, wheel, whir; CONCEPT *152* —*Ant.* straighten

whirlpool [*n*] *spinning water* eddy, maelstrom, stir, undercurrent, undertow, vortex, whirl; CONCEPT *514*

whirlwind [*adj*] *very fast* cyclonic, hasty, headlong, hurricane, impetuous, impulsive, lightning, quick, rapid, rash, short, speedy, swift, tornado; CONCEPTS *588,798* —*Ant.* slow

whisk [*v*] *brush quickly; hasten* barrel, bullet, dart, dash, flick, flit, flutter, fly, hurry, race, rush, shoot, speed, sweep, tear, whip, whiz, wipe, zip; CONCEPT *152*

whisper [*n1*] *rumor; information expressed in soft voice* buzz*, confidence, disclosure, divulgence, gossip, hint, hum, hushed tone, innuendo, insinuation, low voice, mumble, murmur, mutter, report, secret, secret message, sigh, sighing, susurration, undertone, word; CONCEPTS *274,278*

whisper [*n2*] *trace, suggestion* breath, dash, fraction, hint, shade, shadow, soupçon, suspicion, tinge, touch, whiff; CONCEPTS *529,673,831* —*Ant.* information

whisper [*v*] *speak softly* breathe, buzz*, confide, gossip, hint, hiss, insinuate, intimate, mumble, murmur, mutter, say softly, say under one's breath*, sibilate, sigh, speak confidentially, spread rumor, susurrate, talk into someone's ear*, talk low, tell, tell a secret; CONCEPTS *60,266* —*Ant.* shout

whistle [*v*] *make sharp, shrill sound* blare, blast, fife, flute, hiss, pipe, shriek, signal, skirl, sound, toot, tootle, trill, warble, wheeze, whine, whiz*; CONCEPTS *65,77*

whit [*n*] *very tiny bit* atom, crumb, dash, drop, fragment, grain, hoot*, iota, jot, little, mite, modicum, particle, piece, pinch, scrap, shred, speck, trace; CONCEPTS *831,835* —*Ant.* lot

white [*adj*] *extremely pale; lacking color* achromatic, achromic, alabaster, ashen, blanched, bleached, bloodless, chalky, clear, fair, frosted, ghastly, hoary, immaculate, ivory, light, milky, neutral, pallid, pasty, pearly, silver, silvery, snowy, transparent, wan, waxen; CONCEPT 618 —Ant. black, dark, dirty

white-collar [adj] non-manual clerical, executive, office, professional, salaried; CONCEPT 348

whiten [v] make or become extremely pale blanch, bleach, blench, chalk, decolor, decolorize, dull, etiolate, fade, frost, grizzle, lighten, pale, silver, turn pale, white, whitewash; CONCEPT 250 —Ant. blacken, darken, dirty

whitewash [v] cover up the truth blanch, camouflage, conceal, exonerate, extenuate, gloss over, launder*, liberate, make light of*, paint, palliate, sugarcoat*, suppress, varnish, veneer, vindicate, white, whiten; CONCEPTS 49,63 —Ant. expose, reveal, tell truth

whittle [v] cut away at; reduce carve, chip, consume, decrease, diminish, eat away, erode, fashion, form, hew, lessen, model, mold, pare, sculpt, shape, shave, trim, undermine, wear away; CONCEPTS 176,184,236,247 —Ant. build, increase

whiz [n] very intelligent person adept, expert, genius, gifted person, marvel, pro*, prodigy, professional, star, virtuoso, wonder; CONCEPT 416 —Ant. ignoramus, imbecile

whiz [v] move quickly by bullet, buzz, dart, flit, fly, hiss, hum, hurry, hurtle, race, speed, swish, whir, whirl, whisk, whoosh*, zip; CONCEPT 150 —Ant. decelerate

whole [adj1] entire, complete accomplished, aggregate, all, choate, completed, concentrated, conclusive, consummate, every, exclusive, exhaustive, fixed, fulfilled, full, full-length, gross, inclusive, in one piece, integral, outright, perfect, plenary, rounded, total, unabbreviated, unabridged, uncut, undivided, unexpurgated, unqualified, utter; CONCEPT 531 —Ant. fractional, incomplete, part, partial

whole [adj2] unbroken, perfect complete, completed, developed, faultless, flawless, good, in good order*, in one piece*, intact, inviolate, mature, mint, plenary, preserved, replete, safe, ship-shape, solid, sound, thorough, together, undamaged, unharmed, unhurt, unimpaired, uninjured, unmarred, unmutilated, unscathed, untouched, without a scratch; CONCEPTS 485,574 —Ant. broken, deficient, imperfect, insufficient, partial

whole [adj3] healthy able-bodied, better, cured, fit, hale, healed, hearty, in fine fettle, in good health, recovered, right, robust, sane, sound, strong, well, wholesome; CONCEPT 314 —Ant. hurt, impaired, sick, unhealthy

whole [n] total made up of parts aggregate, aggregation, all, amount, assemblage, assembly, being, big picture, body, bulk, coherence, collectivity, combination, complex, ensemble, entirety, entity, everything, fullness, gross, hook line and sinker*, integral, jackpot*, linkage, lock stock and barrel*, lot, lump, oneness, organism, organization, piece, quantity, quantum, result, sum, summation, sum total*, supply, system, the works*, totality, unit, unity, whole ball of wax*, whole enchilada*, whole nine yards*, whole shebang*; CONCEPT 432 —Ant. part

wholehearted/whole-hearted [adj] enthusiastic, sincere abiding, ardent, authentic, bona fide, candid, committed, complete, dedicated, determined, devoted, earnest, emphatic, enduring, fervent, frank, genuine, heartfelt, hearty, impassioned, never-failing, passionate, real, serious, steadfast, steady, sure, true, unfaltering, unfeigned, unqualified, unquestioning, unreserved, unstinting, unwavering, warm, zealous; CONCEPTS 542,548,582 —Ant. disinterested, halfhearted, insincere, unenthusiastic

wholesale [adj] all-inclusive broad, bulk, complete, comprehensive, extensive, far-reaching, general, in bulk, indiscriminate, in quantity, in the mass, large-scale, mass, overall, quantitative, sweeping, total, wide-ranging, widespread; CONCEPTS 771,772 —Ant. part, partial, retail

wholesome [adj] healthy, decent all there, beneficial, clean, edifying, ethical, exemplary, fit, good, hale, healthful, health-giving, helpful, honorable, hygienic, in fine feather*, innocent, in the pink*, invigorating, moral, nice, normal, nourishing, nutritious, nutritive, pure, respectable, restorative, right, righteous, safe, salubrious, salutary, sane, sanitary, sound, strengthening, together, virtuous, well, worthy; CONCEPTS 314,462,537,545 —Ant. bad, impure, indecent, unhealthy, unwholesome

wholly [adv1] completely, entirely all, all in all*, all the way*, altogether, comprehensively, from A to Z*, fully, heart and soul*, in every respect*, in toto, one-hundred percent*, outright, perfectly, quite, roundly, thoroughly, top to bottom*, totally, utterly, well; CONCEPTS 531,772 —Ant. incompletely, partially, partly

wholly [adv2] exclusively individually, just, only, purely, solely, specifically, without exception; CONCEPT 557 —Ant. inclusively

whoop [n/v] hurrah bellow, boo, cheer, cry, cry out, holler, hoot, howl, jeer, scream, shout, shriek, squawk, yell; CONCEPT 77

whopping [adj] enormous big, colossal, extraordinary, gargantuan, giant, gigantic, great, huge, immense, large, mammoth, massive, mighty, monstrous, mountainous, prodigious, tremendous; CONCEPTS 773,781 —Ant. little, small, teeny, tiny

whore [n] prostitute call girl, escort, fallen woman, harlot, hooker*, hustler, lady of the evening*, pro*, slut, streetwalker, strumpet, tramp, working girl*; CONCEPT 412

whorehouse [n] brothel bagnio, bawdy house*, bordello, call house*, cathouse*, den of iniquity*, house of assignation, house of ill fame*, house of ill repute, house of prostitution, house with red doors*, massage parlor, red-light district; CONCEPT 449

whorl [n] spiral coil, corkscrew, curl, eddy, helix, swirl, twirl, twist, vortex, whirlpool; CONCEPT 436

wicked [adj1] corrupt, bad abandoned, abominable, amoral, arch, atrocious, bad news*, base, contemptible, debased, degenerate, depraved, devilish, dissolute, egregious, evil, fiendish, flagitious, foul, gross, guilty, heartless, heinous, immoral, impious, impish, incorrigible, indecent, iniquitous, irreligious, low-down, mean, mischievous, nasty, naughty, nefarious, profane, reprobate, rotten, scandalous, shameful, shameless, sinful, unethical, unprincipled, unrighteous, vicious, vile, villainous, wayward, worthless; CONCEPTS 401,545 —Ant. decent, good, moral, nice

wicked [adj2] *destructive, troublesome* acute, agonizing, awful, barbarous, bothersome; chancy, crashing, dangerous, difficult, distressing, dreadful, fearful, fierce, galling, harmful, hazardous, injurious, intense, mean, mighty, offensive, outrageous, painful, perilous, pesky, risky, severe, terrible, treacherous, troublous, trying, ugly, uncivilized, unconscionable, ungodly, unhealthy, unholy, unpleasant, unsound, vexatious; CONCEPTS 537,565,571 —*Ant.* aiding, assisting, helpful, useful, worthwhile

wicked [adj3] *expert* able, adept, adroit, au fait, capable, clever, competent, deft, good, masterly, mighty, outstanding, powerful, pretty, qualified, skillful, strong; CONCEPT 527 —*Ant.* amateur

wide [adj1] *expansive, roomy* advanced, all-inclusive, ample, baggy, broad, capacious, catholic, commodious, comprehensive, deep, dilated, distended, encyclopedic, expanded, extensive, far-ranging, far-reaching, full, general, immense, inclusive, large, large-scale, liberal, loose, open, outspread, outstretched, progressive, radical, scopic, spacious, splay, squat, sweeping, tolerant, universal, vast, voluminous; CONCEPTS 772,773,796 —*Ant.* cramped, narrow, restricted

wide [adj2] *off-course* astray, away, distant, far, far-off, inaccurate, off, off-target, off the mark, remote; CONCEPTS 581,583 —*Ant.* on-course, straight

wide-awake [adj] *alert* active, all ears*, attentive, bright, bright-eyed and bushy-tailed*, fast on the draw*, heads up*, intelligent, lively, on guard*, on one's toes*, on the ball*, on the job*, on the lookout*, psyched up*, quick, ready, sharp, spirited, vigilant, watchful, wired*; CONCEPTS 402,403

widen [v] *open up* add to, augment, broaden, dilate, distend, enlarge, expand, extend, grow, grow larger, increase, multiply, open, open out, open wide, ream, spread, spread out, stretch, swell, unfold; CONCEPTS 236,245,780 —*Ant.* cramp, narrow, restrict

widespread [adj] *extensive* across the board*, all over the place*, boundless, broad, common, comprehensive, current, diffuse, epidemic, far-flung, far-reaching, general, on a large scale, outspread, overall, pandemic, pervasive, popular, prevailing, prevalent, public, rampant, regnant, rife, ruling, sweeping, universal, unlimited, unrestricted, wall-to-wall*, wholesale; CONCEPTS 530,536,772 —*Ant.* concentrated, limited, local, narrow

widget [n] *gadget* apparatus, appliance, contraption, contrivance, device, doodad*, doohickey*, gizmo*, invention, object, thing*, thingamabob*, thingamajig*, tool, whatchamacallit*; CONCEPTS 463,499

width [n] *breadth, wideness of some amount* amplitude, area, broadness, compass, cross measure, diameter, distance across, expanse, extent, girth, measure, range, reach, scope, span, squatness, stretch, thickness; CONCEPTS 760,788,792 —*Ant.* height, tallness

wield [v] *control, use* apply, brandish, command, conduct, employ, exercise, exert, flourish, handle, have, have at one's disposal, hold, maintain, make use of, manage, maneuver, manipulate, operate, ply, possess, put to use, shake, swing, throw, utilize, wave, work; CONCEPTS 94,147,225

wife [n] *married woman* bride, companion, consort, helpmate, mate, monogamist, other half*, partner, roommate, spouse; CONCEPTS 414,415 —*Ant.* husband

wig [n] *hairpiece* false hair, hair extension, hair implant, hair weaving, periwig, peruke, postiche, rug*, toupee; CONCEPT 392

wiggle [n/v] *shake back and forth* jerk, jiggle, shimmy, squirm, twist, twitch, wag, waggle, wave, worm, wriggle, writhe, zigzag; CONCEPTS 80,150,152

wild [adj1] *untamed* agrarian, barbarian, barbaric, barbarous, dense, desert, deserted, desolate, escaped, feral, ferocious, fierce, free, indigenous, lush, luxuriant, native, natural, neglected, overgrown, overrun, primitive, rampant, rude, savage, unbroken, uncivilized, uncultivated, undomesticated, uninhabited, untouched, vicious, waste; CONCEPTS 406,583 —*Ant.* civilized, controlled, delicate, gentle, manageable, tame

wild [adj2] *disorderly, rowdy* avid, berserk, boisterous, chaotic, crazed, crazy, eager, enthusiastic, extravagant, flighty, foolhardy, foolish, giddy, hysterical, impetuous, impracticable, imprudent, incautious, irrational, lawless, licentious, mad, madcap, noisy, nuts, outrageous, preposterous, profligate, rabid, rash, raving, reckless, riotous, rough, self-willed, turbulent, unbridled, uncontrolled, undisciplined, unfettered, ungovernable, unmanageable, unrestrained, unruly, uproarious, violent, wayward; CONCEPT 401 —*Ant.* behaved, controllable, manageable, orderly

wild [adj3] *intense, stormy* blustering, blustery, choppy, disturbed, furious, howling, inclement, raging, rough, storming, tempestuous, turbulent, violent; CONCEPTS 525,569 —*Ant.* calm, mild, moderate

wilderness/wilds [n] *uninhabited area* back country, back of beyond*, badland, barrens, boondocks, bush, desert, forest, hinterland, jungle, middle of nowhere*, outback, primeval forest, sticks*, waste, wasteland, wild; CONCEPT 517 —*Ant.* city, metropolis

wile [n] *cunning* angle, artfulness, artifice, cheating, chicane, chicanery, con*, contrivance, craft, craftiness, deceit, deception, device, dishonesty, dissimulation, dodge, feint, flimflam*, fraud, gambit, game, gimmick, guile, hoax, horseplay, imposition, little game*, lure, maneuver, monkey business*, monkeyshines*, plot, ploy, racket*, ruse, scam*, scheming, setup*, shenanigans*, skullduggery*, slant, slyness, stratagem, stunt, subterfuge, switch, trick, trickery, twist; CONCEPTS 59,63 —*Ant.* naivety, stupidity

will [n1] *personal choice* aim, appetite, attitude, character, conviction, craving, decision, decisiveness, decree, design, desire, determination, discipline, discretion, disposition, fancy, feeling, hankering, heart's desire*, inclination, intention, liking, longing, mind, option, passion, pining, pleasure, power, preference, prerogative, purpose, resolution, resolve, self-control, self-discipline, self-restraint, temperament, urge, velleity, volition, willfulness, willpower, wish, wishes, yearning; CONCEPTS *20,411,659*

will [n2] *last wishes; command* bequest, bestowal, declaration, decree, device, directions, dispensation, disposition, estate, heritage, inheritance, insistence, instructions, legacy, order, property, testament; CONCEPT *318*

will [v1] *cause* authorize, bid, bring about, command, decide on, decree, demand, determine, direct, effect, enjoin, exert, insist, intend, ordain, order, request, resolve; CONCEPT *242*

will [v2] *choose* be inclined, crave, desire, elect, have a mind to*, incline, like, opt, please, prefer, see fit*, want, wish; CONCEPT *20* —*Ant.* neglect, pass

will [v3] *give, bequeath to another* bequest, confer, cut off, devise, disherit, disinherit, leave, legate, pass on, probate, transfer; CONCEPTS *108,317* —*Ant.* keep, receive

willful [adj1] *stubborn, obstinate* adamant, bullheaded, contumacious, determined, dogged, fractious, froward, headstrong, inflexible, intractable, intransigent, mulish, obdurate, persistent, pertinacious, perverse, pigheaded, refractory, resolved, self-willed, stiff-necked, uncompromising, unyielding; CONCEPTS *401, 542* —*Ant.* flexible, willing, yielding

willful [adj2] *voluntary* conscious, contemplated, deliberate, designed, intended, intentional, planned, premeditated, purposeful, studied, unforced, volitional, willed, willing, witting; CONCEPTS *401,535* —*Ant.* involuntary, unwilling

willing [adj] *agreeable, ready* accommodating, active, amenable, cheerful, compliant, consenting, content, deliberate, desirous, disposed, eager, energetic, enthusiastic, fair, favorable, feeling, forward, game, go along with, happy, in accord with, inclined, in favor, intentional, in the mood, like-minded, obedient, one, pleased, predisposed, prepared, prompt, prone, reliable, responsible, tractable, unasked, unbidden, unforced, voluntary, well-disposed, willful, witting, zealous; CONCEPTS *401,403,576* —*Ant.* disagreeable, unprepared, unwilling

willowy [adj] *graceful, slender* adroit, agile, dainty, delicate, elastic, elegant, flowing, limber, lithe, lithesome, nimble, pliant, shapely, skinny, springy, svelte, thin, trim; CONCEPTS *579,584,589*

willpower [n] *personal determination* discipline, drive, firmness, fixity, force, grit, resolution, resolve, self-control, self-discipline, self-government, self-restraint, single-mindedness, strength, will; CONCEPT *411*

wilt [v] *sag, fail* become limp, break down, cave in, collapse, diminish, droop, drop, dry up, dwindle, ebb, fade, faint, flag, give out, languish, melt, mummify, shrivel, sink, succumb, wane, waste, waste away, weaken, wither, wizen; CONCEPTS *181,427,469,699* —*Ant.* bloom, rise

wily [adj] *crafty, clever* arch, artful, astute, cagey, crazy like a fox*, crooked, cunning, deceitful, deceptive, deep, designing, foxy, greasy*, guileful, insidious, intriguing, knowing, sagacious, scheming, sharp, shifty, shrewd, slick*, slippery*, sly, smooth, sneaky, streetwise, tricky, underhanded; CONCEPTS *401,545*

wimp [n] *weakling* baby, caitiff, chicken*, chicken heart*, chicken liver*, coward, cream puff*, crybaby, daisy*, featherweight*, fraidy-cat*, jellyfish*, lily liver, loser, milksop, momma's boy*, namby-pamby, pansy, pantywaist*, puppy*, pushover, scaredy-cat*, schlemiel*, sissy, wuss*, wussy*, yellow belly*; CONCEPTS *412,423*

win [n] *victory* accomplishment, achievement, conquest, gain, gold*, gold star*, kill*, killing*, pay dirt*, score, slam, success, sweep, triumph*; CONCEPTS *95,141,832* —*Ant.* failure, forfeit, loss

win [v1] *finish first; succeed* achieve, beat, be first, be victorious, carry the day*, come in first, conquer, edge, finish in front*, finish off, gain, gain victory, overcome, overwhelm, prevail, run circles around*, shut out*, sink*, take the prize, triumph, upset, walk away with*, walk off with*; CONCEPTS *95,141,363* —*Ant.* fail, forfeit, lose

win [v2] *achieve, obtain* accomplish, acquire, annex, approach, attain, bag*, bring in, catch, collect, come away with*, derive, earn, effect, gain, get, harvest, have, make, net, pick up, procure, rack up*, reach, realize, receive, score, secure; CONCEPTS *120,706* —*Ant.* fail

win/win over [v3] *influence, persuade* allure, argue into, attract, bring around, carry, charm, convert, convince, disarm, draw, get, induce, overcome, prevail upon, prompt, slay, sway, talk into, wow*; CONCEPTS *11,68* —*Ant.* disenchant, turn off

wince [v] *draw back* back off, blanch, blench, cower, cringe, dodge, duck, flinch, grimace, jib, make a face*, quail, recoil, shrink, shy, start, swerve, turn; CONCEPTS *154,185*

wind [n1] *air currents* air, blast, blow, breath, breeze, chinook, cyclone, draft, draught, flurry, flutter, gale, gust, mistral, puff, tempest, typhoon, wafting, whiff, whirlwind, whisk, zephyr; CONCEPT *524*

wind [n2] *warning, report* babble, clue, cue, gossip, hint, hot air*, idle talk, inkling, intimation, notice, rumor, suggestion, talk, tidings, whisper; CONCEPT *278*

wind [v] *bend, turn* coil, convolute, corkscrew, cover, crook, curl, curve, deviate, distort, encircle, enclose, entwine, envelop, fold, furl, loop, meander, ramble, reel, roll, screw, slither, snake, spiral, swerve, twine, twist, weave, wrap, wreathe, wriggle, zigzag; CONCEPTS *201,738* —*Ant.* straighten

windbag [n] *bigmouth, chatterer* bag of wind*, big talker*, blabberer, blowhard*, boaster, braggart, bragger, gasbag*, gascon*, jabberer, know-it-all, motor-mouth*; CONCEPTS *412,423*

winded [adj] *out of breath* breathless, gasping, huffing and puffing*, panting, puffing; CONCEPT *163*

windfall [n] *jackpot, profit* bonanza, bonus, find, fortune, gift from the gods*, godsend, gravy*, lucky find, money from heaven*, pennies from heaven*, stroke of luck*; CONCEPTS *337,679*

winding [adj] *bending, turning* ambiguous, anfractuous, circuitous, convoluted, crooked, curving, devious, flexuous, gyrating, indirect, intricate, involved, labyrinthine, mazy, meandering, roundabout, serpentine, sinuous, snaky, spiraling, tortuous, twisting, wriggly, zigzag; CONCEPT 581 —Ant. straight, unbent

wind up [v] finish be through with, bring to a close, clean up*, close, close down, come to the end, complete, conclude, determine, do, end, end up*, finalize, finish up, halt, liquidate, settle, terminate, tie up loose ends*, wrap up*; CONCEPT 234 —Ant. begin, commence, open, start

windy [adj1] breezy airy, blowing, blowy, blustering, blustery, boisterous, brisk, drafty, fresh, gusty, raw, squally, stormy, tempestuous, wild, windswept; CONCEPT 525 —Ant. calm

windy [adj2] talkative; boastful bombastic, diffuse, empty, garrulous, inflated, lengthy, long-winded, loquacious, meandering, palaverous, pompous, prolix, rambling, redundant, turgid, verbose, wordy; CONCEPT 267 —Ant. uncommunicative, unresponsive

wing [n1] organ, device of flight aileron, airfoil, appendage, feather, pennon, pinion; CONCEPTS 399,502

wing [n2] section; extension addition, adjunct, annex, arm, block, branch, bulge, circle, clique, coterie, detachment, division, ell, expansion, faction, group, part, projection, prolongation, protrusion, protuberance, segment, set, side, unit; CONCEPTS 440,441,824,835 —Ant. base, headquarters

wing it [v] improvise ad-lib, concoct, devise, do offhand, do off the top of your head*, fake it, improv*, invent, make do*, make up, play it by ear*, speak off the cuff*, throw together*; CONCEPTS 173,266

wink [n1/v] flutter, flick bat, blink, flash, gleam, glimmer, glitter, nictate, nictitate, sparkle, squinch, squint, twinkle; CONCEPTS 185,624

wink [n2] moment flash*, instant, jiffy*, minute, second, shake*, split second*, twinkle*, twinkling*; CONCEPTS 808,821

winner [n] someone or something that succeeds champ, champion, conquering hero, conqueror, first, hero, medalist, medalwinner, number one*, prizewinner, title-holder, top dog*, vanquisher, victor; CONCEPTS 366,416 —Ant. failure, loser

winning/winsome [adj1] attractive, charming acceptable, adorable, agreeable, alluring, amiable, bewitching, captivating, cute, delectable, delightful, disarming, enchanting, endearing, engaging, fascinating, fetching, gratifying, lovable, lovely, pleasing, prepossessing, sweet, taking; CONCEPTS 401,404 —Ant. disenchanting, ugly, unappealing, unattractive

winning [adj2] triumphant champion, conquering, leading, successful, victorious; CONCEPTS 528,632 —Ant. failing, forfeiting, losing

wino [n] drunk alcoholic, boozer*, bum*, carouser*, dipsomaniac, drinker, drunkard, guzzler*, hobo, inebriate, lush*, sot*, sponge*; CONCEPT 423

winsome [adj] charming absorbing, alluring, appealing, attractive, captivating, charismatic, cute, dainty, delicate, delightful, desirable, elegant, enamoring, engaging, enthralling, eye-catching, fascinating, glamorous, inviting, irresistible, lovable, pleasant, pleasing, pretty, rapturous, ravishing, seducing, seductive, sweet, tantalizing, titillating, winning; CONCEPT 404

winter [n] cold season of the year chill, cold, frost, Jack Frost*, wintertide, wintertime; CONCEPT 814

wintry [adj] cold, snowy biting, bleak, brumal, chilly, cutting, desolate, dismal, freezing, frigid, frosty, frozen, harsh, hibernal, hiemal, icebox*, icy, raw, snappy, three-dog night*; CONCEPTS 525,605 —Ant. hot, summery

wipe [v] brush, swab clean, clean off, clear, dry, dust, erase, mop, obliterate, remove, rub, sponge, take away, towel, wash; CONCEPT 165

wipeout [n] fall collapse, crash, destruction, dive, downfall, drop, spill, tumble, yard sale*; CONCEPTS 116,230,674,699

wipe out [v] destroy; get rid of abate, abolish, annihilate, black out, blot out, cancel, decimate, delete, efface, eliminate, eradicate, erase, expunge, exterminate, extinguish, extirpate, kill, massacre, obliterate, remove, root out, slaughter, slay, uproot, X-out*; CONCEPT 252 —Ant. build, create

wiry [adj] thin and strong agile, athletic, bristly, fibrous, lean, light, limber, muscular, ropy, sinewy, stiff, strapping, stringy, supple, tough; CONCEPTS 490,491 —Ant. small, tiny

wisdom [n] insight, common sense acumen, astuteness, balance, brains*, caution, circumspection, clear thinking, comprehension, discernment, discrimination, enlightenment, erudition, experience, foresight, good judgment, gumption*, horse sense*, information, intelligence, judgment, judiciousness, knowledge, learning, pansophy, penetration, perspicacity, poise, practicality, prudence, reason, sagacity, sageness, sanity, sapience, savoir faire, savvy*, shrewdness, solidity, sophistication, stability, understanding; CONCEPT 409 —Ant. ignorance, stupidity

wise [adj] intelligent, reasonable astute, aware, calculating, careful, clever, cogitative, contemplative, crafty, cunning, discerning, discreet, educated, enlightened, erudite, experienced, foresighted, grasping, informed, insightful, intuitive, judicious, keen, knowing, knowledgeable, perceptive, perspicacious, politic, prudent, rational, reflective, sagacious, sage, sane, sapient, scholarly, sensible, sensing, sharp, shrewd, smart, sophic, sound, tactful, taught, thoughtful, understanding, wary, well-informed, witty; CONCEPT 402 —Ant. foolish, ignorant, stupid, unintelligent, unreasonable, unwise

wisecrack [n] joke antic, caper, clowning, dig, escapade, farce, frolic, gag, lark, laugh, mischief, monkeyshine*, one-liner*, parody, prank, put-on, quip, remark, retort, rib, shenanigan*, smart crack*, stunt, trick, witticism, yarn, zinger*; CONCEPT 273

wise guy [n] smart-aleck; gangster bigmouth*, criminal, crook, hood, hoodlum, know-it-all*, Mafioso*, member of the family, mobster, smart ass*, smarty-pants*, wiseacre, wiseass, wisenheimer; CONCEPT 412

wish [n] desire ambition, aspiration, choice, disposition, hankering, hope, hunger, inclination, intention, invocation, itch, liking, longing, pleasure, prayer, preference, request, thirst, urge, want, whim, will, yearning, yen; CONCEPTS 20,709 —Ant. dislike, hate, hatred

wish [v] *desire* aspire, beg, choose, command, covet, crave, desiderate, elect, entreat, envy, expect, fancy, hanker*, hope, hunger, invoke, itch, like, long, look forward to*, need, order, please, pray for, solicit, spoil for*, thirst, want, will, yearn, yen; CONCEPT 20 —*Ant.* dislike, hate

wishful [adj] *desirous* acquisitive, ambitious, aspiring, craving, daydreaming, desiring, greedy, hankering, hopeful, itchy*, keen, longful, longing, lustful, wishing, yearning; CONCEPTS 403,529

wishy-washy [adj] *bland, dull* banal, characterless, cowardly, enervated, feeble, flat, flavorless, indecisive, ineffective, ineffectual, insipid, irresolute, jejune, languid, listless, mediocre, namby-pamby*, sapless, spiritless, tasteless, thin, vacillating, vapid, watered-down, watery, wavering, weak, weak-kneed*; CONCEPT 404 —*Ant.* dynamic, exciting, interesting, lively

wisp [n] *strand* bit, lock, piece, shock, shred, snippet, string, thread, tuft, twist; CONCEPTS 392,831

wistful [adj] *daydreaming, longing* contemplative, desirous, disconsolate, dreaming, dreamy, forlorn, hopeless, meditative, melancholy, mournful, musing, nostalgic, pensive, plaintive, reflective, sad, thoughtful, wishful, yearning; CONCEPT 403 —*Ant.* uncaring

wit [n1] *humor* aphorism, badinage, banter, bon mot, burlesque, drollery, facetiousness, fun, gag, jest, jocularity, joke, lark, levity, pleasantry, practical joke, prank, pun, quip, raillery, repartee, sally, satire, trick, whimsicality, wisecrack, wittiness, wordplay; CONCEPTS 59, 273,411 —*Ant.* seriousness

wit [n2] *person who is very funny* a million laughs*, banterer, card, comedian, comic, cutup*, epigrammatist, farceur, funster, gag person, humorist, jester, joker, jokesmith, jokester, life of the party*, madcap, punster, quipster, trickster, wag, wisecracker; CONCEPTS 352,416

witch [n] *person who casts spells over others* conjurer, enchanter, magician, necromancer, occultist, sorcerer; CONCEPTS 361,412,415

witchcraft [n] *spell-casting, magic* abracadabra*, bewitchment, black art, black magic, charisma, conjuring, divination, enchantment, hocus-pocus*, hoodoo*, incantation, jinx, magnetism, mumbo jumbo*, necromancy, occult, occultism, sorcery, spell, thaumaturgy, voodoo, voodooism, whammy*, witchery, witching; CONCEPTS 367,370,689

witch doctor [n] *shaman* healer, medicine man, priest, sorcerer, wizard; CONCEPT 361

withdraw [v1] *remove something or someone from situation* abjure, absent oneself, back out, bail out, blow, book, bow out, check out, depart, detach, disengage, draw away, draw back, drop out, ease out, eliminate, exfiltrate, exit, extract, fall back, get away, get lost, get off, give ground, give way, go, keep aloof, keep apart, leave, make oneself scarce*, phase out, pull back, pull out, quail, quit, recede, recoil, retire, retreat, run along, secede, seclude oneself, shrink, switch, take a hike*, take away, take leave, take off, take out, vacate; CONCEPTS 195,211 —*Ant.* remain, stay

withdraw [v2] *retract; declare void* abjure, abolish, abrogate, annul, ban, bar, call off, disavow, disclaim, dissolve, forswear, invalidate, nullify, quash, recall, recant, renege, renig, repress, repudiate, rescind, retire, reverse, revoke, stamp out, suppress, take back, unsay; CONCEPTS 50,88,121,697 —*Ant.* advance, allow, permit

withdrawal [n] *removal; retraction* abandonment, abdication, abjuration, alienation, departure, disavowal, disclaimer, disengagement, egress, egression, exit, exiting, exodus, extraction, marooning, palinode, recall, recantation, relinquishment, repudiation, rescission, resignation, retirement, retreat, revocation, revulsion, secession; CONCEPTS 195,211,685 —*Ant.* remainder, stay

withdrawn [adj1] *unsociable* aloof, aseptic, casual, cool, detached, disinterested, distant, incurious, indifferent, introverted, nongregarious, offish, quiet, recluse, reclusive, remote, reserved, restrained, retired, retiring, retreated, shrinking, shy, silent, solitary, standoffish, taciturn, timorous, uncommunicative, uncompanionable, unconcerned, uncurious, undemonstrative, unforthcoming, uninterested; CONCEPT 401 —*Ant.* extroverted, friendly, outgoing, sociable

withdrawn [adj2] *hidden, remote* cloistered, departed, isolated, out-of-the-way, private, recluse, removed, retreated, secluded, solitary, taken out; CONCEPT 583 —*Ant.* known, seen, visible

wither [v] *droop, decline* atrophy, become stale, blast, blight, collapse, constrict, contract, decay, deflate, desiccate, deteriorate, die, disintegrate, dry, dry up, fade, fold, languish, perish, shrink, shrivel, wane, waste, waste away, wilt, wizen; CONCEPTS 427,698 —*Ant.* bloom, grow

withhold [v] *keep back* abstain, bridle, check, clam up*, conceal, constrain, curb, deduct, deny, detain, disallow, dummy up*, hide, hold, hold back, hold down, hold out, hold out on, inhibit, keep, keep secret, keep to oneself*, keep under one's hat*, keep under wraps*, kill, refrain, refuse, repress, reserve, resist, restrain, retain, sit on, spike, stop oneself, suppress; CONCEPTS 35,121,188 —*Ant.* let go, release

within [adv] *inside* in, in a period, indoors, inner, in reach, interior, inward, not beyond, not outside, not over; CONCEPTS 586,772 —*Ant.* outside

with it [adj] *cognizant; stylish* alive, apprehensive, au courant, awake, aware, chic, conscious, cool*, familiar, groovy*, hep to*, hip to*, in, in fashion, informed, in on, in the know, in vogue, knowing, knowledgeable, latest, mod*, now*, observant, on to*, perceptive, plugged in, savvy, switched on*, trendy, tuned in*, turned on*, up on*, versed, wise to*; CONCEPTS 402,579,589

without [adv] *outside* after, beyond, externally, left out, on the outside, out, outdoors, out-of-doors, outwardly, past; CONCEPTS 586,772 —*Ant.* inside

withstand [v] *endure, bear* brace, brave, buck, combat, confront, contest, cope, cross, defy, dispute, duel, face, fight, fly in the face of*, grapple with, hang on*, hang tough*, hold off*,

hold one's ground*, hold out*, oppose, prevail
against, put up struggle*, put up with*, remain
firm, repel, resist, ride out*, sit and take it*,
stand, stand fast*, stand firm*, stand one's
ground*, stand up against*, stand up to*,
stick*, stick fast*, suffer, take, take it*, take on,
thwart, tolerate, traverse, violate, weather, win
out; CONCEPTS 23,96 —*Ant.* surrender, yield

witless [adj] foolish absurd, asinine, birdbrained*, brainless, cockamamy*, crazy,
daffy*, doltish*, dotty*, dumb, feebleminded*,
half-baked*, half-witted*, harebrained*, idiotic,
ill-advised, irrational, jerky*, kooky*, loony*,
ludicrous, lunatic, mad, mindless, moronic,
nonsensical, nutty*, ridiculous, senseless, silly,
stupid, unintelligent, unwise, wacky*, zany*;
CONCEPTS 401,542,544

witness [n] person who observes an event
attestant, attestor, beholder, bystander,
corroborator, deponent, eyewitness, gawker,
looker-on, observer, onlooker, proof, rubber-
necker*, signatory, signer, spectator, testifier,
testimony, viewer, watcher; CONCEPTS 355,423
—*Ant.* participant

witness [vI] observe attend, be a witness,
behold, be on hand*, be on the scene*, be
present, eyeball*, flash on*, get a load of*,
look on, mark, note, notice, perceive, pick up
on, pipe*, read, see, sight, spot, spy, take in,
view, watch; CONCEPT 626 —*Ant.* participate

witness [v2] testify; authenticate affirm,
announce, argue, attest, bear out, bear witness,
be a witness, bespeak, betoken, certify, confirm, corroborate, countersign, depone, depose,
endorse, give evidence, give testimony, indicate, say under oath, sign, stand for, subscribe,
vouch for; CONCEPTS 49,50,88,317 —*Ant.*
deny, refute

witty [adj] funny and clever amusing, bright,
brilliant, campy*, crazy*, diverting, droll,
entertaining, epigrammatic, facetious, fanciful,
gay, humorous, ingenious, intelligent, jocose,
jocular, joshing, keen, lively, original, penetrating, piercing, piquant, quick-witted, ridiculous,
scintillating, screaming*, slapstick, sparkling,
waggish, whimsical; CONCEPTS 267,542 —*Ant.*
serious, unamusing, unfunny

wit/wits [n3] judgment, intelligence acumen,
acuteness, astucity, astuteness, awareness,
balance, brainpower, brains*, cleverness,
common sense, comprehension, depth of
perception, discernment, discrimination,
esprit, grasp, ingenuity, insight, keenness,
lucidity, marbles*, mentality, mind, perception,
perspicacity, practicality, prudence, rationality,
reason, sagaciousness, sagacity, sageness,
saneness, sanity, sapience, sense, shrewdness,
soundness, understanding, wisdom; CONCEPT
409 —*Ant.* ignorance, stupidity

wizard [n1] person who can perform magic
astrologer, augurer, clairvoyant, conjurer,
diviner, enchanter, fortuneteller, hypnotist, magician, magus, medium, necromancer, occultist,
palmist, seer, shaman, soothsayer, sorcerer,
thaumaturge, warlock, witch; CONCEPT 361

wizard [n2] person who is highly skilled ace*,
adept, artist, authority, crackerjack*, expert,
genius, hot shot*, pro*, prodigy, professional,
proficient, shark*, star, virtuoso, whiz*, whiz

kid*, wiz*; CONCEPTS 348,423 —*Ant.* amateur,
rookie

wizened [adj] dried, shriveled up diminished,
gnarled, lean, macerated, mummified, old,
reduced, shrunk, shrunken, wilted, withered,
worn, wrinkled; CONCEPTS 485,603 —*Ant.*
moist, smooth, unwrinkled

wobble [†] stagger, quake be unsteady, careen,
falter, flounder, lurch, oscillate, quiver, reel,
rock, roll, seesaw, shake, shimmy, stumble,
sway, swing, teeter, totter, tremble, vacillate,
vibrate, waver, weave, wiggle; CONCEPTS
150,152

wobbly [adj] shaky fluctuant, insecure,
precarious, rattletrap, rickety, rocky, teetering,
tottering, unbalanced, uneven, unsafe, unstable,
unsteady, unsure, vacillating, wavering, wavy,
weak, wiggling; CONCEPT 488 —*Ant.* stable,
steady, unshaky

woe [n] suffering adversity, affliction, agony,
anguish, bemoaning, blues*, burden, calamity,
care, cataclysm, catastrophe, curse, dejection,
deploring, depression, disaster, distress,
dole, drag, gloom, grief, grieving, hardship,
headache*, heartache*, heartbreak, lamentation,
melancholy, misadventure, misery, misfortune,
pain, rain*, regret, rue, sadness, sorrow,
tragedy, trial, tribulation, trouble, unhappiness,
wretchedness; CONCEPTS 410,532,690,728
—*Ant.* happiness, joy

woebegone [adj] depressed, troubled black,
bleak, blue*, bummed out*, chapfallen,
cheerless, crestfallen, dejected, despondent,
disconsolate, dismal, dispirited, doleful, down,
downcast, downhearted, down-in-the-mouth*,
dreary, forlorn, gloomy, grief-stricken, grim,
hangdog*, hurting, in pain*, long-faced*, low,
lugubrious, melancholy, miserable, mournful,
sad, shot down*, sorrowful, unhappy, woeful,
wretched; CONCEPT 403 —*Ant.* enthused,
excited, happy, untroubled

woeful [adj] terrible, sad afflicted, agonized,
anguished, appalling, awful, bad, calamitous,
catastrophic, cruel, deplorable, disappointing,
disastrous, disconsolate, disgraceful, distressing, doleful, dreadful, feeble, gloomy, grieving,
grievous, grim, heartbreaking, heartrending,
heartsick, hopeless, inadequate, lamentable,
lousy*, mean, miserable, mournful, paltry, pathetic, piteous, pitiable, pitiful, plaintive, poor,
racked, rotten, shocking, sorrowful, sorry, tortured, tragic, unfortunate, unhappy, wretched;
CONCEPTS 548,571 —*Ant.* glad, happy, joyful

wolf [v] consume sloppily and fast bolt, cram,
devour, gobble, gorge, gulp, guzzle, ingurgitate,
pack, slop, slosh, stuff, swallow; CONCEPT 169
—*Ant.* nibble

woman [n] female human aunt, daughter,
gentlewoman, girl, girlfriend, grandmother,
matron, mother, Ms./Miss/Mrs., niece, she,
spouse, wife; CONCEPTS 414,415 —*Ant.* man

womanizer [n] philanderer Casanova,
Don Juan, gigolo, heartbreaker, ladies' man,
lady-killer, lecher, libertine, lothario, lover,
lover-boy*, rake, Romeo, seducer, skirt chaser,
stud*, wolf*; CONCEPT 423

womanly [adj] feminine female, girlish, ladylike, maidenly, matronly, motherly, womanish;
CONCEPTS 371,372,408,648

wonder [n1] *amazement* admiration, astonishment, awe, bewilderment, concern, confusion, consternation, curiosity, doubt, fascination, fear, incredulity, jar, jolt, marveling, perplexity, perturbation, puzzlement, reverence, shock, skepticism, start, stupefaction, stupor, surprise, suspicion, uncertainty, wondering, wonderment; CONCEPTS 410,532,690 —*Ant.* expectation

wonder [n2] *something that is amazing* act of God*, curiosity, cynosure, freak, marvel, miracle, nonpareil, oddity, phenomenon, portent, prodigy, rara avis, rarity, sensation, sight, spectacle, stunner*, wonderment; CONCEPTS 529,687

wonder [v1] *doubt; ponder* ask oneself, be curious, be inquisitive, conjecture, disbelieve, inquire, meditate, puzzle, query, question, speculate, think; CONCEPTS 17,21 —*Ant.* believe, know

wonder [v2] *be amazed* admire, be astonished, be awestruck, be confounded, be dumbstruck, be fascinated, be flabbergasted, be startled, be taken aback, boggle, gape, gawk, look aghast, marvel, stare; CONCEPT 34 —*Ant.* anticipate, expect

wonderful [adj] *great, extraordinary* admirable, amazing, astonishing, astounding, awe-inspiring, awesome, brilliant, cool*, divine*, dynamite*, enjoyable, excellent, fabulous, fantastic, fine, groovy*, incredible, magnificent, marvelous, miraculous, outstanding, peachy*, phenomenal, pleasant, pleasing, prime, remarkable, sensational, something else*, staggering, startling, strange, stupendous, super, superb, surprising, swell, terrific, too much*, tremendous, unheard-of, wondrous; CONCEPTS 529,574 —*Ant.* bad, lousy, poor, rotten

wonderment [n] *astonishment* amazement, astoundment, awe, bewilderment, curiosity, fascination, marvel, shock, stunner, surprise, wonder; CONCEPTS 230,410

wonk [n] *excessive studier* bookworm, brain*, dweeb*, geek*, greasy grind*, grind*, grub*, nerd, poindexter, swotter*; CONCEPT 350

wont [adj] *in the habit of* accustomed, given, inclined, used, used to; CONCEPT 547

woo [v] *seek as romantic partner* address, aim for, beg, bill and coo*, butter up*, caress, charm, chase, court, cultivate, curry favor*, date, entreat, go steady, importune, keep company, make advances, make love, press one's suit with*, propose, pursue, run after, rush, seek in marriage*, seek the hand of*, set one's cap for*, solicit, spark*, spoon*; CONCEPTS 297,375,384 —*Ant.* ignore

wooden [adj1] *made of timber* board, clapboard, frame, ligneous, log, peg, plant, slab, timber, timbered, woody; CONCEPT 485

wooden [adj2] *stiff, inflexible* awkward, bumbling, clumsy, gauche, gawky, graceless, heavy, heavy-handed, inelegant, inept, maladroit, obstinate, ponderous, rigid, stilted, unbending, ungainly, ungraceful, unhandy, unyielding, weighty; CONCEPTS 488,542 —*Ant.* bending, flexible, pliable

wood/woods [n] *forest* copse, grove, lumber, thicket, timber, timberland, trees, weald, woodland; CONCEPTS 430,509,517

woozy [adj] *dizzy* befuddled, bemused, bewildered, confused, dazed, dazzled, dumbfounded, faint, gaga*, giddy, groggy*, hazy, light-headed, muddled, off balance*, punch-drunk*, punchy*, puzzled, queasy, reeling, seeing stars*, shaky, slap-happy*, staggered, staggering, tipsy, unsteady, weak in the knees*, weak-kneed*, wobbly; CONCEPTS 314,480

word [n1] *discussion* chat, chitchat*, colloquy, confab*, confabulation, consultation, conversation, discussion, talk, tête-à-tête; CONCEPT 56 —*Ant.* silence

word [n2] *statement* account, adage, advice, announcement, bulletin, byword, comment, communication, communiqué, declaration, directive, discourse, dispatch, expression, gossip, hearsay, information, intelligence, intimation, introduction, message, news, notice, pronouncement, proverb, remark, report, rumble, rumor, saw, saying, scuttlebutt, speech, talk, tidings, utterance; CONCEPTS 274,278

word [n3] *unit of language* concept, designation, expression, idiom, lexeme, locution, morpheme, name, phrase, sound, term, usage, utterance, vocable; CONCEPT 275

word [n4] *command* behest, bidding, charge, commandment, decree, dictate, edict, go-ahead*, green light*, injunction, mandate, order, signal, ukase, will; CONCEPT 685 —*Ant.* question

word [n5] *promise* affirmation, assertion, assurance, commitment, declaration, engagement, guarantee, oath, parole, pledge, plight, solemn oath*, solemn word*, vow, warrant, word of honor; CONCEPTS 71,278, 689 —*Ant.* breach, break

word [n6] *password* countersign, slogan, watchword; CONCEPTS 684,685

wording [n] *way of expressing a thought* choice of words, diction, language, locution, manner, mode, parlance, phraseology, phrasing, style, terminology, turn of phrase, wordage, words; CONCEPTS 278,682

wordy [adj] *talkative* bombastic, chatty*, diffuse, discursive, flatulent, gabby*, garrulous, inflated, lengthy, long-winded, loquacious, palaverous, pleonastic, prolix, rambling, redundant, rhetorical, tedious, turgid, verbose, voluble, windy*; CONCEPT 267 —*Ant.* concise, untalkative

work [n1] *labor, chore* assignment, attempt, commission, daily grind*, drudge, drudgery, effort, elbow grease*, endeavor, exertion, functioning, grind, grindstone*, industry, job, moil, muscle, obligatioh, pains*, performance, production, push, salt mines*, servitude, slogging, stint, stress, striving, struggle, sweat*, task, toil, travail, trial, trouble, undertaking; CONCEPTS 87,362,677 —*Ant.* entertainment, fun, pastime

work [n2] *business, occupation* activity, art, calling, commitment, contract, craft, do*, duty, employment, endeavor, gig*, grind*, industry, job, line, line of business, livelihood, métier, nine-to-five*, obligation, office, practice, profession, pursuit, racket*, responsibility, skill, slot*, specialization, stint, swindle, task, thing*, trade, vocation, walk; CONCEPTS 349,351,360 —*Ant.* entertainment, fun, pastime

work [n3] *achievement* act, application, article, composition, creation, deed, end product, function, handiwork, handiwork, oeuvre, opus, output, performance, piece, product, production; CONCEPTS 260,706 —*Ant.* failure, loss

work [v1] *be employed; exert oneself* apply oneself, be gainfully employed, buckle down*, carry on, dig, do a job, do business, drive, drudge, earn a living*, freelance, have a job, hold a job, hustle*, knuckle down*, labor, manage, manufacture, moil, moonlight*, nine-to-five it*, peg away*, plug away*, ply, punch a clock*, pursue, report, scratch, slave, slog*, specialize, strain, strive, sweat*, take on, toil, try; CONCEPTS 100,351 —*Ant.* idle, laze, relax, rest

work [v2] *manipulate, operate* accomplish, achieve, act, behave, bring about, carry out, cause, contrive, control, create, direct, drive, effect, execute, force, function, go, handle, implement, manage, maneuver, move, perform, ply, progress, react, run, serve, take, tick, use, wield; CONCEPTS 94,117,199,204

work [v3] *cultivate, form* care for, dig, dress, farm, fashion, handle, knead, labor, make, manipulate, mold, process, shape, tend, till; CONCEPTS 173,184,257 —*Ant.* destroy

workable [adj] *feasible* applicable, breeze*, cinch*, doable, duck soup*, easy, easy as pie*, exploitable, functional, no sweat*, piece of cake*, possible, practicable, practical, simple as ABC*, snap, usable, useful, viable, working; CONCEPTS 538,552,560 —*Ant.* impractical, unfeasible, unworkable

worker [n] *person who is employed* artisan, blue collar*, breadwinner, company person, craftsperson, employee, hand, help, laborer, nine-to-fiver*, operative, peasant, proletarian, serf, slave, stiff, toiler, trader, tradesperson, wage earner, white collar*, working person, working stiff*; CONCEPT 348 —*Ant.* unemployed

working [adj] *active, occupied* alive, busy, dynamic, effective, employed, engaged, functioning, going, hot*, in a job, in force, in full swing, in gear, in process, laboring, live, moving, on fire*, on the job, on track*, operative, practical, running, useful, viable; CONCEPTS 538,560 —*Ant.* idle, inoperative, passive, unoccupied, unworking

workmanship [n] *craftsmanship* artisanship, artistry, artwork, craft, design, expertise, handicraft, handiwork, know-how*, skill, skillfulness, technique; CONCEPTS 259,409,630

workout [n] *exercise, practice* conditioning, constitutional, drill, rehearsal, routine, session, test, training, tryout, warm-up, work; CONCEPTS 290,363 —*Ant.* inactivity

work out [v] *solve; satisfy* accomplish, achieve, arrange, attain, be effective, bring off, clear, come out, come to terms*, complete, compromise, construct, contrive, develop, devise, elaborate, evolve, figure out, find out, finish, fix, form, formulate, get something done*, go, go well, handle, happen, manipulate, pan out*, plan, prosper, pull off*, put together, reach agreement, resolve, result, succeed, swing*, turn out, up, win; CONCEPTS 706,713

work up [v] *stimulate* agitate, animate, arouse, breed, cause, develop, engender, excite, generate, get up, hatch, improve, incite, induce, inflame, instigate, move, muster up, occasion, produce, rouse, spur, stir up; CONCEPTS 14,242 —*Ant.* discourage, dissuade

world [n1] *planet, globe* cosmos, creation, earth, heavenly body, macrocosm, microcosm, nature, sphere, star, terrene, universe; CONCEPTS 511,770

world [n2] *class of existing beings* class, division, everybody, everyone, group, humanity, humankind, human race, race, realm; CONCEPTS 378,391

world [n3] *person's environment, experience* ambience, area, atmosphere, business, domain, field, life, matters, memory, province, pursuits, realm, sphere, system; CONCEPT 678

worldly [adj1] *material, nonreligious* carnal, earthly, earthy, fleshly, human, lay, materialistic, mundane, natural, physical, practical, profane, secular, sublunary, telluric, temporal, terrene, terrestrial, ungodly; CONCEPTS 536,582 —*Ant.* immaterial, otherworldly, religious

worldly [adj2] *sophisticated, materialistic* avaricious, been around, blasé, callous, cool*, cosmopolitan, covetous, disenchanted, grasping, greedy, hardened, knowing, opportunistic, power-loving, practical, self-centered, selfish, unprincipled, uptown*, urbane, worldly wise; CONCEPT 401 —*Ant.* low, unrefined, unsophisticated

worldwide [adj] *general* catholic, common, comprehensive, cosmic, ecumenical, extensive, global, international, multinational, omnipresent, pandemic, planetary, ubiquitous, universal; CONCEPT 536 —*Ant.* limited, local

worn/worn-out [adj] *used, tired* beat, burned out*, bushed*, busted*, clichéd, consumed, depleted, destroyed, deteriorated, drained, drawn, effete, exhausted, fatigued, frayed, gone, hackneyed, had it*, haggard, jaded, kaput*, knocked out*, old, out of gas*, overused, overworked, pinched, played out*, pooped*, ragged, ruined, shabby, shot, spent, stale, tattered, the worse for wear*, threadbare, timeworn, tired out, totaled*, used up, useless, wearied, weary, well-worn, wiped out, worn down, wrung out*; CONCEPTS 485,560 —*Ant.* fresh, new, unused

worried [adj] *anxious, troubled* afraid, apprehensive, beside oneself, bothered, clutched, concerned, distracted, distraught, distressed, disturbed, fearful, fretful, frightened, hung up*, ill at ease, nervous, on edge*, on pins and needles*, overwrought, perturbed, solicitous, tense, tormented, uneasy, upset, uptight, worried stiff*; CONCEPT 403 —*Ant.* calm, untroubled, unworried

worrisome [adj] *troublesome* agonizing, alarming, annoying, anxious, apprehensive, bothersome, burdensome, disquieting, disturbing, inconvenient, irksome, irritating, nervous, taxing, tiresome, trying, uneasy, unnerving, upsetting, vexing, wearisome, worrying; CONCEPTS 529,565

worry [n] *anxiety, trouble* anguish, annoyance, apprehension, bad news*, care, concern, disquiet, distress, disturbance, doubt, fear, headache*, heartache*, irritation, misery, misgiving, nag*, pain*, perplexity, pest, plague, presentiment, problem, torment, torture, trial, uncertainty, uneasiness, vexation, woe, worriment; CONCEPTS *532,690* —*Ant.* calmness, reassurance

worry [v] *be or make anxious, troubled* afflict, aggrieve, agonize, ail, annoy, attack, bedevil, beleaguer, beset, bite one's nails*, bother, brood, bug*, chafe, concern oneself, depress, despair, disquiet, distress, disturb, dun, feel uneasy, fret, gnaw at, goad, go for*, harass, harry, hassle, have qualms, hector, importune, irritate, needle, oppress, persecute, perturb, pester, plague, stew*, sweat out*, take on, tantalize, tear, tease, test, torment, torture, trouble, try, unsettle, upset, vex, wince, writhe, wrong; CONCEPTS *7,14,19,410* —*Ant.* reassure

worsen [v] *diminish, decay* aggravate, corrode, damage, decline, degenerate, depress, descend, deteriorate, disintegrate, exacerbate, fall off, get worse, go downhill*, impair, lower, retrograde, retrogress, rot, sink; CONCEPTS *240,698* —*Ant.* improve, increase

worship [n] *honoring, glorification* adoration, adulation, awe, beatification, benediction, chapel, church service, deification, devotion, exaltation, genuflection, glory, homage, honor, idolatry, idolization, invocation, laudation, love, offering, praise, prayer, prostration, regard, respect, reverence, rite, ritual, service, supplication, veneration, vespers; CONCEPTS *69*

worship [v] *honor, glorify* admire, adore, adulate, bow down to, canonize, celebrate, chant, deify, dote on, esteem, exalt, extol, idolize, laud, love, magnify, offer prayers to, pay homage to, praise, pray to, put on a pedestal*, respect, revere, reverence, sanctify, sing, sing praises to*, venerate; CONCEPTS *69, 367* —*Ant.* dishonor, disrespect, hate

worth [n] *value, estimation associated with something* account, aid, assistance, avail, benefit, caliber, class, consequence, cost, credit, desirability, dignity, equivalence, excellence, goodness, help, importance, mark, meaningfulness, merit, moment, note, perfection, price, quality, rate, significance, stature, use, usefulness, utility, valuation, virtue, weight, worthiness; CONCEPTS *335,346* —*Ant.* worthlessness

worthless [adj] *of no use; without value* abandoned, abject, barren, base, bogus, cheap, contemptible, counterproductive, despicable, empty, futile, good-for-nothing*, ignoble, inconsequential, ineffective, ineffectual, inferior, insignificant, inutile, meaningless, mediocre, miserable, no-account*, no-good*, nothing, nugatory, paltry, pointless, poor, profitless, sterile, trashy, trifling, trivial, unavailing, unessential, unimportant, unproductive, unprofitable, unusable, useless, valueless, waste, wretched; CONCEPTS *560,570,575* —*Ant.* valuable, worthwhile, worthy

worthwhile [adj] *helpful* advantageous, beneficial, constructive, estimable, excellent, gainful, good, important, invaluable, justifiable, lucrative, meritorious, money-making, paying, priceless, productive, profitable, remunerative, rewarding, serviceable, useful, valuable, worthy; CONCEPTS *560,567,572* —*Ant.* unhelpful, valueless, worthless

worthy [adj] *honorable, respectable* A-1*, aces*, admirable, best, blameless, choice, commendable, creditable, decent, dependable, deserving, desirable, divine, estimable, ethical, excellent, exemplary, first-class*, first-rate*, good, honest, incorrupt, invaluable, laudable, meritorious, model, moral, noble, pleasing, praiseworthy, precious, priceless, pure, reliable, reputable, righteous, right-minded, salt of the earth*, satisfying, sterling, top-drawer*, top-notch*, true, trustworthy, upright, valuable, virtuous, winning, worthwhile; CONCEPTS *545,567,572* —*Ant.* dishonorable, disreputable, unrespected, unworthy

would-be [adj] *aspiring* ambitious, budding, eager, enterprising, hopeful, keen, potential, promising, prospective, striving, wannabe*, wishful; CONCEPT *403*

wound [n] *injury* anguish, bruise, cut, damage, distress, gash, grief, harm, heartbreak, hurt, insult, laceration, lesion, pain, pang, shock, slash, torment, torture, trauma; CONCEPT *309*

wound [v1] *cause bodily damage* bruise, carve, clip*, contuse, cut, damage, ding*, gash, harm, hit, hurt, injure, irritate, lacerate, nick, open up, ouch*, pierce, rough up*, scrape, scratch, slash, slice, stick, total*; CONCEPTS *137,246,313* —*Ant.* aid, cure, heal, help

wound [v2] *cause mental hurt* bother, cut to the quick*, distress, do in*, dump on*, get*, grieve, hurt, hurt one's feelings, mortify, offend, outrage, pain, put down*, shake up*, sting, traumatize, trouble, upset; CONCEPTS *7,14,19* —*Ant.* appease, help

wow [v] *amuse, delight* bowl over*, break one up*, charm, cheer, crack up*, entertain, go over big*, kill*, knock dead*, knock someone's socks off*, make laugh, make roll in the aisles*, slay*, tickle, tickle pink*, tickle to death*; CONCEPTS *7,9,22,292,384*

wrangle [n] *fight, argument* altercation, battle royal*, bickering, blow-off*, blowup*, brannigan*, brawl, brouhaha*, clash, contest, controversy, disagreement, dispute, exchange, falling-out*, flap*, fracas, hassle, knock-down drag-out*, quarrel, row, ruckus*, ruction, rumble, rumpus, scene, set-to*, squabble, tiff; CONCEPTS *46,106* —*Ant.* agreement, peace

wrangle [v] *fight, argue* altercate, bicker, brawl, bump heads*, contend, cross swords*, disagree, dispute, fall out*, hassle, have at it*, have words*, lock horns*, pick a bone*, put up a fight, quarrel, quibble, row, scrap, spat, squabble, take on, tangle, tiff; CONCEPTS *46, 106* —*Ant.* agree, give in

wrap [n] *clothing that is worn over for warmth* blanket, cape, cloak, coat, cover, fur, jacket, mantle, shawl, stole; CONCEPT *451*

wrap [v] *surround with a covering* absorb, bandage, bind, bundle, bundle up, camouflage, cloak, clothe, cover, drape, encase, encircle, enclose, enfold, envelop, fold, gift-wrap*, hide, immerse, invest, mask, muffle, pack, package, protect, roll up, sheathe, shelter, shroud, swaddle, swathe, twine, veil, wind; CONCEPT *172* —*Ant.* uncover, unwrap

wrap up [v] *finish* bring to a close, close, complete, conclude, determine, end, halt, polish off, terminate, wind up; CONCEPT *234* —*Ant.* begin, introduce, start

wrath [n] *extreme anger* acrimony, asperity, boiling point*, conniption*, dander, displeasure, exasperation, flare-up, fury, hate, hatefulness, huff, indignation, ire, irritation, mad, madness, offense, passion, rage, resentment, rise, stew*, storm, temper, vengeance; CONCEPTS 29,410 —Ant. happiness, love

wrathful [adj] *very angry* beside oneself, displeased, enraged, furious, heated, incensed, indignant, infuriated, irate, ireful, mad, on the warpath*, raging, storming; CONCEPT 403 —Ant. happy, pleased

wreak [v] *force, cause* bring about, carry out, create, effect, execute, exercise, force upon, inflict, unleash, vent, visit, work, wreck; CONCEPT 242

wreath [n] *circular decoration* band, bay, bouquet, chaplet, circlet, coronal, coronet, crown, festoon, garland, laurel, lei, loop, ring, ringlet; CONCEPTS 259,260,429

wreck [n] *severe damage or severely damaged goods* collapse, crash, crate, debacle, débris, derelict, destruction, devastation, disruption, fender bender*, heap*, hulk*, jalopy*, junk*, junker*, litter, mess, pile-up*, rear-ender*, relic, ruin, ruins, shipwreck, smashup*, total*, waste, wreckage; CONCEPTS 260,674 —Ant. creation

wreck [v] *ruin, destroy* bash, batter, beach, break, capsize, crack up*, crash, cripple, dash, decimate, demolish, devastate, dilapidate, disable, do in*, efface, founder, impair, injure, mangle, mar, mess up*, pile up*, put out of commission*, ravage, raze, run aground, sabotage, scuttle, shatter, shipwreck, sink, smash, smash up, spoil, strand, subvert, take apart, take out, tear up, torpedo*, total*, trash*, undermine, vandalize, wrack*, wrack up*; CONCEPT 252 —Ant. build, create, repair

wrench [v] *jerk, force violently* bend, coerce, compel, contort, dislocate, dislodge, distort, drag, exact, extract, pervert, pinch, pull, rend, rip, screw, sprain, squeeze, strain, tear, tug, tweak, twist, wrest, wring, yank; CONCEPT 80

wrestle [v] *struggle physically or mentally with something* battle, combat, contend, endeavor, essay, exert, fight, grapple, grunt, scuffle, strain, strive, tangle, tussle, work; CONCEPTS 17,191,208

wretched [adj] *terrible, very bad* abject, afflicted, base, bummed, calamitous, cheap, contemptible, dejected, deplorable, depressed, despicable, disconsolate, distressed, dolorous, down, down-and-out*, downcast, faulty, flimsy, forlorn, gloomy, hapless, hopeless, hurting, inferior, in the pits*, low, low-down*, mean, melancholy, miserable, paltry, pathetic, pitiable, pitiful, poor, shabby, shameful, sordid, sorrowful, sorry, spiritless, tragic, unfortunate, unhappy, vile, weak, woebegone, woeful, worthless; CONCEPTS 403,571 —Ant. good, nice

wriggle [v] *maneuver out of; wiggle* convulse, crawl, dodge, extricate oneself, glide, jerk, jiggle, ooze, skew, slink, slip, snake, sneak, squirm, turn, twist, twitch, wag, waggle, worm, writhe, zigzag; CONCEPTS 30,149

wring [v] *twist, contort* choke, coerce, compress, draw out, exact, extort, extract, force, gouge, hurt, pain, pinch, pry, push, screw, shake down, squeeze, strain, strangle, throttle, turn, wrench, wrest; CONCEPTS 142,206,208 —Ant. untwist

wrinkle [n] *crinkle, fold* contraction, corrugation, crease, crow's-foot*, crumple, depression, furrow, gather, line, pleat, plica, pucker, ridge, rimple, rumple, tuck; CONCEPTS 418,513 —Ant. smoothness

wrinkle [v] *crinkle, fold* compress, corrugate, crease, crimp, crisp, crumple, furrow, gather, line, prune up, pucker, purse, rimple, ruck, rumple, screw up, scrunch, seam, shrivel, twist; CONCEPTS 185,201 —Ant. smooth, straighten, unfold

writ [n] *court order* command, decree, document, habeas corpus, mandate, paper, prescript, process, replevin, subpoena, summons, warrant; CONCEPT 318

write [v] *put language down on paper* address, author, autograph, bang out*, chalk*, commit, communicate, comp*, compose, copy, correspond, create, dash off*, draft, draw up*, drop a line*, drop a note*, engross, formulate, ghost, indite, ink, inscribe, jot down, knock off*, knock out*, letter, note, note down*, pen, pencil, print, push a pencil*, put in writing, record, reproduce, rewrite, scrawl, scribble, scribe, scriven, set down, set forth, sign, take down, tell, transcribe, turn out, typewrite, write down, write up; CONCEPTS 79,203 —Ant. read

write off [v] *devalue; forget about* cancel, cross out, decry, depreciate, disregard, downgrade, give up, lower, mark down, shelve, take a loss on, underrate, undervalue; CONCEPT 54 —Ant. figure

writer [n] *person who composes with language* author, biographer, columnist, contributor, correspondent, critic, dramatist, editor, essayist, freelancer, ghostwriter, journalist, newspaper person, novelist, person of letters, poet, reporter, screenwriter, scribbler, scribe, scripter, stenographer, stringer, wordsmith; CONCEPTS 348,356 —Ant. reader

writhe [v] *contort; toss back and forth* agonize, bend, distort, jerk, recoil, squirm, struggle, suffer, thrash, thresh, twist, wiggle, wince, worm, wriggle; CONCEPTS 80,150 —Ant. be still

writing [n1] *printing on paper* autograph, calligraphy, chirography, cuneiform, hand, handwriting, hieroglyphics, longhand, manuscription, print, scrawl, scribble, script, shorthand; CONCEPTS 79,284

writing [n2] *printed composition* article, belles-lettres, book, discourse, dissertation, document, editorial, essay, letter, literature, manuscript, novel, ode, opus, pamphlet, paper, piece, play, poem, prose, publication, record, review, signature, theme, thesis, tract, treatise, work; CONCEPT 271

wrong [adj] *incorrect* amiss, askew, astray, at fault, awry, bad, counterfactual, defective, erratic, erring, erroneous, fallacious, false, , faulty, fluffed, goofed*, inaccurate, in error, inexact, miscalculated, misconstrued, misfigured, misguided, mishandled, mistaken, not precise, not right, not working, off-target*, on the wrong track*, out, out of commission*, out of line*, out of order*, perverse, rotten*, sophistical, specious, spurious, ungrounded,

unsatisfactory, unsound, unsubstantial, untrue, wide; CONCEPTS *571,582* —**Ant.** correct, right
wrong [*adj2*] *immoral, dishonest* amoral, bad, base, blamable, blameworthy, blasphemous, censurable, corrupt, criminal, crooked, debauched, depraved, dishonorable, dissipated, dissolute, evil, felonious, illegal, illicit, indecent, iniquitous, naughty, profane, profligate, reprehensible, reprobate, risqué, sacrilegious, salacious, shady, sinful, smutty, unethical, unfair, ungodly, unholy, unjust, unlawful, unrighteous, vicious, wanton, wicked, wrongful; CONCEPT *545* —**Ant.** decent, good, honest, moral
wrong [*adj3*] *inappropriate, not suitable* amiss, awkward, bad, disproportionate, funny, gauche, ill-advised, improper, inapt, incongruous, incorrect, indecorous, infelicitous, malapropos, misplaced, not done*, off-balance, rotten*, unacceptable, unbecoming, unconventional, undesirable, unfit, unfitted, unfitting, unhappy, unsatisfactory, unseemly, unsuitable; CONCEPT *558* —**Ant.** acceptable, appropriate, correct, ok, suitable
wrong [*adj4*] *reverse, opposite* back, inside, inverse, obverse; CONCEPT *586*
wrong [*adv*] *astray* afield, amiss, askew, badly, erroneously, inaccurately, incorrectly, mistakenly, unfavorably, wrongly; CONCEPTS *544,548*
wrong [*n*] *offense, sin* abuse, bad deed, bias, blunder, crime, cruelty, damage, delinquency, discourtesy, error, evil, faux pas, favor, foul play, grievance, harm, hurt, immorality, imposition, indecency, inequity, inhumanity, iniquity, injury, injustice, insult, libel, malevolence, miscarriage, misdeed, misdemeanor, misdoing, mistake, oppression, persecution, prejudice, sinfulness, slander, slight, spite, tort, transgression, trespass, turpitude, unfairness, vice, villainy, violation, wickedness, wrongdoing; CONCEPT *645* —**Ant.** goodness, kindness, right, virtue
wrong [*v*] *hurt, mistreat another* abuse, aggrieve, cheat, damage, defame, discredit, dishonor, harm, hurt, ill-treat, impose upon, injure, malign, maltreat, misrepresent, mistreat, offend, oppress, outrage, persecute, take advantage of; CONCEPTS *7,19,246,313* —**Ant.** aid, assist, help, sympathize
wrongful [*adj*] *evil, illegal* blameworthy, criminal, dishonest, dishonorable, felonious, illegitimate, illicit, immoral, improper, lawless, reprehensible, unethical, unfair, unjust, unlawful, wicked; CONCEPTS *319,545* —**Ant.** ethical, fair, good, just, legal, rightful
wry [*adj*] *sarcastic, distorted* askew, aslant, awry, contorted, crooked, cynical, derisive, droll, dry, ironic, mocking, sardonic, twisted, uneven, warped; CONCEPTS *267,581* —**Ant.** straight, straightforward

X

Xanadu [*n*] *utopia* Arcadia, dreamland, dreamworld, Eden, heaven, land of milk and honey*, never-never land*, paradise, promised land*, Shangri-La*, wonderland; CONCEPTS *370,689*
xerophagy [*n*] *fasting* hunger strike, keeping fast, Lenten fast, strict fast, without food, xerophagia; CONCEPT *169*

Xerox [*v*] *copy* carbon, clone, counterfeit, ditto, duplicate, forge, mimeograph, photocopy, photostat, replicate, reprint, reproduce, trace; CONCEPT *171*
Xmas [*n*] *Christmas* Christmastide, Christmastime, festive season, Nativity, Noel, Yule, Yuletide; CONCEPT *802*
X-rated [*adj*] *pornographic* adult, bawdy, dirty, erotic, fleshy, hard-core, immoral, indecent, lascivious, lewd, obscene, off-color, offensive, porn*, porno*, raunchy, sensual, sexual, sexy, smutty*, steamy*; CONCEPTS *267,372,545*
X ray [*n*] *picture of inside a body* actinism, cathode rays, encephalogram, fluoroscope, radioactivity, radiograph, refractometry, Roentgen rays, ultraviolet rays; CONCEPT *311*

Y

yacht [*n*] *pleasure boat* cabin cruiser, cruiser, ketch, racer, sailboat, sailing boat, sloop, yawl; CONCEPT *506*
yak/yap [*n/v*] *talk a lot* babble, blather, chat, chatter, clack, confabulate, gab, gossip, jabber, jaw*, prate, prattle, run on*, tattle; yammer; CONCEPTS *51,266*
yammer [*v*] *whine* bellyache, carp, complain, fuss, gripe, grumble, howl, moan, repine, wail, whimper, yowl; CONCEPTS *54,77*
yank [*v*] *pull hard and fast* draw, evulse, extract, hitch, jerk, lug, snap, snatch, tear, tug, twitch, vellicate, wrench; CONCEPT *206* —**Ant.** push
yap [*v1*] *bark* bay, woof, yelp; CONCEPT *64*
yap [*v2*] *chatter* babble, blather, chit-chat, gab, gibber, go on, gossip, jabber, jaw, prate, prattle, ramble, run off at the mouth*, talk a lot, twaddle; CONCEPT *266*
yard [*n*] *grassy area around a structure* backyard, barnyard, clearing, close, corral, court, courtyard, enclosure, fold, garden, grass, lawn, lot, patch, patio, playground, quadrangle, terrace; CONCEPT *509*
yardstick [*n*] *gauge* barometer, basis, benchmark, criterion, example, guide, guideline, indicator, mark, measure, meter, model, norm, rule, sample, scale, standard, tape measure, test; CONCEPTS *647,680,688,792*
yarn [*n1*] *fiber for knitting* cotton fiber, flaxen thread, fleece, spun wool, thread, twist, wool; CONCEPT *473*
yarn [*n2*] *story, often long and made-up* adventure, alibi, anecdote, fable, fabrication, fairy tale, lie, line, narrative, potboiler*, prose, sea story*, song*, song and dance*, string*, tale, tall story*, tall tale; CONCEPT *282*
yawn [*v*] *open mouth wide, usually sign of fatigue* catch flies*, divide, doze, drowse, expand, gap, gape, give, nap, part, sleep, snooze, spread, yaw, yawp*; CONCEPTS *163, 185*
yearly [*adj*] *every twelve months* annual, annually, once a year, per annum, perennial, regularly, year by year, yearlong; CONCEPTS *541,823*
yearn [*v*] *desire strongly* ache, be desirous of, be eager for, be passionate, chafe, covet, crave, dream, hanker, have a crush on*, have a yen for, hunger, itch, languish, long, lust, pine, set

one's heart on*, thirst, want, wish for; CONCEPT 20 —*Ant.* dislike, hate

yearning [*n*] *desire* ache, ambition, appetite, aspiration, craving, craze, eagerness, fancy, fascination, hankering*, hunger, infatuation, liking, longing, love, need, passion, thirst, urge, want; CONCEPTS 20,709

years [*n*] *age; old age* agedness, caducity, dotage, elderliness, generation, lifespan, lifetime, oldness, senescence, senility; CONCEPT 715 —*Ant.* youth

yell [*n/v*] *loud communication* bawl, bellow, call, cheer, complain, cry, holler*, hoot, howl, lament, roar, scream, screech, shout, shriek, shrill, squawk, squeal, ululate, vociferate, wail, weep, whoop, yap, yelp, yip; CONCEPTS 47,595 —*Ant.* whisper

yellow [*adj1*] *cowardly* chicken*, craven, deceitful, gutless, lily-livered*, low, offensive, pusillanimous, sneaking, treacherous, tricky, unethical, unprincipled; CONCEPTS 267,401 —*Ant.* bold, brave, confident

yellow [*n/adj2*] *sunny color* amber, bisque, blond, buff, chrome, cream, gold, ivory, lemon, saffron, sand, tawny; CONCEPTS 618,622

yelp [*n/v*] *short, high cry* bark, hoot, howl, screech, yap, yip, yowl; CONCEPT 64

yen [*n*] *strong want* craving, desire, hankering, hunger, itch, longing, lust, passion, thirst, urge, yearning; CONCEPTS 20,709 —*Ant.* dislike, hate, hatred

yes [*adv*] *agreed* affirmative, all right*, amen, aye*, beyond a doubt, by all means, certainly, definitely, even so, exactly, fine, gladly, good, good enough, granted, indubitably, just so, most assuredly, naturally, of course, okay*, positively, precisely, surely, sure thing*, true, undoubtedly, unquestionably, very well, willingly, without fail, yea*, yep*; CONCEPTS 535,572 —*Ant.* disagreed

yes-person [*n*] *sycophant* apple-polisher*, backscratcher*, backslapper*, bootlicker*, brownnoser*, doormat*, fan, fawner, flatterer, flunky*, groupie*, hanger-on*, lackey, minion, puppet, toady; CONCEPT 423

yesterday [*n*] *the day before today* bygone, foretime, lang syne*, last day, not long ago, past, recently, the other day*; CONCEPT 815 —*Ant.* tomorrow

yet [*adv1*] *up until now* as yet, earlier, hitherto, prior to, so far, still, thus far, till, until now, up to now; CONCEPT 820

yet [*adv2*] *in spite of* after all, although, at any rate, but, despite, even though, howbeit, however, nevertheless, nonetheless, notwithstanding, on the other hand, still, still and all, though, withal; CONCEPT 544

yet [*adv3*] *in addition* additionally, along, also, as well, besides, further, furthermore, likewise, more, moreover, over and above*, still, still further, to boot*, too; CONCEPT 548

yet [*adv4*] *in the future* after a while, at some future time, beyond this, even, eventually, finally, in due course, in the course of time, someday, sometime, sooner or later, still, ultimately; CONCEPT 799

yield [*n*] *production of labor* crop, earnings, harvest, income, output, outturn, produce, profit, return, revenue, takings, turnout; CONCEPT 260

yield [*v1*] *produce* accrue, admit, afford, allow, beam, bear, blossom, bring forth, bring in, discharge, earn, furnish, generate, give, give off, hold out, net, offer, pay, proffer, provide, return, sell for, supply, tender, turn out; CONCEPT 205 —*Ant.* disallow, withhold

yield [*v2*] *give in, surrender* abandon, abdicate, admit defeat, back down, bend, bow, break, buy, call it quits*, capitulate, cave in, cede, collapse, come to terms*, crumple, defer, fold, fold up, give oneself over, give up, give way*, go, hand over, knuckle, knuckle under*, lay down arms*, leave, let go*, part with, relax, relent, relinquish, resign, sag, submit, succumb, suffer defeat, throw in the towel*; CONCEPTS 14,18,35 —*Ant.* deny, oppose, prevent, refuse, reject

yield [*v3*] *grant, allow* accede, accept, acknowledge, acquiesce, admit, agree, assent, bow, break, comply, concede, concur, consent, defer, fail, fit in, go along with*, go with the flow*, permit, play the game*, surrender, toe the line*, toe the mark*, waive; CONCEPT 8 —*Ant.* counter, disallow, disapprove, veto

yielding [*adj1*] *accommodating* acquiescent, biddable, compliant, docile, easy, flexible, humble, nonresistant, obedient, passive, pliable, pliant, putty in one's hands, resigned, submissive, tractable; CONCEPTS 401,404 —*Ant.* obstinate, resistant, unflexible

yielding [*adj2*] *soft, flexible* elastic, malleable, mushy, pappy, plastic, pliable, pulpy, quaggy, resilient, spongy, springy, squishy, supple, tractable, tractile, unresisting; CONCEPTS 488, 606 —*Ant.* hard, rigid, solid, unflexible

yoke [*n*] *bondage, bond* burden, chain, coupling, enslavement, helotry, knot, ligament, ligature, link, nexus, oppression, peonage, serfdom, service, servility, servitude, slavery, tie; CONCEPTS 513,677

yoke [*v*] *bond together; join* associate, attach, bracket, buckle, combine, conjoin, conjugate, connect, couple, fasten, fix, harness, hitch, link, secure, splice, strap, tack, tie, unite, wed; CONCEPTS 85,160 —*Ant.* disconnect, disjoin

yokel [*n*] *person who is mired in local custom* backwoods person, boor*, country cousin*, country person, hayseed*, peasant, rustic; CONCEPT 413

yonder [*adv*] *faraway* away, beyond, distant, farther, further, remote, yon; CONCEPTS 586, 778 —*Ant.* close, near, nearby

young [*adj*] *immature* adolescent, blooming, blossoming, boyish, boylike, budding, burgeoning, callow, childish, childlike, crude, developing, early, fledgling, fresh, girlish, girllike, green*, growing, half-grown, ignorant, inexperienced, infant, inferior, junior, juvenile, little, modern, new, newborn, newish, not aged, pubescent, puerile, punk, raw, recent, tender, tenderfoot*, undeveloped, undisciplined, unfinished, unfledged, unlearned, unpracticed, unripe, unseasoned, untried, unversed, vernal, youthful; CONCEPTS 578,678,715,797 —*Ant.* mature, old, older

young [*n*] *animate beings that are not mature* babies, baby, brood, family, infants, issue, litter, little ones*, offspring, progeny; CONCEPTS 394,414,424 —*Ant.* parent

youngster/youth [n] *person before the age of maturity* boy, chick*, cub*, fledgling, girl, junior, juvenile, juvenile delinquent*, kid*, lad, lass, pup, pupil, student, teenager, young person; CONCEPTS *414,424* —*Ant.* adult

youth [n] *early period in life of animate being* adolescence, awkward age, bloom, boyhood, childhood, girlhood, greenness, ignorance, immaturity, inexperience, innocence, juvenescence, minority, prime, puberty, salad days*, springtide, springtime of life, teens, tender age*, youthfulness; CONCEPT *817* —*Ant.* adulthood, maturity

youthful [adj] *new, immature* active, adolescent, boyish, budding, buoyant, callow, childish, childlike, enthusiastic, fresh, full of life, girlish, green*, inexperienced, infant, juvenile, keen, pubescent, puerile, tender, underage, vernal, vigorous, young; CONCEPTS *542,578, 797* —*Ant.* experienced, mature, old

yowl [n/v] *long, loud animate sound* bawl, bay, caterwaul, cry, holler*, howl, mewl, scream, screech, squall, squeal, ululate, wail, whine, yell, yelp, yip; CONCEPT *77*

yucky [adj] *disgusting* abominable, awful, beastly, crappy*, creepy, cruddy*, crummy*, detestable, distasteful, foul, funky*, grody*, gross, gruesome, hideous, icky*, loathsome, lousy, nasty, nauseating, odious, offensive, raunchy, repugnant, repulsive, revolting, rotten, scuzzy*, sickening, skanky*, sleazy*, stinking, vile, vulgar, yecchy*; CONCEPTS *485,548*

yummy [adj] *delicious* ambrosial, appetizing, choice, delectable, delightful, divine, enticing, fit for a king*, good, heavenly, juicy, luscious, mouthwatering, nectarous, out of this world*, palatable, piquant, pleasant, rich, sapid, savory, scrumptious, spicy, succulent, super, sweet, tasteful, tasty, tempting, toothsome; CONCEPTS *572,613*

yuppie [n/adj] *young upwardly mobile professional* button-down, clone, conspicuous consumer, suit, three-piecer, urban professional, white-collar worker; CONCEPT *348*

Z

zany [adj] *crazy, funny* camp*, campy*, clownish, comical, dumb, eccentric, fool, foolish, goofy, hare-brained*, humorous, joshing, kooky*, loony*, madcap*, nutty*, sappy*, wacky*, witty; CONCEPT *267* —*Ant.* serious

zany [n] *person who is wildly funny* buffoon, card*, clown, comedian, comic, cutup*, farceur, funny person, gag person, humorist, idiot, jester, joker, madcap*, moron, nut*, practical joker, prankster, screwball*, showoff, simpleton*, wag*, wisecracker*; CONCEPTS *352,423*

zap [v] *destroy* exterminate, kill, kill off, slaughter, terminate; CONCEPT *252*

zeal [n] *enthusiasm* alacrity, ardor, bustle, determination, devotion, diligence, dispatch, drive, eagerness, earnestness, enterprise, fanaticism, fervor, fierceness, fire, gusto, hustle, inclination, initiative, intensity, intentness, keenness, mania, passion, perseverance, push, readiness,

sincerity, spirit, stick-to-itiveness*, urgency, vehemence, verve, warmth, what-it-takes*, yen, zest; CONCEPTS *32,410,411* —*Ant.* apathy, indifference, lethargy

zealot [n] *enthusiast* activist, diehard, extremist, fanatic, fiend, maniac, militant, nut, radical, ultra*, young Turk; CONCEPT *423* —*Ant.* moderate

zealous [adj] *enthusiastic* afire, antsy*, ardent, avid, burning, coming on strong*, dedicated, devoted, eager, earnest, fanatic, fanatical, fervent, fervid, fireball*, fired, frenetic, gung-ho*, hot*, impassioned, itchy*, keen, obsessed, passionate, possessed, pushy*, rabid, ripe, self-starting, spirited, wild-eyed*; CONCEPTS *326,401,404* —*Ant.* apathetic, indifferent, lethargic, unenthusiastic

zenith [n] *top* acme, altitude, apex, apogee, cap, capper, capstone, climax, crest, crown, culmination, elevation, eminence, height, high noon*, high point, meridian, payoff*, peak, pinnacle, roof, summit, tiptop*, topper*, vertex; CONCEPTS *706,832,836* —*Ant.* bottom, nadir

zero [n] *nothing* aught, blank, bottom, cipher, insignificancy, love*, lowest point, nada*, nadir, naught, nil*, nix*, nobody*, nonentity, nought, nullity, oblivion, ought, rock bottom*, scratch, shutout, void, zilch*, zip*, zot*; CONCEPTS *407,784* —*Ant.* anything, being, something, thing

zero hour [n] *vital moment* appointed hour*, climax, contingency, countdown, crisis, crossroad, D-day*, emergency, exigency, jumping-off point*, juncture, moment of truth*, pinch, strait, target, the time*, turning point*; CONCEPTS *668,815,832*

zest [n1] *taste, flavor* bite, body, charm, flavoring, ginger, guts*, interest, kick*, nip, piquancy, punch*, pungency, relish, salt, savor, seasoning, smack*, snap*, spice, tang, zap*, zip*; CONCEPT *614* —*Ant.* blandness, dullness

zest [n2] *energy, gusto* appetite, ardor, bliss, bounce, cheer, delectation, delight, eagerness, ecstasy, elation, enjoyment, enthusiasm, fervor, guts*, happiness, keenness, moxie*, passion, pep*, pleasure, relish*, satisfaction, zeal, zing*; CONCEPTS *410,411* —*Ant.* apathy, indifference, laziness, lethargy

zigzag [adj] *moving side to side* askew, awry, bent, crinkled, crooked, devious, diagonal, erratic, fluctuating, inclined, indirect, irregular, jagged, meandering, oblique, oscillating, rambling, serrated, sinuous, sloping, snaking, tortuous, transverse, twisted, twisting, undulating, waggling, winding; CONCEPT *581* —*Ant.* straight

zilch [n] *nothing* blank, diddly-squat*, goose egg*, hill of beans*, insignificancy, nada*, naught, not anything, nothingness, nought, void, zero, zip, zippo*; CONCEPTS *407,707*

zing [n] *liveliness* brio, dash, drive, élan, energy, enthusiasm, get-up-and-go*, go, gusto, life, oomph*, pep, pizzazz, punch, sparkle, spirit, verve, vigor, vim, vitality, zest, zip; CONCEPTS *411,633*

zip [n] *enthusiasm, energy* brio, drive, get-up-and-go*, go*, gusto, life, liveliness, oomph*, pep, pizzazz*, punch, sparkle, spirit, verve, vigor, vim, vitality, zest, zing*; CONCEPTS *411,*

ye
zi

633 —*Ant.* apathy, enervation, idleness, laziness, lethargy

zip [*v*] *move about quickly* bustle, dash, flash, fly, hasten, hurry, run, rush, shoot, speed, tear, waltz, whisk, whiz, zoom; CONCEPT *150* —*Ant.* decelerate, slow

zippy [*adj*] *energetic* active, animated, ball of fire*, brisk, chipper, dashing, dynamic, enterprising, full of energy, full of life, full of pep, high-powered, kinetic, lively, peppy, potent, powerful, snappy, speedy, spirited, sprightly, spry, strong, tireless, untiring, vigorous, vital, vivacious, zestful, zingy*; CONCEPTS *404,542*

zit [*n*] *pimple* abscess, acne, blackhead, blemish, bump, carbuncle, excrescence, goober*, goophead*, papula, papule, pustule, whitehead; CONCEPT *306*

zone [*n*] *district* area, band, belt, circuit, ground, realm, region, section, sector, segment, sphere, territory, tract; CONCEPTS *508,513*

zonked [*adj*] *drunk, intoxicated; stunned* amazed, astonished, bashed, boozed up*, buzzed*, crocked*, dazed, dumbfounded, feeling no pain*, flying*, groggy, high*, inebriated, juiced*, laced*, liquored up*, lit*, plastered*, seeing double*, sloshed*, stewed*, stoned*, tanked*, three sheets to the wind*, thunderstruck, tipsy, totaled*, under the influence, under the table*, wasted*; CONCEPTS *314,545*

zoom [*v*] *move very quickly* buzz, dart, dash, dive, flash, fly, hum, hurtle, outstrip, rip, rocket, rush, shoot, shoot up, skyrocket, speed, streak, surge, tear, whirl, whiz, zip*; CONCEPT *150* —*Ant.* decelerate, slow

ROGET'S 21ST CENTURY CONCEPT INDEX

HOW TO USE THE CONCEPT INDEX

Simply put, a thesaurus is a collection of words grouped according to idea. Appearing in the A to Z listings of *Roget's 21st Century Thesaurus, Second Edition* are about 20,000 words and 500,000 synonyms to choose from. This selection alone would seem generous enough to satisfy the lexicographer's expectation of what a thesaurus should contain. But a wealth of new alternatives is created when we begin to think about the higher connections that can be made between words and ideas in the language. This is the purpose of *Roget's 21st Century*'s Concept Index.

The Concept Index not only helps writers and thinkers to *organize* their ideas but leads them from those very ideas to the words that can best express them. It is a semantic hierarchy of the most common concepts we use in American English as it is spoken and written today.

There are 837 concepts classified according to their subject and usage, and grouped under ten general categories of interest: Actions, Fields of Human Activity, Objects, Qualities, States, and Weights and Measures.

All of *Roget's 21st Century Thesaurus*'s 20,000 main entries are cross-referenced to related concepts. For example, when you look up the entry for "knowledgeable" in the A to Z listing, it is referenced to concept #402. Turning in the index to concept #402, "attribute of intelligence," you will see over 50 other main entries that are also related to this concept:

MAIN ENTRY

with synonym list as it appears in the A to Z listing

> **knowledgeable** [*adj*] *aware, educated*
> abreast, acquainted, alert, appreciative, apprised, au courant, au fait, brainy*, bright, brilliant, clever, cognizant, conscious, conversant, discerning, erudite, experienced, familiar, informed, insightful, intelligent, in the know, knowing, learned, lettered, omniscient, perceptive, plugged in*, posted, prescient, privy, quick-witted, sagacious, sage, savvy, scholarly, sensible, sharp, smart, sophic, sophisticated, tuned-in*, understanding, versed, well-informed, well-rounded, wise, with-it; CONCEPT 402 —*Ant.* ignorant, unaware, uneducated, uninformed

CONCEPT

with collection of main entry words referenced to it in the index

402 attribute of intelligence: able, abstruse, accident-prone, acute, alert, analytic/analytical, apt, astute, aware, bewildered, blind, brilliant, canny, cerebral, clairvoyant, clever, cognizant, common-sense, comprehensible, considered, conversant, cunning, deducible, delirious, designedly, dim, dizzy, down-to-earth, dumb, eagle-eyed, efficient, empty, empty-headed, erudite, expert, far-sighted, feebleminded, frivolous, gullible, hazy, idiotic, illiterate, impressionable, incomprehensible, ineligible, inexperienced, ingenious, inquisitive, insipid, intelligent, inventive, judicious, knowing, learned, logical, lucid, mindful, moronic, not born yesterday, observant, omniscient, penetrating, perceptive, philosophical/philosophic, privy, proficient, psychic, quick-witted, rational, reasonable, sagacious, sane, savvy, scholarly, seasoned, sensible, shallow, shrewd, skillful, slow, soft, studious, subtle, thick, thoughtless, unaware, uneducated, uninformed, unknowing, vacant, versed, veteran, weak, well-balanced, well-defined, wide-awake, with-it

Any of these main entry words appearing together as attributes of intelligence in the Concept Index— from "able" to "ingenious" to "perceptive" to "with-it"—may be the perfect word you are looking for. Or, intrigued by the associations the word "veteran" brings to mind, you could return to the A to Z listing to explore its synonyms:

veteran [*adj*] *experienced, seasoned* adept, battle-scarred*, been around*, disciplined, exercised, expert, from way back*, hardened, inured, knows one's stuff*, long-serving, long-time, not born yesterday*, of the old school*, old, old-time, practical, practiced, pro*, proficient, skilled, sophisticated, steady, trained, up to speed*, versed, vet*, weathered, wise, wise to ways*, worldly; CONCEPTS 402,527,678 —*Ant.* amateur, green, inexperienced

Even further possibilities exist, when you realize that "veteran" is referenced to two additional concepts: #527, the quality of "ability" and #678, the state of "experience." Many main entries are referenced to as many as three or four different concepts.

Simple to use, the Concept Index becomes invaluable in the effort to turn an idea into a specific word. By linking together the main entries that share similar concepts, the index makes possible creative semantic connections between words in our language, stimulating thought and broadening vocabulary. Whether you begin by browsing through the Concept Index for ideas, you will find that *Roget's 21st Century Thesaurus, Second Edition* goes beyond traditional thesauri and synonymfinders to offer thousands of word choices through access to its unique Concept Index.

QUICK REFERENCE GUIDE TO CONCEPTS

ACTIONS

CLASS OF

1 action: act, activity, doings, spurt, tour de force

2 event: affair, be, eventuate, fact, locomotion, move, occasion, pass, proceeding

3 occurrence: development, occurrence, recur, transpire

4 occurrence with one participant: act, behave, chance, come, deed, fall out, go, happening, occur, result, rise

5 occurrence with two participants: boundary, limit, obstruct, restraint, test

6 series of related actions: channel, disposition, esplanade, instrument, manner, mechanism, methodology, modus operandi, pattern, procedure, routine, rut, technique, usage, way

COGNITIVE

7 affect: abandon, acerbate, affront, agitate, alarm, allay, allure, annoy, appall/appal, appease, arouse, assuage, awaken, baffle, beckon, befuddle, beleaguer, beset, bewitch, bombard, bother, bring down, bug, buoy (up), captivate, chagrin, cheer, clear, comfort, compose, console, cow, cross, crush, dash, debase, deception, deflate, degrade, demean, deprecate, depress, disaffect, disarm, discomfort, discompose, discountenance, dishearten, disoblige, displease, distress, divert, double-cross, draw, electrify, embarrass, embolden, enamor, encourage, encroach, energize, enrage, enthrall, enticement, estrange, exasperate, exercise, fail, faze, flurry, fortify, fret, fulfill, galling, get, govern, gratify, grip, harass, harry, henpeck, horrify, hurt, inflame, inspire, interest, intrigue, irk, jar, kindle, lighten, lull, matter, miff, molest, mortify, nag, nerve, nonaggression, offend, outrage, pain, peeve, perk up, perturb, petrify, pick at/pick on, placate, please, pressure, prod, puncture, quell, rack, rankle, reach, reduce, register, repay, revolt, rile, rub the wrong way, sadden, satisfy, scare, send, shake, shatter, slight, smooth, soothe, spook, startle, strain, stress, sugarcoat, sweeten, tantalize, tease, terrify, threaten, tickle, torment, touch, transport, try, turn off, two-time, unnerve, uplift, vex, wake/waken, weigh, whet, wound, wrong

8 agree: accede, acceptance, accord, acknowledgment, acquiescence, align, avowal, bear, cohere, compromise, consent, contract, draft, enlist, give in/give up, go along/go along with, grant, negotiate, unanimous, yield

9 amuse: divert, humor, wow

10 approve: acquiesce, advocate, applaud, approbation, blessing, concur, countenance, deference, envy, exalt, excuse, favor, go to bat for, idolize, nod, overlook, pity, prize, recognition, regard, revere/reverence, sanctify, support, venerate

11 attract: grip, intrigue, kid around, mesmerize, ravish, send, take, tease, titillate, turn on, win/win over

12 believe: accept, acknowledge, appreciation, authenticate, bear, bleed, convert, count on/count upon, deem, eat up, esteem, extrapolate, forgive, glory, imagine, lean, misjudge, opine, postulate, presume, rate, regard, sanctify, suppose, think, underestimate, view

13 change conception: ache, awakening, catharsis, conform, crack, fit, flip out, give, go back on, oscillate, recharge, resuscitate, revert, sway, tire, vagary, weary

14 compel: abet, alarm, badger, bewilder, bind, brainwash, brutality, bully, butt in, coercion, conjure, constraint, corrupt, debauch, demoralize, discourage, dispel, domineer, embitter, enrage, entrance, fan, foist, force, frighten, get back at, grate, harass, hassle, horrify, humiliate, impel, imposition, incite, inculcate, induce, inflame, instill, intimidate, inveigle, jinx, kindle, lumber, manipulate, mesmerize, molest, nauseate, nettle, oblige, oppress, panic, pervert, pique, poison, predispose, press, prey on, push, put out, ride, scourge, sell/sell out, shame, sour, spook, stimulate, sway, task, terrorize, transfix, unnerve, visit, wake/waken, work up, wound, yield

15 comprehend: appreciate, apprehend, catch, conceive, decode, deduction, determine, dig, discern, distinguish, draw, extrapolate, fathom, figure, gather, grasp, have someone's number, identify with, inure, make, misapprehend, mistake, outwit/outsmart, perceive, recognize, see, take, tell, understand

16 confuse: confound, daze, decoy, disconcert, distract, floor, foul up, hassle, jumble, muddle, nonplus, obscure, perplex, puzzle, snarl, throw

17 consider: absorb, balance, bleed, buckle down, commune, contemplate, cram, deliberate, devote, dream up, dwell on/dwell upon, entertain, envisage/envision, eye, fantasize, focus, grieve, heed, hindsight, marvel, meditate, muse, picture, puzzle, reflect, reminisce, revolve, think, treat, visualize, wrestle

18 decide: abnegation, adopt, appraisal, call off, circumscribe, classify, convict, credit, define, destine, disapprove, dispose of, evaluate, figure, go along/go along with, ground, have someone's number, impose, intend, make out, moderate, plant, provide, referee, resolve, set, solve, stipulate, turn down, waver, yield

19 depress: abandon, acerbate, afflict, aggravate, agonize, alienate, annoy, appall/appal, arouse, awaken, baffle, befuddle, beleaguer, beset, bias, bore, bring down, bug, chafe, chill, complicate, cow, cross, crush, dash, debase, deception, deflate, demean, deprecate, disappoint, discomfit, discommode, disconcert, disgust, dismay, disparage, disquiet, disturb, double-cross, draw, embarrass, embroil, enrage, entice, estrange, exasperate, exercise, faze, flurry, freak, frustrate, galling, govern, grieve, harass, harry, hoodwink, hound, impress, instigate, irk, jar, lower, matter, miff, molest, move, needle, occupy, oppress, pain, peeve, perturb, petrify, pick at/pick on, plague, pressure, prod, puncture, quicken, rankle, reach, register, repay, revolt, rile, ruffle, scar, seduction, shame, sink, slur, stagger, strain, strike, take down, taunt, terrify, threaten, torture, trouble, turn, two-time, unnerve, upset, visit, weigh, worry, wrong

20 **desire:** addiction, advance(s), aim, ambition, appetite, aspire, behest, care, crave, crush, curiosity, dependence/dependency, drool, envy, expect, fancy, fascination, free will, goad, hanker after/hanker for, hope, hungry, inclination, insatiable, itch, languish, leaning, libido, liking, longing, malnutrition, mind, moon, motivation, need, notion, one-track mind, penchant, pipe dream, pleasure, predisposition, preference, propensity, purpose, relish, sigh, substance abuse, temptation, urge, voracious, will, yearn, yen

21 **doubt:** begrudge, controvert, despair, disapprove, disbelieve, discountenance, dissent, doubt, fume, hesitate, lovelorn, mind, mistrust, objection, oppugn, question, reject, repudiate, rue, scruple, skepticism, suspect, wonder

22 **elated:** affect, alleviate, appeal, appeasement, arrest, attract, awe, bedazzle, bemuse, brighten, buoy (up), charm, clear, compose, console, defuse, depressant, divert, elevate, enamor, encourage, endear, enliven, enthrall, enticement, excite, fascinate, fortify, galvanize, gladden, gratify, hearten, inflame, inspire, interest, invigorate, lighten, matter, move, nonaggression, pacify, perk up, placate, pressure, prod, quell, rally, reassure, register, rouse, satisfy, settle, solace, still, strike, sugarcoat, tantalize, temper, tickle, touch, transport, wake/waken, whet

23 **endure:** abide, accommodate, bear, bear with, bow, brook, come through, cope, digest, face the music, go through, hang tough, keep at, linger, make out, mind, pay, receive, remain, resistance, stand/stand for, stomach, subsist, support, sustain, take, tolerate, wear, withstand

24 **examine:** analysis, assay, assessment, canvass, chew, compare, consider, debate, deduce, deliberate, dissect, enquire, evaluate, experiment, go over, inquiry, meditation, ponder, reflect, resolve, ruminate, scrutiny, soul-searching, speculation, view, weigh

25 **exclude:** abnegation, blackball, boycott, deactivate, disallow, disinherit, exception, exclusion, omission, ostracism, oust, pass, pass over, recant, rule out, shut off/shut out, take back

26 **expect:** anticipate, assume, bargain for, count, count on/count upon, depend, foresee, lean, mean, plan, predispose, propose, rely, think

27 **fear:** apprehension, cold feet, dismay, horror, panic, terror, trepidation

28 **guess:** accounting, bet, call, deem, estimate, forecast, implication, presume, projection, speculation, surmise, wager

29 **hate:** abhor, abominate, aggression, anger, antagonism, atrocity, bad blood, blow up, burn, deplore, detest, disdain, disinclination, disrespect, dissent, enmity, execrate, frown, fury, horror, incivility, inhumanity, lament/lamentation, loathe, malice, odium, outrage, pique, rancor, resent, revulsion, seethe, spite, umbrage, venom, wrath

30 **ignore:** abjure, blink, brush aside/brush off, cold shoulder, discount, disobey, disregard, eliminate, eschew, except, exclude, fence, forsake, get off someone's back, goof off, lose, lovesick, negligence, parry, pass by, rebuff, reject, relegate, renunciation, repudiate, run-around, shirk, skip, skulk, sneer, snub, weasel, wriggle

31 **learn:** absorb, ascertain, decipher, determine, discover, edification, get, hear, master, pick up, research, study, turn up

32 **love:** acceptance, admiration, adoration, adulation, affection, amour, appreciate, approval, attention, bask, bewitched, canonize, charity, consideration, constancy, delight in, dig, discrimination, dote on/dote upon, enamored, enjoy, esteem, exult, fall for, fascinated, favor, flame, fond, get a kick out of, gratitude, idolize, leaning, like, mad, mercy, passion, predilection, prize, rapture, respect, revere/reverence, savor, taste, thrill, treasure, venerate, zeal

33 **mental event:** learn, shock, think

34 **mental perception:** ascertain, behold, burn, empathize, gnaw, grope, learn, note, observe, pity, seethe, sense, sorrow, visualize, wonder

35 **mental preparation:** abide, adjust, brainstorm, center, comply, conceive, convert, crawl, deign, design, dismiss, face, get over, habituate, look out, melt, plan, prepare, quail, reform, rehabilitate, relent, resist, season, sink, steel, stoop, succumb, sweat, train, withhold, yield

36 **plan:** arrange, base, book, budget, chart, concoct, conspire, contrive, coordinate, delineate, devise, dream up, fabricate, finesse, formulate, hatch, intrigue, lay, machinate, manufacture, organize, parlay, plot, project, purpose, rough out, shape, synchronize

37 **reason:** analyze, clear up, construe, criticize, decipher, do, equate, figure, gauge, induction, judgment, make, overview, premise, rank, reckon, speculate, survey

38 **recognize:** acknowledge, come across, conjure up, cut, detection, differentiate, discriminate, elude, familiarize, feel, inure, mark, pinpoint, recognition, remark, salute/salutation, spot, stereotype

39 **relate:** ascribe, association, class, classify, compare, contrast, equate, implication, pigeonhole

40 **remember:** block out, flashback, hindsight, mind, recollect, remembrance, reminisce, retrospect, think

41 **select:** aim, allot, appoint, assign, cast, choose, designate, elect, excerpt, finger, name, nominate, opt, prefer, relegate, turn, vote

42 **surprise:** alarm, appall/appal, astound, backfire, bedazzle, bewilder, confound, dazzle, dumbfound, electrify, frighten, overwhelm, petrify, shock, startle, stun/stupefy, terrify

43 **think:** count, devise, envisage/envision, imagine, occur, picture, see, thought

COMMUNICATIVE

44 **accuse:** affront, bastardize, betrayal, blow up, charge, condemnation, denounce, forswear, groan, heckle, humble, impeach, impute, indict, invective, malign, persecute, rant, reprimand, reprove, scold, tax, tirade, vilify, vituperate

45 **answer:** acknowledge, decline, disclaimer, give in/give up, reaction, repartee, respond, return

46 **argue:** ado, altercation, argument, battle, bicker, cause celebre, conflict, confrontation, contend, contest, contradiction, controversy, demur, dicker, difference, disagree, dispute, dissent, divide, double standard, expostulate, falling out, fight, friction, haggle, hue and cry, imbroglio, misunderstanding, object, protest, quibble, rebut, rift, row, run-in, sass, squabble, tiff, vendetta, wrangle

47 **articulate:** catcall, delivery, elocution, exclaim, hail, holler, mumble, pipe, put, slur, speech, talk, utterance, yell

48 **ask:** accost, apology, application, approach, beg, canvass, charter, consult, crave, cross-examine, desire, enquiry, examine, grill, implore, inquire, interrogate, investigate, invitation, invocation, pester, plead, pray, propose, pump, quest, quiz, requisition, seek, survey

49 **assert:** accredit, adduce, advocate, affirmation, allege, announcement, attest, bemoan, bluster, brag, bring out, come clean, crow, declaim, declare, deny, drum into, emphasize, exclaim, exult, gloat, gloss, gush, impute, insist, justify, level, maintain, mockery, overrate, play down, plead, point out, proclaim, promote, pronounce, punctuate, push, rave, retract, rumor, speak out/speak up, state, stress, support, swear, testify, testimony, underscore, vindicate, vouch, whitewash, witness

50 **authorize:** accede, accredit, acknowledgment, affirm, appoint, approve, assign, back, bar, bless, certify, chicken out, concession, constitute, countenance, crown, dedicate, delegation, disown, enable, endorse, enjoin, entrust, exempt, forgive, induct, invest, lay, let off, make, negate, nominate, notarize, okay, order, overrule, permission, place, prohibit, recall, release, repeal, revoke, spare, subscribe, validate, veto, warrant, witness

51 **comment:** accost, add, annotate, babble, bemoan, bravado, broach, congratulate, couch, declaim, deliver, editorial, express, fumigate, greeting, hearsay, interrupt, jaw, observation, pontificate, ramble, rave, report, say, state, throw out, vent, voice, yak/yap

52 **criticize:** abuse, admonition, aspersion, assault, bad-mouth, baste, beef, berate, browbeat, castigate, chasten, chew out, come down on, complaint, condemnation, correct, criticism, critique, cut, damn, debase, denigrate, denunciation, deprecate, deride, detract, diatribe, disparage, dress down, flak, fulminate, gainsay, gird, gripe, grouch, hiss, humiliate, impugn, invective, jaw, knock, lament, lay into, malign, mortify, mug, nag, offense, pick at/pick on, protest, rail, rap, reflection, reprimand, reprove, revile, row, sarcasm, scorn, sit-in, sneer, storm, swear, tell off, upbraid, vituperate

53 **demand:** adjure, beckon, behest, bidding, call, charge, command, crave, cross-examine, debrief, demand, direct, enjoin, exact, extortion, grease, importune, inflict, instruct, necessitate, order, petition, query, request, requisition, solicit, squeeze, supplicate, take on

54 **deny:** abjure, abuse, affront, attack, backstab, bad-mouth, belie, blacken, blemish, confront, curse, darn, defamation, defile, demur, denigrate, detract, dig, disclaim, discountenance, disgrace, disown, disparagement, downplay, explode, flout, fulminate, gainsay, gird, invective, jeer, lament, lecture, malign, minimize, mouth, needle, oppose, protest, put down, put-down, rebuff, refute, remonstrate, renunciation, run down, satirize, scold, show up, sit-in, slander, smear, snap, snub, squeal, sully, swearing, taunt, tirade, turn, underestimate, vituperation, write off, yammer

55 **describe:** articulate, blab, delineate, mean, narration, paraphrase, portray, recount, signify, state, sum up, translate, unfold, utter

56 **discuss:** argue, belabor, communicate, conference, debate, deliberation, dialogue/dialog, gossip, intercede, jabber, negotiate, powwow, reason, repartee, symposium, treat, word

57 **explain:** account for, admit, apprise, cite, clarify, come clean, concede, confirm, corroborate, defense, demonstrate, dilate, elucidate, enlighten, evidence, expand, explicate, gloss, illustrate, itemize, let on, palliate, plea, prove, recite, simplify, speak out/speak up, spell out, translator, warrant

58 **fabricate:** aspersion, belie, disprove, profane

59 **fool:** adulate, artifice, bamboozle, beguile, blow up, brownnose, cajole, cheat, circumvent, con, corner, cross, deceive, decoy, defraud, dirty tricks, dishonesty, dissimulate, dodge, double-cross, double-dealing, dupe, elude, ensnare, entrap, excuse, fake, fence, finesse, flatterer, fleece, forge, fraud, fudge, game, gimmick, grift, hanky-panky, hoax, hocus-pocus, impersonate, imposture, invent, kid, make believe, masquerade, mince, mock, outwit/outsmart, palliate, parlay, play dirty, ploy, posture, pretend, pretext, renege, ruse, scam, sham, shirk, sidestep, skulk, sport, string along, take, trap, trickery, welsh, wit

60 **inform:** acknowledge, address, advertise, allow, allusion, apprise, bare, betrayal, blab, breathe, briefing, broadcast, chronicle, clue, come out with, confession, convey, debunk, define, detail, dictate, divulge, expose, feature, furnish, give, gossip, hint, intimate, issue, lecture, newscaster, orate, out of the closet, pass, post, proclaim, promulgate, publication, publish, release, reveal, show up, speak, spill, squeal, talk, tip, uncover, unveil, weatherperson, whisper

61 **instruct:** bar, educate, prescribe

62 **label:** attach, call, define, dub, identify, name, style, term, title

63 **lie:** backbiting, bunk, casuistry, default, distort, duplicity, equivocate, evasion, exaggeration, fabrication, falsify, fib, fudge, gloss, humbug, invent, juggle, misinform, misrepresent/misquote, misstatement, obscure, pad, perjury, play down, pretend, prevaricate, profess, sell/sell out, simulate, slant, twist, whitewash, wile

64 **noise, animal:** bark, call, chirp, peep, squawk, squeal, yelp

65 **noisemaking:** bang, blast, boom, cadence, chime, clash, click, clump, crash, crinkle, drum, gurgle, honk, hullabaloo, hush, intonation, jar, measure, muffle, mute, peal, pitch, quiet, rattle, resonate, reverberate, roll, rustle, sizzle, squeak, stillness, swing, tempo, thud/thump, tick, toll, tranquility, tune/tune up, uproar, whistle

66 **offer:** allude, lay, pose, proffer, put, volunteer

67 **offer to give:** amends, apology, bidding, concession, extend, offer, present, put, volunteer

68 **persuade:** advance, argument, bend, budge, carry, coerce, convince, discourage, draw, drum up, elicit, entice, forward, goad, hammer away/hammer into, induce, influence, invite, lobby, motivate, negotiation, pitch, prevail upon/prevail on, prompt, reason, spur, sway, urge, win/win over

69 **praise:** accent, acclamation, accredit, adulation, apotheosis, applause, benediction, bless, champion, citation, commend, compliment, congratulations, credit, dedicate, deify, elevate, endorse, eulogize, exalt, extol, flatter, flattery, glorify, homage, laud, lionize, obsequy, plaudits, puff, salute, thanks, tribute, worship

70 **predict:** announce, astrology, augury, divination, forecast, foresee, foretell, oracle, presage, project, prophesy

71 **promise:** assurance, avow, commitment, ensure, go back/go back on, oath, portend, vouch, warrant, word

72 **read:** leaf, narrate, peruse, read, recitation, refer, skim

73 **refer:** attach, drive at, intend, mention, point out

74 **signal:** beckon, call, flag, gesture/gesticulate, harbinger, indicate, nod, page, sign, spell, symbolize, wave

75 **suggest:** advice, advocate, ask, come up with, connote, drum into, exhort, fish for, get at, guide, imply, insinuate, moralize, move, nomination, pontificate, preach, propose, recommend, urge

76 **thank:** appreciate

77 **vocalize:** accent, bark, bellow, cackle, chant, chortle, clamor, cry, drone, giggle, growl, guffaw, harmonize, howl, laugh/laughter, locution, mumble, mutter, parrot, roar, shout, shut up, snap, snicker/snigger/sniggle, squawk, stutter, voice, whimper, whistle, yammer, yowl

78 **warn:** admonish, alert, caution, caveat, defy, enjoin, exhortation, foreboding, foretell, page, remind, warning

79 **write:** abstract, annotate, brand, compile, correspond, cover, dot, draw, edit, endorse, engraving, extract, fleck, graffiti, inscribe, line, mark, page, picture, point, punctuate, quote, revise, rough out, scratch, scribble, sign, stamp, trace, type, underscore, writing

GENERAL

80 **act abstractly:** freak, lurch, wiggle, writhe

81 **act over an area:** decree, tour, veto

82 **admit:** accede, acquiesce, allow, concur, grant

83 **allow:** absolve, acquit, admit, approve, capitulate, contribute, enable, excuse, get off someone's back, have, let, liberate, overlook, permission, pity, reception, suffer, tolerate

84 **arrange:** adjust, antedate, arrangement, center, codify, collocate, concentrate, coordinate, dispose, distribute, divide, graduate, index, line, muddle, organization, organized, pile, program, rank, remodel, synchronize, tabulate, type

85 **attach:** adhere, adjoin, anchor, append, batten, bond, chain, clasp, cohere, engage, fix, hitch, knot, lock, nail, peg, screw, secure, stick, tag, tether, yoke

86 **attack:** aggression, assail, beat up, blast, blind-side, bomb, brutality, charge, come at, *coup d'état*, embroil, encroach, fire, foray, go for, infest, insurrection, invasion, lay into, mug, occupation, offensive, onslaught, overrun, pillage, pounce, raid, ravage, rush, sortie, subvert, waylay

87 **attempt:** acid test, angle for, apply, bother, campaign, commit, counterbalance, dabble, defy, dip into, drill, drudge, elbow grease, emulate, engage, essay, exert, experiment, function, go, hammer away/hammer into, hush, keep at, labor, monkey, overdo, persevere, plod, presume, purpose, putter, risk, seek, slog, strain, struggle, tackle, take a crack at, tinker, try, undertake, venture, whack, work

88 **authorize:** accede, accredit, acknowledgment, affirm, appoint, approve, assign, avowal, ban, bear out, blessing, charter, commission, consent, contract, countermand, decree, delegate, detail, empower, enact, enforce, entitle, establish, fire, grant, inflict, invoke, let, license, name, nod, nomination, nullify, ordain, override, pardon, permit, prescribe, ratify, receive, relieve, reprieve, sanction, station, underwrite, vest, void, withdraw, witness

89 **borrow:** lease, mooch, rent

90 **capture:** abducted, apprehend, arrest, besiege, catch, commandeer, conquer, *coup d'état*, enslave, entangle, expropriate, foray, grab, hijack, hog, incarcerate, nab, net, occupy, pull in, seizure, shanghai, snare, tackle, trap

91 **carry out:** accomplish, actualize, assure, clone, complete, conclude, discharge, duplicate, effect, execute, fill, finish, follow through, get the lead out, handle, implement, make out, meet, obey, offender, perfect, perpetrate, practice, prosecute, realize, render, resonate, rush, specialize, wage

92 **compete:** bout, contend, contest, pit, rival, take on, vie

93 **contract:** catch, incur, waterloo

94 **control:** aegis, contain, deal/deal with, deregulate, discipline, domineer, manage, monopolize, order about, overlook, preside, regulate, ride, steer, wield, work

95 **defeat:** beat, confute, conquest, crush, discomfit, edge, finish, landslide, outdo, overpower, overtake, overwhelm, prostrate, quash, reduce, smash, subjugate, surmount, top, trim, trounce, vanquish, wallop, win

96 **defend:** beard, bulwark, counteract, cover, ensure, fend off, fight back/fight off, parapet, repulse, resistance, save, secure, ward/ward off, withstand

97 **demonstrate:** advertising, demonstrate, evidence, give, imply

98 **divide:** allocate, bestow, cleave, disconnect, disrupt, distribute, divvy up, fragment, mete, partition, portion, quarter, ration, sever, slice, split

99 **enable:** allow, implement, qualify

100 **engage in:** address, apply, dig in, elbow grease, exist, fare, fight, go about, go into, grub, labor, participate, plunge, practice, reiterate, share, step in, take, trouble, undertake, work

101 **err:** Achilles' heel, boo-boo, botch, butcher, err, fault, flounder, frailty, gaffe, goof, impropriety, indiscretion, malpractice, mishandle/mismanage, miss, mistake, neglect, oversight, sin, slip up, stray, transgression, trip, violation, wander

102 **escape:** abscond, avoidance, break, bypass, close call, disappear, dodge, elude, evade, extricate, flight, fly, get out, lose, pussy foot, sidestep, skirt, weasel

103 **examine:** adjudication, analyze, audit, autopsy, check, confirm, decompose, dig, evaluation, explore, go into, go through, graduate, inspect, investigate, judgment, mapmaker, nose, overview, peruse, pore, probe, quest, reconnaissance, review, scan, scrutinize, sift, spy, surveillance, test, try on/try out, weigh

104 **exchange:** alternate, barter, reciprocate, replace, substitute, swap/swop, transpose

105 **existential change:** age, awaken, begin, date, disappear, dissipate, dissolve, fade, go, languish, originate, perish, run out, succumb, wake/waken

106 **fight:** act up, altercation, bout, brawl, clamor, combat, confrontation, contention, contravene, donnybrook, engage, faction, feud, fight back/fight off, fracas, free-for-all, fuss, hassle, mayhem, misunderstanding, opposition, racket, rebellion, resistance, revolution, riot, row, run-in, scuffle, skirmish, spat, struggle, tussle, uproar, war, wrangle

107 **fuel:** charge, fill, supply

108 **give:** administer, allocate, allow, atone, bequeath, cast, commend, compensate, consign, contribute, defray, delivery, devote, disseminate, donate, emit, entrust, furnish, give away, hand over, kick in, mete, pass off, provide, render, reward, sacrifice, show, transfer, will

109 **group:** aggregate, amass, blend, cluster, collection, compilation, compound, confluence, consolidate, cull, flock, gather, herd, pick, rake, recruit, round up, store

110 **help:** abet, alleviate, assistance, baby, bail out, benefit, boost, care, coddle, contribute, cover, cultivation, defend, doctor, ease, encourage, facilitate, fawn, foster, further, go straight, guide, indulge, intervene, keep, lavish, lift, mind, nurse, oblige, patronize, play ball, promote, provide, reform, serve, shore, simplify, speed, sponsor, synchronize, support, sympathize, temper, toady, underwrite, uphold

111 **imitate:** ape, mimic, mock, parallel, pattern, repeat, sham, takeoff, take off

112 **involve:** attack, confuse, cooperate, count, embody, encapsulate, encompass, entangle, figure in, include, interpolate, overdo, synchronize, task, teamwork

113 **join:** accompany, adhere, affiliate, alloy, annex, append, articulation, assembly, band, butt, close, cohere, compound, converge, desegregate, embody, fasten, fuse, get together, hitch, integrate, intersect, intertwine/ interweave, knit, lace, meeting, merge, mix, piece, reunion, synthesis, unify, unite, wed

114 **join socially:** affiliate, assemble, attach, band, bump into, call, chaperon, collusion, congregate, consultation, convention, convocation, dalliance, dally/dally with, desegregate, enter, fraternize, group, hang about/hang around/hang out, huddle, intermingle, intertwine/interweave, league, matriculate, mix, session, take

115 **lend:** defray, fund, invest, loan, rent, trust

116 **lose:** deliver, forfeit, leak, misplace, sacrifice, wipeout

117 **manage:** adjust, administration, carry on, compose, control, deal/deal with, direct, dispose, drill, face, farm, fend for, get by, guide, handling, lead, management, monitor, operate, order about, overlook, oversight, preside, regulate, reign, run, save, subjugate, supervision, treatment, work

118 **manifest:** agree, connote, embody, evince, exude, indicate, point, promise, radiate

119 **modify an event:** abide, advent, birth, cessation, closure, come out, coming, complement, conception, conclusion, dawn, develop, disposal, end, end up, entrance, expire, finish, give in/give up, halt, lapse, matriculate, pass, pull out, quit, relinquish, resign, result, resurrection, revival, secede, standstill, stop, suspend, terminate, termination

120 **obtain:** acquire, amass, capitalize, gain, get at, land, lay up/lay by, possess, pull in, reap, recruit, repossess, save, strike, win

121 **prevent:** abolish, abort, abstain, adjournment, arrest, avert, avoidance, balk, banish, birth control, bog down, break, censor, check, circumvent, close, constrain, contravene, counter, cross, cut short, deactivate, defeat, deferment/deferral, deprivation, deter, discontinue, dispossess, dissolve, drop out, exclude, foil, forbid, freeze, gag, hesitate, hinder, hold back/hold off, impede, incapacitate, intercept, interference, invalidate, keep one's cool, localize, muffle, negate, neutralize, nullify, obviate, omit, override/overrule, parry, pigeonhole, preempt, privation, prohibit, proscribe, pull up, put off, quell, refrain, remove, repress, respite, retard, rule out, run-around, scratch, seclude, shut, shut off/shut out, slowpoke, squash, stall, stem, still, stymie, suppress, table, thwart, turn off, veto, void, waiver, withdraw, withhold

122 **punish:** avenge, chastise, correction, evict, expel, pay, scourge, sentence

123 **punishment:** blackmail, damage(s), dressing-down, fine, lesson, rap, reproach, sanction, whipping

124 **receive:** accept, acquire, bring in, come in for, find, have, make, profit, reap, recoup, retrieve, take

125 **record:** enroll, enumerate, list, register, score, tally, transcribe

126 **rectify:** accommodate, appease, arbitrate, atone, avenge, compensate, correct, counteract, cover, debug, edit, equalize, fix, iron out, mediate, mend, overhaul, placate, quiet, recoup, redeem, reform, remedy, restore, retribution, revision, satisfy, square, suit, temper, tune/tune up, untangle

127 **release:** acquittal, clear, delivery, disentangle, dismissal, exculpate, exonerate, free, loose/loosen, redeem, relinquish, save

128 **replace:** change, follow, supplant

129 **reserve:** allocate, assignment, claim, come by, deserve, earmark, engage, entitle, intend, put away/put aside/put by, spare, subscribe

130 **restrict:** bar, bind, bound, brake, circumscribe, cocoon, constrain, constrict, control, curb, dam, defer, deferment/deferral, desensitize, embargo, enjoin, expatriate, expulsion, fetters, forbear, gag, grind, hamper, handicap, hem/hem in, hobble, hold back/hold off, impair, imposition, inhibit, keep one's cool, localize, moderate, obligate, ostracism, prohibit, rein, restrain, retard, shackle, slowdown, squelch, strangle, subdue, suspend, tie/tie up

131 **return:** deliver, hand over, recall, regain, requite, retrieve, return

132 **reward:** award, confer, reward

133 **rule:** abdicate, command, deposition, displace, enforcement, impose, rule, supremacy

134 **save:** cocoon, conserve, deposit, guard, lay up/lay by, maintenance, patrol, preserve, put away/put aside/put by, rescue, salvation, shelter, spare, ward/ward off, watch

135 **separate:** abstract, appropriate, assign, classification, dedicate, dichotomy, disconnect, disentangle, dismantle, disperse, dissociate, division, fragment, garner, hoard, loneliness, part, quarantine, secession, seclusion, segregation, separation, split up, sunder, unlock

136 **serve:** accommodate, board, cater, obey, pamper, provide, spoon-feed, wait on

137 **shape change:** beat, bruise, chip, cleave, compact, crinkle, depreciation, disfigure, distort, divide, edge, enlarge, file, fragment, hack, lacerate, mow, nick, pierce, puncture, roll, scar, sculpture, sharpen, shear, shrink, skew, slice, stiffen, taper/taper off, thin, truncate, whet, wound

138 **show:** advertising, circulate, point, represent, symbolize, trot out, unveil

139 **steal:** abduct, abduction, appropriation, bilk, burglary, confiscate, divest, embezzle, extort, filch, flimflam, heist, hijacker, kidnap, larceny, loot, milk, pilfer, pinch, plagiarism, plunder, pocket, ransack, rip off, rip-off, sack, shoplift, snitch, swindle, take, unmask, welsh

140 **supply:** appoint, deal, dish out, dispense, distribute, divide, dole out, feed, fuel, glut, infuse, keep, larder, maintain, nourish, nurture, provide, publish, ration, render, rig, serve, stockpile, support, sustain

141 **surpass:** abound, better, cap, eclipse, excel, get ahead, hack it, lick, outdistance, outflank, outweigh, pass, prevail, supersede, surpass, tower, triumph, win

142 **take:** acquire, arrogate, assumption, burn,

compass, cull, deprivation, disarm, dispossess, drain, educe, exact, exfoliate, extract, harvest, leach, molt, peel, pocket, privation, ransack, sap, usurp, wring

143 transfer abstractly: afford, bring, consign, conveyance, delegation, recall, relay, relegate, turn over

MOTION

144 be moved: earthquake, flop, lap

145 change of place: flicker, motion, onrush, pop, sway, swing, swivel, tremor

146 flow: run, seep, surge, teem, trickle

147 move: bob, careen, circulate, contort, curl, dandle, descend, dislocate, displace, drift, entwine, fidget, flourish, haul, loop, oscillate, paddle, pivot, pulsate/pulse, revolve, rock, rotate, skirt, topple, transport, tumble, twine, uproot, waft, waver, wheel, wield

148 move mechanically: aviation, carriage, cart, fly, mobilize, operate, park, rocket, skyrocket, takeoff, veer

149 move oneself: ascend, bend, flap, flounce, gait, gambol, go for, hike, lope, mount, mountaineering, negotiate, pad, patter, quail, rock, round, stamp, stir, stride, stump, tilt, tread, tumble, wallow, wriggle

150 move oneself quickly: barge in/barge into, bolt, bustle, coast, dart, decamp, flash, flinch, flutter, gallop, glide, hurry, hustle, jiggle, make off, plunge, prance, rebound, ricochet, run, scamper, scramble, shake, shudder, skedaddle, skip, slide, slither, speed, sprint, storm, swerve, tear, twirl, wag, whiz, wobble, zip, zoom

151 move oneself slowly: amble, creep, dalliance, decline, dilly-dally, hobble, knock about/knock around, laggard, linger, lumber, meander, plod, prowl, ramble, reel, saunter, slink/slither, sneak, steal, stroll, tarry, tramp, waddle, wander

152 move quickly: advance, agitate, capsize, course, dispatch, ejaculate, flicker, flutter, jerk, jostle, lurch, plunge, quake, rattle, shake, shoot, skate, skim, slip, speed, stampede, tear, tremble, vibrate, wag, whirl, wiggle, wobble

153 move slowly: agitation, dawdle, lag, reel

154 position oneself: arise, cant, get down, get up, huddle, kneel, list, lounge, nestle, perch, pose, recline, rest, seat, slouch, wince

155 travelling: lift, procession, transit, voyage

PHYSICAL

156 abuse: consumption, corrode, dissipate, enervate, exploit, force, fritter, lose, milk, mishandle/mismanage, misuse, pervert, riddle, sap, squander, throw away, wear

157 anatomical change: distend, neuter

158 arrange: agitation, collate, crease, dispose, group, lay, located, mix up, order, position, rank, ruffle, separate, snarl, split up, stack, straighten, weave

159 arrive: admission, alight, appearance, arrival, billow, butt in, come in, cross, disembark, embark, enter, foray, get back, get on, go ahead, immigrate, influx, intrude, invasion, lance, light, lunge, penetrate, pierce, progress, reach, return, stalk, trespass, turn up

160 attach: adhere, adjoin, anchor, append, batten, bond, chain, clasp, cohere, engage, fix, hitch, latch, moor, paste, pin, seal, shut, tack, tape, tie, yoke

161 bathe: ablution, decontaminate, wet

162 beautify: accessorize, adornment, decorate, doll up, emblazon, face-lift, fix up, furbish, ornament, shave, trim

163 breathe: breath, draw, expire, heave, inhale, puff, suffocate, yawn

164 catch: intercept, tackle

165 clean: ablution, bath, brush, clarify, cleanse, decontaminate, distill, do up, expurgate, flush, gut, lather, mop, purification, rake, refinement, scour, scrub, sweep, wipe

166 climb: arise, ascension, mount, scale, surface

167 clothe: array, disrobe, dress, garb, ornament, primp, sport, stuff, try on/try out, wear

168 construct: build, dismantle, establish, forge, found, make, pave, put up, rear, remodel, revamp, ultramodern

169 consume: absorption, chew, contract, crunch, deplete, diet, dig in, dispatch, draft, eat, exhaust, feast, finish, glut, gobble, gormandize, graze, guzzle, ingest, nibble, nosh, peck, polish off, prey on, quaff, sip, stuff, take, tear down, wolf, xerophagy

170 cook: agitation, barbecue, beat, brew, butcher, churn, distill, flavor, fry, honeyed, knead, microwave, pickle, preserve, season, sizzle, sweeten, warm, whip

171 copy: ape, duplicate, emulate, forge, imitate, mimic, multiply, parrot, pretend, reconstruct, reiterate, reproduce, simulate, take after, Xerox

172 cover: blanket, camouflage, disguise, drape, dust, enshroud, face, funeral, glaze, inter, laminate, line, masquerade, muzzle, oil, paint, paper, pervade, sheet, smother, spread, varnish, veneer, wrap

173 create: bear, brainstorm, coin, compose, concoct, construct, design, engineer, establishment, fashion, film, form, formulate, generate, hatch, institute, make, materialize, mold, piece, procreate, regenerate, reproduction, wing it, work

174 create art: chart, depict, draw, engraving, illustrate, imprint, mount, paint, picture, portray, pottery, printer, sculpture, stamp, trace

175 create with effort: beat, mold

176 cut: amputate, ax/axe, bisect, chisel, cleave, crop, cut up, dent, dissect, engrave, etch, fell, hack, lacerate, mangle, molt, mutilate, notch, peel, pink, scar, scratch, shave, shred, slash, slit, trim, whittle

177 decorate: accessorize, adornment, decoration, embellishment, embroider, enrich, furnish, modernize, paper, renovate, trim, varnish

178 dig: bore, claw, dredge, excavate, exhume, hollow, mine, plow, root, tunnel, uproot

179 discharge: blast, blow up, burst, come from, detonate, drain, drop, ejaculate, ejection, emanation, emit, eruption, excrete, expel, explosion, exude, flare, flow, gag, give off/give out, gush, impregnate, infiltrate, infuse, inundate, jet, leak, mushroom, ouster, outflow, overrun, penetrate, permeate, pour, project, scatter, seep, shoot, spew, spit, spout, sprinkle, squirt, surge, teem, torrent, vent, vomit

180 dispose: boot, chuck, disposal, dispose of, do away with, elimination, kick out, rejection, scrap, throw away, void

181 drop: alight, crash, decline, descent, dive, droop, duck, fall, flop, fumble, go under, keel over, light, percolate, plumb, plunge, sag, settle, sink, slump, stoop, submerge, suspend, thud/thump, tumble, wilt

182 equip: arm, do up, fit, gear, rig, stockpile

183 find: come across, detection, discovery, find, learn, meet, pinpoint, repossess, strike, track/track down, uncover, unearth

184 form: arch, bloat, carve, constitute, crumple, curve, form, model, pat, sculpture, twist, work

185 gesture: bawl, beat, bite, blink, chew, disgorge, dribble, drool, expire, grimace, guffaw, hemorrhage, kink, laugh/laughter, lick, necking, perspire, puff, pulsate/pulse, purse, scowl, slobber, smirk, sob, spit, sweat, tear/tears, twitch, wail, whimper, wink, yawn

186 grind: abrade, corrode, crunch, frazzle, granulate, mill, powder, rasp, scrape

187 guide: aviation, conduct, direct, drive, ferry, inject, lay, level, marshal, navigate, point, round, row, show, sled, steer, transport, usher

188 hide: ambush, bury, camouflage, conceal, cover, cover-up, cringe, disguise, dissimulate, embed, ensconce, envelop, isolation, lurk, masquerade, palliate, screen, seclusion, sequester, shrink, shut off/shut out, sneak, withhold

189 hit: applaud, bang, baste, batter, beat, blindside, boot, buffet, bunt, chip, clash, clip, clout, collide, concussion, crash, cuff, deflect, drive, flail, glance, hammer, jab, jostle, knock, lick, nail, peck, plaudits, pound, punch, rap, scourge, slap, smack, sock, strike, swipe, tap, thud/thump, tip, whack, whip

190 hold: anchor, clog, cradle, dandle, embrace, grab, hug, nuzzle, prop, retard, shore, support, sustain, tangle

191 hold forcefully: apprehend, cage, clasp, clinch, confinement, constriction, cramp, detain, embrace, enslave, fetters, grasp, gripe, hold, incarcerate, overpower, press, shackle, snatch, strangle, throttle, wrestle

192 illegal behavior: backstab, bleed, break, bribe, buy, conspire, contravene, delin-

quency, disobey, extortion, felony, foul, graft, hara-kiri, holdup, imposture, infringe, intrigue, kickback, larceny, loot, misconduct, misdeed/misdemeanor, offense, pick, piracy, poach, rape, rip off, rip-off, robbery, sexual assault, shenanigans, smear campaign, speculation, stick up, take, theft, treason, victimize, violation

193 join physically: link, merge, mingle, piece, splice, tuck, unite, weld, yoke

194 jump: bounce, clear, dive, gallop, hop, lunge, plunge, rear, recoil, skip, start, vault

195 leave: abandon, back, blow, bolt, break, break out, cringe, dart, depart, desert, deviate, digress, disappearance, distance, draw back, ebb, embark, exit, fall back, flee, fly, get along, get out, goodbye, go out, jilt, light out, maroon, parting, push off/push on, quit, recoil, renunciation, resign, retire, run, scram, segregation, shake off, shrink, strike out, takeoff, threads, trousers, vacate, withdrawal

196 lift: boost, elevate, heave, pry, rear

197 measure: balance, survey

198 move living quarters: anyplace, approach, battlefield, colonization, defect, deport, destination, element, empire, evict, exile, expel, jurisdiction, locale/locality, lookout, move, neighborhood, outdoors, point, post, province, region, rendezvous, seat, site, soil, spot, stop, terminal, turn, where

199 perform: fan, work

200 physical action: application, bash, drop, hold, plunk, slug

201 position: aim, bow, cant, cock, deposit, dip, disseminate, entwine, hang, insert, installation, intersperse, jut, lay, lie, located, loop, occlude, pile, place, point, post, put, recline, seat, set, slant, slouch, sprawl, squat, station, stoop, tip, train, turn, twist, wallow, wrinkle

202 prepare physically: acclimate, accustom, braid, brush up, bundle, coat, disguise, domesticate, dress, embattle, fine-tune, fix up, fortify, gear, gild, gloss, grease, habituate, knit, make up, modulate, overhaul, pad, plaster, polish, prepare, preserve, primp, reform, refrigerate, regenerate, rejuvenate, renovate, round, set, shine, smear, square, strain, toughen, training, weather

203 print: edit, printer, write

204 process: gnash, work

205 produce: agriculture, fabrication, forge, generate, horticulture, make, mint, print, production, turn out, yield

206 pull: drag, extract, lug, pluck, schlep, strain, tow, twist, wrench, yank

207 pursue: chase, dragnet, hound, shadow, tag, trace, track/track down, trail

208 push: advance, back, barge in/barge into, billow, blow up, bulge, burst, compress, crowd, crush, depress, drive, extrude, force, indent, insinuate, jam, jolt, knead, mash, mob, notch, poke, prod, protrude, pump, repel, roll, shove, slam, squish, tax, tip, trample, wrestle, wring

209 **put in container:** box, enclose, flood, glut, inject, interpolate, load, plug, ram, stow, surfeit

210 **relax:** asleep, dalliance, dawdle, dilly-dally, kick back, loiter, lounge, nap, putter, relaxation, rest, slack/slacken, stay, trifle, unwind, wait

211 **remove:** abstract, blot, break off, cancel, clear, cut out, denude, deportation, disarmament, distill, doff, drain, eliminate, eradicate, evict, except, excerpt, excoriate, expulsion, extirpate, extraction, gut, leach, oust, pry, relegate, replace, shed, skin, subtract, top, unburden, unload, void, withdrawal

212 **repair:** adjust, debug, fine-tune, overhaul, remedy, restore, tinker, troubleshooter

213 **reposition:** bank, bump, crinkle, crouch, curve, descend, dislocate, displace, drag, invert, reverse, sidetrack, squirm, turn, veer, warp

214 **rip:** claw, lacerate, snag, tear

215 **rub:** bite, burnish, creak, erase, file, friction, glaze, grate, polish, smear

216 **search:** comb, dig, explore, forage, grope, hunt, investigation, nose, plumb, prospect, quest, ransack, rummage, scout, snoop, track/track down

217 **send:** banish, carry, channel, consign, convey, delivery, deportation, dismiss, dispatch, distribute, download, extradite, forward, mail, pass, pipe, remit, route, sled, take, transmit, waft

218 **sew:** baste, embroidery, line, sew, tack, tuck

219 **squeeze:** choke, clinch, constriction, crush, enfold, pinch, pulp, rumple, squash

220 **stab:** claw, gore, impale, lacerate, perforate, prick, puncture, spike, stick, tap, transfix

221 **start:** actuate, emanate, embark on, engender, establish, fall to, found, impel, inaugurate, initiate, inspire, installation, instill, introduce, kindle, lead, mobilize, open, pioneer, preface, provoke, recharge, renew, resurgence, resuscitate, revive, set up, take on, turn on, whip up

222 **throw:** buck, chuck, dash, disseminate, eject, extrude, fling, heave, intersperse, launch, lob, pelt, powder, propagate, scatter, sling, splatter, toss

223 **transfer of an object:** download, send, transaction, transfer

224 **travel:** accompany, cover, cruise, double back, embark, expedition, explore, flight, gad, hike, journey, knock about/knock around, migrate, mountaineering, navigation, odyssey, passage, pilgrimage, range, roam, safari, shuttle, takeoff, tour, tramp, trip, voyage, wander

225 **use:** apply, bolt, broach, consumption, devour, drain, eat, employment, exercise, exhaust, exploit, fatigue, gormandize, maneuver, milk, partake, polish off, run, squander, telephone, wear, wield

226 **use living quarters:** abide, cohabit, exist, hang about/hang around/hang out, live, lodge, reside, situate, stay, visit

227 **visit:** call, drop in, see, stay, tour

CAUSES

ABSTRACT

228 **affect:** change, evoke

229 **event that causes another:** account, cause, precipitous/precipitate

230 **state of causation:** abortion, Achilles' heel, aftermath, anticlimax, astonishment, backlash, bang, bereavement, blessing, blot, booboo, boom, break, by-product, cease-fire, change, check, coincidence, collision, complication, congestion, consternation, corollary, decay, decomposition, degeneracy, descent, deterioration, disappointment, disaster area, disposal, dissipation, effect, ending, error, eventuality, flap, flurry, frenzy, fulfillment, gaffe, glitch, gridlock, hubbub, humbug, imperfection, impression, impurity, infection, issue, jitters, lather, malarky, miscarriage, mix-up, muddle, nonsense, outcome, payoff, piffle, portent, price, product, racket, rash, resolution, rigmarole, scare, settlement, shortfall, snafu, stain, stigma, stir, taint, tempest, to-do, tomfoolery, trip, truce, turmoil, twaddle, unification, upshot, whirl, wonderment

231 **to be:** alienate, antagonize, awaken, calm, compound, energize, materialize, sterilize, threaten

232 **to change:** adapt, alter, assimilate, break even, change, conversion, co-opt, distort, double back, expurgate, fit, invert, neutralize, overturn, shift, tamper, translate, turn

233 **to change abstractly:** demote, intensify, mitigate

234 **to change an event:** abbreviate, acceleration, actuate, approach, bed, break off, build, cease, commence, conclude, continue, cut in, cut short, determine, discontinue, dispose of, dissolve, enter, floor it, graduate, hurry, invalidate, knock off, leave, lift, nip, pause, preclude, put off, quell, quit, remit, retire, revoke, ruin, scrub, slow, stall, terminate, turn out, waive, wrap up

235 **to change cognitively:** agree, concede, lay

236 **to change number or quantity:** abbreviate, abstract, add, advance, alleviate, amplify, blow up, build, bump, compress, contract, cut, deduct, deflate, digest, discount, downsize, encapsulate, epitomize, evolve, extend, fatten, imbue, inflate, lengthen, lop, magnify, narrow, prune, reduce, shorten, step up, supplement, take, truncate, widen

237 **to change or affect an event:** delay, protract, stop, weigh

238 **to change state of being:** dispatch, do for

239 **to continue:** abide, broaden, come, drag on/drag out, drawl, dwell on/ dwell upon, elongate, extend, go, hammer away/hammer into, hold, lengthen, perpetuate, persist, protract, remain, scam, take up

240 **to diminish:** abate, aggravate, alloy, blot, break, cheapen, compromise, corrupt, cut, debase, debilitate, decline, decrease, depress, disarrange, doctor, downplay, emas-

culate, fatigue, impair, let up, minimize, moderate, muffle, pale, pick-me-up, provocation, reduce, retard, sap, slash, stimulus, tax, undermine, wear, worsen

241 to function: animate, cause, start

242 to happen: accelerate, breathe, copy, ensue, eventuate, expedite, facilitate, follow, incite, induce, influence, instigate, intervene, motivate, muddle, oblige, occur, pass, prod, prompt, put, result, stimulate, unsettle, work up, wreak

243 to have: accent, give, transfer

244 to improve: advance, ameliorate, assuage, augmentation, benefit, betterment, brighten, brush up, confirm, cultivate, dignify, enrich, garnish, lighten, mend, pad, perk up, quench, raise, relieve, revise, rouse, strengthen, touch up, update, upgrade

245 to increase quantity: accumulate, addition, aggrandize, amplify, augmentation, boost, build up, deepen, double, enlarge, evolve, extend, fatten, imbue, inflate, lengthen, magnify, reinforce, supplement, widen

246 to injure: abuse, ail, batter, beat, bruise, cost, crush, debilitate, deface, deform, desecrate, devastate, disagree, disfigure, expose, fragment, gripe, handicap, hurt, incapacitate, jeopardize, lacerate, maim, mar, mistreat, mutilate, outrage, paralyze, poison, pummel, repay, ruin, sabotage, scar, shatter, shoot, smart, snap, spoil, stress, taint, torture, turn, violate, vitiate, wrong

247 to reduce quantity: abbreviate, abstract, commute, condense, curtail, cut back, deflate, digest, downsize, epitomize, lessen, minimize, narrow, prune, shorten, summarize, trim, whittle

PHYSICAL

248 to break: collide, crash, dash

249 to burn: arson, conflagration, flame, glow, incinerate, kindle, light, scorch, singe, smolder

250 to change physically: awake, blacken, bleach, brighten, buttress, color, confirm, consolidate, crimp, cross, daub, deepen, dehydrate, dilute, disarrange, disfigure, disorganize, disturb, douse, dye, edge, emasculate, exhaust, fatigue, ferment, flatten, fog, geld, harden, hone, intensify, lay, light, liquefy, loose/loosen, melt, neaten, numb, pacify, petrify, prostrate, quicken, redden, roll, rumple, set, shadow, shrivel, slow, soften, sour, stain, stiffen, strengthen, sully, temper, thin, tighten, tint, turn, vitiate, weary, whiten

251 to create: bear, breed, concoct, construct, engineer, fabricate, form, hatch, mint, originate, procreate, regenerate, spawn

252 to destroy: ablate, abolition, annul, batter, bomb, bring down, burst, butcher, clobber, come unglued, consumption, coup de grâce, crumple, cut down, decimate, deforestation, demolition, desecrate, desolate, devastate, dismantle, dispatch, do away with, do in, end, endanger, eradicate, erosion, execute, expunge, exterminate, extinguish, finish, genocide, hara-kiri, homicide, jeopardize, kill, knock off, liquidate, mangle, massacre, murder, obliterate, paralyze, pillage, poison, prostrate, pulverize, put away, put out, quench, raze, ruin, sack, shiver, slaughter, smash, stamp out, subdue, suppress, undo, vandalism, violation, wipe out, wreck

253 to grow: cultivate, farm, flower, raise, till, vegetate

254 to make dirty: adulterate, clutter, mess up, smudge, stain, tarnish

255 to make hot or cold: air, chill, freeze, heat, melt, numb, refrigerate, shrivel, warm

256 to make wet: absorb, dampen, dip, drench, drool, dunk, extinguish, marinate, oil, permeate, saturate, souse, splash, spray, squirt, submerge

FIELDS OF HUMAN ACTIVITY

AGRICULTURE

257 action: agriculture, bury, cross, cultivation, deforestation, erosion, gather, harvest, preservation, reap, round up, sprout, till, work

258 organization: cowboy, grange, ranch

THE ARTS

259 art object: antique, canvas, coat, composition, decal, depiction, dye, embroidery, etching, figure, glaze, illustration, insignia, landscape, logo, medium, monument, pattern, piece, pigment, portrait, print, pyramid, silhouette, statue, workmanship, wreath

260 created object: alloy, apparatus, ash(es), brew, by-product, capsule, change, cinder, composition, concoction, creation, debris, derivative, dip, dregs, dung, enamel, excrement, fake, fertilizer, flotsam, folder, froth, fuzz, garland, glass, grit, half-breed, hodgepodge, huddle, imitation, invention, junk, lather, litter, mess, mix/mixture, oddity, offshoot, outgrowth, pack, paper, patchwork, placebo, potpourri, quantum leap, remainder, replica, rest, scum, sewage, slime, smashup, spin-off, surplus, trash, waste, work, wreck, yield

261 exhibition: appear, boast, declassify, demonstration, display, exhibit, exhibitionism, exposure, flaunt, glitz, impress, loom, mark, parade, peep/peer, point out, posture, present, produce, reflect, render, show, showpiece, simplify, sport, strut, typify, unfold

262 musical instrument: accompaniment, baton, compact disc, harmony, measure, melody, note, requiem, song, strain

263 performance: anthem, ballet, burlesque, chant, comedy, concert, dramatization, event, farce, lampoon, medium, movie, music hall, part, piece, premiere, preview, recital, rendition, role, scene, script, setting, skit, takeoff, theater/theatre

264 performance part: act, encore, ovation, prelude, refrain, scene, stunt, tune

265 photograph: observe, portray, proof

COMMUNICATIONS

266 communication: address, ad-lib, arrogate, babble, beam, bid, call, censor, chatter, colloquy, communicate, contact, converse, debrief, discourse, drivel, e-mail, exult, gab, give, improvise, interact, interplay, intrude, magnify, monologue, patter, punctuate, quiet, reach, recant, recitation, recount, rehearse, render, say, shoot the breeze, silence, speak, stammer, talk, telephone, tête-à-tête, transpire, wander, whisper, yak/yap

267 communicative quality: abusive, acid, acrid, ad-lib, amusing, articulate, behind one's back, bitter, blunt, bombastic, brief, brusque, captious, censorious, classified, closemouthed, communicative, confidential, convincing, crisp, crude, curt, cynical, defamatory, demonstrative, derogatory, destructive, direct, dirty, discursive, disjointed, doctrinaire, droll, effusive, embittered, encyclopedic, et cetera, even, expansive, explicit, expressive, extemporaneous/extemporary, fallacious, falsely, fault-finding, fictitious, filthy, firsthand, flatulent, florid, fluent, forcible, forensic, foul, frank, fresh, funny, gabby, genuine, glowing, graphic, grouchy, gruff, hackneyed, hard-line, hateful, heated, hollow, honorable, hypercritical, idle, illustrative, imperious, implied, impromptu, imprudent, incisive, indescribable, ineffable, inexplicable, informative, inoffensive, insistent, instructive, ironic/ironical, jocular/jocose/jocund, keen, laudatory, legendary, lengthy, lip service, literally, long-winded, loose, lurid, malicious, matter-of-fact, meaningful, mendacious, misleading, mouthy, musty, mythical/mythological, nameless, natural, noncommittal, obnoxious, offensive, off the cuff, oily, openhearted, opinionated, oracular, ornery, overblown, parting, penetrating, persuasive, plain, poignant, pompous, pornographic, priceless, privileged, profane, prosaic, pulp, quick-witted, racy, redolent, rhetorical, rich, rough, rude, sarcastic, satirical/satiric, scathing, secretive, sensational, sharp, sharp-tongued, sidesplitting, silent, sincere, smut, snappy, snippy, spicy, square, stilted, straightforward, succinct, summary, symptomatic, talkative, telltale, threadbare, tongue-in-cheek, tongue-tied, trenchant, truculent, truly, trustworthy/trusty, unabridged, unattached, uncommunicative, uninhibited, unsaid, untruthful, unwritten, valedictory, verbal, verbose, vernacular, viperous, vocal, voluble, warm, windy, wordy, X-rated, zany

268 description: appellation, denotation, exposition, formula, hermeneutical, hyperbole, illustration, label, moniker, news, nom de plume, notes, ode, paraphrase, plan, poetry, profile, pseudonym, sobriquet, translation

269 devices used for: alarm, calculator, copy, distress signal, fax, foghorn, photocopy, software, telephone, transcript

270 document, part: addendum, amendment, article, body, clause, condition, epilogue, extract, foreword, item, leaf, margin, passage, prologue, provision/proviso, sheet, sound bite, stipulation, supplement, tag, text

271 document, physical object: act, agreement, analysis, annal(s), annual, article, bill, book, card, catalog/catalogue, chronicle, commitment, composition, constitution, convention, credentials, critique, deed, digest, direction(s), dispatch, docket, documentary, draft, enclosure, epistle, essay, exposition, fiction, form, guarantee, history, injunction, ledger, life, log, manifesto, material, memorandum/memo, missive, narrative, note/notes, notice, opus, pamphlet, paper/papers, pass, patent, petition, placard, poker, poster, proclamation, pronouncement, prose, reading, record, release, résumé, schedule, script, sign, survey, theme, ticket, timetable, voucher, writing

272 document quality: readable, summary, terse

273 humorous tale: banter, crack, joke, lampoon, parody, pun, spoof, take off, trick, wit

274 information: ace in the hole, advice, analysis, announcement, back door, broadcast, buzz, calendar, cautionary tale, charge, clue, confession, construction, cybernetics, data bank, definition, digital library, direction(s), dirt, dope, excerpt, explanation, fact, freeware, grounds, guidance, guideline, hint, illumination, intelligence, key, lead, lesson, lore, material, minutiae, news, notification, online, plug, pointer, prognosis, prompt, proof, publicity, quotation/quote, rebuttal, recommendation, rejoinder, resolution, rumor, science, scuttlebutt, sign, sound bite, story, tidings, tip/tipoff, tutelage, warning, word

275 integral language parts: adjective, antonym, bad form, barbarism, byword, catchword, cliché, euphemism, figure of speech, grammar, jargon, neologism, parlance, proverb, term, word

276 language: adage, alphabet, code, dialect, expression, grammar, lingo, patter, speech, style, tongue, vocabulary, voice

277 media: advertisement, correspondence, desktop publishing, infomercial, memorandum/memo, pen, prattle, rejoinder, rumor, sass, scuttlebutt, small talk, spiel, terminology, tripe, video, videocassette

278 object used in: address, alert, anathema, aphorism, assertion, axiom, back talk, banter, bunk, cant, cause celebre, chatter, cliché, comment, commonplace, congratulations, contention, controversy, criticism, cue, decision, defense, derision, dialogue/dialog, dictum, dirt, dispatch, dispute, dissidence, divination, double standard, double-talk, dressing-down, edict, eloquence, epigram, epitaph, eulogy, exaggeration, fabrication, falsity, feedback, figure of speech, fulmination, gibberish, goodbye, grace, grievance, groan, harangue, hiss, hocus-pocus, honor, impropriety, indignity, instruction, invective, invocation, issue, lament/lamentation, lecture, letter, line, litany, maxim, memorandum/memo, missive, monologue, motif, motto, negation, notice, obscenity, observation, offer, oracle, order, overtone, password, phrase, platform, plea, pledge, praise, prediction, proclamation, profession, promise, propaganda, proverb, pun, put-down, quotation/quote, rebuke, reference, regards, reminder, reply, reprimand, response, return, rhyme, rubbish, sarcasm, scandal, shadow, slander, slur, story, swearing, talk, testimony, theme, tirade, translation, tribute, utterance, veracity, voice, welcome, wind, wording

279 organization: bandwidth, media, newspaper, radio, television

280 publication: advertisement, anthology, authority, bible, biography, brochure, cartoon, catalog/catalogue, dictionary, edition, fiction, guidebook, issue, journalism, lexicon, magazine, memoir, newspaper, organ, paper, press, reference, review, satire, text, thesaurus, treatise, volume

281 record: annal(s), calendar, itinerary, program, register, roster

282 story: account, anecdote, chronicle, epic, fib, folklore, lore, mystery, mythology, narrative, old wives' tale, phenomenology, poem, report, scenario, tale, version, yarn

283 summary: abbreviation, abstract, annotation, breakdown, caption, citation, condensation, diagnosis, directory, heading, inventory, moral, profile, prospectus, résumé, review, rundown, schedule, summary, synopsis, tally, title

284 symbol: arms, autograph, beep, capital, charm, code, cue, device, emblem, ensign, flag, flourish, graffiti, handwriting, herald, imprint, indication, John Hancock, landmark, letter, logo, notation, numeral, script, sign, spot, stripe, tag, tick, trademark, type, writing

EDUCATION

285 educate: address, breed, catechize, domesticate, form, ground, inculcate, initiate, instruct, lesson, orator, preach, school, speech, teach, train, tutelage, tutor

286 education level: class, level, rating

287 objects used in: academia, college, dissertation, education, lesson, preschool, teaching, text, thesis, tuition

288 organization: academia, alma mater, college, faculty, institute/institution, school

289 place of: academy, class, preschool, school

290 test: acid test, audition, dissection, examination, experiment, index, inquiry, investigation, probe, reconnaissance, trial, workout

291 testing: fiddle, pace, survey, trial, try on/try out, verify

ENTERTAINMENT

292 action: act, amuse, antic, arrange, bill, cruise, diversion, emote, enactment, featuring, game, hype, interpret, overplay, parody, play, pretend, produce, publicize, regale, rehearse, revel, score, spotlight, takeoff, tape, translator, travesty, weatherperson

293 object: absentmindedness, balloon, broadcast, butt, circus, disco, drama, elegy, farce, firecracker, humor, medium, movie, news, picture, red herring, sequel, sight, telecast, theater/theatre, videocassette

294 organization: band, chorus, ensemble, gallery, orchestra

FAMILY

295 child raising: au pair, baby-sit, bring up, coddle, cultivate, form, mind, nanny, nurse, nurture, raise, spoon-feed, tend

296 family: aristocracy, blood, bridegroom, clan, consanguinity, descendant, doll, family, folk, genealogy, house, issue, kindred, line, mate, origin, people, progeny, relation, strain, tribe

297 marriage: annul, betroth, couple, desertion, elope, engagement, estrange, jilt, marry, mate, nuptials, parting, propose, separate, sever, vow, wedding, woo

GOVERNMENT AND POLITICS

298 government action: abdicate, abolition, administer, amnesty, cease-fire, command, depose, dethrone, dominate, enforce, exile, filibuster, override/overrule, reign, run in, second, tax, veto

299 government organization: administration, cabinet, capitol, confederacy, cop, court, democracy, dictatorship, empire, government, jury, police/police officer, regime, sovereignty, tyranny

300 political action: amnesty, arbitration, campaign, crusade, demonstration, drive, elect, endorse, mutiny, nomination, picket, poll, reaction, revolt, riot, sedition, vote

301 political organization: alliance, caucus, communism, delegation, fascism, party, side, tyranny

HEALTH

302 birth: bear, breed, conception, spring

303 change in: ache, come down with, fit, mend, recover, remission, swoon, weary

304 death: abort, curtains, decease, die, end, expire, mortician, pass away, perish, undertaker

305 deathplace: boneyard, crypt, graveyard, monument, tomb

306 disease: abscess, AIDS, bacteria, bug, canker, complaint, contagion, cyst, disease, epidemic, growth, impurity, infection, inflammation, microbe, pest, pimple, rash, sickness, swelling, syndrome, virus, zit

307 drug: acid, analgesic, anesthetic/anaesthetic, antibiotic, antiseptic, balm, cocaine, contraceptive, dope, hashish, heroin, LSD, medicine/medication, nostrum, painkiller, pick-me-up, poison, potion, remedy, stimulant, tablet, toxin, vaccination

308 event: abort, ache, cardiac arrest, contract, cough, crick, gag, heal, massage, palpitate, pass out, rubdown, seizure, spew, suffer, take, tic, wheeze

309 injury: abrasion, affliction, blister, boo boo, concussion, corrosion, damage, detriment, disadvantage, fracture, harm, inflammation, laceration, prick, rip, rust, shock, swelling, wound

310 medical action: alter, autopsy, castrate, diagnose, doctor, dress, ease, heal, inoculation, massage, operation, postmortem, remedy, therapy, transplant, treatment, vaccinate

311 medical instruments: bandage, elixir, injection, lotion, moisturizer, ointment, prescription, salve, X ray

312 medical organization: asylum, delivery room, headquarters, laboratory, madhouse, nursing home, office

313 pain: ache, anesthesia/anaesthesia, distress, harassment, hurt, pinch, strain, suffer, torture, wrong

314 quality of: able-bodied, ailing, bad, benign, burning, clean, congenital, convalescent, curable, delicate, diseased, dizzy, done in, drunk, epidemic, faint, fit, full-blooded, genetic, gory, groggy, hale, healthy, high, ill, incapacitated, inebriated, infirm, invalid, lame, light-headed, lusty, mental, nauseating, neurotic, out cold, paralytic, pestilent/ pestilential, pooped, poorly, queer, robust, rugged, run-down, salutary, senile, sickly, slaphappy, solvent, sound, spent, stoned, sturdy, terminal, tough, tuckered out, unfeeling, unhealthy, unsound, vertigo, wan, weak, well, wholesome, zoned

315 sleep: anesthesia/anaesthesia, awake, doze, hibernate, languor, lethargy, nightmare, quiet, sleep, slumber, snore, stupor

316 state of: ache, ailment, beat, complaint, cough, dementia, dislocation, epidemic, fatigue, form, hangover, health, hygiene, immunity, insanity, madness, maternity, nausea, pain, pestilence, shape, substance abuse, syndrome, trim, tumor, welfare/well-being

LEGAL

317 legal action: absolve, acquittal, adjudicate, adoption, annulment, apprehension, arrest, bequeath, bring, charge, collar, condemn, convict, counsel, cross-examine, decree, detain, disinherit, enforce, evidence, exculpate, extradite, impeach, incarcerate, indictment, insure, judge, legalize, lift, moderate, nail, outlaw, override/overrule, pass, pick up, plead, prohibit, prosecute, put away, rap, represent, rescind, sentence, sortie, sue, transport, try, verify, vitiate, waive, witness

318 objects used in legal practice: acquittal, affidavit, bail, bench, bill, brief, case, code, court, decree, deposition, dictate, enactment, evidence, injunction, institute, jury, lawsuit, libel, mandate, ordinance, paper/papers, passage, plea, precept, principle, repeal, ruling, statute, subpoena, terms, testimonial, tribunal, waiver, writ

319 quality of law: administrative, authoritative, canonical, constitutional, democratic, egalitarian, forensic, high-handed, illegitimate, inadmissible, just, lawful, legal, legitimate, on the level, punitive, unconstitutional, unprejudiced, wrongful

MILITARY

320 military action: action, barrage, blow up, conflict, *coup d'état*, deploy, deposition, dethrone, disarm, draft, engage, enlist, explosion, incursion, induction, invade, maneuver, occupation, offensive, overthrow, rebellion, revolt, salute, station, volley, warfare

321 object used by military: armory, battery, citadel, draft, fort/fortress, magazine, rampart, service

322 organization: ally, artillery, brigade, corps, detachment, enemy, flotilla, legion, navy, platoon, troop/troops

MONETARY AND FINANCIAL AFFAIRS

323 association: board, conglomerate, federation, grocery store, mall, market/ mart, patronage, syndicate, trust

324 business action: advertise, annexation, appointment, aviation, commercialize, conclave, consultation, convention, cut a deal, dealings, depression, discharge, drudge, exchange, farm, fold, hold, incorporate, malpractice, manufacture/manufacturing, mediate, meet, merge, monopolize, patronage, pioneer, position, practice, project, promotion, publicize, push, sale, second, service, shake up, sit, specialize, stock, table, traffic, transaction, undertaking, wait on

325 business organization: agency, association, bar, bureau, bureaucracy, cartel, commerce, concern, corporation, department store, dispensation, establishment, field, house, labor, management, outfit, personnel, red tape, ring, staff, syndicate, union

326 business quality: accomplished, businesslike, careful, diligent, eager, enterprising, greedy, methodical/methodic, ordered, painstaking, persistent, practical, proper, rapacious, relentless, tenacious, up-and-coming, zealous

327 buying: buy, lavish, order, pay, purchase, shop, shower, spree, take, traffic, truck

328 cost: appraisal, expense

329 fee: amount, bill, charge, damage(s), duty, expense, levy, overhead, price, rent, stake, tab, tax, wager

330 financial action: assess, bank, bet, bidding, bring, budget, cash, deduct, deficit spending, depress, devalue, discount, economize, endorse, frugality, hock, invest, levy, mutual fund, pawn, pinch, profit, return, save, scrimp, skimp, speculation, stint, trade, transact, truck, venture

331 financial document: account, book, entente, return, statement

332 financial object: account, arrears, asset(s), bail, balance sheet, bill, budget, cheap, equity, insurance, investment, liability, lucre, mortgage, order, patronage, pay, pension, principal, quotation/quote, revenue, stock, treasure, voucher

333 financial organization: bank, grocery store, market/mart, stock market

334 financial quality: affluent, bankrupt, broke, charitable, close, commercial, costly, dear, destitute, disadvantageous, down-and-out, economic, exorbitant, extravagant, financial, fiscal, free, gainful, ghetto, good, gratis, high, impecunious, improvident, indigent, insolvent, invaluable, liberal, low, marketable, miserly, monetary, moneymaking, narrow, net, on the house, outstanding, owing, paltry, patrician, pecuniary, penurious, poor, poverty-stricken, priceless, prodigal, profligate, prosperous, rich, second-rate/ second-class, self-sufficient, sleazy, sparing, squalid, stingy, substantial, tawdry, thriving, underprivileged, unpaid, unsettled, valuable, wealthy, well-bred, well-off, well-to-do

335 financial state: afford, avarice, boom, circumstances, cutback, deficit, devalue, economy, fail, frugality, inadequacy, inflation, living, need, owe, panic, pile, poverty, recession, savings, slum, squalor, thrift, value, worth

336 financial value state: cost, downturn, value

337 gift: acquisition, alms, atonement, balm, bequest, bonus, booty, charity, comfort, compensation, courtesy, diploma, dividend, donation, endowment, find, fruit, gain, good, gratuity, heirloom, indulgence, laurels, loot, medal, memorabilia, offering, plum, present, prize, recognition, reparation, scholarship, spoils, token, trophy, windfall

338 merchandise: bargain, commodity, contraband, freight, hardware, haul, line, product, truck, wares, yield

339 monetary container: bag, purse, till, treasury

340 money: ace in the hole, affluence, appropriation, asset(s), bread, change, chips, contribution, deposit, donation, endowment, finances, fund, income, investment, loot,

maintenance, mint, offering, pay, pile, recompense, reserve, resources, riches, support, wealth

341 money giving: advance, buy, disburse, endow, finance, fund, lavish, misappropriate, patronize, play, recompense, reimburse, remunerate, requite, satisfy, shell out, sponsor, subscribe, support, underwrite

342 money taking: bill, bleed, collect, extortion, fleece, squeeze

343 ownership part: hold, possession, proprietor

344 payment: advance, bounty, commission, consideration, deal, deficit spending, disbursement, dividend, draft, earnings, expenditure, fee, gain, grant, gross, installment, kickback, pay, pension, perquisite, premium, proceeds, purse, ransom, receipts, redress, reparation, revenue, safety net, satisfaction, stake, subsidy, take, upkeep, wage/wages

345 selling: auction, charge, market, peddle, sell, trade, truck

346 value state: appreciation, decline, import, mark, value, worth

PROFESSIONS

347 business manager: administrator, best shot, bureaucrat, capitalist, chief, conductor, director, emir, employer, entrepreneur, executive, financier, founder, hawker, huckster, investor, leader, manager, merchant, mover and shaker, officer, overseer, pacesetter, peasant, prime minister, professional, ringleader, shopkeeper, storekeeper, superior, taskmaster, upstart, warden

348 businessperson: abettor, adjutant, adviser/ advisor, aid/aide, announcer, apprentice, archaeologist, assistant, astronaut, auditor, authority, baker, barber, bearer, broker, businessperson, buyer, caretaker, cartoonist, chair, chef, client, colleague, computer geek, conservator, consumer, correspondent, court, creator, curator, customer, dabbler, desk jockey, developer, devil's advocate, drudge, employee, envoy, espionage, explorer, fellow, flier, flyer, fortuneteller, freshman, gatekeeper, go-between, gourmet, guard, guru, hacker, hand, hawker, helper, hooker, huckster, inferior, informant/informer, inspector, interviewer, investigator, janitor, labor, liaison, machine, maverick, messenger, miser, moderator, monitor, navigator, newsman/woman, opposition, page, patron, peddler, picket, pioneer, poet, practitioner, prodigal, protégé, rat, referee, representative, reviewer, rival, sailor, scout, seaman/ woman, seller, serf, shopper, slave, snitch, speaker, spokesperson, spy, subordinate, tailor, tightwad, traveler, underling, virtuoso, wayfarer, wizard, writer, yuppie

349 discipline: affair, anthropology, archaeology, arithmetic, astronomy, botany, bulletin board, chat room, communications, cyberspace, department, domain, ergonomics, geography, journalism, line, logic, matter, occupation, passion, philosopher, poetry, press, province, pursuit, research, school, scientist, specialty, stage, territory, undertaking, walk, work

350 educator: academic, adviser/advisor, alumnus/alumna, coach, conductor, cretin, disciplinarian, egghead, faculty, freshman, graduate, half-wit, intellectual, learner, martinet, mastermind, monitor, practitioner, professor, rookie, savant, school, swami, trainer, wonk

351 employment: ax/axe, can, commission, discharge, dismissal, elevate, employ, engage, gross, hire, job, labor, lay off, livelihood, make, occupation, oust, picket, promote, raise, relieve, resignation, retire, sack, spot, strike, work

352 entertainer: acrobat, actress, aficionado, ballet dancer, character, comic, creator, director, fan, fledgling, freak, groupie, hero/heroine, humorist, inventor, luminary, magician, minion, name, originator, participant, personage/personality, player, protagonist, star, troubadour, virtuoso, zany

353 financier: accountant, bean counter, broker, investor, spendthrift

354 government officer: administrator, ambassador, authoritarian, autocracy, bureaucrat, consul, delegate, despot, diplomat, emir, empress, establishment, exile, fascist, figurehead, front runner, informant/informer, intermediary, leader, liaison, magistrate, master, mogul, mouthpiece, officer, oppressor, pacifist, patrol, personage/personality, police/police officer, prime minister, representative, snitch, spokesperson, tyrant, weasel

355 legal practitioner: attorney, beneficiary, counsel, heir, judge, lawyer, officer, proponent, witness

356 media person: commentator, journalist, newsman/woman, reporter, writer

357 medical practitioner: analyst, druggist, nurse, patient, physician, researcher, therapist

358 military person: combatant, conqueror, fighter, gladiator, lookout, militant, patrol, recruit, scout, seaman/woman, truant, warmonger, warrior

359 politician: advocate, anarchist, apostle, arbitrator, bigot, conservative, diehard, dissident, extremist, firebrand, hostage, idealist, militant, mouthpiece, nonconformist, patron, picket, proponent, racist, reactionary, refugee, sectarian, warmonger

360 profession: business, career, employment, hacker, labor, line, mission, place, science, trade, walk, work

361 religious person: acolyte, angel, atheist, chaplain, conformist, creator, deacon, doubter, dreamer, evangelism, father, genie, inventor, loner, minister, monk, pagan, pastor, priest, saint, skeptic, visionary, witch, wizard

362 task: affair, bee, chore, concern, duty, enterprise, exercise, function, groove, labor, office, picnic, project, realm, role, scientist, stint, toil, work

RECREATION

363 action: acrobatics, aerobics/aerobic, athletics, boating, boxing, championship, coach, contest, dance, defeat, diversion, event, fish, gamble, game, hike, hunt, lay, lottery, match, meeting, oppose, pit, race, recreation, rehearse, rivalry, shuffle, speculation, stake, tournament, turn, venture, wager, workout

364 objects used in: amusement, bicycle, equipment, game, hobby, lap, point, raffle, round, standoff, wager

365 organization: conference, league, squad, team

366 participants: abolitionist, aficionado, aspirant, aviator, coach, contestant, dark horse, entrant, fan, fighter, follower, geek, groupie, jock, master, moderator, observer, opposition, pedestrian, player, referee, sailor, star, underdog, winner

RELIGIOUS

367 action: anoint, baptism, bless, burial, canonize, communion, dedicate, defect, deify, enshrine, excommunicate, inter, penance, prayer, purification, wake, worship

368 objects used in: abbey, bible, casket, cemetery, cloister, convent, denomination, faith, holiness, litany, monastery, necropolis, pulpit, requiem, sanctuary, service, synagogue, temple

369 organization: church, congregation, Jewish, priesthood

370 supernatural: abracadabra, angel, black magic, deep space, demon, divinity, elf, fairy, galaxy, ghoul, god, hell, hex, incantation, inferno, Lucifer, monster, paradise, phantom, poltergeist, purgatory, Satan, shade, Shangri-la, specter, spirit, utopia, voodoo, witchcraft, Xanadu

SEX AND REPRODUCTION

371 attribute of gender: female, femininity/feminine, he-man, macho, male, masculinity/masculine, womanly

372 attribute of sexuality: AC-DC, amatory, androgynous, bisexual, celibate, close, erotic, femininity/feminine, fertility, gay, horny, kinky, lecherous, libidinous, loose, loving, masculinity/masculine, naughty, passion, peccadillo, pornography, promiscuous, prurient, raunchy, salicious, sensual, sexual, smut, spicy, sultry, thought-provoking, vice, virgin/virginal, virility, vulgar, womanly, X-rated

373 birth: bear, breed, conception, spring

374 child bearing: beget, delivery, generate, get, labor, procreate, propagate, spawn

375 sex act: affair, assignation, caress, cohabit, copulate, couple, dalliance, dally/dally with,

deflower, fertilize, flirtation, foreplay, fornication, impregnate, kiss, love affair, mate,
necking, paw, proposition, ravish, seduce,
sexual assault, smooch, violate, woo

SOCIAL INTERACTIONS

376 **authority:** aegis, agent, ascendancy/
ascendency, carte blanche, chair, chief,
civil rights, clearance, command, control,
custody, domination, duty, empire, green
card, impunity, jurisdiction, leadership,
office, permission, power, privilege, reign,
rule, supremacy, title, voice, warrant

377 **celebration:** acclamation, banquet, carnival,
commemoration, entertain, fanfare, festival,
fete, gaiety, have a ball, keep, observe,
pageant, parade, rally, revelry, sacrament,
spree, wassail

378 **class:** branch, breed, category, classification, denomination, division, estate, folks,
genre/genus, grade, kind, mob, mold,
nobility, position, rabble, rating, sort,
stock, tier, variety, world

379 **community:** colony, country, hoi polloi,
people, public, society

380 **ethnic group:** nationality, race, tribe

381 **organization:** affiliate, agency, assembly,
brigade, combination, committee, crew,
department, foundation, guild, institute/
institution, league, movement, partnership,
ring, society, union

382 **part of a group:** chapter, plurality, sect

383 **party:** affair, blowout, entertainment, gala,
orgy, reception, show business, tear

384 **social action:** abuse, advance(s), amends,
appeal, associate, betray, blackball, booking,
break the ice, carouse, cohabit, come upon,
compel, conduct, cool, court, cultivate,
disaffect, disgrace, disorganize, encounter,
engagement, entertain, escapade, estrange,
faux pas, fete, flirt, flock, fornication, fraternize, frisk, get a kick out of, go together/go
with, hanky-panky, hold, host, induct, infringe, interfere, interrupt, invitation, jilt,
know, lose, make up, mask, mediate, meet,
mingle, mishandle/mismanage, network,
oblige, observe, overture, part, pass, patronize, pick up, poke, powwow, prank, program,
prostrate, pursue, rampage, reception, reconcile, regale, rendezvous, reprisal, respond,
retribution, revelry, riot, romp, seat, second,
separate, share, show business, sit, snoop,
socialize, spree, squire, step in, stunt,
tantrum, throw over, toy, trespass, truckle,
usurp, wallow, woo

385 **social change:** breakup, give in/give up,
succumb

386 **social event:** adventure, ball, bells and
whistles, binge, bustle, caricature, ceremony, clown, conference, debut, dissipation, entertainment, exhibition, exposition,
feature, fiesta, frolic, function, gathering,
inauguration, memorial, merriment/
merrymaking, occasion, parade, rally, rite,
rumpus, sacrament

387 **social organization:** association, brotherhood, clan, clique, congregation, crowd,
fraternity, entourage, fellowship, gang,
high society, league, order, society

388 **social state:** abasement, affirmative action,
association, awkwardness, behind, belonging, bond, breach, breeding, calm, care,
celebrity, censorship, circumstances, class,
coherence, companionship, complicity,
concord, conjunction, consanguinity, contact,
cooperation, courtesy, credit, culture, degree,
détente, dignitary, diplomacy, disagreement,
disfavor, disharmony, disorder, dissolution,
disturbance, duty, echelon, eminence, entertainment, entry, estate, excitement, falling-
out, familiarity, fellowship, fidelity, foreplay,
friendship, fun, fuss, genre/genus, get along,
glory, height, hit it off, hospitality, hubbub,
humiliation, immunity, infidelity, intrigue,
juncture, laissez-faire, lather, level, liberty,
luxury, marriage, men's movement,
mortification, mutiny, nepotism, nobility,
nonviolence, notoriety, odium, opprobrium,
partnership, piffle, place, pleasure, polygamy,
popularity, predicament, prestige, rage,
rapport, rate, relationship, reproach, reputation, ruckus, rupture, seclusion, servitude,
shame, situation, society, sophistication,
split, standing, state, status, stillness, stink,
support, sympathy, taste, terms, tomfoolery,
uncertainty, variance, whirl

LIFE FORMS

BEINGS

389 **beings:** being, cell, creature, egg, individual,
organism, soul

390 **former beings:** body, carcass/carcase,
corpse

391 **group of beings:** band, group, world

392 **limb or appendage of:** ankle, back, beak,
branch, butt/buttocks, chest, derriere, duff,
extremity, fanny, finger, flesh, freckle,
hair, head, leg, lip, microorganism, mouth,
posterior, rump, skin, tail, trunk, wig, wisp

393 **organ:** abdomen, bacteria, blood, bowels,
dentures, false teeth, heart, mind, muscle,
seed, spine, tummy, vein

BEINGS, ANIMAL

394 **animal:** adult, beast, buck, cat, chicken,
cock, cur, father, frog, goat, half-breed,
horse, hybrid, litter, mongrel, monster,
parasite, pig, stock, young

395 **bird:** bird, chicken

396 **fish:** aquarium, aquatic

397 **group of animals:** drove, herd, insect,
pack, stock, team

398 **insect:** bee, grub, pest

399 **limb or appendage of:** bill, coat, feather,
fur, manure, mop, pelt, scale, trunk, wing

400 **mammal:** cat, dog, father, goat, hound,
mother, pig

GENERAL CHARACTERISTICS

401 attribute of behavior: abstemious, accident-prone, acid, acrimonious, adamant, affable, affectionate, agreeable, aimless, aloof, amuck, animated, anxious, arbitrary,ardent, arrogant, ascetic, attentive, austere, avid, backhanded, bad, barbarian, barbarous, beaming, belligerent, big, blindly, boisterous, bossy, brassy, brazen, brusque, cagey, calm, capricious, casual, cavalier, cheeky, chill, chummy, clumsy, cocky/cocksure, combative, comic/comical, compassionate, complaisant, compulsive, conciliatory, considerate, contemptuous, contrary, convivial, cordial, corrupt, courageous, courtly, cowardly, crabby/crabbed, cranky, craven, crotchety, cruel, cunning, daring, dauntless, debonair, decent, decided, defensive, defiant, deliberately, delightful, delirious, demure, detached, diffident, disagreeable, disarming, discreet, disgruntled, disinterested, disobedient, disorderly, disputatious, disruptive, dissolute, distraught, divisive, doctrinaire, dolorous, doting, double-dealing, draconian, eager, easy, edgy, effervescent, emotionless, envious, equable, evasive, even-tempered, excitable, exuberant, faithful, fake, false, fanatical, favorably, fearful, feigned, ferocious, fervent/fervid, fickle, fiery, finicky, flamboyant, flighty, flirtatious, foolhardy, foolishly, forceful, forward, fractious, freely, fretful, frivolous, fussy, gamely, genteel, glacial, gluttonous, goody-goody, graceless, grandiose, gritty, gruff, gung ho, halfhearted, hardhearted, haram-scarum, headstrong, hearty, helpless, high and mighty, high-handed, high-strung, holier-than-thou, hot, huffy, humble, hypocritical, idle, ill-mannered, ill-natured, ill-tempered, impatient, impertinent, impolite, importunate, impudent, inactive, inconsiderate, ingratiating, inhuman/inhumane, innocuous, insidious, insubordinate, intractable/intransigent, introverted, invidious, irreconcilable, irreverent, jaded, jaunty, jazzed-up, jovial, jumpy, keen, kittenish, lax, lecherous, lethargic, liberal, lifeless, light-headed, litigious, lofty, loquacious, loud, loving, Machiavellian, maladroit, malicious, mannered, martial, mean, meat-eating, menacing, merciful, mercurial, militant, mischievous, miserly, mousy, munificent, naive, nasty, naughty, neglectful, neighborly, nervy, nomadic, noncompliant, nonconformist, nosy, obedient, obliging, obsequious, obtrusive, offhand, on edge, on purpose, orderly, ostentatious, overbearing, overwrought, parsimonious, passionate, peevish, pent-up, peppy, peripatetic, permissive, pert, petulant, philosophical/philosophic, phobic, pitiless, plaintive, playful, plucky, politic, pompous, pragmatic, precipitous/precipitate, predatory, presumptuous, prickly, prissy, profane, prompt, propitious, provident, prudish, puerile, pumped, puritanical, quarrelsome, quick-tempered, racy, raffish, rash, ready, rebellious, reckless, regardful, relentless, remiss, remorseless, renegade, repugnant, resigned, responsible, restful, restrained, retiring, revolutionary, rocky, rollicking, rootin'-tootin', rousing, rude, runaway, ruthless, safe, sanctimonious, sassy, savage, scintillating, secluded, self-conscious, self-righteous, sentimental, serpentine, severe, shameful, sheepish, shifty, short-sighted, shy, simple, sincere, skittish, slippery, sluggish, small, smooth, snappy, snide, snooty, sober, soft, solid, sophomoric, spineless, spontaneous, sporting/sportive, sprightly, square, staid, starchy, staunch, stealthy, stiff, stingy, stoic/stoical, stony, strained, strait-laced, strenuous, stringent, stuck-up, suave, submissive, subversive, supercilious, supine, surly, sympathetic, tactful, tame, tearful, tempestuous, tender, tense, thankful, theatrical, thieving/thievish, thoughtless, tight, tipsy, touchy, traitorous, treasonous, truculent, true-blue, turbulent, two-faced, unaffected, unasked, unattached, unbridled, uncivilized, uncontrollable, uncouth, undependable, underhand, unemotional, unfriendly, unguarded, unintentional/unintended, unkind, unmerciful, unprejudiced, unreasonable, unrelenting, unruly, unseemly, unsettled, unsophisticated, unsympathetic, untoward, unwary, unwise, unworldly, uppity, urbane, vainglorious, valorous, vengeful, vibrant, vicious, vigilant, violent, virile, vital, volatile, wacky, wanton, warm, wary, watchful, wayward, well-bred, wicked, willful, wily, winning/winsome, witless, yellow, zany, zealous

402 attribute of intelligence: able, abstruse, accident-prone, acute, alert, analytic/analytical, apt, astute, aware, bewildered, blind, brilliant, canny, cerebral, clairvoyant, clever, cognizant, common-sense, comprehensible, considered, conversant, cunning, deducible, delirious, designedly, dim, dizzy, down-to-earth, dumb, eagle-eyed, efficient, empty, empty-headed, erudite, expert, far-sighted, feebleminded, frivolous, gullible, hazy, idiotic, illiterate, impressionable, incomprehensible, ineligible, inexperienced, ingenious, inquisitive, insipid, intelligent, inventive, judicious, knowing, learned, logical, lucid, mindful, moronic, not born yesterday, observant, omniscient, penetrating, perceptive, philosophical/philosophic, privy, proficient, psychic, quick-witted, rational, reasonable, sagacious, sane, savvy, scholarly, seasoned, sensible, shallow, shrewd, skillful, slow, soft, studious, subtle, thick, thoughtless, unaware, uneducated, uninformed, unknowing, vacant, versed, veteran, weak, well-balanced, well-defined, wide-awake, with-it

403 attribute of mentality: aback, absconder, absent-minded, absorbing, accustomed, affected, afraid, aghast, alert, amatory, angry, apathetic, apprehensive, assumed, attentive, averse, bad, beaten, believable, berserk, bewildered, bigoted, bleak, blue, breathless, broad-minded, brokenhearted, burning, captive, cautious, cheerful, chipper, clairvoyant, compassionate, concerned, confused, contemplative, contented, crabby/crabbed, crazy, cross, curious, daffy, dearly, dejected, delirious, depressed, desolate, desperately, disaffected, disbelieving, disconcerted, discontented/discontent, discouraging, disenchanted, disgusted, disillusioned, disinterested, dispirited, dissident, distressed, doleful, dotty, down, downcast, dumbfounded, elated, emotional, enamored, enraged, excited, exultant, fed up, firm, flushed, forgetful, forlorn, frenetic, frightened, fulfilled, furious, glad, gleeful, glum, grateful, grief-stricken, gut, half-baked, happily, hard, hard-boiled, harried, headstrong, heartsick, high, hopeful, huffy, hysterical, ill-tempered, impassioned, inattentive, inconsolable, indifferent, indiscriminate, insane, insecure, intent, interested, intoxicated, irate, irresolute, jaundiced, jovial, joyful/joyous, jubilant, keen, languid, lethargic, livid, lonesome, loony, low, lukewarm, mad, malleable, manic/maniacal, mental, mindful, mirthful, mixed-up, morbid, mournful, narrow-minded,nerveless, neurotic, new age, normal, numb, nuts/nutty, objectivity, observant, obsessed, off-guard, one-sided, on the fence, opposed/opposing, overjoyed, partial, pensive, pent-up, petrified, phlegmatic, platonic, pooped, predisposed, prepared, profound, provincial, psyched, psychological, pumped, punch-drunk, puzzled, rabid, radical, rapacious, realistic, regretful, restless, rigid, rueful, salacious, sanguine, saturnine, sectarian, self-assured, sensitive, sick, skeptical, small-minded, solicitous, sore, sorry, sound, spellbound, steady, strong, stupefied, sulky, susceptible, tearful, tender, testy, thirsty, thoughtless, tired, torn, tough, ugly, unbalanced, uncaring, uncommitted, undecided, unemotional, unfeeling, uninterested, unsound, untroubled, upbeat, versed, wacky, wary, weary, wide-awake, wishful, woebegone, wrathful, wretched

404 attribute of personality: aboveboard, adventurous, airy, amenable, approachable, arrogant, assertive, assured, august, bashful, belonging to, big-hearted, blasé, blithe, boastful, boorish, brash, buoyant, callous, captious, catty, charming, cheeky, childlike, chilly, churlish, clear, clinical, cocky/cocksure, co-dependent, colorful, combative, confident, cool, coy, culpable, cute, dainty, dastardly, dedicated, delicate, demonic/demoniac/demoniacal, dependent, despicable, determined, dewy-eyed, die-hard, dignified, dispassionate, distant, dynamic, easygoing, egocentric, egotistic/

egoistic, embittered, endearing, engaging, even-tempered, exalted, exemplary, feckless, finicky, flatulent, forbearing, forward, free, frigid, gallant, garrulous, generous, genteel, glacial, good, good-humored, good-natured, gregarious, gutless, halcyon, happy-go-lucky, hardhearted, hard-nosed/hardheaded, hell-bent, high and mighty, high-strung, hyperactive, icy, ill-natured, immovable, imperturbable, individual, indulgent, infamous, inherent, innocent, insouciant, intrinsic, inveterate, irresponsible, jazzed-up, kindhearted, kosher, laid-back, latent, liberal, likable, loutish, low, loyal, magnetic, matronly, meritorious, mincing, miserly, mulish, native, nice, nonchalant, obedient, obsequious, odd/oddball, officious, open-hearted, open-minded, opprobrious, ossified, outspoken, particular, peculiar, perfidious, persistent, personable, philanthropic, pig-headed, predictable, prim, proper, pushy, quick-tempered, recluse/reclusive, reserved, rotten, saintly, Satanic, selective, self-assured, self-centered, self-confident, self-conscious, self-satisfied, self-suffcient, shabby, shifty, slothful, snotty, spick-and-span, spotless, spunky, squeamish, staid, standoffish, stoic/stoical, stubborn, suave, sweet, thick-skinned, trustworthy/trusty, unapproachable, unpretentious, unsuspecting, uppity, vain, valorous, virile, vocal, winning, wishy-washy, zealous, zippy

405 essential property of life forms: allergy, body, dotage, hygiene, sense, sensitivity

406 essential quality of life forms: adult, animal, awake, barefoot, blank, breathless, brunette/brunet, buxom, corpulent, curvaceous, deadpan, drowsy, exhausted, expecting, fair, fleshy, full, glassy, hairless, high, hungry, inborn/inbred, innate, intestinal/intestine, intrinsic, light, lumbering, predatory, primitive, promising, ravenous, rich, sensory, smooth, starving/starved, thin-skinned, tipsy, untamed, wild

407 existential state: be, casualty, endangered, exist, fettle, gone, loss, matter, nature, nothing/nothingness, outlast, presence, spirit, subsist, threaten, zero, zilch

408 gender: female, femininity/feminine, he-man, macho, male, masculinity/masculine

409 intelligence: acquaintance, anticipation, apprehension, attention, bent, capacity, clarity, cognizance/cognition, comprehension, consciousness, creativity, darkness, depth, education, empathy, erudition, expertise/expertness, familiarity, feeling, foresight, genius, grasp, head, ignorance, imagination, innocence, intellect, interpretation, invention, ken, know-how, learning, literacy, mentality, misconception, nirvana, observation, perception, proficiency, sagacity, sanity, scholarship, sensibility, skill, soul, understanding, wit/wits, workmanship

410 mentality: abhorrence, absentmindedness, abstraction, ache, aggravation, agonize, alarm, allergy, amazement, angst, anticipa-

tion, apathy, assurance, attention, attrition,
awe, bathos, behalf, belonging, bitterness,
boast, bosom, breast, buoyancy/buoyance,
capitulation, care, censure, cheer, clemency,
cogitation, comfort, complex, compulsion,
conception, confusion, consideration, constancy, content, contrition, corollary, credit,
curiosity, darkness, decision, deference,
delight, delirium, dementia, dependence/
dependency, design, despair, difficulty,
disaffection, discipline, discomfiture,
discontent, discrimination, disinclination,
disorder, disquiet, distraction, disturbance,
dolor, dumps, ecstasy, elation, emotion,
enjoyment, envy, esprit de corps, exaltation,
excitement, exhilaration, expectation,
exultation, fat city, felicity, firmness, fog,
forbearance, foresight, forgetfulness, frame
of mind, free will, fret, frustration, funk,
fury, glee, gratification, grief, happiness,
heart, heartbreak, heaven, hoopla, huff,
humanity, humor, idiocy, impulse, indignity,
insight, introspection, jealousy, joy, kick,
lament/lamentation, letdown, levity,
madness, mania, melancholy, merriment/
merrymaking, mirth, monotony, mope,
mortification, mourning, nausea, neglect,
nervous breakdown, neurosis, objection,
observance, obsession, optimism, outlook,
panic, paroxysm, pathos, penance, perception, pessimism, pity, Pollyanna, pout, precognition, premonition, presence, psyche,
push, qualm, rage, rapture, red herring,
rejoice, repent, repose, resent, resignation,
resolution, restlessness, ruckus, sadness,
satisfaction, security, self-satisfaction,
sensibility, sentiment, servitude, simmer,
slump, solace, sorrow, soul-searching,
status quo, strain, stress, surprise, sympathy,
telepathy, temperament, tension, tolerance,
torpor, trance, triumph, umbrage, unrest,
vanity, waver, wonder, worry, zeal, zest

411 personality: aggression, arrogance, artifice,
atrocity, audacity, bearing, best, bravery,
buoyancy/buoyance, calm, character,
charisma, charm, compliance, confidence,
courage, dash, dedication, determination,
disposition, distinction, effrontery, egoism/
egotism, empathy, endurance, enterprise,
esprit de corps, eye, fettle, fight, foible,
fortitude, gall, generosity, gentility, go,
good will/goodwill, grit, gusto, hauteur,
heroism, hubris, identity, ilk, individuality,
inhibition, innocence, kind, laziness,
longevity, magnetism, manner, martyrdom,
mettle, might, monstrosity, morale, motivation, mystique, nerve, obedience, oomph,
patience, penchant, perseverance, pizzazz,
point, potency, presence of mind, prima
donna, proclivity, property, psyche, qualify,
reputation, savor, self-respect/self-esteem,
shortcoming, soul, spirit, spunk, stamina,
staying power, taste, temper, tenacity, thing,
trick, twist, valor, verve, vigor, vitality,
weakness, willpower, zeal, zing, zip

HUMANS

412 bad person: accessory, accurser, adversary,
aggressor, alarmist, antagonist, ass, assassin,
authoritarian, barbarian, bigmouth, bottom
feeder, bum, burglar, cad, captive, charlatan,
clod, cold fish, conspirator, criminal, crook,
culprit, deadbeat, delinquent, demon, derelict,
desperado, devil, dirty old man, dolt,
do-nothing, dope, dregs, drone, dumbbell,
dunce, enemy, espionage, exile, failure, fall
guy, femme fatale, fighter, firebrand, fool,
fugitive, gangster, glutton, good-for-nothing,
gossip, grump, hellion, hobo, hot dog,
hypocrite, imbecile, impostor, incubus,
insurgent, intruder, Judas, killer, klutz,
know-it- all, lawbreaker, lemon, loafer,
loser, lummox, mad person, maniac, menace,
misanthrope, miser, mole, mountebank,
naysayer, ne' er-do-well, nuisance, nut, ogre,
organized crime, parasite, pawn, pessimist,
pill, placebo, prodigal, prostitute, psychopath,
quack, rascal, renegade, rogue, ruffian, sap,
scamp, schlemiel, Scrooge, shirked, shyster,
simpleton, skinflint, sleazebag, sneak,
sourpuss, spy, swindler, tattletale/tattler,
thug, tool, traitor, troll, truant, tyrant,
vandal, wanton, whipping boy, wimp, witch

413 community group member: aborigine,
denizen, émigré, foreigner, hick, immigrant,
innovator, migrant, newcomer, outsider,
pioneer, proletariat, refugee, rustic, subject,
yokel

414 family member: ancestor, antecedent(s),
baby, brother, conservationist, descendant,
father, fiancé/fiancée, forefather, guardian,
heir, he-man, hybrid, issue, kid, kindred,
man, newborn, occupant, orphan, paramedic,
partner, progeny, relative, scion, senior,
spitting image, successor, sweetheart,
trustee, ward, young, youngster/youth

415 female: bachelor, broad, dated, dish,
girlfriend, Jezebel, nymph, sister, wife,
woman

416 good person: ace, benefactor, do-gooder,
dreamer, expert, hero/heroine, idealist,
intellectual, missionary, peacemaker, pet,
prodigy, pundit, victor, visionary, whiz, wit

417 group of people: anybody, army, attendance, band, board, cadre, circle, class,
clique, company, contingent, corps, crew,
crush, elite, entourage, everybody/everyone,
federation, flesh, force, gathering, horde,
huddle, humanity, legion, member, mob,
mortality, muster, pack, people, personnel,
practice, rabble, set, squad, swarm, throng,
troop/troops, turnout

418 limb or appendage: ankle, bosom, braid,
bristle, can, coiffure, elbow, pore, wrinkle

419 male: bachelor, boyfriend, brother,
father, groom, he-man, husband, lad,
man, wanton

420 organ: backbone, bone, heart, spine,
tummy, vein

421 racial group member: kin, relation, tribe
422 royalty: crown, noble, potentate

423 social group member: accurser, addict, adventurer, alarmist, alien, alter ego, apprentice, aristocrat, aspirant, associate, augur, bachelor, beau, beginner, beloved, beneficiary, best-seller, bigot, birds of a feather, black sheep, boor, boyfriend, brownnose, buddy, buffoon, bum, busybody, butterfingers, captive, celebrity, character, chum, civilian, clod, cohort, colleague, comic, company, comrade, conformist, conquest, consort, correspondent, coward, cretin, cynic, daredevil, date, dear, deserter, devil's advocate, diehard, disciple, dissident, do-gooder, dolt, donor, do-nothing, dope, doubting Thomas, driver, drunk/drunkard, dullard, dummy, dupe, elitist, emissary, entrant, epicurean, escort, exile, exponent, extremist, eyewitness, fan, favorite, fiancé/fiancée, figure, fink, flame, follower, fop, fortune-teller, freak, fuddy-duddy, gigolo, go-between, gourmet, grouch, guardian, guide, half-wit, hanger-on, helper, herald, hippie, homeboy, humanitarian, iconoclast, idol, informant/informer, intimate, intruder, jester, joker, killjoy, know-it-all, layperson, liaison, loner, lout, lover, machine, marionette, mate, mediator, mind reader, misfit, mother, namby-pamby, name-dropper, negotiator, neophyte, noble, nobody/nonentity, notable, nouveau riche, nut, oddity/oddball, odds-on-favorite, onlooker, outcast, pagan, pantywaist, pariah, partisan, passenger, patron, peer, personage/personality, philanderer, pill, plebeian, prey, proletariat, prophet, protagonist, pundit, pushover, ragamuffin, recluse, rival, second, seer, sidekick, sissy, slacker, snoop, somebody, sourpuss, spendthrift, sponsor, square, stick-in-the-mud, stranger, subordinate, suitor, support/supporter, sweetheart, target, tattletale/tattler, tenant, tool, trainee, trustee, umpire, underling, urchin, vagabond, veteran, visitor, waif, wayfarer, weirdo, windbag, witness, womanizer, yes-person, zany

424 traits: adolescent, babe, beauty, boy, child, colossus, debutante, doll, elder, fetus, freak, girl, grown-up, invalid, kid, midget, mossback, neophyte, nymph, old-timer, pip-squeak, senior, toddler, tyro, young, youngster/youth

PLANTS

425 flower: bloom, bouquet, flower
426 fruit: berry, produce
427 growth or death of: bloom, bud, germinate, growth, wilt, wither
428 part: bark, branch, cereal, flavoring, foliage, grain, juice, limb, nut, pod, scion, shell, stalk, trunk
429 plant: algae, bramble, bush, crop, fossil, grass, harvest, hybrid, organism, produce, wreath
430 tree: timber, wood/woods
431 vegetable: produce

OBJECTS

ARTICLES, PHYSICAL

432 group of: accrual, admixture, aggregate, anthology, armada, arsenal, assortment, bale, battery, blend, bolt, bundle, canon, cavalcade, clot, clump, clutter, column, compilation, composite, concentration, concourse, conglomeration, crush, deposit, drove, everything, flock, fusion, gridlock, hash, herd, host, jumble, knot, load, lump, mass, mélange, mishmash, mix/mixture, mob, mound, multitude, navy, odds and ends, pack, pair, party, pile, potpourri, queue, residue, scads, score/scores, set, stew, stuff, surge, throng, tuft, variety, whole
433 object: anything, entity, individual, matter, something, tableware, thing
434 part of: aspect, carcass/carcase, cubicle, pigeonhole
435 place: asylum, base, center, depot, haunt, heaven, inferno, mecca, repository, storeroom
436 shape: angle, arch, bead, bulb, check, coil, contortion, convolution, crescent, curve, dogleg, effigy, globe, kink, labyrinth, line, loop, mold, orbit, rainbow, ring, rod, round, sphere, streak, wave, whorl

ATMOSPHERE

437 air: billow, breath, bubble, draft, effervescence, fumes, puff, vapor

BUILDINGS, POSSESSIONS

438 arena: aquarium, bazaar, coliseum, field, hall, mecca, stage
439 building: abbey, architecture, armory, asylum, bakery, bar, booth, cathedral, club, construction, court, department store, dock, edifice, emergency room, factory, food court, fort/fortress, framework, garrison, greasy spoon, hacienda, hangout, headquarters, hotel, inn, institute/institution, jetty, laboratory, mansion, mental hospital, monastery, mosque, museum, nursing home, office, pavilion, penitentiary, plant, prison, rampart, repository, ruins, sanctuary, shrine, skyscraper, stockade, storeroom, structure, temple, theater/theatre, treasury, warehouse, wharf
440 building part: aisle, annex, attic, balcony, bay, bleachers, buttress, ceiling, chimney, closet, concourse, corridor, den, dome, egress, entry, fireplace, flue, gallery, gazebo, hall, locker, nook, passage/passageway, platform, post, recess, stack, step, threshold, vent, wing
441 business place: agency, boutique, bureau, foyer, lobby, shop, store, wing
442 foundation: backbone, basis, bottom, cornerstone, foot, groundwork, kiosk, nitty-gritty, rock, seat, support

479 wood: beam, cane, fence, girder, paddle, picket, pole, rack, rail/railing, splinter, stake, timber

MATTER, QUALITIES OF

480 balance: asymmetrical, dizzy, inequitable, odd, proportionate/proportional, slaphappy, symmetrical, unequal, vertigo, woozy

481 capacity: brimming/brimful, compact, crowded, full, spacious, teeming, void

482 continuity: broken, continuous, disconnected, disjointed, durable, endless, episodic, fitful, indelible, lengthy, never-ending, numberless, ongoing, perfect, sequential, solid, spasmodic, through, timeless, unbroken, unending, uninterrupted

483 density: airtight, close, concentrated, cramped, dense, fraught, hollow, impermeable, petrified, solid, teeming, tight

484 exteriority: adjunct, annex, bound/bounds, brink, casing, circumference, confines, cover, cushion, exterior, extremity, fringe, horizon, husk, lip, membrane, outer, outside, perimeter, pod, rim, sheet, skin, surface, verge

485 physical: abhorrent, acid, adulterated, aesthetic/esthetic, alimentary, atomic, bad, bare, bearded, bedridden, blank, blunt, broken, burning, chintzy, combustible, corrugated, cozy, crumbly, curable, decayed, deformed, desolate, dilapidated, diluted/dilute, dirty, disheveled, disorderly, disrepair, done in, drawn, ducky, effervescent, erect, expectant, exposed, faint, fat, fatty, fertile, fireproof, flaccid, flammable, foamy, formless, fragile, free, frothy, gaping, ghetto, gnarled, good, grimy, gruesome, hardy, immature, impalpable, impotent, inconspicuous, incurable, infirm, insubstantial, invisible, knurled, leafy, lifeless, livable, loose, magnificent, mangy, material, mean, mild, misshapen, moth-eaten, muscular, nasty, neat, noxious, oblique, obvious, on-the-blink, open-and-shut, orderly, pacific, palpable, paltry, pathetic, pendulous/pendent, perishable, physical, pitiful, plain, premature, prickly, prolific, prostrate, pure, quizzical, rambling, rank, rocky, rough, run-down, savage, scraggly, seedy, shabby, shaggy, shoddy, slack, slimy, slovenly, snug, somber, speckled, splendid, squalid, stark, stony, surface, symmetrical, tacky, tense, thorny, tidy, topsy-turvy, tousled, tumescent, unblemished, uncomfortable, unfinished, unorganized, untouched, vague, visual, watery, weary, wizened, worn/worn-out

486 shape: angular, beaten, billowy, checkered, concave, conical/conic, crescent, curly, deformed, elliptical, flat, gnarled, kinky, misshapen, obtuse, round, shapeless, spiral, straight

487 similarity: akin, analogous, closely, comparable, comparative, different, equivalent, homogenous, interchangeable, like-minded, related, same, similar, tantamount, uniform, virtually

488 stability: adhesive, brittle, choppy, ductile, fast, firmly, flexible, immobile, insecure, lissom, motionless, moving, ramshackle, rickety, secure, shaky, soft, solvent, stable, steady, supple, taut, tractable, unstable/unsteady, weak, wooden, yielding

489 strength: able-bodied, athletic, breakable, durable, feeble, flimsy, frail, full-blooded, full-bodied, hardy, impregnable, indomitable, invincible, leathery, mighty, potent, powerless, resilient, rocky, stalwart, strapping, sturdy, tenuous, tough, unsuccessful, weak

490 structure: airtight, amorphous, baggy, beaten, blind, cavernous, clean-cut, cleft, conglomerate, crooked, curved, delicate, detached, ductile, emaciated, flabby, flush, gaping, hollow, irregular, level, oblique, pointed, rude, scrawny, sheer, slender/slim, spare, stout, sunken, trim, wiry

491 weight: anorexic, beaten, cadaverous, chunky, dainty, emaciated, fat, fleshy, gargantuan, giant, haggard, hefty, lean, lightweight, meager, overweight, ponderous, portly, rangy, roly-poly, round, skinny, slender/slim, spare, stocky, stubby, tenuous, thin, trim, underweight, weighty, wiry

TOOLS

492 cleaner: antiseptic, deodorant, polish

493 cooking: barbecue, china, pan, scoop, utensil

494 container: bag, barrel, basket, bowl, briefcase, cabinet, can, carton, cask, cell, chest, coffin, crate, decanter, envelope, frying pan, hamper, jug, kettle, luggage, mug, package, pan, pitcher, pot, pouch, receptacle, trunk, vessel

495 cutting: blade, dagger, knife

496 equipment: harness, kit, pack, plant, tackle, trappings

497 grasping: bond, catch, curb, manacle

498 part: ammunition, hook, pivot, round, shot

499 tool: accordion, ax/axe, brace, brush, chain, clamp, conduit, contraption, dagger, device, doodad, drill, fastener, gadgetry, hardware, instrument, knife, lock, night stick, paddle, pipe, ruler, tableware, valve, wedge, widget

500 weapon: A-bomb, armament(s), arrow, atom bomb, battery, bullet, catapult, defense, explosive, firearm, gun, missile, nuclear weapon, ordnance, rocket

TRANSPORTATION

501 object used for: access, approach, artery, boulevard, career, circuit, conduit, course, detour, drain, esplanade, flume, heading, intersection, line, passage/passageway, road, street, trail, turnpike, way

502 part, vehicle: anchor, fender, portal, wheel, wing

503 vehicle: camper, conveyance, motorcade, transport

504 vehicle, air: aircraft, armada, blimp, dirigible, helicopter, shuttle, UFO

505 vehicle, land: ambulance, bicycle, car, cherry-picker, dolly, excavator, model, traffic, truck

506 vehicle, water: armada, boat, craft, fleet, sailboat, yacht

THE PLANET

GEOGRAPHY

507 city: capital, metropolis, town, village

508 geographic division: area, county, desert, dynasty, kingdom, outskirts, quarter, sector, suburb, territory, tract, zone

509 land: abyss, avalanche, bank, bay, bed, bluff, campus, cape, cavern, cliff, compost, cove, crevice/crevasse, dirt, downgrade, dune, elevation, estuary, expanse, field, fossil, garden, glacier, gorge, green, ground, gulf, harbor, hillock, inlet, knoll, landscape, lawn, lot, marshy, menagerie, mine, moat, mound, mountainous, nature, outlook, park, patio, pit, plateau, plaza, porch, prairie, projection, property, quagmire, ravine, ridge, savanna, shelf, soil, stack, table, trench, tundra, valley, well, wood/woods, yard

510 nation: country, home, land, nationality, soil, state

511 planet: cosmos, Earth, galaxy, moon, planet, sphere, world

512 region: capital, commonwealth, quarter, region, settlement, suburb

513 section: acreage, across-the-board, alcove, barrier, bed, berth, border, brink, cavity, chasm, clearance, cleavage, corner, county, crack, crevice/crevasse, deadline, depression, ditch, enclosure, expanse, fracture, furrow, green, gulch, gully, hem, hole, interstice, leak, limit, margin, menagerie, mouth, nook, opening, outlet, parcel, pass, patio, playground, plot, porch, precinct, projection, puncture, recess, repair, rift, rupture, scratch, side, slack, slot, subdivision, threshold, tract, trough, vacancy, valley, ward, wrinkle, zone

514 water: abyss, aqueduct, basin, beach, blackball, brook, cape, channel, condensation, creek, deep, estuary, fountain, gulf, heading, inlet, lake, oasis, pond, promontory, reservoir, sea, spray, strait, tide, wash, wave, whirlpool

HABITATS

515 habitat: abode, ecosystem, environmentalist, habitat/habitation, harbor, home, land, nest, paradise, premises, refuge, settlement, tent

516 habitat, human: accommodations, apartment, barracks, cabin, castle, condominium, convent, domesticity, dungeon, element, encampment, estate, grange, hacienda, home, house, housing, hut, jail, lodging, madhouse, monastery, neighborhood, old country, palace, prison, reservation, resort, sanctuary, shanty, suite, vacancy, villa

517 habitat, rural: barn, burrow, conservatory, desert, farm, forest, grange, jungle, sanctuary, wilderness/wilds, wood/woods

518 state of: domain, eco-rich, occupancy, presence

NATURAL RESOURCES

519 electricity: beam, spark

520 energy: electricity, fuel, nuclear energy, petroleum, power

521 expression of energy: blast, bonfire, chill, concussion, discharge, fire, flash, noise, thunder

522 natural event: eclipse, meteorology, weather

523 resources: fuel, resource, rock, substance

WEATHER

524 object connected with: avalanche, breeze, climate, cold, dew, film, flurry, frost, gust, haze, hurricane, meteorology, moisture, puff, thunder, weather, wind

525 quality of: breezy, clear, close, crisp, dismal, fair, fiercely, fine, furious, gloomy, hazy, humid, intimidating, misty, oppressive, raw, rugged, soft, stormy, sultry, temperate, thick, tranquil, turbulent, wild, wintry

526 type of: blizzard, cloud, drizzle, fog, hail, mist, puff, rain, shower, tempest, torrent, tremor

QUALITIES

ABSTRACT

527 ability: able, accountable, adroit, all-around, artistic, barren, commendable, deft, dilettante, easy as pie, efficient, executive, expert, feeble, good, handy, inapt, incapacitated, inefficient, inexperienced, masterful, nimble, powerful, practical, proficient, raw, rusty, short, talented, unaccustomed, unprofessional, unskilled, versed, veteran, well, wicked

528 achievement: able, achievable, ace, attainable, complete, crack, done, efficacious, fine, flourishing, fruitful, futile, great, operable, potential, professional, prosperous, swimmingly, triumphant, victorious, washed-up, winning

529 cognitive: academic, affective, afterthought, alternative, anathema, attractive, bad, balm, bearable, beta, boring, breast, burdensome, cheering, comforting, comic/comical, complex, conceivable, considering, crazy, deducible, déjà vu, deplorable, derivable, detestable, difficult, disputable, dissatisfactory, doleful, dream, dull, elusive, engrossing, enigmatic/enigmatical, entertaining, esoteric, exalted, exhilarating, eye-catching, fanciful, far-fetched, favored, fearful, figment, flat, forerunner, foul, frightful/frightening, funny, ghoulish, golden, grating, hair-raising, half-baked, harbinger, harebrained, haunting, heady, heartrending, hellish, hilarious, hopeless, horrible/horrendous/horrid, hypnotic, idea, idealistic, illogical, illusory/illusive, imaginable, imaginative, impenetrable, inadvisable, inconceivable, incredulous, indicator, inner, innovative, inside, inspiration, insufferable, interesting, intolerable, inviting, irksome, irrefutable, itch, jocular/jocose/jocund, knotty, known, leery, left-wing, liking, loathsome, loose, luminous, mad, make-believe, manifest, marvelous, maudlin, measurable, memory, miraculous, mistaken, monotonous, mutinous, mystic/mystical, nauseating, nemesis, new age, nondescript, note, notion, observable, obvious, on paper, opaque, open-and-shut, otherworldly, palatable, panorama, pedagogic, perceptible, pesky, phenomenon, pick, piquant, pitiful, plaintive, pointless, ponderous, portentous, preference, premonition, presage, problematic, provocative, pure, putative, questionable, radical, ravishing, readable, rebellious, recondite, remembrance, reminiscent, reputed, revolting, rich, right, rosy, sad, scary, scintillating, scrumptious, secular, selection, self-evident/self-explanatory, shock, sidesplitting, signal, slight, smidgen, somber, sorry, soupçon, spectacular, speculative, stimulating, strain, subject, suggestion, surmise, suspect, suspicious, tactile, tame, taste, tedious, tempting, theorem, theory, thick, thinkable, thought-provoking, tinge, token, touch, trace, troublesome, unaccountable, unbelievable, uncomfortable, understood, unexciting, unfavorable, ungodly, uninteresting, unlucky, unpleasant, unquestionable, unsatisfactory, unwelcome, vapid, vile, vision, whim, wishful, wonderful, worrisome

530 commonality: accidental, antiquated, au courant, banal, common, commonplace, current, customary, dogmatic, everyday, familiar, frequently, generally, habitual, infrequent, less, mainly, much, natural, occasional, off and on, old school, once in a while, ordinary, popular, prevalent, public, rarely, routine, stereotyped, time-honored, trite, ubiquitous, unexceptional, used to, usually, widespread

531 completeness: absolutely, all-out, altogether, bodily, clean, completely, conscientious, dead, deficient, demonstrative, downright, entirely, exhaustive, final, fulfilled, full-scale, halfway, incomplete, intact, intensive, out-and-out, over, partial, partly, perfectly, plenary, pretty, principally, pure, quite, right, round, sheer, sketchy, solid, superficially, sweeping, thorough/thoroughgoing, through, total, unabridged, undivided, unmitigated, utmost, utterly, washed-up, wholly

532 concerned with: about, angst, appertain, apropos, barrier, bear on/bear upon, behalf,

belong, bug, business, care, catch-22, charge, concept, consideration, craze, difficulty, disputation, distraction, duel, encumbrance, fancy, feeling, focus, guilt, hang-up, horror, interest, keynote/keystone, millstone, notice, object, obstruction, pain, part, passion, pertain, place, priority, province, qualm, question, regard, reverie, scruple, suspicion, temptation, touch, toward/towards, urge, weight, wonder, worry

533 conformity: acceptable, admissible, classic, formal, mediocre, middle-of-the-road, old school, orthodox, proper, so-so, time-honored, typical, unwritten

534 constancy: adjustable, arbitrary, changeable, consistent, continual, firmly, fluid, formative, grim, hesitant, immutable, incessant, inconstant, indecisive, indomitable, insistent, intractable/intransigent, inveterate, irregular, monotonous, relentless, same, slippery, spotty, staunch, steady, unbending, uncertain, unchanging, unforeseeable, unpredictable, unstable/unsteady, varying, wanton, weak-minded

535 definiteness: absolute, accurate, ad hoc, airtight, apparent, assured, canonical, certain, clean, clean-cut, clear-cut, close, conclusive, conscious, dead-on, decided, decisive, deep-seated, definitely, demonstrable, desultory, discernible, disorderly, distinct, doubtless, easily, emphatic, equivocal, especial, evident, exact, experimental, express, factual, fail-safe, finally, fixed, foolproof, for sure, gross, haphazard, hard-core, hit-or-miss, impeccable, implied, incalculable, indecisive, indefinite, indisputable, indubitably, infallible, intangible, ironclad, irresolute, legible, main, markedly, moot, necessarily, obviously, only, outright, palpable, peremptory, plain, positive, precarious, precisely, pure, random, really, right, rigorous, secure, set, sharp, simply, sound, straight, strict, strong, surely, tentative, thorough/thoroughgoing, tried, tried-and-true, truly, trustworthy/trusty, unavoidable, uncertain, undeniable, undisputed/undisputable, unequivocal, unfailing, unmistakable, unorganized, unquestionable, unsettled, unsure, utter, very, weak-minded, yes

536 domain: absolute, administrative, agricultural, athletic, autocratic, bridal, captive, chemical, civic, classical, commanding, communal, constituent, democratic, domestic, earthly, economic, egalitarian, fleshly, free, God-fearing, homegrown, homespun, industrial, internal, itinerant, local, marine/maritime, military, municipal, native, nautical/ naval, oceanic, personal, psychological, religious, sovereign, spiritual, technical, theatrical, totalitarian, universal, urban, worldly, worldwide

537 effects: advantageous, aphrodisiac, awry, baleful, beastly, bitter, bracing, burning, charismatic, combustible, consequent, corrective, costly, curative, deadly, deep, deleterious, desperate, destructive, dire, disadvantageous, disastrous, divisive, doomed, drastic, dreadful, ecumenical, effective, efficacious, emergent, epidemic, expressive, faint, fateful, favorably, fecund, fierce, flat, fooled, forcible, for kicks, formidable, foul, frightful/frightening, fruitless, funereal, furious, gentle, ghostly, gold mine, gory, grave, grievous, gross, harmful, harsh, healthful/healthy, heartrending, helpful, highly, horrible/horrendous/horrid, hypnotic, ill-fated/ill-starred, imposing, inconclusive, ineffective/ineffectual, influential, injurious, insufferable, intoxicating, inviting, juicy, lethal, lucky, macabre, magic/magical, malign, menacing, mild, morbid, moving, nasty, neutral, noisome, noticeable, noxious, oppressive, painful, pallid, penetrating, pernicious, pesky, pestilent/pestilential, pleasing/pleasurable, poison/poisonous, prepossessing, profitable, provocative, remedial, rugged, safe, sedative, sensuous, sick, slow, soporific, spectral, star-crossed, strong, tangy, therapeutic, touching, trenchant, unbearable, uncomfortable, unholy, unspoiled, venomous, virtual, vivid, wholesome, wicked

538 efforts: amateurish, applied, automated, backbreaking, conscientious, difficult, employed, go-ahead, heavy, idle, industrious, jobless, laborious, light, mechanize, murderous, onerous, persistent, rugged, scrupulous, serious, slack, softly, strenuous, studious, thorough/thoroughgoing, tireless, together, torpid, unemployed, unfaltering, unpaid, unsolicited, uphill, vicarious, voluntary, workable, working

539 existential: alive, animate, conscious, dead, deceased, departed, drowsy, extant, fallen, immaterial, inanimate, late, live, lost, missing, nil, obsolete, out cold, present, sleepy, soporific, unconscious, vital, wakeful

540 forcefulness: almighty, blatant, brute, desperate, dynamic, electric/electrical, fiercely, high-powered, insistent, invulnerable, mightily, potent, powerfully, stiff, violent

541 frequency: annual, casual, daily, nightly, occasional, off and on, on and off, periodic, rarely, scarce, seldom, sporadic, usually, yearly

542 inclination: abrupt, acquisitive, addicted, adventurous, aggressive, agreeable, allaround, aloof, amicable, anxious, arbitrary, assiduous, avaricious, beastly, big-hearted, brisk, careful, careless, characteristic, cheap, co-dependent, cold-blooded, conducive, conflicting, conspicuous, contentious, corporal, correct, cost-effective, creditable, decent, deep, deliberately, delicately, dependable, designing, detestable, devout, dewy-eyed, die-hard, dilatory, dim, dirty, disinclined, disposed, distrustful, dog-eat-dog, dogmatic, doubtful, downtrodden, dutiful, eager, eagleeyed, earthy, economical, effusive, emotional, energetic, engrossed, enthusiastic, equal, errant, evasive, even-handed, exaggerated, execrable, exotic, explosive,

fail-safe, fairly, farcical, fastidious, feisty, ferocious, fervent/fervid, firm, flexible, flyby-night, foolish, footloose, forced, frantic, frenzied, frisky, funereal, gailant, generous, genuine, given to, go-ahead, godly, gracious, grasping, greedy, guarded, gullible, gutless, hair-raising, happily, happy-go-lucky, hardboiled, hard-core, hard-nosed/hardheaded, harum-scarum, headlong, heartwarming, hell-bent, hesitant, hooked, hostile, humane, hurtful, hysterical, ignoble, imaginative, impartial, impatient, impetuous, improper, imprudent, inadvertent, inattentive, inclined, indifferent, indiscreet, indisposed, indulgent, inert, infant/infantile, ingenuous, innocent, inquiring, insidious, insincere, intent, intractable/intransigent, inventive, irate, jealous, joyful/joyous, judicious, kindhearted, kinky, lackluster, largesse, left-wing, levelheaded, liable, lifeless, lighthearted, litigious, lively, loath, loving, low-key, magnanimous, malicious, materialistic, mawkish, melodramatic, merciless, methodical/methodic, mindful, naive, narrow-minded, neglectful, nerveless, neutral, nonchalant, noncompliant, nonpartisan, objective, objectivity, obnoxious, obtrusive, odd/oddball, off-guard, one-sided, open, openhearted, opposed/opposing, opprobrious, ossified, overrated, pacific, parental, partial, partisan, passive, peaceful, penitent, perceptive, perfunctory, perverse, philanthropic, plastic, pleasant, pompous, poor, practical, precipitous/precipitate, predictable, premeditated, presumptuous, productive, prolific, prostrate, proud, pugnacious, purposeful, querulous, raging, raunchy, ready, rebellious, reliable, resigned, responsive, restless, revolutionary, romantic, sadistic, sanctioned, sappy, scheming, scurrilous, sedentary, selective, self-righteous, self-satisfied, sentimental, seriously, set, short-sighted, simple, slapdash, sly, small-minded, smug, sober, solemn, sour, spirited, spiteful, sporty, spunky, staunch, steady, stimulating, straight, strict, subjective, susceptible, sweet, tame, temperate, tenacious, tenderhearted, tepid, thickskinned, thoughtless, together, torn, touchy, tractable, true, truthful, unbiased, uncommitted, unconcerned, uncritical, unfeeling, ungodly, unimaginative, unprejudiced, unrehearsed, unrestricted, unstable/ unsteady, untoward, unwavering, unyielding, up-andcoming, vehement, venomous, vicious, vindictive, voucher, wanton, weak, wellbalanced, well-preserved, wholehearted/ whole-hearted, witless, wooden, zippy

543 is an attribute of: appear, belong, quality, seem, trivia

544 manner: abominable, advisedly, although, anyway, backhanded, blah, breezy, brutal, busily, busy, by hand, camp, catchy, circumspect, covert, cumbersome, deluxe, dreary, eat high on the hog, ergo, foolish, for, forthwith, freely, frequently, gradually, grim, hastily, helter-skelter, however, ill-advised, immoderate, impolitic, incautious, indelicate, individually, instant, instinctive, intently, irregularly, just, kindly, largely, less, little, low-key, luxuriate, madly, manual, mechanical, methodical/methodic, mightily, misspent, monotonous, moreover, most, motorized, mutually, naturally, nevertheless, objectively, one by one, otherwise, over, parenthetical, pell-mell, perfunctory, personally, poorly, possibly, powerfully, primarily, progressive, providing/provided, purely, purposely, rampant, rather, recurrent, regular, reliable, ritzy, seriously, simply, softly, somehow, straight, subtle, superficially, swimmingly, though, thus, too, ulterior, unconditional, undercover, unduly, unfair, unusually, venomous, via, violent, virtually, voluntarily, well, wrong, yet

545 morality: abandoned, answerable, astray, bad, bawdy, blasphemous, broad, coarse, conscientious, corrupt, crooked, cunning, damned, dastardly, decadent, demonic/demoniac/demoniacal, devilish, dirty, dissipated, drunk, elevated, equitable, errant, evil, faithless, faultless, fickle, filthy, fleshly, frightful, God-fearing, gross, guiltless, heathen, high-minded, honest, hood, hooligan, ill, illicit, immodest, impious, impure, indecent, indelicate, infamous, inhuman/inhumane, irreligious, insincere, irreproachable, justifiable, lawful, lewd, libidinous, loose, Machiavellian, miscreant, nasty, nefarious, off-color, perverted, pornographic, prejudicial, profane, promiscuous, rakish, raw, reprobate, responsible, righteous, risqué, rotten, satanic, scurrilous, secret, shady, shameless, sinful, sordid, soused, suggestive, true-blue, unconstitutional, unethical, unfaithful, unforgivable, unjust, unprincipled, untrue, unwarranted, upstanding, venal, vicious, vile, vulgar, wholesome, wily, wrong, zonked

546 necessity: absent, auxiliary, bereft, capital, collateral, compulsory, deciding, dire, dispensable, enough, expendable, extraneous, fresh, gratuitous, inadequate, indebted, insatiable, integral, introductory, main, marketable, necessary, nonessential, piddle, prerequisite, providing/provided, radical, required/requisite, shy, starving/starved, superfluous, uncalled for, undue, unessential, vital, wanting

547 normality: aberrant, accepted, addictive, amazing, astonishing, average, characteristic, common, curious, customary, eccentric, exorbitant, familiar, formal, generally, habitual, incongruous, lowly, maladjusted, mediocre, middle, mind-blowing, mind-boggling, modest, natural, normal, ordinary, plain, prosaic, regular, run-of-the-mill, spacey/spacy, temperate, unaccustomed, uninspired, used to, veiled

548 occurrence: abhorrent, accursed, asinine, atrocious, behind one's back, ceremonious,

chronological, coincident, consequent, covertly, cumulative, dangerous, dark, desultory, dire, disastrous, dismal, dramatic, ducky, dullsville, embarrassing, empirical/empiric, enjoyable, eventful, excruciating, exigent, express, feebleminded, forbidden, forcibly, fortuitous, furious, futile, ghoulish, grateful, grievous, hairy, half-baked, happily, hazardous, heavy, heinous, historical, hit-or-miss, hopeful, humdrum, ill-advised, ill-fated/ill-starred, ill-timed, impending, inauspicious, inconclusive, incurable, informal, ironic/ironical, intimidating, joyful, joyous, juicy, lass, limit, low-key, madcap, magic/magical, memorable, meritorious, meteoric, mirthful, misleading, mostly, murderous, nearing, nefarious, nerve-racking, oafish, offensive, oncoming, oppressive, over, overblown, partisan, penal, perilous, pernicious, pleasant, pointless, predetermined, premeditated, pressing, privileged, propitious, prosperous, random, realistic, regrettable, ridiculous, risky, rollicking, rosy, ruinous, safe, secretive, self-evident/self-explanatory, sequential, simpleminded, sinful, slow, somewhat, speedy, staggering, star-crossed, stupid, surprising, swell, tacit, tardy, tender, terminal, then, threatening, through, tight, tolerable, topsy-turvy, tragic, trying, tumultous/tumultuous, ugly, unaffected, unavailing, unbelievable, uneasy, unexpected, unforeseen, unfortunate, ungodly, unholy, unimaginative, unintelligent, unintentional/unintended, uninviting, unlucky, unreasonable, unsophisticated, untimely, untroubled, unwise, urgent, warlike, well, wholehearted/whole-hearted, wrong, yet

549 original: aboriginal, automated, bastard, born, built-in, colonial, constitutional, deep-seated, domestic, ethereal, exotic, extrinsic, from, hereditary, humble, illegitimate, imported, inborn/inbred, ingrained, inherited, intimate, lowly, medieval, mortal, mystic/mystical, noble, patrician, plebeian, premature, primary/prime, provincial, radical, rudimentary, secular, thoroughbred, unprecedented, vernacular

550 peculiarity: ablaze, aggressive, ashamed, authoritative, born, clement, contemptible, conventional, craven, dead, dreadful, forbidding, forgetful, gingerly, hokey, laughable, on guard, punctual, shamefaced

551 permanency: abiding, carved in stone, endless, fixed, fly-by-night, fugitive, invulnerable, lasting, long-standing, passing, perpetual, stationary, temporary, unchanging

552 probability: absurd, accidentally, alleged, apparently, chance, clearly, contingent, credible, dicey, doubtless, earthly, eventual, far-fetched, feasible, fluky, fortuitous, groundless, hypothetical, iffy, illusory/illusive, immune, impossible, impractical/impracticable, inclined, incredible, insurmountable, invalid, liable, logical, maybe, obviously, off, optional, out, perhaps, possible, potential, presumably, probably, prospective, ridiculous, slender/slim, so-called, specious, starry-eyed, tenable, unlikely, unreliable, viable, workable

553 **repetition:** again, away, repeatedly, repetitious

554 **restrictiveness:** absolute, autonomous, binding, bounded, captive, concentrated, confined, dye-in-the-wool, exclusively, exempt, fixed, independent, ironclad, narrow, numbered, obliged, off-limits, permissible, prohibitive, qualified, self-reliant

555 **social:** accommodating, amorous, aristo-cratic, bigoted, brotherly, busy, civilian, clannish, commemorative, compatible, conjugal, cooperative, dear, degrading, difficult, disadvantageous, disgraceful, elite, engaged, familiar, friendless, frisky, homeless, hot, inelegant, intimate, lone-some, matrimonial, meddlesome, noble, palsy-walsy, popular, prestigious, recluse/reclusive, single, solitary, thoughtful, top-level, unapproachable, uninvited, unpopu-lar, unsociable, unworldly, valued, welcome

556 **specialization:** alone, express, finicky, respective

557 **specificity:** accurate, ad hoc, approximate, catholic, closely, definite, detailed, exactly, fine, just, limited, literally, minute, nice, particularly, peculiar, photographic, pre-cisely, punctilious, right, rough, sectional, simply, skin-deep, special, specific, strict, superficial, thorough/thoroughgoing, topical, wholly

558 **suitability:** absurd, accepted, accordingly, adequately, agreeable, ample, applicable, apropos, awkward, befitting, conformable, correct, cut out for, decorous, discordant, done, down-to-earth, duly, enough, exorbi-tant, extreme, favorably, felicitous, fit, fitting, full-grown/full-fledged, germane, granted, ill-suited, improper, inadvisable, inappropriate, incongruous, ineligible, inopportune, justifiable, lame, livable, nice, okay, on the level, passable, perfect, prehistoric, previous, reasonable, relevant, rightful, satisfactory, seemly, sound, suit-able, tailor-made, timely, unasked, undue, unsatisfactory, unsuitable, unwarranted, venial, well, wrong

559 **transmission:** infectious, roundabout

560 **usefulness:** acting, barren, convenient, dead, defunct, derelict, desirable, dilapi-dated, drained, effete, employed, excessive, expedient, faded, faulty, fitted, fruitful, funetional, futility, good, helpful, idle, impaired, inactive, ineffective/ ineffectual, infallible, instead, interim, irrelevant, live, lost, make-shift, neither here nor there, obsolete, old, on the blink, operational, outmoded, practical, prepared, productive, purposeless, ready, ripe, salubrious, service-able, spent, starry-eyed, subservient, substi-tute, superfluous, surplus, trial, under, unrealistic, useful, user-friendly, vacant,

viable, virgin/virginal, void, washed-out, working, worn/worn-out, worthwhile

COMPARATIVE

561 **compared with:** contrast, touch

562 **complexity:** abstruse, backward, baroque, blank, clarion, complex, crude, elaborate, exaggerated, folksy, high-flown, involved, pell-mell, simply, tortuous, ultra, unwieldy, well-defined

563 **correspondence:** accordant, allied, applicable, commensurate, concerning, conformable, congruous, consonant, corporate, euphonious, kindred, moderate, proportionate/proportional, relative, truant, unanimous, united, unrelated

564 **difference:** against, altered, ambivalent, assorted, avant-garde, bizarre, converse, deviant, diametric/diametrical, differently, discrepant, disparate, dissimilar, distinct, divergent, eccentric, especially, extraordi-nary, flaky, funny, heterogeneous, inconsis-tent, inverse, manifold, mixed, motley, multiple/multifarious, new, odd/oddball, opposed/opposing, other, peculiar, plural, preternatural, queer, remote, rival, separate, single, sole, spacey/spacy, specific, strange, suspicious, unaccustomed, uncommon, underground, unequal, unheard-of, unlike, unorthodox, unrelated, unusual, varied, various, weird

565 **difficulty:** agonizing, awkward, defective, delicate, easily, easy as pie, facile, grueling, heavy, insurmountable, laborious, mortally, nerve-racking, onerous, prickly, rugged, seriously, sticky, tall, thorny, tight, treacher-ous, trying, uphill, wicked, worrisome

566 **equivalence:** alike, approximately, balanced, comparable, coordinate, disproportionate, equal, even, indistinguishable, matching, model, nearly, regular, uneven

567 **importance:** above, below, beneficial, bush-league, chiefly, climactic/climacteric, component, costly, dogmatic, essential, exclusive, fundamental, high, immediate, inferior, life-and-death, majestic, meaning-ful, noteworthy, operative, pregnant, primary/prime, reputable, second-rate/second-class, special, telling, towering, used, worthwhile, worthy

568 **importance, extreme:** acclaimed, basic, beloved, better, big league, bright, burning, cardinal, chief, considerable, crucial, dire, dominant, eminent, fabled, fatal, favored, first, glorious, great, head, high-class, illus-trious, influential, key, legendary, master, monumental, notable, noteworthy, outstand-ing, paramount, pivotal, predominant, premier, prestigious, principal, renowned, serious, signal, sovereign, star, supreme, unsurpassed, urgent, weighty, well-known

569 **intensity:** acute, awfully, badly, blatant, concentrated, desperate, drastic, exquisite, extreme, greatly, heavy, highly, insanely, mightily, notably, powerfully, profound,

severe, sharp, stark, stringent, substantially, terrific, ultra, undue, unmitigated, very, vivid, wild

570 negative: adverse, amiss, awful, bad, baneful, beside oneself, conflicting, cruel, damned, degenerate, delinquent, derogatory, detrimental, direful, egregious, erroneous, fallacious, faulty, filthy, grisly, hellish, ill, inadequate, incendiary, incorrigible, infamous, inordinate, lame, miserable, misspent, nerd, objectionable, poor, rancid, ruinous, run-down, slipshod, tasteless, threatening, trumped up, unforgivable, ungodly, unsatisfactory, unwelcome, weak, worthless

571 negative, extreme: abject, accursed, astounding, awful, bad, crappy, cursed, nasty, outrageous, perverse, regrettable, repugnant, rotten, shocking, sick, sickly, sordid, terrible, ugly, unfavorable, unsavory, unworthy, vile, wicked, wretched, wrong

572 positive: admirable, agreeable, all right, angelic, auspicious, beloved, benign, better, comfort, commendable, cool, delicious, estimable, exemplary, fabulous, fantastic, far-out, favorable, for kicks, fortunately, good, groovy, high-class, idyllic, innocuous, intriguing, lucky, majestic, merry, mind-blowing, mind-boggling, nice, noble, pleasant, pleasing/pleasurable, prodigious, propitious, proud, rewarding, salubrious, terrific, toothsome, utopian, well, worthy, yummy

573 similarity: akin, analogous, closely, comparable, conformable, equal, faithful, identical, like, like-minded, related, same, similar, tantamount, uniform, virtually

574 superiority: absolute, admirable, advantage, all right, all-time, below par, cardinal, chief, chosen, classic/classical, commanding, crack, definitive, delicate, dependent, dignified, distinguished, dominant, elite, enviable, especially, exceptional, exquisite, fine, first-class/first-rate, flat-out, glorious, golden, great, high-powered, ideal, imperative, imperious, imposing, incomparable, infallible, inimitable, irresistible, laudable, less, low, lush, luxurious, major, matchless, menial, model, optimal, outstanding, peerless, perfectly, phenomenal, poorly, praiseworthy, preeminent, premium, primary/prime, privileged, prodigious, rare, renowned, ritzy, royal, sacred, secondary, second-rate/second-class, senior, signal, spectacular, stately, striking, stupendous, substandard, super, superior, supreme, tasteful, top-level, top-notch, transcendent/ transcendental, ultimate, unequaled, unique, unparalleled, unrivaled, upper hand, utopian, vintage, wonderful

575 unimportance: beside the point, expendable, hand-me-down, inconsequential/inconsiderable, irrelevant, lightweight, meaningless, middle-of-the-road, minute, needless, neither here nor there, nonessential, peripheral, picayune, puny, second, side, small, small-time, so-so, subordinate,

subsidiary, tenuous, trivial, undistinguished, unimportant, vapid, worthless

PHYSICAL

576 accessibility: accessible, approachable, arrant, bereft, broad, classified, closed, confidential, cryptic, defenseless, discernible, distant, engaged, enigmatic/enigmatical, exposed, far-flung, furtive, graphic, hush-hush, impenetrable, incognito, inner, inside, known, legible, manifest, mobile, nameless, observable, occult, off-course, off-limits, on call, optional, outward, passable, perceptible, plain, private, prohibited, public, ready, reserved, secret, strange, ulterior, unarmed, uncovered, underground, unheard-of, unknown, unreadable, unsung, user-friendly, vigilant, visual, willing

577 accompaniment: abandoned, alone, also, attendant, concomitant, corporate, each, en route, et cetera, furthermore, including, joint, left, mutually, one, parenthetical, personally, related, separately, single-handed, singular, solely, solo, unaccompanied, unified, united

578 age: adolescent, afresh, ancient, antiquarian, antique, big, childish, crude, doddering, elderly, fresh, full-grown/full-fledged, green, hoary, immemorial, infant/infantile, junior, late, medieval, mint, modish, new, novel, older, old-fashioned, originally, outdated/out-of-date, passé, quaint, refreshing, secondhand, stale, state-of-the-art, undeveloped, up-to-date, well-preserved, youthful

579 appearance: adorable, aesthetic/esthetic, artistic, beautiful, comely, crisp, dapper, decorative, desirable, dressy, exquisite, eye-catching, fancy, fetching, flawless, glorious, good-looking, graceful, grungy, hideous, homely, irresistible, natty, ornate, plain, pretty, refreshing, resplendent, seductive, spiffy, striking, stylish, ugly, unbecoming, willowy, with-it

580 deformity: acne, birthmark, blot, bug, contortion, distortion, flaw, freak, malformation, misstatement, mutant, scar

581 direction: about, adrift, around, astern, at, awry, below, circuitous, crooked, crosswise/crossways, diagonal, direct, due, errant, forked, forward, horizontal, inward, left, off-center, outward, perpendicular, plumb, right, roundabout, sheer, sinuous, steep, thereabout, tortuous, upright, wide, wry, zigzag

582 genuineness: abstract, actually, alias, apocryphal, apparently, arty, authentic, baseless, beta, bona fide, circumstantial, concrete, contrived, credible, deceptive, delusive, dreamy, ecclesiastical, empirical/empiric, enigmatic/enigmatical, ersatz, ethereal, factual, fallacious, fantastic, far-fetched, fictitious, foolproof, fraudulent, good, hard, historical, honest-to-God, illusory/illusive, imitative, indisputable, invisible, just, lifelike, made-up, magic/

magical, make-believe, matter-of-fact, metaphysical, monstrous, mystic/mystical, mythical/mythological, nonexistent, open-hearted, ostensibly, paranormal, physical, positive, pretended, quack, quite, realistic, right, sincerely, specious, spurious, super-natural, synthetic, tangible, true, unearthly, unnatural, unthinkable, unvarnished, unworldly, valid, veritable, wholehearted/whole-hearted, wrong

583 location: aboard, abroad, absent, advance, agricultural, airy, ashore, astride, beached, center, civic, cloistered, diffuse, every-where, external, forward, front, horizontal, insular, isolated, leafy, lonely, middle, off, off-center, off-course, out, outer, outlying, outward, overseas, penal, perpendicular, populous, precipitous, private, prone, quiet, recumbent, restful, roughly, rustic, side-ways, single-handed, solo, stray, surface, through, topical, uncomfortable, untamed, uppermost, upside-down, void, where/wherever, wild, withdrawn

584 movement: ambulatory, brisk, clumsy, fleet, fluent, frozen, gawky, graceless, immobile, indolent, itinerant, leisurely, lifeless, liquid, lithe, maladroit, migrant/migratory, motion-less, moving, nomadic, oafish, passive, pendulous/pendent, portable, restless, roundabout, sedentary, slow, speedy, static, vibrant, winding

585 order: advance, alphabetical, avant-garde, center, collective, consecutive, disjointed, first, fore, foremost, formerly, from scratch, hand-me-down, incipient, initial, internal, jumbled, last, latter, least, mean, methodi-cal/methodic, neatly, older, onward/onwards, original, past, pell-mell, posterior, prelimi-nary, preparatory, primary/prime, second, sequential, shipshape, subsequent, succeed-ing/successive, tidy, topsy-turvy, uttermost

586 relative placement: abaft, abreast, adjoin-ing, ahead, almost, alongside, amid/amidst, apart, around, askew, below, beside, bottom, close, contiguous, direct, downhill, en route, faraway, farthest, gone, handy, immediate, near, next, overhead, preceding, toward/towards, underneath, without, yonder

587 safety: chancy, perilous, sacred, secure, unharmed, unsafe, vulnerable, weak

588 speed: agile, expeditious, fast, gradual, hastily, headlong, instant, one by one, posthaste, precipitous/precipitate, quickly, rapidly, snappy, swift, swiftly/swift, whirl-wind

589 style: adorable, baroque, becoming, black, bold, brassy, cheap, class, classy, contempo-rary, country, cultural, dashing, dowdy, eat high on the hog, exquisite, featureless, flam-boyant, floral, flowery, formless, futuristic, garish, gay, glamorous, gorgeous, grand, graphic, hot, improvised, informal, innova-tive, kinky, loud, lush, luxurious, mean, meretricious, modish, neat, new, obsolete, old-fashioned, orderly, ornamental, ostenta-tious, outdated/out-of-date, palatial,

picturesque, plush, posh, prevalent, quaint, refined, resplendent, rustic, scruffy, sharp, simple, sleazy, smart, snazzy, spiffy, spruce, stately, state-of-the-art, stylish, swank/swanky, tacky, tasteless, tousled, two-bit, unbecoming, unworldly, up-to-date, vogue

SENSES

ASPECTS OF PERCEPTION

590 physical: burn, hear, smell, touch

AUDITORY

591 attribute of hearing: acoustic, deaf, distinct

592 attribute of noise: blatant, cacophonous, deafening, dissonant, grating, noisy, pierc-ing, raucous, shrill, soft-spoken, strident, vociferous

593 attribute of noisemaking: dumb, mute

594 attribute of sound: acoustic, audible, brassy, clarion, deep, dissonant, dull, faint, gentle, gruff, high, hollow, inaudible, low, lyrical, mellow, melodious/melodic, mum, noiseless, noisy, off-key, quiet, raucous, rich, round, silent, soft-spoken, soundproof, subdued, tight-lipped, tuneful, vocal, weak

595 audible object: acknowledgment, air, anthem, arrangement, bang, blast, buzz, carol, clamor, clap, click, clump, crash, din, discord, ditty, echo, groan, gurgle, hiss, howl, inflection, jangle, melody, music, peal, psalm, report, rhythm, roar, rumpus, scream, shriek, song, strain, tick, yell

596 hearing: attend, commiserate, hear, mind, regard

597 sound perception: hearing

OLFACTORY

598 attribute of odor: aromatic, fetid, gamy, malodorous, noisome, odorous, rancid, scented, smelly, stinking, sweet, tangy

599 object that can be smelled: aroma, breath, incense, perfume, smell, stink, whiff

600 odor: cologne, fumes, perfume, smell, stink, tang

601 olfactory perception: breathe, nose, smell, whiff

602 smelling: scent, sniff, whiff

TACTILE

603 attribute of dryness: absorbent, balmy, damp, dry, fluid, juicy, misty, moldy, musty, parched, soaked soggy, thirsty, watery, wizened

604 attribute of hardness: adamant, downy, firm, flaccid, hard, impermeable, inflexible, limp, mushy, permeable, plastic, solid, supple, tender, unbending

605 attribute of temperature: ablaze, balmy, biting, boiling, brisk, burning, chilly, cold, cozy, febrile, fiery, frigid, frozen, heated, icy, polar, sweltering, thermal, tropical, wintry

606 attribute of texture: abrasive, beaten, breakable, bumpy, coarse, cozy, creamy, crumbly, crusty, delicate, diluted/dilute, elastic, fibrous, fine, fleecy, fluff, fuzzy, gelatinous, glossy, gossamer, gritty, irregular, knurled, leathery, lucid, mottled, mushy, oily, paper, permeable, porous, rough, sheer, sleek, slippery, soft, springy, tenacious, thick, threadbare, uneven, yielding

607 dryness: drought, humidity, wet

608 tactile perception: feeling, touch

609 tactile quality: excruciating, numb

610 temperature: cold, frost, heat, temperature

611 texture: consistency, feel, finish, grain, nap, texture

612 touching: brush, dab, finger, graze, handle, lick, meet, nestle, nuzzle, paw, reach, tickle, toothsome, yummy

TASTING

613 attribute of taste: acerbic, acid, acrid, astringent, bitter, corrupt, delicious, done, edible, full-bodied, insipid, mouth-watering, peppery, poignant, racy, rich, salty, scrumptious, sour, succulent, tart, tasty, yummy

614 taste: acidity, bitterness, savor, tang, zest

615 taste perception: taste

616 tasting: bite, sample, taste

VISUAL

617 attribute of brightness: ablaze, bold, brilliant, colorful, dark, dim, drab, dusky, faded, glaring, glossy, incandescent, light, luminescent, lustrous, murky, obscure, radiant, scintillating, shady, sunny, washed-out

618 attribute of color: amber, ashen, black, blond/blonde, blue, bright, brown, brunette/brunet, cadaverous, clear, colorful, crystal, dark, deep, dusky, fair, flushed, gay, glowing, gold/golden, gray/grey, hoary, jet, livid, milky, mottled, muddy, murky, opaque, pale, pallor, pasty, pearly, red, rosy, sable, sanguine, smoky, speckled, swarthy, translucent, variegated, vibrant, wan, white, yellow

619 attribute of vision: appreciable, clear, conspicuous, disguised, fuzzy, glassy, impalpable, lucid, nearsighted, pronounced, visual

620 brightness: dark, gleam, gloom, glow, lamp, light, murk, overshadow, polish, radiate, shadow, shimmer, splendor

621 clean: grimy, hygienic, impeccable, mangy, neat, pure, sanitary, slimy, slovenly, spick-and-span, stagnant, straight, trim, unblemished, unkempt, untidy, untouched

622 color: auburn, blush, color, decor, flush, glow, orange, pink, red, shadow, stripe, tinge, tone, yellow

623 looking: attend, bear in mind, contemplate, dip into, face, fixate, gape, gaze, glare, glower, inspect, leer, lookout, mind, ogle, peek/peep, point, regard, scan, scrutinize, skim, spy, stare, vigil, watch

624 occurrence of light: beam, bolt, eclipse, flicker, glare, glimmer, glisten, glow, illuminate, lamp, light, ray, shimmer, spark, spotlight, wink

625 picture: arms, caricature, chart, diagram, emblem, facsimile, flowchart, graphics, impression, layout, model, pattern, plaid, portrait, reproduction, scheme, sketch, tableau

626 seeing: behold, eye, make out, meet, notice, perceive, remark, sight, view, witness

627 visibility change: blur, dim, fog

628 visible object: acknowledgment, aspect, beam, buoy, footprint, glare, halo, light, model, panorama, ray, scene, sparkle, track, vista

629 visual perception: blindness, perspective, vision

STATES

ABSTRACT

630 ability: artifice, awkwardness, can, capacity, dexterity, ease, eloquence, expertise/expertness, faculty, flair, hand, head, inclination, know-how, literacy, mastery, modus operandi, performance, power, proficiency, propensity, qualification, readiness, skill, technique, touch, turn

631 accessibility: access, circulation, cover-up, seclusion, secret

632 be ahead: ahead, front, winning

633 behavior: abandon, abstinence, acrimony, act up, affectation, alacrity, amenity, apathy, asperity, austerity, bad manners, barbarism, bearing, betrayal, bluster, bravery, carry on, cheek, chutzpah, cold shoulder, complaisance, condescension, conduct, cordiality, corruption, courage, cruelty, custom, debauchery, decency, deference, demeanor, desperation, diffidence, dirty tricks, disloyalty, disregard, dissidence, distance, eagerness, ebullience, effrontery, enthusiasm, excess, exuberance, faithfulness, falderal, flare-up, feint, firmness, flippancy, foolishness, formality, frivolity, fuss, geniality, grit, haughtiness, heroism, honor, hubris, humility, impatience, incivility, indiscretion, insubordination, kindness, lethargy, lifestyle, lunacy, manhood/womanhood, manners, misbehave, mischief, misdeed/misdemeanor, modesty, moxie, naiveté, nonconformity, obedience, observance, ostentation, pep, piety, polish, precaution, pretense, pride, prowess, purpose, radiance, react, readiness, rebellion, refusal, reserve, restraint, scene, self-control, shenanigans, simplicity, sloth, sophistication, steam, sympathy, technicality, temperance, treat, vainglory, veneer, vitality, zing, zip

634 commonality: diffusion, ritual

635 **completeness:** bulk, complement, deficiency, finality, integrity, whole

636 **conformity:** adequacy, archetype, fidelity, par

637 **constancy:** consistency, continuance, monotony

638 **definiteness:** accuracy, certainty, correctness, finality, rigor, truth

639 **exist in a condition:** blame, existence, status quo

640 **extension:** addition, continuation

641 **forcefulness:** clasp, dictatorship, force, impact, impulse, kick, momentum, power, propulsion, swamp, violence

642 **made of:** compose, inclusion, manifestation

643 **make up:** accompany, consist of, form, make up

644 **mannerism:** air, attention(s), characterize, courtesy, earmark, epitomize, foible, habit, manner, mark, mien, mores, purpose, regard, vigilance

645 **morality:** abandon, affirmative action, blasphemy, conscience, craft, decadence, delinquency, dirt, enormity, equality, ethics/ethic, excess, faithfulness, falsity, favoritism, good, good will/goodwill, guile, guise, honesty, ideals, imposture, infamy, infraction, iniquity, innocence, liability, loyalty, misbehavior, misconduct, misdeed/misdemeanor, morals, obscenity, outrage, principle/principles, profanity, responsibility, sacrilege, scandal, score, sin, treachery, trespass, trickery, turpitude, validity, veracity, virtue, wrong

646 **necessity:** absence, call for, defect, demand, do without, enough, essential, exigency/exigence, go without, lack, must, obligate, paucity, provide, require, requirement/requisite, shortage, subsistence, void, want

647 **normality:** aberration, anomaly, eccentricity, norm, rut, yardstick

648 **origin:** ancestry, bottom, cradle, derivation, emanate, extraction, femininity/feminine, fountain, germ, hail, heredity, home, issue, masculinity/masculine, mortality, parent, root(s), sex, spring, stem, threshold

649 **permanency:** constant, forever, perpetual, unchanging

650 **probability:** absurdity, contingency, eventuality, likelihood, odds, possibility, probability, tend

651 **range:** area, circulation, continuation, degree, dissemination, distance, expanse, gamut, jurisdiction, length, overrun, play, realm, run, scope, stretch, sweep

652 **restrictiveness:** abbreviation, autonomy, block, bondage, constraint, exemption, prohibition, qualification

653 **specialization:** alone, express, select

654 **specificity:** accuracy, exactness, point, property, rigor

655 **style:** appeal, artistry, clash, classicism, cut, dernier cri, elegance, fashion, frill, genre/genus, glitter, look, ostentation, pomp, rage, simplicity, splendor, taste, touch, vogue

656 **suitability:** absurdity, agree, blend, correctness, expediency/expedience, propriety, serve, suit

657 **tendency:** acrimony, alms, aptitude, cabin fever, charity, dedication, determination, diligence, discretion, disinclination, earnestness, enterprise, equity, fairness, fervor, fundraiser, generosity, guile, guts, hospitality, humility, hypocrisy, impatience, indifference, indulgence, inhibition, kindness, mind, monstrosity, neglect, nonconformity, philanthropy, posture, pretension, resignation, restlessness, sincerity, tenacity, thing, trend, truth, vice, vigilance

658 **usefulness:** abend, agent, efficiency, expediency/expedience, help, malfunction, operation, purpose, serve, surplus, use, value, wear

COGNITIVE

659 **goal:** aim, aspiration, dream, function, intent/intention, meaning, object, pleasure, prize, purpose, reason, sake, taste, will

660 **plan:** angle, architecture, calculation, chart, collusion, concoction, contrivance, deceit, device, diet, disposition, draft, expediency/expedience, feint, form, freeware, game, groundwork, innovation, invention, layout, machination, manner, move, plot, program, purpose, scenario, scheme, strategem, tactics

661 **reason:** alibi, asset, basis, blame, cause, essence, excuse, footing, goad, groundwork, idea, incentive, inspiration, keynote/keystone, meaning, motive, occasion, pretext, raison d'être, reason, sake, spring, stimulant, whim

662 **request:** command, desire, edict, petition, prayer, proposition, recall, requisition, ultimatum

COMPARATIVE

663 **complexity:** complexity, labyrinth, snarl

664 **correspondence:** accord, approximate, clash, community, conformity, consonance, correspond, double, duplicate, flatter, go together/go with, harmony, jibe, look-alike, match, proportion, resemble, spitting image, sympathy, union, unity

665 **difference:** aberration, assortment, contradict, contrast, converse, departure, deviation, difference, disagree, discrepancy, disparity, dissension, dissimilarity, distinction, divergence, eccentricity, flip side, gap, grade, innovation, mismatch, multiculturalism, novelty, oddity, opposition, rent, shade, variant, variety, wander

666 **difficulty:** abomination, bottleneck, deficiency, disadvantage(s), drawback, entanglement, handicap, hitch, labyrinth, matter, muddle, obstruction, pressure, quagmire, restraint, rigor, shortcoming, snarl, stumbling block, tax, trouble, wall

667 **equivalence:** alternate, balance, cancel, cohere, coincidence, copy, counterpart,

ditto, equal, equate, equivalent, image, match, par, parity, sameness, tie, transcript

668 importance: accent, bearing, berth, celebrity, cipher, core, cream, cutting edge, dignity, element, eminence, essence, forefront/foreground, glory, gravity, height, honorary, immortality, key, magnitude, matter, name, nothingness, peak, pride, prominence, renown, sense, significance, situation, stardom, status, stuff, tedium, trifle, weight, zero hour

669 intensity: violence

670 similarity: affinity, analogy, consistency, equivalent, likeness, parity, reproduction, resemble, second, tune, twin

671 superiority: ascendancy/ascendency, elegance, excel, hairsplitting, imperfection, jewel, marvel, paragon, pick, precedence, prodigy, seniority, victory

OF BEING

672 abstraction: manifestation, oblivion

673 aura: abracadabra, allure, appeal, aspect, attribute, background, blaze, charm, climate, dash, ease, environmentalist, feeling, glory, hex, look, milieu, mood, presence, romance, serenity, solitude, spice, splendor, surroundings, tone, undercurrent, vein, vestige, whisper

674 bad situation: abend, accident, adversity, anarchy, apocalypse, backwash, bad scene, bane, bedlam, bind, blooper, bottleneck, bug, bummer, can of worms, cataclysm, catch, chaos, clog, cobweb, collision, commotion, conflict, contempt, crisis, crunch, damage, deadlock, debacle, decline, deficiency, detriment, difficulty, disadvantage(s), disaster, discomfiture, disorganization, disservice, disturbance, downfall, drag, drawback, duress, emergency, error, exigency/exigence, failing, famine, fiasco, fix, flash point, flip-flop, flotsam, friction, gadfly, hang-up, harm, havoc, hell, histrionics, holdup, hurdle, impasse, impropriety, inconvenience, infirmity, jalopy, jump, lapse, limitation, lose, madhouse, malfunction, maze, mire, misery, misfortune/mishap, mix-up, neglect, nightmare, obstacle, onus, ordeal, pall, pass, pell-mell, pickle, pitfall, plague, poison, press, problem, quagmire, question, restraint, reverse, ruin, scandal, scrape, shambles, showdown, smash, snare, spot, storm, strife, syndrome, tiff, to-do, trap, trouble, turmoil, undoing, uprising, upset, weight, wreck

675 danger: act of God, bad trip, calamity, cataclysm, crapshoot, curse, dilemma, emergency, hardship, ill, mayhem, peril, risk, seriousness, threat, trouble, violence

676 effect: amount, because, combustion, culmination, efficacy, magnetism, proceed, sex appeal, tell, wash

677 effort: concentration, difficulty, direct, exertion, go, headache, industry, sweat, trouble, work, yoke

678 experience: background, career, heritage, ignorance, lead (a life), live, mellow, naive, phenomenon, readiness, sustain, training, unfamiliar, veteran, world, young

679 fate: accident, break, bummer, chaff, contingency, damnation, destiny, doom, downfall, duty, flip-flop, fortune, future, good, judgment, limbo, lot, misfortune/mishap, outlook, penalty, plague, predestination, setback, suspense, undoing, windfall

680 function: application, bar, bolt, closure, cushion, deterrent, dump, operate, run, tie, yardstick

681 inaction: abeyance, asleep, dalliance, dawdle, drag, forbear, hang, hesitation, inertia, linger, loiter, neglect, procrastinate, relief, repose, rest, sit tight, slack/slacken, wait

682 meaning: ambiguity, content, cryptic, denote, drift, emphasis, fiber, imply, importance, matter, message, nature, point, purport, represent, sense, signify, stand for, strength, substance, symbolize, terminology, texture, thrust, typify, undertone, value, weigh, wording

683 name: alias, appellation, designation, handle, nom de plume, pen name, sobriquet, term, title

684 of agreement: accord, alliance, arrangement, bargain, charter, coherence, communion, compliance, concert, consensus, contract, covenant, debenture, give-and-take, negotiation, order, protocol, provision/proviso, stipulation, transaction, truce, warranty, word

685 of authorization: absolution, Annie Oakley, authority, charter, consent, decree, determination, doorbell, enactment, enforcement, entry, fiat, forgiveness, go-ahead, guarantee, leave, mandate, nod, pardon, passage, patent, permit, release, repeal, sanction, signal, treaty, waiver, warranty, word

686 of being an example: archetype, classic, embodiment, example, exponent, ideal, instance, light, model, original, paragon, picture, prototype, representative, specimen, type

687 of being an influence: bolt, effect, fetish, gush, instrument, leverage, muscle, persuasion, preponderance, rudiments, squeeze, wonder

688 of being a rule: authority, ban, benchmark, code, convention, criterion, democracy, doctrine, edict, ethics/ethic, form, formula, gauge, ideology, keynote/keystone, line, model, norm, parameter, policy, precept, protocol, ritual, standard, tenet, tradition

689 of belief: absolution, adjudication, ageism, allegiance, apartheid, apparition, assumed, atheism, attrition, ax to grind, belief, black magic, case, chauvinism, commonplace, concept, conclusion, conformity, connotation, consensus, conviction, creed, culture, deduction, delusion, denomination, dependence/dependency, determination, dictum, disbelief, dissent, dissonance, divinity, dogma, estimate, ethics/ethic, expectancy, eye, faith, fallacy, fantasy, fatalism, feeling, foreboding, frame of mind, gospel, guess, honor, hunch, idea, ideology, illusion, impression, induction, instinct, intuition, leaning, logic, make-believe, millstone, mindset, misconception, misogynist, motive, necromancy, nihilism, notion, obsession, old wives' tale, opinion, oracle, patriotism, perspective, pessimism, piety, Pollyanna, preconception, prejudice, premonition, presentiment, pride, principle/principles, prophecy, purport, racism, reality, regard, religion, resolve, right, self-respect/self-esteem, self-satisfaction, sexism, Shangri-la, sign, slant, speculation, stance, standpoint, stock, substance, superstition, surmise, taste, theme, theory, trust, utopia, values, viewpoint, voodoo, witchcraft, Xanadu

690 of concern: afraid, alarm, anxiety, apprehension, concern, craze, dismay, distraction, distress, encumbrance, feeling, foreboding, guilt, hang-up, horror, jitters, jumpy, misgiving, obsession, one-track mind, passion, petrified, puzzled, question, suspicion, terror, trouble, weight, wonder, worry

691 of law: abomination, autocracy, détente, exemption, freedom, justice, laissez-faire, liberty, offense, peace, trespass, validity, ward

692 on a course: career, ramble, tendency, traverse

693 opportunity: big win, contingency, duck soup, fluke, handicap, hearing, juncture, leverage, merit, occasion, opening, outlet, plus, preference, profit, pushover, remedy, risk, serendipity, snap, strength, success, treat, vacancy, welfare/well-being

694 purpose: application, help, role, vehicle

695 repetition: boomerang, repeat, return, verbiage

696 situation: case, condition, ecosystem, experience, landmark, medium, occurrence, position, state, uncertainty

OF CHANGE

697 abstract: about-face, adapt, adjust, back down, backslide, deepen, departure, deviation, digression, diversify, flux, interchange, metamorphosis, mutation, oscillate, reconcile, refresh, retract, reverse, revolution, rotate, suit, tighten, transformation, transpose, turnabout, variation, vicissitude, withdraw

698 diminish: abate, come down, cutback, decrease, depreciate, deterioration, drain, drop off, dwindle, entropy, evaporate, extenuate, fester, go, lapse, let up, mollify, plummet, recede, regress, relax, remission, revert, sag, sink, slack/slacken, stagnate, taper/taper off, wane, wear, worsen

699 fail: abortion, blow over, comedown, decline, disappoint, downfall, error, failure, fault, flag, flounder, founder, go down, miscarriage, miss, neglect, overlook, slump, wilt

700 improve: accession, advancement, boom, clear up, correction, development, edification, embellish, energize, furbish, lift, mend, pick up, pull through, recoup, recuperate, repair, rise, upgrade

701 of state: acclimate, aging, alternate, assimilate, become, change, come about, convert, co-opt, metamorphosis, state

702 of structure: buckle, degenerate, flatten

703 organizational: adjournment, expansionism, merger

704 progress: advance, batten, breakthrough, bring off, click, coast, consummate, develop, evolution, expansion, fare, flower, fruition, gestation, get on, go ahead, grow, headway, jump, mellow, mushroom, passage, progress, push off/push on, score, thrive, wax

705 unchanged: abeyance, limbo, quiet

OF NEED OR ACHIEVEMENT

706 achievement: ability, accomplishment, action, arrive, attain, background, bloom, bring about, carry, climax, come at, come through, completion, conquest, consummation, craft, crown, degree, distinction, doing, drive, eager beaver, efficacy, execute, exercise, extreme, failure, find, flair, fruition, fulfillment, get, gift, go far, graduation, hairsplitting, hit, manage, milestone, orgasm, pass, perfection, pinnacle, prodigy, progress, prosper, pull off, rack up, record, smash, succeed, take, tour de force, triumph, welfare/well-being, work, zenith

707 lack: nothing/nothingness, zilch

708 mutual possession: communal, mutual

709 need: addiction, alcoholism, call, claim, cupidity, default, dependence/dependency, desire, exigency/exigence, hankering, hunger, lack, libido, lust, must, penchant, predilection, preference, prize, requirement/requisite, slum, sustenance, thirst, void, wish, yen

710 possession: abundance, asset(s), boast, buy, capital, clutches, custody, desolation, domain, due, effects, enjoyment, estate, finances, fund, gain, grasp, hoard, keep, lot, monopoly, occupancy, opulence, ownership, plunder, possession, prize, property, reservation, reserved, resources, return, savings, spoils, store, title, wealth

711 requirement: depend, larder, provision/proviso, reservation, safekeeping, stockpile, understudy

712 resource: amenity, bastion, comfort, edge, expediency/expedience, facility, guard, indulgence, mainstay, makeshift, mine, nurture, organ, plum, provision, redress, remedy, repertory, reservoir, resource, rock, safekeeping, shelter, solution, stopgap, substitute, support, vehicle

713 satisfaction: afford, work out

PHYSICAL

714 accompaniment: attend, chaperon, coincidence, escort, go, relation, solidarity, squire, union, unity

715 age: antiquity, freshness, manhood/womanhood, novelty, years, young

716 appearance: appear, beard, braid, color, countenance, dissemble, double, duplicate, expression, facade, facsimile, fax, front, grimace, guise, image, likeness, look-alike, mask, mug, pose, presence, pretext, represent, resemblance, rise, scowl, show, stand out, surface, symmetry, veneer

717 balance: awkwardness, proportion, symmetry

718 beauty: Afro, coiffure, elegance, fright, glory, hairstyle, pulchritude

719 capacity: content, hold, volume

720 condition: abhorrence, apoplexy, calm, comfort, corrosion, disgust, dissipation, disturbance, exhaustion, frazzle, maturity, pollutant, repose, satisfaction, smog, state, tangle

721 continuity: alignment, concatenation, durability, length, sequence, spread, stretch

722 density: consistency, firmness

723 essential: austerity, corruption, fat, fitness, love handles, posture, tension

724 force: combustion, push

725 genuineness: actuality, certainty, credibility, fait accompli, falsity, funny money, make-believe, sure thing, validity, verisimilitude

726 hardness: firmness, tension

727 order: alignment, chain, concatenation, confusion, course, dislocation, distribution, form, grade, hierarchy, line, median, pattern, precede, precursor, procession, range, round, run, sequence, stage, streak, succeed, tier, train

728 pain: ache, agony, anesthesia/anaesthesia, bad time, boo-boo, crick, distress, harm, heartbreak, injury, kink, misery, pain, pinch, repentance, spasm, strain, suffering, torture, trial, trouble, woe

729 safety: buffer, fortification, precaution, safekeeping, security, shield

730 size: brevity, caliber, dimensions/dimension, extent, greatness, magnitude, miniature, proportion(s), size

731 stability: anchor, equilibrium, flexibility, spring, traction

732 strength: brawn, feebleness, infirmity, might, power, staying power, tolerance, weakness

733 structure: anatomy, composition, easel, fabric, frame, mesh, skeleton

734 weight: buoyancy/buoyance, fatness, love handles, pressure

---

: down, under, underneath
nment: capacity, fill
deep, shallow
n: ascent, crook, current, decline,
divergence, downgrade, grade,

inclination, intersect, level, list, orbit, reverse, revolve, rotate, slant, swirl, tendency, trend, twist, way, wind

739 distance: altitude, bearing/bearings, leeway, space, way

740 fill: brim, cloy, cram, flood, hollow, packed, satiate, teem, vacuum, volume

741 height: dominate, elevation, stature

742 inside: contain, hold, twine

743 length: extent, range

744 level: gradation, layer, line, notch, plateau, row, scale, tier

745 limits, physical: abutment, confines, deadline, end, extreme, frontier, limit, periphery, range, terminal

746 location: absence, bearing/bearings, front, junction/juncture, look, middle, space, stretch

747 location, relative: adjoin, butt, cross, face, near miss, precedence, project, vicinity

748 motion: activity, convulsion, ejection, lassitude, onrush, restlessness, spin, still, swing, turn, vibration, wash

749 nearness: abut, intersect, succeed, verge

750 on: casing, top, traverse

751 outside: band, skirt, stick out

752 over: above, dominate, overlook, tower, vault

753 sequential: line, wake

754 shape: bag, curvature, entwine, fold, hollow, pucker, turn, twist

755 speed: celerity, expedition, hurry, rapidity, velocity

756 spread: balloon, branch off/branch out, bridge, latitude, reach, space, sweep

757 structure: aperture, attitude, beef, build, condition, constitution, crease, even, figure, form, grade, makeup, plane, set, slope, stoop

758 surrounding: circle, compass, edge, enclose, fence, gird, hem/hem in, pen, surround

759 touching: meet, overlap

760 width: breadth

761 within a group: middle, range

WEIGHTS AND MEASURES

MATHEMATICS

762 attribute of a number: abounding, apiece, calculable, dual, flat-out, infinite, just about, less, limitless, many, maximum, minimum, multiple/multifarious, myriad, numberless, numeric/numerical, one, plentiful/plenty, plus, round, short, single, slight, steep, tiny, unreasonable, wee

763 change in number: accrue, appreciation, discount, increment, jump, plummet, reach, slump

764 mathematic reasoning: accounting, addition, arithmetic, balance, calculation, computation, count, estimate, gauge, measure, pace, reckon, score, subtract, tally, total, underestimate

765 numeric symbol: digit, number

766 **numeric value:** appraisal, couple, maximum, percentage, scant/scanty
767 **quantity:** abundance, enough, greatness, paucity, plenty, preponderance, scant/scanty, superabundance
768 **ratio:** quota, ratio
769 **series:** array, range, set, string
770 **system:** apparatus, board, bulletin board, business, channel, circuit, communications, cosmos, dispensation, finance, Internet, mail, method, network, post, routine, world

QUANTIFIERS

771 **attribute of quantity:** about, affluent, altogether, below, better, bountiful, brimming/brimful, depleted, double, elephantine, excessive, exiguous, extravagant, extremely, flush, further, hardly, inadequate, just about, leftover, limited, lush, many, most, new, other, over, residual, rich, slender/slim, spent, supplementary, thin, unreasonable, wholesale
772 **attribute of range:** abysmal, across-the-board, all-out, besides, blanket, bounded, broad, catholic, comprehensive, dead, deeply, diffuse, eclectic, encyclopedic, expansive, extensive, far-reaching, full-scale, general, global, inclusive, indiscriminate, international, lower, mixed, more, most, motley, multinational, multiple/multifarious, overall, pervasive, primarily, quite, rampant, relatively, slightly, substantially, sweeping, universal, utmost, very, wholesale, wide, within, without
773 **attribute of size:** angular, baby, better, brief, burly, capsule, chubby, commodious, compendious, corpulent, cumbersome, elephantine, extensive, full, giant, grand, gross, hefty, hulking, immeasurable, imposing, incalculable, inflated, large, major, massive, midget, miniature, miniscule/minuscule, minute, monstrous, narrow, pocket, prodigious, puny, roly-poly, scrawny, small, small-time, stocky, strapping, stunted, teeny/teensy, thin, titanic, vast, wee, wide
774 **capacity:** brimming/brimful, compact, crowded, full, spacious, vacant, void
775 **change of quantity:** accession, develop, grow, growth
776 **decreasing:** attrition, cut, deduction, depreciate, diminution, drop off, fall, recede, sag, sink, taper/taper off, wane
777 **depth:** abysmal, profound, skin-deep, unfathomable
778 **distance:** about, away, contiguous, distant, far, far-flung, farthest, immediate, near, off, onward/onwards, yonder
779 **height:** alpine, elongated, gigantic, lanky, long, midget, precipitous, short, squat, stubby, tall, towering
780 **increasing:** accretion, accrue, amplification, bulge, enlarge, expansion, increase, inflate, leap, peak, reach, swell, widen

781 **large:** abounding, aggregate, appreciable, colossal, considerable, excessive, extremely, fantastic, generous, gigantic, great, handsome, hulking, incalculable, inordinate, legion, massive, mighty, monstrous, multitudinous, numberless, opulent, plentiful/plenty, prodigious, redundant, stupendous, surplus, tremendous, unwieldy, voluminous, whopping
782 **length:** extended, lengthy, short, tall
783 **measurement:** degree, mark, proportion
784 **number:** amount, estimate, number, pair, point, quotation/quote, sum, trio/triple, zero
785 **portion:** among, asunder, fragmentary, half, sectional
786 **quantity:** agglomeration, amount, avalanche, backlog, batch, bundle, cascade, cipher, deluge, duo, extravagance, figure, flow, gust, lot, mass, minimum, myriad, oodles, pile, plenty, surge, total, trio/triple, turnout
787 **range:** bound/bounds, compass, expanse, gamut, length, scads, scope, superabundance, waterfall, width
788 **relative:** cumulative, fairly, influx
789 **small:** compendious, dinky, few, infinitesimal, less, little, marginal, measly, miniature, minimum, miniscule/minuscule, minute, nominal, outside, piddling, scant/scanty, scarcely, skimpy, teeny/teensy, trifling
790 **unit of distance measure:** depth, foot, mile
791 **unit of height measure:** altitude, height, mile
792 **unit of measure:** acre, degree, dimensions/dimension, mass, measurement, proportions, size, volume, width
793 **unit of scalar measure:** above, lesser, over, under
794 **unit of volume measure:** capacity, volume
795 **unit of weight measure:** ounce, weight
796 **width:** broad, wide

TIME

797 **attribute of age:** adolescent, afresh, ancient, antiquarian, antique, behind the times, callow, contemporary, dated, elder, embryonic, full-grown/full-fledged, green, immemorial, infant/infantile, junior, late, medieval, mint, modish, musty, newfangled, old, old-fashioned, originally, outdated/out-of-date, passé, quaint, ripe, senior, tender, up-to-date, young, youthful
798 **attribute of duration:** ad infinitum, all-time, annual, brief, chronic, concise, constant, continuous, endless, eternal, evanescent, everlasting, fleeting, for keeps, immortal, indefinitely, interminable, laconic, lifelong, long, long-standing, momentary, never-ending, old, ongoing, perennial, perpetual, running, short, short-lived, steady, through, timeless, transient/transitory, unbroken, undying, unflagging, unrelenting, whirlwind

799 **attribute of time:** actual, afterward/afterwards, almost, antediluvian, at, behind the times, colonial, concurrent, dilatory, due, early, ever, extemporaneous/extempory, felicitous, foremost, for keeps, forward, from scratch, gradually, hence, hurried, initial, instantly, irregular, just about, lastly, later, leisurely, meanwhile, narrowly, next, nocturnal, old-fashioned, once and for all, on the double, overdue, pell-mell, perpetual, posthaste, preceding, precipitous/precipitate, previous, primarily, primary/prime, primitive, pristine, promptly, quickly, rapidly, right, sharp, simultaneous, sudden, summarily, swiftly/swift, temporal, thereafter, ultimate, untimely, up-to-date, while, yet

800 **date:** anniversary
801 **day:** afternoon, anniversary, date, ephemeral, journal, morning, nightly, noon, time
802 **definite period:** date, furlough, instant, midnight, noon, sabbatical, shift
803 **division of:** day, second
804 **duration:** brevity, continuation, endure, extent, halt, remain
805 **frequency:** rapidity, sometimes
806 **hour:** afternoon, morning, noon, time
807 **indefinite period:** age, anytime, bout, breath, convenience, eon, era, future, hiatus, infinity, interlude, interruption, lapse, leisure, lull, millenium, moment, past, period, recess, respite, round, semester, space, spell, stint, suspension, tour, vacation, while
808 **minute:** flash, jiffy, tick, wink
809 **month:** almanac, gestation, moon, time
810 **part of a day:** afternoon, dawn, daybreak, dusk, gloom, morning, nightfall, sunset, twilight
811 **past or future:** following, past, previous, succeeding/successive
812 **proximity:** immediate, now, succeeding/successive
813 **relative order:** follow, succeed
814 **season:** autumn, spring, winter
815 **specific:** anniversary, date, daybreak, instance, point, yesterday, zero hour
816 **stage of existence:** administration, childhood, day, generation, millenium, phase, stage, tenure
817 **stage of life form:** adolescence, babyhood, cradle, landmark, lifetime, maternity, prime, spell, youth
818 **temporal association:** anachronism, dispatch, eternity, following, haste, past, precedence, previous, rush, succeeding/successive
819 **temporal object:** anytime, time
820 **time relative to present:** abaft, after, ahead, amid/amidst, antecedent, back, beforehand, belated, bygone, coincident, current, destined, during, ensuing, eventual, fated, first, fore, former, forthwith, historical,

immediately, impending, infant/infantile, just, momentarily, nearing, newly, once, present, previous, prior, recent, shortly, soon, subsequent, succeeding/successive, ultimate, until, yet
821 **unit of time measure:** day, minute, wink
822 **within a time period:** epoch, interval, semester, spell, stretch, while
823 **year:** almanac, annual, time, yearly

WHOLENESS OR DIVISION

824 **added part:** arm, auxiliary, complement, excess, extra, flap, frill, furthermore, new, outgrowth, ramification, sequel, spin-off, supplement, trim, wing
825 **bottom part:** fringe, rest, seat, stub, tail
826 **core part:** base, bottom, core, crux, essential, filling/filler, foundation, germ, hub, inner, internal, marrow, nerve center, nucleus, root, trunk
827 **end part:** abutment, back, butt, point, rear, stub, tail
828 **first part:** appetizer, hors d'oeuvre, introduction, nucleus, precursor, preliminary, spark
829 **main part:** bells and whistle, bulk, chief, feature, focus, hulk, main, nerve center, plurality, root
830 **middle part:** aisle, axle, center, filling/filler, inside, intermediate, joint, junction/juncture, median, midst, pivot
831 **minor part:** atom, breath, chip, component, dandruff, detail, drop, factor, fiber, fleck, glimmer, grit, iota, joint, ligature, modicum, morsel, nibble, node/nodule, patch, pinch, powder, scrap, sliver, soupçon, specimen, splinter, sprinkling, tinge, trace, whisper, wisp
832 **of an event:** chapter, conclusion, dawn, end, finale, finish, germ, height, inception, interruption, leg, meridian, opening, origin, outbreak, particular, period, prelude, prevention, prime, snatch, standstill, stay, stop, suspension, term, threshold, turning point, twist, win, zero hour
833 **of an order:** back, end, front, middle
834 **part:** accessory, attribute, constituent, feature, piece, thing, trash, unit
835 **portion:** accompaniment, adjunct, allotment, appendage, bit, branch, contents, deal, dollop, drop, excerpt, extract, factor, fraction, front, ingredient, interest, layer, little, majority, measure, morsel, pat, piece, precinct, quota, remainder, rest, scrap, sector, share, slab, stake, taste, whit, wing
836 **top part:** acme, apex, brim, citadel, crescendo, crown, extremity, front, height, maximum, orgasm, pinnacle, point, rim, tip, vertex, zenith
837 **whole:** all, entirety, gross, system, unit